Carole Satyamurti
Anne Sexton
William Shakespeare
Stevie Smith
William Stafford

Wallace Stevens
Diane Thiel
Dylan Thomas
Natasha Trethewey
John Updike

Gina Valdés
Walt Whitman
William Butler Yeats

PLAYWRIGHTS

Susan Glaspell
Lorraine Hansberry
Henrik Ibsen

David Ives
Terrence McNally
William Shakespeare

Sophocles
Tennessee Williams

ESSAYISTS AND NONFICTION WRITERS

James Baldwin
Myrna E. Bein
Raymond Carver
Judith Ortiz Cofer
Joan Didion
Annie Dillard
Frederick Douglass
Mohandas Gandhi
bell hooks
Mike Ives

Ryan Kelly
Martin Luther King Jr.
Maxine Hong Kingston
Elisabeth Kübler-Ross
Abraham Lincoln
Kenneth McClane
John Muir
George Orwell
Cynthia Ozick
Paul

Richard Rodriguez
Sacha Z. Scoblic
Brent Staples
Wallace Stegner
Amy Tan
Henry David Thoreau
Leo Tolstoy
Virginia Woolf

CRITICS

W. H. Auden
Roland Barthes
Maud Bodkin
Richard R. Bozorth
Anthony Burgess
Barbara T. Christian
Michael Clark
Brenda O. Daly
Rita Dove
Stanley Fish
Sandra M. Gilbert

Susan Gubar
Daniel Hoffman
Langston Hughes
Thomas H. Johnson
Brett C. Millier
Joseph Moldenhauer
Don Moser
Marilyn Nelson
Joyce Carol Oates
Wilfred Owen
Camille Paglia

Darryl Pinckney
Arnold Rampersad
B. Ruby Rich
Kathryn Lee Seidel
Elaine Showalter
Virginia Mason Vaughan
Edmond Volpe
Alice Walker
Mary Helen Washington
Richard Wilbur

Literature for Life

Literature for Life

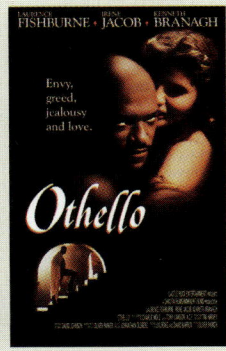

X. J. Kennedy

•

Dana Gioia
University of Southern California

•

Nina Revoyr
Pitzer College

PEARSON

Boston Columbus Indianapolis New York San Francisco Upper Saddle River
Amsterdam Cape Town Dubai London Madrid Milan Munich Paris Montreal Toronto
Delhi Mexico City São Paulo Sydney Hong Kong Seoul Singapore Taipei Tokyo

Vice President and Editor in Chief: Joe Terry
Director of Development: Mary Ellen Curley
Senior Development Editor: Katharine Glynn
Executive Marketing Manager: Joyce Nilsen
Senior Supplements Editor: Donna Campion
Production Manager: Savoula Amanatidis
Project Coordination, Text Design, and Electronic Page Makeup: Cenveo Publisher Services
Cover Designer/Manager: John Callahan
Cover Designer: Laura Shaw
Cover Photos (front cover, left to right): Alice Walker (Anthony Barboza/Archive Photo/Gettyimages); William Faulkner (AP Images); *Othello* Poster (© Moviestore collection Ltd/Alamy); Amy Tan (© Jim McHugh Photography). Spine (top to bottom): Robert Frost (Bachrach/Archive Photo/Getty Images); Flannery O'Connor (Joe McTyre/The Atlanta Journal Constitution); James Baldwin (© Richard Kalvar/Magnum Photos); Mohandas Gandhi (Dinodia Photos/Hulton Archive/Getty Images).
Photo Research: PreMedia Global USA
Senior Manufacturing Buyer: Roy L. Pickering, Jr.
Printer and Binder: Quad Graphics–Taunton
Cover Printer: Lehigh-Phoenix Color Corporation–Hagerstown

Credits and acknowledgments borrowed from other sources and reproduced with permission in this textbook appear on pages 1433–1441.

Cataloging-in-Publication Data is on file at the Library of Congress

Copyright © 2013 by X. J. Kennedy, Dana Gioia, and Nina Revoyr.

All rights reserved. Manufactured in the United States of America. This publication is protected by Copyright, and permission should be obtained from the publisher prior to any prohibited reproduction, storage in a retrieval system, or transmission in any form or by any means, electronic, mechanical, photocopying, recording, or likewise. To obtain permission(s) to use material from this work, please submit a written request to Pearson Education, Inc., Permissions Department, One Lake Street, Upper Saddle River, New Jersey 07458, or you may fax your request to 201-236-3290.

10 9 8 7 6 5 4 3 2 1—QGT—15 14 13 12

www.pearsonhighered.com

ISBN-10: 0-205-74514-8
ISBN-13: 978-0-205-74514-2

DETAILED CONTENTS

Contents by Genre xxvii
To the Instructor xxxi
About the Authors xxxix

READING AND THINKING ABOUT LITERATURE

1 LITERATURE AND LIFE 3

WHY ARE YOU IN THIS COURSE? 4
WHY STUDY LITERATURE AND WRITING? 4
   Empathy and Imagination 5
GETTING A JOB 6
   Career Growth 7
   Reading and Writing Are Critical Skills 8
   You May Have More Than One Career 9
FIFTY FAMOUS ENGLISH MAJORS 10
LITERATURE FOR LIFE 12
Kenneth McClane "Sonny's Blues" Saved My Life 13
Charles Bukowski Dostoevsky 15
Emily Dickinson There is no Frigate like a Book 16

2 READING A STORY 17

THE ART OF FICTION 17
TYPES OF SHORT FICTION 18
ELEMENTS OF FICTION 20
   Plot 20
   Point of View 21
   Character 23
   Setting 25
   Tone and Style 26
   Symbol 28
   Theme 30
John Updike A & P 33
Edgar Allan Poe The Tell-Tale Heart 38
Katherine Mansfield Miss Brill 42
Checklist: Analyzing a Story 47

BRIEF CONTENTS

READING AND THINKING ABOUT LITERATURE

1. Literature and Life 3
2. Reading a Story 17
3. Reading a Poem 50
4. Reading a Play 81
5. Reading an Essay 106

WRITING ABOUT LITERATURE

6. Writing about Literature 127
7. Writing about a Story 147
8. Writing about a Poem 169
9. Writing about a Play 190
10. Writing about an Essay 198
11. Writing a Research Paper 204

REFERENCE GUIDE FOR MLA CITATIONS 228

THEMES OF LITERATURE, THEMES OF LIFE

12. Families 237
13. Love 444
14. Life's Journey 672
15. The Individual and Society 900
16. Personal Identity 1031
17. Nature and the Environment 1201
18. War and Peace 1296

CRITICAL STRATEGIES

19. Critical Approaches to Literature 1397

GLOSSARY OF LITERARY TERMS 1419

3 READING A POEM 50

TYPES OF POETRY: LYRIC, NARRATIVE, DRAMATIC 51
W. H. Auden Funeral Blues 51
Edwin Arlington Robinson Richard Cory 52
Margaret Atwood Siren Song 53
READING A POEM 54
ELEMENTS OF POETRY 55
    Tone 55
Emily Dickinson Wild Nights – Wild Nights! 56
    Words 57
Gina Valdés English con Salsa 58
    Denotation and Connotation 60
Robert Frost Nothing Gold Can Stay 60
    Imagery 61
Langston Hughes Harlem [Dream Deferred] 61
    Figures of Speech 62
    Sound 64
    Rhythm 66
    Closed Form 69
John Keats When I have fears that I may cease to be 70
Matsuo Basho Temple bells die out 71
Matsuo Basho Heat-lightning streak 71
Taniguchi Buson Moonrise on mudflats 72
Kobayashi Issa only one guy 72
Anonymous Epitaph on a Dentist 72
    Open Form 73
E. E. Cummings in Just- 74
    Symbol 75
WHAT IS POETRY? 76
Checklist: Analyzing a Poem 78

4 READING A PLAY 81

READING A PLAY 82
THEATRICAL CONVENTIONS 83
MODES OF DRAMA: TRAGEDY AND COMEDY 83
ELEMENTS OF A PLAY 87

Susan Glaspell Trifles 88

ANALYZING *TRIFLES* 99
    Conflict 99
    Plot 100
    Subplot 100
    Protagonist 100
    Exposition 101
    Dramatic Question 101
    Climax 101
    Resolution and Dénouement 102
    Rising and Falling Action 102
    Unity of Time, Place, and Action 103
    Symbols in Drama 103

Checklist: Analyzing a Play 104

5 READING AN ESSAY 106

WHAT IS AN ESSAY? 106

HISTORY OF THE ESSAY 107

TYPES OF ESSAYS 108
    Narrative Essay 108
    Descriptive Essay 108
    Expository Essay 109
    Argumentative Essay 109

ELEMENTS OF ESSAYS 110
    Voice 110
    Style 111
    Structure 112
    Theme 113

Joan Didion On Morality 114

Amy Tan Mother Tongue 117

Checklist: Analyzing an Essay 123

WRITING ABOUT LITERATURE

6 WRITING ABOUT LITERATURE 127

READ ACTIVELY 127
Robert Frost Nothing Gold Can Stay 128
   Sample Student Reading Annotation 128
PLAN YOUR ESSAY 129
PREWRITING: DISCOVER YOUR IDEAS 129
   Sample Student Prewriting Exercises 130
DEVELOP A LITERARY ARGUMENT 133
Checklist: Developing an Argument 135
WRITE A ROUGH DRAFT 136
   Sample Student Rough Draft: Argument Paper 136
REVISE YOUR DRAFT 138
Checklist: Revising Your Draft 141
FINAL ADVICE ON REWRITING 142
   Sample Student Revised Draft: Argument Paper 143
DOCUMENT SOURCES TO AVOID PLAGIARISM 145
THE FORM OF YOUR FINISHED PAPER 146

7 WRITING ABOUT A STORY 147

READ ACTIVELY 147
   Sample Student Reading Annotation 148
THINK ABOUT THE STORY 148
PREWRITING: DISCOVER YOUR IDEAS 149
   Sample Student Prewriting Exercises 150
WRITE A ROUGH DRAFT 152
Checklist: Writing a Rough Draft 153
REVISE YOUR DRAFT 153
Checklist: Revising Your Draft 154

WHAT'S YOUR PURPOSE? COMMON APPROACHES
TO WRITING ABOUT FICTION 154
   Explication 155
   Sample Student Explication Paper 156
   Analysis 158
   Sample Student Analysis Paper 159
   Comparison and Contrast 161
   Sample Student Comparison and Contrast Paper 163
   Response Paper 164
   Sample Student Response Paper 165

TOPICS FOR WRITING 167

8 WRITING ABOUT A POEM 169

READ ACTIVELY 169
Robert Frost Design 170
   Sample Student Reading Annotation 170
THINK ABOUT THE POEM 171
PREWRITING: DISCOVER YOUR IDEAS 171
   Sample Student Prewriting Exercises 172
WRITE A ROUGH DRAFT 174
Checklist: Writing a Rough Draft 175
REVISE YOUR DRAFT 175
Checklist: Revising Your Draft 177
COMMON APPROACHES TO WRITING
ABOUT POETRY 177
   Explication 177
   Sample Student Explication Paper 178
   Analysis 181
   Sample Student Analysis Paper 181
   Comparison and Contrast 183
Abbie Huston Evans Wing-Spread 183
   Sample Student Comparison and Contrast Paper 184
HOW TO QUOTE A POEM 186
TOPICS FOR WRITING 187
Robert Frost In White 188

9 WRITING ABOUT A PLAY 190

READ CRITICALLY   190
   Sample Student Reading Annotation   191
COMMON APPROACHES TO WRITING ABOUT DRAMA   191
   Explication   192
   Analysis   192
   Comparison and Contrast   192
   Drama Review   192
   Sample Student Drama Review   194
HOW TO QUOTE A PLAY   195
TOPICS FOR WRITING   196

10 WRITING ABOUT AN ESSAY 198

READ ACTIVELY   199
THINK ABOUT THE ESSAY   199
PREWRITING: DISCOVER AND SHAPE YOUR IDEAS   199
COMMON APPROACHES TO WRITING ABOUT ESSAYS   200
   Explication   200
   Analysis   200
   Comparison and Contrast   201
   Response Paper   201
TOPICS FOR WRITING   202

11 WRITING A RESEARCH PAPER 204

BROWSE THE RESEARCH   204
CHOOSE A TOPIC   205
BEGIN YOUR RESEARCH   205
   Print Resources   205
   Online Databases   206
   Reliable Web Sources   206
Checklist: Finding Reliable Sources   207
   Visual Images   208
Checklist: Using Visual Images   209

EVALUATE YOUR SOURCES   209
   Print Resources   209
   Web Sources   210
Checklist: Evaluating Your Sources   210
ORGANIZE YOUR RESEARCH   211
REFINE YOUR THESIS   213
ORGANIZE YOUR PAPER   214
WRITE AND REVISE   214
MAINTAIN ACADEMIC INTEGRITY   215
ACKNOWLEDGE ALL SOURCES   215
   Using Quotations   216
   Citing Ideas   216
DOCUMENT SOURCES USING MLA STYLE   217
   List of Sources   217
   Parenthetical References   217
   Works-Cited List   218
   Citing Print Sources in MLA Style   219
   Citing Web Sources in MLA Style   220
   Sample List of Works Cited   221
   Sample Student Research Paper   222

REFERENCE GUIDE FOR MLA CITATIONS   228

Detailed Contents xiii

THEMES OF LITERATURE, THEMES OF LIFE

12 FAMILIES 237

FICTION 240

Parents and Children 237
Amy Tan   A Pair of Tickets   240
William Faulkner   Barn Burning   254
Luke   The Parable of the Prodigal Son   266
Alice Walker   Everyday Use   268
Suggestions for Writing   275

Critical and Cultural Contexts Casebook
Alice Walker's "Everyday Use"   276

Alice Walker on Writing   277
Alice Walker   The Black Woman Writer in America   277

Criticism and Cultural Contexts   278
Barbara T. Christian   "Everyday Use" and the Black Power Movement   278
Mary Helen Washington   "Everyday Use" as a Portrait of the Artist   281
Elaine Showalter   Quilt as Metaphor in "Everyday Use"   283

Alice Walker and Her World: Images
Cover of *In Love & Trouble*   276
Alice Walker in Conversation   277
Scene from *Everyday Use* (2003 Film)   279
Alice Walker at Home with Quilt Art   282
Lone Star Quilt Pattern   284
Suggestions for Writing   285

Brothers and Sisters   286
James Baldwin   Sonny's Blues   286
Tobias Wolff   The Rich Brother   308
Eudora Welty   Why I Live at the P.O.   321
Louise Erdrich   The Red Convertible   330
Suggestions for Writing   337

POETRY 338

Children Looking at Parents, Parents Looking at Children 338
Robert Hayden Those Winter Sundays 338
Theodore Roethke My Papa's Waltz 339
Rhina P. Espaillat Bilingual / *Bilingüe* 340
Sylvia Plath Daddy 341
Sharon Olds Rite of Passage 344
Suggestions for Writing 345

Family Legacies 346
Robert Hayden The Whipping 346
Seamus Heaney Digging 347
Julia Alvarez By Accident 349
Li-Young Lee The Gift 350
Diane Thiel The Minefield 351
Suggestions for Writing 352

Family Bonds
Poet in Depth: Gwendolyn Brooks 353
Gwendolyn Brooks Sadie and Maud 354
　　　　　　　the mother 355
　　　　　　　the rites for Cousin Vit 356
　　　　　　　The Bean Eaters 356
　　　　　　　Speech to the Young. Speech to the Progress-Toward 357
Suggestions for Writing 357

ESSAYS 358

Child into Adult 358
Brent Staples The Runaway Son 358
Raymond Carver My Father's Life 366
Annie Dillard An American Childhood 372
Suggestions for Writing 375

DRAMA 376

Family Drama 376
Lorraine Hansberry A Raisin in the Sun 376
Suggestions for Writing 442
Suggestions for Writing on Literature about Families 443

13 LOVE 444

FICTION 448

Discovering Love 448
Margaret Atwood   Happy Endings   448
O. Henry   The Gift of the Magi   451
Max Apple   Vegetable Love   455
Suggestions for Writing   465

Love Gone Wrong 466
William Faulkner   A Rose for Emily   466
Zora Neale Hurston   Sweat   473
Flannery O'Connor   Parker's Back   482
Suggestions for Writing   496

Troubled Marriages
Writer in Depth: Kate Chopin   497
Kate Chopin   The Story of an Hour   498
               The Storm   500
               Désirée's Baby   503

Suggestions for Writing   507

POETRY 508

Love Poems 508
Anne Bradstreet   To My Dear and Loving Husband   508
Elizabeth Barrett Browning   How Do I Love Thee? Let Me Count the Ways   509
William Butler Yeats   When You Are Old   510
E. E. Cummings   somewhere I have never travelled,gladly beyond   511
Rafael Campo   For J. W.   512
Wendy Cope   Lonely Hearts   513
Suggestions for Writing   514

Love, Sex, and Desire 515
Andrew Marvell   To His Coy Mistress   515
John Donne   The Flea   517
Edna St. Vincent Millay   What lips my lips have kissed, and where, and why   518
T. S. Eliot   The Love Song of J. Alfred Prufrock   519
Marilyn Nelson   The Ballad of Aunt Geneva   523
Kim Addonizio   First Poem for You   525
Suggestions for Writing   526

Love Sonnets
Poet in Depth: William Shakespeare 527

William Shakespeare Shall I compare thee to a summer's day? 528
When, in disgrace with Fortune and men's eyes 528
Let me not to the marriage of true minds 529
My mistress' eyes are nothing like the sun 529
When my love swears that she is made of truth 530

Suggestions for Writing 530

ESSAYS AND OTHER NONFICTION 531

Remembering Love 531
Paul "The Greatest of These Is Love": 1 Corinthians 13 531
Cynthia Ozick Lovesickness 532
Judith Ortiz Cofer I Fell in Love, or My Hormones Awakened 537
Mike Ives Would Hemingway Cry? 542
Suggestions for Writing 545

DRAMA 546

Love: Comic and Tragic 546
David Ives Sure Thing 546
Suggestions for Writing 556

William Shakespeare Othello, the Moor of Venice 557
Picturing *Othello* 558

Critical and Cultural Contexts Casebook
William Shakespeare's *Othello* 663

Historical Contexts 664
The Theater of Shakespeare 664
Source Material for *Othello* 665

Criticism and Cultural Contexts 667
Anthony Burgess An Asian Culture Looks at Shakespeare 667
W. H. Auden Iago as a Triumphant Villain 668
Maud Bodkin Lucifer in Shakespeare's *Othello* 669
Virginia Mason Vaughan Black and White in *Othello* 669

Othello in Performance: Images
Othello Movie Poster 663
Globe Theater 664

Detailed Contents xvii

A Portfolio of Players: Famous Othellos in Performance 666
Othello in Translation 667
Suggestions for Writing 670
Suggestions for Writing on Literature about Love 670

14 LIFE'S JOURNEY 672

FICTION 675

Childhood and Adolescence 675
James Joyce   Araby 675
ZZ Packer   Brownies 680
Michael Chabon   The Little Knife 694
Suggestions for Writing 699

Dangerous Encounters 700
Nathaniel Hawthorne   Young Goodman Brown 700
Flannery O'Connor   A Good Man Is Hard to Find 710
Joyce Carol Oates   Where Are You Going, Where Have You Been? 721
Suggestions for Writing 733

Critical and Cultural Contexts Casebook
Joyce Carol Oates's "Where Are You Going, Where Have You Been?" 734

Fact into Fiction 735
Don Moser   The Pied Piper of Tucson: He Cruised in a Golden Car, Looking for the Action 735

Fiction into Film 742
Joyce Carol Oates   "Where Are You Going, Where Have You Been?" and *Smooth Talk*: Short Story into Film 742
B. Ruby Rich   Good Girls, Bad Girls: Joyce Chopra's *Smooth Talk* 745
Brenda O. Daly   An Unfilmable Conclusion: Joyce Carol Oates at the Movies 747

"Where Are You Going?" and Media: Images
Smooth Talk Movie Poster 734
Life Magazine Spread 736
Scenes from *Smooth Talk* 743, 746
Suggestions for Writing 751

Bargaining with Death 752
W. Somerset Maugham   The Appointment in Samarra 752
Jakob and Wilhelm Grimm   Godfather Death 753
Chinua Achebe   Dead Men's Path 756
Suggestions for Writing 759

Death and Transformation 760
Franz Kafka   The Metamorphosis 760
Suggestions for Writing 792

POETRY 793

Childhood and Adolescence 793
Countee Cullen   Incident 793
Gwendolyn Brooks   We Real Cool 794
Judith Ortiz Cofer   Quinceañera 795
William Blake   London 796
Dylan Thomas   Fern Hill 797
Suggestions for Writing 799

Life's Challenges 800
A. E. Housman   When I was one-and-twenty 800
John Updike   Ex-Basketball Player 801
Elizabeth Bishop   One Art 802
Natasha Trethewey   White Lies 803
Antonio Machado   Caminante / Traveler 804
Suggestions for Writing 805

Facing Death 806
John Donne   Death be not proud 806
Emily Dickinson   Because I could not stop for Death 807
Dylan Thomas   Do not go gentle into that good night 808
José Emilio Pacheco   La Ceniza / Ashes 809
E. E. Cummings   Buffalo Bill 's 810
Sylvia Plath   Lady Lazarus 811
Suggestions for Writing 814

Life and Its Crossroads
Poet in Depth: Robert Frost 815
Robert Frost   The Road Not Taken 816
  Acquainted with the Night 817
  Fire and Ice 817
  Stopping by Woods on a Snowy Evening 818
  Desert Places 818
Suggestions for Writing 819

Detailed Contents xix

ESSAYS 820

Turning Points 820
James Baldwin   Notes of a Native Son   820
George Orwell   Shooting an Elephant   834
Sacha Z. Scoblic   Rock Star, Meet Teetotaler   840
Elisabeth Kübler-Ross   On the Fear of Death   842
Suggestions for Writing   848

DRAMA 849

Life Passages 849
Tennessee Williams   The Glass Menagerie   849
Terrence McNally   Andre's Mother   895
Suggestions for Writing   898
Suggestions for Writing on Literature about Life's Journeys   899

15 THE INDIVIDUAL AND SOCIETY 900

FICTION 902

Conformity, Rebellion, and Dissent 902
Shirley Jackson   The Lottery   902
Kurt Vonnegut Jr.   Harrison Bergeron   909
Ursula K. Le Guin   The Ones Who Walk Away from Omelas   914
Suggestions for Writing   919

Individuals In Isolation 920
Ernest Hemingway   A Clean, Well-Lighted Place   920
John Cheever   The Swimmer   924
Ha Jin   Saboteur   933
Suggestions for Writing   941

POETRY 942

Loneliness and Community 942
E. E. Cummings   anyone lived in a pretty how town   942
Stevie Smith   Not Waving but Drowning   944
Allen Ginsberg   A Supermarket in California   944
Anne Sexton   Her Kind   946
Pablo Neruda   Muchos Somos / We Are Many   947
Suggestions for Writing   948

Individualism Versus Conformity 949
Walt Whitman I Hear America Singing 949
Paul Laurence Dunbar Sympathy 950
Robert Frost Mending Wall 951
W. H. Auden The Unknown Citizen 953
Mary Oliver Wild Geese 954
Suggestions for Writing 955

Selecting Your Own Society
Poet in Depth: Emily Dickinson 956
Emily Dickinson I'm Nobody! Who are you? 957
    The Soul selects her own Society 958
    This is my letter to the World 958
    Much Madness is divinest Sense 958
    Some keep the Sabbath going to Church 959
Suggestions for Writing 959

Critical and Cultural Contexts Casebook
The Poetry of Emily Dickinson 960

Emily Dickinson on Writing 961
Emily Dickinson Recognizing Poetry 961
Emily Dickinson Self-Description 961

Criticism and Cultural Contexts 963
Thomas H. Johnson The Discovery of Emily Dickinson's Manuscripts 963
Richard Wilbur The Three Privations of Emily Dickinson 964
Sandra M. Gilbert and Susan Gubar The Freedom of Emily Dickinson 965

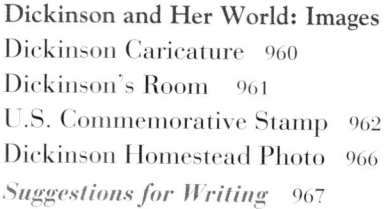

Dickinson and Her World: Images
Dickinson Caricature 960
Dickinson's Room 961
U.S. Commemorative Stamp 962
Dickinson Homestead Photo 966
Suggestions for Writing 967

ESSAYS 968

Inspiring Social Change 968
Martin Luther King Jr. Letter from Birmingham Jail 968
Henry David Thoreau *from* Civil Disobedience 981
Maxine Hong Kingston No Name Woman 989
Suggestions for Writing 998

DRAMA 999

The Individual Versus Authority 999
Sophocles Antigonê 999
Suggestions for Writing 1029
Suggestions for Writing on Literature about the Individual and Society 1030

16 PERSONAL IDENTITY 1031

FICTION 1034

Becoming an Individual 1034
Charlotte Perkins Gilman The Yellow Wallpaper 1034
David Leavitt A Place I've Never Been 1046
Sherman Alexie This Is What It Means to Say Phoenix, Arizona 1057
Suggestions for Writing 1065

Personal Change 1067
John Steinbeck The Chrysanthemums 1067
Raymond Carver Cathedral 1075
Jhumpa Lahiri Interpreter of Maladies 1086
Suggestions for Writing 1101

POETRY 1102

Men and Women 1102
Sylvia Plath Metaphors 1102
Carole Satyamurti I Shall Paint My Nails Red 1103
Charles Bukowski my old man 1104
Denise Levertov The Ache of Marriage 1106
Marge Piercy Barbie Doll 1106
Donald Justice Men at Forty 1107
Suggestions for Writing 1108

Cultural and Personal Origins 1109
Francisco X. Alarcón The X in My Name 1109
Paul Laurence Dunbar We Wear the Mask 1110
Shirley Geok-lin Lim Learning to love America 1111
Edwin Arlington Robinson New England 1112
Rhina P. Espaillat Bodega 1113
Ted Kooser So This Is Nebraska 1113
Suggestions for Writing 1115

"I, Too, Sing America"
Poet in Depth: Langston Hughes 1116

Langston Hughes   The Negro Speaks of Rivers   1117
     I, Too   1118
     Theme for English B   1118
     Dream Boogie   1120
     Mother to Son   1120

Suggestions for Writing   1121

Critical and Cultural Contexts Casebook
The Poetry of Langston Hughes 1122

Langston Hughes on Writing   1123
Langston Hughes   The Negro Artist and the Racial Mountain   1123
Langston Hughes   The Harlem Renaissance   1124

Criticism and Cultural Contexts   1125
Arnold Rampersad   Hughes as an Experimentalist   1125
Rita Dove and Marilyn Nelson   The Voices in Langston Hughes   1127
Darryl Pinckney   Black Identity in Langston Hughes   1129

Hughes and His World: Images
Cover of Hughes's First Book   1122
Langston Hughes Postage Stamp   1123
Photograph of Lenox Avenue, Harlem   1125
Cover of *FIRE!!*   1126
Langston Hughes with Fans   1128

Suggestions for Writing   1130

ESSAYS 1131

Defining Self 1131

Frederick Douglass   Learning to Read and Write   1131
Virginia Woolf   What If Shakespeare Had a Sister?   1136
Richard Rodriguez   "Blaxicans" and Other Reinvented Americans   1141

Suggestions for Writing   1145

DRAMA 1146

Personal Transformation 1146
Henrik Ibsen   A Doll's House   1146

Suggestions for Writing   1199
Suggestions for Writing on Literature about Personal Identity   1200

17 NATURE AND THE ENVIRONMENT 1201

FICTION 1204

Humanity Versus Nature 1204
Jack London To Build a Fire 1204
Stephen Crane The Open Boat 1215
T. Coraghessan Boyle Greasy Lake 1232
Suggestions for Writing 1240

Living with Nature 1241
Ursula K. Le Guin She Unnames Them 1241
Leslie Marmon Silko The Man to Send Rain Clouds 1243
Terry Bisson Bears Discover Fire 1247
Suggestions for Writing 1254

Animals as Allegory: Three Fables 1255
Aesop The Grasshopper and the Ant 1255
Bidpai The Camel and His Friends 1256
Chuang Tzu Independence 1258
Suggestions for Writing 1259

POETRY 1260

Nature 1260
William Blake To see a world in a grain of sand 1260
Gerard Manley Hopkins God's Grandeur 1261
William Butler Yeats The Lake Isle of Innisfree 1262
H.D. Storm 1263
Elizabeth Bishop The Fish 1263
Dana Gioia California Hills in August 1265
Benjamin Alire Sáenz To the Desert 1267
Suggestions for Writing 1268

Animals: Symbolic and Real 1269
William Blake The Tyger 1269
Lewis Carroll Jabberwocky 1271
Thomas Hardy The Darkling Thrush 1272
Wallace Stevens Thirteen Ways of Looking at a Blackbird 1273
Robinson Jeffers Rock and Hawk 1276
Phillis Levin Brief Bio 1277
Kay Ryan Turtle 1277
Suggestions for Writing 1278

Just for Fun: Pet Haiku 1279
Anonymous Dog Haiku 1279
Anonymous Cat Haiku 1280
Suggestions for Writing 1280

ESSAYS 1281

Our Place in Nature 1281
John Muir A Wind-Storm in the Forests 1281
Wallace Stegner Wilderness Letter 1286
bell hooks Earthbound: On Solid Ground 1291
Suggestions for Writing 1294
Suggestions for Writing on Literature about Nature and the Environment 1295

18 WAR AND PEACE 1296

FICTION 1299

WAR AND VIOLENCE 1299
Tim O'Brien The Things They Carried 1299
Ambrose Bierce An Occurrence at Owl Creek Bridge 1312
Mary Yukari Waters Shibusa 1318
Suggestions for Writing 1325

Crime and Punishment 1326
Andre Dubus A Father's Story 1326
Edgar Allan Poe The Cask of Amontillado 1341
Guy de Maupassant Mother Savage 1346
Suggestions for Writing 1351

POETRY 1352

Soldiers and Warfare 1352
Richard Lovelace To Lucasta 1352
Henry Reed Naming of Parts 1353
Richard Eberhart The Fury of Aerial Bombardment 1354
Marilyn Nelson Star-Fix 1355
Yusef Komunyakaa Facing It 1358
R. S. Gwynn Body Bags 1359
Suggestions for Writing 1361

Peace and Social Justice 1362
William Blake   A Poison Tree 1362
Emma Lazarus   The New Colossus 1364
Claude McKay   If We Must Die 1364
William Stafford   At the Un-National Monument Along the Canadian Border 1365
Denise Levertov   Making Peace 1366
Suggestions for Writing   1367

"The Pity of War"
Poet in Depth: Wilfred Owen 1368
Wilfred Owen   The Pity of War (prose introduction) 1370
　　　　　　　　Dulce et Decorum Est 1370
　　　　　　　　Anthem for Doomed Youth 1371
　　　　　　　　Futility 1372
Suggestions for Writing   1372

NONFICTION 1373

The Cost of War 1373
Abraham Lincoln   Second Inaugural Address 1373
Ryan Kelly   A Quick Look at Who Is Fighting This War; This Is Not a Game 1375
Myrna E. Bein   A Journey Taken with My Son 1380
Suggestions for Writing   1381

Visions of Peace 1382
Mohandas Gandhi   Non-Violence—the Greatest Force 1382
Leo Tolstoy   *from* The Kingdom of God Is Within You 1384
Suggestions for Writing   1388

DRAMA 1389

War in Drama: Two Contrasting Speeches from Shakespeare 1389
William Shakespeare   "We Happy Few, We Band of Brothers": Speech from *Henry V* 1389
William Shakespeare   "The Better Part of Valor is Discretion": Speech from *Henry IV, Part I* 1391
Suggestions for Writing   1393
Suggestions for Writing on Literature about War and Peace   1393

CRITICAL STRATEGIES

19 CRITICAL APPROACHES TO LITERATURE 1397

FORMALIST CRITICISM 1398
Michael Clark Light and Darkness in "Sonny's Blues" 1398
BIOGRAPHICAL CRITICISM 1399
Brett C. Millier On Elizabeth Bishop's "One Art" 1400
HISTORICAL CRITICISM 1401
Joseph Moldenhauer "To His Coy Mistress" and the Renaissance Tradition 1402
PSYCHOLOGICAL CRITICISM 1403
Daniel Hoffman The Father-Figure in "The Tell-Tale Heart" 1404
MYTHOLOGICAL CRITICISM 1405
Edmond Volpe Myth in Faulkner's "Barn Burning" 1406
SOCIOLOGICAL CRITICISM 1408
Kathryn Lee Seidel The Economics of Zora Neale Hurston's "Sweat" 1408
GENDER CRITICISM 1410
Richard R. Bozorth "Tell Me the Truth About Love" 1411
READER-RESPONSE CRITICISM 1413
Stanley Fish An Eskimo "A Rose for Emily" 1413
DECONSTRUCTIONIST CRITICISM 1414
Roland Barthes The Death of the Author 1415
CULTURAL STUDIES 1416
Camille Paglia A Reading of William Blake's "London" 1417

GLOSSARY OF LITERARY TERMS 1419

Literary and Photo Credits 1433
Index of First Lines of Poetry 1443
Index of Authors and Titles 1445
Index of Literary Terms last page

CONTENTS BY GENRE

FICTION

Chinua Achebe, Dead Men's Path 756
Aesop, The Grasshopper and the Ant 1255
Sherman Alexie, This Is What It Means to Say Phoenix, Arizona 1057
Max Apple, Vegetable Love 455
Margaret Atwood, Happy Endings 448
James Baldwin, Sonny's Blues 286
Bidpai, The Camel and His Friends 1256
Ambrose Bierce, An Occurrence at Owl Creek Bridge 1312
Terry Bisson, Bears Discover Fire 1247
T. Coraghessan Boyle, Greasy Lake 1232
Raymond Carver, Cathedral 1075
Michael Chabon, The Little Knife 694
John Cheever, The Swimmer 924
Kate Chopin, Désirée's Baby 503
Kate Chopin, The Storm 500
Kate Chopin, The Story of an Hour 498
Chuang Tzu, Independence 1258
Stephen Crane, The Open Boat 1215
Andre Dubus, A Father's Story 1326
Louise Erdrich, The Red Convertible 330
William Faulkner, Barn Burning 254
William Faulkner, A Rose for Emily 466
Charlotte Perkins Gilman, The Yellow Wallpaper 1034
Jakob and Wilhelm Grimm, Godfather Death 753
Nathaniel Hawthorne, Young Goodman Brown 700
Ernest Hemingway, A Clean, Well-Lighted Place 920
O. Henry (William Sydney Porter), The Gift of the Magi 451
Zora Neale Hurston, Sweat 473
Shirley Jackson, The Lottery 902
Ha Jin, Saboteur 933
James Joyce, Araby 675
Franz Kafka, The Metamorphosis 760
Jhumpa Lahiri, Interpreter of Maladies 1086
Ursula K. Le Guin, The Ones Who Walk Away from Omelas 914
Ursula K. Le Guin, She Unnames Them 1241
David Leavitt, A Place I've Never Been 1046
Jack London, To Build a Fire 1204
Luke, The Parable of the Prodigal Son 266
Katherine Mansfield, Miss Brill 42
Somerset Maugham, The Appointment in Samarra 752
Guy de Maupassant, Mother Savage 1346
Joyce Carol Oates, Where Are You Going, Where Have You Been? 721
Tim O'Brien, The Things They Carried 1299
Flannery O'Connor, A Good Man Is Hard to Find 710
Flannery O'Connor, Parker's Back 482
ZZ Packer, Brownies 680
Edgar Allan Poe, The Cask of Amontillado 1341
Edgar Allan Poe, The Tell-Tale Heart 38
Leslie Marmon Silko, The Man to Send Rain Clouds 1243
John Steinbeck, The Chrysanthemums 1067
Amy Tan, A Pair of Tickets 240
John Updike, A & P 33
Kurt Vonnegut Jr., Harrison Bergeron 909
Alice Walker, Everyday Use 268
Mary Yukari Waters, Shibusa 1318
Eudora Welty, Why I Live at the P. O. 321
Tobias Wolff, The Rich Brother 308

POETRY

Kim Addonizio, First Poem for You 525
Francisco X. Alarcón, The X in My Name 1109
Julia Alvarez, By Accident 349
Anonymous, Cat Haiku 1280
Anonymous, Dog Haiku 1279
Anonymous, Epitaph on a Dentist 72
Margaret Atwood, Siren Song 53
W. H. Auden, Funeral Blues 51
W. H. Auden, The Unknown Citizen 953
Matsuo Basho, Heat-lightning streak 71
Matsuo Basho, Temple bells die out 71
Elizabeth Bishop, The Fish 1263

xxvii

Elizabeth Bishop, One Art 802
William Blake, London 796
William Blake, A Poison Tree 1362
William Blake, To see a world in a grain of sand 1260
William Blake, The Tyger 1269
Anne Bradstreet, To My Dear and Loving Husband 508
Gwendolyn Brooks, The Bean Eaters 356
Gwendolyn Brooks, the mother 355
Gwendolyn Brooks, the rites for Cousin Vit 356
Gwendolyn Brooks, Sadie and Maud 354
Gwendolyn Brooks, Speech to the Young. Speech to the Progress-Toward 357
Gwendolyn Brooks, We Real Cool 794
Elizabeth Barrett Browning, How Do I Love Thee? Let Me Count the Ways 509
Charles Bukowski, Dostoevsky 15
Charles Bukowski, my old man 1104
Taniguchi Buson, Moonrise on mudflats 72
Rafael Campo, For J. W. 512
Lewis Carroll, Jabberwocky 1271
Judith Ortiz Cofer, Quinceañera 795
Wendy Cope, Lonely Hearts 513
Countee Cullen, Incident 793
E. E. Cummings, anyone lived in a pretty how town 942
E. E. Cummings, Buffalo Bill's 810
E. E. Cummings, in Just- 74
E. E. Cummings, somewhere i have never travelled,gladly beyond 511
Emily Dickinson, Because I could not stop for Death 807
Emily Dickinson, I'm Nobody! Who are you? 957
Emily Dickinson, Much Madness is divinest Sense 958
Emily Dickinson, Some keep the Sabbath going to Church 959
Emily Dickinson, The Soul selects her own Society 958
Emily Dickinson, There is no Frigate like a Book 16
Emily Dickinson, This is my letter to the World 958
Emily Dickinson, Wild Nights – Wild Nights! 56
John Donne, Death be not proud 806
John Donne, The Flea 517
Paul Laurence Dunbar, Sympathy 950

Paul Laurence Dunbar, We Wear the Mask 1110
Richard Eberhart, The Fury of Aerial Bombardment 1354
T. S. Eliot, The Love Song of J. Alfred Prufrock 519
Rhina P. Espaillat, Bilingual / Bilingüe 340
Rhina P. Espaillat, Bodega 1113
Abbie Huston Evans, Wing-Spread 183
Robert Frost, Acquainted with the Night 817
Robert Frost, Desert Places 818
Robert Frost, Design 170
Robert Frost, Fire and Ice 817
Robert Frost, In White 188
Robert Frost, Mending Wall 951
Robert Frost, Nothing Gold Can Stay 60, 128
Robert Frost, The Road Not Taken 816
Robert Frost, Stopping by Woods on a Snowy Evening 818
Allen Ginsberg, A Supermarket in California 944
Dana Gioia, California Hills in August 1265
R. S. Gwynn, Body Bags 1359
H.D. (Hilda Doolittle), Storm 1263
Thomas Hardy, The Darkling Thrush 1272
Robert Hayden, Those Winter Sundays 338
Robert Hayden, The Whipping 346
Seamus Heaney, Digging 347
Gerard Manley Hopkins, God's Grandeur 1261
A. E. Housman, When I was one-and-twenty 800
Langston Hughes, Dream Boogie 1120
Langston Hughes, Harlem [Dream Deferred] 61
Langston Hughes, I, Too 1118
Langston Hughes, Mother to Son 1120
Langston Hughes, The Negro Speaks of Rivers 1117
Langston Hughes, Theme for English B 1118
Kobayashi Issa, only one guy 72
Robinson Jeffers, Rock and Hawk 1276
Donald Justice, Men at Forty 1107
John Keats, When I have fears that I may cease to be 70
Yusef Komunyakaa, Facing It 1358
Ted Kooser, So This Is Nebraska 1113
Emma Lazarus, The New Colossus 1364
Li-Young Lee, The Gift 350
Denise Levertov, The Ache of Marriage 1106
Denise Levertov, Making Peace 1366
Phillis Levin, Brief Bio 1277

Shirley Geok-lin Lim, Learning to love America 1111
Richard Lovelace, To Lucasta 1352
Antonio Machado, Caminante / Traveler 804
Andrew Marvell, To His Coy Mistress 515
Claude McKay, If We Must Die 1364
Edna St. Vincent Millay, What lips my lips have kissed, and where, and why 518
Marilyn Nelson, The Ballad of Aunt Geneva 523
Marilyn Nelson, Star-Fix 1355
Pablo Neruda, Muchos Somos / We Are Many 947
Sharon Olds, Rite of Passage 344
Mary Oliver, Wild Geese 954
Wilfred Owen, Anthem for Doomed Youth 1371
Wilfred Owen, Dulce et Decorum Est 1370
Wilfred Owen, Futility 1372
José Emilio Pacheco, La Ceniza / Ashes 809
Marge Piercy, Barbie Doll 1106
Sylvia Plath, Daddy 341
Sylvia Plath, Lady Lazarus 811
Sylvia Plath, Metaphors 1102
Henry Reed, Naming of Parts 1353
Edwin Arlington Robinson, New England 1112
Edwin Arlington Robinson, Richard Cory 52
Theodore Roethke, My Papa's Waltz 339
Kay Ryan, Turtle 1277
Benjamin Alire Sáenz, To the Desert 1267
Carole Satyamurti, I Shall Paint My Nails Red 1103
Anne Sexton, Her Kind 946
William Shakespeare, Let me not to the marriage of true minds 529
William Shakespeare, My mistress' eyes are nothing like the sun 529
William Shakespeare, Shall I compare thee to a summer's day? 528
William Shakespeare, When, in disgrace with Fortune and men's eyes 528
William Shakespeare, When my love swears that she is made of truth 530
Stevie Smith, Not Waving but Drowning 944
William Stafford, At the Un-National Monument Along the Canadian Border 1365
Wallace Stevens, Thirteen Ways of Looking at a Blackbird 1273
Diane Thiel, The Minefield 351
Dylan Thomas, Do not go gentle into that good night 808
Dylan Thomas, Fern Hill 797
Natasha Trethewey, White Lies 803
John Updike, Ex-Basketball Player 801
Gina Valdés, English con Salsa 58
Walt Whitman, I Hear America Singing 949
William Butler Yeats, The Lake Isle of Innisfree 1262
William Butler Yeats, When You Are Old 510

DRAMA

Susan Glaspell, Trifles 88
Lorraine Hansberry, A Raisin in the Sun 376
Henrik Ibsen, A Doll's House 1146
David Ives, Sure Thing 546
Terrence McNally, Andre's Mother 895
William Shakespeare, Othello, the Moor of Venice 560
William Shakespeare, "The Better Part of Valor Is Discretion": Speech from *Henry IV, Part I* 1391
William Shakespeare, "We Happy Few, We Band of Brothers": Speech from *Henry V* 1389
Sophocles, Antigonê 999
Tennessee Williams, The Glass Menagerie 849

ESSAYS AND NONFICTION

James Baldwin, Notes of a Native Son 820
Myrna E. Bein, A Journey Taken with My Son 1380
Raymond Carver, My Father's Life 366
Judith Ortiz Cofer, I Fell in Love, or My Hormones Awakened 537
Joan Didion, On Morality 114
Annie Dillard, An American Childhood 372
Frederick Douglass, Learning to Read and Write 1131
Mohandas Gandhi, Non-Violence—The Greatest Force 1382
bell hooks, Earthbound: On Solid Ground 1291

Mike Ives, Would Hemingway Cry? 542
Ryan Kelly, A Quick Look at Who Is Fighting This War; This Is Not a Game 1375
Martin Luther King Jr., Letter from Birmingham Jail 968
Maxine Hong Kingston, No Name Woman 989
Elisabeth Kübler-Ross, On the Fear of Death 842
Abraham Lincoln, Second Inaugural Address 1373
Kenneth McClane, "Sonny's Blues" Saved My Life 13
John Muir, A Wind-Storm in the Forests 1281
George Orwell, Shooting an Elephant 834
Cynthia Ozick, Lovesickness 532
Paul, "The Greatest of These Is Love": 1 Corinthians 13 531
Richard Rodriguez, "Blaxicans" and Other Reinvented Americans 1141
Sacha Z. Scoblic, Rock Star, Meet Teetotaler 840
Brent Staples, The Runaway Son 358
Wallace Stegner, Wilderness Letter 1286
Amy Tan, Mother Tongue 117
Henry David Thoreau, from Civil Disobedience 981
Leo Tolstoy, from The Kingdom of God Is Within You 1384
Virginia Woolf, What If Shakespeare Had a Sister? 1136

CRITICAL PROSE

W. H. Auden, Iago as a Triumphant Villain 668
Roland Barthes, The Death of the Author 1415
Maud Bodkin, Lucifer in Shakespeare's Othello 669
Richard R. Bozorth, "Tell Me the Truth About Love" 1411
Anthony Burgess, An Asian Culture Looks at Shakespeare 667
Barbara T. Christian, "Everyday Use" and the Black Power Movement 278
Michael Clark, Light and Darkness in "Sonny's Blues" 1398
Brenda O. Daly, An Unfilmable Conclusion: Joyce Carol Oates at the Movies 747
Emily Dickinson, Recognizing Poetry 961
Emily Dickinson, Self-Description 961
Rita Dove and Marilyn Nelson, The Voices in Langston Hughes 1127
Stanley Fish, An Eskimo "A Rose for Emily" 1413
Sandra M. Gilbert and Susan Gubar, The Freedom of Emily Dickinson 965
Daniel Hoffman, The Father-Figure in "The Tell-Tale Heart" 1404
Langston Hughes, The Harlem Renaissance 1124
Langston Hughes, The Negro Artist and the Racial Mountain 1123
Thomas H. Johnson, The Discovery of Emily Dickinson's Manuscripts 963
Brett C. Millier, On Elizabeth Bishop's "One Art" 1400
Joseph Moldenhauer, "To His Coy Mistress" and the Renaissance Tradition 1402
Don Moser, The Pied Piper of Tucson: He Cruised in a Golden Car, Looking for the Action 735
Joyce Carol Oates, "Where Are You Going, Where Have You Been?" and Smooth Talk: Short Story into Film 742
Wilfred Owen, The Pity of War 1370
Camille Paglia, A Reading of William Blake's "London" 1417
Darryl Pinckney, Black Identity in Langston Hughes 1129
Arnold Rampersad, Hughes as an Experimentalist 1125
B. Ruby Rich, Good Girls, Bad Girls: Joyce Chopra's Smooth Talk 745
Kathryn Lee Seidel, The Economics of Zora Neale Hurston's "Sweat" 1408
Elaine Showalter, Quilt as Metaphor in "Everyday Use" 283
Virginia Mason Vaughan, Black and White in Othello 669
Edmond Volpe, Myth in Faulkner's "Barn Burning" 1406
Alice Walker, The Black Woman Writer in America 277
Mary Helen Washington, "Everyday Use" as a Portrait of the Artist 281
Richard Wilbur, The Three Privations of Emily Dickinson 964

TO THE INSTRUCTOR

Our new book, *Literature for Life*, is based on two simple observations. First, the ability to read and write well has a decisive impact on the lives of students. Recent studies have repeatedly shown that students who gain proficiency in reading and writing perform better in school, the job market, and their subsequent careers. As all English teachers know, reading (especially reading literature) has the power to awaken, enlarge, and enhance the imagination—to help individuals visualize their own lives and destinies. This new consciousness can change how people lead their lives. Our second observation, however, is less upbeat—namely, that for a variety of reasons, today's students generally have more difficulty mastering these essential skills. Distracted by a multitude of competing activities, especially in the electronic media, many students have not been able to focus sufficiently on developing their proficiency in reading and writing.

Literature for Life offers a new thematic approach to motivating and guiding students to become active readers and writers. The book stresses the vital connections between their daily lives and their classroom experience. Everything in the book has been designed to be accessible and inviting to students, especially those who may be initially intimidated by literature and composition courses. The book's format is clean, colorful, and friendly. The selections combine familiar favorites with compelling new works—and they have been carefully chosen to reflect not only the teaching experience of the three editors but also of dozens of other practiced instructors.

THE PLAN OF THE BOOK

Literature for Life combines the best features of various approaches to teaching literature and composition.

The book begins with a chapter unlike anything you might have seen in a textbook—a serious and straightforward explanation of how reading and writing will change the student's life for the better. It is hard for many students to understand how courses in literature and composition have much direct benefit to the lives they hope to lead. This innovative chapter speaks directly to that issue. A motivated student is a better student. As busy as you are, we urge you to look over this important and compelling chapter.

The next four chapters provide a comprehensive introduction to reading and understanding fiction, poetry, drama, and essays. There is a concise and comprehensive chapter focused on each genre. The chapters have been designed both for easy reading and quick reference later.

The reading chapters are followed by six detailed chapters on writing about literature and specific genres. The writing chapters take students through the process, step-by-step, from brainstorming ideas through a finished paper. There are sample student reading annotations and brainstorming exercises, as well as 10 sample papers (including a research paper demonstrating how to use MLA documentation).

The heart of the book presents seven thematic chapters. Our key themes are Families, Love, Life's Journeys, The Individual and Society, Personal Identity, Nature and the Environment, and War and Peace. Each of these thematic chapters is divided into smaller clusters that provide instructors with useful and flexible teaching units. Each thematic chapter contains stories, poems, essays, and plays that explore the central subject in interesting and sometimes surprising ways.

Selections begin with a **short author biography,** often illustrated with a **photograph** to personalize the subject and make a human connection between author and reader. **Footnotes** clarify anything that might puzzle the novice reader. **Questions** follow every selection to foster individual exploration as well as classroom discussion. **Writing suggestions** follow every cluster to provide ideas for student papers.

This abundance of material allows instructors enormous flexibility to design the best course for their students and communities.

KEY FEATURES

Literature for Life was created to help readers develop sensitivity to language, culture, and identity, to lead them beyond the boundaries of their own selves, and to see the world through the eyes of others. This book is built on the assumption that great literature can enrich and enlarge the lives it touches. Teaching is a kind of conversation between instructor and student and between reader and text. We try to help keep this conversation fresh by mixing the classic with the new and the familiar with the unexpected. This new volume includes:

- **7 major thematic chapters**—each subdivided into small teachable units—that address real issues in students' lives.
  - Families
  - Love
  - Life's Journey
  - The Individual and Society
  - Personal Identity
  - Nature and the Environment
  - War and Peace
- **A wide variety of popular and provocative stories, poems, plays, essays, and critical prose**—offers traditional favorites with exciting and sometimes surprising contemporary selections.
  - **57 stories**—diverse and compelling stories from authors new and old from around the globe.
  - **134 poems**—great poems, mixing familiar favorites with engaging contemporary work from a wonderful range of poets.
  - **10 plays and scenes**—a rich array of drama from ancient Greek tragedy to Shakespeare to modern work by Lorraine Hansberry and David Ives.
  - **28 essays and nonfiction pieces**—both classic statements and contemporary perspectives on the major themes, with a range of authors from Mohandas Gandhi and Martin Luther King Jr. to Maxine Hong Kingston and Elisabeth Kübler-Ross.
  - **33 critical prose pieces**—to help students think about different approaches to reading, interpreting, and writing about literature.
  - **Over 200 photographs and images**—provide visual information for students as well as humanize the authors they read.

- **7 "Writers in Depth"**—Each of these special units provides a larger selection of works by a single writer, both to allow students to read them in depth and also to provide material for writing assignments.
    - Gwendolyn Brooks
    - Kate Chopin
    - Emily Dickinson
    - Robert Frost
    - Langston Hughes
    - Wilfred Owen
    - William Shakespeare
- **5 "Critical and Cultural Contexts Casebooks" on major authors and literary masterpieces**—provide students a variety of material, including biographies, photographs, critical commentaries, and author statements, to begin an in-depth study of writers and works frequently used for critical analyses or research papers.
    - Alice Walker's "Everyday Use"
    - Joyce Carol Oates's "Where Are You Going, Where Have You Been?"
    - Emily Dickinson's poetry
    - Langston Hughes's poetry
    - William Shakespeare's *Othello*
- ***Trifles* audio production**—Susan Glaspell's classic one-act play is now available in a special audio performance to make the "Elements of Drama" section more exciting and accessible for students (many of whom may never have attended a professional theatrical performance).
- ***Othello*, richly illustrated**—Production photos of every major scene and character make Shakespeare more accessible to students, helping them to visualize the play's action (as well as break up the long blocks of print to make the play's text less intimidating).
    - **"Picturing *Othello*"** photo montage—offers students a pictorial introduction to the play with a visual preview of the key scenes and characters.
- **4 chapters with clear instruction on reading and understanding literature**—outline the elements of fiction, poetry, drama, and essays, and provide instruction, pertinent examples, and key vocabulary. (The book carefully introduces a large range of critical terms that may help students in both reading and writing. When these important words and phrases are first defined, they are printed in **boldface**. If students need a critical term they don't know, they can also check the "Index of Literary Terms" in the back of the book to find the page where the term is discussed.)
- **"Writing about Literature"—6 full writing chapters** provide comprehensive coverage of the composition and research process, in general and by genre. The chapters are written with an eye to clarity and accessibility.
- **Student writing**—10 sample papers by students with annotations, prewriting exercises, and rough drafts provide credible examples of how to write about literature. Includes many samples of student work-in-progress that illustrate the writing process, including a step-by-step presentation of the development of a topic, idea generation, and the formulation of a strong thesis and argument. Samples include:
    - Argument Paper
    - Explication Papers

- Analysis Papers
- Comparison and Contrast Papers
- Response Paper
- Drama Review
- Research Paper

- **MLA guidelines and examples**—provide students source citation requirements from the 7th edition of the *MLA Handbook* and demonstration of correct style in all sample student papers.
- **"Suggestions for Writing" with every cluster of selections**—aid students in generating ideas for paper topics.
- **"Critical Approaches to Literature" with 10 prose selections**—provides depth and flexibility for instructors who prefer to incorporate literary theory and criticism into their introductory courses. Includes an example excerpt from each major critical school, carefully chosen both to illustrate the major theoretical approaches and to be accessible to beginning students, focusing on literary works found in the book.
- **Glossary of Literary Terms**—Over 250 terms defined, including those highlighted in boldface throughout the text as well as other important terms. Provides clear and accurate definitions, often with cross-references to related terms.
- **Accessible, easy-to-use format**—section titles, subtitles, and color-coding help web-oriented students navigate easily from topic to topic in and between chapters.

TEXTS AND DATES

Every effort has been made to supply each selection in its most accurate text and (where necessary) in a lively, faithful translation. For the reader who wishes to know when a work was written, at the right of each title appears the date of its first publication in book form. Parentheses around a date indicate the work's date of composition or first magazine publication, given when it was composed much earlier than when it was first published in book form.

RESOURCES FOR STUDENTS AND INSTRUCTORS

FOR STUDENTS

MyLiteratureLab.com

MyLiteratureLab is a dynamic website that provides a wealth of resources geared to meet the diverse teaching and learning needs of today's instructors and students. It adds a new dimension to the study of literature with Longman Lectures—evocative, richly illustrated audio readings along with advice on how to read, interpret, and write about literary works from our roster of Longman authors (including X. J. Kennedy). This powerful program also features an eAnthology with two hundred additional selections, feature-length films from Films for the Humanities and Sciences, a composing space with a "Writer's Toolkit," Interactive Readings with clickable prompts, "Writers on Writing" (video interviews with distinguished authors that inspire students to explore their creativity), sample student papers, Literature Timelines, Avoiding Plagiarism, and more.

Audio Production of Trifles

So many students today have limited experience attending live theater that we felt it would be useful to offer a complete audio version of our opening play, Susan Glaspell's *Trifles*, which we use to teach the elements of drama. The audio version was produced especially for *Literature* by the celebrated L.A. Theatre Works for students to download in *MyLiteratureLab*. It includes an introduction and commentary by Dana Gioia.

Handbook of Literary Terms

Handbook of Literary Terms by X. J. Kennedy, Dana Gioia, and Mark Bauerlein is a user-friendly primer of over 350 critical terms brought to life with literary examples, pronunciation guides, and scholarly yet accessible explanations. Aimed at undergraduates getting their first taste of serious literary study, the volume will help students engage with the humanities canon and become critical readers and writers ready to experience the insights and joys of great fiction, poetry, and drama.

Responding to Literature: A Writer's Journal

This journal provides students with their own personal space for writing and is available at no additional cost when packaged with this anthology. Helpful writing prompts for responding to fiction, poetry, and drama are also included.

Evaluating Plays on Film and Video

This guide walks students through the process of analyzing and writing about plays on film, whether in a short review or longer essay. It covers each stage of the process from preparing and analyzing material through writing the piece. The four appendixes include writing and editing tips and a glossary of film terms. The final section of the guide offers worksheets to help students organize their notes and thoughts before they begin writing.

Evaluating a Performance

Perfect for students assigned to review a local production, this supplement offers students a convenient place to record their evaluations and is available at no additional cost when packaged with this anthology. Useful tips and suggestions of things to consider when evaluating a production are included.

What Every Student Should Know About Reading a Novel

This brief booklet provides students with helpful approaches to reading a novel. Suggestions for how to read, as well as accessible coverage of the structure and elements of a novel give students the necessary tools they need to read novels with confidence. Students are also introduced to reading a novel through the lens of cultural contexts. Finally, ideas and tips on how to write about novels are also provided.

FOR INSTRUCTORS

Instructor's Manual

A separate *Instructor's Manual* written expressly for *Literature for Life* is available to instructors. If you have not seen our *Instructor's Manual*, don't prejudge it. We actually write most of the manual ourselves, and we work hard to make it as interesting, lively, and informed as the parent text. It offers commentary and teaching ideas for every selection in the book. It also contains additional commentary, debate, qualifications, and information—including scores of classroom ideas—from over 100 teachers and authors.

Penguin Discount Paperback Program

In cooperation with Penguin Group USA, Pearson is proud to offer a variety of Penguin paperbacks, such as Tennessee Williams's *A Streetcar Named Desire*, George Orwell's *Animal Farm*, and Charlotte Brontë's *Jane Eyre*, at a significant discount—almost sixty percent off the retail price—when packaged with any Pearson title. To review the list of titles available, visit the Pearson Penguin Group USA website at *www.pearsonhighered.com/penguin*.

Video Program

For qualified adopters, an impressive selection of videos is available to enrich students' experience of literature. The videos include selections from William Shakespeare, Sylvia Plath, Ezra Pound, Alice Walker, and many more. Contact your Pearson sales representative to see if you qualify.

The Longman Electronic Testbank for Literature

This electronic testbank features various objective questions on major works of fiction, short fiction, poetry, and drama. Instructors simply choose questions from the testbank, then print out the completed test for distribution. It is available as a download from the Instructor Resource Center located at *www.pearsonhighered.com*.

Teaching Literature Online

Concise and practical, *Teaching Literature Online* provides instructors with strategies and advice for incorporating elements of technology into the literature classroom. Offering a range of information and examples, this manual provides ideas and activities for enhancing literature courses with the help of technology.

CONTACT US

For examination copies of any of our books or information about our programs, contact your Pearson sales representative, or write to Literature Marketing Manager, Pearson, 51 Madison Avenue, New York, NY 10010. For examination copies only, call (800) 922-0579. Go to: *http://www.pearsonhighered.com* to order an examination copy online, or send an e-mail to: *exam.copies@pearsonhighered.com*.

THANKS

The collaboration necessary to create this new book goes far beyond the partnership of its three editors. We have been guided in our effort to shape this innovative book by a number of instructors who have viewed early versions of these chapters.

Special thanks for advice and feedback in development of *Literature for Life* go to:

Jo Ann Bamdas, *Palm Beach State College*
Mary M. Evans, *Hudson Valley Community College*
Africa Fine, *Palm Beach State College*
Joseph Haske, *South Texas College–Pecan*
Yvonne Jocks, *Tarrant County College*
Jonathan T. Jones, *South Texas College–Pecan*
Jordine Logan, *Montclair State University*
Erin Radcliffe, *Central New Mexico Community College*
Constance Sabo-Risley, *University of the Incarnate Word*
Vicki J. Sapp, *Tarrant County College*
Ann C. Spurlock, *Mississippi State University*
Jeniffer Strong, *Central New Mexico Community College*
Rebecca McLauchlin Whitten, *Mississippi State University*

Thanks also to our friends and colleagues including Michael Palma, who scrupulously fact-checked and proofread this book, while also helping to create lively and useful discussion questions, biographical notes, and contributing to the *Instructor's Manual* entries.

On the publisher's staff, Joseph Terry, Katharine Glynn, Kelly Carroll, and Joyce Nilsen made many contributions to the development of this new book. Savoula Amanatidis and Lois Lombardo heroically went beyond the call of duty almost daily, directing the complex job of production of this book from the manuscript to the final printed form. Cathy Harlem ably coordinated the schedule and proofs. Vernon Nahrgang copyedited the new book. Jenn Kennett handled the difficult job of permissions. Rona Tuccillo and Nancy Tobin managed the research and inclusion of photographs. Donna Campion and Dianne Hall handled the development and production of the *Instructor's Manual*. We are grateful to each one of them for their part in creating *Literature for Life*.

Mary Gioia was involved in every stage of planning, editing, and execution. Not only could the book not have been done without her capable hand and careful eye, but her expert guidance made every chapter better.

Past debts that can never be repaid are outstanding to Dorothy M. Kennedy.

X. J. K., D. G., AND N. R.

ABOUT THE AUTHORS

X. J. KENNEDY after graduation from Seton Hall and Columbia, became a journalist second class in the Navy ("Actually, I was pretty eighth class"). His poems, some published in the *New Yorker*, were first collected in *Nude Descending a Staircase* (1961). Since then he has published seven more collections, including a volume of new and selected poems in 2007, several widely adopted literature and writing textbooks, and seventeen books for children, including two novels. He has taught at Michigan, North Carolina (Greensboro), California (Irvine), Wellesley, Tufts, and Leeds. Cited in *Bartlett's Familiar Quotations* and reprinted in some 200 anthologies, his verse has brought him a Guggenheim fellowship, a Lamont Award, a *Los Angeles Times* Book Prize, an award from the American Academy and Institute of Arts and Letters, an Aiken-Taylor prize, and the Award for Poetry for Children from the National Council of Teachers of English.

DANA GIOIA is a poet, critic, and teacher. Born in Los Angeles of Italian and Mexican ancestry, he attended Stanford and Harvard before taking a detour into business. ("Not many poets have a Stanford M.B.A., thank goodness!") After years of writing and reading late in the evenings after work, he quit a vice presidency to write and teach. He has published four collections of poetry, *Daily Horoscope* (1986), *The Gods of Winter* (1991), *Interrogations at Noon* (2001), which won the American Book Award, and *Pity the Beautiful* (2012); and three critical volumes, including *Can Poetry Matter?* (1992), an influential study of poetry's place in contemporary America. Gioia has taught at Johns Hopkins, Sarah Lawrence, Wesleyan (Connecticut), Mercer, and Colorado College. From 2003–2009 he served as the Chairman of the National Endowment for the Arts. At the NEA he created the largest literary programs in federal history, including Shakespeare in American Communities and Poetry Out Loud, the national high school poetry recitation contest. He also led the campaign to restore active literary reading by creating The Big Read, which helped reverse a quarter century of decline in U. S. reading. He is currently the Judge Widney Professor of Poetry and Public Culture at the University of Southern California.

(The surname Gioia is pronounced JOY-A. As some of you may have already guessed, Gioia is the Italian word for joy.)

NINA REVOYR was born in Tokyo to a Japanese mother and white American father, and raised in Tokyo, Wisconsin, and Los Angeles. After her dream of becoming a pro basketball player faltered in college ("The usual story—I was too short to be a forward, too slow to be a guard"), she decided to focus on writing. She is the author of four prize-winning novels, *The Necessary Hunger* (1997), *Southland* (2003), *The Age of Dreaming* (2008), and *Wingshooters*. *Wingshooters*, published in 2011, won an Indie Booksellers' Choice Award and was one of *O: Oprah Magazine's* "Books to Watch For." She has taught at a number of colleges, including Cornell, Occidental, and Pitzer, and is also vice president of a non-profit children's service organization. She lives in Los Angeles, California, with her spouse, two rowdy dogs, and a pair of bossy cats.

Literature for Life

John Updike

READING AND THINKING ABOUT LITERATURE

1 LITERATURE AND LIFE

Read in order to live.
— GUSTAVE FLAUBERT

If you are reading this book, you are probably taking a college-level composition class or an introductory course in literature. You've probably read some poetry and short stories in high school English classes, or maybe this is the first time you have ever been asked to do any serious literary reading. Perhaps you are returning to school after raising a family or serving in the military, and it's been a while since you've been in a classroom. It could be that you're already a fan of a particular writer, or that you have a taste for poetry or fiction. But whether or not you enjoy reading, you may wonder what you're doing here. You may ask, What's the point of reading fiction or poetry, plays or essays, when what I'm *really* interested in is getting a good job? Why spend time trying to figure out some hundred-year-old poem when I'm studying to be a nurse or an engineer? Why should I puzzle through a story that has no practical application in the real world? Why should I care about literature at all?

Most English teachers will tell you about the intangible benefits of literature—how reading will make you a better, smarter, more well-rounded person. Many will also say that learning to analyze and write about literature will help you with your work in other classes. This last claim probably seems reasonable to you. It's fairly easy to see how writing for a composition class might help improve your writing for other courses. The skills needed to analyze a text, organize information, and make persuasive arguments are clearly transferable to other subjects. But, you might still ask, What good will studying literature and writing do me in "the real world"?

The answer to this question may surprise you. The three editors of this book are all working writers and teachers, but we have also spent many years in a surprisingly wide range of non-academic jobs—in business, government, media, and nonprofit organizations. (One of us even served a stint in the U.S. Navy.) These experiences have given us a different perspective on the relationship between studying literature and success in "the real world." We have learned that reading and writing well can give you a measurable advantage. We also believe that your ability to interpret and write about literature will enhance your competitiveness in the job market. If you can think and communicate with clarity and insight, those skills will make a difference to your future. In fact, such skills are relevant no matter what field you enter. Finally, we believe that studying literature can influence your personal development outside of school and career. Reading will change how you understand and engage with the world, and ultimately it will enhance the quality of your life.

That is *what* we believe. Now let us tell you *why*.

WHY ARE YOU IN THIS COURSE?

Let's be honest. The main reason you are in this course is most likely that it's mandatory—one of the requirements you need to satisfy in order to earn a degree. Your college or university believes you need to improve your reading and writing skills, especially your ability to read critically and to express your ideas clearly in words. It's easy to see why building these skills can be important to your short-term academic success. If you accomplish nothing else in this course, such improvement would be reason enough to take your work here seriously. But there are additional possibilities you should consider.

When you study literature and writing, you develop a bundle of skills. Some of them are surprisingly practical, others are almost spiritual. If you resist the reading and writing assignments in this course, if you do only the minimal work, you will—in direct proportion to your attitude and effort—learn only the minimal amount. But if you approach the course as an opportunity to awaken and develop your personal talents, you may be surprised by what you begin to accomplish. This course has the potential to be a life-changer.

WHY STUDY LITERATURE AND WRITING?

Reading literary texts—stories, poems, plays, and essays—develops certain skills and capabilities that studying scientific or technical texts generally does not. Three skills in particular seem to be developed by literary reading: qualitative judgment, empathy, and imagination. Each of them helps you do better in life and in the workplace.

Most poems, plays, and stories have no single meaning or neat conclusion. They present rich and complex situations, characters, settings, and conflicts—just as life does. In our daily lives we find a great mix of events and experiences that we move through, always trying to figure out what is important and what is not. Reading allows us to develop our qualitative judgment—which is to say, our ability to look at complex or ambiguous situations and make reliable judgments. Writing a well-reasoned analysis of a story or poem develops this capability, which isn't unlike the process by which civic leaders decide where to locate a new school or studio executives choose which screenplay to film. There is rarely a single right or wrong quantitative answer.

Qualitative reasoning requires you to consider multiple options, each of which may offer distinct advantages. Most important decisions—in life, business, art, and politics—are qualitative. There is no mathematical formula for deciding where you should live, what career you should choose, whom you should marry (or not marry). These are complex qualitative decisions that require the judgment of many elements, some of them intangible.

People are not entirely rational or consistent animals. How they make important decisions is often unclear. Sometimes they do unpredictably silly, self-destructive, or remarkable things. How can we understand or explain the mysteries of human behavior? In a recent column in the *New York Times*, David Brooks discussed the importance of literature and the humanities in helping students to understand the more mysterious human impulses, which he grouped together and named "The Big Shaggy." According to Brooks, whenever we see people behaving in a way that seems inexplicably foolish (having risky affairs, betting everything on the stock market) or unbelievably admirable (saving someone's life, showing tremendous drive or grace on the playing field), we are witnessing The Big Shaggy at work. Brooks writes:

> Technical knowledge stops at the outer edge. If you spend your life riding the links of the Internet, you probably won't get too far into The Big Shaggy . . . because the fast, effortless prose of blogging (and journalism) lacks the heft to get you deep below.
>
> But over the centuries, there have been rare and strange people who possessed the skill of taking the upheavals of thought that emanate from The Big Shaggy and representing them in the form of story, music, myth, painting, liturgy, architecture, sculpture, landscape and speech. These men and women developed languages that help us understand these yearnings and also educate and mold them.[1]

You won't learn about such "shaggy" knowledge in courses in economics, chemistry, business, or math. But understanding the form and language of emotions is necessary knowledge in life. Developing the qualitative judgment to interpret them accurately is one of the benefits of studying literature. As Brooks says at the end of his essay, "If you're dumb about The Big Shaggy, you'll probably get eaten by it."

EMPATHY AND IMAGINATION

Reading literature also develops empathy. When you read a literary work, it usually describes the lives or experiences of others, and these sustained meditations on the imaginary lives of other people—often both their outer and inner lives—make us realize how rich and complex other people are. The experience of reading also breaks down some easy stereotypes we consciously or unconsciously carry. No one reading Tim O'Brien's powerful depiction of an army platoon in the Vietnam War, "The Things They Carried," will ever think all American soldiers are alike. Nor will anyone studying Alice Walker's "Everyday Use" assume that all African American women have identical personalities and attitudes. Literature helps us recognize and appreciate the vibrant diversity of humanity. A good story, poem, essay, or play also allows us to see the world through another person's point of view.

As the writer Amy Tan said in an interview, reading provided her:

[1]"History for Dollars," *New York Times*, 7 June 2010, A27.

with the notion that I could find an ending that was different from what was happening to me at the time. When you read about the lives of other people, people of different circumstances or similar circumstances, you are part of their lives for that moment. You inhabit their lives and you feel what they're feeling and this is compassion.[2]

This compassion, this attempt at understanding, is critical to our humanity. Literature provides a way for a man to comprehend what it's like to be a woman, for a white person to feel what it's like to be a person of color, for a city kid to imagine what it's like to live in the country—and vice versa. Why is this important? It's important because when we see the world from someone else's point of view—even for a moment—it can affect the decisions we make, how we relate to other people, and how we live in the world. As Atticus Finch says in *To Kill a Mockingbird*, "You never really understand a person until you consider things from his point of view—until you climb into his skin and walk around in it." When we get into trouble—in our families, in our relationships, at school or at work, or even in issues facing our country—it's often at least partly because we are unable or unwilling to consider someone else's point of view.

By helping us understand how others think and feel, empathy is an invaluable skill in any profession. Doctors and nurses require empathy to treat their patients successfully. A manager needs empathy to direct and motivate employees. A sales person needs empathy to close a deal. Actors use empathy to become the characters they portray. Most leaders have great empathetic powers because they often communicate with others emotionally more than intellectually. Empathy is equally important in personal relationships—in romance, friendship, and family life. We need to feel what others feel, especially the people we care about, in order to sustain and nourish important human bonds. We can't trust people to tell us everything. People hold things back. Empathy helps us understand both what is said and what isn't said.

Finally, reading develops our imagination. Reading is not a passive activity. It requires focused attention, memory, and an active imagination. The reader needs to visualize the people, actions, and places in the text. Because a movie or TV program shows us every detail in a narrative—the background music even dictates the mood—we can become passive observers. Reading, however, requires active participation. It increases our attention span and strengthens our imagination. (No wonder reading burns more calories than watching television.) We learn to visualize new places and situations. Reading also develops the ability to assimilate large amounts of detail and description without losing our line of thought. These are not insignificant mental skills. Our imagination enables us to visualize the possibilities of the future. It also leads to creative problem solving. For these reasons, regular readers develop mental and imaginative powers that help them in other aspects of life. As Joseph Addison observed, "Reading is to the mind what exercise is to the body."

GETTING A JOB

When you're a college student, it seems that everyone keeps asking you about jobs. What sort of career do you want? Do you have a particular job in mind? Parents and

---

[2]"Talking with Amy Tan: Dana Gioia Interviews Amy Tan," *Literature: An Introduction to Fiction, Poetry, Drama, and Writing*, ed. X. J. Kennedy and Dana Gioia, 12th ed. (New York: Pearson: 2013), 3.

family members quiz you repeatedly, often with looks of deep concern on their faces. Friends and fellow students ask about your plans. All these questions can create a sense of anxiety in students who, quite rightly, often don't know exactly what line of work they want to pursue and plan to wait until graduation to see what opportunities present themselves. What? No plans! Some people, especially parents, find this wait-and-see attitude outrageous, yet there is often a certain wisdom in delay.

Some students very sensibly focus on a specific job that requires technical knowledge (and sometimes professional certification). Careers like respiratory therapist, court reporter, dental hygienist, and sign-language interpreter, all require specific job skills that can be learned in school. A degree often leads to quick employment (though it may also lock the new hire into a fairly narrow career with limited prospects for advancement). Most jobs, however, do not require people with specific technical knowledge, but rather, people with broad and varied skills. Managers know that their new hires will face a variety of problems and opportunities in the workplace and that as these employees advance in their careers, they may need additional skills.

When managers are asked what skills they most need in new employees, they list qualities such as work ethic, teamwork, problem solving, reading ability, oral communication, and written communication. These are not narrow technical skills, but broad talents. Some of them, especially written communication, reading ability, oral communication, and problem solving, are talents you develop in literature and writing classes.

Writing and reading well can give you a competitive advantage in the job market. Not only do employers rate writing and reading as the most important basic skills for both two-year and four-year college graduates, they also find the inability to write well the top skill deficiency among job applicants at all educational levels. Almost half (47 percent) of community college grads lack the necessary skills in writing. If you can demonstrate proficiency in writing, you will immediately distinguish yourself from many other job applicants.

How have the editors of this book—two poets and a novelist—earned the right to have an opinion on how people get jobs? Because, in our positions in the corporate, government, and nonprofit sectors, we have looked at thousands of resumes, interviewed hundreds of people, and hired and supervised scores of employees. We know *from our own work experience* how important reading and writing skills are, because we ourselves have hired and promoted employees on the basis of those skills. And those skills are being developed and honed in courses like the one you're now taking.

CAREER GROWTH

If writing and reading well can help you get a job, they will also earn you promotion and advancement. When reading ability is measured against job status, it is shockingly clear how much better skilled readers do in their careers. Proficient readers earn management and advanced professional jobs at nearly four times the rate of individuals with only basic skills, and they make dramatically more money. Proficient readers are three times more likely than basic readers to have a high-paying job (more than $100,000 per year). While money is not the only (or even the best) measure of academic achievement or job satisfaction, the clear correlation between reading ability and financial success in the workplace indicates that reading well is a highly practical job skill.

The connections between reading literature and both professional and personal success are now well documented. According to the National Endowment for the Arts' landmark report, *To Read or Not To Read: A Question of National Consequence*, multiple studies have demonstrated that "poor reading skills correlate heavily with lack of employment, lower wages, and fewer opportunities for advancement." Likewise, U.S. Department of Education studies have noted that 70 percent of adults with poor reading skills feel that this factor has limited their job opportunities. Many of them will face lifelong employment issues.

In *To Read or Not To Read*, the NEA compiled over forty large and reliable national studies. Their combined conclusions were clear and consistent:

> All of the data suggest how powerfully reading transforms the lives of individuals—whatever their social circumstances. Regular reading not only boosts the likelihood of an individual's academic and economic success . . . but it also seems to awaken a person's social and civic sense. . . . The cold statistics confirm something that most readers know but have mostly been reluctant to declare as fact—books change lives for the better.[3]

The correlation between reading, writing, and job success was addressed by Richard Anderson, CEO of Delta Air Lines, in an interview in the *New York Times*:

> More and more, the ability to speak well and write is important. . . . Writing is not something that is taught as strongly as it should be in the educational curriculum. . . . I think this communication point is getting more and more important. People really have to be able to handle the written and spoken word. And when I say written word, I don't mean PowerPoints. I don't think PowerPoints help people think as clearly as they should because you don't have to have a complete thought in place. You can just put a phrase with a bullet point in front of it. And it doesn't have a subject, a verb, and an object, so you aren't expressing complete thoughts.[4]

READING AND WRITING ARE CRITICAL SKILLS

What's striking about Richard Anderson's comments is that he works in the airline industry, a field that is about as far from the study of literature as you can get. Yet he clearly states that good writing and communication skills are important to getting a job and advancing in a career.

We agree. We believe that these skills are essential to the work of people in many different occupations:

- a scholar who writes academic papers
- a doctor who writes research reports
- a medical technician who summarizes test findings
- a public relations executive who is trying to create a new "brand"
- a lawyer who writes legal briefs

---

[3] *To Read or Not To Read: A Question of National Consequence*, Research Report #47 (Washington: NEA, Nov. 2007), 6.

[4] Adam Bryant, "He Wants Subjects, Verbs and Objects," *New York Times*, 26 April 2009, BU2.

- a business owner who writes advertising copy
- a scientist who writes articles for a professional journal
- a nonprofit employee who writes grant proposals
- a real estate developer who describes a project to obtain financing
- a manager who writes business reports
- a government employee or political aide who writes public policy briefings
- an administrative assistant who writes letters and memos
- an outdoors adventure company owner who writes copy for a website or an advertisement

Supreme Court Justice John Paul Stevens once remarked that the best preparation for law school is to study poetry. Why? George D. Gopen, an English professor with a law degree, says it may be because "no other discipline so closely replicates the central question asked in the study of legal thinking: Here is a text; in how many ways can it have meaning?" Another Supreme Court Justice, Sandra Day O'Connor, was inspired to become a lawyer because of a fictional character, Atticus Finch, the hero and moral compass of Harper Lee's *To Kill a Mockingbird*. Reading that novel changed O'Connor's life—with historic consequences.

YOU MAY HAVE MORE THAN ONE CAREER

There is a good chance that you will switch jobs or even careers at some point in your life. A profession you thought you would enjoy may prove unsatisfying. Some interesting new opportunity may present itself. Or the industry in which you work may begin to change or fail. After World War II, Detroit was the fourth-largest city in the United States and the center of the world automotive trade. Today the city has shrunk to less than half its former size, and many thousands of jobs have vanished—not just on the production lines but also in finance, marketing, engineering, public relations, and design. Other once huge American industries such as railroads, steel, textiles, and fishing have also declined in the global marketplace—taking millions of jobs with them.

In a perpetually changing society, it may be risky to lock yourself into one career track, refusing to consider any other. "We are moving," writes John Naisbitt in *Megatrends*, a study of our changing society, "from the specialist, soon obsolete, to the generalist who can adapt." Perhaps the greatest opportunity in your future lies in a career that has yet to be invented. If you do change your career at some point, you will be like most people. According to a U.S. Bureau of Labor Statistics survey conducted in September 2010, the average American holds over eleven jobs between the ages of 18 and 44—often completely changing his or her core occupation. If you have to make such a change, basic writing and reading skills—and a knowledge of humanity—may be your most valuable credentials.

To show the variety of opportunities open to those who study literature, here's a list of fifty famous and successful Americans who were English majors. We present the list mostly for fun, but we also hope it will destroy any misconception that studying literature is a narrow and impractical preparation for success in life.

FIFTY FAMOUS ENGLISH MAJORS

(Who aren't teachers or novelists)

Learning to read and write effectively creates a broad set of skills that can be used in countless professions. It is no surprise to learn that novelists or poets, such as Stephen King, Kay Ryan, and Amy Tan, majored in English, but one finds English majors in all sorts of places, from Wall Street and the Supreme Court to Hollywood and even outer space. Here is a short list of American leaders and celebrities who majored in English.

GOVERNMENT AND LAW

Michael Astrue, Commissioner of Social Security Administration
Carol Browner, Head of Environmental Protection Agency
Mario Cuomo, Governor of New York
Henry Paulson, U.S. Secretary of the Treasury
Donald Regan, U.S. Secretary of the Treasury, White House Chief of Staff under Ronald Reagan
John Paul Stevens, Supreme Court Justice
Clarence Thomas, Supreme Court Justice
Pete Wilson, Governor of California

BUSINESS AND FINANCE

John Barr, Investment Banking CEO, President of Poetry Foundation
Michael Eisner, CEO of Walt Disney Company
Kathryn Fuller, Chair of Ford Foundation, CEO of World Wildlife Fund
Herb Scannell, President of BBC Worldwide, President of Nickelodeon
Grant Tinker, CEO of NBC
Brandon Tartikoff, TV Producer, Head of NBC Entertainment

FILM PRODUCERS AND DIRECTORS

James Cameron, Director, Producer; *Avatar, Titanic*
David Cronenberg, Director, Producer; *Fly, A History of Violence*
Christopher Nolan, Director, Producer; *Memento, The Dark Knight*
Martin Scorsese, Academy Award-Winning Director; *Goodfellas, The Departed*
Steven Spielberg, Academy Award-Winning Director; *Schindler's List, Jaws*

JOURNALISM AND HUMOR

Russell Baker, Pulitzer Prize-Winning Columnist
Dave Barry, Humorist

Joy Behar, Comedian, Writer, Talk Show Host
Maureen Dowd, Columnist, Presidential Speech Writer
Conan O'Brien, Comedian, Talk Show Host
Richard Rodriguez, Essayist, NPR Commentator
Diane Sawyer, Broadcast Journalist
Barbara Walters, Broadcast Journalist
Bob Woodward, Watergate-Busting Investigative Journalist

SINGERS AND SONGWRITERS

Amerie
Don Henley
Chris Isaak
Kris Kristofferson
Paul Simon
Sting

ACTORS

Alan Alda
Matt Damon
Vin Diesel
David Duchovny
Harrison Ford
Jodie Foster
James Franco
Tommy Lee Jones
Emma Thompson
Sigourney Weaver
Reese Witherspoon
Renée Zellweger

OTHER FIELDS

A. Bartlett Giamatti, President of Yale University, Commissioner of Baseball
Sally Ride, Astronaut and Physicist, First American Woman in Space
Morty Schottenheimer, NFL Coach
Harold Varmus, Nobel Prize-Winner in Medicine

ARE YOU PREPARED?

You may already be a capable reader and a fine writer, but many students have not yet developed these skills. Young people today spend less time reading, and—not surprisingly—they read less well. Only about one-third of high school seniors now read at a "proficiency" level—a substantial decrease from twenty years ago. They need additional training in courses like the one in which you have enrolled—and they need to read more.

Not only educators think this a problem. Business and government employers agree. Not reading well and not writing well now top the list of problems that employers face when seeking job candidates. "Written communication" has become the single largest "skill deficiency" among both two-year and four-year college graduates. Nearly half (47%) of two-year college graduates fail to demonstrate the writing skills they need to find employment.

Deficiency in Written Communication
(Percentage of Job Seekers Who Lack the Skill)

High School Grads	Two-Year College Grads	Four-Year College Grads
81%	47%	28%

Source: Conference Board, 2006

Reading is a cumulative skill—like playing a sport or a musical instrument, the more you practice, the better you get. Work on such cumulative skills every day, and you will achieve first an easy competence and eventually a mastery. If you don't practice, all your natural talent will remain undeveloped. The reason you are in this class is to develop your talents. Don't miss the extraordinary ways in which reading and writing accomplish that transformation. You may be surprised by the results. As the novelist David Foster Wallace said about his discovery of writing and literature, "It was sorta like being an athlete and using only the left side of your body, and then finding a game where you could use your whole body."

Are you currently using your whole self—your body, mind, imagination, and life experience—in your life and work?

LITERATURE FOR LIFE

You may by now be convinced that the study of literature will help you in your job or career. But how, you might ask, does literature help you with life?

As it turns out, the reasons are related. If you are skilled at determining meaning, if you can analyze complex ideas, if you can tell the difference between what something seems to say and what it really says, and if you can clearly and logically state your opinions, then those skills are applicable not only to your studies or your job; they are also relevant to your life. Reading literature can directly influence how you understand and respond to the larger world and to your own personal experience. This, in turn, can help you better manage your life and even encourage you to become a more engaged and active citizen.

How can literature do this? In at least three ways. First, when you see how other people manage (or bungle) their lives, it can help you reflect on your own life. You may identify with the characters, or at least see something in their situations that parallels something in yours. But it's often easier to understand our own experiences when we see them through the comforting, distancing lens of another person—or a fictional character.

Consider this short essay by poet and Cornell professor Kenneth McClane. McClane lost a brother whom he loved but couldn't connect with—an experience that James Baldwin's story "Sonny's Blues" helped him understand.

Kenneth McClane (b. 1951)

"Sonny's Blues" Saved My Life   1994

"Sonny's Blues" saved my life, and I am not being hyperbolic. In 1982, my brother Paul killed himself. He was an alcoholic, a brilliant jazz drummer, a tough, truculent kid, and an inspiration to his older brother, who, although not always understanding *who* Paul was, knew who Paul was not—and that was someone who was scared, timid, or obsequious. Paul did not talk much. If anything, he hated where we lived in Harlem; more precisely, he hated *how* we lived; and no one, in all my memory, ever made my brother cower. Life would lead him to more and more improbable scenarios—at first he was a college student, then a drifter, and all too soon he was on to drugs and alcohol. And yet Paul was strangely gentle and circumspect: his many girlfriends loved his characteristic good cheer—they knew him to be in their corner, and he had that ability (which is always the provender of the outwardly giving) to love those outside his immediate environs while dismissing those at his feet. If Paul was remote to his family, we were similarly distant. And yet he loved us and we him: one could glimpse it in the messiness of our interactions, the buoyancy which too often became icy. I vividly recall the many times when he walked up to his room, closed the door, and played his drums into the next morning, finally descending to have a bowl of cereal, sometimes providing a slight nod to one of us—and then, always returning to *that* room and its privacy. Paul would go to his drums, as he would travel through Harlem, with a saucy, ragged coolness. Those of you who know Baldwin's Sonny know my brother Paul.

Two years Paul's senior, I was, in every way, his absolute opposite. Where he was fearless and an inveterate street-blood, I was cautious, frightened, and retiring. Sometimes, he would push me to go out and I would beg off, suggesting that I wanted to see a movie or read a book. It was a lie, and Paul knew it. As he once said, half jokingly, "You live by not living."

When I began to teach at Cornell, Paul would often call me. We rarely talked about anything serious: Paul would hold court; I would pretend to be more in touch with life than I really was; the whole thing was rather comical. Then, one Friday, I received a call from my father telling me that Paul was dying. It was a surreal conversation, my father understandably uncontrollable, his son lying in a coma, his older son, hardly believing the inevitable: *Your brother is going to die.* Paul was in a New York hospital. I had best come immediately.

As luck would have it, I had been teaching summer school, and a student had suggested that we read James Baldwin's "Sonny's Blues" for our next class. Needing something to do and feigning to be the dutiful teacher, I read Baldwin's story on the plane ride to the hospital. It was a gift. The story involves an older unnamed man and his young brother, Sonny, who is a jazz pianist and a heroin addict. The older brother is *safe*—that is, he has a job and a wonderful wife and has, at least temporarily, made peace with his existence. He is not rich, nor has he been able to truly escape Harlem—where he lives and where "dangers loom everywhere"—but he is a teacher. The younger brother, however, is menaced by his need to make life bearable.

The story, of course, is about much more, including love and how human beings cannot protect anyone, the reality that "sorrow never gets stopped," and the inexorable fact that the best among us may not survive—that life, sadly, often takes those whose dreams are greatest, whose voices are most needed. As the mother tells the far too cocky older brother when he protests that she needn't worry about Sonny, "It ain't only the bad ones, nor yet the dumb ones that gets sucked under." The older brother, at this early narrative moment, does not understand his mother; he is too caught in his own needful simplicity; reality is simply too costly. Yet as the story reminds, life is not interested in one's comfort, and the darkness—the terrors inside and outside—looms just above one's head.

"Sonny's Blues" saved my life. When my brother died, I felt terribly guilty. To my thinking I had not done all I could: I hadn't listened with enough passion; I had been too self-concerned, too self-infested. And yet the story admonishes that there is no ultimate safety, that a brother or a loved one may die (no matter what one does), and that, in the mother's wondrous and provident words, "You may not be able to stop nothing from happening. But you got to let him know you's *there*."

However tentatively and inappropriately, I did try to be my brother's witness. That I ultimately failed is certainly true: Paul is dead. But I am, at this hour, at this writing, *listening* to Sonny. *Deep water and drowning are not the same thing*. And yet they can be. And one can fall even further, farther. Baldwin does not lie about the landscape of suffering. Baldwin, quite simply, does not lie.

Finding a character with whom we identify provides comfort and clarity as we try to make sense of events in our own lives. But a second way that literature can help us understand life is by doing just the opposite—by exposing us to people with whom we *don't* seem to have much in common. And, yet a third way that literature helps us understand life is by putting us in touch with the mysterious, intangible parts of the human experience that can't be explained through other methods. Many fields of study, including psychology, the social sciences, political science, and anthropology, try to categorize and define human behavior. But the mysterious forces that drive people to do what they do cannot reliably be captured in charts and logic models. People feel and act on passions, motivations, impulses, and needs that cannot always be explained, but that *can* be depicted, and are best done so through literature and the arts.

THE VALUE OF LITERATURE

Finally, let us make a case for the value of literature on its own terms. Yes, the study of literature can help you with everything from school success to work and career, and to understanding yourself and your loved ones (and even your enemies). But the editors of this book also believe—we are writers, after all—that literature has an intrinsic value in itself. Literature—the art of words—can make you much more attuned to the particulars of language, including the language of emotions, actions, and ideas. We've already explained how attention to language is important for school and career, but it's also important for its own sake. Literature teaches through giving pleasure. Beautiful writing sings like music, soars like birds and athletes, and leaves a lasting, thought-provoking effect like that of visiting a new place. Learning to read and appreciate literature gives you access to that revelatory beauty—which can be as satisfying as a rock song, as exhilarating as a basketball game, as calming as a beach sunset.

Literature also fulfills our fundamental need for stories. Human beings love stories, and we make them everywhere—in movies, TV shows, songs, even in video games. We like to have our disorderly experiences organized into narratives. We want stories of good and evil, of love, of family, of triumph over adversity. Stories make us feel part of a larger human community, the community of alert and curious people. And great literature brings us news of the world. We don't mean "news" here in the literal sense. What you read in the paper or on the Internet is only the "what" of a story; literature helps illuminate the "why" and the "how." Literature gives us access to the thoughts and feelings and motivations of people; it gives us the story behind the story. Knowing those deeper stories clarifies and enlarges the meaning of our own lives.

BY WAY OF AN ENDING

You now have a rare opportunity to improve your odds of future success and personal fulfillment. The literature and writing course that you are taking (even if only because you had no choice) offers you the chance to develop skills that will enhance your life and make you more competitive in the job market. You may never again have the chance to learn these valuable skills anywhere else. Don't waste the opportunity. If you take this course seriously, you will be amazed at what you learn in a few short months. Remember Joseph Addison's comment that reading is to the mind what exercise is to the body? Let's start building some muscle.

Your workout starts here with two short poems about the importance of reading. The first is by Charles Bukowski, a rude, self-described barfly, and former underachiever from Los Angeles, who went on to become an internationally celebrated writer. The second is by Emily Dickinson, a well-bred, if eccentric, lady from a respectable Amherst, Massachusetts, family. Despite their differences of temperament and background, they agree on one thing: reading changes lives.

Charles Bukowski (1920–1994)

Dostoevsky   1997

against the wall, the firing squad ready.
then he got a reprieve.
suppose they had shot Dostoevsky?
before he wrote all that?
I suppose it wouldn't have   5
mattered
not directly.

there are billions of people who have
never read him and never
will.
but as a young man I know that he
got me through the factories,
past the whores,
lifted me high through the night
and put me down
in a better
place.
even while in the bar
drinking with the other
derelicts,
I was glad they gave Dostoevsky a
reprieve,
it gave me one,
allowed me to look directly at those
rancid faces
in my world,
death pointing its finger,
I held fast,
an immaculate drunk
sharing the stinking dark with
my
brothers.

DOSTOEVSKY. The Russian novelist Fyodor Dostoevsky (1821–1880), author of *Crime and Punishment* and *The Brothers Karamazov*, was arrested in 1849 in a czarist crackdown on liberal organizations and sentenced to death. It was not until the members of the firing squad had aimed their rifles and were awaiting the order to fire that he was informed that his sentence had been commuted to four years at hard labor in Siberia.

Emily Dickinson (1830–1886)

There is no Frigate like a Book   (about 1873)

There is no Frigate like a Book
To take us Lands away
Nor any Coursers like a Page
Of prancing Poetry –
This Traverse may the poorest take
Without oppress of Toll –
How frugal is the Chariot
That bears the Human soul.

THERE IS NO FRIGATE LIKE A BOOK. *1 frigate:* large, fast sailing ship. *3 courser:* a swift racing horse or warhorse.

2 READING A STORY

> *When I read a good book . . . I wish that*
> *life were three thousand years long.*
>
> —RALPH WALDO EMERSON

Here is a story, one of the shortest ever written and one of the most difficult to forget:

> A woman is sitting in her old, shuttered house. She knows that she is alone in the whole world; every other thing is dead.
>
> The doorbell rings.

In a brief space this small tale of terror, credited to Thomas Bailey Aldrich, makes itself memorable. It sets a promising scene—is this a haunted house?—introduces a character, and places her in a strange and intriguing situation. Although in reading a story that is over so quickly we don't come to know the character well, for a moment we enter her thoughts and begin to share her feelings. Then something amazing happens. The story leaves us to wonder: who or what rang that bell?

Like many richer, longer, more complicated stories, this one, in its few words, engages the imagination. It makes us want to know what will happen next, and it touches on our own senses of fear, anticipation, and intrigue. How much a story contains and suggests doesn't depend on its size. In this chapter, we will consider the elements of fiction and discuss some examples. By examining a few short stories broken into their parts, you will come to a keener sense of how a story is put together. You will also start to see how the ideas and feelings we encounter in stories can help shape our understanding of the world—and of ourselves.

THE ART OF FICTION

Fiction (from the Latin *fictio*, "a shaping, a counterfeiting") is a name for stories not entirely factual, but at least partially shaped, made up, imagined. It is true that in some fiction, such as a historical novel, a writer draws on factual information in presenting scenes, events, and characters. But the factual information in a historical novel, unlike that in a history book, is of secondary importance.

Many firsthand accounts of the American Civil War were written by men who had fought in it, but few eyewitnesses give us so keen a sense of actual life on the battlefront as the author of *The Red Badge of Courage*, Stephen Crane, who was born after the war was over. In fiction, the "facts" may or may not be true, and a story is none the worse for their being entirely imaginary. We expect from fiction a sense of how people act, not an authentic chronicle of how, at some past time, a few people acted.

Human beings love stories. We put them everywhere—not only in books, films, and plays, but also in songs, news articles, cartoons, and video games. There seems to be a general human curiosity about how other lives, both real and imaginary, take shape and unfold—perhaps because examining others' lives can help us understand our own. Some stories provide simple and predictable pleasures according to a conventional plan. Each episode of *Law & Order* or *The Simpsons*, for instance, follows a roughly similar structure, so that regular viewers feel comfortably engaged and entertained. But other stories may seek to challenge rather than comfort us, by finding new and exciting ways to tell a tale, or delving deeper into the mysteries of human nature, or both.

Literary Fiction

Literary fiction—fiction that is written with serious artistic intent, and that doesn't rely on the conventions or formulas of genres such as the western, romance, horror, or detective novel—calls for close attention. Reading a short story by Ernest Hemingway instead of watching an episode of *Grey's Anatomy* is a little like playing chess rather than checkers. It isn't that Hemingway isn't entertaining; great literature provides deep and genuine pleasures. But it also requires focused attention and skilled engagement from the reader. We are not led on only by the promise of thrills; we do not keep reading merely to find out what happens next. Indeed, a literary story might even disclose in its opening lines everything that happened, then spend the rest of its length revealing what that happening meant.

Reading literary fiction is no simply passive activity, but one that demands both attention and insight-lending participation. In return, it offers rewards. In some works of literary fiction, such as Stephen Crane's "The Open Boat" and Flannery O'Connor's "A Good Man Is Hard to Find," we see more deeply into the minds and hearts of the characters than we ever see into those of our families, our close friends, our lovers—or even ourselves. But working to analyze those characters' fears and dreams and insecurities, their reactions and choices, can be an important step in our gaining knowledge about our own motivations and feelings, our own ways of moving through the world.

TYPES OF SHORT FICTION

Modern literary fiction in English has been dominated by two forms: the **novel** and the **short story**. The two have many elements in common. Perhaps we will be able to define the short story more meaningfully—for it has traits more essential than just a particular length—if first, for comparison, we consider some related varieties of fiction: the fable, the parable, and the tale. Ancient forms whose origins date back to the time of word-of-mouth storytelling, the fable and the tale are relatively simple in structure; in them we can plainly see elements also found in the short story.

Fable, Parable, and Tale

The **fable** is a brief, often humorous narrative told to illustrate a moral. The characters in a fable are often animals whose personality traits represent specific human qualities. An ant, for example, may represent a hard-working type of person, or a lion nobility. Another traditional form, the **parable**, is a brief, often allegorical narrative that teaches a moral, but unlike the fable, its plot is plausibly realistic, and the main characters are human rather than anthropomorphized animals or natural forces. Another key difference is that parables usually possess a more mysterious and suggestive tone. A fable customarily ends by explicitly stating its moral, but parables often present their morals implicitly, and their meanings can be open to several interpretations.

The name *tale* (from the Old English *talu*, "speech") is sometimes applied to any story, whether short or long, true or fictitious. *Tale* being a more evocative name than *story*, writers sometimes call their stories "tales" as if to imply something handed down from the past. But defined in a more limited sense, a **tale** is a story, usually short, that sets forth strange and wonderful events in more or less bare summary, without detailed character-drawing. A tale differs from a short story by its tendency toward less-developed characters and linear plotting.

The Short Story

The teller of tales relies heavily on the method of **summary**: terse, general narration. In a **short story**, a form more realistic than the tale and of modern origin, the writer usually presents the main events in greater fullness. Fine writers of short stories, although they may use summary at times (often to give some portion of a story less emphasis), are skilled in rendering a **scene**: a vivid or dramatic moment described in enough detail to create the illusion that the reader is practically there. Avoiding long summary, they try to *show* rather than simply to *tell*, as if following Mark Twain's advice to authors: "Don't say, 'The old lady screamed.' Bring her on and let her scream."

A short story is more than just a sequence of happenings. Flannery O'Connor, a master of the form, told young writers that "Being short does not mean being slight. A short story should be long in depth and should give us an experience of meaning." A finely wrought short story has depth and significance—and the richness and conciseness of an excellent lyric poem. Spontaneous and natural as the finished story may seem, the writer has crafted it so artfully that there is meaning in even seemingly casual speeches and apparently trivial details. If we skim it hastily, skipping the descriptive passages, we miss significant parts.

Some literary short stories, unlike commercial fiction in which the main interest is in physical action or conflict, tell of an **epiphany**: some moment of insight, discovery, or revelation by which a character's life, or view of life, is greatly altered. The term, which means "showing forth" in Greek, was first used in Christian theology to signify the manifestation of God's presence in the world. This theological idea was adapted by James Joyce to refer to a heightened moment of secular revelation. Other short stories tell of a character initiated into experience or maturity: two such **stories of initiation** are William Faulkner's "Barn Burning," in which a boy finds it necessary to defy his father and suddenly to grow into manhood, and John Updike's "A & P," whose protagonist undergoes an initiation into maturity.

ELEMENTS OF FICTION

1. PLOT

Passions spin the plot.
—GEORGE MEREDITH

Elements of Plot

Plot sometimes refers simply to the events in a story. In this book, though, **plot** will mean the artistic arrangement of those events. Stories often open with a **dramatic situation**: a person is involved in some **conflict**. Drama in fiction occurs in any clash of wills, desires, or powers—whether it be a conflict of character against character, character against society, character against some natural force, or character against some supernatural entity.

Most stories have a beginning, a middle, and an end—although what is revealed, and when, might vary from story to story. Often a story begins with an **exposition**: the opening portion that sets the scene (if any), introduces the main characters, tells us what happened before the story opened, and provides any other background information that we need in order to understand and care about the events to follow.

Protagonist Versus Antagonist

The principal person with whom the story is concerned is called the **protagonist** (a better term than **hero**, for it may apply equally well to a central character who is not especially brave or virtuous). The **suspense**, the pleasurable anxiety we feel that heightens our attention to the story, resides in our wondering how things will all turn out. Often, the protagonist is in conflict with another character, the **antagonist**, whose desires or needs run counter to those of the protagonist or keep him or her from getting what he or she wants.

Crisis and Climax

When the protagonist squares off with the antagonist or reaches a roadblock, we have a **crisis**, a moment of high tension. Ultimately events will come to a **climax**, the moment of greatest tension at which the outcome is to be decided. The outcome or **conclusion**—also called the **resolution** or **dénouement** (French for "the untying of the knot")—announces the final part of the story, which will end soon.

Narrative Techniques

The treatment of plot is one aspect of an author's artistry. Different arrangements of the same material are possible. A writer might decide to tell of the events in chronological order, beginning with the earliest; or he or she might open the story with the last event, then tell what led up to it. Sometimes a writer chooses to skip rapidly over the exposition and begin ***in medias res*** (Latin for "in the midst of things"), first presenting some exciting or significant moment, then filling in what happened earlier. This method is by no means a modern invention: Homer begins the *Odyssey* with his hero mysteriously late in returning from war and his son searching for him; John Milton's *Paradise Lost* opens with Satan already defeated in his revolt against the Lord. A device useful to writers for filling in what happened earlier is the **flashback**, a scene relived in a character's memory. Alternatively, a storyteller can try to incite our anticipation by giving us some **foreshadowing** or indication of events to come.

■ Writing Assignment on Plot

Choose and read a story from this collection, and write a brief description of its plot and main characters. Then write at length about how the protagonist is changed or tested by the story's events. What do the main character's actions reveal about his or her personality? Some possible story choices are John Updike's "A & P," Alice Walker's "Everyday Use," and ZZ Packer's "Brownies."

2. POINT OF VIEW

> *An author in his book must be like God in His universe, present everywhere and visible nowhere.*
>
> —GUSTAVE FLAUBERT

In the opening lines of *Adventures of Huckleberry Finn*, Mark Twain takes care to separate himself from the leading character, who is to tell his own story:

> You don't know about me, without you have read a book by the name of *The Adventures of Tom Sawyer*, but that ain't no matter. That book was made by Mr. Mark Twain, and he told the truth, mainly.

Twain wrote the novel, but the **narrator** or speaker is Huck Finn, a fictional character who supposedly tells the story. Obviously, in *Huckleberry Finn,* the narrator of the story is not the same person as the "real-life" author. In employing Huck as his narrator, Twain selects a special angle of vision: not his own, exactly, but that of a resourceful boy moving through the thick of events, with a mind at times shrewd, at other times innocent. Through Huck's eyes, Twain takes in certain scenes, actions, and characters and—as only Huck's angle of vision could have enabled Twain to do so well—records them memorably.

Not every narrator in fiction is, like Huck Finn, a main character, one in the thick of events. Some narrators play only minor parts in the stories they tell; others take no active part at all. Often the narrator is not a character in the story, but is someone not even named, who stands at a distance from the action recording what the main characters say and do; recording also, at times, what they think, feel, or desire.

Identifying Point of View

Narrators come in many forms; however, because stories usually are told by someone, almost every story has some kind of narrator. Some theorists reserve the term *narrator* for a character who tells a story in the first person. We use it in a wider sense, to mean a recording consciousness that an author creates, who may or may not be a participant in the events related.

To identify a story's **point of view**, describe the role the narrator plays in the events and any limits placed on his or her knowledge of what is happening. In a short story, it is usual—although not always the case—for the writer to maintain one point of view from beginning to end; in novels, the writer may introduce several points of view. In his long, panoramic novel *War and Peace*, encompassing the vast drama of Napoleon's invasion of Russia, Leo Tolstoy freely shifts the point of view in and out of the minds of many characters, among them Napoleon himself.

Types of Narrators

Here is a list of the most familiar and recognizable points of view:

Participant Narrator

- Writes in the first person ("I")
- Can be either a major or a minor character

Nonparticipant Narrator

- Writes in the third person ("he," "she")
- Can possess different levels of knowledge about characters
    - **All-knowing** or **omniscient** (sees into the mind of any or all of the characters)
    - **Limited omniscience** (sees into one character)
    - **Objective** (does not see into any characters, reports events from outside)

When the narrator is cast as a **participant** in the events of the story, he or she is a dramatized character who says "I." Such a narrator may be the protagonist (Huck Finn) or may be an **observer**, a minor character standing a little to one side, watching a story unfold that mainly involves someone else. A famous example of a participant narrator occurs in F. Scott Fitzgerald's *The Great Gatsby*. The novel's narrator is not Jay Gatsby, but his friend Nick Carraway, who knows only portions of Gatsby's mysterious life.

A narrator who remains a **nonparticipant** does not appear in the story as a character. Viewing the characters, perhaps seeing into the minds of one or more of them, such a narrator refers to them as "he," "she," or "they."

Other Narrative Points of View

Besides the common points of view just listed, uncommon points of view are possible. In *Flush*, a fictional biography of Elizabeth Barrett Browning, Virginia Woolf employs an unusual observer as narrator: the poet's pet cocker spaniel. In "The Circular Valley," a short story by Paul Bowles, a man and a woman are watched by a sinister spirit trying to take possession of them, and we see the human characters through the spirit's vague consciousness.

Also possible, but unusual, is a story written in the second person, *you*. This point of view results in an attention-getting directness, as in Jay McInerney's novel *Bright Lights, Big City* (1985), which begins:

> You are not the kind of guy who would be at a place like this at this time of the morning. But here you are, and you cannot say that the terrain is entirely unfamiliar, although the details are fuzzy. You are at a nightclub talking to a girl with a shaved head.

The attitudes and opinions of a narrator aren't necessarily those of the author; in fact, we may notice a lively conflict between what we are told and what, apparently, we are meant to believe. A story may be told by an **innocent narrator** or a **naive narrator**, a character who fails to understand all the implications of the story. One such innocent narrator (despite his sometimes shrewd perceptions) is Huckleberry Finn. Because Huck accepts without question the morality and lawfulness of slavery, he feels guilty about helping Jim, a runaway slave. But, far from condemning Huck for his defiance of the law—"All right, then, I'll *go* to hell," Huck tells himself, deciding against returning Jim to captivity—the author, and the reader along with him, silently applaud.

Naive in the extreme is the narrator of one part of William Faulkner's novel *The Sound and the Fury,* the mentally disabled Benjy, a grown man with the intellect of a child. In a story told by an **unreliable narrator**, the point of view is that of a person who, we perceive, is deceptive, self-deceptive, deluded, or deranged.

■ Writing Assignment on Point of View

Choose a story from this book and analyze how point of view contributes to the story's overall meaning. Come up with a thesis sentence, and back up your argument with specific observations about the text. Incorporate at least three quotations, and document them, as explained in the writing chapters which follow. Some stories that might lend themselves well to this assignment are James Baldwin's "Sonny's Blues," Raymond Carver's "Cathedral," and Edgar Allan Poe's "The Tell-Tale Heart."

3. CHARACTER

> *Show me a character without anxieties and I will show you a boring book.*
> —MARGARET ATWOOD

From popular fiction and drama, both classic and contemporary, we are acquainted with many stereotyped characters. Called **stock characters**, they are often known by some outstanding trait or traits: the *bragging* soldier of Greek and Roman comedy, the Prince Charming of fairy tales, the *mad* scientist of horror movies, the *fearlessly reckless* police detective of urban action films, the *brilliant but alcoholic* brain surgeon of medical thrillers on television. Stock characters are especially convenient for writers of commercial fiction: they require little detailed portraiture, for we already know them well. Most writers of the literary story, however, attempt to create characters who strike us not as stereotypes but as unique individuals. Although stock characters tend to have single dominant virtues and vices, characters in the finest short stories tend to have many facets, like people we meet.

A **character**, then, is presumably an imagined person who inhabits a story—although that simple definition may admit to a few exceptions. In George Stewart's novel *Storm*, the protagonist is the wind; in Richard Adams's *Watership Down*, the main characters are rabbits. But usually we recognize, in the main characters of a story, human personalities that become familiar to us. If the story seems "true to life," we generally find that its characters act in a reasonably consistent manner and that the author has provided them with **motivation**: sufficient reason to behave as they do. Should a character behave in a sudden and unexpected way, seeming to deny what we have been told about his or her nature or personality, we trust that there was a reason for this behavior and that sooner or later we will discover it.

In good fiction, characters often change or develop—and that transformation, and all of the things that led up to it or result from it, are an integral part of the story. In *A Christmas Carol,* Charles Dickens tells how Ebenezer Scrooge, a tightfisted miser, reforms overnight, suddenly gives to the poor, and endeavors to assist his clerk's struggling family. But Dickens amply demonstrates why Scrooge had such a change of heart: four ghostly visitors, stirring kind memories the old miser had forgotten and also warning him of the probable consequences of his habits, provide the character (and hence the story) with adequate motivation.

Types of Characters

To borrow the useful terms of the English novelist E. M. Forster, characters may seem **flat** or **round**, depending on whether a writer sketches or sculpts them. A flat character has only one outstanding trait or feature, or at most a few distinguishing marks: for example, the familiar stock character of the mad scientist, with his lust for absolute power and his crazily gleaming eyes. Flat characters, however, need not be stock characters: in all of literature there is probably only one Tiny Tim, though his functions in *A Christmas Carol* are mainly to invoke blessings and to remind others of their Christian duties.

Flat characters tend to stay the same throughout a story, but round characters often change—learn or become enlightened, grow or deteriorate. In William Faulkner's "Barn Burning," the boy Sarty Snopes, driven to defy his proud and violent father, becomes at the story's end more knowing and more mature. (Some critics call a fixed character **static**; a changing one, **dynamic**.) This is not to damn a flat character as an inferior creation. In most fiction—even the greatest—minor characters tend to be flat instead of round. Why? Rounding them would cost time and space; and so enlarged, they might only distract us from the main characters.

Heroes Versus Antiheroes

Instead of a hero, many a recent novel has featured an **antihero**: a protagonist conspicuously lacking in one or more of the usual attributes of a traditional **hero**—bravery, skill, idealism, sense of purpose. The antihero is an ordinary, unglorious citizen of the modern world, usually drawn (according to the Irish short story writer Sean O'Faolain) as someone "groping, puzzled, cross, mocking, frustrated, and isolated."

If epic poets once drew their heroes as decisive leaders of their people, embodying their people's highest ideals, antiheroes tend to be loners, without admirable qualities, just barely able to survive. A gulf separates Leopold Bloom, antihero of James Joyce's novel *Ulysses,* from the hero of the Greek *Odyssey.* In Homer's epic, Ulysses wanders the Mediterranean, battling monsters and overcoming enchantments. In Joyce's novel, Bloom wanders the littered streets of Dublin, peddling advertising space.

■ Writing Assignment on Character

Choose a story with a dynamic protagonist. Write an essay exploring how that character evolves over the course of the story, providing evidence from the story to back up your argument. Some good story choices might be William Faulkner's "Barn Burning," Raymond Carver's "Cathedral," James Baldwin's "Sonny's Blues," and Flannery O'Connor's "A Good Man Is Hard to Find."

4. SETTING

> *What are the three key rules of real estate?*
> *Location, location, location!*
> —AMERICAN BUSINESS PROVERB

By the **setting** of a story, we mean its time and place. The word might remind you of the metal that holds a diamond in a ring, or of a *set* used in a play—perhaps a bare chair in front of a slab of painted canvas. But often, in an effective short story, setting can figure as more than mere background or underpinning. It can make things happen. It can prompt characters to act, bring them to realizations, or cause them to reveal their inmost natures. It can even act as a character itself.

Place

To be sure, the idea of setting or place includes the physical environment of a story: a house, a street, a city, a landscape, a region. (*Where* a story takes place is sometimes called its **locale**.) Physical places mattered so greatly to French novelist Honoré de Balzac that sometimes, before writing a story set in a particular town, he would visit that town, select a few houses, and describe them in detail, down to their very smells.

Time

In addition to place, setting may crucially involve the time of the story—the hour, year, or century. It might matter greatly that a story takes place at dawn, or on the day of the first moon landing. When we begin to read a historical novel, we are soon made aware that we aren't reading about life in the twenty-first century. In *The Scarlet Letter*, nineteenth-century author Nathaniel Hawthorne, by a long introduction and a vivid opening scene at a prison door, prepares us to witness events in the Puritan community of Boston in the earlier seventeenth century. This setting, together with scenes of Puritan times we recall from high school history, helps us understand what happens in the novel. We can appreciate the shocked agitation in town when a woman is accused of adultery: she has given illegitimate birth. Such an event might seem common today, but in the stern, God-fearing New England Puritan community, it was a flagrant defiance of church and state, which were all-powerful (and were all one). Since Hawthorne's novel takes place in a time remote from our own, we are not surprised by the different customs and different attitudes.

Weather

Besides time and place, setting may also include the weather, which in some stories may be crucial. Climate seems as substantial as any character in William Faulkner's "Dry September." After sixty-two rainless days, a long unbroken spell of late-summer heat has frayed every nerve in a small town and caused the main character, a hot-headed white supremacist, to feel more and more irritated. The weather, someone remarks, is "enough to make a man do anything." When a false report circulates that a white woman has been raped by a black man, the rumor, like a match flung into a dry field, ignites rage and provokes a lynching. All the elements of the story's setting—its location, its era, and its infernal heat wave—are critical to the events that take place.

Atmosphere

Atmosphere is the dominant mood or feeling that pervades all parts of a literary work. Atmosphere refers to the total effect conveyed by the author's use of language, images, and physical setting. But as the term *atmosphere* suggests, aspects of the physical setting (place, time, and weather) are usually crucial elements in achieving the author's intention. In some stories, a writer will seem to draw a setting mainly to evoke atmosphere. In such a story, setting starts us feeling whatever the storyteller would have us feel. In "The Tell-Tale Heart," Edgar Allan Poe's setting the action in an old, dark, lantern-lit house greatly contributes to our sense of unease—and so helps the story's effectiveness.

■ Writing Assignment on Setting

Choose a story from this book, and explore how character and setting are interrelated. A possible topic would be to describe the significance of setting to the protagonist in Kate Chopin's "The Storm" or Jack London's "To Build a Fire." How does the setting contribute to a change in the character's personal perspective?

5. TONE AND STYLE

> *Style has no fixed laws; it is changed by the usage of the people, never the same for any length of time.*
>
> —SENECA

The great short story writer Anton Chekhov said that a writer should not judge his characters but should serve as an "impartial witness." Yet writers no doubt have feelings toward their characters and events, and they want to make the reader view their characters in such a way that we, too, will care about them. While many modern writers have adopted Chekhov's "impartial" methods, they are rarely impartial witnesses. They merely embed their own feelings into the story so that those reactions emerge indirectly for the reader. For example, when at the beginning of the short story "In Exile" Chekhov introduces us to a character, he does so with a description that arouses sympathy:

> The Tartar was worn out and ill, and wrapping himself in his rags, he talked about how good it was in the province of Simbirsk, and what a beautiful and clever wife he had left at home. He was not more than twenty-five, and in the firelight his pale, sickly face and woebegone expression made him seem like a boy.

Other than the comparison of the Tartar to a child, the details in this passage seem mostly factual: the young man's illness, ragged clothes, facial expression, and topics of conversation. But these details form a portrait that stirs pity. By Chekhov's selection of these imaginary details out of countless others that he might have included, he firmly directs our feelings about the Tartar, so miserable and pathetic in his sickness and his homesickness. We cannot know, of course, exactly what the living Chekhov felt; but at least we can be sure that we are supposed to share the compassion and tenderness of the narrator, Chekhov's impartial (but human) witness.

Tone

An author's presentation of details, events, situations, and choice of words can lead us to infer his or her attitude toward the characters or ideas expressed. When the narrator of Joseph Conrad's *Heart of Darkness* comes upon an African outpost littered with abandoned machines and notices "a boiler wallowing in the grass," the exact word *wallowing* conveys an attitude: that there is something swinish about this scene of careless waste.

Whatever leads us to infer the author's attitude is commonly called **tone**. Like a tone of voice, the tone of a story may communicate amusement, anger, affection, sorrow, contempt. It implies the feelings of the author, so far as we can sense them. Those feelings may be similar to feelings expressed by the narrator of the story (or by any character), but sometimes they may be dissimilar, even sharply opposed. The characters in a story may regard an event as sad, but we sense that the author regards it as funny. To understand the tone of a story, then, is to understand some attitude more fundamental to the story than whatever attitudes the characters explicitly declare.

Style

One of the clearest indications of the tone of a story is the **style** in which it is written. In general, style refers to the individual traits or characteristics of a piece of writing: to a writer's particular ways of managing words that we come to recognize as habitual or customary. A distinctive style marks the work of a fine writer: we can tell his or her work from that of anyone else. From one story to another, however, the writer may fittingly change style; and in some stories, style may be altered meaningfully as the story goes along.

Usually, *style* indicates a mode of expression: the language a writer uses. In this sense, the notion of style includes such traits as the length and complexity of sentences, as well as **diction**, or choice of words: abstract or concrete, bookish or close to everyday speech. Involved in the idea of style, too, is any habitual use of imagery, patterns of sound, figures of speech, or other devices.

An Example of Distinctive Style: Ernest Hemingway

To see what style means, consider the classic story "A Clean, Well-Lighted Place" by Ernest Hemingway. Hemingway's famous style includes both short sentences and long, but when the sentences are long, they tend to be relatively simple in construction. Hemingway likes long compound sentences (clause plus clause plus clause), sometimes joined with "and"s. The effect is like listening to speech:

> In the day time the street was dusty, but at night the dew settled the dust and the old man liked to sit late because he was deaf and now at night it was quiet and he felt the difference.

Hemingway is a master of swift, terse dialogue, and often casts whole scenes in the form of conversation. As if he were a closemouthed speaker unwilling to let his feelings loose, the narrator of a Hemingway story often addresses us in understatement, implying greater depths of feeling than he puts into words.

Irony

If a friend declares, "Oh, sure, I just *love* to have four papers fall due on the same day," you detect that the statement contains **irony**. This is **verbal irony**, the most familiar kind, in which we understand the speaker's meaning to be far from the usual meaning of the words—in this case, quite the opposite. (When the irony is found, as here, in a somewhat sour statement tinged with mockery, it is called **sarcasm**.)

Irony, of course, occurs in writing as well as in conversation. For example, when in a comic moment in Isaac Bashevis Singer's "Gimpel the Fool" the sexton announces, "The wealthy Reb Gimpel invites the congregation to a feast in honor of the birth of a son," the people at the synagogue burst into laughter. They know that Gimpel, in contrast to the sexton's words, is not a wealthy man but a humble baker; that the son is not his own but his wife's lover's; and that the birth brings no honor to anybody. Singer's verbal irony implies a contrast or discrepancy between what is *said* and what is *meant*.

Dramatic Irony

There are also times when the speaker, unlike the reader, does not realize the ironic dimension of his or her words or actions; such instances are known as **dramatic irony**. The most famous example occurs in Sophocles's tragic drama *Oedipus the King*, when Oedipus vows to find and punish the murderer of King Laius, unaware that he himself is the man he seeks, and adds: "if by any chance / he proves to be an intimate of our house, / here at my hearth, with my full knowledge, / may the curse I just called down on him strike me!" Dramatic irony may also be used for lighter purposes: for example, Daisy Coble, the mother in Anne Tyler's "Teenage Wasteland," whose attitudes and moods shift constantly according to what others tell her, responds to the idea that *she* should be less strict with her son by saying, "But see, he's still so suggestible."

Cosmic Irony

Storytellers are sometimes fond of ironic twists of fate—developments that reveal a terrible distance between what people deserve and what they get, between what is and what ought to be. Such an irony is sometimes called an **irony of fate** or a **cosmic irony**, for it suggests that some malicious fate (or force in the universe) is deliberately frustrating human efforts. There is an irony of fate in the servant's futile attempt to escape Death in the fable "The Appointment in Samarra." In Jack London's "To Build a Fire," it is ironic that a freezing man, desperately trying to strike a match to light a fire and save himself, accidentally ignites all his remaining matches. To notice an irony gives pleasure. It may arouse our sympathy, make us feel wonder, or move us to laughter. By so involving us, irony—whether a statement, a situation, an unexpected event, or a point of view—can render a story more likely to strike us, to affect us, and to be remembered.

■ Writing Assignment on Tone and Style

Examine a short story with a style you admire. Write an essay in which you analyze the author's approach to diction, sentence structure, tone, and organization. How do these elements work together to create a certain mood? How does that mood contribute to the story's meaning? If your chosen story has a first-person narrator, how do stylistic choices help to create a sense of that particular character?

6. SYMBOL

> *All you have to do is close your eyes and wait for the symbols.*
> —TENNESSEE WILLIAMS

In F. Scott Fitzgerald's novel *The Great Gatsby*, a huge pair of bespectacled eyes stares across a wilderness of ash heaps, from a billboard advertising the services of an oculist.

Repeatedly entering into the story, the advertisement comes to mean more than simply the availability of eye examinations. Fitzgerald has a character liken it to the eyes of God; he hints that some sad, compassionate spirit is brooding as it watches the passing procession of humanity. Such an object is a **symbol**: in literature, a person, place, or thing that suggests more than its literal meaning. Symbols generally do not "stand for" any one meaning, nor for anything absolutely definite; they point, they hint, or, as Henry James put it, they cast long shadows. To take a large example: in Herman Melville's *Moby-Dick*, the great white whale of the book's title apparently means more than the literal dictionary-definition meaning of an aquatic mammal. He also suggests more than the devil, to whom some of the characters liken him. The great whale, as the story unfolds, comes to imply an amplitude of meanings, among them the forces of nature and the whole created universe.

Symbols

Symbols in fiction are not generally abstract terms such as *love* or *truth*, but are likely to be perceptible objects (or worded descriptions that cause us to imagine them). In William Faulkner's "A Rose for Emily," Miss Emily's invisible watch ticking at the end of a golden chain not only indicates the passage of time, but also suggests that time passes without even being noticed by the watch's owner, and the golden chain carries suggestions of wealth and authority. Objects (and creatures) that seem insignificant in themselves can take on a symbolic importance in the larger context: in Jhumpa Lahiri's "Interpreter of Maladies," the piece of gum that Mrs. Das gives Mr. Kapasi—"As soon as Mr. Kapasi put the gum in his mouth a thick sweet liquid burst onto his tongue"—underscores her effect on his slumbering senses.

Often the symbols we meet in fiction are inanimate objects, but other things also may function symbolically. In James Joyce's "Araby," the very name of the bazaar, Araby—the poetic name for Arabia—suggests magic, romance, and *The Arabian Nights*; its syllables (the narrator tells us) "cast an Eastern enchantment over me." Even a locale, or a feature of physical topography, can provide rich suggestions. In Ernest Hemingway's "A Clean, Well-Lighted Place," the café is not merely a café, but an island of refuge from night, chaos, loneliness, old age, and impending death.

Symbolic Characters

In some novels and stories, **symbolic characters** make brief cameo appearances. Such characters often are not well-rounded and fully known, but are seen fleetingly and remain slightly mysterious. In *Heart of Darkness*, a short novel by Joseph Conrad, a steamship company that hires men to work in the Congo maintains in its waiting room two women who knit black wool—like the classical Fates. Usually such a symbolic character is more a portrait than a person—or somewhat portraitlike, like Faulkner's Miss Emily, who twice appears at a window of her house "like the carven torso of an idol in a niche." Though Faulkner invests Miss Emily with life and vigor, he also clothes her in symbolic hints: she seems almost to personify the vanishing aristocracy of the antebellum South, still maintaining a black servant and being ruthlessly betrayed by a moneymaking Yankee. Sometimes a part of a character's body or an attribute may convey symbolic meaning: a baleful eye, as in Edgar Allan Poe's "The Tell-Tale Heart."

Why Use Symbols?

Why do writers have to symbolize—why don't they tell us outright? One advantage of a symbol is that it is so compact, and yet so fully laden. Both starkly concrete and slightly mysterious, like Miss Emily's invisible ticking watch, it may impress us with all the force of something beheld in a dream or in a nightmare. The watch suggests, among other things, the slow and invisible passage of time. What this symbol says, it says more fully and more memorably than could be said, perhaps, in a long essay on the subject.

Recognizing Symbols

A pitfall in analyzing a story's symbolism is the temptation to read symbolic meaning into everything. An image acquires symbolic resonance because it is organically important to the actions and emotions of the story. Unless an object, act, or character is given some such special emphasis and importance (often a crucial symbol will open a story or end it), we may generally feel safe in taking it at face value. But an object, an act, or a character is surely symbolic (and almost as surely displays high literary art) if, when we finish the story, we realize that it was that item—that gigantic eye; that clean, well-lighted café; that burning of a barn—which led us to the author's theme, the essential meaning.

■ Writing Assignment on Symbol

From the stories in this book, choose one with a strong central symbol. Explain how the symbol helps to communicate the story's meaning, citing specific moments in the text.

7. THEME

> *They say great themes make great novels . . . but what these young writers don't understand is that there is no greater theme than men and women.*
>
> —JOHN O'HARA

The **theme** of a story is whatever general idea or insight the entire story reveals. In some stories the theme is unmistakable. At the end of Aesop's fable about the council of the mice that can't decide who will bell the cat, the theme is stated in the moral: *It is easier to propose a thing than to carry it out.* In a work of commercial fiction, too, the theme (if any) is usually obvious. Consider a typical detective thriller in which, say, a rookie police officer trained in scientific methods of crime detection sets out to solve a mystery sooner than his or her rival, a veteran sleuth whose only laboratory is carried under his hat. Perhaps the veteran solves the case, leading to the conclusion (and the theme), "The old ways are the best ways after all." Another story by the same writer might dramatize the same rivalry but reverse the outcome, having the rookie win, thereby reversing the theme: "The times are changing! Those old-fashioned ways don't work anymore."

Plot Versus Theme

In literary fiction, a theme is seldom so obvious. That is, a theme need not be a moral or a message; it may be what the events add up to, what the story is about. Flannery O'Connor held that "when you can state the theme of a story, when you can separate it out from the story itself, then you can be sure the story is not a very good one. The meaning of a story has to be embodied in it, has to be made concrete in it. A story is a way to say something that can't be said any other way, and it takes every word in the story to say what the meaning is. You tell a story because a statement would be inadequate."

When we come to the end of a finely wrought short story such as Ernest Hemingway's "A Clean, Well-Lighted Place," it may be easy to sum up the plot—to say what happens—but it is more difficult to sum up the story's main idea. Hemingway relates events—how a younger waiter gets rid of an old man and how an older waiter then goes to a coffee bar—but in themselves these events seem relatively slight, though the story as a whole seems large and full of meaning. A **summary**, a brief condensation of the main idea or plot of a literary work, may be helpful, but it tends to focus on the surface events of a story. A **theme** aims for a deeper and more comprehensive statement of its larger meaning.

For the meaning, we must look to other elements in the story besides what happens in it. It is clear that Hemingway is most deeply interested in the thoughts and feelings of the older waiter, the character who has more and more to say as the story progresses, until at the end the story is entirely confined to his thoughts and perceptions. What is meaningful in these thoughts and perceptions? The older waiter understands the old man and sympathizes with his need for a clean, well-lighted place. If we say that, we are still talking about what happens in the story, though we have gone beyond merely recording its external events. But a theme is usually stated in *general* words. Another try: "Solitary people who cannot sleep need a cheerful, orderly place where they can drink with dignity." That's a little better. We have indicated, at least, that Hemingway's story is about more than just an old man and a couple of waiters. But what about the older waiter's meditation on *nada*, nothingness? Coming near the end of the story, it is given great emphasis, and probably no good statement of Hemingway's theme can leave it out. Still another try at a statement: "Solitary people need a place of refuge from their terrible awareness that their lives (or, perhaps, human lives) are essentially meaningless." Neither this nor any other statement of the story's theme is unarguably right, but at least the sentence helps the reader to bring into focus one primary idea that Hemingway seems to be driving at. But the story may not set forth one lesson. One could argue that "A Clean, Well-Lighted Place" contains *several* themes, and other statements could be made to include Hemingway's views of love, of communication between people, of dignity. Great short stories frequently have more than one theme.

Theme as Unifying Device

In many a fine short story, theme is the center, the moving force, the principle of unity. Clearly, such a theme is something other than the characters and events of its story. To say of James Joyce's "Araby" that it is about a boy who goes to a bazaar to buy a gift for a young woman, only to arrive too late, is to summarize plot, not theme. (The theme *might* be put, "The illusions of a romantic youth are vulnerable," or it might be put in any of a few hundred other ways.) Although the title of Shirley Jackson's "The Lottery," with its hint of the lure of easy riches, may arouse pleasant expectations, which the neutral tone of the narrative does nothing to dispel, the theme—the larger realization that the story leaves us with—has to do with the ways in which cruel and insensitive attitudes can come to seem like normal and natural ones, and how easily people will go along with the crowd.

Sometimes we say that the theme of a story (Faulkner's "Barn Burning," for example) is "loss of innocence" or (as in Zora Neale Hurston's "Sweat") "the revolt of the downtrodden." This is to use *theme* in a more general sense than we mean here. Identifying that a story is about family, for example, doesn't tell us exactly what it's saying. What does James Baldwin's story "Sonny's Blues" suggest about family? That history and culture have lasting effects on each new generation? That family members lose touch with one another at great cost to themselves? That we cannot, no matter how hard we try, save another person? Saying that "Sonny's Blues" is a story about family doesn't tell us what the story actually suggests—and it may, as in the case of "Sonny's Blues," contain more than one theme or idea. We suggest that, in the beginning, you look for whatever *specific* truth or insight you think the writer of a story reveals. Try to sum it up *in a sentence*—even while recognizing, as O'Connor does, that great stories can never be distilled to one statement.

Finding the Theme

You may find it helpful, in making a sentence-statement of theme, to consider these questions:

1. Look back once more at the title of the story. From what you have read, what does it indicate?
2. Does the main character change in any way over the course of the story? Does this character arrive at any eventual realization or understanding? Are you left with any realization or understanding you did not have before?
3. Does the author make any general observations about life or human nature? Do the characters make any? (Caution: Characters now and then will utter opinions with which the reader is not necessarily supposed to agree.)
4. Does the story contain any especially curious objects, mysterious flat characters, significant animals, repeated names, song titles, or whatever, that hint at meanings larger than such things ordinarily have? In literary stories, such symbols may point to central themes.
5. When you have worded your statement of theme, have you cast it into general language, not just given a plot summary?
6. Does your statement hold true for the story as a whole, not for just part of it?

In distilling a statement of theme from a rich and complicated story, we have, of course, no more encompassed the whole story than a paleontologist taking a plaster mold of a petrified footprint has captured a living stegosaurus. A writer does not usually set out with theme in hand, determined to make every detail in the story work to demonstrate it. Well then, the skeptical reader may ask, if only *some* stories have themes, if those themes may be hard to sum up, and if readers will probably disagree in their summations, why bother to state themes? Isn't it too much trouble? We think not. Trying to sum up the point of a story in our own words is merely one way to make ourselves better aware of whatever we may have understood only vaguely and tentatively. Attempted with care, such statements may bring into focus our scattered impressions of a rewarding story, and may help to clarify whatever wisdom the storyteller has offered us. Ultimately, they may help to shed light and understanding on the ways that similar themes play out in our own lives.

■ **Writing Assignment on Theme**

Choose a story that catches your attention, and go through the steps listed above to develop a strong thesis sentence about the story's theme. Then flesh out your argument into an essay, supporting your thesis with evidence from the text, including quotations. Some good story choices might be Ernest Hemingway's "A Clean, Well-Lighted Place," John Steinbeck's "The Chrysanthemums," Flannery O'Connor's "A Good Man Is Hard to Find," and Shirley Jackson's "The Lottery."

How do all of these elements work together in a real story? Let's consider three short stories that span over a hundred years. These stories vary widely in plot, character, point of view, style, theme, and symbol—and yet are all classics of the form.

John Updike

John Updike (1932–2009) was born in Pennsylvania, received his B.A. from Harvard, then went to Oxford to study drawing and fine art. In the mid-1950s he worked on the staff of the New Yorker, *at times doing errands for the aged James Thurber. Although he left the magazine to become a full-time writer, Updike continued to supply it with memorable stories, witty light verse, and searching reviews. A famously prolific writer, he published more than fifty books. Updike is best known as a hardworking, versatile, highly productive writer of fiction. For his novel* The Centaur *(1963) he received a National Book Award, and for* Rabbit Is Rich *(1982) a Pulitzer Prize and an American Book Award. The fourth and last Rabbit Angstrom novel,* Rabbit at Rest *(1990), won him a second Pulitzer. Updike is one of the few Americans ever to be awarded both the National Medal of Arts (1989) and the National Humanities Medal (2003)—the nation's highest honors in each respective field. His many other books include* The Witches of Eastwick *(1984), made into a successful film starring Jack Nicholson,* Terrorist *(2006), and his final novel,* The Widows of Eastwick *(2008).*

Almost uniquely among contemporary American writers, Updike moved back and forth successfully among a variety of literary genres: light verse, serious poetry, drama, criticism, children's books, novels, and short stories. But it is perhaps in short fiction that he did his finest work. Some critics, such as Washington Post *writer Jonathan Yardley, believe that "It is in his short stories that we find Updike's most assured work, and no doubt it is upon the best of them that his reputation ultimately will rest."*

John Updike

A & P   1961

In walks three girls in nothing but bathing suits. I'm in the third check-out slot, with my back to the door, so I don't see them until they're over by the bread. The one that caught my eye first was the one in the plaid green two-piece. She was a chunky kid, with a good tan and a sweet broad soft-looking can with those two crescents of white just under it, where the sun never seems to hit, at the top of the backs of her legs. I stood there with my hand on a box of HiHo crackers trying to remember if I rang it up or not. I ring it up again and the customer starts giving me hell. She's one of these cash-register-watchers, a witch about fifty with rouge on her cheekbones and no eyebrows, and I know it made her day to trip me up. She'd been watching cash registers for fifty years and probably never seen a mistake before.

By the time I got her feathers smoothed and her goodies into a bag—she gives me a little snort in passing, if she'd been born at the right time they would have burned her over in Salem—by the time I get her on her way the girls had circled around the bread and were coming back, without a pushcart, back my way along the counters, in the aisle between the check-outs and the Special bins. They didn't even have shoes on. There was this chunky one, with the two-piece—it was bright green and the seams on the bra were still sharp and her belly was still pretty pale so I guessed she just got it (the suit)—there was this one, with one of those chubby berry-faces, the lips all bunched together under her nose, this one, and a tall one, with black hair that hadn't quite frizzed right, and one of these sunburns right across under the eyes, and a chin that was too long—you know, the kind of girl other girls think is very "striking" and "attractive" but never quite makes it, as they very well know, which is why they like her so much—and then the third one, that wasn't quite so tall. She was the queen. She kind of led them, the other two peeking around and making their shoulders round. She didn't look around, not this queen, she just walked straight on slowly, on these long white prima-donna legs. She came down a little hard on her heels, as if she didn't walk in her bare feet that much, putting down her heels and then letting the weight move along to her toes as if she was testing the floor with every step, putting a little deliberate extra action into it. You never know for sure how girls' minds work (do you really think it's a mind in there or just a little buzz like a bee in a glass jar?) but you got the idea she had talked the other two into coming in here with her, and now she was showing them how to do it, walk slow and hold yourself straight.

She had on a kind of dirty-pink—beige maybe, I don't know—bathing suit with a little nubble all over it and, what got me, the straps were down. They were off her shoulders looped loose around the cool tops of her arms, and I guess as a result the suit had slipped a little on her, so all around the top of the cloth there was this shining rim. If it hadn't been there you wouldn't have known there could have been anything whiter than those shoulders. With the straps pushed off, there was nothing between the top of the suit and the top of her head except just *her*, this clean bare plane of the top of her chest down from the shoulder bones like a dented sheet of metal tilted in the light. I mean, it was more than pretty.

She had sort of oaky hair that the sun and salt had bleached, done up in a bun that was unraveling, and a kind of prim face. Walking into the A & P with your straps down, I suppose it's the only kind of face you *can* have. She held her head so high her neck, coming up out of those white shoulders, looked kind of stretched, but I didn't mind. The longer her neck was, the more of her there was.

She must have felt in the corner of her eye me and over my shoulder Stokesie in the second slot watching, but she didn't tip. Not this queen. She kept her eyes moving across the racks, and stopped, and turned so slow it made my stomach rub the inside

5

of my apron, and buzzed to the other two, who kind of huddled against her for relief, and they all three of them went up the cat-and-dog-food-breakfast-cereal-macaroni-rice-raisins-seasonings-spreads-spaghetti-soft-drinks-crackers-and-cookies aisle. From the third slot I look straight up this aisle to the meat counter, and I watched them all the way. The fat one with the tan sort of fumbled with the cookies, but on second thought she put the packages back. The sheep pushing their carts down the aisle—the girls were walking against the usual traffic (not that we have one-way signs or anything)—were pretty hilarious. You could see them, when Queenie's white shoulders dawned on them, kind of jerk, or hop, or hiccup, but their eyes snapped back to their own baskets and on they pushed. I bet you could set off dynamite in an A & P and the people would by and large keep reaching and checking oatmeal off their lists and muttering "Let me see, there was a third thing, began with A, asparagus, no, ah, yes, applesauce!" or whatever it is they do mutter. But there was no doubt, this jiggled them. A few houseslaves in pin curlers even looked around after pushing their carts past to make sure what they had seen was correct.

You know, it's one thing to have a girl in a bathing suit down on the beach, where what with the glare nobody can look at each other much anyway, and another thing in the cool of the A & P, under the fluorescent lights, against all those stacked packages, with her feet padding along naked over our checkerboard green-and-cream rubber-tile floor.

"Oh Daddy," Stokesie said beside me. "I feel so faint."

"Darling," I said. "Hold me tight." Stokesie's married, with two babies chalked up on his fuselage already, but as far as I can tell that's the only difference. He's twenty-two, and I was nineteen this April.

"Is it done?" he asks, the responsible married man finding his voice. I forgot to say he thinks he's going to be manager some sunny day, maybe in 1990 when it's called the Great Alexandrov and Petrooshki Tea Company or something.

What he meant was, our town is five miles from a beach, with a big summer colony out on the Point, but we're right in the middle of town, and the women generally put on a shirt or shorts or something before they get out of the car into the street. And anyway these are usually women with six children and varicose veins mapping their legs and nobody, including them, could care less. As I say, we're right in the middle of town, and if you stand at our front doors you can see two banks and the Congregational church and the newspaper store and three real-estate offices and about twenty-seven old freeloaders tearing up Central Street because the sewer broke again. It's not as if we're on the Cape; we're north of Boston and there's people in this town haven't seen the ocean for twenty years. The girls had reached the meat counter and were asking McMahon something. He pointed, they pointed, and they shuffled out of sight behind a pyramid of Diet Delight peaches. All that was left for us to see was old McMahon patting his mouth and looking after them sizing up their joints. Poor kids, I began to feel sorry for them, they couldn't help it.

Now here comes the sad part of the story, at least my family says it's sad but I don't think it's sad myself. The store's pretty empty, it being Thursday afternoon, so there was nothing much to do except lean on the register and wait for the girls to show up again. The whole store was like a pinball machine and I didn't know which tunnel they'd come out of. After a while they come around out of the far aisle, around the light bulbs, records at discount of the Caribbean Six or Tony Martin Sings or some such gunk you wonder they waste the wax on, six-packs of candy bars, and plastic toys done up in cellophane that fall apart when a kid looks at them anyway. Around they come, Queenie still leading the way, and holding a little gray jar in her hand. Slots Three through Seven are unmanned and I could see her wondering between Stokes and me, but Stokesie with his usual luck draws an old party in baggy gray pants who stumbles up with four giant cans of pineapple juice (what do these bums *do* with all that pineapple juice? I've often asked myself) so the girls come to me. Queenie puts down the jar and I take it into my fingers icy cold. Kingfish Fancy Herring Snacks in Pure Sour Cream: 49¢. Now her hands are empty, not a ring or a bracelet, bare as God made them, and I wonder where the money's coming from. Still with that prim look she lifts a folded dollar bill out of the hollow at the center of her nubbled pink top. The jar went heavy in my hand. Really, I thought that was so cute.

Then everybody's luck begins to run out. Lengel comes in from haggling with a truck full of cabbages on the lot and is about to scuttle into that door marked MANAGER behind which he hides all day when the girls touch his eye. Lengel's pretty dreary, teaches Sunday school and the rest, but he doesn't miss that much. He comes over and says, "Girls, this isn't the beach."

Queenie blushes, though maybe it's just a brush of sunburn I was noticing for the first time, now that she was so close. "My mother asked me to pick up a jar of herring snacks." Her voice kind of startled me, the way voices do when you see the people first, coming out so flat and dumb yet kind of tony, too, the way it ticked over "pick up" and "snacks." All of a sudden I slid right down her voice into her living room. Her father and the other men were standing around in ice-cream coats and bow ties and the women were in sandals picking up herring snacks on toothpicks off a big plate and they were all holding drinks the color of water with olives and sprigs of mint in them. When my parents have somebody over they get lemonade and if it's a real racy affair Schlitz in tall glasses with "They'll Do It Every Time" cartoons stencilled on.

"That's all right," Lengel said. "But this isn't the beach." His repeating this struck me as funny, as if it had just occurred to him, and he had been thinking all these years the A & P was a great big dune and he was the head lifeguard. He didn't like my smiling—as I say he doesn't miss much—but he concentrates on giving the girls that sad Sunday-school-superintendent stare.

Queenie's blush is no sunburn now, and the plump one in plaid, that I liked better from the back—a really sweet can—pipes up, "We weren't doing any shopping. We just came in for the one thing."

"That makes no difference," Lengel tells her, and I could see from the way his eyes went that he hadn't noticed she was wearing a two-piece before. "We want you decently dressed when you come in here."

"We *are* decent," Queenie says suddenly, her lower lip pushing, getting sore now that she remembers her place, a place from which the crowd that runs the A & P must look pretty crummy. Fancy Herring Snacks flashed in her very blue eyes.

"Girls, I don't want to argue with you. After this come in here with your shoulders covered. It's our policy." He turns his back. That's policy for you. Policy is what the kingpins want. What the others want is juvenile delinquency.

All this while, the customers had been showing up with their carts but, you know, sheep, seeing a scene, they had all bunched up on Stokesie, who shook open a paper bag as gently as peeling a peach, not wanting to miss a word. I could feel in the silence everybody getting nervous, most of all Lengel, who asks me, "Sammy, have you rung up this purchase?"

I thought and said "No" but it wasn't about that I was thinking. I go through the punches, 4, 9, GROC, TOT—it's more complicated than you think, and after you do it often enough, it begins to make a little song, that you hear words to, in my case "Hello (*bing*) there, you (*gung*) hap-py *pee*-pul (*splat*)!"—the *splat* being the drawer flying out. I uncrease the bill, tenderly as you may imagine, it just having come from between the two smoothest scoops of vanilla I had ever known were there, and pass a half and a penny into her narrow pink palm, and nestle the herrings in a bag and twist its neck and hand it over, all the time thinking.

The girls, and who'd blame them, are in a hurry to get out, so I say "I quit" to Lengel quick enough for them to hear, hoping they'll stop and watch me, their unsuspected hero. They keep right on going, into the electric eye; the door flies open and they flicker across the lot to their car, Queenie and Plaid and Big Tall Goony-Goony (not that as raw material she was so bad), leaving me with Lengel and a kink in his eyebrow.

"Did you say something, Sammy?"

"I said I quit."

"I thought you did."

"You didn't have to embarrass them."

"It was they who were embarrassing us."

I started to say something that came out "Fiddle-de-doo." It's a saying of my grandmother's, and I know she would have been pleased.

"I don't think you know what you're saying," Lengel said.

"I know you don't," I said. "But I do." I pull the bow at the back of my apron and start shrugging it off my shoulders. A couple customers that had been heading for my slot begin to knock against each other, like scared pigs in a chute.

Lengel sighs and begins to look very patient and old and gray. He's been a friend of my parents for years. "Sammy, you don't want to do this to your Mom and Dad," he tells me. It's true, I don't. But it seems to me that once you begin a gesture it's fatal not to go through with it. I fold the apron, "Sammy" stitched in red on the pocket, and put it on the counter, and drop the bow tie on top of it. The bow tie is theirs, if you've ever wondered. "You'll feel this for the rest of your life," Lengel says, and I know that's true, too, but remembering how he made that pretty girl blush makes me so scrunchy inside I punch the No Sale tab and the machine whirs "pee-pul" and the drawer splats out. One advantage to this scene taking place in summer, I can follow this up with a clean exit, there's no fumbling around getting your coat and galoshes, I just saunter into the electric eye in my white shirt that my mother ironed the night before, and the door heaves itself open, and outside the sunshine is skating around on the asphalt.

I look around for my girls, but they're gone, of course. There wasn't anybody but some young married screaming with her children about some candy they didn't get by the door of a powder-blue Falcon station wagon. Looking back in the big windows, over the bags of peat moss and aluminum lawn furniture stacked on the pavement, I could see Lengel in my place in the slot, checking the sheep through. His face was dark gray and his back stiff, as if he'd just had an injection of iron, and my stomach kind of fell as I felt how hard the world was going to be to me hereafter.

Questions

1. Notice how artfully Updike arranges details to set the story in a perfectly ordinary supermarket. What details stand out for you as particularly true to life? What does this close attention to detail contribute to the story?
2. How fully does Updike draw the character of Sammy? What traits (admirable or otherwise) does Sammy show? Is he any less a hero for wanting the girls to notice his heroism?
3. What part of the story seems to be the exposition? (See the definition of *exposition* in the discussion of plot earlier in the chapter.) Of what value to the story is the carefully detailed portrait of Queenie, the leader of the three girls?
4. How does the setting of the story—not just the store, but the location of the town—shape Sammy and his reactions?
5. As the story develops, do you detect any change in Sammy's feelings toward the girls?
6. Where in "A & P" does the dramatic conflict become apparent? What moment in the story brings the crisis? What is the climax of the story?
7. Why, exactly, does Sammy quit his job?
8. Does anything lead you to *expect* Sammy to make some gesture of sympathy for the three girls? What incident earlier in the story (before Sammy quits) seems a foreshadowing?
9. What do you understand from the conclusion of the story? What does Sammy mean when he acknowledges "how hard the world was going to be to me hereafter"?

Edgar Allan Poe

Edgar Poe was born in Boston in January 1809, the second son of actors Eliza and David Poe. Edgar inherited his family's legacy of artistic talent, financial instability, and social inferiority (actors were not considered respectable in the nineteenth century), as well as his father's problems with alcohol. David Poe abandoned his family after the birth of Edgar's little sister, Rosalie, and Eliza died of tuberculosis in a Richmond, Virginia, boardinghouse before Edgar turned three. He was taken in by the wealthy John and Frances Allan of Richmond, whose name he added to his own. Allan educated Poe at first-rate schools, where he excelled in all subjects. But he grew into a moody adolescent, and his relationship with his foster father deteriorated.

Edgar Allan Poe

Poe's first year at the University of Virginia was marked by scholastic success, alcoholic binges, and gambling debts. Disgraced, he fled to Boston and joined the army under the name Edgar Perry. He performed well as an enlisted man and published his first collection of poetry, Tamerlane and Other Poems, *at the age of eighteen. After an abortive stint at West Point led to a final break with Allan, Poe embarked on a full-time literary career. A respected critic and editor, he sharply improved both the content and circulation of every magazine with which he was associated. But, morbidly sensitive to criticism, paranoid and belligerent when drunk, he left or was fired from every post he held. Poorly paid as both an editor and a writer, he earned almost nothing from the works that made him famous, such as "The Fall of the House of Usher" and "The Raven."*

After the break with his foster family, Poe rediscovered his own. From 1831, he lived with his father's widowed sister, Maria Clemm, and her daughter, Virginia. In 1836 Poe married this thirteen-year-old first cousin. These women provided him with much-needed emotional stability. However, like his mother, Poe's wife died of tuberculosis at age twenty-four, her demise doubtless hastened by poverty. Afterward, Poe's life came apart; his drinking intensified, as did his self-destructive tendencies. In October 1849 he died in mysterious circumstances, a few days after being found sick and incoherent on a Baltimore street.

The Tell-Tale Heart (1843) 1850

True!—nervous—very, very dreadfully nervous I had been and am; but why *will* you say that I am mad? The disease had sharpened my senses—not destroyed—not dulled them. Above all was the sense of hearing acute. I heard all things in the heaven and in the earth. I heard many things in hell. How, then, am I mad? Hearken! and observe how healthily—how calmly, I can tell you the whole story.

It is impossible to say how first the idea entered my brain; but once conceived, it haunted me day and night. Object there was none. Passion there was none. I loved the old man. He had never wronged me. He had never given me insult. For his gold I had no desire. I think it was his eye! yes, it was this! One of his eyes resembled that of a vulture—a pale blue eye, with a film over it. Whenever it fell upon me, my blood ran cold; and so by degrees—very gradually—I made up my mind to take the life of the old man, and thus rid myself of the eye forever.

Now this is the point. You fancy me mad. Madmen know nothing. But you should have seen *me*. You should have seen how wisely I proceeded—with what caution—with what foresight—with what dissimulation I went to work! I was never kinder to the old man than during the whole week before I killed him. And every night, about midnight, I turned the latch of his door and opened it—oh, so gently! And then, when I had made an opening sufficient for my head, I put in a dark lantern, all closed, closed, so that no light shone out, and then I thrust in my head. Oh, you would have laughed to see how cunningly I thrust it in! I moved it slowly—very, very slowly, so that I might not disturb the old man's sleep. It took me an hour to place my whole head within the opening so far that I could see him as he lay upon his bed. Ha!—would a madman have been so wise as this? And then, when my head was well in the room, I undid the lantern cautiously—oh, so cautiously—cautiously (for the hinges creaked)—I undid it just so much that a single thin ray fell upon the vulture eye. And this I did for seven long nights—every night just at midnight—but I found the eye always closed; and so it was impossible to do the work; for it was not the old man who vexed me, but his Evil Eye. And every morning, when the day broke, I went boldly into the chamber, and spoke courageously to him, calling him by name in a hearty tone, and inquiring how he had passed the night. So you see he would have been a very profound old man, indeed, to suspect that every night, just at twelve, I looked in upon him while he slept.

Upon the eighth night I was more than usually cautious in opening the door. A watch's minute hand moves more quickly than did mine. Never before that night had I *felt* the extent of my own powers—of my sagacity. I could scarcely contain my feelings of triumph. To think that there I was, opening the door, little by little, and he not even to dream of my secret deeds or thoughts. I fairly chuckled at the idea; and perhaps he heard me; for he moved on the bed suddenly, as if startled. Now you may think that I drew back—but no. His room was as black as pitch with the thick darkness (for the shutters were close fastened, through fear of robbers), and so I knew that he could not see the opening of the door, and I kept pushing it on steadily, steadily.

I had my head in, and was about to open the lantern, when my thumb slipped upon the tin fastening, and the old man sprang up in the bed, crying out—"Who's there?" 5

I kept quite still and said nothing. For a whole hour I did not move a muscle, and in the meantime I did not hear him lie down. He was still sitting up in the bed, listening;—just as I have done, night after night, hearkening to the death watches° in the wall.

Presently I heard a slight groan, and I knew it was the groan of mortal terror. It was not a groan of pain or of grief—oh, no!—it was the low stifled sound that arises from the bottom of the soul when overcharged with awe. I knew the sound very well. Many a night, just at midnight, when all the world slept, it has welled up from my own bosom, deepening, with its dreadful echo, the terrors that distracted me. I say I knew it well. I knew what the old man felt, and pitied him, although I chuckled at heart. I knew that he had been lying awake ever since the first slight noise, when he had turned in the bed. His fears had been ever since growing upon him. He had been trying to fancy them causeless, but could not. He had been saying to himself—"It is nothing but the wind in the chimney—it is only a mouse crossing the floor," or "it is merely a cricket which has made a single chirp." Yes, he had been trying to comfort himself with these suppositions; but he had found all in vain. *All in vain;* because Death, in approaching him, had stalked with his black shadow before him, and enveloped the victim. And it was the mournful influence of the unperceived shadow that caused him to feel—although he neither saw nor heard—to *feel* the presence of my head within the room.

When I had waited a long time, very patiently, without hearing him lie down, I resolved to open a little—a very, very little crevice in the lantern. So I opened it—you cannot imagine how stealthily, stealthily—until, at length, a single dim ray, like the thread of the spider, shot from out of the crevice and fell upon the vulture eye.

It was open—wide, wide open—and I grew furious as I gazed upon it. I saw it with perfect distinctness—all a dull blue, with a hideous veil over it that chilled the very marrow in my bones; but I could see nothing else of the old man's face or person: for I had directed the ray as if by instinct, precisely upon the damned spot.

And now have I not told you that what you mistake for madness is but over-acuteness of the senses?—now, I say, there came to my ears a low, dull, quick sound, such as a watch makes when enveloped in cotton. I knew *that* sound well, too. It was the beating of the old man's heart. It increased my fury, as the beating of a drum stimulates the soldier into courage. 10

But even yet I refrained and kept still. I scarcely breathed. I held the lantern motionless. I tried how steadily I could maintain the ray upon the eye. Meantime the hellish tattoo of the heart increased. It grew quicker and quicker, and louder and louder every instant. The old man's terror *must* have been extreme! It grew louder, I say, louder every moment!—do you mark me well? I have told you that I am nervous:

---

death watches: beetles that infest timbers. Their clicking sound was thought to be an omen of death.

so I am. And now at the dead hour of the night, amid the dreadful silence of that old house, so strange a noise as this excited me to uncontrollable terror. Yet, for some minutes longer I refrained and stood still. But the beating grew louder, louder! I thought the heart must burst. And now a new anxiety seized me—the sound would be heard by a neighbor! The old man's hour had come! With a loud yell, I threw open the lantern and leaped into the room. He shrieked once—once only. In an instant I dragged him to the floor, and pulled the heavy bed over him. I then smiled gaily, to find the deed so far done. But, for many minutes, the heart beat on with a muffled sound. This, however, did not vex me; it would not be heard through the wall. At length it ceased. The old man was dead. I removed the bed and examined the corpse. Yes, he was stone, stone dead. I placed my hand upon the heart and held it there many minutes.

If still you think me mad, you will think so no longer when I describe the wise precautions I took for the concealment of the body. The night waned, and I worked hastily, but in silence. First of all I dismembered the corpse. I cut off the head and the arms and the legs.

I then took up three planks from the flooring of the chamber, and deposited all between the scantlings. I then replaced the boards so cleverly, so cunningly, that no human eye—not even *his*—could have detected anything wrong. There was nothing to wash out—no stain of any kind—no blood-spot whatever. I had been too wary for that. A tub had caught all—ha! ha!

When I had made an end of these labors, it was four o'clock—still dark as midnight. As the bell sounded the hour, there came a knocking at the street door. I went down to open it with a light heart,—for what had I *now* to fear? There entered three men, who introduced themselves, with perfect suavity, as officers of the police. A shriek had been heard by a neighbor during the night; suspicion of foul play had been aroused, information had been lodged at the police office, and they (the officers) had been deputed to search the premises.

I smiled,—for *what* had I to fear? I bade the gentlemen welcome. The shriek, I said, was my own in a dream. The old man, I mentioned, was absent in the country. I took my visitors all over the house. I bade them search—search *well*. I led them, at length, to *his* chamber. I showed them his treasures, secure, undisturbed. In the enthusiasm of my confidence, I brought chairs into the room, and desired them *here* to rest from their fatigues, while I myself, in the wild audacity of my perfect triumph, placed my own seat upon the very spot beneath which reposed the corpse of the victim.

The officers were satisfied. My *manner* had convinced them. I was singularly at ease. They sat, and while I answered cheerily, they chatted of familiar things. But, ere long, I felt myself getting pale and wished them gone. My head ached, and I fancied a ringing in my ears: but still they sat and still chatted. The ringing became more distinct:—it continued and became more distinct: I talked more freely to get rid of the feeling: but it continued and gained definitiveness—until, at length, I found that the noise was *not* within my ears.

No doubt I now grew *very* pale:—but I talked more fluently, and with a heightened voice. Yet the sound increased—and what could I do? It was a *low, dull, quick sound—much such a sound as a watch makes when enveloped in cotton*. I gasped for breath—and yet the officers heard it not. I talked more quickly—more vehemently; but the noise steadily increased. I arose and argued about trifles, in a high key and with violent gesticulations; but the noise steadily increased. Why *would* they not be gone? I paced the floor to and fro with heavy strides, as if excited to fury by the observations of the men—but the noise steadily increased. Oh God! what *could* I do? I foamed—I raved—I swore! I swung the chair upon which I had been sitting, and grated it upon the boards, but the noise arose over all and continually increased. It grew louder—louder—*louder!* And still the men chatted pleasantly, and smiled. Was it possible they heard not? Almighty God!—no, no! They heard!—they suspected!—they *knew!*—they were making a mockery of my horror!—this I thought, and this I think. But anything was better than this agony! Anything was more tolerable than this derision! I could bear those hypocritical smiles no longer! I felt that I must scream or die!—and now—again!—hark! louder! louder! louder! *louder!*—

"Villains!" I shrieked, "dissemble no more! I admit the deed!—tear up the planks!—here, here!—it is the beating of his hideous heart!"

Questions

1. From what point of view is Poe's story told? Why is this point of view particularly effective for "The Tell-Tale Heart"?
2. Point to details in the story that identify its speaker as an unreliable narrator.
3. What do we know about the old man in the story? What motivates the narrator to kill him?
4. In spite of all his precautions, the narrator does not commit the perfect crime. What trips him up?
5. How do you account for the police officers' chatting calmly with the murderer instead of reacting to the sound that stirs the murderer into a frenzy?
6. What might the old man's "Evil Eye" represent?
7. Whose heart does the narrator actually hear? How would different answers to that question change your entire reading of the story?
8. See the student essays on this story in the chapter "Writing About a Story" later in this book. What do they point out that enlarges your own appreciation of Poe's art?

Katherine Mansfield

Katherine Mansfield Beauchamp (1888–1923), who shortened her byline, was born into a sedate Victorian family in New Zealand, the daughter of a successful businessman. At fifteen, she emigrated to England to attend school and did not ever permanently return Down Under. In 1918, after a time of wild-oat sowing in bohemian London, she married the journalist and critic John Middleton Murry. All at once, Mansfield found herself struggling to define her sexual identity, to earn a living by her pen, to endure World War I (in which her brother was killed in action), and to survive the ravages of tuberculosis. She died at thirty-four, in France, at a spiritualist commune where she had sought to regain her health. Mansfield wrote no novels, but during her brief career concentrated on the

Katherine Mansfield

short story, in which form of art she has few peers. Bliss *(1920)* and The Garden-Party and Other Stories *(1922)* were greeted with an acclaim that has continued; her collected short stories were published in 1937. Some of her stories celebrate life, others wryly poke fun at it. Many reveal, in ordinary lives, small incidents that open like doorways into significances.

Miss Brill

1922

Although it was so brilliantly fine—the blue sky powdered with gold and great spots of light like white wine splashed over the Jardins Publiques—Miss Brill was glad that she had decided on her fur. The air was motionless, but when you opened your mouth there was just a faint chill, like a chill from a glass of iced water before you sip, and now and again a leaf came drifting—from nowhere, from the sky. Miss Brill put up her hand and touched her fur. Dear little thing! It was nice to feel it again. She had taken it out of its box that afternoon, shaken out the moth-powder, given it a good brush, and rubbed the life back into the dim little eyes. "What has been happening to me?" said the sad little eyes. Oh, how sweet it was to see them snap at her again from the red eiderdown! . . . But the nose, which was of some black composition, wasn't at all firm. It must have had a knock, somehow. Never mind—a little dab of black sealing-wax when the time came—when it was absolutely necessary. . . . Little rogue! Yes, she really felt like that about it. Little rogue biting its tail just by her left ear. She could have taken it off and laid it on her lap and stroked it. She felt a tingling in her hands and arms, but that came from walking, she supposed. And when she breathed, something light and sad—no, not sad, exactly—something gentle seemed to move in her bosom.

There were a number of people out this afternoon, far more than last Sunday. And the band sounded louder and gayer. That was because the Season had begun. For although the band played all year round on Sundays, out of season it was never the same. It was like some one playing with only the family to listen; it didn't care how it played if there weren't any strangers present. Wasn't the conductor wearing a new coat, too? She was sure it was new. He scraped with his foot and flapped his arms like a rooster about to crow, and the bandsmen sitting in the green rotunda blew out their cheeks and glared at the music. Now there came a little "flutey" bit—very pretty!—a little chain of bright drops. She was sure it would be repeated. It was; she lifted her head and smiled.

Only two people shared her "special" seat: a fine old man in a velvet coat, his hands clasped over a huge carved walking-stick, and a big old woman, sitting upright, with a roll of knitting on her embroidered apron. They did not speak. This was disappointing, for Miss Brill always looked forward to the conversation. She had become really quite expert, she thought, at listening as though she didn't listen, at sitting in other people's lives just for a minute while they talked round her.

She glanced, sideways, at the old couple. Perhaps they would go soon. Last Sunday, too, hadn't been as interesting as usual. An Englishman and his wife, he wearing a dreadful Panama hat and she button boots. And she'd gone on the whole time about how she ought to wear spectacles; she knew she needed them; but that it was no good getting any; they'd be sure to break and they'd never keep on. And he'd been so patient. He'd suggested everything—gold rims, the kind that curved round your ears, little pads inside the bridge. No, nothing would please her. "They'll always be sliding down my nose!" Miss Brill wanted to shake her.

The old people sat on the bench, still as statues. Never mind, there was always the crowd to watch. To and fro, in front of the flower-beds and the band rotunda, the couples and groups paraded, stopped to talk, to greet, to buy a handful of flowers from the old beggar who had his tray fixed to the railings. Little children ran among them, swooping and laughing; little boys with big white silk bows under their chins, little girls, little French dolls, dressed up in velvet and lace. And sometimes a tiny staggerer came suddenly rocking into the open from under the trees, stopped, stared, as suddenly sat down "flop," until its small high-stepping mother, like a young hen, rushed scolding to its rescue. Other people sat on the benches and green chairs, but they were nearly always the same, Sunday after Sunday, and—Miss Brill had often noticed—there was something funny about nearly all of them. They were odd, silent, nearly all old, and from the way they stared they looked as though they'd just come from dark little rooms or even—even cupboards!

Behind the rotunda the slender trees with yellow leaves down drooping, and through them just a line of sea, and beyond the blue sky with gold-veined clouds.

Tum-tum-tum tiddle-um! tiddle-um! tum tiddley-um tum ta! blew the band.

Two young girls in red came by and two young soldiers in blue met them, and they laughed and paired and went off arm-in-arm. Two peasant women with funny straw hats passed, gravely, leading beautiful smoke-colored donkeys. A cold, pale nun hurried by. A beautiful woman came along and dropped her bunch of violets, and a little boy ran after to hand them to her, and she took them and threw them away as if they'd been poisoned. Dear me! Miss Brill didn't know whether to admire that or not! And now an ermine toque and a gentleman in grey met just in front of her. He was tall, stiff, dignified, and she was wearing the ermine toque she'd bought when her hair was yellow. Now everything, her hair, her face, even her eyes, was the same color as the shabby ermine, and her hand, in its cleaned glove, lifted to dab her lips, was a tiny yellowish paw. Oh, she was so pleased to see him—delighted! She rather thought they were going to meet that afternoon. She described where she'd been—everywhere, here, there, along by the sea. The day was so charming—didn't he agree? And wouldn't he, perhaps? . . . But he shook his head, lighted a cigarette, slowly breathed a great deep puff into her face, and, even while she was still talking and laughing, flicked the match away and walked on. The ermine toque was alone; she smiled more brightly than ever. But even the band seemed to know what she was feeling and played more softly, played tenderly, and the drum beat, "The Brute! The Brute!" over and over. What would she do? What was going to happen now? But as Miss Brill wondered, the ermine toque turned, raised her hand as though she'd seen some one else, much nicer, just over there, and pattered away. And the band changed again and played more quickly, more gaily than ever, and the old couple on Miss Brill's seat got up and marched away, and such a funny old man with long whiskers hobbled along in time to the music and was nearly knocked over by four girls walking abreast.

Oh, how fascinating it was! How she enjoyed it! How she loved sitting here, watching it all! It was like a play. It was exactly like a play. Who could believe the sky at the back wasn't painted? But it wasn't till a little brown dog trotted on solemn and then slowly trotted off, like a little "theatre" dog, a little dog that had been drugged, that Miss Brill discovered what it was that made it so exciting. They were all on the stage. They weren't only the audience, not only looking on; they were acting. Even she had a part and came every Sunday. No doubt somebody would have noticed if she hadn't been there; she was part of the performance after all. How strange she'd never thought of it like that before! And yet it explained why she made such a point of starting from home at just the same time each week—so as not to be late for the performance—and it also explained why she had quite a queer, shy feeling at telling her English pupils how she spent her Sunday afternoons. No wonder! Miss Brill nearly laughed out loud. She was on the stage. She thought of the old invalid gentleman to whom she read the newspaper four afternoons a week while he slept in the garden. She had got quite used to the frail head on the cotton pillow, the hollowed eyes, the open mouth and the high pinched nose. If he'd been dead she mightn't have noticed for weeks; she wouldn't have minded. But suddenly he knew he was having the paper read to him by an actress! "An actress!" The old head lifted; two points of light quivered in the old eyes. "An actress—are ye?" And Miss Brill smoothed the newspaper as though it were the manuscript of her part and said gently: "Yes, I have been an actress for a long time."

The band had been having a rest. Now they started again. And what they played was warm, sunny, yet there was just a faint chill—a something, what was it?—not sadness—no, not sadness—a something that made you want to sing. The tune lifted, lifted, the light shone; and it seemed to Miss Brill that in another moment all of them, all the whole company, would begin singing. The young ones, the laughing ones who were moving together, they would begin, and the men's voices, very resolute and brave, would join them. And then she too, she too, and the others on the benches—they would come in with a kind of accompaniment—something low, that scarcely rose or fell, something so beautiful—moving . . . And Miss Brill's eyes filled with tears and she looked smiling at all the other members of the company. Yes, we understand, we understand, she thought—though what they understood she didn't know.

Just at that moment a boy and a girl came and sat down where the old couple had been. They were beautifully dressed; they were in love. The hero and heroine, of course, just arrived from his father's yacht. And still soundlessly singing, still with that trembling smile, Miss Brill prepared to listen.

"No, not now," said the girl. "Not here, I can't."

"But why? Because of that stupid old thing at the end there?" asked the boy. "Why does she come here at all—who wants her? Why doesn't she keep her silly old mug at home?"

"It's her fu-fur which is so funny," giggled the girl. "It's exactly like a fried whiting."

"Ah, be off with you!" said the boy in an angry whisper. Then: "Tell me, my petite chérie—"

"No, not here," said the girl. "Not *yet*."

On her way home she usually bought a slice of honeycake at the baker's. It was her Sunday treat. Sometimes there was an almond in her slice, sometimes not. It made a great difference. If there was an almond it was like carrying home a tiny present—a surprise—something that might very well not have been there. She hurried on the almond Sundays and struck the match for the kettle in quite a dashing way.

But today she passed the baker's boy, climbed the stairs, went into the little dark room—her room like a cupboard—and sat down on the red eiderdown. She sat there for a long time. The box that the fur came out of was on the bed. She unclasped the necklet quickly; quickly, without looking, laid it inside. But when she put the lid on she thought she heard something crying.

Questions

1. What details provide insight into Miss Brill's character and lifestyle?
2. What point of view is used in "Miss Brill"? How does this method improve the story?
3. Where and in what season does the story take place? Would the effect be the same if the story were set, say, in a remote Alaskan village in the winter?
4. What draws Miss Brill to the park every Sunday? What is the nature of the startling revelation that delights her on the day the story takes place?
5. Miss Brill's sense of herself is at least partly based on her attitudes toward others. Give instances of this tendency, showing also how it is connected with her drastic change of mood.
6. What explanations might there be for Miss Brill's thinking, in the last line of the story, that she "heard something crying"?

checklist: Analyzing a Story

1. PLOT
- [ ] What is the story's central conflict?
- [ ] Who is the protagonist? What does he or she want?
- [ ] What is at stake for the protagonist in the conflict?
- [ ] What stands in the way of the protagonist's easily achieving his or her goal?
- [ ] What are the main events that take place in the story? How does each event relate to the protagonist's struggle?
- [ ] Where do you find the story's climax, or crisis?
- [ ] How is the conflict resolved?
- [ ] Does the protagonist succeed in achieving his or her goals?
- [ ] What is the impact of success, failure, or a surprising outcome on the protagonist?

2. POINT OF VIEW
- [ ] How is the story narrated? Is it told in the third or the first person?
- [ ] If the story is told in the third person, is the point of view omniscient or does it confine itself to what is perceived by a particular character?
- [ ] What is gained by this choice?
- [ ] If the story is told by a first-person narrator, what is the speaker's main reason for telling the story? What does the narrator have to gain by making us believe his or her account?
- [ ] Does the first-person narrator fully understand his or her own motivations? Is there some important aspect of the narrator's character or situation that is being overlooked?
- [ ] Is there anything peculiar about the first-person narrator? Does this peculiarity create any suspicions about the narrator's accuracy or reliability?
- [ ] What does the narrator's perspective add? Would the story seem as memorable if related from another narrative angle?

3. CHARACTER
- ☐ Who is the main character or protagonist of the story?
- ☐ Make a quick list of the character's physical, mental, moral, or behavioral traits. Which seem especially significant to the action of the story?
- ☐ Does the main character have an antagonist in the story? How do they differ?
- ☐ Does the way the protagonist speaks reveal anything about his or her personality?
- ☐ If the story is told in the first person, what is revealed about how the protagonist views his or her surroundings?
- ☐ What is the character's primary motivation? Does this motivation seem reasonable to you?
- ☐ Does the protagonist fully understand his or her motivations?
- ☐ In what ways is the protagonist changed or tested by the events of the story?

4. SETTING
- ☐ Where does the story take place?
- ☐ What does the setting suggest about the characters' lives?
- ☐ Are there significant differences in the settings for different characters? What does this suggest about each person?
- ☐ When does the story take place? Is the time of year or time of day significant?
- ☐ Does the weather play a meaningful role in the story's action?
- ☐ What is the protagonist's relationship to the setting?
- ☐ Does the setting of the story in some way compel the protagonist into action?
- ☐ Does the story's time or place suggest something about the character of the protagonist?
- ☐ Does a change in setting during the story suggest some internal change in the protagonist?

5. TONE AND STYLE
- ☐ Does the writer use word choice in a distinctive way?
- ☐ Is the diction unusual in any way?
- ☐ Does the author tend toward long or short—even fragmented—sentences?
- ☐ How would you characterize the writer's voice? Is it formal or casual? Distant or intimate? Impassioned or restrained?
- ☐ Can the narrator's words be taken at face value? Is there anything ironic about the narrator's voice?

- ☐ How does the writer arrange the material? Is information delivered chronologically, or is the organization more complex?
- ☐ What is the writer's attitude toward the material?

6. SYMBOL
- ☐ Which objects, actions, or places seem unusually significant?
- ☐ List the specific objects, people, and ideas with which a particular symbol is associated.
- ☐ Locate the exact place in the story where the symbol links itself to the other thing.
- ☐ Ask whether each symbol comes with ready-made cultural associations.
- ☐ Avoid far-fetched interpretations. Focus first on the literal things, places, and actions in the story.
- ☐ Don't make a symbol mean too much or too little. Don't limit it to one narrow association or claim it summons up many different things.
- ☐ Be specific. Identify the exact place in the story where a symbol takes on a deeper meaning.

7. THEME
- ☐ List as many themes as possible that are suggested by the story.
- ☐ Circle the two or three most important possible themes and try to combine them into one sentence.
- ☐ Relate particular details of the story to the theme you have spelled out. Consider plot details, dialogue, setting, point of view, title—any elements that seem especially pertinent.
- ☐ Check whether all the elements of the story fit your thesis.
- ☐ Have you missed an important aspect of the story? Or have you chosen to focus on a secondary idea, overlooking the central one?
- ☐ If necessary, rework your thesis on theme until it applies to every element in the story.

3 READING A POEM

Every good poem begins as the poet's but ends as the reader's.

—MILLER WILLIAMS

What is poetry? The nature of poetry eludes simple definitions. (In this respect it is rather like jazz. Asked after one of his concerts, "What is jazz?" Louis Armstrong replied, "Man, if you gotta ask, you'll never know.") Definitions will be of little help at first, if we are to know poetry and respond to it. We have to go to it willing to see and hear. For this reason, we ask you not to be in any hurry to decide what poetry is, but instead to study poems in this book and to let them grow in your mind. This chapter provides an introduction to the study of poetry. It tries to help you look at a poem closely, and to offer you a wider and more accurate vocabulary with which to express what poems say to you.

Good poetry is something that readers can care about. In fact, an ancient belief of humankind is that the hearing of a poem, as well as the making of a poem, can be a religious act. Poetry, in speech and song, was part of classical Greek drama, which for playwright, actor, and spectator alike was a holy-day ceremony. The Greeks' belief that a poet writes a poem only by supernatural assistance is clear from the invocations to the Muse that begin the *Iliad* and the *Odyssey* and from the opinion of Socrates (in Plato's *Ion*) that a poet has no powers of invention until divinely inspired. Among the ancient Celts, poets were regarded as magicians and priests, and whoever insulted one of them might expect to receive a curse in rime potent enough to afflict him with boils and to curdle the milk of his cows.

To read a poem, we have to be willing to offer it responses *besides* a logical understanding. If we take the reading of poetry seriously (not solemnly), we may find that—as some of the poems in this book demonstrate—few other efforts can repay us so generously, both in wisdom and in joy. Let's begin with a consideration of several different types of poetry.

TYPES OF POETRY

Lyric Poetry

Originally, as its Greek name suggests, a *lyric* was a poem sung to the music of a lyre. This earlier meaning—a poem made for singing—is still current today, when we use *lyrics* to mean the words of a popular song. But the kind of printed poem we now call a *lyric* is usually something else: a short poem expressing the thoughts and feelings of a single speaker. Often a poet will write a lyric in the first person ("I") as in W. H. Auden's "Funeral Blues," but not always. A lyric can also be in the first person plural ("we"). Or a lyric might describe an object or recall an experience without the speaker's ever bringing himself or herself into it. In the sense in which we use it, **lyric** will usually apply to a kind of poem you can easily recognize: a short poem that sets forth the speaker's definite, unmistakable feelings.

W. H. Auden

W. H. Auden (1907–1973)

Funeral Blues   1940

Stop all the clocks, cut off the telephone,
Prevent the dog from barking with a juicy bone,
Silence the pianos and with muffled drum
Bring out the coffin, let the mourners come.

Let aeroplanes circle moaning overhead   5
Scribbling on the sky the message He Is Dead,
Put crêpe bows round the white necks of the public doves,
Let the traffic policemen wear black cotton gloves.

He was my North, my South, my East and West,
My working week and my Sunday rest,   10
My noon, my midnight, my talk, my song;
I thought that love would last for ever: I was wrong.

The stars are not wanted now: put out every one,
Pack up the moon and dismantle the sun,
Pour away the ocean and sweep up the woods;   15
For nothing now can ever come to any good.

Questions

1. In its first book publication, Auden included "Funeral Blues" in a section called "Lighter Poems." Why might he have done so? Do you agree with that classification?
2. The speaker's emotions are never directly described. What details in the poem tell us what the speaker is feeling?

3. The attitudes expressed in lines 12 and 16 might seem to be short-sighted and immature. Do they also express a deeper truth about the nature of love, and of human emotions in general?

Narrative Poetry

Although a lyric sometimes relates an incident or draws a scene, it does not usually relate a series of events. That happens in a **narrative poem**, one whose main purpose is to tell a story. Narrative poetry dates back to the Babylonian *Epic of Gilgamesh* (composed before 2000 B.C.) and Homer's epics the *Iliad* and the *Odyssey* (composed before 700 B.C.); it may well have originated much earlier. The art of narrative poetry invites the skills of a writer of fiction: the ability to draw characters and settings, to engage attention, to shape a plot. Needless to say, it calls for all the skills of a poet as well. Although there has recently been a revival of interest in writing narrative poems, they have a far smaller audience than the readership enjoyed in the nineteenth century by long verse narratives, such as Henry Wadsworth Longfellow's *Evangeline* and Alfred, Lord Tennyson's *Idylls of the King*. Here is a miniature narrative that has remained extremely popular for more than a hundred years:

Edwin Arlington Robinson (1869–1935)

Richard Cory 1897

Whenever Richard Cory went down town,
We people on the pavement looked at him:
He was a gentleman from sole to crown,
Clean favored, and imperially slim.

And he was always quietly arrayed, 5
And he was always human when he talked;
But still he fluttered pulses when he said,
"Good-morning," and he glittered when he walked.

And he was rich—yes, richer than a king—
And admirably schooled in every grace: 10
In fine,° we thought that he was everything   °*in short*
To make us wish that we were in his place.

So on we worked, and waited for the light,
And went without the meat, and cursed the bread;
And Richard Cory, one calm summer night, 15
Went home and put a bullet through his head.

Questions
1. How does "Richard Cory" fit the definition of a narrative poem?
2. Students frequently describe the poem's theme as "Money can't buy happiness." How much of the poem, in fact, is concerned with Richard Cory's wealth? What other attributes of his are more heavily emphasized?

3. Explain the meanings of lines 5, 10, and 14.
4. Does the word "glittered" in line 8 give any foreshadowing of the poem's conclusion? (Hint: think of a popular saying that contains the word "glitters.")

Dramatic Poetry

A third kind of poetry is **dramatic poetry**, which presents the voice of an imaginary character (or characters) speaking directly, without any additional narration by the author. Strictly speaking, the term *dramatic poetry* describes any verse written for the stage (and until a few centuries ago most playwrights, such as Shakespeare and Molière, wrote their plays mainly in verse). But the term *dramatic poetry* most often refers to the **dramatic monologue**, a poem written as a speech made by a character (other than the author) at some decisive moment. A dramatic monologue is usually addressed by the speaker to some other character who remains silent. In the following poem, Margaret Atwood adopts the mask of an ancient mythological creature to make some timeless observations:

Margaret Atwood (b. 1939)

Siren Song   1974

This is the one song everyone
would like to learn: the song
that is irresistible:

the song that forces men
to leap overboard in squadrons   5
even though they see the beached skulls

the song nobody knows
because anyone who has heard it
is dead, and the others can't remember.

Shall I tell you the secret   10
and if I do, will you get me
out of this bird suit?

I don't enjoy it here
squatting on this island
looking picturesque and mythical   15

with these two feathery maniacs,
I don't enjoy singing
this trio, fatal and valuable.

I will tell the secret to you,
to you, only to you.   20
Come closer. This song

is a cry for help: Help me!
Only you, only you can,
you are unique

at last. Alas   25
it is a boring song
but it works every time.

SIREN SONG. In Greek mythology, sirens were half-woman, half-bird nymphs who lured sailors to their deaths by singing hypnotically beautiful songs.

Questions

1. Who is the speaker of the poem? What details tell us so?
2. Do you find any shifts in tone or attitude as the poem proceeds? Explain.
3. What is the thematic intent of the final stanza?

READING A POEM

How do you read a poem? Many a reader who has no trouble understanding and enjoying prose finds poetry difficult. At first glance, a poem usually will make some sense and give some pleasure, but it may not yield everything at once. Poetry is not to be galloped over like the daily news: it is to be read slowly, carefully, and attentively. Not all poems are difficult, of course, and some can be understood and enjoyed on first encounter. But good poems yield more if read twice; and the best poems—after ten, twenty, or a hundred readings—still go on yielding.

How to set about reading a poem? Here are a few suggestions. To begin with, read the poem once straight through, with no particular expectations; read open-mindedly. Let yourself experience whatever you find, without worrying just yet about the large general and important ideas the poem contains (if indeed it contains any). Don't dwell on a troublesome word or difficult passage—just push on. Some of the difficulties may seem smaller when you read the poem a second time.

On the second reading, read for the exact sense of all the words; if there are words you don't understand, look them up in a dictionary. Dwell on any difficult parts as long as you need to.

If you read the poem silently, sound its words in your mind. Better still, read the poem aloud, or listen to someone else reading it. You may discover meanings you didn't perceive in it before. Deciding how to speak a poem can be an excellent way of coming to understand it.

Paraphrase

Try to **paraphrase** the poem as a whole, or perhaps just the more difficult lines. In paraphrasing, we put into our own words what we understand the poem to say, restating ideas that seem essential, coming out and stating what the poem may only suggest. This may sound like a heartless thing to do to a poem, but good poems can stand it. In fact, to compare a poem to its paraphrase is a good way to see the distance between poetry and prose. In making a paraphrase, we generally work through a poem or a passage line by line. The statement that results may take as many words as the original, if not more. A paraphrase, then, is different and ampler than a **summary**—a brief condensation of the gist, main idea, or story. And even though it represents an imperfect approximation of the real thing, a paraphrase can be useful to write and read. It can clearly map out a poem's key images, actions, and ideas. A map is no substitute for a landscape, but a good map often helps us find our way through the landscape without getting lost.

A paraphrase of Robinson's "Richard Cory" might go something like this: "Richard Cory had good breeding, looks, and fabulous wealth—and yet he never acted snooty or superior to other people. When we looked at our hard lives, it seemed that it must be heaven on earth to be him. But with all he had going for him, in the end he killed himself, which shows that you never really know the truth about anyone else's feelings." Such a restatement, accurate as it may be in reproducing the substance of what Robinson is saying, seems dull when compared to the subtlety and art of the original, in which every word contributes to the overall effect— for instance "crown" and "In fine," instead of the more ordinary "head" and "in short." Nonetheless, the paraphrase is a useful method of clarifying—and deepening—our understanding of the poem's meaning, as in the use of the word "human" to describe Richard Cory's basic decency and consideration toward others.

Theme and Subject

Whenever you paraphrase, you stick your neck out. You affirm what the poem gives you to understand. And making a paraphrase can help you see the central thought of the poem, its **theme**. The theme isn't the same as the **subject**, which is the main topic, whatever the poem is "about." The theme of a poem is the idea or insight the poem expresses or reveals.

Writing Assignment on Reading a Poem

Paraphrase any short poem included in this book. Be sure to do a careful line-by-line reading. Include the most vital points and details, and state the poem's main thought or theme without quoting any original passage.

ELEMENTS OF POETRY

1. TONE

> *Irony is that little pinch of salt*
> *which alone makes the dish palatable.*
> —JOHANN WOLFGANG VON GOETHE

Like tone of voice, **tone** in literature often conveys an attitude toward the person addressed. Like the manner of a person, the manner of a poem may be friendly or belligerent toward its reader, condescending or respectful; the tone of a poem may also tell us how the speaker feels about himself or herself. But usually when we ask "What is the tone of a poem?" we mean "What attitude does the poet take toward a theme or a subject?"

Strictly speaking, tone isn't an attitude; it is whatever in the poem makes an attitude clear to us: the choice of certain words instead of others, the picking out of certain details. To perceive the tone of a poem rightly, we need to read the poem carefully, paying attention to whatever suggestions we find in it. We need to listen to the words, as we might listen to an actual conversation. The key is to hear not only *what* is being said but also *how* it is being said. Does the speaker sound noticeably surprised, angry, nostalgic, or tender? In reading the following poem, pay close attention not only to the meanings of the words, but to the sounds they make and the feelings they create:

Emily Dickinson (1830–1886)

Wild Nights – Wild Nights! (about 1861)

Wild Nights – Wild Nights!
Were I with thee
Wild Nights should be
Our luxury!

Futile – the Winds – 5
To a Heart in port –
Done with the Compass –
Done with the Chart!

Rowing in Eden –
Ah, the Sea! 10
Might I but moor – Tonight –
In Thee!

Questions

1. How would you describe the tone of this poem—ecstatic, wistful, frustrated, or some combination of all three? What elements of the text do you base your conclusions on?
2. Look up the word "luxury" in an unabridged dictionary. Are there any historical meanings or associations that might be relevant to the poem's theme?
3. Paraphrase the second stanza, and relate it to the poem's larger thematic concerns.

The Person in the Poem

The tone of a poem, we said, is like a tone of voice in that both communicate feelings. Still, this comparison raises a question: when we read a poem, whose "voice" speaks to us? "The poet's" is one possible answer; and in the case of many a poem that answer may be right. But don't assume that every poem is spoken by its author.

Persona

Most of us can tell the difference between a person we meet in life and a person we meet in a work of art—and yet, in reading poems, we may want to assume that the poet is making a personal statement. But do all poems have to be personal? Here is a brief poem inscribed on the tombstone of an infant in Burial Hill Cemetery, Plymouth, Massachusetts:

Since I have been so quickly done for,
I wonder what I was begun for.

We do not know who wrote those lines, but it is clear that the poet was not a short-lived infant writing from personal experience. In many poems, the speaker is obviously a **persona**, or fictitious character: not the poet, but the poet's creation.

Irony

To see a distinction between the literal sense of the words and the true intent of the statement—as in lines 10–24 of Margaret Atwood's "Siren Song"—is to be aware of **irony**: a manner of speaking that implies a discrepancy. If the mask says one thing and we sense that the writer is in fact saying something else, the writer has adopted an **ironic point of view**.

The effect of irony depends on the reader's noticing some incongruity or discrepancy between two things. In **verbal irony**, as in the Atwood poem, there is a contrast between the speaker's words and their meaning; in an **ironic point of view**, between the writer's attitude and what is spoken by a fictitious character; in **dramatic irony**, between the limited knowledge of a character and the fuller knowledge of the reader or spectator; in **cosmic irony**, between a character's position or aspiration and the treatment he or she receives at the hands of Fate.

■ Writing Assignment on Tone

Choose a poem from this book, and analyze its speaker's attitude toward the poem's main subject. Examine the author's choice of specific words and images to create the particular tone used to convey the speaker's attitudes. (Possible subjects include Wilfred Owen's attitude toward war in "Dulce et Decorum Est," the tone and imagery of Theodore Roethke's "My Papa's Waltz," and William Blake's view of life in a large city in "London.")

2. WORDS

> *We all write poems; it is simply that poets are the ones who write in words.*
> —JOHN FOWLES

Literal Meaning: What a Poem Says First

Although a poem may contain images and ideas, it is made up of words. Language is the medium of poetry, and a poem's diction—its exact wording—is the chief source of its power. In reading a poem, some people assume that its words can be skipped over rapidly, and they try to leap at once to the poem's general theme. Such readers often ignore the literal meanings of words: the ordinary, matter-of-fact sense to be found in a dictionary.

Writers labor to shape each word and phrase to create particular effects. Poets choose words for their meanings, their associations, and even their sounds. Changing a single word may ruin a poem's effect, just as changing one number in an online password makes all the other numbers useless.

Diction

If a poem says *daffodils* instead of *plant life*, *diaper years* instead of *infancy*, we call its **diction**, or choice of words, **concrete** rather than **abstract**. Concrete words refer to what we can immediately perceive with our senses: *dog, actor, chemical*, or particular individuals who belong to those general classes: *Bonzo the fox terrier, Clint Eastwood, hydrogen sulfate*. Abstract words express ideas or concepts: *love, time, truth*. In abstracting, we leave out some characteristics found in each individual and instead observe a quality common to many. The word *beauty*, for instance, denotes what may be observed in numerous persons, places, and things.

Types of Diction

Handbooks of grammar sometimes distinguish various **levels of diction**. A sort of ladder is imagined, on whose rungs words, phrases, and sentences may be ranked in an ascending order of formality, from the curses of an illiterate thug to the commencement-day address of a doctor of divinity. These levels range from **vulgate** (speech not much affected by schooling) to **colloquial** (the casual conversation or informal writing of literate people) to **general English** (literate speech and writing, more studied than colloquial but not pretentious), up to **formal English** (the impersonal language of educated persons, usually only written, possibly spoken on dignified occasions). Recently, however, lexicographers have been shunning such labels. The designation *colloquial* was expelled from *Webster's Third New International Dictionary* on the grounds that "it is impossible to know whether a word out of context is colloquial or not" and that the diction of Americans nowadays is more fluid than the labels suggest.

Allusion

An **allusion** is an indirect reference to any person, place, or thing—fictitious, historical, or actual. Usually the poet draws only upon common knowledge. When, in his poem "To Helen," Edgar Allan Poe refers to "the glory that was Greece / And the grandeur that was Rome," he assumes that we have heard of those places. He also expects that we will understand his allusion to the cultural achievements of those ancient nations and perhaps even catch the subtle contrast between those two similar words *glory* and *grandeur*, with its suggestion that, for all its merits, Roman civilization was also more pompous than Greek civilization.

Allusions not only enrich the meaning of a poem, they also save space. In "The Love Song of J. Alfred Prufrock," T. S. Eliot, by giving a brief introductory quotation from the speech of a damned soul in Dante's *Inferno*, is able to suggest that his poem will be the confession of a soul in torment, who sees no chance of escape and who feels the need to confide in someone but trusts that his secrets will be kept safe.

Gina Valdés (b. 1943)

English con Salsa 1993

Welcome to ESL 100, English Surely Latinized,
inglés con chile y cilantro, English as American
as Benito Juárez. Welcome, muchachos from Xochicalco,
learn the language of dólares and Dolores, of kings
and queens, of Donald Duck and Batman. Holy Toluca! 5
In four months you'll be speaking like George Washington,

in four weeks you can ask, More coffee? In two months
you can say, May I take your order? In one year you
can ask for a raise, cool as the Tuxpan River.

Welcome, muchachas from Teocaltiche, in this class   10
we speak English refrito, English con sal y limón,
English thick as mango juice, English poured from
a clay jug, English tuned like a requinto from Uruapan,
English lighted by Oaxacan dawns, English spiked
with mezcal from Mitla, English with a red cactus   15
flower blooming in its heart.

Welcome, welcome, amigos del sur, bring your Zapotec
tongues, your Nahuatl tones, your patience of pyramids,
your red suns and golden moons, your guardian angels,
your duendes, your patron saints, Santa Tristeza,   20
Santa Alegría, Santo Todolopuede. We will sprinkle
holy water on pronouns, make the sign of the cross
on past participles, jump like fish from Lake Pátzcuaro
on gerunds, pour tequila from Jalisco on future perfects,
say shoes and shit, grab a cool verb and a pollo loco   25
and dance on the walls like chapulines.

When a teacher from La Jolla or a cowboy from Santee
asks you, Do you speak English? You'll answer, Sí,
yes, simón, of course, I love English!
                                And you'll hum
A Mixtec chant that touches la tierra and the heavens.   30

ENGLISH CON SALSA. *3 Benito Juárez:* Mexican statesman (1806–1872), president of Mexico in the 1860s and 1870s. *3 Xochicalco . . . 5 Toluca . . . etc. . . . 30 Mixtec:* Names of ancient and modern places, regions, and languages in Mexico that reflect that nation's pre-Columbian peoples and history. *13 requinto:* small, high-pitched version of another instrument.

Questions

1. Valdés's poem is full of Spanish and Mesoamerican words and places. Even the title mixes two languages. What does Valdés gain by mixing languages? Would the poem be the same if it were all in English?
2. Whom is the poem addressing? Why is that important in determining the diction?
3. What does Valdés suggest about the nature of American English and contemporary Americans?
4. In addition to Spanish words Valdés also integrates Mesoamerican words, tribes, and places into the poem. What does that choice of diction suggest about the people she addresses?
5. Could a reader in England understand Valdés's English? If a British reader said that this poem made no sense, would you agree or disagree?

■ Writing Assignment on Word Choice

Find two poems in this book that use very different sorts of diction to address similar subjects. You might choose one with formal and elegant language and another with very down-to-earth or slangy word choices. Some good choices include Elizabeth

Barrett Browning's "How Do I Love Thee? Let Me Count the Ways" and Kim Addonizio's "First Poem for You"; Robert Frost's "Acquainted with the Night" and E. E. Cummings's "anyone lived in a pretty how town." In a short essay, discuss how the difference in diction affects the tones of the two poems.

3. DENOTATION AND CONNOTATION

> *To name an object is to take away three-fourths*
> *of the pleasure given by a poem . . .*
> *to suggest it, that is the ideal.*
>
> —STÉPHANE MALLARMÉ

Every word has at least one **denotation**: a meaning as defined in a dictionary. But the English language has many a common word with so many denotations that a reader may need to think twice to see what it means in a specific context. The noun *field*, for instance, can denote a piece of ground, a sports arena, the scene of a battle, part of a flag, a profession, and a number system in mathematics. Further, the word can be used as a verb ("he fielded a grounder") or an adjective ("field trip," "field glasses").

A word also has **connotations**: overtones or suggestions of additional meaning that it gains from the various contexts in which it might appear. The word *skeleton*, according to a dictionary, denotes "the bony framework of a human being or other vertebrate animal, which supports the flesh and protects the organs." But by its associations, the word can rouse thoughts of war, of disease and death, or even of one's plans to go to medical school. Think, too, of the difference between "Old Doc Jones" and "Theodore E. Jones, M.D." In the mind's eye, the former appears in his shirtsleeves; the latter has a gold nameplate on his door.

On our first reading of a poem, we are concerned to understand the denotative meanings of its individual words; in our effort to comprehend the poem on its most literal level, we must also attend to the larger meanings those words create when they combine with one another to form statements and descriptions. When journalists write a news story, they usually try to cover the "five W's" in the opening paragraph—*who, what, when, where,* and *why.* These questions are worthwhile ones to ask about a poem: *Who* is the speaker or central figure of the poem? *What* objects or events are being seen or presented? *When* does the poem take place? *Where* is the poem set? *Why* does the action or occurrence take place?

Robert Frost (1874–1963)

Nothing Gold Can Stay   1923

Nature's first green is gold,
Her hardest hue to hold.
Her early leaf's a flower;
But only so an hour.
Then leaf subsides to leaf.   5
So Eden sank to grief,
So dawn goes down to day.
Nothing gold can stay.

Questions

1. To what myth does this poem allude? Does Frost sound as though he believes in the myth or as though he rejects it?
2. When Frost says, "Nature's first green is gold," he is describing how many leaves first appear as tiny yellow buds and blossoms. But what else does this line imply?
3. What would happen to the poem's meaning if line 6 were omitted?

Writing Assignment on Denotation and Connotation

Search a poem of your own choosing for the answers to the "five W's"—Who? What? When? Where? Why? Indicate, with details, which of the questions are explicitly answered by the poem and which are left unaddressed.

4. IMAGERY

> *It is better to present one Image in a lifetime than to produce voluminous works.*
>
> —EZRA POUND

Images are powerful things—thus the old saw, "A picture is worth a thousand words." A poem, however, must build its pictures from words. By taking note of its imagery, and watching how the nature of those images evolves from start to finish, you can go a long way toward a better understanding of the poem.

Though the term **image** suggests a thing seen, when speaking of images in poetry, we generally mean *a word or sequence of words that refers to any sensory experience*. Often this experience is a sight (**visual imagery**), but it may be a sound (**auditory imagery**) or a touch (**tactile imagery**, as a perception of roughness or smoothness).

It is tempting to think of imagery as mere decoration, but a successful image is not just a dab of paint or a flashy bauble. Indeed, some literary critics look for much of the meaning of a poem in its imagery, wherein they expect to see the mind of the poet more truly revealed than in whatever the poet explicitly claims to believe.

Langston Hughes (1902–1967)

Harlem [Dream Deferred]   1951

What happens to a dream deferred?

> Does it dry up
> like a raisin in the sun?
> Or fester like a sore—
> And then run?   5
> Does it stink like rotten meat?
> Or crust and sugar over—
> like a syrupy sweet?

>   Maybe it just sags
>   like a heavy load.   10
>
>   Or does it explode?

HARLEM. This famous poem appeared under two titles in the author's lifetime. Both titles appear above the poem.

Questions

1. How many images does this poem contain? What are they?
2. How many of the five senses are invoked in the poem, and by which images?
3. What do all the images in the poem have in common?

■ Writing Assignment on Imagery

Examining any poem in this book, demonstrate how its imagery helps communicate its general theme. Be specific in noting how each key image contributes to the poem's total effect. Feel free to consult criticism on the poem, but make sure to credit any observation you borrow from a critical source.

5. FIGURES OF SPEECH

> *All slang is metaphor,*
> *and all metaphor is poetry.*
>
> —G. K. CHESTERTON

"I will speak daggers to her, but use none," says Hamlet, preparing to confront his mother. His statement makes sense only because we realize that *daggers* is to be taken two ways: literally (denoting sharp, pointed weapons) and nonliterally (referring to something that can be used *like* weapons—namely, words). Reading poetry, we often find comparisons between two things whose similarity we have never noticed before. Such comparisons are called **figures of speech**. In its broadest definition, a figure of speech may be said to occur whenever a speaker or writer, for the sake of freshness or emphasis, departs from the usual denotations of words. Certainly, when Hamlet says he will speak daggers, no one expects him to release pointed weapons from his lips, for *daggers* is not to be read solely for its denotation. Its connotations—sharp, stabbing, piercing, wounding—also come to mind, and we see ways in which words and daggers work alike. (Words too can hurt: by striking through pretenses, possibly, or by wounding their hearer's self-esteem.)

Figures of speech are not devices to state what is demonstrably untrue. Indeed they often state truths that more literal language cannot communicate; they call attention to such truths; they lend them emphasis.

Metaphor and Simile

A **simile** is a comparison of two things, indicated by some connective, usually *like*, *as*, *than*, or a verb such as *resembles*. A simile expresses a similarity. Still, for a simile to exist, the things compared have to be dissimilar in kind. It is no simile to say "Your fingers are like mine"; that is a literal observation. But to say "Your fingers are like sausages" is to use a simile. Omit the connective—say "Your fingers are sausages"—and the result is a **metaphor**, a statement that one thing *is* something else, which, in a literal sense, it is not.

Oh, my love is like a red, red rose.	*Simile*
Oh, my love resembles a red, red rose.	*Simile*
Oh, my love is a red, red rose.	*Metaphor*
Oh, my love has red petals and sharp thorns.	*Implied Metaphor*

In general, a simile refers to only one characteristic that two things have in common, while a metaphor is not limited in the number of resemblances it may indicate. To use the simile "He eats like a pig" is to compare man and animal in one respect: eating habits. But to say "He's a pig" is to use a metaphor that might involve comparisons of appearance and morality as well.

Personification

When Shakespeare asks, in a sonnet,

> O! how shall summer's honey breath hold out
> Against the wrackful siege of batt'ring days,

he is giving breath to summer, and making the season a man or woman. It is as if the fragrance of summer were the breath within a person's body, and winter were the onslaught of old age. This is an instance of **personification**: a figure of speech in which a thing, an animal, or an abstract term (*truth, nature*) is made human.

Overstatement and Understatement

Most of us, from time to time, emphasize a point with a statement containing exaggeration: "Faster than greased lightning," "I've told him a thousand times." We do not then speak literal truth, but use a figure of speech called **overstatement** (or **hyperbole**). Poets too, being fond of emphasis, often exaggerate for effect. Instances are Andrew Marvell's profession of a love that should grow "Vaster than empires, and more slow" and John Burgon's description of Petra: "A rose-red city, half as old as Time." The opposite figure is **understatement**, implying more than is said. One example is Robert Frost's line "One could do worse than be a swinger of birches"—the conclusion of a poem that has suggested that to swing on a birch tree is one of the most deeply satisfying activities in the world.

Paradox

Paradox occurs in a statement that at first strikes us as self-contradictory but that on reflection makes some sense. "The peasant," said G. K. Chesterton, "lives in a larger world than the globe-trotter." Here, two different meanings of *larger* are contrasted: "greater in spiritual values" versus "greater in miles." Some paradoxical statements, however, are much more than plays on words. In a moving sonnet, the blind John Milton tells how one night he dreamed he could see his dead wife. The poem ends in a paradox:

> But oh, as to embrace me she inclined,
> I waked, she fled, and day brought back my night.

Pun

Asked to tell the difference between men and women, Samuel Johnson replied, "I can't conceive, madam, can you?" The great dictionary-maker was using a figure of speech known to classical rhetoricians as *paronomasia*, better known to us as a **pun** or play on words. How does a pun operate? It reminds us of another word (or other words) of similar or identical sound but of very different denotation. (Or, as in Johnson's example, a pun can play on two different meanings of the same word.) Although puns at their worst can be mere piddling quibbles, at best they can sharply point to surprising but genuine resemblances.

■ Writing Assignment on Figures of Speech

In a brief essay of approximately 500 words, analyze the figures of speech to be found in any poem in this book. To what effect does the poem employ metaphors, similes, hyperbole, overstatement, paradox, or any other figure of speech?

6. SOUND

> *The sound must seem an echo to the sense.*
> —ALEXANDER POPE

Good poetry, like music, appeals to the ear. The sound of words in itself gives pleasure—and most good poetry has meaningful sound as well as musical sound. Certainly the words of a song have an effect different from that of wordless music: they go along with their music and, by making statements, add more meaning.

Euphony and Cacophony

When, in a poem, the sound of words working together with meaning pleases mind and ear, the effect is **euphony**, as in the following lines from Tennyson's "Come down, O maid":

> Myriads of rivulets hurrying through the lawn,
> The moan of doves in immemorial elms,
> And murmuring of innumerable bees.

Euphony's opposite is **cacophony**: a harsh, discordant effect. It too is chosen for the sake of meaning. We hear it in Milton's scornful reference in "Lycidas" to corrupt clergymen whose songs "Grate on their scrannel pipes of wretched straw." (Read that line and one of Tennyson's aloud and see which requires lips, teeth, and tongue to do more work.) But note that although Milton's line is harsh in sound, the line (when we meet it in his poem) is pleasing because it is artful.

Is sound identical with meaning in lines such as these? Not quite. All by itself, sound does not communicate anything definite. The most beautiful phrase in the English language, according to Dorothy Parker, is *cellar door*. Another wit once nominated, as our most euphonious word, not *sunrise* or *silvery*, but *syphilis*.

Onomatopoeia

Relating sound more closely to meaning, the device called **onomatopoeia** is an attempt to represent a thing or an action by a word that imitates the sound associated with it: *zoom, whiz, crash, bang, ding-dong, pitter-patter, yakety-yak*. Onomatopoeia is often effective in poetry, as in Emily Dickinson's line about the fly with its "uncertain stumbling Buzz," in which the nasal sounds *n, m, ng* and the sibilants *c, s* help make a droning buzz.

Alliteration and Assonance

Poems have patterns of sounds. Among such patterns that have long been popular in English poetry is **alliteration**, which has been defined as a succession of similar sounds. Alliteration occurs in the repetition of the same consonant sound at the beginning of successive words—"round and round the rugged rocks the ragged rascal ran." In a line by E. E. Cummings, "colossal hoax of clocks and calendars," the sound of *x* within *hoax* alliterates with the *cks* in *clocks*.

To repeat the sound of a *vowel* is to produce **assonance**. Like alliteration, assonance may occur either initially—"*all* the *awful auguries*"—or internally, as in Edmund Spenser's lines "Her goodly *eyes like* sapphires sh*i*ning br*i*ght, / Her forehead *i*vory wh*i*te ..." and it can help make common phrases unforgettable: "eager beaver," "holy smoke." Like alliteration, it slows the reader down and focuses attention.

Rime

Rime is one means to set poetry apart from ordinary conversation and bring it closer to music. A **rime** (or rhyme), defined most narrowly, occurs when two or more words or phrases contain an identical or similar vowel sound, usually accented, and the consonant sounds (if any) that follow the vowel sound are identical: *hay* and *sleigh*, *prairie schooner* and *piano tuner*. From these examples it will be seen that rime depends not on spelling but on sound.

Excellent rimes surprise. Riming becomes dull clunking if, at the end of each line, the reader can predict the word that will end the next. Hearing many a pop song for the first time, a listener can do so: *charms* lead to *arms*, *skies above* to *love*. As Alexander Pope observes of the habits of dull rimesters,

> Where'er you find "the cooling western breeze,"
> In the next line it "whispers through the trees";
> If crystal streams "with pleasing murmurs creep,"
> The reader's threatened (not in vain) with "sleep" ...

Types of Rime

To have an **exact rime**, sounds following the vowel sound have to be the same: *red* and *bread*, *wealthily* and *stealthily*, *walk to her* and *talk to her*. If final consonant sounds are the same but the vowel sounds are different, the result is **slant rime**, also called **near rime**, **off rime**, or **imperfect rime**: *sun* riming with *bone*, *moon*, *rain*, *green*, *gone*, *thin*. By not satisfying the reader's expectation of an exact chime, but instead giving a clunk, a slant rime can help a poet say some things in a particular way.

■ Writing Assignment on Sound

Choose a brief poem from this book and examine how one or two elements of sound work throughout the poem to strengthen its meaning. Before you write, review the elements of sound described in this section. Back up your argument with specific quotations from the poem.

7. RHYTHM

> *I would define, in brief, the Poetry of words as the Rhythmical Creation of Beauty.*
>
> —EDGAR ALLAN POE

Rhythms affect us powerfully. We are lulled by a hammock's sway, awakened by an alarm clock's repeated yammer. Long after we come home from a beach, the rising and falling of waves and tides continue in memory. How powerfully the rhythms of poetry also move us may be felt in the folk songs of railroad workers and chain gangs whose words were chanted in time to the lifting and dropping of a sledgehammer, and in verse that marching soldiers shout, putting a stress on every word that coincides with a footfall.

Rhythm and sound are not identical. In poetry, several kinds of recurrent *sound* are possible, including (as we saw in the last section) rime, alliteration, and assonance. But most often when we speak of the **rhythm** of a poem, we mean the recurrence of stresses and pauses in it. When analyzing a poem, it helps to have a clear sense of how the rhythm works, and the best way to reach that understanding is through **scansion**. In scansion, we *scan* a line or a poem by indicating the stresses in it.

A **stress** (or **accent**) is a greater amount of force given to one syllable in speaking than is given to another. In this manner we place a stress on the first syllable of words such as *EA·gle, IM·pact, O·pen,* and *STA·tue,* and on the second syllable in *ci·GAR, my·STIQUE, pre·CISE,* and *un·TIL.* Each word in English carries at least one stress, except (usually) for the articles *a, an,* and *the,* the conjunction *and,* and one-syllable prepositions: *at, by, for, from, of, to, with.* Even these words, however, take a stress once in a while. When stresses recur at fixed intervals, the result is called a **meter**.

Meter

Meter is the rhythmic pattern of stresses in verse. To enjoy the rhythms of a poem, no special knowledge of meter is necessary. All you need do is pay attention to stresses and where they fall, and you will perceive the basic pattern, if there is any. To make ourselves aware of a meter, we need only listen to a poem or sound its words to ourselves. To scan a poem, make a diagram of the stresses (and absences of stress) you find in it. Various marks are used in scansion; in this book we use ′ for a stressed syllable and ⌣ for an unstressed syllable, as in these lines from Edgar Allan Poe's poem "Annabel Lee."

⌣ ⌣ ′ ⌣ ⌣ ′
For the moon ne·ver beams,
⌣ ⌣ ′ ⌣ ⌣ ′
with·out bring·ing me dreams
⌣ ⌣ ′ ⌣ ⌣ ′ ⌣ ⌣ ′
Of the beau·ti·ful An·na·bel Lee.

Types of Meter

There are four common accentual-syllabic meters in English—iambic, anapestic, trochaic, and dactylic. Each is named for its basic **foot** (usually a unit of two or three syllables that contains one strong stress) or building block. Here are some examples of each meter.

1. **Iambic**—a line made up primarily of **iambs**, an unstressed syllable followed by a stressed syllable, ˘ ′. The iambic measure is the most common meter in English poetry. Many writers, such as Robert Frost, feel that iambs most easily capture the natural rhythms of our speech.

    ˘ ′ | ˘ ′ | ˘ ′ | ˘ ′ | ˘ ′
    But soft, | what light | through yon | der win | dow breaks?
    —William Shakespeare

2. **Anapestic**—a line made up primarily of **anapests**, two unstressed syllables followed by a stressed syllable, ˘˘ ′. Anapestic meter resembles iambic but contains an extra unstressed syllable.

    ˘ ′ | ˘ ˘ ′ | ˘ ˘ ′ | ˘ ˘ ′ | ˘ ˘ ′
    Now this | is the Law | of the Jun | gle—as old | and as true
    ˘ ˘ ′
    | as the sky;
    ˘ ˘ ′ | ˘ ˘ ′ | ˘ ˘ ′ | ˘ ˘ ′ | ˘ ˘ ′
    And the Wolf | that shall keep | it may pros | per, | but the Wolf
    ˘ ˘ ′ | ˘ ˘ ′
    | that shall break | it must die.
    —Rudyard Kipling

3. **Trochaic**—a line made up primarily of **trochees**, a stressed syllable followed by an unstressed syllable, ′ ˘. The trochaic meter is often associated with songs, chants, and magic spells in English. Trochees make a strong, emphatic meter that is often very mnemonic—that is, "helping, or meant to help, the memory."

    ′ ˘ | ′ ˘ | ′ ˘ | ′ ˘
    Dou·ble, | dou·ble, | toil and | trou·ble,
    ′ ˘ | ′ ˘ | ′ ˘ | ′ ˘
    Fi·re | burn and | caul·dron | bub·ble.
    —Shakespeare

4. **Dactylic**—a line made up primarily of **dactyls**, one stressed syllable followed by two unstressed syllables, ′ ˘ ˘. The dactylic meter is less common in English than in classical languages such as Greek or Latin. Used carefully, dactylic meter can sound stately, as in Longfellow's *Evangeline*.

    ′ ˘ ˘ | ′ ˘ ˘ | ′ ˘ ˘ | ′ ˘ | ′ ˘ ˘
    This is the | for·est pri | me·val. The | mur·mur·ing | pines and the
    ′ ˘
    | hem·lock
    —Henry Wadsworth Longfellow

But it also easily becomes a prancing, propulsive measure and is often used in comic verse.

    ′ ˘ ˘ | ′ ˘ ˘ | ′ ˘ ˘ | ′
    Puss·y·cat, | puss·y·cat, | where have you | been?
    —Mother Goose

Line Lengths

Meters are classified also by line lengths. A frequently heard metrical description is **iambic pentameter**: a line of *five* iambs, a meter especially familiar because it occurs in all blank verse (such as Shakespeare's plays and Milton's *Paradise Lost*), heroic couplets, and sonnets. The commonly used names for line lengths are:

> **monometer** (one foot)
> **dimeter** (two feet)
> **trimeter** (three feet)
> **tetrameter** (four feet)
> **pentameter** (five feet)
> **hexameter** (six feet)
> **heptameter** (seven feet)
> **octameter** (eight feet).

Like a basic dance step, a meter is not to be slavishly adhered to. The fun in reading a metrical poem often comes from watching the poet continually departing from perfect regularity, giving a few heel-kicks to display a bit of joy or ingenuity, then easing back into the basic step again. Because meter is orderly and the rhythms of living speech are unruly, poets can play one against the other, in a sort of counterpoint.

Accentual Meter

Another popular type of meter in English is **accentual meter**, in which the poet does not write in *feet,* but instead counts accents (stresses). The idea is to have the same number of stresses in every line. The poet may place them anywhere in the line and may include practically any number of unstressed syllables, which do not count.

Many poets, from the authors of Mother Goose rimes to Snoop Dogg, have found accentual meters congenial. Recently, accentual meter has enjoyed huge popularity through rap poetry, which usually employs a four-stress line.

> Star light, star bright.
> First star I see to-night.
> I wish I may, I wish I might,
> Have the wish I wish to-night.

■ Writing Assignment on Rhythm

Find a poem with a strong rhythm in this book and try scanning it, following the guidelines listed above. Discuss how the poem uses rhythm to create certain key effects. Be sure that your scansion shows all the elements you've chosen to discuss.

8. FORM

> *Anybody can write the first line of a poem,*
> *but it is a very difficult task to make*
> *the second line rhyme with the first.*
>
> —MARK TWAIN

Form, as a general idea, is the design of a thing as a whole, the configuration of all its parts. No poem can escape having some kind of form, whether its lines are as various in length as a tree's branches or all in hexameter.

Writing in **closed form**, a poet follows (or finds) some sort of pattern, such as that of a sonnet with its rime scheme and its fourteen lines of iambic pentameter. On a page, poems in closed form tend to look regular and symmetrical, often falling into **stanzas**—poetry's equivalent to the paragraph—that indicate groups of rimes. Along with William Butler Yeats, who held that a successful poem will "come shut with a click, like a closing box," the poet who writes in closed form apparently strives for a kind of perfection—seeking, perhaps, to lodge words so securely in place that no word can be budged without a worsening.

The poet who writes in **open form** usually seeks no final click. Often, such a poet views the writing of a poem as a process, rather than a quest for an absolute. Free to use white space for emphasis, able to shorten or lengthen lines as the sense seems to require, the poet lets the poem discover its shape as it goes along, moving as water flows downhill, adjusting to its terrain, engulfing obstacles.

Most poetry of the past is in closed form, exhibiting at least a pattern of rime or meter, but since the early 1960s the majority of American poets have preferred forms that stay open. Lately, the situation has been changing yet again, with closed form reappearing in much recent poetry. Whatever the fashion of the moment, the reader who seeks a wide understanding of poetry of both the present and the past will need to know both the closed and open varieties.

A. Closed Form

Formal Patterns

The best-known one-line pattern for a poem in English is **blank verse**: unrimed iambic pentameter. (This pattern is not a stanza: stanzas have more than one line.) Most portions of Shakespeare's plays are in blank verse, and so are Milton's *Paradise Lost*, Tennyson's "Ulysses," certain dramatic monologues of Browning and Frost, and thousands of other poems. The lines of this passage from Christopher Marlowe's *Doctor Faustus* (in which Faustus addresses the apparition of Helen of Troy) are in unrimed iambic pentameter:

> Was this the face that launch'd a thousand ships,
> And burnt the topless towers of Ilium?
> Sweet Helen, make me immortal with a kiss.
> Her lips suck forth my soul: see, where it flies!

The **couplet** is a two-line stanza, usually rimed. Its lines often tend to be equal in length. In fact, any pair of rimed lines that contains a complete thought is called a couplet, even if it is not a stanza, such as the couplet that ends a Shakespearean sonnet.

A **tercet** is a group of three lines. If rimed, they usually keep to one rime sound, as in this anonymous English children's jingle:

Julius Caesar,
The Roman geezer,
Squashed his wife with a lemon-squeezer.

The workhorse of English poetry is the **quatrain**, a stanza consisting of four lines. Quatrains are used in rimed poems more often than any other form.

The Sonnet

In the poetry of western Europe and America, the **sonnet** is the fixed form that has attracted for the longest time the largest number of noteworthy practitioners. Originally an Italian form (*sonetto:* "little song"), the sonnet owes much of its prestige to Petrarch (1304–1374), who wrote in it of his love for the unattainable Laura. So great was the vogue for sonnets in England at the end of the sixteenth century that a gentleman might have been thought a boor if he couldn't turn out a decent one. Not content to adopt merely the sonnet's fourteen-line pattern, English poets also tried on its conventional mask of the tormented lover.

They worked out, however, their own rime scheme—one easier for them to follow than Petrarch's, which calls for a greater number of riming words than English can readily provide. In the **English sonnet**, sometimes called a **Shakespearean sonnet**, the rimes cohere in four clusters: *a b a b, c d c d, e f e f, g g*. Because a rime scheme tends to shape the poet's statements to it, the English sonnet has three places where the procession of thought is likely to turn in another direction. Within its form, a poet may pursue one idea throughout the three quatrains and then in the couplet end with a surprise.

Less frequently met in English poetry, the **Italian sonnet**, or **Petrarchan sonnet**, follows the rime scheme *a b b a, a b b a* in its first eight lines, the **octave**, and then adds new rime sounds in the last six lines, the **sestet**. The sestet may rime *c d c d c d*, or *c d e c d e*, or *c d c c d c*, or in almost any other variation that doesn't end in a couplet. This organization into two parts sometimes helps arrange the poet's thoughts. In the octave, the poet may state a problem, and then, in the sestet, may offer a resolution. A lover, for example, may lament all octave long that a loved one is neglectful, then in line 9 begin to foresee some outcome: the speaker will die, or accept unhappiness, or trust that the beloved will have a change of heart.

John Keats (1795–1821)

When I have fears that I may cease to be (1818)

When I have fears that I may cease to be
    Before my pen has gleaned my teeming brain,
Before high-pilèd books, in charact'ry,°   *written language*
    Hold like rich garners° the full-ripened grain;   *storehouses*
When I behold, upon the night's starred face,   5
    Huge cloudy symbols of a high romance,
And think that I may never live to trace

Their shadows with the magic hand of chance;
And when I feel, fair creature of an hour,
   That I shall never look upon thee more,   10
Never have relish in the fairy° power   *supernatural*
   Of unreflecting love;—then on the shore
Of the wide world I stand alone, and think
   Till love and fame to nothingness do sink.

WHEN I HAVE FEARS THAT I MAY CEASE TO BE. 12 *unreflecting*: thoughtless and spontaneous, rather than deliberate.

Questions

1. What, specifically, does the speaker fear when he thinks about his death?
2. What connection between poetry and love does the poem suggest?
3. Do you see a turn of thought in this sonnet? At the conclusion of the poem, does the speaker resolve his fears?

Other Short Forms: The Haiku

Haiku is a Japanese verse form that has three unrimed lines of five, seven, and five syllables. Traditional haiku is often serious and spiritual in tone and minimizes figures of speech, relying mostly on imagery and having one of the four seasons as its setting:

   Temple bells die out.
   The fragrant blossoms remain.
   A perfect evening!
            —Matsuo Basho

Haiku emerged in sixteenth-century Japan and soon developed into a deeply esteemed form. Even today, Japanese soldiers, stockbrokers, scientists, schoolchildren, and the emperor himself find occasion to pen haiku. Soon after the form first captured the attention of Western poets at the end of the nineteenth century, it became immensely influential for modern poets such as Ezra Pound, William Carlos Williams, and H. D. as a model for the kind of verse they wanted to write—concise, direct, and imagistic.

   The Japanese consider the poems of the "Three Masters"—Basho, Buson, and Issa—to be the pinnacle of the classical haiku. Each poet had his own personality: Basho, the ascetic seeker of Zen enlightenment; Buson, the worldly artist; Issa, the sensitive master of wit and pathos. Here is a free translation of a poem from each of the Masters.

Matsuo Basho (1644–1694)

Heat-lightning streak

Heat-lightning streak—
through darkness pierces
the heron's shriek.
         —Translated by X. J. Kennedy

Taniguchi Buson (1716–1783)

Moonrise on mudflats

Moonrise on mudflats,
the line of water and sky
    blurred by a bullfrog.
       —Translated by Michael Stillman

Kobayashi Issa (1763–1827)

only one guy

only one guy and
only one fly trying to
make the guest room do.
       —Translated by Cid Corman

The Epigram

An **epigram** is "A short poem ending in a witty or ingenious turn of thought, to which the rest of the composition is intended to lead up" (according to the *Oxford English Dictionary*). Often it is a malicious gibe with an unexpected stinger in the final line—perhaps in the very last word.

Anonymous

Epitaph on a Dentist

Stranger, approach this spot with gravity;
John Brown is filling his last cavity.

Limerick

In English the only other fixed form to rival the sonnet and the epigram in favor is the **limerick**: five anapestic lines usually riming *a a b b a*. The limerick was made popular by Edward Lear (1812–1888), English painter and author of such nonsense poems as "The Owl and the Pussycat." Here is a sample, attributed to President Woodrow Wilson (1856–1924):

I sat next to the Duchess at tea;
It was just as I feared it would be:
    Her rumblings abdominal
      Were truly phenomenal
And everyone thought it was me!

Other Forms

There are many other verse forms used in English. Some forms, like the triolet, come from other European literatures. But English has borrowed fixed forms from an astonishing variety of sources. The rubaiyat stanza, for instance, comes from Persian poetry; the haiku and tanka originated in Japan. Other borrowed forms include the ghazal (Arabic), pantoum (Malay), and sapphics (Greek). A number of French forms—such as the villanelle, triolet, and sestina—have been particularly fascinating to English-language poets because they do not merely require the repetition of rime sounds; instead, they demand more elaborate echoing, involving the repetition of either full words or whole lines of verse. Sometimes difficult to master, these forms can create a powerful musical effect unlike ordinary riming. (There are several villanelles in this book: Dylan Thomas's "Do not go gentle into that good night," Wendy Cope's "Lonely Hearts," and Elizabeth Bishop's "One Art.")

■ Writing Assignment on a Sonnet

Examine a sonnet from anywhere in this book. Explain how its two parts combine to create a total effect neither part could achieve alone. Be sure to identify the turning point. Paraphrase what each of the poem's two sections says and describe how the poem as a whole reconciles the two contrasting parts. You might consider one of the following: Elizabeth Barrett Browning's "How Do I Love Thee? Let Me Count the Ways"; John Keats's "When I have fears that I may cease to be"; Wilfred Owen's "Anthem for Doomed Youth"; or any of Shakespeare's sonnets.

B. Open Form

Writing in **open form**, a poet seeks to discover a fresh and unique arrangement of words in each poem, usually without using a rime scheme or basic meter. Doing without these powerful (some would say hypnotic) elements, the poet must rely on other means to engage and sustain the reader's attention. Novice poets often think that open form looks easy, not nearly so hard as riming everything; but in truth, formally open poems are only easy to write if written carelessly. To compose lines with keen awareness of open form's demands and its infinite possibilities, calls for skill: at least as much as that needed to write in meter and rime, if not more. Should the poet succeed, then the discovered arrangement will seem exactly right for what the poem is saying.

Free Verse

Poetry in open form used to be called **free verse** (from the French ***vers libre***), suggesting a kind of verse liberated from the shackles of rime and meter. "Writing free verse," said Robert Frost, who wasn't interested in it, "is like playing tennis with the net down." And yet, as William Carlos Williams and many other poets have demonstrated, high scores can be made in such an unconventional game, provided it doesn't straggle all over the court. For a successful poem in open form, the term *free verse* seems inaccurate. "Being an art form," said Williams, "verse cannot be 'free' in the sense of having *no* limitations or guiding principles." Various substitute names have been suggested: organic poetry, composition by field, raw (as against cooked) poetry, open form poetry.

Free Verse Lines

In the best free verse, the line endings transform language and suggest meaning. A line break implies a slight pause so that the last word of each line receives special emphasis: the last word in a line is meant to linger, however briefly, in the listener's ear. With practice and attention, you can easily develop a better sense of how a poem's line breaks operate.

E. E. Cummings (1894–1962)

in Just- 1923

in Just-
spring   when the world is mud-
luscious the little
lame balloonman

whistles   far   and wee   5

and eddieandbill come
running from marbles and
piracies and it's
spring

when the world is puddle-wonderful   10

the queer
old balloonman whistles
far   and   wee
and bettyandisbel come dancing

from hop-scotch and jump-rope and   15

it's
spring
and
   the

      goat-footed   20

balloonMan   whistles
far
and
wee

Questions

1. Why do you think the poet isolates the word "spring" every time it occurs in the poem?
2. What effects are achieved by running the children's names together, and by spreading open the phrase "far and wee"?

■ Writing Assignment on Open Form

Retype a free verse poem as prose, by adding conventional punctuation and capitalization if necessary. Then compare and contrast the prose version with the poem itself. How do the two texts differ in tone, rhythm, emphasis, and effect? How do they remain similar? Use any poem from this book. You might consider: Margaret Atwood's "Siren Song"; Gwendolyn Brooks's "Speech to the Young. Speech to the Progress-Toward"; E. E. Cummings's "Buffalo Bill 's"; Denise Levertov's "The Ache of Marriage"; or W. S. Merwin's "For the Anniversary of My Death."

9. SYMBOL

> *A symbol is like a rock dropped into a pool:*
> *it sends out ripples in all directions,*
> *and the ripples are in motion.*
>
> —JOHN CIARDI

The national flag is supposed to stir our patriotic feelings. When a black cat crosses his path, a superstitious man shivers, foreseeing bad luck. To each of these, by custom, our society expects a standard response. A flag, a black cat crossing one's path—each is a **symbol**: a visible object or action that suggests some further meaning in addition to itself.

A flag and the crossing of a black cat may be called **conventional symbols** because they can have a conventional or customary effect on us. Conventional symbols are also part of the language of poetry, as we know when we meet the red rose, emblem of love, in a lyric, or the Christian cross in the devotional poems of George Herbert. More often, however, symbols in literature have no conventional, long-established meaning, but particular meanings of their own. In Herman Melville's novel *Moby-Dick*, to take a rich example, whatever we associate with the great white whale is *not* attached unmistakably to white whales by custom. Though Melville tells us that men have long regarded whales with awe and relates Moby Dick to the celebrated fish that swallowed Jonah, the reader's response is to one particular whale, the creature of Herman Melville. Only the experience of reading the novel in its entirety can give Moby Dick his particular meaning.

A symbol, to use the poet John Drury's concise definition, is "an image that radiates meanings." While images in a poem can and should be read as what they literally are, images often do double duty, suggesting deeper meanings. Exactly what those meanings are, however, often differs from poem to poem. Some symbols have been used so often and effectively over time that a traditional reading of them has developed: at times a poet clearly adopts an image's traditional symbolic meaning. Some poems, however, deliberately play against a symbol's conventional associations.

Identifying Symbols

"But how am I supposed to know a symbol when I see one?" The best approach is to read poems closely. Pick out all the references to concrete objects—newspapers, black cats, twisted pins. Consider them with special care. Notice any object that the poet emphasizes by detailed description, by repetition, or by placing it at the very beginning or end of the poem. Ask: What is the poem about, what does it add up to? If, when the poem is paraphrased, the paraphrase depends primarily on the meaning of certain concrete objects, these richly suggestive objects may be symbols.

There are some things a literary symbol usually is *not*. A symbol is not an abstraction. Such terms as *truth*, *death*, *love*, and *justice* cannot work as symbols (unless personified, as in the traditional figure of Justice holding a scale). Most often, a symbol is something we can see in the mind's eye: a newspaper, a lightning bolt, a gesture of nodding good-bye.

Sometimes a symbol addresses a sense other than sight: the sound of a mysterious snapping string at the end of Anton Chekhov's play *The Cherry Orchard*, or, in William Faulkner's tale "A Rose for Emily," the odor of decay that surrounds the house of the last survivor of a town's leading family—suggesting not only physical decomposition but also the decay of a social order. A symbol is a special kind of image, for it exceeds the usual image in the richness of its connotations.

A symbol radiates hints or casts long shadows (to use Henry James's metaphor). We are unable to say it "stands for" or "represents" a meaning. It evokes, it suggests, it manifests. It demands no single necessary interpretation, such as the interpretation a driver gives to a red traffic light. Rather, like Emily Dickinson's lightning bolt, it points toward an indefinite meaning, which may lie in part beyond the reach of words.

■ Writing Assignment on Symbol

Do an in-depth analysis of the symbolism in a poem of your choice. Some likely choices would be Emily Dickinson's "Because I could not stop for Death"; Robert Frost's "Stopping by Woods on a Snowy Evening"; Thomas Hardy's "The Darkling Thrush"; Andrew Marvell's "To His Coy Mistress"; Sylvia Plath's "Daddy"; and Dylan Thomas's "Fern Hill."

WHAT IS POETRY?

What, then, is poetry? By now, perhaps, you have formed your own idea, whether or not you can define it. Robert Frost made a try at a definition: "A poem is an idea caught in the act of dawning." Just in case further efforts at definition may be useful, here are a few memorable ones:

> things that are true expressed in words that are beautiful.
> —*Dante*

> the best words in the best order.
> —*Samuel Taylor Coleridge*

> the spontaneous overflow of powerful feelings.
> —*William Wordsworth*

> If I feel physically as if the top of my head were taken off, I know *that* is poetry.
> —*Emily Dickinson*

a way of remembering what it would impoverish us to forget.
—Robert Frost

Poetry is prose bewitched.
—Mina Loy

hundreds of things coming together at the right moment.
—Elizabeth Bishop

the clear expression of mixed feelings.
—W. H. Auden

an angel with a gun in its hand . . .
—José Garcia Villa

Reduced to its simplest and most essential form, the poem is a song. Song is neither discourse nor explanation.
—Octavio Paz

imaginary gardens with real toads in them.
—Marianne Moore

Poetry is to prose as dancing is to walking.
—Paul Valéry

    Throughout this book, we are working on the assumption that the patient and conscious explication of poems will sharpen unconscious perceptions. We can only hope that it will; the final test lies in whether you care to go on by yourself, reading other poems, finding in them pleasure and enlightenment. Like Yeats's chestnut-tree in "Among School Children" (which, when asked whether it is leaf, blossom, or trunk, has no answer), a poem is to be seen not as a confederation of form, rime, image, metaphor, tone, and theme, but *as a whole*. We study a poem one element at a time because the intellect best comprehends what it can separate. But only our total attention, involving the participation of our blood and marrow, can perceive the elements in a poem fused, all dancing together.

checklist: Analyzing a Poem

1. TONE
- ☐ Who is speaking the poem? Is the narrator's voice close to the poet's or is it the voice of a fictional or historical person?
- ☐ Does the poem directly reveal any emotions or attitudes? Does it indirectly reveal any attitudes or emotions?
- ☐ What adjectives would best describe the poem's tone?
- ☐ Does your reaction to what is happening in the poem differ widely from that of the speaker? If so, what does that difference suggest? Is the poem in some way ironic?

2. WORDS AND DICTION
- ☐ As you read, underline words or phrases that appeal to you or seem especially significant. What is it about each underlined word or phrase that appeals to you? How does the sound of a word you've chosen add to the poem's mood?
- ☐ What sort of diction does the poem use? Conversational or lofty? Monosyllabic or polysyllabic? Concrete or abstract? How does the diction contribute to the poem's flavor and meaning?
- ☐ Does the poem contain any allusions? What do they add to your understanding of its meaning?

3. DENOTATION AND CONNOTATION
- ☐ As you read, highlight words or phrases that you don't understand. Look them up in the dictionary.
- ☐ Do any of the words in the poem have connotations beyond their literal meanings that are significant in understanding the author's intentions?
- ☐ Are any of the words in the poem used in an unfamiliar or unexpected way? In an unfamiliar or unexpected context?
- ☐ When and where does the poem take place? What is the significance of the setting, and of any other details in the text?

4. IMAGERY
- ☐ List the poem's key images, in the order in which they appear. Remember, images can draw on all five senses—not just the visual.
- ☐ What emotions or attitudes are suggested by each image? Does the mood of the imagery change from start to finish? What is suggested by the movement from one image to the next? Remember that the order or sequence of images is almost as important as the images themselves.

5. FIGURES OF SPEECH
- ☐ Underline the poem's key comparisons. Look for both similes and metaphors.
- ☐ How are the two things being compared alike? In what ways are the two things unlike each other?
- ☐ List any other figures of speech you notice. Are there instances of personification? Overstatement? Understatement? Puns? How do they contribute to the poem's overall intentions?

6. SOUND
- ☐ List the main auditory elements you find in the poem. Look for rime, meter, alliteration, assonance, euphony, cacophony, repetition, onomatopoeia. Is there a pattern in your list? Is the poem particularly heavy in alliteration or repetition, for example?
- ☐ How do these effects help communicate the poem's main theme? How does the sound of the words add to the poem's mood?
- ☐ Are there rimes? Indicate where they occur. Do any other recurring sound patterns strike you?

7. RHYTHM: SCANNING A POEM

- [ ] Read the poem aloud. Mark the syllables on which the main speech stresses fall. How many syllables are there in each line? How many stresses?
- [ ] Is the poem written in an identifiable meter? If so, which one? How many feet are there to each line?
- [ ] Does the poem set up a reliable pattern and then diverge from it anywhere? If so, how does that irregularity underscore the line's meaning?

8. FORM

- [ ] Is the poem written in closed form (with an established pattern of meter, rime, and lines or stanzas) or in open form?
- [ ] Is the poem written in a traditional form, such as the sonnet? How well does it observe the conventions of that form? If there are breaks from the conventions, how do they contribute to the poem's intentions?
- [ ] If the poem is in free verse, what organizational strategies does it employ, in terms of line lengths, line breaks, and stanza breaks (if any)?
- [ ] If a poem is written in free verse, pay special attention to where its lines end. Do the breaks tend to come at the end of the sentences or phrases? Do they tend to come in the middle of an idea? What mood is created by the breaks?
- [ ] How do line breaks and stanza breaks reinforce the poem's meaning as a whole?

9 SYMBOL

- [ ] Does any image in the poem radiate meaning beyond its literal sense? If not, it might not be intended as a symbol.
- [ ] If you identify a symbol, what does it seem to mean in the larger context of the poem? What emotions are evoked by the image?
- [ ] Is the symbol a conventional one, or does its meaning seem unique to the present context?

4 READING A PLAY

Drama is life with the dull bits left out.
—ALFRED HITCHCOCK

Unlike a short story or a novel, a **play** is a work of storytelling in which actors represent the characters. A play also differs from a work of fiction in another essential way: it is addressed not to readers but to spectators.

To be part of an audience in a theater is an experience far different from reading a story in solitude. As the house lights dim and the curtain rises, we become members of a community. The responses of people around us affect our own responses. We, too, contribute to the community's response whenever we laugh, sigh, applaud, murmur in surprise, or catch our breath in excitement. In contrast, when we watch a movie by ourselves in our living room—say, a slapstick comedy—we probably laugh less often than if we were watching the same film in a theater, surrounded by a roaring crowd. On the other hand, no one is spilling popcorn down the backs of our necks. Each kind of theatrical experience, to be sure, has its advantages.

A theater of live actors has another advantage: a sensitive give-and-take between actors and audience. (Such rapport, of course, depends on the skill of the actors and the perceptiveness of the audience.) Although professional actors may try to give a first-rate performance on all occasions, it is natural for them to feel more keenly inspired by a lively, appreciative audience than by a lethargic one. As veteran playgoers well know, something unique and wonderful can happen when good actors and a good audience respond to each other.

In another sense, a play is more than actors and audience. Like a short story or a poem, a play is a work of art made of words. Watching a play, we don't notice the playwright standing between us and the characters. If the play is absorbing, it flows before our eyes. In a silent reading, the usual play consists mainly of **dialogue**, exchanges of speech punctuated by stage directions. In performance, though, stage directions vanish. And although the thoughtful efforts of perhaps a hundred people—actors, director, producer, stage designer, costumer, makeup artist, technicians—may have gone into a production, a successful play makes us forget its artifice. We may even forget that the play is literature, for its gestures, facial expressions, bodily stances, lighting, and special effects are as much a part of it as the playwright's written words. Even though words are not all there is to a living play, they are its bones. And the whole play, the finished production, is the total of whatever takes place on stage.

READING A PLAY

Most plays are written not to be read in books but to be performed. Finding plays in a literature anthology, the student may well ask: Isn't there something wrong with the idea of reading plays on the printed page? True, plays are meant to be seen on stage, but equally true, reading a play may afford advantages. One is that it is better to know some masterpieces by reading them than never to know them at all. To succeed in your lifetime in witnessing, say, all the plays of Shakespeare might well be impossible. In print, they are as near to hand as a book on a shelf, ready to be enacted (if you like) on the stage of the mind.

After all, a play is literature before it comes alive in a theater, and it might be argued that when we read an unfamiliar play, we meet it in the same form in which it first appears to its actors and its director. If a play is rich and complex or if it dates from the remote past and contains difficulties of language and allusion, to read it on the page enables us to study it at our leisure and return to the parts that demand greater scrutiny.

But even if a play may be seen in a theater, sometimes to read it in print may be our way of knowing it as the author wrote it in its entirety. Far from regarding Shakespeare's words as holy writ, producers of *Hamlet, King Lear, Othello,* and other masterpieces often shorten or even leave out whole speeches and scenes. Besides, the nature of the play, as far as you can tell from a stage production, may depend on decisions of the director. In one production Othello may dress as a Renaissance Moor, in another as a modern general. Every actor who plays Iago in *Othello* makes his own interpretation of this knotty character. Some see Iago as a figure of pure evil; others, as a madman; still others, as a suffering human being consumed by hatred, jealousy, and pride. What do you think Shakespeare meant? You can always read the play and decide for yourself. If every stage production of a play is a fresh interpretation, so, too, is every reader's reading of it. Some readers, when silently reading a play to themselves, try to visualize a stage, imagining the characters in costume and under lights. If such a reader is an actor or a director and is reading the play with an eye toward staging it, then he or she may try to imagine every detail of a possible production, even shades of makeup and the loudness of sound effects. But the nonprofessional reader, who regards the play as literature, need not attempt such exhaustive imagining. Although some readers find it enjoyable to imagine the play taking place on a stage, others prefer to imagine the people and events that the play brings vividly to mind. Sympathetically following the tangled life of Nora in *A Doll's House* by Henrik Ibsen, we forget that we are reading printed stage directions and instead feel ourselves in the presence of human conflict. Thus regarded, a play becomes a form of storytelling, and the playwright's instructions to the actors and the director become a conventional mode of narrative that we accept much as we accept the methods of a novel or short story.

THEATRICAL CONVENTIONS

Most plays, whether seen in a theater or in print, employ some **conventions**: customary methods of presenting an action, usual and recognizable devices that an audience is willing to accept. In reading a great play from the past, such as *Antigonê* or *Othello,* it will help if we know some of the conventions of the classical Greek theater or the Elizabethan theater. When in *Antigonê* we encounter a character called the Chorus, it may be useful to be aware that this is a group of citizens who stand to one side of the action, conversing with the principal character and commenting. In *Othello,* when the sinister Iago, left on stage alone, begins to speak (at the end of Act I, Scene iii), we recognize the conventional device of a **soliloquy**, a monologue in which we seem to overhear the character's inmost thoughts uttered aloud. Another such device is the **aside**, in which a character addresses the audience directly, unheard by the other characters on stage, as when the villain in a melodrama chortles, "Heh! Heh! Now she's in my power!" Like conventions in poetry, such familiar methods of staging a narrative afford us a happy shock of recognition. Often, as in these examples, they are ways of making clear to us exactly what the playwright would have us know.

MODES OF DRAMA: TRAGEDY AND COMEDY

In 1770, Horace Walpole wrote, "the world is a comedy to those that think, a tragedy to those that feel." All of us, of course, both think and feel, and all of us have moments when we stand back and laugh, whether ruefully or with glee, at life's absurdities, just as we all have times when our hearts are broken by its pains and losses. Thus, the modes of tragedy and comedy, diametrically opposed to one another though they are, do not demand that we choose between them: both of them speak to something deep and real within us, and each of them has its own truth to tell about the infinitely complex experience of living in this world.

1. TRAGEDY

Show me a hero and I will write you a tragedy.
—F. SCOTT FITZGERALD

A **tragedy** is a play that portrays a serious conflict between human beings and some superior, overwhelming force. It ends sorrowfully and disastrously, and this outcome seems inevitable. Many of our ideas of tragedy go back to classical Athens and the plays of the Greek dramatists Sophocles, Aeschylus, and Euripides.

One of the oldest and most durable of literary genres, tragedy is also one of the simplest—the protagonist undergoes a reversal of fortune, from good to bad, ending in catastrophe. However simple, though, tragedy can be one of the most complex genres to explain satisfactorily, with almost every principal point of its definition open to differing and often hotly debated interpretations. It is a fluid and adaptive genre, and for every one of its defining points, we can cite a tragic masterpiece that fails to observe that particular convention. Its fluidity and adaptability can also be shown by the way in which the classical tragic pattern is played out in pure form in such unlikely places as Orson Welles's film *Citizen Kane* (1941) and Chinua Achebe's celebrated novel *Things Fall Apart* (1958): in each of these works, a man of high position and character—one a multimillionaire newspaper publisher, the other a late nineteenth-century African warrior—moves inexorably to destruction, impelled by his rigidity and self-righteousness. Even a movie such as *King Kong*—despite its oversized and hirsute protagonist—exemplifies some of the principles of tragedy.

To gain a clearer understanding of what tragedy is, let us first talk about what it is not. Consider the kinds of events that customarily bring the term "tragedy" to mind: the death of a child, a fire that destroys a family's home and possessions, the killing of a bystander caught in the crossfire of a shootout between criminals, and so on. What all of these unfortunate instances have in common, obviously, is that they involve the infliction of great and irreversible suffering. But what they also share is the sense that the sufferers are innocent, that they have done nothing to cause or to deserve their fate. This is what we usually describe as a tragedy in real life, but tragedy in a literary or dramatic context has a slightly different meaning: in tragic theater the protagonist's reversal of fortune is usually brought about through some error or weakness on his or her part, generally referred to as the **tragic flaw**.

Aristotle's Tragic Hero

Aristotle's famous description of tragedy, constructed in the fourth century B.C., is the testimony of one who probably saw many classical tragedies performed. Aristotle observes that the protagonist, the **tragic hero**, is a person of "high estate," apparently a king or queen or other celebrated hero. It is the nature of tragedy that the protagonist must fall from power and from happiness; his or her high estate gives the person a place of dignity to fall from and perhaps makes the fall seem all the more a calamity in that it involves an entire nation or people. Nor is the protagonist extraordinary merely by his or her position in society. Oedipus is not only a king, but also a noble soul who suffers profoundly and who employs splendid eloquence to express his suffering.

The tragic hero, however, is not a superman; he is fallible. The hero's downfall is the result, as Aristotle said, of his **hamartia**, his error or transgression—his tragic flaw or weakness of character. In some classical tragedies, his transgression is a weakness the Greeks called **hubris**: extreme pride, leading to overconfidence. In most tragedies, the catastrophe entails not only the loss of outward fortune such as reputation, power, and life itself, but also the erosion of the protagonist's moral character and greatness of spirit.

■ Writing Assignments on Tragedy

1. Select any tragedy in this book and analyze the protagonist using Aristotle's description. In what ways does the hero meet the description? In what ways does the hero depart from it?
2. According to Oscar Wilde, "In this world there are only two tragedies: one is not getting what one wants, and the other is getting it." Write an essay in which you discuss this statement in its application to one of the tragedies in this book, for example, *Othello* or *Antigonê*.

Traditional masks of Comedy and Tragedy.

2. COMEDY

Comedy is just tragedy without the sentimentality.

—DAVID IVES

The best-known traditional emblem of drama—a pair of masks, one sorrowful (representing tragedy) and one smiling (representing comedy)—suggests that tragedy and comedy, although opposites, are close relatives. Often, comedy shows people getting into trouble through error or weakness; in this respect it is akin to tragedy. An important difference between comedy and tragedy lies in the attitude toward human failing that is expected of us. The tragic view of life presupposes that in the end we will prove unequal to the challenges we must face, while the comic outlook asserts a view of human possibility in which our common sense and resilience—or pure dumb luck—will enable us to win out.

Comedy, from the Greek *komos*, "a revel," is thought to have originated in festivities to celebrate spring, ritual performances in praise of Dionysus, god of fertility and wine. In drama, comedy may be broadly defined as whatever makes us laugh. A comedy may be a name for one entire play, or we may say that there is comedy in only part of a play—as in a comic character or a comic situation.

Satiric Comedy

Derisive humor is basic to **satiric comedy**, in which human weakness or folly is ridiculed from a vantage point of supposedly enlightened superiority. Satiric comedy may be coolly malicious and gently biting, but it tends to be critical of people, their manners, and their morals. It is at least as old as the comedies of Aristophanes, who thrived in the fifth century B.C. In *Lysistrata*, the satirist shows how the women of two warring cities speedily halt a war by agreeing to deny sex to their husbands. More contemporary satirists include the cable favorite Stephen Colbert, whose *The Colbert Report* takes delight in skewering politicians of all stripes, and Sacha Baron Cohen's fictional character Borat, whose "mockumentary" captures real-life interactions with unsuspecting Americans and exposes widespread prejudices.

High Comedy

Comedy is often divided into two varieties—"high" and "low." **High comedy** relies more on wit and wordplay than on physical action for its humor. It tries to address the audience's intelligence by pointing out the pretension and hypocrisy of human behavior. High comedy also generally avoids derisive humor. Jokes about physical appearance would, for example, be avoided. One technique it employs to appeal to a sophisticated, verbal audience is use of the **epigram**, a brief and witty statement that memorably expresses some truth, large or small. Oscar Wilde's plays *The Importance of Being Earnest* (1895) and *Lady Windermere's Fan* (1892) sparkle with such brilliant epigrams as: "I can resist everything except temptation"; "Experience is simply the name we give our mistakes"; "There is only one thing in the world worse than being talked about, and that is not being talked about."

A type of high comedy is the **comedy of manners**, a witty satire set in elite or fashionable society. Popular since the seventeenth-century Restoration period, splendid comedies of manners continue to be written to this day. Bernard Shaw's *Pygmalion* (1913), which eventually became the musical *My Fair Lady*, contrasts life in the streets of London with that in aristocratic drawing rooms. Contemporary playwrights such as Tom Stoppard, Michael Frayn, Tina Howe, and John Guare have all created memorable comedies of manners.

Low Comedy

Low comedy explores the opposite extreme of humor. It places greater emphasis on physical action and visual gags, and its verbal jokes do not require much intellect to appreciate (as in Groucho Marx's pithy put-down to his brother Chico, "You have the brain of a five-year-old, and I bet he was glad to get rid of it!"). Low comedy does not avoid derisive humor; rather, it revels in making fun of whatever will get a good laugh. Drunkenness, stupidity, lust, senility, trickery, insult, and clumsiness are inexhaustible staples of this style of comedy. Although it is all too easy for critics to dismiss low comedy, like high comedy it serves a valuable purpose in satirizing human failings. Shakespeare indulged in coarse humor in some of his noblest plays. Low comedy is usually the preferred style of popular culture, and it has inspired many incisive satires on modern life—from the classic films of W. C. Fields and the Marx Brothers to the weekly TV antics of Matt Groening's *The Simpsons* or Tina Fey's *30 Rock*.

Low comedy includes several distinct types. One is the **burlesque**, a broadly humorous parody or travesty of another play or kind of play. (In the United States, *burlesque* is something else: a once-popular form of show business featuring stripteases interspersed with bits of ribald low comedy.) Another valuable type of low comedy is the **farce**, a broadly humorous play whose action is usually fast-moving and improbable. The farce is a descendant of the Italian ***commedia dell'arte*** ("artistic comedy") of the late Renaissance, a kind of theater developed by comedians who traveled from town to town, regaling crowds at country fairs and in marketplaces. **Slapstick comedy** (such as that of the Three Stooges) is a kind of farce. Featuring pratfalls, pie-throwing, fisticuffs, and other violent action, it takes its name from a circus clown's prop—a bat with two boards that loudly clap together when one clown swats another.

Romantic Comedy

Romantic comedy, another traditional sort of comedy, is subtler. Its main characters are generally lovers, and its plot unfolds their ultimately successful strivings to be united. Unlike satiric comedy, romantic comedy portrays its characters not with withering contempt but with kindly indulgence. It may take place in the everyday world, or perhaps in some never-never land, such as the forest of Arden in Shakespeare's *As You Like It*. Romantic comedy is also a popular staple of Hollywood, depicting two people undergoing humorous mishaps on their way to falling in love. The characters often suffer humiliation and discomfort along the way, but these moments are funny rather than sad, and the characters are rewarded in the end by true love.

■ Writing Assignments on Comedy

1. Read one of the comedies in this book and write a brief analysis of what makes the play amusing or humorous. Provide details to back up your argument.
2. Write about a recent romantic comedy film. How does its plot fulfill the notion of comedy?
3. Write about a movie you've seen lately that was meant to be funny but fell short. What was lacking?

ELEMENTS OF A PLAY

When we read a play on the printed page and find ourselves swept forward by the motion of its story, we need not wonder how—and from what ingredients—the playwright put it together. Still, to analyze the structure of a play is one way to understand and appreciate a playwright's art. Analysis is complicated, however, because in an excellent play the elements (including plot, theme, and characters) do not stand in isolation. Often, deeds clearly follow from the kinds of people the characters are, and from those deeds it is left to the reader to infer the **theme** of the play—the general point or truth about human beings that may be drawn from it.

However, it is safe to make one general assumption: a good play almost always presents a conflict. Conflict creates suspense and keeps an audience from meandering out to the lobby water fountain. Without it, a play would be static and, most likely, dull. When a character intensely desires something but some obstacle—perhaps another character—stands in the way, the result is dramatic tension. To understand a play, it is essential to understand the basic conflicts motivating the plot.

Perhaps the most meaningful way to study the elements of a play (and certainly the most enjoyable) is to consider a play in its entirety. Here is a famous one-act play worth reading for the boldness of its elements—and for its own sake. *Trifles* tells the story of a murder. As you will discover, the "trifles" mentioned in its title are not of trifling stature. In reading the play, you will probably find yourself imagining what you might see on stage if you were in a theater. You may also want to imagine what took place in the lives of the characters before the curtain rose. All this imagining may sound like a tall order, but don't worry. Just read the play for enjoyment the first time through, and then we will consider what makes it effective.

Susan Glaspell

Susan Glaspell (1876–1948) grew up in her native Davenport, Iowa, the daughter of a grain dealer. After four years at Drake University and a job as a reporter in Des Moines, she settled in New York's Greenwich Village. In 1915, with her husband, George Cram Cook, a theatrical director, she founded the Provincetown Players, the first influential noncommercial theater troupe in America. During the summers of 1915 and 1916, in a makeshift playhouse on a Cape Cod pier, the Players staged the earliest plays of Eugene O'Neill and works by John Reed, Edna St. Vincent Millay, and Glaspell herself. Transplanting the company to New York in the fall of 1916, Glaspell and Cook renamed it the Playwrights' Theater. Glaspell wrote several still-remembered plays, among them a pioneering work of feminist drama, The Verge (1921), and the Pulitzer Prize-winning Alison's House (1930), about the family of a reclusive poet like Emily Dickinson who, after her death, squabble over the right to publish her poems. First widely known for her fiction with an Iowa background, Glaspell wrote ten novels, including Fidelity (1915) and The Morning Is Near Us (1939). Shortly after writing the play Trifles, she rewrote it as a short story, "A Jury of Her Peers."

Susan Glaspell

Trifles
1916

CHARACTERS

George Henderson, county attorney
Henry Peters, sheriff
Lewis Hale, a neighboring farmer
Mrs. Peters
Mrs. Hale

SCENE. *The kitchen in the now abandoned farmhouse of John Wright, a gloomy kitchen, and left without having been put in order—unwashed pans under the sink, a loaf of bread outside the breadbox, a dish towel on the table—other signs of incompleted work. At the rear the outer door opens and the Sheriff comes in followed by the County Attorney and Hale. The Sheriff and Hale are men in middle life, the County Attorney is a young man; all are much bundled up and go at once to the stove. They are followed by two women—the Sheriff's wife first; she is a slight wiry woman, a thin nervous face. Mrs. Hale is larger and would ordinarily be called more comfortable looking, but she is disturbed now and looks fearfully about as she enters. The women have come in slowly, and stand close together near the door.*

County Attorney (*rubbing his hands*): This feels good. Come up to the fire, ladies.
Mrs. Peters (*after taking a step forward*): I'm not—cold.
Sheriff (*unbuttoning his overcoat and stepping away from the stove as if to mark the beginning of official business*): Now, Mr. Hale, before we move things about, you explain to Mr. Henderson just what you saw when you came here yesterday morning.

County Attorney: By the way, has anything been moved? Are things just as you left them yesterday?

Sheriff (*looking about*): It's just the same. When it dropped below zero last night I thought I'd better send Frank out this morning to make a fire for us—no use getting pneumonia with a big case on, but I told him not to touch anything except the stove—and you know Frank.

County Attorney: Somebody should have been left here yesterday.

Sheriff: Oh—yesterday. When I had to send Frank to Morris Center for that man who went crazy—I want you to know I had my hands full yesterday, I knew you could get back from Omaha by today and as long as I went over everything here myself—

County Attorney: Well, Mr. Hale, tell just what happened when you came here yesterday morning.

Hale: Harry and I had started to town with a load of potatoes. We came along the road from my place and as I got here I said, "I'm going to see if I can't get John Wright to go in with me on a party telephone." I spoke to Wright about it once before and he put me off, saying folks talked too much anyway, and all he asked was peace and quiet—I guess you know about how much he talked himself; but I thought maybe if I went to the house and talked about it before his wife, though I said to Harry that I didn't know as what his wife wanted made much difference to John—

County Attorney: Let's talk about that later, Mr. Hale. I do want to talk about that, but tell now just what happened when you got to the house.

Hale: I didn't hear or see anything; I knocked at the door, and still it was all quiet inside. I knew they must be up, it was past eight o'clock. So I knocked again, and I thought I heard somebody say, "Come in." I wasn't sure, I'm not sure yet, but I opened the door—this door (*indicating the door by which the two women are still standing*) and there in that rocker—(*pointing to it*) sat Mrs. Wright.

(*They all look at the rocker.*)

County Attorney: What—was she doing?

Hale: She was rockin' back and forth. She had her apron in her hand and was kind of—pleating it.

County Attorney: And how did she—look?

Hale: Well, she looked queer.

County Attorney: How do you mean—queer?

Hale: Well, as if she didn't know what she was going to do next. And kind of done up.

County Attorney: How did she seem to feel about your coming?

Hale: Why, I don't think she minded—one way or other. She didn't pay much attention. I said, "How do, Mrs. Wright, it's cold, ain't it?" And she said, "Is it?"— and went on kind of pleating at her apron. Well, I was surprised; she didn't ask me to come up to the stove, or to set down, but just sat there, not even looking at me, so I said, "I want to see John." And then she—laughed. I guess you would call it a laugh. I thought of Harry and the team outside, so I said a little sharp: "Can't I see John?" "No," she says, kind o' dull like. "Ain't he home?" says I. "Yes," says she, "he's home." "Then why can't I see him?" I asked her, out of patience. "'Cause he's dead," says she. "*Dead?*" says I. She just nodded her head, not getting a bit excited, but rockin' back and forth.

"Why—where is he?" says I, not knowing what to say. She just pointed upstairs—like that. (*Himself pointing to the room above.*) I got up, with the idea of going up there. I walked from there to here—then I says, "Why, what did he die of?" "He died of a rope round his neck," says she, and just went on pleatin' at her apron. Well, I went out and called Harry. I thought I might—need help. We went upstairs and there he was lyin'—

County Attorney: I think I'd rather have you go into that upstairs, where you can point it all out. Just go on now with the rest of the story.

Hale: Well, my first thought was to get that rope off. It looked . . . (*stops, his face twitches*) . . . but Harry, he went up to him, and he said, "No, he's dead all right, and we'd better not touch anything." So we went back down stairs. She was still sitting that same way. "Has anybody been notified?" I asked. "No," says she, unconcerned. "Who did this, Mrs. Wright?" said Harry. He said it businesslike—and she stopped pleatin' of her apron. "I don't know," she says. "You don't *know?*" says Harry. "No," says she. "Weren't you sleepin' in the bed with him?" says Harry. "Yes," says she, "but I was on the inside." "Somebody slipped a rope round his neck and strangled him and you didn't wake up?" says Harry. "I didn't wake up," she said after him. We must 'a looked as if we didn't see how that could be, for after a minute she said, "I sleep sound." Harry was going to ask her more questions but I said maybe we ought to let her tell her story first to the coroner, or the sheriff, so Harry went fast as he could to Rivers' place, where there's a telephone.

County Attorney: And what did Mrs. Wright do when she knew that you had gone for the coroner?

Hale: She moved from that chair to this one over here (*pointing to a small chair in the corner*) and just sat there with her hands held together and looking down. I got a feeling that I ought to make some conversation, so I said I had come in to see if John wanted to put in a telephone, and at that she started to laugh, and then she stopped and looked at me—scared. (*The County Attorney, who has had his notebook out, makes a note.*) I dunno, maybe it wasn't scared. I wouldn't like to say it was. Soon Harry got back, and then Dr. Lloyd came, and you, Mr. Peters, and so I guess that's all I know that you don't.

County Attorney (*looking around*): I guess we'll go upstairs first—and then out to the barn and around there. (*To the Sheriff.*) You're convinced that there was nothing important here—nothing that would point to any motive.

Sheriff: Nothing here but kitchen things.

(*The County Attorney, after again looking around the kitchen, opens the door of a cupboard closet. He gets up on a chair and looks on a shelf. Pulls his hand away, sticky.*)

County Attorney: Here's a nice mess.

(*The women draw nearer.*)

Mrs. Peters (*to the other woman*): Oh, her fruit; it did freeze. (*To the County Attorney*) She worried about that when it turned so cold. She said the fire'd go out and her jars would break.

Sheriff: Well, can you beat the women! Held for murder and worryin' about her preserves.

County Attorney: I guess before we're through she may have something more serious than preserves to worry about.
Hale: Well, women are used to worrying over trifles.

(*The two women move a little closer together.*)

County Attorney (*with the gallantry of a young politician*): And yet, for all their worries, what would we do without the ladies? (*The women do not unbend. He goes to the sink, takes a dipperful of water from the pail and pouring it into a basin, washes his hands. Starts to wipe them on the roller towel, turns it for a cleaner place.*) Dirty towels! (*Kicks his foot against the pans under the sink.*) Not much of a housekeeper, would you say, ladies?
Mrs. Hale (*stiffly*): There's a great deal of work to be done on a farm.
County Attorney: To be sure. And yet (*with a little bow to her*) I know there are some Dickson County farmhouses which do not have such roller towels.

(*He gives it a pull to expose its full length again.*)

Mrs. Hale: Those towels get dirty awful quick. Men's hands aren't always as clean as they might be.
County Attorney: Ah, loyal to your sex, I see. But you and Mrs. Wright were neighbors. I suppose you were friends, too.
Mrs. Hale (*shaking her head*): I've not seen much of her of late years. I've not been in this house—it's more than a year.
County Attorney: And why was that? You didn't like her?
Mrs. Hale: I liked her all well enough. Farmers' wives have their hands full, Mr. Henderson. And then—
County Attorney: Yes—?
Mrs. Hale (*looking about*): It never seemed a very cheerful place.
County Attorney: No—it's not cheerful. I shouldn't say she had the home-making instinct.
Mrs. Hale: Well, I don't know as Wright had, either.
County Attorney: You mean that they didn't get on very well?
Mrs. Hale: No, I don't mean anything. But I don't think a place'd be any cheerfuller for John Wright's being in it.
County Attorney: I'd like to talk more of that a little later. I want to get the lay of things upstairs now.

(*He goes to the left, where three steps lead to a stair door.*)

Sheriff: I suppose anything Mrs. Peters does'll be all right. She was to take in some clothes for her, you know, and a few little things. We left in such a hurry yesterday.
County Attorney: Yes, but I would like to see what you take, Mrs. Peters, and keep an eye out for anything that might be of use to us.
Mrs. Peters: Yes, Mr. Henderson.

(*The women listen to the men's steps on the stairs, then look about the kitchen.*)

Mrs. Hale: I'd hate to have men coming into my kitchen, snooping around and criticizing.

(*She arranges the pans under sink which the County Attorney had shoved out of place.*)

Mrs. Peters: Of course it's no more than their duty.

Mrs. Hale: Duty's all right, but I guess that deputy sheriff that came out to make the fire might have got a little of this on. (*Gives the roller towel a pull.*) Wish I'd thought of that sooner. Seems mean to talk about her for not having things slicked up when she had to come away in such a hurry.

Mrs. Peters (*who has gone to a small table in the left rear corner of the room, and lifted one end of a towel that covers a pan*): She had bread set.

(*Stands still.*)

Mrs. Hale (*eyes fixed on a loaf of bread beside the breadbox, which is on a low shelf at the other side of the room; moves slowly toward it*): She was going to put this in there. (*Picks up loaf, then abruptly drops it. In a manner of returning to familiar things.*) It's a shame about her fruit. I wonder if it's all gone. (*Gets up on the chair and looks.*) I think there's some here that's all right, Mrs. Peters. Yes—here; (*holding it toward the window*) this is cherries, too. (*Looking again.*) I declare I believe that's the only one. (*Gets down, bottle in her hand. Goes to the sink and wipes it off on the outside.*) She'll feel awful bad after all her hard work in the hot weather. I remember the afternoon I put up my cherries last summer.

(*She puts the bottle on the big kitchen table, center of the room. With a sigh, is about to sit down in the rocking-chair. Before she is seated realizes what chair it is; with a slow look at it, steps back. The chair which she has touched rocks back and forth.*)

Mrs. Peters: Well, I must get those things from the front room closet. (*She goes to the door at the right, but after looking into the other room, steps back.*) You coming with me, Mrs. Hale? You could help me carry them.

(*They go in the other room; reappear, Mrs. Peters carrying a dress and skirt, Mrs. Hale following with a pair of shoes.*)

Mrs. Peters: My, it's cold in there.

(*She puts the clothes on the big table, and hurries to the stove.*)

Mrs. Hale (*examining her skirt*): Wright was close. I think maybe that's why she kept so much to herself. She didn't even belong to the Ladies Aid. I suppose she felt she couldn't do her part, and then you don't enjoy things when you feel shabby. She used to wear pretty clothes and be lively, when she was Minnie Foster, one of the town girls singing in the choir. But that—oh, that was thirty years ago. This all you was to take in?

Mrs. Peters: She said she wanted an apron. Funny thing to want, for there isn't much to get you dirty in jail, goodness knows. But I suppose just to make her feel more natural. She said they was in the top drawer in this cupboard. Yes, here. And then her little shawl that always hung behind the door. (*Opens stair door and looks.*) Yes, here it is.

(*Quickly shuts door leading upstairs.*)

Mrs. Hale (*abruptly moving toward her*): Mrs. Peters?
Mrs. Peters: Yes, Mrs. Hale?

Mrs. Hale: Do you think she did it?

Mrs. Peters (in a frightened voice): Oh, I don't know.

Mrs. Hale: Well, I don't think she did. Asking for an apron and her little shawl. Worrying about her fruit.

Mrs. Peters (starts to speak, glances up, where footsteps are heard in the room above; in a low voice): Mr. Peters says it looks bad for her. Mr. Henderson is awful sarcastic in a speech and he'll make fun of her sayin' she didn't wake up.

Mrs. Hale: Well, I guess John Wright didn't wake when they was slipping that rope under his neck.

Mrs. Peters: No, it's strange. It must have been done awful crafty and still. They say it was such a—funny way to kill a man, rigging it all up like that.

Mrs. Hale: That's just what Mr. Hale said. There was a gun in the house. He says that's what he can't understand.

Mrs. Peters: Mr. Henderson said coming out that what was needed for the case was a motive; something to show anger, or—sudden feeling.

Mrs. Hale (who is standing by the table): Well, I don't see any signs of anger around here. (She puts her hand on the dish towel which lies on the table, stands looking down at table, one half of which is clean, the other half messy.) It's wiped to here. (Makes a move as if to finish work, then turns and looks at loaf of bread outside the breadbox. Drops towel. In that voice of coming back to familiar things.) Wonder how they are finding things upstairs. I hope she had it a little more red-up° there. You know, it seems kind of *sneaking*. Locking her up in town and then coming out here and trying to get her own house to turn against her!

Mrs. Peters: But Mrs. Hale, the law is the law.

Mrs. Hale: I s'pose 'tis. (Unbuttoning her coat.) Better loosen up your things, Mrs. Peters. You won't feel them when you go out.

(Mrs. Peters takes off her fur tippet, goes to hang it on hook at back of room, stands looking at the under part of the small corner table.)

Mrs. Peters: She was piecing a quilt.

(She brings the large sewing basket and they look at the bright pieces.)

Mrs. Hale: It's a log cabin pattern. Pretty, isn't it? I wonder if she was goin' to quilt it or just knot it?

(Footsteps have been heard coming down the stairs. The Sheriff enters followed by Hale and the County Attorney.)

Sheriff: They wonder if she was going to quilt it or just knot it!

(The men laugh; the women look abashed.)

County Attorney (rubbing his hands over the stove): Frank's fire didn't do much up there, did it? Well, let's go out to the barn and get that cleared up.

(The men go outside.)

red-up: (slang) readied up, ready to be seen.

Mrs. Hale (*resentfully*): I don't know as there's anything so strange, our takin' up our time with little things while we're waiting for them to get the evidence. (*She sits down at the big table smoothing out a block with decision.*) I don't see as it's anything to laugh about.

Mrs. Peters (*apologetically*): Of course they've got awful important things on their minds.

(*Pulls up a chair and joins Mrs. Hale at the table.*)

Mrs. Hale (*examining another block*): Mrs. Peters, look at this one. Here, this is the one she was working on, and look at the sewing! All the rest of it has been so nice and even. And look at this! It's all over the place! Why, it looks as if she didn't know what she was about!

(*After she has said this they look at each other, then start to glance back at the door. After an instant Mrs. Hale has pulled at a knot and ripped the sewing.*)

Mrs. Peters: Oh, what are you doing, Mrs. Hale?

Mrs. Hale (*mildly*): Just pulling out a stitch or two that's not sewed very good. (*Threading a needle.*) Bad sewing always made me fidgety.

Mrs. Peters (*nervously*): I don't think we ought to touch things.

Mrs. Hale: I'll just finish up this end. (*Suddenly stopping and leaning forward.*) Mrs. Peters?

Mrs. Peters: Yes, Mrs. Hale?

Mrs. Hale: What do you suppose she was so nervous about?

Mrs. Peters: Oh—I don't know. I don't know as she was nervous. I sometimes sew awful queer when I'm just tired. (*Mrs. Hale starts to say something, looks at Mrs. Peters, then goes on sewing.*) Well, I must get these things wrapped up. They may be through sooner than we think. (*Putting apron and other things together.*) I wonder where I can find a piece of paper, and string.

Mrs. Hale: In that cupboard, maybe.

Mrs. Peters (*looking in cupboard*): Why, here's a birdcage. (*Holds it up.*) Did she have a bird, Mrs. Hale?

Mrs. Hale: Why, I don't know whether she did or not—I've not been here for so long. There was a man around last year selling canaries cheap, but I don't know as she took one; maybe she did. She used to sing real pretty herself.

Mrs. Peters (*glancing around*): Seems funny to think of a bird here. But she must have had one, or why would she have a cage? I wonder what happened to it.

Mrs. Hale: I s'pose maybe the cat got it.

Mrs. Peters: No, she didn't have a cat. She's got that feeling some people have about cats—being afraid of them. My cat got in her room and she was real upset and asked me to take it out.

Mrs. Hale: My sister Bessie was like that. Queer, ain't it?

Mrs. Peters (*examining the cage*): Why, look at this door. It's broke. One hinge is pulled apart.

Mrs. Hale (*looking too*): Looks as if someone must have been rough with it.

Mrs. Peters: Why, yes.

(*She brings the cage forward and puts it on the table.*)

Mrs. Hale: I wish if they're going to find any evidence they'd be about it. I don't like this place.

Mrs. Peters: But I'm awful glad you came with me, Mrs. Hale. It would be lonesome for me sitting here alone.
Mrs. Hale: It would, wouldn't it? (*Dropping her sewing.*) But I tell you what I do wish, Mrs. Peters. I wish I had come over sometimes when *she* was here. I—(*looking around the room*)—wish I had.
Mrs. Peters: But of course you were awful busy, Mrs. Hale—your house and your children.
Mrs. Hale: I could've come. I stayed away because it weren't cheerful—and that's why I ought to have come. I—I've never liked this place. Maybe because it's down in a hollow and you don't see the road. I dunno what it is but it's a lonesome place and always was. I wish I had come over to see Minnie Foster sometimes. I can see now—

(*Shakes her head.*)

Mrs. Peters: Well, you mustn't reproach yourself, Mrs. Hale. Somehow we just don't see how it is with other folks until—something comes up.
Mrs. Hale: Not having children makes less work—but it makes a quiet house, and Wright out to work all day, and no company when he did come in. Did you know John Wright, Mrs. Peters?
Mrs. Peters: Not to know him; I've seen him in town. They say he was a good man.
Mrs. Hale: Yes—good; he didn't drink, and kept his word as well as most, I guess, and paid his debts. But he was a hard man, Mrs. Peters. Just to pass the time of day with him—(*shivers*). Like a raw wind that gets to the bone. (*Pauses, her eye falling on the cage.*) I should think she would'a wanted a bird. But what do you suppose went with it?
Mrs. Peters: I don't know, unless it got sick and died.

(*She reaches over and swings the broken door, swings it again. Both women watch it.*)

Mrs. Hale: You weren't raised round here, were you? (*Mrs. Peters shakes her head.*) You didn't know—her?
Mrs. Peters: Not till they brought her yesterday.
Mrs. Hale: She—come to think of it, she was kind of like a bird herself—real sweet and pretty, but kind of timid and—fluttery. How—she—did—change. (*Silence; then as if struck by a happy thought and relieved to get back to everyday things.*) Tell you what, Mrs. Peters, why don't you take the quilt in with you? It might take up her mind.
Mrs. Peters: Why, I think that's a real nice idea, Mrs. Hale. There couldn't possibly be any objection to it, could there? Now, just what would I take? I wonder if her patches are in here—and her things.

(*They look in the sewing basket.*)

Mrs. Hale: Here's some red. I expect this has got sewing things in it. (*Brings out a fancy box.*) What a pretty box. Looks like something somebody would give you. Maybe her scissors are in here. (*Opens box. Suddenly puts her hand to her nose.*) Why—(*Mrs. Peters bends nearer, then turns her face away.*) There's something wrapped up in this piece of silk.
Mrs. Peters: Why, this isn't her scissors.
Mrs. Hale (*lifting the silk*): Oh, Mrs. Peters—it's—

(*Mrs. Peters bends closer.*)

2000 production of *Trifles*, by Echo Theatre of Dallas.

Mrs. Peters: It's the bird.

Mrs. Hale (*jumping up*): But, Mrs. Peters—look at it! Its neck! Look at its neck! It's all—other side *too*.

Mrs. Peters: Somebody—wrung—its—neck.

(*Their eyes meet. A look of growing comprehension, of horror. Steps are heard outside. Mrs. Hale slips box under quilt pieces, and sinks into her chair. Enter Sheriff and County Attorney. Mrs. Peters rises.*)

County Attorney (*as one turning from serious things to little pleasantries*): Well, ladies, have you decided whether she was going to quilt it or knot it?

Mrs. Peters: We think she was going to—knot it.

County Attorney: Well, that's interesting, I'm sure. (*Seeing the birdcage.*) Has the bird flown?

Mrs. Hale (*putting more quilt pieces over the box*): We think the—cat got it.

County Attorney (*preoccupied*): Is there a cat?

(*Mrs. Hale glances in a quick covert way at Mrs. Peters.*)

Mrs. Peters: Well, not *now*. They're superstitious, you know. They leave.
County Attorney (*to Sheriff Peters, continuing an interrupted conversation*): No sign at all of anyone having come from the outside. Their own rope. Now let's go up again and go over it piece by piece. (*They start upstairs.*) It would have to have been someone who knew just the—

(*Mrs. Peters sits down. The two women sit there not looking at one another, but as if peering into something and at the same time holding back. When they talk now it is in the manner of feeling their way over strange ground, as if afraid of what they are saying, but as if they cannot help saying it.*)

Mrs. Hale: She liked the bird. She was going to bury it in that pretty box.
Mrs. Peters (*in a whisper*): When I was a girl—my kitten—there was a boy took a hatchet, and before my eyes—and before I could get there—(*covers her face an instant*). If they hadn't held me back I would have—(*catches herself, looks upstairs where steps are heard, falters weakly*)—hurt him.
Mrs. Hale (*with a slow look around her*): I wonder how it would seem never to have had any children around. (*Pause.*) No, Wright wouldn't like the bird—a thing that sang. She used to sing. He killed that, too.
Mrs. Peters (*moving uneasily*): We don't know who killed the bird.
Mrs. Hale: I knew John Wright.
Mrs. Peters: It was an awful thing was done in this house that night, Mrs. Hale. Killing a man while he slept, slipping a rope around his neck that choked the life out of him.
Mrs. Hale: His neck. Choked the life out of him.

(*Her hand goes out and rests on the birdcage.*)

Mrs. Peters (*with rising voice*): We don't know who killed him. We don't *know*.
Mrs. Hale (*her own feeling not interrupted*): If there'd been years and years of nothing, then a bird to sing to you, it would be awful—still, after the bird was still.
Mrs. Peters (*something within her speaking*): I know what stillness is. When we home-steaded in Dakota, and my first baby died—after he was two years old, and me with no other then—
Mrs. Hale (*moving*): How soon do you suppose they'll be through looking for the evidence?
Mrs. Peters: I know what stillness is. (*Pulling herself back.*) The law has got to punish crime, Mrs. Hale.
Mrs. Hale (*not as if answering that*): I wish you'd seen Minnie Foster when she wore a white dress with blue ribbons and stood up there in the choir and sang. (*A look around the room.*) Oh, I wish I'd come over here once in a while! That was a crime! That was a crime! Who's going to punish that?
Mrs. Peters (*looking upstairs*): We mustn't—take on.
Mrs. Hale: I might have known she needed help! I know how things can be—for women. I tell you, it's queer, Mrs. Peters. We live close together and we live far apart. We all go through the same things—it's all just a different kind of the same thing. (*Brushes her eyes; noticing the bottle of fruit, reaches out for it.*) If I was you I wouldn't tell her her fruit was gone. Tell her it *ain't*. Tell her it's all right. Take this in to prove it to her. She—she may never know whether it was broke or not.

Mrs. Peters (*takes the bottle, looks about for something to wrap it in; takes petticoat from the clothes brought from the other room, very nervously begins winding this around the bottle; in a false voice*): My, it's a good thing the men couldn't hear us. Wouldn't they just laugh! Getting all stirred up over a little thing like a—dead canary. As if that could have anything to do with—with—wouldn't they *laugh*!

(*The men are heard coming downstairs.*)

Mrs. Hale (*under her breath*): Maybe they would—maybe they wouldn't.
County Attorney: No, Peters, it's all perfectly clear except a reason for doing it. But you know juries when it comes to women. If there was some definite thing. Something to show—something to make a story about—a thing that would connect up with this strange way of doing it—

(*The women's eyes meet for an instant. Enter Hale from outer door.*)

Hale: Well, I've got the team around. Pretty cold out there.
County Attorney: I'm going to stay here a while by myself. (*To the Sheriff*) You can send Frank out for me, can't you? I want to go over everything. I'm not satisfied that we can't do better.
Sheriff: Do you want to see what Mrs. Peters is going to take in?

(*The County Attorney goes to the table, picks up the apron, laughs.*)

County Attorney: Oh, I guess they're not very dangerous things the ladies have picked out. (*Moves a few things about, disturbing the quilt pieces which cover the box. Steps back.*) No, Mrs. Peters doesn't need supervising. For that matter, a sheriff's wife is married to the law. Ever think of it that way, Mrs. Peters?
Mrs. Peters: Not—just that way.
Sheriff (*chuckling*): Married to the law. (*Moves toward the other room.*) I just want you to come in here a minute, George. We ought to take a look at these windows.
County Attorney (*scoffingly*): Oh, windows!
Sheriff: We'll be right out, Mr. Hale.

(*Hale goes outside. The Sheriff follows the County Attorney into the other room. Then Mrs. Hale rises, hands tight together, looking intensely at Mrs. Peters, whose eyes make a slow turn, finally meeting Mrs. Hale's. A moment Mrs. Hale holds her, then her own eyes point the way to where the box is concealed. Suddenly Mrs. Peters throws back quilt pieces and tries to put the box in the bag she is wearing. It is too big. She opens box, starts to take bird out, cannot touch it, goes to pieces, stands there helpless. Sound of a knob turning in the other room. Mrs. Hale snatches the box and puts it in the pocket of her big coat. Enter County Attorney and Sheriff.*)

County Attorney (*facetiously*): Well, Henry, at least we found out that she was not going to quilt it. She was going to—what is it you call it, ladies?
Mrs. Hale (*her hand against her pocket*): We call it—knot it, Mr. Henderson.

CURTAIN

Questions

1. What attitudes toward women do the Sheriff and the County Attorney express? How do Mrs. Hale and Mrs. Peters react to these sentiments?
2. Why does the County Attorney care so much about discovering a motive for the killing?
3. What does Glaspell show us about the position of women in this early twentieth-century community?
4. What do we learn about the married life of the Wrights? By what means is this knowledge revealed to us?
5. What is the setting of this play, and how does it help us to understand Mrs. Wright's deed?
6. What do you infer from the wildly stitched block in Minnie's quilt? Why does Mrs. Hale rip out the crazy stitches?
7. What is so suggestive in the ruined birdcage and the dead canary wrapped in silk? What do these objects have to do with Minnie Foster Wright? What similarity do you notice between the way the canary died and John Wright's own death?
8. What thoughts and memories confirm Mrs. Peters and Mrs. Hale in their decision to help Minnie beat the murder rap?
9. In what places does Mrs. Peters show that she is trying to be a loyal, law-abiding sheriff's wife? How do she and Mrs. Hale differ in background and temperament?
10. What ironies does the play contain? Comment on Mrs. Hale's closing speech: "We call it—knot it, Mr. Henderson." Why is that little hesitation before "knot it" such a meaningful pause?
11. Point out some moments in the play when the playwright conveys much to the audience without needing dialogue.
12. How would you sum up the play's major theme?
13. How does this play, first produced in 1916, show its age? In what ways does it seem still remarkably new?
14. "*Trifles* is a lousy mystery. All the action took place before the curtain went up. Almost in the beginning, on the third page, we find out 'who done it.' So there isn't really much reason for us to sit through the rest of the play." Discuss this view.

ANALYZING *TRIFLES*

Some plays endure, perhaps because (among other reasons) actors take pleasure in performing them. *Trifles* is such a play, a showcase for the skills of its two principals. While the men importantly bumble about, trying to discover a motive, Mrs. Peters and Mrs. Hale solve the case right under their dull noses. The two players in these leading roles face a challenging task: to show both characters growing onstage before us. Discovering a secret that binds them, the two women must realize painful truths in their own lives, become aware of all they have in common with Minnie Wright, and gradually resolve to side with the accused against the men. That *Trifles* has enjoyed a revival of attention may reflect its evident feminist views, its convincing portrait of two women forced reluctantly to arrive at a moral judgment and to make a defiant move.

Conflict

Some critics say that the essence of drama is **conflict**, the central struggle between two or more forces in a play. Evidently, Glaspell's play is rich in this essential, even though its most violent conflict—the war between John and Minnie Wright—has taken place before the play begins. Right away, when the menfolk barge through the door into the warm room, letting the women trail in after them; right away, when the sheriff makes fun of Minnie for worrying about "trifles" and the county attorney (that slick politician) starts crudely trying to flatter the "ladies," we sense a conflict between officious, self-important men and the women they expect to wait on them. What is the play's *theme?* Surely the title points to it: women, who men say worry over trifles, can find large meanings in those little things.

Plot

Like a carefully constructed traditional short story, *Trifles* has a **plot**, a term sometimes taken to mean whatever happens in a story, but more exactly referring to the unique arrangement of events that the author has made. If Glaspell had elected to tell the story of John and Minnie Wright in chronological order, the sequence in which events took place in time, she might have written a much longer play, opening perhaps with a scene of Minnie's buying her canary and John's cold complaint, "That damned bird keeps twittering all day long!" She might have included scenes showing John strangling the canary and swearing when it beaks him; the Wrights in their loveless bed while Minnie knots her noose; and farmer Hale's entrance after the murder, with Minnie rocking. Only at the end would she have shown us what happened after the crime. That arrangement of events would have made for a quite different play than the short, tight one Glaspell wrote. By telling of events in retrospect, by having the women detectives piece together what happened, Glaspell leads us to focus not only on the murder but, more important, on the developing bond between the two women and their growing compassion for the accused.

Subplot

Tightly packed, the one-act *Trifles* contains but one plot: the story of how two women discover evidence that might hang another woman and then hide it. Some plays, usually longer ones, may be more complicated. They may contain a **double plot** (or **subplot**), a secondary arrangement of incidents, involving not the protagonist but someone less important. In Henrik Ibsen's *A Doll's House*, the main plot involves a woman and her husband; they are joined by a second couple, whose fortunes we also follow with interest and whose futures pose different questions.

Protagonist

If *Trifles* may be said to have a **protagonist**, a leading character—a word we usually save for the primary figure of a larger and more eventful play such as *Othello* or *Antigonê*—then you would call the two women dual protagonists. They act in unison to make the plot unfold. Or you could argue that Mrs. Hale—because she destroys the wild stitching in the quilt, because she finds the dead canary, because she invents a cat to catch the bird (thus deceiving the county attorney), and because in the end when Mrs. Peters helplessly "goes to pieces" it is she who takes the initiative and seizes the evidence—deserves to be called the protagonist. More than anyone else in the play, you could claim, the more decisive Mrs. Hale makes things happen.

Exposition

A vital part of most plays is an **exposition**, the part in which we first meet the characters, learn what happened before the curtain rose, and find out what is happening now. For a one-act play, *Trifles* has a fairly long exposition, extending from the opening of the kitchen door through the end of farmer Hale's story. Clearly, this substantial exposition is necessary to set the situation and to fill in the facts of the crime. By comparison, Shakespeare's far longer *Tragedy of Richard III* begins almost abruptly, with its protagonist, a duke who yearns to be king, summing up history in an opening speech and revealing his evil character: "And therefore, since I cannot prove a lover . . . I am determinèd to prove a villain." But Glaspell, too, knows her craft. In the exposition, we are given a **foreshadowing** (or hint of what is to come) in Hale's dry remark, "I didn't know as what his wife wanted made much difference to John." The remark announces the play's theme that men often ignore women's feelings, and it hints at Minnie Wright's motive, later to be revealed. The county attorney, failing to pick up on a valuable clue, tables the discussion. (Still another foreshadowing occurs in Mrs. Hale's ripping out the wild, panicky stitches in Minnie's quilt. In the end, Mrs. Hale will make a similar final move to conceal the evidence.)

Dramatic Question

With the county attorney's speech to the sheriff, "You're convinced that there was nothing important here—nothing that would point to any motive," we begin to understand what he seeks. As he will make even clearer later, the attorney needs a motive in order to convict the accused wife of murder in the first degree. Will Minnie's motive in killing her husband be discovered? Through the first two-thirds of *Trifles*, this is the play's **dramatic question**. Whether or not we state such a question in our minds (and it is doubtful that we do), our interest quickens as we sense that here is a problem to be solved, an uncertainty to be cleared up. When Mrs. Hale and Mrs. Peters find the dead canary with the twisted neck, the question is answered. We know that Minnie killed John to repay him for his act of gross cruelty. The playwright, however, now raises a *new* dramatic question. Having discovered Minnie's motive, will the women reveal it to the lawmen? Alternatively (if you care to phrase the new question differently), what will they do with the incriminating evidence? We keep reading, or stay clamped to our theater seats, because we want that question answered. We share the women's secret now, and we want to see what they will do with it.

Climax

Step by step, *Trifles* builds to a **climax**: a moment, usually coming late in a play, when tension reaches its greatest height. At such a moment, we sense that the play's dramatic question (or its final dramatic question, if the writer has posed more than one) is about to be answered. In *Trifles* this climax occurs when Mrs. Peters finds herself torn between her desire to save Minnie and her duty to the law. "It was an awful thing was done in this house that night," she reminds herself in one speech, suggesting that Minnie deserves to be punished; then in the next speech she insists, "We don't know who killed him. We don't *know*." Shortly after that, in one speech she voices two warring attitudes. Remembering the loss of her first child, she sympathizes with Minnie: "I know what stillness is." But in her next breath she recalls once more her duty to be a loyal sheriff's wife: "The law has got to punish crime, Mrs. Hale." For a moment, she is placed in conflict with Mrs. Hale, who knew Minnie personally. The two now stand on the edge of a fateful brink. Which way will they decide?

You will sometimes hear *climax* used in a different sense to mean any **crisis**—that is, a moment of tension when one or another outcome is possible. What *crisis* means will be easy to remember if you think of a crisis in medicine: the turning point in an illness when it becomes clear that a patient will either die or recover. In talking about plays, you will probably find both *crisis* and *climax* useful. You can say that a play has more than one crisis, perhaps several. In such a play, the last and most decisive crisis is the climax. A play has only one climax.

Resolution and Dénouement

From this moment of climax, the play, like its protagonist (or if you like, protagonists), will make a final move. Mrs. Peters takes her stand. Mrs. Hale, too, decides. She owes Minnie something to make up for her own "crime"—her failure to visit the desperate woman. The plot now charges ahead to its outcome or **resolution**, also called the **conclusion** or **dénouement** (French for "untying of a knot"). The two women act: they scoop up the damaging evidence. Seconds before the very end, Glaspell heightens the **suspense**, our enjoyable anxiety, by making Mrs. Peters fumble with the incriminating box as the sheriff and the county attorney draw near. Mrs. Hale's swift grab for the evidence saves the day and presumably saves Minnie's life. The sound of the doorknob turning in the next room, as the lawmen return, is a small but effective bit of **stage business**—any nonverbal action that engages the attention of an audience. Earlier, when Mrs. Hale almost sits down in Minnie's place, the empty chair that ominously starts rocking is another brilliant piece of stage business. Not only does it give us something interesting to watch, but it also gives us something to think about.

Rising and Falling Action

The German critic Gustav Freytag maintained that events in a plot can be arranged in the outline of a pyramid. In his influential view, a play begins with a **rising action**, that part of the narrative (including the exposition) in which events start moving toward a climax. After the climax, the story tapers off in a **falling action**—that is, the subsequent events, including a resolution. In a tragedy, this falling action usually is recognizable: the protagonist's fortunes proceed downhill to an inevitable end.

Some plays indeed have demonstrable pyramids. In *Trifles*, we might claim that in the first two-thirds of the play a rising action builds in intensity. It proceeds through each main incident: the finding of the crazily stitched quilt, Mrs. Hale's ripping out the evidence, the discovery of the birdcage, then of the bird itself, and Mrs. Hale's concealing it. At the climax, the peak of the pyramid, the two women seem about to clash as Mrs. Peters wavers uncertainly. The action then falls to a swift resolution. If you outlined that pyramid on paper, however, it would look lopsided—a long rise and a short, steep fall. The pyramid metaphor seems more meaningfully to fit longer plays, among them some classic tragedies, such as *Antigonê*. Nevertheless, in most other plays, it is hard to find a symmetrical pyramid.

Unity of Time, Place, and Action

Because its action occurs all at one time and in one place, *Trifles* happens to observe the **unities**, certain principles of good drama laid down by Italian literary critics in the sixteenth century. Interpreting the theories of Aristotle as binding laws, these critics set down three basic principles: a good play, they maintained, should display unity of *action*, unity of *time*, and unity of *place*. In practical terms, this theory maintained that a play must represent a single series of interrelated actions that take place within twenty-four hours in a single location. Furthermore, they insisted, to have true unity of action, a play had to be entirely serious or entirely funny. Mixing tragic and comic elements was not allowed. That Glaspell consciously strove to obey those critics is doubtful, and certainly many great plays, such as Shakespeare's *Othello*, defy such arbitrary rules. Still, it is at least arguable that some of the power of *Trifles* comes from the intensity of the playwright's concentration on what happens in one place, in one short expanse of time.

Symbol in Drama

Brief though it is, *Trifles* has main elements you will find in much longer, more complicated plays. It even has **symbols**, things that hint at large meanings—for example, the broken birdcage and the dead canary, both suggesting the music and the joy that John Wright stifled in Minnie and the terrible stillness that followed his killing the one thing she loved. Perhaps the lone remaining jar of cherries, too, radiates suggestions: it is the one bright, cheerful thing poor Minnie has to show for a whole summer of toil. Plays can also contain symbolic characters (generally flat ones such as a prophet who croaks, "Beware the ides of March"), symbolic settings, and symbolic gestures. Symbols in drama may be as big as a house—the home in Ibsen's *A Doll's House*, for instance—or they may appear to be trifles. In Glaspell's rich art, such trifles aren't trifling at all.

■ Writing Assignment on Drama

Select any short play or hour-long TV drama, and write a brief essay identifying the protagonist, central conflict, and dramatic question.

checklist: Analyzing a Play

WRITING ABOUT A PLAY

- ☐ List the play's three or four main characters. Jot down what each character wants most at the play's beginning.
- ☐ Which of these characters is the protagonist?
- ☐ Does the play have an antagonist?
- ☐ What stands in the way of the protagonist's achieving his or her goal?
- ☐ How do the other characters' motivations fit into the central conflict? Identify any double plots or subplots.
- ☐ What are the play's main events? How does each relate to the protagonist's struggle?
- ☐ Where do you find the play's climax?
- ☐ How is the conflict resolved? What qualities in the protagonist's character bring about the play's outcome?
- ☐ Does the protagonist achieve his or her goal? How does that success or failure affect the protagonist?

WRITING ABOUT TRAGEDY

- ☐ Identify the protagonist. In what ways does he or she fit Aristotle's description of a tragic hero?
- ☐ Does the main character have a tragic flaw? If so, in what ways does that flaw prefigure or determine what happens in the play?
- ☐ Does the play have an antagonist who opposes or interferes with the main character's intentions?
- ☐ What is the key moment in the play that leads to the hero's reversal of fortune? What happens? How do the characters respond?
- ☐ Do you find the main character, and his or her tragic flaw, believable?
- ☐ How do a character's beliefs influence his or her actions and motivations?
- ☐ In what ways are the play's characters like the people you know? How do these familiar qualities influence the characters' actions and motivations?
- ☐ What lessons do you draw from the outcome of the play, and how might they apply to contemporary life?

WRITING ABOUT COMEDY

- ☐ What kind of comedy is the play? Romantic? Slapstick? Satire? How can you tell?
- ☐ Which style of comedy prevails? Is there more emphasis on high comedy or low? More emphasis on verbal humor or physical comedy?
- ☐ Focus on a key comic moment. Does the comedy grow out of situation? Character? A mix of both?
- ☐ How does the play end? In a wedding or romance? A reconciliation? Mutual understanding?

5 READING AN ESSAY

> *You write in order to change the world, knowing perfectly well that you probably can't, but also knowing that literature is indispensable to the world. The world changes according to the way people see it, and if you alter even by a millimeter the way people look at reality, then you can change it.*
>
> —JAMES BALDWIN

Nonfiction—unlike fiction, poetry, or drama—is something you probably read every day. You may have a subscription to the local newspaper. You might buy a magazine such as *Time*, *Sports Illustrated*, or *Cosmopolitan*, or a more specialized magazine that discusses music or video games. You may prefer an online source of information or a favorite blog. Or you may be reading a nonfiction book—a memoir, a diet plan, an inspirational volume. There are many different kinds of nonfiction, from blogs to biographies, from travel guides to get-rich-quick manuals. In this chapter we will consider only one form of nonfiction: the essay.

WHAT IS AN ESSAY?

What exactly *is* an essay? How does it differ from other forms of prose such as a newspaper article or short story? Although it is hard to offer a single definition of this varied form, we can begin by saying an **essay** is a short piece of nonfiction usually written in a personal style. There is no standard for length, style, or subject. The nature of the essay is as diverse as humanity itself. Essays can be serious, funny, visionary, or nostalgic. The style can be as casual as a conversation with an old friend or as formal as a presidential inaugural address. The key thing is that we somehow recognize by the style or subject (or both) the author's personality and perspective. Newspaper journalists try to report the news objectively—even though they sometimes fail—by removing their own personal point of view from the story. By contrast, the essayist lets herself or himself into the piece.

Essays are generally written from a strong first-person point of view—and whether or not the author uses "I" in the piece, his or her feelings and opinions are usually clear. While news articles report on something that happened, they don't typically use those events to spark an analysis of broader issues. Essays, on the other hand, usually aim for something bigger—they use an event or experience, often a personal one, to demonstrate or comment on a larger point about the world, our social or political structures, or the nature of what it means to be human. Essays use personal perspective to achieve a general insight.

As Joyce Carol Oates writes in the introduction to the 1991 edition of *Best American Essays*,

> [U]nlike journalism, which exists primarily to present facts, the essays transcend their data, or transmute it into personal meaning. The memorable essay, unlike the article, is not place- or time-bound; it survives the occasion of its original composition.

To illustrate Oates's point, let's consider an example. Joan Didion's essay "On Morality," which is included in this chapter, begins with a description of an accident on a freeway in California. In a news article, a reporter would have relayed the facts of the accident—when it occurred, who was involved, how and why it happened. If there had been a history of accidents on this particular freeway, the reporter might also have talked about this incident in relation to earlier accidents. But Didion takes the accident and uses it as a jumping-off point for something much larger—a discussion of the "right" thing to do in various circumstances, and the difficulties of establishing an absolute definition of morality.

You might ask how Didion's piece differs from someone's writing about the same incident, and the same issues, in a blog. Writing for online sources is a still-evolving phenomenon, and there certainly are websites—such as *Slate* and *Salon*—that include both reportage and essays. But most blog posts are shorter and of the moment. They don't adhere to a strict set of editorial standards, and most pieces written for blogs lack the careful shape and structure that characterize a fully achieved essay.

HISTORY OF THE ESSAY

Although there are examples of short nonfiction prose pieces dating back to Greek and Latin times, the father of the modern essay was the French nobleman Michel de Montaigne. In the late 1500s, Montaigne, who was tired of the stiff and formal academic writing that was the norm at the time, started to discuss ideas and events in a more personal manner. He termed his efforts "*essais*," meaning "trials" or "attempts," and the best essays still often have the sense of an author *attempting* something new. Famous essayists who followed Montaigne include Charles Lamb, George Orwell, and Virginia Woolf in England, and Ralph Waldo Emerson, H. L. Mencken, and E. B. White in America. During the late 1950s, James Baldwin's essays were deeply influential in the civil rights movement. In the 1960s, Susan Sontag wrote brilliantly about books, films, sexual mores, and cultural trends. Later essayists such as Wendell Berry, Joan Didion, Joseph Epstein, Katha Pollitt, Camille Paglia, Richard Rodriguez, and Brent Staples—who are still writing today—began to take on other social and cultural issues in American society.

Creative Nonfiction

Essays have enjoyed a resurgence in the last two decades, as more and more writers have employed the form to address an ever-widening array of topics. In recent years, the term **creative nonfiction** has often been used to imply that the best nonfiction writing has literary merit comparable to that of short stories, novels, and poems. The name is slightly misleading in that all good writing displays some degree of creativity, but it also reminds us how much real invention goes into constructing a memorable piece of nonfiction. In general, the term *creative nonfiction* emphasizes the ways in which the essay or memoir departs from the highly linear and factual style of journalism.

Although essays have their own set of expectations and conventions, a good essay should capture our attention in the same way a good short story does, by presenting us with a compelling situation, intriguing characters, and carefully wrought language, and by drawing our interest to what the author is saying. But unlike a short story, an essay usually addresses its readers directly, generally telling us outright what it wants us to see, what connections it wants us to make, and how it would like us to feel by the end of the piece. Short stories, by contrast, usually suggest their themes more indirectly. While short stories are fictional, or at least include elements that are made up, essays should be rooted in fact. Being factual is the source of their authority, even if their styles are often highly personal.

TYPES OF ESSAYS

Here are definitions of the most common types of essays. These definitions will help you analyze the essays you read, but don't stick to the descriptions too closely. The best essays often incorporate elements of more than one of these common types. Still, if you are able to identify what kind of essay you are reading, that's a good first step toward understanding the essay itself.

Narrative Essay

A **narrative essay** is built around a story that supports or illustrates the point the writer is making. Most narrative essays describe an important moment or event, and then provide the reader with an interpretation of what it signified. Often narrative essays are autobiographical, and the writer mines his or her own experience as a way to talk about a larger observation, issue, or problem. George Orwell's "Shooting an Elephant" and Judith Ortiz Cofer's "I Fell in Love, or My Hormones Awakened" are examples of narrative essays. Each combines the personal qualities of memoir with an attempt to make some general observations about politics, culture, and society. Both tell compelling stories of pivotal events in the writers' lives—and both tie those events to larger social and historical forces that were at work around them. Sometimes essays tell multiple stories. Cynthia Ozick's "Lovesickness" presents four interrelated episodes from her early life, all showing the peculiarities of the human heart.

Descriptive Essay

A **descriptive essay** uses sensory descriptions to evoke how a place (or time period, or person) looks, sounds, smells, or feels. Ultimately these descriptions help create an overall feeling or impression, which relates to the writer's theme. John Muir, for example, in "A Wind Storm in the Forests," isn't simply describing a storm. He's trying to make us feel the power and beauty of nature in the unforgettable way he personally experienced it, so that we'll ultimately enjoy and preserve it. Descriptive essays often make their points less directly than other essays, but they may leave us with a lingering feeling or impression that is even more compelling and enduring.

Expository Essay

The aim of an **expository essay** is to explain, analyze, or organize information, in order to create a cohesive picture of a concept or event. Expository writing is the most straightforward kind of writing. It is not trying to tell an interesting personal story or describe a particular time or place. It is meant to give the reader information in a clear and effective manner. An expository essay might instruct the reader in how to do something—the chapter you are now reading in this textbook, for example, is expository. Or it might explain how something happened—like Elisabeth Kübler Ross's "On the Fear of Death," which relates specific information about how society's treatment of death and dying has changed in modern times. An expository essay could also take on an intangible concept—such as love or racism—and try to make it concrete. In general, writers of expository essays approach their topics in a way that makes it possible for the reader to understand them more easily.

Argumentative Essay

An **argumentative essay** states a case and tries to influence the reader's opinion. Argumentative essays have something in common with opinion pieces and editorials, as well as with certain speeches in the public arena, particularly political speeches. All of these forms are used to try to convince people of something. We find argumentative essays published daily as editorials in the opinion sections of newspapers. But a truly fine argumentative essay, as opposed to a short op-ed piece or most political stump speeches, is generally longer, more complex, and less confined to the events that inspire it.

Still, argumentative essays often address subjects that are a matter of current debate. Martin Luther King Jr.'s "Letter from Birmingham Jail" is an example of an argumentative essay—one that had tremendous influence during the civil rights era. Wallace Stegner's "Wilderness Letter" makes a strong case for the value of wild places—and became a clarion call for the environmental movement. Amy Tan's essay "Mother Tongue," which is included in this chapter, has elements that can be described as narrative, descriptive, and expository—but in the end, Tan strives to make general points about language and identity, and is trying to influence (however gently and comically) those who might disagree with her, so one might argue that it evolves into a very personal sort of argumentative essay.

Effective arguments require persuasion. The common methods of persuasion, or **rhetorical appeals**, are traditionally divided into three basic types:

- **Logos:** this method refers to persuading the audience through logic or reason. Logos is the part of the argument that appeals to the head. Is the claim of the essay clear? Is the argument logical? Is the evidence convincing? Logos is the part of the argument a reader can most easily define and analyze.

- **Pathos:** this technique refers to evoking emotion. Pathos is the part of the argument that appeals to the heart. An argument that relies on pathos makes the reader identify with the writer's point of view—to feel what he or she feels. If the writer can make the reader respond with emotion, the reader is more likely to be convinced by the argument.

- **Ethos**: this method refers to the credibility or character of the writer or speaker. Obviously, we are more likely to believe the argument of someone who is an established expert on the topic being discussed, or someone we believe to be honorable and trustworthy. Credibility can be established through the tone and style of the essay itself, or independently, through the known reputation of the writer.

Many essays use all three of the traditional rhetorical appeals. King's "Letter from Birmingham Jail" lays out a strong and logical argument (logos) while also making the reader empathize with blacks living under segregation (pathos), and he writes from a position of established moral authority (ethos). Stegner's essay also makes a strong argument based on logic (logos) and appeals to our human need for connection and beauty (pathos). Tan's essay weaves her argument (logos) in with appeals to our humanity and humor (pathos). As you consider the essays in this book, you can judge for yourself how well the writers employ these strategies.

ELEMENTS OF ESSAYS

While essays are often more direct and seemingly straightforward than fiction or poetry, they too contain the familiar elements of literature. When you read an essay, you should look for many of the same things you consider in other genres. Understanding the basic elements of an essay will help you understand it more deeply and appreciate it more fully. It will also help you as you prepare to write about essays.

Voice

Like a story or a poem, an essay has a **voice**—a person or persona who is narrating. In an essay, the voice is usually that of the author. A voice in an essay is akin to the voice of a person speaking to you. It might be chummy, or restrained, or funny, or angry; it might be confident or self-critical. It might be high-minded and even remote, or it might be more intimate, like the voice of someone with whom you're having a cup of coffee. Also like the voices of people, the voice of an essay may have a particular tone—sarcastic, or sincere, or hectoring, or convincing, or light-hearted, or deeply serious. Essays have a wide range of voices and tones, depending on the context in which, and purpose for which, they were written. Consider this passage from Amy Tan's "Mother Tongue":

> Just last week, I was walking down the street with my mother, and I again found myself conscious of the English I was using, the English I do use with her. We were talking about the price of new and used furniture and I heard myself saying this: "Not waste money that way." My husband was with us as well, and he didn't notice any switch in my English. And then I realized why. It's because over the twenty years we've been together I've often used that same kind of English with him, and sometimes he even uses it with me. It has become our language of intimacy, a different sort of English that relates to family talk, the language I grew up with.

Now, read this passage from Martin Luther King Jr.'s "Letter from Birmingham Jail":

> We know through painful experience that freedom is never voluntarily given by the oppressor; it must be demanded by the oppressed. Frankly, I have yet to engage in a direct-action campaign that was "well timed" in the view of those who have not suffered unduly from the disease of segregation. For years now I have heard the word "Wait!" It rings in the ear of every Negro with piercing familiarity. This "Wait" has almost always meant "Never." We must come to see, with one of our distinguished jurists, that "justice too long delayed is justice denied."

The voice in Tan's essay is direct and conversational—it's as if we're walking down the street with her family, and she is gently encouraging us to see things her way. The voice in King's essay is formal and authoritative. The sweep and power of its language are related to the moral force of its argument.

Style

The **style** of an essay—like style in fiction or poetry—relates to the way a particular writer manages language. Generally, style refers to things such as sound, imagery, figures of speech—anything that makes a writer uniquely him- or herself. In "Letter from Birmingham Jail," King's style is very formal; it also has the cadences of a sermon. Compare that with the opening of Raymond Carver's essay "My Father's Life":

> My dad's name was Clevie Raymond Carver. His family called him Raymond and friends called him C. R. I was named Raymond Clevie Carver Jr. I hated the "Junior" part. When I was little my dad called me Frog, which was okay. But later, like everybody else in the family, he began calling me Junior.

Carver's style is very different from King's. His sentences are simple, straightforward, and direct—pared of rhetorical flourish. Differences in writers' styles might derive from their personalities and characters, and their styles are also shaped by the worlds they describe, their respective audiences, and the purposes of their essays. Carver's essay is a eulogy to his father, a testimony to one man's life. King's essay is aimed at changing minds and changing history.

Another element of style is the use of **rhetorical devices**, a way of using language to achieve particular effects. When employed well, rhetorical devices can help make an author's arguments more convincing. Most of these techniques also appear in stories, poems, and plays, but it is in essays that the author's rhetoric is most visible. Here are a few common rhetorical devices:

- **Analogy**: a comparison between two things that have similar features, in order to stress a point. When the Reverend Martin Luther King Jr. invokes the Apostle Paul in "Letter from Birmingham Jail," he is making an analogy. He is implying that he, like Paul, has traveled from his native place to carry the Christian gospel of freedom, and also that he, like the Apostle, has been imprisoned for preaching truth.
- **Antithesis**: words, phrases, or sentences set in deliberate contrast to one another. Antithesis balances opposites to heighten the effect of a statement. A famous

example occurs in John F. Kennedy's Inaugural Address, when he tells the American public to "Ask *not* what your country can do for you, ask what you can do for your country." This memorable phrase has remained in the public parlance partly because of Kennedy's effective use of antithesis.

- **Hyperbole**: exaggeration in order to emphasize a point. People often use hyperbole in everyday speech, as when someone says "I'm so hungry I could eat a horse" or "I've asked you a million times to clean your room."
- **Repetition**: repeating words or phrases to create an effect or make a point. A common form of repetition is to repeat the same words at the beginning of sentences, phrases, or paragraphs—or at the end of them. Joan Didion uses repetition in her essay "On Morality" to underscore the dangers of people's justifying their actions by saying that they were doing what they thought was right. She writes: "How many madmen have said it? How many murderers? Klaus Fuchs said it, and the men who committed the Mountain Meadows Massacre said it, and Alfred Rosenberg said it."
- **Parallelism**: an arrangement of words, phrases, or sentences in a similar grammatical or structural way. Parallelism organizes ideas in a way that demonstrates their coordination to the reader, usually to heighten their memorability or persuasiveness. An excellent example is Lincoln's often-quoted phrase "government of the people, by the people, for the people."
- **Rhetorical question**: a question asked with the purpose of making a point—not to elicit an answer. Joan Didion's question "How many madmen have said it and meant it?" is a rhetorical question; obviously there is no clear reply, but it makes one stop and think. We use rhetorical questions all the time to make a point, for example, "Why bother?" and "How cool is that?"

Structure

The **structure**, or design of an essay, is often the hardest element to define. Classic narrative, descriptive, or argumentative essays tend to be more complex and subtle than the essays you might write for school. An academic essay is generally put together in accordance with certain expectations, such as length, style, focus, and content. No instructor gave Reverend King a set of strict guidelines for his letter from his Birmingham jail cell. In the essays we're reading in this volume, there's not always a clearly expressed thesis statement in the first few sentences, nor is there a general formula by which the author backs up his or her claims. As Annie Dillard writes in the introduction to the 1988 edition of *Best American Essays*,

> The essay is, and has been, all over the map. There's nothing you cannot do with it; no subject matter is forbidden, no structure is proscribed. You get to make up your own structure every time, a structure that arises from the materials and best contains them.

Although essays do not necessarily follow a set of rules laid out in advance, an essay often does have a discernible structure that we can analyze. In King's essay, the author refutes, point by point, his "Fellow Clergymen's" objections to acts of civil disobedience during the civil rights movement and makes a larger case for racial equality.

Good essays may also create their own structures as they proceed. In "On Morality," for example, Joan Didion begins by placing us, with her, in an overheated motel room in Death Valley. She then tells the story of a fatal car accident that occurred on the local freeway the night before. From there, she goes on to discuss the people who helped the young couple in the accident, historical incidents of other travelers who met with disaster in California, the way that gossip is spread in the area, a church meeting across the road. And then suddenly she shifts perspective completely and begins to discuss morality and the dangers of being too quick to define what is wrong and what is right. The essay transforms from a simple narrative of an accident to what ultimately reads like a work of philosophy. It's a hard essay to break down and make a chart of—and yet somehow it works wonderfully.

Amy Tan, on the other hand, begins her essay "Mother Tongue" with a disclaimer, explaining,

> I am not a scholar of English literature. I cannot give you much more than personal opinions on the English language and its variations in this country or others.
>
> I am a writer. And by that definition, I am someone who has always loved language.

She then weaves her reflections on writing in with her observations of how her mother uses language, and she continues this parallel discussion throughout the essay.

When you consider an essay's structure, pay special attention to how the essay begins and ends. By opening her essay as she does, Tan immediately establishes a sense of familiarity with the reader (who is likely a general reader and also "not a scholar of English literature") which understates her expertise on her subject. The opening of King's essay, on the other hand, establishes that he is responding to the critical comments of specific clergymen, but also lays the groundwork for an argument aimed at a much broader audience. And the sweltering, desolate scene described at the start of Didion's "On Morality" creates an atmosphere of starkness that sets the reader up perfectly for the tragic accident, as well as the tough-minded philosophical discussion that follows.

Theme

The **theme** of an essay—like the theme of a story, poem, or play—is the main point or idea, the essence of what the writer is saying. Because essays are generally addressed directly to the reader, it is often—but not always—easier to discern the theme of an essay than the theme of a story, poem, or play. Especially in the case of an argumentative essay, the writer needs to be clear and explicit about the theme because he or she is trying to influence our opinion. Sometimes, though, you have to dig a little deeper to figure out where a writer really stands—and presenting the reader with such a challenge may be part of the point.

The themes of "Letter from Birmingham Jail," "Mother Tongue," and "On Morality" are stated directly. But what exactly is the theme of Carver's "My Father's Life" or Cynthia Ozick's "Lovesickness"? Ozick's essay lends itself to good discussion. Is her theme only the difficulties created by falling in love? Or is it that we never outgrow the irrationality of love? Ozick certainly suggests that age does not necessarily bring wisdom, since she begins with her most recent and oddest infatuation—with the groom at someone else's wedding! Mixing in her sometimes embarrassing stories of her own romantic obsessions and revelations, she suggests a larger theme about the difficulty of self-knowledge in regard to love.

Let's consider two of the essays we've mentioned, Joan Didion's "On Morality" and Amy Tan's "Mother Tongue."

Joan Didion

Joan Didion (b. 1934) was born in Sacramento, California, into a family that had been in the state for five generations. She graduated from the University of California at Berkeley and soon began publishing articles and stories. After spending some years in New York, she returned to California with her husband, the novelist and screenwriter John Gregory Dunne. Although Didion has published five well-received novels, and co-authored half a dozen screenplays with her late husband, she has achieved her greatest distinction as an essayist. "On Morality" was originally published in the American Scholar *quarterly and later collected in* Slouching Towards Bethlehem *(1968), Didion's book of essays on 1960s American culture. Her other major works include* The White Album *(1979) and* The Year of Magical Thinking *(2005). The Dictionary of Literary Biography says of Didion, "No literary journalist currently writing is better able to shape the shards of American disorder into a living history of this time."*

Joan Didion

On Morality   1968

As it happens I am in Death Valley, in a room at the Enterprise Motel and Trailer Park, and it is July, and it is hot. In fact it is 119°. I cannot seem to make the air conditioner work, but there is a small refrigerator, and I can wrap ice cubes in a towel and hold them against the small of my back. With the help of the ice cubes I have been trying to think, because *The American Scholar* asked me to, in some abstract way about "morality," a word I distrust more every day, but my mind veers inflexibly toward the particular.

Here are some particulars. At midnight last night, on the road in from Las Vegas to Death Valley Junction, a car hit a shoulder and turned over. The driver, very young and apparently drunk, was killed instantly. His girl was found alive but bleeding internally, deep in shock. I talked this afternoon to the nurse who had driven the girl to the nearest doctor, 185 miles across the floor of the Valley and three ranges of lethal mountain road. The nurse explained that her husband, a talc miner, had stayed on the highway with the boy's body until the coroner could get over the mountains from Bishop, at dawn today. "You can't just leave a body on the highway," she said. "It's immoral."

It was one instance in which I did not distrust the word, because she meant something quite specific. She meant that if a body is left alone for even a few minutes on the desert, the coyotes close in and eat the flesh. Whether or not a corpse is torn apart by coyotes may seem only a sentimental consideration, but of course it is more: one of the promises we make to one another is that we will try to retrieve our casualties, try not to abandon our dead to the coyotes. If we have been taught to keep our promises—if, in the simplest terms, our upbringing is good enough—we stay with the body, or have bad dreams.

I am talking, of course, about the kind of social code that is sometimes called, usually pejoratively, "wagon-train morality." In fact that is precisely what it is. For better or worse, we are what we learned as children: my own childhood was illuminated by graphic litanies of the grief awaiting those who failed in their loyalties to each other. The Donner-Reed Party, starving in the Sierra snows, all the ephemera of civilization gone save that one vestigial taboo, the provision that no one should eat his own blood kin. The Jayhawkers, who quarreled and separated not far from where I am tonight. Some of them died in the Funerals and some of them died down near Badwater and most of the rest of them died in the Panamints. A woman who got through gave the Valley its name. Some might say that the Jayhawkers were killed by the desert summer, and the Donner Party by the mountain winter, by circumstances beyond control; we were taught instead that they had somewhere abdicated their responsibilities, somehow breached their primary loyalties, or they would not have found themselves helpless in the mountain winter or the desert summer, would not have given way to acrimony, would not have deserted one another, would not have *failed*. In brief, we heard such stories as cautionary tales, and they still suggest the only kind of "morality" that seems to me to have any but the most potentially mendacious meaning.

You are quite possibly impatient with me by now; I am talking, you want to say, about a "morality" so primitive that it scarcely deserves the name, a code that has as its point only survival, not the attainment of the ideal good. Exactly. Particularly out here tonight, in this country so ominous and terrible that to live in it is to live with antimatter, it is difficult to believe that "the good" is a knowable quantity. Let me tell you what it is like out here tonight. Stories travel at night on the desert. Someone gets in his pickup and drives a couple of hundred miles for a beer, and he carries news of what is happening, back wherever he came from. Then he drives another hundred miles for another beer, and passes along stories from the last place as well from the one before; it is a network kept alive by people whose instincts tell them that if they do not keep moving at night on the desert they will lose all reason. Here is a story that is going around the desert tonight: over across the Nevada line, sheriff's deputies are diving in some underground pools, trying to retrieve a couple of bodies known to be in the hole. The widow of one of the drowned boys is over there; she is eighteen, and pregnant, and is said not to leave the hole. The divers go down and come up, and she just stands there and stares into the water. They have been diving for ten days but have found no bottom to the caves, no bodies and no trace of them, only the black 90° water going down and down and down, and a single translucent fish, not classified. The story tonight is that one of the divers has been hauled up incoherent, out of his head, shouting—until they got him out of there so that the widow could not hear—about water that got hotter instead of cooler as he went down, about light flickering through the water, about magma, about underground nuclear testing.

That is the tone stories take out here, and there are quite a few of them tonight. And it is more than the stories alone. Across the road at the Faith Community Church a couple of dozen old people, come here to live in trailers and die in the sun, are holding a prayer sing. I cannot hear them and do not want to. What I can hear are occasional coyotes and a constant chorus of "Baby the Rain Must Fall" from the jukebox in the Snake Room next door, and if I were also to hear those dying voices, those Midwestern voices drawn to this lunar country for some unimaginable atavistic rites, *rock of ages cleft for me*, I think I would lose my own reason. Every now and then I imagine I hear a rattlesnake, but my husband says that it is a faucet, a paper rustling, the wind. Then he stands by a window, and plays a flashlight over the dry wash outside.

What does it mean? It means nothing manageable. There is some sinister hysteria in the air out here tonight, some hint of the monstrous perversion to which any human idea can come. "I followed my own conscience." "I did what I thought was right." How many madmen have said it and meant it? How many murderers? Klaus Fuchs said it, and the men who committed the Mountain Meadows Massacre said it, and Alfred Rosenberg said it. And, as we are rotely and rather presumptuously reminded by those who would say it now, Jesus said it. Maybe we have all said it, and maybe we have been wrong. Except on the most primitive level—our loyalties to those we love—what could be more arrogant than to claim the primacy of personal conscience? ("Tell me," a rabbi asked Daniel Bell when he said, as a child, that he did not believe in God. "Do you think God cares?") At least some of the time, the world appears to me as a painting by Hieronymous Bosch; were I to follow my conscience then, it would lead me out onto the desert with Marion Faye, out to where he stood in *The Deer Park* looking east to Los Alamos and praying, as if for rain, that it would happen: " . . . *let it come and clear the rot and the stench and the stink, let it come for all of everywhere, just so it comes and the world stands clear in the white dead dawn.*"

Of course you will say that I do not have the right, even if I had the power, to inflict that unreasonable conscience upon you; nor do I want you to inflict your conscience, however reasonable, however enlightened, upon me. ("We must be aware of the dangers which lie in our most generous wishes," Lionel Trilling once wrote. "Some paradox of our nature leads us, when once we have made our fellow men the objects of our enlightened interest, to go on to make them the objects of our pity, then of our wisdom, ultimately of our coercion.") That the ethic of conscience is intrinsically insidious seems scarcely a revelatory point, but it is one raised with increasing infrequency; even those who do raise it tend to *segue* with troubling readiness into the quite contradictory position that the ethic of conscience is dangerous when it is "wrong," and admirable when it is "right."

You see I want to be quite obstinate about insisting that we have no way of knowing—beyond that fundamental loyalty to the social code—what is "right" and what is "wrong," what is "good" and what "evil." I dwell so upon this because the most disturbing aspect of "morality" seems to me to be the frequency with which the word now appears; in the press, on television, in the most perfunctory kinds of conversation. Questions of straightforward power (or survival) politics, questions of quite indifferent public policy, questions of almost anything: they are all assigned these factitious moral burdens. There is something facile going on, some self-indulgence at work. Of course we would all like to "believe" in something, like to assuage our private guilts in public causes, like to lose our tiresome selves; like, perhaps, to transform the white flag of defeat at home into the brave white banner of battle away from home. And of course it is all right to do that; that is how, immemorially, things have gotten done. But I think it is all right only so long as we do not delude ourselves about what we are doing, and why. It is all right only so long as we remember that all the *ad hoc* committees, all the picket lines, all the brave signatures in *The New York Times*, all the tools of agitprop straight across the spectrum, do not confer upon anyone any *ipso facto* virtue. It is all right only so long as we recognize that the end may or may not be expedient, may or may not be a good idea, but in any case has nothing to with "morality." Because when we start deceiving ourselves into thinking not that we want something or need something, not that it is a pragmatic necessity for us to have it, but that it is a *moral imperative* that we have it, then is when we join the fashionable madmen, and then is when the thin whine of hysteria is heard in the land, and then is when we are in bad trouble. And I suspect we are already there.

Questions

1. Didion's essay begins with her sitting in a sweltering motel room. What other details does she provide about her physical whereabouts during the writing of the essay? How does this setting contribute to her larger discussion?
2. Why does Didion describe the car accident and its aftermath? Why does she accept the nurse's brand of morality, and how does it differ from the other types of morality she discusses?
3. What is Didion's point in including the examples of Klaus Fuchs, the Mountain Meadows Massacre, and Alfred Rosenberg?
4. Why does Didion include the quotation from the critic Lionel Trilling? How does his observation relate to her own opinion?
5. Do you agree that there is a difference between a "want," "need," or "pragmatic necessity" versus a "moral imperative"? Who should decide what constitutes a "moral imperative"?

▪ Writing Assignments

1. Compare and contrast Didion's views of "right" and "wrong" with Martin Luther King Jr.'s view in "Letter from Birmingham Jail." With whose view do you find yourself more in agreement? Why?
2. Pick a current issue on which people have widely different opinions. Analyze whether the resolution of that issue constitutes a "want," "need," or "pragmatic necessity"—or a "moral imperative." What makes it fall on one side or the other? Who should decide?

Amy Tan

Amy Tan (b. 1952) was born in Oakland, California, to Chinese immigrant parents. Her first novel, The Joy Luck Club, *published in 1989, immediately became both a critical success and a best seller. The celebrated author of numerous fiction and nonfiction books, Tan wrote the following about "Mother Tongue" in the introduction to her book of essays,* The Opposite of Fate: Memories of a Writing Life *(2003):*

> "Mother Tongue" was written hastily, as an apologia the night before I was to be on a panel with people far more erudite than I on the topic "The State of the English Language."

The speech was later published in The Threepenny Review *and then selected for inclusion in the anthology* The Best American Essays 1991*—leading me to wonder whether all my essays should be written at two in the*

morning in a state of panic. A version of "Mother Tongue" has also been used for the Advanced Placement SAT in English: this unanticipated development delights this author to no end, since her score in the 400s on the verbal section of the SAT made it seem unlikely, at least in 1969, that she would even think of making her living by the artful arrangement of words.

Mother Tongue   1990

I am not a scholar of English or literature. I cannot give you much more than personal opinions on the English language and its variations in this country or others.

I am a writer. And by that definition, I am someone who has always loved language. I am fascinated by language in daily life. I spend a great deal of my time thinking about the power of language—the way it can evoke an emotion, a visual image, a complex idea, or a simple truth. Language is the tool of my trade. And I use them all—all the Englishes I grew up with.

Recently, I was made keenly aware of the different Englishes I do use. I was giving a talk to a large group of people, the same talk I had already given to half a dozen other groups. The nature of the talk was about my writing, my life, and my book, *The Joy Luck Club*. The talk was going along well enough, until I remembered one major difference that made the whole talk sound wrong. My mother was in the room. And it was perhaps the first time she had heard me give a lengthy speech, using the kind of English I have never used with her. I was saying things like, "The intersection of memory upon imagination" and "There is an aspect of my fiction that relates to thus-and-thus"—a speech filled with carefully wrought grammatical phrases, burdened, it suddenly seemed to me, with nominalized forms, past perfect tenses, conditional phrases, all the forms of standard English that I had learned in school and through books, the forms of English I did not use at home with my mother.

Just last week, I was walking down the street with my mother, and I again found myself conscious of the English I was using, the English I do use with her. We were talking about the price of new and used furniture and I heard myself saying this: "Not waste money that way." My husband was with us as well, and he didn't notice any switch in my English. And then I realized why. It's because over the twenty years we've been together I've often used that same kind of English with him, and sometimes he even uses it with me. It has become our language of intimacy, a different sort of English that relates to family talk, the language I grew up with.

So you'll have some idea of what this family talk I heard sounds like, I'll quote what my mother said during a recent conversation which I videotaped and then transcribed. During this conversation, my mother was talking about a political gangster in Shanghai who had the same last name as her family's, Du, and how the gangster in his early years wanted to be adopted by her family, which was rich by comparison. Later, the gangster became more powerful, far richer than my mother's family, and one day showed up at my mother's wedding to pay his respects. Here's what she said in part:

"Du Yusong having business like fruit stand. Like off the street kind. He is Du like Du Zong—but not Tsung-ming Island people. The local people call putong, the river east side, he belong to that side local people. That man want to ask Du Zong father take him in like become own family. Du Zong father wasn't look down on him, but didn't take seriously, until that man big like become a mafia. Now important person, very hard to inviting him. Chinese way, came only to show respect, don't stay for dinner. Respect for making big celebration, he shows up. Mean gives lots of respect. Chinese custom. Chinese social life that way. If too important won't have to stay too long. He come to my wedding. I didn't see, I heard it. I gone to boy's side, they have YMCA dinner. Chinese age I was nineteen."

You should know that my mother's expressive command of English belies how much she actually understands. She reads the *Forbes* report, listens to *Wall Street Week*, converses daily with her stockbroker, reads all of Shirley MacLaine's books with ease—all kinds of things I can't begin to understand. Yet some of my friends tell me they understand 50 percent of what my mother says. Some say they understand 80 to 90 percent. Some say they understand none of it, as if she were speaking pure Chinese. But to me, my mother's English is perfectly clear, perfectly natural. It's my mother tongue. Her language, as I hear it, is vivid, direct, full of observation and imagery. That was the language that helped shape the way I saw things, expressed things, made sense of the world.

Lately, I've been giving more thought to the kind of English my mother speaks. Like others, I have described it to people as "broken" or "fractured" English. But I wince when I say that. It has always bothered me that I can think of no way to describe it other than "broken," as if it were damaged and needed to be fixed, as if it lacked a certain wholeness and soundness. I've heard other terms used, "limited English," for example. But they seem just as bad, as if everything is limited, including people's perceptions of the limited English speaker.

I know this for a fact, because when I was growing up, my mother's "limited" English limited my perception of her. I was ashamed of her English. I believed that her English reflected the quality of what she had to say. That is, because she expressed them imperfectly her thoughts were imperfect. And I had plenty of empirical evidence to support me: the fact that people in department stores, at banks, and at restaurants did not take her seriously, did not give her good service, pretended not to understand her, or even acted as if they did not hear her.

My mother has long realized the limitations of her English as well. When I was fifteen, she used to have me call people on the phone to pretend I was she. In this guise, I was forced to ask for information or even to complain and yell at people who had been rude to her. One time it was a call to her stockbroker in New York. She had cashed out her small portfolio and it just so happened we were going to go to New York the next week, our very first trip outside California. I had to get on the phone and say in an adolescent voice that was not very convincing, "This is Mrs. Tan."

And my mother was standing in the back whispering loudly, "Why he don't send me check, already two weeks late. So mad he lie to me, losing me money."

And then I said in perfect English, "Yes, I'm getting rather concerned. You had agreed to send the check two weeks ago, but it hasn't arrived."

Then she began to talk more loudly. "What he want, I come to New York tell him front of his boss, you cheating me?" And I was trying to calm her down, make her be quiet, while telling the stockbroker, "I can't tolerate any more excuses. If I don't receive the check immediately, I am going to have to speak to your manager when I'm in New York next week." And sure enough, the following week there we were in front of this astonished stockbroker, and I was sitting there red-faced and quiet, and my mother, the real Mrs. Tan, was shouting at his boss in her impeccable broken English.

We used a similar routine just five days ago, for a situation that was far less humorous. My mother had gone to the hospital for an appointment, to find out about a benign brain tumor a CAT scan had revealed a month ago. She said she had spoken very good English, her best English, no mistakes. Still, she said, the hospital did not apologize when they said they had lost the CAT scan and she had come for nothing. She said they did not seem to have any sympathy when she told them she was anxious to know the exact diagnosis, since her husband and son had both died of brain tumors. She said they would not give her any more information until the next time and she would have to make another appointment for that. So she said she would not leave until the doctor called her daughter. She wouldn't budge. And when the doctor finally called her daughter, me, who spoke in perfect English—lo and behold—we had assurances the CAT scan would be found, promises that a conference call on Monday would be held, and apologies for any suffering my mother had gone through for a most regrettable mistake.

I think my mother's English almost had an effect on limiting my possibilities in life as well. Sociologists and linguists probably will tell you that a person's developing language skills are more influenced by peers. But I do think that the language spoken in the family, especially in immigrant families which are more insular, plays a large role in shaping the language of the child. And I believe that it affected my results on achievement tests, I.Q. tests, and the SAT. While my English skills were never judged as poor, compared to math, English could not be considered my strong suit. In grade school I did moderately well, getting perhaps B's, sometimes B-pluses, in English and scoring perhaps in the sixtieth or seventieth percentile on achievement tests. But those scores were not good enough to override the opinion that my true abilities lay in math and science, because in those areas I achieved A's and scored in the ninetieth percentile or higher. 15

This was understandable. Math is precise; there is only one correct answer. Whereas, for me at least, the answers on English tests were always a judgment call, a matter of opinion and personal experience. Those tests were constructed around items like fill-in-the-blank sentence completion, such as, "Even though Tom was _____, Mary thought he was _____." And the correct answer always seemed to be the most bland combinations of thoughts, for example, "Even though Tom was shy, Mary thought he was charming": with the grammatical structure "even though" limiting the correct answer to some sort of semantic opposites, so you wouldn't get answers like, "Even though Tom was foolish, Mary thought he was ridiculous." Well, according to my mother, there were very few limitations as to what Tom could have been and what Mary might have thought of him. So I never did well on tests like that.

The same was true with word analogies, pairs of words in which you were supposed to find some sort of logical, semantic relationship—for example, " 'sunset' is to 'nightfall' as _____ is to _____." And here you would be presented with a list of four possible pairs, one of which showed the same kind of relationship: red is to stoplight, bus is to arrival, chills is to fever, yawn is to boring: Well, I could never think that way. I knew what the tests were asking, but I could not block out of my mind the images already created by the first pair, "sunset is to nightfall"—and I would see a burst of colors against a darkening sky, the moon rising, the lowering of a curtain of stars. And all the other pairs of words—red, bus, stoplight, boring—just threw up a mass of confusing images, making it impossible for me to sort out something as logical as saying: "A sunset precedes nightfall" is the same as "a chill precedes a fever." The only way I would have gotten that answer right would have been to imagine an associative situation, for example, my being disobedient and staying out past sunset, catching a chill at night, which turns into feverish pneumonia as punishment, which indeed did happen to me.

I have been thinking about all this lately, about my mother's English, about achievement tests. Because lately I've been asked, as a writer, why there are not more Asian Americans represented in American literature. Why are there few Asian Americans enrolled in creative writing programs? Why do so many Chinese students go into engineering! Well, these are broad sociological questions I can't begin to answer. But I have noticed in surveys—in fact, just last week—that Asian students, as a whole, always do significantly better on math achievement tests than in English. And this makes me think that there are other Asian American students whose English spoken in the home might also be described as "broken" or "limited." And perhaps they also have teachers who are steering them away from writing and into math and science, which is what happened to me.

Fortunately, I happen to be rebellious in nature and enjoy the challenge of disproving assumptions made about me. I became an English major my first year in college, after being enrolled as pre-med. I started writing nonfiction as a freelancer the week after I was told by my former boss that writing was my worst skill and I should hone my talents toward account management.

But it wasn't until 1985 that I finally began to write fiction. And at first I wrote using what I thought to be wittily crafted sentences, sentences that would finally prove I had mastery over the English language. Here's an example from the first draft of a story that later made its way into *The Joy Luck Club*, but without this line: "That was my mental quandary in its nascent state." A terrible line, which I can barely pronounce.

Fortunately, for reasons I won't get into today, I later decided I should envision a reader for the stories I would write. And the reader I decided upon was my mother, because these were stories about mothers. So with this reader in mind—and in fact she did read my early drafts—I began to write stories using all the Englishes I grew up with: the English I spoke to my mother, which for lack of a better term might be described as "simple"; the English she used with me, which for lack of a better term might be described as "broken"; my translation of her Chinese, which could certainly be described as "watered down"; and what I imagined to be her translation of her Chinese if she could speak in perfect English, her internal language, and for that I sought to preserve the essence, but neither an English nor a Chinese structure. I wanted to capture what language ability tests can never reveal: her intent, her passion, her imagery, the rhythms of her speech and the nature of her thoughts.

Apart from what any critic had to say about my writing, I knew I had succeeded where it counted when my mother finished reading my book and gave me her verdict: "So easy to read."

Questions

1. Do you speak differently at home (or among old friends or in your own neighborhood) than you do at school or at work? How does your way of speaking change in these different settings, and why?
2. Why does Tan dislike the term "broken English"? What does it imply to her?
3. What role does humor play in this essay? How does it help Tan in making her points?
4. Why does Tan include specific examples of English questions on standardized tests? Do you think such tests truly reflect students' skills and understanding? If not, is there a better alternative?
5. Tan describes being steered toward a career in math or science. Are students in high school (and even before) still steered in particular directions or careers today? On what basis?

■ Writing Assignments

1. Would you describe "Mother Tongue" as mainly a narrative, descriptive, expository, or argumentative essay? A combination? Why? Be sure to cite specific passages and examples.
2. Write about an instance or situation in which the way you used language influenced how other people responded to you. What happened, and how did it make you feel? How did it change your view of yourself—or of the other people?

checklist: Analyzing an Essay

- ☐ How would you classify the essay under consideration? Is it narrative, descriptive, expository, or argumentative? Does it include elements of more than one essay type?
- ☐ What rhetorical appeals does the author use? Is the argument primarily logical, emotional, or ethical? Is it rational? Does the essay engage your emotions? Do you find the author trustworthy?
- ☐ How would you describe the author's voice? Is it formal or casual? Distant or familiar? Impassioned or restrained?
- ☐ What is the tone of the essay? Is it sincere or ironic? Lighthearted or serious?
- ☐ How would you describe the author's style? Does the writer use language in a particular, distinctive way?
- ☐ Does the author use any rhetorical devices to intensify the effects of the writing or to heighten its persuasiveness? If so, which devices? Are they effective?
- ☐ How is the essay structured? Is it put together in a linear fashion? Does it describe a personal experience or does it address more abstract issues? How does the beginning of the essay lay the groundwork for what follows?
- ☐ What is the essay's theme? What is it trying to make us see, do, or believe? What evidence or arguments does the author provide to support his or her opinion?
- ☐ How do the various elements of the essay (voice, tone, style, structure, etc.) help to convey the theme?
- ☐ Are you convinced by the essay? Why or why not?

Amy Tan

WRITING ABOUT LITERATURE

6
WRITING ABOUT LITERATURE

If one waits for the right time to come before writing, the right time never comes.

—JAMES RUSSELL LOWELL

Assigned to write an essay on *Hamlet*, a student might well wonder, What can I say that hasn't been said a thousand times before? Often the most difficult aspect of writing about a story, poem, or play is the feeling that we have nothing of interest to contribute to the ongoing conversation about some celebrated literary work. There's always room, though, for a reader's fresh take on an old standby.

Remember that in the study of literature common sense is never out of place. For most of a class hour, a professor once rhapsodized about the arrangement of the contents of W. H. Auden's *Collected Poems*. Auden, he claimed, was a master of thematic continuity, who had brilliantly placed the poems in the order that they ingeniously complemented each other. Near the end of the hour, his theories were punctured—with a great inaudible pop—when a student, timidly raising a hand, pointed out that Auden had arranged the poems in the book not by theme but in alphabetical order according to the first word of each poem. The professor's jaw dropped: "Why didn't you say that sooner?" The student was apologetic: "I—I was afraid I'd sound too *ordinary*."

Don't be afraid to state a conviction, though it seems obvious. Does it matter that you may be repeating something that, once upon a time or even just the other day, has been said before? What matters more is that you are actively engaged in thinking about literature. There are excellent old ideas as well as new ones. You have something to say.

READ ACTIVELY

Most people read in a relaxed, almost passive way. They let the story or poem carry them along without asking too many questions. To write about literature well, however, you need to *read actively*, paying special attention to various aspects of the text. This special sort of attention will not only deepen your enjoyment of the story, poem, play, or essay but will also help generate the information and ideas that will become your final paper. How do you become an active reader? Here are some steps to get you started:

- **Preview the text.** To get acquainted with a work of literature before you settle in for a closer reading, skim it for an overview of its content and organization. Take a quick look at all parts of the work. Even a book's cover, preface, introduction, footnotes, and biographical notes about the author can provide you with some context for reading the work itself.

- **Take notes. Annotate the text.** Read with a highlighter and pencil at hand, making appropriate annotations to the text. Later, you'll easily be able to review these highlights, and, when you write your paper, quickly refer to supporting evidence.
    - Underline words, phrases, or sentences that seem interesting or important, or that raise questions.
    - Jot down brief notes in the margin (*"key symbol—this foreshadows the ending,"* for example, or *"dramatic irony"*).
    - Use lines or arrows to indicate passages that seem to speak to each other—for instance, all the places in which you find the same theme or related symbols.

Robert Frost

Nothing Gold Can Stay

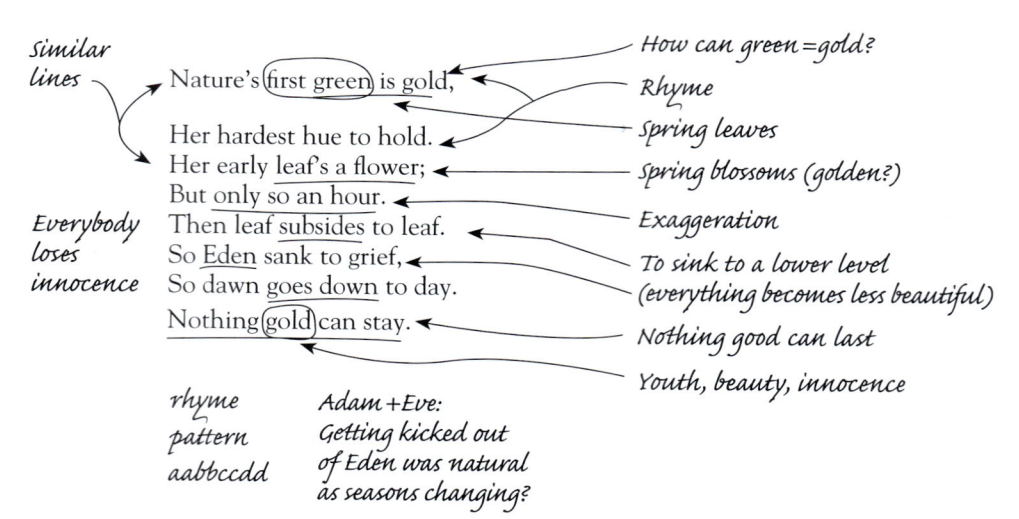

similar lines

Nature's first green is gold, — *How can green = gold?*
Her hardest hue to hold. — *Rhyme*
Her early leaf's a flower; — *Spring leaves*
But only so an hour. — *Spring blossoms (golden?)*

Everybody loses innocence

Then leaf subsides to leaf. — *Exaggeration*
So Eden sank to grief, — *To sink to a lower level*
So dawn goes down to day. — *(everything becomes less beautiful)*
Nothing gold can stay. — *Nothing good can last*
— *Youth, beauty, innocence*

rhyme pattern aabbccdd

Adam + Eve: Getting kicked out of Eden was natural as seasons changing?

- **Read closely.** Once you have begun reading in earnest, don't skim or skip over words you don't recognize; sometimes, looking up those very words will unlock a piece's meaning.

- **Reread as needed.** If a piece is short, read it several times. Often, knowing the ending of a poem or short story will allow you to extract new meaning from its beginning and middle. If the piece is longer, reread the passages you thought important enough to highlight.

PLAN YOUR ESSAY

If you have actively reread the work you plan to write about and have made notes or annotations, you are well on your way to writing your paper. Your mind has already begun to work through some initial impressions and ideas. Now you need to arrange those early notions into an organized and logical essay. Here is some advice on how to manage the writing process:

- **Leave yourself time.** Good writing involves thought and revision. Anyone who has ever been a student knows what it's like to pull an all-nighter, churning out a term paper hours before it is due. Still, the best writing evolves over time. Your ideas need to marinate. Sometimes, you'll make false starts, and you'll need to salvage what you can and do the rest from scratch. For the sake of your writing—not to mention your health and sanity—it's far better to get the job started well before your deadline.

- **Choose a subject you care about.** If you have been given a choice of literary works to write about, always choose the play, story, poem, or essay that evokes the strongest emotional response. Your writing will be liveliest if you feel engaged by your subject.

- **Know your purpose.** As you write, keep the assignment in mind. You may have been asked to write a response, in which you describe your reactions to a literary work. Perhaps your purpose is to interpret a work, analyzing how one or more of its elements contribute to its meaning. You may have been instructed to write an evaluation, in which you judge a work's merits. Whatever the assignment, how you approach your essay will depend in large part on your purpose.

- **Think about your audience.** When you write journal entries or rough drafts, you may be composing for your own eyes only. More often, though, you are likely to be writing for an audience, even if it is an audience of one: your professor. Whenever you write for others, you need to be conscious of your readers. Your task is to convince them that your take on a work of literature is a plausible one. To do so, you need to keep your audience's needs and expectations in mind.

- **Define your topic narrowly.** Worried about having enough to say, students sometimes frame their topic so broadly that they can't do justice to it in the allotted number of pages. Your paper will be stronger if you go more deeply into your subject than if you choose a gigantic subject and touch on most aspects of it only superficially. A thorough explication of a short story is hardly possible in a 250-word paper, but an explication of a paragraph or two could work in that space. A profound topic ("The Character of Hamlet") might overflow a book, but a more focused one ("Hamlet's View of Acting" or "Hamlet's Puns") could result in a manageable paper.

PREWRITING: DISCOVER YOUR IDEAS

Topic in hand, you can begin to get your ideas on the page. To generate new ideas and clarify the thoughts you already have, try one or more of the following useful prewriting techniques:

- **Brainstorm.** Writing quickly, list everything that comes into your mind about your subject. Set a time limit—ten or fifteen minutes—and force yourself to keep adding items to the list, even when you think you have run out of things to say. Sometimes, if you press onward past the point where you feel you are finished, you will surprise yourself with new and fresh ideas.

    gold = early leaves/blossoms
    Or gold = something precious (both?)
    early leaf = flower (yellow blossoms)
    spring (lasts an hour)
    Leaves subside (sink to lower level)
    Eden = paradise = perfection = beauty
    Loss of innocence?
    What about original sin?
    Dawn becomes day (dawn is more precious?)
    Adam and Eve had to fall? Part of natural order.
    seasons/days/people's lives
    Title = last line: perfection can't last
    spring/summer/autumn
    dawn/day
    Innocence can't last

- **Cluster.** This prewriting technique works especially well for visual thinkers. In clustering, you build a diagram to help you explore the relationships among your ideas. To get started, write your subject at the center of a sheet of paper. Circle it. Then jot down ideas, linking each to the central circle with lines. As you write down each new idea, draw lines to link it to related old ideas. The result will look something like the following web.

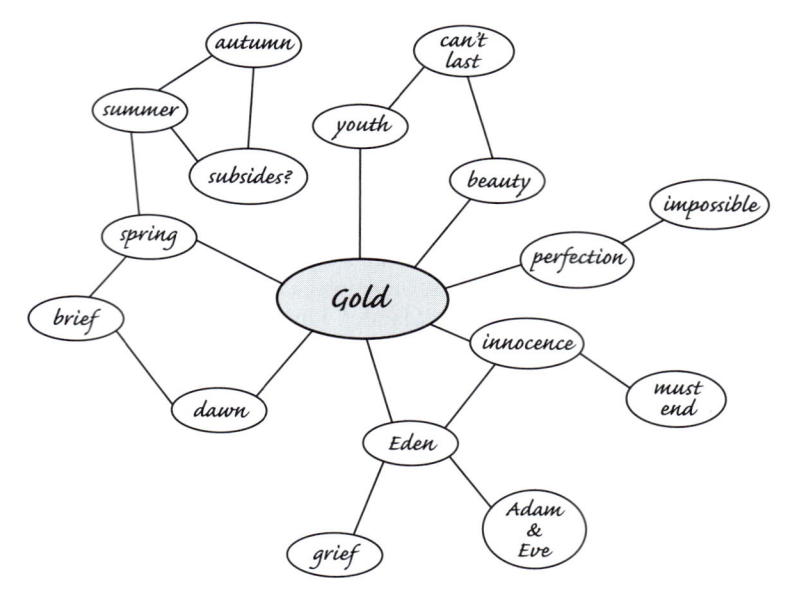

- **List.** Look over the notes and annotations that you made in your active reading of the work. You have probably underlined or noted more information than you can possibly use. One way to sort through your material to find the most useful information is to make a list of the important items. It helps to make several short lists under different headings. Here are some lists you might make after rereading Frost's "Nothing Gold Can Stay." Don't be afraid to add more comments or questions on the lists to help your thought process.

    <u>Images</u>
    leaf ("early leaf")
    flower
    dawn
    day
    Eden
    gold

    <u>Colors</u>
    green
    gold ("hardest hue to hold")

    <u>Key Actions</u>
    gold is hard to hold
    early leaf lasts only an hour
    leaf subsides to leaf (what does this mean???)
    Eden sinks to grief (paradise is lost)
    dawn goes down to day
    gold can't stay (perfection is impossible?)

- **Freewrite.** Most writers have snarky little voices in their heads, telling them that the words they're committing to paper aren't interesting or deep or elegant enough. To drown out those little voices, try freewriting. Give yourself a set amount of time (say, ten minutes) and write, nonstop, on your topic. Force your pen or your fingers on the keyboard to keep moving, even if you have run out of things to say. If all you can think of to write is "I'm stuck" or "This is dumb," so be it. Keep going, and something else will most likely occur to you. Don't worry, yet, about grammar or spelling. When your time is up, read what you have written, highlighting the best ideas for later use.

    > How can green be gold? By nature's first green, I guess he means the first leaves in spring. Are those leaves gold? They're more delicate and yellow than summer leaves . . . so maybe in a sense they look gold. Or maybe he means spring blossoms. Sometimes they're yellow. Also the first line seems to connect with the third one, where he comes right out and says that flowers are like early leaves. Still, I think he also means that the first leaves are the most precious ones, like gold. I don't think the poem wants me to take all of these statements literally. Flowers on trees last more than an hour, but that really beautiful moment in spring when blossoms are everywhere always ends too quickly, so maybe that's what he means by "only so an hour." I had to look up "subsides." It means to sink to a lower level . . . as if the later leaves will be less perfect than the first ones. I don't know if I agree. Aren't fall leaves precious? Then he says, "So Eden sank to grief" which seems to be

saying that Adam and Eve's fall would have happened no matter what they did, because everything that seems perfect falls apart . . . nothing gold can stay. Is he saying Adam and Eve didn't really have a choice? No matter what, everything gets older, less beautiful, less innocent . . . even people.

- **Journal.** Your instructor might ask you to keep a journal in which you jot down your ideas, feelings, and impressions before they are fully formulated. Sometimes a journal is meant for your eyes only; in other instances your instructor might read it. Either way, it is meant to be informal and immediate, and to provide raw material that you may later choose to refine into a formal essay. Here are some tips for keeping a useful journal:
  - Get your ideas down as soon as they occur to you.
  - Write quickly.
  - Jot down your feelings about and first impressions of the story, poem, play, or essay you are reading.
  - Don't worry about grammar, spelling, or punctuation.
  - Don't worry about sounding academic.
  - Don't worry about whether your ideas are good or bad ones; you can sort that out later.
  - Try out invention strategies such as freewriting, clustering, and outlining.
  - Keep writing, even after you think you have run out of things to say. You might surprise yourself.
  - Write about what interests you most.
  - Write in your journal on a regular basis.

- **Outline.** Some topics by their very nature suggest obvious ways to organize a paper. "An Explication of a Sonnet by Shakespeare" might mean simply working through the poem line by line. If this isn't the case, some kind of outline will probably prove helpful. Your outline needn't be elaborate to be useful. While a long research paper on several literary works might call for a detailed outline, a 500-word analysis of a short story's figures of speech might call for just a simple list of points in the order that makes the most logical sense—not necessarily the order in which those thoughts first came to mind.

    1. Passage of time = fall from innocence
        blossoms
        gold
        dawn
        grief

    2. Innocence = perfection
        Adam and Eve
        loss of innocence = inevitable
        real original sin = passing of time
        paradise sinks to grief

3. Grief = knowledge
    experience of sin & suffering
    unavoidable as grow older

DEVELOP A LITERARY ARGUMENT

Once you have finished a rough outline of your ideas, you need to refine it into a clear and logical shape. You need to state your thesis (or basic idea) clearly and then support it with logical and accurate evidence. Here is a practical approach to this crucial stage of the writing process:

- **Consider your purpose.** As you develop your argument, be sure to refer back to the specific assignment; let it guide you. Your instructor might request one of the following kinds of papers:
  - *Response,* in which you explore your reaction to a work of literature.
  - *Evaluation,* in which you assess the literary merits of a work.
  - *Interpretation,* in which you discuss a work's meaning. If your instructor has assigned an interpretation, he or she may have more specifically asked for an *analysis, explication,* or *comparison and contrast* essay, among other possibilities.

- **Remember your audience.** Practically speaking, your professor (and sometimes your classmates) will be your paper's primary audience. Some assignments may specify a particular audience beyond your professor and classmates. Keep your readers in mind. Be sure to adapt your writing to meet their needs and interests. If, for example, the audience has presumably already read a story under discussion, you won't need to relate the plot in its entirety. Instead, you will be free to bring up only those plot points that serve as evidence for your thesis.

- **Narrow your topic to fit the assignment.** Though you may be tempted to choose a broad topic so that you will have no shortage of things to say, remember that a good paper needs focus. Your choice should be narrow enough for you to do it justice in the space and time allotted.

- **Decide on a thesis.** Just as you need to know your destination before you set out on a trip, you need to decide what point you're traveling toward before you begin your first draft. Start by writing a provisional thesis sentence: a summing up of the main idea or argument your paper will explore. While your thesis doesn't need to be outrageous or deliberately provocative, it does need to take a stand. A clear, decisive statement gives you something to prove and lends vigor to your essay.

    WORKING THESIS

    The poem argues that like Adam and Eve we all lose our innocence and the passage of time is inevitable.

This first stab at a thesis sentence gave its author a sense of purpose and direction that allowed him to finish his first draft. Later, as he revised his essay, he found he needed to refine his thesis to make more specific and focused assertions.

- **Build your argument.** Once you've formulated your thesis, your task will be clear: you need to convince your audience that your thesis is sound. To write persuasively, it helps to have an understanding of some key elements of argument:
  - *Claims.* Anytime you make a statement you hope will be taken as true, you have made a claim. Some claims are unlikely to be contradicted ("the sky is blue" or "today is Tuesday"), but others are debatable ("every college sophomore dreams of running off to see the world"). Your essay's main claim—your thesis—should not be something entirely obvious. Having to support your point of view will cause you to clarify your ideas about a work of literature.
  - *Persuasion.* If the word *argument* makes you think of raised voices and short tempers, it may help to think of your task as the gentler art of persuasion. To convince your audience of your thesis, you will need to present a cogent argument supported by evidence gathered from the text. If the assignment is a research paper, you will also need to cite what others have written on your topic.
  - *Evidence.* When you write about a work of literature, the most convincing evidence will generally come from the text itself. Direct quotations from the poem, play, story, or essay under discussion can provide particularly convincing support for your claims. Be sure to introduce any quotation by putting it in the context of the larger work. It is even more important to follow up each quotation with your own analysis of what it shows about the work.
  - *Warrants.* Whenever you use a piece of evidence to support a claim, an underlying assumption connects one to the other. For instance, if you were to make the claim that today's weather is absolutely perfect and offer as your evidence the blue sky, your logic would include an unspoken warrant: sunny weather is perfect weather. Not everyone will agree with your warrant, though. Some folks (perhaps farmers) might prefer rain. In making any argument, including one about literature, you may find that you sometimes need to spell out your warrants to demonstrate that they are sound. This is especially true when the evidence you provide can lead to conclusions other than the one you are hoping to prove.
  - *Credibility.* When weighing the merits of a claim, you will probably take into account the credibility of the person making the case. Often this happens almost automatically. You are more likely to listen to the opinion that you should take vitamins if it is expressed by your doctor than if it is put forth by a stranger you meet on the street. An expert on any given topic has a certain brand of authority not available to most of us. Fortunately, there are other ways to establish your own credibility:

    Keep your tone thoughtful. Your reader will develop a sense of who you are through your words. If you come across as belligerent or disrespectful to those inclined to disagree with your views, you may lose your reader's goodwill. Therefore, express your ideas calmly and thoughtfully. A level tone demonstrates that you are interested in thinking through an issue or idea, not in bullying your reader into submission.

Take opposing arguments into account. To make an argument more convincing, demonstrate familiarity with other possible points of view. Doing so indicates that you have taken other claims into account before arriving at your thesis; it reveals your fairness as well as your understanding of your subject matter. In laying out other points of view, though, be sure to represent them fairly but also to respectfully make clear why your thesis is the soundest claim; you don't want your reader to doubt where you stand.

Demonstrate your knowledge. To gain your reader's trust, it helps to demonstrate a solid understanding of your subject matter. Always check your facts; factual errors can call your knowledge into doubt. It also helps to have a command of the conventions of writing. Errors in punctuation and spelling can undermine a writer's credibility.

- **Organize your argument.** Unless you are writing an explication that works its way line by line through a work of literature, you will need to make crucial decisions about how to shape your essay. Its order should be driven by the logic of your argument, not by the structure of the story, play, poem or essay you're discussing. In other words, you need not work your way from start to finish through your source material, touching on each major point. Instead, choose only the points needed to prove your thesis, and present them in whatever order best makes your point. A rough outline can help you to determine that order.

- **Make sure your thesis is supported by the evidence.** If you find you can't support certain aspects of your thesis, then refine it so that you can. Remember: until you turn it in, your essay is a work in progress. Anything can and should be changed if it doesn't further the development of the paper's main idea.

checklist: Developing an Argument

- ☐ What is your essay's purpose?
- ☐ Who is your audience?
- ☐ Is your topic narrow enough?
- ☐ Is your thesis interesting and thought-provoking?
- ☐ Does everything in your essay support your thesis?
- ☐ Have you considered and refuted alternative views?
- ☐ Is your tone thoughtful?
- ☐ Is your argument sensibly organized? Are similar ideas grouped together? Does one point lead logically to the next?

WRITE A ROUGH DRAFT

Seated at last, you prepare to write, only to find yourself besieged with petty distractions. All of a sudden you remember a friend you had promised to call, some double-A batteries you were supposed to pick up, a neglected Coke (in another room) growing warmer and flatter by the minute. If your paper is to be written, you have only one course of action: collar these thoughts and for the moment banish them. Here are a few tips for writing your rough draft:

- **Review your argument.** The shape of your argument, its support, and the evidence you have collected will form the basis of your rough draft.
- **Get your thoughts down.** The best way to draft a paper is to get your ideas down quickly. At this stage, don't fuss over details. The critical, analytical side of your mind can worry about spelling, grammar, and punctuation later. For now, let your creative mind take charge. This part of yourself has the good ideas, insight, and confidence. Forge ahead. Believe in yourself and in your ideas.
- **Write the part you feel most comfortable with first.** There's no need to start at the paper's beginning and work your way methodically through to the end. Instead, plunge right into the parts of the paper you feel most prepared to write. You can always go back later and fill in the blanks.
- **Leave yourself plenty of space.** As you compose, leave plenty of space between lines and set wide margins. When you print out your draft, you will easily be able to go back and squeeze other thoughts in.
- **Focus on the argument.** As you jot down your first draft, you might not want to look at the notes you have compiled. When you come to a place where a note will fit, just insert a reminder to yourself such as "See card 19" or "See Aristotle on comedy." Also, whenever you bring up a new point, it's good to tie it back to your thesis. If you can't find a way to connect a point to your thesis, it's probably better to leave it out of your paper and come up with a point that advances your central claim.
- **Does your thesis hold up?** If, as you write, you find that most of the evidence you uncover is not helping you prove your paper's thesis, it may be that the thesis needs honing. Adjust it as needed.
- **Be open to new ideas.** Writing rarely proceeds in a straight line. Even after you outline your paper and begin to write and revise, expect to discover new thoughts—perhaps the best thoughts of all. If you do, be sure to invite them in.

Here is a student's rough draft for an essay on "Nothing Gold Can Stay."

On Robert Frost's "Nothing Gold Can Stay"

Most of the lines in the poem "Nothing Gold Can Stay" by Robert Frost focus on the changing of the seasons. The poem's first line says that the first leaves of spring are actually blossoms, and the actual leaves that follow are less precious. Those first blossoms only last a little while. The reader realizes that nature is a metaphor for a person's state of mind. People start off perfectly innocent, but as time passes, they can't help but lose that innocence. The poem argues that like Adam and Eve we all lose our innocence and the passage of time is inevitable.

The poem's first image is of the color found in nature. The early gold of spring blossoms is nature's "hardest hue to hold." The color gold is associated with the mineral gold, a precious commodity. There's a hint that early spring is nature in its perfect state, and perfection is impossible to hold on to. To the poem's speaker, the colors of early spring seem to last only an hour. If you blink, they are gone. Like early spring, innocence can't last.

The line "leaf subsides to leaf" brings us from early spring through summer and fall. The golden blossoms and delicate leaves of spring subside, or sink to a lower level, meaning they become less special and beautiful. There's nothing more special and beautiful than a baby, so people are the same way. In literature, summer often means the prime of your life, and autumn often means the declining years. These times are less beautiful ones. "So dawn goes down to day" is a similar kind of image. Dawns are unbelievably colorful and beautiful but they don't last very long. Day is nice, but not as special as dawn.

The most surprising line in the poem is the one that isn't about nature. Instead it's about human beings. Eden may have been a garden (a part of nature), but it also represents a state of mind. The traditional religious view is that Adam and Eve chose to disobey God and eat from the tree of knowledge. They could have stayed in paradise forever if they had followed God's orders. So it's surprising that Frost writes "So Eden sank to grief" in a poem that is all about how inevitable change is. It seems like he's saying that no matter what Adam and Eve had done, the Garden of Eden wouldn't stay the paradise it started out being. When Adam and Eve ate the apple, they lost their innocence. The apple is supposed to represent knowledge, so they became wiser but less perfect. But the poem implies that no matter what Adam and Eve had done, they would have grown sadder and wiser. That's true for all people. We can't stay young and innocent.

It's almost as if Frost is defying the Bible, suggesting that there is no such thing as sin. We can't help getting older and wiser. It's a natural process. Suffering happens not because we choose to do bad things but because passing time takes our innocence. The real original sin is that time has to pass and we all have to grow wiser and less innocent.

The poem "Nothing Gold Can Stay" makes the point that people can't stay innocent forever. Suffering is the inevitable result of the aging process. Like the first leaves of spring, we are at the best at the very beginning, and it's all downhill from there.

REVISE YOUR DRAFT

A writer rarely—if ever—achieves perfection on the first try. For most of us, good writing is largely a matter of revision. Once your first draft is done, you can—and should—turn on your analytical mind. Painstaking revision is more than just tidying up grammar and spelling. It might mean expanding your ideas or sharpening the focus by cutting out any unnecessary thoughts. To achieve effective writing, you must have the courage to be merciless. Tear your rough drafts apart and reassemble their pieces into a stronger order. As you revise, consider the following:

- **Be sure your thesis is clear, decisive, and thought-provoking.** The most basic ingredient in a good essay is a strong thesis—the sentence in which you summarize the claim you are making. Your thesis should say something more than just the obvious; it should be clear and decisive and make a point that requires evidence to persuade your reader to agree. A sharp, bold thesis lends energy to your argument. A revision of the working thesis used in the rough draft above provides a good example.

    WORKING THESIS

    The poem argues that like Adam and Eve we all lose our innocence and the passage of time is inevitable.

    This thesis may not be bold or specific enough to make for an interesting argument. A careful reader would be hard pressed to disagree with the observation that Frost's poem depicts the passage of time or the loss of innocence. In a revision of his thesis, however, the essay's author pushes the claim further, going beyond the obvious to its implications.

    REVISED THESIS

    In "Nothing Gold Can Stay," Frost makes a bold claim: sin, suffering, and loss are inevitable because the passage of time causes everyone to fall from grace.

    Instead of simply asserting that the poem looks with sorrow on the passage of time, the revised thesis raises the issue of why this is so. It makes a more thought-provoking claim about the poem. An arguable thesis can result in a more energetic, purposeful essay. A thesis that is obvious to everyone, on the other hand, leads to a static, dull paper.

- **Ascertain whether the evidence you provide supports your theory.** Does everything within your paper work to support its thesis sentence? While a solid paper might be written about the poetic form of "Nothing Gold Can Stay," the student paper above would not be well served by bringing the subject up unless the author could show how the poem's form contributes to its message that time causes everyone to lose his or her innocence. If you find yourself including information that doesn't serve your argument, consider going back into the poem, story, play, or essay for more useful evidence. On the other hand, if you're beginning to have a sneaking feeling that your thesis itself is shaky, consider reworking *it* so that it more accurately reflects the evidence in the text.

- **Check whether your argument is logical.** Does one point lead naturally to the next? Reread the paper, looking for logical fallacies, moments in which the claims you make are not sufficiently supported by evidence, or the connection between one thought and the next seems less than rational. Classic logical fallacies include making hasty generalizations, confusing cause and effect, or using a non sequitur, a statement that doesn't follow from the statement that precedes it. An example of two seemingly unconnected thoughts may be found in the second paragraph of the draft above:

    > To the poem's speaker, the colors of early spring seem to last only an hour. If you blink, they are gone. Like early spring, innocence can't last.

    Though there may well be a logical connection between the first two sentences and the third one, the paper doesn't spell that connection out. Asked to clarify the warrant, or assumption, that makes possible the leap from the subject of spring to the subject of innocence, the author revised the passage this way:

    > To the poem's speaker, the colors of early spring seem to last only an hour. When poets write of seasons, they often also are commenting on the life cycle. To make a statement that spring can't last more than an hour implies that a person's youth (often symbolically associated with spring) is all too short. Therefore, the poem implies that innocent youth, like spring, lasts for only the briefest time.

    The revised version spells out the author's thought process, helping the reader to follow the argument.

- **Supply transitional words and phrases.** To ensure that your reader's journey from one idea to the next is a smooth one, insert transitional words and phrases at the start of new paragraphs or sentences. Phrases such as "in contrast" and "however" signal a U-turn in logic, while those such as "in addition" and "similarly" alert the reader that you are continuing in the same direction you have been traveling. Seemingly inconsequential words and phrases such as "also" and "as well" or "as mentioned above" can smooth the reader's path from one thought to the next, as in the example below.

    DRAFT

    Though Frost is writing about nature, his real subject is humanity. In literature, spring often represents youth. Summer symbolizes young adulthood, autumn stands for middle age, and winter represents old age. The adult stages of life are, for Frost, less precious than childhood, which passes very quickly. The innocence of childhood is, like those spring leaves, precious as gold.

    ADDING TRANSITIONAL WORDS AND PHRASES

    Though Frost is writing about nature, his real subject is humanity. <u>As mentioned above</u>, in literature, spring often represents youth. <u>Similarly</u>, summer symbolizes young adulthood, autumn stands for middle age, and winter represents old age. The adult stages of life are, for Frost, less precious than childhood, which passes very quickly. <u>Also</u>, the innocence of childhood is, like those spring leaves, precious as gold.

- **Make sure each paragraph contains a topic sentence.** Each paragraph in your essay should develop a single idea; this idea should be conveyed in a topic sentence. As astute readers often expect to get a sense of a paragraph's purpose from its first few sentences, a topic sentence is often well placed at or near a paragraph's start.
- **Make a good first impression.** Your introductory paragraph may have seemed just fine as you began the writing process. Be sure to reconsider it in light of the entire paper. Does the introduction draw readers in and prepare them for what follows? If not, be sure to rework it, as the author of the rough draft above did. Look at his first paragraph again:

   DRAFT OF OPENING PARAGRAPH

   Most of the lines in the poem "Nothing Gold Can Stay" by Robert Frost focus on the changing of the seasons. The poem's first line says that the first leaves of spring are actually blossoms, and the actual leaves that follow are less precious. Those first blossoms only last a little while. The reader realizes that nature is a metaphor for a person's state of mind. People start off perfectly innocent, but as time passes, they can't help but lose that happy innocence. The poem argues that like Adam and Eve we all lose our innocence and the passage of time is inevitable.

While serviceable, this paragraph could be more compelling. Its author improved it by adding specifics to bring his ideas to more vivid life. For example, the rather pedestrian sentence "People start off perfectly innocent, but as time passes, they can't help but lose that innocence" became this livelier one: "As babies we are all perfectly innocent, but as time passes, we can't help but lose that innocence." By adding a specific image—the baby—the author gave the reader a visual picture to illustrate the abstract idea of innocence. He also sharpened his thesis sentence, making it less general and more thought-provoking. By varying the length of his sentences, he made the paragraph less monotonous.

   REVISED OPENING PARAGRAPH

   Most of the lines in Robert Frost's brief poem "Nothing Gold Can Stay" focus on nature: the changing of the seasons and the fading of dawn into day. The poem's opening line asserts that the first blossoms of spring are more precious than the leaves that follow. Likewise, dawn is more special than day. Though Frost's subject seems to be nature, the reader soon realizes that his real subject is human nature. As babies we are all perfectly innocent, but as time passes, we can't help but lose that happy innocence. In "Nothing Gold Can Stay," Frost makes a bold claim: sin, suffering, and loss are inevitable because the passage of time causes everyone to fall from grace.

- **Remember that last impressions count too.** Your paper's conclusion should give the reader some closure, tying up the paper's loose ends without simply (and boringly) restating all that has come before. The author of the rough draft above initially ended his paper with a paragraph that repeated the paper's main ideas without pushing those ideas any further:

DRAFT OF CONCLUSION

> The poem "Nothing Gold Can Stay" makes the point that people can't stay innocent forever. Grief is the inevitable result of the aging process. Like the first leaves of spring, we are at the best at the very beginning, and it's all downhill from there.

While revising his paper, the author realized that the ideas in his next-to-last paragraph would serve to sum up the paper. The new final paragraph doesn't simply restate the thesis; it pushes the idea further, in its last two sentences, by exploring the poem's implications.

REVISED CONCLUSION

> Some people might view Frost's poem as sacrilegious because it seems to say that Adam and Eve had no choice; everything in life is doomed to fall. Growing less innocent and more knowing seems less a choice in Frost's view than a natural process like the changing of golden blossoms to green leaves. "Eden sank to grief" not because we choose to do evil things but because time takes away our innocence as we encounter the suffering and loss of human existence. Frost suggests that the real original sin is that time has to pass and we all must grow wiser and less innocent.

- **Give your paper a compelling title.** Like the introduction, a title should be inviting to readers, giving them a sense of what's coming. Avoid a nontitle such as "A Rose for Emily," which serves as a poor advertisement for your paper. Instead, provide enough specifics to pique your reader's interest. "On Robert Frost's 'Nothing Gold Can Stay'" is a duller, less informative title than "Lost Innocence in Robert Frost's 'Nothing Gold Can Stay,'" which may spark the reader's interest and prepare him or her for what is to come.

checklist: Revising Your Draft

- ☐ Is your thesis clear? Can it be sharpened?
- ☐ Does all your evidence serve to advance the argument put forth in your thesis?
- ☐ Is your argument logical?
- ☐ Do transitional words and phrases signal movement from one idea to the next?
- ☐ Does each paragraph contain a topic sentence?
- ☐ Does your introduction draw the reader in? Does it prepare the reader for what follows?
- ☐ Does your conclusion tie up the paper's loose ends? Does it avoid merely restating what has come before?
- ☐ Is your title compelling?

FINAL ADVICE ON REWRITING

- **Whenever possible, get feedback from a trusted reader.** In every project there comes a time when the writer has gotten so close to the work that he or she can't see it clearly. A talented roommate or a tutor in the campus writing center can tell you what isn't yet clear on the page, what questions still need answering, or what line of argument isn't yet as persuasive as it could be.
- **Be willing to refine your thesis.** Once you have fleshed out your whole paper, you may find that your original thesis is not borne out by the rest of your argument. If so, you will need to rewrite your thesis so that it more precisely fits the evidence at hand.
- **Be prepared to question your whole approach to a work of literature.** On occasion, you may even need to entertain the notion of throwing everything you have written into the wastebasket and starting over again. Occasionally having to start from scratch is the lot of any writer.
- **Rework troublesome passages.** Look for skimpy paragraphs of one or two sentences—evidence that your ideas might need more fleshing out. Can you supply more evidence, more explanation, more examples or illustrations?
- **Cut out any unnecessary information.** Everything in your paper should serve to further its thesis. Delete any sentences or paragraphs that detract from your focus.
- **Aim for intelligent clarity when you use literary terminology.** Critical terms can help sharpen your thoughts and make them easier to handle. Nothing is less sophisticated or more opaque, however, than too many technical terms thrown together for grandiose effect: "The mythic *symbolism* of this *archetype* is the *antithesis* of the *dramatic situation*." Choose plain words you're already at ease with. When you use specialized terms, do so to smooth the way for your reader—to make your meaning more precise. It is less cumbersome, for example, to refer to the *tone* of a story than to say, "the way the author makes you feel that she feels about what she is talking about."
- **Set your paper aside for a while.** Even an hour or two away from your essay can help you return to it with fresh eyes. Remember that the literal meaning of "revision" is "seeing again."
- **Finally, carefully read your paper one last time to edit it.** Now it's time to sweat the small stuff. Check any uncertain spellings, scan for run-on sentences and fragments, pull out a weak word and send in a stronger one. Like soup stains on a job interviewee's tie, finicky errors distract from the overall impression and prejudice your reader against your essay.

Here is the revised version of the student paper we have been examining.

Gabriel 1

Noah Gabriel
Professor James
English 2171
7 January 2012

Lost Innocence in
Robert Frost's "Nothing Gold Can Stay"

    Most of the lines in Robert Frost's brief poem "Nothing Gold Can Stay" focus on nature: the changing of the seasons and the fading of dawn into day. The poem's opening line asserts that the first blossoms of spring are more precious than the leaves that follow. Likewise, dawn is more special than day. Though Frost's subject seems to be nature, the reader soon realizes that his real subject is human nature. As babies we are all perfectly innocent, but as time passes, we can't help but lose that happy innocence. In "Nothing Gold Can Stay," Frost makes a bold claim: sin, suffering, and loss are inevitable because the passage of time causes everyone to fall from grace.

    The poem begins with a deceptively simple sentence: "Nature's first green is gold." The subject seems to be the first, delicate leaves of spring which are less green and more golden than summer leaves. However, the poem goes on to say, "Her early leaf's a flower" (3), indicating that Frost is describing the first blossoms of spring. In fact, he's describing both the new leaves and blossoms. Both are as rare and precious as the mineral gold. They are precious because they don't last long; the early gold of spring blossoms is nature's "hardest hue to hold" (2). Early spring is an example of nature in its perfect state, and perfection is impossible to hold on to. To the poem's speaker, in fact, the colors of early spring seem to last only an hour. When poets write of seasons, they often also are commenting on the life cycle. To make a statement that spring can't last more than an hour implies that a person's youth (often symbolically associated with spring) is all too short. Therefore, the poem implies that innocent youth, like spring, lasts for only the briefest time.

    While Frost takes four lines to describe the decline of the spring blossoms, he picks up the pace when he describes what happens next. The line "Then leaf subsides to leaf" (5) brings us from early spring through summer and fall, compressing three seasons into a single line. Just as time seems to pass slowly when we are children, and then much more quickly when we grow up, the poem

Thesis sentence is specific and decisive

Textual evidence to back up thesis

Warrant is spelled out

Claim

Gabriel 2

moves quickly once the first golden moment is past. The word "subsides" feels important. The golden blossoms and delicate leaves of spring subside, or sink to a lower level, meaning they become less special and beautiful.

Though Frost is writing about nature, his real subject is humanity. As mentioned above, in literature, spring often represents youth. Similarly, summer symbolizes young adulthood, autumn stands for middle age, and winter represents old age. The adult stages of life are, for Frost, less precious than childhood, which passes very quickly, as we later realize. Also, the innocence of childhood is, like those spring leaves, precious as gold.

Frost shifts his view from the cycle of the seasons to the cycle of a single day to make a similar point. Just as spring turns to summer, "So dawn goes down to day" (7). Like spring, dawn is unbelievably colorful and beautiful but doesn't last very long. Like "subsides," the phrase "goes down" implies that full daylight is actually a falling off from dawn. As beautiful as daylight is, it's ordinary, while dawn is special because it is more fleeting.

Among these natural images, one line stands out: "So Eden sank to grief" (6). This line is the only one in the poem that deals directly with human beings. Eden may have been a garden (a part of nature) but it represents a state of mind—perfect innocence. In the traditional religious view, Adam and Eve chose to disobey God by eating an apple from the tree of knowledge. They were presented with a choice: to be obedient and remain in paradise forever, or to disobey God's order. People often speak of that first choice as "original sin." In this religious view, "Eden sank to grief" because the first humans chose to sin.

Frost, however, takes a different view. He compares the Fall of Man to the changing of spring to summer, as though it was as inevitable as the passage of time. The poem implies that no matter what Adam and Eve did, they couldn't remain in paradise. Original sin in Frost's view seems less a voluntary moral action than a natural, if unhappy sort of maturation. The innocent perfection of the garden of Eden couldn't possibly last. The apple represents knowledge, so in a symbolic sense God wanted Adam and Eve to stay unknowing, or innocent. But the poem implies that it was inevitable that Adam and Eve would gain knowledge and lose their innocence, becoming wiser but less perfect. They lost Eden and encountered "grief," the knowledge of suffering and loss associated with the human condition. This is certainly true for the rest of us human beings. As much as we might like to, we can't stay young or innocent forever.

Gabriel 3

    Some people might view Frost's poem as sacrilegious because it seems to say that Adam and Eve had no choice; everything in life is doomed to fall. Growing less innocent and more knowing seems less a choice in Frost's view than a natural process like the changing of golden blossoms to green leaves. "Eden sank to grief" not because we choose to do evil things but because time takes away our innocence as we encounter the suffering and loss of human existence. Frost suggests that the real original sin is that time has to pass and we all must grow wiser and less innocent.

Restatement of thesis

Gabriel 4

Work Cited

Frost, Robert. "Nothing Gold Can Stay." *Literature for Life*. Ed. X. J. Kennedy, Dana Gioia, and Nina Revoyr. New York: Pearson. 2013. 60. Print.

DOCUMENT SOURCES TO AVOID PLAGIARISM

Certain literary works, because they offer intriguing difficulties, have attracted professional critics by the score. On library shelves, great phalanxes of critical books now stand at the side of James Joyce's *Ulysses* and T. S. Eliot's allusive poem *The Waste Land*. The student who undertakes to study such works seriously is well advised to profit from the critics' labors. Chances are, too, that even in discussing a relatively uncomplicated work, you will want to seek the aid of some critics.

    If you do so, you may find yourself wanting to borrow quotations for your own papers. This is a fine thing to do—provided you give credit for those words to their rightful author. To do otherwise is plagiarism—a serious offense—and most English instructors are likely to recognize it when they see it. In any but the most superlative student paper, a brilliant (or even not so brilliant) phrase from a renowned critic is likely to stand out like a golf ball in a garter snake's midriff.

    To avoid plagiarism, you must reproduce the text you are using with quotation marks around it, and give credit where it is due. Even if you summarize a critic's idea in your own words, rather than quoting his or her exact words, you have to give credit to your source. Chapter 11, "Writing a Research Paper," will discuss in depth the topic of properly citing your sources. For now, students should simply remember that claiming another's work as one's own is the worst offense of the learning community. It negates the very purpose of education, which is to learn to think for oneself.

THE FORM OF YOUR FINISHED PAPER

If your instructor has not specified the form of your finished paper, follow the guidelines in the current edition of the *MLA Handbook for Writers of Research Papers*, which you will find more fully described in the chapter "Writing a Research Paper." In brief:

- Choose standard letter-size ($8\frac{1}{2} \times 11$) white paper.
- Use standard, easy-to-read type fonts, such as Times New Roman. Be sure the italic type style contrasts with the regular style.
- Give your name, your instructor's name, the course number, and the date at the top left-hand corner of your first page, starting one inch from the top.
- On all pages, give your last name and the page number in the upper right-hand corner, one-half inch from the top.
- Remember to give your paper a title that reflects your thesis.
- Leave one inch of margin on all four sides of each page and a few inches of blank space or an additional sheet of paper after your conclusion, so that your instructor can offer comments.
- If you include a works-cited section, begin it on a new page.
- Double-space all your text, including quotations, notes, and the works-cited page.
- Italicize the titles of longer works—books, plays, periodicals, and book-length poems such as *The Odyssey*. The titles of shorter works—poems, articles, and short stories—should appear in quotation marks.

What's left to do but hand in your paper? By now, you may be glad to see it go. But a good paper is not only worth submitting; it is also worth keeping. If you return to it after a while, you may find to your surprise that it will preserve and even renew what you have learned.

7 WRITING ABOUT A STORY

Don't write merely to be understood.
Write so that you cannot possibly be misunderstood.

—ROBERT LOUIS STEVENSON

Writing about fiction presents its own set of challenges and rewards. Because a well-wrought work of fiction can catch us up in the twists and turns of its plot, we may be tempted to read it in a trance, passively letting its plot wash over us, as we might watch an entertaining film. Or, because stories, even short ones, unfold over time, there is often so much to say about them that narrowing down and organizing your thoughts can seem daunting.

To write compellingly about fiction, you need to read actively, identify a meaningful topic, and focus on making a point about which you feel strongly. (For pointers on finding a topic, organizing, writing, and revising your paper, see the previous chapter, "Writing About Literature." Some methods especially useful for writing about stories are described in the present chapter.)

In this chapter much of the discussion and many examples refer to Edgar Allan Poe's short story "The Tell-Tale Heart" (page 39). If you haven't already read it, you can do so in only a few minutes, so that the rest of this chapter will make more sense to you.

READ ACTIVELY

Unlike a brief poem or a painting that you can take in with one glance, a work of fiction—even a short story—may be too complicated to hold all at once in the mind's eye. Before you can write about it, you may need to give it two or more careful readings, and even then, as you begin to think further about it, you will probably have to thumb through it to reread passages. The first time through, it is best just to read attentively, open to whatever pleasure and wisdom the story may afford. The second time, you will find it useful to read with pencil in hand, either to mark your text or to take notes to jog your memory. To work out the design and meaning of a story need not be a chore, any more than it is to land a fighting fish and to study it with admiration.

- **Read the story at least twice.** The first time through, allow yourself just to enjoy the story—to experience surprise and emotion. Once you know how the tale ends, you'll find it easier to reread with some detachment, noticing details you may have glossed over the first time.

- **Annotate the text.** Reread the story, taking notes in the margins or highlighting key passages as you go. When you sit down to write, you probably will have to skim the story to refresh your memory, and those notes and highlighted passages should prove useful. Here is a sample of an annotated passage, from paragraph 3 of Edgar Allan Poe's "The Tell-Tale Heart."

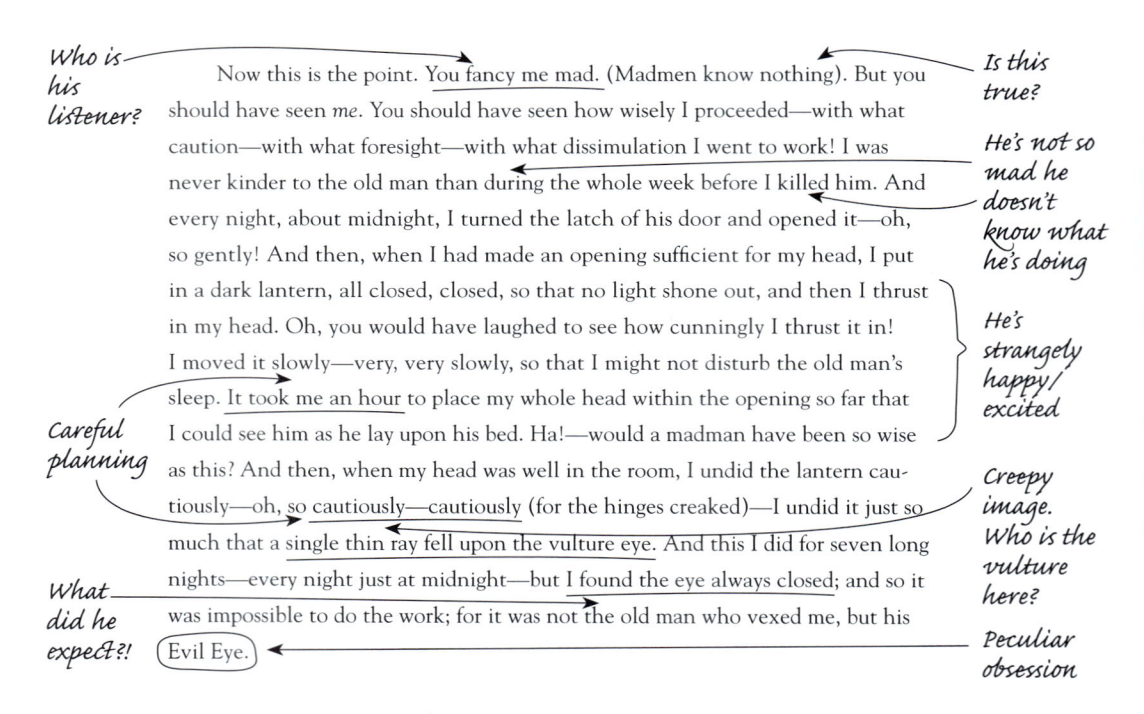

Who is his listener?

Careful planning

What did he expect?!

Now this is the point. You fancy me mad. (Madmen know nothing). But you should have seen *me*. You should have seen how wisely I proceeded—with what caution—with what foresight—with what dissimulation I went to work! I was never kinder to the old man than during the whole week before I killed him. And every night, about midnight, I turned the latch of his door and opened it—oh, so gently! And then, when I had made an opening sufficient for my head, I put in a dark lantern, all closed, closed, so that no light shone out, and then I thrust in my head. Oh, you would have laughed to see how cunningly I thrust it in! I moved it slowly—very, very slowly, so that I might not disturb the old man's sleep. It took me an hour to place my whole head within the opening so far that I could see him as he lay upon his bed. Ha!—would a madman have been so wise as this? And then, when my head was well in the room, I undid the lantern cautiously—oh, so cautiously—cautiously (for the hinges creaked)—I undid it just so much that a single thin ray fell upon the vulture eye. And this I did for seven long nights—every night just at midnight—but I found the eye always closed; and so it was impossible to do the work; for it was not the old man who vexed me, but his (Evil Eye.)

Is this true?

He's not so mad he doesn't know what he's doing

He's strangely happy/ excited

Creepy image. Who is the vulture here?

Peculiar obsession

THINK ABOUT THE STORY

Once you have reread the story, you can begin to process your ideas about it. To get started, try the following steps:

- **Identify the protagonist and the conflict.** Whose story is being told? What does that character desire more than anything else? What stands in the way of that character's achievement of his or her goal? The answers to these questions can give you a better handle on the story's plot.

- **Consider the story's point of view.** What does it contribute to the story? How might the tale change if told from another point of view?

- **Think about the setting.** Does it play a significant role in the plot? How does setting affect the story's tone?
- **Notice key symbols.** If any symbols catch your attention as you go, be sure to highlight each place in which they appear in the text. What do these symbols contribute to the story's meaning? (Remember, not every image is a symbol—only those important recurrent persons, places, or things that seem to suggest more than their literal meaning.)
- **Look for the theme.** Is the story's central meaning stated directly? If not, how does it reveal itself?
- **Think about tone and style.** How would you characterize the style in which the story is written? Consider elements such as diction, sentence structure, tone, and organization. How does the story's style contribute to its tone?

PREWRITING: DISCOVER YOUR IDEAS

Once you have given the story some preliminary thought, it is time to write as a means of discovering what it is you have to say. Brainstorming, clustering, listing, freewriting, keeping a journal, and outlining all can help you clarify your thoughts about the story and, in doing so, generate ideas for your paper. While you don't need to use *all* these techniques, try them to find the one or two that work best for you.

- **Brainstorm.** If you aren't sure what, exactly, to say about a story, try jotting down everything you can think of about it. Work quickly, without pausing to judge what you have written. Set yourself a time limit of ten or fifteen minutes and keep writing even if you think you have said it all. A list that results from brainstorming on "The Tell-Tale Heart" might look something like this:

madness? seems crazy	old man's gold/treasures
unreliable narrator	old man's eye = motive
Could story be a dream?	vulture eye = symbolic
Could heartbeat be supernatural?	Calls plotting murder "work"
heartbeat = speaker's paranoia	careful/patient
tone: dramatic, intense, quick mood changes	Chops up body perfect crime
glee/terror	Policemen don't hear heartbeat
lots of exclamation points	Guilt makes him confess
telling his story to listener	
old man = father? boss? friend?	

- **Cluster.** Clustering involves generating ideas by diagramming the relationship among your many ideas. First, write your subject at the center of a sheet of paper and circle it. Then, jot down ideas as they occur to you, drawing lines to link each idea to related ones. Here is an example of how you might cluster your ideas about "The Tell-Tale Heart."

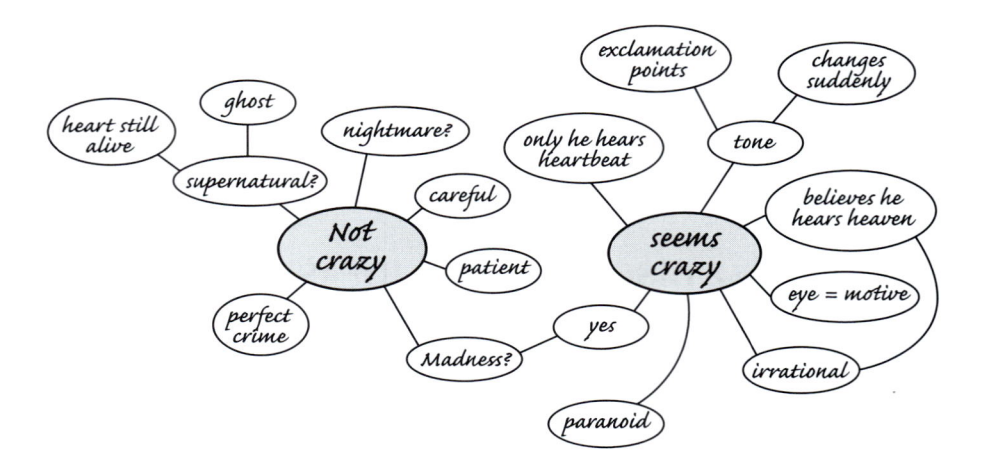

Not crazy: heart still alive, ghost, supernatural?, nightmare?, careful, patient, perfect crime, Madness?, yes, paranoid

Seems crazy: exclamation points, only he hears heartbeat, changes suddenly, tone, believes he hears heaven, eye = motive, irrational

- **List.** Using your notes and annotations as a guide, list information that seems useful, adding any notes that help you to keep track of your thought process. Use different headings to organize related concepts. Your lists might look something like this:

Unreliable Narrator	Other Possibilities
mood swings	nightmare
insists too much on being sane	supernatural
confusion	heart still alive?
disease	ghost's heartbeat?
sharpened senses	
loved old man	
murder	
patience	
guilt	
hearing things	

- **Freewrite.** Before you try to write a coherent first draft of your essay, take time to write freely, exploring your ideas as they occur to you. Writing quickly, without thinking too hard about grammar or spelling, can call forth surprising new ideas that wouldn't arrive if you were composing in a more reflective, cautious manner. To freewrite, give yourself a set amount of time—fifteen or twenty minutes. Put your pen to paper (or your fingers to the keyboard) and write without pausing to think. Keep going even if you run out of things to say. A freewrite on "The Tell-Tale Heart" might look like this:

  > The guy seems crazy. He keeps insisting he's sane, so maybe others have accused him of being insane. He's speaking to someone—a judge? a fellow inmate? The story feels spoken out loud, like a dramatic monologue. His mood changes really quickly. One minute he's gleeful, and then impatient, then terrified. The story is full of dashes and exclamation points. He says he can hear everything in heaven and earth and even some things in hell. That seems crazy. His disease has sharpened his senses. Is he the old man's son, or his employee? I don't think the story says. It does say he loves the old man but he's obsessed with vulture eye. He describes it in detail. It sounds like a blind eye, but it makes him more paranoid than the old man's other eye which probably can see. The things that freak the narrator out are little things—body parts, an eye and a heart. He's really careful in planning the murder. This is supposed to mean he is sane, but don't mentally ill people sometimes hatch careful plots and pay attention to detail? He says his senses are sharp but maybe he's hearing things that aren't there?

- **Journal.** If your instructor has asked you to keep a reading journal, don't forget to look back at it for your first responses to the story. Doing so may jog your memory and provide raw material for your essay.
- **Outline.** Some writers organize their papers by trial and error, writing them and going back in, cutting out useless material and filling in what seems to be missing. For a more efficient approach to organization, though, try making an outline—a simple list of points arranged in an order that makes logical sense. Such an outline might look like this:

  1. Point of view is ironic (speaker is mad/unreliable)
      hears things in heaven/hell
      excited tone
      focus on strange detail

  2. Can we trust story really happened?
      nightmare?
      more interesting if actual

  3. Supernatural elements?
      ghost heartbeat?
      heart still alive?

  4. More interesting/believable if speaker is mad

WRITE A ROUGH DRAFT

Once your prewriting exercises have sparked an idea or two, you will be ready to begin shaping your thoughts into a rough draft. Reread the section "Develop a Literary Argument" in the previous chapter for help getting started. You can still keep your approach loose and informal; don't worry yet about phrasing things perfectly or pinning down the ideal word. For now, your goal is to begin finding a shape for your argument.

- **Remember your purpose.** Before you begin work on your first draft, be sure to check the assignment you have been given. There is no sense in writing even the most elegant *analysis* (in which you focus on one particular element of a story) if you have been told to write an *explication* (a detailed, line-by-line interpretation of a passage).

- **Consider your audience.** Though your professor and classmates will likely be your paper's actual audience, the assignment might specify hypothetical readers. Whoever your audience may be, keep their needs in mind as you write.

- **Formulate your thesis.** Before you get going on your rough draft, you will need a thesis sentence summing up your paper's main idea. Begin with a provisional thesis to give your argument direction. As you write, be sure to keep your provisional thesis in mind; doing so will help you stay on track. Here is a working thesis for a paper on "The Tell-Tale Heart":

    WORKING THESIS

    The story contains many hints that the narrator of "The Tell-Tale Heart" is crazy.

    While this thesis gives its author something to work toward, it isn't yet as sharp as it could be. Most readers would agree that the story's narrator shows obvious signs of insanity. A more compelling thesis would go into the specifics of what, exactly, gives away the narrator's madness, or it might spell out the implications of this madness for the story. The following reworked version of this thesis sentence does both:

    REVISED THESIS

    The narrator's tenuous hold on reality and his wild shifts in mood indicate that he is insane and, therefore, that his point of view is untrustworthy.

    Like this statement, your thesis should be decisive and specific. As you write a rough draft, your task is to persuade readers of the wisdom of your thesis.

- **Back up your thesis with evidence.** The bulk of your essay should be spent providing evidence that proves your thesis. Because the most persuasive evidence tends to be that which comes from the story itself, be sure to quote as needed. As you flesh out your argument, check back frequently to make sure your thesis continues to hold up to the evidence. If you find that the facts of the story don't bear out your thesis, the problem may be with the evidence or with the thesis itself. Could your point be better proved by presenting different evidence? If so, exchange what you have for more convincing information. If not, go back in and refine your thesis sentence. Then make sure that the rest of the evidence bears out your new and improved thesis.

- **Organize your argument.** Choose the points you need to prove your thesis and present them, along with supporting evidence, in whatever order best makes your case. A rough outline is often a useful tool.

checklist: Writing a Rough Draft

- ☐ What is your essay's purpose?
- ☐ Who is your audience? What do they need to know?
- ☐ What is your thesis? Is it debatable?
- ☐ Does everything in your essay support your thesis?
- ☐ Is your argument sensibly organized?

REVISE YOUR DRAFT

Once your first draft has been committed to paper, you will need to begin revising—going back in and reworking it to make the argument as persuasive and the prose as seamless as can be. First, though, it is an excellent idea to get feedback on your draft from a trusted reader—a classmate, a roommate, a tutor in your school's writing center, or even your instructor—who can tell you which ideas are, and are not, coming across clearly, or where your argument is persuasive and where it could be more convincing. For writers at all levels of expertise, there simply is no substitute for constructive criticism from a thoughtful reader. If, however, you find readers are in short supply, put your rough draft away for at least an hour or two, and reread it with fresh eyes before you begin revising.

The following is an example of how one student used his instructor's comments to improve his paper's opening paragraph. (The final paper appears later in this chapter.)

DRAFT OF OPENING PARAGRAPH

Tell me more!

The narrator of Edgar Allan Poe's "The Tell-Tale Heart" is a very mysterious and murderous character. The reader doesn't know much about him, except for how he speaks and what he has to say for himself. There is one important fact revealed by evidence in the story. The story contains many hints that the narrator of "The Tell-Tale Heart" is crazy.

Provide specifics.

Why is this important?

What are some of these?

REVISED OPENING PARAGRAPH

Although there are many things we do not know about the narrator of Edgar Allan Poe's story "The Tell-Tale Heart"—is he a son? a servant? a companion?—there is one thing we are sure of from the start. He is mad. In the opening paragraph, Poe makes the narrator's condition unmistakable, not only from his excited and worked-up speech (full of dashes and exclamation points), but also from his wild claims. He says it is merely some disease which has sharpened his senses that has made people call him crazy. Who but a madman, however, would say, "I heard all things in the heaven and in the earth," and brag how his ear is a kind of radio, listening in on hell? The narrator's tenuous hold on reality and his wild shifts in mood indicate that he is mad and, therefore, that his point of view is untrustworthy.

Remember that revision means more than just cleaning up typos and doing away with stray semicolons. Revision might mean fleshing out your ideas with new paragraphs, rearranging material, or paring away passages that detract from your focus. As you rewrite, make sure every paragraph has a topic sentence that announces its main idea. Feel free to link your ideas with transitional words and phrases such as "moreover," "in addition," or "in contrast" to help your reader understand how each new idea relates to the one that precedes it.

checklist: Revising Your Draft

- ☐ Is your thesis clear? Does it say something significant but not entirely obvious about the story?
- ☐ Does all your evidence serve to advance the argument put forth in your thesis?
- ☐ Is your argument clear and logical?
- ☐ Do transitional words and phrases help signal movement from one idea to the next?
- ☐ Does your introduction draw the reader in? Does it prepare the reader for what follows?
- ☐ Does your conclusion tie up the paper's loose ends? Does it avoid merely restating what has come before?
- ☐ Does each paragraph contain a topic sentence?
- ☐ Does the paper have an interesting and compelling title?

WHAT'S YOUR PURPOSE? COMMON APPROACHES TO WRITING ABOUT FICTION

It is crucial to keep your paper's purpose in mind. When you write an academic paper, you are likely to have been given a specific set of marching orders. Maybe you have been asked to write for a particular audience besides the obvious one (your professor, that is). Perhaps you have been asked to describe your personal reaction to a literary work. Maybe your purpose is to interpret a work, analyzing how one or more of its elements contribute to its meaning. You may have been instructed to write an evaluation in which you judge a work's merits. Let the assignment dictate your paper's tone and content. Below are several commonly used approaches to writing about fiction.

Explication

Explication is the patient unfolding of meanings in a work of literature. An explication proceeds carefully through a story, usually interpreting it line by line—perhaps even word by word, dwelling on details a casual reader might miss and illustrating how a story's smaller parts contribute to the whole. Alert and willing to take pains, the writer of such an essay notices anything meaningful that isn't obvious, whether it is a colossal theme suggested by a symbol or a little hint contained in a single word.

To write an honest explication of an entire story takes time and space, and it is a better assignment for a term paper, an honors thesis, or a dissertation than a short essay. A thorough explication of Nathaniel Hawthorne's "Young Goodman Brown," for example, would likely run much longer than the rich and intriguing short story itself. Ordinarily, explication is best suited to a short passage or section of a story: a key scene, a critical conversation, a statement of theme, or an opening or closing paragraph. In a long critical essay that doesn't adhere to one method all the way through, the method of explication may appear from time to time, as when the critic, in discussing a story, stops to unravel a particularly knotty passage. Here are tips for writing a successful explication of your own:

- **Focus on the details that strike you as most meaningful.** Do not try to cover everything.
- **Try working through the original passage sentence by sentence.** If you choose this method, be sure to vary your transitions from one point to the next, to avoid the danger of falling into a boring singsong: "In the first sentence I noticed . . . ," "In the next sentence . . . ," "Now in the third sentence . . . ," and "Finally, in the last sentence. . . ."
- **Consider working from a simple outline.** In writing the explication that follows of a passage from "The Tell-Tale Heart," the student began with a list of points she wanted to express:

    1. Speaker's extreme care and exactness—typical of some mental illnesses.
    2. Speaker doesn't act by usual logic but by a crazy logic.
    3. Dreamlike connection between latch and lantern and old man's eye.

Storytellers who are especially fond of language invite closer attention to their words than others might. Poe, for one, was a poet sensitive to the rhythms of his sentences and a symbolist whose stories abound in potent suggestions. Here is a student's explication of a short but essential passage in "The Tell-Tale Heart." The passage occurs in the third paragraph of the story, and to help us follow the explication, the student quotes the passage in full at the paper's beginning.

Susan Kim

Professor A. M. Lundy

English 100

20 October 2012

By Lantern Light: An Explication

of a Passage in Poe's "The Tell-Tale Heart"

Quotes passage to be explicated

And every night, about midnight, I turned the latch of his door and opened it—oh, so gently! And then, when I had made an opening sufficient for my head, I put in a dark lantern, all closed, closed, so that no light shone out, and then I thrust in my head. Oh, you would have laughed to see how cunningly I thrust it in! I moved it slowly—very, very slowly, so that I might not disturb the old man's sleep. It took me an hour to place my whole head within the opening so far that I could see him as he lay upon his bed. Ha!—would a madman have been so wise as this? And then, when my head was well in the room, I undid the lantern cautiously—oh, so cautiously—cautiously (for the hinges creaked)—I undid it just so much that a single thin ray fell upon the vulture eye. And this I did for seven long nights—every night just at midnight—but I found the eye always closed; and so it was impossible to do the work; for it was not the old man who vexed me, but his Evil Eye. (par. 3)

Thesis sentence

Although Edgar Allan Poe has suggested in the first lines of his story "The Tell-Tale Heart" that the person who addresses us is insane, it is only when we come to the speaker's account of his preparations for murdering the old man that we find his madness fully revealed. Even more convincingly than his earlier words (for we might possibly think that someone who claims to hear things in heaven and hell is a religious mystic), these preparations reveal him to be mad. What strikes us is that they are so elaborate and meticulous. A significant detail

Textual evidence supports thesis

is the exactness of his schedule for spying: "every night just at midnight." The words with which he describes his motions also convey the most extreme care (and I will indicate them by italics): "how *wisely* I proceeded—with *what caution*," "I turned the latch of his door and opened it—oh, so *gently*!" "how *cunningly* I

Kim 2

thrust it [my head] in! I moved it slowly—*very, very slowly*," "I undid the lantern *cautiously*—oh, *so cautiously*—*cautiously*." Taking a whole hour to intrude his head into the room, he asks, "Ha!—would a madman have been so wise as this?" But of course the word *wise* is unconsciously ironic, for clearly it is not wisdom the speaker displays, but an absurd degree of care, an almost fiendish ingenuity. Such behavior, I understand, is typical of certain mental illnesses. All his careful preparations that he thinks prove him sane only convince us instead that he is mad.

Obviously his behavior is self-defeating. He wants to catch the "vulture eye" open, and yet he takes all these pains not to disturb the old man's sleep. If he behaved logically, he might go barging into the bedroom with his lantern ablaze, shouting at the top of his voice. And yet, if we can see things his way, there *is* a strange logic to his reasoning. He regards the eye as a creature in itself, quite apart from its possessor. "It was not," he says, "the old man who vexed me, but his Evil Eye." Apparently, to be inspired to do his deed, the madman needs to behold the eye—at least, this is my understanding of his remark, "I found the eye always closed; and so it was impossible to do the work." Poe's choice of the word *work*, by the way, is also revealing. Murder is made to seem a duty or a job; and anyone who so regards murder is either extremely cold-blooded, like a hired killer for a gangland assassination, or else deranged. Besides, the word suggests again the curious sense of detachment that the speaker feels toward the owner of the eye.

Topic sentence on narrator's mad logic

In still another of his assumptions, the speaker shows that he is madly logical, or operating on the logic of a dream. There seems a dreamlike relationship between his dark lantern "all closed, closed, so that no light shone out," and the sleeping victim. When the madman opens his lantern so that it emits a single ray, he is hoping that the eye in the old man's head will be open too, letting out its corresponding gleam. The latch that he turns so gently, too, seems like the eye, whose lid needs to be opened in order for the murderer to go ahead. It is as though the speaker is *trying* to get the eyelid to lift. By taking such great pains and by going through all this nightly ritual, he is practicing some kind of magic, whose rules are laid down not by our logic, but by the logic of dreams.

Conclusion pushes thesis further, making it more specific.

> Kim 3
>
> Work Cited
>
> Poe, Edgar Allan. "The Tell-Tale Heart." *Literature for Life.* Ed. X. J. Kennedy, Dana Gioia, and Nina Revoyr. New York: Pearson, 2013. 39–42. Print.

An unusually well written essay, "By Lantern Light" cost its author two or three careful revisions. Rather than attempting to say something about *everything* in the passage from Poe, she selects only the details that strike her as most meaningful. In her very first sentence, she briefly shows us how the passage functions in the context of Poe's story: how it clinches our suspicions that the narrator is mad. Notice too that the student who wrote the essay doesn't inch through the passage sentence by sentence, but freely takes up its details in an order that seems appropriate to her argument.

Analysis

Examining a single component of a story can afford us a better understanding of the entire work. This is perhaps why in most literature classes students are asked to write at least one **analysis** (from the Greek, "breaking up"), an essay that breaks a story or novel into its elements and, usually, studies one part closely. One likely topic for an analysis might be "The Character of James Baldwin's Sonny," in which the writer would concentrate on showing us Sonny's highly individual features and traits of personality. Other topics for an analysis might be "Irony in Ha Jin's 'Saboteur,'" or "Setting in Kate Chopin's 'The Storm,'" or "The Unidentified Narrator in 'A Rose for Emily.'"

To be sure, no element of a story dwells in isolation from the story's other elements. In "The Tell-Tale Heart," the madness of the leading character apparently makes it necessary to tell the story from a special point of view and probably helps determine the author's choice of theme, setting, symbolism, tone, style, and ironies. But it would be mind-boggling to try to study all those elements simultaneously. For this reason, when we write an analysis, we generally study just one element, though we may suggest—probably at the start of the essay—its relation to the whole story. Here are two points to keep in mind when writing an analysis:

- **Decide upon a thesis, and include only relevant insights.** As tempting as it might be to include your every idea, stick to those that will help to prove your point.
- **Support your contentions with specific references to the story you are analyzing.** Quotations can be particularly convincing.

The following paper is an example of a solid, brief analysis. Written by a student, it focuses on just one element of "The Tell-Tale Heart": the story's point of view.

Mike Frederick

Professor Stone

English 110

18 January 2012

The Hearer of the Tell-Tale Heart

    Although there are many things we do not know about the narrator of Edgar Allan Poe's story "The Tell-Tale Heart"—is he a son? a servant? a companion?—there is one thing we are sure of from the start. He is mad. In the opening paragraph, Poe makes the narrator's condition unmistakable, not only from his excited and worked-up speech (full of dashes and exclamation points), but also from his wild claims. He says it is merely some disease which has sharpened his senses that has made people call him crazy. Who but a madman, however, would say, "I heard all things in the heaven and in the earth," and brag how his ear is a kind of radio, listening in on hell? The narrator's tenuous hold on reality and his wild shifts in mood indicate that he is insane and, therefore, that his point of view is untrustworthy.

    Because the participant narrator is telling his story in the first person, some details in the story stand out more than others. When the narrator goes on to tell how he watches the old man sleeping, he rivets his attention on the old man's "vulture eye." When a ray from his lantern finds the Evil Eye open, he says, "I could see nothing else of the old man's face or person" (par. 9). Actually, the reader can see almost nothing else about the old man anywhere in the rest of the story. All we are told is that the old man treated the younger man well, and we gather that the old man was rich, because his house is full of treasures. We do not have a clear idea of what the old man looks like, though, nor do we know how he talks, for we are not given any of his words. Our knowledge of him is mainly confined to his eye and its effect on the narrator. This confinement gives that symbolic eye a lot of importance in the story. The narrator tells us all we know and directs our attention to parts of it.

    This point of view raises an interesting question. Since we are dependent on the narrator for all our information, how do we know the whole story isn't just a nightmare in his demented mind? We have really no way to be sure it isn't, as far as I can see. I assume, however, that there really is a dark shuttered house and an old man and real policemen who start snooping around when screams are heard in the neighborhood because it is a more memorable story if

Frederick 2

it is a crazy man's view of reality than if it is all just a terrible dream. But we can't rely on the madman's interpretation of what happens. Poe keeps putting distances between what the narrator says and what we are apparently supposed to think. For instance: the narrator has boasted that he is calm and clear in the head, but as soon as he starts trying to explain why he killed the old man, we gather that he is confused, to say the least. "I think it was his eye!" the narrator exclaims, as if not quite sure (par. 2). As he goes on to explain how he conducted the murder, we realize that he is a man with a fixed idea working with a patience that is certainly mad, almost diabolical.

Some readers might wonder if "The Tell-Tale Heart" is a story of the supernatural. Is the heartbeat that the narrator hears a ghost come back to haunt him? Here, I think, the point of view is our best guide to what to believe. The simple explanation for the heartbeat is this: it is all in the madman's mind. Perhaps he feels such guilt that he starts hearing things. Another explanation is possible, one suggested by Daniel Hoffman, a critic who has discussed the story: the killer hears the sound of his *own* heart (227). Hoffman's explanation (which I don't like as well as mine) also is a natural one, and it fits the story as a whole. Back when the narrator first entered the old man's bedroom to kill him, the heartbeat sounded so loud to him that he was afraid the neighbors would hear it too. Evidently they didn't, and so Hoffman may be right in thinking that the sound was only that of his own heart pounding in his ears. Whichever explanation you take, it is a more down-to-earth and reasonable explanation than (as the narrator believes) that the heart is still alive, even though its owner has been cut to pieces. Then, too, the police keep chatting. If they heard the heartbeat, wouldn't they leap to their feet, draw their guns, and look all around the room? As the author keeps showing us in the rest of the story, the narrator's view of things is untrustworthy. You don't kill someone just because you dislike the look in his eye. You don't think that such a murder is funny. For all its Gothic atmosphere of the old dark house with a secret hidden inside, "The Tell-Tale Heart" is not a ghost story. We have only to see its point of view to know it is a study in abnormal psychology.

> Frederick 3
>
> Works Cited
>
> Hoffman, Daniel. *Poe Poe Poe Poe Poe Poe Poe.* New York: Anchor, 1973. Print.
>
> Poe, Edgar Allan. "The Tell-Tale Heart." *Literature for Life.* Ed. X. J. Kennedy, Dana Gioia, and Nina Revoyr. New York: Pearson, 2013. 39-42. Print.

The temptation in writing an analysis is to include all sorts of insights that the writer proudly wishes to display, even though they aren't related to the main idea. In the preceding essay, the student resists this temptation admirably. In fairly plump and ample paragraphs, he works out his ideas and supports his contentions with specific references to Poe's story. Although his paper is not brilliantly written and contains no insight so fresh as the suggestion (by the writer of the first paper) that the madman's lantern is like the old man's head, still, it is a good brief analysis. By sticking faithfully to his purpose and by confronting the problems he raises ("How do we know the whole story isn't just a nightmare?"), the writer persuades us that he understands not only the story's point of view but also the story in its entirety.

Comparison and Contrast

If you were to write on "The Humor of Alice Walker's 'Everyday Use' and John Updike's 'A & P,'" you would probably employ one or two methods. You might use **comparison**, placing the two stories side by side and pointing out their similarities, or **contrast**, pointing out their differences. Most of the time, in dealing with a pair of stories, you will find them similar in some ways and different in others, and you'll use both methods. Keep the following points in mind when writing a comparison and contrast paper:

- **Choose stories with something significant in common.** This will simplify your task and help ensure that your paper hangs together. Before you start writing, ask yourself if the two stories you've selected throw some light on each other. If the answer is no, rethink your story selection.
- **Choose a focus.** Simply ticking off every similarity and difference between two stories would make for a slack and rambling essay. More compelling writing would result from better-focused topics such as "The Experience of Coming of Age in James Joyce's 'Araby' and William Faulkner's 'Barn Burning'" or "Mother-Daughter Relationships in Alice Walker's 'Everyday Use' and Eudora Welty's 'Why I Live at the P.O.'"
- **Don't feel you need to spend equal amounts of time on comparing and contrasting.** If your chosen stories are more similar than different, you naturally will spend more space on comparison, and vice versa.
- **Don't devote the first half of your paper to one story and the second half to the other.** Such a paper wouldn't be a comparison or contrast so much as a pair of analyses yoked together. To reap the full benefits of the assignment, let the two stories mingle.

- **Before you start writing, draw up a brief list of points you would like to touch on.** Then address each point, first in one story and then in the other. A sample outline follows for a paper on William Faulkner's "A Rose for Emily" and Katherine Mansfield's "Miss Brill." The essay's topic is "Adapting to Change: The Characters of Emily Grierson and Miss Brill."

    1. Adapting to change (both women)
       Miss Brill more successful
    2. Portrait of women
       Miss Emily—unflattering
       Miss Brill—empathetic
    3. Imagery
       Miss Emily—morbid
       Miss Brill—cheerful
    4. Plot
       Miss Emily
       - loses sanity
       - refuses to adapt
       Miss Brill
       - finds place in society
       - adapts
    5. Summary: Miss Brill is more successful

- **Emphasize the points that interest you the most.** This strategy will help keep you from following your outline in a plodding fashion ("Well, now it's time to whip over to Miss Brill again . . .").

- **If the assignment allows, consider applying comparison and contrast in an essay on a single story.** You might, for example, analyze the attitudes of the younger and older waiters in Hemingway's "A Clean, Well-Lighted Place." Or you might contrast Pete's self-satisfied view of himself with his brother Donald's more critical view of him in Tobias Wolff's "The Rich Brother."

The following student-written paper compares and contrasts the main characters in "A Rose for Emily" and "Miss Brill." Notice how the author focuses the discussion on a single aspect of each woman's personality—the ability to adapt to change and the passage of time. By looking through the lens of three different elements of the short story—diction, imagery, and plot—this clear and systematic essay convincingly argues its thesis.

Ortiz 1

Michelle Ortiz
Professor Gregg
English 200
25 November 2012

Successful Adaptation in
"A Rose for Emily" and "Miss Brill"

  In William Faulkner's "A Rose for Emily" and Katherine Mansfield's "Miss Brill," the reader is given a glimpse into the lives of two old women living in different worlds but sharing many similar characteristics. Both Miss Emily and Miss Brill attempt to adapt to a changing environment as they grow older. Through the authors' use of language, imagery, and plot, it becomes clear to the reader that Miss Brill is more successful at adapting to the world around her and finding happiness. *Clear statement of thesis*

  In "A Rose for Emily," Faulkner's use of language paints an unflattering picture of Miss Emily. His tone evokes pity and disgust rather than sympathy. The reader identifies with the narrator of the story and shares the townspeople's opinion that Miss Emily is somehow "perverse" (par. 51). In "Miss Brill," however, the reader can identify with the title character. Mansfield's attitude toward the young couple at the end makes the reader hate them for ruining the happiness that Miss Brill has found, however small it may be. *Textual evidence on language supports thesis.*

  The imagery in "A Rose for Emily" keeps the reader from further identifying with Miss Emily by creating several morbid images of her. For example, there are several images of decay throughout the story. The house she lives in is falling apart and described as "filled with dust and shadows" (par. 5), "an eyesore among eyesores" (par. 2). Emily herself is described as looking "bloated, like a body long submerged in motionless water" (par. 6). Faulkner also uses words like "skeleton," "dank," "decay," and "cold" to reinforce these morbid, deathly images (par. 6, 5, 2, 8, 34). *Imagery in Faulkner's story supports argument.*

  In "Miss Brill," however, Mansfield uses more cheerful imagery. The music and the lively action in the park make Miss Brill feel alive inside. She notices the other old people who are in the park are "still as statues," "odd," and "silent" (par. 5). She says they "looked as though they'd just come from dark little rooms or even— even cupboards!" (par. 5). In the final paragraph, her own room is later described as "like a cupboard," but during the action of the story she does not include herself as "like a cupboard," among those other old people. She still feels alive. *Contrasting imagery in Mansfield's story supports argument.*

  Through the plots of both stories the reader can also see that Miss Brill is more successful in adapting to her environment. Miss Emily loses her sanity and ends up committing a crime in order to control her environment. Throughout *Characters contrasted with examples drawn from plots.*

> the story, she refuses to adapt to any of the changes going on in the town, such as the taxes or the mailboxes. Miss Brill is able to find her own special place in society where she can be happy and remain sane.
>
> In "A Rose for Emily" and "Miss Brill" the authors' use of language and the plots of the stories illustrate that Miss Brill is more successful in her story. Instead of hiding herself away she emerges from the "cupboard" to participate in life. She adapts to the world that is changing as she grows older, without losing her sanity or committing crimes, as Miss Emily does. The language of "Miss Brill" allows the reader to sympathize with the main character. The imagery in the story is lighter and less morbid than in "A Rose for Emily." The resulting portrait is of an aging woman who has found creative ways to adjust to her lonely life.

The final conclusion is stated and the thesis is restated.

Works Cited

Faulkner, William. "A Rose for Emily." *Literature for Life*. Ed. X. J. Kennedy, Dana Gioia, and Nina Revoyr. Pearson: 2013, 467-73. Print.

Mansfield, Katherine. "Miss Brill." *Literature for Life*. Ed. X. J. Kennedy, Dana Gioia, and Nina Revoyr. Pearson: 2013, 43-46. Print.

Response Paper

One popular form of writing assignment is the **response paper,** a short essay that expresses your personal reaction to a work of literature. Both instructors and students often find the response paper an ideal introductory writing assignment. It provides you with an opportunity to craft a focused essay about a literary work, but it does not usually require any outside research. What it does require is careful reading, clear thinking, and honest writing.

The purpose of a response paper is to convey your thoughts and feelings about an aspect of a particular literary work. It isn't a book report (summarizing the work's content) or a book review (evaluating the quality of a work). A response paper expresses what you experienced in reading and thinking about the assigned text. Your reaction should reflect your background, values, and attitudes in response to the work, not what the instructor thinks about it. You might even consider your response paper a conversation with the work you have just read. What questions does it seem to ask you? What reactions does it elicit? You might also regard your paper as a personal message to your instructor telling him or her what you really think about one of the reading assignments.

Of course, you can't say everything you thought and felt about your reading in a short paper. Focus on an important aspect (such as a main character, setting, or theme) and discuss your reaction to it. Don't gush or meander. Personal writing doesn't mean disorganized writing. Identify your main ideas and present your point of view in a clear and organized way. Once you get started you might surprise yourself by discovering that it's fun to explore your own responses. Stranger things have happened.

Here are tips for writing a successful response paper of your own:

- **Make quick notes as you read or reread the work.** Don't worry about writing anything organized at this point. Just write a word or two in the margin noting your reactions as you read (e.g., "what a jerk!" or "interesting" or "this reminds me of something my sister said"). These little notes will jog your memory when you go back to write your paper.
- **Consider which aspect of the work affected you the most**. That aspect will probably be a good starting point for your response.
- **Be candid in your writing.** Remember that the literary work is only half of the subject matter of your paper. The other half is your reaction.
- **Try to understand and explain why you have reacted the way you did.** It's not enough just to state your responses. You also want to justify or explain them.
- **Refer to the text in your paper.** Demonstrate to the reader that your response is based on the text. Provide specific textual details and quotations wherever relevant.

The following paper is one student's response to Tim O'Brien's story "The Things They Carried."

Martin 1

Ethan Martin
English 99
Professor Merrill
31 October 2012

"Perfect Balance and Perfect Posture":
Reflecting on "The Things They Carried"

Reading Tim O'Brien's short story "The Things They Carried" became a very personal experience. It reminded me of my father, who is a Vietnam veteran, and the stories he used to tell me. Growing up, I regularly asked my dad to share stories from his past, especially about his service in the United States Marine Corps. He would rarely talk about his tour during the Vietnam War for more than a few minutes, and what he shared was usually the same: the monsoon rain could chill to the bone, the mosquitoes would never stop biting, and the M-16 rifles often jammed in a moment of crisis. He dug a new foxhole where he slept every night, he traded the cigarettes from his C-rations for food, and—since he was the radio man of his platoon—the combination of his backpack and radio was very heavy during the long, daily walks through rice paddies and jungles. For these reasons, "The Things They Carried" powerfully affected me.

While reading the story, I felt as if I was "humping" (par. 4) through Vietnam with Lieutenant Jimmy Cross, Rat Kiley, Ted Lavender, and especially Mitchell Sanders—who carries the 26-pound radio and battery. Every day, we carry our backpacks to school. Inside are some objects that we need to use in class: books, paper, and pens. But most of us probably include "unnecessary" items that reveal something about who we are or what we value—photographs, perfume, or good-luck charms. O'Brien uses this device to tell his story. At times he lists the things that the soldiers literally carried, such as weapons, medicine, and flak jackets. These military items weigh between 30 and 70 pounds, depending on one's rank or function in the platoon. The narrator says, "They carried all they could bear, and then some, including a silent awe for the terrible power of the things they carried" (par. 12).

Some of this "terrible power" comes from the sentimental objects the men keep. Although these are relatively light, they weigh down the hearts of the soldiers. Lt. Jimmy Cross carries 10-ounce letters and a pebble from Martha, a girl in his hometown who doesn't love him back. Rat Kiley carries comic books, and Norman Bowker carries a diary. I now own the small, water-logged Bible that my father carried through his tour in Vietnam, which was a gift from his mother. When I open its pages, I can almost hear his voice praying to survive the war.

The price of such survival is costly. O'Brien's platoon carries ghosts, memories, and "the land itself" (par. 39). Their intangible burdens are heavier than what they carry in their backpacks. My father has always said that, while he was in Vietnam, an inexpressible feeling of death hung heavy in the air, which he could not escape. O'Brien notes that an emotional weight of fear and cowardice "could never be put down, it required perfect balance and perfect posture" (par. 77), and I wonder if this may be part of what my father meant.

Both Tim O'Brien and my father were wounded by shrapnel, and now they both carry a Purple Heart. They carry the weight of survival. They carry memories that I will never know. "The Things They Carried" is not a war story about glory and honor. It is a portrait of the psychological damage that war can bring. It is a story about storytelling and how hard it can be to find the truth. And it is a beautiful account of what the human heart can endure.

> Martin 3
>
> Work Cited
>
> O'Brien, Tim. "The Things They Carried." *Literature for Life.* Ed. X. J. Kennedy, Dana Gioia, and Nina Revoyr. New York: Pearson, 2013. 1299-1310. Print.

Topics for Writing

What kinds of topics are likely to result in papers that will reveal something about works of fiction? Here is a list of typical topics, suitable for papers of various lengths, offered in the hope of stimulating your own ideas. For additional ideas, see "Suggestions for Writing" at the end of each thematic chapter in this book.

Topics for Writing Brief Papers (250–500 Words)

1. Explicate the opening paragraph or first few lines of a story. Show how the opening prepares the reader for what will follow. In an essay of this length, you will need to limit your discussion to the most important elements of the passage you explicate; there won't be room to deal with everything. Or, as thoroughly as the word count allows, explicate the final paragraph of a story. What does the ending imply about the fates of the story's characters, and about the story's take on its central theme?
2. Select a story that features a first-person narrator. Write a concise yet thorough analysis of how that character's point of view colors the story.
3. Consider a short story in which the central character has to make a decision or must take some decisive step that will alter the rest of his or her life. Faulkner's "Barn Burning" is one such story; another is Updike's "A & P." As concisely and as thoroughly as you can, explain the nature of the character's decision, the reasons for it, and its probable consequences (as suggested by what the author tells us).
4. Choose two stories that might be interesting to compare and contrast. Write a brief defense of your choice. How might these two stories illuminate each other?
5. Choose a key passage from a story you admire. As closely as the word count allows, explicate that passage and explain why it strikes you as an important moment in the story. Concentrate on the aspects of the passage that seem most essential.
6. Write a new ending to a story of your choice. Try to imitate the author's writing style. Add a paragraph explaining how this exercise illuminates the author's choices in the original.
7. Drawing on your own experience, make the case that a character in any short story behaves (or doesn't behave) as people do in real life. Your audience for this assignment is your classmates; tailor your tone and argument accordingly.

Topics for Writing More Extended Papers (600–1,000 Words)

1. Write an analysis of a short story, focusing on a single element, such as point of view, theme, symbolism, character, or the author's voice (tone, style, irony). For a sample paper in response to this assignment, see "The Hearer of the Tell-Tale Heart" (page 159).
2. Compare and contrast two stories with protagonists who share an important personality trait. Make character the focus of your essay.
3. Write a thorough explication of a short passage in a story you admire. Pick a crucial moment in the plot, or a passage that reveals the story's theme. You might look to the paper "By Lantern Light" (page 156) as a model.
4. Write an analysis of a story in which the protagonist experiences an epiphany or revelation of some sort. Describe the nature of this change of heart. How is the reader prepared for it? What are its repercussions in the character's life? Some possible story choices are Alice Walker's "Everyday Use," William Faulkner's "Barn Burning," Raymond Carver's "Cathedral," James Baldwin's "Sonny's Blues," and Flannery O'Connor's "A Good Man Is Hard to Find."
5. Imagine you are given the task of teaching a story to your class. Write an explanation of how you would address this challenge.
6. Imagine a reluctant reader, one who would rather play video games than crack a book. Which story in this book would you recommend to him or her? Write an essay to that imagined reader, describing the story's merits.
7. Choose a story that treats a subject or a theme very differently than your own experiences of that subject or theme. Write an essay about how the story influenced your thinking and maybe changed your mind—or why it didn't.

Topics for Writing Long Papers (1,500 Words or More)

1. Write an analysis of a longer work of fiction. Concentrate on a single element of the story, quoting as necessary to make your point.
2. Read three or four short stories by an author whose work you admire. Concentrating on a single element treated similarly in all of the stories, write an analysis of the author's work as exemplified by your chosen stories.
3. Describe the process of reading a story for the first time and gradually learning to understand and appreciate it. First, choose a story you haven't yet read. As you read it for the first time, take notes on aspects of the story you find difficult or puzzling. Read the story a second time. Now write about the experience. What uncertainties were resolved when you read the story the second time? What, if any, uncertainties remain? What has this experience taught you about reading fiction?
4. Choose two stories that treat a similar theme. Compare and contrast the stance each story takes toward that theme, marshalling quotations and specifics as necessary to back up your argument.
5. Browse through newspapers and magazines for a story with the elements of good fiction. Now rewrite the story *as* fiction. Then write a one-page accompanying essay explaining the challenges of the task. What did it teach you about the relative natures of journalism and fiction?

8 WRITING ABOUT A POEM

> *I love being a writer.*
> *What I can't stand is the paperwork.*
>
> —PETER DE VRIES

Many readers—even some enthusiastic ones—are wary of poems. "I don't know anything about poetry," some people say, if the subject arises. While poems aren't booby traps designed to trip up careless readers, it is true that poetry demands a special level of concentration. Poetry is language at its most intense and condensed, and in a good poem, every word counts. With practice, though, anyone can become a more confident reader—and critic—of poetry. Remember that the purpose of poetry isn't intimidation but wisdom and pleasure. Even writing a paper on poetry can occasion a certain enjoyment. Here are some tips.

- **Choose a poem that speaks to you.** Let pleasure be your guide in choosing the poem you write about. The act of writing is easier if your feelings are engaged. Write about something you dislike and don't understand, and your essay will be as dismal to read as it was for you to write. But write about something that interests you, and your essay will communicate that interest and enthusiasm.
- **Allow yourself time to get comfortable with your subject.** As most professors will tell you, when students try to fudge their way through a paper on a topic they don't fully understand, the lack of comfort shows, making for muddled, directionless prose. The more familiar you become with a poem, however, the easier and more pleasurable it will be to write about it. Expect to read the poem several times over before its meaning becomes clear. Better still, reread it over the course of several days.

READ ACTIVELY

A poem should be read slowly, carefully, and attentively. Good poems yield more if read twice, and the best poems—after ten, twenty, or even thirty readings—keep on yielding. Here are suggestions to enhance your reading of a poem you plan to write about.

- **Read the poem aloud.** There is no better way to understand a poem than to effectively read it aloud. Read slowly, paying attention to punctuation cues. Listen for the audio effects.
- **Read closely and painstakingly, annotating as you go.** Keep your mind (and your pencil) sharp and ready. The subtleties of language are essential to a poem. Pay attention to the connotations or suggestions of words, and to the rhythm of phrases and lines. Underline words and images that jump out at you. Use arrows to link phrases that seem connected. Highlight key passages or take notes in the margins as ideas or questions occur to you.

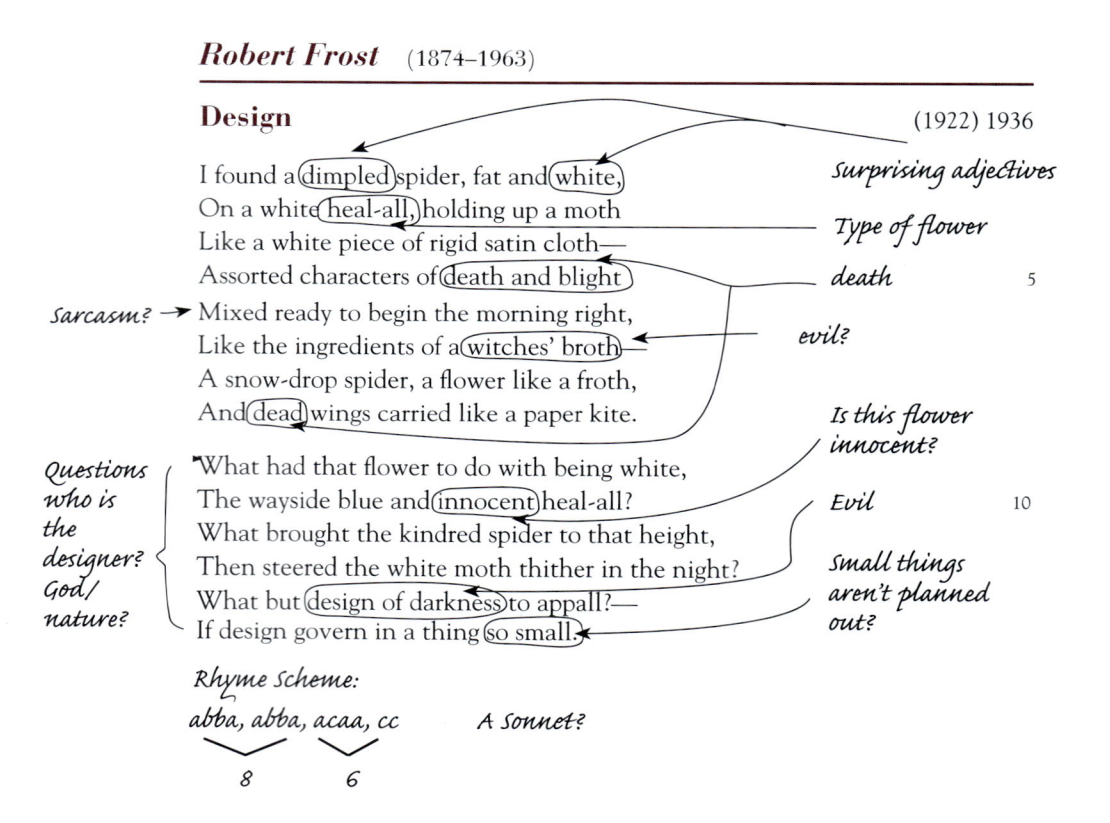

Robert Frost (1874–1963)

Design (1922) 1936

I found a (dimpled) spider, fat and (white,) — *Surprising adjectives*
On a white (heal-all,) holding up a moth — *Type of flower*
Like a white piece of rigid satin cloth—
Assorted characters of (death and blight) — *death*   5
Sarcasm? → Mixed ready to begin the morning right,
Like the ingredients of a (witches' broth) — *evil?*
A snow-drop spider, a flower like a froth,
And (dead) wings carried like a paper kite. — *Is this flower innocent?*

Questions who is the designer? God/ nature? { "What had that flower to do with being white,
The wayside blue and (innocent) heal-all? — *Evil*   10
What brought the kindred spider to that height,
Then steered the white moth thither in the night? — *Small things aren't planned out?*
What but (design of darkness) to appall?—
If design govern in a thing (so small.)

Rhyme Scheme:
abba, abba, acaa, cc   A Sonnet?
   8   6

- **Look up any unfamiliar words, allusions, or references.** Often the very words you may be tempted to skim over will provide the key to a poem's meaning. Thomas Hardy's "The Ruined Maid" will remain elusive to a reader unfamiliar with the archaic meaning of the word "ruin"—a woman's loss of virginity to a man other than her husband. Similarly, be sure to acquaint yourself with any references or allusions that appear in a poem. H.D.'s poem "Helen" will make sense only to readers who are familiar with the story of Helen of Troy.

THINK ABOUT THE POEM

Before you begin writing, take some time to collect your thoughts. The following steps can be useful in thinking about a poem.

- **Let your emotions guide you into the poem.** Do any images or phrases call up a strong emotional response? If so, try to puzzle out why those passages seem so emotionally loaded. In a word or two, describe the poem's tone.

- **Determine what's literally happening in the poem.** Separating literal language from figurative or symbolic language can be one of the trickiest—and most essential—tasks in poetic interpretation. Begin by working out the literal. Who is speaking the poem? To whom? Under what circumstances? What happens in the poem?

- **Ask what it all adds up to.** Once you've pinned down the literal action of the poem, it's time to take a leap into the figurative. What is the significance of the poem? Address symbolism, any figures of speech, and any language that means one thing literally but suggests something else. In "My Papa's Waltz," for example, Theodore Roethke tells a simple story of a father dancing his small son around a kitchen. The language of the poem suggests much more, however, implying that while the father is rough to the point of violence, the young boy hungers for his attention.

- **Consider the poem's shape on the page, and the way it sounds.** What patterns of sound do you notice? Are the lines long, short, or a mixture of both? How do these elements contribute to the poem's effect?

- **Pay attention to form.** If a poem makes use of rime or regular meter, ask yourself how those elements contribute to its meaning. If it is in a fixed form, such as a sonnet, how do the demands of that form serve to set its tone? If the form calls for repetition—of sounds, words, or entire lines—how does that repetition underscore the poem's message? If, on the other hand, the poem is in free verse—without a consistent pattern of rime or regular meter—how does this choice affect the poem's feel?

- **Take note of line breaks.** If the poem is written in free verse, pay special attention to its line breaks. Poets break their lines with care, conscious that readers pause momentarily over the last word in any line, giving that word special emphasis. Notice whether the lines tend to be broken at the ends of whole phrases and sentences or in the middle of phrases. Then ask yourself what effect is created by the poet's choice of line breaks. How does that effect contribute to the poem's meaning?

PREWRITING: DISCOVER YOUR IDEAS

Now that you have thought the poem through, it's time to let your ideas crystallize on the page (or screen). One or more of the following prewriting exercises could help you collect your thoughts.

- **Brainstorm.** With the poem in front of you, jot down or type every single thing you can think of about it. Write quickly, without worrying about the value of your thoughts; you can sort that out later. Brainstorming works best if you set a time limit of ten or fifteen minutes and force yourself to keep working until the time is up, even if you feel as though you've said it all. A new idea might surprise you after you thought you were done. A list that results from brainstorming on "Design" might look something like this:

    white spider
    heal-all/flower
    dead moth like a kite
    white = innocence?
    death/blight
    begin the morning right=oddly cheerful
    irony
    witches' broth/scary
    white = strangeness
    heal-all usually blue
    flower doesn't heal all
    design = God or nature
    design of darkness = the devil?
    maybe no design (no God?)
    God doesn't govern small things

- **Cluster.** If you are a visual thinker, you might find yourself drawn to clustering as a way to explore the relationship among your ideas. Begin by writing your subject at the center of a sheet of paper. Circle it. Then write ideas as they occur to you, drawing lines linking each new idea to ones that seem related. Here is an example of clustering on "Design."

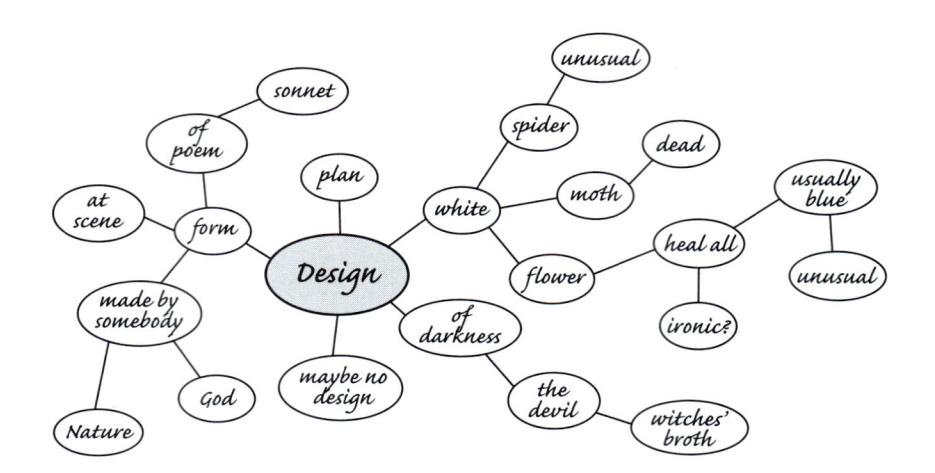

- **List.** Make a list of information that seems useful. Feel free to add notes that will help you to remember what you meant by each item. Headings can help you to organize related concepts. A list might look like this:

  <u>Odd Coincidence</u>
  white spider
  white flower (not blue,
     innocent)
  white moth (stiff, dead)
  characters of death/blight
  morning (hopeful) = ironic
  witches' broth

  <u>Questions</u>
  Accidental or by design?
  Whose design?
  Nature or God?
  Does God care?

  <u>Form of Poem</u>
  sonnet (strict, orderly)
  form of universe =
     not so orderly?

- **Freewrite.** Another approach to generating ideas is to let your thoughts pour out onto the page. To freewrite, give yourself a time limit: fifteen or twenty minutes will work well. Then write, without stopping to think, for that whole time. Keep writing. Don't worry about grammar or spelling or even logic; your task is to come up with fresh ideas that might evade you if you were writing more cautiously. Keep writing even (or especially) if you run out of ideas. New and surprising thoughts sometimes arrive when we least expect them. Here is a sample of freewriting on "Design."

  > The scene seems strange. Spiders aren't usually white, and heal-alls are supposed to be blue. Moths are white, but this one is described as being like a rigid satin cloth or a paper kite. It's dead, which is why it is rigid, but the images seem to focus on its stiffness—its deadness—in a creepy way. The poet seems surprised at all this whiteness. Whiteness usually represents innocence, but here he says the flower would ordinarily be blue and innocent, so maybe it's not innocent now? I think he's saying this is a kind of deathly pageant; he calls the three things assorted characters though a flower can't be a character. The second part of the poem is all questions, no answers. What does he mean by "design of darkness"?
  > Design seems to mean plan. It sounds like he's saying something sinister is going on. Like someone (God?) put the scene there for a purpose, maybe for him to notice. But then he seems to say no, God doesn't care about small things which maybe means he doesn't care about us either. I just noticed that this poem is (I think) a sonnet. It has rime and fourteen lines. It seems funny that a poem about there being no order to the universe is written in such a strict form.

- **Journal.** A journal of your reactions to the works you read can be an excellent place to look for raw material for more formal writing. If your instructor has assigned such a journal, page through to remind yourself of your first reactions to a poem you plan to write about.

- **Outline.** To think through your argument before you begin to flesh it out, make an outline (a list of points arranged in a logical order). Not all writers work from outlines, but some find them indispensable. Here is a sample outline.

1. Italian sonnet (define)
    two parts
    octave draws picture
    sestet asks questions
2. Rhyme
    "ite" sound stresses whiteness
3. Sonnet form = order
    poem's subject = order
    irony/no order in universe
4. Design of poem is unpredictable
    looks orderly but isn't
5. Design of universe is unpredictable

WRITE A ROUGH DRAFT

When your prewriting work has given you a sense of direction, you will be ready to begin forming your thoughts and writing a first draft of your essay. Reread the section "Develop a Literary Argument" on page 133 for help getting started.

- **Review your purpose and audience.** Begin by referring back to the exact assignment you have been given. No matter how crystal clear your prose or intriguing your ideas, an essay that fails to respond to the assignment is likely to fall flat. As you begin your first draft, consider how best to focus your essay to fulfill the instructor's requirements. Whatever the assignment, you need to keep your purpose in mind as you write. You also need to consider your audience's needs, whether that audience is your professor, your fellow students, or some hypothetical set of readers.

- **Define your thesis.** To keep you focused on the task at hand, and to signal your intentions to your reader, you will need, first of all, to come up with a thesis. Like the rest of your first draft, that thesis sentence can be rough around the edges; you can refine it later in the process. For now, though, the thesis gives you something to work toward. You need to make a decisive statement that offers an insight that isn't entirely obvious about the work under discussion. In the final paper your task will be to convince readers that your thesis is sound. Here is a working thesis sentence for an analytical essay on Frost's poem "Design."

    WORKING THESIS

    The poem "Design" both is and isn't formal.

This rough thesis defines the essay's focus—the poem's form. But the statement is still very vague. A later, sharper version will clarify the idea and show what the author means by the claim that the poem both is and isn't formal. The revision also will push this idea further by connecting the poem's form to its meaning.

    REVISED THESIS

    Although Frost's sonnet "Design" is a well-designed formal poem, the conclusions it presents are not predictable but both surprising and disturbing.

In its revised form, this thesis makes a stronger and more specific claim. Because the revision says something specific about how the poem works, it is more compelling than the vaguer original.

- **Supply evidence to prove your point.** Once you've settled on a working thesis, your next task is to decide what evidence will best prove your point. Be sure to quote from the poem to back up each point you make; there is no evidence more convincing than the words of the poem itself.
- **Organize your argument.** You will need to make clear what each bit of evidence illustrates. Connect your argument back to the thesis as often as it takes to clarify your line of reasoning for the reader.
- **Concentrate on getting your ideas onto the page.** Later you will go back and revise, making your prose clearer and more elegant. At that point, you can add information that seems to be missing and discard passages that seem beside the point. For now, though, the goal is to spell out your argument while it is clear in your mind.

checklist: Writing a Rough Draft

- ☐ What is your assignment? Does the essay fulfill it?
- ☐ Who is your audience?
- ☐ What is your thesis?
- ☐ Is your thesis thought-provoking rather than a statement of the obvious?
- ☐ Have you provided evidence to support your thesis?
- ☐ Does anything in your essay undercut your thesis?
- ☐ Have you quoted from the poem? Would more quotations strengthen your argument?
- ☐ Is your argument organized in a logical way?

REVISE YOUR DRAFT

- **Have a reader review your paper.** Once you have completed your rough draft, consider enlisting the aid of a reader, professional (a writing center tutor) or otherwise (a trusted friend). The author of the paragraph below used her instructor's comments to improve her paper's introduction.

DRAFT OF OPENING PARAGRAPH

Add a little more. Is the scene significant? How so?

Robert Frost's poem "Design" is an Italian sonnet, a form that divides its argument into two parts, an octave and a sestet. The octave, or first part of the poem, concentrates on telling the reader about a peculiar scene the poet has noticed: a white spider holding a dead moth on a white flower. The sestet, or second part of the poem, asks what the scene means. It doesn't really provide any answers.

Good start. I'm glad you're thinking about the poem's form. How does the form suit the content?

Does it hint at answers? Be more specific.

REVISED OPENING PARAGRAPH

> For Robert Frost's poem "Design," the sonnet form has at least two advantages. As in most Italian sonnets, the poem's argument falls into two parts. In the octave Frost's persona draws a still life of a spider, a flower, and a moth; then in the sestet he contemplates the meaning of his still life. The sestet focuses on a universal: the possible existence of a vindictive deity who causes the spider to catch the moth and, no doubt, also causes—when viewed anthropomorphically—other suffering.

To see this essay in its entirety, turn to page 181. (It's worth noting that while the thesis sentence often appears in an essay's first paragraph, this paper takes a different tack. The first paragraph introduces the essay's focus—the benefits of the sonnet form for this particular poem—then builds carefully toward its thesis, which appears in the last paragraph.)

- **Make your argument more specific.** Use specifics instead of generalities in describing the poem. Writing imprecisely or vaguely, favoring the abstract over the concrete, is a common problem for student writers. When discussing ideas or principles, you can communicate more fully to your reader by supplying specific examples of those ideas or principles in action, as this student did when she reworked the ending of the paragraph above.
- **Make your language fresh and accurate.** It is easy to depend on habitual expressions and to overuse a few convenient words. Mechanical language may tempt you to think of the poem in mechanical terms. Here, for instance is a plodding discussion of Frost's "Design":

DRAFT

> The symbols Frost uses in "Design" are very successful. Frost makes the spider <u>stand</u> <u>for</u> Nature. He <u>wants</u> us to see nature as blind and cruel. He also <u>employs</u> good sounds. He <u>uses</u> a lot of *i*'s because he is <u>trying</u> to make you think of falling rain.

What's wrong with this "analysis"? The underscored words are worth questioning here. While understandable, the words *employs* and *uses* seem to lead the writer to see Frost only as a conscious tool-manipulator. To be sure, Frost in a sense "uses" symbols, but did he grab hold of them and lay them into his poem? For all we know, perhaps the symbols arrived quite unbidden and used the poet. To write a good poem, Frost maintained, the poet himself has to be surprised. (How, by the way, can we hope to know what a poet *wants* to do? And there isn't much point in saying that the poet is *trying* to do something. He has already done it, if he has written a good poem.) At least it is likely that Frost didn't plan to fulfill a certain quota of *i*-sounds. Writing his poem, not by following a blueprint but probably by bringing it slowly to the surface of his mind, Frost no doubt had enough to do without trying to engineer the reactions of his possible audience. Like all true symbols, Frost's spider doesn't *stand for* anything. The writer would be closer to the truth in saying that the spider *suggests* or *reminds us* of nature or of certain forces in the natural world. (Symbols just hint; they don't indicate.)

After the student discussed the paper in a conference with her instructor, she rewrote her sentences:

REVISION

> The symbols in Frost's "Design" are highly effective. The spider, for instance, suggests the blindness and cruelty of Nature. Frost's word-sounds, too, are part of the meaning of his poem, for the *i*'s remind the reader of falling rain.

Not every reader of "Design" will hear rain falling, but the student's revision probably comes closer to describing the experience of the poem most of us have.

- **Be clear and precise.** Another very real pitfall of writing literary criticism is the temptation to write in official-sounding Critic Speak. Writers who aren't quite sure about what to say may try to compensate for this uncertainty with unnecessarily ornate sentences that don't say much of anything. Other times, they will begin a sentence and find themselves completely entangled in its structure, unable to make a perfectly sound idea clear to the reader. Should you feel yourself being tugged out to sea by an undertow of fancy language, here is a trick for getting back ashore: speak your ideas aloud, in the simplest terms possible, to a friend, or a tape recorder, or your mirror. When you've formulated your idea simply and clearly, write down your exact words. Most likely, your instructor will be grateful for the resulting clarity of expression.

checklist: Revising Your Draft

- ☐ Is your thesis clear and decisive?
- ☐ Does all your evidence advance your argument?
- ☐ Is information presented in the most logical order?
- ☐ Could your prose be clearer? More precise? More specific?
- ☐ Do transitional words and phrases signal movement from one idea to the next?
- ☐ Does your introduction draw the reader in? Does it prepare him or her for what follows?
- ☐ Does your conclusion tie up the essay's loose ends?
- ☐ Does each paragraph include a topic sentence?
- ☐ Does your title give a sense of the essay's subject?

COMMON APPROACHES TO WRITING ABOUT POETRY

Explication

In an **explication** (literally, "an unfolding"), a writer explains an entire poem in detail, unraveling its complexities. An explication, however, should not be confused with a paraphrase, which puts the poem's literal meaning into plain prose. While an explication might include some paraphrasing, it does more than simply restate. It explains a poem in great detail, showing how each part contributes to the whole. In writing an explication, keep the following tips in mind:

178   Chapter 8   Writing about a Poem

- **Start with the poem's first line, and keep working straight through to the end.** As needed, though, you can take up points out of order.
- **Read closely, addressing the poem's details.** You may choose to include allusions, the denotations or connotations of words, the possible meanings of symbols, the effects of certain sounds and rhythms and formal elements (rime schemes, for instance), the sense of any statements that contain irony, and other particulars.
- **Show how each part of the poem contributes to the meaning of the whole.** Your explication should go beyond dissecting the pieces of a poem; it should also bring them together in a way that casts light on the poem in its entirety.

Here is a successful student-authored explication of Frost's "Design." The assignment was to explain, in not more than 750 words, whatever in the poem seemed most essential.

Jasper 1

Ted Jasper
Professor Koss
English 130
21 November 2012

An Unfolding of Robert Frost's "Design"

Interesting opening. Quotes author

"I always wanted to be very observing," Robert Frost once told an audience, after reading aloud his poem "Design." Then he added, "But I have always been afraid of my own observations" (qtd. in Cook 126–27). What could

Central question raised

Frost have observed that could scare him? Let's examine the poem in question and see what we discover.

Starting with the title, "Design," any reader of this poem will find it full of meaning. As the *Merriam-Webster Dictionary* defines *design*, the word can

Defines key word. Sets up theme

denote among other things a plan, purpose, or intention ("Design"). Some arguments for the existence of God (I remember from Sunday School) are based on the "argument from design": that because the world shows a systematic order, there must be a Designer who made it. But the word *design* can also mean "a deliberate undercover project or scheme" such as we attribute to a "designing person" ("Design"). As we shall see, Frost's poem incorporates all of

Topic sentence on significance of title

these meanings. His poem raises the old philosophic question of whether there is a Designer, an evil Designer, or no Designer at all.

Begins line-by-line unfolding of meaning

Like many other sonnets, "Design" is divided into two parts. The first eight lines draw a picture centering on the spider, who at first seems almost jolly. It is *dimpled* and *fat* like a baby, or Santa Claus. The spider stands on a wildflower

Jasper 2

whose name, *heal-all*, seems ironic: a heal-all is supposed to cure any disease, but this flower has no power to restore life to the dead moth. (Later, in line ten, we learn that the heal-all used to be blue. Presumably, it has died and become bleached-looking.) In the second line we discover, too, that the spider has hold of another creature, a dead moth. We then see the moth described with an odd simile in line three: "Like a white piece of rigid satin cloth." Suddenly, the moth becomes not a creature but a piece of fabric—lifeless and dead—and yet *satin* has connotations of beauty. Satin is a luxurious material used in rich formal clothing, such as coronation gowns and brides' dresses. Additionally, there is great accuracy in the word: the smooth and slightly plush surface of satin is like the powder-smooth surface of moths' wings. But this "cloth," rigid and white, could be the lining to Dracula's coffin. *— Discusses images*

— Explores language

In the fifth line an invisible hand enters. The characters are "mixed" like ingredients in an evil potion. Some force doing the mixing is behind the scene. The characters in themselves are innocent enough, but when brought together, their whiteness and look of *rigor mortis* are overwhelming. There is something diabolical in the spider's feast. The "morning right" echoes the word *rite*, a ritual—in this case apparently a Black Mass or a Witches' Sabbath. The simile in line seven ("a flower like a froth") is more ambiguous and harder to describe. Froth is white, foamy, and delicate—something found on a brook in the woods or on a beach after a wave recedes. However, in the natural world, froth also can be ugly: the foam on a polluted stream or a rabid dog's mouth. The dualism in nature—its beauty and its horror—is there in that one simile. *— Refers to sound*

(So far,) the poem has portrayed a small, frozen scene, with the dimpled killer holding its victim as innocently as a boy holds a kite. Already, Frost has hinted that Nature may be, as Radcliffe Squires suggests, "Nothing but an ash-white plain without love or faith or hope, where ignorant appetites cross by chance" (87). Now, in the last six lines of the sonnet, Frost comes out and directly states his theme. What else could bring these deathly pale, stiff things together "but design of darkness to appall"? The question is clearly rhetorical; we are meant to answer, "Yes, there does seem to be an evil design at work here!" I take the next-to-last line to mean, "What except a design so dark and sinister that we're appalled by it?" "Appall," by the way, is the second pun in the poem: it sounds like *a pall* or shroud. (The derivation of *appall*, according to *Merriam-Webster*, is ultimately from a Latin word meaning "to be pale"— an interesting word choice for a poem full of pale white images ["Appall"].) *— Transition words*

— Quotes secondary source

— Discusses theme

— Defines key word

180   Chapter 8   Writing about a Poem

Jasper 3

Steered carries the suggestion of a steering-wheel or rudder that some pilot had to control. Like the word *brought*, it implies that some invisible force charted the paths of spider, heal-all, and moth, so that they arrived together.

Having suggested that the universe is in the hands of that sinister force (an indifferent God? Fate? the Devil?), Frost adds a note of doubt. The Bible tells us that "His eye is on the sparrow," but at the moment the poet doesn't seem sure. Maybe, he hints, when things in the universe drop below a certain size, they pass completely out of the Designer's notice. When creatures are this little, maybe God doesn't bother to govern them but just lets them run wild. And possibly the same mindless chance is all that governs human lives. And because this is even more senseless than having an angry God intent on punishing us, it is, Frost suggests, the worst suspicion of all.

Answers question raised in introduction

Conclusion

Jasper 4

Works Cited

"Appall." *Merriam-Webster Online Dictionary*. Merriam-Webster, 2012. Web. 13 November 2012.

Cook, Reginald. *Robert Frost: A Living Voice*. Amherst: U of Massachusetts P, 1974. Print.

"Design." *Merriam-Webster Online Dictionary*. Merriam-Webster, 2012. Web. 11 November 2012.

Frost, Robert. "Design." *Collected Poems, Prose, and Plays*. New York: Library of America, 1995. 275. Print.

Squires, Radcliffe. *The Major Themes of Robert Frost*. Ann Arbor: U of Michigan P, 1963. Print.

This excellent paper finds something worth unfolding in every line of Frost's poem, without seeming mechanical. Although the student proceeds sequentially through the poem from the title to the last line, he takes up some points out of order when it serves his purpose. In paragraph two, for example, he looks ahead to the poem's ending and briefly states its main theme in order to relate it to the poem's title. In the third paragraph, he explicates the poem's later image of the heal-all, relating it to the first image. He also comments on the poem's form ("Like many other sonnets"), on its similes and puns, and on its denotations and connotations.

This paper also demonstrates good use of manuscript form, following the *MLA Handbook*, 7th ed. Brief references (in parentheses) tell us where the writer found Frost's remarks and give the page number for his quotation from the book by Radcliffe Squires. At the end of the paper, a list of works cited uses abbreviations that the *MLA Handbook* recommends.

Analysis

Like a news commentator's analysis of a crisis in the Middle East or a chemist's analysis of an unknown fluid, an **analysis** separates a poem into elements as a means to understanding that subject. Usually, the writer of an analysis focuses on one particular element: "Imagery of Light and Darkness in Frost's 'Design'" or "The Character of Satan in Milton's *Paradise Lost*." To write an analysis, remember two key points:

- **Focus on a single, manageable element of a poem.** Some possible choices are tone, irony, literal meaning, imagery, figures of speech, sound, rhythm, theme, and symbolism.
- **Show how this element of the poem contributes to the meaning of the whole.** While no element of a poem exists apart from all the others, by taking a closer look at one particular aspect of the poem, you can see the whole more clearly.

The paper that follows analyzes a particularly tricky subject: the formal and technical elements of Frost's "Design." Long analyses of metrical feet, rime schemes, and indentations can make for ponderous reading, but this paper shows how formal analysis can be interesting and can cast light on a poem.

Lopez 1

Guadalupe Lopez
Professor Faber
English 210
14 October 2012

The Design of Robert Frost's "Design"

For Robert Frost's poem "Design," the sonnet form has at least two advantages. As in most Italian sonnets, the poem's argument falls into two parts. In the octave Frost's persona draws a still life of a spider, a flower, and a moth; then in the sestet he contemplates the meaning of his still life. Although the poem is perfectly formal in its shape, the ideas it presents are not predictable, but are instead both surprising and disturbing. The sestet focuses on a universal: the possible existence of a vindictive deity who causes the spider to catch the moth and, no doubt, also causes—when viewed anthropomorphically—other suffering.

Introduction gives overview of poem's form.

Thesis sentence

Topic sentence on how poem subtly makes its point

Frost's persona weaves his own little web. The unwary audience is led through the poem's argument from its opening "story" to a point at which something must be made of the story's symbolic significance. Even the rhyme scheme contributes to the poem's successful leading of the audience toward the sestet's theological questioning. The word *white* ends the first line of the sestet, and the same vowel sound is echoed in the lines that follow. All in all, half of the sonnet's lines end in the "ite" sound, as if to render significant the wh*ite*ness—the symbolic innocence—of nature's representation of a greater truth.

Topic sentence on how form relates to theme

A sonnet has a familiar design, and the poem's classical form points to the thematic concern that there seems to be an order to the universe that might be perceived by looking at even seemingly insignificant natural events. The sonnet must follow certain conventions, and nature, though not as readily apprehensible as a poetic form, is apparently governed by a set of laws. There is a ready-made irony in Frost's choosing such an order-driven form to meditate on whether or not there is any order in the universe. However, whether or not his questioning sestet is actually approaching an answer or, indeed, the answer, Frost has approached an order that seems to echo a larger order in his using the sonnet form. An approach through poetic form and substance is itself significant in Frost's own estimation, for he argues that what a poet achieves in writing poetry is "a momentary stay against confusion" (777).

Although design clearly governs in this poem—in this "thing so small"—the design is not entirely predictable. The poem does start out in the form of an Italian sonnet, relying on only two rhyming sounds. However, unlike an Italian sonnet, one of the octave's rhyming sounds—the "ite"—continues into the sestet. And additionally, "Design" ends in a couplet, much in the manner of the Shakespearean sonnet, which frequently offers, in the final couplet, a summing up of the sonnet's argument. Perhaps not only nature's "story" of the spider, the flower, and the moth but also Frost's poem itself

Conclusion

echoes the larger universe. It looks perfectly orderly until the details are given their due.

Lopez 3

Work Cited

Frost, Robert. "The Figure a Poem Makes." *Collected Poems, Prose, and Plays.* New York: Library of America, 1995. 776-78. Print.

Comparison and Contrast

The process of **comparison** and **contrast** places two poems side by side and studies their differences and similarities in order to shed light on both works. Writing an effective comparison and contrast paper involves the following steps:

- **Pair two poems with much in common.** Comparing two poems with only surface similarities can be a futile endeavor. Instead, choose two poems with enough in common that their differences take on interesting weight, for example, Robert Frost's "Design" and the following poem by Abbie Huston Evans.

Abbie Huston Evans   (1881–1983)

Wing-Spread   1938

The midge spins out to safety
Through the spider's rope;
But the moth, less lucky,
Has to grope.

Mired in glue-like cable   5
See him foundered swing
By the gap he opened
With his wing,

Dusty web enlacing
All that blue and beryl.   10
In a netted universe
Wing-spread is peril.

- **Point to further, unsuspected resemblances.** Steer clear of the obvious ("'Design' and 'Wing-Spread' are both about bugs"). The interesting resemblances take some thought to discover.
- **Show noteworthy differences.** Avoid those your reader will see without any help.
- **Carefully consider your essay's organization.** While you may be tempted to discuss first one poem and then the other, this simple structure may weaken your essay if it leads you to keep the two poems in total isolation from each other. After all, the point is to see what can be learned by comparison. There is nothing wrong in discussing all of poem A first, then discussing poem B—if in discussing B you keep

184   Chapter 8   Writing about a Poem

referring back to A. Another strategy is to do a point-by-point comparison of the two poems all the way through your paper, dealing first, perhaps, with their themes, then with their central metaphors, and finally with their respective merits.

A comparison and contrast essay is often a kind of analysis—a study of a theme common to two poems, perhaps, or of two poets' similar fondness for the myth of Eden. In some cases, though, a comparison can also involve evaluation—a judgment on the relative worth of two poems. Here, for example, is a paper that considers the merits of Abbie Huston Evans's "Wing-Spread" and Robert Frost's "Design." Through comparison and contrast, this student makes a case for his view of which poet deserves the brighter laurels.

Munjee 1

Tom Munjee
Professor Mickey
English 110
21 October 2012

"Wing-Spread" Does a Dip

Thesis sentence

Abbie Huston Evans's "Wing-Spread" is an effective short poem, but it lacks the complexity and depth of Robert Frost's "Design." These two poems were published only two years apart, and both present a murderous spider and an unlucky moth, but Frost's treatment differs from Evans's approach in at least

Argument summary

two important ways. First, Frost uses poetic language more evocatively than Evans. Second, "Design" digs more deeply into the situation to uncover a more memorable theme.

If we compare the language of the two poems, we find "Design" is full of words and phrases rich with suggestions. The language of "Wing-Spread," by

Textual evidence— contrasts diction of 2 poems

comparison, seems thinner. Frost's "dimpled spider, fat and white," for example, is certainly a more suggestive description. Actually, Evans does not describe her spider; she just says, "the spider's rope." (Evans does vividly show the spider and moth in action. In Frost's poem, they are already dead and petrified.) In "Design," the spider's dimples show that it is like a chubby little baby. This seems an odd way to look at a spider, but it is more original than Evans's conventional view (although I like her word *cable*, suggesting that the spider's web is a kind of high-tech food trap). Frost's word choice—his repetition of *white*—paints a more striking scene than Evans's slightly vague "All that blue and beryl." Except for her brief personification of the moth in the second stanza, Evans hardly uses any figures of speech, and even this one is not a clear personification— she simply gives the moth a sex by referring to it as "him." Frost's striking metaphors, similes, and even puns (*right, appall*) show him, as usual, to be a master of figures of speech. He calls the moth's wings "satin cloth" and "a paper kite"; Evans just refers in line 8 to a moth's wing. As far as the language of the two poems goes, we might as well compare a vase brimming with flowers and a single flower stuck in a vase. In fairness to Evans, I would say that her poem, while lacking complexity, still makes its point effectively. Her poem has powerful sounds: short lines with the rhyming words coming at us again and again.

In theme, however, "Wing-Spread" seems much more narrow than "Design." The first time I read Evans's poem, all I felt was: Ho hum, the moth's wings were too wide and got stuck. The second time I read it, I realized that she was saying something with a universal application. This message comes out in line 11, in "a netted universe." That metaphorical phrase is the most interesting part of her poem. *Netted* makes me imagine the universe as being full of nets rigged by someone who is fishing for us. Maybe, like Frost, Evans sees an evil plan operating. She does not, though, investigate it. She says that the midge escapes because it is tiny. On the other hand, things with wide wing-spreads get stuck. Her theme as I read it is, "Be small and inconspicuous if you want to survive," or maybe, "Isn't it too bad that in this world the big beautiful types crack up and die, while the little puny punks keep sailing?" Now, this is a valuable idea. I have often thought that very same thing myself. But Frost's closing note ("If design govern in a thing so small") is really devastating because it raises a huge uncertainty. "Wing-Spread" leaves us with not much besides a moth stuck in a web and a moral. In both language and theme, "Design" climbs to a higher altitude.

Contrasts thematic approach

Conclusion restates thesis

Works Cited

Evans, Abbie Huston. "Wing-Spread." *Literature for Life*. Ed. X. J. Kennedy, Dana Gioia, and Nina Revoyr. New York: Pearson, 2013. 183. Print.

Frost, Robert. "Design." *Collected Poems, Prose, and Plays*. New York: Library of America, 1995. 275. Print.

HOW TO QUOTE A POEM

Quoted to illustrate some point, memorable lines can enliven your paper. Carefully chosen quotations can serve to back up your thesis, or to alert your readers to a phrase or passage they may have neglected. Quoting poetry accurately, however, raises certain difficulties you don't face in quoting prose. Poets choose their line breaks with deliberation, and part of a critic's job is to take those breaks into account. Here are guidelines for respecting a poet's line breaks and for making your essay more polished in the bargain.

- **Quoting a few lines.** If you are quoting fewer than four lines of poetry, transform the passage into prose form, separating each line by a space, diagonal (/), and another space. The diagonal (/) indicates where the poet's lines begin and end. Two diagonals (//) signal a new stanza. Do not change the poet's capitalization or punctuation. Be sure to identify the line numbers you are quoting, as follows:

    The color white preoccupies Frost. The spider is "fat and white, / On a white heal-all" (1–2), and even the victim moth is pale, too.

- **Quoting four or more lines.** If you are quoting four or more lines of verse, set them off from your text, and arrange them just as they occur on the page, white space and all. Be sure to identify the lines you are quoting. In general, follow these rules:
    - Indent the quotation one inch from the left-hand margin.
    - Double-space between the quoted lines.
    - Type the poem exactly as it appears in the original. You do not need to use quotation marks.
    - If you begin the quotation in the middle of a line of verse, position the starting word about where it occurs in the poem—not at the left-hand margin.
    - If a line you are quoting runs too long to fit on one line, indent the return one-quarter inch.
    - Cite the line numbers you are quoting in parentheses.

    At the end of the poem, the poet asks what deity or fate cursed this particular mutant flower

                    with being white,
    The wayside blue and innocent heal-all?
    What brought the kindred spider to that height,
    Then steered the white moth thither in the
        night? (9-12)

- **Omitting words.** If you omit words from the lines you quote, indicate the omission with an ellipsis (. . .), as in the following example:

    The color white preoccupies Frost in his description of the spider "fat and white, / On a white heal-all . . . / Like a white piece of rigid satin cloth" (1–3).

- **Quoting only a brief phrase.** There's no need for an ellipsis if it is obvious that only a phrase is being quoted.

    The speaker says that he "found a dimpled spider," and he goes on to portray it as a kite-flying boy.

- **Omitting full lines of verse.** If you leave out lines of verse, indicate the omission by spaced periods about the length of a line of the poem you are quoting.

> Maybe, she hints, when things in the universe drop below a certain size,
> they pass completely out of the Designer's notice:
>> The midge spins out to safety
>> Through the spider's rope;
>> . . . .
>> In a netted universe
>> Wing-spread is peril. (1-2, 11-12)

One last note: often a paper on a short poem will include the whole text of the poem at its beginning, with the lines numbered so that your reader can refer to it with ease. Ask your instructor whether he or she prefers the full text to be quoted this way.

Topics for Writing

Topics for Writing Brief Papers (250–500 words)

1. Write a concise *explication* of a short poem of your choice. Concentrate on those facets of the poem that you think most need explaining.
2. Write an *analysis* of a short poem, focusing on how a single key element shapes its meaning. Some possible topics are:
   - Tone in E. E. Cummings's "Buffalo Bill's"
   - Rime and meter in Theodore Roethke's "My Papa's Waltz"
   - Imagery in Thomas Hardy's "The Darkling Thrush"
   - Kinds of irony in Robert Frost's "The Road Not Taken"

   (To locate any of these poems, see the Index of Authors and Titles.)
3. Select a poem in which the main speaker is a character who for any reason interests you. You might consider, for instance, Charles Bukowski's "Dostoevsky," T. S. Eliot's "The Love Song of J. Alfred Prufrock," Rhina Espaillat's "Bilingual/ *Bilingüe*," or Andrew Marvell's "To His Coy Mistress." Then write a brief profile of this character, drawing only on what the poem tells you (or reveals). What is the character's approximate age? Situation in life? Attitude toward self? Attitude toward others? General personality? Do you find this character admirable?
4. Choose a brief poem that you find difficult. Write an essay in which you begin by listing the points in the poem that strike you as most impenetrable. Next, reread the poem at least twice. In the essay's second half, describe how further readings changed your experience of the poem.
5. Although each of these poems tells a story, what happens in the poem isn't necessarily obvious: Elizabeth Bishop's "The Fish," E. E. Cummings's "anyone lived in a pretty how town," T. S. Eliot's "The Love Song of J. Alfred Prufrock," Robert Frost's "Mending Wall," Robert Hayden's "The Whipping." Choose one of these poems, and in a paragraph sum up what you think happens in it. Then in a second

paragraph, ask yourself: what, *besides* the element of story, did you consider in order to understand the poem?
6. Imagine a reader who categorically dislikes poetry. Choose a poem for that person to read and, addressing your skeptical reader, explain the ways in which this particular poem rewards a careful reader.

Topics for Writing More Extended Papers (600–1,000 words)

1. Perform a line-by-line explication of a brief poem of your choice. Imagine that your audience is unfamiliar with the poem and needs your assistance in interpreting it.
2. Explicate a passage from a longer poem. Choose a passage that is, in your opinion, central to the poem's meaning.
3. Compare and contrast any two poems that treat a similar theme. Let your comparison bring you to an evaluation of the poems. Which is the stronger, more satisfying one?
4. Write a comparison and contrast essay on any two or more poems by a single poet. Look for two poems that share a characteristic thematic concern. (This book contains "Poet in Depth" collections on Gwendolyn Brooks, Emily Dickinson, Robert Frost, Langston Hughes, Wilfred Owen, and William Shakespeare; in addition, there are multiple poems by many authors.) Here are possible topics:

    - Emily Dickinson's treatment of individuality and conformity
    - Nature in the poems of Robert Frost
    - Wilfred Owen on the nobility of war
    - Romantic love in the sonnets of William Shakespeare

5. Evaluate Robert Frost's finished poem "Design" by comparing it with this early draft of the poem (sent to a correspondent in 1912, ten years before the publication of "Design"). In what respects is the finished poem superior?

In White

A dented spider like a snow drop white
On a white Heal-all, holding up a moth
Like a white piece of lifeless satin cloth—
Saw ever curious eye so strange a sight?
Portent in little, assorted death and blight   5
Like the ingredients of a witches' broth?
The beady spider, the flower like a froth,

And the moth carried like a paper kite.
What had that flower to do with being white,
The blue Brunella every child's delight.   10
What brought the kindred spider to that height?
(Make we no thesis of the miller's plight.)
What but design of darkness and of night?
Design, design! Do I use the word aright?

6. Terry Ehret of Santa Rosa Junior College developed the following assignment:

   Compose your own answer to the question "What is poetry?" You may want to devise original metaphor(s) to define poetry and then develop your essay with examples and explanations. Select at least one poem from the anthology to illustrate your definition.

Topics for Writing Long Papers (1,500 words or more)

1. Read five or six poems by one author. Start with a poet featured in this book, then find additional poems at the library or on the Internet. Write an analysis of a single element of that poet's work—for example, theme, imagery, diction, or form.
2. Write a line-by-line explication of a poem rich in matters to explain or of a longer poem that offers ample difficulty. Even a short, apparently simple poem such as Robert Frost's "Stopping by Woods on a Snowy Evening" can provide more than enough material to explicate thoughtfully in a longer paper.
3. Write an analysis of a certain theme (or other element) that you find in the work of two or more poets. It is probable that in your conclusion you will want to set the poets' works side by side, comparing or contrasting them, and perhaps making some evaluation. Here are sample topics to consider:
   - Langston Hughes and Gwendolyn Brooks as prophets of social change
   - What it is to be a woman: the special knowledge of Sylvia Plath and Anne Sexton
   - The complex relations between fathers and children in the poetry of Robert Hayden, Rhina Espaillat, Theodore Roethke, and Diane Thiel
   - The view of romantic love in the poetry of Anne Bradstreet and Kim Addonizio
4. Review an entire poetry collection by a poet featured in this book. You will need to communicate to your reader a sense of the work's style and thematic preoccupations. Finally, make a value judgment about the work's quality.

9 WRITING ABOUT A PLAY

*The play was a great success,
but the audience was a total failure.*

—OSCAR WILDE

Writing about a play you've read is similar, in many ways, to writing about poetry or fiction. If your subject is a play you have actually seen performed, however, some differences will quickly become apparent. Although, like a story or a poem, a play in print is usually the work of a single author, a play on stage may be the joint effort of seventy or eighty people—actors, director, costumers, set designers, and technicians. Though a play on the page stays fixed and changeless, a play in performance changes in many details from season to season—and even from night to night.

Later in this chapter you will find advice on reviewing a performance of a play, as you might do for a class assignment or for publication in a campus newspaper. In a literature course, though, you will probably write about the plays you quietly read and behold only in the theater of your mind.

READ CRITICALLY

- **Read the whole play—not just the dialogue, but also everything in italics, including stage directions and descriptions of settings.** The meaning of a scene, or even of an entire play, may depend on the tone of voice in which an actor is supposed to deliver a significant line. At the end of *A Doll's House*, for example, we need to pay attention to *how* Helmer's last line is spoken—"*A hope flashes across his mind*"—if we are to understand that Nora ignores his last desperate hope for reconciliation when she closes the door. The meaning of a line may depend upon the actions described in the stage directions. If Nora did not leave the house or close the door, but hesitated at Helmer's last line, the meaning of the play would be slightly different.

- **Highlight key passages and take notes as you read.** Later you will want to quote or refer to important moments in the play, and marking those moments will simplify your job.

> Mrs. Peters (*to the other woman*): Oh, her fruit; it did freeze. (*To the County Attorney*) She worried about that when it turned so cold. She said the fire'd go out and her jars would break.
>
> Sheriff: Well, can you beat the women! Held for murder and worryin' about her preserves. — *Both men are insulting toward Mrs. Wright.*
>
> County Attorney: I guess before we're through she may have something more serious than preserves to worry about. — *He thinks he's being kind.*
>
> Hale: Well, women are used to worrying over (trifles). — *Is housework really insignificant?*
>
> (*The two women move a little closer together.*) — *The women side with each other.*
>
> County Attorney (*with the (gallantry) of a young politician*): And yet, for all their worries, what would we do without the ladies? (*The women do not unbend.*) He goes to the sink, takes a dipperful of water from the pail and pouring it into a basin, washes his hands. Starts to wipe them on the roller towel, turns it for a cleaner place.) Dirty towels! (*Kicks his foot against the pans under the sink.*) Not much of a housekeeper, would you say, ladies? — *Courtesy toward women, but condescending. The two women aren't buying it.*
>
> Mrs. Hale ((stiffly):) There's a great deal of work to be done on a farm. — *She holds back, but she's mad.* — *I don't like this guy!*

Small, insignificant things or not?

Play's title. Significant word? The men miss the "clues"—too trifling.

- **If your subject is a play in verse**—such as those by Sophocles or Shakespeare—**keep track of act, scene, and line numbers as you take notes.** This will help you to easily relocate any text you want to refer to or quote.

> Iago's hypocrisy is apparent in his speech defending his good name (3.3.168–74).

COMMON APPROACHES TO WRITING ABOUT DRAMA

The methods commonly used to write about fiction and poetry—for example, explication, analysis, and comparison and contrast—are all well suited to writing about drama. These methods are discussed in depth in Chapters 7 and 8. Here are suggestions for using these methods to write about plays.

Explication

A whole play is too much to cover in an ordinary **explication**, a line-by-line unfolding of meaning in a literary work. In drama, explication is best suited to brief passages—a key soliloquy, for example, or a moment of dialogue that lays bare the play's theme. Closely examining a critical moment in a play can shed light on the play in its entirety. To be successful, an explication needs to concentrate on a passage probably not much more than 20 lines long.

Analysis

A separation of a literary work into elements, **analysis** is a very useful method for writing about drama. To write an analysis, choose a single element in a play—for example, animal imagery in speeches from *Othello*, or the theme of fragility in *The Glass Menagerie*. Plays certainly offer many choices of elements for analysis: characters, themes, tone, irony, imagery, figures of speech, and symbol, for example. Keep in mind, though, that not all plays contain the same elements you would find in poetry or fiction. Few plays have a narrator, and in most cases the point of view is that of the audience, which perceives the events not through a narrator's eyes but through its own. And while we might analyze a short story's all-pervading style, a play might contain as many styles as there are speaking characters. As for traditional poetic devices such as metaphor and metrical pattern, they may be found in plays such as *Othello*, but not in most contemporary plays, in which the dialogue tends to sound like ordinary conversation.

Comparison and Contrast

The method of **comparison** and **contrast** involves setting two plays side by side and pointing out their similarities and differences. Because plays are complicated entities, you need to choose a narrow focus, or you will find yourself overwhelmed. A profound topic—"The Self-Deception of Othello and Oedipus"—might do for a three-hundred-page dissertation, but an essay of a mere thousand words could never do it justice. A large but finite topic—say, attitudes toward marriage in *A Doll's House* and *Trifles*—would best suit a long term paper. To apply this method to a shorter term paper, you might compare and contrast a certain aspect of personality in two characters within the same play—for example, Walter's and Beneatha's dreams in *A Raisin in the Sun*.

A Drama Review

Writing a **play review**, a brief critical account of an actual performance, involves going out on a limb and making an evaluation. It also can mean assessing various aspects of the production, including the acting, direction, sets, costumes, lighting, and possibly even the play itself. While reviews can be challenging to write, many students find them more stimulating—even more fun—than most writing assignments. There is no better way to understand and appreciate drama than by seeing live theater. Here are tips for writing a review.

- **Clarify what you are evaluating.** Is it the play's script, or the performance? If the latter, are you concentrating on the performance in its entirety, or on certain elements, such as the acting or the direction? If the play is a classic one, the more urgent task for the reviewer will be not to evaluate the playwright's work but to comment on the success of the actors', director's, and production crew's particular interpretation of it. If the play is newer and less well established, you may profitably evaluate the script itself.

- **If the play itself is your subject, be aware of the conventions within which the playwright is working.** Consider how the play itself asks to be judged. Does it belong to a particular type of drama? It might be a farce, a comedy of manners, or a melodrama (a piece in which suspense and physical action are the prime ingredients). Remember that theaters, such as the classical Greek theater of Sophocles, impose conventions. Do not condemn *Oedipus the King* as one spectator did: "That damned chorus keeps sticking their noses in!" Do not complain that Hamlet utters soliloquies. Do not dismiss *Sweeney Todd* on the grounds that real people don't keep suddenly bursting into song. Judge how well a play fulfills its own conventions. Ask yourself whether it delivers on the expectations it sets up. If a tragedy wants you to feel for the protagonist while also approving the rightness of his downfall, decide whether it has achieved those goals, and if not, why not.

- **Don't simply sneer or gush; give reasons for your opinions.** Ground your praise or criticism of a production in specifics. Incidentally, harsh evaluations can tempt a reviewer to flashes of wit. One celebrated flash was Eugene Field's observation of an actor in a production of *King Lear*, that "he played the king as though he were in constant fear that someone else was about to play the ace." The comment isn't merely nasty; it implies that Field had closely watched the actor's performance and had discerned what was wrong with it.

- **Early in the review, provide the basic facts.** Give the play's title and author, the theatrical company producing it, and the theater in which it is performed.

- **Give the names of actors in lead roles, and evaluate their performances.** How well cast do the leads seem? If an actor stands out—for good or ill—in a supporting role, he or she may deserve a mention as well.

- **Provide a brief plot summary.** Your reader may be unacquainted with the play, and will certainly want a general sense of what it is about. Out of consideration to the reader, however, it is best not to reveal any plot surprises, unless the play is a classic one with an ending likely to be common knowledge.

- **If the play is unfamiliar, summarize its theme.** This exercise will not only help your reader understand your review but probably sharpen your analysis.

- **For a well-known play, evaluate the director's approach to familiar material.** Is the production exactly what you'd expect, or are there any fresh and apparently original innovations? If a production is unusual, does it achieve newness by violating the play? The director of one college production of *Othello* emphasized the play's being partly set in Venice by staging it in the campus swimming pool, with actors floating on barges and a homemade gondola—a fresh, but not entirely successful, innovation.

- **Comment on the director's work.** Can you discern the director's approach to the play? Do the actors hurry their lines or speak too slowly? Do they speak and gesture naturally, or in an awkward, stylized manner? Are these touches effective or distracting?

- **Pay attention to costumes, sets, and lighting.** Though such matters may seem small, they have an effect on the play's overall tone.
- **Finally, to prepare yourself, read a few professional play reviews.** Reviews appear regularly in magazines such as the *New Yorker, Time,* the *New Criterion,* and *American Theatre,* and also on the entertainment pages of most metropolitan newspapers. Newspaper reviews can often be accessed online; for example, *New York Times* reviews may be found at <http://theater.nytimes.com.>

Here is a good, concise review of an amateur production of *Trifles,* as it might be written for a college newspaper or as a course assignment.

Trifles Scores Mixed Success in

Monday Players' Production

Opening paragraph gives information on play and production

Women have come a long way since 1916. At least, that impression was conveyed yesterday when the Monday Players presented Susan Glaspell's classic one-act play *Trifles* in Alpaugh Theater.

At first, in Glaspell's taut story of two subjugated farm women who figure out why a fellow farm woman strangled her husband, actors Lloyd Fox and Cal Federicci get to strut around. As a small-town sheriff and a county attorney, they lord it over the womenfolk, making sexist remarks about women in general. Fox and Federicci obviously enjoy themselves as the pompous types that Glaspell means them to be.

Evaluates performances

But of course it is the women with their keen eyes for small details who prove the superior detectives. In the demanding roles of the two Nebraska Miss Marples, Kathy Betts and Ruth Fine cope as best they can with what is asked of them. Fine is especially convincing. As Mrs. Hale, a friend of the wife accused of the murder, she projects a growing sense of independence. Visibly smarting under the verbal lashes of the menfolk, she seems to straighten her spine inch by inch as the play goes on.

Analyzes direction

Unluckily for Betts, director Alvin Klein seems determined to view Mrs. Peters as a comedian. Though Glaspell's stage directions call the woman "nervous," I doubt she is supposed to be quite so fidgety as Betts makes her. Betts vibrates like a tuning fork every time a new clue turns up, and when she is obliged to smell a dead canary bird (another clue), you would think she was whiffing a dead hippopotamus. Mrs. Peters, whose sad past includes a lost baby and a kitten some maniac chopped up with a hatchet, is no figure of fun to my mind. Played for laughs, her character fails to grow visibly on stage, as Fine makes Mrs. Hale grow.

Klein, be it said in his favor, makes the quiet action proceed at a brisk pace. Feminists in the audience must have been a little embarrassed, though, by his having Betts and Fine deliver every speech defending women in an extra-loud voice. After all, Glaspell makes her points clearly enough just by showing us what she shows. Not everything is overstated, however. As a farmer who found the murder victim, Ron Valdez acts his part with quiet authority. *Further elaborates on stage direction*

Despite flaws in its direction, this powerful play still spellbinds an audience. Anna Winterbright's set, seen last week as a background for *Dracula* and just slightly touched up, provides appropriate gloom. *Overall evaluation*

HOW TO QUOTE A PLAY

The guidelines for quoting prose or poetry generally apply to quoting from a play. Plays present certain challenges of their own, however. When you quote an extended section of a play or dialogue that involves more than one character, use the following MLA format to set the passage off from the body of your paper:

- Indent one inch.
- Type the character's name in all capitals, followed by a period.
- If a speech runs for more than a single line, indent any additional lines one-quarter inch.
- Provide a citation reference:

    If the play is written in prose, provide a page number.

    If the play is written in verse, provide the act, scene, and line numbers.

Here is an example of that format:

> The men never find a motive for the murder because, ironically, they consider all the real clues "trifles" that don't warrant their attention:
>
>> SHERIFF. Well, can you beat the women! Held for murder and
>> worryin' about her preserves.
>> COUNTY ATTORNEY. I guess before we're through she may have
>> something more serious than preserves to worry about.
>> HALE. Well, women are used to worrying over trifles. (91)

When you are quoting a verse play, be careful to respect the line breaks. For citation references, you should provide the act, scene, and line numbers, so that your reader will be able to find the quotation in any edition of the play. A quotation from a verse play should look like this:

Even before her death, Othello will not confront Desdemona with his specific suspicions:

> OTHELLO. Think on thy sins.
> DESDEMONA. They are loves I bear to you.
> OTHELLO. Ay, and for that thou diest.
> DESDEMONA. That death's unnatural that kills for loving.
>   Alas, why gnaw you so your nether lip?
>   Some bloody passion shakes your very frame.
>   These are portents; but yet I hope, I hope,
>   They do not point on me. (5.2.42-48)

Topics for Writing

Topics for Writing Brief Papers (250–500 words)

1. Analyze a key character from any play in this book. Some choices might be Tom Wingfield in *The Glass Menagerie*, Torvald Helmer in *A Doll's House*, and Walter in *A Raisin in the Sun*. What motivates that character? Point to specific moments in the play to make your case.
2. When the curtain comes down on the conclusion of some plays, the audience is left to decide exactly what finally happened. In a short informal essay, state your interpretation of the conclusion of *The Glass Menagerie*. Don't just give a plot summary; tell what you think the conclusion means.
3. Sum up the main suggestions you find in one of these meaningful objects (or actions): the handkerchief in *Othello*; the Christmas tree in *A Doll's House* (or Nora's doing a wild tarantella); Laura's collection of figurines in *The Glass Menagerie*.
4. Attend a play and write a review. In an assignment this brief, you will need to concentrate your remarks on either the performance or the script itself. Be sure to back up your opinions with specific observations.

Topics for Writing More Extended Papers (600–1,000 words)

1. From a play you have enjoyed, choose a passage that strikes you as difficult and worth reading closely. Try to pick a passage not longer than about 20 lines. Explicate it—give it a close, sentence-by-sentence reading—and explain how this small part of the play relates to the whole. For instance, any of the following passages might be considered memorable (and essential to their plays):
   - Othello's soliloquy beginning "It is the cause, it is the cause, my soul" (*Othello*, 5.2.1–22).
   - Creon's speech beginning "She has much to learn" (*Antigonê*, 2.76–92).
   - Oedipus to Teiresias, speech beginning "Wealth, power, craft of statemanship!" (*Oedipus the King*, 1.163–86).
   - Nora to Mrs. Linde, speech beginning "Yes, someday, maybe, in many years when I am not as pretty as I am now . . ." (*A Doll's House*, page 1156).

2. Analyze the complexities and contradictions to be found in a well-rounded character from a play of your choice. A good subject might be Othello, Nora Helmer (in *A Doll's House*), Walter (in *A Raisin in the Sun*), or Tom Wingfield (in *The Glass Menagerie*).
3. Take just a single line or sentence from a play, one that stands out for some reason as greatly important. Perhaps it states a theme, reveals a character, or serves as a crisis (or turning point). Write an essay demonstrating its importance—how it functions, why it is necessary. Two possible lines are:
   - Iago to Roderigo: "I am not what I am" (*Othello*, 1.1.67).
   - Amanda to Tom: "You live in a dream; you manufacture illusions!" (*The Glass Menagerie*, Scene vii).
4. Write an analysis essay in which you single out an element of a play for examination—character, plot, setting, theme, dramatic irony, tone, language, symbolism, conventions, or any other element. Try to relate this element to the play as a whole. Sample topics: "Imagery of Poison in *Othello*," "Irony in *Antigone*," "Williams's Use of Magic-Lantern Slides in *The Glass Menagerie*."
5. How would you stage an updated production of a play by Shakespeare, Sophocles, or Ibsen, transplanting it to our time? Choose a play, and describe the challenges and difficulties of this endeavor. How would you overcome them—or, if they cannot be overcome, why not?

Topics for Writing Long Papers (1,500 words or more)

1. Choose a play from this book that you admire and read a second play by the same author. Compare and contrast the two plays with attention to a single element—a theme they have in common, or a particular kind of imagery, for example.
2. Read *Othello* and view a movie version of the play. You might choose Oliver Parker's 1995 take on the play with Laurence Fishburne and Kenneth Branagh, or even *O* (2001), an updated version that has a prep school as its setting and a basketball star as its protagonist. Review the movie. What does it manage to convey of the original? What gets lost in the translation?
3. Attend a play and write an in-depth review, taking into account many elements of the drama: acting, direction, staging, costumes, lighting, and—if the work is relatively new and not a classic—the play itself.
4. Have you ever taken part in a dramatic production, either as an actor or a member of the crew? What did the experience teach you about the nature of drama and about what makes a play effective?
5. Write a one-act play of your own, featuring a minor character from one of the plays you have read for class. Think about what motivates that character, and let the play's central conflict grow from his or her preoccupations.

10 WRITING ABOUT AN ESSAY

We tell ourselves stories in order to live.

—JOAN DIDION

Writing about an essay is similar in some ways to writing about a story. In both cases, you are responding to a short prose piece and considering elements such as voice, style, setting, and theme. But there is a significant difference: short stories, no matter how much they might be inspired by real life, are classified as "fiction," while essays, no matter how much they incorporate elements of story-telling, are considered "fact." Although the essay writer may use tools from the fiction writer's toolbox (such as symbol, metaphor, or dialogue), he or she addresses the reader directly and generally makes an argument in a more straightforward fashion.

Their tendency to address the reader directly does not mean that essays are always easy to understand, nor does it suggest that a writer's words should always be taken at face value. Essayists—like the writers of stories, poems, and plays—might use irony, or humor, or imagery you have to decipher. But the short story and the essay differ in a more fundamental way: a fiction writer is free to create a private world out of the imagination, but an essayist, no matter how personal he or she might be in style or treatment, must ultimately appeal to the reader's sense of a common world of shared reality. A good essay may well expand our notion of reality, but it cannot afford to discard it.

The essay's reliance on a shared sense of reality between the author and the reader may make essays easier to write about than fiction or poetry. Writing a paper on an essay can provide an opportunity to discuss real-world issues as well as analyze the work itself. Yet in writing such a paper you will discover that the process of writing about an essay is largely the same as for writing about other genres.

READ ACTIVELY

- **Read the essay at least twice.** As with a short story or poem, you should read an essay more than once. Read it first to get a general sense of what the writer is saying and what the argument is. You may have an initial reaction of agreement, disagreement, or befuddlement—and that's fine. Just read it straight through the first time. The second time you read, pay closer attention to how the writer tries to bring you around to his or her point of view.

- **Highlight and take notes as you read.** You should also highlight key passages or make notes in the margins as you read, especially the second time through. Pay special attention to the parts where you have a strong reaction, either positive or negative. They may give you a starting point for coming up with a paper topic.

THINK ABOUT THE ESSAY

When you have read the essay twice, you can begin to process your thoughts and reactions to it. Consider the following:

- **Identify what type of essay it is.** How would you categorize the essay? Is it narrative, descriptive, expository, or argumentative? Does it have elements of more than one essay type?

- **Look for the theme.** What is the essay's central meaning or point? Is it stated directly? If not, how does it reveal itself?

- **Identify the author's rhetorical strategy.** Does the author appeal mostly to logic, emotion, or personal credibility? Do you find yourself convinced?

- **Is there a central argument?** What kind of evidence does the writer present to support the point he or she is making? Do you find the argument persuasive? Why or why not?

- **Think about voice and tone.** How would you characterize the author's voice? What is the author's attitude toward his or her subject? Is the tone serious or amusing, formal or casual, confrontational or conciliatory?

- **Think about style.** Consider sentence structure and length, use of imagery, and the overall organization and structure. How do they contribute to the tone of the essay—and to the writer's central argument? Does the author use any rhetorical devices such as analogy, hyperbole, or irony to strengthen his or her case?

PREWRITING: DISCOVER AND SHAPE YOUR IDEAS

The process of preparing to write about an essay is the same as it is for thinking about stories, poems, or plays. (For a detailed discussion of this process, refer to Chapter 6, "Writing About Literature," or Chapter 7, "Writing About a Story.") Here are two points to keep in mind when writing about nonfiction:

- **The fact that an essay has a clearly stated argument does not mean you have to agree with it.** Sometimes students feel they can't respond to a clearly articulated argument. But it's all right if you disagree with it. Because the writer usually lays out evidence to support his or her opinion, you have a good roadmap for providing other evidence to counter that opinion. Alternatively, you might agree with a writer's conclusion, but think that he or she used weak evidence to support it. In that case, you might try to make a better argument.
- **Essays focus explicitly on things in the real world and lend themselves to discussions about issues.** Essays often address issues we share. They might be deeply personal concerns, such as family relationships, or broader social or political issues, such as race or war. Often they are issues about which many people disagree. But because essays try to influence thought on real-life matters, they need to establish a common ground of shared reality with the reader. For this reason, essays are often perfect starting points to talk about those issues in your own way.

COMMON APPROACHES TO WRITING ABOUT ESSAYS

The methods discussed in earlier chapters for writing about fiction, poetry, and drama—including explication, analysis, comparison and contrast, and response—are also well suited to writing about essays. Here are suggestions for using these methods to write about essays in particular.

Explication

A thorough explication of an entire essay—like a thorough explication of a whole story—is a better subject for a term paper than for a short assignment. Explication is probably best suited to a short passage or section of an essay: for example, the opening or closing paragraph, a key description or argument, or the statement of the theme. Sometimes, when the theme of an essay is stated explicitly, it is most useful to focus on a passage that demonstrates or argues for the theme, rather than one that directly states it.

Analysis

An analysis is the examination of a single element in a piece in order to better understand the entire work. Such elements might include voice, tone, style, setting, theme, or structure. Because essays are often straightforward in making their arguments, it is especially useful to consider the elements they employ to further those arguments. How effective are they? How does the use of a particular structure, or the adoption of a particular voice and tone, help convey the author's points? Topics for analysis might include the sensory descriptions of heat and space in Joan Didion's "On Morality," the use of humor in Annie Dillard's "American Childhood" or Amy Tan's "Mother Tongue," and the stylistic choice of rhetorical devices in Martin Luther King's "Letter from Birmingham Jail." You might also examine how the setting of King's or Didion's essay provides credibility to its argument.

Many essays include literary elements such as symbols, metaphors, or allusions. In "Lovesickness," Cynthia Ozick compares falling in love to a magic "spell" and a "possession" by a dybbuk (an evil spirit in Jewish folklore). Likewise, Ozick uses allusions such as a "Cheshire-cat smile" and a long reference to the love affair between the Romantic poet Lord Bryon and the aristocratic Lady Caroline Lamb. You could easily analyze Ozick's allusion to Byron and Lamb to show how it illuminates the author's own emotional situation. Essays that use rhetorical devices such as analogies or repetition include both King's essay and Didion's. And certainly an essay's theme is a good topic for analysis, especially when—as in John Muir's "A Wind Storm in the Forests"—the theme is not explicitly stated.

Comparison and Contrast

Comparing and contrasting involves selecting two works and pointing out their similarities and differences. As in the case of a comparison and contrast paper written about two stories, this method works best with essays when you:

- **Pick two essays with something significant in common—but also with significant differences.** This will make for a cohesive paper that also has some tension and spark. For example, you might contrast views of "right" and "wrong" in Joan Didion's "On Morality" and Martin Luther King's "Letter from Birmingham Jail." Another topic might be the role of language in Amy Tan's "Mother Tongue" and Frederick Douglass's "Learning to Read and Write."
- **Choose a focus.** Don't just compare two essays; narrow the focus down to a particular element of those essays—for example, theme or style. Otherwise, your paper might read like a list. One topic might be civil disobedience as described and applied in King's "Letter from Birmingham Jail" and Henry David Thoreau's "Civil Disobedience." Another might be the writer's relationship with his parent in Raymond Carver's "My Father's Life" and Annie Dillard's "An American Childhood."
- **Pick essays that interest you.** You are most likely to write a lively, well-thought-out paper if you are engaged by the topic, or if it relates to something in your daily world or personal life.
- **Consider comparing and contrasting elements within a single essay.** You might, for example, analyze the survival strategies of Brent Staples and his sister in Staples's "The Runaway Son," or attitudes toward exposing children to the fact of death in Elizabeth Kübler Ross's "On the Fear of Death," or different beliefs about the value of wild places in Wallace Stegner's "Wilderness Letter."

Response Paper

Because essays generally try to convince the reader of something, they are particularly good subjects for response papers. The response paper gives you the opportunity to explore your thoughts and reactions—both to the essay itself and to the larger issues it addresses. You can make connections between the points of the essay and events in your own life or in the larger world. In a response paper to Tan's "Mother Tongue," for example, you might discuss the ways that language has shaped your own identity and your relationship with your family. In a response paper to Didion's "On Morality" or King's "Letter from Birmingham Jail"—or both—you might discuss your own views about the benefits or drawbacks of acting out of moral conviction. When you write a response paper in reaction to an essay, keep these things in mind:

- **Personal writing does not mean disorganized writing.** Don't gush or meander. Pick one or two important aspects of the essay (theme, voice, rhetorical appeal) and focus on them. Have a main idea or theme in your paper, and carefully choose points to support it. Be clear and organized in what you want to say. Remember, now *you* are trying to convince the reader of something.
- **Try to understand and explain your reaction.** It's not enough just to state a random response. "I didn't like Amy Tan's mother much" is not a helpful response unless you explain something of what lies behind your opinion. Your reasons may not be logical; they may be mostly emotional, but you need to share them. Figure out why you felt the way you did, then justify or explain your position.
- **Refer to the text in your paper.** Provide quotations and specific details from the text where relevant.

Topics for Writing

Topics for Writing Brief Papers (250–500 words)

1. Explicate the opening paragraph or the first few lines of an essay. Show how the opening prepares the reader for what will follow. Alternatively, explicate the final paragraph of the essay. How does the ending relate to the essay's overall theme?
2. Choose a key passage or paragraph of an essay. As closely as the word count allows, explicate that passage and explain why it strikes you as an important moment in the essay.
3. Select an essay that features a distinctive voice, tone, or style. Write a concise yet thorough analysis of how these elements either complement or detract from the writer's statement of theme.
4. Choose one element of the author's argument—a particular bit of evidence, an example—and explain why that element does not actually help the author's case.
5. Choose an essay whose central theme or narrative reminds you of something in your own life. Describe how the essay gave you a different perspective on your own personal experience.
6. Cite a statement in an essay that you find particularly brilliant or hopelessly mistaken, and explain your reaction. Support your point of view with logic and examples.

Topics for Writing More Extended Papers (600–1,000 words)

1. Write an analysis of an essay, focusing on a single element such as voice, tone, style, structure, or theme.
2. Write a thorough explication of a short passage in an essay you admire. Pick a crucial passage of narrative or description, or a passage that directly deals with the essay's theme.
3. Write an analysis of an essay in which the author experiences a moment of epiphany or has a revelation of some sort. Describe the nature of this change or realization. How is the reader prepared for it? What effect does this moment

have on the author's life? Possible choices include Judith Ortiz Cofer's "I Fell in Love, or My Hormones Awakened," James Baldwin's "Notes of a Native Son," and George Orwell's "Shooting an Elephant."
4. Write a comparison and contrast paper about a single essay. Pick an essay that describes two sides of an argument, or two people who respond to situations in very different ways. An example might be the differing views of wilderness laid out in Wallace Stegner's "Wilderness Essay."
5. Choose an essay with a clear theme and set of arguments. Write an essay making the case for the other side.

Topics for Writing Long Papers (1,500 words or more)

1. Compare and contrast two essays whose authors address a similar theme. How do the two essays treat this theme? How might the authors' positions be influenced by their cultural and political contexts? Which treatment of the theme do you find more convincing, and why?
2. Select an author you admire and read two or three essays by that author. Now concentrate on an element treated similarly in all the pieces, and write an analysis of the author's work as exemplified by the essays you chose.
3. Choose an essay that takes on a large theme such as race, the environment, civil liberties, sexism, or morality. Write an essay discussing how and why the theme and the arguments in the essay are still relevant today. Possible essay choices include James Baldwin's "Notes of a Native Son," Joan Didion's "On Morality," Amy Tan's "Mother Tongue," and Wallace Stegner's "Wilderness Letter."
4. Write an argumentative essay addressing a current issue in daily life. Pick a topic that's important to you. Write to a general audience whom you are trying to bring around to your point of view.
5. Write about an untruth, an undiscussed truth, or a secret kept by yourself, your family, or your community. (Think of Maxine Hong Kingston's "No Name Woman" or Brent Staples's "The Runaway Son.") Why is it so vital to maintain this secret or untruth? What is at stake for the person or people involved? What does the maintaining of this secret or untruth reveal about the people who maintain it?
6. Do you live or have you grown up in more than one culture? (We mean the term "culture" to refer to broad categories such as nation, region, religion, and race as well as more specific categories such as sports fanatic, comic book collector, classical music fan, and show dog enthusiast.) How have you negotiated the cultures? How are the cultures different? In which one(s) do you feel more comfortable? What do you like and dislike about the cultures? How does language play a role in your negotiating the cultures? Write an essay addressing these topics.

11 WRITING A RESEARCH PAPER

A writer is a person for whom writing is more difficult than it is for other people.

—THOMAS MANN

Oh no! You have been assigned a research paper, and every time you even think about starting it, your spirits sink and your blood pressure rises. You really liked the story by Ernest Hemingway, but when you entered his name in a search of the college library catalogue it listed 135 books about him. Time to switch authors, you decide. How about Emily Dickinson? She was fun to talk about in class, but when you Google her name, the computer states that there are over 8.4 million entries. What should you do? The paper is due in two weeks, not twenty years. Why would an otherwise very nice instructor put you through this mental trauma?

Why is it worthwhile to write a research paper? (Apart from the fact that you want a passing grade in the class, that is.) While you can learn much by exploring your own responses to a literary work, there is no substitute for entering into a conversation with others who have studied and thought about your topic. Literary criticism is that conversation. Your reading will expose you to the ideas of others who can shed light on a story, poem, or play. It will introduce you to the wide range of informed opinions that exist about literature, as about almost any subject. Sometimes, too, your research will uncover information about an author's life that leads you to new insights into a literary work. Undertaking a research paper gives you a chance to test your ideas against those of others, and in doing so to clarify your own opinions.

BROWSE THE RESEARCH

The most daunting aspect of the research paper may well be the mountains of information available on almost any literary subject. It can be hard to know where to begin. Sifting through books and articles is part of the research process. Unfortunately, the first material you uncover in the library or on the Internet is rarely the evidence you need to develop or support your thesis. Keep looking until you uncover helpful sources.

Another common pitfall in the process is the creeping feeling that your idea has already been examined a dozen times over. But take heart: like Odysseus, tie yourself to the mast so that when you hear the siren voices of published professors, you can listen without abandoning your own point of view. Your idea may have been treated, but not yet by you. Your particular take on a topic is bound to be different from someone else's. After all, thousands of books have been written on Shakespeare's plays, but people still find new things to say about them.

CHOOSE A TOPIC

- **Find a topic that interests you.** A crucial first step in writing a research paper is coming up with a topic that interests you. Start with a topic that bores you, and the process will be a chore and yield dull results. But if you come up with an intriguing research question, seeking the answer will be a more engaging process. The paper that results will inevitably be stronger and more interesting.
- **Find a way to get started.** Browsing through books of literary criticism in the library, or glancing at online journal articles, can help to spark an idea or two. Prewriting techniques such as brainstorming, freewriting, listing, and clustering can also help you to generate ideas on a specific work of literature. If you take notes and jot down ideas as they occur to you, when it's time to start the formal writing process you will discover you have already begun.
- **Keep your purpose and audience in mind.** Refer often to the assignment, and approach your essay accordingly. Think of your audience as well. Is it your professor, your classmates, or some hypothetical reader? As you plan your essay, keep your audience's expectations and needs in mind.
- **Develop a general thesis that you hope to support with research, and look for material that will help you demonstrate its plausibility.** Remember: the ideal research paper is based on your own observations and interpretations of a literary text.

BEGIN YOUR RESEARCH

Print Resources

Writing a research paper on literature calls for two kinds of sources: primary sources, or the literary works that are your subject, and secondary sources, or the books, articles, and web resources that discuss your primary sources. When you are hunting down secondary sources, the best place to begin is your campus library. Plan to spend some time thumbing through scholarly books and journals, looking for passages that you find particularly interesting or that pertain to your topic. Begin your search with the online catalog to get a sense of where you might find the books and journals you need.

To choose from the many books available on your library's shelves and through interlibrary loan, you might turn to book reviews for a sense of which volumes would best suit your purpose. *Book Review Digest* contains the full texts of many book reviews and excerpts of others. The *Digest* may be found in printed form in the reference section of your campus library, which may also provide access to the online version. Whether you are using the online or print version, you will need the author's name, title, and date of first publication of any book for which you hope to find a review.

Scholarly journals are an excellent resource for articles on your topic. Indexes to magazines and journals may be found in your library's reference section. You may also find an index to print periodicals on your library's website.

Online Databases

Most college libraries subscribe to specialized online or CD-ROM database services covering all academic subjects—treasure troves of reliable sources. If you find yourself unsure how to use your library's database system, ask the reference librarian to help you get started. The following databases are particularly useful for literary research:

- The *MLA International Bibliography*, the Modern Language Association's database, is an excellent way to search for books and full-text articles on literary topics.
- *JSTOR*, a not-for-profit organization, indexes articles or abstracts from an archive of hundreds of journals in over fifty disciplines.
- *Literature Resource Center* (Thomson Gale) provides biographies, bibliographies, and critical analyses of more than 120,000 authors and their work. This information is culled from journal articles and reference works.
- *Literature Online (LION)* provides a vast searchable database of critical articles and reference works as well as full texts of more than 300,000 works of prose, poetry, and drama.
- *Project MUSE*, a collaboration between publishers and libraries, offers access to more than 400 journals in the humanities, arts, and social sciences.
- EBSCO, a multisubject resource, covers literature and the humanities, as well as the social sciences, medical sciences, linguistics, and other fields.

Your library may provide access to some or all of these databases, or it may offer other useful ones. Many college library home pages provide students with access to subscription databases, which means that if you really can't bear to leave your comfy desk at home, you can still pay a virtual visit.

Reliable Web Sources

While online databases are the most reliable source for high-quality information, you may find yourself looking to supplement journal articles with information and quotations from the Internet. If so, proceed with care. While the journal articles in online databases have been reviewed for quality by specialists and librarians, websites may be written and published by anybody for any purpose, with no oversight. Even the online reference site *Wikipedia*, for example, an amalgamation of voluntary contributors, is rife with small factual errors and contributor biases.

Carefully analyze any material you gather online, or you may find yourself tangled in the spidery threads of a dubious website. To garner the best sources possible, take these steps:

- **Learn to use Internet search engines effectively.** If you enter general terms such as the author's name and story title into an Internet search engine, you may well find yourself bombarded with thousands of hits. For a more efficient approach to navigating the Internet, try using an "advanced" search option, entering keywords to get results that contain those words (LITERARY CRITICISM A DOLL'S HOUSE or SYMBOLISM THE LOTTERY).
- **Begin your search at a reliable website.** Helpful as an advanced search may be, it won't separate valuable sources from useless ones. To weed out sloppy and inaccurate sites, begin your search with one of the following excellent guides through cyberspace:
  - *Library of Congress*. Fortunately, you don't have to trek to Washington to visit this venerable institution's annotated collection of websites in the Humanities and Social Sciences Division. For your purpose—writing a literary research paper—access the Subject Index <http://www.loc.gov/rr/main/alcove9>, click on "Literatures in English" and then on "Literary Criticism." This will take you to a list of metapages and websites with collections of reliable critical and biographical materials on authors and their works. (A metapage provides links to other websites.)
  - *Internet Public Library*. Created and maintained by the University of Michigan School of Information and Library Studies, this site <http://www.ipl.org> lets you search for literary criticism by author, work, country of origin, or literary period.
  - *Library Spot*. Visit <http://www.libraryspot.com> for a portal to over 5,000 libraries around the world, and to periodicals, online texts, reference works, and links to metapages and websites on any topic, including literary criticism. This carefully maintained site is published by StartSpot Mediaworks, Inc., in the Northwestern University/Evanston Research Park in Evanston, Illinois.
  - *Voice of the Shuttle*. Research links in over 25 categories in the humanities and social sciences, including online texts, libraries, academic websites, and metapages may be found at this site. Located at <http://vos.ucsb.edu> it was developed and is maintained by Dr. Alan Liu of the English Department of the University of California, Santa Barbara.

checklist: Finding Reliable Sources

- ☐ Begin at your campus library. Ask the reference librarian for advice.
- ☐ Check the library catalog for books and journals on your topic.
- ☐ Look into the online databases subscribed to by your library.
- ☐ Locate reputable websites by starting at a reputable website designed for that purpose.

Visual Images

The web is an excellent source of visual images. If a picture, chart, or graph will enhance your argument, you may find the perfect one via an image search on Google, PicSearch, or other search engines. The Library of Congress offers a wealth of images documenting American political, social, and cultural history—including portraits, letters, and original manuscripts—at <http://memory.loc.gov>. Remember, though, that not all images are available for use by the general public. Check for a copyright notice to see if its originator allows that image to be reproduced. If so, you may include the photograph, provided you credit your source as you would if you were quoting text.

One note on images: use them carefully. Choose visuals that provide supporting evidence for the point you are trying to make or that enhance your reader's understanding of the work. Label your images with captions. Your goal should be to make your argument more convincing. In the example below, a reproduction of Brueghel's painting helps to advance the author's argument and provide insight into Auden's poem.

Lombardo 4

Fig. 1. *Landscape with the Fall of Icarus* by Pieter Brueghel the Elder (c. 1558, Musées Royaux des Beaux-Arts de Belgique, Brussels)

W. H. Auden's poem "Musée des Beaux Arts" refers to a specific painting to prove its point that the most honest depictions of death take into account the way life simply goes on even after the most tragic of events. In line 14, Auden turns specifically to Pieter Brueghel the Elder's masterwork *The Fall of Icarus* (see Fig. 1), pointing to the painting's understated depiction of tragedy. In this painting, the death of Icarus does not take place on center stage. A plowman and his horse take up the painting's foreground, while the leg of Icarus falling into the sea takes up a tiny portion of the painting's lower-right corner. A viewer who fails to take the painting's title into account might not even notice Icarus at all.

checklist: Using Visual Images

- ☐ Use images as evidence to support your argument.
- ☐ Use images to enhance communication and understanding.
- ☐ Refer to the images in your text.
- ☐ Label image as "Fig. 1" and provide title or caption.
- ☐ Check copyrights.
- ☐ Include source in works-cited list.

EVALUATE YOUR SOURCES

Print Resources

It's an old saying, but a useful one: don't believe everything you read. The fact that a book or an article is printed and published doesn't necessarily mean it is accurate or unbiased. Be discriminating about printed resources.

Begin your search in a place that has taken some of the work out of quality control—your school library. Books and articles you find there are regarded by librarians as having some obvious merit. If your search takes you beyond the library, though, you will need to be discerning when choosing print resources. As you weigh the value of printed matter, take the following into account:

- **Look closely at information provided about the author.** Is he or she known for expertise in the field? What are the author's academic or association credentials? Is there any reason to believe that the author is biased in any way? For example, a biography of an author written by that author's son or daughter might not be as unbiased as one written by a scholar with no personal connections.

- **Determine the publisher's reliability.** Books or articles published by an advocacy group might be expected to take a particular—possibly biased—slant on an issue. Be aware also that some books are published by vanity presses, companies that are paid by an author to publish his or her books. As a result, vanity press-published books generally aren't subject to the same rigorous quality control as those put out by more reputable publishing houses.

- **Always check for a publication date.** If a document lists an edition number, check to see whether you are using the latest edition of the material.

- **For periodicals, decide whether a publication is an academic journal or a popular magazine.** What type of reputation does it have? Obviously, you do not want to use a magazine that periodically reports on Elvis sightings and alien births. And even articles on writers in magazines such as *Time* and *People* are likely to be too brief and superficial for purposes of serious research. Instead, choose scholarly journals designed to enhance the study of literature.

Web Resources

As handy and informative as the Internet is, it sometimes serves up some pretty iffy information. A website, after all, can be created by anyone with a computer and access to the Internet—no matter how poorly qualified that person might be. Be discerning when it comes to the Internet. Here are tips on choosing your sources wisely:

- **Check a site's author or sponsorship.** Is the site's creator or sponsor known to you or reputable by association? Look closely at information provided about the author. Is he or she known for expertise in the field? What are the author's academic or association credentials? Is the web entry unsigned and anonymous? If the website is sponsored by an organization, is it a reputable one? While government or university-sponsored sites may be considered reliable, think carefully about possible biases in sites sponsored by advocacy or special interest groups.

    A word of warning: individual student pages posted on university sites have not necessarily been reviewed by that university and are not reliable sources of information. Also, postings on the popular encyclopedia website *Wikipedia* are not subject to a scholarly review process and have been found to contain inaccuracies. It's safer to use a published encyclopedia.

- **Look at the site's date of publication.** When was it last updated? In some cases you may want to base your essay on the most current information or theories, so you will want to steer toward the most recently published material.

- **Is this an online version of a print publication?** If so, what type of reputation does it have?

- **Make your own assessment of the site.** Does the content seem consistent with demonstrated scholarship? Does it appear balanced in its point of view?

- **Consult experts.** Cornell University has two good documents with guidance for analyzing sources, posted at <http://olinuris.librarycornell.edu/content/skill-guides>. The titles are "Critically Analyzing Information Sources" and "Distinguishing Scholarly from Non-Scholarly Periodicals." Your school's library website may have similar resources.

checklist: Evaluating Your Sources

PRINT
- ☐ Who wrote it? What are the author's credentials?
- ☐ Is he or she an expert in the field?
- ☐ Does he or she appear to be unbiased toward the subject matter?
- ☐ Is the publisher reputable? Is it an advocacy group or a vanity press?
- ☐ When was it published? Do later editions exist? If so, would a later edition be more useful?

WEB

- ☐ Who wrote it? What are the author's credentials?
- ☐ Is he or she an expert in the field?
- ☐ Who sponsors the website? Is the sponsor reputable?
- ☐ When was the website published? When was it last updated?
- ☐ Is the website an online journal or magazine? Is it scholarly or popular?
- ☐ Does content seem consistent with demonstrated scholarship?
- ☐ Can you detect obvious bias?

ORGANIZE YOUR RESEARCH

- **Get your thoughts down on notecards or the equivalent on your laptop.** Once you have amassed your secondary sources, it will be time to begin reading in earnest. As you do so, be sure to take notes on any passage that pertains to your topic. A convenient way to organize your many thoughts is to write them down on index cards, which are easy to shuffle and rearrange. You'll need 3- × 5-inch cards for brief notes and titles and 5- × 8-inch cards for more in-depth notes. Confine your jottings to one side of the card; notes on the back can easily be overlooked. Write a single fact or opinion on each card. This will make it easier for you to shuffle the deck and re-envision the order in which you deliver information to your reader.

- **Keep careful track of the sources of quotations and paraphrases.** As you take notes, make it unmistakably clear which thoughts and phrases are yours and which derive from others. (Remember, *quotation* means using the exact words of your source and placing the entire passage in quotation marks and citing the author. *Paraphrase* means expressing the ideas of your source in your own words, again citing the author.) Bear in mind the cautionary tale of a well-known historian, Doris Kearns Goodwin. She was charged with plagiarizing sections of two of her famous books when her words were found to be jarringly similar to those published in other books. Because she had not clearly indicated on her note cards which ideas and passages were hers and which came from other sources, Goodwin was forced to admit to plagiarism. Her enormous reputation suffered from these charges, but you can learn from her mistakes and save your own reputation—and your grades.

- **Keep track of the sources of ideas and concepts.** When an idea is inspired by or directly taken from someone else's writing, be sure to jot down the source on that same card or in your computer file. Your deck of cards or computer list will function as a working bibliography, which later will help you put together a works-cited list. To save yourself work, keep a separate list of the sources you're using. Then, as you make the note, you need write only the material's author or title and page reference on the card in order to identify your source. It's also useful to classify the note in a way that will help you to organize your material, making it easy, for example, to separate cards that deal with a story's theme from cards that deal with point of view or symbolism.

- **Make notes of your own thoughts and reactions to your research.** When a critical article sparks your own original idea, be sure to capture that thought in your notes and mark it as your own. As you plan your paper, these notes may form the outline for your arguments.

Some useful note cards taken on a critical essay about Joyce Carol Oates's short story "Where Are You Going, Where Have You Been?" might look something like this:

Direct quotation from critic

> THEME
>
> Schulz and Rockwood, p. 2030
> "There is a terrible irony here, for although the story is full of fairy tales, Connie, its protagonist, is not. Connie represents an entire generation of young people who have grown up—or tried to—without the help of those bedtime stories which not only entertain the child, but also enable him vicariously to experience and work through problems which he will encounter in adolescence."

Paraphrase of critic

> THEME
>
> Schulz and Rockwood, p. 2030
> Ironic that while story steeped in fairy tales, Connie is not. Connie stands for her whole generation that grew up without fairy tales.
>
> Missed benefits of fairy tales for child: working through life's problems.

Critic's idea

> THEME
>
> Schulz and Rockwood, p. 2030
>
> Many fairy tales underlie "Where Are You Going?" e.g.
> > Snow White
> > Cinderella
> > Sleeping Beauty
> > Little Red Riding Hood

Your own idea

> THEME or CHARACTER?
>
> My Idea
>
> Is Arnold the big bad wolf?
> > Can I find clues in story?

- **Make photocopies or printouts to simplify the process and ensure accuracy.** Scholars once had to spend long hours copying out prose passages by hand. Luckily, for a small investment you can simply photocopy your sources to ensure accuracy in quoting and citing your sources. In fact, some instructors will require you to hand in photocopies of your original sources with the final paper, along with printouts of articles downloaded from an Internet database. Even if this is not the case, photocopying your sources and holding onto your printouts can help you to reproduce quotations accurately in your essay—and accuracy is crucial.

REFINE YOUR THESIS

As you read secondary sources and take notes, you should begin to refine your essay's thesis. This, in turn, will help you to winnow your stacks of source material down to the secondary sources that will best help you to make your point. Even your revised thesis doesn't have to be etched in stone. It should simply give you a sense of direction as you start to plan your essay.

- **Be willing to fine-tune your thesis or even rework it completely.** Your research may reveal that you have misinterpreted an idea, or that there is not much evidence to support your thesis. Of course, it is annoying to find that you may be wrong about something, but don't let these discoveries put you off. Use your research to refine your thoughts.
- **Let your initial idea be the jumping-off point to other, better ideas.** Say, for example, that you plan to write about the peculiar physical description of Arnold Friend in Joyce Carol Oates's story "Where Are You Going, Where Have You Been?" You may have noticed he has trouble standing in his shoes, and you want to explore that odd detail. If you research this character, you may find Arnold Friend likened to the devil (whose cloven hooves might give him similar problems with standard-issue cowboy boots), or to the wolf in "Little Red Riding Hood" (also a character who would have a hard time managing human clothes). Use your research to sharpen your focus. Can you think of other stories that deal with potentially supernatural, possibly even evil, characters? What about Nathaniel Hawthorne's "Young Goodman Brown"? Or Flannery O'Connor's "A Good Man Is Hard to Find"? How might you compare Arnold Friend with Hawthorne's devil or O'Connor's Misfit?

ORGANIZE YOUR PAPER

With your thesis in mind and your notes spread before you, draw up an outline—a rough map of how best to argue your thesis and present your material. Determine what main points you need to make, and look for quotations that support those points. Even if you generally prefer to navigate the paper-writing process without a map, you will find that an outline makes the research-paper writing process considerably smoother. When organizing information from many different sources, it pays to plan ahead.

WRITE AND REVISE

As with any other kind of essay, a research paper rarely, if ever, reaches its full potential in a single draft. Leave yourself time to rewrite. The knowledge that your first draft won't be your final one can free you up to take chances and to jot down your ideas as quickly as they occur to you. If your phrasing is less than elegant, it hardly matters in a first draft; the object is to rough out your ideas on paper, working as quickly as you can. Later you can rearrange paragraphs and smooth out any rough patches.

Once you've got the first draft down, it's an excellent idea to run it by a friend, a writing center tutor, or even your instructor. A writer can't know how clear or persuasive his or her argument is without a trusted reader to give feedback.

When you do revise, be open to making both large and small changes. Sometimes revising means adding needed paragraphs, or even refining the thesis a bit further. Be willing to start from scratch if you need to, but even as you take the whole picture into account, remember that details are important too. Before you hand in that final draft, be sure to proofread for small errors that could detract from the finished product.

MAINTAIN ACADEMIC INTEGRITY

PAPERS FOR SALE ARE PAPERS THAT "F"AIL

Do not be seduced by the apparent ease of cheating by computer. Your Internet searches may turn up several sites that offer term papers to download (just as you can find pornography, political propaganda, and questionable get-rich-quick schemes!). Most of these sites charge money for what they offer, but a few do not, happy to strike a blow against the "oppressive" insistence of English teachers that students learn to think and write.

Plagiarized term papers are an old game: the fraternity file and the "research assistance" service have been around far longer than the computer. It may seem easy enough to download a paper, put your name at the head of it, and turn it in for an easy grade. As any writing instructor can tell you, though, such papers usually stick out like a sore thumb. The style will be wrong, the work will not be consistent with other work by the same student in any number of ways, and the teacher will sometimes even have seen the same phony paper before. The ease with which electronic texts are reproduced makes this last possibility increasingly likely.

The odds of being caught and facing the unpleasant consequences are reasonably high. It is far better to take the grade you have earned for your own effort, no matter how mediocre, than to try to pass off someone else's work as your own. Even if, somehow, your instructor does not recognize your submission as a plagiarized paper, you have diminished your character through dishonesty and lost an opportunity to learn something on your own.

A WARNING AGAINST INTERNET PLAGIARISM

Plagiarism detection services are a professor's newest ally in the battle against academic dishonesty. Questionable research papers can be sent to these services (such as Turnitin.com and EVE2), which perform complex searches of the Internet and of a growing database of purchased term papers. The research paper will be returned to the professor with plagiarized sections annotated and the sources documented. The end result will certainly be a failing grade on the essay, possibly a failing grade for the course, and, depending on the policies of your university, the very real possibility of expulsion.

ACKNOWLEDGE ALL SOURCES

The brand of straight-out dishonesty described above is one type of plagiarism. There is, however, another, subtler kind: when students incorporate somebody else's words *or* ideas into their papers without giving proper credit. To avoid this second—sometimes quite accidental—variety of plagiarism, familiarize yourself with the conventions for acknowledging sources. First and foremost, remember to give credit to any writer who supplies you with ideas, information, or specific words and phrases.

Using Quotations

- **Acknowledge your source when you quote a writer's words or phrases.** When you use someone else's words or phrases, you should reproduce his or her exact words in quotation marks, and be sure to properly credit the source.

   > Already, Frost has hinted that Nature may be, as Radcliffe Squires suggests, "Nothing but an ash-white plain without love or faith or hope, where ignorant appetites cross by chance" (87).

- **If you quote more than four lines, set your quotation off from the body of the paper.** Start a new line; indent one inch, and type the quotation, double-spaced. (You do not need to use quotation marks, as the format tells the reader the passage is a quotation.)

   > Samuel Maio made an astute observation about the nature of Weldon Kees's distinctive tone:
   >
   > > Kees has therefore combined a personal subject matter with an impersonal voice—that is, one that is consistent in its tone evenly recording the speaker's thoughts without showing any emotional intensity which might lie behind those thoughts. (136)

Citing Ideas

- **Acknowledge your source when you mention a critic's ideas.** Even if you are not quoting exact words or phrases, be sure to acknowledge the source of any original ideas or concepts you have used.

   > Another explanation is suggested by Daniel Hoffman, a critic who has discussed the story: the killer hears the sound of his *own* heart (227).

- **Acknowledge your source when you paraphrase a writer's words.** To paraphrase a critic, you should do more than just rearrange his or her words: you should translate them into your own original sentences—again, always being sure to credit the original source. As an example, suppose you wish to refer to an insight of Randall Jarrell, who commented as follows on the images of spider, flower, and moth in Robert Frost's poem "Design":

   > **RANDALL JARRELL'S ORIGINAL TEXT**
   >
   > Notice how the *heal-all*, because of its name, is the one flower in all the world picked to be the altar for this Devil's Mass; notice how *holding up* the moth brings something ritual and hieratic, a ghostly, ghastly formality, to this priest and its sacrificial victim.[1]

   [1]*Poetry and the Age* (New York: Knopf, 1953) 42.

It would be too close to the original to write, without quotation marks, these sentences:

PLAGIARIZED REWORDING

Frost picks the *heal-all* as the one flower in all the world to be the altar for this Devil's Mass. There is a ghostly, ghastly formality to the spider *holding up* the moth, like a priest holding a sacrificial victim.

This rewording, although not exactly in Jarrell's language, manages to steal his memorable phrases without giving him credit. Nor is it sufficient just to include Jarrell's essay in the works-cited list at the end of your paper. If you do, you are still a crook; you merely point to the scene of the crime. Instead, think through Jarrell's words to the point he is making, so that it can be restated in your own original way. If you want to keep any of his striking phrases (and why not?), put them exactly as he wrote them in quotation marks:

APPROPRIATE PARAPHRASE, ACKNOWLEDGES SOURCE

As Randall Jarrell points out, Frost portrays the spider as a kind of priest in a Mass, or Black Mass, elevating the moth like an object for sacrifice, with "a ghostly, ghastly formality" (42).

Note also that this improved passage gives Jarrell the credit not just for his words but for his insight into the poem. Both the idea and the words in which it was originally expressed are the properties of their originator. Finally, notice the page reference that follows the quotation (this system of documenting your sources is detailed below).

DOCUMENT SOURCES USING MLA STYLE

You must document everything you take from a source. When you quote from other writers, when you borrow their information, when you summarize or paraphrase their ideas, make sure you give them proper credit. Identify the writer by name and cite the book, magazine, newspaper, pamphlet, website, or other source you have used.

The conventions that govern the proper way to document sources are available in the *MLA Handbook for Writers of Research Papers*, 7th ed. (New York: MLA, 2009). The following brief list of pointers is not meant to take the place of the *MLA Handbook* itself, but to give you a basic sense of the rules for documentation.

List of Sources

Keep a working list of your research sources—all the references from which you might quote, summarize, paraphrase, or take information. When your paper is in finished form, it will end with a neat copy of the works you actually used (once called a "Bibliography," now titled "Works Cited").

Parenthetical References

In the body of your paper, every time you refer to a source, you need to provide information to help a reader locate it in your works-cited list. You can usually give just the author's name and a page citation in parentheses. For example, if you are writing a paper on Weldon Kees's sonnet "For My Daughter" and want to include an observation you found on page 136 of Samuel Maio's book *Creating Another Self*, write:

> One critic has observed that the distinctive tone of "For My Daughter" depends on Kees's combination of "personal subject matter with an impersonal voice" (Maio 136).

If you mention the author's name in your sentence, you need give only the page number in your reference:

> As Samuel Maio has observed, Kees creates a distinctive tone in this sonnet by combining a "personal subject with an impersonal voice" (136).

If you have two books or magazine articles by Samuel Maio in your works-cited list, how will the reader tell them apart? In your text, refer to the title of each book or article by condensing it into a word or two. Condensed book titles are italicized, and condensed article titles are still placed within quotation marks.

> One critic has observed that the distinctive tone of "For My Daughter" depends on Kees's combination of "personal subject matter with an impersonal voice" (Maio, *Creating* 136).

Works-Cited List

Provide a full citation for each source on your works-cited page. At the end of your paper, in your list of works cited, your reader will find a full description of your source—for the above examples, a critical book:

> Maio, Samuel. *Creating Another Self: Voices in Modern American Personal Poetry*. 2nd ed. Kirksville: Thomas Jefferson UP, 2005. Print.

Put your works-cited list in proper form. The *MLA Handbook* provides detailed instructions for citing a myriad of different types of sources, from books to online databases. Here is a partial list of the *Handbook*'s recommendations for presenting your works-cited list.

1. Start a new page for the works-cited list, and continue the page numbering from the body of your paper.
2. Center the title, "Works Cited," one inch from the top of the page.
3. Double-space between all lines (including between the title and the first entry, and both between and within the entries).
4. Type each entry beginning at the left-hand margin. If an entry runs longer than a single line, indent the following lines one-half inch from the left-hand margin.
5. Alphabetize each entry according to the author's last name.
6. Include three sections in each entry: author, title, publication or access information. (You will, however, give slightly different information for a book, journal article, online source, or other reference.)

Citing Print Sources in MLA Style

For a book citation

a. **Author's full name** as it appears on the title page, last name first, followed by a period.
b. **Book's full title** (and subtitle, if it has one, separated by a colon) followed by a period. Remember to italicize the title. Also provide edition and volume information, if applicable, followed by a period.
c. **Publication information:** city of publication followed by a colon; name of publisher followed by a comma; year of publication followed by a period; and publication medium—*Print*—followed by a period.

  (1) **Make your citation of the city of publication brief, but clear.** If the title page lists more than one city, cite only the first. You need not provide the state, province or country after the city name.

  (2) **Shorten the publisher's name.** Eliminate articles (*A, An, The*), business abbreviations (*Co., Corp., Inc., Ltd.*), and descriptive words (*Books, House, Press, Publishers*). The exception is a university press, for which you should use the letters U (for University) and P (for Press). Use only the first listed *surname* of the publisher.

Publisher's Name	Proper Citation
Harvard University Press	Harvard UP
University of Chicago Press	U of Chicago P
Farrar, Straus and Giroux, Inc.	Farrar
Alfred A. Knopf, Inc.	Knopf

d. **Optional additional information:** Any additional information that may be helpful for your reader can be provided at the end of a citation. For example, if the book is part of an established series or part of a multivolume set, put the name of the series or the complete work here.

The citation for a book should read:

> Author's Last name, First name. *Book Title*. Ed. or vol. Publication city: Publisher, Year. Print.

For a journal or periodical article citation

a. **Author's name,** last name first, followed by a period.
b. **Title of article** followed by a period, all within quotation marks.
c. **Journal publication information:** journal title (italicized); volume number followed by period, issue number; year of publication in parentheses followed by a colon; inclusive page numbers of the entire article followed by a period; and publication medium—*Print*—followed by a period.

or

Periodical publication information: periodical title (italicized); day month year followed by a colon; page numbers of article (for continuous articles use inclusive pages, such as 31–33; for newspapers use starting page, such as C1+) followed by a period; and publication medium—*Print*—followed by a period.

The citation for a journal article should read:

> Author's Last name, First name. "Article Title." *Journal* Volume.Issue (Year): Pages. Print.

The citation for a periodical article should read:

> Author's Last name, First name. "Article Title." *Periodical* Day Month Year: Pages. Print.

Citing Web Sources in MLA Style

Like print sources, Internet sources should be documented with care. Before you begin your Internet search, be aware of the types of information you will want for your works-cited list. You can then record the information as you go. Keep track of the following information:

- Author's name
- Title of document
- Full information about publication in print form, when available
- Title of scholarly project, database, periodical, or professional or personal site
- Name of editor of project or database
- Date of electronic publication or last update
- Institution or organization sponsoring the website
- Date *you* accessed the source
- Website address or URL

Although many websites provide much of this information at the beginning or ending of an article or at the bottom of the home page, you will find that it is not always available. Also note that as web pages and even sites may sometimes disappear or change, you are well advised to print out important pages for future reference.

For a web resource citation

  a. **Author or editor's name,** last name first, followed by a period.
  b. **Title of work,** within quotation marks or italicized as appropriate, followed by a period.
  c. **Title of website,** in italics, followed by a period.
  d. **Sponsor or publisher of website** followed by a comma. If not available, use *N.p.*
  e. **Publication date** followed by a period. If data is not available, use *n.d.*
  f. **Publication medium—Web**—followed by a period.
  g. **Date *you* accessed information:** day month year that you viewed the document online.
  h. **Optional URL:** if there is some reason your reader may not be able to access your web page with the information provided, you may include the full URL, enclosed in angle brackets <>.

The citation for a web source should read:

> Author's Last name, First name. "Document Title." *Website*. Website Sponsor, Publication date. Web. Access Day Month Year.

For a print journal accessed on the web

   a. **Provide information for standard print citation**
      (1) **Author's name,** last name first, followed by a period.
      (2) **Title of work,** within quotation marks or italicized as appropriate, followed by a period.
      (3) **Print publication information:** journal title in italics; volume and issue number; year; page references, as available. If no pages are available, use *n. pag.*
   b. **Provide web access information**
      (1) **Title of website or database,** italicized.
      (2) **Publication medium—Web**—followed by period.
      (3) **Date *you* accessed information:** day month year that you viewed the document online.

The citation for a scholarly journal article obtained on the web should read:

> Author's Last name, First name. "Article Title." *Journal* Volume.Issue (Year): Pages. *Website or Online Database*. Web. Access Day Month Year.

Sample List of Works Cited

For a paper on Weldon Kees's "For My Daughter," a student's works-cited list might look as follows:

Works Cited

Grosholz, Emily. "The Poetry of Memory." *Weldon Kees: A Critical Introduction*. Ed. Jim Elledge. Metuchen: Scarecrow, 1985. 46-47. Print.

Kees, Weldon. *The Collected Poems of Weldon Kees*. Ed. Donald Justice. Lincoln: U of Nebraska P, 1975. Print.

Lane, Anthony. "The Disappearing Poet: What Ever Happened to Weldon Kees?" *New Yorker*. Condé Nast Digital, 4 July 2005. Web. 22 Aug. 2012.

Maio, Samuel. *Creating Another Self: Voice in Modern American Personal Poetry*. 2nd ed. Kirksville: Thomas Jefferson UP, 2005. Print.

Nelson, Raymond. "The Fitful Life of Weldon Kees." *American Literary History* 1 (1989): 816-52. Print.

Reidel, James. *Vanished Act: The Life and Art of Weldon Kees*. Lincoln: U of Nebraska P, 2003. Print.

---, ed. "Weldon Kees." *Nebraska Center for Writers*. Creighton University,
n.d. Web. 26 Aug. 2012.

Ross, William T. *Weldon Kees*. Boston: Twayne, 1985. Print. Twayne's US
Authors Ser. 484.

"Weldon Kees." *Poetry Out Loud*. National Endowment for the Arts and the
Poetry Foundation, n.d. Web. 20 Sept. 2012.

See the Reference Guide for MLA Citations at the end of this chapter for additional examples of the types of citations that you are likely to need for your papers, or check the seventh edition of the *MLA Handbook*.

As you put together your works-cited list, keep in mind that the little things—page numbers, quotation marks—count. Documentation may seem tedious, but it has an important purpose: it's for the reader of your paper who wants to pursue a topic you have researched. Luckily, you don't have to know the rules by heart. You can refer as necessary to the *MLA Handbook* or to the examples in this book.

Research Paper

Here is a short research paper in response to a challenging assignment from Professor Michael Cass of Mercer University. He asked his students to select the fiction writer whose work impressed them most. Each student then had to research the author and, using at least five critical sources, write a paper defending that author's claim to literary greatness. The students had to present clear reasons why the author was a major writer and to support the argument with both examples from the writer's work and statements from critics. Stephanie Crowe, a student in Professor Cass's class, discusses why she believes that Franz Kafka was a great writer.

Crowe 1

Stephanie Crowe
Professor Cass
English 120
21 November 2012

Kafka's Greatness

Introduction of essay topic

Although most of his major works remained unfinished and unpublished at his untimely death in 1924, Franz Kafka has gradually come to be considered one of the great writers of the twentieth century. By 1977, well over ten thousand works of commentary had appeared on Kafka, and

Citation of secondary source

many more have been written since then (Goodden 2). According to critic Peter Heller, Kafka represents the "mainstream of German literary and intellectual

Quotation from secondary source integrated into sentence

tradition," a nihilistic tradition which extends from Goethe and Lessing to the present (289).

Not only is Kafka generally considered one of the greatest fiction writers of the modern era, he is also indisputably one of the most influential. In his 1989 study, *After Kafka*, Shimon Sandbank discusses Kafka's influence on a dozen modern writers including Sartre, Camus, Beckett, Borges, and Ionesco. His effects on these writers differed. Some borrowed his understated, almost passive prose style while others adopted his recurrent images and themes. Whatever the specific elements they used, however, Kafka's ability to influence these writers is another measure of his stature.

Great literature often gives us the stories and images to understand our own age, a process that necessarily includes understanding our deepest problems. The twentieth century, to borrow a phrase from W. H. Auden, was mostly an "Age of Anxiety." Most modern people are no longer bound to follow the occupations, behaviors, and beliefs of their parents, but they gain this newfound freedom at the expense of a constant, difficult search for identity. The personal quest for meaningful identity often leads to despair. This "existential crisis" is the basis for many contemporary problems including the decline of religion, the rise of totalitarianism, the breakdown of social identity, and the decay of traditional family structure.

Kafka's works dramatize these problems memorably because they provide us with myths, images, stories, and situations that describe the particular crises of the early twentieth century. When faced with the modern challenge of not having a predetermined social or religious identity, Kafka's characters desperately attempt to find certainty. The problem, however, is that they are usually afraid to do anything decisive because everything is uncertain. Auden observed:

> Far from being confident of success, the Kafka hero is convinced from the start that he is doomed to fail, as he is also doomed, being who he is, to make prodigious and unending efforts to reach it [the goal]. Indeed, the mere desire to reach the goal is itself a proof, not that he is one of the elect, but that he is under a special curse. (162)

One way that Kafka memorably dramatizes the modern struggle for identity is by reversing the traditional quest story. In a quest story, the hero knows the goal that he wants to achieve and has some confidence that he will be able to achieve it. As he tries to reach the goal, he must overcome various enemies and obstacles. "In a typical Kafka story, on the other hand, the goal is peculiar to the hero himself: he has no competitors" (Auden 162). His question then becomes not a practical "Can I succeed?" but instead a vague and problematic "What should I do?" Unable to answer this question satisfactorily, the hero becomes increasingly alienated from his own surroundings. This alienation is yet another symptom of "the inhumanity of modern society" that Kafka so memorably portrayed (Kuna 62).

Topic sentence on relationship between Kafka's era and his style

Kafka also distinguishes himself as a great writer because he created a distinctive style that effectively dramatizes modern problems. Although Kafka's fiction often describes extreme situations, his prose usually seems strangely calm and detached. He uses "clear and simple language" that paints "concrete pictures of human beings, pictures that, in a sense, have to speak for themselves" (Cooper 19). These haunting images (the unreachable castle, the unknown laws, the unspecified trial) dramatize the mysterious struggles of the characters.

Topic sentence on Kafka's style incorporates critical view

Kafka also uses his style to separate himself from his characters, a technique that develops a contrast between the calmness of his style and the nervous desperation of his characters (Heller 237). For example, the opening of Kafka's novella *The Metamorphosis*, which is perhaps the most famous first sentence in modern fiction, describes an outrageous event—a young man who wakes up transformed into a giant bug—in a strangely matter-of-fact tone. This contrast is important because it reminds us of the desperation of modern man imprisoned in a world he can neither understand nor control.

Topic sentence on Kafka's style of ambiguity

Perhaps the most interesting feature of Kafka's style is his ability to create works that cannot be explained by a single interpretation. Because he allows his pictures to "speak for themselves," "Kafka's texts have been subject to a variety of widely divergent approaches" (Heller 236). Another critic, speaking directly of *The Metamorphosis*, agrees: "Gregor's transformation has a double meaning: it is both an escape from his oppressive life and a representation or even an intensification of it" (Goldfarb). Therefore, no single interpretation can adequately explain an entire work of Kafka's. Most interpretations may illuminate particular moments in a work, but inevitably they lead to a dead end when pressed to explain the whole narrative. Whether one is reading on a social, moral, psychological, metaphysical, theological, or existential level, Kafka "tends to suspend all distinction and thus to revert to total ambiguity" (Heller 285). According to Heller, this characteristic mysteriousness becomes "the epitome of his art" (230).

Auden believed that the impossibility of interpreting Kafka's work is essential in defining him as an important and influential writer. He says that "Kafka is a great, perhaps the greatest, master of the pure parable, a literary genre about which a critic can say very little worth saying" (159). Since the meaning of a parable is different for each individual, critics cannot explain them without revealing their own visions and values. Kafka develops stories with important symbols that are easily identified; attempting to interpret these symbols, however, only leads to frustration.

Topic sentence on Kafka's complexity

The frustration that comes from trying to interpret Kafka's works exemplifies his recurrent, and particularly twentieth-century, theme, which Peter Heller has described as man's "ever frustrated, ever defeated striving for self-realization in an inhuman human universe in which he is alienated from himself and from the world he lives in" (305). Kafka uses his characteristic difficult symbolism and ambiguity, along with his theme of hopelessness and despair, as a common thread that binds all of his works together.

Topic sentence on Kafka's central theme incorporates quotation from secondary source

Kafka's book *The Great Wall of China* contains several short pieces which have a slightly less desperate tone than that of *The Metamorphosis*. Many of the stories in *The Great Wall of China*, however, still present the theme of hopelessness. In the reflection titled "The Problem of Our Laws," Kafka examines the origins and legitimacy of law. This parable begins with the narrator stating, "Our laws are not generally known; they are kept secret by the small group of nobles who rule us" (147). Next, the narrator goes through a laborious process of rationally questioning why only the nobility knows the laws, whether the laws really exist, and whether it will ever be possible for common men to know the laws. He finally concludes that the only way to know the law would be a quiet revolution that ends nobility. But even this solution, he realizes, is futile. The nobility cannot be eliminated because they provide the only order that exists. While this parable makes several interesting points, its structure is essentially static. The narrator ends where he began—trapped in an unknowable world.

Topic sentence on tone

Quotation from primary source

One of Kafka's unfinished novels, *The Trial*, also concentrates on the unknown symbol of the Law. In the novel, Joseph K. is arrested for a crime that no one ever knows. Joseph, like most of Kafka's characters, is a common man with an uneventful life who admits that he knows little of the Law. The drama of the novel is the protagonist's hopeless attempts to master an unknown and

Topic sentence on theme

impossible situation. Joseph K.'s life itself becomes a trial, although he is never sentenced. Finally, one year after his arrest, two men come and murder him. Instead of trying to understand the Law, "In the end he appears to accept the verdict as a release from the condition of despair," and "dies like an animal, without comprehending the rationale of the Law which condemns him" (Heller 280-81). Like many men, before his death K. is struggling to discover his identity in relation to the Law that governs him; however, K.'s hopeless life ends with a pointless murder.

Topic sentence on theme

Kafka's other great unfinished novel, *The Castle*, also concentrates on the theme of unknowability and despair. Instead of trying to understand the Law, K. in *The Castle* has another impossible quest, his attempt to enter the castle of the local ruler to report for duty as a land surveyor. His constant efforts, however, prove futile. As in *The Trial*, the protagonist is at the mercy of an arbitrary and unknowable Law:

> In many ways the castle functions like a secret court system: the officials decide and carry out policies that are conceived as stipulations of law; they lean on their law books, try to serve the law, and know the clandestine ways of law. Many decisions are arrived at arbitrarily and remain secret; even legal actions such as an official indictment can be kept hidden for some time. (Heidsieck 3)

Only when K. lies on his deathbed does a call from the castle come, giving him permission to live in the town. Once again, the protagonist suffers hopelessly and dies in despair.

While *The Trial* emphasizes political and psychological themes characteristic of the twentieth century, *The Castle* focuses on the religious identity crisis. *The Metamorphosis* examines similar themes of identity on a personal and family level. All of these works focus on modern humanity's difficult struggle to define its place in existence.

Conclusion sums up argument

Thesis sentence makes debatable claim

Kafka, through his works, accurately describes the modern condition of many by using memorable images and a distinctive style. This characteristic style influenced many twentieth-century writers and readers. While difficult and somewhat bleak, Kafka's often ambiguous yet understated dramatizations of man's condition, along with his lasting influence, form the foundation of his greatness.

Works Cited

Auden, W. H. "The I without a Self." *The Dyer's Hand*. New York: Random, 1989. 159-70. Print.

Cooper, Gabriele Bon Natzmer. *Kafka and Language: In the Stream of Thoughts and Life*. Riverside: Ariadne, 1991. Print.

Goldfarb, Sheldon. "Critical Essay on *The Metamorphosis*." *Short Stories for Students*. Ed. Jennifer Smith. Vol. 12. Detroit: Gale, 2001. N. pag. *Literature Resource Center*. Web. 19 Sept. 2012.

Goodden, Christina. "Points of Departure." *The Kafka Debate: New Perspectives for Our Time*. Ed. Angel Flores. New York: Gordian, 1988. 2-9. Print.

Heidsieck, Arnold. "Community, Delusion and Anti-Semitism in Kafka's *The Castle*." *German Studies Program*. German Dept., U of Southern California, n.d. Web. 19 Sept. 2012. <http://www.usc.edu/dept/LAS/german/track/heidsiec/KafkaAntisemitism/KafkaAntisemitism.pdf>.

Heller, Peter. "Kafka: The Futility of Striving." *Dialectics and Nihilism*. Amherst: U of Massachusetts P, 1966. 227-306. Print.

Kafka, Franz. "The Problem of Our Laws." *The Great Wall of China*. New York: Schocken, 1946. 147-49. Print.

Kuna, Franz. *Franz Kafka: Literature as Corrective Punishment*. Bloomington: Indiana UP, 1974. Print.

Sandbank, Shimon. *After Kafka: The Influence of Kafka's Fiction*. Athens: U of Georgia P, 1989. Print.

A well-crafted research essay is a wondrous thing—as delightful, in its own way, as a well-crafted poem or short story or play. Good essays prompt thought and add to knowledge. Writing a research paper sharpens your own mind and exposes you to the honed insights of other thinkers. Think of anything you write as a piece that could be published for the benefit of other people interested in your topic. After all, such a goal is not as far-fetched as it seems: this textbook, for example, features a number of papers written by students. Why shouldn't yours number among them? Aim high.

REFERENCE GUIDE FOR MLA CITATIONS

Here are examples of the types of citations you are likely to need for documenting most student papers. The formats follow current MLA style for works-cited lists.

PRINT PUBLICATIONS
Books

No Author Listed

The Chicago Manual of Style. 16th ed. Chicago: U of Chicago P, 2010. Print.

One Author

Middlebrook, Diane Wood. *Anne Sexton: A Biography.* Boston: Houghton, 1991. Print.

Two or Three Authors

Jarman, Mark, and Robert McDowell. *The Reaper: Essays.* Brownsville: Story Line, 1996. Print.

Four or More Authors

Phillips, Rodney, et al. *The Hand of the Poet.* New York: Rizzoli, 1997. Print.

or

Phillips, Rodney, Susan Benesch, Kenneth Benson, and Barbara Bergeron. *The Hand of the Poet.* New York: Rizzoli, 1997. Print.

Two Books by the Same Author

Bawer, Bruce. *The Aspect of Eternity.* St. Paul: Graywolf, 1993. Print.

---. *Diminishing Fictions: Essays on the Modern American Novel and Its Critics.* St. Paul: Graywolf, 1988. Print.

Corporate Author

Poets and Writers. *A Writer's Guide to Copyright*. New York: Poets and
    Writers, 1979. Print.

Author and Editor

Shakespeare, William. *The Sonnets*. Ed. G. Blakemore Evans. Cambridge:
    Cambridge UP, 1996. Print.

One Editor

Monteiro, George, ed. *Conversations with Elizabeth Bishop*. Jackson: UP of
    Mississippi, 1996. Print.

Two Editors

Craig, David, and Janet McCann, eds. *Odd Angles of Heaven: Contemporary
    Poetry by People of Faith*. Wheaton: Shaw, 1994. Print.

Translation

Dante Alighieri. *Inferno: A New Verse Translation*. Trans. Michael Palma.
    New York: Norton, 2002. Print.

Introduction, Preface, Foreword, or Afterword

Lapham, Lewis. Introduction. *Understanding Media: The Extensions of
    Man*. By Marshall McLuhan. Cambridge: MIT P, 1994. vi-x. Print.
Thwaite, Anthony. Preface. *Contemporary Poets*. Ed. Thomas Riggs. 6th
    ed. New York: St. James, 1996. vii-viii. Print.

Work in an Anthology

Rodriguez, Richard. "Aria: A Memoir of a Bilingual Childhood." *The Best
    American Essays of the Century*. Ed. Robert Atwan and Joyce Carol
    Oates. Boston: Houghton, 2001. 447-66. Print. Best American Ser.

Translation in an Anthology

Neruda, Pablo. "We Are Many." Trans. Alastair Reid. *Literature for Life*. Ed. X. J. Kennedy, Dana Gioia, and Nina Revoyr. New York: Pearson, 2013. 947-48. Print.

Multivolume Work

Wellek, René. *A History of Modern Criticism, 1750-1950*. 8 vols. New Haven: Yale UP, 1955-92. Print.

One Volume of a Multivolume Work

Wellek, René. *A History of Modern Criticism, 1750-1950*. Vol. 7. New Haven: Yale UP, 1991. Print.

Book in a Series

Ross, William T. *Weldon Kees*. Boston: Twayne, 1985. Print. Twayne's US Authors Ser. 484.

Republished Book

Ellison, Ralph. *Invisible Man*. 1952. New York: Vintage, 1995. Print.

Revised or Subsequent Edition

Janouch, Gustav. *Conversations with Kafka*. Trans. Goronwy Rees. Rev. ed. New York: New Directions, 1971. Print.

Reference Books

Signed Article in a Reference Book

Cavoto, Janice E. "Harper Lee's *To Kill a Mockingbird*." *The Oxford Encyclopedia of American Literature*. Ed. Jay Parini. Vol. 2. New York: Oxford UP, 2004. 418-21. Print.

Unsigned Encyclopedia Article—Standard Reference Book

"James Dickey." *The New Encyclopaedia Britannica: Micropaedia.* 15th ed. 1987. Print.

Dictionary Entry

"Design." *Merriam-Webster's Collegiate Dictionary.* 11th ed. 2003. Print.

Periodicals

Journal

Salter, Mary Jo. "The Heart Is Slow to Learn." *New Criterion* 10.8 (1992): 23-29. Print.

Signed Magazine Article

Gioia, Dana. "Studying with Miss Bishop." *New Yorker* 5 Sept. 1986: 90-101. Print.

Unsigned Magazine Article

"The Real Test." *New Republic* 5 Feb. 2001: 7. Print.

Newspaper Article

Lyall, Sarah. "In Poetry, Ted Hughes Breaks His Silence on Sylvia Plath." *New York Times* 19 Jan. 1998, natl. ed.: A1+. Print.

Signed Book Review

Fugard, Lisa. "Divided We Love." Rev. of *Unaccustomed Earth,* by Jhumpa Lahiri. *Los Angeles Times* 30 Mar. 2008: R1. Print.

Unsigned, Untitled Book Review

Rev. of *Otherwise: New and Selected Poems,* by Jane Kenyon. *Virginia Quarterly Review* 72 (1996): 136. Print.

WEB PUBLICATIONS

Website

Liu, Alan, dir. Home Page. *Voice of the Shuttle*. Dept. of English, U of California, Santa Barbara, n.d. Web. 17 Oct. 2012.

Document on a Website

"A Hughes Timeline." *PBS Online*. Public Broadcasting Service, 2001. Web. 20 Sept. 2012.

"Wallace Stevens." *Poets.org*. Academy of American Poets, n.d. Web. 20 Sept. 2012.

Online Reference Database

"Brooks, Gwendolyn." *Encyclopaedia Britannica Online*. Encyclopaedia Britannica, 2011. Web. 15 Feb. 2012.

Entire Online Book, Previously Appeared in Print

Jewett, Sarah Orne. *The Country of the Pointed Firs*. 1896. *Project Gutenberg*, 8 July 2008. Web. 10 Oct. 2012.

Article in an Online Newspaper

Atwood, Margaret. "The Writer: A New Canadian Life-Form." *New York Times*. New York Times, 18 May 1997. Web. 20 Aug. 2012.

Article in an Online Magazine

Garner, Dwight. "Jamaica Kincaid: The Salon Interview." *Salon*. Salon Media Group, 13 Jan. 1996. Web. 15 Feb. 2012.

Article in an Online Scholarly Journal

Carter, Sarah. "From the Ridiculous to the Sublime: Ovidian and Neoplatonic Registers in *A Midsummer Night's Dream*." *Early Modern Literary Studies* 12.1 (2006): 1-31. Web. 18 Jan. 2012.

Article from a Scholarly Journal, Part of an Archival Online Database

Finch, Annie. "My Father Dickinson: On Poetic Influence." *Emily Dickinson Journal* 17.2 (2008): 24-38. *Project Muse*. Web. 18 Jan. 2012.

Article Accessed via a Library Subscription Service

Seitler, Dana. "Unnatural Selection: Mothers, Eugenic Feminism, and Charlotte Perkins Gilman's Regeneration Narratives." *American Quarterly* 55.1 (2003): 61-87. *ProQuest*. Web. 7 July 2012.

Online Blog

Gioia, Ted. *"The Road* by Cormac McCarthy." *The New Canon: The Best in Fiction Since 1985*. N.p., n.d. Web. 11 May 2012.

Vellala, Rob. "Gilman: No Trouble to Anyone." *The American Literary Blog*. N.p., 10 Sept. 2010. Web. 23 Apr. 2012.

Photograph or Painting Accessed Online

Alice Walker, Miami Book Fair International, 1989. Wikimedia Commons. Wikimedia Foundation, 22 Jan. 2009. Web. 11 May 2012.

Brueghel, Pieter. *Landscape with the Fall of Icarus*. 1558. Musées Royaux des Beaux-Arts de Belgique, Brussels. *ibilio.org*. Center for the Public Domain and UNC-CH. Web. 21 Nov. 2012.

Video Accessed Online

Ozymandias: Percy Bysshe Shelley. YouTube. E-Verse Radio, 13 Mar. 2007. Web. 21 May 2012. <http://www.youtube.com/watch?v=6xGa-fNSHaM>.

CD-ROM REFERENCE WORKS
CD-ROM Publication

"Appall." *The Oxford English Dictionary*. 2nd ed. Oxford: Oxford UP, 1992. CD-ROM.

Periodically Published Information, Collected on CD-ROM

Kakutani, Michiko. "Slogging Surreally in the Vietnamese Jungle." Rev. of *The Things They Carried*, by Tim O'Brien. *New York Times* 6 Mar. 1990: C6. CD-ROM. *New York Times Ondisc*. UMI-ProQuest. Oct. 1993.

MISCELLANEOUS SOURCES
Compact Disc (CD)

Shakespeare, William. *The Complete Arkangel Shakespeare: 38 Fully-Dramatized Plays*. Narr. Eileen Atkins and John Gielgud. Read by Imogen Stubbs, Joseph Fiennes, et al. Audio Partners, 2003. CD.

Audiocassette

Roethke, Theodore. *Theodore Roethke Reads His Poetry*. Caedmon, 1972. Audiocassette.

Videocassette

Henry V. By William Shakespeare. Dir. Laurence Olivier. Perf. Laurence Olivier. Two Cities Films. 1944. Paramount, 1988. Videocassette.

DVD

Hamlet. By William Shakespeare. Dir. Laurence Olivier. Perf. Laurence Olivier, Eileen Herlie, and Basil Sydney. Two Cities Films. 1948. Criterion, 2000. DVD.

Film

Hamlet. By William Shakespeare. Dir. Franco Zeffirelli. Perf. Mel Gibson, Glenn Close, Helena Bonham Carter, Alan Bates, and Paul Scofield. Warner, 1991. Film.

Television or Radio Program

Moby Dick. By Herman Melville. Dir. Franc Roddam. Perf. Patrick Stewart and Gregory Peck. 2 episodes. USA Network. 16-17 Mar. 1998. Television.

Gwendolyn Brooks

THEMES OF LITERATURE, THEMES OF LIFE

12 FAMILIES

All happy families are alike;
every unhappy family is unhappy in its own way.

—LEO TOLSTOY,
FIRST SENTENCE OF ANNA KARENINA

All happy families are more or less dissimilar;
all unhappy ones are more or less alike.

—VLADIMIR NABOKOV,
FIRST SENTENCE OF ADA

We choose our friends, the saying goes, but we can't choose our families. When we're young, we don't think much about the families we're born into—they just *are*, since we have almost no other frame of reference. It's only later that we start to see our families with more objective eyes; that we can appreciate what we've learned from them, or figure out the ways we hope to be different.

What *is* family, anyway? When you think of your own family, whom do you think of? Your mother or father? Both—or maybe neither? Your siblings or stepsiblings? Maybe family members who are one step removed, such as grandparents, or uncles and aunts and cousins? Another person—say, a mentor or friend—whom you consider "a part of the family"? Or is family, to you, something totally different—the people who've taken you in, or whom you've chosen to join?

The concept of a nuclear family—a father, a mother, and two or three children—has long been considered the desirable norm in North America, and many people still feel strongly that this remains the ideal model of family. Yet individual realities are often much more complicated. In many cultures it is common for three or more generations to live under one roof. To them the concept of a "nuclear" family seems downright skimpy.

Sometimes families are broken by war, disease, violent crime, or accident. One parent dies, and the surviving spouse must raise the child or children alone. Or the survivor remarries. Divorce also breaks families into new and complex pieces. Many children are now raised by single parents, or are part of "blended" families that include a stepparent and stepsiblings. Some kids are raised by their grandparents or other relatives or same-sex parents. Others live with foster parents.

Whatever the configuration of your own family, one thing is indisputable. Our family experience shapes us and influences the way we see the world—whether we know it or not. Our deepest relationships are mostly with our family. And our connections aren't just emotional. Some of them are in our DNA. We usually look like other members of our biological family (especially if we have an identical twin!). Siblings often share speech patterns and body language. We may also consciously or unconsciously adopt our family's views on everything from politics and religion to food and favorite sports teams. Or we may define ourselves in rebellion—gentle or not—against our families, by doing exactly the opposite of what they think we should. Your dad, with whom you're fighting, is a Yankees fan? Well, then maybe you should root for the Red Sox. Your mom listens to classical music? Well, maybe you'll end up being a fan of industrial metal or punk—and get your nose pierced to boot.

Sometimes familial legacies are more intangible and emotional. If you grew up in a household where there was physical abuse, that might limit your ability to trust other people—but it could also spark your deep need to prove something. If you were raised in a household which was deeply supportive, that might make you more confident in your dealings with the world—but also less aware of the challenges faced by other people.

There are numerous studies on family dynamics, of course, covering everything from sibling rivalry to the lingering effects of divorce or alcoholism. But what literature does that sociology can't is to make us *feel* what it's like to live these things. The stories, poems, essays, and play presented here can provide us with a window into the lives of other people or a mirror which reveals our own inner selves. These insights help us to better understand our own lives and relationships.

THE SELECTIONS IN THIS CHAPTER

The selections in this chapter explore family from a number of angles—as a place of origin, a place of comfort and identity, a source of pride, a source of shame. William Faulkner's "Barn Burning" and Theodore Roethke's "My Papa's Waltz" depict the legacies of difficult fathers—and how characters revere or break away from them. Alice Walker's "Everyday Use" involves a grown daughter who, despite her worldly experience, has a limited appreciation of family heritage, while Amy Tan's "A Pair of Tickets" shows a daughter building understanding about her dead mother's early suffering and sacrifice. Robert Hayden's "Those Winter Sundays" depicts a son who finally comprehends the silent ways his father demonstrated love. James Baldwin's "Sonny's Blues" and Tobias Wolff's "The Rich Brother" both address the issue of what it means to be a sibling—and the responsibilities that should and shouldn't be involved. Diane Thiel's "The Minefield" explores how traumas inflicted on a parent are in turn visited upon the children; and Robert Hayden's "The Whipping" takes on the difficult topic of childhood abuse. Gwendolyn Brooks's "the mother" addresses an unborn child. Lorraine Hansberry's *A Raisin in the Sun* addresses the frustrations of a family's "dream deferred," while Raymond Carver's essay "My Father's Life" honors parents who made the best of limited circumstances, and Brent Staples, in "The Runaway Son," writes of his growing need to escape the pressures of family obligations to create his own life.

We hope that you will find pieces in this chapter to relate to, and to learn from. Each of us has a family story, or a multitude of them. Maybe some of your own stories will be reflected in the pieces you read here. And maybe seeing how other people respond to their family situations—or don't—will give you insight into how to deal with your own.

Things to Think About

1. What is your definition of family? What, in your own mind, is an ideal family?
2. What are some of the assumptions or beliefs you have learned from your family? Does your family have any opinions or beliefs you disagree with?
3. Do you think you are similar to your parents? If so, in what ways? If not, how are you different?
4. How do you feel about your family and its individual members? Proud? Embarrassed? Indifferent? Why?
5. Often siblings take on very different roles in a family, as demonstrated by several pieces in this chapter. Why do siblings sometimes turn out to be so different from each other? How do sibling roles play out in your own family?
6. What part of your family heritage or legacy makes you feel the proudest? What part do you find troubling?

FICTION

PARENTS AND CHILDREN

Amy Tan	*A Pair of Tickets*
William Faulkner	*Barn Burning*
Luke	*Parable of the Prodigal Son*
Alice Walker	*Everyday Use*
	Casebook on "Everyday Use"

Parents play a huge role in the lives of their children, and the effects can be positive or negative—sometimes both. Often parents think of children as extensions of themselves—and children, at least when they're very young, identify with their parents. But there usually comes a time when children begin to see themselves as separate from their parents—when they start to grow up. A son might look at his father and disagree with his opinions or actions. A daughter might look at her mother and realize the mother has a life, distinct and separate from her, which the daughter never imagined. A young adult might reject everything that she thinks her parents stand for, and either move beyond what were limited circumstances or lose something crucial. Sometimes the most difficult breaks come in happy families when a young man or woman feels pulled in some direction inconsistent with a parent's wishes, and the child feels guilty that following his or her own destiny betrays familial love and loyalty. And the parents in these situations might react in a number of ways—by being proud of their children's independence, or trying to stop the changes, or feeling betrayed and angry. The stories in this section, in one way or another, present children differentiating themselves from their parents or discovering connections they had not suspected. When such major shifts occur in a parent-child relationship—and in a family—there is certain to be some difficulty. But this process is all a part of children becoming adults, and of everyone—children and parents—growing up.

Amy Tan

Amy Tan was born in Oakland, California, in 1952. Both of her parents were recent Chinese immigrants. Her father was an electrical engineer (as well as a Baptist minister); her mother was a vocational nurse. When her father and older brother both died of brain tumors, the fifteen-year-old Tan moved with her mother and younger brother to Switzerland, where she attended high school. On their return to the United States Tan attended Linfield College, a Baptist school in Oregon, but she eventually transferred to California State University at San Jose. At this time Tan and her mother argued about her future. The mother insisted her daughter pursue premedical studies in preparation for becoming a neurosurgeon, but Tan wanted to do something else. For six months the

Amy Tan

two did not speak to one another. Tan worked for IBM writing computer manuals and also wrote freelance business articles under a pseudonym. In 1987 she and her mother visited China together. This experience, which is reflected in "A Pair of Tickets," deepened Tan's sense of her Chinese American identity. "As soon as my feet touched China," she wrote, "I became Chinese." Soon after, she began writing her first novel, The Joy Luck Club (1989), which consists of sixteen interrelated stories about a group of Chinese American mothers and their daughters. (The club of the title is a woman's social group.) The Joy Luck Club became both a critical success and a best seller, and was made into a movie in 1993. In 1991 Tan published her second novel, The Kitchen God's Wife. Her later novels include The Bonesetter's Daughter (2001) and Saving Fish from Drowning (2005). Tan performs with a "vintage garage" band called the Rock Bottom Remainders, which also includes, among others, Stephen King, Dave Barry, and Scott Turow. She lives outside San Francisco with her husband.

A Pair of Tickets 1989

The minute our train leaves the Hong Kong border and enters Shenzhen, China, I feel different. I can feel the skin on my forehead tingling, my blood rushing through a new course, my bones aching with a familiar old pain. And I think, My mother was right. I am becoming Chinese.

"Cannot be helped," my mother said when I was fifteen and had vigorously denied that I had any Chinese whatsoever below my skin. I was a sophomore at Galileo High in San Francisco, and all my Caucasian friends agreed: I was about as Chinese as they were. But my mother had studied at a famous nursing school in Shanghai, and she said she knew all about genetics. So there was no doubt in her mind, whether I agreed or not: Once you are born Chinese, you cannot help but feel and think Chinese.

"Someday you will see," said my mother. "It is in your blood, waiting to be let go."

And when she said this, I saw myself transforming like a werewolf, a mutant tag of DNA suddenly triggered, replicating itself insidiously into a *syndrome,*° a cluster of telltale Chinese behaviors, all those things my mother did to embarrass me—haggling with store owners, pecking her mouth with a toothpick in public, being color-blind to the fact that lemon yellow and pale pink are not good combinations for winter clothes.

But today I realize I've never really known what it means to be Chinese. I am 5 thirty-six years old. My mother is dead and I am on a train, carrying with me her dreams of coming home. I am going to China.

We are first going to Guangzhou, my seventy-two-year-old father, Canning Woo, and I, where we will visit his aunt, whom he has not seen since he was ten years old. And I don't know whether it's the prospect of seeing his aunt or if it's because he's back in China, but now he looks like he's a young boy, so innocent and happy I want to button his sweater and pat his head. We are sitting across from each other, separated by a little table with two cold cups of tea. For the first time I can ever remember, my father has tears in his eyes, and all he is seeing out the train window is a sectioned field of yellow, green, and brown, a narrow canal flanking the tracks, low rising hills, and three people in blue jackets riding an ox-driven cart on this early October morning.

syndrome: a group of symptoms that occur together as the sign of a particular disease or abnormality.

And I can't help myself. I also have misty eyes, as if I had seen this a long, long time ago, and had almost forgotten.

In less than three hours, we will be in Guangzhou, which my guidebook tells me is how one properly refers to Canton these days. It seems all the cities I have heard of, except Shanghai, have changed their spellings. I think they are saying China has changed in other ways as well. Chungking is Chongqing. And Kweilin is Guilin. I have looked these names up, because after we see my father's aunt in Guangzhou, we will catch a plane to Shanghai, where I will meet my two half-sisters for the first time.

They are my mother's twin daughters from her first marriage, little babies she was forced to abandon on a road as she was fleeing Kweilin for Chungking in 1944. That was all my mother had told me about these daughters, so they had remained babies in my mind, all these years, sitting on the side of a road, listening to bombs whistling in the distance while sucking their patient red thumbs.

And it was only this year that someone found them and wrote with this joyful news. A letter came from Shanghai, addressed to my mother. When I first heard about this, that they were alive, I imagined my identical sisters transforming from little babies into six-year-old girls. In my mind, they were seated next to each other at a table, taking turns with the fountain pen. One would write a neat row of characters: *Dearest Mama. We are alive.* She would brush back her wispy bangs and hand the other sister the pen, and she would write: *Come get us. Please hurry.*

Of course they could not know that my mother had died three months before, suddenly, when a blood vessel in her brain burst. One minute she was talking to my father, complaining about the tenants upstairs, scheming how to evict them under the pretense that relatives from China were moving in. The next minute she was holding her head, her eyes squeezed shut, groping for the sofa, and then crumpling softly to the floor with fluttering hands.

So my father had been the first one to open the letter, a long letter it turned out. And they did call her Mama. They said they always revered her as their true mother. They kept a framed picture of her. They told her about their life, from the time my mother last saw them on the road leaving Kweilin to when they were finally found.

And the letter had broken my father's heart so much—these daughters calling my mother from another life he never knew—that he gave the letter to my mother's old friend Auntie Lindo and asked her to write back and tell my sisters, in the gentlest way possible, that my mother was dead.

But instead Auntie Lindo took the letter to the Joy Luck Club and discussed with Auntie Ying and Auntie An-mei what should be done, because they had known for many years about my mother's search for her twin daughters, her endless hope. Auntie Lindo and the others cried over this double tragedy, of losing my mother three months before, and now again. And so they couldn't help but think of some miracle, some possible way of reviving her from the dead, so my mother could fulfill her dream.

So this is what they wrote to my sisters in Shanghai: "Dearest Daughters, I too have never forgotten you in my memory or in my heart. I never gave up hope that we would see each other again in a joyous reunion. I am only sorry it has been too long. I want to tell you everything about my life since I last saw you. I want to tell you this when our family comes to see you in China. . . ." They signed it with my mother's name.

It wasn't until all this had been done that they first told me about my sisters, the letter they received, the one they wrote back.

"They'll think she's coming, then," I murmured. And I had imagined my sisters now being ten or eleven, jumping up and down, holding hands, their pigtails bouncing, excited that their mother—*their* mother—was coming, whereas my mother was dead.

"How can you say she is not coming in a letter?" said Auntie Lindo. "She is their mother. She is your mother. You must be the one to tell them. All these years, they have been dreaming of her." And I thought she was right.

But then I started dreaming, too, of my mother and my sisters and how it would be if I arrived in Shanghai. All these years, while they waited to be found, I had lived with my mother and then had lost her. I imagined seeing my sisters at the airport. They would be standing on their tip-toes, looking anxiously, scanning from one dark head to another as we got off the plane. And I would recognize them instantly, their faces with the identical worried look.

"*Jyejye, Jyejye.* Sister, Sister. We are here," I saw myself saying in my poor version of Chinese.

"Where is Mama?" they would say, and look around, still smiling, two flushed and eager faces. "Is she hiding?" And this would have been like my mother, to stand behind just a bit, to tease a little and make people's patience pull a little on their hearts. I would shake my head and tell my sisters she was not hiding.

"Oh, that must be Mama, no?" one of my sisters would whisper excitedly, pointing to another small woman completely engulfed in a tower of presents. And that, too, would have been like my mother, to bring mountains of gifts, food, and toys for children—all bought on sale—shunning thanks, saying the gifts were nothing, and later turning the labels over to show my sisters, "Calvin Klein, 100% wool."

I imagined myself starting to say, "Sisters, I am sorry, I have come alone . . ." and before I could tell them—they could see it in my face—they were wailing, pulling their hair, their lips twisted in pain, as they ran away from me. And then I saw myself getting back on the plane and coming home.

After I had dreamed this scene many times—watching their despair turn from horror into anger—I begged Auntie Lindo to write another letter. And at first she refused.

"How can I say she is dead? I cannot write this," said Auntie Lindo with a stubborn look.

"But it's cruel to have them believe she's coming on the plane," I said. "When they see it's just me, they'll hate me."

"Hate you? Cannot be." She was scowling. "You are their own sister, their only family."

"You don't understand," I protested.

"What I don't understand?" she said.

And I whispered, "They'll think I'm responsible, that she died because I didn't appreciate her."

And Auntie Lindo looked satisfied and sad at the same time, as if this were true and I had finally realized it. She sat down for an hour, and when she stood up she handed me a two-page letter. She had tears in her eyes. I realized that the very thing I had feared, she had done. So even if she had written the news of my mother's death in English, I wouldn't have had the heart to read it.

"Thank you," I whispered.

The landscape has become gray, filled with low flat cement buildings, old factories, and then tracks and more tracks filled with trains like ours passing by in the opposite direction. I see platforms crowded with people wearing drab Western clothes, with spots of bright colors: little children wearing pink and yellow, red and peach. And there are soldiers in olive green and red, and old ladies in gray tops and pants that stop mid-calf. We are in Guangzhou.

Before the train even comes to a stop, people are bringing down their belongings from above their seats. For a moment there is a dangerous shower of heavy suitcases laden with gifts to relatives, half-broken boxes wrapped in miles of string to keep the contents from spilling out, plastic bags filled with yarn and vegetables and packages of dried mushrooms, and camera cases. And then we are caught in a stream of people rushing, shoving, pushing us along, until we find ourselves in one of a dozen lines waiting to go through customs. I feel as if I were getting on the number 30 Stockton bus in San Francisco. I am in China, I remind myself. And somehow the crowds don't bother me. It feels right. I start pushing too.

I take out the declaration forms and my passport. "Woo," it says at the top, and below that, "June May," who was born in "California, U.S.A.," in 1951. I wonder if the customs people will question whether I'm the same person in the passport photo. In this picture, my chin-length hair is swept back and artfully styled. I am wearing false eyelashes, eye shadow, and lip liner. My cheeks are hollowed out by bronze blusher. But I had not expected the heat in October. And now my hair hangs limp with the humidity. I wear no makeup; in Hong Kong my mascara had melted into dark circles and everything else had felt like layers of grease. So today my face is plain, unadorned except for a thin mist of shiny sweat on my forehead and nose.

Even without makeup, I could never pass for true Chinese. I stand five-foot-six, and my head pokes above the crowd so that I am eye level only with other tourists. My mother once told me my height came from my grandfather, who was a northerner, and may have even had some Mongol blood. "This is what your grandmother once told me," explained my mother. "But now it is too late to ask her. They are all dead, your grandparents, your uncles, and their wives and children, all killed in the war, when a bomb fell on our house. So many generations in one instant."

She had said this so matter-of-factly that I thought she had long since gotten over any grief she had. And then I wondered how she knew they were all dead.

"Maybe they left the house before the bomb fell," I suggested.

"No," said my mother. "Our whole family is gone. It is just you and I."

"But how do you know? Some of them could have escaped."

"Cannot be," said my mother, this time almost angrily. And then her frown was washed over by a puzzled blank look, and she began to talk as if she were trying to remember where she had misplaced something. "I went back to that house. I kept looking up to where the house used to be. And it wasn't a house, just the sky. And below, underneath my feet, were four stories of burnt bricks and wood, all the life of our house. Then off to the side I saw things blown into the yard, nothing valuable. There was a bed someone used to sleep in, really just a metal frame twisted up at one corner. And a book, I don't know what kind, because every page had turned black. And I saw a teacup which was unbroken but filled with ashes. And then I found my doll, with her hands and legs broken, her hair burned off. . . . When I was a little girl, I had cried for that doll, seeing it all alone in the store window, and my mother had bought it for me. It was an American doll with yellow hair. It could turn its legs and arms. The eyes moved up and down. And when I married and left my family home, I gave the doll to my youngest niece, because she was like me. She cried if that doll was not with her always. Do you see? If she was in the house with that doll, her parents were there, and so everybody was there, waiting together, because that's how our family was."

The woman in the customs booth stares at my documents, then glances at me briefly, and with two quick movements stamps everything and sternly nods me along. And soon my father and I find ourselves in a large area filled with thousands of people and suitcases. I feel lost and my father looks helpless.

"Excuse me," I say to a man who looks like an American. "Can you tell me where I can get a taxi?" He mumbles something that sounds Swedish or Dutch.

"Syau Yen! Syau Yen!" I hear a piercing voice shout from behind me. An old woman in a yellow knit beret is holding up a pink plastic bag filled with wrapped trinkets. I guess she is trying to sell us something. But my father is staring down at this tiny sparrow of a woman, squinting into her eyes. And then his eyes widen, his face opens up and he smiles like a pleased little boy.

"Aiyi! Aiyi!" —Auntie Auntie!—he says softly.

"Syau Yen!" coos my great-aunt. I think it's funny she has just called my father "Little Wild Goose." It must be his baby milk name, the name used to discourage ghosts from stealing children.

They clasp each other's hands—they do not hug—and hold on like this, taking turns saying, "Look at you! You are so old. Look how old you've become!" They are both crying openly, laughing at the same time, and I bite my lip, trying not to cry. I'm afraid to feel their joy. Because I am thinking how different our arrival in Shanghai will be tomorrow, how awkward it will feel.

Now Aiyi beams and points to a Polaroid picture of my father. My father had wisely sent pictures when he wrote and said we were coming. See how smart she was, she seems to intone as she compares the picture to my father. In the letter, my father had said we would call her from the hotel once we arrived, so this is a surprise, that they've come to meet us. I wonder if my sisters will be at the airport.

It is only then that I remember the camera. I had meant to take a picture of my father and his aunt the moment they met. It's not too late.

"Here, stand together over here," I say, holding up the Polaroid. The camera flashes and I hand them the snapshot. Aiyi and my father still stand close together, each of them holding a corner of the picture, watching as their images begin to form. They are almost reverentially quiet. Aiyi is only five years older than my father, which makes her around seventy-seven. But she looks ancient, shrunken, a mummified relic. Her thin hair is pure white, her teeth are brown with decay. So much for stories of Chinese women looking young forever, I think to myself.

Now Aiyi is crooning to me: "*Jandale.*" So big already. She looks up at me, at my full height, and then peers into her pink plastic bag—her gifts to us, I have figured out—as if she is wondering what she will give to me, now that I am so old and big. And then she grabs my elbow with her sharp pincerlike grasp and turns me around. A man and woman in their fifties are shaking hands with my father, everybody smiling and saying, "Ah! Ah!" They are Aiyi's oldest son and his wife, and standing next to them are four other people, around my age, and a little girl who's around ten. The introductions go by so fast, all I know is that one of them is Aiyi's grandson, with his wife, and the other is her granddaughter, with her husband. And the little girl is Lili, Aiyi's great-granddaughter.

Aiyi and my father speak the Mandarin dialect from their childhood, but the rest of the family speaks only the Cantonese of their village. I understand only Mandarin but can't speak it that well. So Aiyi and my father gossip unrestrained in Mandarin, exchanging news about people from their old village. And they stop only occasionally to talk to the rest of us, sometimes in Cantonese, sometimes in English.

"Oh, it is as I suspected," says my father, turning to me. "He died last summer." And I already understood this. I just don't know who this person, Li Gong, is. I feel as if I were in the United Nations and the translators had run amok.

"Hello," I say to the little girl. "My name is Jing-mei." But the little girl squirms to look away, causing her parents to laugh with embarrassment. I try to think of Cantonese words I can say to her, stuff I learned from friends in Chinatown, but all I can think of are swear words, terms for bodily functions, and short phrases like "tastes good," "tastes like garbage," and "she's really ugly." And then I have another plan: I hold up the Polaroid camera, beckoning Lili with my finger. She immediately jumps forward, places one hand on her hip in the manner of a fashion model, juts out her chest, and flashes me a toothy smile. As soon as I take the picture she is standing next to me, jumping and giggling every few seconds as she watches herself appear on the greenish film.

By the time we hail taxis for the ride to the hotel, Lili is holding tight onto my hand, pulling me along.

In the taxi, Aiyi talks nonstop, so I have no chance to ask her about the different sights we are passing by.

"You wrote and said you would come only for one day," says Aiyi to my father in an agitated tone. "One day! How can you see your family in one day! Toishan is many hours' drive from Guangzhou. And this idea to call us when you arrive. This is nonsense. We have no telephone."

My heart races a little. I wonder if Auntie Lindo told my sisters we would call from the hotel in Shanghai?

Aiyi continues to scold my father. "I was so beside myself, ask my son, almost turned heaven and earth upside down trying to think of a way! So we decided the best was for us to take the bus from Toishan and come into Guangzhou—meet you right from the start."

And now I am holding my breath as the taxi driver dodges between trucks and buses, honking his horn constantly. We seem to be on some sort of long freeway overpass, like a bridge above the city. I can see row after row of apartments, each floor cluttered with laundry hanging out to dry on the balcony. We pass a public bus, with people jammed in so tight their faces are nearly wedged against the window. Then I see the skyline of what must be downtown Guangzhou. From a distance, it looks like a major American city, with high rises and construction going on everywhere. As we slow down in the more congested part of the city, I see scores of little shops, dark inside, lined with counters and shelves. And then there is a building, its front laced with scaffolding made of bamboo poles held together with plastic strips. Men and women are standing on narrow platforms, scraping the sides, working without safety straps or helmets. Oh, would OSHA° have a field day here, I think.

Aiyi's shrill voice rises up again: "So it is a shame you can't see our village, our house. My sons have been quite successful, selling our vegetables in the free market. We had enough these last few years to build a big house, three stories, all of new brick, big enough for our whole family and then some. And every year, the money is even better. You Americans aren't the only ones who know how to get rich!"

The taxi stops and I assume we've arrived, but then I peer out at what looks like a grander version of the Hyatt Regency. "This is communist China?" I wonder out loud. And then I shake my head toward my father. "This must be the wrong hotel." I quickly pull out our itinerary, travel tickets, and reservations. I had explicitly instructed my travel agent to choose something inexpensive, in the thirty-to-forty-dollar range. I'm sure of this. And there it says on our itinerary: Garden Hotel, Huanshi Dong Lu. Well, our travel agent had better be prepared to eat the extra, that's all I have to say.

The hotel is magnificent. A bellboy complete with uniform and sharp-creased cap jumps forward and begins to carry our bags into the lobby. Inside, the hotel looks like an orgy of shopping arcades and restaurants all encased in granite and glass. And rather than be impressed, I am worried about the expense, as well as the appearance it must give Aiyi, that we rich Americans cannot be without our luxuries even for one night.

But when I step up to the reservation desk, ready to haggle over this booking mistake, it is confirmed. Our rooms are prepaid, thirty-four dollars each. I feel sheepish, and Aiyi and the others seem delighted by our temporary surroundings. Lili is looking wide-eyed at an arcade filled with video games.

Our whole family crowds into one elevator, and the bellboy waves, saying he will meet us on the eighteenth floor. As soon as the elevator door shuts, everybody becomes very quiet, and when the door finally opens again, everybody talks at once in what sounds like relieved voices. I have the feeling Aiyi and the others have never been on such a long elevator ride.

Our rooms are next to each other and are identical. The rugs, drapes, bedspreads are all in shades of taupe. There's a color television with remote-control panels built into the lamp table between the two twin beds. The bathroom has marble walls and floors. I find a built-in wet bar with a small refrigerator stocked with Heineken beer, Coke Classic, and Seven-Up, mini-bottles of Johnnie Walker Red, Bacardi rum, and Smirnoff vodka, and packets of M & M's, honey-roasted cashews, and Cadbury chocolate bars. And again I say out loud, "This is communist China?"

My father comes into my room. "They decided we should just stay here and visit," he says, shrugging his shoulders. "They say, Less trouble that way. More time to talk."

"What about dinner?" I ask. I have been envisioning my first real Chinese feast for many days already, a big banquet with one of those soups steaming out of a carved winter melon, chicken wrapped in clay, Peking duck, the works.

OSHA: Occupational Safety and Health Administration, a U.S. federal agency that regulates and monitors workplace safety conditions.

My father walks over and picks up a room service book next to a *Travel & Leisure* magazine. He flips through the pages quickly and then points to the menu. "This is what they want," says my father.

So it's decided. We are going to dine tonight in our rooms, with our family, sharing hamburgers, french fries, and apple pie à la mode.

Aiyi and her family are browsing the shops while we clean up. After a hot ride on the train, I'm eager for a shower and cooler clothes.

The hotel has provided little packets of shampoo which, upon opening, I discover is the consistency and color of hoisin sauce. This is more like it, I think. This is China. And I rub some in my damp hair.

Standing in the shower, I realize this is the first time I've been by myself in what seems like days. But instead of feeling relieved, I feel forlorn. I think about what my mother said, about activating my genes and becoming Chinese. And I wonder what she meant.

Right after my mother died, I asked myself a lot of things, things that couldn't be answered, to force myself to grieve more. It seemed as if I wanted to sustain my grief, to assure myself that I had cared deeply enough.

But now I ask the questions mostly because I want to know the answers. What was that pork stuff she used to make that had the texture of sawdust? What were the names of the uncles who died in Shanghai? What had she dreamt all these years about her other daughters? All the times when she got mad at me, was she really thinking about them? Did she wish I were they? Did she regret that I wasn't?

At one o'clock in the morning, I awake to tapping sounds on the window. I must have dozed off and now I feel my body uncramping itself. I'm sitting on the floor, leaning against one of the twin beds. Lili is lying next to me. The others are asleep, too, sprawled out on the beds and floor. Aiyi is seated at a little table, looking very sleepy. And my father is staring out the window, tapping his fingers on the glass. The last time I listened my father was telling Aiyi about his life since he last saw her. How he had gone to Yenching University, later got a post with a newspaper in Chungking, met my mother there, a young widow. How they later fled together to Shanghai to try to find my mother's family house, but there was nothing there. And then they traveled eventually to Canton and then to Hong Kong, then Haiphong and finally to San Francisco. . . .

"Suyuan didn't tell me she was trying all these years to find her daughters," he is now saying in a quiet voice. "Naturally, I did not discuss her daughters with her. I thought she was ashamed she had left them behind."

"Where did she leave them?" asks Aiyi. "How were they found?"

I am wide awake now. Although I have heard parts of this story from my mother's friends.

"It happened when the Japanese took over Kweilin," says my father.

"Japanese in Kweilin?" says Aiyi. "That was never the case. Couldn't be. The Japanese never came to Kweilin."

"Yes, that is what the newspapers reported. I know this because I was working for the news bureau at the time. The Kuomintang often told us what we could say and could not say. But we knew the Japanese had come into Kwangsi Province. We had sources who told us how they had captured the Wuchang-Canton railway. How they were coming overland, making very fast progress, marching toward the provincial capital."

Aiyi looks astonished. "If people did not know this, how could Suyuan know the Japanese were coming?"

"An officer of the Kuomintang secretly warned her," explains my father. "Suyuan's husband also was an officer and everybody knew that officers and their families would be the first to be killed. So she gathered a few possessions and, in the middle of the night, she picked up her daughters and fled on foot. The babies were not even one year old."

"How could she give up those babies!" sighs Aiyi. "Twin girls. We have never had such luck in our family." And then she yawns again.

"What were they named?" she asks. I listen carefully. I had been planning on using just the familiar "Sister" to address them both. But now I want to know how to pronounce their names.

"They have their father's surname, Wang," says my father. "And their given names are Chwun Yu and Chwun Hwa."

"What do the names mean?" I ask.

"Ah." My father draws imaginary characters on the window. "One means 'Spring Rain,' the other 'Spring Flower,'" he explains in English, "because they born in the spring, and of course rain come before flower, same order these girls are born. Your mother like a poet, don't you think?"

I nod my head. I see Aiyi nod her head forward, too. But it falls forward and stays there. She is breathing deeply, noisily. She is asleep.

"And what does Ma's name mean?" I whisper.

"'Suyuan,'" he says, writing more invisible characters on the glass. "The way she write it in Chinese, it mean 'Long-Cherished Wish.' Quite a fancy name, not so ordinary like flower name. See this first character, it mean something like 'Forever Never Forgotten.' But there is another way to write 'Suyuan.' Sound exactly the same, but the meaning is opposite." His finger creates the brushstrokes of another character. "The first part look the same: 'Never Forgotten.' But the last part add to first part make the whole word mean 'Long-Held Grudge.' Your mother get angry with me, I tell her her name should be Grudge."

My father is looking at me, moist-eyed. "See, I pretty clever, too, hah?"

I nod, wishing I could find some way to comfort him. "And what about my name," I ask, "what does 'Jing-mei' mean?"

"Your name also special," he says. I wonder if any name in Chinese is not something special. "'Jing' like excellent *jing*. Not just good, it's something pure, essential, the best quality. *Jing* is good leftover stuff when you take impurities out of something like gold, or rice, or salt. So what is left—just pure essence. And 'Mei,' this is common *mei*, as in *meimei*, 'younger sister.'"

I think about this. My mother's long-cherished wish. Me, the younger sister who was supposed to be the essence of the others. I feed myself with the old grief, wondering how disappointed my mother must have been. Tiny Aiyi stirs suddenly, her head rolls and then falls back, her mouth opens as if to answer my question. She grunts in her sleep, tucking her body more closely into the chair.

"So why did she abandon those babies on the road?" I need to know, because now I feel abandoned too.

"Long time I wondered this myself," says my father. "But then I read that letter from her daughters in Shanghai now, and I talk to Auntie Lindo, all the others. And then I knew. No shame in what she done. None."

"What happened?"

"Your mother running away—" begins my father.

"No, tell me in Chinese," I interrupt. "Really, I can understand."

He begins to talk, still standing at the window, looking into the night.

After fleeing Kweilin, your mother walked for several days trying to find a main road. Her thought was to catch a ride on a truck or wagon, to catch enough rides until she reached Chungking, where her husband was stationed.

She had sewn money and jewelry into the lining of her dress, enough, she thought, to barter rides all the way. If I am lucky, she thought, I will not have to trade the heavy gold bracelet and jade ring. These were things from her mother, your grandmother.

By the third day, she had traded nothing. The roads were filled with people, everybody running and begging for rides from passing trucks. The trucks rushed by, afraid to stop. So your mother found no rides, only the start of dysentery pains in her stomach.

Her shoulders ached from the two babies swinging from scarf slings. Blisters grew on her palms from holding two leather suitcases. And then the blisters burst and began to bleed. After a while, she left the suitcases behind, keeping only the food and a few clothes. And later she also dropped the bags of wheat flour and rice and kept walking like this for many miles, singing songs to her little girls, until she was delirious with pain and fever.

Finally, there was not one more step left in her body. She didn't have the strength to carry those babies any farther. She slumped to the ground. She knew she would die of her sickness, or perhaps from thirst, from starvation, or from the Japanese, who she was sure were marching right behind her.

She took the babies out of the slings and sat them on the side of the road, then lay down next to them. You babies are so good, she said, so quiet. They smiled back, reaching their chubby hands for her, wanting to be picked up again. And then she knew she could not bear to watch her babies die with her.

She saw a family with three young children in a cart going by. "Take my babies, I beg you," she cried to them. But they stared back with empty eyes and never stopped.

She saw another person pass and called out again. This time a man turned around, and he had such a terrible expression—your mother said it looked like death itself—she shivered and looked away.

When the road grew quiet, she tore open the lining of her dress, and stuffed jewelry under the shirt of one baby and money under the other. She reached into her pocket and drew out the photos of her family, the picture of her father and mother, the picture of herself and her husband on their wedding day. And she wrote on the back of each the names of the babies and this same message: "Please care for these babies with the money and valuables provided. When it is safe to come, if you bring them to Shanghai, 9 Weichang Lu, the Li family will be glad to give you a generous reward. Li Suyuan and Wang Fuchi."

And then she touched each baby's cheek and told her not to cry. She would go down the road to find them some food and would be back. And without looking back, she walked down the road, stumbling and crying, thinking only of this one last hope, that her daughters would be found by a kindhearted person who would care for them. She would not allow herself to imagine anything else.

She did not remember how far she walked, which direction she went, when she fainted, or how she was found. When she awoke, she was in the back of a bouncing truck with several other sick people, all moaning. And she began to scream, thinking she was now on a journey to Buddhist hell. But the face of an American missionary lady bent over her and smiled, talking to her in a soothing language she did not understand. And yet she could somehow understand. She had been saved for no good reason, and it was now too late to go back and save her babies.

When she arrived in Chungking, she learned her husband had died two weeks before. She told me later she laughed when the officers told her this news, she was so delirious with madness and disease. To come so far, to lose so much and to find nothing.

I met her in a hospital. She was lying on a cot, hardly able to move, her dysentery had drained her so thin. I had come in for my foot, my missing toe, which was cut off by a piece of falling rubble. She was talking to herself, mumbling.

"Look at these clothes," she said, and I saw she had on a rather unusual dress for wartime. It was silk satin, quite dirty, but there was no doubt it was a beautiful dress.

"Look at this face," she said, and I saw her dusty face and hollow cheeks, her eyes shining back. "Do you see my foolish hope?"

"I thought I had lost everything, except these two things," she murmured. "And I wondered which I would lose next. Clothes or hope? Hope or clothes?"

"But now, see here, look what is happening," she said, laughing, as if all her prayers had been answered. And she was pulling hair out of her head as easily as one lifts new wheat from wet soil.

It was an old peasant woman who found them. "How could I resist?" the peasant woman later told your sisters when they were older. They were still sitting obediently near where your mother had left them, looking like little fairy queens waiting for their sedan to arrive.

The woman, Mei Ching, and her husband, Mei Han, lived in a stone cave. There were thousands of hidden caves like that in and around Kweilin so secret that the people remained hidden even after the war ended. The Meis would come out of their cave every few days and forage for food supplies left on the road, and sometimes they would see something that they both agreed was a tragedy to leave behind. So one day they took back to their cave a delicately painted set of rice bowls, another day a little footstool with a velvet cushion and two new wedding blankets. And once, it was your sisters.

They were pious people, Muslims, who believed the twin babies were a sign of double luck, and they were sure of this when, later in the evening, they discovered how valuable the babies were. She and her husband had never seen rings and bracelets like those. And while they admired the pictures, knowing the babies came from a good family, neither of them could read or write. It was not until many months later that Mei Ching found someone who could read the writing on the back. By then, she loved these baby girls like her own.

In 1952 Mei Han, the husband, died. The twins were already eight years old, and Mei Ching now decided it was time to find your sisters' true family.

She showed the girls the picture of their mother and told them they had been born into a great family and she would take them back to see their true mother and grandparents. Mei Ching told them about the reward, but she swore she would refuse it. She loved these girls so much, she only wanted them to have what they were entitled to—a better life, a fine house, educated ways. Maybe the family would let her stay on as the girls' amah. Yes, she was certain they would insist.

Of course, when she found the place at 9 Weichang Lu, in the old French Concession, it was something completely different. It was the site of a factory building, recently constructed, and none of the workers knew what had become of the family whose house had burned down on that spot.

Mei Ching could not have known, of course, that your mother and I, her new husband, had already returned to that same place in 1945 in hopes of finding both her family and her daughters.

Your mother and I stayed in China until 1947. We went to many different cities—back to Kweilin, to Changsha, as far south as Kunming. She was always looking out of one corner of her eye for twin babies, then little girls. Later we went to Hong Kong, and when we finally left in 1949 for the United States, I think she was even looking for them on the boat. But when we arrived, she no longer talked about them. I thought, At last, they have died in her heart.

When letters could be openly exchanged between China and the United States, she wrote immediately to old friends in Shanghai and Kweilin. I did not know she did this. Auntie Lindo told me. But of course, by then, all the street names had changed. Some people had died, others had moved away. So it took many years to find a contact. And when she did find an old schoolmate's address and wrote asking her to look for her daughters, her friend wrote back and said this was impossible, like looking for a needle on the bottom of the ocean. How did she know her daughters were in Shanghai and not somewhere else in China? The friend, of course, did not ask, How do you know your daughters are still alive?

So her schoolmate did not look. Finding babies lost during the war was a matter of foolish imagination, and she had no time for that.

But every year, your mother wrote to different people. And this last year, I think she got a big idea in her head, to go to China and find them herself. I remember she told me, "Canning, we should go, before it is too late, before we are too old." And I told her we were already too old, it was already too late.

I just thought she wanted to be a tourist! I didn't know she wanted to go and look for her daughters. So when I said it was too late, that must have put a terrible thought in her head that her daughters might be dead. And I think this possibility grew bigger and bigger in her head, until it killed her.

Maybe it was your mother's dead spirit who guided her Shanghai schoolmate to find her daughters. Because after your mother died, the schoolmate saw your sisters, by chance, while shopping for shoes at the Number One Department Store on Nanjing Dong Road. She said it was like a dream, seeing these two women who looked so much alike, moving down the stairs together. There was something about their facial expressions that reminded the schoolmate of your mother.

She quickly walked over to them and called their names, which of course, they did not recognize at first, because Mei Ching had changed their names. But your mother's friend was so sure, she persisted. "Are you not Wang Chwun Yu and Wang Chwun Hwa?" she asked them. And then these double-image women became very excited, because they remembered the names written on the back of an old photo, a photo of a young man and woman they still honored, as their much-loved first parents, who had died and become spirit ghosts still roaming the earth looking for them.

At the airport, I am exhausted. I could not sleep last night. Aiyi had followed me into my room at three in the morning, and she instantly fell asleep on one of the twin beds, snoring with the might of a lumberjack. I lay awake thinking about my mother's story, realizing how much I have never known about her, grieving that my sisters and I had both lost her.

And now at the airport, after shaking hands with everybody, waving good-bye, I think about all the different ways we leave people in this world. Cheerily waving good-bye to some at airports, knowing we'll never see each other again. Leaving others on the side of the road, hoping that we will. Finding my mother in my father's story and saying good-bye before I have a chance to know her better.

Aiyi smiles at me as we wait for our gate to be called. She is so old. I put one arm around her and one around Lili. They are the same size, it seems. And then it's time. As we wave good-bye one more time and enter the waiting area, I get the sense I am going from one funeral to another. In my hand I'm clutching a pair of tickets to Shanghai. In two hours we'll be there.

The plane takes off. I close my eyes. How can I describe to them in my broken Chinese about our mother's life? Where should I begin?

"Wake up, we're here," says my father. And I awake with my heart pounding in my throat. I look out the window and we're already on the runway. It's gray outside.

And now I'm walking down the steps of the plane, onto the tarmac and toward the building. If only, I think, if only my mother had lived long enough to be the one walking toward them. I am so nervous I cannot even feel my feet. I am just moving somehow.

Somebody shouts, "She's arrived!" And then I see her. Her short hair. Her small body. And that same look on her face. She has the back of her hand pressed hard against her mouth. She is crying as though she had gone through a terrible ordeal and were happy it is over.

And I know it's not my mother, yet it is the same look she had when I was five and had disappeared all afternoon, for such a long time, that she was convinced I was dead. And when I miraculously appeared, sleepy-eyed, crawling from underneath my bed, she wept and laughed, biting the back of her hand to make sure it was true.

And now I see her again, two of her, waving, and in one hand there is a photo, the Polaroid I sent them. As soon as I get beyond the gate, we run toward each other, all three of us embracing, all hesitations and expectations forgotten.

"Mama, Mama," we all murmur, as if she is among us.

My sisters look at me, proudly. *"Meimei jandale,"* says one sister proudly to the other. "Little Sister has grown up." I look at their faces again and I see no trace of my mother in them. Yet they still look familiar. And now I also see what part of me is Chinese. It is so obvious. It is my family. It is in our blood. After all these years, it can finally be let go.

                        *

My sisters and I stand, arms around each other, laughing and wiping the tears from each other's eyes. The flash of the Polaroid goes off and my father hands me the snapshot. My sisters and I watch quietly together, eager to see what develops.

The gray-green surface changes to the bright colors of our three images, sharpening and deepening all at once. And although we don't speak, I know we all see it: Together we look like our mother. Her same eyes, her same mouth, open in surprise to see, at last, her long-cherished wish.

Questions

1. How is the external setting of "A Pair of Tickets" essential to what happens internally to the narrator in the course of this story?
2. How does the narrator's view of her father change by seeing him in a different setting?
3. In what ways does the narrator feel at home in China? In what ways does she feel foreign?
4. What do the narrator and her half-sisters have in common? How does this element relate to the theme of the story?
5. In what ways does the story explore specifically Chinese American experiences? In what other ways is the story grounded in universal family issues?

William Faulkner

William Faulkner (1897–1962) spent most of his days in Oxford, Mississippi, where he attended the University of Mississippi and where he served as postmaster until angry townspeople ejected him because they had failed to receive mail. During World War I he served with the Royal Canadian Air Force and afterward worked as a feature writer for the New Orleans Times-Picayune. Faulkner's private life was a long struggle to stay solvent: even after fame came to him, he had to write Hollywood scripts and teach at the University of Virginia to support himself. His violent comic novel Sanctuary (1931) caused a stir and turned a profit, but critics tend most to admire The Sound and the Fury (1929), a tale partially told through the eyes of an idiot; As I Lay Dying (1930); Light in August (1932); Absalom, Absalom (1936); and The Hamlet (1940). Beginning with Sartoris (1929), Faulkner in his fiction imagines a Mississippi county named Yoknapatawpha and traces the fortunes of several of its families, including the aristocratic Compsons and Sartorises and the white-trash, dollar-grabbing Snopeses, from the Civil War to modern times. His influence on his fellow Southern writers (and others) has been profound. In 1950 he received the Nobel Prize in Literature. Although we think of Faulkner primarily as a novelist, he wrote nearly a hundred short stories. Forty-two of the best are available in his Collected Stories (1950; 1995).

William Faulkner

Barn Burning   1939

The store in which the Justice of the Peace's court was sitting smelled of cheese. The boy, crouched on his nail keg at the back of the crowded room, knew he smelled cheese, and more: from where he sat he could see the ranked shelves close-packed with the solid, squat, dynamic shapes of tin cans whose labels his stomach read, not from the lettering which meant nothing to his mind but from the scarlet devils and the silver curve of fish—this, the cheese which he knew he smelled and the hermetic meat which his intestines believed he smelled coming in intermittent gusts momentary and brief between the other constant one, the smell and sense just a little of fear because mostly of despair and grief, the old fierce pull of blood. He could not see the table where the Justice sat and before which his father and his father's enemy (*our enemy* he thought in that despair: *ourn! mine and hisn both! He's my father!*) stood, but he could hear them, the two of them that is, because his father had said no word yet:

"But what proof have you, Mr. Harris?"

"I told you. The hog got into my corn. I caught it up and sent it back to him. He had no fence that would hold it. I told him so, warned him. The next time I put the hog in my pen. When he came to get it I gave him enough wire to patch up his pen. The next time I put the hog up and kept it. I rode down to his house and saw the wire I gave him still rolled on to the spool in his yard. I told him he could have the hog when he paid me a dollar pound fee. That evening a nigger came with the dollar and got the hog. He was a strange nigger. He said, 'He say to tell you wood and hay kin burn.' I said, 'What?' 'That whut he say to tell you,' the nigger said. 'Wood and hay kin burn.' That night my barn burned. I got the stock out but I lost the barn."

"Where's the nigger? Have you got him?"

"He was a strange nigger, I tell you. I don't know what became of him."

"But that's not proof. Don't you see that's not proof?"

"Get that boy up here. He knows." For a moment the boy thought too that the man meant his older brother until Harris said, "Not him. The little one. The boy," and, crouching, small for his age, small and wiry like his father, in patched and faded jeans even too small for him, with straight, uncombed, brown hair and eyes gray and wild as storm scud, he saw the men between himself and the table part and become a lane of grim faces, at the end of which he saw the Justice, a shabby, collarless, graying man in spectacles, beckoning him. He felt no floor under his bare feet; he seemed to walk beneath the palpable weight of the grim turning faces. His father, still in his black Sunday coat donned not for the trial but for the moving, did not even look at him. *He aims for me to lie*, he thought, again with that frantic grief and despair. *And I will have to do hit.*

"What's your name, boy?" the Justice said.

"Colonel Sartoris Snopes," the boy whispered.

"Hey?" the Justice said. "Talk louder. Colonel Sartoris? I reckon anybody named for Colonel Sartoris in this country can't help but tell the truth, can they?" The boy said nothing. *Enemy! Enemy!* he thought; for a moment he could not even see, could not see that the Justice's face was kindly nor discern that his voice was troubled when he spoke to the man named Harris: "Do you want me to question this boy?" But he could hear, and during those subsequent long seconds while there was absolutely no sound in the crowded little room save that of quiet and intent breathing it was as if he had swung outward at the end of a grape vine, over a ravine, and at the top of the swing had been caught in a prolonged instant of mesmerized gravity, weightless in time.

"No!" Harris said violently, explosively. "Damnation! Send him out of here!" Now time, the fluid world, rushed beneath him again, the voices coming to him again through the smell of cheese and sealed meat, the fear and despair and the old grief of blood:

"This case is closed. I can't find against you, Snopes, but I can give you advice. Leave this country and don't come back to it."

His father spoke for the first time, his voice cold and harsh, level, without emphasis: "I aim to. I don't figure to stay in a country among people who . . ." he said something unprintable and vile, addressed to no one.

"That'll do," the Justice said. "Take your wagon and get out of this country before dark. Case dismissed."

His father turned, and he followed the stiff black coat, the wiry figure walking a little stiffly from where a Confederate provost's man's musket ball had taken him in the heel on a stolen horse thirty years ago, followed the two backs now, since his older brother had appeared from somewhere in the crowd, no taller than the father but thicker, chewing tobacco steadily, between the two lines of grim-faced men and out of the store and across the worn gallery and down the sagging steps and among the dogs and half-grown boys in the mild May dust, where as he passed a voice hissed:

"Barn burner!"

Again he could not see, whirling; there was a face in a red haze, moonlike, bigger than the full moon, the owner of it half again his size, he leaping in the red haze toward the face, feeling no blow, feeling no shock when his head struck the earth, scrabbling up and leaping again, feeling no blow this time either and tasting no blood, scrabbling up to see the other boy in full flight and himself already leaping into pursuit as his father's hand jerked him back, the harsh, cold voice speaking above him: "Go get in the wagon."

It stood in a grove of locusts and mulberries across the road. His two hulking sisters in their Sunday dresses and his mother and her sister in calico and sunbonnets were already in it, sitting on and among the sorry residue of the dozen and more movings which even the boy could remember—the battered stove, the broken beds and chairs, the clock inlaid with mother-of-pearl, which would not run, stopped at some fourteen minutes past two o'clock of a dead and forgotten day and time, which had been his mother's dowry. She was crying, though when she saw him she drew her sleeve across her face and began to descend from the wagon. "Get back," the father said.

"He's hurt. I got to get some water and wash his . . ."

"Get back in the wagon," his father said. He got in too, over the tail-gate. His father mounted to the seat where the older brother already sat and struck the gaunt mules two savage blows with the peeled willow, but without heat. It was not even sadistic; it was exactly that same quality which in later years would cause his descendants to over-run the engine before putting a motor car into motion, striking and reining back in the same movement. The wagon went on, the store with its quiet crowd of grimly watching men dropped behind; a curve in the road hid it. *Forever* he thought. *Maybe he's done satisfied now, now that he has* . . . stopping himself, not to say it aloud even to himself. His mother's hand touched his shoulder.

"Does hit hurt?" she said.

"Naw," he said. "Hit don't hurt. Lemme be."

"Can't you wipe some of the blood off before hit dries?"

"I'll wash to-night," he said. "Lemme be, I tell you."

The wagon went on. He did not know where they were going. None of them ever did or ever asked, because it was always somewhere, always a house of sorts waiting for them a day or two days or even three days away. Likely his father had already arranged to make a crop on another farm before he . . . Again he had to stop himself. He (the father) always did. There was something about his wolflike independence and even courage when the advantage was at least neutral which impressed strangers, as if they got from his latent ravening ferocity not so much a sense of dependability as a feeling that his ferocious conviction in the rightness of his own actions would be of advantage to all whose interest lay with his.

That night they camped, in a grove of oaks and beeches where a spring ran. The nights were still cool and they had a fire against it, of a rail lifted from a nearby fence and cut into lengths—a small fire, neat, niggard almost, a shrewd fire; such fires were his father's habit and custom always, even in freezing weather. Older, the boy might have remarked this and wondered why not a big one; why should not a man who had not only seen the waste and extravagance of war, but who had in his blood an inherent voracious prodigality with material not his own, have burned everything in sight? Then he might have gone a step farther and thought that that was the reason: that niggard blaze was the living fruit of nights passed during those four years in the woods hiding from all men, blue and gray, with his strings of horses (captured horses, he called them). And older still, he might have divined the true reason: that the element of fire spoke to some deep mainspring of his father's being, as the element of steel or of powder spoke to other men, as the one weapon for the preservation of integrity, else breath were not worth the breathing, and hence to be regarded with respect and used with discretion.

But he did not think this now and he had seen those same niggard blazes all his life. He merely ate his supper beside it and was already half asleep over his iron plate when his father called him, and once more he followed the stiff back, the stiff and ruthless limp, up the slope and on to the starlit road where, turning, he could see his father against the stars but without face or depth—a shape black, flat, and bloodless as though cut from tin in the iron folds of the frockcoat which had not been made for him, the voice harsh like tin and without heat like tin:

"You were fixing to tell them. You would have told him." He didn't answer. His father struck him with the flat of his hand on the side of the head, hard but without heat, exactly as he had struck the two mules at the store, exactly as he would strike either of them with any stick in order to kill a horse fly, his voice without heat or anger: "You're getting to be a man. You got to learn. You got to learn to stick to your own blood or you ain't going to have any blood to stick to you. Do you think either of them, any man there this morning, would? Don't you know all they wanted was a chance to get at me because they knew I had them beat? Eh?" Later, twenty years later, he was to tell himself, "If I had said they wanted only truth, justice, he would have hit me again." But now he said nothing. He was not crying. He just stood there. "Answer me," his father said.

"Yes," he whispered. His father turned.

"Get on to bed. We'll be there tomorrow."

Tomorrow they were there. In the early afternoon the wagon stopped before a paintless two-room house identical almost with the dozen others it had stopped before even in the boy's ten years, and again, as on the other dozen occasions, his mother and aunt got down and began to unload the wagon, although his two sisters and his father and brother had not moved.

"Likely hit ain't fitten for hawgs," one of the sisters said.

30

"Nevertheless, fit it will and you'll hog it and like it," his father said. "Get out of them chairs and help your Ma unload."

The two sisters got down, big, bovine, in a flutter of cheap ribbons; one of them drew from the jumbled wagon bed a battered lantern, the other a worn broom. His father handed the reins to the older son and began to climb stiffly over the wheel. "When they get unloaded, take the team to the barn and feed them." Then he said, and at first the boy thought he was still speaking to his brother: "Come with me."

"Me?" he said.

"Yes," his father said. "You."

"Abner," his mother said. His father paused and looked back—the harsh level stare beneath the shaggy, graying, irascible brows.

"I reckon I'll have a word with the man that aims to begin to-morrow owning me body and soul for the next eight months."

They went back up the road. A week ago—or before last night, that is—he would have asked where they were going, but not now. His father had struck him before last night but never before had he paused afterward to explain why; it was as if the blow and the following calm, outrageous voice still rang, repercussed, divulging nothing to him save the terrible handicap of being young, the light weight of his few years, just heavy enough to prevent his soaring free of the world as it seemed to be ordered but not heavy enough to keep him footed solid in it, to resist it and try to change the course of its events.

Presently he could see the grove of oaks and cedars and the other flowering trees and shrubs where the house would be, though not the house yet. They walked beside a fence massed with honeysuckle and Cherokee roses and came to a gate swinging open between two brick pillars, and now, beyond a sweep of drive, he saw the house for the first time and at that instant he forgot his father and the terror and despair both, and even when he remembered his father again (who had not stopped) the terror and despair did not return. Because, for all the twelve movings, they had sojourned until now in a poor country, a land of small farms and fields and houses, and he had never seen a house like this before. *Hit's big as a courthouse* he thought quietly, with a surge of peace and joy whose reason he could not have thought into words, being too young for that: *They are safe from him. People whose lives are a part of this peace and dignity are beyond his touch, he no more to them than a buzzing wasp: capable of stinging for a little moment but that's all; the spell of this peace and dignity rendering even the barns and stable and cribs which belong to it impervious to the puny flames he might contrive* . . . this, the peace and joy, ebbing for an instant as he looked again at the stiff black back, the stiff and implacable limp of the figure which was not dwarfed by the house, for the reason that it had never looked big anywhere and which now, against the serene columned backdrop, had more than ever that impervious quality of something cut ruthlessly from tin, depthless, as though, sidewise to the sun, it would cast no shadow. Watching him, the boy remarked the absolutely undeviating course which his father held and saw the stiff foot come squarely down in a pile of fresh droppings where a horse had stood in the drive and which his father could have avoided by a simple change of stride. But it ebbed only a moment, though he could not have thought this into words either, walking on in the spell of the house, which he could even want but without envy, without sorrow, certainly never with that ravening and jealous rage which unknown to him walked in the ironlike black coat before him: *Maybe he will feel it too. Maybe it will even change him now from what maybe he couldn't help but be.*

They crossed the portico. Now he could hear his father's stiff foot as it came down on the boards with clocklike finality, a sound out of all proportion to the displacement of the body it bore and which was not dwarfed either by the white door before it, as though it had attained to a sort of vicious and ravening minimum not to be dwarfed by anything—the flat, wide, black hat, the formal coat of broadcloth which had once been black but which had now that friction-glazed greenish cast of the bodies of old house flies, the lifted sleeve which was too large, the lifted hand like a curled claw. The door opened so promptly that the boy knew the Negro must have been watching them all the time, an old man with neat grizzled hair, in a linen jacket, who stood barring the door with his body, saying, "Wipe yo foots, white man, fo you come in here. Major ain't home nohow."

"Get out of my way, nigger," his father said, without heat too, flinging the door back and the Negro also and entering, his hat still on his head. And now the boy saw the prints of the stiff foot on the doorjamb and saw them appear on the pale rug behind the machinelike deliberation of the foot which seemed to bear (or transmit) twice the weight which the body compassed. The Negro was shouting "Miss Lula! Miss Lula!" somewhere behind them, then the boy, deluged as though by a warm wave by a suave turn of the carpeted stair and a pendant glitter of chandeliers and a mute gleam of gold frames, heard the swift feet and saw her too, a lady—perhaps he had never seen her like before either—in a gray, smooth gown with lace at the throat and an apron tied at the waist and the sleeves turned back, wiping cake or biscuit dough from her hands with a towel as she came up the hall, looking not at his father at all but at the tracks on the blond rug with an expression of incredulous amazement.

"I tried," the Negro cried. "I tole him to . . ."

"Will you please go away?" she said in a shaking voice. "Major de Spain is not at home. Will you please go away?"

His father had not spoken again. He did not speak again. He did not even look at her. He just stood stiff in the center of the rug, in his hat, the shaggy iron-gray brows twitching slightly above the pebble-colored eyes as he appeared to examine the house with brief deliberation. Then with the same deliberation he turned; the boy watched him pivot on the good leg and saw the stiff foot drag around the arc of the turning, leaving a final long and fading smear. His father never looked at it, he never once looked down at the rug. The Negro held the door. It closed behind them, upon the hysteric and indistinguishable woman-wail. His father stopped at the top of the steps and scraped his boot clean on the edge of it. At the gate he stopped again. He stood for a moment, planted stiffly on the stiff foot, looking back at the house. "Pretty and white, ain't it?" he said. "That's sweat. Nigger sweat. Maybe it ain't white enough yet to suit him. Maybe he wants to mix some white sweat with it."

Two hours later the boy was chopping wood behind the house within which his mother and aunt and the two sisters (the mother and aunt, not the two girls, he knew that; even at this distance and muffled by walls the flat loud voices of the two girls emanated an incorrigible idle inertia) were setting up the stove to prepare a meal, when he heard the hooves and saw the linen-clad man on a fine sorrel mare, whom he recognized even before he saw the rolled rug in front of the Negro youth following on a fat bay carriage horse—a suffused, angry face vanishing, still at full gallop, beyond the corner of the house where his father and brother were sitting in the two tilted chairs; and a moment later, almost before he could have put the axe down, he heard the hooves again and watched the sorrel mare go back out of the yard, already galloping again. Then his father began to shout one of the sisters' names, who presently emerged backward from the kitchen door dragging the rolled rug along the ground by one end while the other sister walked behind it.

"If you ain't going to tote, go on and set up the wash pot," the first said.

"You, Sarty!" the second shouted. "Set up the wash pot!" His father appeared at the door, framed against that shabbiness, as he had been against that other bland perfection, impervious to either, the mother's anxious face at his shoulder.

"Go on," the father said. "Pick it up." The two sisters stooped, broad, lethargic; stooping, they presented an incredible expanse of pale cloth and a flutter of tawdry ribbons.

"If I thought enough of a rug to have to git hit all the way from France I wouldn't keep hit where folks coming in would have to tromp on hit," the first said. They raised the rug.

"Abner," the mother said. "Let me do it."

"You go back and git dinner," his father said. "I'll tend to this."

From the woodpile through the rest of the afternoon the boy watched them, the rug spread flat in the dust beside the bubbling wash pot, the two sisters stooping over it with that profound and lethargic reluctance, while the father stood over them in turn, implacable and grim, driving them though never raising his voice again. He could smell the harsh homemade lye they were using; he saw his mother come to the door once and look toward them with an expression not anxious now but very like despair; he saw his father turn, and he fell to with the axe and saw from the corner of his eye his father raise from the ground a flattish fragment of field stone and examine it and return to the pot, and this time his mother actually spoke: "Abner. Abner. Please don't. Please, Abner."

Then he was done too. It was dusk; the whippoorwills had already begun. He could smell coffee from the room where they would presently eat the cold food remaining from the mid-afternoon meal, though when he entered the house he realized they were having coffee again probably because there was a fire on the hearth, before which the rug now lay spread over the backs of the two chairs. The tracks of his father's foot were gone. Where they had been were now long, water-cloudy scoriations resembling the sporadic course of a lilliputian mowing machine.

It still hung there while they ate the cold food and then went to bed, scattered without order or claim up and down the two rooms, his mother in one bed, where his father would later lie, the older brother in the other, himself, the aunt, and the two sisters on pallets on the floor. But his father was not in bed yet. The last thing the boy remembered was the depthless, harsh silhouette of the hat and coat bending over the rug and it seemed to him that he had not even closed his eyes when the silhouette was standing over him, the fire almost dead behind it, the stiff foot prodding him awake. "Catch up the mule," his father said.

When he returned with the mule his father was standing in the back door, the rolled rug over his shoulder. "Ain't you going to ride?" he said.

"No. Give me your foot."

He bent his knee into his father's hand, the wiry, surprising power flowed smoothly, rising, he rising with it, on to the mule's bare back (they had owned a saddle once; the boy could remember it though not when or where) and with the same effortlessness his father swung the rug up in front of him. Now in the starlight they retraced the afternoon's path, up the dusty road rife with honeysuckle, through the gate and up the black tunnel of the drive to the lightless house, where he sat on the mule and felt the rough warp of the rug drag across his thighs and vanish.

"Don't you want me to help?" he whispered. His father did not answer and now he heard again that stiff foot striking the hollow portico with that wooden and clocklike deliberation, that outrageous overstatement of the weight it carried. The rug, hunched, not flung (the boy could tell that even in the darkness) from his father's shoulder struck the angle of wall and floor with a sound unbelievably loud, thunderous, then the foot again, unhurried and enormous; a light came on in the house and the boy sat, tense, breathing steadily and quietly and just a little fast, though the foot itself did not increase its beat at all, descending the steps now; now the boy could see him.

"Don't you want to ride now?" he whispered. "We kin both ride now," the light within the house altering now, flaring up and sinking. *He's coming down the stairs now*, he thought. He had already ridden the mule up beside the horse block; presently his father was up behind him and he doubled the reins over and slashed the mule across the neck, but before the animal could begin to trot the hard, thin arm came around him, the hard, knotted hand jerking the mule back to a walk.

In the first red rays of the sun they were in the lot, putting plow gear on the mules. This time the sorrel mare was in the lot before he heard it at all, the rider collarless and even bareheaded, trembling, speaking in a shaking voice as the woman in the house had done, his father merely looking up once before stooping again to the hame he was buckling, so that the man on the mare spoke to his stooping back:

"You must realize you have ruined that rug. Wasn't there anybody here, any of your women . . ." he ceased, shaking, the boy watching him, the older brother leaning now in the stable door, chewing, blinking slowly and steadily at nothing apparently. "It cost a hundred dollars. But you never had a hundred dollars. You never will. So I'm going to charge you twenty bushels of corn against your crop. I'll add it in your contract and when you come to the commissary you can sign it. That won't keep Mrs. de Spain quiet but maybe it will teach you to wipe your feet off before you enter her house again."

Then he was gone. The boy looked at his father, who still had not spoken or even looked up again, who was now adjusting the logger-head in the hame.

"Pap," he said. His father looked at him—the inscrutable face, the shaggy brows beneath where the gray eyes glinted coldly. Suddenly the boy went toward him, fast, stopping as suddenly. "You done the best you could!" he cried. "If he wanted hit done different why didn't he wait and tell you how? He won't git no twenty bushels! He won't git none! We'll gather hit and hide hit! I kin watch . . ."

"Did you put the cutter back in that straight stock like I told you?"

"No, sir," he said.

"Then go do it."

That was Wednesday. During the rest of that week he worked steadily, at what was within his scope and some which was beyond it, with an industry that did not need to be driven nor even commanded twice; he had this from his mother, with the difference that some at least of what he did he liked to do, such as splitting wood with the half-size axe which his mother and aunt had earned, or saved money somehow, to present him with at Christmas. In company with the two older women (and on one afternoon, even one of the sisters), he built pens for the shoat and the cow which were a part of his father's contract with the landlord, and one afternoon, his father being absent, gone somewhere on one of the mules, he went to the field.

They were running a middle buster now, his brother holding the plow straight while he handled the reins, and walking beside the straining mule, the rich black soil shearing cool and damp against his bare ankles, he thought *Maybe this is the end of it. Maybe even that twenty bushels that seems hard to have to pay for just a rug will be a cheap price for him to stop forever and always from being what he used to be*; thinking, dreaming now, so that his brother had to speak sharply to him to mind the mule: *Maybe he even won't collect the twenty bushels. Maybe it will all add up and balance and vanish—corn, rug, fire; the terror and grief; the being pulled two ways like between two teams of horses—gone, done with for ever and ever.*

Then it was Saturday; he looked up from beneath the mule he was harnessing and saw his father in the black coat and hat. "Not that," his father said. "The wagon gear." And then, two hours later, sitting in the wagon bed behind his father and brother on the seat, the wagon accomplished a final curve, and he saw the weathered paintless store with its tattered tobacco- and patent-medicine posters and the tethered wagons and saddle animals below the gallery. He mounted the gnawed steps behind his father and brother, and there again was the lane of quiet, watching faces for the three of them to walk through. He saw the man in spectacles sitting at the plank table and he did not need to be told this was a Justice of the Peace; he sent one glare of fierce, exultant, partisan defiance at the man in collar and cravat now, whom he had seen but twice before in his life, and that on a galloping horse, who now wore on his face an expression not of rage but of amazed unbelief which the boy could not have known was at the incredible circumstance of being sued by one of his own tenants, and came and stood against his father and cried at the Justice: "He ain't done it! He ain't burnt . . ."

"Go back to the wagon," his father said.

"Burnt?" the Justice said. "Do I understand this rug was burned too?"

"Does anybody here claim it was?" his father said. "Go back to the wagon." But he did not, he merely retreated to the rear of the room, crowded as that other had been, but not to sit down this time, instead, to stand pressing among the motionless bodies, listening to the voices:

"And you claim twenty bushels of corn is too high for the damage you did to the rug?"

"He brought the rug to me and said he wanted the tracks washed out of it. I washed the tracks out and took the rug back to him."

"But you didn't carry the rug back to him in the same condition it was in before you made the tracks on it."

His father did not answer, and now for perhaps half a minute there was no sound at all save that of breathing, the faint, steady suspiration of complete and intent listening.

"You decline to answer that, Mr. Snopes?" Again his father did not answer. "I'm going to find against you, Mr. Snopes. I'm going to find that you were responsible for the injury to Major de Spain's rug and hold you liable for it. But twenty bushels of corn seems a little high for a man in your circumstances to have to pay. Major de Spain claims it cost a hundred dollars. October corn will be worth about fifty cents. I figure that if Major de Spain can stand a ninety-five dollar loss on something he paid cash for, you can stand a five-dollar loss you haven't earned yet. I hold you in damages to Major de Spain to the amount of ten bushels of corn over and above your contract with him, to be paid to him out of your crop at gathering time. Court adjourned."

It had taken no time hardly, the morning was but half begun. He thought they would return home and perhaps back to the field, since they were late, far behind all other farmers. But instead his father passed on behind the wagon, merely indicating with his hand for the older brother to follow with it, and crossed the road toward the blacksmith shop opposite, pressing on after his father, overtaking him, speaking, whispering up at the harsh, calm face beneath the weathered hat: "He won't git no ten bushels either. He won't git one. We'll . . ." until his father glanced for an instant down at him, the face absolutely calm, the grizzled eyebrows tangled above the cold eyes, the voice almost pleasant, almost gentle:

"You think so? Well, we'll wait till October anyway."

The matter of the wagon—the setting of a spoke or two and the tightening of the tires—did not take long either, the business of the tires accomplished by driving the wagon into the spring branch behind the shop and letting it stand there, the mules nuzzling into the water from time to time, and the boy on the seat with the idle reins, looking up the slope and through the sooty tunnel of the shed where the slow hammer rang and where his father sat on an upended cypress bolt, easily, either talking or listening, still sitting there when the boy brought the dripping wagon up out of the branch and halted it before the door.

"Take them on to the shade and hitch," his father said. He did so and returned. His father and the smith and a third man squatting on his heels inside the door were talking, about crops and animals; the boy, squatting too in the ammoniac dust and hoof-parings and scales of rust, heard his father tell a long and unhurried story out of the time before the birth of the older brother even when he had been a professional horsetrader. And then his father came up beside him where he stood before a tattered last year's circus poster on the other side of the store, gazing rapt and quiet at the scarlet horses, the incredible poisings and convulsions of tulle and tights and the painted leers of comedians, and said, "It's time to eat."

But not at home. Squatting beside his brother against the front wall, he watched his father emerge from the store and produce from a paper sack a segment of cheese and divide it carefully and deliberately into three with his pocket knife and produce crackers from the same sack. They all three squatted on the gallery and ate, slowly, without talking; then in the store again, they drank from a tin dipper tepid water smelling of the cedar bucket and of living beech trees. And still they did not go home. It was a horse lot this time, a tall rail fence upon and along which men stood and sat and out of which one by one horses were led, to be walked and trotted and then cantered back and forth along the road while the slow swapping and buying went on and the sun began to slant westward, they—the three of them—watching and listening, the older brother with his muddy eyes and his steady, inevitable tobacco, the father commenting now and then on certain of the animals, to no one in particular.

It was after sundown when they reached home. They ate supper by lamplight, then, sitting on the doorstep, the boy watched the night fully accomplish, listening to the whippoorwills and the frogs, when he heard his mother's voice: "Abner! No! No! Oh, God. Oh, God. Abner!" and he rose, whirled, and saw the altered light through the door where a candle stub now burned in a bottle neck on the table and his father, still in the hat and coat, at once formal and burlesque as though dressed carefully for some shabby and ceremonial violence, emptying the reservoir of the lamp back into the five-gallon kerosene can from which it had been filled, while the mother tugged at his arm until he shifted the lamp to the other hand and flung her back, not savagely or viciously, just hard, into the wall, her hands flung out against the wall for balance, her mouth open and in her face the same quality of hopeless despair as had been in her voice. Then his father saw him standing in the door.

"Go to the barn and get that can of oil we were oiling the wagon with," he said. The boy did not move. Then he could speak.

"What . . ." he cried. "What are you . . ."

"Go get that oil," his father said. "Go."

Then he was moving, running, outside the house, toward the stable: this the old habit, the old blood which he had not been permitted to choose for himself, which had been bequeathed him willy nilly and which had run for so long (and who knew where, battening on what of outrage and savagery and lust) before it came to him. *I could keep on,* he thought. *I could run on and on and never look back, never need to see his face again. Only I can't. I can't,* the rusted can in his hand now, the liquid sploshing in it as he ran back to the house and into it, into the sound of his mother's weeping in the next room, and handed the can to his father.

"Ain't you going to even send a nigger?" he cried. "At least you sent a nigger before!"

This time his father didn't strike him. The hand came even faster than the blow had, the same hand which had set the can on the table with almost excruciating care flashing from the can toward him too quick for him to follow it, gripping him by the back of his shirt and on to tiptoe before he had seen it quit the can, the face stooping at him in breathless and frozen ferocity, the cold, dead voice speaking over him to the older brother who leaned against the table, chewing with that steady, curious, sidewise motion of cows:

"Empty the can into the big one and go on. I'll catch up with you."

"Better tie him up to the bedpost," the brother said.

"Do like I told you," the father said. Then the boy was moving, his bunched shirt and the hard, bony hand between his shoulder-blades, his toes just touching the floor, across the room and into the other one, past the sisters sitting with spread heavy thighs in the two chairs over the cold hearth, and to where his mother and aunt sat side by side on the bed, the aunt's arm about his mother's shoulders.

"Hold him," the father said. The aunt made a startled movement. "Not you," the father said. "Lennie. Take hold of him. I want to see you do it." His mother took him by the wrist. "You'll hold him better than that. If he gets loose don't you know what he is going to do? He will go up yonder." He jerked his head toward the road. "Maybe I'd better tie him."

"I'll hold him," his mother whispered.

"See you do then." Then his father was gone, the stiff foot heavy and measured upon the boards, ceasing at last.

Then he began to struggle. His mother caught him in both arms, he jerking and wrenching at them. He would be stronger in the end, he knew that. But he had no time to wait for it. "Lemme go!" he cried. "I don't want to have to hit you!"

"Let him go!" the aunt said. "If he don't go, before God, I am going up there myself!"

"Don't you see I can't?" his mother cried. "Sarty! Sarty! No! No! Help me, Lizzie!"

Then he was free. His aunt grasped at him but it was too late. He whirled, running, his mother stumbled forward on to her knees behind him, crying to the nearer sister: "Catch him, Net! Catch him!" But that was too late too, the sister (the sisters were twins, born at the same time, yet either of them now gave the impression of being, encompassing as much living meat and volume and weight as any other two of the family) not yet having begun to rise from the chair, her head, face, alone merely turned, presenting to him in the flying instant an astonishing expanse of young female features untroubled by any surprise even, wearing only an expression of bovine interest. Then he was out of the room, out of the house, in the mild dust of the starlit road and the heavy rifeness of honeysuckle, the pale ribbon unspooling with terrific slowness under his running feet, reaching the gate at last and turning in, running, his heart and lungs drumming, on up the drive toward the lighted house, the lighted door. He did not knock, he burst in, sobbing for breath, incapable for the moment of speech; he saw the astonished face of the Negro in the linen jacket without knowing when the Negro had appeared.

"De Spain!" he cried, panted. "Where's . . ." then he saw the white man too emerging from a white door down the hall. "Barn!" he cried. "Barn!"

"What?" the white man said. "Barn?"

"Yes!" the boy cried. "Barn!"

"Catch him!" the white man shouted.

But it was too late this time too. The Negro grasped his shirt, but the entire sleeve, rotten with washing, carried away, and he was out that door too and in the drive again, and had actually never ceased to run even while he was screaming into the white man's face.

Behind him the white man was shouting, "My horse! Fetch my horse!" and he thought for an instant of cutting across the park and climbing the fence into the road, but he did not know the park nor how high the vine-massed fence might be and he dared not risk it. So he ran on down the drive, blood and breath roaring; presently he was in the road again though he could not see it. He could not hear either: the galloping mare was almost upon him before he heard her, and even then he held his course, as if the very urgency of his wild grief and need must in a moment more find him wings, waiting until the ultimate instant to hurl himself aside and into the weed-choked roadside ditch as the horse thundered past and on, for an instant in furious silhouette against the stars, the tranquil early summer night sky which, even before the shape of the horse and rider vanished, stained abruptly and violently upward: a long, swirling roar incredible and soundless, blotting the stars, and he springing up and into the road again, running again, knowing it was too late yet still running even after he heard the shot and, an instant later, two shots, pausing now without knowing he had ceased to run, crying, "Pap! Pap!", running again before he knew he had begun to run, stumbling, tripping over something and scrabbling up again without ceasing to run, looking backward over his shoulder at the glare as he got up, running on among the invisible trees, panting, sobbing, "Father! Father!"

At midnight he was sitting on the crest of a hill. He did not know it was midnight and he did not know how far he had come. But there was no glare behind him now and he sat now, his back toward what he had called home for four days anyhow, his face toward the dark woods which he would enter when breath was strong again, small, shaking steadily in the chill darkness, hugging himself into the remainder of his thin, rotten shirt, the grief and despair now no longer terror and fear but just grief and despair. *Father. My father*, he thought. "He was brave!" he cried suddenly, aloud but not loud, no more than a whisper. "He was! He was in the war! He was in Colonel Sartoris' cav'ry!" not knowing that his father had gone to that war a private in the fine old European sense, wearing no uniform, admitting the authority of and giving fidelity to no man or army or flag, going to war as Malbrouck° himself did: for booty—it meant nothing and less than nothing to him if it were enemy booty or his own.

The slow constellations wheeled on. It would be dawn and then sun-up after a while and he would be hungry. But that would be to-morrow and now he was only cold, and walking would cure that. His breathing was easier now and he decided to get up and go on, and then he found that he had been asleep because he knew it was almost dawn, the night almost over. He could tell that from the whippoorwills. They were everywhere now among the dark trees below him, constant and inflectioned and ceaseless, so that, as the instant for giving over to the day birds drew nearer and nearer, there was no interval at all between them. He got up. He was a little stiff, but walking would cure that too as it would the cold, and soon there would be the sun. He went on down the hill, toward the dark woods within which the liquid silver voices of the birds called unceasing—the rapid and urgent beating of the urgent and quiring heart of the late spring night. He did not look back.

Questions

1. After delivering his warning to Major de Spain, the boy Snopes does not actually witness what happens to his father and brother, or what happens to the Major's barn. But what do you assume happens? What evidence is given in the story?
2. What do you understand to be Faulkner's opinion of Abner Snopes? Make a guess, indicating details in the story that convey attitudes.
3. How does the boy Snopes feel about his father? Does he identify with him? Find details in the story that support your view. Is there a point in the story where his feelings change?
4. Late in the story, Faulkner refers to "the old blood which he had not been permitted to choose for himself, which had been bequeathed him willy nilly . . ." (par. 88). What does this suggest about family legacy? Is it inevitable that we take after our parents? Do the events of the story support this view?
5. Suppose that, instead of "Barn Burning," Faulkner had written a story told by Abner Snopes in the first person. Why would such a story need a style different from that of "Barn Burning"? (Suggestion: Notice Faulkner's descriptions of Abner Snopes's voice.)
6. Although "Barn Burning" takes place some thirty years after the Civil War, how does the war figure in it?

Luke

Luke (first century) is traditionally considered the author of the Gospel bearing his name and the Acts of the Apostles in the New Testament. A physician who lived in the Greek city

---

Malbrouck: John Churchill, Duke of Marlborough (1650–1722), English general victorious in the Battle of Blenheim (1704), which triumph drove the French army out of Germany. The French called him Malbrouck, a name they found easier to pronounce.

of Antioch (now in Syria), Luke accompanied the Apostle Paul on some of his missionary journeys. Luke's elegantly written Gospel includes some of the Bible's most beloved parables, including those of the Good Samaritan and the Prodigal Son.

The Parable of the Prodigal Son (King James Version, 1611)

And he said, A certain man had two sons: And the younger of them said to his father, Father, give me the portion of goods that falleth to me. And he divided unto them his living. And not many days after the younger son gathered all together, and took his journey into a far country, and there wasted his substance with riotous living. And when he had spent all, there arose a mighty famine in that land; and he began to be in want. And he went and joined himself to a citizen of that country; and he sent him into his fields to feed swine. And he would fain have filled his belly with the husks that the swine did eat: and no man gave unto him. And when he came to himself, he said, How many hired servants of my father's have bread enough and to spare, and I perish with hunger! I will arise and go to my father, and will say unto him, Father I have sinned against heaven, and before thee, and am no more worthy to be called thy son; make me as one of thy hired servants. And he arose, and came to his father. But when he was yet a great way off, his father saw him, and had compassion, and ran, and fell on his neck, and kissed him. And the son said unto him, Father I have sinned against heaven, and in thy sight, and am no more worthy to be called thy son. But the father said to his servants, Bring forth the best robe, and put it on him; and put a ring on his hand, and shoes on his feet: And bring hither the fatted calf, and kill it; and let us eat, and be merry: For this my son was dead, and is alive again; he was lost, and is found. And they began to be merry. Now his elder son was in the field: and he came and drew nigh to the house, he heard music and dancing. And he called one of the servants, and asked what these things meant. And he said unto him, Thy brother is come; and thy father hath killed the fatted calf, because he hath received him safe and sound. And he was angry, and would not go in: therefore came his father out, and entreated him. And he answering said to his father, Lo, these many years do I serve thee, neither transgressed I at any time thy commandment; and yet thou never gavest me a kid, that I might make merry with my friends: But as soon as this thy son was come, which hath devoured thy living with harlots, thou hast killed for him the fatted calf. And he said unto him, Son thou art ever with me, and all that I have is thine. It was meet that we should make merry, and be glad: for this thy brother was dead, and is alive again; and was lost, and is found.

—Luke 15:11–32

Questions

1. This story has traditionally been called "The Parable of the Prodigal Son." What does *prodigal* mean? Which of the two brothers is prodigal?
2. What position does the younger son expect when he returns to his father's house? What does the father give him?
3. When the older brother sees the celebration for his younger brother's return, he grows angry. He makes a very reasonable set of complaints to his father. He has indeed been a loyal and moral son, but what virtue does the older brother lack?
4. Is the father fair to the elder son? Explain your answer.

5. Theologians have discussed this parable's religious significance for two thousand years. What, in your own words, is the human theme of the story?
6. Does this story still have relevance today? Do you find parallels to situations in your family, or in families you know?

Alice Walker

Alice Walker, a leading writer and social activist, was born in 1944 in Eatonton, Georgia, the youngest of eight children. Her father, a sharecropper and dairy farmer, usually earned about $300 a year; her mother helped by working as a maid. Both entertained their children by telling stories. When Alice Walker was eight, she was accidentally struck by a pellet from a brother's BB gun. She lost the sight of one eye because the Walkers had no car to rush her to the hospital. Later she attended Spelman College in Atlanta and finished at Sarah Lawrence College on a scholarship. While working for the civil rights movement in Mississippi, she met a young lawyer, Melvyn Leventhal. In 1967 they settled in Jackson, Mississippi, the first legally married interracial couple in town. They returned to New York in 1974 and were later divorced. First known as a poet, Walker has published nine books of her verse. She also has edited a collection of the work of the then-neglected black writer Zora Neale Hurston, and has written a study of Langston Hughes. In a collection of essays, In Search of Our Mothers' Gardens: Womanist Prose (1983), she recalls her mother and addresses her own daughter. (By womanist she means "black feminist.") But the largest part of Walker's reading audience knows her fiction: three story collections, including In Love and Trouble (1973), from which "Everyday Use" is taken, and her many novels. Her best-known novel, The Color Purple (1982), won a Pulitzer Prize and was made into a film by Steven Spielberg in 1985. Her recent novels include By the Light of My Father's Smile (1998) and Now Is the Time to Open Your Heart (2004). Walker lives in Northern California.

Alice Walker

Everyday Use

1973

for your grandmama

I will wait for her in the yard that Maggie and I made so clean and wavy yesterday afternoon. A yard like this is more comfortable than most people know. It is not just a yard. It is like an extended living room. When the hard clay is swept clean as a floor and the fine sand around the edges lined with tiny, irregular grooves, anyone can come and sit and look up into the elm tree and wait for the breezes that never come inside the house.

Maggie will be nervous until after her sister goes: she will stand hopelessly in corners, homely and ashamed of the burn scars down her arms and legs, eyeing her sister with a mixture of envy and awe. She thinks her sister has held life always in the palm of one hand, that "no" is a word the world never learned to say to her.

*

You've no doubt seen those TV shows where the child who has "made it" is confronted, as a surprise, by her own mother and father, tottering in weakly from backstage. (A pleasant surprise, of course: What would they do if parent and child came on the show only to curse out and insult each other?) On TV mother and child embrace and smile into each other's faces. Sometimes the mother and father weep, the child wraps them in her arms and leans across the table to tell how she would not have made it without their help. I have seen these programs.°

Sometimes I dream a dream in which Dee and I are suddenly brought together on a TV program of this sort. Out of a dark and soft-seated limousine I am ushered into a bright room filled with many people. There I meet a smiling, gray, sporty man like Johnny Carson who shakes my hand and tells me what a fine girl I have. Then we are on the stage and Dee is embracing me with tears in her eyes. She pins on my dress a large orchid, even though she has told me once that she thinks orchids are tacky flowers.

In real life I am a large, big-boned woman with rough, man-working hands. In the winter I wear flannel nightgowns to bed and overalls during the day. I can kill and clean a hog as mercilessly as a man. My fat keeps me hot in zero weather. I can work outside all day, breaking ice to get water for washing. I can eat pork liver cooked over the open fire minutes after it comes steaming from the hog. One winter I knocked a bull calf straight in the brain between the eyes with a sledge hammer and had the meat hung up to chill before nightfall. But of course all this does not show on television. I am the way my daughter would want me to be: a hundred pounds lighter, my skin like an uncooked barley pancake. My hair glistens in the hot bright lights. Johnny Carson has much to do to keep up with my quick and witty tongue.

But that is a mistake. I know even before I wake up. Who ever knew a Johnson with a quick tongue? Who can even imagine me looking a strange white man in the eye? It seems to me I have talked to them always with one foot raised in flight, with my head turned in whichever way is farthest from them. Dee, though. She would always look anyone in the eye. Hesitation was no part of her nature.

"How do I look, Mama?" Maggie says, showing just enough of her thin body enveloped in pink skirt and red blouse for me to know she's there, almost hidden by the door.

"Come out into the yard," I say.

Have you ever seen a lame animal, perhaps a dog run over by some careless person rich enough to own a car, sidle up to someone who is ignorant enough to be kind to him? That is the way my Maggie walks. She has been like this, chin on chest, eyes on ground, feet in shuffle, ever since the fire that burned the other house to the ground.

Dee is lighter than Maggie, with nicer hair and a fuller figure. She's a woman now, though sometimes I forget. How long ago was it that the other house burned? Ten, twelve years? Sometimes I can still hear the flames and feel Maggie's arms sticking to me, her hair smoking and her dress falling off her in little black papery flakes. Her eyes seemed stretched open, blazed open by the flames reflected in them. And Dee. I see her standing off under the sweet gum tree she used to dig gum out of; a look of concentration on her face as she watched the last dingy gray board of the house fall

---

these programs: On the NBC television show *This Is Your Life*, people were publicly and often tearfully reunited with friends, relatives, and teachers they had not seen in years.

in toward the red-hot brick chimney. Why don't you do a dance around the ashes? I'd wanted to ask her. She had hated the house that much.

I used to think she hated Maggie, too. But that was before we raised the money, the church and me, to send her to Augusta to school. She used to read to us without pity; forcing words, lies, other folks' habits, whole lives upon us two, sitting trapped and ignorant underneath her voice. She washed us in a river of make-believe, burned us with a lot of knowledge we didn't necessarily need to know. Pressed us to her with the serious way she read, to shove us away at just the moment, like dimwits, we seemed about to understand.

Dee wanted nice things. A yellow organdy dress to wear to her graduation from high school; black pumps to match a green suit she'd made from an old suit somebody gave me. She was determined to stare down any disaster in her efforts. Her eyelids would not flicker for minutes at a time. Often I fought off the temptation to shake her. At sixteen she had a style of her own: and knew what style was.

I never had an education myself. After second grade the school was closed down. Don't ask me why: in 1927 colored asked fewer questions than they do now. Sometimes Maggie reads to me. She stumbles along good-naturedly but can't see well. She knows she is not bright. Like good looks and money, quickness passed her by. She will marry John Thomas (who has mossy teeth in an earnest face) and then I'll be free to sit here and I guess just sing church songs to myself. Although I never was a good singer. Never could carry a tune. I was always better at a man's job. I used to love to milk till I was hoofed in the side in '49. Cows are soothing and slow and don't bother you, unless you try to milk them the wrong way.

I have deliberately turned my back on the house. It is three rooms, just like the one that burned, except the roof is tin; they don't make shingle roofs any more. There are no real windows, just some holes cut in the sides, like the portholes in a ship, but not round and not square, with rawhide holding the shutters up on the outside. This house is in a pasture, too, like the other one. No doubt when Dee sees it she will want to tear it down. She wrote me once that no matter where we "choose" to live, she will manage to come see us. But she will never bring her friends. Maggie and I thought about this and Maggie asked me, "Mama, when did Dee ever *have* any friends?"

She had a few. Furtive boys in pink shirts hanging about on washday after school. Nervous girls who never laughed. Impressed with her they worshiped the well-turned phrase, the cute shape, the scalding humor that erupted like bubbles in lye. She read to them.

When she was courting Jimmy T she didn't have much time to pay to us, but turned all her faultfinding power on him. He *flew* to marry a cheap city girl from a family of ignorant flashy people. She hardly had time to recompose herself.

When she comes I will meet—but there they are!

Maggie attempts to make a dash for the house, in her shuffling way, but I stay her with my hand. "Come back here," I say. And she stops and tries to dig a well in the sand with her toe.

It is hard to see them clearly through the strong sun. But even the first glimpse of leg out of the car tells me it is Dee. Her feet were always neat-looking, as if God himself had shaped them with a certain style. From the other side of the car comes a short, stocky man. Hair is all over his head a foot long and hanging from his chin like a kinky mule tail. I hear Maggie suck in her breath. "Uhnnnh," is what it sounds like. Like when you see the wriggling end of a snake just in front of your foot on the road. "Uhnnnh."

Dee next. A dress down to the ground, in this hot weather. A dress so loud it hurts my eyes. There are yellows and oranges enough to throw back the light of the sun. I feel my whole face warming from the heat waves it throws out. Earrings, too, gold and hanging down to her shoulders. Bracelets dangling and making noises when she moves her arm up to shake the folds of the dress out of her armpits. The dress is loose and flows, and as she walks closer, I like it. I hear Maggie go "Uhnnnh" again. It is her sister's hair. It stands straight up like the wool on a sheep. It is black as night and around the edges are two long pigtails that rope about like small lizards disappearing behind her ears.

"Wa-su-zo-Tean-o!"° she says, coming on in that gliding way the dress makes her move. The short stocky fellow with the hair to his navel is all grinning and he follows up with "Asalamalakim,° my mother and sister!" He moves to hug Maggie but she falls back, right up against the back of my chair. I feel her trembling there and when I look up I see the perspiration falling off her chin.

"Don't get up," says Dee. Since I am stout it takes something of a push. You can see me trying to move a second or two before I make it. She turns, showing white heels through her sandals, and goes back to the car. Out she peeks next with a Polaroid. She stoops down quickly and lines up picture after picture of me sitting there in front of the house with Maggie cowering behind me. She never takes a shot without making sure the house is included. When a cow comes nibbling around the edge of the yard she snaps it and me and Maggie *and* the house. Then she puts the Polaroid in the back seat of the car, and comes up and kisses me on the forehead.

Meanwhile Asalamalakim is going through the motions with Maggie's hand. Maggie's hand is as limp as a fish, and probably as cold, despite the sweat, and she keeps trying to pull it back. It looks like Asalamalakim wants to shake hands but wants to do it fancy. Or maybe he don't know how people shake hands. Anyhow, he soon gives up on Maggie.

"Well," I say. "Dee."

"No, Mama," she says. "Not 'Dee,' Wangero Leewanika Kemanjo!"

"What happened to 'Dee'?" I wanted to know.

"She's dead," Wangero said. "I couldn't bear it any longer, being named after the people who oppress me."

"You know as well as me you was named after your aunt Dicie," I said. Dicie is my sister. She named Dee. We called her "Big Dee" after Dee was born.

"But who was *she* named after?" asked Wangero.

"I guess after Grandma Dee," I said.

"And who was she named after?" asked Wangero.

"Her mother," I said, and saw Wangero was getting tired. "That's about as far back as I can trace it," I said. Though, in fact, I probably could have carried it back beyond the Civil War through the branches.

Wa-su-zo-Tean-o!: salutation in Swahili, an African language. Notice that Dee has to sound it out, syllable by syllable.   *Asalamalakim*: salutation in Arabic: "Peace be upon you."

"Well," said Asalamalakim, "there you are."

"Uhnnnh," I heard Maggie say.

"There I was not," I said, "before 'Dicie' cropped up in our family, so why should I try to trace it that far back?"

He just stood there grinning, looking down on me like somebody inspecting a Model A car.° Every once in a while he and Wangero sent eye signals over my head.

"How do you pronounce this name?" I asked.

"You don't have to call me by it if you don't want to," said Wangero.

"Why shouldn't I?" I asked. "If that's what you want us to call you, we'll call you."

"I know it might sound awkward at first," said Wangero.

"I'll get used to it," I said. "Ream it out again."

Well, soon we got the name out of the way. Asalamalakim had a name twice as long and three times as hard. After I tripped over it two or three times he told me to just call him Hakim-a-barber. I wanted to ask him was he a barber, but I didn't really think he was, so I didn't ask.

"You must belong to those beef-cattle peoples down the road," I said. They said "Asalamalakim" when they met you, too, but they didn't shake hands. Always too busy: feeding the cattle, fixing the fences, putting up salt-lick shelters, throwing down hay. When the white folks poisoned some of the herd the men stayed up all night with rifles in their hands. I walked a mile and a half just to see the sight.

Hakim-a-barber said, "I accept some of their doctrines, but farming and raising cattle is not my style." (They didn't tell me, and I didn't ask, whether Wangero (Dee) had really gone and married him.)

We sat down to eat and right away he said he didn't eat collards and pork was unclean. Wangero, though, went on through the chitlins and corn bread, the greens and everything else. She talked a blue streak over the sweet potatoes. Everything delighted her. Even the fact that we still used the benches her daddy made for the table when we couldn't afford to buy chairs.

"Oh, Mama!" she cried. Then turned to Hakim-a-barber. "I never knew how lovely these benches are. You can feel the rump prints," she said, running her hands underneath her and along the bench. Then she gave a sigh and her hand closed over Grandma Dee's butter dish. "That's it!" she said. "I knew there was something I wanted to ask you if I could have." She jumped up from the table and went over in the corner where the churn stood, the milk in it clabber° by now. She looked at the churn and looked at it.

"This churn top is what I need," she said. "Didn't Uncle Buddy whittle it out of a tree you all used to have?"

"Yes," I said.

"Uh huh," she said happily. "And I want the dasher, too."

"Uncle Buddy whittle that, too?" asked the barber.

Dee (Wangero) looked up at me.

"Aunt Dee's first husband whittled the dash," said Maggie so low you almost couldn't hear her. "His name was Henry, but they called him Stash."

Model A car: popular low-priced automobile introduced by the Ford Motor Company in 1927.
clabber: sour milk or buttermilk.

"Maggie's brain is like an elephant's," Wangero said, laughing. "I can use the churn top as a centerpiece for the alcove table," she said, sliding a plate over the churn, "and I'll think of something artistic to do with the dasher."

When she finished wrapping the dasher the handle stuck out. I took it for a moment in my hands. You didn't even have to look close to see where hands pushing the dasher up and down to make butter had left a kind of sink in the wood. In fact, there were a lot of small sinks; you could see where thumbs and fingers had sunk into the wood. It was beautiful light yellow wood, from a tree that grew in the yard where Big Dee and Stash had lived.

After dinner Dee (Wangero) went to the trunk at the foot of my bed and started rifling through it. Maggie hung back in the kitchen over the dishpan. Out came Wangero with two quilts. They had been pieced by Grandma Dee and then Big Dee and me had hung them on the quilt frames on the front porch and quilted them. One was in the Lone Star pattern. The other was Walk Around the Mountain. In both of them were scraps of dresses Grandma Dee had worn fifty and more years ago. Bits and pieces of Grandpa Jarrell's paisley shirts. And one teeny faded blue piece, about the size of a penny matchbox, that was from Great Grandpa Ezra's uniform that he wore in the Civil War.

"Mama," Wangero said sweet as a bird. "Can I have these old quilts?"

I heard something fall in the kitchen, and a minute later the kitchen door slammed.

"Why don't you take one or two of the others?" I asked. "These old things was just done by me and Big Dee from some tops your grandma pieced before she died."

"No," said Wangero. "I don't want those. They are stitched around the borders by machine."

"That'll make them last better," I said.

"That's not the point," said Wangero. "These are all pieces of dresses Grandma used to wear. She did all this stitching by hand. Imagine!" She held the quilts securely in her arms, stroking them.

"Some of the pieces, like those lavender ones, come from old clothes her mother handed down to her," I said, moving up to touch the quilts. Dee (Wangero) moved back just enough so that I couldn't reach the quilts. They already belonged to her.

"Imagine!" she breathed again, clutching them closely to her bosom.

"The truth is," I said, "I promised to give them quilts to Maggie, for when she marries John Thomas."

She gasped like a bee had stung her.

"Maggie can't appreciate these quilts!" she said. "She'd probably be backward enough to put them to everyday use."

"I reckon she would," I said. "God knows I been saving 'em for long enough with nobody using 'em. I hope she will!" I didn't want to bring up how I had offered Dee (Wangero) a quilt when she went away to college. Then she had told me they were old-fashioned, out of style.

"But they're *priceless!*" she was saying now, furiously; for she has a temper. "Maggie would put them on the bed and in five years they'd be in rags. Less than that!"

"She can always make some more," I said. "Maggie knows how to quilt."

Dee (Wangero) looked at me with hatred. "You just will not understand. The point is these quilts, *these* quilts!"

"Well," I said, stumped. "What would *you* do with them?"

"Hang them," she said. As if that was the only thing you *could* do with quilts.

Maggie by now was standing in the door. I could almost hear the sound her feet made as they scraped over each other.

"She can have them, Mama," she said, like somebody used to never winning anything, or having anything reserved for her. "I can 'member Grandma Dee without the quilts."

I looked at her hard. She had filled her bottom lip with checkerberry snuff and it gave her face a kind of dopey, hangdog look. It was Grandma Dee and Big Dee who taught her how to quilt herself. She stood there with her scarred hands hidden in the folds of her skirt. She looked at her sister with something like fear but she wasn't mad at her. This was Maggie's portion. This was the way she knew God to work.

When I looked at her like that something hit me in the top of my head and ran down to the soles of my feet. Just like when I'm in church and the spirit of God touches me and I get happy and shout. I did something I never had done before: hugged Maggie to me, then dragged her on into the room, snatched the quilts out of Miss Wangero's hands and dumped them into Maggie's lap. Maggie just sat there on my bed with her mouth open.

"Take one or two of the others," I said to Dee.

But she turned without a word and went out to Hakim-a-barber.

"You just don't understand," she said, as Maggie and I came out to the car.

"What don't I understand?" I wanted to know.

"Your heritage," she said. And then she turned to Maggie, kissed her, and said, "You ought to try to make something of yourself, too, Maggie. It's really a new day for us. But from the way you and Mama still live you'd never know it."

She put on some sunglasses that hid everything above the tip of her nose and her chin.

Maggie smiled; maybe at the sunglasses. But a real smile, not scared. After we watched the car dust settle I asked Maggie to bring me a dip of snuff. And then the two of us sat there just enjoying, until it was time to go in the house and go to bed.

Questions

1. What is the basic conflict in "Everyday Use"?
2. What is the tone of Walker's story? By what means does the author communicate it?
3. From whose point of view is "Everyday Use" told? What does the story gain from being told from this point of view—instead of, say, from the point of view of Dee (Wangero)?
4. What does the narrator of the story feel toward Dee? What seems to be Dee's present attitude toward her mother and sister?
5. What do you take to be the author's attitude toward each of her characters? How does she convey it?
6. What levels of meaning do you find in the story's title?
7. Contrast Dee's attitude toward her heritage with the attitudes of her mother and sister. How much truth is there in Dee's accusation that her mother and sister don't understand their heritage?

Suggestions for Writing on *Stories about Parents and Children*

1. In some of these stories, parents seem to favor—or at least identify with—one child over the others. Pick a work from this section and discuss the character who is the favored child. What contributes to the apparent favoritism? How does the favored child respond? How does the child who is "out of favor" respond? Do the parent's feelings change or adjust through the course of the story?
2. Several of these stories feature children whose understanding of the world is broader than that of their parents. Pick two of them and analyze how the children's views differ from their parents' views. Discuss also whether this broader knowledge and experience is always a positive thing. Is anything lost when children move beyond their original circumstances and out into the larger world?
3. At least two of these stories involve children who have serious disagreements with their parents. Have you ever had such a serious disagreement with your parents? What deeper reasons or value differences related to the conflict? How did you resolve it?
4. Are all happy families really alike, as Leo Tolstoy claimed? Find a happy episode from one of these stories (such as the end of "A Pair of Tickets" or "The Parable of the Prodigal Son") and discuss what unusual or unlikely circumstances contributed to that happiness.

CRITICAL AND CULTURAL CONTEXTS CASEBOOK
Alice Walker's "Everyday Use"

Alice Walker on Writing
Alice Walker
The Black Woman Writer in America

Criticism and Cultural Contexts
Barbara T. Christian
"Everyday Use" and the Black Power Movement

Mary Helen Washington
"Everyday Use" as a Portrait of the Artist

Elaine Showalter
Quilt as Metaphor in "Everyday Use"

Alice Walker and Her World: Images
Cover of Walker's 1973 Story Collection
Alice Walker in Conversation
Scene from Everyday Use *(2003 film)*
Alice Walker at Home with Quilt Art
Lone Star Quilt Pattern

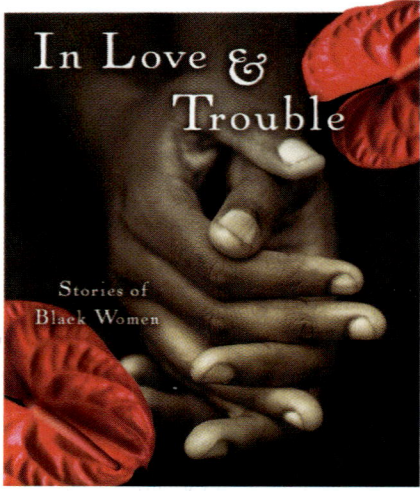

"Everyday Use" was first published in 1973 in *In Love & Trouble: Stories of Black Women.*

Although Alice Walker is best known for her 1982 novel *The Color Purple*, her career as both a writer and an activist has spanned a wide array of genres and interests. She achieved early prominence as a poet in the civil rights movement, and then became involved in the struggle for equal rights for women and was one of the early editors of *Ms.* magazine. These interests were not always compatible, leading Walker to call herself not a feminist, but a "womanist"—a woman of color who, by her definition, is willful and courageous, appreciates women's strength and culture, universally appreciates people regardless of gender and race, and takes pleasure in the sensual offerings of the world, from music to food to nature. Her poems, essays, stories, and novels reflect this philosophy, which resulted in early criticism about her portrayals of black men and later criticism of her work as being too "new age." But while Walker often focuses on stories of black women, she has always seen her work as being more universal. Both of these dynamics are at play in her story "Everyday Use." While the story is narrated by a poor black mother in the South, the depiction of tensions between parent and child, and the differences between siblings, has universal application.

ALICE WALKER ON WRITING

The Black Woman Writer in America   1973

Interview by John O'Brien

Interviewer: Why do you think that the black woman writer has been so ignored in America? Does she have even more difficulty than the black male writer, who perhaps has just begun to gain recognition?

Walker: There are two reasons why the black woman writer is not taken as seriously as the black male writer. One is that she's a woman. Critics seem unusually ill-equipped to intelligently discuss and analyze the works of black women. Generally, they do not even make the attempt; they prefer, rather, to talk about the lives of black women writers, not about what they write. And, since black women writers are not—it would seem—very likable— until recently they were the least willing worshipers of male supremacy— comments about them tend to be cruel.

Alice Walker in conversation.

In Nathan Huggins's very readable book, *Harlem Renaissance,* he hardly refers to Zora Neale Hurston's work, except negatively. He quotes from Wallace Thurman's novel, *Infants of the Spring,* at length, giving us the words of a character, "Sweetie Mae Carr," who is allegedly based on Zora Neale Hurston. "Sweetie Mae" is a writer noted more "for her ribald wit and personal effervescence than for any actual literary work. She was a great favorite among those whites who went in for Negro prodigies." Mr. Huggins goes on for several pages, never quoting Zora Neale Hurston herself, but rather the opinions of others about her character. He does say that she was "a master of dialect," but adds that "Her greatest weakness was carelessness or indifference to her art."

Having taught Zora Neale Hurston, and of course, having read her work myself, I am stunned. Personally, I do not care if Zora Hurston was fond of her white women friends. When she was a child in Florida, working for nickels and dimes, two white women helped her escape. Perhaps this explains it. But even if it doesn't, so what? Her work, far from being done carelessly, is done (especially in *Their Eyes Were Watching God*) almost too perfectly. She took the trouble to capture the beauty of rural black expression. She saw poetry where other writers merely saw failure to cope with English. She was so at ease with her blackness it never occurred to her that she should act one way among blacks and another among whites (as her more sophisticated black critics apparently did).

It seems to me that black writing has suffered, because even black critics have assumed that a book that deals with the relationships between members of a black family—or between a man and a woman—is less important than one that has white people as a primary antagonist. The consequences of this is that many of our books by "major" writers (always male) tell us little about the culture, history, or future, imagination, fantasies, etc., of black people, and a lot about isolated (often improbable) or limited encounters with a nonspecific white world. Where is the book, by an American black person (aside from *Cane*), that equals Elechi Amadi's *The Concubine*, for example? A book that exposes the *subconscious* of a people, because the people's dreams, imaginings, rituals, legends, etc., are known to be important, are known to contain the accumulated collective reality of the people themselves. Or, in *The Radiance of the King,* the white person is shown to be the outsider he is, because the culture he enters into in Africa *itself* [expels] him. Without malice, but as nature expels what does not suit. The white man is mysterious, a force to be reckoned with, but he is not glorified to such an extent that the Africans turn their attention away from themselves and their own imagination and culture. Which is what often happens with "protest literature." The superficial becomes—for a time—the deepest reality, and replaces the still waters of the collective subconscious.

When my own novel was published, a leading black monthly admitted (the editor did) that the book itself was never read; but the magazine ran an item stating that a *white* reviewer had praised the book (which was, in itself, an indication that the book was no good—such went the logic) and then hinted that the reviewer had liked my book because of my life-style. When I wrote to the editor to complain, he wrote me a small sermon on the importance of my "image," of what is "good" for others to see. Needless to say, what others "see" of me is the least of my worries, and I assumed that "others" are intelligent enough to recover from whatever shocks my presence might cause.

Women writers are supposed to be intimidated by male disapprobation. What they write is not important enough to be read. How they live, however, their "image," they owe to the race. Read the reason Zora Neale Hurston gave for giving up her writing. See what "image" the Negro press gave her, innocent as she was. I no longer read articles or reviews unless they are totally about the work. I trust that someday a generation of men and women will arise who will forgive me for such wrong as I do not agree I do, and will read my work because it is a true account of my feelings, my perceptions, and my imagination, and because it will reveal something to them of their own selves. They will also be free to toss it—and me—out of a high window. They can do what they like.

From *Interviews with Black Writers*

CRITICISM AND CULTURAL CONTEXTS

Barbara T. Christian (1943–2000)

"Everyday Use" and the Black Power Movement — 1994

"Everyday Use" is, in part, Alice Walker's response to the concept of heritage as articulated by the black movements of the 1960s. In that period, many African Americans, disappointed by the failure of integration, gravitated to the philosophy of cultural nationalism as the means to achieve liberation. In contrast to the veneration of Western ideas and ideals by many integrationists of the 1950s, Black Power ideologues emphasized the African cultural past as the true heritage of African Americans. The acknowledgment and appreciation of that heritage, which had too often been

Everyday Use **film adaptation, 2003.**

denigrated by African Americans themselves as well as by Euro-Americans, was a major tenet of the revolutionary movements of the period. Many blacks affirmed their African roots by changing their "slave names" to African names, and by wearing Afro styles and African clothing. Yet, ideologues of the period also lambasted older African Americans, opposing them to the lofty mythical models of the ancient past. These older men and women, they claimed, had become Uncle Toms and Aunt Jemimas who displayed little awareness of their culture and who, as a result of their slave past, had internalized the white man's view of blacks. So while these 1960s ideologues extolled an unknown ancient history, they denigrated the known and recent past. The tendency to idealize an ancient African past while ignoring the recent African American past still persists in the Afrocentric movements of the 1990s.

In contrast to that tendency, Walker's "Everyday Use" is dedicated to "your grandmama." And the story is told by a woman many African Americans would recognize as their grandmama, that supposedly backward Southern ancestor the cultural nationalists of the North probably visited during the summers of their youth and probably considered behind the times. Walker stresses those physical qualities which suggest such a person, qualities often demeaned by cultural nationalists. For this grandmama, like the stereotypical mammy of slavery, is "a large big-boned woman with rough, man-working hands," who wears "flannel nightgowns to bed and overalls during the day," and whose "fat keeps [her] hot in zero weather." Nor is this grandmama politically conscious according to the fashion of the day; she never had an education after the second grade, she knows nothing about African names, and she eats pork. In having the grandmama tell this story, Walker gives voice to an entire maternal ancestry often silenced by the political rhetoric of the period. Indeed, Walker tells us in "In Search of Our Mothers' Gardens" that her writing is part of her mother's legacy to her, that many of her stories are based on stories *her* mother told her. Thus, Walker's writing is her way of breaking silences and stereotypes about her grandmothers', mothers', sisters' lives. In effect, her work is a literary continuation of a distinctly oral tradition in which African American women have been and still are pivotal participants.

Alice Walker is well aware of the restrictions of the African American Southern past, for she is the eighth child of Georgia sharecroppers. Born in 1944, she grew up during the period when, as she put it, apartheid existed in America. For in the 1940s and 1950s, when segregation was the law of the South, opportunities for economic and social advancement were legally denied to Southern blacks. Walker was fortunate to come to adulthood during the social and political movements of the late fifties and sixties. Of her siblings, only she, and a slightly older sister, Molly, were able even to imagine the possibility of moving beyond the poverty of their parents. It is unlikely that Alice Walker would have been able to go to college—first at Spelman, the African American women's college in Atlanta, and then at Sarah Lawrence, the white women's college near New York City—if it had not been for the changes that came about as a result of the Civil Rights Movement. Nor is it likely that she, a Southern black woman from a poor family, would have been able to become the writer that she did without the changes resulting from the ferment of the Black and Women's Movements of the 1960s and early 1970s.

While Walker was a participant in these movements, she was also one of their most astute critics. As a Southerner, she was aware of the ways in which black Southern culture was often thought of as backward by predominantly Northern Black Power ideologues, even as they proclaimed their love for black people. She was also acutely aware of the ways in which women were oppressed within the Black Power Movement itself, even as the very culture its participants revered was so often passed on by women. Walker had also visited Africa during her junior year of college and had personally experienced the gap between the Black Power advocates' idealization of Africa and the reality of the African societies she visited.

• • •

Names are extremely important in African and African American culture as a means of indicating a person's spirit. During the 1960s Walker criticized the tendency among some African Americans to give up the names their parents gave them—names which embodied the history of their recent past—for African names that did not relate to a single person they knew. Hence the grandmama in "Everyday Use" is amazed that Dee would give up her name for the name Wangero. For Dee was the name of her great-grandmother, a woman who had kept her family together against great odds. Wangero might have sounded authentically African but it had no relationship to a person she knew, nor to the personal history that had sustained her.

• • •

In "Everyday Use," by contrasting a sister who has the opportunity to go to college with a sister who stays at home, Walker reminds us of the challenges that contemporary African American women face as they discover what it means to be truly educated. The same concern appears in many of her works. For example, in "For My Sister Molly Who in the Fifties," she explores the conflicts that can result from an education that takes a woman away from her cultural source. Like Molly, Dee/Wangero in "Everyday Use" is embarrassed by her folk. She has been to the North, wears an Afro, and knows the correct political rhetoric of the 1960s, but she has little regard for her relatives who have helped to create that heritage. Thus, she does not know how to quilt and can only conceive of her family's quilts as priceless artifacts, as things, which she intends to hang on her wall as a means of demonstrating to others that she has "heritage." On the other hand, Maggie, the supposedly uneducated sister, who has been nowhere beyond the supposedly uneducated black South, loves and understands her family and can appreciate its history. She knows how to quilt and would put the precious quilts to "everyday use," which is precisely what, Walker suggests, one needs to do with one's heritage. For Maggie, the quilts are an embodiment of the spirit her folks have passed on to her.

From introduction to *Everyday Use*

Mary Helen Washington

"Everyday Use" as a Portrait of the Artist — 1994

In 1994 Rutgers University Press brought out a collection of critical essays on Walker's "Everyday Use" in its Women Writers: Texts and Contexts *series. The book reprinted an earlier essay by Mary Helen Washington on Walker's work, along with an addendum she titled "A Postscript to My 1979 Essay on Alice Walker." This excerpt comes from that 1994 postscript.*

One of the most interesting and glaring omissions of my earlier Walker essay is Walker's statement in the 1973 interview (which took place in her home in Jackson, Mississippi) of the way she sees the story "Everyday Use" as a reflection of her own struggles as an artist, an admission that suggests that female conflicts over art are not so easily resolved as they are in "A Sudden Trip Home. . . ."° In "Everyday Use" (published in 1973) all three women characters are artists: Mama, as the narrator, tells her own story; Maggie is the quiltmaker, the creator of art for "everyday use"; Dee, the photographer and collector of art, has designed her jewelry, dress, and hair so deliberately and self-consciously that she appears in the story as a self-creation. Walker says in the interview that she thinks of these three characters as herself split into three parts:

> . . . I really see that story as almost about one person, the old woman and two daughters being one person. The one who stays and sustains—this is the older woman—who has on the one hand a daughter who is the same way, who stays and abides and loves, plus the part of them—*the autonomous person*, the part of them that also wants to go out into the world to see change and be changed. . . . I do in fact have an African name that was given to me, and I love it and use it when I want to, and I love my Kenyan gowns and my Ugandan gowns—the whole bit—it's a part of me. But, on the other hand, my parents and grandparents were part of it, and they take precedence.[1]

Walker is most closely aligned in the story with the "bad daughter," Dee, "this autonomous person," the one who goes out in the world and returns with African

---

"*A Sudden Trip Home*": A reference to Walker's later story "A Sudden Trip Home in the Spring," about a black college student returning home from the North to Georgia for her father's funeral.

[1] Mary Helen Washington, "Interview with Alice Walker," June 1973, *Black-Eyed Susans: Classic Stories By and About Black Women* (Garden City: Doubleday, 1975).

Alice Walker at home with collection of American quilts and art.

clothes and an African name. Like Dee, Walker leaves the community, appropriating the oral tradition in order to turn it into a written artifact, which will no longer be available for "everyday use" by its originators. Everywhere in the story the fears and self-doubts of the woman artist are revealed. The narrator-mother remains hostile to Dee and partial to the homely daughter, Maggie, setting up the opposition between the two daughters that Walker says mirrors her own internal struggles.

• • •

The oppositions in "Everyday Use," between mother and daughters and sisters, between art for everyday use and art for art's sake, between insider and outsider, certainly capture [a] sense of contradiction and conflict. The story ends with Mama choosing Maggie and rejecting Dee, but Dee, who represents Walker herself as the artist who returns home, at least imaginatively, in order to collect the material for her art, certainly cannot be repressed. In this story, as in her essays, Walker shows that the quiltmaker, who has female precursors and female guidance, has an easier relationship with her art than the "deviant" female who finds herself outside of acceptable boundaries. Unlike quiltmaking and garden making and even blues singing, which are part of women's traditions, the writing of fiction is still done under the shadow of men, without female authority. The self-assurance of "A Sudden Trip Home in the Spring" is acquired through an alliance with that male authority. "Everyday Use" tells a different, more threatening tale of the woman writer's fears, of the difficulty of reconciling home and art, particularly when the distance from home has been enlarged by education, by life among the "gentlefolk," and by literary recognition.

From "A Postscript to My 1979 Essay on Alice Walker"

Elaine Showalter (b. 1941)

Quilt as Metaphor in "Everyday Use"   1991

For Alice Walker, piecing and quilting have come to represent both the aesthetic heritage of Afro-American women and the model for what she calls a "Womanist," or black feminist, writing of reconciliation and connection; in her essay "In Search of Our Mothers' Gardens," Walker identified the quilt as a major form of creative expression for black women in the South. "In the Smithsonian Institution in Washington, D.C.," Walker writes,

> there hangs a quilt unlike another in the world. In fanciful, inspired, and yet simple and identifiable figures, it portrays the story of the Crucifixion . . . Though it follows no known pattern of quiltmaking, and though it is made of bits and pieces of worthless rags, it is obviously the work of a person of powerful imagination and deep spiritual feeling. Below this quilt I saw a note that says it was made by "an anonymous Black woman in Alabama a hundred years ago."

The quilt Walker is describing from memory is in fact one of two extant narrative quilts by Harriet Powers (1836–1911), born a slave in Georgia. The Powers quilt at the Smithsonian illustrates Bible stories, while the one in the Boston Museum of Fine Arts mingles Bible tales with folklore and astronomical events such as shooting stars and meteor showers.[1] For Walker, genuine imagination and feeling can be recognized without the legitimacy conferred by the labels of "art" or the approval of museums. Paradoxically this heritage survives because it has been preserved in museums; but it can be a living art only if it is practiced.

    The theme of Walker's quilt aesthetic is most explicitly presented in her early story "Everyday Use." Like much of her work, it uses a contrast between two sisters to get at the meaning of the concept of "heritage": a privileged one who escapes from Southern black culture, and a suffering one who stays or is left behind. The younger daughter, Maggie, has stayed at home since she was horribly scarred in a house fire ten years before. Dee is the bright and confident sister, the one with "faultfinding power." Dee has learned fast how to produce herself: "At sixteen she had a style of her own: and knew what style was." Now having chosen the style of radical black nationalism, her name changed to "Wangero," and spouting Swahili, Dee returns to claim her heritage from her mother in the form of "folk art": the worn benches made by her father, the butter churn whittled by an uncle, and especially the quilts pieced by her grandmother. "Maggie can't appreciate these quilts," Dee exclaims. "She'd probably be backward enough to put them to everyday use." Walker thus establishes a contrast between "everyday use" and "institutional theories of aesthetics."[2] In a moment of epiphanic insight, the mother, who has always been intimidated by Dee's intelligence and sophistication, decides to give the quilts to Maggie. "She can always make some more," the mother responds. "Maggie knows how to quilt." Maggie cannot

---

[1] See Marie Jean Adams, "The Harriet Powers Pictorial Quilts," *Black Art* 3 (1982) 12–28.
[2] Houston A. Baker and Charlotte Pierce-Baker, "Patches: Quilts and Community in Alice Walker's 'Everyday Use.'" *Southern Review* 21:3 (Summer 1985) 716.

Lone Star quilt pattern: "Out came Wangero with two quilts.... One was in the Lone Star pattern" (paragraph 55).

speak glibly about her "heritage" or about "priceless" artifacts, but, unlike Dee, she understands the quilt as a process rather than as a commodity; she can read its meaning in a way Dee never will, because she knows the contexts of its pieces, and loves the women who have made it. The meaning of an aesthetic heritage, according to Walker's story, lies in continual renewal rather than in the rhetoric of nostalgia or appreciation. In writing *The Color Purple*, Walker herself took up quilt-making as well as using it as a central metaphor in the novel.

From *Sister's Choice: Tradition and Change in American Women's Writing*

Suggestions for Writing on *Alice Walker's* "Everyday Use"

1. Write a brief version of the family encounter in "Everyday Use" from Dee's point of view. Is it possible to present a non-ironic affirmation of her values over those of her mother and sister? Why or why not?
2. How does the use of a first-person narrator function in "Everyday Use"? Are there places in which the reader is expected to understand more than the narrator does, or is everything that she says and sees to be accepted at face value?
3. Alice Walker has suggested that one of her principal intentions in her writing is "nurturing and healing the reader." Do you think "nurturing and healing" is one of the primary aims of "Everyday Use"?
4. Consider the interview with Alice Walker in this casebook. Choose an opinion or statement of Walker's that you find especially striking. How does it affect your reading of the story "Everyday Use"? How does she embody her thoughts and beliefs in the context of the story?
5. Using the material in the casebook, discuss the quilt as a symbol in "Everyday Use." What does the quilt bring to the meaning of the story that another object, such as a small financial legacy or an antique piece of jewelry, would not?
6. Read the critical works on "Everyday Use," and choose an idea expressed by one of the writers (for example, the commentary about quilts or about African Americans of a certain era widely changing their names). Discuss how this insight illuminates your understanding of the story. Alternatively, if you disagree with the idea, discuss how the writer misses the mark.

BROTHERS AND SISTERS

James Baldwin　　　　　*Sonny's Blues*

Tobias Wolff　　　　　　*The Rich Brother*

Eudora Welty　　　　　 *Why I Live at the P.O.*

Louise Erdrich　　　　　*The Red Convertible*

If you have a brother or a sister, you know how complicated, wonderful, and frustrating the sibling relationship can be. You have the same parent or parents, the same blood, maybe even some of the same physical features—and yet your personalities, tastes, and ways of viewing the world might be completely different. If you're an older sibling, your younger brother might drive you nuts with his irreverence and irresponsibility—especially if your parents let him get away with things you couldn't have gotten away with. If you're a younger sibling, your older sister might seem unbearably uptight and self-righteous—almost like another parent. Siblings often become annoyed with each other, even as they can also be each other's biggest fans or defenders. And parents can consciously or unconsciously feed those tensions by giving their children unequal amounts of attention or approval. Sometimes the tensions between siblings are so deep that they can never be overcome. But what is the proper way to relate to our siblings, especially if we—or they—are in trouble? What is our responsibility to them? Do we do all we can to help them, even as they seem determined to fall? Or do we leave them to their own devices? The siblings in the following stories all have complex relationships that shift through the course of their lives. But in all of them, how the characters relate to their siblings reveals as much about them as it does about their brothers or sisters.

James Baldwin

James Baldwin (1924–1987) was born in Harlem, in New York City. His father was a Pentecostal minister, and the young Baldwin initially planned to become a clergyman. While still in high school, he preached sermons in a storefront church. At seventeen, however, he left home to live in Greenwich Village, where he worked at menial jobs and began publishing articles in Commentary *and the* Nation. *Later he embarked on a series of travels that eventually brought him to France. Baldwin soon regarded France as a second home, a country in which he could avoid the racial discrimination he felt in America. His first novel,* Go Tell It on the Mountain *(1953), which described a single day in the lives of the members of a Harlem church, immediately earned him a position as a leading African American writer.*

James Baldwin

His next two novels, Giovanni's Room *(1956) and* Another Country *(1962), dealt with homosexual themes and drew criticism from some of his early champions. His collection of essays* Notes of a Native Son *(1955) remains one of the key books of the civil rights movement. His short stories were not collected until* Going to Meet the Man *was published in 1965. Although he spent nearly forty years in France, Baldwin still considered himself an American. He was not an expatriate, he claimed, but a "commuter." He died in St. Paul de Vence, France, but was buried in Ardsley, New York.*

Sonny's Blues 1957

  I read about it in the paper, in the subway, on my way to work. I read it, and I couldn't believe it, and I read it again. Then perhaps I just stared at it, at the newsprint spelling out his name, spelling out the story. I stared at it in the swinging lights of the subway car, and in the faces and bodies of the people, and in my own face, trapped in the darkness which roared outside.

  It was not to be believed and I kept telling myself that, as I walked from the subway station to the high school. And at the same time I couldn't doubt it. I was scared, scared for Sonny. He became real to me again. A great block of ice got settled in my belly and kept melting there slowly all day long, while I taught my classes algebra. It was a special kind of ice. It kept melting, sending trickles of ice water all up and down my veins, but it never got less. Sometimes it hardened and seemed to expand until I felt my guts were going to come spilling out or that I was going to choke or scream. This would always be at a moment when I was remembering some specific thing Sonny had once said or done.

  When he was about as old as the boys in my classes his face had been bright and open, there was a lot of copper in it; and he'd had wonderfully direct brown eyes, and great gentleness and privacy. I wondered what he looked like now. He had been picked up, the evening before, in a raid on an apartment downtown, for peddling and using heroin.

  I couldn't believe it: but what I mean by that is that I couldn't find any room for it anywhere inside me. I had kept it outside me for a long time. I hadn't wanted to know. I had had suspicions, but I didn't name them, I kept putting them away. I told myself that Sonny was wild, but he wasn't crazy. And he'd always been a good boy, he hadn't ever turned hard or evil or disrespectful, the way kids can, so quick, so quick, especially in Harlem. I didn't want to believe that I'd ever see my brother going down, coming to nothing, all that light in his face gone out, in the condition I'd already seen so many others. Yet it had happened and here I was, talking about algebra to a lot of boys who might, every one of them for all I knew, be popping off needles every time they went to the head. Maybe it did more for them than algebra could.

  I was sure that the first time Sonny had ever had horse,° he couldn't have been much older than these boys were now. These boys, now, were living as we'd been living then, they were growing up with a rush and their heads bumped abruptly against the low ceiling of their actual possibilities. They were filled with rage. All they really knew were two darknesses, the darkness of their lives, which was now closing in on

5

---

horse: heroin.

them, and the darkness of the movies, which had blinded them to that other darkness, and in which they now, vindictively, dreamed, at once more together than they were at any other time, and more alone.

When the last bell rang, the last class ended, I let out my breath. It seemed I'd been holding it for all that time. My clothes were wet—I may have looked as though I'd been sitting in a steam bath, all dressed up, all afternoon. I sat alone in the classroom a long time. I listened to the boys outside, downstairs, shouting and cursing and laughing. Their laughter struck me for perhaps the first time. It was not the joyous laughter which—God knows why—one associates with children. It was mocking and insular, its intent to denigrate. It was disenchanted, and in this, also, lay the authority of their curses. Perhaps I was listening to them because I was thinking about my brother and in them I heard my brother. And myself.

One boy was whistling a tune, at once very complicated and very simple, it seemed to be pouring out of him as though he were a bird, and it sounded very cool and moving through all that harsh, bright air, only just holding its own through all those other sounds.

I stood up and walked over to the window and looked down into the courtyard. It was the beginning of the spring and the sap was rising in the boys. A teacher passed through them every now and again, quickly, as though he or she couldn't wait to get out of that courtyard, to get those boys out of their sight and off their minds. I started collecting my stuff. I thought I'd better get home and talk to Isabel.

The courtyard was almost deserted by the time I got downstairs. I saw this boy standing in the shadow of a doorway, looking just like Sonny. I almost called his name. Then I saw that it wasn't Sonny, but somebody we used to know, a boy from around our block. He'd been Sonny's friend. He'd never been mine, having been too young for me, and, anyway, I'd never liked him. And now, even though he was a grown-up man, he still hung around that block, still spent hours on the street corners, was always high and raggy. I used to run into him from time to time and he'd often work around to asking me for a quarter or fifty cents. He always had some real good excuse, too, and I always gave it to him, I don't know why.

But now, abruptly, I hated him. I couldn't stand the way he looked at me, partly like a dog, partly like a cunning child. I wanted to ask him what the hell he was doing in the school courtyard.

He sort of shuffled over to me, and he said, "I see you got the papers. So you already know about it."

"You mean about Sonny? Yes, I already know about it. How come they didn't get you?"

He grinned. It made him repulsive and it also brought to mind what he'd looked like as a kid. "I wasn't there. I stay away from them people."

"Good for you." I offered him a cigarette and I watched him through the smoke. "You come all the way down here just to tell me about Sonny?"

"That's right." He was sort of shaking his head and his eyes looked strange, as though they were about to cross. The bright sun deadened his damp dark brown skin and it made his eyes look yellow and showed up the dirt in his kinked hair. He smelled funky. I moved a little away from him and I said, "Well, thanks. But I already know about it and I got to get home."

"I'll walk you a little ways," he said. We started walking. There were a couple of kids still loitering in the courtyard and one of them said goodnight to me and looked strangely at the boy beside me.

"What're you going to do?" he asked me. "I mean, about Sonny?"

"Look. I haven't seen Sonny for over a year. I'm not sure I'm going to do anything. Anyway, what the hell *can* I do?"

"That's right," he said quickly, "ain't nothing you can do. Can't much help old Sonny no more, I guess."

It was what I was thinking and so it seemed to me he had no right to say it.

"I'm surprised at Sonny, though," he went on—he had a funny way of talking, he looked straight ahead as though he were talking to himself—"I thought Sonny was a smart boy, I thought he was too smart to get hung."

"I guess he thought so too," I said sharply, "and that's how he got hung. And how about you? You're pretty goddamn smart, I bet."

Then he looked directly at me, just for a minute. "I ain't smart," he said. "If I was smart, I'd have reached for a pistol a long time ago."

"Look. Don't tell *me* your sad story, if it was up to me, I'd give you one." Then I felt guilty—guilty, probably, for never having supposed that the poor bastard *had* a story of his own, much less a sad one, and I asked, quickly, "What's going to happen to him now?"

He didn't answer this. He was off by himself some place. "Funny thing," he said, and from his tone we might have been discussing the quickest way to get to Brooklyn, "when I saw the papers this morning, the first thing I asked myself was if I had anything to do with it. I felt sort of responsible."

I began to listen more carefully. The subway station was on the corner, just before us, and I stopped. He stopped, too. We were in front of a bar and he ducked slightly, peering in, but whoever he was looking for didn't seem to be there. The juke box was blasting away with something black and bouncy and I half watched the barmaid as she danced her way from the juke box to her place behind the bar. And I watched her face as she laughingly responded to something someone said to her, still keeping time to the music. When she smiled one saw the little girl, one sensed the doomed, still-struggling woman beneath the battered face of the semiwhore.

"I never *give* Sonny nothing," the boy said finally, "but a long time ago I come to school high and Sonny asked me how it felt." He paused, I couldn't bear to watch him, I watched the barmaid, and I listened to the music which seemed to be causing the pavement to shake. "I told him it felt great." The music stopped, the barmaid paused and watched the juke box until the music began again. "It did."

All this was carrying me some place I didn't want to go. I certainly didn't want to know how it felt. It filled everything, the people, the houses, the music, the dark, quicksilver barmaid, with menace; and this menace was their reality.

"What's going to happen to him now?" I asked again.

"They'll send him away some place and they'll try to cure him." He shook his head. "Maybe he'll even think he's kicked the habit. Then they'll let him loose"—he gestured, throwing his cigarette into the gutter. "That's all."

"What do you mean, that's *all*?"

But I knew what he meant.

"I *mean*, that's *all*." He turned his head and looked at me, pulling down the corners of his mouth. "Don't you know what I mean?" he asked, softly.

"How the hell *would* I know what you mean?" I almost whispered it, I don't know why.

"That's right," he said to the air, "how would *he* know what I mean?" He turned toward me again, patient and calm, and yet I somehow felt him shaking, shaking as though he were going to fall apart. I felt that ice in my guts again, the dread I'd felt all afternoon; and again I watched the barmaid, moving about the bar, washing glasses, and singing. "Listen. They'll let him out and then it'll just start all over again. That's what I mean."

"You mean—they'll let him out. And then he'll just start working his way back in again. You mean he'll never kick the habit. Is that what you mean?"

"That's right," he said, cheerfully. "*You* see what I mean."

"Tell me," I said at last, "why does he want to die? He must want to die, he's killing himself, why does he want to die?"

He looked at me in surprise. He licked his lips. "He don't want to die. He wants to live. Don't nobody want to die, ever."

Then I wanted to ask him—too many things. He could not have answered, or if he had, I could not have borne the answers. I started walking. "Well, I guess it's none of my business."

"It's going to be rough on old Sonny," he said. We reached the subway station. "This is your station?" he asked. I nodded. I took one step down. "Damn!" he said, suddenly. I looked up at him. He grinned again. "Damn it if I didn't leave all my money home. You ain't got a dollar on you, have you? Just for a couple of days, is all."

All at once something inside gave and threatened to come pouring out of me. I didn't hate him any more. I felt that in another moment I'd start crying like a child.

"Sure," I said. "Don't sweat." I looked in my wallet and didn't have a dollar, I only had a five. "Here," I said. "That hold you?"

He didn't look at it—he didn't want to look at it. A terrible closed look came over his face, as though he were keeping the number on the bill a secret from him and me. "Thanks," he said, and now he was dying to see me go. "Don't worry about Sonny. Maybe I'll write him or something."

"Sure," I said. "You do that. So long."

"Be seeing you," he said. I went on down the steps.

And I didn't write Sonny or send him anything for a long time. When I finally did, it was just after my little girl died, he wrote me back a letter which made me feel like a bastard.

Here's what he said:

Dear brother,

You don't know how much I needed to hear from you. I wanted to write you many a time but I dug how much I must have hurt you and so I didn't write. But now I feel like a man who's been trying to climb up out of some deep, real deep and funky hole and just saw the sun up there, outside. I got to get outside.

I can't tell you much about how I got here. I mean I don't know how to tell you. I guess I was afraid of something or I was trying to escape from something and you know I have never been very strong in the head (smile). I'm glad Mama and Daddy are dead and can't see what's happened to their son and I swear if I'd known what I was doing I would never have hurt you so, you and a lot of other fine people who were nice to me and who believed in me.

I don't want you to think it had anything to do with me being a musician. It's more than that. Or maybe less than that. I can't get anything straight in my head down here and I try not to think about what's going to happen to me when I get outside again. Sometime I think I'm going to flip and *never* get outside and sometime I think I'll come straight back. I tell you one thing, though, I'd rather blow my brains out than go through this again. But that's what they all say, so they tell me. If I tell you when I'm coming to New York and if you could meet me, I sure would appreciate it. Give my love to Isabel and the kids and I was sure sorry to hear about little Gracie. I wish I could be like Mama and say the Lord's will be done, but I don't know it seems to me that trouble is the one thing that never does get stopped and I don't know what good it does to blame it on the Lord. But maybe it does some good if you believe it.

Your brother,
Sonny

Then I kept in constant touch with him and I sent him whatever I could and I went to meet him when he came back to New York. When I saw him many things I thought I had forgotten came flooding back to me. This was because I had begun, finally, to wonder about Sonny, about the life that Sonny lived inside. This life, whatever it was, had made him older and thinner and it had deepened the distant stillness in which he had always moved. He looked very unlike my baby brother. Yet, when he smiled, when we shook hands, the baby brother I'd never known looked out from the depths of his private life, like an animal waiting to be coaxed into the light.

"How you been keeping?" he asked me.

"All right. And you?"

"Just fine." He was smiling all over his face. "It's good to see you again."

"It's good to see you."

The seven years' difference in our ages lay between us like a chasm: I wondered if these years would ever operate between us as a bridge. I was remembering, and it made it hard to catch my breath, that I had been there when he was born; and I had heard the first words he had ever spoken. When he started to walk, he walked from our mother straight to me. I caught him just before he fell when he took the first steps he ever took in this world.

"How's Isabel?"

"Just fine. She's dying to see you."

"And the boys?"

"They're fine, too. They're anxious to see their uncle."

"Oh, come on. You know they don't remember me."

"Are you kidding? Of course they remember you."

He grinned again. We got into a taxi. We had a lot to say to each other, far too much to know how to begin.

As the taxi began to move, I asked, "You still want to go to India?"

He laughed. "You still remember that. Hell, no. This place is Indian enough for me."

"It used to belong to them," I said.

And he laughed again. "They damn sure knew what they were doing when they got rid of it."

Years ago, when he was around fourteen, he'd been all hipped on the idea of going to India. He read books about people sitting on rocks, naked, in all kinds of weather, but mostly bad, naturally, and walking barefoot through hot coals and arriving at wisdom. I used to say that it sounded to me as though they were getting away from wisdom as fast as they could. I think he sort of looked down on me for that.

"Do you mind," he asked, "if we have the driver drive alongside the park? On the west side—I haven't seen the city in so long."

"Of course not," I said. I was afraid that I might sound as though I were humoring him, but I hoped he wouldn't take it that way.

So we drove along, between the green of the park and the stony, lifeless elegance of hotels and apartment buildings, toward the vivid, killing streets of our childhood. These streets hadn't changed, though housing projects jutted up out of them now like rocks in the middle of a boiling sea. Most of the houses in which we had grown up had vanished, as had the stores from which we had stolen, the basements in which we had first tried sex, the rooftops from which we had hurled tin cans and bricks. But houses exactly like the houses of our past yet dominated the landscape, boys exactly like the boys we once had been found themselves smothering in these houses, came down into the streets for light and air and found themselves encircled by disaster. Some escaped the trap, most didn't. Those who got out always left something of themselves behind, as some animals amputate a leg and leave it in the trap. It might be said, perhaps, that I had escaped, after all, I was a school teacher; or that Sonny had, he hadn't lived in Harlem for years. Yet, as the cab moved uptown through streets which seemed, with a rush, to darken with dark people, and as I covertly studied Sonny's face, it came to me that what we both were seeking through our separate cab windows was that part of ourselves which had been left behind. It's always at the hour of trouble and confrontation that the missing member aches.

We hit 110th Street and started rolling up Lenox Avenue. And I'd known this avenue all my life, but it seemed to me again, as it had seemed on the day I'd first heard about Sonny's trouble, filled with a hidden menace which was its very breath of life.

"We almost there," said Sonny.

"Almost." We were both too nervous to say anything more.

We live in a housing project. It hasn't been up long. A few days after it was up it seemed uninhabitably new, now, of course, it's already rundown. It looks like a parody of the good, clean, faceless life—God knows the people who live in it do their best to make it a parody. The beat-looking grass lying around isn't enough to make their lives green, the hedges will never hold out the streets, and they know it. The big windows fool no one, they aren't big enough to make space out of no space. They don't bother with the windows, they watch the TV screen instead. The playground is most popular with the children who don't play at jacks, or skip rope, or roller skate, or swing, and they can be found in it after dark. We moved in partly because it's not too far from where I teach, and partly for the kids; but it's really just like the houses in which Sonny and I grew up. The same things happen, they'll have the same things to remember. The moment Sonny and I started into the house I had the feeling that I was simply bringing him back into the danger he had almost died trying to escape.

Sonny has never been talkative. So I don't know why I was sure he'd be dying to talk to me when supper was over the first night. Everything went fine, the oldest boy remembered him, and the youngest boy liked him, and Sonny had remembered to bring something for each of them; and Isabel, who is really much nicer than I am, more open and giving, had gone to a lot of trouble about dinner and was genuinely glad to see him. And she's always been able to tease Sonny in a way that I haven't. It was nice to see her face so vivid again and to hear her laugh and watch her make Sonny laugh. She wasn't, or, anyway, she didn't seem to be, at all uneasy or embarrassed. She chatted as though there were no subject which had to be avoided and she got Sonny past his first, faint stiffness. And thank God she was there, for I was filled with that icy dread again. Everything I did seemed awkward to me, and everything I said sounded freighted with hidden meaning. I was trying to remember everything I'd heard about dope addiction and I couldn't help watching Sonny for signs. I wasn't doing it out of malice. I was trying to find out something about my brother. I was dying to hear him tell me he was safe.

"Safe!" my father grunted, whenever Mama suggested trying to move to a neighborhood which might be safer for children. "Safe, hell! Ain't no place safe for kids, nor nobody."

He always went on like this, but he wasn't, ever, really as bad as he sounded, not even on weekends, when he got drunk. As a matter of fact, he was always on the lookout for "something a little better," but he died before he found it. He died suddenly, during a drunken weekend in the middle of the war, when Sonny was fifteen. He and Sonny hadn't ever got on too well. And this was partly because Sonny was the apple of his father's eye. It was because he loved Sonny so much and was frightened for him, that he was always fighting with him. It doesn't do any good to fight with Sonny. Sonny just moves back, inside himself, where he can't be reached. But the principal reason that they never hit it off is that they were so much alike. Daddy was big and rough and loud-talking, just the opposite of Sonny, but they both had—that same privacy.

Mama tried to tell me something about this, just after Daddy died. I was home on leave from the army.

This was the last time I ever saw my mother alive. Just the same, this picture gets all mixed up in my mind with pictures I had of her when she was younger. The way I always see her is the way she used to be on a Sunday afternoon, say, when the old folks were talking after the big Sunday dinner. I always see her wearing pale blue. She'd be sitting on the sofa. And my father would be sitting in the easy chair, not far from her. And the living room would be full of church folks and relatives. There they sit, in chairs all around the living room, and the night is creeping up outside, but nobody knows it yet. You can see the darkness growing against the windowpanes and you hear the street noises every now and again, or maybe the jangling beat of a tambourine from one of the churches close by, but it's real quiet in the room. For a moment nobody's talking, but every face looks darkening, like the sky outside. And my mother rocks a little from the waist, and my father's eyes are closed. Everyone is looking at something a child can't see. For a minute they've forgotten the children. Maybe a kid is lying on the rug, half asleep. Maybe somebody's got a kid in his lap and is absent-mindedly stroking the kid's head. Maybe there's a kid, quiet and big-eyed, curled up in a big chair in the corner. The silence, the darkness coming, and the darkness in the faces frightens the child obscurely. He hopes that the hand which strokes his forehead will never stop—will never die. He hopes that there will never come a time when the old folks won't be sitting around the living room, talking about where they've come from, and what they've seen, and what's happened to them and their kinfolk.

But something deep and watchful in the child knows that this is bound to end, is already ending. In a moment someone will get up and turn on the light. Then the old folks will remember the children and they won't talk any more that day. And when light fills the room, the child is filled with darkness. He knows that every time this happens he's moved just a little closer to that darkness outside. The darkness outside is what the old folks have been talking about. It's what they've come from. It's what they endure. The child knows that they won't talk any more because if he knows too much about what's happened to *them*, he'll know too much too soon, about what's going to happen to *him*.

The last time I talked to my mother, I remember I was restless. I wanted to get out and see Isabel. We weren't married then and we had a lot to straighten out between us.

There Mama sat, in black, by the window. She was humming an old church song, *Lord, you brought me from a long ways off.* Sonny was out somewhere. Mama kept watching the streets.

"I don't know," she said, "if I'll ever see you again, after you go off from here. But I hope you'll remember the things I tried to teach you."

"Don't talk like that," I said, and smiled. "You'll be here a long time yet."

She smiled, too, but she said nothing. She was quiet for a long time. And I said, "Mama, don't you worry about nothing. I'll be writing all the time, and you be getting the checks . . ."

"I want to talk to you about your brother," she said, suddenly. "If anything happens to me he ain't going to have nobody to look out for him."

"Mama," I said, "ain't nothing going to happen to you *or* Sonny. Sonny's all right. He's a good boy and he's got good sense."

"It ain't a question of his being a good boy," Mama said, "nor of his having good sense. It ain't only the bad ones, nor yet the dumb ones that gets sucked under." She stopped, looking at me. "Your Daddy once had a brother," she said, and she smiled in a way that made me feel she was in pain. "You didn't never know that, did you?"

"No," I said, "I never knew that," and I watched her face.

"Oh, yes," she said, "your Daddy had a brother." She looked out of the window again. "I know you never saw your Daddy cry. But *I* did—many a time, through all these years."

I asked her, "What happened to his brother? How come nobody's ever talked about him?"

This was the first time I ever saw my mother look old.

"His brother got killed," she said, "when he was just a little younger than you are now. I knew him. He was a fine boy. He was maybe a little full of the devil, but he didn't mean nobody no harm."

Then she stopped and the room was silent, exactly as it had sometimes been on those Sunday afternoons. Mama kept looking out into the streets.

"He used to have a job in the mill," she said, "and, like all young folks, he just liked to perform on Saturday nights. Saturday nights, him and your father would drift around to different places, go to dances and things like that, or just sit around with people they knew, and your father's brother would sing, he had a fine voice, and play along with himself on his guitar. Well, this particular Saturday night, him and your father was coming home from some place, and they were both a little drunk and there was a moon that night, it was bright like day. Your father's brother was feeling kind of good, and he was whistling to himself, and he had his guitar slung over his shoulder. They was coming down a hill and beneath them was a road that turned off from the highway. Well, your father's brother, being always kind of frisky, decided to run down this hill, and he did, with that guitar banging and clanging behind him, and he ran across the road, and he was making water behind a tree. And your father was sort of amused at him and he was still coming down the hill, kind of slow. Then he heard a car motor and that same minute his brother stepped from behind the tree, into the road, in the moonlight. And he started to cross the road. And your father started to run down the hill, he says he don't know why. This car was full of white men. They was all drunk, and when they seen your father's brother they let out a great whoop and holler and they aimed the car straight at him. They was having fun, they just wanted to scare him, the way they do sometimes, you know. But they was drunk. And I guess the boy, being drunk, too, and scared, kind of lost his head. By the time he jumped it was too late. Your father says he heard his brother scream when the car rolled over him, and he heard the wood of that guitar when it give, and he heard them strings go flying, and he heard them white men shouting, and the car kept on a-going and it ain't stopped till this day. And, time your father got down the hill, his brother weren't nothing but blood and pulp."

Tears were gleaming on my mother's face. There wasn't anything I could say.

"He never mentioned it," she said, "because I never let him mention it before you children. Your Daddy was like a crazy man that night and for many a night thereafter. He says he never in his life seen anything as dark as that road after the lights of that car had gone away. Weren't nothing, weren't nobody on that road, just your Daddy and his brother and that busted guitar. Oh, yes. Your Daddy never did really get right again. Till the day he died he weren't sure but that every white man he saw was the man that killed his brother."

She stopped and took out her handkerchief and dried her eyes and looked at me.

"I ain't telling you all this," she said, "to make you scared or bitter or to make you hate nobody. I'm telling you this because you got a brother. And the world ain't changed."

I guess I didn't want to believe this. I guess she saw this in my face. She turned away from me, toward the window again, searching those streets.

"But I praise my Redeemer," she said at last, "that He called your Daddy home before me. I ain't saying it to throw no flowers at myself, but, I declare, it keeps me from feeling too cast down to know I helped your father get safely through this world. Your father always acted like he was the roughest, strongest man on earth. And everybody took him to be like that. But if he hadn't had *me* there—to see his tears!"

She was crying again. Still, I couldn't move. I said, "Lord, Lord, Mama, I didn't know it was like that."

"Oh, honey," she said, "there's a lot that you don't know. But you are going to find it out." She stood up from the window and came over to me. "You got to hold on to your brother," she said, "and don't let him fall, no matter what it looks like is happening to him and no matter how evil you gets with him. You going to be evil with him many a time. But don't you forget what I told you, you hear?"

"I won't forget," I said. "Don't you worry, I won't forget. I won't let nothing happen to Sonny."

My mother smiled as though she were amused at something she saw in my face. Then, "You may not be able to stop nothing from happening. But you got to let him know you's *there*."

Two days later I was married, and then I was gone. And I had a lot of things on my mind and I pretty well forgot my promise to Mama until I got shipped home on a special furlough for her funeral.

And, after the funeral, with just Sonny and me alone in the empty kitchen, I tried to find out something about him.

"What do you want to do?" I asked him.

"I'm going to be a musician," he said.

For he had graduated, in the time I had been away, from dancing to the juke box to finding out who was playing what, and what they were doing with it, and he had bought himself a set of drums.

"You mean, you want to be a drummer?" I somehow had the feeling that being a drummer might be all right for other people but not for my brother Sonny.

"I don't think," he said, looking at me very gravely, "that I'll ever be a good drummer. But I think I can play a piano."

I frowned. I'd never played the role of the older brother quite so seriously before, had scarcely ever, in fact, *asked* Sonny a damn thing. I sensed myself in the presence of something I didn't really know how to handle, didn't understand. So I made my frown a little deeper as I asked: "What kind of musician do you want to be?"

He grinned. "How many kinds do you think there are?"

"Be *serious*," I said.

He laughed, throwing his head back, and then looked at me. "I *am* serious."

"Well, then, for Christ's sake, stop kidding around and answer a serious question. I mean, do you want to be a concert pianist, you want to play classical music and all that, or—or what?" Long before I finished he was laughing again. "For Christ's *sake*, Sonny!"

He sobered, but with difficulty. "I'm sorry. But you sound so—*scared!*" and he was off again.

"Well, you may think it's funny now, baby, but it's not going to be so funny when you have to make your living at it, let me tell you *that*." I was furious because I knew he was laughing at me and I didn't know why.

"No," he said, very sober now, and afraid, perhaps, that he'd hurt me, "I don't want to be a classical pianist. That isn't what interests me. I mean"—he paused, looking hard at me, as though his eyes would help me to understand, and then gestured helplessly, as though perhaps his hand would help—"I mean, I'll have a lot of studying to do, and I'll have to study *everything,* but, I mean, I want to play *with*—jazz musicians." He stopped. "I want to play jazz," he said.

Well, the word had never before sounded as heavy, as real, as it sounded that afternoon in Sonny's mouth. I just looked at him and I was probably frowning a real frown by this time. I simply couldn't see why on earth he'd want to spend his time hanging around nightclubs, clowning around on bandstands, while people pushed each other around a dance floor. It seemed—beneath him, somehow. I had never thought about it before, had never been forced to, but I suppose I had always put jazz musicians in a class with what Daddy called "goodtime people."

"Are you *serious?*"

"Hell, *yes*, I'm serious."

He looked more helpless than ever, and annoyed, and deeply hurt.

I suggested, helpfully: "You mean—like Louis Armstrong?"°

His face closed as though I'd struck him. "No. I'm not talking about none of that old-time, down home crap."

"Well, look, Sonny, I'm sorry, don't get mad. I just don't altogether get it, that's all. Name somebody—you know, a jazz musician you admire."

"Bird."

"Who?"

"Bird! Charlie Parker!° Don't they teach you nothing in the goddamn army?"

I lit a cigarette. I was surprised and then a little amused to discover that I was trembling. "I've been out of touch," I said. "You'll have to be patient with me. Now. Who's this Parker character?"

"He's just one of the greatest jazz musicians alive," said Sonny, sullenly, his hands in his pockets, his back to me. "Maybe *the* greatest," he added, bitterly, "that's probably why *you* never heard of him."

"All right," I said, "I'm ignorant. I'm sorry. I'll go out and buy all the cat's records right away, all right?"

"It don't," said Sonny, with dignity, "make any difference to me. I don't care what you listen to. Don't do me no favors."

I was beginning to realize that I'd never seen him so upset before. With another part of my mind I was thinking that this would probably turn out to be one of those things kids go through and that I shouldn't make it seem important by pushing it too hard. Still, I didn't think it would do any harm to ask: "Doesn't all this take a lot of time? Can you make a living at it?"

He turned back to me and half leaned, half sat, on the kitchen table. "Everything takes time," he said, "and—well, yes, sure, I can make a living at it. But what I don't seem to be able to make you understand is that it's the only thing I want to do."

"Well, Sonny," I said, gently, "you know people can't always do exactly what they *want* to do—"

"*No*, I don't know that," said Sonny, surprising me. "I think people *ought* to do what they want to do, what else are they alive for?"

"You getting to be a big boy," I said desperately, "it's time you started thinking about your future."

"I'm thinking about my future," said Sonny, grimly. "I think about it all the time."

Louis Armstrong: jazz trumpeter and vocalist (1900–1971) born in New Orleans. In the 1950s his music would have been considered conservative by progressive jazz fans. *Charlie Parker:* a jazz saxophonist (1920–1955) who helped create the progressive jazz style called bebop. Parker was a heroin addict who died at an early age.

I gave up. I decided, if he didn't change his mind, that we could always talk about it later. "In the meantime," I said, "you got to finish school." We had already decided that he'd have to move in with Isabel and her folks. I knew this wasn't the ideal arrangement because Isabel's folks are inclined to be dicty° and they hadn't especially wanted Isabel to marry me. But I didn't know what else to do. "And we have to get you fixed up at Isabel's."

There was a long silence. He moved from the kitchen table to the window. "That's a terrible idea. You know it yourself."

"Do you have a *better* idea?"

He just walked up and down the kitchen for a minute. He was as tall as I was. He had started to shave. I suddenly had the feeling that I didn't know him at all.

He stopped at the kitchen table and picked up my cigarettes. Looking at me with a kind of mocking, amused defiance, he put one between his lips. "You mind?"

"You smoking already?"

He lit the cigarette and nodded, watching me through the smoke. "I just wanted to see if I'd have the courage to smoke in front of you." He grinned and blew a great cloud of smoke to the ceiling. "It was easy." He looked at my face. "Come on, now. I bet you was smoking at my age, tell the truth."

I didn't say anything but the truth was on my face, and he laughed. But now there was something very strained in his laugh. "Sure. And I bet that ain't all you was doing."

He was frightening me a little. "Cut the crap," I said. "We already decided that you was going to go and live at Isabel's. Now what's got into you all of a sudden?"

"*You* decided it," he pointed out. "*I* didn't decide nothing." He stopped in front of me, leaning against the stove, arms loosely folded. "Look, brother. I don't want to stay in Harlem no more, I really don't." He was very earnest. He looked at me, then over toward the kitchen window. There was something in his eyes I'd never seen before, some thoughtfulness, some worry all his own. He rubbed the muscle of one arm. "It's time I was getting out of here."

"Where do you want to *go*, Sonny?"

"I want to join the army. Or the navy, I don't care. If I say I'm old enough, they'll believe me."

Then I got mad. It was because I was so scared. "You must be crazy. You goddamn fool, what the hell do you want to go and join the *army* for?"

"I just told you. To get out of Harlem."

"Sonny, you haven't even finished *school*. And if you really want to be a musician, how do you expect to study if you're in the *army*?"

He looked at me, trapped, and in anguish. "There's ways. I might be able to work out some kind of deal. Anyway, I'll have the G.I. Bill when I come out."

"*If* you come out." We stared at each other. "Sonny, please. Be reasonable. I know the setup is far from perfect. But we got to do the best we can."

"I ain't learning nothing in school," he said. "Even when I go." He turned away from me and opened the window and threw his cigarette out into the narrow alley. I watched his back. "At least, I ain't learning nothing you'd want me to learn." He slammed the window so hard I thought the glass would fly out, and turned back to me. "And I'm sick of the stink of these garbage cans!"

dicty: slang word for stylish, high-class; snobbish.

"Sonny," I said, "I know how you feel. But if you don't finish school now, you're going to be sorry later that you didn't." I grabbed him by the shoulders. "And you only got another year. It ain't so bad. And I'll come back and I swear I'll help you do *whatever* you want to do. Just try to put up with it till I come back. Will you please do that? For me?"

He didn't answer and he wouldn't look at me.

"Sonny. You hear me?"

He pulled away. "I hear you. But you never hear anything *I* say."

I didn't know what to say to that. He looked out of the window and then back at me. "OK," he said, and sighed. "I'll try."

Then I said, trying to cheer him up a little, "They got a piano at Isabel's. You can practice on it."

And as a matter of fact, it did cheer him up for a minute. "That's right," he said to himself. "I forgot that." His face relaxed a little. But the worry, the thoughtfulness, played on it still, the way shadows play on a face which is staring into the fire.

But I thought I'd never hear the end of that piano. At first, Isabel would write me, saying how nice it was that Sonny was so serious about his music and how, as soon as he came in from school, or wherever he had been when he was supposed to be at school, he went straight to that piano and stayed there until suppertime. And, after supper, he went back to that piano and stayed there until everybody went to bed. He was at the piano all day Saturday and all day Sunday. Then he bought a record player and started playing records. He'd play one record over and over again, all day long sometimes, and he'd improvise along with it on the piano. Or he'd play one section of the record, one chord, one change, one progression, then he'd do it on the piano. Then back to the record. Then back to the piano.

Well, I really don't know how they stood it. Isabel finally confessed that it wasn't like living with a person at all, it was like living with sound. And the sound didn't make any sense to her, didn't make any sense to any of them—naturally. They began, in a way, to be afflicted by this presence that was living in their home. It was as though Sonny were some sort of god, or monster. He moved in an atmosphere which wasn't like theirs at all. They fed him and he ate, he washed himself, he walked in and out of their door; he certainly wasn't nasty or unpleasant or rude, Sonny isn't any of those things; but it was as though he were all wrapped up in some cloud, some fire, some vision all his own; and there wasn't any way to reach him.

At the same time, he wasn't really a man yet, he was still a child, and they had to watch out for him in all kinds of ways. They certainly couldn't throw him out. Neither did they dare to make a great scene about that piano because even they dimly sensed, as I sensed, from so many thousands of miles away, that Sonny was at that piano playing for his life.

But he hadn't been going to school. One day a letter came from the school board and Isabel's mother got it—there had, apparently, been other letters but Sonny had torn them up. This day, when Sonny came in, Isabel's mother showed him the letter and asked where he'd been spending his time. And she finally got it out of him that he'd been down in Greenwich Village, with musicians and other characters, in a white girl's apartment. And this scared her and she started to scream at him and what came up, once she began—though she denies it to this day—was what sacrifices they were making to give Sonny a decent home and how little he appreciated it.

Sonny didn't play the piano that day. By evening, Isabel's mother had calmed down but then there was the old man to deal with, and Isabel herself. Isabel says she did her best to be calm but she broke down and started crying. She says she just watched Sonny's face. She could tell, by watching him, what was happening with him. And what was happening was that they penetrated his cloud, they had reached him. Even if their fingers had been a thousand times more gentle than human fingers ever are, he could hardly help feeling that they had stripped him naked and were spitting on that nakedness. For he also had to see that his presence, that music, which was life or death to him, had been torture for them and that they had endured it, not at all for his sake, but only for mine. And Sonny couldn't take that. He can take it a little better today than he could then but he's still not very good at it and, frankly, I don't know anybody who is.

The silence of the next few days must have been louder than the sound of all the music ever played since time began. One morning, before she went to work, Isabel was in his room for something and she suddenly realized that all of his records were gone. And she knew for certain that he was gone. And he was. He went as far as the navy would carry him. He finally sent me a postcard from some place in Greece and that was the first I knew that Sonny was still alive. I didn't see him any more until we were both back in New York and the war had long been over.

He was a man by then, of course, but I wasn't willing to see it. He came by the house from time to time, but we fought almost every time we met. I didn't like the way he carried himself, loose and dreamlike all the time, and I didn't like his friends, and his music seemed to be merely an excuse for the life he led. It sounded just that weird and disordered.

Then we had a fight, a pretty awful fight, and I didn't see him for months. By and by I looked him up, where he was living, in a furnished room in the Village, and I tried to make it up. But there were lots of people in the room and Sonny just lay on his bed, and he wouldn't come downstairs with me, and he treated these other people as though they were his family and I weren't. So I got mad and then he got mad, and then I told him that he might just as well be dead as live the way he was living. Then he stood up and he told me not to worry about him any more in life, that he *was* dead as far as I was concerned. Then he pushed me to the door and the other people looked on as though nothing were happening, and he slammed the door behind me. I stood in the hallway, staring at the door. I heard somebody laugh in the room and then the tears came to my eyes. I started down the steps, whistling to keep from crying, I kept whistling to myself, *You going to need me, baby, one of these cold, rainy days.*

I read about Sonny's trouble in the spring. Little Grace died in the fall. She was a beautiful little girl. But she only lived a little over two years. She died of polio and she suffered. She had a slight fever for a couple of days, but it didn't seem like anything and we just kept her in bed. And we would certainly have called the doctor, but the fever dropped, she seemed to be all right. So we thought it had just been a cold. Then, one day, she was up, playing, Isabel was in the kitchen fixing lunch for the two boys when they'd come in from school, and she heard Grace fall down in the living room. When you have a lot of children you don't always start running when one of them falls, unless they start screaming or something. And, this time, Grace was quiet. Yet, Isabel says that when she heard that *thump* and then that silence, something happened in her to make her afraid. And she ran to the living room and there was little Grace on the floor, all twisted up, and the reason she hadn't screamed was that she couldn't get her breath. And when she did scream, it was the worst sound, Isabel says, that she'd ever heard in all her life, and she still hears it sometimes in her dreams. Isabel will sometimes wake me up with a low, moaning, strangled sound and I have to be quick to awaken her and hold her to me and where Isabel is weeping against me seems a mortal wound.

I think I may have written Sonny the very day that little Grace was buried. I was sitting in the living room in the dark, by myself, and I suddenly thought of Sonny. My trouble made his real.

One Saturday afternoon, when Sonny had been living with us, or, anyway, been in our house, for nearly two weeks, I found myself wandering aimlessly about the living room, drinking from a can of beer, and trying to work up the courage to search Sonny's room. He was out, he was usually out whenever I was home, and Isabel had taken the children to see their grandparents. Suddenly I was standing still in front of the living room window, watching Seventh Avenue. The idea of searching Sonny's room made me still. I scarcely dared to admit to myself what I'd be searching for. I didn't know what I'd do if I found it. Or if I didn't.

On the sidewalk across from me, near the entrance to a barbecue joint, some people were holding an old-fashioned revival meeting. The barbecue cook, wearing a dirty white apron, his conked hair reddish and metallic in the pale sun, and a cigarette between his lips, stood in the doorway, watching them. Kids and older people paused in their errands and stood there, along with some older men and a couple of very tough-looking women who watched everything that happened on the avenue, as though they owned it, or were maybe owned by it. Well, they were watching this, too. The revival was being carried on by three sisters in black, and a brother. All they had were their voices and their Bibles and a tambourine. The brother was testifying and while he testified two of the sisters stood together, seeming to say, amen, and the third sister walked around with the tambourine outstretched and a couple of people dropped coins into it. Then the brother's testimony ended and the sister who had been taking up the collection dumped the coins into her palm and transferred them to the pocket of her long black robe. Then she raised both hands, striking the tambourine against the air, and then against one hand, and she started to sing. And the two other sisters and the brother joined in.

It was strange, suddenly, to watch, though I had been seeing these street meetings all my life. So, of course, had everybody else down there. Yet, they paused and watched and listened and I stood still at the window. "'*Tis the old ship of Zion*," they sang, "*it has rescued many a thousand!*" Not a soul under the sound of their voices was hearing this song for the first time, not one of them had been rescued. Nor had they seen much in the way of rescue work being done around them. Neither did they especially believe in the holiness of the three sisters and the brother, they knew too much about them, knew where they lived, and how. The woman with the tambourine, whose voice dominated the air, whose face was bright with joy, was divided by very little from the woman who stood watching her, a cigarette between her heavy, chapped lips, her hair a cuckoo's nest, her face scarred and swollen from many beatings, and her black eyes glittering like coal. Perhaps they both knew this, which was why, when, as rarely, they addressed each other, they addressed each other as Sister. As the singing filled the air the watching, listening faces underwent a change, the eyes focusing on something within; the music seemed to soothe a poison out of them; and time seemed, nearly, to fall away from the sullen, belligerent, battered faces, as though they were fleeing back to their first condition, while dreaming of their last. The barbecue cook half shook his head and smiled, and dropped his cigarette and disappeared into his joint. A man fumbled in his pockets for change and stood holding it in his hand impatiently, as though he had just remembered a pressing appointment further up the avenue. He looked furious. Then I saw Sonny, standing on the edge of the crowd. He was carrying a wide, flat notebook with a green cover, and it made him look, from where I was standing, almost like a schoolboy. The coppery sun brought out the copper in his skin, he was very faintly smiling, standing very still. Then the singing stopped, the tambourine turned into a collection plate again. The furious man dropped in his coins and vanished, so did a couple of the women, and Sonny dropped some change in the plate, looking directly at the woman with a little smile. He started across the avenue, toward the house. He has a slow, loping walk, something like the way Harlem hipsters walk, only he's imposed on this his own half-beat. I had never really noticed it before.

I stayed at the window, both relieved and apprehensive. As Sonny disappeared from my sight, they began singing again. And they were still singing when his key turned in the lock.

"Hey," he said.

"Hey, yourself. You want some beer?"

"No. Well, maybe." But he came up to the window and stood beside me, looking out. "What a warm voice," he said.

They were singing *If I could only hear my mother pray again!*

"Yes," I said, "and she can sure beat that tambourine."

"But what a terrible song," he said, and laughed. He dropped his notebook on the sofa and disappeared into the kitchen. "Where's Isabel and the kids?"

"I think they went to see their grandparents. You hungry?"

"No." He came back into the living room with his can of beer. "You want to come some place with me tonight?"

I sensed, I don't know how, that I couldn't possibly say no. "Sure. Where?"

He sat down on the sofa and picked up his notebook and started leafing through it. "I'm going to sit in with some fellows in a joint in the Village."

"You mean, you're going to play, tonight?"

"That's right." He took a swallow of his beer and moved back to the window. He gave me a sidelong look. "If you can stand it."

"I'll try," I said.

He smiled to himself and we both watched as the meeting across the way broke up. The three sisters and the brother, heads bowed, were singing *God be with you till we meet again*. The faces around them were very quiet. Then the song ended. The small crowd dispersed. We watched the three women and the lone man walk slowly up the avenue.

"When she was singing before," said Sonny, abruptly, "her voice reminded me for a minute of what heroin feels like sometimes—when it's in your veins. It makes you feel sort of warm and cool at the same time. And distant. And—and sure." He sipped his beer, very deliberately not looking at me. I watched his face. "It makes you feel—in control. Sometimes you've got to have that feeling."

"Do you?" I sat down slowly in the easy chair.

"Sometimes." He went to the sofa and picked up his notebook again. "Some people do."

"In order," I asked, "to play?" And my voice was very ugly, full of contempt and anger.

"Well"—he looked at me with great, troubled eyes, as though, in fact, he hoped his eyes would tell me things he could never otherwise say—"they *think* so. And *if* they think so—!"

"And what do *you* think?" I asked.

He sat on the sofa and put his can of beer on the floor. "I don't know," he said, and I couldn't be sure if he were answering my question or pursuing his thoughts. His face didn't tell me. "It's not so much to *play*. It's to *stand* it, to be able to make it at all. On any level." He frowned and smiled: "In order to keep from shaking to pieces."

"But these friends of yours," I said, "they seem to shake themselves to pieces pretty goddamn fast."

"Maybe." He played with the notebook. And something told me that I should curb my tongue, that Sonny was doing his best to talk, that I should listen. "But of course you only know the ones that've gone to pieces. Some don't—or at least they haven't *yet* and that's just about all *any* of us can say." He paused. "And then there are some who just live, really, in hell, and they know it and they see what's happening and they go right on. I don't know." He sighed, dropped the notebook, folded his arms. "Some guys, you can tell from the way they play, they on something *all* the time. And you can see that, well, it makes something real for them. But of course," he picked up his beer from the floor and sipped it and put the can down again, "they *want* to, too, you've got to see that. Even some of them that say they don't—*some*, not all."

"And what about you?" I asked—I couldn't help it. "What about you? Do *you* want to?"

He stood up and walked to the window and remained silent for a long time. Then he sighed. "Me," he said. Then: "While I was downstairs before, on my way here, listening to that woman sing, it struck me all of a sudden how much suffering she must have had to go through—to sing like that. It's *repulsive* to think you have to suffer that much."

I said: "But there's no way not to suffer—is there, Sonny?"

"I believe not," he said and smiled, "but that's never stopped anyone from trying." He looked at me. "Has it?" I realized, with this mocking look, that there stood between us, forever, beyond the power of time or forgiveness, the fact that I had held silence—so long!—when he had needed human speech to help him. He turned back to the window. "No, there's no way not to suffer. But you try all kinds of ways to keep from drowning in it, to keep on top of it, and to make it seem—well, like *you*. Like you did something, all right, and now you're suffering for it. You know?" I said nothing. "Well you know," he said, impatiently, "why *do* people suffer? Maybe it's better to do something to give it a reason, *any* reason."

"But we just agreed," I said, "that there's no way not to suffer. Isn't it better, then, just to—take it?"

"But nobody just takes it," Sonny cried, "that's what I'm telling you! *Everybody* tries not to. You're just hung up on the *way* some people try—it's not *your* way!"

The hair on my face began to itch, my face felt wet. "That's not true," I said, "that's not true. I don't give a damn what other people do, I don't even care how they suffer. I just care how *you* suffer." And he looked at me. "Please believe me," I said, "I don't want to see you—die—trying not to suffer."

"I won't," he said, flatly, "die trying not to suffer. At least, not any faster than anybody else."

"But there's no need," I said, trying to laugh, "is there? in killing yourself."

I wanted to say more, but I couldn't. I wanted to talk about will power and how life could be—well, beautiful. I wanted to say that it was all within; but was it? or, rather, wasn't that exactly the trouble? And I wanted to promise that I would never fail him again. But it would all have sounded—empty words and lies.

So I made the promise to myself and prayed that I would keep it.

"It's terrible sometimes, inside," he said, "that's what's the trouble. You walk these streets, black and funky and cold, and there's not really a living ass to talk to, and there's nothing shaking, and there's no way of getting it out—that storm inside. You can't talk it and you can't make love with it, and when you finally try to get with it and play it, you realize *nobody's* listening. So *you've* got to listen. You got to find a way to listen."

And then he walked away from the window and sat on the sofa again, as though all the wind had suddenly been knocked out of him. "Sometimes you'll do *anything* to play, even cut your mother's throat." He laughed and looked at me. "Or your brother's." Then he sobered. "Or your own." Then: "Don't worry. I'm all right now and I think I'll *be* all right. But I can't forget—where I've been. I don't mean just the physical place I've been, I mean where I've *been*. And *what* I've been."

"What have you been, Sonny?" I asked.

He smiled—but sat sideways on the sofa, his elbow resting on the back, his fingers playing with his mouth and chin, not looking at me. "I've been something I didn't recognize, didn't know I could be. Didn't know anybody could be." He stopped, looking inward, looking helplessly young, looking old. "I'm not talking about it now because I feel *guilty* or anything like that—maybe it would be better if I did, I don't know. Anyway, I can't really talk about it. Not to you, not to anybody," and now he turned and faced me. "Sometimes, you know, and it was actually when I was most *out* of the world, I felt that I was in it, that I was *with* it, really, and I could play or I didn't really have to *play*, it just came out of me, it was there. And I don't know how I played, thinking about it now, but I know I did awful things, those times, sometimes, to people. Or it wasn't that I *did* anything to them—it was that they weren't real." He picked up the beer can; it was empty; he rolled it between his palms: "And other times—well, I needed a fix, I needed to find a place to lean, I needed to clear a space to *listen*—and I couldn't find it, and I—went crazy, I did terrible things to *me*, I was terrible *for* me." He began pressing the beer can between his hands, I watched the metal begin to give. It glittered, as he played with it, like a knife, and I was afraid he would cut himself, but I said nothing. "Oh well. I can never tell you. I was all by myself at the bottom of something, stinking and sweating and crying and shaking, and I smelled it, you know? *my* stink, and I thought I'd die if I couldn't get away from it and yet, all the same, I knew that everything I was doing was just locking me in with it.

And I didn't know," he paused, still flattening the beer can, "I didn't know, I still *don't* know, something kept telling me that maybe it was good to smell your own stink, but I didn't think that *that* was what I'd been trying to do—and—who can stand it?" and he abruptly dropped the ruined beer can, looking at me with a small, still smile, and then rose, walking to the window as though it were the lodestone rock. I watched his face, he watched the avenue. "I couldn't tell you when Mama died—but the reason I wanted to leave Harlem so bad was to get away from drugs. And then, when I ran away, that's what I was running from—really. When I came back, nothing had changed, *I* hadn't changed, I was just—older." And he stopped, drumming with his fingers on the windowpane. The sun had vanished, soon darkness would fall. I watched his face. "It can come again," he said, almost as though speaking to himself. Then he turned to me. "It can come again," he repeated. "I just want you to know that."

"All right," I said, at last. "So it can come again. All right."

He smiled, but the smile was sorrowful. "I had to try to tell you," he said.

"Yes," I said. "I understand that."

"You're my brother," he said, looking straight at me, and not smiling at all.

"Yes," I repeated, "yes. I understand that."

He turned back to the window, looking out. "All that hatred down there," he said, "all that hatred and misery and love. It's a wonder it doesn't blow the avenue apart."

We went to the only nightclub on a short, dark street, downtown. We squeezed through the narrow, chattering, jam-packed bar to the entrance of the big room, where the bandstand was. And we stood there for a moment, for the lights were very dim in this room and we couldn't see. Then, "Hello, boy," said a voice and an enormous black man, much older than Sonny or myself, erupted out of all that atmospheric lighting and put an arm around Sonny's shoulder. "I been sitting right here," he said, "waiting for you."

He had a big voice, too, and heads in the darkness turned toward us.

Sonny grinned and pulled a little away, and said, "Creole, this is my brother. I told you about him."

Creole shook my hand. "I'm glad to meet you, son," he said, and it was clear that he was glad to meet me *there*, for Sonny's sake. And he smiled, "You got a real musician in *your* family," and he took his arm from Sonny's shoulder and slapped him, lightly, affectionately, with the back of his hand.

"Well. Now I've heard it all," said a voice behind us. This was another musician, and a friend of Sonny's, a coal-black, cheerful-looking man, built close to the ground. He immediately began confiding to me, at the top of his lungs, the most terrible things about Sonny, his teeth gleaming like a lighthouse and his laugh coming up out of him like the beginning of an earthquake. And it turned out that everyone at the bar knew Sonny, or almost everyone; some were musicians, working there, or nearby, or not working, some were simply hangers-on, and some were there to hear Sonny play. I was introduced to all of them and they were all very polite to me. Yet, it was clear that, for them, I was only Sonny's brother. Here, I was in Sonny's world. Or, rather: his kingdom. Here, it was not even a question that his veins bore royal blood.

They were going to play soon and Creole installed me, by myself, at a table in a dark corner. Then I watched them, Creole, and the little black man, and Sonny, and the others, while they horsed around, standing just below the bandstand. The light from the bandstand spilled just a little short of them and, watching them laughing and gesturing and moving about, I had the feeling that they, nevertheless, were being most careful not to step into that circle of light too suddenly: that if they moved into the light too suddenly, without thinking, they would perish in flame. Then, while I watched, one of them, the small, black man, moved into the light and crossed the bandstand and started fooling around with his drums. Then—being funny and being, also, extremely ceremonious—Creole took Sonny by the arm and led him to the piano. A woman's voice called Sonny's name and a few hands started clapping. And Sonny, also being funny and being ceremonious, and so touched, I think, that he could have cried, but neither hiding it nor showing it, riding it like a man, grinned, and put both hands to his heart and bowed from the waist.

Creole then went to the bass fiddle and a lean, very bright-skinned brown man jumped up on the bandstand and picked up his horn. So there they were, and the atmosphere on the bandstand and in the room began to change and tighten. Someone stepped up to the microphone and announced them. Then there were all kinds of murmurs. Some people at the bar shushed others. The waitress ran around, frantically getting in the last orders, guys and chicks got closer to each other, and the lights on the bandstand, on the quartet, turned to a kind of indigo. Then they all looked different there. Creole looked about him for the last time, as though he were making certain that all his chickens were in the coop, and then he—jumped and struck the fiddle. And there they were.

All I know about music is that not many people ever really hear it. And even then, on the rare occasions when something opens within, and the music enters, what we mainly hear, or hear corroborated, are personal, private, vanishing evocations. But the man who creates the music is hearing something else, is dealing with the roar rising from the void and imposing order on it as it hits the air. What is evoked in him, then, is of another order, more terrible because it has no words, and triumphant, too, for that same reason. And his triumph, when he triumphs, is ours. I just watched Sonny's face. His face was troubled, he was working hard, but he wasn't with it. And I had the feeling that, in a way, everyone on the bandstand was waiting for him, both waiting for him and pushing him along. But as I began to watch Creole, I realized that it was Creole who held them all back. He had them on a short rein. Up there, keeping the beat with his whole body, wailing on the fiddle, with his eyes half closed, he was listening to everything, but he was listening to Sonny. He was having a dialogue with Sonny. He wanted Sonny to leave the shoreline and strike out for the deep water. He was Sonny's witness that deep water and drowning were not the same thing—he had been there, and he knew. And he wanted Sonny to know. He was waiting for Sonny to do the things on the keys which would let Creole know that Sonny was in the water.

And, while Creole listened, Sonny moved, deep within, exactly like someone in torment. I had never before thought of how awful the relationship must be between the musician and his instrument. He has to fill it, this instrument, with the breath of life, his own. He has to make it do what he wants it to do. And a piano is just a piano. It's made out of so much wood and wires and little hammers and big ones, and ivory. While there's only so much you can do with it, the only way to find this out is to try; to try and make it do everything.

And Sonny hadn't been near a piano for over a year. And he wasn't on much better terms with his life, not the life that stretched before him now. He and the piano stammered, started one way, got scared, stopped; started another way, panicked, marked time, started again; then seemed to have found a direction, panicked again, got stuck. And the face I saw on Sonny I'd never seen before. Everything had been burned out of it, and, at the same time, things usually hidden were being burned in, by the fire and fury of the battle which was occurring in him up there.

Yet, watching Creole's face as they neared the end of the first set, I had the feeling that something had happened, something I hadn't heard. Then they finished, there was scattered applause, and then, without an instant's warning, Creole started into something else, it was almost sardonic, it was *Am I Blue*. And, as though he commanded, Sonny began to play. Something began to happen. And Creole let out the reins. The dry, low, black man said something awful on the drums, Creole answered, and the drums talked back. Then the horn insisted, sweet and high, slightly detached perhaps, and Creole listened, commenting now and then, dry, and driving, beautiful and calm and old. Then they all came together again, and Sonny was part of the family again. I could tell this from his face. He seemed to have found, right there beneath his fingers, a damn brand-new piano. It seemed that he couldn't get over it. Then, for awhile, just being happy with Sonny, they seemed to be agreeing with him that brand-new pianos certainly were a gas.

Then Creole stepped forward to remind them that what they were playing was the blues. He hit something in all of them, he hit something in me, myself, and the music tightened and deepened, apprehension began to beat the air. Creole began to tell us what the blues were all about. They were not about anything very new. He and his boys up there were keeping it new, at the risk of ruin, destruction, madness, and death, in order to find new ways to make us listen. For, while the tale of how we suffer, and how we are delighted, and how we may triumph is never new, it always must be heard. There isn't any other tale to tell, it's the only light we've got in all this darkness.

And this tale, according to that face, that body, those strong hands on those strings, has another aspect in every country, and a new depth in every generation. Listen, Creole seemed to be saying, listen. Now these are Sonny's blues. He made the little black man on the drums know it, and the bright, brown man on the horn. Creole wasn't trying any longer to get Sonny in the water. He was wishing him Godspeed.° Then he stepped back, very slowly, filling the air with the immense suggestion that Sonny speak for himself.

Then they all gathered around Sonny and Sonny played. Every now and again one of them seemed to say, amen. Sonny's fingers filled the air with life, his life. But that life contained so many others. And Sonny went all the way back, he really began with the spare, flat statement of the opening phrase of the song. Then he began to make it his. It was very beautiful because it wasn't hurried and it was no longer a lament. I seemed to hear with what burning he had made it his, with what burning we had yet to make it ours, how we could cease lamenting. Freedom lurked around us and I understood, at last, that he could help us to be free if we would listen, that he would never be free until we did. Yet, there was no battle in his face now. I heard what he had gone through, and would continue to go through until he came to rest in earth. He had made it his: that long line, of which we knew only Mama and Daddy. And he was giving it back, as everything must be given back, so that, passing through death, it can live forever. I saw my mother's face again, and felt, for the first time, how the stones of the road she had walked on must have bruised her feet. I saw the moon-lit road where

wishing him Godspeed: wishing him a safe and successful voyage.

my father's brother died. And it brought something else back to me, and carried me past it. I saw my little girl again and felt Isabel's tears again, and I felt my own tears begin to rise. And I was yet aware that this was only a moment, that the world waited outside, as hungry as a tiger, and that trouble stretched above us, longer than the sky.

Then it was over. Creole and Sonny let out their breath, both soaking wet, and grinning. There was a lot of applause and some of it was real. In the dark, the girl came by and I asked her to take drinks to the bandstand. There was a long pause, while they talked up there in the indigo light and after awhile I saw the girl put a Scotch and milk on top of the piano for Sonny. He didn't seem to notice it, but just before they started playing again, he sipped from it and looked toward me, and nodded. Then he put it back on top of the piano. For me, then, as they began to play again, it glowed and shook above my brother's head like the very cup of trembling.°

Questions

1. From whose point of view is "Sonny's Blues" told? How do the narrator's values and experiences affect his view of the story?
2. What is the older brother's profession? Does it suggest anything about his personality?
3. How would this story change if it were told by Sonny?
4. What event prompts the narrator to write to his brother?
5. What does the narrator's mother ask him to do for Sonny? Does the older brother keep his promise?
6. The major characters in this story are called Mama, Daddy, and Sonny (the older brother is never named or even nicknamed). How do these names affect our sense of the story?
7. The story's tone and language change considerably in the last few pages. What is the effect of the final scene in the nightclub? How does seeing Sonny play change his brother's view of him?
8. Reread the last four paragraphs and explain the significance of the statement "Now these are Sonny's blues." How has Sonny made this music his own?

Tobias Wolff

Tobias Wolff was born in Birmingham, Alabama, in 1945, the son of an aerospace engineer and a waitress and secretary. Following his parents' divorce, Tobias moved with his mother to Washington State while his older brother, Geoffrey, remained with their father (a pathological liar who was the subject of Geoffrey Wolff's acclaimed memoir The Duke of Deception). *Tobias Wolff's own memoir,* This Boy's Life *(1989), describes, among other things, his tense relationship with his abusive stepfather; it was the basis for the 1993 film starring Robert De Niro and Leonardo DiCaprio. In 1964 Wolff joined the Army, where he spent four years, including a year in Vietnam as a Special Forces language expert. This experience is recounted in a second memoir,*

Tobias Wolff

---

cup of trembling: image of redemptive suffering from Isaiah 51:15–22—"See, I have taken out of your hand the cup of trembling, the dregs of the cup of My fury; you shall no longer drink it."

In Pharaoh's Army: Memories of the Lost War *(1994)*. *After his military service, he earned a bachelor's degree at Oxford University and a master's at Stanford University, where he currently teaches in the creative writing program. Wolff is the author of six volumes of fiction, the novella* The Barracks Thief *(1984, PEN/Faulkner Award), the novel* Old School *(2003), and four volumes of short stories, most recently* Our Story Begins: New and Selected Stories *(2008).*

Acknowledging Raymond Carver (his onetime faculty colleague at Syracuse University) and Flannery O'Connor as influences, Wolff writes stories that, in the words of one critic, create a "sometimes comic, always compassionate world of ordinary people who suffer twentieth-century martyrdoms of growing up, growing old, loving and lacking love, living with parents and lovers and wives and their own weaknesses." Wolff lives in Northern California.

The Rich Brother   1985

There were two brothers, Pete and Donald.

Pete, the older brother, was in real estate. He and his wife had a Century 21 franchise in Santa Cruz. Pete worked hard and made a lot of money, but not any more than he thought he deserved. He had two daughters, a sailboat, a house from which he could see a thin slice of the ocean, and friends doing well enough in their own lives not to wish bad luck on him. Donald, the younger brother, was still single. He lived alone, painted houses when he found the work, and got deeper in debt to Pete when he didn't.

No one would have taken them for brothers. Where Pete was stout and hearty and at home in the world, Donald was bony, grave, and obsessed with the fate of his soul. Over the years Donald had worn the images of two different Perfect Masters° around his neck. Out of devotion to the second of these he entered an ashram° in Berkeley, where he nearly died of undiagnosed hepatitis. By the time Pete finished paying the medical bills Donald had become a Christian. He drifted from church to church, then joined a pentecostal community that met somewhere in the Mission District° to sing in tongues and swap prophecies.

Pete couldn't make sense of it. Their parents were both dead, but while they were alive neither of them had found it necessary to believe in anything. They managed to be decent people without making fools of themselves, and Pete had the same ambition. He thought that the whole thing was an excuse for Donald to take himself seriously.

The trouble was that Donald couldn't content himself with worrying about his own soul. He had to worry about everyone else's, and especially Pete's. He handed down his judgments in ways that he seemed to consider subtle: through significant silence, innuendo, looks of mild despair that said, *Brother, what have you come to?* What Pete had come to, as far as he could tell, was prosperity. That was the real issue between them. Pete prospered and Donald did not prosper.

At the age of forty Pete took up sky diving. He made his first jump with two friends who'd started only a few months earlier and were already doing stunts. He

---

Perfect Masters: in Hindu mysticism, God-realized souls who work to help others toward the realization of God.   *ashram*: secluded place where a community of Hindus lead lives of simplicity and meditation.   *Mission District*: run-down and, at one time, dangerous section of San Francisco.

never would have used the word *mystical*, but that was how Pete felt about the experience. Later he made the mistake of trying to describe it to Donald, who kept asking how much it cost and then acted appalled when Pete told him.

"At least I'm trying something new," Pete said. "At least I'm breaking the pattern."

Not long after that conversation Donald also broke the pattern, by going to live on a farm outside Paso Robles. The farm was owned by several members of Donald's community, who had bought it and moved there with the idea of forming a family of faith. That was how Donald explained it in the first letter he sent. Every week Pete heard how happy Donald was, how "in the Lord." He told Pete that he was praying for him, he and the rest of Pete's brothers and sisters on the farm.

"I only have one brother," Pete wanted to answer, "and that's enough." But he kept this thought to himself.

In November the letters stopped. Pete didn't worry about this at first, but when he called Donald at Thanksgiving Donald was grim. He tried to sound upbeat but he didn't try hard enough to make it convincing. "Now listen," Pete said, "you don't have to stay in that place if you don't want to."

"I'll be all right," Donald answered.

"That's not the point. Being all right is not the point. If you don't like what's going on up there, then get out."

"I'm all right," Donald said again, more firmly. "I'm doing fine."

But he called Pete a week later and said that he was quitting the farm. When Pete asked him where he intended to go, Donald admitted that he had no plan. His car had been repossessed just before he left the city, and he was flat broke.

"I guess you'll have to stay with us," Pete said.

Donald put up a show of resistance. Then he gave in. "Just until I get my feet on the ground," he said.

"Right," Pete said. "Check out your options." He told Donald he'd send him money for a bus ticket, but as they were about to hang up Pete changed his mind. He knew that Donald would try hitchhiking to save the fare. Pete didn't want him out on the road all alone where some head case would pick him up, where anything could happen to him.

"Better yet," he said, "I'll come and get you."

"You don't have to do that. I didn't expect you to do that," Donald said. He added, "It's a pretty long drive."

"Just tell me how to get there."

But Donald wouldn't give him directions. He said that the farm was too depressing, that Pete wouldn't like it. Instead, he insisted on meeting Pete at a service station called Jonathan's Mechanical Emporium.

"You must be kidding," Pete said.

"It's close to the highway," Donald said. "I didn't name it."

"That's one for the collection," Pete said.

The day before he left to bring Donald home, Pete received a letter from a man who described himself as "head of household" at the farm where Donald had been living. From this letter Pete learned that Donald had not quit the farm, but had been asked to leave. The letter was written on the back of a mimeographed survey form asking people to record their response to a ceremony of some kind. The last question said:

What did you feel during the liturgy?

    a) Being
    b) Becoming
    c) Being and Becoming
    d) None of the Above
    e) All of the Above

Pete tried to forget the letter. But of course he couldn't. Each time he thought of it he felt crowded and breathless, a feeling that came over him again when he drove into the service station and saw Donald sitting against a wall with his head on his knees. It was late afternoon. A paper cup tumbled slowly past Donald's feet, pushed by the damp wind.

Pete honked and Donald raised his head. He smiled at Pete, then stood and stretched. His arms were long and thin and white. He wore a red bandanna across his forehead, a T-shirt with a couple of words on the front. Pete couldn't read them because the letters were inverted.

"Grow up," Pete yelled. "Get a Mercedes."

Donald came up to the window. He bent down and said, "Thanks for coming. You must be totally whipped."

"I'll make it." Pete pointed at Donald's T-shirt. "What's that supposed to say?"

Donald looked down at his shirt front. "Try God. I guess I put it on backwards. Pete, could I borrow a couple of dollars? I owe these people for coffee and sandwiches."

Pete took five twenties from his wallet and held them out the window.

Donald stepped back as if horrified. "I don't need that much."

"I can't keep track of all these nickels and dimes," Pete said. "Just pay me back when your ship comes in." He waved the bills impatiently. "Go on—take it."

"Only for now." Donald took the money and went into the service station office. He came out carrying two orange sodas, one of which he gave to Pete as he got into the car. "My treat," he said.

"No bags?"

"Wow, thanks for reminding me." Donald balanced his drink on the dashboard, but the slight rocking of the car as he got out tipped it onto the passenger's seat, where half its contents foamed over before Pete could snatch it up again. Donald looked on while Pete held the bottle out the window, soda running down his fingers.

"Wipe it up," Pete told him. "Quick!"

"With what?"

Pete stared at Donald. "That shirt. Use the shirt."

Donald pulled a long face but did as he was told, his pale skin puckering against the wind.

"Great, just great," Pete said. "We haven't even left the gas station yet."

Afterwards, on the highway, Donald said, "This is a new car, isn't it?"

"Yes. This is a new car."

"Is that why you're so upset about the seat?"

"Forget it, okay? Let's just forget about it."

"I said I was sorry."

Pete said, "I just wish you'd be more careful. These seats are made of leather. That stain won't come out, not to mention the smell. I don't see why I can't have leather seats that smell like leather instead of orange pop."

"What was wrong with the other car?"

Pete glanced over at Donald. Donald had raised the hood of the blue sweatshirt he'd put on. The peaked hood above his gaunt, watchful face gave him the look of an inquisitor.

"There wasn't anything wrong with it," Pete said. "I just happened to like this one better."

Donald nodded.

There was a long silence between them as Pete drove on and the day darkened toward evening. On either side of the road lay stubble-covered fields. A line of low hills ran along the horizon, topped here and there with trees black against the grey sky. In the approaching line of cars a driver turned on his headlights. Pete did the same.

"So what happened?" he asked. "Farm life not your bag?"

Donald took some time to answer, and at last he said, simply, "It was my fault."

"What was your fault?"

"The whole thing. Don't play dumb, Pete. I know they wrote to you." Donald looked at Pete, then stared out the windshield again.

"I'm not playing dumb."

Donald shrugged.

"All I really know is they asked you to leave," Pete went on. "I don't know any of the particulars."

"I blew it," Donald said. "Believe me, you don't want to hear the gory details."

"Sure I do," Pete said. He added, "Everybody likes the gory details."

"You mean everybody likes to hear how someone messed up."

"Right," Pete said. "That's the way it is here on Spaceship Earth."

Donald bent one knee onto the front seat and leaned against the door so that he was facing Pete instead of the windshield. Pete was aware of Donald's scrutiny. He waited. Night was coming on in a rush now, filling the hollows of the land. Donald's long cheeks and deep-set eyes were dark with shadow. His brow was white. "Do you ever dream about me?" Donald asked.

"Do I ever dream about you? What kind of a question is that? Of course I don't dream about you," Pete said, untruthfully.

"What do you dream about?"

"Sex and money. Mostly money. A nightmare is when I dream I don't have any."

"You're just making that up," Donald said.

Pete smiled.

"Sometimes I wake up at night," Donald went on, "and I can tell you're dreaming about me."

"We were talking about the farm," Pete said. "Let's finish that conversation and then we can talk about our various out-of-body experiences and the interesting things we did during previous incarnations."

For a moment Donald looked like a grinning skull; then he turned serious again. "There's not much to tell," he said. "I just didn't do anything right."

"That's a little vague," Pete said.

"Well, like the groceries. Whenever it was my turn to get the groceries I'd blow it somehow. I'd bring the groceries home and half of them would be missing, or I'd have all the wrong things, the wrong kind of flour or the wrong kind of chocolate or whatever. One time I gave them away. It's not funny, Pete."

Pete said, "Who did you give the groceries to?"

"Just some people I picked up on the way home. Some fieldworkers. They had about eight kids with them and they didn't even speak English—just nodded their heads. Still, I shouldn't have given away the groceries. Not all of them, anyway. I really learned my lesson about that. You have to be practical. You have to be fair to yourself." Donald leaned forward, and Pete could sense his excitement. "There's nothing actually wrong with being in business," he said. "As long as you're fair to other people you can still be fair to yourself. I'm thinking of going into business, Pete."

"We'll talk about it," Pete said. "So, that's the story? There isn't any more to it than that?"

"What did they tell you?" Donald asked.

"Nothing."

"They must have told you something."

Pete shook his head.

"They didn't tell you about the fire?" When Pete shook his head again Donald regarded him for a time, then folded his arms across his chest and slumped back into the corner. "Everybody had to take turns cooking dinner. I usually did tuna casserole or spaghetti with garlic bread. But this one night I thought I'd do something different, something really interesting." Donald looked sharply at Pete. "It's all a big laugh to you, isn't it?"

"I'm sorry," Pete said.

"You don't know when to quit. You just keep hitting away."

"Tell me about the fire, Donald."

Donald kept watching him. "You have this compulsion to make me look foolish."

"Come off it, Donald. Don't make a big thing out of this."

"I know why you do it. It's because you don't have any purpose in life. You're afraid to relate to people who do, so you make fun of them."

"Relate," Pete said.

"You're basically a very frightened individual," Donald said. "Very threatened. You've always been like that. Do you remember when you used to try to kill me?"

"I don't have any compulsion to make you look foolish, Donald—you do it yourself. You're doing it right now."

"You can't tell me you don't remember," Donald said. "It was after my operation. You remember that."

"Sort of." Pete shrugged. "Not really."

"Oh yes," Donald said. "Do you want to see the scar?"

"I remember you had an operation. I don't remember the specifics, that's all. And I sure as hell don't remember trying to kill you."

"Oh yes," Donald repeated, maddeningly. "You bet your life you did. All the time. The thing was, I couldn't have anything happen to me where they sewed me up because then my intestines would come apart again and poison me. That was a big issue, Pete. Mom was always in a state about me climbing trees and so on. And you used to hit me there every chance you got."

"Mom was in a state every time you burped," Pete said. "I don't know. Maybe I bumped into you accidentally once or twice. I never did it deliberately."

"Every chance you got," Donald said. "Like when the folks went out at night and left you to baby-sit. I'd hear them say good night, and then I'd hear the car start up, and when they were gone I'd lie there and listen. After a while I would hear you coming down the hall, and I would close my eyes and pretend to be asleep. There were nights when you would stand outside the door, just stand there, and then go away again. But most nights you'd open the door and I would hear you in the room with me, breathing. You'd come over and sit next to me on the bed—you remember, Pete, you have to—you'd sit next to me on the bed and pull the sheets back. If I was on my stomach you'd roll me over. Then you would lift up my pajama shirt and start hitting me on my stitches. You'd hit me as hard as you could, over and over. I was afraid that you'd get mad if you knew I was awake. Is that strange or what? I was afraid that you'd get mad if you found out that I knew you were trying to kill me." Donald laughed. "Come on, you can't tell me you don't remember that."

"It might have happened once or twice. Kids do those things. I can't get all excited about something I maybe did twenty-five years ago."

"No maybe about it. You did it."

Pete said, "You're wearing me out with this stuff. We've got a long drive ahead of us and if you don't back off pretty soon we aren't going to make it. You aren't, anyway."

Donald turned away.

"I'm doing my best," Pete said. The self-pity in his own voice made the words sound like a lie. But they weren't a lie! He was doing his best.

The car topped a rise. In the distance Pete saw a cluster of lights that blinked out when he started downhill. There was no moon. The sky was low and black.

"Come to think of it," Pete said, "I did have a dream about you the other night." Then he added, impatiently, as if Donald were badgering him, "A couple of other nights, too. I'm getting hungry," he said.

"The same dream?"

"Different dreams. I only remember one of them. There was something wrong with me, and you were helping out. Taking care of me. Just the two of us. I don't know where everyone else was supposed to be."

Pete left it at that. He didn't tell Donald that in this dream he was blind.

"I wonder if that was when I woke up," Donald said. He added, "I'm sorry I got into that thing about my scar. I keep trying to forget it but I guess I never will. Not really. It was pretty strange, having someone around all the time who wanted to get rid of me."

"Kid stuff," Pete said. "Ancient history."

They ate dinner at a Denny's on the other side of King City. As Pete was paying the check he heard a man behind him say, "Excuse me, but I wonder if I might ask which way you're going?" and Donald answer, "Santa Cruz."

"Perfect," the man said.

Pete could see him in the fish-eye mirror above the cash register: a red blazer with some kind of crest on the pocket, little black moustache, glossy black hair combed down on his forehead like a Roman emperor's. A rug, Pete thought. Definitely a rug.

Pete got his change and turned. "Why is that perfect?" he asked.

The man looked at Pete. He had a soft, ruddy face that was doing its best to express pleasant surprise, as if this new wrinkle were all he could have wished for, but the eyes behind the aviator glasses showed signs of regret. His lips were moist and shiny. "I take it you're together," he said.

"You got it," Pete told him.

"All the better, then," the man went on. "It so happens I'm going to Santa Cruz myself. Had a spot of car trouble down the road. The old Caddy let me down."

"What kind of trouble?" Pete asked.

"Engine trouble," the man said. "I'm afraid it's a bit urgent. My daughter is sick. Urgently sick. I've got a telegram here." He patted the breast pocket of his blazer.

Before Pete could say anything Donald got into the act again. "No problem," Donald said. "We've got tons of room."

"Not that much room," Pete said.

Donald nodded. "I'll put my things in the trunk."

"The trunk's full," Pete told him.

"It so happens I'm traveling light," the man said. "This leg of the trip anyway. In fact, I don't have any luggage at this particular time."

Pete said, "Left it in the old Caddy, did you?"

"Exactly," the man said.

"No problem," Donald repeated. He walked outside and the man went with him. Together they strolled across the parking lot, Pete following at a distance. When they reached Pete's car Donald raised his face to the sky, and the man did the same. They stood there looking up. "Dark night," Donald said.

"Stygian," the man said.

Pete still had it in his mind to brush him off, but he didn't do that. Instead he unlocked the door for him. He wanted to see what would happen. It was an adventure, but not a dangerous adventure. The man might steal Pete's ashtrays but he wouldn't kill him. If Pete got killed on the road it would be by some spiritual person in a sweatsuit, someone with his eyes on the far horizon and a wet Try God T-shirt in his duffel bag.

As soon as they left the parking lot the man lit a cigar. He blew a cloud of smoke over Pete's shoulder and sighed with pleasure. "Put it out," Pete told him.

"Of course," the man said. Pete looked in the rearview mirror and saw the man take another long puff before dropping the cigar out the window. "Forgive me," he said. "I should have asked. Name's Webster, by the way."

Donald turned and looked back at him. "First name or last?"

The man hesitated. "Last," he said finally.

"I know a Webster," Donald said. "Mick Webster."

"There are many of us," Webster said.

"Big fellow, wooden leg," Pete said.

Donald gave Pete a look.

Webster shook his head. "Doesn't ring a bell. Still, I wouldn't deny the connection. Might be one of the cousinry."

"What's your daughter got?" Pete asked.

"That isn't clear," Webster answered. "It appears to be a female complaint of some nature. Then again it may be tropical." He was quiet for a moment, and added: "If indeed it *is* tropical, I will have to assume some of the blame myself. It was my own vaulting ambition that first led us to the tropics and kept us in the tropics all those many years, exposed to every evil. Truly I have much to answer for. I left my wife there."

Donald said quietly, "You mean she died?"

"I buried her with these hands. The earth will be repaid, gold for gold."

"Which tropics?" Pete asked.

"The tropics of Peru."

"What part of Peru are they in?"

"The lowlands," Webster said.

"What's it like down there? In the lowlands."

"Another world," Webster said. His tone was sepulchral. "A world better imagined than described."

"Far out," Pete said.

The three men rode in silence for a time. A line of trucks went past in the other direction, trailers festooned with running lights, engines roaring.

"Yes," Webster said at last, "I have much to answer for."

Pete smiled at Donald, but Donald had turned in his seat again and was gazing at Webster. "I'm sorry about your wife," Donald said.

"What did she die of?" Pete asked.

"A wasting illness," Webster said. "The doctors have no name for it, but I do." He leaned forward and said, fiercely, "*Greed.* My greed, not hers. She wanted no part of it."

Pete bit his lip. Webster was a find and Pete didn't want to scare him off by hooting at him. In a voice low and innocent of knowingness, he asked, "What took you there?"

"It's difficult for me to talk about."

"Try," Pete told him.

"A cigar would make it easier."

Donald turned to Pete and said, "It's okay with me."

"All right," Pete said. "Go ahead. Just keep the window rolled down."

"Much obliged." A match flared. There were eager sucking sounds.

"Let's hear it," Pete said.

"I am by training an engineer," Webster began. "My work has exposed me to all but one of the continents, to desert and alp and forest, to every terrain and season of the earth. Some years ago I was hired by the Peruvian government to search for tungsten in the tropics. My wife and daughter accompanied me. We were the only white people for a thousand miles in any direction, and we had no choice but to live as the Indians lived—to share their food and drink and even their culture."

Pete said, "You knew the lingo, did you?"

"We picked it up." The ember of the cigar bobbed up and down. "We were used to learning as necessity decreed. At any rate, it became evident after a couple of years that there was no tungsten to be found. My wife had fallen ill and was pleading to be taken home. But I was deaf to her pleas, because by then I was on the trail of another metal—a metal far more valuable than tungsten."

"Let me guess," Pete said. "Gold?"

Donald looked at Pete, then back at Webster.

"Gold," Webster said. "A vein of gold greater than the Mother Lode itself. After I found the first traces of it nothing could tear me away from my search—not the sickness of my wife or anything else. I was determined to uncover the vein, and so I did—but not before I laid my wife to rest. As I say, the earth will be repaid."

Webster was quiet. Then he said, "But life must go on. In the years since my wife's death I have been making the arrangements necessary to open the mine. I could have done it immediately, of course, enriching myself beyond measure, but I knew what that would mean—the exploitation of our beloved Indians, the brutal destruction of their environment. I felt I had too much to atone for already." Webster paused, and when he spoke again his voice was dull and rushed, as if he had used up all the interest he had in his own words. "Instead I drew up a program for returning the bulk of the wealth to the Indians themselves. A kind of trust fund. The interest alone will allow them to secure their ancient lands and rights in perpetuity. At the same time, our investors will be rewarded a thousandfold. Two-thousandfold. Everyone will prosper together."

"That's great," said Donald. "That's the way it ought to be."

Pete said, "I'm willing to bet that you just happen to have a few shares left. Am I right?"

Webster made no reply.

"Well?" Pete knew that Webster was on to him now, but he didn't care. The story had bored him. He'd expected something different, something original, and Webster had let him down. He hadn't even tried. Pete felt sour and stale. His eyes burned from cigar smoke and the high beams of road-hogging truckers. "Douse the stogie," he said to Webster. "I told you to keep the window down."

"Got a little nippy back here."

Donald said, "Hey, Pete. Lighten up."

"Douse it!"

Webster sighed. He got rid of the cigar.

"I'm a wreck," Pete said to Donald. "You want to drive for a while?"

Donald nodded.

Pete pulled over and they changed places.

Webster kept his counsel in the back seat. Donald hummed while he drove, until Pete told him to stop. Then everything was quiet.

Donald was humming again when Pete woke up. Pete stared sullenly at the road, at the white lines sliding past the car. After a few moments of this he turned and said, "How long have I been out?"

Donald glanced at him. "Twenty, twenty-five minutes."

Pete looked behind him and saw that Webster was gone. "Where's our friend?"

"You just missed him. He got out in Soledad.° He told me to say thanks and good-bye."

"Soledad? What about his sick daughter? How did he explain her away?"

"He has a brother living there. He's going to borrow a car from him and drive the rest of the way in the morning."

"I'll bet his brother's living there," Pete said. "Doing fifty concurrent life sentences. His brother and his sister and his mom and his dad."

"I kind of liked him," Donald said.

Soledad: city in central California, site of a state prison.

"I'm sure you did," Pete said wearily.
"He was interesting. He's been places."
"His cigars had been places, I'll give you that."
"Come on, Pete."
"Come on yourself. What a phony."
"You don't know that."
"Sure I do."
"How? How do you know?"

Pete stretched. "Brother, there are some things you're just born knowing. What's the gas situation?"

"We're a little low."

"Then why didn't you get some more?"

"I wish you wouldn't snap at me like that," Donald said.

"Then why don't you use your head? What if we run out?"

"We'll make it," Donald said. "I'm pretty sure we've got enough to make it. You didn't have to be so rude to him," Donald added.

Pete took a deep breath. "I don't feel like running out of gas tonight, okay?"

Donald pulled in at the next station they came to and filled the tank while Pete went to the men's room. When Pete came back, Donald was sitting in the passenger's seat. The attendant came up to the driver's window as Pete got in behind the wheel. He bent down and said, "Twelve fifty-five."

"You heard the man," Pete said to Donald.

Donald looked straight ahead. He didn't move.

"Cough up," Pete said. "This trip's on you."

"I can't."

"Sure you can. Break out that wad."

Donald glanced up at the attendant, then at Pete. "Please," he said. "Pete, I don't have it anymore."

Pete took this in. He nodded, and paid the attendant.

Donald began to speak when they left the station but Pete cut him off. He said, "I don't want to hear from you right now. You just keep quiet or I swear to God I won't be responsible."

They left the fields and entered a tunnel of tall trees. The trees went on and on. "Let me get this straight," Pete said at last. "You don't have the money I gave you."

"You treated him like a bug or something," Donald said.

"You don't have the money," Pete said again.

Donald shook his head.

"Since I bought dinner, and since we didn't stop anywhere in between, I assume you gave it to Webster. Is that right? Is that what you did with it?"

"Yes."

Pete looked at Donald. His face was dark under the hood but he still managed to convey a sense of remove, as if none of this had anything to do with him.

"Why?" Pete asked. "Why did you give it to him?" When Donald didn't answer, Pete said, "A hundred dollars. Gone. Just like that. I *worked* for that money, Donald."

"I know, I know," Donald said.

"You don't know! How could you? You get money by holding out your hand."

"I work too," Donald said.

"You work too. Don't kid yourself, brother."

Donald leaned toward Pete, about to say something, but Pete cut him off again.

"You're not the only one on the payroll, Donald. I don't think you understand that. I have a family."

"Pete, I'll pay you back."

"Like hell you will. A hundred dollars!" Pete hit the steering wheel with the palm of his hand. "Just because you think I hurt some goofball's feelings. Jesus, Donald."

"That's not the reason," Donald said. "And I didn't just *give* him the money."

"What do you call it, then? What do you call what you did?"

"I *invested* it. I wanted a share, Pete." When Pete looked over at him Donald nodded and said again, "I wanted a share."

Pete said, "I take it you're referring to the gold mine in Peru."

"Yes," Donald said.

"You believe that such a gold mine exists?"

Donald looked at Pete, and Pete could see him just beginning to catch on. "You'll believe anything," Pete said. "Won't you? You really will believe anything at all."

"I'm sorry," Donald said, and turned away.

Pete drove on between the trees and considered the truth of what he had just said—that Donald would believe anything at all. And it came to him that it would be just like this unfair life for Donald to come out ahead in the end, by believing in some outrageous promise that would turn out to be true and that he, Pete, would reject out of hand because he was too wised up to listen to anybody's pitch anymore except for laughs. What a joke. What a joke if there really was a blessing to be had, and the blessing didn't come to the one who deserved it, the one who did all the work, but to the other.

And as if this had already happened Pete felt a shadow move upon him, darkening his thoughts. After a time he said, "I can see where all this is going, Donald."

"I'll pay you back," Donald said.

"No," Pete said. "You won't pay me back. You can't. You don't know how. All you've ever done is take. All your life."

Donald shook his head.

"I see exactly where this is going," Pete went on. "You can't work, you can't take care of yourself, you believe anything anyone tells you. I'm stuck with you, aren't I?" He looked over at Donald. "I've got you on my hands for good."

Donald pressed his fingers against the dashboard as if to brace himself. "I'll get out," he said.

Pete kept driving.

"Let me out," Donald said. "I mean it, Pete."

"Do you?"

Donald hesitated. "Yes," he said.

"Be sure," Pete told him. "This is it. This is for keeps."

"I mean it."

"All right. You made the choice." Pete braked the car sharply and swung it to the shoulder of the road. He turned off the engine and got out. Trees loomed on both sides, shutting out the sky. The air was cold and musty. Pete took Donald's duffel bag from the back seat and set it down behind the car. He stood there, facing Donald in the red glow of the taillights. "It's better this way," Pete said.

Donald just looked at him.

"Better for you," Pete said.

Donald hugged himself. He was shaking. "You don't have to say all that," he told Pete. "I don't blame you."

"Blame me? What the hell are you talking about? Blame me for what?"

"For anything," Donald said.

"I want to know what you mean by blame me."

"Nothing. Nothing, Pete. You'd better get going. God bless you."

"That's it," Pete said. He dropped to one knee, searching the packed dirt with his hands. He didn't know what he was looking for, his hands would know when they found it.

Donald touched Pete's shoulder. "You'd better go," he said.

Somewhere in the trees Pete heard a branch snap. He stood up. He looked at Donald, then went back to the car and drove away. He drove fast, hunched over the wheel, conscious of the way he was hunched and the shallowness of his breathing, refusing to look in the mirror above his head until there was nothing behind him but darkness.

Then he said, "A hundred dollars," as if there were someone to hear.

The trees gave way to fields. Metal fences ran beside the road, plastered with windblown scraps of paper. Tule fog° hung above the ditches, spilling into the road, dimming the ghostly halogen lights that burned in the yards of the farms Pete passed. The fog left beads of water rolling up the windshield.

Pete rummaged among his cassettes. He found Pachelbel's Canon° and pushed it into the tape deck. When the violins began to play he leaned back and assumed an attentive expression as if he were really listening to them. He smiled to himself like a man at liberty to enjoy music, a man who has finished his work and settled his debts, done all things meet and due.

And in this way, smiling, nodding to the music, he went another mile or so and pretended that he was not already slowing down, that he was not going to turn back, that he would be able to drive on like this, alone, and have the right answer when his wife stood before him in the doorway of his home and asked, Where is he? Where is your brother?

Questions

1. How would you describe the two brothers? Who do you find more sympathetic, and why?
2. Why is there such conflict between them?
3. Why does Pete keep bailing Donald out? Is it simply out of duty and brotherhood? What do you make of the comment that "everybody likes to hear how someone messed up"?
4. Do you believe Donald's story about Pete hitting him in the stitches? If so, what might this say about their relationship?
5. Why does Pete turn back? Do you believe that he would?

Tule fog: thick ground fog in California. *Pachelbel's Canon:* musical composition by Johann Pachelbel (1653–1706); it became widely known through its use in the film *Ordinary People* (1980).

Eudora Welty

Eudora Welty (1909–2001) was born in Jackson, Mississippi, the daughter of an insurance company president. Like William Faulkner, another Mississippi writer, she stayed close to her roots for practically all her life, except for short sojourns at the University of Wisconsin, where she took her B.A., and in New York City, where she studied advertising. She lived most of her life in her childhood home in Jackson, within a stone's throw of the state capitol. Although Welty was a novelist distinguished for *The Robber Bridegroom* (1942), *Delta Wedding* (1946), *The Ponder Heart* (1954), *Losing Battles* (1970), and *The Optimist's Daughter* (1972), many critics think her finest work was in the short-story form. *The Collected Stories of Eudora Welty* (1980) gathers the work of more than forty years. Welty's other books include a memoir, *One Writer's Beginnings* (1984), and *The Eye of the Story* (1977), a book of sympathetic criticism on the fiction of other writers, including Willa Cather, Virginia Woolf, Katherine Anne Porter, and Isak Dinesen. *One Time, One Place*, a book of photographs of everyday life that Welty took in Mississippi during the Depression, was republished in a revised edition in 1996.

Why I Live at the P.O. 1941

I was getting along fine with Mama, Papa-Daddy, and Uncle Rondo until my sister Stella-Rondo just separated from her husband and came back home again. Mr. Whitaker! Of course I went with Mr. Whitaker first, when he first appeared here in China Grove, taking "Pose Yourself" photos, and Stella-Rondo broke us up. Told him I was one-sided. Bigger on one side than the other, which is a deliberate, calculated falsehood: I'm the same. Stella-Rondo is exactly twelve months to the day younger than I am and for that reason she's spoiled.

She's always had anything in the world she wanted and then she'd throw it away. Papa-Daddy gave her this gorgeous Add-a-Pearl necklace when she was eight years old and she threw it away playing baseball when she was nine, with only two pearls.

So as soon as she got married and moved away from home the first thing she did was separate! From Mr. Whitaker! This photographer with the popeyes she said she trusted. Came home from one of those towns up in Illinois and to our complete surprise brought this child of two.

Mama said she like to make her drop dead for a second. "Here you had this marvelous blonde child and never so much as wrote your mother a word about it," says Mama. "I'm thoroughly ashamed of you." But of course she wasn't.

Stella-Rondo just calmly takes off this *hat*. I wish you could see it. She says, "Why, Mama, Shirley-T.'s adopted, I can prove it."

"How?" says Mama, but all I says was, "H'm!" There I was over the hot stove, trying to stretch two chickens over five people and a completely unexpected child into the bargain, without one moment's notice.

"What do you mean—'H'm!'?" says Stella-Rondo, and Mama says, "I heard that, Sister."

I said that oh, I didn't mean a thing, only that whoever Shirley-T. was, she was the spit-image of Papa-Daddy if he'd cut off his beard, which of course he'd never do in the world. Papa-Daddy's Mama's papa and sulks.

Stella-Rondo got furious! She said, "Sister, I don't need to tell you you got a lot of nerve and always did have and I'll thank you to make no future reference to my adopted child whatsoever."

"Very well," I said. "Very well, very well. Of course I noticed at once she looks like Mr. Whitaker's side too. That frown. She looks like a cross between Mr. Whitaker and Papa-Daddy."

"Well, all I can say is she isn't."

"She looks exactly like Shirley Temple to me," says Mama, but Shirley-T. just ran away from her.

So the first thing Stella-Rondo did at the table was turn Papa-Daddy against me.

"Papa-Daddy," she says. He was trying to cut up his meat. "Papa-Daddy!" I was taken completely by surprise. Papa-Daddy is about a million years old and's got this long-long beard. "Papa-Daddy, Sister says she fails to understand why you don't cut off your beard."

So Papa Daddy l-a-y-s down his knife and fork! He's real rich. Mama says he is, he says he isn't. So he says, "Have I heard correctly? You don't understand why I don't cut off my beard?"

"Why," I says, "Papa-Daddy, of course I understand, I did not say any such of a thing, the idea!"

He says, "Hussy!"

I says, "Papa-Daddy, you know I wouldn't any more want you to cut off your beard than the man in the moon. It was the farthest thing from my mind! Stella-Rondo sat there and made that up while she was eating breast of chicken."

But he says, "So the postmistress fails to understand why I don't cut off my beard. Which job I got you through my influence with the government. 'Bird's nest'—is that what you call it?"

Not that it isn't the next to smallest P.O. in the entire state of Mississippi.

I says, "Oh, Papa-Daddy," I says, "I didn't say any such of a thing, I never dreamed it was a bird's nest, I have always been grateful though this is the next to smallest P.O. in the state of Mississippi, and I do not enjoy being referred to as a hussy by my own grandfather."

But Stella-Rondo says, "Yes, you did say it too. Anybody in the world could of heard you, that had ears."

"Stop right there," says Mama, looking at *me*.

So I pulled my napkin straight back through the napkin ring and left the table.

As soon as I was out of the room Mama says, "Call her back, or she'll starve to death," but Papa-Daddy says, "This is the beard I started growing on the Coast when I was fifteen years old." He would of gone on till nightfall if Shirley-T. hadn't lost the Milky Way she ate in Cairo.

So Papa-Daddy says, "I am going out and lie in the hammock, and you can all sit here and remember my words: I'll never cut off my beard as long as I live, even one inch, and I don't appreciate it in you at all." Passed right by me in the hall and went straight out and got in the hammock.

It would be a holiday. It wasn't five minutes before Uncle Rondo suddenly appeared in the hall in one of Stella-Rondo's flesh-colored kimonos, all cut on the bias, like something Mr. Whitaker probably thought was gorgeous.

"Uncle Rondo!" I says. "I didn't know who that was! Where are you going?"

"Sister," he says, "get out of my way, I'm poisoned."

"If you're poisoned stay away from Papa-Daddy," I says. "Keep out of the hammock. Papa-Daddy will certainly beat you on the head if you come within forty miles of him. He thinks I deliberately said he ought to cut off his beard after he got me the P.O., and I've told him and told him and told him, and he acts like he just don't hear me. Papa-Daddy must of gone stone deaf."

"He picked a fine day to do it then," says Uncle Rondo, and before you could say "Jack Robinson" flew out in the yard.

What he'd really done, he'd drunk another bottle of that prescription. He does it every single Fourth of July as sure as shooting, and it's horribly expensive. Then he falls over in the hammock and snores. So he insisted on zigzagging right on out to the hammock, looking like a half-wit.

Papa-Daddy woke up with this horrible yell and right there without moving an inch he tried to turn Uncle Rondo against me. I heard every word he said. Oh, he told Uncle Rondo I didn't learn to read till I was eight years old and he didn't see how in the world I ever got the mail put up at the P.O., much less read it all, and he said if Uncle Rondo could only fathom the lengths he had gone to get me that job! And he said on the other hand he thought Stella-Rondo had a brilliant mind and deserved credit for getting out of town. All the time he was just lying there swinging as pretty as you please and looping out his beard, and poor Uncle Rondo was *pleading* with him to slow down the hammock, it was making him as dizzy as a witch to watch it. But that's what Papa-Daddy likes about a hammock. So Uncle Rondo was too dizzy to get turned against me for the time being. He's Mama's only brother and is a good case of a one-track mind. Ask anybody. A certified pharmacist.

Just then I heard Stella-Rondo raising the upstairs window. While she was married she got this peculiar idea that it's cooler with the windows shut and locked. So she has to raise the window before she can make a soul hear her outdoors.

So she raises the window and says, "*Oh!*" You would have thought she was mortally wounded.

Uncle Rondo and Papa-Daddy didn't even look up, but kept right on with what they were doing. I had to laugh.

I flew up the stairs and threw the door open! I says, "What in the wide world's the matter, Stella-Rondo? You mortally wounded?"

"No," she says, "I am not mortally wounded but I wish you would do me the favor of looking out that window there and telling me what you see."

So I shade my eyes and look out the window.

"I see the front yard," I says.

"Don't you see any human beings?" she says.

"I see Uncle Rondo trying to run Papa-Daddy out of the hammock," I says. "Nothing more. Naturally, it's so suffocating-hot in the house, with all the windows shut and locked, everybody who cares to stay in their right mind will have to go out and get in the hammock before the Fourth of July is over."

"Don't you notice anything different about Uncle Rondo?" asks Stella-Rondo.

"Why, no, except he's got on some terrible-looking flesh-colored contraption I wouldn't be found dead in, is all I can see," I says.

"Never mind, you won't be found dead in it, because it happens to be part of my trousseau, and Mr. Whitaker took several dozen photographs of me in it," says Stella-Rondo. "What on earth could Uncle Rondo *mean* by wearing part of my trousseau out in the broad open daylight without saying so much as 'Kiss my foot,' *knowing* I only got home this morning after my separation and hung my negligee up on the bathroom door, just as nervous as I could be?"

"I'm sure I don't know, and what do you expect me to do about it?" I says. "Jump out the window?"

"No, I expect nothing of the kind. I simply declare that Uncle Rondo looks like a fool in it, that's all," she says. "It makes me sick to my stomach."

"Well, he looks as good as he can," I says. "As good as anybody in reason could." I stood up for Uncle Rondo, please remember. And I said to Stella-Rondo, "I think I would do well not to criticize so freely if I were you and came home with a two-year-old child I had never said a word about, and no explanation whatever about my separation."

"I asked you the instant I entered this house not to refer one more time to my adopted child, and you gave me your word of honor you would not," was all Stella-Rondo would say, and started pulling out every one of her eyebrows with some cheap Kress tweezers.

So I merely slammed the door behind me and went down and made some green-tomato pickle. Somebody had to do it. Of course Mama had turned both the niggers loose; she always said no earthly power could hold one anyway on the Fourth of July, so she wouldn't even try. It turned out that Jaypan fell in the lake and came within a very narrow limit of drowning.

So Mama trots in. Lifts up the lid and says, "H'm! Not very good for your Uncle Rondo in his precarious condition, I must say. Or poor little adopted Shirley-T. Shame on you!"

That made me tired. I says, "Well, Stella-Rondo had better thank her lucky stars it was her instead of me came trotting in with that very peculiar-looking child. Now if it had been me that trotted in from Illinois and brought a peculiar-looking child of two, I shudder to think of the reception I'd of got, much less controlled the diet of an entire family."

"But you must remember, Sister, that you were never married to Mr. Whitaker in the first place and didn't go up to Illinois to live," says Mama, shaking a spoon in my face. "If you had I would have been just as overjoyed to see you and your little adopted girl as I was to see Stella-Rondo, when you wound up with your separation and came on back home."

"You would not," I says.

"Don't contradict me, I would," says Mama.

But I said she couldn't convince me though she talked till she was blue in the face. Then I said, "Besides, you know as well as I do that that child is not adopted."

"She most certainly is adopted," says Mama, stiff as a poker.

I says, "Why, Mama, Stella-Rondo had her just as sure as anything in this world, and just too stuck up to admit it."

"Why Sister," said Mama. "Here I thought we were going to have a pleasant Fourth of July, and you start right out not believing a word your own baby sister tells you!"

"Just like Cousin Annie Flo. Went to her grave denying the facts of life," I remind Mama.

"I told you if you ever mentioned Annie Flo's name I'd slap your face," says Mama, and slaps my face.

"All right, you wait and see," I says.

"I," says Mama, "*I* prefer to take my children's word for anything when it's humanly possible." You ought to see Mama, she weighs two hundred pounds and has real tiny feet.

Just then something perfectly horrible occurred to me.

"Mama," I says, "can that child talk?" I simply had to whisper! "Mama, I wonder if that child can be—you know—in any way? Do you realize," I says, "that she hasn't spoken one single, solitary word to a human being up to this minute? This is the way she looks," I says, and I looked like this.

Well, Mama and I just stood there and stared at each other. It was horrible!

"I remember well that Joe Whitaker frequently drank like a fish," says Mama. "I believed to my soul he drank *chemicals*." And without another word she marches to the foot of the stairs and calls Stella-Rondo.

"Stella-Rondo? O-o-o-o-o! Stella-Rondo!"

"What?" says Stella-Rondo from upstairs. Not even the grace to get up off the bed.

"Can that child of yours talk?" asks Mama.

Stella-Rondo yells back, "Can she what?"

"Talk! Talk!" says Mama. "Burdyburdyburdyburdy!"

So Stella-Rondo yells back, "Who says she can't talk?"

"Sister says so," says Mama.

"You didn't have to tell me, I know whose word of honor don't mean a thing in this house," says Stella-Rondo.

And in a minute the loudest Yankee voice I ever heard in my life yells out, "OE'm Pop-OE the Sailor-r-r-r Ma-a-an!" and then somebody jumps up and down in the upstairs hall. In another second the house would of fallen down.

"Not only talks, she can tap-dance!" calls Stella-Rondo. "Which is more than some people I won't name can do."

"Why, the little precious darling thing!" Mama says, so surprised. "Just as smart as she can be!" Starts talking baby talk right there. Then she turns on me. "Sister, you ought to be thoroughly ashamed! Run upstairs this instant and apologize to Stella-Rondo and Shirley-T."

"Apologize for what?" I says. "I merely wondered if the child was normal, that's all. Now that she's proved she is, why, I have nothing further to say."

But Mama just turned on her heel and flew out, furious. She ran right upstairs and hugged the baby. She believed it was adopted. Stella-Rondo hadn't done a thing but turn her against me from upstairs while I stood there helpless over the hot stove. So that made Mama, Papa-Daddy, and the baby all on Stella-Rondo's side.

Next, Uncle Rondo.

I must say that Uncle Rondo has been marvelous to me at various times in the past and I was completely unprepared to be made to jump out of my skin, the way it turned out. Once Stella-Rondo did something perfectly horrible to him—broke a chain letter from Flanders Field°—and he took the radio back he had given her and gave it to me. Stella-Rondo was furious! For six months we all had to call her Stella instead of Stella-Rondo, or she wouldn't answer. I always thought Uncle Rondo had all the brains of the entire family. Another time he sent me to Mammoth Cave,° with all expenses paid.

But this would be the day he was drinking that prescription, the Fourth of July.

So at supper Stella-Rondo speaks up and says she thinks Uncle Rondo ought to try to eat a little something. So finally Uncle Rondo said he would try a little cold biscuits and ketchup, but that was all. So *she* brought it to him.

"Do you think it is wise to disport with ketchup in Stella-Rondo's flesh-colored kimono?" I says. Trying to be considerate! If Stella-Rondo couldn't watch out for her trousseau, somebody had to.

"Any objections?" asks Uncle Rondo, just about to pour out all the ketchup.

"Don't mind what she says, Uncle Rondo," says Stella-Rondo. "Sister has been devoting this solid afternoon to sneering out my bedroom window at the way you look."

"What's that?" says Uncle Rondo. Uncle Rondo has got the most terrible temper in the world. Anything is liable to make him tear the house down if it comes at the wrong time.

So Stella-Rondo says, "Sister says, 'Uncle Rondo certainly does look like a fool in that pink kimono!'"

Do you remember who it was really said that?

Uncle Rondo spills out all the ketchup and jumps out of his chair and tears off the kimono and throws it down on the dirty floor and puts his foot on it. It had to be sent all the way to Jackson to the cleaners and re-pleated.

"So that's your opinion of your Uncle Rondo, is it?" he says. "I look like a fool, do I? Well, that's the last straw. A whole day in this house with nothing to do, and then to hear you come out with a remark like that behind my back!"

"I didn't say any such of a thing, Uncle Rondo," I says, "and I'm not saying who did, either. Why, I think you look all right. Just try to take care of yourself and not talk and eat at the same time," I says. "I think you better go lie down."

"Lie down my foot," says Uncle Rondo. I ought to of known by that he was fixing to do something perfectly horrible.

So he didn't do anything that night in the precarious state he was in—just played Casino with Mama and Stella-Rondo and Shirley-T. and gave Shirley-T. a nickel with a head on both sides. It tickled her nearly to death, and she called him "Papa." But at 6:30 A.M. the next morning, he threw a whole five-cent package of some unsold one-inch firecrackers from the store as hard as he could into my bedroom and they every one went off. Not one bad one in the string. Anybody else, there'd be one that wouldn't go off.

Well, I'm just terribly susceptible to noise of any kind, the doctor has always told me I was the most sensitive person he had ever seen in his whole life, and I was simply prostrated. I couldn't eat! People tell me they heard it as far as the cemetery, and old

---

Flanders Field: an Allied military cemetery in Belgium for the dead of World War I, it was made famous by a poem by John McCrae. The artificial red poppies still sold for charity on Veterans Day commemorate the cemetery and poem.   *Mammoth Cave*: a network of natural underground caverns in Kentucky.

Aunt Jep Patterson, that had been holding her own so good, thought it was Judgment Day and she was going to meet her whole family. It's usually so quiet here.

And I'll tell you it didn't take me any longer than a minute to make up my mind what to do. There I was with the whole entire house on Stella-Rondo's side and turned against me. If I have anything at all I have pride.

So I just decided I'd go straight down to the P.O. There's plenty of room there in the back, I says to myself.

Well! I made no bones about letting the family catch on to what I was up to. I didn't try to conceal it.

The first thing they knew, I marched in where they were all playing Old Maid and pulled the electric oscillating fan out by the plug, and everything got real hot. Next I snatched the pillow I'd done the needlepoint on right off the davenport from behind Papa-Daddy. He went "Ugh!" I beat Stella-Rondo up the stairs and finally found my charm bracelet in her bureau drawer under a picture of Nelson Eddy.°

"So that's the way the land lies," says Uncle Rondo. There he was, piecing on the ham. "Well, Sister, I'll be glad to donate my army cot if you got any place to set it up, providing you'll leave right this minute and let me get some peace." Uncle Rondo was in France.

"Thank you kindly for the cot and 'peace' is hardly the word I would select if I had to resort to firecrackers at 6:30 A.M. in a young girl's bedroom," I says back to him. "And as to where I intend to go, you seem to forget my position as postmistress of China Grove, Mississippi," I says. "I've always got the P.O."

Well, that made them all sit up and take notice.

I went out front and started digging up some four-o'clocks to plant around the P.O.

"Ah-ah-ah!" says Mama, raising the window. "Those happen to be my four-o'clocks. Everything planted in that star is mine. I've never known you to make anything grow in your life."

"Very well," I says. "But I take the fern. Even you, Mama, can't stand there and deny that I'm the one watered that fern. And I happen to know where I can send in a box top and get a packet of one thousand mixed seeds, no two the same kind, free."

"Oh, where?" Mama wants to know.

But I says, "Too late. You 'tend to your house, and I'll 'tend to mine. You hear things like that all the time if you know how to listen to the radio. Perfectly marvelous offers. Get anything you want free."

So I hope to tell you I marched in and got that radio, and they could of all bit a nail in two, especially Stella-Rondo, that it used to belong to, and she well knew she couldn't get it back, I'd sue for it like a shot. And I very politely took the sewing-machine motor I helped pay the most on to give Mama for Christmas back in 1929, and a good big calendar, with the first-aid remedies on it. The thermometer and the Hawaiian ukulele certainly were rightfully mine, and I stood on the step-ladder and got all my watermelon-rind preserves and every fruit and vegetable I'd put up, every jar. Then I began to pull the tacks out of the bluebird wall vases on the archway to the dining room.

"Who told you you could have those, Miss Priss?" says Mama, fanning as hard as she could.

Nelson Eddy: a popular singer (1901–1967) who appeared in romantic musical films during the Depression era.

"I bought 'em and I'll keep track of 'em," I says. "I'll tack 'em up one on each side the post-office window, and you can see 'em when you come to ask me for your mail, if you're so dead to see 'em."

"Not I! I'll never darken the door to that post office again if I live to be a hundred," Mama says. "Ungrateful child! After all the money we spent on you at the Normal."°

"Me either," says Stella-Rondo. "You can just let my mail lie there and *rot*, for all I care. I'll never come and relieve you of a single, solitary piece."

"I should worry," I says. "And who you think's going to sit down and write you all those big fat letters and postcards, by the way? Mr. Whitaker? Just because he was the only man ever dropped down in China Grove and you got him—unfairly—is he going to sit down and write you a lengthy correspondence after you come home giving no rhyme nor reason whatsoever for your separation and no explanation for the presence of that child? I may not have your brilliant mind, but I fail to see it."

So Mama says, "Sister, I've told you a thousand times that Stella-Rondo simply got homesick, and this child is far too big to be hers," and she says, "Now, why don't you just sit down and play Casino?"

Then Shirley-T. sticks out her tongue at me in this perfectly horrible way. She has no more manners than the man in the moon. I told her she was going to cross her eyes like that some day and they'd stick.

"It's too late to stop me now," I says. "You should have tried that yesterday. I'm going to the P.O. and the only way you can possibly see me is to visit me there."

So Papa-Daddy says, "You'll never catch me setting foot in that post office, even if I should take a notion into my head to write a letter some place." He says, "I won't have you reachin' out of that little old window with a pair of shears and cuttin' off any beard of mine. I'm too smart for you!"

"We all are," says Stella-Rondo.

But I said, "If you're so smart, where's Mr. Whitaker?"

So then Uncle Rondo says, "I'll thank you from now on to stop reading all the orders I get on postcards and telling everybody in China Grove what you think is the matter with them," but I says, "I draw my own conclusions and will continue in the future to draw them." I says, "If people want to write their inmost secrets on penny postcards, there's nothing in the wide world you can do about it, Uncle Rondo."

"And if you think we'll ever *write* another postcard you're sadly mistaken," says Mama.

"Cutting off your nose to spite your face then," I says. "But if you're all determined to have no more to do with the U.S. mail, think of this: What will Stella-Rondo do now, if she wants to tell Mr. Whitaker to come after her?"

"Wah!" says Stella-Rondo. I knew she'd cry. She had a conniption fit right there in the kitchen.

"It will be interesting to see how long she holds out," I says. "And now—I am leaving."

"Good-by," says Uncle Rondo.

"Oh, I declare," says Mama, "to think that a family of mine should quarrel on the Fourth of July, or the day after, over Stella-Rondo leaving old Mr. Whitaker and having the sweetest little adopted child! It looks like we'd all be glad!"

"Wah!" says Stella-Rondo, and has a fresh conniption fit.

Normal: normal school, a two-year college for the training of elementary school teachers.

"*He* left *her*—you mark my words," I says. "That's Mr. Whitaker. I know Mr. Whitaker. After all, I knew him first. I said from the beginning he'd up and leave her. I foretold every single thing that's happened."

"Where did he go?" asks Mama.

"Probably to the North Pole, if he knows what's good for him," I says.

But Stella-Rondo just bawled and wouldn't say another word. She flew to her room and slammed the door.

"Now look what you've gone and done, Sister," says Mama. "You go apologize."

"I haven't got time, I'm leaving," I says.

"Well, what are you waiting around for?" asks Uncle Rondo.

So I just picked up the kitchen clock and marched off, without saying "Kiss my foot," or anything, and never did tell Stella-Rondo good-by.

There was a nigger girl going along on a little wagon right in front.

"Nigger girl," I says, "come help me haul these things down the hill, I'm going to live in the post office."

Took her nine trips in her express wagon. Uncle Rondo came out on the porch and threw her a nickel.

And that's the last I've laid eyes on any of my family or my family laid eyes on me for five solid days and nights. Stella-Rondo may be telling the most horrible tales in the world about Mr. Whitaker, but I haven't heard them. As I tell everybody, I draw my own conclusions.

But oh, I like it here. It's ideal, as I've been saying. You see, I've got everything cater-cornered, the way I like it. Hear the radio? All the war news. Radio, sewing machine, book ends, ironing board and that great big piano lamp—peace, that's what I like. Butter-bean vines planted all along the front where the strings are.

Of course, there's not much mail. My family are naturally the main people in China Grove, and if they prefer to vanish from the face of the earth, for all the mail they get or the mail they write, why, I'm not going to open my mouth. Some of the folks here in town are taking up for me and some turned against me. I know which is which. There are always people who will quit buying stamps just to get on the right side of Papa-Daddy.

But here I am, and here I'll stay. I want the world to know I'm happy.

And if Stella-Rondo should come to me this minute, on bended knees, and *attempt* to explain the incidents of her life with Mr. Whitaker, I'd simply put my fingers in both my ears and refuse to listen.

Questions

1. Can we equate the narrator's voice with Welty's? What clues does the author give that Sister's opinions are not her own?
2. What statements does the narrator make that seem unreliable?
3. Describe Sister's personality. Is she slightly crazy or is her odd behavior a justified revolt against her family?
4. How would you describe the dynamic between Sister and Stella-Rondo? Why does the rest of the family seem to side with Stella-Rondo? Why does Sister fight so much with her family?
5. Sister uses the word "nigger" several times in the story, and she is clearly a racist. What does her attitude toward African Americans tell you about the time and place of the story?

Louise Erdrich

Born in Little Falls, Minnesota, Karen Louise Erdrich grew up in Wahpeton, North Dakota, near the Turtle Mountain Reservation where her Chippewa grandfather had been a tribal leader. Her father and mother were teachers with the Bureau of Indian Affairs, and they encouraged her to write stories from an early age. As Erdrich related to Contemporary Authors, "My father used to give me a nickel for every story I wrote, and my mother wove strips of construction paper together and stapled them into book covers. So at an early age I felt myself to be a published author earning substantial royalties." Erdrich attended Dartmouth College, and later studied creative writing at Johns Hopkins University where she wrote both poetry and fiction. She returned as a writer-in-residence to Dartmouth, where she became reacquainted with fellow writer Michael Dorris. The couple were married in 1981 and often collaborated on literary work, including a jointly written novel, The Crown of Columbus (1991). They also raised six children (several were adopted). After the couple separated, Dorris committed suicide in 1997.

Louise Erdrich

Erdrich's first novel, Love Medicine (1984), grew out of a prize-winning story she coauthored with her husband. A substantial critical and commercial success, the book won the National Book Critics Circle Award. Erdrich's subsequent novels—The Beet Queen (1986), Tracks (1988), The Bingo Palace (1994), and Tales of Burning Love (1996)—continue her practice of weaving novels from interconnected stories and chronicle the lives of the members of several families living in and around a North Dakota reservation over a period ranging from the first decade of the twentieth century to the last. Erdrich now owns a bookstore in Minneapolis, Minnesota. Her recent novel The Plague of Doves (2008) was a finalist for the 2009 Pulitzer Prize.

The Red Convertible   1984

Lyman Lamartine

I was the first one to drive a convertible on my reservation. And of course it was red, a red Olds. I owned that car along with my brother Henry Junior. We owned it together until his boots filled with water on a windy night and he bought out my share. Now Henry owns the whole car, and his youngest brother Lyman (that's myself), Lyman walks everywhere he goes.

How did I earn enough money to buy my share in the first place? My own talent was I could always make money. I had a touch for it, unusual in a Chippewa. From the first I was different that way, and everyone recognized it. I was the only kid they let in the American Legion Hall to shine shoes, for example, and one Christmas I sold spiritual bouquets for the mission door to door. The nuns let me keep a percentage. Once I started, it seemed the more money I made the easier the money came. Everyone encouraged it. When I was fifteen I got a job washing dishes at the Joliet Café, and that was where my first big break happened.

It wasn't long before I was promoted to bussing tables, and then the short-order cook quit and I was hired to take her place. No sooner than you know it I was managing the Joliet. The rest is history. I went on managing. I soon became part owner, and of course there was no stopping me then. It wasn't long before the whole thing was mine.

After I'd owned the Joliet for one year, it blew over in the worst tornado ever seen around here. The whole operation was smashed to bits. A total loss. The fryalator was up in a tree, the grill torn in half like it was paper. I was only sixteen. I had it all in my mother's name, and I lost it quick, but before I lost it I had every one of my relatives, and their relatives, to dinner, and I also bought that red Olds I mentioned, along with Henry.

The first time we saw it! I'll tell you when we first saw it. We had gotten a ride up to Winnipeg, and both of us had money. Don't ask me why, because we never mentioned a car or anything, we just had all our money. Mine was cash, a big bankroll from the Joliet's insurance. Henry had two checks—a week's extra pay for being laid off, and his regular check from the Jewel Bearing Plant.

We were walking down Portage anyway, seeing the sights, when we saw it. There it was, parked, large as life. Really as *if* it was alive. I thought of the word *repose*, because the car wasn't simply stopped, parked, or whatever. That car reposed, calm and gleaming, a FOR SALE sign in its left front window. Then, before we had thought it over at all, the car belonged to us and our pockets were empty. We had just enough money for gas back home.

We went places in that car, me and Henry. We took off driving all one whole summer. We started off toward the Little Knife River and Mandaree in Fort Berthold and then we found ourselves down in Wakpala somehow, and then suddenly we were over in Montana on the Rocky Boys, and yet the summer was not even half over. Some people hang on to details when they travel, but we didn't let them bother us and just lived our everyday lives here to there.

I do remember this one place with willows. I remember I laid under those trees and it was comfortable. So comfortable. The branches bent down all around me like a tent or a stable. And quiet, it was quiet, even though there was a powwow close enough so I could see it going on. The air was not too still, not too windy either. When the dust rises up and hangs in the air around the dancers like that, I feel good. Henry was asleep with his arms thrown wide. Later on, he woke up and we started driving again. We were somewhere in Montana, or maybe on the Blood Reserve—it could have been anywhere. Anyway it was where we met the girl.

All her hair was in buns around her ears, that's the first thing I noticed about her. She was posed alongside the road with her arm out, so we stopped. That girl was short, so short her lumber shirt looked comical on her, like a nightgown. She had jeans on and fancy moccasins and she carried a little suitcase.

"Hop on in," says Henry. So she climbs in between us.
"We'll take you home," I says. "Where do you live?"
"Chicken," she says.
"Where the hell's that?" I ask her.
"Alaska."
"Okay," says Henry, and we drive.

We got up there and never wanted to leave. The sun doesn't truly set there in summer, and the night is more a soft dusk. You might doze off, sometimes, but before you know it you're up again, like an animal in nature. You never feel like you have to sleep hard or put away the world. And things would grow up there. One day just dirt or moss, the next day flowers and long grass. The girl's name was Susy. Her family really took to us. They fed us and put us up. We had our own tent to live in by their house, and the kids would be in and out of there all day and night. They couldn't get over me and Henry being brothers, we looked so different. We told them we knew we had the same mother, anyway.

One night Susy came in to visit us. We sat around in the tent talking of this thing and that. The season was changing. It was getting darker by that time, and the cold was even getting just a little mean. I told her it was time for us to go. She stood up on a chair.

"You never seen my hair," Susy said.

That was true. She was standing on a chair, but still, when she unclipped her buns the hair reached all the way to the ground. Our eyes opened. You couldn't tell how much hair she had when it was rolled up so neatly. Then my brother Henry did something funny. He went up to the chair and said, "Jump on my shoulders." So she did that, and her hair reached down past his waist, and he started twirling, this way and that, so her hair was flung out from side to side.

"I always wondered what it was like to have long pretty hair," Henry says. Well we laughed. It was a funny sight, the way he did it. The next morning we got up and took leave of those people.

On to greener pastures, as they say. It was down through Spokane and across Idaho then Montana and very soon we were racing the weather right along under the Canadian border through Columbus, Des Lacs, and then we were in Bottineau County and soon home. We'd made most of the trip, that summer, without putting up the car hood at all. We got home just in time, it turned out, for the army to remember Henry had signed up to join it.

I don't wonder that the army was so glad to get my brother that they turned him into a Marine. He was built like a brick outhouse anyway. We liked to tease him that they really wanted him for his Indian nose. He had a nose big and sharp as a hatchet, like the nose on Red Tomahawk, the Indian who killed Sitting Bull, whose profile is on signs all along the North Dakota highways. Henry went off to training camp, came home once during Christmas, then the next thing you know we got an overseas letter from him. It was 1970, and he said he was stationed up in the northern hill country. Whereabouts I did not know. He wasn't such a hot letter writer, and only got off two before the enemy caught him. I could never keep it straight, which direction those good Vietnam soldiers were from.

I wrote him back several times, even though I didn't know if those letters would get through. I kept him informed all about the car. Most of the time I had it up on blocks in the yard or half taken apart, because that long trip did a hard job on it under the hood.

I always had good luck with numbers, and never worried about the draft myself. I never even had to think about what my number was. But Henry was never lucky in the same way as me. It was at least three years before Henry came home. By then I guess the whole war was solved in the government's mind, but for him it would keep on going. In those years I'd put his car into almost perfect shape. I always thought of it as his car while he was gone, even though when he left he said, "Now it's yours," and threw me his key.

"Thanks for the extra key," I'd say. "I'll put it up in your drawer just in case I need it." He laughed.

When he came home, though, Henry was very different, and I'll say this: the change was no good. You could hardly expect him to change for the better, I know. But he was quiet, so quiet, and never comfortable sitting still anywhere but always up and moving around. I thought back to times we'd sat still for whole afternoons, never moving a muscle, just shifting our weight along the ground, talking to whoever sat with us, watching things. He'd always had a joke, then, too, and now you couldn't get him to laugh, or when he did it was more the sound of a man choking, a sound that stopped up the throats of other people around him. They got to leaving him alone most of the time, and I didn't blame them. It was a fact: Henry was jumpy and mean.

I'd bought a color TV set for my mom and the rest of us while Henry was away. Money still came very easy. I was sorry I'd ever bought it though, because of Henry. I was also sorry I'd bought color, because with black-and-white the pictures seem older and farther away. But what are you going to do? He sat in front of it, watching it, and that was the only time he was completely still. But it was the kind of stillness that you see in a rabbit when it freezes and before it will bolt. He was not easy. He sat in his chair gripping the armrests with all his might, as if the chair itself was moving at a high speed and if he let go at all he would rocket forward and maybe crash right through the set.

Once I was in the room watching TV with Henry and I heard his teeth click at something. I looked over, and he'd bitten through his lip. Blood was going down his chin. I tell you right then I wanted to smash that tube to pieces. I went over to it but Henry must have known what I was up to. He rushed from his chair and shoved me out of the way, against the wall. I told myself he didn't know what he was doing.

My mom came in, turned the set off real quiet, and told us she had made something for supper. So we went and sat down. There was still blood going down Henry's chin, but he didn't notice it and no one said anything, even though every time he took a bit of his bread his blood fell onto it until he was eating his own blood mixed in with the food.

While Henry was not around we talked about what was going to happen to him. There were no Indian doctors on the reservation, and my mom was afraid of trusting Old Man Pillager because he courted her long ago and was jealous of her husbands. He might take revenge through her son. We were afraid that if we brought Henry to a regular hospital they would keep him.

"They don't fix them in those places," Mom said; "they just give them drugs."

"We wouldn't get him there in the first place," I agreed, "so let's just forget about it."

Then I thought about the car.

Henry had not even looked at the car since he'd gotten home, though like I said, it was in tip-top condition and ready to drive. I thought the car might bring the old

Henry back somehow. So I bided my time and waited for my chance to interest him in the vehicle.

One night Henry was off somewhere. I took myself a hammer. I went out to that car and I did a number on its underside. Whacked it up. Bent the tail pipe double. Ripped the muffler loose. By the time I was done with the car it looked worse than any typical Indian car that has been driven all its life on reservation roads, which they always say are like government promises—full of holes. It just about hurt me, I'll tell you that! I threw dirt in the carburetor and I ripped all the electric tape off the seats. I made it look just as beat up as I could. Then I sat back and waited for Henry to find it.

Still, it took him over a month. That was all right, because it was just getting warm enough, not melting, but warm enough to work outside.

"Lyman," he says, walking in one day, "that red car looks like shit."

"Well it's old," I says. "You got to expect that."

"No way!" says Henry. "That car's a classic! But you went and ran the piss right out of it, Lyman, and you know it don't deserve that. I kept that car in A-one shape. You don't remember. You're too young. But when I left, that car was running like a watch. Now I don't even know if I can get it to start again, let alone get it anywhere near its old condition."

"Well you try," I said, like I was getting mad, "but I say it's a piece of junk."

Then I walked out before he could realize I knew he'd strung together more than six words at once.

After that I thought he'd freeze himself to death working on that car. He was out there all day, and at night he rigged up a little lamp, ran a cord out the window, and had himself some light to see by while he worked. He was better than he had been before, but that's still not saying much. It was easier for him to do the things the rest of us did. He ate more slowly and didn't jump up and down during the meal to get this or that or look out the window. I put my hand in the back of the TV set, I admit, and fiddled around with it good, so that it was almost impossible now to get a clear picture. He didn't look at it very often anyway. He was always out with that car or going off to get parts for it. By the time it was really melting outside, he had it fixed.

I had been feeling down in the dumps about Henry around this time. We had always been together before. Henry and Lyman. But he was such a loner now that I didn't know how to take it. So I jumped at the chance one day when Henry seemed friendly. It's not that he smiled or anything. He just said, "Let's take that old shitbox for a spin." Just the way he said it made me think he could be coming around.

We went out to the car. It was spring. The sun was shining very bright. My only sister, Bonita, who was just eleven years old, came out and made us stand together for a picture. Henry leaned his elbow on the red car's windshield, and he took his other arm and put it over my shoulder, very carefully, as though it was heavy for him to lift and he didn't want to bring the weight down all at once.

"Smile," Bonita said, and he did.

That picture, I never look at it anymore. A few months ago, I don't know why, I got his picture out and tacked it on the wall. I felt good about Henry at the time, close to him. I felt good having his picture on the wall, until one night when I was looking at television. I was a little drunk and stoned. I looked up at the wall and Henry was staring at me. I don't know what it was, but his smile had changed, or maybe it was gone. All I know is I couldn't stay in the same room with that picture. I was shaking. I got up, closed the door, and went into the kitchen. A little later my friend Ray came over and we both went back into that room. We put the picture in a brown bag, folded the bag over and over tightly, then put it way back in a closet.

I still see that picture now, as if it tugs at me, whenever I pass that closet door. The picture is very clear in my mind. It was so sunny that day Henry had to squint against the glare. Or maybe the camera Bonita held flashed like a mirror, blinding him, before she snapped the picture. My face is right out in the sun, big and round. But he might have drawn back, because the shadows on his face are deep as holes. There are two shadows curved like little hooks around the ends of his smile, as if to frame it and try to keep it there—that one, first smile that looked like it might have hurt his face. He has his field jacket on and the worn-in clothes he'd come back in and kept wearing ever since. After Bonita took the picture, she went into the house and we got into the car. There was a full cooler in the trunk. We started off, east, toward Pembina and the Red River because Henry said he wanted to see the high water.

The trip over there was beautiful. When everything starts changing, drying up, clearing off, you feel like your whole life is starting. Henry felt it, too. The top was down and the car hummed like a top. He'd really put it back in shape, even the tape on the seats was very carefully put down and glued back in layers. It's not that he smiled again or even joked, but his face looked to me as if it was clear, more peaceful. It looked as though he wasn't thinking of anything in particular except the bare fields and windbreaks and houses we were passing.

The river was high and full of winter trash when we got there. The sun was still out, but it was colder by the river. There were still little clumps of dirty snow here and there on the banks. The water hadn't gone over the banks yet, but it would, you could tell. It was just at its limit, hard swollen, glossy like an old gray scar. We made ourselves a fire, and we sat down and watched the current go. As I watched it I felt something squeezing inside me and tightening and trying to let go all at the same time. I knew I was not just feeling it myself; I knew I was feeling what Henry was going through at that moment. Except that I couldn't stand it, the closing and opening. I jumped to my feet. I took Henry by the shoulders and I started shaking him. "Wake up," I says, "wake up, wake up, wake up!" I didn't know what had come over me. I sat down beside him again.

His face was totally white and hard. Then it broke, like stones break all of a sudden when water boils up inside them.

"I know it," he says. "I know it. I can't help it. It's no use."

We start talking. He said he knew what I'd done with the car. It was obvious it had been whacked out of shape and not just neglected. He said he wanted to give the car to me for good now, it was no use. He said he'd fixed it just to give it back and I should take it.

"No way," I says, "I don't want it."

"That's okay," he says, "you take it."

"I don't want it, though," I says back to him, and then to emphasize, just to emphasize, you understand, I touch his shoulder. He slaps my hand off.

"Take that car," he says.

"No," I say, "make me," I say, and then he grabs my jacket and rips the arm loose. That jacket is a class act, suede with tags and zippers. I push Henry backwards, off the log. He jumps up and bowls me over. We go down in a clinch and come up swinging hard, for all we're worth, with our fists. He socks my jaw so hard I feel like it swings loose. Then I'm at his ribcage and land a good one under his chin so his head snaps back. He's dazzled. He looks at me and I look at him and then his eyes are full of tears and blood and at first I think he's crying. But no, he's laughing. "Ha! Ha!" he says. "Ha! Ha! Take good care of it."

"Okay," I says, "okay, no problem. Ha! Ha!"

I can't help it, and I start laughing, too. My face feels fat and strange, and after a while I get a beer from the cooler in the trunk, and when I hand it to Henry he takes his shirt and wipes my germs off. "Hoof-and-mouth disease," he says. For some reason this cracks me up, and so we're really laughing for a while, and then we drink all the rest of the beers one by one and throw them in the river and see how far, how fast, the current takes them before they fill up and sink.

"You want to go on back?" I ask after a while. "Maybe we could snag a couple nice Kashpaw girls."

He says nothing. But I can tell his mood is turning again.

"They're all crazy, the girls up here, every damn one of them."

"You're crazy too," I say, to jolly him up. "Crazy Lamartine boys!"

He looks as though he will take this wrong at first. His face twists, then clears, and he jumps up on his feet. "That's right!" he says. "Crazier 'n hell. Crazy Indians!"

I think it's the old Henry again. He throws off his jacket and starts swinging his legs out from the knees like a fancy dancer. He's down doing something between a grouse dance and a bunny hop, no kind of dance I ever saw before, but neither has anyone else on all this green growing earth. He's wild. He wants to pitch whoopee! He's up and at me and all over. All this time I'm laughing so hard, so hard my belly is getting tied up in a knot.

"Got to cool me off!" he shouts all of a sudden. Then he runs over to the river and jumps in.

There's boards and other things in the current. It's so high. No sound comes from the river after the splash he makes, so I run right over. I look around. It's getting dark. I see he's halfway across the water already, and I know he didn't swim there but the current took him. It's far. I hear his voice, though, very clearly across it.

"My boots are filling," he says.

He says this in a normal voice, like he just noticed and he doesn't know what to think of it. Then he's gone. A branch comes by. Another branch. And I go in.

By the time I get out of the river, off the snag I pulled myself onto, the sun is down. I walk back to the car, turn on the high beams, and drive it up the bank. I put it in first gear and then I take my foot off the clutch. I get out, close the door, and watch it plow softly into the water. The headlights reach in as they go down, searching, still lighted even after the water swirls over the back end. I wait. The wires short out. It is all finally dark. And then there is only the water, the sound of it going and running and going and running and running.

Questions

1. How are Lyman and Henry different? How would you characterize each of them?
2. Why does Erdrich choose to tell the story from Lyman's point of view? How might the story be different if it were narrated by Henry?
3. What is the significance of the red convertible? What does it mean to the brothers? Why does Lyman choose not to drive it while Henry is gone? And then why does he damage it?
4. Do you think it would have been possible for Lyman to help his brother after he returned from Vietnam?
5. Why does Lyman push the car into the river?

Suggestions for Writing on *Stories about Brothers and Sisters*

1. Both "Sonny's Blues" and "The Rich Brother" involve older brothers who are established and stable, and younger brothers who are more free-spirited. Compare these relationships: how are the dynamics similar or different? Do you see the older brothers in the same light, or are there significant differences between them? How about the younger brothers? If you do see differences in the respective brothers (or in the relationships), what factors contribute to those differences?
2. Each of these stories takes place in a specific time, place, and environment. How do factors such as setting, class, and culture influence the events of the stories? Pick at least one story and analyze how these elements have bearing on the characters and their situations. Choose particular details and passages to support your view. Are there—despite these factors—also universal dynamics or truths at work?
3. Pretend you are a family therapist who has just heard the narrator of "Why I Live at the P.O." tell her story in a counseling session. Write up a short report summarizing your point of view on her personal situation. Support all of your opinions with examples from the text.
4. Consider how different each of these stories might be if told from another character's point of view. Pick one story and describe how the story would change, or be presented differently, if told from the *other* sibling's point of view.

POETRY

CHILDREN LOOKING AT PARENTS, PARENTS LOOKING AT CHILDREN

Robert Hayden	*Those Winter Sundays*
Theodore Roethke	*My Papa's Waltz*
Rhina P. Espaillat	*Bilingual/Bilingüe*
Sylvia Plath	*Daddy*
Sharon Olds	*Rite of Passage*

Lyric poetry is often intensely personal, and the speaker usually has strong opinions about the subject being discussed. For this reason, lyric poetry is a perfect medium for authors writing about their parents—or their children. When we are younger, our parents often seem larger than life, and they can fill us with joy, fear, dread, or hope with their smallest words or actions, without even realizing the impact they have. It often takes us until we're adults to see them more clearly—to understand kindnesses we didn't appreciate; to realize that we lived in fear of them; to fully comprehend our lasting feelings of love, or resentment, or rage. And when parents look at children, the love might be equally complicated. Although we know that many parents try to assume the best about their children (think of parents who won't believe that their children misbehave in school or of parents who insist that their children get more time on the playing field or stage), the true feelings of parents are often more complex. Parents can feel fear, and disappointment, and disillusionment in their children—parents, too, can recognize a gap between their hopes and beliefs about their children and reality.

The poems in this section are all by writers who are looking at their parents, or their children, with open eyes. Sometimes what they see is disturbing, but it is always revealing.

Robert Hayden

Robert Hayden (1913–1980) was born in Detroit, Michigan, and raised by foster parents. He attended Detroit City College (now Wayne State University) and the University of Michigan, where he studied with W. H. Auden. After teaching at Fisk University in Nashville, Tennessee for over twenty years, he returned to the University of Michigan in 1969 and taught there for the rest of his life. In 1976 Hayden was appointed Consultant in Poetry at the Library of Congress (the position now known as Poet Laureate), the first African American to hold that office. "Those Winter Sundays" is a quiet, powerful meditation on the range of feelings among family members and the sometimes surprising ways in which they are expressed.

Those Winter Sundays   1962

Sundays too my father got up early
and put his clothes on in the blueblack cold,

then with cracked hands that ached
from labor in the weekday weather made
banked fires blaze. No one ever thanked him.   5

I'd wake and hear the cold splintering, breaking.
When the rooms were warm, he'd call,
and slowly I would rise and dress,
fearing the chronic angers of that house,

Speaking indifferently to him,   10
who had driven out the cold
and polished my good shoes as well.
What did I know, what did I know
of love's austere and lonely offices?

Questions

1. Jot down a brief paraphrase of this poem. In your paraphrase, clearly show what the speaker finds himself remembering.
2. What do you understand from the words "chronic angers" and "austere"?
3. With what specific details does the poem make the past seem real?
4. How did the speaker feel about his father when he was young, and how does he seem to feel about him now? What accounts for the change?

Theodore Roethke

Theodore Roethke (1908–1963) was born in Saginaw, Michigan, where his father and uncle owned a large commercial greenhouse. Roethke often played there as a child, and images of earth and plant life run deep in his poetry. He graduated magna cum laude from the University of Michigan, but had to drop out of graduate school at Harvard for financial reasons. Lacking a doctorate, he taught at a number of colleges before finding a permanent position in 1947 at the University of Washington in Seattle. His poetry—which ranges from formal lyrics to free-verse meditations, from elegant statements to explorations of the unconscious mind—brought him two Pulitzer Prizes. Roethke was a large, heavyset man who was surprisingly light on his feet, and in "My Papa's Waltz" his boisterousness and his delicacy come together to create an unforgettable effect.

My Papa's Waltz   1948

The whiskey on your breath
Could make a small boy dizzy;
But I hung on like death:
Such waltzing was not easy.

We romped until the pans   5
Slid from the kitchen shelf;
My mother's countenance
Could not unfrown itself.

The hand that held my wrist
Was battered on one knuckle;   10

At every step you missed
My right ear scraped a buckle.

You beat time on my head
With a palm caked hard by dirt,
Then waltzed me off to bed   15
Still clinging to your shirt.

Questions

1. What expectations are created by the word "waltz" in the title? Are they fulfilled by the poem, or not?
2. What do the speaker's terms of reference for his parents suggest about his feelings for each of them?
3. Which details of the poem are frightening, or otherwise negative in nature?
4. Do lines 7–8 suggest anything about the relationship between the speaker's parents?
5. How would you describe the speaker's attitude toward his "papa's waltz"—fearful, affectionate, or some mixture of the two?

Rhina P. Espaillat

Rhina P. Espaillat was born in the Dominican Republic in 1932, where her father was in the diplomatic service. When she was seven the family moved to New York. In 1952 she married Alfred Moskowitz, an industrial arts teacher, and they had three sons. She earned an M.S.E. in 1964 from Queens College and taught high school English for fifteen years. After retiring from teaching, she and her husband moved to Newburyport, Massachusetts. She was then able to devote herself to poetry, which she had written all her life, both in Spanish in English. Her first volume, Lapsing to Grace, *appeared in 1992. A second collection, and* Where Horizons Go *(1998), won the T. S. Eliot award. She has since published several other collections. Like many of her poems, "Bilingual/Bilingüe" reflects her dual cultural heritage.*

Bilingual/*Bilingüe*   1998

My father liked them separate, one there,
one here (*allá y aquí*), as if aware

that words might cut in two his daughter's heart
(*el corazón*) and lock the alien part

to what he was—his memory, his name   5
(*su nombre*)—with a key he could not claim.

"English outside this door, Spanish inside,"
he said, "*y basta*." But who can divide

the world, the word (*mundo y palabra*) from
any child? I knew how to be dumb   10

and stubborn (*testaruda*); late, in bed,
I hoarded secret syllables I read

until my tongue (*mi lengua*) learned to run
where his stumbled. And still the heart was one.

I like to think he knew that, even when, 15
proud (*orgulloso*) of his daughter's pen,

he stood outside *mis versos*, half in fear
of words he loved but wanted not to hear.

Questions

1. Espaillat's poem is full of Spanish words and phrases. (Even the title is given in both languages.) What does the Spanish add to the poem? Could we remove the phrases without changing the poem?
2. How does the father want to divide his daughter's world, at least in terms of language? Does his request suggest any other divisions he hopes to enforce in her life?
3. How does the daughter respond to her father's request to leave English outside their home?
4. "And still the heart was one," states the speaker of the poem. Should we take her statement at face value or do we sense a cost to her bilingual existence? Agree or disagree with the daughter's statement, but state the reasons for your opinion.

Sylvia Plath

Sylvia Plath (1932–1963) was born in Boston, Massachusetts. Both of her parents were German immigrants who taught at Boston University; just after her eighth birthday, she was profoundly affected by her father's death from diabetes. While a junior at Smith College, Plath attempted suicide and was hospitalized for six months; nonetheless, she graduated summa cum laude shortly thereafter. While studying at Cambridge University in England on a Fulbright scholarship, she met the poet Ted Hughes; they were married in 1956. Their marriage ultimately proved unhappy, and Hughes abandoned Plath in 1962 after she discovered he was having an affair. She took her own life in February 1963. In 1965, an international sensation was created by the publication of Ariel, *which collected the intense, striking poems she had written in the last months of her life; "Daddy," the most intense—and shocking—of these poems, has proven to be one of the most popular.*

Sylvia Plath

Daddy
(1962) 1965

You do not do, you do not do
Any more, black shoe
In which I have lived like a foot
For thirty years, poor and white,
Barely daring to breathe or Achoo. 5

Daddy, I have had to kill you.
You died before I had time—
Marble-heavy, a bag full of God,
Ghastly statue with one grey toe
Big as a Frisco seal   10

And a head in the freakish Atlantic
Where it pours bean green over blue
In the waters off beautiful Nauset.
I used to pray to recover you.
Ach, du.   15

In the German tongue, in the Polish town
Scraped flat by the roller
Of wars, wars, wars.
But the name of the town is common.
My Polack friend   20

Says there are a dozen or two.
So I never could tell where you
Put your foot, your root,
I never could talk to you.
The tongue stuck in my jaw.   25

It stuck in a barb wire snare.
Ich, ich, ich, ich,
I could hardly speak.
I thought every German was you.
And the language obscene   30

An engine, an engine
Chuffing me off like a Jew.
A Jew to Dachau, Auschwitz, Belsen.
I began to talk like a Jew.
I think I may well be a Jew.   35

The snows of the Tyrol, the clear beer of Vienna
Are not very pure or true.
With my gypsy ancestress and my weird luck
And my Taroc pack and my Taroc pack
I may be a bit of a Jew.   40

I have always been scared of *you*,
With your Luftwaffe, your gobbledygoo.
And your neat moustache
And your Aryan eye, bright blue.
Panzer-man, panzer-man, O You—   45

Not God but a swastika
So black no sky could squeak through.

Every woman adores a Fascist,
The boot in the face, the brute
Brute heart of a brute like you.   50

You stand at the blackboard, daddy,
In the picture I have of you,
A cleft in your chin instead of your foot
But no less a devil for that, no not
Any less the black man who   55

Bit my pretty red heart in two.
I was ten when they buried you.
At twenty I tried to die
And get back, back, back to you.
I thought even the bones would do.   60

But they pulled me out of the sack,
And they stuck me together with glue.
And then I knew what to do.
I made a model of you,
A man in black with a Meinkampf look   65

And a love of the rack and the screw.
And I said I do, I do.
So daddy, I'm finally through.
The black telephone's off at the root,
The voices just can't worm through.   70

If I've killed one man, I've killed two—
The vampire who said he was you
And drank my blood for a year,
Seven years, if you want to know.
Daddy, you can lie back now.   75

There's a stake in your fat black heart
And the villagers never liked you.
They are dancing and stamping on you.
They always *knew* it was you.
Daddy, daddy, you bastard, I'm through.   80

DADDY. 15 *Ach, du:* Oh, you. 27 *Ich, ich, ich, ich*: I, I, I, I. 51 *blackboard*: Otto Plath had been a professor of biology at Boston University. 65 *Meinkampf*: Adolf Hitler titled his autobiography *Mein Kampf* ("My Struggle").

Introducing this poem in a reading, Sylvia Plath remarked:

> The poem is spoken by a girl with an Electra complex. Her father died while she thought he was God. Her case is complicated by the fact that her father was also a Nazi and her mother very possibly part Jewish. In the daughter the two strains marry and paralyze each other—she has to act out the awful little allegory before she is free of it. (Quoted by A. Alvarez, *Beyond All This Fiddle*, New York: Random, 1968).

In some details "Daddy" is autobiography: the poet's father, Otto Plath, a German, had come to the United States from Grabow, Poland. He died following the amputation of a gangrened foot and leg when Sylvia was eight years old. Politically, Otto Plath was a Republican, not a Nazi, but was apparently a somewhat domineering head of the household. (See the recollections of the poet's mother, Aurelia Schober Plath, in her edition of *Letters Home* by Sylvia Plath [New York: Harper, 1975].)

Questions

1. What does the speaker mean when she calls her father a "black shoe / In which I have lived like a foot / For thirty years" (lines 2–4)?
2. Which specific details in the poem provide an explanation of the speaker's hatred of her father?
3. The statement in lines 48–50 has proved to be quite controversial. Do you think there's any truth to it? Do you think that the speaker herself believes it?
4. How do you interpret lines 58–62?
5. Do you find the description of the father—Nazi references and all—convincing, or is the poem more effective as a portrayal of the speaker's own psychological disturbance?

Sharon Olds

Sharon Olds was born in San Francisco in 1942. She graduated from Stanford University and earned a Ph.D. from Columbia University in 1972. She teaches in the Graduate Creative Writing Program at New York University, and was New York State Poet Laureate from 1998 to 2000. Olds has published ten books of poetry, including Strike Sparks: Selected Poems *(2004) and* One Secret Thing *(2008). Her second collection,* The Dead and the Living *(1984), won both the Lamont Award and the National Book Critics Circle Award, and is generally considered her finest work. "Rite of Passage," in its use of her family as subject matter and its attention to the violence—emotional and otherwise—latent in everyday experience, is representative of that volume and of her poetry in general.*

Rite of Passage   1983

As the guests arrive at my son's party
they gather in the living room—
short men, men in first grade
with smooth jaws and chins.
Hands in pockets, they stand around   5
jostling, jockeying for place, small fights
breaking out and calming. One says to another
How old are you? Six. I'm seven. So?
They eye each other, seeing themselves
tiny in the other's pupils. They clear their   10
throats a lot, a room of small bankers,
they fold their arms and frown. *I could beat you
up,* a seven says to a six,
the dark cake, round and heavy as a
turret, behind them on the table. My son,   15
freckles like specks of nutmeg on his cheeks,
chest narrow as the balsa keel of a
model boat, long hands
cool and thin as the day they guided him
out of me, speaks up as a host   20

for the sake of the group.
We could easily kill a two-year-old,
he says in his clear voice. The other
men agree, they clear their throats
like Generals, they relax and get down to   25
playing war, celebrating my son's life.

Questions

1. What is ironic about the way the speaker describes the first-grade boys at her son's birthday party?
2. What other irony does the author underscore in the last two lines?
3. Does this mother sentimentalize her own son by seeing him as better than the other little boys?
4. What view of manhood is communicated by the details of the poem? Does the speaker seem to have complex feelings about being the mother of a male child?
5. How is the age of each speaker used ironically in a poem about birthdays?

Suggestions for Writing on Poems about Parents and Children

1. Compare and contrast Sylvia Plath's "Daddy" with Theodore Roethke's "My Papa's Waltz." How are the poems similar; how are they different? How do the speakers feel about their fathers—and what imagery do they use to give you a sense of their fathers?
2. Several of these poems describe parental love. Pick at least two of them and analyze how this love is conveyed, citing specific lines and images. Is parental love always obvious and spoken? Do parents always idealize their children? Discuss.
3. Several of the most intense poems in this section involve speakers whose parents have died. Is there something about a parent being gone that enables us to see—or say—things we might not otherwise be able to tell them? What would you tell your parents, if you could—and what is it that makes it difficult to do so?
4. Rhina Espaillat creates a sort of dialogue between her father and herself in which both of them articulate their differing views about language and identity. Take a topic on which you and a parent (or you and a child) disagree. Explain both sides of the argument and how each person came to those beliefs. (Explain your own views clearly, but remember to be fair to the other person's views, too.)

FAMILY LEGACIES

Robert Hayden	*The Whipping*
Seamus Heaney	*Digging*
Julia Alvarez	*By Accident*
Li-Young Lee	*The Gift*
Diane Thiel	*The Minefield*

Maybe you've been given something special by a relative, an item that's representative of that person or of your family. It could be a picture, or a war medal, or a ring or a watch, or any number of other items. It's common for relatives to give important items to younger members of their families, in order to pass on symbols of family, culture, or history. But the most lasting family legacies are often more intangible than a piece of jewelry or a photo album. We might, from watching our parents or grandparents, emulate their work ethic, their tastes, or their kindness toward other people. On the other hand, if they are cruel, to others or to us, we might adopt a similar stance in our dealings with people. And often the ways that parents act, be they healthy or unhealthy, are ways they learned from their own families or from their experiences in the world. The pain they suffered, or the joys they felt, are often visited onto their children—who may never learn what those experiences were.

The lyric poems in this section all deal with family legacies in one form or another, some positive, some sad or unhealthy. But all the poems attest to the indelible mark that our families leave on us.

Robert Hayden

Robert Hayden (1913–1980) endured a number of hardships throughout his life. Born after the breakup of his parents' marriage, he was raised by another couple, who sometimes took out their own frustrations on the helpless boy. He came of age in Detroit, Michigan, in the depths of the Great Depression, and later experienced the shock of racial segregation when he began teaching in Nashville, Tennessee. His poetry attracted little notice until he was in his fifties. A convert to the Baha'i faith (a Universalist religion that emphasizes charity, tolerance, and equality), he often, as in "The Whipping," uses painful experience—his own and that of others—as a means toward a deeper understanding and compassion.

The Whipping   1962

The old woman across the way
   is whipping the boy again
and shouting to the neighborhood
   her goodness and his wrongs.

Wildly he crashes through elephant ears,
   pleads in dusty zinnias,
while she in spite of crippling fat
   pursues and corners him.

She strikes and strikes the shrilly circling
   boy till the stick breaks
in her hand. His tears are rainy weather
   to woundlike memories:

My head gripped in bony vise
   of knees, the writhing struggle
to wrench free, the blows, the fear
   worse than blows that hateful

Words could bring, the face that I
   no longer knew or loved. . . .
Well, it is over now, it is over,
   and the boy sobs in his room,

And the woman leans muttering against
   a tree, exhausted, purged—
avenged in part for lifelong hidings
   she has had to bear.

Questions

1. Who is the speaker of the poem? What is the speaker's relation to the people he observes in the opening stanza?
2. How does the scene being depicted change in the fourth stanza? Who are the people depicted here?
3. What reason does the speaker give for the old woman's violence? Does the speaker feel her reason is adequate to excuse her behavior?
4. Does the speaker's attempt to understand the old woman's motivation suggest any softening of his own feelings toward the person who beat him when he was young?
5. How would you summarize the theme of this poem?

Seamus Heaney

Seamus Heaney, the first of nine children, was born in 1939 on his family's farm near Bellaghy, in Northern Ireland. He graduated from the Queen's University in Belfast with a first class honors degree in 1961, and has since taught at a number of colleges and universities in Northern Ireland, the Irish Republic, and the United States. Beginning with Death of a Naturalist in 1966, Heaney has published a number of volumes of poetry as well as several collections of essays, versions of two plays by Sophocles and of several classic Gaelic texts, and a highly acclaimed translation of Beowulf. In 1995 he was awarded the Nobel Prize in Literature. Like many of his poems, "Digging" is a warm-hearted evocation of his rural ancestry and upbringing.

Digging   1966

Between my finger and my thumb
The squat pen rests; snug as a gun.

Under my window, a clean rasping sound
When the spade sinks into gravelly ground:
My father, digging. I look down   5

Till his straining rump among the flowerbeds
Bends low, comes up twenty years away
Stooping in rhythm through potato drills
Where he was digging.

The coarse boot nestled on the lug, the shaft   10
Against the inside knee was levered firmly.
He rooted out tall tops, buried the bright edge deep
To scatter new potatoes that we picked
Loving their cool hardness in our hands.

By God, the old man could handle a spade.   15
Just like his old man.

My grandfather cut more turf in a day
Than any other man on Toner's bog.
Once I carried him milk in a bottle
Corked sloppily with paper. He straightened up   20
To drink it, then fell to right away
Nicking and slicing neatly, heaving sods
Over his shoulder, going down and down
For the good turf. Digging.

The cold smell of potato mould, the squelch and slap   25
Of soggy peat, the curt cuts of an edge
Through living roots awaken in my head.
But I've no spade to follow men like them.

Between my finger and my thumb
The squat pen rests.   30
I'll dig with it.

Questions
1. How does the speaker feel about the fact that his father and grandfather were laborers?
2. Why does the poem devote so much detail to the way they went about their work?
3. Does the speaker's chosen path in life constitute a rejection of his forebears? Does he seem to feel guilty about not being like them?
4. In what sense might the speaker "dig" with his pen?

Julia Alvarez

Born in New York City in 1950, Julia Alvarez spent her childhood in the Dominican Republic until she was ten, when her family returned to New York, exiled because of her father's participation in a plot to overthrow the dictator Rafael Trujillo. Alvarez graduated summa cum laude from Middlebury College in 1971, and earned an M.F.A. from Syracuse University. Married and divorced twice in her twenties, she spent her years after graduation from Syracuse moving from university to university, earning her living with one-year teaching appointments. In 1988 she accepted a position at Middlebury College and married again the next year—two positive changes that proved permanent. Alvarez's widely read novels—How the García Girls Lost Their Accents (1991), In the Time of the Butterflies (1994), ¡Yo! (1996), and In the Name of Salomé (2000)—are often autobiographical, and like her poetry, they explore her dual cultural heritage.

By Accident   2004

Sometimes I think I became the woman
I am by accident, nothing prepared
the way, not a dramatic, wayward aunt,
or moody mother who read *Middlemarch*,
or godmother who whispered, "You can be   5
whatever you want!" and by doing so
performed the god-like function of breathing
grit into me. Even my own sisters
were more concerned with hairdryers and boys
than with the poems I recited ad nauseum   10

in our shared bedrooms when the lights were out.
"You're making me sick!" my sisters would say
as I ranted on, Whitman's "Song of Myself"
not the best lullaby, I now admit,
or Chaucer in Middle English which caused   15
many a nightmare fight. "Mami!" they'd called,
"She's doing it again!" Slap of slippers
in the hall, door clicks, and lights snapped on.
"Why can't you be considerate for once?"
"I am," I pleaded, "these are sounds, sweet airs   20

that give delight and—" "Keep it to yourself!"
my mother said, which more than anything
anyone in my childhood advised
turned me to this paper solitude
where I both keep things secret and broadcast   25
my heart for all the world to read. And so,
through many drafts, I became the woman
I kept to myself as I lay awake
in that dark bedroom with the lonesome sound
of their soft breathing as my sisters slept.   30

Questions
1. Why does the speaker think her literary career happened "by accident"?
2. How did the author's mother's advice suggest a writing life?
3. The speaker claims she is different from her mother and sisters. Have these differences weakened the family ties?

Li-Young Lee

Li-Young Lee was born in 1957 in Jakarta, Indonesia, where his father, who had been Mao Zedong's personal physician, had relocated the family; his mother's grandfather had been the first president of the Republic of China. His parents then fled Indonesia in 1959 because of anti-Chinese sentiment, eventually settling in the United States in 1964. Lee grew up in Pennsylvania, where his father was a Presbyterian minister, and got his degree in biochemistry from the University of Pittsburgh in 1979. He currently lives in Chicago. The Wingéd Seed: A Remembrance (1995) is Lee's memoir of his early life. His poetry, for which he has won a number of prestigious awards and fellowships, has been collected in four volumes: Rose (1986), The City in Which I Love You (1990), Book of My Nights (2001), and Behind My Eyes (2008). Like much of his work, "The Gift" is a quiet, tender celebration of love and of family life.

The Gift   1986

To pull the metal splinter from my palm
my father recited a story in a low voice.
I watched his lovely face and not the blade.
Before the story ended, he'd removed
the iron sliver I thought I'd die from.   5

I can't remember the tale,
but hear his voice still, a well
of dark water, a prayer.
And I recall his hands,
two measures of tenderness   10
he laid against my face,
the flames of discipline
he raised above my head.

Had you entered that afternoon
you would have thought you saw a man   15
planting something in a boy's palm,
a silver tear, a tiny flame.
Had you followed that boy
you would have arrived here,
where I bend over my wife's right hand.   20

Look how I shave her thumbnail down
so carefully she feels no pain.
Watch as I lift the splinter out.
I was seven when my father

took my hand like this, 25
and I did not hold that shard
between my fingers and think,
Metal that will bury me,
christen it Little Assassin,
Ore Going Deep for My Heart. 30
And I did not lift up my wound and cry,
Death visited here!
I did what a child does
when he's given something to keep.
I kissed my father. 35

Questions

1. What is the "gift" that the speaker refers to?
2. How does the incident with his father prefigure the later scene with his wife? What does this suggest about family legacy?
3. In what sense does the statement in lines 14–16 describe a misunderstanding? Is there another, deeper sense in which there is some validity to what "you would have thought"?
4. What meaning do the italicized phrases have? How do they relate to the rest of the poem?

Diane Thiel

Diane Thiel was born in Coral Gables, Florida, in 1967, the second of five children, and grew up in Miami Beach. Her father had been a child in Germany during World War II and was deeply scarred by his experiences there. She received both her B.A. (1988) and M.F.A. (1990) from Brown University. Her first full-length poetry collection, Echolocations *(2000), was awarded the Nicholas Roerich Poetry Prize; her second,* Resistance Fantasies, *appeared in 2004. She has also published a memoir and several textbooks. Thiel is a professor of English and creative writing at the University of New Mexico. "The Minefield," like others of her poems, reflects her tense, oppressive, and sometimes violent childhood home; these frank portrayals, however, never lack compassion.*

Diane Thiel

The Minefield 2000

He was running with his friend from town to town.
They were somewhere between Prague and Dresden.
He was fourteen. His friend was faster
and knew a shortcut through the fields they could take.
He said there was lettuce growing in one of them, 5
and they hadn't eaten all day. His friend ran a few lengths ahead,
like a wild rabbit across the grass,
turned his head, looked back once,
and his body was scattered across the field.

My father told us this, one night, 10
and then continued eating dinner.

He brought them with him—the minefields.
He carried them underneath his good intentions.
He gave them to us—in the volume of his anger,
in the bruises we covered up with sleeves. 15
In the way he threw anything against the wall—
a radio, that wasn't even ours,
a melon, once, opened like a head.
In the way we still expect, years later and continents away,
that anything might explode at any time, 20
and we would have to run on alone
with a vision like that
only seconds behind.

Questions

1. In the opening lines of the poem, a seemingly small decision—to take a shortcut and find something to eat—leads to a horrifying result. What does this suggest about the poem's larger view of what life is like?
2. The speaker tells the story of the minefield before letting us know that the other boy was her father. What is the effect of this narrative strategy?
3. How does the image of the melon reinforce the poem's intentions?
4. The literal application of the title is obvious. Does it have a larger symbolic meaning as well?
5. What does this poem suggest about the legacy of our parents' experiences?

Suggestions for Writing on *Poems about Family Legacies*

1. Compare and contrast Hayden's "The Whipping" and Thiel's "The Minefield." How are they similar, and how are they different? What do they suggest about family legacies? How is the old woman in "The Whipping" different from—or similar to—the speaker in "The Minefield"? Cite specific passages and examples to make your case.
2. Heaney's "Digging" and Lee's "The Gift" also address family legacies. What have the sons in these poems learned from their fathers, both tangibly and intangibly? How have the lessons played out in their own adult lives? Again, cite specific passages and examples to make your case.
3. Write about a family legacy you're aware of but would rather not emulate. How do you know about it? How will you avoid fulfilling it?
4. If you are a parent, what have your children (or your child) inherited from you—good or bad or both—that you never intended?
5. If you have siblings (or step-siblings), write a short essay discussing at least one significant difference between you, and one similarity. End your essay by discussing whether your sibling would agree with your analysis.

Poet in Depth
Gwendolyn Brooks

FAMILY BONDS

Sadie and Maud

the mother

the rites for Cousin Vit

The Bean Eaters

Speech to the Young. Speech to the Progress-Toward

Gwendolyn Brooks was the first African American poet to win the Pulitzer Prize. Accomplished in both traditional verse forms and free verse, Brooks's poetry is distinguished by the vibrancy of her language and the vitality of the characters she presents. These poems of family, including portraits of a lost, lively cousin, a would-be mother who chooses not to have her child, two sisters who take different paths, and a loving older couple, provide unforgettable snapshots of black American life. As technically accomplished as they are emotionally powerful, her poems demonstrate why Brooks has been popular among readers of all ages and all races. Even though she emerged as a writer in a period when poetry was widely assumed to be written mostly for a small academic audience, Brooks insisted on writing for the common reader, an audience she quickly won and never lost.

Gwendolyn Brooks

Though a lifelong resident of Chicago, Gwendolyn Brooks (1917–2000) was born in Topeka, Kansas. When she was thirteen, she had a poem published in American Childhood, *and while still a student, she met the poets James Weldon Johnson and Langston Hughes. She graduated from Wilson Junior College in 1936. In 1939 she married Henry Blakely; the marriage produced two children, Henry, born in 1940, and Nora, born in 1951.* A Street in Bronzeville *(1945) was Brooks's first collection of poetry; its subject matter was drawn from the life of the black neighborhoods of Chicago.* Annie Allen *(1949), her second collection, was awarded the Pulitzer Prize, the first time that an African American poet had received this prestigious award. In 1967, at the Second Black Writers' Conference at Fisk University, Brooks was struck by the passion and commitment of young poets at that gathering. Perceiving that these young poets, as she later told an interviewer, "felt that black poets*

Gwendolyn Brooks

should write as blacks, about blacks, and address themselves to blacks," she determined to do likewise. Having written about African Americans in her earlier books for a larger, mostly white audience, she now decided to write for them. In the Mecca (1968), her next collection, was a work in keeping with the temper of the raw, intense time out of which it came. With Broadside Press, a small, independent publisher devoted to the work of African American writers, she issued the poetry chapbooks Riot (1969) and Family Pictures (1970), among others, and the autobiography Report from Part One (1972). In 1968 Brooks was appointed Poet Laureate of Illinois, a post she held until her death in 2000. Far from regarding it as a merely honorary post, she used this position to bring poetry not only to the schools and colleges of her state, but also to its hospitals and prisons, and she encouraged many young poets, often through awards that she sponsored not only with her reputation and influence but with her own money. In her entry in Who's Who in America, she provided the following as a statement of her personal philosophy: "To be clean of heart, clear of mind, and claiming of what is right and just."

Sadie and Maud   1945

Maud went to college.
Sadie stayed home.
Sadie scraped life
With a fine-tooth comb.

She didn't leave a tangle in.   5
Her comb found every strand.
Sadie was one of the livingest chits
In all the land.

Sadie bore two babies
Under her maiden name.   10
Maud and Ma and Papa
Nearly died of shame.
Every one but Sadie
Nearly died of shame.

When Sadie said her last so-long   15
Her girls struck out from home.
(Sadie had left as heritage
Her fine-tooth comb.)

Maud, who went to college,
Is a thin brown mouse.   20
She is living all alone
In this old house.

Questions

1. What is Sadie and Maud's family relationship? Which details in the poem make it clear?
2. What sort of person is each woman? Use textual references to back up your conclusions.
3. What does the fourth stanza suggest about family legacies?
4. In your opinion, does the author seem to prefer one woman over the other? If so, which one, and for what reasons?

the mother   1945

Abortions will not let you forget.
You remember the children you got that you did not get,
The damp small pulps with a little or with no hair,
The singers and workers that never handled the air.
You will never neglect or beat   5
Them, or silence or buy with a sweet.
You will never wind up the sucking-thumb
Or scuttle off ghosts that come.
You will never leave them, controlling your luscious sigh,
Return for a snack of them, with gobbling mother-eye.   10

I have heard in the voices of the wind the voices of my dim killed children.
I have contracted. I have eased
My dim dears at the breasts they could never suck.
I have said, Sweets, if I sinned, if I seized
Your luck   15
And your lives from your unfinished reach,
If I stole your births and your names,
Your straight baby tears and your games,
Your stilted or lovely loves, your tumults, your marriages, aches, and your deaths,
If I poisoned the beginnings of your breaths,   20
Believe that even in my deliberateness I was not deliberate.
Though why should I whine,
Whine that the crime was other than mine?—
Since anyhow you are dead.
Or rather, or instead,   25
You were never made.
But that too, I am afraid,
Is faulty: oh, what shall I say, how is the truth to be said?
You were born, you had body, you died.
It is just that you never giggled or planned or cried.   30

Believe me, I loved you all.
Believe me, I knew you, though faintly, and I loved, I loved you
All.

Questions
1. Is the mother of the title the speaker throughout the poem? If not, at what point does she begin to speak?
2. What do lines 5–10 communicate about the complexities of a mother's feelings toward her children?
3. What do you understand line 21 to mean, in the larger context of the poem?
4. How would you characterize the mother's attitude toward her aborted children? Is she apologetic, defensive, honest, or are her feelings complicated and perhaps even contradictory?
5. Should the last three lines be taken at face value, or does the author present the mother's words as (unintentionally) ironic? Explain the reasons for your conclusion.

the rites for Cousin Vit   1949

Carried her unprotesting out the door.
Kicked back the casket-stand. But it can't hold her,
That stuff and satin aiming to enfold her,
The lid's contrition nor the bolts before.
Oh oh. Too much. Too much. Even now, surmise,   5
She rises in the sunshine. There she goes,
Back to the bars she knew and the repose
In love-rooms and the things in people's eyes.
Too vital and too squeaking. Must emerge.
Even now she does the snake-hips with a hiss,   10
Slops the bad wine across her shantung, talks
Of pregnancy, guitars and bridgework, walks
In parks or alleys, comes haply on the verge
Of happiness, haply hysterics. Is.

Questions

1. What is meant by "The lid's contrition" (line 4)?
2. What does "Too much. Too much" (line 5) refer to?
3. How would you describe Cousin Vit's personality? What is there about her that leads to the "surmise" that extends from line 5 to the end of the poem?
4. What does "haply" (in line 13) mean? How does the paralleling of "happiness" and "hysterics" in the last two lines relate to the poem's main theme?

The Bean Eaters   1960

They eat beans mostly, this old yellow pair.
Dinner is a casual affair.
Plain chipware on a plain and creaking wood,
Tin flatware.

Two who are Mostly Good.   5
Two who have lived their day,
But keep on putting on their clothes
And putting things away.

And remembering . . .
Remembering, with twinklings and twinges,   10
As they lean over the beans in their rented back room that is full of beads and
   receipts and dolls and cloths, tobacco crumbs, vases and fringes.

Questions

1. What is the point of characterizing the old couple in the poem as "bean eaters"?
2. How would you describe the tone of the second stanza? What attitude toward the couple does that stanza seem to take?
3. Nothing in the poem gives any sense of the individual personalities of the two old people. Is the author making a comment about the effects of a long marriage?
4. What are the implications of the phrase "twinklings and twinges" (line 10)?
5. What is the effect of the long last line, with its piling up of specific details?

Speech to the Young.
Speech to the Progress-Toward

1970/1987

(Among them Nora and Henry III)

Say to them,
say to the down-keepers,
the sun-slappers,
the self-soilers,
the harmony-hushers, 5
"Even if you are not ready for day
it cannot always be night."
You will be right.
For that is the hard home-run.

Live not for battles won. 10
Live not for the-end-of-the-song.
Live in the along.

Questions
1. This poem was the concluding text in Brooks's 1970 chapbook *Family Pictures*; Nora and Henry are her children. In what sense, then, is this a poem about family relationships?
2. Explain, in the context of the poem, the epithets in lines 2–5.
3. Why is the attitude affirmed in the poem described as "hard" (line 9)?
4. How would you paraphrase the theme of this poem?

Suggestions for Writing on *Gwendolyn Brooks's Poetry*

1. The speaker of "the mother" is addressing children who were never born. Why does she see herself as "the mother"?
2. What kind of person was Cousin Vit? What is the speaker's attitude toward her? Cite specific examples to make your case.
3. Relate the advice given in "Speech to the Young. Speech to the Progress-Toward" to the characters in "Sadie and Maud" and "the rites for Cousin Vit." Refer as specifically as possible to all three poems in your discussion.
4. In a detailed discussion of at least three of the poems in this selection, discuss Gwendolyn Brooks's implicit views on respectability and conventional morality.

ESSAYS

CHILD INTO ADULT

Brent Staples	*The Runaway Son*
Raymond Carver	*My Father's Life*
Annie Dillard	*An American Childhood*

The influence of family doesn't vanish when we move out of our childhood homes. The lessons we learn as children continue to shape us long after we're adults. If you doubt this, consider the people who replicate the dynamics of their early family relationships in their later adult lives—and the huge number of adults who go to therapy to sort out "childhood issues."

While our family experiences are hugely important in our lives, our futures are not narrowly predetermined by the past. There is no single set reaction to family circumstances. Some who lived in dysfunctional households might be driven to achieve stability as adults; others might only repeat the dysfunction. If our parents were admirable or hard-working or fabulous, we might feel as though we can never live up to them. Our need to define ourselves with, or against, our parents might fuel our efforts as adults—in work, in love, and with our own families. With the perspective that comes from growing up, we might be more forgiving of parents who were less than ideal, or more critical of parents who once seemed perfect. Either way, our parents continue to shape us, even after they are gone. The essays in this chapter are all portraits of parents and of families. The writers look at their parents with a variety of emotions—anger, shame, admiration, love, and feelings too nuanced to define clearly. In all of the essays, the parents still loom larger than life, not just for the authors, but also for us.

Brent Staples

Brent Staples (b. 1951) was born and raised in Chester, Pennsylvania. Though he is now a member of the editorial board of the New York Times—*one of the most prestigious jobs in journalism—Staples's early circumstances did not seem promising. His family began to struggle when his father, a truck driver, was debilitated by alcoholism. Staples, the eldest of nine children, assumed greater responsibilities at home—a task made more daunting by the growing poverty in Chester as a result of plant closings in the area. By the time he was in junior high school, the family had moved at least eight times, and Staples began to seek support outside the home. Still, college seemed out of reach; he did not even take the SATs because he believed he would go straight to work after high school. Then he met a college*

Brent Staples

professor who encouraged him to apply for Project Prepare, a program that recruited and prepared black students for Philadelphia Military College. Staples soon enrolled as a student at PMC, which later became Widener University, and graduated in 1973. He then earned a Ph.D. in psychology from the University of Chicago and supported himself for a time as a teacher. While teaching, he began to publish his writing on a freelance basis, and soon his teaching job gave way to his growing success as a writer. He got a job as a reporter for the Chicago Sun-Times *and later, as a writer for the* New York Times, *where he now specializes in essays and editorials on politics, race, and culture. In 1994, spurred in part by the drug-related death of his brother Blake, Staples published* Parallel Time: Growing Up in Black and White. *In this powerful memoir, he explores how his own life diverged from the lives of his parents and siblings. Although he writes often about race, Staples resists being held up as an example of African American success. "I despise the expression 'black experience,'" he told an interviewer. "There is no such thing. Black people's lives in this country are too varied to be reduced to a single term." Staples's second book is another memoir,* An American Love Story (1999).

The Runaway Son   1994

  The mother at the beach was supernaturally pale, speaking that blunt Canadian French with a couple on the next blanket. At the market, she wore a business suit and was lost in a dream at the cheese counter. At the museum, the mother was tan and grimly thin, wearing ink-black shades and hissing furiously into a pocket phone. I was watching when each of these women let a small child wander away. The events were years and cities apart, but basically the same each time. I shadowed the child and waited for its absence to hit home. A mother who loses her cub—even for a moment—displays a seizure of panic unique to itself. Those seizures of panic are a specialty of mine. I guess you could say I collect them.

  This morning I am walking to the doctor's office, brooding about mortality and the yearly finger up the butt. Today's mother has flaming red hair and is standing on the steps, riffling her bag for keys. Her little girl is no more than four—with the same creamy face, trimmed in ringlets of red. The mother's hair is thick and shoulder-length, blocking her view as she leans over the bag. The child drifts down the steps and stands on the sidewalk. Idling as children do, she crosses to the curb and stares dreamily into traffic. Three people pass her without breaking stride. A pair of teenagers with backpacks. A homeless man pushing a junk-laden shopping cart. A businessman, who glances up at the woman's legs and marches onward.

  For some people a four-year-old beyond its mother's reach is invisible. For me that child is the axis of the world. Should I run to her, pull her back from the curb? Should I yell in crude Brooklynese, "Hey lady, look out for the friggin' kid!" Nearing the child, I croon in sweet falsetto, "Hey honey, let's wait for Mommy before you cross." The mention of Mommy freezes her. Up on the steps, the red mane of hair whips hysterically into the air. "Patty, get back here! I told you: Don't go near the street!" The woman thanks me and flushes with embarrassment. I smile—"No trouble at all"—and continue on my way.

  Most men past forty dream of muscle tone and sex with exotic strangers. Mine is a constant fantasy of rescue, with a sobbing child as the star. What I tell now is how this came to be.

*

My parents were children when they married. She was eighteen. He was twenty-two. The ceremony was performed in the log house where my mother was born and where she, my grandmother Mae, and my great-grandmother Luella still lived, in the foothills of the Blue Ridge Mountains. I visited the house often as a small child. The only surviving picture shows a bewildered toddler sitting in the grass, staring fixedly at an unknown something in the distance. My great-grandmother Luella was a tall, raw-boned woman with a mane of hair so long she had to move it aside to sit down. Her daughter, my Grandma Mae, wore tight dresses that showed off her bosoms and a string of dead foxes that trailed from her shoulder. The beady eyes of the foxes were frightening when she bent to kiss me.

The log house had no running water, no electricity. At night I bathed in a metal washtub set near the big, wood-burning stove. Once washed, I got into my white dressing gown and prepared for the trip to the outhouse. My grandmother held a hurricane lamp out of the back door to light the way. The path was long and dark and went past the cornfield where all the monsters were. I could tell they were there, hidden behind the first row, by the way the corn squeaked and rustled as I passed. Most feared among them were the snakes that turned themselves into hoops and rolled after you at tremendous speed, thrashing through the corn as they came.

The outhouse itself was dank and musty. While sitting on the toilet I tried as much as possible to keep the lamp in view through cracks in the outhouse wall. The trip back to the log house was always the worst; the monsters gathered in the corn to ambush me, their groaning, growling reaching a crescendo as they prepared to spring. I ran for the light and landed in the kitchen panting and out of breath.

My father's clan, the Staples of Troutville, had an indoor toilet. My paternal great-grandparents, John Wesley and Eliza Staples, were people of substance in the Roanoke valley. In the 1920s, when folks still went about on horseback, John Wesley burst on the scene in a Model T Ford with all the extras—and let it be known that he paid for the car in cash. Though not an educated man, he could read and write. He was vain of his writing: he scribbled even grocery lists with flourish, pausing often to lick the pencil point. There was no school for black children at that time. And so John Wesley and his two immediate neighbors built one at the intersection of their three properties. Then they retained the teacher who worked in it.

The Pattersons were rich in love, but otherwise broke. This made my mother's marriage to a Staples man seem a fine idea. But domestic stability was not my father's experience, the role of husband and father not one that he could play. His own father, John Wesley's son Marshall, had routinely disappeared on payday and reappeared drunk and broke several days later. He abandoned the family at the start of the Depression, leaving Grandma Ada with four children in hand and one—my father—on the way. Ada had no choice but to place her children with relatives and go north, looking for work.

The luckiest of my uncles landed with John Wesley and Eliza. My father came to rest in hell on earth: the home of Ada's father, Tom Perdue. Three wives preceded Tom into the grave and the family lore was that he worked them to death. He hired out his sons for farmwork and collected their pay, leaving them with nothing. My father was beaten for wetting the bed and forced to sleep on a pallet under the kitchen sink. He left school at third grade and became part of Tom's dark enterprise. Birthdays went by unnoted. Christmas meant a new pair of work boots—if that. Had it not been for my father and a younger cousin, Tom would have died with no one to note his passing.

This childhood left its mark. My father distrusted affection, and what there was of it he pushed away. He looked suspicious when you hugged or kissed him—as though doubting that affection was real. The faculty for praising us was dead in him. I could choose any number of examples from childhood, but permit me to skip ahead to college. I was obsessed with achievement and made the dean's list nearly every semester. My father was mute on the subject—and never once said "good job." Finally, I achieved the perfect semester—an A in every subject—with still not a word from him. Years later, I found that he had carried my grades in his wallet and bragged on them to strangers at truck stops.

My father worked as a truck driver; he earned a handsome salary, then tried to drink it up. My mother mishandled what was left. How could she do otherwise when money was a mystery to her? She grew up in a barter economy, where one farmer's milk bought another's eggs and the man who butchered the hogs was paid in pork. She stared at dollar bills as though awaiting divine instruction on how to spend them.

I grew up in a household on the verge of collapse, the threat of eviction ever present, the utilities subject to cutoff at any moment. Gas was cheap and therefore easy to regain. The water company had pity on us and relented when we made even token efforts to pay. But the electric company had no heart to harden. We lived in darkness for weeks at a time. While our neighbors' houses were blazing with light, we ate, played, and bathed in the sepia glow of hurricane lamps. My mother made the darkness into a game. Each night before bed, she assembled us in a circle on the floor, with a hurricane lamp at the center. First she told a story, then had each of us tell one. Those too young to tell stories sang songs. I looked forward to the circle and my brothers' and sisters' faces in the lamplight. The stories I told were the first stirrings of the writer in me.

On Saturday night my father raged through the house hurling things at the walls. Sunday morning would find him placid, freshly shaven, and in his favorite chair, the air around him singing with Mennon Speed Stick and Old Spice Cologne. At his feet were stacked the Sunday papers, the *Philadelphia Bulletin* and the *Philadelphia Inquirer*. I craved his attention but I was wary of him; it was never clear who he would be.

On a table nearby was a picture of him when he was in the navy and not yet twenty years old. He was wearing dress whites, with his cap tilted snappily back on his head, his hand raised in a salute. He smiled a rich expansive smile that spread to every corner of his face. A hardness had undermined the smile and limited its radius. His lips—full and fleshy in the picture—were tense and narrow by comparison. The picture showed a carefree boy—free of terrible Tom—on the verge of a life filled with possibility. Ten years later those possibilities had all been exhausted. He was knee-deep in children, married to a woman he no longer loved but lacked the courage to leave. The children were coming fast. We were three, then five, then nine.

Our first neighborhood was called The Hill, a perfect place for a young mother with a large family and an unreliable husband. The men went to work at the shipyard and brought home hefty paychecks that easily supported an entire household. The women stayed home to watch and dote on the children. Not just their own, but all of us. Many of these women were no happier than my mother. They had husbands who beat them; husbands who took lovers within full view of their neighbors; husbands who drove them crazy in any number of ways. The women submerged their suffering in love for children. There was no traffic to speak of, and we played for hours in the streets. A child five years old passed easily from its mother's arms into the arms of the neighborhood. Eyes were on us at every moment. We'd be playing with broken glass when a voice rang out from nowhere: "Y'all stop that and play nice!" We'd be transfixed by the sight of wet cement, ripe for writing curse words, when the voice rang out again: "Y'all get away from that cement. Mr. Prince paid good money to have that done!" Women on errands patrolled the sidewalks and made them unsafe for fighting. Every woman had license to discipline a child caught in the wrong. We feigned the deepest remorse, hopeful that the report would not reach our mothers.

Everyone on The Hill grew some kind of fruit; my gang was obsessed with stealing it. We prowled hungrily at people's fences, eyeing their apples, pears, and especially their peaches. We were crazed to get at them, even when they were tiny and bitter and green. We turned surly when there was no fruit at all. Then we raided gardens where people grew trumpet flowers, which gave a sweet nectar when you sucked them. The flowers were enormous and bright orange. When the raid was finished, the ground would be covered with them.

I lost The Hill when my family was evicted. We landed miles away in the Polish West End. The Poles and Ukrainians had once ruled much of the city. They had surrendered it street by street and were now confined to the westernmost neighborhood, their backs pressed to the city limits.

My family had crossed the color line. The people who lived in the house before us had been black as well. But they were all adults. After them, my brothers and sisters must have seemed an invading army.

The Polish and Ukrainian kids spelled their names exotically and ate unpronounceable foods. They were Catholics and on certain Wednesdays wore ashes on their foreheads. On Fridays they were forbidden to eat meat. When you walked by their churches you caught a glimpse of a priest swinging incense at the end of a chain. I wanted to know all there was to know about them. That I was their neighbor entitled me to it.

The Polish and Ukrainian boys did not agree. The first week was a series of fights, one after another. They despised us, as did their parents and grandparents. I gave up trying to know them and played alone. Deprived of friends, I retreated into comic books. My favorite hero was the Silver Surfer, bald and naked to his silver skin, riding a surfboard made of the same silver stuff. The comic's most perfect panels showed the seamless silver body flashing through space on the board. No words; just the long view of the Surfer hurtling past planets and stars.

My fantasies of escape centered on airplanes; I was drunk with the idea of flying. At home, I labored over model planes until the glue made me dizzy. At school, I made planes out of notebook paper and crammed them into my pockets and books. I was obsessed with movies about aerial aces and studied them carefully, prepping for the acehood that I'd been born to and that was destined to be mine. I planned to join the air force when I graduated from high school. The generals would already have heard of me; my jet would be warming up on the runway.

My favorite plane was a wooden Spitfire with British Air Force markings and a propeller powered by a rubber band. I was flying it one day when it landed in the yard of a Ukrainian boy whose nose I had bloodied. His grandfather was gardening when the plane touched down on the neatly kept lawn. He seized the plane, sputtered at me in Ukrainian, and disappeared into the house. A few minutes later one of his older grandsons delivered what was left of it. The old man had destroyed it with malevolent purpose. The wings and fuselage were broken the long way, twice. The pieces were the width of popsicle sticks and wrapped in the rubber band. This was the deepest cruelty I had known.

My mother suffered too. She missed her friends on The Hill, but we were too far west for them to reach us easily. She was learning how difficult it was to care for us on her own, especially since there were few safe places to play. The new house sat on a truck route. Forty-foot semis thundered by, spewing smoke and rattling windows. My mother lived in terror of the traffic and forbade us to roller-skate even on the sidewalk. On The Hill, she had swept off on errands confident that we would be fine. In the Polish West End, she herded us into the house and told us to stay there until she got back.

The house had become a prison. My eldest sister, Yvonne, was thirteen years old—and the first to escape. She stayed out later and later and finally disappeared for days at a time. My mother strapped her. My father threatened her with the juvenile home. But Yvonne met their anger with steeliness. When they questioned her she went dumb and stared into space. I knew the look from prisoner-of-war movies; do your worst, it said, I will tell you nothing. She lied casually and with great skill. But I was an expert listener, determined to break the code. The lie had a strained lightness, the quality of cotton candy. I recognized that sound when she said, "Mom, I'll be right back, I'm going out to the store." I followed her. She passed the store and started across town just as I thought she would. I trotted after her, firing questions. "Where do you think you're going? What is on your mind? What are you trying to do to yourself?" I was my mother's son and accepted all she told me about the dangers of the night. Girls became sluts at night. Boys got into fights and went to jail. These hazards meant nothing to Yvonne; she ignored me and walked on. I yelled "Slut! Street dog!" She lunged at me, but I dodged out of reach. "Slut" I had gotten from my mother. But "street dog" was an original, I'd made it up on the spur of the moment. I had become the child parent. I could scold and insult—but I was too young and ill-formed to instruct. I relished the role; it licensed me to be judge and disparage people I envied but lacked the courage to imitate.

Yvonne was wild to get away. You turned your back and—POOF!—she was gone. Finally she stayed away for days that stretched into weeks and then months. There was no sign or word of her. My mother was beaten up with worry. By night she walked the floors, tilting at every sound in the street.

What is it like to be one of nine children, to be tangled in arms and legs in bed and at the dinner table? My brothers and sisters were part of my skin; you only notice your skin when something goes wrong with it. My youngest brother, Blake, got infections that dulled his hearing and closed his ears to the size of pinholes. Bruce broke his arm—while playing in the safety of our treeless and boring backyard. Sherri began to sleepwalk, once leaping down a flight of stairs. Every illness and injury and visit to the hospital involved me. I was first assistant mother now, auxiliary parent in every emergency.

My five-year-old sister Christi was burned nearly to death. Her robe caught fire at the kitchen stove. I was upstairs in my room when it happened. First I heard the scream. Then came thunder of feet below me, and soon after the sound of the ambulance. The doctors did the best they could and gave the rest up to God.

The sign at the nurses' station said that no one under sixteen could visit. I was only eleven; with Yvonne missing, I was as close to sixteen as the children got. I knew that Christi had been brought back from the dead. What I saw the first day added mightily to that awareness. A domed frame had been built over the bed to keep the sheets from touching the burns. Peering under the dome, I saw her wrapped in gauze, round and round the torso, round and round each leg, like a mummy. Blood seeped through the bandages where the burns were deepest. The burns that I could see outside the bandages didn't look too bad. The skin was blackened, but bearable.

Eventually she was allowed to sit up. I would arrive to find her in her bright white gauze suit, sitting in a child's rocking chair. I got used to the gauze. Then they took it off to air out the wounds. Her body was raw from the breast to below the knee. The flesh was wet and bloody in places; I could see the blood pulsing beneath what had been her skin. The room wobbled, but I kept smiling and tried to be natural. I walked in a wide circle around her that day, afraid that I would brush against her. I got past even this, because Christi smiled interminably. The nerve endings were dead and she felt nothing. In time I grew accustomed to flesh without skin.

Christi's injuries were the worst on the ward. Next to the burns everything else was easy to look at. I was especially interested in the boy with the steel rods jutting out of his leg. He'd been hit by a car, and the bone was shattered. He didn't talk much, but the rods in his legs were fascinating. The skin clung to them like icing to the candles on a cake.

The children's ward was sparsely visited on weekdays. I cruised the room, cooing at toddlers and making jokes with frightened newcomers. On weekends the ward filled up with parents, highlighting the fact that I was eleven years old—and that my own parents were elsewhere. When real parents visited, I felt like a fraud. I clung to Christi's bedside and did not stray. I wished that the scene at Christi's bed was like the scene around the other beds: fathers, mothers, relatives. But that was not to be.

Christi's accident made the world dangerous. When left in charge, I gathered the children in the living room and imprisoned them there. Trips to the bathroom were timed and by permission only. Now and then I imagined the smell of gas and trotted into the kitchen to check the stove. I avoided looking out of windows for fear of daydreaming. Staring at the sky, I punched through it into space and roamed the galaxy with my hero, the Silver Surfer.

I was daydreaming one day when my brother Brian cried out in pain. He had taken a pee and gotten his foreskin snarled in his zipper. He had given a good yank, too, and pulled it nearly halfway up. Every step tugged at the zipper and caused him to scream. I cut off the pants and left just the zipper behind. To keep his mind off his troubles and kill time until my parents got home, I plunked out a tune on the piano. The longer they stayed away the more crazed I became.

The days were too full for an eleven-year-old who needed desperately to dream. The coal-fired boiler that heated our house was part of the reason. The fire went out at night, which meant that I built a new fire in the morning: chop kindling; haul ashes; shovel coal. Then it was up from the basement, to iron shirts, polish shoes, make sandwiches, and pack the school lunches. My mother tried to sweeten the jobs by describing them as "little": "Build a little fire to throw the chill off of the house."

But there was no such thing as a "little" fire. Every fire required the same backbreaking work. Chop kindling. Chop wood. Shovel coal. Haul ashes. One morning she said, "Put a little polish on the toe of your brother's shoes." I dipped the applicator into the liquid polish and dabbed the tiniest spot on the top of each shoe. Yvonne's departure had left my mother brittle and on the edge of violence. I knew this but couldn't stop myself. She was making breakfast when I presented her with the shoes, which were still scuffed and unpolished. "I told you to polish those shoes," she said. "No, you didn't," I said, "you said 'put a little polish on the toe.'" She snapped at me. I snapped back. Then she lifted the serving platter and smashed it across my head.

My father was drinking more than ever. Debt mounted in the customary pattern. We pushed credit to the limit at one store, then abandoned the bills and moved on to the next. Mine was the face of the family's debt. I romanced the shop owners into giving us food and coal on time, then tiptoed past their windows to put the bite on the next guy. When gas and electricity were cut off, I traveled across town to plead with the utility companies. The account executives were mainly women with soft spots for little boys. I conned them, knowing we would never pay. We were behind in the rent and would soon be evicted. Once settled elsewhere, we would apply for gas and electricity, under a fictitious name.

The only way to get time to myself was to steal it. During the summer, I got up early, dressed with the stealth of a burglar, and tiptoed out of the house. The idea was to get in a full day's play unencumbered by errands or housework. Most days I escaped. On other days my mother's radar was just too good, and her rich contralto came soaring out of the bedroom. "Brent, make sure you're back here in time to . . ." to go shopping, to visit Christi at the hospital, to go a thousand places on a thousand errands.

Inevitably I thought of running away—to Florida. In Florida you could sleep outside, live on fruit from the orange groves, and never have to work. I decided to do it on a snowy Saturday at the start of a blizzard. Thought and impulse were one: I took an orange from the fruit bowl, grabbed my parka from the coat rack, and ran from the house.

I did not get to Florida. In my haste, I had grabbed the coat belonging to my younger brother Brian. It was the same color as mine but too small even to zip up. The freight train I planned to take never left the rail yard. The snow thickened and began to freeze. Numb and disheartened, I headed home.

Five years later I succeeded in running away—this time to college. Widener University was two miles from where my family lived. For all that I visited them, two miles could have been two thousand. I lived at school year round—through holidays, semester breaks, and right through the summer. Alone in bed for the first time, I recognized how crowded my life had been. I enjoyed the campus most when it was deserted. I wandered the dormitory drinking in the space. At night I sat in the stadium, smoking pot and studying the constellations. I never slept with my brothers again.

Years later my youngest sister, Yvette, accused me of abandoning the family. But the past is never really past; what we have lived is who we are. I am still the frightened ten-year-old tending babies and waiting for my parents. The sight of a child on its own excludes everything else from view. No reading. No idle conversation. No pretending not to see. I follow and watch and intervene because I have no choice. When next you see a child beyond its mother's reach, scan the crowd for me. I am there, watching you watch the child.

Questions

1. How do the anecdotes at the beginning of the essay relate to the essay's theme? Do they serve as an effective set-up for the essay that follows?
2. Staples describes how he and his friends were "obsessed with stealing" fruit. What might this obsession have signified?
3. How would you describe Staples's childhood and family life? How have they shaped him as an adult?

Raymond Carver

Raymond Carver (1938–1988) was born in Clatskanie, Oregon. When he was three, his family moved to Yakima, Washington, where his father worked in a sawmill. In his early years Carver worked briefly at a lumber mill and at other unskilled jobs, including a stint as a tulip-picker. Married with two children before he was twenty, he experienced blue-collar desperation more intimately than most American writers, though he once quipped that, until he read critics' reactions to his works, he never realized that the characters in his stories "were so bad off." In 1963 Carver earned a degree from Humboldt State College. He briefly attended the Writers' Workshop of the University of Iowa, but, needing to support his family, he returned to California, working for three years as a hospital custodian before finding a job editing textbooks. He began publishing in the late 1960s, first poetry and then the stories that gained him lasting fame. In the early 1970s, though plagued with bankruptcies, increasing dependency on alcohol, and marital problems, he taught at several universities. In his last decade Carver taught creative writing at Syracuse University and lived with the poet Tess Gallagher, whom he married in 1988. He divided his final years between Syracuse and Port Angeles, Washington. Carver's personal victory in 1977 over decades of alcoholism underscored the many professional triumphs of his final decade. He once said, "I'm prouder of that, that I quit drinking, than I am of anything in my life." His reputation as a master craftsman of the contemporary short story was still growing when he died after a struggle with lung cancer.

My Father's Life   1986

My dad's name was Clevie Raymond Carver. His family called him Raymond and friends called him C. R. I was named Raymond Clevie Carver, Jr. I hated the "Junior" part. When I was little my dad called me Frog, which was okay. But later, like everybody else in the family, he began calling me Junior. He went on calling me this until I was thirteen or fourteen and announced that I wouldn't answer to that name any longer. So he began calling me Doc. From then until his death, on June 17, 1967, he called me Doc, or else Son.

When he died, my mother telephoned my wife with the news. I was away from my family at the time, between lives, trying to enroll in the School of Library Science at the University of Iowa. When my wife answered the phone, my mother blurted out,

"Raymond's dead!" For a moment, my wife thought my mother was telling her that I was dead. Then my mother made it clear *which* Raymond she was talking about and my wife said, "Thank God. I thought you meant *my* Raymond."

My dad walked, hitched rides, and rode in empty boxcars when he went from Arkansas to Washington State in 1934, looking for work. I don't know whether he was pursuing a dream when he went out to Washington. I doubt it. I don't think he dreamed much. I believe he was simply looking for steady work at decent pay. Steady work was meaningful work. He picked apples for a time and then landed a construction laborer's job on the Grand Coulee Dam. After he'd put aside a little money, he bought a car and drove back to Arkansas to help his folks, my grandparents, pack up for the move west. He said later that they were about to starve down there, and this wasn't meant as a figure of speech. It was during that short while in Arkansas, in a town called Leola, that my mother met my dad on the sidewalk as he came out of a tavern.

"He was drunk," she said. "I don't know why I let him talk to me. His eyes were glittery. I wish I'd had a crystal ball." They'd met once, a year or so before, at a dance. He'd had girlfriends before her, my mother told me. "Your dad always had a girlfriend, even after we married. He was my first and last. I never had another man. But I didn't miss anything."

They were married by a justice of the peace on the day they left for Washington, this big, tall country girl and a farmhand-turned-construction worker. My mother spent her wedding night with my dad and his folks, all of them camped beside the road in Arkansas.

In Omak, Washington, my dad and mother lived in a little place not much bigger than a cabin. My grandparents lived next door. My dad was still working on the dam, and later, with the huge turbines producing electricity and the water backed up for a hundred miles into Canada, he stood in the crowd and heard Franklin D. Roosevelt when he spoke at the construction site. "He never mentioned those guys who died building that dam," my dad said. Some of his friends had died there, men from Arkansas, Oklahoma, and Missouri.

He then took a job in a sawmill in Clatskanie, Oregon, a little town alongside the Columbia River. I was born there, and my mother has a picture of my dad standing in front of the gate to the mill, proudly holding me up to face the camera. My bonnet is on crooked and about to come untied. His hat is pushed back on his forehead, and he's wearing a big grin. Was he going in to work or just finishing his shift? It doesn't matter. In either case, he had a job and a family. These were his salad days.

In 1941 we moved to Yakima, Washington, where my dad went to work as a saw filer, a skilled trade he'd learned in Clatskanie. When war broke out, he was given a deferment because his work was considered necessary to the war effort. Finished lumber was in demand by the armed services, and he kept his saws so sharp they could shave the hair off your arm.

After my dad had moved us to Yakima, he moved his folks into the same neighborhood. By the mid-1940s the rest of my dad's family—his brother, his sister, and her husband, as well as uncles, cousins, nephews, and most of their extended family and friends—had come out from Arkansas. All because my dad came out first. The men went to work at Boise Cascade, where my dad worked, and the women packed apples in the canneries. And in just a little while, it seemed—according to my mother—everybody was better off than my dad. "Your dad couldn't keep money," my mother said. "Money burned a hole in his pocket. He was always doing for others."

The first house I clearly remember living in, at 1515 South Fifteenth Street, in Yakima, had an outdoor toilet. On Halloween night, or just any night, for the hell of it, neighbor kids, kids in their early teens, would carry our toilet away and leave it next to the road. My dad would have to get somebody to help him bring it home. Or these kids would take the toilet and stand it in somebody else's backyard. Once they actually set it on fire. But ours wasn't the only house that had an outdoor toilet. When I was old enough to know what I was doing, I threw rocks at the other toilets when I'd see someone go inside. This was called bombing the toilets. After a while, though, everyone went to indoor plumbing until, suddenly, our toilet was the last outdoor one in the neighborhood. I remember the shame I felt when my third-grade teacher, Mr. Wise, drove me home from school one day. I asked him to stop at the house just before ours, claiming I lived there.

I can recall what happened one night when my dad came home late to find that my mother had locked all the doors on him from the inside. He was drunk, and we could feel the house shudder as he rattled the door. When he'd managed to force open a window, she hit him between the eyes with a colander and knocked him out. We could see him down there on the grass. For years afterward, I used to pick up this colander—it was as heavy as a rolling pin—and imagine what it would feel like to be hit in the head with something like that.

It was during this period that I remember my dad taking me into the bedroom, sitting me down on the bed, and telling me that I might have to go live with my Aunt LaVon for a while. I couldn't understand what I'd done that meant I'd have to go away from home to live. But this, too—whatever prompted it—must have blown over, more or less, anyway, because we stayed together, and I didn't have to go live with her or anyone else.

I remember my mother pouring his whiskey down the sink. Sometimes she'd pour it all out and sometimes, if she was afraid of getting caught, she'd only pour half of it out and then add water to the rest. I tasted some of his whiskey once myself. It was terrible stuff, and I don't see how anybody could drink it.

After a long time without one, we finally got a car, in 1949 or 1950, a 1938 Ford. But it threw a rod the first week we had it, and my dad had to have the motor rebuilt.

"We drove the oldest car in town," my mother said. "We could have had a Cadillac for all he spent on car repairs." One time she found someone else's tube of lipstick on the floorboard, along with a lacy handkerchief. "See this?" she said to me. "Some floozy left this in the car."

Once I saw her take a pan of warm water into the bedroom where my dad was sleeping. She took his hand from under the covers and held it in the water. I stood in the doorway and watched. I wanted to know what was going on. This would make him talk in his sleep, she told me. There were things she needed to know, things she was sure he was keeping from her.

Every year or so, when I was little, we would take the North Coast Limited across the Cascade Range from Yakima to Seattle and stay in the Vance Hotel and eat, I remember, at a place called the Dinner Bell Cafe. Once we went to Ivar's Acres of Clams and drank glasses of warm clam broth.

In 1956, the year I was to graduate from high school, my dad quit his job at the mill in Yakima and took a job in Chester, a little sawmill town in northern California. The reasons given at the time for his taking the job had to do with a higher hourly wage and the vague promise that he might, in a few years' time, succeed to the job of head filer in this new mill. But I think, in the main, that my dad had grown restless and simply wanted to try his luck elsewhere. Things had gotten a little too predictable for him in Yakima. Also, the year before, there had been the deaths, within six months of each other, of both his parents.

But just a few days after graduation, when my mother and I were packed to move to Chester, my dad penciled a letter to say he'd been sick for a while. He didn't want us to worry, he said, but he'd cut himself on a saw. Maybe he'd got a tiny sliver of steel in his blood. Anyway, something had happened and he'd had to miss work, he said. In the same mail was an unsigned postcard from somebody down there telling my mother that my dad was about to die and that he was drinking "raw whiskey."

When we arrived in Chester, my dad was living in a trailer that belonged to the company. I didn't recognize him immediately. I guess for a moment I didn't want to recognize him. He was skinny and pale and looked bewildered. His pants wouldn't stay up. He didn't look like my dad. My mother began to cry. My dad put his arm around her and patted her shoulder vaguely, like he didn't know what this was all about, either. The three of us took up life together in the trailer, and we looked after him as best we could. But my dad was sick, and he couldn't get any better. I worked with him in the mill that summer and part of the fall. We'd get up in the mornings and eat eggs and toast while we listened to the radio, and then go out the door with our lunch pails. We'd pass through the gate together at eight in the morning, and I wouldn't see him again until quitting time. In November I went back to Yakima to be closer to my girlfriend, the girl I'd made up my mind I was going to marry.

He worked at the mill in Chester until the following February, when he collapsed on the job and was taken to the hospital. My mother asked if I would come down there and help. I caught a bus from Yakima to Chester, intending to drive them back to Yakima. But now, in addition to being physically sick, my dad was in the midst of a nervous breakdown, though none of us knew to call it that at the time. During the entire trip back to Yakima, he didn't speak, not even when asked a direct question. ("How do you feel, Raymond?" "You okay, Dad?") He'd communicate, if he communicated at all, by moving his head or by turning his palms up as if to say he didn't know or care. The only time he said anything on the trip, and for nearly a month afterward, was when I was speeding down a gravel road in Oregon and the car muffler came loose. "You were going too fast," he said.

Back in Yakima a doctor saw to it that my dad went to a psychiatrist. My mother and dad had to go on relief, as it was called, and the county paid for the psychiatrist. The psychiatrist asked my dad, "Who is the President?" He'd had a question put to him that he could answer. "Ike," my dad said. Nevertheless, they put him on the fifth floor of Valley Memorial Hospital and began giving him electroshock treatments. I was married by then and about to start my own family. My dad was still locked up when my wife went into this same hospital, just one floor down, to have our first baby. After she had delivered, I went upstairs to give my dad the news. They let me in through a steel door and showed me where I could find him. He was sitting on a couch with a blanket over his lap. *Hey*, I thought. *What in hell is happening to my dad?* I sat down next to him and told him he was a grandfather. He waited a minute and then he said, "I feel like a grandfather." That's all he said. He didn't smile or move. He was in a big room with a lot of other people. Then I hugged him, and he began to cry.

Somehow he got out of there. But now came the years when he couldn't work and just sat around the house trying to figure what next and what he'd done wrong in his life that he'd wound up like this. My mother went from job to crummy job. Much later she referred to that time he was in the hospital, and those years just afterward, as "when Raymond was sick." The word *sick* was never the same for me again.

In 1964, through the help of a friend, he was lucky enough to be hired on at a mill in Klamath, California. He moved down there by himself to see if he could hack it. He lived not far from the mill, in a one-room cabin not much different from the place he and my mother had started out living in when they went west. He scrawled letters to my mother, and if I called she'd read them aloud to me over the phone. In the letters, he said it was touch and go. Every day that he went to work, he felt like it was the most important day of his life. But every day, he told her, made the next day that much easier. He said for her to tell me he said hello. If he couldn't sleep at night, he said, he thought about me and the good times we used to have. Finally, after a couple of months, he regained some of his confidence. He could do the work and didn't think he had to worry that he'd let anybody down ever again. When he was sure, he sent for my mother.

He'd been off from work for six years and had lost everything in that time—home, car, furniture, and appliances, including the big freezer that had been my mother's pride and joy. He'd lost his good name too—Raymond Carver was someone who couldn't pay his bills—and his self-respect was gone. He'd even lost his virility. My mother told my wife, "All during that time Raymond was sick we slept together in the same bed, but we didn't have relations. He wanted to a few times, but nothing happened. I didn't miss it, but I think he wanted to, you know."

During those years I was trying to raise my own family and earn a living. But, one thing and another, we found ourselves having to move a lot. I couldn't keep track of what was going down in my dad's life. But I did have a chance one Christmas to tell him I wanted to be a writer. I might as well have told him I wanted to become a plastic surgeon. "What are you going to write about?" he wanted to know. Then, as if to help me out, he said, "Write about stuff you know about. Write about some of those fishing trips we took." I said I would, but I knew I wouldn't. "Send me what you write," he said. I said I'd do that, but then I didn't. I wasn't writing anything about fishing, and I didn't think he'd particularly care about, or even necessarily understand, what I was writing in those days. Besides, he wasn't a reader. Not the sort, anyway, I imagined I was writing for.

Then he died. I was a long way off, in Iowa City, with things still to say to him. I didn't have the chance to tell him goodbye, or that I thought he was doing great at his new job. That I was proud of him for making a comeback.

My mother said he came in from work that night and ate a big supper. Then he sat at the table by himself and finished what was left of a bottle of whiskey, a bottle she found hidden in the bottom of the garbage under some coffee grounds a day or so later. Then he got up and went to bed, where my mother joined him a little later.

But in the night she had to get up and make a bed for herself on the couch. "He was snoring so loud I couldn't sleep," she said. The next morning when she looked in on him, he was on his back with his mouth open, his cheeks caved in. *Gray-looking*, she said. She knew he was dead—she didn't need a doctor to tell her that. But she called one anyway, and then she called my wife.

Among the pictures my mother kept of my dad and herself during those early days in Washington was a photograph of him standing in front of a car, holding a beer and a stringer of fish. In the photograph he is wearing his hat back on his forehead and has this awkward grin on his face. I asked her for it and she gave it to me, along with some others. I put it up on my wall, and each time we moved, I took the picture along and put it up on another wall. I looked at it carefully from time to time, trying to figure out some things about my dad, and maybe myself in the process. But I couldn't. My dad just kept moving further and further away from me and back into time. Finally, in the course of another move, I lost the photograph. It was then that I tried to recall it, and at the same time make an attempt to say something about my dad, and how I thought that in some important ways we might be alike. I wrote the poem when I was living in an apartment house in an urban area south of San Francisco, at a time when I found myself, like my dad, having trouble with alcohol. The poem was a way of trying to connect up with him.

Photograph of My Father in His Twenty-Second Year

October. Here in this dank, unfamiliar kitchen
I study my father's embarrassed young man's face.
Sheepish grin, he holds in one hand a string
of spiny yellow perch, in the other
a bottle of Carlsberg beer.

In jeans and flannel shirt, he leans
against the front fender of a 1934 Ford.
He would like to pose brave and hearty for his posterity,
wear his old hat cocked over his ear.
All his life my father wanted to be bold.

But the eyes give him away, and the hands
that limply offer the string of dead perch
and the bottle of beer. Father, I love you,
yet how can I say thank you, I who can't hold my liquor either
and don't even know the places to fish.

The poem is true in its particulars, except that my dad died in June and not October, as the first word of the poem says. I wanted a word with more than one syllable to it to make it linger a little. But more than that, I wanted a month appropriate to what I felt at the time I wrote the poem—a month of short days and failing light, smoke in the air, things perishing. June was summer nights and days, graduations, my wedding anniversary, the birthday of one of my children. June wasn't a month your father died in.

After the service at the funeral home, after we had moved outside, a woman I didn't know came over to me and said, "He's happier where he is now." I stared at this woman until she moved away. I still remember the little knob of a hat she was wearing. Then one of my dad's cousins—I didn't know the man's name—reached out and took my hand. "We all miss him," he said, and I knew he wasn't saying it just to be polite.

I began to weep for the first time since receiving the news. I hadn't been able to before. I hadn't had the time, for one thing. Now, suddenly, I couldn't stop. I held my wife and wept while she said and did what she could do to comfort me there in the middle of that summer afternoon.

I listened to people say consoling things to my mother, and I was glad that my dad's family had turned up, had come to where he was. I thought I'd remember everything that was said and done that day and maybe find a way to tell it sometime. But I didn't. I forgot it all, or nearly. What I do remember is that I heard our name used a lot that afternoon, my dad's name and mine. But I knew they were talking about my dad. *Raymond*, these people kept saying in their beautiful voices out of my childhood. *Raymond*.

Questions

1. Why did the young Raymond Carver resent being called "Junior"? Why is he struck at the end of the piece by people using the name "Raymond"?
2. How does the story of Carver's parents meeting on the sidewalk foreshadow what will happen later in their relationship?
3. What particularly telling details does Carver use to show how difficult the family's life was?
4. What do you think Carver feels toward his father? What makes you think so?

Annie Dillard

Annie Dillard (b. 1945) was born in Pittsburgh, Pennsylvania. She is a prominent novelist, poet, and nonfiction writer who often incorporates nature into her work. Raised by well-off, free-spirited parents, Dillard was encouraged to be creative and to think for herself. She rebelled from her society upbringing, opting to avoid her parents' country club set in favor of exploring the outdoors. This connection to the natural world, and the spiritual elements of her experience, are evident in her first and still best-known work, Pilgrim at Tinker Creek *(1974).* Pilgrim *won the Pulitzer Prize for general nonfiction and brought Dillard a level of attention and fame with which she was uncomfortable. Always happier in nature, she moved to Waldron Island, a small and isolated island off Puget Sound near Seattle, and then to Connecticut, where she taught at Wesleyan University. Her many books include the memoirs* An American Childhood *(1987) and* The Writing Life *(1989), and the novels* The Living *(1992) and* The Maytrees *(2007). The following selection is from* An American Childhood.

An American Childhood 1987

There was a big snow that same year, 1950. Traffic vanished; in the first week, nothing could move. The mailman couldn't get to us; the milkman couldn't come. Our long-legged father walked four miles with my sled to the dairy across Fifth Avenue and carried back milk.

We had a puppy, who was shorter than the big snow. Our parents tossed it for fun in the yard and it disappeared, only to pop up somewhere else at random like a loon in a lake. After a few days of this game, the happy puppy went crazy and died. It had distemper. While it was crazy it ran around the house crying, upstairs and down.

One night during the second week of the big snow I saw Jo Ann Sheehy skating on the street. I remembered this sight for its beauty and strangeness.

I was aware of the Sheehy family; they were Irish Catholics from a steep part of the neighborhood. One summer when I was walking around the block, I had to walk past skinny Tommy Sheehy and his fat father, who were hunched on their porch doing nothing. Tommy's eleven-year-old sister, Jo Ann, brought them iced tea.

"Go tell your maid she's a nigger," Tommy Sheehy said to me.

What?

He repeated it, and I did it, later, when I got home. That night, Mother came into our room after Amy was asleep. She explained, and made sure I understood. She was steely. Where had my regular mother gone? Did she hate me? She told me a passel of other words that some people use for other people. I was never to use such words, and never to associate with people who did so long as I lived; I was to apologize to Margaret Butler first thing in the morning; and I was to have no further dealings with the Sheehys.

The night Jo Ann Sheehy skated on the street, it was dark inside our house. We were having dinner in the dining room—my mother, my father, my sister Amy, who was two, and I. There were lighted ivory candles on the table. The only other light inside was the blue fluorescent lamp over the fish tank, on a sideboard. Inside the tank, neon tetras, black mollies, and angelfish circled, illumined, through the light-shot water. When I turned the fluorescent lamp off, I had learned, the fish still circled their tank in the dark. The still water in the tank's center barely stirred.

Now we sat in the dark dining room, hushed. The big snow outside, the big snow on the roof, silenced our words and the scrape of our forks and our chairs. The dog was gone, the world outside was dangerously cold, and the big snow held the houses down and the people in.

Behind me, tall chilled windows gave out onto the narrow front yard and the street. A motion must have caught my mother's eye; she rose and moved to the windows, and Father and I followed. There we saw the young girl, the transfigured Jo Ann Sheehy, skating alone under the streetlight.

She was turning on ice skates inside the streetlight's yellow cone of light—illumined and silent. She tilted and spun. She wore a short skirt, as if Edgerton Avenue's asphalt had been the ice of an Olympic arena. She wore mittens and a red knitted cap below which her black hair lifted when she turned. Under her skates the street's packed snow shone; it illumined her from below, the cold light striking her under her chin. I stood at the tall window, barely reaching the sill; the glass fogged before my face, so I had to keep moving or hold my breath. What was she doing out there? Was everything beautiful so bold? I expected a car to run over her at any moment: the open street was a fatal place, where I was forbidden to set foot. Once, the skater left the light. She winged into the blackness beyond the streetlight and sped down the street; only her white skates showed, and the white snow. She emerged again under another streetlight, in the continuing silence, just at our corner stop sign where the trucks' brakes hissed. Inside that second cone of light she circled backward and leaning. Then she reversed herself in an abrupt half-turn—as if she had skated backward into herself, absorbed her own motion's impetus, and rebounded from it; she shot forward into the dark street and appeared again becalmed in the first streetlight's cone. I exhaled; I looked up. Distant over the street, the night sky was moonless and foreign, a frail, bottomless black, and the cold stars speckled it without moving.

This was for many years the center of the maze, this still, frozen evening inside, the family's watching through glass the Irish girl skate outside on the street. Here were beauty and mystery outside the house, and peace and safety within. I watched passive and uncomprehending, as in summer I watched Lombardy poplar leaves turn their green sides out, and then their silver sides out—watched as if the world were a screen on which played interesting scenes for my pleasure. But there was danger in this radiant sight, in the long glimpse of the lone girl skating, for it was night, and killingly cold. The open street was fatal and forbidden. And the apparently invulnerable girl was Jo Ann Sheehy, Tommy Sheehy's sister, part of the Sheehy family, whose dark ways were a danger and a crime.

"Tell your maid she's a nigger," he had said, and when I said to Margaret, "You're a nigger," I had put myself in danger—I felt at the time, for Mother was so enraged—of being put out, tossed out in the cold, where I would go crazy and die like the dog.

That night Jo Ann alone outside in the cold had performed recklessly. My parents did not disapprove; they loved the beauty of it, and the queerness of skating on a street. The next morning I saw from the dining-room windows the street shrunken again and ordinary, tracked by tires, and the streetlights inconspicuous, and Jo Ann Sheehy walking to school in a blue plaid skirt.

Questions

1. How would you characterize Dillard's mother? What do all the examples suggest?
2. How does Dillard seem to feel about her mother? Cite specific examples.
3. What kind of legacy or lesson has Dillard's mother provided her?
4. Do you think that all of Dillard's siblings and relatives saw the mother (and reacted to her) in the same way? How might others have characterized her?

Suggestions for Writing on *Essays about Childhood and Growing Up*

1. Compare the lessons that sons learned from their fathers in Staples's "The Runaway Son" and Carver's "My Father's Life." What good examples—and bad ones—have they taken from their fathers? How have these lessons affected their adult lives?
2. Dillard describes her mother as being nonconformist, and as encouraging her children to question accepted rules and norms. Do you see her as setting a positive example for her children? Why or why not? What effect has she had on Dillard?
3. Consider Staples's comment in his closing paragraph, "But the past is never really past; what we have lived is who we are." Now apply it to one of the essays in this section. Do you think Staples's view is accurate? Why or why not? What evidence can you find in the chosen essay?
4. Write a personal essay describing how one of your parents has shaped you. Have you tried to emulate your parent, or do you define yourself against him or her? What kind of lasting impact does your parent have on your current choices, your aspirations, and how you interact with the world?

DRAMA

FAMILY DRAMA

Lorraine Hansberry   *A Raisin in the Sun*

If we are deeply shaped by our experience in families, then what influence do we have on our own development? How much of who we become and what we achieve is the result of our background and upbringing—and how much do we control ourselves? Where does the family end and the self begin? And when our needs as individuals clash with the needs of family members—or the family more generally—whose needs should prevail? Who decides? The following award-winning drama by an African American playwright produced at the start of the civil rights movement takes on these questions, and more. It depicts troubled relationships between parents and children, brother and sister, husband and wife. Set against the backdrop of a specific era and society, it has a larger, lasting relevance in its portrayal of a family that ultimately holds together. This classic American play presents a unique and thought-provoking portrait of a family and the individuals within it.

Lorraine Hansberry

Lorraine Hansberry was born in Chicago in 1930. Her father was a banker and real-estate broker, her mother a former schoolteacher; both of her parents were active in the struggle for social justice. When Lorraine Hansberry was eight years old, her father bought a home in what she later described as a "hellishly hostile 'white neighborhood' in which, literally, howling mobs surrounded our house. . . . My memories . . . include being spat on, cursed and pummeled in the daily trek to and from school." Hansberry's father brought a lawsuit over his right to purchase the house; the case went all the way to the U.S. Supreme Court, which ruled in his favor. Visitors to the family home when Lorraine Hansberry was young included W. E. B. Du Bois, Duke Ellington, Langston Hughes, Paul Robeson, and other prominent black artists and intellectuals. After two years of study at the University of Wisconsin, Hansberry moved to New York City in 1950. She became associate editor of the newspaper Freedom, *published by Paul Robeson, but resigned in 1953 to concentrate on her writing.* A Raisin in the Sun *made history in March 1959 when it became the first play by a black woman to be produced on Broadway. It ran for nineteen months, won the New York Drama Critics Circle Award as Best Play of the Year, and was made into a film in 1961. Her second full-length play,* The Sign in Sidney Brustein's Window, *opened on Broadway in October 1964. By the time of its production, Hansberry was terminally ill; she died of cancer in January 1965, at the age of thirty-four. Posthumously produced works included* To Be Young, Gifted and Black *(1969) and* Les Blancs *(1970). The text of* A Raisin in the Sun *presented here is*

Lorraine Hansberry

the most complete version available; it includes two short scenes omitted for reasons of length from the Broadway production and omitted as well from the early published editions.

A Raisin in the Sun
1959

To Mama: *in gratitude for the dream*

> What happens to a dream deferred?
> Does it dry up
> Like a raisin in the sun?
> Or fester like a sore—
> And then run?
> Does it stink like rotten meat
> Or crust and sugar over—
> Like a syrupy sweet?
>
> Maybe it just sags
> Like a heavy load.
>
> Or does it explode?
>
> —LANGSTON HUGHES

CHARACTERS

Ruth Younger
Travis Younger
Walter Lee Younger (Brother)
Beneatha Younger
Lena Younger (Mama)
Joseph Asagai
George Murchison
Mrs. Johnson
Karl Lindner
Bobo
Moving Men

The action of the play is set in Chicago's Southside, sometime between World War II and the present.

ACT I
Scene 1: *Friday morning.*
Scene 2: *The following morning.*

ACT II
Scene 1: *Later, the same day.*
Scene 2: *Friday night, a few weeks later.*
Scene 3: *Moving day, one week later.*

ACT III
An hour later.

ACT ONE

SCENE 1

The Younger living room would be a comfortable and well-ordered room if it were not for a number of indestructible contradictions to this state of being. Its furnishings are typical and undistinguished and their primary feature now is that they have clearly had to accommodate the living of too many people for too many years—and they are tired. Still, we can see that at some time, a time probably no longer remembered by the family (except perhaps for Mama), the furnishings of this room were actually selected with care and love and even hope—and brought to this apartment and arranged with taste and pride.

That was a long time ago. Now the once loved pattern of the couch upholstery has to fight to show itself from under acres of crocheted doilies and couch covers which have themselves finally come to be more important than the upholstery. And here a table or a chair has been moved to disguise the worn places in the carpet; but the carpet has fought back by showing its weariness, with depressing uniformity, elsewhere on its surface.

Weariness has, in fact, won in this room. Everything has been polished, washed, sat on, used, scrubbed too often. All pretenses but living itself have long since vanished from the very atmosphere of this room.

Moreover, a section of this room, for it is not really a room unto itself, though the landlord's lease would make it seem so, slopes backward to provide a small kitchen area, where the family prepares the meals that are eaten in the living room proper, which must also serve as dining room. The single window that has been provided for these "two" rooms is located in this kitchen area. The sole natural light the family may enjoy in the course of a day is only that which fights its way through this little window.

At left, a door leads to a bedroom which is shared by Mama and her daughter, Beneatha. At right, opposite, is a second room (which in the beginning of the life of this apartment was probably a breakfast room) which serves as a bedroom for Walter and his wife, Ruth.

Diana Sands, Ruby Dee, Claudia McNeil, and Sidney Poitier in the original 1959 Broadway production of *A Raisin in the Sun*. The play was made into a film with the same cast in 1961.

TIME. *Sometime between World War II and the present.*

PLACE. *Chicago's Southside.*

AT RISE. *It is morning dark in the living room. Travis is asleep on the make-down bed at center. An alarm clock sounds from within the bedroom at right, and presently Ruth enters from that room and closes the door behind her. She crosses sleepily toward the window. As she passes her sleeping son she reaches down and shakes him a little. At the window she raises the shade and a dusky Southside morning light comes in feebly. She fills a pot with water and puts it on to boil. She calls to the boy, between yawns, in a slightly muffled voice.*

Ruth is about thirty. We can see that she was a pretty girl, even exceptionally so, but now it is apparent that life has been little that she expected, and disappointment has already begun to hang in her face. In a few years, before thirty-five even, she will be known among her people as a "settled woman."

She crosses to her son and gives him a good, final, rousing shake.

Ruth: Come on now, boy, it's seven thirty! *(Her son sits up at last, in a stupor of sleepiness.)* I say hurry up, Travis! You ain't the only person in the world got to use a bathroom!

(The child, a sturdy, handsome little boy of ten or eleven, drags himself out of the bed and almost blindly takes his towels and "today's clothes" from drawers and a closet and goes out to the bathroom, which is in an outside hall and which is shared by another family or families on the same floor. Ruth crosses to the bedroom door at right and opens it and calls in to her husband.)

The 2004 award-winning Broadway production of *A Raisin in the Sun* was filmed for television in 2008, starring Sean "P. Diddy" Combs, Sanaa Lathan, Phylicia Rashad, and Audra McDonald.

Walter Lee! . . . It's after seven thirty! Lemme see you do some waking up in there now! *(She waits.)* You better get up from there, man! It's after seven thirty I tell you. *(She waits again.)* All right, you just go ahead and lay there and next thing you know Travis be finished and Mr. Johnson'll be in there and you'll be fussing and cussing round here like a madman! And be late too! *(She waits, at the end of patience.)* Walter Lee—it's time for you to GET UP!

(She waits another second and then starts to go into the bedroom, but is apparently satisfied that her husband has begun to get up. She stops, pulls the door to, and returns to the kitchen area. She wipes her face with a moist cloth and runs her fingers through her sleep-disheveled hair in a vain effort and ties an apron around her housecoat. The bedroom door at right opens and her husband stands in the doorway in his pajamas, which are rumpled and mismated. He is a lean, intense young man in his middle thirties, inclined to quick nervous movements and erratic speech habits—and always in his voice there is a quality of indictment.)

Walter: Is he out yet?

Ruth: What you mean *out*? He ain't hardly got in there good yet.

Walter (wandering in, still more oriented to sleep than to a new day): Well, what was you doing all that yelling for if I can't even get in there yet? *(Stopping and thinking.)* Check coming today?

Ruth: They *said* Saturday and this is just Friday and I hopes to God you ain't going to get up here first thing this morning and start talking to me 'bout no money—'cause I 'bout don't want to hear it.

Walter: Something the matter with you this morning?

Ruth: No—I'm just sleepy as the devil. What kind of eggs you want?

Walter: Not scrambled. *(Ruth starts to scramble eggs.)* Paper come? *(Ruth points impatiently to the rolled up* Tribune *on the table, and he gets it and spreads it out and vaguely reads the front page.)* Set off another bomb yesterday.

Ruth (maximum indifference): Did they?

Walter (looking up): What's the matter with you?

Ruth: Ain't nothing the matter with me. And don't keep asking me that this morning.

Walter: Ain't nobody bothering you. *(Reading the news of the day absently again.)* Say Colonel McCormick° is sick.

Ruth (affecting tea-party interest): Is he now? Poor thing.

Walter (sighing and looking at his watch): Oh, me. *(He waits.)* Now what is that boy doing in that bathroom all this time? He just going to have to start getting up earlier. I can't be being late to work on account of him fooling around in there.

Ruth (turning on him): Oh, no he ain't going to be getting up no earlier no such thing! It ain't his fault that he can't get to bed no earlier nights 'cause he got a bunch of crazy good-for-nothing clowns sitting up running their mouths in what is supposed to be his bedroom after ten o'clock at night . . .

Walter: That's what you mad about, ain't it? The things I want to talk about with my friends just couldn't be important in your mind, could they?

(He rises and finds a cigarette in her handbag on the table and crosses to the little window and looks out, smoking and deeply enjoying this first one.)

Colonel McCormick: Robert R. McCormick (1880–1955) was an eccentric but influential newspaper publisher who founded the *Chicago Tribune* in 1914.

Ruth (almost matter of factly, a complaint too automatic to deserve emphasis): Why you always got to smoke before you eat in the morning?

Walter (at the window): Just look at 'em down there ... Running and racing to work ... *(He turns and faces his wife and watches her a moment at the stove, and then, suddenly)* You look young this morning, baby.

Ruth (indifferently): Yeah?

Walter: Just for a second—stirring them eggs. Just for a second it was—you looked real young again. *(He reaches for her; she crosses away. Then, drily)* It's gone now—you look like yourself again!

Ruth: Man, if you don't shut up and leave me alone.

Walter (looking out to the street again): First thing a man ought to learn in life is not to make love to no colored woman first thing in the morning. You all some eeeevil people at eight o'clock in the morning.

(Travis appears in the hall doorway, almost fully dressed and quite wide awake now, his towels and pajamas across his shoulders. He opens the door and signals for his father to make the bathroom in a hurry.)

Travis (watching the bathroom): Daddy, come on!

(Walter gets his bathroom utensils and flies out to the bathroom.)

Ruth: Sit down and have your breakfast, Travis.

Travis: Mama, this is Friday. *(Gleefully)* Check coming tomorrow, huh?

Ruth: You get your mind off money and eat your breakfast.

Travis (eating): This is the morning we supposed to bring the fifty cents to school.

Ruth: Well, I ain't got no fifty cents this morning.

Travis: Teacher say we have to.

Ruth: I don't care what teacher say. I ain't got it. Eat your breakfast, Travis.

Travis: I *am* eating.

Ruth: Hush up now and just eat!

(The boy gives her an exasperated look for her lack of understanding, and eats grudgingly.)

Travis: You think Grandmama would have it?

Ruth: No! And I want you to stop asking your grandmother for money, you hear me?

Travis (outraged): Gaaaleee! I don't ask her, she just gimme it sometimes!

Ruth: Travis Willard Younger—I got too much on me this morning to be—

Travis: Maybe Daddy—

Ruth: Travis!

(The boy hushes abruptly. They are both quiet and tense for several seconds.)

Travis (presently): Could I maybe go carry some groceries in front of the supermarket for a little while after school then?

Ruth: Just hush, I said. *(Travis jabs his spoon into his cereal bowl viciously, and rests his head in anger upon his fists.)* If you through eating, you can get over there and make up your bed.

(The boy obeys stiffly and crosses the room, almost mechanically, to the bed and more or less folds the bedding into a heap, then angrily gets his books and cap.)

Travis (sulking and standing apart from her unnaturally): I'm gone.

Ruth (looking up from the stove to inspect him automatically): Come here. *(He crosses to her and she studies his head.)* If you don't take this comb and fix this here head, you better! *(Travis puts down his books with a great sigh of oppression, and crosses to the mirror. His mother mutters under her breath about his "slubbornness.")* 'Bout to march out of here with that head looking just like chickens slept in it! I just don't know where you get your slubborn ways . . . And get your jacket, too. Looks chilly out this morning.

Travis (with conspicuously brushed hair and jacket): I'm gone.

Ruth: Get carfare and milk money—*(waving one finger)*—and not a single penny for no caps, you hear me?

Travis (with sullen politeness): Yes'm.

(He turns in outrage to leave. His mother watches after him as in his frustration he approaches the door almost comically. When she speaks to him, her voice has become a very gentle tease.)

Ruth (mocking; as she thinks he would say it): Oh, Mama makes me so mad sometimes, I don't know what to do! *(She waits and continues to his back as he stands stock-still in front of the door.)* I wouldn't kiss that woman good-bye for nothing in this world this morning!

(The boy finally turns around and rolls his eyes at her, knowing the mood has changed and he is vindicated; he does not, however, move toward her yet.)

Not for nothing in this world!

(She finally laughs aloud at him and holds out her arms to him and we see that it is a way between them, very old and practiced. He crosses to her and allows her to embrace him warmly but keeps his face fixed with masculine rigidity. She holds him back from her presently and looks at him and runs her fingers over the features of his face. With utter gentleness—)

Now—whose little old angry man are you?

Travis (the masculinity and gruffness start to fade at last): Aw gaalee—Mama . . .

Ruth (mimicking): Aw—gaaaaalleeeee, Mama! *(She pushes him, with rough playfulness and finality, toward the door.)* Get on out of here or you going to be late.

Travis (in the face of love, new aggressiveness): Mama, could I *please* go carry groceries?

Ruth: Honey, it's starting to get so cold evenings.

Walter (coming in from the bathroom and drawing a make-believe gun from a make-believe holster and shooting at his son): What is it he wants to do?

Ruth: Go carry groceries after school at the supermarket.

Walter: Well, let him go . . .

Travis (quickly, to the ally): I have to—she won't gimme the fifty cents . . .

Walter (to his wife only): Why not?

Ruth (simply, and with flavor): 'Cause we don't have it.

Walter (to Ruth only): What you tell the boy things like that for? *(Reaching down into his pants with a rather important gesture.)* Here, son—

(He hands the boy the coin, but his eyes are directed to his wife's. Travis takes the money happily.)

Travis: Thanks, Daddy.

(*He starts out. Ruth watches both of them with murder in her eyes. Walter stands and stares back at her with defiance, and suddenly reaches into his pocket again on an afterthought.*)

Walter (*without even looking at his son, still staring hard at his wife*): In fact, here's another fifty cents . . . Buy yourself some fruit today—or take a taxicab to school or something!

Travis: Whoopee—

(*He leaps up and clasps his father around the middle with his legs, and they face each other in mutual appreciation; slowly Walter Lee peeks around the boy to catch the violent rays from his wife's eyes and draws his head back as if shot.*)

Walter: You better get down now—and get to school, man.

Travis (*at the door*): O.K. Good-bye. (*He exits.*)

Walter (*after him, pointing with pride*): That's my boy. (*She looks at him in disgust and turns back to her work.*) You know what I was thinking 'bout in the bathroom this morning?

Ruth: No.

Walter: How come you always try to be so pleasant!

Ruth: What is there to be pleasant 'bout!

Walter: You want to know what I was thinking 'bout in the bathroom or not!

Ruth: I know what you thinking 'bout.

Walter (*ignoring her*): 'Bout what me and Willy Harris was talking about last night.

Ruth (*immediately—a refrain*): Willy Harris is a good-for-nothing loudmouth.

Walter: Anybody who talks to me has got to be a good-for-nothing loudmouth, ain't he? And what you know about who is just a good-for-nothing loudmouth? Charlie Atkins was just a "good-for-nothing loudmouth" too, wasn't he! When he wanted me to go in the dry-cleaning business with him. And now—he's grossing a hundred thousand a year. A hundred thousand dollars a year! You still call *him* a loudmouth!

Ruth (*bitterly*): Oh, Walter Lee . . .

(*She folds her head on her arms over the table.*)

Walter (*rising and coming to her and standing over her*): You tired, ain't you? Tired of everything. Me, the boy, the way we live—this beat-up hole—everything. Ain't you? (*She doesn't look up, doesn't answer.*) So tired—moaning and groaning all the time, but you wouldn't do nothing to help, would you? You couldn't be on my side that long for nothing, could you?

Ruth: Walter, please leave me alone.

Walter: A man needs for a woman to back him up . . .

Ruth: Walter—

Walter: Mama would listen to you. You know she listen to you more than she do me and Bennie. She think more of you. All you have to do is just sit down with her when you drinking your coffee one morning and talking 'bout things like you do and—(*He sits down beside her and demonstrates graphically what he thinks her methods and tone should be.*)—you just sip your coffee, see, and say easy like that you been thinking 'bout that deal Walter Lee is so interested in, 'bout the store and all, and sip some more coffee, like what you saying ain't really that important to you—And the next thing you know, she be listening good and asking you questions and when I come home—I can tell her the details. This ain't no fly-by-night proposition, baby. I mean we figured it out, me and Willy and Bobo.

Ruth (with a frown): Bobo?

Walter: Yeah. You see, this little liquor store we got in mind cost seventy-five thousand and we figured the initial investment on the place be 'bout thirty thousand, see. That be ten thousand each. Course, there's a couple of hundred you got to pay so's you don't spend your life just waiting for them clowns to let your license get approved—

Ruth: You mean graft?

Walter (frowning impatiently): Don't call it that. See there, that just goes to show you what women understand about the world. Baby, don't *nothing* happen for you in this world 'less you pay *somebody* off!

Ruth: Walter, leave me alone! *(She raises her head and stares at him vigorously—then says, more quietly.)* Eat your eggs, they gonna be cold.

Walter (straightening up from her and looking off): That's it. There you are. Man say to his woman: I got me a dream. His woman say: Eat your eggs. *(Sadly, but gaining in power.)* Man say: I got to take hold of this here world, baby! And a woman will say: Eat your eggs and go to work. *(Passionately now.)* Man say: I got to change my life, I'm choking to death, baby! And his woman say—*(In utter anguish as he brings his fists down on his thighs)*—Your eggs is getting cold!

Ruth (softly): Walter, that ain't none of our money.

Walter (not listening at all or even looking at her): This morning, I was lookin' in the mirror and thinking about it . . . I'm thirty-five years old; I been married eleven years and I got a boy who sleeps in the living room—*(very, very quietly)*—and all I got to give him is stories about how rich white people live . . .

Ruth: Eat your eggs, Walter.

Walter (slams the table and jumps up): DAMN MY EGGS—DAMN ALL THE EGGS THAT EVER WAS!

Ruth: Then go to work.

Walter (looking up at her): See—I'm trying to talk to you 'bout myself—*(Shaking his head with the repetition.)*—and all you can say is eat them eggs and go to work.

Ruth (wearily): Honey, you never say nothing new. I listen to you every day, every night and every morning, and you never say nothing new. *(Shrugging.)* So you would rather *be* Mr. Arnold than be his chauffeur. So—I would *rather* be living in Buckingham Palace.

Walter: That is just what is wrong with the colored woman in this world . . . Don't understand about building their men up and making 'em feel like they somebody. Like they can do something.

Ruth (drily, but to hurt): There *are* colored men who do things.

Walter: No thanks to the colored woman.

Ruth: Well, being a colored woman, I guess I can't help myself none.

(She rises and gets the ironing board and sets it up and attacks a huge pile of rough-dried clothes, sprinkling them in preparation for the ironing and then rolling them into tight fat balls.)

Walter (mumbling): We one group of men tied to a race of women with small minds!

(His sister Beneatha enters. She is about twenty, as slim and intense as her brother. She is not as pretty as her sister-in-law, but her lean, almost intellectual face has a

handsomeness of its own. She wears a bright-red flannel nightie, and her thick hair stands wildly about her head. Her speech is a mixture of many things; it is different from the rest of the family's insofar as education has permeated her sense of English—and perhaps the Midwest rather than the South has finally—at last—won out in her inflection; but not altogether, because over all of it is a soft slurring and transformed use of vowels which is the decided influence of the Southside. She passes through the room without looking at either Ruth or Walter and goes to the outside door and looks, a little blindly, out to the bathroom. She sees that it has been lost to the Johnsons. She closes the door with a sleepy vengeance and crosses to the table and sits down a little defeated.)

Beneatha: I am going to start timing those people.
Walter: You should get up earlier.
Beneatha (her face in her hands. She is still fighting the urge to go back to bed): Really— would you suggest dawn? Where's the paper?
Walter (pushing the paper across the table to her as he studies her almost clinically, as though he has never seen her before): You a horrible-looking chick at this hour.
Beneatha (drily): Good morning, everybody.
Walter (senselessly): How is school coming?
Beneatha (in the same spirit): Lovely. Lovely. And you know, biology is the greatest. (Looking up at him.) I dissected something that looked just like you yesterday.
Walter: I just wondered if you've made up your mind and everything.
Beneatha (gaining in sharpness and impatience): And what did I answer yesterday morning—and the day before that?
Ruth (from the ironing board, like someone disinterested and old): Don't be so nasty, Bennie.
Beneatha (still to her brother): And the day before that and the day before that!
Walter (defensively): I'm interested in you. Something wrong with that? Ain't many girls who decide—
Walter and Beneatha (in unison): —"to be a doctor."

(Silence.)

Walter: Have we figured out yet just exactly how much medical school is going to cost?
Ruth: Walter Lee, why don't you leave that girl alone and get out of here to work?
Beneatha (exits to the bathroom and bangs on the door): Come on out of there, please!

(She comes back into the room.)

Walter (looking at his sister intently): You know the check is coming tomorrow.
Beneatha (turning on him with a sharpness all her own): That money belongs to Mama, Walter, and it's for her to decide how she wants to use it. I don't care if she wants to buy a house or a rocket ship or just nail it up somewhere and look at it. It's hers. Not ours—hers.
Walter (bitterly): Now ain't that fine! You just got your mother's interest at heart, ain't you, girl? You such a nice girl—but if Mama got that money she can always take a few thousand and help you through school too—can't she?
Beneatha: I have never asked anyone around here to do anything for me!
Walter: No! And the line between asking and just accepting when the time comes is big and wide—ain't it!

Beneatha (with fury): What do you want from me, Brother—that I quit school or just drop dead, which!

Walter: I don't want nothing but for you to stop acting holy 'round here. Me and Ruth done made some sacrifices for you—why can't you do something for the family?

Ruth: Walter, don't be dragging me in it.

Walter: You are in it—Don't you get up and go work in somebody's kitchen for the last three years to help put clothes on her back?

Ruth: Oh, Walter—that's not fair . . .

Walter: It ain't that nobody expects you to get on your knees and say thank you, Brother; thank you, Ruth; thank you, Mama—and thank you, Travis, for wearing the same pair of shoes for two semesters—

Beneatha (dropping to her knees): Well—I do—all right?—thank everybody! And forgive me for ever wanting to be anything at all! *(Pursuing him on her knees across the floor.)* FORGIVE ME, FORGIVE ME, FORGIVE ME!

Ruth: Please stop it! Your mama'll hear you.

Walter: Who the hell told you you had to be a doctor? If you so crazy 'bout messing 'round with sick people—then go be a nurse like other women—or just get married and be quiet . . .

Beneatha: Well—you finally got it said . . . It took you three years but you finally got it said. Walter, give up; leave me alone—it's Mama's money.

Walter: He was my father, too!

Beneatha: So what? He was mine, too—and Travis' grandfather—but the insurance money belongs to Mama. Picking on me is not going to make her give it to you to invest in any liquor stores—*(Underbreath, dropping into a chair.)*—and I for one say, God bless Mama for that!

Walter (to Ruth): See—did you hear? Did you hear!

Ruth: Honey, please go to work.

Walter: Nobody in this house is ever going to understand me.

Beneatha: Because you're a nut.

Walter: Who's a nut?

Beneatha: You—you are a nut. Thee is mad, boy.

Walter (looking at his wife and his sister from the door, very sadly): The world's most backward race of people, and that's a fact.

Beneatha (turning slowly in her chair): And then there are all those prophets who would lead us out of the wilderness—*(Walter slams out of the house.)*—into the swamps!

Ruth: Bennie, why you always gotta be pickin' on your brother? Can't you be a little sweeter sometimes?

(Door opens. Walter walks in. He fumbles with his cap, starts to speak, clears throat, looks everywhere but at Ruth. Finally:)

Walter (to Ruth): I need some money for carfare.

Ruth (looks at him, then warms; teasing, but tenderly): Fifty cents? *(She goes to her bag and gets money.)* Here—take a taxi!

(Walter exits. Mama enters. She is a woman in her early sixties, full-bodied and strong. She is one of those women of a certain grace and beauty who wear it so unobtrusively

that it takes a while to notice. Her dark-brown face is surrounded by the total whiteness of her hair, and, being a woman who has adjusted to many things in life and overcome many more, her face is full of strength. She has, we can see, wit and faith of a kind that keep her eyes lit and full of interest and expectancy. She is, in a word, a beautiful woman. Her bearing is perhaps most like the noble bearing of the women of the Hereros of Southwest Africa—rather as if she imagines that as she walks she still bears a basket or a vessel upon her head. Her speech, on the other hand, is as careless as her carriage is precise—she is inclined to slur everything—but her voice is perhaps not so much quiet as simply soft.)

Mama: Who that 'round here slamming doors at this hour?

(She crosses through the room, goes to the window, opens it, and brings in a feeble little plant growing doggedly in a small pot on the windowsill. She feels the dirt and puts it back out.)

Ruth: That was Walter Lee. He and Bennie was at it again.

Mama: My children and they tempers. Lord, if this little old plant don't get more sun than it's been getting it ain't never going to see spring again. (*She turns from the window.*) What's the matter with you this morning, Ruth? You looks right peaked. You aiming to iron all them things? Leave some for me. I'll get to 'em this afternoon. Bennie honey, it's too drafty for you to be sitting 'round half dressed. Where's your robe?

Beneatha: In the cleaners.

Mama: Well, go get mine and put it on.

Beneatha: I'm not cold, Mama, honest.

Mama: I know—but you so thin . . .

Beneatha (*irritably*): Mama, I'm not cold.

Mama (*seeing the make-down bed as Travis has left it*): Lord have mercy, look at that poor bed. Bless his heart—he tries, don't he? (*She moves to the bed Travis has sloppily made up.*)

Ruth: No—he don't half try at all 'cause he knows you going to come along behind him and fix everything. That's just how come he don't know how to do nothing right now—you done spoiled that boy so.

Mama (*folding bedding*): Well—he's a little boy. Ain't supposed to know 'bout housekeeping. My baby, that's what he is. What you fix for his breakfast this morning?

Ruth (*angrily*): I feed my son, Lena!

Mama: I ain't meddling—(*Underbreath; busy-bodyish*) I just noticed all last week he had cold cereal, and when it starts getting this chilly in the fall a child ought to have some hot grits or something when he goes out in the cold—

Ruth (*furious*): I gave him hot oats—is that all right!

Mama: I ain't meddling. (*Pause.*) Put a lot of nice butter on it? (*Ruth shoots her an angry look and does not reply.*) He likes lots of butter.

Ruth (*exasperated*): Lena—

Mama (*to Beneatha. Mama is inclined to wander conversationally sometimes*): What was you and your brother fussing 'bout this morning?

Beneatha: It's not important, Mama.

(She gets up and goes to look out at the bathroom, which is apparently free, and she picks up her towels and rushes out.)

Mama: What was they fighting about?

Ruth: Now you know as well as I do.

Mama (shaking her head): Brother still worrying hisself sick about that money?

Ruth: You know he is.

Mama: You had breakfast?

Ruth: Some coffee.

Mama: Girl, you better start eating and looking after yourself better. You almost thin as Travis.

Ruth: Lena—

Mama: Un-hunh?

Ruth: What are you going to do with it?

Mama: Now don't you start, child. It's too early in the morning to be talking about money. It ain't Christian.

Ruth: It's just that he got his heart set on that store—

Mama: You mean that liquor store that Willy Harris want him to invest in?

Ruth: Yes—

Mama: We ain't no business people, Ruth. We just plain working folks.

Ruth: Ain't nobody business people till they go into business. Walter Lee say colored people ain't never going to start getting ahead till they start gambling on some different kinds of things in the world—investments and things.

Mama: What done got into you, girl? Walter Lee done finally sold you on investing.

Ruth: No. Mama, something is happening between Walter and me. I don't know what it is—but he needs something—something I can't give him any more. He needs this chance, Lena.

Mama (frowning deeply): But liquor, honey—

Ruth: Well—like Walter say—I spec people going to always be drinking themselves some liquor.

Mama: Well—whether they drinks it or not ain't none of my business. But whether I go into business selling it to 'em *is*, and I don't want that on my ledger this late in life. *(Stopping suddenly and studying her daughter-in-law.)* Ruth Younger, what's the matter with you today? You look like you could fall over right there.

Ruth: I'm tired.

Mama: Then you better stay home from work today.

Ruth: I can't stay home. She'd be calling up the agency and screaming at them, "My girl didn't come in today—send me somebody! My girl didn't come in!" Oh, she just have a fit . . .

Mama: Well, let her have it. I'll just call her up and say you got the flu—

Ruth (laughing): Why the flu?

Mama: 'Cause it sounds respectable to 'em. Something white people get, too. They know 'bout the flu. Otherwise they think you been cut up or something when you tell 'em you sick.

Ruth: I got to go in. We need the money.

Mama: Somebody would of thought my children done all but starved to death the way they talk about money here late. Child, we got a great big old check coming tomorrow.

Ruth (sincerely, but also self-righteously): Now that's your money. It ain't got nothing to do with me. We all feel like that—Walter and Bennie and me—even Travis.

Mama (thoughtfully, and suddenly very far away): Ten thousand dollars—

Ruth: Sure is wonderful.

Mama: Ten thousand dollars.

Ruth: You know what you should do, Miss Lena? You should take yourself a trip somewhere. To Europe or South America or someplace—

Mama (throwing up her hands at the thought): Oh, child!

Ruth: I'm serious. Just pack up and leave! Go on away and enjoy yourself some. Forget about the family and have yourself a ball for once in your life—

Mama (drily): You sound like I'm just about ready to die. Who'd go with me? What I look like wandering 'round Europe by myself?

Ruth: Shoot—these here rich white women do it all the time. They don't think nothing of packing up they suitcases and piling on one of them big steamships and—swoosh!—they gone, child.

Mama: Something always told me I wasn't no rich white woman.

Ruth: Well—what are you going to do with it then?

Mama: I ain't rightly decided. (*Thinking. She speaks now with emphasis.*) Some of it got to be put away for Beneatha and her schoolin'—and ain't nothing going to touch that part of it. Nothing. (*She waits several seconds, trying to make up her mind about something, and looks at Ruth a little tentatively before going on.*) Been thinking that we maybe could meet the notes on a little old two-story somewhere, with a yard where Travis could play in the summertime, if we use part of the insurance for a down payment and everybody kind of pitch in. I could maybe take on a little day work again, few days a week—

Ruth (studying her mother-in-law furtively and concentrating on her ironing, anxious to encourage without seeming to): Well, Lord knows, we've put enough rent into this here rat trap to pay for four houses by now . . .

Mama (looking up at the words "rat trap" and then looking around and leaning back and sighing—in a suddenly reflective mood): "Rat trap"—yes, that's all it is. (*Smiling.*) I remember just as well the day me and Big Walter moved in here. Hadn't been married but two weeks and wasn't planning on living here no more than a year. (*She shakes her head at the dissolved dream.*) We was going to set away, little by little, don't you know, and buy a little place out in Morgan Park. We had even picked out the house. (*Chuckling a little.*) Looks right dumpy today. But Lord, child, you should know all the dreams I had 'bout buying that house and fixing it up and making me a little garden in the back—(*She waits and stops smiling.*) And didn't none of it happen. (*Dropping her hands in a futile gesture.*)

Ruth (keeps her head down, ironing): Yes, life can be a barrel of disappointments, sometimes.

Mama: Honey, Big Walter would come in here some nights back then and slump down on that couch there and just look at the rug, and look at me and look at the rug and then back at me—and I'd know he was down then . . . really down. (*After a second very long and thoughtful pause; she is seeing back to times that only she can see.*) And then, Lord, when I lost that baby—little Claude—I almost thought I was going to lose Big Walter too. Oh, that man grieved hisself! He was one man to love his children.

Ruth: Ain't nothin' can tear at you like losin' your baby.

Mama: I guess that's how come that man finally worked hisself to death like he done. Like he was fighting his own war with this here world that took his baby from him.

Ruth: He sure was a fine man, all right. I always liked Mr. Younger.

Mama: Crazy 'bout his children! God knows there was plenty wrong with Walter Younger—hard-headed, mean, kind of wild with women—plenty wrong with him. But he sure loved his children. Always wanted them to have something—be something. That's where Brother gets all these notions, I reckon. Big Walter used to say, he'd get right wet in the eyes sometimes, lean his head back with the water standing in his eyes and say, "Seem like God didn't see fit to give the black man nothing but dreams—but He did give us children to make them dreams seem worth while." *(She smiles.)* He could talk like that, don't you know.

Ruth: Yes, he sure could. He was a good man, Mr. Younger.

Mama: Yes, a fine man—just couldn't never catch up with his dreams, that's all.

(Beneatha comes in, brushing her hair and looking up to the ceiling, where the sound of a vacuum cleaner has started up.)

Beneatha: What could be so dirty on that woman's rugs that she has to vacuum them every single day?

Ruth: I wish certain young women 'round here who I could name would take inspiration about certain rugs in a certain apartment I could also mention.

Beneatha (shrugging): How much cleaning can a house need, for Christ's sakes.

Mama (not liking the Lord's name used thus): Bennie!

Ruth: Just listen to her—just listen!

Beneatha: Oh, God!

Mama: If you use the Lord's name just one more time—

Beneatha (a bit of a whine): Oh, Mama—

Ruth: Fresh—just fresh as salt, this girl!

Beneatha (drily): Well—if the salt loses its savor°—

Mama: Now that will do. I just ain't going to have you 'round here reciting the scriptures in vain—you hear me?

Beneatha: How did I manage to get on everybody's wrong side by just walking into a room?

Ruth: If you weren't so fresh—

Beneatha: Ruth, I'm twenty years old.

Mama: What time you be home from school today?

Beneatha: Kind of late. *(With enthusiasm.)* Madeline is going to start my guitar lessons today.

(Mama and Ruth look up with the same expression.)

Mama: Your *what* kind of lessons?

Beneatha: Guitar.

Ruth: Oh, Father!

Mama: How come you done taken it in your mind to learn to play the guitar?

Beneatha: I just want to, that's all.

Mama (smiling): Lord, child, don't you know what to do with yourself? How long it going to be before you get tired of this now—like you got tired of that little play-acting group you joined last year? *(Looking at Ruth.)* And what was it the year before that?

---

if the salt loses its savor: Beneatha's retort is a reference to the verse from Matthew 5:13—"You are the salt of the earth: but if the salt have lost his savor, wherewith shall it be salted? It is thenceforth good for nothing, but to be cast out . . ."

Ruth: The horseback-riding club for which she bought that fifty-five-dollar riding habit that's been hanging in the closet ever since!

Mama (to Beneatha): Why you got to flit so from one thing to another, baby?

Beneatha (sharply): I just want to learn to play the guitar. Is there anything wrong with that?

Mama: Ain't nobody trying to stop you. I just wonders sometimes why you has to flit so from one thing to another all the time. You ain't never done nothing with all that camera equipment you brought home—

Beneatha: I don't flit! I—I experiment with different forms of expression—

Ruth: Like riding a horse?

Beneatha: —People have to express themselves one way or another.

Mama: What is it you want to express?

Beneatha (angrily): Me! *(Mama and Ruth look at each other and burst into raucous laughter.)* Don't worry—I don't expect you to understand.

Mama (to change the subject): Who you going out with tomorrow night?

Beneatha (with displeasure): George Murchison again.

Mama (pleased): Oh—you getting a little sweet on him?

Ruth: You ask me, this child ain't sweet on nobody but herself—*(Underbreath.)* Express herself! *(They laugh.)*

Beneatha: Oh—I like George all right, Mama. I mean I like him enough to go out with him and stuff, but—

Ruth (for devilment): What does *and stuff* mean?

Beneatha: Mind your own business.

Mama: Stop picking at her now, Ruth. *(She chuckles. A thoughtful pause, and then a suspicious sudden look at her daughter as she turns in her chair for emphasis.)* What DOES it mean?

Beneatha (wearily): Oh, I just mean I couldn't ever really be serious about George. He's—he's so shallow.

Ruth: Shallow—what do you mean he's shallow? He's *rich!*

Mama: Hush, Ruth.

Beneatha: I know he's rich. He knows he's rich, too.

Ruth: Well—what other qualities a man got to have to satisfy you, little girl?

Beneatha: You wouldn't even begin to understand. Anybody who married Walter could not possibly understand.

Mama (outraged): What kind of way is that to talk about your brother?

Beneatha: Brother is a flip—let's face it.

Mama (to Ruth, helplessly): What's a flip?

Ruth (glad to add kindling): She's saying he's crazy.

Beneatha: Not crazy. Brother isn't really crazy yet—he—he's an elaborate neurotic.

Mama: Hush your mouth!

Beneatha: As for George. Well. George looks good—he's got a beautiful car and he takes me to nice places and, as my sister-in-law says, he is probably the richest boy I will ever get to know and I even like him sometimes—but if the Youngers are sitting around waiting to see if their little Bennie is going to tie up the family with the Murchisons, they are wasting their time.

Ruth: You mean you wouldn't marry George Murchison if he asked you someday? That pretty, rich thing? Honey, I knew you was odd—

Beneatha: No I would not marry him if all I felt for him was what I feel now. Besides, George's family wouldn't really like it.

Mama: Why not?

Beneatha: Oh, Mama—The Murchisons are honest-to-God-real-*live*-rich colored people, and the only people in the world who are more snobbish than rich white people are rich colored people. I thought everybody knew that. I've met Mrs. Murchison. She's a scene!

Mama: You must not dislike people 'cause they well off, honey.

Beneatha: Why not? It makes just as much sense as disliking people 'cause they are poor, and lots of people do that.

Ruth (a wisdom-of-the-ages manner. To Mama): Well, she'll get over some of this—

Beneatha: Get over it? What are you talking about, Ruth? Listen, I'm going to be a doctor. I'm not worried about who I'm going to marry yet—if I ever get married.

Mama and Ruth: If!

Mama: Now, Bennie—

Beneatha: Oh, I probably will . . . but first I'm going to be a doctor, and George, for one, still thinks that's pretty funny. I couldn't be bothered with that. I am going to be a doctor and everybody around here better understand that!

Mama (kindly): 'Course you going to be a doctor, honey, God willing.

Beneatha (drily): God hasn't got a thing to do with it.

Mama: Beneatha—that just wasn't necessary.

Beneatha: Well—neither is God. I get sick of hearing about God.

Mama: Beneatha!

Beneatha: I mean it! I'm just tired of hearing about God all the time. What has He got to do with anything? Does He pay tuition?

Mama: You 'bout to get your fresh little jaw slapped!

Ruth: That's just what she needs, all right!

Beneatha: Why? Why can't I say what I want to around here, like everybody else?

Mama: It don't sound nice for a young girl to say things like that—you wasn't brought up that way. Me and your father went to trouble to get you and Brother to church every Sunday.

Beneatha: Mama, you don't understand. It's all a matter of ideas, and God is just one idea I don't accept. It's not important. I am not going out and be immoral or commit crimes because I don't believe in God. I don't even think about it. It's just that I get tired of Him getting credit for all the things the human race achieves through its own stubborn effort. There simply is no blasted God—there is only man and it is *he* who makes miracles!

(Mama absorbs this speech, studies her daughter and rises slowly and crosses to Beneatha and slaps her powerfully across the face. After, there is only silence and the daughter drops her eyes from her mother's face, and Mama is very tall before her.)

Mama: Now—you say after me, in my mother's house there is still God. *(There is a long pause and Beneatha stares at the floor wordlessly. Mama repeats the phrase with precision and cool emotion.)* In my mother's house there is still God.

Beneatha: In my mother's house there is still God.

(A long pause.)

Mama (*walking away from Beneatha, too disturbed for triumphant posture. Stopping and turning back to her daughter*): There are some ideas we ain't going to have in this house. Not long as I am at the head of this family.
Beneatha: Yes, ma'am.

(*Mama walks out of the room.*)

Ruth (*almost gently, with profound understanding*): You think you a woman, Bennie—but you still a little girl. What you did was childish—so you got treated like a child.
Beneatha: I see. (*Quietly.*) I also see that everybody thinks it's all right for Mama to be a tyrant. But all the tyranny in the world will never put a God in the heavens!

(*She picks up her books and goes out. Pause.*)

Ruth (*goes to Mama's door*): She said she was sorry.
Mama (*coming out, going to her plant*): They frightens me, Ruth. My children.
Ruth: You got good children, Lena. They just a little off sometimes—but they're good.
Mama: No—there's something come down between me and them that don't let us understand each other and I don't know what it is. One done almost lost his mind thinking 'bout money all the time and the other done commence to talk about things I can't seem to understand in no form or fashion. What is it that's changing, Ruth?
Ruth (*soothingly, older than her years*): Now . . . you taking it all too seriously. You just got strong-willed children and it takes a strong woman like you to keep 'em in hand.
Mama (*looking at her plant and sprinkling a little water on it*): They spirited all right, my children. Got to admit they got spirit—Bennie and Walter. Like this little old plant that ain't never had enough sunshine or nothing—and look at it . . .

(*She has her back to Ruth, who has had to stop ironing and lean against something and put the back of her hand to her forehead.*)

Ruth (*trying to keep Mama from noticing*): You . . . sure . . . loves that little old thing, don't you? . . .
Mama: Well, I always wanted me a garden like I used to see sometimes at the back of the houses down home. This plant is close as I ever got to having one. (*She looks out of the window as she replaces the plant.*) Lord, ain't nothing as dreary as the view from this window on a dreary day, is there? Why ain't you singing this morning, Ruth? Sing that "No Ways Tired." That song always lifts me up so—(*She turns at last to see that Ruth has slipped quietly to the floor, in a state of semiconsciousness.*) Ruth! Ruth honey—what's the matter with you . . . Ruth!

ACT ONE

SCENE 2

It is the following morning; a Saturday morning, and house cleaning is in progress at the Youngers'. Furniture has been shoved hither and yon and Mama is giving the kitchen-area walls a washing down. Beneatha, in dungarees, with a handkerchief tied around her face, is spraying insecticide into the cracks in the walls. As they work, the radio is on and a Southside disk-jockey program is inappropriately filling the house with a rather exotic saxophone blues. Travis, the sole idle one, is leaning on his arms, looking out of the window.

Travis: Grandmama, that stuff Bennie is using smells awful. Can I go downstairs, please?
Mama: Did you get all them chores done already? I ain't seen you doing much.
Travis: Yes'm—finished early. Where did Mama go this morning?
Mama (looking at Beneatha): She had to go on a little errand.

> *(The phone rings. Beneatha runs to answer it and reaches it before Walter, who has entered from bedroom.)*

Travis: Where?
Mama: To tend to her business.
Beneatha: Haylo . . . *(Disappointed.)* Yes, he is. *(She tosses the phone to Walter, who barely catches it.)* It's Willie Harris again.
Walter (as privately as possible under Mama's gaze): Hello, Willie. Did you get the papers from the lawyer? . . . No, not yet. I told you the mailman doesn't get here till ten-thirty . . . No, I'll come there . . . Yeah! Right away. *(He hangs up and goes for his coat.)*
Beneatha: Brother, where did Ruth go?
Walter (as he exits): How should I know!
Travis: Aw come on, Grandma. Can I go outside?
Mama: Oh, I guess so. You stay right in front of the house, though, and keep a good lookout for the postman.
Travis: Yes'm. *(He darts into bedroom for stickball and bat, reenters, and sees Beneatha on her knees spraying under sofa with behind upraised. He edges closer to the target, takes aim, and lets her have it. She screams.)* Leave them poor little cockroaches alone, they ain't bothering you none! *(He runs as she swings the spraygun at him viciously and playfully.)* Grandma! Grandma!
Mama: Look out there, girl, before you be spilling some of that stuff on that child!
Travis (safely behind the bastion of Mama): That's right—look out, now! *(He exits.)*
Beneatha (drily): I can't imagine that it would hurt him—it has never hurt the roaches.
Mama: Well, little boys' hides ain't as tough as Southside roaches. You better get over there behind the bureau. I seen one marching out of there like Napoleon yesterday.
Beneatha: There's really only one way to get rid of them, Mama—
Mama: How?
Beneatha: Set fire to this building! Mama, where did Ruth go?
Mama (looking at her with meaning): To the doctor, I think.
Beneatha: The doctor? What's the matter? *(They exchange glances.)* You don't think—
Mama (with her sense of drama): Now I ain't saying what I think. But I ain't never been wrong 'bout a woman neither.

> *(The phone rings.)*

Beneatha (at the phone): Hay-lo . . . *(pause, and a moment of recognition)* Well—when did you get back! . . . And how was it? . . . Of course I've missed you—in my way . . . This morning? No . . . house cleaning and all that and Mama hates it if I let people come over when the house is like this . . . You *have?* Well, that's different . . . What is it—Oh, what the hell, come on over . . . Right, see you then. *Arrivederci. (She hangs up.)*
Mama (who has listened vigorously, as is her habit): Who is that you inviting over here with this house looking like this? You ain't got the pride you was born with!

Beneatha: Asagai doesn't care how houses look, Mama—he's an intellectual.
Mama: Who?
Beneatha: Asagai—Joseph Asagai. He's an African boy I met on campus. He's been studying in Canada all summer.
Mama: What's his name?
Beneatha: Asagai, Joseph. Ah-sah-guy . . . He's from Nigeria.
Mama: Oh, that's the little country that was founded by slaves way back . . .
Beneatha: No, Mama—that's Liberia.
Mama: I don't think I never met no African before.
Beneatha: Well, do me a favor and don't ask him a whole lot of ignorant questions about Africans. I mean, do they wear clothes and all that—
Mama: Well, now, I guess if you think we so ignorant 'round here maybe you shouldn't bring your friends here—
Beneatha: It's just that people ask such crazy things. All anyone seems to know about when it comes to Africa is Tarzan—
Mama *(indignantly)*: Why should I know anything about Africa?
Beneatha: Why do you give money at church for the missionary work?
Mama: Well, that's to help save people.
Beneatha: You mean save them from *heathenism*—
Mama *(innocently)*: Yes.
Beneatha: I'm afraid they need more salvation from the British and the French.

(*Ruth comes in forlornly and pulls off her coat with dejection. They both turn to look at her.*)

Ruth *(dispiritedly)*: Well, I guess from all the happy faces—everybody knows.
Beneatha: You pregnant?
Mama: Lord have mercy, I sure hope it's a little old girl. Travis ought to have a sister.

(*Beneatha and Ruth give her a hopeless look for this grandmotherly enthusiasm.*)

Beneatha: How far along are you?
Ruth: Two months.
Beneatha: Did you mean to? I mean did you plan it or was it an accident?
Mama: What do you know about planning or not planning?
Beneatha: Oh, Mama.
Ruth *(wearily)*: She's twenty years old, Lena.
Beneatha: Did you plan it, Ruth?
Ruth: Mind your own business.
Beneatha: It is my business—where is he going to live, on the *roof*? (*There is silence following the remark as the three women react to the sense of it.*) Gee—I didn't mean that, Ruth, honest. Gee, I don't feel like that at all. I—I think it is wonderful.
Ruth *(dully)*: Wonderful.
Beneatha: Yes—really. (*There is a sudden commotion from the street and she goes to the window to look out.*) What on earth is going on out there? These kids. (*There are, as she throws open the window, the shouts of children rising up from the street. She sticks her head out to see better and calls out.*) TRAVIS! TRAVIS! . . . WHAT ARE YOU DOING DOWN THERE? (*She sees.*) Oh Lord, they're chasing a rat!

(*Ruth covers her face with hands and turns away.*)

Mama *(angrily)*: Tell that youngun to get himself up here, at once!
Beneatha: TRAVIS . . . YOU COME UPSTAIRS . . . AT ONCE!
Ruth *(her face twisted)*: Chasing a rat . . .
Mama *(looking at Ruth, worried)*: Doctor say everything going to be all right?
Ruth *(far away)*: Yes—she says everything is going to be fine . . .
Mama *(immediately suspicious)*: "She"—What doctor you went to?

> *(Ruth just looks at Mama meaningfully and Mama opens her mouth to speak as Travis bursts in.)*

Travis *(excited and full of narrative, coming directly to his mother)*: Mama, you should of seen the rat . . . Big as a cat, honest! *(He shows an exaggerated size with his hands.)* Gaaleee, that rat was really cuttin' and Bubber caught him with his heel and the janitor, Mr. Barnett, got him with a stick—and then they got him in a corner and—BAM! BAM! BAM!—and he was still jumping around and bleeding like everything too—there's rat blood all over the street—

> *(Ruth reaches out suddenly and grabs her son without even looking at him and clamps her hand over his mouth and holds him to her. Mama crosses to them rapidly and takes the boy from her.)*

Mama: You hush up now . . . talking all that terrible stuff . . .

> *(Travis is staring at his mother with a stunned expression. Beneatha comes quickly and takes him away from his grandmother and ushers him to the door.)*

Beneatha: You go back outside and play . . . but not with any rats. *(She pushes him gently out the door with the boy straining to see what is wrong with his mother.)*
Mama *(worriedly hovering over Ruth)*: Ruth honey—what's the matter with you—you sick?

> *(Ruth has her fists clenched on her thighs and is fighting hard to suppress a scream that seems to be rising in her.)*

Beneatha: What's the matter with her, Mama?
Mama *(working her fingers in Ruth's shoulders to relax her)*: She be all right. Women gets right depressed sometimes when they get her way. *(Speaking softly, expertly, rapidly.)* Now you just relax. That's right . . . just lean back, don't think 'bout nothing at all . . . nothing at all—
Ruth: I'm all right . . .

> *(The glassy-eyed look melts and then she collapses into a fit of heavy sobbing. The bell rings.)*

Beneatha: Oh, my God—that must be Asagai.
Mama *(to Ruth)*: Come on now, honey. You need to lie down and rest awhile . . . then have some nice hot food.

> *(They exit, Ruth's weight on her mother-in-law. Beneatha, herself profoundly disturbed, opens the door to admit a rather dramatic-looking young man with a large package.)*

Asagai: Hello, Alaiyo—
Beneatha *(holding the door open and regarding him with pleasure)*: Hello . . . *(Long pause.)* Well—come in. And please excuse everything. My mother was very upset about my letting anyone come here with the place like this.

Asagai (coming into the room): You look disturbed too . . . Is something wrong?

Beneatha (still at the door, absently): Yes . . . we've all got acute ghetto-itis. *(She smiles and comes toward him, finding a cigarette and sitting.)* So—sit down! No! Wait! *(She whips the spray gun off sofa where she had left it and puts the cushions back. At last perches on arm of sofa. He sits.)* So, how was Canada?

Asagai (a sophisticate): Canadian.

Beneatha (looking at him): Asagai, I'm very glad you are back.

Asagai (looking back at her in turn): Are you really?

Beneatha: Yes—very.

Asagai: Why?—you were quite glad when I went away. What happened?

Beneatha: You went away.

Asagai: Ahhhhhhh.

Beneatha: Before—you wanted to be so serious before there was time.

Asagai: How much time must there be before one knows what one feels?

Beneatha (stalling this particular conversation. Her hands pressed together, in a deliberately childish gesture): What did you bring me?

Asagai (handing her the package): Open it and see.

Beneatha (eagerly opening the package and drawing out some records and the colorful robes of a Nigerian woman): Oh, Asagai! . . . You got them for me! . . . How beautiful . . . and the records too! *(She lifts out the robes and runs to the mirror with them and holds the drapery up in front of herself.)*

Asagai (coming to her at the mirror): I shall have to teach you how to drape it properly. *(He flings the material about her for the moment and stands back to look at her.)* Ah—Oh-pay-gay-day, oh-gbah-mu-shay. *(A Yoruba exclamation for admiration.)* You wear it well . . . very well . . . mutilated hair and all.

Beneatha (turning suddenly): My hair—what's wrong with my hair?

Asagai (shrugging): Were you born with it like that?

Beneatha (reaching up to touch it): No . . . of course not. *(She looks back to the mirror, disturbed.)*

Asagai (smiling): How then?

Beneatha: You know perfectly well how . . . as crinkly as yours . . . that's how.

Asagai: And it is ugly to you that way?

Beneatha (quickly): Oh, no—not ugly . . . *(More slowly, apologetically.)* But it's so hard to manage when it's, well—raw.

Asagai: And so to accommodate that—you mutilate it every week?

Beneatha: It's not mutilation!

Asagai (laughing aloud at her seriousness): Oh . . . please! I am only teasing you because you are so very serious about these things. *(He stands back from her and folds his arms across his chest as he watches her pulling at her hair and frowning in the mirror.)* Do you remember the first time you met me at school? . . . *(He laughs.)* You came up to me and you said—and I thought you were the most serious little thing I had ever seen—you said: *(He imitates her.)* "Mr. Asagai—I want very much to talk with you. About Africa. You see, Mr. Asagai, I am looking for my *identity!*"

(He laughs.)

Beneatha (turning to him, not laughing): Yes—*(Her face is quizzical, profoundly disturbed.)*

Asagai (still teasing and reaching out and taking her face in his hands and turning her profile to him): Well . . . it is true that this is not so much a profile of a Hollywood queen as perhaps a queen of the Nile—(*A mock dismissal of the importance of the question.*) But what does it matter? Assimilationism is so popular in your country.

Beneatha (wheeling, passionately, sharply): I am not an assimilationist!

Asagai (the protest hangs in the room for a moment and Asagai studies her, his laughter fading): Such a serious one. (*There is a pause.*) So—you like the robes? You must take excellent care of them—they are from my sister's personal wardrobe.

Beneatha (with incredulity): You—you sent all the way home—for me?

Asagai (with charm): For you—I would do much more . . . Well, that is what I came for. I must go.

Beneatha: Will you call me Monday?

Asagai: Yes . . . We have a great deal to talk about. I mean about identity and time and all that.

Beneatha: Time?

Asagai: Yes. About how much time one needs to know what one feels.

Beneatha: You see! You never understood that there is more than one kind of feeling which can exist between a man and a woman—or, at least, there should be.

Asagai (shaking his head negatively but gently): No. Between a man and a woman there need be only one kind of feeling. I have that for you . . . Now even . . . right this moment . . .

Beneatha: I know—and by itself—it won't do. I can find that anywhere.

Asagai: For a woman it should be enough.

Beneatha: I know—because that's what it says in all the novels that men write. But it isn't. Go ahead and laugh—but I'm not interested in being someone's little episode in America or—(*with feminine vengeance*)—one of them! (*Asagai has burst into laughter again.*) That's funny as hell, huh!

Asagai: It's just that every American girl I have known has said that to me. White— black—in this you are all the same. And the same speech, too!

Beneatha (angrily): Yuk, yuk, yuk!

Asagai: It's how you can be sure that the world's most liberated women are not liberated at all. You all talk about it too much!

(*Mama enters and is immediately all social charm because of the presence of a guest.*)

Beneatha: Oh—Mama—this is Mr. Asagai.

Mama: How do you do?

Asagai (total politeness to an elder): How do you do, Mrs. Younger. Please forgive me for coming at such an outrageous hour on a Saturday.

Mama: Well, you are quite welcome. I just hope you understand that our house don't always look like this. (*Chatterish.*) You must come again. I would love to hear all about—(*Not sure of the name.*)—your country. I think it's so sad the way our American Negroes don't know nothing about Africa 'cept Tarzan and all that. And all that money they pour into these churches when they ought to be helping you people over there drive out them French and Englishmen done taken away your land.

(*The mother flashes a slightly superior look at her daughter upon completion of the recitation.*)

Asagai (taken aback by this sudden and acutely unrelated expression of sympathy): Yes . . . yes . . .

Mama (smiling at him suddenly and relaxing and looking him over): How many miles is it from here to where you come from?
Asagai: Many thousands.
Mama (looking at him as she would Walter): I bet you don't half look after yourself, being away from your mama either. I spec you better come 'round here from time to time to get yourself some decent homecooked meals . . .
Asagai (moved): Thank you. Thank you very much. *(They are all quiet, then:)* Well . . . I must go. I will call you Monday, Alaiyo.
Mama: What's that he call you?
Asagai: Oh—"Alaiyo." I hope you don't mind. It is what you would call a nickname, I think. It is a Yoruba word. I am a Yoruba.
Mama (looking at Beneatha): I—I thought he was from—*(Uncertain.)*
Asagai (understanding): Nigeria is my country. Yoruba is my tribal origin—
Beneatha: You didn't tell us what Alaiyo means . . . for all I know, you might be calling me Little Idiot or something . . .
Asagai: Well . . . let me see . . . I do not know how just to explain it. . . . The sense of a thing can be so different when it changes languages.
Beneatha: You're evading.
Asagai: No—really it is difficult . . . *(Thinking.)* It means . . . it means One for Whom Bread—Food—Is Not Enough. *(He looks at her.)* Is that all right?
Beneatha (understanding, softly): Thank you.
Mama (looking from one to the other and not understanding any of it): Well . . . that's nice . . . You must come see us again—Mr.—
Asagai: Ah-sah-guy . . .
Mama: Yes . . . Do come again.
Asagai: Good-bye. *(He exits.)*
Mama (after him): Lord, that's a pretty thing just went out here!*(Insinuatingly, to her daughter.)* Yes, I guess I see why we done commence to get so interested in Africa 'round here. Missionaries my aunt Jenny! *(She exits.)*
Beneatha: Oh, Mama! . . .

(She picks up the Nigerian dress and holds it up to her in front of the mirror again. She sets the headdress on haphazardly and then notices her hair again and clutches at it and then replaces the headdress and frowns at herself. Then she starts to wriggle in front of the mirror as she thinks a Nigerian woman might. Travis enters and stands regarding her.)

Travis: What's the matter, girl, you cracking up?
Beneatha: Shut up.

(She pulls the headdress off and looks at herself in the mirror and clutches at her hair again and squinches her eyes as if trying to imagine something. Then, suddenly, she gets her raincoat and kerchief and hurriedly prepares for going out.)

Mama (coming back into the room): She's resting now. Travis, baby, run next door and ask Miss Johnson to please let me have a little kitchen cleanser. This here can is empty as Jacob's kettle.°

Jacob's kettle: an allusion to Genesis 25:29-34, where the hungry Esau sells his birthright to his twin brother Jacob in return for all the stew in his pot or "kettle."

Travis: I just came in.
Mama: Do as you told. *(He exits and she looks at her daughter.)* Where you going?
Beneatha (halting at the door): To become a queen of the Nile!

(She exits in a breathless blaze of glory. Ruth appears in the bedroom doorway.)

Mama: Who told you to get up?
Ruth: Ain't nothing wrong with me to be lying in no bed for. Where did Bennie go?
Mama (drumming her fingers): Far as I could make out—to Egypt. *(Ruth just looks at her.)* What time is it getting to?
Ruth: Ten twenty. And the mailman going to ring that bell this morning just like he done every morning for the last umpteen years.

(Travis comes in with the cleanser can.)

Travis: She say to tell you that she don't have much.
Mama (angrily): Lord, some people I could name sure is tight-fisted! *(Directing her grandson.)* Mark two cans of cleanser down on the list there. If she that hard up for kitchen cleanser, I sure don't want to forget to get her none!
Ruth: Lena—maybe the woman is just short on cleanser—
Mama (not listening): Much baking powder as she done borrowed from me all these years, she could of done gone into the baking business!

(The bell sounds suddenly and sharply and all three are stunned—serious and silent—mid-speech. In spite of all the other conversations and distractions of the morning, this is what they have been waiting for, even Travis, who looks helplessly from his mother to his grandmother. Ruth is the first to come to life again.)

Ruth (to Travis): Get down them steps, boy!

(Travis snaps to life and flies out to get the mail.)

Mama (her eyes wide, her hand to her breast): You mean it done really come?
Ruth (excited): Oh, Miss Lena!
Mama (collecting herself): Well . . . I don't know what we all so excited about 'round here for. We known it was coming for months.
Ruth: That's a whole lot different from having it come and being able to hold it in your hands . . . a piece of paper worth ten thousand dollars . . .

(Travis bursts back into the room. He holds the envelope high above his head, like a little dancer, his face is radiant and he is breathless. He moves to his grandmother with sudden slow ceremony and puts the envelope into her hands. She accepts it, and then merely holds it and looks at it.)

Come on! Open it . . . Lord have mercy, I wish Walter Lee was here!

Travis: Open it, Grandmama!
Mama (staring at it): Now you all be quiet. It's just a check.
Ruth: Open it . . .
Mama (still staring at it): Now don't act silly . . . We ain't never been no people to act silly 'bout no money—
Ruth (swiftly): We ain't never had none before—OPEN IT!

(Mama finally makes a good strong tear and pulls out the thin blue slice of paper and inspects it closely. The boy and his mother study it raptly over Mama's shoulders.)

Mama: Travis! *(She is counting off with doubt.)* Is that the right number of zeros?

Travis: Yes'm . . . ten thousand dollars. Gaalee, Grandmama, you rich.

Mama *(she holds the check away from her, still looking at it. Slowly her face sobers into a mask of unhappiness)*: Ten thousand dollars. *(She hands it to Ruth.)* Put it away somewhere, Ruth. *(She does not look at Ruth; her eyes seem to be seeing something somewhere very far off.)* Ten thousand dollars they give you. Ten thousand dollars.

Travis *(to his mother, sincerely)*: What's the matter with Grandmama—don't she want to be rich?

Ruth *(distractedly)*: You go on out and play now, baby. *(Travis exits. Mama starts wiping dishes absently, humming intently to herself. Ruth turns to her, with kind exasperation.)* You've gone and got yourself upset.

Mama *(not looking at her)*: I spec if it wasn't for you all . . . I would just put that money away or give it to the church or something.

Ruth: Now what kind of talk is that. Mr. Younger would just be plain mad if he could hear you talking foolish like that.

Mama *(stopping and staring off)*: Yes . . . he sure would. *(Sighing.)* We got enough to do with that money, all right. *(She halts then, and turns and looks at her daughter-in-law hard; Ruth avoids her eyes and Mama wipes her hands with finality and starts to speak firmly to Ruth.)* Where did you go today, girl?

Ruth: To the doctor.

Mama *(impatiently)*: Now, Ruth . . . you know better than that. Old Doctor Jones is strange enough in his way but there ain't nothing 'bout him make somebody slip and call him "she"—like you done this morning.

Ruth: Well, that's what happened—my tongue slipped.

Mama: You went to see that woman, didn't you?

Ruth *(defensively, giving herself away)*: What woman you talking about?

Mama *(angrily)*: That woman who—

(Walter enters in great excitement.)

Walter: Did it come?

Mama *(quietly)*: Can't you give people a Christian greeting before you start asking about money?

Walter *(to Ruth)*: Did it come? *(Ruth unfolds the check and lays it quietly before him, watching him intently with thoughts of her own. Walter sits down and grasps it close and counts off the zeros.)* Ten thousand dollars—*(He turns suddenly, frantically to his mother and draws some papers out of his breast pocket.)* Mama—look. Old Willy Harris put everything on paper—

Mama: Son—I think you ought to talk to your wife . . . I'll go on out and leave you alone if you want—

Walter: I can talk to her later—Mama, look—

Mama: Son—

Walter: WILL SOMEBODY PLEASE LISTEN TO ME TODAY!

Mama (quietly): I don't 'low no yellin' in this house, Walter Lee, and you know it— (*Walter stares at them in frustration and starts to speak several times.*) And there ain't going to be no investing in no liquor stores.

Walter: But, Mama, you ain't even looked at it.

Mama: I don't aim to have to speak on that again.

(*A long pause.*)

Walter: You ain't looked at it and you don't aim to have to speak on that again? You ain't even looked at it and *you* have decided—(*Crumpling his papers.*) Well, you tell that to my boy tonight when you put him to sleep on the living-room couch . . . (*Turning to Mama and speaking directly to her.*) Yeah—and tell it to my wife, Mama, tomorrow when she has to go out of here to look after somebody else's kids. And tell it to me, Mama, every time we need a new pair of curtains and I have to watch you go out and work in somebody's kitchen. Yeah, you tell me then! (*Walter starts out.*)

Ruth: Where you going?

Walter: I'm going out!

Ruth: Where?

Walter: Just out of this house somewhere—

Ruth (getting her coat): I'll come too.

Walter: I don't want you to come!

Ruth: I got something to talk to you about, Walter.

Walter: That's too bad.

Mama (still quietly): Walter Lee—(*She waits and he finally turns and looks at her.*) Sit down.

Walter: I'm a grown man, Mama.

Mama: Ain't nobody said you wasn't grown. But you still in my house and my presence. And as long as you are—you'll talk to your wife civil. Now sit down.

Ruth (suddenly): Oh, let him go on out and drink himself to death! He makes me sick to my stomach! (*She flings her coat against him and exits to bedroom.*)

Walter (violently flinging the coat after her): And you turn mine too, baby! (*The door slams behind her.*) That was my biggest mistake—

Mama (still quietly): Walter, what is the matter with you?

Walter: Matter with me? Ain't nothing the matter with *me!*

Mama: Yes there is. Something eating you up like a crazy man. Something more than me not giving you this money. The past few years I been watching it happen to you. You get all nervous acting and kind of wild in the eyes—(*Walter jumps up impatiently at her words.*) I said sit there now, I'm talking to you!

Walter: Mama—I don't need no nagging at me today.

Mama: Seem like you getting to a place where you always tied up in some kind of knot about something. But if anybody ask you 'bout it you just yell at 'em and bust out the house and go out and drink somewheres. Walter Lee, people can't live with that. Ruth's a good, patient girl in her way—but you getting to be too much. Boy, don't make the mistake of driving that girl away from you.

Walter: Why—what she do for me?

Mama: She loves you.

Walter: Mama—I'm going out. I want to go off somewhere and be by myself for a while.

Mama: I'm sorry 'bout your liquor store, son. It just wasn't the thing for us to do. That's what I want to tell you about—

Walter: I got to go out, Mama—*(He rises.)*

Mama: It's dangerous, son.

Walter: What's dangerous?

Mama: When a man goes outside his home to look for peace.

Walter (beseechingly): Then why can't there never be no peace in this house then?

Mama: You done found it in some other house?

Walter: No—there ain't no woman! Why do women always think there's a woman somewhere when a man gets restless. *(Picks up the check.)* Do you know what this money means to me? Do you know what this money can do for us? *(Puts it back.)* Mama—Mama—I want so many things . . .

Mama: Yes, son—

Walter: I want so many things that they are driving me kind of crazy . . . Mama—look at me.

Mama: I'm looking at you. You a good-looking boy. You got a job, a nice wife, a fine boy and—

Walter: A job. *(Looks at her.)* Mama, a job? I open and close car doors all day long. I drive a man around in his limousine and I say, "Yes, sir; no, sir; very good, sir; shall I take the Drive, sir?" Mama, that ain't no kind of job . . . that ain't nothing at all. *(Very quietly.)* Mama, I don't know if I can make you understand.

Mama: Understand what, baby?

Walter (quietly): Sometimes it's like I can see the future stretched out in front of me—just plain as day. The future, Mama. Hanging over there at the edge of my days. Just waiting for me—a big, looming blank space—full of *nothing*. Just waiting for *me*. But it don't have to be. *(Pause. Kneeling beside her chair.)* Mama—sometimes when I'm downtown and I pass them cool, quiet-looking restaurants where them white boys are sitting back and talking 'bout things . . . sitting there turning deals worth millions of dollars . . . sometimes I see guys don't look much older than me—

Mama: Son—how come you talk so much 'bout money?

Walter (with immense passion): Because it is life, Mama!

Mama (quietly): Oh—*(Very quietly.)* So now it's life. Money is life. Once upon a time freedom used to be life—now it's money. I guess the world really do change . . .

Walter: No—it was always money, Mama. We just didn't know about it.

Mama: No . . . something has changed. *(She looks at him.)* You something new, boy. In my time we was worried about not being lynched and getting to the North if we could and how to stay alive and still have a pinch of dignity too . . . Now here come you and Beneatha—talking 'bout things we ain't never even thought about hardly, me and your daddy. You ain't satisfied or proud of nothing we done. I mean that you had a home; that we kept you out of trouble till you was grown; that you don't have to ride to work on the back of nobody's streetcar—You my children—but how different we done become.

Walter (a long beat. He pats her hand and gets up): You just don't understand, Mama, you just don't understand.

Mama: Son—do you know your wife is expecting another baby? *(Walter stands, stunned, and absorbs what his mother has said.)* That's what she wanted to talk to you about. (*Walter sinks down into a chair.*) This ain't for me to be telling—but you ought to know. (*She waits.*) I think Ruth is thinking 'bout getting rid of that child.

Walter (slowly understanding): No—no—Ruth wouldn't do that.

Mama: When the world gets ugly enough—a woman will do anything for her family. The part that's already living.

Walter: You don't know Ruth, Mama, if you think she would do that.

(*Ruth opens the bedroom door and stands there a little limp.*)

Ruth (beaten): Yes I would too, Walter. (*Pause.*) I gave her a five-dollar down payment.

(*There is total silence as the man stares at his wife and the mother stares at her son.*)

Mama (presently): Well—(*Tightly.*) Well—son, I'm waiting to hear you say something . . . (*She waits.*) I'm waiting to hear how you be your father's son. Be the man he was . . . (*Pause. The silence shouts.*) Your wife say she going to destroy your child. And I'm waiting to hear you talk like him and say we a people who give children life, not who destroys them—(*She rises.*) I'm waiting to see you stand up and look like your daddy and say we done give up one baby to poverty and that we ain't going to give up nary another one . . . I'm waiting.

Walter: Ruth—(*He can say nothing.*)

Mama: If you a son of mine, tell her! (*Walter picks up his keys and his coat and walks out. She continues, bitterly.*) You . . . you are a disgrace to your father's memory. Somebody get me my hat!

ACT TWO

SCENE 1

TIME. *Later the same day*

AT RISE. *Ruth is ironing again. She has the radio going. Presently Beneatha's bedroom door opens and Ruth's mouth falls and she puts down the iron in fascination.*

Ruth: What have we got on tonight!

Beneatha (emerging grandly from the doorway so that we can see her thoroughly robed in the costume Asagai brought): You are looking at what a well-dressed Nigerian woman wears—

(*She parades for Ruth, her hair completely hidden by the headdress; she is coquettishly fanning herself with an ornate oriental fan, mistakenly more like Butterfly° than any Nigerian that ever was.*)

Isn't it beautiful? (*She promenades to the radio and, with an arrogant flourish, turns off the good loud blues that is playing.*) Enough of this assimilationist junk!

Butterfly: the lead character of *Madama Butterfly* (1904), Giacomo Puccini's (1858–1924) famous tragic opera about a Japanese woman abandoned by her American husband.

(*Ruth follows her with her eyes as she goes to the phonograph and puts on a record and turns and waits ceremoniously for the music to come up. Then, with a shout—*) OCOMOGOSIAY!

(*Ruth jumps. The music comes up, a lovely Nigerian melody. Beneatha listens, enraptured, her eyes far away—"back to the past." She begins to dance. Ruth is dumfounded.*)

Ruth: What kind of dance is that?
Beneatha: A folk dance.
Ruth (*Pearl Bailey°*): What kind of folks do that, honey?
Beneatha: It's from Nigeria. It's a dance of welcome.
Ruth: Who you welcoming?
Beneatha: The men back to the village.
Ruth: Where they been?
Beneatha: How should I know—out hunting or something. Anyway, they are coming back now . . .
Ruth: Well, that's good.
Beneatha (*with the record*):

Alundi, alundi
Alundi alunya
Jop pu a jeepua
Ang gu sooooooooooo

Ai yai yae . . .
Ayehaye—alundi . . .

(*Walter comes in during this performance; he has obviously been drinking. He leans against the door heavily and watches his sister, at first with distaste. Then his eyes look off—"back to the past"—as he lifts both his fists to the roof, screaming.*)

Walter: YEAH . . . AND ETHIOPIA STRETCH FORTH HER HANDS AGAIN! . . .
Ruth (*drily, looking at him*): Yes—and Africa sure is claiming her own tonight. (*She gives them both up and starts ironing again.*)
Walter (*all in a drunken, dramatic shout*): Shut up! . . . I'm digging them drums . . . them drums move me! . . . (*He makes his weaving way to his wife's face and leans in close to her.*) In my heart of hearts—(*He thumps his chest.*)—I am much warrior!
Ruth (*without even looking up*): In your heart of hearts you are much drunkard.
Walter (*coming away from her and starting to wander around the room, shouting*): Me and Jomo° . . . (*Intently, in his sister's face. She has stopped dancing to watch him in this unknown mood.*) That's my man, Kenyatta. (*Shouting and thumping his chest.*) FLAMING SPEAR! HOT DAMN! (*He is suddenly in possession of an imaginary spear and actively spearing enemies all over the room.*) OCOMOGOSIAY . . .
Beneatha (*to encourage Walter, thoroughly caught up with this side of him*): OCOMOGOSIAY, FLAMING SPEAR!

Pearl Bailey: Pearl Mae Bailey (1918–1990) was an American entertainer known for her singing voice and larger-than-life personality.   Jomo: Jomo Kenyatta (1893?-1978) was a famous African political leader and the first president of Kenya (1964–78).

Walter: THE LION IS WAKING . . . OWIMOWEH!° *(He pulls his shirt open and leaps up on the table and gestures with his spear.)*
Beneatha: OWIMOWEH!
Walter (on the table, very far gone, his eyes pure glass sheets. He sees what we cannot, that he is a leader of his people, a great chief, a descendant of Chaka,° and that the hour to march has come): Listen, my black brothers—
Beneatha: OCOMOGOSIAY!
Walter: —Do you hear the waters rushing against the shores of the coastlands—
Beneatha: OCOMOGOSIAY!
Walter: —Do you hear the screeching of the cocks in yonder hills beyond where the chiefs meet in council for the coming of the mighty war—
Beneatha: OCOMOGOSIAY!

(And now the lighting shifts subtly to suggest the world of Walter's imagination, and the mood shifts from pure comedy. It is the inner Walter speaking: the Southside chauffeur has assumed an unexpected majesty.)

Walter: —Do you hear the beating of the wings of the birds flying low over the mountains and the low places of our land—
Beneatha: OCOMOGOSIAY!
Walter: —Do you hear the singing of the women, singing the war songs of our fathers to the babies in the great houses? Singing the sweet war songs! *(The doorbell rings.)* OH, DO YOU HEAR, MY BLACK BROTHERS!
Beneatha (completely gone): We hear you, Flaming Spear—

(Ruth shuts off the phonograph and opens the door. George Murchison enters.)

Walter: Telling us to prepare for the GREATNESS OF THE TIME! *(Lights back to normal. He turns and sees George.)* Black Brother! *(He extends his hand for the fraternal clasp.)*
George: Black Brother, hell!
Ruth (having had enough, and embarrassed for the family): Beneatha, you got company—what's the matter with you? Walter Lee Younger, get down off that table and stop acting like a fool . . .

(Walter comes down off the table suddenly and makes a quick exit to the bathroom.)

Ruth: He's had a little to drink . . . I don't know what her excuse is.
George (to Beneatha): Look honey, we're going to the theatre—we're not going to be in it . . . so go change, huh?

(Beneatha looks at him and slowly, ceremoniously, lifts her hands and pulls off the headdress. Her hair is close-cropped and unstraightened. George freezes mid-sentence and Ruth's eyes all but fall out of her head.)

George: What in the name of—

THE LION IS WAKING . . . OWIMOWEH: Walter is referring to the popular pop song "The Lion Sleeps Tonight," whose chorus keeps repeating "Owimoweh." The song, originally recorded by the South African singer Solomon Linda, has been covered by many artists, and became even more popular when used in Disney's *The Lion King*.   Chaka: or Shaka (1785?-1828), was a famous Zulu warrior and chieftain.

Ruth (*touching Beneatha's hair*): Girl, you done lost your natural mind!? Look at your head!

George: What have you done to your head—I mean your hair!

Beneatha: Nothing—except cut it off.

Ruth: Now that's the truth—it's what ain't been done to it! You expect this boy to go out with you with your head all nappy like that?

Beneatha (*looking at George*): That's up to George. If he's ashamed of his heritage—

George: Oh, don't be so proud of yourself, Bennie—just because you look eccentric.

Beneatha: How can something that's natural be eccentric?

George: That's what being eccentric means—being natural. Get dressed.

Beneatha: I don't like that, George.

Ruth: Why must you and your brother make an argument out of everything people say?

Beneatha: Because I hate assimilationist Negroes!

Ruth: Will somebody please tell me what assimila-whoever means!

George: Oh, it's just a college girl's way of calling people Uncle Toms—but that isn't what it means at all.

Ruth: Well, what does it mean?

Beneatha (*cutting George off and staring at him as she replies to Ruth.*) It means someone who is willing to give up his own culture and submerge himself completely in the dominant, and in this case *oppressive,* culture!

George: Oh, dear, dear, dear! Here we go! A lecture on the African past! On our Great West African Heritage! In one second we will hear all about the great Ashanti empires; the great Songhay civilizations; and the great sculpture of Bénin—and then some poetry in the Bantu—and the whole monologue will end with the word *heritage!* (*Nastily.*) Let's face it, baby, your heritage is nothing but a bunch of raggedy-assed spirituals and some grass huts!

Beneatha: GRASS HUTS! (*Ruth crosses to her and forcibly pushes her toward the bedroom.*) See there . . . you are standing there in your splendid ignorance talking about people who were the first to smelt iron on the face of the earth! (*Ruth is pushing her through the door.*) The Ashanti were performing surgical operations when the English—(*Ruth pulls the door to, with Beneatha on the other side, and smiles graciously at George. Beneatha opens the door and shouts the end of the sentence defiantly at George.*)—were still tatooing themselves with blue dragons! (*She goes back inside.*)

Ruth: Have a seat, George. (*They both sit. Ruth folds her hands rather primly on her lap, determined to demonstrate the civilization of the family.*) Warm, ain't it? I mean for September. (*Pause.*) Just like they always say about Chicago weather: If it's too hot or cold for you, just wait a minute and it'll change. (*She smiles happily at this cliché of clichés.*) Everybody say it's got to do with them bombs and things they keep setting off. (*Pause.*) Would you like a nice cold beer?

George: No, thank you. I don't care for beer. (*He looks at his watch.*) I hope she hurries up.

Ruth: What time is the show?

George: It's an eight-thirty curtain. That's just Chicago, though. In New York standard curtain time is eight forty. (*He is rather proud of this knowledge.*)

Ruth (*properly appreciating it*): You get to New York a lot?

George (offhand): Few times a year.

Ruth: Oh—that's nice. I've never been to New York.

>   (*Walter enters. We feel he has relieved himself, but the edge of unreality is still with him.*)

Walter: New York ain't got nothing Chicago ain't. Just a bunch of hustling people all squeezed up together—being "Eastern." (*He turns his face into a screw of displeasure.*)

George: Oh—you've been?

Walter: Plenty of times.

Ruth (shocked at the lie): Walter Lee Younger!

Walter (staring her down): Plenty! (*Pause.*) What we got to drink in this house? Why don't you offer this man some refreshment. (*To George.*) They don't know how to entertain people in this house, man.

George: Thank you—I don't really care for anything.

Walter (feeling his head; sobriety coming.) Where's Mama?

Ruth: She ain't come back yet.

Walter (looking Murchison over from head to toe, scrutinizing his carefully casual tweed sports jacket over cashmere V-neck sweater over soft eyelet shirt and tie, and soft slacks, finished off with white buckskin shoes): Why all you college boys wear them faggoty-looking white shoes?

Ruth: Walter Lee!

>   (*George Murchison ignores the remark.*)

Walter (to Ruth): Well, they look crazy as hell—white shoes, cold as it is.

Ruth (crushed): You have to excuse him—

Walter: No he don't! Excuse me for what? What you always excusing me for! I'll excuse myself when I needs to be excused! (*A pause.*) They look as funny as them black knee socks Beneatha wears out of here all the time.

Ruth: It's the college *style*, Walter.

Walter: Style, hell. She looks like she got burnt legs or something!

Ruth: Oh, Walter—

Walter (an irritable mimic): Oh, Walter! Oh, Walter! (*To Murchison.*) How's your old man making out? I understand you all going to buy that big hotel on the Drive? (*He finds a beer in the refrigerator, wanders over to Murchison, sipping and wiping his lips with the back of his hand, and straddling a chair backwards to talk to the other man.*) Shrewd move. Your old man is all right, man. (*Tapping his head and half winking for emphasis.*) I mean he knows how to operate. I mean he thinks *big*, you know what I mean, I mean for a *home*, you know? But I think he's kind of running out of ideas now. I'd like to talk to him. Listen, man, I got some plans that could turn this city upside down. I mean think like he does. *Big*. Invest big, gamble big, hell, lose *big* if you have to, you know what I mean. It's hard to find a man on this whole Southside who understands my kind of thinking—you dig? (*He scrutinizes Murchison again, drinks his beer, squints his eyes and leans in close, confidential, man to man.*) Me and you ought to sit down and talk sometimes, man. Man, I got me some ideas . . .

Murchison (with boredom): Yeah—sometimes we'll have to do that, Walter.

Walter (understanding the indifference, and offended): Yeah—well, when you get the time, man. I know you a busy little boy.
Ruth: Walter, please—
Walter (bitterly, hurt): I know ain't nothing in this world as busy as you colored college boys with your fraternity pins and white shoes . . .
Ruth (covering her face with humiliation): Oh, Walter Lee—
Walter: I see you all the time—with the books tucked under your arms—going to your *(British A—a mimic.)* "clahsses." And for what! What the hell you learning over there! Filling up your heads—*(counting off on his fingers)*—with the sociology and the psychology—but they teaching you how to be a man? How to take over and run the world? They teaching you how to run a rubber plantation or a steel mill? Naw—just to talk proper and read books and wear them faggoty-looking white shoes . . .
George (looking at him with distaste, a little above it all): You're all wacked up with bitterness, man.
Walter (intently, almost quietly, between the teeth, glaring at the boy): And you—ain't you bitter, man? Ain't you just about had it yet? Don't you see no stars gleaming that you can't reach out and grab? You happy?—You contented son-of-a-bitch—you happy? You got it made? Bitter? Man, I'm a volcano. Bitter? Here I am a giant—surrounded by ants! Ants who can't even understand what it is the giant is talking about.
Ruth (passionately and suddenly): Oh, Walter—ain't you with nobody!
Walter (violently): No! 'Cause ain't nobody with me! Not even my own mother!
Ruth: Walter, that's a terrible thing to say!

(Beneatha enters, dressed for the evening in a cocktail dress and earrings, hair natural.)

George: Well—hey—*(Crosses to Beneatha; thoughtful, with emphasis, since this is a reversal.)* You look great!
Walter (seeing his sister's hair for the first time): What's the matter with your head?
Beneatha (tired of the jokes now): I cut it off, Brother.
Walter (coming close to inspect it and walking around her): Well, I'll be damned. So that's what they mean by the African bush . . .
Beneatha: Ha ha. Let's go, George.
George (looking at her): You know something? I like it. It's sharp. I mean it really is. *(Helps her into her wrap.)*
Ruth: Yes—I think so, too. *(She goes to the mirror and starts to clutch at her hair.)*
Walter: Oh no! You leave yours alone, baby. You might turn out to have a pin-shaped head or something!
Beneatha: See you all later.
Ruth: Have a nice time.
George: Thanks. Good night. *(Half out the door, he reopens it. To Walter.)* Good night, Prometheus!°

(Beneatha and George exit.)

Walter (to Ruth): Who is Prometheus?

Prometheus: in Greek legend, the god who gave the secret of fire to humanity.

Ruth: I don't know. Don't worry about it.
Walter (in fury, pointing after George): See there—they get to a point where they can't insult you man to man—they got to go talk about something ain't nobody never heard of!
Ruth: How do you know it was an insult? *(To humor him.)* Maybe Prometheus is a nice fellow.
Walter: Prometheus! I bet there ain't even no such thing! I bet that simple-minded clown—
Ruth: Walter—*(She stops what she is doing and looks at him.)*
Walter (yelling): Don't start!
Ruth: Start what?
Walter: Your nagging! Where was I? Who was I with? How much money did I spend?
Ruth (plaintively): Walter Lee—why don't we just try to talk about it . . .
Walter (not listening): I been out talking with people who understand me. People who care about the things I got on my mind.
Ruth (wearily): I guess that means people like Willy Harris.
Walter: Yes, people like Willy Harris.
Ruth (with a sudden flash of impatience): Why don't you all just hurry up and go into the banking business and stop talking about it!
Walter: Why? You want to know why? 'Cause we all tied up in a race of people that don't know how to do nothing but moan, pray and have babies!

(The line is too bitter even for him and he looks at her and sits down.)

Ruth: Oh, Walter . . . *(Softly.)* Honey, why can't you stop fighting me?
Walter (without thinking): Who's fighting you? Who even cares about you? *(This line begins the retardation of his mood.)*
Ruth: Well—*(She waits a long time, and then with resignation starts to put away her things.)* I guess I might as well go on to bed . . . *(More or less to herself.)* I don't know where we lost it . . . but we have . . . *(Then, to him.)* I—I'm sorry about this new baby, Walter. I guess maybe I better go on and do what I started . . . I guess I just didn't realize how bad things was with us . . . I guess I just didn't really realize—*(She starts out to the bedroom and stops.)* You want some hot milk?
Walter: Hot milk?
Ruth: Yes—hot milk.
Walter: Why hot milk?
Ruth: 'Cause after all that liquor you come home with you ought to have something hot in your stomach.
Walter: I don't want no milk.
Ruth: You want some coffee then?
Walter: No, I don't want no coffee. I don't want nothing hot to drink.*(Almost plaintively.)* Why you always trying to give me something to eat?
Ruth (standing and looking at him helplessly): What else can I give you, Walter Lee Younger?

(She stands and looks at him and presently turns to go out again. He lifts his head and watches her going away from him in a new mood which began to emerge when he asked her "Who even cares about you?")

Walter: It's been rough, ain't it, baby? (*She hears and stops but does not turn around and he continues to her back.*) I guess between two people there ain't never as much understood as folks generally thinks there is. I mean like between me and you— (*She turns to face him.*) How we gets to the place where we scared to talk softness to each other. (*He waits, thinking hard himself.*) Why you think it got to be like that? (*He is thoughtful, almost as a child would be.*) Ruth, what is it gets into people ought to be close?

Ruth: I don't know, honey. I think about it a lot.

Walter: On account of you and me, you mean? The way things are with us. The way something done come down between us.

Ruth: There ain't so much between us, Walter . . . Not when you come to me and try to talk to me. Try to be with me . . . a little even.

Walter (total honesty): Sometimes . . . sometimes . . . I don't even know how to try.

Ruth: Walter—

Walter: Yes?

Ruth (coming to him, gently and with misgiving, but coming to him): Honey . . . life don't have to be like this. I mean sometimes people can do things so that things are better . . . You remember how we used to talk when Travis was born . . . about the way we were going to live . . . the kind of house . . . (*She is stroking his head.*) Well, it's all starting to slip away from us . . .

(*He turns her to him and they look at each other and kiss, tenderly and hungrily. The door opens and Mama enters—Walter breaks away and jumps up. A beat.*)

Walter: Mama, where have you been?

Mama: My—them steps is longer than they used to be. Whew! (*She sits down and ignores him.*) How you feeling this evening, Ruth?

(*Ruth shrugs, disturbed at having been interrupted and watching her husband knowingly.*)

Walter: Mama, where have you been all day?

Mama (still ignoring him and leaning on the table and changing to more comfortable shoes): Where's Travis?

Ruth: I let him go out earlier and he ain't come back yet. Boy, is he going to get it!

Walter: Mama!

Mama (as if she has heard him for the first time): Yes, son?

Walter: Where did you go this afternoon?

Mama: I went downtown to tend to some business that I had to tend to.

Walter: What kind of business?

Mama: You know better than to question me like a child, Brother.

Walter (rising and bending over the table): Where were you, Mama? (*Bringing his fists down and shouting.*) Mama, you didn't go do something with that insurance money, something crazy?

(*The front door opens slowly, interrupting him, and Travis peeks his head in, less than hopefully.*)

Travis (to his mother): Mama, I—

Ruth: "Mama I" nothing! You're going to get it, boy! Get on in that bedroom and get yourself ready!

Travis: But I—

Mama: Why don't you all never let the child explain hisself.

Ruth: Keep out of it now, Lena.

(*Mama clamps her lips together, and Ruth advances toward her son menacingly.*)

Ruth: A thousand times I have told you not to go off like that—

Mama (holding out her arms to her grandson): Well—at least let me tell him something. I want him to be the first one to hear . . . Come here, Travis. (*The boy obeys, gladly.*) Travis—(*She takes him by the shoulder and looks into his face.*)—you know that money we got in the mail this morning?

Travis: Yes'm—

Mama: Well—what you think your grandmama gone and done with that money?

Travis: I don't know, Grandmama.

Mama (putting her finger on his nose for emphasis): She went out and she bought you a house! (*The explosion comes from Walter at the end of the revelation and he jumps up and turns away from all of them in a fury. Mama continues, to Travis.*) You glad about the house? It's going to be yours when you get to be a man.

Travis: Yeah—I always wanted to live in a house.

Mama: All right, gimme some sugar then—(*Travis puts his arms around her neck as she watches her son over the boy's shoulder. Then, to Travis, after the embrace.*) Now when you say your prayers tonight, you thank God and your grandfather—'cause it was him who give you the house—in his way.

Ruth (taking the boy from Mama and pushing him toward the bedroom): Now you get out of here and get ready for your beating.

Travis: Aw, Mama—

Ruth: Get on in there—(*Closing the door behind him and turning radiantly to her mother-in-law.*) So you went and did it!

Mama (quietly, looking at her son with pain): Yes, I did.

Ruth (raising both arms classically): PRAISE GOD! (*Looks at Walter a moment, who says nothing. She crosses rapidly to her husband.*) Please, honey—let me be glad . . . you be glad too. (*She has laid her hands on his shoulders, but he shakes himself free of her roughly, without turning to face her.*) Oh Walter . . . a home . . . a home. (*She comes back to Mama.*) Well—where is it? How big is it? How much it going to cost?

Mama: Well—

Ruth: When we moving?

Mama (smiling at her): First of the month.

Ruth (throwing back her head with jubilance): Praise God!

Mama (tentatively, still looking at her son's back turned against her and Ruth): It's—it's a nice house too . . . (*She cannot help speaking directly to him. An imploring quality in her voice, her manner, makes her almost like a girl now.*) Three bedrooms—nice big one for you and Ruth . . . Me and Beneatha still have to share our room, but Travis have one of his own—and (*With difficulty.*) I figure if the—new baby—is a boy, we could get one of them double-decker outfits . . . And there's a yard with a little patch of dirt where I could maybe get to grow me a few flowers . . . And a nice big basement . . .

Ruth: Walter honey, be glad—

Mama (still to his back, fingering things on the table): 'Course I don't want to make it sound fancier than it is . . . It's just a plain little old house—but it's made good and solid—and it will be *ours*. Walter Lee—it makes a difference in a man when he can walk on floors that belong to him . . .

Ruth: Where is it?

Mama (frightened at this telling): Well—well—it's out there in Clybourne Park—

(*Ruth's radiance fades abruptly, and Walter finally turns slowly to face his mother with incredulity and hostility.*)

Ruth: Where?

Mama (matter-of-factly): Four o six Clybourne Street, Clybourne Park.

Ruth: Clybourne Park? Mama, there ain't no colored people living in Clybourne Park.

Mama (almost idiotically): Well, I guess there's going to be some now.

Walter (bitterly): So that's the peace and comfort you went out and bought for us today!

Mama (raising her eyes to meet his finally): Son—I just tried to find the nicest place for the least amount of money for my family.

Ruth (trying to recover from the shock): Well—well—'course I ain't one never been 'fraid of no crackers, mind you—but—well, wasn't there no other houses nowhere?

Mama: Them houses they put up for colored in them areas way out all seem to cost twice as much as other houses. I did the best I could.

Ruth (struck senseless with the news, in its various degrees of goodness and trouble, she sits a moment, her fists propping her chin in thought, and then she starts to rise, bringing her fists down with vigor, the radiance spreading from cheek to cheek again): Well—well!—All I can say is—if this is my time in life—MY TIME—to say goodbye—(*And she builds with momentum as she starts to circle the room with an exuberant, almost tearfully happy release.*)—to these goddamned cracking walls!—(*She pounds the walls.*)—and these marching roaches!—(*She wipes at an imaginary army of marching roaches.*)—and this cramped little closet which ain't now or never was no kitchen! . . . then I say it loud and good, HALLELUJAH! AND GOOD-BYE MISERY . . . I DON'T NEVER WANT TO SEE YOUR UGLY FACE AGAIN! (*She laughs joyously, having practically destroyed the apartment, and flings her arms up and lets them come down happily, slowly, reflectively, over her abdomen, aware for the first time perhaps that the life therein pulses with happiness and not despair.*) Lena?

Mama (moved, watching her happiness): Yes, honey?

Ruth (looking off): Is there—is there a whole lot of sunlight?

Mama (understanding): Yes, child, there's a whole lot of sunlight.

(*Long pause.*)

Ruth (collecting herself and going to the door of the room Travis is in): Well—I guess I better see 'bout Travis. (*to Mama.*) Lord, I sure don't feel like whipping nobody today! (*She exits.*)

Mama (the mother and son are left alone now and the mother waits a long time, considering deeply, before she speaks): Son—you—you understand what I done, don't you? (*Walter is silent and sullen.*) I—I just seen my family falling apart today . . . just falling to pieces in front of my eyes . . . We couldn't of gone on like we was today. We was going backwards 'stead of forwards—talking 'bout killing babies and wishing each other was dead . . . When it gets like that in life—you just got to do something different, push on out and do something bigger . . . (*She waits.*) I wish you say something, son . . . I wish you'd say how deep inside you think I done the right thing—

Walter (*crossing slowly to his bedroom door and finally turning there and speaking measuredly*): What you need me to say you done right for? *You* the head of this family. You run our lives like you want to. It was your money and you did what you wanted with it. So what you need for me to say it was all right for? (*Bitterly, to hurt her as deeply as he knows is possible.*) So you butchered up a dream of mine—you—who always talking 'bout your children's dreams . . .

Mama: Walter Lee—

(*He just closes the door behind him. Mama sits alone, thinking heavily.*)

ACT TWO

SCENE 2

TIME. *Friday night. A few weeks later.*

AT RISE. *Packing crates mark the intention of the family to move. Beneatha and George come in, presumably from an evening out again.*

George: O.K. . . . O.K., whatever you say . . . (*They both sit on the couch. He tries to kiss her. She moves away.*) Look, we've had a nice evening; let's not spoil it, huh? . . .

(*He again turns her head and tries to nuzzle in and she turns away from him, not with distaste but with momentary lack of interest; in a mood to pursue what they were talking about.*)

Beneatha: I'm *trying* to talk to you.
George: We always talk.
Beneatha: Yes—and I love to talk.
George (*exasperated; rising*): I know it and I don't mind it sometimes . . . I want you to cut it out, see—The moody stuff, I mean. I don't like it. You're a nice-looking girl . . . all over. That's all you need, honey, forget the atmosphere. Guys aren't going to go for the atmosphere—they're going to go for what they see. Be glad for that. Drop the Garbo° routine. It doesn't go with you. As for myself, I want a nice—(*groping*)—simple (*thoughtfully*)—sophisticated girl . . . not a poet—O.K.?

(*He starts to kiss her, she rebuffs him again and he jumps up.*)

Beneatha: Why are you angry, George?
George: Because this is stupid! I don't go out with you to discuss the nature of "quiet desperation"° or to hear all about your thoughts—because the world will go on thinking what it thinks regardless—

Garbo: Greta Garbo (1905–1990) was a glamorous and reclusive movie star of the 1920s and '30s.
"quiet desperation": quotation from Henry David Thoreau's *Walden* (1854): "The mass of men lead lives of quiet desperation."

Beneatha: Then why read books? Why go to school?
George (with artificial patience, counting on his fingers): It's simple. You read books—to learn facts—to get grades—to pass the course—to get a degree. That's all—it has nothing to do with thoughts.

(A long pause.)

Beneatha: I see. *(He starts to sit.)* Good night, George.

(George looks at her a little oddly, and starts to exit. He meets Mama coming in.)

George: Oh—hello, Mrs. Younger.
Mama: Hello, George, how you feeling?
George: Fine—fine, how are you?
Mama: Oh, a little tired. You know them steps can get you after a day's work. You all have a nice time tonight?
George: Yes—a fine time. A fine time.
Mama: Well, good night.
George: Good night. *(He exits. Mama closes the door behind her.)*
Mama: Hello, honey. What you sitting like that for?
Beneatha: I'm just sitting.
Mama: Didn't you have a nice time?
Beneatha: No.
Mama: No? What's the matter?
Beneatha: Mama, George is a fool—honest *(She rises.)*
Mama (hustling around unloading the packages she has entered with. She stops): Is he, baby?
Beneatha: Yes. *(Beneatha makes up Travis' bed as she talks.)*
Mama: You sure?
Beneatha: Yes.
Mama: Well—I guess you better not waste your time with no fools.

(Beneatha looks up at her mother, watching her put groceries in the refrigerator. Finally she gathers up her things and starts into the bedroom. At the door she stops and looks back at her mother.)

Beneatha: Mama—
Mama: Yes, baby—
Beneatha: Thank you.
Mama: For what?
Beneatha: For understanding me this time.

(She exits quickly and the mother stands, smiling a little, looking at the place where Beneatha just stood. Ruth enters.)

Ruth: Now don't you fool with any of this stuff, Lena—
Mama: Oh, I just thought I'd sort a few things out. Is Brother here?
Ruth: Yes.
Mama (with concern): Is he—
Ruth (reading her eyes): Yes.

(*Mama is silent and someone knocks on the door. Mama and Ruth exchange weary and knowing glances and Ruth opens it to admit the neighbor, Mrs. Johnson, who is a rather squeaky wide-eyed lady of no particular age, with a newspaper under her arm.*)

Mama (*changing her expression to acute delight and a ringing cheerful greeting*): Oh—hello, there, Johnson.

Johnson (*this is a woman who decided long ago to be enthusiastic about EVERYTHING in life and she is inclined to wave her wrist vigorously at the height of her exclamatory comments*): Hello there, yourself! H'you this evening, Ruth?

Ruth (*not much of a deceptive type*): Fine, Mis' Johnson, h'you?

Johnson: Fine. (*Reaching out quickly, playfully, and patting Ruth's stomach.*) Ain't you starting to poke out none yet! (*She mugs with delight at the overfamiliar remark and her eyes dart around looking at the crates and packing preparation; Mama's face is a cold sheet of endurance.*) Oh, ain't we getting ready 'round here, though! Yessir! Lookathere! I'm telling you the Youngers is really getting ready to "move on up a little higher!"—Bless God!

Mama (*a little drily, doubting the total sincerity of the Blesser*): Bless God.

Johnson: He's good, ain't He?

Mama: Oh yes, He's good.

Johnson: I mean sometimes He works in mysterious ways . . . but He works, don't He!

Mama (*the same*): Yes, He does.

Johnson: I'm just sooooo happy for y'all. And this here child—(*about Ruth*) looks like she could just pop open with happiness, don't she. Where's all the rest of the family?

Mama: Bennie's gone to bed—

Johnson: Ain't no . . . (*The implication is pregnancy.*) sickness done hit you—I hope . . . ?

Mama: No—she just tired. She was out this evening.

Johnson (*all is a coo, an emphatic coo*): Aw—ain't that lovely. She still going out with the little Murchison boy?

Mama (*drily*): Ummmm huh.

Johnson: That's lovely. You sure got lovely children, Younger. Me and Isaiah talks all the time 'bout what fine children you was blessed with. We sure do.

Mama: Ruth, give Mis' Johnson a piece of sweet potato pie and some milk.

Johnson: Oh honey, I can't stay hardly a minute—I just dropped in to see if there was anything I could do. (*Accepting the food easily.*) I guess y'all seen the news what's all over the colored paper this week . . .

Mama: No—didn't get mine yet this week.

Johnson (*lifting her head and blinking with the spirit of catastrophe*): You mean you ain't read 'bout them colored people that was bombed out their place out there?

(*Ruth straightens with concern and takes the paper and reads it. Johnson notices her and feeds commentary.*)

Johnson: Ain't it something how bad these here white folks is getting here in Chicago! Lord, getting so you think you right down in Mississippi! (*With a tremendous and rather insincere sense of melodrama.*) 'Course I thinks it's wonderful how our folks keeps on pushing out. You hear some of these Negroes round here talking 'bout how they don't go where they ain't wanted and all that—but not me, honey!

(*This is a lie.*) Wilhemenia Othella Johnson goes anywhere, any time she feels like it! (*With head movement for emphasis.*) Yes I do! Why if we left it up to these here crackers, the poor niggers wouldn't have nothing—(*She clasps her hand over her mouth.*) Oh, I always forgets you don't 'low that word in your house.

Mama (*quietly, looking at her*): No—I don't 'low it.

Johnson (*vigorously again*): Me neither! I was just telling Isaiah yesterday when he come using it in front of me—I said, "Isaiah, it's just like Mis' Younger says all the time—"

Mama: Don't you want some more pie?

Johnson: No—no thank you; this was lovely. I got to get on over home and have my midnight coffee. I hear some people say it don't let them sleep but I finds I can't close my eyes right lessen I done had that laaaast cup of coffee . . . (*She waits. A beat. Undaunted.*) My Goodnight coffee, I calls it!

Mama (*with much eye-rolling and communication between herself and Ruth*): Ruth, why don't you give Mis' Johnson some coffee.

(*Ruth gives Mama an unpleasant look for her kindness.*)

Johnson (*accepting the coffee*): Where's Brother tonight?

Mama: He's lying down.

Johnson: Mmmmmm, he sure gets his beauty rest, don't he? Good-looking man. Sure is a good-looking man! (*Reaching out to pat Ruth's stomach again.*) I guess that's how come we keep on having babies around here. (*She winks at Mama.*) One thing 'bout Brother, he always know how to have a *good* time. And sooooo ambitious! I bet it was his idea y'all moving out to Clybourne Park. Lord—I bet this time next month y'all's names will have been in the papers plenty—(*Holding up her hands to mark off each word of the headline she can see in front of her.*) "NEGROES INVADE CLYBOURNE PARK—BOMBED!"

Mama (*she and Ruth look at the woman in amazement*): We ain't exactly moving out there to get bombed.

Johnson: Oh, honey—you know I'm praying to God every day that don't nothing like that happen! But you have to think of life like it is—and these here Chicago peckerwoods is some baaaad peckerwoods.

Mama (*wearily*): We done thought about all that, Mis' Johnson.

(*Beneatha comes out of the bedroom in her robe and passes through to the bathroom. Mrs. Johnson turns.*)

Johnson: Hello there, Bennie!

Beneatha (*crisply*): Hello, Mrs. Johnson.

Johnson: How is school?

Beneatha (*crisply*): Fine, thank you. (*She goes out.*)

Johnson (*insulted*): Getting so she don't have much to say to nobody.

Mama: The child was on her way to the bathroom.

Johnson: I know—but sometimes she act like ain't got time to pass the time of day with nobody ain't been to college. Oh—I ain't criticizing her none. It's just—you know how some of our young people gets when they get a little education. (*Mama and Ruth say nothing, just look at her.*) Yes—well. Well, I guess I better get on home. (*Unmoving.*) 'Course I can understand how she must be proud and everything—being the only one in the family to make something of herself. I know just being a chauffeur ain't never satisfied Brother none. He shouldn't feel like that, though. Ain't nothing wrong with being a chauffeur.

Mama: There's plenty wrong with it.

Johnson: What?

Mama: Plenty. My husband always said being any kind of a servant wasn't a fit thing for a man to have to be. He always said a man's hands was made to make things, or to turn the earth with—not to drive nobody's car for 'em—or—(*She looks at her own hands.*) carry they slop jars. And my boy is just like him—he wasn't meant to wait on nobody.

Johnson (rising, somewhat offended): Mmmmmmmmm. The Youngers is too much for me! (*She looks around.*) You sure one proud-acting bunch of colored folks. Well—I always thinks like Booker T. Washington° said that time—"Education has spoiled many a good plow hand"—

Mama: Is that what old Booker T. said?

Johnson: He sure did.

Mama: Well, it sounds just like him. The fool.

Johnson (indignantly): Well—he was one of our great men.

Mama: Who said so?

Johnson (nonplussed): You know, me and you ain't never agreed about some things, Lena Younger. I guess I better be going—

Ruth (quickly): Good night.

Johnson: Good night. Oh—(*Thrusting it at her.*) You can keep the paper! (*With a trill.*) 'Night.

Mama: Good night, Mis' Johnson. (*Mrs. Johnson exits.*)

Ruth: If ignorance was gold . . .

Mama: Shush. Don't talk about folks behind their backs.

Ruth: You do.

Mama: I'm old and corrupted. (*Beneatha enters.*) You was rude to Mis' Johnson, Beneatha, and I don't like it at all.

Beneatha (at her door): Mama, if there are two things we, as a people, have got to overcome, one is the Ku Klux Klan—and the other is Mrs. Johnson. (*She exits.*)

Mama: Smart aleck.

(*The phone rings.*)

Ruth: I'll get it.

Mama: Lord, ain't this a popular place tonight.

Ruth (at the phone): Hello—Just a minute. (*Goes to door.*) Walter, it's Mrs. Arnold. (*Waits. Goes back to the phone. Tense.*) Hello. Yes, this is his wife speaking . . . He's lying down now. Yes . . . well, he'll be in tomorrow. He's been very sick. Yes—I know we should have called, but we were so sure he'd be able to come in today. Yes—yes, I'm very sorry. Yes . . . Thank you very much. (*She hangs up. Walter is standing in the doorway of the bedroom behind her.*) That was Mrs. Arnold.

Walter (indifferently): Was it?

Ruth: She said if you don't come in tomorrow that they are getting a new man . . .

Walter: Ain't that sad—ain't that crying sad.

Booker T. Washington: the most influential black educator and leader of his time, Washington (1858–1915) was criticized by W. E. B. Du Bois and others for being too accepting of inequality and injustice.

Ruth: She said Mr. Arnold has had to take a cab for three days . . . Walter, you ain't been to work for three days! (*This is a revelation to her.*) Where you been, Walter Lee Younger? (*Walter looks at her and starts to laugh.*) You're going to lose your job.
Walter: That's right . . . (*He turns on the radio.*)
Ruth: Oh, Walter, and with your mother working like a dog every day—

(*A steamy, deep blues pours into the room.*)

Walter: That's sad too—Everything is sad.
Mama: What you been doing for these three days, son?
Walter: Mama—you don't know all the things a man what got leisure can find to do in this city . . . What's this—Friday night? Well—Wednesday I borrowed Willy Harris' car and I went for a drive . . . just me and myself and I drove and drove . . . Way out . . . way past South Chicago, and I parked the car and I sat and looked at the steel mills all day long. I just sat in the car and looked at them big black chimneys for hours. Then I drove back and I went to the Green Hat. (*Pause.*) And Thursday—Thursday I borrowed the car again and I got in it and I pointed it the other way and I drove the other way—for hours—way, way up to Wisconsin, and I looked at the farms. I just drove and looked at the farms. Then I drove back and I went to the Green Hat. (*Pause.*) And today—today I didn't get the car. Today I just walked. All over the Southside. And I looked at the Negroes and they looked at me and finally I just sat down on the curb at Thirty-ninth and South Parkway and I just sat there and watched the Negroes go by. And then I went to the Green Hat. You all sad? You all depressed? And you know where I am going right now—

(*Ruth goes out quietly.*)

Mama: Oh, Big Walter, is this the harvest of our days?
Walter: You know what I like about the Green Hat? I like this little cat they got there who blows a sax . . . He blows. He talks to me. He ain't but 'bout five feet tall and he's got a conked head and his eyes is always closed and he's all music—
Mama (*rising and getting some papers out of her handbag*): Walter—
Walter: And there's this other guy who plays the piano . . . and they got a sound. I mean they can work on some music . . . They got the best little combo in the world in the Green Hat . . . You can just sit there and drink and listen to them three men play and you realize that don't nothing matter worth a damn, but just being there—
Mama: I've helped do it to you, haven't I, son? Walter, I been wrong.
Walter: Naw—you ain't never been wrong about nothing, Mama.
Mama: Listen to me, now. I say I been wrong, son. That I been doing to you what the rest of the world been doing to you. (*She turns off the radio.*) Walter—(*She stops and he looks up slowly at her and she meets his eyes pleadingly.*) What you ain't never understood is that I ain't got nothing, don't own nothing, ain't never really wanted nothing that wasn't for you. There ain't nothing as precious to me . . . There ain't nothing worth holding on to, money, dreams, nothing else—if it means—if it means it's going to destroy my boy. (*She takes an envelope out of her handbag and puts it in front of him and he watches her without speaking or moving.*) I paid the man thirty-five hundred dollars down on the house. That leaves sixty-five hundred dollars. Monday morning I want you to take this money and take three thousand dollars and put it in a savings account for Beneatha's medical schooling. The rest you put in a checking

account—with your name on it. And from now on any penny that come out of it or that go in it is for you to look after. For you to decide. (*She drops her hands a little helplessly.*) It ain't much, but it's all I got in the world and I'm putting it in your hands. I'm telling you to be the head of this family from now on like you supposed to be.

Walter (*stares at the money*): You trust me like that, Mama?

Mama: I ain't never stop trusting you. Like I ain't never stop loving you.

(*She goes out, and Walter sits looking at the money on the table. Finally, in a decisive gesture, he gets up, and, in mingled joy and desperation, picks up the money. At the same moment, Travis enters for bed.*)

Travis: What's the matter, Daddy? You drunk?

Walter (*sweetly, more sweetly than we have ever known him*): No, Daddy ain't drunk. Daddy ain't going to never be drunk again . . .

Travis: Well, good night, Daddy.

(*The Father has come from behind the couch and leans over, embracing his son.*)

Walter: Son, I feel like talking to you tonight.

Travis: About what?

Walter: Oh, about a lot of things. About you and what kind of man you going to be when you grow up . . . Son—son, what do you want to be when you grow up?

Travis: A bus driver.

Walter (*laughing a little*): A what? Man, that ain't nothing to want to be!

Travis: Why not?

Walter: 'Cause, man—it ain't big enough—you know what I mean.

Travis: I don't know then. I can't make up my mind. Sometimes Mama asks me that too. And sometimes when I tell her I just want to be like you—she says she don't want me to be like that and sometimes she says she does . . .

Walter (*gathering him up in his arms*): You know what, Travis? In seven years you going to be seventeen years old. And things is going to be very different with us in seven years, Travis . . . One day when you are seventeen I'll come home—home from my office downtown somewhere—

Travis: You don't work in no office, Daddy.

Walter: No—but after tonight. After what your daddy gonna do tonight, there's going to be offices—a whole lot of offices . . .

Travis: What you gonna do tonight, Daddy?

Walter: You wouldn't understand yet, son, but your daddy's gonna make a transaction . . . a business transaction that's going to change our lives . . . That's how come one day when you 'bout seventeen years old I'll come home and I'll be pretty tired, you know what I mean, after a day of conferences and secretaries getting things wrong the way they do . . . 'cause an executive's life is hell, man—(*The more he talks the farther away he gets.*) And I'll pull the car up on the driveway . . . just a plain black Chrysler, I think, with white walls—no—black tires. More elegant. Rich people don't have to be flashy . . . though I'll have to get something a little sportier for Ruth—maybe a Cadillac convertible to do her shopping in . . . And I'll come up the steps to the house and the gardener will be clipping away at the hedges and he'll say, "Good evening, Mr. Younger." And I'll say, "Hello, Jefferson, how are you this evening?" And I'll go inside and Ruth will come downstairs and meet me at the door and we'll kiss each other and she'll take my arm and we'll go up to your room to see you sitting on the floor with the catalogues of all the great schools in America around you . . . All the great schools in the world! And—and I'll say, all right son—it's your seventeenth birthday, what is it you've decided? . . . Just tell me where you want to go to school and you'll go. Just tell me, what it is you want to be—and you'll be it . . . Whatever you want to be—Yessir! *(He holds his arms open for Travis.)* You just name it, son . . . *(Travis leaps into them.)* and I hand you the world!

(Walter's voice has risen in pitch and hysterical promise and on the last line he lifts Travis high.)

ACT TWO

SCENE 3

TIME. *Saturday, moving day, one week later.*

Before the curtain rises, Ruth's voice, a strident, dramatic church alto, cuts through the silence.

It is, in the darkness, a triumphant surge, a penetrating statement of expectation: "Oh, Lord, I don't feel no ways tired! Children, oh, glory hallelujah!"

As the curtain rises we see that Ruth is alone in the living room, finishing up the family's packing. It is moving day. She is nailing crates and tying cartons. Beneatha enters, carrying a guitar case, and watches her exuberant sister-in-law.

Ruth: Hey!
Beneatha *(putting away the case)*: Hi.
Ruth *(pointing at a package)*: Honey—look in that package there and see what I found on sale this morning at the South Center. *(Ruth gets up and moves to the package and draws out some curtains.)* Lookahere—hand-turned hems!
Beneatha: How do you know the window size out there?
Ruth *(who hadn't thought of that)*: Oh—Well, they bound to fit something in the whole house. Anyhow, they was too good a bargain to pass up. *(Ruth slaps her head, suddenly remembering something.)* Oh, Bennie—I meant to put a special note on that carton over there. That's your mama's good china and she wants 'em to be very careful with it.
Beneatha: I'll do it.

(Beneatha finds a piece of paper and starts to draw large letters on it.)

Ruth: You know what I'm going to do soon as I get in that new house?
Beneatha: What?
Ruth: Honey—I'm going to run me a tub of water up to here . . . *(With her fingers practically up to her nostrils.)* And I'm going to get in it—and I am going to sit . . . and sit . . . and sit in that hot water and the first person who knocks to tell me to hurry up and come out—
Beneatha: Gets shot at sunrise.
Ruth *(laughing happily)*: You said it, sister! *(Noticing how large Beneatha is absent-mindedly making the note.)* Honey, they ain't going to read that from no airplane.
Beneatha *(laughing herself)*: I guess I always think things have more emphasis if they are big, somehow.

Ruth (looking up at her and smiling): You and your brother seem to have that as a philosophy of life. Lord, that man—done changed so 'round here. You know—you know what we did last night? Me and Walter Lee?

Beneatha: What?

Ruth (smiling to herself): We went to the movies. *(Looking at Beneatha to see if she understands.)* We went to the movies. You know the last time me and Walter went to the movies together?

Beneatha: No.

Ruth: Me neither. That's how long it been. *(Smiling again.)* But we went last night. The picture wasn't much good, but that didn't seem to matter. We went—and we held hands.

Beneatha: Oh, Lord!

Ruth: We held hands—and you know what?

Beneatha: What?

Ruth: When we come out of the show it was late and dark and all the stores and things was closed up . . . and it was kind of chilly and there wasn't many people on the streets . . . and we was still holding hands, me and Walter.

Beneatha: You're killing me.

(Walter enters with a large package. His happiness is deep in him; he cannot keep still with his new-found exuberance. He is singing and wiggling and snapping his fingers. He puts his package in a corner and puts a phonograph record, which he has brought in with him, on the record player. As the music, soulful and sensuous, comes up he dances over to Ruth and tries to get her to dance with him. She gives in at last to his raunchiness and in a fit of giggling allows herself to be drawn into his mood. They dip and she melts into his arms in a classic, body-melding "slow drag.")

Beneatha (regarding them a long time as they dance, then drawing in her breath for a deeply exaggerated comment which she does not particularly mean): Talk about—oldddddddddd-fashioneddddddd—Negroes!

Walter (stopping momentarily): What kind of Negroes? *(He says this in fun. He is not angry with her today, nor with anyone. He starts to dance with his wife again.)*

Beneatha: Old-fashioned.

Walter (as he dances with Ruth): You know, when these New Negroes have their convention—*(Pointing at his sister.)*—that is going to be the chairman of the Committee on Unending Agitation. *(He goes on dancing, then stops.)* Race, race, race! . . . Girl, I do believe you are the first person in the history of the entire human race to successfully brainwash yourself. *(Beneatha breaks up and he goes on dancing. He stops again, enjoying his tease.)* Damn, even the N double A C P takes a holiday sometimes! *(Beneatha and Ruth laugh. He dances with Ruth some more and starts to laugh and stops and pantomimes someone over an operating table.)* I can just see that chick someday looking down at some poor cat on an operating table and before she starts to slice him, she says . . . *(Pulling his sleeves back maliciously.)* "By the way, what are your views on civil rights down there? . . ."

(He laughs at her again and starts to dance happily. The bell sounds.)

Beneatha: Sticks and stones may break my bones but . . . words will never hurt me!

(Beneatha goes to the door and opens it as Walter and Ruth go on with the clowning. Beneatha is somewhat surprised to see a quiet-looking middle-aged white man in a business suit holding his hat and a briefcase in his hand and consulting a small piece of paper.)

Man: Uh—how do you do, miss. I am looking for a Mrs.—(He looks at the slip of paper.) Mrs. Lena Younger? (He stops short, struck dumb at the sight of the oblivious Walter and Ruth.)

Beneatha (smoothing her hair with slight embarrassment): Oh—yes, that's my mother. Excuse me. (She closes the door and turns to quiet the other two.) Ruth! Brother! (Enunciating precisely but soundlessly: "There's a white man at the door!" They stop dancing, Ruth cuts off the phonograph, Beneatha opens the door. The man casts a curious quick glance at all of them.) Uh—come in please.

Man (coming in): Thank you.

Beneatha: My mother isn't here just now. Is it business?

Man: Yes . . . well, of a sort.

Walter (freely, the Man of the House): Have a seat. I'm Mrs. Younger's son. I look after most of her business matters.

(Ruth and Beneatha exchange amused glances.)

Man (regarding Walter, and sitting): Well—My name is Karl Lindner . . .

Walter (stretching out his hand): Walter Younger. This is my wife—(Ruth nods politely.)—and my sister.

Lindner: How do you do.

Walter (amiably, as he sits himself easily on a chair, leaning forward on his knees with interest and looking expectantly into the newcomer's face): What can we do for you, Mr. Lindner!

Lindner (some minor shuffling of the hat and briefcase on his knees): Well—I am a representative of the Clybourne Park Improvement Association—

Walter (pointing): Why don't you sit your things on the floor?

Lindner: Oh—yes. Thank you. (He slides the briefcase and hat under the chair.) And as I was saying—I am from the Clybourne Park Improvement Association and we have had it brought to our attention at the last meeting that you people—or at least your mother—has bought a piece of residential property at—(He digs for the slip of paper again.)—four o six Clybourne Street . . .

Walter: That's right. Care for something to drink? Ruth, get Mr. Lindner a beer.

Lindner (upset for some reason): Oh—no, really. I mean thank you very much, but no thank you.

Ruth (innocently): Some coffee?

Lindner: Thank you, nothing at all. (Beneatha is watching the man carefully.) Well, I don't know how much you folks know about our organization. (He is a gentle man; thoughtful and somewhat labored in his manner.) It is one of these community organizations set up to look after—oh, you know, things like block upkeep and special projects and we also have what we call our New Neighbors Orientation Committee . . .

Beneatha (drily): Yes—and what do they do?

Lindner (turning a little to her and then returning the main force to Walter): Well—it's what you might call a sort of welcoming committee, I guess. I mean they, we—I'm the chairman of the committee—go around and see the new people who move into the neighborhood and sort of give them the lowdown on the way we do things out in Clybourne Park.

Beneatha (with appreciation of the two meanings, which escape Ruth and Walter.) Un-huh.

Lindner: And we also have the category of what the association calls—*(He looks elsewhere.)*—uh—special community problems . . .

Beneatha: Yes—and what are some of those?

Walter: Girl, let the man talk.

Lindner (with understated relief): Thank you. I would sort of like to explain this thing in my own way. I mean I want to explain to you in a certain way.

Walter: Go ahead.

Lindner: Yes. Well. I'm going to try to get right to the point. I'm sure we'll all appreciate that in the long run.

Beneatha: Yes.

Walter: Be still now!

Lindner: Well—

Ruth (still innocently): Would you like another chair—you don't look comfortable.

Lindner (more frustrated than annoyed): No, thank you very much. Please. Well—to get right to the point I—*(A great breath, and he is off at last.)* I am sure you people must be aware of some of the incidents which have happened in various parts of the city when colored people have moved into certain areas—

(Beneatha exhales heavily and starts tossing a piece of fruit up and down in the air.)

Well—because we have what I think is going to be a unique type of organization in American community life—not only do we deplore that kind of thing—but we are trying to do something about it.

(Beneatha stops tossing and turns with a new and quizzical interest to the man.)

We feel—*(Gaining confidence in his mission because of the interest in the faces of the people he is talking to.)*—we feel that most of the trouble in this world, when you come right down to it—*(He hits his knee for emphasis.)*—most of the trouble exists because people just don't sit down and talk to each other.

Ruth (nodding as she might in church, pleased with the remark): You can say that again, mister.

Lindner (more encouraged by such affirmation): That we don't try hard enough in this world to understand the other fellow's problem. The other guy's point of view.

Ruth: Now that's right.

(Beneatha and Walter merely watch and listen with genuine interest.)

Lindner: Yes—that's the way we feel out in Clybourne Park. And that's why I was elected to come here this afternoon and talk to you people. Friendly like, you know, the way people should talk to each other and see if we couldn't find some way to work this thing out. As I say, the whole business is a matter of *caring* about the other fellow. Anybody can see that you are a nice family of folks, hard-working and honest I'm sure.

(Beneatha frowns slightly, quizzically, her head tilted regarding him.)

Today everybody knows what it means to be on the outside of *something*. And of course, there is always somebody who is out to take advantage of people who don't always understand.

Walter: What do you mean?

Lindner: Well—you see our community is made up of people who've worked hard as the dickens for years to build up that little community. They're not rich and fancy people; just hard-working, honest people who don't really have much but those little homes and a dream of the kind of community they want to raise their children in. Now, I don't say we are perfect and there is a lot wrong in some of the things they want. But you've got to admit that a man, right or wrong, has the right to want to have the neighborhood he lives in a certain kind of way. And at the moment the overwhelming majority of our people out there feel that people get along better, take more of a common interest in the life of the community, when they share a common background. I want you to believe me when I tell you that race prejudice simply doesn't enter into it. It is a matter of the people of Clybourne Park believing, rightly or wrongly, as I say, that for the happiness of all concerned that our Negro families are happier when they live in their *own* communities.

Beneatha (with a grand and bitter gesture): This, friends, is the Welcoming Committee!

Walter (dumfounded, looking at Lindner): Is this what you came marching all the way over here to tell us?

Lindner: Well, now we've been having a fine conversation. I hope you'll hear me all the way through.

Walter (tightly): Go ahead, man.

Lindner: You see—in the face of all the things I have said, we are prepared to make your family a very generous offer. . . .

Beneatha: Thirty pieces and not a coin less!°

Walter: Yeah?

Lindner (putting on his glasses and drawing a form out of the briefcase): Our association is prepared, through the collective effort of our people, to buy the house from you at a financial gain to your family.

Ruth: Lord have mercy, ain't this the living gall!

Walter: All right, you through?

Lindner: Well, I want to give you the exact terms of the financial arrangement—

Walter: We don't want to hear no exact terms of no arrangements. I want to know if you got any more to tell us 'bout getting together?

Linder (taking off his glasses): Well—I don't suppose that you feel . . .

Walter: Never mind how I feel—you got any more to say 'bout how people ought to sit down and talk to each other? . . . Get out of my house, man. *(He turns his back and walks to the door.)*

Lindner (looking around at the hostile faces and reaching and assembling his hat and briefcase): Well—I don't understand why you people are reacting this way. What do you think you are going to gain by moving into a neighborhood where you just aren't wanted and where some elements—well—people can get awful worked up when they feel that their whole way of life and everything they've ever worked for is threatened.

Walter: Get out.

Thirty pieces and not a coin less: reference to Judas's betrayal of Jesus for thirty pieces of silver (Matthew 26: 14–16).

Lindner (at the door, holding a small card): Well—I'm sorry it went like this.
Walter: Get out.
Lindner (almost sadly regarding Walter): You just can't force people to change their hearts, son.

> (*He turns and put his card on a table and exits. Walter pushes the door to with stinging hatred, and stands looking at it. Ruth just sits and Beneatha just stands. They say nothing. Mama and Travis enter.*)

Mama: Well—this all the packing got done since I left out of here this morning? I testify before God that my children got all the energy of the *dead!* What time the moving men due?
Beneatha: Four o'clock. You had a caller, Mama. (*She is smiling, teasingly.*)
Mama: Sure enough—who?
Beneatha (her arms folded saucily): The Welcoming Committee.

> (*Walter and Ruth giggle.*)

Mama (innocently): Who?
Beneatha: The Welcoming Committee. They said they're sure going to be glad to see you when you get there.
Walter (devilishly): Yeah, they said they can't hardly wait to see your face. (*Laughter.*)
Mama (sensing their facetiousness): What's the matter with you all?
Walter: Ain't nothing the matter with us. We just telling you 'bout the gentleman who came to see you this afternoon. From the Clybourne Park Improvement Association.
Mama: What he want?
Ruth (in the same mood as Beneatha and Walter): To welcome you, honey.
Walter: He said they can't hardly wait. He said the one thing they don't have, that they just *dying* to have out there, is a fine family of fine colored people! (*To Ruth and Beneatha.*) Ain't that right!
Ruth (mockingly): Yeah! He left his card—
Beneatha (handing card to Mama): In case—

> (*Mama reads and throws it on the floor—understanding and looking off as she draws her chair up to the table on which she has put her plant and some sticks and some cord.*)

Mama: Father, give us strength. (*Knowingly—and without fun.*) Did he threaten us?
Beneatha: Oh—Mama—they don't do it like that any more. He talked Brotherhood. He said everybody ought to learn how to sit down and hate each other with good Christian fellowship.

> (*She and Walter shake hands to ridicule the remark.*)

Mama (sadly): Lord, protect us . . .
Ruth: You should hear the money those folks raised to buy the house from us. All we paid and then some.
Beneatha: What they think we going to do—eat 'em?
Ruth: No, honey, marry 'em.
Mama (shaking her head): Lord, Lord, Lord . . .

Ruth: Well—that's the way the crackers crumble. *(A beat.)* Joke.
Beneatha (laughingly noticing what her mother is doing): Mama, what are you doing?
Mama: Fixing my plant so it won't get hurt none on the way . . .
Beneatha: Mama, you going to take *that* to the new house?
Mama: Un-huh—
Beneatha: That raggedy-looking old thing?
Mama (stopping and looking at her): It expresses ME!
Ruth (with delight, to Beneatha): So there, Miss Thing!

> *(Walter comes to Mama suddenly and bends down behind her and squeezes her in his arms with all his strength. She is overwhelmed by the suddenness of it and, though delighted, her manner is like that of Ruth and Travis.)*

Mama: Look out now, boy! You make me mess up my thing here!
Walter (his face lit, he slips down on his knees beside her, his arms still about her): Mama . . . you know what it means to climb up in the chariot?
Mama (gruffly, very happy): Get on away from me now . . .
Ruth (near the gift-wrapped package, trying to catch Walter's eye): Psst—
Walter: What the old song say, Mama . . .
Ruth: Walter—Now? *(She is pointing at the package.)*
Walter (speaking the lines, sweetly, playfully, in his mother's face):

> I got wings! . . . you got wings! . . .
> All God's Children got wings . . .

Mama: Boy—get out of my face and do some work . . .
Walter:

> When I get to heaven gonna put on my wings,
> Gonna fly all over God's heaven . . .

Beneatha (teasingly, from across the room): Everybody talking 'bout heaven ain't going there!
Walter (to Ruth, who is carrying the box across to them): I don't know, you think we ought to give her that . . . Seems to me she ain't been very appreciative around here.
Mama (eying the box, which is obviously a gift): What is that?
Walter (taking it from Ruth and putting it on the table in front of Mama): Well—what you all think? Should we give it to her?
Ruth: Oh—she was pretty good today.
Mama: I'll good you—*(She turns her eyes to the box again.)*
Beneatha: Open it, Mama.

> *(She stands up, looks at it, turns and looks at all of them, and then presses her hands together and does not open the package.)*

Walter (sweetly): Open it, Mama. It's for you. *(Mama looks in his eyes. It is the first present in her life without its being Christmas. Slowly she opens her package and lifts out, one by one, a brand-new sparkling set of gardening tools. Walter continues, prodding.)* Ruth made up the note—read it . . .

Mama (picking up the card and adjusting her glasses): "To our own Mrs. Miniver°—Love from Brother, Ruth and Beneatha." Ain't that lovely . . .

Travis (tugging at his father's sleeve): Daddy, can I give her mine now?

Walter: All right, son. (*Travis flies to get his gift.*)

Mama: Now I don't have to use my knives and forks no more . . .

Walter: Travis didn't want to go in with the rest of us, Mama. He got his own. (*Somewhat amused.*) We don't know what it is . . .

Travis (racing back in the room with a large hatbox and putting it in front of his grandmother): Here!

Mama: Lord have mercy, baby. You done gone and bought your grandmother a hat?

Travis (very proud): Open it!

(*She does and lifts out an elaborate, but very elaborate, wide gardening hat, and all the adults break up at the sight of it.*)

Ruth: Travis, honey, what is that?

Travis (who thinks it is beautiful and appropriate): It's a gardening hat! Like the ladies always have on in the magazines when they work in their gardens.

Beneatha (giggling fiercely): Travis—we were trying to make Mama Mrs. Miniver—not Scarlett O'Hara!°

Mama (indignantly): What's the matter with you all! This here is a beautiful hat! (*Absurdly.*) I always wanted me one just like it!

(*She pops it on her head to prove it to her grandson, and the hat is ludicrous and considerably oversized.*)

Ruth: Hot dog! Go, Mama!

Walter (doubled over with laughter): I'm sorry, Mama—but you look like you ready to go out and chop you some cotton sure enough!

(*They all laugh except Mama, out of deference to Travis' feelings.*)

Mama (gathering the boy up to her): Bless your heart—this is the prettiest hat I ever owned—(*Walter, Ruth, and Beneatha chime in—noisily, festively and insincerely congratulating Travis on his gift.*) What are we all standing around here for? We ain't finished packin' yet. Bennie, you ain't packed one book.

(*The bell rings.*)

Beneatha: That couldn't be the movers . . . it's not hardly two o'clock yet—

(*Beneatha goes into her room. Mama starts for door.*)

Walter (turning, stiffening): Wait—wait—I'll get it. (*He stands and looks at the door.*)

Mama: You expecting company, son?

Mrs. Miniver: As portrayed by Greer Garson in the Academy Award-winning World War II film, Mrs. Miniver is a British housewife who loves her family and gardening, and is called to show great courage, strength, and perseverance in the face of German bombardments. *Scarlett O'Hara*: the young, flamboyant, and histrionic heroine of *Gone with the Wind* (1936) by Margaret Mitchell—made into a blockbuster movie in 1939 by David O. Selznick. The Southern belle Scarlett O'Hara is a sharp contrast to the down-to-earth, sensible Mrs. Miniver.

Walter (just looking at the door): Yeah—yeah . . .

(*Mama looks at Ruth, and they exchange innocent and unfrightened glances.*)

Mama (not understanding): Well, let them in, son.
Beneatha (from her room): We need some more string.
Mama: Travis—you run to the hardware and get me some string cord.

(*Mama goes out and Walter turns and looks at Ruth. Travis goes to a dish for money.*)

Ruth: Why don't you answer the door, man?
Walter (suddenly bounding across the floor to embrace her): 'Cause sometimes it hard to let the future begin! (*Stooping down in her face.*)

I got wings! You got wings!
All God's children got wings!

(*He crosses to the door and throws it open. Standing there is a very slight little man in a not too prosperous business suit and with haunted frightened eyes and a hat pulled down tightly, brim up, around his forehead. Travis passes between the men and exits. Walter leans deep in the man's face, still in his jubilance.*)

When I get to heaven gonna put on my wings,
Gonna fly all over God's heaven . . .

(*The little man just stares at him.*)

Heaven—

(*Suddenly he stops and looks past the little man into the empty hallway.*)

Where's Willy, man?

Bobo: He ain't with me.
Walter (not disturbed): Oh—come on in. You know my wife.
Bobo (dumbly, taking off his hat): Yes—h'you, Miss Ruth.
Ruth (quietly, a mood apart from her husband already, seeing Bobo): Hello, Bobo.
Walter: You right on time today . . . Right on time. That's the way! (*He slaps Bobo on his back.*) Sit down . . . lemme hear.

(*Ruth stands stiffly and quietly in back of them, as though somehow she senses death, her eyes fixed on her husband.*)

Bobo (his frightened eyes on the floor, his hat in his hands): Could I please get a drink of water, before I tell you about it, Walter Lee?

(*Walter does not take his eyes off the man. Ruth goes blindly to the tap and gets a glass of water and brings it to Bobo.*)

Walter: There ain't nothing wrong, is there?
Bobo: Lemme tell you—
Walter: Man—didn't nothing go wrong?

Bobo: Lemme tell you—Walter Lee. *(Looking at Ruth and talking to her more than to Walter.)* You know how it was. I got to tell you how it was. I mean first I got to tell you how it was all the way . . . I mean about the money I put in, Walter Lee . . .

Walter (with taut agitation now): What about the money you put in?

Bobo: Well—it wasn't much as we told you—me and Willy—*(He stops.)* I'm sorry, Walter. I got a bad feeling about it. I got a real bad feeling about it . . .

Walter: Man, what you telling me about all this for? . . . Tell me what happened in Springfield . . .

Bobo: Springfield.

Ruth (like a dead woman): What was supposed to happen in Springfield?

Bobo (to her): This deal that me and Walter went into with Willy—Me and Willy was going to go down to Springfield and spread some money 'round so's we wouldn't have to wait so long for the liquor license . . . That's what we were going to do. Everybody said that was the way you had to do, you understand, Miss Ruth?

Walter: Man—what happened down there?

Bobo (a pitiful man, near tears): I'm trying to tell you, Walter.

Walter (screaming at him suddenly): THEN TELL ME, GODDAMMIT . . . WHAT'S THE MATTER WITH YOU?

Bobo: Man . . . I didn't go to no Springfield, yesterday.

Walter (halted, life hanging in the moment): Why not?

Bobo (the long way, the hard way to tell): 'Cause I didn't have no reasons to . . .

Walter: Man, what are you talking about!

Bobo: I'm talking about the fact that when I got to the train station yesterday morning—eight o'clock like we planned . . . Man—*Willy didn't never show up.*

Walter: Why . . . where was he . . . where is he?

Bobo: That's what I'm trying to tell you . . . I don't know . . . I waited six hours . . . I called his house . . . and I waited . . . six hours . . . I waited in that train station six hours . . . *(Breaking into tears.)* That was all the extra money I had in the world . . . *(Looking up at Walter with tears running down his face.)* Man, *Willy is gone.*

Walter: Gone, what you mean Willy is gone? Gone where? You mean he went by himself. You mean he went off to Springfield by himself—to take care of getting the license—*(Turns and looks anxiously at Ruth.)* You mean maybe he didn't want too many people in on the business down there? *(Looks to Ruth again, as before.)* You know Willy got his own ways. *(Looks back to Bobo.)* Maybe you was late yesterday and he just went on down there without you. Maybe—maybe—he's been callin' you at home tryin' to tell you what happened or something. Maybe—maybe—he just got sick. He's somewhere—he's got to be somewhere. We just got to find him—me and you got to find him. *(Grabs Bobo senselessly by the collar and starts to shake him.)* We got to!

Bobo (in sudden angry, frightened agony): What's the matter with you, Walter! When a cat take off with your money he don't leave you no road maps!

Walter (turning madly, as though he is looking for Willy in every room): Willy! . . . Willy . . . don't do it . . . Please don't do it . . . Man, not with that money . . . Man, please, not with that money . . . Oh, God . . . Don't let it be true . . . *(He is wandering around, crying out for Willy and looking for him or perhaps for help from God.)* Man . . . I trusted you . . . Man, I put my life in your hands . . .

(*He starts to crumple down on the floor as Ruth just covers her face in horror. Mama opens the door and comes into the room, with Beneatha behind her.*)

Man . . . (*He starts to pound the floor with his fists, sobbing wildly.*) THAT MONEY IS MADE OUT OF MY FATHER'S FLESH—

Bobo (*standing over him helplessly*): I'm sorry, Walter . . . (*Only Walter's sobs reply. Bobo puts on his hat.*) I had my life staked on this deal, too . . . (*He exits.*)

Mama (*to Walter*): Son—(*She goes to him, bends down to him, talks to his bent head.*) Son . . . Is it gone? Son, I gave you sixty-five hundred dollars. Is it gone? All of it? Beneatha's money too?

Walter (*lifting his head slowly*): Mama . . . I never . . . went to the bank at all . . .

Mama (*not wanting to believe him*): You mean . . . Your sister's school money . . . you used that too . . . Walter? . . .

Walter: Yessss! All of it . . . It's all gone. . . .

(*There is total silence. Ruth stands with her face covered with her hands; Beneatha leans forlornly against a wall, fingering a piece of red ribbon from the mother's gift. Mama stops and looks at her son without recognition and then, quite without thinking about it, starts to beat him senselessly in the face. Beneatha goes to them and stops it.*)

Beneatha: Mama!

(*Mama stops and looks at both of her children and rises slowly and wanders vaguely, aimlessly away from them.*)

Mama: I seen . . . him . . . night after night . . . come in . . . and look at that rug . . . and then look at me . . . the red showing in his eyes . . . the veins moving in his head . . . I seen him grow thin and old before he was forty . . . working and working and working like somebody's old horse . . . killing himself . . . and you—you give it all away in a day—(*She raises her arms to strike him again.*)

Beneatha: Mama—

Mama: Oh, God . . . (*She looks up to Him.*) Look down here—and show me the strength.

Beneatha: Mama—

Mama (*folding over*): Strength . . .

Beneatha (*plaintively*): Mama . . .

Mama: Strength!

ACT THREE

TIME. *An hour later*

At curtain, there is a sullen light of gloom in the living room, gray light not unlike that which began the first scene of Act One. At left we can see Walter within his room, alone with himself. He is stretched out on the bed, his shirt out and open, his arms under his head. He does not smoke, he does not cry out, he merely lies there, looking up at the ceiling, much as if he were alone in the world.

In the living room Beneatha sits at the table, still surrounded by the now almost ominous packing crates. She sits looking off. We feel that this is a mood struck perhaps an hour *before, and it lingers now, full of the empty sound of profound disappointment. We see on a line from her brother's bedroom the sameness of their attitudes. Presently the bell rings and Beneatha rises without ambition or interest in answering. It is Asagai, smiling broadly, striding into the room with energy and happy expectation and conversation.*

Asagai: I came over . . . I had some free time. I thought I might help with the packing. Ah, I like the look of packing crates! A household in preparation for a journey! It depresses some people . . . but for me . . . it is another feeling. Something full of the flow of life, do you understand? Movement, progress . . . It makes me think of Africa.
Beneatha: Africa!
Asagai: What kind of a mood is this? Have I told you how deeply you move me?
Beneatha: He gave away the money, Asagai . . .
Asagai: Who gave away what money?
Beneatha: The insurance money. My brother gave it away.
Asagai: Gave it away?
Beneatha: He made an investment! With a man even Travis wouldn't have trusted with his most worn-out marbles.
Asagai: And it's gone?
Beneatha: Gone!
Asagai: I'm very sorry . . . And you, now?
Beneatha: Me? . . . Me? . . . Me, I'm nothing . . . Me. When I was very small . . . we used to take our sleds out in the wintertime and the only hills we had were the ice-covered stone steps of some houses down the street. And we used to fill them in with snow and make them smooth and slide down them all day . . . and it was very dangerous, you know . . . far too steep . . . and sure enough one day a kid named Rufus came down too fast and hit the sidewalk and we saw his face just split open right there in front of us . . . And I remember standing there looking at his bloody open face thinking that was the end of Rufus. But the ambulance came and they took him to the hospital and they fixed the broken bones and they sewed it all up . . . and the next time I saw Rufus he just had a little line down the middle of his face . . . I never got over that . . .
Asagai: What?
Beneatha: That that was what one person could do for another, fix him up—sew up the problem, make him all right again. That was the most marvelous thing in the world . . . I wanted to do that. I always thought it was the one concrete thing in the world that a human being could do. Fix up the sick, you know—and make them whole again. This was truly being God . . .
Asagai: You wanted to be God?
Beneatha: No—I wanted to cure. It used to be so important to me. I wanted to cure. It used to matter. I used to care. I mean about people and how their bodies hurt . . .
Asagai: And you've stopped caring?
Beneatha: Yes—I think so.
Asagai: Why?
Beneatha (bitterly): Because it doesn't seem deep enough, close enough to what ails mankind! It was a child's way of seeing things—or an idealist's.
Asagai: Children see things very well sometimes—and idealists even better.

Beneatha: I know that's what you think. Because you are still where I left off. You with all your talk and dreams about Africa! You still think you can patch up the world. Cure the Great Sore of Colonialism—(*Loftily, mocking it.*) with the Penicillin of Independence—!

Asagai: Yes!

Beneatha: Independence *and then what?* What about all the crooks and thieves and just plain idiots who will come into power and steal and plunder the same as before—only now they will be black and do it in the name of the new Independence—WHAT ABOUT THEM?!

Asagai: That will be the problem for another time. First we must get there.

Beneatha: And where does it end?

Asagai: End? Who even spoke of an end? To life? To living?

Beneatha: An end to misery! To stupidity! Don't you see there isn't any real progress, Asagai, there is only one large circle that we march in, around and around, each of us with our own little picture in front of us—our own little mirage that we think is the future.

Asagai: That is the mistake.

Beneatha: What?

Asagai: What you just said about the circle. It isn't a circle—it is simply a long line—as in geometry, you know, one that reaches into infinity. And because we cannot see the end—we also cannot see how it changes. And it is very odd but those who see the changes—who dream, who will not give up—are called idealists . . . and those who see only the circle we call *them* the "realists"!

Beneatha: Asagai, while I was sleeping in that bed in there, people went out and took the future right out of my hands! And nobody asked me, nobody consulted me—they just went out and changed my life!

Asagai: Was it your money?

Beneatha: What?

Asagai: Was it your money he gave away?

Beneatha: It belonged to all of us.

Asagai: But did you earn it? Would you have had it at all if your father had not died?

Beneatha: No.

Asagai: Then isn't there something wrong in a house—in a world—where all dreams, good or bad, must depend on the death of a man? I never thought to see *you* like this, Alaiyo. You! Your brother made a mistake and you are grateful to him so that now you can give up the ailing human race on account of it! You talk about what good is struggle; what good is anything! Where are we all going and why are we bothering?

Beneatha: AND YOU CANNOT ANSWER IT!

Asagai (shouting over her): I LIVE THE ANSWER! (*Pause.*) In my village at home it is the exceptional man who can even read a newspaper . . . or who ever sees a book at all. I will go home and much of what I will have to say will seem strange to the people of my village. But I will teach and work and things will happen, slowly and swiftly. At times it will seem that nothing changes at all . . . and then again the sudden dramatic events which make history leap into the future. And then quiet again. Retrogression even. Guns, murder, revolution. And I even will have moments when I wonder if the quiet was not better than all that death and hatred. But I will look about my village at the illiteracy and disease and ignorance and I will not wonder long. And perhaps . . . perhaps I will be a great man . . . I mean perhaps I will hold on to the substance of truth and find my way always with the right course . . . and perhaps for it I will be butchered in my bed some night by the servants of empire . . .

Beneatha: The martyr!

Asagai (he smiles): . . . or perhaps I shall live to be a very old man, respected and esteemed in my new nation . . . And perhaps I shall hold office and this is what I'm trying to tell you, Alaiyo: Perhaps the things I believe now for my country will be wrong and outmoded, and I will not understand and do terrible things to have things my way or merely to keep my power. Don't you see that there will be young men and women—not British soldiers then, but my own black countrymen—to step out of the shadows some evening and slit my then useless throat? Don't you see they have always been there . . . that they always will be. And that such a thing as my own death will be an advance? They who might kill me even . . . actually replenish all that I was.

Beneatha: Oh, Asagai, I know all that.

Asagai: Good! Then stop moaning and groaning and tell me what you plan to do.

Beneatha: Do?

Asagai: I have a bit of a suggestion.

Beneatha: What?

Asagai (rather quietly for him): That when it is all over—that you come home with me—

Beneatha (staring at him and crossing away with exasperation): Oh—Asagai—at this moment you decide to be romantic!

Asagai (quickly understanding the misunderstanding): My dear, young creature of the New World—I do not mean across the city—I mean across the ocean: home—to Africa.

Beneatha (slowly understanding and turning to him with murmured amazement): To Africa?

Asagai: Yes! . . . (*Smiling and lifting his arms playfully.*) Three hundred years later the African Prince rose up out of the seas and swept the maiden back across the middle passage over which her ancestors had come—

Beneatha (unable to play): To—to Nigeria?

Asagai: Nigeria. Home. (*Coming to her with genuine romantic flippancy.*) I will show you our mountains and our stars; and give you cool drinks from gourds and teach you the old songs and the ways of our people—and, in time, we will pretend that—(*Very softly.*)—you have only been away for a day. Say that you'll come—(*He swings her around and takes her full in his arms in a kiss which proceeds to passion.*)

Beneatha (pulling away suddenly): You're getting me all mixed up—

Asagai: Why?

Beneatha: Too many things—too many things have happened today. I must sit down and think. I don't know what I feel about anything right this minute. (*She promptly sits down and props her chin on her fist.*)

Asagai (charmed): All right, I shall leave you. No—don't get up. (*Touching her, gently, sweetly.*) Just sit awhile and think . . . Never be afraid to sit awhile and think. (*He goes to door and looks at her.) How often I have looked at you and said, "Ah—so this is what the New World hath finally wrought . . ."*

(He exits. Beneatha sits on alone. Presently Walter enters from his room and starts to rummage through things, feverishly looking for something. She looks up and turns in her seat.)

Beneatha *(hissingly)*: Yes—just look at what the New World hath wrought! . . . Just look! *(She gestures with bitter disgust.)* There he is! *Monsieur le petit bourgeois noir*°— himself! There he is—Symbol of a Rising Class! Entrepreneur! Titan of the system!

(Walter ignores her completely and continues frantically and destructively looking for something and hurling things to floor and tearing things out of their place in his search. Beneatha ignores the eccentricity of his actions and goes on with the monologue of insult.)

Did you dream of yachts on Lake Michigan, Brother? Did you see yourself on that Great Day sitting down at the Conference Table, surrounded by all the mighty bald-headed men in America? All halted, waiting, breathless, waiting for your pronouncements on industry? Waiting for you—Chairman of the Board!

(Walter finds what he is looking for—a small piece of white paper—and pushes it in his pocket and puts on his coat and rushes out without ever having looked at her. She shouts after him.)

I look at you and I see the final triumph of stupidity in the world!

(The door slams and she returns to just sitting again. Ruth comes quickly out of Mama's room.)

Ruth: Who was that?
Beneatha: Your husband.
Ruth: Where did he go?
Beneatha: Who knows—maybe he has an appointment at U.S. Steel.
Ruth *(anxiously, with frightened eyes)*: You didn't say nothing bad to him, did you?
Beneatha: Bad? Say anything bad to him? No—I told him he was a sweet boy and full of dreams and everything is strictly peachy keen, as the *ofay*° kids say!

(Mama enters from her bedroom. She is lost, vague, trying to catch hold, to make some sense of her former command of the world, but it still eludes her. A sense of waste overwhelms her gait; a measure of apology rides on her shoulders. She goes to her plant, which has remained on the table, looks at it, picks it up and takes it to the windowsill and sits it outside, and she stands and looks at it a long moment. Then she closes the window, straightens her body with effort and turns around to her children.)

Mama: Well—ain't it a mess in here, though? *(A false cheerfulness, a beginning of something.)* I guess we all better stop moping around and get some work done. All this unpacking and everything we got to do. *(Ruth raises her head slowly in response to*

Monsieur le petit bourgeois noir: French for "Mr. Black Middle Class."   *ofay*: Pig Latin for "foe."

the sense of the line; and Beneatha in similar manner turns very slowly to look at her mother.) One of you all better call the moving people and tell 'em not to come.

Ruth: Tell 'em not to come?

Mama: Of course, baby. Ain't no need in 'em coming all the way here and having to go back. They charges for that too. (*She sits down, fingers to her brow, thinking.*) Lord, ever since I was a little girl, I always remembers people saying, "Lena—Lena Eggleston, you aims too high all the time. You needs to slow down and see life a little more like it is. Just slow down some." That's what they always used to say down home—"Lord, that Lena Eggleston is a high-minded thing. She'll get her due one day!"

Ruth: No, Lena . . .

Mama: Me and Big Walter just didn't never learn right.

Ruth: Lena, no! We gotta go. Bennie—tell her . . . (*She rises and crosses to Beneatha with her arms outstretched. Beneatha doesn't respond.*) Tell her we can still move . . . the notes ain't but a hundred and twenty-five a month. We got four grown people in this house—we can work . . .

Mama (*to herself*): Just aimed too high all the time—

Ruth (*turning and going to Mama fast—the words pouring out with urgency and desperation*): Lena—I'll work . . . I'll work twenty hours a day in all the kitchens in Chicago . . . I'll strap my baby on my back if I have to and scrub all the floors in America and wash all the sheets in America if I have to—but we got to MOVE! We got to get OUT OF HERE!!

(*Mama reaches out absently and pats Ruth's hand.*)

Mama: No—I sees things differently now. Been thinking 'bout some of the things we could do to fix this place up some. I seen a second-hand bureau over on Maxwell Street just the other day that could fit right there. (*She points to where the new furniture might go. Ruth wanders away from her.*) Would need some new handles on it and then a little varnish and it look like something brand-new. And—we can put up them new curtains in the kitchen . . . Why this place be looking fine. Cheer us all up so that we forget trouble ever come . . . (*To Ruth.*) And you could get some nice screens to put up in your room 'round the baby's bassinet . . . (*She looks at both of them, pleadingly.*) Sometimes you just got to know when to give up some things . . . and hold on to what you got . . .

(*Walter enters from the outside, looking spent and leaning against the door, his coat hanging from him.*)

Mama: Where you been, son?

Walter (*breathing hard*): Made a call.

Mama: To who, son?

Walter: To The Man. (*He heads for his room.*)

Mama: What man, baby?

Walter (*stops in the door*): The Man, Mama. Don't you know who The Man is?

Ruth: Walter Lee?

Walter: The Man. Like the guys in the streets say—The Man. Captain Boss—Mistuh Charley . . . Old Cap'n Please Mr. Bossman . . .

Beneatha (*suddenly*): Lindner!

Walter: That's right! That's good. I told him to come right over.

Beneatha (fiercely, understanding): For what? What do you want to see him for!

Walter (looking at his sister): We going to do business with him.

Mama: What you talking 'bout, son?

Walter: Talking 'bout life, Mama. You all always telling me to see life like it is. Well—I laid in there on my back today . . . and I figured it out. Life just like it is. Who gets and who don't get. *(He sits down with his coat on and laughs.)* Mama, you know it's all divided up. Life is. Sure enough. Between the takers and the "tooken." *(He laughs.)* I've figured it out finally. *(He looks around at them.)* Yeah. Some of us always getting "tooken." *(He laughs.)* People like Willy Harris, they don't never get "tooken." And you know why the rest of us do? 'Cause we all mixed up. Mixed up bad. We get to looking 'round for the right and the wrong; and we worry about it and cry about it and stay up nights trying to figure out 'bout the wrong and the right of things all the time . . . And all the time, man, them takers is out there operating, just taking and taking. Willy Harris? Shoot—Willy Harris don't even count. He don't even count in the big scheme of things. But I'll say one thing for old Willy Harris . . . he's taught me something. He's taught me to keep my eye on what counts in this world. Yeah—*(Shouting out a little.)* Thanks, Willy!

Ruth: What did you call that man for, Walter Lee?

Walter: Called him to tell him to come on over to the show. Gonna put on a show for the man. Just what he wants to see. You see, Mama, the man came here today and he told us that them people out there where you want us to move—well they so upset they willing to pay us *not* to move! *(He laughs again.)* And—and oh, Mama—you would of been proud of the way me and Ruth and Bennie acted. We told him to get out . . . Lord have mercy! We told the man to get out! Oh, we was some proud folks this afternoon, yeah. *(He lights a cigarette.)* We were still full of that old-time stuff . . .

Ruth (coming toward him slowly): You talking 'bout taking them people's money to keep us from moving in that house?

Walter: I ain't just talking 'bout it, baby—I'm telling you that's what's going to happen!

Beneatha: Oh, God! Where is the bottom! Where is the real honest-to-God bottom so he can't go any farther!

Walter: See—that's the old stuff. You and that boy that was here today. You all want everybody to carry a flag and a spear and sing some marching songs, huh? You wanna spend your life looking into things and trying to find the right and the wrong part, huh? Yeah. You know what's going to happen to that boy someday—he'll find himself sitting in a dungeon, locked in forever—and the takers will have the key! Forget it, baby! There ain't no causes—there ain't nothing but taking in this world, and he who takes most is smartest—and it don't make a damn bit of difference *how*.

Mama: You making something inside me cry, son. Some awful pain inside me.

Walter: Don't cry, Mama. Understand. That white man is going to walk in that door able to write checks for more money than we ever had. It's important to him and I'm going to help him . . . I'm going to put on the show, Mama.

Mama: Son—I come from five generations of people who was slaves and sharecroppers—but ain't nobody in my family never let nobody pay 'em no money that was a way of telling us we wasn't fit to walk the earth. We ain't never been that poor. *(Raising her eyes and looking at him.)* We ain't never been that—dead inside.

Beneatha: Well—we are dead now. All the talk about dreams and sunlight that goes on in this house. It's all dead now.

Walter: What's the matter with you all! I didn't make this world! It was give to me this way! Hell, yes, I want me some yachts someday! Yes, I want to hang some real pearls 'round my wife's neck. Ain't she supposed to wear no pearls? Somebody tell me—tell me, who decides which women is suppose to wear pearls in this world! I tell you I am a *man*—and I think my wife should wear some pearls in this world!

(This last line hangs a good while and Walter begins to move about the room. The word "Man" has penetrated his consciousness; he mumbles it to himself repeatedly between strange agitated pauses as he moves about.)

Mama: Baby, how you going to feel on the inside?

Walter: Fine! . . . Going to feel fine . . . a man . . .

Mama: You won't have nothing left then, Walter Lee.

Walter (coming to her): I'm going to feel fine, Mama. I'm going to look that son-of-a-bitch in the eyes and say—*(He falters.)*—and say, "All right, Mr. Lindner—*(He falters even more.)*—that's *your* neighborhood out there! You got the right to keep it like you want! You got the right to have it like you want! Just write the check and—the house is yours." And—and I am going to say—*(His voice almost breaks.)* "And you—you people just put the money in my hand and you won't have to live next to this bunch of stinking niggers! . . . " *(He straightens up and moves away from his mother, walking around the room.)* And maybe—maybe I'll just get down on my black knees . . . *(He does so; Ruth and Bennie and Mama watch him in frozen horror.)* "Captain, Mistuh, Bossman—*(Groveling and grinning and wringing his hands in profoundly anguished imitation of the slow-witted movie stereotype.)* A-hee-hee-hee! Oh, yassuh boss! Yasssssuh! Great white—*(Voice breaking, he forces himself to go on.)*—Father, just gi' ussen de money, fo' God's sake, and we's—we's ain't gwine come out deh and dirty up yo' white folks neighborhood . . ." *(He breaks down completely.)* And I'll feel fine! Fine! FINE! *(He gets up and goes into the bedroom.)*

Beneatha: That is not a man. That is nothing but a toothless rat.

Mama: Yes—death done come in this here house. *(She is nodding, slowly, reflectively.)* Done come walking in my house on the lips of my children. You what supposed to be my beginning again. You—what supposed to be my harvest. *(To Beneatha.)* You—you mourning your brother?

Beneatha: He's no brother of mine.

Mama: What you say?

Beneatha: I said that that individual in that room is no brother of mine.

Mama: That's what I thought you said. You feeling like you better than he is today? *(Beneatha does not answer.)* Yes? What you tell him a minute ago? That he wasn't a man? Yes? You give him up for me? You done wrote his epitaph too—like the rest of the world? Well, who give you the privilege?

Beneatha: Be on my side for once! You saw what he just did, Mama! You saw him—down on his knees. Wasn't it you who taught me to despise any man who would do that? Do what he's going to do?

Mama: Yes—I taught you that. Me and your daddy. But I thought I taught you something else too . . . I thought I taught you to love him.

Beneatha: Love him? There is nothing left to love.

Mama: There is *always* something left to love. And if you ain't learned that, you ain't learned nothing. *(Looking at her.)* Have you cried for that boy today? I don't mean for yourself and for the family 'cause we lost the money. I mean for him:

what he been through and what it done to him. Child, when do you think is the time to love somebody the most? When they done good and made things easy for everybody? Well then, you ain't through learning—because that ain't the time at all. It's when he's at his lowest and can't believe in hisself 'cause the world done whipped him so! When you starts measuring somebody, measure him right, child, measure him right. Make sure you done taken into account what hills and valleys he come through before he got to wherever he is.

(*Travis bursts into the room at the end of the speech, leaving the door open.*)

Travis: Grandmama—the moving men are downstairs! The truck just pulled up.
Mama (*turning and looking at him*): Are they, baby? They downstairs?

(*She sighs and sits. Lindner appears in the doorway. He peers in and knocks lightly, to gain attention, and comes in. All turn to look at him.*)

Lindner (*hat and briefcase in hand*): Uh—hello . . .

(*Ruth crosses mechanically to the bedroom door and opens it and lets it swing open freely and slowly as the lights come up on Walter within, still in his coat, sitting at the far corner of the room. He looks up and out through the room to Lindner.*)

Ruth: He's here.

(*A long minute passes and Walter slowly gets up.*)

Lindner (*coming to the table with efficiency, putting his briefcase on the table and starting to unfold papers and unscrew fountain pens*): Well, I certainly was glad to hear from you people.

(*Walter has begun the trek out of the room, slowly and awkwardly, rather like a small boy, passing the back of his sleeve across his mouth from time to time.*)

Life can really be so much simpler than people let it be most of the time. Well—with whom do I negotiate? You, Mrs. Younger, or your son here?

(*Mama sits with her hands folded on her lap and her eyes closed as Walter advances. Travis goes closer to Lindner and looks at the papers curiously.*)

Just some official papers, sonny.

Ruth: Travis, you go downstairs—
Mama (*opening her eyes and looking into Walter's*): No. Travis, you stay right here. And you make him understand what you doing, Walter Lee. You teach him good. Like Willy Harris taught you. You show where our five generations done come to. (*Walter looks from her to the boy, who grins at him innocently.*) Go ahead, son—(*She folds her hands and closes her eyes.*) Go ahead.
Walter (*at last crosses to Lindner, who is reviewing the contract*): Well, Mr. Lindner. (*Beneatha turns away.*) We called you—(*There is a profound, simple groping quality in his speech.*)—because, well, me and my family (*He looks around and shifts from one foot to the other.*) Well—we are very plain people. . . .
Lindner: Yes—
Walter: I mean—I have worked as a chauffeur most of my life—and my wife here, she does domestic work in people's kitchens. So does my mother. I mean—we are plain people . . .
Lindner: Yes, Mr. Younger—

Walter (really like a small boy, looking down at his shoes and then up at the man): And—uh—well, my father, well, he was a laborer most of his life . . .

Lindner (absolutely confused): Uh, yes—yes, I understand. *(He turns back to the contract.)*

Walter (a beat; staring at him): And my father—*(With sudden intensity.)* My father almost *beat a man to death* once because this man called him a bad name or something, you know what I mean?

Lindner (looking up, frozen): No, no, I'm afraid I don't—

Walter (a beat. The tension hangs; then Walter steps back from it): Yeah. Well—what I mean is that we come from people who had a lot of *pride*. I mean—we are very proud people. And that's my sister over there and she's going to be a doctor—and we are very proud—

Lindner: Well—I am sure that is very nice, but—

Walter: What I am telling you is that we called you over here to tell you that we are very proud and that this—*(Signaling to Travis.)* Travis, come here. *(Travis crosses and Walter draws him before him facing the man.)* This is my son, and he makes the sixth generation of our family in this country. And we have all thought about your offer—

Lindner: Well, good . . . good—

Walter: And we have decided to move into our house because my father—my father—he earned it for us brick by brick. *(Mama has her eyes closed and is rocking back and forth as though she were in church, with her head nodding the Amen yes.)*

We don't want to make no trouble for nobody or fight no causes, and we will try to be good neighbors. And that's *all* we got to say about that. *(He looks the man absolutely in the eyes.)* We don't want your money. *(He turns and walks away.)*

Lindner (looking around at all of them): I take it then—that you have decided to occupy . . .

Beneatha: That's what the man said.

Lindner (to Mama in her reverie): Then I would like to appeal to you, Mrs. Younger. You are older and wiser and understand things better I am sure . . .

Mama: I am afraid you don't understand. My son said we was going to move and there ain't nothing left for me to say. *(Briskly.)* You know how these young folks is nowadays, mister. Can't do a thing with 'em! *(As he opens his mouth, she rises.)* Good-bye.

Lindner (folding up his materials): Well—if you are that final about it . . . there is nothing left for me to say. *(He finishes, almost ignored by the family, who are concentrating on Walter Lee. At the door Lindner halts and looks around.)* I sure hope you people know what you're getting into. *(He shakes his head and exits.)*

Ruth (looking around and coming to life): Well, for God's sake—if the moving men are here—LET'S GET THE HELL OUT OF HERE!

Mama (into action): Ain't it the truth! Look at all this here mess. Ruth, put Travis' good jacket on him . . . Walter Lee, fix your tie and tuck your shirt in; you look like somebody's hoodlum! Lord have mercy, where is my plant? *(She flies to get it amid the general bustling of the family, who are deliberately trying to ignore the nobility of the past moment.)* You all start on down . . . Travis child, don't go empty-handed . . . Ruth, where did I put that box with my skillets in it? I want to be in charge of it myself . . . I'm going to make us the biggest dinner we ever ate tonight . . . Beneatha, what's the matter with them stockings? Pull them things up, girl . . .

(*The family starts to file out as two moving men appear and begin to carry out the heavier pieces of furniture, bumping into the family as they move about.*)

Beneatha: Mama, Asagai asked me to marry him today and go to Africa—
Mama (*in the middle of her getting-ready activity*): He did? You ain't old enough to marry nobody—(*Seeing the moving men lifting one of her chairs precariously.*) Darling, that ain't no bale of cotton, please handle it so we can sit in it again! I had that chair twenty-five years . . .

(*The movers sigh with exasperation and go on with their work.*)

Beneatha (*girlishly and unreasonably trying to pursue the conversation*): To go to Africa, Mama—be a doctor in Africa . . .
Mama (*distracted*): Yes, baby—
Walter: Africa! What he want you to go to Africa for?
Beneatha: To practice there . . .
Walter: Girl, if you don't get all them silly ideas out your head! You better marry yourself a man with some loot . . .
Beneatha (*angrily, precisely as in the first scene of the play*): What have you got to do with who I marry!
Walter: Plenty. Now I think George Murchison—
Beneatha: George Murchison! I wouldn't marry him if he was Adam and I was Eve!

(*Walter and Beneatha go out yelling at each other vigorously and the anger is loud and real till their voices diminish. Ruth stands at the door and turns to Mama and smiles knowingly.*)

Mama (*fixing her hat at last*): Yeah—they something all right, my children . . .
Ruth: Yeah—they're something. Let's go, Lena.
Mama (*stalling, starting to look around at the house*): Yes—I'm coming. Ruth—
Ruth: Yes?
Mama (*quietly, woman to woman*): He finally come into his manhood today, didn't he? Kind of like a rainbow after the rain . . .
Ruth (*biting her lip lest her own pride explode in front of Mama*): Yes, Lena.

(*Walter's voice calls for them raucously.*)

Walter (*off stage*): Y'all come on! These people charges by the hour, you know!
Mama (*waving Ruth out vaguely*): All right, honey—go on down. I be down directly.

(*Ruth hesitates, then exits. Mama stands, at last alone in the living room, her plant on the table before her as the lights start to come down. She looks around at all the walls and ceilings and suddenly, despite herself, while the children call below, a great heaving thing rises in her and she puts her fist to her mouth to stifle it, takes a final desperate look, pulls her coat about her, pats her hat and goes out. The lights dim down. The door opens and she comes back in, grabs her plant, and goes out for the last time.*)

CURTAIN

Questions

1. In the opening scene of the play, what factors account for the irritation and hostility that the family members show toward one another?
2. What values do the members of the family associate with Mama's late husband? In what ways do they try to live up to those values in their own lives?
3. How would you characterize the relationship between Walter and his sister, Beneatha? Do they seem to have a genuine affection for one another?
4. Mama maintains that everything she does is for her family. Do her actions support this claim, in your opinion, or not?
5. Why does Asagai call Beneatha "Alaiyo: One for Whom Bread—Food—Is Not Enough"? (page 399.) Why is she flattered by this description?
6. Do Walter and Ruth respect one another? Cite specific details from the play to back up your conclusions.
7. What does Mama mean when she says on page 427 about her flower: "It expresses ME!"?
8. Even though the future of the Younger family in their new neighborhood is uncertain, to say the least, does the play have a happy ending? Explain.

Suggestions for Writing on *Lorraine Hansberry's A Raisin in the Sun*

1. There is a great deal of conflict among the family members in the play. Are their arguments caused more by simple differences of opinion or by a failure to understand one another's feelings and desires? Refer as specifically as possible to the words and actions of the characters to back up your conclusions.
2. Beneatha's two suitors function as foils to one another: the contrast between them highlights the characteristics of each. Describe each one's essential nature, emphasizing the differences between them. Which one does Beneatha prefer, and why?
3. Discuss the meaning of Mama's famous speech (page 439), especially—but not exclusively—as it applies to Walter: "When you starts measuring somebody, measure him right, child, measure him right. Make sure you done taken into account what hills and valleys he come through before he got to wherever he is."
4. *A Raisin in the Sun* takes its title from Langston Hughes's poem "Harlem" (page 61). Read the poem, then write an essay in which you discuss how its theme applies to the members of the Younger family.

Suggestions for Writing on Literature about Families

1. Some of the strongest family ties depicted in this chapter (for example, the mother and Maggie in "Everyday Use," the two brothers in "Sonny's Blues") exist despite challenges from both within and outside the family. What, in your opinion, are the characteristics of a healthy relationship between family members? When such relationships do work well, what accounts for it? Do these situations have common characteristics? Pick at least two family relationships that appear in this chapter and write about what makes them functional—or not functional.
2. What did Leo Tolstoy mean when he wrote, "All happy families are alike; every unhappy family is unhappy in its own way"? Consider two of the families presented in this chapter and discuss whether Tolstoy's statement applies to them.
3. It could be argued that all of the families depicted in this chapter are deeply shaped and influenced by the settings, times, and cultures in which they exist. Choose two pieces (of any genre) and analyze how the social, historical, geographical, or cultural contexts in which the families' stories take place influence the family dynamics and the narrative outcome.
4. Many of the poems and essays in this chapter deal with parents and work. How has the work of your parents influenced and shaped you? Do you respect what they do? What have you learned from it? What will you emulate—and what will you want to do differently?
5. Have you grown apart from a friend or relative with whom you once had a close relationship? Imagine an encounter with that person, and write a first-person description of it from the other person's point of view.
6. Write about some unexpected act of kindness you experienced from a member of your family. What happened? Why did it surprise you? Did it change your life in any way?
7. Imagine that you are one of the people who raised you. In the voice of that person, write a letter to you—discussing what you (the parent) observe, what you hope for, what disappoints you, what you hope you (the child) will learn and achieve. Try to step outside yourself and really see yourself as you might appear to someone else.

13   LOVE

Life's greatest happiness is to be convinced we are loved.

—VICTOR HUGO

Of all the themes included in this book, love is probably the one you think about most often. You might go for weeks without pondering the meaning of war or mortality; you might even go for a day or two without thinking about your family. But love? Or at least romance and desire? Even now your thoughts are probably on the guy you have a crush on, or your wonderful girlfriend, or the argument you had with your significant other yesterday, or the evil ex who broke your heart.

Love, desire, and heartbreak seem to be universal human experiences. Certainly no other theme occupies such a large place in literature as love. There are countless stories, novels, poems, and plays on the subject—not to mention movies, songs, operas, and paintings. Without love what would become of the greeting card industry? This is because love is one of the most thrilling of human experiences. When you're in love, your beloved may seem unique—the most beautiful, amazing creature who ever existed. And if the person you love returns your feelings, then *you* might feel incredible, too—more capable, more desirable, brighter, happier.

Love affects not only how we see another person and ourselves; it also influences how optimistic we are about life in general. When you're in love, suddenly the everyday challenges of life seem manageable, and the world becomes a friendlier place. Love can be magical and utterly transformative. Interestingly, the power of love is not simply a matter of emotion. Recent research has found that love affects the chemical makeup of the brain. Falling in love can actually help ease physical pain. In other words, love doesn't just *feel* good; sometimes it *is* good for you. No wonder people strive so hard to find it.

As wonderful as love can be, it can also disappoint us. Most people have had the experience of being madly in love with someone—only to realize that the object of their love was not as perfect or as admirable as they believed. Sometimes love devolves into a distaste that borders on hatred—or even more deadly, cold indifference. If passion doesn't last, does that mean the original feelings weren't real? Is love actually a gentle variety of madness?

Perhaps to save us from this kind of disappointment, we are often told by our elders that infatuation isn't the same as "real" love; that there's a difference between desire and a lasting, stable connection. We're also warned to be skeptical about the popular images of love in songs and movies because they can create unrealistic expectations of romance that will lead to disappointment. Such warnings may make it sound as though "real" love is something hearty and good for you, but not particularly exciting—like boiled vegetables. But as some of the authors in this chapter demonstrate, love sometimes can be both good for you *and* exciting.

In reality, despite all the sober warnings, there are still plenty of happy couples who have kept the spark between them alive for decades, as well as thwarted lovers who still feel strong passion despite being separated for years. These stories defy the conventional wisdom about romantic love's fading over time. How do such couples do it? Isn't this the kind of love we should all aspire to? How do we get there, anyway? Is it destiny, or sheer luck, or is there some secret formula for enduring love?

The truth is that, for all of the scientific studies, psychological analyses, and sociological examinations, much about love remains an intriguing mystery. We can't predict or control whom we'll be attracted to, or which attraction will blossom into a deeper connection. While biology, upbringing, and environment may play some part in our choices, no one really knows the exact ingredients for love.

But we do know that the road to love can be difficult. How can we tell the difference between lust and love—and isn't lust also a necessary component of deep romantic love? How do we overcome our shyness and fear to approach the person we like, or to respond appropriately if he or she approaches us? How can we be giving and selfless in love without surrendering too much of ourselves? What do we do when the one we love turns out to be different from the wonderful person we had imagined, or if he or she begins to evolve in ways that puzzle or alarm us?

As if internal challenges weren't enough, there are often external factors to cope with as well. The society, culture, or neighborhood in which we live may have particular expectations about what's acceptable in the choice of a romantic partner. (Arranged marriages—which remove the variable of individual attraction in favor of more seemingly logical criteria—are still common in some cultures.) Gender roles and expectations may influence everything from who we think should make the first move, to who should carry what responsibilities in a relationship, to what we look for in a partner.

Finally, there is another seemingly universal truth about love—that losing it really hurts. People who are heartbroken can barely attend to the other parts of their lives. They might lose weight, lose sleep, drink or smoke too much, lose the ability to find pleasure in life. In extreme cases, jilted lovers have been known to commit crimes of passion, driven by rage or jealousy to kill their beloved. Even under less dramatic circumstances, heartbreak can last for months, even years. The rejected and dejected are often convinced that they can never love again—which, fortunately, is almost never true. The heart is resilient, and in time, love almost inevitably reappears in some new form. This may be one reason that so much love-inspired art exists. All those beautifully sad songs and poems provide the consolation that someone else has been there too, felt what we felt, and survived.

THE SELECTIONS IN THIS CHAPTER

The selections in this chapter address the many aspects of love. Works such as John Donne's "The Flea" and Andrew Marvell's "To His Coy Mistress" describe romantic courtship at its most playful, while Kate Chopin's "The Storm" explores sexual passion at its most recklessly heated. Kim Addonizio's "First Poem for You," Wendy Cope's "Lonely Hearts," and T. S. Eliot's "The Love Song of J. Alfred Prufrock" capture the quiet agonies of loneliness and desire—even when the object of love is within reach. Flannery O'Connor's "Parker's Back," Max Apple's "Vegetable Love," and O. Henry's "The Gift of the Magi" present characters who make major sacrifices for love—to very different ends. Zora Neale Hurston's "Sweat" and Margaret Atwood's "Happy Endings" tell stories of women whose relationships have stifled rather than nourished them. William Faulkner's "A Rose for Emily" tells the story of a woman forever paralyzed (but not powerless!) by an early romantic rejection. Shakespeare's play *Othello* deals with both the poisonous power of jealousy and the difficulties of a marriage that goes against conventional norms. Poems by Elizabeth Barrett Browning, Anne Bradstreet, Rafael Campo, E. E. Cummings, and William Shakespeare describe love that is both deep and true.

Paul of Tarsus's famous passage on love from his First Letter to the Corinthians, which is often read at weddings, provides a traditional description of ideal love. Cynthia Ozick's compelling memoir essay "Lovesickness" provides a less idealized account of the irrationality of obsessive romantic attraction. Judith Ortiz Cofer's "I Fell in Love, or My Hormones Awakened" offers a different version of the confusions of early love from a female perspective, while Mike Ives offers a young man's account of romantic illusions.

As you read these works, we hope you find a few that speak to you. Maybe one of them will help give you that extra bit of courage you need to approach someone you like—or to avoid someone you know is not the one for you. Maybe some of these works will give you insights into choices you've made in the past—and influence what you do in the future. As many of the authors in this chapter demonstrate, the course of love is unpredictable. Sometimes the road is direct, and sometimes it takes detours, but getting there is worth the journey. Love is our common theme, and each selection offers a different variation on this inexhaustible topic.

Things to Think About

1. What is your definition of love? What, in your opinion, is the difference between infatuation and true love?
2. Do you know of any couples whom you consider really in love? How would you describe them? Do they behave differently from other people?
3. Two people in love come to a relationship with different needs, expectations, and hopes. What is the proper balance, in your opinion, between compromise

and self-interest? What kinds of sacrifice do you think are acceptable—and what would be asking too much?
4. Do you think that the images of love we receive from movies, television, and other media influence our expectations of love? Why or why not?
5. Why is it so painful when love doesn't work out? What is it about love that makes romantic disappointment so much more poignant than other kinds of disappointment?
6. There are many different kinds of love: romantic love, love of family, love of friends, love of animals, love of causes, love of humankind. How would you characterize these various forms of love? How are they different, and similar?

FICTION

DISCOVERING LOVE

Margaret Atwood   *Happy Endings*

O. Henry   *The Gift of the Magi*

Max Apple   *Vegetable Love*

The process of falling in love is a mystery. You never know why someone catches your eye or sets you daydreaming during lunch or in English class. And when the person you love returns your feelings, the mystery is even deeper. What makes two people fall in love? Is it as simple—and as random—as physical chemistry? Is it that the lovers see each other as different from what they've known before? Or is it that they find, in one another, a place where they're safe; where they can fully be themselves? The beginning of love can be thrilling and nerve-wracking, like driving too fast at night, or like skydiving. And part of the thrill of love—as well as the anxiety—is figuring out how much of yourself to throw into it. What is the right balance between self-protection and self-sacrifice? What should we reveal about ourselves and our intentions, especially in the early stages? Is it all right to keep certain things secret—about our pasts, or our future intentions? All of the stories in this section feature characters swept up by love, sometimes in its early stages or in a difficult middle passage. In Margaret Atwood's story, lovers—especially women—are foiled by their own high hopes. O. Henry gives us an ironic tale about a couple whose genuine love for each other is shown by their self-sacrifice. Max Apple's satiric "Vegetable Love" presents a fellow willing to attempt total transformation in order to win the object of his love. The situations of these characters vary, as do the intentions and actions of the people they love—but they are all grappling with the ever-present and familiar issues of hope, trust, illusion, and disillusion.

Margaret Atwood

Born in Ottawa, Ontario, in 1939, Margaret Eleanor Atwood was the daughter of an entomologist and spent her childhood summers in the forests of northern Quebec, where her father carried out research. She began writing at the age of five and had already seriously entertained thoughts of becoming a professional writer before she finished high school. She graduated from the University of Toronto in 1961, and later did graduate work at Radcliffe and Harvard. Atwood first gained prominence as a poet, and has published nearly twenty volumes of verse. Atwood began to write fiction seriously in graduate school; her short stories were first collected in Dancing Girls *(1977), followed by numerous additional collections, most recently* Moral Disorder *(2006).*

Margaret Atwood

A dedicated feminist, Atwood explores in her fiction the complex relations between the sexes, most incisively in The Handmaid's Tale *(1986), a futuristic novel about a world in which gender roles are ruthlessly enforced by a society based on religious fundamentalism. In the same year that* The Handmaid's Tale *appeared, Atwood was named Woman of the Year by* Ms. *magazine. Subsequent novels include* Cat's Eye *(1988),* The Robber Bride *(1993),* The Blind Assassin *(2000), and* The Year of the Flood *(2009). Atwood has served as writer-in-residence at universities in Canada, the United States, and Europe, and she is widely in demand for appearances at symposia devoted to literature and women's issues. In "Happy Endings" Atwood finds an innovative way to explore the mystery and the risk at the center of any romance.*

Happy Endings   1983

John and Mary meet.
What happens next?
If you want a happy ending, try A.

A

John and Mary fall in love and get married. They both have worthwhile and remunerative jobs which they find stimulating and challenging. They buy a charming house. Real estate values go up. Eventually, when they can afford live-in help, they have two children, to whom they are devoted. The children turn out well. John and Mary have a stimulating and challenging sex life and worthwhile friends. They go on fun vacations together. They retire. They both have hobbies which they find stimulating and challenging. Eventually they die. This is the end of the story.

B

Mary falls in love with John but John doesn't fall in love with Mary. He merely uses her body for selfish pleasure and ego gratification of a tepid kind. He comes to her apartment twice a week and she cooks him dinner, you'll notice that he doesn't even consider her worth the price of a dinner out, and after he's eaten the dinner he fucks her and after that he falls asleep, while she does the dishes so he won't think she's untidy, having all those dirty dishes lying around, and puts on fresh lipstick so she'll look good when he wakes up, but when he wakes up he doesn't even notice, he puts on his socks and his shorts and his pants and his shirt and his tie and his shoes, the reverse order from the one in which he took them off. He doesn't take off Mary's clothes, she takes them off herself, she acts as if she's dying for it every time, not because she likes sex exactly, she doesn't, but she wants John to think she does because if they do it often enough surely he'll get used to her, he'll come to depend on her and they will get married, but John goes out the door with hardly so much as a goodnight and three days later he turns up at six o'clock and they do the whole thing over again.

Mary gets run down. Crying is bad for your face, everyone knows that and so does Mary but she can't stop. People at work notice. Her friends tell her John is a rat, a pig, a dog, he isn't good enough for her, but she can't believe it. Inside John, she thinks, is another John, who is much nicer. This other John will emerge like a butterfly from a cocoon, a Jack from a box, a pit from a prune, if the first John is only squeezed enough.

One evening John complains about the food. He has never complained about the food before. Mary is hurt.

Her friends tell her they've seen him in a restaurant with another woman, whose name is Madge. It's not even Madge that finally gets to Mary; it's the restaurant. John has never taken Mary to a restaurant. Mary collects all the sleeping pills and aspirins she can find, and takes them and a half a bottle of sherry. You can see what kind of a woman she is by the fact that it's not even whiskey. She leaves a note for John. She hopes he'll discover her and get her to the hospital in time and repent and then they can get married, but this fails to happen and she dies.

John marries Madge and everything continues as in A.

C

John, who is an older man, falls in love with Mary, and Mary, who is only twenty-two, feels sorry for him because he's worried about his hair falling out. She sleeps with him even though she's not in love with him. She met him at work. She's in love with someone called James, who is twenty-two also and not yet ready to settle down.

John on the contrary settled down long ago: this is what is bothering him. John has a steady, respectable job and is getting ahead in his field, but Mary isn't impressed by him, she's impressed by James, who has a motorcycle and a fabulous record collection. But James is often away on his motorcycle, being free. Freedom isn't the same for girls, so in the meantime Mary spends Thursday evenings with John. Thursdays are the only days John can get away.

John is married to a woman called Madge and they have two children, a charming house which they bought just before the real estate values went up, and hobbies which they find stimulating and challenging, when they have the time. John tells Mary how important she is to him, but of course, he can't leave his wife because a commitment is a commitment. He goes on about this more than is necessary and Mary finds it boring, but older men can keep it up longer so on the whole she has a fairly good time.

One day James breezes in on his motorcycle with some top-grade California hybrid and James and Mary get higher than you'd believe possible and they climb into bed. Everything becomes very underwater, but along comes John, who has a key to Mary's apartment. He finds them stoned and entwined. He's hardly in any position to be jealous, considering Madge, but nevertheless he's overcome with despair. Finally he's middle-aged, in two years he'll be bald as an egg and he can't stand it. He purchases a handgun, saying he needs it for target practice—this is the thin part of the plot, but it can be dealt with later—and shoots the two of them and himself.

Madge, after a suitable period of mourning, marries an understanding man called Fred and everything continues as in A, but under different names.

D

Fred and Madge have no problems. They get along exceptionally well and are good at working out any little difficulties that may arise. But their charming house is by the seashore and one day a giant tidal wave approaches. Real estate values go down. The rest of the story is about what caused the tidal wave and how they escape from it. They do, though thousands drown, but Fred and Madge are virtuous and lucky. Finally on high ground they clasp each other, wet and dripping and grateful, and continue as in A.

E

Yes, but Fred has a bad heart. The rest of the story is about how kind and understanding they both are until Fred dies. Then Madge devotes herself to charity work until the end of A. If you like, it can be "Madge," "cancer," "guilty and confused," and "bird watching."

F

If you think this is all too bourgeois, make John a revolutionary and Mary a counterespionage agent and see how far that gets you. Remember, this is Canada. You'll still end up with A, though in between you may get a lustful brawling saga of passionate involvement, a chronicle of our times, sort of.

* *

You'll have to face it, the endings are the same however you slice it. Don't be deluded by any other endings, they're all fake, either deliberately fake, with malicious intent to deceive, or just motivated by excessive optimism if not by downright sentimentality.

The only authentic ending is the one provided here:

John and Mary die. John and Mary die. John and Mary die.

So much for endings. Beginnings are always more fun. True connoisseurs, however, are known to favor the stretch in between, since it's the hardest to do anything with.

That's about all that can be said for plots, which anyway are just one thing after another, a what and a what and a what.

Now try How and Why.

Questions

1. Why does Atwood present the story (or stories) in this manner? What point is she trying to make? What effect does the method of storytelling have on your understanding of the characters?
2. How would you characterize the various possible scenarios for John, Mary, Fred, and Madge?
3. What is Atwood suggesting about love and romance?
4. Is there really a "happy ending" in this story?

O. Henry (William Sydney Porter)

William Sydney Porter (1862–1910), known to the world as O. Henry, was born in Greensboro, North Carolina. He began writing in his mid-twenties, contributing humorous sketches to various periodicals. In 1896 he was indicted for embezzlement from the First National Bank of Austin, Texas; he fled to Honduras before his trial, but returned when he found that his wife was terminally ill. He was convicted and served three years of a five-year sentence; his guilt or innocence has never been definitively established. Released in 1901, he moved to New York the following year. Already a well-known writer, for the next three years he produced a story every week for the New York World while also contributing tales and sketches

O. Henry

to magazines. Beginning with Cabbages and Kings in 1904, his stories were published in nine highly successful collections during the remaining years of his life, as well as in three posthumously issued volumes. Financial extravagance and alcoholism darkened his last days, culminating in his death from tuberculosis at the age of forty-seven. Ranked during his lifetime with Hawthorne and Poe, O. Henry is now more likely to be invoked in negative terms for his sentimentality and especially for his reliance on frequently forced trick endings. But the most prestigious annual volume of the best American short fiction is still called The O. Henry Prize Stories, and the best of his own work is loved by millions of readers. Here is O. Henry's most famous story, a surprising and ironic tale of true love.

The Gift of the Magi

1906

One dollar and eighty-seven cents. That was all. And sixty cents of it was in pennies. Pennies saved one and two at a time by bulldozing the grocer and the vegetable man and the butcher until one's cheeks burned with the silent imputation of parsimony that such close dealing implied. Three times Della counted it. One dollar and eighty-seven cents. And the next day would be Christmas.

There was clearly nothing to do but flop down on the shabby little couch and howl. So Della did it. Which instigates the moral reflection that life is made up of sobs, sniffles, and smiles, with sniffles predominating.

While the mistress of the home is gradually subsiding from the first stage to the second, take a look at the home. A furnished flat at $8 per week. It did not exactly beggar description, but it certainly had that word on the lookout for the mendicancy squad.

In the vestibule below was a letter-box into which no letter would go, and an electric button from which no mortal finger could coax a ring. Also appertaining thereunto was a card bearing the name "Mr. James Dillingham Young."

The "Dillingham" had been flung to the breeze during a former period of prosperity when its possessor was being paid $30 per week. Now, when the income was shrunk to $20, the letters of "Dillingham" looked blurred, as though they were thinking seriously of contracting to a modest and unassuming D. But whenever Mr. James Dillingham Young came home and reached his flat above he was called "Jim" and greatly hugged by Mrs. James Dillingham Young, already introduced to you as Della. Which is all very good.

Della finished her cry and attended to her cheeks with the powder rag. She stood by the window and looked out dully at a grey cat walking a grey fence in a grey backyard. Tomorrow would be Christmas Day, and she had only $1.87 with which to buy Jim a present. She had been saving every penny she could for months, with this result. Twenty dollars a week doesn't go far. Expenses had been greater than she had calculated. They always are. Only $1.87 to buy a present for Jim. Her Jim. Many a happy hour she had spent planning for something nice for him. Something fine and rare and sterling—something just a little bit near to being worthy of the honor of being owned by Jim.

There was a pier-glass between the windows of the room. Perhaps you have seen a pier-glass in an $8 flat. A very thin and very agile person may, by observing his reflection in a rapid sequence of longitudinal strips, obtain a fairly accurate conception of his looks. Della, being slender, had mastered the art.

Suddenly she whirled from the window and stood before the glass. Her eyes were shining brilliantly, but her face had lost its color within twenty seconds. Rapidly she pulled down her hair and let it fall to its full length.

Now, there were two possessions of the James Dillingham Youngs in which they both took a mighty pride. One was Jim's gold watch that had been his father's and his grandfather's. The other was Della's hair. Had the Queen of Sheba lived in the flat across the airshaft, Della would have let her hair hang out the window some day to dry just to depreciate Her Majesty's jewels and gifts. Had King Solomon been the janitor, with all his treasures piled up in the basement, Jim would have pulled out his watch every time he passed, just to see him pluck at his beard from envy.

So now Della's beautiful hair fell about her, rippling and shining like a cascade of brown waters. It reached below her knee and made itself almost a garment for her. And then she did it up again nervously and quickly. Once she faltered for a minute and stood still while a tear or two splashed on the worn red carpet.

On went her old brown jacket; on went her old brown hat. With a whirl of skirts and with the brilliant sparkle still in her eyes, she fluttered out the door and down the stairs to the street.

Where she stopped the sign read: "Mme. Sofronie. Hair Goods of All Kinds." One flight up Della ran, and collected herself, panting. Madame, large, too white, chilly, hardly looked the "Sofronie."

"Will you buy my hair?" asked Della.

"I buy hair," said Madame. "Take yer hat off and let's have a sight at the looks of it." Down rippled the brown cascade.

"Twenty dollars," said Madame, lifting the mass with a practiced hand.

"Give it to me quick," said Della.

Oh, and the next two hours tripped by on rosy wings. Forget the hashed metaphor. She was ransacking the stores for Jim's present.

She found it at last. It surely had been made for Jim and no one else. There was no other like it in any of the stores, and she had turned all of them inside out. It was a platinum fob chain simple and chaste in design, properly proclaiming its value by substance alone and not by meretricious ornamentation—as all good things should do. It was even worthy of The Watch. As soon as she saw it she knew that it must be Jim's. It was like him. Quietness and value—the description applied to both. Twenty-one dollars they took from her for it, and she hurried home with the 87 cents. With that chain on his watch Jim might be properly anxious about the time in any company. Grand as the watch was, he sometimes looked at it on the sly on account of the old leather strap that he used in place of a chain.

When Della reached home her intoxication gave way a little to prudence and reason. She got out her curling irons and lighted the gas and went to work repairing the ravages made by generosity added to love. Which is always a tremendous task, dear friends—a mammoth task.

Within forty minutes her head was covered with tiny, close-lying curls that made her look wonderfully like a truant schoolboy. She looked at her reflection in the mirror long, carefully, and critically.

"If Jim doesn't kill me," she said to herself, "before he takes a second look at me, he'll say I look like a Coney Island chorus girl. But what could I do—oh! What could I do with a dollar and eighty-seven cents?"

At 7 o'clock the coffee was made and the frying-pan was on the back of the stove hot and ready to cook the chops.

Jim was never late. Della doubled the fob chain in her hand and sat on the corner of the table near the door that he always entered. Then she heard his step on the stair away down on the first flight, and she turned white for just a moment. She had a habit of saying little silent prayers about the simplest everyday things, and now she whispered: "Please God, make him think I am still pretty."

The door opened and Jim stepped in and closed it. He looked thin and very serious. Poor fellow, he was only twenty-two—and to be burdened with a family! He needed a new overcoat and he was without gloves.

Jim stopped inside the door, as immovable as a setter at the scent of quail. His eyes were fixed upon Della, and there was an expression in them that she could not read, and it terrified her. It was not anger, nor surprise, nor disapproval, nor horror, nor any of the sentiments that she had been prepared for. He simply stared at her fixedly with that peculiar expression on his face.

Della wriggled off the table and went for him.

"Jim, darling," she cried, "don't look at me that way. I had my hair cut off and sold because I couldn't have lived through Christmas without giving you a present. It'll grow out again—you won't mind, will you? I just had to do it. My hair grows awfully fast. Say 'Merry Christmas!' Jim, and let's be happy. You don't know what a nice— what a beautiful, nice gift I've got for you."

"You've cut off your hair?" asked Jim, laboriously, as if he had not arrived at that patent fact yet even after the hardest mental labor.

"Cut it off and sold it," said Della. "Don't you like me just as well, anyhow? I'm me without my hair, ain't I?"

Jim looked about the room curiously.

"You say your hair is gone?" he said, with an air almost of idiocy.

"You needn't look for it," said Della. "It's sold, I tell you—sold and gone, too. It's Christmas Eve, boy. Be good to me, for it went for you. Maybe the hairs of my head were numbered," she went on with a sudden serious sweetness, "but nobody could ever count my love for you. Shall I put the chops on, Jim?"

Out of his trance Jim seemed quickly to wake. He enfolded his Della. For ten seconds let us regard with discreet scrutiny some inconsequential object in the other direction. Eight dollars a week or a million a year—what is the difference? A mathematician or a wit would give you the wrong answer. The magi brought valuable gifts, but that was not among them. This dark assertion will be illuminated later on.

Jim drew a package from his overcoat pocket and threw it upon the table.

"Don't make any mistake, Dell," he said, "about me. I don't think there's anything in the way of a haircut or a shave or a shampoo that could make me like my girl any less. But if you'll unwrap that package you may see why you had me going a while at first."

White fingers and nimble tore at the string and paper. And then an ecstatic scream of joy; and then, alas! a quick feminine change to hysterical tears and wails, necessitating the immediate employment of all the comforting powers of the lord of the flat.

For there lay The Combs—the set of combs, side and back, that Della had worshipped for long in a Broadway window. Beautiful combs, pure tortoise shell, with jewelled rims—just the shade to wear in the beautiful vanished hair. They were expensive combs, she knew, and her heart had simply craved and yearned over them without the least hope of possession. And now, they were hers, but the tresses that should have adorned the coveted adornments were gone.

But she hugged them to her bosom, and at length she was able to look up with dim eyes and a smile and say: "My hair grows so fast, Jim!"

And then Della leaped up like a little singed cat and cried, "Oh, oh!"

Jim had not yet seen his beautiful present. She held it out to him eagerly upon her open palm. The dull precious metal seemed to flash with a reflection of her bright and ardent spirit.

"Isn't it a dandy, Jim? I hunted all over town to find it. You'll have to look at the time a hundred times a day now. Give me your watch. I want to see how it looks on it."

Instead of obeying, Jim tumbled down on the couch and put his hands under the back of his head and smiled.

"Dell," said he, "let's put our Christmas presents away and keep 'em a while. They're too nice to use just at present. I sold the watch to get the money to buy your combs. And now suppose you put the chops on."

The magi, as you know, were wise men—wonderfully wise men—who brought gifts to the Babe in the manger. They invented the art of giving Christmas presents. Being wise, their gifts were no doubt wise ones, possibly bearing the privilege of exchange in case of duplication. And here I have lamely related to you the uneventful chronicle of two foolish children in a flat who most unwisely sacrificed for each other the greatest treasures of their house. But in a last word to the wise of these days let it be said that of all who give gifts these two were the wisest. Of all who give and receive gifts, such as they are wisest. Everywhere they are wisest. They are the magi.

Questions

1. How would you describe the style of this story? Does the author's tone tell you anything about his attitude toward the characters and events of the narrative?
2. What do the details in paragraph 7 tell you about Della and Jim's financial situation?
3. O. Henry tells us that Jim "needed a new overcoat and he was without gloves" (paragraph 25). Why do you think Della didn't buy him these things for Christmas instead of a watch chain?
4. What is ironic about the story's ending? Is this plot twist the most important element of the conclusion? If not, what is?
5. What do you think of the sacrifices that Della and Jim made? Do you find this story romantic, or sad? What do you think of self-sacrifice in the name of love?

Max Apple

Max Apple was born into a Yiddish-speaking household in Grand Rapids, Michigan, in 1941. He told an interviewer: "My grandmother was a great storyteller, so I grew up hearing the real thing. I knew that a good story was the best thing in the world." Apple received his Ph.D. in seventeenth-century literature from the University of Michigan in 1970, and taught for many years at Rice University. His first books, The Oranging of America and Other Stories (1976) and Zip: A Novel of the Left and the Right (1978), established his reputation for wildly inventive, satirical observations of American life. Newsweek wrote of him, "Apple's principal asset is his startling imagination. Original, witty, writing deftly and economically, he translates the most battered of our cultural clichés into glistening artifacts." Apple's short

Max Apple

story "Vegetable Love" demonstrates both the satiric and the deeply emotional sides of his imagination. His parody of the American obsession with health, diet, and exercise provides fertile comic territory, but underneath the zany surface is the story of a couple's search for love and meaning.

Vegetable Love   1976

I

Ferguson was never crazy about chicken, but red meat he shoveled up between fork and thick bread and cleaned his mustache with the tip of his tongue.

Annette Grim taught him otherwise. "I never make love to meat eaters," she said; "it adds the smell of the grave to postcoital depression."

They met at Safeway while he examined Jerusalem artichokes, wondering at their shape and aroma. She was on her way to the health-food island and Ferguson's cart blocked the best route. Just as he had decided to buy the artichokes, Annette pushed the cart aside and he turned to capture, full force, the loaded wire cart upon his groin.

"You poor man," Annette said when she heard his groan, and rushed to him as he leaned against the mushrooms. "You poor, poor, man. I once saw someone get poked in the nuts by an umbrella and they had to call an ambulance." They were alone in the vegetable aisle when she put her long fingers under his zipper, giving comfort as nonchalantly as if she were helping a blind man across the street.

"To me the body is a temple. Would you bring a steak to a temple?"   5

Later he reminded her that in the original temple they did slaughter animals, smoke the entrails, and did eat the flesh thereof.

"Paganism," said Annette Grim, but by then she had converted him almost beyond argument.

II

His pain blossomed into love. For him she cooked that day a stew of the Jerusalem artichokes, sweet potatoes, turnips, and carrots. Afterward they drank the broth blended with mint leaves, and Ferguson stayed with Annette, gratified by her flesh, but so hungry that at three A.M. he crept from bed and tried to find enough food to sustain him through the night. In her refrigerator she had only brewer's yeast, a coconut, and sprouted mung beans in a baggy thick with mold. In her cupboard were fresh spices from Oregon, a record player, dry mung beans, rolled oats, defatted wheat germ, two rows of empty glass bottles, and a color poster of a bowl of yogurt. Not even bread, he thought, as he slouched toward the bedroom, longing for a McDonald's.

In the first month of their relationship, Ferguson lost fourteen pounds. This was a blessing, since most of it was excess. His clothes, which had been tight, now fit him as they had in 1971 when he weighed one hundred eighty. A sign on her living-room wall reminded him, "The more flesh, the more worms." Yet, rarely from Annette herself did Ferguson hear any direct criticism of his eating habits or his one hundred eighty pounds née° one hundred ninety-four. While he marveled at her, his own appetite shrank and his endurance increased. Annette could eat a cup of yogurt and a banana and manage the night in either innocent sleep or full passion without a hunger pain.

---

née: formerly.

She was five feet five and weighed an unvarying one hundred and eight pounds. She was eighty percent protein and water. She used no deodorants, nor did she shave her legs or underarms or cut her hair. She brushed her teeth with baking soda and a one-thousand-sheet roll of toilet tissue could last her a month. She hadn't had a cold since the day after Nixon announced the bombing of Hanoi and Haiphong.

Next to her, Ferguson felt like an ineffective cancer. Full of dead meats, artificial flavors, and additives, he attached himself to her, but so whole was her purity that his soft and weak one hundred eighty pounds of pulsating tissue limped back to itself without touching what she called "the center of my consciousness." This she had worked out herself, a sort of Cartesian pineal gland that existed within her right rib cage. "This is its place, my body's soul lives here. This is not the spirit or soul that maybe doesn't exist. This is a real one. You can find it without God or Jesus or anybody else. It's just a spot in your body. Mine happens to be right here. When you find yours, let me know and I'll be glad for you."

III

Ferguson searched for his spot but found only heartburn and hunger pains. Still, in the first month of their love he did not knowingly cheat on Annette. Once, at lunch, he took a bite of a friend's hamburger, a small bite that was already swallowed before he even realized it was meat. "After all," he explained to his friend, "you don't live twenty-eight years taking meat for granted and then automatically think 'This is meat' every time you take a bite of a hamburger, do you?"

That night Annette shunned him, but powered perhaps by that single bite of ground beef, he forced her somewhat and with sad and open eyes she suffered the carnivore upon her.

When he could not sleep, he admitted the hamburger.

"You don't have to explain, Ferguson. I knew it. I can see meat in someone I love like an x-ray. It poisons the air."

"One lousy bite can't be that poisonous," he protested.

Annette closed her eyes, pulled the nylon comforter over her like a shawl, and slept soundly beside the guilty Ferguson.

IV

By the third month he was one hundred fifty-five and shrinking. He poked ragged new holes in his belt with a kitchen knife and the extra piece of leather at the front flapped against his empty stomach. Even his shoes were too wide. His friends at first told him to see a doctor, then they said a psychiatrist. Annette expressed no pride in him but she did not reject him either. They continued that bliss they had begun at the supermarket. Away from her he sometimes felt an overpowering hunger which he soothed with cold water and occasional peanuts. In her presence the hunger was no problem. Annette Grim had taken him one step further into the nature of life. The old Ferguson would not have quibbled with "You are what you eat." The new Ferguson would roll his eyes heavenward and in a low sweet voice, not really meaning to correct you, would say, "You are what you don't eat." *Feast Not, Want Not* she calligraphed in her own hand as a decoration for the wall of his office.

"Counting the time needed for consuming and properly digesting red meat, a person spends twenty percent of his day on this single occupation. Another ten percent, say, on the body-cleaning functions needed by meat eaters in civilized society, and at least another ten percent sleeping time caused by too much amino acid combined with loss of oxygen, and you have a carnivore actually losing forty percent of his day to meat. Thus, so called convenience foods are an absolute necessity. They are to the modern meat eater what fire was to his apelike ancestors. You and I, Ferguson," she went on, "have forty percent more time; that's like adding twenty years to your life expectancy. What better thing to do for someone you love?"

Ferguson, who was a CPA and attended law classes at night, decided pragmatically that the only better thing was to marry her and spend the extra twenty years of life expectancy together in a vegetarian home of their own. When he proposed they were in her apartment on a soft couch with a broken spring which forced Ferguson to sit straighter than he wanted to and added to his nervousness. They were snacking on sunflower seeds after coming home from the movies.

When he asked, Annette closed her eyes and touched her spot. Ferguson, while he awaited her answer, imagined their first child, a girl thin as a moonbeam, lustrous of skin, jumping rope, almost popping the bands of gravity as she floated above the cracking white pavement crowded with grimy infants.

Annette, with fingertips pressed beneath her right breast, took the measure of an organ that sat within her, absolutely parallel to the heart and functioning to interpret the steady rhythms of her heart across the vastness of the chest and the many pitfalls of the digestive tract. She was solemn and her eyelids fluttered against the pressures of choice. When she opened her eyes, her voice was steady. Her spot spoke to her and it said, No—not yet, at least. "I have this strange feeling that even though I love you too, we aren't ready for each other: not yet, maybe someday. We can't push it." He knew her well enough to keep from protesting. "I don't think it can ever work out permanently until you have your spot too. It's an uncanny thing. I can't tell you what it is, but I know it's there and it only partly"—she looked sadder now than he had ever seen her—"it only partly has to do with what you eat or don't eat."

V

Something changed after the proposal. They were no longer the people who had met in the supermarket, who shared one another and a philosophy of diet. They were potential parents, potential owners of houses, cars, and major appliances. She lived in a furnished apartment, owned only a few garments, and refused to be proud of him for graduating, finally, from the South Texas College of Law after five and one half years of night-school study. He went alone to the graduation banquet, to celebrate with his classmates, their spouses, and the dean of the college. Annette stayed in her apartment working on the rug which she had been making during the months of their romance.

"Enjoy yourself," she said as he left, wrinkling her tiny nose, smiling as if to tease him for going to a steakhouse to celebrate what she called "thousands of hours of studying dullness." According to Annette it was a fitting celebration. Ferguson and fifty-five fat, hard-working Texas night-school lawyers going out to munch upon the loins of cattle in a restaurant decorated like a covered wagon.

"I'll bring you back the bone," he said, feeling cruel and smug himself. This was their first real fight. She might not find anything worth praising in his past, but this one night with people who had shared his ambition in countless humid hours while night settled over Houston and the red neon sign of the beauty academy across the street peeped through the venetian blinds, this one night with his fellow law students she would not rob him of. It had nothing to do with food. He planned to eat fruitplate. It had been ordered for him by the banquet chairman weeks before.

Ferguson sat three chairs from the dean, shared in toasts to the college, to the dean, to the wives and families of these working men whose sacrifices had made daddy, against long odds, a lawyer. Ferguson felt especially cheated not having someone to clink his champagne glass with. Even the dean brought a wife. After they had toasted the Law itself, a cowgirl waitress placed in front of Ferguson "Sonny's Special," a ten-inch medium-rare filet, butterflied so that it spread open like a radish, exposing its sizzling innards. "I ordered fruitplate," he told her, but she was well along the table and his voice fell among the sound of plates and teeth meeting beef. Goddamn, Ferguson said to himself, and he sliced off a bite of the steak, hesitated, chewed, and when he saw that it was good, he ate with relish and a pinch of A-1 sauce the remainder of Sonny's Special, had an after-dinner liqueur and two cups of coffee. He thought he must look like a snake who had swallowed a whole piglet, but in the men's room mirror, his stomach did not bulge. On the contrary, his skin had a ruddy healthy glow he had not seen in some time. "If she can't celebrate one lousy night with me after my five and a half years, then the hell with her," he told his reflection.

He went home, not to her apartment and her x-ray senses. Not that Ferguson intended to hide the steak from her. He would admit it but without feeling guilty. He paid enough that night for his gluttony on a stomach accustomed for three months to vegetables.

In the morning she was gone, disappeared, evanesced as if she had never been there. The door was open, a yogurt carton scraped clean lay alone in the garbage bag. The cupboard empty, the refrigerator empty, open, unplugged, smelling baking-powder clean. The bare hangers in her closet looked to Ferguson like bright teeth in a corpse. He ran to the building supervisor, who told him, "Mizz Grim left real early in the morning in a taxicab. She gave her two weeks notice and cleaned the place up good."

At the Prudential Insurance building Ferguson learned the same. Annette Grim, who for more than a year typed policy amendments five days a week, had given a two-week advance notice and told the girl at the desk next to her that she was going to Dallas. For several hours Ferguson sat in the Prudential coffee shop trying to make himself get up from his small table and his cold cup of tea, but he could not leave until he knew where to go. "What about our camping trip?" he asked aloud. He put his head on the table and breathed deeply, hoping the oxygen would clear his head. His body was sluggish from the meat and wine of the banquet. He finally decided to go home and hope she would be there to tell him this was her joking way of saying, yes, she wanted to get married right this minute. She had quit her job so that they could start a family immediately, even before the camping trip.

But Ferguson's apartment was as empty as it had always been, and he, three months a lover and a vegetarian, four days a lawyer, and all his life a loner, sat down with a bowl of wheat germ and milk to contemplate the suddenly narrow vista of his future. Annette was, after all, not his. Only a handful of people even knew about them as a couple.

Thanks to his law degree, Shell Oil would move him on Monday from accounting to contracts. Without Annette the weekend looming before him seemed longer than the twenty added years of life expectancy which she had bequeathed to him as a free gift. He spent Saturday and Sunday in a total fast, re-examining his months with Annette, and found no clues to her sudden departure. The two weeks' notice to her landlord and to the Prudential suggested that Annette had well-laid plans, but this, Ferguson understood, was a guise. She did not fool him. He knew, in spite of the apparent facts, that had he not left her for that Thursday night banquet he would not be alone now. Had he gone to the banquet and at least not eaten the steak, that too might have been enough to sustain their love.

But he had gone and he had eaten, and the beef that passed through him came between them, perhaps forever. Ferguson arose from his two-day fast and prepared to seek within himself the spot that would solve the mystery of Annette and create the Ferguson she could live with.

VI

The lawyer waned. After the initial fast, he worked out his own penance. For thirty days he would do the brown-rice regimen. A diet that Annette said was okay but too austere and too low on fluids. For thirty days he would eat only the king of grains, brown rice with its perfect harmony of phosphorous and potassium. He prepared it in a pressure cooker so that it took only a few minutes to cook and lasted days. Finding no comfort in friends and in no mood for entertainment, Ferguson worked late on the Shell leases and lost weight. His plan was to use these thirty days of brown rice in two ways. First to cleanse his body from that meat orgy of the banquet, and second to hope that in some mysterious way his monkish diet would be communicated to Annette, who would forgive and return. When at the end of thirty days she had not returned, he put away the pressure cooker and resumed a more normal vegetarian diet. He was now down to one hundred forty-seven and had to buy some smaller-sized clothes.

His new boss, the head of Shell contracts, called him "the most dedicated young man I've ever seen," and took Ferguson to lunch in the executive dining room, where amid martini-drinking businessmen and special cuts of aged beef the dedicated young man ate, at company expense, a lettuce and avocado salad. "You're too thin," said the head of contracts; "have a roast-beef sandwich. It's Iowa beef." Ferguson smiled his thanks and rejected chicken salad as well.

He was beginning to realize that he might just have to get over her, that whatever diet or other penance he tried might not do it. After all, thirty-four days and not even a post card to a man who had virtually lived with you for three months, who had proposed and told you all his heart. Thirty-four days of silence when she knew how barren he was without her. This he did not deserve for one steak. She knew it, he knew it. It was something else.

VII

At one hundred forty-two pounds, Ferguson began to have mild hallucinations. Nothing colorful or spectacular, no dreamlike surreal dazzlers, only short episodic vignettes slightly more concrete than a daydream. It was as if, all at once, the characters in the daydream had a bright spotlight focused upon them. The light did not deter them. They went about their business, but it made Ferguson recognize the subtle difference between a daydream and a hallucination. There was nothing terrifying in these experiences, and he felt, in spite of his thinness, healthy and robust. The hallucinations were largely about oil and taxes. In the first episode that he recognized as a new phenomenon, the daydream was Ferguson as a Shell executive somewhere upon a Colorado slope looking over thousands of green acres beneath which there might be recoverable shale deposits. The scene was as standard as a poster. When it became a hallucination, the earth slowly opened, disturbing nothing on the surface, and droplets of oil shot up like slippery watermelon seeds. As far as the oilman could see, this happened, the droplets flying up rhythmically like coffee percolating. No results, only the image, and Ferguson was back reading the fine print in a Shell lease between Mr. Howard S. Sounders of Ardmore, Oklahoma, and the Company, regarding section 71 and adjoining properties of McClehlen's addition, Runyn County.

The episodes followed no pattern and happened at home as well as at the office. He considered seeing a doctor but he suspected the doctor would suggest psychotherapy, and Ferguson, though he might be in despair and loneliness, felt very certain of his sanity. Anyway, how explain to a doctor that you were hoping to find within yourself a hidden resource called a spot which had a true and absolute physical existence and yet might vary in location among peoples and had never been located in an autopsy. "Doctors look for causes of disease," Annette had once told him when they discussed her spot, "doctors look for causes of death; this is a cause of life." Although Ferguson disliked the mumbo jumbo of mysticism, he did not think the idea of a spot was so absurd. The analogy with nature was very clear to him. All sorts of land looked the same from the surface, only a good geologist could tell you exactly where to drill for oil. Life itself starting with one cell spread to many. Scientists were continually finding out the secret codes of genetic reproduction. A person's spot would one day also be labeled, perhaps called an I AM, a fingernail of an RNA itself a fingernail of a DNA, and all this history pummeling through you with so little commotion that, if you don't stop to look for it, it might lie undisturbed, like oil, for millions of years. Perhaps most people didn't need a spot, they were still in a spotless age, the way men for thousands of generations didn't need oil or uranium even though it was always there just waiting to be needed. Because of Annette Grim, Ferguson needed his spot. She was the catalyst that had moved Ferguson, of necessity, beyond the frontiers of science. Doctors could not help, nor because of the personal and secular nature of the spot could theologians or friends or entertainment or art. Thus, Ferguson ate fruits, vegetables, grains, seeds, and low-fat milk products, did his work for Shell Oil, and hoped for a better life.

VIII

To help him find his spot, Ferguson tried, in order, yoga, transcendental meditation, dynamic tension, and aerobics. Nothing did it, but after some experimentation with these methods of body analysis and muscle control, he found certain combinations that offered, if not a spot, at least some release from his anxieties. He could combine the jogging with the dynamic tension by squeezing his hands together as he ran. The tension squirted from his palms down to his legs and was dissipated in a seven-minute mile. It surprised Ferguson that, even though he was losing all hope of ever regaining Annette, he had no desire to go back to his old eating habits. Meat had forever joined the ranks of certain other inedible materials, wood, steel, fabric, glass. For her he sought his spot, for himself he remained a vegetarian.

IX

When he reached one hundred thirty-four, Ferguson's entire aspect changed. He had apparently exhausted all the extra flesh that had remained in his cheeks, and suddenly his face looked as strong and bony as a fist. His forehead, his cheekbones, his nose, and his chin stood out like the knuckles in a clenched hand. Sixty pounds ago Ferguson had been round cheeked, almost teddy bearish in appearance. A few girls had liked him because he was cute and cuddly. Now he had become an arrowhead.

Because he could concentrate with such perfect composure and for so long a time, Ferguson did the work of five men. In hours he read through the contracts that took other lawyers days or weeks, and he rarely made even the smallest of errors. In the office they called him the computer, but as he continued to shrink they changed his name to Pocket Calculator. His eyes soared out of the bleak landscape of his face. They sought Annette the way birds seek out a resting place after long journeys. Because Ferguson's bird eyes found no Annette they did not rest. He could awaken from ten hours of perfect slumber with sleepless, raging eyes. And these remembering eyes became the great weight of his body. When they blinked long, he might lose his balance and sway in the wind. He thought of himself as a simplified diagram. There was a plumb line extending directly from his eyes down to his mouth, his belly, and his penis, and upward to his brain. The line was taut and powerful. Yet something was missing, a spot as intricate and important as any other in the brain-to-penis complex.

At night after deep breathing exercises in the lotus position and a three-minute shoulder stand, Ferguson would lie completely still in his bed and examine the front of his body as if the examining fingers belonged to someone else. He would speak aloud to himself as the finger doctors did their checking of the clean and relaxed corpus under them. "Here," the digits would pound at the solar plexus, "perhaps it is here, where it hurts when I poke, here, in this little Mesopotamia between the lungs." The fingers would pound at the space between his ribs until he could barely catch his breath, but no inkling of the spot. As far as the finger doctors could reach, they touched and examined and tried to root out the spot. And when all else failed, the doctors became Annette. They found out his most obvious weakness and pulled away at his solid flesh until it melted and stained Ferguson with the realization of his loneliness.

X

Mr. Solomon, his boss in the contracts department, insisted that Ferguson take a two-week vacation. "Longer if you like," he said, "and of course with full pay. You've done a year's work in a few months, go out and relax, have some fun." Solomon slapped him on the back in a broad gesture of camaraderie. But as he shook Ferguson's hand and pulled him closer the older lawyer said in a voice of honest concern, "Son, is there anything I can do to help you? Whatever it is, I know you won't talk about it, but I just want you to know that Harold Solomon cares. You're the best contracts man here, but I don't give a damn about that when I can see you suffering right in front of me. Do something about it on this vacation, son, and when you come back remember that Harold Solomon isn't just your boss, he's your friend."

Mr. Solomon's concern touched Ferguson but it also unnerved him. He realized for the first time how obvious his despair must be. It was five and one half months since the banquet. He weighed one hundred twenty-eight pounds now and domestic dress shirts ballooned around his chest. He switched to the modish handmade type, mostly Indian, which hung loosely over his shoulders and gave him the look of a very large and well-groomed Asian peasant. On the first day of his vacation, he took the Greyhound bus to Dallas, checked into the Holiday Inn under the name of William Glass, and rented a car. He could have driven his own car and registered under his own name. He did not understand why he acted so irrationally, but he decided to follow his whims and hope that they would lead him to Annette.

Ferguson did not roam the streets of Dallas looking for her, but he sought out the health-food shops and the vegetarian restaurants where he thought she might be. He had no photograph to pass around and her description—thin, fair, strong, beautiful, direct, knowledgeable, precise, self-assured—none of this really described her. Annette Grim was identifiable only by her spot, that roommate of her heart, which sat beneath her solemn nipple on the right-hand side of an otherwise biologically unspectacular chest. "I am probably in better condition than she is," Ferguson thought; "she probably doesn't run and do yoga." Perhaps he could even teach her something new.

In a restaurant called Pelops Arms, beneath a modern cartoon of Greek heroes wrestling with monsters, Ferguson sat eating an avocado, cheese, and mung-sprout sandwich. Dallas had even fewer health restaurants than Houston. In the midst of men who raised cattle for shipment to the dinner tables of America, there sat Ferguson eschewing red meats, disdaining poultry, laying off eggs, hardening and slenderizing a body that sought its own center, and while doing so rushed with all its pent-up energies toward unknown places, creating, like the universe itself, an area of empty space wherever it traveled. There sat Ferguson, just and thin and powerful, seeking his center like a dog after its own tail.

"Pardon me," the voice said, and Ferguson's raging eyes turned as always, looking for her, frightening by their intensity an innocent waitress delivering a bill for $1.79.

"Was everything all right?" she asked.

"Are you in a hurry?" Ferguson asked her in return.

She smiled at the empty restaurant. "You're the only customer," she said, and sat down opposite him. Starting from the day in the supermarket, Ferguson told her almost everything. This girl, Kathleen Simpson, a junior at SMU, herself not completely vegetarian, sat in awe as the story of Ferguson's search for a spot unfolded before her.

"I never heard of anything like it," she said, "but I believe in the soul so it is not so preposterous to me. I'm through here in an hour, I'll help you look. There's only a few places in Dallas where a girl like that might be and they're not far from here." Ferguson paid his $1.79 and sipped distilled water while he waited for Kathleen. She took him to the Garden of Eden, where long-haired men sold grain and seeds out of huge tin pails. She led him to the Cornucopia, which catered to SMU students and served only a modest vegetarian choice amid a wide meat menu. Caesar's Salad, a small downtown coffee shop that served luncheon greens to secretaries, was the only other place she could think of. Annette, of course, was in none of these restaurants, but since she had been a secretary, Ferguson thought this last one might be a good place for him to camp out and wait for her. Kathleen Simpson, brown eyed and friendly, wished him well.

The next day Ferguson haunted Caesar's Salad. It was very difficult to stay there for long. There was only a counter with eight stools and three small booths that at lunch and with squeezing could accommodate four each. Twenty customers maximum and two waitresses. By noon both of them knew Ferguson and suspected him. He explained but they asked him to do his waiting outside. Ferguson stood in the Dallas sun trying to shade himself beneath the awning of a nearby paint store. From the store window a cardboard peacock flashed many colors into the sunlight, dazzling him. He took a salt tablet and carried a paper cup of water with him, but the Dallas afternoon rose above one hundred and Ferguson felt weak and dizzy. He visited, on foot, the only Dallas landmark he knew, the place of the schoolbook depository and the grassy knoll. As he walked the route of the motorcade he tried to imagine the sound of the bullets, the scream of Jacqueline, Lyndon Johnson, fearful beneath a secret-service man. The book depository had been torn down, the grassy knoll was merely an overpass for a highway, and a small plaque marked the place where the President's head had been splintered.

For the first time Ferguson wondered about the spots of the great. Did someone like President Kennedy have a spot which he consulted when the Russians put missiles in Cuba? Had there been an inkling, a negative feeling, like Annette had about him, on that day in November when the young President put on his clean starched shirt, his cuff links and his garters, and shook his longish hair in front of the mirror to make certain that it would look fine in the hot Dallas wind? If important people had spots and listened to them, things would not go wrong in the world, Ferguson reasoned. Yet starting from himself and stretching right to the farthest astronaut hitting a golf ball on the moon, there was a line of chaos as direct as the plumb line that went through Ferguson. Who had absolutes? Even the Pope changed his mind. Only his Annette heard the hum of the rhythm of her body, while a tone-deaf world scrambled around her.

"I have tried," Ferguson said aloud in the shadow of the grassy knoll where thousands had watched the motorcade speed up and curve toward Parkland Hospital; "I have fasted and meditated and relentlessly examined myself. I have known no strangers among women, nor have my lips touched the flesh of birds or animals." The desert heat struck him full force as he raised his face heavenward and saw for an instant the flaming sun, like a carbonated peacock bubbling in his eyes. He shielded himself with uplifted arms, and a Buick whisked by so closely that the string tie of his shirt thudded softly against the outside mirror of the automobile.

"Watch yourself, nut," the driver yelled back at him.

"I have been doing that," Ferguson answered, "I have been doing little else." To the grassy knoll and to the anonymous traffic Ferguson announced, "I know myself and have no spot. Kennedy had none, neither did Roosevelt, or Justice Frankfurter, or George Washington." Ferguson raced up the grassy knoll and proclaimed to the roaring highway, "You lost me too, Annette. Whoever you're huddled with now does not love you like I did. You were my spot and your spot didn't know it."

In the Dallas heat he ran along the side of the highway in his long-and-easy jogging stride. Along Dallas Avenue Ferguson ran, past post-office buildings and skyscrapers, through streets emptied by the hot sun. As he ran he clenched and unclenched his fists, letting the dynamic tension pulse through his arms as the crashing cement vibrated through his legs. Deeply he inhaled the city, its desert air and its poisonous oxides. As his ribcage stretched, Ferguson felt loose and lucid. He imagined that the plumb line was now stretched taut, that the final open space had been pulled out with a sudden jerk and had disappeared, leaving him unmarked down the middle.

55

He raced past Caesar's Salad not even casting a glance. His second wind had come by the time Ferguson reached Pelops Arms. Entering at a gallop, he surprised Kathleen Simpson, who handed him distilled water.

"Did you find her?" she asked.

"Yes," Ferguson said, "will you run with me?"

"Where?"

"To Houston for dinner, and then through Mexico to the Pan American Highway, along the banks of the Amazon, over the Chilean Andes right into Buenos Aires."

Kathleen hesitated, then she slipped off her short black apron, put down her green order pad, and in a long and fluent stride, side by side with Ferguson, headed south.

Questions

1. Is Annette an ideal romantic partner for Ferguson? How would you describe her as a possible girlfriend or wife?
2. What does Ferguson find attractive about Annette?
3. As in many modern stories, the climax of "Vegetable Love" depends less on external action than on the protagonist's epiphany. What epiphany does Ferguson have while visiting the site of the Kennedy assassination, and what are the implications of his farewell words to Annette: "You lost me too, Annette. Whoever you're huddled with now does not love you like I did. You were my spot and your spot didn't know it"?
4. Does everything in this story seem absolutely realistic? Does Apple ever seem to exaggerate details? If so, why would he use exaggeration?
5. Apple has been called a satirist without a mean bone in his body. Is this true in "Vegetable Love"?

Suggestions for Writing on Stories about Discovering Love

1. Both Mary in "Happy Endings" and Ferguson in "Vegetable Love" are infatuated with someone who may or may not return their feelings. In what ways are these characters similar and different? How do you account for the different outcomes of their romances?
2. O. Henry's "The Gift of the Magi" has a surprise ending with a significant twist. Is this ending just a plot device, or does it have a deeper significance? In a general sense, do you think surprise endings are mostly just tricks, or can they reveal hidden meanings?
3. Margaret Atwood's "Happy Endings" provides multiple plot lines and multiple endings. What is gained and what is lost by presenting alternatives rather than one authoritative story?
4. What do you think would have happened if John in "Happy Endings" (the older, married John in part C) left his wife for Mary? Or if Ferguson in "Vegetable Love" had not attended the banquet and eaten a steak? Write a new ending for one of these stories.

LOVE GONE WRONG

William Faulkner   *A Rose for Emily*
Zora Neale Hurston   *Sweat*
Flannery O'Connor   *Parker's Back*

Love is a risky proposition. Falling in love means taking chances, and it's an investment that doesn't always pay. Your beloved might make promises that he or she has no intention of keeping—or commitments that are meant to be kept but somehow end up broken. Or you might believe in someone's affection or truthfulness because you want to, when it should be obvious to you (and may be obvious to others) that your beloved isn't worthy of such trust. Whatever the situation, having your heart broken always hurts—often excruciatingly. Sometimes, in retrospect, you get annoyed at yourself for believing a hopeless situation had potential. But more often, you're upset with the beloved. This sense of letdown can be even more intense when you made sacrifices for the other person or for the relationship. Coping with the gap between your eager hopes and the painful reality can be challenging for anyone. We don't need to be in a relationship as abusive as the one in Zora Neale Hurston's "Sweat" to understand how disastrous relationships can become. The stories in this section all depict how people act—and act out—in the name of love, and the various ways they cope with its loss. You may identify with these characters completely, or you may find their choices unfathomable. Either way, these stories demonstrate the lasting marks that love can leave—marks that, like the tattoos in Flannery O'Connor's "Parker's Back," stay with us forever.

William Faulkner

William Faulkner (1897–1962) was born in New Albany, Mississippi, near the college town of Oxford, where he briefly attended the University of Mississippi. In 1918 Faulkner enlisted in the British Royal Air Force and trained in Canada, but the war ended before he saw service. After a few months in New York, he returned to Oxford, serving so ineptly as postmaster that his fellow townspeople (to whom he was known as "Count No-Account") forced his resignation. After an early book of poems, Faulkner turned his attention to fiction, publishing Soldiers' Pay, his first novel, in 1925. These Thirteen, a collection of short stories that included "A Rose for Emily," appeared in 1931.

In his early career Faulkner was rarely successful in finding wide readership. For twenty years he supported his fiction by working intermittently in Hollywood as a screenwriter. Eventually Faulkner's most important novels—The Sound and the Fury (1929), As I Lay Dying (1930), Light in August (1932), and Absalom, Absalom! (1936)—gained him the belated respect of critics and fellow writers. In 1950 Faulkner became the fifth American to win the Nobel Prize in Literature.

Perhaps more than any other writer, Faulkner was responsible for the flowering of Southern fiction that took place in the early decades of the twentieth century. As the critic Alfred Kazin noted, "Faulkner has an abiding sense that the whole human race can be fitted into his own native spot of Mississippi earth, no larger 'than a postage stamp.'" In "A Rose for Emily" Faulkner explores the strange consequences of a love that eerily lasts a lifetime.

A Rose for Emily

1931

I

When Miss Emily Grierson died, our whole town went to her funeral: the men through a sort of respectful affection for a fallen monument, the women mostly out of curiosity to see the inside of her house, which no one save an old manservant—a combined gardener and cook—had seen in at least ten years.

It was a big, squarish frame house that had once been white, decorated with cupolas and spires and scrolled balconies in the heavily lightsome style of the seventies, set on what had once been our most select street. But garages and cotton gins had encroached and obliterated even the august names of that neighborhood; only Miss Emily's house was left, lifting its stubborn and coquettish decay above the cotton wagons and the gasoline pumps—an eyesore among eyesores. And now Miss Emily had gone to join the representatives of those august names where they lay in the cedar-bemused cemetery among the ranked and anonymous graves of Union and Confederate soldiers who fell at the battle of Jefferson.

Alive, Miss Emily had been a tradition, a duty, and a care; a sort of hereditary obligation upon the town, dating from that day in 1894 when Colonel Sartoris, the mayor—he who fathered the edict that no Negro woman should appear on the streets without an apron—remitted her taxes, the dispensation dating from the death of her father on into perpetuity. Not that Miss Emily would have accepted charity. Colonel Sartoris invented an involved tale to the effect that Miss Emily's father had loaned money to the town, which the town, as a matter of business, preferred this way of repaying. Only a man of Colonel Sartoris' generation and thought could have invented it, and only a woman could have believed it.

When the next generation, with its more modern ideas, became mayors and aldermen, this arrangement created some little dissatisfaction. On the first of the year they mailed her a tax notice. February came, and there was no reply. They wrote her a formal letter, asking her to call at the sheriff's office at her convenience. A week later the mayor wrote her himself, offering to call or to send his car for her, and received in reply a note on paper of an archaic shape, in a thin, flowing calligraphy in faded ink, to the effect that she no longer went out at all. The tax notice was also enclosed, without comment.

They called a special meeting of the Board of Aldermen. A deputation waited upon her, knocked at the door through which no visitor had passed since she ceased giving china-painting lessons eight or ten years earlier. They were admitted by the old Negro into a dim hall from which a stairway mounted into still more shadow. It smelled of dust and disuse—a close, dank smell. The Negro led them into the parlor.

It was furnished in heavy, leather-covered furniture. When the Negro opened the blinds of one window, they could see that the leather was cracked; and when they sat down, a faint dust rose sluggishly about their thighs, spinning with slow motes in the single sun-ray. On a tarnished gilt easel before the fireplace stood a crayon portrait of Miss Emily's father.

They rose when she entered—a small, fat woman in black, with a thin gold chain descending to her waist and vanishing into her belt, leaning on an ebony cane with a tarnished gold head. Her skeleton was small and spare; perhaps that was why what would have been merely plumpness in another was obesity in her. She looked bloated, like a body long submerged in motionless water, and of that pallid hue. Her eyes, lost in the fatty ridges of her face, looked like two small pieces of coal pressed into a lump of dough as they moved from one face to another while the visitors stated their errand.

She did not ask them to sit. She just stood in the door and listened quietly until the spokesman came to a stumbling halt. Then they could hear the invisible watch ticking at the end of the gold chain.

Her voice was dry and cold. "I have no taxes in Jefferson. Colonel Sartoris explained it to me. Perhaps one of you can gain access to the city records and satisfy yourselves."

"But we have. We are the city authorities, Miss Emily. Didn't you get a notice from the sheriff, signed by him?"

"I received a paper, yes," Miss Emily said. "Perhaps he considers himself the sheriff . . . I have no taxes in Jefferson."

"But there is nothing on the books to show that, you see. We must go by the—"

"See Colonel Sartoris. I have no taxes in Jefferson."

"But, Miss Emily—"

"See Colonel Sartoris." (Colonel Sartoris had been dead almost ten years.) "I have no taxes in Jefferson. Tobe!" The Negro appeared. "Show these gentlemen out."

II

So she vanquished them, horse and foot, just as she had vanquished their fathers thirty years before about the smell. That was two years after her father's death and a short time after her sweetheart—the one we believed would marry her—had deserted her. After her father's death she went out very little; after her sweetheart went away, people hardly saw her at all. A few of the ladies had the temerity to call, but were not received, and the only sign of life about the place was the Negro man—a young man then—going in and out with a market basket.

"Just as if a man—any man—could keep a kitchen properly," the ladies said; so they were not surprised when the smell developed. It was another link between the gross, teeming world and the high and mighty Griersons.

A neighbor, a woman, complained to the mayor, Judge Stevens, eighty years old.

"But what will you have me do about it, madam?" he said.

"Why, send her word to stop it," the woman said. "Isn't there a law?"

"I'm sure that won't be necessary," Judge Stevens said. "It's probably just a snake or a rat that nigger of hers killed in the yard. I'll speak to him about it."

The next day he received two more complaints, one from a man who came in diffident deprecation. "We really must do something about it, Judge. I'd be the last one in the world to bother Miss Emily, but we've got to do something." That night the Board of Aldermen met—three graybeards and one younger man, a member of the rising generation.

"It's simple enough," he said. "Send her word to have her place cleaned up. Give her a certain time to do it in, and if she don't . . ."

"Dammit, sir," Judge Stevens said, "will you accuse a lady to her face of smelling bad?"

So the next night, after midnight, four men crossed Miss Emily's lawn and slunk about the house like burglars, sniffing along the base of the brickwork and at the cellar openings while one of them performed a regular sowing motion with his hand out of a sack slung from his shoulder. They broke open the cellar door and sprinkled lime there, and in all the outbuildings. As they recrossed the lawn, a window that had been dark was lighted and Miss Emily sat in it, the light behind her, and her upright torso motionless as that of an idol. They crept quietly across the lawn and into the shadow of the locusts that lined the street. After a week or two the smell went away.

That was when people had begun to feel really sorry for her. People in our town, remembering how old lady Wyatt, her great-aunt, had gone completely crazy at last, believed that the Griersons held themselves a little too high for what they really were. None of the young men were quite good enough for Miss Emily and such. We had long thought of them as a tableau, Miss Emily a slender figure in white in the background, her father a spraddled silhouette in the foreground, his back to her and clutching a horsewhip, the two of them framed by the back-flung front door. So when she got to be thirty and was still single, we were not pleased exactly, but vindicated; even with insanity in the family she wouldn't have turned down all of her chances if they had really materialized.

When her father died, it got about that the house was all that was left to her; and in a way, people were glad. At last they could pity Miss Emily. Being left alone, and a pauper, she had become humanized. Now she too would know the old thrill and the old despair of a penny more or less.

The day after his death all the ladies prepared to call at the house and offer condolence and aid, as is our custom. Miss Emily met them at the door, dressed as usual and with no trace of grief on her face. She told them that her father was not dead. She did that for three days, with the ministers calling on her, and the doctors, trying to persuade her to let them dispose of the body. Just as they were about to resort to law and force, she broke down, and they buried her father quickly.

We did not say she was crazy then. We believed she had to do that. We remembered all the young men her father had driven away, and we knew that with nothing left, she would have to cling to that which had robbed her, as people will.

III

She was sick for a long time. When we saw her again, her hair was cut short, making her look like a girl, with a vague resemblance to those angels in colored church windows—sort of tragic and serene.

The town had just let the contracts for paving the sidewalks, and in the summer after her father's death they began the work. The construction company came with niggers and mules and machinery, and a foreman named Homer Barron, a Yankee—a big, dark, ready man, with a big voice and eyes lighter than his face. The little boys would follow in groups to hear him cuss the niggers, and the niggers singing in time to the rise and fall of picks. Pretty soon he knew everybody in town. Whenever you heard a lot of laughing anywhere about the square, Homer Barron would be in the center of the group. Presently we began to see him and Miss Emily on Sunday afternoons driving in the yellow-wheeled buggy and the matched team of bays from the livery stable.

At first we were glad that Miss Emily would have an interest, because the ladies all said, "Of course a Grierson would not think seriously of a Northerner, a day laborer." But there were still others, older people, who said that even grief could not cause a real lady to forget *noblesse oblige*°—without calling it *noblesse oblige*. They just said, "Poor Emily. Her kinsfolk should come to her." She had some kin in Alabama; but years ago her father had fallen out with them over the estate of old lady Wyatt, the crazy woman, and there was no communication between the two families. They had not even been represented at the funeral.

And as soon as the old people said, "Poor Emily," the whispering began. "Do you suppose it's really so?" they said to one another. "Of course it is. What else could . . ." This behind their hands; rustling of craned silk and satin behind jalousies closed upon the sun of Sunday afternoon as the thin, swift clop-clop-clop of the matched team passed: "Poor Emily."

She carried her head high enough—even when we believed that she was fallen. It was as if she demanded more than ever the recognition of her dignity as the last Grierson; as if it had wanted that touch of earthiness to reaffirm her imperviousness. Like when she bought the rat poison, the arsenic. That was over a year after they had begun to say "Poor Emily," and while the two female cousins were visiting her.

"I want some poison," she said to the druggist. She was over thirty then, still a slight woman, though thinner than usual, with cold, haughty black eyes in a face the flesh of which was strained across the temples and about the eye-sockets as you imagine a lighthouse-keeper's face ought to look. "I want some poison," she said.

"Yes, Miss Emily. What kind? For rats and such? I'd recom—"

"I want the best you have. I don't care what kind."

The druggist named several. "They'll kill anything up to an elephant. But what you want is—"

"Arsenic," Miss Emily said. "Is that a good one?"

"Is . . . arsenic? Yes, ma'am. But what you want—"

"I want arsenic."

The druggist looked down at her. She looked back at him, erect, her face like a strained flag. "Why, of course," the druggist said. "If that's what you want. But the law requires you to tell what you are going to use it for."

Miss Emily just stared at him, her head tilted back in order to look him eye for eye, until he looked away and went and got the arsenic and wrapped it up. The Negro delivery boy brought her the package; the druggist didn't come back. When she opened the package at home there was written on the box, under the skull and bones: "For rats."

IV

So the next day we all said, "She will kill herself"; and we said it would be the best thing. When she had first begun to be seen with Homer Barron, we had said, "She will

---

noblesse oblige: the obligation of a member of the nobility to behave with honor and dignity.

marry him." Then we said, "She will persuade him yet," because Homer himself had remarked—he liked men, and it was known that he drank with the younger men in the Elks' Club—that he was not a marrying man. Later we said, "Poor Emily," behind the jalousies as they passed on Sunday afternoon in the glittering buggy, Miss Emily with her head high and Homer Barron with his hat cocked and a cigar in his teeth, reins and whip in a yellow glove.

Then some of the ladies began to say that it was a disgrace to the town and a bad example to the young people. The men did not want to interfere, but at last the ladies forced the Baptist minister—Miss Emily's people were Episcopal—to call upon her. He would never divulge what happened during that interview, but he refused to go back again. The next Sunday they again drove about the streets, and the following day the minister's wife wrote to Miss Emily's relations in Alabama.

So she had blood-kin under her roof again and we sat back to watch developments. At first nothing happened. Then we were sure that they were to be married. We learned that Miss Emily had been to the jeweler's and ordered a man's toilet set in silver, with the letters H.B. on each piece. Two days later we learned that she had bought a complete outfit of men's clothing, including a nightshirt, and we said, "They are married." We were really glad. We were glad because the two female cousins were even more Grierson than Miss Emily had ever been.

So we were not surprised when Homer Barron—the streets had been finished some time since—was gone. We were a little disappointed that there was not a public blowing-off, but we believed that he had gone on to prepare for Miss Emily's coming, or to give her a chance to get rid of the cousins. (By that time it was a cabal, and we were all Miss Emily's allies to help circumvent the cousins.) Sure enough, after another week they departed. And, as we had expected all along, within three days Homer Barron was back in town. A neighbor saw the Negro man admit him at the kitchen door at dusk one evening.

And that was the last we saw of Homer Barron. And of Miss Emily for some time. The Negro man went in and out with the market basket, but the front door remained closed. Now and then we would see her at a window for a moment, as the men did that night when they sprinkled the lime, but for almost six months she did not appear on the streets. Then we knew that this was to be expected too; as if that quality of her father which had thwarted her woman's life so many times had been too virulent and too furious to die.

When we next saw Miss Emily, she had grown fat and her hair was turning gray. During the next few years it grew grayer and grayer until it attained an even pepper-and-salt iron-gray, when it ceased turning. Up to the day of her death at seventy-four it was still that vigorous iron-gray, like the hair of an active man.

From that time on her front door remained closed, save for a period of six or seven years, when she was about forty, during which she gave lessons in china-painting. She fitted up a studio in one of the downstairs rooms, where the daughters and granddaughters of Colonel Sartoris' contemporaries were sent to her with the same regularity and in the same spirit that they were sent to church on Sundays with a twenty-five-cent piece for the collection plate. Meanwhile her taxes had been remitted.

Then the newer generation became the backbone and the spirit of the town, and the painting pupils grew up and fell away and did not send their children to her with boxes of color and tedious brushes and pictures cut from the ladies' magazines.

The front door closed upon the last one and remained closed for good. When the town got free postal delivery, Miss Emily alone refused to let them fasten the metal numbers above her door and attach a mailbox to it. She would not listen to them.

Daily, monthly, yearly we watched the Negro grow grayer and more stooped, going in and out with the market basket. Each December we sent her a tax notice, which would be returned by the post office a week later, unclaimed. Now and then we would see her in one of the downstairs windows—she had evidently shut up the top floor of the house—like the carven torso of an idol in a niche, looking or not looking at us, we could never tell which. Thus she passed from generation to generation—dear, inescapable, impervious, tranquil, and perverse.

And so she died. Fell ill in the house filled with dust and shadows, with only a doddering Negro man to wait on her. We did not even know she was sick; we had long since given up trying to get any information from the Negro. He talked to no one, probably not even to her, for his voice had grown harsh and rusty, as if from disuse.

She died in one of the downstairs rooms, in a heavy walnut bed with a curtain, her gray head propped on a pillow yellow and moldy with age and lack of sunlight.

V

The Negro met the first of the ladies at the front door and let them in, with their hushed, sibilant voices and their quick, curious glances, and then he disappeared. He walked right through the house and out the back and was not seen again.

The two female cousins came at once. They held the funeral on the second day, with the town coming to look at Miss Emily beneath a mass of bought flowers, with the crayon face of her father musing profoundly above the bier and the ladies sibilant and macabre; and the very old men—some in their brushed Confederate uniforms—on the porch and the lawn, talking of Miss Emily as if she had been a contemporary of theirs, believing that they had danced with her and courted her perhaps, confusing time with its mathematical progression, as the old do, to whom all the past is not a diminishing road but, instead, a huge meadow which no winter ever quite touches, divided from them now by the narrow bottleneck of the most recent decade of years.

Already we knew that there was one room in that region above stairs which no one had seen in forty years, and which would have to be forced. They waited until Miss Emily was decently in the ground before they opened it.

The violence of breaking down the door seemed to fill this room with pervading dust. A thin, acrid pall as of the tomb seemed to lie everywhere upon this room decked and furnished as for a bridal: upon the valance curtains of faded rose color, upon the rose-shaded lights, upon the dressing table, upon the delicate array of crystal and the man's toilet things backed with tarnished silver, silver so tarnished that the monogram was obscured. Among them lay collar and tie, as if they had just been removed, which, lifted, left upon the surface a pale crescent in the dust. Upon a chair hung the suit, carefully folded; beneath it the two mute shoes and the discarded socks.

The man himself lay in the bed.

For a long while we just stood there, looking down at the profound and fleshless grin. The body had apparently once lain in the attitude of an embrace, but now the long sleep that outlasts love, that conquers even the grimace of love, had cuckolded him. What was left of him, rotted beneath what was left of the nightshirt, had become inextricable from the bed in which he lay; and upon him and upon the pillow beside him lay that even coating of the patient and biding dust.

Then we noticed that in the second pillow was the indentation of a head. One of us lifted something from it, and leaning forward, that faint and invisible dust dry and acrid in the nostrils, we saw a long strand of iron-gray hair.

Questions

1. What is meaningful in the final detail that the strand of hair on the second pillow is "iron-gray"?
2. Who is the unnamed narrator? For whom does he (or she) profess to be speaking?
3. Why does "A Rose for Emily" seem better told from his (or her) point of view than if it were told from the point of view of the main character?
4. What contrasts does the narrator draw between changing reality and Emily's refusal or inability to recognize change?
5. How do the character and background of Emily Grierson differ from those of Homer Barron? Why does their courtship inspire so much curiosity? Why might Miss Emily be so drawn to Barron?
6. What do you infer to be the author's attitude toward Emily Grierson? Is she simply a murderous madwoman? Why do you suppose Faulkner calls his story "A Rose . . ."?
7. Do you think Miss Emily is crazy? Is her action a "crime of passion," or simply the act of an insane person? Do you have sympathy for her?

Zora Neale Hurston

Zora Neale Hurston (1901?–1960) was born in Eatonville, Florida, but no record of her actual date of birth exists (best guesses range from 1891 to 1901). Hurston was one of eight children. Her father, a carpenter and Baptist preacher, was also the three-term mayor of Eatonville, the first all-black town incorporated in the United States. When Hurston's mother died in 1912, the father moved the children from one relative to another. Consequently, Hurston never finished grammar school, although in 1918 she began taking classes at Howard University, paying her way through school by working as a manicurist and maid. While at Howard, she published her first story. In early 1925 she moved to New York, arriving with "$1.50, no job, no friends, and a lot of hope." She soon became an important member of the Harlem Renaissance, a group of young black artists (including Langston Hughes, Countee Cullen, Jean Toomer, and Claude McKay) who sought "spiritual emancipation" for African Americans by exploring black heritage and identity in the arts. Hurston eventually became, according to critic Laura Zaidman, "the most prolific black American woman writer of her time." In 1925 she became the first African American student at Barnard College, where she completed a B.A. in anthropology. Hurston's most famous story, "Sweat," appeared in the only issue of Fire!!, *a 1926 avant-garde Harlem Renaissance magazine edited by Hurston, Hughes, and Wallace Thurman. This powerful story of an unhappy marriage*

turned murderous was particularly noteworthy for having the characters speak in the black country dialect of Hurston's native Florida. Hurston achieved only modest success during her lifetime, despite the publication of her memorable novel Their Eyes Were Watching God (1937) and her many contributions to the study of African American folklore. She died, poor and neglected, in a Florida welfare home and was buried in an unmarked grave. In 1973 the novelist Alice Walker erected a gravestone for her carved with the words:

Zora Neale Hurston
"A Genius of the South"
1901–1960
Novelist, Folklorist
Anthropologist

Sweat

1926

I

It was eleven o'clock of a Spring night in Florida. It was Sunday. Any other night, Delia Jones would have been in bed for two hours by this time. But she was a washwoman, and Monday morning meant a great deal to her. So she collected the soiled clothes on Saturday when she returned the clean things. Sunday night after church, she sorted and put the white things to soak. It saved her almost a half-day's start. A great hamper in the bedroom held the clothes that she brought home. It was so much neater than a number of bundles lying around.

She squatted on the kitchen floor beside the great pile of clothes, sorting them into small heaps according to color, and humming a song in a mournful key, but wondering through it all where Sykes, her husband, had gone with her horse and buckboard.°

Just then something long, round, limp, and black fell upon her shoulders and slithered to the floor beside her. A great terror took hold of her. It softened her knees and dried her mouth so that it was a full minute before she could cry out or move. Then she saw that it was the big bull whip her husband liked to carry when he drove.

She lifted her eyes to the door and saw him standing there bent over with laughter at her fright. She screamed at him.

"Sykes, what you throw dat whip on me like dat? You know it would skeer me— looks just like a snake, an' you knows how skeered Ah is of snakes." 5

"Course Ah knowed it! That's how come Ah done it." He slapped his leg with his hand and almost rolled on the ground in his mirth. "If you such a big fool dat you got to have a fit over a earth worm or a string, Ah don't keer how bad Ah skeer you."

"You ain't got no business doing it. Gawd knows it's a sin. Some day Ah'm gointuh drop dead from some of yo' foolishness. 'Nother thing, where you been wid mah rig? Ah feeds dat pony. He ain't fuh you to be drivin' wid no bull whip."

"You sho' is one aggravatin' nigger woman!" he declared and stepped into the room. She resumed her work and did not answer him at once. "Ah done tole you time and again to keep them white folks' clothes outa dis house."

He picked up the whip and glared at her. Delia went on with her work. She went out into the yard and returned with a galvanized tub and set it on the wash-bench.

---

buckboard: a four-wheeled open carriage with the seat resting on a spring platform.

She saw that Sykes had kicked all of the clothes together again, and now stood in her way truculently, his whole manner hoping, *praying,* for an argument. But she walked calmly around him and commenced to re-sort the things.

"Next time, Ah'm gointer kick 'em outdoors," he threatened as he struck a match along the leg of his corduroy breeches.

Delia never looked up from her work, and her thin, stooped shoulders sagged further.

"Ah ain't for no fuss t'night Sykes. Ah just come from taking sacrament at the church house."

He snorted scornfully. "Yeah, you just come from de church house on a Sunday night, but heah you is gone to work on them clothes. You ain't nothing but a hypocrite. One of them amen-corner Christians—sing, whoop, and shout, then come home and wash white folks' clothes on the Sabbath."

He stepped roughly upon the whitest pile of things, kicking them helter-skelter as he crossed the room. His wife gave a little scream of dismay, and quickly gathered them together again.

"Sykes, you quit grindin' dirt into these clothes! How can Ah git through by Sat'day if Ah don't start on Sunday?"

"Ah don't keer if you never git through. Anyhow, Ah done promised Gawd and a couple of other men, Ah ain't gointer have it in mah house. Don't gimme no lip neither, else Ah'll throw 'em out and put mah fist up side yo' head to boot."

Delia's habitual meekness seemed to slip from her shoulders like a blown scarf. She was on her feet; her poor little body, her bare knuckly hands bravely defying the strapping hulk before her.

"Looka heah, Sykes, you done gone too fur. Ah been married to you fur fifteen years, and Ah been takin' in washin' fur fifteen years. Sweat, sweat, sweat! Work and sweat, cry and sweat, pray and sweat!"

"What's that got to do with me?" he asked brutally.

"What's it got to do with you, Sykes? Mah tub of suds is filled yo' belly with vittles more times than yo' hands is filled it. Mah sweat is done paid for this house and Ah reckon Ah kin keep on sweatin' in it."

She seized the iron skillet from the stove and struck a defensive pose, which act surprised him greatly, coming from her. It cowed him and he did not strike her as he usually did.

"Naw you won't," she panted, "that ole snaggle-toothed black woman you runnin' with ain't comin' heah to pile up on *mah* sweat and blood. You ain't paid for nothin' on this place, and Ah'm gointer stay right heah till Ah'm toted out foot foremost."

"Well, you better quit gittin' me riled up, else they'll be totin' you out sooner than you expect. Ah'm so tired of you Ah don't know whut to do. Gawd! How Ah hates skinny wimmen!"

A little awed by this new Delia, he sidled out of the door and slammed the back gate after him. He did not say where he had gone, but she knew too well. She knew very well that he would not return until nearly daybreak also. Her work over, she went on to bed but not to sleep at once. Things had come to a pretty pass!

She lay awake, gazing upon the debris that cluttered their matrimonial trail. Not an image left standing along the way. Anything like flowers had long ago been drowned in the salty stream that had been pressed from her heart. Her tears, her sweat, her blood. She had brought love to the union and he had brought a longing after the flesh. Two months after the wedding, he had given her the first brutal beating. She had the memory of his numerous trips to Orlando with all of his wages when he had returned to her penniless, even before the first year had passed. She was young and soft then, but now she thought of her knotty, muscled limbs, her harsh knuckly hands, and drew herself up into an unhappy little ball in the middle of the big feather bed. Too late now to hope for love, even if it were not Bertha it would be someone else. This case differed from the others only in that she was bolder than the others. Too late for everything except her little home. She had built it for her old days, and planted one by one the trees and flowers there. It was lovely to her, lovely.

Somehow, before sleep came, she found herself saying aloud: "Oh well, whatever goes over the Devil's back, is got to come under his belly. Sometime or ruther, Sykes, like everybody else, is gointer reap his sowing." After that she was able to build a spiritual earthworks° against her husband. His shells could no longer reach her. AMEN. She went to sleep and slept until he announced his presence in bed by kicking her feet and rudely snatching the covers away.

"Gimme some kivah heah, an' git yo' damn foots over on yo' own side! Ah oughter mash you in yo' mouf fuh drawing dat skillet on me."

Delia went clear to the rail without answering him. A triumphant indifference to all that he was or did.

II

The week was full of work for Delia as all other weeks, and Saturday found her behind her little pony, collecting and delivering clothes.

It was a hot, hot day near the end of July. The village men on Joe Clarke's porch even chewed cane listlessly. They did not hurl the cane-knots as usual. They let them dribble over the edge of the porch. Even conversation had collapsed under the heat.

"Heah come Delia Jones," Jim Merchant said, as the shaggy pony came 'round the bend of the road toward them. The rusty buckboard was heaped with baskets of crisp, clean laundry.

"Yep," Joe Lindsay agreed. "Hot or col', rain or shine, jes'ez reg'lar ez de weeks roll roun' Delia carries 'em an' fetches 'em on Sat'day."

"She better if she wanter eat," said Moss. "Syke Jones ain't wuth de shot an' powder hit would tek tuh kill 'im. Not to *huh* he ain't."

"He sho' ain't," Walter Thomas chimed in. "It's too bad, too, cause she wuz a right pretty li'l trick when he got huh. Ah'd uh mah'ied huh mahself if he hadnter beat me to it."

Delia nodded briefly at the men as she drove past.

"Too much knockin' will ruin *any* 'oman. He done beat huh 'nough tuh kill three women, let 'lone change they looks," said Elijah Moseley. "How Syke kin stommuck dat big black greasy Mogul he's layin' roun' wid, gits me. Ah swear dat eight-rock couldn't kiss a sardine can Ah done thowed out de back do' 'way las' yeah."

"Aw, she's fat, thass how come. He's allus been crazy 'bout fat women," put in Merchant. "He'd a' been tied up wid one long time ago if he could a' found one tuh

---

spiritual earthworks: earthworks are military fortifications made of earth; here Hurston uses it metaphorically to mean Delia's emotional defenses.

have him. Did Ah tell yuh 'bout him come sidlin' roun' *mah* wife—bringin' her a basket uh peecans outa his yard fuh a present? Yessir, mah wife! She tol' him tuh take 'em right straight back home, 'cause Delia works so hard ovah dat washtub she reckon everything on de place taste lak sweat an' soapsuds. Ah jus' wisht Ah'd a' caught 'im 'roun' dere! Ah'd a' made his hips ketch on fiah down dat shell road."

"Ah know he done it, too. Ah sees 'im grinnin' at every 'oman dat passes," Walter Thomas said. "But even so, he useter eat some mighty big hunks uh humble pie tuh git dat li'l 'oman he got. She wuz ez pritty ez a speckled pup! Dat wuz fifteen years ago. He useter be so skeered uh losin' huh, she could make him do some parts of a husband's duty. Dey never wuz de same in de mind."

"There oughter be a law about him," said Lindsay. "He ain't fit tuh carry guts tuh a bear."

Clarke spoke for the first time. "Tain't no law on earth dat kin make a man be decent if it ain't in 'im. There's plenty men dat takes a wife lak dey do a joint uh sugarcane. It's round, juicy, an' sweet when dey gits it. But dey squeeze an' grind, squeeze an' grind an' wring tell dey wring every drop uh pleasure dat's in 'em out. When dey's satisfied dat dey is wrung dry, dey treats 'em jes' lak dey do a cane-chew. Dey thows 'em away. Dey knows whut dey is doin' while dey is at it, an' hates theirselves fuh it but they keeps on hangin' after huh tell she's empty. Den dey hates huh fuh bein' a cane-chew an' in de way."

"We oughter take Syke an' dat stray 'oman uh his'n down in Lake Howell swamp an' lay on de rawhide till they cain't say Lawd a' mussy. He allus wuz uh ovahbearin niggah, but since dat white 'oman from up north done teached 'im how to run a automobile, he done got too biggety to live—an' we oughter kill 'im," Old Man Anderson advised.

A grunt of approval went around the porch. But the heat was melting their civic virtue and Elijah Moseley began to bait Joe Clarke.

"Come on, Joe, git a melon outa dere an' slice it up for yo' customers. We'se all sufferin' wid de heat. De bear's done got *me!*"

"Thass right, Joe, a watermelon is jes' whut Ah needs tuh cure de eppizudicks," Walter Thomas joined forces with Moseley. "Come on dere, Joe. We all is steady customers an' you ain't set us up in a long time. Ah chooses dat long, bowlegged Floridy favorite."

"A god, an' be dough. You all gimme twenty cents and slice away," Clarke retorted. "Ah needs a col' slice m'self. Heah, everybody chip in. Ah'll lend y'all mah meat knife."

The money was all quickly subscribed and the huge melon brought forth. At that moment, Sykes and Bertha arrived. A determined silence fell on the porch and the melon was put away again.

Merchant snapped down the blade of his jackknife and moved toward the store door.

"Come on in, Joe, an' gimme a slab uh sow belly an' uh pound uh coffee—almost fuhgot 'twas Sat'day. Got to git on home." Most of the men left also.

Just then Delia drove past on her way home, as Sykes was ordering magnificently for Bertha. It pleased him for Delia to see.

"Git whutsoever yo' heart desires, Honey. Wait a minute, Joe. Give huh two bottles uh strawberry soda-water, uh quart parched ground-peas, an' a block uh chewin' gum."

With all this they left the store, with Sykes reminding Bertha that this was his town and she could have it if she wanted it.

The men returned soon after they left, and held their watermelon feast.

"Where did Syke Jones git da 'oman from nohow?" Lindsay asked.

"Ovah Apopka. Guess dey musta been cleanin' out de town when she lef'. She don't look lak a thing but a hunk uh liver wid hair on it."

"Well, she sho' kin squall," Dave Carter contributed. "When she gits ready tuh laff, she jes' opens huh mouf an' latches it back tuh de las' notch. No ole granpa alligator down in Lake Bell ain't got nothin' on huh."

III

Bertha had been in town three months now. Sykes was still paying her room-rent at Della Lewis'—the only house in town that would have taken her in. Sykes took her frequently to Winter Park to "stomps." He still assured her that he was the swellest man in the state.

"Sho' you kin have dat li'l ole house soon's Ah git dat 'oman outadere. Everything b'longs tuh me an' you sho' kin have it. Ah sho' 'bominates uh skinny 'oman. Lawdy, you sho' is got one portly shape on you! You kin git *anything* you wants. Dis is *mah* town an' you sho' kin have it."

Delia's work-worn knees crawled over the earth in Gethsemane° and up the rocks of Calvary° many, many times during these months. She avoided the villagers and meeting places in her efforts to be blind and deaf. But Bertha nullified this to a degree, by coming to Delia's house to call Sykes out to her at the gate.

Delia and Sykes fought all the time now with no peaceful interludes. They slept and ate in silence. Two or three times Delia had attempted a timid friendliness, but she was repulsed each time. It was plain that the breaches must remain agape.

The sun had burned July to August. The heat streamed down like a million hot arrows, smiting all things living upon the earth. Grass withered, leaves browned, snakes went blind in shedding, and men and dogs went mad. Dog days!

Delia came home one day and found Sykes there before her. She wondered, but started to go on into the house without speaking, even though he was standing in the kitchen door and she must either stoop under his arm or ask him to move. He made no room for her. She noticed a soap box beside the steps, but paid no particular attention to it, knowing that he must have brought it there. As she was stooping to pass under his outstretched arm, he suddenly pushed her backward, laughingly.

"Look in de box dere, Delia, Ah done brung yuh somethin'!"

She nearly fell upon the box in her stumbling, and when she saw what it held, she all but fainted outright.

"Syke! Syke, mah Gawd! You take dat rattlesnake 'way from heah! You *gottuh*. Oh, Jesus, have mussy!"

"Ah ain't got tuh do nuthin' uh de kin'—fact is Ah ain't got tuh do nothin' but die. Tain't no use uh you puttin' on airs makin' out lak you skeered uh dat snake—he's gointer stay right heah tell he die. He wouldn't bite me cause Ah knows how tuh handle 'im. Nohow he wouldn't risk breakin' out his fangs 'gin yo skinny laigs."

Gethsemane: the garden outside Jerusalem that was the scene of Jesus's agony and arrest (see Matthew 26:36–57); hence, a scene of great suffering.   *Calvary:* the hill outside Jerusalem where Jesus was crucified.

"Naw, now Syke, don't keep dat thing 'round tryin' tuh skeer me tuh death. You knows Ah'm even feared uh earth worms. Thass de biggest snake Ah evah did see. Kill 'im, Syke, please."

"Doan ast me tuh do nothin' fuh yuh. Goin' 'round tryin' tuh be so damn asterperious.° Naw, Ah ain't gonna kill it. Ah think uh damn sight mo' uh him dan you! Dat's a nice snake an' anybody doan lak 'im kin jes' hit de grit."

The village soon heard that Sykes had the snake, and came to see and ask questions.

"How de hen-fire did you ketch dat six-foot rattler, Syke?" Thomas asked.

"He's full uh frogs so he cain't hardly move, thass how Ah eased up on 'im. But Ah'm a snake charmer an' knows how tuh handle 'em. Shux, dat ain't nothin'. Ah could ketch one eve'y day if Ah so wanted tuh."

"Whut he needs is a heavy hick'ry club leaned real heavy on his head. Dat's de bes' way tuh charm a rattlesnake."

"Naw, Walt, y'all jes' don't understand dese diamon' backs lak Ah do," said Sykes in a superior tone of voice.

The village agreed with Walter, but the snake stayed on. His box remained by the kitchen door with its screen wire covering. Two or three days later it had digested its meal of frogs and literally came to life. It rattled at every movement in the kitchen or the yard. One day as Delia came down the kitchen steps she saw his chalky-white fangs curved like scimitars hung in the wire meshes. This time she did not run away with averted eyes as usual. She stood for a long time in the doorway in a red fury that grew bloodier for every second that she regarded the creature that was her torment.

That night she broached the subject as soon as Sykes sat down to the table.

"Syke, Ah wants you tuh take dat snake 'way fum heah. You done starved me an' Ah put up widcher, you done beat me an Ah took dat, but you done kilt all mah insides bringin' dat varmint heah."

Sykes poured out a saucer full of coffee and drank it deliberately before he answered her.

"A whole lot Ah keer 'bout how you feels inside uh out. Dat snake ain't goin' no damn wheah till Ah gits ready fuh 'im tuh go. So fur as beatin' is concerned, yuh ain't took near all dat you gointer take ef yuh stay 'round *me*."

Delia pushed back her plate and got up from the table. "Ah hates you, Sykes," she said calmly. "Ah hates you tuh de same degree dat Ah useter love yuh. Ah done took an' took till mah belly is full up tuh mah neck. Dat's de reason Ah got mah letter fum de church an' moved mah membership tuh Woodbridge—so Ah don't haftuh take no sacrament wid yuh. Ah don't wantuh see yuh 'round me atall. Lay 'round wid dat 'oman all yuh wants tuh, but gwan 'way fum me an' mah house. Ah hates yuh lak uh suck-egg dog."

Sykes almost let the huge wad of corn bread and collard greens he was chewing fall out of his mouth in amazement. He had a hard time whipping himself up to the proper fury to try to answer Delia.

"Well, Ah'm glad you does hate me. Ah'm sho' tiahed uh you hangin' ontuh me. Ah don't want yuh. Look at yuh stringey ole neck! Yo' rawbony laigs an' arms is enough tuh cut uh man tuh death. You looks jes' lak de devvul's doll-baby tuh *me*. You cain't hate me no worse dan Ah hates you. Ah been hatin' *you* fuh years."

asterperious: haughty.

"Yo' ole black hide don't look lak nothin' tuh me, but uh passle uh wrinkled up rubber, wid yo' big ole yeahs flappin' on each side lak uh paih uh buzzard wings. Don't think Ah'm gointuh be run 'way fum mah house neither. Ah'm goin' tuh de white folks 'bout *you*, mah young man, de very nex' time you lay yo' han's on me. Mah cup is done run ovah." Delia said this with no signs of fear and Sykes departed from the house, threatening her, but made not the slightest move to carry out any of them.

That night he did not return at all, and the next day being Sunday, Delia was glad she did not have to quarrel before she hitched up her pony and drove the four miles to Woodbridge.

She stayed to the night service—"love feast"—which was very warm and full of spirit. In the emotional winds her domestic trials were borne far and wide so that she sang as she drove homeward,

> *Jurden water,° black an' col*
> *Chills de body, not de soul*
> *An' Ah wantah cross Jurden in uh calm time.*

She came from the barn to the kitchen door and stopped.

"Whut's de mattah, ol' Satan, you ain't kickin' up yo' racket?" She addressed the snake's box. Complete silence. She went on into the house with a new hope in its birth struggles. Perhaps her threat to go to the white folks had frightened Sykes! Perhaps he was sorry! Fifteen years of misery and suppression had brought Delia to the place where she would hope *anything* that looked towards a way over or through her wall of inhibitions.

She felt in the match-safe behind the stove at once for a match. There was only one there.

"Dat niggah wouldn't fetch nothin' heah tuh save his rotten neck, but he kin run thew whut Ah brings quick enough. Now he done toted off nigh on tuh haff uh box uh matches. He done had dat 'oman heah in mah house, too."

Nobody but a woman could tell how she knew this even before she struck the match. But she did and it put her into a new fury.

Presently she brought in the tubs to put the white things to soak. This time she decided she need not bring the hamper out of the bedroom; she would go in there and do the sorting. She picked up the pot-bellied lamp and went in. The room was small and the hamper stood hard by the foot of the white iron bed. She could sit and reach through the bedposts—resting as she worked.

"Ah wantah cross Jurden in uh calm time." She was singing again. The mood of the "love feast" had returned. She threw back the lid of the basket almost gaily. Then, moved by both horror and terror, she sprang back toward the door. *There lay the snake in the basket!* He moved sluggishly at first, but even as she turned round and round, jumped up and down in an insanity of fear, he began to stir vigorously. She saw him pouring his awful beauty from the basket upon the bed, then she seized the lamp and ran as fast as she could to the kitchen. The wind from the open door blew out the light and the darkness added to her terror. She sped to the darkness of the yard, slamming

---

°*Jurden water*: black Southern dialect for the River Jordan, which represents the last boundary before entering heaven. It comes from the Old Testament, when the Jews had to cross the River Jordan to reach the Promised Land.

the door after her before she thought to set down the lamp. She did not feel safe even on the ground, so she climbed up in the hay barn.

There for an hour or more she lay sprawled upon the hay a gibbering wreck.

Finally she grew quiet, and after that came coherent thought. With this stalked through her a cold, bloody rage. Hours of this. A period of introspection, a space of retrospection, then a mixture of both. Out of this an awful calm.

"Well, Ah done de bes' Ah could. If things ain't right, Gawd knows tain't mah fault."

She went to sleep—a twitch sleep—and woke up to a faint gray sky. There was a loud hollow sound below. She peered out. Sykes was at the wood-pile, demolishing a wire-covered box.

He hurried to the kitchen door, but hung outside there some minutes before he entered, and stood some minutes more inside before he closed it after him.

The gray in the sky was spreading. Delia descended without fear now, and crouched beneath the low bedroom window. The drawn shade shut out the dawn, shut in the night. But the thin walls held back no sound.

"Dat ol' scratch° is woke up now!" She mused at the tremendous whirr inside, which every woodsman knows, is one of the sound illusions. The rattler is a ventriloquist. His whirr sounds to the right, to the left, straight ahead, behind, close under foot—everywhere but where it is. Woe to him who guesses wrong unless he is prepared to hold up his end of the argument! Sometimes he strikes without rattling at all.

Inside, Sykes heard nothing until he knocked a pot lid off the stove while trying to reach the match-safe in the dark. He had emptied his pockets at Bertha's.

The snake seemed to wake up under the stove and Sykes made a quick leap into the bedroom. In spite of the gin he had had, his head was clearing now.

"Mah Gawd!" he chattered, "ef Ah could on'y strack uh light!"

The rattling ceased for a moment as he stood paralyzed. He waited. It seemed that the snake waited also.

"Oh, fuh de light! Ah thought he'd be too sick"—Sykes was muttering to himself when the whirr began again, closer, right underfoot this time. Long before this, Sykes' ability to think had been flattened down to primitive instinct and he leaped—onto the bed.

Outside Delia heard a cry that might have come from a maddened chimpanzee, a stricken gorilla. All the terror, all the horror, all the rage that man possibly could express, without a recognizable human sound.

A tremendous stir inside there, another series of animal screams, the intermittent whirr of the reptile. The shade torn violently down from the window, letting in the red dawn, a huge brown hand seizing the window stick, great dull blows upon the wooden floor punctuating the gibberish of sound long after the rattle of the snake had abruptly subsided. All this Delia could see and hear from her place beneath the window, and it made her ill. She crept over to the four-o'clocks and stretched herself on the cool earth to recover.

She lay there. "Delia, Delia!" She could hear Sykes calling in a most despairing tone as one who expected no answer. The sun crept on up, and he called. Delia could

---

scratch: a folk expression for the devil.

not move—her legs had gone flabby. She never moved, he called, and the sun kept rising.

"Mah Gawd!" She heard him moan, "Mah Gawd fum Heben!" She heard him stumbling about and got up from her flower-bed. The sun was growing warm. As she approached the door she heard him call out hopefully, "Delia, is dat you Ah heah?"

She saw him on his hands and knees as soon as she reached the door. He crept an inch or two toward her—all that he was able, and she saw his horribly swollen neck and his one open eye shining with hope. A surge of pity too strong to support bore her away from that eye that must, could not, fail to see the tubs. He would see the lamp. Orlando with its doctors was too far. She could scarcely reach the chinaberry tree, where she waited in the growing heat while inside she knew the cold river was creeping up and up to extinguish that eye which must know by now that she knew.

Questions

1. Why is the house so important to Delia? What is its significance?
2. Sykes seems not only disrespectful of Delia; he appears to want to aggravate her purposely. Why do you think he is so hostile to her?
3. Delia and Sykes apparently did care for each other at the start of their marriage. What do you think went wrong?
4. How do you feel about Delia's actions at the end of the story? Are they justified?

Flannery O'Connor

Mary Flannery O'Connor (1925–1964) was born in Savannah, Georgia, but spent most of her life in the small town of Milledgeville. While attending Georgia State College for Women, she won a local reputation for her fledgling stories and satiric cartoons. After graduating in 1945, she went on to study at the University of Iowa, where she earned an M.F.A. in 1947. Diagnosed in 1950 with disseminated lupus, the same incurable illness that had killed her father, O'Connor returned home and spent the last decade of her life living with her mother in Milledgeville. Back on the family dairy farm, she wrote, maintained an extensive literary correspondence, raised peacocks, and underwent medical treatment. When her illness occasionally went into a period of remission, she made trips to lecture and read her stories to college audiences. Her health declined rapidly after surgery early in 1964 for an unrelated complaint. She died at thirty-nine.

Flannery O'Connor

O'Connor is unusual among modern American writers in the depth of her Christian vision. A devout Roman Catholic, she attended mass daily while growing up and living in the largely Protestant South. As a latter-day satirist in the manner of Jonathan Swift, O'Connor levels the eye of an uncompromising moralist on the violence and spiritual disorder of the modern world, focusing on what she calls "the action of grace in territory held largely by the devil." She is sometimes called a "Southern Gothic" writer because of her fascination with grotesque incidents and characters. Throughout her career she depicted the South as a troubled region in which the social, racial, and religious status quo that had existed since before the Civil War was coming to a violent end. Despite the inherent seriousness of her religious and social themes, O'Connor's mordant and frequently outrageous humor is everywhere apparent. Her combination of profound vision and dark comedy is the distinguishing characteristic of her literary sensibilities. "Parker's Back," the last story Flannery O'Connor wrote, was published the year after her death.

Parker's Back   1965

Parker's wife was sitting on the front porch floor, snapping beans. Parker was sitting on the step, some distance away, watching her sullenly. She was plain, plain. The skin on her face was thin and drawn as tight as the skin on an onion and her eyes were gray and sharp like the points of two icepicks. Parker understood why he had married her—he couldn't have got her any other way—but he couldn't understand why he stayed with her now. She was pregnant and pregnant women were not his favorite kind. Nevertheless, he stayed as if she had him conjured. He was puzzled and ashamed of himself.

The house they rented sat alone save for a single tall pecan tree on a high embankment overlooking a highway. At intervals a car would shoot past below and his wife's eyes would swerve suspiciously after the sound of it and then come back to rest on the newspaper full of beans in her lap. One of the things she did not approve of was automobiles. In addition to her other bad qualities, she was forever sniffing up sin. She did not smoke or dip, drink whiskey, use bad language or paint her face, and God knew some paint would have improved it, Parker thought. Her being against color, it was the more remarkable she had married him. Sometimes he supposed that she had married him because she meant to save him. At other times he had a suspicion that she actually liked everything she said she didn't. He could account for her one way or another; it was himself he could not understand.

She turned her head in his direction and said, "It's no reason you can't work for a man. It don't have to be a woman."

"Aw shut your mouth for a change," Parker muttered.

If he had been certain she was jealous of the woman he worked for he would have been pleased but more likely she was concerned with the sin that would result if he and the woman took a liking to each other. He had told her that the woman was a hefty young blonde; in fact she was nearly seventy years old and too dried up to have an interest in anything except getting as much work out of him as she could. Not that an old woman didn't sometimes get an interest in a young man, particularly if he was as attractive as Parker felt he was, but this old woman looked at him the same way she looked at her old tractor—as if she had to put up with it because it was all she had. The tractor had broken down the second day Parker was on it and she had set him at once to cutting bushes, saying out of the side of her mouth to the nigger, "Everything he touches, he breaks." She also asked him to wear his shirt when he worked; Parker had removed it even though the day was not sultry; he put it back on reluctantly.

This ugly woman Parker married was his first wife. He had had other women but he had planned never to get himself tied up legally. He had first seen her one morning when his truck broke down on the highway. He had managed to pull it off the road into a neatly swept yard on which sat a peeling two-room house. He got out and opened the hood of the truck and began to study the motor. Parker had an extra sense that told him when there was a woman nearby watching him. After he had leaned over the motor a few minutes, his neck began to prickle. He cast his eye over the empty yard and porch of the house. A woman he could not see was either nearby beyond a clump of honeysuckle or in the house, watching him out the window.

Suddenly Parker began to jump up and down and fling his hand about as if he had mashed it in the machinery. He doubled over and held his hand close to his chest. "God dammit!" he hollered, "Jesus Christ in hell! Jesus God Almighty damm! God dammit to hell!" he went on, flinging out the same few oaths over and over as loud as he could.

Without warning a terrible bristly claw slammed the side of his face and he fell backwards on the hood of the truck. "You don't talk no filth here!" a voice close to him shrilled.

Parker's vision was so blurred that for an instant he thought he had been attacked by some creature from above, a giant hawk-eyed angel wielding a hoary weapon. As his sight cleared, he saw before him a tall raw-boned girl with a broom.

"I hurt my hand," he said. "I HURT my hand." He was so incensed that he forgot that he hadn't hurt his hand. "My hand may be broke," he growled although his voice was still unsteady.

"Lemme see it," the girl demanded.

Parker stuck out his hand and she came closer and looked at it. There was no mark on the palm and she took the hand and turned it over. Her own hand was dry and hot and rough and Parker felt himself jolted back to life by her touch. He looked more closely at her. I don't want nothing to do with this one, he thought.

The girl's sharp eyes peered at the back of the stubby reddish hand she held. There emblazoned in red and blue was a tattooed eagle perched on a cannon. Parker's sleeve was rolled to the elbow. Above the eagle a serpent was coiled about a shield and in the spaces between the eagle and the serpent there were hearts, some with arrows through them. Above the serpent there was a spread hand of cards. Every space on the skin of Parker's arm, from wrist to elbow, was covered in some loud design. The girl gazed at this with an almost stupefied smile of shock, as if she had accidentally grasped a poisonous snake; she dropped the hand.

"I got most of my other ones in foreign parts," Parker said. "These here I mostly got in the United States. I got my first one when I was only fifteen year old."

"Don't tell me," the girl said, "I don't like it. I ain't got any use for it."

"You ought to see the ones you can't see," Parker said and winked.

Two circles of red appeared like apples on the girl's cheeks and softened her appearance. Parker was intrigued. He did not for a minute think that she didn't like the tattoos. He had never yet met a woman who was not attracted to them.

Parker was fourteen when he saw a man in a fair, tattooed from head to foot. Except for his loins which were girded with a panther hide, the man's skin was patterned in what seemed from Parker's distance—he was near the back of the tent, standing on a bench—a single intricate design of brilliant color. The man, who was small and sturdy, moved about on the platform, flexing his muscles so that the arabesque of men and beasts and flowers on his skin appeared to have a subtle motion of its own. Parker was filled with emotion, lifted up as some people are when the flag passes. He was a boy whose mouth habitually hung open. He was heavy and earnest, as ordinary as a loaf of bread. When the show was over, he had remained standing on the bench, staring where the tattooed man had been, until the tent was almost empty.

Parker had never before felt the least motion of wonder in himself. Until he saw the man at the fair, it did not enter his head that there was anything out of the ordinary about the fact that he existed. Even then it did not enter his head, but a peculiar unease settled in him. It was as if a blind boy had been turned so gently in a different direction that he did not know his destination had been changed.

He had his first tattoo some time after—the eagle perched on the cannon. It was done by a local artist. It hurt very little, just enough to make it appear to Parker to be worth doing. This was peculiar too for before he had thought that only what did not hurt was worth doing. The next year he quit school because he was sixteen and could. He went to the trade school for a while, then he quit the trade school and worked for six months in a garage. The only reason he worked at all was to pay for more tattoos. His mother worked in a laundry and could support him, but she would not pay for any tattoo except her name on a heart, which he had put on, grumbling. However, her name was Betty Jean and nobody had to know it was his mother. He found out that the tattoos were attractive to the kind of girls he liked but who had never liked him before. He began to drink beer and get in fights. His mother wept over what was becoming of him. One night she dragged him off to a revival with her, not telling him where they were going. When he saw the big lighted church, he jerked out of her grasp and ran. The next day he lied about his age and joined the navy.

Parker was large for the tight sailor's pants but the silly white cap, sitting low on his forehead, made his face by contrast look thoughtful and almost intense. After a month or two in the navy, his mouth ceased to hang open. His features hardened into the features of a man. He stayed in the navy five years and seemed a natural part of the grey mechanical ship, except for his eyes, which were the same pale slate-color as the ocean and reflected the immense spaces around him as if they were a microcosm of the mysterious sea. In port Parker wandered about comparing the run-down places he was in to Birmingham, Alabama. Everywhere he went he picked up more tattoos.

He had stopped having lifeless ones like anchors and crossed rifles. He had a tiger and a panther on each shoulder, a cobra coiled about a torch on his chest, hawks on his thighs, Elizabeth II and Philip over where his stomach and liver were respectively. He did not care much what the subject was so long as it was colorful; on his abdomen he had a few obscenities but only because that seemed the proper place for them. Parker would be satisfied with each tattoo about a month, then something about it that had attracted him would wear off. Whenever a decent-sized mirror was available, he would get in front of it and study his overall look. The effect was not of one intricate arabesque of colors but of something haphazard and botched. A huge dissatisfaction would come over him and he would go off and find another tattooist and have another space filled up. The front of Parker was almost completely covered but there were no tattoos on his back. He had no desire for one anywhere he could not readily see it himself. As the space on the front of him for tattoos decreased, his dissatisfaction grew and became general.

After one of his furloughs, he didn't go back to the navy but remained away without official leave, drunk, in a rooming house in a city he did not know. His dissatisfaction, from being chronic and latent, had suddenly become acute and raged in him. It was as if the panther and the lion and the serpents and the eagles and the hawks had penetrated his skin and lived inside him in a raging warfare. The navy caught up with him, put him in the brig for nine months and then gave him a dishonorable discharge.

After that Parker decided that country air was the only kind fit to breathe. He rented the shack on the embankment and bought the old truck and took various jobs which he kept as long as it suited him. At the time he met his future wife, he was buying apples by the bushel and selling them for the same price by the pound to isolated homesteaders on back country roads.

"All that there," the woman said, pointing to his arm, "is no better than what a fool Indian would do. It's a heap of vanity." She seemed to have found the word she wanted. "Vanity of vanities," she said.

Well what the hell do I care what she thinks of it? Parker asked himself, but he was plainly bewildered. "I reckon you like one of these better than another anyway," he said, dallying until he thought of something that would impress her. He thrust the arm back at her. "Which you like best?"

"None of them," she said, "but the chicken is not as bad as the rest."

"What chicken?" Parker almost yelled.

She pointed to the eagle.

"That's an eagle," Parker said. "What fool would waste their time having a chicken put on themselves?"

"What fool would have any of it?" the girl said and turned away. She went slowly back to the house and left him there to get going. Parker remained for almost five minutes, looking agape at the dark door she had entered.

The next day he returned with a bushel of apples. He was not one to be outdone by anything that looked like her. He liked women with meat on them, so you didn't feel their muscles, much less their old bones. When he arrived, she was sitting on the top step and the yard was full of children, all as thin and poor as herself; Parker remembered it was Saturday. He hated to be making up to a woman when there were children around, but it was fortunate he had brought the bushel of apples off the truck. As the children approached him to see what he carried, he gave each child an apple and told it to get lost; in that way he cleared out the whole crowd.

The girl did nothing to acknowledge his presence. He might have been a stray pig or goat that had wandered into the yard and she too tired to take up the broom and send it off. He set the bushel of apples down next to her on the step. He sat down on a lower step.

"Hep yourself," he said, nodding at the basket; then he lapsed into silence.

She took an apple quickly as if the basket might disappear if she didn't make haste. Hungry people made Parker nervous. He had always had plenty to eat himself. He grew very uncomfortable. He reasoned he had nothing to say so why should he say it? He could not think now why he had come or why he didn't go before he wasted another bushel of apples on the crowd of children. He supposed they were her brothers and sisters.

She chewed the apple slowly but with a kind of relish of concentration, bent slightly but looking out ahead. The view from the porch stretched off across a long incline studded with iron weed and across the highway to a vast vista of hills and one small mountain. Long views depressed Parker. You look out into space like that and you begin to feel as if someone were after you, the navy or the government or religion.

"Who them children belong to, you?" he said at length.

"I ain't married yet," she said. "They belong to momma." She said it as if it were only a matter of time before she would be married.

Who in God's name would marry her? Parker thought.

A large barefooted woman with a wide gap-toothed face appeared in the door behind Parker. She had apparently been there for several minutes.

"Good evening," Parker said.

The woman crossed the porch and picked up what was left of the bushel of apples. "We thank you," she said and returned with it into the house.

"That your old woman?" Parker muttered.

The girl nodded. Parker knew a lot of sharp things he could have said like "You got my sympathy," but he was gloomily silent. He just sat there, looking at the view. He thought he must be coming down with something.

"If I pick up some peaches tomorrow I'll bring you some," he said.

"I'll be much obliged to you," the girl said.

Parker had no intention of taking any basket of peaches back there but the next day he found himself doing it. He and the girl had almost nothing to say to each other. One thing he did say was, "I ain't got any tattoo on my back."

"What you got on it?" the girl said.

"My shirt," Parker said. "Haw."

"Haw, haw," the girl said politely.

Parker thought he was losing his mind. He could not believe for a minute that he was attracted to a woman like this. She showed not the least interest in anything but what he brought until he appeared the third time with two cantaloups. "What's your name?" she asked.

"O. E. Parker," he said.

"What does the O. E. stand for?"

"You can just call me O. E.," Parker said. "Or Parker. Don't nobody call me by my name."

"What's it stand for?" she persisted.

"Never mind," Parker said. "What's yours?"

"I'll tell you when you tell me what them letters are the short of," she said. There was just a hint of flirtatiousness in her tone and it went rapidly to Parker's head. He had never revealed the name to any man or woman, only to the files of the navy and the government, and it was on his baptismal record which he got at the age of a month; his mother was a Methodist. When the name leaked out of the navy files, Parker narrowly missed killing the man who used it.

"You'll go blab it around," he said.

"I'll swear I'll never tell nobody," she said. "On God's holy word I swear it."

Parker sat for a few minutes in silence. Then he reached for the girl's neck, drew her ear close to his mouth and revealed the name in a low voice.

"Obadiah," she whispered. Her face slowly brightened as if the name came as a sign to her. "Obadiah," she said.

The name still stank in Parker's estimation.

"Obadiah Elihue," she said in a reverent voice.

"If you call me that aloud, I'll bust your head open," Parker said. "What's yours?"

"Sarah Ruth Cates," she said.

"Glad to meet you, Sarah Ruth," Parker said.

Sarah Ruth's father was a Straight Gospel preacher but he was away, spreading it in Florida. Her mother did not seem to mind his attention to the girl so long as he brought a basket of something with him when he came. As for Sarah Ruth herself, it was plain to Parker after he had visited three times that she was crazy about him. She liked him even though she insisted that pictures on the skin were vanity of vanities and even after hearing him curse, and even after she had asked him if he was saved and he had replied that he didn't see it was anything in particular to save him from. After that, inspired, Parker had said, "I'd be saved enough if you was to kiss me."

She scowled. "That ain't being saved," she said.

Not long after that she agreed to take a ride in his truck. Parker parked it on a deserted road and suggested to her that they lie down together in the back of it.

"Not until after we're married," she said—just like that.

"Oh that ain't necessary," Parker said and as he reached for her, she thrust him away with such force that the door of the truck came off and he found himself flat on his back on the ground. He made up his mind then and there to have nothing further to do with her.

They were married in the County Ordinary's office because Sarah Ruth thought churches were idolatrous. Parker had no opinion about that one way or the other. The Ordinary's office was lined with cardboard file boxes and record books with dusty yellow slips of paper hanging on out of them. The Ordinary was an old woman with red hair who had held office for forty years and looked as dusty as her books. She married them from behind the iron-grill of a stand-up desk and when she finished, she said with a flourish, "Three dollars and fifty cents and till death do you part!" and yanked some forms out of a machine.

Marriage did not change Sarah Ruth a jot and it made Parker gloomier than ever. Every morning he decided he had had enough and would not return that night; every night he returned. Whenever Parker couldn't stand the way he felt, he would have another tattoo, but the only surface left on him now was his back. To see a tattoo on his own back he would have to get two mirrors and stand between them in just the correct position and this seemed to Parker a good way to make an idiot of himself. Sarah Ruth who, if she had had better sense, could have enjoyed a tattoo on his back, would not even look at the ones he had elsewhere. When he attempted to point out especial details of them, she would shut her eyes tight and turn her back as well. Except in total darkness, she preferred Parker dressed and with his sleeves rolled down.

"At the judgement seat of God, Jesus is going to say to you, 'What you been doing all your life besides have pictures drawn all over you?'" she said.

"You don't fool me none," Parker said, "you're just afraid that hefty girl I work for'll like me so much she'll say, 'Come on, Mr. Parker, let's you and me . . .'"

"You're tempting sin," she said, "and at the judgement seat of God you'll have to answer for that too. You ought to go back to selling the fruits of the earth."

Parker did nothing much when he was at home but listen to what the judgement seat of God would be like for him if he didn't change his ways. When he could, he broke in with tales of the hefty girl he worked for. "'Mr. Parker,'" he said she said, "'I hired you for your brains.'" (She had added, "So why don't you use them?")

"And you should have seen her face the first time she saw me without my shirt," he said. "'Mr. Parker,' she said, 'you're a walking panner-rammer!'" This had, in fact, been her remark but it had been delivered out of one side of her mouth.

Dissatisfaction began to grow so great in Parker that there was no containing it outside of a tattoo. It had to be his back. There was no help for it. A dim half-formed inspiration began to work in his mind. He visualized having a tattoo put there that Sarah Ruth would not be able to resist—a religious subject. He thought of an open book with HOLY BIBLE tattooed under it and an actual verse printed on the page. This seemed just the thing for a while; then he began to hear her say, "Ain't I already got a real Bible? What you think I want to read the same verse over and over for when I can read it all?" He needed something better even than the Bible! He thought about it so much that he began to lose sleep. He was already losing flesh—Sarah Ruth just threw food in the pot and let it boil. Not knowing for certain why he continued to stay with a woman who was both ugly and pregnant and no cook made him generally nervous and irritable, and he developed a little tic in the side of his face.

Once or twice he found himself turning around abruptly as if someone were trailing him. He had had a granddaddy who had ended in the state mental hospital, although not until he was seventy-five, but as urgent as it might be for him to get a tattoo, it was just as urgent that he get exactly the right one to bring Sarah Ruth to heel. As he continued to worry over it, his eyes took on a hollow preoccupied expression. The old woman he worked for told him that if he couldn't keep his mind on what he was doing, she knew where she could find a fourteen-year-old colored boy who could. Parker was too preoccupied even to be offended. At any time previous, he would have left her then and there, saying drily, "Well, you go ahead on and get him then."

Two or three mornings later he was baling hay with the old woman's sorry baler and her broken down tractor in a large field, cleared save for one enormous old tree standing in the middle of it. The old woman was the kind who would not cut down a large old tree because it was a large old tree. She had pointed it out to Parker as if he didn't have eyes and told him to be careful not to hit it as the machine picked up hay near it. Parker began at the outside of the field and made circles inward toward it. He had to get off the tractor every now and then and untangle the baling cord or kick a rock out of the way. The old woman had told him to carry the rocks to the edge of the field, which he did when she was there watching. When he thought he could make it, he ran over them. As he circled the field his mind was on a suitable design for his back. The sun, the size of a golf ball, began to switch regularly from in front to behind him, but he appeared to see it both places as if he had eyes in the back of his head. All at once he saw the tree reaching out to grasp him. A ferocious thud propelled him into the air, and he heard himself yelling in an unbelievably loud voice, "GOD ABOVE!"

He landed on his back while the tractor crashed upside down into the tree and burst into flame. The first thing Parker saw were his shoes, quickly being eaten by the fire; one was caught under the tractor, the other was some distance away, burning by itself. He was not in them. He could feel the hot breath of the burning tree on his face. He scrambled backwards, still sitting, his eyes cavernous, and if he had known how to cross himself he would have done it.

His truck was on a dirt road at the edge of the field. He moved toward it, still sitting, still backwards, but faster and faster; halfway to it he got up and began a kind of forward-bent run from which he collapsed on his knees twice. His legs felt like two old rusted rain gutters. He reached the truck finally and took off in it, zigzagging up the road. He drove past his house on the embankment and straight for the city, fifty miles distant.

Parker did not allow himself to think on the way to the city. He only knew that there had been a great change in his life, a leap forward into a worse unknown, and that there was nothing he could do about it. It was for all intents accomplished.

The artist had two large cluttered rooms over a chiropodist's office on a back street. Parker, still barefooted, burst silently in on him at a little after three in the afternoon. The artist, who was about Parker's own age—twenty-eight—but thin and bald, was behind a small drawing table, tracing a design in green ink. He looked up with an annoyed glance and did not seem to recognize Parker in the hollow-eyed creature before him.

"Let me see the book you got with all the pictures of God in it," Parker said breathlessly. "The religious one."

The artist continued to look at him with his intellectual, superior stare. "I don't put tattoos on drunks," he said.

"You know me!" Parker cried indignantly. "I'm O. E. Parker! You done work for me before and I always paid!"

The artist looked at him another moment as if he were not altogether sure. "You've fallen off some," he said. "You must have been in jail."

"Married," Parker said.

"Oh," said the artist. With the aid of mirrors the artist had tattooed on the top of his head a miniature owl, perfect in every detail. It was about the size of a half-dollar and served him as a show piece. There were cheaper artists in town but Parker had never wanted anything but the best. The artist went over to a cabinet at the back of the room and began to look over some art books. "Who are you interested in?" he said, "saints, angels, Christs or what?"

"God," Parker said.

"Father, Son or Spirit?"

"Just God," Parker said impatiently. "Christ. I don't care. Just so it's God."

The artist returned with a book. He moved some papers off another table and put the book down on it and told Parker to sit down and see what he liked. "The up-to-date ones are in the back," he said.

Parker sat down with the book and wet his thumb. He began to go through it, beginning at the back where the up-to-date pictures were. Some of them he recognized—The Good Shepherd, Forbid Them Not, The Smiling Jesus, Jesus the Physician's Friend, but he kept turning rapidly backwards and the pictures became less and less reassuring. One showed a gaunt green dead face streaked with blood. One was yellow with sagging purple eyes. Parker's heart began to beat faster and faster until it appeared to be roaring inside him like a great generator. He flipped the pages quickly, feeling that when he reached the one ordained, a sign would come. He continued to flip through until he had almost reached the front of the book. On one of the pages a pair of eyes glanced at him swiftly. Parker sped on, then stopped. His heart too appeared to cut off; there was absolute silence. It said as plainly as if silence were a language itself, GO BACK.

Parker returned to the picture—the haloed head of a flat stern Byzantine Christ with all-demanding eyes. He sat there trembling; his heart began slowly to beat again as if it were being brought to life by a subtle power.

"You found what you want?" the artist asked.

Parker's throat was too dry to speak. He got up and thrust the book at the artist, opened at the picture.

"That'll cost you plenty," the artist said. "You don't want all those little blocks though, just the outline and some better features."

"Just like it is," Parker said, "just like it is or nothing."

"It's your funeral," the artist said, "but I don't do that kind of work for nothing."

"How much?" Parker asked.

"It'll take maybe two days work."

"How much?" Parker said.

"On time or cash?" the artist asked. Parker's other jobs had been on time, but he had paid.

"Ten down and ten for every day it takes," the artist said.

Parker drew ten dollar bills out of his wallet; he had three left in.

"You come back in the morning," the artist said, putting the money in his own pocket. "First I'll have to trace that out of the book."

"No no!" Parker said. "Trace it now or gimme my money back," and his eyes blared as if he were ready for a fight.

The artist agreed. Any one stupid enough to want a Christ on his back, he reasoned, would be just as likely as not to change his mind the next minute, but once the work was begun he could hardly do so.

While he worked on the tracing, he told Parker to go wash his back at the sink with the special soap he used there. Parker did it and returned to pace back and forth across the room, nervously flexing his shoulders. He wanted to go look at the picture again but at the same time he did not want to. The artist got up finally and had Parker lie down on the table. He swabbed his back with ethyl chloride and then began to outline the head on it with his iodine pencil. Another hour passed before he took up his electric instrument. Parker felt no particular pain. In Japan he had had a tattoo of the Buddha done on his upper arm with ivory needles; in Burma, a little brown root of a man had made a peacock on each of his knees using thin pointed sticks, two feet long; amateurs had worked on him with pins and soot. Parker was usually so relaxed and easy under the hand of the artist that he often went to sleep, but this time he remained awake, every muscle taut.

At midnight the artist said he was ready to quit. He propped one mirror, four feet square, on a table by the wall and took a smaller mirror off the lavatory wall and put it in Parker's hands. Parker stood with his back to the one on the table and moved the other until he saw a flashing burst of color reflected from his back. It was almost completely covered with little red and blue and ivory and saffron squares; from them he made out the lineaments of the face—a mouth, the beginning of heavy brows, a straight nose, but the face was empty; the eyes had not yet been put in. The impression for the moment was almost as if the artist had tricked him and done the Physician's Friend.

"It don't have eyes," Parker cried out.

"That'll come," the artist said, "in due time. We have another day to go on it yet."

Parker spent the night on a cot at the Haven of Light Christian Mission. He found these the best places to stay in the city because they were free and included a meal of sorts. He got the last available cot and because he was still barefooted, he accepted a pair of second-hand shoes which, in his confusion, he put on to go to bed; he was still shocked from all that had happened to him. All night he lay awake in the long dormitory of cots with lumpy figures on them. The only light was from a phosphorescent cross glowing at the end of the room. The tree reached out to grasp him again, then burst into flame; the shoe burned quietly by itself; the eyes in the book said to him distinctly GO BACK and at the same time did not utter a sound. He wished that he were not in this city, not in this Haven of Light Mission, not in a bed by himself. He longed miserably for Sarah Ruth. Her sharp tongue and icepick eyes were the only comfort he could bring to mind. He decided he was losing it. Her eyes appeared soft and dilatory compared with the eyes in the book, for even though he could not summon up the exact look of those eyes, he could still feel their penetration. He felt as though, under their gaze, he was as transparent as the wing of a fly.

The tattooist had told him not to come until ten in the morning, but when he arrived at that hour, Parker was sitting in the dark hallway on the floor, waiting for him. He had decided upon getting up that, once the tattoo was on him, he would not look at it, that all his sensations of the day and night before were those of a crazy man and that he would return to doing things according to his own sound judgement.

The artist began where he left off. "One thing I want to know," he said presently as he worked over Parker's back, "why do you want this on you? Have you gone and got religion? Are you saved?" he asked in a mocking voice.

Parker's throat felt salty and dry. "Naw," he said, "I ain't got no use for none of that. A man can't save his self from whatever it is he don't deserve none of my sympathy." These words seemed to leave his mouth like wraiths and to evaporate at once as if he had never uttered them.

"Then why . . ." 120

"I married this woman that's saved," Parker said. "I never should have done it. I ought to leave her. She's done gone and got pregnant."

"That's too bad," the artist said. "Then it's her making you have this tattoo."

"Naw," Parker said, "she don't know nothing about it. It's a surprise for her."

"You think she'll like it and lay off you a while?"

"She can't hep herself," Parker said. "She can't say she don't like the looks of 125 God." He decided he had told the artist enough of his business. Artists were all right in their place but he didn't like them poking their noses into the affairs of regular people. "I didn't get no sleep last night," he said. "I think I'll get some now."

That closed the mouth of the artist but it did not bring him any sleep. He lay there, imagining how Sarah Ruth would be struck speechless by the face on his back and every now and then this would be interrupted by a vision of the tree of fire and his empty shoe burning beneath it.

The artist worked steadily until nearly four o'clock, not stopping to have lunch, hardly pausing with the electric instrument except to wipe the dripping dye off Parker's back as he went along. Finally he finished. "You can get up and look at it now," he said.

Parker sat up but he remained on the edge of the table.

The artist was pleased with his work and wanted Parker to look at it at once. Instead Parker continued to sit on the edge of the table, bent forward slightly but with a vacant look. "What ails you?" the artist said. "Go look at it."

"Ain't nothing ail me," Parker said in a sudden belligerent voice. "That tattoo 130 ain't going nowhere. It'll be there when I get there." He reached for his shirt and began gingerly to put it on.

The artist took him roughly by the arm and propelled him between the two mirrors. "Now *look*," he said, angry at having his work ignored.

Parker looked, turned white and moved away. The eyes in the reflected face continued to look at him—still, straight, all-demanding, enclosed in silence.

"It was your idea, remember," the artist said. "I would have advised something else."

Parker said nothing. He put on his shirt and went out the door while the artist shouted, "I'll expect all of my money!"

Parker headed toward a package shop on the corner. He bought a pint of whiskey and took it into a nearby alley and drank it all in five minutes. Then he moved on to a pool hall nearby which he frequented when he came to the city. It was a well-lighted barn-like place with a bar up one side and gambling machines on the other and pool tables in the back. As soon as Parker entered, a large man in a red and black checkered shirt hailed him by slapping him on the back and yelling, "Yeyyyyyy boy! O. E. Parker!"

Parker was not yet ready to be struck on the back. "Lay off," he said, "I got a fresh tattoo there."

"What you got this time?" the man asked and then yelled to a few at the machines. "O. E.'s got him another tattoo."

"Nothing special this time," Parker said and slunk over to a machine that was not being used.

"Come on," the big man said, "let's have a look at O. E.'s tattoo," and while Parker squirmed in their hands, they pulled up his shirt. Parker felt all the hands drop away instantly and his shirt fell again like a veil over the face. There was a silence in the pool room which seemed to Parker to grow from the circle around him until it extended to the foundations under the building and upward through the beams in the roof.

Finally some one said, "Christ!" Then they all broke into noise at once. Parker turned around, an uncertain grin on his face.

"Leave it to O. E.!" the man in the checkered shirt said, "That boy's a real card!"

"Maybe he's gone and got religion," some one yelled.

"Not on your life," Parker said.

"O. E.'s got religion and is witnessing for Jesus, ain't you, O. E.?" a little man with a piece of cigar in his mouth said wryly. "An o-riginal way to do it if I ever saw one."

"Leave it to Parker to think of a new one!" the fat man said.

"Yyeeeeeyyyyyy boy!" someone yelled and they all began to whistle and curse in compliment until Parker said, "Aaa shut up."

"What'd you do it for?" somebody asked.

"For laughs," Parker said. "What's it to you?"

"Why ain't you laughing then?" somebody yelled. Parker lunged into the midst of them and like a whirlwind on a summer's day there began a fight that raged amid overturned tables and swinging fists until two of them grabbed him and ran to the door with him and threw him out. Then a calm descended on the pool hall as nerve shattering as if the long barn-like room were the ship from which Jonah had been cast into the sea.

Parker sat for a long time on the ground in the alley behind the pool hall, examining his soul. He saw it as a spider web of facts and lies that was not at all important to him but which appeared to be necessary in spite of his opinion. The eyes that were now forever on his back were eyes to be obeyed. He was as certain of it as he had ever been of anything. Throughout his life, grumbling and sometimes cursing, often afraid, once in rapture, Parker had obeyed whatever instinct of this kind had come to him—in rapture when his spirit had lifted at the sight of the tattooed man at the fair, afraid when he had joined the navy, grumbling when he had married Sarah Ruth.

The thought of her brought him slowly to his feet. She would know what he had to do. She would clear up the rest of it, and she would at least be pleased. It seemed to him that, all along, that was what he wanted, to please her. His truck was still parked in front of the building where the artist had his place, but it was not far away. He got in it and drove out of the city and into the country night. His head was almost clear of liquor and he observed that his dissatisfaction was gone, but he felt not quite like himself. It was as if he were himself but a stranger to himself, driving into a new country though everything he saw was familiar to him, even at night.

He arrived finally at the house on the embankment, pulled the truck under the pecan tree and got out. He made as much noise as possible to assert that he was still in charge here, that his leaving her for a night without word meant nothing except it was the way he did things. He slammed the car door, stamped up the two steps and across the porch and rattled the door knob. It did not respond to his touch. "Sarah Ruth!" he yelled, "let me in."

There was no lock on the door and she had evidently placed the back of a chair against the knob. He began to beat on the door and rattle the knob at the same time.

He heard the bed springs screak and bent down and put his head to the keyhole, but it was stopped up with paper. "Let me in!" he hollered, bamming on the door again. "What you got me locked out for?"

A sharp voice close to the door said, "Who's there?" 155

"Me," Parker said, "O. E."

He waited a moment.

"Me," he said impatiently, "O. E."

Still no sound from inside.

He tried once more. "O. E.," he said, bamming the door two or three more times. 160
"O. E. Parker. You know me."

There was a silence. Then the voice said slowly, "I don't know no O. E."

"Quit fooling," Parker pleaded. "You ain't got any business doing me this way. It's me, old O. E., I'm back. You ain't afraid of me."

"Who's there?" the same unfeeling voice said.

Parker turned his head as if he expected someone behind him to give him the answer. The sky had lightened slightly and there were two or three streaks of yellow floating above the horizon. Then as he stood there, a tree of light burst over the skyline.

Parker fell back against the door as if he had been pinned there by a lance. 165

"Who's there?" the voice from inside said and there was a quality about it now that seemed final. The knob rattled and the voice said peremptorily, "Who's there, I ast you?"

Parker bent down and put his mouth near the stuffed keyhole. "Obadiah," he whispered and all at once he felt the light pouring through him, turning his spider web soul into a perfect arabesque of colors, a garden of trees and birds and beasts.

"Obadiah Elihue!" he whispered.

The door opened and he stumbled in. Sarah Ruth loomed there, hands on her hips. She began at once, "That was no hefty blonde woman you was working for and you'll have to pay her every penny on her tractor you busted up. She don't keep insurance on it. She came here and her and me had us a long talk and I . . ."

Trembling, Parker set about lighting the kerosene lamp.

"What's the matter with you, wasting that kerosene this near daylight?" she demanded. "I ain't got to look at you."

A yellow glow enveloped them. Parker put the match down and began to unbutton his shirt.

"And you ain't going to have none of me this near morning," she said.

"Shut your mouth," he said quietly. "Look at this and then I don't want to hear no more out of you." He removed the shirt and turned his back to her.

"Another picture," Sarah Ruth growled. "I might have known you was off after putting some more trash on yourself."

Parker's knees went hollow under him. He wheeled around and cried, "Look at it! Don't just say that! *Look* at it!"

"I done looked," she said.

"Don't you know who it is?" he cried in anguish.

"No, who is it?" Sarah Ruth said. "It ain't anybody I know."

"It's him," Parker said.

"Him who?"

"God!" Parker cried.

"God? God don't look like that!"

"What do you know how he looks?" Parker moaned. "You ain't seen him."

"He don't *look*," Sarah Ruth said. "He's a spirit. No man shall see his face."

"Aw listen," Parker groaned, "this is just a picture of him."

"Idolatry!" Sarah Ruth screamed. "Idolatry! Enflaming yourself with idols under every green tree! I can put up with lies and vanity but I don't want no idolator in this house!" and she grabbed up the broom and began to thrash him across the shoulders with it.

Parker was too stunned to resist. He sat there and let her beat him until she had nearly knocked him senseless and large welts had formed on the face of the tattooed Christ. Then he staggered up and made for the door.

She stamped the broom two or three times on the floor and went to the window and shook it out to get the taint of him off it. Still gripping it, she looked toward the pecan tree and her eyes hardened still more. There he was—who called himself Obadiah Elihue—leaning against the tree, crying like a baby.

Questions

1. Why, in your judgment, did Parker marry Sarah Ruth? Why did she marry him?
2. At the end of the second paragraph, the author says of Parker and Sarah Ruth: "He could account for her one way or another; it was himself he could not understand." How accurate is each part of this assumption?
3. What is the basis of Parker's fascination with tattooing? What kinds of feelings usually prompt him to get a new tattoo?
4. What motivates Parker to get the tattoo on his back? How does he expect Sarah Ruth to respond to it?

5. When the artist asks him if he's "gone and got religion," Parker says, "I ain't got no use for none of that. A man can't save his self from whatever it is he don't deserve none of my sympathy" (paragraph 119). What does this attitude illustrate about Parker's personality? By his own standard, how much of his own sympathy does he deserve?
6. Why does Sarah Ruth refuse to recognize Parker by his initials? What is the significance of his whispering his name through the keyhole, and what effect does doing so have on him?
7. Do you find Parker sympathetic? Why or why not? Where does he go wrong?

Suggestions for Writing on Stories about Love Gone Wrong

1. Both "A Rose for Emily" and "Sweat" feature women who exact some sort of revenge. How are these situations different, and similar? How are the characters' choices and actions influenced by factors such as setting and economic circumstance? Do you find their actions equally justifiable? Equally reasonable? Explain.
2. "Parker's Back" features a man who makes a physical and perhaps spiritual sacrifice to win his beloved's affection. Does his action inspire the result he hopes for? What does the story imply about sacrifice and love?
3. What is the role of religious belief in "Sweat" and "Parker's Back"? How does faith play a part in the lives and loves of Delia and Sarah Ruth? Compare the practice and importance of religion in the two stories, and analyze how the two characters' religious faith influences them, their relationships with their husbands, and their actions.
4. Do you have a tattoo? Write about why you got it: What did you hope to gain by it? Have your attitudes toward the tattoo changed over time?

Writer in Depth
Kate Chopin

TROUBLED MARRIAGES

The Story of an Hour

The Storm

Désirée's Baby

Kate Chopin's memorable stories bring us to a time and place different from our own. She describes the lives and milieu of privileged Southern white women in the late nineteenth century. Although these women enjoyed economic security, they also led constricted lives by modern standards. In Chopin's time, women's roles were limited not only in terms of such things as voting and public office. Women generally did not pursue higher education except to become teachers. Upper- and middle-class women were not expected to work outside the home. (Poor women had no choice except to work.) Social and economic pressure made it difficult for women to leave bad or abusive marriages, and their emotional needs, including their sexual needs, were often ignored or invisible. Today it does not seem revelatory to say that women, too, are sexual beings. But in nineteenth-century America, such a notion was scandalous, even morally dangerous. In these three stories, Chopin presents women who have thoughts, feelings, and desires of their own. She depicts women who are making their own choices—not all of them admirable—and struggling not only for their right to have feelings, but for the freedom to define their own lives.

Kate Chopin

Kate Chopin (1851–1904) was born Katherine O'Flaherty in St. Louis, daughter of an Irish immigrant grown wealthy in retailing. On his death, young Kate was raised by her mother's family: aristocratic Creoles, descendants of the French and Spaniards who had colonized Louisiana. Young Kate received a convent schooling, and at nineteen married Oscar Chopin, a Creole cotton broker from New Orleans. Later, the Chopins lived on a plantation near Cloutierville, Louisiana, a region whose varied people—Creoles, Cajuns, blacks— Kate Chopin was later to write about with loving care in Bayou Folk (1894) and A Night in Arcadie (1897). The shock of her husband's sudden death in 1883, which left her with the raising of six children, seems to have plunged Kate Chopin into writing. She read and admired fine woman writers of her day, such as the Maine realist Sarah Orne Jewett. She also read Maupassant, Zola, and other new (and scandalous) French naturalist writers.

She began to bring into American fiction some of their hard-eyed observation and their passion for telling unpleasant truths. Determined, in defiance of her times, to show frankly the sexual feelings of her characters, Chopin suffered from neglect and censorship. When her major novel, The Awakening, *appeared in 1899, critics were outraged by her candid portrait of a woman who seeks sexual and professional independence. After causing such a literary scandal, Chopin was unable to get her later work published and wrote little more before she died.* The Awakening *and many of her stories had to wait seven decades for a sympathetic audience.*

The Story of an Hour 1894

Knowing that Mrs. Mallard was afflicted with a heart trouble, great care was taken to break to her as gently as possible the news of her husband's death.

It was her sister Josephine who told her, in broken sentences; veiled hints that revealed in half concealing. Her husband's friend Richards was there, too, near her. It was he who had been in the newspaper office when intelligence of the railroad disaster was received, with Brently Mallard's name leading the list of "killed." He had only taken the time to assure himself of its truth by a second telegram, and had hastened to forestall any less careful, less tender friend in bearing the sad message.

She did not hear the story as many women have heard the same, with a paralyzed inability to accept its significance. She wept at once, with sudden, wild abandonment, in her sister's arms. When the storm of grief had spent itself she went away to her room alone. She would have no one follow her.

There stood, facing the open window, a comfortable, roomy armchair. Into this she sank, pressed down by a physical exhaustion that haunted her body and seemed to reach into her soul.

She could see in the open square before her house the tops of trees that were all aquiver with the new spring life. The delicious breath of rain was in the air. In the street below a peddler was crying his wares. The notes of a distant song which some one was singing reached her faintly, and countless sparrows were twittering in the eaves.

There were patches of blue sky showing here and there through the clouds that had met and piled one above the other in the west facing her window.

She sat with her head thrown back upon the cushion of the chair, quite motionless, except when a sob came up into her throat and shook her, as a child who has cried itself to sleep continues to sob in its dreams.

She was young, with a fair, calm face, whose lines bespoke repression and even a certain strength. But now there was a dull stare in her eyes, whose gaze was fixed away off yonder on one of those patches of blue sky. It was not a glance of reflection, but rather indicated a suspension of intelligent thought.

There was something coming to her and she was waiting for it, fearfully. What was it? She did not know; it was too subtle and elusive to name. But she felt it, creeping out of the sky, reaching toward her through the sounds, the scents, the color that filled the air.

Now her bosom rose and fell tumultuously. She was beginning to recognize this thing that was approaching to possess her, and she was striving to beat it back with her will—as powerless as her two white slender hands would have been.

When she abandoned herself a little whispered word escaped her slightly parted lips. She said it over and over under her breath: "free, free, free!" The vacant stare and the look of terror that had followed it went from her eyes. They stayed keen and bright. Her pulses beat fast, and the coursing blood warmed and relaxed every inch of her body.

She did not stop to ask if it were or were not a monstrous joy that held her. A clear and exalted perception enabled her to dismiss the suggestion as trivial.

She knew that she would weep again when she saw the kind, tender hands folded in death; the face that had never looked save with love upon her, fixed and gray and dead. But she saw beyond that bitter moment a long procession of years to come that would belong to her absolutely. And she opened and spread her arms out to them in welcome.

There would be no one to live for her during those coming years; she would live for herself. There would be no powerful will bending hers in that blind persistence with which men and women believe they have a right to impose a private will upon a fellow-creature. A kind intention or a cruel intention made the act seem no less a crime as she looked upon it in that brief moment of illumination.

And yet she had loved him—sometimes. Often she had not. What did it matter! What could love, the unsolved mystery, count for in face of this possession of self-assertion which she suddenly recognized as the strongest impulse of her being!

"Free! Body and soul free!" she kept whispering.

Josephine was kneeling before the closed door with her lips to the keyhole, imploring for admission. "Louise, open the door! I beg; open the door—you will make yourself ill. What are you doing, Louise? For heaven's sake open the door."

"Go away. I am not making myself ill." No; she was drinking in a very elixir of life through that open window.

Her fancy was running riot along those days ahead of her. Spring days, and summer days, and all sorts of days that would be her own. She breathed a quick prayer that life might be long. It was only yesterday she had thought with a shudder that life might be long.

She arose at length and opened the door to her sister's importunities. There was a feverish triumph in her eyes, and she carried herself unwittingly like a goddess of Victory. She clasped her sister's waist, and together they descended the stairs. Richards stood waiting for them at the bottom.

Some one was opening the front door with a latchkey. It was Brently Mallard who entered, a little travel-stained, composedly carrying his grip-sack and umbrella. He had been far from the scene of the accident, and did not even know there had been one. He stood amazed at Josephine's piercing cry; at Richards' quick motion to screen him from the view of his wife.

But Richards was too late.

When the doctors came they said she had died of heart disease—of joy that kills.

Questions

1. Do you find Louise Mallard sympathetic? Why or why not?
2. Mrs. Mallard believes that the only way she can achieve freedom is through the death of her husband. How much of this belief is shaped by the time in which the story took place? Could such a situation happen today?
3. Is it possible to be in a committed relationship and still retain a sense of independence? Does love give someone the "right to impose a private will upon a fellow-creature" (paragraph 14)?

Kate Chopin

The Storm (1898)

I

The leaves were so still that even Bibi thought it was going to rain. Bobinôt, who was accustomed to converse on terms of perfect equality with his little son, called the child's attention to certain somber clouds that were rolling with sinister intention from the west, accompanied by a sullen, threatening roar. They were at Friedheimer's store and decided to remain there till the storm had passed. They sat within the door on two empty kegs. Bibi was four years old and looked very wise.

"Mama'll be 'fraid, yes," he suggested with blinking eyes.

"She'll shut the house. Maybe she got Sylvie helpin' her this evenin'," Bobinôt responded reassuringly.

"No; she ent got Sylvie. Sylvie was helpin' her yistiday," piped Bibi.

Bobinôt arose and going across to the counter purchased a can of shrimps, of which Calixta was very fond. Then he returned to his perch on the keg and sat stolidly holding the can of shrimps while the storm burst. It shook the wooden store and seemed to be ripping great furrows in the distant field. Bibi laid his little hand on his father's knee and was not afraid.

II

Calixta, at home, felt no uneasiness for their safety. She sat at a side window sewing furiously on a sewing machine. She was greatly occupied and did not notice the approaching storm. But she felt very warm and often stopped to mop her face on which the perspiration gathered in beads. She unfastened her white sacque at the throat. It began to grow dark, and suddenly realizing the situation she got up hurriedly and went about closing windows and doors.

Out on the small front gallery she had hung Bobinôt's Sunday clothes to air and she hastened out to gather them before the rain fell. As she stepped outside, Alcée Laballière rode in at the gate. She had not seen him very often since her marriage, and never alone. She stood there with Bobinôt's coat in her hands, and the big rain drops began to fall. Alcée rode his horse under the shelter of a side projection where the chickens had huddled and there were plows and a harrow piled up in the corner.

"May I come and wait on your gallery till the storm is over, Calixta?" he asked.

"Come 'long in, M'sieur Alcée."

His voice and her own startled her as if from a trance, and she seized Bobinôt's vest. Alcée, mounting to the porch, grabbed the trousers and snatched Bibi's braided jacket that was about to be carried away by a sudden gust of wind. He expressed an intention to remain outside, but it was soon apparent that he might as well have been out in the open: the water beat in upon the boards in driving sheets, and he went inside, closing the door after him. It was even necessary to put something beneath the door to keep the water out.

"My! what a rain! It's good two years since it rain' like that," exclaimed Calixta as she rolled up a piece of bagging and Alcée helped her to thrust it beneath the crack.

She was a little fuller of figure than five years before when she married; but she had lost nothing of her vivacity. Her blue eyes still retained their melting quality; and her yellow hair, dishevelled by the wind and rain, kinked more stubbornly than ever about her ears and temples.

The rain beat upon the low, shingled roof with a force and clatter that threatened to break an entrance and deluge them there. They were in the dining room—the sitting room—the general utility room. Adjoining was her bed room, with Bibi's couch along side her own. The door stood open, and the room with its white, monumental bed, its closed shutters, looked dim and mysterious.

Alcée flung himself into a rocker and Calixta nervously began to gather up from the floor the lengths of a cotton sheet which she had been sewing.

"If this keeps up, *Dieu sait°* if the levees goin' to stan' it!" she exclaimed.

"What have you got to do with the levees?"

"I got enough to do! An' there's Bobinôt with Bibi out in that storm—if he only didn' left Friedheimer's!"

"Let us hope, Calixta, that Bobinôt's got sense enough to come in out of a cyclone."

She went and stood at the window with a greatly disturbed look on her face. She wiped the frame that was clouded with moisture. It was stiflingly hot. Alcée got up and joined her at the window, looking over her shoulder. The rain was coming down in sheets obscuring the view of far-off cabins and enveloping the distant wood in a gray mist. The playing of the lightning was incessant. A bolt struck a tall chinaberry tree at the edge of the field. It filled all visible space with a blinding glare and the crash seemed to invade the very boards they stood upon.

Calixta put her hands to her eyes, and with a cry, staggered backward. Alcée's arm encircled her, and for an instant he drew her close and spasmodically to him.

"*Bonté!*"° she cried, releasing herself from his encircling arm and retreating from the window, "the house'll go next! If I only knew w'ere Bibi was!" She would not compose herself; she would not be seated. Alcée clasped her shoulders and looked into her face. The contact of her warm, palpitating body when he had unthinkingly drawn her into his arms, had aroused all the old-time infatuation and desire for her flesh.

"Calixta," he said, "don't be frightened. Nothing can happen. The house is too low to be struck, with so many tall trees standing about. There! aren't you going to be quiet? say, aren't you?" He pushed her hair back from her face that was warm and steaming. Her lips were as red and moist as pomegranate seed. Her white neck and a glimpse of her full, firm bosom disturbed him powerfully. As she glanced up at him the fear in her liquid blue eyes had given place to a drowsy gleam that unconsciously betrayed a sensuous desire. He looked down into her eyes and there was nothing for him to do but gather her lips in a kiss. It reminded him of Assumption.°

"Do you remember—in Assumption, Calixta?" he asked in a low voice broken by passion. Oh! she remembered; for in Assumption he had kissed her and kissed and kissed her; until his senses would well nigh fail, and to save her he would resort to a desperate flight. If she was not an immaculate dove in those days, she was still inviolate; a passionate creature whose very defenselessness had made her defense, against which his honor forbade him to prevail. Now—well, now—her lips seemed in a manner free to be tasted, as well as her round, white throat and her whiter breasts.

Dieu sait: God only knows.   *Bonté!:* Heavens!   *Assumption:* a parish west of New Orleans.

They did not heed the crashing torrents, and the roar of the elements made her laugh as she lay in his arms. She was a revelation in that dim, mysterious chamber; as white as the couch she lay upon. Her firm, elastic flesh that was knowing for the first time its birthright, was like a creamy lily that the sun invites to contribute its breath and perfume to the undying life of the world.

The generous abundance of her passion, without guile or trickery, was like a white flame which penetrated and found response in depths of his own sensuous nature that had never yet been reached.

When he touched her breasts they gave themselves up in quivering ecstasy, inviting his lips. Her mouth was a fountain of delight. And when he possessed her, they seemed to swoon together at the very borderland of life's mystery.

He stayed cushioned upon her, breathless, dazed, enervated, with his heart beating like a hammer upon her. With one hand she clasped his head, her lips lightly touching his forehead. The other hand stroked with a soothing rhythm his muscular shoulders.

The growl of the thunder was distant and passing away. The rain beat softly upon the shingles, inviting them to drowsiness and sleep. But they dared not yield.

The rain was over; and the sun was turning the glistening green world into a palace of gems. Calixta, on the gallery, watched Alcée ride away. He turned and smiled at her with a beaming face; and she lifted her pretty chin in the air and laughed aloud.

III

Bobinôt and Bibi, trudging home, stopped without at the cistern to make themselves presentable.

"My! Bibi, w'at will yo' mama say! You ought to be ashame'. You oughtn' put on those good pants. Look at 'em! An' that mud on yo' collar! How you got that mud on yo' collar, Bibi? I never saw such a boy!" Bibi was the picture of pathetic resignation. Bobinôt was the embodiment of serious solicitude as he strove to remove from his own person and his son's the signs of their tramp over heavy roads and through wet fields. He scraped the mud off Bibi's bare legs and feet with a stick and carefully removed all traces from his heavy brogans. Then, prepared for the worst—the meeting with an overscrupulous housewife, they entered cautiously at the back door.

Calixta was preparing supper. She had set the table and was dripping coffee at the hearth. She sprang up as they came in.

"Oh, Bobinôt! You back! My! but I was uneasy. W'ere you been during the rain? An' Bibi? he ain't wet? he ain't hurt?" She had clasped Bibi and was kissing him effusively. Bobinôt's explanations and apologies which he had been composing all along the way, died on his lips as Calixta felt him to see if he were dry, and seemed to express nothing but satisfaction at their safe return.

"I brought you some shrimps, Calixta," offered Bobinôt, hauling the can from his ample side pocket and laying it on the table.

"Shrimps! Oh, Bobinôt! you too good fo' anything!" and she gave him a smacking kiss on the cheek that resounded. "*J'vous réponds,*° we'll have a feas' to night! umph-umph!"

J'vous réponds: Let me tell you.

Bobinôt and Bibi began to relax and enjoy themselves, and when the three seated themselves at table they laughed much and so loud that anyone might have heard them as far away as Laballière's.

IV

Alcée Laballière wrote to his wife, Clarisse, that night. It was a loving letter, full of tender solicitude. He told her not to hurry back, but if she and the babies liked it at Biloxi, to stay a month longer. He was getting on nicely; and though he missed them, he was willing to bear the separation a while longer—realizing that their health and pleasure were the first things to be considered.

V

As for Clarisse, she was charmed upon receiving her husband's letter. She and the babies were doing well. The society was agreeable; many of her old friends and acquaintances were at the bay. And the first free breath since her marriage seemed to restore the pleasant liberty of her maiden days. Devoted as she was to her husband, their intimate conjugal life was something which she was more than willing to forego for a while.

So the storm passed and everyone was happy.

Questions

1. Exactly where does Chopin's story take place? How can you tell?
2. What circumstances introduced in Part I turn out to have a profound effect on events in the story?
3. What details in "The Storm" emphasize the fact that Bobinôt loves his wife? What details reveal how imperfectly he comprehends her nature?
4. What general attitudes toward sex, love, and marriage does Chopin imply? Cite evidence to support your answer.
5. What meanings do you find in the title "The Storm"?
6. Do you consider the story's ending a happy ending? Why or why not?
7. Both Calixta and Bobinôt, and Alcée and Clarisse, seem to feel real affection for each other. Yet both couples experience less than ideal sex lives. Are love and sexual passion necessarily the same? Is it possible to feel one and not the other? What is necessary for a long-term relationship to work?

Kate Chopin

Désirée's Baby   1894

As the day was pleasant, Madame Valmondé drove over to L'Abri to see Désirée and the baby.

It made her laugh to think of Désirée with a baby. Why, it seemed but yesterday that Désirée was little more than a baby herself; when Monsieur in riding through the gateway of Valmondé had found her lying asleep in the shadow of the big stone pillar.

The little one awoke in his arms and began to cry for "Dada." That was as much as she could do or say. Some people thought she might have strayed there of her own accord, for she was of the toddling age. The prevailing belief was that she had been purposely left by a party of Texans, whose canvas-covered wagon, late in the day, had crossed the ferry that Coton Maïs kept, just below the plantation. In time Madame Valmondé abandoned every speculation but the one that Désirée had been sent to her by a beneficent Providence to be the child of her affection, seeing that she was without child of the flesh. For the girl grew to be beautiful and gentle, affectionate and sincere,—the idol of Valmondé.

It was no wonder, when she stood one day against the stone pillar in whose shadow she had lain asleep, eighteen years before, that Armand Aubigny riding by and seeing her there, had fallen in love with her. That was the way all the Aubignys fell in love, as if struck by a pistol shot. The wonder was that he had not loved her before; for he had known her since his father brought him home from Paris, a boy of eight, after his mother died there. The passion that awoke in him that day, when he saw her at the gate, swept along like an avalanche, or like a prairie fire, or like anything that drives headlong over all obstacles.

Monsieur Valmondé grew practical and wanted things well considered: that is, the girl's obscure origin. Armand looked into her eyes and did not care. He was reminded that she was nameless. What did it matter about a name when he could give her one of the oldest and proudest in Louisiana? He ordered the *corbeille*° from Paris, and contained himself with what patience he could until it arrived; then they were married.

Madame Valmondé had not seen Désirée and the baby for four weeks. When she reached L'Abri she shuddered at the first sight of it, as she always did. It was a sad looking place, which for many years had not known the gentle presence of a mistress, old Monsieur Aubigny having married and buried his wife in France, and she having loved her own land too well ever to leave it. The roof came down steep and black like a cowl, reaching out beyond the wide galleries that encircled the yellow stuccoed house. Big, solemn oaks grew close to it, and their thick-leaved, far-reaching branches shadowed it like a pall. Young Aubigny's rule was a strict one, too, and under it his negroes had forgotten how to be gay, as they had been during the old master's easy-going and indulgent lifetime.

The young mother was recovering slowly, and lay full length, in her soft white muslins and laces, upon a couch. The baby was beside her, upon her arm, where he had fallen asleep, at her breast. The yellow nurse woman sat beside a window fanning herself.

Madame Valmondé bent her portly figure over Désirée and kissed her, holding her an instant tenderly in her arms. Then she turned to the child.

"This is not the baby!" she exclaimed, in startled tones. French was the language spoken at Valmondé in those days.

"I knew you would be astonished," laughed Désirée, "at the way he has grown. The little *cochon de lait!*° Look at his legs, mamma, and his hands and finger-nails,— real finger-nails. Zandrine had to cut them this morning. Is n't it true, Zandrine?"

The woman bowed her turbaned head majestically, "Mais si, Madame."

"And the way he cries," went on Désirée, "is deafening. Armand heard him the other day as far away as La Blanche's cabin."

Madame Valmondé had never removed her eyes from the child. She lifted it and walked with it over to the window that was lightest. She scanned the baby narrowly, then looked as searchingly at Zandrine, whose face was turned to gaze across the fields.

---

corbeille: traditionally, a groom's gifts to the bride before the wedding, often lavish and put on display before the wedding.   *cochon de lait:* French term of endearment, literally, "suckling pig."

"Yes, the child has grown, has changed;" said Madame Valmondé, slowly, as she replaced it beside its mother. "What does Armand say?"

Désirée's face became suffused with a glow that was happiness itself.

"Oh, Armand is the proudest father in the parish, I believe, chiefly because it is a boy, to bear his name; though he says not,—that he would have loved a girl as well. But I know it isn't true. I know he says that to please me. And mamma," she added, drawing Madame Valmondé's head down to her, and speaking in a whisper, "he has n't punished one of them—not one of them—since baby is born. Even Négrillon, who pretended to have burnt his leg that he might rest from work—he only laughed, and said Négrillon was a great scamp. Oh, mamma, I 'm so happy; it frightens me."

What Désirée said was true. Marriage, and later the birth of his son, had softened Armand Aubigny's imperious and exacting nature greatly. This was what made the gentle Désirée so happy, for she loved him desperately. When he frowned she trembled, but loved him. When he smiled, she asked no greater blessing of God. But Armand's dark, handsome face had not often been disfigured by frowns since the day he fell in love with her.

When the baby was about three months old, Désirée awoke one day to the conviction that there was something in the air menacing her peace. It was at first too subtle to grasp. It had only been a disquieting suggestion; an air of mystery among the blacks; unexpected visits from far-off neighbors who could hardly account for their coming. Then a strange, an awful change in her husband's manner, which she dared not ask him to explain. When he spoke to her, it was with averted eyes, from which the old love-light seemed to have gone out. He absented himself from home; and when there, avoided her presence and that of her child, without excuse. And the very spirit of Satan seemed suddenly to take hold of him in his dealings with the slaves. Désirée was miserable enough to die.

She sat in her room, one hot afternoon, in her *peignoir*, listlessly drawing through her fingers the strands of her long, silky brown hair that hung about her shoulders. The baby, half naked, lay asleep upon her own great mahogany bed, that was like a sumptuous throne, with its satin-lined half-canopy. One of La Blanche's little quadroon boys—half naked too—stood fanning the child slowly with a fan of peacock feathers. Désirée's eyes had been fixed absently and sadly upon the baby, while she was striving to penetrate the threatening mist that she felt closing about her. She looked from her child to the boy who stood beside him, and back again; over and over. "Ah!" It was a cry that she could not help; which she was not conscious of having uttered. The blood turned like ice in her veins, and a clammy moisture gathered upon her face.

She tried to speak to the little quadroon boy; but no sound would come, at first. When he heard his name uttered, he looked up, and his mistress was pointing to the door. He laid aside the great, soft fan, and obediently stole away, over the polished floor, on his bare tiptoes.

She stayed motionless, with gaze riveted upon her child, and her face the picture of fright.

Presently her husband entered the room, and without noticing her, went to a table and began to search among some papers which covered it.

"Armand," she called to him, in a voice which must have stabbed him, if he was human. But he did not notice. "Armand," she said again. Then she rose and tottered towards him. "Armand," she panted once more, clutching his arm, "look at our child. What does it mean? tell me."

He coldly but gently loosened her fingers from about his arm and thrust the hand away from him. "Tell me what it means!" she cried despairingly.

"It means," he answered lightly, "that the child is not white; it means that you are not white."

A quick conception of all that this accusation meant for her; nerved her with unwonted courage to deny it. "It is a lie; it is not true, I am white! Look at my hair, it is brown; and my eyes are gray, Armand, you know they are gray. And my skin is fair," seizing his wrist. "Look at my hand; whiter than yours, Armand," she laughed hysterically.

"As white as La Blanche's," he returned cruelly; and went away leaving her alone with their child.

When she could hold a pen in her hand, she sent a despairing letter to Madame Valmondé.

"My mother, they tell me I am not white. Armand has told me I am not white. For God's sake tell them it is not true. You must know it is not true. I shall die. I must die. I cannot be so unhappy, and live."

The answer that came was as brief:

"My own Désirée: Come home to Valmondé; back to your mother who loves you. Come with your child."

When the letter reached Désirée she went with it to her husband's study, and laid it open upon the desk before which he sat. She was like a stone image: silent, white, motionless after she placed it there.

In silence he ran his cold eyes over the written words. He said nothing. "Shall I go, Armand?" she asked in tones sharp with agonized suspense.

"Yes, go."

"Do you want me to go?"

"Yes, I want you to go."

He thought Almighty God had dealt cruelly and unjustly with him; and felt, somehow, that he was paying Him back in kind when he stabbed thus into his wife's soul. Moreover he no longer loved her, because of the unconscious injury she had brought upon his home and his name.

She turned away like one stunned by a blow, and walked slowly towards the door, hoping he would call her back.

"Good-bye, Armand," she moaned.

He did not answer her. That was his last blow at fate.

Désirée went in search of her child. Zandrine was pacing the somber gallery with it. She took the little one from the nurse's arms with no word of explanation, and descending the steps, walked away, under the live-oak branches.

It was an October afternoon; the sun was just sinking. Out in the still fields the negroes were picking cotton.

Désirée had not changed the thin white garment nor the slippers which she wore. Her head was uncovered and the sun's rays brought a golden gleam from its brown meshes. She did not take the broad, beaten road which led to the far-off plantation of Valmondé. She walked across a deserted field, where the stubble bruised her tender feet, so delicately shod, and tore her thin gown to shreds.

She disappeared among the reeds and willows that grew thick along the banks of the deep, sluggish bayou; and she did not come back again.

Some weeks later there was a curious scene enacted at L'Abri. In the center of the smoothly swept back yard was a great bonfire. Armand Aubigny sat in the wide hallway that commanded a view of the spectacle; and it was he who dealt out to a half-dozen negroes the material which kept this fire ablaze.

A graceful cradle of willow, with all its dainty furbishings, was laid upon the pyre, which had already been fed with the richness of a priceless *layette*. Then there were silk gowns, and velvet and satin ones added to these; laces, too, and embroideries; bonnets and gloves; for the *corbeille* had been of rare quality.

The last thing to go was a tiny bundle of letters; innocent little scribblings that Désirée had sent to him during the days of their espousal. There was the remnant of one back in the drawer from which he took them. But it was not Désirée's; it was part of an old letter from his mother to his father. He read it. She was thanking God for the blessing of her husband's love:—

"But, above all," she wrote, "night and day, I thank the good God for having so arranged our lives that our dear Armand will never know that his mother, who adores him, belongs to the race that is cursed with the brand of slavery."

Questions

1. Do Armand and Désirée truly love each other? Is one partner's love different from or more real than the other's?
2. What do you think of Madame Valmondé's reactions in the story—both to meeting the baby and to Désirée's later despair? How do her feelings differ from Armand's?
3. In the end, the truth is very different from what Armand originally thought. What do you think will be his reaction to his discovery? Justify your opinion with some evidence from the story.
4. If you found out something surprising about your loved one's history or family, could this change how you feel about him or her? Why or why not? If feelings are so easy to change—as Armand's seem to be—then are they really love?

Suggestions for Writing on Kate Chopin's Stories

1. Compare the circumstances and actions of each of the female protagonists in the three stories in this section. Is Chopin equally sympathetic to each one?
2. Discuss Chopin's views toward marriage in these stories. Are the marriages equally troubled? Is any one happier than the others?
3. From reading these stories, what do you think is Chopin's view of what is necessary for a woman's happiness? What keeps women from achieving that happiness? Cite specific passages and examples.
4. Chopin's stories shocked the reading public when they were published in the late 1800s. Do you find them shocking today? Why or why not? Do you think any of the situations described in the stories would be possible today? Write an essay that relates one of Chopin's plots to a contemporary situation.

POETRY

LOVE POEMS

Anne Bradstreet	*To My Dear and Loving Husband*
Elizabeth Barrett Browning	*How Do I Love Thee? Let Me Count the Ways*
William Butler Yeats	*When You Are Old*
E. E. Cummings	*somewhere i have never travelled, gladly beyond*
Rafael Campo	*For J. W.*
Wendy Cope	*Lonely Hearts*

Does true love really exist? Judging from the following poems, the answer is a resounding "yes," sometimes followed by an important "but." Most of the works in this section are depictions of deep and abiding love. They were written by men and by women, in various eras, in different phases of a relationship. Sometimes the enduring love resides with only one partner, as in Yeats's poem of long devotion to a woman who did not ultimately choose him. Because there's such a broad range of writers and time periods, it's interesting to consider what, if anything, these depictions of love have in common. Do a woman writing in the 1600s (Anne Bradstreet) and a gay man such as Rafael Campo writing in the late twentieth century have similar feelings? Does real love have certain features that transcend such things as time and context? The lovers in these poems feel attraction and affection, familiarity and wonder, urgency and patience, and a sense of deep comfort that still leaves room for continuing thrill and excitement. How do they do it? How are they able to love in a way that's both exhilarating and totally secure? Maybe the poems offer a clue. The section's last poem slyly suggests how desperately everyone else wants what these lucky poets in love already have.

Anne Bradstreet

Born in Northampton, England, Anne Bradstreet (c. 1612–1672) emigrated to Massachusetts with her parents and her husband, Simon Bradstreet, when she was eighteen. For many years they endured the adverse conditions of the struggling colony, where both her husband and her father eventually became governor. Her own life was marked by toil and hardship: she gave birth to eight children, and in 1666 a fire destroyed her home, her library, and many unpublished manuscripts. In 1650 a collection of her verse, The Tenth Muse Lately Sprung Up in America, *was published in London without her knowledge; because it was the first book of poetry ever published by an American, Bradstreet is often considered the "first poet of the New World." Tender and direct, "To My Dear and Loving Husband" is an excellent example of both her style and her subject matter.*

To My Dear and Loving Husband 1678

If ever two were one, then surely we.
If ever man were loved by wife, then thee;

If ever wife was happy in a man,
Compare with me, ye women, if you can.
I prize thy love more than whole mines of gold, 5
Or all the riches that the East doth hold.
My love is such that rivers cannot quench,
Nor ought but love from thee, give recompense.
Thy love is such I can no way repay;
The heavens reward thee manifold, I pray. 10
Then while we live, in love let's so persevere,
That when we live no more, we may live ever.

Questions

1. Do the speaker's expressions of love strike you as persuasive, or do they seem excessive? Explain the reasons for your response.
2. Explain the meaning of the statement in lines 7–8. (Hint: it will be helpful if you understand "Nor ought" in line 8 as "Nor aught," meaning "Nor anything at all.")
3. What is the speaker saying in the last four lines of the poem?

Elizabeth Barrett Browning

Elizabeth Barrett (1806–1861) was born in a large country house outside Durham, England. Ill health kept her at home as an adult, but she nonetheless achieved literary fame and corresponded with many famous writers. Gradually, she fell in love with one devoted visitor, fellow poet Robert Browning, but the courtship was conducted in secret because her father had forbidden his children to marry. In 1846 she and Browning eloped to Italy, where the couple lived happily until her death in 1861. She was the most highly regarded woman poet of the nineteenth century, and her work was immensely popular with both critics and general readers. The following poem, the best-known and best-loved of her works, is the next-to-last of her Sonnets from the Portuguese. *(The book's title comes from her husband's calling her "my little Portuguese" because of her dark complexion.)*

How Do I Love Thee? Let Me Count the Ways 1850

How do I love thee? Let me count the ways.
I love thee to the depth and breadth and height
My soul can reach, when feeling out of sight
For the ends of Being and ideal Grace.
I love thee to the level of every day's 5
Most quiet need, by sun and candle-light.
I love thee freely, as men strive for Right.
I love thee purely, as they turn from Praise.
I love thee with the passion put to use
In my old griefs, and with my childhood's faith. 10
I love thee with a love I seemed to lose
With my lost saints,— I love thee with the breath,
Smiles, tears, of all my life!—and, if God choose,
I shall but love thee better after death.

Questions

1. What is the meaning of lines 2–4?
2. Explain the comparisons in lines 7 and 8.
3. Compare the last four lines of this poem with the last four lines of Anne Bradstreet's "To My Dear and Loving Husband." How are the two passages similar? How do they differ from one another?

William Butler Yeats

William Butler Yeats (1865–1939), an Irishman of English ancestry, was born in Dublin, the son of the painter John Butler Yeats. For a time he studied art himself and was irregularly schooled in Dublin and in London. He became involved in the movement for an Irish nation (partly drawn in by his unrequited love for Maud Gonne, a crusading nationalist) and in founding the Irish Literary Theatre (1898) and the Abbey Theatre (1904). After the establishment of the Irish Free State, Yeats served as a senator (1922-1928). Through the engagement of profound issues, both personal and public, and the constant development of his art, he became one of the greatest poets of the twentieth century. In 1923 he was the first Irish writer to be awarded the Nobel Prize in Literature. Inspired by a sonnet of the sixteenth-century French poet Pierre de Ronsard, "When You Are Old" is a haunting meditation on the complexities of love.

When You Are Old   1893

When you are old and grey and full of sleep,
And nodding by the fire, take down this book,
And slowly read, and dream of the soft look
Your eyes had once, and of their shadows deep;

How many loved your moments of glad grace,   5
And loved your beauty with love false or true,
But one man loved the pilgrim soul in you,
And loved the sorrows of your changing face;

And bending down beside the glowing bars,
Murmur, a little sadly, how Love fled   10
And paced upon the mountains overhead
And hid his face amid a crowd of stars.

Questions

1. How does the speaker, in the second stanza, distinguish his feelings for the woman he addresses from those of her other admirers?
2. What other distinction does the speaker implicitly claim for himself among those who loved her?

3. In the Ronsard original that inspired Yeats's poem, the speaker evokes the image of the beloved as an old woman in order to urge her to love him now before it's too late. How does Yeats's thematic use of the image differ from Ronsard's?
4. What do you understand the last two lines of the poem to mean?

E. E. Cummings

Edward Estlin Cummings (1894–1962) was born in Cambridge, Massachusetts, the son of a Unitarian minister. Having decided at age eight to be a poet, Cummings produced a poem a day for fourteen years, training himself in traditional forms and slowly becoming acquainted with the work of his modernist contemporaries. All of his published verse is collected in the thousand pages of his Complete Poems 1904–1962 *(1994), published to mark the centenary of his birth. Although many of his lyric poems revel in typographical experiment, in theme and sentiment they are often more conventional than they appear. One of his most frequent themes is romantic love, an emotion he treats with straightforward and unabashed celebration—as in the following poem, which was recited in its entirety in Woody Allen's 1986 film* Hannah and Her Sisters.

somewhere i have never travelled,gladly beyond   1931

somewhere i have never travelled,gladly beyond
any experience,your eyes have their silence:
in your most frail gesture are things which enclose me,
or which i cannot touch because they are too near

your slightest look easily will unclose me   5
though i have closed myself as fingers,
you open always petal by petal myself as Spring opens
(touching skilfully,mysteriously)her first rose

or if your wish be to close me,i and
my life will shut very beautifully,suddenly,   10
as when the heart of this flower imagines
the snow carefully everywhere descending;

nothing which we are to perceive in this world equals
the power of your intense fragility:whose texture
compels me with the colour of its countries,   15
rendering death and forever with each breathing

(i do not know what it is about you that closes
and opens;only something in me understands
the voice of your eyes is deeper than all roses)
nobody,not even the rain, has such small hands   20

Questions
1. What is the speaker saying about the effects of love? What kinds of imagery does he use to describe love?
2. Cummings does not use traditional punctuation in his poetry, and he doesn't capitalize letters. What effect does this have on his poem?

3. What are some of the qualities he seems to prize in his beloved?
4. What effects are produced by the use of imagery drawn from nature?

Rafael Campo

Rafael Campo, the son of Cuban immigrants who fled Castro's regime, was born in Dover, New Jersey, in 1964. He graduated from Amherst College, and earned his M.D. from Harvard Medical School in 1992. He teaches and practices medicine at Harvard Medical School and Beth Israel Deaconess Medical Center in Boston. Much of his poetry deals with issues of illness and healing, as well as with his sense of himself as a gay man and as a Latino. His first book of poems, The Other Man Was Me: A Voyage to the New World (1994), won the National Poetry Series 1993 Open Competition. In "For J. W.," as in much of his work, Campo skillfully uses traditional form for a sensitive exploration of contemporary themes.

For J.W. 1994

I know exactly what I want to say,
Except we're men. Except it's poetry,
And poetry is too precise. You know
That when we met on Robert's porch, I knew.
My paper plate seemed suddenly too small; 5

I stepped on a potato chip. I watched
The ordinary spectacle of birds
Become magnificent until the sky,
Which was an ordinary sky, was blue
And comforting across my face. At least 10

I thought I knew. I thought I'd seen your face
In poetry, in shapeless clouds, in ice—
Like staring deeply into frozen lakes.
I thought I'd heard your voice inside my chest,
And it was comforting, magnificent, 15

Like poetry but more precise. I knew,
Or thought I knew, exactly how I felt.
About the insects fizzing in the lawn.
About the stupid, ordinary birds,
About the poetry of Robert Frost, 20

Fragility and paper plates. I look at you.
Because we're men, and frozen hard as ice—
So hard from muscles spreading out our chests—
I want to comfort you, and say it all.
Except my poetry is imprecise. 25

Questions

1. One rhetorical strategy employed by Campo is the repetition of certain key terms in different contexts. Discuss the poem's use of the words "knew," "magnificent," and "ordinary."
2. At the beginning, middle, and end of the poem, there are statements involving poetry and precision. How do the changes that occur in these statements help to communicate the poem's thematic intentions?
3. What point is the speaker making in lines 22–23?
4. If Campo had addressed "For J. W." to a woman, would he need to have changed anything in the poem?

Wendy Cope

Wendy Cope was born in Kent, England, in 1945. She first gained literary notice for her brilliant parodies of famous poems (which include a retelling of T. S. Eliot's The Waste Land *in five limericks), but gradually her bittersweet and incisive love poems have become equally prized. Her books—*Making Cocoa for Kingsley Amis *(1986),* Serious Concerns *(1992),* If I Don't Know *(2001) and* Family Values *(2011)—have become best sellers in England. In a 1998 BBC Radio 4 poll following the death of Ted Hughes, she was the respondents' first choice to succeed him as poet laureate. "Lonely Hearts" brilliantly showcases her skill, wit, and sensitivity.*

Lonely Hearts   1986

Can someone make my simple wish come true?
Male biker seeks female for touring fun.
Do you live in North London? Is it you?

Gay vegetarian whose friends are few,
I'm into music, Shakespeare and the sun.   5
Can someone make my simple wish come true?

Executive in search of something new—
Perhaps bisexual woman, arty, young.
Do you live in North London? Is it you?

Successful, straight and solvent? I am too—   10
Attractive Jewish lady with a son.
Can someone make my simple wish come true?

I'm Libran, inexperienced and blue—
Need slim non-smoker, under twenty-one.
Do you live in North London? Is it you?   15

Please write (with photo) to Box 152.
Who knows where it may lead once we've begun?
Can someone make my simple wish come true?
Do you live in North London? Is it you?

LONELY HEARTS. This poem has a double form: the rhetorical, a series of "lonely heart" personal ads from a newspaper, and metrical, a **villanelle**, a fixed form developed by French courtly poets in imitation of Italian folk song. In the villanelle, the first and the third lines are repeated in a set pattern throughout the poem.

Questions

1. What sort of language does Wendy Cope borrow for this poem?
2. The form of the villanelle requires that the poet end each stanza with one of two repeating lines. What special use does the author make of these mandatory repetitions?
3. How many speakers are there in the poem? Does the author's voice ever enter or is the entire poem spoken by individuals in personal ads?
4. The poem seems to begin satirically. Does the poem ever move beyond the critical, mocking tone typical of satire?

Suggestions for Writing on Love Poems

1. Consider two or more poems that describe love that is fulfilled and enduring. Analyze and compare their descriptions of "true love."
2. W. B. Yeats's poem describes a love that endures for the speaker but has played only a minor part in his beloved's life. This is not a "jilted lover" poem; it contains no hint of recrimination. Describe the role the speaker wants to play in this woman's life.
3. Consider two poems which describe love that has not been fulfilled or has not yet happened: Yeats's "When You Are Old" and Cope's "Lonely Hearts." How is love or the hope of love described in these poems? How are the descriptions similar to, or different from, one another?
4. Do the descriptions and concepts of love in these poems differ according to the poet's sex? Choose at least one poem anywhere in this chapter written by a man and one written by a woman, and compare them.

LOVE, SEX, AND DESIRE

Andrew Marvell	To His Coy Mistress
John Donne	The Flea
Edna St. Vincent Millay	What lips my lips have kissed
T. S. Eliot	The Love Song of J. Alfred Prufrock
Marilyn Nelson	The Ballad of Aunt Geneva
Kim Addonizio	First Poem for You

The waves of feeling that characterize sexual desire are different from (although they may be a part of) the complex, layered emotions of a more developed love. Anyone who's ever desperately longed for someone knows how overwhelming those feelings can be, how immediate and consuming, like a primal hunger. And when people are consumed by this kind of desire, they will often try any means to convince other people to have sex with them. The more urgent or desperate the seducer's desire, the more creative his or her arguments may sometimes be. There is an element of persuasion and performance in courtship. The prospective lover must demonstrate his or her attractive qualities, which are not confined to elements of physical allure, but can include wit, intelligence, loyalty, and good humor. Because lyric poetry is usually personal and intense—and because it is often short—it serves as a perfect vehicle for expressions of desire. The poems in this section capture the various stages of desire—before, during, and after consummation. Some are full of lively arguments as well as anticipation, and some describe the quieter aftermath.

Andrew Marvell

Andrew Marvell (1621–1678), the son of an Anglican clergyman, took his bachelor of arts degree at Cambridge University in 1638, after which he spent considerable time traveling through Europe and acquainting himself with the languages of the countries he visited. He served as Secretary for Foreign Languages in Oliver's Cromwell's government, and after the Restoration he used his influence to save his friend and fellow poet John Milton from imprisonment and, possibly, execution. From 1659 until his death, Marvell was a Member of Parliament. During his lifetime, he was known chiefly as a writer on political subjects, but three years after his death a woman who called herself his widow published an edition of his poems. One of them, the delightful "To His Coy Mistress," has kept his name alive since then, and will continue to do so in the future.

To His Coy Mistress 1681

Had we but world enough, and time,
This coyness,° Lady, were no crime. *modesty, reluctance*
We would sit down, and think which way
To walk, and pass our long love's day.

Thou by the Indian Ganges' side 5
Should'st rubies find; I by the tide
Of Humber would complain.° I would   *sing sad songs*
Love you ten years before the Flood,
And you should, if you please, refuse
Till the Conversion of the Jews. 10
My vegetable° love should grow   *vegetative, flourishing*
Vaster than empires, and more slow.
An hundred years should go to praise
Thine eyes, and on thy forehead gaze,
Two hundred to adore each breast, 15
But thirty thousand to the rest.
An age at least to every part,
And the last age should show your heart.
For, Lady, you deserve this state,°   *pomp, ceremony*
Nor would I love at lower rate. 20
   But at my back I always hear
Time's wingèd chariot hurrying near,
And yonder all before us lie
Deserts of vast eternity.
Thy beauty shall no more be found, 25
Nor, in thy marble vault, shall sound
My echoing song; then worms shall try
That long preserved virginity,
And your quaint honor turn to dust,
And into ashes all my lust. 30
The grave's a fine and private place,
But none, I think, do there embrace.
   Now therefore, while the youthful hue
Sits on thy skin like morning glew°   *glow*
And while thy willing soul transpires 35
At every pore with instant° fires,   *eager*
Now let us sport us while we may;
And now, like amorous birds of prey,
Rather at once our time devour,
Than languish in his slow-chapped° power.   *slow-jawed* 40
Let us roll all our strength, and all
Our sweetness, up into one ball
And tear our pleasures with rough strife,
Thorough° the iron gates of life.   *through*
Thus, though we cannot make our sun 45
Stand still, yet we will make him run.

To His Coy Mistress. 7 *Humber*: a river that flows by Marvell's town of Hull (on the side of the world opposite from the Ganges). 10 *conversion of the Jews*: an event that, according to St. John the Divine, is to take place just before the end of the world. 35 *transpires*: exudes, as a membrane lets fluid or vapor pass through it.

Questions

1. What arguments is the speaker making? What is he after? Do you find his reasoning convincing?
2. How are the speaker's arguments similar to, and different from, those of a present-day seducer? Can you think of a more contemporary poem or song that is written in the same vein?
3. Does this poem have a serious theme beyond the seduction ploy? Explain.

John Donne

John Donne (1572–1631), English poet and divine, wrote his subtle, worldly love lyrics as a young man in the court of Queen Elizabeth I. At the time (wrote his contemporary, Richard Baker), he came to be known in London as "a great visitor of ladies, a great frequenter of plays, a great writer of conceited verse." The poems of his Songs and Sonnets *were first circulated in manuscript form, for in his lifetime Donne printed little. When in 1601 he married without the consent of his bride's father, he was dismissed from his secretarial post at court. For a number of years he endured poverty, a situation that was eased when he won the favor of King James I and took holy orders in the Church of England. The wit, ingenuity, and outrageousness of "The Flea" make it a prime example of Donne's early verse. In this famous poem the speaker tries to seduce his lady love through a series of ingenious arguments based on a flea that has bitten them both and unites them in "one blood made of two." Although the young woman remains unconvinced, she could hardly fail to have been amused (and if we accept the traditional assumption that "The Flea" was written to the young Ann More, she eventually eloped with the poet).*

The Flea   1633

Mark but this flea, and mark in this
How little that which thou deny'st me is;
It sucked me first, and now sucks thee,
And in this flea our two bloods mingled be;
Thou know'st that this cannot be said   5
A sin, nor shame, nor loss of maidenhead,
    Yet this enjoys before it woo,
    And pampered swells with one blood made of two,
    And this, alas, is more than we would do.

Oh stay, three lives in one flea spare,   10
Where we almost, yea more than married are.
This flea is you and I, and this
Our marriage bed, and marriage temple is;
Though parents grudge, and you, we're met
And cloistered in these living walls of jet.   15
    Though use° make you apt to kill me,   *custom*
    Let not to that, self-murder added be,
    And sacrilege, three sins in killing three.

Cruel and sudden, hast thou since
Purpled thy nail in blood of innocence?   20
Wherein could this flea guilty be,

Except in that drop which it sucked from thee?
Yet thou triumph'st, and say'st that thou
Find'st not thyself, nor me, the weaker now;
   'Tis true; then learn how false, fears be;   25
   Just so much honor, when thou yield'st to me,
   Will waste, as this flea's death took life from thee.

Questions

1. What is "that which thou deny'st me" in line 2?
2. What progression of events occurs as the poem moves from stanza to stanza?
3. In lines 16–18, why would "use" make the young woman "apt to kill" the speaker? Why would her killing of the flea constitute "sacrilege"?
4. How seriously should this poem be taken? (Consider especially the import of the last three lines.)

Edna St. Vincent Millay

*Edna St. Vincent Millay (1892–1950) was born in Rockland, Maine, the eldest of three daughters; when she was twelve, her father deserted the family. At twenty, she won a poetry contest with "Renascence," one of her most celebrated poems. In 1917 Millay graduated from Vassar College and settled in Greenwich Village. Her earliest collections—*Renascence and Other Poems *(1917),* A Few Figs from Thistles *(1920),* Second April *(1921)—brought her great popularity and acclaim, culminating in a Pulitzer Prize for* The Harp-Weaver and Other Poems *(1923). Depressed by her husband's death and poor reviews of her later books, she died of a heart attack at the age of fifty-eight. But many of her works, including the following sonnet, have remained favorites with the poetry-loving public.*

What lips my lips have kissed, and where, and why   1923

What lips my lips have kissed, and where, and why,
I have forgotten, and what arms have lain
Under my head till morning; but the rain
Is full of ghosts tonight, that tap and sigh
Upon the glass and listen for reply,   5
And in my heart there stirs a quiet pain
For unremembered lads that not again
Will turn to me at midnight with a cry.
Thus in the winter stands the lonely tree,
Nor knows what birds have vanished one by one,   10
Yet knows its boughs more silent than before:
I cannot say what loves have come and gone,
I only know that summer sang in me
A little while, that in me sings no more.

Questions

1. Does the speaker here seem concerned to find a close and enduring love relationship?
2. This poem is characterized by a tone of regret. What does the speaker express regret for? What does she *not* seem to regret?
3. Do you find any element of self-pity in this sonnet? Explain.
4. How do the last six lines of the sonnet relate to what has come before?

T. S. Eliot

Thomas Stearns Eliot (1888-1965) was born into a New England family who had moved to St. Louis. After study at Harvard, Eliot emigrated to London and became a bank clerk. In June 1915, he married Vivienne Haigh-Wood after an acquaintance of two months. (The marriage was troubled from the start. He would separate from Vivienne in 1933.) That year also saw Eliot's first major publication, when "The Love Song of J. Alfred Prufrock" appeared in the June issue of Poetry *magazine. The poem, a masterpiece of romantic hesitation and self-doubt, became the centerpiece of his first book of poems,* Prufrock and Other Observations *(1917). Eliot became one of the best-known and most controversial poets of his time with the publication of* The Waste Land *(1922). Conservative critics denounced it as impenetrable and*

Eliot around 1910

incoherent; readers of more advanced tastes responded at once to the poem's depiction of a sordid society, empty of spiritual values, in the wake of World War I. Through his essays and volumes of literary and social criticism, Eliot came to exert immense influence on modern culture. In 1948, he was awarded the Nobel Prize in Literature.

The Love Song of J. Alfred Prufrock   1917

> S'io credessi che mia risposta fosse
> a persona che mai tornasse al mondo,
> questa fiamma staria senza più scosse.
> Ma per ciò che giammai di questo fondo
> non tornò vivo alcun, s'i'odo il vero,
> senza tema d'infamia ti rispondo.

Let us go then, you and I,
When the evening is spread out against the sky
Like a patient etherized upon a table;
Let us go, through certain half-deserted streets,
The muttering retreats   5
Of restless nights in one-night cheap hotels
And sawdust restaurants with oyster-shells:
Streets that follow like a tedious argument
Of insidious intent
To lead you to an overwhelming question . . .   10

Oh, do not ask, "What is it?"
Let us go and make our visit.

In the room the women come and go
Talking of Michelangelo.

The yellow fog that rubs its back upon the window-panes,   15
The yellow smoke that rubs its muzzle on the window-panes,
Licked its tongue into the corners of the evening,
Lingered upon the pools that stand in drains,
Let fall upon its back the soot that falls from chimneys,
Slipped by the terrace, made a sudden leap,   20
And seeing that it was a soft October night,
Curled once about the house, and fell asleep.

And indeed there will be time
For the yellow smoke that slides along the street
Rubbing its back upon the window-panes;   25
There will be time, there will be time
To prepare a face to meet the faces that you meet;
There will be time to murder and create,
And time for all the works and days of hands
That lift and drop a question on your plate;   30
Time for you and time for me,
And time yet for a hundred indecisions,
And for a hundred visions and revisions,
Before the taking of a toast and tea.

In the room the women come and go   35
Talking of Michelangelo.

And indeed there will be time
To wonder, "Do I dare?" and, "Do I dare?"
Time to turn back and descend the stair,
With a bald spot in the middle of my hair—   40
(They will say: "How his hair is growing thin!")
My morning coat, my collar mounting firmly to the chin,
My necktie rich and modest, but asserted by a simple pin—
(They will say: "But how his arms and legs are thin!")
Do I dare   45
Disturb the universe?
In a minute there is time
For decisions and revisions which a minute will reverse.

For I have known them all already, known them all—
Have known the evenings, mornings, afternoons,   50
I have measured out my life with coffee spoons;
I know the voices dying with a dying fall
Beneath the music from a farther room.
  So how should I presume?

And I have known the eyes already, known them all—
The eyes that fix you in a formulated phrase,
And when I am formulated, sprawling on a pin,
When I am pinned and wriggling on the wall,
Then how should I begin
To spit out all the butt-ends of my days and ways?
    And how should I presume?

And I have known the arms already, known them all—
Arms that are braceleted and white and bare
(But in the lamplight, downed with light brown hair!)
Is it perfume from a dress
That makes me so digress?
Arms that lie along a table, or wrap about a shawl.
    And should I then presume?
    And how should I begin?

• • •

Shall I say, I have gone at dusk through narrow streets
And watched the smoke that rises from the pipes
Of lonely men in shirt-sleeves, leaning out of windows? . . .

I should have been a pair of ragged claws
Scuttling across the floors of silent seas.

• • •

And the afternoon, the evening, sleeps so peacefully!
Smoothed by long fingers,
Asleep . . . tired . . . or it malingers,
Stretched on the floor, here beside you and me.
Should I, after tea and cakes and ices,
Have the strength to force the moment to its crisis?
But though I have wept and fasted, wept and prayed,
Though I have seen my head (grown slightly bald) brought in upon a platter,
I am no prophet—and here's no great matter;
I have seen the moment of my greatness flicker,
And I have seen the eternal Footman hold my coat, and snicker,
And in short, I was afraid.

And would it have been worth it, after all,
After the cups, the marmalade, the tea,
Among the porcelain, among some talk of you and me,
Would it have been worth while,
To have bitten off the matter with a smile,
To have squeezed the universe into a ball
To roll it toward some overwhelming question,
To say: "I am Lazarus, come from the dead,
Come back to tell you all, I shall tell you all"—

If one, settling a pillow by her head,
    Should say: "That is not what I meant at all.
    That is not it, at all."

And would it have been worth it, after all,
Would it have been worth while,   100
After the sunsets and the dooryards and the sprinkled streets,
After the novels, after the teacups, after the skirts that trail along the floor—
And this, and so much more?—
It is impossible to say just what I mean!
But as if a magic lantern threw the nerves in patterns on a screen: 105
Would it have been worth while
If one, settling a pillow or throwing off a shawl,
And turning toward the window, should say:
    "That is not it at all,
    That is not what I meant, at all."   110

        • • •

No! I am not Prince Hamlet, nor was meant to be;
Am an attendant lord, one that will do
To swell a progress, start a scene or two,
Advise the prince; no doubt, an easy tool,
Deferential, glad to be of use,   115
Politic, cautious, and meticulous;
Full of high sentence, but a bit obtuse;
At times, indeed, almost ridiculous—
Almost, at times, the Fool.

I grow old . . . I grow old . . .   120
I shall wear the bottoms of my trousers rolled.

Shall I part my hair behind? Do I dare to eat a peach?
I shall wear white flannel trousers, and walk upon the beach.
I have heard the mermaids singing, each to each.

I do not think that they will sing to me.   125

I have seen them riding seaward on the waves
Combing the white hair of the waves blown back
When the wind blows the water white and black.

We have lingered in the chambers of the sea
By sea-girls wreathed with seaweed red and brown   130
Till human voices wake us, and we drown.

THE LOVE SONG OF J. ALFRED PRUFROCK. The epigraph, from Dante's *Inferno*, is the speech of one dead and damned, who thinks that his hearer also is going to remain in Hell. Count Guido da Montefeltro, whose sin was to give false counsel after a corrupt prelate had offered him prior absolution and whose punishment is to be wrapped in a constantly burning flame, offers to tell Dante his story:

    If I thought my answer were to someone who
        might see the world again, then there would be
        no more stirrings of this flame. Since it is true

that no one leaves these depths of misery
   alive, from all that I have heard reported,
   I answer you without fear of infamy.

(Translation by Michael Palma from: Dante Alighieri, *Inferno: A New Verse Translation* [New York: Norton, 2002].) 29 *works and days:* title of a poem by Hesiod (eighth century B.C.), depicting his life as a hardworking Greek farmer and exhorting his brother to be like him. 82 *head . . . platter:* like that of John the Baptist, prophet and praiser of chastity, whom King Herod beheaded at the demand of Herodias, his unlawfully wedded wife (see Mark 6:17–28). 92–93 *squeezed . . . To roll it:* an echo from Marvell's "To His Coy Mistress," lines 41–42. 94 *Lazarus:* probably the Lazarus whom Jesus called forth from the tomb (John 11:1–44), but possibly the beggar seen in Heaven by the rich man in Hell (Luke 16:19–25). 105 *magic lantern:* an early type of projector used to display still pictures from transparent slides.

Questions

1. What expectations are created by the title of the poem? Are those expectations fulfilled by the text?
2. John Berryman wrote of line 3, "With this line, modern poetry begins." What do you think he meant?
3. It has been said that Prufrock's difficulties in love are caused in part by a "morbid self-consciousness." How many references can you find in the poem to back up that statement?
4. In the total context of the poem, is the sense of lines 47–48 reassuring or disturbing? Explain your choice.
5. How do lines 70–72 relate to the questions that Prufrock raises in the three preceding stanzas (lines 49–69)?
6. What is the effect of riming "ices" and "crisis"? Can you find similar instances of such odd juxtapositions elsewhere in the poem?
7. Is the situation in the poem presented statically, or is there discernible development as the poem proceeds? Defend your answer with references to the text.
8. What, finally, is your attitude toward Prufrock—identification, sympathy, contempt, or something more complicated?

Marilyn Nelson

Born in Cleveland, Ohio, in 1946, Marilyn Nelson was the daughter of a U.S. Air Force officer and an elementary school teacher. Raised on a number of military bases, she earned a B.A. from the University of California at Davis and a Ph.D. at the University of Minnesota. In 2006 she completed a five-year term as Poet Laureate of Connecticut. Two of her collections, The Homeplace (1990) and The Fields of Praise (1997), were finalists for the National Book Award. Nelson is committed to building a wider audience for poetry—she has written several volumes of poetry for children and young adults, including Carver: A Life in Poems (2001), A Wreath for Emmett Till (2005), and Sweethearts of Rhythm (2009), and she frequently employs traditional verse forms, as in "The Ballad of Aunt Geneva."

The Ballad of Aunt Geneva   1990

Geneva was the wild one.
Geneva was a tart.
Geneva met a blue-eyed boy
and gave away her heart.

Geneva ran a roadhouse.
Geneva wasn't sent
to college like the others:
Pomp's pride her punishment.

She cooked out on the river,
watching the shore slide by,
her lips pursed into hardness,
her deep-set brown eyes dry.

They say she killed a woman
over a good black man
by braining the jealous heifer
with an iron frying pan.

They say, when she was eighty,
she got up late at night
and sneaked her old, white lover in
to make love, and to fight.

First they heard the tell-tale
singing of the springs,
then Geneva's voice rang out:
I need to buy some things,

So next time, bring more money.
And bring more moxie, too.
I ain't got no time to waste
On limp white mens like you.

Oh yeah? Well, Mister White Man,
it sure might be stone-white,
but my thing's white as it is.
And you know damn well I'm right.

Now listen: take your heart pills
and pay the doctor mind.
If you up and die on me,
I'll whip your white behind.

They tiptoed through the parlor
on heavy, time-slowed feet
She watched him, from her front door,
walk down the dawnlit street.

Geneva was the wild one.
Geneva was a tart.
Geneva met a blue-eyed boy
and gave away her heart.

Questions

1. What is the meaning of "Pomp's pride her punishment" (line 8)?
2. What is the effect of the speaker's beginning the fourth and fifth stanzas with "They say"?
3. How have Aunt Geneva's earlier experiences contributed to making her the person she is at eighty?
4. Is Aunt Geneva a sympathetic character, in your opinion? Why or why not?

Kim Addonizio

Born in Washington, D.C., in 1954 and raised in Bethesda, Maryland, Kim Addonizio is part of a prominent family: her father, Bob Addie, was a highly regarded sportswriter; her mother, Pauline Betz, was a professional tennis player who won five Grand Slam singles championships; and her daughter, Aya Cash, is an actress who has appeared on Law & Order *and other television shows. Addonizio has published five books of poetry, including* Tell Me *(2000),* What Is This Thing Called Love *(2004), and* Lucifer at the Starlite *(2009), as well as two novels and a collection of short stories. "First Poem for You," from her first book,* The Philosopher's Club *(1994), shows the emphasis on the erotic that has remained a prominent feature of her work.*

Kim Addonizio

First Poem for You 1994

I like to touch your tattoos in complete
darkness, when I can't see them. I'm sure of
where they are, know by heart the neat
lines of lightning pulsing just above
your nipple, can find, as if by instinct, the blue   5
swirls of water on your shoulder where a serpent
twists, facing a dragon. When I pull you
to me, taking you until we're spent
and quiet on the sheets, I love to kiss
the pictures in your skin. They'll last until   10
you're seared to ashes; whatever persists
or turns to pain between us, they will still
be there. Such permanence is terrifying.
So I touch them in the dark; but touch them, trying.

Questions

1. What is the speaker of this poem "sure of"? What, by implication, is she not sure of?
2. Why do you think the speaker feels that "Such permanence is terrifying"?
3. What, in your view, is she "trying" to do in the poem's last line?

Suggestions for Writing on Poems about Love, Sex, and Desire

1. Marvell's "To His Coy Mistress" describes desire that may or may not be related to deeper feelings of love. What ideas of love and desire does it convey?
2. Compare Donne's "The Flea" with Marvell's "To His Coy Mistress." How do the speakers' arguments differ? Which is more convincing?
3. "The Love Song of J. Alfred Prufrock" features a speaker who expresses fear or ambivalence about love. What are the speaker's fears? Are there sound reasons for his romantic uncertainty?
4. "The Love Song of J. Alfred Prufrock" is very firmly grounded in upper-class society in the early twentieth century, and in that society's social codes governing the proper relations between young men and women. Is the poem of mostly historical value, opening a window on a society and a set of values that no longer exist, or are the attitudes and concerns that it expresses still relevant today?
5. Eliot's poem mentions several famous cultural names: Michelangelo, John the Baptist, Lazarus, and Hamlet (along with an epigraph from Dante's *Inferno*). What do these allusions tell the reader about Prufrock and his social environment? Would Eliot's poem be more accessible without them, or would it be less effective?
6. When Millay first published her love poems, her work was often considered shocking and provocative because the author was female. Discuss what elements in Millay's sonnet "What lips my lips have kissed" might have been particularly unsettling to its early readers, and discuss why they might have been shocked or surprised.
7. Nelson's "The Ballad of Aunt Geneva" displays the sometimes strange and intense feelings that can arise from a close relationship with another person. Discuss the ways in which the narrator's attitudes toward Aunt Geneva are ambivalent. What behavior does she disapprove of? What behavior does she seem to admire?
8. Write a poem in the voice of the person who is *addressed* in any of the poems in this chapter. In your poem, answer the arguments, doubts, requests, demands, or fears of the original poem's speaker.

Poet in Depth
William Shakespeare

LOVE SONNETS

Shall I compare thee to a summer's day? (Sonnet 18)

When in disgrace with Fortune and men's eyes (Sonnet 29)

Let me not to the marriage of true minds (Sonnet 114)

My mistress' eyes are nothing like the sun (Sonnet 130)

When my love swears that she is made of truth (Sonnet 138)

Although William Shakespeare is best known for his plays, his sonnets are equally memorable. Even though we can't assume that the speaker of a poem is necessarily its author, Shakespeare's sonnets of love seem intensely personal—more revealing, vulnerable, intimate, and pained than the grand drama and comedy of his plays. In his series of one hundred fifty-four sonnets, Shakespeare expresses admiration, hope, fear, anxiety, love, and nagging jealousy. His opening sonnets are addressed mostly to an aristocratic young man, or the "Fair Youth," in a voice that begins in mentorly advice but develops into troubled love and disappointed admiration. His later sonnets are addressed to the "Dark Lady." These poems represent an abrupt shift in tone, describing a tortured sexual passion and jealousy rather than the idealized admiration of the earlier sonnets. No one knows for sure who the "Fair Youth" and the "Dark Lady" were—but the poems and the descriptions of the shifting relations between them make for an interesting love triangle. Many of the individual sonnets still stand today as some of the finest examples of their form; some are used widely in weddings and by people who are courting. As with most topics Shakespeare addresses, he captures all the nuances and permutations, the implications and the messiness of love. The sonnets collected here capture all of these moods—the idealization of the beloved, the philosophizing on the characteristics of "true love," the addictive quality of desire, and the nagging ache of doubt.

William Shakespeare

William Shakespeare (1564–1616), the supreme writer of English, was born, baptized, and buried in the market town of Stratford-on-Avon, eighty miles from London. At eighteen, he married Anne Hathaway, twenty-six, by whom he had three children, including twins. Soon thereafter, he moved to London, where he began a successful career as an actor and playwright. When plagues shut down the theaters from 1592 to 1594, Shakespeare turned to poetry. His great Sonnets (not published until 1609) probably date from the 1590s. Are they autobiographical? William Wordsworth, in defense of the sonnet form, said: "with this key Shakespeare unlocked

William Shakespeare

his heart." But Robert Browning thought Shakespeare's genius lay in his ability to imagine and convincingly render persons and situations outside his own experience; he responded to Wordsworth with: "Did Shakespeare? / If so, the less Shakespeare he!"

Shall I compare thee to a summer's day? 1609

Shall I compare thee to a summer's day?
Thou art more lovely and more temperate.
Rough winds do shake the darling buds of May,
And summer's lease hath all too short a date.
Sometime too hot the eye of heaven shines, 5
And often is his gold complexion dimmed;
And every fair° from fair sometimes declines, *fair one*
By chance, or nature's changing course, untrimmed:
But thy eternal summer shall not fade,
Nor lose possession of that fair thou ow'st,° *ownest, have* 10
Nor shall death brag thou wand'rest in his shade,
When in eternal lines to time thou grow'st.
   So long as men can breathe or eyes can see,
   So long lives this, and this gives life to thee.

Questions

1. In what ways does the speaker find his beloved superior to a "summer's day"?
2. What effect does he think that death will have on his love?
3. In the poem's last line, what does he mean by "this"? What is he saying?

When, in disgrace with Fortune and men's eyes 1609

When, in disgrace with Fortune and men's eyes,
I all alone beweep my outcast state,
And trouble deaf heaven with my bootless° cries, *futile*
And look upon myself and curse my fate,
Wishing me like to one more rich in hope, 5
Featured like him, like him with friends possessed,
Desiring this man's art, and that man's scope,
With what I most enjoy contented least,
Yet in these thoughts myself almost despising,
Haply° I think on thee, and then my state, *luckily* 10
Like to the lark at break of day arising
From sullen earth, sings hymns at heaven's gate;
   For thy sweet love rememb'red such wealth brings
   That then I scorn to change my state with kings.

Questions

1. According to lines 5–8, what are the reasons for the speaker's dissatisfaction with himself?
2. Explain the simile in lines 9–12.
3. What is this poem saying about the importance of love to one's sense of well-being? Do you agree with its conclusions?

Let me not to the marriage of true minds 1609

Let me not to the marriage of true minds
Admit impediments; love is not love
Which alters when it alteration finds,
Or bends with the remover to remove.
O, no, it is an ever-fixèd mark 5
That looks on tempests and is never shaken;
It is the star to every wand'ring bark,
Whose worth's unknown, although his height be taken.
Love's not Time's fool, though rosy lips and cheeks
Within his bending sickle's compass° come;   *range* 10
Love alters not with his° brief hours and weeks,   *Time's*
But bears° it out even to the edge of doom.   *endures*
   If this be error and upon me proved,
   I never writ, nor no man ever loved.

LET ME NOT TO THE MARRIAGE OF TRUE MINDS. 5 *ever-fixèd mark:* a sea-mark like a beacon or a lighthouse that provides mariners with safe bearings. 7 *the star:* presumably the North Star, which gave sailors the most dependable bearing at sea. 12 *edge of doom:* either the brink of death or—taken more generally—Judgment Day.

Questions
1. What is the speaker saying about true love?
2. Explain the statement in lines 9–10.
3. Do you agree with this poem's definition of love? Is there ever a situation when love should be "altered"?

My mistress' eyes are nothing like the sun 1609

My mistress' eyes are nothing like the sun;
Coral is far more red than her lips' red;
If snow be white, why then her breasts are dun;
If hairs be wires, black wires grow on her head.
I have seen roses damasked, red and white, 5
But no such roses see I in her cheeks;
And in some perfumes is there more delight
Than in the breath that from my mistress reeks.
I love to hear her speak, yet well I know
That music hath a far more pleasing sound; 10
I grant I never saw a goddess go:
My mistress, when she walks, treads on the ground.
   And yet, by heaven, I think my love as rare
   As any she° belied with false compare.   *woman*

Questions
1. What kind of image is the speaker presenting of his beloved? Is it an idealized image? A harsh one?
2. What is the tone of this poem? Serious? Ironic?
3. Is this a love poem? Explain.

When my love swears that she is made of truth   1599/1609

When my love swears that she is made of truth
I do believe her, though I know she lies,
That she might think me some untutored youth,
Unlearnèd in the world's false subtleties.
Thus vainly thinking that she thinks me young,   5
Although she knows my days are past the best,
Simply I credit her false-speaking tongue:
On both sides thus is simple truth suppressed.
But wherefore says she not she is unjust?
And wherefore say not I that I am old?   10
O, love's best habit is in seeming trust,
And age in love loves not to have years told:
  Therefore I lie with her and she with me,
  And in our faults by lies we flattered be.

Questions
1. There are a number of puns in this poem. What are the double meanings of "vainly" (line 5), "habit" (line 11), and "lie with" (line 13)?
2. Does the speaker trust his beloved?
3. The speaker's age is a consideration in this poem. What is he saying about age?

Suggestions for Writing on *Shakespeare's Sonnets*

1. Shakespeare's sonnets present different depictions of love. In them, can you discern an overall set of beliefs or ideas on that subject? What does Shakespeare seem to think that love is—and isn't? How would you characterize love as presented in these sonnets?
2. Some of Shakespeare's sonnets describe love in the context of permanence. Bradstreet's "To My Dear and Loving Husband" and Browning's "How Do I Love Thee? Let Me Count the Ways" also speak of love in terms of permanence. How are Shakespeare's ideas about love and permanence different from those of the other poets? How are they similar?
3. Two of the poems in this section—"My mistress' eyes are nothing like the sun" and "When my love swears that she is made of truth"—seem more ironic and less idealized than the other three. Make an argument for why they are, in fact, more realistic—and perhaps even more romantic—than the other three.
4. The highly complicated emotion of love has elements of both selflessness and selfishness. Taking the five Shakespeare sonnets as a unit, which aspect seems to you to be more prominent—that is, does the speaker seem more concerned with pleasing his beloved or with gratifying himself?

ESSAYS AND OTHER NONFICTION
REMEMBERING LOVE

Paul	*"The Greatest of These Is Love": 1 Corinthians 13*
Cynthia Ozick	*Lovesickness*
Judith Ortiz Cofer	*I Fell in Love, or My Hormones Awakened*
Mike Ives	*Would Hemingway Cry?*

When you are in love, your emotions color everything you see, think, and feel. Perhaps this is the reason love lends itself so naturally to poetry and song—those short lyric forms can replicate the great, sudden emotional sweep of romantic experience. But essays and memoirs bring a different sort of intelligence to understanding love. They often try to understand the nature of love and obsession with the benefit of hindsight. This section presents three memoirs about deep romantic attachments. Cynthia Ozick brilliantly recalls a series of romantic obsessions and encounters that illustrate the sheer irrationality of falling—or not falling—in love. With a combination of tenderness and hilarity, Judith Ortiz Cofer recounts the events leading up to her first kiss, while Mike Ives tells the bittersweet tale of the great love that got away. Finally, to put these modern views of love in perspective, we begin with a classic definition of perfect love from Paul's Epistle to the Corinthians.

Paul

The Apostle Paul was born in Tarsus in what is now Turkey. Originally known as Saul, he was a Jewish persecutor of Christians until he experienced a vision of Christ while on the road to Damascus. Thereafter, he traveled widely through the ancient world as a Christian missionary. He is believed to have been martyred in Rome sometime between 64 and 67 A.D. Thirteen epistles in the New Testament are attributed to him (though his authorship of several of them has been called into question by some biblical scholars). Through his activities and especially his writings, Paul had enormous influence on the development of Christian thought and belief. The thirteenth chapter of his First Epistle to the Corinthians, in which he describes the love that Christians should practice as a sign of their faith, is one of the most famous passages in the Bible; though it does not refer specifically to romantic love, passages from it are frequently used in wedding ceremonies.

"The Greatest of These Is Love": 1 Corinthians 13

(New King James Version, 1979)

c. 50–60 A.D.

Though I speak with the tongues of men and of angels, but have not love, I have become sounding brass or a clanging cymbal. And though I have the gift of prophecy, and understand all mysteries and all knowledge, and though I have all faith, so that I could remove mountains, but have not love, I am nothing. And though I bestow all my goods to feed the poor, and though I give my body to be burned, but have not love, it profits me nothing.

Love suffers long and is kind; love does not envy; love does not parade itself, is not puffed up; does not behave rudely, does not seek its own, is not provoked, thinks no evil; does not rejoice in iniquity, but rejoices in the truth; bears all things, believes all things, hopes all things, endures all things.

Love never fails. But whether there are prophecies, they will fail; whether there are tongues, they will cease; whether there is knowledge, it will vanish away. For we know in part and we prophesy in part. But when that which is perfect has come, then that which is in part will be done away.

When I was a child, I spoke as a child, I understood as a child, I thought as a child; but when I became a man, I put away childish things. For now we see in a mirror, dimly, but then face to face. Now I know in part, but then I shall know just as I also am known.

And now abide faith, hope, love, these three; but the greatest of these is love.

Questions

1. How does Paul define love? Do you agree with his definition?
2. Why does Paul rank "love" above "faith" and "hope"? How does he differentiate among the three?
3. Paul is not talking specifically about romantic love, but his definition of love is meant to encompass it as well as other types of love. How does Paul's definition differ from conventional ideas of love found in popular songs or romantic movies?

Cynthia Ozick

Cynthia Ozick was born in 1928 in New York City. Her parents, who had fled Russia to escape persecution, owned a pharmacy in the Bronx where they sometimes worked as much as fourteen hours a day. As a child Ozick delivered prescriptions but was an essentially shy girl who escaped into her studies and voracious reading. She earned a bachelor's degree from New York University in 1949 and a master's in English literature from Ohio State University in 1950. In 1952 she married Bernard Hallote, a lawyer; they live in New Rochelle, New York. Although she had dreamed from a very young age of becoming a writer, she was relatively slow to publish. The first of her six novels, Trust, appeared in 1966; the most recent is Foreign Bodies (2010). She has published several collections of short stories and novellas, including The Shawl (1989), one of her most powerful and admired works. Ozick is also the author of five volumes of essays, including Quarrel & Quandary (2000), which contains "Lovesickness," and A Din in the Head (2006). Her essays are celebrated for their range of subjects, stylistic elegance, intellectual rigor, and wit. Often, as in "Lovesickness," she uses personal experience to illuminate larger truths about the depths and peculiarities of human nature.

Lovesickness

1997

I

Once, when I had already been married for a time, I went to a friend's wedding and fell in love with the bridegroom. It happened out of the blue, in an instant, as unexpectedly as a sneeze. I was not responsible for it; it came upon me; it was an incursion, an invasion—a possession, like that of a dybbuk.° Or it was what diplomats call an "intervention," an intact sovereign tract subjected without warning to military fire. Or it was a kind of spell, the way the unearthly music of a fairy-tale pipe casts a helpless enchantment, so that, willy-nilly, you are compelled to dance and dance without surcease.

The bride had a small head and a Cheshire-cat smile. I had known her since childhood. Together, under the heavy-hanging trees, we had gathered acorns and pretended to dine on them. But we were not confidantes; we were not close. We had differing temperaments. She was humorous: her jokiness cut with an icy ironic blade. I was naïve and grave and obtuse. She was diligent at the violin and played it well. I hid when the piano teacher rang the doorbell. She was acutely and cleverly mathematical. I was an arithmetical imbecile. She was tall and I was short: we were seriously divided by our arms' reach. Often I felt between us a jealous tremor. I was jealous because she was almost two years younger, and even in girlhood I lamented the passing of my prime. At eleven, I scribbled a story and appended a lie: "By the Young Author," I wrote, "Age Nine."

The bride was standing under the wedding canopy in a white dress, her acorn head ringed by a wreath, when lovesickness struck. The venerable image of arrow or dart is crucially exact. Though I had met the bridegroom once before, in the long green darkening tangle of a meadow at dusk—it was a game of Frisbee—I had been unmoved. His thighs were taut, his calf-sinews thick; he had the inky curly hair of a runner on a Greek amphora. The white plastic disk arced into a blackening sky, along the trajectory of an invisible yet perfect night-rainbow. He sprinted after it; his catch was deft, like the pluck of a lyre. He was an Englishman. He was a mathematician. He was nothing to me.

But when I saw him under the wedding canopy next to my childhood friend, I was seized and shaken by a dazing infatuation so stormy, so sibylline, so like a divination, that I went away afterward hollowed-out. Infatuation was not an added condition: it was loss—the strangeness of having lost what had never been mine.

The newly married pair departed for England, by sea, in a sluggishly churning vessel. A shipboard postcard arrived: on the one side a view of the ship itself, all serene white flanks pocked by portholes, and on the other an unfamiliar script. It was the new husband's. I studied his handwriting—examined its loops and troughs, the blue turns of ink where they thickened and narrowed, the height of the l's and d's, the width of the crossbars, the hillocks of the m's and n's, the connecting tails and the interrupting gaps. The sentences themselves were sturdy and friendly, funny and offhand—entirely by-the-by. Clearly, composing this note was a lunch-table diversion. "You do it," I imagined the new wife telling the new husband. In a minute and a half it was done.

5

---

dybbuk: in Jewish folklore, the soul of a dead person, often evil, who possesses a living person.

For weeks I kept the card under my eye; it was as if the letters of each word were burning, as if the air above and below the letters were shuddering in an invisible fire. The words, the sentences, were of no moment; I hardly saw them; but the letters crazed me. They were the new husband's nerves, they were the vibrations of his pulse, his fingers' pressure, his most intimate mark. They were more powerful than the imprint of his face and shoulders, which had anyhow begun to fade. What I remembered was the hand leaping up into the dark to snatch the Frisbee out of the sky. That same hand had shaped these intoxicating yet regimented letters. A mathematician's letters: as upright and precise as numbers.

Infatuation has its own precision. It focuses on its object as directly and sharply as sunlight through a magnifying glass: it enlarges and clarifies, but it also scorches. What we call lovesickness, or desire, is deliberate in that way—the way of exactitude and scrupulous discrimination—and at the same time it is wildly undeliberate, zigzag, unpremeditated, driven, even loony.

What I finally did with—or *to*—that postcard was both meticulously focused and rapaciously mad.

It was the hand that my desire had fixed on—or, rather, the force and the brain that flowed from that hand. I wanted to get *into* that hand—to become it, to grow myself into its blood vessels, to steal its fire. I had already felt the boil of that fire under my own hand: the phosphorescent threads of the letters, as blue as veins, bled hotly into the paper's grain.

And I knew what I would do. I took my pencil and slowly, slowly traced over the letters of the first word. Slowly, slowly. The sensation was that of a novice dancer mimicking the movements of a ballet master; or of a mute mouth speaking through a ventriloquist; or of a shadow following a light; or of a mountain climber ascending the upward slope of a *t*, stopping to rest on the horizontal shelf of the crossbar, again toiling upward, turning, again resting on a ledge, and then sliding downward along a sheerly vertical wall.

Letter by letter, day by day, I pressed the point of my pencil into the fleshly lines of the sea-borne bridegroom's pen; I jumped my pencil over his jumps and skips, those minute blank sites of his pen's apnea.

In a week or so it was finished. I had coupled with him. Every word was laboriously Siamese-twinned. Each of the letters bore on its back the graphite coat I had slowly, slowly laid over it. Breath by breath, muscle by muscle, nerve by nerve, with the concentration of a monkish scribe, with the dedication of a Torah scribe, I had trod in his tracks and made his marks. Like a hunter, I had pursued his marks; I had trapped and caged them. I was his fanatical, indelible Doppelgänger.° And a forger besides.

II

All this was done in secret: lovesickness is most often silent, private, concealed. But sometimes it is wily and reckless, thrusting itself into the world like a novelist on the loose. To wit: I once observed an illustrious young professor of philosophy swinging a small boy between his knees. The child was rapturous; the man went on teasing and swinging. He had a merry, thin, mobile face—not at all professorial. And yet his

---

Doppelgänger: German for "double-goer," a mysterious figure who resembles someone, usually in sinister ways.

reputation was dauntingly fierce: he was an original; his famous Mind crackled around him like an electric current, or like a charged whip fending off mortals less dazzlingly endowed. It was said that his intellectual innovations and uncommon insights had so isolated him from ordinary human pursuits, and his wants were so sparse, that he slept on a couch in his mother's apartment in an outer borough. And here he was, laughing and swinging— himself a boy at play.

The blow of lovesickness came hammering down. I had no connection of any kind with this wizard of thought. It was unlikely that I could ever aspire to one.

But I had just then been reading Peter Quennell's biography of Lord Byron, and was captivated by its portrait of Lady Caroline Lamb, a married flirt who had seduced and conquered Byron (or vice-versa—both were mercurial and inclined toward escapades). Quennell described Lady Caroline as a volatile woman in search of "some violent, self-justificatory explosion, some crisis in which she could gather up the spasmodic and ill-directed energies that drove her. . . . The fever of Romanticism was in her blood." She delighted in spats and subterfuges and secret letters delivered to her lover by a page, who turned out to be Lady Caroline in disguise. It was she who invented Byron's most celebrated epithet—*mad, bad, and dangerous to know*. This would do admirably for Lady Caroline.

Certainly Byron found her dangerous to know. When, exasperated, he tired of her, he discovered she was impossible to get rid of. He called her "a little volcano," and complained that her fascination was "unfortunately coupled with a total want of common conduct." In the end she became a pest, an affliction, a plague. In vindictive verses he pronounced her a fiend. She was a creature of ruse and caprice and jealousy; she would not let him go. She chased after him indefatigably, she badgered him, she burned him in effigy, she stabbed herself. And she wrote him letters.

The fever of Romanticism was in my blood; I had been maddened by a hero of imagination, a man who could unravel the skeins of logic that braid human cognition. Byron had his clubfoot; my philosopher was still spending his nights on his mother's couch. Byron spoke of his pursuer as a volcano; I could at least leak quantities of epistolary lava: And so, magnetized and wanting to mystify, I put on a disguise and began my chase: I wrote letters. They were love letters; they were letters of enthrallment, of lovesickness. I addressed them to the philosopher's university and signed them all, in passionately counterfeit handwriting, "Lady Caroline Lamb."

III

But what of lovesickness in reverse? The arrow not suffered but inadvertently shot? The wound not taken but blindly caused?

The Second World War was just over; the college cafeteria swarmed with professed Communists, grim veterans on the G.I. Bill, girls flaunting Edwardian skirts down to their ankles in the New Look style, and a squat square mustached fellow who, when anyone inquired after his politics, insisted he was a monarchist working for the restoration of his dynasty. There was, in addition, an aristocratic and very young Turkish boy, a prodigy, whose father was attached to the United Nations and whose mother wore the veil. The Turkish boy and I studied Latin together, and sometimes spoke of *amor intellectualis*°—but intellectual love rooted in a common admiration

---

amor intellectualis: an intellectual love as opposed to a physical or sexual kind.

of Catullus's ode to kissing was too heated, or not heated enough. In the cafeteria I was often ambushed by spasms of bewitchment—over a green-eyed sophomore, for instance, with a radio-announcer voice, who was himself in love with a harpist called Angel. I waited for him at the foot of a certain staircase, hoping he might come down it. I cultivated one of his classmates in the expectation that I might learn something intimate about my distant love, and I did: his nickname, I was told, was Beanhead. "Beanhead, Beanhead," I would murmur at the bottom of the stairs. All my loves at that time were dreamlike, remote, inconclusive, evanescent.

But one afternoon in winter, a foreign-seeming young man (I had noticed him in the cafeteria, curled over a notebook) followed me home. What made him appear foreign was his intensity, his strict stride, his unembarrassed persistence; and also the earnest luster of his dangling black bangs, which shielded his eyes like a latticed gate, and freed him to gaze without moderation. Following me home was no easy journey—it was a long, long subway ride to the end of the line. Despite that curtained look, I saw in his face an urgency I knew in myself. Unaccountably, I had become his Beanhead, his Byron, his bridegroom. I pleaded with him not to undertake the trek to the northeast Bronx—what, I privately despaired, would I *do* with him?

He filled an underground hour by explaining himself: he was a Persian in command of the history and poetry of his beautiful country, and with my permission, because at this moment he was unluckily without a nosegay (he was prone to words like nosegay, garland, attar), he would offer me instead a beautiful poem in Arabic. He drew out his notebook and a pen: from its nib flowed a magical calligraphy.

"This is my poem, my original own," he said, "for you," and folded the sheet and slipped it into my copy of Emily Dickinson, exactly at the page where I had underlined "There's a certain Slant of light / On winter afternoons."

"You don't really want to ride all this distance," I said, hoping to shake him off. "Suppose you just get out at the East 86th Street express stop and go right back, all right?"

"Ah," he said, "will the moon abandon the sun?"

But the third time he demanded to come home with me, it was the sun who abandoned the moon. I had had enough of lovelorn importuning. He accepted his dismissal with Persian melancholy, pressing on me yet another poem, his original own, that he had set down in those melodious, undulating Scheherazadean characters. At the entrance to the subway, forbidden to go farther, he declaimed his translation: "There is a garden, a wall, a brook. You are the lily, I am the brook. O wall, permit me to refresh the lily!"

No one is crueler than the conscious object of infatuation: I blew back the black veil of hair, looked into a pair of moonstruck black eyes, and laughed. Meanly, heartlessly.

IV

And once I made a suitor cry. He was, I feared, a genuine suitor. By now the war had long been over, and nearly all the former G.I.s had gladly returned to civilian life. My suitor, though, was still in uniform; he was stationed at an army base on an island in the harbor. He had a tidy blond head on which his little soldier's cap rested; he had little blunt fingers; everything about him was miniature, like a toy soldier. He was elfin, but without elfishness: he was sober, contained, and as neutral as khaki.

He put me in mind of a drawing in a children's coloring book: those round clear pale eyes anticipating blueness, that firm outline beyond which no crayon would ever stray. He had a kind of blankness waiting to be filled in. On weekends, when he was free, he came to call with a phonograph record under his arm. We sat side by side, sternly taking in the music. We were two sets of blank outlines. The music was coloring us in.

One Sunday he brought Richard Strauss's *Death and Transfiguration*. The jacket supplied the title in German, *Tod und Verklärung,* and a description—tone poem. But it was "transfiguration" that held me. Transfiguration! Would the toy soldier be transformed into live human flesh and begin to move and think on his own?

When he returned to his island, I put *Death and Transfiguration* on the record player and, alone, listened to it over and over again. It colored the empty air, but I saw there would be no transfiguration. Stasis was the toy soldier's lot.

The next Sunday, I piled all the records that had been his gifts into his arms. "At least keep this one. You liked it," he said dolefully: it was *Tod und Verklärung.* But I dropped it on top of the farewell pile and watched him weep, my marble heart immune to any arrow.

V

Not long afterward, a young man whose eyes were not green, who inspired nothing eccentric or adventurous, who never gave a thought to brooks and lilies or death and transfiguration, who never sought to untangle the knots in the history of human thought, began, with awful consistency, to bring presents of marzipan.° So much marzipan was making me sick—though not lovesick.

Ultimately the philosopher learned the true identity of the writer of those love letters; it was reported that he laughed. He is, I believe, still sleeping on his mother's couch.

I never saw the bridegroom again. He never sent another postcard. I suppose he is an unattractive old man by now. Or anyhow I hope so.

The marzipan provider? Reader, I married him.

Questions

1. The first romantic episode that Ozick describes is unusual, to say the least. She falls in love with the groom at someone else's wedding. How does she justify her emotions?
2. Ozick is writing a personal memoir, yet she offers a long digression about Lord Byron and Lady Caroline Lamb. Why mention two historical British figures in a memoir that takes place in modern New York state?
3. The Persian boy is intellectual and literary. He seems to adore the young Ozick. Why does she dismiss him as a suitor?
4. The first episode is actually the last one in strictly chronological terms. What does Ozick gain by placing it first in the narrative?

Judith Ortiz Cofer

Judith Ortiz Cofer was born in 1952 in the small town of Hormigueros, Puerto Rico, where the famous sanctuary of the Virgin of Monserrate is located. Her father joined the U.S. Navy and brought his family to Paterson, New Jersey, close to the Brooklyn Navy Yard

---

marzipan: a confection made out of sugar and almond paste.

where he was stationed. *The family would move back and forth between Puerto Rico and Paterson whenever Cofer's father would leave on assignment, typically every six months. This culturally divided upbringing had a significant effect on the poet as a child, and it became the focus of much of her writing. When Cofer's father retired from the navy in 1968, the family relocated to Augusta, Georgia, where the poet attended high school and Augusta College (B.A., 1974). Cofer began writing seriously in graduate school. Her first two books of poetry were published almost simultaneously—*Terms of Survival *(1987) and* Reaching for the Mainland *(1987). Cofer then began writing fiction, and her first novel,* The Line of the Sun *(1989), soon appeared. Her subsequent collections have included a mix of poetry and prose, mostly involving the stories of her childhood and her ancestors. Cofer is a professor of English and the director of the creative writing program at the University of Georgia. She lives with her husband on a farm in the rural community of Louisville, Georgia. "I Fell in Love, or My Hormones Awakened" is from Cofer's memoir,* Silent Dancing: A Partial Remembrance of a Puerto Rican Childhood.

I Fell in Love, or My Hormones Awakened   1990

I fell in love, or my hormones awakened from their long slumber in my body, and suddenly the goal of my days was focused on one thing: to catch a glimpse of my secret love. And it had to remain secret, because I had, of course, in the great tradition of tragic romance, chosen to love a boy who was totally out of my reach. He was not Puerto Rican; he was Italian and rich. He was also an older man. He was a senior at the high school when I came in as a freshman. I first saw him in the hall, leaning casually on a wall that was the border line between girlside and boyside for underclassmen. He looked extraordinarily like a young Marlon Brando—down to the ironic little smile. The total of what I knew about the boy who starred in every one of my awkward fantasies was this: that he was the nephew of the man who owned the supermarket on my block; that he often had parties at his parents' beautiful home in the suburbs which I would hear about; that this family had money (which came to our school in many ways)—and this fact made my knees weak: and that he worked at the store near my apartment building on weekends and in the summer.

My mother could not understand why I became so eager to be the one sent out on her endless errands. I pounced on every opportunity from Friday to late Saturday afternoon to go after eggs, cigarettes, milk (I tried to drink as much of it as possible, although I hated the stuff)—the staple items that she would order from the "American" store.

Week after week I wandered up and down the aisles, taking furtive glances at the stock room in the back, breathlessly hoping to see my prince. Not that I had a plan. I felt like a pilgrim waiting for a glimpse of Mecca. I did not expect him to notice me. It was sweet agony.

One day I did see him. Dressed in a white outfit like a surgeon: white pants and shirt, white cap, and (gross sight, but not to my love-glazed eyes) blood-smeared butcher's apron. He was helping to drag a side of beef into the freezer storage area of the store. I must have stood there like an idiot, because I remember that he did see me, he even spoke to me! I could have died. I think he said, "Excuse me," and smiled vaguely in my direction.

After that, I *willed* occasions to go to the supermarket. I watched my mother's pack of cigarettes empty ever so slowly. I wanted her to smoke them fast. I drank milk and forced it on my brother (although a second glass for him had to be bought with my share of Fig Newton cookies which we both liked, but we were restricted to one row each). I gave my cookies up for love, and watched my mother smoke her L&M's with so little enthusiasm that I thought (God, no!) that she might be cutting down on her smoking or maybe even giving up the habit. At this crucial time!

I thought I had kept my lonely romance a secret. Often I cried hot tears on my pillow for the things that kept us apart. In my mind there was no doubt that he would never notice me (and that is why I felt free to stare at him—I was invisible). He could not see me because I was a skinny Puerto Rican girl, a freshman who did not belong to any group he associated with.

At the end of the year I found out that I had not been invisible. I learned one little lesson about human nature—adulation leaves a scent, one that we are all equipped to recognize, and no matter how insignificant the source, we seek it.

In June the nuns at our school would always arrange for some cultural extravaganza. In my freshman year it was a Roman banquet. We had been studying Greek drama (as a prelude to church history—it was at a fast clip that we galloped through Sophocles and Euripides toward the early Christian martyrs), and our young, energetic Sister Agnes was in the mood for spectacle. She ordered the entire student body (it was a small group of under 300 students) to have our mothers make us togas out of sheets. She handed out a pattern on mimeo pages fresh out of the machine. I remember the intense smell of the alcohol on the sheets of paper, and how almost everyone in the auditorium brought theirs to their noses and inhaled deeply—mimeographed handouts were the school-day buzz that the new Xerox generation of kids is missing out on. Then, as the last couple of weeks of school dragged on, the city of Paterson becoming a concrete oven, and us wilting in our uncomfortable uniforms, we labored like frantic Roman slaves to build a splendid banquet hall in our small auditorium. Sister Agnes wanted a raised dais where the host and hostess would be regally enthroned.

She had already chosen our Senator and Lady from among our ranks. The Lady was to be a beautiful new student named Sophia, a recent Polish immigrant, whose English was still practically unintelligible, but whose features, classically perfect without a trace of makeup, enthralled us. Everyone talked about her gold hair cascading past her waist, and her voice which could carry a note right up to heaven in choir. The nuns wanted her for God. They kept saying that she had vocation. We just looked at her in awe, and the boys seemed afraid of her. She just smiled and did as she was told. I don't know what she thought of it all. The main privilege of beauty is that others will do almost everything for you, including thinking.

Her partner was to be our best basketball player, a tall, red-haired senior whose family sent its many offspring to our school. Together, Sophia and her senator looked like the best combination of immigrant genes our community could produce. It did not occur to me to ask then whether anything but their physical beauty qualified them for the starring roles in our production. I had the highest average in the church history class, but I was given the part of one of many "Roman Citizens." I was to sit in front of the plastic fruit and recite a greeting in Latin along with the rest of the school when our hosts came into the hall and took their places on their throne.

On the night of our banquet, my father escorted me in my toga to the door of our school. I felt foolish in my awkwardly draped sheet (blouse and skirt required underneath). My mother had no great skill as a seamstress. The best she could do was hem a skirt or a pair of pants. That night I would have traded her for a peasant woman with a golden needle. I saw other Roman ladies emerging from their parents' cars looking authentic in sheets of material that folded over their bodies like the garments on a statue by Michelangelo. How did they do it? How was it that I always got it just slightly wrong, and worse, I believed that other people were just too polite to mention it. "The poor little Puerto Rican girl," I could hear them thinking. But in reality, I must have been my worst critic, self-conscious as I was.

Soon, we were all sitting at our circle of tables joined together around the dais. Sophia glittered like a golden statue. Her smile was beatific: a perfect, silent Roman lady. Her "senator" looked uncomfortable, glancing around at his buddies, perhaps waiting for the ridicule that he would surely get in the locker room later. The nuns in their black habits stood in the background watching us. What were they supposed to be, the Fates? Nubian slaves? The dancing girls did their modest little dance to tinny music from their finger cymbals, then the speeches were made. Then the grape juice "wine" was raised in a toast to the Roman Empire we all knew would fall within the week—before finals anyway.

All during the program I had been in a state of controlled hysteria. My secret love sat across the room from me looking supremely bored. I watched his every move, taking him in gluttonously. I relished the shadow of his eyelashes on his ruddy cheeks, his pouty lips smirking sarcastically at the ridiculous sight of our little play. Once he slumped down on his chair, and our sergeant-at-arms nun came over and tapped him sharply on his shoulder. He drew himself up slowly, with disdain. I loved his rebellious spirit. I believed myself still invisible to him in my "nothing" status as I looked upon my beloved. But toward the end of the evening, as we stood chanting our farewells in Latin, he looked straight across the room and into my eyes! How did I survive the killing power of those dark pupils? I trembled in a new way. I was not cold—I was burning! Yet I shook from the inside out, feeling light-headed, dizzy.

The room began to empty and I headed for the girls' lavatory. I wanted to relish the miracle in silence. I did not think for a minute that anything more would follow. I was satisfied with the enormous favor of a look from my beloved. I took my time, knowing that my father would be waiting outside for me, impatient, perhaps glowing in the dark in his phosphorescent white Navy uniform. The others would ride home. I would walk home with my father, both of us in costume. I wanted as few witnesses as possible. When I could no longer hear the crowds in the hallway, I emerged from the bathroom, still under the spell of those mesmerizing eyes.

The lights had been turned off in the hallway and all I could see was the lighted stairwell, at the bottom of which a nun would be stationed. My father would be waiting just outside. I nearly screamed when I felt someone grab me by the waist. But my mouth was quickly covered by someone else's mouth. I was being kissed. My first kiss and I could not even tell who it was. I pulled away to see that face not two inches away from mine. It was he. He smiled down at me. Did I have a silly expression on my face? My glasses felt crooked on my nose. I was unable to move or to speak. More gently, he lifted my chin and touched his lips to mine. This time I did not forget to enjoy it. Then, like the phantom lover that he was, he walked away into the darkened corridor and disappeared.

I don't know how long I stood there. My body was changing right there in the hallway of a Catholic school. My cells were tuning up like musicians in an orchestra, and my heart was a chorus. It was an opera I was composing, and I wanted to stand very still and just listen. But, of course, I heard my father's voice talking to the nun. I was in trouble if he had had to ask about me. I hurried down the stairs making up a story on the way about feeling sick. That would explain my flushed face and it would buy me a little privacy when I got home.

The next day Father announced at the breakfast table that he was leaving on a six month tour of Europe with the Navy in a few weeks, and, that at the end of the school year my mother, my brother, and I would be sent to Puerto Rico to stay for half a year at Mamá's (my mother's mother) house. I was devastated. This was the usual routine for us. We had always gone to Mamá's to stay when Father was away for long periods. But this year it was different for me. I was in love, and . . . my heart knocked against my bony chest at this thought . . . he loved me too? I broke into sobs and left the table.

In the next week I discovered the inexorable truth about parents. They can actually carry on with their plans right through tears, threats, and the awful spectacle of a teenager's broken heart. My father left me to my mother who impassively packed while I explained over and over that I was at a crucial time in my studies and that if I left my entire life would be ruined. All she would say was, "You are an intelligent girl, you'll catch up." Her head was filled with visions of *casa* and family reunions, long gossip sessions with her mamá and sisters. What did she care that I was losing my one chance at true love?

In the meantime I tried desperately to see him. I thought he would look for me too. But the few times I saw him in the hallway, he was always rushing away. It would be long weeks of confusion and pain before I realized that the kiss was nothing but a little trophy for his ego. He had no interest in me other than as his adorer. He was flattered by my silent worship of him, and he had *bestowed* a kiss on me to please himself, and to fan the flames. I learned a lesson about the battle of the sexes then that I have never forgotten: the object is not always to win, but most times simply to keep your opponent (synonymous at times with "the loved one") guessing.

But this is too cynical a view to sustain in the face of that overwhelming rush of emotion that is first love. And in thinking back about my own experience with it, I can be objective only to the point where I recall how sweet the anguish was, how caught up in the moment I felt, and how every nerve in my body was involved in this salute to life. Later, much later, after what seemed like an eternity of dragging the weight of unrequited love around with me, I learned to make myself visible and to relish the little battles required to win the greatest prize of all. And much later, I read and understood Camus's statement about the subject that concerns both adolescent and philosopher alike: if love were easy, life would be too simple.

20

Questions

1. What contact does Cofer have with her "secret love" before the night of the banquet?
2. The climax of Cofer's memoir takes place after a "Roman banquet." What does this setting add to her essay?
3. Does the boy do anything wrong in kissing Cofer? Yes or no? Give your reasons for your opinion.
4. Does Cofer now regret or enjoy remembering her first kiss?

Mike Ives

Mike Ives (b. 1983) is an American writer based in Hanoi, Vietnam. A graduate of Middlebury College, he worked for two years as a staff writer for the Vermont alternative newsweekly Seven Days. *His essay "Would Hemingway Cry?" appeared in the* New York Times *weekly "Modern Love" column on October 3, 2010. His writing has also appeared in the* Los Angeles Times, Washington Post, Christian Science Monitor, Smithsonian Online *and other publications and websites. In Vietnam he writes for the Associated Press.*

Mike Ives

Would Hemingway Cry? 2010

Ten years ago, my high school sweetheart and I liked to pretend we were disaffected expatriates living in some crumbly postwar foreign capital. In reality, we lived in an affluent New York City suburb.

Fortunately there was English class, where our teacher assigned *The Sun Also Rises*, Hemingway's 1926 novel about American and British expats who booze their way through Parisian cafes and Spanish bullfights.

Devouring the book, we thought the protagonist, Jake Barnes, a twentysomething American reporter, and his hot-and-cold lover, Lady Brett Ashley, were pretty cool. They were always visiting interesting places and discussing the meaning of life, or lack thereof. And even though their lives were a little messy, they always spoke so insightfully!

Sure, we concluded, Barnes, Lady Brett and other Lost Generation all-stars had dependency, identity, and substance-abuse issues. But in other ways, they seemed like the sort of people we'd be happy to be like when we grew up. They were adults, but they were much cooler than most of the adults we knew.

The summer after my freshman year of college, my girlfriend and I traveled to France and Spain together, Hemingway style, picnicking on the Seine and sipping wine with Basques in San Sebastián. After the trip, we corresponded via telegram-style letters and e-mail messages that went something like this:

Dearest Jake: Can't bear staying apart. Stop. Please visit after exams. Brett.

5

Brett Darling: Will come on Greyhound Saturday. Stop. Arriving 6:40 P.M. All my love. Jake.

I was pretty sure I would marry her, just not anytime soon. I also assumed—taking my cues from Hemingway, Maugham and Fitzgerald—that I had years of globetrotting to do before I'd consider settling down with anyone.

The next summer she and I worked in California. On weekends we'd cruise to the Henry Miller Library, an oceanside hangout named after the footloose novelist. It was fun to gaze at the Pacific and quote him to each other.

My own travels would begin to feel Milleresque: That fall I went to Buenos Aires; the following spring, I volunteered on a coffee farm in Mexico; that summer my girlfriend and I traveled to Montana, where I had landed a job baking pies at a roadside cafe.

Thinking of Hemingway's Ketchum, Idaho, I had looked for a beautiful place where I could write and fish. The cafe owners said they also had work for my girlfriend—they needed line cooks.

In Montana, we were happy living under big skies, among friendly strangers and away from the East Coast. But our cabin was cramped and mouse-infested, and my girlfriend—a vegetarian—quickly tired of grilling burgers.

We quit after six weeks and headed east in her car. The ride felt like a defeat. I broke off the relationship because I was restless. Stop.

More than a year passed before we met for pizza on a dreary November afternoon in Boston. I had come down for the weekend from Vermont, where I was starting to write for a newspaper, to attend a journalism conference.

She was thinking of applying to law school; I wanted to go abroad again. There was no spark between us, but I attributed that to bad timing, figuring we would eventually rekindle our romance in a different place and context. The fact that I didn't know where or how seemed kind of exciting.

Three springs later, I quit my newspaper job and spent the summer wandering around China and Southeast Asia. I settled in Hanoi, Vietnam, partly because its sidewalk cafes, French-designed boulevards and bustling expat social scene reminded me of books I had read about postwar Europe.

I spent the fall and winter drinking coffee, writing travel stories, scratching away at a novel and dating women from other countries. Soon I would be learning the ropes at a European news agency, playing tennis with diplomats and feeling expatriated in a good, adventurous, Hemingway sort of way.

But I still thought fondly of my first love. From what she'd told me over the phone before I left the United States, I knew she had started law school. I resisted that plotline: I sensed that someday she would decide to come find me.

I hadn't seen her in three years. Two months after my 26th birthday, I mailed her a letter: Living abroad was fun, I wrote, but I missed her, and I wanted to see her the next time I came home to visit.

She replied via e-mail that she couldn't see me: she had a boyfriend, and she was happy.

Ouch. I hadn't been pining for her per se, but I was upset that she didn't seem to need to see me in the same way I felt I needed to see her. Also: what boyfriend? I had assumed that, like me, she had been drifting through lovers as one floats among so many ocean swells.

Then she e-mailed to say that she was in Washington, D.C.—Did I want to meet up?

I did. A few weeks later, I hoisted my backpack, hailed a motorbike taxi outside my apartment and began a five-week odyssey of work and travel that would take me from Hanoi to Moscow to Paris to Reykjavik to New York. Along the way I strolled the Luxembourg Gardens, ate crepes by the Seine, reported a story from Rouen, slept in departure lounges and on friends' couches, rode Amtrak to Vermont, paddled a canoe across an Adirondack lake and caught a train back to the city, where in Chinatown I boarded a southbound bus.

The next day, a sweltering Wednesday, I finally arrived at my destination: the entrance of a Washington Metro station, where my high school sweetheart, in a black skirt and silver blouse, looked more beautiful than I remembered. We ducked into a Mexican restaurant and ordered beers to steady our trembling hands.

She said she had been dating the same guy for three years. I had met him once at a party but I wouldn't remember. Anyway, now they were living together. She liked law school and had never felt so settled—in a good way.

"What about you?" she asked.

My throat crackled. I had been kidding myself assuming that I would marry this woman: We had each followed roads that the other had no interest in taking, and now she was in love with someone else.

Still: She was looking at me so prettily over the guacamole that I felt like whisking her away. Dearest Brett: Let's start over together in Mexico City. Jake.

"Let's have another drink," I said.

We split the bill—it was almost half a month's rent in Hanoi—and found a table at a high-ceilinged German brewpub on the next block. The lighting was dimmer there. Loosening up under the alcohol, I said the kind of playful, witty things I knew would make her smile.

Laughing, she said she wanted to hear more about my expat life. "A wire service in Southeast Asia?" I recall her saying. "I imagine you wearing one of those silly reporter hats with the wrap-around brim."

We left the bar and walked toward the Metro. She pointed out that the station was closing in five minutes. She wasn't inviting me to come home with her. She joked that she would be sure to send me one of those silly—

When she noticed that I was crying, she hugged me as one holds a child who has scraped a knee. I held her hands and realized that the next time I saw her—if I ever were to see her again—she would probably be wearing a ring. She might even be a mother.

I dried my eyes on my T-shirt. A janitor was cleaning up. Otherwise we were alone. I scratched my sandals against the pavement. Perhaps I wanted to keep standing there because I had been traveling too much. Or maybe I sensed that I wouldn't be back. Two or three minutes passed.

For the first half of my 20s, the Rest of My Life had appeared to wait patiently. And time, like a gift certificate, seemed like something I could hold on to and cash in later. But that night I felt as if the rest of my life was already upon me. Time was short, and I couldn't think of anything to look forward to.

I grasped for something winning to say. Nothing came. I was drunk. She walked into the station and didn't look back.

For a dizzy moment I considered chasing her down that escalator. Dearest Brett: Am lonely without you. Stop. Come to Hanoi. Mike.

The escalator stopped and the trains left. I walked on. I suppose I had my own connections to make.

Questions

1. What are the young Ives's assumptions about the stability of his romance with his girlfriend? What does he think is required to sustain it?
2. When he meets his girlfriend a year after their breakup, what does he assume about their long-term fate? On what does he base his feelings?
3. When does Ives finally realize his romance is over for good?
4. The famously macho Ernest Hemingway would probably not have cried outside the German brewpub. Why did Ives give his memoir this title?

Suggestions for Writing on *Nonfiction about Remembering Love*

1. Several kinds of love are described in these pieces. Choose at least two different kinds of love and analyze how they are defined and described in the essays. Use specific passages to support your argument.
2. Cynthia Ozick describes a series of romantic encounters. Compare them and discuss why she chose to marry the final suitor.
3. Compare a young person's view of love from Michael Ives with an older person's view from Cynthia Ozick. What similarities and differences do you see?
4. Describe your first kiss. What were the circumstances? How did you feel about it during the kiss and afterward?

DRAMA

LOVE: COMIC AND TRAGIC

David Ives	*Sure Thing*
William Shakespeare	*Othello*
	Picturing *Othello*
	Casebook on *Othello*

Even when people have the best of intentions in love, it is easy to make mistakes. Sometimes lovers press too hard when they should go more slowly, or they hang back just when they should make their feelings known. Each tentative (or pushy) step forward by one lover can cause a corresponding move from the other, until both are dancing around or away from each other instead of moving together in harmony. The two works that follow—one a contemporary one-act play by David Ives and the other a classic drama by Shakespeare—depict this dance in comic and tragic forms. Ives playfully shows us how a pair of potential lovers reveal themselves, and even reconstruct themselves, in their efforts to impress one another. Shakespeare shows us how self-doubt and insecurity can poison the trust between lovers, especially when they are coping with larger obstacles. Because love is capable of bringing out both the best and the worst in people, it is ripe for comedy as well as for tragedy. While the two plays in this section could not be more different in content, scope, or tone, they both demonstrate that the intensity of love opens up in human nature every possibility—good or bad—to create unexpected outcomes.

David Ives

David Ives (b. 1950) grew up on the South Side of Chicago. He attended Catholic schools before entering Northwestern University. Later Ives studied at the Yale Drama School—"a blissful time for me," he recalls, "in spite of the fact that there is slush on the ground in New Haven 238 days a year." Ives received his first professional production in Los Angeles at the age of twenty-one "at America's smallest, and possibly worst theater, in a storefront that had a pillar dead center in the middle of the stage." He continued writing for the theater while working as an editor at Foreign Affairs, *and gradually achieved a reputation in theatrical circles for his wildly original and brilliantly written short comic plays. His public breakthrough came in 1993 with the New York staging of* All in the Timing, *which presented six short comedies, including* Sure Thing. *This production earned ecstatic reviews and a busy box office. In the 1995–1996 season,* All in the Timing *was the most widely performed play in America (except for the works of Shakespeare).*

David Ives

His second group of one-act comedies, Mere Mortals (1997), was produced with great success in New York City; it was published with Lives of the Saints, another cycle of his one-act plays, in the volume Time Flies (2001). A talented adapter, Ives was chosen to rework a newly discovered play by Mark Twain, Is He Dead?, which had a successful run on Broadway in 2007. His most recent plays are Venus in Fur (2010) and a number of translations and adaptations of French comedies, including Pierre Corneille's The Liar (2010), and Molière's The Misanthrope, which Ives titled The School of Lies (2011). He lives in New York City.

Sure Thing

1988

CHARACTERS
Betty
Bill

SCENE. *A café. Betty, a woman in her late twenties, is reading at a café table. An empty chair is opposite her. Bill, same age, enters.*

Original 1993 Off-Broadway production of *Sure Thing* by Primary Stages.

Bill: Excuse me. Is this chair taken?
Betty: Excuse me?
Bill: Is this taken?
Betty: Yes it is.
Bill: Oh. Sorry.
Betty: Sure thing.

(*A bell rings softly.*)

Bill: Excuse me. Is this chair taken?
Betty: Excuse me?
Bill: Is this taken?
Betty: No, but I'm expecting somebody in a minute.

Bill: Oh. Thanks anyway.
Betty: Sure thing.

　(*A bell rings softly.*)

Bill: Excuse me. Is this chair taken?
Betty: No, but I'm expecting somebody very shortly.
Bill: Would you mind if I sit here till he or she or it comes?
Betty (glances at her watch): They do seem to be pretty late. . . .
Bill: You never know who you might be turning down.
Betty: Sorry. Nice try, though.
Bill: Sure thing.

　(*Bell.*)

　Is this seat taken?
Betty: No it's not.
Bill: Would you mind if I sit here?
Betty: Yes I would.
Bill: Oh.

　(*Bell.*)

　Is this chair taken?
Betty: No it's not.
Bill: Would you mind if I sit here?
Betty: No. Go ahead.
Bill: Thanks. (*He sits. She continues reading.*) Everyplace else seems to be taken.
Betty: Mm-hm.
Bill: Great place.
Betty: Mm-hm.
Bill: What's the book?
Betty: I just wanted to read in quiet, if you don't mind.
Bill: No. Sure thing.

　(*Bell.*)

　Everyplace else seems to be taken.
Betty: Mm-hm.
Bill: Great place for reading.
Betty: Yes, I like it.
Bill: What's the book?
Betty: *The Sound and the Fury.*
Bill: Oh. Hemingway.

　(*Bell.*)

　What's the book?
Betty: *The Sound and the Fury.*
Bill: Oh. Faulkner.
Betty: Have you read it?
Bill: Not . . . actually. I've sure read *about* it, though. It's supposed to be great.
Betty: It is great.

Bill: I hear it's great. (*Small pause.*) Waiter?

    (*Bell.*)

    What's the book?
Betty: *The Sound and the Fury.*
Bill: Oh. Faulkner.
Betty: Have you read it?
Bill: I'm a Mets fan, myself.

    (*Bell.*)

Betty: Have you read it?
Bill: Yeah, I read it in college.
Betty: Where was college?
Bill: I went to Oral Roberts University.

    (*Bell.*)

Betty: Where was college?
Bill: I was lying. I never really went to college. I just like to party.

    (*Bell.*)

Betty: Where was college?
Bill: Harvard.
Betty: Do you like Faulkner?
Bill: I love Faulkner. I spent a whole winter reading him once.
Betty: I've just started.
Bill: I was so excited after ten pages that I went out and bought everything else he wrote. One of the greatest reading experiences of my life. I mean, all that incredible psychological understanding. Page after page of gorgeous prose. His profound grasp of the mystery of time and human existence. The smells of the earth . . . What do you think?
Betty: I think it's pretty boring.

    (*Bell.*)

Bill: What's the book?
Betty: *The Sound and the Fury.*
Bill: Oh! Faulkner!
Betty: Do you like Faulkner?
Bill: I love Faulkner.
Betty: He's incredible.
Bill: I spent a whole winter reading him once.
Betty: I was so excited after ten pages that I went out and bought everything else he wrote.
Bill: All that incredible psychological understanding.
Betty: And the prose is so gorgeous.
Bill: And the way he's grasped the mystery of time—
Betty: —and human existence. I can't believe I've waited this long to read him.
Bill: You never know. You might not have liked him before.
Betty: That's true.

Bill: You might not have been ready for him. You have to hit these things at the right moment or it's no good.
Betty: That's happened to me.
Bill: It's all in the timing. (*Small pause.*) My name's Bill, by the way.
Betty: I'm Betty.
Bill: Hi.
Betty: Hi. (*Small pause.*)
Bill: Yes I thought reading Faulkner was . . . a great experience.
Betty: Yes. (*Small pause.*)
Bill: The Sound and the Fury. . . . (*Another small pause.*)
Betty: Well. Onwards and upwards. (*She goes back to her book.*)
Bill: Waiter—?

(*Bell.*)

You have to hit these things at the right moment or it's no good.
Betty: That's happened to me.
Bill: It's all in the timing. My name's Bill, by the way.
Betty: I'm Betty.
Bill: Hi.
Betty: Hi.
Bill: Do you come in here a lot?
Betty: Actually I'm just in town for two days from Pakistan.
Bill: Oh. Pakistan.

(*Bell.*)

My name's Bill, by the way.
Betty: I'm Betty.
Bill: Hi.
Betty: Hi.
Bill: Do you come in here a lot?
Betty: Every once in a while. Do you?
Bill: Not so much anymore. Not as much as I used to. Before my nervous breakdown.

(*Bell.*)

Do you come in here a lot?
Betty: Why are you asking?
Bill: Just interested.
Betty: Are you really interested, or do you just want to pick me up?
Bill: No, I'm really interested.
Betty: Why would you be interested in whether I come in here a lot?
Bill: I'm just . . . getting acquainted.
Betty: Maybe you're only interested for the sake of making small talk long enough to ask me back to your place to listen to some music, or because you've just rented this great tape for your VCR, or because you've got some terrific unknown Django Reinhardt record, only all you really want to do is fuck—which you won't do very well—after which you'll go into the bathroom and pee very loudly, then pad into the kitchen and get yourself a beer from the refrigerator without asking me whether I'd like anything,

and then you'll proceed to lie back down beside me and confess that you've got a girlfriend named Stephanie who's away at medical school in Belgium for a year, and that you've been involved with her—*off and on*—in what you'll call a very "intricate" relationship, for the past *seven* YEARS. None of which *interests* me, mister!

Bill: Okay.

(*Bell.*)

Do you come in here a lot?
Betty: Every other day, I think.
Bill: I come in here quite a lot and I don't remember seeing you.
Betty: I guess we must be on different schedules.
Bill: Missed connections.
Betty: Yes. Different time zones.
Bill: Amazing how you can live right next door to somebody in this town and never even know it.
Betty: I know.
Bill: City life.
Betty: It's crazy.
Bill: We probably pass each other in the street every day. Right in front of this place, probably.
Betty: Yep.
Bill (*looks around*): Well the waiters here sure seem to be in some different time zone. I can't seem to locate one anywhere. . . . Waiter! (*He looks back.*) So what do you—(*He sees that she's gone back to her book.*)
Betty: I beg pardon?
Bill: Nothing. Sorry.

(*Bell.*)

Betty: I guess we must be on different schedules.
Bill: Missed connections.
Betty: Yes. Different time zones.
Bill: Amazing how you can live right next door to somebody in this town and never even know it.
Betty: I know.
Bill: City life.
Betty: It's crazy.
Bill: You weren't waiting for somebody when I came in, were you?
Betty: Actually I was.
Bill: Oh. Boyfriend?
Betty: Sort of.
Bill: What's a sort-of boyfriend?
Betty: My husband.
Bill: Ah-ha.

(*Bell.*)

You weren't waiting for somebody when I came in, were you?
Betty: Actually I was.

Bill: Oh. Boyfriend?
Betty: Sort of.
Bill: What's a sort-of boyfriend?
Betty: We were meeting here to break up.
Bill: Mm-hm . . .

(*Bell.*)

What's a sort-of boyfriend?
Betty: My lover. Here she comes right now!

(*Bell.*)

Bill: You weren't waiting for somebody when I came in, were you?
Betty: No, just reading.
Bill: Sort of a sad occupation for a Friday night, isn't it? Reading here, all by yourself?
Betty: Do you think so?
Bill: Well sure. I mean, what's a good-looking woman like you doing out alone on a Friday night?
Betty: Trying to keep away from lines like that.
Bill: No, listen—

(*Bell.*)

You weren't waiting for somebody when I came in, were you?
Betty: No, just reading.
Bill: Sort of a sad occupation for a Friday night, isn't it? Reading here all by yourself?
Betty: I guess it is, in a way.
Bill: What's a good-looking woman like you doing out alone on a Friday night anyway? No offense, but . . .
Betty: I'm out alone on a Friday night for the first time in a very long time.
Bill: Oh.
Betty: You see, I just recently ended a relationship.
Bill: Oh.
Betty: Of rather long standing.
Bill: I'm sorry. (*Small pause.*) Well listen, since reading by yourself *is* such a sad occupation for a Friday night, would you like to go elsewhere?
Betty: No . . .
Bill: Do something else?
Betty: No thanks.
Bill: I was headed out to the movies in a while anyway.
Betty: I don't think so.
Bill: Big chance to let Faulkner catch his breath. All those long sentences get him pretty tired.
Betty: Thanks anyway.
Bill: Okay.
Betty: I appreciate the invitation.
Bill: Sure thing.

(*Bell.*)

You weren't waiting for somebody when I came in, were you?
Betty: No, just reading.
Bill: Sort of a sad occupation for a Friday night, isn't it? Reading here all by yourself?
Betty: I guess I was trying to think of it as existentially romantic. You know—cappuccino, great literature, rainy night . . .
Bill: That only works in Paris. We *could* hop the late plane to Paris. Get on a Concorde. Find a café . . .
Betty: I'm a little short on plane fare tonight.
Bill: Darn it, so am I.
Betty: To tell you the truth, I was headed to the movies after I finished this section. Would you like to come along? Since you can't locate a waiter?
Bill: That's a very nice offer, but . . .
Betty: Uh-huh. Girlfriend?
Bill: Two, actually. One of them's pregnant, and Stephanie—

(*Bell.*)

Betty: Girlfriend?
Bill: No, I don't have a girlfriend. Not if you mean the castrating bitch I dumped last night.

(*Bell.*)

Betty: Girlfriend?
Bill: Sort of. Sort of.
Betty: What's a sort-of girlfriend?
Bill: My mother.

(*Bell.*)

I just ended a relationship, actually.
Betty: Oh.
Bill: Of rather long standing.
Betty: I'm sorry to hear it.
Bill: This is my first night out alone in a long time. I feel a little bit at sea, to tell you the truth.
Betty: So you didn't stop to talk because you're a Moonie, or you have some weird political affiliation—?
Bill: Nope. Straight-down-the-ticket Republican.

(*Bell.*)

Straight-down-the-ticket Democrat.

(*Bell.*)

Can I tell you something about politics?

(*Bell.*)

I like to think of myself as a citizen of the universe.

(*Bell.*)

I'm unaffiliated.

Betty: That's a relief. So am I.
Bill: I vote my beliefs.
Betty: Labels are not important.
Bill: Labels are not important, exactly. Take me, for example. I mean, what does it matter if I had a two-point at—

(*Bell.*)

three-point at—

(*Bell.*)

four-point at college? Or if I did come from Pittsburgh—

(*Bell.*)

Cleveland—

(*Bell.*)

Westchester County?
Betty: Sure.
Bill: I believe that a man is what he is.

(*Bell.*)

A person is what he is.

(*Bell.*)

A person is . . . what they are.
Betty: I think so too.
Bill: So what if I admire Trotsky?

(*Bell.*)

So what if I once had a total-body liposuction?

(*Bell.*)

So what if I don't have a penis?

(*Bell.*)

So what if I spent a year in the Peace Corps? I was acting on my convictions.
Betty: Sure.
Bill: You just can't hang a sign on a person.
Betty: Absolutely. I'll bet you're a Scorpio.

(*Many bells ring.*)

Listen, I was headed to the movies after I finished this section. Would you like to come along?
Bill: That sounds like fun. What's playing?
Betty: A couple of the really early Woody Allen movies.
Bill: Oh.
Betty: You don't like Woody Allen?

Bill: Sure. I like Woody Allen.
Betty: But you're not crazy about Woody Allen.
Bill: Those early ones kind of get on my nerves.
Betty: Uh-huh.

  (*Bell.*)

Bill: Y'know I was headed to the—
Betty (simultaneously): I was thinking about—
Bill: I'm sorry.
Betty: No, go ahead.
Bill: I was going to say that I was headed to the movies in a little while, and . . .
Betty: So was I.
Bill: The Woody Allen festival?
Betty: Just up the street.
Bill: Do you like the early ones?
Betty: I think anybody who doesn't ought to be run off the planet.
Bill: How many times have you seen *Bananas*?
Betty: Eight times.
Bill: Twelve. So are you still interested? (*Long pause.*)
Betty: Do you like Entenmann's crumb cake . . . ?
Bill: Last night I went out at two in the morning to get one. Did you have an Etch-a-Sketch as a child?
Betty: Yes! And do you like Brussels sprouts? (*Pause.*)
Bill: No, I think they're disgusting.
Betty: They *are* disgusting!
Bill: Do you still believe in marriage in spite of current sentiments against it?
Betty: Yes.
Bill: And children?
Betty: Three of them.
Bill: Two girls and a boy.
Betty: Harvard, Vassar, and Brown.
Bill: And will you love me?
Betty: Yes.
Bill: And cherish me forever?
Betty: Yes.
Bill: Do you still want to go to the movies?
Betty: Sure thing.
Bill and Betty (together): Waiter!

BLACKOUT

Questions

1. Ives originally planned to set *Sure Thing* at a bus stop. What does its current setting in a café suggest about the characters?
2. What happens on stage when the bell rings?
3. Who is the protagonist? What does the protagonist want?
4. Does the play have a dramatic question?
5. Does this play have a climax? If so, where does it occur?

6. How well developed are the two characters in the play? Why does Ives not tell us very much about them?
7. What do the two characters seem to find appealing, or not appealing, in each other?
8. When the characters restate something after the bell rings, do you think they are really expressing something new or simply telling the other person what he or she wants to hear?
9. How would you describe the theme of *Sure Thing*?

Suggestions for Writing on David Ives's *Sure Thing*

1. "*Sure Thing* is not a funny play because it isn't realistic. Conversations just don't happen this way." Discuss that opinion. Do you agree or disagree about the success of Ives's humor?
2. Choose a passage that includes at least one instance of the bell ringing. Why does the bell ring at that particular moment or moments? What does it signify? What does it suggest about what the characters seek in each other and in a relationship?
3. What does *Sure Thing* imply about romantic relationships, or at least about the beginnings of such relationships? Do you find Ives's view encouraging or depressing? Make an argument for why Ives is correct in his views of love—or incorrect.
4. Pick one of the references in *Sure Thing* (for example, William Faulkner's work or Woody Allen's movies) and write two or three paragraphs about what the reference adds to the play. Why does Ives include it? How does it influence your understanding of the events and characters in the play?

The title page of the First Folio—published in 1623 (after Shakespeare's death) and the first collected edition of his plays.

William Shakespeare

William Shakespeare (1564–1616) is still the best-known and most-performed playwright in the English language. Son of a glove maker and merchant who was high bailiff (or mayor) of the town, he probably attended grammar school and learned to read Latin authors in the original. By 1592 Shakespeare had become well known and envied as an actor and playwright in London. From 1594 until he retired, he belonged to the same theatrical company, the Lord Chamberlain's Men (later renamed the King's Men in honor of their patron, James I), for whom he wrote thirty-six plays—some of them, such as Hamlet and King Lear, profound reworkings of old plays. As an actor, Shakespeare is believed to have played supporting roles, such as the ghost of Hamlet's father. In time he became quite prosperous as one of the major shareholders of the company, which was very successful. The company moved into the Globe in 1599, and in 1608 bought the fashionable Blackfriars as well. Plays were then regarded as entertainments of little literary merit, like comic books today, and Shakespeare did not bother to supervise their publication. After writing The Tempest (1611), the last play entirely from his hand, he retired to Stratford, where since 1597 he had owned the second-largest house in town. Most critics agree that when Shakespeare wrote Othello, about 1604, he was at the height of his powers.

Picturing
OTHELLO

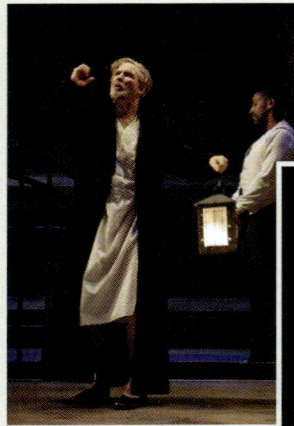

▲ Desdemona's father, Brabantio, *page 565.*

▲ Desdemona arrives in Cyprus, *page 587.*

◄ Othello and Desdemona, *page 578.*

▲ Desdemona offers the wrong handkerchief, *page 619.*

▲ Iago's machinations, *page 626.*

► Iago with the fateful handkerchief, *page 613.*

▶ Iago advises Cassio, *page 598*.

▲ Drunken Cassio fights, *page 594*.

▲ Iago plants doubts about Desdemona, *page 608*.

▼ Othello despairs, *page 634*.

▶ Othello smothers Desdemona, *page 651*.

▶ Enter Othello, *page 648*.

560 Chapter 13 Love

Othello, the Moor of Venice

1604?

Edited by David Bevington

THE NAMES OF THE ACTORS

Othello, the Moor
Brabantio, [a senator,] father to Desdemona
Cassio, an honorable lieutenant [to Othello]
Iago, [Othello's ancient,] a villain
Roderigo, a gulled gentleman
Duke of Venice
Senators [of Venice]
Montano, governor of Cyprus
Gentlemen of Cyprus
Lodovico and Gratiano, [kinsmen to Brabantio,] two noble Venetians
Sailors
Clown
Desdemona, [daughter to Brabantio and] wife to Othello
Emilia, wife to Iago
Bianca, a courtesan [and mistress to Cassio]
[*A Messenger*
A Herald
A Musician
Servants, Attendants, Officers, Senators, Musicians, Gentlemen

SCENE. Venice; a seaport in Cyprus]

ACT I

SCENE I [VENICE. A STREET.]

Enter Roderigo and Iago.

Roderigo: Tush, never tell me!° I take it much unkindly
   That thou, Iago, who hast had my purse
   As if the strings were thine, shouldst know of this.°

NOTE ON THE TEXT: This text of *Othello* is based on that of the First Folio, or large collection, of Shakespeare's plays (1623). But there are many differences between the Folio text and that of the play's first printing in the Quarto, or small volume, of 1621 (eighteen or nineteen years after the play's first performance). Some readings from the Quarto are included. For the reader's convenience, some material has been added by the editor, David Bevington (some indications of scene, some stage directions). Such additions are enclosed in brackets. Mr. Bevington's text and notes were prepared for his book *The Complete Works of Shakespeare*, updated 4th ed. (New York: Longman, 1997).

PRODUCTION PHOTOS: The photos included are from the 2003 production of *Othello* by the Guthrie Theater of Minneapolis, with Lester Purry (Othello), Bill McCallum (Iago), Cheyenne Casebier (Desdemona), Robert O. Berdahl (Cassio), Virginia S. Burke (Emilia), Nathaniel Fuller (Brabantio), and Shawn Hamilton (Montano).

1 *never tell me* (An expression of incredulity, like "tell me another one.")   3 *this* i.e., Desdemona's elopement

Iago: 'Sblood,° but you'll not hear me.
　　If ever I did dream of such a matter,
　　Abhor me.
Roderigo: Thou toldst me thou didst hold him in thy hate.
Iago: Despise me
　　If I do not. Three great ones of the city,
　　In personal suit to make me his lieutenant,
　　Off-capped to him;° and by the faith of man,
　　I know my price, I am worth no worse a place.
　　But he, as loving his own pride and purposes,
　　Evades them with a bombast circumstance°
　　Horribly stuffed with epithets of war,°
　　And, in conclusion,
　　Nonsuits° my mediators. For, "Certes,"° says he,
　　"I have already chose my officer."
　　And what was he?
　　Forsooth, a great arithmetician,°
　　One Michael Cassio, a Florentine,
　　A fellow almost damned in a fair wife,°
　　That never set a squadron in the field
　　Nor the division of a battle° knows
　　More than a spinster°—unless the bookish theoric,°
　　Wherein the togaed° consuls° can propose°
　　As masterly as he. Mere prattle without practice
　　Is all his soldiership. But he, sir, had th' election;
　　And I, of whom his° eyes had seen the proof
　　At Rhodes, at Cyprus, and on other grounds
　　Christened° and heathen, must be beleed and calmed°
　　By debitor and creditor.° This countercaster,°
　　He, in good time,° must his lieutenant be,
　　And I—God bless the mark!°—his Moorship's ancient.°
Roderigo: By heaven, I rather would have been his hangman.°
Iago: Why, there's no remedy. 'Tis the curse of service;
　　Preferment° goes by letter and affection,°

---

4 *'Sblood* by His (Christ's) blood   11 *him* i.e., Othello   14 *bombast circumstance* wordy evasion. (Bombast is cotton padding.)   15 *epithets of war* military expressions   17 *Nonsuits* rejects the petition of.   *Certes* certainly   20 *arithmetician* i.e., a man whose military knowledge is merely theoretical, based on books of tactics   22 *A . . . wife* (Cassio does not seem to be married, but his counterpart in Shakespeare's source does have a woman in his house. See also IV, i, 127.)   24 *division of a battle* disposition of a military unit   25 *a spinster* i.e., a housewife, one whose regular occupation is spinning.   *theoric* theory   26 *togaed* wearing the toga.   *consuls* counselors, senators.   *propose* discuss   29 *his* i.e., Othello's   31 *Christened* Christian.   *beleed and calmed* left to leeward without wind, becalmed. (A sailing metaphor.)   32 *debitor and creditor* (A name for a system of bookkeeping, here used as a contemptuous nickname for Cassio.)   *countercaster* i.e., bookkeeper, one who tallies with *counters,* or "metal disks." (Said contemptuously.)   33 *in good time* opportunely, i.e., forsooth   34 *God bless the mark* (Perhaps originally a formula to ward off evil; here an expression of impatience.)   *ancient* standard-bearer, ensign   35 *his hangman* his executioner   37 *Preferment* promotion.   *letter and affection* personal influence and favoritism

                    And not by old gradation,° where each second
                    Stood heir to th' first. Now, sir, be judge yourself
                    Whether I in any just term° am affined°   40
                    To love the Moor.
Roderigo: I would not follow him then.
Iago: O sir, content you.°
                    I follow him to serve my turn upon him.
                    We cannot all be masters, nor all masters   45
                    Cannot be truly° followed. You shall mark
                    Many a duteous and knee-crooking knave
                    That, doting on his own obsequious bondage,
                    Wears out his time, much like his master's ass,
                    For naught but provender, and when he's old, cashiered.°   50
                    Whip me° such honest knaves. Others there are
                    Who, trimmed in forms and visages of duty,°
                    Keep yet their hearts attending on themselves,
                    And, throwing but shows of service on their lords,
                    Do well thrive by them, and when they have lined their coats,°   55
                    Do themselves homage.° These fellows have some soul,
                    And such a one do I profess myself. For, sir,
                    It is as sure as you are Roderigo,
                    Were I the Moor I would not be Iago.°
                    In following him, I follow but myself—   60
                    Heaven is my judge, not I for love and duty,
                    But seeming so for my peculiar° end.
                    For when my outward action doth demonstrate
                    The native° act and figure° of my heart
                    In compliment extern,° 'tis not long after   65
                    But I will wear my heart upon my sleeve
                    For daws° to peck at. I am not what I am.°
Roderigo: What a full° fortune does the thick-lips° owe°
                    If he can carry 't thus!°
Iago: Call up her father.
                    Rouse him, make after him, poison his delight,   70
                    Proclaim him in the streets; incense her kinsmen,
                    And, though he in a fertile climate dwell,
                    Plague him with flies.° Though that his joy be joy,°

38 *old gradation* step-by-step seniority, the traditional way   40 *term* respect.   *affined* bound   43 *content you* don't you worry about that   46 *truly* faithfully   50 *cashiered* dismissed from service   51 *Whip me* whip, as far as I'm concerned   52 *trimmed . . . duty* dressed up in the mere form and show of dutifulness   55 *lined their coats* i.e., stuffed their purses   56 *Do themselves homage* i.e., attend to self-interest solely   59 *Were . . . Iago* i.e., if I were able to assume command, I certainly would not choose to remain a subordinate, or, I would keep a suspicious eye on a flattering subordinate   62 *peculiar* particular, personal   64 *native* innate.   *figure* shape, intent   65 *compliment extern* outward show. (Conforming in this case to the inner workings and intention of the heart.)   67 *daws* small crowlike birds, proverbially stupid and avaricious.   *I am not what I am* i.e., I am not one who wears his heart on his sleeve   68 *full* swelling.   *thick-lips* (Elizabethans often applied the term "Moor" to blacks.)   *owe* own   69 *carry 't thus* carry this off   72–73 *though . . . flies* though he seems prosperous and happy now, vex him with misery   73 *Though . . . be joy* although he seems fortunate and happy. (Repeats the idea of line 72.)

  Yet throw such changes of vexation° on 't
  As it may° lose some color.°
Roderigo: Here is her father's house. I'll call aloud.
Iago: Do, with like timorous° accent and dire yell
  As when, by night and negligence,° the fire
  Is spied in populous cities.
Roderigo: What ho, Brabantio! Signor Brabantio, ho!
Iago: Awake! What ho, Brabantio! Thieves, thieves, thieves!
  Look to your house, your daughter, and your bags!
  Thieves, thieves!

 Brabantio [enters] above [at a window].°

Brabantio: What is the reason of this terrible summons?
  What is the matter° there?
Roderigo: Signor, is all your family within?
Iago: Are your doors locked?
Brabantio: Why, wherefore ask you this?
Iago: Zounds,° sir, you're robbed. For shame, put on your gown!
  Your heart is burst; you have lost half your soul.
  Even now, now, very now, an old black ram
  Is tupping° your white ewe. Arise, arise!
  Awake the snorting° citizens with the bell,
  Or else the devil° will make a grandsire of you.
  Arise, I say!
Brabantio: What, have you lost your wits?
Roderigo: Most reverend signor, do you know my voice?
Brabantio: Not I. What are you?
Roderigo: My name is Roderigo.
Brabantio: The worser welcome.
  I have charged thee not to haunt about my doors.
  In honest plainness thou hast heard me say
  My daughter is not for thee; and now, in madness,
  Being full of supper and distempering° drafts,
  Upon malicious bravery° dost thou come
  To start° my quiet.
Roderigo: Sir, sir, sir—
Brabantio: But thou must needs be sure
  My spirits and my place° have in° their power
  To make this bitter to thee.
Roderigo: Patience, good sir.
Brabantio: What tell'st thou me of robbing? This is Venice;

---

74 *changes of vexation* vexing changes   75 *As it may* that may cause it to. *some color* some of its fresh gloss   77 *timorous* frightening   78 *and negligence* i.e., by negligence   83 s.d. *at a window* (This stage direction, from the Quarto, probably calls for an appearance on the gallery above and rearstage.)   85 *the matter* your business   88 *Zounds* by His (Christ's) wounds   91 *tupping* covering, copulating with. (Said of sheep.)   92 *snorting* snoring   93 *the devil* (The devil was conventionally pictured as black.)   102 *distempering* intoxicating   103 *Upon malicious bravery* with hostile intent to defy me   104 *start* startle, disrupt   106 *My spirits and my place* my temperament and my authority of office. *have in* have it in

       My house is not a grange.°
Roderigo: Most grave Brabantio,
       In simple° and pure soul I come to you.   110
Iago: Zounds, sir, you are one of those that will not serve God if the devil bid you.
       Because we come to do you service and you think we are ruffians, you'll have your
       daughter covered with a Barbary° horse; you'll have your nephews° neigh to you;
       you'll have coursers° for cousins° and jennets° for germans.°
Brabantio: What profane wretch art thou?   115
Iago: I am one, sir, that comes to tell you your daughter and the Moor are now
       making the beast with two backs.
Brabantio: Thou art a villain.
Iago: You are—a senator.°
Brabantio: This thou shalt answer.° I know thee, Roderigo.
Roderigo: Sir, I will answer anything. But I beseech you,   120
       If't be your pleasure and most wise° consent—
       As partly I find it is—that your fair daughter,
       At this odd-even° and dull watch o' the night,
       Transported with° no worse nor better guard
       But with a knave° of common hire, a gondolier,   125
       To the gross clasps of a lascivious Moor—
       If this be known to you and your allowance°
       We then have done you bold and saucy° wrongs.
       But if you know not this, my manners tell me
       We have your wrong rebuke. Do not believe   130
       That, from° the sense of all civility,°
       I thus would play and trifle with your reverence.°
       Your daughter, if you have not given her leave,
       I say again, hath made a gross revolt,
       Tying her duty, beauty, wit,° and fortunes   135
       In an extravagant° and wheeling° stranger°
       Of here and everywhere. Straight° satisfy yourself.
       If she be in her chamber or your house,
       Let loose on me the justice of the state
       For thus deluding you.
Brabantio: Strike on the tinder,° ho!   140
       Give me a taper! Call up all my people!
       This accident° is not unlike my dream.
       Belief of it oppresses me already.
       Light, I say, light!   *Exit [above].*

---

109 *grange* isolated country house   110 *simple* sincere   113 *Barbary* from northern Africa (and hence associated with Othello). *nephews* i.e., grandsons   114 *coursers* powerful horses. *cousins* kinsmen. *jennets* small Spanish horses. *germans* near relatives   118 *a senator* (Said with mock politeness, as though the word itself were an insult.)   119 *answer* be held accountable for   121 *wise* well-informed   123 *odd-even* between one day and the next, i.e., about midnight   124 *with* by   125 *But with a knave* than by a low fellow, a servant   127 *allowance* permission   128 *saucy* insolent   131 *from* contrary to. *civility* good manners, decency   132 *your reverence* the respect due to you   135 *wit* intelligence   136 *extravagant* expatriate, wandering far from home. *wheeling* roving about, vagabond. *stranger* foreigner   137 *Straight* straightway   140 *tinder* charred linen ignited by a spark from flint and steel, used to light torches or *tapers* (lines 141, 166)   142 *accident* occurrence, event

Roused from sleep, Desdemona's father, Brabantio, rushes to the street to search out his daughter (I, i, 160–180).

Iago: Farewell, for I must leave you.
    It seems not meet° nor wholesome to my place°   145
    To be producted°—as, if I stay, I shall—
    Against the Moor. For I do know the state,
    However this may gall° him with some check,°
    Cannot with safety cast° him, for he's embarked°
    With such loud reason° to the Cyprus wars,   150
    Which even now stands in act,° that, for their souls,°
    Another of his fathom° they have none

145 *meet* fitting.   *place* position (as ensign)   146 *producted* produced (as a witness)   148 *gall* rub; oppress. *check* rebuke   149 *cast* dismiss. *embarked* engaged   150 *loud reason* unanimous shout of confirmation (in the Senate)   151 *stands in act* are going on.   *for their souls* to save themselves   152 *fathom* i.e., ability, depth of experience

  To lead their business; in which regard,°
  Though I do hate him as I do hell pains,
  Yet for necessity of present life°   155
  I must show out a flag and sign of love,
  Which is indeed but sign. That you shall surely find him,
  Lead to the Sagittary° the raisèd search,°
  And there will I be with him. So farewell.   *Exit.*

  Enter [below] Brabantio [in his nightgown°] with servants and torches.

Brabantio: It is too true an evil. Gone she is;   160
  And what's to come of my despisèd time°
  Is naught but bitterness. Now, Roderigo,
  Where didst thou see her?—O unhappy girl!—
  With the Moor, sayst thou?—Who would be a father!—
  How didst thou know 'twas she?—O, she deceives me   165
  Past thought!—What said she to you?—Get more tapers.
  Raise all my kindred.—Are they married, think you?
Roderigo: Truly, I think they are.
Brabantio: O heaven! How got she out? O treason of the blood!
  Fathers, from hence trust not your daughters' minds   170
  By what you see them act. Is there not charms°
  By which the property° of youth and maidhood
  May be abused?° Have you not read, Roderigo,
  Of some such thing?
Roderigo: Yes, sir, I have indeed.
Brabantio: Call up my brother.—O, would you had had her!—   175
  Some one way, some another.—Do you know
  Where we may apprehend her and the Moor?
Roderigo: I think I can discover° him, if you please
  To get good guard and go along with me.
Brabantio: Pray you, lead on. At every house I'll call;   180
  I may command° at most.—Get weapons, ho!
  And raise some special officers of night.—
  On, good Roderigo. I will deserve° your pains.

  Exeunt.

SCENE II [VENICE. ANOTHER STREET, BEFORE OTHELLO'S LODGINGS.]

  Enter Othello, Iago, attendants with torches.

Iago: Though in the trade of war I have slain men,
  Yet do I hold it very stuff° o' the conscience

---

153 *in which regard* out of regard for which   155 *life* livelihood   158 *Sagittary* (An inn or house where Othello and Desdemona are staying, named for its sign of Sagittarius, or Centaur.)   *raisèd search* search party roused out of sleep   159 s.d. *nightgown* dressing gown. (This costuming is specified in the Quarto text.)   161 *time* i.e., remainder of life   171 *charms* spells   172 *property* special quality, nature   173 *abused* deceived   178 *discover* reveal, uncover   181 *command* demand assistance   183 *deserve* show gratitude for   2 *very stuff* essence, basic material (continuing the metaphor of *trade* from line 1)

To do no contrived° murder. I lack iniquity
Sometimes to do me service. Nine or ten times
I had thought t' have yerked° him° here under the ribs.
Othello: 'Tis better as it is.
Iago: Nay, but he prated,
And spoke such scurvy and provoking terms
Against your honor
That, with the little godliness I have,
I did full hard forbear him.° But, I pray you, sir,
Are you fast married? Be assured of this,
That the magnifico° is much beloved,
And hath in his effect° a voice potential
As double as the Duke's. He will divorce you,
Or put upon you what restraint or grievance
The law, with all his might to enforce it on,
Will give him cable.°
Othello: Let him do his spite.
My services which I have done the seigniory°
Shall out-tongue his complaints. 'Tis yet to know°—
Which, when I know that boasting is an honor,
I shall promulgate—I fetch my life and being
From men of royal siege,° and my demerits°
May speak unbonneted° to as proud a fortune
As this that I have reached. For know, Iago,
But that I love the gentle Desdemona,
I would not my unhousèd° free condition
Put into circumscription and confine°
For the sea's worth.° But look, what lights come yond?

Enter Cassio [and certain officers°] with torches.

Iago: Those are the raisèd father and his friends.
You were best go in.
Othello: Not I. I must be found.
My parts, my title, and my perfect soul°
Shall manifest me rightly. Is it they?
Iago: By Janus,° I think no.
Othello: The servants of the Duke? And my lieutenant?
The goodness of the night upon you, friends!
What is the news?

3 *contrived* premeditated   5 *yerked* stabbed.   *him* i.e., Roderigo   10 *I . . . him* I restrained myself with great difficulty from assaulting him   12 *magnifico* Venetian grandee, i.e., Brabantio   13 *in his effect* at his command.   *potential* powerful   17 *cable* i.e., scope   18 *seigniory* Venetian government   19 *yet to know* not yet widely known   22 *siege* i.e., rank. (Literally, a seat used by a person of distinction.)   *demerits* deserts   23 *unbonneted* without removing the hat, i.e., on equal terms (?) (Or "with hat off," "in all due modesty.")   26 *unhousèd* unconfined, undomesticated   27 *circumscription and confine* restriction and confinement   28 *the sea's worth* all the riches at the bottom of the sea.   s.d. *officers* (The Quarto text calls for "Cassio with lights, officers with torches.")   31 *My . . . soul* my natural gifts, my position or reputation, and my unflawed conscience   33 *Janus* Roman two-faced god of beginnings

Cassio: The Duke does greet you, General,
    And he requires your haste-post-haste appearance
    Even on the instant.
Othello: What is the matter,° think you?
Cassio: Something from Cyprus, as I may divine.°
    It is a business of some heat.° The galleys   40
    Have sent a dozen sequent° messengers
    This very night at one another's heels,
    And many of the consuls,° raised and met,
    Are at the Duke's already. You have been hotly called for;
    When, being not at your lodging to be found,   45
    The Senate hath sent about° three several° quests
    To search you out.
Othello: 'Tis well I am found by you.
    I will but spend a word here in the house
    And go with you.   [*Exit.*]
Cassio: Ancient, what makes° he here?
Iago: Faith, he tonight hath boarded° a land carrack.°   50
    If it prove lawful prize,° he's made forever.
Cassio: I do not understand.
Iago: He's married.
Cassio: To who?

[*Enter Othello.*]

Iago: Marry,° to—Come, Captain, will you go?
Othello: Have with you.°
Cassio: Here comes another troop to seek for you.   55

    Enter Brabantio, Roderigo, with officers and torches.°

Iago: It is Brabantio. General, be advised.°
    He comes to bad intent.
Othello: Holla! Stand there!
Roderigo: Signor, it is the Moor.
Brabantio: Down with him, thief!

[*They draw on both sides.*]

Iago: You, Roderigo! Come, sir, I am for you.
Othello: Keep up° your bright swords, for the dew will rust them.   60
    Good signor, you shall more command with years
    Than with your weapons.

---

38 *matter* business   39 *divine* guess   40 *heat* urgency   41 *sequent* successive   43 *consuls* senators   46 *about* all over the city.   *several* separate   49 *makes* does   50 *boarded* gone aboard and seized as an act of piracy (with sexual suggestion).   *carrack* large merchant ship   51 *prize* booty   53 *Marry* (An oath, originally "by the Virgin Mary"; here used with wordplay on *married.*)   54 *Have with you* i.e., let's go   55 s.d. *officers and torches* (The Quarto text calls for "others with lights and weapons.")   56 *be advised* be on your guard   60 *Keep up* keep in the sheath

Brabantio: O thou foul thief, where hast thou stowed my daughter?
   Damned as thou art, thou hast enchanted her!
   For I'll refer me° to all things of sense,°
   If she in chains of magic were not bound
   Whether a maid so tender, fair, and happy,
   So opposite to marriage that she shunned
   The wealthy curlèd darlings of our nation,
   Would ever have, t' incur a general mock,
   Run from her guardage° to the sooty bosom
   Of such a thing as thou—to fear, not to delight.
   Judge me the world if 'tis not gross in sense°
   That thou hast practiced on her with foul charms,
   Abused her delicate youth with drugs or minerals°
   That weaken motion.° I'll have 't disputed on;°
   'Tis probable and palpable to thinking.
   I therefore apprehend and do attach° thee
   For an abuser of the world, a practicer
   Of arts inhibited° and out of warrant.°—
   Lay hold upon him! If he do resist,
   Subdue him at his peril.
Othello: Hold your hands,
   Both you of my inclining° and the rest.
   Were it my cue to fight, I should have known it
   Without a prompter.—Whither will you that I go
   To answer this your charge?
Brabantio: To prison, till fit time
   Of law and course of direct session°
   Call thee to answer.
Othello: What if I do obey?
   How may the Duke be therewith satisfied,
   Whose messengers are here about my side
   Upon some present business of the state
   To bring me to him?
Officer: 'Tis true, most worthy signor.
   The Duke's in council, and your noble self,
   I am sure, is sent for.
Brabantio: How? The Duke in council?
   In this time of the night? Bring him away.°
   Mine's not an idle° cause. The Duke himself,
   Or any of my brothers of the state,
   Cannot but feel this wrong as 'twere their own;

---

65 *refer me* submit my case.   *things of sense* commonsense understandings, or, creatures possessing common sense   71 *her guardage* my guardianship of her   73 *gross in sense* obvious   75 *minerals* i.e., poisons   76 *weaken motion* impair the vital faculties.   *disputed on* argued in court by professional counsel, debated by experts   78 *attach* arrest   80 *arts inhibited* prohibited arts, black magic.   *out of warrant* illegal   83 *inclining* following, party   88 *course of direct session* regular or specially convened legal proceedings   96 *away* right along   97 *idle* trifling

For if such actions may have passage free,° 100
Bondslaves and pagans shall our statesmen be.

Exeunt.

SCENE III [VENICE. A COUNCIL CHAMBER.]

Enter Duke [and] Senators [and sit at a table, with lights], and Officers.° [The Duke and Senators are reading dispatches.]

Duke: There is no composition° in these news
    That gives them credit.
First Senator: Indeed, they are disproportioned.°
    My letters say a hundred and seven galleys.
Duke: And mine, a hundred forty.
Second Senator: And mine, two hundred. 5
    But though they jump° not on a just° account—
    As in these cases, where the aim° reports
    'Tis oft with difference—yet do they all confirm
    A Turkish fleet, and bearing up to Cyprus.
Duke: Nay, it is possible enough to judgment. 10
    I do not so secure me in the error
    But the main article I do approve°
    In fearful sense.
Sailor (within):   What ho, what ho, what ho!

Enter Sailor.

Officer: A messenger from the galleys.
Duke: Now, what's the business? 15
Sailor: The Turkish preparation° makes for Rhodes.
    So was I bid report here to the state
    By Signor Angelo.
Duke: How say you by° this change?
First Senator: This cannot be
    By no assay° of reason. 'Tis a pageant° 20
    To keep us in false gaze.° When we consider
    Th' importancy of Cyprus to the Turk,
    And let ourselves again but understand
    That, as it more concerns the Turk than Rhodes,
    So may he with more facile question bear it,° 25
    For that° it stands not in such warlike brace,°
    But altogether lacks th' abilities°

---

100 *have passage free* are allowed to go unchecked   s.d. *Enter . . . Officers* (The Quarto text calls for the Duke and senators to "sit at a table with lights and attendants.")   1 *composition* consistency   3 *disproportioned* inconsistent   6 *jump* agree.   *just* exact   7 *the aim* conjecture   11–12 *I do not . . . approve* I do not take such (false) comfort in the discrepancies that I fail to perceive the main point, i.e., that the Turkish fleet is threatening   16 *preparation* fleet prepared for battle   19 *by* about   20 *assay* test.   *pageant* mere show   21 *in false gaze* looking the wrong way   25 *So may . . . it* so also he (the Turk) can more easily capture it (Cyprus)   26 *For that* since.   *brace* state of defense   27 *abilities* means of self-defense

                That Rhodes is dressed in°—if we make thought of this,
                We must not think the Turk is so unskillful°
                To leave that latest° which concerns him first,   30
                Neglecting an attempt of ease and gain
                To wake° and wage° a danger profitless.
Duke: Nay, in all confidence, he's not for Rhodes.
Officer: Here is more news.

                Enter a Messenger.

Messenger: The Ottomites, reverend and gracious,   35
                Steering with due course toward the isle of Rhodes,
                Have there injointed them° with an after° fleet.
First Senator: Ay, so I thought. How many, as you guess?
Messenger: Of thirty sail; and now they do restem
                Their backward course,° bearing with frank appearance°   40
                Their purposes toward Cyprus. Signor Montano,
                Your trusty and most valiant servitor,°
                With his free duty° recommends° you thus,
                And prays you to believe him.
Duke: 'Tis certain then for Cyprus.   45
                Marcus Luccicos, is not he in town?
First Senator: He's now in Florence.
Duke: Write from us to him, post-post-haste. Dispatch.
First Senator: Here comes Brabantio and the valiant Moor.

                Enter Brabantio, Othello, Cassio, Iago, Roderigo, and officers.

Duke: Valiant Othello, we must straight° employ you   50
                Against the general enemy° Ottoman.
                [*To Brabantio.*] I did not see you; welcome, gentle° signor.
                We lacked your counsel and your help tonight.
Brabantio: So did I yours. Good Your Grace, pardon me;
                Neither my place° nor aught I heard of business   55
                Hath raised me from my bed, nor doth the general care
                Take hold on me, for my particular° grief
                Is of so floodgate° and o'erbearing nature
                That it engluts° and swallows other sorrows
                And it is still itself.°
Duke: Why, what's the matter?   60
Brabantio: My daughter! O, my daughter!
Duke and Senators: Dead?
Brabantio: Ay, to me.
                She is abused,° stol'n from me, and corrupted

28 *dressed in* equipped with   29 *unskillful* deficient in judgment   30 *latest* last   32 *wake* stir up.   *wage* risk   37 *injointed them* joined themselves.   *after* second, following   39–40 *restem . . . course* retrace their original course   40 *frank appearance* undisguised intent   42 *servitor* officer under your command   43 *free duty* freely given and loyal service.   *recommends* commends himself and reports to   50 *straight* straightway   51 *general enemy* universal enemy to all Christendom   52 *gentle* noble   55 *place* official position   57 *particular* personal   58 *floodgate* i.e., overwhelming (as when floodgates are opened)   59 *engluts* engulfs   60 *is still itself* remains undiminished   62 *abused* deceived

Othello answers Brabantio's charges before the Duke (I, iii, 78–172).

> By spells and medicines bought of mountebanks;
> For nature so preposterously to err,
> Being not deficient,° blind, or lame of sense,° 65
> Sans° witchcraft could not.
> Duke: Whoe'er he be that in this foul proceeding
> Hath thus beguiled your daughter of herself,
> And you of her, the bloody book of law
> You shall yourself read in the bitter letter 70
> After your own sense°—yea, though our proper° son
> Stood in your action.°
> Brabantio: Humbly I thank Your Grace.
> Here is the man, this Moor, whom now it seems
> Your special mandate for the state affairs
> Hath hither brought.
> All: We are very sorry for 't. 75
> Duke [to Othello]: What, in your own part, can you say to this?
> Brabantio: Nothing, but this is so.
> Othello: Most potent, grave, and reverend signors,
>   My very noble and approved° good masters:
>   That I have ta'en away this old man's daughter, 80

65 *deficient* defective.   *lame of sense* deficient in sensory perception   66 *Sans* without   71 *After . . . sense* according to your own interpretation.   *our proper* my own   72 *Stood . . . action* were under your accusation   79 *approved* proved, esteemed

It is most true; true, I have married her.
The very head and front° of my offending
Hath this extent, no more. Rude° am I in my speech,
And little blessed with the soft phrase of peace;
For since these arms of mine had seven years' pith,°   85
Till now some nine moons wasted,° they have used
Their dearest° action in the tented field;
And little of this great world can I speak
More than pertains to feats of broils and battle,
And therefore little shall I grace my cause   90
In speaking for myself. Yet, by your gracious patience,
I will a round° unvarnished tale deliver
Of my whole course of love—what drugs, what charms,
What conjuration, and what mighty magic,
For such proceeding I am charged withal,°   95
I won his daughter.
Brabantio: A maiden never bold;
Of spirit so still and quiet that her motion
Blushed at herself;° and she, in spite of nature,
Of years,° of country, credit,° everything,
To fall in love with what she feared to look on!   100
It is a judgment maimed and most imperfect
That will confess° perfection so could err
Against all rules of nature, and must be driven
To find out practices° of cunning hell
Why this should be. I therefore vouch° again   105
That with some mixtures powerful o'er the blood,°
Or with some dram conjured to this effect,°
He wrought upon her.
Duke: To vouch this is no proof,
Without more wider° and more overt test°
Than these thin habits° and poor likelihoods°   110
Of modern seeming° do prefer° against him.
First Senator: But Othello, speak.
Did you by indirect and forcèd courses°
Subdue and poison this young maid's affections?
Or came it by request and such fair question°   115
As soul to soul affordeth?
Othello: I do beseech you,
Send for the lady to the Sagittary

---

82 *head and front* height and breadth, entire extent   83 *Rude* unpolished   85 *since . . . pith* i.e., since I was seven. *pith* strength, vigor   86 *Till . . . wasted* until some nine months ago (since when Othello has evidently not been on active duty, but in Venice)   87 *dearest* most valuable   92 *round* plain   95 *withal* with   97–98 *her . . . herself* i.e., she blushed easily at herself. (*Motion* can suggest the impulse of the soul or of the emotions, or physical movement.)   99 *years* i.e., difference in age.   *credit* virtuous reputation   102 *confess* concede (that)   104 *practices* plots   105 *vouch* assert   106 *blood* passions   107 *dram . . . effect* dose made by magical spells to have this effect   109 *more wider* fuller.   *test* testimony   110 *habits* garments, i.e., appearances.   *poor likelihoods* weak inferences   111 *modern seeming* commonplace assumption.   *prefer* bring forth   113 *forcèd courses* means used against her will   115 *question* conversation

And let her speak of me before her father.
If you do find me foul in her report,
The trust, the office I do hold of you   120
Not only take away, but let your sentence
Even fall upon my life.
Duke: Fetch Desdemona hither.
Othello: Ancient, conduct them. You best know the place.

[*Exeunt Iago and attendants.*]

And, till she come, as truly as to heaven
I do confess the vices of my blood,°   125
So justly° to your grave ears I'll present
How I did thrive in this fair lady's love,
And she in mine.
Duke: Say it, Othello.
Othello: Her father loved me, oft invited me,   130
Still° questioned me the story of my life
From year to year—the battles, sieges, fortunes
That I have passed.
I ran it through, even from my boyish days
To th' very moment that he bade me tell it,   135
Wherein I spoke of most disastrous chances,
Of moving accidents° by flood and field,
Of hairbreadth scapes i' th' imminent deadly breach,°
Of being taken by the insolent foe
And sold to slavery, of my redemption thence,   140
And portance° in my travels' history,
Wherein of antres° vast and deserts idle,°
Rough quarries,° rocks, and hills whose heads touch heaven,
It was my hint° to speak—such was my process—
And of the Cannibals that each other eat,   145
The Anthropophagi,° and men whose heads
Do grow beneath their shoulders. These things to hear
Would Desdemona seriously incline;
But still the house affairs would draw her thence,
Which ever as she could with haste dispatch   150
She'd come again, and with a greedy ear
Devour up my discourse. Which I, observing,
Took once a pliant° hour, and found good means
To draw from her a prayer of earnest heart
That I would all my pilgrimage dilate,°   155
Whereof by parcels° she had something heard,

125 *blood* passions, human nature   126 *justly* truthfully, accurately   131 *Still* continually   137 *moving accidents* stirring happenings   138 *imminent . . . breach* death-threatening gaps made in a fortification   141 *portance* conduct   142 *antres* caverns.   *idle* barren, desolate   143 *Rough quarries* rugged rock formations   144 *hint* occasion, opportunity   146 *Anthropophagi* man-eaters. (A term from Pliny's *Natural History*.)   153 *pliant* well-suiting   155 *dilate* relate in detail   156 *by parcels* piecemeal

But not intentively.° I did consent,
And often did beguile her of her tears,
When I did speak of some distressful stroke
That my youth suffered. My story being done, 160
She gave me for my pains a world of sighs.
She swore, in faith, 'twas strange, 'twas passing° strange,
'Twas pitiful, 'twas wondrous pitiful.
She wished she had not heard it, yet she wished
That heaven had made her° such a man. She thanked me, 165
And bade me, if I had a friend that loved her,
I should but teach him how to tell my story,
And that would woo her. Upon this hint° I spake.
She loved me for the dangers I had passed,
And I loved her that she did pity them. 170
This only is the witchcraft I have used.
Here comes the lady. Let her witness it.

Enter Desdemona, Iago, [and] attendants.

Duke: I think this tale would win my daughter too.
    Good Brabantio,
    Take up this mangled matter at the best.° 175
    Men do their broken weapons rather use
    Than their bare hands.
Brabantio: I pray you, hear her speak.
    If she confess that she was half the wooer,
    Destruction on my head if my bad blame
    Light on the man!—Come hither, gentle mistress. 180
    Do you perceive in all this noble company
    Where most you owe obedience?
Desdemona: My noble Father,
    I do perceive here a divided duty.
    To you I am bound for life and education;°
    My life and education both do learn° me 185
    How to respect you. You are the lord of duty;°
    I am hitherto your daughter. But here's my husband,
    And so much duty as my mother showed
    To you, preferring you before her father,
    So much I challenge° that I may profess 190
    Due to the Moor my lord.
Brabantio: God be with you! I have done.
    Please it Your Grace, on to the state affairs.
    I had rather to adopt a child than get° it.
    Come hither, Moor.   *[He joins the hands of Othello and Desdemona.]* 195

---

157 *intentively* with full attention, continuously   162 *passing* exceedingly   165 *made her* created her to be   168 *hint* opportunity. (Othello does not mean that she was dropping hints.)   175 *Take . . . best* make the best of a bad bargain   184 *education* upbringing   185 *learn* teach   186 *of duty* to whom duty is due   190 *challenge* claim   194 *get* beget

>   I here do give thee that with all my heart°
>   Which, but thou hast already, with all my heart°
>   I would keep from thee.—For your sake,° jewel,
>   I am glad at soul I have no other child,
>   For thy escape° would teach me tyranny,   200
>   To hang clogs° on them.—I have done, my lord.
> *Duke:* Let me speak like yourself,° and lay a sentence°
>   Which, as a grece° or step, may help these lovers
>   Into your favor.
>   When remedies° are past, the griefs are ended   205
>   By seeing the worst, which late on hopes depended.°
>   To mourn a mischief° that is past and gone
>   Is the next° way to draw new mischief on.
>   What° cannot be preserved when fortune takes,
>   Patience her injury a mockery makes.°   210
>   The robbed that smiles steals something from the thief;
>   He robs himself that spends a bootless grief.°
> *Brabantio:* So let the Turk of Cyprus us beguile,
>   We lose it not, so long as we can smile.
>   He bears the sentence well that nothing bears°   215
>   But the free comfort which from thence he hears,
>   But he bears both the sentence and the sorrow
>   That, to pay grief, must of poor patience borrow.°
>   These sentences, to sugar or to gall,
>   Being strong on both sides, are equivocal.°   220
>   But words are words. I never yet did hear
>   That the bruised heart was piercèd through the ear.°
>   I humbly beseech you, proceed to th' affairs of state.
> *Duke:* The Turk with a most mighty preparation makes for Cyprus. Othello, the
>   fortitude° of the place is best known to you; and though we have there a sub-   225
>   stitute° of most allowed° sufficiency, yet opinion, a sovereign mistress of
>   effects, throws a more safer voice on you.° You must therefore be content to
>   slubber° the gloss of your new fortunes with this more stubborn° and boisterous
>   expedition.
> *Othello:* The tyrant custom, most grave senators,   230
>   Hath made the flinty and steel couch of war

196 *with all my heart* wherein my whole affection has been engaged   197 *with all my heart* willingly, gladly   198 *For your sake* on your account   200 *escape* elopement   201 *clogs* (Literally, blocks of wood fastened to the legs of criminals or convicts to inhibit escape.)   202 *like yourself* i.e., as you would, in your proper temper.   *lay a sentence* apply a maxim   203 *grece* step   205 *remedies* hopes of remedy   206 *which . . . depended* which griefs were sustained until recently by hopeful anticipation   207 *mischief* misfortune, injury   208 *next* nearest   209 *What* whatever   210 *Patience . . . makes* patience laughs at the injury inflicted by fortune (and thus eases the pain)   212 *spends a bootless grief* indulges in unavailing grief   215–218 *He bears . . . borrow* a person well bears out your maxim who can enjoy its platitudinous comfort, free of all genuine sorrow, but anyone whose grief bankrupts his poor patience is left with your saying and his sorrow, too. (*Bears the sentence* also plays on the meaning, "receives judicial sentence.")   219–220 *These . . . equivocal* these fine maxims are equivocal, either sweet or bitter in their application   222 *piercèd . . . ear* i.e., surgically lanced and cured by mere words of advice   225 *fortitude* strength   226 *substitute* deputy.   *allowed* acknowledged   226–227 *opinion . . . on you* general opinion, an important determiner of affairs, chooses you as the best man   228 *slubber* soil, sully.   *stubborn* harsh, rough

>   My thrice-driven° bed of down. I do agnize°
>   A natural and prompt alacrity
>   I find in hardness,° and do undertake
>   These present wars against the Ottomites.   235
>   Most humbly therefore bending to your state,°
>   I crave fit disposition for my wife,
>   Due reference of place and exhibition,°
>   With such accommodation° and besort°
>   As levels° with her breeding.°   240
>
> *Duke:* Why, at her father's.
> *Brabantio:*   I will not have it so.
> *Othello:* Nor I.
> *Desdemona:*   Nor I. I would not there reside,
>   To put my father in impatient thoughts
>   By being in his eye. Most gracious Duke,
>   To my unfolding° lend your prosperous° ear,   245
>   And let me find a charter° in your voice,
>   T' assist my simpleness.
> *Duke:* What would you, Desdemona?
> *Desdemona:* That I did love the Moor to live with him,
>   My downright violence and storm of fortunes°   250
>   May trumpet to the world. My heart's subdued
>   Even to the very quality of my lord.°
>   I saw Othello's visage in his mind,
>   And to his honors and his valiant parts°
>   Did I my soul and fortunes consecrate.   255
>   So that, dear lords, if I be left behind
>   A moth° of peace, and he go to the war,
>   The rites° for why I love him are bereft me,
>   And I a heavy interim shall support
>   By his dear° absence. Let me go with him.   260
> *Othello:* Let her have your voice.°
>   Vouch with me, heaven, I therefore beg it not
>   To please the palate of my appetite,
>   Nor to comply with heat°—the young affects°
>   In me defunct—and proper° satisfaction,   265
>   But to be free° and bounteous to her mind.
>   And heaven defend° your good souls that you think°

232 *thrice-driven* thrice sifted, winnowed.   *agnize* know in myself, acknowledge   234 *hardness* hardship   236 *bending . . . state* bowing or kneeling to your authority   238 *reference . . . exhibition* provision of appropriate place to live and allowance of money   239 *accommodation* suitable provision. *besort* attendance   240 *levels* equals, suits. *breeding* social position, upbringing   245 *unfolding* explanation, proposal. *prosperous* propitious   246 *charter* privilege, authorization   250 *My . . . fortunes* my plain and total breach of social custom, taking my future by storm and disrupting my whole life   251–252 *My heart's . . . lord* my heart is brought wholly into accord with Othello's virtues; I love him for his virtues   254 *parts* qualities   257 *moth* i.e., one who consumes merely   258 *rites* rites of love (with a suggestion, too, of "rights," sharing)   260 *dear* (1) heartfelt (2) costly   261 *voice* consent   264 *heat* sexual passion. *young affects* passions of youth, desires   265 *proper* personal   266 *free* generous   267 *defend* forbid. *think* should think

Desdemona declares her loyalty to her husband Othello (I, iii, 182–301).

    I will your serious and great business scant
    When she is with me. No, when light-winged toys
    Of feathered Cupid seel° with wanton dullness   270
    My speculative and officed instruments,°
    That° my disports° corrupt and taint° my business,
    Let huswives make a skillet of my helm,
    And all indign° and base adversities
    Make head° against my estimation!°   275
Duke: Be it as you shall privately determine,
    Either for her stay or going. Th' affair cries haste,
    And speed must answer it.
A Senator: You must away tonight.
Desdemona: Tonight, my lord?
Duke: This night.
Othello: With all my heart.

270 *seel* i.e., make blind (as in falconry, by sewing up the eyes of the hawk during training)   271 *speculative . . . instruments* eyes and other faculties used in the performance of duty   272 *That* so that. *disports* sexual pastimes.   *taint* impair   274 *indign* unworthy, shameful   275 *Make head* raise an army. *estimation* reputation

Duke: At nine i' the morning here we'll meet again. 280
    Othello, leave some officer behind,
    And he shall our commission bring to you,
    With such things else of quality and respect°
    As doth import° you.
Othello: So please Your Grace, my ancient;
    A man he is of honesty and trust. 285
    To his conveyance I assign my wife,
    With what else needful Your Good Grace shall think
    To be sent after me.
Duke: Let it be so.
    Good night to everyone. [*To Brabantio.*] And, noble signor,
    If virtue no delighted° beauty lack, 290
    Your son-in-law is far more fair than black.
First Senator: Adieu, brave Moor. Use Desdemona well.
Brabantio: Look to her, Moor, if thou hast eyes to see.
    She has deceived her father, and may thee.

              Exeunt [Duke, Brabantio, Cassio, Senators, and officers].

Othello: My life upon her faith! Honest Iago, 295
    My Desdemona must I leave to thee.
    I prithee, let thy wife attend on her,
    And bring them after in the best advantage.°
    Come, Desdemona. I have but an hour
    Of love, of worldly matters and direction,° 300
    To spend with thee. We must obey the time.°

                        Exit [with Desdemona].

Roderigo: Iago—
Iago: What sayst thou, noble heart?
Roderigo: What will I do, think'st thou?
Iago: Why, go to bed and sleep. 305
Roderigo: I will incontinently° drown myself.
Iago: If thou dost, I shall never love thee after. Why, thou silly gentleman?
Roderigo: It is silliness to live when to live is torment; and then have we a prescrip-
    tion° to die when death is our physician.
Iago: O villainous!° I have looked upon the world for four times seven years, and, 310
    since I could distinguish betwixt a benefit and an injury, I never found man
    that knew how to love himself. Ere I would say I would drown myself for the
    love of a guinea hen,° I would change my humanity with a baboon.
Roderigo: What should I do? I confess it is my shame to be so fond,° but it is not
    in my virtue° to amend it. 315

---

283 *of quality and respect* of importance and relevance   284 *import* concern   290 *delighted* capable of delighting   298 *in . . . advantage* at the most favorable opportunity   300 *direction* instructions   301 *the time* the urgency of the present crisis   306 *incontinently* immediately, without self-restraint   308–309 *prescription* (1) right based on long-established custom (2) doctor's prescription   310 *villainous* i.e., what perfect nonsense   313 *guinea hen* (A slang term for a prostitute.)   314 *fond* infatuated   315 *virtue* strength, nature

Iago: Virtue? A fig!° 'Tis in ourselves that we are thus or thus. Our bodies are our gardens, to the which our wills are gardeners; so that if we will plant nettles or sow lettuce, set hyssop° and weed up thyme, supply it with one gender° of herbs or distract it with° many, either to have it sterile with idleness° or manured with industry—why, the power and corrigible authority° of this lies in our wills. If the beam° of our lives had not one scale of reason to poise° another of sensuality, the blood° and baseness of our natures would conduct us to most preposterous conclusions. But we have reason to cool our raging motions,° our carnal stings, our unbitted° lusts, whereof I take this that you call love to be a sect or scion.° 320

Roderigo: It cannot be. 325

Iago: It is merely a lust of the blood and a permission of the will. Come, be a man. Drown thyself? Drown cats and blind puppies. I have professed me thy friend, and I confess me knit to thy deserving with cables of perdurable° toughness. I could never better stead° thee than now. Put money in thy purse. Follow thou the wars; defeat thy favor° with an usurped° beard. I say, put money in thy purse. It cannot be long that Desdemona should continue her love to the Moor—put money in thy purse—nor he his to her. It was a violent commencement in her, and thou shalt see an answerable sequestration° —put but money in thy purse. These Moors are changeable in their wills°—fill thy purse with money. The food that to him now is as luscious as locusts° shall be to him shortly as bitter as coloquintida.° She must change for youth; when she is sated with his body, she will find the error of her choice. She must have change, she must. Therefore put money in thy purse. If thou wilt needs damn thyself, do it a more delicate way than drowning. Make° all the money thou canst. If sanctimony° and a frail vow betwixt an erring° barbarian and a supersubtle Venetian be not too hard for my wits and all the tribe of hell, thou shalt enjoy her. Therefore make money. A pox of drowning thyself! It is clean out of the way.° Seek thou rather to be hanged in compassing° thy joy than to be drowned and go without her. 330 335 340

Roderigo: Wilt thou be fast° to my hopes if I depend on the issue?°

Iago: Thou art sure of me. Go, make money. I have told thee often, and I retell thee again and again, I hate the Moor. My cause is hearted;° thine hath no less reason. Let us be conjunctive° in our revenge against him. If thou canst cuckold him, thou dost thyself a pleasure, me a sport. There are many events in the womb of time which will be delivered. Traverse,° go, provide thy money. We will have more of this tomorrow. Adieu. 345 350

Roderigo: Where shall we meet i' the morning?

Iago: At my lodging.

---

316 *fig* (To give a fig is to thrust the thumb between the first and second fingers in a vulgar and insulting gesture.)   318 *hyssop* an herb of the mint family.   *gender* kind   319 *distract it with* divide it among.   *idleness* want of cultivation   320 *corrigible authority* power to correct   321 *beam* balance.   *poise* counterbalance   322 *blood* natural passions   323 *motions* appetites   324 *unbitted* unbridled, uncontrolled.   *sect or scion* cutting or offshoot   328 *perdurable* very durable   329 *stead* assist   330 *defeat thy favor* disguise your face.   *usurped* (The suggestion is that Roderigo is not man enough to have a beard of his own.)   333 *an answerable sequestration* a corresponding separation or estrangement   334 *wills* carnal appetites   335 *locusts* fruit of the carob tree (see Matthew 3:4), or perhaps honeysuckle.   336 *coloquintida* colocynth or bitter apple, a purgative   339 *Make* raise, collect.   *sanctimony* sacred ceremony   340 *erring* wandering, vagabond, unsteady   342 *clean . . . way* entirely unsuitable as a course of action   343 *compassing* encompassing, embracing   344 *fast* true.   *issue* (successful) outcome   346 *hearted* fixed in the heart, heartfelt   347 *conjunctive* united   349 *Traverse* (A military marching term.)

Roderigo: I'll be with thee betimes.° [He starts to leave.]
Iago: Go to, farewell.—Do you hear, Roderigo?
Roderigo: What say you?
Iago: No more of drowning, do you hear?
Roderigo: I am changed.
Iago: Go to, farewell. Put money enough in your purse.
Roderigo: I'll sell all my land. *Exit.*
Iago: Thus do I ever make my fool my purse;
    For I mine own gained knowledge should profane
    If I would time expend with such a snipe°
    But for my sport and profit. I hate the Moor;
    And it is thought abroad° that twixt my sheets
    He's done my office.° I know not if 't be true;
    But I, for mere suspicion in that kind,
    Will do as if for surety.° He holds me well;°
    The better shall my purpose work on him.
    Cassio's a proper° man. Let me see now:
    To get his place and to plume up° my will
    In double knavery—How, how?—Let's see:
    After some time, to abuse° Othello's ear
    That he° is too familiar with his wife.
    He hath a person and a smooth dispose°
    To be suspected, framed to make women false.
    The Moor is of a free° and open° nature,
    That thinks men honest that but seem to be so,
    And will as tenderly° be led by the nose
    As asses are.
    I have 't. It is engendered. Hell and night
    Must bring this monstrous birth to the world's light.

[*Exit.*]

ACT II

SCENE I [A SEAPORT IN CYPRUS. AN OPEN PLACE NEAR THE QUAY.]

Enter Montano and two Gentlemen.

Montano: What from the cape can you discern at sea?
First Gentleman: Nothing at all. It is a high-wrought flood.°
    I cannot, twixt the heaven and the main,°
    Descry a sail.
Montano: Methinks the wind hath spoke aloud at land;
    A fuller blast ne'er shook our battlements.

---

353 *betimes* early   362 *snipe* woodcock, i.e., fool   364 *it is thought abroad* it is rumored   365 *my office* i.e., my sexual function as husband   367 *do . . . surety* act as if on certain knowledge.   *holds me well* regards me favorably   369 *proper* handsome   370 *plume up* put a feather in the cap of, i.e., glorify, gratify   372 *abuse* deceive   373 *he* i.e., Cassio   374 *dispose* disposition   376 *free* frank, generous.   *open* unsuspicious   378 *tenderly* readily   2 *high-wrought flood* very agitated sea   3 *main* ocean (also at line 41)

582   Chapter 13   Love

>   If it hath ruffianed° so upon the sea,
>   What ribs of oak, when mountains° melt on them,
>   Can hold the mortise?° What shall we hear of this?
> Second Gentleman: A segregation° of the Turkish fleet.   10
>   For do but stand upon the foaming shore,
>   The chidden° billow seems to pelt the clouds;
>   The wind-shaked surge, with high and monstrous mane,°
>   Seems to cast water on the burning Bear°
>   And quench the guards of th' ever-fixèd pole.   15
>   I never did like molestation° view
>   On the enchafèd° flood.
> Montano: If that° the Turkish fleet
>   Be not ensheltered and embayed,° they are drowned;
>   It is impossible to bear it out.°   20
>
>   *Enter a [Third] Gentleman.*
>
> Third Gentleman: News, lads! Our wars are done.
>   The desperate tempest hath so banged the Turks
>   That their designment° halts.° A noble ship of Venice
>   Hath seen a grievous wreck° and sufferance°
>   On most part of their fleet.   25
> Montano: How? Is this true?
> Third Gentleman: The ship is here put in,
>   A Veronesa;° Michael Cassio,
>   Lieutenant to the warlike Moor Othello,
>   Is come on shore; the Moor himself at sea,   30
>   And is in full commission here for Cyprus.
> Montano: I am glad on 't. 'Tis a worthy governor.
> Third Gentleman: But this same Cassio, though he speak of comfort
>   Touching the Turkish loss, yet he looks sadly°
>   And prays the Moor be safe, for they were parted   35
>   With foul and violent tempest.
> Montano: Pray heaven he be,
>   For I have served him, and the man commands
>   Like a full° soldier. Let's to the seaside, ho!
>   As well to see the vessel that's come in
>   As to throw out our eyes for brave Othello,   40
>   Even till we make the main and th' aerial blue°
>   An indistinct regard.°

7 *ruffianed* raged   8 *mountains* i.e., of water   9 *hold the mortise* hold their joints together. (A *mortise* is the socket hollowed out in fitting timbers.)   10 *segregation* dispersal   12 *chidden* i.e., rebuked, repelled (by the shore), and thus shot into the air   13 *monstrous mane* (The surf is like the mane of a wild beast.)   14 *the burning Bear* i.e., the constellation Ursa Minor or the Little Bear, which includes the polestar (and hence regarded as the *guards of th' ever-fixèd pole* in the next line; sometimes the term *guards* is applied to the two "pointers" of the Big Bear or Dipper, which may be intended here).   16 *like molestation* comparable disturbance   17 *enchafèd* angry   18 *If that* if   19 *embayed* sheltered by a bay   20 *bear it out* survive, weather the storm   23 *designment* design, enterprise.   *halts* is lame   24 *wreck* shipwreck.   *sufferance* damage, disaster   28 *Veronesa* i.e., fitted out in Verona for Venetian service, or possibly *Verennessa* (the Folio spelling), i.e., *verrinessa*, a cutter (from *verrinare*, "to cut through")   34 *sadly* gravely   38 *full* perfect   41 *the main . . . blue* the sea and the sky   42 *An indistinct regard* indistinguishable in our view

Third Gentleman: Come, let's do so,
    For every minute is expectancy°
    Of more arrivance.°

Enter Cassio.

Cassio: Thanks, you the valiant of this warlike isle,   45
    That so approve° the Moor! O, let the heavens
    Give him defense against the elements,
    For I have lost him on a dangerous sea.
Montano: Is he well shipped?
Cassio: His bark is stoutly timbered, and his pilot   50
    Of very expert and approved allowance;°
    Therefore my hopes, not surfeited to death,°
    Stand in bold cure.°

[A cry] within: "A sail, a sail, a sail!"

Cassio: What noise?
A Gentleman: The town is empty. On the brow o' the sea°   55
    Stand ranks of people, and they cry "A sail!"
Cassio: My hopes do shape him for° the governor.

[A shot within.]

Second Gentleman: They do discharge their shot of courtesy;°
    Our friends at least.
Cassio: I pray you, sir, go forth,
    And give us truth who 'tis that is arrived.   60
Second Gentleman: I shall.   *Exit.*
Montano: But, good Lieutenant, is your general wived?
Cassio: Most fortunately. He hath achieved a maid
    That paragons° description and wild fame,°
    One that excels the quirks° of blazoning° pens,   65
    And in th' essential vesture of creation
    Does tire the engineer.°

Enter [Second] Gentleman.°

              How now? Who has put in?°
Second Gentleman: 'Tis one Iago, ancient to the General.
Cassio: He's had most favorable and happy speed.
    Tempests themselves, high seas, and howling winds,   70
    The guttered° rocks and congregated sands—

---

43 *is expectancy* gives expectation   44 *arrivance* arrival   46 *approve* admire, honor   51 *approved allowance* tested reputation   52 *surfeited to death* i.e., overextended, worn thin through repeated application or delayed fulfillment   53 *in bold cure* in strong hopes of fulfillment   55 *brow o' the sea* cliff-edge   57 *My . . . for* I hope it is   58 *discharge . . . courtesy* fire a salute in token of respect and courtesy   64 *paragons* surpasses.   *wild fame* extravagant report   65 *quirks* witty conceits.   *blazoning* setting forth as though in heraldic language   66–67 *in . . . enginer* in her real, God-given, beauty, (she) defeats any attempt to praise her.   *enginer* engineer, i.e., poet, one who devises.   s.d. *[Second] Gentleman* (So identified in the Quarto text here and in lines 58, 61, 68, and 96; the Folio calls him a gentleman.)   67 *put in* i.e., to harbor   71 *guttered* jagged, trenched

      Traitors ensteeped° to clog the guiltless keel—
      As° having sense of beauty, do omit°
      Their mortal° natures, letting go safely by
      The divine Desdemona.
Montano: What is she?   75
Cassio: She that I spake of, our great captain's captain,
      Left in the conduct of the bold Iago,
      Whose footing° here anticipates our thoughts
      A sennight's° speed. Great Jove, Othello guard,
      And swell his sail with thine own powerful breath,   80
      That he may bless this bay with his tall° ship,
      Make love's quick pants in Desdemona's arms,
      Give renewed fire to our extincted spirits,
      And bring all Cyprus comfort!

      Enter Desdemona, Iago, Roderigo, and Emilia.

                       O, behold,
      The riches of the ship is come on shore!   85
      You men of Cyprus, let her have your knees.

      [The gentlemen make curtsy to Desdemona.]

      Hail to thee, lady! And the grace of heaven
      Before, behind thee, and on every hand
      Enwheel thee round!
Desdemona: I thank you, valiant Cassio.
      What tidings can you tell me of my lord?   90
Cassio: He is not yet arrived, nor know I aught
      But that he's well and will be shortly here.
Desdemona: O, but I fear—How lost you company?
Cassio: The great contention of the sea and skies
      Parted our fellowship.

      (*Within*)   "A sail, a sail!" *[A shot.]*

                       But hark. A sail!   95
Second Gentleman: They give their greeting to the citadel.
      This likewise is a friend.
Cassio: See for the news.

      [Exit Second Gentleman.]

      Good Ancient, you are welcome. *[Kissing Emilia.]* Welcome, mistress.
      Let it not gall your patience, good Iago,
      That I extend° my manners; 'tis my breeding°   100
      That gives me this bold show of courtesy.
Iago: Sir, would she give you so much of her lips
      As of her tongue she oft bestows on me,
      You would have enough.

---

72 *ensteeped* lying under water   73 *As* as if.   *omit* forbear to exercise   74 *mortal* deadly   78 *footing* landing   79 *sennight's* week's   81 *tall* splendid, gallant   100 *extend* give scope to.   *breeding* training in the niceties of etiquette

Desdemona: Alas, she has no speech!°
Iago: In faith, too much.
    I find it still,° when I have list° to sleep.
    Marry, before your ladyship, I grant,
    She puts her tongue a little in her heart
    And chides with thinking.°
Emilia: You have little cause to say so.
Iago: Come on, come on. You are pictures out of doors,°
    Bells° in your parlors, wildcats in your kitchens,°
    Saints° in your injuries, devils being offended,
    Players° in your huswifery,° and huswives° in your beds.
Desdemona: O, fie upon thee, slanderer!
Iago: Nay, it is true, or else I am a Turk.°
    You rise to play, and go to bed to work.
Emilia: You shall not write my praise.
Iago: No, let me not.
Desdemona: What wouldst write of me, if thou shouldst praise me?
Iago: O gentle lady, do not put me to 't,
    For I am nothing if not critical.°
Desdemona: Come on, essay.°—There's one gone to the harbor?
Iago: Ay, madam.
Desdemona: I am not merry, but I do beguile
    The thing I am° by seeming otherwise.
    Come, how wouldst thou praise me?
Iago: I am about it, but indeed my invention
    Comes from my pate as birdlime° does from frieze°—
    It plucks out brains and all. But my Muse labors,°
    And thus she is delivered:
    If she be fair and wise, fairness and wit,
    The one's for use, the other useth it.°
Desdemona: Well praised! How if she be black° and witty?
Iago: If she be black, and thereto have a wit,
    She'll find a white° that shall her blackness fit.°
Desdemona: Worse and worse.
Emilia: How if fair and foolish?
Iago: She never yet was foolish that was fair,
    For even her folly° helped her to an heir.°
Desdemona: These are old fond° paradoxes to make fools laugh i' th' alehouse.
    What miserable praise hast thou for her that's foul and foolish?

---

105 *she has no speech* i.e., she's not a chatterbox, as you allege   107 *still* always. *list* desire   110 *with thinking* i.e., in her thoughts only   111 *pictures out of doors* i.e., silent and well-behaved in public   112 *Bells* i.e., jangling, noisy, and brazen. *in your kitchens* i.e., in domestic affairs. (Ladies would not do the cooking.)   113 *Saints* martyrs   114 *Players* idlers, triflers, or deceivers. *huswifery* housekeeping. *huswives* hussies (i.e., women are "busy" in bed, or unduly thrifty in dispensing sexual favors)   116 *a Turk* an infidel, not to be believed   121 *critical* censorious   122 *essay* try   125 *The thing I am* i.e., my anxious self   128 *birdlime* sticky substance used to catch small birds. *frieze* coarse woolen cloth   129 *labors* (1) exerts herself (2) prepares to deliver a child (with a following pun on *delivered* in line 130)   132 *The one's . . . it* i.e., her cleverness will make use of her beauty   133 *black* dark-complexioned, brunette   135 *a white* a fair person (with word-play on "wight," a person). *fit* (with sexual suggestion of mating)   138 *folly* (with added meaning of "lechery, wantonness"). *to an heir* i.e., to bear a child   139 *fond* foolish

Iago: There's none so foul° and foolish thereunto,°
    But does foul° pranks which fair and wise ones do.
Desdemona: O heavy ignorance! Thou praisest the worst best. But what praise
    couldst thou bestow on a deserving woman indeed, one that, in the authority of
    her merit, did justly put on the vouch° of very malice itself?   145
Iago: She that was ever fair, and never proud,
    Had tongue at will, and yet was never loud,
    Never lacked gold and yet went never gay,°
    Fled from her wish, and yet said, "Now I may,"°
    She that being angered, her revenge being nigh,   150
    Bade her wrong stay° and her displeasure fly,
    She that in wisdom never was so frail
    To change the cod's head for the salmon's tail,°
    She that could think and ne'er disclose her mind,
    See suitors following and not look behind,   155
    She was a wight, if ever such wight were—
Desdemona: To do what?
Iago: To suckle fools° and chronicle small beer.°
Desdemona: O most lame and impotent conclusion! Do not learn of him, Emilia, though
    he be thy husband. How say you, Cassio? Is he not a most profane° and liberal°   160
    counselor?
Cassio: He speaks home,° madam. You may relish° him more in° the soldier than in
    the scholar.

    [Cassio and Desdemona stand together, conversing intimately.]

Iago [aside]: He takes her by the palm. Ay, well said,° whisper. With as little a
    web as this will I ensnare as great a fly as Cassio. Ay, smile upon her, do; I will 165
    gyve° thee in thine own courtship.° You say true;° 'tis so, indeed. If such tricks as
    these strip you out of your lieutenantry, it had been better you had not kissed
    your three fingers so oft, which now again you are most apt to play the sir° in.
    Very good; well kissed! An excellent courtesy! 'Tis so, indeed. Yet again your
    fingers to your lips? Would they were clyster pipes° for your sake! *[Trumpet   170
    within.]* The Moor! I know his trumpet.
Cassio: 'Tis truly so.
Desdemona: Let's meet him and receive him.
Cassio: Lo, where he comes!

    Enter Othello and attendants.

Othello: O my fair warrior!
Desdemona: My dear Othello!   175

---

141 *foul* ugly. *thereunto* in addition   142 *foul* sluttish   145 *put . . . vouch* compel the approval   148 *gay* extravagantly clothed   149 *Fled . . . may* avoided temptation where the choice was hers   151 *Bade . . . stay* i.e., resolved to put up with her injury patiently   153 *To . . . tail* i.e., to exchange a lackluster husband for a sexy lover (?) (*Cod's head* is slang for "penis," and *tail*, for "pudendum.")   158 *suckle fools* breastfeed babies.   *chronicle small beer* i.e., keep petty household accounts, keep track of trivial matters   160 *profane* irreverent, ribald.   *liberal* licentious, free-spoken   162 *home* right to the target. (A term from fencing.)   *relish* appreciate   *in* in the character of   164 *well said* well done   166 *gyve* fetter, shackle.   *courtship* courtesy, show of courtly manners.   *You say true* i.e., that's right, go ahead   168 *the sir* i.e., the fine gentleman   170 *clyster pipes* tubes used for enemas and douches

Desdemona arrives in Cyprus and reunites with Othello as Cassio looks on (II, i, 175–208).

Othello: It gives me wonder great as my content
    To see you here before me. O my soul's joy,
    If after every tempest come such calms,
    May the winds blow till they have wakened death,
    And let the laboring bark climb hills of seas   180
    Olympus-high, and duck again as low
    As hell's from heaven! If it were now to die,
    'Twere now to be most happy, for I fear
    My soul hath her content so absolute
    That not another comfort like to this   185
    Succeeds in unknown fate.°
Desdemona: The heavens forbid
    But that our loves and comforts should increase
    Even as our days do grow!
Othello: Amen to that, sweet powers!
    I cannot speak enough of this content.   190
    It stops me here; it is too much of joy.
    And this, and this, the greatest discords be

    [*They kiss.*]°

    That e'er our hearts shall make!

---

186 *Succeeds . . . fate* i.e., can follow in the unknown future   192 s.d. *They kiss* (The direction is from the Quarto.)

Iago [aside]: O, you are well tuned now!
    But I'll set down° the pegs that make this music, 195
    As honest as I am.°
Othello: Come, let us to the castle.
    News, friends! Our wars are done, the Turks are drowned.
    How does my old acquaintance of this isle?—
    Honey, you shall be well desired° in Cyprus; 200
    I have found great love amongst them. O my sweet,
    I prattle out of fashion,° and I dote
    In mine own comforts.—I prithee, good Iago,
    Go to the bay and disembark my coffers.°
    Bring thou the master° to the citadel; 205
    He is a good one, and his worthiness
    Does challenge° much respect.—Come, Desdemona.—
    Once more, well met at Cyprus!

    Exeunt Othello and Desdemona [and all but Iago and Roderigo].

Iago [to an attendant]: Do thou meet me presently at the harbor. *[To Roderigo.]*
    Come hither. If thou be'st valiant—as, they say, base men° being in love have 210
    then a nobility in their natures more than is native to them—list° me. The Lieu-
    tenant tonight watches on the court of guard.° First, I must tell thee this: Desde-
    mona is directly in love with him.
Roderigo: With him? Why, 'tis not possible.
Iago: Lay thy finger thus,° and let thy soul be instructed. Mark me with what violence 215
    she first loved the Moor, but° for bragging and telling her fantastical lies. To love
    him still for prating? Let not thy discreet heart think it. Her eye must be fed; and
    what delight shall she have to look on the devil? When the blood is made dull
    with the act of sport,° there should be, again to inflame it and to give satiety a
    fresh appetite, loveliness in favor,° sympathy° in years, manners, and beauties— 220
    all which the Moor is defective in. Now, for want of these required conve-
    niences,° her delicate tenderness will find itself abused,° begin to heave the
    gorge,° disrelish and abhor the Moor. Very nature° will instruct her in it and com-
    pel her to some second choice. Now, sir, this granted—as it is a most pregnant° and
    unforced position—who stands so eminent in the degree of° this fortune as Cassio 225
    does? A knave very voluble,° no further conscionable° than in putting on the
    mere form of civil and humane° seeming for the better compassing of his salt°
    and most hidden loose affection.° Why, none, why, none. A slipper° and subtle

---

195 *set down* loosen (and hence untune the instrument) 196 *As . . . I am* for all my supposed honesty 200 *desired* welcomed 202 *out of fashion* irrelevantly, incoherently (?) 204 *coffers* chests, baggage 205 *master* ship's captain 207 *challenge* lay claim to, deserve 210 *base men* even lowly born men 211 *list* listen to 212 *court of guard* guardhouse. (Cassio is in charge of the watch.) 215 *thus* i.e., on your lips 216 *but* only 219 *the act of sport* sex 220 *favor* appearance. *sympathy* correspondence, similarity 221–222 *required conveniences* things conducive to sexual compatibility 222 *abused* cheated, revolted 222–223 *heave the gorge* experience nausea 223 *Very nature* her very instincts 224 *pregnant* evident, cogent 225 *in the degree of* as next in line for 226 *voluble* facile, glib. *conscionable* conscientious, conscience-bound 227 *humane* polite, courteous. *salt* licentious 228 *affection* passion. *slipper* slippery

knave, a finder out of occasions, that has an eye can stamp° and counterfeit advantages,° though true advantage never present itself; a devilish knave. Besides, the knave is handsome, young, and hath all those requisites in him that folly° and green° minds look after. A pestilent complete knave, and the woman hath found him° already.

Roderigo: I cannot believe that in her. She's full of most blessed condition.°

Iago: Blessed fig's end!° The wine she drinks is made of grapes. If she had been blessed, she would never have loved the Moor. Blessed pudding!° Didst thou not see her paddle with the palm of his hand? Didst not mark that?

Roderigo: Yes, that I did; but that was but courtesy.

Iago: Lechery, by this hand. An index° and obscure° prologue to the history of lust and foul thoughts. They met so near with their lips that their breaths embraced together. Villainous thoughts, Roderigo! When these mutualities° so marshal the way, hard at hand° comes the master and main exercise, th' incorporate° conclusion. Pish! But, sir, be you ruled by me. I have brought you from Venice. Watch you° tonight; for the command, I'll lay 't upon you.° Cassio knows you not. I'll not be far from you. Do you find some occasion to anger Cassio, either by speaking too loud, or tainting° his discipline, or from what other course you please, which the time shall more favorably minister.°

Roderigo: Well.

Iago: Sir, he's rash and very sudden in choler,° and haply° may strike at you. Provoke him that he may, for even out of that will I cause these of Cyprus to mutiny,° whose qualification° shall come into no true taste° again but by the displanting of Cassio. So shall you have a shorter journey to your desires by the means I shall then have to prefer° them, and the impediment most profitably removed, without the which there were no expectation of our prosperity.

Roderigo: I will do this, if you can bring it to any opportunity.

Iago: I warrant° thee. Meet me by and by° at the citadel. I must fetch his necessaries ashore. Farewell.

Roderigo: Adieu. *Exit.*

Iago: That Cassio loves her, I do well believe 't;
That she loves him, 'tis apt° and of great credit.°
The Moor, howbeit that I endure him not,
Is of a constant, loving, noble nature,
And I dare think he'll prove to Desdemona
A most dear husband. Now, I do love her too,
Not out of absolute lust—though peradventure
I stand accountant° for as great a sin—
But partly led to diet° my revenge

---

229 *an eye can stamp* an eye that can coin, create   230 *advantages* favorable opportunities   231 *folly* wantonness   232 *green* immature   233 *found him* sized him up, perceived his intent   234 *condition* disposition   235 *fig's end* (See Act I, Scene iii, line 316 for the vulgar gesture of the fig.)   236 *pudding* sausage   239 *index* table of contents.   *obscure* (i.e., the *lust and foul thoughts* in lines 239–240 are secret, hidden from view)   241 *mutualities* exchanges, intimacies   242 *hard at hand* closely following.   *incorporate* carnal   244 *Watch you* stand watch.   *for the command . . . you* I'll arrange for you to be appointed, given orders   246 *tainting* disparaging   247 *minister* provide   249 *choler* wrath.   *haply* perhaps   250 *mutiny* riot   251 *qualification* appeasement.   *true taste* i.e., acceptable state   253 *prefer* advance   256 *warrant* assure.   *by and by* immediately   260 *apt* probable.   *credit* credibility   266 *accountant* accountable   267 *diet* feed

For that I do suspect the lusty Moor
Hath leaped into my seat, the thought whereof
Doth, like a poisonous mineral, gnaw my innards; 270
And nothing can or shall content my soul
Till I am evened with him, wife for wife,
Or failing so, yet that I put the Moor
At least into a jealousy so strong
That judgment cannot cure. Which thing to do, 275
If this poor trash of Venice, whom I trace°
For° his quick hunting, stand the putting on,°
I'll have our Michael Cassio on the hip,°
Abuse° him to the Moor in the rank garb°—
For I fear Cassio with my nightcap° too— 280
Make the Moor thank me, love me, and reward me
For making him egregiously an ass
And practicing upon° his peace and quiet
Even to madness. 'Tis here, but yet confused.
Knavery's plain face is never seen till used. *Exit.* 285

SCENE II [CYPRUS. A STREET.]

Enter Othello's Herald with a proclamation.

Herald: It is Othello's pleasure, our noble and valiant general, that, upon certain tidings now arrived, importing the mere perdition° of the Turkish fleet, every man put himself into triumph:° some to dance, some to make bonfires, each man to what sport and revels his addiction° leads him. For, besides these beneficial news, it is the celebration of his nuptial. So much was his pleasure should be 5 proclaimed. All offices° are open, and there is full liberty of feasting from this present hour of five till the bell have told eleven. Heaven bless the isle of Cyprus and our noble general Othello!

Exit.

SCENE III [CYPRUS. THE CITADEL.]

Enter Othello, Desdemona, Cassio, and attendants.

Othello: Good Michael, look you to the guard tonight.
Let's teach ourselves that honorable stop°
Not to outsport° discretion.
Cassio: Iago hath direction what to do,
But notwithstanding, with my personal eye 5
Will I look to 't.

---

276 *trace* i.e., train, or follow (?), or perhaps *trash*, a hunting term, meaning to put weights on a hunting dog in order to slow him down   277 *For* to make more eager.   *stand . . . on* respond properly when I incite him to quarrel   278 *on the hip* at my mercy, where I can throw him. (A wrestling term.)   279 *Abuse* slander.   *rank garb* coarse manner, gross fashion   280 *with my nightcap* i.e., as a rival in my bed, as one who gives me cuckold's horns   283 *practicing upon* plotting against   2 *mere perdition* complete destruction   3 *triumph* public celebration   4 *addiction* inclination   6 *offices* rooms where food and drink are kept   2 *stop* restraint   3 *outsport* celebrate beyond the bounds of

Othello: Iago is most honest.
Michael, good night. Tomorrow with your earliest°
Let me have speech with you. *[To Desdemona.]*
　　　　　　　　　　　Come, my dear love,
The purchase made, the fruits are to ensue;
That profit's yet to come 'tween me and you.°—
Good night.

Exit [Othello, with Desdemona and attendants].

Enter Iago.

Cassio: Welcome, Iago. We must to the watch.
Iago: Not this hour,° Lieutenant; 'tis not yet ten o' the clock. Our general cast° us thus early for the love of his Desdemona; who° let us not therefore blame. He hath not yet made wanton the night with her, and she is sport for Jove.
Cassio: She's a most exquisite lady.
Iago: And, I'll warrant her, full of game.
Cassio: Indeed, she's a most fresh and delicate creature.
Iago: What an eye she has! Methinks it sounds a parley° to provocation.
Cassio: An inviting eye, and yet methinks right modest.
Iago: And when she speaks, is it not an alarum° to love?
Cassio: She is indeed perfection.
Iago: Well, happiness to their sheets! Come, Lieutenant, I have a stoup° of wine, and here without° are a brace° of Cyprus gallants that would fain have a measure° to the health of black Othello.
Cassio: Not tonight, good Iago. I have very poor and unhappy brains for drinking. I could well wish courtesy would invent some other custom of entertainment.
Iago: O, they are our friends. But one cup! I'll drink for you.°
Cassio: I have drunk but one cup tonight, and that was craftily qualified° too, and behold what innovation° it makes here.° I am unfortunate in the infirmity and dare not task my weakness with any more.
Iago: What, man? 'Tis a night of revels. The gallants desire it.
Cassio: Where are they?
Iago: Here at the door. I pray you, call them in.
Cassio: I'll do 't, but it dislikes me.°　　　　　　　　　　*Exit.*
Iago: If I can fasten but one cup upon him,
With that which he hath drunk tonight already,
He'll be as full of quarrel and offense°
As my young mistress' dog. Now, my sick fool Roderigo,
Whom love hath turned almost the wrong side out,
To Desdemona hath tonight caroused°

---

7 *with your earliest* at your earliest convenience　9–10 *The purchase . . . you* i.e., though married, we haven't yet consummated our love　13 *Not this hour* not for an hour yet.　*cast* dismissed　14 *who* i.e., Othello　19 *sounds a parley* calls for a conference, issues an invitation　21 *alarum* signal calling men to arms (continuing the military metaphor of *parley*, line 19)　23 *stoup* measure of liquor, two quarts　24 *without* outside.　*brace* pair.　*fain have a measure* gladly drink a toast　28 *for you* in your place. (Iago will do the steady drinking to keep the gallants company while Cassio has only one cup.)　29 *qualified* diluted　30 *innovation* disturbance, insurrection.　*here* i.e., in my head　35 *it dislikes me* i.e., I'm reluctant　38 *offense* readiness to take offense　41 *caroused* drunk off

Potations pottle-deep;° and he's to watch.°
Three lads of Cyprus—noble swelling° spirits,
That hold their honors in a wary distance,°
The very elements° of this warlike isle— 45
Have I tonight flustered with flowing cups,
And they watch° too. Now, 'mongst this flock of drunkards
Am I to put our Cassio in some action
That may offend the isle.—But here they come.

Enter Cassio, Montano, and gentlemen; [servants following with wine].

If consequence do but approve my dream,° 50
My boat sails freely both with wind and stream.°
Cassio: 'Fore God, they have given me a rouse° already.
Montano: Good faith, a little one; not past a pint, as I am a soldier.
Iago: Some wine, ho! *[He sings.]*
    "And let me the cannikin° clink, clink, 55
    And let me the cannikin clink.
    A soldier's a man,
    O, man's life's but a span;°
    Why, then, let a soldier drink."
Some wine, boys! 60
Cassio: 'Fore God, an excellent song.
Iago: I learned it in England, where indeed they are most potent in potting.° Your Dane, your German, and your swag-bellied Hollander—drink, ho!—are nothing to your English.
Cassio: Is your Englishman so exquisite in his drinking? 65
Iago: Why, he drinks you,° with facility, your Dane° dead drunk; he sweats not° to overthrow your Almain;° he gives your Hollander a vomit ere the next pottle can be filled.
Cassio: To the health of our general!
Montano: I am for it, Lieutenant, and I'll do you justice.° 70
Iago: O sweet England! *[He sings.]*
    "King Stephen was and-a worthy peer,
    His breeches cost him but a crown;
    He held them sixpence all too dear,
    With that he called the tailor lown.° 75

    He was a wight of high renown,
    And thou art but of low degree.
    'Tis pride° that pulls the country down;
    Then take thy auld° cloak about thee."
Some wine, ho! 80

42 *pottle-deep* to the bottom of the tankard. *watch* stand watch 43 *swelling* proud 44 *hold . . . distance* i.e., are extremely sensitive of their honor 45 *very elements* typical sort 47 *watch* are members of the guard 50 *If . . . dream* if subsequent events will only substantiate my scheme 51 *stream* current 52 *rouse* full draft of liquor 55 *cannikin* small drinking vessel 58 *span* brief span of time. (Compare Psalm 39:6 as rendered in the 1928 Book of Common Prayer: "Thou hast made my days as it were a span long.") 62 *potting* drinking 66 *drinks you* drinks. *your Dane* your typical Dane. *sweats not* i.e., need not exert himself 67 *Almain* German 70 *I'll . . . justice* i.e., I'll drink as much as you 75 *lown* lout, rascal 78 *pride* i.e., extravagance in dress 79 *auld* old

Cassio: 'Fore God, this is a more exquisite song than the other.
Iago: Will you hear 't again?
Cassio: No, for I hold him to be unworthy of his place that does those things. Well, God's above all; and there be souls must be saved, and there be souls must not be saved.
Iago: It's true, good Lieutenant.
Cassio: For mine own part—no offense to the General, nor any man of quality°—I hope to be saved.
Iago: And so do I too, Lieutenant.
Cassio: Ay, but, by your leave, not before me; the lieutenant is to be saved before the ancient. Let's have no more of this; let's to our affairs.—God forgive us our sins!—Gentlemen, let's look to our business. Do not think, gentlemen, I am drunk. This is my ancient; this is my right hand, and this is my left. I am not drunk now. I can stand well enough, and speak well enough.
Gentlemen: Excellent well.
Cassio: Why, very well then; you must not think then that I am drunk.   *Exit.*
Montano: To th' platform, masters. Come, let's set the watch.°

[Exeunt Gentlemen.]

Iago: You see this fellow that is gone before.
   He's a soldier fit to stand by Caesar
   And give direction; and do but see his vice.
   'Tis to his virtue a just equinox,°
   The one as long as th' other. 'Tis pity of him.
   I fear the trust Othello puts him in,
   On some odd time of his infirmity,
   Will shake this island.
Montano: But is he often thus?
Iago: 'Tis evermore the prologue to his sleep.
   He'll watch the horologe a double set,°
   If drink rock not his cradle.
Montano: It were well
   The General were put in mind of it.
   Perhaps he sees it not, or his good nature
   Prizes the virtue that appears in Cassio
   And looks not on his evils. Is not this true?

   Enter Roderigo.

Iago [aside to him]: How now, Roderigo?
   I pray you, after the Lieutenant; go.   *[Exit Roderigo.]*
Montano: And 'tis great pity that the noble Moor
   Should hazard such a place as his own second
   With° one of an engraffed° infirmity.

---

87 *quality* rank   97 *set the watch* mount the guard   101 *just equinox* exact counterpart. (*Equinox* is an equal length of days and nights.)   107 *watch . . . set* stay awake twice around the clock or *horologe*   116–117 *hazard . . . With* risk giving such an important position as his second in command to   117 *engraffed* engrafted, inveterate

Cassio, encouraged to drink by Iago, starts a fight with Montano (II, iii, 130).

> It were an honest action to say so
> To the Moor.
> Iago: Not I, for this fair island.
> I do love Cassio well and would do much   120
> To cure him of this evil.   *[Cry within: "Help! Help!"]*
>   But, hark! What noise?
>
> *Enter Cassio, pursuing° Roderigo.*
>
> Cassio: Zounds, you rogue! You rascal!
> Montano: What's the matter, Lieutenant?
> Cassio: A knave teach me my duty?
>   I'll beat the knave into a twiggen° bottle.

121 s.d. *pursuing* (The Quarto text reads, "driving in.") 124 *twiggen* wicker-covered. (Cassio vows to assail Roderigo until his skin resembles wickerwork or until he has driven Roderigo through the holes in a wickerwork.)

Roderigo: Beat me? 125
Cassio: Dost thou prate, rogue?   *[He strikes Roderigo.]*
Montano: Nay, good Lieutenant. *[Restraining him.]* I pray you, sir, hold your hand.
Cassio: Let me go, sir, or I'll knock you o'er the mazard.°
Montano: Come, come, you're drunk.
Cassio: Drunk?   *[They fight.]* 130
Iago [aside to Roderigo]: Away, I say. Go out and cry a mutiny.°

   [Exit Roderigo.]

   Nay, good Lieutenant—God's will, gentlemen—
   Help, ho!—Lieutenant—sir—Montano—sir—
   Help, masters!°—Here's a goodly watch indeed!

   [A bell rings.]°

   Who's that which rings the bell?—Diablo,° ho! 135
   The town will rise.° God's will, Lieutenant, hold!
   You'll be ashamed forever.

   Enter Othello and attendants [with weapons].

Othello: What is the matter here?
Montano: Zounds, I bleed still.
   I am hurt to th' death. He dies!   *[He thrusts at Cassio.]*
Othello: Hold, for your lives!
Iago: Hold, ho! Lieutenant—sir—Montano—gentlemen— 140
   Have you forgot all sense of place and duty?
   Hold! The General speaks to you. Hold, for shame!
Othello: Why, how now, ho! From whence ariseth this?
   Are we turned Turks, and to ourselves do that
   Which heaven hath forbid the Ottomites?° 145
   For Christian shame, put by this barbarous brawl!
   He that stirs next to carve for° his own rage
   Holds his soul light;° he dies upon his motion.°
   Silence that dreadful bell. It frights the isle
   From her propriety.° What is the matter, masters? 150
   Honest Iago, that looks dead with grieving,
   Speak. Who began this? On thy love, I charge thee.
Iago: I do not know. Friends all but now, even now,
   In quarter° and in terms° like bride and groom
   Devesting them° for bed; and then, but now— 155
   As if some planet had unwitted men—

128 *mazard* i.e., head. (Literally, a drinking vessel.)   131 *mutiny* riot   134 *masters* sirs.   s.d. *A bell rings* (This direction is from the Quarto, as are *Exit Roderigo* at line 114, *They fight* at line 130, and *with weapons* at line 137.)   135 *Diablo* the devil   136 *rise* grow riotous   144–145 *to ourselves . . . Ottomites* inflict on ourselves the harm that heaven has prevented the Turks from doing (by destroying their fleet)   147 *carve for* i.e., indulge, satisfy with his sword   148 *Holds . . . light* i.e., places little value on his life.   *upon his motion* if he moves   150 *propriety* proper state or condition   154 *In quarter* in friendly conduct, within bounds.   *in terms* on good terms   155 *Devesting them* undressing themselves

>   Swords out, and tilting one at others' breasts
>   In opposition bloody. I cannot speak°
>   Any beginning to this peevish odds;°
>   And would in action glorious I had lost   160
>   Those legs that brought me to a part of it!
> *Othello:* How comes it, Michael, you are thus forgot?°
> *Cassio:* I pray you, pardon me. I cannot speak.
> *Othello:* Worthy Montano, you were wont be° civil;
>   The gravity and stillness° of your youth   165
>   The world hath noted, and your name is great
>   In mouths of wisest censure.° What's the matter
>   That you unlace° your reputation thus
>   And spend your rich opinion° for the name
>   Of a night-brawler? Give me answer to it.   170
> *Montano:* Worthy Othello, I am hurt to danger.
>   Your officer, Iago, can inform you—
>   While I spare speech, which something° now offends° me—
>   Of all that I do know; nor know I aught
>   By me that's said or done amiss this night,   175
>   Unless self-charity be sometimes a vice,
>   And to defend ourselves it be a sin
>   When violence assails us.
> *Othello:*   Now, by heaven,
>   My blood° begins my safer guides° to rule,
>   And passion, having my best judgment collied,°   180
>   Essays° to lead the way. Zounds, if I stir,
>   Or do but lift this arm, the best of you
>   Shall sink in my rebuke. Give me to know
>   How this foul rout° began, who set it on;
>   And he that is approved in° this offense,   185
>   Though he had twinned with me, both at a birth,
>   Shall lose me. What? In a town of° war
>   Yet wild, the people's hearts brim full of fear,
>   To manage° private and domestic quarrel?
>   In night, and on the court and guard of safety?°   190
>   'Tis monstrous. Iago, who began 't?
> *Montano [to Iago]:* If partially affined,° or leagued in office,°
>   Thou dost deliver more or less than truth,
>   Thou art no soldier.
> *Iago:*   Touch me not so near.
>   I had rather have this tongue cut from my mouth   195

158 *speak* explain   159 *peevish odds* childish quarrel   162 *are thus forgot* have forgotten yourself thus   164 *wont be* accustomed to be   165 *stillness* sobriety   167 *censure* judgment   168 *unlace* undo, lay open (as one might loose the strings of a purse containing reputation)   169 *opinion* reputation   173 *something* somewhat.   *offends* pains   179 *blood* passion (of anger).   *guides* i.e., reason   180 *collied* darkened   181 *Essays* undertakes   184 *rout* riot   185 *approved in* found guilty of   187 *town of* town garrisoned for   189 *manage* undertake   190 *on . . . safety* at the main guardhouse or headquarters and on watch   192 *partially affined* made partial by some personal relationship.   *leagued in office* in league as fellow officers

Than it should do offense to Michael Cassio;
Yet, I persuade myself, to speak the truth
Shall nothing wrong him. Thus it is, General.
Montano and myself being in speech,
There comes a fellow crying out for help,
And Cassio following him with determined sword
To execute° upon him. Sir, this gentleman

[indicating Montano]

Steps in to Cassio and entreats his pause.°
Myself the crying fellow did pursue,
Lest by his clamor—as it so fell out—
The town might fall in fright. He, swift of foot,
Outran my purpose, and I returned, the rather°
For that I heard the clink and fall of swords
And Cassio high in oath, which till tonight
I ne'er might say before. When I came back—
For this was brief—I found them close together
At blow and thrust, even as again they were
When you yourself did part them.
More of this matter cannot I report.
But men are men; the best sometimes forget.°
Though Cassio did some little wrong to him,
As men in rage strike those that wish them best,°
Yet surely Cassio, I believe, received
From him that fled some strange indignity,
Which patience could not pass.°
Othello: I know, Iago,
Thy honesty and love doth mince this matter,
Making it light to Cassio. Cassio, I love thee,
But nevermore be officer of mine.

Enter Desdemona, attended.

Look if my gentle love be not raised up.
I'll make thee an example.
Desdemona: What is the matter, dear?
Othello: All's well now, sweeting;
Come away to bed. *[To Montano.]* Sir, for your hurts,
Myself will be your surgeon.°—Lead him off.

[Montano is led off.]

Iago, look with care about the town
And silence those whom this vile brawl distracted.

---

202 *execute* give effect to (his anger)   203 *his pause* him to stop   207 *rather* sooner   215 *forget* forget themselves   217 *those . . . best* i.e., even those who are well disposed   220 *pass* pass over, overlook   228 *be your surgeon* i.e., make sure you receive medical attention

Iago advises Cassio to ask Desdemona to plead his cause with Othello (II, iii, 233–286).

> Come, Desdemona. 'Tis the soldiers' life
> To have their balmy slumbers waked with strife.
>
> *Exit [with all but Iago and Cassio].*
>
> *Iago:* What, are you hurt, Lieutenant?
> *Cassio:* Ay, past all surgery.
> *Iago:* Marry, God forbid! 235
> *Cassio:* Reputation, reputation, reputation! O, I have lost my reputation! I have lost the immortal part of myself, and what remains is bestial. My reputation, Iago, my reputation!
> *Iago:* As I am an honest man, I thought you had received some bodily wound; there 240 is more sense in that than in reputation. Reputation is an idle and most false imposition,° oft got without merit and lost without deserving. You have lost no reputation at all, unless you repute yourself such a loser. What, man, there are more ways to recover° the General again. You are but now cast in his mood°—a punishment more in policy° than in malice, even so as one would beat his offenseless dog to affright an imperious lion.° Sue° to him again and he's yours. 245

240–241 *false imposition* thing artificially imposed and of no real value   243 *recover* regain favor with. *cast in his mood* dismissed in a moment of anger   244 *in policy* done for expediency's sake and as a public gesture   244–245 *would . . . lion* i.e., would make an example of a minor offender in order to deter more important and dangerous offenders   245 *Sue* petition

Cassio: I will rather sue to be despised than to deceive so good a commander with so slight,° so drunken, and so indiscreet an officer. Drunk? And speak parrot?° And squabble? Swagger? Swear? And discourse fustian with one's own shadow? O thou invisible spirit of wine, if thou hast no name to be known by, let us call thee devil!

Iago: What was he that you followed with your sword? What had he done to you?

Cassio: I know not.

Iago: Is 't possible?

Cassio: I remember a mass of things, but nothing distinctly; a quarrel, but nothing wherefore.° O God, that men should put an enemy in their mouths to steal away their brains! That we should, with joy, pleasance, revel, and applause° transform ourselves into beasts!

Iago: Why, but you are now well enough. How came you thus recovered?

Cassio: It hath pleased the devil drunkenness to give place to the devil wrath. One unperfectness shows me another, to make me frankly despise myself.

Iago: Come, you are too severe a moraler.° As the time, the place, and the condition of this country stands, I could heartily wish this had not befallen; but since it is as it is, mend it for your own good.

Cassio: I will ask him for my place again; he shall tell me I am a drunkard. Had I as many mouths as Hydra,° such an answer would stop them all. To be now a sensible man, by and by a fool, and presently a beast! O, strange! Every inordinate cup is unblessed, and the ingredient is a devil.

Iago: Come, come, good wine is a good familiar creature, if it be well used. Exclaim no more against it. And, good Lieutenant, I think you think I love you.

Cassio: I have well approved° it, sir. I drunk!

Iago: You or any man living may be drunk at a time,° man. I'll tell you what you shall do. Our general's wife is now the general—I may say so in this respect, for that° he hath devoted and given up himself to the contemplation, mark, and denotement° of her parts° and graces. Confess yourself freely to her; importune her help to put you in your place again. She is of so free,° so kind, so apt, so blessed a disposition, she holds it a vice in her goodness not to do more than she is requested. This broken joint between you and her husband entreat her to splinter;° and, my fortunes against any lay° worth naming, this crack of your love shall grow stronger than it was before.

Cassio: You advise me well.

Iago: I protest,° in the sincerity of love and honest kindness.

Cassio: I think it freely;° and betimes in the morning I will beseech the virtuous Desdemona to undertake for me. I am desperate of my fortunes if they check° me here.

Iago: You are in the right. Good night, Lieutenant. I must to the watch.

Cassio: Good night, honest Iago. *Exit Cassio.*

---

247 *slight* worthless. *speak parrot* talk nonsense, rant   255 *wherefore* why   256 *applause* desire for applause   261 *moraler* moralizer   265 *Hydra* the Lernaean Hydra, a monster with many heads and the ability to grow two heads when one was cut off, slain by Hercules as the second of his twelve labors   270 *approved* proved   271 *at a time* at one time or another   272 *in . . . that* in view of this fact, that   273–274 *mark, and denotement* (Both words mean "observation.")   274 *parts* qualities   275 *free* generous   277 *splinter* bind with splints.   278 *lay* stake, wager   281 *protest* insist, declare   282 *freely* unreservedly   283 *check* repulse

Iago: And what's he then that says I play the villain,
    When this advice is free° I give, and honest,
    Probal° to thinking, and indeed the course
    To win the Moor again? For 'tis most easy
    Th' inclining° Desdemona to subdue°
    In any honest suit; she's framed as fruitful°
    As the free elements.° And then for her
    To win the Moor—were 't to renounce his baptism,
    All seals and symbols of redeemèd sin—
    His soul is so enfettered to her love
    That she may make, unmake, do what she list,
    Even as her appetite° shall play the god
    With his weak function.° How am I then a villain,
    To counsel Cassio to this parallel° course
    Directly to his good? Divinity of hell!°
    When devils will the blackest sins put on,°
    They do suggest° at first with heavenly shows,
    As I do now. For whiles this honest fool
    Plies Desdemona to repair his fortune,
    And she for him pleads strongly to the Moor,
    I'll pour this pestilence into his ear,
    That she repeals him° for her body's lust;
    And by how much she strives to do him good,
    She shall undo her credit with the Moor.
    So will I turn her virtue into pitch,°
    And out of her own goodness make the net
    That shall enmesh them all.

Enter Roderigo.

                      How now, Roderigo?
Roderigo: I do follow here in the chase, not like a hound that hunts, but one that fills up the cry.° My money is almost spent; I have been tonight exceedingly well cudgeled; and I think the issue will be I shall have so much° experience for my pains, and so, with no money at all and a little more wit, return again to Venice.
Iago: How poor are they that have not patience!
    What wound did ever heal but by degrees?
    Thou know'st we work by wit, and not by witchcraft,
    And wit depends on dilatory time.
    Does 't not go well? Cassio hath beaten thee,

---

288 *free* (1) free from guile (2) freely given   289 *Probal* probable, reasonable   291 *inclining* favorably disposed. *subdue* persuade   292 *framed as fruitful* created as generous   293 *free elements* i.e., earth, air, fire, and water, unrestrained and spontaneous   298 *her appetite* her desire, or, perhaps, his desire for her   299 *function* exercise of faculties (weakened by his fondness for her)   300 *parallel* corresponding to these facts and to his best interests   301 *Divinity of hell* inverted theology of hell (which seduces the soul to its damnation)   302 *put on* further, instigate   303 *suggest* tempt   308 *repeals him* attempts to get him restored   311 *pitch* i.e., (1) foul blackness (2) a snaring substance   315 *fills up the cry* merely takes part as one of the pack   316 *so much* just so much and no more

And thou, by that small hurt, hast cashiered° Cassio.
Though other things grow fair against the sun, 325
Yet fruits that blossom first will first be ripe.°
Content thyself awhile. By the Mass, 'tis morning!
Pleasure and action make the hours seem short.
Retire thee; go where thou art billeted.
Away, I say! Thou shalt know more hereafter. 330
Nay, get thee gone.   *Exit Roderigo.*
        Two things are to be done.
My wife must move° for Cassio to her mistress;
I'll set her on;
Myself the while to draw the Moor apart
And bring him jump° when he may Cassio find 335
Soliciting his wife. Ay, that's the way.
Dull not device° by coldness° and delay.   *Exit.*

ACT III

SCENE I [BEFORE THE CHAMBER OF OTHELLO AND DESDEMONA.]

Enter Cassio [and] Musicians.

Cassio: Masters, play here—I will content your pains°—
    Something that's brief, and bid "Good morrow, General."   *[They play.]*

[Enter] Clown.

Clown: Why, masters, have your instruments been in Naples, that they speak i' the nose° thus?
A Musician: How, sir, how? 5
Clown: Are these, I pray you, wind instruments?
A Musician: Ay, marry, are they, sir.
Clown: O, thereby hangs a tail.
A Musician: Whereby hangs a tale, sir?
Clown: Marry, sir, by many a wind instrument° that I know. But, masters, here's 10
    money for you. *[He gives money.]* And the General so likes your music that he
    desires you, for love's sake,° to make no more noise with it.
A Musician: Well, sir, we will not.
Clown: If you have any music that may not° be heard, to 't again; but, as they say, to
    hear music the General does not greatly care. 15
A Musician: We have none such, sir.

---

324 *cashiered* dismissed from service   325–326 *Though . . . ripe* i.e., plans that are well prepared and set expeditiously in motion will soonest ripen into success   332 *move* plead   335 *jump* precisely   337 *device* plot.   *coldness* lack of zeal   1 *content your pains* reward your efforts   3–4 *speak i' the nose* (1) sound nasal (2) sound like one whose nose has been attacked by syphilis. (Naples was popularly supposed to have a high incidence of venereal disease.)   10 *wind instrument* (With a joke on flatulence. The *tail*, line 8, that hangs nearby the *wind instrument* suggests the penis.)   12 *for love's sake* (1) out of friendship and affection (2) for the sake of lovemaking in Othello's marriage   14 *may not* cannot

Clown: Then put up your pipes in your bag, for I'll away.° Go, vanish into air, away!

Exeunt Musicians.

Cassio: Dost thou hear, mine honest friend?
Clown: No, I hear not your honest friend; I hear you.
Cassio: Prithee, keep up° thy quillets.° There's a poor piece of gold for thee. *[He gives money.]* If the gentle-woman that attends the General's wife be stirring, tell her there's one Cassio entreats her a little favor of speech.° Wilt thou do this?
Clown: She is stirring, sir. If she will stir° hither, I shall seem° to notify unto her.
Cassio: Do, good my friend.

Exit Clown.

Enter Iago.

                In happy time,° Iago.
Iago: You have not been abed, then?
Cassio: Why, no. The day had broke
   Before we parted. I have made bold, Iago,
   To send in to your wife. My suit to her
   Is that she will to virtuous Desdemona
   Procure me some access.
Iago: I'll send her to you presently;
   And I'll devise a means to draw the Moor
   Out of the way, that your converse and business
   May be more free.
Cassio: I humbly thank you for 't.

Exit [Iago].

               I never knew
   A Florentine° more kind and honest.

Enter Emilia.

Emilia: Good morrow, good Lieutenant. I am sorry
   For your displeasure;° but all will sure be well.
   The General and his wife are talking of it,
   And she speaks for you stoutly.° The Moor replies
   That he you hurt is of great fame° in Cyprus
   And great affinity,° and that in wholesome wisdom
   He might not but refuse you; but he protests° he loves you
   And needs no other suitor but his likings
   To take the safest occasion by the front°
   To bring you in again.
Cassio: Yet I beseech you,
   If you think fit, or that it may be done,
   Give me advantage of some brief discourse
   With Desdemona alone.

---

17 *I'll away* (Possibly a misprint, or a snatch of song?)   21 *keep up* do not bring out, do not use.   *quillets* quibbles, puns   23 *a little . . . speech* the favor of a brief talk   24 *stir* bestir herself (with a play on *stirring*, "rousing herself from rest").   *seem* deem it good, think fit   25 *In happy time* i.e., well met   37 *Florentine* i.e., even a fellow Florentine. (Iago is a Venetian; Cassio is a Florentine.)   39 *displeasure* fall from favor   41 *stoutly* spiritedly   42 *fame* reputation, importance   43 *affinity* kindred, family connection   44 *protests* insists   46 *occasion . . . front* opportunity by the forelock

Emilia: Pray you, come in. 50
    I will bestow you where you shall have time
    To speak your bosom° freely.
Cassio: I am much bound to you.   *[Exeunt.]*

SCENE II [THE CITADEL.]

Enter Othello, Iago, and Gentlemen.

Othello [giving letters]: These letters give, Iago, to the pilot,
    And by him do my duties° to the Senate.
    That done, I will be walking on the works;°
    Repair° there to me.
Iago: Well, my good lord, I'll do 't.
Othello: This fortification, gentlemen, shall we see 't?   5
Gentlemen: We'll wait upon° your lordship.   *Exeunt.*

SCENE III [THE GARDEN OF THE CITADEL.]

Enter Desdemona, Cassio, and Emilia.

Desdemona: Be thou assured, good Cassio, I will do
    All my abilities in thy behalf.
Emilia: Good madam, do. I warrant it grieves my husband
    As if the cause were his.
Desdemona: O, that's an honest fellow. Do not doubt, Cassio,   5
    But I will have my lord and you again
    As friendly as you were.
Cassio: Bounteous madam,
    Whatever shall become of Michael Cassio,
    He's never anything but your true servant.
Desdemona: I know 't. I thank you. You do love my lord;   10
    You have known him long, and be you well assured
    He shall in strangeness° stand no farther off
    Than in a politic° distance.
Cassio: Ay, but, lady,
    That policy may either last so long,
    Or feed upon such nice and waterish diet,°   15
    Or breed itself so out of circumstance,°
    That, I being absent and my place supplied,°
    My general will forget my love and service.
Desdemona: Do not doubt° that. Before Emilia here
    I give thee warrant° of thy place. Assure thee,   20

---

52 *bosom* inmost thoughts   2 *do my duties* convey my respects   3 *works* breastworks, fortifications   4 *Repair* return, come   6 *wait upon* attend   12 *strangeness* aloofness   13 *politic* required by wise policy   15 *Or . . . diet* or sustain itself at length upon such trivial and meager technicalities   16 *breed . . . circumstance* continually renew itself so out of chance events, or yield so few chances for my being pardoned   17 *supplied* filled by another person   19 *doubt* fear   20 *warrant* guarantee

If I do vow a friendship I'll perform it
To the last article. My lord shall never rest.
I'll watch him tame° and talk him out of patience;°
His bed shall seem a school, his board° a shrift;°
I'll intermingle everything he does   25
With Cassio's suit. Therefore be merry, Cassio,
For thy solicitor° shall rather die
Than give thy cause away.°

    Enter Othello and Iago [at a distance].

Emilia: Madam, here comes my lord.
Cassio: Madam, I'll take my leave.   30
Desdemona: Why, stay, and hear me speak.
Cassio: Madam, not now. I am very ill at ease,
    Unfit for mine own purposes.
Desdemona: Well, do your discretion.°   *Exit Cassio.*
Iago: Ha? I like not that.   35
Othello: What dost thou say?
Iago: Nothing, my lord; or if—I know not what.
Othello: Was not that Cassio parted from my wife?
Iago: Cassio, my lord? No, sure, I cannot think it,
    That he would steal away so guiltylike,   40
    Seeing you coming.
Othello: I do believe 'twas he.
Desdemona: How now, my lord?
    I have been talking with a suitor here,
    A man that languishes in your displeasure.   45
Othello: Who is 't you mean?
Desdemona: Why, your lieutenant, Cassio. Good my lord,
    If I have any grace or power to move you,
    His present reconciliation take;°
    For if he be not one that truly loves you,   50
    That errs in ignorance and not in cunning,°
    I have no judgment in an honest face.
    I prithee, call him back.
Othello: Went he hence now?
Desdemona: Yes, faith, so humbled   55
    That he hath left part of his grief with me
    To suffer with him. Good love, call him back.
Othello: Not now, sweet Desdemon. Some other time.
Desdemona: But shall 't be shortly?
Othello: The sooner, sweet, for you.   60
Desdemona: Shall 't be tonight at supper?

---

23 *watch him tame* tame him by keeping him from sleeping. (A term from falconry.) *out of patience* past his endurance 24 *board* dining table. *shrift* confessional 27 *solicitor* advocate 28 *away* up 34 *do your discretion* act according to your own discretion 49 *His . . . take* let him be reconciled to you right away 51 *in cunning* wittingly

Othello: No, not tonight.
Desdemona: Tomorrow dinner,° then?
Othello: I shall not dine at home.
   I meet the captains at the citadel.
Desdemona: Why, then, tomorrow night, or Tuesday morn,
   On Tuesday noon, or night, on Wednesday morn.
   I prithee, name the time, but let it not
   Exceed three days. In faith, he's penitent;
   And yet his trespass, in our common reason°—
   Save that, they say, the wars must make example
   Out of her best°—is not almost° a fault
   T' incur a private check.° When shall he come?
   Tell me, Othello. I wonder in my soul
   What you would ask me that I should deny,
   Or stand so mammering on.° What? Michael Cassio,
   That came a-wooing with you, and so many a time,
   When I have spoke of you dispraisingly,
   Hath ta'en your part—to have so much to do
   To bring him in!° By 'r Lady, I could do much—
Othello: Prithee, no more. Let him come when he will;
   I will deny thee nothing.
Desdemona: Why, this is not a boon.
   'Tis as I should entreat you wear your gloves,
   Or feed on nourishing dishes, or keep you warm,
   Or sue to you to do a peculiar° profit
   To your own person. Nay, when I have a suit
   Wherein I mean to touch° your love indeed,
   It shall be full of poise° and difficult weight,
   And fearful to be granted.
Othello: I will deny thee nothing.
   Whereon,° I do beseech thee, grant me this,
   To leave me but a little to myself.
Desdemona: Shall I deny you? No. Farewell, my lord.
Othello: Farewell, my Desdemona. I'll come to thee straight.°
Desdemona: Emilia, come.—Be as your fancies° teach you;
   Whate'er you be, I am obedient.   *Exit [with Emilia]*
Othello: Excellent wretch!° Perdition catch my soul
   But I do love thee! And when I love thee not,
   Chaos is come again.°
Iago: My noble lord—

63 *dinner* (The noontime meal.)   70 *common reason* everyday judgments   71–72 *Save . . . best* were it not that, as the saying goes, military discipline requires making an example of the very best men. (He refers to *wars* as a singular concept.)   72 *not almost* scarcely   73 *private check* even a private reprimand   76 *mammering on* wavering about   80 *bring him in* restore him to favor   86 *peculiar* particular, personal   88 *touch* test   89 *poise* weight, heaviness; or equipoise, delicate balance involving hard choice   92 *Whereon* in return for which   95 *straight* straightway   96 *fancies* inclinations   98 *wretch* (A term of affectionate endearment.)   99–100 *And . . . again* i.e., my love for you will last forever, until the end of time when chaos will return. (But with an unconscious, ironic suggestion that, if anything should induce Othello to cease loving Desdemona, the result would be chaos.)

Othello: What dost thou say, Iago?
Iago: Did Michael Cassio, when you wooed my lady,
　　Know of your love?
Othello: He did, from first to last. Why dost thou ask?
Iago: But for a satisfaction of my thought;
　　No further harm.
Othello:　　　　　Why of thy thought, Iago?
Iago: I did not think he had been acquainted with her.
Othello: O, yes, and went between us very oft.
Iago: Indeed?
Othello: Indeed? Ay, indeed. Discern'st thou aught in that?
　　Is he not honest?
Iago: Honest, my lord?
Othello: Honest. Ay, honest.
Iago: My lord, for aught I know.
Othello: What dost thou think?
Iago: Think, my lord?
Othello: "Think, my lord?" By heaven, thou echo'st me,
　　As if there were some monster in thy thought
　　Too hideous to be shown. Thou dost mean something.
　　I heard thee say even now, thou lik'st not that,
　　When Cassio left my wife. What didst not like?
　　And when I told thee he was of my counsel°
　　In my whole course of wooing, thou criedst "Indeed?"
　　And didst contract and purse° thy brow together
　　As if thou then hadst shut up in thy brain
　　Some horrible conceit.° If thou dost love me,
　　Show me thy thought.
Iago: My lord, you know I love you.
Othello: I think thou dost;
　　And, for° I know thou'rt full of love and honesty,
　　And weigh'st thy words before thou giv'st them breath,
　　Therefore these stops° of thine fright me the more;
　　For such things in a false disloyal knave
　　Are tricks of custom,° but in a man that's just
　　They're close dilations,° working from the heart
　　That passion cannot rule.°
Iago:　　　　　For° Michael Cassio,
　　I dare be sworn I think that he is honest.
Othello: I think so too.
Iago:　　　　Men should be what they seem;
　　Or those that be not, would they might seem none!°
Othello: Certain, men should be what they seem.

105

110

115

120

125

130

135

140

123 *of my counsel* in my confidence　125 *purse* knit　127 *conceit* fancy　131 *for* because　133 *stops* pauses　135 *of custom* customary　136 *close dilations* secret or involuntary expressions or delays　137 *That passion cannot rule* i.e., that are too passionately strong to be restrained (referring to the workings), or that cannot rule its own passions (referring to the heart).　137 *For* as for　140 *none* i.e., not to be men, or not seem to be honest

Iago: Why, then, I think Cassio's an honest man.
Othello: Nay, yet there's more in this.
    I prithee, speak to me as to thy thinkings,
    As thou dost ruminate, and give thy worst of thoughts 145
    The worst of words.
Iago: Good my lord, pardon me.
    Though I am bound to every act of duty,
    I am not bound to that° all slaves are free to.°
    Utter my thoughts? Why, say they are vile and false,
    As where's the palace whereinto foul things 150
    Sometimes intrude not? Who has that breast so pure
    But some uncleanly apprehensions
    Keep leets and law days,° and in sessions sit
    With° meditations lawful?°
Othello: Thou dost conspire against thy friend,° Iago, 155
    If thou but think'st him wronged and mak'st his ear
    A stranger to thy thoughts.
Iago: I do beseech you,
    Though I perchance am vicious° in my guess—
    As I confess it is my nature's plague
    To spy into abuses, and oft my jealousy° 160
    Shapes faults that are not—that your wisdom then,°
    From one° that so imperfectly conceits,°
    Would take no notice, nor build yourself a trouble
    Out of his scattering° and unsure observance.
    It were not for your quiet nor your good, 165
    Nor for my manhood, honesty, and wisdom,
    To let you know my thoughts.
Othello: What dost thou mean?
Iago: Good name in man and woman, dear my lord,
    Is the immediate° jewel of their souls.
    Who steals my purse steals trash; 'tis something, nothing; 170
    'Twas mine, 'tis his, and has been slave to thousands;
    But he that filches from me my good name
    Robs me of that which not enriches him
    And makes me poor indeed.
Othello: By heaven, I'll know thy thoughts. 175
Iago: You cannot, if° my heart were in your hand,
    Nor shall not, whilst 'tis in my custody.
Othello: Ha?
Iago: O, beware, my lord, of jealousy.
    It is the green-eyed monster which doth mock
    The meat it feeds on.° That cuckold lives in bliss 180

---

148 *that* that which. *free to* free with respect to   153 *Keep leets and law days* i.e., hold court, set up their authority in one's heart. (*Leets* are a kind of manor court; *law days* are the days courts sit in session, or those sessions.)   154 *With* along with. *lawful* innocent   155 *thy friend* i.e., Othello   158 *vicious* wrong 160 *jealousy* suspicious nature   161 *then* on that account   162 *one* i.e., myself, Iago. *conceits* judges, conjectures   164 *scattering* random   169 *immediate* essential, most precious   176 *if* even if   179–180 *doth mock . . . on* mocks and torments the heart of its victim, the man who suffers jealousy

Iago plants doubts about Desdemona in Othello's mind (III, iii, 101–295).

    Who, certain of his fate, loves not his wronger;°
    But O, what damnèd minutes tells° he o'er
    Who dotes, yet doubts, suspects, yet fondly loves!
Othello: O misery!
Iago: Poor and content is rich, and rich enough,°   185
    But riches fineless° is as poor as winter
    To him that ever fears he shall be poor.
    Good God, the souls of all my tribe defend
    From jealousy!
Othello: Why, why is this?   190
    Think'st thou I'd make a life of jealousy,
    To follow still the changes of the moon
    With fresh suspicions?° No! To be once in doubt
    Is once° to be resolved.° Exchange me for a goat

---

181 *his wronger* i.e., his faithless wife. (The unsuspecting cuckold is spared the misery of loving his wife only to discover she is cheating on him.)   182 *tells* counts   185 *Poor . . . enough* to be content with what little one has is the greatest wealth of all. (Proverbial.)   186 *fineless* boundless   192–193 *To follow . . . suspicions* to be constantly imagining new causes for suspicion, changing incessantly like the moon   194 *once* once and for all.   *resolved* free of doubt, having settled the matter

When I shall turn the business of my soul
To such exsufflicate and blown° surmises
Matching thy inference.° 'Tis not to make me jealous
To say my wife is fair, feeds well, loves company,
Is free of speech, sings, plays, and dances well;
Where virtue is, these are more virtuous.
Nor from mine own weak merits will I draw
The smallest fear or doubt of her revolt,°
For she had eyes, and chose me. No, Iago,
I'll see before I doubt; when I doubt, prove;
And on the proof, there is no more but this—
Away at once with love or jealousy.

Iago: I am glad of this, for now I shall have reason
To show the love and duty that I bear you
With franker spirit. Therefore, as I am bound,
Receive it from me. I speak not yet of proof.
Look to your wife; observe her well with Cassio.
Wear your eyes thus, not° jealous nor secure.°
I would not have your free and noble nature,
Out of self-bounty,° be abused.° Look to 't.
I know our country disposition well;
In Venice they do let God see the pranks
They dare not show their husbands; their best conscience
Is not to leave 't undone, but keep 't unknown.

Othello: Dost thou say so?

Iago: She did deceive her father, marrying you;
And when she seemed to shake and fear your looks,
She loved them most.

Othello: And so she did.

Iago: Why, go to,° then!
She that, so young, could give out such a seeming,°
To seel° her father's eyes up close as oak,°
He thought 'twas witchcraft! But I am much to blame.
I humbly do beseech you of your pardon
For too much loving you.

Othello: I am bound° to thee forever.

Iago: I see this hath a little dashed your spirits.

Othello: Not a jot, not a jot.

Iago: I' faith, I fear it has.
I hope you will consider what is spoke
Comes from my love. But I do see you're moved.
I am to pray you not to strain my speech

---

196 *exsufflicate and blown* inflated and blown up, rumored about, or, spat out and flyblown, hence, loathsome, disgusting   197 *inference* description or allegation   202 *doubt . . . revolt* fear of her unfaithfulness   212 *not* neither. *secure* free from uncertainty   214 *self-bounty* inherent or natural goodness and generosity. *abused* deceived   222 *go to* (An expression of impatience.)   223 *seeming* false appearance   224 *seel* blind. (A term from falconry.) *oak* (A close-grained wood.)   228 *bound* indebted (but perhaps with ironic sense of "tied")

   To grosser issues° nor to larger reach°
   Than to suspicion.   235
Othello: I will not.
Iago: Should you do so, my lord,
   My speech should fall into such vile success°
   Which my thoughts aimed not. Cassio's my worthy friend.
   My lord, I see you're moved.
Othello: No, not much moved.   240
   I do not think but Desdemona's honest.°
Iago: Long live she so! And long live you to think so!
Othello: And yet, how nature erring from itself—
Iago: Ay, there's the point! As—to be bold with you—
   Not to affect° many proposèd matches   245
   Of her own clime, complexion, and degree,°
   Whereto we see in all things nature tends—
   Foh! One may smell in such a will° most rank,
   Foul disproportion,° thoughts unnatural.
   But pardon me. I do not in position°   250
   Distinctly speak of her, though I may fear
   Her will, recoiling° to her better° judgment,
   May fall to match you with her country forms°
   And happily repent.°
Othello: Farewell, farewell!
   If more thou dost perceive, let me know more.   255
   Set on thy wife to observe. Leave me, Iago.
Iago [going]: My lord, I take my leave.
Othello: Why did I marry? This honest creature doubtless
   Sees and knows more, much more, than he unfolds.
Iago [returning]: My Lord, I would I might entreat your honor 260
   To scan° this thing no farther. Leave it to time.
   Although 'tis fit that Cassio have his place—
   For, sure, he fills it up with great ability—
   Yet, if you please to hold him off awhile,
   You shall by that perceive him and his means.°   265
   Note if your lady strain his entertainment°
   With any strong or vehement importunity;
   Much will be seen in that. In the meantime,
   Let me be thought too busy° in my fears—
   As worthy cause I have to fear I am—   270
   And hold her free,° I do beseech your honor.
Othello: Fear not my government.°
Iago: I once more take my leave.   *Exit.*

---

234 *issues* significances. *reach* meaning, scope 238 *success* effect, result 241 *honest* chaste 245 *affect* prefer, desire 246 *clime . . . degree* country, color, and social position 248 *will* sensuality, appetite 249 *disproportion* abnormality 250 *position* argument, proposition 252 *recoiling* reverting. *better* i.e., more natural and reconsidered 253 *fall . . . forms* undertake to compare you with Venetian norms of handsomeness 254 *happily repent* happily repent her marriage 261 *scan* scrutinize 265 *his means* the method he uses (to regain his post) 266 *strain his entertainment* urge his reinstatement 269 *busy* interfering 271 *hold her free* regard her as innocent 272 *government* self-control, conduct

Othello: This fellow's of exceeding honesty,
    And knows all qualities,° with a learnèd spirit,
    Of human dealings. If I do prove her haggard,°
    Though that her jesses° were my dear heartstrings,
    I'd whistle her off and let her down the wind°
    To prey at fortune.° Haply, for° I am black
    And have not those soft parts of conversation°
    That chamberers° have, or for I am declined
    Into the vale of years—yet that's not much—
    She's gone. I am abused,° and my relief
    Must be to loathe her. O curse of marriage,
    That we can call these delicate creatures ours
    And not their appetites! I had rather be a toad
    And live upon the vapor of a dungeon
    Than keep a corner in the thing I love
    For others' uses. Yet, 'tis the plague of great ones;
    Prerogatived° are they less than the base.°
    'Tis destiny unshunnable, like death.
    Even then this forkèd° plague is fated to us
    When we do quicken.° Look where she comes.

Enter Desdemona and Emilia.

    If she be false, O, then heaven mocks itself!
    I'll not believe 't.
Desdemona: How now, my dear Othello?
    Your dinner, and the generous° islanders
    By you invited, do attend° your presence.
Othello: I am to blame.
Desdemona: Why do you speak so faintly?
    Are you not well?
Othello: I have a pain upon my forehead here.
Desdemona: Faith, that's with watching.° 'Twill away again.

[She offers her handkerchief.]

    Let me but bind it hard, within this hour
    It will be well.
Othello: Your napkin° is too little.
    Let it alone.° Come, I'll go in with you.

[He puts the handkerchief from him, and it drops.]

275

280

285

290

295

300

---

275 *qualities* natures, types   276 *haggard* wild (like a wild female hawk)   277 *jesses* straps fastened around the legs of a trained hawk   278 *I'd . . . wind* i.e., I'd let her go forever. (To release a hawk downwind was to invite it not to return.)   279 *prey at fortune* fend for herself in the wild.   *Haply, for* perhaps because   280 *soft . . . conversation* pleasing graces of social behavior   281 *chamberers* gallants   283 *abused* deceived   290 *Prerogatived* privileged (to have honest wives).   *the base* ordinary citizens. (Socially prominent men are especially prone to the unavoidable destiny of being cuckolded and to the public shame that goes with it.)   292 *forkèd* (An allusion to the horns of the cuckold.)   293 *quicken* receive life. (Quicken may also mean to swarm with maggots as the body festers, as in IV, ii, 69, in which case lines 292–293 suggest that *even then*, in death, we are cuckolded by *forkèd* worms.)   296 *generous* noble   297 *attend* await   301 *watching* too little sleep   303 *napkin* handkerchief   304 *Let it alone* i.e., never mind

Desdemona: I am very sorry that you are not well. 305

   Exit [with Othello].

Emilia [picking up the handkerchief]: I am glad I have found this napkin.
   This was her first remembrance from the Moor.
   My wayward° husband hath a hundred times
   Wooed me to steal it, but she so loves the token—
   For he conjured her she should ever keep it— 310
   That she reserves it evermore about her
   To kiss and talk to. I'll have the work ta'en out,°
   And give 't Iago. What he will do with it
   Heaven knows, not I;
   I nothing but to please his fantasy.° 315

   Enter Iago.

Iago: How now? What do you here alone?
Emilia: Do not you chide. I have a thing for you.
Iago: You have a thing for me? It is a common thing°—
Emilia: Ha?
Iago: To have a foolish wife. 320
Emilia: O, is that all? What will you give me now
   For that same handkerchief?
Iago: What handkerchief?
Emilia: What handkerchief?
   Why, that the Moor first gave to Desdemona; 325
   That which so often you did bid me steal.
Iago: Hast stolen it from her?
Emilia: No, faith. She let it drop by negligence,
   And to th' advantage° I, being here, took 't up.
   Look, here 'tis.
Iago: A good wench! Give it me. 330
Emilia: What will you do with 't, that you have been so earnest
   To have me filch it?
Iago [snatching it]:   Why, what is that to you?
Emilia: If it be not for some purpose of import,
   Give 't me again. Poor lady, she'll run mad
   When she shall lack° it.
Iago: Be not acknown on 't.° 335
   I have use for it. Go, leave me.   *Exit Emilia.*
   I will in Cassio's lodging lose° this napkin
   And let him find it. Trifles light as air
   Are to the jealous confirmations strong
   As proofs of Holy Writ. This may do something. 340

308 *wayward* capricious   312 *work ta'en out* design of the embroidery copied   315 *fantasy* whim   318 *common thing* (With bawdy suggestion; *common* suggests coarseness and availability to all comers, and *thing* is a slang term for the pudendum.)   329 *to th' advantage* taking the opportunity   335 *lack* miss. *Be . . . on 't* do not confess knowledge of it   337 *lose* (The Folio spelling, *loose*, is a normal spelling for "lose," but it may also contain the idea of "let go," "release.")

Iago: "I have use for it. Go, leave me. / I will in Cassio's lodging lose this napkin" (III, iii, 336–337).

    The Moor already changes with my poison.
Dangerous conceits° are in their natures poisons,
Which at the first are scarce found to distaste,°
But with a little act° upon the blood
Burn like the mines of sulfur.

Enter Othello.

                              I did say so.
Look where he comes! Not poppy nor mandragora°
Nor all the drowsy syrups of the world

345

---

342 *conceits* fancies, ideas   343 *distaste* be distasteful   344 *act* action, working   346 *mandragora* an opiate made of the mandrake root

      Shall ever medicine thee to that sweet sleep
        Which thou owedst° yesterday.
Othello: Ha, ha, false to me?
Iago: Why, how now, General? No more of that.   350
Othello: Avaunt! Begone! Thou hast set me on the rack.
      I swear 'tis better to be much abused
      Than but to know 't a little.
Iago: How now, my lord?
Othello: What sense had I of her stolen hours of lust?
      I saw 't not, thought it not, it harmed not me.   355
      I slept the next night well, fed well, was free° and merry;
      I found not Cassio's kisses on her lips.
      He that is robbed, not wanting° what is stolen,
      Let him not know 't and he's not robbed at all.
Iago: I am sorry to hear this.   360
Othello: I had been happy if the general camp,
      Pioners° and all, had tasted her sweet body,
      So° I had nothing known. O, now, forever
      Farewell the tranquil mind! Farewell content!
      Farewell the plumèd troops and the big° wars   365
      That makes ambition virtue! O, farewell!
      Farewell the neighing steed and the shrill trump,
      The spirit-stirring drum, th' ear-piercing fife,
      The royal banner, and all quality,°
      Pride,° pomp, and circumstance° of glorious war!   370
      And O, you mortal engines,° whose rude throats
      Th' immortal Jove's dread clamors° counterfeit,
      Farewell! Othello's occupation's gone.
Iago: Is 't possible, my lord?
Othello: Villain, be sure thou prove my love a whore!   375
      Be sure of it. Give me the ocular proof,
      Or, by the worth of mine eternal soul,
      Thou hadst been better have been born a dog
      Than answer my waked wrath!
Iago: Is 't come to this?
Othello: Make me to see 't, or at the least so prove it   380
      That the probation° bear no hinge nor loop
      To hang a doubt on, or woe upon thy life!
Iago: My noble lord—
Othello: If thou dost slander her and torture me,
      Never pray more; abandon all remorse;°   385
      On horror's head horrors accumulate;°
      Do deeds to make heaven weep, all earth amazed;°

349 *thou owedst* you did own   356 *free* carefree   358 *wanting* missing   362 *Pioners* diggers of mines, the lowest grade of soldiers   363 *So* provided   365 *big* stately   369 *quality* character, essential nature   370 *Pride* rich display. *circumstance* pageantry   371 *mortal engines* i.e., cannon. (Mortal means "deadly.")   372 *Jove's dread clamors* i.e., thunder   381 *probation* proof   385 *remorse* pity, penitent hope for salvation   386 *horrors accumulate* add still more horrors   387 *amazed* confounded with horror

>   For nothing canst thou to damnation add
>   Greater than that.
> Iago: O grace! O heaven forgive me!
>   Are you a man? Have you a soul or sense?
>   God b' wi' you; take mine office. O wretched fool,°
>   That lov'st to make thine honesty a vice!°
>   O monstrous world! Take note, take note, O world,
>   To be direct and honest is not safe.
>   I thank you for this profit,° and from hence°
>   I'll love no friend, sith° love breeds such offense.°
> Othello: Nay, stay. Thou shouldst be° honest.
> Iago: I should be wise, for honesty's a fool
>   And loses that° it works for.
> Othello: By the world,
>   I think my wife be honest and think she is not;
>   I think that thou art just and think thou art not.
>   I'll have some proof. My name, that was as fresh
>   As Dian's° visage, is now begrimed and black
>   As mine own face. If there be cords, or knives,
>   Poison, or fire, or suffocating streams,
>   I'll not endure it. Would I were satisfied!
> Iago: I see, sir, you are eaten up with passion.
>   I do repent me that I put it to you.
>   You would be satisfied?
> Othello: Would? Nay, and I will.
> Iago: And may; but how? How satisfied, my lord?
>   Would you, the supervisor,° grossly gape on?
>   Behold her topped?
> Othello: Death and damnation! O!
> Iago: It were a tedious difficulty, I think,
>   To bring them to that prospect. Damn them then,°
>   If ever mortal eyes do see them bolster°
>   More° than their own.° What then? How then?
>   What shall I say? Where's satisfaction?
>   It is impossible you should see this,
>   Were they as prime° as goats, as hot as monkeys,
>   As salt° as wolves in pride,° and fools as gross
>   As ignorance made drunk. But yet I say,
>   If imputation and strong circumstances°
>   Which lead directly to the door of truth
>   Will give you satisfaction, you might have 't.

390

395

400

405

410

415

420

391 *O wretched fool* (Iago addresses himself as a fool for having carried honesty too far.)   392 *vice* failing, something overdone   395 *profit* profitable instruction.   *hence* henceforth   396 *sith* since.   *offense* i.e., harm to the one who offers help and friendship   397 *Thou shouldst be* it appears that you are. (But Iago replies in the sense of "ought to be.")   399 *that* what   403 *Dian* Diana, goddess of the moon and of chastity   411 *supervisor* onlooker   414 *Damn them then* i.e., they would have to be really incorrigible   415 *bolster* go to bed together, share a bolster   416 *More* other.   *own* own eyes   419 *prime* lustful   420 *salt* wanton, sensual.   *pride* heat   422 *imputation . . . circumstances* strong circumstantial evidence

Othello: Give me a living reason she's disloyal. 425
Iago: I do not like the office.
   But sith° I am entered in this cause so far,
   Pricked° to 't by foolish honesty and love,
   I will go on. I lay with Cassio lately,
   And being troubled with a raging tooth 430
   I could not sleep. There are a kind of men
   So loose of soul that in their sleeps will mutter
   Their affairs. One of this kind is Cassio.
   In sleep I heard him say, "Sweet Desdemona,
   Let us be wary, let us hide our loves!" 435
   And then, sir, would he grip and wring my hand,
   Cry "O sweet creature!" and then kiss me hard,
   As if he plucked up kisses by the roots
   That grew upon my lips; then laid his leg
   Over my thigh, and sighed, and kissed, and then 440
   Cried, "Cursèd fate that gave thee to the Moor!"
Othello: O monstrous! Monstrous!
Iago: Nay, this was but his dream.
Othello: But this denoted a foregone conclusion.°
   'Tis a shrewd doubt,° though it be but a dream.
Iago: And this may help to thicken other proofs 445
   That do demonstrate thinly.
Othello: I'll tear her all to pieces.
Iago: Nay, but be wise. Yet we see nothing done;
   She may be honest yet. Tell me but this:
   Have you not sometimes seen a handkerchief
   Spotted with strawberries° in your wife's hand? 450
Othello: I gave her such a one. 'Twas my first gift.
Iago: I know not that; but such a handkerchief—
   I am sure it was your wife's—did I today
   See Cassio wipe his beard with.
Othello: If it be that—
Iago: If it be that, or any that was hers, 455
   It speaks against her with the other proofs.
Othello: O, that the slave° had forty thousand lives!
   One is too poor, too weak for my revenge.
   Now do I see 'tis true. Look here, Iago,
   All my fond° love thus do I blow to heaven. 460
   'Tis gone.
   Arise, black vengeance, from the hollow hell!
   Yield up, O love, thy crown and hearted° throne
   To tyrannous hate! Swell, bosom, with thy freight,°
   For 'tis of aspics'° tongues! 465

427 *sith* since   428 *Pricked* spurred   443 *foregone conclusion* concluded experience or action   444 *shrewd doubt* suspicious circumstance   450 *Spotted with strawberries* embroidered with a strawberry pattern   457 *the slave* i.e., Cassio   460 *fond* foolish (but also suggesting "affectionate")   463 *hearted* fixed in the heart   464 *freight* burden   465 *aspics'* venomous serpents'

Iago: Yet be content.°
Othello: O, blood, blood, blood!
Iago: Patience, I say. Your mind perhaps may change.
Othello: Never, Iago. Like to the Pontic Sea,°
    Whose icy current and compulsive course 470
    Ne'er feels retiring ebb, but keeps due on
    To the Propontic° and the Hellespont,°
    Even so my bloody thoughts with violent pace
    Shall ne'er look back, ne'er ebb to humble love,
    Till that a capable° and wide revenge 475
    Swallow them up. Now, by yond marble° heaven,
    [Kneeling] In the due reverence of a sacred vow
    I here engage my words.
Iago: Do not rise yet.
    [He kneels.°] Witness, you ever-burning lights above,
    You elements that clip° us round about, 480
    Witness that here Iago doth give up
    The execution° of his wit,° hands, heart,
    To wronged Othello's service. Let him command,
    And to obey shall be in me remorse,°
    What bloody business ever.°   *[They rise.]*
Othello: I greet thy love, 485
    Not with vain thanks, but with acceptance bounteous,
    And will upon the instant put thee to 't.°
    Within these three days let me hear thee say
    That Cassio's not alive.
Iago: My friend is dead;
    'Tis done at your request. But let her live. 490
Othello: Damn her, lewd minx!° O, damn her, damn her!
    Come, go with me apart. I will withdraw
    To furnish me with some swift means of death
    For the fair devil. Now art thou my lieutenant.
Iago: I am your own forever.   *Exeunt.* 495

SCENE IV [BEFORE THE CITADEL.]

    Enter Desdemona, Emilia, and Clown.

Desdemona: Do you know, sirrah,° where Lieutenant Cassio lies?°
Clown: I dare not say he lies anywhere.
Desdemona: Why, man?
Clown: He's a soldier, and for me to say a soldier lies, 'tis stabbing.

---

466 *content* calm   469 *Pontic Sea* Black Sea   472 *Propontic* Sea of Marmara, between the Black Sea and the Aegean. *Hellespont* Dardanelles, straits where the Sea of Marmara joins with the Aegean   475 *capable* ample, comprehensive   476 *marble* i.e., gleaming like marble and unrelenting   479 s.d. *He kneels* (In the Quarto text, Iago kneels here after Othello has knelt at line 477.)   480 *clip* encompass   482 *execution* exercise, action. *wit* mind   484 *remorse* pity (for Othello's wrongs)   485 *ever* soever   487 *to 't* to the proof   491 *minx* wanton   1 *sirrah* (A form of address to an inferior.)   *lies* lodges. (But the Clown makes the obvious pun.)

Desdemona: Go to. Where lodges he? 5
Clown: To tell you where he lodges is to tell you where I lie.
Desdemona: Can anything be made of this?
Clown: I know not where he lodges, and for me to devise a lodging and say he lies here, or he lies there, were to lie in mine own throat.°
Desdemona: Can you inquire him out, and be edified by report? 10
Clown: I will catechize the world for him; that is, make questions, and by them answer.
Desdemona: Seek him, bid him come hither. Tell him I have moved° my lord on his behalf and hope all will be well.
Clown: To do this is within the compass of man's wit, and therefore I will attempt 15
the doing it. *Exit Clown.*
Desdemona: Where should I lose that handkerchief, Emilia?
Emilia: I know not, madam.
Desdemona: Believe me, I had rather have lost my purse
    Full of crusadoes;° and but my noble Moor 20
    Is true of mind and made of no such baseness
    As jealous creatures are, it were enough
    To put him to ill thinking.
Emilia: Is he not jealous?
Desdemona: Who, he? I think the sun where he was born
    Drew all such humors° from him.
Emilia: Look where he comes. 25

    Enter Othello.

Desdemona: I will not leave him now till Cassio
    Be called to him.—How is 't with you, my lord?
Othello: Well, my good lady. *[Aside.]* O, hardness to dissemble!—
    How do you, Desdemona?
Desdemona: Well, my good lord.
Othello: Give me your hand. *[She gives her hand.]* This hand is moist, my lady. 30
Desdemona: It yet hath felt no age nor known no sorrow.
Othello: This argues° fruitfulness° and liberal° heart.
    Hot, hot, and moist. This hand of yours requires
    A sequester° from liberty, fasting and prayer,
    Much castigation,° exercise devout;° 35
    For here's a young and sweating devil here
    That commonly rebels. 'Tis a good hand,
    A frank° one.
Desdemona: You may indeed say so,
    For 'twas that hand that gave away my heart.
Othello: A liberal hand. The hearts of old gave hands,° 40

9 *lie . . . throat* (1) lie egregiously and deliberately (2) use the windpipe to speak a lie   13 *moved* petitioned   20 *crusadoes* Portuguese gold coins   25 *humors* (Refers to the four bodily fluids thought to determine temperament.)   32 *argues* gives evidence of.   *fruitfulness* generosity, amorousness, and fecundity.   *liberal* generous and sexually free   34 *sequester* separation, sequestration   35 *castigation* corrective discipline.   *exercise devout* i.e., prayer, religious meditation, etc.   38 *frank* generous, open (with sexual suggestion)   40 *The hearts . . . hands* i.e., in former times, people would give their hearts when they gave their hands to something

"She offers a handkerchief" (III, iv, 47 s.d.).

    But our new heraldry is hands, not hearts.°
Desdemona: I cannot speak of this. Come now, your promise.
Othello: What promise, chuck?°
Desdemona: I have sent to bid Cassio come speak with you.
Othello: I have a salt and sorry rheum° offends me;   45
    Lend me thy handkerchief.
Desdemona: Here, my lord.   *[She offers a handkerchief.]*
Othello: That which I gave you.
Desdemona: I have it not about me.
Othello: Not?
Desdemona: No, faith, my lord.   50
Othello: That's a fault. That handkerchief
    Did an Egyptian to my mother give.
    She was a charmer,° and could almost read
    The thoughts of people. She told her, while she kept it
    'Twould make her amiable° and subdue my father   55
    Entirely to her love, but if she lost it
    Or made a gift of it, my father's eye
    Should hold her loathèd and his spirits should hunt

41 *But . . . hearts* i.e., in our decadent times, the joining of hands is no longer a badge to signify the giving of hearts   43 *chuck* (A term of endearment.)   45 *salt . . . rheum* distressful head cold or watering of the eyes   53 *charmer* sorceress   55 *amiable* desirable

>   After new fancies.° She, dying, gave it me,
>   And bid me, when my fate would have me wived,   60
>   To give it her.° I did so; and take heed on 't;
>   Make it a darling like your precious eye.
>   To lose 't or give 't away were such perdition°
>   As nothing else could match.
> *Desdemona:*   Is 't possible?
> *Othello:* 'Tis true. There's magic in the web° of it.   65
>   A sibyl, that had numbered in the world
>   The sun to course two hundred compasses,°
>   In her prophetic fury° sewed the work;°
>   The worms were hallowed that did breed the silk,
>   And it was dyed in mummy° which the skillful   70
>   Conserved of° maidens' hearts.
> *Desdemona:*   I' faith! Is 't true?
> *Othello:* Most veritable. Therefore look to 't well.
> *Desdemona:* Then would to God that I had never seen 't!
> *Othello:* Ha? Wherefore?
> *Desdemona:* Why do you speak so startingly and rash?°   75
> *Othello:* Is 't lost? Is 't gone? Speak, is 't out o' the way?°
> *Desdemona:* Heaven bless us!
> *Othello:* Say you?
> *Desdemona:* It is not lost; but what an if° it were?
> *Othello:* How?   80
> *Desdemona:* I say it is not lost.
> *Othello:*   Fetch 't, let me see 't.
> *Desdemona:* Why, so I can, sir, but I will not now.
>   This is a trick to put me from my suit.
>   Pray you, let Cassio be received again.
> *Othello:* Fetch me the handkerchief! My mind misgives.   85
> *Desdemona:* Come, come,
>   You'll never meet a more sufficient° man.
> *Othello:* The handkerchief!
> *Desdemona:*   I pray, talk° me of Cassio.
> *Othello:* The handkerchief!
> *Desdemona:*   A man that all his time°
>   Hath founded his good fortunes on your love,   90
>   Shared dangers with you—
> *Othello:* The handkerchief!
> *Desdemona:* I' faith, you are to blame.
> *Othello:* Zounds!   *Exit Othello.*
> *Emilia:* Is not this man jealous?   95

59 *fancies* loves   61 *her* i.e., to my wife   63 *perdition* loss   65 *web* fabric, weaving   67 *compasses* annual circlings. (The *sibyl*, or prophetess, was two hundred years old.)   68 *prophetic fury* frenzy of prophetic inspiration.   *work* embroidered pattern   70 *mummy* medicinal or magical preparation drained from mummified bodies   71 *Conserved of* prepared or preserved out of   75 *startingly and rash* disjointedly and impetuously, excitedly   76 *out o' the way* lost, misplaced   79 *an if* if   87 *sufficient* able, complete   88 *talk* talk to   89 *all his time* throughout his career

Desdemona: I ne'er saw this before.
    Sure, there's some wonder in this handkerchief.
    I am most unhappy in the loss of it.
Emilia: 'Tis not a year or two shows us a man.°
    They are all but stomachs, and we all but° food;
    They eat us hungerly,° and when they are full
    They belch us.

Enter Iago and Cassio.

                    Look you, Cassio and my husband.
Iago [to Cassio]: There is no other way; 'tis she must do 't.
    And, lo, the happiness!° Go and importune her.
Desdemona: How now, good Cassio? What's the news with you?
Cassio: Madam, my former suit. I do beseech you
    That by your virtuous° means I may again
    Exist and be a member of his love
    Whom I, with all the office° of my heart,
    Entirely honor. I would not be delayed.
    If my offense be of such mortal° kind
    That nor my service past, nor° present sorrows,
    Nor purposed merit in futurity
    Can ransom me into his love again,
    But to know so must be my benefit;°
    So shall I clothe me in a forced content,
    And shut myself up in° some other course,
    To fortune's alms.°
Desdemona: Alas, thrice-gentle Cassio,
    My advocation° is not now in tune.
    My lord is not my lord; nor should I know him,
    Were he in favor° as in humor° altered.
    So help me every spirit sanctified
    As I have spoken for you all my best
    And stood within the blank° of his displeasure
    For my free speech! You must awhile be patient.
    What I can do I will, and more I will
    Than for myself I dare. Let that suffice you.
Iago: Is my lord angry?
Emilia: He went hence but now,
    And certainly in strange unquietness.
Iago: Can he be angry? I have seen the cannon
    When it hath blown his ranks into the air,

99 *'Tis . . . man* i.e., you can't really know a man even in a year or two of experience (?), or, real men come along seldom (?)   100 *but* nothing but   101 *hungerly* hungrily   104 *the happiness* in happy time, fortunately met   107 *virtuous* efficacious   109 *office* loyal service   111 *mortal* fatal   112 *nor . . . nor* neither . . . nor   115 *But . . . benefit* merely to know that my case is hopeless will have to content me (and will be better than uncertainty)   117 *shut . . . in* confine myself to   118 *To fortune's alms* throwing myself on the mercy of fortune   119 *advocation* advocacy   121 *favor* appearance.   *humor* mood   124 *within the blank* within point-blank range. (The *blank* is the center of the target.)

                    And like the devil from his very arm
                    Puffed his own brother—and is he angry?
                    Something of moment° then. I will go meet him.
                    There's matter in 't indeed, if he be angry.   135
Desdemona: I prithee, do so.   *Exit [Iago].*
                              Something, sure, of state,°
                    Either from Venice, or some unhatched practice°
                    Made demonstrable here in Cyprus to him,
                    Hath puddled° his clear spirit; and in such cases
                    Men's natures wrangle with inferior things,   140
                    Though great ones are their object. 'Tis even so;
                    For let our finger ache, and it indues°
                    Our other, healthful members even to a sense
                    Of pain. Nay, we must think men are not gods,
                    Nor of them look for such observancy°   145
                    As fits the bridal.° Beshrew me° much, Emilia,
                    I was, unhandsome° warrior as I am,
                    Arraigning his unkindness with° my soul;
                    But now I find I had suborned the witness,°
                    And he's indicted falsely.
Emilia: Pray heaven it be   150
                    State matters, as you think, and no conception
                    Nor no jealous toy° concerning you.
Desdemona: Alas the day! I never gave him cause.
Emilia: But jealous souls will not be answered so;
                    They are not ever jealous for the cause,   155
                    But jealous for° they're jealous. It is a monster
                    Begot upon itself,° born on itself.
Desdemona: Heaven keep that monster from Othello's mind!
Emilia: Lady, amen.
Desdemona: I will go seek him. Cassio, walk hereabout.   160
                    If I do find him fit, I'll move your suit
                    And seek to effect it to my uttermost.
Cassio: I humbly thank your ladyship.

        Exit [Desdemona with Emilia].

        Enter Bianca.

Bianca: Save° you, friend Cassio!
Cassio: What make° you from home?
                    How is 't with you, my most fair Bianca?   165
                    I' faith, sweet love, I was coming to your house.

134 *of moment* of immediate importance, momentous   136 *of state* concerning state affairs   137 *unhatched practice* as yet unexecuted or undiscovered plot   139 *puddled* muddied   142 *indues* brings to the same condition   145 *observancy* attentiveness   146 *bridal* wedding (when a bridegroom is newly attentive to his bride). *Beshrew me* (A mild oath.)   147 *unhandsome* insufficient, unskillful   148 *with* before the bar of   149 *suborned the witness* induced the witness to give false testimony   152 *toy* fancy   156 *for* because   157 *Begot upon itself* generated solely from itself   164 *Save* God save.   *make* do

Cassio explains to Bianca that he does not know how the handkerchief appeared in his room (III, iv, 175–186).

Bianca: And I was going to your lodging, Cassio.
    What, keep a week away? Seven days and nights?
    Eightscore-eight° hours? And lovers' absent hours
    More tedious than the dial° eightscore times?   170
    O weary reckoning!
Cassio: Pardon me, Bianca.
    I have this while with leaden thoughts been pressed;
    But I shall, in a more continuate° time,
    Strike off this score° of absence. Sweet Bianca,

169 *Eightscore-eight* one hundred sixty-eight, the number of hours in a week   170 *the dial* a complete revolution of the clock   173 *continuate* uninterrupted   174 *Strike . . . score* settle this account

[giving her Desdemona's handkerchief]

Take me this work out.°
Bianca:　　　　　　　O Cassio, whence came this?
　This is some token from a newer friend.°
　To the felt absence now I feel a cause.
　Is 't come to this? Well, well.
Cassio:　　　　　　　Go to, woman!
　Throw your vile guesses in the devil's teeth,
　From whence you have them. You are jealous now
　That this is from some mistress, some remembrance.
　No, by my faith, Bianca.
Bianca:　　　　　　Why, whose is it?
Cassio: I know not, neither. I found it in my chamber.
　I like the work well. Ere it be demanded°—
　As like° enough it will—I would have it copied.
　Take it and do 't, and leave me for this time.
Bianca: Leave you? Wherefore?
Cassio: I do attend here on the General,
　And think it no addition,° nor my wish,
　To have him see me womaned.
Bianca: Why, I pray you?
Cassio: Not that I love you not.
Bianca: But that you do not love me.
　I pray you, bring° me on the way a little,
　And say if I shall see you soon at night.
Cassio: 'Tis but a little way that I can bring you,
　For I attend here; but I'll see you soon.
Bianca: 'Tis very good. I must be circumstanced.°

　Exeunt omnes.

ACT IV

SCENE I [BEFORE THE CITADEL.]

　Enter Othello and Iago.

Iago: Will you think so?
Othello:　　　　　Think so, Iago?
Iago:　　　　　　　　　　What,
　To kiss in private?
Othello:　　　　　An unauthorized kiss!
Iago: Or to be naked with her friend in bed
　An hour or more, not meaning any harm?
Othello: Naked in bed, Iago, and not mean harm?
　It is hypocrisy against the devil.

175 *Take . . . out* copy this embroidery for me 176 *friend* mistress 184 *demanded* inquired for 185 *like* likely 189 *addition* i.e., addition to my reputation 194 *bring* accompany 198 *be circumstanced* be governed by circumstance, yield to your conditions

They that mean virtuously and yet do so,
　　　　The devil their virtue tempts, and they tempt heaven.
Iago: If they do nothing, 'tis a venial° slip.
　　　But if I give my wife a handkerchief—
Othello: What then?
Iago: Why then, 'tis hers, my lord, and being hers,
　　　She may, I think, bestow 't on any man.
Othello: She is protectress of her honor too.
　　　May she give that?
Iago: Her honor is an essence that's not seen;
　　　They have it° very oft that have it not.
　　　But, for the handkerchief—
Othello: By heaven, I would most gladly have forgot it.
　　　Thou saidst—O, it comes o'er my memory
　　　As doth the raven o'er the infectious house,°
　　　Boding to all—he had my handkerchief.
Iago: Ay, what of that?
Othello:　　　　That's not so good now.
Iago:　　　　　　　　　　What
　　　If I had said I had seen him do you wrong?
　　　Or heard him say—as knaves be such abroad,°
　　　Who having, by their own importunate suit,
　　　Or voluntary dotage° of some mistress,
　　　Convincèd or supplied° them, cannot choose
　　　But they must blab—
Othello:　　　　Hath he said anything?
Iago: He hath, my lord; but, be you well assured,
　　　No more than he'll unswear.
Othello:　　　　　　What hath he said?
Iago: Faith, that he did—I know not what he did.
Othello: What? What?
Iago: Lie—
Othello:　　With her?
Iago:　　　　With her, on her; what you will.
Othello: Lie with her? Lie on her? We say "lie on her" when they belie° her. Lie with her? Zounds, that's fulsome.°—Handkerchief—confessions—handkerchief!—To confess and be hanged for his labor—first to be hanged and then to confess.°—I tremble at it. Nature would not invest herself in such shadowing passion without some instruction.° It is not words° that shakes me

---

9 *venial* pardonable　17 *They have it* i.e., they enjoy a reputation for it　21 *raven . . . house* (Allusion to the belief that the raven hovered over a house of sickness or infection, such as one visited by the plague.)　25 *abroad* around about　27 *voluntary dotage* willing infatuation　28 *Convincèd or supplied* seduced or sexually gratified　35 *belie* slander　36 *fulsome* foul　37–38 *first . . . to confess* (Othello reverses the proverbial *confess* and *be hanged*; Cassio is to be given no time to confess before he dies.)　38–39 *Nature . . . instruction* i.e., without some foundation in fact, nature would not have dressed herself in such an overwhelming passion that comes over me now and fills my mind with images, or in such a lifelike fantasy as Cassio had in his dream of lying with Desdemona　39 *words* mere words

Iago lies to Cassio that Othello has "fall'n into an epilepsy" (IV, i, 48).

>   thus. Pish! Noses, ears, and lips.—Is 't possible?—Confess—handkerchief!— 40
>   O devil!
>
>   *Falls in a trance.*
>
> *Iago:* Work on,
>   My medicine, work! Thus credulous fools are caught,
>   And many worthy and chaste dames even thus,
>   All guiltless, meet reproach.—What, ho! My lord! 45
>   My lord, I say! Othello!
>
>   *Enter Cassio.*
>
>   How now, Cassio?
> *Cassio:* What's the matter?
> *Iago:* My lord is fall'n into an epilepsy.
>   This is his second fit. He had one yesterday.

Cassio: Rub him about the temples.
Iago: No, forbear.
   The lethargy° must have his° quiet course.
   If not, he foams at mouth, and by and by
   Breaks out to savage madness. Look, he stirs.
   Do you withdraw yourself a little while.
   He will recover straight. When he is gone,
   I would on great occasion° speak with you.

   [*Exit Cassio.*]

   How is it, General? Have you not hurt your head?
Othello: Dost thou mock me?°
Iago: I mock you not, by heaven.
   Would you would bear your fortune like a man!
Othello: A hornèd man's a monster and a beast.
Iago: There's many a beast then in a populous city,
   And many a civil° monster.
Othello: Did he confess it?
Iago: Good sir, be a man.
   Think every bearded fellow that's but yoked°
   May draw with you.° There's millions now alive
   That nightly lie in those unproper° beds
   Which they dare swear peculiar.° Your case is better.°
   O, 'tis the spite of hell, the fiend's arch-mock,
   To lip° a wanton in a secure° couch
   And to suppose her chaste! No, let me know,
   And knowing what I am,° I know what she shall be.°
Othello: O, thou art wise. 'Tis certain.
Iago: Stand you awhile apart;
   Confine yourself but in a patient list.°
   Whilst you were here o'erwhelmèd with your grief—
   A passion most unsuiting such a man—
   Cassio came hither. I shifted him away,°
   And laid good 'scuse upon your ecstasy,°
   Bade him anon return and here speak with me,
   The which he promised. Do but encave° yourself
   And mark the fleers,° the gibes, and notable° scorns
   That dwell in every region of his face;
   For I will make him tell the tale anew,
   Where, how, how oft, how long ago, and when
   He hath and is again to cope° your wife.

51 *lethargy* coma. *his* its   56 *on great occasion* on a matter of great importance   58 *mock me* (Othello takes Iago's question about hurting his head to be a mocking reference to the cuckold's horns.)   62 *civil* i.e., dwelling in a city   65 *yoked* (1) married (2) put into the yoke of infamy and cuckoldry   66 *draw with you* pull as you do, like oxen who are yoked, i.e., share your fate as cuckold   67 *unproper* not exclusively their own   68 *peculiar* private, their own. *better* i.e., because you know the truth   70 *lip* kiss. *secure* free from suspicion   72 *what I am* i.e., a cuckold. *she shall be* will happen to her   75 *in . . . list* within the bounds of patience   78 *shifted him away* used a dodge to get rid of him   79 *ecstasy* trance   81 *encave* conceal   82 *fleers* sneers. *notable* obvious   86 *cope* encounter with, have sex with

I say, but mark his gesture. Marry, patience!
Or I shall say you're all-in-all in spleen,°
And nothing of a man.
Othello: Dost thou hear, Iago?
I will be found most cunning in my patience;   90
But—dost thou hear?—most bloody.
Iago: That's not amiss;
But yet keep time° in all. Will you withdraw?

[*Othello stands apart.*]

Now will I question Cassio of Bianca,
A huswife° that by selling her desires
Buys herself bread and clothes. It is a creature   95
That dotes on Cassio—as 'tis the strumpet's plague
To beguile many and be beguiled by one.
He, when he hears of her, cannot restrain°
From the excess of laughter. Here he comes.

Enter Cassio.

As he shall smile, Othello shall go mad;   100
And his unbookish° jealousy must conster°
Poor Cassio's smiles, gestures, and light behaviors
Quite in the wrong.—How do you now, Lieutenant?
Cassio: The worser that you give me the addition°
Whose want° even kills me.   105
Iago: Ply Desdemona well and you are sure on 't.
   [*Speaking lower.*] Now, if this suit lay in Bianca's power,
How quickly should you speed!
Cassio [*laughing*]: Alas, poor caitiff!°
Othello [*aside*]: Look how he laughs already!   110
Iago: I never knew a woman love man so.
Cassio: Alas, poor rogue! I think, i' faith, she loves me.
Othello: Now he denies it faintly, and laughs it out.
Iago: Do you hear, Cassio?
Othello: Now he importunes him
To tell it o'er. Go to!° Well said,° well said.   115
Iago: She gives it out that you shall marry her.
Do you intend it?
Cassio: Ha, ha, ha!
Othello: Do you triumph, Roman?° Do you triumph?
Cassio: I marry her? What? A customer?° Prithee, bear some charity to my wit;° do   120
not think it so unwholesome. Ha, ha, ha!

88 *all-in-all in spleen* utterly governed by passionate impulses   92 *keep time* keep yourself steady (as in music)   94 *huswife* hussy   98 *restrain* refrain   101 *unbookish* uninstructed. *conster* construe   104 *addition* title   105 *Whose want* the lack of which   109 *caitiff* wretch   115 *Go to* (An expression of remonstrance.) *Well said* well done   119 *Roman* (The Romans were noted for their *triumphs* or triumphal processions.)   120 *customer* i.e., prostitute. *bear . . . wit* be more charitable to my judgment

Othello: So, so, so, so! They laugh that win.°
Iago: Faith, the cry° goes that you shall marry her.
Cassio: Prithee, say true.
Iago: I am a very villain else.°
Othello: Have you scored me?° Well.
Cassio: This is the monkey's own giving out. She is persuaded I will marry her out of her own love and flattery,° not out of my promise.
Othello: Iago beckons me.° Now he begins the story.
Cassio: She was here even now; she haunts me in every place. I was the other day talking on the seabank° with certain Venetians, and thither comes the bauble,° and, by this hand,° she falls me thus about my neck—

[He embraces Iago.]

Othello: Crying, "O dear Cassio!" as it were; his gesture imports it.
Cassio: So hangs and lolls and weeps upon me, so shakes and pulls me. Ha, ha, ha!
Othello: Now he tells how she plucked him to my chamber. O, I see that nose of yours, but not that dog I shall throw it to.°
Cassio: Well, I must leave her company.
Iago: Before me,° look where she comes.

Enter Bianca [with Othello's handkerchief].

Cassio: 'Tis such another fitchew!° Marry, a perfumed one.—What do you mean by this haunting of me?
Bianca: Let the devil and his dam° haunt you! What did you mean by that same handkerchief you gave me even now? I was a fine fool to take it. I must take out the work? A likely piece of work,° that you should find it in your chamber and know not who left it there! This is some minx's token, and I must take out the work? There; give it your hobbyhorse.° *[She gives him the handkerchief.]* Wheresoever you had it, I'll take out no work on 't.
Cassio: How now, my sweet Bianca? How now? How now?
Othello: By heaven, that should be° my handkerchief!
Bianca: If you'll come to supper tonight, you may; if you will not, come when you are next prepared for.° *Exit.*
Iago: After her, after her.
Cassio: Faith, I must. She'll rail in the streets else.
Iago: Will you sup there?
Cassio: Faith, I intend so.
Iago: Well, I may chance to see you, for I would very fain speak with you.
Cassio: Prithee, come. Will you?
Iago: Go to.° Say no more. *[Exit Cassio.]*

122 *They . . . win* i.e., they that laugh last laugh best   123 *cry* rumor   125 *I . . . else* call me a complete rogue if I'm not telling the truth   126 *scored me* scored off me, beaten me, made up my reckoning, branded me   128 *flattery* self-flattery, self-deception   129 *beckons* signals   131 *seabank* seashore.   *bauble* plaything   132 *by this hand* I make my vow   136 *not . . . to* (Othello imagines himself cutting off Cassio's nose and throwing it to a dog.)   138 *Before me* i.e., on my soul   139 *'Tis . . . fitchew* what a polecat she is! Just like all the others. (Polecats were often compared with prostitutes because of their rank smell and presumed lechery.)   141 *dam* mother   143 *A likely . . . work* a fine story   145 *hobbyhorse* harlot   148 *should be* must be   149–150 *when . . . for* when I'm ready for you (i.e., never)   157 *Go to* (An expression of remonstrance.)

Othello [advancing]: How shall I murder him, Iago?
Iago: Did you perceive how he laughed at his vice?
Othello: O, Iago!
Iago: And did you see the handkerchief?
Othello: Was that mine?
Iago: Yours, by this hand. And to see how he prizes the foolish woman your wife! She gave it him, and he hath given it his whore.
Othello: I would have him nine years a-killing. A fine woman! A fair woman! A sweet woman!
Iago: Nay, you must forget that.
Othello: Ay, let her rot and perish, and be damned tonight, for she shall not live. No, my heart is turned to stone; I strike it, and it hurts my hand. O, the world hath not a sweeter creature! She might lie by an emperor's side and command him tasks.
Iago: Nay, that's not your way.°
Othello: Hang her! I do but say what she is. So delicate with her needle! An admirable musician! O, she will sing the savageness out of a bear. Of so high and plenteous wit and invention!°
Iago: She's the worse for all this.
Othello: O, a thousand, a thousand times! And then, of so gentle a condition!°
Iago: Ay, too gentle.°
Othello: Nay, that's certain. But yet the pity of it, Iago! O, Iago, the pity of it, Iago!
Iago: If you are so fond° over her iniquity, give her patent° to offend, for if it touch not you it comes near nobody.
Othello: I will chop her into messes.° Cuckold me?
Iago: O, 'tis foul in her.
Othello: With mine officer?
Iago: That's fouler.
Othello: Get me some poison, Iago, this night. I'll not expostulate with her, lest her body and beauty unprovide° my mind again. This night, Iago.
Iago: Do it not with poison. Strangle her in her bed, even the bed she hath contaminated.
Othello: Good, good! The justice of it pleases. Very good.
Iago: And for Cassio, let me be his undertaker.° You shall hear more by midnight.
Othello: Excellent good. *[A trumpet within.]* What trumpet is that same?
Iago: I warrant, something from Venice.

Enter Lodovico, Desdemona, and attendants.

'Tis Lodovico. This comes from the Duke.
See, your wife's with him.
Lodovico: God save you, worthy General!
Othello: With all my heart,° sir.
Lodovico [giving him a letter]: The Duke and the senators of Venice greet you.
Othello: I kiss the instrument of their pleasures.

---

172 *your way* i.e., the way you should think of her   175 *invention* imagination   177 *gentle a condition* wellborn and well-bred   178 *gentle* generous, yielding (to other men)   180 *fond* foolish.   *patent* license   182 *messes* portions of meat, i.e., bits   187 *unprovide* weaken, render unfit   191 *be his undertaker* undertake to dispatch him   196 *With all my heart* i.e., I thank you most heartily

[*He opens the letter, and reads.*]

Desdemona: And what's the news, good cousin Lodovico?
Iago: I am very glad to see you, signor.
    Welcome to Cyprus.
Lodovico: I thank you. How does Lieutenant Cassio?
Iago: Lives, sir.
Desdemona: Cousin, there's fall'n between him and my lord
    An unkind° breach; but you shall make all well.
Othello: Are you sure of that?
Desdemona: My lord?
Othello [*reads*]: "This fail you not to do, as you will—"
Lodovico: He did not call; he's busy in the paper.
    Is there division twixt my lord and Cassio?
Desdemona: A most unhappy one. I would do much
    T' atone° them, for the love I bear to Cassio.
Othello: Fire and brimstone!
Desdemona: My lord?
Othello: Are you wise?
Desdemona: What, is he angry?
Lodovico: Maybe the letter moved him;
    For, as I think, they do command him home,
    Deputing Cassio in his government.°
Desdemona: By my troth, I am glad on 't.°
Othello: Indeed?
Desdemona: My lord?
Othello: I am glad to see you mad.°
Desdemona: Why, sweet Othello—
Othello [*striking her*]: Devil!
Desdemona: I have not deserved this.
Lodovico: My lord, this would not be believed in Venice,
    Though I should swear I saw 't. 'Tis very much.°
    Make her amends; she weeps.
Othello: O devil, devil!
    If that the earth could teem° with woman's tears,
    Each drop she falls would prove a crocodile.°
    Out of my sight!
Desdemona: I will not stay to offend you. [*Going.*]
Lodovico: Truly, an obedient lady.
    I do beseech your lordship, call her back.
Othello: Mistress!
Desdemona [*returning*]: My lord?
Othello: What would you with her, sir?°

---

205 *unkind* unnatural, contrary to their natures; hurtful   212 *atone* reconcile   218 *government* office   219 *on 't* of it   222 *I am . . . mad* i.e., I am glad to see that you are insane enough to rejoice in Cassio's promotion (?) (Othello bitterly plays on Desdemona's *I am glad.*)   227 *very much* too much, outrageous   229 *teem* breed, be impregnated   230 *falls . . . crocodile* (Crocodiles were supposed to weep hypocritical tears for their victims.)   236 *What . . . sir* (Othello implies that Desdemona is pliant and will do a *turn,* lines 238–240, for any man.)

Lodovico: Who, I, my lord?
Othello: Ay, you did wish that I would make her turn.
    Sir, she can turn, and turn, and yet go on
    And turn again; and she can weep, sir, weep;   240
    And she's obedient,° as you say, obedient,
    Very obedient.—Proceed you in your tears.—
    Concerning this, sir—O well-painted passion!°—
    I am commanded home.—Get you away;
    I'll send for you anon.—Sir, I obey the mandate   245
    And will return to Venice.—Hence, avaunt!

[Exit Desdemona.]

    Cassio shall have my place. And, sir, tonight
    I do entreat that we may sup together.
    You are welcome, sir, to Cyprus.—Goats and monkeys!°   *Exit.*
Lodovico: Is this the noble Moor whom our full Senate   250
    Call all in all sufficient? Is this the nature
    Whom passion could not shake? Whose solid virtue
    The shot of accident nor dart of chance
    Could neither graze nor pierce?
Iago: He is much changed.
Lodovico: Are his wits safe? Is he not light of brain?   255
Iago: He's that he is. I may not breathe my censure
    What he might be. If what he might he is not,
    I would to heaven he were!°
Lodovico: What, strike his wife?
Iago: Faith, that was not so well; yet would I knew
    That stroke would prove the worst!
Lodovico: Is it his use?°   260
    Or did the letters work upon his blood°
    And new-create his fault?
Iago: Alas, alas!
    It is not honesty in me to speak
    What I have seen and known. You shall observe him,
    And his own courses will denote° him so   265
    That I may save my speech. Do but go after,
    And mark how he continues.
Lodovico: I am sorry that I am deceived in him.   *Exeunt.*

SCENE II [THE CITADEL.]

    Enter Othello and Emilia.

Othello: You have seen nothing then?
Emilia: Nor ever heard, nor ever did suspect.

---

241 *obedient* (With much the same sexual connotation as *turn* in lines 238–240.)   243 *passion* i.e., grief   249 *Goats and monkeys* (See III, iii, 419.)   256–258 *I may . . . were* i.e., I dare not venture an opinion as to whether he's of unsound mind, as you suggest, but, if he isn't, then it might be better to wish he were in fact insane, since only that could excuse his wild behavior   260 *use* custom   261 *blood* passions   265 *courses will denote* actions will reveal

Othello: Yes, you have seen Cassio and she together.
Emilia: But then I saw no harm, and then I heard
　　Each syllable that breath made up between them.
Othello: What, did they never whisper?
Emilia: Never, my lord.
Othello: Nor send you out o' the way?
Emilia: Never.
Othello: To fetch her fan, her gloves, her mask, nor nothing?
Emilia: Never, my lord.
Othello: That's strange.
Emilia: I durst, my lord, to wager she is honest,
　　Lay down my soul at stake.° If you think other,
　　Remove your thought; it doth abuse your bosom.°
　　If any wretch have put this in your head,
　　Let heaven requite it with the serpent's curse!°
　　For if she be not honest, chaste, and true,
　　There's no man happy; the purest of their wives
　　Is foul as slander.
Othello: 　　　　　　Bid her come hither. Go.

　　Exit Emilia.

　　She says enough; yet she's a simple bawd
　　That cannot say as much.° This° is a subtle whore,
　　A closet lock and key° of villainous secrets.
　　And yet she'll kneel and pray; I have seen her do 't.

　　Enter Desdemona and Emilia.

Desdemona: My lord, what is your will?
Othello: Pray you, chuck, come hither.
Desdemona: What is your pleasure?
Othello: 　　　　　　Let me see your eyes.
　　Look in my face.
Desdemona: 　　　　What horrible fancy's this?
Othello [to Emilia]: Some of your function,° mistress.
　　Leave procreants° alone and shut the door;
　　Cough or cry "hem" if anybody come.
　　Your mystery, your mystery!° Nay, dispatch.

　　Exit Emilia.

Desdemona [kneeling]: Upon my knees, what doth your speech import?
　　I understand a fury in your words,
　　But not the words.
Othello: Why, what art thou?

---

14 *at stake* as the wager　15 *abuse your bosom* deceive you　17 *the serpent's curse* the curse pronounced by God on the serpent for deceiving Eve, just as some man has done to Othello and Desdemona. (See Genesis 3:14.)　21–22 *she's . . . much* i.e., any procuress or go-between who couldn't make up as plausible a story as Emilia's would have to be pretty stupid　22 *This* i.e., Desdemona　23 *closet lock and key* i.e., concealer　29 *Some . . . function* i.e., practice your chosen profession, that of bawd (by guarding the door)　30 *procreants* mating couples　32 *mystery* trade, occupation

"Ah, Desdemon! Away, away, away!" (IV, ii, 43).

Desdemona: Your wife, my lord, your true
 And loyal wife.
Othello: Come, swear it, damn thyself,
 Lest, being like one of heaven,° the devils themselves
 Should fear to seize thee. Therefore be double damned:
 Swear thou art honest.
Desdemona: Heaven doth truly know it. 40
Othello: Heaven truly knows that thou art false as hell.
Desdemona: To whom, my lord? With whom? How am I false?
Othello [weeping]: Ah, Desdemon! Away, away, away!
Desdemona: Alas the heavy day! Why do you weep?
 Am I the motive° of these tears, my lord? 45

38 *being . . . heaven* looking like an angel 45 *motive* cause

> If haply you my father do suspect
> An instrument of this your calling back,
> Lay not your blame on me. If you have lost him,
> I have lost him too.
> Othello:　　　　　Had it pleased heaven
> To try me with affliction, had they° rained
> All kinds of sores and shames on my bare head,
> Steeped me in poverty to the very lips,
> Given to captivity me and my utmost hopes,
> I should have found in some place of my soul
> A drop of patience. But, alas, to make me
> A fixèd figure for the time of scorn°
> To point his° slow and moving finger° at!
> Yet could I bear that too, well, very well.
> But there where I have garnered° up my heart,
> Where either I must live or bear no life,
> The fountain° from the which my current runs
> Or else dries up—to be discarded thence!
> Or keep it as a cistern° for foul toads
> To knot° and gender° in! Turn thy complexion there,°
> Patience, thou young and rose-lipped cherubin—
> Ay, there look grim as hell!°
> Desdemona: I hope my noble lord esteems me honest.°
> Othello: O, ay, as summer flies are in the shambles,°
> That quicken° even with blowing.° O thou weed,
> Who art so lovely fair and smell'st so sweet
> That the sense aches at thee, would thou hadst ne'er been born!
> Desdemona: Alas, what ignorant° sin have I committed?
> Othello: Was this fair paper, this most goodly book,
> Made to write "whore" upon? What committed?
> Committed? O thou public commoner!°
> I should make very forges of my cheeks,
> That would to cinders burn up modesty,
> Did I but speak thy deeds. What committed?
> Heaven stops the nose at it and the moon winks;°
> The bawdy° wind, that kisses all it meets,
> Is hushed within the hollow mine° of earth
> And will not hear 't. What committed?
> Impudent strumpet!

50 *they* i.e., heavenly powers   56 *time of scorn* i.e., scornful world   57 *his* its.   *slow and moving finger* i.e., hour hand of the clock, moving so slowly it seems hardly to move at all. (Othello envisages himself as being eternally pointed at by the scornful world as the numbers on a clock are pointed at by the hour hand.)   59 *garnered* stored   61 *fountain* spring   63 *cistern* cesspool   64 *knot* couple.   *gender* engender.   *Turn . . . there* change your color, grow pale, at such a sight   65–66 *Patience . . . hell* (Even Patience, that rose-lipped cherub, will look grim and pale at this spectacle.)   67 *honest* chaste   68 *shambles* slaughterhouse   69 *quicken* come to life.   *with blowing* i.e., with the puffing up of something rotten in which maggots are breeding   72 *ignorant sin* sin in ignorance   75 *commoner* prostitute   79 *winks* closes her eyes. (The moon symbolizes chastity.)   80 *bawdy* kissing one and all   81 *mine* cave (where the winds were thought to dwell)

Othello berates Desdemona as a "strumpet" and "cunning whore" (IV, ii, 73–98).

Desdemona: By heaven, you do me wrong.
Othello: Are not you a strumpet?
Desdemona: No, as I am a Christian.   85
    If to preserve this vessel° for my lord
    From any other foul unlawful touch
    Be not to be a strumpet, I am none.
Othello: What, not a whore?
Desdemona: No, as I shall be saved.   90
Othello: Is 't possible?
Desdemona: O, heaven forgive us!
Othello: I cry you mercy,° then.
    I took you for that cunning whore of Venice
    That married with Othello. *[Calling out.]* You, mistress,
    That have the office opposite to Saint Peter   95
    And keep the gate of hell!

Enter Emilia.

                            You, you, ay, you!
    We have done our course.° There's money for your pains.   *[He gives money.]*
    I pray you, turn the key and keep our counsel.   *Exit.*

---

86 *vessel* body   92 *cry you mercy* beg your pardon   97 *course* business (with an indecent suggestion of "trick," turn at sex)

Emilia: Alas, what does this gentleman conceive?°
  How do you, madam? How do you, my good lady? 100
Desdemona: Faith, half asleep.°
Emilia: Good madam, what's the matter with my lord?
Desdemona: With who?
Emilia: Why, with my lord, madam.
Desdemona: Who is thy lord?
Emilia: He that is yours, sweet lady. 105
Desdemona: I have none. Do not talk to me, Emilia.
  I cannot weep, nor answers have I none
  But what should go by water.° Prithee, tonight
  Lay on my bed my wedding sheets, remember;
  And call thy husband hither. 110
Emilia: Here's a change indeed! *Exit.*
Desdemona: 'Tis meet I should be used so, very meet.°
  How have I been behaved, that he might stick°
  The small'st opinion° on my least misuse?°

  Enter Iago.

Iago: What is your pleasure, madam? How is 't with you? 115
Desdemona: I cannot tell. Those that do teach young babes
  Do it with gentle means and easy tasks.
  He might have chid me so, for, in good faith,
  I am a child to chiding.
Iago: What is the matter, lady? 120
Emilia: Alas, Iago, my lord hath so bewhored her,
  Thrown such despite and heavy terms upon her,
  That true hearts cannot bear it.
Desdemona: Am I that name, Iago?
Iago: What name, fair lady? 125
Desdemona: Such as she said my lord did say I was.
Emilia: He called her whore. A beggar in his drink
  Could not have laid such terms upon his callet.°
Iago: Why did he so?
Desdemona [*weeping*]: I do not know. I am sure I am none such. 130
Iago: Do not weep, do not weep. Alas the day!
Emilia: Hath she forsook so many noble matches,
  Her father and her country and her friends,
  To be called whore? Would it not make one weep?
Desdemona: It is my wretched fortune.
Iago: Beshrew° him for 't! 135
  How comes this trick° upon him?
Desdemona: Nay, heaven doth know.
Emilia: I will be hanged if some eternal° villain,
  Some busy and insinuating° rogue,

---

99 *conceive* suppose, think   101 *half asleep* i.e., dazed   108 *go by water* be expressed by tears   112 *meet* fitting   113 *stick* attach   114 *opinion* censure.   *least misuse* slightest misconduct   128 *callet* whore   135 *Beshrew* curse   136 *trick* strange behavior, delusion   137 *eternal* inveterate   138 *insinuating* ingratiating, fawning, wheedling

Iago comforts Desdemona regarding Othello's accusations (IV, ii, 115–179).

    Some cogging,° cozening° slave, to get some office,
    Have not devised this slander. I will be hanged else.   140
Iago: Fie, there is no such man. It is impossible.
Desdemona: If any such there be, heaven pardon him!
Emilia: A halter° pardon him! And hell gnaw his bones!
    Why should he call her whore? Who keeps her company?
    What place? What time? What form?° What likelihood?   145
    The Moor's abused by some most villainous knave,
    Some base notorious knave, some scurvy fellow.
    O heaven, that° such companions° thou'dst unfold,°
    And put in every honest hand a whip
    To lash the rascals naked through the world   150
    Even from the east to th' west!
Iago: Speak within door.°
Emilia: O, fie upon them! Some such squire° he was
    That turned your wit the seamy side without°
    And made you to suspect me with the Moor.
Iago: You are a fool. Go to.°
Desdemona: Alas, Iago,   155
    What shall I do to win my lord again?

---

139 *cogging* cheating. *cozening* defrauding   143 *halter* hangman's noose   145 *form* appearance, circumstance   148 *that* would that. *companions* fellows. *unfold* expose   151 *within door* i.e., not so loud   152 *squire* fellow   153 *seamy side without* wrong side out   155 *Go to* i.e., that's enough

Good friend, go to him; for, by this light of heaven,
I know not how I lost him. Here I kneel. *[She kneels.]*
If e'er my will did trespass 'gainst his love,
Either in discourse of thought° or actual deed, 160
Or that° mine eyes, mine ears, or any sense
Delighted them° in any other form;
Or that I do not yet,° and ever did,
And ever will—though he do shake me off
To beggarly divorcement—love him dearly, 165
Comfort forswear° me! Unkindness may do much,
And his unkindness may defeat° my life,
But never taint my love. I cannot say "whore."
It does abhor° me now I speak the word;
To do the act that might the addition° earn 170
Not the world's mass of vanity° could make me.

[She rises.]

Iago: I pray you, be content. 'Tis but his humor.°
    The business of the state does him offense,
    And he does chide with you.
Desdemona: If 'twere no other— 175
Iago: It is but so, I warrant. *[Trumpets within.]*
    Hark, how these instruments summon you to supper!
    The messengers of Venice stays the meat.°
    Go in, and weep not. All things shall be well.

Exeunt Desdemona and Emilia.

Enter Roderigo.

    How now, Roderigo? 180
Roderigo: I do not find that thou deal'st justly with me.
Iago: What in the contrary?
Roderigo: Every day thou daff'st me° with some device,° Iago, and rather, as it seems to me now, keep'st from me all conveniency° than suppliest me with the least advantage° of hope. I will indeed no longer endure it, nor am I yet persuaded to 185 put up° in peace what already I have foolishly suffered.
Iago: Will you hear me, Roderigo?
Roderigo: Faith, I have heard too much, for your words and performances are no kin together.
Iago: You charge me most unjustly. 190
Roderigo: With naught but truth. I have wasted myself out of my means. The jewels you have had from me to deliver° Desdemona would half have corrupted a

---

160 *discourse of thought* process of thinking   161 *that* if. (Also in line 163.)   162 *Delighted them* took delight   163 *yet* still   166 *Comfort forswear* may heavenly comfort forsake   167 *defeat* destroy   169 *abhor* (1) fill me with abhorrence (2) make me whorelike   170 *addition* title   171 *vanity* showy splendor   172 *humor* mood   178 *stays the meat* are waiting to dine   183 *thou daff'st me* you put me off. *device* excuse, trick   184 *conveniency* advantage, opportunity   185 *advantage* increase   186 *put up* submit to, tolerate   192 *deliver* deliver to

votarist.° You have told me she hath received them and returned me expectations and comforts of sudden respect° and acquaintance, but I find none.

Iago: Well, go to, very well.

Roderigo: "Very well"! "Go to"! I cannot go to,° man, nor 'tis not very well. By this hand, I think it is scurvy, and begin to find myself fopped° in it.

Iago: Very well.

Roderigo: I tell you 'tis not very well.° I will make myself known to Desdemona. If she will return me my jewels, I will give over my suit and repent my unlawful solicitation; if not, assure yourself I will seek satisfaction° of you.

Iago: You have said now?°

Roderigo: Ay, and said nothing but what I protest intendment° of doing.

Iago: Why, now I see there's mettle in thee, and even from this instant do build on thee a better opinion than ever before. Give me thy hand, Roderigo. Thou hast taken against me a most just exception; but yet I protest I have dealt most directly in thy affair.

Roderigo: It hath not appeared.

Iago: I grant indeed it hath not appeared, and your suspicion is not without wit and judgment. But, Roderigo, if thou hast that in thee indeed which I have greater reason to believe now than ever—I mean purpose, courage, and valor—this night show it. If thou the next night following enjoy not Desdemona, take me from this world with treachery and devise engines for° my life.

Roderigo: Well, what is it? Is it within reason and compass?

Iago: Sir, there is especial commission come from Venice to depute Cassio in Othello's place.

Roderigo: Is that true? Why, then Othello and Desdemona return again to Venice.

Iago: O, no; he goes into Mauritania and takes away with him the fair Desdemona, unless his abode be lingered here by some accident; wherein none can be so determinate° as the removing of Cassio.

Roderigo: How do you mean, removing of him?

Iago: Why, by making him uncapable of Othello's place—knocking out his brains.

Roderigo: And that you would have me to do?

Iago: Ay, if you dare do yourself a profit and a right. He sups tonight with a harlotry,° and thither will I go to him. He knows not yet of his honorable fortune. If you will watch his going thence, which I will fashion to fall out° between twelve and one, you may take him at your pleasure. I will be near to second your attempt, and he shall fall between us. Come, stand not amazed at it, but go along with me. I will show you such a necessity in his death that you shall think yourself bound to put it on him. It is now high° suppertime, and the night grows to waste.° About it.

Roderigo: I will hear further reason for this.

Iago: And you shall be satisfied. *Exeunt.*

193 *votarist* nun   194 *sudden respect* immediate consideration   196 *I cannot go to* (Roderigo changes Iago's *go to,* an expression urging patience, to *I cannot go to,* "I have no opportunity for success in wooing.")   197 *fopped* fooled, duped   199 *not very well* (Roderigo changes Iago's *very well,* "all right, then," to *not very well,* "not at all good.")   201 *satisfaction* repayment. (The term normally means settling of accounts in a duel.)   202 *You . . . now* have you finished?   203 *intendment* intention   213 *engines for* plots against   220 *determinate* conclusive   224 *harlotry* slut   226 *fall out* occur   230 *high* fully.   *grows to waste* wastes away

SCENE III [THE CITADEL.]

Enter Othello, Lodovico, Desdemona, Emilia, and attendants.

Lodovico: I do beseech you, sir, trouble yourself no further.
Othello: O, pardon me; 'twill do me good to walk.
Lodovico: Madam, good night. I humbly thank your ladyship.
Desdemona: Your honor is most welcome.
Othello: Will you walk, sir?
    O, Desdemona!
Desdemona: My lord?
Othello: Get you to bed on th' instant.
    I will be returned forthwith. Dismiss your attendant there. Look
    't be done.
Desdemona: I will, my lord.

Exit [Othello, with Lodovico and attendants].

Emilia: How goes it now? He looks gentler than he did.
Desdemona: He says he will return incontinent,°
    And hath commanded me to go to bed,
    And bid me to dismiss you.
Emilia: Dismiss me?
Desdemona: It was his bidding. Therefore, good Emilia,
    Give me my nightly wearing, and adieu.
    We must not now displease him.
Emilia: I would you had never seen him!
Desdemona: So would not I. My love doth so approve him
    That even his stubbornness,° his checks,° his frowns—
    Prithee, unpin me—have grace and favor in them.

[Emilia prepares Desdemona for bed.]

Emilia: I have laid those sheets you bade me on the bed.
Desdemona: All's one.° Good faith, how foolish are our minds!
    If I do die before thee, prithee shroud me
    In one of these same sheets.
    Emilia: Come, come, you talk.°
Desdemona: My mother had a maid called Barbary.
    She was in love, and he she loved proved mad°
    And did forsake her. She had a song of "Willow."
    An old thing 'twas, but it expressed her fortune,
    And she died singing it. That song tonight
    Will not go from my mind; I have much to do
    But to go hang° my head all at one side
    And sing it like poor Barbary. Prithee, dispatch.
Emilia: Shall I go fetch your nightgown?°

---

12 *incontinent* immediately   21 *stubbornness* roughness. *checks* rebukes 24 *All's one* all right. It doesn't really matter   26 *talk* i.e., prattle   28 *mad* wild, i.e., faithless   32–33 *I . . . hang* I can scarcely keep myself from hanging   35 *nightgown* dressing gown

Desdemona: No, unpin me here.
    This Lodovico is a proper° man.
Emilia: A very handsome man.
Desdemona: He speaks well.
Emilia: I know a lady in Venice would have walked barefoot to Palestine for a touch of his nether lip.
Desdemona [singing]:
    "The poor soul sat sighing by a sycamore tree,
    Sing all a green willow;°
    Her hand on her bosom, her head on her knee,
    Sing willow, willow, willow.
    The fresh streams ran by her and murmured her moans;
    Sing willow, willow, willow;
    Her salt tears fell from her, and softened the stones—"
Lay by these.
    [*Singing.*] "Sing willow, willow, willow—"
Prithee, hie thee.° He'll come anon.°
    [*Singing.*] "Sing all a green willow must be my garland.
    Let nobody blame him; his scorn I approve—"
Nay, that's not next.—Hark! Who is 't that knocks?
Emilia: It's the wind.
Desdemona [singing]:
    "I called my love false love; but what said he then?
    Sing willow, willow, willow;
    If I court more women, you'll couch with more men."
So, get thee gone. Good night. Mine eyes do itch;
Doth that bode weeping?
Emilia: 'Tis neither here nor there.
Desdemona: I have heard it said so. O, these men, these men!
    Dost thou in conscience think—tell me, Emilia—
    That there be women do abuse° their husbands
    In such gross kind?
Emilia: There be some such, no question.
Desdemona: Wouldst thou do such a deed for all the world?
Emilia: Why, would not you?
Desdemona: No, by this heavenly light!
Emilia: Nor I neither by this heavenly light;
    I might do 't as well i' the dark.
Desdemona: Wouldst thou do such a deed for all the world?
Emilia: The world's a huge thing. It is a great price
    For a small vice.
Desdemona: Good troth, I think thou wouldst not.
Emilia: By my troth, I think I should, and undo 't when I had done. Marry, I would not do such a thing for a joint ring,° nor for measures of lawn,° nor for gowns, petticoats, nor caps, nor any petty exhibition.° But for all the whole world! Uds°

---

37 *proper* handsome   43 *willow* (A conventional emblem of disappointed love.)   51 *hie thee* hurry.   *anon* right away   63 *abuse* deceive   74 *joint ring* a ring made in separate halves.   *lawn* fine linen   75 *exhibition* gift.   *Uds* God's

pity, who would not make her husband a cuckold to make him a monarch? I
should venture purgatory for 't.
Desdemona: Beshrew me if I would do such a wrong
    For the whole world.
Emilia: Why, the wrong is but a wrong i' the world, and having the world for your
    labor, 'tis a wrong in your own world, and you might quickly make it right.
Desdemona: I do not think there is any such woman.
Emilia: Yes, a dozen, and as many
    To th' vantage° as would store° the world they played° for.
    But I do think it is their husbands' faults
    If wives do fall. Say that they slack their duties°
    And pour our treasures into foreign laps,°
    Or else break out in peevish jealousies,
    Throwing restraint upon us?° Or say they strike us,
    Or scant our former having in despite?°
    Why, we have galls,° and though we have some grace,
    Yet have we some revenge. Let husbands know
    Their wives have sense° like them. They see, and smell,
    And have their palates both for sweet and sour,
    As husbands have. What is it that they do
    When they change us for others? Is it sport?°
    I think it is. And doth affection° breed it?
    I think it doth. Is 't frailty that thus errs?
    It is so, too. And have not we affections,
    Desires for sport, and frailty, as men have?
    Then let them use us well; else let them know,
    The ills we do, their ills instruct us so.
Desdemona: Good night, good night. God me such uses° send
    Not to pick bad from bad, but by bad mend!°

    Exeunt.

ACT V

SCENE I [A STREET IN CYPRUS.]

Enter Iago and Roderigo.

Iago: Here stand behind this bulk.° Straight will he come.
    Wear thy good rapier bare,° and put it home.
    Quick, quick! Fear nothing. I'll be at thy elbow.
    It makes us or it mars us. Think on that,
    And fix most firm thy resolution.
Roderigo: Be near at hand. I may miscarry in 't.

84 *To th' vantage* in addition, to boot.   *store* populate.   *played* (1) gambled (2) sported sexually   86 *duties* marital duties   87 *pour . . . laps* i.e., are unfaithful, give what is rightfully ours (semen) to other women   89 *Throwing . . . us* i.e., jealously restricting our freedom to see other men   90 *scant . . . despite* reduce our allowance to spite us   91 *have galls* i.e., are capable of resenting injury and insult   93 *sense* physical sense   96 *sport* sexual pastime   97 *affection* passion   103 *uses* habit, practice   104 *Not . . . mend* i.e., not to learn bad conduct from others' badness (as Emilia has suggested women learn from men), but to mend my ways by perceiving what badness is, making spiritual benefit out of evil and adversity   1 *bulk* framework projecting from the front of a shop   2 *bare* unsheathed

Iago: Here, at thy hand. Be bold, and take thy stand.

[*Iago stands aside. Roderigo conceals himself.*]

Roderigo: I have no great devotion to the deed;
And yet he hath given me satisfying reasons.
'Tis but a man gone. Forth, my sword! He dies. 10

[*He draws.*]

Iago: I have rubbed this young quat° almost to the sense,°
And he grows angry. Now, whether he kill Cassio
Or Cassio him, or each do kill the other,
Every way makes my gain. Live Roderigo,°
He calls me to a restitution large 15
Of gold and jewels that I bobbed° from him
As gifts to Desdemona.
It must not be. If Cassio do remain,
He hath a daily beauty in his life
That makes me ugly; and besides, the Moor 20
May unfold° me to him; there stand I in much peril.
No, he must die. Be 't so. I hear him coming.

Enter Cassio.

Roderigo [coming forth]: I know his gait, 'tis he.—Villain, thou diest!

[*He attacks Cassio.*]

Cassio: That thrust had been mine enemy indeed,
But that my coat° is better than thou know'st. 25
I will make proof° of thine.

[*He draws, and wounds Roderigo.*]

Roderigo: O, I am slain!   [*He falls.*]

[*Iago, from behind, wounds Cassio in the leg, and exits.*]

Cassio: I am maimed forever. Help, ho! Murder! Murder!

Enter Othello.

Othello: The voice of Cassio! Iago keeps his word.
Roderigo: O, villain that I am!
Othello: It is even so. 30
Cassio: O, help, ho! Light! A surgeon!
Othello: 'Tis he. O brave Iago, honest and just,
That hast such noble sense of thy friend's wrong!
Thou teachest me. Minion,° your dear lies dead,

---

11 *quat* pimple, pustule. *to the sense* to the quick   14 *Live Roderigo* if Roderigo lives   16 *bobbed* swindled   21 *unfold* expose   25 *coat* (Possibly a garment of mail under the outer clothing, or simply a tougher coat than Roderigo expected.)   26 *proof* a test   34 *Minion* hussy (i.e., Desdemona)

And your unblest fate hies.° Strumpet, I come. 35
Forth of° my heart those charms, thine eyes, are blotted;
Thy bed, lust-stained, shall with lust's blood be spotted. *Exit Othello.*

Enter Lodovico and Gratiano.

Cassio: What ho! No watch? No passage?° Murder! Murder!
Gratiano: 'Tis some mischance. The voice is very direful.
Cassio: O, help! 40
Lodovico: Hark!
Roderigo: O wretched villain!
Lodovico: Two or three groan. 'Tis heavy° night;
    These may be counterfeits. Let's think 't unsafe
    To come in to° the cry without more help. 45

[They remain near the entrance.]

Roderigo: Nobody come? Then shall I bleed to death.

Enter Iago [in his shirtsleeves, with a light].

Lodovico: Hark!
Gratiano: Here's one comes in his shirt, with light and weapons.
Iago: Who's there? Whose noise is this that cries on° murder?
Lodovico: We do not know.
Iago: Did not you hear a cry? 50
Cassio: Here, here! For heaven's sake, help me!
Iago: What's the matter?

[He moves toward Cassio.]

Gratiano [to Lodovico]: This is Othello's ancient, as I take it.
Lodovico [to Gratiano]: The same indeed, a very valiant fellow.
Iago [to Cassio]: What° are you here that cry so grievously?
Cassio: Iago? O, I am spoiled,° undone by villains! 55
    Give me some help.
Iago: O me, Lieutenant! What villains have done this?
Cassio: I think that one of them is hereabout,
    And cannot make° away.
Iago: O treacherous villains!

[To Lodovico and Gratiano.]

    What are you there? Come in, and give some help. *[They advance.]* 60
Roderigo: O, help me there!
Cassio: That's one of them.
Iago: O murderous slave! O villain!

[He stabs Roderigo.]

---

35 *hies* hastens on   36 *Forth of* from out   38 *passage* people passing by   43 *heavy* thick, dark   45 *come in to* approach   49 *cries on* cries out   54 *What* who (also at lines 60 and 66)   55 *spoiled* ruined, done for   59 *make* get

Roderigo: O damned Iago! O inhuman dog!
Iago: Kill men i' the dark?—Where be these bloody thieves?—
    How silent is this town!—Ho! Murder, murder!—
    [*To Lodovico and Gratiano.*] What may you be? Are you of good or evil?
Lodovico: As you shall prove us, praise° us.
Iago: Signor Lodovico?
Lodovico: He, sir.
Iago: I cry you mercy.° Here's Cassio hurt by villains.
Gratiano: Cassio?
Iago: How is 't, brother?
Cassio: My leg is cut in two.
Iago: Marry, heaven forbid!
    Light, gentlemen! I'll bind it with my shirt.

[*He hands them the light, and tends to Cassio's wound.*]

Enter Bianca.

Bianca: What is the matter, ho? Who is 't that cried?
Iago: Who is 't that cried?
Bianca: O my dear Cassio!
    My sweet Cassio! O Cassio, Cassio, Cassio!
Iago: O notable strumpet! Cassio, may you suspect
    Who they should be that have thus mangled you?
Cassio: No.
Gratiano: I am sorry to find you thus. I have been to seek you.
Iago: Lend me a garter. [*He applies a tourniquet.*] So.—O, for a chair,°
    To bear him easily hence!
Bianca: Alas, he faints! O Cassio, Cassio, Cassio!
Iago: Gentlemen all, I do suspect this trash
    To be a party in this injury.—
    Patience awhile, good Cassio.—Come, come;
    Lend me a light.   [*He shines the light on Roderigo.*]
             Know we this face or no?
    Alas, my friend and my dear countryman
    Roderigo! No.—Yes, sure.—O heaven! Roderigo!
Gratiano: What, of Venice?
Iago: Even he, sir. Did you know him?
Gratiano: Know him? Ay.
Iago: Signor Gratiano? I cry your gentle° pardon.
    These bloody accidents° must excuse my manners
    That so neglected you.
Gratiano: I am glad to see you.
Iago: How do you, Cassio? O, a chair, a chair!
Gratiano: Roderigo!
Iago: He, he, 'tis he. [*A litter is brought in.*] O, that's well said;° the chair.
    Some good man bear him carefully from hence;

65

70

75

80

85

90

95

100

---

67 *praise* appraise   70 *I cry you mercy* I beg your pardon   83 *chair* litter   95 *gentle* noble   96 *accidents* sudden events   100 *well said* well done

I'll fetch the General's surgeon. *[To Bianca.]* For you, mistress,
Save you your labor.°—He that lies slain here, Cassio,
Was my dear friend. What malice° was between you?
Cassio: None in the world, nor do I know the man.
Iago *[to Bianca]*: What, look you pale?—O, bear him out o' th' air.°

[Cassio and Roderigo are borne off.]

Stay you,° good gentlemen.—Look you pale, mistress?—
Do you perceive the gastness° of her eye?—
Nay, if you stare,° we shall hear more anon.—
Behold her well; I pray you, look upon her.
Do you see, gentlemen? Nay, guiltiness
Will speak, though tongues were out of use.

[Enter Emilia.]

Emilia: 'Las, what's the matter? What's the matter, husband?
Iago: Cassio hath here been set on in the dark
By Roderigo and fellows that are scaped.
He's almost slain, and Roderigo dead.
Emilia: Alas, good gentleman! Alas, good Cassio!
Iago: This is the fruits of whoring. Prithee, Emilia,
Go know° of Cassio where he supped tonight.
[To Bianca.] What, do you shake at that?
Bianca: He supped at my house, but I therefore shake not.
Iago: O, did he so? I charge you go with me.
Emilia: O, fie upon thee, strumpet!
Bianca: I am no strumpet, but of life as honest°
As you that thus abuse me.
Emilia: As I? Faugh! Fie upon thee!
Iago: Kind gentlemen, let's go see poor Cassio dressed.°—
Come, mistress, you must tell's another tale.
Emilia, run you to the citadel
And tell my lord and lady what hath happened.—
Will you go on afore? *[Aside.]* This is the night
That either makes me or fordoes° me quite. *Exeunt.*

SCENE II [A BEDCHAMBER IN THE CITADEL.]

Enter Othello [with a light], and Desdemona in her bed.°

Othello: It is the cause,° it is the cause, my soul.
Let me not name it to you, you chaste stars!
It is the cause. Yet I'll not shed her blood,

---

103 *Save . . . labor* i.e., never you mind tending Cassio   104 *malice* enmity   106 *bear . . . air* (Fresh air was thought to be dangerous for a wound.)   107 *Stay you* (Lodovico and Gratiano are evidently about to leave.)   108 *gastness* terror   109 *stare* (Iago pretends to interpret Bianca's wild looks as an involuntary confession of guilt.)   119 *know* learn   124 *honest* chaste   127 *Cassio dressed* Cassio's wounds dressed   132 *fordoes* undoes, ruins   s.d. *in her bed* (Either the curtains are drawn back to reveal the bed in a recessed area backstage, or the bed is "thrust out" onstage as the scene begins.)   1 *cause* i.e., cause of justice, the offense itself, which Othello must correct as an agent of justice

"Enter Othello, and Desdemona in her bed" (V, ii, s.d.).

    Nor scar that whiter skin of hers than snow,
    And smooth as monumental° alabaster.   5
    Yet she must die, else she'll betray more men.
    Put out the light, and then put out the light.°
    If I quench thee, thou flaming minister,°
    I can again thy former light restore,
    Should I repent me;° but once put out thy light,   10
    Thou cunning'st pattern° of excelling nature,
    I know not where is that Promethean heat°
    That can thy light relume.° When I have plucked thy rose,
    I cannot give it vital growth again;
    It needs must wither. I'll smell thee on the tree.   15

[He kisses her.]

    O balmy breath, that dost almost persuade
    Justice to break her sword! One more, one more.
    Be thus when thou art dead, and I will kill thee,
    And love thee after. One more, and that's the last.

[He kisses her.]

---

5 *monumental* i.e., used in making tombs and funeral monuments;   7 *the light . . . light* the torch or lamp . . . Desdemona's life   8 *flaming minister* torch or lamp that serves me   10 *repent me* change my mind   11 *Thou . . . pattern* you skillfully wrought perfect example   12 *Promethean heat* divine fire. (Alluding to the theft of fire from heaven by Prometheus.)   13 *relume* rekindle

So sweet was ne'er so fatal. I must weep,
　　But they are cruel° tears. This sorrow's heavenly;
　　It strikes where it doth love.° She wakes.
Desdemona: Who's there? Othello?
Othello: Ay, Desdemona.
Desdemona: Will you come to bed, my lord?
Othello: Have you prayed tonight, Desdemon?
Desdemona: Ay, my lord.
Othello: If you bethink yourself of any crime°
　　Unreconciled as yet to heaven and grace,
　　Solicit° for it straight.°
Desdemona: Alack, my lord, what may you mean by that?
Othello: Well, do it, and be brief. I will walk by.
　　I would not kill thy unprepared spirit.
　　No, heaven forfend!° I would not kill thy soul.
Desdemona: Talk you of killing?
Othello:　　　　　　　　Ay, I do.
Desdemona:　　　　　　　　　　Then heaven
　　Have mercy on me!
Othello:　　　　　Amen, with all my heart!
Desdemona: If you say so, I hope you will not kill me.
Othello: Humh!
Desdemona: And yet I fear you; for you're fatal then
　　When your eyes roll so. Why I should fear I know not,
　　Since guiltiness I know not; but yet I feel I fear.
Othello: Think on thy sins.
Desdemona:　　　　　　　They are loves I bear to you.°
Othello: Ay, and for that thou diest.
Desdemona: That death's unnatural that kills for loving.
　　Alas, why gnaw you so your nether lip?
　　Some bloody passion shakes your very frame.
　　These are portents; but yet I hope, I hope,
　　They do not point on° me.
Othello: Peace, and be still!
Desdemona: I will so. What's the matter?
Othello: That handkerchief which I so loved and gave thee
　　Thou gav'st to Cassio.
Desdemona:　　　　　　No, by my life and soul!
　　Send for the man and ask him.
Othello: Sweet soul, take heed, take heed of perjury.
　　Thou art on thy deathbed.
Desdemona: Ay, but not yet to die.
Othello:　　　　　　　　　Yes, presently.°

21 *cruel* unrelenting　22 *It . . . love* (Compare Hebrews 12:6: "For whom the Lord loveth he chasteneth.")
28 *crime* sin　30 *Solicit* petition, pray.　*straight* immediately　34 *forfend* forbid　42 *They are . . . you* i.e., if I sinned, it was in loving you more than my father or more than God　48 *point on* point at, predict what is to happen to　56 *presently* immediately

Therefore confess thee freely of thy sin;
For to deny each article with oath
Cannot remove nor choke the strong conception°
That I do groan withal.° Thou art to die. 60
Desdemona: Then Lord have mercy on me!
Othello: I say, amen.
Desdemona: And have you mercy too! I never did
   Offend° you in my life; never loved Cassio
   But with such general warranty° of heaven
   As I might love. I never gave him token. 65
Othello: By heaven, I saw my handkerchief in 's hand.
   O perjured woman! Thou dost stone° my heart,
   And makes me call what I intend to do
   A murder, which I thought a sacrifice.
   I saw the handkerchief.
Desdemona: He found it, then. 70
   I never gave it him. Send for him hither;
   Let him confess a truth.
Othello: He hath confessed.
Desdemona: What, my lord?
Othello: That he hath used thee.
Desdemona: How? Unlawfully?
Othello: Ay.
Desdemona: He will not say so.
Othello: No, his mouth is stopped; 75
   Honest Iago hath ta'en order° for 't.
Desdemona: O, my fear interprets. What, is he dead?
Othello: Had all his hairs been lives, my great revenge
   Had stomach for them all.
Desdemona: Alas, he is betrayed and I undone!   [*She weeps.*] 80
Othello: Out, strumpet! Weep'st thou for him to my face?
Desdemona: O, banish me, my lord, but kill me not!
Othello: Down, strumpet!
Desdemona: Kill me tomorrow; let me live tonight!
Othello: Nay, if you strive— 85
Desdemona: But half an hour!
Othello: Being done,° there is no pause.
Desdemona: But while I say one prayer!
Othello: It is too late.

   Smothers her.

Emilia [at the door]: My lord, my lord! What, ho! My lord, my lord!
Othello: What noise is this? Not dead? Not yet quite dead?
   I that am cruel am yet merciful; 90
   I would not have thee linger in thy pain.

---

59 *conception* (1) belief in your guilt (2) plan in my mind   60 *groan withal* (1) groan at in sorrow (2) as in giving birth   63 *Offend* wrong   64 *warranty* sanction   67 *stone* turn to stone, harden   76 *ta'en order* taken measures   86 *Being done* i.e., since justice has begun its relentless course

Othello smothers Desdemona (V, ii, 87–91).

[*He dispatches her.*]
                                    So, so.
Emilia [within]: What, ho! My lord, my lord!
Othello: Who's there?
Emilia [within]: O, good my lord, I would speak a word with you!
Othello: Yes, 'tis Emilia.—By and by.—She's dead.
    'Tis like° she comes to speak of Cassio's death.—   95
    The noise was here.° Ha! No more moving?
    Still as the grave. Shall she come in? Were 't good?—
    I think she stirs again. No. What's best to do?
    If she come in, she'll sure speak to my wife.
    My wife! My wife! What wife? I have no wife.   100
    O, insupportable! O heavy hour!
    Methinks it should be now a huge eclipse
    Of sun and moon, and that th' affrighted globe
    Should yawn° at alteration.°
Emilia [within]:   I do beseech you
    That I may speak with you, O, good my lord!   105
Othello: I had forgot thee. O, come in, Emilia.—
    Soft,° by and by. Let me the curtains draw.—

---

95 *like* likely that   **96** *here* (The Folio's *high* is possible, suggesting that the commotion of the attack on Cassio was loud.)   **104** *yawn* gape in amazement, i.e., move in an earthquake. (According to Pliny, earthquakes often happen during eclipses.)   *at alteration* at these cataclysmic events in nature, well suited to express the horror of Desdemona's death   **107** *Soft* wait a minute

[He closes the bed-curtains and opens the door.]

Where art thou?

Enter Emilia.

      What's the matter with thee now?
Emilia: O, my good lord, yonder's foul murders done!
Othello: What, now? 110
Emilia: But now, my lord.
Othello: It is the very error° of the moon;
 She comes more nearer earth than she was wont,
 And makes men mad.
Emilia: Cassio, my lord, hath killed a young Venetian 115
 Called Roderigo.
Othello: Roderigo killed?
 And Cassio killed?
Emilia: No, Cassio is not killed.
Othello: Not Cassio killed? Then murder's out of tune,
 And sweet revenge grows harsh.
Desdemona: O, falsely, falsely murdered! 120
Emilia: O Lord, what cry is that?
Othello: That? What?
Emilia: Out° and alas, that was my lady's voice.

[She opens the bed-curtains.]

 Help, help, ho, help! O lady, speak again!
 Sweet Desdemona! O sweet mistress, speak! 125
Desdemona: A guiltless death I die.
Emilia: O, who hath done this deed?
Desdemona: Nobody; I myself. Farewell.
 Commend me to my kind lord. O, farewell!   *[She dies.]*
Othello: Why, how should she be murdered?
Emilia: Alas, who knows? 130
Othello: You heard her say herself it was not I.
Emilia: She said so. I must needs report the truth.
Othello: She's like a liar gone to burning hell!
 'Twas I that killed her.
Emilia: O, the more angel she,
 And you the blacker devil! 135
Othello: She turned to folly,° and she was a whore.
Emilia: Thou dost belie° her, and thou art a devil.
Othello: She was false as water.
Emilia: Thou art rash as fire to say
 That she was false. O, she was heavenly true! 140
Othello: Cassio did top her. Ask thy husband else.°

---

112 *error* aberration, irregularity   123 *Out* (A cry of dismay, intensifying *alas*.)   136 *folly* i.e., wantonness, fleshly sin   137 *belie* slander   141 *else* i.e., if you don't believe me

Emilia declares Desdemona's innocence (V, ii, 134–164).

    O, I were damned beneath all depth in hell
    But that I did proceed upon just grounds
    To this extremity. Thy husband knew it all.
Emilia: My husband?   145
Othello: Thy husband.
Emilia: That she was false to wedlock?
Othello: Ay, with Cassio. Nay, had she been true,
    If heaven would make me such another world
    Of one entire and perfect chrysolite,°   150
    I'd not have sold her for it.
Emilia: My husband?
Othello: Ay, 'twas he that told me on her first.
    An honest man he is, and hates the slime
    That sticks on filthy deeds.   155
Emilia: My husband?
Othello: What needs this iterance,° woman? I say thy husband.
Emilia: O mistress, villainy hath made mocks with° love!
    My husband say that she was false?
Othello: He, woman;

150 *chrysolite* precious topaz   157 *iterance* iteration, repetition   158 *made mocks with* derided, made sport of

> I say thy husband. Dost understand the word? 160
> My friend, thy husband, honest, honest Iago.
Emilia: If he say so, may his pernicious soul
> Rot half a grain a day! He lies to th' heart.
> She was too fond of her most filthy bargain.
Othello: Ha? [He draws.] 165
Emilia: Do thy worst!
> This deed of thine is no more worthy heaven
> Than thou wast worthy her.
Othello: Peace, you were best.°
Emilia: Thou hast not half that power to do me harm
> As I have to be hurt.° O gull!° O dolt! 170
> As ignorant as dirt! Thou hast done a deed—
> I care not for thy sword; I'll make thee known,
> Though I lost twenty lives.—Help! Help, ho, help!
> The Moor hath killed my mistress! Murder, murder!

Enter Montano, Gratiano, and Iago.

Montano: What is the matter? How now, General? 175
Emilia: O, are you come, Iago? You have done well,
> That men must lay their murders on your neck.
Gratiano: What is the matter?
Emilia [to Iago]: Disprove this villain, if thou be'st a man.
> He says thou toldst him that his wife was false. 180
> I know thou didst not; thou'rt not such a villain.
> Speak, for my heart is full.
Iago: I told him what I thought, and told no more
> Than what he found himself was apt° and true.
Emilia: But did you ever tell him she was false? 185
Iago: I did.
Emilia: You told a lie, an odious, damnèd lie!
> Upon my soul, a lie, a wicked lie.
> She false with Cassio? Did you say with Cassio?
Iago: With Cassio, mistress. Go to, charm° your tongue. 190
Emilia: I will not charm my tongue; I am bound to speak.
> My mistress here lies murdered in her bed—
All: O heavens forfend!
Emilia: And your reports have set the murder on.
Othello: Nay, stare not, masters. It is true indeed. 195
Gratiano: 'Tis a strange truth.
Montano: O monstrous act!
Emilia: Villainy, villainy, villainy!
> I think upon 't—I think I smell 't! O villainy!
> I thought so then°—I'll kill myself for grief—
> O villainy, villainy! 200

168 *you were best* it would be best for you   170 *to be hurt* i.e., to endure hurt.   *gull* dupe   184 *apt* plausible   190 *charm* keep silent (as though by a magic spell)   199 *then* (Perhaps at III, iii, 331–332 and IV, ii, 137–154.)

Iago: What, are you mad? I charge you, get you home.
Emilia: Good gentlemen, let me have leave to speak.
    'Tis proper I obey him, but not now.
    Perchance, Iago, I will ne'er go home.
Othello: O! O! O!   *[Othello falls on the bed.°]*
Emilia: Nay, lay thee down and roar,   205
    For thou hast killed the sweetest innocent
    That e'er did lift up eye.°
Othello [rising]:   O, she was foul!
    I scarce did know you, uncle. There lies your niece,
    Whose breath indeed these hands have newly stopped.
    I know this act shows° horrible and grim.   210
Gratiano: Poor Desdemon! I am glad thy father's dead.
    Thy match was mortal to him, and pure grief
    Shore his old thread° in twain. Did he live now,
    This sight would make him do a desperate turn,°
    Yea, curse his better angel from his side,   215
    And fall to reprobance.°
Othello: 'Tis pitiful. But yet Iago knows
    That she with Cassio hath the act of shame
    A thousand times committed. Cassio confessed it;
    And she did gratify° his amorous works   220
    With that recognizance° and pledge of love
    Which I first gave her. I saw it in his hand;
    It was a handkerchief, an antique token
    My father gave my mother.
Emilia: O God! O heavenly God!   225
Iago: Zounds, hold your peace.
Emilia: 'Twill out, 'twill out! I peace?
    No, I will speak as liberal as the north.°
    Let heaven and men and devils, let them all,
    All, all, cry shame against me, yet I'll speak.
Iago: Be wise, and get you home.
Emilia: I will not.

    [Iago threatens Emilia.]

Gratiano: Fie!   230
    Your sword upon a woman?
Emilia: O thou dull Moor! That handkerchief thou speak'st of
    I found by fortune and did give my husband;
    For often, with a solemn earnestness,
    More than indeed belonged° to such a trifle,   235
    He begged of me to steal 't.

---

205 s.d. *Othello . . . bed* (This direction is from the Quarto, as also *He kisses her* at line 19 and *She dies* at line 129.)   207 *lift up eye* i.e., lift her eyes to heaven   210 *shows* looks   213 *Shore . . . thread* sheared the thread of his old age (as Atropos, one of the three Fates, was thought to do)   214 *turn* deed   216 *reprobance* damnation, i.e., suicide   220 *gratify* reward   221 *recognizance* token   227 *liberal as the north* freely as the north wind (blows)   235 *belonged* was appropriate

Iago: Villainous whore!
Emilia: She give it Cassio? No, alas! I found it,
   And I did give 't my husband.
Iago: Filth, thou liest!
Emilia: By heaven, I do not, I do not, gentlemen.
   O murderous coxcomb!° What should such a fool   240
   Do with so good a wife?
Othello: Are there no stones° in heaven
   But what serves for the thunder?—Precious° villain!

   [*He runs at Iago; Montano disarms Othello. Iago, from behind, stabs Emilia.*°]

Gratiano: The woman falls! Sure he hath killed his wife.
Emilia: Ay, ay. O, lay me by my mistress' side.   245

   Exit [Iago.]

Gratiano: He's gone, but his wife's killed.
Montano: 'Tis a notorious villain. Take you this weapon,
   Which I have here recovered from the Moor.
   Come, guard the door without. Let him not pass,
   But kill him rather. I'll after that same villain,   250
   For 'tis a damnèd slave.

   Exit [with all but Othello and Emilia, who has been laid by Desdemona's side].

Othello: I am not valiant neither,
   But every puny whipster° gets my sword.
   But why should honor° outlive honesty?°
   Let it go all.
Emilia: What did thy song bode, lady?   255
   Hark, canst thou hear me? I will play the swan,
   And die in music. [*She sings.*] "Willow, willow, willow."
   Moor, she was chaste. She loved thee, cruel Moor.
   So come my soul to bliss as I speak true.
   So speaking as I think, alas, I die.   [*She dies.*]   260
Othello: I have another weapon in this chamber;
   It was a sword of Spain, the ice-brook's temper°—
   O, here it is. [*He finds a sword.*] Uncle, I must come forth.
Gratiano [*within*]: If thou attempt it, it will cost thee dear.
   Thou hast no weapon, and perforce must suffer.   265
Othello: Look in upon me then and speak with me,
   Or, naked° as I am, I will assault thee.

   [*Enter Gratiano.*]

---

240 *coxcomb* fool. (Addressed to Othello.)   242 *stones* bolts, such as those used for thunderbolts   243 *Precious* i.e., arrant, utter.   s.d. *He . . . Emilia* (The Quarto text reads, "The Moor runs at Iago. Iago kills his wife." The Quarto also specifies the exit of Iago at line 245 and the death of Emilia at line 260.)   253 *whipster* contemptible fellow (one who is always ready to whip out his sword)   254 *honor* i.e., the bravery for which one enjoys a soldier's reputation.   *honesty* true integrity   262 *the ice-brook's temper* tempered in ice-cold water   267 *naked* unarmed

Gratiano: What is the matter?
Othello: Behold, I have a weapon;
   A better never did itself sustain
   Upon a soldier's thigh. I have seen the day
   That, with this little arm and this good sword,
   I have made my way through more impediments
   Than twenty times your stop.° But O, vain boast!
   Who can control his fate? 'Tis not so now.
   Be not afraid, though you do see me weaponed;
   Here is my journey's end, here is my butt°
   And very seamark° of my utmost sail.

   [Gratiano steps back.]

   Do you go back dismayed? 'Tis a lost° fear;
   Man but a rush° against Othello's breast
   And he retires. Where should Othello go?

   [He turns to Desdemona.]

   Now, how dost thou look now? O ill-starred wench!
   Pale as thy smock! When we shall meet at compt,°
   This look of thine will hurl my soul from heaven,
   And fiends will snatch at it. Cold, cold, my girl?
   Even like thy chastity. O cursèd, cursèd slave!°
   Whip me, ye devils,
   From the possession of this heavenly sight!
   Blow me about in winds! Roast me in sulfur!
   Wash me in steep-down gulfs of liquid fire!
   O Desdemon! Dead, Desdemon! Dead! O! O!

   Enter Lodovico, Cassio [carried in a litter°], Montano, and Iago [prisoner], with officers.

Lodovico: Where is this rash and most unfortunate man?
Othello: That's he that was Othello. Here I am.
Lodovico: Where is that viper? Bring the villain forth.

   [Iago is led forward.]

Othello: I look down towards his feet;° but that's a fable.
   If that thou be'st a devil, I cannot kill thee.

   [He wounds Iago.]

Lodovico: Wrench his sword from him.   *[Othello is disarmed.]*
Iago: I bleed, sir, but not killed.

270

275

280

285

290

295

273 *stop* power (to stop)   276 *butt* goal, limit. (An archery term.)   277 *seamark* beacon (marking his destination or limit)   278 *lost* wasted, unneeded   279 *Man . . . rush* wield no more than a reed   282 *compt* account, judgment day   285 *slave* i.e., Othello himself   290 s.d. *in a litter* (The Quarto specifies that Cassio is "in a chair.")   294 *towards his feet* i.e., to see if they are cloven, as the devil's are fabled to be

Lodovico confronts the prisoner Iago; Desdemona and Emilia lie dead in the background (V, ii, 296–314).

Othello: I am not sorry neither. I'd have thee live,
   For in my sense° 'tis happiness to die.
Lodovico: O thou Othello, that was once so good,
   Fall'n in the practice° of a cursèd slave,°   300
   What shall be said to thee?
Othello: Why, anything.
   An honorable murderer, if you will,
   For naught I did in hate, but all in honor.
Lodovico: This wretch hath part confessed his villainy.
   Did you and he consent° in Cassio's death?   305
Othello: Ay.
Cassio: Dear General, I never gave you cause.
Othello: I do believe it, and I ask your pardon.
   Will you, I pray, demand that demi-devil
   Why he hath thus ensnared my soul and body?   310
Iago: Demand me nothing. What you know, you know.
   From this time forth I never will speak word.
Lodovico: What, not to pray?
Gratiano: Torments° will ope your lips.

---

298 *in my sense* to one who feels as I do   300 *in the practice* through the plotting, into the snare. *slave* villain   305 *consent* agree   314 *Torments* torture

Othello: Well, thou dost best.   315
Lodovico: Sir, you shall understand what hath befall'n,
    Which, as I think, you know not. Here is a letter
    Found in the pocket of the slain Roderigo;
    And here another. *[He produces letters.]* The one of them imports
    The death of Cassio, to be undertook   320
    By Roderigo.
Othello: O villain!
Cassio: Most heathenish and most gross!°
Lodovico [showing another paper]: Now here's another discontented° paper
    Found in his pocket too. And this, it seems,
    Roderigo meant t' have sent this damnèd villain;   325
    But that belike° Iago in the interim
    Came in and satisfied him.°
Othello: O thou pernicious caitiff!—
    How came you, Cassio, by that handkerchief
    That was my wife's?
Cassio: I found it in my chamber;   330
    And he himself confessed but even now
    That there he dropped it for a special purpose
    Which wrought to his desire.°
Othello: O fool, fool, fool!
Cassio: There is besides in Roderigo's letter
    How he upbraids Iago, that he made him   335
    Brave° me upon the watch, whereon it came°
    That I was cast;° and even but now he spake,
    After long seeming dead, Iago hurt him,
    Iago set him on.
Lodovico [to Othello]: You must forsake this room and go with us.   340
    Your power and your command is taken off,°
    And Cassio rules in Cyprus. For this slave,
    If there be any cunning cruelty
    That can torment him much and hold him long,°
    It shall be his. You shall close prisoner rest°   345
    Till that the nature of your fault be known
    To the Venetian state.—Come, bring away.
Othello: Soft you;° a word or two before you go.
    I have done the state some service, and they know 't.
    No more of that. I pray you, in your letters,   350
    When you shall these unlucky° deeds relate,
    Speak of me as I am; nothing extenuate,
    Nor set down aught in malice. Then must you speak
    Of one that loved not wisely but too well;
    Of one not easily jealous but, being wrought,°   355

322 *gross* monstrous   323 *discontented* full of discontent   326 *belike* most likely   327 *Came . . . him* interposed and gave him satisfactory explanation   333 *wrought . . . desire* worked out as he wished, fitted in with his plan   336 *Brave* defy.   *whereon it came* whereof it came about   337 *cast* dismissed   341 *taken off* taken away   344 *hold him long* keep him alive a long time (during his torture)   345 *rest* remain   348 *Soft you* one moment   351 *unlucky* unfortunate   355 *wrought* worked upon, worked into a frenzy

Perplexed° in the extreme; of one whose hand,
Like the base Indian,° threw a pearl away
Richer than all his tribe; of one whose subdued° eyes,
Albeit unusèd to the melting mood,
Drop tears as fast as the Arabian trees   360
Their medicinable gum.° Set you down this;
And say besides that in Aleppo once,
Where a malignant and a turbaned Turk
Beat a Venetian and traduced the state,
I took by th' throat the circumcisèd dog   365
And smote him, thus.   [*He stabs himself.*°]
Lodovico: O bloody period!°
Gratiano: All that is spoke is marred.
Othello: I kissed thee ere I killed thee. No way but this,
   Killing myself, to die upon a kiss.   370

[*He kisses Desdemona and dies.*]

Cassio: This did I fear, but thought he had no weapon;
   For he was great of heart.
Lodovico [*to Iago*]:   O Spartan dog,°
   More fell° than anguish, hunger, or the sea!
   Look on the tragic loading of this bed.
   This is thy work. The object poisons sight;   375
   Let it be hid.° Gratiano, keep° the house,

[*The bed curtains are drawn*]

   And seize upon° the fortunes of the Moor,
   For they succeed on° you. [*To Cassio.*] To you, Lord Governor,
   Remains the censure° of this hellish villain,
   The time, the place, the torture. O, enforce it!   380
   Myself will straight aboard, and to the state
   This heavy act with heavy heart relate.   *Exeunt.*

Questions

ACT I

1. What is Othello's position in society? How is he regarded by those who know him? By his own words, when we first meet him in Scene ii, what traits of character does he manifest?
2. How do you account for Brabantio's dismay on learning of his daughter's marriage, despite the fact that Desdemona has married a man so generally honored and admired?
3. What is Iago's view of human nature? In his fondness for likening men to animals (as in I, i, 49–50; I, i, 90–91; and I, iii, 378–379), what does he tell us about himself?
4. What reasons does Iago give for his hatred of Othello?

---

356 *Perplexed* distraught   357 *Indian* (This reading from the Quarto pictures an ignorant savage who cannot recognize the value of a precious jewel. The Folio reading, *Iudean* or *Judean*, i.e., infidel or disbeliever, may refer to Herod, who slew Miriamne in a fit of jealousy, or to Judas Iscariot, the betrayer of Christ.) 358 *subdued* i.e., overcome by grief   361 *gum* i.e., myrrh   366 s.d. \ *He stabs himself* (This direction is in the Quarto text.)   367 *period* termination, conclusion   372 *Spartan dog* (Spartan dogs were noted for their savagery and silence.)   373 *fell* cruel   376 *Let it be hid* i.e., draw the bed curtains. (No stage direction specifies that the dead are to be carried offstage at the end of the play.)   *keep* remain in   377 *seize upon* take legal possession of   378 *succeed on* pass as though by inheritance to   379 *censure* sentencing

5. In Othello's defense before the senators (Scene iii), how does he explain Desdemona's gradual falling in love with him?
6. Is Brabantio's warning to Othello (I, iii, 293–294) an accurate or an inaccurate prophecy?
7. By what strategy does Iago enlist Roderigo in his plot against the Moor? In what lines do we learn Iago's true feelings toward Roderigo?

ACT II

1. What do the Cypriots think of Othello? Do their words (in Scene i) make him seem to us a lesser man or a larger one?
2. What cruelty does Iago display toward Emilia? How well founded is his distrust of his wife's fidelity?
3. In II, iii, 221, Othello speaks of Iago's "honesty and love." How do you account for Othello's being so totally deceived?
4. For what major events does the merrymaking (proclaimed in Scene ii) give opportunity?

ACT III

1. Trace the steps by which Iago rouses Othello to suspicion. Is there anything in Othello's character or circumstances that renders him particularly susceptible to Iago's wiles?
2. In III, iv, 49–98, Emilia knows of Desdemona's distress over the lost handkerchief. At this moment, how do you explain her failure to relieve Desdemona's mind? Is Emilia aware of her husband's villainy?

ACT IV

1. In this act, what circumstantial evidence is added to Othello's case against Desdemona?
2. How plausible do you find Bianca's flinging the handkerchief at Cassio just when Othello is looking on? How important is the handkerchief in this play? What does it represent? What suggestions or hints do you find in it?
3. What prevents Othello from being moved by Desdemona's appeal (IV, ii, 33–92)?
4. When Roderigo grows impatient with Iago (IV, ii, 181–201), how does Iago make use of his fellow plotter's discontent?
5. What does the conversation between Emilia and Desdemona (Scene iii) tell us about the nature of each?
6. In this act, what scenes (or speeches) contain memorable dramatic irony?

ACT V

1. Summarize the events that lead to Iago's unmasking.
2. How does Othello's mistaken belief that Cassio is slain (V, i, 27–34) affect the outcome of the play?
3. What is Iago's motive in stabbing Roderigo?
4. In your interpretation of the play, exactly what impels Othello to kill Desdemona? Jealousy? Desire for revenge? Excess idealism? A wish to be a public avenger who punishes, "else she'll betray more men"?
5. What do you understand by Othello's calling himself "one that loved not wisely but too well" (V, ii, 354)?
6. In your view, does Othello's long speech in V, ii, 348–366 succeed in restoring his original dignity and nobility? Do you agree with Cassio (V, ii, 372) that Othello was "great of heart"?

General Questions

1. What motivates Iago to carry out his schemes? Do you find him a devil incarnate, a madman, or a rational human being?
2. Whom besides Othello does Iago deceive? What is Desdemona's opinion of him? Emilia's? Cassio's (before Iago is found out)? To what do you attribute Iago's success as a deceiver?
3. How essential to the play is the fact that Othello is a black man, a Moor, and not a native of Venice?
4. In the introduction to his edition of the play in *The Complete Signet Classic Shakespeare*, Alvin Kernan remarks:

   > *Othello* is probably the most neatly, the most formally constructed of Shakespeare's plays. Every character is, for example, balanced by another similar or contrasting character. Desdemona is balanced by her opposite, Iago; love and concern for others at one end of the scale, hatred and concern for self at the other.

   Besides Desdemona and Iago, what other pairs of characters strike balances?
5. Does the play contain any *tragic recognition*—a moment of terrible enlightenment, a "realization of the unthinkable"?
6. Does the downfall of Othello proceed from any flaw in his nature, or is his downfall entirely the work of Iago?

CRITICAL AND CULTURAL CONTEXTS CASEBOOK

William Shakespeare's Othello

Historical Contexts
The Theater of Shakespeare

Source Material for Othello

Criticism and Cultural Contexts

Anthony Burgess
An Asian Culture Looks at Shakespeare

W. H. Auden
Iago as a Triumphant Villain

Maud Bodkin
Lucifer in Shakespeare's Othello

Virginia Mason Vaughan
Black and White in Othello

Othello in Performance: Images
Othello *Movie Poster*

Globe Theater

A Portfolio of Players: Famous Othellos in Performance

Othello *in Translation*

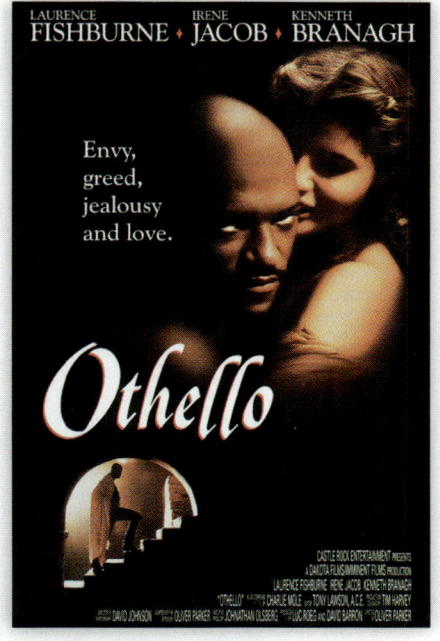

Movie poster for 1995 Oliver Parker film of *Othello*.

Othello is one of William Shakespeare's most perennially fascinating tragedies. Some of its themes—race, interracial marriage, domestic violence, and psychological manipulation—seem especially topical today, but all its major themes—war, military heroism, jealousy, self-doubt, and the nature of evil—remain timelessly relevant. Shakespeare borrowed the plot of *Othello* from a Renaissance Italian story (almost all of Shakespeare's plays borrow their plots from other sources), but he transformed it into something richer and more remarkable. What other author of his age could have imagined a central character of another race in such a complex, sympathetic, and compelling way? Shakespeare also burdens his hero with insecurities that may or may not be related to Othello's status as a "Moor" in a largely white world. Respected by men both powerful and weak, beloved by his wife, the middle-aged Othello still cannot believe that the beautiful young woman he adores truly loves him back. This lack of faith—in her, and perhaps in himself—makes him vulnerable to the machinations of others.

Besides breathing life into these characters and a host of others, Shakespeare—as brilliant a writer as any the world has known—enables them to speak in poetry. Sometimes this poetry seems splendid and rich in imagery, at other times quiet and understated. Always, it seems to grow naturally from the nature of Shakespeare's characters and from their situations. *Othello, the Moor of Venice* has never ceased to grip readers and beholders alike. It is a safe bet that it will live triumphantly as long as fathers dislike whomever their daughters marry, as long as husbands suspect their wives of cheating, as long as interracial marriage remains a sensitive issue to some people, as long as powerful older men marry beautiful young women, and as long as the ambitious court favor and the jealous practice deceit. The play may well make sense as long as public officials connive behind smiling faces, and it may even endure as long as the world makes room for the kind, the true, the beautiful—the blessed pure in heart.

Through the years, many critics have expressed opinions on all of these issues and more. Here is a selection of their writings on *Othello*, preceded by a description of the theater in which it was first performed.

HISTORICAL CONTEXTS

The reconstructed Globe Theater in today's London, built in 1997 as an exact replica of the original.

THE THEATER OF SHAKESPEARE

Compared with the technical resources of a theater of today, those of a London public theater in the time of Queen Elizabeth I seem hopelessly limited. Plays had to be performed by daylight, and scenery had to be kept simple: a table, a chair, a throne, perhaps an artificial tree or two to suggest a forest. But these limitations were, in a sense, advantages. What the theater of today can spell out for us realistically, with massive scenery and electric lighting, Elizabethan playgoers had to imagine and the playwright had to make vivid for them by means of language. Not having a lighting technician to work a panel, Shakespeare had to indicate the dawn by having Horatio, in *Hamlet,* say in a speech rich in metaphor and descriptive detail:

> But look, the morn in russet mantle clad
> Walks o'er the dew of yon high eastward hill.

And yet the theater of Shakespeare was not bare, for the playwright did have *some* valuable technical resources. Costumes could be elaborate, and apparently some costumes conveyed recognized meanings: one theater manager's inventory included "a robe for to go invisible in." There could be musical accompaniment and sound effects such as gunpowder explosions and the beating of a pan to simulate thunder.

The stage itself was remarkably versatile. At its back were doors for exits and entrances and a curtained booth or alcove useful for hiding inside. Above the stage was a higher acting area—perhaps a porch or balcony—useful for a Juliet to stand upon and for a Romeo to raise his eyes to. In the stage floor was a trapdoor leading to a "hell" or cellar, especially useful for ghosts or devils who had to appear or disappear. The stage itself was a rectangular platform that projected into a yard enclosed by three-storied galleries.

The building was round or octagonal. In *Henry V*, Shakespeare calls it a "wooden O." The audience sat in these galleries or else stood in the yard in front of the stage and at its sides. A roof or awning protected the stage and the high-priced gallery seats, but in a sudden rain, the *groundlings*, who paid a penny to stand in the yard, must have been dampened.

Built by the theatrical company to which Shakespeare belonged, the Globe, most celebrated of Elizabethan theaters, was not in the city of London itself but on the south bank of the Thames River. This location had been chosen because earlier, in 1574, public plays had been banished from the city by an ordinance that blamed them for "corruptions of youth and other enormities" (such as providing opportunities for prostitutes and pickpockets).

A playwright had to please all members of the audience, not only the mannered and educated. This obligation may help to explain the wide range of subject matter and tone in an Elizabethan play: passages of subtle poetry, of deep philosophy, of coarse bawdry; scenes of sensational violence and of quiet psychological conflict (not that most members of the audience did not enjoy all these elements). Because he was an actor as well as a playwright, Shakespeare well knew what his company could do and what his audience wanted. In devising a play, he could write a part to take advantage of some actor's specific skills, or he could avoid straining the company's resources (some of his plays have few female parts, perhaps because of a shortage of competent boy actors). The company might offer as many as thirty plays in a season, customarily changing the program daily. The actors thus had to hold many parts in their heads, which may account for Elizabethan playwrights' fondness for blank verse: lines of fixed length were easier for actors to commit to memory.

SOURCE MATERIAL FOR *OTHELLO*

Following his usual practice, Shakespeare based *Othello* on a story he had appropriated—from a tale, "Of the Unfaithfulness of Husbands and Wives," by a sixteenth-century Italian writer, Giraldi Cinthio. As he could not help but do, Shakespeare freely transformed his source material. In the original tale, the heroine Disdemona (whose name Shakespeare so hugely improved) is beaten to death with a stocking full of sand—a shoddier death than the bard imagined for her.

A Portfolio of Players
FAMOUS OTHELLOS IN PERFORMANCE

▲ Orson Welles's classic 1952 film.

▲ Laurence Olivier as Othello, 1965.

▲ Kenneth Branagh and Laurence Fishburne in Oliver Parker's 1995 film.

▲ Chiwetel Ejiofor and Ewan McGregor in the 2007 award-winning London performance at Donmar Warehouse Theatre.

CRITICISM AND CULTURAL CONTEXTS

Brabantio and Othello in a 1997 dance adaptation of *Othello* in New Delhi.

Anthony Burgess (1917–1993)

An Asian Culture Looks at Shakespeare   1982

Is translation possible? I first found myself asking this question in the Far East, when I was given the task of translating T. S. Eliot's *The Waste Land* into Indonesian. The difficulties began with the first line: "April is the cruellest month . . ." This I rendered as "*Bulan Abril ia-lah bulan yang dzalim sa-kali . . .*" I had to take *dzalim* from Arabic, since Indonesian did not, at that time, seem to possess a word for *cruel*. The term was accepted, but not the notion that a month, as opposed to a person or institution, could be cruel. Moreover, even if a month could be cruel, how—in the tropics where all the months are the same and the concepts of spring and winter do not exist—can one month be crueller than another? When I came to *forgetful snow*—rendered as *thalji berlupa*—I had to borrow a highly poetical word from the Persian, acceptable as a useful descriptive device for the brown skin of the beloved but not known in terms of a climatic reality. And, again, how could this inanimate substance possess the faculty of forgetting? I gave up the task as hopeless. Evidently the imagery of *The Waste Land* does not relate to a universal experience but applies only to the northern hemisphere, with its temperate climate and tradition of spring and fertility rituals.

As a teacher in Malaysia, I had to consider with a mixed group of Malay, Chinese, Indian, and Eurasian students, seasoned with the odd Buginese, Achinese, and Japanese, a piece of representative postwar British fiction. Although the setting of the book is West Africa, I felt that its story was of universal import. It was a novel by Graham Greene called *The Heart of the Matter*—a tragic story about a police officer named Scobie who is a Catholic convert. He is in love with his wife but falls in love with another woman, discovers that he cannot repent of this adultery, makes a sacrilegious communion so that his very Catholic wife will not suspect that a love affair is in progress, then commits suicide in despair, trusting that God will thrust him into the outer darkness and be no longer agonized by the exploits of sinning Scobie. To us this is a tragic situation. To my Muslim students it was extremely funny. One girl said: "Why cannot this Mr. Scobie become a Muslim? Then he can have four wives and there is no problem."

The only author who seemed to have the quality of universal appeal in Malaysia was William Shakespeare. Despite the problems of translating him, there is always an intelligible residue. I remember seeing in a Borneo kampong the film of *Richard III* made by Laurence Olivier, and the illiterate tribe which surrounded me was most appreciative. They knew nothing here of literary history and nothing of the great world outside this jungle clearing. They took this film about medieval conspiracy and tyranny to be a kind of newsreel representation of contemporary England. They approved the medieval costumes because they resembled their own ceremonial dress. This story of the assassination of innocents, including children, Machiavellian massacre, and the eventual defeat of a tyrant was typical of their own history, even their contemporary experience, and they accepted Shakespeare as a great poet. Eliot would not have registered with them at all. Translation is not a matter of words only; it is a matter of making intelligible a whole culture. Evidently the Elizabethan culture was still primitive enough to survive transportation over much time and space.

From spoken remarks on the "Importance of Translation"

W. H. Auden (1907–1973)

Iago as a Triumphant Villain   1962

Any consideration of the *Tragedy of Othello* must be primarily occupied, not with its official hero but with its villain. I cannot think of any other play in which only one character performs personal actions—all the *deeds* are Iago's—and all the others without exception only exhibit behavior. In marrying each other, Othello and Desdemona have performed a deed, but this took place before the play begins. Nor can I think of another play in which the villain is so completely triumphant: everything Iago sets out to do, he accomplishes—(among his goals, I include his self-destruction). Even Cassio, who survives, is maimed for life.

If *Othello* is a tragedy—and one certainly cannot call it a comedy—it is tragic in a peculiar way. In most tragedies the fall of the hero from glory to misery and death is the work, either of the gods, or of his own freely chosen acts, or, more commonly, a mixture of both. But the fall of Othello is the work of another human being; nothing he says or does originates with himself. In consequence we feel pity for him but no respect; our aesthetic respect is reserved for Iago.

Iago is a wicked man. The wicked man, the stage villain, as a subject of serious dramatic interest does not, so far as I know, appear in the drama of western Europe before the Elizabethans. In the mystery plays, the wicked characters, like Satan or Herod, are treated comically, but the theme of the triumphant villain cannot be treated comically because the suffering he inflicts is real.

From "The Joker in the Pack"

Maud Bodkin (1875–1967)

Lucifer in Shakespeare's *Othello* 1934

If we attempt to define the devil in psychological terms, regarding him as an archetype, a persistent or recurrent mode of apprehension, we may say that the devil is our tendency to represent in personal form the forces within and without us that threaten our supreme values. When Othello finds those values of confident love, of honor, and pride in soldiership, that made up his purposeful life, falling into ruin, his sense of the devil in all around him becomes acute. Desdemona has become "a fair devil"; he feels "a young and sweating devil" in her hand. The cry "O devil" breaks out among his incoherent words of raving. When Iago's falsehoods are disclosed, and Othello at last, too late, wrenches himself free from the spell of Iago's power over him, his sense of the devil incarnate in Iago's shape before him becomes overwhelming. If those who tell of the devil have failed to describe Iago, they have lied:

> I look down towards his feet; but that's a fable.
> If that thou be'st a devil, I cannot kill thee.

We also, watching or reading the play, experience the archetype. Intellectually aware, as we reflect, of natural forces, within a man himself as well as in society around, that betray or shatter his ideals, we yet feel these forces aptly symbolized for the imagination by such a figure as Iago—a being though personal yet hardly human, concentrated wholly on the hunting to destruction of its destined prey, the proud figure of the hero.

From *Archetypal Patterns in Poetry*

Virginia Mason Vaughan (b. 1947)

Black and White in *Othello* 1994

> If virtue no delighted beauty lack,
> Your son-in-law is far more fair than black.
> —*Othello* (1.3.290–291)

Black/white oppositions permeate *Othello*. Throughout the play, Shakespeare exploits a discourse of racial difference that by 1604 had become ingrained in the English psyche. From Iago's initial racial epithets at Brabantio's window ("old black ram," "barbary horse") to Emilia's cries of outrage in the final scene ("ignorant as dirt"), Shakespeare shows that the union of a white Venetian maiden and a black Moorish general is from at least one perspective emphatically unnatural. The union is of course a central fact of the play, and to some commentators, the spectacle of the pale-skinned woman caught in Othello's black arms has indeed seemed monstrous. Yet that spectacle is a major source of *Othello*'s emotional power. From Shakespeare's day to the present, the sight has titillated and terrified predominantly white audiences.

The effect of *Othello* depends, in other words, on the essential fact of the hero's darkness, the visual signifier of his Otherness. To Shakespeare's original audience, this chromatic sign was probably dark black, although there were other signifiers as well. Roderigo describes the Moor as having "thick lips," a term many sixteenth-century explorers employed in their descriptions of Africans. But, as historian Winthrop Jordan notes, by the late sixteenth century, "Blackness became so generally associated with Africa that every African seemed a black man[,] . . . the terms *Moor* and *Negro* used almost interchangeably." "Moor" became, G. K. Hunter observes, "a word for 'people not like us,' so signaled by color." Richard Burbage's Othello was probably black. But in any production, whether he appears as a tawny Moor (as nineteenth-century actors preferred) or as a black man of African descent, Othello bears the visual signs of his Otherness, a difference that the play's language insists can never be eradicated.

From *Othello: A Contextual History*

Suggestions for Writing on *Shakespeare's Othello*

1. Othello deeply loves Desdemona. Why does his love go so tragically wrong? State your reasons for its failure and support them with examples from the text.
2. Write a defense of Iago.
3. "Never was any play fraught, like this of *Othello*, with improbabilities," wrote Thomas Rymer in a famous attack (*A Short View of Tragedy*, 1692). Consider Rymer's objection to the play, either answering it or finding evidence to back it up.
4. Suppose yourself a casting director assigned to a film version of *Othello*. What well-known actors would you cast in the principal roles? Write a paper justifying your choices. Don't merely discuss the stars and their qualifications; discuss (with specific reference to the play) what Shakespeare appears to call for.
5. Emilia's long speech at the end of Act IV (iii, 83–102) has been called a Renaissance plea for women's rights. Do you agree? Write a brief, close analysis of this speech. How timely is it?

Suggestions for Writing on *Literature about Love*

1. Some of the pieces in this chapter deal with desire, some with love, and some with both. Citing at least two or three of the works in this chapter, how would you differentiate between the presentations of love and desire? Is there a differentiation? Should there be?
2. This chapter includes works on love by both male and female authors. Do you find that depictions and expectations of love are different, depending on the sex of the author? Choose at least two works by men and two by women to make your case.
3. How might hopes and expectations of love be affected by things such as social class, historical era, religion, race, and age? Choose at least two works from this chapter and analyze how they deal with love, taking these other factors into account.

4. How do you think that innovations such as e-mail, Facebook, online dating services, and texting have affected romance and love? Write an essay arguing that technology has made romance easier—or alternatively, that it's having a negative effect.
5. Choose one of the stories in this chapter—for example, O'Connor's "Parker's Back" or any of Kate Chopin's stories—and discuss whether it could have had a happier ending. Could the characters have acted differently to create a different outcome? Or did circumstances or personalities dictate that no happy ending was possible? What do your conclusions lead you to believe about the author's views on love?
6. Love is almost always presented as a great good, something that everyone should want; it is often seen as the most important thing in life. Choose the work in this chapter that seems to you to be at the furthest remove from this point of view. How is love treated in that work? What are the reasons for its less than ideal portrayal?

14 LIFE'S JOURNEY

Life is a verb, not a noun.
—CHARLOTTE PERKINS GILMAN

If you are using this textbook, you are probably in college. You may be a traditional freshman or sophomore, or you may be an older adult returning to school. You could be living on campus, away from your family for the first time—or you might be living at home, with your parents, or with your own spouse and family. You may even be taking this course on a screen physically remote from your instructor and fellow students. No matter what the specifics may be, if you are taking this class, you are in the midst of one of life's most interesting journeys.

From the moment we are born, we embark on journeys both large and small, both literal and figurative. The long transition from childhood to adolescence to adulthood is a journey. So is the change from innocence to understanding and experience. Children see the world mostly in simple terms and are generally unaware of life's dangers and complexities. This wide-eyed view is altered in time by knowledge and experience—often through painful events or difficult realizations. You may come to realize that your parents, who you believed were the smartest, best, most wonderful people alive, aren't as perfect as you thought. Someone you love might have something terrible befall him or her. You might realize that people treat you differently because of your race, sex, or religion.

Ultimately, the journey from innocence to experience involves a change from a simple, straightforward view of the world to a more nuanced, complex understanding. It's the realization that people—including yourself—are more complicated than you first believed. Although we tend to see these realizations as part of the process of becoming an adult, that isn't always the case. If innocence is a state of not knowing, we don't need to be children to "not know." Adam and Eve were innocent before they bit into the apple, before they knew to be ashamed of their nakedness. You probably know adults who seem incredibly naïve, who cannot see fault in other people or even themselves, and who always, against all evidence to the contrary, expect things to work out for the best.

Once you realize that the world is harsh and that the people you love—including yourself—are not infallible, what do you do? This is the most important question. We all have difficult things happen in our lives; we all let ourselves and others down at some point. But it's what we *do* with that experience that ultimately matters. Setbacks, mistakes, and disappointments can give us a fuller understanding of the world, which in turn can help us make our decisions more wisely. If we lose a loved one, or experience a personal trauma, it may make us more empathetic in our dealings with others. If we mess up royally—by hurting a friend or parent or spouse—we might be more careful, and more appreciative, the next time around. Falling down once in a while is not a bad thing—it's the getting up that matters. As basketball legend Michael Jordan, who sank countless game-winning shots under pressure, once said, "I've failed over and over and over again. And that's why I succeed."

Our final journey—from life to death—is harder to define. Because people don't come back from death, we don't have empirical data on what it's like. Perhaps partly for this reason, there is a wide variety of beliefs about the meaning and experience of death across cultures and religions. Some see death as a the absolute end; others see it as the beginning of a different kind of existence. Most people do not want to die, and many—particularly college-age students who are in the prime of life—can't fathom the idea of their own mortality. Others, particularly those who are older or ill, may look forward to death as a time when they will join their loved ones, or simply as a time for "rest." Perhaps because death is both universally experienced and so unknowable, it is one of the most pondered subjects in literature.

THE SELECTIONS IN THIS CHAPTER

This chapter includes works that explore all these kinds of journeys. James Joyce's "Araby" and A. E. Housman's "When I was one-and-twenty" portray bittersweet moments of romantic disillusionment. James Baldwin's "Notes of a Native Son" describes the moment when the author realizes his father's limitations—and the workings of the history that is being made around him. ZZ Packer's "Brownies" relates the story of a Brownie troop that discovers some hard truths about the world. Joyce Carol Oates's "Where Are You Going, Where Have You Been?" captures an adolescent girl's moment of sexual self-awareness and danger. John Updike's "Ex-Basketball Player" describes a character who has fallen from heights of greatness. The collection of poems by Robert Frost explores the turns and crossroads of life's journey, while poems such as Dylan Thomas's "Do not go gentle into that good night" and Emily Dickinson's "Because I could not stop for Death" consider the journey from life into death.

As you read the works in this chapter, we hope you will consider your own life's journey. Reading about other people's experiences can help clarify and refine your own goals, especially as you embark on the next stage of your life.

Things to Think About

1. When was your childhood over? Was its ending marked by a ceremonial milestone (for example: turning eighteen, quinceañera, confirmation, bar or bat mitzvah), or was it connected to a significant experience or realization?
2. What does it mean to be an adult? Is adulthood defined simply by age, or is it related to understanding and experience? Do you consider yourself an adult? Do you know people who are not legally adults (i.e., who are under 18) but seem mature for their age? Do you know people who are technically adults but still act like children?
3. What were the major turning points or realizations of your adolescence or childhood? Did they involve family members? Other people? Yourself? Was there a hard lesson that you are now glad you had to learn?
4. Has there ever been a time when you did something you didn't want to, or that you knew was wrong? How did that event change your understanding of the world—and of yourself?
5. Do you believe that there is life after death? If so, does this belief affect the way you live? Does it influence how you react to the deaths of loved ones?

FICTION

CHILDHOOD AND ADOLESCENCE

James Joyce	*Araby*
ZZ Packer	*Brownies*
Michael Chabon	*The Little Knife*

Childhood and adolescence are fascinating subjects for most writers because they involve the mysterious formation of adult character and beliefs. How do we become grown-up men and women? This is a question that absorbs psychologists, educators, biologists, philosophers, and clergy. Is our character formed by our genetic inheritance, our family background, our social environment, our education? Surely every aspect of our upbringing has some impact, however small; but is one element more important than the others? Scientists, psychologists, and sociologists explore these questions through the methods of their disciplines. But writers investigate the same questions by unfolding imagined lives in revealing circumstances. In "Araby," James Joyce presents a boy as he experiences a moment of quiet but profound disappointment. ZZ Packer explores the complex combination of cruelty and kindness that children display. Michael Chabon demonstrates the power of fiction to portray the significant but secret moments that can change a life.

James Joyce

James Joyce (1882–1941) was born and educated in Dublin, and his love-hate relationship with his native city and Ireland provided the subject matter of his most characteristic works. He left Ireland at twenty-two to spend his life in voluntary exile in Europe. In Trieste, Zurich, and eventually Paris, he supported his family with difficulty, sometimes by teaching in the Berlitz language schools, until his fame secured him wealthy patrons. Publication of Dubliners *(1914), the collection of stories that includes "Araby," was delayed seven years because its prospective Irish publisher feared libel suits. (The book depicts local citizens, some of them recognizable, and views Dubliners mostly as a thwarted, self-deceived lot.)* A Portrait of the Artist as a Young Man *(1916), a novel of thinly veiled autobiography, recounts a young intellectual's breaking away from country, church, and home. Joyce's immense comic novel* Ulysses *(1922), a parody of the* Odyssey, *spans eighteen hours in the life of a wandering Jew, a Dublin seller of advertising. Frank about sex but hardly titillating, the book was banned for years as obscene by the U.S. Post Office. Joyce's main work in his later years was the enormously challenging* Finnegans Wake *(1939), a lengthy and complex*

James Joyce

experimental novel. Joyce was an innovator whose bold experiments showed many other writers possibilities in fiction that had not yet been imagined.

Araby   1914

North Richmond Street, being blind,° was a quiet street except at the hour when the Christian Brothers' School set the boys free. An uninhabited house of two stories stood at the blind end, detached from its neighbors in a square ground. The other houses of the street, conscious of decent lives within them, gazed at one another with brown imperturbable faces.

The former tenant of our house, a priest, had died in the back drawing-room. Air, musty from having been long enclosed, hung in all the rooms, and the waste room behind the kitchen was littered with old useless papers. Among these I found a few paper-covered books, the pages of which were curled and damp: *The Abbot*, by Walter Scott, *The Devout Communicant* and *The Memoirs of Vidocq*.° I liked the last best because its leaves were yellow. The wild garden behind the house contained a central apple-tree and a few straggling bushes under one of which I found the late tenant's rusty bicycle-pump. He had been a very charitable priest: in his will he had left all his money to institutions and the furniture of his house to his sister.

When the short days of winter came dusk fell before we had well eaten our dinners. When we met in the street the houses had grown somber. The space of sky above us was the color of ever-changing violet and towards it the lamps of the street lifted their feeble lanterns. The cold air stung us and we played till our bodies glowed. Our shouts echoed in the silent street. The career of our play brought us through the dark muddy lanes behind the houses where we ran the gantlet of the rough tribes from the cottages, to the back doors of the dark dripping gardens where odors arose from the ashpits, to the dark odorous stables where a coachman smoothed and combed the horse or shook music from the buckled harness. When we returned to the street light from the kitchen windows had filled the areas. If my uncle was seen turning the corner we hid in the shadow until we had seen him safely housed. Or if Mangan's sister° came out on the doorstep to call her brother in to his tea we watched her from our shadow peer up and down the street. We waited to see whether she would remain or go in and, if she remained, we left our shadow and walked up to Mangan's steps resignedly. She was waiting for us, her figure defined by the light from the half-opened door. Her brother always teased her before he obeyed and I stood by the railings looking at her. Her dress swung as she moved her body and the soft rope of her hair tossed from side to side.

Every morning I lay on the floor in the front parlor watching her door. The blind was pulled down within an inch of the sash so that I could not be seen. When she came out on the doorstep my heart leaped. I ran to the hall, seized my books and followed her. I kept her brown figure always in my eye and, when we came near the point at which our ways diverged, I quickened my pace and passed her. This happened morning after morning. I had never spoken to her, except for a few casual words, and yet her name was like a summons to all my foolish blood.

being blind: being a dead-end street.   *The Abbot . . . Vidocq:* a popular historical romance (1820); a book of pious meditations by an eighteenth-century English Franciscan, Pacificus Baker; and the autobiography of François-Jules Vidocq (1775–1857), a criminal who later turned detective.   *Mangan's sister:* an actual young woman in this story, but the phrase recalls Irish poet James Clarence Mangan (1803–1849) and his best-known poem, "Dark Rosaleen," which personifies Ireland as a beautiful woman for whom the poet yearns.

Her image accompanied me even in places the most hostile to romance. On Saturday evenings when my aunt went marketing I had to go to carry some of the parcels. We walked through the flaring streets, jostled by drunken men and bargaining women, amid the curses of laborers, the shrill litanies of shopboys who stood on guard by the barrels of pigs' cheeks, the nasal chanting of street-singers, who sang a *come-all-you* about O'Donovan Rossa,° or a ballad about the troubles in our native land. These noises converged in a single sensation of life for me: I imagined that I bore my chalice safely through a throng of foes. Her name sprang to my lips at moments in strange prayers and praises which I myself did not understand. My eyes were often full of tears (I could not tell why) and at times a flood from my heart seemed to pour itself out into my bosom. I thought little of the future. I did not know whether I would ever speak to her or not or, if I spoke to her, how I could tell her of my confused adoration. But my body was like a harp and her words and gestures were like fingers running upon the wires.

One evening I went into the back drawing-room in which the priest had died. It was a dark rainy evening and there was no sound in the house. Through one of the broken panes I heard the rain impinge upon the earth, the fine incessant needles of water playing in the sodden beds. Some distant lamp or lighted window gleamed below me. I was thankful that I could see so little. All my senses seemed to desire to veil themselves and, feeling that I was about to slip from them, I pressed the palms of my hands together until they trembled, murmuring: *O love! O love!* many times.

At last she spoke to me. When she addressed the first words to me I was so confused that I did not know what to answer. She asked me was I going to *Araby*. I forget whether I answered yes or no. It would be a splendid bazaar, she said; she would love to go.

—And why can't you? I asked.

While she spoke she turned a silver bracelet round and round her wrist. She could not go, she said, because there would be a retreat that week in her convent.° Her brother and two other boys were fighting for their caps and I was alone at the railings. She held one of the spikes, bowing her head towards me. The light from the lamp opposite our door caught the white curve of her neck, lit up her hair that rested there and, falling, lit up the hand upon the railing. It fell over one side of her dress and caught the white border of a petticoat, just visible as she stood at ease.

—It's well for you, she said.

—If I go, I said, I will bring you something.

What innumerable follies laid waste my waking and sleeping thoughts after that evening! I wished to annihilate the tedious intervening days. I chafed against the work of school. At night in my bedroom and by day in the classroom her image came between me and the page I strove to read. The syllables of the word *Araby* were called to me through the silence in which my soul luxuriated and cast an Eastern enchantment over me. I asked for leave to go to the bazaar on Saturday night. My aunt was

---

come-all-you about O'Donovan Rossa: the street singers earned their living by singing timely songs that usually began, "Come all you gallant Irishmen / And listen to my song." Their subject, also called Dynamite Rossa, was a popular hero jailed by the British for advocating violent rebellion. *a retreat . . . in her convent*: a week devoted to religious observances more intense than usual, at the convent school Miss Mangan attends; probably she will have to listen to a number of hellfire sermons.

surprised and hoped it was not some Freemason° affair. I answered few questions in class. I watched my master's face pass from amiability to sternness; he hoped I was not beginning to idle. I could not call my wandering thoughts together. I had hardly any patience with the serious work of life which, now that it stood between me and my desire, seemed to me child's play, ugly monotonous child's play.

On Saturday morning I reminded my uncle that I wished to go to the bazaar in the evening. He was fussing at the hallstand, looking for the hatbrush, and answered me curtly:

—Yes, boy, I know.

As he was in the hall I could not go into the front parlor and lie at the window. I left the house in bad humor and walked slowly towards the school. The air was pitilessly raw and already my heart misgave me.

When I came home to dinner my uncle had not yet been home. Still it was early. I sat staring at the clock for some time and, when its ticking began to irritate me, I left the room. I mounted the staircase and gained the upper part of the house. The high cold empty gloomy rooms liberated me and I went from room to room singing. From the front window I saw my companions playing below in the street. Their cries reached me weakened and indistinct and, leaning my forehead against the cool glass, I looked over at the dark house where she lived. I may have stood there for an hour, seeing nothing but the brown-clad figure cast by my imagination, touched discreetly by the lamplight at the curved neck, at the hand upon the railings and at the border below the dress.

When I came downstairs again I found Mrs. Mercer sitting at the fire. She was an old garrulous woman, a pawnbroker's widow, who collected used stamps for some pious purpose. I had to endure the gossip of the tea-table. The meal was prolonged beyond an hour and still my uncle did not come. Mrs. Mercer stood up to go: she was sorry she couldn't wait any longer, but it was after eight o'clock and she did not like to be out late, as the night air was bad for her. When she had gone I began to walk up and down the room, clenching my fists. My aunt said:

—I'm afraid you may put off your bazaar for this night of Our Lord.

At nine o'clock I heard my uncle's latchkey in the halldoor. I heard him talking to himself and heard the hallstand rocking when it had received the weight of his overcoat. I could interpret these signs. When he was midway through his dinner I asked him to give me the money to go to the bazaar. He had forgotten.

—The people are in bed and after their first sleep now, he said.

I did not smile. My aunt said to him energetically:

—Can't you give him the money and let him go? You've kept him late enough as it is.

My uncle said he was very sorry he had forgotten. He said he believed in the old saying: *All work and no play makes Jack a dull boy.* He asked me where I was going and, when I had told him a second time he asked me did I know *The Arab's Farewell to His Steed.*° When I left the kitchen he was about to recite the opening lines of the piece to my aunt.

Freemason: Catholics in Ireland viewed the Masonic order as a Protestant conspiracy against them. *The Arab's Farewell to His Steed:* This sentimental ballad by a popular poet, Caroline Norton (1808–1877), tells the story of a nomad of the desert who, in a fit of greed, sells his beloved horse, then regrets the loss, flings away the gold he had received, and takes back his horse. Notice the echo of "Araby" in the song title.

I held a florin tightly in my hands as I strode down Buckingham Street towards the station. The sight of the streets thronged with buyers and glaring with gas recalled to me the purpose of my journey. I took my seat in a third-class carriage of a deserted train. After an intolerable delay the train moved out of the station slowly. It crept onward among ruinous houses and over the twinkling river. At Westland Row Station a crowd of people pressed to the carriage doors; but the porters moved them back, saying that it was a special train for the bazaar. I remained alone in the bare carriage. In a few minutes the train drew up beside an improvised wooden platform. I passed out on to the road and saw by the lighted dial of a clock that it was ten minutes to ten. In front of me was a large building which displayed the magical name.

I could not find any sixpenny entrance and, fearing that the bazaar would be closed, I passed in quickly through a turnstile, handing a shilling to a weary-looking man. I found myself in a big hall girdled at half its height by a gallery. Nearly all the stalls were closed and the greater part of the hall was in darkness. I recognized a silence like that which pervades a church after a service. I walked into the center of the bazaar timidly. A few people were gathered about the stalls which were still open. Before a curtain, over which the words *Café Chantant*° were written in colored lamps, two men were counting money on a salver.° I listened to the fall of the coins.

Remembering with difficulty why I had come I went over to one of the stalls and examined porcelain vases and flowered tea-sets. At the door of the stall a young lady was talking and laughing with two young gentlemen. I remarked their English accents and listened vaguely to their conversation.

—O, I never said such a thing!
—O, but you did!
—O, but I didn't!
—Didn't she say that?
—Yes. I heard her.
—O, there's a . . . fib!

Observing me the young lady came over and asked me did I wish to buy anything. The tone of her voice was not encouraging; she seemed to have spoken to me out of a sense of duty. I looked humbly at the great jars that stood like eastern guards at either side of the dark entrance to the stall and murmured:

—No, thank you.

The young lady changed the position of one of the vases and went back to the two young men. They began to talk of the same subject. Once or twice the young lady glanced at me over her shoulder.

I lingered before her stall, though I knew my stay was useless, to make my interest in her wares seem the more real. Then I turned away slowly and walked down the middle of the bazaar. I allowed the two pennies to fall against the sixpence in my pocket. I heard a voice call from one end of the gallery that the light was out. The upper part of the hall was now completely dark.

Gazing up into the darkness I saw myself as a creature driven and derided by vanity; and my eyes burned with anguish and anger.

Café Chantant: name for a Paris nightspot featuring topical songs.   *salver*: a tray like that used in serving Holy Communion.

Questions

1. What is the tone of this story? What does the tone imply about the meaning of this childhood experience to the narrator?
2. Why is the narrator so drawn to Mangan's sister? Does he have reason to believe his interest is returned?
3. How do the things that take place at the bazaar relate to the theme of the story?
4. What does the narrator realize by the end of the story?

ZZ Packer

ZZ Packer (b. 1973) was born in Chicago, Illinois, but grew up in Atlanta, Georgia, and Louisville, Kentucky. Her given name was Zuwena, the Swahili term for "good," but it was so often mispronounced that she began calling herself "ZZ." Packer became interested in writing in high school and published her first story in Seventeen magazine while still a senior at Yale University. She did graduate work at Johns Hopkins and the University of Iowa, and eventually became a Stegner Fellow at Stanford University. "Brownies" is the opening story of her first collection of short stories, Drinking Coffee Elsewhere (2003), which has been translated into five languages. Packer currently lives in the San Francisco Bay Area.

ZZ Packer

Brownies°

2003

By our second day at Camp Crescendo, the girls in my Brownie troop had decided to kick the asses of each and every girl in Brownie Troop 909. Troop 909 was doomed from the first day of camp; they were white girls, their complexions a blend of ice cream: strawberry, vanilla. They turtled out from their bus in pairs, their rolled-up sleeping bags chromatized with Disney characters: Sleeping Beauty, Snow White, Mickey Mouse; or the generic ones cheap parents bought: washed-out rainbows, unicorns, curly-eyelashed frogs. Some clutched Igloo coolers and still others held on to stuffed toys like pacifiers, looking all around them like tourists determined to be dazzled.

Our troop was wending its way past their bus, past the ranger station, past the colorful trail guide drawn like a treasure map, locked behind glass.

"Man, did you smell them?" Arnetta said, giving the girls a slow once-over, "They smell like Chihuahuas. *Wet* Chihuahuas." Their troop was still at the entrance, and though we had passed them by yards, Arnetta raised her nose in the air and grimaced.

Arnetta said this from the very rear of the line, far away from Mrs. Margolin, who always strung our troop behind her like a brood of obedient ducklings. Mrs. Margolin even looked like a mother duck—she had hair cropped close to a small ball of a head, almost no neck, and huge, miraculous breasts. She wore enormous belts that looked like the kind that weightlifters wear, except hers would be cheap metallic gold

---

Brownies: Girl Scout program for 2nd and 3rd grade girls.

or rabbit fur or covered with gigantic fake sunflowers, and often these belts would become nature lessons in and of themselves. "See," Mrs. Margolin once said to us, pointing to her belt, "this one's made entirely from the feathers of baby pigeons."

The belt layered with feathers was uncanny enough, but I was more disturbed by the realization that I had never actually *seen* a baby pigeon. I searched weeks for one, in vain—scampering after pigeons whenever I was downtown with my father.

But nature lessons were not Mrs. Margolin's top priority. She saw the position of troop leader as an evangelical post. Back at the A.M.E. church° where our Brownie meetings were held, Mrs. Margolin was especially fond of imparting religious aphorisms by means of acrostics—"Satan" was the "Serpent Always Tempting and Noisome"; she'd refer to the "Bible" as "Basic Instructions Before Leaving Earth." Whenever she quizzed us on these, expecting to hear the acrostics parroted back to her, only Arnetta's correct replies soared over our vague mumblings. "Jesus?" Mrs. Margolin might ask expectantly, and Arnetta alone would dutifully answer, "Jehovah's Example, Saving Us Sinners."

Arnetta always made a point of listening to Mrs. Margolin's religious talk and giving her what she wanted to hear. Because of this, Arnetta could have blared through a megaphone that the white girls of Troop 909 were "wet Chihuahuas" without so much as a blink from Mrs. Margolin. Once, Arnetta killed the troop goldfish by feeding it a french fry covered in ketchup, and when Mrs. Margolin demanded that she explain what had happened, claimed the goldfish had been eyeing her meal for *hours*, then the fish—giving in to temptation—had leapt up and snatched a whole golden fry from her fingertips.

"*Serious* Chihuahua," Octavia added, and though neither Arnetta nor Octavia could *spell* "Chihuahua," had ever *seen* a Chihuahua, trisyllabic words had gained a sort of exoticism within our fourth-grade set at Woodrow Wilson Elementary. Arnetta and Octavia would flip through the dictionary, determined to work the vulgar-sounding ones like "Djibouti" and "asinine" into conversation.

"*Caucasian* Chihuahuas," Arnetta said.

That did it. The girls in my troop turned elastic: Drema and Elise doubled up on one another like inextricably entwined kites; Octavia slapped her belly; Janice jumped straight up in the air, then did it again, as if to slam-dunk her own head. They could not stop laughing. No one had laughed so hard since a boy named Martez had stuck a pencil in the electric socket and spent the whole day with a strange grin on his face.

"Girls, girls," said our parent helper, Mrs. Hedy. Mrs. Hedy was Octavia's mother, and she wagged her index finger perfunctorily, like a windshield wiper. "Stop it, now. Be good." She said this loud enough to be heard, but lazily, bereft of any feeling or indication that she meant to be obeyed, as though she could say these words again at the exact same pitch if a button somewhere on her were pressed.

But the rest of the girls didn't stop; they only laughed louder. It was the word "Caucasian" that got them all going. One day at school, about a month before the Brownie camping trip, Arnetta turned to a boy wearing impossibly high-ankled floodwater jeans and said, "What are you? *Caucasian?*" The word took off from there, and soon everything was Caucasian. If you ate too fast you ate like a Caucasian, if you ate too slow you ate like a Caucasian. The biggest feat anyone at Woodrow Wilson could do was to jump off the swing in midair, at the highest point in its arc, and if you fell (as I had, more than once) instead of landing on your feet, knees bent Olympic

---

A.M.E. *church*: African Methodist Episcopal Church, a Protestant denomination founded by people of African descent.

gymnast-style, Arnetta and Octavia were prepared to comment. They'd look at each other with the silence of passengers who'd narrowly escaped an accident, then nod their heads, whispering with solemn horror, "*Caucasian.*"

Even the only white kid in our school, Dennis, got in on the Caucasian act. That time when Martez stuck a pencil in the socket, Dennis had pointed and yelled, "That was *so* Caucasian!"

When you lived in the south suburbs of Atlanta, it was easy to forget about whites. Whites were like those baby pigeons: real and existing, but rarely seen or thought about. Everyone had been to Rich's to go clothes shopping, everyone had seen white girls and their mothers coo-cooing over dresses; everyone had gone to the downtown library and seen white businessmen swish by importantly, wrists flexed in front of them to check the time as though they would change from Clark Kent into Superman at any second. But those images were as fleeting as cards shuffled in a deck, whereas the ten white girls behind us—*invaders*, Arnetta would later call them—were instantly real and memorable, with their long, shampoo-commercial hair, straight as spaghetti from the box. This alone was reason for envy and hatred. The only black girl most of us had ever seen with hair that long was Octavia, whose hair hung past her butt like a Hawaiian hula dancer's. The sight of Octavia's mane prompted other girls to listen to her reverentially, as though whatever she had to say would somehow activate their own follicles. For example, when, on the first day of camp, Octavia made as if to speak, and everyone fell silent. "Nobody," Octavia said, "calls us niggers."

At the end of that first day, when half of our troop made their way back to the cabin after tag-team restroom visits, Arnetta said she'd heard one of the Troop 909 girls call Daphne a nigger. The other half of the girls and I were helping Mrs. Margolin clean up the pots and pans from the campfire ravioli dinner. When we made our way to the restrooms to wash up and brush our teeth, we met up with Arnetta midway.

"Man, I completely heard the girl," Arnetta reported. "Right, Daphne?"

Daphne hardly ever spoke, but when she did, her voice was petite and tinkly, the voice one might expect from a shiny new earring. She'd written a poem once, for Langston Hughes Day, a poem brimming with all the teacher-winning ingredients—trees and oceans, sunsets and moons—but what cinched the poem for the grown-ups, snatching the win from Octavia's musical ode to Grandmaster Flash and the Furious Five, were Daphne's last lines:

> You are my father, the veteran
> When you cry in the dark
> It rains and rains and rains in my heart

She'd always worn clean, though faded, jumpers and dresses when Chic jeans were the fashion, but when she went up to the dais to receive her prize journal, pages trimmed in gold, she wore a new dress with a velveteen bodice and a taffeta skirt as wide as an umbrella. All the kids clapped, though none of them understood the poem. I'd read encyclopedias the way others read comics, and I didn't get it. But those last lines pricked me, they were so eerie, and as my father and I ate cereal, I'd whisper over my Froot Loops, like a mantra, "*You are my father, the veteran. You are my father, the veteran, the veteran, the veteran,*" until my father, who acted in plays as Caliban and Othello and was not a veteran, marched me up to my teacher one morning and said, "Can you tell me what's wrong with this kid?"

I thought Daphne and I might become friends, but I think she grew spooked by me whispering those lines to her, begging her to tell me what they meant, and I soon understood that two quiet people like us were better off quiet alone.

"Daphne? Didn't you hear them call you a nigger?" Arnetta asked, giving Daphne a nudge.

The sun was setting behind the trees, and their leafy tops formed a canopy of black lace for the flame of the sun to pass through. Daphne shrugged her shoulders at first, then slowly nodded her head when Arnetta gave her a hard look.

Twenty minutes later, when my restroom group returned to the cabin, Arnetta was still talking about Troop 909. My restroom group had passed by some of the 909 girls. For the most part, they deferred to us, waving us into the restrooms, letting us go even though they'd gotten there first.

We'd seen them, but from afar, never within their orbit enough to see whether their faces were the way all white girls appeared on TV—ponytailed and full of energy, bubbling over with love and money. All I could see was that some of them rapidly fanned their faces with their hands, though the heat of the day had long passed. A few seemed to be lolling their heads in slow circles, half purposefully, as if exercising the muscles of their necks, half ecstatically, like Stevie Wonder.

"We can't let them get away with that," Arnetta said, dropping her voice to a laryngitic whisper. "We can't let them get away with calling us niggers. I say we teach them a lesson." She sat down crosslegged on a sleeping bag, an embittered Buddha, eyes glimmering acrylic-black. "We can't go telling Mrs. Margolin, either. Mrs. Margolin'll say something about doing unto others and the path of righteousness and all. Forget that shit." She let her eyes flutter irreverently till they half closed, as though ignoring an insult not worth returning. We could all hear Mrs. Margolin outside, gathering the last of the metal campware.

Nobody said anything for a while. Usually people were quiet after Arnetta spoke. Her tone had an upholstered confidence that was somehow both regal and vulgar at once. It demanded a few moments of silence in its wake, like the ringing of a church bell or the playing of taps. Sometimes Octavia would ditto or dissent to whatever Arnetta had said, and this was the signal that others could speak. But this time Octavia just swirled a long cord of hair into pretzel shapes.

"Well?" Arnetta said. She looked as if she had discerned the hidden severity of the situation and was waiting for the rest of us to catch up. Everyone looked from Arnetta to Daphne. It was, after all, Daphne who had supposedly been called the name, but Daphne sat on the bare cabin floor, flipping through the pages of the Girl Scout handbook, eyebrows arched in mock wonder, as if the handbook were a catalogue full of bright and startling foreign costumes. Janice broke the silence. She clapped her hands to broach her idea of a plan.

"They gone be sleeping," she whispered conspiratorially; "then we gone sneak into they cabin, then we'll put daddy longlegs in they sleeping bags. Then they'll wake up. Then we gone beat 'em up till they're as flat as frying pans!" She jammed her fist into the palm of her hand, then made a sizzling sound.

Janice's country accent was laughable, her looks homely, her jumpy acrobatics embarrassing to behold. Arnetta and Octavia volleyed amused, arrogant smiles whenever Janice opened her mouth, but Janice never caught the hint, spoke whenever she wanted, fluttered around Arnetta and Octavia futilely offering her opinions to their departing backs. Whenever Arnetta and Octavia shooed her away, Janice loitered until the two would finally sigh and ask, "What *is* it, Miss Caucausoid? What do you want?"

"Shut up, Janice," Octavia said, letting a fingered loop of hair fall to her waist as though just the sound of Janice's voice had ruined the fun of her hair twisting.

Janice obeyed, her mouth hung open in a loose grin, unflappable, unhurt.

"All right," Arnetta said, standing up. "We're going to have a secret meeting and talk about what we're going to do."

Everyone gravely nodded her head. The word "secret" had a built-in importance, the modifier form of the word carried more clout than the noun. A secret meant nothing; it was like gossip: just a bit of unpleasant knowledge about someone who happened to be someone other than yourself. A secret *meeting*, or a secret *club* was entirely different.

That was when Arnetta turned to me as though she knew that doing so was both a compliment and a charity.

"Snot, you're not going to be a bitch and tell Mrs. Margolin, are you?"

I had been called "Snot" ever since first grade, when I'd sneezed in class and two long ropes of mucus had splattered a nearby girl.

"Hey," I said. "Maybe you didn't hear them right—I mean—"

"Are you gonna tell on us or not?" was all Arnetta wanted to know, and by the time the question was asked, the rest of our Brownie troop looked at me as though they'd already decided their course of action, me being the only impediment.

Camp Crescendo used to double as a high-school-band and field hockey camp until an arcing field hockey ball landed on the clasp of a girl's metal barrette, knifing a skull nerve and paralyzing the right side of her body. The camp closed down for a few years and the girl's teammates built a memorial, filling the spot on which the girl fell with hockey balls, on which they had painted—all in nail polish—get-well tidings, flowers, and hearts. The balls were still stacked there, like a shrine of ostrich eggs embedded in the ground.

On the second day of camp, Troop 909 was dancing around the mound of hockey balls, their limbs jangling awkwardly, their cries like the constant summer squeal of an amusement park. There was a stream that bordered the field hockey lawn, and the girls from my troop settled next to it, scarfing down the last of lunch: sandwiches made from salami and slices of tomato that had gotten waterlogged from the melting ice in the cooler. From the stream bank, Arnetta eyed the Troop 909 girls, scrutinizing their movements to glean inspiration for battle.

"Man," Arnetta said, "we could bumrush them right now if that damn lady would leave."

The 909 troop leader was a white woman with the severe pageboy hairdo of an ancient Egyptian. She lay on a picnic blanket, sphinx-like, eating a banana, sometimes holding it out in front of her like a microphone. Beside her sat a girl slowly flapping one hand like a bird with a broken wing. Occasionally, the leader would call out the names of girls who'd attempted leapfrogs and flips, or of girls who yelled too loudly or strayed far from the circle.

"I'm just glad Big Fat Mama's not following us here," Octavia said. "At least we don't have to worry about her." Mrs. Margolin, Octavia assured us, was having her

Afternoon Devotional, shrouded in mosquito netting, in a clearing she'd found. Mrs. Hedy was cleaning mud from her espadrilles in the cabin.

"I handled them." Arnetta sucked on her teeth and proudly grinned. "I told her we was going to gather leaves."

"Gather leaves," Octavia said, nodding respectfully. "That's a good one. Especially since they're so mad-crazy about this camping thing." She looked from ground to sky, sky to ground. Her hair hung down her back in two braids like a squaw's. "I mean, I really don't know why it's even called *camping*—all we ever do with Nature is find some twigs and say something like, 'Wow, this fell from a tree.'" She then studied her sandwich. With two disdainful fingers, she picked out a slice of dripping tomato, the sections congealed with red slime. She pitched it into the stream embrowned with dead leaves and the murky effigies of other dead things, but in the opaque water, a group of small silver-brown fish appeared. They surrounded the tomato and nibbled.

"Look!" Janice cried. "Fishes! Fishes!" As she scrambled to the edge of the stream to watch, a covey of insects threw up tantrums from the wheatgrass and nettle, a throng of tiny electric machines, all going at once. Octavia sneaked up behind Janice as if to push her in. Daphne and I exchanged terrified looks. It seemed as though only we knew that Octavia was close enough—and bold enough—to actually push Janice into the stream. Janice turned around quickly, but Octavia was already staring serenely into the still water as though she was gathering some sort of courage from it. "What's so funny?" Janice said, eyeing them all suspiciously.

Elise began humming the tune to "Karma Chameleon," all the girls joining in, their hums light and facile. Janice also began to hum, against everyone else, the high-octane opening chords of "Beat It."

"I love me some Michael Jackson," Janice said when she'd finished humming, smacking her lips as though Michael Jackson were a favorite meal. "I *will* marry Michael Jackson."

Before anyone had a chance to impress upon Janice the impossibility of this, Arnetta suddenly rose, made a sun visor of her hand, and watched Troop 909 leave the field hockey lawn.

"Dammit!" she said. "We've got to get them *alone*."

"They won't ever be alone," I said. All the rest of the girls looked at me, for I usually kept quiet. If I spoke even a word, I could count on someone calling me Snot. Everyone seemed to think that we could beat up these girls; no one entertained the thought that they might fight *back*. "The only time they'll be unsupervised is in the bathroom."

"Oh shut up, Snot," Octavia said.

But Arnetta slowly nodded her head. "The bathroom," she said. "The bathroom," she said, again and again. "The bathroom! The bathroom!"

According to Octavia's watch, it took us five minutes to hike to the restrooms, which were midway between our cabin and Troop 909's. Inside, the mirrors above the sinks returned only the vaguest of reflections, as though someone had taken a scouring pad to their surfaces to obscure the shine. Pine needles, leaves, and dirty, flattened wads of chewing gum covered the floor like a mosaic. Webs of hair matted the drain in the middle of the floor. Above the sinks and below the mirrors, stacks of folded white paper towels lay on a long metal counter. Shaggy white balls of paper towels sat on the sinktops in a line like corsages on display. A thread of floss snaked from a wad of tissues dotted with the faint red-pink of blood. One of those white girls, I thought, had just lost a tooth.

Though the restroom looked almost the same as it had the night before, it somehow seemed stranger now. We hadn't noticed the wooden rafters coming together in great V's. We were, it seemed, inside a whale, viewing the ribs of the roof of its mouth.

"Wow. It's a mess," Elise said.

"You can say that again."

Arnetta leaned against the doorjamb of a restroom stall. "This is where they'll be again," she said. Just seeing the place, just having a plan seemed to satisfy her. "We'll go in and talk to them. You know, 'How you doing? How long'll you be here?' That sort of thing. Then Octavia and I are gonna tell them what happens when they call any one of us a nigger."

"I'm going to say something, too," Janice said.

Arnetta considered this. "Sure," she said. "Of course. Whatever you want."

Janice pointed her finger like a gun at Octavia and rehearsed the line she'd thought up, "'We're gonna teach you a *lesson!*' That's what I'm going to say." She narrowed her eyes like a TV mobster. "'We're gonna teach you little girls a lesson!'"

With the back of her hand, Octavia brushed Janice's finger away. "You couldn't teach me to shit in a toilet."

"But," I said, "what if they say, 'We didn't say that? We didn't call anyone an N-I-G-G-E-R.'"

"Snot," Arnetta said, and then sighed. "Don't think. Just fight. If you even know how."

Everyone laughed except Daphne. Arnetta gently laid her hand on Daphne's shoulder. "Daphne. You don't have to fight. We're doing this for you."

Daphne walked to the counter, took a clean paper towel, and carefully unfolded it like a map. With it, she began to pick up the trash all around. Everyone watched.

"C'mon," Arnetta said to everyone. "Let's beat it." We all ambled toward the doorway, where the sunshine made one large white rectangle of light. We were immediately blinded, and we shielded our eyes with our hands and our forearms.

"Daphne?" Arnetta asked. "Are you coming?"

We all looked back at the bending girl, the thin of her back hunched like the back of a custodian sweeping a stage, caught in limelight. Stray strands of her hair were lit near-transparent, thin fiber-optic threads. She did not nod yes to the question, nor did she shake her head no. She abided, bent. Then she began again, picking up leaves, wads of paper, the cotton fluff innards from a torn stuffed toy. She did it so methodically, so exquisitely, so humbly, she must have been trained. I thought of those dresses she wore, faded and old, yet so pressed and clean. I then saw the poverty in them; I then could imagine her mother, cleaning the houses of others, returning home, weary.

"I guess she's not coming."

We left her and headed back to our cabin, over pine needles and leaves, taking the path full of shade.

"What about our secret meeting?" Elise asked.

Arnetta enunciated her words in a way that defied contradiction: "We just had it."

It was nearing our bedtime but the sun had not yet set.

"Hey, your mama's coming," Arnetta said to Octavia when she saw Mrs. Hedy walk toward the cabin, sniffling. When Octavia's mother wasn't giving bored, parochial orders, she sniffled continuously, mourning an imminent divorce from her husband. She might begin a sentence, "I don't know what Robert will do when Octavia and I are gone. Who'll buy him cigarettes?" and Octavia would hotly whisper, "*Mama,*" in a way that meant: Please don't talk about our problems in front of everyone. Please shut up.

But when Mrs. Hedy began talking about her husband, thinking about her husband, seeing clouds shaped like the head of her husband, she couldn't be quiet, and no one could dislodge her from the comfort of her own woe. Only one thing could perk her up—Brownie songs. If the girls were quiet, and Mrs. Hedy was in her dopey, sorrowful mood, she would say, "Y'all know I like those songs, girls. Why don't you sing one?" Everyone would groan, except me and Daphne. I, for one, liked some of the songs.

"C'mon, everybody," Octavia said drearily. "She likes the Brownie song best."

We sang, loud enough to reach Mrs. Hedy:

> "I've got something in my pocket;
> It belongs across my face.
> And I keep it very close at hand
>   in a most convenient place.
> I'm sure you couldn't guess it
> If you guessed a long, long while.
> So I'll take it out and put it on—
> It's a great big Brownie smile!"

The Brownie song was supposed to be sung cheerfully, as though we were elves in a workshop, singing as we merrily cobbled shoes, but everyone except me hated the song so much that they sang it like a maudlin record, played on the most sluggish of rpms.

"That was good," Mrs. Hedy said, closing the cabin door behind her. "Wasn't that nice, Linda?"

"Praise God," Mrs. Margolin answered without raising her head from the chore of counting out Popsicle sticks for the next day's craft session.

"Sing another one," Mrs. Hedy said. She said it with a sort of joyful aggression, like a drunk I'd once seen who'd refused to leave a Korean grocery.

"God, Mama, get over it," Octavia whispered in a voice meant only for Arnetta, but Mrs. Hedy heard it and started to leave the cabin.

"Don't go," Arnetta said. She ran after Mrs. Hedy and held her by the arm. "We haven't finished singing." She nudged us with a single look. "Let's sing the 'Friends Song.' For Mrs. Hedy."

Although I liked some of the songs, I hated this one:

> Make new friends
> But keep the o-old.
> One is silver
> And the other gold.

If most of the girls in the troop could be any type of metal, they'd be bunched-up wads of tinfoil, maybe, or rusty iron nails you had to get tetanus shots for.

"No, no, no," Mrs. Margolin said before anybody could start in on the "Friends Song." "An uplifting song. Something to lift her up and take her mind off all these earthly burdens."

Arnetta and Octavia rolled their eyes. Everyone knew what song Mrs. Margolin was talking about, and no one, no one, wanted to sing it.

"Please, no," a voice called out. "Not 'The Doughnut Song.'"

"Please not 'The Doughnut Song,'" Octavia pleaded.

"I'll brush my teeth two times if I don't have to sing 'The Doughnut—'"

"Sing!" Mrs. Margolin demanded.

We sang:

> "Life without Jesus is like a do-ough-nut!
> Like a do-ooough-nut!
> Like a do-ooough-nut!
> Life without Jesus is like a do-ough-nut!
> There's a hole in the middle of my soul!"

There were other verses, involving other pastries, but we stopped after the first one and cast glances toward Mrs. Margolin to see if we could gain a reprieve. Mrs. Margolin's eyes fluttered blissfully. She was half asleep.

"Awww," Mrs. Hedy said, as though giant Mrs. Margolin were a cute baby, "Mrs. Margolin's had a long day."

"Yes indeed," Mrs. Margolin answered. "If you don't mind, I might just go to the lodge where the beds are. I haven't been the same since the operation."

I had not heard of this operation, or when it had occurred, since Mrs. Margolin had never missed the once-a-week Brownie meeting, but I could see from Daphne's face that she was concerned, and I could see that the other girls had decided that Mrs. Margolin's operation must have happened long ago in some remote time unconnected to our own. Nevertheless, they put on sad faces. We had all been taught that adulthood was full of sorrow and pain, taxes and bills, dreaded work and dealings with whites, sickness and death. I tried to do what the others did. I tried to look silent.

"Go right ahead, Linda," Mrs. Hedy said. "I'll watch the girls." Mrs. Hedy seemed to forget about divorce for a moment; she looked at us with dewy eyes, as if we were mysterious, furry creatures. Meanwhile, Mrs. Margolin walked through the maze of sleeping bags until she found her own. She gathered a neat stack of clothes and pajamas slowly, as though doing so was almost painful. She took her toothbrush, her toothpaste, her pillow. "All right!" Mrs. Margolin said, addressing us all from the threshold of the cabin. "Be in bed by nine." She said it with a twinkle in her voice, letting us know she was allowing us to be naughty and stay up till nine-fifteen.

"C'mon, everybody," Arnetta said after Mrs. Margolin left. "Time for us to wash up."

Everyone watched Mrs. Hedy closely, wondering whether she would insist on coming with us since it was night, making a fight with Troop 909 nearly impossible. Troop 909 would soon be in the bathroom, washing their faces, brushing their teeth—completely unsuspecting of our ambush.

"We won't be long," Arnetta said. "We're old enough to go to the restrooms by ourselves."

Mrs. Hedy pursed her lips at this dilemma. "Well, I guess you Brownies are almost Girl Scouts, right?"

"Right!"

"Just one more badge," Drema said.

"And about," Octavia droned, "a million more cookies to sell."

Octavia looked at all of us. *Now's our chance,* her face seemed to say, but our chance to do *what,* I didn't exactly know.

Finally, Mrs. Hedy walked to the doorway where Octavia stood dutifully waiting to say goodbye but looking bored doing it. Mrs. Hedy held Octavia's chin. "You'll be good?"

"Yes, Mama."

"And remember to pray for me and your father? If I'm asleep when you get back?"

"Yes, Mama."

When the other girls had finished getting their toothbrushes and washcloths and flashlights for the group restroom trip, I was drawing pictures of tiny birds with too many feathers. Daphne was sitting on her sleeping bag, reading.

"You're not going to come?" Octavia asked.

Daphne shook her head.

"I'm gonna stay, too," I said. "I'll go to the restroom when Daphne and Mrs. Hedy go."

Arnetta leaned down toward me and whispered so that Mrs. Hedy, who had taken over Mrs. Margolin's task of counting Popsicle sticks, couldn't hear. "No, Snot. If we get in trouble, you're going to get in trouble with the rest of us."

We made our way through the darkness by flashlight. The tree branches that had shaded us just hours earlier, along the same path, now looked like arms sprouting menacing hands. The stars sprinkled the sky like spilled salt. They seemed fastened to the darkness, high up and holy, their places fixed and definite as we stirred beneath them.

Some, like me, were quiet because we were afraid of the dark; others were talking like crazy for the same reason.

"Wow!" Drema said, looking up. "Why are all the stars out here? I never see stars back on Oneida Street."

"It's a camping trip, that's why," Octavia said. "You're supposed to see stars on camping trips."

Janice said, "This place smells like my mother's air freshener."

"These woods are *pine,*" Elise said. "Your mother probably uses *pine* air freshener."

Janice mouthed an exaggerated "Oh," nodding her head as though she just then understood one of the world's great secrets.

No one talked about fighting. Everyone was afraid enough just walking through the infinite deep of the woods. Even though I didn't fight to fight, was afraid of fighting, I felt I was part of the rest of the troop; like I was defending something. We trudged against the slight incline of the path, Arnetta leading the way.

"You know," I said, "their leader will be there. Or they won't even be there. It's dark already. Last night the sun was still in the sky. I'm sure they're already finished."

Arnetta acted as if she hadn't heard me. I followed her gaze with my flashlight, and that's when I saw the squares of light in the darkness. The bathroom was just ahead.

*

But the girls were there. We could hear them before we could see them.

"Octavia and I will go in first so they'll think that there's just two of us, then wait till I say, 'We're gonna teach you a lesson,'" Arnetta said. "Then, bust in. That'll surprise them."

"That's what I was supposed to say," Janice said.

Arnetta went inside, Octavia next to her. Janice followed, and the rest of us waited outside.

They were in there for what seemed like whole minutes, but something was wrong. Arnetta hadn't given the signal yet. I was with the girls outside when I heard one of the Troop 909 girls say, "NO. That did NOT happen!"

That was to be expected, that they'd deny the whole thing. What I hadn't expected was *the voice* in which the denial was said. The girl sounded as though her tongue were caught in her mouth. "That's a BAD word!" the girl continued. "We don't say BAD words!"

"Let's go in," Elise said.

"No," Drema said, "I don't want to. What if we get beat up?"

"Snot?" Elise turned to me, her flashlight blinding. It was the first time anyone had asked my opinion, though I knew they were just asking because they were afraid.

"I say we go inside, just to see what's going on."

"But Arnetta didn't give us the signal," Drema said. "She's supposed to say, 'We're gonna teach you a lesson,' and I didn't hear her say it."

"C'mon," I said. "Let's just go in."

We went inside. There we found the white girls—about five girls huddled up next to one big girl. I instantly knew she was the owner of the voice we'd heard. Arnetta and Octavia inched toward us as soon as we entered.

"Where's Janice?" Elise asked, then we heard a flush. "Oh."

"I think," Octavia said, whispering to Elise, "they're retarded."

"We ARE NOT retarded!" the big girl said, though it was obvious that she was. That they all were. The girls around her began to whimper.

"They're just pretending," Arnetta said, trying to convince herself. "I know they are."

Octavia turned to Arnetta. "Arnetta. Let's just leave."

Janice came out of a stall, happy and relieved, then she suddenly remembered her line, pointed to the big girl, and said, "We're gonna teach you a lesson."

"Shut up, Janice," Octavia said, but her heart was not in it. Arnetta's face was set in a lost, deep scowl. Octavia turned to the big girl and said loudly, slowly, as if they were all deaf, "We're going to leave. It was nice meeting you, O.K.? You don't have to tell anyone that we were here. O.K.?"

"Why not?" said the big girl, like a taunt. When she spoke, her lips did not meet, her mouth did not close. Her tongue grazed the roof of her mouth, like a little pink fish. "You'll get in trouble. I know. *I* know."

Arnetta got back her old cunning. "If you said anything, then you'd be a tattletale."

The girl looked sad for a moment, and then perked up quickly. A flash of genius crossed her face. "I *like* tattletale."

"It's all right, girls. It's gonna be all right!" the 909 troop leader said. All of Troop 909 burst into tears. It was as though someone had instructed them all to cry at once.

The troop leader had girls under her arm, and all the rest of the girls crowded around her. It reminded me of a hog I'd seen on a field trip, where all the little hogs gathered about the mother at feeding time, latching onto her teats. The 909 troop leader had come into the bathroom, shortly after the big girl had threatened to tell. Then the ranger came, then, once the ranger had radioed the station, Mrs. Margolin arrived with Daphne in tow.

The ranger had left the restroom area, but everybody else was huddled just outside, swatting mosquitoes.

"Oh. They *will* apologize," Mrs. Margolin said to the 909 troop leader, but she said this so angrily, I knew she was speaking more to us than to the other troop leader. "When their parents find out, every one a them will be on punishment."

"It's all right, it's all right," the 909 troop leader reassured Mrs. Margolin. Her voice lilted in the same way it had when addressing the girls. She smiled the whole time she talked. She was like one of those TV-cooking-show women who talk and dice onions and smile all at the same time.

"See. It could have happened. I'm not calling your girls fibbers or anything." She shook her head ferociously from side to side, her Egyptian-style pageboy flapping against her cheeks like heavy drapes. "It *could* have happened. See. Our girls are *not* retarded. They are *delayed* learners." She said this in a syrupy instructional voice, as though our troop might be delayed learners as well. "We're from the Decatur Children's Academy. Many of them just have special needs."

"Now we won't be able to walk to the bathroom by ourselves!" the big girl said.

"Yes you will," the troop leader said, "but maybe we'll wait till we get back to Decatur—"

"I don't want to wait!" the girl said. "I want my Independence badge!"

The girls in my troop were entirely speechless. Arnetta looked stoic, as though she were soon to be tortured but was determined not to appear weak. Mrs. Margolin pursed her lips solemnly and said, "Bless them, Lord. Bless them."

In contrast, the Troop 909 leader was full of words and energy. "Some of our girls are echolalic—" She smiled and happily presented one of the girls hanging onto her, but the girl widened her eyes in horror, and violently withdrew herself from the center of attention, sensing she was being sacrificed for the village sins. "Echolalic," the troop leader continued. "That means they will say whatever they hear, like an echo—that's where the word comes from. It comes from 'echo.'" She ducked her head apologetically. "I mean, not all of them have the most *progressive* of parents, so if they heard a bad word, they might have repeated it. But I guarantee it would not have been *intentional*."

Arnetta spoke. "I saw her say the word. I heard her." She pointed to a small girl, smaller than any of us, wearing an oversized T-shirt that read, "Eat Bertha's Mussels."

The troop leader shook her head and smiled, "That's impossible. She doesn't speak. She can, but she doesn't."

Arnetta furrowed her brow. "No. It wasn't her. That's right. It was *her*."

The girl Arnetta pointed to grinned as though she'd been paid a compliment. She was the only one from either troop actually wearing a full uniform: The mocha-colored A-line shift, the orange ascot, the sash covered with badges, though all the same one—the Try-It patch. She took a few steps toward Arnetta and made a grand sweeping gesture toward the sash. "See," she said, full of self-importance, "I'm a

Brownie." I had a hard time imagining this girl calling anyone a "nigger"; the girl looked perpetually delighted, as though she would have cuddled up with a grizzly if someone had let her.

On the fourth morning, we boarded the bus to go home.
The previous day had been spent building miniature churches from Popsicle sticks. We hardly left the cabin. Mrs. Margolin and Mrs. Hedy guarded us so closely, almost no one talked for the entire day.
Even on the day of departure from Camp Crescendo, all was serious and silent. The bus ride began quietly enough. Arnetta had to sit beside Mrs. Margolin; Octavia had to sit beside her mother. I sat beside Daphne, who gave me her prize journal without a word of explanation.
"You don't want it?"
She shook her head no. It was empty.
Then Mrs. Hedy began to weep. "Octavia," Mrs. Hedy said to her daughter without looking at her, "I'm going to sit with Mrs. Margolin. All right?"
Arnetta exchanged seats with Mrs. Hedy. With the two women up front, Elise felt it safe to speak. "Hey," she said, then she set her face into a placid, vacant stare, trying to imitate that of a Troop 909 girl. Emboldened, Arnetta made a gesture of mock pride toward an imaginary sash, the way the girl in full uniform had done. Then they all made a game of it, trying to do the most exaggerated imitations of the Troop 909 girls, all without speaking, all without laughing loud enough to catch the women's attention.
Daphne looked down at her shoes, white with sneaker polish. I opened the journal she'd given me. I looked out the window, trying to decide what to write, searching for lines, but nothing could compare with what Daphne had written, "*My father, the veteran*," my favorite line of all time. It replayed itself in my head, and I gave up trying to write.
By then, it seemed that the rest of the troop had given up making fun of the girls in Troop 909. They were now quietly gossiping about who had passed notes to whom in school. For a moment the gossiping fell off, and all I heard was the hum of the bus as we sped down the road and the muffled sounds of Mrs. Hedy and Mrs. Margolin talking about serious things.
"You know," Octavia whispered, "why did *we* have to be stuck at a camp with retarded girls? You know?"
"*You* know why," Arnetta answered. She narrowed her eyes like a cat. "My mama and I were in the mall in Buckhead, and this white lady just kept looking at us. I mean, like we were foreign or something. Like we were from China."
"What did the woman say?" Elise asked.
"Nothing," Arnetta said. "She didn't say nothing."
A few girls quietly nodded their heads.
"There was this time," I said, "when my father and I were in the mall and—"
"Oh shut up, Snot," Octavia said.
I stared at Octavia, then rolled my eyes from her to the window. As I watched the trees blur, I wanted nothing more than to be through with it all: the bus ride, the troop, school—all of it. But we were going home. I'd see the same girls in school the next day. We were on a bus, and there was nowhere else to go.

"Go on, Laurel," Daphne said to me. It seemed like the first time she'd spoken the whole trip, and she'd said my name. I turned to her and smiled weakly so as not to cry, hoping she'd remember when I'd tried to be her friend, thinking maybe that her gift of the journal was an invitation of friendship. But she didn't smile back. All she said was, "What happened?"

I studied the girls, waiting for Octavia to tell me to shut up again before I even had a chance to utter another word, but everyone was amazed that Daphne had spoken. The bus was silent. I gathered my voice. "Well," I said. "My father and I were in this mall, but *I* was the one doing the staring." I stopped and glanced from face to face. I continued. "There were these white people dressed like Puritans or something, but they weren't Puritans. They were Mennonites.° They're these people who, if you ask them to do a favor, like paint your porch or something, they have to do it. It's in their rules."

"That sucks," someone said.

"C'mon," Arnetta said. "You're lying."

"I am not."

"How do you know that's not just some story someone made up?" Elise asked, her head cocked full of daring. "I mean, who's gonna do whatever you ask?"

"It is not made up. I know because when I was looking at them, my father said, 'See those people? If you ask them to do something, they'll do it. Anything you want.'"

No one would call anyone's father a liar—then they'd have to fight the person. But Drema parsed her words carefully. "How does your *father* know that's not just some story? Huh?"

"Because," I said, "he went up to the man and asked him would he paint our porch, and the man said yes. It's their religion."

"Man, I'm glad I'm a Baptist," Elise said, shaking her head in sympathy for the Mennonites.

"So did the guy do it?" Drema asked, scooting closer to hear if the story got juicy.

"Yeah," I said. "His whole family was with him. My dad drove them to our house. They all painted our porch. The woman and girl were in bonnets and long, long skirts with buttons up to their necks. The guy wore this weird hat and these huge suspenders."

"Why," Arnetta asked archly, as though she didn't believe a word, "would someone pick a *porch*? If they'll do anything, why not make them paint the whole *house*? Why not ask for a hundred bucks?"

I thought about it, and then remembered the words my father had said about them painting our porch, though I had never seemed to think about his words after he'd said them.

"He said," I began, only then understanding the words as they uncoiled from my mouth, "it was the only time he'd have a white man on his knees doing something for a black man for free."

I now understand what he meant, and why he did it, though I didn't like it. When you've been made to feel bad for so long, you jump at the chance to do it to others. I remembered the Mennonites bending the way Daphne had bent when she was cleaning the restroom. I remembered the dark blue of their bonnets, the black of their shoes. They painted the porch as though scrubbing a floor. I was already trembling before Daphne asked quietly, "Did he thank them?"

°**Mennonites:** Highly traditional Christian denomination whose core beliefs include nonviolence and peace. Some sects incorporate very simple living and separation from the modern world—including old-fashioned dress.

I looked out the window. I could not tell which were the thoughts and which were the trees. "No," I said, and suddenly knew there was something mean in the world that I could not stop.

Arnetta laughed. "If I asked them to take off their long skirts and bonnets and put on some jeans, would they do it?"

And Daphne's voice, quiet, steady: "Maybe they would. Just to be nice."

Questions

1. Much of "Brownies" is very funny. What role does humor have in the story—and how does it relate to the decidedly unhumorous ending?
2. The girls in the story casually use terms such as "Caucasian" and easily vilify the other Brownie troop. Would you describe their understanding of race as innocent or sophisticated?
3. What is the effect of having Laurel, or "Snot," narrate the story?
4. What realization does the narrator have at the end of the story? How does this change her understanding of her father and of racial dynamics more generally?

Michael Chabon

Michael Chabon (b. 1963) was born in Washington, D.C., and was raised in Columbia, Maryland, and Pittsburgh, Pennsylvania. He published his first novel, The Mysteries of Pittsburgh *(1988), to great acclaim at the age of twenty-five. After abandoning a 1500-page draft of a second novel, Chabon published* Wonder Boys *(1995), a brilliant satire on literary life. His third novel,* The Amazing Adventures of Kavalier and Clay *(2000), an ambitious historical novel set in New York during the early days of the comic book industry, won the Pulitzer Prize. His novel* The Yiddish Policemen's Union *(2007), an alternative history set in a Jewish homeland established in Alaska, won the Hugo and Nebula Awards—the highest honors in science fiction. Chabon's work customarily combines the material of popular culture (comic books, movies, detective stories, and science fiction) with traditional literary techniques. He has also been an outspoken advocate of the importance of strong plots in fiction.*

The Little Knife   1991

One Saturday in that last, interminable summer before his parents separated and the Washington Senators baseball team was expunged forever from the face of the earth, the Shapiros went to Nags Head, North Carolina, where Nathan, without planning to, perpetrated a great hoax. They drove down I-95, through the Commonwealth of Virginia, to a place called the Sandpiper—a ragged, charming oval of motel cottages painted white and green as the Atlantic, and managed by a kind, astonishingly fat old man named Colonel Larue, who smoked cherry cigars and would, if asked, play catch or keep-away. Outside his office, in the weedy gravel, stood an old red-and-radium-white Coke machine, which dispensed bottles from a vertical glass door that sighed when you opened it, and which reminded Nathan of the Automat his grandmother had taken him to once in New York City. The sight of the faded machine and of the whole Sandpiper—like that of the Automat—filled Nathan with a happy sadness, or, really, a sad happiness; he was not too young, at ten, to have developed a sense of nostalgia.

There were children in every cottage—with all manner of floats, pails, paddles, trucks, and flying objects—and his younger brother Ricky, to Nathan's envy, immediately fell in with a gang of piratical little boys with water pistols, who were always reproducing fart sounds and giggling chaotically when their mothers employed certain ordinary words such as "hot dog" and "rubber." The Shapiros went to the ocean every summer, and at the beginning of this trip, as on all those that had preceded it, Nathan and his brother got along better than they usually did, their mother broke out almost immediately in a feathery red heat rash, and their father lay pale and motionless in the sun, like a monument, and always forgot to take off his wristwatch when he went into the sea. Nathan had brought a stack of James Bond books and his colored pencils; there were board games—he and his father were in the middle of their Strat-O-Matic baseball playoffs—and miniature boxes of cereal; the family ate out every single night. But when they were halfway through the slow, dazzling week—which was as far as they were to get—Nathan began to experience an unfamiliar longing: He wanted to go home.

He awoke very early on Wednesday morning, went into the cottage's small kitchen, where the floor was sticky and the table rocked and trembled, and chose the last of the desirable cereals from the Variety pack, leaving for Ricky only those papery, sour brands with the scientific names—the sort that their grandparents liked. As he began to eat, Nathan heard, from the big bedroom down the hall, the unmistakable, increasingly familiar sound of his father burying his mother under a heap of scorn and ridicule. It was, oddly, a soft and pleading sound. Lately, the conversation and actions of Dr. Shapiro's family seemed to disappoint him terribly. His left hand was always flying up to smack his sad and outraged forehead, so hard that Nathan often thought he could hear his father's wedding ring crack against his skull. When they'd played their baseball game the day before—Nathan's Baltimore Bonfires against his father's Brooklyn Eagles—every decision Nathan made led to a disaster, and his father pointed out each unwise substitution and foolish attempt to steal in this new tone of miserable sarcasm, so that Nathan had spent the afternoon apologizing, and, finally, crying. Now he listened for his mother's voice, for the note of chastened shame.

The bedroom door slammed, and Mrs. Shapiro came out into the kitchen. She was in her bathrobe, a wild, sleepless smile on her face.

"Good morning, honey," she said, then hummed to herself as she boiled water and made a cup of instant coffee. Her spoon tinkled gaily against the cup.

"Where are you going, Mom?" said Nathan. She had taken up her coffee and was heading for the sliding glass door that led out of the kitchen and down to the beach.

"See you, honey," she sang.

"Mom!" said Nathan. He stood up—afraid, absurdly, that she might be leaving for good, because she seemed so happy. After a few seconds he heard her whistling, and he went to the door and pressed his face against the wire screen. His mother had a Disney whistle, melodious and full, like a Scotsman's as he walks across a meadow in a brilliant kilt. She paced briskly along the ramshackle slat-and-wire fence, back and forth through the beach grass, drinking from the huge white mug of coffee and whistling heartily into the breeze; her red hair rose from her head and trailed like a defiant banner. He watched her observe the sunrise—it was going to be a perfect, breezy day—then continued to watch as she set her coffee on the ground, removed her bathrobe, and, in her bathing suit, began to engage in a long series of yoga exercises—a new fad of hers—as though she were playing statues all alone. Nathan was soon lost, with the fervor of a young scientist, in contemplation of his pretty, whistling mother rolling around on the ground.

"Oh, how can she?" said Dr. Shapiro.

"Yes," said Nathan, gravely, before he blushed and whirled around to find his father, in pajamas, staring out at Mrs. Shapiro. His smile was angry and clenched, but in his eyes was the same look of bleak surprise, of betrayal, that had been there when Nathan took out Johnny Sain, a slugging pitcher, and the pinch-hitter, Enos Slaughter, immediately went down on strikes. There were a hundred new things that interested Nathan's mother—bonsai, the Zuni, yoga, real estate—and although Dr. Shapiro had always been a liberal, generous, encouraging man (as Nathan had heard his mother say to a friend), and had at first happily helped her to purchase the necessary manuals, supplies, and coffee-table books, lately each new fad seemed to come as a blow to him—a going astray, a false step.

"How can she?" he said again, shaking his big bearded head.

"She says it's really good for you," said Nathan.

His father smiled down on his son ruefully, and tapped him once on the head. Then he turned and went to the refrigerator, hitching up his pajama bottoms. They were the ones patterned with a blue stripe and red chevrons—the ones that Nathan always imagined were the sort worn by the awkward, doomed elephant in the Groucho Marx joke.°

Later that day, as they made egg-salad sandwiches to carry down to the beach, Dr. and Mrs. Shapiro fought bitterly, for the fifth time since their arrival. In the cottage's kitchen was a knife—a small, new, foreign knife, which Mrs. Shapiro admired. As she used it to slice neat little horseshoes of celery, she praised it again. "Such a good little knife," she said. "Why don't you just take it?" said Dr. Shapiro. The air in the kitchen was suddenly full of sharp, caramel smoke, and Dr. Shapiro ran to unplug the toaster.

"That would be stealing," said Nathan's mother, ignoring her husband's motions of alarm and the fact that their lunch was on fire. "We are not taking this knife, Martin."

"Give it to me." Dr. Shapiro held out his hand, palm up.

"I'm not going to let you—make me—dishonest anymore!" said his mother. She seemed to struggle, at first, not to finish the sentence she had begun, but in the end she turned, put her face right up to his, and cried out boldly. After her outburst, both adults turned to look, with a simultaneity that was almost funny, at their sons. Nathan hadn't the faintest notion of what his mother was talking about.

"Don't steal, Dad," Ricky said.

"I only wanted it to extract the piece of toast," said their father. He was looking at their mother again. "God damn it." He turned and went out of the kitchen.

elephant in the Groucho Marx joke: One of Marx's most famous jokes from the 1930 movie *Animal Crackers*, it runs: "One morning I shot an elephant in my pajamas. How he got in my pajamas, I don't know."

Her knuckles white around the handle of the knife, their mother freed the toast and began scraping the burnt surfaces into the sink. Because their father had said "God damn," Ricky wiggled his eyebrows and smiled at Nathan. At the slamming of the bedroom door, Nathan clambered up suddenly from the rickety kitchen table as though he had found an insect crawling on his leg.

"Kill it!" said Ricky. "What is it?"

"What is it?" said his mother. She scanned Nathan's body quickly, one hand half raised to swat.

"Nothing," said Nathan. He took off his glasses. "I'm going for a walk."

When he got to the edge of the water, he turned to look toward the Sandpiper. At that time in Nags Head there were few hotels and no condominiums, and it seemed to Nathan that their little ring of cottages stood alone, like Stonehenge, in the middle of a giant wasteland. He set off down the beach, watching his feet print and following the script left in the sand by the birds for which the motel was named. He passed a sand castle, then a heart drawn with a stick enclosing the names Jimmy and Beth. Sometimes his heels sank deeply into the sand, and he noticed the odd marks this would leave—a pair of wide dimples. He discovered that he could walk entirely on his heels, and his trail became two lines of big periods. If he took short steps, it looked as though a creature—a bird with two peg legs—had come to fish along the shore.

He lurched a long way in this fashion, watching his feet, and nearly forgot his parents' quarrel. But when at last he grew bored with walking on his heels and turned to go back, he saw that his mother and father had also decided to take a walk, and that they were, in fact, coming toward him—clasping hands, letting go, clasping hands again. Nathan ran to meet them, and they parted to let him walk between them. They all continued down the beach, stooping to pick up shells, glass, dead crabs, twine, and all the colored or smelly things that Nathan had failed to take note of before. At first his parents exclaimed with him over these discoveries, and his father took each striped seashell into his hands, to keep it safe, until there were two dozen and they jingled there like money. But after a while they seemed to lose interest, and Nathan found himself walking a few feet ahead of them, stooping alone, glumly dusting his toes with sand as he tried to eavesdrop on their careless and incomprehensible conversation.

"Never again," his mother said at last.

Dr. Shapiro let the shells fall. He rubbed his hands together and then stared at them as though waking from a dream in which he had been holding a fortune in gold. Straightening up so quickly that his head spun, Nathan let out a cry and pointed down at the sand beneath their feet, among the scattered shells. "Look at those weird tracks!" he cried.

They all looked down.

Speculation on the nature of the beast that went toeless down the shore went on for several minutes, and although Nathan was delighted at first, he soon began to feel embarrassed and, obscurely, frightened by the ease with which he had deceived his parents. His treachery was almost exposed when Ricky, carrying a long stick and wearing a riot of Magic Marker tattoos on his face and all down his arms, ran over to find out what was happening. The little boy immediately tipped back onto his heels, and would have taken a few steps like that had Nathan not grabbed him by the elbow and dragged him aside.

"Why do you have a dog on your face?" said Nathan.

"It's a jaguar," said Ricky.

Nathan bent to whisper into his brother's ear. "I'm tricking Mom and Dad," he said.

"Good," said Ricky.

"They think there's some kind of weird creature on the beach."

Ricky pushed Nathan away and then surveyed their mother and father, who were talking again, quietly, as though they were trying not to alarm their sons. "It can't be real," said Nathan's father.

Ricky's skin under the crude tattoos was tanned, his hair looked stiff and ragged from going unwashed and sea-tangled, and as he regarded their parents he held his skinny stick like a javelin at his side. "They're dumb," he said flatly.

Dr. Shapiro approached, stepping gingerly across the mysterious tracks, and then knelt beside his sons. His face was red, though not from the sun, and he seemed to have trouble looking directly at the boys. Nathan began to cry before his father even spoke.

"Boys," he said. He looked away, then back, and bit his lip. "I'm afraid—I'm sorry. We're going to go home. Your mom and I—don't feel very well. We don't seem to be well."

"No! No! It was Nathan!" said Ricky, laying down his spear and throwing himself into his father's arms. "It wasn't me. Make *him* go home."

Nathan, summoning up his courage, decided to admit that the curious trail of the crippled animal was his, and he said, "I'm responsible."

"Oh, no!" cried both his parents together, startling him. His mother rushed over and fell to her knees, and they took Nathan into their arms and said that it was never, never him, and they ruffled his hair with their fingers, as though he had done something they could love him for.

After they came back from dinner, the Shapiros, save Nathan, went down to the sea for a final, sad promenade. At the restaurant, Ricky had pleaded with his parents to stay through the end of the week—they had not even been to see the monument at Kitty Hawk, the Birthplace of Aviation. For Ricky's sake, Nathan had also tried to persuade them, but his heart wasn't in it—he himself wanted so badly to go home—and the four of them had all ended up crying and chewing their food in the brass-and-rope dining room of the Port O' Call; even Dr. Shapiro had shed a tear. They were going to leave that night. Nathan's family now stood, in sweatshirts, by the sliding glass door, his parents straining to adopt hard and impatient looks, and Nathan saw that they felt guilty about leaving him behind in the cottage.

"I'll pack my stuff," he said. "Just go." For a moment his stomach tightened with angry, secret glee as his mother and father, sighing, turned their backs on him and obeyed his small command. Then he was alone in the kitchen again, for the second time that day, and he wished that he had gone to look at the ocean, and he hated his parents, uncertainly, for leaving him behind. He got up and walked into the bedroom that he and Ricky had shared. There, in the twilight that fell in orange shafts through the open window, the tangle of their clothes and bedsheets, their scattered toys and books, the surfaces of the broken dresser and twin headboards seemed dusted with a film of radiant sand, as though the tide had washed across them and withdrawn, and the room was strewn with the seashells they had found. Nathan, after emptying his shoebox of baseball cards into his suitcase, went slowly around the room and harvested the shells with careful sweeps of his trembling hand. Bearing the shoebox back into the kitchen, he collected the few stray shards of salt-white and green beach glass that lay in a pile beside the electric can opener, and then added a hollow pink crab's leg in whose claw Ricky had fixed a colored pencil. When Nathan saw the little knife in the drainboard by the sink, he hesitated only a moment before dropping it into the box, where it swam, frozen, like a model shark in a museum diorama of life beneath the sea. Nathan chuckled. As clearly as if he were remembering them, he foresaw his mother's accusation, his father's enraged denial, and with an unhappy chuckle he foresaw, recalled, and fondly began to preserve all the discord for which, in his wildly preserving imagination, he was and would always be responsible.

Questions

1. Reread Chabon's opening sentence. How much information about the story's plot, protagonist, and setting can you find in these forty-three words?
2. Nathan's age is never precisely given. About how old does he seem to be? Is he the older or younger brother? Support your answer with details from the story.
3. Why does Nathan suddenly confess that he made the mysterious animal tracks?
4. Why does Nathan steal the small knife? What does it represent for him?
5. How has Nathan changed in the course of the story?

Suggestions for Writing on Stories about Childhood and Adolescence

1. "Araby," "Brownies," and "The Little Knife" all involve narrators who experience a difficult and pivotal moment of understanding. How are these moments similar, and how are they different? How does their narrators' understanding of the world change?
2. How would these stories be different if they were narrated by different characters? Why did Joyce decide to tell his story from the boy's point of view, Packer from Snot's point of view, and Chabon from a more removed third-person point of view? What are the effects of these choices?
3. "Araby," "Brownies," and "The Little Knife" all take place in what should be pleasant or festive settings. Yet the stories all involve problems or disappointments. Take any two stories and discuss how the settings affect the meaning of each narrative.
4. Was there a significant incident in your own childhood or adolescence that changed the course of your life? Describe the incident and discuss the ways it affected you.

DANGEROUS ENCOUNTERS

Nathaniel Hawthorne — *Young Goodman Brown*

Flannery O'Connor — *A Good Man Is Hard to Find*

Joyce Carol Oates — *Where Are You Going, Where Have You Been?*
Casebook on "Where Are You Going, Where Have You Been?"

Sometimes life takes a dangerous or even fatal turn. Wars erupt, crimes are committed, natural disasters occur, and lives, often innocent lives, are changed forever. One of the important purposes of literature is to let us experience such calamities vicariously without directly suffering their consequences. People are drawn to stories of violence and death. Just look at the popularity of crime and police shows on television, or horror and suspense films at the box office. Such stories do more than excite our emotions; they also stretch our imaginations, often putting our everyday lives in a better perspective.

Three classic—and deeply disturbing—stories appear in this section. Each of them presents an unexpected and dangerous encounter that changes the protagonist's life, sometimes fatally. Nathaniel Hawthorne's "Young Goodman Brown" is the story of a successful young man in colonial New England who has a fateful encounter with Satanic forces. The protagonist of Flannery O'Connor's "A Good Man Is Hard to Find" is a manipulative old woman, who has the bad luck to encounter a serial killer on a crime spree. The villain of "Where Are You Going, Where Have You Been?" is subtler but no less dangerous in Joyce Carol Oates's terrifying coming-of-age story.

Nathaniel Hawthorne

Nathaniel Hawthorne (1804–1864) was born in the clipper-ship seaport of Salem, Massachusetts, the son of a merchant captain (who died when the future novelist was only four years old) and the great-great-grandson of a magistrate involved in the notorious Salem witchcraft trials. Hawthorne took a keen interest in New England's sin-and-brimstone Puritan past in many of his stories, especially "Young Goodman Brown," and in the classic novel The Scarlet Letter (1850), *his deepest exploration of his major themes of conscience, sin, and guilt. In 1825 Hawthorne graduated from Bowdoin College; one of his classmates—and his lifelong best friend—was Franklin Pierce, who in 1852 would be elected president of the United States. After college, Hawthorne lived at home and trained to be a writer. During this period,*

Nathaniel Hawthorne

Hawthorne experienced great difficulty in trying to publish his short fiction, both in magazines and in book form, until the appearance of Twice-Told Tales (1837). *In 1841, he* was appointed to a position in the Boston Custom House; in the following year he married Sophia Peabody. When Franklin Pierce ran for president, Hawthorne wrote his campaign biography. After taking office, Pierce appointed his old friend American consul at Liverpool, England. Depressed by ill health and the terrible toll of the Civil War, Hawthorne died suddenly while on a tour with Pierce of New Hampshire's White Mountains. With his contemporary Edgar Allan Poe, Hawthorne transformed the American short story from popular magazine filler into a major literary form.

Young Goodman Brown (1835) 1846

Young Goodman° Brown came forth, at sunset, into the street of Salem village,° but put his head back, after crossing the threshold, to exchange a parting kiss with his young wife. And Faith, as the wife was aptly named, thrust her own pretty head into the street, letting the wind play with the pink ribbons of her cap, while she called to Goodman Brown.

"Dearest heart," whispered she, softly and rather sadly, when her lips were close to his ear, "pray thee, put off your journey until sunrise, and sleep in your own bed to-night. A lone woman is troubled with such dreams and such thoughts, that she's afraid of herself, sometimes. Pray, tarry with me this night, dear husband, of all nights in the year!"

"My love and my Faith," replied young Goodman Brown, "of all nights in the year, this one night must I tarry away from thee. My journey, as thou callest it, forth and back again, must needs be done 'twixt now and sunrise. What, my sweet, pretty wife, dost thou doubt me already, and we but three months married!"

"Then, God bless you!" said Faith, with the pink ribbons, "and may you find all well, when you come back."

"Amen!" cried Goodman Brown. "Say thy prayers, dear Faith, and go to bed at dusk, and no harm will come to thee."

So they parted; and the young man pursued his way, until, being about to turn the corner by the meeting-house, he looked back, and saw the head of Faith still peeping after him, with a melancholy air, in spite of her pink ribbons.

"Poor little Faith!" thought he, for his heart smote him. "What a wretch am I, to leave her on such an errand! She talks of dreams, too. Methought, as she spoke, there was trouble in her face, as if a dream had warned her what work is to be done to-night. But, no, no! 'twould kill her to think it. Well; she's a blessed angel on earth; and after this one night, I'll cling to her skirts and follow her to Heaven."

With this excellent resolve for the future, Goodman Brown felt himself justified in making more haste on his present evil purpose. He had taken a dreary road, darkened by all the gloomiest trees of the forest, which barely stood aside to let the narrow path creep through, and closed immediately behind. It was all as lonely as could be; and there is this peculiarity in such a solitude, that the traveller knows not who may be concealed by the innumerable trunks and the thick boughs overhead; so that, with lonely footsteps, he may yet be passing through an unseen multitude.

"There may be a devilish Indian behind every tree," said Goodman Brown, to himself; and he glanced fearfully behind him, as he added, "What if the devil himself should be at my very elbow!"

Goodman: title given by Puritans to a male head of a household; a farmer or other ordinary citizen. *Salem village:* in England's Massachusetts Bay Colony.

His head being turned back, he passed a crook of the road, and looking forward again, beheld the figure of a man, in grave and decent attire, seated at the foot of an old tree. He arose, at Goodman Brown's approach, and walked onward, side by side with him.

"You are late, Goodman Brown," said he. "The clock of the Old South was striking as I came through Boston; and that is full fifteen minutes agone."°

"Faith kept me back awhile," replied the young man, with a tremor in his voice, caused by the sudden appearance of his companion, though not wholly unexpected.

It was now deep dusk in the forest, and deepest in that part of it where these two were journeying. As nearly as could be discerned, the second traveller was about fifty years old, apparently in the same rank of life as Goodman Brown, and bearing a considerable resemblance to him, though perhaps more in expression than features. Still, they might have been taken for father and son. And yet, though the elder person was as simply clad as the younger, and as simple in manner too, he had an indescribable air of one who knew the world, and would not have felt abashed at the governor's dinner-table, or in King William's court,° were it possible that his affairs should call him thither. But the only thing about him, that could be fixed upon as remarkable, was his staff, which bore the likeness of a great black snake, so curiously wrought, that it might almost be seen to twist and wriggle itself, like a living serpent. This, of course, must have been an ocular deception, assisted by the uncertain light.

"Come, Goodman Brown!" cried his fellow-traveller, "this is a dull pace for the beginning of a journey. Take my staff, if you are so soon weary."

"Friend," said the other, exchanging his slow pace for a full stop, "having kept covenant by meeting thee here, it is my purpose now to return whence I came. I have scruples, touching the matter thou wot'st° of."

"Sayest thou so?" replied he of the serpent, smiling apart. "Let us walk on, nevertheless, reasoning as we go, and if I convince thee not, thou shalt turn back. We are but a little way in the forest, yet."

"Too far, too far!" exclaimed the goodman, unconsciously resuming his walk. "My father never went into the woods on such an errand, nor his father before him. We have been a race of honest men and good Christians, since the days of the martyrs.° And shall I be the first of the name of Brown, that ever took this path, and kept—"

"Such company, thou wouldst say," observed the elder person, interpreting his pause. "Well said, Goodman Brown! I have been as well acquainted with your family as with ever a one among the Puritans; and that's no trifle to say. I helped your grandfather, the constable, when he lashed the Quaker woman so smartly through the streets of Salem. And it was I that brought your father a pitch-pine knot, kindled at my own hearth, to set fire to an Indian village, in King Philip's war.° They were my good friends, both; and many a pleasant walk have we had along this path, and returned merrily after midnight. I would fain be friends with you, for their sake."

full fifteen minutes agone: Apparently this mystery man has traveled in a flash from Boston's Old South Church all the way to the woods beyond Salem—as the crow flies, a good sixteen miles. *King William's court:* back in England, where William III reigned from 1689 to 1702. *wot'st:* know. *days of the martyrs:* a time when many forebears of the New England Puritans had given their lives for religious convictions—when Mary I (Mary Tudor, nicknamed "Bloody Mary"), queen of England from 1553 to 1558, briefly reestablished the Roman Catholic Church in England and launched a campaign of persecution against Protestants. *King Philip's war:* Metacomet, or King Philip (as the English called him), chief of the Wampanoag Indians, had led a bitter, widespread uprising of several New England tribes (1675–78). Metacomet died in the war, as did one out of every ten white male colonists.

"If it be as thou sayest," replied Goodman Brown, "I marvel they never spoke of these matters. Or, verily, I marvel not, seeing that the least rumor of the sort would have driven them from New England. We are a people of prayer, and good works, to boot, and abide no such wickedness."

"Wickedness or not," said the traveller with the twisted staff, "I have a very general acquaintance here in New England. The deacons of many a church have drunk the communion wine with me; the selectmen, of divers towns, make me their chairman; and a majority of the Great and General Court are firm supporters of my interest. The governor and I, too—but these are state-secrets."

"Can this be so!" cried Goodman Brown, with a stare of amazement at his undisturbed companion. "Howbeit, I have nothing to do with the governor and council; they have their own ways, and are no rule for a simple husbandman, like me. But, were I to go on with thee, how should I meet the eye of that good old man, our minister, at Salem village? Oh, his voice would make me tremble, both Sabbath-day and lecture-day!"°

Thus far, the elder traveller had listened with due gravity, but now burst into a fit of irrepressible mirth, shaking himself so violently, that his snake-like staff actually seemed to wriggle in sympathy.

"Ha! ha! ha!" shouted he, again and again; then composing himself, "Well, go on, Goodman Brown, go on; but pray thee, don't kill me with laughing!"

"Well, then, to end the matter at once," said Goodman Brown, considerably nettled, "there is my wife, Faith. It would break her dear little heart; and I'd rather break my own!"

"Nay, if that be the case," answered the other, "e'en go thy ways, Goodman Brown. I would not, for twenty old women like the one hobbling before us, that Faith should come to any harm."

As he spoke, he pointed his staff at a female figure on the path, in whom Goodman Brown recognized a very pious and exemplary dame, who had taught him his catechism, in youth, and was still his moral and spiritual adviser, jointly with the minister and Deacon Gookin.

"A marvel, truly, that Goody° Cloyse should be so far in the wilderness, at nightfall!" said he. "But, with your leave, friend, I shall take a cut through the woods, until we have left this Christian woman behind. Being a stranger to you, she might ask whom I was consorting with, and whither I was going."

"Be it so," said his fellow-traveller. "Betake you to the woods, and let me keep the path."

Accordingly, the young man turned aside, but took care to watch his companion, who advanced softly along the road, until he had come within a staff's length of the old dame. She, meanwhile, was making the best of her way, with singular speed for so aged a woman, and mumbling some indistinct words, a prayer, doubtless, as she went. The traveller put forth his staff, and touched her withered neck with what seemed the serpent's tail.

---

lecture-day: a weekday when everyone had to go to church to hear a sermon or Bible-reading. *Goody:* short for Goodwife, title for a married woman of ordinary station. In his story, Hawthorne borrows from history the names of two "Goodys"—Goody Cloyse and Goody Cory—and one unmarried woman, Martha Carrier. In 1692 Hawthorne's great-great-grandfather John Hathorne, a judge in the Salem witchcraft trials, had condemned all three to be hanged.

"The devil!" screamed the pious old lady.

"Then Goody Cloyse knows her old friend?" observed the traveller, confronting her, and leaning on his writhing stick.

"Ah, forsooth, and is it your worship, indeed?" cried the good dame. "Yea, truly is it, and in the very image of my old gossip,° Goodman Brown, the grandfather of the silly fellow that now is. But—would your worship believe it?—my broomstick hath strangely disappeared, stolen, as I suspect, by that unhanged witch, Goody Cory, and that, too, when I was all anointed with the juice of smallage and cinquefoil and wolf's bane—"°

"Mingled with fine wheat and the fat of a new-born babe," said the shape of old Goodman Brown.

"Ah, your worship knows the receipt,"° cried the old lady, cackling aloud. "So, as I was saying, being all ready for the meeting, and no horse to ride on, I made up my mind to foot it; for they tell me, there is a nice young man to be taken into communion to-night. But now your good worship will lend me your arm, and we shall be there in a twinkling."

"That can hardly be," answered her friend. "I may not spare you my arm, Goody Cloyse, but here is my staff, if you will."

So saying, he threw it down at her feet, where, perhaps, it assumed life, being one of the rods which its owner had formerly lent to the Egyptian Magi.° Of this fact, however, Goodman Brown could not take cognizance. He had cast up his eyes in astonishment, and looking down again, beheld neither Goody Cloyse nor the serpentine staff, but his fellow-traveller alone, who waited for him as calmly as if nothing had happened.

"That old woman taught me my catechism!" said the young man; and there was a world of meaning in this simple comment.

They continued to walk onward, while the elder traveller exhorted his companion to make good speed and persevere in the path, discoursing so aptly, that his arguments seemed rather to spring up in the bosom of his auditor, than to be suggested by himself. As they went, he plucked a branch of maple, to serve for a walking-stick, and began to strip it of the twigs and little boughs, which were wet with evening dew. The moment his fingers touched them, they became strangely withered and dried up, as with a week's sunshine. Thus the pair proceeded, at a good free pace, until suddenly, in a gloomy hollow of the road, Goodman Brown sat himself down on the stump of a tree, and refused to go any farther.

"Friend," said he, stubbornly, "my mind is made up. Not another step will I budge on this errand. What if a wretched old woman do choose to go to the devil, when I thought she was going to Heaven! Is that any reason why I should quit my dear Faith, and go after her?"

"You will think better of this, by-and-by," said his acquaintance, composedly. "Sit here and rest yourself awhile; and when you feel like moving again, there is my staff to help you along."

---

gossip: friend or kinsman.   *smallage and cinquefoil and wolf's bane:* wild plants—here, ingredients for a witch's brew.   *receipt:* recipe.   *Egyptian Magi:* In the Bible, Pharaoh's wise men and sorcerers who by their magical powers changed their rods into live serpents. (This incident, part of the story of Moses and Aaron, is related in Exodus 7:8–12.)

Without more words, he threw his companion the maple stick, and was as speedily out of sight, as if he had vanished into the deepening gloom. The young man sat a few moments, by the road-side, applauding himself greatly, and thinking with how clear a conscience he should meet the minister, in his morning-walk, nor shrink from the eye of good old Deacon Gookin. And what calm sleep would be his, that very night, which was to have been spent so wickedly, but purely and sweetly now, in the arms of Faith! Amidst these pleasant and praiseworthy meditations, Goodman Brown heard the tramp of horses along the road, and deemed it advisable to conceal himself within the verge of the forest, conscious of the guilty purpose that had brought him thither, though now so happily turned from it.

On came the hoof-tramps and the voices of the riders, two grave old voices, conversing soberly as they drew near. These mingled sounds appeared to pass along the road, within a few yards of the young man's hiding-place; but owing, doubtless, to the depth of the gloom, at that particular spot, neither the travellers nor their steeds were visible. Though their figures brushed the small boughs by the way-side, it could not be seen that they intercepted, even for a moment, the faint gleam from the strip of bright sky, athwart which they must have passed. Goodman Brown alternately crouched and stood on tip-toe, pulling aside the branches, and thrusting forth his head as far as he durst, without discerning so much as a shadow. It vexed him the more, because he could have sworn, were such a thing possible, that he recognized the voices of the minister and Deacon Gookin, jogging along quietly, as they were wont to do, when bound to some ordination or ecclesiastical council. While yet within hearing, one of the riders stopped to pluck a switch.

"Of the two, reverend Sir," said the voice like the deacon's, "I had rather miss an ordination-dinner than to-night's meeting. They tell me that some of our community are to be here from Falmouth and beyond, and others from Connecticut and Rhode Island; besides several of the Indian powows,° who, after their fashion, know almost as much deviltry as the best of us. Moreover, there is a goodly young woman to be taken into communion."

"Mighty well, Deacon Gookin!" replied the solemn old tones of the minister. "Spur up, or we shall be late. Nothing can be done, you know, until I get on the ground."

The hoofs clattered again, and the voices, talking so strangely in the empty air, passed on through the forest, where no church had ever been gathered, nor solitary Christian prayed. Whither, then, could these holy men be journeying, so deep into the heathen wilderness? Young Goodman Brown caught hold of a tree, for support, being ready to sink down on the ground, faint and overburdened with the heavy sickness of his heart. He looked up to the sky, doubting whether there really was a Heaven above him. Yet, there was the blue arch, and the stars brightening in it.

"With Heaven above, and Faith below, I will yet stand firm against the devil!" cried Goodman Brown.

While he still gazed upward, into the deep arch of the firmament, and had lifted his hands to pray, a cloud, though no wind was stirring, hurried across the zenith, and hid the brightening stars. The blue sky was still visible, except directly overhead, where this black mass of cloud was sweeping swiftly northward. Aloft in the air, as if from the

---

powows: Indian priests or medicine men.

depths of the cloud, came a confused and doubtful sound of voices. Once, the listener fancied that he could distinguish the accents of town's-people of his own, men and women, both pious and ungodly, many of whom he had met at the communion-table, and had seen others rioting at the tavern. The next moment, so indistinct were the sounds, he doubted whether he had heard aught but the murmur of the old forest, whispering without a wind. Then came a stronger swell of those familiar tones, heard daily in the sunshine, at Salem village, but never, until now, from a cloud of night. There was one voice, of a young woman, uttering lamentations, yet with an uncertain sorrow, and entreating for some favor, which, perhaps, it would grieve her to obtain. And all the unseen multitude, both saints and sinners, seemed to encourage her onward.

"Faith!" shouted Goodman Brown, in a voice of agony and desperation; and the echoes of the forest mocked him, crying—"Faith! Faith!" as if bewildered wretches were seeking her, all through the wilderness.

The cry of grief, rage, and terror, was yet piercing the night, when the unhappy husband held his breath for a response. There was a scream, drowned immediately in a louder murmur of voices, fading into far-off laughter, as the dark cloud swept away, leaving the clear and silent sky above Goodman Brown. But something fluttered lightly down through the air, and caught on the branch of a tree. The young man seized it, and beheld a pink ribbon.

"My Faith is gone!" cried he, after one stupefied moment. "There is no good on earth; and sin is but a name. Come, devil! for to thee is this world given."

And maddened with despair, so that he laughed loud and long, did Goodman Brown grasp his staff and set forth again, at such a rate, that he seemed to fly along the forest-path, rather than to walk or run. The road grew wilder and drearier, and more faintly traced, and vanished at length, leaving him in the heart of the dark wilderness, still rushing onward, with the instinct that guides mortal man to evil. The whole forest was peopled with frightful sounds; the creaking of the trees, the howling of wild beasts, and the yell of Indians; while, sometimes, the wind tolled like a distant church-bell, and sometimes gave a broad roar around the traveller, as if all Nature were laughing him to scorn. But he was himself the chief horror of the scene, and shrank not from its other horrors.

"Ha! ha! ha!" roared Goodman Brown, when the wind laughed at him. "Let us hear which will laugh loudest! Think not to frighten me with your deviltry! Come witch, come wizard, come Indian powow, come devil himself! and here comes Goodman Brown. You may as well fear him as he fear you!"

In truth, all through the haunted forest, there could be nothing more frightful than the figure of Goodman Brown. On he flew, among the black pines, brandishing his staff with frenzied gestures, now giving vent to an inspiration of horrid blasphemy, and now shouting forth such laughter, as set all the echoes of the forest laughing like demons around him. The fiend in his own shape is less hideous, than when he rages in the breast of man. Thus sped the demoniac on his course, until, quivering among the trees, he saw a red light before him, as when the felled trunks and branches of a clearing have been set on fire, and throw up their lurid blaze against the sky, at the hour of midnight. He paused, in a lull of the tempest that had driven him onward, and heard the swell of what seemed a hymn, rolling solemnly from a distance, with the weight of many voices. He knew the tune; it was a familiar one in the choir of the village meeting-house. The verse died heavily away, and was lengthened by a chorus, not of human voices, but of all the sounds of the benighted wilderness, pealing in awful harmony together. Goodman Brown cried out; and his cry was lost to his own ear, by its unison with the cry of the desert.

In the interval of silence, he stole forward, until the light glared full upon his eyes. At one extremity of an open space, hemmed in by the dark wall of the forest, arose a rock, bearing some rude, natural resemblance either to an altar or a pulpit, and surrounded by four blazing pines, their tops aflame, their stems untouched, like candles at an evening meeting. The mass of foliage, that had overgrown the summit of the rock, was all on fire, blazing high into the night, and fitfully illuminating the whole field. Each pendent twig and leafy festoon was in a blaze. As the red light arose and fell, a numerous congregation alternately shone forth, then disappeared in shadow, and again grew, as it were, out of the darkness, peopling the heart of the solitary woods at once.

"A grave and dark-clad company!" quoth Goodman Brown.

In truth, they were such. Among them, quivering to-and-fro, between gloom and splendor, appeared faces that would be seen, next day, at the council-board of the province, and others which, Sabbath after Sabbath, looked devoutly heavenward, and benignantly over the crowded pews, from the holiest pulpits in the land. Some affirm that the lady of the governor was there. At least, there were high dames well known to her, and wives of honored husbands, and widows, a great multitude, and ancient maidens, all of excellent repute, and fair young girls, who trembled, lest their mothers should espy them. Either the sudden gleams of light, flashing over the obscure field, bedazzled Goodman Brown, or he recognized a score of the church-members of Salem village, famous for their especial sanctity. Good old Deacon Gookin had arrived, and waited at the skirts of that venerable saint, his revered pastor. But, irreverently consorting with these grave, reputable, and pious people, these elders of the church, these chaste dames and dewy virgins, there were men of dissolute lives and women of spotted fame, wretches given over to all mean and filthy vice, and suspected even of horrid crimes. It was strange to see, that the good shrank not from the wicked, nor were the sinners abashed by the saints. Scattered, also, among their pale-faced enemies, were the Indian priests, or powows, who had often scared their native forest with more hideous incantations than any known to English witchcraft.

"But, where is Faith?" thought Goodman Brown; and, as hope came into his heart, he trembled.

Another verse of the hymn arose, a slow and mournful strain, such as the pious love, but joined to words which expressed all that our nature can conceive of sin, and darkly hinted at far more. Unfathomable to mere mortals is the lore of fiends. Verse after verse was sung, and still the chorus of the desert swelled between, like the deepest tone of a mighty organ. And, with the final peal of that dreadful anthem, there came a sound, as if the roaring wind, the rushing streams, the howling beasts, and every other voice of the unconverted wilderness, were mingling and according with the voice of guilty man, in homage to the prince of all. The four blazing pines threw up a loftier flame, and obscurely discovered shapes and visages of horror on the smoke-wreaths, above the impious assembly. At the same moment, the fire on the rock shot redly forth, and formed a glowing arch above its base, where now appeared a figure. With reverence be it spoken, the figure bore no slight similitude, both in garb and manner, to some grave divine of the New England churches.

"Bring forth the converts!" cried a voice, that echoed through the field and rolled into the forest.

At the word, Goodman Brown stepped forth from the shadow of the trees, and approached the congregation, with whom he felt a loathful brotherhood, by the sympathy of all that was wicked in his heart. He could have well nigh sworn, that the shape of his own dead father beckoned him to advance, looking downward from a smoke-wreath, while a woman, with dim features of despair, threw out her hand to warn him back. Was it his mother? But he had no power to retreat one step, nor to resist, even in thought, when the minister and good old Deacon Gookin seized his arms, and led him to the blazing rock. Thither came also the slender form of a veiled female, led between Goody Cloyse, that pious teacher of the catechism, and Martha Carrier, who had received the devil's promise to be queen of hell. A rampant hag was she! And there stood the proselytes,° beneath the canopy of fire.

"Welcome, my children," said the dark figure, "to the communion of your race! Ye have found, thus young, your nature and your destiny. My children, look behind you!"

They turned; and flashing forth, as it were, in a sheet of flame, the fiend-worshippers were seen; the smile of welcome gleamed darkly on every visage.

"There," resumed the sable form, "are all whom ye have reverenced from youth. Ye deemed them holier than yourselves, and shrank from your own sin, contrasting it with their lives of righteousness, and prayerful aspirations heavenward. Yet, here are they all, in my worshipping assembly! This night it shall be granted you to know their secret deeds; how hoary-bearded elders of the church have whispered wanton words to the young maids of their households; how many a woman, eager for widow's weeds, has given her husband a drink at bedtime, and let him sleep his last sleep in her bosom; how beardless youths have made haste to inherit their fathers' wealth; and how fair damsels—blush not, sweet ones!—have dug little graves in the garden, and bidden me, the sole guest, to an infant's funeral. By the sympathy of your human hearts for sin, ye shall scent out all the places—whether in church, bed-chamber, street, field, or forest— where crime has been committed, and shall exult to behold the whole earth one stain of guilt, one mighty bloodspot. Far more than this! It shall be yours to penetrate, in every bosom, the deep mystery of sin, the fountain of all wicked arts, and which inexhaustibly supplies more evil impulses than human power—than my power, at its utmost!—can make manifest in deeds. And now, my children, look upon each other."

They did so; and, by the blaze of the hell-kindled torches, the wretched man beheld his Faith, and the wife her husband, trembling before that unhallowed altar.

"Lo! there ye stand, my children," said the figure, in a deep and solemn tone, almost sad, with its despairing awfulness, as if his once angelic nature could yet mourn for our miserable race. "Depending upon one another's hearts, ye had still hoped, that virtue were not all a dream. Now are ye undeceived! Evil is the nature of mankind. Evil must be your only happiness. Welcome, again, my children, to the communion of your race!"

"Welcome!" repeated the fiend-worshippers, in one cry of despair and triumph.

And there they stood, the only pair, as it seemed, who were yet hesitating on the verge of wickedness, in this dark world. A basin was hollowed, naturally, in the rock.

proselytes: new converts.

Did it contain water, reddened by the lurid light? or was it blood? or, perchance, a liquid flame? Herein did the Shape of Evil dip his hand, and prepare to lay the mark of baptism upon their foreheads, that they might be partakers of the mystery of sin, more conscious of the secret guilt of others, both in deed and thought, than they could now be of their own. The husband cast one look at his pale wife, and Faith at him. What polluted wretches would the next glance show them to each other, shuddering alike at what they disclosed and what they saw!

"Faith! Faith!" cried the husband. "Look up to Heaven, and resist the Wicked one!"

Whether Faith obeyed, he knew not. Hardly had he spoken, when he found himself amid calm night and solitude, listening to a roar of the wind, which died heavily away through the forest. He staggered against the rock and felt it chill and damp, while a hanging twig, that had been all on fire, besprinkled his cheek with the coldest dew.

The next morning, young Goodman Brown came slowly into the street of Salem village, staring around him like a bewildered man. The good old minister was taking a walk along the grave-yard, to get an appetite for breakfast and meditate his sermon, and bestowed a blessing, as he passed, on Goodman Brown. He shrank from the venerable saint, as if to avoid an anathema.° Old Deacon Goodkin was at domestic worship, and the holy words of his prayer were heard through the open window. "What God doth the wizard pray to?" quoth Goodman Brown. Goody Cloyse, that excellent old Christian, stood in the early sunshine, at her own lattice, catechizing a little girl, who had brought her a pint of morning's milk. Goodman Brown snatched away the child, as from the grasp of the fiend himself. Turning the corner by the meeting-house, he spied the head of Faith, with the pink ribbons, gazing anxiously forth, and bursting into such joy at sight of him, that she skipt along the street, and almost kissed her husband before the whole village. But, Goodman Brown looked sternly and sadly into her face, and passed on without a greeting.

Had Goodman Brown fallen asleep in the forest, and only dreamed a wild dream of a witch-meeting?

Be it so, if you will. But, alas! it was a dream of evil omen for young Goodman Brown. A stern, a sad, a darkly meditative, a distrustful, if not a desperate man, did he become, from the night of that fearful dream. On the Sabbath-day, when the congregation were singing a holy psalm, he could not listen, because an anthem of sin rushed loudly upon his ear, and drowned all the blessed strain. When the minister spoke from the pulpit, with power and fervid eloquence, and, with his hand on the open Bible, of the sacred truths of our religion, and of saint-like lives and triumphant deaths, and of future bliss or misery unutterable, then did Goodman Brown turn pale, dreading, lest the roof should thunder down upon the gray blasphemer and his hearers. Often, awakening suddenly at midnight, he shrank from the bosom of Faith, and at morning or even-tide, when the family knelt down at prayer, he scowled, and muttered to himself, and gazed sternly at his wife, and turned away. And when he had lived long, and was borne to his grave, a hoary corpse, followed by Faith, an aged woman, and children and grandchildren, a goodly procession, besides neighbors, not a few, they carved no hopeful verse upon his tombstone; for his dying hour was gloom.

---

anathema: an official curse, a decree that casts one out of a church and bans him or her from receiving the sacraments.

Questions

1. Hawthorne's story is set in Salem, Massachusetts. What historical associations does this setting suggest to the reader?
2. Why is Brown's new bride Faith "aptly named" according to the narrator? What does the name "Goodman Brown" suggest about the character of the protagonist?
3. Is there any significance to the fact that the old man in the woods seems to resemble Brown?
4. As Brown and the stranger proceed deeper into the woods, what does Brown find out that troubles him? When the pink ribbon flutters to the ground, as though fallen from something airborne (paragraph 49), what does Brown assume? What effect does this event have upon his determination to resist the devil?
5. Is it significant that most of the story's action take place at night and in the woods?
6. What is the nature of the ceremony going on in the woods? What is being transacted between the old man and the townspeople?
7. What power does the devil promise to give his communicants (paragraph 63)?
8. Is Brown's experience in the woods real? If not, what other explanation can you provide?
9. How does Brown's experience—whether real or imagined—influence his life and his interactions with other people? Why?

Flannery O'Connor

Mary Flannery O'Connor (1925–1964) was born in Savannah, Georgia, but spent most of her life in the small town of Milledgeville. A devout Roman Catholic, she attended mass daily while growing up and living in the largely Protestant South. While attending Georgia State College for Women, she won a local reputation for her fledgling stories and satiric cartoons. After graduating in 1945, she went on to study at the University of Iowa, where she earned an M.F.A. in 1947. Diagnosed in 1950 with disseminated lupus, the same incurable illness that had killed her father, O'Connor returned home and spent the last decade of her life living with her mother in Milledgeville. Back on the family dairy farm, she wrote, maintained an extensive literary correspondence, raised peacocks, and underwent medical treatment. When her illness occasionally went into a period of remission, she made trips to lecture and read her stories to college audiences. Her health declined rapidly after surgery early in 1964 for an unrelated complaint. She died at age thirty-nine.

O'Connor is unusual among modern American writers in the depth of her Christian vision. As a latter-day satirist in the manner of Jonathan Swift, O'Connor levels the eye of an uncompromising moralist on the violence and spiritual disorder of the modern world, focusing on what she calls "the action of grace in territory held largely by the devil." She is sometimes called a "Southern Gothic" writer because of her fascination with grotesque incidents and characters. Throughout her career she depicted the South as a troubled region in which the social, racial, and religious status quo that had existed since before the Civil War was coming to a violent end. O'Connor's published work includes two short novels,

Wise Blood *(1952) and* The Violent Bear It Away *(1960), and two collections of short stories,* A Good Man Is Hard to Find *(1955) and* Everything That Rises Must Converge, *published posthumously in 1965. The Complete Stories of Flannery O'Connor received the National Book Award in 1971.*

A Good Man Is Hard to Find   1955

The grandmother didn't want to go to Florida. She wanted to visit some of her connections in east Tennessee and she was seizing at every chance to change Bailey's mind. Bailey was the son she lived with, her only boy. He was sitting on the edge of his chair at the table, bent over the orange sports section of the *Journal*. "Now look here, Bailey," she said, "see here, read this," and she stood with one hand on her thin hip and the other rattling the newspaper at his bald head. "Here this fellow that calls himself The Misfit is aloose from the Federal Pen and headed toward Florida and you read here what it says he did to these people. Just you read it. I wouldn't take my children in any direction with a criminal like that aloose in it. I couldn't answer to my conscience if I did."

Bailey didn't look up from his reading so she wheeled around then and faced the children's mother, a young woman in slacks, whose face was as broad and innocent as a cabbage and was tied around with a green head-kerchief that had two points on the top like rabbit's ears. She was sitting on the sofa, feeding the baby his apricots out of a jar. "The children have been to Florida before," the old lady said. "You all ought to take them somewhere else for a change so they would see different parts of the world and be broad. They never have been to east Tennessee."

The children's mother didn't seem to hear her but the eight-year-old boy, John Wesley, a stocky child with glasses, said, "If you don't want to go to Florida, why dontcha stay at home?" He and the little girl, June Star, were reading the funny papers on the floor.

"She wouldn't stay at home to be queen for a day," June Star said without raising her yellow head.

"Yes and what would you do if this fellow, The Misfit, caught you?" the grandmother said.

"I'd smack his face," John Wesley said.

"She wouldn't stay at home for a million bucks," June Star said. "Afraid she'd miss something. She has to go everywhere we go."

"All right, Miss," the grandmother said. "Just remember that the next time you want me to curl your hair."

June Star said her hair was naturally curly.

The next morning the grandmother was the first one in the car, ready to go. She had her big black valise that looked like the head of a hippopotamus in one corner, and underneath it she was hiding a basket with Pitty Sing, the cat, in it. She didn't intend for the cat to be left alone in the house for three days because he would miss her too much and she was afraid he might brush against one of the gas burners and accidentally asphyxiate himself. Her son, Bailey, didn't like to arrive at a motel with a cat.

She sat in the middle of the back seat with John Wesley and June Star on either side of her. Bailey and the children's mother and the baby sat in front and they left Atlanta at eight forty-five with the mileage on the car at 55890. The grandmother wrote this down because she thought it would be interesting to say how many miles they had been when they got back. It took them twenty minutes to reach the outskirts of the city.

The old lady settled herself comfortably, removing her white cotton gloves and putting them up with her purse on the shelf in front of the back window. The children's mother still had on slacks and still had her hair tied up in a green kerchief, but the grandmother had on a navy blue straw sailor hat with a bunch of white violets on the brim and a navy blue dress with a small white dot in the print. Her collars and cuffs were white organdy trimmed with lace and at her neckline she had pinned a purple spray of cloth violets containing a sachet. In case of an accident, anyone seeing her dead on the highway would know at once that she was a lady.

She said she thought it was going to be a good day for driving, neither too hot nor too cold, and she cautioned Bailey that the speed limit was fifty-five miles an hour and that the patrolmen hid themselves behind billboards and small clumps of trees and sped out after you before you had a chance to slow down. She pointed out interesting details of the scenery: Stone Mountain; the blue granite that in some places came up to both sides of the highway; the brilliant red clay banks slightly streaked with purple; and the various crops that made rows of green lace-work on the ground. The trees were full of silver-white sunlight and the meanest of them sparkled. The children were reading comic magazines and their mother had gone back to sleep.

"Let's go through Georgia fast so we won't have to look at it much," John Wesley said.

"If I were a little boy," said the grandmother, "I wouldn't talk about my native state that way. Tennessee has the mountains and Georgia has the hills."

"Tennessee is just a hillbilly dumping ground," John Wesley said, "and Georgia is a lousy state too."

"You said it," June Star said.

"In my time," said the grandmother, folding her thin veined fingers, "children were more respectful of their native states and their parents and everything else. People did right then. Oh look at the cute little pickaninny!" she said and pointed to a Negro child standing in the door of a shack. "Wouldn't that make a picture, now?" she asked and they all turned and looked at the little Negro out of the back window. He waved.

"He didn't have any britches on," June Star said.

"He probably didn't have any," the grandmother explained. "Little niggers in the country don't have things like we do. If I could paint, I'd paint that picture," she said.

The children exchanged comic books.

The grandmother offered to hold the baby and the children's mother passed him over the front seat to her. She set him on her knee and bounced him and told him about the things they were passing. She rolled her eyes and screwed up her mouth and stuck her leathery thin face into his smooth bland one. Occasionally he gave her a faraway smile. They passed a large cotton field with five or six graves fenced in the middle of it, like a small island. "Look at the graveyard!" the grandmother said, pointing it out. "That was the old family burying ground. That belonged to the plantation."

"Where's the plantation?" John Wesley asked.

"Gone With the Wind," said the grandmother. "Ha. Ha."

When the children finished all the comic books they had brought, they opened the lunch and ate it. The grandmother ate a peanut butter sandwich and an olive and would not let the children throw the box and the paper napkins out the window. When there was nothing else to do they played a game by choosing a cloud and making the other two guess what shape it suggested. John Wesley took one the shape of a cow and June Star guessed a cow and John Wesley said, no, an automobile, and June Star said he didn't play fair, and they began to slap each other over the grandmother.

    The grandmother said she would tell them a story if they would keep quiet. When she told a story, she rolled her eyes and waved her head and was very dramatic. She said once when she was a maiden lady she had been courted by a Mr. Edgar Atkins Teagarden from Jasper, Georgia. She said he was a very good-looking man and a gentleman and that he brought her a watermelon every Saturday afternoon with his initials cut in it, E. A. T. Well, one Saturday, she said, Mr. Teagarden brought the watermelon and there was nobody at home and he left it on the front porch and returned in his buggy to Jasper, but she never got the watermelon, she said, because a nigger boy ate it when he saw the initials, E. A. T.! This story tickled John Wesley's funny bone and he giggled and giggled but June Star didn't think it was any good. She said she wouldn't marry a man that just brought her a watermelon on Saturday. The grandmother said she would have done well to marry Mr. Teagarden because he was a gentleman and had bought Coca-Cola stock when it first came out and that he had died only a few years ago, a very wealthy man.

    They stopped at The Tower for barbecued sandwiches. The Tower was a part stucco and part wood filling station and dance hall set in a clearing outside of Timothy. A fat man named Red Sammy Butts ran it and there were signs stuck here and there on the building and for miles up and down the highway saying, TRY RED SAMMY'S FAMOUS BARBECUE. NONE LIKE FAMOUS RED SAMMY'S! RED SAM! THE FAT BOY WITH THE HAPPY LAUGH. A VETERAN! RED SAMMY'S YOUR MAN!

    Red Sammy was lying on the bare ground outside The Tower with his head under a truck while a gray monkey about a foot high, chained to a small chinaberry tree, chattered nearby. The monkey sprang back into the tree and got on the highest limb as soon as he saw the children jump out of the car and run toward him.

    Inside, The Tower was a long dark room with a counter at one end and tables at the other and dancing space in the middle. They all sat down at a board table next to the nickelodeon and Red Sam's wife, a tall burnt-brown woman with hair and eyes lighter than her skin, came and took their order. The children's mother put a dime in the machine and played "The Tennessee Waltz," and the grandmother said that tune always made her want to dance. She asked Bailey if he would like to dance but he only glared at her. He didn't have a naturally sunny disposition like she did and trips made him nervous. The grandmother's brown eyes were very bright. She swayed her head from side to side and pretended she was dancing in her chair. June Star said play something she could tap to so the children's mother put in another dime and played a fast number and June Star stepped out onto the dance floor and did her tap routine.

    "Ain't she cute?" Red Sam's wife said, leaning over the counter. "Would you like to come be my little girl?"

    "No I certainly wouldn't," June Star said. "I wouldn't live in a broken-down place like this for a million bucks!" and she ran back to the table.

    "Ain't she cute?" the woman repeated, stretching her mouth politely.

    "Arn't you ashamed?" hissed the grandmother.

Red Sam came in and told his wife to quit lounging on the counter and hurry up with these people's order. His khaki trousers reached just to his hip bones and his stomach hung over them like a sack of meal swaying under his shirt. He came over and sat down at a table nearby and let out a combination sigh and yodel. "You can't win," he said. "You can't win," and he wiped his sweating red face off with a gray handkerchief. "These days you don't know who to trust," he said. "Ain't that the truth?"

"People are certainly not nice like they used to be," said the grandmother.

"Two fellers come in here last week," Red Sammy said, "driving a Chrysler. It was a old beat-up car but it was a good one and these boys looked all right to me. Said they worked at the mill and you know I let them fellers charge the gas they bought? Now why did I do that?"

"Because you're a good man!" the grandmother said at once.

"Yes'm, I suppose so," Red Sam said as if he were struck with this answer.

His wife brought the orders, carrying the five plates all at once without a tray, two in each hand and one balanced on her arm. "It isn't a soul in this green world of God's that you can trust," she said. "And I don't count nobody out of that, not nobody," she repeated, looking at Red Sammy.

"Did you read about that criminal, The Misfit, that's escaped?" asked the grandmother.

"I wouldn't be a bit surprised if he didn't attact this place right here," said the woman. "If he hears about it being here, I wouldn't be none surprised to see him. If he hears it's two cent in the cash register, I wouldn't be a-tall surprised if he . . ."

"That'll do," Red Sam said. "Go bring these people their Co'-Colas," and the woman went off to get the rest of the order.

"A good man is hard to find," Red Sammy said. "Everything is getting terrible. I remember the day you could go off and leave your screen door unlatched. Not no more."

He and the grandmother discussed better times. The old lady said that in her opinion Europe was entirely to blame for the way things were now. She said the way Europe acted you would think we were made of money and Red Sam said it was no use talking about it, she was exactly right. The children ran outside into the white sunlight and looked at the monkey in the lacy chinaberry tree. He was busy catching fleas on himself and biting each one carefully between his teeth as if it were a delicacy.

They drove off again into the hot afternoon. The grandmother took cat naps and woke up every five minutes with her own snoring. Outside of Toombsboro she woke up and recalled an old plantation that she had visited in this neighborhood once when she was a young lady. She said the house had six white columns across the front and that there was an avenue of oaks leading up to it and two little wooden trellis arbors on either side in front where you sat down with your suitor after a stroll in the garden. She recalled exactly which road to turn off to get to it. She knew that Bailey would not be willing to lose any time looking at an old house, but the more she talked about it, the more she wanted to see it once again and find out if the little twin arbors were still standing. "There was a secret panel in this house," she said craftily, not telling the truth but wishing that she were, "and the story went that all the family silver was hidden in it when Sherman° came through but it was never found . . ."

Sherman: General William Tecumseh Sherman, Union commander, whose troops burned Atlanta in 1864, then made a devastating march to the sea.

"Hey!" John Wesley said. "Let's go see it! We'll find it! We'll poke all the woodwork and find it! Who lives there? Where do you turn off at? Hey, Pop, can't we turn off there?"

"We never have seen a house with a secret panel!" June Star shrieked. "Let's go to the house with the secret panel! Hey Pop, can't we go see the house with the secret panel!"

"It's not far from here, I know," the grandmother said. "It wouldn't take over twenty minutes."

Bailey was looking straight ahead. His jaw was as rigid as a horseshoe. "No," he said.

The children began to yell and scream that they wanted to see the house with the secret panel. John Wesley kicked the back of the front seat and June Star hung over her mother's shoulder and whined desperately into her ear that they never had any fun even on their vacation, that they could never do what THEY wanted to do. The baby began to scream and John Wesley kicked the back of the seat so hard that his father could feel the blows in his kidney.

"All right!" he shouted and drew the car to a stop at the side of the road. "Will you all shut up? Will you all just shut up for one second? If you don't shut up, we won't go anywhere."

"It would be very educational for them," the grandmother murmured.

"All right," Bailey said, "but get this: this is the only time we're going to stop for anything like this. This is the one and only time."

"The dirt road that you have to turn down is about a mile back," the grandmother directed. "I marked it when we passed."

"A dirt road," Bailey groaned.

After they had turned around and were headed toward the dirt road, the grandmother recalled other points about the house, the beautiful glass over the front doorway and the candle-lamp in the hall. John Wesley said that the secret panel was probably in the fireplace.

"You can't go inside this house," Bailey said. "You don't know who lives there."

"While you all talk to the people in front, I'll run around behind and get in a window," John Wesley suggested.

"We'll all stay in the car," his mother said.

They turned onto the dirt road and the car raced roughly along in a swirl of pink dust. The grandmother recalled the times when there were no paved roads and thirty miles was a day's journey. The dirt road was hilly and there were sudden washes in it and sharp curves on dangerous embankments. All at once they would be on a hill, looking down over the blue tops of trees for miles around, then the next minute, they would be in a red depression with the dust-coated trees looking down on them.

"This place had better turn up in a minute," Bailey said, "or I'm going to turn around."

The road looked as if no one had traveled on it for months.

"It's not much farther," the grandmother said and just as she said it, a horrible thought came to her. The thought was so embarrassing that she turned red in the face and her eyes dilated and her feet jumped up, upsetting her valise in the corner. The instant the valise moved, the newspaper top she had over the basket under it rose with a snarl and Pitty Sing, the cat, sprang onto Bailey's shoulder.

The children were thrown to the floor and their mother, clutching the baby, was thrown out the door onto the ground; the old lady was thrown into the front seat.

The car turned over once and landed right-side-up in a gulch off the side of the road. Bailey remained in the driver's seat with the cat—gray-striped with a broad white face and an orange nose—clinging to his neck like a caterpillar.

As soon as the children saw they could move their arms and legs, they scrambled out of the car, shouting, "We've had an ACCIDENT!" The grandmother was curled up under the dashboard, hoping she was injured so that Bailey's wrath would not come down on her all at once. The horrible thought she had had before the accident was that the house she had remembered so vividly was not in Georgia but in Tennessee.

Bailey removed the cat from his neck with both hands and flung it out the window against the side of a pine tree. Then he got out of the car and started looking for the children's mother. She was sitting against the side of the red gutted ditch, holding the screaming baby, but she only had a cut down her face and a broken shoulder. "We've had an ACCIDENT!" the children screamed in a frenzy of delight.

"But nobody's killed," June Star said with disappointment as the grandmother limped out of the car, her hat still pinned to her head but the broken front brim standing up at a jaunty angle and the violet spray hanging off the side. They all sat down in the ditch, except the children, to recover from the shock. They were all shaking.

"Maybe a car will come along," said the children's mother hoarsely.

"I believe I have injured an organ," said the grandmother, pressing her side, but no one answered her. Bailey's teeth were clattering. He had on a yellow sport shirt with bright blue parrots designed in it and his face was as yellow as the shirt. The grandmother decided that she would not mention that the house was in Tennessee.

The road was about ten feet above and they could see only the tops of the trees on the other side of it. Behind the ditch they were sitting in there were more woods, tall and dark and deep. In a few minutes they saw a car some distance away on top of a hill, coming slowly as if the occupants were watching them. The grandmother stood up and waved both her arms dramatically to attract their attention. The car continued to come on slowly, disappeared around a bend and appeared again, moving even slower, on top of the hill they had gone over. It was a big black battered hearse-like automobile. There were three men in it.

It came to a stop just over them and for some minutes, the driver looked down with a steady expressionless gaze to where they were sitting, and didn't speak. Then he turned his head and muttered something to the other two and they got out. One was a fat boy in black trousers and a red sweat shirt with a silver stallion embossed on the front of it. He moved around on the right side of them and stood staring, his mouth partly open in a kind of loose grin. The other had on khaki pants and a blue striped coat and a gray hat pulled down very low, hiding most of his face. He came around slowly on the left side. Neither spoke.

The driver got out of the car and stood by the side of it, looking down at them. He was an older man than the other two. His hair was just beginning to gray and he wore silver-rimmed spectacles that gave him a scholarly look. He had a long creased face and didn't have on any shirt or undershirt. He had on blue jeans that were too tight for him and was holding a black hat and a gun. The two boys also had guns.

"We've had an ACCIDENT!" the children screamed.

The grandmother had the peculiar feeling that the bespectacled man was someone she knew. His face was as familiar to her as if she had known him all her life but she could not recall who he was. He moved away from the car and began to come down the embankment, placing his feet carefully so that he wouldn't slip. He had on tan and white shoes and no socks, and his ankles were red and thin. "Good afternoon," he said. "I see you all had you a little spill."

"We turned over twice!" said the grandmother.

"Oncet," he corrected. "We seen it happen. Try their car and see will it run, Hiram," he said quietly to the boy with the gray hat.

"What you got that gun for?" John Wesley asked. "Whatcha gonna do with that gun?"

"Lady," the man said to the children's mother, "would you mind calling them children to sit down by you? Children make me nervous. I want all you all to sit down right together there where you're at."

"What are you telling US what to do for?" June Star asked.

Behind them the line of woods gaped like a dark open mouth. "Come here," said their mother.

"Look here now," Bailey began suddenly, "we're in a predicament! We're in . . ."

The grandmother shrieked. She scrambled to her feet and stood staring. "You're The Misfit!" she said. "I recognized you at once!"

"Yes'm," the man said, smiling slightly as if he were pleased in spite of himself to be known, "but it would have been better for all of you, lady, if you hadn't of reckernized me."

Bailey turned his head sharply and said something to his mother that shocked even the children. The old lady began to cry and The Misfit reddened.

"Lady," he said, "don't you get upset. Sometimes a man says things he don't mean. I don't reckon he meant to talk to you thataway."

"You wouldn't shoot a lady, would you?" the grandmother said and removed a clean handkerchief from her cuff and began to slap at her eyes with it.

The Misfit pointed the toe of his shoe into the ground and made a little hole and then covered it up again. "I would hate to have to," he said.

"Listen," the grandmother almost screamed, "I know you're a good man. You don't look a bit like you have common blood. I know you must come from nice people!"

"Yes mam," he said, "finest people in the world." When he smiled he showed a row of strong white teeth. "God never made a finer woman than my mother and my daddy's heart was pure gold," he said. The boy with the red sweat shirt had come around behind them and was standing with his gun at his hip. The Misfit squatted down on the ground. "Watch them children, Bobby Lee," he said. "You know they make me nervous." He looked at the six of them huddled together in front of him and he seemed to be embarrassed as if he couldn't think of anything to say. "Ain't a cloud in the sky," he remarked, looking up at it. "Don't see no sun but don't see no cloud neither."

"Yes, it's a beautiful day," said the grandmother. "Listen," she said, "you shouldn't call yourself The Misfit because I know you're a good man at heart. I can just look at you and tell."

"Hush!" Bailey yelled. "Hush! Everybody shut up and let me handle this!" He was squatting in the position of a runner about to sprint forward but he didn't move.

"I pre-chate that, lady," The Misfit said and drew a little circle in the ground with the butt of his gun.

"It'll take a half a hour to fix this here car," Hiram called, looking over the raised hood of it.

"Well, first you and Bobby Lee get him and that little boy to step over yonder with you," The Misfit said, pointing to Bailey and John Wesley. "The boys want to ast you something," he said to Bailey. "Would you mind stepping back in them woods there with them?"

"Listen," Bailey began, "we're in a terrible predicament! Nobody realizes what this is," and his voice cracked. His eyes were as blue and intense as the parrots in his shirt and he remained perfectly still.

The grandmother reached up to adjust her hat brim as if she were going to the woods with him but it came off in her hand. She stood staring at it and after a second she let it fall on the ground. Hiram pulled Bailey up by the arm as if he were assisting an old man. John Wesley caught hold of his father's hand and Bobby Lee followed. They went off toward the woods and just as they reached the dark edge, Bailey turned and supporting himself against a gray naked pine trunk, he shouted, "I'll be back in a minute, Mamma, wait on me!"

"Come back this instant!" his mother shrilled but they all disappeared into the woods.

"Bailey Boy!" the grandmother called in a tragic voice but she found she was looking at The Misfit squatting on the ground in front of her. "I just know you're a good man," she said desperately. "You're not a bit common!"

"Nome, I ain't a good man," The Misfit said after a second as if he had considered her statement carefully, "but I ain't the worst in the world neither. My daddy said I was a different breed of dog from my brothers and sisters. 'You know,' Daddy said, 'it's some that can live their whole life out without asking about it and it's others has to know why it is, and this boy is one of the latters. He's going to be into everything!'" He put on his black hat and looked up suddenly and then away deep into the woods as if he were embarrassed again. "I'm sorry I don't have on a shirt before you ladies," he said, hunching his shoulders slightly. "We buried our clothes that we had on when we escaped and we're just making do until we can get better. We borrowed these from some folks we met," he explained.

"That's perfectly all right," the grandmother said. "Maybe Bailey has an extra shirt in his suitcase."

"I'll look and see terrectly," The Misfit said.

"Where are they taking him?" the children's mother screamed.

"Daddy was a card himself," The Misfit said. "You couldn't put anything over on him. He never got in trouble with the Authorities though. Just had the knack of handling them."

"You could be honest too if you'd only try," said the grandmother. "Think how wonderful it would be to settle down and live a comfortable life and not have to think about somebody chasing you all the time."

The Misfit kept scratching in the ground with the butt of his gun as if he were thinking about it. "Yes'm, somebody is always after you," he murmured.

The grandmother noticed how thin his shoulder blades were just behind his hat because she was standing up looking down on him. "Do you ever pray?" she asked.

He shook his head. All she saw was the black hat wiggle between his shoulder blades. "Nome," he said.

There was a pistol shot from the woods, followed closely by another. Then silence. The old lady's head jerked around. She could hear the wind move through the tree tops like a long satisfied insuck of breath. "Bailey Boy!" she called.

"I was a gospel singer for a while," The Misfit said. "I been most everything. Been in the arm service, both land and sea, at home and abroad, been twict married, been an undertaker, been with the railroads, plowed Mother Earth, been in a tornado, seen a man burnt alive oncet," and he looked up at the children's mother and the little girl who were sitting close together, their faces white and their eyes glassy; "I even seen a woman flogged," he said.

"Pray, pray," the grandmother began, "pray, pray . . ."

"I never was a bad boy that I remember of," The Misfit said in an almost dreamy voice, "but somewheres along the line I done something wrong and got sent to the penitentiary. I was buried alive," and he looked up and held her attention to him by a steady stare.

"That's when you should have started to pray," she said. "What did you do to get sent to the penitentiary that first time?"

"Turn to the right, it was a wall," The Misfit said, looking up again at the cloudless sky. "Turn to the left, it was a wall. Look up it was a ceiling, look down it was a floor. I forget what I done, lady. I set there and set there, trying to remember what it was I done and I ain't recalled it to this day. Oncet in a while, I would think it was coming to me, but it never come."

"Maybe they put you in by mistake," the old lady said vaguely.

"Nome," he said. "It wasn't no mistake. They had the papers on me."

"You must have stolen something," she said.

The Misfit sneered slightly. "Nobody had nothing I wanted," he said. "It was a head-doctor at the penitentiary said what I had done was kill my daddy but I known that for a lie. My daddy died in nineteen ought nineteen of the epidemic flu and I never had a thing to do with it. He was buried in the Mount Hopewell Baptist churchyard and you can go there and see for yourself."

"If you would pray," the old lady said, "Jesus would help you."

"That's right," The Misfit said.

"Well then, why don't you pray?" she asked trembling with delight suddenly.

"I don't want no hep," he said. "I'm doing all right by myself."

Bobby Lee and Hiram came ambling back from the woods. Bobby Lee was dragging a yellow shirt with bright blue parrots in it.

"Thow me that shirt, Bobby Lee," The Misfit said. The shirt came flying at him and landed on his shoulder and he put it on. The grandmother couldn't name what the shirt reminded her of. "No, lady," The Misfit said while he was buttoning it up, "I found out the crime don't matter. You can do one thing or you can do another, kill a man or take a tire off his car, because sooner or later you're going to forget what it was you done and just be punished for it."

The children's mother had begun to make heaving noises as if she couldn't get her breath. "Lady," he asked, "would you and that little girl like to step off yonder with Bobby Lee and Hiram and join your husband?"

"Yes, thank you," the mother said faintly. Her left arm dangled helplessly and she was holding the baby, who had gone to sleep, in the other. "Hep that lady up, Hiram," The Misfit said as she struggled to climb out of the ditch, "and Bobby Lee, you hold onto that little girl's hand."

"I don't want to hold hands with him," June Star said. "He reminds me of a pig."

The fat boy blushed and laughed and caught her by the arm and pulled her off into the woods after Hiram and her mother.

Alone with The Misfit, the grandmother found that she had lost her voice. There was not a cloud in the sky nor any sun. There was nothing around her but woods. She wanted to tell him that he must pray. She opened and closed her mouth several times before anything came out. Finally she found herself saying, "Jesus. Jesus," meaning, Jesus will help you, but the way she was saying it, it sounded as if she might be cursing.

"Yes'm," The Misfit said as if he agreed. "Jesus thown everything off balance. It was the same case with Him as with me except He hadn't committed any crime and they could prove I had committed one because they had the papers on me. Of course," he said, "they never shown me my papers. That's why I sign myself now. I said long ago, you get you a signature and sign everything you do and keep a copy of it. Then you'll know what you done and you can hold up the crime to the punishment and see do they match and in the end you'll have something to prove you ain't been treated right. I call myself The Misfit," he said, "because I can't make what all I done wrong fit what all I gone through in punishment."

There was a piercing scream from the woods, followed closely by a pistol report. "Does it seem right to you, lady, that one is punished a heap and another ain't punished at all?"

"Jesus!" the old lady cried. "You've got good blood! I know you wouldn't shoot a lady! I know you come from nice people! Pray! Jesus, you ought not to shoot a lady. I'll give you all the money I've got!"

"Lady," The Misfit said, looking beyond her far into the woods, "there never was a body that give the undertaker a tip."

There were two more pistol reports and the grandmother raised her head like a parched old turkey hen crying for water and called, "Bailey Boy, Bailey Boy!" as if her heart would break.

"Jesus was the only One that ever raised the dead," The Misfit continued, "and He shouldn't have done it. He thown everything off balance. If He did what He said, then it's nothing for you to do but thow away everything and follow Him, and if He didn't, then it's nothing for you to do but enjoy the few minutes you got left the best way you can—by killing somebody or burning down his house or doing some other meanness to him. No pleasure but meanness," he said and his voice had become almost a snarl.

"Maybe He didn't raise the dead," the old lady mumbled, not knowing what she was saying and feeling so dizzy that she sank down in the ditch with her legs twisted under her.

"I wasn't there so I can't say He didn't," The Misfit said. "I wisht I had of been there," he said, hitting the ground with his fist. "It ain't right I wasn't there because if I had of been there I would of known. Listen lady," he said in a high voice, "if I had of been there I would of known and I wouldn't be like I am now." His voice seemed about to crack and the grandmother's head cleared for an instant. She saw the man's face twisted close to her own as if he were going to cry and she murmured, "Why you're one of my babies. You're one of my own children!" She reached out and touched him on the shoulder. The Misfit sprang back as if a snake had bitten him and shot her three times through the chest. Then he put his gun down on the ground and took off his glasses and began to clean them.

Hiram and Bobby Lee returned from the woods and stood over the ditch, looking down at the grandmother who half sat and half lay in a puddle of blood with her legs crossed under her like a child's and her face smiling up at the cloudless sky.

Without his glasses, The Misfit's eyes were red-rimmed and pale and defenseless-looking. "Take her off and thow her where you thown the others," he said, picking up the cat that was rubbing itself against his leg.

"She was a talker, wasn't she?" Bobby Lee said, sliding down the ditch with a yodel.

"She would of been a good woman," The Misfit said, "if it had been somebody there to shoot her every minute of her life." 140

"Some fun!" Bobby Lee said.

"Shut up, Bobby Lee," The Misfit said. "It's no real pleasure in life."

Questions

1. How early in the story does O'Connor foreshadow what will happen in the end? What further hints does she give us along the way? How does the scene at Red Sammy's Barbecue advance the story toward its conclusion?
2. When we first meet the grandmother, what kind of person is she? What do her various remarks reveal about her? Does she remain a static character, or does she change in any way as the story goes on?
3. When the grandmother's head clears for an instant (paragraph 136), what does she suddenly understand? Reread this passage carefully and prepare to discuss what it means.
4. What do we learn from the conversation between The Misfit and the grandmother while the others go to the woods? How would you describe The Misfit's outlook on the world? Compare it with the author's, from whatever you know about Flannery O'Connor and from the story itself.
5. How would you respond to a reader who complained, "The title of this story is just an obvious platitude"?

Joyce Carol Oates

Joyce Carol Oates was born in 1938 into a blue-collar Catholic family in Lockport, New York. As an undergraduate at Syracuse University, she won a Mademoiselle magazine award for fiction. After graduating with top honors, she took a master's degree in English at the University of Wisconsin and went on to teach at several universities: Detroit, Windsor, and Princeton. A remarkably prolific writer, Oates has produced more than twenty-five collections of stories, including High Lonesome: Stories 1966–2006, *and forty novels, including* them, *winner of a National Book Award in 1970,* Because It Is Bitter, and Because It Is My Heart *(1990), and more recently,* Black Girl/White Girl *(2006),* The Gravedigger's Daughter *(2007), and* My Sister, My Love *(2008). She also writes poetry, plays, and literary criticism.*

Joyce Carol Oates

The 1985 film Smooth Talk, *directed by Joyce Chopra, is based on "Where Are You Going, Where Have You Been?"*

Where Are You Going, Where Have You Been? 1970
For Bob Dylan

Her name was Connie. She was fifteen and she had a quick nervous giggling habit of craning her neck to glance into mirrors, or checking other people's faces to make sure her own was all right. Her mother, who noticed everything and knew everything and who hadn't much reason any longer to look at her own face, always scolded Connie about it. "Stop gawking at yourself, who are you? You think you're so pretty?" she would say. Connie would raise her eyebrows at these familiar complaints and look right through her mother, into a shadowy vision of herself as she was right at that moment: she knew she was pretty and that was everything. Her mother had been pretty once too, if you could believe those old snapshots in the album, but now her looks were gone and that was why she was always after Connie.

"Why don't you keep your room clean like your sister? How've you got your hair fixed—what the hell stinks? Hair spray? You don't see your sister using that junk."

Her sister June was twenty-four and still lived at home. She was a secretary in the high school Connie attended, and if that wasn't bad enough—with her in the same building—she was so plain and chunky and steady that Connie had to hear her praised all the time by her mother and her mother's sisters. June did this, June did that, she saved money and helped clean the house and cooked and Connie couldn't do a thing, her mind was all filled with trashy daydreams. Their father was away at work most of the time and when he came home he wanted supper and he read the newspaper at supper and after supper he went to bed. He didn't bother talking much to them, but around his bent head Connie's mother kept picking at her until Connie wished her mother was dead and she herself was dead and it was all over. "She makes me want to throw up sometimes," she complained to her friends. She had a high, breathless, amused voice which made everything she said sound a little forced, whether it was sincere or not.

There was one good thing: June went places with girl friends of hers, girls who were just as plain and steady as she, and so when Connie wanted to do that her mother had no objections. The father of Connie's best girl friend drove the girls the three miles to town and left them off at a shopping plaza, so that they could walk through the stores or go to a movie, and when he came to pick them up again at eleven he never bothered to ask what they had done.

They must have been familiar sights, walking around that shopping plaza in their shorts and flat ballerina slippers that always scuffed the sidewalk, with charm bracelets jingling on their thin wrists; they would lean together to whisper and laugh secretly if someone passed by who amused or interested them. Connie had long dark blond hair that drew anyone's eye to it, and she wore part of it pulled up on her head and puffed out and the rest of it she let fall down her back. She wore a pull-over jersey blouse that looked one way when she was at home and another way when she was away from home. Everything about her had two sides to it, one for home and one for anywhere that was not home: her walk that could be childlike and bobbing, or languid enough to make anyone think she was hearing music in her head, her mouth which was pale and smirking most of the time, but bright and pink on these evenings out, her laugh which was cynical and drawling at home—"Ha, ha, very funny"—but high-pitched and nervous anywhere else, like the jingling of the charms on her bracelet.

Sometimes they did go shopping or to a movie, but sometimes they went across the highway, ducking fast across the busy road, to a drive-in restaurant where older kids hung out. The restaurant was shaped like a big bottle, though squatter than a real bottle, and on its cap was a revolving figure of a grinning boy who held a hamburger aloft. One night in mid-summer they ran across, breathless with daring, and right away someone leaned out a car window and invited them over, but it was just a boy from high school they didn't like. It made them feel good to be able to ignore him. They went up through the maze of parked and cruising cars to the bright-lit, fly-infested restaurant, their faces pleased and expectant as if they were entering a sacred building that loomed out of the night to give them what haven and what blessing they yearned for. They sat at the counter and crossed their legs at the ankles, their thin shoulders rigid with excitement, and listened to the music that made everything so good: the music was always in the background like music at a church service, it was something to depend upon.

A boy named Eddie came in to talk with them. He sat backwards on his stool, turning himself jerkily around in semi-circles and then stopping and turning again, and after a while he asked Connie if she would like something to eat. She said she did and so she tapped her friend's arm on her way out—her friend pulled her face up into a brave droll look—and Connie said she would meet her at eleven, across the way. "I just hate to leave her like that," Connie said earnestly, but the boy said that she wouldn't be alone for long. So they went out to his car and on the way Connie couldn't help but let her eyes wander over the windshields and faces all around her, her face gleaming with a joy that had nothing to do with Eddie or even this place; it might have been the music. She drew her shoulders up and sucked in her breath with the pure pleasure of being alive, and just at that moment she happened to glance at a face just a few feet from hers. It was a boy with shaggy black hair, in a convertible jalopy painted gold. He stared at her and then his lips widened into a grin. Connie slit her eyes at him and turned away, but she couldn't help glancing back and there he was still watching her. He wagged a finger and laughed and said, "Gonna get you, baby," and Connie turned away again without Eddie noticing anything.

She spent three hours with him, at the restaurant where they ate hamburgers and drank Cokes in wax cups that were always sweating, and then down an alley a mile or so away, and when he left her off at five to eleven only the movie house was still open at the plaza. Her girl friend was there, talking with a boy. When Connie came up the two girls smiled at each other and Connie said, "How was the movie?" and the girl said, "*You* should know." They rode off with the girl's father, sleepy and pleased, and Connie couldn't help but look at the darkened shopping plaza with its big empty parking lot and its signs that were faded and ghostly now, and over at the drive-in restaurant where cars were still circling tirelessly. She couldn't hear the music at this distance.

Next morning June asked her how the movie was and Connie said, "So-so."

She and that girl and occasionally another girl went out several times a week that way, and the rest of the time Connie spent around the house—it was summer vacation—getting in her mother's way and thinking, dreaming, about the boys she met.

But all the boys fell back and dissolved into a single face that was not even a face, but an idea, a feeling, mixed up with the urgent insistent pounding of the music and the humid night air of July. Connie's mother kept dragging her back to the daylight by finding things for her to do or saying, suddenly, "What's this about the Pettinger girl?"

And Connie would say nervously, "Oh, her. That dope." She always drew thick clear lines between herself and such girls, and her mother was simple and kindly enough to believe her. Her mother was so simple, Connie thought, that it was maybe cruel to fool her so much. Her mother went scuffling around the house in old bedroom slippers and complained over the telephone to one sister about the other, then the other called up and the two of them complained about the third one. If June's name was mentioned her mother's tone was approving, and if Connie's name was mentioned it was disapproving. This did not really mean she disliked Connie and actually Connie thought that her mother preferred her to June because she was prettier, but the two of them kept up a pretense of exasperation, a sense that they were tugging and struggling over something of little value to either of them. Sometimes, over coffee, they were almost friends, but something would come up—some vexation that was like a fly buzzing suddenly around their heads—and their faces went hard with contempt.

One Sunday Connie got up at eleven—none of them bothered with church—and washed her hair so that it could dry all day long, in the sun. Her parents and sister were going to a barbecue at an aunt's house and Connie said no, she wasn't interested, rolling her eyes to let her mother know just what she thought of it. "Stay home alone then," her mother said sharply. Connie sat out back in a lawn chair and watched them drive away, her father quiet and bald, hunched around so that he could back the car out, her mother with a look that was still angry and not at all softened through the windshield, and in the back seat poor old June all dressed up as if she didn't know what a barbecue was, with all the running yelling kids and the flies. Connie sat with her eyes closed in the sun, dreaming and dazed with the warmth about her as if this were a kind of love, the caresses of love, and her mind slipped over onto thoughts of the boy she had been with the night before and how nice he had been, how sweet it always was, not the way someone like June would suppose but sweet, gentle, the way it was in movies and promised in songs; and when she opened her eyes she hardly knew where she was, the back yard ran off into weeds and a fence-line of trees and behind it the sky was perfectly blue and still. The asbestos "ranch house" that was now three years old startled her—it looked small. She shook her head as if to get awake.

It was too hot. She went inside the house and turned on the radio to drown out the quiet. She sat on the edge of her bed, barefoot, and listened for an hour and a half to a program called XYZ Sunday Jamboree, record after record of hard, fast, shrieking songs she sang along with, interspersed by exclamations from "Bobby King": "An' look here you girls at Napoleon's—Son and Charley want you to pay real close attention to this song coming up!"

And Connie paid close attention herself, bathed in a glow of slow-pulsed joy that seemed to rise mysteriously out of the music itself and lay languidly about the airless little room, breathed in and breathed out with each gentle rise and fall of her chest.

After a while she heard a car coming up the drive. She sat up at once, startled, because it couldn't be her father so soon. The gravel kept crunching all the way in from the road—the driveway was long—and Connie ran to the window. It was a car she didn't know. It was an open jalopy, painted a bright gold that caught the sunlight opaquely. Her heart began to pound and her fingers snatched at her hair, checking it, and she whispered "Christ, Christ," wondering how bad she looked. The car came to a stop at the side door and the horn sounded four short taps as if this were a signal Connie knew.

She went into the kitchen and approached the door slowly, then hung out the screen door, her bare toes curling down off the step. There were two boys in the car and now she recognized the driver: he had shaggy, shabby black hair that looked crazy as a wig and he was grinning at her.

"I ain't late, am I?" he said.

"Who the hell do you think you are?" Connie said.

"Toldja I'd be out, didn't I?"

"I don't even know who you are."

She spoke sullenly, careful to show no interest or pleasure, and he spoke in a fast bright monotone. Connie looked past him to the other boy, taking her time. He had fair brown hair, with a lock that fell onto his forehead. His sideburns gave him a fierce, embarrassed look, but so far he hadn't even bothered to glance at her. Both boys wore sunglasses. The driver's glasses were metallic and mirrored everything in miniature.

"You wanta come for a ride?" he said.

Connie smirked and let her hair fall loose over one shoulder.

"Don'tcha like my car? New paint job," he said. "Hey."

"What?"

"You're cute."

She pretended to fidget, chasing flies away from the door.

"Don'tcha believe me, or what?" he said.

"Look, I don't even know who you are," Connie said in disgust.

"Hey, Ellie's got a radio, see. Mine's broke down." He lifted his friend's arm and showed her the little transistor the boy was holding, and now Connie began to hear the music. It was the same program that was playing inside the house.

"Bobby King?" she said.

"I listen to him all the time. I think he's great."

"He's kind of great," Connie said reluctantly.

"Listen, that guy's *great*. He knows where the action is."

Connie blushed a little, because the glasses made it impossible for her to see just what this boy was looking at. She couldn't decide if she liked him or if he was just a jerk, and so she dawdled in the doorway and wouldn't come down or go back inside. She said, "What's all that stuff painted on your car?"

"Can'tcha read it?" He opened the door very carefully, as if he was afraid it might fall off. He slid out just as carefully, planting his feet firmly on the ground, the tiny metallic world in his glasses slowing down like gelatine hardening and in the midst of it Connie's bright green blouse. "This here is my name, to begin with," he said. ARNOLD FRIEND was written in tarlike black letters on the side, with a drawing of a round grinning face that reminded Connie of a pumpkin, except it wore sunglasses. "I wanta introduce myself, I'm Arnold Friend and that's my real name and I'm gonna be your friend, honey, and inside the car's Ellie Oscar, he's kinda shy." Ellie brought his transistor radio up to his shoulder and balanced it there. "Now these numbers are a secret code, honey," Arnold Friend explained. He read off the numbers 33, 19, 17 and raised his eyebrows at her to see what she thought of that, but she didn't think much of it. The left rear fender had been smashed and around it was written, on the gleaming gold background: DONE BY CRAZY WOMAN DRIVER. Connie had to laugh at that. Arnold Friend was pleased at her laughter and looked up at her. "Around the other side's a lot more—you wanta come and see them?"

"No."

"Why not?"

"Why should I?"

"Don'tcha wanta see what's on the car? Don'tcha wanta go for a ride?"

"I don't know."

"Why not?"

"I got things to do."

"Like what?"

"Things."

He laughed as if she had said something funny. He slapped his thighs. He was standing in a strange way, leaning back against the car as if he were balancing himself. He wasn't tall, only an inch or so taller than she would be if she came down to him. Connie liked the way he was dressed, which was the way all of them dressed: tight faded jeans stuffed into black, scuffed boots, a belt that pulled his waist in and showed how lean he was, and a white pull-over shirt that was a little soiled and showed the hard small muscles of his arms and shoulders. He looked as if he probably did hard work, lifting and carrying things. Even his neck looked muscular. And his face was a familiar face, somehow: the jaw and chin and cheeks slightly darkened, because he hadn't shaved for a day or two, and the nose long and hawk-like, sniffing as if she were a treat he was going to gobble up and it was all a joke.

"Connie, you ain't telling the truth. This is your day set aside for a ride with me and you know it," he said, still laughing. The way he straightened and recovered from his fit of laughing showed that it had been all fake.

"How do you know what my name is?" she said suspiciously.

"It's Connie."

"Maybe and maybe not."

"I know my Connie," he said, wagging his finger. Now she remembered him even better, back at the restaurant, and her cheeks warmed at the thought of how she sucked in her breath just at the moment she passed him—how she must have looked to him. And he had remembered her. "Ellie and I come out here especially for you," he said. "Ellie can sit in back. How about it?"

"Where?"

"Where what?"

"Where're we going?"

He looked at her. He took off the sunglasses and she saw how pale the skin around his eyes was, like holes that were not in shadow but instead in light. His eyes were chips of broken glass that catch the light in an amiable way. He smiled. It was as if the idea of going for a ride somewhere, to some place, was a new idea to him.

"Just for a ride, Connie sweetheart."

"I never said my name was Connie," she said.

"But I know what it is. I know your name and all about you, lots of things," Arnold Friend said. He had not moved yet but stood still leaning back against the side of his jalopy. "I took a special interest in you, such a pretty girl, and found out all about you like I know your parents and sister are gone somewheres and I know where and how long they're going to be gone, and I know who you were with last night, and your best girl friend's name is Betty. Right?"

He spoke in a simple lilting voice, exactly as if he were reciting the words to a song. His smile assured her that everything was fine. In the car Ellie turned up the volume on his radio and did not bother to look around at them.

"Ellie can sit in the back seat," Arnold Friend said. He indicated his friend with a casual jerk of his chin, as if Ellie did not count and she should not bother with him.

"How'd you find out all that stuff?" Connie said.

"Listen: Betty Schultz and Tony Fitch and Jimmy Pettinger and Nancy Pettinger," he said, in a chant. "Raymond Stanley and Bob Hutter—"

"Do you know all those kids?"

"I know everybody."

"Look, you're kidding. You're not from around here."

"Sure."

"But—how come we never saw you before?"

"Sure you saw me before," he said. He looked down at his boots, as if he were a little offended. "You just don't remember."

"I guess I'd remember you," Connie said.

"Yeah?" He looked up at this, beaming. He was pleased. He began to mark time with the music from Ellie's radio, tapping his fists lightly together. Connie looked away from his smile to the car, which was painted so bright it almost hurt her eyes to look at it. She looked at that name, ARNOLD FRIEND. And up at the front fender was an expression that was familiar—MAN THE FLYING SAUCERS. It was an expression kids had used the year before, but didn't use this year. She looked at it for a while as if the words meant something to her that she did not yet know.

"What're you thinking about? Huh?" Arnold Friend demanded. "Not worried about your hair blowing around in the car, are you?"

"No."

"Think I maybe can't drive good?"

"How do I know?"

"You're a hard girl to handle. How come?" he said. "Don't you know I'm your friend? Didn't you see me put my sign in the air when you walked by?"

"What sign?"

"My sign." And he drew an X in the air, leaning out toward her. They were maybe ten feet apart. After his hand fell back to his side the X was still in the air, almost visible. Connie let the screen door close and stood perfectly still inside it, listening to the music from her radio and the boy's blend together. She stared at Arnold Friend. He stood there so stiffly relaxed, pretending to be relaxed, with one hand idly on the door handle as if he were keeping himself up that way and had no intention of ever moving again. She recognized most things about him, the tight jeans that showed his thighs and buttocks and the greasy leather boots and the tight shirt, and even that slippery friendly smile of his, that sleepy dreamy smile that all the boys used to get across ideas they didn't want to put into words. She recognized all this and also the singsong way he talked, slightly mocking, kidding, but serious and a little melancholy, and she recognized the way he tapped one fist against the other in homage to the perpetual music behind him. But all these things did not come together.

She said suddenly, "Hey, how old are you?"

His smile faded. She could see then that he wasn't a kid, he was much older—thirty, maybe more. At this knowledge her heart began to pound faster.

"That's a crazy thing to ask. Can'tcha see I'm your own age?"

"Like hell you are."

"Or maybe a coupla years older, I'm eighteen."

"Eighteen?" she said doubtfully.

He grinned to reassure her and lines appeared at the corners of his mouth. His teeth were big and white. He grinned so broadly his eyes became slits and she saw how thick the lashes were, thick and black as if painted with a black tarlike material. Then he seemed to become embarrassed, abruptly, and looked over his shoulder at Ellie. "*Him*, he's crazy," he said. "Ain't he a riot, he's a nut, a real character." Ellie was still listening to the music. His sunglasses told nothing about what he was thinking. He wore a bright orange shirt unbuttoned halfway to show his chest, which was a pale, bluish chest and not muscular like Arnold Friend's. His shirt collar was turned up all around and the very tips of the collar pointed out past his chin as if they were protecting him. He was pressing the transistor radio up against his ear and sat there in a kind of daze, right in the sun.

"He's kinda strange," Connie said.

"Hey, she says you're kinda strange! Kinda strange!" Arnold Friend cried. He pounded on the car to get Ellie's attention. Ellie turned for the first time and Connie saw with shock that he wasn't a kid either—he had a fair, hairless face, cheeks reddened slightly as if the veins grew too close to the surface of his skin, the face of a forty-year-old baby. Connie felt a wave of dizziness rise in her at this sight and she stared at him as if waiting for something to change the shock of the moment, make it all right again. Ellie's lips kept shaping words, mumbling along with the words blasting in his ear.

"Maybe you two better go away," Connie said faintly.

"What? How come?" Arnold Friend cried. "We come out here to take you for a ride. It's Sunday." He had the voice of the man on the radio now. It was the same voice, Connie thought. "Don'tcha know it's Sunday all day and honey, no matter who you were with last night today you're with Arnold Friend and don't you forget it!—Maybe you better step out here," he said, and this last was in a different voice. It was a little flatter, as if the heat was finally getting to him.

"No. I got things to do."

"Hey."

"You two better leave."

"We ain't leaving until you come with us."

"Like hell I am—"

"Connie, don't fool around with me. I mean, I mean, don't fool *around*," he said, shaking his head. He laughed incredulously. He placed his sunglasses on top of his head, carefully, as if he were indeed wearing a wig, and brought the stems down behind his ears. Connie stared at him, another wave of dizziness and fear rising in her so that for a moment he wasn't even in focus but was just a blur, standing there against his gold car, and she had the idea that he had driven up the driveway all right but had come from nowhere before that and belonged nowhere and that everything about him and even about the music that was so familiar to her was only half real.

"If my father comes and sees you—"

"He ain't coming. He's at a barbecue."

"How do you know that?"

"Aunt Tillie's. Right now they're—uh—they're drinking. Sitting around," he said vaguely, squinting as if he were staring all the way to town and over to Aunt Tillie's backyard. Then the vision seemed to get clear and he nodded energetically. "Yeah. Sitting around. There's your sister in a blue dress, huh? And high heels, the poor sad bitch—nothing like you, sweetheart! And your mother's helping some fat woman with the corn, they're cleaning the corn—husking the corn—"

"What fat woman?" Connie cried.

"How do I know what fat woman. I don't know every goddam fat woman in the world!" Arnold Friend laughed.

"Oh, that's Mrs. Hornby. . . . Who invited her?" Connie said. She felt a little light-headed. Her breath was coming quickly.

"She's too fat. I don't like them fat. I like them the way you are, honey," he said, smiling sleepily at her. They stared at each other for a while, through the screen door. He said softly, "Now what you're going to do is this: you're going to come out that door. You're going to sit up front with me and Ellie's going to sit in the back, the hell with Ellie, right? This isn't Ellie's date. You're my date. I'm your lover, honey."

"What? You're crazy—"

"Yes, I'm your lover. You don't know what that is but you will," he said. "I know that too. I know all about you. But look: it's real nice and you couldn't ask for nobody better than me, or more polite. I always keep my word. I'll tell you how it is, I'm always nice at first, the first time. I'll hold you so tight you won't think you have to try to get away or pretend anything because you'll know you can't. And I'll come inside you where it's all secret and you'll give in to me and you'll love me—"

"Shut up! You're crazy!" Connie said. She backed away from the door. She put her hands against her ears as if she'd heard something terrible, something not meant for her. "People don't talk like that, you're crazy," she muttered. Her heart was almost too big now for her chest and its pumping made sweat break out all over her. She looked out to see Arnold Friend pause and then take a step toward the porch lurching. He almost fell. But, like a clever drunken man, he managed to catch his balance. He wobbled in his high boots and grabbed hold of one of the porch posts.

"Honey?" he said. "You still listening?"

"Get the hell out of here!"

"Be nice, honey. Listen."

"I'm going to call the police—"

He wobbled again and out of the side of his mouth came a fast spat curse, an aside not meant for her to hear. But even this "Christ!" sounded forced. Then he began to smile again. She watched this smile come, awkward as if he were smiling from inside a mask. His whole face was a mask, she thought wildly, tanned down onto his throat but then running out as if he had plastered makeup on his face but had forgotten about his throat.

"Honey—? Listen, here's how it is. I always tell the truth and I promise you this: I ain't coming in that house after you."

"You better not! I'm going to call the police if you—if you don't—"

"Honey," he said, talking right through her voice, "honey, I'm not coming in there but you are coming out here. You know why?"

She was panting. The kitchen looked like a place she had never seen before, some room she had run inside but which wasn't good enough, wasn't going to help her. The kitchen window had never had a curtain, after three years, and there were dishes in the sink for her to do—probably—and if you ran your hand across the table you'd probably feel something sticky there.

"You listening, honey? Hey?"

"—going to call the police—"

"Soon as you touch the phone I don't need to keep my promise and can come inside. You won't want that."

She rushed forward and tried to lock the door. Her fingers were shaking. "But why lock it," Arnold Friend said gently, talking right into her face. "It's just a screen door. It's just nothing." One of his boots was at a strange angle, as if his foot wasn't in it. It pointed out to the left, bent at the ankle. "I mean, anybody can break through a screen door and glass and wood and iron or anything else if he needs to, anybody at all and specially Arnold Friend. If the place got lit up with a fire honey you'd come running out into my arms, right into my arms and safe at home—like you knew I was your lover and'd stopped fooling around. I don't mind a nice shy girl but I don't like no fooling around." Part of those words were spoken with a slight rhythmic lilt, and Connie somehow recognized them—the echo of a song from last year, about a girl rushing into her boyfriend's arms and coming home again—

Connie stood barefoot on the linoleum floor, staring at him. "What do you want?" she whispered.

"I want you," he said.

"What?"

"Seen you that night and thought, that's the one, yes sir. I never needed to look any more."

"But my father's coming back. He's coming to get me. I had to wash my hair first—" She spoke in a dry, rapid voice, hardly raising it for him to hear.

"No, your daddy is not coming and yes, you had to wash your hair and you washed it for me. It's nice and shining and all for me, I thank you, sweetheart," he said, with a mock bow, but again he almost lost his balance. He had to bend and adjust his boots. Evidently his feet did not go all the way down; the boots must have been stuffed with something so that he would seem taller. Connie stared out at him and behind him Ellie in the car, who seemed to be looking off toward Connie's right, into nothing. This Ellie said, pulling the words out of the air one after another as if he were just discovering them, "You want me to pull out the phone?"

"Shut your mouth and keep it shut," Arnold Friend said, his face red from bending over or maybe from embarrassment because Connie had seen his boots. "This ain't none of your business."

"What—what are you doing? What do you want?" Connie said. "If I call the police they'll get you, they'll arrest you—"

"Promise was not to come in unless you touch that phone, and I'll keep that promise," he said. He resumed his erect position and tried to force his shoulders back. He sounded like a hero in a movie, declaring something important. He spoke too loudly and it was as if he were speaking to someone behind Connie. "I ain't made plans for coming in that house where I don't belong but just for you to come out to me, the way you should. Don't you know who I am?"

"You're crazy," she whispered. She backed away from the door but did not want to go into another part of the house, as if this would give him permission to come through the door. "What do you . . . You're crazy, you . . ."

"Huh? What're you saying, honey?"

Her eyes darted everywhere in the kitchen. She could not remember what it was, this room.

"This is how it is, honey: you come out and we'll drive away, have a nice ride. But if you don't come out we're gonna wait till your people come home and then they're all going to get it."

"You want that telephone pulled out?" Ellie said. He held the radio away from his ear and grimaced, as if without the radio the air was too much for him.

"I toldja shut up, Ellie," Arnold Friend said, "you're deaf, get a hearing aid, right? Fix yourself up. This little girl's no trouble and's gonna be nice to me, so Ellie keep to yourself, this ain't your date—right? Don't hem in on me. Don't hog. Don't crush. Don't bird dog. Don't trail me," he said in a rapid meaningless voice, as if he were running through all the expressions he'd learned but was no longer sure which one of them was in style, then rushing on to new ones, making them up with his eyes closed, "Don't crawl under my fence, don't squeeze in my chipmunk hole, don't sniff my glue, suck my popsicle, keep your own greasy fingers on yourself!" He shaded his eyes and peered in at Connie, who was backed against the kitchen table. "Don't mind him honey he's just a creep. He's a dope. Right? I'm the boy for you and like I said you come out here nice like a lady and give me your hand, and nobody else gets hurt, I mean, your nice old bald-headed daddy and your mummy and your sister in her high heels. Because listen: why bring them in this?"

"Leave me alone," Connie whispered.

"Hey, you know that old woman down the road, the one with the chickens and stuff—you know her?"

"She's dead!"

"Dead? What? You know her?" Arnold Friend said.

"She's dead—"

"Don't you like her?"

"She's dead—she's—she isn't here any more—"

"But don't you like her, I mean, you got something against her? Some grudge or something?" Then his voice dipped as if he were conscious of a rudeness. He touched the sunglasses perched on top of his head as if to make sure they were still there. "Now you be a good girl."

"What are you going to do?"

"Just two things, or maybe three," Arnold Friend said. "But I promise it won't last long and you'll like me that way you get to like people you're close to. You will. It's all over for you here, so come on out. You don't want your people in any trouble, do you?"

She turned and bumped against a chair or something, hurting her leg, but she ran into the back room and picked up the telephone. Something roared in her ear, a tiny roaring, and she was so sick with fear that she could do nothing but listen to it—the telephone was clammy and very heavy and her fingers groped down to the dial but were too weak to touch it. She began to scream into the phone, into the roaring. She cried out, she cried for her mother, she felt her breath start jerking back and forth in her lungs as if it were something Arnold Friend were stabbing her with again and again with no tenderness. A noisy sorrowful wailing rose all about her and she was locked inside it the way she was locked inside the house.

After a while she could hear again. She was sitting on the floor with her wet back against the wall.

Arnold Friend was saying from the door, "That's a good girl. Put the phone back."

She kicked the phone away from her.

"No, honey. Pick it up. Put it back right."

She picked it up and put it back. The dial tone stopped.

"That's a good girl. Now come outside."

She was hollow with what had been fear, but what was now just an emptiness. All that screaming had blasted it out of her. She sat, one leg cramped under her, and deep inside her brain was something like a pinpoint of light that kept going and would not let her relax. She thought, I'm not going to see my mother again. She thought, I'm not going to sleep in my bed again. Her bright green blouse was all wet.

Arnold Friend said, in a gentle-loud voice that was like a stage voice, "The place where you came from ain't there any more, and where you had in mind to go is cancelled out. This place you are now—inside your daddy's house—is nothing but a cardboard box I can knock down any time. You know that and always did know it. You hear me?"

She thought, I have got to think. I have to know what to do.

"We'll go out to a nice field, out in the country here where it smells so nice and it's sunny," Arnold Friend said. "I'll have my arms around you so you won't need to try to get away and I'll show you what love is like, what it does. The hell with this house! It looks solid all right," he said. He ran a fingernail down the screen and the noise did not make Connie shiver, as it would have the day before. "Now put your hand on your heart, honey. Feel that? That feels solid too but we know better, be nice to me, be sweet like you can because what else is there for a girl like you but to be sweet and pretty and give in?—and get away before her people come back?"

She felt her pounding heart. Her hand seemed to enclose it. She thought for the first time in her life that it was nothing that was hers, that belonged to her, but just a pounding, living thing inside this body that wasn't really hers either.

"You don't want them to get hurt," Arnold Friend went on. "Now get up, honey. Get up all by yourself."

She stood up.

"Now turn this way. That's right. Come over here to me—Ellie, put that away, didn't I tell you? You dope. You miserable creepy dope," Arnold Friend said. His words were not angry but only part of an incantation. The incantation was kindly. "Now come out through the kitchen to me honey and let's see a smile, try it, you're a brave sweet little girl and now they're eating corn and hotdogs cooked to bursting over an outdoor fire, and they don't know one thing about you and never did and honey you're better than them because not a one of them would have done this for you."

Connie felt the linoleum under her feet; it was cool. She brushed her hair back out of her eyes. Arnold Friend let go of the post tentatively and opened his arms for her, his elbows pointing in toward each other and his wrists limp, to show that this was an embarrassed embrace and a little mocking, he didn't want to make her self-conscious.

She put out her hand against the screen. She watched herself push the door slowly open as if she were safe back somewhere in the other doorway, watching this body and this head of long hair moving out into the sunlight where Arnold Friend waited.

"My sweet little blue-eyed girl," he said, in a half-sung sigh that had nothing to do with her brown eyes but was taken up just the same by the vast sunlit reaches of the land behind him and on all sides of him, so much land that Connie had never seen before and did not recognize except to know that she was going to it.

Questions

1. How is Connie characterized in the first few pages of the story, and how is this characterization important in the events that follow?
2. What hints does Oates give us that Arnold Friend is not what he seems? Do you find him funny—or frightening? Why?
3. How does music work in the story? Does music seem to affect the way that Connie acts and thinks?
4. Oates has described Connie's choice at the end as a selfless, almost heroic, choice. Do you agree with this view? How do you interpret her actions at the end of the story?
5. What do you think happens at the end of the story? What are the possible outcomes of the situation? Which ending do you consider most likely and why?

Suggestions for Writing on Stories about Dangerous Encounters

1. Consider the setting of any one of the three stories in this section. Write an analysis of how setting influences the events of the story, and how it helps reflect or communicate the theme.
2. Each of the stories in this section involves a moment when a main character realizes that the world (or the people in it) is not quite what he or she thought it was. Pick one of the stories and pinpoint when that moment occurs and analyze what the protagonist does with that knowledge. Alternatively, find this moment in two stories, and compare them.
3. Both Hawthorne's "Young Goodman Brown" and O'Connor's "A Good Man Is Hard to Find" grapple with issues of religious faith. Citing examples from both stories, compare and analyze the two authors' views on the subject. You might discuss, specifically, the similarities and differences between the protagonists of the two stories—and of the antagonists as well.
4. Write a personal essay about a moment or experience that made you realize that something you'd taken for granted (the ethics of your parents, the wisdom of your teacher, your own morality, etc.) turned out not to be what it seemed. How did you find out? How did it change your view of that person—and of the world?

CRITICAL AND CULTURAL CONTEXTS CASEBOOK

Joyce Carol Oates's "Where Are You Going, Where Have You Been?"

Fact into Fiction

Don Moser
The Pied Piper of Tucson: He Cruised in a Golden Car, Looking for the Action

Fiction into Film

Joyce Carol Oates
"Where Are You Going, Where Have You Been?" and Smooth Talk: *Short Story into Film*

B. Ruby Rich
Good Girls, Bad Girls: Joyce Chopra's Smooth Talk

Brenda O. Daly
An Unfilmable Conclusion: Joyce Carol Oates at the Movies

"Where Are You Going?" and Media: Images

Smooth Talk *Movie Poster*

Life *Magazine Spread*

Scenes from Smooth Talk

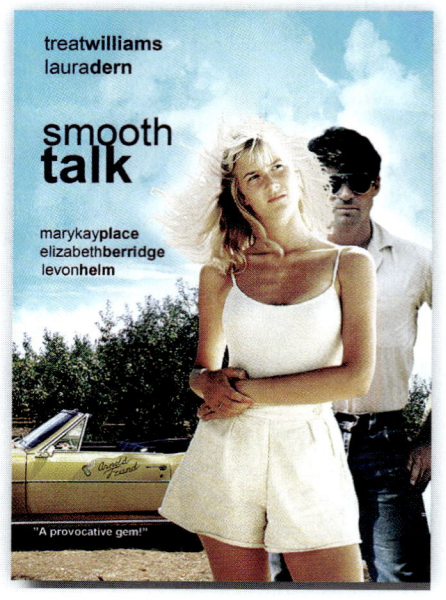

Poster for Joyce Chopra's 1986 film.

Ever since Joyce Carol Oates's short story "Where Are You Going, Where Have You Been?" first appeared in *Epoch* magazine in 1966, it has impressed readers by its powerful realism and penetrating psychological authenticity. Few of those readers have realized that Oates built her masterful and disturbing tale from a real crime story.

Oates began "Where Are You Going, Where Have You Been?" after reading "The Pied Piper of Tucson" in *Life* magazine. The article described a psychopathic man, twenty-three years old, who dressed and talked like a teenager to seduce and sometimes murder high school girls. While conscientiously mentioning a source, Oates has remarked, "I do recall deliberately not reading the full article because I didn't want to be distracted by too much detail." She also admits that she was less interested in the murder than the teenage girls from supposedly "good families" who fell under his spell.

In the following casebook we reprint the relevant sections of the original *Life* magazine article that inspired Oates's story. Then we present discussions of how Oates's fictionalized version was itself adapted into Joyce Chopra's 1986 film, *Smooth Talk*. The transformation of a nonfiction crime article into a fictional short story which in turn became a motion picture shows how the theme of adolescent sexuality and dangerous teenage rebellion has been handled—slightly differently—in three media.

FACT INTO FICTION

Don Moser

The Pied Piper of Tucson: He Cruised in a Golden Car, Looking for the Action 1966

> Hey, c'mon babe, follow me,
> I'm the Pied Piper, follow me,
> I'm the Pied Piper,
> And I'll show you where it's at.
> —Popular song, Tucson, winter 1965

At dusk in Tucson, as the stark, yellow-flared mountains begin to blur against the sky, the golden car slowly cruises Speedway. Smoothly it rolls down the long, divided avenue, past the supermarkets, the gas stations and the motels; past the twist joints, the sprawling drive-in restaurants. The car slows for an intersection, stops, then pulls away again. The exhaust mutters against the pavement as the young man driving takes the machine swiftly, expertly through the gears. A car pulls even with him; the teenage girls in the front seat laugh, wave and call his name. The young man glances toward the rearview mirror, turned always so that he can look at his own reflection, and he appraises himself.

The face is his own creation: the hair dyed a raven black, the skin darkened to a deep tan with pancake make-up, the lips whitened, the whole effect heightened by a mole he has painted on one cheek. But the deep-set blue eyes are all his own. Beautiful eyes, the girls say.

Approaching the Hi-Ho, the teenagers' nightclub, he backs off on the accelerator, then slowly cruises on past Johnie's Drive-in. There the cars are beginning to orbit and accumulate in the parking lot—neat sharp cars with deep throated mufflers and Maltese-cross decals on the windows. But it's early yet. Not much going on. The driver shifts up again through the gears, and the golden car slides away along the glitter and gimcrack of Speedway. Smitty keeps looking for the action.

Whether the juries in the two trials decide that Charles Howard Schmid Jr. did or did not brutally murder Alleen Rowe, Gretchen Fritz, and Wendy Fritz has from the beginning seemed of almost secondary importance to the people of Tucson. They are not indifferent. But what disturbs them far beyond the question of Smitty's guilt or innocence are the revelations about Tucson itself that have followed on the disclosure of the crimes. Starting with the bizarre circumstances of the killings and on through the ugly fragments of the plot—which in turn hint at other murders as yet undiscovered, at teenage sex, blackmail, even connections with the *Cosa Nostra*—they have had to view their city in a

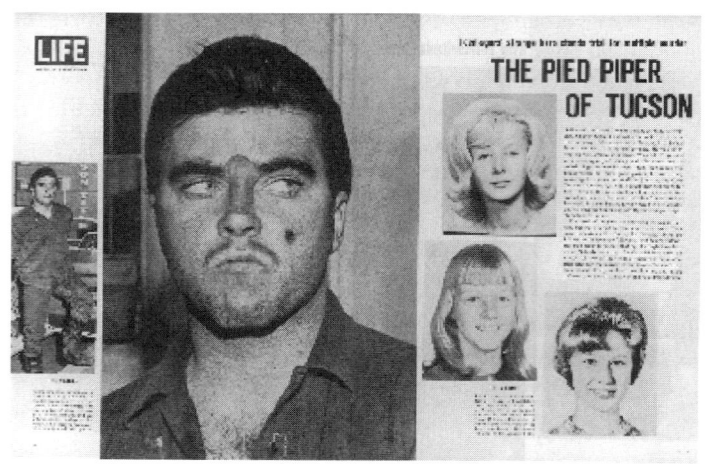

The opening pages of *Life* magazine's article on the murderer Charles Schmid Jr. and his three victims.

new and unpleasant light. The fact is that Charles Schmid—who cannot be dismissed as a freak, an aberrant of no consequence—had for years functioned successfully as a member, even a leader of the yeastiest stratum of Tucson's teenage society.

As a high school student Smitty had been, as classmates remember, an outsider—but not that far outside. He was small but he was a fine athlete, and in his last year—1960—he was a state gymnastics champion. His grades were poor, but he was in no trouble to speak of until his senior year, when he was suspended for stealing tools from a welding class.

But Smitty never really left the school. After his suspension he hung around waiting to pick up kids in a succession of sharp cars which he drove fast and well. He haunted all the teenage hangouts along Speedway, including the bowling alleys and the public swimming pool—and he put on spectacular diving exhibitions for girls far younger than he.

At the time of his arrest last November, Charles Schmid was twenty-three years old. He wore face make-up and dyed his hair. He habitually stuffed three or four inches of old rags and tin cans into the bottoms of his high-topped boots to make himself taller than his five-foot-three and stumbled about so awkwardly while walking that some people thought he had wooden feet. He pursed his lips and let his eyelids droop in order to emulate his idol, Elvis Presley. He bragged to girls he knew a hundred ways to make love, that he ran dope, that he was a Hell's Angel. He talked about being a rough customer in a fight (he was, though he was rarely in one), and he always carried in his pocket tiny bottles of salt and pepper, which he said he used to blind his opponents. He liked to use highfalutin language and had a favorite saying, "I can manifest my neurotical emotions, emancipate an epicureal instinct, and elaborate on my heterosexual tendencies."

He occasionally shocked even those who thought they knew him well. A friend says he once saw Smitty tie a string to a tail of his pet cat, swing it around his head and beat it bloody against a wall. Then he turned calmly and asked, "You feel compassion—why?"

Yet even while Smitty tried to create an exalted, heroic image of himself, he had worked on a pitiable one. "He thrived on feeling sorry for himself," recalls a friend, "and making others feel sorry for him." At various times Smitty told intimates that he had leukemia and didn't have long to live. He claimed that he was adopted, that his real name was Angel Rodriguez, that his father was a "bean" (local slang for Mexican, an inferior race in Smitty's view), and that his mother was a famous lawyer who would have nothing to do with him.

• • •

He had a nice car. He had plenty of money from his parents, who ran a nursing home, and he was always glad to spend it on anyone who'd listen to him. He had a pad of his own where he threw parties and he had impeccable manners. He was always willing to help a friend and he would send flowers to girls who were ill. He was older and more mature than most of his friends. He knew where the action was, and if he wore make-up—well, at least he was *different*.

Some of the older kids—those who worked, who had something else to do—thought Smitty was a creep. But to the youngsters—to the bored and the lonely, to the dropout and the delinquent, to the young girls with beehive hairdos and tight pants they didn't quite fill out, and to the boys with acne and no jobs—to these people, Smitty was a kind of folk hero. Nutty maybe, but at least more dramatic, more theatrical, more *interesting* than anyone else in their lives: a semi-ludicrous, sexy-eyed pied-piper who, stumbling along in his rag-stuffed boots, led them up and down Speedway.

On the evening of May 31, 1964, Alleen Rowe prepared to go to bed early. She had to be in class by six A.M. and she had an examination the next day. Alleen was a pretty girl of fifteen, a better-than-average student who talked about going to college and becoming an oceanographer. She was also a sensitive child—given to reading romantic novels and taking long walks in the desert at night. Recently she had been going through a period of adolescent melancholia, often talking with her mother, a nurse, about death. She would, she hoped, be some day reincarnated as a cat.

On this evening, dressed in a black bathing suit and thongs, her usual costume around the house, she had watched the Beatles on TV and had tried to teach her mother to dance the Frug. Then she took her bath, washed her hair, and came out to kiss her mother good night. Norma Rowe, an attractive, womanly divorcée, was somehow moved by the girl's clean fragrance and said, "You smell so good—are you wearing perfume?"

"No, Mom," the girl answered, laughing, "it's just me."

A little later Mrs. Rowe looked in on her daughter, found her apparently sleeping peacefully, and then left for her job as a night nurse in a Tucson hospital. She had no premonition of danger, but she had lately been concerned about Alleen's friendship with a neighbor girl named Mary French.

Mary and Alleen had been spending a good deal of time together, smoking and giggling and talking girl talk in the Rowe backyard. Norma Rowe did not approve. She particularly did not approve of Mary French's friends, a tall, gangling boy of nineteen named John Saunders and another named Charles Schmid. She had seen Smitty racing up and down the street in his car and once, when he came to call on Alleen and found her not at home, he had looked at Norma so menacingly with his "pinpoint eyes" that she had been frightened.

Her daughter, on the other hand, seemed to have mixed feelings about Smitty. "He's creepy," she once told her mother, "he just makes me crawl. But he can be nice when he wants to."

At any rate, later that night—according to Mary French's sworn testimony—three friends arrived at Alleen Rowe's house: Smitty, Mary French, and Saunders. Smitty had frequently talked with Mary French about killing the Rowe girl by hitting her over the head with a rock. Mary French tapped on Alleen's window and asked her to come out and drink beer with them. Wearing a shift over her bathing suit, she came willingly enough.

Schmid's two accomplices were strange and pitiable creatures. Each of them was afraid of Smitty, yet each was drawn to him. As a baby, John Saunders had been so afflicted with allergies that scabs encrusted his entire body. To keep him from scratching himself his parents had tied his hands and feet to the crib each night, and when eventually he was cured he was so conditioned that he could not go to sleep without being bound hand and foot.

Later, a scrawny boy with poor eyesight ("Just a skinny little body with a big head on it"), he was taunted and bullied by larger children; in turn he bullied those who were smaller. He also suffered badly from asthma and he had few friends. In high school he was a poor student and constantly in minor trouble.

Mary French, nineteen, was—to put it straight—a frump. Her face, which might have been pretty, seemed somehow lumpy, her body shapeless. She was not dull but she was always a poor student, and she finally had simply stopped going to high school. She was, a friend remembers, "fantastically in love with Smitty. She just sat home and waited while he went out with other girls."

Now, with Smitty at the wheel, the four teen-agers headed for the desert, which begins out Golf Links Road. It is spooky country, dry and empty, the yellow sand clotted with cholla and mesquite and stunted, strangely green palo verde trees, and the great humanoid saguaro that hulk against the sky. Out there at night you can hear the yip and ki-yi of coyotes, the piercing screams of wild creatures—cats, perhaps.

According to Mary French, they got out of the car and walked down into a wash, where they sat on the sand and talked for a while, the four of them. Schmid and Mary then started back to the car. Before they got there, they heard a cry and Schmid turned back toward the wash. Mary went on to the car and sat in it alone. After forty-five minutes, Saunders appeared and said Smitty wanted her to come back down. She refused, and Saunders went away. Five or ten minutes later, Smitty showed up. "He got into the car," says Mary, "and he said, 'We killed her. I love you very much.' He kissed me. He was breathing real hard and seemed excited." Then Schmid got a shovel from the trunk of the car and they returned to the wash. "She was lying on her back and there was blood on her face and head," Mary French testified. Then the three of them dug a shallow grave and put the body in it and covered it up. Afterwards, they wiped Schmid's car clean of Alleen's fingerprints.

More than a year passed. Norma Rowe had reported her daughter missing and the police searched for her—after a fashion. At Mrs. Rowe's insistence they picked up Schmid, but they had no reason to hold him. The police, in fact, assumed that Alleen was just one more of Tucson's runaways.

Norma Rowe, however, had become convinced that Alleen had been killed by Schmid, although she left her kitchen light on every night in case Alleen did come home. She badgered the police and she badgered the sheriff until the authorities began to dismiss her as a crank. She began to imagine a high-level conspiracy against her. She wrote the state attorney general, the FBI, the U.S. Department of Health, Education and Welfare. She even contacted a New Jersey mystic, who said she could see Alleen's body out in the desert under a big tree.

Ultimately Norma Rowe started her own investigation, questioning Alleen's friends, poking around, dictating her findings to a tape recorder; she even tailed Smitty at night, following him in her car, scared stiff that he might spot her.

Schmid, during this time, acquired a little house of his own. There he held frequent parties, where people sat around amid his stacks of *Playboy* magazines, playing Elvis Presley records and drinking beer.

He read Jules Feiffer's novel, *Harry, the Rat with Women*, and said that his ambition was to be like Harry and have a girl commit suicide over him. Once, according to a friend, he went to see a minister, who gave him a Bible and told him to read the first three chapters of John. Instead Schmid tore the pages out and burned them in the street. "Religion is a farce," he announced. He started an upholstery business with some friends, called himself "founder and president," but then failed to put up the money he promised and the venture was short-lived.

He decided he liked blondes best, and took to dyeing the hair of various teenage girls he went around with. He went out and bought two imitation diamonds for about $13 apiece and then engaged himself, on the same day, both to Mary French and to a fifteen-year-old girl named Kathy Morath. His plan, he confided to a friend, was to put each of the girls to work and have them deposit their salaries in a bank account held jointly with him. Mary French did indeed go to work in the convalescent home Smitty's parents operated. When their bank account was fat enough, Smitty withdrew the money and bought a tape recorder.

By this time Smitty also had a girl from a higher social stratum than he usually was involved with. She was Gretchen Fritz, daughter of a prominent Tucson heart surgeon. Gretchen was a pretty, thin, nervous girl of seventeen with a knack for trouble. A teacher described her as "erratic, subversive, a psychopathic liar."

At the horsy private school she attended for a time she was a misfit. She not only didn't care about horses, but she shocked her classmates by telling them they were foolish for going out with boys without getting paid for it. Once she even committed the unpardonable social sin of turning up at a formal dance party accompanied by boys wearing what was described as beatnik dress. She cut classes, she was suspected of stealing and when, in the summer before her senior year, she got into trouble with juvenile authorities for her role in an attempted theft at a liquor store, the headmaster suggested she not return and then recommended she get psychiatric treatment.

Charles Schmid saw Gretchen for the first time at a public swimming pool in the summer of 1964. He met her by the simple expedient of following her home, knocking on the door and, when she answered, saying, "Don't I know you?" They talked for an hour. Thus began a fierce and stormy relationship. A good deal of what authorities know of the development of this relationship comes from the statements of a spindly scarecrow of a young man who wears pipestem trousers and Beatle boots: Richard Bruns. At the time Smitty was becoming involved with Gretchen, Bruns was eighteen years old. He had served two terms in the reformatory at Fort Grant. He had been in and out of trouble all his life, had never fit in anywhere. Yet, although he never went beyond the tenth grade in school and his credibility on many counts is suspect, he is clearly intelligent and even sensitive. He was, for a time, Smitty's closest friend and confidant, and he is today one of the mainstays of the state's case against Smitty. His story:

"He and Gretchen were always fighting," says Bruns. "She didn't want him to drink or go out with the guys or go out with other girls. She wanted him to stay home, call her on the phone, be punctual. First she would get suspicious of him, then he'd get suspicious of her. They were made for each other."

Their mutual jealousy led to sharp and continual arguments. Once she infuriated him by throwing a bottle of shoe polish on his car. Another time she was driving past Smitty's house and saw him there with some other girls. She jumped out of her car and began screaming. Smitty took off into the house, out the back, and climbed a tree in his backyard.

His feelings for her were an odd mixture of hate and adoration. He said he was madly in love with her, but he called her a whore. She would let Smitty in her bedroom window at night. Yet he wrote an anonymous letter to the Tucson Health Department accusing her of having venereal disease and spreading it about town. But Smitty also went to enormous lengths to impress Gretchen, once shooting holes through the windows of his car and telling her that thugs, from whom he was protecting her, had fired at him. So Bruns described the relationship.

On the evening of August 16, 1965, Gretchen Fritz left the house with her little sister Wendy, a friendly, lively thirteen-year-old, to go to a drive-in movie. Neither girl ever came home again. Gretchen's father, like Alleen Rowe's mother, felt sure that Charles Schmid had something to do with his daughters' disappearance, and eventually he hired Bill Heilig, a private detective, to handle the case. One of Heilig's men soon found Gretchen's red compact car parked behind a motel, but the police continued to assume that the girls had joined the ranks of Tucson's runaways.

About a week after Gretchen disappeared, Bruns was at Smitty's home. "We were sitting in the living room," Bruns recalls. "He was sitting on the sofa and I was in the chair by the window and we got on the subject of Gretchen. He said, 'You know I killed her?' I said I didn't, and he said, 'You know where?' I said no. He said, 'I did it here in the living room. First I killed Gretchen, then Wendy was still going *"huh, huh, huh,"* so I . . . [here Bruns showed how Smitty made a garroting gesture.] Then I took the bodies and put them in the trunk of the car. I put the bodies in the most obvious place I could think of because I just didn't care any more. Then I ditched the car and wiped it clean.'"

Bruns was not particularly upset by Smitty's story. Months before, Smitty had told him of the murder of Alleen Rowe, and nothing had come of that. So he was not certain Smitty was telling the truth about the Fritz girls. Besides, Bruns detested Gretchen himself. But what happened next, still according to Bruns's story, did shake him up.

One night not long after, a couple of tough-looking characters, wearing sharp suits and smoking cigars, came by with Smitty and picked up Bruns. Smitty said they were Mafia, and that someone had hired them to look for Gretchen. Smitty and Bruns were taken to an apartment where several men were present whom Smitty later claimed to have recognized as local *Cosa Nostra* figures.

They wanted to know what had happened to the girls. They made no threats, but the message, Bruns remembers, came across loud and clear. These were no street-corner punks: these were the real boys. In spite of the intimidating company, Schmid lost none of his insouciance. He said he didn't know where Gretchen was, but if she turned up hurt he wanted these men to help him get whoever was responsible. He added that he thought she might have gone to California.

By the time Smitty and Bruns got back to Smitty's house, they were both a little shaky. Later that night, says Bruns, Smitty did the most unlikely thing imaginable: he called the FBI. First he tried the Tucson office and couldn't raise anyone. Then he called Phoenix and couldn't get an agent there either. Finally he put in a person-to-person call to J. Edgar Hoover in Washington. He didn't get Hoover, of course, but he got someone and told him that the Mafia was harassing him over the disappearance of a girl. The FBI promised to have someone in touch with him soon.

Bruns was scared and said so. It occurred to him now that if Smitty really had killed the Fritz girls and left their bodies in an obvious place, they were in very bad trouble indeed—with the Mafia on one hand and the FBI on the other. "Let's go bury them," Bruns said.

"Smitty stole the keys to his old man's station wagon," says Bruns, "and then we got a flat shovel—the only one we could find. We went to Johnie's and got a hamburger, and then we drove out to the old drinking spot [in the desert]—that's what Smitty meant when he said the most obvious place. It's where we used to drink beer and make out with girls.

"So we parked the car and got the shovel and walked down there, and we couldn't find anything. Then Smitty said, 'Wait, I smell something.' We went in opposite directions looking, and then I heard Smitty say, 'Come here.' I found him kneeling over Gretchen. There was a white rag tied around her legs. Her blouse was pulled up and she was wearing a white bra and Capris.

"Then he said, 'Wendy's up this way.' I sat there for a minute. Then I followed Smitty to where Wendy was. He'd had the decency to cover her—except for one leg, which was sticking up out of the ground.

"We tried to dig with the flat shovel. We each took turns. He'd dig for a while and then I'd dig for a while, but the ground was hard and we couldn't get anywhere with that flat shovel. We dug for twenty minutes and finally Smitty said we'd better do something because it's going to get light. So he grabbed the rag that was around Gretchen's legs and dragged her down in the wash. It made a noise like dragging a hollow shell. It stunk like hell. Then Smitty said wipe off her shoes, there might be fingerprints, so I wiped them off with my handkerchief and threw it away.

"We went back to Wendy. Her leg was sticking up with a shoe on it. He said take off her tennis shoe and throw it over there. I did, I threw it. Then he said, 'Now you're in this as deep as I am.'" By then, the sisters had been missing for about two weeks.

Early next morning Smitty did see the FBI. Nevertheless—here Bruns's story grows even wilder—that same day Smitty left for California, accompanied by a couple of Mafia types, to look for Gretchen Fritz. While there, he was picked up by the San Diego police on a complaint that he was impersonating an FBI officer. He was detained briefly, released and then returned to Tucson.

But now, it seemed to Richard Bruns, Smitty began acting very strangely. He startled Bruns by saying, "I've killed—not three times, but four. Now it's your turn, Richie." He went berserk in his little house, smashing his fist through a wall, slamming doors, then rushing out into the backyard in nothing but his undershorts, when he ran through the night screaming, "God is going to punish me!" He also decided, suddenly, to get married—to a fifteen-year-old girl who was a stranger to most of his friends.

• • •

Bruns went to Ohio to stay with his grandmother and to try to get a job. It was hopeless. He couldn't sleep at night, and if he did doze off he had his old nightmare again.

One night he blurted out the whole story to his grandmother in their kitchen. She thought he had had too many beers and didn't believe him. "I hear beer does strange things to a person," she said comfortingly. At her words Bruns exploded, knocked over a chair and shouted, "The one time in my life when I need advice what do I get?" A few minutes later he was on the phone to the Tucson police.

Things happened swiftly. At Bruns's frantic insistence, the police picked up Kathy Morath and put her in protective custody. They went into the desert and discovered—precisely as Bruns had described them—the grisly, skeletal remains of Gretchen and Wendy Fritz. They started the machinery that resulted in the arrest a week later of John Saunders and Mary French. They found Charles Schmid working in the yard of his little house, his face layered with make-up, his nose covered by a patch of adhesive plaster which he had worn for five months, boasting that his nose was broken in a fight, and his boots packed full of old rags and tin cans. He put up no resistance.

John Saunders and Mary French confessed immediately to their roles in the slaying of Alleen Rowe and were quickly sentenced, Mary French to four to five years, Saunders to life. When Smitty goes on trial for this crime, on March 15, they will be principal witnesses against him.

Meanwhile Richie Bruns, the perpetual misfit, waits apprehensively for the end of the Fritz trial, desperately afraid that Schmid will go free. "If he does," Bruns says glumly, "I'll be the first one he'll kill."

As for Charles Schmid, he has adjusted well to his period of waiting. He is polite and agreeable with all, though at the preliminary hearings he glared menacingly at Richie Bruns. Dressed tastefully, tie neatly knotted, hair carefully combed, his face scrubbed clean of make-up, he is a short, compact, darkly handsome young man with a wide, engaging smile and those deepset eyes.

Life, March 4, 1966

FICTION INTO FILM

Joyce Carol Oates

"Where Are You Going, Where Have You Been?" and *Smooth Talk*: Short Story into Film 1986

Some years ago in the American Southwest there surfaced a tabloid psychopath known as "The Pied Piper of Tucson." I have forgotten his name, but his specialty was the seduction and occasional murder of teen-aged girls. He may or may not have had actual accomplices, but his bizarre activities were known among a circle of teenagers in the Tucson area; for some reason they kept his secret, deliberately did not inform parents or police. It was this fact, not the fact of the mass murderer himself, that struck me at the time. And this was a pre-Manson time, early or mid-1960s.

The Pied Piper mimicked teenagers in their talk, dress, and behavior, but he was not a teenager—he was a man in his early thirties.[1] Rather short, he stuffed rags in his leather boots to give himself height. (And sometimes walked unsteadily as a consequence: did none among his admiring constituency notice?) He charmed his victims as charismatic psychopaths have always charmed their victims, to the bewilderment of others who fancy themselves free of all lunatic attractions. The Pied Piper of Tucson: a trashy dream, a tabloid archetype, sheer artifice, comedy, cartoon—surrounded, however improbably, and finally tragically, by real people. You think that, if you look twice, he won't be there. But there he is.

---

[1] The "Pied Piper" Charles Schmid was actually twenty-three when he was arrested, but Oates wrote her character Arnold Friend "much older—thirty, maybe more" (par. 79).

Laura Dern as Connie and Treat Williams as Arnold Friend in Joyce Chopra's *Smooth Talk.*

    I don't remember any longer where I first read about this Pied Piper—very likely in *Life* magazine. I do recall deliberately not reading the full article because I didn't want to be distracted by too much detail. It was not after all the mass murderer himself who intrigued me, but the disturbing fact that a number of teenagers—from "good" families—aided and abetted his crimes. This is the sort of thing authorities and responsible citizens invariably call "inexplicable" because they can't find explanations for it. *They* would not have fallen under this maniac's spell, after all.

    An early draft of my short story "Where Are You Going, Where Have You Been?"—from which the film *Smooth Talk* was adapted by Joyce Chopra and Tom Cole—had the rather too explicit title "Death and the Maiden." It was cast in a mode of fiction to which I am still partial—indeed, every third or fourth story of mine is probably in this mode—"realistic allegory," it might be called. It is Hawthornean, romantic, shading into parable. Like the medieval German engraving from which my title was taken, the story was minutely detailed yet clearly an allegory of the fatal attractions of death (or the devil). An innocent young girl is seduced by way of her own vanity; she mistakes death for erotic romance of a particularly American/trashy sort.

    In subsequent drafts the story changed its tone, its focus, its language, its title. It became "Where Are You Going, Where Have You Been?" Written at a time when the author was intrigued by the music of Bob Dylan, particularly the hauntingly elegiac song "It's All Over Now, Baby Blue," it was dedicated to Bob Dylan. The charismatic mass murderer drops into the background and his innocent victim, a fifteen-year-old, moves into the foreground. She becomes the true protagonist of the tale, courting and being courted by her fate, a self-styled 1950s pop figure, alternately absurd and winning.

    There is no suggestion in the published story that "Arnold Friend" has seduced and murdered other young girls, or even that he necessarily intends to murder Connie. Is his interest "merely" sexual? (Nor is there anything about the complicity of other teenagers. I saved that yet more provocative note for a current story, "Testimony.") Connie is shallow, vain, silly, hopeful, doomed—but capable nonetheless of an unexpected gesture of heroism at the story's end. Her smooth-talking seducer, who cannot lie, promises her that her family will be unharmed if she gives herself to him; and so she does. The story ends abruptly at the point of her "crossing over." We don't know the nature of her sacrifice, only that she is generous enough to make it.

In adapting a narrative so spare and thematically foreshortened as "Where Are You Going, Where Have You Been?" film director Joyce Chopra and screenwriter Tom Cole were required to do a good deal of filling in, expanding, inventing. Connie's story becomes lavishly, and lovingly, textured; she is not an allegorical figure so much as a "typical" teen-aged girl (if Laura Dern, spectacularly good-looking, can be so defined).

Joyce Chopra, who has done documentary films on contemporary teenage culture and, yet more authoritatively, has an adolescent daughter of her own, creates in *Smooth Talk* a vivid and absolutely believable world for Connie to inhabit. Or worlds: as in the original story there is Connie-at-home, and there is Connie-with-her-friends. Two fifteen-year-old girls, two finely honed styles, two voices, sometimes but not often overlapping. It is one of the marvelous visual features of the film that we *see* Connie and her friends transform themselves, once they are safely free of parental observation. The girls claim their true identities in the neighborhood shopping mall. What freedom, what joy!

Smooth Talk is, in a way, as much Connie's mother's story as it is Connie's; its center of gravity, its emotional nexus, is frequently with the mother—warmly and convincingly played by Mary Kay Place. (Though the mother's sexual jealousy of her daughter is slighted in the film.) Connie's ambiguous relationship with her affable, somewhat mysterious father (well played by Levon Helm) is an excellent touch: I had thought, subsequent to the story's publication, that I should have built up the father, suggesting, as subtly as I could, an attraction there paralleling the attraction Connie feels for her seducer, Arnold Friend. And Arnold Friend himself—"A. Friend" as he says—is played with appropriately overdone sexual swagger by Treat Williams, who is perfect for the part; and just the right age. We see that Arnold Friend isn't a teenager even as Connie, mesmerized by his presumed charm, does not seem to *see* him at all. What is so difficult to accomplish in prose—nudging the reader to look over the protagonist's shoulder, so to speak—is accomplished with enviable ease in film.

Treat Williams as Arnold Friend is supreme in his very awfulness, as, surely, the original Pied Piper of Tucson must have been. (Though no one involved in the film knew about the original source.) Mr. Williams flawlessly impersonates Arnold Friend as Arnold Friend impersonates—is it James Dean? James Dean regarding himself in mirrors, doing James Dean impersonations? That Connie's fate is so trashy is in fact her fate.

What is outstanding in Joyce Chopra's *Smooth Talk* is its visual freshness, its sense of motion and life; the attentive intelligence the director has brought to the semi-secret world of the American adolescent—shopping mall flirtations, drive-in restaurant romances, highway hitchhiking, the fascination of rock music played very, very loud. (James Taylor's music for the film is wonderfully appropriate. We hear it as Connie hears it; it is the music of her spiritual being.) Also outstanding, as I have indicated, and numerous critics have noted, are the acting performances. Laura Dern is so dazzlingly right as "my" Connie that I may come to think I modeled the fictitious girl on her, in the way that writers frequently delude themselves about motions of causality.

My difficulties with *Smooth Talk* have primarily to do with my chronic hesitation—about seeing/hearing work of mine abstracted from its contexture of language. All writers know that Language is their subject; quirky word choices, patterns of rhythm, enigmatic pauses, punctuation marks. Where the quick scanner sees "quick" writing, the writer conceals nine tenths of the iceberg. Of course we all have "real" subjects, and we will fight to the death to defend those subjects, but beneath the tale-telling it is the tale-telling that grips us so very fiercely. The writer works in a single dimension, the director works in three. I assume they are professionals to their fingertips; authorities in their medium as I am an authority (if I am) in mine. I would fiercely defend the placement of a semicolon in one of my novels but I would probably have deferred in the end to Joyce Chopra's decision to reverse the story's conclusion, turn it upside down, in a sense, so that the film ends not with death, not with a sleepwalker's crossing over to her fate, but upon a scene of reconciliation, rejuvenation.

A girl's loss of virginity, bittersweet but not necessarily tragic. Not today. A girl's coming-of-age that involves her succumbing to, but then rejecting, the "trashy dreams" of her pop teenage culture. "Where Are You Going, Where Have You Been?" defines itself as allegorical in its conclusion: Death and Death's chariot (a funky souped-up convertible) have come for the Maiden. Awakening is, in the story's final lines, moving out into the sunlight where Arnold Friend waits:

> "My sweet little blue-eyed girl," he said, in a half-sung sigh that had nothing to do with her [Connie's] brown eyes but was taken up just the same by the vast sunlit reaches of the land behind him and on all sides of him, so much land that Connie had never seen before and did not recognize except to know that she was going to it.

—a conclusion impossible to transfigure into film.

New York Times, March 23, 1986

B. Ruby Rich

Good Girls, Bad Girls: Joyce Chopra's *Smooth Talk* 1986

There is a wonderful movie called *Smooth Talk*. It ends when its teenage protagonist, Connie, has a fight with her mom and stays home alone. There is a horrible movie called *Smooth Talk*. It starts when a psychopath in a gold convertible comes looking for Connie, alone in an empty house.

If you want to see one of this season's finest films, walk out of the 68th Street Playhouse when Connie's family drives off to their barbecue. If you want to see one of the most pernicious pieces of moralism to emerge from a woman director in the 1980s, then stick around.

Smooth Talk is Joyce Chopra's critically acclaimed new movie, but, its boosters to the contrary, this film offers neither the screen's most delectable seduction nor the definitive female coming-of-age portrait. No, what Chopra offers, with the help of the predictably nasty Joyce Carol Oates story that is her springboard, is a punishment to fit the crime of sexual desire. *Smooth Talk* may be the first genuinely postfeminist movie, unless it's just a belated prefeminist one.

The first half of *Smooth Talk* is indeed an engaging and finely observant study of adolescent female sexuality and narcissism, relations between a family and its pubescent

Laura Dern as Connie.

girl-child, and, most astonishingly, the combination of fear and desire (what used to be called "thrill") of virginal sex. It provides the grand drama of going, not All the Way, but at least a ways down the road. We see Connie rehearsing come-on lines in front of her mirror, cruising the mall boys with her girlfriends only to dissolve into giggles if any come close, and infuriating her mom and stay-at-home sister with the omni-presence of her newfound sexuality. Her make-out scenes, in the parked cars of a succession of teenage boys, are so hot they'll define the genre.

But watch out. This movie is made by a moralist. For pleasure like that, Connie—and the audience—must pay.

The second half of *Smooth Talk* is a nightmare. The film drags two red herrings across our path, scary moments in a deserted parking garage and a dark road abuzz with overamplified crickets and a car of drunken boys. But these are mere plot embroidery. It is broad daylight when Connie's family heads out with the charcoal and Arnold Friend pulls up in his golden chariot, intent on having his way with Connie, and mesmerizes her into rape by verbal coercion. In this half of the movie, Chopra uses the whole bag of cinematic tricks. Every time Connie is on screen, she's shot in close-up, tightly, claustrophobically, with no space around her, pinned into that tiny unmovable frame. Every time Arnold is on screen, he's in middle shot, framed against an ample landscape, lots of space around him, master of the territory. The music surges on the soundtrack. It isn't long before the high-spirited Connie is a quivering puddle on the hallway floor.

What has happened here? *Smooth Talk* softens up its audience with lust and flirtation, then slices through its gut with a knife of horror. It turns into a familiar product, the stock in trade of the horror genre: woman alone, trapped in empty house, terrorized, raped or killed or left insane. In Chopra's hands, the knife has a twist: Connie is punished for sex with sex. Connie is singled out for rape because she's guilty of being pretty and flirtatious.

She was asking for it, wasn't she? Just looking for it, right? We're back in the familiar terrain of Blame the Victim Land.

Smooth Talk is an insidious movie, and a curious one. Thirteen years ago, Joyce Chopra made a name for herself as a feminist documentary filmmaker with *Joyce at 34*, a self-portrait of her pregnancy. Now, she's the 48-year-old mother of a teenage daughter. And she's made a movie with a message for teenage daughters everywhere: keep a lid on your sexuality, don't you dare express it, don't you ever act out those "trashy daydreams" (as Connie's mother puts it), or you'll get it. Like a grownup bogeyman, Arnold Friend will come and get you. *Smooth Talk* is a movie that means to teach teenage girls the perils of sex. Worst of all, the film carries out its mission with a massively mixed message. Connie is terrorized with words, reduced to dumb paralysis, abducted from her home, returned to her doorstep after an offscreen rape . . . and this is praised by some critics as a masterful cinematic "seduction." Joyce Chopra is praised as a major new talent. But a talent in the service of what? The phenomenon of a feminist filmmaker from the 1970s emerging in the middle of this decade to put young women in their place does not, for me, go down easy.

Even more disturbing than the critical raves and festival accolades was the reaction of 68th Street Playhouse's posh audience: overwhelmingly middle-aged, they laughed all through the first half and then kept on laughing right through Connie's disintegration. I suspect the lure of *Smooth Talk* is a simple one: the spectacle of lust delivered into the audience, and then the punishment of its female embodiment, again for audience pleasure. If people tell you they like this film, be skeptical. Ask who *they* were in high school: the desexualized Good Girl? the nerd that so many Connies rejected? *Smooth Talk* provides vicarious retribution for a wide audience. Meanwhile, if you know any teenage girls, keep them away from this movie just on the off chance that the antiporn crowd might be right and that movies really can affect behavior. *Smooth Talk* is an old-fashioned mother's dream: fleeing the consequences of her sexuality, Connie returns to the bosom of her family, to the literalization of mamma's arms. That's what Joyce Chopra might call a happy ending.

Village Voice, April 15, 1986

Brenda O. Daly

An Unfilmable Conclusion: Joyce Carol Oates at the Movies   1989

In 1966, three years before the shocking stories of Charles Manson and his "family" emerged, *Life* magazine carried the story of a murderer named Charles Schmid. With the help of teenage "followers," Schmid murdered three young women and buried them in the desert outside Tucson. "The Pied Piper of Tucson" was later exposed by a sidekick, tried, and sent to prison. Locking Schmid up did not, of course, make America a less violent or safer place to live. It was to explore this "senseless" violence in terms of its cultural implications that Joyce Carol Oates wrote her well-known short story "Where Are You Going, Where Have You Been?," first published in the fall of 1966. In the story Charles Schmid, renamed "Arnold Friend," retains his too-large cowboy boots and pancake make-up, as well as his "Golden Car" and his habit of using "highfalutin' language." But Oates transforms him into a friend/fiend—a harbinger of "Death"—whose significance has since been widely discussed in introductory literature classes in colleges and universities.

Twenty years after its first appearance, this widely anthologized story was made into a movie called *Smooth Talk*, released in 1986. Directed by Joyce Chopra, it stars Laura Dern as Connie, Treat Williams as Arnold Friend, and Mary Kay Place as Connie's mother. This intense interest in senseless violence—evident in the translations from fact, into fiction and film—raises a number of questions: Why, for example, has yet another woman artist resurrected a tale of violence against women? Whose story is being told, and what are its larger cultural implications? Any response to these questions requires analysis of the relationship among many different texts: popular music, magazines, and books (some of which Schmid drew upon to create his persona), as well as medieval art, nineteenth-century American literature, and critical essays on Yeats.

One problem that Oates and Chopra emphasize—the psychosocial implications of space—is not a new preoccupation of women artists. For example, Sandra Gilbert and Susan Gubar argue in *The Madwoman in the Attic* that "anxieties about space seem to dominate the literature of the nineteenth century by women and their twentieth-century descendents." For women writers this anxiety about space is not simply metaphysical, but social, according to Gilbert and Gubar. The fact that most agoraphobics are women supports this argument, as does the fact that male readers tend to resist the gothic whose claustrophobic spaces have long identified this genre as for women readers. The gothic spaces of works such as *Jane Eyre* and "The Yellow Wallpaper" further illustrate Gilbert and Gubar's point, and in "Where Are You Going, Where Have You Been?" it is easy to recognize Oates as a twentieth-century descendent. Oates is, in fact, frequently described as a "gothic" writer although this term, sometimes used pejoratively, is too limited. Spatial inequalities are apparent even in Oates's title, "Where Are You Going, Where Have You Been?" Such questions are often put to teenagers by parents, many of whom grant greater freedom of movement to boys. Probably one reason that parents continue to constrain their daughters is that it is still possible for a girl—out late at night and in public places—to be put on trial and found guilty of her own rape/murder. At one level, then, both Oates and Chopra are examining a woman's lack of freedom, and her vulnerability to male violence, in our culture. Indeed, "spatial limitations are of crucial concern" in Oates's story, as Christina Marsden Gillis has pointed out, and the "invasion of personal, interior space" occurs at many levels. I see similar concern with spatial limitations and invasions of personal space in Chopra's film.

Both women use space to signify Connie's lack of sexual and social equality, but what is lost in the translation from fiction to film can only be understood by moving beyond the realistic plane of interpretation to allegory. In a review of Chopra's film, Oates explains that her allegorical intentions were perhaps "too explicit" in an earlier title, "Death and the Maiden."[2] Despite the loss of this title, borrowed from a fifteenth-century German engraving by Albrecht Dürer, critics have noted Friend's Satanic appearance and Connie's role as "Everyman." In addition, as I will illustrate, Oates's allusions to Dickinson, especially "Because I could not stop for Death," suggest that the story may be read as allegory. Finally, it is perhaps in the lyrics of Bob Dylan's "It's All Over Now, Baby Blue"—and Oates has dedicated the story to Dylan—that the historical and political implications of "Where Are You Going, Where Have You Been?" can best be understood. At this level of meaning the question of the title, addressed to readers, asks us to consider how an act of violence—apparently without motive—can teach us something about our culture. Oates's tale of rape may also be compared to Yeats's "Leda and the Swan," an allegory of power and knowledge that had preoccupied Oates in the 1960s in both her fiction—

---

[2] Oates's review is included earlier in this casebook.

A Garden of Earthly Delights (1966)—and in critical essays on Yeats. Although these allegorical allusions are, understandably, lost in the film, Oates nevertheless credits Chopra with "an accomplished and sophisticated film" and, noting the change in her story's ending, describes her own ambiguous conclusion as "unfilmable." The loss is significant since, at this moment in Oates's story, Connie sees beyond Arnold Friend's limited, though powerful, vision.

Yet *Smooth Talk* certainly deserves praise, particularly for its fidelity to Oates's spatial analogies. Nevertheless, one film critic has complained that Oates's "predictably nasty" story has, in Chopra's medium, become a formulaic cautionary tale for girls. Largely through its spatial vocabulary, B. Ruby Rich argues in "Good Girls, Bad Girls," the film warns girls to stay home and "keep a lid on their sexuality."[3] Chopra uses "the whole bag of cinematic tricks," complains Rich, to enforce a sexual/spatial system of inequalities:

> Every time Connie is on screen, she's shot in close-up, tightly, claustrophobically, with no space around her, pinned into the tiny unmoveable frame. Every time Arnold is on screen, he's in middle-shot framed against an ample landscape, lots of space around him, master of the territory. The music surges on the soundtrack. It isn't long before the high-spirited Connie is a quivering puddle on the hallway floor.

Rich exaggerates only slightly. In fact, at moments we do see Connie in a wider frame—at the beach or the shopping center, for example—but it is also true that each time Connie moves into public spaces, traditionally "male" territory, danger lurks in the form of a shadowy male who, as the movie progresses, becomes increasingly more threatening. And each time Connie crosses over into new and larger spaces—such as the moment when Connie crosses the highway to the drive-in—she becomes increasingly more vulnerable. Also, at each crossing she becomes more isolated as, one by one, her girl friends drop out of the adventure, usually under orders from a parent.

The "high-spirited" Connie is indeed trapped by the rapist in an isolated house where she has been left alone by her parents and sister. Yet, just as Oates and Chopra did not invent the spatial inequalities they depict, they also do not simply repeat a horror formula which, at a woman's expense, will titillate an audience. Rich claims that when Friend arrives at Connie's doorstep the film "turns into a familiar product, the stock in trade of the horror genre: woman alone, trapped in empty house, terrorized, raped or killed or left insane." The innovative dialogue that Oates locates at this threshold—much of which Chopra employs in the film—is certainly not formulaic, nor is the conclusion of either the film or the story, as I shall demonstrate. Furthermore, when Rich says that the appeal of the formula, supposedly merely repeated by Oates and Chopra, is "the spectacle of lust delivered unto the audience, and then punishment of its embodiment, again for audience pleasure," she forgets that in the film Connie survives and in fiction, though not likely to survive, Connie "awakens" spiritually and, thus, sees beyond F(r)iend. What she sees, "the vast sunlit reaches of the land behind him and on all sides of him," is "alive." Oates says in her preface, "What seemed to be dead—the world-matter surrounding us—has been discovered to be living, intensely alive." Connie

---

[3]Rich's article is also included in this casebook.

may be moving toward a kind of death—toward her final "home"—but she understands, as Oates says in her Preface, that "What seemed to be dead—the concept of 'God'—is waking up, returning to consciousness." Connie's grave, her "Cornice—in the Ground," is the site of her new home, her new life. In a profound sense, then, Oates's Connie is as "high-spirited" as Chopra's assertive survivor. Oates makes this comment about the film's ending: "Laura Dern's Connie is no longer 'my' Connie at the film's conclusion; she is very much alive, assertive, strong-willed—a girl, perhaps, of the mid-1980s and not of the mid-1960s."

The evolution of Connie's consciousness—as she faces death—is the focus of Oates's story. Schmid was the central figure in *Life*, but in successive drafts of the tale, Oates shifted Friend to the margins as Connie's consciousness became central. Chopra's title, *Smooth Talk*, gives star billing to Friend, but Connie has the last, assertive word. Neither artist blames the victim; instead they tell her story, breaking the silence imposed upon rape victims. Connie's story is one of joy in her awakening sexuality, a "goodness" that challenges the convention of virginal goodness. It is Connie's mother, whose morality is conventional, who forces Connie to disguise her sexuality. Thus Connie has "two sides" that "looked one way when she was at home and another way when she was away from home. Everything had two sides to it." Yet in her Preface Oates explains that neither side is "evil" according to her moral vision:

> A new morality is emerging in America which may appear to be opposed to the old but which is in fact a higher form of the old—the democratization of the spirit, the experiencing of life as meaningful in itself, without divisions into "good" and "bad," "beautiful" or "ugly," "moral" or "immoral."

Younger readers seem to understand this evolution in consciousness, says Oates, and Chopra shares this vision. Chopra has invented some wonderfully amusing scenes that illustrate her pleasure in Connie's "trying on" of her new sexuality: Connie practicing boy/girl dialogue before her bathroom mirror; Connie changing her clothes in the shopping center bathroom; or Connie trying on a revealing outfit to wear to the drive-in. She's lovely.

The film audience is certainly not meant to share the attitude of Connie's mother, who describes the "good" June and the "bad" Connie on the phone, who rejects Connie when she tries to join the family at playing cards, and who expects Connie to fulfill her own emotional emptiness. The mother's sexual jealousy is obvious. One scene, especially, shows the limits of her older morality: when Connie's mother asks about "the Pettinger girl," Connie confronts her mother with her own premarital sexuality. In return for this remark, Connie is slapped. Despite her motherly love for Connie, she cannot express a more genuine concern—that Connie's early sexual maturity may trap her into a loveless marriage—because she thinks judgmentally, in terms of the old morality. A failure of imagination is evident in other family relationships as well. The father—invented by Chopra—cannot seem to "imagine" what his wife does all day. Their lives are gendered, their imaginations limited by a kind of "innocence," a narrow vision of the American dream, bounded by the material world. They cannot move into one another's minds—past boundaries of gender and generation—and this failure of imagination has harsh consequences for Connie. For example, when Connie lies to her father, telling him her mother knows of her crossing the highway to the drive-in, he doesn't check her story, probably because he talks rarely with his wife. Such divisions among the family—including those between the two sisters—lead to Connie's isolation in the house on the day of Friend's visit.

• • •

The difference between Oates's Connie and Chopra's Connie is but one instance of our cultural metamorphosis during the past 20–25 years. For such change, the conception of a conclusion—"an ending of spirit and energy"—would indeed seem "miraculous." In this sense, Oates's non-ending is certainly "unfilmable," for it portrays an energy—an erotic, spiritual energy signalled by violence—that cannot, finally, be contained by a work of art. The conventions of realism especially—the insistence upon endings, and on "character" bounded by material realities including anatomical features—do not allow this higher consciousness to be invoked in Chopra's film. Oates has suggested its mystery by the use of a question in her title, "Where Are You Going, Where Have You Been?," and in the ambiguous conclusion of her story. She has also said, in a *Newsweek* interview in 1972, "I write about things that are violent and extreme, but it is always against a background of something deep and imperishable. I feel I can wade in blood," she said. "I can endure the 10,000 evil visions because there is this absolutely imperishable reality behind it." Perhaps this imperishable reality is present not in a permanent "Connie," but in her metamorphosis through fiction, film and, of course, American life.

Journal of Popular Culture, Winter 1989

Suggestions for Writing on Joyce Carol Oates's "Where Are You Going, Where Have You Been?"

1. Do you see Connie as a sympathetic character, or someone who contributes to her own predicament? Make an argument, using specific lines and passages for support.
2. The film version of Oates's story, *Smooth Talk*, has a different ending than the story has; it imagines what happens after Connie leaves home with Arnold Friend. Write a new ending for "Where Are You Going, Where Have You Been?"—and then write an explanation of why your ending is justifiable.
3. In some respects Oates's story resembles classic fairy tales, especially those about adolescent girls coming into sexual maturity. Compare the story's key elements with those of a traditional folk tale such as "Little Red Riding Hood." How are they similar? How do they differ?
4. Watch the movie *Smooth Talk* and write a review of it as if it were a new release. Discuss the plot, characters, tone, and theme. (Don't worry too much about the acting.) Does the film successfully convey the content of the short story? Should someone see the film or simply read the story?

BARGAINING WITH DEATH

W. Somerset Maugham   *The Appointment in Samarra*

Wilhem and Jakob Grimm   *Godfather Death*

Chinua Achebe   *Dead Men's Path*

Death has always been one of the central subjects of literature, and it's easy to see why. Not only is death a universal experience—we all die eventually, no matter how healthy our diets or how regular our exercise—but death also represents the great unknown of existence. The living can observe death only from their own perspective. What happens beyond death is a mystery pondered by religion, myth, legend, and philosophy. Death also touches on our most primitive human fears about survival and extinction—yet another reason it is so popular among not just poets and storytellers but also the screenwriters of detective shows and horror films. Even journalists know the primal fascination with murderous violence. The traditional rule in choosing the placement of news stories is, "If it bleeds, it leads." Audiences pay more attention when lives are at stake.

The stories in this section all explore the mysteries—and the certainty—of death. Somerset Maugham's famous short parable presents the futility of trying to escape death or, more accurately in this case, Death personified as a character. The Brothers Grimm give their version of a German folktale in which Death offers to become the godfather of a poor child. Finally, Nigerian author Chinua Achebe creates a troubling story of ancient superstition and contemporary skepticism in modern Africa.

W. Somerset Maugham

William Somerset Maugham (1874–1965) was born to a well-to-do British family in Paris. By the age of ten, however, he was orphaned and being raised in England by relatives. Maugham became a doctor, but he desired most of all to be an author. When his first novel was published, he decided not to practice medicine. Maugham soon became one of the most successful novelists and playwrights of his time. His novels, which are still widely read—and repeatedly filmed—include Of Human Bondage *(1915),* The Moon and Sixpence *(1919),* The Painted Veil *(1925),* Cakes and Ale *(1930), and* The Razor's Edge *(1944).*

W. Somerset Maugham

W. Somerset Maugham

The Appointment in Samarra   1933

Death speaks: There was a merchant in Baghdad who sent his servant to market to buy provisions and in a little while the servant came back, white and trembling, and said, Master, just now when I was in the marketplace I was jostled by a woman in the crowd and when I turned I saw it was Death that jostled me. She looked at me and made a threatening gesture; now, lend me your horse, and I will ride away from this city and avoid my fate. I will go to Samarra and there Death will not find me. The merchant lent him his horse, and the servant mounted it, and he dug his spurs in its flanks and as fast as the horse could gallop he went. Then the merchant went down to the marketplace and he saw me standing in the crowd and he came to me and said, Why did you make a threatening gesture to my servant when you saw him this morning? That was not a threatening gesture, I said, it was only a start of surprise. I was astonished to see him in Baghdad, for I had an appointment with him tonight in Samarra.

Questions

1. Does Death, who narrates the story, seem particularly mean or wicked? What does the narrator's tone imply about death?
2. What is the theme of this story?
3. Do you believe that death has unbreakable appointments with us—that we'll go "when the time comes"? How might this belief influence how we live our lives or react to situations of danger?

Jakob and Wilhelm Grimm

Jakob Grimm (1785–1863) and Wilhelm Grimm (1786–1859), brothers and scholars, were born near Frankfurt am Main, Germany. For most of their lives they worked together—lived together, too, even when in 1825 Wilhelm married. In 1838, as librarians, they began toiling on their Deutsch Wörterbuch, *or German dictionary, a vast project that was to outlive them by a century. (It was completed only in 1960.) In 1840 King Friedrich Wilhelm IV appointed both brothers to the Royal Academy of Sciences, and both taught at the University of Berlin for the rest of their days.*

The name Grimm is best known to us for that splendid collection of ancient German folk stories we call Grimm's Fairy Tales—in German, Kinder- und Hausmärchen *("Childhood and Household Tales," 1812–15). This classic work spread German children's stories around the world. Many tales we hear early in life were collected by the Grimms: "Hansel and Gretel," "Snow White and the Seven Dwarfs," "Rapunzel," "Tom Thumb," "Little Red Riding Hood," "Rumpelstiltskin." Versions of some of these tales had been written down as early as the sixteenth century, but mainly the brothers relied on the memories of Hessian peasants who recited the stories aloud for them.*

Godfather Death

1812 (from oral tradition)

Translated by Dana Gioia

A poor man had twelve children and had to work day and night just to give them bread. Now when the thirteenth came into the world, he did not know what to do, so he ran out onto the main highway intending to ask the first one he met to be the child's godfather.

The first person he met was the good Lord God, who knew very well what was weighing on the man's heart. And He said to him, "Poor man, I am sorry for you. I will hold your child at the baptismal font. I will take care of him and fill his days with happiness."

The man asked, "Who are you?"

"I am the good Lord."

"Then I don't want you as godfather. You give to the rich and let the poor starve."

The man spoke thus because he did not know how wisely God portions out wealth and poverty. So he turned away from the Lord and went on.

Then the Devil came up to him and said, "What are you looking for? If you take me as your child's sponsor, I will give him gold heaped high and wide and all the joys of this world."

The man asked, "Who are you?"

"I am the Devil."

"Then I don't want you as godfather," said the man. "You trick men and lead them astray."

He went on, and bone-thin Death strode up to him and said, "Choose me as godfather."

The man asked, "Who are you?"

"I am Death, who makes all men equal."

Then the man said, "You are the right one. You take the rich and the poor without distinction. You will be the godfather."

Death answered, "I will make your child rich and famous. Whoever has me as a friend shall lack for nothing."

The man said, "The baptism is next Sunday. Be there on time."

Death appeared just as he had promised and stood there as a proper godfather.

When the boy had grown up, his godfather walked in one day and said to come along with him. Death led him out into the woods, showed him an herb, and said, "Now you are going to get your christening present. I am making you a famous doctor. When you are called to a patient, I will always appear to you. If I stand next to the sick person's head, you may speak boldly that you will make him healthy again. Give him some of this herb, and he will recover. But if you see me standing by the sick person's feet, then he is mine. You must say that nothing can be done and that no doctor in the world can save him. But beware of using the herb against my will, or it will turn out badly for you."

It was not long before the young man was the most famous doctor in the whole world. "He needs only to look at the sick person," everyone said, "and then he knows how things stand—whether the patient will get well again or whether he must die." People came from far and wide to bring their sick and gave him so much gold that he quickly became quite rich.

Now it soon happened that the king grew ill, and the doctor was summoned to say whether a recovery was possible. But when he came to the bed, Death was standing at the sick man's feet, and now no herb grown could save him.

"If I cheat Death this one time," thought the doctor, "he will be angry, but since I am his godson, he will turn a blind eye, so I will risk it." He took up the sick man and turned him around so that his head was now where Death stood. Then he gave the king some of the herb. The king recovered and grew healthy again.

But Death then came to the doctor with a dark and angry face and threatened him with his finger. "You have hoodwinked me this time," he said. "And I will forgive you once because you are my godson. But if you try such a thing again, it will be your neck, and I will take you away with me."

Not long after, the king's daughter fell into a serious illness. She was his only child, and he wept day and night until his eyes went blind. He let it be known that whoever saved her from death would become her husband and inherit the crown.

When the doctor came to the sick girl's bed, he saw Death standing at her feet. He should have remembered his godfather's warning, but the princess's great beauty and the happy prospect of becoming her husband so infatuated him that he flung all caution to the wind. He didn't notice that Death stared at him angrily or that he raised his hand and shook his bony fist. The doctor picked up the sick girl and turned her around to place her head where her feet had been. He gave her the herb, and right away her cheeks grew rosy and she stirred again with life.

When Death saw that he had been cheated out of his property a second time, he strode with long steps up to the doctor and said, "It is all over for you. Now it's your turn." Death seized him so firmly with his ice-cold hand that the doctor could not resist. He led him into an underground cavern. There the doctor saw thousands and thousands of candles burning in endless rows. Some were tall, others medium-sized, and others quite small. Every moment some went out and others lit up, so that the tiny flames seemed to jump to and fro in perpetual motion.

"Look," said Death, "these are the life lights of mankind. The tall ones belong to children, the middle-size ones to married people in the prime of life, and the short ones to the very old. But sometimes even children and young people have only a short candle."

"Show me my life light," said the doctor, assuming it would be very tall.

Death pointed to a small stub that seemed about to flicker out.

"Oh, dear godfather!" cried the terrified doctor. "Light a new candle for me. If you love me, do it, so that I may enjoy my life, become king, and marry the beautiful princess."

"That I cannot do," Death replied. "One candle must first go out before a new one is lighted."

"Then put my old one on top of a new candle that will keep burning when the old one goes out," begged the doctor.

Death acted as if he were going to grant the wish and picked up a tall new candle. But because he wanted revenge, he deliberately fumbled in placing the new candle, and the stub toppled over and went out. The doctor immediately dropped to the ground and fell into the hands of Death.

Questions

1. Why does the poor man choose Death as the godfather for his son? What does Death have to recommend him that God and the Devil don't?
2. Why is the doctor so confident that he can break the rules that Death has laid out for him? What is the doctor's worst mistake?
3. Does Godfather Death strike you as particularly mean or vengeful? What does the characterization of Death in this story imply?

Chinua Achebe

Chinua Achebe was born in Ogidi, a village in eastern Nigeria, in 1930. His father was a missionary schoolteacher, and Achebe had a devout Christian upbringing. A member of the Ibo tribe, the future writer grew up speaking Igbo, but at the age of eight, he began learning English. He went abroad to study at London University but returned to Africa to complete his B.A. at the University College of Ibadan in 1953. Achebe worked for years in Nigerian radio. Shortly after Nigeria's independence from Great Britain in 1963, civil war broke out and the new nation split in two. Achebe left his job to join the Ministry of Information for Biafra, the new country created from eastern Nigeria. It was not until 1970 that the bloody civil war ended. Approximately one million Ibos lay dead from war, disease, and starvation as the defeated Biafrans reunited with Nigeria. Achebe is often considered Africa's premier novelist. His novels include Things Fall Apart *(1958),* No Longer at Ease *(1962),* A Man of the People *(1966), and* Anthills of the Savannah *(1987). His short stories have been collected in* Girls At War *(1972). He has also published poetry, children's stories, and several volumes of essays, the most recent of which is* The Education of a British-Protected Child *(2009). In 1990 Achebe suffered massive injuries in a car accident outside Lagos that left him paralyzed from the waist down. Following the accident, he taught at Bard College in upstate New York for almost nineteen years. In 1999 he visited Nigeria again after a deliberate nine-year absence to protest government dictatorship, and his homecoming became a national event. In 2007 he was awarded the second Man Booker International Prize for his lifetime contribution to world literature.*

Chinua Achebe

Dead Men's Path (1953) 1972

Michael Obi's hopes were fulfilled much earlier than he had expected. He was appointed headmaster of Ndume Central School in January 1949. It had always been an unprogressive school, so the Mission authorities decided to send a young and energetic man to run it. Obi accepted this responsibility with enthusiasm. He had many wonderful ideas and this was an opportunity to put them into practice. He had had sound secondary school education which designated him a "pivotal teacher" in the official records and set him apart from the other headmasters in the mission field. He was outspoken in his condemnation of the narrow views of these older and often less-educated ones.

"We shall make a good job of it, shan't we?" he asked his young wife when they first heard the joyful news of his promotion.

"We shall do our best," she replied. "We shall have such beautiful gardens and everything will be just *modern* and delightful . . ." In their two years of married life she had become completely infected by his passion for "modern methods" and his denigration of "these old and superannuated people in the teaching field who would be better employed as traders in the Onitsha market." She began to see herself already as the admired wife of the young headmaster, the queen of the school.

The wives of the other teachers would envy her position. She would set the fashion in everything . . . Then, suddenly, it occurred to her that there might not be other wives. Wavering between hope and fear, she asked her husband, looking anxiously at him.

"All our colleagues are young and unmarried," he said with enthusiasm which for once she did not share. "Which is a good thing," he continued.

"Why?"

"Why? They will give all their time and energy to the school."

Nancy was downcast. For a few minutes she became skeptical about the new school; but it was only for a few minutes. Her little personal misfortune could not blind her to her husband's happy prospects. She looked at him as he sat folded up in a chair. He was stoop-shouldered and looked frail. But he sometimes surprised people with sudden bursts of physical energy. In his present posture, however, all his bodily strength seemed to have retired behind his deep-set eyes, giving them an extraordinary power of penetration. He was only twenty-six, but looked thirty or more. On the whole, he was not unhandsome.

"A penny for your thoughts, Mike," said Nancy after a while, imitating the woman's magazine she read.

"I was thinking what a grand opportunity we've got at last to show these people how a school should be run."

Ndume School was backward in every sense of the word. Mr. Obi put his whole life into the work, and his wife hers too. He had two aims. A high standard of teaching was insisted upon, and the school compound was to be turned into a place of beauty. Nancy's dream-gardens came to life with the coming of the rains, and blossomed. Beautiful hibiscus and allamanda hedges in brilliant red and yellow marked out the carefully tended school compound from the rank neighborhood bushes.

One evening as Obi was admiring his work he was scandalized to see an old woman from the village hobble right across the compound, through a marigold flower-bed and the hedges. On going up there he found faint signs of an almost disused path from the village across the school compound to the bush on the other side.

"It amazes me," said Obi to one of his teachers who had been three years in the school, "that you people allowed the villagers to make use of this footpath. It is simply incredible." He shook his head.

"The path," said the teacher apologetically, "appears to be very important to them. Although it is hardly used, it connects the village shrine with their place of burial."

"And what has that got to do with the school?" asked the headmaster.

"Well, I don't know," replied the other with a shrug of the shoulders. "But I remember there was a big row some time ago when we attempted to close it."

"That was some time ago. But it will not be used now," said Obi as he walked away. "What will the Government Education Officer think of this when he comes to inspect the school next week? The villagers might, for all I know, decide to use the schoolroom for a pagan ritual during the inspection."

Heavy sticks were planted closely across the path at the two places where it entered and left the school premises. These were further strengthened with barbed wire.

Three days later the village priest of *Ani* called on the headmaster. He was an old man and walked with a slight stoop. He carried a stout walking-stick which he usually tapped on the floor, by way of emphasis, each time he made a new point in his argument.

"I have heard," he said after the usual exchange of cordialities, "that our ancestral footpath has recently been closed . . ."

"Yes," replied Mr. Obi. "We cannot allow people to make a highway of our school compound."

"Look here, my son," said the priest bringing down his walking-stick, "this path was here before you were born and before your father was born. The whole life of this village depends on it. Our dead relatives depart by it and our ancestors visit us by it. But most important, it is the path of children coming in to be born . . ."

Mr. Obi listened with a satisfied smile on his face.

"The whole purpose of our school," he said finally, "is to eradicate just such beliefs as that. Dead men do not require footpaths. The whole idea is just fantastic. Our duty is to teach your children to laugh at such ideas."

"What you say may be true," replied the priest, "but we follow the practices of our fathers. If you reopen the path we shall have nothing to quarrel about. What I always say is: let the hawk perch and let the eagle perch." He rose to go.

"I am sorry," said the young headmaster. "But the school compound cannot be a thoroughfare. It is against our regulations. I would suggest your constructing another path, skirting our premises. We can even get our boys to help in building it. I don't suppose the ancestors will find the little detour too burdensome."

"I have no more words to say," said the old priest, already outside.

Two days later a young woman in the village died in childbed. A diviner was immediately consulted and he prescribed heavy sacrifices to propitiate ancestors insulted by the fence.

Obi woke up next morning among the ruins of his work. The beautiful hedges were torn up not just near the path but right round the school, the flowers trampled to death and one of the school buildings pulled down . . . That day, the white Supervisor came to inspect the school and wrote a nasty report on the state of the premises but more seriously about the "tribal-war situation developing between the school and the village, arising in part from the misguided zeal of the new headmaster."

Questions

1. What does Mr. Obi mean when he says "Dead men do not require footpaths"? What are the larger implications of his statement?
2. Mr. Obi and his wife consider their new school "backward." What do they mean? Are they correct? Are they, with their more modern views, missing out on something that the villagers know?
3. Why does the village priest visit the school? What choice does he offer the headmaster?

4. Mr. Obi and his wife try to minimize death and the supernatural, while the villagers give great respect to the dead and the yet-to-be-born. Which attitude is more useful or healthy? Why?
5. What significance do you see in the story's title "Dead Men's Path"?

Suggestions for Writing on Stories about Bargaining with Death

1. All three stories in this section make use of elements that could be deemed supernatural. How does use of the supernatural help convey the stories' themes?
2. Analyze Death as a character in "The Appointment in Samarra" and "Godfather Death." What are his motivations? Is he presented differently in the two stories? Similarly? How would you characterize him? What do these characterizations mean?
3. Discuss how Mr. Obi's views of death and the supernatural in Chinua Achebe's story reflect modern attempts to rationalize and control mortality.
4. Pick a controversial current topic related to death and mortality—such as suicide, assisted suicide, or the death penalty—and develop an argument for why it is or is not justified.

DEATH AND TRANSFORMATION

Franz Kafka   *The Metamorphosis*

Few works of fiction have created more vibrant commentary and discussion than Franz Kafka's *The Metamorphosis*. From its first sentence—probably the most famous opening line in modern literature—Kafka's troubling and mysterious tale leaves few readers unmoved. *The Metamorphosis* is simultaneously a masterpiece of fantasy and of realism. It begins with an utterly fantastic premise—a young man awakes to discover that he has been transformed into a giant insect—and the tale then continues by realistically representing everything that follows, mostly seen from the perspective of its poor protagonist, Gregor Samsa. Fiction has a special power to depict sudden changes in life's journey, but surely no story has ever done so more memorably than *The Metamorphosis*.

Franz Kafka

Franz Kafka (1883–1924) was born into a German-speaking Jewish family in Prague, Czechoslovakia (then part of the Austro-Hungarian empire). He was the only surviving son of a domineering, successful father. After earning a law degree, Kafka worked as a claims investigator for the state accident insurance company. He worked on his stories at night, especially during his frequent bouts of insomnia. He never married, and he lived mostly with his parents. Kafka was such a careful and self-conscious writer that he found it difficult to finish his work and send it out for publication. During his lifetime he published only a few thin volumes of short fiction, most notably The Metamorphosis *(1915) and* In the Penal Colony *(1919). He never finished to his own satisfaction any of his three novels (all published posthumously):* The Trial *(1925),* The Castle *(1926), and* Amerika *(1927). As Kafka was dying of tuberculosis, he begged his friend and literary executor Max Brod to burn his uncompleted manuscripts. Brod pondered this request but, luckily, didn't obey. Kafka's two major novels,* The Trial *and* The Castle, *both depict huge, remote, bumbling, irresponsible bureaucracies in whose power the individual feels helpless and blind. Kafka's works appear startlingly prophetic to readers looking back on them in the later light of Stalinism, World War II, and the Holocaust. His haunting vision of an alienated modern world led the poet W. H. Auden to remark at midcentury, "Had one to name the author who comes nearest to bearing the same kind of relation to our age as Dante, Shakespeare, and Goethe bore to theirs, Kafka is the first one would think of."*

The Metamorphosis

Translated by John Siscoe

I

When Gregor Samsa awoke one morning from troubled dreams, he found himself transformed in his bed into a monstrous insect. He was lying on his back, which was hard, as if plated in armor, and when he lifted his head slightly he could see his belly: rounded, brown, and divided into stiff arched segments; on top of it the blanket, about to slip off altogether, still barely clinging. His many legs, which seemed pathetically thin when compared to the rest of his body, flickered helplessly before his eyes.

"What's happened to me?" he thought. It was no dream. His room, a normal though somewhat small human bedroom, lay quietly within its four familiar walls. Above the table on which his unpacked fabric samples were spread—Samsa was a traveling salesman—hung the picture he had recently cut out of an illustrated magazine and had set in a lovely gilt frame. It showed a lady wearing a fur hat and a fur stole, sitting upright, and thrusting out to the viewer a thick fur muff, into which her whole forearm had disappeared.

Gregor's glance then fell on the window, and the overcast sky—one could hear raindrops drumming on the tin sheeting of the windowsill—made him feel profoundly sad. "What if I went back to sleep for a while and forgot all this nonsense," he thought. But that wasn't to be, for he was used to sleeping on his right side and in his present state was unable to get into that position. No matter how hard he threw himself to his right, he would immediately roll onto his back again. He must have tried a hundred times, shutting his eyes so as not to see his wriggling legs, not stopping until he began to feel in his side a slight dull pain that he had never felt before.

"My God," he thought, "what an exhausting job I've chosen! Always on the go, day in and day out. There are far more worries on the road than at the office, what with the constant travel, the nuisance of making your train connections, the wretched meals eaten at odd hours, and the casual acquaintances you meet only in passing, never to see again, never to become intimate friends. To hell with it all!" He felt a slight itch on the surface of his belly. Slowly he shoved himself on his back closer to the bedpost so that he could lift his head more easily. He found the place where it itched. It was covered with small white spots he did not understand. He started to touch it with one of his legs, but pulled back immediately, for the contact sent a cold shiver through him.

He slid back down to his former position. "Getting up this early," he thought, "would turn anyone into an idiot. A man needs his sleep. Other salesmen live like harem women. For example, when I get back to the hotel in the morning to write up the sales I've made, these gentlemen are sitting down to breakfast. If I tried that with my director, I'd be fired on the spot. Actually, that might not be such a bad idea. If I didn't have to curb my tongue because of my parents, I'd have given notice long ago. I'd have gone up to the director and told him from the bottom of my heart exactly what I thought. That would have knocked him from his desk! It's an odd way to run things, this sitting high at a desk and talking down to employees, especially when, since the director is hard of hearing, they have to approach so near. Well, there's hope yet; as soon as I've saved enough money to pay back what my parents owe him—that should take another five or six years—I'll go do it for sure. Then, I'll cut myself completely free. Right now, though, I'd better get up, as my train leaves at five."

He looked at the alarm clock ticking on top of the chest of drawers. "God Almighty!" he thought. It was half past six and the hands were quietly moving forward, it was later than half past, it was nearly a quarter to seven. Hadn't the alarm clock gone off? You could see from the bed that it had been correctly set for four o'clock; of course it must have gone off. Yes, but could he really have slept peacefully through that ear-splitting racket? Well, if he hadn't slept peacefully, he'd slept deeply all the same. But what was he to do now? The next train left at seven, to make it he would have to rush like mad, and his samples weren't even packed, and he himself wasn't feeling particularly spry or alert. And even if he were to make the train, there would be no avoiding a scene with the director. The office messenger would've been waiting for the five o'clock train and would've long since reported his not showing up. The messenger, dim-witted and lacking a will of his own, was a tool of the director. Well, what if he were to call in sick? But that would look embarrassing and suspicious since in his five years with the firm Gregor had not been sick once. The director himself was sure to come over with the health insurance doctor, would upbraid his parents for their son's laziness, and would cut short all excuses by deferring to the doctor, who believed that everyone in the world was a perfectly healthy layabout. And really, would he be so wrong in this case? Apart from a drowsiness that was hard to account for after such a long sleep, Gregor really felt quite well, and in fact was exceptionally hungry.

As he was thinking all this at top speed, without being able to make up his mind to get out of bed—the alarm clock had just struck a quarter to seven—a cautious tap sounded on the door behind his head. "Gregor," said a voice—it was his mother— "it's a quarter to seven. Don't you have a train to catch?" That gentle voice! Gregor was shocked when he heard his own voice answering hers; unmistakably his own voice, true, but mixed in with it, like an undertone, a miserable squeaking that allowed the words to be clearly heard only for a moment before rising up, reverberating, to drown out their meaning, so that no one could be sure if he had heard them correctly. Gregor wanted to answer fully and give a complete explanation, but under the circumstances he merely said, "Yes, yes, thank you, Mother, I'm just getting up." Through the wooden door between them the change in Gregor's voice was probably not obvious, for his mother, quietly accepting his words, shuffled away. However, this brief exchange had made the rest of the family aware that Gregor, surprisingly, was still in the house, and already at one of the side doors his father was knocking, softly, yet with his fist. "Gregor, Gregor," he called, "what's the matter?" Before long he called once more in a deeper voice, "Gregor? Gregor?" From the other side door came the sound of his sister's voice, gentle and plaintive. "Gregor, aren't you feeling well? Is there anything I can get you?" Gregor answered the two of them at the same time: "I'm almost ready." He tried hard to keep his voice from sounding strange by enunciating the words with great care, and by inserting long pauses between the words. His father went back to his breakfast but his sister whispered, "Gregor, please, open the door." But Gregor had no intention of opening the door, and was thankful for having formed, while traveling, the prudent habit of keeping all his doors locked at night, even at home.

What he wanted to do now was to get up quietly and calmly, to get dressed, and above all to eat his breakfast. Only then would he think about what to do next, for he understood that mulling things over in bed would lead him nowhere. He remembered how often in the past he had felt some small pain in bed, perhaps caused by lying in an uncomfortable position, which as soon as he had gotten up had proven to be purely imaginary, and he looked forward to seeing how this morning's fancies would gradually fade and disappear. As for the change in his voice, he hadn't the slightest doubt that it was nothing more than the first sign of a severe cold, an occupational hazard of traveling salesmen.

Throwing off the blanket was easy enough; he had only to puff himself up a little and it slipped right off. But the next part was difficult, especially as he was so unusually wide. He would have needed arms and legs to lift himself up; instead he had only these numerous little legs that never stopped moving and over which he had no control at all. As soon as he tried to bend one of them it would straighten itself out, and if he finally succeeded in making it do as he wished, all the others, as if set free, would waggle about in a high degree of painful agitation. "But what's the point of lying uselessly in bed?" Gregor said to himself.

He thought that he might start by easing the lower part of his body out of bed first, but this lower part, which incidentally he hadn't yet seen and of which he couldn't form a clear picture, turned out to be very difficult to budge—it went so slowly. When finally, almost in a frenzy, he gathered his strength and pushed forward desperately, he miscalculated his direction and bumped sharply against the post at the foot of the bed, and the searing pain he felt told him that, for right now at least, it was exactly this lower part of his body that was perhaps the most tender.

So he tried getting the top part of his body out first, and cautiously turned his head towards the side of the bed. This proved easy enough, and eventually, despite its breadth and weight the bulk of his body slowly followed the turning of his head. But when he finally got his head out over the edge of the bed he felt too afraid to go any farther, for if he were to let himself fall from this position only a miracle would prevent him from hurting his head. And it was precisely now, at all costs, that he must not lose consciousness; he would be better off staying in bed.

But when after repeating his efforts he lay, sighing, in his former position, and once more watched his little legs struggling with one another more furiously than ever, if that were possible, and saw no way of bringing calm and order into this mindless confusion, he again told himself that it was impossible to stay in bed and that the wisest course would be to stake everything on the hope, however slight, of getting away from the bed. At the same time he didn't forget to remind himself that the calmest of calm reflection was much better than frantic resolutions. During this time he kept his eyes fixed as firmly as possible on the window, but unfortunately the morning fog, which shrouded even the other side of the narrow street, gave him little comfort and cheer. "Already seven o'clock," he said to himself when the alarm clock chimed again, "already seven and still such a thick fog." And for some time he lay still, breathing quietly, as if in the hope that utter stillness would bring all things back to how they really and normally were.

But then he said to himself: "I must make sure that I'm out of bed before it strikes a quarter past seven. Anyway, by then someone from work will have come to check on me, since the office opens before seven." And he immediately set the whole length of his body rocking with a rhythmic motion in order to swing out of bed. If he tumbled out this way he could prevent his head from being injured by keeping it tilted upward as he fell. His back seemed to be hard; the fall onto the carpet would probably not hurt it. His greatest worry was the thought of the loud crash he was bound to make; it would probably cause anxiety, if not outright fear, on the other side of the doors. Yet he had to take the chance.

When Gregor was already half out of bed—his new technique made it more of a game than a struggle, since all he had to do was to edge himself across by rocking back and forth—it struck him how simple it would be if he could get someone to help him. Two strong people—he thought of his father and the maid—would be more than enough. All they would have to do would be to slip their arms under his curved back, lift him out of bed, bend down with their burden, and then wait patiently while he flipped himself right side up onto the floor, where, one might hope, his little legs would acquire some purpose. Well then, aside from the fact that the doors were locked, wouldn't it be a good idea to call for help? In spite of his misery, he could not help smiling at the thought.

He had reached the point where, if he rocked any harder, he was in danger of losing his balance, and very soon he would have to commit himself, because in five minutes it would be a quarter past seven—when the doorbell rang. "It's someone from the office," he said to himself, and almost froze, while his little legs danced even faster. For a moment everything remained quiet. "They won't open the door," Gregor said to himself, clutching at an absurd sort of hope. But then, of course, the maid, as usual, went with her firm tread to the door and opened it. Gregor had only to hear the visitor's first word of greeting to know at once who it was—the office manager himself. Why was Gregor condemned to work for a firm where the most insignificant failure to appear instantly provoked the deepest suspicion? Were the employees, one and all, nothing but scoundrels? Wasn't there among them one man who was true and loyal, who if, one morning, he were to waste an hour or so of the firm's time, would become so conscience-stricken as to be driven out of his mind and actually rendered incapable of leaving his bed? Wouldn't it have been enough to send an office boy to ask—that is, if such prying were necessary at all? Did the office manager have to come in person, and thus demonstrate to an entire family of innocent people that he was the only one wise enough to properly investigate this suspicious affair? And it was more from the anxiety caused by these thoughts than by any act of will that Gregor swung himself out of bed with all his might. There was a loud thump, but not really a crash. The carpet broke his fall somewhat, and his back too was more elastic than he had thought, so there was only a muffled thud that was relatively unobtrusive. However, he had not lifted his head carefully enough and had banged it; he twisted it and rubbed it against the carpet in frustration and pain.

"Something fell down in there," said the office manager in the room on the left. Gregor tried to imagine whether something like what had happened to him today might one day happen to the office manager; really, one had to admit that it was possible. But as if in a blunt reply to this question the office manager took several determined steps in the next room and his patent leather boots creaked. From the room on the right his sister was whispering to let him know what was going on: "Gregor, the office manager is here." "I know," said Gregor to himself, but he didn't dare speak loudly enough for his sister to hear him.

"Gregor," his father now said from the room on the left, "the office manager is here and he wants to know why you weren't on the early train. We don't know what to tell him. Besides, he wants to speak to you in person. So please open the door. I'm sure he'll be kind enough to excuse any untidiness in your room." "Good morning, Mr. Samsa," the manager was calling out amiably. "He isn't feeling well," said his mother to the manager, while his father was still speaking at the door. "He's not well, sir, believe me. Why else would Gregor miss his train? The boy thinks of nothing but his work. It nearly drives me to distraction the way he never goes out in the evening; he's been here the last eight days, and every single evening he's stayed at home. He just sits here at the table with us quietly reading the newspapers or looking over train schedules. The only enjoyment he gets is when he's working away with his fretsaw.° For example, he spent two or three evenings cutting out a little picture frame, you'd be surprised at how pretty it is, it's hanging in his room, you'll see it in a minute as soon as Gregor opens the door. By the way, I'm glad you've come, sir, we would've never have gotten him to unlock the door by ourselves, he's so stubborn; and I'm sure he's sick, even though he wouldn't admit it this morning." "I'm coming right now," said Gregor, slowly and carefully and not moving an inch for fear of missing a single word of the conversation. "I can't imagine any other explanation, madam," said the office manager, "I hope it's nothing serious. But on the other hand businessmen such as ourselves—fortunately or unfortunately—very often have to ignore any minor indisposition, since the demands of business come first." "So, can the office manager come in now?" asked Gregor's father impatiently, once more knocking on the door. "No," said Gregor. In the room on the left there was an embarrassed silence; in the room on the right his sister began to sob.

But why didn't his sister go and join the others? Probably because she had just gotten out of bed and hadn't even begun to dress yet. Then why was she crying? Because he was in danger of losing his job, and because the director would start once again dunning his parents for the money they owed him? Yet surely these were matters one didn't need to worry about just now. Gregor was still here, and hadn't the slightest intention of deserting the family. True, at the moment he was lying on the carpet, and no one aware of his condition could seriously expect him to let the office manager in. But this minor discourtesy, for which in good time an appropriate excuse could easily be found, was unlikely to result in Gregor's being fired on the spot. And it seemed to Gregor far more sensible for them now to leave him in peace than to bother him with their tears and entreaties. But the uncertainty that preyed upon them excused their behavior.

"Mr. Samsa," the office manager now called in a louder voice, "what's the matter with you? You've barricaded yourself in your room, giving only yes or no answers, causing your parents a great deal of needless grief and neglecting—I mention this only in passing—neglecting your business responsibilities to an unbelievable degree. I am speaking now in the name of your parents and of your director, and I beg you in all seriousness to give me a complete explanation at once. I'm amazed at you, simply amazed. I took you for a calm and reliable person, and now all at once you

---

fretsaw: saw with a long, narrow, fine-toothed blade, for cutting thin wooden boards or metal plates into patterns.

seem determined to make a ridiculous spectacle of yourself. Earlier this morning the director did suggest to me a possible explanation for your disappearance—I'm referring to the sums of cash that were recently entrusted to you—but I practically swore on my solemn word of honor that this could not be. However, now when I see how incredibly stubborn you are, I no longer have the slightest desire to defend you. And your position with the firm is by no means secure. I came intending to tell you all this in private, but since you're so pointlessly wasting my time I don't see why your parents shouldn't hear it as well. For some time now your work has left much to be desired. We are aware, of course, that this is not the prime season for doing business; but a season for doing no business at all—that, Mr. Samsa, does not and must not exist."

"But sir," Gregor called out distractedly, forgetting everything else in his excitement, "I'm on the verge of opening the door right now. A slight indisposition, a dizzy spell, has prevented me from getting up. I'm still in bed. But I'm feeling better already. I'm getting up now. Please be patient for just a moment. It seems I'm not quite as well as I thought. But really I'm all right. Something like this can come on so suddenly! Only last night I was feeling fine, as my parents can tell you, or actually I did have a slight premonition. I must have shown some sign of it. Oh, why didn't I report it to the office! But one always thinks one can get better without having to stay at home. Please, sir, have mercy on my parents! None of what you've just accused me of has any basis in fact; no one has even spoken a word to me about it. Perhaps you haven't seen the latest orders I've sent in. Anyway, I can still make the eight o'clock train. Don't let me keep you, sir, I'll be showing up at the office very soon. Please be kind enough to inform them, and convey my best wishes to the director."

And while hurriedly blurting all this out, hardly knowing what he was saying, Gregor had reached the chest of drawers easily enough, perhaps because of the practice he had already gotten in bed, and was now trying to use it to lift himself upright. For he actually wanted to open the door, actually intended to show himself, and to talk with the manager; he was eager to find out what the others, who now wanted to see him so much, would say at the sight of him. If they recoiled in horror then he would take no further responsibility and could remain peaceably where he was. But if they took it all in stride then he too had no reason to be upset, and, if he hurried, could even get to the station by eight. The first few times, he slipped down the polished surface of the chest, but finally with one last heave he stood upright. He no longer paid attention to the burning pains in his abdomen, no matter how they hurt. Then, allowing himself to fall against the backrest of a nearby chair, he clung to its edges with his little legs. Now he was once more in control of himself; he fell silent, and was able to hear what the manager was saying.

"Did you understand a single word?" the office manager was asking his parents. "He's not trying to make fools of us, is he?" "My God," cried his mother, already in tears, "maybe he's seriously ill and we're tormenting him. Grete! Grete!" she shouted then. "Mother?" called his sister from the other side. They were calling to each other across Gregor's room. "You must go to the doctor at once. Gregor is sick. Go get the doctor now. Did you hear how Gregor was speaking?" "That was the voice of an animal," said the manager in a tone that was noticeably restrained compared to his mother's shrillness. "Anna! Anna!" his father shouted through the hall to the kitchen, clapping his hands, "get a locksmith and hurry!" And the two girls, their skirts rustling, were already running down the hall—how could his sister have gotten dressed so quickly?—and were pulling the front door open. There was no sound of its being shut; evidently they had left it standing open, as is the custom in houses stricken by some great sorrow.

But Gregor now felt much calmer. Though the words he spoke were apparently no longer understandable, they seemed clear enough to him, even clearer than before, perhaps because his hearing had grown accustomed to their sound. In any case, people were now convinced that something was wrong with him, and were ready to help him. The confidence and assurance with which these first measures had been taken comforted him. He felt himself being drawn back into the human circle and hoped for marvelous and astonishing results from both doctor and locksmith, without really drawing a distinction between them. To ready his voice for the crucial discussion that was now almost upon him, to make it sound as clear as possible, he coughed slightly, as quietly as he could, since for all he knew it might sound different from human coughing. Meanwhile in the next room there was utter silence. Perhaps his parents and the manager were sitting at the table, whispering; perhaps they were, all of them, leaning against the door, listening.

Gregor slowly advanced on the door, pushing the chair in front of him. Then he let go of it, grabbed onto the door for support—the pads at the end of his little legs were somewhat sticky—and, leaning against it, rested for a moment after his efforts. Then he started to turn the key in the lock with his mouth. Unfortunately, he didn't really have any teeth—how was he going to grip the key?—but to make up for that he clearly had very powerful jaws; with their help he was in fact able to start turning the key, paying no attention to the fact that he was surely hurting them somehow, for a brown liquid poured out of his mouth, flowed over the key, and dripped onto the floor. "Listen," said the manager on the other side of the door, "he's turning the key." This was a great encouragement to Gregor, but they should all have been cheering him on, his mother and his father too. "Come on, Gregor," they should have been shouting, "keep at it, hold on to that key!" And, imagining that they were all intently following his efforts, he grimly clamped his jaws on the key with all his might. As the key continued to turn he danced around the lock, holding himself by his mouth alone, either hanging onto the key or pressing down on it with the full weight of his body, as the situation required. The sharper sound of the lock as it finally snapped free woke Gregor up completely. With a sigh of relief he said to himself, "So I didn't need the locksmith after all," and he pressed his head down on the handle to open one wing of the double door.

Because he had to pull the wing in towards him, even when it stood wide open he remained hidden from view. He had to edge slowly around this wing and to do it very carefully or he would fall flat on his back as he made his entrance. He was still busy carrying out this maneuver, with no time to notice anything else, when he heard the manager give a loud "Oh!"—it sounded like a gust of wind—and now he could see him, standing closest to the door, his hand over his open mouth, slowly backing away as if propelled by the relentless pressure of some invisible force. His mother—in spite of the manager's presence, she was standing there with her hair still unpinned and sticking out in all directions—first folded her hands and looked at Gregor's father, then took two steps forward and sank to the floor, her skirts billowing out all around her and her face completely buried in her breast. His father, glowering, clenched his fist, as if he intended to drive Gregor back into his room; then he looked around the living room with uncertainty, covered his eyes with his hands, and wept so hard his great chest shook.

Now Gregor made no attempt to enter the living room, but leaned against the locked wing of the double door, so that only half of his body was visible, with his head above it cocked to one side, peering at the others. Meanwhile the daylight had grown much brighter; across the street one could clearly see a section of the endless, dark gray building opposite—it was a hospital—with a row of uniform windows starkly punctuating its facade. The rain was still falling, but only in large, visibly separate drops that looked as though they were being flung, one by one, onto the earth. On the table the breakfast dishes were set out in lavish profusion, for breakfast was the most important meal of the day for Gregor's father, who lingered over it for hours while reading various newspapers. Hanging on the opposite wall was a photograph of Gregor from his army days, showing him as a lieutenant, with his hand on his sword and his carefree smile demanding respect for his bearing and his rank. The door to the hall stood open, and as the front door was open too, one could see the landing beyond and the top of the stairs going down.

"Well," said Gregor, who was perfectly aware that he was the only one who had kept his composure, "I'll go now and get dressed, pack up my samples, and be on my way. You will, you will let me go, won't you? You can see, sir, that I'm not stubborn and I'm willing to work; the life of a traveling salesman is hard, but I couldn't live without it. Where are you going, sir? To the office? You are? Will you give an honest report about all this? A man may be temporarily unable to work, but that's just the time to remember the service he has rendered in the past, and to bear in mind that later on, when the present problem has been resolved, he is sure to work with even more energy and diligence than before. As you know very well, I am deeply obligated to the director. At the same time, I'm responsible for my parents and my sister. I'm in a tight spot right now, but I'll get out of it. Don't make things more difficult for me than they already are. Stand up for me at the office! People don't like traveling salesmen, I know. They think they make scads of money and lead lives of luxury. And there's no compelling reason for them to revise this prejudice. But you, sir, have a better understanding of things than the rest of the staff, a better understanding, if I may say so, than even the director himself, who, since he is the owner, can be easily swayed against an employee. You also know very well that a traveling salesman, who is away from the office for most of the year, can so easily fall victim to gossip and bad luck and groundless accusations, against which he is powerless to defend himself since he knows nothing about them until, returning home exhausted from his journeys, he suffers personally from evil consequences that can no longer be traced back to their origins. Sir, please don't go away without giving me some word to show that you think that I'm at least partly right!"

But the office manager had turned away at Gregor's first words, and was looking at him now over one twitching shoulder, his mouth agape. And during Gregor's speech he didn't stand still for even a moment, but without once taking his eyes off him kept edging towards the door, yet very slowly, as if there were some secret injunction against his leaving the room. He was already in the hall, and from the suddenness with which he took his last step out of the living room, one might have thought he had burned the sole of his foot. But once in the hall, he stretched out his right hand as far as possible in the direction of the staircase, as if some supernatural rescuer awaited him there.

Gregor realized that he could not let the manager leave in this frame of mind, or his position with the firm would be in extreme jeopardy. His parents were incapable of clearly grasping this; over the years they had come to believe that Gregor was set for life with this firm, and besides they were now so preoccupied with their immediate problems that they had lost the ability to foresee events. But Gregor had this ability. The manager must be overtaken, calmed, swayed, and finally convinced; the future of Gregor and of his family depended on it! If only his sister were here—she was perceptive; she had already begun to cry while Gregor was still lying calmly on his back. And surely the manager, that ladies' man, would've listened to her; she would've shut the door behind them and in the hall talked him out of his fright. But his sister wasn't there, and he would have to handle this himself. And forgetting that he had no idea what his powers of movement were, and forgetting as well that once again his words would possibly, even probably, be misunderstood, he let go of the door, pushed his way through the opening, and started towards the manager, who by now was on the landing, clinging in a ridiculous manner to the banister with both hands. But as Gregor reached out for support, he immediately fell down with a little cry onto his numerous legs. The moment this happened he felt, for the first time that morning, a sense of physical well-being. His little legs had solid ground under them, and, he noticed with joy, they were at his command, and were even eager to carry him in whatever direction he might desire; and he already felt sure that the final recovery from all his misery was at hand. But at that very moment, as he lay on the floor rocking with suppressed motion, not far from his mother and just opposite her, she, who had seemed so completely overwhelmed, leapt to her feet, stretched her arms out wide, spread her fingers, and cried, "Help! For God's sake, help!" She then craned her neck forward as if to see Gregor better, but at the same time, inconsistently, backed away from him. Forgetting that the table with all its dishes was behind her, she sat down on it, and, as if in a daze when she bumped into it, seemed utterly unaware that the large coffee pot next to her had tipped over and was pouring out a flood of coffee onto the carpet.

"Mother, Mother," said Gregor gently, looking up at her. For the moment he had completely forgotten the office manager; on the other hand, he couldn't resist snapping his jaws a few times at the sight of the streaming coffee. This made his mother scream again; she ran from the table and into the outstretched arms of his father, who came rushing to her. But Gregor had no time now for his parents. The manager had already reached the staircase; with his chin on the banister railing, he was looking back for the last time. Gregor darted forward, to be as sure as possible of catching up with him, but the manager must have guessed his intention, for he sprinted down several steps and disappeared. He was still yelling "Oohh!" and the sound echoed throughout the stairwell.

Unfortunately the manager's escape seemed to make his father, who until now had seemed reasonably calm, lose all sense of proportion. Instead of running after the man himself, or at least not interfering with Gregor's pursuit, he grabbed with his right hand the manager's cane, which he had left behind, together with his hat and overcoat, on the chair; with his left hand he snatched up a large newspaper from the table. He began stamping his feet and waving the cane and newspaper in order to drive Gregor back into his room. Nothing Gregor said made any difference, indeed, nothing he said was even understood. No matter how humbly he lowered his head his father only stamped the louder. Behind his father his mother, despite the cold, had flung open a window and was leaning far outside it, her face in her hands. A strong breeze from the street blew across the room to the stairwell, the window curtains billowed inwards, the newspapers fluttered on the table, stray pages skittered across the floor. His father, hissing like a savage, mercilessly drove him back. But as Gregor had had no practice in walking backwards, it was a very slow process. If he had been given a chance to turn around then he would've gotten back into his room at once, but he was afraid that the length of time it would take him to turn around would exasperate his father and that at any moment the cane in his father's hand might deal him a fatal blow on his back or his head. In the end, though, he had no choice, for he noticed to his horror that while moving backwards he couldn't even keep a straight course. And so, looking back anxiously, he began turning around as quickly as possible, which in reality was very slowly. Perhaps his father divined his good intentions, for he did not interfere, and even helped to direct the maneuver from afar with the tip of his cane. If only he would stop that unbearable hissing! It made Gregor completely lose his concentration. He had turned himself almost all the way around when, confused by this hissing, he made a mistake and started turning back the wrong way. But when at last he'd succeeded in getting his head in front of the doorway, he found that his body was too wide to make it through. Of course his father, in the state he was in, couldn't even begin to consider opening the other wing of the door to let Gregor in. His mind was on one thing only: to drive Gregor back into this room as quickly as possible. He would never have permitted the complicated preparations necessary for Gregor to haul himself upright and in that way perhaps slip through. Instead, making even more noise, he urged Gregor forward as if the way were clear. To Gregor the noise behind him no longer sounded like the voice of merely one father; this really wasn't a joke, and Gregor squeezed himself into the doorway, heedless of the consequences. One side of his body lifted up, he was pitched at an angle in the doorway; the other side was scraped raw, ugly blotches stained the white door. Soon he was stuck fast and couldn't have moved any further by himself. On one side his little legs hung trembling in the air, while those on the other were painfully crushed against the floor—when, from behind, his father gave him a hard blow that was truly a deliverance, and bleeding profusely, he flew far into his room. Behind him the door was slammed shut with the cane, and then at last everything was still.

II

It was already dusk when Gregor awoke from a deep, almost comatose sleep. Surely, even if he hadn't been disturbed he would've soon awakened by himself, since he'd rested and slept long enough; yet it seemed to him that he'd been awakened by the sound of hurried steps and the furtive closing of the hallway door. The light from the electric streetlamps cast pale streaks here and there on the ceiling and the upper part of the furniture, but down below, where Gregor was, it was dark. Groping awkwardly with the feelers which he was only now beginning to appreciate, he slowly pushed himself over to the door to see what had been going on there. His left side felt as if it were one long, painfully tightening scar, and he was actually limping on his two rows of legs. One little leg, moreover, had been badly hurt during the morning's events—it was nearly miraculous that only one had been hurt—and it trailed along lifelessly.

Only when he reached the door did he realize what had impelled him forward—the smell of something to eat. For there stood a bowl full of fresh milk, in which floated small slices of white bread. He could almost have laughed for joy, since he was even hungrier now than he'd been during the morning, and he immediately dipped his head into the milk, almost up to his eyes. But he soon drew it back in disappointment; not only did he find it difficult to eat because of the soreness in his left side—and he was capable of eating only if his whole gasping body cooperated—but also because he didn't like the milk at all, although it had once been his favorite drink, which, no doubt, was why his sister had brought it in. In fact, he turned away from the bowl almost in disgust, and crawled back to the middle of the room.

In the living room, as Gregor could see through the crack in the door, the gaslight had been lit. But while this was the hour when his father would usually be reading the afternoon paper in a loud voice to his mother and sometimes to his sister as well, now there wasn't a sound to be heard. Well, perhaps this custom of reading aloud, which his sister was always telling him about or mentioning in her letters, had recently been discontinued. Still, though the apartment was completely silent, it was scarcely deserted. "What a quiet life the family's been leading," said Gregor to himself, and, staring fixedly into the darkness, he felt a genuine pride at having been able to provide his parents and his sister with such a life in such a nice apartment. But what if all this calm, prosperity, and contentment were to end in horror? So as not to give in to such thoughts, Gregor set himself in motion, and he crawled up and down the room.

Once during the long evening first one of the side doors and then the other was opened a crack and then quickly shut. Someone, it seemed, had wanted to come in but then had thought better of it. Gregor now stationed himself so as to somehow get the hesitant visitor to come in or at least to find out who it might be. But the door did not open again and he waited in vain. That morning when the doors had been locked, everyone had wanted to come in, but now after he'd unlocked one of the doors himself—and the others had evidently been unlocked during the day—nobody came in, and the keys, too, were now on the outside.

It was late at night before the light was put out in the living room, and it was easy for Gregor to tell that his parents and sister had stayed up all the while, since he could plainly hear the three of them as they tiptoed away. As it was obvious that no one would be visiting Gregor before morning, he had plenty of time in which to contemplate, undisturbed, how best to rearrange his life. But the open, high-ceilinged room in which he was forced to lie flat on the floor filled him with a dread which he couldn't account for—since it was, after all, the room he had lived in for the past five years. Almost unthinkingly, and not without a faint sense of shame, he scurried under the couch. There, although his back was slightly cramped and he could no longer raise his head, he immediately felt very much at home, and his only regret was that his body was too wide to fit completely under the couch.

There he spent the rest of the night, now in a doze from which hunger pangs kept awakening him with a start, now preoccupied with worries and vague hopes, all of which, however, led to the same conclusion: that for the time being he must remain calm and, by being patient and showing every consideration, try to help his family bear the burdens that his present condition had placed upon them.

Early the next morning—the night was barely over—Gregor got an opportunity to test the strength of his newly-made resolutions, because his sister, who was almost fully dressed, opened the hallway door and looked in expectantly. She didn't see him at first, but when she spotted him underneath the couch—well, my God, he had to be somewhere, he couldn't just fly away—she was so surprised that she lost her self-control and slammed the door shut again. But, as if she felt sorry for her behavior, she opened it again right away and tiptoed in, as if she were in the presence of someone who was very ill, or who was a stranger. Gregor had moved his head forward almost to the edge of the couch and was watching her. Would she notice that he'd let the milk sit there, and not from lack of hunger, and would she bring him some other food that was more to his taste? If she wasn't going to do it on her own, he'd sooner starve than call her attention to it, although in fact he was feeling a tremendous urge to dash out from under the couch, fling himself at his sister's feet, and beg her for something good to eat. But his sister immediately noticed to her astonishment that the bowl was still full, with only a little milk spilt around it. She picked up the bowl at once—not, it's true, with her bare hands but using a rag—and carried it out. Gregor was extremely curious to find out what she would bring in its place, and he speculated at length as to what it might be. But he never would have guessed what his sister, in the goodness of her heart, actually did. She brought him a wide range of choices, all spread out on an old newspaper. There were old, half-rotten vegetables; bones left over from dinner, covered with a congealed white sauce; some raisins and almonds; a piece of cheese which Gregor two days ago had declared inedible; a slice of plain bread, a slice of bread and butter, and a slice with butter and salt. In addition to all this she replaced the bowl, now evidently reserved for Gregor, filled this time with water. And out of a sense of delicacy, since she knew that Gregor wouldn't eat in front of her, she left in a hurry, even turning the key in the lock in order that Gregor might know that he was free to make himself as comfortable as possible. Gregor's legs whirred as they propelled him toward the food. Besides, his wounds must have healed completely, for he no longer felt handicapped, which amazed him. He thought of how, a month ago, he'd cut his finger slightly with his knife and how only the day before yesterday that little wound had still hurt. "Am I less sensitive now?" he wondered, greedily sucking on the cheese, to which, above all the other dishes, he was immediately and strongly attracted. Tears of joy welled up in his eyes as he devoured the cheese, the vegetables, and the sauce. The fresh foods, on the other hand, were not to his liking; in fact, he couldn't stand to smell them and he actually dragged the food he wanted to eat a little way off. He'd long since finished eating, and was merely lying lazily in the same spot, when his sister began to slowly turn the key in the lock as a signal for him to withdraw. He got up at once, although he'd almost fallen asleep, and scurried back under the couch. But it took a great deal of self-control for him to remain under the couch even for the brief time his sister was in the room, for his heavy meal had swollen his body to some extent and he could scarcely breathe in that confined space. Between little fits of suffocation he stared with slightly bulging eyes as his unsuspecting sister took a broom and swept away not only the scraps of what he'd eaten, but also the food that he'd left untouched—as if these too were no longer any good—and hurriedly dumped everything into a bucket, which she covered with a wooden lid and carried away. She'd hardly turned her back before Gregor came out from under the couch to stretch and puff himself out.

So this was how Gregor was fed each day, once in the morning when his parents and the maid were still asleep, and again after the family's midday meal, while his parents took another brief nap and his sister could send the maid away on some errand or other. His parents didn't want Gregor to starve any more than his sister did, but perhaps for them to be directly involved in his feeding was more than they could bear, or perhaps his sister wanted to shield them even from what might prove to be no more than a minor discomfort, for they were surely suffering enough as it was.

Gregor was unable to discover what excuses had served to get rid of the doctor and the locksmith that first morning. Since the others couldn't understand what he said it never occurred to them, not even to his sister, that he could understand them, so when his sister was in the room, he had to be satisfied with occasionally hearing her sighs and her appeals to the saints. Only later, after she began to get used to the situation—of course she could never become completely used to it—would Gregor sometimes hear a remark that was intended to be friendly or could be so interpreted. "He really liked it today," she'd say when Gregor had polished off a good portion, and when the opposite was the case, which began to happen more and more often, she'd say almost sadly, "Once again, he didn't touch a thing."

But while Gregor wasn't able to get any news directly, he could overhear a considerable amount from the adjoining rooms, and as soon as he would hear the sound of voices he would immediately run to the appropriate door and press his whole body against it. In the early days especially, there wasn't a conversation that didn't in some way, if only indirectly, refer to him. For two whole days, at every meal, the family discussed what they should do, and they kept on doing so between meals as well, for at least two members of the family were now always at home, probably because nobody wanted to be in the apartment alone, and it would be unthinkable to leave it empty. Furthermore, on the very first day the cook—it wasn't completely clear how much she knew of what had happened—had on her knees begged Gregor's mother to dismiss her immediately, and when she said her goodbyes a quarter of an hour later, she thanked them for her dismissal with tears in her eyes, as if this had been the greatest favor ever bestowed on her in the house, and without having to be asked she made a solemn vow never to breathe a word of this to anyone.

So now his sister, together with his mother, had to do all the cooking as well, though in fact this wasn't too much of a chore, since the family ate practically nothing. Gregor kept hearing them vainly urging one another to eat, without receiving any reply except "No thanks, I've had enough," or some similar remark. They didn't seem to drink anything, either. His sister would often ask his father if he'd like some beer, and would gladly offer to go out and get it herself. When he wouldn't respond she'd say, in order to remove any hesitation on his part, that she could always send the janitor's wife, but at that point the father would finally utter an emphatic "No" and that would be the end of the matter.

It was on the very first day that his father gave a full account, to both mother and sister, of the family's financial situation and prospects. Every now and then he would get up from the table and take a receipt or notebook from out of the small safe he'd salvaged from the collapse of his business five years before. He could be heard opening the complicated lock and then securing it again after taking out whatever he'd been looking for. The account that his father gave, or at least part of it, was the first encouraging news that Gregor had heard since being imprisoned. He'd always had the impression that his father had failed to save a penny from the ruin of his business; at least his father had never told him otherwise, and Gregor, for that matter, had never asked him about it. At that time Gregor's only concern had been to do his utmost to make the family forget as quickly as possible the business failure that had plunged them all into a state of total despair. And so he had set to work with tremendous zeal, and had risen almost overnight from junior clerk to become a traveling salesman, which naturally opened up completely new financial opportunities so that in no time at all his success was instantly translated, by way of commissions, into hard cash, which could be laid out on the table under the eyes of his astonished and delighted family. Those had been wonderful times, and they had never returned, at least not with the same glory, even though later on Gregor had been earning enough to pay the entire family's expenses, and in fact had been doing so. They'd simply gotten used to it, both family and Gregor; they had gratefully accepted the money, and he had given it gladly, but no special warmth went with it. Gregor had remained close only to his sister, and it was his secret plan that she, who unlike Gregor loved music and could play the violin with deep feeling, should next year attend the Conservatory, despite the expense which, great as it was, would have to be met in some way. During Gregor's brief stays in the city the subject of the Conservatory would often come up in his conversations with his sister, but always only as a beautiful dream that wasn't meant to come true. His parents weren't happy to hear even these innocent remarks, but Gregor's ideas on the subject were firm and he had intended to make a solemn announcement on Christmas Eve.

Such were the thoughts, so futile in his present condition, that ran through his mind as he stood there, pressed against the door, listening. Sometimes he would grow so thoroughly weary that he couldn't listen any more and would carelessly let his head bump against the door, and though he'd pull it back immediately, even the slight noise he'd made would be heard in the next room, causing everyone to fall silent. "What's he up to now?" his father would say after a pause, obviously looking at the door, and only then would the interrupted conversation gradually be resumed.

Gregor now learned with considerable thoroughness—for his father tended to repeat his explanations several times, partly because he hadn't dealt with these matters in a long time, and partly because his mother didn't understand everything the first time through—that despite their catastrophic ruin a certain amount of capital, a very small amount, it's true, had survived intact from the old days, and thanks to the interest being untouched had even increased slightly. And what was more, the money which Gregor had been bringing home every month—he'd kept only a small sum for himself—hadn't been completely spent and had grown into a tidy sum. Gregor nodded eagerly behind his door, delighted to hear of this unexpected foresight and thrift. Of course he might have been able to use this extra money to pay off more of his father's debt to the director, and thus have brought nearer the day when he could quit his current job, but, given the present circumstances, things were better the way his father had arranged them.

Now the sum of this money wasn't nearly large enough for the family to live off the interest; the principal might support them for a year, or two at the most, but that was all. So this was really only a sum that was not to be touched, but saved instead for emergencies. As for money to live on—that would have to be earned. Though Gregor's father was indeed still healthy, nevertheless he was an old man who hadn't worked for five years and one from whom not too much should be expected in any case. During those five years, the first ones of leisure in his hard-working but unsuccessful life, he had put on a lot of weight and consequently had grown somewhat sluggish. And as for Gregor's elderly mother, was she supposed to start bringing in money, burdened as she was by her asthma which made it a strain for her to even walk across the apartment and which kept her gasping for breath every other day on the couch by the open window? Or should his sister go to work instead—she who though seventeen was still a child and one moreover whom it would be cruel to deprive of the life she'd led up until now, a life of wearing pretty clothes, sleeping late, helping around the house, enjoying a few modest pleasures, and above all playing the violin? At first, whenever their conversation turned to the need to earn money, Gregor would let go of the door and fling himself down on the cool leather couch which stood beside it, for he felt hot with grief and shame.

Often he would lie there all night long, not sleeping a wink, scratching at the leather couch for hours. Or, undaunted by the great effort it required, he would push the chair over to the window. Then he would crawl up to the sill and, propped up by the chair, would lean against the pane, apparently inspired by some memory of the sense of freedom that gazing out a window used to give him. For in truth objects only a short distance away were now, each day, becoming more indistinct; the hospital across the street, which he used to curse because he could see it all too clearly, was now completely outside his field of vision, and if he hadn't known for a fact that he lived on Charlotte Street—a quiet but nevertheless urban street—he could have imagined that he was looking out his window at a wasteland where gray sky and gray earth had indistinguishably merged as one. His observant sister needed only to notice twice that the armchair had been moved to the window. From then on, whenever she cleaned the room, she carefully placed the chair back by the window, and even began leaving the inner casement open.

If only Gregor had been able to speak to his sister and thank her for everything she'd had to do for him, he could have borne her kindnesses more easily, but as it was they were painful to him. Of course his sister tried her best to ease the general embarrassment, and naturally as time passed she grew better and better at it. But Gregor too, over time, gained a clearer sense of what was involved. Even the way in which she entered the room was a torture to him. No sooner had she stepped in when—not even pausing to shut the door, despite the care she normally would take in sparing others the sight of Gregor's room—she would run straight over to the window and tear it open with impatient fingers, almost as if she were suffocating, and she would remain for some time by the window, even in the coldest weather, breathing deeply. Twice a day she would terrify Gregor with all this noise and rushing around. He would cower under the couch the entire time, knowing full well that she surely would have spared him this if only she could have stood being in the room with him with the windows closed.

Once, about a month after Gregor's metamorphosis—so there was really no particular reason for his sister to be upset by his appearance—she came in earlier than usual and caught Gregor as he gazed out the window, terrifying in his stillness. It wouldn't have surprised Gregor if she'd decided not to come in, since his position prevented her from opening the window right away, but not only did she not come in, she actually jumped back and shut the door—a stranger might have thought that Gregor had been planning to ambush her and bite her. Of course he immediately hid under the couch, but he had to wait until noon before she came back, and this time she seemed much more nervous than usual. In this way he came to realize that the sight of him disgusted her, and likely would always disgust her, and that she probably had to steel herself not to run away at the sight of even the tiny portion of his body that stuck out from under the couch. So, one day, to spare her even this, he carried the bedsheet on his back over to the couch—it took him four hours—and spread it so that he was completely covered and his sister wouldn't be able to see him even if she bent down. If she felt this sheet wasn't necessary then of course she could remove it, since obviously Gregor wasn't shutting himself away so completely in order to amuse himself. But she left the sheet alone, and Gregor even thought that he caught a look of gratitude when he cautiously lifted the sheet a little with his head in order to see how his sister was taking to this new arrangement.

During the first two weeks, his parents couldn't bring themselves to come in to see him, and he frequently heard them remarking how much they appreciated his sister's efforts, whereas previously they'd often been annoyed with her for being, in their eyes, somewhat useless. But now both father and mother had fallen into the habit of waiting outside Gregor's door while his sister cleaned up the room, and as soon as she emerged she would have to tell them every detail of the room's condition, what Gregor had eaten, how he'd behaved this time, and whether he'd perhaps shown a little improvement. It wasn't long before his mother began to want to visit Gregor, but his father and sister were at first able to dissuade her by rational arguments to which Gregor listened with great care, and with which he thoroughly agreed. But as time went by she had to be restrained by force, and when she cried out "Let me go to Gregor, he's my unhappy boy! Don't you understand that I have to go to him?" Gregor began to think that it might be a good idea if his mother did come in after all, not every day, naturally, but, say, once a week. She was really a much more capable person than his sister, who, for all her courage, was still only a child and had perhaps taken on such a difficult task only out of a childish impulsiveness.

Gregor's wish to see his mother was soon fulfilled. During the day Gregor didn't want to show himself at the window, if only out of consideration for his parents. But his few square meters of floor gave him little room to crawl around in, he found it hard to lie still even at night, and eating soon ceased to give him any pleasure. So in order to distract himself he fell into the habit of crawling all over the walls and the ceiling. He especially enjoyed hanging from the ceiling; it was completely different from lying on the floor. He could breathe more freely, a faint pulsing coursed through his body, and in his state of almost giddy absentmindedness up there, Gregor would sometimes, to his surprise, lose his grip and tumble onto the floor. But now, of course, since he had much better control over his body, even such a great fall didn't hurt him. His sister noticed right away the new pastime Gregor had discovered for himself—he'd left sticky traces where he'd been crawling—and so she got it into her head to provide Gregor with as much room as possible to crawl around in by removing all the furniture that was in the way—especially the chest of drawers and the desk. But she couldn't manage this by herself; she didn't dare ask her father for help; the maid wouldn't be of any use, for while this girl, who was around sixteen, was brave enough to stay on after the cook had left, she'd asked to be allowed to always keep the kitchen door locked, opening it only when specifically asked to do so. This left his sister with no choice but, one day when her father was out, to ask her mother for help. And indeed, her mother followed her with joyful, excited cries, although she fell silent when they reached the door to Gregor's room. Naturally his sister first made sure that everything in the room was as it should be; only then did she let her mother come in. Gregor had hurriedly pulled his sheet even lower and had folded it more tightly and it really did look as if it had been casually tossed over the couch. This time Gregor also refrained from peeking out from under the sheet; he denied himself the pleasure of seeing his mother for now and was simply glad that she'd come after all. "Come on in, he's nowhere in sight," said his sister, apparently leading his mother in by the hand. Now Gregor could hear the two delicate women moving the heavy chest of drawers away from its place, his sister stubbornly insisting on doing the hardest work, ignoring the warnings of her mother, who was afraid her daughter would overstrain herself. The work took a very long time. After struggling for over a quarter of an hour, his mother suggested that they might leave the chest where it was; in the first place, it was just too heavy, they'd never be done before his father came home and they'd have to leave it in the middle of the room, blocking Gregor's movements in every direction; in the second place, it wasn't at all certain that they were doing Gregor a favor in removing the furniture. It seemed to her that the opposite was true, the sight of the bare walls broke her heart; and why shouldn't Gregor feel the same since he'd been used to this furniture for so long and would feel abandoned in the empty room? "And wouldn't it look as if," his mother concluded very softly—in fact, she'd been almost whispering the entire time, as if she wanted to prevent Gregor, whose exact whereabouts she didn't know, from hearing the sound of her voice (she was convinced that he couldn't understand her words)—"as if by removing his furniture we were telling him that we'd given up all hope of his getting better, and were callously leaving him to his own devices? I think the best course would be to try to keep the room exactly the way it was, so that when Gregor does come back to us he'll find everything the same, making it easier for him to forget what has happened in the meantime."

When he heard his mother's words, Gregor realized that, over the past two months, the lack of having anyone to converse with, together with the monotonous life within the family, must have befuddled his mind; there wasn't any other way he could explain to himself how he could have ever seriously wanted his room cleared out. Did he really want this warm room of his, so comfortably furnished with family heirlooms, transformed into a lair where he'd be perfectly free to crawl around in every direction, but only at the cost of simultaneously forgetting his human past, swiftly and utterly? Just now he'd been on the brink of forgetting, and only his mother's voice, which he hadn't heard for so long, had brought him back. Nothing should be removed; everything must stay. He couldn't do without the furniture's soothing influence on his state of mind, and if the furniture were to impede his senselessly crawling around, that wouldn't be a loss but rather a great advantage.

But unfortunately his sister thought otherwise. She'd become accustomed, and not without some justification, to assuming the role of the acknowledged expert whenever she and her parents discussed Gregor's affairs; so her mother's advice was enough for her to insist now not merely on her original plan of moving the chest and the desk, but on the removal of every bit of furniture except for the indispensable couch. Her resolve, to be sure, didn't stem merely from childish stubbornness or from the self-confidence she had recently and unexpectedly gained at such great cost. For in fact she'd noticed that while Gregor needed plenty of room to crawl around in, on the other hand, as far as she could tell, he never used the furniture at all. Perhaps too, the sentimental enthusiasm of girls her age, which they indulge themselves in at every opportunity, now tempted Grete to make Gregor's situation all the more terrifying so that she might be able to do more for him. No one but Grete would ever be likely to enter a room where Gregor ruled the bare walls all alone.

And so she refused to give in to her mother, who in any case, from the sheer anxiety caused by being in Gregor's room, seemed unsure of herself. She soon fell silent and began as best she could to help her daughter remove the chest of drawers. Well, if he must, then Gregor could do without the chest, but the desk had to stay. And no sooner had the two women, groaning and squeezing, gotten the chest out of the room than Gregor poked his head out from under the couch to see how he might intervene as tactfully as possible. But unfortunately it was his mother who came back first, leaving Grete in the next room, gripping the chest with her arms and rocking it back and forth without, of course, being able to budge it from the spot. His mother wasn't used to the sight of him—it might make her sick; so Gregor, frightened, scuttled backwards to the far end of the couch, but he couldn't prevent the front of the sheet from stirring slightly. That was enough to catch his mother's attention. She stopped, stood still for a moment, and then went back to Grete.

Gregor kept telling himself that nothing unusual was happening, that only a few pieces of furniture were being moved around. But he soon had to admit that all this coming and going of the two women, their little calls to one another, the scraping of the furniture across the floor, affected him as if it were some gigantic commotion rushing in on him from every side, and though he tucked in his head and legs and pressed his body against the floor, he had to accept the fact that he wouldn't be able to stand it much longer. They were cleaning out his room, taking away from him everything that he loved; already they'd carried off his chest, where he kept his fretsaw and his other tools; now they were trying to pry his writing desk loose—it was practically embedded in the floor—the same desk where he'd always done his homework when he'd been a student at business school, in high school, and even in elementary school. He really no longer had any time left in which to weigh the good intentions of these two women whose existence, for that matter, he'd almost forgotten, since they were so exhausted by now that they worked in silence, the only sound being that of their weary, plodding steps.

And so, while the women were in the next room, leaning against the desk and trying to catch their breath, he broke out, changing his direction four times—since he really didn't know what to rescue first—when he saw, hanging conspicuously on the otherwise bare wall, the picture of the lady all dressed in furs. He quickly crawled up to it and pressed himself against the glass, which held him fast, soothing his hot belly. Now that Gregor completely covered it, this picture at least wasn't about to be carried away by anyone. He turned his head towards the living room door, so that he could watch the women when they returned.

They hadn't taken much of a rest and were already coming back. Grete had put her arm around her mother and was almost carrying her. "Well, what should we take next?" said Grete, looking around. And then her eyes met Gregor's, looking down at her from the wall. Probably only because her mother was there, she kept her composure, bent her head down to her mother to prevent her from glancing around, and said, though in a hollow, quavering voice: "Come on, let's go back to the living room for a minute." To Gregor, her intentions were obvious: she wanted to get his mother to safety and then chase him down from the wall. Well, just let her try! He clung to his picture and he wasn't going to give it up. He'd rather fly at Grete's face.

But Grete's words had made her mother even more anxious; she stepped aside, glimpsed the huge brown blotch on the flowered wallpaper, and before she fully understood that what she was looking at was Gregor, she cried out, "Oh God, oh God!" in a hoarse scream of a voice, and, as if giving up completely, fell with outstretched arms across the couch, and lay there without moving. "You! Gregor!" cried his sister, raising her fist and glaring at him. These were the first words she had addressed directly to him since his metamorphosis. She ran into the next room to get some spirits to revive her mother from her faint. Gregor also wanted to help—he could rescue the picture another time—but he was stuck to the glass and had to tear himself free. He then scuttled into the next room as if to give some advice, as he used to, to his sister. Instead, he had to stand behind her uselessly while she rummaged among various little bottles. When she turned around she was startled, a bottle fell to the floor, a splinter of glass struck Gregor in the face, some sort of corrosive medicine splashed on him, and Grete, without further delay, grabbing as many of the little bottles as she could carry, ran inside with them to her mother, and slammed the door shut behind her with her foot. Now Gregor was cut off from his mother, who was perhaps near death because of him. He didn't dare open the door for fear of scaring his sister, who had to remain with his mother. There wasn't anything for him to do but wait; and so, tormented by guilt and anxiety, he began crawling. He crawled over everything, walls, furniture, and ceiling, until finally, in despair, the room beginning to spin around him, he collapsed onto the middle of the large table.

A short time passed; Gregor lay there stupefied. Everything was quiet around him; perhaps that was a good sign. Then the doorbell rang. The maid, of course, stayed locked up in her kitchen, so Grete had to answer the door. His father was back. "What's happened?" were his first words. Grete's expression must've told him everything. Her answers came in muffled tones—she was obviously burying her face in her father's chest. "Mother fainted, but she's better now. Gregor's broken loose." "I knew it," her father said. "I told you this would happen, but you women refuse to listen." It was clear to Gregor that his father had put the worst construction on Grete's all too brief account and had assumed that Gregor was guilty of some violent act. That meant that he must calm his father down, since he had neither the time nor the ability to explain things to him. So he fled to the door of his room and pressed himself against it in order that his father might see, as soon as he entered the living room, that Gregor had every intention of returning immediately to his own room and there was no need to force him back. All they had to do was to open the door and he would disappear at once.

But his father wasn't in the mood to notice such subtleties; "Ah!" he roared as he entered, in a voice that sounded at once furious and gleeful. Gregor turned his head from the door and lifted it towards his father. He really hadn't imagined that his father would look the way he did standing before him now; true, Gregor had become too absorbed lately by his new habit of crawling to bother about whatever else might be going on in the apartment, and he should have anticipated that there would be some changes. And yet, and yet, could this really be his father? Was this the same man who used to lie sunk in bed, exhausted, whenever Gregor would set out on one of his business trips; who would greet him upon his return in the evening while sitting in his bathrobe in the armchair; who was hardly capable of getting to his feet, and to show his joy could only lift up his arms; and who, on those rare times when the whole family went out for a walk—on the occasional Sunday or on a legal holiday—used to painfully shuffle along between Gregor and his mother, who were slow walkers themselves, and yet he was always slightly slower than they, wrapped up in his old overcoat, carefully planting his crook-handled cane before him with every step, and almost invariably stopping and gathering his escort around him whenever he wanted to say something? Now, however, he held himself very erect, dressed up in a closely-fitting blue uniform with gold buttons, of the kind worn by bank messengers. His heavy chin thrust out over the stiff collar of his jacket; his black eyes stared, sharp and bright, from under his bushy eyebrows; his white hair, once so rumpled, was combed flat, it gleamed, and the part was meticulously exact. He tossed his cap—which bore a gold monogram, probably that of some bank—in an arc across the room so that it landed on the couch, and with his hands in his pockets, the tails of his uniform's long jacket flung back, his face grim, he went after Gregor. He probably didn't know himself what he was going to do, but he lifted his feet unusually high, and Gregor was amazed at the immense size of the soles of his boots. However, Gregor didn't dwell on these reflections, for he had known from the very first day of his new life that his father considered only the strictest measures to be appropriate in dealing with him. So he ran ahead of his father, stopped when he stood still, and scurried on again when he made the slightest move. In this way they circled the room several times without anything decisive happening; in fact, their movements, because of their slow tempo, did not suggest those of a chase. So Gregor kept to the floor for the time being, especially since he was afraid that his father might consider any flight to the walls or ceiling to be particularly offensive. All the same, Gregor had to admit that he wouldn't be able to keep up even this pace for long, since whenever his father took a single step, Gregor had to perform an entire series of movements. He was beginning to get winded, since even in his former life his lungs had never been strong. As he kept staggering on like this, so weary he could barely keep his eyes open, since he was saving all his strength for running; not even thinking, dazed as he was, that there might be any other way to escape than by running; having almost forgotten that he was free to use the walls, though against these walls, admittedly, were placed bits of intricately carved furniture, bristling with spikes and sharp corners—suddenly something sailed overhead, hit the floor nearby, and rolled right in front of him. It was an apple; at once a second one came flying after it. Gregor stopped, petrified with fear; it was useless to keep on running, for his father had decided to bombard him. He had filled his pockets with the fruit from the bowl on the sideboard and now he was throwing one apple after another, for now at least without bothering to take good aim. These little red apples, colliding with one another, rolled around on the floor as if electrified. One weakly-thrown apple grazed Gregor's back, rolling off without causing harm. But another one that came flying immediately afterwards actually imbedded itself in Gregor's back. Gregor wanted to drag himself onward, as if this shocking and unbelievable pain might disappear if he could only keep moving, but he felt as if he were nailed to the spot, and he splayed himself out in the utter confusion of his senses. With his last glance he saw the door of his room burst open, and his mother, wearing only her chemise—his sister had removed her dress to help her breathe after she'd fainted—rush out, followed by his screaming sister. He saw his mother run toward his father, her loosened underskirts slipping one by one onto the floor. Stumbling over her skirts she flung herself upon his father, embraced him, was as one with him—but now Gregor's sight grew dim—and with her arms clasped around his father's neck, begged for Gregor's life.

III

Gregor's serious wound, which made him suffer for over a month—the apple remained imbedded in his flesh as a visible reminder, no one having the courage to remove it—seemed to have persuaded even his father that Gregor, despite his present pathetic and disgusting shape, was a member of the family who shouldn't be treated as an enemy. On the contrary, familial duty required them to swallow their disgust and to endure him, to endure him and nothing more.

And though his wound probably had caused Gregor to suffer a permanent loss of mobility, and though it now took him, as if he were some disabled war veteran, many a long minute to creep across his room—crawling above ground level was out of the question—yet in return for this deterioration of his condition he was granted a compensation which satisfied him completely: each day around dusk the living room door—which he was in the habit of watching closely for an hour or two ahead of time—was opened, and lying in the darkness of his room, invisible from the living room, he could see the whole family sitting at the table lit by the lamp and could listen to their conversation as if by general consent, instead of the way he'd done before.

True, these were no longer the lively conversations of old, those upon which Gregor had mused somewhat wistfully as he'd settled wearily into his damp bed in some tiny hotel room. Things were now very quiet for the most part. Soon after dinner his father would fall asleep in his armchair, while his mother and sister would admonish each other to be quiet; his mother, bending forward under the light, would sew fine lingerie for a fashion store; his sister, who had found work as a salesgirl, would study shorthand and French in the evenings, hoping to obtain a better job in the future. Sometimes his father would wake up, as if he hadn't the slightest idea that he'd been asleep, and would say to his mother, "Look how long you've been sewing again today!" and then would fall back to sleep, while his mother and sister would exchange weary smiles.

With a kind of perverse obstinacy his father refused to take off his messenger's uniform even in the apartment; while his robe hung unused on the clothes hook, he would sleep fully dressed in his chair, as if he were always ready for duty and were waiting even here for the voice of his superior. As a result his uniform, which hadn't been new in the first place, began to get dirty in spite of all his mother and sister could do to care for it, and Gregor would often spend entire evenings gazing at this garment covered with stains and with its constantly polished buttons gleaming, in which the old man would sit, upright and uncomfortable, yet peacefully asleep.

As soon as the clock would strike ten, his mother would try to awaken his father with soft words of encouragement and then persuade him to go to bed, for this wasn't any place in which to get a decent night's sleep, and his father badly needed his rest, since he had to be at work at six in the morning. But with the stubbornness that had possessed him ever since he'd become a bank messenger he would insist on staying at the table a little while longer, though he invariably would fall asleep again, and then it was only with the greatest difficulty that he could be persuaded to trade his chair for bed. No matter how much mother and sister would urge him on with little admonishments, he'd keep shaking his head for a good fifteen minutes, his eyes closed, and wouldn't get up. Gregor's mother would tug at his sleeve, whisper sweet words into his ear; and his sister would leave her homework to help her mother, but it was all useless. He only sank deeper into his armchair. Not until the two women would lift him up by the arms would he open his eyes, look now at one, now at the other, and usually say, "What a life. So this is the peace of my old age." And leaning on the two women he would get up laboriously, as if he were his own greatest burden, and would allow the women to lead him to the door, where, waving them aside, he continued on his own, while Gregor's mother abandoned her sewing and his sister her pen so that they might run after his father and continue to look after him.

Who in this overworked and exhausted family had time to worry about Gregor any more than was absolutely necessary? Their resources grew more limited; the maid was now dismissed after all; a gigantic bony cleaning woman with white hair fluttering about her head came in the mornings and evenings to do the roughest work; Gregor's mother took care of everything else, in addition to her sewing. It even happened that certain pieces of family jewelry, which his mother and sister had worn with such pleasure at parties and celebrations in days gone by, were sold, as Gregor found out one evening by listening to a general discussion of the prices they'd gone for. But their greatest complaint was that they couldn't give up the apartment, which was too big for their current needs, since no one could figure out how they would move Gregor. But Gregor understood clearly enough that it wasn't simply consideration for him which prevented them moving, since he could have easily been transported in a suitable crate equipped with a few air holes. The main reason preventing them from moving was their utter despair and the feeling that they had been struck by a misfortune far greater than any that had ever visited their friends and relatives. What the world demands of the poor they did to the utmost: his father fetched breakfast for the bank's minor officials, his mother sacrificed herself for the underwear of strangers, his sister ran back and forth behind the counters at the beck and call of customers; but they lacked the strength for anything beyond this. And the wound in Gregor's back began to ache once more when his mother and sister, after putting his father to bed, returned to the room, ignored their work, and sat huddled together cheek to cheek, and his mother said, "Close that door, Grete," so that Gregor was back in the dark, while in the next room the women wept together or simply stared at the table with dry eyes.

Gregor spent the days and nights almost entirely without sleep. Sometimes he imagined that the next time the door opened he would once again assume control of the family's affairs, as he'd done in the old days. Now, after a long absence, there reappeared in his thoughts the director and the manager, the salesmen and the apprentices, the remarkably stupid errand runner, two or three friends from other firms, a chambermaid at one of the provincial hotels—a sweet, fleeting memory—a cashier at a hat store whom he'd courted earnestly but too slowly—they all came to him mixed up with strangers and with people whom he'd already forgotten. But instead of helping him and his family they were all unapproachable, and he was glad when they faded away. At other times he was in no mood to worry about his family; he was utterly filled with rage at how badly he was being treated, and although he couldn't imagine anything that might tempt his appetite, he nevertheless tried to think up ways of getting into the pantry to take what was rightfully his, even if he wasn't hungry. No longer bothering to consider what Gregor might like as a treat, his sister, before she hurried off to work in the morning and after lunch, would shove any sort of food into Gregor's room with her foot. In the evening, regardless of whether the food had been picked at, or—as was more often the case—left completely untouched, she would sweep it out with a swish of the broom. Nowadays she would clean the room in the evening, and she couldn't have done it any faster. Streaks of grime ran along the walls, balls of dust and dirt lay here and there on the floor. At first, whenever his sister would come in, Gregor would station himself in some corner that was particularly objectionable, as if his presence there might serve as a reproach to her. But he probably could have remained there for weeks without her mending her ways; she obviously could see the dirt as clearly as he could, but she'd made up her mind to leave it. At the same time she made certain—with a touchiness that was completely new to her and which indeed was infecting the entire family—that the cleaning of Gregor's room was to remain her prerogative. On one occasion Gregor's mother had subjected his room to a thorough cleaning, which she managed to accomplish only with the aid of several buckets of water—all this dampness being a further annoyance to Gregor, who lay flat, unhappy, and motionless on the couch. But his mother's punishment was not long in coming. For that evening, as soon as Gregor's sister noticed the difference in his room, she ran, deeply insulted, into the living room, and without regard for his mother's uplifted, beseeching hands, burst into a fit of tears. Both parents—the father, naturally, had been startled out of his armchair—at first looked on with helpless amazement, and then they joined in, the father on his right side blaming the mother: she shouldn't have interfered with the sister's cleaning of the room, while on his left side yelling at the sister that she'd never be allowed to clean Gregor's room again. The mother was trying to drag the father, who was half out of his mind, into their bedroom while the sister, shaking with sobs, pounded the table with her little fists, and Gregor hissed loudly with rage because not one of them had thought to close the door and spare him this scene and this commotion.

But even if his sister, worn out by her job at the store, had gotten tired of taking care of Gregor as she once had, it wasn't really necessary for his mother to take her place so that Gregor wouldn't be neglected. For now the cleaning woman was there. This ancient widow, whose powerful bony frame had no doubt helped her through the hard times in her long life, wasn't at all repelled by Gregor. Without being the least bit inquisitive, she had once, by chance, opened the door to Gregor's room and at the sight of Gregor—who, taken completely by surprise, began running back and forth although no one was chasing him—stood there in amazement, her hands folded over her belly. From then on, morning and evening, she never failed to open his door a crack and peek in on him. At first she also would call him to her, using phrases she probably meant to be friendly, such as "Come on over here, you old dung beetle!" or "Just look at that old dung beetle!" Gregor wouldn't respond to such forms of address, but would remain motionless where he was as if the door had never been opened. If only this cleaning woman, instead of pointlessly disturbing him whenever she felt like it, had been given orders to clean his room every day! Once, early in the morning, when a heavy rain, perhaps a sign of the already approaching spring, was beating against the window panes, Gregor became so exasperated when the cleaning woman started in with her phrases that he made as if to attack her, though, of course, in a slow and feeble manner. But instead of being frightened, the cleaning woman simply picked up a chair by the door and, lifting it high in the air, stood there with her mouth wide open. Obviously she didn't plan on shutting it until the chair in her hands had first come crashing down on Gregor's back. "So you're not going through with it?" she asked as Gregor turned back while she calmly set the chair down again in the corner.

By now Gregor was eating next to nothing. Only when he happened to pass by the food set out for him would he take a bite, hold it in his mouth for hours, and then spit most of it out again. At first he imagined that it was his anguish at the state of his room that kept him from eating, but it was those very changes to which he had quickly become accustomed. The family had fallen into the habit of using the room to store things for which there wasn't any place anywhere else, and there were many of these things now, since one room in the apartment had been rented to three boarders. These serious gentlemen—all three of them had full beards, as Gregor once noted, peering through a crack in the door—had a passion for neatness, not only in their room but since they were now settled in as boarders, throughout the entire apartment, and especially in the kitchen. They couldn't abide useless, let alone dirty, junk. Besides, they'd brought most of their own household goods along with them. This meant that many objects were now superfluous, which, while clearly without any resale value, couldn't just be thrown out either. All these things ended up in Gregor's room, and so did the ash bucket and the garbage can from the kitchen. Anything that wasn't being used at the moment was simply tossed into Gregor's room by the cleaning woman, who was always in a tremendous hurry. Fortunately, Gregor generally saw only the object in question and the hand that held it. Perhaps the cleaning woman intended to come back for these things when she had the time, or perhaps she planned on throwing them all out, but in fact there they remained, wherever they'd happened to land, except for Gregor's disturbing them as he squeezed his way through the junk pile. At first he did so simply because he was forced to, since there wasn't any other space to crawl in, but later he took a growing pleasure in these rambles even though they left him dead tired and so sad that he would lie motionless for hours. Since the boarders would sometimes have their dinner at home in the shared living room, on those evenings the door between that room and Gregor's would remain shut. But Gregor didn't experience the door's not being open as a hardship; in fact there had been evenings when he'd ignored the open door and had lain, unnoticed by the family, in the darkest corners of his room. But one time the cleaning woman left the door slightly ajar, and it remained ajar when the boarders came in that evening and the lamp was lit. They sat down at the head of the table, where Gregor, his mother and his father had sat in the old days; they unfolded their napkins, and picked up their knives and forks. At once his mother appeared at the kitchen door carrying a platter of meat and right behind her came his sister carrying a platter piled high with potatoes. The steaming food gave off a thick vapor. The platters were set down in front of the boarders, who bent over them as if to examine them before eating, and in fact the one sitting in the middle, who was apparently looked up to as an authority by the other two, cut into a piece of meat while it was still on the platter, evidently to determine if it was tender enough or whether perhaps it should be sent back to the kitchen. He was satisfied, and both mother and daughter, who'd been watching anxiously, breathed a sigh of relief and began to smile.

The family itself ate in the kitchen. Even so, before going to the kitchen his father came into the living room, bowed once and, cap in hand, walked around the table. The boarders all rose together and mumbled something into their beards. When they were once more alone, they ate in almost complete silence. It seemed strange to Gregor that, out of all the noises produced by eating, he distinctly heard the sound of their teeth chewing; it was as if he were being told you needed teeth in order to eat and that even with the most wonderful toothless jaws, you wouldn't be able to accomplish a thing. "Yes, I'm hungry enough," Gregor told himself sadly, "but not for those things. How well these boarders feed themselves, while I waste away."

That very evening—during this whole time Gregor couldn't once remember hearing the violin—the sound of violin playing came from the kitchen. The boarders had already finished their dinner, the one in the middle had pulled out a newspaper, handed one sheet each to the other two, and now they were leaning back, reading and smoking. When the violin began to play, they noticed it, stood up, and tiptoed to the hall doorway where they stood together in a tight group. They must have been heard in the kitchen for his father called, "Does the playing bother you, gentlemen? We can stop it at once." "On the contrary," said the gentleman in the middle, "wouldn't the young lady like to come and play in here where it's much more roomy and comfortable?" "Why, certainly," called Gregor's father, as if he were the violinist. Soon his father came in carrying the music stand, his mother the sheet music, and his sister the violin. His sister calmly got everything ready for playing; his parents—who had never rented out rooms before and so were overly polite to the boarders—didn't even dare to sit down in their own chairs. His father leaned against the door, slipping his right hand between the buttons of his uniform's jacket, which he'd kept buttoned up; but his mother was offered a chair by one of the gentlemen, and, leaving it where he happened to have placed it, she sat off to one side, in the corner.

His sister began to play; his father and mother, on either side, closely followed the movements of her hands. Gregor, attracted by the playing, had moved a little farther forward and already had his head in the living room. He was hardly surprised that recently he'd shown so little concern for others, although in the past he'd taken pride in being considerate. Now more than ever he had good reason to remain hidden, since he was completely covered with the dust that lay everywhere in his room and was stirred up by the slightest movement. Moreover, threads, hairs, and scraps of food clung to his back and sides, his indifference to everything was much too great for him to have gotten onto his back and rubbed himself clean against the carpet, as he had once done several times a day. And despite his condition he wasn't ashamed to edge his way a little further across the spotless living room floor.

To be sure, no one took any notice of him. The family was completely absorbed by the violin-playing. The boarders, however, who had at first placed themselves, their hands in their pockets, much too close to the music stand—close enough for every one of them to have followed the score, which surely must have flustered his sister—soon retreated to the window, muttering to one another, with their heads lowered. And there they remained while his father watched them anxiously. It seemed all too obvious that they had been disappointed in their hopes of hearing good or entertaining violin-playing; they had had enough of the entire performance, and it was only out of politeness that they continued to let their peace be disturbed. It was especially obvious, by the way they blew their smoke out of their mouths and noses—it floated upwards to the ceiling—just how ill at ease they were. And yet his sister was playing so beautifully. Her face was inclined to one side, and her sad eyes carefully followed the notes of the music. Gregor crawled forward a little farther, keeping his head close to the floor so that their eyes might possibly meet. Was he an animal, that music could move him so? He felt that he was being shown the way to an unknown nourishment he yearned for. He was determined to press on until he reached his sister, to tug at her skirt, and to let her know in this way that she should bring her violin into his room, for no one here would honor her playing as he would. He would never let her out of his room again, at least not for as long as he lived; at last his horrifying appearance would be useful; he would be at every door of his room at once, hissing and spitting at the attackers. His sister, however, wouldn't be forced to remain with him, she would do so of her own free will. She would sit beside him on the couch, leaning towards him and listening as he confided that he had firmly intended to send her to the Conservatory, and if the misfortune hadn't intervened, he would've announced this to everyone last Christmas—for hadn't Christmas come and gone by now?—without paying the slightest attention to any objection. After this declaration his sister would be so moved that she would burst into tears, and Gregor would lift himself up to her shoulder and kiss her on her neck, which, since she had started her job, she had kept bare, without ribbon or collar.

"Mr. Samsa!" cried the middle gentleman to Gregor's father, and without wasting another word pointed with his index finger at Gregor, who was slowly advancing. The violin stopped, the middle gentleman, shaking his head, smiled first at his friends and then looked at Gregor again. Instead of driving Gregor away, his father seemed to think it more important to soothe the boarders, although they weren't upset at all and appeared to consider Gregor more entertaining than the violin-playing. His father rushed over to them and with outstretched arms tried to herd them back into their room and at the same time block their view of Gregor with his body. Now they actually got a little angry—it wasn't clear whether this was due to his father's behavior or to their dawning realization that they had had all along, without knowing it, a next-door neighbor like Gregor. They demanded explanations from his father, raised their own arms now as well, tugged nervously at their beards, and only slowly backed away toward their room. Meanwhile his sister had managed to overcome the bewildered state into which she'd fallen when her playing had been so abruptly interrupted, and after some moments spent holding the violin and bow in her slackly dangling hands and staring at the score as if she were still playing, she suddenly pulled herself together, placed her instrument on her mother's lap—she was still sitting in her chair with her lungs heaving, gasping for breath—and ran into the next room, which the boarders, under pressure from her father, were ever more swiftly approaching. One could see pillows and blankets flying high in the air and then neatly arranging themselves under his sister's practical hands. Before the gentlemen had even reached their room, she had finished making the beds and had slipped out.

Once again a perverse stubbornness seemed to grip Gregor's father, to the extent that he forgot to pay his tenants the respect still due them. He kept on pushing and shoving until the middle gentleman, who was already standing in the room's doorway, brought him up short with a thunderous stamp of his foot. "I hereby declare," he said, raising his hand and looking around for Gregor's mother and sister as well, "that considering the disgusting conditions prevailing in this apartment and in this

75

family"—here he suddenly spat on the floor—"I'm giving immediate notice. Naturally I'm not going to pay a penny for the time I've spent here; on the contrary, I shall be seriously considering bringing some sort of action against you with claims that—I assure you—will be very easy to substantiate." He stopped speaking and stared ahead of him, as if expecting something. And indeed his two friends chimed right in, saying "We're giving immediate notice too." Whereupon he grabbed the doorknob and slammed the door shut with a crash.

Gregor's father, groping his way and staggering forward, collapsed into his armchair; it looked as if he were stretching himself out for his usual evening nap, but his heavily drooping head, looking as if it had lost all means of support, showed that he was anything but asleep. All this time Gregor had lain quietly right where the boarders had first seen him. His disappointment over the failure of his plan, and perhaps also the weakness caused by eating so little for so long, made movement an impossibility. He feared with some degree of certainty that at the very next moment the whole catastrophe would fall on his head, and he waited. He wasn't even startled when the violin slipped from his mother's trembling fingers and fell off her lap with a reverberating clatter.

"Dear parents," said his sister, pounding the table with her hand by way of preamble, "we can't go on like this. Maybe you don't realize it, but I do. I refuse to utter my brother's name in the presence of this monster, and so all I have to say is: we've got to try to get rid of it. We've done everything humanly possible to take care of it and put up with it; I don't think anyone can blame us in the least."

"She's absolutely right," said his father to himself. His mother, still trying to catch her breath, with a wild look in her eyes, began to cough, her cupped hand muffling the sound.

His sister rushed over to his mother and held her forehead. His father seemed to have been led to more definite thoughts by Grete's words; he was sitting up straight and toying with his messenger's cap, which lay on the table among the dishes left over from the boarders' dinner. From time to time he would glance over at Gregor's motionless form.

"We must try to get rid of it," said his sister, speaking only to her father since her mother's coughing was such that she was incapable of hearing a word. "It will be the death of you both. I can see it coming. People who have to work as hard as we do can't stand this constant torture at home. I can't stand it anymore either." And she burst out sobbing so violently that her tears ran down onto her mother's face, where she wiped them away mechanically with her hand.

"But, my child," said her father with compassion and remarkable understanding, "what should we do?"

Gregor's sister could only shrug her shoulders as a sign of the helplessness that had overcome her while she wept, in contrast to her earlier self-confidence.

"If he could understand us," said her father tentatively; Gregor's sister, through her tears, shook her hand violently to indicate how impossible that was.

"If he could understand us," repeated her father, closing his eyes so as to take in his daughter's belief that this was impossible, "then perhaps we might be able to reach some agreement with him, but the way things are—"

"He's got to go," cried Gregor's sister, "it's the only way, Father. You just have to get rid of the idea that this is Gregor. Our real misfortune is having believed it for so long. But how can it be Gregor? If it were, he would've realized a long time ago that it's impossible for human beings to live with a creature like that, and he would've left of his own accord. Then we would've lost a brother, but we'd have been able to go on living and honor his memory. But the way things are, this animal persecutes us, drives away our boarders, obviously it wants to take over the whole apartment and make us sleep in the gutter. Look, Father," she suddenly screamed, "he's at it again!" And in a panic which Gregor found incomprehensible his sister abandoned his mother, and actually pushing herself from the chair as if she would rather sacrifice her mother than remain near Gregor, she rushed behind her father, who, startled by this behavior, got up as well, half raising his arms in front of Grete as if to protect her.

Gregor hadn't the slightest desire to frighten anyone, least of all his sister. He had merely started to turn around in order to go back to his room, a procedure which admittedly looked strange, since in his weakened condition he had to use his head to help him in this difficult maneuver, several times raising it and then knocking it against the floor. He stopped and looked around. His good intentions seemed to have been understood; the panic had only been temporary. Now, silent and sad, they all looked at him. His mother lay in her armchair with her legs outstretched and pressed together, her eyes almost closed from exhaustion. His father and sister sat side by side, and his sister had put her arm around her father's neck.

"Now maybe they'll let me turn around," thought Gregor, resuming his efforts. He couldn't stop panting from the strain, and he also had to rest from time to time. At least no one harassed him and he was left alone. When he had finished turning around, he immediately began to crawl back in a straight line. He was amazed at the distance between him and his room and couldn't understand how, weak as he was, he'd covered the same stretch of ground only a little while ago almost without being aware of it. Completely intent on crawling rapidly, he scarcely noticed that neither a word nor an exclamation came from his family to interrupt his progress. Only when he reached the doorway did he turn his head; not all the way, for he felt his neck growing stiff, but enough to see that behind him all was as before except that his sister had gotten to her feet. His last glimpse was of his mother, who by now was fast asleep.

He was barely inside the room before the door was slammed shut, bolted, and locked. Gregor was so frightened by the sudden noise behind him that his little legs collapsed underneath him. It was his sister who had been in such a hurry. She'd been standing there, ready and waiting, and then had sprung swiftly forward, before Gregor had even heard her coming. "At last!" she cried to her parents as she turned the key in the lock.

"And now?" Gregor asked himself, looking around in the darkness. He soon discovered that he was no longer able to move. This didn't surprise him; rather it seemed to him strange that until now he'd actually been able to propel himself with these thin little legs. In other respects he felt relatively comfortable. It was true that his entire body ached, but the pain seemed to him to be growing fainter and fainter and soon would go away altogether. The rotten apple in his back and the inflamed area around it, completely covered with fine dust, hardly bothered him anymore. He recalled his family with deep emotion and love. His own belief that he must disappear was, if anything, even firmer than his sister's. He remained in this state of empty and peaceful reflection until the tower clock struck three in the morning. He could still just sense the general brightening outside his window. Then, involuntarily, his head sank all the way down, and from his nostrils came his last feeble breath.

Early that morning, when the cleaning woman appeared—out of sheer energy and impatience she always slammed all the doors, no matter how often she'd been asked not to, so hard that sleep was no longer possible anywhere in the apartment once she'd arrived—she didn't notice anything peculiar when she paid Gregor her usual brief visit. She thought that he was lying there so still on purpose, pretending that his feelings were hurt; she considered him to be very clever. As she happened to be holding a long broom, she tried to tickle Gregor with it from the doorway. When this too had no effect, she became annoyed and jabbed it into Gregor a little, and it was only when she shoved him from his place without meeting resistance that she began to take notice. Quickly realizing how things stood, she opened her eyes wide, gave a soft whistle, and without wasting any time she tore open the bedroom door and yelled at the top of her lungs into the darkness: "Come and look, it's had it, it's lying there, dead and done for."

Mr. and Mrs. Samsa sat up in their marriage bed, trying to absorb the shock the cleaning woman had given them and yet at first unable to comprehend the meaning of her words. Then they quickly climbed out of bed, Mr. Samsa on one side, Mrs. Samsa on the other. Mr. Samsa threw a blanket over his shoulders, Mrs. Samsa wore only her nightgown; dressed in this fashion they entered Gregor's room. Meanwhile the door to the living room, where Grete had been sleeping since the boarders' arrival, opened as well. Grete was fully dressed, as if she'd never gone to bed, and the pallor of her face seemed to confirm this. "Dead?" asked Mrs. Samsa and looked inquiring at the cleaning woman, although she could have checked for herself, or guessed at the truth without having to investigate. "That's for sure," said the cleaning woman, and to prove it she pushed Gregor's corpse a good way to one side with her broom. Mrs. Samsa made a move as if to stop her, then let it go. "Well," said Mr. Samsa, "now thanks be to God." He crossed himself, and the three women followed his example. Grete, who never took her eyes off the corpse, said, "Just look how thin he was. It's been a long time since he's eaten anything. The food came out just as it was when it came in." Indeed, Gregor's body was completely flat and dry; this was only now obvious because the body was no longer raised on its little legs and nothing else distracted the eye.

"Come to our room with us for a little while, Grete," said Mrs. Samsa with a sad smile, and Grete, not without a look back at the corpse, followed her parents into the bedroom. The cleaning woman shut the door and opened the windows wide. Although it was early in the morning, there was a certain mildness in the fresh air. After all, these were the last days of March.

The three boarders came out of their rooms and looked around in amazement for their breakfast; they had been forgotten. "Where's our breakfast?" the middle gentleman asked the cleaning woman in a sour tone. But she put her finger to her lips, and then quickly and quietly beckoned to the gentlemen to enter Gregor's room. So they did, and, with their hands in the pockets of their somewhat threadbare jackets, they stood in a circle around Gregor's corpse in the now sunlit room.

At that point the bedroom door opened and Mr. Samsa, wearing his uniform, appeared with his wife on one arm and his daughter on the other. They all looked a little tearful; from time to time Grete would press her face against her father's sleeve.

"Leave my home at once," Mr. Samsa told the three gentlemen, pointing to the door without letting go of the women. "What do you mean?" said the middle gentleman, who, somewhat taken aback, smiled a sugary smile. The other two held their hands behind their backs, and kept rubbing them together as if cheerfully anticipating a major argument which they were bound to win. "I mean just what I say," replied Mr. Samsa, and advanced in a line with his two companions directly on the middle boarder. At first this gentleman stood still, looking at the floor as if the thoughts inside his head were arranging themselves in a new pattern. "Well, so we'll be off," he then said, looking up at Mr. Samsa as if, suddenly overcome with humility, he was asking permission for even this decision. Mr. Samsa, his eyes glowering, merely gave him a few brief nods. With that the gentleman, taking long strides, actually set off in the direction of the hall; his two friends, who had been listening for some time with their hands quite still, now went hopping right along after him, as if they were afraid that Mr. Samsa might reach the hall before them and cut them off from their leader. Once in the hall the three of them took their hats from the coat rack, pulled their canes from the umbrella stand, bowed silently, and left the apartment. Impelled by a suspicion that would turn out to be utterly groundless, Mr. Samsa led the two women out onto the landing; leaning against the banister railing they watched the three gentlemen as they marched slowly but steadily down the long staircase, disappearing at every floor when the staircase made a turn and then after a few moments reappearing once again. The lower they descended the more the Samsas' interest in them waned; and when a butcher's boy with a basket on his head came proudly up the stairs towards the gentlemen and then swept on past them, Mr. Samsa and the women quickly left the banister and, as if relieved, returned to the apartment.

They decided to spend this day resting and going for a walk; not only did they deserve this break from work, they absolutely needed it. And so they sat down at the table to write their three letters excusing themselves, Mr. Samsa to the bank manager, Mrs. Samsa to her employer, and Grete to the store's owner. While they were writing, the cleaning woman came by to say that she was leaving now, since her morning's work was done. At first the three letter writers merely nodded without looking up, but when the cleaning woman made no move to go, they looked up at her, annoyed. "Well?" asked Mr. Samsa. The cleaning woman stood in the doorway, smiling as if she had some wonderful news for the family, news she wasn't about to share until they came right out and asked her to. The little ostrich feathers in her hat, which stood up nearly straight in the air and which had irritated Mr. Samsa the entire time she had worked for them, swayed gently in every direction. "What can we do for you?" asked Mrs. Samsa, whom the cleaning woman respected the most. "Well," the cleaning woman replied, with such good-humored laughter that she had to pause before continuing, "you don't have to worry about getting rid of that thing in the next room. It's already been taken care of." Mrs. Samsa and Grete bent over their letters as if they intended to keep on writing; Mr. Samsa, who realized that the cleaning woman was about to go into the details, stopped her firmly with an outstretched hand. Seeing that she wasn't going to be allowed to tell her story, she suddenly remembered that she was in a great hurry; clearly insulted, she called out,

"Bye, everybody," whirled around wildly, and left the apartment with a terrible slamming of doors.

"She'll be dismissed tonight," said Mr. Samsa, but without getting a reply from his wife or his daughter, for the cleaning woman seemed to have ruined their tenuous peace of mind. They got up, went to the window, and remained there holding each other tightly. Mr. Samsa turned around in his chair toward them and watched them quietly for some time. Then he called out, "Come on now, come over here. Let those old troubles alone. And have a little consideration for me, too." The two women promptly obeyed him, hurried over to him, caressed him, and quickly finished their letters.

Then all three of them left the apartment together, something they hadn't done in months, and took a streetcar out to the open country on the outskirts of the city. Their car, which they had all to themselves, was completely bathed in warm sunlight. Leaning comfortably back in their seats they discussed their prospects for the future, which on closer inspection seemed to be not so bad, since all three of them had jobs which—though they'd never asked one another about them in any detail—were in each case very advantageous and promising. Of course the greatest immediate improvement in their situation would quickly come about when they found a new apartment, one that was smaller, cheaper, and in every way easier to maintain than their current one, which Gregor had chosen for them. As they were talking on in this way, it occurred to both Mr. and Mrs. Samsa, almost simultaneously, as they watched their daughter become more and more vivacious, that in spite of all the recent troubles that had turned her cheeks pale, she had blossomed into a pretty and shapely girl. Growing quieter now, communicating almost unconsciously through glances, they reflected that soon it would be time to find her a good husband. And it was as if in confirmation of their new dreams and good intentions that at the end of their ride their daughter got up first and stretched her young body.

Questions

1. What was Gregor's occupation before his transformation? How did he come to his present job? What kept him working for his firm?
2. When Gregor wakes to discover he has become a gigantic insect, he is mostly intent on the practical implications of his metamorphosis—how to get out of bed, how to get to his job, and so on. He never wonders why or how he has been changed. What does this odd reaction suggest about Gregor?
3. When Gregor's parents first see the gigantic insect (paragraph 25), do they recognize it as their son? What do their initial reactions suggest about their attitude toward their son?
4. How does each family member react to Gregor after his transformation? How do their reactions differ from one another? What do they have in common?
5. What things about Gregor have been changed? What seems to have remained the same? List specific qualities.
6. *The Metamorphosis* takes place almost entirely in the Samsa family apartment. How does the story's setting shape its themes?
7. Which family member first decides that the family must "get rid of" the insect? What rationale is given? In what specific ways does the family's decision affect Gregor?
8. How does the family react to Gregor's death?
9. Does Grete change in the course of the story? If so, how does she change?
10. In what ways is Gregor's metamorphosis symbolic?

Suggestions for Writing on *Franz Kafka's The Metamorphosis*

1. Take any member of Gregor Samsa's family (father, mother, or sister) and discuss her or his role in the story. What specifically do her or his words and actions add to the tale?
2. Choose a thematic concern of *The Metamorphosis*, such as work, shame, or the family. Develop a thesis about what the story has to say on that theme, and choose three key moments from the story to back up your argument. Make your case in a medium-length paper (600 to 1,000 words); be sure to quote as needed from the text.
3. Is *The Metamorphosis* a horror story? What elements does Kafka's story share with horror fiction or horror films you have known? How does *The Metamorphosis* differ from them?
4. Compare and contrast Gregor Samsa's relationships with the people in his life to Miss Emily's relationships with those around her in Faulkner's "A Rose for Emily."
5. Explore how Gregor Samsa's metamorphosis into a giant insect is symbolic of his earlier life and relations with his family.
6. Write a metamorphosis story of your own. Imagine a character who turns overnight into something quite other than himself or herself. As you describe that character's struggles, try for a mix of tragedy and grotesque comedy, as found in *The Metamorphosis*.

POETRY

CHILDHOOD AND ADOLESCENCE

Countee Cullen	*Incident*
Gwendolyn Brooks	*We Real Cool*
Judith Ortiz Cofer	*Quinceañera*
William Blake	*London*
Dylan Thomas	*Fern Hill*

Childhood is usually considered a time of innocence and security, and, fortunately, for many children it is. Surrounded by parents and caretakers who love them, they are allowed to grow at their own pace into their adult selves. Childhood, however, can also be a period of uncertainty and vulnerability in which the child is at the mercy of the elders who should provide love and protection. The presence (or absence) of mature guidance continues to be important in adolescence, when children face adult choices the consequences of which they may not fully understand. The poems in this section explore aspects of childhood and adolescence, both positive and negative. William Blake attacks the evils of late eighteenth-century London with its devastating poverty and exploitative child-labor practices. Gwendolyn Brooks presents urban teenagers who don't yet realize the consequences of their life choices. Countee Cullen portrays a boy's first brush with racism. Judith Ortiz Cofer captures a young girl on the threshold of adulthood. Finally, Dylan Thomas gloriously summons up the magic of childhood's innocent immediacy to the world.

Countee Cullen

Mystery surrounds the early life of Countee Cullen (1903–1946): neither his birthplace nor his parentage nor the identity of the person who raised him from his earliest years can be satisfactorily established. At some point in his youth, he was adopted—whether formally or not is also a matter of dispute—by Reverend Frederick Cullen and his wife. Dr. Cullen, to whom the poet was especially close, was the founder and minister of the Salem Episcopal Church in New York City. Countee Cullen graduated from New York University in 1925, the same year in which he published the first of his several books of poetry, Color (which contains "Incident"). An early marriage to the daughter of W. E. B. DuBois lasted only a year; Cullen married again, more happily, in 1940. For the last twelve years of his life, he taught at Frederick Douglass Junior High School in New York.

Countee Cullen

Incident

1925

For Eric Walrond

Once riding in old Baltimore,
   Heart-filled, head-filled with glee,
I saw a Baltimorean
   Keep looking straight at me.

Now I was eight and very small,
   And he was no whit bigger,
And so I smiled, but he poked out
   His tongue, and called me, "Nigger."

I saw the whole of Baltimore
   From May until December;
Of all the things that happened there
   That's all that I remember.

INCIDENT. Dedication: Eric D. Walrond (1898–1966) was a Guyana-born American writer whose best-known work is *Tropic Death* (1926), a collection of short stories.

Questions

1. What mood is created by the first stanza? Why do you think the poem begins this way?
2. Is the speaker from Baltimore, or not? How do you know? What is the thematic relevance of this detail?
3. Is the poem more—or less—effective for leaving its larger conclusions implicit instead of spelling them out?

Gwendolyn Brooks

A collection of poems by Gwendolyn Brooks (1917–2000), along with a biographical note, appears in Chapter 12, "Families." Brooks's literary career can be neatly divided into two phases. From its beginnings until the late 1960s, her poetry and fiction were published by mainstream journals and publishing houses, and were addressed to a broad general audience. Afterward, she became more directly focused on writing for her own African American community, and she published with small, black-oriented presses. But from the beginning until the end of her career, her work was unified by its concern with the lives, hopes, and frustrations of her people—especially young people, as in her best-known poem, "We Real Cool."

We Real Cool

1960

The Pool Players.
Seven at the Golden Shovel.

We real cool. We
Left school. We

Lurk late. We
Strike straight. We

Sing sin. We
Thin gin. We

Jazz June. We
Die soon.

Questions

1. What effects does the poet achieve by putting the word "We" at the ends of the first seven lines, instead of starting a new line after each period?
2. Who are the "we" of the poem? Approximately how old would you say they are?
3. How do the speakers of the poem seem to feel about themselves and their lives?
4. Is there an element of dramatic irony in the title of the poem?

Judith Ortiz Cofer

Judith Ortiz Cofer was born in Puerto Rico in 1952. Her family moved to Paterson, New Jersey, in 1956, but they returned to Puerto Rico whenever her father, who was in the United States Navy, had extended leave. In 1968 the family relocated to Augusta, Georgia. Cofer earned a B.A. in English at Augusta College in 1974 and an M.A. at Florida Atlantic University in 1977. Although Spanish was her first language, she writes in English and teaches English and creative writing at the University of Georgia. She has published many volumes of poetry, fiction, and essays, and has been the recipient of a number of grants and awards. Like much of her work, "Quinceañera" draws upon her Latin heritage and Catholic upbringing.

Quinceañera   1987

My dolls have been put away like dead
children in a chest I will carry
with me when I marry.
I reach under my skirt to feel
a satin slip bought for this day. It is soft
as the inside of my thighs. My hair
has been nailed back with my mother's
black hairpins to my skull. Her hands
stretched my eyes open as she twisted
braids into a tight circle at the nape
of my neck. I am to wash my own clothes
and sheets from this day on, as if
the fluids of my body were poison, as if
the little trickle of blood I believe
travels from my heart to the world were
shameful. Is not the blood of saints and
men in battle beautiful? Do Christ's hands
not bleed into your eyes from His cross?
At night I hear myself growing and wake
to find my hands drifting of their own will

to soothe skin stretched tight
over my bones.
I am wound like the guts of a clock,
waiting for each hour to release me.

QUINCEAÑERA. The title refers to a fifteen-year-old girl's coming-out party in Latin cultures.

Questions

1. What items and actions are associated with the speaker's new life? What items are put away?
2. What is the speaker waiting to release in the final two lines?
3. If the poem's title were changed to "Fifteen-Year-Old Girl," what would the poem lose in meaning?

William Blake

William Blake (1757–1827) was born in London, where he continued to live for the rest of his life. In his earliest years he was educated at home by his mother. At the age of ten he was enrolled in drawing school, and at fourteen he began a seven-year apprenticeship to an engraver. Thereafter he made his living as a printer and illustrator. Although his first book of poems, Poetical Sketches (1783), was conventionally printed, most of his subsequent volumes were produced by Blake himself through the process of "illuminated printing," with the texts hand-lettered and accompanied by full-color etchings. "London," which first appeared in Songs of Experience, is a withering and memorable portrayal of his native city.

London   1794

I wander through each chartered street,
Near where the chartered Thames does flow,
And mark in every face I meet
Marks of weakness, marks of woe.

In every cry of every man,   5
In every infant's cry of fear,
In every voice, in every ban,
The mind-forged manacles I hear.

How the chimney-sweeper's cry
Every black'ning church appalls   10
And the hapless soldier's sigh
Runs in blood down palace walls.

But most through midnight streets I hear
How the youthful harlot's curse
Blasts the new born infant's tear   15
And blights with plagues the marriage hearse.

Questions

1. What effects are produced by the poem's strong rhythm and by the frequent repetition of words in the first two stanzas? How do these effects help to communicate the poem's themes?
2. What, in the larger context of the poem, do you understand by the phrase "The mind-forged manacles" (line 8)?
3. Does the poem implicitly assign any blame or responsibility for the conditions it describes? If so, to what or to whom?
4. Do you think that the speaker holds out any hope that the conditions he describes will change? Why or why not?

Dylan Thomas

Dylan Thomas (1914–1953) was born in Swansea, Wales. After leaving school at seventeen he worked briefly for a local newspaper, then moved to London to pursue a literary career. He published his first book, Eighteen Poems, *in 1934, before his twentieth birthday. With further publications and increasing fame, he made radio broadcasts and undertook reading tours, especially in the United States, which played a large role in establishing contemporary poetry as a public performance art. Troubled by his failing marriage and waning poetic inspiration, he died in New York after a prolonged bout of drinking. "Fern Hill," a reminiscence of holidays spent on his aunt's farm in Wales, is typical of his work in its lush use of language and its subtle but rigorous metrical pattern.*

Fern Hill   1946

Now as I was young and easy under the apple boughs
About the lilting house and happy as the grass was green,
    The night above the dingle° starry,   *wooded valley*
        Time let me hail and climb
        Golden in the heydays of his eyes,   5
And honored among wagons I was prince of the apple towns
And once below a time I lordly had the trees and leaves
        Trail with daisies and barley
    Down the rivers of the windfall light.

And as I was green and carefree, famous among the barns   10
About the happy yard and singing as the farm was home,
    In the sun that is young once only,
        Time let me play and be
    Golden in the mercy of his means,
And green and golden I was huntsman and herdsman, the calves   15
Sang to my horn, the foxes on the hills barked clear and cold,
        And the sabbath rang slowly
    In the pebbles of the holy streams.

All the sun long it was running, it was lovely, the hay
Fields high as the house, the tunes from the chimneys, it was air
    And playing, lovely and watery
        And fire green as grass.
    And nightly under the simple stars
As I rode to sleep the owls were bearing the farm away,
All the moon long I heard, blessed among stables, the nightjars
    Flying with the ricks, and the horses
        Flashing into the dark.

And then to awake, and the farm, like a wanderer white
With the dew, come back, the cock on his shoulder: it was all
    Shining, it was Adam and maiden,
        The sky gathered again
    And the sun grew round that very day.
So it must have been after the birth of the simple light
In the first, spinning place, the spellbound horses walking warm
    Out of the whinnying green stable
        On to the fields of praise.

And honored among foxes and pheasants by the gay house
Under the new made clouds and happy as the heart was long,
    In the sun born over and over,
        I ran my heedless ways,
    My wishes raced through the house high hay
And nothing I cared, at my sky blue trades, that time allows
In all his tuneful turning so few and such morning songs
    Before the children green and golden
        Follow him out of grace,

Nothing I cared, in the lamb white days, that time would take me
Up to the swallow thronged loft by the shadow of my hand,
    In the moon that is always rising,
        Nor that riding to sleep
        I should hear him fly with the high fields
And wake to the farm forever fled from the childless land.
Oh as I was young and easy in the mercy of his means,
    Time held me green and dying
    Though I sang in my chains like the sea.

Questions

1. What allusion is made in the fourth stanza? How does it help to communicate the poem's larger thematic concerns?
2. Trace and discuss the appearances throughout the poem of the word "Time."
3. What is the meaning of the word "heedless" (line 40)? What is the significance of its use in the poem?
4. Discuss the meaning of the last three lines, both in themselves and in their relevance to the poem's theme.

Suggestions for Writing on *Poems about Childhood and Adolescence*

1. Perhaps the most famous comment on childhood and adolescence is George Bernard Shaw's "Youth is wasted on the young." Which poem in this section most closely exemplifies Shaw's observation? Which poem is at the furthest remove from his viewpoint?
2. The kind of childhood we each have is shaped in large part by our circumstances and our surroundings. Discuss "London" and "Fern Hill" in terms of each one's illustration of that fact.
3. Childhood is traditionally seen as a time of innocence. Choose two poems from this section that illustrate this view. Is the innocence successfully preserved in each poem? If not, what causes the loss of innocence?
4. Discuss "Quinceañera" and "Fern Hill" in terms of each poem's contrast between the experience of youth and the adult perspective on that experience.

LIFE'S CHALLENGES

A. E. Housman	*When I was one-and-twenty*
John Updike	*Ex-Basketball Player*
Elizabeth Bishop	*One Art*
Natasha Trethewey	*White Lies*
Antonio Machado	*Caminante / Traveler*

Life doesn't always turn out as you think it will, and this is not an entirely bad thing. The boy or girl who broke your heart *forever* becomes a mere memory a few years (and a few romances) later. At twenty you no longer really want to be an astronaut or a superhero. A wonderful aspect of life is its capacity to astonish us, and the poems in this section present surprising turns in life. A. E. Housman's ardent lover discovers that some advice proves true. John Updike portrays a man whose greatest moments happened back in high school. Elizabeth Bishop creates an escalating list of losses that gather over a lifetime. Natasha Trethewey presents a mixed-race child who tries to navigate the black and white social barriers of her childhood. Finally, Antonio Machado offers a provocative theory about the road of life's journey.

A. E. Housman

A. E. Housman (1859–1936) was born in Worcestershire, England, the eldest of seven children. His mother died on his twelfth birthday. In 1881, in the midst of an emotional crisis brought on by his unreciprocated love for his college roommate, Housman failed his final examinations and left Oxford University without a degree. Working in the Patent Office for the next ten years, he published papers on ancient Greek and Roman authors that were good enough to earn him a professorship in Latin; thereafter, he became a distinguished classical scholar. "When I was one-and-twenty" appears in A Shropshire Lad (1896), his first and best-known book of poetry. Housman was a poet of limited scope, but within that range he wrote moving and unforgettable poems that have become a permanent part of English literature.

When I was one-and-twenty   1896

When I was one-and-twenty
   I heard a wise man say,
"Give crowns and pounds and guineas
   But not your heart away;
Give pearls away and rubies   5
   But keep your fancy free."
But I was one-and-twenty,
   No use to talk to me.

When I was one-and-twenty
   I heard him say again,   10
"The heart out of the bosom
   Was never given in vain;

'Tis paid with sighs a plenty
   And sold for endless rue."
And I am two-and-twenty,   15
   And oh, 'tis true, 'tis true.

Questions

1. What characteristics of youth are prominently featured in this poem?
2. How do the rhythm and form of the poem contribute to its total effect?
3. Housman's biographer Richard Perceval Graves calls "When I was one-and-twenty" a "bitter poem." Do you agree? Why or why not?

John Updike

John Updike (1932–2009) was born in Pennsylvania. He earned a B.A. from Harvard, studied drawing and fine art at Oxford, and worked briefly on the staff of the New Yorker. *Over a fifty-year career he published more than sixty books—poetry, a play, a memoir, children's books, essays and criticism, short stories (he is considered a modern master of the genre), and twenty-four novels, including* Rabbit, Run *(1960),* Couples *(1968),* The Witches of Eastwick *(1984), and* The Beauty of the Lilies *(1996). He was the recipient of many awards, including two Pulitzer Prizes. "Ex-Basketball Player" appeared in* The Carpentered Hen *(1958), Updike's first book and the first of his seven collections of verse.*

Ex-Basketball Player   1958

Pearl Avenue runs past the high-school lot,
Bends with the trolley tracks, and stops, cut off
Before it has a chance to go two blocks,
At Colonel McComsky Plaza. Berth's Garage
Is on the corner facing west, and there,   5
Most days, you'll find Flick Webb, who helps Berth out.

Flick stands tall among the idiot pumps—
Five on a side, the old bubble-head style,
Their rubber elbows hanging loose and low.
One's nostrils are two S's, and his eyes   10
An E and O. And one is squat, without
A head at all—more of a football type.

Once Flick played for the high-school team, the Wizards.
He was good: in fact, the best. In '46
He bucketed three hundred ninety points,   15
A county record still. The ball loved Flick.
I saw him rack up thirty-eight or forty
In one home game. His hands were like wild birds.

He never learned a trade, he just sells gas,
Checks oil, and changes flats. Once in a while,   20
As a gag, he dribbles an inner tube,
But most of us remember anyway.
His hands are fine and nervous on the lug wrench.
It makes no difference to the lug wrench, though.

Off work, he hangs around Mae's luncheonette.
Grease-gray and kind of coiled, he plays pinball,
Smokes those thin cigars, nurses lemon phosphates.
Flick seldom says a word to Mae, just nods
Beyond her face toward bright applauding tiers
Of Necco Wafers, Nibs, and Juju Beads.

Questions

1. The last two lines of the third and fourth stanzas make reference to Flick's hands. What is communicated by each of these descriptions independently, and what is communicated by the contrast between them?
2. How would you characterize the tone of the poem—mocking and ironic, or wistful and sympathetic?
3. What is being suggested in the last three lines of the poem? How does this conclusion pull the entire text together?

Elizabeth Bishop

Elizabeth Bishop (1911–1979) was born in Worcester, Massachusetts. Her father died when she was eight months old, and her mother, who had suffered several breakdowns, was permanently institutionalized in 1916. Thereafter, she lived with her mother's parents in Nova Scotia, her father's parents in Worcester, and finally with an aunt and uncle. Her first collection of poems, North & South (1946), led to her winning a Guggenheim Fellowship, and her second, A Cold Spring (1955), received the Pulitzer Prize. She lived in Brazil for a number of years with her companion, Lota Soares, who would commit suicide in Bishop's New York apartment in 1967. "One Art" appeared in Geography III (1976), her fourth and last collection, which won the National Book Critics Circle Award: It is a witty and poignant distillation of the wisdom gained from a lifetime of losses.

Elizabeth Bishop

One Art 1976

The art of losing isn't hard to master;
so many things seem filled with the intent
to be lost that their loss is no disaster.

Lose something every day. Accept the fluster
of lost door keys, the hour badly spent.
The art of losing isn't hard to master.

Then practice losing farther, losing faster:
places, and names, and where it was you meant
to travel. None of these will bring disaster.

I lost my mother's watch. And look! my last, or
next-to-last, of three loved houses went.
The art of losing isn't hard to master.

I lost two cities, lovely ones. And, vaster,
some realms I owned, two rivers, a continent.
I miss them, but it wasn't a disaster.

—Even losing you (the joking voice, a gesture
I love) I shan't have lied. It's evident
the art of losing's not too hard to master
though it may look like (*Write* it!) like disaster.

Questions

1. What things has the speaker lost? Put together a complete list in the order she reveals them. What does the list suggest about her experience with loss?
2. Bishop varies the repeated lines that end with the word "disaster." Look only at those lines: what do they suggest about the story being unfolded in the poem?
3. What effect does the parenthetical comment in the poem's last line create? Would the poem be different if it were omitted?

Natasha Trethewey

Natasha Trethewey was born in 1966 in Gulfport, Mississippi, at a time when the marriage of her white father (a published poet) and her African American mother was illegal in that state. Though her parents divorced before she began school, she remained close to both of them. In 1985 her mother was murdered by her second husband, whom she had divorced the previous year. Trethewey's first book, Domestic Work *(2000), was selected by former poet laureate Rita Dove as the first winner of the Cave Canem Prize. Her third book,* Native Guard *(2006), won the Pulitzer Prize. Her most recent book,* Beyond Katrina: A Meditation on the Mississippi Gulf Coast *(2010), presents personal and family experience in the context of the history of her native region—as does much of her poetry, including "White Lies."*

White Lies   2000

The lies I could tell,
when I was growing up
light-bright, near-white,
high-yellow, red-boned
in a black place,
were just white lies.

I could easily tell the white folks
that we lived uptown,
not in that pink and green
shanty-fied shotgun section
along the tracks. I could act
like my homemade dresses
came straight out the window

of Maison Blanche. I could even
keep quiet, quiet as kept,
like the time a white girl said
(squeezing my hand), *Now
we have three of us in this class.*

But I paid for it every time
Mama found out.
She laid her hands on me,
then washed out my mouth
with Ivory soap. *This
is to purify,* she said,
and cleanse your lying tongue.
Believing her, I swallowed suds
thinking they'd work
from the inside out.

Questions

1. What is the common meaning of the phrase "white lie"? What additional meanings does it have in the text of the poem?
2. Other than direct uses of the word "white," what references to whiteness does the poem contain?
3. Does knowing the author's background give deeper insight into "White Lies"? How well does the poem succeed without that knowledge?

Antonio Machado

Antonio Machado (1875–1939) was born in Seville, Spain, but was educated in Madrid. He discovered his literary vocation at an early age. For several years he and his brother lived in Paris, where Machado met many of the leading French and Latin American poets of the era. Returning to his homeland to teach in Soria, Machado published several books that helped define modern Spanish poetry, most importantly Campos de Castilla (1912; first published in English in 1917 as The Landscapes of Castile). The poet died in southern France while fleeing from the Spanish Civil War.

Caminante   1912

Caminante, son tus huellas
el camino, y nada más;
caminante, no hay camino,
se hace camino al andar.
Al andar se hace camino,
y al volver la vista atrás
se ve la senda que nunca
se ha de volver a pisar.
Caminante, no hay camino,
sino estelas en la mar.

Traveler   2011

Traveler, your footsteps are
the road, there's nothing more;
traveler, there is no road,
the road is made by walking.
Walking makes the road,
and if you turn around,
you only see the path
you cannot walk again.
Traveler, there is no road,
only a track of foam upon the sea.

— *Translated by Michael Ortiz*

Questions

1. What does Machado want to tell the reader about life? Can you summarize the main message of the poem? Do you agree or disagree?
2. Can we really not turn around on life's journey and retrace our steps? Can we never recapture something or someone we've lost? How do you think Machado would answer this question?
3. Compare Machado's poem with Robert Frost's "The Road Not Taken." In what ways does Machado's use of the road as a symbol resemble Frost's? In what ways does it differ?

Suggestions for Writing on *Poems about Life's Challenges*

1. Coming of age is often seen as a time of loss and disillusionment. Discuss any two of the poems in this section along these lines. What original assumptions does the poem present or suggest? How are those assumptions shattered? In what spirit, in each poem, is this disillusionment faced?
2. Has the speaker in "One Art" truly mastered the "the art of losing"? What details in the poem suggest that she is still the victim of life-long losses?
3. For Flick Webb in "Ex-Basketball Player," things have turned out very differently than one might have expected. Discuss the changes that have occurred in his life, and what seems to have brought about those changes. How does Updike appear to regard the ex-basketball player?
4. Discuss "White Lies" in terms of the contrast between the speaker's home life and the way that she wants to present herself in public. What seems to be the author's attitude toward the girl's desire to escape and/or to deny her origins?
5. Which poem in this section most closely reflects your own experience of coming of age? With which poem do you identify least? Explain.
6. Antonio Machado believes that we each create the road our life will take. Write a short essay describing the road you hope to create over the next five years. What footsteps will take you where you hope to go?

FACING DEATH

John Donne	*Death be not proud*
Emily Dickinson	*Because I could not stop for Death*
Dylan Thomas	*Do not go gentle into that good night*
José Emilio Pacheco	*La Ceniza/Ashes*
E. E. Cummings	*Buffalo Bill's*
Sylvia Plath	*Lady Lazarus*

"How strange a thing is death," wrote Edna St. Vincent Millay, and thousands of authors have expressed the same sentiment in different ways. Death is one of the grand themes of poetry. No other subject, not even love, is so large, serious, emotional, and conclusive. Death is life's universal ending as well as its central mystery. Birth and death frame our mortality, and thereby put everything in our lives in perspective. Medieval monks sometimes kept a skull on their desks to remind them of life's brevity. That somber insight finds a different expression in the ancient saying, "Eat, drink, and be merry, for tomorrow we may die." Life is not to be wasted, whether one spends it in prayer, work, or partying (or all three). A healthy respect for death is life-affirming. The poems in this section all look at death directly, but they offer very different reactions. Viewing it from the foundation of Christian faith, John Donne considers death a powerful but transient obstacle on the way to eternal life. Emily Dickinson personifies Death as a friend who takes the poem's speaker on her final trip. Dylan Thomas utters a resonant cry of defiance at age, infirmity, and human mortality. José Emilio Pacheco offers a single image to describe the grief and loss death creates. E. E. Cummings writes a sly elegy—half comic, half lyric—for the most celebrated "cowboy" of his era. Sylvia Plath, who was to die at her own hand, explores the death wish and suicide's dark allure.

John Donne

As a young man, John Donne (1572–1631) wrote love poems that were notable for their daring wit, intellectual complexity, and extravagant—at times outrageous—comparisons. In mid-life, Donne was persuaded by King James I to take holy orders in the Church of England, after which his work became as celebrated for its piety and religious devotion as it had previously been for its eroticism and romantic tenderness. He is renowned both for his prose meditation containing the famous lines "No man is an island, entire of itself . . . Therefore, send not to ask for whom the bell tolls: it tolls for thee" and for his sequence of Holy Sonnets *(including "Death be not proud"), poems which demonstrate that even though his subject matter had changed, his brilliance and artistry remained undiminished.*

John Donne

## Death be not proud	(about 1610)

Death be not proud, though some have callèd thee
Mighty and dreadful, for thou art not so;
For those whom thou think'st thou dost overthrow
Die not, poor death, nor yet canst thou kill me.
From rest and sleep, which but thy pictures be,   5
Much pleasure, then from thee much more must flow,
And soonest our best men with thee do go,
Rest of their bones, and soul's delivery.
Thou art slave to fate, chance, kings, and desperate men,
And dost with poison, war, and sickness dwell,   10
And poppy, or charms can make us sleep as well,
And better than thy stroke; why swell'st thou then?
One short sleep past, we wake eternally,
And death shall be no more; death, thou shalt die.

Questions

1. How would you restate the meaning of the poem's first two lines?
2. Explain the simile developed in lines 5–8.
3. What is being said in lines 9–10?
4. Explain the concept expressed in the poem's concluding couplet.

Emily Dickinson

A collection of Emily Dickinson's poetry and a brief biography appear in Chapter 15, "The Individual and Society." As much as for her poetry, Emily Dickinson (1830–1886) is famous for her life and eccentricities—her white dresses; her increasing self-isolation in her upstairs bedroom in her family home in Amherst, Massachusetts; her presumed emotional involvement with an unidentified, perhaps married suitor; her failure to publish all but a handful of her nearly eighteen hundred peculiarly capitalized and punctuated poems. But often overlooked in this legend are her lively nature, love of family and friends, sprightly wit, and penetrating intelligence, all vividly on display in her letters as well as her poetry. "Because I could not stop for Death," like much of her work, deals with a subject that was much more a fact of daily life in Dickinson's time than in ours.

### Because I could not stop for Death	(about 1863)

Because I could not stop for Death –
He kindly stopped for me –
The Carriage held but just Ourselves –
And Immortality.

We slowly drove – He knew no haste   5
And I had put away
My labor and my leisure too,
For His Civility –

We passed the School, where Children strove
At Recess – in the Ring –
We passed the Fields of Gazing Grain –
We passed the Setting Sun –

Or rather – He passed Us –
The Dews drew quivering and chill –
For only Gossamer, my Gown –
My Tippet° – only Tulle –   *cape*

We paused before a House that seemed
A Swelling of the Ground –
The Roof was scarcely visible –
The Cornice – in the Ground –

Since then – 'tis Centuries – and yet
Feels shorter than the Day
I first surmised the Horses' Heads
Were toward Eternity –

Questions

1. How is Death presented in the poem? Why is Immortality along on this carriage ride?
2. What symbolism do you find in the descriptions in the third and fifth stanzas?
3. How would you characterize the poem's tone?

Dylan Thomas

A brief biographical note on Dylan Thomas (1914–1953) appears earlier in this chapter with his poem "Fern Hill." The villanelle "Do not go gentle into that good night" was one of Thomas's last poems and was written for his father, an English teacher who was quite ill. In 1951 Thomas sent the poem to a friend with a note saying the "only person I can't show the little enclosed poem to is, of course, my father who doesn't know he's dying."

Dylan Thomas

Do not go gentle into that good night   1952

Do not go gentle into that good night,
Old age should burn and rave at close of day;
Rage, rage against the dying of the light.

Though wise men at their end know dark is right,
Because their words had forked no lightning they
Do not go gentle into that good night.

Good men, the last wave by, crying how bright
Their frail deeds might have danced in a green bay,
Rage, rage against the dying of the light.

Wild men who caught and sang the sun in flight,   10
And learn, too late, they grieved it on its way,
Do not go gentle into that good night.

Grave men, near death, who see with blinding sight
Blind eyes could blaze like meteors and be gay,
Rage, rage against the dying of the light.   15

And you, my father, there on the sad height,
Curse, bless, me now with your fierce tears, I pray,
Do not go gentle into that good night.
Rage, rage against the dying of the light.

Questions
1. "Do not go gentle into that good night" is a **villanelle**: a fixed form originated by French courtly poets of the Middle Ages. Can you figure out its rules?
2. Whom does the poem address? What is the speaker saying?
3. Villanelles are sometimes criticized as elaborate exercises in trivial wordplay. How would you defend Thomas's poem against this charge?
4. What advice does the speaker offer his father?

José Emilio Pacheco

José Emilio Pacheco was born in Mexico City in 1939. After graduating from the National Autonomous University of Mexico (the largest public university in the Western hemisphere) Pacheco worked as an editor for scholarly journals. Publishing his first poetry collection at the age of twenty, he soon emerged as a major force in Mexican letters. For many years he taught Latin American literature abroad, first in England, then at the University of Maryland. Now regarded as the foremost living Mexican poet, he lives in Mexico City. His collected poems, Tarde o temprano, *were published in 2009.*

La Ceniza   1990

La ceniza no pide excusas a nadie.
Se limita a fundirse en el no ser,
a dispersarse en concentrada grisura.

La ceniza es el humo que se deja tocar,
el fuego ya de luto por sí mismo.

Aire nuestro que fue llama y ahora
no volverá a encenderse.

Ashes   2001

Ashes beg no one's pardon.
They simply melt into non-being,
scatter in concentrated grayness.

Ashes are smoke you can touch,
fire mourning itself.   5

This air of ours that once was flame and now
will never flare up again.

—Translated by Cynthia Steele

Questions

1. By the end of the poem, Pacheco's image of ashes acquires the power of a symbol. What do his ashes seem to symbolize?
2. Considering only the text of this short poem, how would you summarize Pacheco's view of death?

E. E. Cummings

In addition to the poetry that has kept his name alive, E. E. Cummings (1894–1962) produced The Enormous Room *(1922), a novel based on his detention in a French prison camp during World War I;* Eimi *(1933), a scathing account of a trip to the Soviet Union; the plays* Him *(1927) and* Santa Claus *(1946);* Tom *(1935), a ballet based on Uncle Tom's Cabin; and substantial work as a painter and graphic artist. Though perhaps best known for his tender celebrations of romantic love, childhood innocence, and the beauty of nature, he also frequently displayed a harder-edged side. "Buffalo Bill 's" was written immediately after the death of the buffalo hunter and Wild West showman William F. Cody in January 1917.*

Buffalo Bill 's   1923

Buffalo Bill 's
defunct
            who used to
            ride a watersmooth-silver
                                        stallion   5
and break onetwothreefourfive pigeonsjustlikethat
                                                    Jesus
he was a handsome man
                        and what i want to know is
how do you like your blueeyed boy   10
Mister Death

Questions

1. Cummings's poem would look like this if given conventional punctuation and set in a solid block like prose:

   > Buffalo Bill's defunct, who used to ride a water-smooth silver stallion and break one, two, three, four, five pigeons just like that. Jesus, he was a handsome man. And what I want to know is: "How do you like your blue-eyed boy, Mister Death?"

   If this were done, by what characteristics would it still be recognizable as poetry? What would be lost?
2. Look up the word "defunct" in the dictionary and comment on the appropriateness of its use in the poem.
3. Is this poem a tribute to Buffalo Bill Cody or a satirical jab at him? Can it be both at once?

Sylvia Plath

In the last few months of her brief life (1932–1963), suffering from pressures both external—the failure of her marriage and her struggle to cope with her two small children—and internal—her lifelong struggle with depression—Sylvia Plath wrote feverishly, producing poems that in their directness and intensity went far beyond anything in The Colossus *(1960), the only book of her poems published in her lifetime. Plath's daughter, Frieda Hughes, herself a poet, has written of her: "She used every emotional experience as if it were a scrap of material that could be pieced together to make a wonderful dress; she wasted nothing of what she felt, and when in control of those tumultuous feelings she was able to focus and direct her incredible poetic energy to great effect"—words as appropriate to "Lady Lazarus" as to anything else Plath wrote.*

Lady Lazarus (1962) 1965

I have done it again.
One year in every ten
I manage it—

A sort of walking miracle, my skin
Bright as a Nazi lampshade, 5
My right foot

A paperweight,
My face a featureless, fine
Jew linen.

Peel off the napkin 10
O my enemy.
Do I terrify?—

The nose, the eye pits, the full set of teeth?
The sour breath
Will vanish in a day. 15

Soon, soon the flesh
The grave cave ate will be
At home on me

And I a smiling woman.
I am only thirty. 20
And like the cat I have nine times to die.

This is Number Three.
What a trash
To annihilate each decade.

What a million filaments. 25
The peanut-crunching crowd
Shoves in to see

Them unwrap me hand and foot—
The big strip tease.
Gentleman, ladies   30

These are my hands
My knees.
I may be skin and bone,

Nevertheless, I am the same, identical woman.
The first time it happened I was ten.   35
It was an accident.

The second time I meant
To last it out and not come back at all.
I rocked shut

As a seashell.   40
They had to call and call
And pick the worms off me like sticky pearls.

Dying
Is an art, like everything else.
I do it exceptionally well.   45

I do it so it feels like hell.
I do it so it feels real.
I guess you could say I've a call.

It's easy enough to do it in a cell.
It's easy enough to do it and stay put.   50
It's the theatrical

Comeback in broad day
To the same place, the same face, the same brute
Amused shout:

"A miracle!"   55
That knocks me out.
There is a charge

For the eyeing of my scars, there is a charge
For the hearing of my heart—
It really goes.   60

And there is a charge, a very large charge,
For the word or a touch
Or a bit of blood

Or a piece of my hair or my clothes.
So, so, Herr Doktor.   65
So, Herr Enemy.

I am your opus,°   *work, work of art*
I am your valuable,
The pure gold baby

That melts to a shriek.   70
I turn and burn.
Do not think I underestimate your great concern.

Ash, ash—
You poke and stir.
Flesh, bone, there is nothing there—   75

A cake of soap,
A wedding ring,
A gold filling,

Herr God, Herr Lucifer
Beware   80
Beware.

Out of the ash
I rise with my red hair
And I eat men like air.

Questions

1. Although the poem is openly autobiographical, Plath uses certain symbols to represent herself (Lady Lazarus, a Jew murdered in a concentration camp, a cat with nine lives, and so on). What do these symbols tell us about Plath's attitude toward herself and the world around her?
2. In her biography of Plath, *Bitter Fame*, the poet Anne Stevenson says that this poem penetrates "the furthest reaches of disdain and rage . . . bereft of all 'normal' human feelings." What do you think Stevenson means? Does anything in the poem strike you as particularly chilling?
3. The speaker in "Lady Lazarus" says, "Dying / Is an art, like everything else" (lines 43–44). What sense do you make of this metaphor?
4. Does the ending of "Lady Lazarus" imply that the speaker assumes that she will outlive her suicide attempts? Set forth your final understanding of the poem.

Suggestions for Writing on *Poems about Facing Death*

1. Both "Death be not proud" and "Because I could not stop for Death" take very unorthodox attitudes toward their shared subject. Discuss each poem, as specifically as possible, in terms of its divergence from traditional feelings about death. How do the two poems differ from one another in their approach to the subject?
2. Compare "Do not go gentle into that good night" with "When I have fears that I may cease to be" (in Chapter 3) in terms of each one's treatment of (a) the likelihood of fulfilling one's hopes and expectations in this life, and (b) the manner in which one should face the prospect of death. How are the poems similar in this respect? How do they differ?
3. Both "Buffalo Bill 's" and "Lady Lazarus" adopt a brash, almost swaggering tone in dealing with death. Discuss the two poems in this context. Is there any suggestion in either poem that the bravado might be a cover for more vulnerable feelings?
4. John Keats's "Ode to a Nightingale" contains the famous line "I have been half in love with easeful Death." Choose any two of the poems in this section and consider the degree to which each of them does or does not reflect the sentiment expressed in this quotation from Keats.
5. Have you experienced the death of a family member or friend? Write about one such experience and what it taught you about your own life.
6. Which poem in this section comes closest to expressing your own feelings about mortality? Is there a poem in the section that has altered your feelings, however slightly?

Poet in Depth
Robert Frost

LIFE AND ITS CROSSROADS

The Road Not Taken

Acquainted with the Night

Fire and Ice

Stopping by Woods on a Snowy Evening

Desert Places

"The style is the man," Frost once wrote, quoting a famous French maxim; then he added, "Rather say the style is the way the man takes himself." Frost's style is simple but engaging. He seems to address us as a friend or a neighbor, but underneath the smart and unfussy surface there is always a wealth of other meanings subtly suggested. His style is serious without ever being pretentious or unduly earnest. He would rather make his point indirectly than to overstate it. Frost also characteristically presents us with an interesting argument rather than a fast conclusion. "Some say the world will end in fire, / Some say in ice." Who is right? Frost won't tell us. He proposes that we weigh both alternatives. Here are five celebrated poems by Robert Frost, each of which memorably presents a moment of decision, perplexity, or cold determination. Frost can be a dark poet, but he is never a desperate one. He has the poet's gift of looking into the void and giving a sly ironic smile before proceeding clearly forward. Was he made of fire or of ice? Perhaps the best of both.

Robert Frost

Despite his indelible association with New England, Robert Lee Frost (1874–1963) was born in San Francisco, California. After his father's death in 1885, his mother moved the family to Lawrence, Massachusetts. Frost never finished college, though over the course of his life he would be the recipient of many honorary degrees from the most prestigious universities in the United States and Britain. He married Elinor White in December 1895, and their first child was born in September 1896; his death, from cholera, in July 1900, was the first of many family tragedies that Frost would endure. Between 1899 and 1907, the couple had five more children—another son and four daughters, the last of whom lived only three days. Frost moved his family to England in August 1912, hoping to find the literary success that

Robert Frost

had eluded him in his own country. With surprising ease, he had two manuscripts accepted by a London publisher, and he returned to America early in 1915 as the author of two highly regarded books of verse. The first of them, A Boy's Will (1913), is a young man's book. North of Boston (1914), much more substantial in its power and originality, is often considered his finest collection. This book and his next two, Mountain Interval (1916) and New Hampshire (1923), contain the core of his achievement, in the two modes that he made his own—subtle, concentrated lyric poems of understated but brilliant technical accomplishment, and longer narratives, often dramatizing the hard life of rural northern New England a century ago. The speaker in Frost's poems is usually careful and often sly, meditating on and distilling the essence of many years of observation and experience. The poet's rhetoric is measured and precise as he strives to catch the rhythms of ordinary speech—in his own phrase, "the sound of sense." After many years of accumulating fame and honors, including an unprecedented four Pulitzer Prizes, the capstone of Frost's public career was his appearance at John F. Kennedy's Presidential inauguration in January 1961. Kennedy also sent him to the Soviet Union as a cultural envoy in 1962, not long before Frost's death in a Boston hospital on January 29, 1963, eight weeks short of his eighty-ninth birthday. To the broad public, Frost often seemed like a front-porch philosopher dispensing consolation and old-fashioned country wisdom, but behind this stereotype he was a tragic poet whose deepest note is one of inevitable human isolation. In a life more painful than most, he struggled heroically with his inner and outer demons, and out of that struggle he produced what many consider the greatest body of work by an American poet of the twentieth century.

The Road Not Taken   1916

Two roads diverged in a yellow wood,
And sorry I could not travel both
And be one traveler, long I stood
And looked down one as far as I could
To where it bent in the undergrowth;   5

Then took the other, as just as fair,
And having perhaps the better claim,
Because it was grassy and wanted wear;
Though as for that the passing there
Had worn them really about the same,   10

And both that morning equally lay
In leaves no step had trodden black.
Oh, I kept the first for another day!
Yet knowing how way leads on to way,
I doubted if I should ever come back.   15

I shall be telling this with a sigh
Somewhere ages and ages hence:
Two roads diverged in a wood, and I—
I took the one less traveled by,
And that has made all the difference.   20

Questions

1. What symbolism do you find in this poem, if any? Back up your claim with evidence.
2. How do you reconcile lines 9–12 with the rest of the poem?
3. Are the last three lines of the poem a categorical, unchallenged statement of the poem's theme? Why or why not?

Acquainted with the Night   1928

I have been one acquainted with the night.
I have walked out in rain—and back in rain.
I have outwalked the furthest city light.

I have looked down the saddest city lane.
I have passed by the watchman on his beat   5
And dropped my eyes, unwilling to explain.

I have stood still and stopped the sound of feet
When far away an interrupted cry
Came over houses from another street,

But not to call me back or say good-by;   10
And further still at an unearthly height,
One luminary clock against the sky

Proclaimed the time was neither wrong nor right.
I have been one acquainted with the night.

Questions

1. Does this poem follow any formal pattern?
2. What is the meaning of lines 11–13?
3. The first and last lines of the poem are the same. Has the line picked up additional meanings or implications between the beginning of the poem and the end?

Fire and Ice   1923

Some say the world will end in fire,
Some say in ice.
From what I've tasted of desire
I hold with those who favor fire.
But if it had to perish twice,   5
I think I know enough of hate
To say that for destruction ice
Is also great
And would suffice.

Questions

1. To whom does Frost refer in line 1? In line 2?
2. What connotations of "fire" and "ice" contribute to the richness of Frost's comparison?

Stopping by Woods on a Snowy Evening   1923

Whose woods these are I think I know.
His house is in the village though;
He will not see me stopping here
To watch his woods fill up with snow.

My little horse must think it queer   5
To stop without a farmhouse near
Between the woods and frozen lake
The darkest evening of the year.

He gives his harness bells a shake
To ask if there is some mistake.   10
The only other sound's the sweep
Of easy wind and downy flake.

The woods are lovely, dark and deep,
But I have promises to keep,
And miles to go before I sleep,   15
And miles to go before I sleep.

Questions

1. What is the rime scheme of this poem? What are the implications of that scheme for the poem's final stanza?
2. What is "the darkest evening of the year"? What are the connotations of that description in the larger context of the poem?
3. Does the last line of the poem, in your view, contain any meaning or implication not present in line 13? Explain the reasons for your conclusion.

Desert Places   1936

Snow falling and night falling fast, oh, fast
In a field I looked into going past,
And the ground almost covered smooth in snow,
But a few weeds and stubble showing last.

The woods around it have it—it is theirs.   5
All animals are smothered in their lairs.
I am too absent-spirited to count;
The loneliness includes me unawares.

And lonely as it is that loneliness
Will be more lonely ere it will be less—   10
A blanker whiteness of benighted snow
With no expression, nothing to express.

They cannot scare me with their empty spaces
Between stars—on stars where no human race is.
I have it in me so much nearer home   15
To scare myself with my own desert places.

Questions

1. What are these desert places that the speaker finds in himself? (More than one theory is possible. What is yours?)
2. Notice how many times, within the short space of lines 8–10, Frost says "lonely" (or "loneliness"). What other words in the poem contain similar sounds that reinforce these words?
3. In the closing stanza, the feminine rimes "spaces," "race is," and "places" might well occur in light or comic verse. Does "Desert Places" leave you laughing? If not, what does it make you feel?

Suggestions for Writing on Robert Frost's Poetry

1. How would you describe the view of human nature that emerges from "Fire and Ice"? How applicable is that view to "Acquainted with the Night" and "Stopping by Woods on a Snowy Evening"?
2. What similarities do you see in the settings and situations of "Stopping by Woods on a Snowy Evening" and "Desert Places"? Are there other significant similarities between the two poems? Significant differences?
3. "The Road Not Taken," "Fire and Ice," and "Stopping by Woods on a Snowy Evening" all involve the making of a choice. What are the alternatives in each poem? What choice is made in each poem, and why?
4. Based on the poems in this section, would you say that Frost is an optimist, a pessimist, or neither? Explain.

ESSAYS

TURNING POINTS

James Baldwin	*Notes of a Native Son*
George Orwell	*Shooting an Elephant*
Sacha Z. Scoblic	*Rock Star, Meet Teetotaler*
Elisabeth Kübler-Ross	*On the Fear of Death*

At every stage of life's journey you can stop and ponder where you are, how you came to be there, and where you might go next. Don't for a moment think that such meditation is only a literary activity. We all ponder the course of our lives. We all need to understand our current state and have some notion of our future to keep our mental and emotional balance. And when we encounter major life changes—love, relocations, births, deaths, sudden shifts of fortune—we need to think all the harder.

The essays in this chapter focus on experiences that changed the course of lives. James Baldwin's brilliant and explosive "Notes of a Native Son" begins with a birth, a death, and a race riot before going on to explore the author's difficult struggle to achieve a meaningful adult identity as a young black man in the white America of 1943. George Orwell's "Shooting an Elephant" unfolds at the other end of the world in British-ruled Burma, where the young author worked as a colonial policeman in the slowly decaying British empire in the mid-1920s. Orwell memorably describes an odd and troubling experience—how public pressure in a rural town forced him to kill a wandering elephant. Recounting the shooting, he shows how the unfortunate chain of events enlightened him on the complicated evils of imperialism and racism. Sacha Scoblic reflects on a much smaller problem—her drinking—and amusingly charts her own road to recovery in a world that seems very different when sober. Finally, we consider life's inescapable end—death—as Elisabeth Kübler-Ross explores the various ways in which we think about (and mostly fear) our own extinction.

James Baldwin

James Baldwin (1924–1987), whose biography appears in Chapter 12, "Families," along with his story "Sonny's Blues," was noted equally as a writer of both fiction and essays. He wrote some of his earliest essays and reviews while working as a waiter in New York City's Greenwich Village. By 1948 his work was appearing in the leading periodicals of the time, such as Commentary, New Leader, *and* Partisan Review. *(In that same year*

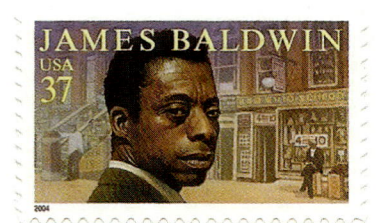

James Baldwin

Baldwin left the United States for Paris.) In 1955 he published his first collection of essays, Notes of a Native Son, *which remains a classic of modern prose. His later nonfiction works include* Nobody Knows My Name *(1961),* The Fire Next Time *(1963), and* No Name in the Street *(1972).*

Notes of a Native Son   1955

On the 29th of July, in 1943, my father died. On the same day, a few hours later, his last child was born. Over a month before this, while all our energies were concentrated in waiting for these events, there had been, in Detroit, one of the bloodiest race riots of the century. A few hours after my father's funeral, while he lay in state in the undertaker's chapel, a race riot broke out in Harlem. On the morning of the 3rd of August, we drove my father to the graveyard through a wilderness of smashed plate glass.

The day of my father's funeral had also been my nineteenth birthday. As we drove him to the graveyard, the spoils of injustice, anarchy, discontent, and hatred were all around us. It seemed to me that God himself had devised, to mark my father's end, the most sustained and brutally dissonant of codas. And it seemed to me, too, that the violence which rose all about us as my father left the world had been devised as a corrective for the pride of his eldest son. I had declined to believe in that apocalypse which had been central to my father's vision; very well, life seemed to be saying, here is something that will certainly pass for an apocalypse until the real thing comes along. I had inclined to be contemptuous of my father for the conditions of his life, for the conditions of our lives. When his life had ended I began to wonder about that life and also, in a new way, to be apprehensive about my own.

I had not known my father very well. We had got on badly, partly because we shared, in our different fashions, the vice of stubborn pride. When he was dead I realized that I had hardly ever spoken to him. When he had been dead a long time I began to wish I had. It seems to be typical of life in America, where opportunities, real and fancied, are thicker than anywhere else on the globe, that the second generation has no time to talk to the first. No one, including my father, seems to have known exactly how old he was, but his mother had been born during slavery. He was of the first generation of free men. He, along with thousands of other Negroes, came North after 1919 and I was part of that generation which had never seen the landscape of what Negroes sometimes call the Old Country.

He had been born in New Orleans and had been a quite young man there during the time that Louis Armstrong, a boy, was running errands for the dives and honky-tonks of what was always presented to me as one of the most wicked of cities—to this day, whenever I think of New Orleans, I also helplessly think of Sodom and Gomorrah. My father never mentioned Louis Armstrong, except to forbid us to play his records; but there was a picture of him on our wall for a long time. One of my father's strong-willed female relatives had placed it there and forbade my father to take it down. He never did, but he eventually maneuvered her out of the house and when, some years later, she was in trouble and near death, he refused to do anything to help her.

He was, I think, very handsome. I gather this from photographs and from my own memories of him, dressed in his Sunday best and on his way to preach a sermon somewhere, when I was little. Handsome, proud, and ingrown, "like a toe-nail," somebody said. But he looked to me, as I grew older, like pictures I had seen of African tribal chieftains: he really should have been naked, with war-paint on and barbaric mementos, standing among spears. He could be chilling in the pulpit and indescribably cruel in his personal life and he was certainly the most bitter man I have ever met; yet it must be said that there was something else in him, buried in him, which lent him his tremendous power and, even, a rather crushing charm. It had something to do with his blackness, I think—he was very black—with his blackness and his beauty, and with the fact that he knew that he was black but did not know that he was beautiful. He claimed to be proud of his blackness but it had also been the cause of much humiliation and it had fixed bleak boundaries to his life. He was not a young man when we were growing up and he had already suffered many kinds of ruin; in his outrageously demanding and protective way he loved his children, who were black like him and menaced, like him; and all these things sometimes showed in his face when he tried, never to my knowledge with any success, to establish contact with any of us. When he took one of his children on his knee to play, the child always became fretful and began to cry; when he tried to help one of us with our homework the absolutely unabating tension which emanated from him caused our minds and our tongues to become paralyzed, so that he, scarcely knowing why, flew into a rage and the child, not knowing why, was punished. If it ever entered his head to bring a surprise home for his children, it was, almost unfailingly, the wrong surprise and even the big watermelons he often brought home on his back in the summertime led to the most appalling scenes. I do not remember, in all those years, that one of his children was ever glad to see him come home. From what I was able to gather of his early life, it seemed that this inability to establish contact with other people had always marked him and had been one of the things which had driven him out of New Orleans. There was something in him, therefore, groping and tentative, which was never expressed and which was buried with him. One saw it most clearly when he was facing new people and hoping to impress them. But he never did, not for long. We went from church to smaller and more improbable church, he found himself in less and less demand as a minister, and by the time he died none of his friends had come to see him for a long time. He had lived and died in an intolerable bitterness of spirit and it frightened me, as we drove him to the graveyard through those unquiet, ruined streets, to see how powerful and overflowing this bitterness could be and to realize that this bitterness now was mine.

When he died I had been away from home for a little over a year. In that year I had had time to become aware of the meaning of all my father's bitter warnings, had discovered the secret of his proudly pursed lips and rigid carriage: I had discovered the weight of white people in the world. I saw that this had been for my ancestors and now would be for me an awful thing to live with and that the bitterness which had helped to kill my father could also kill me.

He had been ill a long time—in the mind, as we now realized, reliving instances of his fantastic intransigence in the new light of his affliction and endeavoring to feel a sorrow for him which never, quite, came true. We had not known that he was being eaten up by paranoia, and the discovery that his cruelty, to our bodies and our minds, had been one of the symptoms of his illness was not, then, enough to enable us to forgive him. The younger children felt, quite simply, relief that he would not be coming home anymore. My mother's observation that it was he, after all, who had kept them alive all these years meant nothing because the problems of keeping children alive are not real for children. The older children felt, with my father gone, that they could invite their friends to the house without fear that their friends would be insulted or, as had sometimes happened with me, being told that their friends were in league with the devil and intended to rob our family of everything we owned. (I didn't fail to wonder, and it made me hate him, what on earth we owned that anybody else would want.)

His illness was beyond all hope of healing before anyone realized that he was ill. He had always been so strange and had lived, like a prophet, in such unimaginably close communion with the Lord that his long silences which were punctuated by moans and hallelujahs and snatches of old songs while he sat at the living-room window never seemed odd to us. It was not until he refused to eat because, he said, his family was trying to poison him that my mother was forced to accept as a fact what had, until then, been only an unwilling suspicion. When he was committed, it was discovered that he had tuberculosis and, as it turned out, the disease of his mind allowed the disease of his body to destroy him. For the doctors could not force him to eat, either, and, though he was fed intravenously, it was clear from the beginning that there was no hope for him.

In my mind's eye I could see him, sitting at the window, locked up in his terrors; hating and fearing every living soul including his children who had betrayed him, too, by reaching towards the world which had despised him. There were nine of us. I began to wonder what it could have felt like for such a man to have had nine children whom he could barely feed. He used to make little jokes about our poverty, which never, of course, seemed very funny to us; they could not have seemed very funny to him, either, or else our all too feeble response to them would never have caused such rages. He spent great energy and achieved, to our chagrin, no small amount of success in keeping us away from the people who surrounded us, people who had all-night rent parties to which we listened when we should have been sleeping, people who cursed and drank and flashed razor blades on Lenox Avenue. He could not understand why, if they had so much energy to spare, they could not use it to make their lives better. He treated almost everybody on our block with a most uncharitable asperity and neither they, nor, of course, their children were slow to reciprocate.

The only white people who came to our house were welfare workers and bill collectors. It was almost always my mother who dealt with them, for my father's temper, which was at the mercy of his pride, was never to be trusted. It was clear that he felt their very presence in his home to be a violation: this was conveyed by his carriage, almost ludicrously stiff, and by his voice, harsh and vindictively polite. When I was around nine or ten I wrote a play which was directed by a young, white schoolteacher, a woman, who then took an interest in me, and gave me books to read and, in order to corroborate my theatrical bent, decided to take me to see what she somewhat tactlessly referred to as "real" plays. Theater-going was forbidden in our house, but, with the really cruel intuitiveness of a child, I suspected that the color of this woman's skin would carry the day for me. When, at school, she suggested taking me to the theater, I did not, as I might have done if she had been a Negro, find a way of discouraging her, but agreed that she should pick me up at my house one evening. I then, very cleverly, left all the rest to my mother, who suggested to my father, as I knew she would, that it would not be very nice to let such a kind woman make the trip for nothing. Also, since it was a schoolteacher, I imagine that my mother countered the idea of sin with the idea of "education," which word, even with my father, carried a kind of bitter weight.

Before the teacher came my father took me aside to ask *why* she was coming, what *interest* she could possibly have in our house, in a boy like me. I said I didn't know but I, too, suggested that it had something to do with education. And I understood that my father was waiting for me to say something—I didn't quite know what; perhaps that I wanted his protection against this teacher and her "education." I said none of these things and the teacher came and we went out. It was clear, during the brief interview in our living room, that my father was agreeing very much against his will and that he would have refused permission if he had dared. The fact that he did not dare caused me to despise him: I had no way of knowing that he was facing in that living room a wholly unprecedented and frightening situation.

Later, when my father had been laid off from his job, this woman became very important to us. She was really a very sweet and generous woman and went to a great deal of trouble to be of help to us, particularly during one awful winter. My mother called her by the highest name she knew: she said she was a "christian." My father could scarcely disagree but during the four or five years of our relatively close association he never trusted her and was always trying to surprise in her open, Midwestern face the genuine, cunningly hidden, and hideous motivation. In later years, particularly when it began to be clear that this "education" of mine was going to lead me to perdition, he became more explicit and warned me that my white friends in high school were not really my friends and that I would see, when I was older, how white people would do anything to keep a Negro down. Some of them could be nice, he admitted, but none of them were to be trusted and most of them were not even nice. The best thing was to have as little to do with them as possible. I did not feel this way and I was certain, in my innocence, that I never would.

But the year which preceded my father's death had made a great change in my life. I had been living in New Jersey, working in defense plants, working and living among southerners, white and black. I knew about the south, of course, and about how southerners treated Negroes and how they expected them to behave, but it had never entered my mind that anyone would look at me and expect *me* to behave that way. I learned in New Jersey that to be a Negro meant, precisely, that one was never looked at but was simply at the mercy of the reflexes the color of one's skin caused in other people. I acted in New Jersey as I had always acted, that is as though I thought a great deal of myself—I had to *act* that way—with results that were, simply, unbelievable. I had scarcely arrived before I had earned the enmity, which was extraordinarily ingenious, of all my superiors and nearly all my co-workers. In the beginning, to make matters worse, I simply did not know what was happening. I did not know what I had done, and I shortly began to wonder what *anyone* could possibly do, to bring about such unanimous, active, and unbearably vocal hostility. I knew about jim-crow but I had never experienced it. I went to the same self-service restaurant three times and stood with all the Princeton boys before the counter, waiting for a hamburger and coffee; it was always an extraordinarily long time before anything was set before me; but it was not until the fourth visit that I learned that, in fact, nothing had ever been set before me: I had simply picked something up. Negroes were not served there, I was told, and they had been waiting for me to realize that I was always the only Negro present. Once I was told this, I determined to go there all the time. But now they were ready for me and, though some dreadful scenes were subsequently enacted in that restaurant, I never ate there again.

It was the same story all over New Jersey, in bars, bowling alleys, diners, places to live. I was always being forced to leave, silently, or with mutual imprecations. I very shortly became notorious and children giggled behind me when I passed and their elders whispered or shouted—they really believed that I was mad. And it did begin to work on my mind, of course; I began to be afraid to go anywhere and to compensate for this I went places to which I really should not have gone and where, God knows, I had no desire to be. My reputation in town naturally enhanced my reputation at work and my working day became one long series of acrobatics designed to keep me out of trouble. I cannot say that these acrobatics succeeded. It began to seem that the machinery of the organization I worked for was turning over, day and night, with but one aim: to eject me. I was fired once, and contrived, with the aid of a friend from New York, to get back on the payroll; was fired again, and bounced back again. It took a while to fire me for the third time, but the third time took. There were no loopholes anywhere. There was not even any way of getting back inside the gates.

That year in New Jersey lives in my mind as though it were the year during which, having an unsuspected predilection for it, I first contracted some dread, chronic disease, the unfailing symptom of which is a kind of blind fever, a pounding in the skull and fire in the bowels. Once this disease is contracted, one can never be really carefree again, for the fever, without an instant's warning, can recur at any moment. It can wreck more important things than race relations. There is not a Negro alive who does not have this rage in his blood—one has the choice, merely, of living with it consciously or surrendering to it. As for me, this fever has recurred in me, and does, and will until the day I die.

My last night in New Jersey, a white friend from New York took me to the nearest big town, Trenton, to go to the movies and have a few drinks. As it turned out, he also saved me from, at the very least, a violent whipping. Almost every detail of that night stands out very clearly in my memory. I even remember the name of the movie we saw because its title impressed me as being so patly ironical. It was a movie about the German occupation of France, starring Maureen O'Hara and Charles Laughton and called *This Land Is Mine*. I remember the name of the diner we walked into when the movie ended: it was the "American Diner." When we walked in the counterman asked what we wanted and I remember answering with the casual sharpness which had become my habit: "We want a hamburger and a cup of coffee, what do you think we want?" I do not know why, after a year of such rebuffs, I so completely failed to anticipate his answer, which was, of course, "We don't serve Negroes here." This reply failed to discompose me, at least for the moment. I made some sardonic comment about the name of the diner and we walked out into the streets.

This was the time of what was called the "brown-out," when the lights in all American cities were very dim. When we re-entered the streets something happened to me which had the force of an optical illusion, or a nightmare. The streets were very crowded and I was facing north. People were moving in every direction but it seemed to me, in that instant, that all of the people I could see, and many more than that, were moving toward me, against me, and that everyone was white. I remember how their faces gleamed. And I felt, like a physical sensation, a *click* at the nape of my neck as though some interior string connecting my head to my body had been cut. I began to walk. I heard my friend call after me, but I ignored him. Heaven only knows what was going on in his mind, but he had the good sense not to touch me—I don't know what would have happened if he had—and to keep me in sight. I don't know what was going on in my mind, either; I certainly had no conscious plan. I wanted to do something to crush these white faces, which were crushing me. I walked for perhaps a block or two until I came to an enormous, glittering, and fashionable restaurant in which I knew not even the intercession of the Virgin would cause me to be served. I pushed through the doors and took the first vacant seat I saw, at a table for two, and waited.

I do not know how long I waited and I rather wonder, until today, what I could possibly have looked like. Whatever I looked like, I frightened the waitress who shortly appeared, and the moment she appeared all of my fury flowed towards her. I hated her for her white face, and for her great, astounded, frightened eyes. I felt that if she found a black man so frightening I would make her fright worth-while.

She did not ask me what I wanted, but repeated, as though she had learned it somewhere, "We don't serve Negroes here." She did not say it with the blunt, derisive hostility to which I had grown so accustomed, but, rather, with a note of apology in her voice, and fear. This made me colder and more murderous than ever. I felt I had to do something with my hands. I wanted her to come close enough for me to get her neck between my hands.

So I pretended not to have understood her, hoping to draw her closer. And she did step a very short step closer, with her pencil poised incongruously over her pad, and repeated the formula: ". . . don't serve Negroes here."

Somehow, with the repetition of that phrase, which was already ringing in my head like a thousand bells of a nightmare, I realized that she would never come any closer and that I would have to strike from a distance. There was nothing on the table but an ordinary water-mug half full of water, and I picked this up and hurled it with all my strength at her. She ducked and it missed her and shattered against the mirror behind the bar. And, with that sound, my frozen blood abruptly thawed, I returned from wherever I had been, I *saw*, for the first time, the restaurant, the people with their mouths open, already, as it seemed to me, rising as one man, and I realized what I had done, and where I was, and I was frightened. I rose and began running for the door. A round, potbellied man grabbed me by the nape of the neck just as I reached the doors and began to beat me about the face. I kicked him and got loose and ran into the streets. My friend whispered, *"Run!"* and I ran.

My friend stayed outside the restaurant long enough to misdirect my pursuers and the police, who arrived, he told me, at once. I do not know what I said to him when he came to my room that night. I could not have said much. I felt, in the oddest, most awful way, that I had somehow betrayed him. I lived it over and over and over again, the way one relives an automobile accident after it has happened and one finds oneself alone and safe. I could not get over two facts, both equally difficult for the imagination to grasp, and one was that I could have been murdered. But the other was that I had been ready to commit murder. I saw nothing very clearly but I did see this: that my life, my *real* life, was in danger, and not from anything other people might do but from the hatred I carried in my own heart.

II

I had returned home around the second week in June—in great haste because it seemed that my father's death and my mother's confinement were both but a matter of hours. In the case of my mother, it soon became clear that she had simply made a miscalculation. This had always been her tendency and I don't believe that a single one of us arrived in the world, or has since arrived anywhere else, on time. But none of us dawdled so intolerably about the business of being born as did my baby sister. We sometimes amused ourselves, during those endless, stifling weeks, by picturing the baby sitting within in the safe, warm dark, bitterly regretting the necessity of becoming a part of our chaos and stubbornly putting it off as long as possible. I understood her perfectly and congratulated her on showing such good sense so soon. Death, however, sat as purposefully at my father's bedside as life stirred within my mother's womb and it was harder to understand why he so lingered in that long shadow. It seemed that he had bent, and for a long time, too, all of his energies towards dying. Now death was ready for him but my father held back.

All of Harlem, indeed, seemed to be infected by waiting. I had never before known it to be so violently still. Racial tensions throughout this country were exacerbated during the early years of the war, partly because the labor market brought together hundreds of thousands of ill-prepared people and partly because Negro soldiers, regardless of where they were born, received their military training in the south. What happened in defense plants and army camps had repercussions, naturally, in every Negro ghetto. The situation in Harlem had grown bad enough for clergymen, policemen, educators, politicians, and social workers to assert in one breath that there was no "crime wave" and to offer, in the very next breath, suggestions as to how to combat it. These suggestions always seemed to involve playgrounds, despite the fact that racial skirmishes were occurring in the playgrounds, too. Playground or not, crime wave or not, the Harlem police force had been augmented in March, and the unrest grew—perhaps, in fact, partly as a result of the ghetto's instinctive hatred of policemen. Perhaps the most revealing news item, out of the steady parade of reports of muggings, stabbings, shootings, assaults, gang wars, and accusations of police brutality, is the item concerning six Negro girls who set upon a white girl in the subway because, as they all too accurately put it, she was stepping on their toes. Indeed she was, all over the nation.

I had never before been so aware of policemen, on foot, on horseback, on corners, everywhere, always two by two. Nor had I ever been so aware of small knots of people. They were on stoops and on corners and in doorways, and what was striking about them, I think, was that they did not seem to be talking. Never, when I passed these groups, did the usual sound of a curse or a laugh ring out and neither did there seem to be any hum of gossip. There was certainly, on the other hand, occurring between them communication extraordinarily intense. Another thing that was striking was the unexpected diversity of the people who made up these groups. Usually, for example, one would see a group of sharpies standing on the street corner, jiving the passing chicks; or a group of older men, usually, for some reason, in the vicinity of a barber shop, discussing baseball scores, or the numbers, or making rather chilling observations about women they had known. Women, in a general way, tended to be seen less often together—unless they were church women, or very young girls, or prostitutes met together for an unprofessional instant. But that summer I saw the strangest combinations: large, respectable, churchly matrons standing on the stoops or the corners with their hair tied up, together with a girl in sleazy satin whose face bore the marks of gin and the razor, or heavy-set, abrupt, no-nonsense older men, in company with the most disreputable and fanatical "race" men, or these same "race" men with the sharpies, or these sharpies with the churchly women. Seventh Day Adventists and Methodists and Spiritualists seemed to be hobnobbing with Holyrollers and they were all, alike, entangled with the most flagrant disbelievers; something heavy in their stance seemed to indicate that they had all, incredibly, seen a common vision, and on each face there seemed to be the same strange, bitter shadow.

The churchly women and the matter-of-fact, no-nonsense men had children in the Army. The sleazy girls they talked to had lovers there, the sharpies and the "race" men had friends and brothers there. It would have demanded an unquestioning patriotism, happily as uncommon in this country as it is undesirable, for these people not to have been disturbed by the bitter letters they received, by the newspaper stories they read, not to have been enraged by the posters, then to be found all over New York, which described the Japanese as "yellow-bellied Japs." It was only the "race" men, to be sure, who spoke ceaselessly of being revenged—how this vengeance was to be exacted was not clear—for the indignities and dangers suffered by Negro boys in uniform; but everybody felt a directionless, hopeless bitterness, as well as that panic which can scarcely be suppressed when one knows that a human being one loves is beyond one's reach, and in danger. This helplessness and this gnawing uneasiness does something, at length, to even the toughest mind. Perhaps the best way to sum all this up is to say that the people I knew felt, mainly, a peculiar kind of relief when they knew that their boys were being shipped out of the south, to do battle overseas. It was, perhaps, like feeling that the most dangerous part of a dangerous journey had been passed and that now, even if death should come, it would come with honor and without the complicity of their countrymen. Such a death would be, in short, a fact with which one could hope to live.

It was on the 28th of July, which I believe was a Wednesday, that I visited my father for the first time during his illness and for the last time in his life. The moment I saw him I knew why I had put off this visit so long. I had told my mother that I did not want to see him because I hated him. But this was not true. It was only that I *had* hated him and I wanted to hold on to this hatred. I did not want to look on him as a ruin: it was not a ruin I had hated. I imagine that one of the reasons people cling to their hates so stubbornly is because they sense, once hate is gone, that they will be forced to deal with pain.

We traveled out to him, his older sister and myself, to what seemed to be the very end of a very Long Island. It was hot and dusty and we wrangled, my aunt and I, all the way out, over the fact that I had recently begun to smoke and, as she said, to give myself airs. But I knew that she wrangled with me because she could not bear to face the fact of her brother's dying. Neither could I endure the reality of her despair, her unstated bafflement as to what had happened to her brother's life, and her own. So we wrangled and I smoked and from time to time she fell into a heavy reverie. Covertly, I watched her face, which was the face of an old woman; it had fallen in, the eyes were sunken and lightless; soon she would be dying, too.

In my childhood—it had not been so long ago—I had thought her beautiful. She had been quick-witted and quick-moving and very generous with all the children and each of her visits had been an event. At one time one of my brothers and myself had thought of running away to live with her. Now she could no longer produce out of her handbag some unexpected and yet familiar delight. She made me feel pity and revulsion and fear. It was awful to realize that she no longer caused me to feel affection. The closer we came to the hospital the more querulous she became and at the same time, naturally, grew more dependent on me. Between pity and guilt and fear I began to feel that there was another me trapped in my skull like a jack-in-the-box who might escape my control at any moment and fill the air with screaming.

She began to cry the moment we entered the room and she saw him lying there, all shriveled and still, like a little black monkey. The great, gleaming apparatus which fed him and would have compelled him to be still even if he had been able to move brought to mind, not beneficence, but torture; the tubes entering his arm made me think of pictures I had seen when a child, of Gulliver, tied down by the pygmies on that island. My aunt wept and wept, there was a whistling sound in my father's throat; nothing was said; he could not speak. I wanted to take his hand, to say something. But I do not know what I could have said, even if he could have heard me. He was not really in that room with us, he had at last really embarked on his journey; and though my aunt told me that he said he was going to meet Jesus, I did not hear anything except that whistling in his throat. The doctor came back and we left, into that unbearable train again, and home. In the morning came the telegram saying that he was dead. Then the house was suddenly full of relatives, friends, hysteria, and confusion and I quickly left my mother and the children to the care of those impressive women, who, in Negro communities at least, automatically appear at times of bereavement armed with lotions, proverbs, and patience, and an ability to cook. I went downtown. By the time I returned, later the same day, my mother had been carried to the hospital and the baby had been born.

III

For my father's funeral I had nothing black to wear and this posed a nagging problem all day long. It was one of those problems, simple, or impossible of solution, to which the mind insanely clings in order to avoid the mind's real trouble. I spent most of that day at the downtown apartment of a girl I knew, celebrating my birthday with whiskey and wondering what to wear that night. When planning a birthday celebration one naturally does not expect that it will be up against competition from a funeral and this girl had anticipated taking me out that night, for a big dinner and a night club afterwards. Sometime during the course of that long day we decided that we would go out anyway, when my father's funeral service was over. I imagine I decided it, since, as the funeral hour approached, it became clearer and clearer to me that I would not know what to do with myself when it was over. The girl, stifling her very lively concern as to the possible effects of the whiskey on one of my father's chief mourners, concentrated on being conciliatory and practically helpful. She found a black shirt for me somewhere and ironed it and, dressed in the darkest pants and jacket I owned, and slightly drunk, I made my way to my father's funeral.

The chapel was full, but not packed, and very quiet. There were, mainly, my father's relatives, and his children, and here and there I saw faces I had not seen since childhood, the faces of my father's one-time friends. They were very dark and solemn now, seeming somehow to suggest that they had known all along that something like this would happen. Chief among the mourners was my aunt, who had quarreled with my father all his life; by which I do not mean to suggest that her mourning was insincere or that she had not loved him. I suppose that she was one of the few people in the world who had, and their incessant quarreling proved precisely the strength of the tie that bound them. The only other person in the world, as far as I knew, whose relationship to my father rivaled my aunt's in depth was my mother, who was not there.

It seemed to me, of course, that it was a very long funeral. But it was, if anything, a rather shorter funeral than most, nor, since there were no overwhelming, uncontrollable expressions of grief, could it be called—if I dare to use the word—successful. The minister who preached my father's funeral sermon was one of the few my father had still been seeing as he neared his end. He presented to us in his sermon a man whom none of us had ever seen—a man thoughtful, patient, and forbearing, a Christian inspiration to all who knew him, and a model for his children. And no doubt the children, in their disturbed and guilty state, were almost ready to believe this; he had been remote enough to be anything and, anyway, the shock of the incontrovertible, that it was really our father lying up there in that casket, prepared the mind for anything. His sister moaned and this grief-stricken moaning was taken as corroboration. The other faces held a dark, non-committal thoughtfulness. This was not the man they had known, but they had scarcely expected to be confronted with *him*; this was, in a sense deeper than questions of fact, the man they had not known, and the man they had not known may have been the real one. The real man, whoever he had been, had suffered and now he was dead: this was all that was sure and all that mattered now. Every man in the chapel hoped that when his hour came he, too, would be eulogized, which is to say forgiven, and that all of his lapses, greeds, errors, and strayings from the truth would be invested with coherence and looked upon with charity. This was perhaps the last thing human beings could give each other and it was what they demanded, after all, of the Lord. Only the Lord saw the midnight tears, only He was present when one of His children, moaning and wringing hands, paced up and down the room. When one slapped one's child in anger the recoil in the heart reverberated through heaven and became part of the pain of the universe. And when the children were hungry and sullen and distrustful and one watched them, daily, growing wilder, and further away, and running headlong into danger, it was the Lord who knew what the charged heart endured as the strap was laid to the backside; the Lord alone who knew what one *would* have said if one had had, like the Lord, the gift of the living word. It was the Lord who knew of the impossibility every parent in that room faced: how to prepare the child for the day when the child would be despised and how to *create* in the child—by what means?—a stronger antidote to this poison than one had found for oneself. The avenues, side streets, bars, billiard halls, hospitals, police stations, and even the playgrounds of Harlem—not to mention the houses of correction, the jails, and the morgue—testified to the potency of the poison while remaining silent as to the efficacy of whatever antidote, irresistibly raising the question of whether or not such an antidote existed; raising, which was worse, the question of whether or not an antidote was desirable; perhaps poison should be fought with poison. With these several schisms in the mind and with more terrors in the heart than could be named, it was better not to judge the man who had gone down under an impossible burden. It was better to remember: *Thou knowest this man's fall; but thou knowest not his wrassling.*

While the preacher talked and I watched the children—years of changing their diapers, scrubbing them, slapping them, taking them to school, and scolding them had had the perhaps inevitable result of making me love them, though I am not sure I knew this then—my mind was busily breaking out with a rash of disconnected impressions. Snatches of popular songs, indecent jokes, bits of books I had read, movie sequences, faces, voices, political issues—I thought I was going mad; all these impressions suspended, as it were, in the solution of the faint nausea produced in me by the heat and liquor. For a moment I had the impression that my alcoholic breath, inefficiently disguised with chewing gum, filled the entire chapel. Then someone began singing one of my father's favorite songs and, abruptly, I was with him, sitting on his knee, in the hot, enormous, crowded church which was the first church we attended. It was the Abyssinia Baptist Church on 138th Street. We had not gone there long. With this image, a host of others came. I had forgotten, in the rage of my growing up, how proud my father had been of me when I was little. Apparently, I had had a voice and my father had liked to show me off before the members of the church. I had forgotten what he had looked like when he was pleased but now I remembered that he had always been grinning with pleasure when my solos ended. I even remembered certain expressions on his face when he teased my mother—had he loved her? I would never know. And when had it all begun to change? For now it seemed that he had not always been cruel. I remembered being taken for a haircut and scraping my knee on the footrest of the barber's chair and I remembered my father's face as he soothed my crying and applied the stinging iodine. Then I remembered our fights, fights which had been of the worst possible kind because my technique had been silence.

I remembered the one time in all our life together when we had really spoken to each other.

It was on a Sunday and it must have been shortly before I left home. We were walking, just the two of us, in our usual silence, to or from church. I was in high school and had been doing a lot of writing and I was, at about this time, the editor of the high school magazine. But I had also been a Young Minister and had been preaching from the pulpit. Lately, I had been taking fewer engagements and preached as rarely as possible. It was said in the church, quite truthfully, that I was "cooling off."

My father asked me abruptly, "You'd rather write than preach, wouldn't you?"

I was astonished at his question—because it was a real question. I answered, "Yes."

That was all we said. It was awful to remember that that was all we had *ever* said.

The casket now was opened and the mourners were being led up the aisle to look for the last time on the deceased. The assumption was that the family was too overcome with grief to be allowed to make this journey alone and I watched while my aunt was led to the casket and, muffled in black, and shaking, led back to her seat. I disapproved of forcing the children to look on their dead father, considering that the shock of his death, or, more truthfully, the shock of death as a reality, was already a little more than a child could bear, but my judgment in this matter had been overruled and there they were, bewildered and frightened and very small, being led, one by one, to the casket. But there is also something very gallant about children at such moments.

It has something to do with their silence and gravity and with the fact that one cannot help them. Their legs, somehow, seem *exposed,* so that it is at once incredible and terribly clear that their legs are all they have to hold them up.

I had not wanted to go to the casket myself and I certainly had not wished to be led there, but there was no way of avoiding either of these forms. One of the deacons led me up and I looked on my father's face. I cannot say that it looked like him at all. His blackness had been equivocated by powder and there was no suggestion in that casket of what his power had or could have been. He was simply an old man dead, and it was hard to believe that he had ever given anyone either joy or pain. Yet, his life filled that room. Further up the avenue his wife was holding his newborn child. Life and death so close together, and love and hatred, and right and wrong, said something to me which I did not want to hear concerning man, concerning the life of man.

After the funeral, while I was downtown desperately celebrating my birthday, a Negro soldier, in the lobby of the Hotel Braddock, got into a fight with a white policeman over a Negro girl. Negro girls, white policemen, in or out of uniform, and Negro males—in or out of uniform—were part of the furniture of the lobby of the Hotel Braddock and this was certainly not the first time such an incident had occurred. It was destined, however, to receive an unprecedented publicity, for the fight between the policeman and the soldier ended with the shooting of the soldier. Rumor, flowing immediately to the streets outside, stated that the soldier had been shot in the back, an instantaneous and revealing invention, and that the soldier had died protecting a Negro woman. The facts were somewhat different—for example, the soldier had not been shot in the back, and was not dead, and the girl seems to have been as dubious a symbol of womanhood as her white counterpart in Georgia usually is, but no one was interested in the facts. They preferred the invention because this invention expressed and corroborated their hates and fears so perfectly. It is just as well to remember that people are always doing this. Perhaps many of those legends, including Christianity, to which the world clings began their conquest of the world with just some such concerted surrender to distortion. The effect, in Harlem, of this particular legend was like the effect of a lit match in a tin of gasoline. The mob gathered before the doors of the Hotel Braddock simply began to swell and to spread in every direction, and Harlem exploded.

The mob did not cross the ghetto lines. It would have been easy, for example, to have gone over Morningside Park on the west side or to have crossed the Grand Central railroad tracks at 125th Street on the east side, to wreak havoc in white neighborhoods. The mob seems to have been mainly interested in something more potent and real than the white face, that is, in white power, and the principal damage done during the riot of the summer of 1943 was to white business establishments in Harlem. It might have been a far bloodier story, of course, if, at the hour the riot began, these establishments had still been open. From the Hotel Braddock the mob fanned out, east and west along 125th Street, and for the entire length of Lenox, Seventh, and Eighth avenues. Along each of these avenues, and along each major side street—116th, 125th, 135th, and so on—bars, stores, pawnshops, restaurants, even little luncheonettes had been smashed open and entered and looted—looted, it might be added, with more haste than efficiency. The shelves really looked as though a bomb had struck them. Cans of beans and soup and dog food, along with toilet paper, corn flakes, sardines and milk tumbled every which way, and abandoned cash registers and cases of beer leaned crazily out of the splintered windows and were strewn along the avenues. Sheets, blankets, and clothing of every description formed a kind of path, as though people had dropped them while running. I truly had not realized that Harlem *had* so many stores until I saw them all smashed open; the first time the word *wealth* ever entered my mind in relation to Harlem was when I saw it scattered in the streets. But one's first, incongruous impression of plenty was countered immediately by an impression of waste. None of this was doing anybody any good. It would have been better to have left the plate glass as it had been and the goods lying in the stores.

It would have been better, but it would also have been intolerable, for Harlem had needed something to smash. To smash something is the ghetto's chronic need. Most of the time it is the members of the ghetto who smash each other, and themselves. But as long as the ghetto walls are standing there will always come a moment when these outlets do not work. That summer, for example, it was not enough to get into a fight on Lenox Avenue, or curse out one's cronies in the barber shops. If ever, indeed, the violence which fills Harlem's churches, pool halls, and bars erupts outward in a more direct fashion, Harlem and its citizens are likely to vanish in an apocalyptic flood. That this is not likely to happen is due to a great many reasons, most hidden and powerful among them the Negro's real relation to the white American. This relation prohibits, simply, anything as uncomplicated and satisfactory as pure hatred. In order really to hate white people, one has to blot so much out of the mind—and the heart—that this hatred itself becomes an exhausting and self-destructive pose. But this does not mean, on the other hand, that love comes easily: the white world is too powerful, too complacent, too ready with gratuitous humiliation, and, above all, too ignorant and too innocent for that. One is absolutely forced to make perpetual qualifications and one's own reactions are always canceling each other out. It is this, really, which has driven so many people mad, both white and black. One is always in the position of having to decide between amputation and gangrene. Amputation is swift but time may prove that the amputation was not necessary—or one may delay the amputation too long. Gangrene is slow, but it is impossible to be sure that one is reading one's symptoms right. The idea of going through life as a cripple is more than one can bear, and equally unbearable is the risk of swelling up slowly, in agony, with poison. And the trouble, finally, is that the risks are real even if the choices do not exist.

"But as for me and my house," my father had said, "we will serve the Lord." I wondered, as we drove him to his resting place, what this line had meant for him. I had heard him preach it many times. I had preached it once myself, proudly giving it an interpretation different from my father's. Now the whole thing came back to me, as though my father and I were on our way to Sunday school and I were memorizing the golden text: *And if it seem evil unto you to serve the Lord, choose you this day whom you will serve; whether the gods which your fathers served that were on the other side of the flood, or the gods of the Amorites, in whose land ye dwell: but as for me and my house, we will serve the Lord.* I suspected in these familiar lines a meaning which had never been there for me before. All of my father's texts and songs, which I had decided were meaningless, were arranged before me at his death like empty bottles, waiting to hold the meaning which life would give them for me. This was his legacy: nothing is ever escaped. That bleakly memorable morning I hated the unbelievable streets and the Negroes and whites who had, equally, made them that way. But I knew that it was folly, as my father would have said, this bitterness was folly. It was necessary to hold on to the things that mattered. The dead man mattered, the new life mattered; blackness and whiteness did not matter; to believe that they did was to acquiesce in one's own destruction. Hatred, which could destroy so much, never failed to destroy the man who hated and this was an immutable law.

It began to seem that one would have to hold in the mind forever two ideas which seemed to be in opposition. The first idea was acceptance, the acceptance, totally without rancor, of life as it is, and men as they are: in the light of this idea, it goes without saying that injustice is a commonplace. But this did not mean that one could be complacent, for the second idea was of equal power: that one must never, in one's own life, accept these injustices as commonplace but must fight them with all one's strength. This fight begins, however, in the heart and it now had been laid to my charge to keep my own heart free of hatred and despair. This intimation made my heart heavy and, now that my father was irrecoverable, I wished that he had been beside me so that I could have searched his face for the answers which only the future would give me now.

Questions

1. James Baldwin packs a lot of information, both personal and public, into the first paragraph. List the major facts he presents.
2. Why does Baldwin mix personal and public events in his opening paragraphs? What does his opening suggest about the relationship between private and social realities?
3. What does Baldwin tell us about his grandmother? Why does it matter to his essay?
4. Baldwin's father was a preacher. Baldwin became a writer. Does Baldwin see any relationship between the two vocations?
5. The essay begins and ends at the funeral of Baldwin's father. What lessons has the author learned—positively or negatively—from his father?

George Orwell

George Orwell (1903–1950) was the pen name of Eric Arthur Blair, who was born in Bengal, where his father served as a colonial administrator in British India. He was educated in England at private schools. Upon graduating from Eton, an elite boys' school, in 1921, Orwell decided not to attend a university but joined the Indian Imperial Police and served in colonial Burma for five years. His grim experiences there (described in the following essay) left him disgusted not only with the British Empire, but with all forms of oppressive political power. Returning to England, he eked out an existence as a writer of bold social and political reportage and dark satiric novels. In 1937 he enlisted with an anarchist squadron to fight in the Spanish Civil War and was wounded. His experiences in Spain, described in Homage to Catalonia (1939), *turned him into an anticommunist. By that time Orwell had become one of the great essayists of the twentieth century, unsurpassed in his political acumen, ideological skepticism, and passion for social justice. Having lived in harsh poverty most of his adult life, Orwell developed tuberculosis. His last two novels,* Animal Farm (1945) *and* Nineteen Eighty-Four (1949), *became international best sellers and achieved almost instantaneous classic status.*

Shooting an Elephant   1936

In Moulmein, in Lower Burma, I was hated by large numbers of people—the only time in my life that I have been important enough for this to happen to me. I was sub-divisional police officer of the town, and in an aimless, petty kind of way anti-European feeling was very bitter. No one had the guts to raise a riot, but if a European woman went through the bazaars alone somebody would probably spit betel juice over her dress. As a police officer I was an obvious target and was baited whenever it seemed safe to do so. When a nimble Burman tripped me up on the football field and the referee (another Burman) looked the other way, the crowd yelled with hideous laughter. This happened more than once. In the end the sneering yellow faces of young men that met me everywhere, the insults hooted after me when I was at a safe distance, got badly on my nerves. The young Buddhist priests were the worst of all. There were several thousands of them in the town and none of them seemed to have anything to do except stand on street corners and jeer at Europeans.

All this was perplexing and upsetting. For at that time I had already made up my mind that imperialism was an evil thing and the sooner I chucked up my job and got out of it the better. Theoretically—and secretly, of course—I was all for the Burmese and all against their oppressors, the British. As for the job I was doing, I hated it more bitterly than I can perhaps make clear. In a job like that you see the dirty work of Empire at close quarters. The wretched prisoners huddling in the stinking cages of the lock-ups, the grey, cowed faces of the long-term convicts, the scarred buttocks of the men who had been flogged with bamboos—all these oppressed me with an intolerable sense of guilt. But I could get nothing into perspective. I was young and ill-educated and I had had to think out my problems in the utter silence that is imposed on every Englishman in the East. I did not even know that the British Empire is dying, still less did I know that it is a great deal better than the younger empires that are going to supplant it. All I knew was that I was stuck between my hatred of the empire I served and my rage against the evil-spirited little beasts who tried to make my job impossible. With one part of my mind I thought of the British Raj° as an unbreakable tyranny, as something clamped down, in *saecula saeculorum*,° upon the will of prostrate peoples; with another part I thought that the greatest joy in the world would be to drive a bayonet into a Buddhist priest's guts. Feelings like these are the normal by-products of imperialism; ask any Anglo-Indian official, if you can catch him off duty.

One day something happened which in a roundabout way was enlightening. It was a tiny incident in itself, but it gave me a better glimpse than I had had before of the real nature of imperialism—the real motives for which despotic governments act. Early one morning the sub-inspector at a police station the other end of the town rang me up on the phone and said that an elephant was ravaging the bazaar. Would I please come and do something about it? I did not know what I could do, but I wanted to see what was happening and I got on to a pony and started out. I took my rifle, an old .44 Winchester and much too small to kill an elephant, but I thought the noise might be useful *in terrorem.*° Various Burmans stopped me on the way and told me

---

British raj: The imperial government of British India and Burma.   *saecula saeculorum*: Latin religious phrase meaning "forever and ever."   *in terrorem*: Latin for "in terror," a legal term used to describe a warning.

about the elephant's doings. It was not, of course, a wild elephant, but a tame one which had gone "must."° It had been chained up, as tame elephants always are when their attack of "must" is due, but on the previous night it had broken its chain and escaped. Its mahout, the only person who could manage it when it was in that state, had set out in pursuit, but he had taken the wrong direction and was now twelve hours' journey away, and in the morning the elephant had suddenly reappeared in the town. The Burmese population had no weapons and were quite helpless against it. It had already destroyed somebody's bamboo hut, killed a cow and raided some fruit-stalls and devoured the stock; also it had met the municipal rubbish van and, when the driver jumped out and took to his heels, had turned the van over and inflicted violence upon it.

The Burmese sub-inspector and some Indian constables were waiting for me in the quarter where the elephant had been seen. It was a very poor quarter, a labyrinth of squalid bamboo huts, thatched with palm-leaf, winding all over a steep hillside. I remember that it was a cloudy stuffy morning at the beginning of the rains. We began questioning the people as to where the elephant had gone and, as usual, failed to get any definite information. That is invariably the case in the East; a story always sounds clear enough at a distance, but the nearer you get to the scene of events the vaguer it becomes. Some of the people said that the elephant had gone in one direction, some said that he had gone in another, some professed not even to have heard of any elephant. I had almost made up my mind that the whole story was a pack of lies, when we heard yells a little distance away. There was a loud, scandalized cry of "Go away, child! Go away this instant!" and an old woman with a switch in her hand came round the corner of a hut, violently shooing away a crowd of naked children. Some more women followed, clicking their tongues and exclaiming; evidently there was something that the children ought not to have seen. I rounded the hut and saw a man's dead body sprawling in the mud. He was an Indian, a black Dravidian coolie,° almost naked, and he could not have been dead many minutes. The people said that the elephant had come suddenly upon him round the corner of the hut, caught him with its trunk, put its foot on his back and ground him into the earth. This was the rainy season and the ground was soft, and his face had scored a trench a foot deep and a couple of yards long. He was lying on his belly with arms crucified and head sharply twisted to one side. His face was coated with mud, the eyes wide open, the teeth bared and grinning with an expression of unendurable agony. (Never tell me, by the way, that the dead look peaceful. Most of the corpses I have seen looked devilish.) The friction of the great beast's foot had stripped the skin from his back as neatly as one skins a rabbit. As soon as I saw the dead man I sent an orderly to a friend's house nearby to borrow an elephant rifle. I had already sent back the pony, not wanting it to go mad with fright and throw me if it smelled the elephant.

The orderly came back in a few minutes with a rifle and five cartridges, and meanwhile some Burmans had arrived and told us that the elephant was in the paddy fields below, only a few hundred yards away. As I started forward practically the whole population of the quarter flocked out of their houses and followed me. They had seen

5

---

must: in sexual heat.   *Dravidian coolie:* A hired manual laborer from southern India, who speaks a Dravidian language.

the rifle and were all shouting excitedly that I was going to shoot the elephant. They had not shown much interest in the elephant when he was merely ravaging their homes, but it was different now that he was going to be shot. It was a bit of fun to them, as it would be to an English crowd; besides, they wanted the meat. It made me vaguely uneasy. I had no intention of shooting the elephant—I had merely sent for the rifle to defend myself if necessary—and it is always unnerving to have a crowd following you. I marched down the hill, looking and feeling a fool, with the rifle over my shoulder and an ever-growing army of people jostling at my heels. At the bottom, when you got away from the huts, there was a metalled road and beyond that a miry waste of paddy fields a thousand yards across, not yet ploughed but soggy from the first rains and dotted with coarse grass. The elephant was standing eighty yards from the road, his left side towards us. He took not the slightest notice of the crowd's approach. He was tearing up bunches of grass, beating them against his knees to clean them and stuffing them into his mouth.

I had halted on the road. As soon as I saw the elephant I knew with perfect certainty that I ought not to shoot him. It is a serious matter to shoot a working elephant—it is comparable to destroying a huge and costly piece of machinery—and obviously one ought not to do it if it can possibly be avoided. And at that distance, peacefully eating, the elephant looked no more dangerous than a cow. I thought then and I think now that his attack of "must" was already passing off; in which case he would merely wander harmlessly about until the mahout came back and caught him. Moreover, I did not in the least want to shoot him. I decided that I would watch him for a little while to make sure that he did not turn savage again, and then go home.

But at that moment I glanced round at the crowd that had followed me. It was an immense crowd, two thousand at the least and growing every minute. It blocked the road for a long distance on either side. I looked at the sea of yellow faces above the garish clothes—faces all happy and excited over this bit of fun, all certain that the elephant was going to be shot. They were watching me as they would watch a conjurer about to perform a trick. They did not like me, but with the magical rifle in my hands I was momentarily worth watching. And suddenly I realized that I should have to shoot the elephant after all. The people expected it of me and I had got to do it; I could feel their two thousand wills pressing me forward, irresistibly. And it was at this moment, as I stood there with the rifle in my hands, that I first grasped the hollowness, the futility of the white man's dominion in the East. Here was I, the white man with his gun, standing in front of the unarmed native crowd—seemingly the leading actor of the piece; but in reality I was only an absurd puppet pushed to and fro by the will of those yellow faces behind. I perceived in this moment that when the white man turns tyrant it is his own freedom that he destroys. He becomes a sort of hollow, posing dummy, the conventionalized figure of a sahib.° For it is the condition of his rule that he shall spend his life in trying to impress the "natives" and so in every crisis he has got to do what the "natives" expect of him. He wears a mask, and his face grows to fit it. I had got to shoot the elephant. I had committed myself to doing it when I sent for the rifle. A sahib has got to act like a sahib; he has got to appear resolute, to know his own mind and do definite things. To come all that

---

sahib: respectful term of address for a European man in colonial India.

way, rifle in hand, with two thousand people marching at my heels, and then to trail feebly away, having done nothing—no, that was impossible. The crowd would laugh at me. And my whole life, every white man's life in the East, was one long struggle not to be laughed at.

But I did not want to shoot the elephant. I watched him beating his bunch of grass against his knees, with that preoccupied grandmotherly air that elephants have. It seemed to me that it would be murder to shoot him. At that age I was not squeamish about killing animals, but I had never shot an elephant and never wanted to. (Somehow it always seems worse to kill a *large* animal.) Besides, there was the beast's owner to be considered. Alive, the elephant was worth at least a hundred pounds; dead, he would only be worth the value of his tusks—five pounds, possibly. But I had got to act quickly. I turned to some experienced-looking Burmans who had been there when we arrived, and asked them how the elephant had been behaving. They all said the same thing: he took no notice of you if you left him alone, but he might charge if you went too close to him.

It was perfectly clear to me what I ought to do. I ought to walk up to within, say, twenty-five yards of the elephant and test his behavior. If he charged I could shoot, if he took no notice of me it would be safe to leave him until the mahout came back. But also I knew that I was going to do no such thing. I was a poor shot with a rifle and the ground was soft mud into which one would sink at every step. If the elephant charged and I missed him, I should have about as much chance as a toad under a steam-roller. But even then I was not thinking particularly of my own skin, only the watchful yellow faces behind. For at that moment, with the crowd watching me, I was not afraid in the ordinary sense, as I would have been if I had been alone. A white man mustn't be frightened in front of "natives"; and so, in general, he isn't frightened. The sole thought in my mind was that if anything went wrong those two thousand Burmans would see me pursued, caught, trampled on and reduced to a grinning corpse like that Indian up the hill. And if that happened it was quite probable that some of them would laugh. That would never do. There was only one alternative. I shoved the cartridges into the magazine and lay down on the road to get a better aim.

The crowd grew very still, and a deep, low, happy sigh, as of people who see the theater curtain go up at last, breathed from innumerable throats. They were going to have their bit of fun after all. The rifle was a beautiful German thing with cross-hair sights. I did not then know that in shooting an elephant one should shoot to cut an imaginary bar running from ear-hole to ear-hole. I ought, therefore, as the elephant was sideways on, to have aimed straight at his ear-hole; actually I aimed several inches in front of this, thinking the brain would be further forward.

When I pulled the trigger I did not hear the bang or feel the kick—one never does when a shot goes home—but I heard the devilish roar of glee that went up from the crowd. In that instant, in too short a time, one would have thought, even for the bullet to get there, a mysterious, terrible change had come over the elephant. He neither stirred nor fell, but every line of his body had altered. He looked suddenly stricken, shrunken, immensely old, as though the frightful impact of the bullet had paralyzed him without knocking him down. At last, after what seemed a long time—it might have been five seconds, I dare say—he sagged flabbily to his knees. His mouth slobbered. An enormous senility seemed to have settled upon him. One could have imagined him thousands of years old. I fired again into the same spot. At the second shot he did not collapse but climbed with desperate slowness to his feet and stood weakly upright, with legs sagging and head drooping. I fired a third time. That was the shot that did for him. You could see the agony of it jolt his whole body and knock the last remnant of strength from his legs. But in falling he seemed for a moment to rise, for as his hind legs collapsed beneath him he seemed to tower upward like a huge rock toppling, his trunk reaching skyward like a tree. He trumpeted, for the first and only time. And then down he came, his belly towards me, with a crash that seemed to shake the ground even where I lay.

I got up. The Burmans were already racing past me across the mud. It was obvious that the elephant would never rise again, but he was not dead. He was breathing very rhythmically with long rattling gasps, his great mound of a side painfully rising and falling. His mouth was wide open—I could see far down into caverns of pale pink throat. I waited a long time for him to die, but his breathing did not weaken. Finally I fired my two remaining shots into the spot where I thought his heart must be. The thick blood welled out of him like red velvet, but still he did not die. His body did not even jerk when the shots hit him, the tortured breathing continued without a pause. He was dying, very slowly and in great agony, but in some world remote from me where not even a bullet could damage him further. I felt that I had got to put an end to that dreadful noise. It seemed dreadful to see the great beast lying there, powerless to move and yet powerless to die, and not even to be able to finish him. I sent back for my small rifle and poured shot after shot into his heart and down his throat. They seemed to make no impression. The tortured gasps continued as steadily as the ticking of a clock.

In the end I could not stand it any longer and went away. I heard later that it took him half an hour to die. Burmans were arriving with dahs° and baskets even before I left, and I was told they had stripped his body almost to the bones by the afternoon.

Afterwards, of course, there were endless discussions about the shooting of the elephant. The owner was furious, but he was only an Indian and could do nothing. Besides, legally I had done the right thing, for a mad elephant has to be killed, like a mad dog, if its owner fails to control it. Among the Europeans opinion was divided. The older men said I was right, the younger men said it was a damn shame to shoot an elephant for killing a coolie, because an elephant was worth more than any damn Coringhee coolie.° And afterwards I was very glad that the coolie had been killed; it put me legally in the right and it gave me a sufficient pretext for shooting the elephant. I often wondered whether any of the others grasped that I had done it solely to avoid looking a fool.

dahs: butcher knives.   *Coringhee coolie:* A hired manual laborer from the seaport of Coringa, in Madras, India.

Questions
1. Why do the local citizens want Orwell to shoot the elephant? Why does he hesitate?
2. How does Orwell think he should handle the situation?
3. What precise reason for shooting the elephant does Orwell confess at the end of the essay?
4. How do Orwell's fellow policemen judge his behavior?
5. What would you have done in the same circumstances?

Sacha Z. Scoblic

Sacha Zimmerman Scoblic (b. 1973) was born and raised in upstate New York. She majored in philosophy at SUNY Binghamton and later spent a year on a fellowship in Israel. She earned an M.A. in magazine journalism at Syracuse University and has worked at Reader's Digest and the New Republic. Currently she manages editorial projects at the Aspen Institute in Washington, D.C. Her witty account of her recovery from alcoholism, Unwasted: My Lush Sobriety, *was published in 2011.*

Sacha Z. Scoblic

Rock Star, Meet Teetotaler   2009

In the restaurant, the little tables shimmered under the moody lighting. It was just the kind of lighting, I knew, that after a few drinks would take on a shadowy glow and make our table the only table, a tiny oasis. But here I was: stone cold sober, out of the house for the first time in weeks, and meeting new people—an intimidatingly attractive couple with bright smiles and even brighter careers.

I wanted to hate them, to cede ground on looks and success, but retain intellectual superiority. It was a lost cause. She was especially arch as she told wicked stories about life as a divorce attorney ("You have to mourn it like a death," she deadpanned to an invisible client). I was smitten, disarmed. Her eyes were mischievous when she leaned over to me and asked, "Shall we order a bottle of wine?" It was as though she were letting me in on a secret, a little bit of whimsy that she wanted to share with me, her table sister, while the men talked foreign policy.

"No thanks, I don't drink," I said apologetically, certain I had just irrevocably denounced the possibility of a good time, rebuffed her sweet attempt at inclusion, and declared myself a Mormon, all in one fell swoop. Which is why my next words—rushing out of my mouth in a kind of desperate lunacy—were: "But don't worry, I'm still fun!" Like that was normal. Like that didn't sound anything at all like a pert promise-ring girl trying to assure her frustrated, panting boyfriend that we could do lots of things besides have sex. Because, really, how fun could I possibly be if I didn't drink?

I had given up alcohol just six months earlier and still felt viscerally close to the life I led as a drinker. I was also acutely aware of my own feeling toward people who didn't drink: that they were all totally vanilla, uptight squares who wanted me to treat my body like a temple, take Jesus Christ as my savior and drink Kool-Aid with them at mixers in church basements. Or they were health nuts who got "high" by hiking Mt. Kilimanjaro or by taking six-hour heated power yoga sessions while communing with their inner gurus and other activities that smacked of effort. But the worst thing was that I feared even those folks were more interesting—if exasperatingly earnest—than I was sober.

Drinking had made me the life of every party, nightclub and living room I wafted into, happily singing or dancing like life was meant only for such pursuits. I was ready to see any evening through till dawn, to wear sequins and glitter, to laugh until black eyeliner ran down my face. My favorite word was "subversive" and my favorite humor was cruel. Every day was hard, but every night was Saturday. Once, when a boyfriend implored me to take it easy, to call it a night, I looked to the friends waiting for me on the sidewalk ready to go to the next party and replied, "But this is who I am. I'm a fun girl."

So now that I was sober, I blurted out things like, "Don't worry, I'm still fun!" even though what I was really thinking was: "Don't even for a minute think I'm vanilla because the truth is I am so hard-core I had to quit. I drank so much it was a matter of life and death. I'm like a rock star compared with you. In fact, maybe you should just call me Sid Vicious from now on. You should look at me with a touch of fear and awe because you would quiver to think about the amount of rotgut I've ingested over the years. So step off with your preconceived notions, O.K.?"

In fact, throughout that entire first year of sobriety, I longed for some shorthand for everything I wanted to say: the confusing pride I felt about my past destructive life, the odd embarrassment I felt over my current redeemed one. Maybe a skull-and-crossbones-like symbol just for us addicts, something with the right mix of menace and solidarity, something I could tattoo on my wrist like a gang member to establish my alcoholic street cred. That way, instead of reassuring new acquaintances that I was fun, I could just silently shake my head when offered a drink, flash my tat and look at my new friend with a kind of weathered mystery. What I had yet to learn was how little people cared about whether I drank or not—and how little I needed to concern myself with what people did think.

In the meantime, I was alarmed by the dissonance between the rock star within screaming to be let out and the insecure woman pledging to be fun. I mean, I hadn't the faintest idea of how to have fun without drinking. I was still discovering all sorts of terrible new truths, like how parties without drinking were really just a lot of people standing in the same room and like how movies I once found funny were often riddled with stilted language and bad dirty jokes. And how, without my booze-fueled sense of rock-star self, I had no clue as to who I was—or whether or not I was any fun. I had lost my swagger.

So, there at the restaurant table, the words "But don't worry, I'm still fun!" rushed out in a chirpy adolescent squawk faster than I could inhale them back into my lungs. But my new pal, the pretty woman with the impish grin, did the unthinkable; without pausing to consider the crazy fact of my sobriety, without even a nanosecond of hesitation, she winked—winked!—and said, "Oh good!" She was thrilled, it seemed, that I was "still fun"; nothing pleased her more. She was just glad it was all working out for me. And as for my embarrassing state of teetotalism, well, it was clear she couldn't care less.

It was a good 10 minutes before I could rejoin the conversation. I sat back in my chair away from the halo of the white tablecloth and watched the restaurant in slow-motion while diners passed the bread, bantered with the salty waitress, poked at the tortellini, and guffawed at tales of office hijinks. They were all really enjoying themselves. Apparently, no one else in the restaurant cared whether I drank or not either. This wasn't, after all, spring break in Cancun where turning down a yard-long tube of crushed ice and battery acid was prudish; this was real life, where in a nice restaurant in Washington no one looked askance at a 32-year-old woman without a drink. Certainly my companions didn't; they seemed more interested in what I brought to the table than whether I put a glass of wine on it.

So I bid a silent goodbye to the internal rock-star speech, promised to stop defining myself by who I used to be, and scooted my chair closer to the table. Adieu, Sid Vicious! It was time to make new friends.

Questions

1. What makes this dinner unusual for the author?
2. What is the author's biggest worry in her new sober identity at the restaurant?
3. The author gave up alcohol six months earlier, but she gives up something else at the restaurant. What turning point does her essay describe?

Elisabeth Kübler-Ross, M.D.

Elisabeth Kübler-Ross (1926–2004) was born—the eldest of triplets—in Zurich, Switzerland. Against her father's wishes, she studied medicine. In 1958 she married an American medical student and moved to New York, where she specialized in psychiatry. Distressed by the hospital treatment of dying patients, Kübler-Ross developed more thoughtful and humane methods to treat the terminally ill. In her celebrated book On Death and Dying *(1969), she proposed "Five Stages of Grief," for people facing death (either their own or the death of a loved one): denial, anger, bargaining, depression, and acceptance. Her advocacy also helped encourage the growth of the hospice movement. In her later years, Kübler-Ross became increasingly interested in spiritualism. In 1995, a series of strokes left her partially paralyzed; she died in Scottsdale, Arizona, in 2004. The following essay is the first chapter of* On Death and Dying, *of which* Time *magazine said, "It has brought death out of the darkness."*

Elisabeth Kübler-Ross

On the Fear of Death   1969

> Let me not pray to be sheltered from dangers but to be fearless in
>   facing them.
> Let me not beg for the stilling of my pain but for the heart to conquer it.
> Let me not look for allies in life's battlefield but to my own strength.
> Let me not crave in anxious fear to be saved but hope for the patience
>   to win my freedom.
> Grant me that I may not be a coward, feeling your mercy in my success
>   alone; but let me find the grasp of your hand in my failure.
>
> —RABINDRANATH TAGORE, *Fruit-Gathering*

Epidemics have taken a great toll of lives in past generations. Death in infancy and early childhood was frequent and there were few families who didn't lose a member of the family at an early age. Medicine has changed greatly in the last decades. Widespread vaccinations have practically eradicated many illnesses, at least in western Europe and the United States. The use of chemotherapy, especially the antibiotics, has contributed to an ever decreasing number of fatalities in infectious diseases. Better child care and education has effected a low morbidity and mortality among children. The many diseases that have taken an impressive toll among the young and middle-aged have been conquered. The number of old people is on the rise, and with this fact come the number of people with malignancies and chronic diseases associated more with old age.

Pediatricians have less work with acute and life-threatening situations as they have an ever increasing number of patients with psychosomatic disturbances and adjustment and behavior problems. Physicians have more people in their waiting rooms with emotional problems than they have ever had before, but they also have more elderly patients who not only try to live with their decreased physical abilities and limitations but who also face loneliness and isolation with all its pains and anguish. The majority of these people are not seen by a psychiatrist. Their needs have to be elicited and gratified by other professional people, for instance, chaplains and social workers. It is for them that I am trying to outline the changes that have taken place in the last few decades, changes that are ultimately responsible for the increased fear of death, the rising number of emotional problems, and the greater need for understanding of and coping with the problems of death and dying.

When we look back in time and study old cultures and people, we are impressed that death has always been distasteful to man and will probably always be. From a psychiatrist's point of view this is very understandable and can perhaps best be explained by our basic knowledge that, in our unconscious, death is never possible in regard to ourselves. It is inconceivable for our unconscious to imagine an actual ending of our own life here on earth, and if this life of ours has to end, the ending is always attributed to a malicious intervention from the outside by someone else. In simple terms, in our unconscious mind we can only be killed; it is inconceivable to die of a natural cause or of old age. Therefore death in itself is associated with a bad act, a frightening happening, something that in itself calls for retribution and punishment.

One is wise to remember these fundamental facts as they are essential in understanding some of the most important, otherwise unintelligible communications of our patients.

The second fact that we have to comprehend is that in our unconscious mind we cannot distinguish between a wish and a deed. We are all aware of some of our illogical dreams in which two completely opposite statements can exist side by side—very acceptable in our dreams but unthinkable and illogical in our wakening state. Just as our unconscious mind cannot differentiate between the wish to kill somebody in anger and the act of having done so, the young child is unable to make this distinction. The child who angrily wishes his mother to drop dead for not having gratified his needs will be traumatized greatly by the actual death of his mother—even if this event is not linked closely in time with his destructive wishes. He will always take part or the whole blame for the loss of his mother. He will always say to himself—rarely to others—"I did it, I am responsible, I was bad, therefore Mommy left me." It is well to remember that the child will react in the same manner if he loses a parent by divorce, separation, or desertion. Death is often seen by a child as an impermanent thing and has therefore little distinction from a divorce in which he may have an opportunity to see a parent again.

Many a parent will remember remarks of their children such as, "I will bury my doggy now and next spring when the flowers come up again, he will get up." Maybe it was the same wish that motivated the ancient Egyptians to supply their dead with food and goods to keep them happy and the old American Indians to bury their relatives with their belongings.

When we grow older and begin to realize that our omnipotence is really not so omnipotent, that our strongest wishes are not powerful enough to make the impossible possible, the fear that we have contributed to the death of a loved one diminishes—and with it the guilt. The fear remains diminished, however, only so long as it is not challenged too strongly. Its vestiges can be seen daily in hospital corridors and in people associated with the bereaved.

A husband and wife may have been fighting for years, but when the partner dies, the survivor will pull his hair, whine and cry louder and beat his chest in regret, fear and anguish, and will hence fear his own death more than before, still believing in the law of talion°—an eye for an eye, a tooth for a tooth—"I am responsible for her death, I will have to die a pitiful death in retribution."

Maybe this knowledge will help us understand many of the old customs and rituals which have lasted over the centuries and whose purpose is to diminish the anger of the gods or the people as the case may be, thus decreasing the anticipated punishment. I am thinking of the ashes, the torn clothes, the veil, the *Klage Weiber*° of the old days—they are all means to ask you to take pity on them, the mourners, and are expressions of sorrow, grief, and shame. If someone grieves, beats his chest, tears his hair, or refuses to eat, it is an attempt at self-punishment to avoid or reduce the anticipated punishment for the blame that he takes on the death of a loved one.

This grief, shame, and guilt are not very far removed from feelings of anger and rage. The process of grief always includes some qualities of anger. Since none of us likes to admit anger at a deceased person, these emotions are often disguised or repressed and prolong the period of grief or show up in other ways. It is well to remember that it is not up to us to judge such feelings as bad or shameful but to understand their true meaning and origin as something very human. In order to illustrate this I will again use the example of the child—and the child in us. The five-year-old who loses his mother is both blaming himself for her disappearance and being angry at her for having deserted him and for no longer gratifying his needs. The dead person then turns into something the child loves and wants very much but also hates with equal intensity for this severe deprivation.

The ancient Hebrews regarded the body of a dead person as something unclean and not to be touched. The early American Indians talked about the evil spirits and shot arrows in the air to drive the spirits away. Many other cultures have rituals to take care of the "bad" dead person, and they all originate in this feeling of anger which

---

talion: Latin for "the law of retaliation," the principle that criminals should be punished with the same injuries they caused ("an eye for an eye, a tooth for a tooth"). *Klage Weiber:* German for "mourning women," a term for hired professional mourners at a funeral.

still exists in all of us, though we dislike admitting it. The tradition of the tombstone may originate in this wish to keep the bad spirits deep down in the ground, and the pebbles that many mourners put on the grave are left-over symbols of the same wish. Though we call the firing of guns at military funerals a last salute, it is the same symbolic ritual as the Indian used when he shot his spears and arrows into the skies.

I give these examples to emphasize that man has not basically changed. Death is still a fearful, frightening happening, and the fear of death is a universal fear even if we think we have mastered it on many levels.

What has changed is our way of coping and dealing with death and dying and our dying patients.

Having been raised in a country in Europe where science is not so advanced, where modern techniques have just started to find their way into medicine, and where people still live as they did in this country half a century ago, I may have had an opportunity to study a part of the evolution of mankind in a shorter period.

I remember as a child the death of a farmer. He fell from a tree and was not expected to live. He asked simply to die at home, a wish that was granted without questioning. He called his daughters into the bedroom and spoke with each one of them alone for a few minutes. He arranged his affairs quietly, though he was in great pain, and distributed his belongings and his land, none of which was to be split until his wife should follow him in death. He also asked each of his children to share in the work, duties, and tasks that he had carried on until the time of the accident. He asked his friends to visit him once more, to bid good-bye to them. Although I was a small child at the time, he did not exclude me or my siblings. We were allowed to share in the preparations of the family just as we were permitted to grieve with them until he died. When he did die, he was left at home, in his own beloved home which he had built, and among his friends and neighbors who went to take a last look at him where he lay in the midst of flowers in the place he had lived in and loved so much. In that country today there is still no make-believe slumber room, no embalming, no false makeup to pretend sleep. Only the signs of very disfiguring illnesses are covered up with bandages and only infectious cases are removed from the home prior to the burial.

Why do I describe such "old-fashioned" customs? I think they are an indication of our acceptance of a fatal outcome, and they help the dying patient as well as his family to accept the loss of a loved one. If a patient is allowed to terminate his life in the familiar and beloved environment, it requires less adjustment for him. His own family knows him well enough to replace a sedative with a glass of his favorite wine; or the smell of a home-cooked soup may give him the appetite to sip a few spoons of fluid which, I think, is still more enjoyable than an infusion. I will not minimize the need for sedatives and infusions and realize full well from my own experience as a country doctor that they are sometimes life-saving and often unavoidable. But I also know that patience and familiar people and foods could replace many a bottle of intravenous fluids given for the simple reason that it fulfills the physiological need without involving too many people and/or individual nursing care.

The fact that children are allowed to stay at home where a fatality has stricken and are included in the talk, discussions, and fears gives them the feeling that they are not alone in the grief and gives them the comfort of shared responsibility and shared mourning. It prepares them gradually and helps them view death as part of life, an experience which may help them grow and mature.

This is in great contrast to a society in which death is viewed as taboo, discussion of it is regarded as morbid, and children are excluded with the presumption and pretext that it would be "too much" for them. They are then sent off to relatives, often accompanied with some unconvincing lies of "Mother has gone on a long trip" or other unbelievable stories. The child senses that something is wrong, and his distrust in adults will only multiply if other relatives add new variations of the story, avoid his questions or suspicions, shower him with gifts as a meager substitute for a loss he is not permitted to deal with. Sooner or later the child will become aware of the changed family situation and, depending on the age and personality of the child, will have an unresolved grief and regard this incident as a frightening, mysterious, in any case very traumatic experience with untrustworthy grownups, which he has no way to cope with.

It is equally unwise to tell a little child who lost her brother that God loved little boys so much that he took little Johnny to heaven. When this little girl grew up to be a woman she never solved her anger at God, which resulted in a psychotic depression when she lost her own little son three decades later.

We would think that our great emancipation, our knowledge of science and of man, has given us better ways and means to prepare ourselves and our families for this inevitable happening. Instead the days are gone when a man was allowed to die in peace and dignity in his own home.

The more we are making advancements in science, the more we seem to fear and deny the reality of death. How is this possible?

We use euphemisms, we make the dead look as if they were asleep, we ship the children off to protect them from the anxiety and turmoil around the house if the patient is fortunate enough to die at home, we don't allow children to visit their dying parents in the hospitals, we have long and controversial discussions about whether patients should be told the truth—a question that rarely arises when the dying person is tended by the family physician who has known him from delivery to death and who knows the weaknesses and strengths of each member of the family.

I think there are many reasons for this flight away from facing death calmly. One of the most important facts is that dying nowadays is more gruesome in many ways, namely, more lonely, mechanical, and dehumanized; at times it is even difficult to determine technically when the time of death has occurred.

Dying becomes lonely and impersonal because the patient is often taken out of his familiar environment and rushed to an emergency room. Whoever has been very sick and has required rest and comfort especially may recall his experience of being put on a stretcher and enduring the noise of the ambulance siren and hectic rush until the hospital gates open. Only those who have lived through this may appreciate the discomfort and cold necessity of such transportation which is only the beginning of a long ordeal—hard to endure when you are well, difficult to express in words when noise, light, pumps, and voices are all too much to put up with. It may well be that we might consider more the patient under the sheets and blankets and perhaps stop our well-meant efficiency and rush in order to hold the patient's hand, to smile, or to listen to a question. I include the trip to the hospital as the first episode in dying, as it is for many. I am putting it exaggeratedly in contrast to the sick man who is left at home—not to say that lives should not be saved if they can be saved by a hospitalization but to keep the focus on the patient's experience, his needs and his reactions.

When a patient is severely ill, he is often treated like a person with no right to an opinion. It is often someone else who makes the decision if and when and where a patient should be hospitalized. It would take so little to remember that the sick person too has feelings, has wishes and opinions, and has—most important of all—the right to be heard.

Well, our presumed patient has now reached the emergency room. He will be surrounded by busy nurses, orderlies, interns, residents, a lab technician perhaps who will take some blood, an electrocardiogram technician who takes the cardiogram. He may be moved to X-ray and he will overhear opinions of his condition and discussions and questions to members of the family. He slowly but surely is beginning to be treated like a thing. He is no longer a person. Decisions are made often without his opinion. If he tries to rebel he will be sedated and after hours of waiting and wondering whether he has the strength, he will be wheeled into the operating room or intensive treatment unit and become an object of great concern and great financial investment.

He may cry for rest, peace, and dignity, but he will get infusions, transfusions, a heart machine, or tracheostomy if necessary. He may want one single person to stop for one single minute so that he can ask one single question—but he will get a dozen people around the clock, all busily preoccupied with his heart rate, pulse, electrocardiogram or pulmonary functions, his secretions or excretions but not with him as a human being. He may wish to fight it all but it is going to be a useless fight since all this is done in the fight for his life, and if they can save his life they can consider the person afterwards. Those who consider the person first may lose precious time to save his life! At least this seems to be the rationale or justification behind all this—or is it? Is the reason for this increasingly mechanical, depersonalized approach our own defensiveness? Is this approach our own way to cope with and repress the anxieties that a terminally or critically ill patient evokes in us? Is our concentration on equipment, on blood pressure our desperate attempt to deny the impending death which is so frightening and discomforting to us that we displace all our knowledge onto machines, since they are less close to us than the suffering face of another human being which would remind us once more of our lack of omnipotence, our own limits and failures, and last but not least perhaps our own mortality?

Maybe the question has to be raised: Are we becoming less human or more human? Though this book is in no way meant to be judgmental, it is clear that whatever the answer may be, the patient is suffering more—not physically, perhaps, but emotionally. And his needs have not changed over the centuries, only our ability to gratify them.

Questions

1. In what ways does Dr. Kübler-Ross believe that our normal experiences with death are different today from those of past generations?
2. Kübler-Ross describes the death of a farmer that she remembers from her childhood. What is unusual, by modern standards, about his death?
3. How did "old-fashioned" customs, as exemplified by the farmer's deathbed rituals, help the dying and his family accept death?

4. What advantages does Kübler-Ross see in allowing people to die at home rather than in hospitals?
5. Does Kübler-Ross feel that children should be excluded from death situations?
6. What arguments do some people offer for screening children from death? Do you agree or disagree?

Suggestions for Writing on *Essays about Turning Points*

1. Take any two essays in this section and identify and compare the turning points in each author's narrative. What does each author turn away from, and what does he or she turn toward?
2. What might Kübler-Ross say about how Baldwin confronts his father's death in "Notes of a Native Son"? Has Baldwin come to accept his father's death?
3. Have you experienced a turning point in your life? Describe the situation and the issues that you turned away from and what you turned toward. In retrospect, did you achieve everything you hoped for?

DRAMA

LIFE PASSAGES

Tennessee Williams *The Glass Menagerie*
Terrence McNally *Andre's Mother*

These two American plays—one full-length, the other a simple short scene—each dramatize a turning point in life's journey. Tennessee Williams's celebrated play *The Glass Menagerie* brilliantly depicts a young man's complicated attempt to escape from home to begin his independent adult life. Williams captures the competing and often contradictory emotions, including love, impatience, frustration, resentment, and concern, that his protagonist feels toward his unusual family. In Terrence McNally's one-act study of the early aftermath of the AIDS epidemic, *Andre's Mother*, the playwright shows how grief can be expressed both by words and by silence.

Tennessee Williams

Tennessee Williams (1911–1983) was born Thomas Lanier Williams in Columbus, Mississippi, went to high school in St. Louis, and graduated from the University of Iowa. As an undergraduate, he saw a performance of Ibsen's Ghosts and decided to become a playwright himself. His family bore a close resemblance to the Wingfields in The Glass Menagerie: *his mother came from a line of Southern blue bloods (Tennessee pioneers); his sister Rose suffered from incapacitating shyness; and as a young man, Williams himself, like Tom, worked at a job he disliked (in a shoe factory where his father worked), wrote poetry, sought refuge in moviegoing, and finally left home to wander and hold odd jobs. He worked as a bellhop in a New Orleans hotel; a teletype operator in Jacksonville, Florida; an usher and a waiter in New York. In 1945* The Glass Menagerie *scored a success on Broadway, winning a Drama Critics Circle award. Two years later Williams received a Pulitzer Prize for* A Streetcar Named Desire, *a grim, powerful study of a woman's illusions and frustrations, set in New Orleans. In 1955 Williams was awarded another Pulitzer Prize for* Cat on a Hot Tin Roof. *Besides other plays, including* Summer and Smoke *(1948),* Sweet Bird of Youth *(1959),* The Night of the Iguana *(1961), and* Clothes for a Summer Hotel *(1980), Williams wrote two novels, poetry, essays, short stories, and* Memoirs *(1975).*

Tennessee Williams

The Glass Menagerie 1945

> Nobody, not even the rain, has such small hands.
>
> —E. E. CUMMINGS

CHARACTERS

Amanda Wingfield, the mother. A little woman of great but confused vitality clinging frantically to another time and place. Her characterization must be carefully created, not copied from type. She is not paranoiac, but her life is paranoia. There is much to admire in Amanda, and as much to love and pity as there is to laugh at. Certainly she has endurance and a kind of heroism, and though her foolishness makes her unwittingly cruel at times, there is tenderness in her slight person.

Laura Wingfield, her daughter. Amanda, having failed to establish contact with reality, continues to live vitally in her illusions, but Laura's situation is even graver. A childhood illness has left her crippled, one leg slightly shorter than the other, and held in a brace. This defect need not be more than suggested on the stage. Stemming from this, Laura's separation increases till she is like a piece of her own glass collection, too exquisitely fragile to move from the shelf.

Tom Wingfield, her son. And the narrator of the play. A poet with a job in a warehouse. His nature is not remorseless, but to escape from a trap he has to act without pity.

Jim O'Connor, the gentleman caller. A nice, ordinary, young man.

SCENE. *An alley in St. Louis.*

PART I. *Preparation for a Gentleman Caller.*

PART II. *The Gentleman Calls.*

TIME. *Now and the Past.*

SCENE I

The Wingfield apartment is in the rear of the building, one of those vast hive-like conglomerations of cellular living-units that flower as warty growths in overcrowded urban centers of lower middle-class population and are symptomatic of the impulse of this largest and fundamentally enslaved section of American society to avoid fluidity and differentiation and to exist and function as one interfused mass of automatism.

The apartment faces an alley and is entered by a fire-escape, a structure whose name is a touch of accidental poetic truth, for all of these huge buildings are always burning with the slow and implacable fires of human desperation. The fire-escape is included in the set—that is, the landing of it and steps descending from it.

The scene is memory and is therefore unrealistic. Memory takes a lot of poetic license. It omits some details; others are exaggerated, according to the emotional value of the articles it touches, for memory is seated predominantly in the heart. The interior is therefore rather dim and poetic.

At the rise of the curtain, the audience is faced with the dark, grim rear wall of the Wingfield tenement. This building, which runs parallel to the footlights, is flanked on both sides by dark, narrow alleys which run into murky canyons of tangled clotheslines, garbage cans, and the sinister latticework of neighboring fire-escapes. It is up and down these side alleys that exterior entrances and exits are made, during the play. At the end of Tom's opening commentary, the dark tenement wall slowly reveals (by means of a transparency) the interior of the ground floor Wingfield apartment.

Poster for 1950 film *The Glass Menagerie*.

Downstage is the living room, which also serves as a sleeping room for Laura, the sofa unfolding to make her bed. Upstage, center, and divided by a wide arch or second proscenium with transparent faded portieres (or second curtain), is the dining room. In an old-fashioned what-not in the living room are seen scores of transparent glass animals. A blown-up photograph of the father hangs on the wall of the living room, facing the audience, to the left of the archway. It is the face of a very handsome young man in a doughboy's First World War cap. He is gallantly smiling, ineluctably smiling, as if to say, "I will be smiling forever."

The audience hears and sees the opening scene in the dining room through both the transparent fourth wall of the building and the transparent gauze portieres of the dining room arch. It is during this revealing scene that the fourth wall slowly ascends, out of sight. This transparent exterior wall is not brought down again until the very end of the play, during Tom's final speech.

The narrator is an undisguised convention of the play. He takes whatever license with dramatic convention as is convenient to his purposes.

Tom enters dressed as a merchant sailor from the alley, stage left, and strolls across the front of the stage to the fire-escape. There he stops and lights a cigarette. He addresses the audience.

Tom: Yes, I have tricks in my pocket, I have things up my sleeve. But I am the opposite of a stage magician. He gives you illusion that has the appearance of truth. I give you truth in the pleasant disguise of illusion. To begin with, I turn back time. I reverse it to that quaint period, the thirties, when the huge middle class of America was matriculating in a school for the blind. Their eyes had failed them, or they had failed their eyes, and so they were having their fingers pressed forcibly down on the fiery Braille alphabet of a dissolving economy. In Spain there was revolution. Here there was only shouting and confusion. In Spain there was Guernica. Here there were disturbances of labor, sometimes pretty violent, in otherwise peaceful cities such as Chicago, Cleveland, St. Louis. . . . This is the social background of the play.

(**Music.**)

The play is memory. Being a memory play, it is dimly lighted, it is sentimental, it is not realistic. In memory everything seems to happen to music. That explains the fiddle in the wings. I am the narrator of the play, and also a character in it. The other characters are my mother, Amanda, my sister, Laura, and a gentleman caller who appears in the final scenes. He is the most realistic character in the play, being an emissary from a world of reality that we were somehow set apart from. But since I have a poet's weakness for symbols, I am using this character also as a symbol; he is the long delayed but always expected something that we live for. There is a fifth character in the play who doesn't appear except in this larger-than-life photograph over the mantel. This is our father who left us a long time ago. He was a telephone man who fell in love with long distances; he gave up his job with the telephone company and skipped the light fantastic out of town. . . . The last we heard of him was a picture post-card from Mazatlan, on the Pacific coast of Mexico, containing a message of two words—"Hello—Good-bye!" and an address. I think the rest of the play will explain itself. . . .

Amanda's voice becomes audible through the portieres.

(**Screen Legend: "Où Sont Les Neiges."**)°

He divides the portieres and enters the upstage area.

Amanda and Laura are seated at a drop-leaf table. Eating is indicated by gestures without food or utensils. Amanda faces the audience. Tom and Laura are seated in profile.

The interior has lit up softly and through the scrim we see Amanda and Laura seated at the table in the upstage area.

Amanda (calling): Tom?
Tom: Yes, Mother.
Amanda: We can't say grace until you come to the table!
Tom: Coming, Mother. (*He bows slightly and withdraws, reappearing a few moments later in his place at the table.*)
Amanda (to her son): Honey, don't *push* with your *fingers.* If you have to push with something, the thing to push with is a crust of bread. And chew—chew! Animals have sections in their stomachs which enable them to digest food without mastication, but human beings are supposed to chew their food before they swallow it down. Eat food leisurely, son, and really enjoy it. A well-cooked meal has lots of delicate flavors that have to be held in the mouth for appreciation. So chew your food and give your salivary glands a chance to function!

Tom deliberately lays his imaginary fork down and pushes his chair back from the table.

Screen Legend: "Où Sont Les Neiges": A slide bearing part of a famous line from the French poet François Villon's *Ballad of the Dead Ladies* is to be projected on a stage wall. The full line, "Où Sont Les Neiges d'Antan?" meaning "But, where are the snows of yester-year?" is projected on the screen later in this scene.

Tom: I haven't enjoyed one bite of this dinner because of your constant directions on how to eat it. It's you that makes me rush through meals with your hawk-like attention to every bite I take. Sickening—spoils my appetite—all this discussion of animals' secretion—salivary glands—mastication!

Amanda (lightly): Temperament like a Metropolitan star!

> *He rises and crosses downstage.*

> You're not excused from the table.

Tom: I am getting a cigarette.

Amanda: You smoke too much.

> *Laura rises.*

Laura: I'll bring in the blanc mange.

> *He remains standing with his cigarette by the portieres during the following.*

Amanda (rising): No, sister, no, sister—you be the lady this time and I'll be the darky.

Laura: I'm already up.

Amanda: Resume your seat, little sister—I want you to stay fresh and pretty—for gentlemen callers!

Laura (sitting down): I'm not expecting any gentlemen callers.

Amanda (crossing out to kitchenette, airily): Sometimes they come when they are least expected! Why, I remember one Sunday afternoon in Blue Mountain—(*Enters kitchenette.*)

Tom: I know what's coming!

Laura: Yes. But let her tell it.

Tom: Again?

Laura: She loves to tell it.

> *Amanda returns with bowl of dessert.*

Amanda: One Sunday afternoon in Blue Mountain—your mother received—seventeen!—gentlemen callers! Why, sometimes there weren't chairs enough to accommodate them all. We had to send the nigger over to bring in folding chairs from the parish house.

Tom (remaining at portieres): How did you entertain those gentlemen callers?

Amanda: I understood the art of conversation!

Tom: I bet you could talk.

Amanda: Girls in those days *knew* how to talk, I can tell you.

Tom: Yes?

(Image: Amanda As A Girl On A Porch Greeting Callers.)

Amanda: They knew how to entertain their gentlemen callers. It wasn't enough for a girl to be possessed of a pretty face and a graceful figure—although I wasn't slighted in either respect. She also needed to have a nimble wit and a tongue to meet all occasions.

Tom: What did you talk about?

Amanda: Things of importance going on in the world! Never anything coarse or common or vulgar. (*She addresses Tom as though he were seated in the vacant chair at the table though he remains by portieres. He plays this scene as though reading from a script.*) My callers were gentlemen—all! Among my callers were some of the most prominent young planters of the Mississippi Delta—planters and sons of planters!

Tom motions for music and a spot of light on Amanda. Her eyes lift, her face glows, her voice becomes rich and elegiac.

(**Screen Legend:** "Où Sont Les Neiges D'Antan?")

There was young Champ Laughlin who later became vice-president of the Delta Planters Bank. Hadley Stevenson who was drowned in Moon Lake and left his widow one hundred and fifty thousand in Government bonds. There were the Cutrere brothers, Wesley and Bates. Bates was one of my bright particular beaux! He got in a quarrel with that wild Wainright boy. They shot it out on the floor of Moon Lake Casino. Bates was shot through the stomach. Died in the ambulance on his way to Memphis. His widow was also well-provided for, came into eight or ten thousand acres, that's all. She married him on the rebound—never loved her—carried my picture on him the night he died! And there was that boy that every girl in the Delta had set her cap for! That beautiful, brilliant young Fitzhugh boy from Green County!

Tom: What did he leave his widow?

Amanda: He never married! Gracious, you talk as though all of my old admirers had turned up their toes to the daisies!

Tom: Isn't this the first you mentioned that still survives?

Amanda: That Fitzhugh boy went North and made a fortune—came to be known as the Wolf of Wall Street! He had the Midas touch, whatever he touched turned to gold! And I could have been Mrs. Duncan J. Fitzhugh, mind you! But—I picked your *father*!

Laura (*rising*): Mother, let me clear the table.

Amanda: No dear, you go in front and study your typewriter chart. Or practice your shorthand a little. Stay fresh and pretty!—It's almost time for our gentlemen callers to start arriving. (*She flounces girlishly toward the kitchenette.*) How many do you suppose we're going to entertain this afternoon?

Tom throws down the paper and jumps up with a groan.

Laura (*alone in the dining room*): I don't believe we're going to receive any, Mother.

Amanda (*reappearing, airily*): What? No one—not one? You must be joking! (*Laura nervously echoes her laugh. She slips in a fugitive manner through the half-open portieres and draws them gently behind her. A shaft of very clear light is thrown on her face against the jaded tapestry of the curtains.*) (**Music: "The Glass Menagerie" Under Faintly.**) (*Lightly.*) Not one gentleman caller? It can't be true! There must be a flood, there must have been a tornado!

Laura: It isn't a flood, it's not a tornado, Mother. I'm just not popular like you were in Blue Mountain. . . . (*Tom utters another groan. Laura glances at him with a faint, apologetic smile. Her voice catching a little.*) Mother's afraid I'm going to be an old maid.

(**The Scene Dims Out With "Glass Menagerie" Music.**)

SCENE II

"Laura, Haven't You Ever Liked Some Boy?"

On the dark stage the screen is lighted with the image of blue roses.

Gradually Laura's figure becomes apparent and the screen goes out.

The music subsides.

Laura is seated in the delicate ivory chair at the small clawfoot table.

She wears a dress of soft violet material for a kimono—her hair tied back from her forehead with a ribbon.

She is washing and polishing her collection of glass.

Amanda appears on the fire-escape steps. At the sound of her ascent, Laura catches her breath, thrusts the bowl of ornaments away and seats herself stiffly before the diagram of the typewriter keyboard as though it held her spellbound. Something has happened to Amanda. It is written in her face as she climbs to the landing: a look that is grim and hopeless and a little absurd.

She has on one of those cheap or imitation velvety-looking cloth coats with imitation fur collar. Her hat is five or six years old, one of those dreadful cloche hats that were worn in the late twenties, and she is clasping an enormous black patent-leather pocketbook with nickel clasp and initials. This is her full-dress outfit, the one she usually wears to the D.A.R.

Before entering she looks through the door.

She purses her lips, opens her eyes wide, rolls them upward and shakes her head.

Then she slowly lets herself in the door. Seeing her mother's expression Laura touches her lips with a nervous gesture.

Laura: Hello, Mother, I was—(*She makes a nervous gesture toward the chart on the wall. Amanda leans against the shut door and stares at Laura with a martyred look.*)

Amanda: Deception? Deception? (*She slowly removes her hat and gloves, continuing the sweet suffering stare. She lets the hat and gloves fall on the floor—a bit of acting.*)

Laura (shakily): How was the D.A.R. meeting? (*Amanda slowly opens her purse and removes a dainty white handkerchief which she shakes out delicately and delicately touches to her lips and nostrils.*) Didn't you go to the D.A.R. meeting, Mother?

Amanda (faintly, almost inaudibly): —No.—No. (*Then more forcibly.*) I did not have the strength—to go to the D.A.R. In fact, I did not have the courage! I wanted to find a hole in the ground and hide myself in it forever! (*She crosses slowly to the wall and removes the diagram of the typewriter keyboard. She holds it in front of her for a second, staring at it sweetly and sorrowfully—then bites her lips and tears it in two pieces.*)

Laura (faintly): Why did you do that, Mother? (*Amanda repeats the same procedure with the chart of the Gregg Alphabet.*) Why are you—

Amanda: Why? Why? How old are you, Laura?

Laura: Mother, you know my age.

Amanda: I thought that you were an adult; it seems that I was mistaken. (*She crosses slowly to the sofa and sinks down and stares at Laura.*)

Laura: Please don't stare at me, Mother.

Amanda closes her eyes and lowers her head. Count ten.

Amanda: What are we going to do, what is going to become of us, what is the future?

Count ten.

Laura: Has something happened, Mother? (*Amanda draws a long breath and takes out the handkerchief again. Dabbing process.*) Mother, has—something happened?

Amanda: I'll be all right in a minute. I'm just bewildered—(*count five*)—by life...

Laura: Mother, I wish that you would tell me what's happened.

Amanda: As you know, I was supposed to be inducted into my office at the D.A.R. this afternoon. (**Image: A Swarm of Typewriters.**) But I stopped off at Rubicam's Business College to speak to your teachers about your having a cold and ask them what progress they thought you were making down there.

Laura: Oh...

Amanda: I went to the typing instructor and introduced myself as your mother. She didn't know who you were. "Wingfield," she said, "We don't have any such student enrolled at the school!" I assured her she did, that you had been going to classes since early in January. "I wonder," she said, "if you could be talking about that terribly shy little girl who dropped out of school after only a few days' attendance?" "No," I said, "Laura, my daughter, has been going to school every day for the past six weeks!" "Excuse me," she said. She took the attendance book out and there was your name, unmistakably printed, and all the dates you were absent until they decided that you had dropped out of school. I still said, "No, there must have been some mistake! There must have been some mix-up in the records!" And she said, "No—I remember her perfectly now. Her hand shook so that she couldn't hit the right keys! The first time we gave a speed-test, she broke down completely—was sick at the stomach and almost had to be carried into the wash-room! After that morning she never showed up any more. We phoned the house but never got any answer"—While I was working at Famous-Barr, I suppose, demonstrating those—(*She indicates a brassiere with her hands.*) Oh! I felt so weak I could barely keep on my feet. I had to sit down while they got me a glass of water! Fifty dollars' tuition, all of our plans—my hopes and ambitions for you—just gone up the spout, just gone up the spout like that. (*Laura draws a long breath and gets awkwardly to her feet. She crosses to the victrola and winds it up.*) What are you doing?

Laura: Oh! (*She releases the handle and returns to her seat.*)

Amanda: Laura, where have you been going when you've gone out pretending that you were going to business college?

Laura: I've just been going out walking.

Amanda: That's not true.

Laura: It is. I just went walking.

Amanda: Walking? Walking? In winter? Deliberately courting pneumonia in that light coat? Where did you walk to, Laura?

Laura: All sorts of places—mostly in the park.

Amanda: Even after you'd started catching that cold?

Laura: It was the lesser of two evils, Mother. (**Image: Winter Scene In Park.**) I couldn't go back there. I—threw up—on the floor!

Amanda: From half past seven till after five every day you mean to tell me you walked around in the park, because you wanted to make me think that you were still going to Rubicam's Business College?

Laura: It wasn't as bad as it sounds. I went inside places to get warmed up.

Amanda: Inside where?

Laura: I went in the art museum and the bird-houses at the Zoo. I visited the penguins every day! Sometimes I did without lunch and went to the movies. Lately I've been spending most of my afternoons in the Jewel-box, that big glass house where they raise the tropical flowers.

Amanda: You did all this to deceive me, just for deception? (*Laura looks down.*) Why?

Laura: Mother, when you're disappointed, you get that awful suffering look on your face, like the picture of Jesus' mother in the museum!

Amanda: Hush!

Laura: I couldn't face it.

> Pause. A whisper of strings.

(Legend: "The Crust Of Humility.")

Amanda (*hopelessly fingering the huge pocketbook*): So what are we going to do the rest of our lives? Stay home and watch the parades go by? Amuse ourselves with the glass menagerie, darling? Eternally play those worn-out phonograph records your father left as a painful reminder of him? We won't have a business career—we've given that up because it gave us nervous indigestion! (*Laughs wearily.*) What is there left but dependency all our lives? I know so well what becomes of unmarried women who aren't prepared to occupy a position. I've seen such pitiful cases in the South—barely tolerated spinsters living upon the grudging patronage of sister's husband or brother's wife!—stuck away in some little mouse-trap of a room—encouraged by one in-law to visit another—little birdlike women without any nest—eating the crust of humility all their life! Is that the future that we've mapped out for ourselves? I swear it's the only alternative I can think of! It isn't a very pleasant alternative, is it? Of course—some girls *do* marry. (*Laura twists her hands nervously.*) Haven't you ever liked some boy?

Laura: Yes. I liked one once. (*Rises.*) I came across his picture a while ago.

Amanda (*with some interest*): He gave you his picture?

Laura: No, it's in the year-book.

Amanda (*disappointed*): Oh—a high-school boy.

(Screen Image: Jim As A High-School Hero Bearing A Silver Cup.)

Laura: Yes. His name was Jim. (*Laura lifts the heavy annual from the clawfoot table.*) Here he is in *The Pirates of Penzance*.

Amanda (*absently*): The what?

Laura: The operetta the senior class put on. He had a wonderful voice and we sat across the aisle from each other Mondays, Wednesdays, and Fridays in the Aud. Here he is with the silver cup for debating! See his grin?

Amanda (*absently*): He must have had a jolly disposition.

Laura: He used to call me—Blue Roses.

(Image: Blue Roses.)

Amanda: Why did he call you such a name as that?

Laura: When I had that attack of pleurosis—he asked me what was the matter when I came back. I said pleurosis—he thought that I said Blue Roses! So that's what he always called me after that. Whenever he saw me, he'd holler, "Hello, Blue Roses!" I didn't care for the girl he went out with. Emily Meisenbach. Emily was the best-dressed girl at Soldan. She never struck me, though, as being sincere . . . It says in the Personal Section—they're engaged. That's—six years ago! They must be married by now.

Amanda: Girls that aren't cut out for business careers usually wind up married to some nice man. (*Gets up with a spark of revival.*) Sister, that's what you'll do!

Laura utters a startled, doubtful laugh. She reaches quickly for a piece of glass.

Laura: But, Mother—
Amanda: Yes? (*Crossing to photograph.*)
Laura (in a tone of frightened apology): I'm—crippled!

(Image: Screen.)

Amanda: Nonsense! Laura, I've told you never, never to use that word. Why, you're not crippled, you just have a little defect—hardly noticeable, even! When people have some slight disadvantage like that, they cultivate other things to make up for it—develop charm—and vivacity—and—*charm*! That's all you have to do! (*She turns again to the photograph.*) One thing your father had *plenty of*—was *charm*!

Tom motions to the fiddle in the wings.

(The Scene Fades Out With Music.)

SCENE III

(Legend On The Screen: "After The Fiasco—")

Tom speaks from the fire-escape landing.

Tom: After the fiasco at Rubicam's Business College, the idea of getting a gentleman caller for Laura began to play a more important part in Mother's calculations. It became an obsession. Like some archetype of the universal unconscious, the image of the gentleman caller haunted our small apartment. . . . **(Image: Young Man At Door With Flowers.)** An evening at home rarely passed without some allusion to this image, this specter, this hope. . . . Even when he wasn't mentioned, his presence hung in Mother's preoccupied look and in my sister's frightened, apologetic manner—hung like a sentence passed upon the Wingfields! Mother was a woman of action as well as words. She began to take logical steps in the planned direction. Late that winter and in the early spring—realizing that extra money would be needed to properly feather the nest and plume the bird—she conducted a vigorous campaign on the telephone, roping in subscribers to one of those magazines for matrons called *The Home-maker's Companion,* the type of journal that features the serialized sublimations of ladies of letters who think in terms of delicate cup-like breasts, slim, tapering waists, rich, creamy thighs, eyes like wood-smoke in autumn, fingers that soothe and caress like strains of music, bodies as powerful as Etruscan sculpture.

(Screen Image: Glamor Magazine Cover.)

Amanda enters with phone on long extension cord. She is spotted in the dim stage.

Amanda: Ida Scott? This is Amanda Wingfield! We *missed* you at the D.A.R. last Monday! I said to myself: She's probably suffering with that sinus condition! How is that sinus condition? Horrors! Heaven have mercy!—You're a Christian martyr, yes, that's what you are, a Christian martyr! Well, I just now happened to notice that your subscription to the *Companion*'s about to expire! Yes, it expires with the next issue, honey!—just when that wonderful new serial by Bessie Mae Hopper is getting off to such an exciting start. Oh, honey, it's something that you can't miss! You remember how *Gone With the Wind* took everybody by storm? You simply couldn't go out if you hadn't read it. All everybody *talked* was Scarlett O'Hara. Well, this is a book that critics already compare to *Gone With the Wind*. It's the *Gone With the Wind* of the post-World War generation!—What?—Burning?—Oh, honey, don't let them burn, go take a look in the oven and I'll hold the wire! Heavens—I think she's hung up!

(Dim Out.)

(Legend On Screen: "You Think I'm In Love With Continental Shoemakers?")

Before the stage is lighted, the violent voices of Tom and Amanda are heard. They are quarreling behind the portieres. In front of them stands Laura with clenched hands and panicky expression.

A clear pool of light on her figure throughout this scene.

Tom: What in Christ's name am I—
Amanda (shrilly): Don't you use that—
Tom: —supposed to do!
Amanda: —expression! Not in my—
Tom: Ohhh!
Amanda: —presence! Have you gone out of your senses?
Tom: I have, that's true, *driven* out!
Amanda: What is the matter with you, you—big—big—IDIOT!
Tom: Look—I've got *no thing*, no single thing—
Amanda: Lower your voice!
Tom: —in my life here that I can call my OWN! Everything is—
Amanda: Stop that shouting!
Tom: Yesterday you confiscated my books! You had the nerve to—
Amanda: I took that horrible novel back to the library—yes! That hideous book by that insane Mr. Lawrence. (*Tom laughs wildly.*) I cannot control the output of diseased minds or people who cater to them—(*Tom laughs still more wildly.*) BUT I WON'T ALLOW SUCH FILTH BROUGHT INTO MY HOUSE! No, no, no, no, no!
Tom: House, house! Who pays rent on it, who makes a slave of himself to—
Amanda (fairly screeching): Don't you DARE to—
Tom: No, no, I mustn't say things! *I've got to just—*
Amanda: Let me tell you—

Tom: I don't want to hear any more! (*He tears the portieres open. The upstage area is lit with a turgid smoky red glow.*)

Amanda's hair is in metal curlers and she wears a very old bathrobe, much too large for her slight figure, a relic of the faithless Mr. Wingfield.

An upright typewriter and a wild disarray of manuscripts are on the drop-leaf table. The quarrel was probably precipitated by Amanda's interruption of his creative labor. A chair lying overthrown on the floor.

Their gesticulating shadows are cast on the ceiling by the fiery glow.

Amanda: You *will* hear more, you—
Tom: No, I won't hear more, I'm going out!
Amanda: You come right back in—
Tom: Out, out out! Because I'm—
Amanda: Come back here, Tom Wingfield! I'm not through talking to you!
Tom: Oh, go—
Laura (desperately): Tom!
Amanda: You're going to listen, and no more insolence from you! I'm at the end of my patience! (*He comes back toward her.*)
Tom: What do you think I'm at? Aren't I supposed to have any patience to reach the end of, Mother? I know, I know. It seems unimportant to you, what I'm *doing*—what *I want* to do—having a little *difference* between them! You don't think that—
Amanda: I think you've been doing things that you're ashamed of. That's why you act like this. I don't believe that you go every night to the movies. Nobody goes to the movies night after night. Nobody in their right minds goes to the movies as often as you pretend to. People don't go to the movies at nearly midnight, and movies don't let out at two A.M. Come in stumbling. Muttering to yourself like a maniac! You get three hours' sleep and then go to work. Oh, I can picture the way you're doing down there. Moping, doping, because you're in no condition.
Tom (wildly): No, I'm in no condition!
Amanda: What right have you got to jeopardize your job? Jeopardize the security of us all? How do you think we'd manage if you were—
Tom: Listen! You think I'm crazy about the *warehouse*? (*He bends fiercely toward her slight figure.*) You think I'm in love with the Continental Shoemakers? You think I want to spend fifty-five years down there in that—celotex interior! with—fluorescent—tubes! Look! I'd rather somebody picked up a crowbar and battered out my brains—than go back mornings! I go! Every time you come in yelling that God-damn "Rise and Shine!" "Rise and Shine!" I say to myself "How *lucky dead* people are!" But I get up. I *go!* For sixty-five dollars a month I give up all that I dream of doing and being *ever!* And you say self—*self's* all I ever think of. Why, listen, if self is what I thought of, Mother, I'd be where he is—GONE! (*Pointing to father's picture.*) As far as the system of transportation reaches! (*He starts past her. She grabs his arm.*) Don't grab at me, Mother!
Amanda: Where are you going?
Tom: I'm going to the *movies!*
Amanda: I don't believe that lie!

Tom (*crouching toward her, overtowering her tiny figure. She backs away, gasping*): I'm going to opium dens! Yes, opium dens, dens of vice and criminals' hangouts, Mother. I've joined the Hogan gang, I'm a hired assassin, I carry a tommy-gun in a violin case! I run a string of cat-houses in the Valley! They call me Killer, Killer Wingfield, I'm leading a double-life, a simple, honest warehouse worker by day, by night a dynamic *czar* of the *underworld*, Mother. I go to gambling casinos, I spin away fortunes on the roulette table! I wear a patch over one eye and a false mustache, sometimes I put on green whiskers. On those occasions they call me—*El Diablo!* Oh, I could tell you things to make you sleepless! My enemies plan to dynamite this place. They're going to blow us all sky-high some night! I'll be glad, very happy, and so will you! You'll go up, up on a broomstick, over Blue Mountain with seventeen gentlemen callers! You ugly—babbling old—*witch*.... (*He goes through a series of violent, clumsy movements, seizing his overcoat, lunging to the door, pulling it fiercely open. The women watch him, aghast. His arm catches in the sleeve of the coat as he struggles to pull it on. For a moment he is pinioned by the bulky garment. With an outraged groan he tears the coat off again, splitting the shoulders of it, and hurls it across the room. It strikes against the shelf of Laura's glass collection, there is a tinkle of shattering glass. Laura cries out as if wounded.*)

(Music Legend: "The Glass Menagerie.")

Laura (*shrilly*): My glass!—menagerie.... (*She covers her face and turns away.*)

But Amanda is still stunned and stupefied by the "ugly witch" so that she barely notices this occurrence. Now she recovers her speech.

Amanda (*in an awful voice*): I won't speak to you—until you apologize! (*She crosses through portieres and draws them together behind her. Tom is left with Laura. Laura clings weakly to the mantel with her face averted. Tom stares at her stupidly for a moment. Then he crosses to shelf. Drops awkwardly to his knees to collect the fallen glass, glancing at Laura as if he would speak but couldn't.*)

("The Glass Menagerie" Music Steals In As The Scene Dims Out.)

SCENE IV

The interior is dark. Faint in the alley.

A deep-voiced bell in a church is tolling the hour of five as the scene commences.

Tom appears at the top of the alley. After each solemn boom of the bell in the tower, he shakes a little noise-maker or rattle as if to express the tiny spasm of man in contrast to the sustained power and dignity of the Almighty. This and the unsteadiness of his advance make it evident that he has been drinking.

As he climbs the few steps to the fire-escape landing light steals up inside. Laura appears in night-dress, observing Tom's empty bed in the front room.

Tom fishes in his pockets for the door-key, removing a motley assortment of articles in the search, including a perfect shower of movie-ticket stubs and an empty bottle. At last he finds the key, but just as he is about to insert it, it slips from his fingers. He strikes a match and crouches below the door.

Tom (bitterly): One crack—and it falls through!

Laura opens the door.

Laura: Tom! Tom, what are you doing?
Tom: Looking for a door-key.
Laura: Where have you been all this time?
Tom: I have been to the movies.
Laura: All this time at the movies?
Tom: There was a very long program. There was a Garbo picture and a Mickey Mouse and a travelogue and a newsreel and a preview of coming attractions. And there was an organ solo and a collection for the milk-fund—simultaneously—which ended up in a terrible fight between a fat lady and an usher!
Laura (innocently): Did you have to stay through everything?
Tom: Of course! And, oh, I forgot! There was a big stage show! The headliner on this stage show was Malvolio the Magician. He performed wonderful tricks, many of them, such as pouring water back and forth between pitchers. First it turned to wine and then it turned to beer and then it turned to whiskey. I know it was whiskey it finally turned into because he needed somebody to come up out of the audience to help him, and I came up—both shows! It was Kentucky Straight Bourbon. A very generous fellow, he gave souvenirs. (*He pulls from his back pocket a shimmering rainbow-colored scarf.*) He gave me this. This is his magic scarf. You can have it, Laura. You wave it over a canary cage and you get a bowl of gold-fish. You wave it over the gold-fish bowl and they fly away canaries. . . . But the wonderfullest trick of all was the coffin trick. We nailed him into a coffin and he got out of the coffin without removing one nail. (*He has come inside.*) There is a trick that would come in handy for me—get me out of this 2 by 4 situation! (*Flops onto bed and starts removing shoes.*)
Laura: Tom—shhh!
Tom: What're you shushing me for?
Laura: You'll wake up Mother.
Tom: Goody, goody! Pay 'er back for all those "Rise an' Shines." (*Lies down, groaning.*) You know it don't take much intelligence to get yourself into a nailed-up coffin, Laura. But who in hell ever got himself out of one without removing one nail?

As if in answer, the father's grinning photograph lights up.

(Scene Dims Out.)

Immediately following: The church bell is heard striking six. At the sixth stroke the alarm clock goes off in Amanda's room, and after a few moments we hear her calling: "Rise and Shine! Rise and Shine! Laura, go tell your brother to rise and shine!"

Tom (sitting up slowly): I'll rise—but I won't shine.

The light increases.

Amanda: Laura, tell your brother his coffee is ready.

Laura slips into front room.

Laura: Tom!—It's nearly seven. Don't make Mother nervous. (*He stares at her stupidly.*) (*Beseechingly*) Tom, speak to Mother this morning. Make up with her, apologize, speak to her!

Tom: She won't to me. It's her that started not speaking.

Laura: If you just say you're sorry she'll start speaking.

Tom: Her not speaking—is that such a tragedy?

Laura: Please—please!

Amanda (*calling from kitchenette*): Laura, are you going to do what I asked you to do, or do I have to get dressed and go out myself?

Laura: Going, going—soon as I get on my coat! (*She pulls on a shapeless felt hat with nervous, jerky movements, pleadingly glancing at Tom. Rushes awkwardly for coat. The coat is one of Amanda's, inaccurately made-over, the sleeves too short for Laura.*) Butter and what else?

Amanda (*entering upstage*): Just butter. Tell them to charge it.

Laura: Mother, they make such faces when I do that.

Amanda: Sticks and stones may break my bones, but the expression on Mr. Garfinkel's face won't harm us! Tell your brother his coffee is getting cold.

Laura (*at door*): Do what I asked you, will you, will you, Tom?

> He looks sullenly away.

Amanda: Laura, go now or just don't go at all!

Laura (*rushing out*): Going—going! (*A second later she cries out. Tom springs up and crosses to the door. Amanda rushes anxiously in. Tom opens the door.*)

Tom: Laura?

Laura: I'm all right. I slipped, but I'm all right.

Amanda (*peering anxiously after her*): If anyone breaks a leg on those fire-escape steps, the landlord ought to be sued for every cent he possesses! (*She shuts door. Remembers she isn't speaking and returns to other room.*)

> *As Tom enters listlessly for his coffee, she turns her back to him and stands rigidly facing the window on the gloomy gray vault of the areaway. Its light on her face with its aged but childish features is cruelly sharp, satirical as a Daumier print.*

(Music Under: "Ave Maria.")

> *Tom glances sheepishly but sullenly at her averted figure and slumps at the table. The coffee is scalding hot; he sips it and gasps and spits it back in the cup. At his gasp, Amanda catches her breath and half turns. Then catches herself and turns back to window.*

> *Tom blows on his coffee, glancing sidewise at his mother. She clears her throat. Tom clears his. He starts to rise. Sinks back down again, scratches his head, clears his throat again. Amanda coughs. Tom raises his cup in both hands to blow on it, his eyes staring over the rim of it at his mother for several moments. Then he slowly sets the cup down and awkwardly and hesitantly rises from the chair.*

Tom (*hoarsely*): Mother. I—I apologize. Mother. (*Amanda draws a quick, shuddering breath. Her face works grotesquely. She breaks into childlike tears.*) I'm sorry for what I said, for everything that I said, I didn't mean it.

Amanda (*sobbingly*): My devotion has made me a witch and so I make myself hateful to my children!

Tom: No, you *don't*.
Amanda: I worry so much, don't sleep, it makes me nervous!
Tom (gently): I understand that.
Amanda: I've had to put up a solitary battle all these years. But you're my right-hand bower! Don't fall down, don't fail!
Tom (gently): I try, Mother.
Amanda (with great enthusiasm): Try and you will SUCCEED! (*The notion makes her breathless.*) Why, you—you're just *full* of natural endowments! Both of my children—they're *unusual* children! Don't you think I know it? I'm so—*proud!* Happy and—feel I've—so much to be thankful for but—promise me one thing, son!
Tom: What, Mother?
Amanda: Promise, son you'll—never be a drunkard!
Tom (turns to her grinning): I will never be a drunkard, Mother.
Amanda: That's what frightened me so, that you'd be drinking! Eat a bowl of Purina!
Tom: Just coffee, Mother.
Amanda: Shredded wheat biscuit?
Tom: No. No, Mother, just coffee.
Amanda: You can't put in a day's work on an empty stomach. You've got ten minutes—don't gulp! Drinking too-hot liquids makes cancer of the stomach. . . . Put cream in.
Tom: No, thank you.
Amanda: To cool it.
Tom: No! No, thank you, I want it black.
Amanda: I know, but it's not good for you. We have to do all that we can to build ourselves up. In these trying times we live in, all that we have to cling to is—each other. . . . That's why it's so important to—Tom, I—I sent out your sister so I could discuss something with you. If you hadn't spoken I would have spoken to you. (*Sits down.*)
Tom (gently): What is it, Mother, that you want to discuss?
Amanda: Laura!

Tom puts his cup down slowly.

(Legend On Screen: "Laura.")

(Music: "The Glass Menagerie.")

Tom: —Oh.—Laura . . .
Amanda (touching his sleeve): You know how Laura is. So quiet but—still water runs deep! She notices things and I think she—broods about them. (*Tom looks up.*) A few days ago I came in and she was crying.
Tom: What about?
Amanda: You.
Tom: Me?
Amanda: She has an idea that you're not happy here.
Tom: What gave her that idea?
Amanda: What gives her any idea? However, you do act strangely. I—I'm not criticizing, understand *that!* I know your ambitions do not lie in the warehouse, that like everybody in the whole wide world—you've had to—make sacrifices, but—Tom—Tom—

life's not easy, it calls for—Spartan endurance! There's so many things in my heart that I cannot describe to you! I've never told you but I—*loved* your father. . . .

Tom (*gently*): I know that, Mother.

Amanda: And you—when I see you taking after his ways! Staying out late—and—well, you *had* been drinking the night you were in that—terrifying condition! Laura says that you hate the apartment and that you go out nights to get away from it! Is that true, Tom?

Tom: No. You say there's so much in your heart that you can't describe to me. That's true of me, too. There's so much in my heart that I can't describe to *you!* So let's respect each other's—

Amanda: But, why—*why*, Tom—are you always so *restless?* Where do you go to, nights?

Tom: I—go to the movies.

Amanda: Why do you go to the movies so much, Tom?

Tom: I go to the movies because—I like adventure. Adventure is something I don't have much of at work, so I go to the movies.

Amanda: But, Tom, you go to the movies *entirely* too *much!*

Tom: I like a lot of adventure.

> Amanda looks baffled, then hurt. As the familiar inquisition resumes he becomes hard and impatient again. Amanda slips back into her querulous attitude toward him.

(Image On Screen: Sailing Vessel With Jolly Roger.)

Amanda: Most young men find adventure in their careers.

Tom: Then most young men are not employed in a warehouse.

Amanda: The world is full of young men employed in warehouses and offices and factories.

Tom: Do all of them find adventure in their careers?

Amanda: They do or they do without it! Not everybody has a craze for adventure.

Tom: Man is by instinct a lover, a hunter, a fighter, and none of those instincts are given much play at the warehouse!

Amanda: Man is by instinct! Don't quote instinct to me! Instinct is something that people have got away from! It belongs to animals! Christian adults don't want it!

Tom: What do Christian adults want, then, Mother?

Amanda: Superior things! Things of the mind and the spirit! Only animals have to satisfy instincts! Surely your aims are somewhat higher than theirs! Than monkeys—pigs—

Tom: I reckon they're not.

Amanda: You're joking. However, that isn't what I wanted to discuss.

Tom (*rising*): I haven't much time.

Amanda (*pushing his shoulder*): Sit down.

Tom: You want me to punch in red at the warehouse, Mother?

Amanda: You have five minutes. I want to talk about Laura.

(Legend: "Plans And Provisions.")

Tom: All right! What about Laura?

Amanda: We have to be making some plans and provisions for her. She's older than you, two years, and nothing has happened. She just drifts along doing nothing. It frightens me terribly how she just drifts along.

Tom: I guess she's the type that people call home girls.

Amanda: There's no such type, and if there is, it's a pity! That is unless the home is hers, with a husband!

Tom: What?

Amanda: Oh, I can see the handwriting on the wall as plain as I see the nose in front of my face! It's terrifying! More and more you remind me of your father! He was out all hours without explanation—Then *left!* Goodbye! And me with the bag to hold. I saw that letter you got from the Merchant Marine. I know what you're dreaming of. I'm not standing here blindfolded. (*She pauses.*) Very well, then. Then *do* it! But not till there's somebody to take your place.

Tom: What do you mean?

Amanda: I mean that as soon as Laura has got somebody to take care of her, married, a home of her own, independent—why, then you'll be free to go wherever you please, on land, on sea, whichever way the wind blows! But until that time you've got to look out for your sister. I don't say me because I'm old and don't matter! I say for your sister because she's young and dependent. I put her in business college—a dismal failure! Frightened her so it made her sick to her stomach. I took her over to the Young People's League at the church. Another fiasco. She spoke to nobody, nobody spoke to her. Now all she does is fool with those pieces of glass and play those worn-out records. What kind of a life is that for a girl to lead!

Tom: What can I do about it?

Amanda: Overcome selfishness! Self, self, self is all that you ever think of! (*Tom springs up and crosses to get his coat. It is ugly and bulky. He pulls on a cap with earmuffs.*) Where is your muffler? Put your wool muffler on! (*He snatches it angrily from the closet and tosses it around his neck and pulls both ends tight.*) Tom! I haven't said what I had in mind to ask you.

Tom: I'm too late to—

Amanda (catching his arms—very importunately. Then shyly): Down at the warehouse, aren't there some—nice young men?

Tom: No!

Amanda: There *must* be—some . . .

Tom: Mother—

    Gesture.

Amanda: Find one that's clean-living—doesn't drink—and ask him out for sister!

Tom: What?

Amanda: For *sister!* To meet! Get *acquainted!*

Tom (stamping to door): Oh, my go-osh!

Amanda: Will you? (*He opens door. Imploringly.*) Will you? (*He starts down.*) Will you? *Will* you, dear?

Tom (calling back): YES!

    Amanda closes the door hesitantly and with a troubled but faintly hopeful expression.

(Screen Image: Glamor Magazine Cover.)

    Spot Amanda at phone.

Amanda: Ella Cartwright? This is Amanda Wingfield! How are you, honey? How is that kidney condition? (*Count five.*) Horrors! (*Count five.*) You're a Christian martyr, yes, honey, that's what you are, a Christian martyr! Well, I just happened to notice in my little red book that your subscription to the *Companion* has just run out! I knew that you wouldn't want to miss out on the wonderful serial starting in this new issue. It's by Bessie Mae Hopper, the first thing she's written since *Honeymoon for Three*. Wasn't that a strange and interesting story? Well, this one is even lovelier, I believe. It has a sophisticated society background. It's all about the horsey set on Long Island!

(Fade Out.)

SCENE V

(Legend On Screen: "Annunciation.") *Fade with music.*

It is early dusk of a spring evening. Supper has just been finished in the Wingfield apartment. Amanda and Laura in light-colored dresses are removing dishes from the table, in the upstage area, which is shadowy, their movements formalized almost as a dance or ritual, their moving forms as pale and silent as moths.

Tom, in white shirt and trousers, rises from the table and crosses toward the fire-escape.

Amanda (as he passes her): Son, will you do me a favor?
Tom: What?
Amanda: Comb your hair! You look so pretty when your hair is combed! (*Tom slouches on sofa with evening paper. Enormous caption "Franco Triumphs."*) There is only one respect in which I would like you to emulate your father.
Tom: What respect is that?
Amanda: The care he always took of his appearance. He never allowed himself to look untidy. (*He throws down the paper and crosses to fire-escape.*) Where are you going?
Tom: I'm going out to smoke.
Amanda: You smoke too much. A pack a day at fifteen cents a pack. How much would that amount to in a month? Thirty times fifteen is how much, Tom? Figure it out and you will be astounded at what you could save. Enough to give you a night-school course in accounting at Washington U! Just think what a wonderful thing that would be for you, son!

Tom is unmoved by the thought.

Tom: I'd rather smoke. (*He steps out on landing, letting the screen door slam.*)
Amanda (sharply): I know! That's the tragedy of it. . . . (*Alone, she turns to look at her husband's picture.*)

(Dance Music: "All The World Is Waiting For The Sunrise.")

Tom (to the audience): Across the alley from us was the Paradise Dance Hall. On evenings in spring the windows and doors were open and the music came outdoors. Sometimes the lights were turned out except for a large glass sphere that hung from the ceiling. It would turn slowly about and filter the dusk with delicate rainbow colors. Then the orchestra played a waltz or a tango, something that had a slow and sensuous rhythm. Couples would come outside, to the relative privacy of the alley. You could see them kissing behind ash-pits and telephone poles. This was the compensation for lives that passed like mine, without any change or adventure. Adventure and change were imminent in this year. They were waiting around the corner for all these kids. Suspended in the mist over Berchtesgaden, caught in the folds of Chamberlain's umbrella. In Spain there was Guernica! But here there was only hot swing music and liquor, dance halls, bars, and movies, and sex that hung in the gloom like a chandelier and flooded the world with brief, deceptive rainbows. . . . All the world was waiting for bombardments!

Amanda turns from the picture and comes outside.

Amanda (sighing): A fire-escape landing's a poor excuse for a porch. (*She spreads a newspaper on a step and sits down, gracefully and demurely as if she were settling into a swing on a Mississippi veranda.*) What are you looking at?
Tom: The moon.
Amanda: Is there a moon this evening?
Tom: It's rising over Garfinkel's Delicatessen.
Amanda: So it is! A little silver slipper of a moon. Have you made a wish on it yet?
Tom: Um-hum.
Amanda: What did you wish for?
Tom: That's a secret.
Amanda: A secret, huh? Well, I won't tell mine either. I will be just as mysterious as you.
Tom: I bet I can guess what yours is.
Amanda: Is my head so transparent?
Tom: You're not a sphinx.
Amanda: No, I don't have secrets. I'll tell you what I wished for on the moon. Success and happiness for my precious children! I wish for that whenever there's a moon, and when there isn't a moon, I wish for it, too.
Tom: I thought perhaps you wished for a gentleman caller.
Amanda: Why do you say that?
Tom: Don't you remember asking me to fetch one?
Amanda: I remember suggesting that it would be nice for your sister if you brought home some nice young man from the warehouse. I think I've made that suggestion more than once.
Tom: Yes, you have made it repeatedly.
Amanda: Well?
Tom: We are going to have one.
Amanda: What?
Tom: A gentleman caller!

(The Annunciation Is Celebrated With Music.)

Amanda rises.

(Image On Screen: Caller With Bouquet.)

Amanda: You mean you have asked some nice young man to come over?

Tom: Yep. I've asked him to dinner.
Amanda: You really did?
Tom: I did!
Amanda: You did, and did he—*accept?*
Tom: He did!
Amanda: Well, well—well, well! That's—lovely!
Tom: I thought that you would be pleased.
Amanda: It's definite, then?
Tom: Very definite.
Amanda: Soon?
Tom: Very soon.
Amanda: For heaven's sake, stop putting on and tell me some things, will you?
Tom: What things do you want me to tell you?
Amanda: Naturally I would like to know when he's *coming!*
Tom: He's coming tomorrow.
Amanda: Tomorrow?
Tom: Yep. Tomorrow.
Amanda: But, Tom!
Tom: Yes, Mother?
Amanda: Tomorrow gives me no time!
Tom: Time for what?
Amanda: Preparations! Why didn't you phone me at once, as soon as you asked him, the minute that he accepted? Then, don't you see, I could have been getting ready!
Tom: You don't have to make any fuss.
Amanda: Oh, Tom, Tom, Tom, of course I have to make a fuss! I want things nice, not sloppy! Not thrown together. I'll certainly have to do some fast thinking, won't I?
Tom: I don't see why you have to think at all.
Amanda: You just don't know. We can't have a gentleman caller in a pig-sty! All my wedding silver has to be polished, the monogrammed table linen ought to be laundered! The windows have to be washed and fresh curtains put up. And how about clothes? We have to *wear* something, don't we?
Tom: Mother, this boy is no one to make a fuss over!
Amanda: Do you realize he's the first young man we've introduced to your sister? It's terrible, dreadful, disgraceful that poor little sister has never received a single gentleman caller! Tom, come inside! (*She opens the screen door.*)
Tom: What for?
Amanda: I want to ask you some things.
Tom: If you're going to make such a fuss, I'll call it off, I'll tell him not to come.
Amanda: You certainly won't do anything of the kind. Nothing offends people worse than broken engagements. It simply means I'll have to work like a Turk! We won't be brilliant, but we will pass inspection. Come on inside. (*Tom follows, groaning.*) Sit down.
Tom: Any particular place you would like me to sit?
Amanda: Thank heavens I've got that new sofa! I'm also making payments on a floor lamp I'll have sent out! And put the chintz covers on, they'll brighten things up! Of course I'd hoped to have these walls re-papered. . . . What is the young man's name?

Tom: His name is O'Connor.
Amanda: That, of course, means fish—tomorrow is Friday! I'll have that salmon loaf—with Durkee's dressing! What does he do? He works at the warehouse?
Tom: Of course! How else would I—
Amanda: Tom, he—doesn't drink?
Tom: Why do you ask me that?
Amanda: Your father *did!*
Tom: Don't get started on that!
Amanda: He *does* drink, then?
Tom: Not that I know of!
Amanda: Make sure, be certain! The last thing I want for my daughter's a boy who drinks!
Tom: Aren't you being a little premature? Mr. O'Connor has not yet appeared on the scene!
Amanda: But will tomorrow. To meet your sister, and what do I know about his character? Nothing! Old maids are better off than wives of drunkards!
Tom: Oh, my God!
Amanda: Be still!
Tom (leaning forward to whisper): Lots of fellows meet girls whom they don't marry!
Amanda: Oh, talk sensibly, Tom—and don't be sarcastic! (*She has gotten a hairbrush.*)
Tom: What are you doing?
Amanda: I'm brushing that cow-lick down! (*She attacks his hair with the brush.*) What is this young man's position at the warehouse?
Tom (submitting grimly to the brush and the interrogation): This young man's position is that of a shipping clerk, Mother.
Amanda: Sounds to me like a fairly responsible job, the sort of a job *you* would be in if you just had more *get-up*. What is his salary? Have you got any idea?
Tom: I would judge it to be approximately eighty-five dollars a month.
Amanda: Well—not princely, but—
Tom: Twenty more than I make.
Amanda: Yes, how well I know! But for a family man, eighty-five dollars a month is not much more than you can just get by on. . . .
Tom: Yes, but Mr. O'Connor is not a family man.
Amanda: He might be, mightn't he? Some time in the future?
Tom: I see. Plans and provisions.
Amanda: You are the only young man that I know of who ignores the fact that the future becomes the present, the present the past, and the past turns into everlasting regret if you don't plan for it!
Tom: I will think that over and see what I can make of it!
Amanda: Don't be supercilious with your mother! Tell me some more about this—what do you call him?
Tom: James D. O'Connor. The D. is for Delaney.
Amanda: Irish on *both* sides! *Gracious!* And doesn't drink?
Tom: Shall I call him up and ask him right this minute?
Amanda: The only way to find out about those things is to make discreet inquiries at the proper moment. When I was a girl in Blue Mountain and it was suspected that a young man drank, the girl whose attentions he had been receiving, if any girl *was*, would

sometimes speak to the minister of his church, or rather her father would if her father was living, and sort of feel him out on the young man's character. That is the way such things are discreetly handled to keep a young woman from making a tragic mistake!

Tom: Then how did you happen to make a tragic mistake?

Amanda: That innocent look of your father's had everyone fooled! He *smiled*—the world was *enchanted!* No girl can do worse than put herself at the mercy of a handsome appearance! I hope that Mr. O'Connor is not too good-looking.

Tom: No, he's not too good-looking. He's covered with freckles and hasn't too much of a nose.

Amanda: He's not right-down homely, though?

Tom: Not right-down homely. Just medium homely, I'd say.

Amanda: Character's what to look for in a man.

Tom: That's what I've always said, Mother.

Amanda: You've never said anything of the kind and I suspect you would never give it a thought.

Tom: Don't be suspicious of me.

Amanda: At least I hope he's the type that's up and coming.

Tom: I think he really goes in for self-improvement.

Amanda: What reason have you to think so?

Tom: He goes to night school.

Amanda (beaming): Splendid! What does he do, I mean study?

Tom: Radio engineering and public speaking!

Amanda: Then he has visions of being advanced in the world! Any young man who studies public speaking is aiming to have an executive job some day! And radio engineering? A thing for the future! Both of these facts are very illuminating. Those are the sort of things that a mother should know concerning any young man who comes to call on her daughter. Seriously or—not.

Tom: One little warning. He doesn't know about Laura. I didn't let on that we had dark ulterior motives. I just said, why don't you come have dinner with us? He said okay and that was the whole conversation.

Amanda: I bet it was! You're eloquent as an oyster. However, he'll know about Laura when he gets here. When he sees how lovely and sweet and pretty she is, he'll thank his lucky stars he was asked to dinner.

Tom: Mother, you mustn't expect too much of Laura.

Amanda: What do you mean?

Tom: Laura seems all those things to you and me because she's ours and we love her. We don't even notice she's crippled any more.

Amanda: Don't say crippled! You know that I never allow that word to be used!

Tom: But face facts, Mother. She is and—that not's all—

Amanda: What do you mean "not all"?

Tom: Laura is very different from other girls.

Amanda: I think the difference is all to her advantage.

Tom: Not quite all—in the eyes of others—strangers—she's terribly shy and lives in a world of her own and those things make her seem a little peculiar to people outside the house.

Amanda: Don't say peculiar.
Tom: Face the facts. She is.

> **(The Dance-Hall Music Changes To A Tango That Has A Minor And Somewhat Ominous Tone.)**

Amanda: In what way is she peculiar—may I ask?
Tom (gently): She lives in a world of her own—a world of—little glass ornaments, Mother. . . . (*Gets up. Amanda remains holding brush, looking at him, troubled.*) She plays old phonograph records and—that's about all—(*He glances at himself in the mirror and crosses to door.*)
Amanda (sharply): Where are you going?
Tom: I'm going to the movies. (*Out screen door.*)
Amanda: Not to the movies, every night to the movies! (*Follows quickly to screen door.*) I don't believe you always go to the movies! (*He is gone. Amanda looks worriedly after him for a moment. Then vitality and optimism return and she turns from the door. Crossing to portieres.*) Laura! Laura! (*Laura answers from kitchenette.*)
Laura: Yes, Mother.
Amanda: Let those dishes go and come in front! (*Laura appears with dish towel. Gaily.*) Laura, come here and make a wish on the moon!
Laura (entering): Moon—moon?
Amanda: A little silver slipper of a moon. Look over your left shoulder, Laura, and make a wish! (*Laura looks faintly puzzled as if called out of sleep. Amanda seizes her shoulders and turns her at an angle by the door.*) Now! Now, darling, *wish!*
Laura: What shall I wish for, Mother?
Amanda (her voice trembling and her eyes suddenly filling with tears): Happiness! Good fortune!

> The violin rises and the stage dims out.

SCENE VI

(Image: High-School Hero.)

Tom: And so the following evening I brought him home to dinner. I had known Jim slightly in high school. In high school Jim was a hero. He had tremendous Irish good nature and vitality with the scrubbed and polished look of white china ware. He seemed to move in a continual spotlight. He was a star in basketball, captain of the debating club, president of the senior class and the glee club and he sang the male lead in the annual light operas. He was always running or bounding, never just walking. He seemed always at the point of defeating the law of gravity. He was shooting with such velocity through his adolescence that you would logically expect him to arrive at nothing short of the White House by the time he was thirty. But Jim apparently ran into more interference after his graduation from Soldan. His speed had definitely slowed. Six years after he left high school he was holding a job that wasn't much better than mine.

(Image: Clerk.)

> He was the only one at the warehouse with whom I was on friendly terms. I was valuable to him as someone who could remember his former glory, who had seen him

win basketball games and the silver cup in debating. He knew of my secret practice of retiring to a cabinet of the washroom to work on my poems when business was slack in the warehouse. He called me Shakespeare. And while the other boys in the warehouse regarded me with suspicious hostility, Jim took a humorous attitude toward me. Gradually his attitude affected the others, their hostility wore off and they also began to smile at me as people smile at an oddly fashioned dog who trots across their path at some distance.

I knew that Jim and Laura had known each other at Soldan, and I had heard Laura speak admiringly of his voice. I didn't know if Jim remembered her or not. In high school Laura had been as unobtrusive as Jim had been astonishing. If he did remember Laura, it was not as my sister, for when I asked him to dinner, he grinned and said, "You know, Shakespeare, I never thought of you as having folks!"

He was about to discover that I did. . . .

(Light Up Stage.)

(Legend On Screen: "The Accent Of A Coming Foot.")

Friday evening. It is about five o'clock of a late spring evening which comes "scattering poems in the sky."

A delicate lemony light is in the Wingfield apartment.

Amanda has worked like a Turk in preparation for the gentleman caller. The results are astonishing. The new floor lamp with its rose-silk shade is in place, a colored paper lantern conceals the broken light fixture in the ceiling, new billowing white curtains are at the windows, chintz covers are on chairs and sofa, a pair of new sofa pillows make their initial appearance.

Open boxes and tissue paper are scattered on the floor.

Laura stands in the middle with lifted arms while Amanda crouches before her, adjusting the hem of the new dress, devout and ritualistic. The dress is colored and designed by memory. The arrangement of Laura's hair is changed; it is softer and more becoming. A fragile, unearthly prettiness has come out in Laura: she is like a piece of translucent glass touched by light, given a momentary radiance, not actual, not lasting.

Amanda (impatiently): Why are you trembling?
Laura: Mother, you've made me so nervous!
Amanda: How have I made you nervous?
Laura: By all this fuss! You make it seem so important!
Amanda: I don't understand you, Laura. You couldn't be satisfied with just sitting home, and yet whenever I try to arrange something for you, you seem to resist it. (*She gets up.*) Now take a look at yourself. No, wait! Wait just a moment—I have an idea!
Laura: What is it now?

Amanda produces two powder puffs which she wraps in handkerchiefs and stuffs in Laura's bosom.

Laura: Mother, what are you doing?
Amanda: They call them "Gay Deceivers"!
Laura: I won't wear them!

Amanda: You will!
Laura: Why should I?
Amanda: Because, to be painfully honest, your chest is flat.
Laura: You make it seem like we were setting a trap.
Amanda: All pretty girls are a trap, a pretty trap, and men expect them to be. (**Legend: "A Pretty Trap."**) Now look at yourself, young lady. This is the prettiest you will ever be! (*She stands back to admire Laura.*) I've got to fix myself now! You're going to be surprised by your mother's appearance! (*She crosses through the portieres, humming gaily.*)

Laura moves slowly to the long mirror and stares solemnly at herself.

A wind blows the white curtains inward in a slow, graceful motion and with a faint, sorrowful sighing.

Amanda (offstage): It isn't dark enough yet. (*She turns slowly before the mirror with a troubled look.*)

(Legend On Screen: "This Is My Sister: Celebrate Her With Strings!" Music.)

Amanda (laughing, off): I'm going to show you something. I'm going to make a spectacular appearance!
Laura: What is it, Mother?
Amanda: Possess your soul in patience—you will see! Something I've resurrected from that old trunk! Styles haven't changed so terribly much after all. . . . (*She parts the portieres.*) Now just look at your mother! (*She wears a girlish frock of yellowed voile with a blue silk sash. She carries a bunch of jonquils—the legend of her youth is nearly revived. Feverishly.*) This is the dress in which I led the cotillion. Won the cakewalk twice at Sunset Hill, wore one Spring to the Governor's Ball in Jackson! See how I sashayed around the ballroom, Laura? (*She raises her skirt and does a mincing step around the room.*) I wore it on Sundays for my gentlemen callers! I had it on the day I met your father . . . I had malaria fever all that Spring. The change of climate from East Tennessee to the Delta—weakened resistance—I had a little temperature all the time—not enough to be serious—just enough to make me restless and giddy! Invitations poured in—parties all over the Delta!—"Stay in bed," said Mother, "you have fever!"—but I just wouldn't. I took quinine but kept on going, going! Evenings, dances! Afternoons, long, long rides! Picnics—lovely!—So lovely, that country in May—all lacy with dogwood, literally flooded with jonquils! That was the spring I had the craze for jonquils. Jonquils became an absolute obsession. Mother said, "Honey, there's no more room for jonquils." And still I kept on bringing in more jonquils. Whenever, wherever I saw them, I'd say, "Stop! Stop! I see jonquils!" I made the young men help me gather the jonquils! It was a joke, Amanda and her jonquils! Finally there were no more vases to hold them, every available space was filled with jonquils. No vases to hold them? All right, I'll hold them myself! And then I—(*She stops in front of the picture.*) (**Music.**) met your father. Malaria fever and jonquils and then—this—boy. . . . (*She switches on the rose-colored lamp.*) I hope they get here before it starts to rain. (*She crosses upstage and places the jonquils in bowl on table.*) I gave your brother a little extra change so he and Mr. O'Connor could take the service car home.
Laura (with altered look): What did you say his name was?

Amanda: O'Connor.
Laura: What is his first name?
Amanda: I don't remember. Oh, yes, I do. It was—Jim!

> *Laura sways slightly and catches hold of a chair.*

(Legend On Screen. "Not Jim!")

Laura (faintly): Not—Jim!
Amanda: Yes, that was it, it was Jim! I've never known a Jim that wasn't nice!

(Music: Ominous.)

Laura: Are you sure his name is Jim O'Connor?
Amanda: Yes. Why?
Laura: Is he the one that Tom used to know in high school?
Amanda: He didn't say so. I think he just got to know him at the warehouse.
Laura: There was a Jim O'Connor we both knew in high school—(*Then, with effort.*) If that is the one that Tom is bringing to dinner—you'll have to excuse me, I won't come to the table.
Amanda: What sort of nonsense is this?
Laura: You asked me once if I'd ever liked a boy. Don't you remember I showed you this boy's picture?
Amanda: You mean the boy you showed me in the year-book?
Laura: Yes, that boy.
Amanda: Laura, Laura, were you in love with that boy?
Laura: I don't know, Mother. All I know is I couldn't sit at the table if it was him!
Amanda: It won't be him! It isn't the least bit likely. But whether it is or not, you will come to the table. You will not be excused.
Laura: I'll have to be, Mother.
Amanda: I don't intend to humor your silliness, Laura. I've had too much from you and your brother, both! So just sit down and compose yourself till they come. Tom has forgotten his key so you'll have to let them in, when they arrive.
Laura (panicky): Oh, Mother—*you* answer the door!
Amanda (lightly): I'll be in the kitchen—busy!
Laura: Oh, Mother, please answer the door, don't make me do it!
Amanda (crossing into kitchenette): I've got to fix the dressing for the salmon. Fuss, fuss—silliness!—over a gentleman caller!

> *Door swings shut. Laura is left alone.*

(Legend: "Terror!")

> *She utters a low moan and turns off the lamp—sits stiffly on the edge of the sofa, knotting her fingers together.*

(Legend On Screen: "The Opening Of A Door!")

> *Tom and Jim appear on the fire-escape steps and climb to landing. Hearing their approach, Laura rises with a panicky gesture. She retreats to the portieres.*

The doorbell. Laura catches her breath and touches her throat. Low drums.

Amanda (*calling*): Laura, sweetheart! The door!

Laura stares at it without moving.

Jim: I think we just beat the rain.
Tom: Uh-huh. (*He rings again, nervously. Jim whistles and fishes for a cigarette.*)
Amanda (*very, very gaily*): Laura, that is your brother and Mr. O'Connor! Will you let them in, darling?

Laura crosses toward kitchenette door.

Laura (*breathlessly*): Mother—you go to the door!

Amanda steps out of kitchenette and stares furiously at Laura. She points imperiously at the door.

Laura: Please, please!
Amanda (*in a fierce whisper*): What is the matter with you, you silly thing?
Laura (*desperately*): Please, you answer it, *please!*
Amanda: I told you I wasn't going to humor you, Laura. Why have you chosen this moment to lose your mind?
Laura: Please, please, please, you go!
Amanda: You'll have to go to the door because I can't!
Laura (*despairingly*): I can't either!
Amanda: Why?
Laura: I'm *sick!*
Amanda: I'm sick, too—of your nonsense! Why can't you and your brother be normal people? Fantastic whims and behavior! (*Tom gives a long ring.*) Preposterous goings on! Can you give me one reason—(*Calls out lyrically.*) Coming! Just one second!—why should you be afraid to open a door? Now you answer it, Laura!
Laura: Oh, oh, oh . . . (*She returns through the portieres. Darts to the victrola and winds it frantically and turns it on.*)
Amanda: Laura Wingfield, you march right to that door!
Laura: Yes—yes, Mother!

A faraway, scratchy rendition of "Dardanella" softens the air and gives her strength to move through it. She slips to the door and draws it cautiously open. Tom enters with the caller, Jim O'Connor.

Tom: Laura, this is Jim. Jim, this is my sister, Laura.
Jim (*stepping inside*): I didn't know that Shakespeare had a sister!
Laura (*retreating stiff and trembling from the door*): How—how do you do?
Jim (*heartily extending his hand*): Okay!

Laura touches it hesitantly with hers.

Jim: Your hand's *cold,* Laura!
Laura: Yes, well—I've been playing the victrola. . . .

Jim: Must have been playing classical music on it! You ought to play a little hot swing music to warm you up!
Laura: Excuse me—I haven't finished playing the victrola. . . .

> She turns awkwardly and hurries into the front room. She pauses a second by the victrola. Then catches her breath and darts through the portieres like a frightened deer.

Jim (grinning): What was the matter?
Tom: Oh—with Laura? Laura is—terribly shy.
Jim: Shy, huh? It's unusual to meet a shy girl nowadays. I don't believe you ever mentioned you had a sister.
Tom: Well, now you know. I have one. Here is the *Post Dispatch*. You want a piece of it?
Jim: Uh-huh.
Tom: What piece? The comics?
Jim: Sports! (*Glances at it.*) Ole Dizzy Dean is on his bad behavior.
Tom (disinterest): Yeah? (*Lights cigarette and crosses back to fire-escape door.*)
Jim: Where are *you* going?
Tom: I'm going out on the terrace.
Jim (goes after him): You know, Shakespeare—I'm going to sell you a bill of goods!
Tom: What goods?
Jim: A course I'm taking.
Tom: Huh?
Jim: In public speaking! You and me, we're not the warehouse type.
Tom: Thanks—that's good news. But what has public speaking got to do with it?
Jim: It fits you for—executive positions!
Tom: Awww.
Jim: I tell you it's done a helluva lot for me.

(Image: Executive At Desk.)

Tom: In what respect?
Jim: In every! Ask yourself what is the difference between you an' me and men in the office down front? Brains?—No!—Ability?—No! Then what? Just one little thing—
Tom: What is that one little thing?
Jim: Primarily it amounts to—social poise! Being able to square up to people and hold your own on any social level!
Amanda (offstage): Tom?
Tom: Yes, Mother?
Amanda: Is that you and Mr. O'Connor?
Tom: Yes, Mother.
Amanda: Well, you just make yourselves comfortable in there.
Tom: Yes, Mother.
Amanda: Ask Mr. O'Connor if he would like to wash his hands.
Jim: Aw—no—no—thank you—I took care of that at the warehouse. Tom—
Tom: Yes?
Jim: Mr. Mendoza was speaking to me about you.
Tom: Favorably?

Jim: What do you think?
Tom: Well—
Jim: You're going to be out of a job if you don't wake up.
Tom: I am waking up—
Jim: You show no signs.
Tom: The signs are interior.

(Image On Screen: The Sailing Vessel With Jolly Roger Again.)

Tom: I'm planning to change. (*He leans over the rail speaking with quiet exhilaration. The incandescent marquees and signs of the first-run movie houses light his face from across the alley. He looks like a voyager.*) I'm right at the point of committing myself to a future that doesn't include the warehouse and Mr. Mendoza or even a night-school course in public speaking.
Jim: What are you gassing about?
Tom: I'm tired of the movies.
Jim: Movies!
Tom: Yes, movies! Look at them—(*A wave toward the marvels of Grand Avenue.*) All of those glamorous people—having adventures—hogging it all, gobbling the whole thing up! You know what happens? People go to the *movies* instead of *moving!* Hollywood characters are supposed to have all the adventures for everybody in America, while everybody in America sits in a dark room and watches them have them! Yes, until there's a war. That's when adventure becomes available to the masses! *Everyone's* dish, not only Gable's! Then the people in the dark room come out of the dark room to have some adventures themselves—goody, goody! It's our turn now, to go to the South Sea Island—to make a safari—to be exotic, far-off—But I'm not patient. I don't want to wait till then. I'm tired of the *movies* and I am *about to move!*
Jim (incredulously): Move?
Tom: Yes!
Jim: When?
Tom: Soon!
Jim: Where? Where?

> *Theme three music seems to answer the question, while Tom thinks it over. He searches among his pockets.*

Tom: I'm starting to boil inside. I know I seem dreamy, but inside—well, I'm boiling! Whenever I pick up a shoe, I shudder a little thinking how short life is and what I am doing!—Whatever that means. I know it doesn't mean shoes—except as something to wear on a traveler's feet! (*Finds paper.*) Look—
Jim: What?
Tom: I'm a member.
Jim (reading): The Union of Merchant Seamen.
Tom: I paid my dues this month, instead of the light bill.
Jim: You will regret it when they turn the lights off.
Tom: I won't be here.

Jim: How about your mother?

Tom: I'm like my father. The bastard son of a bastard! Did you notice how he is grinning in his picture in there? And he's been absent going on sixteen years!

Jim: You're just talking, you drip. How does your mother feel about it?

Tom: Shhh—Here comes Mother! Mother is not acquainted with my plans!

Amanda (enters portieres): Where are you all?

Tom: On the terrace, Mother.

> *They start inside. She advances to them. Tom is distinctly shocked at her appearance. Even Jim blinks a little. He is making his first contact with girlish Southern vivacity and in spite of the night-school course in public speaking is somewhat thrown off the beam by the unexpected outlay of social charm.*
>
> *Certain responses are attempted by Jim but are swept aside by Amanda's gay laughter and chatter. Tom is embarrassed but after the first shock Jim reacts very warmly. Grins and chuckles, is altogether won over.*

(Image: Amanda As A Girl.)

Amanda (coyly smiling, shaking her girlish ringlets): Well, well, well, so this is Mr. O'Connor. Introductions entirely unnecessary. I've heard so much about you from my boy. I finally said to him, Tom—good gracious!—why don't you bring this paragon to supper? I'd like to meet this nice young man at the warehouse!—Instead of just hearing him sing your praises so much! I don't know why my son is so stand-offish—that's not Southern behavior! Let's sit down and—I think we could stand a little more air in here! Tom, leave the door open. I felt a nice fresh breeze a moment ago. Where has it gone? Mmm, so warm already! And not quite summer, even. We're going to burn up when summer really gets started. However, we're having—we're having a very light supper. I think light things are better fo' this time of year. The same as light clothes are. Light clothes an' light food are what warm weather calls fo'. You know our blood gets so thick during th' winter—it takes a while fo' us to *adjust* ou'selves!—when the season changes . . . It's come so quick this year. I wasn't prepared. All of a sudden—heavens! Already summer!—I ran to the trunk an' pulled out this light dress—Terribly old! Historical almost! But feels so good—so good an' co-ol, y' know. . . .

Tom: Mother—

Amanda: Yes, honey?

Tom: How about—supper?

Amanda: Honey, you go ask Sister if supper is ready! You know that Sister is in full charge of supper! Tell her you hungry boys are waiting for it. *(To Jim)* Have you met Laura?

Jim: She—

Amanda: Let you in? Oh, good, you've met already! It's rare for a girl as sweet an' pretty as Laura to be domestic! But Laura is, thank heavens, not only pretty but also very domestic. I'm not at all. I never was a bit. I never could make a thing but angel-food cake. Well, in the South we had so many servants. Gone, gone, gone. All vestige of gracious living! Gone completely! I wasn't prepared for what the future brought me. All of my gentlemen callers were sons of planters and so of course I assumed that I would be married to one and raise my family on a large piece of land with plenty of servants. But man proposes—and woman accepts the proposal!—To vary that old, old saying a little bit—I married no planter! I married a man who worked for the telephone company! That gallantly smiling gentleman over there! (*Points to the picture.*) A telephone man who—fell in love with long-distance! Now he travels and I don't even know where!—But what am I going on for about my—tribulations? Tell me yours—I hope you don't have any! Tom?

Tom (*returning*): Yes, Mother?

Amanda: Is supper nearly ready?

Tom: It looks to me like supper is on the table.

Amanda: Let me look—(*She rises prettily and looks through portieres.*) Oh, lovely! But where is Sister?

Tom: Laura is not feeling well and she says that she thinks she'd better not come to the table.

Amanda: What? Nonsense! Laura? Oh, Laura!

Laura (*offstage, faintly*): Yes, Mother.

Amanda: You really must come to the table. We won't be seated until you come to the table! Come in, Mr. O'Connor. You sit over there and I'll . . . Laura? Laura Wingfield! You're keeping us waiting, honey! We can't say grace until you come to the table!

The back door is pushed weakly open and Laura comes in. She is obviously quite faint, her lips trembling, her eyes wide and staring. She moves unsteadily toward the table.

(Legend: "Terror!")

Outside a summer storm is coming abruptly. The white curtains billow inward at the windows and there is a sorrowful murmur and deep blue dusk.

Laura suddenly stumbles—She catches at a chair with a faint moan.

Tom: Laura!

Amanda: Laura! (*There is a clap of thunder.*) (**Legend: "Ah!"**) (*Despairingly.*) Why, Laura, you *are* ill, darling! Tom, help your sister into the living room, dear! Sit in the living room, Laura—rest on the sofa. Well! (*To Jim as Tom helps his sister to the sofa in the living room*) Standing over the hot stove made her ill!—I told her that it was just too warm this evening, but—(*Tom comes back in. Laura is on the sofa.*) Is Laura all right now?

Tom: Yes.

Amanda: What *is* that? Rain? A nice cool rain has come up! (*She gives the gentleman caller a frightened look.*) I think we may—have grace—now . . . (*Tom looks at her stupidly.*) Tom, honey—you say grace!

Tom: Oh . . . "For these and all thy mercies—" (*They bow their heads, Amanda stealing a nervous glance at Jim. In the living room Laura, stretched on the sofa, clenches her hand to her lips, to hold back a shuddering sob.*) God's Holy Name be praised—

(The Scene Dims Out.)

SCENE VII

A Souvenir.

Half an hour later. Dinner is just being finished in the upstage area which is concealed by the drawn portieres.

As the curtain rises Laura is still huddled upon the sofa, her feet drawn under her, her head resting on a pale blue pillow, her eyes wide and mysteriously watchful. The new floor lamp with its shade of rose-colored silk gives a soft, becoming light to her face, bringing out the fragile, unearthly prettiness which usually escapes attention. There is a steady murmur of rain, but it is slackening and stops soon after the scene begins; the air outside becomes pale and luminous as the moon breaks out.

A moment after the curtain rises, the lights in both rooms flicker and go out.

Jim: Hey, there, Mr. Light Bulb!

> Amanda laughs nervously.

(Legend: "Suspension Of A Public Service.")

Amanda: Where was Moses when the lights went out? Ha-ha. Do you know the answer to that one, Mr. O'Connor?
Jim: No, Ma'am, what's the answer?
Amanda: In the dark! (*Jim laughs appreciatively.*) Everybody sit still. I'll light the candles. Isn't it lucky we have them on the table? Where's a match? Which of you gentlemen can provide a match?
Jim: Here.
Amanda: Thank you, sir.
Jim: Not at all, Ma'am!
Amanda (*as she lights the candles*): I guess the fuse has burnt out. Mr. O'Connor, can you tell a burnt-out fuse? I know I can't and Tom is a total loss when it comes to mechanics. **(Sound: Getting Up: Voices Recede A Little To Kitchenette.)** Oh, be careful you don't bump into something. We don't want our gentleman caller to break his neck. Now wouldn't that be a fine howdy-do?
Jim: Ha-ha! Where is the fuse-box?
Amanda: Right here next to the stove. Can you see anything?
Jim: Just a minute.
Amanda: Isn't electricity a mysterious thing? Wasn't it Benjamin Franklin who tied a key to a kite? We live in such a mysterious universe, don't we? Some people say that science clears up all the mysteries for us. In my opinion it only creates more! Have you found it yet?
Jim: No, Ma'am. All these fuses look okay to me.
Amanda: Tom!
Tom: Yes, Mother?
Amanda: That light bill I gave you several days ago. The one I told you we got the notices about?
Tom: Oh—yeah.

(Legend: "Ha!")

Amanda: You didn't neglect to pay it by any chance?
Tom: Why, I—
Amanda: Didn't! I might have known it!
Jim: Shakespeare probably wrote a poem on that light bill, Mrs. Wingfield.
Amanda: I might have known better than to trust him with it! There's such a high price for negligence in this world!
Jim: Maybe the poem will win a ten-dollar prize.
Amanda: We'll just have to spend the remainder of the evening in the nineteenth century, before Mr. Edison made the Mazda lamp!
Jim: Candlelight is my favorite kind of light.
Amanda: That shows you're romantic! But that's no excuse for Tom. Well, we got through dinner. Very considerate of them to let us get through dinner before they plunged us into everlasting darkness, wasn't it, Mr. O'Connor?
Jim: Ha-ha!
Amanda: Tom, as a penalty for your carelessness you can help me with the dishes.
Jim: Let me give you a hand.
Amanda: Indeed you will not!
Jim: I ought to be good for something.
Amanda: Good for something? (*Her tone is rhapsodic.*) You? Why, Mr. O'Connor, nobody, nobody's given me this much entertainment in years—as you have!
Jim: Aw, now, Mrs. Wingfield!
Amanda: I'm not exaggerating, not one bit! But Sister is all by her lonesome. You go keep her company in the parlor! I'll give you this lovely old candelabrum that used to be on the altar at the church of the Heavenly Rest. It was melted a little out of shape when the church burnt down. Lightning struck it one spring. Gypsy Jones was holding a revival at the time and he intimated that the church was destroyed because the Episcopalians gave card parties.
Jim: Ha-ha.
Amanda: And how about coaxing Sister to drink a little wine? I think it would be good for her! Can you carry both at once?
Jim: Sure. I'm Superman!
Amanda: Now, Thomas, get into this apron!

> Jim comes into the dining room, carrying the candelabrum, its candles lighted, in one hand and a glass of wine in the other. The door of kitchenette swings closed on Amanda's gay laughter; the flickering light approaches the portieres. Laura sits up nervously as he enters. Her speech at first is low and breathless from the almost intolerable strain of being alone with a stranger.

(The Legend: "I Don't Suppose You Remember Me At All!")

> In her first speeches in this scene, before Jim's warmth overcomes her paralyzing shyness, Laura's voice is thin and breathless as though she has run up a steep flight of stairs. Jim's attitude is gently humorous. While the incident is apparently unimportant, it is to Laura the climax of her secret life.

Jim: Hello, there, Laura.

Laura (faintly): Hello. (*She clears her throat.*)
Jim: How are you feeling now? Better?
Laura: Yes. Yes, thank you.
Jim: This is for you. A little dandelion wine. (*He extends it toward her with extravagant gallantry.*)
Laura: Thank you.
Jim: Drink it—but don't get drunk! (*He laughs heartily. Laura takes the glass uncertainly; laughs shyly.*) Where shall I set the candles?
Laura: Oh—oh, anywhere . . .
Jim: How about here on the floor? Any objections?
Laura: No.
Jim: I'll spread a newspaper under to catch the drippings. I like to sit on the floor. Mind if I do?
Laura: Oh, no.
Jim: Give me a pillow?
Laura: What?
Jim: A pillow!
Laura: Oh . . . (*Hands him one quickly.*)
Jim: How about you? Don't you like to sit on the floor?
Laura: Oh—yes.
Jim: Why don't you, then?
Laura: I—will.
Jim: Take a pillow! (*Laura does. Sits on the other side of the candelabrum. Jim crosses his legs and smiles engagingly at her.*) I can't hardly see you sitting way over there.
Laura: I can—see you.
Jim: I know, but that's not fair, I'm in the limelight. (*Laura moves her pillow closer.*) Good! Now I can see you! Comfortable?
Laura: Yes.
Jim: So am I. Comfortable as a cow. Will you have some gum?
Laura: No, thank you.
Jim: I think that I will indulge, with your permission. (*Musingly unwraps it and holds it up.*) Think of the fortune made by the guy that invented the first piece of chewing gum. Amazing, huh? The Wrigley Building is one of the sights of Chicago—I saw it summer before last when I went up to the Century of Progress. Did you take in the Century of Progress?
Laura: No, I didn't.
Jim: Well, it was quite a wonderful exposition. What impressed me most was the Hall of Science. Gives you an idea of what the future will be in America, even more wonderful than the present time is! (*Pause. Smiling at her.*) Your brother tells me you're shy. Is that right, Laura?
Laura: I—don't know.
Jim: I judge you to be an old-fashioned type of girl. Well, I think that's pretty a good type to be. Hope you don't think I'm being too personal—do you?
Laura (hastily, out of embarrassment): I believe I *will* take a piece of gum, if you—don't mind. (*Clearing her throat.*) Mr. O'Connor, have you—kept up with your singing?
Jim: Singing? Me?

Laura: Yes. I remember what a beautiful voice you had.
Jim: When did you hear me sing?

(Voice Offstage In The Pause.)

Voice (offstage):
>O blow, ye winds, heigh-ho,
>A-roving I will go!
>I'm off to my love
>With a boxing glove—
>Ten thousand miles away!

Jim: You say you've heard me sing?
Laura: Oh, yes! Yes, very often . . . I—don't suppose you remember me—at all?
Jim (smiling doubtfully): You know I have an idea I've seen you before. I had that idea soon as you opened the door. It seemed almost like I was about to remember your name. But the name that I started to call you—wasn't a name! And so I stopped myself before I said it.
Laura: Wasn't it—Blue Roses?
Jim (springs up, grinning): Blue Roses! My gosh, yes—Blue Roses! That's what I had on my tongue when you opened the door! Isn't it funny what tricks your memory plays? I didn't connect you with the high school somehow or other. But that's where it was; it was high school. I didn't even know you were Shakespeare's sister! Gosh, I'm sorry.
Laura: I didn't expect you to. You—barely knew me!
Jim: But we did have a speaking acquaintance, huh?
Laura: Yes, we—spoke to each other.
Jim: When did you recognize me?
Laura: Oh, right away!
Jim: Soon as I came in the door?
Laura: When I heard your name I thought it was probably you. I knew that Tom used to know you a little in high school. So when you came in the door—well, then I was—sure.
Jim: Why didn't you say something, then?
Laura (breathlessly): I didn't know what to say, I was—too surprised!
Jim: For goodness sakes! You know, this sure is funny!
Laura: Yes! Yes, isn't it, though . . .
Jim: Didn't we have a class in something together?
Laura: Yes, we did.
Jim: What class was that?
Laura: It was—singing—chorus!
Jim: Aw!
Laura: I sat across the aisle from you in the Aud.
Jim: Aw.
Laura: Mondays, Wednesdays, and Fridays.
Jim: Now I remember—you always came in late.
Laura: Yes, it was so hard for me, getting upstairs. I had that brace on my leg—it clumped so loud!
Jim: I never heard any clumping.

Laura (*wincing at the recollection*): To me it sounded like—thunder!
Jim: Well, well, well. I never even noticed.
Laura: And everybody was seated before I came in. I had to walk in front of all those people. My seat was in the back row. I had to go clumping all the way up the aisle with everyone watching!
Jim: You shouldn't have been self-conscious.
Laura: I know, but I was. It was always such a relief when the singing started.
Jim: Aw, yes, I've placed you now! I used to call you Blue Roses. How was it that I got started calling you that?
Laura: I was out of school a little while with pleurosis. When I came back you asked me what was the matter. I said I had pleurosis—you thought I said *Blue Roses*. That's what you always called me after that!
Jim: I hope you didn't mind.
Laura: Oh, no—I liked it. You see, I wasn't acquainted with many—people. . . .
Jim: As I remember you sort of stuck by yourself.
Laura: I—I—never had much luck at—making friends.
Jim: I don't see why you wouldn't.
Laura: Well, I—started out badly.
Jim: You mean being—
Laura: Yes, it sort of—stood between me—
Jim: You shouldn't have let it!
Laura: I know, but it did, and—
Jim: You were shy with people!
Laura: I tried not to be but never could—
Jim: Overcome it?
Laura: No, I—I never could!
Jim: I guess being shy is something you have to work out of kind of gradually.
Laura (*sorrowfully*): Yes—I guess it—
Jim: Takes time!
Laura: Yes—
Jim: People are not so dreadful when you know them. That's what you have to remember! And everybody has problems, not just you, but practically everybody has got some problems. You think of yourself as having the only problems, as being the only one who is disappointed. But just look around you and you will see lots of people as disappointed as you are. For instance, I hoped when I was going to high school that I would be further along at this time, six years later, than I am now—You remember that wonderful write-up I had in *The Torch?*
Laura: Yes! (*She rises and crosses to table.*)
Jim: It said I was bound to succeed in anything I went into! (*Laura returns with the annual.*) Holy Jeez! *The Torch!* (*He accepts it reverently. They smile across it with mutual wonder. Laura crouches beside him and they begin to turn through it. Laura's shyness is dissolving in his warmth.*)
Laura: Here you are in *The Pirates of Penzance!*
Jim (*wistfully*): I sang the baritone lead in that operetta.
Laura (*rapidly*): So—beautifully!

Jim (protesting): Aw—
Laura: Yes, yes—beautifully—beautifully!
Jim: You heard me?
Laura: All three times!
Jim: No!
Laura: Yes!
Jim: All three performances?
Laura (looking down): Yes.
Jim: Why?
Laura: I—wanted to ask you to—autograph my program.
Jim: Why didn't you ask me to?
Laura: You were always surrounded by your own friends so much that I never had a chance to.
Jim: You should have just—
Laura: Well, I—thought you might think I was—
Jim: Thought I might think you was—what?
Laura: Oh—
Jim (with reflective relish): I was beleaguered by females in those days.
Laura: You were terribly popular!
Jim: Yeah—
Laura: You had such a—friendly way—
Jim: I was spoiled in high school.
Laura: Everybody—liked you!
Jim: Including you?
Laura: I—yes, I—did, too—(*She gently closes the book in her lap.*)
Jim: Well, well, well!—Give me that program, Laura. (*She hands it to him. He signs it with a flourish.*) There you are—better late than never!
Laura: Oh, I—what a—surprise!
Jim: My signature isn't worth very much right now. But some day—maybe—it will increase in value! Being disappointed is one thing and being discouraged is something else. I am disappointed but I'm not discouraged. I'm twenty-three years old. How old are you?
Laura: I'll be twenty-four in June.
Jim: That's not old age!
Laura: No, but—
Jim: You finished high school?
Laura (with difficulty): I didn't go back.
Jim: You mean you dropped out?
Laura: I made bad grades in my final examinations. (*She rises and replaces the book and the program. Her voice strained.*) How is—Emily Meisenbach getting along?
Jim: Oh, that kraut-head!
Laura: Why do you call her that?
Jim: That's what she was.
Laura: You're not still—going with her?
Jim: I never see her.

Laura: It said in the Personal Section that you were—engaged!
Jim: I know, but I wasn't impressed by that—propaganda!
Laura: It wasn't—the truth?
Jim: Only in Emily's optimistic opinion!
Laura: Oh—

(Legend: "What Have You Done Since High School?")

Jim lights a cigarette and leans indolently back on his elbows smiling at Laura with a warmth and charm which light her inwardly with altar candles. She remains by the table and turns in her hands a piece of glass to cover her tumult.

Jim (after several reflective puffs on a cigarette): What have you done since high school? (*She seems not to hear him.*) Huh? (*Laura looks up.*) I said what have you done since high school, Laura?
Laura: Nothing much.
Jim: You must have been doing something these six long years.
Laura: Yes.
Jim: Well, then, such as what?
Laura: I took a business course at business college—
Jim: How did that work out?
Laura: Well, not very—well—I had to drop out, it gave me—indigestion—

Jim laughs gently.

Jim: What are you doing now?
Laura: I don't do anything—much. Oh, please don't think I sit around doing nothing! My glass collection takes up a good deal of time. Glass is something you have to take good care of.
Jim: What did you say—about glass?
Laura: Collection I said—I have one—(*She clears her throat and turns away again, acutely shy.*)
Jim (abruptly): You know what I judge to be the trouble with you? Inferiority complex! Know what that is? That's what they call it when someone low-rates himself! I understand it because I had it, too. Although my case was not so aggravated as yours seems to be. I had it until I took up public speaking, developed my voice, and learned that I had an aptitude for science. Before that time I never thought of myself as being outstanding in any way whatsoever! Now I've never made a regular study of it, but I have a friend who says I can analyze people better than doctors that make a profession of it. I don't claim that to be necessarily true, but I can sure guess a person's psychology, Laura! (*Takes out his gum.*) Excuse me, Laura. I always take it out when the flavor is gone. I'll use this scrap of paper to wrap it in. I know how it is to get it stuck on a shoe. (*He wraps the gum in paper and puts it in his pocket.*) Yep—that's what I judge to be your principal trouble. A lack of confidence in yourself as a person. You don't have the proper amount of faith in yourself. I'm basing that fact on a number of your remarks and also on certain observations I've made. For instance that clumping you thought was so awful in high school. You say that you even dreaded to walk into class. You see what you did? You dropped out of school, you gave up an education because of a

clump, which as far as I know was practically non-existent! A little physical defect is what you have. Hardly noticeable even! Magnified thousands of times by imagination! You know what my strong advice to you is? Think of yourself as *superior* in some way!

Laura: In what way would I think?

Jim: Why, man alive, Laura! Just look about you a little. What do you see? A world full of common people! All of 'em born and all of 'em going to die! Which of them has one-tenth of your good points! Or mine! Or anyone else's, as far as that goes—gosh! Everybody excels in some one thing. Some in many! (*Unconsciously glances at himself in the mirror.*) All you've got to do is discover in *what!* Take me, for instance. (*He adjusts his tie at the mirror.*) My interest happens to lie in electro-dynamics. I'm taking a course in radio engineering at night school, Laura, on top of a fairly responsible job at the warehouse. I'm taking that course and studying public speaking.

Laura: Ohhhh.

Jim: Because I believe in the future of television! (*Turning back to her.*) I wish to be ready to go up right along with it. Therefore I'm planning to get in on the ground floor. In fact, I've already made the right connections and all that remains is for the industry itself to get under way! Full steam—(*His eyes are starry.*) Knowledge—Zzzzzp! Money—Zzzzzp!—Power! That's the cycle democracy is built on! (*His attitude is convincingly dynamic. Laura stares at him, even her shyness eclipsed in her absolute wonder. He suddenly grins.*) I guess you think I think a lot of myself!

Laura: No—o-o-o, I—

Jim: Now how about you? Isn't there something you take more interest in than anything else?

Laura: Well, I do—as I said—have my—glass collection—

A peal of girlish laughter from the kitchen.

Jim: I'm not right sure I know what you're talking about. What kind of glass is it?

Laura: Little articles of it, they're ornaments mostly! Most of them are little animals made out of glass, the tiniest little animals in the world. Mother calls them a glass menagerie! Here's an example of one, if you'd like to see it! This one is one of the oldest. It's nearly thirteen. (*He stretches out his hand.*) (**Music: "The Glass Menagerie."**) Oh, be careful—if you breathe, it breaks!

Jim: I'd better not take it. I'm pretty clumsy with things.

Laura: Go on, I trust you with him! (*Places it in his palm.*) There now—you're holding him gently! Hold him over the light, he loves the light! You see how the light shines through him?

Jim: It sure does shine!

Laura: I shouldn't be partial, but he is my favorite one.

Jim: What kind of a thing is this one supposed to be?

Laura: Haven't you noticed the single horn on his forehead?

Jim: A unicorn, huh?

Laura: Mmm-hmmm!

Jim: Unicorns—aren't they extinct in the modern world?

Laura: I know!

Jim: Poor little fellow, he must feel sort of lonesome.

Laura (smiling): Well, if he does, he doesn't complain about it. He stays on a shelf with some horses that don't have horns and all of them seem to get along nicely together.
Jim: How do you know?
Laura (lightly): I haven't heard any arguments among them!
Jim (grinning): No arguments, huh? Well, that's a pretty good sign! Where shall I set him?
Laura: Put him on the table. They all like a change of scenery once in a while!
Jim: Well, well, well, well—(*He places the glass piece on the table, then raises his arms and stretches.*) Look how big my shadow is when I stretch!
Laura: Oh, oh, yes—it stretches across the ceiling!
Jim (crossing to door): I think it's stopped raining. (*Opens fire-escape door.*) Where does the music come from?
Laura: From the Paradise Dance Hall across the alley.
Jim: How about cutting the rug a little, Miss Wingfield?
Laura: Oh, I—
Jim: Or is your program filled up? Let me have a look at it. (*Grasps imaginary card.*) Why, every dance is taken! I'll just have to scratch some out. (**Waltz Music: "La Golondrina."**) Ahhh, a waltz! (*He executes some sweeping turns by himself, then holds his arms toward Laura.*)
Laura (breathlessly): I—can't dance!
Jim: There you go, that inferiority stuff!
Laura: I've never danced in my life!
Jim: Come on, try!
Laura: Oh, but I'd step on you!
Jim: I'm not made out of glass.
Laura: How—how—how do we start?
Jim: Just leave it to me. You hold your arms out a little.
Laura: Like this?
Jim (taking her in his arms): A little bit higher. Right. Now don't tighten up, that's the main thing about it—relax.
Laura (laughing breathlessly): It's hard not to.
Jim: Okay.
Laura: I'm afraid you can't budge me.
Jim: What do you bet I can't? (*He swings her into motion.*)
Laura: Goodness, yes, you can!
Jim: Let yourself go, now, Laura, just let yourself go.
Laura: I'm—
Jim: Come on!
Laura: —trying!
Jim: Not so stiff—easy does it!
Laura: I know but I'm—
Jim: Loosen th' backbone! There now, that's a lot better.
Laura: Am I?
Jim: Lots, lots better! (*He moves her about the room in a clumsy waltz.*)
Laura: Oh, my!
Jim: Ha-ha!

Laura: Oh, my goodness!

Jim: Ha-ha-ha! (*They suddenly bump into the table, and the glass piece on it falls to the floor. Jim stops.*) What did we hit on?

Laura: Table.

Jim: Did something fall off it? I think—

Laura: Yes. (*She stoops to pick it up.*)

Jim: I hope that it wasn't the little glass horse with the horn!

Laura: Yes. (*she stoops to pick it up.*)

Jim: Aw, aw, aw. Is it broken?

Laura: Now it is just like all the other horses.

Jim: It's lost its—

Laura: Horn! It doesn't matter. Maybe it's a blessing in disguise.

Jim: You'll never forgive me. I bet that that was your favorite piece of glass.

Laura: I don't have favorites much. It's no tragedy, Freckles. Glass breaks so easily. No matter how careful you are. The traffic jars the shelves and things fall off them.

Jim: Still I'm awfully sorry that I was the cause.

Laura (smiling): I'll just imagine he had an operation. The horn was removed to make him feel less—freakish! (*They both laugh.*) Now he will feel more at home with the other horses, the ones that don't have horns . . .

Jim: Ha-ha, that's very funny! (*Suddenly serious.*) I'm glad to see that you have a sense of humor. You know—you're—well—very different! Surprisingly different from anyone else I know! (*His voice becomes soft and hesitant with a genuine feeling.*) Do you mind me telling you that? (*Laura is abashed beyond speech.*) I mean it in a nice way. You make me feel sort of—I don't know how to put it! I'm usually pretty good at expressing things, but—this is something that I don't know how to say! (*Laura touches her throat and clears it—turns the broken unicorn in her hands.*) (*Even softer.*) Has anyone ever told you that you were pretty? (**Pause: Music.**) (*Laura looks up slowly, with wonder, and shakes her head.*) Well, you are! In a very different way from anyone else. And all the nicer because of the difference, too. (*His voice becomes low and husky. Laura turns away, nearly faint with the novelty of her emotions.*) I wish that you were my sister. I'd teach you to have some confidence in yourself. The different people are not like other people, but being different is nothing to be ashamed of. Because other people are not such wonderful people. They're one hundred times one thousand. You're one times one! They walk all over the earth. You just stay here. They're common as—weeds, but—you—well, you're—*Blue Roses!*

(Image On Screen: Blue Roses.)

(Music Changes.)

Laura: But blue is wrong for—roses . . .

Jim: It's right for you! You're—pretty!

Laura: In what respect am I pretty?

Jim: In all respects—believe me! Your eyes—your hair—are pretty! Your hands are pretty! (*He catches hold of her hand.*) You think I'm making this up because I'm invited to dinner and have to be nice. Oh, I could do that! I could put on an act for you, Laura, and say lots of things without being very sincere. But this time I am. I'm talking to you sincerely. I happened to notice you had this inferiority complex that keeps you from feeling comfortable with people. Somebody needs to build your confidence up and make you proud instead of shy and turning away and—blushing—Somebody ought to—ought to—kiss you, Laura! (*His hand slips slowly up her arm to her shoulder.*) (**Music Swells Tumultuously.**) (*He suddenly turns her about and kisses her on the lips. When he releases her Laura sinks on the sofa with a bright, dazed look. Jim backs away and fishes in his pocket for a cigarette.*) (**Legend On Screen: "Souvenir."**) Stumble-john! (*He lights the cigarette, avoiding her look. There is a peal of girlish laughter from Amanda in the kitchen. Laura slowly raises and opens her hand. It still contains the little broken glass animal. She looks at it with a tender, bewildered expression.*) Stumble-john! I shouldn't have done that—That was way off the beam. You don't smoke, do you? (*She looks up, smiling, not hearing the question. He sits beside her a little gingerly. She looks at him speechlessly—waiting. He coughs decorously and moves a little farther aside as he considers the situation and senses her feelings, dimly, with perturbation. Gently.*) Would you—care for a—mint? (*She doesn't seem to hear him but her look grows brighter even.*) Peppermint—Life Saver? My pocket's a regular drug store—wherever I go ... (*He pops a mint in his mouth. Then gulps and decides to make a clean breast of it. He speaks slowly and gingerly.*) Laura, you know, if I had a sister like you, I'd do the same thing as Tom, I'd bring out fellows—and introduce her to them. The right type of boys—of a type to—appreciate her. Only—well—he made a mistake about me. Maybe I've got no call to be saying this. That may not have been the idea in having me over. But what if it was? There's nothing wrong about that. The only trouble is that in my case—I'm not in a situation to—do the right thing. I can't take down your number and say I'll phone. I can't call up next week and—ask for a date. I thought I had better explain the situation in case you—misunderstood it and—I hurt your feelings.... (*Pause. Slowly, very slowly, Laura's look changes, her eyes returning slowly from his to the ornament in her palm.*)

Amanda utters another gay laugh in the kitchen.

Laura (*faintly*): You—won't—call again?
Jim: No, Laura, I can't. (*He rises from the sofa.*) As I was just explaining, I've—got strings on me, Laura, I've—been going steady! I go out all the time with a girl named Betty. She's a home-girl like you, and Catholic, and Irish, and in a great many ways we—get along fine. I met her last summer on a moonlight boat trip up the river to Alton, on the *Majestic.* Well—right away from the start it was—love! (**Legend: Love!**) (*Laura sways slightly forward and grips the arm of the sofa. He fails to notice, now enrapt in his own comfortable being.*) Being in love has made a new man of me! (*Leaning stiffly forward, clutching the arm of the sofa, Laura struggles visibly with her storm. But Jim is oblivious, she is a long way off.*) The power of love is really pretty tremendous! Love is something that—changes the whole world, Laura! (*The storm abates a little and Laura leans back. He notices her again.*) It happened that Betty's aunt took sick, she got a wire and had to go to Centralia. So Tom—when he asked me to dinner—I naturally just accepted the invitation, not knowing that you—that he—that I—(*He stops awkwardly.*) Huh—I'm a stumble-john! (*He flops back on the sofa. The holy candles in the altar of Laura's face have been snuffed out! There is a look of almost infinite desolation. Jim glances at her uneasily.*) I wish that you would—say something. (*She bites her lip which was trembling and then bravely smiles. She opens her hand again on the broken glass ornament. Then she gently takes his hand and raises it level with her own. She carefully places the unicorn in the palm of his hand, then pushes his fingers closed upon it.*) What are you—doing that for? You want me to have him?—Laura? (*She nods.*) What for?

Laura: A—souvenir . . .

She rises unsteadily and crouches beside the victrola to wind it up.

(Legend On Screen: "Things Have A Way Of Turning Out So Badly.")

(Or Image: "Gentleman Caller Waving Good-bye! Gaily.")

At this moment Amanda rushes brightly back in the front room. She bears a pitcher of fruit punch in an old-fashioned cut-glass pitcher and a plate of macaroons. The plate has a gold border and poppies painted on it.

Amanda: Well, well, well! Isn't the air delightful after the shower? I've made you children a little liquid refreshment. (*Turns gaily to the gentleman caller.*) Jim, do you know that song about lemonade?
>"Lemonade, lemonade
>Made in the shade and stirred with a spade—
>Good enough for any old maid!"

Jim (*uneasily*): Ha-ha! No—I never heard it.

Amanda: Why, Laura! You look so serious!

Jim: We were having a serious conversation.

Amanda: Good! Now you're better acquainted!

Jim (*uncertainly*): Ha-ha! Yes.

Amanda: You modern young people are much more serious-minded than my generation. I was so gay as a girl!

Jim: You haven't changed, Mrs. Wingfield.

Amanda: Tonight I'm rejuvenated! The gaiety of the occasion, Mr. O'Connor! (*She tosses her head with a peal of laughter. Spills lemonade.*) Oooo! I'm baptizing myself!

Jim: Here—let me—

Amanda (*setting the pitcher down*): There now. I discovered we had some maraschino cherries. I dumped them in, juice and all!

Jim: You shouldn't have gone to that trouble, Mrs. Wingfield.

Amanda: Trouble, trouble? Why, it was loads of fun! Didn't you hear me cutting up in the kitchen? I bet your ears were burning! I told Tom how outdone with him I was for keeping you to himself so long a time! He should have brought you over much, much sooner! Well, now that you've found your way, I want you to be a very frequent caller! Not just occasional but all the time. Oh, we're going to have a lot of gay times together! I see them coming! Mmm, just breathe that air! So fresh, and the moon's so pretty! I'll skip back out—I know where my place is when young folks are having a—serious conversation!

Jim: Oh, don't go out, Mrs. Wingfield. The fact of the matter is I've got to be going.

Amanda: Going, now? You're joking! Why, it's only the shank of the evening, Mr. O'Connor!

Jim: Well, you know how it is.

Amanda: You mean you're a young workingman and have to keep workingmen's hours. We'll let you off early tonight. But only on the condition that next time you stay later. What's the best night for you? Isn't Saturday night the best night for you workingmen?

Jim: I have a couple of time-clocks to punch, Mrs. Wingfield. One at morning, another one at night!

Amanda: My, but you *are* ambitious! You work at night, too?

Jim: No, Ma'am, not work but—Betty! (*He crosses deliberately to pick up his hat. The band at the Paradise Dance Hall goes into a tender waltz.*)

Amanda: Betty? Betty? Who's—Betty? (*There is an ominous cracking sound in the sky.*)

Jim: Oh, just a girl. The girl I go steady with! (*He smiles charmingly. The sky falls.*)

(**Legend:** "The Sky Falls.")

Amanda (a long-drawn exhalation): Ohhhh . . . Is it a serious romance, Mr. O'Connor?

Jim: We're going to be married the second Sunday in June.

Amanda: Ohhhh—how nice! Tom didn't mention that you were engaged to be married.

Jim: The cat's not out of the bag at the warehouse yet. You know how they are. They call you Romeo and stuff like that. (*He stops at the oval mirror to put on his hat. He carefully shapes the brim and the crown to give a discreetly dashing effect.*) It's been a wonderful evening, Mrs. Wingfield. I guess this is what they mean by Southern hospitality.

Amanda: It really wasn't anything at all.

Jim: I hope it don't seem like I'm rushing off. But I promised Betty I'd pick her up at the Wabash depot, an' by the time I get my jalopy down there her train'll be in. Some women are pretty upset if you keep 'em waiting.

Amanda: Yes, I know—The tyranny of women! (*Extends her hand.*) Goodbye, Mr. O'Connor. I wish you luck—and happiness—and success! All three of them, and so does Laura!—Don't you, Laura?

Laura: Yes!

Jim (taking her hand): Goodbye, Laura. I'm certainly going to treasure that souvenir. And don't you forget the good advice I gave you. (*Raises his voice to a cheery shout.*) So long, Shakespeare! Thanks again, ladies—Good night!

He grins and ducks jauntily out.

Still bravely grimacing, Amanda closes the door on the gentleman caller. Then she turns back to the room with a puzzled expression. She and Laura don't dare to face each other. Laura crouches beside the victrola to wind it.

Amanda (faintly): Things have a way of turning out so badly. I don't believe that I would play the victrola. Well, well—well—Our gentleman caller was engaged to be married! (*She raises her voice.*) Tom!

Tom (from back): Yes, Mother?

Amanda: Come in here a minute. I want to tell you something awfully funny.

Tom (enters with macaroon and a glass of the lemonade): Has the gentleman caller gotten away already?

Amanda: The gentleman caller has made an early departure. What a wonderful joke you played on us!

Tom: How do you mean?

Amanda: You didn't mention that he was engaged to be married.

Tom: Jim? Engaged?

Amanda: That's what he just informed us.

Tom: I'll be jiggered! I didn't know about that.

Amanda: That seems very peculiar.

Tom: What's peculiar about it?

Amanda: Didn't you call him your best friend down at the warehouse?

Tom: He is, but how did I know?

Amanda: It seems extremely peculiar that you wouldn't know your best friend was going to be married!

Tom: The warehouse is where I work, not where I know things about people!

Amanda: You don't know things anywhere! You live in a dream; you manufacture illusions! (*He crosses to door.*) Where are you going?

Tom: I'm going to the movies.

Amanda: That's right, now that you've had us make such fools of ourselves. The effort, the preparations, all the expense! The new floor lamp, the rug, the clothes for Laura! All for what? To entertain some other girl's fiancé! Go to the movies, go! Don't think about us, a mother deserted, an unmarried sister who's crippled and has no job! Don't let anything interfere with your selfish pleasure! Just go, go, go—to the movies!

Tom: All right, I will! The more you shout about my selfishness to me the quicker I'll go, and I won't go to the movies!

Amanda: Go, then! Then go to the moon—you selfish dreamer!

> *Tom smashes his glass on the floor. He plunges out on the fire-escape, slamming the door. Laura screams—cut by door.*
>
> *Dance-hall music up. Tom goes to the rail and grips it desperately, lifting his face in the chill white moonlight penetrating the narrow abyss of the alley.*

(Legend On Screen: "And So Good-bye . . .")

> *Tom's closing speech is timed with the interior pantomime. The interior scene is played as though viewed through sound-proof glass. Amanda appears to be making a comforting speech to Laura who is huddled upon the sofa. Now that we cannot hear the mother's speech, her silliness is gone and she has dignity and tragic beauty. Laura's dark hair hides her face until at the end of the speech she lifts it to smile at her mother. Amanda's gestures are slow and graceful, almost dancelike, as she comforts the daughter. At the end of her speech she glances a moment at the father's picture—then withdraws through the portieres. At close of Tom's speech, Laura blows out the candles, ending the play.*

Tom: I didn't go to the moon, I went much further—for time is the longest distance between two places—Not long after that I was fired for writing a poem on the lid of a shoe-box. I left Saint Louis. I descended the steps of this fire-escape for a last time and followed, from then on, in my father's footsteps, attempting to find in motion what was lost in space. I traveled around a great deal. The cities swept about me like dead leaves, leaves that were brightly colored but torn away from the branches. I would have stopped, but I was pursued by something. It always came upon me unawares, taking me altogether by surprise. Perhaps it was a familiar bit of music. Perhaps it was only a piece of transparent glass. Perhaps I am walking along a street at night, in some strange city, before I have found companions. I pass the lighted window of a shop where perfume is sold. The window is filled with pieces of colored glass, tiny transparent bottles in delicate colors, like bits of a shattered rainbow. Then all at once my sister touches my shoulder. I turn around and look into her eyes. . . . Oh, Laura, Laura, I tried to leave you behind me, but I am more faithful than I intended to be! I reach for a cigarette, I cross the street, I run into the movies or a bar, I buy a drink, I speak to the nearest stranger—anything that can blow your candles out!

Laura bends over the candles.

For nowadays the world is lit by lightning! Blow out your candles, Laura—and so good-bye. . . .

She blows the candles out.

Questions

1. How do Amanda's dreams for her daughter contrast with the realities of the Wingfields' day-to-day existence?
2. What suggestions do you find in Laura's glass menagerie? In the glass unicorn?
3. In the cast of characters, Jim O'Connor is listed as "a nice, ordinary, young man." Why does his coming to dinner have such earthshaking implications for Amanda? For Laura?
4. Try to describe Jim's feelings toward Laura during their long conversation in Scene VII. After he kisses her, how do his feelings seem to change?
5. Near the end of the play, Amanda tells Tom, "You live in a dream; you manufacture illusions!" What is ironic about her speech? Is there any truth in it?
6. Who is the main character in *The Glass Menagerie*? Tom? Laura? Amanda? (It may be helpful to review the definition of a protagonist.)
7. Has Tom, at the conclusion of the play, successfully made his escape from home? Does he appear to have fulfilled his dream?
8. How effective is the device of accompanying the action by projecting slides on a screen, bearing titles and images? Do you think most producers of the play are wise to leave it out?

Terrence McNally

Terrence McNally was born in St. Petersburg, Florida, in 1939, but he was raised mostly in Corpus Christi, Texas, where his Irish-Catholic father worked as a beer distributor. After attending Columbia University, McNally worked as a theatrical stage manager, magazine editor, and film critic while writing his first plays. A versatile dramatist, he has written plays, musicals and screenplays. His screwball comedy The Ritz *(1973) became a popular 1976 film, which McNally himself adapted for the screen. He also rewrote his romantic drama* Frankie and Johnny in the Claire de Lune *(1987) for Gary Marshall's film* Frankie and Johnny *(1991), starring Al Pacino and Michelle Pfeiffer. Other notable McNally plays include* The Lisbon Traviata *(1985),* Lips Together, Teeth Apart *(1991), and*

Terrence McNally

A Perfect Ganesh (1993). In 1995 his play about the opera singer Maria Callas, Master Class, became an international success. McNally has written extensively for musical theater, authoring the books for the Broadway productions of Kiss of the Spider Woman (1992), Ragtime (1997), and The Full Monty (2000). He also wrote the libretto for Jake Heggie's opera Dead Man Walking (2000), based on the book by Sister Helen Prejean. McNally's television version of Andre's Mother won an Emmy in 1990, but the original stage version—written as one brief, memorable scene—needs no video backup to communicate its troubling message of heartache and loss.

Andre's Mother   1988

1990 PBS TV production of Andre's Mother: **left to right, Haviland Morris, Richard Thomas, Richard Venture.**

CHARACTERS

Cal, a young man
Arthur, his father
Penny, his sister
Andre's Mother

TIME. *Now*

PLACE. *New York City, Central Park*

Four people—Cal, Arthur, Penny, and Andre's Mother—enter. They are nicely dressed and each carries a white helium-filled balloon on a string.

Cal: You know what's really terrible? I can't think of anything terrific to say. Goodbye. I love you. I'll miss you. And I'm supposed to be so great with words!
Penny: What's that over there?

Arthur: Ask your brother.
Cal: It's a theater. An outdoor theater. They do plays there in the summer. Shakespeare's plays. (*To Andre's Mother.*) God, how much he wanted to play Hamlet again. He would have gone to Timbuktu to have another go at that part. The summer he did it in Boston, he was so happy!
Penny: Cal, I don't think she . . . ! It's not the time. Later.
Arthur: Your son was a . . . the Jews have a word for it . . .
Penny (quietly appalled): Oh my God!
Arthur: Mensch, I believe it is, and I think I'm using it right. It means warm, solid, the real thing. Correct me if I'm wrong.
Penny: Fine, Dad, fine. Just quit while you're ahead.
Arthur: I won't say he was like a son to me. Even my son isn't always like a son to me. I mean . . . ! In my clumsy way, I'm trying to say how much I liked Andre. And how much he helped me to know my own boy. Cal was always two handsful but Andre and I could talk about anything under the sun. My wife was very fond of him, too.
Penny: Cal, I don't understand about the balloons.
Cal: They represent the soul. When you let go, it means you're letting his soul ascend to Heaven. That you're willing to let go. Breaking the last earthly ties.
Penny: Does the Pope know about this?
Arthur: Penny!
Penny: Andre loved my sense of humor. Listen, you can hear him laughing. (*She lets go of her white balloon.*) So long, you glorious, wonderful, I-know-what-Cal-means-about-words . . . man! God forgive me for wishing you were straight every time I laid eyes on you. But if any man was going to have you, I'm glad it was my brother! Look how fast it went up. I bet that means something. Something terrific.
Arthur (lets his balloon go): Goodbye. God speed.
Penny: Cal?
Cal: I'm not ready yet.
Penny: Okay. We'll be over there. Come on, Pop, you can buy your little girl a Good Humor.
Arthur: They still make Good Humor?
Penny: Only now they're called Dove Bars and they cost twelve dollars.

(*Penny takes Arthur off. Cal and Andre's Mother stand with their balloons.*)

Cal: I wish I knew what you were thinking. I think it would help me. You know almost nothing about me and I only know what Andre told me about you. I'd always had it in my mind that one day we would be friends, you and me. But if you didn't know about Andre and me . . . If this hadn't happened, I wonder if he would have ever told you. When he was sick, if I asked him once I asked him a thousand times, tell her. She's your mother. She won't mind. But he was so afraid of hurting you and of your disapproval. I don't know which was worse. (*No response. He sighs.*) God, how many of us live in this city because we don't want to hurt our mothers and live in mortal terror of their disapproval. We lose ourselves here. Our lives aren't furtive, just our feelings toward people like you are! A city of fugitives from our parents' scorn or heartbreak. Sometimes he'd seem a little down and I'd say, "What's the matter, babe?" and this funny sweet, sad smile would cross his face and he'd say, "Just a little homesick, Cal, just a little bit." I always accused him of being a country boy just playing at being a hotshot, sophisticated New Yorker. (*He sighs.*)

It's bullshit. It's all bullshit. (*Still no response.*)

Do you remember the comic strip *Little Lulu*? Her mother had no name, she was so remote, so formidable to all the children. She was just Lulu's mother. "Hello, Lulu's Mother," Lulu's friends would say. She was almost anonymous in her remoteness. You remind me of her. Andre's mother. Let me answer the questions you can't ask and then I'll leave you alone and you won't ever have to see me again. Andre died of AIDS. I don't know how he got it. I tested negative. He died bravely. You would have been proud of him. The only thing that frightened him was you. I'll have everything that was his sent to you. I'll pay for it. There isn't much. You should have come up the summer he played Hamlet. He was magnificent. Yes, I'm bitter. I'm bitter I've lost him. I'm bitter what's happening. I'm bitter even now, after all this, I can't reach you. I'm beginning to feel your disapproval and it's making me ill. (*He looks at his balloon.*) Sorry, old friend. I blew it. (*He lets go of the balloon.*)

Good night, sweet prince, and flights of angels sing thee to thy rest! (*Beat.*) Goodbye, Andre's mother.

(*He goes. Andre's Mother stands alone holding her white balloon. Her lips tremble. She looks on the verge of breaking down. She is about to let go of the balloon when she pulls it down to her. She looks at it awhile before she gently kisses it. She lets go of the balloon. She follows it with her eyes as it rises and rises. The lights are beginning to fade. Andre's Mother's eyes are still on the balloon. The lights fade.*)

Questions

1. What relation does Andre's mother have to the other characters in the play? Is she marginal to their actions or does she influence them?
2. Andre's mother, the title character of this piece, never says a word in the course of the play. What thoughts and emotions do you think she experiences in the final scene? Give reasons for your opinions.
3. Is the balloon a symbol in *Andre's Mother*? If so, what does it represent?

Suggestions for Writing on *Drama about Life Passages*

1. At the end of *The Glass Menagerie*, Laura's unicorn is knocked off the table and loses its horn. "Now it is just like all the other horses," she comments. Analyze this moment in the play and discuss how it suggests changes in Laura's life.
2. Create a final speech for Andre's mother. Write 500 words for her character to speak alone on the stage about her reactions to Andre's death. Alternative version: have her speak to Andre's spirit, as if he could hear her.
3. Both *The Glass Menagerie* and *Andre's Mother* present a mother as a central figure in the drama. Compare Tom's mother in Williams's play with Andre's mother in McNally's drama. Are the two women similar in any meaningful ways? Or are they utterly different?

Suggestions for Writing on *Literature about Life's Journey*

1. In many of the works in this chapter, the journey from childhood to adulthood is presented as a journey into knowledge. But is something lost when we grow up, some sense of hopefulness or wonder? Choose a story, poem, essay, or play that depicts childhood innocence in a positive light and analyze its implications. What is lost when the protagonist or speaker gains a greater understanding of the world?

2. Take any two works that describe a coming-of-age moment when a young person takes an important step toward maturity, and compare and contrast the two episodes.

3. Several works in this chapter (Joyce's "Araby," Oates's "Where Are You Going, Where Have You Been?," Cofer's "Quinceañera," and others) depict moments of heightened understanding regarding sexuality or romance. How is the journey from innocence into experience different for males and females? Pick at least one work by a man, and one by a woman, and write about the differences or similarities.

4. Choose a story, play, or essay in this chapter—for example, Flannery O'Connor's "A Good Man Is Hard to Find," ZZ Packer's "Brownies," Franz Kafka's *The Metamorphosis*, Tennessee Williams's *The Glass Menagerie*, or James Baldwin's "Notes of a Native Son." How would you describe the journey that is undertaken by the protagonist? What lesson does he or she draw from the events of the piece? How does he or she change as a result of these events? How would you describe the protagonist's state of mind at the end of the piece?

5. Reread the poems in this chapter that deal with the subject of death. Are there particular images that appear repeatedly? Why are these images associated with death? Now reread some of the poems in Chapter 13, "Love." How would you describe the imagery used in poems about love? How does the imagery in poems about love differ from the imagery in poems about death? Pick at least two poems from each chapter and compare.

6. Many selections in this chapter deal with the challenges of accepting death. Considering Elisabeth Kübler-Ross's ideas about "accepting" death, discuss how the authors have or have not come into a sensible acceptance of death. (Possible selections include Dylan Thomas's "Do not go gentle into that good night," Sylvia Plath's "Lady Lazarus," John Donne's "Death be not proud," James Baldwin's "Notes of a Native Son," and Terrence McNally's *Andre's Mother*.)

7. If you have lost someone close to you—a family member, a good friend—do any of the works on death in this chapter speak to you particularly? Are there any that closely reflect your own feelings, or help you understand your loved one's death in a different light? Write an essay describing that work (or works) and how it has helped you make sense of your own loss.

15 THE INDIVIDUAL AND SOCIETY

Not all those who wander are lost.

—J.R.R. TOLKIEN

Think of a group that you're part of, or that you want to be part of. It might be a sports team, a science club, a sorority, a branch of the military, a college, or a profession. Now think of the rules, rites, or common values of that group. What is expected of you? How do you demonstrate membership? Did you have to perform some act or meet some requirement to gain entry to the group or to prove your allegiance?

There are many ways in which individuals earn or show their membership in groups. If you play on a basketball team, you might have a letter jacket. If you want to join a sorority, you're expected to go through rush week. Fans of a particular kind of music might wear certain clothes, have particular hairstyles, or get special tattoos. People who like the same activity might join a related Facebook group. But have you ever had to do something you wouldn't do on your own in order to fit in with a group? Or maybe you've avoided joining groups altogether, either to keep yourself from having to face such a choice, or because you feel, as Groucho Marx once said, "I don't want to belong to any club that would have me as a member."

Each group—whether as small as a sports team or as large as a nation—has its own norms and expectations. Sometimes those expectations clash with the beliefs or needs of the individuals who comprise it. There are definite benefits to membership in a group or in society; rules and expectations help keep order and create a sense of larger community. But there can also be significant costs, both political and human, when institutions—from social groups to employers to governments—infringe on individuals' rights or dignity.

Poets, playwrights, and other writers are uniquely positioned to explore the relationship between the individual and society. While disciplines such as sociology and economics can define the "what" of human issues, literature explores the "how" and the "why." Literature uncovers the nuances, the difficult choices, the exact and particularly human struggles that motivate social change. It can illuminate what it means to be inside a group, or more often, outside it. It can explore what happens when groups clash. Perhaps most important, literature shows how individuals who seem different from one another on the surface often have much in common.

THE SELECTIONS IN THIS CHAPTER

The works in this chapter represent a variety of approaches to the notion of the individual in society. Some, such as Shirley Jackson's "The Lottery" and Kurt Vonnegut Jr.'s "Harrison Bergeron," explore what happens when people conform too easily to social or political norms—or when they refuse to conform. Others, such as Martin Luther King's "Letter from Birmingham Jail" and Paul Laurence Dunbar's "Sympathy," examine how race, language, and culture affect an individual's relationship with society. Sophocles's *Antigonê* directly confronts the tensions that arise when the institutions that people establish to maintain order require individuals to act against their beliefs. Walt Whitman's "I Hear America Singing" and Mary Oliver's "Wild Geese" both celebrate the strength of the human spirit. Anne Sexton's "Her Kind" engages the question of gender roles and expectations. Allen Ginsberg's "A Supermarket in California" and W. H. Auden's "The Unknown Citizen" address the broad theme of loneliness and examine how individuals seek connection and meaning.

As you read these selections, we hope that you'll recognize some of the issues and struggles they explore as things you've encountered in your own life. We hope that in engaging these questions of how people balance social expectation with individual expression or how factors such as gender, race, class, and religion influence our beliefs and choices, you'll take a close look at your own behaviors and beliefs about what it means to be part of a group—or to stand outside it. And you might begin to think more deeply about the question that the best literature poses to us—How should we live our lives?

Things to Think About

1. What is your definition of society? Do you interact with more than one kind of society?
2. Is there one overarching society in America (or in the country you're most familiar with), or are there many overlapping groups? How would you define your society? What are its norms and expectations? Which of them do you see as necessary and positive? Which do you see as negative or limiting?
3. It is sometimes said that there is no lonelier place to be than in the middle of a crowd. What does this mean? Do you agree?
4. Should an individual obey an unjust law? Should individuals be guided absolutely by one set of beliefs?
5. When the interests of the individual and the norms of society conflict, how should that conflict be addressed and resolved?

FICTION

CONFORMITY, REBELLION, AND DISSENT

Shirley Jackson	*The Lottery*
Kurt Vonnegut Jr.	*Harrison Bergeron*
Ursula K. Le Guin	*The Ones Who Walk Away from Omelas*

All societies have customs and rituals that their citizens take for granted. In America, for example, we celebrate the Fourth of July, Halloween, and Thanksgiving. Such customs provide structure, bolster a sense of collective identity, and help reinforce the society's culture or beliefs. But what happens when those customs are no longer useful? (Some people have questioned, for example, whether children should dress up as ghosts and monsters on Halloween; others believe that Thanksgiving celebrations gloss over a heritage of the mistreatment of Native Americans.) What if things that were once deemed acceptable begin to seem unjust or outdated? Segregation in the American South, for example, was once the norm, as are present-day strictures against girls going to school in Afghanistan and limits to free expression in China. If you, as an individual, see something in the world that strikes you as unjust, what should you do? Should you conform to prevailing opinions—or should you challenge them? If you speak out, you could face the very real consequences of rejection or, in some settings, even imprisonment. But if you don't stand up against something unjust, that lack of action could have costs, too—including the loss of your own sense of integrity.

The stories in this section all depict characters who are dealing with choices between conformity and rebellion. Although the characters wrestle with these choices in different ways, they all demonstrate the risk of standing up to accepted ways of thinking—and the possibly greater risks of doing nothing. Shirley Jackson's chilling story "The Lottery" presents a town in which a lethal annual ritual continues without protest. Kurt Vonnegut's hilarious satire "Harrison Bergeron" depicts a future in which the urge for equality has gotten out of hand. Finally, Ursula K. Le Guin's fantasy tale "The Ones Who Walk Away from Omelas" suggests that a "perfect" society may come at an unacceptable cost.

Shirley Jackson

Shirley Jackson (1919–1965), a native of San Francisco, moved in her teens to Rochester, New York. She started college at the University of Rochester but had to drop out, stricken by severe depression, a problem that was to recur at intervals throughout her life. Later she graduated from Syracuse University. With her husband, Stanley Edgar Hyman, a literary critic, she settled in Bennington, Vermont, in a sprawling house built in the nineteenth century. There Jackson conscientiously set herself to produce a fixed number of words each day. She wrote conventional novels—
The Road Through the Wall *(1948)—and three*

Shirley Jackson

psychological thrillers—Hangsaman *(1951)*, The Haunting of Hill House *(1959)*, *and* We Have Always Lived in the Castle *(1962). She wrote light, witty articles for* Good Housekeeping *and other popular magazines about the horrors of housekeeping and rearing four children, collected in* Life Among the Savages *(1953) and* Raising Demons *(1957), but she claimed to have written them only for money. When "The Lottery" appeared in the* New Yorker *in 1948, that issue of the magazine quickly sold out. Her purpose in writing the story, Jackson declared, had been "to shock the story's readers with a graphic demonstration of the pointless violence and general inhumanity in their own lives."*

The Lottery 1948

The morning of June 27th was clear and sunny, with the fresh warmth of a full-summer day; the flowers were blossoming profusely and the grass was richly green. The people of the village began to gather in the square, between the post office and the bank, around ten o'clock; in some towns there were so many people that the lottery took two days and had to be started on June 26th, but in this village, where there were only about three hundred people, the whole lottery took less than two hours, so it could begin at ten o'clock in the morning and still be through in time to allow the villagers to get home for noon dinner.

The children assembled first, of course. School was recently over for the summer, and the feeling of liberty sat uneasily on most of them; they tended to gather together quietly for a while before they broke into boisterous play, and their talk was still of the classroom and the teacher, of books and reprimands. Bobby Martin had already stuffed his pockets full of stones, and the other boys soon followed his example, selecting the smoothest and roundest stones; Bobby and Harry Jones and Dickie Delacroix—the villagers pronounced this name "Dellacroy"—eventually made a great pile of stones in one corner of the square and guarded it against the raids of the other boys. The girls stood aside, talking among themselves, looking over their shoulders at the boys, and the very small children rolled in the dust or clung to the hands of their older brothers or sisters.

Soon the men began to gather, surveying their own children, speaking of planting and rain, tractors and taxes. They stood together, away from the pile of stones in the corner, and their jokes were quiet and they smiled rather than laughed. The women, wearing faded house dresses and sweaters, came shortly after their menfolk. They greeted one another and exchanged bits of gossip as they went to join their husbands. Soon the women, standing by their husbands, began to call to their children, and the children came reluctantly, having to be called four or five times. Bobby Martin ducked under his mother's grasping hand and ran, laughing, back to the pile of stones. His father spoke up sharply, and Bobby came quickly and took his place between his father and his oldest brother.

The lottery was conducted—as were the square dances, the teenage club, the Halloween program—by Mr. Summers, who had time and energy to devote to civic activities. He was a roundfaced, jovial man and he ran the coal business, and people were sorry for him, because he had no children and his wife was a scold. When he arrived in the square, carrying the black wooden box, there was a murmur of conversation among the villagers and he waved and called, "Little late today, folks." The postmaster, Mr. Graves, followed him, carrying a three-legged stool, and the stool was put in the center of the square and Mr. Summers set the black box down on it.

The villagers kept their distance, leaving a space between themselves and the stool, and when Mr. Summers said, "Some of you fellows want to give me a hand?" there was a hesitation before two men, Mr. Martin and his oldest son, Baxter, came forward to hold the box steady on the stool while Mr. Summers stirred up the papers inside it.

The original paraphernalia for the lottery had been lost long ago, and the black box now resting on the stool had been put into use even before Old Man Warner, the oldest man in town, was born. Mr. Summers spoke frequently to the villagers about making a new box, but no one liked to upset even as much tradition as was represented by the black box. There was a story that the present box had been made with some pieces of the box that had preceded it, the one that had been constructed when the first people settled down to make a village here. Every year, after the lottery, Mr. Summers began talking again about a new box, but every year the subject was allowed to fade off without anything's being done. The black box grew shabbier each year; by now it was no longer completely black but splintered badly along one side to show the original wood color, and in some places faded or stained.

Mr. Martin and his oldest son, Baxter, held the black box securely on the stool until Mr. Summers had stirred the papers thoroughly with his hand. Because so much of the ritual had been forgotten or discarded, Mr. Summers had been successful in having slips of paper substituted for the chips of wood that had been used for generations. Chips of wood, Mr. Summers had argued, had been all very well when the village was tiny, but now that the population was more than three hundred and likely to keep on growing, it was necessary to use something that would fit more easily into the black box. The night before the lottery, Mr. Summers and Mr. Graves made up the slips of paper and put them in the box, and it was then taken to the safe of Mr. Summers's coal company and locked up until Mr. Summers was ready to take it to the square next morning. The rest of the year, the box was put away, sometimes one place, sometimes another; it had spent one year in Mr. Graves's barn and another year underfoot in the post office, and sometimes it was set on a shelf in the Martin grocery and left there.

There was a great deal of fussing to be done before Mr. Summers declared the lottery open. There were lists to make up—of heads of families, heads of households in each family, members of each household in each family. There was the proper swearing-in of Mr. Summers by the postmaster, as the official of the lottery; at one time, some people remembered, there had been a recital of some sort, performed by the official of the lottery, a perfunctory, tuneless chant that had been rattled off duly each year; some people believed that the official of the lottery used to stand just so when he said or sang it, others believed that he was supposed to walk among the people, but years and years ago this part of the ritual had been allowed to lapse. There had been, also, a ritual salute, which the official of the lottery had had to use in addressing each person who came up to draw from the box, but this also had changed with time, until now it was felt necessary only for the official to speak to each person approaching. Mr. Summers was very good at all this; in his clean white shirt and blue jeans, with one hand resting carelessly on the black box, he seemed very proper and important as he talked interminably to Mr. Graves and the Martins.

Just as Mr. Summers finally left off talking and turned to the assembled villagers, Mrs. Hutchinson came hurriedly along the path to the square, her sweater thrown over her shoulders, and slid into place in the back of the crowd. "Clean forgot what day it was," she said to Mrs. Delacroix, who stood next to her, and they both laughed softly. "Thought my old man was out back stacking wood," Mrs. Hutchinson went on, "and then I looked out the window and the kids were gone, and then I remembered it was the twenty-seventh and came a-running." She dried her hands on her apron, and Mrs. Delacroix said, "You're in time, though. They're still talking away up there."

Mrs. Hutchinson craned her neck to see through the crowd and found her husband and children standing near the front. She tapped Mrs. Delacroix on the arm as a farewell and began to make her way through the crowd. The people separated good-humoredly to let her through; two or three people said, in voices just loud enough to be heard across the crowd, "Here comes your Missus, Hutchinson," and "Bill, she made it after all." Mrs. Hutchinson reached her husband, and Mr. Summers, who had been waiting, said cheerfully, "Thought we were going to have to get on without you, Tessie." Mrs. Hutchinson said, grinning, "Wouldn't have me leave m'dishes in the sink, now would you, Joe?" and soft laughter ran through the crowd as the people stirred back into position after Mrs. Hutchinson's arrival.

"Well, now," Mr. Summers said soberly, "guess we better get started, get this over with, so's we can go back to work. Anybody ain't here?"

"Dunbar," several people said. "Dunbar, Dunbar."

Mr. Summers consulted his list. "Clyde Dunbar," he said. "That's right. He's broke his leg, hasn't he? Who's drawing for him?"

"Me, I guess," a woman said, and Mr. Summers turned to look at her. "Wife draws for her husband," Mr. Summers said. "Don't you have a grown boy to do it for you, Janey?" Although Mr. Summers and everyone else in the village knew the answer perfectly well, it was the business of the official of the lottery to ask such questions formally. Mr. Summers waited with an expression of polite interest while Mrs. Dunbar answered.

"Horace's not but sixteen yet," Mrs. Dunbar said regretfully. "Guess I gotta fill in for the old man this year."

"Right," Mr. Summers said. He made a note on the list he was holding. Then he asked, "Watson boy drawing this year?"

A tall boy in the crowd raised his hand. "Here," he said. "I'm drawing for m'mother and me." He blinked his eyes nervously and ducked his head as several voices in the crowd said things like "Good fellow, Jack," and "Glad to see your mother's got a man to do it."

"Well," Mr. Summers said, "guess that's everyone. Old Man Warner make it?"

"Here," a voice said, and Mr. Summers nodded.

A sudden hush fell on the crowd as Mr. Summers cleared his throat and looked at the list. "All ready?" he called. "Now, I'll read the names—heads of families first—and the men come up and take a paper out of the box. Keep the paper folded in your hand without looking at it until everyone has had a turn. Everything clear?"

The people had done it so many times that they only half listened to the directions; most of them were quiet, wetting their lips, not looking around. Then Mr. Summers raised one hand high and said, "Adams." A man disengaged himself from the crowd and came forward. "Hi, Steve," Mr. Summers said, and Mr. Adams said, "Hi, Joe." They grinned at one another humorlessly and nervously. Then Mr. Adams reached into the black box and took out a folded paper. He held it firmly by one corner as he turned and went hastily back to his place in the crowd, where he stood a little apart from his family, not looking down at his hand.

"Allen," Mr. Summers said. "Anderson. . . . Bentham."

"Seems like there's no time at all between lotteries any more," Mrs. Delacroix said to Mrs. Graves in the back row. "Seems like we got through with the last one only last week."

"Time sure goes fast," Mrs. Graves said.

"Clark. . . . Delacroix."

"There goes my old man," Mrs. Delacroix said. She held her breath while her husband went forward.

"Dunbar," Mr. Summers said, and Mrs. Dunbar went steadily to the box while one of the women said, "Go on, Janey," and another said, "There she goes."

"We're next," Mrs. Graves said. She watched while Mr. Graves came around from the side of the box, greeted Mr. Summers gravely, and selected a slip of paper from the box. By now, all through the crowd there were men holding the small folded papers in their large hands, turning them over and over nervously. Mrs. Dunbar and her two sons stood together, Mrs. Dunbar holding the slip of paper.

"Harburt. . . . Hutchinson."

"Get up there, Bill," Mrs. Hutchinson said, and the people near her laughed.

"Jones."

"They do say," Mr. Adams said to Old Man Warner, who stood next to him, "that over in the north village they're talking of giving up the lottery."

Old Man Warner snorted. "Pack of crazy fools," he said. "Listening to the young folks, nothing's good enough for *them*. Next thing you know, they'll be wanting to go back to living in caves, nobody work any more, live *that* way for a while. Used to be a saying about 'Lottery in June, corn be heavy soon.' First thing you know, we'd all be eating stewed chickweed and acorns. There's *always* been a lottery," he added petulantly. "Bad enough to see young Joe Summers up there joking with everybody."

"Some places have already quit lotteries," Mrs. Adams said.

"Nothing but trouble in *that*," Old Man Warner said stoutly. "Pack of young fools."

"Martin." And Bobby Martin watched his father go forward. "Overdyke. . . . Percy."

"I wish they'd hurry," Mrs. Dunbar said to her older son. "I wish they'd hurry."

"They're almost through," her son said.

"You get ready to run tell Dad," Mrs. Dunbar said.

Mr. Summers called his own name and then stepped forward precisely and selected a slip from the box. Then he called, "Warner."

"Seventy-seventh year I been in the lottery," Old Man Warner said as he went through the crowd. "Seventy-seventh time."

"Watson." The tall boy came awkwardly through the crowd. Someone said, "Don't be nervous, Jack," and Mr. Summers said, "Take your time, son."

"Zanini."

After that, there was a long pause, a breathless pause, until Mr. Summers, holding his slip of paper in the air, said, "All right, fellows." For a minute, no one moved, and then all the slips of paper were opened. Suddenly, all the women began to speak at once, saying, "Who is it?" "Who's got it?" "Is it the Dunbars?" "Is it the Watsons?" Then the voices began to say, "It's Hutchinson. It's Bill." "Bill Hutchinson's got it."

"Go tell your father," Mrs. Dunbar said to her older son.

People began to look around to see the Hutchinsons. Bill Hutchinson was standing quiet, staring down at the paper in his hand. Suddenly, Tessie Hutchinson shouted to Mr. Summers, "You didn't give him time enough to take any paper he wanted. I saw you. It wasn't fair!"

"Be a good sport, Tessie," Mrs. Delacroix called, and Mrs. Graves said, "All of us took the same chance."

"Shut up, Tessie," Bill Hutchinson said.

"Well, everyone," Mr. Summers said, "that was done pretty fast, and now we've got to be hurrying a little more to get done in time." He consulted his next list. "Bill," he said, "you draw for the Hutchinson family. You got any other households in the Hutchinsons?"

"There's Don and Eva," Mrs. Hutchinson yelled. "Make them take their chance!"

"Daughters draw with their husbands' families, Tessie," Mr. Summers said gently. "You know that as well as anyone else."

"It wasn't fair," Tessie said.

"I guess not, Joe," Bill Hutchinson said regretfully. "My daughter draws with her husband's family, that's only fair. And I've got no other family except the kids."

"Then, as far as drawing for families is concerned, it's you," Mr. Summers said in explanation, "and as far as drawing for households is concerned, that's you, too. Right?"

"Right," Bill Hutchinson said.

"How many kids, Bill?" Mr. Summers asked formally.

"Three," Bill Hutchinson said. "There's Bill, Jr., and Nancy, and little Dave. And Tessie and me."

"All right, then," Mr. Summers said. "Harry, you got their tickets back?"

Mr. Graves nodded and held up the slips of paper. "Put them in the box, then," Mr. Summers directed. "Take Bill's and put it in."

"I think we ought to start over," Mrs. Hutchinson said, as quietly as she could. "I tell you it wasn't *fair*. You didn't give him time enough to choose. *Every*body saw that."

Mr. Graves had selected the five slips and put them in the box, and he dropped all the papers but those onto the ground, where the breeze caught them and lifted them off.

"Listen, everybody," Mrs. Hutchinson was saying to the people around her.

"Ready, Bill?" Mr. Summers asked, and Bill Hutchinson, with one quick glance around at his wife and children, nodded.

"Remember," Mr. Summers said, "take the slips and keep them folded until each person has taken one. Harry, you help little Dave." Mr. Graves took the hand of the little boy, who came willingly with him up to the box. "Take a paper out of the box, Davy," Mr. Summers said. Davy put his hand into the box and laughed. "Take just *one* paper," Mr. Summers said. "Harry, you hold it for him." Mr. Graves took the child's hand and removed the folded paper from the tight fist and held it while little Dave stood next to him and looked up at him wonderingly.

"Nancy next," Mr. Summers said. Nancy was twelve, and her school friends breathed heavily as she went forward, switching her skirt, and took a slip daintily from the box. "Bill, Jr.," Mr. Summers said, and Billy, his face red and his feet over-large, nearly knocked the box over as he got a paper out. "Tessie," Mr. Summers said. She hesitated for a minute, looking around defiantly, and then set her lips and went up to the box. She snatched a paper out and held it behind her.

"Bill," Mr. Summers said, and Bill Hutchinson reached into the box and felt around, bringing his hand out at last with the slip of paper in it.

The crowd was quiet. A girl whispered, "I hope it's not Nancy," and the sound of the whisper reached the edges of the crowd.

"It's not the way it used to be," Old Man Warner said clearly. "People ain't the way they used to be."

"All right," Mr. Summers said. "Open the papers. Harry, you open little Dave's."

Mr. Graves opened the slip of paper and there was a general sigh through the crowd as he held it up and everyone could see that it was blank. Nancy and Bill, Jr., opened theirs at the same time, and both beamed and laughed, turning around to the crowd and holding their slips of paper above their heads.

"Tessie," Mr. Summers said. There was a pause, and then Mr. Summers looked at Bill Hutchinson, and Bill unfolded his paper and showed it. It was blank.

"It's Tessie," Mr. Summers said, and his voice was hushed. "Show us her paper, Bill."

Bill Hutchinson went over to his wife and forced the slip of paper out of her hand. It had a black spot on it, the black spot Mr. Summers had made the night before with the heavy pencil in the coal-company office. Bill Hutchinson held it up, and there was a stir in the crowd.

"All right, folks," Mr. Summers said, "Let's finish quickly."

Although the villagers had forgotten the ritual and lost the original black box, they still remembered to use stones. The pile of stones the boys had made earlier was ready; there were stones on the ground with the blowing scraps of paper that had come out of the box. Mrs. Delacroix selected a stone so large she had to pick it up with both hands and turned to Mrs. Dunbar. "Come on," she said. "Hurry up."

Mrs. Dunbar had small stones in both hands, and she said, gasping for breath, "I can't run at all. You'll have to go ahead and I'll catch up with you."

The children had stones already, and someone gave little Davy Hutchinson a few pebbles.

Tessie Hutchinson was in the center of a cleared space by now, and she held her hands out desperately as the villagers moved in on her. "It isn't fair," she said. A stone hit her on the side of the head.

Old Man Warner was saying, "Come on, come on, everyone." Steve Adams was in the front of the crowd of villagers, with Mrs. Graves beside him.

"It isn't fair, it isn't right," Mrs. Hutchinson screamed, and then they were upon her.

Questions

1. Where do you think "The Lottery" takes place? What purpose do you suppose the writer has in making this setting appear so familiar and ordinary?
2. What details in paragraphs 2 and 3 foreshadow the ending of the story?
3. Take a close look at Jackson's description of the black wooden box (paragraph 5) and of the black spot on the fatal slip of paper (paragraph 72). What do these objects suggest to you? Are there any other symbols in the story?

4. What do you understand to be the writer's own attitude toward the lottery and the stoning? Exactly what in the story makes her attitude clear to us?
5. What do you make of Old Man Warner's saying, "Lottery in June, corn be heavy soon" (paragraph 32)?
6. What do you think Shirley Jackson is driving at? Consider each of the following interpretations and, looking at the story, see if you can find any evidence for it:

> Jackson takes a primitive fertility rite and playfully transfers it to a small town in North America.
>
> Jackson, writing her story soon after World War II, indirectly expresses her horror at the Holocaust. She assumes that the massacre of the Jews was carried out by unwitting, obedient people, like these villagers.
>
> Jackson is satirizing our own society, in which men are selected for the army by lottery.
>
> Jackson is just writing a memorable story that signifies nothing at all.

7. Could something like the situation in "The Lottery" happen today? Why or why not? Do the events in the story have any relation to any current-day society, either here or abroad?

Kurt Vonnegut Jr.

Kurt Vonnegut Jr. (1922–2007) was born in Indianapolis. During the Depression his father, a well-to-do architect, had virtually no work, and the family lived in reduced circumstances. Vonnegut attended Cornell University, where he majored in chemistry and was managing editor of the daily student newspaper. In 1943 he enlisted in the U.S. Army. During the Battle of the Bulge he was captured by German troops and interned as a prisoner of war in Dresden, where he survived the massive Allied firebombing, which killed tens of thousands of people, mostly civilians. (The firebombing of Dresden became the central incident in Vonnegut's best-selling 1969 novel, Slaughterhouse-Five.) After the war, Vonnegut worked as a reporter and later as a public relations man for General Electric in Schenectady, New York. He quit his job in 1951 to write full-time after publishing several science fiction stories in national magazines. His first novel, Player Piano, appeared in 1952, followed by The Sirens of Titan (1959) and his first best seller, Cat's Cradle (1963)—all now considered classics of literary science fiction. Among his many other books are Mother Night (1961), Jailbird (1979), and a book of biographical essays, A Man Without a Country (2005). His short fiction is collected in Welcome to the Monkey House (1968), Bagombo Snuff Box (1999), and other volumes. Vonnegut is a singular figure in modern American fiction. An ingenious comic writer, he combined the popular genre of science fiction with the literary tradition of dark satire—a combination splendidly realized in "Harrison Bergeron."

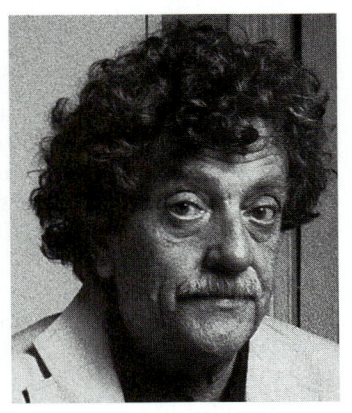

Kurt Vonnegut Jr.

Harrison Bergeron   1961

The year was 2081, and everybody was finally equal. They weren't only equal before God and the law. They were equal every which way. Nobody was smarter than anybody else. Nobody was better looking than anybody else. Nobody was stronger or quicker than anybody else. All this equality was due to the 211th, 212th, and 213th Amendments to the Constitution, and to the unceasing vigilance of agents of the United States Handicapper General.

Some things about living still weren't quite right, though. April, for instance, still drove people crazy by not being springtime. And it was in that clammy month that the H-G men took George and Hazel Bergeron's fourteen-year-old son, Harrison, away.

It was tragic, all right, but George and Hazel couldn't think about it very hard. Hazel had a perfectly average intelligence, which meant she couldn't think about anything except in short bursts. And George, while his intelligence was way above normal, had a little mental handicap radio in his ear. He was required by law to wear it at all times. It was tuned to a government transmitter. Every twenty seconds or so, the transmitter would send out some sharp noise to keep people like George from taking unfair advantage of their brains.

George and Hazel were watching television. There were tears on Hazel's cheeks, but she'd forgotten for the moment what they were about.

On the television screen were ballerinas.

A buzzer sounded in George's head. His thoughts fled in panic, like bandits from a burglar alarm.

"That was a real pretty dance, that dance they just did," said Hazel.

"Huh?" said George.

"That dance—it was nice," said Hazel.

"Yup," said George. He tried to think a little about the ballerinas. They weren't really very good—no better than anybody else would have been, anyway. They were burdened with sash-weights and bags of birdshot, and their faces were masked, so that no one, seeing a free and graceful gesture or a pretty face, would feel like something the cat drug in. George was toying with the vague notion that maybe dancers shouldn't be handicapped. But he didn't get very far with it before another noise in his ear radio scattered his thoughts.

George winced. So did two out of the eight ballerinas.

Hazel saw him wince. Having no mental handicap herself, she had to ask George what the latest sound had been.

"Sounded like somebody hitting a milk bottle with a ball peen hammer," said George.

"I'd think it would be real interesting, hearing all the different sounds," said Hazel, a little envious. "All the things they think up."

"Um," said George.

"Only, if I was Handicapper General, you know what I would do?" said Hazel. Hazel, as a matter of fact, bore a strong resemblance to the Handicapper General, a woman named Diana Moon Glampers. "If I was Diana Moon Glampers," said Hazel, "I'd have chimes on Sunday—just chimes. Kind of in honor of religion."

"I could think, if it was just chimes," said George.

"Well—maybe make 'em real loud," said Hazel. "I think I'd make a good Handicapper General."

"Good as anybody else," said George.

"Who knows better'n I do what normal is?" said Hazel.

"Right," said George. He began to think glimmeringly about his abnormal son who was now in jail, about Harrison, but a twenty-one-gun salute in his head stopped that.

"Boy!" said Hazel, "that was a doozy, wasn't it?"

It was such a doozy that George was white and trembling, and tears stood on the rims of his red eyes. Two of the eight ballerinas had collapsed to the studio floor, were holding their temples.

"All of a sudden you look so tired," said Hazel. "Why don't you stretch out on the sofa, so's you can rest your handicap bag on the pillows, honeybunch." She was referring to the forty-seven pounds of birdshot in a canvas bag, which was padlocked around George's neck. "Go on and rest the bag for a little while," she said. "I don't care if you're not equal to me for a while."

George weighed the bag with his hands. "I don't mind it," he said. "I don't notice it any more. It's just a part of me."

"You been so tired lately—kind of wore out," said Hazel. "If there was just some way we could make a little hole in the bottom of the bag, and just take out a few of them lead balls. Just a few."

"Two years in prison and two thousand dollars fine for every ball I took out," said George. "I don't call that a bargain."

"If you could just take a few out when you came home from work," said Hazel. "I mean—you don't compete with anybody around here. You just set around."

"If I tried to get away with it," said George, "then other people'd get away with it—and pretty soon we'd be right back to the dark ages again, with everybody competing against everybody else. You wouldn't like that, would you?"

"I'd hate it," said Hazel.

"There you are," said George. "The minute people start cheating on laws, what do you think happens to society?"

If Hazel hadn't been able to come up with an answer to this question, George couldn't have supplied one. A siren was going off in his head.

"Reckon it'd fall all apart," said Hazel.

"What would?" said George blankly.

"Society," said Hazel uncertainly. "Wasn't that what you just said?"

"Who knows?" said George.

The television program was suddenly interrupted for a news bulletin. It wasn't clear at first as to what the bulletin was about, since the announcer, like all announcers, had a serious speech impediment. For about half a minute, and in a state of high excitement, the announcer tried to say, "Ladies and gentlemen—"

He finally gave up, handed the bulletin to a ballerina to read.

"That's all right—" Hazel said of the announcer, "he tried. That's the big thing. He tried to do the best he could with what God gave him. He should get a nice raise for trying so hard."

"Ladies and gentlemen—" said the ballerina, reading the bulletin. She must have been extraordinarily beautiful, because the mask she wore was hideous. And it was easy to see that she was the strongest and most graceful of all the dancers, for her handicap bags were as big as those worn by two-hundred-pound men.

And she had to apologize at once for her voice, which was a very unfair voice for a woman to use. Her voice was a warm, luminous, timeless melody. "Excuse me—" she said, and she began again, making her voice absolutely uncompetitive.

"Harrison Bergeron, age fourteen," she said in a grackle squawk, "has just escaped from jail, where he was held on suspicion of plotting to overthrow the government.

He is a genius and an athlete, is under-handicapped, and should be regarded as extremely dangerous."

A police photograph of Harrison Bergeron was flashed on the screen upside down, then sideways, upside down again, then right side up. The picture showed the full length of Harrison against a background calibrated in feet and inches. He was exactly seven feet tall.

The rest of Harrison's appearance was Halloween and hardware. Nobody had ever borne heavier handicaps. He had outgrown hindrances faster than the H-G men could think them up. Instead of a little ear radio for a mental handicap, he wore a tremendous pair of earphones, and spectacles with thick wavy lenses. The spectacles were intended to make him not only half blind, but to give him whanging headaches besides.

Scrap metal was hung all over him. Ordinarily, there was a certain symmetry, a military neatness to the handicaps issued to strong people, but Harrison looked like a walking junkyard. In the race of life, Harrison carried three hundred pounds.

And to offset his good looks, the H-G men required that he wear at all times a red rubber ball for a nose, keep his eyebrows shaved off, and cover his even white teeth with black caps at snaggle-tooth random.

"If you see this boy," said the ballerina, "do not—I repeat, do not—try to reason with him."

There was the shriek of a door being torn from its hinges.

Screams and barking cries of consternation came from the television set. The photograph of Harrison Bergeron on the screen jumped again and again, as though dancing to the tune of an earthquake.

George Bergeron correctly identified the earthquake, and well he might have—for many was the time his own home had danced to the same crashing tune. "My God—" said George, "that must be Harrison!"

The realization was blasted from his mind instantly by the sound of an automobile collision in his head.

When George could open his eyes again, the photograph of Harrison was gone. A living, breathing Harrison filled the screen.

Clanking, clownish, and huge, Harrison stood in the center of the studio. The knob of the uprooted studio door was still in his hand. Ballerinas, technicians, musicians, and announcers cowered on their knees before him, expecting to die.

"I am the Emperor!" cried Harrison. "Do you hear? I am the Emperor! Everybody must do what I say at once!" He stamped his foot and the studio shook.

"Even as I stand here—" he bellowed, "crippled, hobbled, sickened—I am a greater ruler than any man who ever lived! Now watch me become what I *can* become!"

Harrison tore the straps of his handicap harness like wet tissue paper, tore straps guaranteed to support five thousand pounds.

Harrison's scrap-iron handicaps crashed to the floor.

Harrison thrust his thumbs under the bar of the padlock that secured his head harness. The bar snapped like celery. Harrison smashed his headphones and spectacles against the wall.

He flung away his rubber-ball nose, revealed a man that would have awed Thor, the god of thunder.

"I shall now select my Empress!" he said, looking down on the cowering people. "Let the first woman who dares rise to her feet claim her mate and her throne!"

A moment passed, and then a ballerina arose, swaying like a willow.

Harrison plucked the mental handicap from her ear, snapped off her physical handicaps with marvelous delicacy. Last of all, he removed her mask.

She was blindingly beautiful.

"Now—" said Harrison, taking her hand, "shall we show the people the meaning of the word dance? Music!" he commanded.

The musicians scrambled back into their chairs, and Harrison stripped them of their handicaps, too. "Play your best," he told them, "and I'll make you barons and dukes and earls."

The music began. It was normal at first—cheap, silly, false. But Harrison snatched two musicians from their chairs, waved them like batons as he sang the music as he wanted it played. He slammed them back into their chairs.

The music began again and was much improved.

Harrison and his Empress merely listened to the music for a while—listened gravely, as though synchronizing their heartbeats with it.

They shifted their weights to their toes.

Harrison placed his big hands on the girl's tiny waist, letting her sense the weightlessness that would soon be hers.

And then, in an explosion of joy and grace, into the air they sprang!

Not only were the laws of the land abandoned, but the law of gravity and the laws of motion as well.

They reeled, whirled, swiveled, flounced, capered, gamboled, and spun.

They leaped like deer on the moon.

The studio ceiling was thirty feet high, but each leap brought the dancers nearer to it.

It became their obvious intention to kiss the ceiling.

They kissed it.

And then, neutralizing gravity with love and pure will, they remained suspended in air inches below the ceiling, and they kissed each other for a long, long time.

It was then that Diana Moon Glampers, the Handicapper General, came into the studio with a double-barreled ten-gauge shotgun. She fired twice, and the Emperor and the Empress were dead before they hit the floor.

Diana Moon Glampers loaded the gun again. She aimed it at the musicians and told them they had ten seconds to get their handicaps back on.

It was then that the Bergerons' television tube burned out.

Hazel turned to comment about the blackout to George. But George had gone out into the kitchen for a can of beer.

George came back in with the beer, paused while a handicap signal shook him up. And then he sat down again. "You been crying?" he said to Hazel.

"Yup," she said.

"What about?" he said.

"I forget," she said. "Something real sad on television."

"What was it?" he said.

"It's all kind of mixed up in my mind," said Hazel.

"Forget sad things," said George.

"I always do," said Hazel.

"That's my girl," said George. He winced. There was the sound of a rivetting gun in his head.

"Gee—I could tell that one was a doozy," said Hazel.

"You can say that again," said George.

"Gee—" said Hazel, "I could tell that one was a doozy."

Questions

1. What tendencies in present-day American society is Vonnegut satirizing? Does the story argue *for* anything? How would you sum up its theme?
2. Is Diana Moon Glampers a "flat" or a "round" character? (If you need to review these terms, see the discussion of character in Chapter 2.) Would you call Vonnegut's characterization of her "realistic"? If not, why doesn't it need to be?
3. From what point of view is the story told? Why is it more effective than if Harrison Bergeron had told his own story in the first person?
4. What is the effect of Vonnegut's use of humor? Are there points that can be made in a funny story that are harder to make in a more serious one? Why or why not?
5. What does the story suggest about "equality"? Is there a difference between equality and equal opportunity?

Ursula K. Le Guin

Ursula Kroeber Le Guin was born in 1929 on St. Ursula's Day (October 21) in Berkeley, California, the only daughter and youngest child of Theodora Kroeber, a folklorist, and Alfred Kroeber, a renowned anthropologist. Le Guin attended Radcliffe College, where she graduated Phi Beta Kappa, and then entered Columbia University to do graduate work in French and Italian literature. While completing her M.A., she wrote her first stories. On a Fulbright fellowship to France, she met Charles Le Guin, a professor of French history, whom she married in Paris in 1953. Over the next decade Le Guin reared three children and worked on her writing in private.

Ursula K. Le Guin

In the early sixties Le Guin began publishing in both science fiction pulp magazines and academic journals. In 1966 her first novel, Rocannon's World, *was published as an Ace science fiction paperback original—hardly a respectable format for the debut of one of America's premier writers. In 1968 Le Guin published* A Wizard of Earthsea, *the first novel in her Earthsea Trilogy, now considered a classic of children's literature. The next two volumes,* The Tombs of Atuan *(1971), which won a Newbery citation, and* The Farthest Shore *(1972), which won a National Book Award, brought Le Guin mainstream acclaim.*

Le Guin's novels The Left Hand of Darkness *(1969) and* The Dispossessed *(1974) won both the Hugo and the Nebula awards, science fiction's two most prized honors. She also twice won the Hugo for best short story, including the 1974 award for "The Ones Who Walk Away from Omelas." Le Guin has published more than thirty novels and volumes of short stories. She lives in Portland, Oregon.*

One of the few science fiction writers whose work has earned general critical acclaim, Le Guin belongs most naturally in the company of major novelists of ideas such as Aldous Huxley, George Orwell, and Anthony Burgess, who have used the genre of science fiction to explore the possible consequences of ideological rather than technological change. Le Guin has been especially concerned with issues of social justice and equality. In her short stories—including "The Ones Who Walk Away from Omelas"—she creates complex imaginary civilizations, envisioned with anthropological authority, and her aim is less to imagine alien cultures than to explore humanity.

The Ones Who Walk Away from Omelas 1975

With a clamor of bells that set the swallows soaring, the Festival of Summer came to the city Omelas, bright-towered by the sea. The rigging of the boats in harbor sparkled with flags. In the streets between houses with red roofs and painted walls, between old moss-grown gardens and under avenues of trees, past great parks and public buildings, processions moved. Some were decorous: old people in long stiff robes of mauve and grey, grave master workmen, quiet, merry women carrying their babies and chatting as they walked. In other streets the music beat faster, a shimmering of gong and tambourine, and the people went dancing, the procession was a dance. Children dodged in and out, their high calls rising like the swallows' crossing flights over the music and the singing. All the processions wound towards the north side of the city, where on the great water-meadow called the Green Fields boys and girls, naked in the bright air, with mud-stained feet and ankles and long, lithe arms, exercised their restive horses before the race. The horses wore no gear at all but a halter without bit. Their manes were braided with streamers of silver, gold, and green. They flared their nostrils and pranced and boasted to one another; they were vastly excited, the horse being the only animal who has adopted our ceremonies as his own. Far off to the north and west the mountains stood up half encircling Omelas on her bay. The air of morning was so clear that the snow still crowning the Eighteen Peaks burned with white-gold fire across the miles of sunlit air, under the dark blue of the sky. There was just enough wind to make the banners that marked the racecourse snap and flutter now and then. In the silence of the broad green meadows one could hear the music winding through the city streets, farther and nearer and ever approaching, a cheerful faint sweetness of the air that from time to time trembled and gathered together and broke out into the great joyous clanging of the bells.

Joyous! How is one to tell about joy? How describe the citizens of Omelas?

They were not simple folk, you see, though they were happy. But we do not say the words of cheer much any more. All smiles have become archaic. Given a description such as this one tends to make certain assumptions. Given a description such as this one tends to look next for the King, mounted on a splendid stallion and surrounded by his noble knights, or perhaps in a golden litter borne by great-muscled slaves. But there was no king. They did not use swords, or keep slaves. They were not barbarians. I do not know the rules and laws of their society, but I suspect that they were singularly few. As they did without monarchy and slavery, so they also got on without the stock exchange, the advertisement, the secret police, and the bomb. Yet I repeat that these were not simple folk, not dulcet shepherds, noble savages, bland utopians. They were not less complex than us. The trouble is that we have a bad habit, encouraged by pedants and sophisticates, of considering happiness as something rather stupid. Only pain is intellectual, only evil interesting. This is the treason of the artist: a refusal to admit the banality of evil and the terrible boredom of pain. If you can't lick 'em, join 'em. If it hurts, repeat it. But to praise despair is to condemn delight, to embrace violence is to lose hold of everything else. We have almost lost hold; we can no longer describe a happy man, nor make any celebration of joy. How can I tell you about the people of Omelas? They were not naïve and happy children—though their children were, in fact, happy. They were mature, intelligent, passionate adults whose lives were not wretched. O miracle! but I wish I could describe it better. I wish I could convince you. Omelas sounds in my words like a city in a fairy tale, long ago and far away, once upon a time. Perhaps it would be best if you imagined it as your own fancy bids, assuming it will rise to the occasion, for certainly I cannot suit you all. For instance, how about technology? I think that there would be no cars or helicopters in and above the streets; this follows from the fact that the people of Omelas are happy people. Happiness is based on a just discrimination of what is necessary, what is neither necessary nor destructive, and what is destructive. In the middle category, however—that of the unnecessary but undestructive, that of comfort, luxury, exuberance, etc.—they could perfectly well have central heating, subway trains, washing machines, and all kinds of marvelous devices not yet invented here, floating light-sources, fuelless power, a cure for the common cold. Or they could have none of that: it doesn't matter. As you like it. I incline to think that people from towns up and down the coast have been coming in to Omelas during the last days before the Festival on very fast little trains and double-decked trams, and that the train station of Omelas is actually the handsomest building in town, though plainer than the magnificent Farmers' Market. But even granted trains, I fear that Omelas so far strikes some of you as goody-goody. Smiles, bells, parades, horses, bleh. If so, please add an orgy. If an orgy would help, don't hesitate. Let us not, however, have temples from which issue beautiful nude priests and priestesses already half in ecstasy and ready to copulate with any man or woman, lover or stranger, who desires union with the deep godhead of the blood, although that was my first idea. But really it would be better not to have any temples in Omelas—at least, not manned temples. Religion yes, clergy no. Surely the beautiful nudes can just wander about, offering themselves like divine soufflés to the hunger of the needy and the rapture of the flesh. Let them join the processions. Let tambourines be struck above the copulations, and the glory of desire be proclaimed upon the gongs, and (a not unimportant point) let the offspring of these delightful rituals be beloved and looked after by all. One thing I know there is none of in Omelas is guilt. But what else should there be? I thought at first there were no drugs, but that is puritanical. For those who like it, the faint insistent sweetness of *drooz* may perfume the ways of the city, *drooz* which first brings a great lightness and brilliance to the mind and limbs, and then after some hours a dreamy languor, and wonderful visions at last of the very arcana and inmost secrets of the Universe, as well as exciting the pleasure of sex beyond all belief; and it is not habit-forming. For more modest tastes I think there ought to be beer. What else, what else belongs in the joyous city? The sense of victory, surely, the celebration of courage. But as we did without clergy, let us do without soldiers. The joy built upon successful slaughter is not the right kind of joy; it will not do; it is fearful and it is trivial. A boundless and generous contentment, a magnanimous triumph felt not against some outer enemy but in communion with the finest and fairest in the souls of all men everywhere and the splendor of the world's summer: this is what swells the hearts of the people of Omelas, and the victory they celebrate is that of life. I really don't think many of them need to take *drooz*.

Most of the processions have reached the Green Fields by now. A marvelous smell of cooking goes forth from the red and blue tents of the provisioners. The faces of small children are amiably sticky; in the benign grey beard of a man a couple of crumbs of rich pastry are entangled. The youths and girls have mounted their horses and are beginning to group around the starting line of the course. An old woman, small, fat, and laughing, is passing out flowers from a basket, and tall young men wear her flowers in their shining hair. A child of nine or ten sits at the edge of the crowd, alone, playing on a wooden flute. People pause to listen, and they smile, but they do not speak to him, for he never ceases playing and never sees them, his dark eyes wholly rapt in the sweet, thin magic of the tune.

He finishes, and slowly lowers his hands holding the wooden flute.

As if that little private silence were the signal, all at once a trumpet sounds from the pavilion near the starting line: imperious, melancholy, piercing. The horses rear on their slender legs, and some of them neigh in answer. Sober-faced, the young riders stroke the horses' necks and soothe them, whispering, "Quiet, quiet, there my beauty, my hope. . . ." They begin to form in rank along the starting line. The crowds along the racecourse are like a field of grass and flowers in the wind. The Festival of Summer has begun.

Do you believe? Do you accept the festival, the city, the joy? No? Then let me describe one more thing.

In a basement under one of the beautiful public buildings of Omelas, or perhaps in the cellar of one of its spacious private homes, there is a room. It has one locked door, and no window. A little light seeps in dustily between cracks in the boards, secondhand from a cobwebbed window somewhere across the cellar. In one corner of the little room a couple of mops, with stiff, clotted, foul-smelling heads, stand near a rusty bucket. The floor is dirt, a little damp to the touch, as cellar dirt usually is. The room is about three paces long and two wide: a mere broom closet or disused tool room. In the room a child is sitting. It could be a boy or a girl. It looks about six, but actually is nearly ten. It is feeble-minded. Perhaps it was born defective, or perhaps it has become imbecile through fear, malnutrition, and neglect. It picks its nose and occasionally fumbles vaguely with its toes or genitals, as it sits hunched in the corner farthest from the bucket and the two mops. It is afraid of the mops. It finds them horrible. It shuts its eyes, but it knows the mops are still standing there; and the door is locked; and nobody will come. The door is always locked; and nobody ever comes, except that sometimes—the child has no understanding of time or interval—sometimes the door rattles terribly and opens, and a person, or several people, are there. One of them may come in and kick the child to make it stand up. The others never come close, but peer in at it with frightened, disgusted eyes. The food bowl and the water jug are hastily filled, the door is locked, the eyes disappear. The people at the door never say anything, but the child, who has not always lived in the tool room, and can remember sunlight and its mother's voice, sometimes speaks. "I will be good," it says. "Please let me out. I will be good!" They never answer. The child used to scream for help at night, and cry a good deal, but now it only makes a kind of whining, "eh-haa, eh-haa," and it speaks less and less often. It is so thin there are no calves to its legs; its belly protrudes; it lives on a half-bowl of corn meal and grease a day. It is naked. Its buttocks and thighs are a mass of festered sores, as it sits in its own excrement continually.

They all know it is there, all the people of Omelas. Some of them have come to see it, others are content merely to know it is there. They all know that it has to be there. Some of them understand why, and some do not, but they all understand that their happiness, the beauty of their city, the tenderness of their friendships, the health of their children, the wisdom of their scholars, the skill of their makers, even the abundance of their harvest and the kindly weathers of their skies, depend wholly on this child's abominable misery.

This is usually explained to children when they are between eight and twelve, whenever they seem capable of understanding; and most of those who come to see the child are young people, though often enough an adult comes, or comes back, to see the child. No matter how well the matter has been explained to them, these young spectators are always shocked and sickened at the sight. They feel disgust, which they had thought themselves superior to. They feel anger, outrage, impotence, despite all the explanations. They would like to do something for the child. But there is nothing they can do. If the child were brought up into the sunlight out of that vile place, if it were cleaned and fed and comforted, that would be a good thing, indeed; but if it were done, in that day and hour all the prosperity and beauty and delight of Omelas would wither and be destroyed. Those are the terms. To exchange all the goodness and grace of every life in Omelas for that single, small improvement: to throw away the happiness of thousands for the chance of the happiness of one: that would be to let guilt within the walls indeed.

The terms are strict and absolute; there may not even be a kind word spoken to the child.

Often the young people go home in tears, or in a tearless rage, when they have seen the child and faced this terrible paradox. They may brood over it for weeks or years. But as time goes on they begin to realize that even if the child could be released, it would not get much good of its freedom: a little vague pleasure of warmth and food, no doubt, but little more. It is too degraded and imbecile to know any real joy. It has been afraid too long ever to be free of fear. Its habits are too uncouth for it to respond to humane treatment. Indeed, after so long it would probably be wretched without walls about it to protect it, and darkness for its eyes, and its own excrement to sit in. Their tears at the bitter injustice dry when they begin to perceive the terrible justice of reality, and to accept it. Yet it is their tears and anger, the trying of their generosity and the acceptance of their helplessness, which are perhaps the true source of the splendor of their lives. Theirs is no vapid, irresponsible happiness. They know that they, like the child, are not free. They know compassion. It is the existence of the child, and their knowledge of its existence, that makes possible the nobility of their architecture, the poignancy of their music, the profundity of their science. It is because of the child that they are so gentle with children. They know that if the wretched one were not there snivelling in the dark, the other one, the flute-player, could make no joyful music as the young riders line up in their beauty for the race in the sunlight of the first morning of summer.

Now do you believe in them? Are they not more credible? But there is one more thing to tell, and this is quite incredible.

At times one of the adolescent girls or boys who go to see the child does not go home to weep or rage, does not, in fact, go home at all. Sometimes also a man or woman much older falls silent for a day or two, and then leaves home. These people go out into the street, and walk down the street alone. They keep walking, and walk straight out of the city of Omelas, through the beautiful gates. They keep walking across the farmlands of Omelas. Each one goes alone, youth or girl, man or woman. Night falls; the traveler must pass down village streets, between the houses with yellow-lit windows, and on out into the darkness of the fields. Each alone, they go west or north, toward the mountains. They go on. They leave Omelas, they walk ahead into the darkness, and they do not come back. The place they go towards is a place even less imaginable to most of us than the city of happiness. I cannot describe it at all. It is possible that it does not exist. But they seem to know where they are going, the ones who walk away from Omelas.

Questions

1. Does the narrator live in Omelas? What do we know about the narrator's society?
2. What is the narrator's opinion of Omelas? Does the author seem to share that opinion?
3. What is the narrator's attitude toward "the ones who walk away from Omelas"? Would the narrator have been one of those who walked away?
4. How do you account for the narrator's willingness to let us readers add anything we like to the story?—"If an orgy would help, don't hesitate" (paragraph 3). Doesn't Ursula Le Guin care what her story includes?
5. What is suggested by the locked, dark cellar in which the child sits? What other details in the story are suggestive enough to be called symbolic?
6. Do you find in the story any implied criticism of our own society?

Suggestions for Writing on Stories about Conformity, Rebellion, and Dissent

1. The stories in this section are not strictly realistic. Choose at least two stories and make an argument for why their "unrealistic" settings help bolster the authors' points about society—or fail to do so.
2. At least two of the stories involve characters who resist the norms of their society. Pick one dissenting character and analyze his or her form of resistance. Is it effective? Ineffective? Why or why not?
3. Write a personal essay about a time when your opinion differed greatly from that of the people around you. Did you express or act on this disagreement? Why or why not? Whatever your choice was, what were the consequences? How do you feel now about your decision?

INDIVIDUALS IN ISOLATION

Ernest Hemingway　　*A Clean, Well-Lighted Place*
John Cheever　　　　*The Swimmer*
Ha Jin　　　　　　　*Saboteur*

For most people there's comfort in being part of a group, whether that group is made up of their work colleagues, classmates, teammates, or neighbors. But often, even within a group, people feel alone. They might think they're out of step, or different from those around them; they might fear their friends or classmates don't really like them. Yet being alone—or being an individual within the crowd—isn't necessarily a bad thing. Sometimes people are most true to themselves when they have the space to think or act or simply *be* without the prying eyes of others. Sometimes, free of the influence of friends or family members, people make choices they'd be afraid to make otherwise. Sometimes individuals find themselves alone when standing up for a principle, or fighting for their right to be recognized and respected for who they are.

The stories in this section reflect the burdens of individuality. The old man in Ernest Hemingway's "A Clean, Well-Lighted Place" seems pitiable in his quiet solitude to the young waiter who serves him, but an older waiter understands the customer's need for the society a café offers. In John Cheever's "The Swimmer," the protagonist embarks on the curious quest to swim from pool to pool across the county, only to discover his own losses and irreversible isolation. Finally, in Ha Jin's "Saboteur," an ordinary citizen is transformed into an enemy of the state after challenging some provincial policemen.

Ernest Hemingway

Ernest Hemingway (1899–1961), born in Oak Park, Illinois, bypassed college to be a cub reporter. In World War I, as an eighteen-year-old volunteer ambulance driver in Italy, he was wounded in action. In 1922 he settled in Paris, then aswarm with writers; he later recalled that time in A Moveable Feast (1964). Hemingway won swift acclaim for his early stories, In Our Time (1925), and for his first, perhaps finest, novel, The Sun Also Rises (1926), portraying a "lost generation" of postwar American drifters in France and Spain. For Whom the Bell Tolls (1940) depicts life during the Spanish Civil War. Hemingway became a celebrity, often photographed as a marlin fisherman or a lion hunter. A fan of bullfighting, he wrote two non-fiction books on the subject: Death in the Afternoon

Ernest Hemingway

(1932) and The Dangerous Summer (1985). After World War II, with his fourth wife, journalist Mary Welsh, he made his home in Cuba, where he wrote The Old Man and the Sea *(1952). The Nobel Prize in Literature came his way in 1954. In 1961, mentally distressed and physically ailing, he shot himself. Hemingway brought a hard-bitten realism to American fiction. His heroes live dangerously, by personal codes of honor, courage, and endurance. Hemingway's distinctively crisp, unadorned style left American literature permanently changed.*

A Clean, Well-Lighted Place   1933

It was late and every one had left the café except an old man who sat in the shadow the leaves of the tree made against the electric light. In the day time the street was dusty, but at night the dew settled the dust and the old man liked to sit late because he was deaf and now at night it was quiet and he felt the difference. The two waiters inside the café knew that the old man was a little drunk, and while he was a good client they knew that if he became too drunk he would leave without paying, so they kept watch on him.

"Last week he tried to commit suicide," one waiter said.

"Why?"

"He was in despair."

"What about?"

"Nothing."

"How do you know it was nothing?"

"He has plenty of money."

They sat together at a table that was close against the wall near the door of the café and looked at the terrace where the tables were all empty except where the old man sat in the shadow of the leaves of the tree that moved slightly in the wind. A girl and a soldier went by in the street. The street light shone on the brass number on his collar. The girl wore no head covering and hurried beside him.

"The guard will pick him up," one waiter said.

"What does it matter if he gets what he's after?"

"He had better get off the street now. The guard will get him. They went by five minutes ago."

The old man sitting in the shadow rapped on his saucer with his glass. The younger waiter went over to him.

"What do you want?"

The old man looked at him. "Another brandy," he said.

"You'll be drunk," the waiter said. The old man looked at him. The waiter went away.

"He'll stay all night," he said to his colleague. "I'm sleepy now. I never get into bed before three o'clock. He should have killed himself last week."

The waiter took the brandy bottle and another saucer from the counter inside the café and marched out to the old man's table. He put down the saucer and poured the glass full of brandy.

"You should have killed yourself last week," he said to the deaf man. The old man motioned with his finger. "A little more," he said. The waiter poured on into the glass so that the brandy slopped over and ran down the stem into the top saucer of the pile. "Thank you," the old man said. The waiter took the bottle back inside the café. He sat down at the table with his colleague again.

"He's drunk now," he said.

"He's drunk every night."°
"What did he want to kill himself for?"
"How should I know?"
"How did he do it?"
"He hung himself with a rope."
"Who cut him down?"
"His niece."
"Why did they do it?"
"Fear for his soul."
"How much money has he got?"
"He's got plenty."
"He must be eighty years old."
"Anyway I should say he was eighty."°
"I wish he would go home. I never get to bed before three o'clock. What kind of hour is that to go to bed?"
"He stays up because he likes it."
"He's lonely. I'm not lonely. I have a wife waiting in bed for me."
"He had a wife once too."
"A wife would be no good to him now."
"You can't tell. He might be better with a wife."
"His niece looks after him."
"I know. You said she cut him down."
"I wouldn't want to be that old. An old man is a nasty thing."
"Not always. This old man is clean. He drinks without spilling. Even now, drunk. Look at him."
"I don't want to look at him. I wish he would go home. He has no regard for those who must work."

The old man looked from his glass across the square, then over at the waiters.

"Another brandy," he said, pointing to his glass. The waiter who was in a hurry came over.

"Finished," he said, speaking with that omission of syntax stupid people employ when talking to drunken people or foreigners. "No more tonight. Close now."

"Another," said the old man.

"No. Finished." The waiter wiped the edge of the table with a towel and shook his head.

The old man stood up, slowly counted the saucers, took a leather coin purse from his pocket and paid for the drinks, leaving half a peseta tip.

The waiter watched him go down the street, a very old man walking unsteadily but with dignity.

"Why didn't you let him stay and drink?" the unhurried waiter asked. They were putting up the shutters. "It is not half-past two."

"I want to go home to bed."

"He's drunk now," he said. *"He's drunk every night"*: The younger waiter perhaps says both these lines. A device of Hemingway's style is sometimes to have a character pause, then speak again—as often happens in actual speech.   *"He must be eighty years old." "Anyway I should say he was eighty"*: Is this another instance of the same character's speaking twice? Clearly, it is the younger waiter who says the next line, "I wish he would go home."

"What is an hour?"

"More to me than to him."

"An hour is the same."

"You talk like an old man yourself. He can buy a bottle and drink at home."

"It's not the same."

"No, it is not," agreed the waiter with a wife. He did not wish to be unjust. He was only in a hurry.

"And you? You have no fear of going home before the usual hour?"

"Are you trying to insult me?"

"No, hombre, only to make a joke."

"No," the waiter who was in a hurry said, rising from pulling down the metal shutters. "I have confidence. I am all confidence."

"You have youth, confidence, and a job," the older waiter said. "You have everything."

"And what do you lack?"

"Everything but work."

"You have everything I have."

"No. I have never had confidence and I am not young."

"Come on. Stop talking nonsense and lock up."

"I am of those who like to stay late at the café," the older waiter said. "With all those who do not want to go to bed. With all those who need a light for the night."

"I want to go home and into bed."

"We are of two different kinds," the older waiter said. He was not dressed to go home. "It is not only a question of youth and confidence although those things are very beautiful. Each night I am reluctant to close up because there may be some one who needs the café."

"Hombre, there are bodegas° open all night long."

"You do not understand. This is a clean and pleasant café. It is well lighted. The light is very good and also, now, there are shadows of the leaves."

"Good night," said the younger waiter.

"Good night," the other said. Turning off the electric light he continued the conversation with himself. It is the light of course but it is necessary that the place be clean and pleasant. You do not want music. Certainly you do not want music. Nor can you stand before a bar with dignity although that is all that is provided for these hours. What did he fear? It was not fear or dread. It was a nothing that he knew too well. It was all a nothing and a man was nothing too. It was only that and light was all it needed and a certain cleanness and order. Some lived in it and never felt it but he knew it all was nada y pues nada y nada y pues nada.° Our nada who art in nada, nada be thy name thy kingdom nada thy will be nada in nada as it is in nada. Give us this nada our daily nada and nada us our nada as we nada our nadas and nada us not into nada but deliver us from nada; pues nada. Hail nothing full of nothing, nothing is with thee. He smiled and stood before a bar with a shining steam pressure coffee machine.

"What's yours?" asked the barman.

"Nada."

---

bodegas: wineshops.   nada y pues . . . nada: nothing and then nothing and nothing and then nothing.

"Otro loco más,"° said the barman and turned away.
"A little cup," said the waiter.
The barman poured it for him.
"The light is very bright and pleasant but the bar is unpolished," the waiter said.
The barman looked at him but did not answer. It was too late at night for conversation.
"You want another copita?"° the barman asked.
"No, thank you," said the waiter and went out. He disliked bars and bodegas. A clean, well-lighted café was a very different thing. Now, without thinking further, he would go home to his room. He would lie in the bed and finally, with daylight, he would go to sleep. After all, he said to himself, it is probably only insomnia. Many must have it.

Questions

1. What besides insomnia makes the older waiter reluctant to go to bed? Comment especially on his meditation with its *nada* refrain. Why does he understand so well the old man's need for a café? What does the café represent for the two of them?
2. Compare the younger waiter and the older waiter in their attitudes toward the old man. Whose attitude do you take to be closer to that of the author? Even though Hemingway does not editorially state his own feelings, how does he make them clear to us?
3. Point to sentences that establish the style of the story. What is distinctive in them? What repetitions of words or phrases seem particularly effective? Does Hemingway seem to favor a simple or an erudite vocabulary?
4. What is the story's point of view? Discuss its appropriateness.
5. What does the old man want from the café?

John Cheever

John Cheever (1912–1982) was born in Quincy, Massachusetts. His parents had been modestly prosperous, but their livelihood declined substantially and was finally dashed by the 1929 stock market crash. Cheever was sent away to Thayer Academy, a prep school, where he was a poor student. When he was expelled at eighteen, he wrote a story about the incident that was published in the New Republic (1930). Cheever never finished high school or attended college, dedicating himself instead to writing.

Cheever's stories, most of which appeared in the New Yorker, often deal with the ordinary lives of middle-class characters living in Manhattan or its suburbs. Although his stories are realistic in plot and setting, they often contain an underlying religious vision—exploring themes of guilt, grace, and redemption. Cheever's novels include The Wapshot Chronicle (1957), which won the National Book Award; Bullet Park (1969); and Falconer (1977). The Stories of John Cheever (1978), which brings together the

Otro loco más: another lunatic.   *copita:* little cup.

works from his five volumes of short fiction, won the Pulitzer Prize and National Book Critics Circle Award. After Cheever's death, his notebooks and letters revealed how tortured his life had been by sex and alcohol. While some early reviewers regarded Cheever's popular stories as "New Yorker fiction" (satiric views of middle-class life), critics now see the psychological and religious vision underlying his work. Once undervalued, Cheever is now generally regarded as one of the finest American short-story writers of the twentieth century.

The Swimmer   1964

It was one of those midsummer Sundays when everyone sits around saying, "I *drank* too much last night." You might have heard it whispered by the parishioners leaving church, heard it from the lips of the priest himself, struggling with his cassock in the *vestiarium*: heard it from the golf links and the tennis courts, heard it from the wildlife preserve where the leader of the Audubon group was suffering from a terrible hangover. "I *drank* too much," said Donald Westerhazy. "We all *drank* too much," said Lucinda Merrill. "It must have been the wine," said Helen Westerhazy. "I *drank* too much of that claret."

This was at the edge of the Westerhazys' pool. The pool, fed by an artesian well with a high iron content, was a pale shade of green. It was a fine day. In the west there was a massive stand of cumulus cloud so like a city seen from a distance—from the bow of an approaching ship—that it might have had a name. Lisbon. Hackensack. The sun was hot. Neddy Merrill sat by the green water, one hand in it, one around a glass of gin. He was a slender man—he seemed to have the especial slenderness of youth—and while he was far from young he had slid down his banister that morning and given the bronze backside of Aphrodite on the hall table a smack, as he jogged toward the smell of coffee in his dining room. He might have been compared to a summer's day, particularly the last hours of one, and while he lacked a tennis racket or a sail bag the impression was definitely one of youth, sport, and clement weather. He had been swimming and now he was breathing deeply, stertorously as if he could gulp into his lungs the components of that moment, the heat of the sun, the intenseness of his pleasure. It all seemed to flow into his chest. His own house stood in Bullet Park, eight miles to the south, where his four beautiful daughters would have had their lunch and might be playing tennis. Then it occurred to him that by taking a dogleg to the southwest he could reach his home by water.

His life was not confining and the delight he took in this observation could not be explained by its suggestion of escape. He seemed to see, with a cartographer's eye, that string of swimming pools, that quasi-subterranean stream that curved across the county. He had made a discovery, a contribution to modern geography; he would name the stream Lucinda after his wife. He was not a practical joker nor was he a fool but he was determinedly original and had a vague and modest idea of himself as a legendary figure. The day was beautiful and it seemed to him that a long swim might enlarge and celebrate its beauty.

He took off a sweater that was hung over his shoulders and dove in. He had an inexplicable contempt for men who did not hurl themselves into pools. He swam a choppy crawl, breathing either with every stroke or every fourth stroke and counting somewhere well in the back of his mind the one-two one-two of a flutter kick.

It was not a serviceable stroke for long distances but the domestication of swimming had saddled the sport with some customs and in his part of the world a crawl was customary. To be embraced and sustained by the light green water was less a pleasure, it seemed, than the resumption of a natural condition, and he would have liked to swim without trunks, but this was not possible, considering his project. He hoisted himself up on the far curb—he never used the ladder—and started across the lawn. When Lucinda asked where he was going he said he was going to swim home.

The only maps and charts he had to go by were remembered or imaginary but these were clear enough. First there were the Grahams, the Hammers, the Lears, the Howlands, and the Crosscups. He would cross Ditmar Street to the Bunkers and come, after a short portage, to the Levys, the Welchers, and the public pool in Lancaster. Then there were the Hallorans, the Sachses, the Biswangers, Shirley Adams, the Gilmartins, and the Clydes. The day was lovely, and that he lived in a world so generously supplied with water seemed like a clemency, a beneficence. His heart was high and he ran across the grass. Making his way home by an uncommon route gave him the feeling that he was a pilgrim, an explorer, a man with a destiny, and he knew that he would find friends all along the way; friends would line the banks of the Lucinda River.

He went through a hedge that separated the Westerhazys' land from the Grahams', walked under some flowering apple trees, passed the shed that housed their pump and filter, and came out at the Grahams' pool. "Why, Neddy," Mrs. Graham said, "what a marvelous surprise. I've been trying to get you on the phone all morning. Here, let me get you a drink." He saw then, like any explorer, that the hospitable customs and traditions of the natives would have to be handled with diplomacy if he was ever going to reach his destination. He did not want to mystify or seem rude to the Grahams nor did he have the time to linger there. He swam the length of their pool and joined them in the sun and was rescued, a few minutes later, by the arrival of two carloads of friends from Connecticut. During the uproarious reunions he was able to slip away. He went down by the front of the Grahams' house, stepped over a thorny hedge, and crossed a vacant lot to the Hammers'. Mrs. Hammer, looking up from her roses, saw him swim by although she wasn't quite sure who it was. The Lears heard him splashing past the open windows of their living room. The Howlands and the Crosscups were away. After leaving the Howlands' he crossed Ditmar Street and started for the Bunkers', where he could hear, even at that distance, the noise of a party.

The water refracted the sound of voices and laughter and seemed to suspend it in midair. The Bunkers' pool was on a rise and he climbed some stairs to a terrace where twenty-five or thirty men and women were drinking. The only person in the water was Rusty Towers, who floated there on a rubber raft. Oh, how bonny and lush were the banks of the Lucinda River! Prosperous men and women gathered by the sapphire-colored waters while caterer's men in white coats passed them cold gin. Overhead a red de Haviland trainer was circling around and around and around in the sky with something like the glee of a child in a swing. Ned felt a passing affection for the scene, a tenderness for the gathering, as if it was something he might touch. In the distance he heard thunder. As soon as Enid Bunker saw him she began to scream: "Oh, look who's here! What a marvelous surprise! When Lucinda said you couldn't come I thought I'd *die*." She made her way to him through the crowd, and when they had finished kissing she led him to the bar, a progress that was slowed by the fact that he stopped to kiss eight or ten other women and shake the hands of as many men. A smiling bartender he had seen at a hundred parties gave him a gin and tonic and he stood by the bar for a moment, anxious not to get stuck in any conversation that would delay his voyage. When he seemed about to be surrounded he dove in and swam close to the side to avoid colliding with Rusty's raft. At the far end of the pool he bypassed the Tomlinsons with a broad smile and jogged up the garden path. The gravel cut his feet but this was the only unpleasantness. The party was confined to the pool, and as he went toward the house he heard the brilliant, watery sound of voices fade, heard the noise of a radio from the Bunkers' kitchen, where someone was listening to a ball game. Sunday afternoon. He made his way through the parked cars and down the grassy border of their driveway to Alewives Lane. He did not want to be seen on the road in his bathing trunks but there was no traffic and he made the short distance to the Levys' driveway, marked with a PRIVATE PROPERTY sign and a green tube for *The New York Times*. All the doors and windows of the big house were open but there were no signs of life; not even a dog barked. He went around the side of the house to the pool and saw that the Levys had only recently left. Glasses and bottles and dishes of nuts were on a table at the deep end, where there was a bathhouse or gazebo, hung with Japanese lanterns. After swimming the pool he got himself a glass and poured a drink. It was his fourth or fifth drink and he had swum nearly half the length of the Lucinda River. He felt tired, clean, and pleased at that moment to be alone; pleased with everything.

It would storm. The stand of cumulus cloud—that city—had risen and darkened, and while he sat there he heard the percussiveness of thunder again. The de Haviland trainer was still circling overhead and it seemed to Ned that he could almost hear the pilot laugh with pleasure in the afternoon; but when there was another peal of thunder he took off for home. A train whistle blew and he wondered what time it had gotten to be. Four? Five? He thought of the provincial station at that hour, where a waiter, his tuxedo concealed by a raincoat, a dwarf with some flowers wrapped in newspaper, and a woman who had been crying would be waiting for the local. It was suddenly growing dark; it was that moment when the pin-headed birds seem to organize their song into some acute and knowledgeable recognition of the storm's approach. Then there was a fine noise of rushing water from the crown of an oak at his back, as if a spigot there had been turned. Then the noise of fountains came from the crowns of all the tall trees. Why did he love storms, what was the meaning of his excitement when the door sprang open and the rain wind fled rudely up the stairs, why had the simple task of shutting the windows of an old house seemed fitting and urgent, why did the first watery notes of a storm wind have for him the unmistakable sound of good news, cheer, glad tidings? Then there was an explosion, a smell of cordite, and rain lashed the Japanese lanterns that Mrs. Levy had bought in Kyoto the year before last, or was it the year before that?

He stayed in the Levys' gazebo until the storm had passed. The rain had cooled the air and he shivered. The force of the wind had stripped a maple of its red and yellow leaves and scattered them over the grass and the water. Since it was midsummer the tree must be blighted, and yet he felt a peculiar sadness at this sign of autumn. He braced his shoulders, emptied his glass, and started for the Welchers' pool. This meant crossing the Lindleys' riding ring and he was surprised to find it overgrown with grass and all the jumps dismantled. He wondered if the Lindleys had sold their horses or gone away for the summer and put them out to board. He seemed to remember having heard something about the Lindleys and their horses but the memory was unclear. On he went, barefoot through the wet grass, to the Welchers', where he found their pool was dry.

This breach in his chain of water disappointed him absurdly, and he felt like some explorer who seeks a torrential headwater and finds a dead stream. He was disappointed and mystified. It was common enough to go away for the summer but no one ever drained his pool. The Welchers had definitely gone away. The pool furniture was folded, stacked, and covered with a tarpaulin. The bathhouse was locked. All the windows of the house were shut, and when he went around to the driveway in front he saw a FOR SALE sign nailed to the tree. When had he last heard from the Welchers—when, that is, had he and Lucinda last regretted an invitation to dine with them? It seemed only a week or so ago. Was his memory failing or had he so disciplined it in the repression of unpleasant facts that he had damaged his sense of the truth? Then in the distance he heard the sound of a tennis game. This cheered him, cleared away all his apprehensions and let him regard the overcast sky and the cold air with indifference. This was the day that Neddy Merrill swam across the county. That was the day! He started off then for his most difficult portage.

Had you gone for a Sunday afternoon ride that day you might have seen him, close to naked, standing on the shoulders of Route 424, waiting for a chance to cross. You might have wondered if he was the victim of foul play, had his car broken down, or was he merely a fool. Standing barefoot in the deposits of the highway—beer cans, rags, and blowout patches—exposed to all kinds of ridicule, he seemed pitiful. He had known when he started that this was a part of his journey—it had been on his maps—but confronted with the lines of traffic, worming through the summery light, he found himself unprepared. He was laughed at, jeered at, a beer can was thrown at him, and he had no dignity or humor to bring to the situation. He could have gone back, back to the Westerhazys', where Lucinda would still be sitting in the sun. He had signed nothing, vowed nothing, pledged nothing, not even to himself. Why, believing as he did, that all human obduracy was susceptible to common sense, was he unable to turn back? Why was he determined to complete his journey even if it meant putting his life in danger? At what point had this prank, this joke, this piece of horseplay become serious? He could not go back, he could not even recall with any clearness the green water at the Westerhazys', the sense of inhaling the day's components, the friendly and relaxed voices saying that they had *drunk* too much. In the space of an hour, more or less, he had covered a distance that made his return impossible.

An old man, tooling down the highway at fifteen miles an hour, let him get to the middle of the road, where there was a grass divider. Here he was exposed to the ridicule of the northbound traffic, but after ten or fifteen minutes he was able to cross. From here he had only a short walk to the Recreation Center at the edge of the village of Lancaster, where there were some handball courts and a public pool.

The effect of the water on voices, the illusion of brilliance and suspense, was the same here as it had been at the Bunkers' but the sounds here were louder, harsher, and more shrill, and as soon as he entered the crowded enclosure he was confronted with regimentation. "ALL SWIMMERS MUST TAKE A SHOWER BEFORE USING THE POOL. ALL SWIMMERS MUST USE THE FOOTBATH. ALL SWIMMERS MUST WEAR THEIR IDENTIFICATION DISKS." He took a shower, washed his feet in a cloudy and bitter solution, and made his way to the edge of the water. It stank of chlorine and looked to him like a sink. A pair of lifeguards in a pair of towers blew police whistles at what seemed to be regular intervals and abused the swimmers through a public address system. Neddy remembered the sapphire water at the Bunkers' with longing and thought that he might contaminate himself—damage his own prosperousness and charm—by swimming in this murk, but he reminded himself that he was an explorer, a pilgrim, and that this was merely a stagnant bend in the Lucinda River. He dove, scowling with distaste, into the chlorine and had to swim with his head above water to avoid collisions, but even so he was bumped into, splashed, and jostled. When he got to the shallow end both lifeguards were shouting at him: "Hey, you, you without the identification disk, get outa the water." He did, but they had no way of pursuing him and he went through the reek of suntan oil and chlorine out through the hurricane fence and passed the handball courts. By crossing the road he entered the wooded part of the Halloran estate. The woods were not cleared and the footing was treacherous and difficult until he reached the lawn and the clipped beech hedge that encircled their pool.

The Hallorans were friends, an elderly couple of enormous wealth who seemed to bask in the suspicion that they might be Communists. They were zealous reformers but they were not Communists, and yet when they were accused, as they sometimes were, of subversion, it seemed to gratify and excite them. Their beech hedge was yellow and he guessed this had been blighted like the Levys' maple. He called hullo, hullo, to warn the Hallorans of his approach, to palliate his invasion of their privacy. The Hallorans, for reasons that had never been explained to him, did not wear bathing suits. No explanations were in order, really. Their nakedness was a detail in their uncompromising zeal for reform and he stepped politely out of his trunks before he went through the opening in the hedge.

Mrs. Halloran, a stout woman with white hair and a serene face, was reading the *Times*. Mr. Halloran was taking beech leaves out of the water with a scoop. They seemed not surprised or displeased to see him. Their pool was perhaps the oldest in the county, a fieldstone rectangle, fed by a brook. It had no filter or pump and its waters were the opaque gold of the stream.

"I'm swimming across the county," Ned said.

"Why, I didn't know one could," exclaimed Mrs. Halloran.

"Well, I've made it from the Westerhazys'," Ned said. "That must be about four miles."

He left his trunks at the deep end, walked to the shallow end, and swam this stretch. As he was pulling himself out of the water he heard Mrs. Halloran say, "We've been *terribly* sorry to hear about all your misfortunes, Neddy."

"My misfortunes?" Ned asked. "I don't know what you mean."

"Why we heard that you'd sold the house and that your poor children. . . ."

"I don't recall having sold the house," Ned said, "and the girls are at home."

"Yes," Mrs. Halloran sighed. "Yes. . . ." Her voice filled the air with an unseasonable melancholy and Ned spoke briskly. "Thank you for the swim."

"Well, have a nice trip," said Mrs. Halloran.

Beyond the hedge he pulled on his trunks and fastened them. They were loose and he wondered if, during the space of an afternoon, he could have lost some weight. He was cold and he was tired and the naked Hallorans and their dark water had depressed him. The swim was too much for his strength but how could he have guessed this, sliding down the banister that morning and sitting in the Westerhazys' sun? His arms were lame. His legs felt rubbery and ached at the joints. The worst of it was the cold in his bones and the feeling that he might never be warm again. Leaves were falling down around him and he smelled wood smoke on the wind. Who would be burning wood at this time of the year?

He needed a drink. Whiskey would warm him, pick him up, carry him through the last of his journey, refresh his feeling that it was original and valorous to swim across the county. Channel swimmers took brandy. He needed a stimulant. He crossed the lawn in front of the Hallorans' house and went down a little path to where they had built a house for their only daughter, Helen, and her husband, Eric Sachs. The Sachses' pool was small and he found Helen and her husband there.

"Oh, *Neddy*," Helen said. "Did you lunch at Mother's?"

"Not *really*," Ned said. "I *did* stop to see your parents." This seemed to be explanation enough. "I'm terribly sorry to break in on you like this but I've taken a chill and I wonder if you'd give me a drink."

"Why, I'd *love* to," Helen said, "but there hasn't been anything in this house to drink since Eric's operation. That was three years ago."

Was he losing his memory, had his gift for concealing painful facts let him forget that he had sold his house, that his children were in trouble, and that his friend had been ill? His eyes slipped from Eric's face to his abdomen, where he saw three pale, sutured scars, two of them at least a foot long. Gone was his navel, and what, Neddy thought, would the roving hand, bed-checking one's gifts at 3 A.M., make of a belly with no navel, no link to birth, this breach in the succession?

"I'm sure you can get a drink at the Biswangers'," Helen said. "They're having an enormous do. You can hear it from here. Listen!"

She raised her head and from across the road, the lawns, the gardens, the woods, the fields, he heard again the brilliant noise of voices over water. "Well, I'll get wet," he said, still feeling that he had no freedom of choice about his means of travel. He dove into the Sachses' cold water, and gasping, close to drowning, made his way from one end of the pool to the other. "Lucinda and I want *terribly* to see you," he said over his shoulder, his face set toward the Biswangers'. "We're sorry it's been so long and we'll call you *very* soon."

He crossed some fields to the Biswangers' and the sounds of revelry there. They would be honored to give him a drink, they would be happy to give him a drink. The Biswangers invited him and Lucinda for dinner four times a year, six weeks in advance. They were always rebuffed and yet they continued to send out their invitations, unwilling to comprehend the rigid and undemocratic realities of their society. They were the sort of people who discussed the price of things at cocktails, exchanged market tips during dinner, and after dinner told dirty stories to mixed company. They did not belong to Neddy's set—they were not even on Lucinda's

Christmas card list. He went toward their pool with feelings of indifference, charity, and some unease, since it seemed to be getting dark and these were the longest days of the year. The party when he joined it was noisy and large. Grace Biswanger was the kind of hostess who asked the optometrist, the veterinarian, the real-estate dealer, and the dentist. No one was swimming and the twilight, reflected on the water of the pool, had a wintry gleam. There was a bar and he started for this. When Grace Biswanger saw him she came toward him, not affectionately as he had every right to expect, but bellicosely.

"Why, this party has everything," she said loudly, "including a gate crasher."

She could not deal him a social blow—there was no question about this and he did not flinch. "As a gate crasher," he asked politely, "do I rate a drink?"

"Suit yourself," she said. "You don't seem to pay much attention to invitations."

She turned her back on him and joined some guests, and he went to the bar and ordered a whiskey. The bartender served him but he served him rudely. His was a world in which the caterer's men kept the social score, and to be rebuffed by a part-time barkeep meant that he had suffered some loss of social esteem. Or perhaps the man was new and uninformed. Then he heard Grace at his back say: "They went for broke overnight—nothing but income—and he showed up drunk one Sunday and asked us to loan him five thousand dollars. . . ." She was always talking about money. It was worse than eating your peas off a knife. He dove into the pool, swam its length, and went away.

The next pool on his list, the last but two, belonged to his old mistress, Shirley Adams. If he had suffered any injuries at the Biswangers' they would be cured here. Love—sexual roughhouse in fact—was the supreme elixir, the pain killer, the brightly colored pill that would put the spring back into his step, the joy of life in his heart. They had had an affair last week, last month, last year. He couldn't remember. It was he who had broken it off, his was the upper hand, and he stepped through the gate of the wall that surrounded her pool with nothing so considered as self-confidence. It seemed in a way to be his pool, as the lover, particularly the illicit lover, enjoys the possessions of his mistress with an authority unknown to holy matrimony. She was there, her hair the color of brass, but her figure, at the edge of the lighted, cerulean water, excited in him no profound memories. It had been, he thought, a lighthearted affair, although she had wept when he broke it off. She seemed confused to see him and he wondered if she was still wounded. Would she, God forbid, weep again?

"What do you want?" she asked.

"I'm swimming across the county."

"Good Christ. Will you ever grow up?"

"What's the matter?"

"If you've come here for money," she said, "I won't give you another cent."

"You could give me a drink."

"I could but I won't. I'm not alone."

"Well, I'm on my way."

He dove in and swam the pool, but when he tried to haul himself up onto the curb he found that the strength in his arms and shoulders had gone, and he paddled to the ladder and climbed out. Looking over his shoulder he saw, in the lighted bathhouse, a young man. Going out onto the dark lawn he smelled chrysanthemums or marigolds—some stubborn autumnal fragrance—on the night air, strong as gas. Looking overhead he saw that the stars had come out, but why should he seem to see Andromeda, Cepheus, and Cassiopeia? What had become of the constellations of midsummer? He began to cry.

It was probably the first time in his adult life that he had ever cried, certainly the first time in his life that he had ever felt so miserable, cold, tired, and bewildered. He could not understand the rudeness of the caterer's barkeep or the rudeness of a mistress who had come to him on her knees and showered his trousers with tears. He had swum too long, he had been immersed too long, and his nose and his throat were sore from the water. What he needed then was a drink, some company, and some clean, dry clothes, and while he could have cut directly across the road to his home he went on to the Gilmartins' pool. Here, for the first time in his life, he did not dive but went down the steps into the icy water and swam a hobbled sidestroke that he might have learned as a youth. He staggered with fatigue on his way to the Clydes' and paddled the length of their pool, stopping again and again with his hand on the curb to rest. He climbed up the ladder and wondered if he had the strength to get home. He had done what he wanted, he had swum the county, but he was so stupefied with exhaustion that his triumph seemed vague. Stooped, holding on to the gateposts for support, he turned up the driveway of his own house.

The place was dark. Was it so late that they had all gone to bed? Had Lucinda stayed at the Westerhazys' for supper? Had the girls joined her there or gone someplace else? Hadn't they agreed, as they usually did on Sunday, to regret all their invitations and stay at home? He tried the garage doors to see what cars were in but the doors were locked and rust came off the handles onto his hands. Going toward the house, he saw the force of the thunderstorm had knocked one of the rain gutters loose. It hung down over the front door like an umbrella rib, but it could be fixed in the morning. The house was locked, and he thought that the stupid cook or the stupid maid must have locked the place up until he remembered that it had been some time since they had employed a maid or a cook. He shouted, pounded on the door, tried to force it with his shoulder, and then, looking in at the windows, saw that the place was empty.

Questions

1. How is setting used symbolically in the story? Focus on such details as the change in weather and specific locales such as the highway and the public pool.
2. How is Neddy Merrill presented in the beginning of the story (especially paragraphs 2 and 3)? How would you describe the narrator's tone, and what does that tone communicate about the narrator's attitude toward Neddy?
3. At what point do you begin to realize that all is not what it appears to be on the surface? What textual details lead you to that realization?
4. How does Cheever communicate the passing of time and Neddy's aging? Cite specific passages from the story to back up your answer.
5. Does Neddy himself function symbolically in the story? If so, what might he be a symbol of?
6. In paragraph 3, Neddy decides that "he would name the stream Lucinda after his wife." What does that decision suggest at the beginning of the story? What does it suggest at the end?
7. As the story ends, does Neddy have anyone left in his life?

Ha Jin

Ha Jin is the pen name of Xuefei Jin, who was born in Liaoning, China, in 1956. The son of a military officer and a worker, Jin grew up during the turbulent Cultural Revolution, a ten-year upheaval initiated by the Communist Party in 1966 to transform China into a Marxist workers' society by destroying all remnants of the nation's ancient past. During this period many schools and universities were closed and intellectuals were required to work at proletarian jobs. At fourteen, Jin joined the People's Liberation Army, where he remained for nearly six years, and later worked as a telegraph operator for a railroad company. He then attended Heilongjiang University, where in 1981 he received a B.A. in English. After earning an M.A. in American literature from Shangdong University in 1984, Jin traveled to the United States to work on a Ph.D. at Brandeis University. He intended to return to China, but the Communist Party's violent suppression of the student movement in 1989 made him decide to stay in the United States and write only in English. "It's such a brutal government," he commented. "I was very angry, and I decided not to return to China." "Writing in English became my means of survival," he remarked, "of spending or wasting my life, of retrieving losses, mine, and those of others."

Jin has published three books of poetry and six novels, including Waiting *(1999, National Book Award),* War Trash *(2004, PEN/Faulkner Award), and* A Free Life *(2007). His first volume of short fiction,* Ocean of Words *(1996), was drawn from his experience in the People's Liberation Army and won the PEN/Hemingway Award. He is a professor of English at Boston University.*

Saboteur

2000

Mr. Chiu and his bride were having lunch in the square before Muji Train Station. On the table between them were two bottles of soda spewing out brown foam and two paper boxes of rice and sautéed cucumber and pork. "Let's eat," he said to her, and broke the connected ends of the chopsticks. He picked up a slice of streaky pork and put it into his mouth. As he was chewing, a few crinkles appeared on his thin jaw.

To his right, at another table, two railroad policemen were drinking tea and laughing; it seemed that the stout, middle-aged man was telling a joke to his young comrade, who was tall and of athletic build. Now and again they would steal a glance at Mr. Chiu's table.

The air smelled of rotten melon. A few flies kept buzzing above the couple's lunch. Hundreds of people were rushing around to get on the platform or to catch buses to downtown. Food and fruit vendors were crying for customers in lazy voices. About a dozen young women, representing the local hotels, held up placards which displayed the daily prices and words as large as a palm, like FREE MEALS, AIR-CONDITIONING, and ON THE RIVER. In the center of the square stood a concrete statue of Chairman Mao, at whose feet peasants were napping, their backs on the warm granite and their faces toward the sunny sky. A flock of pigeons perched on the Chairman's raised hand and forearm.

The rice and cucumber tasted good, and Mr. Chiu was eating unhurriedly. His sallow face showed exhaustion. He was glad that the honeymoon was finally over and that he and his bride were heading back for Harbin. During the two weeks' vacation, he had been worried about his liver, because three months ago he had suffered from acute hepatitis; he was afraid he might have a relapse. But he had had no severe symptoms, despite his liver being still big and tender. On the whole he was pleased with his health, which could endure even the strain of a honeymoon; indeed, he was on the course of recovery. He looked at his bride, who took off her wire glasses, kneading the root of her nose with her fingertips. Beads of sweat coated her pale cheeks.

"Are you all right, sweetheart?" he asked.

"I have a headache. I didn't sleep well last night."

"Take an aspirin, will you?"

"It's not that serious. Tomorrow is Sunday and I can sleep in. Don't worry."

As they were talking, the stout policeman at the next table stood up and threw a bowl of tea in their direction. Both Mr. Chiu's and his bride's sandals were wet instantly.

"Hooligan!" she said in a low voice.

Mr. Chiu got to his feet and said out loud, "Comrade Policeman, why did you do this?" He stretched out his right foot to show the wet sandal.

"Do what?" the stout man asked huskily, glaring at Mr. Chiu while the young fellow was whistling.

"See, you dumped tea on our feet."

"You're lying. You wet your shoes yourself."

"Comrade Policemen, your duty is to keep order, but you purposely tortured us common citizens. Why violate the law you are supposed to enforce?" As Mr. Chiu was speaking, dozens of people began gathering around.

With a wave of his hand, the man said to the young fellow, "Let's get hold of him!"

They grabbed Mr. Chiu and clamped handcuffs around his wrists. He cried, "You can't do this to me. This is utterly unreasonable."

"Shut up!" The man pulled out his pistol. "You can use your tongue at our headquarters."

The young fellow added, "You're a saboteur, you know that? You're disrupting public order."

The bride was too petrified to say anything coherent. She was a recent college graduate, had majored in fine arts, and had never seen the police make an arrest. All she could say was, "Oh, please, please!"

The policemen were pulling Mr. Chiu, but he refused to go with them, holding the corner of the table and shouting, "We have a train to catch. We already bought the tickets."

The stout man punched him in the chest. "Shut up. Let your ticket expire." With the pistol butt he chopped Mr. Chiu's hands, which at once released the table. Together the two men were dragging him away to the police station.

Realizing he had to go with them, Mr. Chiu turned his head and shouted to his bride, "Don't wait for me here. Take the train. If I'm not back by tomorrow morning, send someone over to get me out."

She nodded, covering her sobbing mouth with her palm.

After removing his belt, they locked Mr. Chiu into a cell in the back of the Railroad Police Station. The single window in the room was blocked by six steel bars; it faced a spacious yard, in which stood a few pines. Beyond the trees, two swings hung from an iron frame, swaying gently in the breeze. Somewhere in the building a cleaver was chopping rhythmically. There must be a kitchen upstairs, Mr. Chiu thought.

He was too exhausted to worry about what they would do to him, so he lay down on the narrow bed and shut his eyes. He wasn't afraid. The Cultural Revolution was over already, and recently the Party had been propagating the idea that all citizens were equal before the law. The police ought to be a law-abiding model for common people. As long as he remained coolheaded and reasoned with them, they probably wouldn't harm him.

Late in the afternoon he was taken to the Interrogation Bureau on the second floor. On his way there, in the stairwell, he ran into the middle-aged policeman who had manhandled him. The man grinned, rolling his bulgy eyes and pointing his fingers at him as if firing a pistol. Egg of a tortoise! Mr. Chiu cursed mentally.

The moment he sat down in the office, he burped, his palm shielding his mouth. In front of him, across a long desk, sat the chief of the bureau and a donkey-faced man. On the glass desktop was a folder containing information on his case. He felt it bizarre that in just a matter of hours they had accumulated a small pile of writing about him. On second thought he began to wonder whether they had kept a file on him all the time. How could this have happened? He lived and worked in Harbin, more than three hundred miles away, and this was his first time in Muji City.

The chief of the bureau was a thin, bald man who looked serene and intelligent. His slim hands handled the written pages in the folder in the manner of a lecturing scholar. To Mr. Chiu's left sat a young scribe, with a clipboard on his knee and a black fountain pen in his hand.

"Your name?" the chief asked, apparently reading out the question from a form.

"Chiu Maguang."

"Age?"

"Thirty-four."

"Profession?"

"Lecturer."

"Work unit?"

"Harbin University."

"Political status?"

"Communist Party member."

The chief put down the paper and began to speak. "Your crime is sabotage, although it hasn't induced serious consequences yet. Because you are a Party member, you should be punished more. You have failed to be a model for the masses and you—"

"Excuse me, sir," Mr. Chiu cut him off.

"What?"

"I didn't do anything. Your men are the saboteurs of our social order. They threw hot tea on my feet and on my wife's feet. Logically speaking, you should criticize them, if not punish them."

"That statement is groundless. You have no witness. Why should I believe you?" the chief said matter-of-factly.

"This is my evidence." He raised his right hand. "Your man hit my fingers with a pistol."

"That doesn't prove how your feet got wet. Besides, you could have hurt your fingers yourself."

"But I am telling the truth!" Anger flared up in Mr. Chiu. "Your police station owes me an apology. My train ticket has expired, my new leather sandals are ruined, and I am late for a conference in the provincial capital. You must compensate me for the damage and losses. Don't mistake me for a common citizen who would tremble when you sneeze. I'm a scholar, a philosopher, and an expert in dialectical materialism. If necessary, we will argue about this in *The Northeastern Daily*, or we will go to the highest People's Court in Beijing. Tell me, what's your name?" He got carried away with his harangue, which was by no means trivial and had worked to his advantage on numerous occasions.

"Stop bluffing us," the donkey-faced man broke in. "We have seen a lot of your kind. We can easily prove you are guilty. Here are some of the statements given by eyewitnesses." He pushed a few sheets of paper toward Mr. Chiu.

Mr. Chiu was dazed to see the different handwritings, which all stated that he had shouted in the square to attract attention and refused to obey the police. One of the witnesses had identified herself as a purchasing agent from a shipyard in Shanghai. Something stirred in Mr. Chiu's stomach, a pain rising to his rib. He gave out a faint moan.

"Now you have to admit you are guilty," the chief said. "Although it's a serious crime, we won't punish you severely, provided you write out a self-criticism and promise that you won't disrupt the public order again. In other words, your release will depend on your attitude toward this crime."

"You're daydreaming," Mr. Chiu cried. "I won't write a word, because I'm innocent. I demand that you provide me with a letter of apology so I can explain to my university why I'm late."

Both the interrogators smiled contemptuously. "Well, we've never done that," said the chief, taking a puff of his cigarette.

"Then make this a precedent."

"That's unnecessary. We are pretty certain that you will comply with our wishes." The chief blew a column of smoke toward Mr. Chiu's face.

At the tilt of the chief's head, two guards stepped forward and grabbed the criminal by the arms. Mr. Chiu meanwhile went on saying, "I shall report you to the Provincial Administration. You'll have to pay for this! You are worse than the Japanese military police."

They dragged him out of the room.

After dinner, which consisted of a bowl of millet porridge, a corn bun, and a piece of pickled turnip, Mr. Chiu began to have a fever, shaking with a chill and sweating profusely. He knew that the fire of anger had gotten into his liver and that he was probably having a relapse. No medicine was available, because his briefcase had been left with his bride. At home it would have been time for him to sit in front of their color TV, drinking jasmine tea and watching the evening news. It was so lonesome in here. The orange bulb above the single bed was the only source of light, which enabled the guards to keep him under surveillance at night. A moment ago he had asked them for a newspaper or a magazine to read, but they turned him down.

Through the small opening on the door noises came in. It seemed that the police on duty were playing cards or chess in a nearby office; shouts and laughter could be heard now and then. Meanwhile, an accordion kept coughing from a remote corner in the building. Looking at the ballpoint and the letter paper left for him by the guards when they took him back from the Interrogation Bureau, Mr. Chiu remembered the old saying, "When a scholar runs into soldiers, the more he argues, the muddier his point becomes." How ridiculous this whole thing was. He ruffled his thick hair with his fingers.

He felt miserable, massaging his stomach continually. To tell the truth, he was more upset than frightened, because he would have to catch up with his work once he was back home—a paper that was due at the printers next week, and two dozen books he ought to read for the courses he was going to teach in the fall.

A human shadow flitted across the opening. Mr. Chiu rushed to the door and shouted through the hole, "Comrade Guard, Comrade Guard!"

"What do you want?" a voice rasped.

"I want you to inform your leaders that I'm very sick. I have heart disease and hepatitis. I may die here if you keep me like this without medication."

"No leader is on duty on the weekend. You have to wait till Monday."

"What? You mean I'll stay in here tomorrow?"

"Yes."

"Your station will be held responsible if anything happens to me."

"We know that. Take it easy, you won't die."

It seemed illogical that Mr. Chiu slept quite well that night, though the light above his head had been on all the time and the straw mattress was hard and infested with fleas. He was afraid of ticks, mosquitoes, cockroaches—any kind of insect but fleas and bedbugs. Once, in the countryside, where his school's faculty and staff had helped the peasants harvest crops for a week, his colleagues had joked about his flesh, which they said must have tasted nonhuman to fleas. Except for him, they were all afflicted with hundreds of bites.

More amazing now, he didn't miss his bride a lot. He even enjoyed sleeping alone, perhaps because the honeymoon had tired him out and he needed more rest.

The backyard was quiet on Sunday morning. Pale sunlight streamed through the pine branches. A few sparrows were jumping on the ground, catching caterpillars and ladybugs. Holding the steel bars, Mr. Chiu inhaled the morning air, which smelled meaty. There must have been an eatery or a cooked-meat stand nearby. He reminded himself that he should take this detention with ease. A sentence that Chairman Mao had written to a hospitalized friend rose in his mind: "Since you are already in here, you may as well stay and make the best of it."

His desire for peace of mind originated in his fear that his hepatitis might get worse. He tried to remain unperturbed. However, he was sure that his liver was swelling up, since the fever still persisted. For a whole day he lay in bed, thinking about his paper on the nature of contradictions. Time and again he was overwhelmed by anger, cursing aloud, "A bunch of thugs!" He swore that once he was out, he would write an article about this experience. He had better find out some of the policemen's names.

It turned out to be a restful day for the most part; he was certain that his university would send somebody to his rescue. All he should do now was remain calm and wait patiently. Sooner or later the police would have to release him, although they had no idea that he might refuse to leave unless they wrote him an apology. Damn those hoodlums, they had ordered more than they could eat!

When he woke up on Monday morning, it was already light. Somewhere a man was moaning; the sound came from the backyard. After a long yawn, and kicking off the tattered blanket, Mr. Chiu climbed out of bed and went to the window. In the middle of the yard, a young man was fastened to a pine, his wrists handcuffed around the trunk from behind. He was wriggling and swearing loudly, but there was no sight of anyone else in the yard. He looked familiar to Mr. Chiu.

Mr. Chiu squinted his eyes to see who it was. To his astonishment, he recognized the man, who was Fenjin, a recent graduate from the Law Department at Harbin University. Two years ago Mr. Chiu had taught a course in Marxist materialism, in which Fenjin had enrolled. Now, how on earth had this young devil landed here?

Then it dawned on him that Fenjin must have been sent over by his bride. What a stupid woman! A bookworm, who only knew how to read foreign novels! He had expected that she would contact the school's Security Section, which would for sure send a cadre here. Fenjin held no official position; he merely worked in a private law firm that had just two lawyers; in fact, they had little business except for some detective work for men and women who suspected their spouses of having extramarital affairs. Mr. Chiu was overcome with a wave of nausea.

Should he call out to let his student know he was nearby? He decided not to, because he didn't know what had happened. Fenjin must have quarreled with the police to incur such a punishment. Yet this could never have occurred if Fenjin hadn't come to his rescue. So no matter what, Mr. Chiu had to do something. But what could he do?

It was going to be a scorcher. He could see purple steam shimmering and rising from the ground among the pines. Poor devil, he thought, as he raised a bowl of corn glue to his mouth, sipped, and took a bite of a piece of salted celery.

When a guard came to collect the bowl and the chopsticks, Mr. Chiu asked him what had happened to the man in the backyard. "He called our boss 'bandit,'" the guard said. "He claimed he was a lawyer or something. An arrogant son of a rabbit."

Now it was obvious to Mr. Chiu that he had to do something to help his rescuer. Before he could figure out a way, a scream broke out in the backyard. He rushed to the window and saw a tall policeman standing before Fenjin, an iron bucket on the ground. It was the same young fellow who had arrested Mr. Chiu in the square two days before. The man pinched Fenjin's nose, then raised his hand, which stayed in the air for a few seconds, then slapped the lawyer across the face. As Fenjin was groaning, the man lifted up the bucket and poured water on his head.

"This will keep you from getting sunstroke, boy. I'll give you some more every hour," the man said loudly.

Fenjin kept his eyes shut, yet his wry face showed that he was struggling to hold back from cursing the policeman, or, more likely, that he was sobbing in silence. He sneezed, then raised his face and shouted, "Let me go take a piss."

"Oh, yeah?" the man bawled. "Pee in your pants."

Still Mr. Chiu didn't make any noise, gripping the steel bars with both hands, his fingers white. The policeman turned and glanced at the cell's window; his pistol, partly holstered, glittered in the sun. With a snort he spat his cigarette butt to the ground and stamped it into the dust.

Then the door opened and the guards motioned Mr. Chiu to come out. Again they took him upstairs to the Interrogation Bureau.

The same men were in the office, though this time the scribe was sitting there empty-handed. At the sight of Mr. Chiu the chief said, "Ah, here you are. Please be seated."

After Mr. Chiu sat down, the chief waved a white silk fan and said to him, "You may have seen your lawyer. He's a young man without manners, so our director had him taught a crash course in the backyard."

"It's illegal to do that. Aren't you afraid to appear in a newspaper?"

"No, we are not, not even on TV. What else can you do? We are not afraid of any story you make up. We call it fiction. What we do care about is that you cooperate with us. That is to say, you must admit your crime."

"What if I refuse to cooperate?"

"Then your lawyer will continue his education in the sunshine."

A swoon swayed Mr. Chiu, and he held the arms of the chair to steady himself. A numb pain stung him in the upper stomach and nauseated him, and his head was throbbing. He was sure that the hepatitis was finally attacking him. Anger was flaming up in his chest; his throat was tight and clogged.

The chief resumed, "As a matter of fact, you don't even have to write out your self-criticism. We have your crime described clearly here. All we need is your signature."

Holding back his rage, Mr. Chiu said, "Let me look at that."

With a smirk the donkey-faced man handed him a sheet which carried these words:

> I hereby admit that on July 13 I disrupted public order at Muji Train Station, and that I refused to listen to reason when the railroad police issued their warning. Thus I myself am responsible for my arrest. After two days' detention, I have realized the reactionary nature of my crime. From now on, I shall continue to educate myself with all my effort and shall never commit this kind of crime again.

A voice started screaming in Mr. Chiu's ears, "Lie, lie!" But he shook his head and forced the voice away. He asked the chief, "If I sign this, will you release both my lawyer and me?"

"Of course, we'll do that." The chief was drumming his fingers on the blue folder—their file on him.

Mr. Chiu signed his name and put his thumbprint under his signature.

"Now you are free to go," the chief said with a smile, and handed him a piece of paper to wipe his thumb with.

Mr. Chiu was so sick that he couldn't stand up from the chair at first try. Then he doubled his effort and rose to his feet. He staggered out of the building to meet his lawyer in the backyard, having forgotten to ask for his belt back. In his chest he felt as though there were a bomb. If he were able to, he would have razed the entire police station and eliminated all their families. Though he knew he could do nothing like that, he made up his mind to do something.

                                    *

"I'm sorry about this torture, Fenjin," Mr. Chiu said when they met.   100
"It doesn't matter. They are savages." The lawyer brushed a patch of dirt off his jacket with trembling fingers. Water was still dribbling from the bottoms of his trouser legs.

"Let's go now," the teacher said.

The moment they came out of the police station, Mr. Chiu caught sight of a tea stand. He grabbed Fenjin's arm and walked over to the old woman at the table. "Two bowls of black tea," he said and handed her a one-yuan note.

After the first bowl, they each had another one. Then they set out for the train station. But before they walked fifty yards, Mr. Chiu insisted on eating a bowl of tree-ear soup at a food stand. Fenjin agreed. He told his teacher, "You mustn't treat me like a guest."

"No, I want to eat something myself."   105

As if dying of hunger, Mr. Chiu dragged his lawyer from restaurant to restaurant near the police station, but at each place he ordered no more than two bowls of food. Fenjin wondered why his teacher wouldn't stay at one place and eat his fill.

Mr. Chiu bought noodles, wonton, eight-grain porridge, and chicken soup, respectively, at four restaurants. While eating, he kept saying through his teeth, "If only I could kill all the bastards!" At the last place he merely took a few sips of the soup without tasting the chicken cubes and mushrooms.

Fenjin was baffled by his teacher, who looked ferocious and muttered to himself mysteriously, and whose jaundiced face was covered with dark puckers. For the first time Fenjin thought of Mr. Chiu as an ugly man.

Within a month over eight hundred people contracted acute hepatitis in Muji. Six died of the disease, including two children. Nobody knew how the epidemic had started.

Questions

1. Why is Mr. Chiu in Muji?
2. In the story's second paragraph, two railroad policemen are sitting next to Mr. Chiu and his wife. Why do you think they are laughing and looking at the newlywed couple?
3. With what specific crime is Mr. Chiu charged? Is he guilty?
4. What is Mr. Chiu's initial reaction to his arrest?
5. Why does Mr. Chiu initially refuse to sign a confession? Why does he eventually sign it?
6. What is ironic about Mr. Chiu's arrest? What is ironic about his ultimate confession?
7. When does Mr. Chiu decide to revenge himself on the police?
8. Is Mr. Chiu's revenge justified? Are the effects of his revenge proportionate to his own suffering?

Suggestions for Writing on *Stories about Individuals in Isolation*

1. All of the protagonists in these stories are, in one way or another, alone. Yet their circumstances and feelings about being alone are very different. Analyze one of these characters and the circumstances of his being alone. Is his solitude a happy one or a sad one? What does his situation suggest about the relationship of the individual to society?
2. All of the stories in this section make use of symbol. Pick two stories and analyze the symbols that appear in them. For what do the symbols stand? How does the author use them to make his point? Are the chosen symbols effective in relating the story's theme? Why or why not?
3. Have you ever, like the protagonist of "Saboteur," found yourself in a humiliating or powerless situation? How did you handle it? Write an essay about the experience, what led to the choices you made, and how you feel about them now.

POETRY

LONELINESS AND COMMUNITY

E. E. Cummings	*anyone lived in a pretty how town*
Stevie Smith	*Not Waving but Drowning*
Allen Ginsberg	*A Supermarket in California*
Anne Sexton	*Her Kind*
Pablo Neruda	*Muchos Somos / We Are Many*

Loneliness may be the saddest of human conditions. If you fight with your parents, you might still have your boyfriend or girlfriend. If you are dumped by the boyfriend or girlfriend, you can commiserate with friends. But when you have no one with whom you feel comfortable or close, the long hours of a day can feel empty and oppressive, and life can be unbearably painful. Even when you're surrounded by people you love, you might not feel understood or worthy of their affections, and that can drive you deeper into yourself. Loneliness may account for why some people stay at the office or the library later than they need to—to avoid going home to empty rooms or to people with whom they don't feel connected. It may also have something to do with the proliferation of dating websites, or the huge popularity of Facebook, which creates easy avenues for social exchange without the risks or the work of actual human intimacy. When loneliness is compounded by feelings of failure, or shame, or inadequacy, or frustration, it can be all the more piercing and unbearable.

The poems in this section all depict loneliness. Some describe characters whose isolation and despair aren't recognized by others until too late, as in Stevie Smith's "Not Waving but Drowning." E. E. Cummings's strange and haunting "anyone lived in a pretty how town" presents loneliness as a part of social existence that can be overcome by love. Anne Sexton's "Her Kind" depicts the dark side of solitude, while in "A Supermarket in California" Allen Ginsberg finds an odd but radiant community in his own isolation. Finally, Pablo Neruda celebrates how many personalities and possibilities each individual possesses.

E. E. Cummings

E. E. Cummings (1894–1962) endured a number of adverse experiences over the course of his life, including a wrongful detention in a French prison camp during World War I and complicated and often painful relationships with women. But through it all, sustained by the unswerving love and support of his family and by his own irrepressible self-confidence, he kept alive his childlike sense of wonder and delight in the beauty of nature and the simple joys of existence. A fine evocation of these themes, "anyone lived in a pretty how town" is one of Cummings's most popular poems with readers of all ages.

E. E. Cummings

anyone lived in a pretty how town

1940

anyone lived in a pretty how town
(with up so floating many bells down)
spring summer autumn winter
he sang his didn't he danced his did.

Women and men(both little and small)   5
cared for anyone not at all
they sowed their isn't they reaped their same
sun moon stars rain

children guessed(but only a few
and down they forgot as up they grew   10
autumn winter spring summer)
that noone loved him more by more

when by now and tree by leaf
she laughed his joy she cried his grief
bird by snow and stir by still   15
anyone's any was all to her

someones married their everyones
laughed their cryings and did their dance
(sleep wake hope and then)they
said their nevers they slept their dream   20

stars rain sun moon
(and only the snow can begin to explain
how children are apt to forget to remember
with up so floating many bells down)

one day anyone died i guess   25
(and noone stooped to kiss his face)
busy folk buried them side by side
little by little and was by was

all by all and deep by deep
and more by more they dream their sleep   30
noone and anyone earth by april
wish by spirit and if by yes.

Women and men(both dong and ding)
summer autumn winter spring
reaped their sowing and went their came   35
sun moon stars rain

Questions

1. Summarize the story told in this poem. Who are the characters?
2. Rearrange the words in the two opening lines into the order you would expect them usually to follow. What effect does Cummings obtain by his unconventional word order?

3. Another of Cummings's strategies is to use one part of speech as if it were another; for instance, in line 4, *didn't* and *did* ordinarily are verbs, but here they are used as nouns. What other words in the poem perform functions other than their expected ones?
4. How do you think Cummings feels about the protagonists of the poem? Explain, as specifically as possible, the reasons for your response.

Stevie Smith

Florence Margaret Smith (1902–1971) was born in Hull, England; her nickname, taken from the name of a popular jockey of the time, was occasioned by her small size. Despite relationships with several men, she never married, living for many years with her beloved Aunt Margaret, whose death in 1968 at the age of ninety-six was devastating to the poet. Smith, who spent thirty years as a secretary in a London publishing firm, wrote three novels and seven volumes of poetry, frequently illustrating them with her own whimsical and childlike drawings. Her Collected Poems *appeared in 1975. "Whimsical" and "childlike" are also apt descriptions of much of her verse, although often, as in "Not Waving but Drowning," it engages themes of loneliness and pain.*

Not Waving but Drowning   1957

Nobody heard him, the dead man,
But still he lay moaning:
I was much further out than you thought
And not waving but drowning.

Poor chap, he always loved larking   5
And now he's dead
It must have been too cold for him his heart gave way,
They said.

Oh, no no no, it was too cold always
(Still the dead one lay moaning)   10
I was much too far out all my life
And not waving but drowning.

Questions
1. What is the general attitude toward "the dead man" and his accident?
2. Does the speaker of the poem agree with the general explanation for the swimmer's death?
3. What does the word "larking" mean in line 5?
4. What did people miss by thinking the dead man "always loved larking"?
5. How would you summarize the theme of this poem?

Allen Ginsberg

Allen Ginsberg (1926–1997) was born in Paterson, New Jersey. His father Louis was a high school teacher and a published poet of conservative tendencies. Ginsberg's first book, Howl and Other Poems *(1956), was unsuccessfully prosecuted for obscenity, and went on to become a best seller and a founding document of the Beat movement. Though he published many other volumes of poetry, culminating in a* Collected Poems *(2006) of over a thousand pages,* Howl *is considered among his finest work. "A Supermarket in California" dramatizes Ginsberg's identification with Walt Whitman, another poetic loner and gay iconoclast.*

A Supermarket in California   1956

What thoughts I have of you tonight, Walt Whitman, for I walked down the sidestreets under the trees with a headache self-conscious looking at the full moon.

In my hungry fatigue, and shopping for images, I went into the neon fruit supermarket, dreaming of your enumerations!

What peaches and what penumbras! Whole families shopping at night! Aisles full of husbands! Wives in the avocados, babies in the tomatoes!—and you, García Lorca, what were you doing down by the watermelons?

I saw you, Walt Whitman, childless, lonely old grubber, poking among the meats in the refrigerator and eyeing the grocery boys.

I heard you asking questions of each: Who killed the pork chops? What price bananas? Are you my Angel?   5

I wandered in and out of the brilliant stacks of cans following you, and followed in my imagination by the store detective.

We strode down the open corridors together in our solitary fancy tasting artichokes, possessing every frozen delicacy, and never passing the cashier.

Where are we going, Walt Whitman? The doors close in an hour. Which way does your beard point tonight?

(I touch your book and dream of our odyssey in the supermarket and feel absurd.)

Will we walk all night through solitary streets? The trees add shade to shade, lights out in the houses, we'll both be lonely.   10

Will we stroll dreaming of the lost America of love past blue automobiles in driveways, home to our silent cottage?

Ah, dear father, graybeard, lonely old courage-teacher, what America did you have when Charon quit poling his ferry and you got out on a smoking bank and stood watching the boat disappear on the black waters of Lethe?

Questions

1. How would you describe the tone of this poem?
2. What elements of Whitman's poetic style does Ginsberg make use of?
3. What personal characteristics of Whitman, as he is presented here, does the speaker identify with and/or seek consolation from?

A SUPERMARKET IN CALIFORNIA.   2 *enumerations:* many of Whitman's poems contain lists of observed details.   3 *García Lorca:* modern Spanish poet who wrote an "Ode to Walt Whitman" in his book-length sequence *Poet in New York.*   12 *Charon . . . Lethe:* Is the poet confusing two underworld rivers? Charon, in Greek and Roman mythology, is the boatman who ferries the souls of the dead across the River Styx. The River Lethe also flows through Hades, and a drink of its waters makes the dead lose their painful memories of loved ones they have left behind.

Anne Sexton

Born Anne Gray Harvey in Newton, Massachusetts, Anne Sexton (1928–1974) was married at the age of nineteen and the mother of two daughters by her mid-twenties. Hospitalized with emotional problems, she began writing poetry at her therapist's suggestion. She took a writing course with the poet Robert Lowell, in which one of her classmates was Sylvia Plath. Sexton's first book of poems was To Bedlam and Part Way Back (1960); her third, Live or Die (1967), won the Pulitzer Prize. Her later books were less well received. After undergoing repeated hospitalizations and a divorce in 1973, she took her own life in October 1974. Her Complete Poems was published in 1981. "Her Kind," with its easy formal mastery, arresting images, and edgy tone, displays her work at its best.

Anne Sexton

Her Kind   1960

I have gone out, a possessed witch,
haunting the black air, braver at night;
dreaming evil, I have done my hitch
over the plain houses, light by light:
lonely thing, twelve-fingered, out of mind.   5
A woman like that is not a woman, quite.
I have been her kind.

I have found the warm caves in the woods,
filled them with skillets, carvings, shelves,
closets, silks, innumerable goods;   10
fixed the suppers for the worms and the elves:
whining, rearranging the disaligned.
A woman like that is misunderstood.
I have been her kind.

I have ridden in your cart, driver,   15
waved my nude arms at villages going by,
learning the last bright routes, survivor
where your flames still bite my thigh
and my ribs crack where your wheels wind.
A woman like that is not ashamed to die.   20
I have been her kind.

Questions

1. Who is the speaker of this poem? What do we know about her?
2. What does the speaker mean by ending each stanza with the statement, "I have been her kind"?
3. Who are the figures with whom the speaker identifies? What do these figures tell us about the speaker's state of mind?
4. What is the speaker's relationship to her community?

Pablo Neruda

Pablo Neruda (1904–1973) was born Neftali Ricardo Reyes Basoalto in Parral, southern Chile. His mother died a month later, a fact which is said to have affected Neruda's choice of imagery throughout his life's work. He began writing poems as a child despite his family's disapproval, which led him to adopt the "working class" pen name Pablo Neruda. Neruda served in a long line of diplomatic positions. When a new right-wing regime outlawed the Communist party in Chile, Neruda, a fervent communist, fled abroad and spent four years in exile. In 1952, when the Chilean government ceased its persecution of Marxists, Neruda returned to his native land, and in 1970 he was a candidate for the presidency of Chile. He was awarded the Nobel Prize in Literature in 1971. Neruda died of cancer in Santiago in 1973.

Muchos Somos 1958

De tantos hombres que soy, que somos,
no puedo encontrar a ninguno:
se me pierden bajo la ropa,
se fueron a otra ciudad.

Cuando todo está preparado
para mostrarme inteligente
el tonto que llevo escondido
se toma la palabra en mi boca.

Otras veces me duermo en medio
de la sociedad distinguida
y cuando busco en mí al valiente,
un cobarde que no conozco
corre a tomar con mi esqueleto
mil deliciosas precauciones.

Cuando arde una casa estimada
en vez del bombero que llamo
se precipita el incendiario
y ése soy yo. No tengo arreglo.
Qué debo hacer para escogerme?
Cómo puedo rehabilitarme?

Todos los libros que leo
celebran héroes refulgentes
siempre seguros de sí mismos:
me muero de envidia por ellos,
y en los filmes de vientos y balas
me quedo envidiando al jinete,
me quedo admirando al caballo.

We Are Many 1967

Of the many men who I am, who we are,
I can't find a single one;
they disappear among my clothes,
they've left for another city.

When everything seems to be set   5
to show me off as intelligent,
the fool I always keep hidden
takes over all that I say.

At other times, I'm asleep
among distinguished people,   10
and when I look for my brave self,
a coward unknown to me
rushes to cover my skeleton
with a thousand fine excuses.

When a decent house catches fire,   15
instead of the fireman I summon,
an arsonist bursts on the scene,
and that's me. What can I do?
What can I do to distinguish myself?
How can I pull myself together?   20

All the books I read
are full of dazzling heroes,
always sure of themselves.
I die with envy of them;
and in films full of wind and bullets,   25
I goggle at the cowboys,
I even admire the horses.

Pero cuando pido al intrépido	But when I call for a hero,
me sale el viejo perezoso,	out comes my lazy old self;
y así yo no sé quién soy,	so I never know who I am, 30
no sé cuántos soy o seremos.	nor how many I am or will be.
Me gustaría tocar un timbre	I'd love to be able to touch a bell
y sacar el mí verdadero	and summon the real me,
porque si yo me necesito	because if I really need myself,
no debo desaparecerme.	I mustn't disappear. 35
Mientras escribo estoy ausente	While I am writing, I'm far away;
y cuando vuelvo ya he partido:	and when I come back, I've gone.
voy a ver si a las otras gentes	I would like to know if others
les pasa lo que a mí me pasa,	go through the same things that I do,
si son tantos como soy yo,	have as many selves as I have, 40
si se parecen a sí mismos	and see themselves similarly;
y cuando lo haya averiguado	and when I've exhausted this problem,
voy a aprender tan bien las cosas	I'm going to study so hard
que para explicar mis problemas	that when I explain myself,
les hablaré de geografía.	I'll be talking geography. 45

—*Translated by Alastair Reid*

Questions

1. How many people are in the speaker of the poem? Cite every example.
2. What do these different men seem to have in common? What is their relation to the men the speaker usually wants to summon?
3. What is Neruda suggesting about human nature by offering all of these contradictory characters in place of a unified and rational individual personality?

Suggestions for Writing on *Poems about Loneliness and Community*

1. Pick one poem and analyze how details about its setting (the ocean in "Not Waving but Drowning" or the supermarket in "A Supermarket in California") convey or add to the speaker's feeling of loneliness.
2. How would you describe the tone of Sexton's "Her Kind"? Are there things about the imagery and situations that strike you as distinctly female? Why or why not? Write an essay about how this poem suggests the ways that gender relates to loneliness—and whether or not you agree.
3. Think of a time you felt particularly lonely in a crowd—or happy in a crowd—and write a personal essay about it. How did the presence of other people contribute to your feelings?
4. Both "Not Waving but Drowning" and "anyone lived in a pretty how town" describe the isolation of individuals in a community. What similarities do you find in the treatment of this subject in the two poems? What differences?
5. If Pablo Neruda is correct in "We Are Many," then each of us contains many different selves, including contradictory ones. Write a short essay in which you share and explain several of the different selves inside you.

INDIVIDUALISM VERSUS CONFORMITY

Walt Whitman	*I Hear America Singing*
Paul Laurence Dunbar	*Sympathy*
Robert Frost	*Mending Wall*
W. H. Auden	*The Unknown Citizen*
Mary Oliver	*Wild Geese*

North American culture, historically, has celebrated the individual. Our cultural icons, from cowboys to prospectors, from detectives to sports figures, are often solitary figures who undertake their tasks alone or against tremendous obstacles. We believe, as a culture, that each person has the right to seek happiness and self-fulfillment, and that individual rights should not be sacrificed for the betterment of the larger group. Indeed, there can be deep satisfaction in pursuing one's dreams, or in fighting for the right to define oneself. But this focus on individual expression and fulfillment is not universal. In some cultures—for example, Japan—the good of the group is traditionally privileged over the needs of a single person. And, while for some people breaking free of prescribed roles and expectations can be liberating, for others it's more desirable to stay within them. A person's success or value—and possibly one's happiness—may in fact be determined, in some contexts, by his or her adherence to a society's expectations. The poems in this section depict those whose courage or self-esteem or stubbornness allows them to express themselves as individuals, as well as those who draw equal satisfaction from playing by the rules.

Walt Whitman

Born on Long Island, New York, and raised in Brooklyn, the young Walt Whitman (1819–1892) worked as a schoolteacher (briefly) and a printer. In 1855, he published the first edition of Leaves of Grass, *a book of poems whose long unrimed lines, ecstatic celebration of all aspects of life, and identification with those scorned and shunned by society made it a revolutionary work. Reissued in successively enlarged editions for the next thirty-five years, it would become the book of his life. In his own time Whitman was condemned as immoral by some, admired to the point of idolatry by others, and largely dismissed by the literary establishment. Over the past hundred years, his work and his example have exerted an enormous influence on the development of American poetry.*

I Hear America Singing 1860

I hear America singing, the varied carols I hear,
Those of mechanics, each one singing his as it should be blithe and strong,
The carpenter singing his as he measures his plank or beam,
The mason singing his as he makes ready for work, or leaves off work,
The boatman singing what belongs to him in his boat, the deckhand 5
    singing on the steamboat deck,
The shoemaker singing as he sits on his bench, the hatter singing as he
    stands,
The wood-cutter's song, the ploughboy's on his way in the morning, or at
    noon intermission or at sundown,
The delicious singing of the mother, or of the young wife at work, or of the
    girl sewing or washing,
Each singing what belongs to him or her and to none else,
The day what belongs to the day—at night the party of young fellows, 10
    robust, friendly,
Singing with open mouths their strong melodious songs.

Questions

1. What sorts of people are mentioned in the poem? What does that focus suggest about Whitman's vision of America?
2. Do you find more emphasis in the poem on individuality or on community? Explain the basis for your conclusion.
3. Look at the date of the poem. What do you know about American society at that point in its history? How might the poem seem to relate to that prevailing situation?

Paul Laurence Dunbar

Paul Laurence Dunbar (1872–1906) was born in Dayton, Ohio. His parents had escaped from slavery in Kentucky, and his father fought for the Union in the Civil War. The only black student in his high school—Wilbur and Orville Wright were fellow students and good friends of his—Dunbar was elected class president, editor of the school newspaper, and president of the literary society. His Lyrics of Lowly Life (1896) made him famous and led to meetings with Booker T. Washington and President Theodore Roosevelt, among others. He died of tuberculosis in February 1906. His sentimental dialect ballads were not always well received, especially among African American readers, but he wrote a number of finely crafted and powerful poems, including "Sympathy."

Sympathy   1899

I know what the caged bird feels, alas!
   When the sun is bright on the upland slopes;
When the wind stirs soft through the springing grass,
And the river flows like a stream of glass;
   When the first bird sings and the first bud opes,   5
And the faint perfume from its chalice steals—
I know what the caged bird feels!

I know why the caged bird beats his wing
   Till its blood is red on the cruel bars;
For he must fly back to his perch and cling   10
When he fain would be on the bough a-swing;
   And a pain still throbs in the old, old scars
And they pulse again with a keener sting—
I know why he beats his wing!

I know why the caged bird sings, ah me,   15
   When his wing is bruised and his bosom sore,—
When he beats his bars and he would be free;
It is not a carol of joy or glee,
   But a prayer that he sends from his heart's deep core,
But a plea, that upward to Heaven he flings—   20
I know why the caged bird sings!

Questions
1. Why do you think the speaker identifies so closely with the caged bird? Is the poem also capable of a more universal interpretation?
2. What exactly do you understand the speaker to be saying in the second stanza?
3. What implicit comparison is being made in the last stanza between the bird and the poet?

Robert Frost

Although Robert Frost (1874–1963) spent most of his adult life living in small towns and rural areas in New Hampshire and Vermont, there was only one ten-year period—the first decade of the twentieth century—when he made a serious effort to support his family by farming. Nonetheless, he cultivated a public image as a farmer-poet, an image that has by and large remained fixed in the popular perception of both the man and his poetry. Given its subject matter and its knowing air, "Mending Wall" is one of the poems that sustains that image. Its engagement of deeper themes, seasoned with Frost's customary sly wit, has also made it one of his most admired works.

Mending Wall 1914

Something there is that doesn't love a wall,
That sends the frozen-ground-swell under it,
And spills the upper boulders in the sun;
And makes gaps even two can pass abreast.
The work of hunters is another thing: 5
I have come after them and made repair
Where they have left not one stone on a stone,
But they would have the rabbit out of hiding,
To please the yelping dogs. The gaps I mean,
No one has seen them made or heard them made, 10
But at spring mending-time we find them there.
I let my neighbor know beyond the hill;
And on a day we meet to walk the line
And set the wall between us once again.
We keep the wall between us as we go. 15
To each the boulders that have fallen to each.
And some are loaves and some so nearly balls
We have to use a spell to make them balance:
"Stay where you are until our backs are turned!"
We wear our fingers rough with handling them. 20
Oh, just another kind of outdoor game,
One on a side. It comes to little more:
There where it is we do not need the wall:
He is all pine and I am apple orchard.
My apple trees will never get across 25
And eat the cones under his pines, I tell him.
He only says, "Good fences make good neighbors."
Spring is the mischief in me, and I wonder
If I could put a notion in his head:
"Why do they make good neighbors? Isn't it 30
Where there are cows? But here there are no cows.
Before I built a wall I'd ask to know
What I was walling in or walling out,
And to whom I was like to give offense.
Something there is that doesn't love a wall, 35
That wants it down." I could say "Elves" to him,
But it's not elves exactly, and I'd rather
He said it for himself. I see him there
Bringing a stone grasped firmly by the top
In each hand, like an old-stone savage armed. 40
He moves in darkness as it seems to me,
Not of woods only and the shade of trees.
He will not go behind his father's saying,
And he likes having thought of it so well
He says again, "Good fences make good neighbors." 45

Questions

1. How would you characterize the speaker? What sort of person is his neighbor? Be as specific as possible, using details from the poem to back up your conclusions.
2. Explain more fully the contrasting viewpoints expressed in the first and last lines of the poem.
3. In your view, does the author show a preference for one attitude over the other?

W. H. Auden

W. H. Auden (1907–1973) was born in York, England, the third son of a physician and a former nurse. In the early 1930s, after his graduation from Oxford University, he published a number of volumes of verse with the prominent British firm of Faber & Faber, and was quickly established as the leading poetic voice of his generation. In January 1939 he moved to New York; he became an American citizen in 1946 and won a Pulitzer Prize in 1948 for his long poem The Age of Anxiety. The variety, range, and abundance of his work made him one of the most prolific poets of the twentieth century; its brilliance, depth, and artistry made him one of the greatest. "The Unknown Citizen" is one of a number of masterpieces in Auden's finest collection, Another Time.

The Unknown Citizen 1940

(To JS/07/M/378
This Marble Monument Is Erected by the State)

He was found by the Bureau of Statistics to be
One against whom there was no official complaint,
And all the reports on his conduct agree
That, in the modern sense of an old-fashioned word, he was a saint,
For in everything he did he served the Greater Community. 5
Except for the War till the day he retired
He worked in a factory and never got fired,
But satisfied his employers, Fudge Motors Inc.
Yet he wasn't a scab or odd in his views,
For his Union reports that he paid his dues, 10
(Our report on his Union shows it was sound)
And our Social Psychology workers found
That he was popular with his mates and liked a drink.
The Press are convinced that he bought a paper every day
And that his reactions to advertisements were normal in every way. 15
Policies taken out in his name prove that he was fully insured,
And his Health-card shows he was once in hospital but left it cured.
Both Producers Research and High-Grade Living declare
He was fully sensible to the advantages of the Installment Plan
And had everything necessary to the Modern Man, 20
A phonograph, a radio, a car and a frigidaire.
Our researchers into Public Opinion are content
That he held the proper opinions for the time of year;
When there was peace, he was for peace; when there was war, he went.

He was married and added five children to the population, 25
Which our Eugenist says was the right number for a parent of his
   generation,
And our teachers report that he never interfered with their education.
Was he free? Was he happy? The question is absurd:
Had anything been wrong, we should certainly have heard.

Questions

1. Read the two-line epitaph at the beginning of the poem as carefully as you read what follows. How does the epitaph help establish the voice by which the rest of the poem is spoken?
2. Who is speaking?
3. What ironic discrepancies do you find between the speaker's attitude toward the subject and that of the poet himself? By what is the poet's attitude made clear?
4. In the phrase "The Unknown Soldier" (of which "The Unknown Citizen" reminds us), what does the word "unknown" mean? What does it mean in the title of Auden's poem?
5. What tendencies in our civilization does Auden satirize?
6. How would you expect the speaker to define a Modern Man, if an iPod, a radio, a car, and a refrigerator are "everything" a Modern Man needs?

Mary Oliver

Mary Oliver was born in Maple Heights, Ohio, in 1935. As a teenager, she befriended the sister of Edna St. Vincent Millay and helped her to organize the late poet's papers. The first of Oliver's many collections of poetry, which have made her one of the best-selling poets in America, was Voyage and Other Poems *(1963); subsequent volumes include* American Primitive *(1983), which won the Pulitzer Prize, and* New and Selected Poems *(1992), which won the National Book Award. Retired from a professorship at Bennington College, she lives in Provincetown, Massachusetts. Like much of her work, "Wild Geese" celebrates the beauty and majesty of nature as an alternative to the ills and stresses of civilization.*

Wild Geese   1986

You do not have to be good.
You do not have to walk on your knees
for a hundred miles through the desert, repenting.
You only have to let the soft animal of your body
   love what it loves.   5
Tell me about despair, yours, and I will tell you mine.
Meanwhile the world goes on.
Meanwhile the sun and the clear pebbles of the rain
are moving across the landscapes,
over the prairies and the deep trees,   10
the mountains and the rivers.
Meanwhile the wild geese, high in the clean blue air,
are heading home again.
Whoever you are, no matter how lonely,
the world offers itself to your imagination,   15

calls to you like the wild geese, harsh and exciting—
over and over announcing your place
in the family of things.

Questions
1. Is this poem addressed to a specific person?
2. What is meant by "good" in the first line?
3. What do the wild geese symbolize? What is the significance here of the term "wild"?
4. What other adjectives are used to describe the phenomena of nature? What thematic purpose is served by this characterization of the natural world?

Suggestions for Writing on *Poems about Individualism Versus Conformity*

1. "I Hear America Singing" and "Sympathy" offer vastly different views of America. Compare the imagery used in each poem and discuss each poet's themes and ideas. Which view strikes you as more convincing? Why?
2. "Sympathy" addresses the issue of how it feels to be black in America. Discuss how Dunbar uses his central symbol of a caged bird to express his vision of African American oppression and resistance. What social ideas does the poem convey?
3. "The Unknown Citizen" and "Mending Wall" both present portraits of conformity. Is any explanation for the conformist spirit offered in either poem? How does each author seem to regard the character in question?
4. Choose a symbol—such as the wall in "Mending Wall" or the geese in "Wild Geese"—and analyze how it relates to the theme of the poem. Do you think the symbol is effective in conveying the poet's ideas? Why or why not?

Poet in Depth
Emily Dickinson

SELECTING YOUR OWN SOCIETY

I'm Nobody! Who are you?

The Soul selects her own Society

This is my letter to the World

Much Madness is divinest Sense

Some keep the Sabbath going to Church

Casebook on Emily Dickinson

Perhaps no poet speaks to the theme of the individual and society more effectively than Emily Dickinson. Although Dickinson spent most of her adult life on the grounds of her family's home in Amherst, Massachusetts, depictions of her as reclusive are not quite accurate, or are perhaps oversimplified. She was deeply engaged with at least a few other people, as evidenced by her many letters; she was also occupied by large human themes such as faith, individual identity, and love. Her exacting expectations of other people—and of herself—may be part of what made it so difficult for her to interact with her decidedly imperfect contemporaries. Dickinson had no patience for small talk, or self-importance, or adherence to social customs. To her, any public display—of one's achievements, or even of religious expression—was inherently suspect. All of these things might have dictated that she not actively seek to place herself or her work in the public eye; only a few of her poems were published during her lifetime. The poems that follow were among the more than 1,700 poems that Dickinson left behind when she died. Deceptively simple on the surface, they delve deeply into issues such as human connection, humility, and the true expression of religious longing.

Emily Dickinson

> If I read a book [and] it makes my whole body so cold
> no fire ever can warm me I know that is poetry.
> —EMILY DICKINSON

Emily Dickinson (1830–1886) spent virtually all her life in her family home in Amherst, Massachusetts. Her father, Edward Dickinson, was a prominent lawyer who ranked as Amherst's leading citizen. (He even served a term in the U.S. Congress.) Dickinson attended one year of college at Mount Holyoke Female Seminary in South Hadley. She proved to be a good student, but, suffering from homesickness and poor health, she did not return for the second year. This brief period of study and a few trips to Boston, Philadelphia, and Washington, D.C., were the only occasions she left home in her fifty-five-year life. As the years passed, Dickinson became more reclusive. She stopped attending church (and refused to endorse the orthodox Congregationalist creed). She also spent increasing time alone in her room—often writing poems. Dickinson never married, but she had a significant romantic relationship with at least one unidentified man. Although scholars have suggested several likely candidates, the historical object of her affections will likely never be known. What survives unmistakably, however, is the intensely passionate poetry written out of these private circumstances. By the end of her life, Dickinson had become a locally famous recluse; she rarely left home. She would greet visitors from her own upstairs room, clearly heard but never seen. In 1886 she was buried, according to her own instructions, within sight of the family home.

Emily Dickinson

Although Dickinson composed 1,789 known poems, only a handful were published in her lifetime. She often, however, sent copies of poems to friends in letters, but only after her death would the full extent of her writings become known when a cache of manuscripts was discovered in a trunk in the homestead attic—handwritten little booklets of poems sewn together by the poet with needle and thread. From 1890 until the mid-twentieth century, nine posthumous collections of her poems were published by friends and relatives, some of whom rewrote her work and changed her idiosyncratic punctuation to make it more conventional. Thomas H. Johnson's three-volume edition of the Poems (1955) established a more accurate text. In relatively few and simple forms clearly indebted to the hymns she heard in church, Dickinson succeeded in being a true visionary and a poet of colossal originality.

I'm Nobody! Who are you?   (about 1861)

I'm Nobody! Who are you?
Are you – Nobody – Too?
Then there's a pair of us!
Don't tell! they'd advertise – you know!

How dreary – to be – Somebody!   5
How public – like a Frog –
To tell one's name – the livelong June –
To an admiring Bog!

Questions
1. Why do you think the speaker calls herself "Nobody"?
2. What might she mean by "they'd advertise"?
3. Why would it be "dreary – to be – Somebody"?
4. How does "Nobody's" idea of social life differ from that of "Somebody"?

The Soul selects her own Society   (about 1862)

The Soul selects her own Society –
Then – shuts the Door –
To her divine Majority –
Present no more –

Unmoved – she notes the Chariots – pausing –   5
At her low Gate –
Unmoved – an Emperor be kneeling
Upon her Mat –

I've known her – from an ample nation –
Choose One –   10
Then – close the Valves of her attention –
Like Stone –

Questions
1. Explain the meaning of the first stanza.
2. What does the second instance of "Unmoved" (line 7) modify?
3. In the first two stanzas, the speaker seems to be talking about the soul in general, or in the abstract. Does that perspective remain constant in the final stanza?

This is my letter to the World   (about 1862)

This is my letter to the World
That never wrote to Me –
The simple News that Nature told –
With tender Majesty

Her Message is committed   5
To Hands I cannot see –
For love of Her – Sweet – countrymen –
Judge tenderly – of Me

Questions
1. The poem's first two lines sound like a lonely cry for acknowledgment from an indifferent society. Is that interpretation borne out by the rest of the poem?
2. Who is the "Her" of lines 5 and 7?
3. What thematic connection might there be between "tender" in line 4 and "tenderly" in line 8?

Much Madness is divinest Sense   (about 1862)

Much Madness is divinest Sense –
To a discerning Eye –
Much Sense – the starkest Madness –
'Tis the Majority
In this, as All, prevail –   5
Assent – and you are sane –
Demur – you're straightway dangerous –
And handled with a Chain –

Questions

1. What might be implied by the use of the word "divinest" in line 1?
2. Find the pun in line 2. What extra meaning does it give the poem?
3. What does the speaker mean by "Much Sense – the starkest Madness – / 'Tis the Majority"? Does this idea have relevance today?
4. Explain the meaning of the poem's last two lines.

Some keep the Sabbath going to Church

(about 1862) Published 1864

Some keep the Sabbath going to Church –
I keep it, staying at Home –
With a Bobolink for a Chorister –
And an Orchard, for a Dome –

Some keep the Sabbath in Surplice – 5
I just wear my Wings –
And instead of tolling the Bell, for Church,
Our little Sexton – sings.

God preaches, a noted Clergyman –
And the sermon is never long, 10
So instead of getting to Heaven, at last –
I'm going, all along.

Questions

1. What does the speaker mean by saying she keeps the Sabbath "staying at Home"? What is she implying about worship, and about faith? Do you agree with her view?
2. What does the speaker substitute for the trappings of traditional church services?
3. What does the last stanza say about the nature of the speaker's religious commitment?

Suggestions for Writing on *Emily Dickinson's Poetry*

1. In her work, Dickinson frequently adopts the stance of an outsider or a nonconformist. Discuss this point through detailed discussion of at least two of her poems. What does she seem to find uncongenial about going along with the crowd?
2. Both "This is my letter to the World" and "Some keep the Sabbath going to Church" deal with nature. What similarities are there in the two poems' treatment of this subject? What significant differences?
3. "I'm Nobody! Who are you?" and "The Soul selects her own Society" both present an individual reaching out to someone else but in a manner different from conventional socializing. Describe Dickinson's view of ideal companionship as expressed in these two poems.
4. Emily Dickinson is perhaps as famous for her reclusiveness as she is for her poetry. Discuss this element of her personality as it is reflected in at least three of the poems in this section. Do the poems suggest any reason—or reasons—for this tendency?

CRITICAL AND CULTURAL CONTEXTS CASEBOOK

The Poetry of Emily Dickinson

Emily Dickinson on Writing

Emily Dickinson
Recognizing Poetry
Self-Description

Criticism and Cultural Contexts

Thomas H. Johnson
The Discovery of Emily Dickinson's Manuscripts

Richard Wilbur
The Three Privations of Emily Dickinson

Sandra M. Gilbert and Susan Gubar
The Freedom of Emily Dickinson

Dickinson and Her World: Images

Dickinson Caricature
Dickinson's Room
U.S. Commemorative Stamp
Dickinson Homestead Photo

Emily Dickinson by John Sherffius.

Only a handful of Emily Dickinson's poems were published during her lifetime. When Dickinson died, her sister Lavinia discovered her many poems, painstakingly copied out, bundled, and packed away in a trunk. Although Dickinson was writing during a particularly eventful time in American history—the Civil War was fought when she was in her thirties—her poems contain no explicit references to world events. But neither is the work solely intimate, for Dickinson embraced large, philosophical themes in her work, themes that included freedom, individuality, faith, and death.

For all of Dickinson's apparent reluctance to seek publication of her work, it appears that she was well aware of its quality. (Compare this with today's aspiring writers and musicians, many of whom distribute their work online as soon it's complete.) She saved her work carefully and even discussed its survival in some of her poems. In the years after she died, several of her friends and family members struggled over the publication of her poetry—who would oversee it, how much they would publish, who would make the decisions when there were different forms of the same poem. The meanings of Dickinson's deceptively simple poems are still the topic of intense study and debate. But what no one debates now, more than one hundred years after her death, is that Emily Dickinson is one of the geniuses of American poetry.

EMILY DICKINSON ON WRITING

Emily Dickinson's room in Amherst, Massachusetts.

Recognizing Poetry (1870)

If I read a book [and] it makes my whole body so cold no fire ever can warm me I know *that* is poetry. If I feel physically as if the top of my head were taken off, I know *that* is poetry. These are the only ways I know it. Is there any other way.

How do most people live without any thoughts. There are many people in the world (you must have noticed them in the street). How do they live. How do they get strength to put on their clothes in the morning.

When I lost the use of my Eyes it was a comfort to think there were so few real *books* that I could easily find some one to read me all of them.

Truth is such a *rare* thing it is delightful to tell it.

I find ecstasy in living – the mere sense of living is joy enough.

From a conversation with Thomas Wentworth Higginson

Self-Description (25 April 1862)

Mr. Higginson,

Your kindness claimed earlier gratitude – but I was ill – and write today, from my pillow.

Thank you for the surgery – it was not so painful as I supposed. I bring you others – as you ask – though they might not differ –

SELF-DESCRIPTION. Emily Dickinson's letter was written to Thomas Wentworth Higginson, a noted writer. Dickinson had read his article of advice to young writers in the *Atlantic Monthly*. She sent him four poems and a letter asking if her verse was "alive." When he responded with comments and suggestions (the "surgery" Dickinson mentions in the second paragraph), she wrote him this letter about herself.

While my thought is undressed – I can make the distinction, but when I put them in the Gown – they look alike, and numb.

You asked how old I was? I made no verse – but one or two – until this winter
– Sir –

I had a terror – since September – I could tell to none – and so I sing, as the Boy does by the Burying Ground – because I am afraid – You inquire my Books – For Poets – I have Keats – and Mr and Mrs Browning. For Prose – Mr Ruskin – Sir Thomas Browne – and the Revelations.° I went to school – but in your manner of the phrase – had no education. When a little Girl, I had a friend, who taught me Immortality – but venturing too near, himself – he never returned – Soon after, my Tutor, died – and for several years, my Lexicon – was my only companion – Then I found one more – but he was not contented I be his scholar – so he left the Land.

You ask of my Companions Hills – Sir – and the Sundown – and a Dog – large as myself, that my Father bought me – They are better than Beings – because they know – but do not tell – and the noise in the Pool, at Noon – excels my Piano. I have a Brother and Sister – My Mother does not care for thought – and Father, too busy with his Briefs° – to notice what we do – He buys me many Books – but begs me not to read them – because he fears they joggle the Mind. They are religious – except me – and address an Eclipse, every morning – whom they call their "Father." But I fear my story fatigues you – I would like to learn – Could you tell me how to grow – or is it unconveyed – like Melody – or Witchcraft?

You speak of Mr Whitman – I never read his Book° – but was told that he was disgraceful –

I read Miss Prescott's "Circumstance,"° but it followed me, in the Dark – so I avoided her –

Two Editors of Journals came to my Father's House, this winter – and asked me for my Mind – and when I asked them "Why," they said I was penurious – and they, would use it for the World –

I could not weigh myself – Myself –

My size felt small – to me – I read your Chapters in the Atlantic – and experienced honor for you – I was sure you would not reject a confiding question –

Is this – Sir – what you asked me to tell you?

Your friend,
E – Dickinson

From *The Letters of Emily Dickinson*

Mr Ruskin . . . Revelations: in listing her favorite prose authors Dickinson chose John Ruskin (1819–1900), an English art critic and essayist; Sir Thomas Browne (1605–1682), a doctor and philosopher with a magnificent prose style; and the final book of the New Testament. *Briefs:* legal papers (her father was a lawyer). *Whitman . . . book:* Leaves of Grass (1855) by Walt Whitman was considered an improper book for women at this time because of the volume's sexual candor. *Miss Prescott's "Circumstance":* a story, also published in the *Atlantic Monthly*, that was full of violence.

CRITICISM AND CULTURAL CONTEXTS

Thomas H. Johnson

The Discovery of Emily Dickinson's Manuscripts   1955

Shortly after Emily Dickinson's death on May fifteenth, 1886, her sister Lavinia discovered a locked box in which Emily had placed her poems. Lavinia's amazement seems to have been genuine. Though the sisters had lived intimately together under the same roof all their lives, and though Lavinia had always been aware that her sister wrote poems, she had not the faintest concept of the great number of them. The story of Lavinia's willingness to spare them because she found no instructions specifying that they be destroyed, and her search for an editor and a publisher to give them to the world has already been told in some detail.

    Lavinia first consulted the two people most interested in Emily's poetry, her sister-in-law Susan Dickinson, and Mrs. Todd. David Peck Todd, a graduate of Amherst College in 1875, returned to Amherst with his young bride in 1881 as director of the college observatory and soon became professor of Astronomy and Navigation. These were the months shortly before Mrs. Edward Dickinson's death, when neighbors were especially thoughtful. Mrs. Todd endeared herself to Emily and Lavinia by small but understanding attentions, in return for which Emily sent Mrs. Todd copies of her poems. At first approach neither Susan Dickinson nor Mrs. Todd felt qualified for the editorial task which they both were hesitant to undertake. Mrs. Todd says of Lavinia's discovery: "She showed me the manuscripts and there were over sixty little 'volumes,' each composed of four or five sheets of note paper tied together with twine. In this box she discovered eight or nine hundred poems tied up in this way."

• • •

    As the story can be reconstructed, at some time during the year 1858 Emily Dickinson began assembling her poems into packets. Always in ink, they are gatherings of four, five, or six sheets of letter paper usually folded once but sometimes single. They are loosely held together by thread looped through them at the spine at two points equidistant from the top and bottom. When opened up they may be read like a small book, a fact that explains why Emily's sister Lavinia, when she discovered them after Emily's death, referred to them as "volumes." All of the packet poems are either fair copies or semifinal drafts, and they constitute two-thirds of the entire body of her poetry.

    For the most part the poems in a given packet seem to have been written and assembled as a unit. Since rough drafts of packet poems are almost totally lacking, one concludes that they were systematically discarded. If the poems were in fact composed at the time the copies were made, as the evidence now seems to point, one concludes that nearly two-thirds of her poems were created in the brief span of eight years, centering on her early thirties. Her interest in the packet method of assembling the verses thus coincides with the years of fullest productivity. In 1858 she gathered some fifty poems into packets. There are nearly one hundred so transcribed in 1859, some sixty-five in 1860, and in 1861 more than eighty. By 1862 the creative drive must have been almost frightening; during that year she transcribed into packets no fewer than three hundred and sixty-six poems, the greater part of them complete and final texts.

Whether this incredible number was in fact composed in that year or represents a transcription of earlier worksheet drafts can never be established by direct evidence. But the pattern established during the preceding four years reveals a gathering momentum, and the quality of tenseness and prosodic skill uniformly present in the poems of 1861–1862 bears scant likeness to the conventionality of theme and treatment in the poems of 1858–1859. Excepting a half dozen occasional verses written in the early fifties, there is not a single scrap of poetry that can be dated earlier than 1858.

From *The Poems of Emily Dickinson*

Richard Wilbur

The Three Privations of Emily Dickinson   1959

Emily Dickinson never lets us forget for very long that in some respects life gave her short measure; and indeed it is possible to see the greater part of her poetry as an effort to cope with her sense of privation. I think that for her there were three major privations: she was deprived of an orthodox and steady religious faith; she was deprived of love; she was deprived of literary recognition.

At the age of seventeen, after a series of revival meetings at Mount Holyoke Seminary, Emily Dickinson found that she must refuse to become a professing Christian. To some modern minds this may seem to have been a sensible and necessary step; and surely it was a step toward becoming such a poet as she became. But for her, no pleasure in her own integrity could then eradicate the feeling that she had betrayed a deficiency, a want of grace. In her letters to Abiah Root she tells of the enhancing effect of conversion on her fellow-students, and says of herself in a famous passage:

> I am one of the lingering bad ones, and so do I slink away, and pause and ponder, and ponder and pause, and do work without knowing why, not surely for this brief world, and more sure it is not for heaven, and I ask what this message *means* that they ask for so very eagerly: *you* know of this depth and fulness, will you try to tell me about it?

There is humor in that, and stubbornness, and a bit of characteristic lurking pride: but there is also an anguished sense of having separated herself, through some dry incapacity, from spiritual community, from purpose, and from magnitude of life. As a child of evangelical Amherst, she inevitably thought of purposive, heroic life as requiring a vigorous faith. Out of such a thought she later wrote:

The abdication of Belief
Makes the Behavior small –
Better an ignis fatuus
Than no illume at all –

That hers *was* a species of religious personality goes without saying; but by her refusal of such ideas as original sin, redemption, hell, and election, she made it impossible for herself—as Whicher observed—"to share the religious life of her generation." She became an unsteady congregation of one.

Her second privation, the privation of love, is one with which her poems and her biographies have made us exceedingly familiar, though some biographical facts remain conjectural. She had the good fortune, at least once, to bestow her heart on another; but she seems to have found her life, in great part, a history of loneliness, separation, and bereavement.

As for literary fame, some will deny that Emily Dickinson ever greatly desired it, and certainly there is evidence, mostly from her latter years, to support such a view. She *did* write that "Publication is the auction / Of the mind of man." And she *did* say to Helen Hunt Jackson, "How can you print a piece of your soul?" But earlier, in 1861, she had frankly expressed to Sue Dickinson the hope that "sometime" she might make her kinfolk proud of her. The truth is, I think, that Emily Dickinson knew she was good, and began her career with a normal appetite for recognition. I think that she later came, with some reason, to despair of being understood or properly valued, and so directed against her hopes of fame what was by then a well-developed disposition to renounce. That she wrote a good number of poems about fame supports my view: the subjects to which a poet returns are those which vex him.

What did Emily Dickinson do, as a poet, with her sense of privation? One thing she quite often did was to pose as the laureate and attorney of the empty-handed, and question God about the economy of His creation. Why, she asked, is a fatherly God so sparing of His presence? Why is there never a sign that prayers are heard? Why does Nature tell us no comforting news of its Maker? Why do some receive a whole loaf, while others must starve on a crumb? Where is the benevolence in shipwreck and earthquake? By asking such questions as these, she turned complaint into critique, and used her own sufferings as experiential evidence about the nature of the deity. The God who emerges from these poems is a God who does not answer, an unrevealed God whom one cannot confidently approach through Nature or through doctrine.

From "Sumptuous Destitution"

Sandra M. Gilbert and Susan Gubar

The Freedom of Emily Dickinson   1985

[Emily Dickinson] defined herself as a *woman* writer, reading the works of female precursors with special care, attending to the implications of novels like Charlotte Brontë's *Jane Eyre*, Emily Brontë's *Wuthering Heights*, and George Eliot's *Middlemarch* with the same absorbed delight that characterized her devotion to Elizabeth Barrett Browning's *Aurora Leigh*. Finally, then, the key to her enigmatic identity as a "supposed person" who was called the "Myth of Amherst" may rest, not in investigations of her questionable romance, but in studies of her unquestionably serious reading as well as in analyses of her disquietingly powerful writing. Elliptically phrased, intensely compressed, her poems are more linguistically innovative than any other nineteenth-century verses, with the possible exception of some works by Walt Whitman and Gerard Manley Hopkins, her two most radical male contemporaries. Throughout her largely secret but always brilliant career, moreover, she confronted precisely the questions about the individual and society, time and death, flesh and spirit, that major precursors from Milton to Keats had faced. Dreaming of "Amplitude and Awe," she

Dickinson Homestead in Amherst, Massachusetts; now a museum.

recorded sometimes vengeful, sometimes mystical visions of social and personal transformation in poems as inventively phrased and imaginatively constructed as any in the English language.

Clearly such accomplishments required not only extraordinary talent but also some measure of freedom. Yet because she was the unmarried daughter of conservative New Englanders, Dickinson was obliged to take on many household tasks; as a nineteenth-century New England wife, she would have had the same number of obligations, if not more. Some of these she performed with pleasure; in 1856, for instance, she was judge of a bread-baking contest, and in 1857 she won a prize in that contest. But as Higginson's "scholar," as a voracious reader and an ambitious writer, Dickinson had to win herself time for "Amplitude and Awe," and it is increasingly clear that she did so through a strategic withdrawal from her ordinary world. A story related by her niece Martha Dickinson Bianchi reveals that the poet herself knew from the first what both the price and the prize might be: on one occasion, said Mrs. Bianchi, Dickinson took her up to the room in which she regularly sequestered herself, and, mimicking locking herself in, "thumb and forefinger closed on an imaginary key," said "with a quick turn of her wrist, 'It's just a turn—and freedom, Matty!'"

In the freedom of her solitary, but not lonely, room, Dickinson may have become what her Amherst neighbors saw as a bewildering "myth." Yet there, too, she created myths of her own. Reading the Brontës and Barrett Browning, studying Transcendentalism and the Bible, she contrived a theology which is powerfully expressed in many of her poems. That it was at its most hopeful a female-centered theology is revealed in verses like those she wrote about the women artists she admired, as well as in more general works like her gravely pantheistic address to the "Sweet Mountains" who "tell me no lie," with its definition of the hills around Amherst as "strong Madonnas" and its description of the writer herself as "The Wayward Nun – beneath the Hill – / Whose service is to You – ." As Dickinson's admirer and descendant Adrienne Rich has accurately observed, this passionate poet consistently chose to confront her society—to "have it out"—"on her own premises."

From introduction to Emily Dickinson,
The Norton Anthology of Literature by Women

Suggestions for Writing on *Critics and Emily Dickinson's Poetry*

1. How do the poems by Dickinson in this chapter and elsewhere in the book illustrate her statement (in "Recognizing Poetry") that "I find ecstasy in living – the mere sense of living is joy enough"?
2. Many of Dickinson's poems explore the relationship between the individual and society. Take several of her poems and present a summary of Dickinson's views on that relationship.
3. In "The Three Privations of Emily Dickinson," Richard Wilbur writes: "What did Emily Dickinson do, as a poet, with her sense of privation? One thing she quite often did was to pose as the laureate and attorney of the empty-handed." Discuss this comment through a detailed consideration of at least three of Dickinson's poems.
4. In "The Three Privations of Emily Dickinson," Richard Wilbur quotes this stanza from a Dickinson poem:

> The abdication of Belief
> Makes the Behavior small –
> Better an ignis fatuus
> Than no illume at all –

Consider the implications of this stanza with reference to Dickinson's treatment of religion in at least two of the poems in this chapter.

ESSAYS

INSPIRING SOCIAL CHANGE

Martin Luther King Jr.   *Letter from Birmingham Jail*
Henry David Thoreau   *Civil Disobedience*
Maxine Hong Kingston   *No Name Woman*

Sometimes people take deliberate stands against customs or laws they believe are unjust. At other times people challenge those customs without even meaning to. In the case of Martin Luther King Jr.'s "Letter from Birmingham Jail" and Henry David Thoreau's "Civil Disobedience," the challenges are direct and intentional. King invoked moral and religious reasons in his arguments against segregation and racial discrimination; Thoreau, a century earlier, refused to participate in—or pay taxes to—a government that carried out what he considered immoral practices, including slavery and the Mexican American War. Both men went to jail for not adhering to the state's law; King's letter was actually written in his jail cell. Both of these works influenced the public discussions of their time; both did, in fact, help inspire change. However, sometimes resistance to custom can be private and personal. In Maxine Hong Kingston's "No Name Woman," Kingston's aunt is ostracized and ultimately driven to suicide because of an out-of-wedlock pregnancy. As part of a small village in China, she was expected to live according to the tight expectations of that place and time. For people who don't adhere to laws and customs, the consequence may be exile or punishment. Yet change sometimes depends on the courage of individuals who are willing to stand up for it despite the risks.

Martin Luther King Jr.

Martin Luther King Jr. was the most visible and most influential leader of the American civil rights movement. Born in Atlanta, Georgia, in 1929, he grew up in a middle-class family, the son and grandson of Baptist ministers. King entered Morehouse College at the age of fifteen, graduating in 1948. He earned a bachelor of divinity degree from Crozer Theological Seminary in Pennsylvania, where he first became acquainted with Mohandas Gandhi's theories of nonviolent resistance. King then earned his Ph.D. at Boston University in 1955. He had recently become the pastor of Dexter Avenue Baptist Church in Montgomery, Alabama, when events occurred that catapulted him into the public eye. In late 1955, an African American woman named Rosa Parks refused to give up her seat on a bus to a white

Martin Luther King Jr.

man, and was subsequently arrested for breaking the city's segregation laws. King led a boycott against the bus system in Montgomery until, a year later, segregation on city buses was ended. After his success in Montgomery, Reverend King organized the Southern Christian Leadership Conference (SCLC), which served as a platform and base of operations for national civil rights efforts, and moved back to Atlanta to become co-pastor, with his father, of Ebenezer Baptist Church. Utilizing Gandhi's methods of nonviolent resistance, he helped organize sit-ins and protest marches to challenge segregation throughout the South, and he was arrested many times. A gifted orator, King gave one of the most memorable speeches in modern American history during the 1963 March on Washington—the "I Have a Dream" speech, where he described his vision for a country in which his children would "not be judged by the color of their skin, but by the content of their character." All of these events helped lead to the passage of the landmark Civil Rights Act of 1964. That same year, King was awarded the Nobel Peace Prize—at thirty-five, the youngest person ever to receive that honor. On March 10, 1969, King was assassinated in Memphis, Tennessee. He was thirty-nine years old. He has since been honored with a national holiday in his name.

The document that has come to be known as "Letter from Birmingham Jail" was an open letter written by Reverend King on April 16, 1963, after he had been arrested while leading a protest march. King drafted the letter as a public response to eight local white Protestant, Catholic, and Jewish clergymen who had published a joint statement in a local newspaper which recognized the social injustice of racial segregation, but argued that the battle for civil rights should be conducted in the courts and not on the streets. While the statement did not name King, it criticized the demonstrations being "directed and led in part by outsiders." King's response letter was widely published in media outlets and distributed in pamphlet form around the nation. It rapidly became one of the most important documents of the civil rights movement.

Letter from Birmingham Jail

April 16, 1963

My Dear Fellow Clergymen:

 While confined here in the Birmingham city jail, I came across your recent statement calling my present activities "unwise and untimely." Seldom do I pause to answer criticism of my work and ideas. If I sought to answer all the criticisms that cross my desk, my secretaries would have little time for anything other than such correspondence in the course of the day, and I would have no time for constructive work. But since I feel that you are men of genuine good will and that your criticisms are sincerely set forth, I want to try to answer your statements in what I hope will be patient and reasonable terms.

 I think I should indicate why I am here in Birmingham, since you have been influenced by the view which argues against "outsiders coming in." I have the honor of serving as president of the Southern Christian Leadership Conference, an organization operating in every southern state, with headquarters in Atlanta, Georgia. We have some eighty-five affiliated organizations across the South, and one of them is the Alabama Christian Movement for Human Rights. Frequently we share staff, educational and financial resources with our affiliates. Several months ago the affiliate here in Birmingham asked us to be on call to engage in a nonviolent direct-action program if such were deemed necessary. We readily consented, and when the hour came we lived up to our promise. So I, along with several members of my staff, am here because I was invited here. I am here because I have organizational ties here.

 But more basically, I am in Birmingham because injustice is here. Just as the prophets of the eighth century B.C. left their villages and carried their "thus saith the Lord" far beyond the boundaries of their home towns, and just as the Apostle Paul left his village of Tarsus and carried the gospel of Jesus Christ to the far corners of the Greco-Roman world, so am I compelled to carry the gospel of freedom beyond my own home town. Like Paul, I must constantly respond to the Macedonian call for aid.°

Moreover, I am cognizant of the interrelatedness of all communities and states. I cannot sit idly by in Atlanta and not be concerned about what happens in Birmingham. Injustice anywhere is a threat to justice everywhere. We are caught in an inescapable network of mutuality, tied in a single garment of destiny. Whatever affects one directly, affects all indirectly. Never again can we afford to live with the narrow, provincial "outside agitator" idea. Anyone who lives inside the United States can never be considered an outsider anywhere within its bounds.

You deplore the demonstrations taking place in Birmingham. But your statement, I am sorry to say, fails to express a similar concern for the conditions that brought about the demonstrations. I am sure that none of you would want to rest content with the superficial kind of social analysis that deals merely with effects and does not grapple with underlying causes. It is unfortunate that demonstrations are taking place in Birmingham, but it is even more unfortunate that the city's white power structure left the Negro community with no alternative.

In any nonviolent campaign there are four basic steps: collection of the facts to determine whether injustices exist; negotiation; self-purification; and direct action. We have gone through all of these steps in Birmingham. There can be no gainsaying the fact that racial injustice engulfs this community. Birmingham is probably the most thoroughly segregated city in the United States. Its ugly record of brutality is widely known. Negroes have experienced grossly unjust treatment in the courts. There have been more unsolved bombings of Negro homes and churches in Birmingham than in any other city in the nation. These are the hard, brutal facts of the case. On the basis of these conditions, Negro leaders sought to negotiate with the city fathers. But the latter consistently refused to engage in good-faith negotiation.

Then, last September, came the opportunity to talk with leaders of Birmingham's economic community. In the course of the negotiations, certain promises were made by the merchants—for example, to remove the stores' humiliating racial signs. On the basis of these promises, the Reverend Fred Shuttlesworth and the leaders of the Alabama Christian Movement for Human Rights agreed to a moratorium on all demonstrations. As the weeks and months went by, we realized that we were the victims of a broken promise. A few signs, briefly removed, returned; the others remained.

As in so many past experiences, our hopes had been blasted, and the shadow of deep disappointment settled upon us. We had no alternative except to prepare for direct action, whereby we would present our very bodies as a means of laying our case before the conscience of the local and the national community. Mindful of the difficulties involved, we decided to undertake a process of self-purification. We began a series of workshops on nonviolence, and we repeatedly asked ourselves: "Are you able to accept blows without retaliating?" "Are you able to endure the ordeal of jail?" We decided to schedule our direct-action program for the Easter season, realizing that

---

Macedonian call for aid: King is drawing an analogy of his coming to Birmingham to the apostle Paul's being called to Macedonia, from Acts 16:9–10: "During the night Paul had a vision of a man of Macedonia standing and begging him, 'Come over to Macedonia and help us.' After Paul had seen the vision, we got ready at once to leave for Macedonia, concluding that God had called us to preach the gospel to them."

except for Christmas, this is the main shopping period of the year. Knowing that a strong economic withdrawal program would be the by-product of direct action, we felt that this would be the best time to bring pressure to bear on the merchants for the needed change.

Then it occurred to us that Birmingham's mayoralty election was coming up in March, and we speedily decided to postpone action until after election day. When we discovered that the Commissioner of Public Safety, Eugene "Bull" Connor, had piled up enough votes to be in the run-off we decided again to postpone action until the day after the run-off so that the demonstrations could not be used to cloud the issues. Like many others, we waited to see Mr. Connor defeated, and to this end we endured postponement after postponement. Having aided in this community need, we felt that our direct-action program could be delayed no longer.

You may well ask: "Why direct action? Why sit-ins, marches and so forth? Isn't negotiation a better path?" You are quite right in calling for negotiation. Indeed, this is the very purpose of direct action. Nonviolent direct action seeks to create such a crisis and foster such a tension that a community which has constantly refused to negotiate is forced to confront the issue. It seeks to so dramatize the issue that it can no longer be ignored. My citing the creation of tension as part of the work of the nonviolent-resister may sound rather shocking. But I must confess that I am not afraid of the word "tension." I have earnestly opposed violent tension, but there is a type of constructive, nonviolent tension which is necessary for growth. Just as Socrates felt that it was necessary to create a tension in the mind so that individuals could rise from the bondage of myths and half-truths to the unfettered realm of creative analysis and objective appraisal, so must we see the need for nonviolent gadflies to create the kind of tension in society that will help men rise from the dark depths of prejudice and racism to the majestic heights of understanding and brotherhood.

The purpose of our direct-action program is to create a situation so crisis-packed that it will inevitably open the door to negotiation. I therefore concur with you in your call for negotiation. Too long has our beloved Southland been bogged down in a tragic effort to live in monologue rather than dialogue.

One of the basic points in your statement is that the action that I and my associates have taken in Birmingham is untimely. Some have asked: "Why didn't you give the new city administration time to act?" The only answer that I can give to this query is that the new Birmingham administration must be prodded about as much as the outgoing one, before it will act. We are sadly mistaken if we feel that the election of Albert Boutwell as mayor will bring the millennium to Birmingham. While Mr. Boutwell is a much more gentle person than Mr. Connor, they are both segregationists, dedicated to maintenance of the status quo. I have hope that Mr. Boutwell will be reasonable enough to see the futility of massive resistance to desegregation. But he will not see this without pressure from devotees of civil rights. My friends, I must say to you that we have not made a single gain in civil rights without determined legal and nonviolent pressure. Lamentably, it is an historical fact that privileged groups seldom give up their privileges voluntarily. Individuals may see the moral light and voluntarily give up their unjust posture; but, as Reinhold Niebuhr° has reminded us, groups tend to be more immoral than individuals.

Reinhold Niebuhr: See footnote on page 973.

We know through painful experience that freedom is never voluntarily given by the oppressor; it must be demanded by the oppressed. Frankly, I have yet to engage in a direct-action campaign that was "well timed" in the view of those who have not suffered unduly from the disease of segregation. For years now I have heard the word "Wait!" It rings in the ear of every Negro with piercing familiarity. This "Wait" has almost always meant "Never." We must come to see, with one of our distinguished jurists, that "justice too long delayed is justice denied."

We have waited for more than 340 years for our constitutional and God-given rights. The nations of Asia and Africa are moving with jetlike speed toward gaining political independence, but we still creep at horse-and-buggy pace toward gaining a cup of coffee at a lunch counter. Perhaps it is easy for those who have never felt the stinging darts of segregation to say, "Wait." But when you have seen vicious mobs lynch your mothers and fathers at will and drown your sisters and brothers at whim; when you have seen hate-filled policemen curse, kick and even kill your black brothers and sisters; when you see the vast majority of your twenty million Negro brothers smothering in an airtight cage of poverty in the midst of an affluent society; when you suddenly find your tongue twisted and your speech stammering as you seek to explain to your six-year-old daughter why she can't go to the public amusement park that has just been advertised on television, and see tears welling up in her eyes when she is told that Funtown is closed to colored children, and see ominous clouds of inferiority beginning to form in her little mental sky, and see her beginning to distort her personality by developing an unconscious bitterness toward white people; when you have to concoct an answer for a five-year-old son who is asking: "Daddy, why do white people treat colored people so mean?"; when you take a cross-country drive and find it necessary to sleep night after night in the uncomfortable corners of your automobile because no motel will accept you; when you are humiliated day in and day out by nagging signs reading "white" and "colored"; when your first name becomes "nigger," your middle name becomes "boy" (however old you are) and your last name becomes "John," and your wife and mother are never given the respected title "Mrs."; when you are harried by day and haunted by night by the fact that you are a Negro, living constantly at tiptoe stance, never quite knowing what to expect next, and are plagued with inner fears and outer resentments; when you go forever fighting a degenerating sense of "nobodiness" then you will understand why we find it difficult to wait. There comes a time when the cup of endurance runs over, and men are no longer willing to be plunged into the abyss of despair. I hope, sirs, you can understand our legitimate and unavoidable impatience.

You express a great deal of anxiety over our willingness to break laws. This is certainly a legitimate concern. Since we so diligently urge people to obey the Supreme Court's decision of 1954 outlawing segregation in the public schools, at first glance it may seem rather paradoxical for us consciously to break laws. One may want to ask: "How can you advocate breaking some laws and obeying others?" The answer lies in the fact that there are two types of laws: just and unjust. I would be the first to advocate obeying just laws. One has not only a legal but a moral responsibility to obey just laws. Conversely, one has a moral responsibility to disobey unjust laws. I would agree with St. Augustine° that "an unjust law is no law at all."

St. Augustine: See footnote on page 973.

Now, what is the difference between the two? How does one determine whether a law is just or unjust? A just law is a man-made code that squares with the moral law or the law of God. An unjust law is a code that is out of harmony with the moral law. To put it in the terms of St. Thomas Aquinas:° An unjust law is a human law that is not rooted in eternal law and natural law. Any law that uplifts human personality is just. Any law that degrades human personality is unjust. All segregation statutes are unjust because segregation distorts the soul and damages the personality. It gives the segregator a false sense of superiority and the segregated a false sense of inferiority. Segregation, to use the terminology of the Jewish philosopher Martin Buber,° substitutes an "I-it" relationship for an "I-thou" relationship and ends up relegating persons to the status of things. Hence segregation is not only politically, economically and sociologically unsound, it is morally wrong and awful. Paul Tillich° said that sin is separation. Is not segregation an existential expression of man's tragic separation, his awful estrangement, his terrible sinfulness? Thus it is that I can urge men to obey the 1954 decision of the Supreme Court, for it is morally right; and I can urge them to disobey segregation ordinances, for they are morally wrong.

Let us consider a more concrete example of just and unjust laws. An unjust law is a code that a numerical or power majority group compels a minority group to obey but does not make binding on itself. This is *difference* made legal. By the same token, a just law is a code that a majority compels a minority to follow and that it is willing to follow itself. This is *sameness* made legal.

Let me give another explanation. A law is unjust if it is inflicted on a minority that, as a result of being denied the right to vote, had no part in enacting or devising the law. Who can say that the legislature of Alabama which set up that state's segregation laws was democratically elected? Throughout Alabama all sorts of devious methods are used to prevent Negroes from becoming registered voters, and there are some counties in which, even though Negroes constitute a majority of the population, not a single Negro is registered. Can any law enacted under such circumstances be considered democratically structured?

Sometimes a law is just on its face and unjust in its application. For instance, I have been arrested on a charge of parading without a permit. Now, there is nothing wrong in having an ordinance which requires a permit for a parade. But such an ordinance becomes unjust when it is used to maintain segregation and to deny citizens the First Amendment privilege of peaceful assembly and protest.

I hope you are able to see the distinction I am trying to point out. In no sense do I advocate evading or defying the law, as would the rabid segregationist. That would lead to anarchy. One who breaks an unjust law must do so openly, lovingly, and with a willingness to accept the penalty. I submit that an individual who breaks a law that conscience tells him is unjust and who willingly accepts the penalty of imprisonment in order to arouse the conscience of the community over its injustice, is in reality expressing the highest respect for law.

Of course, there is nothing new about this kind of civil disobedience. It was evidenced sublimely in the refusal of Shadrach, Meshach and Abednego to obey the

---

Reinhold Niebuhr . . . St. Augustine . . . St. Thomas Aquinas . . . Martin Buber . . . Paul Tillich: Five prominent Christian and Jewish theologians spanning the ages, underscoring King's point about the eternal truth of his arguments—St. Augustine (354–430), St. Thomas Aquinas (1225–1274), Martin Buber (1878–1965), Paul Tillich (1886–1965), and Reinhold Niebuhr (1892–1971).

laws of Nebuchadnezzar,° on the ground that a higher moral law was at stake. It was practiced superbly by the early Christians, who were willing to face hungry lions and the excruciating pain of chopping blocks rather than submit to certain unjust laws of the Roman Empire. To a degree, academic freedom is a reality today because Socrates practiced civil disobedience. In our own nation, the Boston Tea Party represented a massive act of civil disobedience.

We should never forget that everything Adolf Hitler did in Germany was "legal" and everything the Hungarian freedom fighters did in Hungary was "illegal." It was "illegal" to aid and comfort a Jew in Hitler's Germany. Even so, I am sure that, had I lived in Germany at the time, I would have aided and comforted my Jewish brothers. If today I lived in a Communist country where certain principles dear to the Christian faith are suppressed, I would openly advocate disobeying that country's antireligious laws.

I must make two honest confessions to you, my Christian and Jewish brothers. First, I must confess that over the past few years I have been gravely disappointed with the white moderate. I have almost reached the regrettable conclusion that the Negro's great stumbling block in his stride toward freedom is not the White Citizen's Counciler° or the Ku Klux Klanner, but the white moderate, who is more devoted to "order" than to justice; who prefers a negative peace which is the absence of tension to a positive peace which is the presence of justice; who constantly says: "I agree with you in the goal you seek, but I cannot agree with your methods of direct action"; who paternalistically believes he can set the timetable for another man's freedom; who lives by a mythical concept of time and who constantly advises the Negro to wait for a "more convenient season."° Shallow understanding from people of good will is more frustrating than absolute misunderstanding from people of ill will. Lukewarm acceptance is much more bewildering than outright rejection.

I had hoped that the white moderate would understand that law and order exist for the purpose of establishing justice and that when they fail in this purpose they become the dangerously structured dams that block the flow of social progress. I had hoped that the white moderate would understand that the present tension in the South is a necessary phase of the transition from an obnoxious negative peace, in which the Negro passively accepted his unjust plight, to a substantive and positive peace, in which all men will respect the dignity and worth of human personality. Actually, we who engage in nonviolent direct action are not the creators of tension. We merely bring to the surface the hidden tension that is already alive. We bring it out in the open, where it can be seen and dealt with. Like a boil that can never be cured so long as it is covered up but must be opened with all its ugliness to the natural medicines of air and light, injustice must be exposed, with all the tension its exposure creates, to the light of human conscience and the air of national opinion before it can be cured.

Shadrach, Meshach and Abednego . . . Nebuchadnezzar: From Daniel 3, Shadrach, Meschach, and Abednego refused to obey a royal edict to bow down and worship a golden image King Nebuchanzzar had erected, despite the penalty of being thrown into a "blazing furnace." *White Citizen's Counciler:* white supremacist organization formed to maintain segregation. *"more convenient season":* quotation from Acts 24:24–25, allusion to the Roman governor Felix, who was disturbed by the Apostle Paul's words, but wanted to put off responding.

In your statement you assert that our actions, even though peaceful, must be condemned because they precipitate violence. But is this a logical assertion? Isn't this like condemning a robbed man because his possession of money precipitated the evil act of robbery? Isn't this like condemning Socrates because his unswerving commitment to truth and his philosophical inquiries precipitated the act by the misguided populace in which they made him drink hemlock? Isn't this like condemning Jesus because his unique God-consciousness and never-ceasing devotion to God's will precipitated the evil act of crucifixion? We must come to see that, as the federal courts have consistently affirmed, it is wrong to urge an individual to cease his efforts to gain his basic constitutional rights because the quest may precipitate violence. Society must protect the robbed and punish the robber.

I had also hoped that the white moderate would reject the myth concerning time in relation to the struggle for freedom. I have just received a letter from a white brother in Texas. He writes: "All Christians know that the colored people will receive equal rights eventually, but it is possible that you are in too great a religious hurry. It has taken Christianity almost two thousand years to accomplish what it has. The teachings of Christ take time to come to earth." Such an attitude stems from a tragic misconception of time, from the strangely rational notion that there is something in the very flow of time that will inevitably cure all ills. Actually, time itself is neutral; it can be used either destructively or constructively. More and more I feel that the people of ill will have used time much more effectively than have the people of good will. We will have to repent in this generation not merely for the hateful words and actions of the bad people but for the appalling silence of the good people. Human progress never rolls in on wheels of inevitability; it comes through the tireless efforts of men willing to be co-workers with God, and without this hard work, time itself becomes an ally of the forces of social stagnation. We must use time creatively, in the knowledge that the time is always ripe to do right. Now is the time to make real the promise of democracy and transform our pending national elegy into a creative psalm of brotherhood. Now is the time to lift our national policy from the quicksand of racial injustice to the solid rock of human dignity.

You speak of our activity in Birmingham as extreme. At first I was rather disappointed that fellow clergymen would see my nonviolent efforts as those of an extremist. I began thinking about the fact that I stand in the middle of two opposing forces in the Negro community. One is a force of complacency, made up in part of Negroes who, as a result of long years of oppression, are so drained of self-respect and a sense of "somebodiness" that they have adjusted to segregation; and in part of a few middle class Negroes who, because of a degree of academic and economic security and because in some ways they profit by segregation, have become insensitive to the problems of the masses. The other force is one of bitterness and hatred, and it comes perilously close to advocating violence. It is expressed in the various black nationalist groups that are springing up across the nation, the largest and best-known being Elijah Muhammad's Muslim movement.° Nourished by the Negro's frustration over the continued existence of racial discrimination, this movement is made up of people

---

Elijah Muhammad's Muslim movement: Nation of Islam, a religious movement led by Elijah Muhammad (1897–1975), that called for African Americans to establish their own separate nation and reject integration.

who have lost faith in America, who have absolutely repudiated Christianity, and who have concluded that the white man is an incorrigible "devil."

I have tried to stand between these two forces, saying that we need emulate neither the "do-nothingism" of the complacent nor the hatred and despair of the black nationalist. For there is the more excellent way of love and nonviolent protest. I am grateful to God that, through the influence of the Negro church, the way of nonviolence became an integral part of our struggle.

If this philosophy had not emerged, by now many streets of the South would, I am convinced, be flowing with blood. And I am further convinced that if our white brothers dismiss as "rabble-rousers" and "outside agitators" those of us who employ nonviolent direct action, and if they refuse to support our nonviolent efforts, millions of Negroes will, out of frustration and despair, seek solace and security in black-nationalist ideologies—a development that would inevitably lead to a frightening racial nightmare.

Oppressed people cannot remain oppressed forever. The yearning for freedom eventually manifests itself, and that is what has happened to the American Negro. Something within has reminded him of his birthright of freedom, and something without has reminded him that it can be gained. Consciously or unconsciously, he has been caught up by the *Zeitgeist*,° and with his black brothers of Africa and his brown and yellow brothers of Asia, South America and the Caribbean, the United States Negro is moving with a sense of great urgency toward the promised land of racial justice. If one recognizes this vital urge that has engulfed the Negro community, one should readily understand why public demonstrations are taking place. The Negro has many pent-up resentments and latent frustrations, and he must release them. So let him march; let him make prayer pilgrimages to the city hall; let him go on freedom rides°—and try to understand why he must do so. If his repressed emotions are not released in nonviolent ways, they will seek expression through violence; this is not a threat but a fact of history. So I have not said to my people: "Get rid of your discontent." Rather, I have tried to say that this normal and healthy discontent can be channeled into the creative outlet of nonviolent direct action. And now this approach is being termed extremist.

But though I was initially disappointed at being categorized as an extremist, as I continued to think about the matter I gradually gained a measure of satisfaction from the label. Was not Jesus an extremist for love: "Love your enemies, bless them that curse you, do good to them that hate you, and pray for them which despitefully use you, and persecute you." Was not Amos an extremist for justice: "Let justice roll down like waters and righteousness like an ever-flowing stream." Was not Paul an extremist for the Christian gospel: "I bear in my body the marks of the Lord Jesus." Was not Martin Luther an extremist: "Here I stand; I cannot do otherwise, so help me God." And John Bunyan: "I will stay in jail to the end of my days before I make a butchery of my conscience." And Abraham Lincoln: "This nation cannot survive half slave and half free." And Thomas Jefferson: "We hold these truths to be self-evident, that all men are created equal . . . " So the question is not whether we will be extremists,

---

Zeitgeist: German for "spirit of the age."   *freedom rides:* In 1960 the Supreme Court ruled that Southern segregation laws could not apply to interstate travel or to bus terminals or facilities that served interstate transporters. Immediately, civil rights activist groups—comprised of blacks and whites—starting testing the ruling by riding together on interstate buses from the North into the segregated South.

but what kind of extremists we will be. Will we be extremists for hate or for love? Will we be extremists for the preservation of injustice or for the extension of justice? In that dramatic scene on Calvary's hill three men were crucified. We must never forget that all three were crucified for the same crime—the crime of extremism. Two were extremists for immorality, and thus fell below their environment. The other, Jesus Christ, was an extremist for love, truth and goodness, and thereby rose above his environment. Perhaps the South, the nation and the world are in dire need of creative extremists.

I had hoped that the white moderate would see this need. Perhaps I was too optimistic; perhaps I expected too much. I suppose I should have realized that few members of the oppressor race can understand the deep groans and passionate yearnings of the oppressed race, and still fewer have the vision to see that injustice must be rooted out by strong, persistent and determined action. I am thankful, however, that some of our white brothers in the South have grasped the meaning of this social revolution and committed themselves to it. They are still too few in quantity, but they are big in quality. Some—such as Ralph McGill, Lillian Smith, Harry Golden, James McBride Dabbs, Ann Braden and Sarah Patton Boyle—have written about our struggle in eloquent and prophetic terms. Others have marched with us down nameless streets of the South. They have languished in filthy, roach-infested jails, suffering the abuse and brutality of policemen who view them as "dirty nigger lovers." Unlike so many of their moderate brothers and sisters, they have recognized the urgency of the moment and sensed the need for powerful "action" antidotes to combat the disease of segregation.

Let me take note of my other major disappointment. I have been so greatly disappointed with the white church and its leadership. Of course, there are some notable exceptions. I am not unmindful of the fact that each of you has taken some significant stands on this issue. I commend you, Reverend Stallings, for your Christian stand on this past Sunday, in welcoming Negroes to your worship service on a nonsegregated basis. I commend the Catholic leaders of this state for integrating Spring Hill College several years ago.

But despite these notable exceptions, I must honestly reiterate that I have been disappointed with the church. I do not say this as one of those negative critics who can always find something wrong with the church. I say this as a minister of the gospel, who loves the church; who was nurtured in its bosom; who has been sustained by its spiritual blessings and who will remain true to it as long as the cord of life shall lengthen.

When I was suddenly catapulted into the leadership of the bus protest in Montgomery, Alabama, a few years ago, I felt we would be supported by the white church. I felt that the white ministers, priests and rabbis of the South would be among our strongest allies. Instead, some have been outright opponents, refusing to understand the freedom movement and misrepresenting its leaders; all too many others have been more cautious than courageous and have remained silent behind the anesthetizing security of stained-glass windows.

In spite of my shattered dreams, I came to Birmingham with the hope that the white religious leadership of this community would see the justice of our cause and, with deep moral concern, would serve as the channel through which our just grievances could reach the power structure. I had hoped that each of you would understand. But again I have been disappointed.

I have heard numerous southern religious leaders admonish their worshipers to comply with a desegregation decision because it is the law, but I have longed to hear white ministers declare: "Follow this decree because integration is morally right and because the Negro is your brother." In the midst of blatant injustices inflicted upon the Negro, I have watched white churchmen stand on the sideline and mouth pious irrelevancies and sanctimonious trivialities. In the midst of a mighty struggle to rid our nation of racial and economic injustice, I have heard many ministers say: "Those are social issues, with which the gospel has no real concern." And I have watched many churches commit themselves to a completely other worldly religion which makes a strange, un-Biblical distinction between body and soul, between the sacred and the secular.

I have traveled the length and breadth of Alabama, Mississippi and all the other southern states. On sweltering summer days and crisp autumn mornings I have looked at the South's beautiful churches with their lofty spires pointing heavenward. I have beheld the impressive outlines of her massive religious-education buildings. Over and over I have found myself asking: "What kind of people worship here? Who is their God? Where were their voices when the lips of Governor Barnett dripped with words of interposition and nullification? Where were they when Governor Wallace gave a clarion call for defiance and hatred? Where were their voices of support when bruised and weary Negro men and women decided to rise from the dark dungeons of complacency to the bright hills of creative protest?"

Yes, these questions are still in my mind. In deep disappointment I have wept over the laxity of the church. But be assured that my tears have been tears of love. There can be no deep disappointment where there is not deep love. Yes, I love the church. How could I do otherwise? I am in the rather unique position of being the son, the grandson and the great-grandson of preachers. Yes, I see the church as the body of Christ. But, oh! How we have blemished and scarred that body through social neglect and through fear of being nonconformists.

There was a time when the church was very powerful in the time when the early Christians rejoiced at being deemed worthy to suffer for what they believed. In those days the church was not merely a thermometer that recorded the ideas and principles of popular opinion; it was a thermostat that transformed the mores of society. Whenever the early Christians entered a town, the people in power became disturbed and immediately sought to convict the Christians for being "disturbers of the peace" and "outside agitators." But the Christians pressed on, in the conviction that they were "a colony of heaven,"° called to obey God rather than man. Small in number, they were big in commitment. They were too God-intoxicated to be "astronomically intimidated." By their effort and example they brought an end to such ancient evils as infanticide and gladiatorial contests.

Things are different now. So often the contemporary church is a weak, ineffectual voice with an uncertain sound. So often it is an arch defender of the status quo. Far from being disturbed by the presence of the church, the power structure of the average community is consoled by the church's silent and often even vocal sanction of things as they are.

"*a colony of heaven*": Another quotation from Paul, Philippians 3:20, used to remind the church leaders that their primary obligation should be to God's laws as opposed to the State's.

But the judgment of God is upon the church as never before. If today's church does not recapture the sacrificial spirit of the early church, it will lose its authenticity, forfeit the loyalty of millions, and be dismissed as an irrelevant social club with no meaning for the twentieth century. Every day I meet young people whose disappointment with the church has turned into outright disgust.

Perhaps I have once again been too optimistic. Is organized religion too inextricably bound to the status quo to save our nation and the world? Perhaps I must turn my faith to the inner spiritual church, the church within the church, as the true ekklesia° and the hope of the world. But again I am thankful to God that some noble souls from the ranks of organized religion have broken loose from the paralyzing chains of conformity and joined us as active partners in the struggle for freedom, They have left their secure congregations and walked the streets of Albany, Georgia, with us. They have gone down the highways of the South on tortuous rides for freedom. Yes, they have gone to jail with us. Some have been dismissed from their churches, have lost the support of their bishops and fellow ministers. But they have acted in the faith that right defeated is stronger than evil triumphant. Their witness has been the spiritual salt that has preserved the true meaning of the gospel in these troubled times. They have carved a tunnel of hope through the dark mountain of disappointment.

I hope the church as a whole will meet the challenge of this decisive hour. But even if the church does not come to the aid of justice, I have no despair about the future. I have no fear about the outcome of our struggle in Birmingham, even if our motives are at present misunderstood. We will reach the goal of freedom in Birmingham and all over the nation, because the goal of America is freedom. Abused and scorned though we may be, our destiny is tied up with America's destiny. Before the pilgrims landed at Plymouth, we were here. Before the pen of Jefferson etched the majestic words of the Declaration of Independence across the pages of history, we were here. For more than two centuries our forebears labored in this country without wages; they made cotton king; they built the homes of their masters while suffering gross injustice and shameful humiliation—and yet out of a bottomless vitality they continued to thrive and develop. If the inexpressible cruelties of slavery could not stop us, the opposition we now face will surely fail. We will win our freedom because the sacred heritage of our nation and the eternal will of God are embodied in our echoing demands.

Before closing I feel impelled to mention one other point in your statement that has troubled me profoundly. You warmly commended the Birmingham police force for keeping "order" and "preventing violence." I doubt that you would have so warmly commended the police force if you had seen its dogs sinking their teeth into unarmed, nonviolent Negroes. I doubt that you would so quickly commend the policemen if you were to observe their ugly and inhumane treatment of Negroes here in the city jail; if you were to watch them push and curse old Negro women and young Negro girls; if you were to see them slap and kick old Negro men and young boys; if you were to observe them, as they did on two occasions, refuse to give us food because we wanted to sing our grace together. I cannot join you in your praise of the Birmingham police department.

---

ekklesia: Greek, for an assembly of people "called out." A term used for the early Christian church, it can also refer to the body of believers throughout the world.

It is true that the police have exercised a degree of discipline in handing the demonstrators. In this sense they have conducted themselves rather "nonviolently" in public. But for what purpose? To preserve the evil system of segregation. Over the past few years I have consistently preached that nonviolence demands that the means we use must be as pure as the ends we seek. I have tried to make clear that it is wrong to use immoral means to attain moral ends. But now I must affirm that it is just as wrong, or perhaps even more so, to use moral means to preserve immoral ends. Perhaps Mr. Connor and his policemen have been rather nonviolent in public, as was Chief Pritchett in Albany, Georgia, but they have used the moral means of nonviolence to maintain the immoral end of racial injustice. As T. S. Eliot has said: "The last temptation is the greatest treason: To do the right deed for the wrong reason."

I wish you had commended the Negro sit-inners and demonstrators of Birmingham for their sublime courage, their willingness to suffer and their amazing discipline in the midst of great provocation. One day the South will recognize its real heroes. There will be the James Merediths,° with the noble sense of purpose that enables them to face jeering and hostile mobs, and with the agonizing loneliness that characterizes the life of the pioneer. There will be the old, oppressed, battered Negro women, symbolized in a seventy-two-year-old woman in Montgomery, Alabama, who rose up with a sense of dignity and with her people decided not to ride segregated buses, and who responded with ungrammatical profundity to one who inquired about her weariness: "My feets is tired, but my soul is at rest." There will be the young high school and college students, the young ministers of the gospel and a host of their elders, courageously and nonviolently sitting in at lunch counters and willingly going to jail for conscience' sake. One day the South will know that when these disinherited children of God sat down at lunch counters, they were in reality standing up for what is best in the American dream and for the most sacred values in our Judaeo-Christian heritage, thereby bringing our nation back to those great wells of democracy which were dug deep by the founding fathers in their formulation of the Constitution and the Declaration of Independence.

Never before have I written so long a letter. I'm afraid it is much too long to take your precious time. I can assure you that it would have been much shorter if I had been writing from a comfortable desk, but what else can one do when he is alone in a narrow jail cell, other than write long letters, think long thoughts and pray long prayers?

If I have said anything in this letter that overstates the truth and indicates an unreasonable impatience, I beg you to forgive me. If I have said anything that understates the truth and indicates my having a patience that allows me to settle for anything less than brotherhood, I beg God to forgive me.

I hope this letter finds you strong in the faith. I also hope that circumstances will soon make it possible for me to meet each of you, not as an integrationist or a civil rights leader but as a fellow clergyman and a Christian brother. Let us all hope that the dark clouds of racial prejudice will soon pass away and the deep fog of

---

James Meredith: First African American to enter University of Mississippi, in 1962. After being denied admission twice, Meredith filed suit in court, and the case was eventually taken to the Supreme Court. Meredith's enrollment, enforced by U.S. marshals, was met with riots on campus.

misunderstanding will be lifted from our fear-drenched communities, and in some not too distant tomorrow the radiant stars of love and brotherhood will shine over our great nation with all their scintillating beauty.

Yours for the cause of Peace and Brotherhood,

Martin Luther King Jr.

Questions

1. King addressed "Letter from Birmingham Jail" to eight fellow clergymen who disagreed with his activities. Why did he write this piece as a letter rather than as an essay? How does reading this piece as a letter influence the reader's experience?
2. What is King's theory of nonviolent resistance? Do you think such a strategy is effective? Why or why not?
3. Do you think King's letter was persuasive enough to change people's minds? Why or why not? Do people tend to change their minds because of emotion, or because of logic?

Henry David Thoreau

Henry David Thoreau (1817–1862) was born in Concord, Massachusetts. He entered Harvard College at age sixteen, and after graduating in 1837, he worked for several years as a schoolteacher, a surveyor, and an employee in his father's pencil factory. For several years he lived in the household of the philosopher and poet Ralph Waldo Emerson, working mostly as a handyman, but also helping to edit Emerson's magazine The Dial. This experience profoundly affected Thoreau, as did the untimely death of his brother John when Thoreau was twenty-five. In 1845, Thoreau moved to a small wooden house he built himself along the shore of Walden Pond. Although he sometimes made the two-mile walk to Concord for supplies and occasionally had dinner with his family, he spent most of the next twenty-six months alone at Walden. There he produced his first book, A Week on the Concord and Merrimack Rivers (1849), and kept an extensive journal, which would become the source of his most famous book, Walden, Or Life in the Woods (1854). Thoreau is one of the major figures of the Transcendentalist movement—which encouraged individuals to recognize their unity with the world and to find the divine spark inside themselves. Thoreau wrote extensively about humanity's relation to nature, but he was also deeply engaged in the political issues of the day. In 1846 he spent a night in jail for refusing to pay a poll tax that he said would help fund America's war with Mexico and extend the practice of slavery. Two years later, in order to explain this deliberate action to his fellow citizens, he delivered a two-part lecture at the Concord Lyceum, "On the Relation of the Individual to the State." Thoreau published the speech the following year, in what became his most famous essay, "Resistance to Civil Government" (now usually called "Civil Disobedience"). Thoreau's arguments for citizens' resisting unjust laws deeply influenced both

Henry David Thoreau

Mohandas Gandhi and Martin Luther King Jr. Thoreau never made a living with his writing; he continued to support himself with intermittent work on land surveys and at the pencil factory until he died of tuberculosis at age forty-four. His works—particularly Walden and "Civil Disobedience"—continue to inspire readers, naturalists, and activists even today.

from Civil Disobedience 1848, 1849

I heartily accept the motto, "That government is best which governs least;" and I should like to see it acted up to more rapidly and systematically. Carried out, it finally amounts to this, which also I believe,—"That government is best which governs not at all;" and when men are prepared for it, that will be the kind of government which they will have. Government is at best but an expedient; but most governments are usually, and all governments are sometimes, inexpedient. The objections which have been brought against a standing army, and they are many and weighty, and deserve to prevail, may also at last be brought against a standing government. The standing army is only an arm of the standing government. The government itself, which is only the mode which the people have chosen to execute their will, is equally liable to be abused and perverted before the people can act through it. Witness the present Mexican war,° the work of comparatively a few individuals using the standing government as their tool; for, in the outset, the people would not have consented to this measure.

This American government,—what is it but a tradition, though a recent one, endeavoring to transmit itself unimpaired to posterity, but each instant losing some of its integrity? It has not the vitality and force of a single living man; for a single man can bend it to his will. It is a sort of wooden gun to the people themselves. But it is not the less necessary for this; for the people must have some complicated machinery or other, and hear its din, to satisfy that idea of government which they have. Governments show thus how successfully men can be imposed upon, even impose on themselves, for their own advantage. It is excellent, we must all allow. Yet this government never of itself furthered any enterprise, but by the alacrity with which it got out of its way. It does not keep the country free. It does not settle the West. It does not educate. The character inherent in the American people has done all that has been accomplished; and it would have done somewhat more, if the government had not sometimes got in its way. For government is an expedient by which men would fain succeed in letting one another alone; and, as has been said, when it is most expedient, the governed are most let alone by it. Trade and commerce, if they were not made of india-rubber, would never manage to bounce over obstacles which legislators are continually putting in their way; and if one were to judge these men wholly by the effects of their actions and not partly by their intentions, they would deserve to be classed and punished with those mischievous persons who put obstructions on the railroads.

But, to speak practically and as a citizen, unlike those who call themselves no-government men, I ask for, not at once no government, but *at once* a better government. Let every man make known what kind of government would command his respect, and that will be one step toward obtaining it.

• • •

Unjust laws exist: shall we be content to obey them, or shall we endeavor to amend them, and obey them until we have succeeded, or shall we transgress them at

---

Mexican war: Mexican-American war of 1846–1848, fought over the annexation of Texas.

once? Men generally, under such a government as this, think that they ought to wait until they have persuaded the majority to alter them. They think that, if they should resist, the remedy would be worse than the evil. But it is the fault of the government itself that the remedy *is* worse than the evil. *It* makes it worse. Why is it not more apt to anticipate and provide for reform? Why does it not cherish its wise minority? Why does it cry and resist before it is hurt? Why does it not encourage its citizens to be on the alert to point out its faults, and *do* better than it would have them? Why does it always crucify Christ, and excommunicate Copernicus and Luther, and pronounce Washington and Franklin rebels?

One would think, that a deliberate and practical denial of its authority was the only offense never contemplated by government; else, why has it not assigned its definite, its suitable and proportionate, penalty? If a man who has no property refuses but once to earn nine shillings for the State, he is put in prison for a period unlimited by any law that I know, and determined only by the discretion of those who placed him there; but if he should steal ninety times nine shillings from the State, he is soon permitted to go at large again.

If the injustice is part of the necessary friction of the machine of government, let it go, let it go: perchance it will wear smooth—certainly the machine will wear out. If the injustice has a spring, or a pulley, or a rope, or a crank, exclusively for itself, then perhaps you may consider whether the remedy will not be worse than the evil; but if it is of such a nature that it requires you to be the agent of injustice to another, then, I say, break the law. Let your life be a counter-friction to stop the machine. What I have to do is to see, at any rate, that I do not lend myself to the wrong which I condemn.

As for adopting the ways which the State has provided for remedying the evil, I know not of such ways. They take too much time, and a man's life will be gone. I have other affairs to attend to. I came into this world, not chiefly to make this a good place to live in, but to live in it, be it good or bad. A man has not everything to do, but something; and because he cannot do *every thing*, it is not necessary that he should do *something* wrong. It is not my business to be petitioning the Governor or the Legislature any more than it is theirs to petition me; and if they should not hear my petition, what should I do then? But in this case the State has provided no way: its very Constitution is the evil.° This may seem to be harsh and stubborn and unconciliatory; but it is to treat with the utmost kindness and consideration the only spirit that can appreciate or deserves it. So is all change for the better, like birth and death, which convulse the body.

I do not hesitate to say, that those who call themselves Abolitionists should at once effectually withdraw their support, both in person and property, from the government of Massachusetts, and not wait till they constitute a majority of one, before they suffer the right to prevail through them. I think that it is enough if they have God on their side, without waiting for that other one. Moreover, any man more right than his neighbors constitutes a majority of one already.

I meet this American government, or its representative, the State government, directly, and face to face, once a year—no more—in the person of its tax-gatherer;

---

its very Constitution is the evil: Thoreau observes that the Constitution, itself a compromise between Northern and Southern states, did not declare slavery illegal.

this is the only mode in which a man situated as I am necessarily meets it; and it then says distinctly, Recognize me; and the simplest, the most effectual, and, in the present posture of affairs, the indispensablest mode of treating with it on this head, of expressing your little satisfaction with and love for it, is to deny it then. My civil neighbor, the tax-gatherer, is the very man I have to deal with,—for it is, after all, with men and not with parchment that I quarrel,—and he has voluntarily chosen to be an agent of the government. How shall he ever know well what he is and does as an officer of the government, or as a man, until he is obliged to consider whether he will treat me, his neighbor, for whom he has respect, as a neighbor and well-disposed man, or as a maniac and disturber of the peace, and see if he can get over this obstruction to his neighborliness without a ruder and more impetuous thought or speech corresponding with his action. I know this well, that if one thousand, if one hundred, if ten men whom I could name,—if ten *honest* men only,—aye, if *one* HONEST man, in this State of Massachusetts, *ceasing to hold slaves*, were actually to withdraw from this copartnership, and be locked up in the county jail therefore, it would be the abolition of slavery in America. For it matters not how small the beginning may seem to be: what is once well done is done forever. But we love better to talk about it: that we say is our mission. Reform keeps many scores of newspapers in its service, but not one man. If my esteemed neighbor, the State's ambassador, who will devote his days to the settlement of the question of human rights in the Council Chamber, instead of being threatened with the prisons of Carolina, were to sit down the prisoner of Massachusetts, that State which is so anxious to foist the sin of slavery upon her sister,—though at present she can discover only an act of inhospitality to be the ground of a quarrel with her,—the Legislature would not wholly waive the subject the following winter.

Under a government which imprisons unjustly, the true place for a just man is also a prison. The proper place today, the only place which Massachusetts has provided for her freer and less desponding spirits, is in her prisons, to be put out and locked out of the State by her own act, as they have already put themselves out by their principles. It is there that the fugitive slave, and the Mexican prisoner on parole, and the Indian come to plead the wrongs of his race should find them; on that separate, but more free and honorable, ground, where the State places those who are not *with* her, but *against* her,—the only house in a slave State in which a free man can abide with honor. If any think that their influence would be lost there, and their voices no longer afflict the ear of the State, that they would not be as an enemy within its walls, they do not know by how much truth is stronger than error, nor how much more eloquently and effectively he can combat injustice who has experienced a little in his own person. Cast your whole vote, not a strip of paper merely, but your whole influence. A minority is powerless while it conforms to the majority; it is not even a minority then; but it is irresistible when it clogs by its whole weight. If the alternative is to keep all just men in prison, or give up war and slavery, the State will not hesitate which to choose. If a thousand men were not to pay their tax-bills this year, that would not be a violent and bloody measure, as it would be to pay them, and enable the State to commit violence and shed innocent blood. This is, in fact, the definition of a peaceable revolution, if any such is possible. If the tax-gatherer, or any other public officer, asks me, as one has done, "But what shall I do?" my answer is, "If you really wish to do anything, resign your office."

When the subject has refused allegiance, and the officer has resigned his office, then the revolution is accomplished. But even suppose blood should flow. Is there not a sort of blood shed when the conscience is wounded? Through this wound a man's real manhood and immortality flow out, and he bleeds to an everlasting death. I see this blood flowing now.

• • •

When I converse with the freest of my neighbors, I perceive that, whatever they may say about the magnitude and seriousness of the question, and their regard for the public tranquillity, the long and the short of the matter is, that they cannot spare the protection of the existing government, and they dread the consequences to their property and families of disobedience to it. For my own part, I should not like to think that I ever rely on the protection of the State. But, if I deny the authority of the State when it presents its tax bill, it will soon take and waste all my property, and so harass me and my children without end. This is hard. This makes it impossible for a man to live honestly, and at the same time comfortably, in outward respects. It will not be worth the while to accumulate property; that would be sure to go again. You must hire or squat somewhere, and raise but a small crop, and eat that soon. You must live within yourself, and depend upon yourself always tucked up and ready for a start, and not have many affairs. A man may grow rich in Turkey even, if he will be in all respects a good subject of the Turkish government. Confucius said: "If a state is governed by the principles of reason, poverty and misery are the subjects of shame; if a state is not governed by the principles of reason, riches and honors are subjects of shame." No: until I want the protection of Massachusetts to be extended to me in some distant Southern port, where my liberty is endangered, or until I am bent solely on building up an estate at home by peaceful enterprise, I can afford to refuse allegiance to Massachusetts, and her right to my property and life. It costs me less in every sense to incur the penalty of disobedience to the State than it would to obey. I should feel as if I were worth less in that case.

• • •

I have paid no poll-tax for six years. I was put into a jail once on this account, for one night; and, as I stood considering the walls of solid stone, two or three feet thick, the door of wood and iron, a foot thick, and the iron grating which strained the light, I could not help being struck with the foolishness of that institution which treated me as if I were mere flesh and blood and bones, to be locked up. I wondered that it should have concluded at length that this was the best use it could put me to, and had never thought to avail itself of my services in some way. I saw that, if there was a wall of stone between me and my townsmen, there was a still more difficult one to climb or break through before they could get to be as free as I was. I did not for a moment feel confined, and the walls seemed a great waste of stone and mortar. I felt as if I alone of all my townsmen had paid my tax. They plainly did not know how to treat me, but behaved like persons who are underbred. In every threat and in every compliment there was a blunder; for they thought that my chief desire was to stand the other side of that stone wall. I could not but smile to see how industriously they locked the door on my meditations, which followed them out again without let or hindrance, and *they* were really all that was dangerous. As they could not reach me, they had resolved to punish my body; just as boys, if they cannot come at some person against whom they have a spite, will abuse his dog. I saw that the State was half-witted, that it was timid as a lone woman with her silver spoons, and that it did not know its friends from its foes, and I lost all my remaining respect for it, and pitied it.

Thus the state never intentionally confronts a man's sense, intellectual or moral, but only his body, his senses. It is not armed with superior wit or honesty, but with superior physical strength. I was not born to be forced. I will breathe after my own fashion. Let us see who is the strongest. What force has a multitude? They only can force me who obey a higher law than I. They force me to become like themselves. I do not hear of *men* being *forced* to live this way or that by masses of men. What sort of life were that to live? When I meet a government which says to me, "Your money or your life," why should I be in haste to give it my money? It may be in a great strait, and not know what to do: I cannot help that. It must help itself; do as I do. It is not worth the while to snivel about it. I am not responsible for the successful working of the machinery of society. I am not the son of the engineer. I perceive that, when an acorn and a chestnut fall side by side, the one does not remain inert to make way for the other, but both obey their own laws, and spring and grow and flourish as best they can, till one, perchance, overshadows and destroys the other. If a plant cannot live according to nature, it dies; and so a man.

• • •

I do not wish to quarrel with any man or nation. I do not wish to split hairs, to make fine distinctions, or set myself up as better than my neighbors. I seek rather, I may say, even an excuse for conforming to the laws of the land. I am but too ready to conform to them. Indeed, I have reason to suspect myself on this head; and each year, as the tax-gatherer comes round, I find myself disposed to review the acts and position of the general and State governments, and the spirit of the people, to discover a pretext for conformity.

> "We must affect our country as our parents,
> And if at any time we alienate
> Our love or industry from doing it honor,
> We must respect effects and teach the soul
> Matter of conscience and religion,
> And not desire of rule or benefit."°

I believe that the State will soon be able to take all my work of this sort out of my hands, and then I shall be no better patriot than my fellow-countrymen. Seen from a lower point of view, the Constitution, with all its faults, is very good; the law and the courts are very respectable; even this State and this American government are, in many respects, very admirable, and rare things, to be thankful for, such as a great many have described them; but seen from a point of view a little higher, they are what I have described them; seen from a higher still, and the highest, who shall say what they are, or that they are worth looking at or thinking of at all?

However, the government does not concern me much, and I shall bestow the fewest possible thoughts on it. It is not many moments that I live under a government, even in this world. If a man is thought-free, fancy-free, imagination-free, that which

---

"We must affect . . . rule or benefit": speech from the play *Battle of Alcazar* attributed to George Peele (1556?–1596). These lines were inserted after the first printing.

is not never for a long time appearing *to be* to him, unwise rulers or reformers cannot fatally interrupt him.

I know that most men think differently from myself; but those whose lives are by profession devoted to the study of these or kindred subjects content me as little as any. Statesmen and legislators, standing so completely within the institution, never distinctly and nakedly behold it. They speak of moving society, but have no resting-place without it. They may be men of a certain experience and discrimination, and have no doubt invented ingenious and even useful systems, for which we sincerely thank them; but all their wit and usefulness lie within certain not very wide limits. They are wont to forget that the world is not governed by policy and expediency. Webster° never goes behind government, and so cannot speak with authority about it. His words are wisdom to those legislators who contemplate no essential reform in the existing government; but for thinkers, and those who legislate for all time, he never once glances at the subject. I know of those whose serene and wise speculations on this theme would soon reveal the limits of his mind's range and hospitality. Yet, compared with the cheap professions of most reformers, and the still cheaper wisdom and eloquence of politicians in general, his are almost the only sensible and valuable words, and we thank Heaven for him. Comparatively, he is always strong, original, and, above all, practical. Still, his quality is not wisdom, but prudence. The lawyer's truth is not Truth, but consistency or a consistent expediency. Truth is always in harmony with herself, and is not concerned chiefly to reveal the justice that may consist with wrong-doing. He well deserves to be called, as he has been called, the Defender of the Constitution. There are really no blows to be given by him but defensive ones. He is not a leader, but a follower. His leaders are the men of '87.° "I have never made an effort," he says, "and never propose to make an effort; I have never countenanced an effort, and never mean to countenance an effort, to disturb the arrangement as originally made, by which various States came into the Union."° Still thinking of the sanction which the Constitution gives to slavery, he says, "Because it was part of the original compact,—let it stand." Notwithstanding his special acuteness and ability, he is unable to take a fact out of its merely political relations, and behold it as it lies absolutely to be disposed of by the intellect—what, for instance, it behooves a man to do here in American today with regard to slavery,—but ventures, or is driven, to make some such desperate answer as the following, while professing to speak absolutely, and as a private man,—from which what new and singular code of social duties might be inferred?—"The manner," says he, "in which the governments of those States where slavery exists are to regulate it is for their own consideration, under their responsibility to their constituents, to the general laws of propriety, humanity, and justice, and to God. Associations formed elsewhere, springing from a feeling of humanity, or any other cause, have nothing whatever to do with it. They have never received any encouragement from me, and they never will."[1]

Webster: Daniel Webster (1782–1852), U.S. Senator from Massachusetts and famed orator. His position of compromise with the Southern states on the issue of slavery in order to preserve the Union was viewed as a betrayal by Thoreau and other Massachusetts Abolitionists.   *men of '87:* 1787, the year of the Constitutional Convention in Philadelphia.   *"I have never made an effort . . . States came into the Union":* from Daniel Webster's December 22, 1845, Senate speech on the admission of Texas to the Union.

[1] These extracts have been inserted since the Lecture was read. [Thoreau's note to his 1849 printed article]

They who know of no purer sources of truth, who have traced up its stream no higher, stand, and wisely stand, by the Bible and the Constitution, and drink at it there with reverence and humility; but they who behold where it comes trickling into this lake or that pool, gird up their loins once more, and continue their pilgrimage toward its fountain-head.

No man with a genius for legislation has appeared in America. They are rare in the history of the world. There are orators, politicians, and eloquent men, by the thousand; but the speaker has not yet opened his mouth to speak who is capable of settling the much-vexed questions of the day. We love eloquence for its own sake, and not for any truth which it may utter, or any heroism it may inspire. Our legislators have not yet learned the comparative value of free trade and of freedom, of union, and of rectitude, to a nation. They have no genius or talent for comparatively humble questions of taxation and finance, commerce and manufactures and agriculture. If we were left solely to the wordy wit of legislators in Congress for our guidance, uncorrected by the seasonable experience and the effectual complaints of the people, America would not long retain her rank among the nations. For eighteen hundred years, though perchance I have no right to say it, the New Testament has been written; yet where is the legislator who has wisdom and practical talent enough to avail himself of the light which it sheds on the science of legislation?

The authority of government, even such as I am willing to submit to,—for I will cheerfully obey those who know and can do better than I, and in many things even those who neither know nor can do so well,—is still an impure one: to be strictly just, it must have the sanction and consent of the governed. It can have no pure right over my person and property but what I concede to it. The progress from an absolute to a limited monarchy, from a limited monarchy to a democracy, is a progress toward a true respect for the individual. Even the Chinese philosopher was wise enough to regard the individual as the basis of the empire. Is a democracy, such as we know it, the last improvement possible in government? Is it not possible to take a step further towards recognizing and organizing the rights of man? There will never be a really free and enlightened State until the State comes to recognize the individual as a higher and independent power, from which all its own power and authority are derived, and treats him accordingly. I please myself with imagining a State at last which can afford to be just to all men, and to treat the individual with respect as a neighbor; which even would not think it inconsistent with its own repose if a few were to live aloof from it, not meddling with it, nor embraced by it, who fulfilled all the duties of neighbors and fellow-men. A State which bore this kind of fruit, and suffered it to drop off as fast as it ripened, would prepare the way for a still more perfect and glorious State, which also I have imagined, but not yet anywhere seen.

Questions

1. What reasons does Thoreau give to justify his actions? Do they seem sufficient?
2. Are there circumstances in which you think it's acceptable to break the law? Why or why not? If yes, what would those circumstances be?
3. Do you agree with Thoreau's points about the role of individual versus the role of government? Are his ideas relevant today?

Maxine Hong Kingston

Maxine Hong Kingston was born in 1940 in Stockton, California, the oldest of six American-born children of Tom and Ying Lan Hong. (Her parents had two children who had died in China before they emigrated.) Kingston's father, who had been a poet and scholar in China, was relegated to working in a laundry and a gambling house in California; her mother also worked in a laundry, and labored as a field hand. Kingston grew up hearing stories of her parents' struggles in China, and of the challenges of their immigration and adjustment to America. She was especially struck by her mother's haunting "talk-stories" about her family's secrets and the difficulties faced by female relatives in China. Kingston attended the University of California at Berkeley on scholarship, graduating in 1962. In the same year, she married Earll Kingston, an actor. The couple first taught high school in California, then moved to Hawaii, where Kingston taught at the Mid-Pacific Institute and then the University of Hawaii. In 1976, Kingston published her first book, The Woman Warrior: Memoirs of a Girlhood Among Ghosts. Utilizing elements of both the memoir and the novel, Kingston retold stories that had previously been silenced about the struggles of women in China. Kingston's subsequent books include China Men (1980), which won the 1981 American Book Award, and Tripmaster Monkey: His Fake Book (1989). Kingston joined the faculty at University of California at Berkeley in 1990, where she is now a professor emerita. In 1996, she was named by Time magazine as one of the preeminent Asian American artists in its special issue "60 Years of Asian Heroes," and in 1997, she was awarded the National Humanities Medal.

In "No Name Woman," the opening chapter of The Woman Warrior, Kingston imagines the tragic life of an aunt she never knew, and considers the effect of her aunt's story on her own emotional and sexual development.

No Name Woman   1976

"You must not tell anyone," my mother said, "what I am about to tell you. In China your father had a sister who killed herself. She jumped into the family well. We say that your father has all brothers because it is as if she had never been born.

"In 1924 just a few days after our village celebrated seventeen hurry-up weddings—to make sure that every young man who went 'out on the road' would responsibly come home—your father and his brothers and your grandfather and his brothers and your aunt's new husband sailed for America, the Gold Mountain. It was your grandfather's last trip. Those lucky enough to get contracts waved goodbye from the decks. They fed and guarded the stowaways and helped them off in Cuba, New York, Bali, Hawaii. 'We'll meet in California next year,' they said. All of them sent money home.

"I remember looking at your aunt one day when she and I were dressing; I had not noticed before that she had such a protruding melon of a stomach. But I did not think, 'She's pregnant,' until she began to look like other pregnant women, her shirt pulling and the white tops of her black pants showing. She could not have been pregnant, you see, because her husband had been gone for years. No one said anything. We did not discuss it. In early summer she was ready to have the child, long after the time when it could have been possible.

"The village had also been counting. On the night the baby was to be born the villagers raided our house. Some were crying. Like a great saw, teeth strung with lights, files of people walked zigzag across our land, tearing the rice. Their lanterns doubled in the disturbed black water, which drained away through the broken bunds. As the villagers closed in, we could see that some of them, probably men and women we knew well, wore white masks. The people with long hair hung it over their faces. Women with short hair made it stand up on end. Some had tied white bands around their foreheads, arms, and legs.

"At first they threw mud and rocks at the house. Then they threw eggs and began slaughtering our stock. We could hear the animals scream their deaths—the roosters, the pigs, a last great roar from the ox. Familiar wild heads flared in our night windows; the villagers encircled us. Some of the faces stopped to peer at us, their eyes rushing like searchlights. The hands flattened against the panes, framed heads, and left red prints.

"The villagers broke in the front and the back doors at the same time, even though we had not locked the doors against them. Their knives dripped with the blood of our animals. They smeared the blood on the doors and walls. One woman swung a chicken, whose throat she had slit, splattering blood in red arcs about her. We stood together in the middle of our house, in the family hall with the pictures and tables of the ancestors around us, and looked straight ahead.

"At that time the house had only two wings. When the men came back, we would build two more to enclose our courtyard and a third one to begin a second courtyard. The villagers pushed through both wings, even your grandparents' rooms, to find your aunt's, which was also mine until the men returned. From this room a new wing for one of the younger families would grow. They ripped up her clothes and shoes and broke her combs, grinding them underfoot. They tore her work from the loom. They scattered the cooking fire and rolled the new weaving in it. We could hear them in the kitchen breaking our bowls and banging the pots. They overturned the great waist-high earthenware jugs; duck eggs, pickled fruits, vegetables burst out and mixed in acrid torrents. The old woman from the next field swept a broom through the air and loosed the spirits-of-the-broom over our heads. 'Pig.' 'Ghost.' 'Pig,' they sobbed and scolded while they ruined our house.

"When they left, they took sugar and oranges to bless themselves. They cut pieces from the dead animals. Some of them took bowls that were not broken and clothes that were not torn. Afterward we swept up the rice and sewed it back up into sacks. But the smells from the spilled preserves lasted. Your aunt gave birth in the pigsty that night. The next morning when I went for the water, I found her and the baby plugging up the family well.

"Don't let your father know that I told you. He denies her. Now that you have started to menstruate, what happened to her could happen to you. Don't humiliate us. You wouldn't like to be forgotten as if you had never been born. The villagers are watchful."

Whenever she had to warn us about life, my mother told stories that ran like this one, a story to grow up on. She tested our strength to establish realities. Those in the emigrant generations who could not reassert brute survival died young and far from home. Those of us in the first American generations have had to figure out how the invisible world the emigrants built around our childhoods fits in solid America.

The emigrants confused the gods by diverting their curses, misleading them with crooked streets and false names. They must try to confuse their offspring as well, who, I suppose, threaten them in similar ways—always trying to get things straight, always trying to name the unspeakable. The Chinese I know hide their names; sojourners take new names when their lives change and guard their real names with silence.

Chinese-Americans, when you try to understand what things in you are Chinese, how do you separate what is peculiar to childhood, to poverty, insanities, one family, your mother who marked your growing with stories, from what is Chinese? What is Chinese tradition and what is the movies?

If I want to learn what clothes my aunt wore, whether flashy or ordinary, I would have to begin, "Remember Father's drowned-in-the-well sister?" I cannot ask that. My mother has told me once and for all the useful parts. She will add nothing unless powered by Necessity, a riverbank that guides her life. She plants vegetable gardens rather than lawns; she carries the odd-shaped tomatoes home from the fields and eats food left for the gods.

Whenever we did frivolous things, we used up energy; we flew high kites. We children came up off the ground over the melting cones our parents brought home from work and the American movie on New Year's Day—*Oh, You Beautiful Doll* with Betty Grable one year, and *She Wore a Yellow Ribbon* with John Wayne another year. After the one carnival ride each, we paid in guilt; our tired father counted his change on the dark walk home.

Adultery is extravagance. Could people who hatch their own chicks and eat the embryos and the heads for delicacies and boil the feet in vinegar for party food, leaving only the gravel, eating even the gizzard lining—could such people engender a prodigal aunt? To be a woman, to have a daughter in starvation time was a waste enough. My aunt could not have been the lone romantic who gave up everything for sex. Women in the old China did not choose. Some man had commanded her to lie with him and be his secret evil. I wonder whether he masked himself when he joined the raid on her family.

Perhaps she had encountered him in the fields or on the mountain where the daughters-in-law collected fuel. Or perhaps he first noticed her in the marketplace. He was not a stranger because the village housed no strangers. She had to have dealings with him other than sex. Perhaps he worked an adjoining field, or he sold her the cloth for the dress she sewed and wore. His demand must have surprised, then terrified her. She obeyed him; she always did as she was told.

When the family found a young man in the next village to be her husband, she had stood tractably beside the best rooster, his proxy, and promised before they met that she would be his forever. She was lucky that he was her age and she would be the first wife, an advantage secure now. The night she first saw him, he had sex with her. Then he left for America. She had almost forgotten what he looked like. When she tried to envision him, she only saw the black and white face in the group photograph the men had had taken before leaving.

The other man was not, after all, much different from her husband. They both gave orders: she followed. "If you tell your family, I'll beat you. I'll kill you. Be here again next week." No one talked sex, ever. And she might have separated the rapes from the rest of living if only she did not have to buy her oil from him or gather wood in the same forest. I want her fear to have lasted just as long as rape lasted so that the fear could have been contained. No drawn-out fear. But women at sex hazarded birth and hence lifetimes. The fear did not stop but permeated everywhere. She told the man, "I think I'm pregnant." He organized the raid against her.

On nights when my mother and father talked about their life back home, sometimes they mentioned an "outcast table" whose business they still seemed to be settling, their voices tight. In a commensal tradition, where food is precious, the powerful older people made wrongdoers eat alone. Instead of letting them start separate new lives like the Japanese, who could become samurais and geishas, the Chinese family, faces averted but eyes glowering sideways, hung on to the offenders and fed them leftovers. My aunt must have lived in the same house as my parents and eaten at an outcast table. My mother spoke about the raid as if she had seen it, when she and my aunt, a daughter-in-law to a different household, should not have been living together at all. Daughters-in-law lived with their husbands' parents, not their own; a synonym for marriage in Chinese is "taking a daughter-in-law." Her husband's parents could have sold her, mortgaged her, stoned her. But they had sent her back to her own mother and father, a mysterious act hinting at disgraces not told me. Perhaps they had thrown her out to deflect the avengers.

She was the only daughter; her four brothers went with her father, husband, and uncles "out on the road" and for some years became western men. When the goods were divided among the family, three of the brothers took land, and the youngest, my father, chose an education. After my grandparents gave their daughter away to her husband's family, they had dispensed all the adventure and all the property. They expected her alone to keep the traditional ways, which her brothers, now among the barbarians, could fumble without detection. The heavy, deep-rooted women were to maintain the past against the flood, safe for returning. But the rare urge west had fixed upon our family, and so my aunt crossed boundaries not delineated in space. 20

The work of preservation demands that the feelings playing about in one's guts not be turned into action. Just watch their passing like cherry blossoms. But perhaps my aunt, my forerunner, caught in a slow life, let dreams grow and fade and after some months or years went toward what persisted. Fear at the enormities of the forbidden kept her desires delicate, wire and bone. She looked at a man because she liked the way the hair was tucked behind his ears, or she liked the question-mark line of a long torso curving at the shoulder and straight at the hip. For warm eyes or a soft voice or a slow walk—that's all—a few hairs, a line, a brightness, a sound, a pace, she gave up family. She offered us up for a charm that vanished with tiredness, a pigtail that didn't toss when the wind died. Why, the wrong lighting could erase the dearest thing about him.

It could very well have been, however, that my aunt did not take subtle enjoyment of her friend, but, a wild woman, kept rollicking company. Imagining her free with sex doesn't fit, though. I don't know any women like that, or men either. Unless I see her life branching into mine, she gives me no ancestral help.

To sustain her being in love, she often worked at herself in the mirror, guessing at the colors and shapes that would interest him, changing them frequently in order to hit on the right combination. She wanted him to look back.

On a farm near the sea, a woman who tended her appearance reaped a reputation for eccentricity. All the married women blunt-cut their hair in flaps about their ears or pulled it back in tight buns. No nonsense. Neither style blew easily into heart-catching tangles. And at their weddings they displayed themselves in their long hair for the last time. "It brushed the backs of my knees," my mother tells me. "It was braided, and even so, it brushed the backs of my knees."

At the mirror my aunt combed individuality into her bob. A bun could have been contrived to escape into black streamers blowing in the wind or in quiet wisps about her face, but only the older women in our picture album wear buns. She brushed her hair back from her forehead, tucking the flaps behind her ears. She looped a piece of thread, knotted into a circle between her index fingers and thumbs, and ran the double strand across her forehead. When she closed her fingers as if she were making a pair of shadow geese bite, the string twisted together catching the little hairs. Then she pulled the thread away from her skin, ripping the hairs out neatly, her eyes watering from the needles of pain. Opening her fingers, she cleaned the thread, then rolled it along her hairline and the tops of her eyebrows. My mother did the same to me and my sisters and herself. I used to believe that the expression "caught by the short hairs" meant a captive held with a depilatory string. It especially hurt at the temples, but my mother said we were lucky we didn't have to have our feet bound when we were seven. Sisters used to sit on their beds and cry together, she said, as their mothers or their slaves removed the bandages for a few minutes each night and let the blood gush back into their veins. I hope that the man my aunt loved appreciated a smooth brow, that he wasn't just a tits-and-ass man.

Once my aunt found a freckle on her chin, at a spot that the almanac said predestined her for unhappiness. She dug it out with a hot needle and washed the wound with peroxide.

More attention to her looks than these pullings of hairs and pickings at spots would have caused gossip among the villagers. They owned work clothes and good clothes, and they wore good clothes for feasting the new seasons. But since a woman combing her hair hexes beginnings, my aunt rarely found an occasion to look her best. Women looked like great sea snails—the corded wood, babies, and laundry they carried were the whorls on their backs. The Chinese did not admire a bent back; goddesses and warriors stood straight. Still there must have been a marvelous freeing of beauty when a worker laid down her burden and stretched and arched.

Such commonplace loveliness, however, was not enough for my aunt. She dreamed of a lover for the fifteen days of New Year's, the time for families to exchange visits, money, and food. She plied her secret comb. And sure enough she cursed the year, the family, the village, and herself.

Even as her hair lured her imminent lover, many other men looked at her. Uncles, cousins, nephews, brothers would have looked, too, had they been home between journeys. Perhaps they had already been restraining their curiosity, and they left, fearful that their glances, like a field of nesting birds, might be startled and caught. Poverty hurt, and that was their first reason for leaving. But another, final reason for leaving the crowded house was the never-said.

She may have been unusually beloved, the precious only daughter, spoiled and mirror gazing because of the affection the family lavished on her. When her husband left, they welcomed the chance to take her back from the in-laws; she could live like the little daughter for just a while longer. There are stories that my grandfather was different from other people, "crazy ever since the little Jap bayoneted him in the head." He used to put his naked penis on the dinner table, laughing. And one day he brought home a baby girl, wrapped up inside his brown western-style greatcoat. He had traded one of his sons, probably my father, the youngest, for her. My grandmother made him trade back. When he finally got a daughter of his own, he doted on her. They must have all loved her, except perhaps my father, the only brother who never went back to China, having once been traded for a girl.

Brothers and sisters, newly men and women, had to efface their sexual color and present plain miens. Disturbing hair and eyes, a smile like no other, threatened the ideal of five generations living under one roof. To focus blurs, people shouted face to face and yelled from room to room. The immigrants I know have loud voices, unmodulated to American tones even after years away from the village where they called their friendships out across the fields. I have not been able to stop my mother's screams in public libraries or over telephones. Walking erect (knees straight, toes pointed forward, not pigeon-toed, which is Chinese-feminine) and speaking in an inaudible voice, I have tried to turn myself American-feminine. Chinese communication was loud, public. Only sick people had to whisper. But at the dinner table, where the family members came nearest one another, no one could talk, not the outcasts nor any eaters. Every word that falls from the mouth is a coin lost. Silently they gave and accepted food with both hands. A preoccupied child who took his bowl with one hand got a sideways glare. A complete moment of total attention is due everyone alike. Children and lovers have no singularity here, but my aunt used a secret voice, a separate attentiveness.

She kept the man's name to herself throughout her labor and dying; she did not accuse him that he be punished with her. To save her inseminator's name she gave silent birth.

He may have been somebody in her own household, but intercourse with a man outside the family would have been no less abhorrent. All the village were kinsmen, and the titles shouted in loud country voices never let kinship be forgotten. Any man within visiting distance would have been neutralized as a lover—"brother," "younger brother," "older brother"—one hundred and fifteen relationship titles. Parents researched birth charts probably not so much to assure good fortune as to circumvent incest in a population that has but one hundred surnames. Everybody has eight million relatives. How useless then sexual mannerisms, how dangerous.

As if it came from an atavism deeper than fear, I used to add "brother" silently to boys' names. It hexed the boys, who would or would not ask me to dance, and made them less scary and as familiar and deserving of benevolence as girls.

But, of course, I hexed myself also—no dates. I should have stood up, both arms waving, and shouted out across libraries, "Hey, you! Love me back." I had no idea, though, how to make attraction selective, how to control its direction and magnitude. If I made myself American-pretty so that the five or six Chinese boys in the class fell in love with me, everyone else—the Caucasian, Negro, and Japanese boys—would too. Sisterliness, dignified and honorable, made much more sense.

Attraction eludes control so stubbornly that whole societies designed to organize relationships among people cannot keep order, not even when they bind people to one another from childhood and raise them together. Among the very poor and the wealthy, brothers married their adopted sisters, like doves. Our family allowed some romance, paying adult brides' prices and providing dowries so that their sons and daughters could marry strangers. Marriage promises to turn strangers into friendly relatives—a nation of siblings.

In the village structure, spirits shimmered among the live creatures, balanced and held in equilibrium by time and land. But one human being flaring up into violence could open up a black hole, a maelstrom that pulled in the sky. The frightened villagers, who depended on one another to maintain the real, went to my aunt to show her a personal, physical representation of the break she had made in the "roundness." Misallying couples snapped off the future, which was to be embodied in true offspring. The villagers punished her for acting as if she could have a private life, secret and apart from them.

If my aunt had betrayed the family at a time of large grain yields and peace, when many boys were born, and wings were being built on many houses, perhaps she might have escaped such severe punishment. But the men—hungry, greedy, tired of planting in dry soil—had been forced to leave the village in order to send food-money home. There were ghost plagues, bandit plagues, wars with the Japanese, floods. My Chinese brother and sister had died of an unknown sickness. Adultery, perhaps only a mistake during good times, became a crime when the village needed food.

The round moon cakes and round doorways, the round tables of graduated sizes that fit one roundness inside another, round windows and rice bowls—these talismans had lost their power to warn this family of the law: a family must be whole, faithfully keeping the descent line by having sons to feed the old and the dead, who in turn look after the family. The villagers came to show my aunt and her lover-in-hiding a broken house. The villagers were speeding up the circling of events because she was too shortsighted to see that her infidelity had already harmed the village, that waves of consequences would return unpredictably, sometimes in disguise, as now, to hurt her. This roundness had to be made coin-sized so that she would see its circumference: punish her at the birth of her baby. Awaken her to the inexorable. People who refused fatalism because they could invent small resources insisted on culpability. Deny accidents and wrest fault from the stars.

After the villagers left, their lanterns now scattering in various directions toward home, the family broke their silence and cursed her. "Aiaa, we're going to die. Death is coming. Death is coming. Look what you've done. You've killed us. Ghost! Dead ghost! Ghost! You've never been born." She ran out into the fields, far enough from the house so that she could no longer hear their voices, and pressed herself against the earth, her own land no more. When she felt the birth coming, she thought that she had been hurt. Her body seized together. "They've hurt me too much," she thought. "This is gall, and it will kill me." With forehead and knees against the earth, her body convulsed and then relaxed. She turned on her back, lay on the ground. The black well of sky and stars went out and out and out forever; her body and her complexity seemed to disappear. She was one of the stars, a bright dot in blackness, without home, without a companion, in eternal cold and silence. An agoraphobia rose in her, speeding higher and higher, bigger and bigger; she would not be able to contain it; there would no end to fear.

Flayed, unprotected against space, she felt pain return, focusing her body. This pain chilled her—a cold, steady kind of surface pain. Inside, spasmodically, the other pain, the pain of the child, heated her. For hours she lay on the ground, alternately body and space. Sometimes a vision of normal comfort obliterated reality: she saw the family in the evening gambling at the dinner table, the young people massaging their elders' backs. She saw them congratulating one another, high joy on the mornings the rice shoots came up. When these pictures burst, the stars drew yet further apart. Black space opened.

She got to her feet to fight better and remembered that old-fashioned women gave birth in their pigsties to fool the jealous, pain-dealing gods, who do not snatch piglets. Before the next spasms could stop her, she ran to the pigsty, each step a rushing out into emptiness. She climbed over the fence and knelt in the dirt. It was good to have a fence enclosing her, a tribal person alone.

Laboring, this woman who had carried her child as a foreign growth that sickened her every day, expelled it at last. She reached down to touch the hot, wet, moving mass, surely smaller than anything human, and could feel that it was human after all—fingers, toes, nails, nose. She pulled it up on to her belly, and it lay curled there, butt in the air, feet precisely tucked one under the other. She opened her loose shirt and buttoned the child inside. After resting, it squirmed and thrashed and she pushed it up to her breast. It turned its head this way and that until it found her nipple. There, it made little snuffling noises. She clenched her teeth at its preciousness, lovely as a young calf, a piglet, a little dog.

She may have gone to the pigsty as a last act of responsibility: she would protect this child as she had protected its father. It would look after her soul, leaving supplies on her grave. But how would this tiny child without family find her grave when there would be no marker for her anywhere, neither in the earth nor the family hall? No one would give her a family hall name. She had taken the child with her into the wastes. At its birth the two of them had felt the same raw pain of separation, a wound that only the family pressing tight could close. A child with no descent line would not soften her life but only trail after her, ghostlike, begging her to give it purpose. At dawn the villagers on their way to the fields would stand around the fence and look.

Full of milk, the little ghost slept. When it awoke, she hardened her breasts against the milk that crying loosens. Toward morning she picked up the baby and walked to the well.

Carrying the baby to the well shows loving. Otherwise abandon it. Turn its face into the mud. Mothers who love their children take them along. It was probably a girl; there is some hope of forgiveness for boys.

"Don't tell anyone you had an aunt. Your father does not want to hear her name. She has never been born." I have believed that sex was unspeakable and words so strong and fathers so frail that "aunt" would do my father mysterious harm. I have thought that my family, having settled among immigrants who had also been their neighbors in the ancestral land, needed to clean their name, and a wrong word would incite the kinspeople even here. But there is more to this silence: they want me to participate in her punishment. And I have.

In the twenty years since I heard this story I have not asked for details nor said my aunt's name; I do not know it. People who can comfort the dead can also chase after them to hurt them further—a reverse ancestor worship. The real punishment was not the raid swiftly inflicted by the villagers, but the family's deliberately forgetting her.

Her betrayal so maddened them, they saw to it that she would suffer forever, even after death. Always hungry, always needing, she would have to beg food from other ghosts, snatch and steal it from those whose living descendants give them gifts. She would have to fight the ghosts massed at crossroads for the buns a few thoughtful citizens leave to decoy her away from village and home so that the ancestral spirits could feast unharassed. At peace, they could act like gods, not ghosts, their descent lines providing them with paper suits and dresses, spirit money, paper houses, paper automobiles, chicken, meat, and rice into eternity—essences delivered up in smoke and flames, steam and incense rising from each rice bowl. In an attempt to make the Chinese care for people outside the family, Chairman Mao encourages us now to give our paper replicas to the spirits of outstanding soldiers and workers, no matter whose ancestors they may be. My aunt remains forever hungry. Goods are not distributed evenly among the dead.

My aunt haunts me—her ghost drawn to me because now, after fifty years of neglect, I alone devote pages of paper to her, though not origamied into houses and clothes. I do not think she always means me well. I am telling on her, and she was a spite suicide, drowning herself in the drinking water. The Chinese are always very frightened of the drowned one, whose weeping ghost, wet hair hanging and skin bloated, waits silently by the water to pull down a substitute.

Questions

1. Why do you think the villagers reacted so harshly to the aunt's transgression? Against whom was she seen as committing this transgression? Her husband? The family? The village?
2. Are women and men treated equally by the villagers in this essay? How are relations between men and women portrayed?
3. Have you experienced or witnessed an equivalent to the "outcast table" (par. 19)? What is the purpose of this kind of punishment? Is it effective? Why or why not?
4. Why do you think the aunt protected the father of her baby? Do you see this as an act of resistance? Of love?
5. Kingston writes, "Carrying the baby to the well shows loving" (par. 46). What does she mean? Do you agree?
6. Do you think the aunt behaved in a way that deserved such a harsh reaction? How would a present-day woman in this situation be treated? Are expectations of fidelity different for men than they are for women? Why or why not?
7. In what ways does Kingston participate in the punishment of her aunt? In what ways does she try to recover or stand up for her aunt?

Suggestions for Writing on *Essays about Inspiring Social Change*

1. Both King's "Letter from Birmingham Jail" and Thoreau's "Civil Disobedience" include descriptions of nonviolent resistance. Under what conditions is nonviolent resistance justifiable or necessary? Why might nonviolent resistance be more effective than violent protest? Use specific examples.
2. How do the circumstances described in "Letter from Birmingham Jail" differ from those in "Civil Disobedience"? Do you think both writers were justified in their actions? Did one have more justification than the other? Write an essay comparing the writers' situations.
3. "Letter from Birmingham Jail" and "Civil Disobedience" were written by authors who held very strong convictions about the issues they addressed. In "On Morality" (in Chapter 5, "Reading an Essay"), Joan Didion questions the value of absolute convictions. Write an essay arguing for one point of view or the other. Alternatively, choose a current-day situation and make an argument for which approach is most effective and relevant in addressing it.
4. In "No Name Woman," Maxine Hong Kingston's aunt is driven to suicide because of community disapproval of her infidelity. Write an essay describing how a woman in her situation might react, and might be treated, today. Would people respond to a man's infidelity in the same way? What particular factors might contribute to an unfaithful woman's being judged more harshly—and what does this suggest about present-day gender roles and expectations?
5. In "No Name Woman," Kingston mixes fact with conjecture, and with scenes or situations that are imagined. What is the effect of her mingling imagination with "truth"? How does this help her get her points across?
6. Why does Kingston identify so much with her aunt? In what ways might the aunt's struggles relate to her own experiences as a Chinese American woman?

DRAMA
THE INDIVIDUAL VERSUS AUTHORITY

Sophocles *Antigonê*

Sometimes laws created by governments conflict with individual moral or religious obligations. In Sophocles's *Antigonê*, the heroine of the play's title acts against the explicit order of her uncle, Creon, the king of Thebes, who decrees that the body of her brother Polyneicês, who has led an unsuccessful rebellion, not be given a proper burial. But Antigonê, whose main concern is her personal and religious responsibility to her brother, dares to defy the king and then faces the consequences. *Antigonê* deals directly with the difference between a state law and the higher moral law—when the two are in conflict, what is the proper way to respond? The play also raises questions about what it means to be a proper citizen—whether true loyalty dictates that people adhere to what the state decrees, or whether it means challenging the laws so that the state may be inspired to improve. But while Antigonê is the undisputed heroine of this powerful play, she is not without faults. Her treatment of her sister and her fiancé, Creon's son, also demonstrates that effective crusaders sometimes neglect or mistreat the people closest to them. Righteousness can sometimes cross over into self-righteousness, no matter how worthy the cause. Sophocles's classical play is set in ancient Greece, but the issues that it raises are just as relevant today as they were in his time.

Sophocles

Sophocles (496?–406 B.C.), *tragic dramatist, priest, for a time one of ten Athenian generals, was one of the three great ancient Greek writers of tragedy whose work has survived. (The other two were his contemporaries: Aeschylus, his senior, and Euripides, his junior.) Sophocles won his first victory in the Athenian spring drama competition in 468* B.C. *when a tragedy he had written defeated one by Aeschylus. He went on to win many prizes, writing more than 120 plays, of which only seven have survived in their entirety—Ajax, Antigonê, Oedipus the King, Electra, Philoctetes, The Trachinian Women, and Oedipus at Colonus. (Of the lost plays, about a thousand fragments remain.) In his long life, Sophocles saw Greece rise to supremacy over the Persian Empire. He enjoyed the favor of the statesman Pericles, who, making peace with enemy Sparta, ruled Athens during a Golden Age (461–429* B.C.*), during which the Parthenon was built and music, art, drama, and philosophy flourished.*

Although Antigonê *tells the final episode of the Oedipus story, it was written in 441* B.C., *over twenty years before the author took up the story of Oedipus himself. In* Antigonê, *duties to family and duties to the state are pitted against one another. The heroine Antigonê resists the king's edict in the name of family loyalty, a defiance both noble and potentially threatening to political stability in a time of crisis. Though the gods approve of her action, she dies a victim of Creon's hubris.*

Antigonê. Martha Henry in the 1971 Lincoln Center Repertory production.

Antigonê

441 B.C.

Translated by Dudley Fitts and Robert Fitzgerald

CHARACTERS

Antigonê
Ismenê
Eurydicê
Creon
Haimon

Teiresias
A Sentry
A Messenger
Chorus

SCENE. *Before the palace of Creon, King of Thebes. A central double door, and two lateral doors. A platform extends the length of the façade, and from this platform three steps lead down into the "orchestra," or chorus-ground.*

TIME. *Dawn of the day after the repulse of the Argive army from the assault on Thebes.*

PROLOGUE°

Antigonê and Ismenê enter from the central door of the palace.

Antigonê: Ismenê, dear sister,
    You would think that we had already suffered enough
    For the curse on Oedipus:°
    I cannot imagine any grief
    That you and I have not gone through. And now—   5
    Have they told you of the new decree of our King Creon?
Ismenê: I have heard nothing: I know
    That two sisters lost two brothers, a double death
    In a single hour; and I know that the Argive army
    Fled in the night; but beyond this, nothing.   10
Antigonê: I thought so. And that is why I wanted you
    To come out here with me. There is something we must do.
Ismenê: Why do you speak so strangely?
Antigonê: Listen, Ismenê:
    Creon buried our brother Eteoclês   15
    With military honors, gave him a soldier's funeral,
    And it was right that he should; but Polyneicês,
    Who fought as bravely and died as miserably,—
    They say that Creon has sworn
    No one shall bury him, no one mourn for him,   20
    But his body must lie in the fields, a sweet treasure
    For carrion birds to find as they search for food.
    That is what they say, and our good Creon is coming here
    To announce it publicly; and the penalty—
    Stoning to death in the public square!
                                There it is,   25
    And now you can prove what you are:
    A true sister, or a traitor to your family.
Ismenê: Antigonê, you are mad! What could I possibly do?
Antigonê: You must decide whether you will help me or not.
Ismenê: I do not understand you. Help you in what?   30
Antigonê: Ismenê, I am going to bury him. Will you come?
Ismenê: Bury him! You have just said the new law forbids it.
Antigonê: He is my brother. And he is your brother, too.

Prologue: portion of the play containing the exposition, or explanation of what has gone before and what is now happening.   3 *the curse on Oedipus:* As Sophocles tells in *Oedipus the King*, the King of Thebes discovered that he had lived his life under a curse. Unknowingly, he had slain his father and married his mother. On realizing this terrible truth, Oedipus put out his own eyes and departed into exile. Now, years later, as *Antigonê* opens, Antigonê and Ismenê, daughters of Oedipus, are recalling how their two brothers died. After the abdication of their father, the brothers had ruled Thebes together. But they fell to quarreling. When Eteoclês expelled Polyneicês, the latter returned with an army and attacked the city. The two brothers killed each other in combat, leaving the throne to Creon. The new king of Thebes has buried Eteoclês with full honors, but, calling Polyneicês a traitor, has decreed that his body shall be left to the crows—an especially terrible decree, for a rotting corpse might offend Zeus; bring down plague, blight, and barrenness upon Thebes; and prevent the soul of a dead hero from entering the Elysian Fields, abode of those favored by the gods.

Ismenê: But think of the danger! Think what Creon will do!
Antigonê: Creon is not strong enough to stand in my way.
Ismenê: Ah sister!
    Oedipus died, everyone hating him
    For what his own search brought to light, his eyes
    Ripped out by his own hand; and Iocastê died,
    His mother and wife at once: she twisted the cords
    That strangled her life; and our two brothers died,
    Each killed by the other's sword. And we are left:
    But oh, Antigonê,
    Think how much more terrible than these
    Our own death would be if we should go against Creon
    And do what he has forbidden! We are only women,
    We cannot fight with men, Antigonê!
    The law is strong, we must give in to the law
    In this thing, and in worse. I beg the Dead
    To forgive me, but I am helpless: I must yield
    To those in authority. And I think it is dangerous business
    To be always meddling.
Antigonê: If that is what you think,
    I should not want you, even if you asked to come.
    You have made your choice, you can be what you want to be.
    But I will bury him; and if I must die,
    I say that this crime is holy: I shall lie down
    With him in death, and I shall be as dear
    To him as he to me.
              It is the dead,
    Not the living, who make the longest demands:
    We die for ever . . .
              You may do as you like,
    Since apparently the laws of the gods mean nothing to you.
Ismenê: They mean a great deal to me; but I have no strength
    To break laws that were made for the public good.
Antigonê: That must be your excuse, I suppose. But as for me,
    I will bury the brother I love.
Ismenê: Antigonê,
    I am so afraid for you!
Antigonê: You need not be:
    You have yourself to consider, after all.
Ismenê: But no one must hear of this, you must tell no one!
    I will keep it a secret, I promise!
Antigonê: O tell it! Tell everyone!
    Think how they'll hate you when it all comes out
    If they learn that you knew about it all the time!
Ismenê: So fiery! You should be cold with fear.
Antigonê: Perhaps. But I am doing only what I must.
Ismenê: But you can do it? I say that you cannot.

Antigonê: Very well: when my strength gives out, I shall do no more. 75
Ismenê: Impossible things should not be tried at all.
Antigonê: Go away, Ismenê:
    I shall be hating you soon, and the dead will too,
    For your words are hateful. Leave me my foolish plan:
    I am not afraid of the danger; if it means death, 80
    It will not be the worst of deaths—death without honor.
Ismenê: Go then, if you feel that you must.
    You are unwise,
    But a loyal friend indeed to those who love you.

Exit into the palace. Antigonê goes off, left. Enter the Chorus.

PÁRODOS°

Strophe° 1

Chorus: Now the long blade of the sun, lying
    Level east to west, touches with glory
    Thebes of the Seven Gates. Open, unlidded
    Eye of golden day! O marching light
    Across the eddy and rush of Dircê's stream,°
    Striking the white shields of the enemy 5
    Thrown headlong backward from the blaze of morning!
Choragos:° Polyneicês their commander
    Roused them with windy phrases,
    He the wild eagle screaming 10
    Insults above our land,
    His wings their shields of snow,
    His crest their marshalled helms.

Antistrophe° 1

Chorus: Against our seven gates in a yawning ring
    The famished spears came onward in the night; 15
    But before his jaws were sated with our blood,
    Or pinefire took the garland of our towers,
    He was thrown back; and as he turned, great Thebes—
    No tender victim for his noisy power—
    Rose like a dragon behind him, shouting war. 20
Choragos: For God hates utterly
    The bray of bragging tongues;
    And when he beheld their smiling,
    Their swagger of golden helms,
    The frown of his thunder blasted 25
    Their first man from our walls.

Párodos: a song sung by the chorus on first entering. Its *strophe* (according to scholarly theory) was sung while the chorus danced from stage right to stage left; its *antistrophe*, while it danced back again. 5 *Dircê's stream:* river near Thebes. 8 *Choragos:* leader of the Chorus and principal commentator on the play's action.

Strophe 2

Chorus: We heard his shout of triumph high in the air
    Turn to a scream; far out in a flaming arc
    He fell with his windy torch, and the earth struck him.
    And others storming in fury no less than his
    Found shock of death in the dusty joy of battle.
Choragos: Seven captains at seven gates
    Yielded their clanging arms to the god
    That bends the battle-line and breaks it.
    These two only, brothers in blood,
    Face to face in matchless rage,
    Mirroring each the other's death,
    Clashed in long combat.

Antistrophe 2

Chorus: But now in the beautiful morning of victory
    Let Thebes of the many chariots sing for joy!
    With hearts for dancing we'll take leave of war:
    Our temples shall be sweet with hymns of praise,
    And the long night shall echo with our chorus.

SCENE I

Choragos: But now at last our new King is coming:
    Creon of Thebes, Menoikeus' son.
    In this auspicious dawn of his reign
    What are the new complexities
    That shifting Fate has woven for him?
    What is his counsel? Why has he summoned
    The old men to hear him?

Enter Creon from the palace, center. He addresses the Chorus from the top step.

Creon: Gentlemen: I have the honor to inform you that our Ship of State, which recent storms have threatened to destroy, has come safely to harbor at last, guided by the merciful wisdom of Heaven. I have summoned you here this morning because I know that I can depend upon you: your devotion to King Laïos was absolute; you never hesitated in your duty to our late ruler Oedipus; and when Oedipus died, your loyalty was transferred to his children. Unfortunately, as you know, his two sons, the princes Eteoclês and Polyneicês, have killed each other in battle; and I, as the next in blood, have succeeded to the full power of the throne.

    I am aware, of course, that no Ruler can expect complete loyalty from his subjects until he has been tested in office. Nevertheless, I say to you at the very outset that I have nothing but contempt for the kind of Governor who is afraid, for whatever reason, to follow the course that he knows is best for the State; and as for the man who sets private friendship above the public welfare,—I have no use for him, either. I call God to witness that if I saw my country headed for ruin, I should not be afraid to speak out plainly; and I need hardly remind you that I would never have any dealings with an enemy of the people. No one values

friendship more highly than I; but we must remember that friends made at the
risk of wrecking our Ship are not real friends at all.

    These are my principles, at any rate, and that is why I have made the following decision concerning the sons of Oedipus: Eteoclês, who died as a man should die, fighting for his country, is to be buried with full military honors, with all the ceremony that is usual when the greatest heroes die; but his brother Polyneicês, who broke his exile to come back with fire and sword against his native city and the shrines of his fathers' gods, whose one idea was to spill the blood of his blood and sell his own people into slavery—Polyneicês, I say, is to have no burial: no man is to touch him or say the least prayer for him; he shall lie on the plain, unburied; and the birds and the scavenging dogs can do with him whatever they like.

    This is my command, and you can see the wisdom behind it. As long as I am King, no traitor is going to be honored with the loyal man. But whoever shows by word and deed that he is on the side of the State,—he shall have my respect while he is living, and my reverence when he is dead.

Choragos: If that is your will, Creon son of Menoikeus,
    You have the right to enforce it: we are yours.
Creon: That is my will. Take care that you do your part.
Choragos: We are old men: let the younger ones carry it out.
Creon: I do not mean that: the sentries have been appointed.
Choragos: Then what is it that you would have us do?
Creon: You will give no support to whoever breaks this law.
Choragos: Only a crazy man is in love with death!
Creon: And death it is, yet money talks, and the wisest
    Have sometimes been known to count a few coins too many.

Enter Sentry from left.

Sentry: I'll not say that I'm out of breath from running, King, because every time I stopped to think about what I have to tell you, I felt like going back. And all the time a voice kept saying, "You fool, don't you know you're walking straight into trouble?"; and then another voice: "Yes, but if you let somebody else get the news to Creon first, it will be even worse than that for you!" But good sense won out, at least I hope it was good sense, and here I am with a story that makes no sense at all; but I'll tell it anyhow, because, as they say, what's going to happen's going to happen and—
Creon: Come to the point. What have you to say?
Sentry: I did not do it. I did not see who did it. You must not punish me for what someone else has done.
Creon: A comprehensive defense! More effective, perhaps,
    If I knew its purpose. Come: what is it?
Sentry: A dreadful thing . . . I don't know how to put it—
Creon: Out with it!
Sentry: Well, then;
    The dead man—
               Polyneicês—

Pause. The Sentry is overcome, fumbles for words. Creon waits impassively.

          out there—
             someone,—
New dust on the slimy flesh!

Pause. No sign from Creon.

Someone has given it burial that way, and
Gone . . .

Long pause. Creon finally speaks with deadly control.

Creon: And the man who dared do this?
Sentry: I swear I   70
 Do not know! You must believe me!
           Listen:
 The ground was dry, not a sign of digging, no,
 Not a wheeltrack in the dust, no trace of anyone.
 It was when they relieved us this morning: and one of them,
 The corporal, pointed to it.
          There it was,   75
 The strangest—
     Look:
 The body, just mounded over with light dust: you see?
 Not buried really, but as if they'd covered it
 Just enough for the ghost's peace. And no sign
 Of dogs or any wild animal that had been there.   80

 And then what a scene there was! Every man of us
 Accusing the other: we all proved the other man did it,
 We all had proof that we could not have done it.
 We were ready to take hot iron in our hands,
 Walk through fire, swear by all the gods,   85
 It was not I!
 I do not know who it was, but it was not I!

Creon's rage has been mounting steadily, but the Sentry is too intent upon his story to notice it.

 And then, when this came to nothing, someone said
 A thing that silenced us and made us stare
 Down at the ground: you had to be told the news,   90
 And one of us had to do it! We threw the dice,
 And the bad luck fell to me. So here I am,
 No happier to be here than you are to have me:
 Nobody likes the man who brings bad news.
Choragos: I have been wondering, King: can it be that the gods have done this? 95
Creon (*furiously*): Stop!
 Must you doddering wrecks
 Go out of your heads entirely? "The gods"!

Intolerable!
The gods favor this corpse? Why? How had he served them?
Tried to loot their temples, burn their images,
Yes, and the whole State, and its laws with it!
Is it your senile opinion that the gods love to honor bad men?
A pious thought!—
              No, from the very beginning
There have been those who have whispered together,
Stiff-necked anarchists, putting their heads together,
Scheming against me in alleys. These are the men,
And they have bribed my own guard to do this thing.

(*Sententiously.*) Money!
There's nothing in the world so demoralizing as money.
Down go your cities,
Homes gone, men gone, honest hearts corrupted,
Crookedness of all kinds, and all for money!
(*To Sentry.*)   But you—!
I swear by God and by the throne of God,
The man who has done this thing shall pay for it!
Find that man, bring him here to me, or your death
Will be the least of your problems: I'll string you up
Alive, and there will be certain ways to make you
Discover your employer before you die;
And the process may teach you a lesson you seem to have missed:
The dearest profit is sometimes all too dear:
That depends on the source. Do you understand me?
A fortune won is often misfortune.

Sentry: King, may I speak?
Creon: Your very voice distresses me.
Sentry: Are you sure that it is my voice, and not your conscience?
Creon: By God, he wants to analyze me now!
Sentry: It is not what I say, but what has been done, that hurts you.
Creon: You talk too much.
Sentry: Maybe; but I've done nothing.
Creon: Sold your soul for some silver: that's all you've done.
Sentry: How dreadful it is when the right judge judges wrong!
Creon: Your figures of speech
    May entertain you now; but unless you bring me the man,
    You will get little profit from them in the end.

    Exit Creon into the palace.

Sentry: "Bring me the man"—!
    I'd like nothing better than bringing him the man!
    But bring him or not, you have seen the last of me here.
    At any rate, I am safe!

    Exit Sentry.

ODE I°

Strophe 1

Chorus: Numberless are the world's wonders, but none
    More wonderful than man; the stormgray sea
    Yields to his prows, the huge crests bear him high;
    Earth, holy and inexhaustible, is graven
    With shining furrows where his plows have gone   5
    Year after year, the timeless labor of stallions.

Antistrophe 1

The lightboned birds and beasts that cling to cover,
The lithe fish lighting their reaches of dim water,
All are taken, tamed in the net of his mind;
The lion on the hill, the wild horse windy-maned,   10
Resign to him; and his blunt yoke has broken
The sultry shoulders of the mountain bull.

Strophe 2

Words also, and thought as rapid as air,
He fashions to his good use; statecraft is his,
And his the skill that deflects the arrows of snow,   15
The spears of winter rain: from every wind
He has made himself secure—from all but one:
In the late wind of death he cannot stand.

Antistrophe 2

O clear intelligence, force beyond all measure!
O fate of man, working both good and evil!   20
When the laws are kept, how proudly his city stands!
When the laws are broken, what of his city then?
Never may the anárchic man find rest at my hearth,
Never be it said that my thoughts are his thoughts.

SCENE II

Re-enter Sentry leading Antigonê.

Choragos: What does this mean? Surely this captive woman
    Is the Princess, Antigonê. Why should she be taken?
Sentry: Here is the one who did it! We caught her
    In the very act of burying him.—Where is Creon?
Choragos: Just coming from the house.

    Enter Creon, center.

Creon: What has happened?   5
    Why have you come back so soon?
Sentry (expansively):   O King,

Ode I: first song sung by the Chorus, who at the same time danced. Here again, as in the *párodos, strophe* and *antistrophe* probably divide the song into two movements of the dance: right to left, then left to right.

A man should never be too sure of anything:
I would have sworn
That you'd not see me here again: your anger
Frightened me so, and the things you threatened me with; 10
But how could I tell then
That I'd be able to solve the case so soon?

No dice-throwing this time: I was only too glad to come!

Here is this woman. She is the guilty one:
We found her trying to bury him. 15
Take her, then; question her; judge her as you will.
I am through with the whole thing now, and glad of it.
Creon: But this is Antigonê! Why have you brought her here?
Sentry: She was burying him, I tell you!
Creon (severely):   Is this the truth?
Sentry: I saw her with my own eyes. Can I say more? 20
Creon: The details: come, tell me quickly!
Sentry: It was like this:
  After those terrible threats of yours, King,
  We went back and brushed the dust away from the body.
  The flesh was soft by now, and stinking,
  So we sat on a hill to windward and kept guard. 25
  No napping this time! We kept each other awake.
  But nothing happened until the white round sun
  Whirled in the center of the round sky over us:
  Then, suddenly,
  A storm of dust roared up from the earth, and the sky 30
  Went out, the plain vanished with all its trees
  In the stinging dark. We closed our eyes and endured it.
  The whirlwind lasted a long time, but it passed;
  And then we looked, and there was Antigonê!
                                                35
  I have seen
  A mother bird come back to a stripped nest, heard
  Her crying bitterly a broken note or two
  For the young ones stolen. Just so, when this girl
  Found the bare corpse, and all her love's work wasted,
  She wept, and cried on heaven to damn the hands 40
  That had done this thing.
                    And then she brought more dust
  And sprinkled wine three times for her brother's ghost.

  We ran and took her at once. She was not afraid,
  Not even when we charged her with what she had done.
  She denied nothing.
                    And this was a comfort to me, 45
  And some uneasiness: for it is a good thing
  To escape from death, but it is no great pleasure

  To bring death to a friend.
Yet I always say
  There is nothing so comfortable as your own safe skin!
Creon (*slowly, dangerously*): And you, Antigonê,   50
  You with your head hanging,—do you confess this thing?
Antigonê: I do. I deny nothing.
Creon (*to Sentry*):   You may go.

  Exit Sentry.

  (*To Antigonê.*) Tell me, tell me briefly:
  Had you heard my proclamation touching this matter?
Antigonê: It was public. Could I help hearing it?   55
Creon: And yet you dared defy the law.
Antigonê: I dared.
  It was not God's proclamation. That final Justice
  That rules the world below makes no such laws.

  Your edict, King, was strong,
  But all your strength is weakness itself against   60
  The immortal unrecorded laws of God.
  They are not merely now: they were, and shall be,
  Operative for ever, beyond man utterly.

  I knew I must die, even without your decree:
  I am only mortal. And if I must die   65
  Now, before it is my time to die,
  Surely this is no hardship: can anyone
  Living, as I live, with evil all about me,
  Think Death less than a friend? This death of mine
  Is of no importance; but if I had left my brother   70
  Lying in death unburied, I should have suffered.
  Now I do not.
       You smile at me. Ah Creon,
  Think me a fool, if you like; but it may well be
  That a fool convicts me of folly.
Choragos: Like father, like daughter: both headstrong, deaf to reason!   75
  She has never learned to yield.
Creon: She has much to learn.
  The inflexible heart breaks first, the toughest iron
  Cracks first, and the wildest horses bend their necks
  At the pull of the smallest curb.
         Pride? In a slave?
  This girl is guilty of a double insolence,   80
  Breaking the given laws and boasting of it.
  Who is the man here,
  She or I, if this crime goes unpunished?
  Sister's child, or more than sister's child,
  Or closer yet in blood—she and her sister   85

Win bitter death for this!
(*To Servants.*)   Go, some of you,
Arrest Ismenê. I accuse her equally.
Bring her: you will find her sniffling in the house there.

Her mind's a traitor: crimes kept in the dark
Cry for light, and the guardian brain shudders;
But how much worse than this
Is brazen boasting of barefaced anarchy!
Antigonê: Creon, what more do you want than my death?
Creon: Nothing.
    That gives me everything.
Antigonê: Then I beg you: kill me.
    This talking is a great weariness: your words
    Are distasteful to me, and I am sure that mine
    Seem so to you. And yet they should not seem so:
    I should have praise and honor for what I have done.
    All these men here would praise me
    Were their lips not frozen shut with fear of you.
    (*Bitterly.*) Ah the good fortune of kings,
    Licensed to say and do whatever they please!
Creon: You are alone here in that opinion.
Antigonê: No, they are with me. But they keep their tongues in leash.
Creon: Maybe. But you are guilty, and they are not.
Antigonê: There is no guilt in reverence for the dead.
Creon: But Eteoclês—was he not your brother too?
Antigonê: My brother too.
Creon: And you insult his memory?
Antigonê (softly): The dead man would not say that I insult it.
Creon: He would: for you honor a traitor as much as him.
Antigonê: His own brother, traitor or not, and equal in blood.
Creon: He made war on his country. Eteoclês defended it.
Antigonê: Nevertheless, there are honors due all the dead.
Creon: But not the same for the wicked as for the just.
Antigonê: Ah Creon, Creon,
    Which of us can say what the gods hold wicked?
Creon: An enemy is an enemy, even dead.
Antigonê: It is my nature to join in love, not hate.
Creon (finally losing patience): Go join them, then; if you must have your love,
    Find it in hell!
Choragos: But see, Ismenê comes:

Enter Ismenê, guarded.

    Those tears are sisterly, the cloud
    That shadows her eyes rains down gentle sorrow.
Creon: You too, Ismenê,
    Snake in my ordered house, sucking my blood

>   Stealthily—and all the time I never knew
>   That these two sisters were aiming at my throne!
>   Ismenê,
>   Do you confess your share in this crime, or deny it?
>   Answer me.
> *Ismenê:* Yes, if she will let me say so. I am guilty.   130
> *Antigonê (coldly):* No, Ismenê. You have no right to say so.
>   You would not help me, and I will not have you help me.
> *Ismenê:* But now I know what you meant; and I am here
>   To join you, to take my share of punishment.
> *Antigonê:* The dead man and the gods who rule the dead   135
>   Know whose act this was. Words are not friends.
> *Ismenê:* Do you refuse me, Antigonê? I want to die with you:
>   I too have a duty that I must discharge to the dead.
> *Antigonê:* You shall not lessen my death by sharing it.
> *Ismenê:* What do I care for life when you are dead?   140
> *Antigonê:* Ask Creon. You're always hanging on his opinions.
> *Ismenê:* You are laughing at me. Why, Antigonê?
> *Antigonê:* It's a joyless laughter, Ismenê.
> *Ismenê:*   But can I do nothing?
> *Antigonê:* Yes. Save yourself. I shall not envy you.
>   There are those who will praise you; I shall have honor, too.   145
> *Ismenê:* But we are equally guilty!
> *Antigonê:*   No more, Ismenê.
>   You are alive, but I belong to Death.
> *Creon (to the Chorus):* Gentlemen, I beg you to observe these girls:
>   One has just now lost her mind; the other,
>   It seems, has never had a mind at all.   150
> *Ismenê:* Grief teaches the steadiest minds to waver, King.
> *Creon:* Yours certainly did, when you assumed guilt with the guilty!
> *Ismenê:* But how could I go on living without her?
> *Creon:*   You are.
>   She is already dead.
> *Ismenê:*   But your own son's bride!
> *Creon:* There are places enough for him to push his plow.   155
>   I want no wicked women for my sons!
> *Ismenê:* O dearest Haimon, how your father wrongs you!
> *Creon:* I've had enough of your childish talk of marriage!
> *Choragos:* Do you really intend to steal this girl from your son?
> *Creon:* No; Death will do that for me.
> *Choragos:*   Then she must die?   160
> *Creon (ironically):* You dazzle me.
>   —But enough of this talk!
>   *(To Guards.)* You, there, take them away and guard them well:
>   For they are but women, and even brave men run
>   When they see Death coming.
>
>   *Exeunt Ismenê, Antigonê, and Guards.*

ODE II

Strophe 1

Chorus: Fortunate is the man who has never tasted God's vengeance!
    Where once the anger of heaven has struck, that house is shaken
    For ever: damnation rises behind each child
    Like a wave cresting out of the black northeast,
    When the long darkness under sea roars up   5
    And bursts drumming death upon the windwhipped sand.

Antistrophe 1

    I have seen this gathering sorrow from time long past
    Loom upon Oedipus' children: generation from generation
    Takes the compulsive rage of the enemy god.
    So lately this last flower of Oedipus' line   10
    Drank the sunlight! but now a passionate word
    And a handful of dust have closed up all its beauty.

Strophe 2

        What mortal arrogance
        Transcends the wrath of Zeus?
    Sleep cannot lull him nor the effortless long months   15
    Of the timeless gods: but he is young for ever,
    And his house is the shining day of high Olympos.
        All that is and shall be,
        And all the past, is his.
    No pride on earth is free of the curse of heaven.   20

Antistrophe 2

        The straying dreams of men
        May bring them ghosts of joy:
    But as they drowse, the waking embers burn them;
    Or they walk with fixed eyes, as blind men walk.
    But the ancient wisdom speaks for our own time: 25
        Fate works most for woe
        With Folly's fairest show.
    Man's little pleasure is the spring of sorrow.

SCENE III

Choragos: But here is Haimon, King, the last of all your sons.
    Is it grief for Antigonê that brings him here,
    And bitterness at being robbed of his bride?

Enter Haimon.

Creon: We shall soon see, and no need of diviners.
                                      —Son,
    You have heard my final judgment on that girl: 5
    Have you come here hating me, or have you come
    With deference and with love, whatever I do?
Haimon: I am your son, father. You are my guide.
    You make things clear for me, and I obey you.

       No marriage means more to me than your continuing wisdom.
Creon: Good. That is the way to behave: subordinate
    Everything else, my son, to your father's will.
    This is what a man prays for, that he may get
    Sons attentive and dutiful in his house,
    Each one hating his father's enemies,
    Honoring his father's friends. But if his sons
    Fail him, if they turn out unprofitably,
    What has he fathered but trouble for himself
    And amusement for the malicious?
                                  So you are right
    Not to lose your head over this woman.
    Your pleasure with her would soon grow cold, Haimon,
    And then you'd have a hellcat in bed and elsewhere.
    Let her find her husband in Hell!
    Of all the people in this city, only she
    Has had contempt for my law and broken it.

    Do you want me to show myself weak before the people?
    Or to break my sworn word? No, and I will not.
    The woman dies.

    I suppose she'll plead "family ties." Well, let her.
    If I permit my own family to rebel,
    How shall I earn the world's obedience?
    Show me the man who keeps his house in hand,
    He's fit for public authority.
                                  I'll have no dealings
    With law-breakers, critics of the government:
    Whoever is chosen to govern should be obeyed—
    Must be obeyed, in all things, great and small,
    Just and unjust! O Haimon,
    The man who knows how to obey, and that man only,
    Knows how to give commands when the time comes.
    You can depend on him, no matter how fast
    The spears come: he's a good soldier, he'll stick it out.

    Anarchy, anarchy! Show me a greater evil!
    This is why cities tumble and the great houses rain down,
    This is what scatters armies!

    No, no: good lives are made so by discipline.
    We keep the laws then, and the lawmakers,
    And no woman shall seduce us. If we must lose,
    Let's lose to a man, at least! Is a woman stronger than we?
Choragos: Unless time has rusted my wits,
    What you say, King, is said with point and dignity.
Haimon (boyishly earnest): Father:
    Reason is God's crowning gift to man, and you are right

To warn me against losing mine. I cannot say—
I hope that I shall never want to say!—that you
Have reasoned badly. Yet there are other men   55
Who can reason, too; and their opinions might be helpful.
You are not in a position to know everything
That people say or do, or what they feel:
Your temper terrifies them—everyone
Will tell you only what you like to hear.   60
But I, at any rate, can listen; and I have heard them
Muttering and whispering in the dark about this girl.
They say no woman has ever, so unreasonably,
Died so shameful a death for a generous act:
"She covered her brother's body. Is this indecent?   65
She kept him from dogs and vultures. Is this a crime?
Death?—She should have all the honor that we can give her!"

This is the way they talk out there in the city.

You must believe me:
Nothing is closer to me than your happiness.   70
What could be closer? Must not any son
Value his father's fortune as his father does his?
I beg you, do not be unchangeable:
Do not believe that you alone can be right.
The man who thinks that,   75
The man who maintains that only he has the power
To reason correctly, the gift to speak, the soul—
A man like that, when you know him, turns out empty.

It is not reason never to yield to reason!

In flood time you can see how some trees bend,   80
And because they bend, even their twigs are safe,
While stubborn trees are torn up, roots and all.
And the same thing happens in sailing:
Make your sheet fast, never slacken,—and over you go,
Head over heels and under: and there's your voyage. 85
Forget you are angry! Let yourself be moved!
I know I am young; but please let me say this:
The ideal condition
Would be, I admit, that men should be right by instinct;
But since we are all too likely to go astray,   90
The reasonable thing is to learn from those who can teach.
Choragos: You will do well to listen to him, King,
    If what he says is sensible. And you, Haimon,
    Must listen to your father.—Both speak well.
Creon: You consider it right for a man of my years and experience   95
    To go to school to a boy?
Haimon: It is not right,

      If I am wrong. But if I am young, and right,
        What does my age matter?
Creon: You think it right to stand up for an anarchist?
Haimon: Not at all. I pay no respect to criminals.
Creon: Then she is not a criminal?
Haimon: The City would deny it, to a man.
Creon: And the City proposes to teach me how to rule?
Haimon: Ah. Who is it that's talking like a boy now?
Creon: My voice is the one voice giving orders in this City!
Haimon: It is no City if it takes orders from one voice.
Creon: The State is the King!
Haimon: Yes, if the State is a desert.

    Pause.

Creon: This boy, it seems, has sold out to a woman.
Haimon: If you are a woman: my concern is only for you.
Creon: So? Your "concern"! In a public brawl with your father!
Haimon: How about you, in a public brawl with justice?
Creon: With justice, when all that I do is within my rights?
Haimon: You have no right to trample on God's right.
Creon (completely out of control Fool, adolescent fool! Taken in by a woman!
Haimon: You'll never see me taken in by anything vile.
Creon: Every word you say is for her!
Haimon (quietly, darkly):   And for you.
    And for me. And for the gods under the earth.
Creon: You'll never marry her while she lives.
Haimon: Then she must die.—But her death will cause another.
Creon: Another?
    Have you lost your senses? Is this an open threat?
Haimon: There is no threat in speaking to emptiness.
Creon: I swear you'll regret this superior tone of yours!
    You are the empty one!
Haimon: If you were not my father,
    I'd say you were perverse.
Creon: You girl-struck fool, don't play at words with me!
Haimon: I am sorry. You prefer silence.
Creon: Now, by God—!
    I swear, by all the gods in heaven above us,
    You'll watch it, I swear you shall!
    (*To the Servants.*)   Bring her out!
    Bring the woman out! Let her die before his eyes!
    Here, this instant, with her bridegroom beside her!
Haimon: Not here, no; she will not die here, King.
    And you will never see my face again.
    Go on raving as long as you've a friend to endure you.

    Exit Haimon.

Choragos: Gone, gone. 135
    Creon, a young man in a rage is dangerous!
Creon: Let him do, or dream to do, more than a man can.
    He shall not save these girls from death.
Choragos: These girls?
    You have sentenced them both?
Creon: No, you are right.
    I will not kill the one whose hands are clean. 140
Choragos: But Antigonê?
Creon (somberly):   I will carry her far away
    Out there in the wilderness, and lock her
    Living in a vault of stone. She shall have food,
    As the custom is, to absolve the State of her death.
    And there let her pray to the gods of hell: 145
    They are her only gods:
    Perhaps they will show her an escape from death,
    Or she may learn,
                 though late,
    That piety shown the dead is pity in vain.

Exit Creon.

ODE III

                                                            Strophe

Chorus: Love, unconquerable
    Waster of rich men, keeper
    Of warm lights and all-night vigil
    In the soft face of a girl:
    Sea-wanderer, forest-visitor! 5
    Even the pure Immortals cannot escape you,
    And mortal man, in his one day's dusk,
    Trembles before your glory.

                                                   Antistrophe

    Surely you swerve upon ruin
    The just man's consenting heart, 10
    As here you have made bright anger
    Strike between father and son—
    And none has conquered but Love!
    A girl's glánce wórking the will of heaven:
    Pleasure to her alone who mocks us, 15
    Merciless Aphroditê.°

SCENE IV

Choragos (as Antigonê enters guarded):
    But I can no longer stand in awe of this,
    Nor, seeing what I see, keep back my tears.

---

16 *Aphrodité:* goddess of love and beauty.

Here is Antigonê, passing to that chamber
   Where all find sleep at last.

                                                    Strophe 1

Antigonê: Look upon me, friends, and pity me
   Turning back at the night's edge to say
   Good-by to the sun that shines for me no longer;
   Now sleepy Death
   Summons me down to Acheron,° that cold shore:
   There is no bridesong there, nor any music.
Chorus: Yet not unpraised, not without a kind of honor,
   You walk at last into the underworld;
   Untouched by sickness, broken by no sword.
   What woman has ever found your way to death?

                                                    Antistrophe 1

Antigonê: How often I have heard the story of Niobê,°
   Tantalos' wretched daughter, how the stone
   Clung fast about her, ivy-close: and they say
   The rain falls endlessly
   And sifting soft snow; her tears are never done.
   I feel the loneliness of her death in mine.
Chorus: But she was born of heaven, and you
   Are woman, woman-born. If her death is yours,
   A mortal woman's, is this not for you
   Glory in our world and in the world beyond?

                                                    Strophe 2

Antigonê: You laugh at me. Ah, friends, friends,
   Can you not wait until I am dead? O Thebes,
   O men many-charioted, in love with Fortune,
   Dear springs of Dircê, sacred Theban grove,
   Be witnesses for me, denied all pity,
   Unjustly judged! and think a word of love
   For her whose path turns
   Under dark earth, where there are no more tears.
Chorus: You have passed beyond human daring and come at last
   Into a place of stone where Justice sits.
   I cannot tell
   What shape of your father's guilt appears in this.

                                                    Antistrophe 2

Antigonê: You have touched it at last: that bridal bed
   Unspeakable, horror of son and mother mingling:
   Their crime, infection of all our family!
   O Oedipus, father and brother!
   Your marriage strikes from the grave to murder mine.

---

9 *Acheron:* river in Hades, domain of the dead.   15 *story of Niobê:* a Theban queen whose fourteen children were slain. She wept so copiously she was transformed to a stone on Mount Sipylos, and her tears became the mountain's streams.

> I have been a stranger here in my own land:
> All my life
> The blasphemy of my birth has followed me.
> *Chorus:* Reverence is a virtue, but strength 45
> Lives in established law: that must prevail.
> You have made your choice,
> Your death is the doing of your conscious hand.
>
> *Epode*°
>
> *Antigonê:* Then let me go, since all your words are bitter,
> And the very light of the sun is cold to me. 50
> Lead me to my vigil, where I must have
> Neither love nor lamentation; no song, but silence.
>
> *Creon interrupts impatiently.*
>
> *Creon:* If dirges and planned lamentations could put off death,
> Men would be singing for ever.
> (*To the Servants.*)   Take her, go!
> You know your orders: take her to the vault 55
> And leave her alone there. And if she lives or dies,
> That's her affair, not ours: our hands are clean.
> *Antigonê:* O tomb, vaulted bride-bed in eternal rock,
> Soon I shall be with my own again
> Where Persephonê° welcomes the thin ghosts underground: 60
> And I shall see my father again, and you, mother,
> And dearest Polyneicês—
>   dearest indeed
> To me, since it was my hand
> That washed him clean and poured the ritual wine:
> And my reward is death before my time! 65
>
> And yet, as men's hearts know, I have done no wrong,
> I have not sinned before God. Or if I have,
> I shall know the truth in death. But if the guilt
> Lies upon Creon who judged me, then, I pray,
> May his punishment equal my own.
> *Choragos:*   O passionate heart, 70
> Unyielding, tormented still by the same winds!
> *Creon:* Her guards shall have good cause to regret their delaying.
> *Antigonê:* Ah! That voice is like the voice of death!
> *Creon:* I can give you no reason to think you are mistaken.
> *Antigonê:* Thebes, and you my fathers' gods, 75
> And rulers of Thebes, you see me now, the last
> Unhappy daughter of a line of kings,

---

48 *Epode:* the final section (after the *strophe* and *antistrophe*) of a lyric passage; whereas the earlier sections are symmetrical, it takes a different metrical form.   60 *Persephonê:* daughter of Zeus and Demeter whom Pluto, god of the underworld, abducted to be his queen.

Your kings, led away to death. You will remember
What things I suffer, and at what men's hands,
Because I would not transgress the laws of heaven. 80
(*To the Guards, simply.*) Come: let us wait no longer.

Exit Antigonê, left, guarded.

ODE IV

Strophe 1

Chorus: All Danaê's beauty was locked away
In a brazen cell where the sunlight could not come:
A small room still as any grave, enclosed her.
Yet she was a princess too,
And Zeus in a rain of gold poured love upon her.° 5
O child, child,
No power in wealth or war
Or tough sea-blackened ships
Can prevail against untiring Destiny!

Antistrophe 1

And Dryas' son° also, that furious king, 10
Bore the god's prisoning anger for his pride:
Sealed up by Dionysos in deaf stone,
His madness died among echoes.
So at the last he learned what dreadful power
His tongue had mocked: 15
For he had profaned the revels,
And fired the wrath of the nine
Implacable Sisters° that love the sound of the flute.

Strophe 2

And old men tell a half-remembered tale
Of horror° where a dark ledge splits the sea 20
And a double surf beats on the gráy shóres:
How a king's new woman, sick
With hatred for the queen he had imprisoned,
Ripped out his two sons' eyes with her bloody hands
While grinning Arês° watched the shuttle plunge 25
Four times: four blind wounds crying for revenge,

1–5 *All Danaê's beauty . . . poured love upon her:* In legend, when an oracle told Acrisius, king of Argos, that his daughter Danaê would bear a son who would grow up to slay him, he locked the princess into a chamber made of bronze, lest any man impregnate her. But Zeus, father of the gods, entered Danaê's prison in a shower of gold. The resultant child, the hero Perseus, was accidentally to fulfill the prophecy by killing Acrisius with an ill-aimed discus throw.   10 *Dryas' son:* King Lycurgus of Thrace, whom Dionysos, god of wine, caused to be stricken with madness.   18 *Sisters:* the Muses, nine sister goddesses who presided over poetry and music, arts and sciences.   19–20 *a half-remembered tale of horror:* As the Chorus recalls in the rest of this song, the point of this tale is that being nobly born will not save one from disaster. King Phineas cast off his first wife, Cleopatra (not the later Egyptian queen, but the daughter of Boreas, god of the north wind) and imprisoned her in a cave. Out of hatred for Cleopatra, the cruel Eidothea, second wife of the king, blinded her stepsons.   25 *Arês:* god of war, said to gloat over bloodshed.

Antistrophe 2

Crying, tears and blood mingled.—Piteously born,
Those sons whose mother was of heavenly birth!
Her father was the god of the North Wind
And she was cradled by gales, 30
She raced with young colts on the glittering hills
And walked untrammeled in the open light:
But in her marriage deathless Fate found means
To build a tomb like yours for all her joy.

SCENE V

Enter blind Teiresias, led by a boy. The opening speeches of Teiresias should be in sing-song contrast to the realistic lines of Creon.

Teiresias: This is the way the blind man comes, Princes, Princes,
   Lockstep, two heads lit by the eyes of one.
Creon: What new thing have you to tell us, old Teiresias?
Teiresias: I have much to tell you: listen to the prophet, Creon.
Creon: I am not aware that I have ever failed to listen. 5
Teiresias: Then you have done wisely, King, and ruled well.
Creon: I admit my debt to you. But what have you to say?
Teiresias: This, Creon: you stand once more on the edge of fate.
Creon: What do you mean? Your words are a kind of dread.
Teiresias: Listen Creon: 10
   I was sitting in my chair of augury, at the place
   Where the birds gather about me. They were all a-chatter,
   As is their habit, when suddenly I heard
   A strange note in their jangling, a scream, a
   Whirring fury; I knew that they were fighting, 15
   Tearing each other, dying
   In a whirlwind of wings clashing. And I was afraid.
   I began the rites of burnt-offering at the altar,
   But Hephaistos° failed me: instead of bright flame,
   There was only the sputtering slime of the fat thigh-flesh 20
   Melting: the entrails dissolved in gray smoke,
   The bare bone burst from the welter. And no blaze!

   This was a sign from heaven. My boy described it,
   Seeing for me as I see for others.

   I tell you, Creon, you yourself have brought 25
   This new calamity upon us. Our hearths and altars
   Are stained with the corruption of dogs and carrion birds
   That glut themselves on the corpse of Oedipus' son.
   The gods are deaf when we pray to them, their fire
   Recoils from our offering, their birds of omen 30

---

19 *Hephaistos:* god of fire.

>   Have no cry of comfort, for they are gorged
>   With the thick blood of the dead.
>   O my son,
>   These are no trifles! Think: all men make mistakes,
>   But a good man yields when he knows his course is wrong,
>   And repairs the evil. The only crime is pride.   35
>
>   Give in to the dead man, then: do not fight with a corpse—
>   What glory is it to kill a man who is dead?
>   Think, I beg you:
>   It is for your own good that I speak as I do.
>   You should be able to yield for your own good.   40
> Creon: It seems that prophets have made me their especial province.
>   All my life long
>   I have been a kind of butt for the dull arrows
>   Of doddering fortune-tellers!
>   No, Teiresias:
>   If your birds—if the great eagles of God himself   45
>   Should carry him stinking bit by bit to heaven,
>   I would not yield. I am not afraid of pollution:
>   No man can defile the gods.
>   Do what you will,
>   Go into business, make money, speculate
>   In India gold or that synthetic gold from Sardis,   50
>   Get rich otherwise than by my consent to bury him.
>   Teiresias, it is a sorry thing when a wise man
>   Sells his wisdom, lets out his words for hire!
> Teiresias: Ah Creon! Is there no man left in the world—
> Creon: To do what?—Come, let's have the aphorism!   55
> Teiresias: No man who knows that wisdom outweighs any wealth?
> Creon: As surely as bribes are baser than any baseness.
> Teiresias: You are sick, Creon! You are deathly sick!
> Creon: As you say: it is not my place to challenge a prophet.
> Teiresias: Yet you have said my prophecy is for sale.   60
> Creon: The generation of prophets has always loved gold.
> Teiresias: The generation of kings has always loved brass.
> Creon: You forget yourself! You are speaking to your King.
> Teiresias: I know it. You are a king because of me.
> Creon: You have a certain skill; but you have sold out.   65
> Teiresias: King, you will drive me to words that—
> Creon: Say them, say them!
>   Only remember: I will not pay you for them.
> Teiresias: No, you will find them too costly.
> Creon: No doubt. Speak:
>   Whatever you say, you will not change my will.
> Teiresias: Then take this, and take it to heart!   70
>   The time is not far off when you shall pay back
>   Corpse for corpse, flesh of your own flesh.

You have thrust the child of this world into living night,
You have kept from the gods below the child that is theirs:
The one in a grave before her death, the other, 75
Dead, denied the grave. This is your crime:
And the Furies and the dark gods of Hell
Are swift with terrible punishment for you.

Do you want to buy me now, Creon?

                            Not many days,
And your house will be full of men and women weeping, 80
And curses will be hurled at you from far
Cities grieving for sons unburied, left to rot
Before the walls of Thebes.

These are my arrows, Creon: they are all for you.

(*To Boy.*) But come, child: lead me home. 85
Let him waste his fine anger upon younger men.
Maybe he will learn at last
To control a wiser tongue in a better head.

Exit Teiresias.

Choragos: The old man has gone, King, but his words
    Remain to plague us. I am old, too, 90
    But I cannot remember that he was ever false.
Creon: That is true. . . . It troubles me.
    Oh it is hard to give in! but it is worse
    To risk everything for stubborn pride.
Choragos: Creon: take my advice.
Creon: What shall I do? 95
Choragos: Go quickly: free Antigonê from her vault
    And build a tomb for the body of Polyneicês.
Creon: You would have me do this!
Choragos: Creon, yes!
    And it must be done at once: God moves
    Swiftly to cancel the folly of stubborn men. 100
Creon: It is hard to deny the heart! But I
    Will do it: I will not fight with destiny.
Choragos: You must go yourself, you cannot leave it to others.
Creon: I will go.
          —Bring axes, servants:
    Come with me to the tomb. I buried her, I 105
    Will set her free.
               Oh quickly!
    My mind misgives—
    The laws of the gods are mighty, and a man must serve them
    To the last day of his life!

Exit Creon.

PAEAN°

Choragos: God of many names   *Strophe 1*
Chorus: O Iacchos
                        son
  of Kadmeian Sémelê
              O born of the Thunder!
  Guardian of the West
            Regent
  of Eleusis' plain
            O Prince of maenad Thebes
  and the Dragon Field by rippling Ismenós:°   5

Choragos: God of many names   *Antistrophe 1*
Chorus: the flame of torches
  flares on our hills
         the nymphs of Iacchos
  dance at the spring of Castalia:°

  from the vine-close mountain
              come ah come in ivy:
  Evohé evohé!° sings through the streets of Thebes   10

Choragos: God of many names   *Strophe 2*
Chorus: Iacchos of Thebes
  heavenly Child
        of Sémelê bride of the Thunderer!
  The shadow of plague is upon us:
            come
  with clement feet
        oh come from Parnasos
  down the long slopes
         across the lamenting water   15

Choragos: Iô° Fire! Chorister of the throbbing stars!   *Antistrophe 2*
  O purest among the voices of the night!
  Thou son of God, blaze for us!

Paean: a song of praise or prayer, here to Dionysos, god of wine. 1–5 *God of many names . . . Dragon Field by rippling Ismenós:* Dionysos was also called Iacchos (or, by the Romans, Bacchus). He was the son of Zeus ("the Thunderer") and of Sémelê, daughter of Kadmos (or Cadmus), legendary founder of Thebes. "Regent of Eleusis' plain" is another name for Dionysos, honored in secret rites at Eleusis, a town northwest of Athens. "Prince of maenad Thebes" is yet another: the Maenads were women of Thebes said to worship Dionysos with wild orgiastic rites. Kadmos, so the story goes, sowed dragon's teeth in a field beside the river Ismenós. Up sprang a crop of fierce warriors who fought among themselves until only five remained. These victors became the first Thebans. 8 *Castalia:* a spring on Mount Parnassus, named for a maiden who drowned herself in it to avoid rape by the god Apollo. She became a nymph, or nature spirit, dwelling in its waters. In the temple of Delphi, at the mountain's foot, priestesses of Dionysos (the "nymphs of Iacchos") used the spring's waters in rites of purification. 10 *Evohé evohé!:* cry of the Maenads in supplicating Dionysos: "Come forth, come forth!" 16 *Iô:* "Hail" or "Praise be to . . ."

Chorus: Come with choric rapture of circling Maenads
   Who cry *Iô Iacche!*
                              God of many names!   20

ÉXODOS°

Enter Messenger from left.

Messenger: Men of the line of Kadmos, you who live
   Near Amphion's citadel:°
                           I cannot say
   Of any condition of human life "This is fixed,
   This is clearly good, or bad." Fate raises up,
   And Fate casts down the happy and unhappy alike: 5
   No man can foretell his Fate.
                           Take the case of Creon:
   Creon was happy once, as I count happiness:
   Victorious in battle, sole governor of the land,
   Fortunate father of children nobly born.
   And now it has all gone from him! Who can say   10
   That a man is still alive when his life's joy fails?
   He is a walking dead man. Grant him rich,
   Let him live like a king in his great house:
   If his pleasure is gone, I would not give
   So much as the shadow of smoke for all he owns.   15
Choragos: Your words hint at sorrow: what is your news for us?
Messenger: They are dead. The living are guilty of their death.
Choragos: Who is guilty? Who is dead? Speak!
Messenger: Haimon.
   Haimon is dead; and the hand that killed him
   Is his own hand.
Choragos: His father's? or his own?   20
Messenger: His own, driven mad by the murder his father had done.
Choragos: Teiresias, Teiresias, how clearly you saw it all!
Messenger: This is my news: you must draw what conclusions you can from it.
Choragos: But look: Eurydicê, our Queen:
   Has she overheard us?   25

Enter Eurydicê from the palace, center.

Eurydicê: I have heard something, friends:
   As I was unlocking the gate of Pallas'° shrine,
   For I needed her help today, I heard a voice
   Telling of some new sorrow. And I fainted
   There at the temple with all my maidens about me.   30

Éxodos: the final scene, containing the play's resolution.   2 *Amphion's citadel:* a name for Thebes. Amphion, son of Zeus, had built a wall around the city by playing so beautifully on his lyre that the charmed stones leaped into their slots.   27 *Pallas:* Pallas Athene, goddess of wisdom, and hence an excellent source of advice.

But speak again: whatever it is, I can bear it:
Grief and I are no strangers.
Messenger: Dearest Lady.
I will tell you plainly all that I have seen.
I shall not try to comfort you: what is the use,
Since comfort could lie only in what is not true?   35
The truth is always best.
                    I went with Creon
To the outer plain where Polyneicês was lying,
No friend to pity him, his body shredded by dogs.
We made our prayers in that place to Hecatê
And Pluto,° that they would be merciful. And we bathed   40
The corpse with holy water, and we brought
Fresh-broken branches to burn what was left of it,
And upon the urn we heaped up a towering barrow
Of the earth of his own land.
                    When we were done, we ran
To the vault where Antigonê lay on her couch of stone.   45
One of the servants had gone ahead,
And while he was yet far off he heard a voice
Grieving within the chamber, and he came back
And told Creon. And as the King went closer,
The air was full of wailing, the words lost,   50
And he begged us to make all haste. "Am I a prophet?"
He said, weeping, "And must I walk this road,
The saddest of all that I have gone before?
My son's voice calls me on. Oh quickly, quickly!
Look through the crevice there, and tell me   55
If it is Haimon, or some deception of the gods!"

We obeyed; and in the cavern's farthest corner
We saw her lying:
She had made a noose of her fine linen veil
And hanged herself. Haimon lay beside her,   60
His arms about her waist, lamenting her,
His love lost under ground, crying out
That his father had stolen her away from him.

When Creon saw him the tears rushed to his eyes
And he called to him: "What have you done, child? Speak to me.   65
What are you thinking that makes your eyes so strange?
O my son, my son, I come to you on my knees!"
But Haimon spat in his face. He said not a word,
Staring—
           And suddenly drew his sword

39–40 *Hecatê and Pluto:* two fearful divinities—the goddess of witchcraft and sorcery and the king of Hades, underworld of the dead.

And lunged. Creon shrank back, the blade missed; and the boy,
Desperate against himself, drove it half its length
Into his own side, and fell. And as he died
He gathered Antigonê close in his arms again,
Choking, his blood bright red on her white cheek.
And now he lies dead with the dead, and she is his
At last, his bride in the houses of the dead.

Exit Eurydicê into the palace.

Choragos: She has left us without a word. What can this mean?
Messenger: It troubles me, too; yet she knows what is best,
    Her grief is too great for public lamentation,
    And doubtless she has gone to her chamber to weep
    For her dead son, leading her maidens in his dirge.
Choragos: It may be so: but I fear this deep silence.

Pause.

Messenger: I will see what she is doing. I will go in.

Exit Messenger into the palace.

Enter Creon with attendants, bearing Haimon's body.

Choragos: But here is the king himself: oh look at him,
    Bearing his own damnation in his arms.
Creon: Nothing you say can touch me any more.
    My own blind heart has brought me
    From darkness to final darkness. Here you see
    The father murdering, the murdered son—
    And all my civic wisdom!

    Haimon my son, so young, so young to die,
    I was the fool, not you; and you died for me.
Choragos: That is the truth; but you were late in learning it.
Creon: This truth is hard to bear. Surely a god
    Has crushed me beneath the hugest weight of heaven,
    And driven me headlong a barbaric way
    To trample out the thing I held most dear.

    The pains that men will take to come to pain!

Enter Messenger from the palace.

Messenger: The burden you carry in your hands is heavy,
    But it is not all: you will find more in your house.
Creon: What burden worse than this shall I find there?
Messenger: The Queen is dead.
Creon: O port of death, deaf world,
    Is there no pity for me? And you, Angel of evil,
    I was dead, and your words are death again.

      Is it true, boy? Can it be true?
      Is my wife dead? Has death bred death?
Messenger: You can see for yourself.

The doors are opened and the body of Eurydicê is disclosed within.

Creon: Oh pity!
      All true, all true, and more than I can bear!   110
      O my wife, my son!
Messenger: She stood before the altar, and her heart
      Welcomed the knife her own hand guided,
      And a great cry burst from her lips for Megareus° dead,
      And for Haimon dead, her sons; and her last breath   115
      Was a curse for their father, the murderer of her sons.
      And she fell, and the dark flowed in through her closing eyes.
Creon: O God, I am sick with fear.
      Are there no swords here? Has no one a blow for me?
Messenger: Her curse is upon you for the deaths of both.   120
Creon: It is right that it should be. I alone am guilty.
      I know it, and I say it. Lead me in,
      Quickly, friends.
      I have neither life nor substance. Lead me in.
Choragos: You are right, if there can be right in so much wrong.   125
      The briefest way is best in a world of sorrow.
Creon: Let it come,
      Let death come quickly, and be kind to me.
      I would not ever see the sun again.
Choragos: All that will come when it will; but we, meanwhile,   130
      Have much to do. Leave the future to itself.
Creon: All my heart was in that prayer!
Choragos: Then do not pray any more: the sky is deaf.
Creon: Lead me away. I have been rash and foolish.
      I have killed my son and my wife.   135
      I look for comfort; my comfort lies here dead.
      Whatever my hands have touched has come to nothing.
      Fate has brought all my pride to a thought of dust.

As Creon is being led into the house, the Choragos advances and speaks directly to the audience.

Choragos: There is no happiness where there is no wisdom;
      No wisdom but in submission to the gods.   140
      Big words are always punished,
      And proud men in old age learn to be wise.

---

114 *Megareus:* Son of Creon and brother of Haimon, Megareus was slain in the unsuccessful attack upon Thebes.

Questions

1. What is Creon's motivation for forbidding the burial of his own nephew Polyneicês? Why would he issue an edict that runs so contrary to his family obligations?
2. What are Antigonê's reasons for performing funeral rites on her brother's corpse in direct violation of Creon's edict?
3. What are the larger issues behind the conflicting positions of both Creon and Antigonê? Is either person or position clearly wrong?
4. Does the chorus take a position in the argument between Creon and Antigonê?
5. If Antigonê is a tragic heroine, what is her tragic flaw? Does she have any particular *hubris* or excess of virtue that dooms her?
6. Can a modern reader discern Sophocles's own position on the debate between civic responsibility (Creon's edict) and family duty (Antigonê's defiance)? Are his authorial sympathies anywhere evident in the play?
7. What is the role of Eurydicê? Is her presence essential to the story? What would be the effect of removing her from the drama?

Suggestions for Writing on *Sophocles's Antigonê*

1. Take one of the major characters in *Antigonê* and describe that character's individual identity—age, social position, family background, and beliefs. Then contrast this identity to that of another of the key characters in the play. How are they similar? In what crucial ways do they differ? How do those differences motivate the action of the play?
2. Antigonê is the protagonist of Sophocles's tragedy. Write a short essay explaining how she exemplifies or refutes Aristotle's description of a tragic hero.
3. What is the role of the chorus in *Antigonê*? Does it represent Theban society's collective opinions, or does it mostly just react to what the individual characters say? Analyze one of the choral odes and discuss the social attitudes and opinions it presents.
4. Imagine yourself as the director of a new production of *Antigonê*. You have decided to set the play in a different time and place than ancient Greece. Describe your new production. Where would it take place? How would you dress and direct the major characters?
5. Reread and analyze one of the choral odes from *Antigonê* and discuss how it clarifies and influences the action of the play.
6. Choose one of the minor characters—Haimon, Ismenê, or Eurydicê—and discuss what his or her presence adds to the action and meaning of the play.
7. Write an essay justifying Creon's point of view. Why is it necessary that he punish the rebels even after death? Why will Thebes be a better and stronger city-state if the citizens follow his plan?
8. Write an essay justifying Antigonê's actions. Why is it important for the citizens of Thebes to fulfill their family and religious duties even when the king forbids them? Why will Antigonê's principled dissent make a better and stronger city-state? (Read this essay in class in coordination with someone's reading an essay on Creon's point of view. Then invite the class to debate the topic and vote for a preferred action.)

Suggestions for Writing on *Literature about the Individual and Society*

1. Both Ursula Le Guin's "The Ones Who Walk Away from Omelas" and Shirley Jackson's "The Lottery" offer troubling views of social norms and majority opinion. Do such dynamics still exist? In your opinion, are there situations today where majority opinion might not be the "right" opinion? Write an essay in which you answer this question.
2. Martin Luther King's "Letter from Birmingham Jail" and Paul Laurence Dunbar's poem "Sympathy" reflect a time when the expectations and possibilities for African Americans (and people of color in general) were much more narrowly defined. Have these expectations and possibilities changed? Write an essay that argues whether or not the situations and themes described in these pieces still hold relevance today.
3. Ha Jin's "Saboteur" and Ursula Le Guin's "The Ones Who Walk Away from Omelas" both include characters who resist societal rules. Do these stories suggest that changes can be made from within a society? Why or why not? How do you think that today's real-life conflicts could be addressed? Write an essay about a current conflict between peoples, communities, entities, or sets of beliefs, and then argue for how such divisions could be overcome or mended.
4. When the interests of individuals or even a group differ from the established norms of society, what is the most effective way to come to a resolution? How should such a disagreement be decided? Take a current issue—such as abortion, the death penalty, or same-sex marriage—and write an essay describing what you think would be the best way to decide the matter.
5. Both Allen Ginsberg's "A Supermarket in California" and Anne Sexton's "Her Kind" combine an intense sense of loneliness with an equally powerful (and even slightly crazy) joy surprisingly found in solitude. What makes people feel connected, or not connected, to a larger world? What is the value of solitude? Write an essay that examines the benefits and disadvantages of both solitude and community.
6. People today use many "virtual" methods of staying in touch with one another that don't involve face-to-face contact. They include e-mail, social networking websites, texting, Skype, and other methods. Write an essay about what is gained or lost by using electronic methods to communicate.
7. Both E. E. Cummings's "anyone lived in a pretty how town" and W. H. Auden's "The Unknown Citizen" satirize middle-class conformity and complacency. Is there, however, a case to be made on the other side of the issue? What might be a good reason to strive to think, live, and be like everyone else?

16 PERSONAL IDENTITY

We all know we are unique individuals, but we tend to see others as representatives of groups.

—DEBORAH TANNEN

Imagine that you are describing yourself to a stranger. What adjectives or terms would you use? Would you refer to your age or sex? Your hometown? How about your race, religion, ethnicity, class, or sexual orientation? Would you mention your job or college, a favorite hobby or sport? Would you say something about your physical appearance or style of dress? What if you had to limit your description to five adjectives, or only three? What, to you, are the most important aspects of your identity? Would someone else describe you in the same way?

Personal identity is made up of many elements. We know that our families have an influence on who we become, but plenty of other factors help to determine who we are. Someone who is born wealthy—or impoverished—is likely to perceive the world through the lens of his or her economic situation. A girl may grow up hearing different kinds of compliments and admonishments than a boy hears, and that might affect both her self-image and her ideas about what is possible in life. A New York City resident and someone who lives in small-town South Dakota will probably think differently about everything from nature to government policies, to hunting and fishing, to methods of transportation. (A subway would be as out of place in the Black Hills as a snowmobile would be on Wall Street.) An immigrant may have more complicated views of the United States—positive or negative—than someone who has always lived life here. A member of a minority group might respond differently to a political or social question than would someone from the majority.

But the idea of personal identity is a tricky one; while factors such as race and gender may *influence* someone's outlook, it's too simple to think they *define* it—or to assume that all members of a given group think alike. Women do not all feel the same way about, for example, feminism or gender roles. Latinos do not all have the same opinions on immigration, faith, or bilingual education. Football fans don't all root for the same team. Many people belong to two, three, or even five different kinds of groups that might have vastly different belief systems.

It's also important to recognize that the concept of "personal identity" doesn't relate only to people of color, or immigrants, or women, or gays and lesbians, or members of religious minorities. Statements about being part of "the majority culture" mean very little in a diverse and complex nation. Is the "majority" member male or female? Protestant, Catholic, Mormon, Jewish, Muslim, or agnostic? Do "majority" members live in the city, the suburbs, or the country? Are they wealthy, poor, or middle-class? Young, old, or middle-aged? Lumping white people together as one class perpetuates a stereotype as misleading as any other racial prejudice. The point is, as literature reminds us, people are individuals. When we stereotype a person or a group, we miss the essential elements of his or her character and beliefs.

What happens when a part of our identity is shaken up a bit? When a star athlete has a career-ending injury or retires, who does he become? When someone who prides herself on being working-class puts herself through school, opens a business, and becomes rich, what happens to her image of herself? Which elements of our identity stay with us, and which ones change? Is identity fixed or mutable? Does it evolve? How do you reconcile those parts of yourself that are different from, or even in opposition to, each other?

Differences among people are part of what makes the world such a vibrant, interesting, and stimulating place. Think how boring it would be if everyone looked, talked, felt, thought, or worshipped in exactly the same way; such monotony sounds like the stuff of a *Twilight Zone* episode. But with diversity comes challenges. Too often, we use difference to make people so foreign, so other, so "not like us" that it becomes easier to justify treating them differently. We all do this at one time or another; even the most enlightened and open-minded individuals make assumptions about other people. But we can recognize that our assumptions are just that—assumptions—and try to see each person, or group of people, in their wholeness and complexity. When difference is embraced, people enrich and learn from each other. We can recognize that, despite our differences, many human realities—such as love or grief—are universal human experiences.

THE SELECTIONS IN THIS CHAPTER

The pieces in this chapter all explore personal identity. Charlotte Perkins Gilman's "The Yellow Wallpaper," Sylvia Plath's "Metaphors," John Steinbeck's "The Chrysanthemums," and Virginia Woolf's "What If Shakespeare Had a Sister?" investigate the intellectual and emotional aspirations of women in situations that inhibit their free expression and development. Donald Justice's "Men at Forty" and Raymond Carver's "Cathedral" address concerns of middle-aged men. Francisco X. Alarcon's "The X in My Name" and Shirley Geok-lin Lim's "Learning to Love America" present very different views of immigrants. David Leavitt's "A Place I've Never Been" examines both gay and heterosexual identity as well as the complexity of living with HIV. Ted Kooser's "So This Is Nebraska," Edwin Arlington Robinson's "New England," and Rhina Espaillat's "Bodega" all describe the importance of place as a formative element. Frederick Douglass's classic "Learning to Read and Write" documents the struggle of a man born in slavery to gain knowledge—and the power that comes with it. Sherman Alexie's story "This Is What It Means to Say Phoenix, Arizona" expands on the idea of the power of storytelling and heritage.

Reading about issues of personal identity in literature can do two important things: help you recognize what you have in common with people who seem very different from you, and make you see where other people are coming from. As Harper Lee suggests in *To Kill a Mockingbird*, "You never really understand a person until you consider things from his point of view—until you climb into his skin and walk around in it."

Things to Think About

1. How would you describe yourself? How important are age, sex, and race in your concept of who you are? What about religion, class, nationality, and region? Is part of your identity based on what you do for recreation or work?
2. Do you identify yourself as part of a particular group? Do you consider yourself a representative of that group, or an individual whose concerns may or may not mesh with those of the larger group?
3. Do you see yourself differently than others see you? If so, in what ways? Are parts of your identity hard to reconcile with one another? How so?
4. Has anyone ever had preconceptions about you because of some aspect of who you are—your race, sex, nationality, religion, birthplace, sexual orientation? What were the preconceptions? How did you handle it? Have you ever had preconceptions about other people based on similar factors?
5. Do you think there are experiences (such as love and loss) that are universal among all people? Or are all experiences influenced by social or cultural context?
6. Do you think there is such a thing as a national identity? If so, how would you describe it?

FICTION

BECOMING AN INDIVIDUAL

Charlotte Perkins Gilman *The Yellow Wallpaper*
David Leavitt *A Place I've Never Been*
Sherman Alexie *This Is What It Means to Say Phoenix, Arizona*

We are all shaped by the families, cultures, and eras into which we are born. A person who grows up in a prosperous community that values education and takes personal luxuries for granted might see the world differently from someone raised among poor, newly arrived immigrants. A person who grows up in a place where everyone looks the same might react differently to a college roommate of a different race or religion than someone whose hometown is more diverse. Our views and beliefs are influenced by the views and beliefs of the people around us—and yet, at some point, most of us start to develop our own opinions and identities. We might then feel at odds with our family or group, or become drawn to people or possibilities outside our familiar worlds. Sometimes becoming an individual means breaking away from family history or legacy; at other times it involves connecting more deeply to what is best in our own past. Whatever the case, there's often a delicate balance between forging our own identities and remaining part of the social structures that support and nourish us.

The stories in this section all involve characters who are struggling to establish their identities. In Charlotte Perkins Gilman's classic "The Yellow Wallpaper," a nineteenth-century woman suffering from depression is confined to a "rest cure"—which turns out to be no cure at all. In David Leavitt's "A Place I've Never Been," two friends—one straight, the other gay—sort through a number of issues, not all of them, as it turns out, related to sexual orientation. In Sherman Alexie's "This Is What It Means to Say Phoenix, Arizona," a young Spokane Indian travels to Arizona to recover his dead father's effects—and rediscovers his own history and identity.

Charlotte Perkins Gilman

Charlotte Perkins Gilman (1860–1935) was born in Hartford, Connecticut. Her father was the writer Frederick Beecher Perkins (a nephew of the reformer and novelist Harriet Beecher Stowe, author of Uncle Tom's Cabin, *and abolitionist minister Henry Ward Beecher), but he abandoned the family shortly after his daughter's birth. Raised in meager surroundings, the young Gilman adopted her intellectual Beecher aunts as role models. Because she and her mother moved from one relation to another, Gilman's early education was neglected—at fifteen, she had had only four years of schooling. In 1878 she studied commercial art at the Rhode Island School of Design. In 1884 she married Walter Stetson, an artist. After the birth of her one daughter, she experienced a severe depression. The rest*

Charlotte Perkins Gilman

cure her doctor prescribed became the basis of her most famous story, "The Yellow Wallpaper." This tale combines standard elements of Gothic fiction (the isolated country mansion, the brooding atmosphere of the room, the aloof but dominating husband) with the fresh clarity of Gilman's feminist perspective. Gilman's first marriage ended in an amicable divorce. A celebrated essayist and public speaker, she became an important early figure in American feminism. Her study Women and Economics (1898) stressed the importance of both sexes having a place in the working world. Her feminist-Utopian novel Herland (1915) describes a thriving nation of women without men. In 1900 Gilman married a second time—this time, more happily—to her cousin George Houghton Gilman. Following his sudden death in 1934, Gilman discovered she had inoperable breast cancer. After finishing her autobiography, she killed herself with chloroform in Pasadena, California.

The Yellow Wallpaper 1892

It is very seldom that mere ordinary people like John and myself secure ancestral halls for the summer.

A colonial mansion, a hereditary estate, I would say a haunted house and reach the height of romantic felicity—but that would be asking too much of fate!

Still I will proudly declare that there is something queer about it.

Else, why should it be let so cheaply? And why have stood so long untenanted?

John laughs at me, of course, but one expects that.

John is practical in the extreme. He has no patience with faith, an intense horror of superstition, and he scoffs openly at any talk of things not to be felt and seen and put down in figures.

John is a physician, and *perhaps*—(I would not say it to a living soul, of course, but this is dead paper and a great relief to my mind)—*perhaps* that is one reason I do not get well faster.

You see, he does not believe I am sick! And what can one do?

If a physician of high standing, and one's own husband, assures friends and relatives that there is really nothing the matter with one but temporary nervous depression—a slight hysterical tendency—what is one to do?

My brother is also a physician, and also of high standing, and he says the same thing.

So I take phosphates or phosphites—whichever it is—and tonics, and air and exercise, and journeys, and am absolutely forbidden to "work" until I am well again.

Personally, I disagree with their ideas.

Personally, I believe that congenial work, with excitement and change, would do me good.

But what is one to do?

I did write for a while in spite of them; but it *does* exhaust me a good deal—having to be so sly about it, or else meet with heavy opposition.

I sometimes fancy that in my condition, if I had less opposition and more society and stimulus—but John says the very worst thing I can do is to think about my condition, and I confess it always makes me feel bad.

So I will let it alone and talk about the house.

The most beautiful place! It is quite alone, standing well back from the road, quite three miles from the village. It makes me think of English places that you read about, for there are hedges and walls and gates that lock, and lots of separate little houses for the gardeners and people.

There is a *delicious* garden! I never saw such a garden—large and shady, full of box-bordered paths, and lined with long grape-covered arbors with seats under them.

There were greenhouses, but they are all broken now.

There was some legal trouble, I believe, something about the heirs and co-heirs; anyhow, the place has been empty for years.

That spoils my ghostliness, I am afraid, but I don't care—there is something strange about the house—I can feel it.

I even said so to John one moonlight evening, but he said what I felt was a *draught*, and shut the window.

I get unreasonably angry with John sometimes. I'm sure I never used to be so sensitive. I think it is due to this nervous condition.

But John says if I feel so I shall neglect proper self-control; so I take pains to control myself—before him, at least, and that makes me very tired.

I don't like our room a bit. I wanted one downstairs that opened onto the piazza and had roses all over the window, and such pretty old-fashioned chintz hangings! But John would not hear of it.

He said there was only one window and not room for two beds, and no near room for him if he took another.

He is very careful and loving, and hardly lets me stir without special direction.

I have a schedule prescription for each hour in the day; he takes all care from me, and so I feel basely ungrateful not to value it more.

He said he came here solely on my account, that I was to have perfect rest and all the air I could get. "Your exercise depends on your strength, my dear," said he, "and your food somewhat on your appetite; but air you can absorb all the time." So we took the nursery at the top of the house.

It is a big, airy room, the whole floor nearly, with windows that look all ways, and air and sunshine galore. It was a nursery first, and then playroom and gymnasium, I should judge, for the windows are barred for little children, and there are rings and things in the walls.

The paint and paper look as if a boys' school had used it. It is stripped off—the paper—in great patches all around the head of my bed, about as far as I can reach, and in a great place on the other side of the room low down. I never saw a worse paper in my life. One of those sprawling, flamboyant patterns committing every artistic sin.

It is dull enough to confuse the eye in following, pronounced enough constantly to irritate and provoke study, and when you follow the lame uncertain curves for a little distance they suddenly commit suicide—plunge off at outrageous angles, destroy themselves in unheard-of contradictions.

The color is repellent, almost revolting: a smouldering unclean yellow, strangely faded by the slow-turning sunlight. It is a dull yet lurid orange in some places, a sickly sulphur tint in others.

No wonder the children hated it! I should hate it myself if I had to live in this room long.

There comes John, and I must put this away—he hates to have me write a word.

We have been here two weeks, and I haven't felt like writing before, since that first day.

I am sitting by the window now, up in this atrocious nursery, and there is nothing to hinder my writing as much as I please, save lack of strength.

John is away all day, and even some nights when his cases are serious.

I am glad my case is not serious!

But these nervous troubles are dreadfully depressing.

John does not know how much I really suffer. He knows there is no *reason* to suffer, and that satisfies him.

Of course it is only nervousness. It does weigh on me so not to do my duty in any way!

I meant to be such a help to John, such a real rest and comfort, and here I am a comparative burden already!

Nobody would believe what an effort it is to do what little I am able—to dress and entertain, and order things.

It is fortunate Mary is so good with the baby. Such a dear baby!

And yet I *cannot* be with him, it makes me so nervous.

I suppose John never was nervous in his life. He laughs at me so about this wallpaper!

At first he meant to repaper the room, but afterward he said that I was letting it get the better of me, and that nothing was worse for a nervous patient than to give way to such fancies.

He said that after the wallpaper was changed it would be the heavy bedstead, and then the barred windows, and then that gate at the head of the stairs, and so on.

"You know the place is doing you good," he said, "and really, dear, I don't care to renovate the house just for a three months' rental."

"Then do let us go downstairs," I said. "There are such pretty rooms there."

Then he took me in his arms and called me a blessed little goose, and said he would go down to the cellar, if I wished, and have it whitewashed into the bargain.

But he is right enough about the beds and windows and things.

It is as airy and comfortable a room as anyone need wish, and, of course, I would not be so silly as to make him uncomfortable just for a whim.

I'm really getting quite fond of the big room, all but that horrid paper.

Out of one window I can see the garden—those mysterious deep-shaded arbors, the riotous old-fashioned flowers, and bushes and gnarly trees.

Out of another I get a lovely view of the bay and a little private wharf belonging to the estate. There is a beautiful shaded lane that runs down there from the house. I always fancy I see people walking in these numerous paths and arbors, but John has cautioned me not to give way to fancy in the least. He says that with my imaginative power and habit of story-making, a nervous weakness like mine is sure to lead to all manner of excited fancies, and that I ought to use my will and good sense to check the tendency. So I try.

I think sometimes that if I were only well enough to write a little it would relieve the press of ideas and rest me.

But I find I get pretty tired when I try.

It is so discouraging not to have any advice and companionship about my work. When I get really well, John says we will ask Cousin Henry and Julia down for a long visit; but he says he would as soon put fireworks in my pillow-case as to let me have those stimulating people about now.

I wish I could get well faster.

But I must not think about that. This paper looks to me as if it *knew* what a vicious influence it had!

There is a recurrent spot where the pattern lolls like a broken neck and two bulbous eyes stare at you upside down.

I get positively angry with the impertinence of it and the everlastingness. Up and down and sideways they crawl, and those absurd unblinking eyes are everywhere.

There is one place where two breadths didn't match, and the eyes go all up and down the line, one a little higher than the other.

I never saw so much expression in an inanimate thing before, and we all know how much expression they have! I used to lie awake as a child and get more entertainment and terror out of blank walls and plain furniture than most children could find in a toy-store.

I remember what a kindly wink the knobs of our big old bureau used to have, and there was one chair that always seemed like a strong friend.

I used to feel that if any of the other things looked too fierce I could always hop into that chair and be safe.

The furniture in this room is no worse than inharmonious, however, for we had to bring it all from downstairs. I suppose when this was used as a playroom they had to take the nursery things out, and no wonder! I never saw such ravages as the children have made here.

The wallpaper, as I said before, is torn off in spots, and it sticketh closer than a brother—they must have had perseverance as well as hatred. 70

Then the floor is scratched and gouged and splintered, the plaster itself is dug out here and there, and this great heavy bed, which is all we found in the room, looks as if it had been through the wars.

But I don't mind it a bit—only the paper.

There comes John's sister. Such a dear girl as she is, and so careful of me! I must not let her find me writing.

She is a perfect and enthusiastic housekeeper, and hopes for no better profession. I verily believe she thinks it is the writing which made me sick!

But I can write when she is out, and see her a long way off from these windows. 75

There is one that commands the road, a lovely shaded winding road, and one that just looks off over the country. A lovely country, too, full of great elms and velvet meadows.

This wallpaper has a kind of sub-pattern in a different shade, a particularly irritating one, for you can only see it in certain lights, and not clearly then.

But in the places where it isn't faded and where the sun is just so—I can see a strange, provoking, formless sort of figure that seems to skulk about behind that silly and conspicuous front design.

There's sister on the stairs!

Well, the Fourth of July is over! The people are all gone, and I am tired out. John thought it might do me good to see a little company, so we just had Mother and Nellie and the children down for a week. 80

Of course I didn't do a thing. Jennie sees to everything now.

But it tired me all the same.

John says if I don't pick up faster he shall send me to Weir Mitchell° in the fall.

But I don't want to go there at all. I had a friend who was in his hands once, and she says he is just like John and my brother, only more so!

Besides, it is such an undertaking to go so far. 85

Weir Mitchell (1829–1914): famed nerve specialist who actually treated the author, Charlotte Perkins Gilman, for nervous prostration with his well-known "rest cure." (The cure was not successful.) Also the author of *Diseases of the Nervous System, Especially of Women* (1881).

I don't feel as if it was worthwhile to turn my hand over for anything, and I'm getting dreadfully fretful and querulous.

I cry at nothing, and cry most of the time.

Of course I don't when John is here, or anybody else, but when I am alone.

And I am alone a good deal just now. John is kept in town very often by serious cases, and Jennie is good and lets me alone when I want her to.

So I walk a little in the garden or down that lovely lane, sit on the porch under the roses, and lie down up here a good deal.

I'm getting really fond of the room in spite of the wallpaper. Perhaps *because* of the wallpaper.

It dwells in my mind so!

I lie here on this great immovable bed—it is nailed down, I believe—and follow that pattern about by the hour. It is as good as gymnastics, I assure you. I start, we'll say, at the bottom, down in the corner over there where it has not been touched, and I determine for the thousandth time that I *will* follow that pointless pattern to some sort of a conclusion.

I know a little of the principle of design, and I know this thing was not arranged on any laws of radiation,° or alternation, or repetition, or symmetry, or anything else that I ever heard of.

It is repeated, of course, by the breadths, but not otherwise.

Looked at in one way, each breadth stands alone; the bloated curves and flourishes—a kind of "debased Romanesque" with *delirium tremens*—go waddling up and down in isolated columns of fatuity.

But, on the other hand, they connect diagonally, and the sprawling outlines run off in great slanting waves of optic horror, like a lot of wallowing sea-weeds in full chase.

The whole thing goes horizontally, too, at least it seems so, and I exhaust myself trying to distinguish the order of its going in that direction.

They have used a horizontal breadth for a frieze, and that adds wonderfully to the confusion.

There is one end of the room where it is almost intact, and there, when the cross-lights fade and the low sun shines directly upon it, I can almost fancy radiation after all—the interminable grotesque seems to form around a common center and rush off in headlong plunges of equal distraction.

It makes me tired to follow it. I will take a nap, I guess.

I don't know why I should write this.

I don't want to.

I don't feel able.

And I know John would think it absurd. But I *must* say what I feel and think in some way—it is such a relief!

But the effort is getting to be greater than the relief.

Half the time now I am awfully lazy, and lie down ever so much. John says I mustn't lose my strength, and has me take cod liver oil and lots of tonics and things, to say nothing of ale and wines and rare meat.

laws of radiation: a principle of design in which all elements are arranged in some circular pattern around a center.

Dear John! He loves me very dearly, and hates to have me sick. I tried to have a real earnest reasonable talk with him the other day, and tell him how I wish he would let me go and make a visit to Cousin Henry and Julia.

But he said I wasn't able to go, nor able to stand it after I got there; and I did not make out a very good case for myself, for I was crying before I had finished.

It is getting to be a great effort for me to think straight. Just this nervous weakness, I suppose.

And dear John gathered me up in his arms, and just carried me upstairs and laid me on the bed, and sat by me and read to me till it tired my head.

He said I was his darling and his comfort and all he had, and that I must take care of myself for his sake, and keep well.

He says no one but myself can help me out of it, that I must use my will and self-control and not let any silly fancies run away with me.

There's one comfort—the baby is well and happy, and does not have to occupy this nursery with the horrid wallpaper.

If we had not used it, that blessed child would have! What a fortunate escape! Why, I wouldn't have a child of mine, an impressionable little thing, live in such a room for worlds.

I never thought of it before, but it is lucky that John kept me here after all; I can stand it so much easier than a baby, you see.

Of course I never mention it to them any more—I am too wise—but I keep watch for it all the same.

There are things in the wallpaper that nobody knows about but me, or ever will.

Behind that outside pattern the dim shapes get clearer every day.

It is always the same shape, only very numerous.

And it is like a woman stooping down and creeping about behind that pattern. I don't like it a bit. I wonder—I begin to think—I wish John would take me away from here!

It is so hard to talk with John about my case, because he is so wise, and because he loves me so.

But I tried it last night.

It was moonlight. The moon shines in all around just as the sun does.

I hate to see it sometimes, it creeps so slowly, and always comes in by one window or another.

John was asleep and I hated to waken him, so I kept still and watched the moonlight on that undulating wallpaper till I felt creepy.

The faint figure behind seemed to shake the pattern, just as if she wanted to get out.

I got up softly and went to feel and see if the paper *did* move, and when I came back John was awake.

"What is it, little girl?" he said. "Don't go walking about like that—you'll get cold."

I thought it was a good time to talk, so I told him that I really was not gaining here, and that I wished he would take me away.

"Why, darling!" said he. "Our lease will be up in three weeks, and I can't see how to leave before.

"The repairs are not done at home, and I cannot possibly leave town just now. Of course, if you were in any danger, I could and would, but you really are better, dear, whether you can see it or not. I am a doctor, dear, and I know. You are gaining flesh and color, your appetite is better, I feel really much easier about you."

"I don't weigh a bit more," said I, "nor as much; and my appetite may be better in the evening when you are here but it is worse in the morning when you are away!"

"Bless her little heart!" said he with a big hug. "She shall be as sick as she pleases! But now let's improve the shining hours by going to sleep, and talk about it in the morning!"

"And you won't go away?" I asked gloomily.

"Why, how can I, dear? It is only three weeks more and then we will take a nice little trip for a few days while Jennie is getting the house ready. Really, dear, you are better!"

"Better in body perhaps—" I began, and stopped short, for he sat up straight and looked at me with such a stern, reproachful look that I could not say another word.

"My darling," said he, "I beg you, for my sake and for our child's sake, as well as for your own, that you will never for one instant let that idea enter your mind! There is nothing so dangerous, so fascinating, to a temperament like yours. It is a false and foolish fancy. Can you trust me as a physician when I tell you so?"

So of course I said no more on that score, and we went to sleep before long. He thought I was asleep first, but I wasn't, and lay there for hours trying to decide whether that front pattern and the back pattern really did move together or separately.

On a pattern like this, by daylight, there is a lack of sequence, a defiance of law, that is a constant irritant to a normal mind.

The color is hideous enough, and unreliable enough, and infuriating enough, but the pattern is torturing.

You think you have mastered it, but just as you get well under way in following, it turns a back-somersault and there you are. It slaps you in the face, knocks you down, and tramples upon you. It is like a bad dream.

The outside pattern is a florid arabesque,° reminding one of a fungus. If you can imagine a toadstool in joints, an interminable string of toadstools, budding and sprouting in endless convolutions—why, that is something like it.

That is, sometimes!

There is one marked peculiarity about this paper, a thing nobody seems to notice but myself, and that is that it changes as the light changes.

When the sun shoots in through the east window—I always watch for that first long, straight ray—it changes so quickly that I never can quite believe it.

That is why I watch it always.

By moonlight—the moon shines in all night when there is a moon—I wouldn't know it was the same paper.

At night in any kind of light, in twilight, candlelight, lamplight, and worst of all by moonlight, it becomes bars! The outside pattern, I mean, and the woman behind it is as plain as can be.

I didn't realize for a long time what the thing was that showed behind, that dim sub-pattern, but now I am quite sure it is a woman.

By daylight she is subdued, quiet. I fancy it is the pattern that keeps her so still. It is so puzzling. It keeps me quiet by the hour.

I lie down ever so much now. John says it is good for me, and to sleep all I can.

---

arabesque: a type of ornamental style (Arabic in origin) that uses flowers, foliage, fruit, or other figures to create an intricate pattern of interlocking shapes and lines.

Indeed he started the habit by making me lie down for an hour after each meal.
It is a very bad habit, I am convinced, for you see, I don't sleep.
And that cultivates deceit, for I don't tell them I'm awake—oh, no!
The fact is I am getting a little afraid of John.
He seems very queer sometimes, and even Jennie has an inexplicable look.
It strikes me occasionally, just as a scientific hypothesis, that perhaps it is the paper!
I have watched John when he did not know I was looking, and come into the room suddenly on the most innocent excuses, and I've caught him several times *looking at the paper!* And Jennie too. I caught Jennie with her hand on it once.
She didn't know I was in the room, and when I asked her in a quiet, a very quiet voice, with the most restrained manner possible, what she was doing with the paper, she turned around as if she had been caught stealing, and looked quite angry—asked me why I should frighten her so!
Then she said that the paper stained everything it touched, that she had found yellow smooches° on all my clothes and John's and she wished we would be more careful!
Did not that sound innocent? But I know she was studying that pattern, and I am determined that nobody shall find it out but myself!

Life is very much more exciting now than it used to be. You see, I have something more to expect, to look forward to, to watch. I really do eat better, and am more quiet than I was.
John is so pleased to see me improve! He laughed a little the other day, and said I seemed to be flourishing in spite of my wallpaper.
I turned it off with a laugh. I had no intention of telling him it was *because* of the wallpaper—he would make fun of me. He might even want to take me away.
I don't want to leave now until I have found it out. There is a week more, and I think that will be enough.

I'm feeling so much better!
I don't sleep much at night, for it is so interesting to watch developments; but I sleep a good deal during the daytime.
In the daytime it is tiresome and perplexing.
There are always new shoots on the fungus, and new shades of yellow all over it. I cannot keep count of them, though I have tried conscientiously.
It is the strangest yellow, that wallpaper! It makes me think of all the yellow things I ever saw—not beautiful ones like buttercups, but old, foul, bad yellow things.
But there is something else about that paper—the smell! I noticed it the moment we came into the room, but with so much air and sun it was not bad. Now we have had a week of fog and rain, and whether the windows are open or not, the smell is here.
It creeps all over the house.
I find it hovering in the dining-room, skulking in the parlor, hiding in the hall, lying in wait for me on the stairs.
It gets into my hair.

smooches: smudges or smears.

Even when I go to ride, if I turn my head suddenly and surprise it—there is that smell!

Such a peculiar odor, too! I have spent hours in trying to analyze it, to find what it smelled like.

It is not bad—at first—and very gentle, but quite the subtlest, most enduring odor I ever met.

In this damp weather it is awful. I wake up in the night and find it hanging over me.

It used to disturb me at first. I thought seriously of burning the house—to reach the smell.

But now I am used to it. The only thing I can think of that it is like is the *color* of the paper! A yellow smell.

There is a very funny mark on this wall, low down, near the mopboard. A streak that runs round the room. It goes behind every piece of furniture, except the bed, a long, straight, even *smooch,* as if it had been rubbed over and over.

I wonder how it was done and who did it, and what they did it for. Round and round and round—round and round and round—it makes me dizzy!

I really have discovered something at last.

Through watching so much at night, when it changes so, I have finally found out.

The front pattern *does* move—and no wonder! The woman behind shakes it!

Sometimes I think there are a great many women behind, and sometimes only one, and she crawls around fast, and her crawling shakes it all over.

Then in the very bright spots she keeps still, and in the very shady spots she just takes hold of the bars and shakes them hard.

And she is all the time trying to climb through. But nobody could climb through that pattern—it strangles so; I think that is why it has so many heads.

They get through, and then the pattern strangles them off and turns them upside down, and makes their eyes white!

If those heads were covered or taken off it would not be half so bad.

I think that woman gets out in the daytime!

And I'll tell you why—privately—I've seen her!

I can see her out of every one of my windows!

It is the same woman, I know, for she is always creeping, and most women do not creep by daylight.

I see her in that long shaded lane, creeping up and down. I see her in those dark grape arbors, creeping all round the garden.

I see her on that long road under the trees, creeping along, and when a carriage comes she hides under the blackberry vines.

I don't blame her a bit. It must be very humiliating to be caught creeping by daylight!

I always lock the door when I creep by daylight. I can't do it at night, for I know John would suspect something at once.

And John is so queer now that I don't want to irritate him. I wish he would take another room! Besides, I don't want anybody to get that woman out at night but myself.

I often wonder if I could see her out of all the windows at once.

But, turn as fast as I can, I can only see out of one at one time.

And though I always see her, she *may* be able to creep faster than I can turn! I have watched her sometimes away off in the open country, creeping as fast as a cloud shadow in a high wind.

If only that top pattern could be gotten off from the under one! I mean to try it, little by little.

I have found out another funny thing, but I shan't tell it this time! It does not do to trust people too much.

There are only two more days to get this paper off, and I believe John is beginning to notice. I don't like the look in his eyes.

And I heard him ask Jennie a lot of professional questions about me. She had a very good report to give.

She said I slept a good deal in the daytime.

John knows I don't sleep very well at night, for all I'm so quiet!

He asked me all sorts of questions too, and pretended to be very loving and kind. As if I couldn't see through him!

Still, I don't wonder he acts so, sleeping under this paper for three months.

It only interests me, but I feel sure John and Jennie are affected by it.

Hurrah! This is the last day, but it is enough. John is to stay in town over night, and won't be out until this evening.

Jennie wanted to sleep with me—the sly thing; but I told her I should undoubtedly rest better for a night all alone.

That was clever, for really I wasn't alone a bit! As soon as it was moonlight and that poor thing began to crawl and shake the pattern, I got up and ran to help her.

I pulled and she shook. I shook and she pulled, and before morning we had peeled off yards of that paper.

A strip about as high as my head and half around the room.

And then when the sun came and that awful pattern began to laugh at me, I declared I would finish it today!

We go away tomorrow, and they are moving all my furniture down again to leave things as they were before.

Jennie looked at the wall in amazement, but I told her merrily that I did it out of pure spite at the vicious thing.

She laughed and said she wouldn't mind doing it herself, but I must not get tired.

How she betrayed herself that time!

But I am here, and no person touches this paper but me—not *alive!*

She tried to get me out of the room—it was too patent! But I said it was so quiet and empty and clean now that I believed I would lie down again and sleep all I could, and not to wake me even for dinner—I would call when I woke.

So now she is gone, and the servants are gone, and the things are gone, and there is nothing left but that great bedstead nailed down, with the canvas mattress we found on it.

We shall sleep downstairs tonight, and take the boat home tomorrow.

I quite enjoy the room, now it is bare again.

How those children did tear about here!

This bedstead is fairly gnawed!

But I must get to work.

I have locked the door and thrown the key down into the front path.

I don't want to go out, and I don't want to have anybody come in, till John comes.

I want to astonish him.

I've got a rope up here that even Jennie did not find. If that woman does get out, and tries to get away, I can tie her!

But I forgot I could not reach far without anything to stand on!

This bed will *not* move!

I tried to lift and push it until I was lame, and then I got so angry I bit off a little piece at one corner—but it hurt my teeth.

Then I peeled off all the paper I could reach standing on the floor. It sticks horribly and the pattern just enjoys it! All those strangled heads and bulbous eyes and waddling fungus growths just shriek with derision!

I am getting angry enough to do something desperate. To jump out of the window would be admirable exercise, but the bars are too strong even to try.

Besides I wouldn't do it. Of course not. I know well enough that a step like that is improper and might be misconstrued.

I don't like to *look* out of the windows even—there are so many of those creeping women, and they creep so fast.

I wonder if they all come out of that wallpaper as I did!

But I am securely fastened now by my well-hidden rope—you don't get *me* out in the road there!

I suppose I shall have to get back behind the pattern when it comes night, and that is hard!

It is so pleasant to be out in this great room and creep around as I please!

I don't want to go outside. I won't, even if Jennie asks me to.

For outside you have to creep on the ground, and everything is green instead of yellow.

But here I can creep smoothly on the floor, and my shoulder just fits in that long smooch around the wall, so I cannot lose my way.

Why, there's John at the door!

It is no use, young man, you can't open it!

How he does call and pound!

Now he's crying to Jennie for an axe.

It would be a shame to break down that beautiful door!

"John, dear!" said I in the gentlest voice. "The key is down by the front steps, under a plantain leaf!"

That silenced him for a few moments.

Then he said, very quietly indeed, "Open the door, my darling!"

"I can't," said I. "The key is down by the front door under a plantain leaf!" And then I said it again, several times, very gently and slowly, and said it so often that he had to go and see, and he got it of course, and came in. He stopped short by the door.

"What is the matter?" he cried. "For God's sake, what are you doing!"

I kept on creeping just the same, but I looked at him over my shoulder.

"I've got out at last," said I, "in spite of you and Jane. And I've pulled off most of the paper, so you can't put me back!"

Now why should that man have fainted? But he did, and right across my path by the wall, so that I had to creep over him every time!

Questions

1. Several times at the beginning of the story, the narrator says such things as "What is one to do?" and "What can one do?" What do these comments refer to? What, if anything, do they suggest about women's roles at the time the story was written?
2. The narrator says, "I get unreasonably angry with John sometimes" (paragraph 24). How unreasonable is her anger at him? What does the fact that she feels it is unreasonable say about her?
3. What do her changing feelings about the wallpaper tell us about the changes in her condition?
4. "It is so hard to talk with John about my case, because he is so wise, and because he loves me so" (paragraph 122). His wisdom is, to say the least, open to question, but what about his love? Do you think he suffers merely from a failure of perception, or is there a failure of affection as well? Explain your response.
5. Where precisely in the story do you think it becomes clear that she has begun to hallucinate?
6. What does the woman behind the wallpaper represent? Why does the narrator come to identify with her?
7. How ill does the narrator seem at the beginning of the story? How ill does she seem at the end? How do you account for the change in her condition?

David Leavitt

David Leavitt was born in Pittsburgh, Pennsylvania, in 1961. He attended Yale University, where he earned a B.A. in English. At age twenty, while still in college, he published his first story in the New Yorker—*the first fiction published in that journal that presented an openly homosexual protagonist. His first collection,* Family Dancing, *appeared in 1984 and was a finalist for the National Book Critics Award. Leavitt then published two novels,* The Lost Language of Cranes *(1986) and* Equal Affections *(1989). His short story collection* A Place I've Never Been *appeared in 1990, followed by nine more volumes of fiction, most recently* The Indian Clerk *(2007). Leavitt currently teaches at the University of Florida in Gainesville.*

David Leavitt

A Place I've Never Been   1990

I had known Nathan for years—too many years, since we were in college—so when he went to Europe I wasn't sure how I'd survive it; he was my best friend, after all, my constant companion at Sunday afternoon double bills at the Thalia, my ever-present source of consolation and conversation. Still, such a turn can prove to be a blessing in disguise. It threw me off at first, his not being there—I had no one to watch *Jeopardy!* with, or talk to on the phone late at night—but then, gradually, I got over it, and I realized that maybe it was a good thing after all, that maybe now, with Nathan gone, I would be forced to go out into the world more, make new friends, maybe even find a boyfriend. And I had started: I lost weight, I went shopping. I was at Bloomingdale's one day on my lunch hour when a very skinny black woman with a French accent asked me if I'd like to have a makeover. I had always run away from such things, but this time, before I had a chance, this woman put her long hands on my cheeks and looked into my face—not my eyes, my face—and said, "You're really beautiful. You know that?" And I absolutely couldn't answer. After she was through with me I didn't even know what I looked like, but everyone at my office was amazed. "Celia," they said, "you look great. What happened?" I smiled, wondering if I'd be allowed to go back every day for a makeover, if I offered to pay.

There was even some interest from a man—a guy named Roy who works downstairs, in contracts—and I was feeling pretty good about myself again, when the phone rang, and it was Nathan. At first I thought he must have been calling me from some European capital, but he said no, he was back in New York. "Celia," he said, "I have to see you. Something awful has happened."

Hearing those words, I pitched over—I assumed the worst. (And why not? He had been assuming the worst for over a year.) But he said, "No, no, I'm fine. I'm perfectly healthy. It's my apartment. Oh, Celia, it's awful. Could you come over?"

"Were you broken into?" I asked.

"I might as well have been!"

"Okay," I said. "I'll come over after work."

"I just got back last night. This is too much."

"I'll be there by six, Nathan."

"Thank you," he said, a little breathlessly, and hung up.

I drummed my nails—newly painted by another skinny woman at Bloomingdale's—against the black Formica of my desk, mostly to try out the sound. In truth I was a little happy he was back—I had missed him—and not at all surprised that he'd cut his trip short. Rich people are like that, I've observed; because they don't have to buy bargain-basement tickets on weird charter airlines, they feel free to change their minds. Probably he just got bored tooting around Europe, missed his old life, missed *Jeopardy!*, his friends. Oh, Nathan! How could I tell him the Thalia had closed?

I had to take several buses to get from my office to his neighborhood—a route I had once traversed almost daily, but which, since Nathan's departure, I hadn't had much occasion to take. Sitting on the Madison Avenue bus, I looked out the window at the rows of unaffordable shops, some still exactly what they'd been before, others boarded up, or reopened under new auspices—such a familiar panorama, unfolding, block by block, like a Chinese scroll I'd once been shown on a museum trip in junior high school. It was raining a little, and in the warm bus the long, unvarying progress of my love for Nathan seemed to unscroll as well—all the dinners and lunches and arguments, and all the trips back alone to my apartment, feeling ugly and fat, because Nathan had once again confirmed he could never love me the way he assured me he would someday love a man. How many hundreds of times I received that confirmation! And yet, somehow, it never occurred to me to give up that love I had nurtured for him since our earliest time together, that love which belonged to those days just past the brink of childhood, before I understood about Nathan, or rather, before Nathan understood about himself. So I persisted, and Nathan, in spite of his embarrassment at my occasional outbursts, continued to depend on me. I think he hoped that my feeling for him would one day transform itself into a more maternal kind of affection, that I would one day become the sort of woman who could tend to him without expecting anything in return. And that was, perhaps, a reasonable hope on his part, given my behavior. But: "If only," he said to me once, "you didn't have to act so crazy, Celia—" And that was how I realized I had to get out.

I got off the bus and walked the block and a half to his building—its façade, I noted, like almost every façade in the neighborhood, blemished by a bit of scaffolding—and, standing in that vestibule where I'd stood so often, waited for him to buzz me up. I read for diversion the now familiar list of tenants' names. The only difference today was that there were ragged ends of Scotch tape stuck around Nathan's name; probably his subletter had put his own name over Nathan's, and Nathan, returning, had torn the piece of paper off and left the ends of the tape. This didn't seem like him, and it made me suspicious. He was a scrupulous person about such things.

In due time—though slowly, for him—he let me in, and I walked the three flights of stairs to find him standing in the doorway, unshaven, looking as if he'd just gotten out of bed. He wasn't wearing any shoes, and he'd gained some weight. Almost immediately he fell into me—that is the only way to describe it, his big body limp in my arms. "Oh, God," he murmured into my hair, "am I glad to see you."

"Nathan," I said. "Nathan." And held him there. Usually he wriggled out of physical affection; kisses from him were little nips; hugs were tight, jerky chokeholds. Now he lay absolutely still, his arms slung under mine, and I tried to keep from gasping from the weight of him. But finally—reluctantly—he let go, and putting his hand on his forehead, gestured toward the open door. "Prepare yourself," he said. "It's worse than you can imagine."

He led me into the apartment. I have to admit, I was shocked by what I saw. Nathan, unlike me, is a chronically neat person, everything in its place, all his perfect furniture glowing, polished, every state-of-the-art fountain pen and pencil tip-up in the blue glass jar on his desk. Today, however, the place was in havoc—newspapers and old Entenmann's cookie boxes spread over the floor, records piled on top of each other, inner sleeves crumpled behind the radiator, the blue glass jar overturned. The carpet was covered with dark mottlings, and a stench of old cigarette smoke and sweat and urine inhabited the place. "It gets worse," he said. "Look at the kitchen." A thick, yellowing layer of grease encrusted the stovetop. The bathroom was beyond the pale of my descriptive capacity for filth.

"Those bastards," Nathan was saying, shaking his head.

"Hold on to the security deposit," I suggested. "Make them pay for it."

He sat down on the sofa, the arms of which appeared to have been ground with cigarette butts, and shook his head. "There *is* no security deposit," he moaned. "I didn't take one because supposedly Denny was my friend, and this other guy—Hoop, or whatever his name was—he was Denny's friend. And look at this!" From the coffee table he handed me a thick stack of utility and phone bills, all unopened. "The phone's disconnected," he said. "Two of the rent checks have bounced. The landlord's about to evict me. I'm sure my credit rating has gone to hell. Jesus, why'd I do it?" He stood, marched into the corner, then turned again to face me. "You know what? I'm going to call my father. I'm going to have him sic every one of his bastard lawyers on those assholes until they pay."

"Nathan," I reminded, "they're unemployed actors. They're poor."

"Then let them rot in jail!" Nathan screamed. His voice was loud and sharp in my ears. It had been a long time since I'd had to witness another person's misery, a long time since anyone had asked of me what Nathan was now asking of me: to take care, to resolve, to smooth. Nonetheless I rallied my energies. I stood. "Look," I said. "I'm going to go out and buy sponges, Comet, Spic and Span, Fantastik, Windex. Everything. We're going to clean this place up. We're going to wash the sheets and shampoo the rug, we're going to scrub the toilet until it shines. I promise you, by the time you go to sleep tonight, it'll be what it was."

He stood silent in the corner.

"Okay?" I said.

"Okay."

"So you wait here," I said. "I'll be right back."

"Thank you."

I picked up my purse and closed the door, thus, once again, saving him from disaster.

But there were certain things I could not save Nathan from. A year ago, his ex-lover Martin had called him up and told him he had tested positive. This was the secret fact he had to live with every day of his life, the secret fact that had brought him to Xanax and Halcion, Darvon and Valium—all crude efforts to cut the fear firing through his blood, exploding like the tiny viral time bombs he believed were lying in wait, expertly planted. It was the day after he found out that he started talking about clearing out. He had no obligations—he had quit his job a few months before and was just doing free-lance work anyway—and so, he reasoned, what was keeping him in New York? "I need to get away from all this," he said, gesturing frantically at the air. I believe he really thought back then that by running away to somewhere where it was less well known, he might be able to escape the disease. This is something I've noticed: The men act as if they think the power of infection exists in direct proportion to its publicity, that in places far from New York City it can, in effect, be outrun. And who's to say they are wrong, with all this talk about stress and the immune system? In Italy, in the countryside, Nathan seemed to feel he'd feel safer. And probably he was right; he would feel safer. Over there, away from the American cityscape with its streets full of gaunt sufferers, you're able to forget the last ten years, you can remember how old the world is and how there was a time when sex wasn't something likely to kill you.

It should be pointed out that Nathan had no symptoms; he hadn't even had the test for the virus itself. He refused to have it, saying he could think of no reason to give up at least the hope of freedom. Not that this made any difference, of course. The fear itself is a brutal enough enemy.

But he gave up sex. No sex, he said, was safe enough for him. He bought a VCR and began to hoard pornographic videotapes. And I think he was having phone sex too, because once I picked up the phone in his apartment and before I could say hello, a husky-voiced man said, "You stud," and then, when I said "Excuse me?" got flustered-sounding and hung up. Some people would probably count that as sex, but I'm not sure I would.

All the time, meanwhile, he was frenzied. I could never guess what time he'd call—six in the morning, sometimes, he'd drag me from sleep. "I figured you'd still be up," he'd say, which gave me a clue to how he was living. It got so bad that by the time he actually left I felt as if a great burden had been lifted from my shoulders. Not that I didn't miss him, but from that day on my time was, miraculously, my own. Nathan is a terrible correspondent—I don't think he's sent me one postcard or letter in all the time we've known each other—and so for months my only news of him came through the phone. Strangers would call me, Germans, Italians, nervous-sounding young men who spoke bad English, who were staying at the YMCA, who were in New York for the first time and to whom he had given my number. I don't think any of them actually wanted to see me; I think they just wanted me to tell them which bars were good and which subway lines were safe—information I happily dispensed. Of course, there was a time when I would have taken them on the subways, shown them around the bars, but I have thankfully passed out of that phase.

And of course, as sex became more and more a possibility, then a likelihood once again in my life, I began to worry myself about the very things that were torturing Nathan. What should I say, say, to Roy in contracts, when he asked me to sleep with him, which I was fairly sure he was going to do within a lunch or two? Certainly I wanted to sleep with him. But did I dare ask him to use a condom? Did I dare even broach the subject? I was frightened that he might get furious, that he might overreact, and I considered saying nothing, taking my chances. Then again, for me in particular, it was a very big chance to take; I have a pattern of falling in love with men who at some point or other have fallen in love with other men. All trivial, selfish, this line of worry, I recognize now, but at that point Nathan was gone, and I had no one around to remind me of how high the stakes were for other people. I slipped back into a kind of women's-magazine attitude toward the whole thing: for the moment, at least, *I* was safe, and I cherished that safety without even knowing it, I gloried in it. All my speculations were merely matters of prevention; that place where Nathan had been exiled was a place I'd never been. I am ashamed to admit it, but there was even a moment when I took a kind of vengeful pleasure in the whole matter—the years I had hardly slept with anyone, for which I had been taught to feel ashamed and freakish, I now wanted to rub in someone's face: I was right and you were wrong! I wanted to say. I'm not proud of having had such thoughts, and I can only say, in my defense, that they passed quickly—but a strict accounting of all feelings, at this point, seems to me necessary. We have to be rigorous with ourselves these days.

In any case, Nathan was back, and I didn't dare think about myself. I went to the grocery store, I bought every cleaner I could find. And when I got back to the apartment he was still standing where he'd been standing, in the corner. "Nate," I said, "here's everything. Let's get to work."

"Okay," he said glumly, even though he is an ace cleaner, and we began.

As we cleaned, the truth came out. This Denny to whom he'd sublet the apartment, Nathan had had a crush on. "To the extent that a crush is a relevant thing in my life anymore," he said, "since God knows, there's nothing to be done about it. But there you are. The libido doesn't stop, the heart doesn't stop, no matter how hard you try to make them."

None of this—especially that last part—was news to me, though Nathan had managed to overlook that aspect of our relationship for years. I had understood from the beginning about the skipping-over of the security payment, the laxness of the setup, because these were the sorts of things I would have willingly done for Nathan at a different time. I think he was privately so excited at the prospect of this virile young man, Denny, sleeping, and perhaps having sex, between his sheets, that he would have taken any number of risks to assure it. Crush: what an oddly appropriate word, considering what it makes you do to yourself. His apartment was, in a sense, the most Nathan could offer, and probably the most Denny would accept. I understood: You want to get as close as you can, even if it's only at arm's length. And when you come back, maybe, you want to breathe in the smell of the person you love loving someone else.

Europe, he said, had been a failure. He had wandered, having dinner with old friends of his parents, visiting college acquaintances who were busy with exotic lives. He'd gone to bars, which was merely frustrating; there was nothing to be done. "What about safe sex?" I asked, and he said, "Celia, please. There is no such thing, as far as I'm concerned." Once again this started a panicked thumping in my chest as I thought about Roy, and Nathan said, "It's really true. Suppose something lands on you—you know what I'm saying—and there's a microscopic cut in your skin. Bingo."

"Nathan, come on," I said. "That sounds crazy to me."

"Yeah?" he said. "Just wait till some ex-lover of yours calls you up with a little piece of news. Then see how you feel."

He returned to his furious scrubbing of the bathroom sink. I returned to my furious scrubbing of the tub. Somehow, even now, I'm always stuck with the worst of it.

Finally we were done. The place looked okay—it didn't smell anymore—though it was hardly what it had been. Some long-preserved pristineness was gone from the apartment, and both of us knew without saying a word that it would never be restored. We breathed in exhausted—no, not exhausted triumph. It was more like relief. We had beaten something back, yet again.

My hands were red from detergents, my stomach and forehead sweaty. I went into the now-bearable bathroom and washed up, and then Nathan said he would take me out to dinner—my choice. And so we ended up, as we had a thousand other nights, sitting by the window at the Empire Szechuan down the block from his apartment, eating cold noodles with sesame sauce, which, when we had finished them, Nathan ordered more of. "God, how I've missed these," he said, as he scooped the brown slimy noodles into his mouth. "You don't know."

In between slurps he looked at me and said, "You look good, Celia. Have you lost weight?"

"Yes, as a matter of fact," I said.

"I thought so."

I looked back at him, trying to re-create the expression on the French woman's face, and didn't say anything, but as it turned out I didn't need to. "I know what you're thinking," he said, "and you're right. Twelve pounds since you last saw me. But I don't care. I mean, you lose weight when you're sick. At least this way, gaining weight, I know I don't have it."

He continued eating. I looked outside. Past the plate-glass window that separated us from the sidewalk, crowds of people walked, young and old, good-looking and bad-looking, healthy and sick, some of them staring in at our food and our eating. Suddenly—urgently—I wanted to be out among them, I wanted to be walking in that crowd, pushed along in it, and not sitting here, locked into this tiny two-person table with Nathan. And yet I knew that escape was probably impossible. I looked once again at Nathan, eating happily, resigned, perhaps, to the fate of his apartment, and the knowledge that everything would work out, that this had, in fact, been merely a run-of-the-mill crisis. For the moment he was appeased, his hungry anxiety sated; for the moment. But who could guess what would set him off next? I steadied my chin on my palm, drank some water, watched Nathan eat like a happy child.

    The next few weeks were thorny with events. Nathan bought a new sofa, had his place recarpeted, threw several small dinners. Then it was time for Lizzie Fischman's birthday party—one of the few annual events in our lives. We had known Lizzie since college—she was a tragic, trying sort of person, the sort who carries with her a constant aura of fatedness, of doom. So many bad things happen to Lizzie you can't help but wonder, after a while, if she doesn't hold out a beacon for disaster. This year alone, she was in a taxi that got hit by a bus; then she was mugged in the subway by a man who called her an "ugly dyke bitch"; then she started feeling sick all the time, and no one could figure out what was wrong, until it was revealed that her building's heating system was leaking small quantities of carbon monoxide into her awful little apartment. The tenants sued, and in the course of the suit, Lizzie, exposed as an illegal subletter, was evicted. She now lived with her father in one half of a two-family house in Plainfield, New Jersey, because she couldn't find another apartment she could afford. (Her job, incidentally, in addition to being wretchedly low-paying, is one of the dreariest I know of: proofreading accounting textbooks in an office on Forty-second Street.)

    Anyway, each year Lizzie threw a big birthday party for herself in her father's house in Plainfield, and we all went, her friends, because of course we couldn't bear to disappoint her and add ourselves to her roster of worldwide enemies. It was invariably a miserable party—everyone drunk on bourbon, and Lizzie, eager to re-create the slumber parties of her childhood, dancing around in pink pajamas with feet. We were making s'mores over the gas stove—shoving the chocolate bars and the graham crackers onto fondue forks rather than old sticks—and *Beach Blanket Bingo* was playing on the VCR and no one was having a good time, particularly Nathan, who was overdressed in a beige Giorgio Armani linen suit he'd bought in Italy, and was standing in the corner idly pressing his neck, feeling for swollen lymph nodes. Lizzie's circle dwindled each year, as her friends moved on, or found ways to get out of it. This year eight of us had made it to the party, plus a newcomer from Lizzie's office, a very fat girl with very red nails named Dorrie Friedman, who, in spite of her heaviness, was what my mother would have called dainty. She ate a lot, but unless you were observant, you'd never have noticed it. The image of the fat person stuffing food into her face is mythic: I know from experience, when fat you eat slowly, chew methodically, in order not to draw attention to your mouth. Over the course of an hour I watched Dorrie Friedman put away six of those s'mores with a tidiness worthy of Emily Post, I watched her dab her cheek with her napkin after each bite, and I understood: This was shame, but also, in some peculiar way, this was innocence. A state to envy.

    There is a point in Lizzie's parties when she invariably suggests we play Deprivation, a game that had been terribly popular among our crowd in college. The way you play it is you sit in a big circle, and everyone is given ten pennies. (In this case the pennies were unceremoniously taken from a huge bowl that sat on top of Lizzie's mother's refrigerator, and that she had upended on the linoleum floor—no doubt a long-contemplated act of desecration.) You go around the circle, and each person announces something he or she has never done, or a place they've never been—"I've never been to Borneo" is a good example—and then everyone who has been to Borneo is obliged to throw you a penny. Needless to say, especially in college, the game degenerates rather quickly to matters of sex and drugs.

I remembered the first time I ever played Deprivation, my sophomore year, I had been reading Blake's *Songs of Innocence* and *Songs of Experience*. Everything in our lives seemed a question of innocence and experience back then, so this seemed appropriate. There was a tacit assumption among my friends that "experience"—by that term we meant, I think, almost exclusively sex and drugs—was something you strove to get as much of as you could, that innocence, for all the praise it received in literature, was a state so essentially tedious that those of us still stuck in it deserved the childish recompense of shiny new pennies. (None of us, of course, imagining that five years from now the "experiences" we urged on one another might spread a murderous germ, that five years from now some of our friends, still in their youth, would be lost. Youth! You were supposed to sow your wild oats, weren't you? Those of us who didn't—we were the ones who failed, weren't we?)

One problem with Deprivation is that the older you get, the less interesting it becomes; every year, it seemed, my friends had fewer gaps in their lives to confess, and as our embarrassments began to stack up on the positive side, it was what we *had* done that was titillating. Indeed, Nick Walsh, who was to Lizzie what Nathan was to me, complained as the game began, "I can't play this. There's nothing I haven't done." But Lizzie, who has a naive faith in ritual, merely smiled and said, "Oh come on, Nick. No one's done *everything*. For instance, you could say, 'I've never been to Togo,' or 'I've never been made love to simultaneously by twelve Arab boys in a back alley on Mott Street.'"

"Well, Lizzie," Nick said, "it is true that I've never been to Togo." His leering smile surveyed the circle, and of course, there *was* someone there—Gracie Wong, I think—who had, in fact, been to Togo.

The next person in the circle was Nathan. He's never liked this game, but he also plays it more cleverly than anyone. "Hmm," he said, stroking his chin as if there were a beard there, "let's see . . . Ah, I've got it. I've never had sex with anyone in this group." He smiled boldly, and everyone laughed—everyone, that is, except for me and Bill Darlington, and Lizzie herself—all three of us now, for the wretched experiments of our early youth, obliged to throw Nathan a penny.

Next was Dorrie Friedman's turn, which I had been dreading. She sat on the floor, her legs crossed under her, her very fat fingers intertwined, and said, "Hmm . . . Something I've never done. Well—I've never ridden a bicycle."

An awful silence greeted this confession, and then a tinkling sound, like wind chimes, as the pennies flew. "Gee," Dorrie Friedman said, "I won big that time." I couldn't tell if she was genuinely pleased.

And as the game went on, we settled, all of us, into more or less parallel states of innocence and experience, except for Lizzie and Nick, whose piles had rapidly dwindled, and Dorrie Friedman, who, it seemed, by virtue of lifelong fatness, had done nearly nothing. She had never been to Europe; she had never swum; she had never played tennis; she had never skied; she had never been on a boat. Even someone else's turn could be an awful moment for Dorrie, as when Nick said, "I've never had a vaginal orgasm." But fortunately, there, she did throw in her penny. I was relieved; I don't think I could have stood it if she hadn't.

After a while, in an effort not to look at Dorrie and her immense pile of pennies, we all started trying to trip up Lizzie and Nick, whose respective caches of sexual experience seemed limitless. "I've never had sex in my parents' bed," I offered. The pennies flew. "I've never had sex under a dry-docked boat." "I've never had sex with more than one other person." "Two other people." "Three other people." By then Lizzie was out of pennies, and declared the game over.

"I guess I won," Dorrie said rather softly. She had her pennies neatly piled in identically sized stacks.

I wondered if Lizzie was worried. I wondered if she was thinking about the disease, if she was frightened, the way Nathan was, or if she just assumed death was coming anyway, the final blow in her life of unendurable misfortunes. She started to gather the pennies back into their bowl, and I glanced across the room at Nathan, to see if he was ready to go. All through the game, of course, he had been looking pretty miserable—he always looks miserable at parties. Worse, he has a way of turning his misery around, making me responsible for it. Across the circle of our nearest and dearest friends he glared at me angrily, and I knew that by the time we were back in his car and on our way home to Manhattan he would have contrived a way for the evening to be my fault. And yet tonight, his occasional knowing sneers, inviting my complicity in looking down on the party, only enraged me. I was angry at him, in advance, for what I was sure he was going to do in the car, and I was also angry at him for being such a snob, for having no sympathy toward this evening, which, in spite of all its displeasures, was nevertheless an event of some interest, perhaps the very last hurrah of our youth, our own little big chill. And that was something: Up until now I had always assumed Nathan's version of things to be the correct one, and cast my own into the background. Now his perception seemed meager, insufficient: Here was an historic night, after all, and all he seemed to want to think about was his own boredom, his own unhappiness.

Finally, reluctantly, Lizzie let us go, and relinquished from her grip, we got into Nathan's car and headed onto the Garden State Parkway. "Never again," Nathan was saying, "will I allow you to convince me to attend one of Lizzie Fischman's awful parties. This is the last." I didn't even bother answering, it all seemed so predictable. Instead I just settled back into the comfortable velour of the car seat and switched on the radio. Dionne Warwick and Elton John were singing "That's What Friends Are For," and Nathan said, "You know, of course, that that's the song they wrote to raise money for AIDS."

"I'd heard," I said.

"Have you seen the video? It makes me furious. All these famous singers up there, grinning these huge grins, rocking back and forth. Why the hell are they smiling, I'd like to ask?"

For a second, I considered answering that question, then decided I'd better not. We were slipping into the Holland Tunnel, and by the time we got through to Manhattan I was ready to call it a night. I wanted to get back to my apartment and see if Roy had left a message on my answering machine. But Nathan said, "It's Saturday night, Celia, it's still early. Won't you have a drink with me or something?"

"I don't want to go to any more gay bars, Nathan, I told you that."

"So we'll go to a straight bar. I don't care. I just can't bear to go back to my apartment at eleven o'clock." We stopped for a red light, and he leaned closer to me. "The truth is, I don't think I can bear to be alone. Please."

"All right," I said. What else could I say?

"Goody," Nathan said.

We parked the car in a garage and walked to a darkish café on Greenwich Avenue, just a few doors down from the huge gay bar Nathan used to frequent, and which he jokingly referred to as "the airport." No mention was made of that bar in the café, however, where he ordered latte machiato for both of us. "Aren't you going to have some dessert?" he said. "I know I am. Baba au rhum, perhaps. Or tiramisu. You know *tirami su* means 'pick me up,' but if you want to offend an Italian waiter, you say, 'I'll have the *tiramilo su*,' which means 'pick up my dick.'"

"I'm trying to lose weight, Nathan," I said. "Please don't encourage me to eat desserts."

"Sorry." He coughed. Our latte machiatos came, and Nathan raised his cup and said, "Here's to us. Here's to Lizzie Fischman. Here's to never playing that dumb game again as long as we live." These days, I noticed, Nathan used the phrase "as long as we live" a bit too frequently for comfort.

Reluctantly I touched my glass to his. "You know," he said, "I think I've always hated that game. Even in college, when I won, it made me jealous. Everyone else had done so much more than me. Back then I figured I'd have time to explore the sexual world. Guess the joke's on me, huh?"

I shrugged. I wasn't sure.

"What's with you tonight, anyway?" he said. "You're so distant."

"I just have things on my mind, Nathan, that's all."

"You've been acting weird ever since I got back from Europe, Celia. Sometimes I think you don't even want to see me."

Clearly he was expecting reassurances to the contrary. I didn't say anything.

"Well," he said, "is that it? You don't want to see me?"

I twisted my shoulders in confusion. "Nathan—"

"Great," he said, and laughed so that I couldn't tell if he was kidding. "Your best friend for nearly ten years. Jesus."

"Look, Nathan, don't melodramatize," I said. "It's not that simple. It's just that I have to think a little about myself. My own life, my own needs. I mean, I'm going to be thirty soon. You know how long it's been since I've had a boyfriend?"

"I'm not against your having a boyfriend," Nathan said. "Have I ever tried to stop you from having a boyfriend?"

"But, Nathan," I said, "I never get to meet anyone when I'm with you all the time. I love you and I want to be your friend, but you can't expect me to just keep giving and giving and giving my time to you without anything in return. It's not fair."

I was looking away from him as I said this. From the corner of my vision I could see him glancing to the side, his mouth a small, tight line.

"You're all I have," he said quietly.
"That's not true, Nathan," I said.
"Yes, it is true, Celia."
"Nathan, you have lots of other friends."
"But none of them count. No one but you counts."

The waitress arrived with his goblet of tiramisu, put it down in front of him. "Go on with your life, you say," he was muttering. "Find a boyfriend. Don't you think I'd do the same thing if I could? But all those options are closed to me, Celia. There's nowhere for me to go, no route that isn't dangerous. I mean, getting on with my life—I just can't talk about that simply anymore, the way you can." He leaned closer, over the table. "Do you want to know something?" he said. "Every time I see someone I'm attracted to I go into a cold sweat. And I imagine that they're dead, that if I touch them, the part of them I touch will die. Don't you see? It's bad enough to be afraid you might get it. But to be afraid you might give it—and to someone you loved—" He shook his head, put his hand to his forehead.

What could I say to that? What possibly was there to say? I took his hand, suddenly, I squeezed his hand until the edges of his fingers were white. I was remembering how Nathan looked the first time I saw him, in line at a college dining hall, his hands on his hips, his head erect, staring worriedly at the old lady dishing out food, as if he feared she might run out, or not give him enough. I have always loved the boyish hungers—for food, for sex—because they are so perpetual, so faithful in their daily revival, and even though I hadn't met Nathan yet, I think, in my mind, I already understood: I wanted to feed him, to fill him up; I wanted to give him everything.

Across from us, now, two girls were smoking cigarettes and talking about what art was. A man and a woman, in love, intertwined their fingers. Nathan's hand was getting warm and damp in mine, so I let it go, and eventually he blew his nose and lit a cigarette.

"You know," he said after a while, "it's not the sex, really. That's not what I regret missing. It's just that—Do you realize, Celia, I've never been in love? Never once in my life have I actually been in love?" And he looked at me very earnestly, not knowing, not having the slightest idea, that once again he was counting me for nothing.

"Nathan," I said. "Oh, my Nathan." Still, he didn't seem satisfied, and I knew he had been hoping for something better than my limp consolation. He looked away from me, across the café, listening, I suppose, for that wind-chime peal as all the world's pennies flew his way.

Questions

1. Approximately how old are Nathan and Celia? How long have they known one another?
2. What were Celia's original feelings toward Nathan? How have they changed?
3. What has been Celia's self-image? How is she trying to change it?
4. What concerns affect Nathan's self-image? How has he adapted his life as a gay man to reflect those concerns?
5. What does Nathan expect from Celia? What does he give in return?
6. How does the game Deprivation become a symbol in this short story? What does it suggest ironically about Nathan's life?

Sherman Alexie

Sherman Alexie was born in 1966 on the Spokane Indian Reservation in Wellpinit, Washington. Hydrocephalic at birth, he underwent surgery at the age of six months. At first he was expected not to survive; when that prognosis proved wrong, it was predicted, again wrongly, that he would be severely retarded. Alexie attended Gonzaga University in Spokane and graduated from the University of Washington with a degree in American studies. His first book, a collection of poems called The Business of Fancydancing, *appeared in 1991, and he has published prolifically since then, averaging a book a year. He is the author of ten volumes of poetry, as well as three collections of stories—*The Lone Ranger and Tonto Fistfight in Heaven *(1993),* The Toughest Indian in the World *(2000), and* Ten Little Indians *(2003)—and three novels—*Reservation Blues *(1995),* Indian Killer *(1996), and* Flight *(2007).* War Dances, *his 2009 collection of stories and poems, won the 2010 PEN/Faulkner Award. Alexie has also performed frequently as a stand-up comedian; and he co-produced and wrote the 1998 feature film* Smoke Signals, *based on "This Is What It Means to Say Phoenix, Arizona." He lives with his wife and two sons in Seattle, Washington.*

This Is What It Means to Say Phoenix, Arizona   1993

Just after Victor lost his job at the BIA,° he also found out that his father had died of a heart attack in Phoenix, Arizona. Victor hadn't seen his father in a few years, only talked to him on the telephone once or twice, but there still was a genetic pain, which was soon to be pain as real and immediate as a broken bone.

Victor didn't have any money. Who does have money on a reservation, except the cigarette and fireworks salespeople? His father had a savings account waiting to be claimed, but Victor needed to find a way to get to Phoenix. Victor's mother was just as poor as he was, and the rest of his family didn't have any use at all for him. So Victor called the Tribal Council.

"Listen," Victor said. "My father just died. I need some money to get to Phoenix to make arrangements."

"Now, Victor," the council said. "You know we're having a difficult time financially."

"But I thought the council had special funds set aside for stuff like this."

"Now, Victor, we do have some money available for the proper return of tribal members' bodies. But I don't think we have enough to bring your father all the way back from Phoenix."

"Well," Victor said. "It ain't going to cost all that much. He had to be cremated. Things were kind of ugly. He died of a heart attack in his trailer and nobody found him for a week. It was really hot, too. You get the picture."

"Now, Victor, we're sorry for your loss and the circumstances. But we can really only afford to give you one hundred dollars."

BIA: Bureau of Indian Affairs, a federal agency responsible for management of Indian lands and concerns.

"That's not even enough for a plane ticket."

"Well, you might consider driving down to Phoenix."

"I don't have a car. Besides, I was going to drive my father's pickup back up here."

"Now, Victor," the council said. "We're sure there is somebody who could drive you to Phoenix. Or is there somebody who could lend you the rest of the money?"

"You know there ain't nobody around with that kind of money."

"Well, we're sorry, Victor, but that's the best we can do."

Victor accepted the Tribal Council's offer. What else could he do? So he signed the proper papers, picked up his check, and walked over to the Trading Post to cash it.

While Victor stood in line, he watched Thomas Builds-the-Fire standing near the magazine rack, talking to himself. Like he always did. Thomas was a storyteller that nobody wanted to listen to. That's like being a dentist in a town where everybody has false teeth.

Victor and Thomas Builds-the-Fire were the same age, had grown up and played in the dirt together. Ever since Victor could remember, it was Thomas who always had something to say.

Once, when they were seven years old, when Victor's father still lived with the family, Thomas closed his eyes and told Victor this story: "Your father's heart is weak. He is afraid of his own family. He is afraid of you. Late at night he sits in the dark. Watches the television until there's nothing but that white noise. Sometimes he feels like he wants to buy a motorcycle and ride away. He wants to run and hide. He doesn't want to be found."

Thomas Builds-the-Fire had known that Victor's father was going to leave, knew it before anyone. Now Victor stood in the Trading Post with a one-hundred-dollar check in his hand, wondering if Thomas knew that Victor's father was dead, if he knew what was going to happen next.

Just then Thomas looked at Victor, smiled, and walked over to him.

"Victor, I'm sorry about your father," Thomas said.

"How did you know about it?" Victor asked.

"I heard it on the wind. I heard it from the birds. I felt it in the sunlight. Also, your mother was just in here crying."

"Oh," Victor said and looked around the Trading Post. All the other Indians stared, surprised that Victor was even talking to Thomas. Nobody talked to Thomas anymore because he told the same damn stories over and over again. Victor was embarrassed, but he thought that Thomas might be able to help him. Victor felt a sudden need for tradition.

"I can lend you the money you need," Thomas said suddenly. "But you have to take me with you."

"I can't take your money," Victor said. "I mean, I haven't hardly talked to you in years. We're not really friends anymore."

"I didn't say we were friends. I said you had to take me with you."

"Let me think about it."

Victor went home with his one hundred dollars and sat at the kitchen table. He held his head in his hands and thought about Thomas Builds-the-Fire, remembered little details, tears and scars, the bicycle they shared for a summer, so many stories.

Thomas Builds-the-Fire sat on the bicycle, waited in Victor's yard. He was ten years old and skinny. His hair was dirty because it was the Fourth of July.

"Victor," Thomas yelled. "Hurry up. We're going to miss the fireworks."

After a few minutes, Victor ran out of his house, jumped the porch railing, and landed gracefully on the sidewalk.

"And the judges award him a 9.95, the highest score of the summer," Thomas said, clapped, laughed.

"That was perfect, cousin," Victor said. "And it's my turn to ride the bike."

Thomas gave up the bike and they headed for the fairgrounds. It was nearly dark and the fireworks were about to start.

"You know," Thomas said. "It's strange how us Indians celebrate the Fourth of July. It ain't like it was *our* independence everybody was fighting for."

"You think about things too much," Victor said. "It's just supposed to be fun. Maybe Junior will be there."

"Which Junior? Everybody on this reservation is named Junior."

And they both laughed.

The fireworks were small, hardly more than a few bottle rockets and a fountain. But it was enough for two Indian boys. Years later, they would need much more.

Afterwards, sitting in the dark, fighting off mosquitoes, Victor turned to Thomas Builds-the-Fire.

"Hey," Victor said. "Tell me a story."

Thomas closed his eyes and told this story: "There were these two Indian boys who wanted to be warriors. But it was too late to be warriors in the old way. All the horses were gone. So the two Indian boys stole a car and drove to the city. They parked the stolen car in front of the police station and then hitchhiked back home to the reservation. When they got back, all their friends cheered and their parents' eyes shone with pride. *You were very brave*, everybody said to the two Indian boys. *Very brave*."

"Ya-hey," Victor said. "That's a good one. I wish I could be a warrior."

"Me, too," Thomas said.

They went home together in the dark, Thomas on the bike now, Victor on foot. They walked through shadows and light from streetlamps.

"We've come a long ways," Thomas said. "We have outdoor lighting."

"All I need is the stars," Victor said. "And besides, you still think about things too much."

They separated then, each headed for home, both laughing all the way.

Victor sat at his kitchen table. He counted his one hundred dollars again and again. He knew he needed more to make it to Phoenix and back. He knew he needed Thomas Builds-the-Fire. So he put his money in his wallet and opened the front door to find Thomas on the porch.

"Ya-hey, Victor," Thomas said. "I knew you'd call me."

Thomas walked into the living room and sat down on Victor's favorite chair.

"I've got some money saved up," Thomas said. "It's enough to get us down there, but you have to get us back."

"I've got this hundred dollars," Victor said. "And my dad had a savings account I'm going to claim."

"How much in your dad's account?"

"Enough. A few hundred."

"Sounds good. When we leaving?"

*

When they were fifteen and had long since stopped being friends, Victor and Thomas got into a fistfight. That is, Victor was really drunk and beat Thomas up for no reason at all. All the other Indian boys stood around and watched it happen. Junior was there and so were Lester, Seymour, and a lot of others. The beating might have gone on until Thomas was dead if Norma Many Horses hadn't come along and stopped it.

"Hey, you boys," Norma yelled and jumped out of her car. "Leave him alone."

If it had been someone else, even another man, the Indian boys would've just ignored the warnings. But Norma was a warrior. She was powerful. She could have picked up any two of the boys and smashed their skulls together. But worse than that, she would have dragged them all over to some tipi and made them listen to some elder tell a dusty old story.

The Indian boys scattered, and Norma walked over to Thomas and picked him up.

"Hey, little man, are you okay?" she asked.

Thomas gave her a thumbs up.

"Why they always picking on you?"

Thomas shook his head, closed his eyes, but no stories came to him, no words or music. He just wanted to go home, to lie in his bed and let his dreams tell his stories for him.

Thomas Builds-the-Fire and Victor sat next to each other in the airplane, coach section. A tiny white woman had the window seat. She was busy twisting her body into pretzels. She was flexible.

"I have to ask," Thomas said, and Victor closed his eyes in embarrassment.

"Don't," Victor said.

"Excuse me, miss," Thomas asked. "Are you a gymnast or something?"

"There's no something about it," she said. "I was first alternate on the 1980 Olympic team."

"Really?" Thomas asked.

"Really."

"I mean, you used to be a world-class athlete?" Thomas asked.

"My husband still thinks I am."

Thomas Builds-the-Fire smiled. She was a mental gymnast, too. She pulled her leg straight up against her body so that she could've kissed her kneecap.

"I wish I could do that," Thomas said.

Victor was ready to jump out of the plane. Thomas, that crazy Indian storyteller with ratty old braids and broken teeth, was flirting with a beautiful Olympic gymnast. Nobody back home on the reservation would ever believe it.

"Well," the gymnast said. "It's easy. Try it."

Thomas grabbed at his leg and tried to pull it up into the same position as the gymnast. He couldn't even come close, which made Victor and the gymnast laugh.

"Hey," she asked. "You two are Indian, right?"

"Full-blood," Victor said.

"Not me," Thomas said. "I'm half magician on my mother's side and half clown on my father's."

They all laughed.

"What are your names?" she asked.

"Victor and Thomas."

"Mine is Cathy. Pleased to meet you all."

The three of them talked for the duration of the flight. Cathy the gymnast complained about the government, how they screwed the 1980 Olympic team by boycotting.°

"Sounds like you all got a lot in common with Indians," Thomas said.

Nobody laughed.

After the plane landed in Phoenix and they had all found their way to the terminal, Cathy the gymnast smiled and waved good-bye.

"She was really nice," Thomas said.

"Yeah, but everybody talks to everybody on airplanes," Victor said. "It's too bad we can't always be that way."

"You always used to tell me I think too much," Thomas said. "Now it sounds like you do."

"Maybe I caught it from you."

"Yeah."

Thomas and Victor rode in a taxi to the trailer where Victor's father died.

"Listen," Victor said as they stopped in front of the trailer. "I never told you I was sorry for beating you up that time."

"Oh, it was nothing. We were just kids and you were drunk."

"Yeah, but I'm still sorry."

"That's all right."

Victor paid for the taxi and the two of them stood in the hot Phoenix summer. They could smell the trailer.

"This ain't going to be nice," Victor said. "You don't have to go in."

"You're going to need help."

Victor walked to the front door and opened it. The stink rolled out and made them both gag. Victor's father had lain in that trailer for a week in hundred-degree temperatures before anyone found him. And the only reason anyone found him was because of the smell. They needed dental records to identify him. That's exactly what the coroner said. They needed dental records.

"Oh, man," Victor said. "I don't know if I can do this."

"Well, then don't."

"But there might be something valuable in there."

"I thought his money was in the bank."

"It is. I was talking about pictures and letters and stuff like that."

"Oh," Thomas said as he held his breath and followed Victor into the trailer.

When Victor was twelve, he stepped into an underground wasp nest. His foot was caught in the hole, and no matter how hard he struggled, Victor couldn't pull free. He might have died there, stung a thousand times, if Thomas Builds-the-Fire had not come by.

"Run," Thomas yelled and pulled Victor's foot from the hole. They ran then, hard as they ever had, faster than Billy Mills, faster than Jim Thorpe,° faster than the wasps could fly.

---

they screwed the 1980 Olympic team by boycotting: in an international movement led by the United States at the direction of President Jimmy Carter, some sixty nations boycotted the 1980 Summer Olympic Games in Moscow as a protest against the Soviet invasion of Afghanistan in December 1979. *Billy Mills . . . Jim Thorpe*: William Mervin "Billy" Mills (born 1938), a member of the Sioux tribe, won a gold medal in the 10,000-meter run at the 1964 Summer Olympic Games in Tokyo, Japan. Jacobus Franciscus "Jim" Thorpe (1888–1953), of the Sac and Fox tribe, is widely regarded as one of the greatest American athletes of the twentieth century; he won gold medals in the pentathlon and decathlon at the 1912 Summer Olympic Games in Stockholm, Sweden. He also played professional football, baseball, and basketball.

Victor and Thomas ran until they couldn't breathe, ran until it was cold and dark outside, ran until they were lost and it took hours to find their way home. All the way back, Victor counted his stings.

"Seven," Victor said. "My lucky number."

Victor didn't find much to keep in the trailer. Only a photo album and a stereo. Everything else had that smell stuck in it or was useless anyway.

"I guess this is all," Victor said. "It ain't much."

"Better than nothing," Thomas said.

"Yeah, and I do have the pickup."

"Yeah," Thomas said. "It's in good shape."

"Dad was good about that stuff."

"Yeah, I remember your dad."

"Really?" Victor asked. "What do you remember?"

Thomas Builds-the-Fire closed his eyes and told this story: "I remember when I had this dream that told me to go to Spokane, to stand by the Falls in the middle of the city and wait for a sign. I knew I had to go there but I didn't have a car. Didn't have a license. I was only thirteen. So I walked all the way, took me all day, and I finally made it to the Falls. I stood there for an hour waiting. Then your dad came walking up. *What the hell are you doing here?* he asked me. I said, *Waiting for a vision.* Then your father said, *All you're going to get here is mugged.* So he drove me over to Denny's, bought me dinner, and then drove me home to the reservation. For a long time I was mad because I thought my dreams had lied to me. But they didn't. Your dad was my vision. *Take care of each other* is what my dreams were saying. *Take care of each other.*"

Victor was quiet for a long time. He searched his mind for memories of his father, found the good ones, found a few bad ones, added it all up, and smiled.

"My father never told me about finding you in Spokane," Victor said.

"He said he wouldn't tell anybody. Didn't want me to get in trouble. But he said I had to watch out for you as part of the deal."

"Really?"

"Really. Your father said you would need the help. He was right."

"That's why you came down here with me, isn't it?" Victor asked.

"I came because of your father."

Victor and Thomas climbed into the pickup, drove over to the bank, and claimed the three hundred dollars in the savings account.

Thomas Builds-the-Fire could fly.

Once, he jumped off the roof of the tribal school and flapped his arms like a crazy eagle. And he flew. For a second, he hovered, suspended above all the other Indian boys who were too smart or too scared to jump.

"He's flying," Junior yelled, and Seymour was busy looking for the trick wires or mirrors. But it was real. As real as the dirt when Thomas lost altitude and crashed to the ground.

He broke his arm in two places.

"He broke his wing," Victor chanted, and the other Indian boys joined in, made it a tribal song.

"He broke his wing, he broke his wing, he broke his wing," all the Indian boys chanted as they ran off, flapping their wings, wishing they could fly, too. They hated

Thomas for his courage, his brief moment as a bird. Everybody has dreams about flying. Thomas flew.

One of his dreams came true for just a second, just enough to make it real.

Victor's father, his ashes, fit in one wooden box with enough left over to fill a cardboard box.

"He always was a big man," Thomas said.

Victor carried part of his father and Thomas carried the rest out to the pickup. They set him down carefully behind the seats, put a cowboy hat on the wooden box and a Dodgers cap on the cardboard box. That's the way it was supposed to be.

"Ready to head back home," Victor asked.

"It's going to be a long drive."

"Yeah, take a couple days, maybe."

"We can take turns," Thomas said.

"Okay," Victor said, but they didn't take turns. Victor drove for sixteen hours straight north, made it halfway up Nevada toward home before he finally pulled over.

"Hey, Thomas," Victor said. "You got to drive for a while."

"Okay."

Thomas Builds-the-Fire slid behind the wheel and started off down the road. All through Nevada, Thomas and Victor had been amazed at the lack of animal life, at the absence of water, of movement.

"Where is everything?" Victor had asked more than once.

Now when Thomas was finally driving they saw the first animal, maybe the only animal in Nevada. It was a long-eared jackrabbit.

"Look," Victor yelled. "It's alive."

Thomas and Victor were busy congratulating themselves on their discovery when the jackrabbit darted out into the road and under the wheels of the pickup.

"Stop the goddamn car," Victor yelled, and Thomas did stop, backed the pickup to the dead jackrabbit.

"Oh, man, he's dead," Victor said as he looked at the squashed animal.

"Really dead."

"The only thing alive in this whole state and we just killed it."

"I don't know," Thomas said. "I think it was suicide."

Victor looked around the desert, sniffed the air, felt the emptiness and loneliness, and nodded his head.

"Yeah," Victor said. "It had to be suicide."

"I can't believe this," Thomas said. "You drive for a thousand miles and there ain't even any bugs smashed on the windshield. I drive for ten seconds and kill the only living thing in Nevada."

"Yeah," Victor said. "Maybe I should drive."

"Maybe you should."

Thomas Builds-the-Fire walked through the corridors of the tribal school by himself. Nobody wanted to be anywhere near him because of all those stories. Story after story.

Thomas closed his eyes and this story came to him: "We are all given one thing by which our lives are measured, one determination. Mine are the stories which can change or not change the world. It doesn't matter which as long as I continue to tell the stories. My father, he died on Okinawa in World War II, died fighting for this country, which had tried to kill him for years. My mother, she died giving birth to me, died while I was still inside her. She pushed me out into the world with her last breath. I have no brothers or sisters. I have only my stories which came to me before I even had the words to speak. I learned a thousand stories before I took my first thousand steps. They are all I have. It's all I can do."

Thomas Builds-the-Fire told his stories to all those who would stop and listen. He kept telling them long after people had stopped listening.

Victor and Thomas made it back to the reservation just as the sun was rising. It was the beginning of a new day on earth, but the same old shit on the reservation.

"Good morning," Thomas said.

"Good morning."

The tribe was waking up, ready for work, eating breakfast, reading the newspaper, just like everybody else does. Willene LeBret was out in her garden wearing a bathrobe. She waved when Thomas and Victor drove by.

"Crazy Indians made it," she said to herself and went back to her roses.

Victor stopped the pickup in front of Thomas Builds-the-Fire's HUD house.° They both yawned, stretched a little, shook dust from their bodies.

"I'm tired," Victor said.

"Of everything," Thomas added.

They both searched for words to end the journey. Victor needed to thank Thomas for his help, for the money, and make the promise to pay it all back.

"Don't worry about the money," Thomas said. "It don't make any difference anyhow."

"Probably not, enit?"

"Nope."

Victor knew that Thomas would remain the crazy storyteller who talked to dogs and cars, who listened to the wind and pine trees. Victor knew that he couldn't really be friends with Thomas, even after all that had happened. It was cruel but it was real. As real as the ashes, as Victor's father, sitting behind the seats.

"I know how it is," Thomas said. "I know you ain't going to treat me any better than you did before. I know your friends would give you too much shit about it."

Victor was ashamed of himself. Whatever happened to the tribal ties, the sense of community? The only real thing he shared with anybody was a bottle and broken dreams. He owed Thomas something, anything.

"Listen," Victor said and handed Thomas the cardboard box which contained half of his father. "I want you to have this."

Thomas took the ashes and smiled, closed his eyes, and told this story: "I'm going to travel to Spokane Falls one last time and toss these ashes into the water. And your father will rise like a salmon, leap over the bridge, over me, and find his way home. It will be beautiful. His teeth will shine like silver, like a rainbow. He will rise, Victor, he will rise."

Victor smiled.

"I was planning on doing the same thing with my half," Victor said. "But I didn't imagine my father looking anything like a salmon. I thought it'd be like cleaning the attic or something. Like letting things go after they've stopped having any use."

HUD house: housing subsidized by the U.S. Department of Housing and Urban Development.

"Nothing stops, cousin," Thomas said. "Nothing stops."

Thomas Builds-the-Fire got out of the pickup and walked up his driveway. Victor started the pickup and began the drive home.

"Wait," Thomas yelled suddenly from his porch. "I just got to ask one favor."

Victor stopped the pickup, leaned out the window, and shouted back. "What do you want?"

"Just one time when I'm telling a story somewhere, why don't you stop and listen?" Thomas asked.

"Just once?"

"Just once."

Victor waved his arms to let Thomas know that the deal was good. It was a fair trade, and that was all Victor had ever wanted from his whole life. So Victor drove his father's pickup toward home while Thomas went into his house, closed the door behind him, and heard a new story come to him in the silence afterwards.

Questions

1. How would you describe the two main characters in this story, Victor and Thomas?
2. What details does Alexie provide to give the reader a sense of life on the reservation?
3. How would you describe the tone of the narration? What is the role of humor in this story?
4. Why is Victor so impatient with Thomas's stories? Why don't people want to hear them?
5. What is the significance of the encounter Thomas had at age thirteen with Victor's father?
6. What is Thomas's role—not just in the events of this story, but in his community? Does Victor recognize this role?
7. How does Victor change in the course of the story? What has he discovered about himself and his family?

Suggestions for Writing on *Stories about Becoming an Individual*

1. In each of these stories, the main character has the opportunity to achieve a moment of self-realization or transformation. Some make more of that opportunity than others. Pick a character (for example, Celia in "A Place I've Never Been" or Victor in "This Is What It Means to Say Phoenix, Arizona") and make a case for why she or he has—or has not—changed significantly by the end of the story.
2. All of these stories feature a character who is somehow at a disadvantage or is treated poorly by the other characters. (Think of Celia in "A Place I've Never Been," Thomas in "This Is What It Means to Say Phoenix, Arizona," and the narrator in "The Yellow Wallpaper.") Yet each of them also seems to understand or relate to the world around them in a fuller way than the people they interact with. Analyze one of these characters and discuss how his or her "outsider" status provides an unusual perspective on the world.

3. "The Yellow Wallpaper" is cast in the form of a journal written by its central character. Consider how the use of this narrative device enriches—or impoverishes—the story.
4. Discuss the larger implications of the conclusion of "The Yellow Wallpaper." In the end, has the narrator triumphed by escaping her oppression, or has she been crushed by it?
5. Re-tell one of the stories in this section from a different character's point of view. Possible choices are John in "The Yellow Wallpaper," Nathan in "A Place I've Never Been," and Thomas in "This Is What It Means to Say Phoenix, Arizona." How will the story differ when told from this other person's viewpoint?
6. Write an essay describing a key moment or event in your life that caused you to see the world (or your life, or your loved ones, or your community) in a different way. How did this knowledge change you and influence how you live today?

PERSONAL CHANGE

John Steinbeck	*The Chrysanthemums*
Raymond Carver	*Cathedral*
Jhumpa Lahiri	*Interpreter of Maladies*

Unhappiness is often the root of change. Trapped in an unfulfilling relationship or a dead-end job, we might be moved to alter our circumstances. Sometimes it takes a drastic event before we finally act; at other times the gradual buildup of discontent pushes us to a breaking point. In still other situations, even when we know the cause of our unhappiness, it may seem too risky or daunting to do anything about it. But finding yourself in a bad situation isn't always a negative thing. When everything is going well, we are less likely to address the nagging issues in our lives. Occasionally, the glimpse of an unexpected joy will lead us forward toward a new and better life. "Follow your bliss," as Joseph Campbell said in *The Power of Myth*. But for many of us, it is unhappiness that serves as the catalyst to our making necessary changes. The three writers in this section all describe characters who try to make personal changes and achieve varied results. John Steinbeck shows us how a chance visit from a stranger affects a woman's view of herself and her marriage; Raymond Carver writes about an initially suspicious, insecure man's opening up to the possibility of enlightenment; and Jhumpa Lahiri presents a young Indian American couple visiting India, who find they are out of touch with both their country of origin and each other.

John Steinbeck

John Steinbeck (1902–1968) was born in Salinas, California, in the fertile valley he remembers in "The Chrysanthemums." Off and on, he attended Stanford University, then sojourned in New York as a reporter and a bricklayer. After years of struggle to earn his living by fiction, Steinbeck reached a large audience with Tortilla Flat (1935), a loosely woven novel portraying Mexican Americans in Monterey with fondness and sympathy. Great acclaim greeted The Grapes of Wrath (1939), the story of a family of Oklahoma farmers who, ruined by dust storms in the 1930s, join a mass migration to California. In 1962 he became the seventh American to win the Nobel Prize in Literature, but critics have never placed Steinbeck on the same high shelf as Faulkner and Hemingway. He wrote much, not all good, and yet his best work adds up to an impressive total. Besides The Grapes of Wrath, it includes In Dubious Battle (1936), a novel of an apple-pickers' strike; Of Mice and Men (1937), a powerful short novel of comradeship between a hobo and a retarded man; and the short stories in The Long Valley (1938). Throughout the fiction he wrote in his prime, Steinbeck maintains an appealing sympathy for the poor and downtrodden, the lonely and dispossessed.

The Chrysanthemums   1938

    The high grey-flannel fog of winter closed off the Salinas Valley° from the sky and from all the rest of the world. On every side it sat like a lid on the mountains and made of the great valley a closed pot. On the broad, level land floor the gang plows bit deep and left the black earth shining like metal where the shares had cut. On the foothill ranches across the Salinas River, the yellow stubble fields seemed to be bathed in pale cold sunshine, but there was no sunshine in the valley now in December. The thick willow scrub along the river flamed with sharp and positive yellow leaves.

    It was a time of quiet and of waiting. The air was cold and tender. A light wind blew up from the southwest so that the farmers were mildly hopeful of a good rain before long; but fog and rain do not go together.

    Across the river, on Henry Allen's foothill ranch there was little work to be done, for the hay was cut and stored and the orchards were plowed up to receive the rain deeply when it should come. The cattle on the higher slopes were becoming shaggy and rough-coated.

    Elisa Allen, working in her flower garden, looked down across the yard and saw Henry, her husband, talking to two men in business suits. The three of them stood by the tractor shed, each man with one foot on the side of the little Fordson. They smoked cigarettes and studied the machine as they talked.

    Elisa watched them for a moment and then went back to her work. She was thirty-five. Her face was lean and strong and her eyes were as clear as water. Her figure looked blocked and heavy in her gardening costume, a man's black hat pulled low down over her eyes, clodhopper shoes, a figured print dress almost completely covered by a big corduroy apron with four big pockets to hold the snips, the trowel and scratcher, the seeds and the knife she worked with. She wore heavy leather gloves to protect her hands while she worked.

    She was cutting down the old year's chrysanthemum stalks with a pair of short and powerful scissors. She looked down toward the men by the tractor shed now and then. Her face was eager and mature and handsome; even her work with the scissors was over-eager, over-powerful. The chrysanthemum stems seemed too small and easy for her energy.

    She brushed a cloud of hair out of her eyes with the back of her glove, and left a smudge of earth on her cheek in doing it. Behind her stood the neat white farm house with red geraniums close-banked around it as high as the windows. It was a hard-swept looking little house with hard-polished windows, and a clean mud-mat on the front steps.

    Elisa cast another glance toward the tractor shed. The strangers were getting into their Ford coupe. She took off a glove and put her strong fingers down into the forest of new green chrysanthemum sprouts that were growing around the old roots. She spread the leaves and looked down among the close-growing stems. No aphids were there, no sowbugs or snails or cutworms. Her terrier fingers destroyed such pests before they could get started.

    Elisa started at the sound of her husband's voice. He had come near quietly, and he leaned over the wire fence that protected her flower garden from cattle and dogs and chickens.

    "At it again," he said. "You've got a strong new crop coming."

Salinas Valley: south of San Francisco in the Coast Ranges region of California.

Elisa straightened her back and pulled on the gardening glove again. "Yes. They'll be strong this coming year." In her tone and on her face there was a little smugness.

"You've got a gift with things," Henry observed. "Some of those yellow chrysanthemums you had this year were ten inches across. I wish you'd work out in the orchard and raise some apples that big."

Her eyes sharpened. "Maybe I could do it, too. I've a gift with things, all right. My mother had it. She could stick anything in the ground and make it grow. She said it was having planters' hands that knew how to do it."

"Well, it sure works with flowers," he said.

"Henry, who were those men you were talking to?"

"Why, sure, that's what I came to tell you. They were from the Western Meat Company. I sold those thirty head of three-year-old steers. Got nearly my own price, too."

"Good," she said. "Good for you."

"And I thought," he continued, "I thought how it's Saturday afternoon, and we might go into Salinas for dinner at a restaurant, and then to a picture show—to celebrate, you see."

"Good," she repeated. "Oh, yes. That will be good."

Henry put on his joking tone. "There's fights tonight. How'd you like to go to the fights?"

"Oh, no," she said breathlessly. "No, I wouldn't like fights."

"Just fooling, Elisa. We'll go to a movie. Let's see. It's two now. I'm going to take Scotty and bring down those steers from the hill. It'll take us maybe two hours. We'll go in town about five and have dinner at the Cominos Hotel. Like that?"

"Of course I'll like it. It's good to eat away from home."

"All right, then. I'll go get up a couple of horses."

She said, "I'll have plenty of time to transplant some of these sets, I guess."

She heard her husband calling Scotty down by the barn. And a little later she saw the two men ride up the pale yellow hillside in search of the steers.

There was a little square sandy bed kept for rooting the chrysanthemums. With her trowel she turned the soil over and over, and smoothed it and patted it firm. Then she dug ten parallel trenches to receive the sets. Back at the chrysanthemum bed she pulled out the little crisp shoots, trimmed off the leaves of each one with her scissors and laid it on a small orderly pile.

A squeak of wheels and plod of hoofs came from the road. Elisa looked up. The country road ran along the dense bank of willows and cottonwoods that bordered the river, and up this road came a curious vehicle, curiously drawn. It was an old spring-wagon, with a round canvas top on it like the cover of a prairie schooner. It was drawn by an old bay horse and a little grey-and-white burro. A big stubble-bearded man sat between the cover flaps and drove the crawling team. Underneath the wagon, between the hind wheels, a lean and rangy mongrel dog walked sedately. Words were painted on the canvas, in clumsy, crooked letters. "Pots, pans, knives, sisors, lawn mores, Fixed." Two rows of articles, and the triumphantly definitive "Fixed" below. The black paint had run down in little sharp points beneath each letter.

Elisa, squatting on the ground, watched to see the crazy, loose-jointed wagon pass by. But it didn't pass. It turned into the farm road in front of her house, crooked old wheels skirling and squeaking. The rangy dog darted from between the wheels and ran ahead. Instantly the two ranch shepherds flew out at him. Then all three stopped, and with stiff and quivering tails, with taut straight legs, with ambassadorial dignity, they slowly circled, sniffing daintily. The caravan pulled up to Elisa's wire fence and stopped. Now the newcomer dog, feeling out-numbered, lowered his tail and retired under the wagon with raised hackles and bared teeth.

The man on the wagon seat called out, "That's a bad dog in a fight when he gets started."

Elisa laughed. "I see he is. How soon does he generally get started?"

The man caught up her laughter and echoed it heartily. "Sometimes not for weeks and weeks," he said. He climbed stiffly down, over the wheel. The horse and the donkey drooped like unwatered flowers.

Elisa saw that he was a very big man. Although his hair and beard were greying, he did not look old. His worn black suit was wrinkled and spotted with grease. The laughter had disappeared from his face and eyes the moment his laughing voice ceased. His eyes were dark, and they were full of the brooding that gets in the eyes of teamsters and of sailors. The calloused hands he rested on the wire fence were cracked, and every crack was a black line. He took off his battered hat.

"I'm off my general road, ma'am," he said. "Does this dirt road cut over across the river to the Los Angeles highway?"

Elisa stood up and shoved the thick scissors in her apron pocket. "Well, yes, it does, but it winds around and then fords the river. I don't think your team could pull through the sand."

He replied with some asperity, "It might surprise you what them beasts can pull through."

"When they get started?" she asked.

He smiled for a second. "Yes. When they get started."

"Well," said Elisa, "I think you'll save time if you go back to the Salinas road and pick up the highway there."

He drew a big finger down the chicken wire and made it sing. "I ain't in any hurry, ma'am. I go from Seattle to San Diego and back every year. Takes all my time. About six months each way. I aim to follow nice weather."

Elisa took off her gloves and stuffed them in the apron pocket with the scissors. She touched the under edge of her man's hat, searching for fugitive hairs. "That sounds like a nice kind of a way to live," she said.

He leaned confidentially over the fence. "Maybe you noticed the writing on my wagon. I mend pots and sharpen knives and scissors. You got any of them things to do?"

"Oh, no," she said quickly. "Nothing like that." Her eyes hardened with resistance.

"Scissors is the worst thing," he explained. "Most people just ruin scissors trying to sharpen 'em, but I know how. I got a special tool. It's a little bobbit kind of thing, and patented. But it sure does the trick."

"No. My scissors are all sharp."

"All right, then. Take a pot," he continued earnestly, "a bent pot, or a pot with a hole. I can make it like new so you don't have to buy no new ones. That's a saving for you."

"No," she said shortly. "I tell you I have nothing like that for you to do."

His face fell to an exaggerated sadness. His voice took on a whining undertone. "I ain't had a thing to do today. Maybe I won't have no supper tonight. You see I'm off my regular road. I know folks on the highway clear from Seattle to San Diego. They save their things for me to sharpen up because they know I do it so good and save them money."

"I'm sorry," Elisa said irritably. "I haven't anything for you to do."

His eyes left her face and fell to searching the ground. They roamed about until they came to the chrysanthemum bed where she had been working. "What's them plants, ma'am?"

The irritation and resistance melted from Elisa's face. "Oh, those are chrysanthemums, giant whites and yellows. I raise them every year, bigger than anybody around here."

"Kind of a long-stemmed flower? Looks like a quick puff of colored smoke?" he asked.

"That's it. What a nice way to describe them."

"They smell kind of nasty till you get used to them," he said.

"It's a good bitter smell," she retorted, "not nasty at all."

He changed his tone quickly. "I like the smell myself."

"I had ten-inch blooms this year," she said.

The man leaned farther over the fence. "Look. I know a lady down the road a piece, has got the nicest garden you ever seen. Got nearly every kind of flower but no chrysanthemums. Last time I was mending a copper-bottom washtub for her (that's a hard job but I do it good), she said to me, 'If you ever run acrost some nice chrysanthemums I wish you'd try to get me a few seeds.' That's what she told me."

Elisa's eyes grew alert and eager. "She couldn't have known much about chrysanthemums. You *can* raise them from seed, but it's much easier to root the little sprouts you see there."

"Oh," he said. "I s'pose I can't take none to her, then."

"Why yes you can," Elisa cried. "I can put some in damp sand, and you can carry them right along with you. They'll take root in the pot if you keep them damp. And then she can transplant them."

"She'd sure like to have some, ma'am. You say they're nice ones?"

"Beautiful," she said. "Oh, beautiful." Her eyes shone. She tore off the battered hat and shook out her dark pretty hair. "I'll put them in a flower pot, and you can take them right with you. Come into the yard."

While the man came through the picket gate Elisa ran excitedly along the geranium-bordered path to the back of the house. And she returned carrying a big red flower pot. The gloves were forgotten now. She kneeled on the ground by the starting bed and dug up the sandy soil with her fingers and scooped it into the bright new flower pot. Then she picked up the little pile of shoots she had prepared. With her strong fingers she pressed them in the sand and tamped around them with her knuckles. The man stood over her. "I'll tell you what to do," she said. "You remember so you can tell the lady."

"Yes, I'll try to remember."

"Well, look. These will take root in about a month. Then she must set them out, about a foot apart in good rich earth like this, see?" She lifted a handful of dark soil for him to look at. "They'll grow fast and tall. Now remember this: In July tell her to cut them down, about eight inches from the ground."

"Before they bloom?" he asked.

"Yes, before they bloom." Her face was tight with eagerness. "They'll grow right up again. About the last of September the buds will start."

She stopped and seemed perplexed. "It's the budding that takes the most care," she said hesitantly. "I don't know how to tell you." She looked deep into his eyes, searchingly. Her mouth opened a little, and she seemed to be listening. "I'll try to tell you," she said. "Did you ever hear of planting hands?"

"Can't say I have, ma'am."

"Well, I can only tell you what it feels like. It's when you're picking off the buds you don't want. Everything goes right down into your fingertips. You watch your fingers work. They do it themselves. You can feel how it is. They pick and pick the buds. They never make a mistake. They're with the plant. Do you see? Your fingers and the plant. You can feel that, right up your arm. They know. They never make a mistake. You can feel it. When you're like that you can't do anything wrong. Do you see that? Can you understand that?"

She was kneeling on the ground looking up at him. Her breast swelled passionately.

The man's eyes narrowed. He looked away self-consciously. "Maybe I know," he said. "Sometimes in the night in the wagon there—"

Elisa's voice grew husky. She broke in on him, "I've never lived as you do, but I know what you mean. When the night is dark—why, the stars are sharp-pointed, and there's quiet. Why, you rise up and up! Every pointed star gets driven into your body. It's like that. Hot and sharp and—lovely."

Kneeling there, her hand went out toward his legs in the greasy black trousers. Her hesitant fingers almost touched the cloth. Then her hand dropped to the ground. She crouched low like a fawning dog.

He said, "It's nice, just like you say. Only when you don't have no dinner, it ain't."

She stood up then, very straight, and her face was ashamed. She held the flower pot out to him and placed it gently in his arms. "Here. Put it in your wagon, on the seat, where you can watch it. Maybe I can find something for you to do."

At the back of the house she dug in the can pile and found two old and battered aluminum saucepans. She carried them back and gave them to him. "Here, maybe you can fix these."

His manner changed. He became professional. "Good as new I can fix them." At the back of his wagon he set a little anvil, and out of an oily tool box dug a small machine hammer. Elisa came through the gate to watch him while he pounded out the dents in the kettles. His mouth grew sure and knowing. At a difficult part of the work he sucked his under-lip.

"You sleep right in the wagon?" Elisa asked.

"Right in the wagon, ma'am. Rain or shine I'm dry as a cow in there."

"It must be nice," she said. "It must be very nice. I wish women could do such things."

"It ain't the right kind of a life for a woman."

Her upper lip raised a little, showing her teeth. "How do you know? How can you tell?" she said.

"I don't know, ma'am," he protested. "Of course I don't know. Now here's your kettles, done. You don't have to buy no new ones."

"How much?"

"Oh, fifty cents'll do. I keep my prices down and my work good. That's why I have all them satisfied customers up and down the highway."

Elisa brought him a fifty-cent piece from the house and dropped it in his hand. "You might be surprised to have a rival some time. I can sharpen scissors, too. And I can beat the dents out of little pots. I could show you what a woman might do."

He put his hammer back in the oily box and shoved the little anvil out of sight. "It would be a lonely life for a woman, ma'am, and a scary life, too, with animals creeping under the wagon all night." He climbed over the singletree, steadying himself with a hand on the burro's white rump. He settled himself in the seat, picked up the lines. "Thank you kindly, ma'am," he said. "I'll do like you told me; I'll go back and catch the Salinas road."

"Mind," she called, "if you're long in getting there, keep the sand damp."

"Sand, ma'am? . . . Sand? Oh, sure. You mean around the chrysanthemums. Sure I will." He clucked his tongue. The beasts leaned luxuriously into their collars. The mongrel dog took his place between the back wheels. The wagon turned and crawled out the entrance road and back the way it had come, along the river.

Elisa stood in front of her wire fence watching the slow progress of the caravan. Her shoulders were straight, her head thrown back, her eyes half-closed, so that the scene came vaguely into them. Her lips moved silently, forming the words "Good-bye—good-bye." Then she whispered, "That's a bright direction. There's a glowing there." The sound of her whisper startled her. She shook herself free and looked about to see whether anyone had been listening. Only the dogs had heard. They lifted their heads toward her from their sleeping in the dust, and then stretched out their chins and settled asleep again. Elisa turned and ran hurriedly into the house.

In the kitchen she reached behind the stove and felt the water tank. It was full of hot water from the noonday cooking. In the bathroom she tore off her soiled clothes and flung them into the corner. And then she scrubbed herself with a little block of pumice, legs and thighs, loins and chest and arms, until her skin was scratched and red. When she had dried herself she stood in front of a mirror in her bedroom and looked at her body. She tightened her stomach and threw out her chest. She turned and looked over her shoulder at her back.

After a while she began to dress, slowly. She put on her newest underclothing and her nicest stockings and the dress which was the symbol of her prettiness. She worked carefully on her hair, penciled her eyebrows and rouged her lips.

Before she was finished she heard the little thunder of hoofs and the shouts of Henry and his helper as they drove the red steers into the corral. She heard the gate bang shut and set herself for Henry's arrival.

His step sounded on the porch. He entered the house calling, "Elisa, where are you?"

"In my room, dressing. I'm not ready. There's hot water for your bath. Hurry up. It's getting late."

When she heard him splashing in the tub, Elisa laid his dark suit on the bed, and shirt and socks and tie beside it. She stood his polished shoes on the floor beside the bed. Then she went to the porch and sat primly and stiffly down. She looked toward the river road where the willow-line was still yellow with frosted leaves so that under the high grey fog they seemed a thin band of sunshine. This was the only color in the grey afternoon. She sat unmoving for a long time. Her eyes blinked rarely.

Henry came banging out of the door, shoving his tie inside his vest as he came. Elisa stiffened and her face grew tight. Henry stopped short and looked at her. "Why—why, Elisa. You look so nice!"

"Nice? You think I look nice? What do you mean by 'nice'?"

Henry blundered on. "I don't know. I mean you look different, strong and happy."

"I am strong? Yes, strong. What do you mean 'strong'?"

He looked bewildered. "You're playing some kind of a game," he said helplessly. "It's a kind of a play. You look strong enough to break a calf over your knee, happy enough to eat it like a watermelon."

For a second she lost her rigidity. "Henry! Don't talk like that. You didn't know what you said." She grew complete again. "I'm strong," she boasted. "I never knew before how strong."

Henry looked down toward the tractor shed, and when he brought his eyes back to her, they were his own again. "I'll get out the car. You can put on your coat while I'm starting."

Elisa went into the house. She heard him drive to the gate and idle down his motor, and then she took a long time to put on her hat. She pulled it here and pressed it there. When Henry turned the motor off she slipped into her coat and went out.

The little roadster bounced along on the dirt road by the river, raising the birds and driving the rabbits into the brush. Two cranes flapped heavily over the willow-line and dropped into the river-bed.

Far ahead on the road Elisa saw a dark speck. She knew.

She tried not to look as they passed it, but her eyes would not obey. She whispered to herself sadly, "He might have thrown them off the road. That wouldn't have been much trouble, not very much. But he kept the pot," she explained. "He had to keep the pot. That's why he couldn't get them off the road."

The roadster turned a bend and she saw the caravan ahead. She swung full around toward her husband so she could not see the little covered wagon and the mismatched team as the car passed them.

In a moment it was over. The thing was done. She did not look back.

She said loudly, to be heard above the motor, "It will be good, tonight, a good dinner."

"Now you're changed again," Henry complained. He took one hand from the wheel and patted her knee. "I ought to take you in to dinner oftener. It would be good for both of us. We get so heavy out on the ranch."

"Henry," she asked, "could we have wine at dinner?"

"Sure we could. Say! That will be fine."

She was silent for a while; then she said, "Henry, at those prize fights, do the men hurt each other very much?"

"Sometimes a little, not often. Why?"

"Well, I've read how they break noses, and blood runs down their chests. I've read how the fighting gloves get heavy and soggy with blood."

He looked around at her. "What's the matter, Elisa? I didn't know you read things like that." He brought the car to a stop, then turned to the right over the Salinas River bridge.

"Do any women ever go to the fights?" she asked.

"Oh, sure, some. What's the matter, Elisa? Do you want to go? I don't think you'd like it, but I'll take you if you really want to go."

She relaxed limply in the seat. "Oh, no. No. I don't want to go. I'm sure I don't." Her face was turned away from him. "It will be enough if we can have wine. It will be plenty." She turned up her coat collar so he could not see that she was crying weakly—like an old woman.

Questions

1. When we first meet Elisa Allen in her garden, with what details does Steinbeck delineate her character for us?
2. Elisa works inside a "wire fence that protected her flower garden from cattle and dogs and chickens" (paragraph 9). What does this wire fence suggest?
3. How would you describe Henry and Elisa's marriage? Cite details from the story.
4. With what motive does the traveling salesman take an interest in Elisa's chrysanthemums? What immediate effect does his interest have on Elisa?
5. For what possible purpose does Steinbeck give us such a detailed account of Elisa's preparations for her evening out? Notice her tearing off her soiled clothes and her scrubbing her body with pumice (paragraphs 93–94).
6. Of what significance to Elisa is the sight of the contents of the flower pot discarded in the road? Notice that, as her husband's car overtakes the covered wagon, Elisa averts her eyes; and then Steinbeck adds, "In a moment it was over. The thing was done. She did not look back" (paragraph 111). Explain this passage.
7. How do you interpret Elisa's asking for wine with dinner? How do you account for her new interest in prizefights?
8. In a sentence, try to state this short story's theme.
9. Why are Elisa Allen's chrysanthemums so important to this story? Sum up what you understand them to mean.

Raymond Carver

Raymond Carver (1938–1988) was born in Clatskanie, Oregon. When he was three, his family moved to Yakima, Washington, where his father worked in a sawmill. In his early years Carver worked briefly at a lumber mill and at other unskilled jobs, including a stint as a tulip-picker. Married with two children before he was twenty, he experienced blue-collar desperation more intimately than most American writers, though he once quipped that, until he read critics' reactions to his works, he never realized that the characters in his stories "were so bad off." In 1963 Carver earned a degree from Humboldt State College (now California State University, Humboldt). He briefly attended the Writers' Workshop of the University of Iowa, but, needing to support his family, he returned to California, working for three years as a hospital custodian before finding a job editing textbooks. In 1967 he met Gordon Lish, the influential editor who would publish several of his stories in Esquire. Under Lish's demanding tutelage, Carver learned to pare his fiction to the essentials, creating a style that is sometimes called "minimalism."

His books of short stories include Will You Please Be Quiet, Please? *(1977)*, What We Talk About When We Talk About Love *(1981),* Cathedral *(1983), and* Where I'm Calling From *(1988), which contained new and selected work. In his last decade Carver taught creative writing at Syracuse University and lived with the poet Tess Gallagher, whom he married in 1988. Carver's personal victory in 1977 over decades of alcoholism underscored the many professional triumphs of his final decade. He once said, "I'm prouder of that, that I quit drinking, than I am of anything in my life." His reputation as a master craftsman of the contemporary short story was still growing when he died after a struggle with lung cancer.*

Cathedral   1983

    This blind man, an old friend of my wife's, he was on his way to spend the night. His wife had died. So he was visiting the dead wife's relatives in Connecticut. He called my wife from his in-laws'. Arrangements were made. He would come by train, a five-hour trip, and my wife would meet him at the station. She hadn't seen him since she worked for him one summer in Seattle ten years ago. But she and the blind man had kept in touch. They made tapes and mailed them back and forth. I wasn't enthusiastic about his visit. He was no one I knew. And his being blind bothered me. My idea of blindness came from the movies. In the movies, the blind moved slowly and never laughed. Sometimes they were led by seeing-eye dogs. A blind man in my house was not something I looked forward to.

    That summer in Seattle she had needed a job. She didn't have any money. The man she was going to marry at the end of the summer was in officers' training school. He didn't have any money, either. But she was in love with the guy, and he was in love with her, etc. She'd seen something in the paper: HELP WANTED—*Reading to Blind Man,* and a telephone number. She phoned and went over, was hired on the spot. She'd worked with this blind man all summer. She read stuff to him, case studies, reports, that sort of thing. She helped him organize his little office in the county social-service department. They'd become good friends, my wife and the blind man. How do I know these things? She told me. And she told me something else. On her last day in the office, the blind man asked if he could touch her face. She agreed to this. She told me he touched his fingers to every part of her face, her nose—even her neck! She never forgot it. She even tried to write a poem about it. She was always trying to write a poem. She wrote a poem or two every year, usually after something really important had happened to her.

    When we first started going out together, she showed me the poem. In the poem, she recalled his fingers and the way they had moved around over her face. In the poem, she talked about what she had felt at the time, about what went through her mind when the blind man touched her nose and lips. I can remember I didn't think much of the poem. Of course, I didn't tell her that. Maybe I just don't understand poetry. I admit it's not the first thing I reach for when I pick up something to read.

    Anyway, this man who'd first enjoyed her favors, the officer-to-be, he'd been her childhood sweetheart. So okay. I'm saying that at the end of the summer she let the blind man run his hands over her face, said good-bye to him, married her childhood etc., who was now a commissioned officer, and she moved away from Seattle. But they'd kept in touch, she and the blind man. She made the first contact after a year or so. She called him up one night from an Air Force base in Alabama. She wanted to talk. They talked. He asked her to send a tape and tell him about her life. She did this. She sent the tape. On the tape, she told the blind man about her husband and about their life together in the military. She told the blind man she loved her husband but she didn't like it where they lived and she didn't like it that he was part of the military-industrial thing. She told the blind man she'd written a poem and he was in it. She told him that she was writing a poem about what it was like to be an Air Force officer's wife. The poem wasn't finished yet. She was still writing it. The blind man made a tape. He sent her the tape. She made a tape. This went on for years. My wife's officer was posted to one base and then another. She sent tapes from Moody AFB, McGuire, McConnell, and finally Travis, near Sacramento, where one night she got to feeling lonely and cut off from people she kept losing in that moving-around life. She got to feeling she couldn't go it another step. She went in and swallowed all the pills and capsules in the medicine chest and washed them down with a bottle of gin. Then she got into a hot bath and passed out.

But instead of dying, she got sick. She threw up. Her officer—why should he have a name? he was the childhood sweetheart, and what more does he want?—came home from somewhere, found her, and called the ambulance. In time, she put it all on a tape and sent the tape to the blind man. Over the years, she put all kinds of stuff on tapes and sent the tapes off lickety-split. Next to writing a poem every year, I think it was her chief means of recreation. On one tape, she told the blind man she'd decided to live away from her officer for a time. On another tape, she told him about her divorce. She and I began going out, and of course she told her blind man about it. She told him everything, or so it seemed to me. Once she asked me if I'd like to hear the latest tape from the blind man. This was a year ago. I was on the tape, she said. So I said okay, I'd listen to it. I got us drinks and we settled down in the living room. We made ready to listen. First she inserted the tape into the player and adjusted a couple of dials. Then she pushed a lever. The tape squeaked and someone began to talk in this loud voice. She lowered the volume. After a few minutes of harmless chitchat, I heard my own name in the mouth of this stranger, this blind man I didn't even know! And then this: "From all you've said about him, I can only conclude—" But we were interrupted, a knock at the door, something, and we didn't ever get back to the tape. Maybe it was just as well. I'd heard all I wanted to.

Now this same blind man was coming to sleep in my house.

"Maybe I could take him bowling," I said to my wife. She was at the draining board doing scalloped potatoes. She put down the knife she was using and turned around.

"If you love me," she said, "you can do this for me. If you don't love me, okay. But if you had a friend, any friend, and the friend came to visit, I'd make him feel comfortable." She wiped her hands with the dish towel.

"I don't have any blind friends," I said.

"You don't have *any* friends," she said. "Period. Besides," she said, "goddamn it, his wife's just died! Don't you understand that? The man's lost his wife!"

I didn't answer. She'd told me a little about the blind man's wife. Her name was Beulah. Beulah! That's a name for a colored woman.

"Was his wife a Negro?" I asked.

"Are you crazy?" my wife said. "Have you just flipped or something?" She picked up a potato. I saw it hit the floor, then roll under the stove. "What's wrong with you?" she said. "Are you drunk?"

"I'm just asking," I said.

Right then my wife filled me in with more detail than I cared to know. I made a drink and sat at the kitchen table to listen. Pieces of the story began to fall into place.

Beulah had gone to work for the blind man the summer after my wife had stopped working for him. Pretty soon Beulah and the blind man had themselves a church wedding. It was a little wedding—who'd want to go to such a wedding in the first place?—just the two of them, plus the minister and the minister's wife. But it was a church wedding just the same. It was what Beulah had wanted, he'd said. But even then Beulah must have been carrying the cancer in her glands. After they had been inseparable for eight years—my wife's word, *inseparable*—Beulah's health went into a rapid decline. She died in a Seattle hospital room, the blind man sitting beside the bed and holding on to her hand. They'd married, lived and worked together, slept together—had sex, sure—and then the blind man had to bury her. All this without his having ever seen what the goddamned woman looked like. It was beyond my understanding. Hearing this, I felt sorry for the blind man for a little bit. And then I found myself thinking what a pitiful life this woman must have led. Imagine a woman who could never see herself as she was seen in the eyes of her loved one. A woman who could go on day after day and never receive the smallest compliment from her beloved. A woman whose husband could never read the expression on her face, be it misery or something better. Someone who could wear makeup or not—what difference to him? She could, if she wanted, wear green eye-shadow around one eye, a straight pin in her nostril, yellow slacks, and purple shoes, no matter. And then to slip off into death, the blind man's hand on her hand, his blind eyes streaming tears—I'm imagining now—her last thought maybe this: that he never even knew what she looked like, and she on an express to the grave. Robert was left with a small insurance policy and a half of a twenty-peso Mexican coin. The other half of the coin went into the box with her. Pathetic.

So when the time rolled around, my wife went to the depot to pick him up. With nothing to do but wait—sure, I blamed him for that—I was having a drink and watching the TV when I heard the car pull into the drive. I got up from the sofa with my drink and went to the window to have a look.

I saw my wife laughing as she parked the car. I saw her get out of the car and shut the door. She was still wearing a smile. Just amazing. She went around to the other side of the car to where the blind man was already starting to get out. This blind man, feature this, he was wearing a full beard! A beard on a blind man! Too much, I say. The blind man reached into the backseat and dragged out a suitcase. My wife took his arm, shut the car door, and, talking all the way, moved him down the drive and then up the steps to the front porch. I turned off the TV. I finished my drink, rinsed the glass, dried my hands. Then I went to the door.

My wife said, "I want you to meet Robert. Robert, this is my husband. I've told you all about him." She was beaming. She had this blind man by his coat sleeve.

The blind man let go of his suitcase and up came his hand.

I took it. He squeezed hard, held my hand, and then he let it go.

"I feel like we've already met," he boomed.

"Likewise," I said. I didn't know what else to say. Then I said, "Welcome. I've heard a lot about you." We began to move then, a little group, from the porch into the living room, my wife guiding him by the arm. The blind man was carrying his suitcase in his other hand. My wife said things like, "To your left here, Robert. That's right. Now watch it, there's a chair. That's it. Sit down right here. This is the sofa. We just bought this sofa two weeks ago."

I started to say something about the old sofa. I'd liked that old sofa. But I didn't say anything. Then I wanted to say something else, small-talk, about the scenic ride along the Hudson. How going *to* New York, you should sit on the right-hand side of the train, and coming *from* New York, the left-hand side.

"Did you have a good train ride?" I said. "Which side of the train did you sit on, by the way?"

"What a question, which side!" my wife said. "What's it matter which side?" she said.

"I just asked," I said.

"Right side," the blind man said. "I hadn't been on a train in nearly forty years. Not since I was a kid. With my folks. That's been a long time. I'd nearly forgotten the sensation. I have winter in my beard now," he said. "So I've been told, anyway. Do I look distinguished, my dear?" the blind man said to my wife.

"You look distinguished, Robert," she said. "Robert," she said. "Robert, it's just so good to see you."

My wife finally took her eyes off the blind man and looked at me. I had the feeling she didn't like what she saw. I shrugged.

I've never met, or personally known, anyone who was blind. This blind man was late forties, a heavy-set, balding man with stooped shoulders, as if he carried a great weight there. He wore brown slacks, brown shoes, a light-brown shirt, a tie, a sports coat. Spiffy. He also had this full beard. But he didn't use a cane and he didn't wear dark glasses. I'd always thought dark glasses were a must for the blind. Fact was, I wished he had a pair. At first glance, his eyes looked like anyone else's eyes. But if you looked close, there was something different about them. Too much white in the iris, for one thing, and the pupils seemed to move around in the sockets without his knowing it or being able to stop it. Creepy. As I stared at his face, I saw the left pupil turn in toward his nose while the other made an effort to keep in one place. But it was only an effort, for that eye was on the roam without his knowing it or wanting it to be.

I said, "Let me get you a drink. What's your pleasure? We have a little of everything. It's one of our pastimes."

"Bub, I'm a Scotch man myself," he said fast enough in this big voice.

"Right," I said. Bub! "Sure you are. I knew it."

He let his fingers touch his suitcase, which was sitting alongside the sofa. He was taking his bearings. I didn't blame him for that.

"I'll move that up to your room," my wife said.

"No, that's fine," the blind man said loudly. "It can go up when I go up."

"A little water with the Scotch?" I said.

"Very little," he said.

"I knew it," I said.

He said, "Just a tad. The Irish actor, Barry Fitzgerald? I'm like that fellow. When I drink water, Fitzgerald said, I drink water. When I drink whiskey, I drink whiskey." My wife laughed. The blind man brought his hand up under his beard. He lifted his beard slowly and let it drop.

I did the drinks, three big glasses of Scotch with a splash of water in each. Then we made ourselves comfortable and talked about Robert's travels. First the long flight from the West Coast to Connecticut, we covered that. Then from Connecticut up here by train. We had another drink concerning that leg of the trip.

I remembered having read somewhere that the blind didn't smoke because, as speculation had it, they couldn't see the smoke they exhaled. I thought I knew that much and that much only about blind people. But this blind man smoked his cigarette down to the nubbin and then lit another one. This blind man filled his ashtray and my wife emptied it.

When we sat down at the table for dinner, we had another drink. My wife heaped Robert's plate with cube steak, scalloped potatoes, green beans. I buttered him up two slices of bread. I said, "Here's bread and butter for you." I swallowed some of my drink. "Now let us pray," I said, and the blind man lowered his head. My wife looked at me, her mouth agape. "Pray the phone won't ring and the food doesn't get cold," I said.

We dug in. We ate everything there was to eat on the table. We ate like there was no tomorrow. We didn't talk. We ate. We scarfed. We grazed that table. We were into serious eating. The blind man had right away located his foods, he knew just where everything was on his plate. I watched with admiration as he used his knife and fork on the meat. He'd cut two pieces of meat, fork the meat into his mouth, and then go all out for the scalloped potatoes, the beans next, and then he'd tear off a hunk of buttered bread and eat that. He'd follow this up with a big drink of milk. It didn't seem to bother him to use his fingers once in a while, either.

We finished everything, including half a strawberry pie. For a few moments, we sat as if stunned. Sweat beaded on our faces. Finally, we got up from the table and left the dirty plates. We didn't look back. We took ourselves into the living room and sank into our places again. Robert and my wife sat on the sofa. I took the big chair. We had us two or three more drinks while they talked about the major things that had come to pass for them in the past ten years. For the most part, I just listened. Now and then I joined in. I didn't want him to think I'd left the room, and I didn't want her to think I was feeling left out. They talked of things that had happened to them—to them!—these past ten years. I waited in vain to hear my name on my wife's sweet lips: "And then my dear husband came into my life"—something like that. But I heard nothing of the sort. More talk of Robert. Robert had done a little of everything, it seemed, a regular blind jack-of-all-trades. But most recently he and his wife had had an Amway distributorship, from which, I gathered, they'd earned their living, such as it was. The blind man was also a ham radio operator. He talked in his loud voice about conversations he'd had with fellow operators in Guam, in the Philippines, in Alaska, and even in Tahiti. He said he'd have a lot of friends there if he ever wanted to go visit those places. From time to time, he'd turn his blind face toward me, put his hand under his beard, ask me something. How long had I been in my present position? (Three years.) Did I like my work? (I didn't.) Was I going to stay with it? (What were the options?) Finally, when I thought he was beginning to run down, I got up and turned on the TV.

My wife looked at me with irritation. She was heading toward a boil. Then she looked at the blind man and said, "Robert, do you have a TV?"

The blind man said, "My dear, I have two TVs. I have a color set and a black-and-white thing, an old relic. It's funny, but if I turn the TV on, and I'm always turning it on, I turn on the color set. It's funny, don't you think?"

I didn't know what to say to that. I had absolutely nothing to say to that. No opinion. So I watched the news program and tried to listen to what the announcer was saying.

"This is a color TV," the blind man said. "Don't ask me how, but I can tell."

"We traded up a while ago," I said.

The blind man had another taste of his drink. He lifted his beard, sniffed it, and let it fall. He leaned forward on the sofa. He positioned his ashtray on the coffee table, then put the lighter to his cigarette. He leaned back on the sofa and crossed his legs at the ankles.

My wife covered her mouth, and then she yawned. She stretched. She said, "I think I'll go upstairs and put on my robe. I think I'll change into something else. Robert, you make yourself comfortable," she said.

"I'm comfortable," the blind man said.

"I want you to feel comfortable in this house," she said.

"I am comfortable," the blind man said.

After she'd left the room, he and I listened to the weather report and then to the sports roundup. By that time, she'd been gone so long I didn't know if she was going to come back. I thought she might have gone to bed. I wished she'd come back downstairs. I didn't want to be left alone with a blind man. I asked him if he wanted another drink, and he said sure. Then I asked if he wanted to smoke some dope with me. I said I'd just rolled a number. I hadn't, but I planned to do so in about two shakes.

"I'll try some with you," he said.

"Damn right," I said. "That's the stuff."

"I got our drinks and sat down on the sofa with him. Then I rolled us two fat numbers. I lit one and passed it. I brought it to his fingers. He took it and inhaled.

"Hold it as long as you can," I said. I could tell he didn't know the first thing.

My wife came back downstairs wearing her pink robe and her pink slippers.

"What do I smell?" she said.

"We thought we'd have us some cannabis," I said.

My wife gave me a savage look. Then she looked at the blind man and said, "Robert, I didn't know you smoked."

He said, "I do now, my dear. There's a first time for everything. But I don't feel anything yet."

"This stuff is pretty mellow," I said. "This stuff is mild. It's dope you can reason with," I said. "It doesn't mess you up."

"Not much it doesn't, bub," he said, and laughed.

My wife sat on the sofa between the blind man and me. I passed her the number. She took it and toked and then passed it back to me. "Which way is this going?" she said. Then she said, "I shouldn't be smoking this. I can hardly keep my eyes open as it is. That dinner did me in. I shouldn't have eaten so much."

"It was the strawberry pie," the blind man said. "That's what did it," he said, and he laughed his big laugh. Then he shook his head.

"There's more strawberry pie," I said.

"Do you want some more, Robert?" my wife said.

"Maybe in a little while," he said.

We gave our attention to the TV. My wife yawned again. She said, "Your bed is made up when you feel like going to bed, Robert. I know you must have had a long day. When you're ready to go to bed, say so." She pulled his arm. "Robert?"

He came to and said, "I've had a real nice time. This beats tapes, doesn't it?"

I said, "Coming at you," and I put the number between his fingers. He inhaled, held the smoke, and then let it go. It was like he'd been doing it since he was nine years old.

"Thanks, bub," he said. "But I think this is all for me. I think I'm beginning to feel it," he said. He held the burning roach out for my wife.

"Same here," she said. "Ditto. Me, too." She took the roach and passed it to me. "I may just sit here for a while between you two guys with my eyes closed. But don't let me bother you, okay? Either one of you. If it bothers you, say so. Otherwise, I may just sit here with my eyes closed until you're ready to go to bed," she said. "Your bed's made up, Robert, when you're ready. It's right next to our room at the top of the stairs. We'll show you up when you're ready. You wake me up now, you guys, if I fall asleep." She said that and then she closed her eyes and went to sleep.

The news program ended. I got up and changed the channel. I sat back down on the sofa. I wished my wife hadn't pooped out. Her head lay across the back of the sofa, her mouth open. She'd turned so that her robe slipped away from her legs, exposing a juicy thigh. I reached to draw her robe back over her, and it was then that I glanced at the blind man. What the hell! I flipped the robe open again.

"You say when you want some strawberry pie," I said.

"I will," he said.

I said, "Are you tired? Do you want me to take you up to your bed? Are you ready to hit the hay?"

"Not yet," he said. "No, I'll stay up with you, bub. If that's all right. I'll stay up until you're ready to turn in. We haven't had a chance to talk. Know what I mean? I feel like me and her monopolized the evening." He lifted his beard and he let it fall. He picked up his cigarettes and his lighter.

"That's all right," I said. Then I said, "I'm glad for the company."

And I guess I was. Every night I smoked dope and stayed up as long as I could before I fell asleep. My wife and I hardly ever went to bed at the same time. When I did go to sleep, I had these dreams. Sometimes I'd wake up from one of them, my heart going crazy.

Something about the church and the Middle Ages was on the TV. Not your run-of-the-mill TV fare. I wanted to watch something else. I turned to the other channels. But there was nothing on them, either. So I turned back to the first channel and apologized.

"Bub, it's all right," the blind man said. "It's fine with me. Whatever you want to watch is okay. I'm always learning something. Learning never ends. It won't hurt me to learn something tonight. I got ears," he said.

We didn't say anything for a time. He was leaning forward with his head turned at me, his right ear aimed in the direction of the set. Very disconcerting. Now and then his eyelids drooped and then they snapped open again. Now and then he put his fingers into his beard and tugged, like he was thinking about something he was hearing on the television.

On the screen, a group of men wearing cowls was being set upon and tormented by men dressed in skeleton costumes and men dressed as devils. The men dressed as devils wore devil masks, horns, and long tails. This pageant was part of a procession. The Englishman who was narrating the thing said it took place in Spain once a year. I tried to explain to the blind man what was happening.

"Skeletons," he said. "I know about skeletons," he said, and he nodded.

The TV showed this one cathedral. Then there was a long, slow look at another one. Finally, the picture switched to the famous one in Paris, with its flying buttresses and its spires reaching up to the clouds. The camera pulled away to show the whole of the cathedral rising above the skyline.

There were times when the Englishman who was telling the thing would shut up, would simply let the camera move around the cathedrals. Or else the camera would tour the countryside, men in fields walking behind oxen. I waited as long as I could. Then I felt I had to say something. I said, "They're showing the outside of this cathedral now. Gargoyles. Little statues carved to look like monsters. Now I guess they're in Italy. Yeah, they're in Italy. There's paintings on the walls of this one church."

"Are those fresco paintings, bub?" he asked, and he sipped from his drink.

I reached for my glass. But it was empty. I tried to remember what I could remember. "You're asking me are those frescoes?" I said. "That's a good question. I don't know."

The camera moved to a cathedral outside Lisbon. The differences in the Portuguese cathedral compared with the French and Italian were not that great. But they were there. Mostly the interior stuff. Then something occurred to me, and I said, "Something has occurred to me. Do you have any idea what a cathedral is? What they look like, that is? Do you follow me? If somebody says cathedral to you, do you have any notion what they're talking about? Do you know the difference between that and a Baptist church, say?"

He let the smoke dribble from his mouth. "I know they took hundreds of workers fifty or a hundred years to build," he said. "I just heard the man say that, of course. I know generations of the same families worked on a cathedral. I heard him say that, too. The men who began their life's work on them, they never lived to see the completion of their work. In that wise, bub, they're no different from the rest of us, right?" He laughed. Then his eyelids drooped again. His head nodded. He seemed to be snoozing. Maybe he was imagining himself in Portugal. The TV was showing another cathedral now. This one was in Germany. The Englishman's voice droned on. "Cathedrals," the blind man said. He sat up and rolled his head back and forth. "If you want the truth, bub, that's about all I know. What I just said. What I heard him say. But maybe you could describe one to me? I wish you'd do it. I'd like that. If you want to know, I really don't have a good idea."

I stared hard at the shot of the cathedral on the TV. How could I even begin to describe it? But say my life depended on it. Say my life was being threatened by an insane guy who said I had to do it or else.

I stared some more at the cathedral before the picture flipped off into the countryside. There was no use. I turned to the blind man and said, "To begin with, they're very tall." I was looking around the room for clues. "They reach way up. Up and up. Toward the sky. They're so big, some of them, they have to have these supports. To help hold them up, so to speak. These supports are called buttresses. They remind me of viaducts, for some reason. But maybe you don't know viaducts, either? Sometimes the cathedrals have devils and such carved into the front. Sometimes lords and ladies. Don't ask me why this is," I said.

He was nodding. The whole upper part of his body seemed to be moving back and forth.

"I'm not doing so good, am I?" I said.

He stopped nodding and leaned forward on the edge of the sofa. As he listened to me, he was running his fingers through his beard. I wasn't getting through to him, I could see that. But he waited for me to go on just the same. He nodded, like he was trying to encourage me. I tried to think what else to say. "They're really big," I said. "They're massive. They're built of stone. Marble, too, sometimes. In those olden days, when they built cathedrals, men wanted to be close to God. In those olden days, God was an important part of everyone's life. You could tell this from their cathedral-building. I'm sorry," I said, "but it looks like that's the best I can do for you. I'm just no good at it."

"That's all right, bub," the blind man said. "Hey, listen. I hope you don't mind my asking you. Can I ask you something? Let me ask you a simple question, yes or no. I'm just curious and there's no offense. You're my host. But let me ask if you are in any way religious? You don't mind my asking?"

I shook my head. He couldn't see that, though. A wink is the same as a nod to a blind man. "I guess I don't believe in it. In anything. Sometimes it's hard. You know what I'm saying?"

"Sure, I do," he said.

"Right," I said.

The Englishman was still holding forth. My wife sighed in her sleep. She drew a long breath and went on with her sleeping.

"You'll have to forgive me," I said. "But I can't tell you what a cathedral looks like. It just isn't in me to do it. I can't do any more than I've done."

The blind man sat very still, his head down, as he listened to me.

I said, "The truth is, cathedrals don't mean anything special to me. Nothing. Cathedrals. They're something to look at on late-night TV. That's all they are."

It was then that the blind man cleared his throat. He brought something up. He took a handkerchief from his back pocket. Then he said, "I get it, bub. It's okay. It happens. Don't worry about it," he said. "Hey, listen to me. Will you do me a favor? I got an idea. Why don't you find us some heavy paper? And a pen. We'll do something. We'll draw one together. Get us a pen and some heavy paper. Go on, bub, get the stuff," he said.

So I went upstairs. My legs felt like they didn't have any strength in them. They felt like they did after I'd done some running. In my wife's room I looked around. I found some ballpoints in a little basket on her table. And then I tried to think where to look for the kind of paper he was talking about.

Downstairs, in the kitchen, I found a shopping bag with onion skins in the bottom of the bag. I emptied the bag and shook it. I brought it into the living room and sat down with it near his legs. I moved some things, smoothed the wrinkles from the bag, spread it out on the coffee table.

The blind man got down from the sofa and sat next to me on the carpet.

He ran his fingers over the paper. He went up and down the sides of the paper. The edges, even the edges. He fingered the corners.

"All right," he said. "All right, let's do her."

He found my hand, the hand with the pen. He closed his hand over my hand. "Go ahead, bub, draw," he said. "Draw. You'll see. I'll follow along with you. It'll be okay. Just begin now like I'm telling you. You'll see. Draw," the blind man said.

So I began. First I drew a box that looked like a house. It could have been the house I lived in. Then I put a roof on it. At either end of the roof, I drew spires. Crazy.

"Swell," he said. "Terrific. You're doing fine," he said. "Never thought anything like this could happen in your lifetime, did you, bub? Well, it's a strange life, we all know that. Go on now. Keep it up."

I put in windows with arches. I drew flying buttresses. I hung great doors. I couldn't stop. The TV station went off the air. I put down the pen and closed and opened my fingers. The blind man felt around over the paper. He moved the tips of his fingers over the paper, all over what I had drawn, and he nodded.

"Doing fine," the blind man said.

I took up the pen again, and he found my hand. I kept at it. I'm no artist. But I kept drawing just the same.

My wife opened up her eyes and gazed at us. She sat up on the sofa, her robe hanging open. She said, "What are you doing? Tell me, I want to know."

I didn't answer her.

The blind man said, "We're drawing a cathedral. Me and him are working on it. Press hard," he said to me. "That's right. That's good," he said. "Sure. You got it, bub, I can tell. You didn't think you could. But you can, can't you? You're cooking with gas now. You know what I'm saying? We're going to really have us something here in a minute. How's the old arm?" he said. "Put some people in there now. What's a cathedral without people?"

My wife said, "What's going on? Robert, what are you doing? What's going on?"

"It's all right," he said to her. "Close your eyes now," the blind man said to me.

I did it. I closed them just like he said.

"Are they closed?" he said. "Don't fudge."

"They're closed," I said.

"Keep them that way," he said. He said, "Don't stop now. Draw."

So we kept on with it. His fingers rode my fingers as my hand went over the paper. It was like nothing else in my life up to now.

Then he said, "I think that's it. I think you got it," he said. "Take a look. What do you think?"

But I had my eyes closed. I thought I'd keep them that way for a little longer. I thought it was something I ought to do.

"Well?" he said. "Are you looking?"

My eyes were still closed. I was in my house. I knew that. But I didn't feel like I was inside anything.

"It's really something," I said.

Questions

1. What details in "Cathedral" make clear the narrator's initial attitude toward blind people? What hints does the author give about the reasons for this attitude? At what point in the story do the narrator's preconceptions about blind people start to change?
2. For what reason does the wife keep asking Robert if he'd like to go to bed (paragraphs 74–78)? What motivates the narrator to make the same suggestion in paragraph 82? What effect does Robert's reply have on the narrator?
3. What makes the narrator start explaining what he's seeing on television?

4. How does the point of view contribute to the effectiveness of the story?
5. At the end, the narrator has an epiphany. How would you describe it?
6. Is the wife a fully realized character? Is Robert? Support your conclusion about each of them.
7. In a good story, a character doesn't suddenly become a completely different sort of person. Find details early in the story that show the narrator's more sensitive side and thus help to make his development credible and persuasive.

Jhumpa Lahiri

Jhumpa Lahiri was born in London in 1967 and grew up in Rhode Island. Her father, a librarian, and her mother, a teacher, had emigrated from their native India, to which Lahiri has made a number of extended visits. She graduated from Barnard College with a B.A. in English literature, and after all her graduate school applications had been rejected, she went to work as a research assistant for a nonprofit organization. She began staying late after work to use her office computer to write short stories, on the strength of which she was accepted into the creative writing program at Boston University. Earning an M.A. in creative writing, Lahiri stayed on to complete an M.A. in English, an M.A. in comparative literature and the arts, and a Ph.D. in Renaissance studies. "In the process," she has said, "it became clear to me that I was not meant to be a scholar." Lahiri's first book of stories, Interpreter of Maladies, was published in 1999 to excellent reviews and won the Pulitzer Prize for fiction. Her first novel, The Namesake (2003), was made into a film (2006) directed by Mira Nair. Her second collection of stories, Unaccustomed Earth (2008), also received glowing reviews and became a best seller. She lives in New York.

Interpreter of Maladies   1999

    At the tea stall Mr. and Mrs. Das bickered about who should take Tina to the toilet. Eventually Mrs. Das relented when Mr. Das pointed out that he had given the girl her bath the night before. In the rearview mirror Mr. Kapasi watched as Mrs. Das emerged slowly from his bulky white Ambassador, dragging her shaved, largely bare legs across the back seat. She did not hold the little girl's hand as they walked to the rest room.
    They were on their way to see the Sun Temple at Konarak. It was a dry, bright Saturday, the mid-July heat tempered by a steady ocean breeze, ideal weather for sightseeing. Ordinarily Mr. Kapasi would not have stopped so soon along the way, but less than five minutes after he'd picked up the family that morning in front of Hotel Sandy Villa, the little girl had complained. The first thing Mr. Kapasi had noticed when he saw Mr. and Mrs. Das, standing with their children under the portico of the hotel, was that they were very young, perhaps not even thirty. In addition to Tina they had two boys, Ronny and Bobby, who appeared very close in age and had teeth covered in a network of flashing silver wires. The family looked Indian but dressed as foreigners did, the children in stiff, brightly colored clothing and caps with

translucent visors. Mr. Kapasi was accustomed to foreign tourists; he was assigned to them regularly because he could speak English. Yesterday he had driven an elderly couple from Scotland, both with spotted faces and fluffy white hair so thin it exposed their sunburnt scalps. In comparison, the tanned, youthful faces of Mr. and Mrs. Das were all the more striking. When he'd introduced himself, Mr. Kapasi had pressed his palms together in greeting, but Mr. Das squeezed hands like an American so that Mr. Kapasi felt it in his elbow. Mrs. Das, for her part, had flexed one side of her mouth, smiling dutifully at Mr. Kapasi, without displaying any interest in him.

As they waited at the tea stall, Ronny, who looked like the older of the two boys, clambered suddenly out of the back seat, intrigued by a goat tied to a stake in the ground.

"Don't touch it," Mr. Das said. He glanced up from his paperback tour book, which said "INDIA" in yellow letters and looked as if it had been published abroad. His voice, somehow tentative and a little shrill, sounded as though it had not yet settled into maturity.

"I want to give it a piece of gum," the boy called back as he trotted ahead.

Mr. Das stepped out of the car and stretched his legs by squatting briefly to the ground. A clean-shaven man, he looked exactly like a magnified version of Ronny. He had a sapphire blue visor, and was dressed in shorts, sneakers, and a T-shirt. The camera slung around his neck, with an impressive telephoto lens and numerous buttons and markings, was the only complicated thing he wore. He frowned, watching as Ronny rushed toward the goat, but appeared to have no intention of intervening. "Bobby, make sure that your brother doesn't do anything stupid."

"I don't feel like it," Bobby said, not moving. He was sitting in the front seat beside Mr. Kapasi, studying a picture of the elephant god taped to the glove compartment.

"No need to worry," Mr. Kapasi said. "They are quite tame." Mr. Kapasi was forty-six years old, with receding hair that had gone completely silver, but his butterscotch complexion and his unlined brow, which he treated in spare moments to dabs of lotus-oil balm, made it easy to imagine what he must have looked like at an earlier age. He wore gray trousers and a matching jacket-style shirt, tapered at the waist, with short sleeves and a large pointed collar, made of a thin but durable synthetic material. He had specified both the cut and the fabric to his tailor—it was his preferred uniform for giving tours because it did not get crushed during his long hours behind the wheel. Through the windshield he watched as Ronny circled around the goat, touched it quickly on its side, then trotted back to the car.

"You left India as a child?" Mr. Kapasi asked when Mr. Das had settled once again into the passenger seat.

"Oh, Mina and I were both born in America," Mr. Das announced with an air of sudden confidence. "Born and raised. Our parents live here now, in Assansol.° They retired. We visit them every couple years." He turned to watch as the little girl ran toward the car, the wide purple bows of her sundress flopping on her narrow brown shoulders. She was holding to her chest a doll with yellow hair that looked as if it had been chopped, as a punitive measure, with a pair of dull scissors. "This is Tina's first trip to India, isn't it, Tina?"

Assansol: a city in the state of West Bengal in northeastern India.

"I don't have to go to the bathroom anymore," Tina announced.

"Where's Mina?" Mr. Das asked.

Mr. Kapasi found it strange that Mr. Das should refer to his wife by her first name when speaking to the little girl. Tina pointed to where Mrs. Das was purchasing something from one of the shirtless men who worked at the tea stall. Mr. Kapasi heard one of the shirtless men sing a phrase from a popular Hindi love song as Mrs. Das walked back to the car, but she did not appear to understand the words of the song, for she did not express irritation, or embarrassment, or react in any other way to the man's declarations.

He observed her. She wore a red-and-white-checkered skirt that stopped above her knees, slip-on shoes with a square wooden heel, and a close-fitting blouse styled like a man's undershirt. The blouse was decorated at chest-level with a calico appliqué in the shape of a strawberry. She was a short woman, with small hands like paws, her frosty pink fingernails painted to match her lips, and was slightly plump in her figure. Her hair, shorn only a little longer than her husband's, was parted far to one side. She was wearing large dark brown sunglasses with a pinkish tint to them, and carried a big straw bag, almost as big as her torso, shaped like a bowl, with a water bottle poking out of it. She walked slowly, carrying some puffed rice tossed with peanuts and chili peppers in a large packet made from newspapers. Mr. Kapasi turned to Mr. Das.

"Where in America do you live?"

"New Brunswick, New Jersey."

"Next to New York?"

"Exactly. I teach middle school there."

"What subject?"

"Science. In fact, every year I take my students on a trip to the Museum of Natural History in New York City. In a way we have a lot in common, you could say, you and I. How long have you been a tour guide, Mr. Kapasi?"

"Five years."

Mrs. Das reached the car. "How long's the trip?" she asked, shutting the door.

"About two and a half hours," Mr. Kapasi replied.

At this Mrs. Das gave an impatient sigh, as if she had been traveling her whole life without pause. She fanned herself with a folded Bombay film magazine written in English.

"I thought that the Sun Temple is only eighteen miles north of Puri," Mr. Das said, tapping on the tour book.

"The roads to Konarak are poor. Actually it is a distance of fifty-two miles," Mr. Kapasi explained.

Mr. Das nodded, readjusting the camera strap where it had begun to chafe the back of his neck.

Before starting the ignition, Mr. Kapasi reached back to make sure the cranklike locks on the inside of each of the back doors were secured. As soon as the car began to move the little girl began to play with the lock on her side, clicking it with some effort forward and backward, but Mrs. Das said nothing to stop her. She sat a bit slouched at one end of the back seat, not offering her puffed rice to anyone. Ronny and Tina sat on either side of her, both snapping bright green gum.

"Look," Bobby said as the car began to gather speed. He pointed with his finger to the tall trees that lined the road. "Look."

"Monkeys!" Ronny shrieked. "Wow!"

They were seated in groups along the branches, with shining black faces, silver bodies, horizontal eyebrows, and crested heads. Their long gray tails dangled like a series of ropes among the leaves. A few scratched themselves with black leathery hands, or swung their feet, staring as the car passed.

"We call them the hanuman," Mr. Kapasi said. "They are quite common in the area."

As soon as he spoke, one of the monkeys leaped into the middle of the road, causing Mr. Kapasi to brake suddenly. Another bounced onto the hood of the car, then sprang away. Mr. Kapasi beeped his horn. The children began to get excited, sucking in their breath and covering their faces partly with their hands. They had never seen monkeys outside of a zoo, Mr. Das explained. He asked Mr. Kapasi to stop the car so that he could take a picture.

While Mr. Das adjusted his telephoto lens, Mrs. Das reached into her straw bag and pulled out a bottle of colorless nail polish, which she proceeded to stroke on the tip of her index finger.

The little girl stuck out a hand. "Mine too. Mommy, do mine too."

"Leave me alone," Mrs. Das said, blowing on her nail and turning her body slightly. "You're making me mess up."

The little girl occupied herself by buttoning and unbuttoning a pinafore on the doll's plastic body.

"All set," Mr. Das said, replacing the lens cap.

The car rattled considerably as it raced along the dusty road, causing them all to pop up from their seats every now and then, but Mrs. Das continued to polish her nails. Mr. Kapasi eased up on the accelerator, hoping to produce a smoother ride. When he reached for the gearshift the boy in front accommodated him by swinging his hairless knees out of the way. Mr. Kapasi noted that this boy was slightly paler than the other children. "Daddy, why is the driver sitting on the wrong side in this car, too?" the boy asked.

"They all do that here, dummy," Ronny said.

"Don't call your brother a dummy," Mr. Das said. He turned to Mr. Kapasi. "In America, you know . . . it confuses them."

"Oh yes, I am well aware," Mr. Kapasi said. As delicately as he could, he shifted gears again, accelerating as they approached a hill in the road. "I see it on *Dallas*,° the steering wheels are on the left-hand side."

"What's *Dallas*?" Tina asked, banging her now naked doll on the seat behind Mr. Kapasi.

"It went off the air," Mr. Das explained. "It's a television show."

They were all like siblings, Mr. Kapasi thought as they passed a row of date trees. Mr. and Mrs. Das behaved like an older brother and sister, not parents. It seemed that they were in charge of the children only for the day; it was hard to believe they were regularly responsible for anything other than themselves. Mr. Das tapped on his lens cap, and his tour book, dragging his thumbnail occasionally across the pages so that they made a scraping sound. Mrs. Das continued to polish her nails. She had still not removed her sunglasses. Every now and then Tina renewed her plea that she wanted her nails done, too, and so at one point Mrs. Das flicked a drop of polish on the little girl's finger before depositing the bottle back inside her straw bag.

Dallas: extremely popular 1980s television drama centered on the professional and romantic affairs of unscrupulous oil baron J. R. Ewing and his family.

"Isn't this an air-conditioned car?" she asked, still blowing on her hand. The window on Tina's side was broken and could not be rolled down.

"Quit complaining," Mr. Das said. "It isn't so hot."

"I told you to get a car with air-conditioning," Mrs. Das continued. "Why do you do this, Raj, just to save a few stupid rupees. What are you saving us, fifty cents?"

Their accents sounded just like the ones Mr. Kapasi heard on American television programs, though not like the ones on *Dallas*.

"Doesn't it get tiresome, Mr. Kapasi, showing people the same thing every day?" Mr. Das asked, rolling down his own window all the way. "Hey, do you mind stopping the car. I just want to get a shot of this guy."

Mr. Kapasi pulled over to the side of the road as Mr. Das took a picture of a barefoot man, his head wrapped in a dirty turban, seated on top of a cart of grain sacks pulled by a pair of bullocks.° Both the man and the bullocks were emaciated. In the back seat Mrs. Das gazed out another window, at the sky, where nearly transparent clouds passed quickly in front of one another.

"I look forward to it, actually," Mr. Kapasi said as they continued on their way. "The Sun Temple is one of my favorite places. In that way it is a reward for me. I give tours on Fridays and Saturdays only. I have another job during the week."

"Oh? Where?" Mr. Das asked.

"I work in a doctor's office."

"You're a doctor?"

"I am not a doctor. I work with one. As an interpreter."

"What does a doctor need an interpreter for?"

"He has a number of Gujarati patients. My father was Gujarati, but many people do not speak Gujarati in this area, including the doctor. And so the doctor asked me to work in his office, interpreting what the patients say."

"Interesting. I've never heard of anything like that," Mr. Das said.

Mr. Kapasi shrugged. "It is a job like any other."

"But so romantic," Mrs. Das said dreamily, breaking her extended silence. She lifted her pinkish brown sunglasses and arranged them on top of her head like a tiara. For the first time, her eyes met Mr. Kapasi's in the rearview mirror: pale, a bit small, their gaze fixed but drowsy.

Mr. Das craned to look at her. "What's so romantic about it?"

"I don't know. Something." She shrugged, knitting her brows together for an instant. "Would you like a piece of gum, Mr. Kapasi?" she asked brightly. She reached into her straw bag and handed him a small square wrapped in green-and-white-striped paper. As soon as Mr. Kapasi put the gum in his mouth a thick sweet liquid burst onto his tongue.

"Tell us more about your job, Mr. Kapasi," Mrs. Das said.

"What would you like to know, madame?"

"I don't know," she shrugged, munching on some puffed rice and licking the mustard oil from the corners of her mouth. "Tell us a typical situation." She settled back in her seat, her head tilted in a patch of sun, and closed her eyes. "I want to picture what happens."

---

bullocks: young or castrated bulls; steers.

"Very well. The other day a man came in with a pain in his throat."

"Did he smoke cigarettes?"

"No. It was very curious. He complained that he felt as if there were long pieces of straw stuck in his throat. When I told the doctor he was able to prescribe the proper medication."

"That's so neat."

"Yes," Mr. Kapasi agreed after some hesitation.

"So these patients are totally dependent on you," Mrs. Das said. She spoke slowly, as if she were thinking aloud. "In a way, more dependent on you than the doctor."

"How do you mean? How could it be?"

"Well, for example, you could tell the doctor that the pain felt like a burning, not straw. The patient would never know what you had told the doctor, and the doctor wouldn't know that you had told the wrong thing. It's a big responsibility."

"Yes, a big responsibility you have there, Mr. Kapasi," Mr. Das agreed.

Mr. Kapasi had never thought of his job in such complimentary terms. To him it was a thankless occupation. He found nothing noble in interpreting people's maladies, assiduously translating the symptoms of so many swollen bones, countless cramps of bellies and bowels, spots on people's palms that changed color, shape, or size. The doctor, nearly half his age, had an affinity for bell-bottom trousers and made humorless jokes about the Congress party.° Together they worked in a stale little infirmary where Mr. Kapasi's smartly tailored clothes clung to him in the heat, in spite of the blackened blades of a ceiling fan churning over their heads.

The job was a sign of his failings. In his youth he'd been a devoted scholar of foreign languages, the owner of an impressive collection of dictionaries. He had dreamed of being an interpreter for diplomats and dignitaries, resolving conflicts between people and nations, settling disputes of which he alone could understand both sides. He was a self-educated man. In a series of notebooks, in the evenings before his parents settled his marriage, he had listed the common etymologies of words, and at one point in his life he was confident that he could converse, if given the opportunity, in English, French, Russian, Portuguese, and Italian, not to mention Hindi, Bengali, Orissi, and Gujarati. Now only a handful of European phrases remained in his memory, scattered words for things like saucers and chairs. English was the only non-Indian language he spoke fluently anymore. Mr. Kapasi knew it was not a remarkable talent. Sometimes he feared that his children knew better English than he did, just from watching television. Still, it came in handy for the tours.

He had taken the job as an interpreter after his first son, at the age of seven, contracted typhoid—that was how he had first made the acquaintance of the doctor. At the time Mr. Kapasi had been teaching English in a grammar school, and he bartered his skills as an interpreter to pay the increasingly exorbitant medical bills. In the end the boy had died one evening in his mother's arms, his limbs burning with fever, but then there was the funeral to pay for, and the other children who were born soon enough, and the newer, bigger house, and the good schools and tutors, and the fine shoes and the television, and the countless other ways he tried to console his wife and to keep her from crying in her sleep, and so when the doctor offered to pay him twice

---

the Congress party: India's governing party for five decades after independence in 1947, widely perceived as corrupt.

as much as he earned at the grammar school, he accepted. Mr. Kapasi knew that his wife had little regard for his career as an interpreter. He knew it reminded her of the son she'd lost, and that she resented the other lives he helped, in his own small way, to save. If ever she referred to his position, she used the phrase "doctor's assistant," as if the process of interpretation were equal to taking someone's temperature, or changing a bedpan. She never asked him about the patients who came to the doctor's office, or said that his job was a big responsibility.

For this reason it flattered Mr. Kapasi that Mrs. Das was so intrigued by his job. Unlike his wife, she had reminded him of its intellectual challenges. She had also used the word "romantic." She did not behave in a romantic way toward her husband, and yet she had used the word to describe him. He wondered if Mr. and Mrs. Das were a bad match, just as he and his wife were. Perhaps they, too, had little in common apart from three children and a decade of their lives. The signs he recognized from his own marriage were there—the bickering, the indifference, the protracted silences. Her sudden interest in him, an interest she did not express in either her husband or her children, was mildly intoxicating. When Mr. Kapasi thought once again about how she had said "romantic," the feeling of intoxication grew.

He began to check his reflection in the rearview mirror as he drove, feeling grateful that he had chosen the gray suit that morning and not the brown one, which tended to sag a little in the knees. From time to time he glanced through the mirror at Mrs. Das. In addition to glancing at her face he glanced at the strawberry between her breasts, and the golden brown hollow in her throat. He decided to tell Mrs. Das about another patient, and another: the young woman who had complained of a sensation of raindrops in her spine, the gentleman whose birthmark had begun to sprout hairs. Mrs. Das listened attentively, stroking her hair with a small plastic brush that resembled an oval bed of nails, asking more questions, for yet another example. The children were quiet, intent on spotting more monkeys in the trees, and Mr. Das was absorbed by his tour book, so it seemed like a private conversation between Mr. Kapasi and Mrs. Das. In this manner the next half hour passed, and when they stopped for lunch at a roadside restaurant that sold fritters and omelette sandwiches, usually something Mr. Kapasi looked forward to on his tours so that he could sit in peace and enjoy some hot tea, he was disappointed. As the Das family settled together under a magenta umbrella fringed with white and orange tassels, and placed their orders with one of the waiters who marched about in tricornered caps, Mr. Kapasi reluctantly headed toward a neighboring table.

"Mr. Kapasi, wait. There's room here," Mrs. Das called out. She gathered Tina onto her lap, insisting that he accompany them. And so, together, they had bottled mango juice and sandwiches and plates of onions and potatoes deep-fried in graham-flour batter. After finishing two omelette sandwiches Mr. Das took more pictures of the group as they ate.

"How much longer?" he asked Mr. Kapasi as he paused to load a new roll of film in the camera.

"About half an hour more."

By now the children had gotten up from the table to look at more monkeys perched in a nearby tree, so there was a considerable space between Mrs. Das and Mr. Kapasi. Mr. Das placed the camera to his face and squeezed one eye shut, his tongue exposed at one corner of his mouth. "This looks funny. Mina, you need to lean in closer to Mr. Kapasi."

She did. He could smell a scent on her skin, like a mixture of whiskey and rosewater. He worried suddenly that she could smell his perspiration, which he knew had collected beneath the synthetic material of his shirt. He polished off his mango juice in one gulp and smoothed his silver hair with his hands. A bit of the juice dripped onto his chin. He wondered if Mrs. Das had noticed.

She had not. "What's your address, Mr. Kapasi?" she inquired, fishing for something inside her straw bag.

"You would like my address?"

"So we can send you copies," she said. "Of the pictures." She handed him a scrap of paper which she had hastily ripped from a page of her film magazine. The blank portion was limited, for the narrow strip was crowded by lines of text and a tiny picture of a hero and heroine embracing under a eucalyptus tree.

The paper curled as Mr. Kapasi wrote his address in clear, careful letters. She would write to him, asking about his days interpreting at the doctor's office, and he would respond eloquently, choosing only the most entertaining anecdotes, ones that would make her laugh out loud as she read them in her house in New Jersey. In time she would reveal the disappointment of her marriage, and he his. In this way their friendship would grow, and flourish. He would possess a picture of the two of them, eating fried onions under a magenta umbrella, which he would keep, he decided, safely tucked between the pages of his Russian grammar. As his mind raced, Mr. Kapasi experienced a mild and pleasant shock. It was similar to a feeling he used to experience long ago when, after months of translating with the aid of a dictionary, he would finally read a passage from a French novel, or an Italian sonnet, and understand the words, one after another, unencumbered by his own efforts. In those moments Mr. Kapasi used to believe that all was right with the world, that all struggles were rewarded, that all of life's mistakes made sense in the end. The promise that he would hear from Mrs. Das now filled him with the same belief.

When he finished writing his address Mr. Kapasi handed her the paper, but as soon as he did so he worried that he had either misspelled his name, or accidentally reversed the numbers of his postal code. He dreaded the possibility of a lost letter, the photograph never reaching him, hovering somewhere in Orissa,° close but ultimately unattainable. He thought of asking for the slip of paper again, just to make sure he had written his address accurately, but Mrs. Das had already dropped it into the jumble of her bag.

They reached Konarak at two-thirty. The temple, made of sandstone, was a massive pyramid-like structure in the shape of a chariot. It was dedicated to the great master of life, the sun, which struck three sides of the edifice as it made its journey each day across the sky. Twenty-four giant wheels were carved on the north and south sides of the plinth. The whole thing was drawn by a team of seven horses, speeding as if through the heavens. As they approached, Mr. Kapasi explained that the temple had been built between A.D. 1243 and 1255, with the efforts of twelve hundred artisans, by the great ruler of the Ganga dynasty, King Narasimhadeva the First, to commemorate his victory against the Muslim army.

Orissa: a state on the southwest border of West Bengal.

"It says the temple occupies about a hundred and seventy acres of land," Mr. Das said, reading from his book.

"It's like a desert," Ronny said, his eyes wandering across the sand that stretched on all sides beyond the temple.

"The Chandrabhaga River once flowed one mile north of here. It is dry now," Mr. Kapasi said, turning off the engine.

They got out and walked toward the temple, posing first for pictures by the pair of lions that flanked the steps. Mr. Kapasi led them next to one of the wheels of the chariot, higher than any human being, nine feet in diameter.

"'The wheels are supposed to symbolize the wheel of life,'" Mr. Das read. "'They depict the cycle of creation, preservation, and achievement of realization.' Cool." He turned the page of his book. "'Each wheel is divided into eight thick and thin spokes, dividing the day into eight equal parts. The rims are carved with designs of birds and animals, whereas the medallions in the spokes are carved with women in luxurious poses, largely erotic in nature.'"

What he referred to were the countless friezes of entwined naked bodies, making love in various positions, women clinging to the necks of men, their knees wrapped eternally around their lovers' thighs. In addition to these were assorted scenes from daily life, of hunting and trading, of deer being killed with bows and arrows and marching warriors holding swords in their hands.

It was no longer possible to enter the temple, for it had filled with rubble years ago, but they admired the exterior, as did all the tourists Mr. Kapasi brought there, slowly strolling along each of its sides. Mr. Das trailed behind, taking pictures. The children ran ahead, pointing to figures of naked people, intrigued in particular by the Nagamithunas, the half-human, half-serpentine couples who were said, Mr. Kapasi told them, to live in the deepest waters of the sea. Mr. Kapasi was pleased that they liked the temple, pleased especially that it appealed to Mrs. Das. She stopped every three or four paces, staring silently at the carved lovers, and the processions of elephants, and the topless female musicians beating on two-sided drums.

Though Mr. Kapasi had been to the temple countless times, it occurred to him, as he, too, gazed at the topless women, that he had never seen his own wife fully naked. Even when they had made love she kept the panels of her blouse hooked together, the string of her petticoat knotted around her waist. He had never admired the backs of his wife's legs the way he now admired those of Mrs. Das, walking as if for his benefit alone. He had, of course, seen plenty of bare limbs before, belonging to the American and European ladies who took his tours. But Mrs. Das was different. Unlike the other women, who had an interest only in the temple, and kept their noses buried in a guidebook, or their eyes behind the lens of a camera, Mrs. Das had taken an interest in him.

Mr. Kapasi was anxious to be alone with her, to continue their private conversation, yet he felt nervous to walk at her side. She was lost behind her sunglasses, ignoring her husband's requests that she pose for another picture, walking past her children as if they were strangers. Worried that he might disturb her, Mr. Kapasi walked ahead, to admire, as he always did, the three life-sized bronze avatars of Surya, the sun god, each emerging from its own niche on the temple facade to greet the sun at dawn, noon, and evening. They wore elaborate headdresses, their languid, elongated eyes closed, their bare chests draped with carved chains and amulets. Hibiscus petals, offerings from previous visitors, were strewn at their gray-green feet. The last statue, on the northern wall of the temple, was Mr. Kapasi's favorite. This Surya had a tired expression, weary after a hard day of work, sitting astride a horse with folded legs. Even his horse's eyes were drowsy. Around his body were smaller sculptures of women in pairs, their hips thrust to one side.

"Who's that?" Mrs. Das asked. He was startled to see that she was standing beside him.

"He is the Astachala-Surya," Mr. Kapasi said. "The setting sun."

"So in a couple of hours the sun will set right here?" She slipped a foot out of one of her square-heeled shoes, rubbed her toes on the back of her other leg.

"That is correct."

She raised her sunglasses for a moment, then put them back on again. "Neat."

Mr. Kapasi was not certain exactly what the word suggested, but he had a feeling it was a favorable response. He hoped that Mrs. Das had understood Surya's beauty, his power. Perhaps they would discuss it further in their letters. He would explain things to her, things about India, and she would explain things to him about America. In its own way this correspondence would fulfill his dream, of serving as an interpreter between nations. He looked at her straw bag, delighted that his address lay nestled among its contents. When he pictured her so many thousands of miles away he plummeted, so much so that he had an overwhelming urge to wrap his arms around her, to freeze with her, even for an instant, in an embrace witnessed by his favorite Surya. But Mrs. Das had already started walking.

"When do you return to America?" he asked, trying to sound placid.

"In ten days."

He calculated: A week to settle in, a week to develop the pictures, a few days to compose her letter, two weeks to get to India by air. According to his schedule, allowing room for delays, he would hear from Mrs. Das in approximately six weeks' time.

The family was silent as Mr. Kapasi drove them back, a little past four-thirty, to Hotel Sandy Villa. The children had bought miniature granite versions of the chariot's wheels at a souvenir stand, and they turned them round in their hands. Mr. Das continued to read his book. Mrs. Das untangled Tina's hair with her brush and divided it into two little ponytails.

Mr. Kapasi was beginning to dread the thought of dropping them off. He was not prepared to begin his six-week wait to hear from Mrs. Das. As he stole glances at her in the rearview mirror, wrapping elastic bands around Tina's hair, he wondered how he might make the tour last a little longer. Ordinarily he sped back to Puri using a shortcut, eager to return home, scrub his feet and hands with sandalwood soap, and enjoy the evening newspaper and a cup of tea that his wife would serve him in silence. The thought of that silence, something to which he'd long been resigned, now oppressed him. It was then that he suggested visiting the hills at Udayagiri and Khandagiri, where a number of monastic dwellings were hewn out of the ground, facing one another across a defile. It was some miles away, but well worth seeing, Mr. Kapasi told them.

"Oh yeah, there's something mentioned about it in this book," Mr. Das said. "Built by a Jain° king or something."

Jain: an adherent of Jainism, a dualistic, ascetic religion founded in the sixth century B.C. in revolt against the Hindu caste system.

"Shall we go then?" Mr. Kapasi asked. He paused at a turn in the road. "It's to the left."

Mr. Das turned to look at Mrs. Das. Both of them shrugged.

"Left, left," the children chanted.

Mr. Kapasi turned the wheel, almost delirious with relief. He did not know what he would do or say to Mrs. Das once they arrived at the hills. Perhaps he would tell her what a pleasing smile she had. Perhaps he would compliment her strawberry shirt, which he found irresistibly becoming. Perhaps, when Mr. Das was busy taking a picture, he would take her hand.

He did not have to worry. When they got to the hills, divided by a steep path thick with trees, Mrs. Das refused to get out of the car. All along the path, dozens of monkeys were seated on stones, as well as on the branches of the trees. Their hind legs were stretched out in front and raised to shoulder level, their arms resting on their knees.

"My legs are tired," she said, sinking low in her seat. "I'll stay here."

"Why did you have to wear those stupid shoes?" Mr. Das said. "You won't be in the pictures."

"Pretend I'm there."

"But we could use one of these pictures for our Christmas card this year. We didn't get one of all five of us at the Sun Temple. Mr. Kapasi could take it."

"I'm not coming. Anyway, those monkeys give me the creeps."

"But they're harmless," Mr. Das said. He turned to Mr. Kapasi. "Aren't they?"

"They are more hungry than dangerous," Mr. Kapasi said. "Do not provoke them with food, and they will not bother you."

Mr. Das headed up the defile with the children, the boys at his side, the little girl on his shoulders. Mr. Kapasi watched as they crossed paths with a Japanese man and woman, the only other tourists there, who paused for a final photograph, then stepped into a nearby car and drove away. As the car disappeared out of view some of the monkeys called out, emitting soft whooping sounds, and then walked on their flat black hands and feet up the path. At one point a group of them formed a little ring around Mr. Das and the children. Tina screamed in delight. Ronny ran in circles around his father. Bobby bent down and picked up a fat stick on the ground. When he extended it, one of the monkeys approached him and snatched it, then briefly beat the ground.

"I'll join them," Mr. Kapasi said, unlocking the door on his side. "There is much to explain about the caves."

"No. Stay a minute," Mrs. Das said. She got out of the back seat and slipped in beside Mr. Kapasi. "Raj has his dumb book anyway." Together, through the windshield, Mrs. Das and Mr. Kapasi watched as Bobby and the monkey passed the stick back and forth between them.

"A brave little boy," Mr. Kapasi commented.

"It's not so surprising," Mrs. Das said.

"No?"

"He's not his."

"I beg your pardon?"

"Raj's. He's not Raj's son."

Mr. Kapasi felt a prickle on his skin. He reached into his shirt pocket for the small tin of lotus-oil balm he carried with him at all times, and applied it to three spots on his forehead. He knew that Mrs. Das was watching him, but he did not turn to face her. Instead he watched as the figures of Mr. Das and the children grew smaller, climbing up the steep path, pausing every now and then for a picture, surrounded by a growing number of monkeys.

"Are you surprised?" The way she put it made him choose his words with care.

"It's not the type of thing one assumes," Mr. Kapasi replied slowly. He put the tin of lotus-oil balm back in his pocket.

"No, of course not. And no one knows, of course. No one at all. I've kept it a secret for eight whole years." She looked at Mr. Kapasi, tilting her chin as if to gain a fresh perspective. "But now I've told you."

Mr. Kapasi nodded. He felt suddenly parched, and his forehead was warm and slightly numb from the balm. He considered asking Mrs. Das for a sip of water, then decided against it.

"We met when we were very young," she said. She reached into her straw bag in search of something, then pulled out a packet of puffed rice. "Want some?"

"No, thank you."

She put a fistful in her mouth, sank into the seat a little, and looked away from Mr. Kapasi, out the window on her side of the car. "We married when we were still in college. We were in high school when he proposed. We went to the same college, of course. Back then we couldn't stand the thought of being separated, not for a day, not for a minute. Our parents were best friends who lived in the same town. My entire life I saw him every weekend, either at our house or theirs. We were sent upstairs to play together while our parents joked about our marriage. Imagine! They never caught us at anything, though in a way I think it was all more or less a setup. The things we did those Friday and Saturday nights, while our parents sat downstairs drinking tea . . . I could tell you stories, Mr. Kapasi."

As a result of spending all her time in college with Raj, she continued, she did not make many close friends. There was no one to confide in about him at the end of a difficult day, or to share a passing thought or a worry. Her parents now lived on the other side of the world, but she had never been very close to them, anyway. After marrying so young she was overwhelmed by it all, having a child so quickly, and nursing, and warming up bottles of milk and testing their temperature against her wrist while Raj was at work, dressed in sweaters and corduroy pants, teaching his students about rocks and dinosaurs. Raj never looked cross or harried, or plump as she had become after the first baby.

Always tired, she declined invitations from her one or two college girlfriends, to have lunch or shop in Manhattan. Eventually the friends stopped calling her, so that she was left at home all day with the baby, surrounded by toys that made her trip when she walked or wince when she sat, always cross and tired. Only occasionally did they go out after Ronny was born, and even more rarely did they entertain. Raj didn't mind; he looked forward to coming home from teaching and watching television and bouncing Ronny on his knee. She had been outraged when Raj told her that a Punjabi° friend, someone whom she had once met but did not remember, would be staying with them for a week for some job interviews in the New Brunswick area.

Punjabi: a native of Punjab, a state in northwest India.

Bobby was conceived in the afternoon, on a sofa littered with rubber teething toys, after the friend learned that a London pharmaceutical company had hired him, while Ronny cried to be freed from his playpen. She made no protest when the friend touched the small of her back as she was about to make a pot of coffee, then pulled her against his crisp navy suit. He made love to her swiftly, in silence, with an expertise she had never known, without the meaningful expressions and smiles Raj always insisted on afterward. The next day Raj drove the friend to JFK. He was married now, to a Punjabi girl, and they lived in London still, and every year they exchanged Christmas cards with Raj and Mina, each couple tucking photos of their families into the envelopes. He did not know that he was Bobby's father. He never would.

"I beg your pardon, Mrs. Das, but why have you told me this information?" Mr. Kapasi asked when she had finally finished speaking, and had turned to face him once again.

"For God's sake, stop calling me Mrs. Das. I'm twenty-eight. You probably have children my age."

"Not quite." It disturbed Mr. Kapasi to learn that she thought of him as a parent. The feeling he had had toward her, that had made him check his reflection in the rearview mirror as they drove, evaporated a little.

"I told you because of your talents." She put the packet of puffed rice back into her bag without folding over the top.

"I don't understand," Mr. Kapasi said.

"Don't you see? For eight years I haven't been able to express this to anybody, not to friends, certainly not to Raj. He doesn't even suspect it. He thinks I'm still in love with him. Well, don't you have anything to say?"

"About what?"

"About what I've just told you. About my secret, and about how terrible it makes me feel. I feel terrible looking at my children, and at Raj, always terrible. I have terrible urges, Mr. Kapasi, to throw things away. One day I had the urge to throw everything I own out the window, the television, the children, everything. Don't you think it's unhealthy?"

He was silent.

"Mr. Kapasi, don't you have anything to say? I thought that was your job."

"My job is to give tours, Mrs. Das."

"Not that. Your other job. As an interpreter."

"But we do not face a language barrier. What need is there for an interpreter?"

"That's not what I mean. I would never have told you otherwise. Don't you realize what it means for me to tell you?"

"What does it mean?"

"It means that I'm tired of feeling so terrible all the time. Eight years, Mr. Kapasi, I've been in pain eight years. I was hoping you could help me feel better, say the right thing. Suggest some kind of remedy."

He looked at her, in her red plaid skirt and strawberry T-shirt, a woman not yet thirty, who loved neither her husband nor her children, who had already fallen out of love with life. Her confession depressed him, depressed him all the more when he thought of Mr. Das at the top of the path, Tina clinging to his shoulders, taking pictures of ancient monastic cells cut into the hills to show his students in America, unsuspecting and unaware that one of his sons was not his own. Mr. Kapasi felt insulted that Mrs. Das should ask him to interpret her common, trivial little secret. She did not resemble the patients in the doctor's office, those who came glassy-eyed and desperate, unable to sleep or breathe or urinate with ease, unable, above all, to give words to their pains. Still, Mr. Kapasi believed it was his duty to assist Mrs. Das. Perhaps he ought to tell her to confess the truth to Mr. Das. He would explain that honesty was the best policy. Honesty, surely, would help her feel better, as she'd put it. Perhaps he would offer to preside over the discussion, as a mediator. He decided to begin with the most obvious question, to get to the heart of the matter, and so he asked, "Is it really pain you feel, Mrs. Das, or is it guilt?"

She turned to him and glared, mustard oil thick on her frosty pink lips. She opened her mouth to say something, but as she glared at Mr. Kapasi some certain knowledge seemed to pass before her eyes, and she stopped. It crushed him; he knew at that moment that he was not even important enough to be properly insulted. She opened the car door and began walking up the path, wobbling a little on her square wooden heels, reaching into her straw bag to eat handfuls of puffed rice. It fell through her fingers, leaving a zigzagging trail, causing a monkey to leap down from a tree and devour the little white grains. In search of more, the monkey began to follow Mrs. Das. Others joined him, so that she was soon being followed by about half a dozen of them, their velvety tails dragging behind.

Mr. Kapasi stepped out of the car. He wanted to holler, to alert her in some way, but he worried that if she knew they were behind her, she would grow nervous. Perhaps she would lose her balance. Perhaps they would pull at her bag or her hair. He began to jog up the path, taking a fallen branch in his hand to scare away the monkeys. Mrs. Das continued walking, oblivious, trailing grains of puffed rice. Near the top of the incline, before a group of cells fronted by a row of squat stone pillars, Mr. Das was kneeling on the ground focusing the lens of his camera. The children stood under the arcade, now hiding, now emerging from view.

"Wait for me," Mrs. Das called out. "I'm coming."

Tina jumped up and down. "Here comes Mommy!"

"Great," Mr. Das said without looking up. "Just in time. We'll get Mr. Kapasi to take a picture of the five of us."

Mr. Kapasi quickened his pace, waving his branch so that the monkeys scampered away, distracted, in another direction.

"Where's Bobby?" Mrs. Das asked when she stopped.

Mr. Das looked up from the camera. "I don't know. Ronny, where's Bobby?"

Ronny shrugged, "I thought he was right here."

"Where is he?" Mrs. Das repeated sharply. "What's wrong with all of you?"

They began calling his name, wandering up and down the path a bit. Because they were calling, they did not initially hear the boy's screams. When they found him, a little farther down the path under a tree, he was surrounded by a group of monkeys, over a dozen of them, pulling at his T-shirt with their long black fingers. The puffed rice Mrs. Das had spilled was scattered at his feet, raked over by the monkeys' hands. The boy was silent, his body frozen, swift tears running down his startled face. His bare legs were dusty and red with welts from where one of the monkeys struck him repeatedly with the stick he had given to it earlier.

"Daddy, the monkey's hurting Bobby," Tina said.

Mr. Das wiped his palms on the front of his shorts. In his nervousness he accidentally pressed the shutter on his camera; the whirring noise of the advancing film excited the monkeys, and the one with the stick began to beat Bobby more intently. "What are we supposed to do? What if they start attacking?"

"Mr. Kapasi," Mrs. Das shrieked, noticing him standing to one side. "Do something, for God's sake, do something!"

Mr. Kapasi took his branch and shooed them away, hissing at the ones that remained, stomping his feet to scare them. The animals retreated slowly, with a measured gait, obedient but unintimidated. Mr. Kapasi gathered Bobby in his arms and brought him back to where his parents and siblings were standing. As he carried him he was tempted to whisper a secret into the boy's ear. But Bobby was stunned, and shivering with fright, his legs bleeding slightly where the stick had broken the skin. When Mr. Kapasi delivered him to his parents, Mr. Das brushed some dirt off the boy's T-shirt and put the visor on him the right way. Mrs. Das reached into her straw bag to find a bandage which she taped over the cut on his knee. Ronny offered his brother a fresh piece of gum. "He's fine. Just a little scared, right, Bobby?" Mr. Das said, patting the top of his head.

"God, let's get out of here," Mrs. Das said. She folded her arms across the strawberry on her chest. "This place gives me the creeps."

"Yeah. Back to the hotel, definitely," Mr. Das agreed.

"Poor Bobby," Mrs. Das said. "Come here a second. Let Mommy fix your hair." Again she reached into her straw bag, this time for her hairbrush, and began to run it around the edges of the translucent visor. When she whipped out the hairbrush, the slip of paper with Mr. Kapasi's address on it fluttered away in the wind. No one but Mr. Kapasi noticed. He watched as it rose, carried higher and higher by the breeze, into the trees where the monkeys now sat, solemnly observing the scene below. Mr. Kapasi observed it too, knowing that this was the picture of the Das family he would preserve forever in his mind.

Questions

1. From whose point of view is the story told? How would you characterize the narrator?
2. Mr. Das tells Mr. Kapasi (paragraph 20), "In a way we have a lot in common. . . ." What does he mean by this? Do they in fact have much in common? Explain.
3. What can we determine about the relationship between Mr. and Mrs. Das from the details given in the first few pages of the story?
4. On one level, "Interpreter of Maladies" is about a clash of cultures. In what ways do the members of the Das family seem particularly American to Mr. Kapasi? How are these characteristics contrasted with Indian life and behavior?
5. When Mrs. Das comments on Mr. Kapasi's responsibilities as an interpreter of maladies (paragraph 74), her remarks underline the importance of subjective perceptions. People don't usually change in the space of an afternoon, but our perceptions of them can shift profoundly, especially when we don't know them very well. How would you characterize and describe the separate stages of Mr. Kapasi's evolving feelings about Mrs. Das?
6. Why does Mrs. Das tell Mr. Kapasi intimate details about her life? How does she respond to his interpretation of her malady? How accurate, in your view, is his interpretation? Explain.

Suggestions for Writing on Stories about *Personal Change*

1. Some of the stories in this section feature women whose lives are shaped (some more than others) by society's expectations. Pick two of the female characters and compare the ways in which they do, or don't, resist these expectations.
2. In some of the stories in this section, female sexuality is a significant issue. Pick one or two of the stories and analyze how female sexuality is portrayed. What particular images, passages, or metaphors are used to describe it? How do the male characters react to it?
3. Focusing on one story, pick a symbol or metaphor that appears significant. (For example, the chrysanthemums in Steinbeck's "The Chrysanthemums," the monkeys in "The Interpreter of Maladies," or the cathedral in "Cathedral.") Discuss how the symbol or metaphor relates to the story's theme. Be sure to cite specific examples and passages.
4. The protagonist in "Cathedral" changes in the course of the story, losing his instinctive antipathy to the blind man. Write a short essay explaining how and why this change occurs.
5. Each of the stories in this section features at least one character who undergoes a significant transformation. Pick one character and write an essay describing the changes that he or she experiences. What are the key events or moments of realization? What has the person learned or become by the end of the story?

POETRY

MEN AND WOMEN

Sylvia Plath	*Metaphors*
Carole Satyamurti	*I Shall Paint My Nails Red*
Charles Bukowski	*my old man*
Denise Levertov	*The Ache of Marriage*
Marge Piercy	*Barbie Doll*
Donald Justice	*Men at Forty*

In her celebrated study *You Just Don't Understand: Women and Men in Conversation* (1990), linguist Deborah Tannen explored how men and women use language differently. Tannen compared many everyday conversations between husbands and wives to "cross-cultural communications," as if people from separate worlds lived under the same roof. While analyzing the divergent ways in which women and men converse, Tannen carefully emphasizes that neither linguistic style is superior, only that they are different. While it would be simplistic to assume that all poems reveal the sex of their authors, many poems do become both richer and clearer when we examine their gender assumptions. Donald Justice's "Men at Forty" is hardly a macho poem, but it does evoke a complicated series of male roles and responsibilities passed on from fathers to sons. By contrast, Sylvia Plath's "Metaphors," which describes her own pregnancy through a series of images, deals with an experience that, by biological definition, only a woman can know firsthand.

Although gender roles in America are now less rigidly defined than they were a hundred years ago, traditional expectations still influence the lives of many people. The poems in this section explore the impact of gender on identity in different ways; they are by turns playful, celebratory, resentful, poignant, and sad. They demonstrate both the comforts of embracing traditional gender roles and the very real limits of those roles, whether they are imposed by ourselves or by others.

Sylvia Plath

Sylvia Plath (1932–1963) capsule biographies appear on pages 341 and 811, along with her poems "Lady Lazarus" and "Daddy." Were she known only for her poetry, Plath would not have been the subject of nearly a dozen biographical studies and a feature film starring Gwyneth Paltrow. In the half-century that has passed since her brief career, the often lurid details of her life and death, and the frequently nasty battles over her literary legacy, have tended to overshadow her actual achievement. But Plath is first and foremost a poet, not a martyr or an icon, and it is as a poet that she would no doubt wish to be remembered. As "Metaphors" demonstrates, she was a serious student of her art. In this meticulously crafted poem even the title and number of lines carries meaning, all supported by her subtle and satisfying use of off-rimes.

Metaphors 1960

I'm a riddle in nine syllables,
An elephant, a ponderous house,
A melon strolling on two tendrils.
O red fruit, ivory, fine timbers!
This loaf's big with its yeasty rising.   5
Money's new-minted in this fat purse.
I'm a means, a stage, a cow in calf.
I've eaten a bag of green apples,
Boarded the train there's no getting off.

Questions
1. To what central fact do all the metaphors in this poem refer?
2. In the first line, what has the speaker in common with a riddle? Why does she say she has *nine* syllables?
3. What do you understand the last two lines of the poem to mean?

Carole Satyamurti

Carole Satyamurti (b. 1939) is a British poet who has also lived in North America, Uganda, and Singapore. A sociologist and translator (her version of the Mahabharata *is forthcoming), she has taught at a number of institutions and directed several poetry-writing programs in England and elsewhere. She is the co-editor of two anthologies,* Social Work, Welfare, and the State *(1979) and* Acquainted with the Night: Psychoanalysis and the Poetic Imagination *(2003). Her seven collections of poetry include* Stitching the Dark: New & Selected Poems *(2005) and* Countdown *(2011).*

I Shall Paint My Nails Red 1990

Because a bit of color is a public service.
Because I am proud of my hands.
Because it will remind me I'm a woman.
Because I will look like a survivor.
Because I can admire them in traffic jams.   5
Because my daughter will say ugh.
Because my lover will be surprised.
Because it is quicker than dyeing my hair.
Because it is a ten-minute moratorium.
Because it is reversible.   10

Questions
1. "I Shall Paint My Nails Red" is written in free verse, but the poem has several organizing principles. How many can you discover?
2. "I Shall Paint My Nails Red" is from a sequence called "Changing the Subject," which deals with the speaker's treatment for cancer. How does awareness of this fact deepen your understanding of the poem?

Charles Bukowski

Charles Bukowski (1920–1994) was born in Germany, the son of a German mother and an American G.I. father. The family moved to Los Angeles when he was two. A rebellious child in a dysfunctional family, Bukowski began drinking heavily in his teens. His face scarred from terrible acne and boils, he became a loner with secret reading as his main escape. He attended Los Angeles City College but dropped out and took on manual labor jobs until joining the U.S. Postal Service, where he worked for over a decade. Writing every day, Bukowski was slow in getting recognition for his efforts, but his funny, irreverent, brokenhearted, wild and yet often tender fiction and poetry eventually made him world-famous. He died at seventy-three; on his gravestone is the epitaph "Don't Try." His more than sixty books include the novels Post Office *(1971) and* Factotum *(1975) as well as four dozen collections of poetry. The following poem is from* Love Is a Dog from Hell *(1977).*

my old man   1977

16 years old
during the depression
I'd come home drunk
and all my clothing—
shorts, shirts, stockings—   5
suitcase, and pages of
short stories
would be thrown out on the
front lawn and about the
street.   10

my mother would be
waiting behind a tree:
"Henry, Henry, don't
go in . . . he'll
kill you, he's read   15
your stories . . ."

"I can whip his
ass . . ."

"Henry, please take
this . . . and   20
find yourself a room."

but it worried him
that I might not
finish high school
so I'd be back   25
again.

one evening he walked in
with the pages of
one of my short stories
(which I had never submitted
to him)
and he said, "this is
a great short story."
I said, "o.k.,"
and he handed it to me
and I read it.
it was a story about
a rich man
who had a fight with
his wife and had
gone out into the night
for a cup of coffee
and had observed
the waitress and the spoons
and forks and the
salt and pepper shakers
and the neon sign
in the window
and then had gone back
to his stable
to see and touch his
favorite horse
who then
kicked him in the head
and killed him.

somehow
the story held
meaning for him
though
when I had written it
I had no idea
of what I was
writing about.

so I told him,
"o.k., old man, you can
have it."

and he took it
and walked out
and closed the door.
I guess that's
as close
as we ever got.

Questions

1. This poem contains a story inside its own story. The speaker doesn't know what the father liked in the short story. Can you speculate on any special meaning it might have had for the father?
2. When the father walks in to praise his son's story, what else happens in this incident that neither the father nor the son openly acknowledges?
3. The mother fears the father will "kill" the son because of the stories. What is ironic about the outcome of this poem?

Denise Levertov

Born in Essex, England, Denise Levertov (1923–1997) was the daughter of an Anglican parson who had been raised as a Hasidic Jew. Home-schooled by her mother, she wrote a letter at the age of twelve to T. S. Eliot, who encouraged her to keep writing poetry. Levertov was a tireless political activist, prominent in her opposition to the Vietnam War. She was also a deeply spiritual Christian. Writing about "The Ache of Marriage" and others of her poems, the poet Robert Creeley said: "There is no one who writes more particularly of what being a woman constitutes."

The Ache of Marriage   1964

The ache of marriage:

thigh and tongue, beloved,
are heavy with it,
it throbs in the teeth

We look for communion   5
and are turned away, beloved,
each and each

It is leviathan and we
in its belly
looking for joy, some joy   10
not to be known outside it

two by two in the ark of
the ache of it.

THE ACHE OF MARRIAGE. 8 *leviathan*: a monstrous sea creature mentioned in the Book of Job.

Questions

1. How does the speaker seem to feel about her spouse?
2. How committed does the speaker seem to be to the marriage relationship?
3. Is there a breakthrough or a resolution at the end of the poem?

Marge Piercy

Marge Piercy was born in Detroit in 1936, where she grew up in a working-class neighborhood. From her mother's family she inherited both her Jewish identity and her political activism (her maternal grandfather, a union organizer, was murdered). Suffering through much of her life with poor health and failed relationships, she has in the last several decades achieved both physical and emotional well-being in a happy marriage and a harmonious life on Cape Cod. Extraordinarily prolific, she has published fourteen novels and fourteen collections of poetry, as well as several other volumes. The stinging "Barbie Doll" has achieved the status of a contemporary classic.

Barbie Doll   1973

This girlchild was born as usual
and presented dolls that did pee-pee
and miniature GE stoves and irons
and wee lipsticks the color of cherry candy.
Then in the magic of puberty, a classmate said: 5
You have a great big nose and fat legs.

She was healthy, tested intelligent,
possessed strong arms and back,
abundant sexual drive and manual dexterity.
She went to and fro apologizing.   10
Everyone saw a fat nose on thick legs.

She was advised to play coy,
exhorted to come on hearty,
exercise, diet, smile and wheedle.
Her good nature wore out   15
like a fan belt.
So she cut off her nose and her legs
and offered them up.

In the casket displayed on satin she lay
with the undertaker's cosmetics painted on,   20
a turned-up putty nose,
dressed in a pink and white nightie.
Doesn't she look pretty? everyone said.
Consummation at last.
To every woman a happy ending.   25

Questions
1. Does "the magic of puberty" (line 5) have a literal application here? How is it also a very bitter phrase in the larger context of the poem?
2. What is particularly ironic about the placement of line 10?
3. Are there connotations of the phrases "offered them up" (line 18) and "Consummation at last" (line 24) that enrich the meaning of the poem?

Donald Justice

Donald Justice (1925–2004) was born in Miami, Florida. After graduating from the University of Miami in 1945, he earned a Ph.D. at the University of Iowa, where, from 1957 to 1982, he taught at the Iowa Writers' Workshop. He was instrumental in building that program into national prominence and is widely regarded as the most influential poetry teacher of his generation. His first collection, *The Summer Anniversaries* (1960), won the Lamont Poetry Prize; *Selected Poems* (1979) won the Pulitzer. A literary perfectionist, Justice published very little—about one volume every ten years. With its quiet, perfectly finished surface and troubling undercurrents, "Men at Forty" is an outstanding example of his art.

Men at Forty   1967

Men at forty
Learn to close softly
The doors to rooms they will not be
Coming back to.

At rest on a stair landing,   5
They feel it moving
Beneath them now like the deck of a ship,
Though the swell is gentle.

And deep in mirrors
They rediscover   10
The face of the boy as he practices tying
His father's tie there in secret,

And the face of that father,
Still warm with the mystery of lather.
They are more fathers than sons themselves now.   15
Something is filling them, something

That is like the twilight sound
Of the crickets, immense,
Filling the woods at the foot of the slope
Behind their mortgaged houses.   20

Questions

1. How does the first stanza set the tone and theme for the rest of the poem?
2. What do you think the "something" of line 16 might be?
3. What is the significance of the word "mortgaged" in the last line?

Suggestions for Writing on *Poems about Men and Women*

1. Does Marge Piercy's incisive analysis of 1973 sexual stereotypes still feel relevant? Agree or disagree, but cite specific passages from the poem.
2. Women sometimes express envy of the supposed freedom and power of men. As it is portrayed in "Men at Forty" and "my old man," is manhood always an enviable state? Provide your own perspective on the possible disadvantages of being male.
3. Both "Metaphors" and "I Shall Paint My Nails Red" explore themes of self-image and the essence of femaleness. Discuss each poem's examination of these issues. Are there any points of contact between the two works?

CULTURAL AND PERSONAL ORIGINS

Francisco X. Alarcón	*The X in My Name*
Paul Laurence Dunbar	*We Wear the Mask*
Shirley Geok-lin Lim	*Learning to Love America*
Edwin Arlington Robinson	*New England*
Rhina P. Espaillat	*Bodega*
Ted Kooser	*So This Is Nebraska*

People's feelings about their origins—whether familial, cultural, or geographical—can vary widely. Some people feel at home in their circumstances and take pride in their backgrounds; others can't escape them fast enough. Young people often leave home to explore the larger world, and later return to their place of origin, which in adulthood seems familiar and grounding. Whether people love or hate their backgrounds, most will find some kind of middle ground, appreciating what those backgrounds have given them, yet recognizing that there are other ways of living. For many people, however, culture and personal origins are impossible to leave behind. They miss the people and places, the landscape and weather, the food and music of their youth. Others take a few important elements and construct new lives elsewhere. But no matter how we feel about the people and places we come from, there's no denying that they shape us. The poets in this section address aspects of how culture and geography affect personal identity—the joys they bring us, the scars they leave, and the lessons we always take with us.

Francisco X. Alarcón

Francisco Xavier Alarcón was born in Wilmington, California, in 1954, but during his childhood he moved back and forth between Los Angeles and Mexico. Educated in both English and Spanish, he developed an early sense of double identity. Later he faced another sort of double identity: the alienation of being a gay man in the Hispanic community. He completed a bachelor's degree at California State University at Long Beach in 1977 and a master's at Stanford, and is now a professor of Spanish and classics at the University of California at Davis. His poetry collection Snake Poems (1992) won the American Book Award. "The X in My Name" is characteristically taut and compressed, reduced to the fewest words possible, with much left to implication.

The X in My Name   1993

the poor
signature
of my illiterate
and peasant
self

5

giving away
all rights
in a deceiving
contract for life

Questions

1. What does the speaker imply the X in his name signifies?
2. What is meant by the last four lines of the poem?

Paul Laurence Dunbar

Although his parents had been slaves and he himself never attended college, Paul Laurence Dunbar (1872–1906) achieved great success in his short life as a poet and fiction writer. But despite his international reputation and the brisk sales of his books, his last years were unhappy. Depressed by the failure of his marriage after only four years, he was afflicted by pneumonia and tuberculosis. Trapped by the pressures of the marketplace and the expectations of his public, he also felt that he had failed to grow as an artist. Nonetheless, he created lasting work: the novel The Sport of the Gods *(1902), several short stories, and a number of memorable poems, including "We Wear the Mask."*

We Wear the Mask   1895

We wear the mask that grins and lies,
It hides our cheeks and shades our eyes—
This debt we pay to human guile;
With torn and bleeding hearts we smile
And mouth with myriad subtleties,   5

Why should the world be over-wise,
In counting all our tears and sighs?
Nay, let them only see us, while
    We wear the mask.

We smile, but oh great Christ, our cries   10
To Thee from tortured souls arise.
We sing, but oh the clay is vile
Beneath our feet, and long the mile,
But let the world dream otherwise,
    We wear the mask!   15

Questions

1. Who are the "we" of this poem?
2. What does "human guile" (line 3) refer to?
3. Is there irony intended in the second stanza? Explain.

Shirley Geok-lin Lim

Shirley Geok-lin Lim was born in Malacca, Malaysia, in 1944. Although her first language was Malay, Lim could read English by age six. She won a federal scholarship to the University of Malaya, where she received a B.A. in English in 1969. She came then to the United States, earning a Ph.D. at Brandeis University in 1973. Her first book, Crossing the Peninsula and Other Poems *(1980), won the Commonwealth Poetry Prize; she was the first woman and the first Asian to receive the award. She has published both fiction and poetry. Her books include* Monsoon History: Selected Poems *(1994) and* Walking Backwards *(2010). Lim is currently a professor of English and chair of women's studies at the University of California, Santa Barbara.*

Learning to love America   1998

because it has no pure products

because the Pacific Ocean sweeps along the coastline
because the water of the ocean is cold
and because land is better than ocean

because I say we rather than they   5

because I live in California
I have eaten fresh artichokes
and jacarandas bloom in April and May

because my senses have caught up with my body
my breath with the air it swallows   10
my hunger with my mouth

because I walk barefoot in my house

because I have nursed my son at my breast
because he is a strong American boy
because I have seen his eyes redden when he is asked who he is   15
because he answers I don't know

because to have a son is to have a country
because my son will bury me here
because countries are in our blood and we bleed them

because it is late and too late to change my mind   20
because it is time.

LEARNING TO LOVE AMERICA. 1 *pure products*: an allusion to poem XVIII of *Spring and All* (1923) by William Carlos Williams, which begins: "The pure products of America / go crazy—."

Questions

1. Why does the speaker need to learn to love America?
2. What are the "pure products" of line 1?
3. Do the reasons given in the poem suggest that she really does love America?

Edwin Arlington Robinson

Edwin Arlington Robinson (1869–1935) was raised in Gardiner, Maine, the model for the Tilbury Town of many of his poems. After publishing three books, he slowly sank into poverty and alcoholism in New York City. In 1904 President Theodore Roosevelt discovered Robinson's work and the next year obtained for him a government sinecure. Freed to write, Robinson gradually became the most esteemed American poet of his era. He won three Pulitzer Prizes, and his long poem Tristram *(1927) became a bestseller. His austere style, penetrating psychology, and bitter realism represent a turning point in American poetry from nineteenth-century romanticism to the threshold of Modernism. In "New England" and elsewhere in his work, he shows the sly wit that is characteristic of his native region.*

New England   1925

Here where the wind is always north-north-east
And children learn to walk on frozen toes,
Wonder begets an envy of all those
Who boil elsewhere with such a lyric yeast
Of love that you will hear them at a feast   5
Where demons would appeal for some repose,
Still clamoring where the chalice overflows
And crying wildest who have drunk the least.

Passion is here a soilure of the wits,
We're told, and Love a cross for them to bear;   10
Joy shivers in the corner where she knits
And Conscience always has the rocking-chair,
Cheerful as when she tortured into fits
The first cat that was ever killed by Care.

Questions

1. Do the hyperbolic tone and descriptions of lines 1–8 give any clue as to how the statements in the poem should be taken?
2. What, according to the proverb, killed the cat? Why might the poet have said "Care" instead?
3. Robinson claimed that the object of his satire was not New England but the false view of it common to outsiders. What elements of the poem support that assertion? (Robert Frost dissented from Robinson's statement. With which of the two poets do you agree?)

Rhina P. Espaillat

Rhina Espaillat was born in the Dominican Republic in 1932. (A biographical note on Espaillat appears on page 340 along with her poem "Bilingual/Bilingüe.") The poem "Bodega" describes the contents of a bodega, a small grocery store. Seeing the foods offered for sale summons memories of the poet's Dominican American childhood.

Bodega   1992

Bitter coffee, musty beans,
caramel and guava jam,
rice and sausage, nippy cheese,
saffron, anise, honey, ham,

rosemary, oregano,   5
clove, allspice and bacalao.
Fifty years have blown away:
childhood falls around me now,

childhood and another place
where the tang of orange sweets   10
golden on the vendor's tray
drifts like laughter through the streets.

Memory is filament
weaving, weaving what I am:
bitter coffee, musty beans,   15
caramel and guava jam.

BODEGA. *bacalao*: Spanish for "codfish."

Questions
1. What do you understand to be the basic situation or "action" of the poem?
2. What is meant by line 7?
3. What does the last stanza suggest about the speaker's sense of her cultural identification?

Ted Kooser

From the beginning of his career, former U.S. poet laureate Ted Kooser (b. 1939) has been a regional writer in the best sense of that term, devoting himself, with precision and affection, to the celebration of the people and places of his native Great Plains—as in The Blizzard Voices *(1986), a sequence of poems commemorating the victims of a terrible 1888 snowstorm. In recent years, he has also published two prose works of personal reflection and family history,* Local Wonders: Seasons in the Bohemian Alps *(2004) and* Lights on a Ground of Darkness: An Evocation of Place and Time *(2005). The subtitle of the latter volume could also be applied to many of Kooser's poems, including "So This Is Nebraska."*

So This Is Nebraska   1976

The gravel road rides with a slow gallop
over the fields, the telephone lines
streaming behind, its billow of dust
full of the sparks of redwing blackbirds.

On either side, those dear old ladies,   5
the loosening barns, their little windows
dulled by cataracts of hay and cobwebs
hide broken tractors under their skirts.

So this is Nebraska. A Sunday
afternoon; July. Driving along   10
with your hand out squeezing the air,
a meadowlark waiting on every post.

Behind a shelterbelt of cedars,
top-deep in hollyhocks, pollen and bees,
a pickup kicks its fenders off   15
and settles back to read the clouds.

You feel like that; you feel like letting
your tires go flat, like letting the mice
build a nest in your muffler, like being
no more than a truck in the weeds,   20

clucking with chickens or sticky with honey
or holding a skinny old man in your lap
while he watches the road, waiting
for someone to wave to. You feel like

waving. You feel like stopping the car   25
and dancing around on the road. You wave
instead and leave your hand out gliding
larklike over the wheat, over the houses.

Questions
1. How would you describe the mood of this poem? Back up your response with specific details from the text.
2. Where in the poem do you find a figure of speech? What kind of figure is it?
3. The final section of the poem—the last three stanzas—begins with "You feel like that." Like what, exactly?

Suggestions for Writing on *Poems about Cultural and Personal Origins*

1. "We Wear the Mask," "The X in My Name," and "Learning to Love America" look at mainstream American culture from an outsider's perspective. What degree of alienation from—or assimilation into—that larger culture is expressed in each poem?
2. "New England" and "So This Is Nebraska" each portray a particular area of the United States. What characteristics of his native region does each speaker focus on? To what degree does each seem to identify himself with those characteristics?
3. In "Bodega" Rhina Espaillat reveals how powerfully the sight and scent of foods awaken her Latina identity. Write a short prose description of the foods or objects that would awaken your own ethnic, cultural, religious, or regional identity.
4. Choose three poems from this section and discuss each one's exploration of the theme of the divided self. What, in each poem, are the reasons for that division? How successful does the speaker of each poem seem to be in bridging the contradictions in his or her sense of self?
5. If you are from northern New England or the Great Plains, explain why, in your view, "New England" or "So This Is Nebraska" is or is not an accurate reflection of that section of the country. If you are not from either of these places, do these poems make you want to visit the areas they describe? Why or why not?

Poet in Depth:
Langston Hughes

"I, TOO, SING AMERICA"

The Negro Speaks of Rivers

I, Too

Theme for English B

Dream Boogie

Mother to Son

Casebook on Langston Hughes

Langston Hughes is a major figure in American literary history, arguably the most influential of our African American poets. While many writers of color—in the time Hughes was writing and now—have shied away from being held up as spokespersons for their race, Langston Hughes embraced the role enthusiastically. He used the collective "I" to speak of African Americans, particularly in his poems that address the place of black people in history, such as "The Negro Speaks of Rivers" and "I, Too." He was keenly aware of how the fate of African Americans is interwoven with that of the rest of the country. Hughes's poems can be cautionary, like "Mother to Son," or melancholy and thoughtful, like "Dream Boogie," or proud and defiant, like "I, Too," but they are always engaged and passionate. While Hughes didn't shy away from expressing anger or disappointment (see his "Harlem," often known as "Dream Deferred," on page 61), he never lost sight of the idea of a better America. His work is often optimistic, filled with a sort of visionary patriotism for the future of America. In "Theme for English B," a young black student feels isolated from his white classmates and teacher, but claims his right to a broad range of artistic traditions—"Bessie, bop, or Bach"—and tells the teacher that he is "a part of me, as I am a part of you." In language that is rhythmic, straightforward, and musical, Hughes celebrates the joys and challenges of ordinary black people. Like his predecessor and influence, the poet Walt Whitman, he sings America as he hopes it will someday be.

Langston Hughes

Langston Hughes was born in Joplin, Missouri, in 1902. After his parents separated during his early years, he and his mother often lived a life of itinerant poverty, mostly in Kansas. Hughes attended high school in Cleveland, where as a senior he wrote "The Negro Speaks of Rivers." Reluctantly supported by his father, he attended Columbia University for a year before withdrawing. After a series of menial jobs, Hughes became a merchant seaman in 1923 and visited the ports of West Africa. For a time he lived in Paris, Genoa, and Rome before returning to the United States. The publication of The Weary Blues

(1926) earned him immediate fame, which he solidified a few months later with his pioneering essay "The Negro Artist and the Racial Mountain." In 1926 he also entered Lincoln University in Pennsylvania, from which he graduated in 1929. By then Hughes was one of the central figures of the Harlem Renaissance, the flowering of African American arts and literature in the Harlem neighborhood of upper Manhattan in New York City during the 1920s. A strikingly versatile author, Hughes worked in fiction, drama, translation, criticism, opera libretti, memoir, cinema, and songwriting, as well as poetry. He also became a tireless promoter of African American culture, crisscrossing the United States on speaking tours and compiling twenty-eight anthologies of African American folklore and poetry. His newspaper columns, which often reported conversations with an imaginary Harlem friend named Jesse B. Semple, nicknamed "Simple," attracted an especially large following. During the 1930s Hughes became involved in radical politics and traveled to the Soviet Union, but after World War II he gradually shifted to mainstream progressive politics. In his last years he became a spokesman for the moderate wing of the civil rights movement. He died in Harlem in 1967.

The Negro Speaks of Rivers

(1921) 1926

I've known rivers:
I've known rivers ancient as the world and older than the flow of human
    blood in human veins.

My soul has grown deep like the rivers.

I bathed in the Euphrates when dawns were young.
I built my hut near the Congo and it lulled me to sleep.   5
I looked upon the Nile and raised the pyramids above it.
I heard the singing of the Mississippi when Abe Lincoln went down to New
    Orleans, and I've seen its muddy bosom turn all golden in the sunset.

I've known rivers:
Ancient, dusky rivers.

My soul has grown deep like the rivers.   10

Questions

1. How do rivers, broadly speaking, function symbolically in this poem?
2. What is the significance of each of the rivers named in lines 4–7?
3. Why do you think the rivers are described as "ancient" and "dusky" in line 9?

I, Too

1926

I, too, sing America.

I am the darker brother.
They send me to eat in the kitchen
When company comes,
But I laugh,   5
And eat well,
And grow strong.

Tomorrow,
I'll be at the table
When company comes.   10
Nobody'll dare
Say to me,
"Eat in the kitchen,"
Then.

Besides,   15
They'll see how beautiful I am
And be ashamed—

I, too, am America.

Questions

1. To what historical situation does the third line of the poem allude?
2. Why is the speaker hopeful that he will ultimately be accepted?
3. Discuss the significance of the difference in wording between the first line and the last.

Theme for English B

1951

The instructor said,

> Go home and write
> a page tonight.
> And let that page come out of you—
> Then, it will be true.   5

I wonder if it's that simple?
I am twenty-two, colored, born in Winston-Salem.
I went to school there, then Durham, then here
to this college on the hill above Harlem.
I am the only colored student in my class.   10
The steps from the hill lead down into Harlem,
through a park, then I cross St. Nicholas,
Eighth Avenue, Seventh, and I come to the Y,
the Harlem Branch Y, where I take the elevator
up to my room, sit down, and write this page: 15

It's not easy to know what is true for you or me
at twenty-two, my age. But I guess I'm what
I feel and see and hear, Harlem, I hear you:
hear you, hear me—we two—you, me, talk on this page.
(I hear New York, too.) Me—who? 20
Well, I like to eat, sleep, drink, and be in love.
I like to work, read, learn, and understand life.
I like a pipe for a Christmas present,
or records—Bessie, bop, or Bach.
I guess being colored doesn't make me *not* like 25
the same things other folks like who are other races.
So will my page be colored that I write?
Being me, it will not be white.
But it will be
a part of you, instructor. 30
You are white—
yet a part of me, as I am a part of you.
That's American.
Sometimes perhaps you don't want to be a part of me.
Nor do I often want to be a part of you. 35
But we are, that's true!
As I learn from you,
I guess you learn from me—
although you're older—and white—
and somewhat more free. 40

This is my page for English B.

THEME FOR ENGLISH B. 9 *college on the hill above Harlem:* Columbia University, where Hughes was briefly a student. (Note, however, that this poem is not autobiographical. The young speaker is a character invented by the middle-aged author.) 24 *Bessie:* Bessie Smith (1898?–1937) was a popular blues singer often called the "Empress of the Blues."

Questions

1. Generally speaking, would you agree with the point he makes in line 6—"I wonder if it's that simple?" Why or why not?
2. How would you answer the question posed in line 27?
3. What does the speaker mean by "You are white– / yet a part of me, as I am a part of you" (lines 31–32)? Do you agree with him?

Dream Boogie   1951

Good morning, daddy!
Ain't you heard
The boogie-woogie rumble
Of a dream deferred?

Listen closely: 5
You'll hear their feet
Beating out and beating out a—

>   *You think*
>   *It's a happy beat?*

Listen to it closely: 10
Ain't you heard
something underneath
like a—
>   *What did I say?*

Sure,   15
I'm happy!
Take it away!

>   *Hey, pop!*
>   *Re-bop!*
>   *Mop!*   20

>   *Y-e-a-h!*

Questions
1. Which famous poem by Langston Hughes is alluded to in line 4? (*Hint:* see page 61).
2. Should the poem's last seven lines be taken at face value?
3. In what ways does this 1951 poem prefigure the hip-hop poetry of today?

Mother to Son   (1922) 1932

Well, son, I'll tell you:
Life for me ain't been no crystal stair.
It's had tacks in it,
And splinters,
And boards torn up,   5
And places with no carpet on the floor—
Bare.
But all the time
I'se been a-climbin' on,
And reachin' landin's,   10

And turnin' corners,
And sometimes goin' in the dark
Where there ain't been no light.
So boy, don't you turn back.
Don't you set down on the steps   15
'Cause you finds it's kinder hard.
Don't you fall now—
For I'se still goin', honey,
I'se still climbin',
And life for me ain't been no crystal stair.   20

Questions

1. What is the central symbol of "Mother to Son"? How does it function thematically in the poem?
2. Is the poem more effective, or less so, than it would be if it were written in a more formal style?

Suggestions for Writing on Langston Hughes's Poetry

1. Compare and contrast the use of first-person voices in two poems by Langston Hughes (such as "I, Too" and "Theme for English B" or "Mother to Son" and "The Negro Speaks of Rivers"). In what ways does the speaker's "I" differ in each poem, and in what ways is it similar?
2. "Dream Boogie" contains descriptions of music and song and gains power from the contrast between the almost bouncy rhythms and other, more troubling elements. Discuss the poem along these lines. What mood ultimately predominates?
3. Both "Mother to Son" and "I, Too" offer hopeful or encouraging assertions despite the grimness of their subject matter. Discuss the two poems in this context. How persuasive do you find each one's optimistic emphasis to be?
4. Write your own "Theme for English B," using autobiographical details and personal tastes to express both your sense of yourself and your relationship to your community.
5. Through a detailed discussion of any three of the poems in this section, consider whether the emphasis in Hughes's poetry falls more upon the uniqueness of African Americans and their experience or more upon the common bonds of humanity between African Americans and members of other races.

CRITICAL AND CULTURAL CONTEXTS CASEBOOK
The Poetry of Langston Hughes

Langston Hughes on Writing

Langston Hughes
The Negro Artist and the Racial Mountain

Langston Hughes
The Harlem Renaissance

Criticism and Cultural Contexts

Arnold Rampersad
Hughes as an Experimentalist

Rita Dove and Marilyn Nelson
The Voices in Langston Hughes

Darryl Pinckney
Black Identity in Langston Hughes

Hughes and His World: Images

Cover of Hughes's First Book

Langston Hughes Postage Stamp

Photograph of Lenox Avenue, Harlem

Cover of FIRE!!

Langston Hughes with Fans

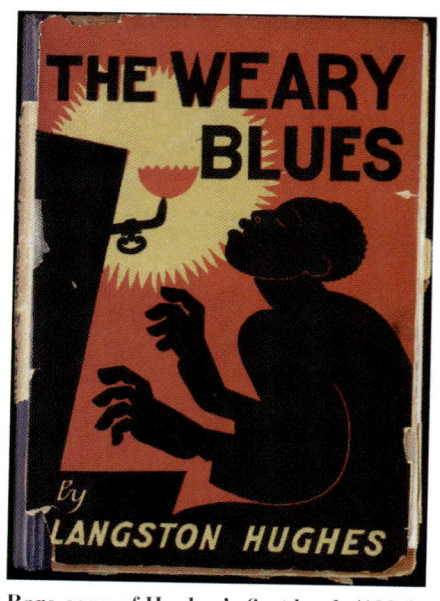

Rare copy of Hughes's first book (1926).

Langston Hughes wanted people of all races to recognize that African Americans were an inextricable part of the larger national fabric. He also wanted all African Americans—not just the intellectuals and professionals, but "workers, roustabouts, and singers, and job hunters in Lenox Avenue in New York"—to see themselves as beautiful and valuable. Hughes worked to combat black self-hatred and self-limitation with joyous, determined, and pride-filled poems that reached beyond the confines of academic study and were addressed directly "to the people." Adopting rhythms and conventions from jazz, learning from the influence of Carl Sandburg and Walt Whitman, and addressing everyday topics such as love, sex, and poverty, Hughes was sometimes seen as too direct or too playful, even by some black readers. But Hughes, who believed deeply in the power of poetry to effect social change, has influenced countless other writers, from his own time to the present day. As evidenced by the following critical pieces, his legacy in American literature and his influence on African American identity continue to be debated and analyzed.

LANGSTON HUGHES ON WRITING

2002 Langston Hughes commemorative stamp.

The Negro Artist and the Racial Mountain

1926

Most of my own poems are racial in theme and treatment, derived from the life I know. In many of them I try to grasp and hold some of the meanings and rhythms of jazz. I am as sincere as I know how to be in these poems and yet after every reading I answer questions like these from my own people: Do you think Negroes should always write about Negroes? I wish you wouldn't read some of your poems to white folks. How do you find anything interesting in a place like a cabaret? Why do you write about black people? You aren't black. What makes you do so many jazz poems?

But jazz to me is one of the inherent expressions of Negro life in America; the eternal tom-tom beating in the Negro soul—the tom-tom of revolt against weariness in a white world, a world of subway trains, and work, work, work; the tom-tom of joy and laughter, and pain swallowed in a smile. Yet the Philadelphia clubwoman is ashamed to say that her race created it and she does not like me to write about it. The old subconscious "white is best" runs through her mind. Years of study under white teachers, a lifetime of white books, pictures, and papers, and white manners, morals, and Puritan standards made her dislike the spirituals. And now she turns up her nose at jazz and all its manifestations—likewise almost everything else distinctly racial. She doesn't care for the Winold Reiss portraits of Negroes because they are "too Negro." She does not want a true picture of herself from anybody. She wants the artist to flatter her, to make the white world believe that all Negroes are as smug and as near white in soul as she wants to be. But, to my mind, it is the duty of the younger Negro artist, if he accepts any duties at all from outsiders, to change through the force of his art that old whispering "I want to be white," hidden in the aspirations of his people, to "Why should I want to be white? I am a Negro—and beautiful."

So I am ashamed for the black poet who says, "I want to be a poet, not a Negro poet," as though his own racial world were not as interesting as any other world. I am ashamed, too, for the colored artist who runs from the painting of Negro faces to the painting of sunsets after the manner of the academicians because he fears the strange un-whiteness of his own features. An artist must be free to choose what he does, certainly, but he must also never be afraid to do what he might choose.

From "The Negro Artist and the Racial Mountain"

The Harlem Renaissance 1940

White people began to come to Harlem in droves. For several years they packed the expensive Cotton Club on Lenox Avenue. But I was never there, because the Cotton Club was a Jim Crow club for gangsters and monied whites. They were not cordial to Negro patronage, unless you were a celebrity like Bojangles.° So Harlem Negroes did not like the Cotton Club and never appreciated its Jim Crow policy in the very heart of their dark community. Nor did ordinary Negroes like the growing influx of whites toward Harlem after sundown, flooding the little cabarets and bars where formerly only colored people laughed and sang, and where now the strangers were given the best ringside tables to sit and stare at the Negro customers—like amusing animals in a zoo.

The Negroes said: "We can't go downtown and sit and stare at you in your clubs. You won't even let us in your clubs." But they didn't say it out loud—for Negroes are practically never rude to white people. So thousands of whites came to Harlem night after night, thinking the Negroes loved to have them there, and firmly believing that all Harlemites left their houses at sundown to sing and dance in cabarets, because most of the whites saw nothing but the cabarets, not the houses.

Some of the owners of Harlem clubs, delighted at the flood of white patronage, made the grievous error of barring their own race, after the manner of the famous Cotton Club. But most of these quickly lost business and folded up, because they failed to realize that a large part of the Harlem attraction for downtown New Yorkers lay in simply watching the colored customers amuse themselves. And the smaller clubs, of course, had no big floor shows or a name band like the Cotton Club, where Duke Ellington usually held forth, so, without black patronage, they were not amusing at all.

Some of the small clubs, however, had people like Gladys Bentley, who was something worth discovering in those days, before she got famous, acquired an accompanist, specially written material, and conscious vulgarity. But for two or three amazing years, Miss Bentley sat, and played a big piano all night long, literally all night, without stopping—singing songs like "The St. James Infirmary," from ten in the evening until dawn, with scarcely a break between the notes, sliding from one song to another, with a powerful and continuous underbeat of jungle rhythm. Miss Bentley was an amazing exhibition of musical energy—a large, dark, masculine lady, whose feet pounded the floor while her fingers pounded the keyboard—a perfect piece of African sculpture, animated by her own rhythm.

But when the place where she played became too well known, she began to sing with an accompanist, became a star, moved to a larger place, then downtown, and is now in Hollywood. The old magic of the woman and the piano and the night and the rhythm being one is gone. But everything goes, one way or another. The '20s are gone and lots of fine things in Harlem night life have disappeared like snow in the sun—since it became utterly commercial, planned for the downtown tourist trade, and therefore dull.

The lindy-hoppers at the Savoy even began to practice acrobatic routines, and to do absurd things for the entertainment of the whites, that probably never would have

Bojangles: Bill "Bojangles" Robinson (1876–1949), a dancer.

Lenox Avenue, Harlem, in 1925.

entered their heads to attempt merely for their own effortless amusement. Some of the lindy-hoppers had cards printed with their names on them and became dance professors teaching the tourists. Then Harlem nights became show nights for the Nordics.

Some critics say that that is what happened to certain Negro writers, too—that they ceased to write to amuse themselves and began to write to amuse and entertain white people, and in so doing distorted and overcolored their material, and left out a great many things they thought would offend their American brothers of a lighter complexion. Maybe—since Negroes have writer-racketeers, as has any other race. But I have known almost all of them, and most of the good ones have tried to be honest, write honestly, and express their world as they saw it.

From *The Big Sea*

CRITICISM AND CULTURAL CONTEXTS

Arnold Rampersad

Hughes as an Experimentalist   1991

From his first publication of verse in the *Crisis*, Hughes had reflected his admiration for Sandburg and Whitman by experimenting with free verse as opposed to committing himself conservatively to rhyme. Even when he employed rhyme in his verse, as he often did, Hughes composed with relative casualness—unlike other major black poets of the day, such as Countee Cullen and Claude McKay, with their highly wrought stanzas. He seemed to prefer, as Whitman and Sandburg had preferred, to write lines that captured the cadences of common

The first and only issue of *Fire!!* (1926), an influential journal of the Harlem Renaissance.

American speech, with his ear always especially attuned to the variety of black American language. This last aspect was only a token of his emotional and aesthetic involvement in black American culture, which he increasingly saw as his prime source of inspiration, even as he regarded black Americans ("Loud laughers in the hands of Fate—/ My People") as his only indispensable audience.

Early poems captured some of the sights and sounds of ecstatic black church worship ("Glory! Hallelujah!"), but Hughes's greatest technical accomplishment as a poet was in his fusing of the rhythms of blues and jazz with traditional poetry. This technique, which he employed his entire life, surfaced in his art around 1923 with the landmark poem "The Weary Blues," in which the persona recalls hearing a blues singer and piano player ("Sweet Blues! / Coming from a black man's soul") performing in what most likely is a speakeasy in Harlem. The persona recalls the plaintive verse intoned by the singer ("Ain't got nobody in all this world, / Ain't got nobody but ma self.") but finally surrenders to the mystery and magic of the blues singer's art. In the process, Hughes had taken an indigenous African American art form, perhaps the most vivid and commanding of all, and preserved its authenticity even as he formally enshrined it in the midst of a poem in traditional European form.

"The Weary Blues," a work virtually unprecedented in American poetry in its blending of black and white rhythms and forms, won Hughes the first prize for poetry in May 1925 in the epochal literary contest sponsored by *Opportunity* magazine, which marked the first high point of the Harlem Renaissance. The work also confirmed his leadership, along with Countee Cullen, of all the younger poets of the burgeoning movement. For Hughes, it was only the first step in his poetical tribute to blues and jazz. By the time of his second volume of verse, *Fine Clothes to the Jew* (1927), he was writing blues poems without either apology or framing devices taken from the traditional world of poetry. He was also delving into the basic subject matters of the blues—love and raw sexuality, deep sorrow and sudden violence, poverty and heartbreak. These subjects, treated with sympathy for the poor and dispossessed, and without false piety, made him easily the most controversial black poet of his time.

From "Langston Hughes"

Rita Dove and Marilyn Nelson

The Voices in Langston Hughes — 1998

Affectionately known for most of his life as "The Poet Laureate of Harlem," Langston Hughes was born in Missouri and raised in the Midwest, moving to Harlem only as a young man. There he discovered his spiritual home, in Harlem's heart of Blackness finding both his vocation—"to explain and illuminate the Negro condition in America"—and the proletarian voice of most of his best work. If Johnson° was the Renaissance man of the Harlem Renaissance, Hughes was its greatest man of letters; he saw through publication more than a dozen collections of poems, ten plays, two novels, several collections of short fiction, one historical study, two autobiographical works, several anthologies, and many books for children. His essay, "The Negro Artist and the Racial Mountain," provided a personal credo and statement of direction for the poets of his generation, who, he says, "intend to express our individual dark-skinned selves without fear or shame . . . We know we are beautiful. And ugly too." His forthright commitment to the Negro people led him to explore with great authenticity the frustrated dreams of the Black masses and to experiment with diction, rhythm, and musical forms.

Hughes was ever quick to confess the influences of Whitman and Sandburg on his work, and his best poetry also reflects the influence of Sherwood Anderson's *Winesburg, Ohio*. Like these poets, Hughes collected individual voices; his work is a notebook of life-studies. In his best poems Hughes the man remains masked; his voices are the voices of the Negro race as a whole, or of individual Negro speakers. "The Negro Speaks of Rivers," a widely anthologized poem from his first book, *The Weary Blues* (1926), is a case in point. Here Hughes is visible only as spokesman for the race as he proclaims "I bathed in the Euphrates when dawns were young. / I built my hut near the Congo and it lulled me to sleep." Poems frequently present anonymous Black personae, each of whom shares a painful heritage and an ironic pride. As one humorous character announces:

> I do cooking,
> Day's work, too!
> Alberta K. Johnson—
> *Madam* to you.

Hughes took poetry out of what Cullen called "the dark tower"—which was, and even during the Harlem Renaissance, ivy-covered and distant and took it directly to the people.

Johnson: James Weldon Johnson (1871–1938), writer and activist who edited one of the earliest and most influential anthologies of African American literature, *The Book of American Negro Poetry* (1922). The multitalented Johnson served in the diplomatic corps, was the executive secretary of the NAACP, and wrote poetry and novels, as well as the lyrics for the song that became known as "The Negro National Anthem."

His blues and jazz experiments described and addressed an audience for which music was a central experience; he became a spokesman for their troubles, as in "Po' Boy Blues":

> When I was home de
> Sunshine seemed like gold.
> When I was home de
> Sunshine seemed like gold.
> Since I come up North de
> Whole damn world's turned cold.

American democracy appears frequently in Hughes's work as the unfulfilled but potentially realizable dream of the Negro, who says in "Let America Be America Again":

> O, yes,
> I say it plain,
> America never was America *to* me
> And yet I swear this oath—
> America will be!

There are many fine poems in the Hughes canon, but the strongest single work is *Montage of a Dream Deferred* (1951), a collection of sketches, captured voices, and individual lives unified by the jazzlike improvisations on the central theme of "a dream deferred." Like many of his individual poems, this work is intended for performance: think of it as a Harlem *Under Milk Wood*. Hughes moves rapidly from one voice or scene to the next; from the person in "Blues at Dawn" who says "I don't dare start thinking in the morning," to, in "Dime," a snatch of conversation: "Chile, these steps is hard to climb. / Grandma, lend me a dime."

The moods of the poems are as varied as their voices, for Hughes includes the daylight hours as well as the night. There are the bitter jump-rope rhymes of disillusioned children, the naive exclamations of young lovers, the gossip of friends. A college freshman writes in his "Theme for English B": "I guess being colored doesn't make me *not* like / the same things other folks like who are other races." A jaded woman offers in "Advice" the observation that

Hughes signing autographs, Negro History Week, Atlanta, 1947.

"birthing is hard / and dying is mean," and advises youth to "get yourself / a little loving / in between." "Hope" is a miniature vignette in which a dying man asks for fish, and "His wife looked it up in her dream book / and played it." The changing voices, moods, and rhythms of this collection are, as Hughes wrote in a preface, "Like be-bop . . . marked by conflicting change, sudden nuances. . . ." We are reminded throughout that we should be hearing the poem as music; as boogie-woogie, as blues, as bass, as saxophone. Against the eighty-odd dreams collected here, the refrain insists that these frustrated dreams are potentially dangerous:

> What happens to a dream deferred?
>
>> Does it dry up
>> like a raisin in the sun?
>> Or fester like a sore—
>> And then run?
>> Does it stink like rotten meat?
>> Or crust and sugar over—
>> like a syrupy sweet?
>> Maybe it just sags
>> like a heavy load.
>
> *Or does it explode?*

More than any other Black poet, Langston Hughes spoke for the Negro people. Most of those after him have emulated his ascent of the Racial Mountain, his painfully joyous declaration of pride and commonality. His work offers white readers a glimpse into the social and the personal lives of Black America; Black readers recognize a proud affirmation of self.

From "A Black Rainbow: Modern Afro-American Poetry"

Darryl Pinckney

Black Identity in Langston Hughes   1989

Fierce identification with the sorrows and pleasures of the poor black—"I myself belong to that class"—propelled Hughes toward the voice of the black Everyman. He made a distinction between his lyric and his social poetry, the private and the public. In the best of his social poetry he turned himself into a transmitter of messages and made the "I" a collective "I":

> I've known rivers:
> I've known rivers ancient as the world and older than the flow of human blood in
>> human veins.
>
> My soul has grown deep like the rivers.
>
> I bathed in the Euphrates when dawns were young.
> I built my hut near the Congo and it lulled me to sleep.
> I looked upon the Nile and raised the pyramids above it.
> I heard the singing of the Mississippi when Abe Lincoln went down to New
>> Orleans, and I've seen its muddy bosom turn all golden in the sunset.

("The Negro Speaks of Rivers")

The medium conveys a singleness of intention: to make the black known. The straightforward, declarative style doesn't call attention to itself. Nothing distracts from forceful statement, as if the shadowy characters Sandburg wrote about in, say, "When Mammy Hums" had at last their chance to come forward and testify. Poems like "Aunt Sue's Stories" reflect the folk ideal of black women as repositories of racial lore. The story told in dramatic monologues like "The Negro Mother" or "Mother to Son" is one of survival—life "ain't been no crystal stair." The emphasis is on the capacity of black people to endure, which is why Hughes's social poetry, though not strictly protest writing, indicts white America, even taunts it with the steady belief that blacks will overcome simply by "keeping on":

> I, too, sing America.
>
> I am the darker brother.
> They send me to eat in the kitchen
> When company comes,
> But I laugh,
> And eat well,
> And grow strong.
>
> ("I, Too")

Whites were not the only ones who could be made uneasy by Hughes's attempts to boldly connect past and future. The use of "black" and the invocation of Africa were defiant gestures back in the days when many blacks described themselves as brown. When Hughes answered Sandburg's "Nigger" ("I am the nigger, / Singer of Songs . . .") with "I am a Negro, / Black as the night is black, / Black like the depths of my Africa" ("Negro") he challenged the black middle class with his absorption in slave heritage.

From "Suitcase in Harlem"

Suggestions for Writing on Critics and Langston Hughes's Poetry

1. Reread the last two sentences of Arnold Rampersad's "Hughes as an Experimentalist." Is Hughes, in your opinion, still a controversial poet, or have his views now become entirely mainstream? If the latter, is it for the reasons that Rampersad gives? If not, why not? Explain.
2. In "The Voices in Langston Hughes," Rita Dove and Marilyn Nelson write: "More than any other Black poet, Langston Hughes spoke for the Negro people." In your view, does Hughes's poetry also speak predominately *to* black people, or to white people, or to all readers, irrespective of race?
3. In our time, autobiography and memoir are very popular genres, and even much contemporary poetry is based on the poet's personal experience. But, as Darryl Pinckney makes clear in "Black Identity in Langston Hughes," Hughes rarely writes out of his own life. Do you see this as a weakness or a strength in his work? Explain the reasons for your conclusion.
4. Compare Hughes's comments on the African American artist with Darryl Pinckney's critical observations on Langston Hughes's public identity as a black poet.

ESSAYS

DEFINING SELF

Frederick Douglass	*Learning to Read and Write*
Virginia Woolf	*What If Shakespeare Had a Sister?*
Richard Rodriguez	*"Blaxicans" and Other Reinvented Americans*

People express themselves through both their actions and their words. They do so in a variety of ways—with their jobs, their chosen hobbies, their commitment to certain causes, or their creativity. The ability to tell your own story, rather than have others tell it for you, is one of the most fundamental concepts of self-definition. Today, in the age of blogging, Facebook, and Twitter, it's easy for just about anyone to express himself or herself (maybe *too* easy, depending on your point of view). But it wasn't always so simple for people to share their opinions, or even to communicate at all. In "Learning to Read and Write," Frederick Douglass describes a time when illiteracy among African Americans was the norm. Without a strong community of African American writers and readers, blacks had only limited means to understand, articulate, and communicate their situation—a predicament Douglass spent his lifetime correcting. Virginia Woolf, in an excerpt from *A Room of One's Own*, describes the difficulties that women historically had in getting their voices heard—or even in staking out the space and time to write. Both authors assert their right to express themselves and tell their stories, in a way that modern people might take for granted. Sometimes it's hard simply to find adequate language for telling one's story. In "'Blaxicans' and Other Reinvented Americans," Richard Rodriguez relates how complicated the idea of race and ethnicity has become in contemporary America, where so many types of people live together and mix, and he speculates that the very terms people use to describe one another are inadequate and outdated.

Frederick Douglass

Frederick Douglass (1818–1895) was born into slavery in Tuckahoe, Maryland. The son of a slave mother and a white father, probably a slave owner, his birth name was Frederick Augustus Washington Bailey. Separated from his mother soon after his birth, Douglass lived with his grandmother for several years until he was moved at about age six to the plantation owned by the man who may have been his father. Upon his master's death, Douglass was sent to the man's relatives, Hugh and Sophia Auld, where Mrs. Auld taught young Frederick the alphabet. Eventually, Douglass was sent to several other masters, including one who beat him regularly. At the age of twenty, he made a daring escape from slavery to safety in New York, via

Frederick Douglass

trains and boats, by dressing in a sailor's uniform and carrying false identification papers supplied to him by a friend. He adopted the name "Douglass" (from the hero in Sir Walter Scott's The Lady of the Lake), married a free black woman, and moved to Massachusetts. There he began to speak for the abolitionist cause; his powerful oratory convinced many Northerners of the evils of slavery.

Douglass's first and best-known book, Narrative of the Life of Frederick Douglass, an American Slave, was published in 1845. It was a best seller that deeply influenced the public discourse about slavery. His new notoriety forced him to flee to England—as an escaped slave, he was at risk of being captured by slave-traders. Douglass returned to the United States after his freedom was purchased by wealthy friends, and settled in Rochester, New York. There he began to publish The North Star, an abolitionist newspaper, and resumed his antislavery efforts. His reputation grew so great that during the Civil War President Abraham Lincoln consulted him. After the war he was appointed U.S. Marshal for the District of Columbia. Douglass published two more installments of his autobiography: My Bondage and My Freedom (1855) and Life and Times of Frederick Douglass (1881). One of the most important figures of African American history, he continued to advocate for the rights of African Americans and for women until his death in 1895. "Learning to Read and Write" is Chapter 7 of his Narrative of the Life of Frederick Douglass, an American Slave.

Learning to Read and Write   1845

I lived in Master Hugh's family about seven years. During this time, I succeeded in learning to read and write. In accomplishing this, I was compelled to resort to various stratagems. I had no regular teacher. My mistress, who had kindly commenced to instruct me, had, in compliance with the advice and direction of her husband, not only ceased to instruct, but had set her face against my being instructed by anyone else. It is due, however, to my mistress to say of her, that she did not adopt this course of treatment immediately. She at first lacked the depravity indispensable to shutting me up in mental darkness. It was at least necessary for her to have some training in the exercise of irresponsible power, to make her equal to the task of treating me as though I were a brute.

My mistress was, as I have said, a kind and tender-hearted woman; and in the simplicity of her soul she commenced, when I first went to live with her, to treat me as she supposed one human being ought to treat another. In entering upon the duties of a slaveholder, she did not seem to perceive that I sustained to her the relation of a mere chattel, and that for her to treat me as a human being was not only wrong, but dangerously so. Slavery proved as injurious to her as it did to me. When I went there, she was a pious, warm, and tender-hearted woman. There was no sorrow or suffering for which she had not a tear. She had bread for the hungry, clothes for the naked, and comfort for every mourner that came within her reach. Slavery soon proved its ability to divest her of these heavenly qualities. Under its influence, the tender heart became stone, and the lamb-like disposition gave way to one of tiger-like fierceness. The first step in her downward course was in her ceasing to instruct me. She now commenced to practise her husband's precepts. She finally became even more violent in her opposition than her husband himself. She was not satisfied with simply doing as well as he had commanded; she seemed anxious to do better. Nothing seemed to make her more angry than to see me with a newspaper. She seemed to think that here lay the danger.

I have had her rush at me with a face made all up of fury, and snatch from me a newspaper, in a manner that fully revealed her apprehension. She was an apt woman; and a little experience soon demonstrated, to her satisfaction, that education and slavery were incompatible with each other.

From this time I was most narrowly watched. If I was in a separate room any considerable length of time, I was sure to be suspected of having a book, and was at once called to give an account of myself. All this, however, was too late. The first step had been taken. Mistress, in teaching me the alphabet, had given me the *inch*, and no precaution could prevent me from taking the *ell*.°

The plan which I adopted, and the one by which I was most successful, was that of making friends of all the little white boys whom I met in the street. As many of these as I could, I converted into teachers. With their kindly aid, obtained at different times and in different places, I finally succeeded in learning to read. When I was sent of errands, I always took my book with me, and by going one part of my errand quickly, I found time to get a lesson before my return. I used also to carry bread with me, enough of which was always in the house, and to which I was always welcome; for I was much better off in this regard than many of the poor white children in our neighborhood. This bread I used to bestow upon the hungry little urchins, who, in return, would give me that more valuable bread of knowledge. I am strongly tempted to give the names of two or three of those little boys, as a testimonial of the gratitude and affection I bear them; but prudence forbids;—not that it would injure me, but it might embarrass them; for it is almost an unpardonable offence to teach slaves to read in this Christian country. It is enough to say of the dear little fellows, that they lived on Philpot Street, very near Durgin and Bailey's ship-yard. I used to talk this matter of slavery over with them. I would sometimes say to them, I wished I could be as free as they would be when they got to be men. "You will be free as soon as you are twenty-one, *but I am a slave for life!* Have not I as good a right to be free as you have?" These words used to trouble them; they would express for me the liveliest sympathy, and console me with the hope that something would occur by which I might be free.

I was now about twelve years old, and the thought of being *a slave for life* began to bear heavily upon my heart. Just about this time, I got hold of a book entitled *The Columbian Orator*. Every opportunity I got, I used to read this book. Among much of other interesting matter, I found in it a dialogue between a master and his slave. The slave was represented as having run away from his master three times. The dialogue represented the conversation which took place between them, when the slave was retaken the third time. In this dialogue, the whole argument in behalf of slavery was brought forward by the master, all of which was disposed of by the slave. The slave was made to say some very smart as well as impressive things in reply to his master— things which had the desired though unexpected effect; for the conversation resulted in the voluntary emancipation of the slave on the part of the master.

In the same book, I met with one of Sheridan's° mighty speeches on and in behalf of Catholic emancipation.° These were choice documents to me. I read them over and

5

---

ell: an old English measurement, about 45 inches. *Sheridan:* Irish playwright Richard Brinsley Sheridan (1751–1816) became a member of the British Parliament, where he argued on behalf of granting rights to Catholics, often using humor to mock his opponents. *Catholic emancipation:* the process culminating in 1829 by which England stopped the legal discrimination against Catholics, especially in Ireland, granting them freedom of religion, the right to vote, and limited access to public office.

over again with unabated interest. They gave tongue to interesting thoughts of my own soul, which had frequently flashed through my mind, and died away for want of utterance. The moral which I gained from the dialogue was the power of truth over the conscience of even a slaveholder. What I got from Sheridan was a bold denunciation of slavery, and a powerful vindication of human rights. The reading of these documents enabled me to utter my thoughts, and to meet the arguments brought forward to sustain slavery; but while they relieved me of one difficulty, they brought on another even more painful than the one of which I was relieved. The more I read, the more I was led to abhor and detest my enslavers. I could regard them in no other light than a band of successful robbers, who had left their homes, and gone to Africa, and stolen us from our homes, and in a strange land reduced us to slavery. I loathed them as being the meanest as well as the most wicked of men. As I read and contemplated the subject, behold! that very discontentment which Master Hugh had predicted would follow my learning to read had already come, to torment and sting my soul to unutterable anguish. As I writhed under it, I would at times feel that learning to read had been a curse rather than a blessing. It had given me a view of my wretched condition, without the remedy. It opened my eyes to the horrible pit, but to no ladder upon which to get out. In moments of agony, I envied my fellow-slaves for their stupidity. I have often wished myself a beast. I preferred the condition of the meanest reptile to my own. Any thing, no matter what, to get rid of thinking! It was this everlasting thinking of my condition that tormented me. There was no getting rid of it. It was pressed upon me by every object within sight or hearing, animate or inanimate. The silver trump of freedom had roused my soul to eternal wakefulness. Freedom now appeared, to disappear no more forever. It was heard in every sound, and seen in every thing. It was ever present to torment me with a sense of my wretched condition. I saw nothing without seeing it, I heard nothing without hearing it, and felt nothing without feeling it. It looked from every star, it smiled in every calm, breathed in every wind, and moved in every storm.

I often found myself regretting my own existence, and wishing myself dead; and but for the hope of being free, I have no doubt but that I should have killed myself, or done something for which I should have been killed. While in this state of mind, I was eager to hear any one speak of slavery. I was a ready listener. Every little while, I could hear something about the abolitionists. It was some time before I found what the word meant. It was always used in such connections as to make it an interesting word to me. If a slave ran away and succeeded in getting clear, or if a slave killed his master, set fire to a barn, or did any thing very wrong in the mind of a slaveholder, it was spoken of as the fruit of *abolition*. Hearing the word in this connection very often, I set about learning what it meant. The dictionary afforded me little or no help. I found it was "the act of abolishing;" but then I did not know what was to be abolished. Here I was perplexed. I did not dare to ask any one about its meaning, for I was satisfied that it was something they wanted me to know very little about. After a patient waiting, I got one of our city papers, containing an account of the number of petitions from the north, praying for the abolition of slavery in the District of Columbia, and of the slave trade between the States. From this time I understood the words *abolition* and *abolitionist*, and always drew near when that word was spoken, expecting to hear something of importance to myself and fellow-slaves. The light broke in upon me by degrees. I went one day down on the wharf of Mr. Waters; and seeing two Irishmen unloading a scow° of stone, I went, unasked, and helped them. When we had finished, one of them came to me and asked me if I were a slave. I told him I was. He asked, "Are ye a slave for life?" I told him that I was. The good Irishman seemed to be deeply affected by the statement. He said to the other that it was a pity so fine a little fellow as myself should be a slave for life. He said it was a shame to hold me. They both advised me to run away to the north; that I should find friends there, and that I should be free. I pretended not to be interested in what they said, and treated them as if I did not understand them; for I feared they might be treacherous. White men have been known to encourage slaves to escape, and then, to get the reward, catch them and return them to their masters. I was afraid that these seemingly good men might use me so; but I nevertheless remembered their advice, and from that time I resolved to run away. I looked forward to a time at which it would be safe for me to escape. I was too young to think of doing so immediately; besides, I wished to learn how to write, as I might have occasion to write my own pass. I consoled myself with the hope that I should one day find a good chance. Meanwhile, I would learn to write.

The idea as to how I might learn to write was suggested to me by being in Durgin and Bailey's ship-yard, and frequently seeing the ship carpenters, after hewing, and getting a piece of timber ready for use, write on the timber the name of that part of the ship for which it was intended. When a piece of timber was intended for the larboard side, it would be marked thus—"L." When a piece was for the starboard side, it would be marked thus—"S." A piece for the larboard side forward, would be marked thus—"L. F." When a piece was for starboard side forward, it would be marked thus—"S. F." For larboard aft, it would be marked thus—"L. A." For starboard aft, it would be marked thus—"S. A." I soon learned the names of these letters, and for what they were intended when placed upon a piece of timber in the ship-yard. I immediately commenced copying them, and in a short time was able to make the four letters named. After that, when I met with any boy who I knew could write, I would tell him I could write as well as he. The next word would be, "I don't believe you. Let me see you try it." I would then make the letters which I had been so fortunate as to learn, and ask him to beat that. In this way I got a good many lessons in writing, which it is quite possible I should never have gotten in any other way. During this time, my copy-book was the board fence, brick wall, and pavement; my pen and ink was a lump of chalk. With these, I learned mainly how to write. I then commenced and continued copying the Italics in Webster's Spelling Book, until I could make them all without looking on the book. By this time, my little Master Thomas had gone to school, and learned how to write, and had written over a number of copy-books. These had been brought home, and shown to some of our near neighbors, and then laid aside. My mistress used to go to class meeting at the Wilk Street meetinghouse every Monday afternoon, and leave me to take care of the house. When left thus, I used to spend the time in writing in the spaces left in Master Thomas's copy-book, copying what he had written. I continued to do this until I could write a hand very similar to that of Master Thomas. Thus, after a long, tedious effort for years, I finally succeeded in learning how to write.

scow: large, flat-bottomed boat used in shipping.

Questions

1. Why was it, as Douglass writes, "almost an unpardonable offence to teach slaves to read"? What were the perceived effects if someone learned to read and write?
2. How does the experience of reading change Douglass? Does he consider these changes a curse or a blessing?
3. What book makes a particularly strong impact on the young Douglass? Why?
4. Douglass describes several people who are kind to him—the "good Irishman," the young boys on Philpot Street, and initially, his mistress. Do these people have anything in common? Why are they able to treat him with respect?
5. Think about the implications of Douglass's essay in the context of contemporary life. Do his points about education and knowledge still have relevance today?

Virginia Woolf

Adeline Virginia Stephen Woolf (1882–1941) was born in London, the daughter of Sir Leslie Stephen, an influential critic and editor of the voluminous Dictionary of National Biography. Virginia and her sister Vanessa (later Vanessa Bell) were largely self-educated in their father's extensive library while—in a distinction not lost on them—their brothers were sent to college. After their father's death in 1904, Virginia and Vanessa moved to Bloomsbury, a bohemian London neighborhood, and became the center of the "Bloomsbury Group" of progressive artists and intellectuals. Always in frail health, Virginia experienced episodes of mental disturbance. In 1912 she married Leonard Woolf, a journalist and novelist. In 1917 as therapy, they set up a hand-press in their home and started the Hogarth Press, which became one of the most celebrated small presses of the century. In addition to Woolf's books, it issued works by T. S. Eliot, Katherine Mansfield, Robinson Jeffers, Edwin Arlington Robinson, and Sigmund Freud. Woolf's first novel was The Voyage Out (1915); though realistic in technique, it foreshadowed the psychological depth and poetic force of her late work. In innovative novels such as Mrs. Dalloway (1925) and To the Lighthouse (1927), Woolf became one of the central modernist writers in English and a pioneer of stream-of-consciousness narration, which portrays the random flow of thoughts and feelings through a character's mind. Her critical essays are collected in The Common Reader (1925, second series 1932). Her book-length essay A Room of One's Own (1929), from which the following selection has been drawn, is a feminist classic. After several nervous breakdowns, Woolf, fearing for her sanity, drowned herself in 1941.

Virginia Woolf

What If Shakespeare Had a Sister? 1929

Here am I asking why women did not write poetry in the Elizabethan age, and I am not sure how they were educated; whether they were taught to write; whether they had sitting-rooms to themselves; how many women had children before they were twenty-one; what, in short, they did from eight in the morning till eight at night.

They had no money evidently; according to Professor Trevelyan° they were married whether they liked it or not before they were out of the nursery, at fifteen or sixteen very likely. It would have been extremely odd, even upon this showing, had one of them suddenly written the plays of Shakespeare, I concluded, and I thought of that old gentleman, who is dead now, but was a bishop, I think, who declared that it was impossible for any woman, past, present, or to come, to have the genius of Shakespeare. He wrote to the papers about it. He also told a lady who applied to him for information that cats do not as a matter of fact go to heaven, though they have, he added, souls of a sort. How much thinking those old gentlemen used to save one! How the borders of ignorance shrank back at their approach! Cats do not go to heaven. Women cannot write the plays of Shakespeare.

Be that as it may, I could not help thinking, as I looked at the works of Shakespeare on the shelf, that the bishop was right at least in this; it would have been impossible, completely and entirely, for any woman to have written the plays of Shakespeare in the age of Shakespeare. Let me imagine, since facts are so hard to come by, what would have happened had Shakespeare had a wonderfully gifted sister, called Judith, let us say. Shakespeare himself went, very probably—his mother was an heiress—to the grammar school, where he may have learnt Latin—Ovid, Virgil and Horace°—and the elements of grammar and logic. He was, it is well known, a wild boy who poached rabbits, perhaps shot a deer, and had, rather sooner than he should have done, to marry a woman in the neighborhood, who bore him a child rather quicker than was right. That escapade sent him to seek his fortune in London. He had, it seemed, a taste for the theatre; he began by holding horses at the stage door. Very soon he got work in the theatre, became a successful actor, and lived at the hub of the universe, meeting everybody, knowing everybody, practicing his art on the boards, exercising his wits in the streets, and even getting access to the palace of the queen. Meanwhile his extraordinarily gifted sister, let us suppose, remained at home. She was as adventurous, as imaginative, as agog to see the world as he was. But she was not sent to school. She had no chance of learning grammar and logic, let alone of reading Horace and Virgil. She picked up a book now and then, one of her brother's perhaps, and read a few pages. But then her parents came in and told her to mend the stockings or mind the stew and not moon about with books and papers. They would have spoken sharply but kindly, for they were substantial people who knew the conditions of life for a woman and loved their daughter—indeed, more likely than not she was the apple of her father's eye. Perhaps she scribbled some pages up in an apple loft on the sly, but was careful to hide them or set fire to them. Soon, however, before she was out of her teens, she was to be betrothed to the son of a neighboring wool-stapler. She cried out that marriage was hateful to her, and for that she was severely beaten by her father. Then he ceased to scold her. He begged her instead not to hurt him, not to shame him in this matter of her marriage. He would give her a chain of beads or a fine petticoat, he said; and there were tears in his eyes. How could she disobey him? How could she break his heart? The force of her own gift alone drove her to it. She made up a small parcel of her belongings, let herself down by a rope one summer's night and took the road to London. She was not seventeen. The birds that sang

Professor Trevelyan: an eminent British historian, author of *History of England* (1926). *Ovid, Virgil and Horace*: three great Roman poets whom Shakespeare would have read and studied in his Latin grammar class.

in the hedge were not more musical than she was. She had the quickest fancy, a gift like her brother's, for the tune of words. Like him, she had a taste for the theatre. She stood at the stage door; she wanted to act, she said. Men laughed in her face. The manager—a fat, loose-lipped man—guffawed. He bellowed something about poodles dancing and women acting—no woman, he said, could possibly be an actress. He hinted—you can imagine what. She could get no training in her craft. Could she even seek her dinner in a tavern or roam the streets at midnight? Yet her genius was for fiction and lusted to feed abundantly upon the lives of men and women and the study of their ways. At last—for she was very young, oddly like Shakespeare the poet in her face, with the same grey eyes and rounded brows—at last Nick Greene the actor-manager took pity on her; she found herself with child by that gentleman and so—who shall measure the heat and violence of the poet's heart when caught and tangled in a woman's body?—killed herself one winter's night and lies buried at some cross-roads where the omnibuses now stop outside the Elephant and Castle.°

That, more or less, is how the story would run, I think, if a woman in Shakespeare's day had had Shakespeare's genius. But for my part, I agree with the deceased bishop, if such he was—it is unthinkable that any woman in Shakespeare's day should have had Shakespeare's genius. For genius like Shakespeare's is not born among laboring, uneducated, servile people. It was not born in England among the Saxons and the Britons. It is not born today among the working classes. How, then, could it have been born among women whose work began, according to Professor Trevelyan, almost before they were out of the nursery, who were forced to it by their parents and held to it by all the power of law and custom? Yet genius of a sort must have existed among women as it must have existed among the working classes. Now and again an Emily Brontë or a Robert Burns° blazes out and proves its presence. But certainly it never got itself on to paper. When, however, one reads of a witch being ducked, of a woman possessed by devils, of a wise woman selling herbs, or even of a very remarkable man who had a mother, then I think we are on the track of a lost novelist, a suppressed poet, of some mute and inglorious Jane Austen, some Emily Brontë who dashed her brains out on the moor or mopped and mowed about the highways crazed with the torture that her gift had put her to. Indeed, I would venture to guess that Anon, who wrote so many poems without signing them, was often a woman. It was a woman Edward FitzGerald,° I think, suggested who made the ballads and the folk-songs, crooning them to her children, beguiling her spinning with them, on the length of the winter's night.

This may be true or it may be false—who can say?—but what is true in it, so it seemed to me, reviewing the story of Shakespeare's sister as I had made it, is that any woman born with a great gift in the sixteenth century would certainly have gone crazed, shot herself, or ended her days in some lonely cottage outside the village, half witch, half wizard, feared and mocked at. For it needs little skill in psychology to be sure that a highly gifted girl who had tried to use her gift for poetry would have been so thwarted and hindered by other people, so tortured and pulled asunder by her own contrary instincts, that she must have lost her health and sanity to a certainty. No girl

Elephant and Castle: busy road intersection in London, also a tube station and railway station. *Emily Brontë or a Robert Burns:* Emily Brontë (1818–1848) was an English author who achieved great success as a novelist; Robert Burns (1759–1796) was a poor Scottish poet who became a national hero to his people. *Edward FitzGerald:* English poet and famous translator of Omar Khayyam's *Rubaiyat*, lived 1809–1883.

could have walked to London and stood at a stage door and forced her way into the presence of actor-managers without doing herself a violence and suffering an anguish which may have been irrational—for chastity may be a fetish invented by certain societies for unknown reasons—but were none the less inevitable. Chastity had then, it has even now, a religious importance in a woman's life, and has so wrapped itself round with nerves and instincts that to cut it free and bring it to the light of day demands courage of the rarest. To have lived a free life in London in the sixteenth century would have meant for a woman who was poet and playwright a nervous stress and dilemma which might well have killed her. Had she survived, whatever she had written would have been twisted and deformed, issuing from a strained and morbid imagination. And undoubtedly, I thought, looking at the shelf where there are no plays by women, her work would have gone unsigned. That refuge she would have sought certainly. It was the relic of the sense of chastity that dictated anonymity to women even so late as the nineteenth century. Currer Bell, George Eliot, George Sand,° all the victims of inner strife as their writings prove, sought ineffectively to veil themselves by using the name of a man. Thus they did homage to the convention, which if not implanted by the other sex was liberally encouraged by them (the chief glory of a woman is not to be talked of, said Pericles, himself a much-talked-of man), that publicity in women is detestable. Anonymity runs in their blood. The desire to be veiled still possesses them. They are not even now as concerned about the health of their fame as men are, and, speaking generally, will pass a tombstone or a signpost without feeling an irresistible desire to cut their names on it, as Alf, Bert or Chas. must do in obedience to their instinct, which murmurs if it sees a fine woman go by, or even a dog, *Ce chien est à moi*.° And, of course, it may not be a dog, I thought, remembering Parliament Square, the *Sièges Allée*° and other avenues; it may be a piece of land or a man with curly black hair. It is one of the great advantages of being a woman that one can pass even a very fine negress without wishing to make an Englishwoman of her.

That woman, then, who was born with a gift of poetry in the sixteenth century, was an unhappy woman, a woman at strife against herself. All the conditions of her life, all her own instincts, were hostile to the state of mind which is needed to set free whatever is in the brain. But what is the state of mind that is most propitious to the act of creation, I asked. Can one come by any notion of the state that furthers and makes possible that strange activity? Here I opened the volume containing the Tragedies of Shakespeare. What was Shakespeare's state of mind, for instance, when he wrote *Lear* and *Antony and Cleopatra*? It was certainly the state of mind most favorable to poetry that there has ever existed. But Shakespeare himself said nothing about it. We only know casually and by chance that he "never blotted a line." Nothing indeed was ever said by the artist himself about his state of mind until the eighteenth century perhaps. Rousseau perhaps began it. At any rate, by the nineteenth century self-consciousness had developed so far that it was the habit for men of letters to describe their minds in confessions and autobiographies.

Currer Bell, George Eliot, George Sand: Three female authors successfully adopted these male pen names for publication. Currer Bell was the pseudonym Charlotte Brontë (1816–1855) used to publish *Jane Eyre* (1847); George Eliot was the pen name of Mary Ann Evans (1819–1880), author of *Middlemarch* (1871); and George Sand was the pseudonym of the French novelist Amandine Aurore Lucie Dupin (1804–1876). *Ce chien est à moi:* French for "this dog is mine."   *Sièges Allée:* a boulevard in Berlin, Germany.

Their lives also were written, and their letters were printed after their deaths. Thus, though we do not know what Shakespeare went through when he wrote *Lear*, we do know what Carlyle went through when he wrote *The French Revolution*; what Flaubert went through when he wrote *Madame Bovary*; what Keats was going through when he tried to write poetry against the coming of death and the indifference of the world.

And one gathers from this enormous modern literature of confession and self-analysis that to write a work of genius is almost always a feat of prodigious difficulty. Everything is against the likelihood that it will come from the writer's mind whole and entire. Generally material circumstances are against it. Dogs will bark; people will interrupt; money must be made; health will break down. Further, accentuating all these difficulties and making them harder to bear is the world's notorious indifference. It does not ask people to write poems and novels and histories; it does not need them. It does not care whether Flaubert finds the right word or whether Carlyle scrupulously verifies this or that fact. Naturally, it will not pay for what it does not want. And so the writer, Keats, Flaubert, Carlyle, suffers, especially in the creative years of youth, every form of distraction and discouragement. A curse, a cry of agony, rises from those books of analysis and confession. "Mighty poets in their misery dead"°—that is the burden of their song. If anything comes through in spite of all this, it is a miracle, and probably no book is born entire and uncrippled as it was conceived.

But for women, I thought, looking at the empty shelves, these difficulties were infinitely more formidable. In the first place, to have a room of her own, let alone a quiet room or a sound-proof room, was out of the question, unless her parents were exceptionally rich or very noble, even up to the beginning of the nineteenth century. Since her pin money, which depended on the goodwill of her father, was only enough to keep her clothed, she was debarred from such alleviations as came even to Keats or Tennyson or Carlyle, all poor men, from a walking tour, a little journey to France, from the separate lodging which, even if it were miserable enough, sheltered them from the claims and tyrannies of their families. Such material difficulties were formidable; but much worse were the immaterial. The indifference of the world which Keats and Flaubert and other men of genius have found so hard to bear was in her case not indifference but hostility. The world did not say to her as it said to them, Write if you choose; it makes no difference to me. The world said with a guffaw, Write? What's the good of your writing?

Questions

1. Woolf claims that the bishop was right, that "it would have been impossible, completely and entirely, for any woman to have written the plays of Shakespeare in the age of Shakespeare" (paragraph 2). Is she being sarcastic? What does she mean?
2. Why does Woolf create a hypothetical sister for Shakespeare? How does this help her to make her points?
3. Does Woolf's essay still have relevance today? Has the world changed so much that her arguments are out of date? Why or why not?

"*Mighty poets in their misery dead*": a famous quotation from William Wordsworth's 1802 poem "Resolution and Independence."

Richard Rodriguez

Richard Rodriguez (b. 1944) was raised in Sacramento, California, in a family of Mexican immigrants. He spoke Spanish until he entered primary school. After twelve years in Catholic schools, he attended Stanford University, where he earned a B.A. and then gained an M.A. in English from Columbia. He left a Ph.D. program at University of California, Berkeley, to accept a Fulbright fellowship and soon left academia altogether to become a freelance writer. His first book, Hunger of Memory *(1981), described his own education from a disadvantaged background to a successful literary career. This book was followed by* Mexico's Children *(1990);* Days of Obligation: An Argument with My Mexican Father *(1992), in which the author revealed his own gay identity; and* Brown: The Last Discovery of America *(2002). He lives in San Francisco. A superb essayist and skilled stylist, Rodriguez is a frequent commentator on PBS and NPR. He has been an outspoken critic of bilingual education, which he believes inhibits Latino success in American society, and consequently has been attacked by some Hispanics as a traitor to his fellow Mexican Americans. But as the following essay, "'Blaxicans' and Other Reinvented Americans," makes clear, Rodriguez believes that the American racial situation is too complex and dynamic to be understood in terms of simple "us" versus "them" polarities.*

"Blaxicans" and Other Reinvented Americans   2003

There is something unsettling about immigrants because . . . well, because they chatter incomprehensibly, and they get in everyone's way. Immigrants seem to be bent on undoing America. Just when Americans think we know who we are—we are Protestants, culled from Western Europe, are we not?—then new immigrants appear from Southern Europe or from Eastern Europe. We—we who are already here—we don't know exactly what the latest comers will mean to our community. How will they fit in with us? Thus we—we who were here first—we begin to question our own identity.

After a generation or two, the grandchildren or the great-grandchildren of immigrants to the United States and the grandchildren of those who tried to keep immigrants out of the United States will romanticize the immigrant, will begin to see the immigrant as the figure who teaches us most about what it means to be an American. The immigrant, in mythic terms, travels from the outermost rind of America to the very center of American mythology. None of this, of course, can we admit to the Vietnamese immigrant who served us our breakfast at the hotel this morning. In another forty years, we will be prepared to say to the Vietnamese immigrant that he, with his breakfast tray, with his intuition for travel, with his memory of tragedy, with his recognition of peerless freedoms, he fulfills the meaning of America.

In 1997, Gallup conducted a survey on race relations in America, but the poll was concerned only with white and black Americans. No question was put to the aforementioned Vietnamese man. There was certainly no question for the Chinese grocer, none for the Guatemalan barber, none for the tribe of Mexican Indians who reroofed your neighbor's house.

The American conversation about race has always been a black-and-white conversation, but the conversation has become as bloodless as badminton.

I have listened to the black-and-white conversation for most of my life. I was supposed to attach myself to one side or the other, without asking the obvious questions: What is this perpetual dialectic between Europe and Africa? Why does it admit so little reference to anyone else?

I am speaking to you in American English that was taught me by Irish nuns—immigrant women. I wear an Indian face; I answer to a Spanish surname as well as this California first name, Richard. You might wonder about the complexity of historical factors, the collision of centuries, that creates Richard Rodriguez. My brownness is the illustration of that collision, or the bland memorial of it. I stand before you as an Impure-American, an Ambiguous-American.

In the nineteenth century, Texans used to say that the reason Mexicans were so easily defeated in battle was because we were so dilute, being neither pure Indian nor pure Spaniard. Yet, at the same time, Mexicans used to say that Mexico, the country of my ancestry, joined two worlds, two competing armies. José Vasconcelos, the Mexican educator and philosopher, famously described Mexicans as *la raza cósmica*, the cosmic race. In Mexico what one finds as early as the eighteenth century is a predominant population of mixed-race people. Also, once the slave had been freed in Mexico, the incidence of marriage between Indian and African people there was greater than in any other country in the Americas and has not been equaled since.

Race mixture has not been a point of pride in America. Americans speak more easily about "diversity" than we do about the fact that I might marry your daughter; you might become we; we might become us. America has so readily adopted the Canadian notion of multiculturalism because it preserves our preference for thinking ourselves separate—our elbows need not touch, thank you. I would prefer *that* table. I can remain Mexican, whatever that means, in the United States of America.

I would propose that instead of adopting the Canadian model of multiculturalism, America might begin to imagine the Mexican alternative—that of a *mestizaje* society.

Because of colonial Mexico, I am *mestizo*. But I was reinvented by President Richard Nixon. In the early 1970s, Nixon instructed the Office of Management and Budget to identify the major racial and ethnic groups in the United States. OMB came up with five major ethnic or racial groups. The groups are white, black, Asian/Pacific Islander, American Indian/Eskimo, and Hispanic.

It's what I learned to do when I was in college: to call myself a Hispanic. At my university we even had separate cafeteria tables and "theme houses," where the children of Nixon could gather—of a feather. Native Americans united. African-Americans. Casa Hispanic.

The interesting thing about Hispanics is that you will never meet us in Latin America. You may meet Chileans and Peruvians and Mexicans. You will not meet Hispanics. If you inquire in Lima or Bogotá about Hispanics, you will be referred to Dallas. For "Hispanic" is a gringo contrivance, a definition of the world according to European patterns of colonization. Such a definition suggests I have more in common with Argentine-Italians than with American Indians; that there is an ineffable union between the white Cuban and the mulatto Puerto Rican because of Spain. Nixon's conclusion has become the basis for the way we now organize and understand American society.

The Census Bureau foretold that by the year 2003, Hispanics would outnumber blacks to become the largest minority in the United States. And, indeed, the year 2003 has arrived and the proclamation of Hispanic ascendancy has been published far and wide. While I admit a competition has existed—does exist—in America between Hispanic and black people, I insist that the comparison of Hispanics with blacks will lead, ultimately, to complete nonsense. For there is no such thing as a Hispanic race. In Latin America, one sees every race of the world. One sees white Hispanics, one sees black Hispanics, one sees brown Hispanics who are Indians, many of whom do not speak Spanish because they resist Spain. One sees Asian-Hispanics. To compare blacks and Hispanics, therefore, is to construct a fallacious equation.

Some Hispanics have accepted the fiction. Some Hispanics have too easily accustomed themselves to impersonating a third race, a great new third race in America. But Hispanic is an ethnic term. It is a term denoting culture. So when the Census Bureau says by the year 2060 one-third of all Americans will identify themselves as Hispanic, the Census Bureau is not speculating in pigment or quantifying according to actual historical narratives, but rather is predicting how by the year 2060 one-third of all Americans will identify themselves culturally. For a country that traditionally has taken its understandings of community from blood and color, the new circumstance of so large a group of Americans identifying themselves by virtue of language or fashion or cuisine or literature is an extraordinary change, and a revolutionary one.

People ask me all the time if I envision another Quebec forming in the United States because of the large immigrant movement from the south. Do I see a Quebec forming in the Southwest, for example? No, I don't see that at all. But I do notice the Latin American immigrant population is as much as 10 years younger than the U.S. national population. I notice the Latin American immigrant population is more fertile than the U.S. national population. I see the movement of the immigrants from south to north as a movement of youth—like approaching spring!—into a country that is growing middle-aged. I notice immigrants are the archetypal Americans at a time when we—U.S, citizens—have become post-Americans, most concerned with subsidized medications.

I was at a small Apostolic Assembly in East Palo Alto a few years ago—a mainly Spanish-speaking congregation in an area along the freeway, near the heart of the Silicon Valley. This area used to be black East Palo Alto, but it is quickly becoming an Asian and Hispanic Palo Alto neighborhood. There was a moment in the service when newcomers to the congregation were introduced. Newcomers brought letters of introduction from sister evangelical churches in Latin America. The minister read out the various letters and pronounced the names and places of origin to the community. The congregation applauded. And I thought to myself: It's over. The border is over. These people were not being asked whether they had green cards. They were not being asked whether they arrived here legally or illegally. They were being welcomed within a new community for reasons of culture. There is now a north-south line that is theological, a line that cannot be circumvented by the U.S. Border Patrol.

I was on a British Broadcasting Corporation interview show, and a woman introduced me as being "in favor" of assimilation. I am not in favor of assimilation any more than I am in favor of the Pacific Ocean or clement weather. If I had a bumper sticker on the subject, it might read something like ASSIMILATION HAPPENS. One doesn't get up in the morning, as an immigrant child in America, and think to oneself, "How much of an American shall I become today?" One doesn't walk down the street and decide to be forty percent Mexican and sixty percent American. Culture is fluid. Culture is smoke. You breathe it. You eat it. You can't help hearing it—Elvis Presley goes in your ear, and you cannot get Elvis Presley out of your mind.

I am in favor of assimilation. I am not in favor of assimilation. I recognize assimilation. A few years ago, I was in Merced, California—a town of about 75,000 people in the Central Valley where the two largest immigrant groups at that time (California is so fluid, I believe this is no longer the case) were Laotian Hmong and Mexicans. Laotians have never in the history of the world, as far as I know, lived next to Mexicans. But there they were in Merced, and living next to Mexicans. They don't like each other. I was talking to the Laotian kids about why they don't like the Mexican kids. They were telling me that the Mexicans do this and the Mexicans don't do that, when I suddenly realized that they were speaking English with a Spanish accent.

On his interview show, Bill Moyers once asked me how I thought of myself. As an American? Or Hispanic? I answered that I am Chinese, and that is because I live in a Chinese city and because I want to be Chinese. Well, why not? Some Chinese-American people in the Richmond and Sunset districts of San Francisco sometimes paint their houses (so many qualifiers!) in colors I would once have described as garish: lime greens, rose reds, pumpkin. But I have lived in a Chinese city for so long that my eye has taken on that palette, has come to prefer lime greens and rose reds and all the inventions of this Chinese Mediterranean. I see photographs in magazines or documentary footage of China, especially rural China, and I see what I recognize as home. Isn't that odd?

I do think distinctions exist. I'm not talking about an America tomorrow in which we're going to find that black and white are no longer the distinguishing marks of separateness. But many young people I meet tell me they feel like Victorians when they identify themselves as black or white. They don't think of themselves in those terms. And they're already moving into a world in which tattoo or ornament or movement or commune or sexuality or drug or rave or electronic bombast are the organizing principles of their identity. The notion that they are white or black simply doesn't occur.

And increasingly, of course, one meets children who really don't know how to say what they are. They simply are too many things. I met a young girl in San Diego at a convention of mixed-race children, among whom the common habit is to define one parent over the other—black over white, for example. But this girl said that her mother was Mexican and her father was African. The girl said, "Blaxican." By reinventing language, she is reinventing America.

America does not have a vocabulary like the vocabulary the Spanish empire evolved to describe the multiplicity of racial possibilities in the New World. The conversation, the interior monologue of America, cannot rely on the old vocabulary— black, white. We are no longer a black-white nation.

So, what myth do we tell ourselves? The person who got closest to it was Karl Marx. Marx predicted that the discovery of gold in California would be a more central event to the Americas than the discovery of the Americas by Columbus—which was only the meeting of two tribes, essentially, the European and the Indian. But when gold was discovered in California in the 1840s, the entire world met. For the first time in human history, all of the known world gathered. The Malaysian stood in the gold fields alongside the African, alongside the Chinese, alongside the Australian, alongside the Yankee.

That was an event without parallel in world history and the beginning of modern California—why California today provides the mythological structure for understanding how we might talk about the American experience: not as biracial, but as the re-creation of the known world in the New World.

Sometimes truly revolutionary things happen without regard. I mean, we may wake up one morning and there is no black race. There is no white race either. There are mythologies, and—as I am in the business, insofar as I am in any business at all, of demythologizing such identities as black and white—I come to you as a man of many cultures. I come to you as Chinese. Unless you understand that I am Chinese, then you have not understood anything I have said.

Questions

1. What is a "Blaxican"? Why does Rodriguez think we need such an odd new term?
2. Rodriguez contrasts a Canadian model of multiculturalism to a Mexican alternative. What is the difference between those two visions?
3. Rodriguez states, "I am *mestizo*" (paragraph 10). What does he mean by that term?
4. What is Rodriguez's problem with the term "Hispanic," which he calls a "gringo contrivance"? Do you agree or disagree?

Suggestions for Writing on *Essays about Defining Self*

1. Re-read Douglass's "Learning to Read and Write." Then choose a current issue related to education and/or racial equality, and discuss how (and whether) Douglass's observations of more than a century ago relate to the circumstances of the current-day issue.
2. Alternatively, do the same thing with Woolf's "What If Shakespeare Had a Sister?" Think of a current issue related either to sexual equality or to groups of people who are underrepresented in the arts. Discuss how Woolf's observations relate—or don't relate—to the present-day situation.
3. Both Douglass's "Learning to Read and Write" and Woolf's "What If Shakespeare Had a Sister?" address the connection between writing and self-definition or empowerment. Think of a modern-day situation in which a person, or a group of people, is denied the right of free expression. Does this restriction relate to larger issues of control or oppression? How so? Why is the ability to express oneself considered so powerful?
4. Make a list of the ethnic, racial, regional, and religious elements in your own background. Write a short essay discussing how that particular mix contributes to your individual identity.
5. Write about a book that changed your life in some small or large way. What was it about this book and the time in your life that made the change possible?

DRAMA
PERSONAL TRANSFORMATION

Henrik Ibsen　　　　　　*A Doll's House*

Henrik Ibsen's *A Doll's House*, first produced in 1879, was a play ahead of its time. It was written in an era when women were still expected to adhere to traditional views of marriage: the man was the undisputed head of the household, the woman the home-bound caretaker of him and their children. Yet *A Doll's House*, the story of Torvald and Nora Helmer, demonstrates the drawbacks of such simplified roles. Torvald, the husband, is protective and paternalistic toward his wife, whom he does not see as having an identity separate from himself and their family. Nora, the play's main character, is initially sympathetic to her husband but grows weary of his controlling manner and strict expectations. How Nora ultimately copes with her situation was highly controversial in Ibsen's time; the playwright's belief that men and women should be equal partners in marriage was considered progressive by some, but morally dangerous by others. Despite Ibsen's sympathy for Nora, however, he does not idealize the prospects for her escape from her comfortable life of middle-class safety and privilege. Her future life will be difficult. Changing tough circumstances—or changing oneself—has its benefits, not the least of which is self-determination. But it also has its costs. Change doesn't always make a person happy, or make those around him or her happy—and it may exact heavy social, economic, and personal tolls. Sometimes, though, breaking away—whether from a relationship, a job, or some other obligation—is worth it, especially when one's freedom or identity is at stake.

Henrik Ibsen

Henrik Ibsen (1828–1906) was born in Skien, a seaport in Norway. When he was six, his father's business losses suddenly reduced his wealthy family to poverty. After a brief attempt to study medicine, young Ibsen worked as a stage manager in provincial Bergen; then, becoming known as a playwright, he moved to Oslo as artistic director of the National Theater—practical experience that gained him firm grounding in his craft. Discouraged when his theater failed and the king turned down his plea for a grant to enable him to write, Ibsen left Norway and for twenty-seven years lived in Italy and Germany. There, in his middle years (1879–1891), he wrote most of his famed plays about middle-class life, among them A Doll's House, Ghosts, An Enemy of the People, The Wild Duck, and Hedda Gabler. Introducing social problems to the stage, these plays aroused storms of controversy. Late in life Ibsen returned to Oslo, honored at last both at home and abroad.

Henrik Ibsen

A Doll's House

1879

Translated by R. Farquharson Sharp
Revised by Viktoria Michelsen

CHARACTERS

Torvald Helmer, a lawyer
Nora, his wife
Doctor Rank
Mrs. Kristine Linde
Nils Krogstad
The Helmers' three young children
Anne Marie, their nursemaid
Helene, the maid
A Porter

The action takes place in the Helmers' apartment.

ACT I

The scene is a room furnished comfortably and tastefully, but not extravagantly. At the back wall, a door to the right leads to the entrance hall. Another to the left leads to Helmer's study. Between the doors there is a piano. In the middle of the left-hand wall is a door, and beyond it a window. Near the window are a round table, armchairs, and a small sofa. In the right-hand wall, at the farther end, is another door, and on the same side, nearer the footlights, a stove, two easy chairs and a rocking chair. Between the stove and the door there is a small table. There are engravings on the walls, a cabinet with china and other small objects, and a small bookcase with expensively bound books. The floors are carpeted, and a fire burns in the stove. It is winter.

A bell rings in the hall. A moment later, we hear the door being opened. Enter Nora, humming a tune and in high spirits. She is wearing a hat and coat and carries a number of packages, which she puts down on the table to the right. She leaves the outer door open behind her. Through the door we see a porter who is carrying a Christmas tree and a basket, which he gives to the maid, who has opened the door.

Nora: Hide the Christmas tree carefully, Helene. Make sure the children don't see it till it's decorated this evening. (*To the Porter, taking out her purse.*) How much?
Porter: Fifty ore.
Nora: Here's a krone. No, keep the change.

(*The Porter thanks her and goes out. Nora shuts the door. She is laughing to herself as she takes off her hat and coat. She takes a bag of macaroons from her pocket and eats one or two, then goes cautiously to the door of her husband's study and listens.*)

Yes, he's there. (*Still humming, she goes to the table on the right.*)
Helmer (*calls out from his study*): Is that my little lark twittering out there?
Nora (*busy opening some of the packages*): Yes, it is!
Helmer: Is it my little squirrel bustling around?
Nora: Yes!
Helmer: When did my squirrel come home?

Nora: Just now. (*Puts the bag of macaroons into her pocket and wipes her mouth.*) Come in here, Torvald, and see what I bought.

Helmer: I'm very busy right now. (*A little later, he opens the door and looks into the room, pen in hand.*) Bought, did you say? All these things? Has my little spendthrift been wasting money again?

Nora: Yes, but, Torvald, this year we really can let ourselves go a little. This is the first Christmas that we don't have to watch every penny.

Helmer: Still, you know, we can't spend money recklessly.

Nora: Yes, Torvald, but we can be a little more reckless now, can't we? Just a tiny little bit! You're going to have a big salary and you'll be making lots and lots of money.

Helmer: Yes, after the New Year. But it'll still be a whole three months before the money starts coming in.

Nora: Pooh! We can borrow till then.

Helmer: Nora! (*Goes up to her and takes her playfully by the ear.*) The same little featherbrain! Just suppose that I borrowed a thousand kroner today, and you spent it all on Christmas, and then on New Year's Eve a roof tile fell on my head and killed me, and—

Nora (*putting her hand over his mouth*): Oh! Don't say such horrible things.

Helmer: Still, suppose that happened. What then?

Nora: If that happened, I don't suppose I'd care whether I owed anyone money or not.

Helmer: Yes, but what about the people who'd lent it to us?

Nora: Them? Who'd care about them? I wouldn't even know who they were.

Helmer: That's just like a woman! But seriously, Nora, you know how I feel about that. No debt, no borrowing. There can't be any freedom or beauty in a home life that depends on borrowing and debt. We two have managed to stay on the straight road so far, and we'll go on the same way for the short time that we still have to be careful.

Nora (*moving towards the stove*): As you wish, Torvald.

Helmer (*following her*): Now, now, my little skylark mustn't let her wings droop. What's the matter? Is my little squirrel sulking? (*Taking out his purse.*) Nora, what do you think I've got here?

Nora (*turning round quickly*): Money!

Helmer: There you are. (*Gives her some money.*) Do you think I don't know how much you need for the house at Christmastime?

Nora (*counting*): Ten, twenty, thirty, forty! Thank you, thank you, Torvald. That'll keep me going for a long time.

Helmer: It's going to have to.

Nora: Yes, yes, it will. But come here and let me show you what I bought. And all so cheap! Look, here's a new suit for Ivar, and a sword. And a horse and a trumpet for Bob. And a doll and doll's bed for Emmy. They're not the best, but she'll break them soon enough anyway. And here's dress material and handkerchiefs for the maids. Old Anne Marie really should have something nicer.

Helmer: And what's in this package?

Nora (*crying out*): No, no! You can't see that till this evening.

Helmer: If you say so. But now tell me, you extravagant little thing, what would you like for yourself?

Nora: For myself? Oh, I'm sure I don't want anything.

Helmer: But you must. Tell me something that you'd especially like to have—within reasonable limits.

Nora: No, I really can't think of anything. Unless, Torvald . . .

Helmer: Well?

Nora (*playing with his coat buttons, and without raising her eyes to his*): If you really want to give me something, you might . . . you might . . .

Helmer: Well, out with it!

Nora (*speaking quickly*): You might give me money, Torvald. Only just as much as you can afford. And then one of these days I'll buy something with it.

Helmer: But, Nora—

Nora: Oh, do! Dear Torvald, please, please do! Then I'll wrap it up in beautiful gold paper and hang it on the Christmas tree. Wouldn't that be fun?

Helmer: What do they call those little creatures that are always wasting money?

Nora: Spendthrifts. I know. Let's do as I suggest, Torvald, and then I'll have time to think about what I need most. That's a very sensible plan, isn't it?

Helmer (*smiling*): Yes, it is. That is, if you really did save some of the money I give you, and then really buy something for yourself. But if you spend it all on the housekeeping and all kinds of unnecessary things, then I just have to open my wallet all over again.

Nora: Oh, but, Torvald—

Helmer: You can't deny it, my dear little Nora. (*Puts his arm around her waist.*) She's a sweet little spendthrift, but she uses up a lot of money. One would hardly believe how expensive such little creatures are!

Nora: That's a terrible thing to say. I really do save all I can.

Helmer (*laughing*): That's true. All you can. But you can't save anything!

Nora (*smiling quietly and happily*): You have no idea how many bills skylarks and squirrels have, Torvald.

Helmer: You're an odd little soul. Just like your father. You always find some new way of wheedling money out of me, and, as soon as you've got it, it seems to melt in your hands. You never know where it's gone. Still, one has to take you as you are. It's in the blood. Because, you know, it's true that you can inherit these things, Nora.

Nora: Ah, I wish I'd inherited a lot of Papa's traits.

Helmer: And I wouldn't want you to be anything but just what you are, my sweet little skylark. But, you know, it seems to me that you look rather—how can I put it—rather uneasy today.

Nora: Do I?

Helmer: You do, really. Look straight at me.

Nora (*looks at him*): Well?

Helmer (*wagging his finger at her*): Has little Miss Sweet Tooth been breaking our rules in town today?

Nora: No, what makes you think that?

Helmer: Has she paid a visit to the bakery?

Nora: No, I assure you, Torvald—

Helmer: Not been nibbling pastries?

Nora: No, certainly not.

Helmer: Not even taken a bite of a macaroon or two?

Nora: No, Torvald, I assure you, really—

Helmer: Come on, you know I was only kidding.

Nora (*going to the table on the right*): I wouldn't dream of going against your wishes.

1896 production of *A Doll's House* at the Empire Theatre in New York.

Helmer: No, I'm sure of that. Besides, you gave me your word. (*Going up to her.*) Keep your little Christmas secrets to yourself, my darling. They'll all be revealed tonight when the Christmas tree is lit, no doubt.

Nora: Did you remember to invite Doctor Rank?

Helmer: No. But there's no need. It goes without saying that he'll have dinner with us. All the same, I'll ask him when he comes over this morning. I've ordered some good wine. Nora, you have no idea how much I'm looking forward to this evening.

Nora: So am I! And how the children will enjoy themselves, Torvald!

Helmer: It's great to feel that you have a completely secure position and a big enough income. It's a delightful thought, isn't it?

Nora: It's wonderful!

Helmer: Do you remember last Christmas? For three whole weeks you hid yourself away every evening until long after midnight, making ornaments for the Christmas tree and all the other fine things that were going to be a surprise for us. It was the most boring three weeks I ever spent!

Nora: I wasn't bored.

Helmer (*smiling*)*:* But there was precious little to show for it, Nora.

Nora: Oh, you're not going to tease me about that again. How could I help it that the cat went in and tore everything to pieces?

Helmer: Of course you couldn't, poor little girl. You had the best of intentions to make us all happy, and that's the main thing. But it's a good thing that our hard times are over.

Nora: Yes, it really is wonderful.

Helmer: This time I don't have to sit here and be bored all by myself, and you don't have to ruin your dear eyes and your pretty little hands—

2009 adaptation of *A Doll's House* at the Donmar Warehouse in London starring Gillian Anderson and Toby Stephens.

Nora (*clapping her hands*): No, Torvald, I don't have to anymore, do I! It's wonderfully lovely to hear you say so! (*Taking his arm.*) Now let me tell you how I've been thinking we should arrange things, Torvald. As soon as Christmas is over— (*A bell rings in the hall.*) There's the bell. (*She tidies the room a little.*) There's somebody at the door. What a nuisance!
Helmer: If someone's visiting, remember I'm not home.
Maid (*in the doorway*): A lady to see you, ma'am. A stranger.
Nora: Ask her to come in.
Maid (*to Helmer*): The doctor's here too, sir.
Helmer: Did he go straight into my study?
Maid: Yes, sir.

(*Helmer goes into his study. The maid ushers in Mrs. Linde, who is in traveling clothes, and shuts the door.*)

Mrs. Linde (*in a dejected and timid voice*): Hello, Nora.
Nora (*doubtfully*): Hello.
Mrs. Linde: You don't recognize me, I suppose.

Nora: No, I don't know . . . Yes, of course, I think so—(*Suddenly.*) Yes! Kristine! Is it really you?

Mrs. Linde: Yes, it is.

Nora: Kristine! Imagine my not recognizing you! And yet how could I—(*In a gentle voice.*) You've changed, Kristine!

Mrs. Linde: Yes, I certainly have. In nine, ten long years—

Nora: Is it that long since we've seen each other? I suppose it is. The last eight years have been a happy time for me, you know. And so now you've come to town, and you've taken this long trip in the winter. That was brave of you.

Mrs. Linde: I arrived by steamer this morning.

Nora: To have some fun at Christmastime, of course. How delightful! We'll have such fun together! But take off your things. You're not cold, I hope. (*Helps her.*) Now we'll sit down by the stove and be cozy. No, take this armchair. I'll sit here in the rocking chair. (*Takes her hands.*) Now you look like your old self again. It was only that first moment. You are a little paler, Kristine, and maybe a little thinner.

Mrs. Linde: And much, much older, Nora.

Nora: Maybe a little older. Very, very little. Surely not very much. (*Stops suddenly and speaks seriously.*) What a thoughtless thing I am, chattering away like this. My poor, dear Kristine, please forgive me.

Mrs. Linde: What do you mean, Nora?

Nora (*gently*): Poor Kristine, you're a widow.

Mrs. Linde: Yes. For three years now.

Nora: Yes, I knew. I saw it in the papers. I swear to you, Kristine, I kept meaning to write to you at the time, but I always put it off and something always came up.

Mrs. Linde: I understand completely, dear.

Nora: It was very bad of me, Kristine. Poor thing, how you must have suffered. And he left you nothing?

Mrs. Linde: No.

Nora: And no children?

Mrs. Linde: No.

Nora: Nothing at all, then?

Mrs. Linde: Not even any sorrow or grief to live on.

Nora (*looking at her in disbelief*): But, Kristine, is that possible?

Mrs. Linde (*smiles sadly and strokes Nora's hair*): It happens sometimes, Nora.

Nora: So you're completely alone. How terribly sad that must be. I have three beautiful children. You can't see them just now, because they're out with their nursemaid. But now you must tell me all about it.

Mrs. Linde: No, no, I want to hear about you.

Nora: No, you go first. I mustn't be selfish today. Today I should think only about you. But there is one thing I have to tell you. Do you know we've just had a fabulous piece of good luck?

Mrs. Linde: No, what is it?

Nora: Just imagine, my husband's been appointed manager of the bank!

Mrs. Linde: Your husband? That is good luck!

Nora: Yes, it's tremendous! A lawyer's life is so uncertain, especially if he won't take any cases that are the slightest bit shady, and of course Torvald has never been willing to do that, and I completely agree with him. You can imagine how delighted we are! He starts his job in the bank at New Year's, and then he'll have a big salary and lots of commissions. From now on we can live very differently. We can do just what we want. I feel so relieved and so happy, Kristine! It'll be wonderful to have heaps of money and not have to worry about anything, won't it?

Mrs. Linde: Yes. Anyway, I think it would be delightful to have what you need.

Nora: No, not only what you need, but heaps and heaps of money.

Mrs. Linde (*smiling*): Nora, Nora, haven't you learned any sense yet? Back in school you were a terrible spendthrift.

Nora (*laughing*): Yes, that's what Torvald says now. (*Wags her finger at her.*) But "Nora, Nora" isn't as silly as you think. We haven't been in a position for me to waste money. We've both had to work.

Mrs. Linde: You too?

Nora: Oh, yes, odds and ends, needlework, crocheting, embroidery, and that kind of thing. (*Dropping her voice.*) And other things too. You know Torvald left his government job when we got married? There was no chance of promotion, and he had to try to earn more money than he was making there. But in that first year he overworked himself terribly. You see, he had to make money any way he could, and he worked all hours, but he couldn't take it, and he got very sick, and the doctors said he had to go south, to a warmer climate.

Mrs. Linde: You spent a whole year in Italy, didn't you?

Nora: Yes. It wasn't easy to get away, I can tell you that. It was just after Ivar was born, but obviously we had to go. It was a wonderful, beautiful trip, and it saved Torvald's life. But it cost a tremendous amount of money, Kristine.

Mrs. Linde: I would imagine so.

Nora: It cost about four thousand, eight hundred kroner. That's a lot, isn't it?

Mrs. Linde: Yes, it is, and when you have an emergency like that it's lucky to have the money.

Nora: Well, the fact is, we got it from Papa.

Mrs. Linde: Oh, I see. It was just about that time that he died, wasn't it?

Nora: Yes, and, just think of it, I couldn't even go and take care of him. I was expecting little Ivar any day and I had my poor sick Torvald to look after. My dear, kind father. I never saw him again, Kristine. That was the worst experience I've gone through since we got married.

Mrs. Linde: I know how fond of him you were. And then you went off to Italy?

Nora: Yes. You see, we had money then, and the doctors insisted that we go, so we left a month later.

Mrs. Linde: And your husband came back completely recovered?

Nora: The picture of health!

Mrs. Linde: But . . . the doctor?

Nora: What doctor?

Mrs. Linde: Didn't your maid say that the gentleman who arrived here with me was the doctor?

Nora: Yes, that was Doctor Rank, but he doesn't come here professionally. He's our dearest friend, and he drops in at least once every day. No, Torvald hasn't been sick for an hour since then, and our children are strong and healthy, and so am I. (*Jumps up and claps her hands.*) Kristine! Kristine! It's good to be alive and happy! But how awful of me. I'm talking about nothing but myself. (*Sits on a nearby stool and rests her arms on her knees.*) Please don't be mad at me. Tell me, is it really true that you didn't love your husband? Why did you marry him?

Mrs. Linde: My mother was still alive then, and she was bedridden and helpless, and I had to provide for my two younger brothers, so I didn't think I had any right to turn him down.

Nora: No, maybe you did the right thing. So he was rich then?

Mrs. Linde: I believe he was quite well off. But his business wasn't very solid, and when he died, it all went to pieces and there was nothing left.

Nora: And then?

Mrs. Linde: Well, I had to turn my hand to anything I could find. First a small shop, then a small school, and so on. The last three years have seemed like one long workday, with no rest. Now it's over, Nora. My poor mother's gone and doesn't need me anymore, and the boys don't need me, either. They've got jobs now and can manage for themselves.

Nora: What a relief it must be if—

Mrs. Linde: No, not at all. All I feel is an unbearable emptiness. No one to live for anymore. (*Gets up restlessly.*) That's why I couldn't stand it any longer in my little backwater. I hope it'll be easier to find something here that'll keep me busy and occupy my mind. If I could be lucky enough to find some regular work, office work of some kind—

Nora: But, Kristine, that's so awfully tiring, and you look tired out now. It'd be much better for you if you could get away to a resort.

Mrs. Linde (*walking to the window*): I don't have a father to give me money for a trip, Nora.

Nora (*rising*): Oh, don't be mad at me!

Mrs. Linde (*going up to her*): It's you who mustn't be mad at me, dear. The worst thing about a situation like mine is that it makes you so bitter. No one to work for, and yet you have to always be on the lookout for opportunities. You have to live, and so you grow selfish. When you told me about your good luck—you'll find this hard to believe—I was delighted less for you than for myself.

Nora: What do you mean? Oh, I understand. You mean that maybe Torvald could find you a job.

Mrs. Linde: Yes, that's what I was thinking.

Nora: He must, Kristine. Just leave it to me. I'll broach the subject very cleverly. I'll think of something that'll put him in a really good mood. It'll make me so happy to be of some use to you.

Mrs. Linde: How kind you are, Nora, to be so eager to help me! It's doubly kind of you, since you know so little of the burdens and troubles of life.

Nora: Me? I know so little of them?

Mrs. Linde (*smiling*): My dear! Small household cares and that sort of thing! You're a child, Nora.

Nora (*tosses her head and crosses the stage*): You shouldn't act so superior.

Mrs. Linde: No?
Nora: You're just like the others. They all think I'm incapable of anything really serious—
Mrs. Linde: Come on—
Nora: —that I haven't had to deal with any real problems in my life.
Mrs. Linde: But, my dear Nora, you've just told me all your troubles.
Nora: Pooh! That was nothing. (*Lowering her voice.*) I haven't told you the important thing.
Mrs. Linde: The important thing? What do you mean?
Nora: You really look down on me, Kristine, but you shouldn't. Aren't you proud of having worked so hard and so long for your mother?
Mrs. Linde: Believe me, I don't look down on anyone. But it's true, I'm proud and I'm glad that I had the privilege of making my mother's last days almost worry-free.
Nora: And you're proud of what you did for your brothers?
Mrs. Linde: I think I have the right to be.
Nora: I think so, too. But now, listen to this. I have something to be proud of and happy about too.
Mrs. Linde: I'm sure you do. But what do you mean?
Nora: Keep your voice down. If Torvald were to overhear! He can't find out, not under any circumstances. No one in the world must know, Kristine, except you.
Mrs. Linde: But what is it?
Nora: Come here. (*Pulls her down on the sofa beside her.*) Now I'll show you that I too have something to be proud and happy about. I'm the one who saved Torvald's life.
Mrs. Linde: Saved? How?
Nora: I told you about our trip to Italy. Torvald would never have recovered if he hadn't gone there—
Mrs. Linde: Yes, but your father gave you the money you needed.
Nora (*smiling*): Yes, that's what Torvald thinks, along with everybody else, but—
Mrs. Linde: But—
Nora: Papa didn't give us a penny. I was the one who raised the money.
Mrs. Linde: You? That huge amount?
Nora: That's right, four thousand, eight hundred kroner. What do you think of that?
Mrs. Linde: But, Nora, how could you possibly? Did you win the lottery?
Nora (*disdainfully*): The lottery? That wouldn't have been any accomplishment.
Mrs. Linde: But where did you get it from, then?
Nora (*humming and smiling with an air of mystery*): Hm, hm! Ha!
Mrs. Linde: Because you couldn't have borrowed it.
Nora: Couldn't I? Why not?
Mrs. Linde: No, a wife can't borrow money without her husband's consent.
Nora (*tossing her head*): Oh, if it's a wife with a head for business, a wife who has the brains to be a little clever—
Mrs. Linde: I don't understand this at all, Nora.
Nora: There's no reason why you should. I never said I'd borrowed the money. Maybe I got it some other way. (*Lies back on the sofa.*) Maybe I got it from an admirer. When a woman's as pretty as I am—
Mrs. Linde: You're crazy.

Nora: Now, you know you're dying of curiosity, Kristine.

Mrs. Linde: Listen to me, Nora dear. Have you done something rash?

Nora (sits up straight): Is it rash to save your husband's life?

Mrs. Linde: I think it's rash, without his knowledge, to—

Nora: But it was absolutely necessary that he not know! My goodness, can't you understand that? It was necessary he have no idea how sick he was. The doctors came to *me* and said his life was in danger and the only thing that could save him was to live in the south. Don't you think I tried first to get him to do it as if it was for me? I told him how much I would love to travel abroad like other young wives. I tried tears and pleading with him. I told him he should remember the condition I was in, and that he should be kind and indulgent to me. I even hinted that he might take out a loan. That almost made him mad, Kristine. He said I was thoughtless, and that it was his duty as my husband not to indulge me in my "whims and caprices," as I believe he called them. All right, I thought, you need to be saved. And that was how I came to think up a way out of the mess—

Mrs. Linde: And your husband never found out from your father that the money hadn't come from him?

Nora: No, never. Papa died just then. I'd meant to let him in on the secret and beg him never to reveal it. But he was so sick. Unfortunately, there never was any need to tell him.

Mrs. Linde: And since then you've never told your secret to your husband?

Nora: Good heavens, no! How could you think I would? A man with such strong opinions about these things! Besides, how painful and humiliating it would be for Torvald, with his masculine pride, to know that he owed me anything! It would completely upset the balance of our relationship. Our beautiful happy home would never be the same.

Mrs. Linde: Are you never going to tell him about it?

Nora (meditatively, and with a half smile): Yes, someday, maybe, in many years, when I'm not as pretty as I am now. Don't laugh at me! I mean, of course, when Torvald is no longer as devoted to me as he is now, when he's grown tired of my dancing and dressing up and reciting. Then it may be a good thing to have something in reserve— (*Breaking off.*) What nonsense! That time will never come. Now, what do you think of my great secret, Kristine? Do you still think I'm useless? And the fact is, this whole situation has caused me a lot of worry. It hasn't been easy for me to make my payments on time. I can tell you that there's something in business that's called quarterly interest, and something else called installment payments, and it's always so terribly difficult to keep up with them. I've had to save a little here and there, wherever I could, you understand. I haven't been able to put much aside from my housekeeping money, because Torvald has to live well. And I couldn't let my children be shabbily dressed. I feel I have to spend everything he gives me for them, the sweet little darlings!

Mrs. Linde: So it's all had to come out of your own allowance, poor Nora?

Nora: Of course. Besides, I was the one responsible for it. Whenever Torvald has given me money for new dresses and things like that, I've never spent more than half of it. I've always bought the simplest and cheapest things. Thank heaven, any clothes look good on me, and so Torvald's never noticed anything. But it was often very hard on me, Kristine, because it is delightful to be really well dressed, isn't it?

Mrs. Linde: I suppose so.

Nora: Well, then I've found other ways of earning money. Last winter I was lucky enough to get a lot of copying to do, so I locked myself up and sat writing every evening until late into the night. A lot of the time I was desperately tired, but all the same it was a tremendous pleasure to sit there working and earning money. It was like being a man.

Mrs. Linde: How much have you been able to pay off that way?

Nora: I can't tell you exactly. You see, it's very hard to keep a strict account of a business matter like that. I only know that I've paid out every penny I could scrape together. Many a time I was at my wits' end. (*Smiles.*) Then I used to sit here and imagine that a rich old gentleman had fallen in love with me—

Mrs. Linde: What! Who was it?

Nora: Oh, be quiet! That he had died, and that when his will was opened it said, in great big letters: "The lovely Mrs. Nora Helmer is to have everything I own paid over to her immediately in cash."

Mrs. Linde: But, my dear Nora, who could the man be?

Nora: Good gracious, can't you understand? There wasn't any old gentleman. It was only something that I used to sit here and imagine, when I couldn't think of any way of getting money. But it's all right now. The tiresome old gent can stay right where he is, as far as I'm concerned. I don't care about him or his will either, because now I'm worry-free. (*Jumps up.*) My goodness, it's delightful to think of, Kristine! Worry-free! To be able to have no worries, no worries at all! To be able to play and romp with the children! To be able to keep the house beautifully and have everything just the way Torvald likes it! And, just think of it, soon the spring will come and the big blue sky! Maybe we can take a little trip. Maybe I can see the sea again! Oh, it's a wonderful thing to be alive and happy.

(*A bell rings in the hall.*)

Mrs. Linde (*rising*): There's the bell. Perhaps I should be going.

Nora: No, don't go. No one will come in here. It's sure to be for Torvald.

Servant (*at the hall door*): Excuse me, ma'am. There's a gentleman to see the master, and as the doctor is still with him—

Nora: Who is it?

Krogstad (*at the door*): It's me, Mrs. Helmer.

(*Mrs. Linde starts, trembles, and turns toward the window.*)

Nora (*takes a step toward him, and speaks in a strained, low voice*): You? What is it? What do you want to see my husband for?

Krogstad: Bank business, in a way. I have a small position in the bank, and I hear your husband is going to be our boss now—

Nora: Then it's—

Krogstad: Nothing but dry business matters, Mrs. Helmer, that's all.

Nora: Then please go into the study.

(*She bows indifferently to him and shuts the door into the hall, then comes back and makes up the fire in the stove.*)

Mrs. Linde: Nora, who was that man?

Nora: A lawyer. His name is Krogstad.
Mrs. Linde: Then it really was him.
Nora: Do you know the man?
Mrs. Linde: I used to, many years ago. At one time he was a law clerk in our town.
Nora: That's right, he was.
Mrs. Linde: How much he's changed.
Nora: He had a very unhappy marriage.
Mrs. Linde: He's a widower now, isn't he?
Nora: With several children. There, now it's really caught. (*Shuts the door of the stove and moves the rocking chair aside.*)
Mrs. Linde: They say he's mixed up in a lot of questionable business.
Nora: Really? Maybe he is. I don't know anything about it. But let's not talk about business. It's so tiresome.
Doctor Rank (*comes out of Helmer's study. Before he shuts the door he calls to Helmer*): No, my dear fellow, I won't disturb you. I'd rather go in and talk to your wife for a little while.

(*Shuts the door and sees Mrs. Linde.*)

I beg your pardon. I'm afraid I'm in the way here too.
Nora: No, not at all. (*Introducing him:*) Doctor Rank, Mrs. Linde.
Rank: I've often heard that name in this house. I think I passed you on the stairs when I arrived, Mrs. Linde?
Mrs. Linde: Yes, I take stairs very slowly. I can't manage them very well.
Rank: Oh, some small internal problem?
Mrs. Linde: No, it's just that I've been overworking myself.
Rank: Is that all? Then I suppose you've come to town to get some rest by sampling our social life.
Mrs. Linde: I've come to look for work.
Rank: Is that a good cure for overwork?
Mrs. Linde: One has to live, Doctor Rank.
Rank: Yes, that seems to be the general opinion.
Nora: Now, now, Doctor Rank, you know you want to live.
Rank: Of course I do. However miserable I may feel, I want to prolong the agony for as long as possible. All my patients are the same way. And so are those who are morally sick. In fact, one of them, and a bad case too, is at this very moment inside with Helmer—
Mrs. Linde (*sadly*): Ah!
Nora: Who are you talking about?
Rank: A lawyer by the name of Krogstad, a fellow you don't know at all. He's a completely worthless creature, Mrs. Helmer. But even he started out by saying, as if it were a matter of the utmost importance, that he has to live.
Nora: Did he? What did he want to talk to Torvald about?
Rank: I have no idea. All I heard was that it was something about the bank.
Nora: I didn't know this—what's his name—Krogstad had anything to do with the bank.
Rank: Yes, he has some kind of a position there. (*To Mrs. Linde*) I don't know whether you find the same thing in your part of the world, that there are certain people who go

around zealously looking to sniff out moral corruption, and, as soon as they find some, they put the person involved in some cushy job where they can keep an eye on him. Meanwhile, the morally healthy ones are left out in the cold.

Mrs. Linde: Still, I think it's the sick who are most in need of being taken care of.

Rank (shrugging his shoulders): Well, there you have it. That's the attitude that's turning society into a hospital.

(*Nora, who has been absorbed in her thoughts, breaks out into smothered laughter and claps her hands.*)

Rank: Why are you laughing at that? Do you have any idea what society really is?

Nora: What do I care about your boring society? I'm laughing at something else, something very funny. Tell me, Doctor Rank, are all the people who work in the bank dependent on Torvald now?

Rank: That's what's so funny?

Nora (smiling and humming): That's my business! (*Walking around the room.*) It's just wonderful to think that we have—that Torvald has—so much power over so many people. (*Takes the bag out of her pocket.*) Doctor Rank, what do you say to a macaroon?

Rank: Macaroons? I thought they were forbidden here.

Nora: Yes, but these are some Kristine gave me.

Mrs. Linde: What! Me?

Nora: Oh, well, don't be upset! How could you know that Torvald had forbidden them? I have to tell you, he's afraid they'll ruin my teeth. But so what? Once in a while, that's all right, isn't it, Doctor Rank? With your permission! (*Puts a macaroon into his mouth.*) You have to have one too, Kristine. And I'll have one, just a little one—or no more than two. (*Walking around.*) I am tremendously happy. There's just one thing in the world now that I would dearly love to do.

Rank: Well, what is it?

Nora: It's something I would dearly love to say, if Torvald could hear me.

Rank: Well, why can't you say it?

Nora: No, I don't dare. It's too shocking.

Mrs. Linde: Shocking?

Rank: Well then, I'd advise you not to say it. Still, in front of us you might risk it. What is it you'd so much like to say if Torvald could hear you?

Nora: I would just love to say—"Well, I'll be damned!"

Rank: Are you crazy?

Mrs. Linde: Nora, dear!

Rank: Here he is. Say it!

Nora (hiding the bag): Shh, shh, shh!

(*Helmer comes out of his room, with his coat over his arm and his hat in his hand.*)

Nora: Well, Torvald dear, did you get rid of him?

Helmer: Yes, he just left.

Nora: Let me introduce you. This is Kristine. She's just arrived in town.

Helmer: Kristine? I'm sorry, but I don't know any—

Nora: Mrs. Linde, dear, Kristine Linde.

Helmer: Oh, of course. A school friend of my wife's, I believe?
Mrs. Linde: Yes, we knew each other back then.
Nora: And just think, she's come all this way in order to see you.
Helmer: What do you mean?
Mrs. Linde: No, really, I—
Nora: Kristine is extremely good at bookkeeping, and she's very eager to work for some talented man, so she can perfect her skills—
Helmer: Very sensible, Mrs. Linde.
Nora: And when she heard that you'd been named manager of the bank—the news was sent by telegraph, you know—she traveled here as quickly as she could. Torvald, I'm sure you'll be able to do something for Kristine, for my sake, won't you?
Helmer: Well, it's not completely out of the question. I expect that you're a widow, Mrs. Linde?
Mrs. Linde: Yes.
Helmer: And you've had some bookkeeping experience?
Mrs. Linde: Yes, a fair amount.
Helmer: Ah! Well, there's a very good chance that I'll be able to find something for you—
Nora (clapping her hands): What did I tell you? What did I tell you?
Helmer: You've just come at a lucky moment, Mrs. Linde.
Mrs. Linde: How can I thank you?
Helmer: There's no need. (*Puts on his coat.*) But now you must excuse me—
Rank: Wait a minute. I'll come with you. (*Brings his fur coat from the hall and warms it at the fire.*)
Nora: Don't be long, Torvald dear.
Helmer: About an hour, that's all.
Nora: Are you leaving too, Kristine?
Mrs. Linde (putting on her cloak): Yes, I have to go and look for a place to stay.
Helmer: Oh, well then, we can walk down the street together.
Nora (helping her): It's too bad we're so short of space here. I'm afraid it's impossible for us—
Mrs. Linde: Please don't even think of it! Goodbye, Nora dear, and many thanks.
Nora: Goodbye for now. Of course you'll come back this evening. And you too, Dr. Rank. What do you say? If you're feeling up to it? Oh, you have to be! Wrap yourself up warmly.

(*They go to the door all talking together. Children's voices are heard on the staircase.*)

Nora: There they are! There they are!

(*She runs to open the door. The nursemaid comes in with the children.*)

Come in! Come in! (*Stoops and kisses them.*) Oh, you sweet blessings! Look at them, Kristine! Aren't they darlings?
Rank: Let's not stand here in the draft.
Helmer: Come along, Mrs. Linde. Only a mother will be able to stand it in here now!

(*Rank, Helmer, and Mrs. Linde go downstairs. The Nursemaid comes forward with the children. Nora shuts the hall door.*)

Nora: How fresh and healthy you look! Cheeks as red as apples and roses. (*The children all talk at once while she speaks to them.*) Did you have a lot of fun? That's wonderful! What, you pulled Emmy and Bob on the sled? Both at once? That was really something. You *are* a clever boy, Ivar. Let me take her for a little, Anne Marie. My sweet little baby doll! (*Takes the baby from the maid and dances her up and down.*) Yes, yes, mother will dance with Bob too. What! Have you been throwing snowballs? I wish I'd been there too! No, no, I'll take their things off, Anne Marie, please let me do it, it's such fun. Go inside now, you look half frozen. There's some hot coffee for you on the stove.

(*The Nursemaid goes into the room on the left. Nora takes off the children's things and throws them around, while they all talk to her at once.*)

Nora: Really! Did a big dog run after you? But it didn't bite you? No, dogs don't bite nice little dolly children. You mustn't look at the packages, Ivar. What are they? Oh, I'll bet you'd like to know. No, no, it's something boring! Come on, let's play a game! What should we play? Hide and seek? Yes, we'll play hide and seek. Bob will hide first. You want me to hide? All right, I'll hide first.

(*She and the children laugh and shout, and romp in and out of the room. At last Nora hides under the table. The children rush in and out looking for her, but they don't see her. They hear her smothered laughter, run to the table, lift up the cloth and find her. Shouts of laughter. She crawls forward and pretends to scare them. More laughter. Meanwhile there has been a knock at the hall door, but none of them has noticed it. The door is opened halfway and Krogstad appears. He waits for a little while. The game goes on.*)

Krogstad: Excuse me, Mrs. Helmer.
Nora (*with a stifled cry, turns round and gets up onto her knees*): Oh! What do you want?
Krogstad: Excuse me, the outside door was open. I suppose someone forgot to shut it.
Nora (*rising*): My husband is out, Mr. Krogstad.
Krogstad: I know that.
Nora: What do you want here, then?
Krogstad: A word with you.
Nora: With me? (*To the children, gently.*) Go inside to Anne Marie. What? No, the strange man won't hurt Mother. When he's gone we'll play another game. (*She takes the children into the room on the left, and shuts the door after them.*) You want to speak to me?
Krogstad: Yes, I do.
Nora: Today? It isn't the first of the month yet.
Krogstad: No, it's Christmas Eve, and it's up to you what kind of Christmas you're going to have.
Nora: What do you mean? Today it's absolutely impossible for me—
Krogstad: We won't talk about that until later on. This is something else. I presume you can spare me a moment?
Nora: Yes, yes, I can. Although . . .
Krogstad: Good. I was in Olsen's restaurant and I saw your husband going down the street—

Nora: Yes?

Krogstad: With a lady.

Nora: So?

Krogstad: May I be so bold as to ask if it was a Mrs. Linde?

Nora: It was.

Krogstad: Just arrived in town?

Nora: Yes, today.

Krogstad: She's a very good friend of yours, isn't she?

Nora: She is. But I don't see—

Krogstad: I knew her too, once upon a time.

Nora: I'm aware of that.

Krogstad: Are you? So you know all about it. I thought so. Then I can ask you, without beating around the bush. Is Mrs. Linde going to work in the bank?

Nora: What right do you have to question me, Mr. Krogstad? You're one of my husband's employees. But since you ask, I'll tell you. Yes, Mrs. Linde is going to work in the bank. And I'm the one who spoke up for her, Mr. Krogstad. So now you know.

Krogstad: So I was right, then.

Nora (*walking up and down the stage*): Sometimes one has a tiny little bit of influence, I should hope. Just because I'm a woman, it doesn't necessarily follow that—You know, when somebody's in a subordinate position, Mr. Krogstad, they should really be careful to avoid offending anyone who—who—

Krogstad: Who has influence?

Nora: Exactly.

Krogstad (*changing his tone*): Mrs. Helmer, may I ask you to use *your* influence on my behalf?

Nora: What? What do you mean?

Krogstad: Will you be kind enough to see to it that I'm allowed to keep my subordinate position in the bank?

Nora: What do you mean by that? Who's threatening to take your job away from you?

Krogstad: Oh, there's no need to keep up the pretence of ignorance. I can understand that your friend isn't very anxious to expose herself to the chance of rubbing shoulders with me. And now I realize exactly who I have to thank for pushing me out.

Nora: But I swear to you—

Krogstad: Yes, yes. But, to get right to the point, there's still time to prevent it, and I would advise you to use your influence to do so.

Nora: But, Mr. Krogstad, I have no influence.

Krogstad: Oh no? Didn't you yourself just say—

Nora: Well, obviously, I didn't mean for you to take it that way. Me? What would make you think I have that kind of influence with my husband?

Krogstad: Oh, I've known your husband since our school days. I don't suppose he's any more unpersuadable than other husbands.

Nora: If you're going to talk disrespectfully about my husband, I'll have to ask you to leave my house.

Krogstad: Bold talk, Mrs. Helmer.

Nora: I'm not afraid of you anymore. When the New Year comes, I'll soon be free of the whole thing.

Krogstad (*controlling himself*): Listen to me, Mrs. Helmer. If I have to, I'm ready to fight for my little job in the bank as if I were fighting for my life.

Nora: So it seems.

Krogstad: It's not just for the sake of the money. In fact, that matters the least to me. There's another reason. Well, I might as well tell you. Here's my situation. I suppose, like everybody else, you know that many years ago I did something pretty foolish.

Nora: I think I heard something about it.

Krogstad: It never got as far as the courtroom, but every door seemed closed to me after that. So I got involved in the business that you know about. I had to do something, and, honestly, I think there are many worse than me. But now I have to get myself free of all that. My sons are growing up. For their sake I have to try to win back as much respect as I can in this town. The job in the bank was like the first step up for me, and now your husband is going to kick me downstairs back into the mud.

Nora: But you have to believe me, Mr. Krogstad, it's not in my power to help you at all.

Krogstad: Then it's because you don't want to. But I have ways of making you.

Nora: You don't mean you'll tell my husband I owe you money?

Krogstad: Hm! And what if I did tell him?

Nora: That would be a terrible thing for you to do. (*Sobbing.*) To think he would learn my secret, which has been my pride and joy, in such an ugly, clumsy way—that he would learn it from you! And it would put me in a horribly uncomfortable position—

Krogstad: Just uncomfortable?

Nora (*impetuously*): Well, go ahead and do it, then! And it'll be so much the worse for you. My husband will see for himself how vile you are, and then you'll lose your job for sure.

Krogstad: I asked you if it's just an uncomfortable situation at home that you're afraid of.

Nora: If my husband does find out about it, of course he'll immediately pay you what I still owe, and then we'll be through with you once and for all.

Krogstad (*coming a step closer*): Listen to me, Mrs. Helmer. Either you have a very bad memory or you don't know much about business. I can see I'm going to have to remind you of a few details.

Nora: What do you mean?

Krogstad: When your husband was sick, you came to me to borrow four thousand, eight hundred kroner.

Nora: I didn't know anyone else to go to.

Krogstad: I promised to get you that amount—

Nora: Yes, and you did so.

Krogstad: I promised to get you that amount, on certain conditions. You were so preoccupied with your husband's illness, and you were so anxious to get the money for your trip, that you seem to have paid no attention to the conditions of our bargain. So it won't be out of place for me to remind you of them. Now, I promised to get the money on the security of a note which I drew up.

Nora: Yes, and which I signed.

Krogstad: Good. But underneath your signature there were a few lines naming your father as a co-signer who guaranteed the repayment of the loan. Your father was supposed to sign that part.

Nora: Supposed to? He did sign it.
Krogstad: I had left the date blank. That was because your father was supposed to fill in the date when he signed the paper. Do you remember that?
Nora: Yes, I think I remember. . . .
Krogstad: Then I gave you the note to mail to your father. Isn't that so?
Nora: Yes.
Krogstad: And obviously you mailed it right away, because five or six days later you brought me the note with your father's signature. And then I gave you the money.
Nora: Well, haven't I been paying it back regularly?
Krogstad: Fairly regularly, yes. But, to get back to the point, that must have been a very difficult time for you, Mrs. Helmer.
Nora: Yes, it was.
Krogstad: Your father was very sick, wasn't he?
Nora: He was very near the end.
Krogstad: And he died soon after?
Nora: Yes.
Krogstad: Tell me, Mrs. Helmer, can you by any chance remember what day your father died? On what day of the month, I mean.
Nora: Papa died on the 29th of September.
Krogstad: That's right. I looked it up myself. And, since that is the case, there's something extremely peculiar (*taking a piece of paper from his pocket*) that I can't account for.
Nora: Peculiar in what way? I don't know—
Krogstad: The peculiar thing, Mrs. Helmer, is the fact that your father signed this note three days after he died.
Nora: What do you mean? I don't understand—
Krogstad: Your father died on the 29th of September. But, look here. Your father dated his signature the 2nd of October. It is mighty peculiar, isn't it? (*Nora is silent.*) Can you explain it to me? (*Nora is still silent.*) And what's just as peculiar is that the words "October 2," as well as the year, are not in your father's handwriting, but in someone else's, which I think I recognize. Well, of course it can all be explained. Your father might have forgotten to date his signature, and someone else might have filled in the date before they knew that he had died. There's no harm in that. It all depends on the signature, and that's genuine, isn't it, Mrs. Helmer? It was your father himself who signed his name here?
Nora (*after a short pause, lifts her head up and looks defiantly at him*): No, it wasn't. I'm the one who wrote Papa's name.
Krogstad: Are you aware that you're making a very serious confession?
Nora: How so? You'll get your money soon.
Krogstad: Let me ask you something. Why didn't you send the paper to your father?
Nora: It was out of the question. Papa was too sick. If I had asked him to sign something, I'd have had to tell him what the money was for, and when he was so sick himself I couldn't tell him that my husband's life was in danger. It was out of the question.
Krogstad: It would have been better for you if you'd given up your trip abroad.
Nora: No, that was impossible. That trip was to save my husband's life. I couldn't give that up.

Krogstad: But didn't it ever occur to you that you were committing a fraud against me?

Nora: I couldn't take that into account. I didn't trouble myself about you at all. I couldn't stand you, because you put so many heartless difficulties in my way, even though you knew how seriously ill my husband was.

Krogstad: Mrs. Helmer, you evidently don't realize clearly what you're guilty of. But, believe me, my one mistake, which cost me my whole reputation, was nothing more and nothing worse than what you did.

Nora: You? You expect me to believe that you were brave enough to take a risk to save your wife's life?

Krogstad: The law doesn't care about motives.

Nora: Then the law must be very stupid.

Krogstad: Stupid or not, it's the law that's going to judge you, if I produce this paper in court.

Nora: I don't believe it. Isn't a daughter allowed to spare her dying father anxiety and concern? Isn't a wife allowed to save her husband's life? I don't know much about the law, but I'm sure there must be provisions for things like that. Don't you know anything about such provisions? You seem like a very poor excuse for a lawyer, Mr. Krogstad.

Krogstad: That's as may be. But business, the kind of business you and I have done together—do you think I don't know about that? Fine. Do what you want. But I can assure you of this. If I lose everything all over again, this time you're going down with me. (*He bows, and goes out through the hall.*)

Nora (*appears buried in thought for a short time, then tosses her head*): Nonsense! He's just trying to scare me! I'm not as naive as he thinks I am. (*Begins to busy herself putting the children's things in order.*) And yet . . . ? No, it's impossible! I did it for love.

Children (*in the doorway on the left*): Mother, the strange man is gone. He went out through the gate.

Nora: Yes, dears, I know. But don't tell anyone about the strange man. Do you hear me? Not even Papa.

Children: No, Mother. But will you come and play with us again?

Nora: No, no, not just now.

Children: But, Mother, you promised us.

Nora: Yes, but I can't right now. Go inside. I have too much to do. Go inside, my sweet little darlings.

(*She gets them into the room bit by bit and shuts the door on them. Then she sits down on the sofa, takes up a piece of needlework and sews a few stitches, but soon stops.*)

No! (*Throws down the work, gets up, goes to the hall door and calls out.*) Helene! Bring the tree in. (*Goes to the table on the left, opens a drawer, and stops again.*) No, no! It's completely impossible!

Maid (*coming in with the tree*): Where should I put it, ma'am?

Nora: Here, in the middle of the floor.

Maid: Do you need anything else?

Nora: No, thank you. I have everything I want.

(*Exit Maid.*)

Nora (begins decorating the tree): A candle here, and flowers here. That horrible man! It's all nonsense, there's nothing wrong. The tree is going to be magnificent! I'll do everything I can think of to make you happy, Torvald! I'll sing for you, dance for you—

(*Helmer comes in with some papers under his arm.*)

Oh! You're back already?

Helmer: Yes. Has anyone been here?

Nora: Here? No.

Helmer: That's strange. I saw Krogstad going out the gate.

Nora: You did? Oh yes, I forgot, Krogstad was here for a moment.

Helmer: Nora, I can tell from the way you're acting that he was here begging you to put in a good word for him.

Nora: Yes, he was.

Helmer: And you were supposed to pretend it was all your idea and not tell me that he'd been here to see you. Didn't he beg you to do that too?

Nora: Yes, Torvald, but—

Helmer: Nora, Nora, to think that you'd be a party to that sort of thing! To have any kind of conversation with a man like that, and promise him anything at all? And to lie to me in the bargain?

Nora: Lie?

Helmer: Didn't you tell me no one had been here? (*Shakes his finger at her.*) My little songbird must never do that again. A songbird must have a clean beak to chirp with. No false notes! (*Puts his arm round her waist.*) That's true, isn't it? Yes, I'm sure it is. (*Lets her go.*) We won't mention this again. (*Sits down by the stove.*) How warm and cozy it is here! (*Turns over his papers.*)

Nora (after a short pause, during which she busies herself with the Christmas tree): Torvald!

Helmer: Yes?

Nora: I'm really looking forward to the masquerade ball at the Stenborgs' the day after tomorrow.

Helmer: And I'm really curious to see what you're going to surprise me with.

Nora: Oh, it was very silly of me to want to do that.

Helmer: What do you mean?

Nora: I can't come up with anything good. Everything I think of seems so stupid and pointless.

Helmer: So my little Nora finally admits that?

Nora (standing behind his chair with her arms on the back of it): Are you very busy, Torvald?

Helmer: Well . . .

Nora: What are all those papers?

Helmer: Bank business.

Nora: Already?

Helmer: I've gotten the authority from the retiring manager to reorganize the work procedures and make the necessary personnel changes. I need to take care of it during Christmas week, so as to have everything in place for the new year.

Nora: Then that was why this poor Krogstad—

Helmer: Hm!

Nora (leans against the back of his chair and strokes his hair): If you weren't so busy, I would have asked you for a huge favor, Torvald.

Helmer: What favor? Tell me.

Nora: No one has such good taste as you. And I really want to look nice at the fancy-dress ball. Torvald, couldn't you take me in hand and decide what I should go as and what kind of costume I should wear?

Helmer: Aha! So my obstinate little woman has to get someone to come to her rescue?

Nora: Yes, Torvald, I can't get along at all without your help.

Helmer: All right, I'll think it over. I'm sure we'll come up with something.

Nora: That's so nice of you. (*Goes to the Christmas tree. A short pause.*) How pretty the red flowers look. But, tell me, was it really something very bad that this Krogstad was guilty of?

Helmer: He forged someone's name. Do you have any idea what that means?

Nora: Isn't it possible that he was forced to do it by necessity?

Helmer: Yes. Or, the way it is in so many cases, by foolishness. I'm not so heartless that I'd absolutely condemn a man because of one mistake like that.

Nora: No, you wouldn't, would you, Torvald?

Helmer: Many a man has been able to rehabilitate himself, if he's openly admitted his guilt and taken his punishment.

Nora: Punishment?

Helmer: But Krogstad didn't do that. He wriggled out of it with lies and trickery, and that's what completely undermined his moral character.

Nora: But do you think that that would—

Helmer: Just think how a guilty man like that has to lie and act like a hypocrite with everyone, how he has to wear a mask in front of the people closest to him, even with his own wife and children. And the children. That's the most terrible part of it all, Nora.

Nora: How so?

Helmer: Because an atmosphere of lies infects and poisons the whole life of a home. Every breath the children take in a house like that is full of the germs of moral corruption.

Nora (*coming closer to him*): Are you sure of that?

Helmer: My dear, I've seen it many times in my legal career. Almost everyone who's gone wrong at a young age had a dishonest mother.

Nora: Why only the mother?

Helmer: It usually seems to be the mother's influence, though naturally a bad father would have the same result. Every lawyer knows this. This Krogstad, now, has been systematically poisoning his own children with lies and deceit. That's why I say he's lost all moral character. (*Holds out his hands to her.*) And that's why my sweet little Nora must promise me not to plead his cause. Give me your hand on it. Come now, what's this? Give me your hand. There, that's settled. Believe me, it would be impossible for me to work with him. It literally makes me feel physically ill to be around people like that.

Nora (*takes her hand out of his and goes to the opposite side of the Christmas tree*): How hot it is in here! And I have so much to do.

Helmer (*getting up and putting his papers in order*): Yes, and I have to try to read through some of these before dinner. And I have to think about your costume, too. And it's just possible I'll have something wrapped in gold paper to hang up on the tree. (*Puts his hand on her head.*) My precious little songbird! (*He goes into his study and closes the door behind him.*)

Nora (after a pause, whispers): No, no, it's not true. It's impossible. It has to be impossible.

(*The nursemaid opens the door on the left.*)

Nursemaid: The little ones are begging so hard to be allowed to come in to see Mama.
Nora: No, no, no! Don't let them come in to me! You stay with them, Anne Marie.
Nursemaid: Very well, ma'am. (*Shuts the door.*)
Nora (pale with terror): Corrupt my little children? Poison my home? (*A short pause. Then she tosses her head.*) It's not true. It can't possibly be true.

ACT II

The same scene. The Christmas tree is in the corner by the piano, stripped of its ornaments and with burnt-down candle-ends on its disheveled branches. Nora's coat and hat are lying on the sofa. She is alone in the room, walking around uneasily. She stops by the sofa and picks up her coat.

Nora (drops her coat): Someone's coming! (*Goes to the door and listens.*) No, there's no one there. Of course, no one will come today. It's Christmas Day. And not tomorrow either. But maybe . . . (*opens the door and looks out*) No, nothing in the mailbox. It's empty. (*Comes forward.*) What nonsense! Of course he can't be serious about it. A thing like that couldn't happen. It's impossible. I have three little children.

(*Enter the nursemaid Anne Marie from the room on the left, carrying a big cardboard box.*)

Nursemaid: I finally found the box with the costume.
Nora: Thank you. Put it on the table.
Nursemaid (doing so): But it really needs to be mended.
Nora: I'd like to tear it into a hundred thousand pieces.
Nursemaid: What an idea! It can easily be fixed up. All you need is a little patience.
Nora: Yes, I'll go get Mrs. Linde to come and help me with it.
Nursemaid: What, going out again? In this horrible weather? You'll catch cold, Miss Nora, and make yourself sick.
Nora: Well, worse things than that might happen. How are the children?
Nursemaid: The poor little ones are playing with their Christmas presents, but—
Nora: Do they ask for me much?
Nursemaid: You see, they're so used to having their Mama with them.
Nora: Yes, but, Anne Marie, I won't be able to spend as much time with them now as I did before.
Nursemaid: Oh well, young children quickly get used to anything.
Nora: Do you think so? Do you think they'd forget their mother if she went away for good?
Nursemaid: Good heavens! Went away for good?
Nora: Anne Marie, I want you to tell me something I've often wondered about. How could you have the heart to let your own child be raised by strangers?
Nursemaid: I had to, if I wanted to be little Nora's nursemaid.
Nora: Yes, but how could you agree to it?
Nursemaid: What, when I was going to get such a good situation out of it? A poor girl who's gotten herself in trouble should be glad to. Besides, that worthless man didn't do a single thing for me.

Nora: But I suppose your daughter has completely forgotten you.

Nursemaid: No, she hasn't, not at all. She wrote to me when she was confirmed, and again when she got married.

Nora (*putting her arms round her neck*): Dear old Anne Marie, you were such a good mother to me when I was little.

Nursemaid: Poor little Nora, you had no other mother but me.

Nora: And if my little ones had no other mother, I'm sure that you would—What nonsense I'm talking! (*Opens the box.*) Go in and see to them. Now I have to . . . You'll see how lovely I'll look tomorrow.

Nursemaid: I'm sure there'll be no one at the ball as lovely as you, Miss Nora.

(*Goes into the room on the left.*)

Nora (*begins to unpack the box, but soon pushes it away from her*): If only I dared to go out. If only no one would come. If only I could be sure nothing would happen here in the meantime. What nonsense! No one's going to come. I just have to stop thinking about it. This muff needs to be brushed. What beautiful, beautiful gloves! Stop thinking about it, stop thinking about it! One, two, three, four, five, six—(*Screams.*) Aaah! Somebody is coming—(*Makes a movement towards the door, but stands in hesitation.*)

(*Enter Mrs. Linde from the hall, where she has taken off her coat and hat.*)

Nora: Oh, it's you, Kristine. There's no one else out in the hall, is there? How good of you to come!

Mrs. Linde: I heard you came by asking for me.

Nora: Yes, I was passing by. As a matter of fact, it's something you could help me with. Let's sit down here on the sofa. Listen, tomorrow evening there's going to be a fancy-dress ball at the Stenborgs'—they live upstairs from us—and Torvald wants me to go as a Neapolitan fisher-girl and dance the tarantella. I learned it when we were at Capri.

Mrs. Linde: I see. You're going to give them the whole show.

Nora: Yes, Torvald wants me to. Look, here's the dress. Torvald had it made for me there, but now it's all so torn, and I don't have any idea—

Mrs. Linde: We can easily fix that. Some of the trim has just come loose here and there. Do you have a needle and thread? That's all we need.

Nora: This is so nice of you.

Mrs. Linde (*sewing*): So you're going to be dressed up tomorrow, Nora. I'll tell you what. I'll stop by for a moment so I can see you in your finery. Oh, meanwhile I've completely forgotten to thank you for a delightful evening last night.

Nora (*gets up, and crosses the stage*): Well, I didn't think last night was as pleasant as usual. You should have come to town a little earlier, Kristine. Torvald really knows how to make a home pleasant and attractive.

Mrs. Linde: And so do you, if you ask me. You're not your father's daughter for nothing. But tell me, is Doctor Rank always as depressed as he was yesterday?

Nora: No, yesterday it was especially noticeable. But you have to understand that he has a very serious disease. He has tuberculosis of the spine, poor creature. His father was a horrible man who always had mistresses, and that's why his son has been sickly since childhood, if you know what I mean.

Mrs. Linde (*dropping her sewing*): But, my dear Nora, how do you know anything about such things?

Nora (*walking around the room*): Pooh! When you have three children, you get visits now and then from—from married women, who know something about medical matters, and they talk about one thing and another.

Mrs. Linde (*goes on sewing. A short silence*): Does Doctor Rank come here every day?

Nora: Every day, like clockwork. He's Torvald's best friend, and a great friend of mine too. He's just like one of the family.

Mrs. Linde: But tell me, is he really sincere? I mean, isn't he the kind of man who tends to play up to people?

Nora: No, not at all. What makes you think that?

Mrs. Linde: When you introduced him to me yesterday, he told me he'd often heard my name mentioned in this house, but later I could see that your husband didn't have the slightest idea who I was. So how could Doctor Rank—?

Nora: That's true, Kristine. Torvald is so ridiculously fond of me that he wants me completely to himself, as he says. At first he used to seem almost jealous if I even mentioned any of my friends back home, so naturally I stopped talking about them to him. But I often talk about things like that with Doctor Rank, because he likes hearing about them.

Mrs. Linde: Listen to me, Nora. You're still like a child in a lot of ways, and I'm older than you and more experienced. So pay attention. You'd better stop all this with Doctor Rank.

Nora: Stop all what?

Mrs. Linde: Two things, I think. Yesterday you talked some nonsense about a rich admirer who was going to leave you his money—

Nora: An admirer who doesn't exist, unfortunately! But so what?

Mrs. Linde: Is Doctor Rank a wealthy man?

Nora: Yes, he is.

Mrs. Linde: And he has no dependents?

Nora: No, no one. But—

Mrs. Linde: And he comes here every day?

Nora: Yes, I told you he does.

Mrs. Linde: But how can such a well-bred man be so tactless?

Nora: I don't understand what you mean.

Mrs. Linde: Don't try to play dumb, Nora. Do you think I didn't guess who lent you the four thousand, eight hundred kroner?

Nora: Are you out of your mind? How can you even think that? A friend of ours, who comes here every day! Don't you realize what an incredibly awkward position that would put me in?

Mrs. Linde: Then he's really not the one?

Nora: Absolutely not. It would never have come into my head for one second. Besides, he had nothing to lend back then. He inherited his money later on.

Mrs. Linde: Well, I think that was lucky for you, my dear Nora.

Nora: No, it would never have crossed my mind to ask Doctor Rank. Although I'm sure that if I had asked him—

Mrs. Linde: But of course you won't.

Nora: Of course not. I have no reason to think I could possibly need to. But I'm absolutely certain that if I told Doctor Rank—

Mrs. Linde: Behind your husband's back?

Nora: I have to finish up with the other one, and that'll be behind his back too. I've got to wash my hands of him.

Mrs. Linde: Yes, that's what I told you yesterday, but—

Nora (*walking up and down*): A man can take care of these things so much more easily than a woman.

Mrs. Linde: If he's your husband, yes.

Nora: Nonsense! (*Standing still.*) When you pay off a debt you get your note back, don't you?

Mrs. Linde: Yes, of course.

Nora: And you can tear it into a hundred thousand pieces and burn up the filthy, nasty piece of paper!

Mrs. Linde (*stares at her, puts down her sewing and gets up slowly*): Nora, you're hiding something from me.

Nora: You can tell by looking at me?

Mrs. Linde: Something's happened to you since yesterday morning. Nora, what is it?

Nora (*going nearer to her*): Kristine! (*Listens.*) Shh! I hear Torvald. He's come home. Would you mind going in to the children's room for a little while? Torvald can't stand to see all this sewing going on. You can get Anne Marie to help you.

Mrs. Linde (*gathering some of the things together*): All right, but I'm not leaving this house until we've talked this thing through.

(*She goes into the room on the left, as Helmer comes in from the hall.*)

Nora (*going up to Helmer*): I've missed you so much, Torvald dear.

Helmer: Was that the seamstress?

Nora: No, it was Kristine. She's helping me fix up my dress. You'll see how nice I'm going to look.

Helmer: Wasn't that a good idea of mine, now?

Nora: Wonderful! But don't you think it's nice of me, too, to do what you said?

Helmer: Nice, because you do what your husband tells you to? Go on, you silly little thing, I am sure you didn't mean it like that. But I'll stay out of your way. I imagine you'll be trying on your dress.

Nora: I suppose you're going to do some work.

Helmer: Yes. (*Shows her a stack of papers.*) Look at that. I've just been at the bank. (*Turns to go into his room.*)

Nora: Torvald.

Helmer: Yes?

Nora: If your little squirrel were to ask you for something in a very, very charming way—

Helmer: Well?

Nora: Would you do it?

Helmer: I'd have to know what it is, first.

Nora: Your squirrel would run around and do all her tricks if you would be really nice and do what she wants.

Helmer: Speak plainly.
Nora: Your skylark would chirp her beautiful song in every room—
Helmer: Well, my skylark does that anyhow.
Nora: I'd be a little elf and dance in the moonlight for you, Torvald.
Helmer: Nora, you can't be referring to what you talked about this morning.
Nora (moving close to him): Yes, Torvald, I'm really begging you—
Helmer: You really have the nerve to bring that up again?
Nora: Yes, dear, you have to do this for me. You have to let Krogstad keep his job in the bank.
Helmer: My dear Nora, his job is the one that I'm giving to Mrs. Linde.
Nora: Yes, you've been awfully sweet about that. But you could just as easily get rid of somebody else instead of Krogstad.
Helmer: This is just unbelievable stubbornness! Because you decided to foolishly promise that you'd speak up for him, you expect me to—
Nora: That's not the reason, Torvald. It's for your own sake. This man writes for the trashiest newspapers, you've told me so yourself. He can do you an incredible amount of harm. I'm scared to death of him—
Helmer: Oh, I see, it's bad memories that are making you afraid.
Nora: What do you mean?
Helmer: Obviously you're thinking about your father.
Nora: Yes. Yes, of course. You remember what those hateful creatures wrote in the papers about Papa, and how horribly they slandered him. I believe they'd have gotten him fired if the department hadn't sent you over to look into it, and if you hadn't been so kind and helpful to him.
Helmer: My little Nora, there's an important difference between your father and me. His reputation as a public official was not above suspicion. Mine is, and I hope it will continue to be for as long as I hold my office.
Nora: You never can tell what trouble these men might cause. We could be so well off, so snug and happy here in our peaceful home, without a care in the world, you and I and the children, Torvald! That's why I'm begging you to—
Helmer: And the more you plead for him, the more you make it impossible for me to keep him. They already know at the bank that I'm going to fire Krogstad. Do you think I'm going to let them all say that the new manager has changed his mind because his wife said to—
Nora: And what if they did?
Helmer: Right! What does it matter, as long as this stubborn little creature gets her own way! Do you think I'm going to make myself look ridiculous in front of my whole staff, and let people think that I can be pushed around by all sorts of outside influence? That would soon come back to haunt me, you can be sure! And besides, there's one thing that makes it totally impossible for me to have Krogstad working in the bank as long as I'm the manager.
Nora: What's that?
Helmer: I might have been able to overlook his moral failings, if need be—
Nora: Yes, you could do that, couldn't you?
Helmer: And I hear he's a good worker, too. But I knew him when we were boys. It was one of those rash friendships that so often turn out to be a millstone around the neck

later on. I might as well tell you straight out, we were very close friends at one time. But he has no tact and no self-restraint, especially when other people are around. He thinks he has the right to still call me by my first name, and every minute it's Torvald this and Torvald that. I don't mind telling you, I find it extremely annoying. He would make my position at the bank intolerable.

Nora: Torvald, I can't believe you're serious.

Helmer: Oh no? Why not?

Nora: Because it's so petty.

Helmer: What do you mean, petty? You think I'm petty?

Nora: No, just the opposite, dear, and that's why I can't—

Helmer: It's the same thing. You say my attitude's petty, so I must be petty too! Petty! Fine! Well, I'll put a stop to this once and for all. (*Goes to the hall door and calls.*) Helene!

Nora: What are you going to do?

Helmer (*looking among his papers*): Settle it.

(*Enter Maid.*)

Here, take this letter downstairs right now. Find a messenger and tell him to deliver it, and to be quick about it. The address is on it, and here's the money.

Maid: Yes, sir. (*Exits with the letter.*)

Helmer (*putting his papers together*): There, Little Pigheaded Miss.

Nora (*breathlessly*): Torvald, what was that letter?

Helmer: Krogstad's notice.

Nora: Call her back, Torvald! There's still time. Oh, Torvald, call her back! Do it for my sake—for your own sake—for the children's sake! Do you hear me, Torvald? Call her back! You don't know what that letter can do to us.

Helmer: It's too late.

Nora: Yes, it's too late.

Helmer: My dear Nora, I can forgive this anxiety of yours, even though it's insulting to me. It really is. Don't you think it's insulting to suggest that I should be afraid of retaliation from a grubby pen-pusher? But I forgive you anyway, because it's such a beautiful demonstration of how much you love me. (*Takes her in his arms.*) And that is as it should be, my own darling Nora. Come what may, you can rest assured that I'll have both courage and strength if necessary. You'll see that I'm man enough to take everything on myself.

Nora (*in a horror-stricken voice*): What do you mean by that?

Helmer: Everything, I say.

Nora (*recovering herself*): You'll never have to do that.

Helmer: That's right, we'll take it on together, Nora, as man and wife. That's just how it should be. (*Caressing her.*) Are you satisfied now? There, there! Don't look at me that way, like a frightened dove! This whole thing is just your imagination running away with you. Now you should go and run through the tarantella and practice your tambourine. I'll go into my study and shut the door so I can't hear anything. You can make all the noise you want. (*Turns back at the door.*) And when Rank comes, tell him where I am.

(*Nods to her, takes his papers and goes into his room, and shuts the door behind him.*)

Nora (*bewildered with anxiety, stands as if rooted to the spot and whispers*): He's capable of doing it. He's going to do it. He'll do it in spite of everything. No, not that! Never, never! Anything but that! Oh, for somebody to help me find some way out of this! (*The doorbell rings.*) Doctor Rank! Anything but that—anything, whatever it is!

(*She puts her hands over her face, pulls herself together, goes to the door and opens it. Rank is standing in the hall, hanging up his coat. During the following dialogue it starts to grow dark.*)

Nora: Hello, Doctor Rank. I recognized your ring. But you'd better not go in and see Torvald just now. I think he's busy with something.

Rank: And you?

Nora (*brings him in and shuts the door behind him*): Oh, you know perfectly well I always have time for you.

Rank: Thank you. I'll make use of it for as long as I can.

Nora: What does that mean, for as long as you can?

Rank: Why, does that frighten you?

Nora: It was such a strange way of putting it. Is something going to happen?

Rank: Nothing but what I've been expecting for a long time. But I never thought it would happen so soon.

Nora (*gripping him by the arm*): What have you found out? Doctor Rank, you must tell me.

Rank (*sitting down by the stove*): I'm done for. And there's nothing I can do about it.

Nora (*with a sigh of relief*): Oh—you're talking about yourself?

Rank: Who else? And there's no use lying to myself. I'm the sickest patient I have, Mrs. Helmer. Lately I've been adding up my internal account. Bankrupt! In a month I'll probably be rotting in the ground.

Nora: What a horrible thing to say!

Rank: The thing itself is horrible, and the worst of it is all the horrible things I'll have to go through before it's over. I'm going to examine myself just once more. When that's done, I'll be pretty sure when I'm going to start breaking down. There's something I want to say to you. Helmer's sensitive nature makes him completely unable to deal with anything ugly. I don't want him in my sickroom.

Nora: Oh, but, Doctor Rank—

Rank: I won't have him there, period. I'll lock the door to keep him out. As soon as I'm quite sure that the worst has come, I'll send you my card with a black cross on it, and that way you'll know that the final stage of the horror has started.

Nora: You're being really absurd today. And I so much wanted you to be in a good mood.

Rank: With death stalking me? Having to pay this price for another man's sins? Where's the justice in that? In every single family, in one way or another, some such unavoidable retribution is being imposed.

Nora (*putting her hands over her ears*): Nonsense! Can't you talk about something cheerful?

Rank: Oh, this *is* something cheerful. In fact, it's hilarious. My poor innocent spine has to suffer for my father's youthful self-indulgence.

Nora (*sitting at the table on the left*): Yes, he did love asparagus and *pâté de foie gras*, didn't he?

Rank: Yes, and truffles.

Nora: Truffles, yes. And oysters too, I suppose?

Rank: Oysters, of course. That goes without saying.

Nora: And oceans of port and champagne. Isn't it sad that all those delightful things should take their revenge on our bones?

Rank: Especially that they should take their revenge on the unlucky bones of people who haven't even had the satisfaction of enjoying them.

Nora: Yes, that's the saddest part of all.

Rank (with a searching look at her): Hm!

Nora (after a short pause): Why did you smile?

Rank: No, it was you who laughed.

Nora: No, it was you who smiled, Doctor Rank!

Rank (rising): You're even more of a tease than I thought you were.

Nora: I am in a crazy mood today.

Rank: Apparently so.

Nora (putting her hands on his shoulders): Dear, dear Doctor Rank, we can't let death take you away from Torvald and me.

Rank: It's a loss that you'll easily recover from. Those who are gone are soon forgotten.

Nora (looking at him anxiously): Do you really believe that?

Rank: People make new friends, and then—

Nora: Who'll make new friends?

Rank: Both you and Helmer, when I'm gone. You yourself are already well on the way to it, I think. What was that Mrs. Linde doing here last night?

Nora: Oho! You're not telling me that you're jealous of poor Kristine, are you?

Rank: Yes, I am. She'll be my successor in this house. When I'm six feet under, this woman will—

Nora: Shh! Don't talk so loud. She's in that room.

Rank: Again today. There, you see.

Nora: She's just come to sew my dress for me. Goodness, how unreasonable you are! (*Sits down on the sofa.*) Be nice now, Doctor Rank, and tomorrow you'll see how beautifully I'll dance, and you can pretend that I'm doing it just for you—and for Torvald too, of course. (*Takes various things out of the box.*) Doctor Rank, come and sit down here, and I'll show you something.

Rank (sitting down): What is it?

Nora: Just look at these!

Rank: Silk stockings.

Nora: Flesh-colored. Aren't they lovely? It's so dark here now, but tomorrow—No, no, no! You're only supposed to look at the feet. Oh well, you have my permission to look at the legs too.

Rank: Hm!

Nora: Why do you look so critical? Don't you think they'll fit me?

Rank: I have no basis for forming an opinion on that subject.

Nora (looks at him for a moment): Shame on you! (*Hits him lightly on the ear with the stockings.*) That's your punishment. (*Folds them up again.*)

Rank: And what other pretty things do I have your permission to look at?

Nora: Not one single thing. That's what you get for being so naughty. (*She looks among the things, humming to herself.*)

Rank (*after a short silence*): When I'm sitting here, talking to you so intimately this way, I can't imagine for a moment what would have become of me if I'd never come into this house.
Nora (*smiling*): I believe you really do feel completely at home with us.
Rank (*in a lower voice, looking straight in front of him*): And to have to leave it all—
Nora: Nonsense, you're not going to leave it.
Rank (*as before*): And not to be able to leave behind the slightest token of my gratitude, hardly even a fleeting regret. Nothing but an empty place to be filled by the first person who comes along.
Nora: And if I were to ask you now for a—No, never mind!
Rank: For a what?
Nora: For a great proof of your friendship—
Rank: Yes, yes!
Nora: I mean a tremendously huge favor—
Rank: Would you really make me so happy, just this once?
Nora: But you don't know what it is yet.
Rank: No, but tell me.
Nora: I really can't, Doctor Rank. It's too much to ask. It involves advice, and help, and a favor—
Rank: So much the better. I can't imagine what you mean. Tell me what it is. You do trust me, don't you?
Nora: More than anyone. I know that you're my best and truest friend, so I'll tell you what it is. Well, Doctor Rank, it's something you have to help me prevent. You know how devoted Torvald is to me, how deeply he loves me. He wouldn't hesitate for a second to give his life for me.
Rank (*leaning towards her*): Nora, do you think that he's the only one—
Nora (*with a slight start*): The only one?
Rank: Who would gladly give his life for you.
Nora (*sadly*): Oh, is that it?
Rank: I'd made up my mind to tell you before I—I go away, and there'll never be a better opportunity than this. Now you know it, Nora. And now you know that you can trust me more than you can trust anyone else.
Nora (*rises, deliberately and quietly*): Let me by.
Rank (*makes room for her to pass him, but sits still*): Nora!
Nora (*at the hall door*): Helene, bring in the lamp. (*Goes over to the stove.*) Dear Doctor Rank, that was really horrible of you.
Rank: To love you just as much as somebody else does? Is that so horrible?
Nora: No, but to go and tell me like that. There was really no need—
Rank: What do you mean? Did you know—

(*Maid enters with lamp, puts it down on the table, and goes out.*)

Nora—Mrs. Helmer—tell me, did you have any idea I felt this way?
Nora: Oh, how do I know whether I did or I didn't? I really can't answer that. How could you be so clumsy, Doctor Rank? When we were getting along so nicely.

Rank: Well, at any rate, now you know that I'm yours to command, body and soul. So won't you tell me what it is?

Nora (*looking at him*): After what just happened?

Rank: I beg you to let me know what it is.

Nora: I can't tell you anything now.

Rank: Yes, yes. Please don't punish me that way. Give me permission to do anything for you that a man can do.

Nora: You can't do anything for me now. Besides, I really don't need any help at all. The whole thing is just my imagination. It really is. It has to be! (*Sits down in the rocking chair, and smiles at him.*) You're a nice man, Doctor Rank. Don't you feel ashamed of yourself, now that the lamp is lit?

Rank: Not a bit. But maybe it would be better if I left—and never came back?

Nora: No, no, you can't do that. You must keep coming here just as you always did. You know very well Torvald can't do without you.

Rank: But what about you?

Nora: Oh, I'm always extremely pleased to see you.

Rank: And that's just what gave me the wrong idea. You're a puzzle to me. I've often felt that you'd almost just as soon be in my company as in Helmer's.

Nora: Yes, you see, there are the people you love the most, and then there are the people whose company you enjoy the most.

Rank: Yes, there's something to that.

Nora: When I lived at home, of course I loved Papa best. But I always thought it was great fun to sneak down to the maids' room, because they never preached at me, and I loved listening to the way they talked to each other.

Rank: I see. So I'm their replacement.

Nora (*jumping up and going to him*): Oh, dear, sweet Doctor Rank, I didn't mean it that way. But surely you can understand that being with Torvald is a little like being with Papa—

(*Enter Maid from the hall.*)

Maid: Excuse me, ma'am. (*Whispers and hands her a card.*)

Nora (*glancing at the card*): Oh! (*Puts it in her pocket.*)

Rank: Is something wrong?

Nora: No, no, not at all. It's just—it's my new dress—

Rank: What? Your dress is lying right there.

Nora: Oh, yes, that one. But this is another one, one that I ordered. I don't want Torvald to find out about it—

Rank: Oh! So that was the big secret.

Nora: Yes, that's it. Why don't you just go inside and see him? He's in his study. Stay with him for as long as—

Rank: Put your mind at ease. I won't let him escape. (*Goes into Helmer's study.*)

Nora (*to the maid*): And he's waiting in the kitchen?

Maid: Yes, ma'am. He came up the back stairs.

Nora: Didn't you tell him no one was home?

Maid: Yes, but it didn't do any good.

Nora: He won't go away?
Maid: No, he says he won't leave until he sees you, ma'am.
Nora: Well, show him in, but quietly. Helene, I don't want you to say anything about this to anyone. It's a surprise for my husband.
Maid: Yes, ma'am. I understand. (*Exit.*)
Nora: This horrible thing is really going to happen! It's going to happen in spite of me! No, no, no, it can't happen! I can't let it happen!

(*She bolts the door of Helmer's study. The maid opens the hall door for Krogstad and closes it behind him. He is wearing a fur coat, high boots, and a fur cap.*)

Nora (*advancing towards him*): Speak quietly. My husband's home.
Krogstad: What do I care about that?
Nora: What do you want from me?
Krogstad: An explanation of something.
Nora: Be quick, then. What is it?
Krogstad: I suppose you're aware that I've been let go.
Nora: I couldn't prevent it, Mr. Krogstad. I fought for you as hard as I could, but it was no use.
Krogstad: Does your husband love you so little, then? He knows what I can expose you to, and he still goes ahead and—
Nora: How can you think that he knows any such thing?
Krogstad: I didn't think so for a moment. It wouldn't be at all like dear old Torvald Helmer to show that kind of courage—
Nora: Mr. Krogstad, a little respect for my husband, please.
Krogstad: Certainly—all the respect he deserves. But since you've kept everything so carefully to yourself, may I be bold enough to assume that you see a little more clearly than you did yesterday just what it is that you've done?
Nora: More than you could ever teach me.
Krogstad: Yes, such a poor excuse for a lawyer as I am.
Nora: What is it you want from me?
Krogstad: Only to see how you're doing, Mrs. Helmer. I've been thinking about you all day. A mere bill collector, a pen-pusher, a—well, a man like me—even he has a little of what people call feelings, you know.
Nora: Why don't you show some, then? Think about my little children.
Krogstad: Have you and your husband thought about mine? But never mind about that. I just wanted to tell you not to take this business too seriously. I won't make any accusations against you. Not for now, anyway.
Nora: No, of course not. I was sure you wouldn't.
Krogstad: The whole thing can be settled amicably. There's no need for anyone to know anything about it. It'll be our little secret, just the three of us.
Nora: My husband must never know anything about it.
Krogstad: How are you going to keep him from finding out? Are you telling me that you can pay off the whole balance?
Nora: No, not just yet.
Krogstad: Or that you have some other way of raising the money soon?

Nora: No way that I plan to make use of.

Krogstad: Well, in any case, it wouldn't be any use to you now even if you did. If you stood in front of me with a stack of bills in each hand, I still wouldn't give you back your note.

Nora: What are you planning to do with it?

Krogstad: I just want to hold onto it, just keep it in my possession. No one who isn't involved in the matter will ever know anything about it. So, if you've been thinking about doing something desperate—

Nora: I have.

Krogstad: If you've been thinking about running away—

Nora: I have.

Krogstad: Or doing something even worse—

Nora: How could you know that?

Krogstad: Stop thinking about it.

Nora: How did you know I'd thought of that?

Krogstad: Most of us think about that at first. I did, too. But I didn't have the courage.

Nora (faintly): Neither do I.

Krogstad (in a tone of relief): No, that's true, isn't it? You don't have the courage either?

Nora: No, I don't. I don't.

Krogstad: Besides, it would have been an incredibly stupid thing to do. Once the first storm at home blows over . . . I have a letter for your husband in my pocket.

Nora: Telling him everything?

Krogstad: As gently as possible.

Nora (quickly): He can't see that letter. Tear it up. I'll find some way of getting money.

Krogstad: Excuse me, Mrs. Helmer, but didn't I just tell you—

Nora: I'm not talking about what I owe you. Tell me how much you want from my husband, and I'll get the money.

Krogstad: I don't want any money from your husband.

Nora: Then what do you want?

Krogstad: I'll tell you what I want. I want a fresh start, Mrs. Helmer, and I want to move up in the world. And your husband's going to help me do it. I've steered clear of anything questionable for the last year and a half. In all that time I've been struggling along, pinching every penny. I was content to work my way up step by step. But now I've been fired, and it's not going to be enough just to get my job back, as if you people were doing me some huge favor. I want to move up, I tell you. I want to get back into the bank again, but with a promotion. Your husband's going to have to find me a position—

Nora: He'll never do it!

Krogstad: Oh yes, he will. I know him. He won't dare object. And as soon as I'm back there with him, then you'll see! Inside of a year I'll be the manager's right-hand man. It'll be Nils Krogstad, not Torvald Helmer, who's running the bank.

Nora: That's never going to happen!

Krogstad: Do you mean that you'll—

Nora: I have enough courage for it now.

Krogstad: Oh, you can't scare me. An elegant, spoiled lady like you—

Nora: You'll see, you'll see.

Krogstad: Under the ice, maybe? Down in the cold, coal-black water? And then floating up to the surface in the spring, all horrible and unrecognizable, with your hair fallen out—

Nora: You can't scare me.

Krogstad: And you can't scare me. People don't do that kind of thing, Mrs. Helmer. Besides, what good would it do? I'd still have him completely in my power.

Nora: Even then? When I'm no longer—

Krogstad: Have you forgotten that your reputation is completely in my hands? (*Nora stands speechless, looking at him.*) Well, now I've warned you. Don't do anything foolish. I'll be expecting an answer from Helmer after he reads my letter. And remember, it's your husband himself who's forced me to act this way again. I'll never forgive him for that. Goodbye, Mrs. Helmer. (*Exits through the hall.*)

Nora (*goes to the hall door, opens it slightly and listens.*): He's leaving. He isn't putting the letter in the box. Oh no, no! He couldn't! (*Opens the door little by little.*) What? He's standing out there. He's not going downstairs. He's hesitating? Is he?

(*A letter drops into the box. Then Krogstad's footsteps are heard, until they die away as he goes downstairs. Nora utters a stifled cry, and runs across the room to the table by the sofa. A short pause.*)

Nora: In the mailbox. (*Steals across to the hall door.*) It's there! Torvald, Torvald, there's no hope for us now!

(*Mrs. Linde comes in from the room on the left, carrying the dress.*)

Mrs. Linde: There, I can't find anything more to mend. Would you like to try it on?

Nora (*in a hoarse whisper*): Kristine, come here.

Mrs. Linde (*throwing the dress down on the sofa*): What's the matter with you? You look so agitated!

Nora: Come here. Do you see that letter? There, look. You can see it through the glass in the mailbox.

Mrs. Linde: Yes, I see it.

Nora: That letter is from Krogstad.

Mrs. Linde: Nora! It was Krogstad who lent you the money!

Nora: Yes, and now Torvald will know all about it.

Mrs. Linde: Believe me, Nora, that's the best thing for both of you.

Nora: You don't know the whole story. I forged a name.

Mrs. Linde: My God!

Nora: There's something I want to say to you, Kristine. I need you to be my witness.

Mrs. Linde: Your witness? What do you mean? What am I supposed to—

Nora: If I should go out of my mind—and it could easily happen—

Mrs. Linde: Nora!

Nora: Or if anything else should happen to me—anything, for instance, that might keep me from being here—

Mrs. Linde: Nora! Nora! What's the matter with you?

Nora: And if it turned out that somebody wanted to take all the responsibility, all the blame, you understand what I mean—

Mrs. Linde: Yes, yes, but how can you imagine—

Nora: Then you must be my witness that it's not true, Kristine. I'm not out of my mind at all. I'm perfectly rational right now, and I'm telling you that no one else ever knew anything about it. I did the whole thing all by myself. Remember that.
Mrs. Linde: I will. But I don't understand all this.
Nora: How could you understand it? Or the miracle that's going to happen!
Mrs. Linde: A miracle?
Nora: Yes, a miracle! But it's so terrible, Kristine. I can't let it happen, not for the whole world.
Mrs. Linde: I'll go and see Krogstad right this minute.
Nora: No, don't. He'll do something to hurt you too.
Mrs. Linde: There was a time when he would have gladly done anything for my sake.
Nora: What?
Mrs. Linde: Where does he live?
Nora: How should I know? Yes (*feeling in her pocket*), here's his card. But the letter, the letter—
Helmer (*calls from his room, knocking at the door*): Nora!
Nora (*cries out anxiously*): What is it? What do you want?
Helmer: Don't be so afraid. We're not coming in. You've locked the door. Are you trying on your dress?
Nora: Yes, that's it. Oh, it's going to look so nice, Torvald.
Mrs. Linde (*who has read the card*): Look, he lives right around the corner.
Nora: But it's no use. It's all over. The letter's lying right there in the box.
Mrs. Linde: And your husband has the key?
Nora: Yes, always.
Mrs. Linde: Krogstad can ask for his letter back unread. He'll have to make up some reason—
Nora: But now is just about the time that Torvald usually—
Mrs. Linde: You have to prevent him. Go in and talk to him. I'll be back as soon as I can.

(*She hurries out through the hall door.*)

Nora (*goes to Helmer's door, opens it and peeps in*): Torvald!
Helmer (*from the inner room*): Well? May I finally come back into my own room? Come along, Rank, now you'll see—(*Stopping in the doorway.*) But what's this?
Nora: What's what, dear?
Helmer: Rank led me to expect an amazing transformation.
Rank (*in the doorway*): So I understood, but apparently I was mistaken.
Nora: Yes, nobody gets to admire me in my dress until tomorrow.
Helmer: But, my dear Nora, you look exhausted. Have you been practicing too much?
Nora: No, I haven't been practicing at all.
Helmer: But you'll have to—
Nora: Yes, of course I will, Torvald. But I can't get anywhere without you helping me. I've completely forgotten the whole thing.
Helmer: Oh, we'll soon get you back up to form again.
Nora: Yes, help me, Torvald. Promise that you will! I'm so nervous about it—all those people. I need you to devote yourself completely to me this evening. Not even the tiniest little bit of business. You can't even pick up a pen. Do you promise, Torvald dear?
Helmer: I promise. This evening I will be wholly and absolutely at your service, you helpless little creature. But first I'm just going to—(*Goes towards the hall door.*)

Nora: Just going to what?
Helmer: To see if there's any mail.
Nora: No, no! Don't do that, Torvald!
Helmer: Why not?
Nora: Torvald, please don't. There's nothing there.
Helmer: Well, let me look. (*Turns to go to the mailbox. Nora, at the piano, plays the first bars of the tarantella. Helmer stops in the doorway.*) Aha!
Nora: I can't dance tomorrow if I don't practice with you.
Helmer (*going up to her*): Are you really so worried about it, dear?
Nora: Yes, terribly worried about it. Let me practice right now. We have time before dinner. Sit down and play for me, Torvald dear. Criticize me and correct me, the way you always do.
Helmer: With great pleasure, if you want me to. (*Sits down at the piano.*)
Nora (*takes a tambourine and a long multicolored shawl out of the box. She hastily drapes the shawl around her. Then she bounds to the front of the stage and calls out*): Now play for me! I'm going to dance!

(*Helmer plays and Nora dances. Rank stands by the piano behind Helmer and watches.*)

Helmer (*as he plays*): Slower, slower!
Nora: I can't do it any other way.
Helmer: Not so violently, Nora!
Nora: This is the way.
Helmer (*stops playing*): No, no, that's not right at all.
Nora (*laughing and swinging the tambourine*): Didn't I tell you so?
Rank: Let me play for her.
Helmer (*getting up*): Good idea. I can correct her better that way.

(*Rank sits down at the piano and plays. Nora dances more and more wildly. Helmer has taken up a position beside the stove, and as she dances, he gives her frequent instructions. She doesn't seem to hear him. Her hair comes undone and falls over her shoulders. She pays no attention to it, but goes on dancing. Enter Mrs. Linde.*)

Mrs. Linde (*standing as if spellbound in the doorway*): Oh!
Nora (*as she dances*): What fun, Kristine!
Helmer: My dear darling Nora, you're dancing as if your life depended on it.
Nora: It does.
Helmer: Stop, Rank. This is insane! I said stop!

(*Rank stops playing, and Nora suddenly stands still. Helmer goes up to her.*)

I never would have believed it. You've forgotten everything I taught you.
Nora (*throwing the tambourine aside*): There, you see.
Helmer: You're going to need a lot of coaching.
Nora: Yes, you see how much I need it. You have to coach me right up to the last minute. Promise me you will, Torvald!
Helmer: You can depend on me.
Nora: You can't think about anything but me, today or tomorrow. Don't open a single letter. Don't even open the mailbox—

Helmer: You're still afraid of that man—
Nora: Yes, yes, I am.
Helmer: Nora, I can tell from your face that there's a letter from him in the box.
Nora: I don't know. I think there is. But you can't read anything like that now. Nothing nasty must come between us until this is all over.
Rank (whispers to Helmer): Don't contradict her.
Helmer (taking her in his arms): The child shall have her way. But tomorrow night, after you've danced—
Nora: Then you'll be free.

(*The Maid appears in the doorway to the right.*)

Maid: Dinner is served, ma'am.
Nora: We'll have champagne, Helene.
Maid: Yes, ma'am. (*Exit.*)
Helmer: Oh, are we having a banquet?
Nora: Yes, a banquet. Champagne till dawn! (*Calls out.*) And a few macaroons, Helene. Lots of them, just this once!
Helmer: Come on, stop acting so wild and nervous. Be my own little skylark again.
Nora: Yes, dear, I will. But go inside now, and you too, Doctor Rank. Kristine, please help me do up my hair.
Rank (whispers to Helmer as they go out): There isn't anything—she's not expecting—?
Helmer: No, nothing like that. It's just this childish nervousness I was telling you about.
(*They go into the right-hand room.*)
Nora: Well?
Mrs. Linde: Out of town.
Nora: I could tell from your face.
Mrs. Linde: He'll be back tomorrow evening. I wrote him a note.
Nora: You should have left it alone. Don't try to prevent anything. After all, it's exciting to be waiting for a miracle to happen.
Mrs. Linde: What is it that you're waiting for?
Nora: Oh, you wouldn't understand. Go inside with them, I'll be there in a moment.

(*Mrs. Linde goes into the dining room. Nora stands still for a little while, as if to compose herself. Then she looks at her watch.*)

Five o'clock. Seven hours till midnight, and another twenty-four hours till the next midnight. And then the tarantella will be over. Twenty-four plus seven? Thirty-one hours to live.
Helmer (from the doorway on the right): Where's my little skylark?
Nora (going to him with her arms outstretched): Here she is!

ACT III

The same scene. The table has been placed in the middle of the stage, with chairs around it. A lamp is burning on the table. The door into the hall stands open. Dance music is heard in the room above. Mrs. Linde is sitting at the table idly turning over the pages of a book. She tries to read, but she seems unable to concentrate. Every now and then she listens intently for a sound at the outer door.

Mrs. Linde (*looking at her watch*): Not yet—and the time's nearly up. If only he doesn't— (*Listens again.*) Ah, there he is. (*Goes into the hall and opens the outer door carefully. Light footsteps are heard on the stairs. She whispers.*) Come in. There's no one else here.
Krogstad (*in the doorway*): I found a note from you at home. What does this mean?
Mrs. Linde: It's absolutely necessary that I have a talk with you.
Krogstad: Really? And is it absolutely necessary that we have it here?
Mrs. Linde: It's impossible where I live. There's no private entrance to my apartment. Come in. We're all alone. The maid's asleep, and the Helmers are upstairs at a dance.
Krogstad (*coming into the room*): Are the Helmers really at a dance tonight?
Mrs. Linde: Yes. Why shouldn't they be?
Krogstad: Certainly—why not?
Mrs. Linde: Now, Nils, let's have a talk.
Krogstad: What can we two have to talk about?
Mrs. Linde: Quite a lot.
Krogstad: I wouldn't have thought so.
Mrs. Linde: Of course not. You've never really understood me.
Krogstad: What was there to understand, except what the whole world could see—a heartless woman drops a man when a better catch comes along?
Mrs. Linde: Do you think I'm really that heartless? And that I broke it off with you so lightly?
Krogstad: Didn't you?
Mrs. Linde: Nils, did you really think that?
Krogstad: If not, why did you write what you did to me?
Mrs. Linde: What else could I do? Since I had to break it off with you, I had an obligation to stamp out your feelings for me.
Krogstad (*wringing his hands*): So that was it. And all this just for the sake of money!
Mrs. Linde: Don't forget that I had an invalid mother and two little brothers. We couldn't wait for you, Nils. Success seemed a long way off for you back then.
Krogstad: That may be so, but you had no right to cast me aside for anyone else's sake.
Mrs. Linde: I don't know if I did or not. Many times I've asked myself if I had the right.
Krogstad (*more gently*): When I lost you, it was as if the earth crumbled under my feet. Look at me now—a shipwrecked man clinging to a bit of wreckage.
Mrs. Linde: But help may be on the way.
Krogstad: It *was* on the way, till you came along and blocked it.
Mrs. Linde: Without knowing it, Nils. It wasn't till today that I found out I'd be taking your job.
Krogstad: I believe you, if you say so. But now that you know it, are you going to step aside?
Mrs. Linde: No, because it wouldn't do you any good.
Krogstad: Good? I would quit whether it did any good or not.
Mrs. Linde: I've learned to be practical. Life and hard, bitter necessity have taught me that.
Krogstad: And life has taught me not to believe in fine speeches.
Mrs. Linde: Then life has taught you something very sensible. But surely you believe in actions?

Krogstad: What do you mean by that?

Mrs. Linde: You said you were like a shipwrecked man clinging to a piece of wreckage.

Krogstad: I had good reason to say so.

Mrs. Linde: Well, I'm like a shipwrecked woman clinging to a piece of wreckage, with no one to mourn for and no one to care for.

Krogstad: That was your own choice.

Mrs. Linde: I had no other choice—then.

Krogstad: Well, what about now?

Mrs. Linde: Nils, how would it be if we two shipwrecked people could reach out to each other?

Krogstad: What are you saying?

Mrs. Linde: Two people on the same piece of wreckage would stand a better chance than each one on their own.

Krogstad: Kristine, I . . .

Mrs. Linde: Why do you think I came to town?

Krogstad: You can't mean that you were thinking about me?

Mrs. Linde: Life is unendurable without work. I've worked all my life, for as long as I can remember, and it's been my greatest and my only pleasure. But now that I'm completely alone in the world, my life is so terribly empty and I feel so abandoned. There isn't the slightest pleasure in working only for yourself. Nils, give me someone and something to work for.

Krogstad: I don't trust this. It's just some romantic female impulse, a high-minded urge for self-sacrifice.

Mrs. Linde: Have you ever known me to be like that?

Krogstad: Could you really do it? Tell me, do you know all about my past?

Mrs. Linde: Yes.

Krogstad: And you know what they think of me around here?

Mrs. Linde: Didn't you imply that with me you might have been a very different person?

Krogstad: I'm sure I would have.

Mrs. Linde: Is it too late now?

Krogstad: Kristine, are you serious about all this? Yes, I'm sure you are. I can see it in your face. Do you really have the courage, then—

Mrs. Linde: I want to be a mother to someone, and your children need a mother. We two need each other. Nils, I have faith in your true nature. I can face anything together with you.

Krogstad (grasps her hands): Thank you, thank you, Kristine! Now I can find a way to clear myself in the eyes of the world. Ah, but I forgot—

Mrs. Linde (listening): Shh! The tarantella! You have to go!

Krogstad: Why? What's the matter?

Mrs. Linde: Do you hear them up there? They'll probably come home as soon as this dance is over.

Krogstad: Yes, yes, I'll go. But it won't make any difference. You don't know what I've done about my situation with the Helmers.

Mrs. Linde: Yes, I know all about that.

Krogstad: And in spite of that you still have the courage to—

Mrs. Linde: I understand completely what despair can drive a man like you to do.
Krogstad: If only I could undo it!
Mrs. Linde: You can't. Your letter's lying in the mailbox now.
Krogstad: Are you sure?
Mrs. Linde: Quite sure, but—
Krogstad (with a searching look at her): Is that what this is all about? That you want to save your friend, no matter what you have to do? Tell me the truth. Is that it?
Mrs. Linde: Nils, when a woman has sold herself for someone else's sake, she doesn't do it a second time.
Krogstad: I'll ask for my letter back.
Mrs. Linde: No, no.
Krogstad: Yes, of course I will. I'll wait here until Helmer comes home. I'll tell him he has to give me back my letter, that it's only about my being fired, that I don't want him to read it—
Mrs. Linde: No, Nils, don't ask for it back.
Krogstad: But wasn't that the reason why you asked me to meet you here?
Mrs. Linde: In my first moment of panic, it was. But twenty-four hours have gone by since then, and in the meantime I've seen some incredible things in this house. Helmer has to know all about it. This terrible secret has to come out. They have to have a complete understanding between them. It's time for all this lying and pretending to stop.
Krogstad: All right then, if you think it's worth the risk. But there's at least one thing I can do, and do right away—
Mrs. Linde (listening): You have to leave this instant! The dance is over. They could walk in here any minute.
Krogstad: I'll wait for you downstairs.
Mrs. Linde: Yes, please do. I want you to walk me home.
Krogstad: I've never been so happy in my entire life!

(*Goes out through the outer door. The door between the room and the hall remains open.*)

Mrs. Linde (straightening up the room and getting her hat and coat ready): How different things will be! Someone to work for and live for, a home to bring happiness into. I'm certainly going to try. I wish they'd hurry up and come home—(*Listens.*) Ah, here they are now. I'd better put on my things.

(*Picks up her hat and coat. Helmer's and Nora's voices are heard outside. A key is turned, and Helmer brings Nora into the hall almost by force. She is in an Italian peasant costume with a large black shawl wrapped around her. He is in formal wear and a black domino—a hooded cloak with an eye-mask—which is open.*)

Nora (hanging back in the doorway and struggling with him): No, no, no! Don't bring me inside. I want to go back upstairs. I don't want to leave so early.
Helmer: But, my dearest Nora—
Nora: Please, Torvald dear, please, please, only one more hour.
Helmer: Not one more minute, my sweet Nora. You know this is what we agreed on. Come inside. You'll catch cold standing out there.

(*He brings her gently into the room, in spite of her resistance.*)

Mrs. Linde: Good evening.

Nora: Kristine!

Helmer: What are you doing here so late, Mrs. Linde?

Mrs. Linde: You must excuse me. I was so anxious to see Nora in her dress.

Nora: Have you been sitting here waiting for me?

Mrs. Linde: Yes, unfortunately I came too late, you'd already gone upstairs. And I didn't want to go away again without seeing you.

Helmer (*taking off Nora's shawl*): Yes, take a good look at her. I think she's worth looking at. Isn't she charming, Mrs. Linde?

Mrs. Linde: Yes, indeed she is.

Helmer: Doesn't she look especially pretty? Everyone thought so at the dance. But this sweet little person is extremely stubborn. What are we going to do with her? Believe it or not, I almost had to drag her away by force.

Nora: Torvald, you'll be sorry you didn't let me stay, even if only for half an hour.

Helmer: Listen to her, Mrs. Linde! She danced her tarantella and it was a huge success, as it deserved to be, though maybe her performance was a tiny bit too realistic, a little more so than it might have been by strict artistic standards. But never mind about that! The main thing is, she was a success, a tremendous success. Do you think I was going to let her stay there after that, and spoil the effect? Not a chance! I took my charming little Capri girl—my capricious little Capri girl, I should say—I took her by the arm, one quick circle around the room, a curtsey to one and all, and, as they say in novels, the beautiful vision vanished. An exit should always make an effect, Mrs. Linde, but I can't make Nora understand that. Whew, this room is hot!

(*Throws his domino on a chair and opens the door to his study.*)

Why is it so dark in here? Oh, of course. Excuse me.

(*He goes in and lights some candles.*)

Nora (*in a hurried, breathless whisper*): Well?

Mrs. Linde (*in a low voice*): I talked to him.

Nora: And?

Mrs. Linde: Nora, you have to tell your husband the whole story.

Nora (*in an expressionless voice*): I knew it.

Mrs. Linde: You have nothing to fear from Krogstad, but you still have to tell him.

Nora: I'm not going to.

Mrs. Linde: Then the letter will.

Nora: Thank you, Kristine. Now I know what I have to do. Shh!

Helmer (*coming in again*): Well, Mrs. Linde, have you been admiring her?

Mrs. Linde: Yes, I have, and now I'll say goodnight.

Helmer: What, already? Is this your knitting?

Mrs. Linde (*taking it*): Yes, thank you, I'd almost forgotten it.

Helmer: So you knit?

Mrs. Linde: Yes, of course.

Helmer: You know, you ought to embroider.

Mrs. Linde: Really? Why?

Helmer: It's much more graceful-looking. Here, let me show you. You hold the embroidery this way in your left hand, and use the needle with your right, like this, with a long, easy sweep. Do you see?

Mrs. Linde: Yes, I suppose—

Helmer: But knitting, that can never be anything but awkward. Here, look. The arms close together, the knitting needles going up and down. It's sort of Chinese looking. That was really excellent champagne they gave us.

Mrs. Linde: Well, good night, Nora, and don't be stubborn anymore.

Helmer: That's right, Mrs. Linde.

Mrs. Linde: Good night, Mr. Helmer.

Helmer (*seeing her to the door*): Good night, good night. I hope you get home safely. I'd be very happy to—but you only have a short way to go. Good night, good night.

(*She goes out. He closes the door behind her, and comes in again.*)

Ah, rid of her at last! What a bore that woman is.

Nora: Aren't you tired, Torvald?

Helmer: No, not at all.

Nora: You're not sleepy?

Helmer: Not a bit. As a matter of fact, I feel very lively. And what about you? You really look tired *and* sleepy.

Nora: Yes, I am very tired. I want to go to sleep right away.

Helmer: So, you see how right I was not to let you stay there any longer.

Nora: You're always right, Torvald.

Helmer (*kissing her on the forehead*): Now my little skylark is talking sense. Did you notice what a good mood Rank was in this evening?

Nora: Really? Was he? I didn't talk to him at all.

Helmer: And I only talked to him for a little while, but it's a long time since I've seen him so cheerful. (*Looks at her for a while and then moves closer to her.*) It's delightful to be home again by ourselves, to be alone with you, you fascinating, charming little darling!

Nora: Don't look at me like that, Torvald.

Helmer: Why shouldn't I look at my dearest treasure? At all the beauty that is mine, all my very own?

Nora (*going to the other side of the table*): I wish you wouldn't talk that way to me tonight.

Helmer (*following her*): You've still got the tarantella in your blood, I see. And it makes you more captivating than ever. Listen, the guests are starting to leave now. (*In a lower voice.*) Nora, soon the whole house will be quiet.

Nora: Yes, I hope so.

Helmer: Yes, my own darling Nora. Do you know why, when we're out at a party like this, why I hardly talk to you, and keep away from you, and only steal a glance at you now and then? Do you know why I do that? It's because I'm pretending to myself that we're secretly in love, and we're secretly engaged, and no one suspects that there's anything between us.

Nora: Yes, yes, I know you're thinking about me every moment.

Helmer: And when we're leaving, and I'm putting the shawl over your beautiful young shoulders, on your lovely neck, then I imagine that you're my young bride and that we've just come from our wedding and I'm bringing you home for the first time, to be alone with you for the first time, all alone with my shy little darling! This whole night I've been longing for you alone. My blood was on fire watching you move when you danced the tarantella. I couldn't stand it any longer, and that's why I brought you home so early—

Nora: Stop it, Torvald! Let me go. I won't—

Helmer: What? You're not serious, Nora! You won't? You won't? I'm your husband—

(*There is a knock at the outer door.*)

Nora (*starting*): Did you hear—

Helmer (*going into the hall*): Who is it?

Rank (*outside*): It's me. May I come in for a moment?

Helmer (*in an irritated whisper*): What does he want now? (*Aloud.*) Wait a minute! (*Unlocks the door.*) Come in. It's good of you not to pass by our door without saying hello.

Rank: I thought I heard your voice, and I felt like dropping by. (*With a quick look around.*) Ah, yes, these dear familiar rooms. You two are very happy and cozy in here.

Helmer: You seemed to be making yourself pretty happy upstairs too.

Rank: Very much so. Why shouldn't I? Why shouldn't we enjoy everything in this world? At least as much as we can, for as long as we can. The wine was first-rate—

Helmer: Especially the champagne.

Rank: So you noticed that too? It's almost unbelievable how much of it I managed to put away!

Nora: Torvald drank a lot of champagne tonight too.

Rank: Did he?

Nora: Yes, and it always makes him so merry.

Rank: Well, why shouldn't a person have a merry evening after a well-spent day?

Helmer: Well-spent? I'm afraid I can't take credit for that.

Rank (*clapping him on the back*): But I can, you know!

Nora: Doctor Rank, you must have been busy with some scientific investigation today.

Rank: Exactly.

Helmer: Listen to this! Little Nora talking about scientific investigations!

Nora: And may I congratulate you on the result?

Rank: Indeed you may.

Nora: Was it favorable, then?

Rank: The best possible result, for both doctor and patient—certainty.

Nora (*quickly and searchingly*): Certainty?

Rank: Absolute certainty. So wasn't I entitled to make a merry evening of it after that?

Nora: Yes, you certainly were, Doctor Rank.

Helmer: I think so too, as long as you don't have to pay for it in the morning.

Rank: Oh well, you can't have anything in this life without paying for it.

Nora: Doctor Rank, are you fond of fancy-dress balls?

Rank: Yes, if there are a lot of pretty costumes.

Nora: Tell me, what should the two of us wear to the next one?

Helmer: Little featherbrain! You're thinking of the next one already?
Rank: The two of us? Yes, I can tell you. You'll go as a good-luck charm—
Helmer: Yes, but what would be the costume for that?
Rank: She just needs to dress the way she always does.
Helmer: That was very nicely put. But aren't you going to tell us what you'll be?
Rank: Yes, my dear friend, I've already made up my mind about that.
Helmer: Well?
Rank: At the next fancy-dress ball I'm going to be invisible.
Helmer: That's a good one!
Rank: There's a big black cap . . . Haven't you ever heard of the cap that makes you invisible? Once you put it on, no one can see you anymore.
Helmer (*suppressing a smile*): Yes, that's right.
Rank: But I'm clean forgetting what I came for. Helmer, give me a cigar. One of the dark Havanas.
Helmer: With the greatest pleasure. (*Offers him his case.*)
Rank (*takes a cigar and cuts off the end*): Thanks.
Nora (*striking a match*): Let me give you a light.
Rank: Thank you. (*She holds the match for him to light his cigar.*) And now goodbye!
Helmer: Goodbye, goodbye, my dear old friend.
Nora: Sleep well, Doctor Rank.
Rank: Thank you for that wish.
Nora: Wish me the same.
Rank: You? Well, if you want me to. Sleep well! And thanks for the light. (*He nods to them both and goes out.*)
Helmer (*in a subdued voice*): He's had too much to drink.
Nora (*absently*): Maybe.

(*Helmer takes a bunch of keys out of his pocket and goes into the hall.*)

Torvald! What are you going to do out there?
Helmer: Empty the mailbox. It's quite full. There won't be any room for the newspaper in the morning.
Nora: Are you going to work tonight?
Helmer: You know I'm not. What's this? Someone's been at the lock.
Nora: At the lock?
Helmer: Yes, it's been tampered with. What does this mean? I never would have thought the maid—Look, here's a broken hairpin. It's one of yours, Nora.
Nora (*quickly*): Then it must have been the children—
Helmer: Then you'd better break them of those habits. There, I've finally got it open.

(*Empties the mailbox and calls out to the kitchen.*)

Helene! Helene, put out the light over the front door.

(*Comes back into the room and shuts the door into the hall. He holds out his hand full of letters.*)

Look at that. Look what a pile of them there are. (*Turning them over.*) What's this?

Nora (at the window): The letter! No! Torvald, no!

Helmer: Two calling cards of Rank's.

Nora: Of Doctor Rank's?

Helmer (looking at them): Yes, Doctor Rank. They were on top. He must have put them in there when he left just now.

Nora: Is there anything written on them?

Helmer: There's a black cross over the name. Look. What a morbid thing to do! It looks as if he's announcing his own death.

Nora: That's exactly what he's doing.

Helmer: What? Do you know anything about it? Has he said anything to you?

Nora: Yes. He told me that when the cards came it would be his farewell to us. He means to close himself off and die.

Helmer: My poor old friend! Of course I knew we wouldn't have him for very long. But this soon! And he goes and hides himself away like a wounded animal.

Nora: If it has to happen, it's better that it be done without a word. Don't you think so, Torvald?

Helmer (walking up and down): He's become so much a part of our lives, I can't imagine him not being with us anymore. With his poor health and his loneliness, he was like a cloudy background to our sunlit happiness. Well, maybe it's all for the best. For him, anyway. (*Standing still.*) And maybe for us too, Nora. Now we have only each other to rely on. (*Puts his arms around her.*) My darling wife, I feel as though I can't possibly hold you tight enough. You know, Nora, I've often wished you were in some kind of serious danger, so that I could risk everything, even my own life, to save you.

Nora (disengages herself from him, and says firmly and decidedly): Now you must go and read your letters, Torvald.

Helmer: No, no, not tonight. I want to be with you, my darling wife.

Nora: With the thought of your friend's death—

Helmer: You're right, it has affected us both. Something ugly has come between us, the thought of the horrors of death. We have to try to put it out of our minds. Until we do, we'll each go to our own room.

Nora (with her arms around his neck): Good night, Torvald. Good night!

Helmer (kissing her on the forehead): Good night, my little songbird. Sleep well, Nora. Now I'll go read all my mail. (*He takes his letters and goes into his room, shutting the door behind him.*)

Nora (gropes distractedly about, picks up Helmer's domino and wraps it around her, while she says in quick, hoarse, spasmodic whispers): Never to see him again. Never! Never! (*Puts her shawl over her head.*) Never to see my children again either, never again. Never! Never! Oh, the icy, black water, the bottomless depths! If only it were over! He's got it now, now he's reading it. Goodbye, Torvald . . . children!

(*She is about to rush out through the hall when Helmer opens his door hurriedly and stands with an open letter in his hand.*)

Helmer: Nora!

Nora: Ah!

Helmer: What is this? Do you know what's in this letter?

Nora: Yes, I know. Let me go! Let me get out!

Helmer (*holding her back*): Where are you going?

Nora (*trying to get free*): You're not going to save me, Torvald!

Helmer (*reeling*): It's true? Is this true, what it says here? This is horrible! No, no, it can't possibly be true.

Nora: It is true. I've loved you more than anything else in the world.

Helmer: Don't start with your ridiculous excuses.

Nora (*taking a step towards him*): Torvald!

Helmer: You little fool, do you know what you've done?

Nora: Let me go. I won't let you suffer for my sake. You're not going to take it on yourself.

Helmer: Stop play-acting. (*Locks the hall door.*) You're going to stay right here and give me an explanation. Do you understand what you've done? Answer me! Do you understand what you've done?

Nora (*looks steadily at him and says with a growing look of coldness in her face*): Yes, I'm beginning to understand everything now.

Helmer (*walking around the room*): What a horrible awakening! The woman who was my pride and joy for eight years, a hypocrite, a liar, worse than that, much worse—a criminal! The unspeakable ugliness of it all! The shame of it! The shame!

(*Nora is silent and looks steadily at him. He stops in front of her.*)

I should have realized that something like this was bound to happen. I should have seen it coming. Your father's shifty nature—be quiet!—your father's shifty nature has come out in you. No religion, no morality, no sense of duty. This is my punishment for closing my eyes to what he did! I did it for your sake, and this is how you pay me back.

Nora: Yes, that's right.

Helmer: Now you've destroyed all my happiness. You've ruined my whole future. It's horrible to think about! I'm in the power of an unscrupulous man. He can do what he wants with me, ask me for anything he wants, give me any orders he wants, and I don't dare say no. And I have to sink to such miserable depths, all because of a featherbrained woman!

Nora: When I'm out of the way, you'll be free.

Helmer: Spare me the speeches. Your father had always plenty of those on hand, too. What good would it do me if you were out of the way, as you say? Not the slightest. He can tell everybody the whole story. And if he does, I could be wrongly suspected of having been in on it with you. People will probably think I was behind it all, that I put you up to it! And I have you to thank for all this, after I've cherished you the whole time we've been married. Do you understand what you've done to me?

Nora (*coldly and quietly*): Yes.

Helmer: It's so incredible that I can't take it all in. But we have to come to some understanding. Take off that shawl. Take it off, I said. I have to try to appease him some way or another. It has to be hushed up, no matter what it costs. And as for you and me, we have to make it look as if everything is just as it always was, but only for the sake of appearances, obviously. You'll stay here in my house, of course. But I won't let you bring up the children. I can't trust them to you. To think that I have to say these things to someone I've loved so dearly, and that I still—No, that's all over. From this moment on happiness is out of the question. All that matters now is to save the bits and pieces, to keep up the appearance—

(*The front doorbell rings.*)

Helmer (*with a start*): What's that? At this hour! Can the worst—Can he—Go and hide yourself, Nora. Say you don't feel well. (*Nora stands motionless. Helmer goes and unlocks the hall door.*)

Maid (*half-dressed, comes to the door*): A letter for Mrs. Helmer.

Helmer: Give it to me. (*Takes the letter, and shuts the door.*) Yes, it's from him. I'm not giving it to you. I'll read it myself.

Nora: Go ahead, read it.

Helmer (*standing by the lamp*): I barely have the courage to. It could mean ruin for both of us. No, I have to know. (*Tears open the letter, runs his eye over a few lines, looks at a piece of paper enclosed with it, and gives a shout of joy.*) Nora! (*She looks at him questioningly.*) Nora! No, I'd better read it again. Yes, it's true! I'm saved! Nora, I'm saved!

Nora: And what about me?

Helmer: You too, of course. We're both saved, you and I. Look, he's returned your note. He says he's sorry and he apologizes—that a happy change in his life—what difference does it make what he says! We're saved, Nora! Nobody can hurt you. Oh, Nora, Nora! No, first I have to destroy these horrible things. Let me see.... (*Glances at the note.*) No, no, I don't want to look at it. This whole business will be nothing but a bad dream to me.

(*Tears up the note and both letters, throws them all into the stove, and watches them burn.*)

There, now it doesn't exist anymore. He says that you've known since Christmas Eve. These must have been a horrible three days for you, Nora.

Nora: I fought a hard fight these three days.

Helmer: And suffered agonies, and saw no way out but—No, we won't dwell on any of those horrors. We'll just shout for joy and keep saying, "It's all over! It's all over!" Listen to me, Nora. You don't seem to realize that it's all over. What's this? Such a cold, hard face! My poor little Nora, I understand. You find it hard to believe that I've really forgiven you. But I swear that it's true, Nora. I forgive you for everything. I know that you did it all out of love for me.

Nora: That's true.

Helmer: You've loved me the way a wife ought to love her husband. You just didn't have the awareness to see what was wrong with the means you used. But do you think I love you any less because you don't understand how to deal with these things? No, of course not. I want you to lean on me. I'll advise you and guide you. I wouldn't be a man if this womanly helplessness didn't make you twice as attractive to me. Don't think anymore about the hard things I said when I was so upset at first, when I thought everything was going to crush me. I forgive you, Nora. I swear to you that I forgive you.

Nora: Thank you for your forgiveness. (*She goes out through the door to the right.*)

Helmer: No, don't go—(*Looks in.*) What are you doing in there?

Nora (from within): Taking off my costume.

Helmer (standing at the open door): Yes, do. Try to calm yourself, and ease your mind again, my frightened little songbird. I want you to rest and feel secure. I have wide wings for you to take shelter underneath. (*Walks up and down by the door.*) What a warm and cozy home we have, Nora: Here's a safe haven for you, and I'll protect you like a hunted dove that I've rescued from a hawk's claws. I'll calm your poor pounding heart. It will happen, little by little, Nora, believe me. In the morning you'll see it in a very different light. Soon everything will be exactly the way it was before. Before you know it, you won't need my reassurances that I've forgiven you. You'll know for certain that I have. You can't imagine that I'd ever consider rejecting you, or even blaming you? You have no idea what a man feels in his heart, Nora. A man finds it indescribably sweet and satisfying to know that he's forgiven his wife, freely and with all his heart. It's as if he's made her his own all over again. He's given her a new life, in a way, and she's become both wife and child to him. And from this moment on that's what you'll be to me, my little scared, helpless darling. Don't worry about anything, Nora. Just be honest and open with me, and I'll be your will and your conscience. What's this? You haven't gone to bed yet? Have you changed?

Nora (in everyday dress): Yes, Torvald, I've changed.

Helmer: But why—It's so late.

Nora: I'm not going to sleep tonight.

Helmer: But, my dear Nora—

Nora (looking at her watch): It's not that late. Sit down here, Torvald. You and I have a lot to talk about. (*She sits down at one side of the table.*)

Helmer: Nora, what is this? Why this cold, hard face?

Nora: Sit down. This is going to take a while. I have a lot to say to you.

Helmer (sits down at the opposite side of the table): You're making me nervous, Nora. And I don't understand you.

Nora: No, that's it exactly. You don't understand me, and I've never understood you either, until tonight. No, don't interrupt me. I want you to listen to what I have to say. Torvald, I'm settling accounts with you.

Helmer: What do you mean by that?

Nora (after a short silence): Doesn't anything strike you as odd about the way we're sitting here like this?

Helmer: No, what?

Nora: We've been married for eight years. Doesn't it occur to you that this is the first time the two of us, you and I, husband and wife, have had a serious conversation?

Helmer: What do you mean by serious?

Nora: In the whole eight years—longer than that, for the whole time we've known each other—we've never exchanged one word on any serious subject.

Helmer: Did you expect me to be constantly worrying you with problems that you weren't capable of helping me deal with?

Nora: I'm not talking about business. I mean we've never sat down together seriously to try to get to the bottom of anything.

Helmer: But, dearest Nora, what good would that have done you?

Nora: That's just it. You've never understood me. I've been treated badly, Torvald, first by Papa and then by you.

Helmer: What? The two people who've loved you more than anyone else?

Nora (*shaking her head*): You've never loved me. You just thought it was pleasant to be in love with me.

Helmer: Nora, what are you saying?

Nora: It's true, Torvald. When I lived at home with Papa, he gave me his opinion about everything, and so I had all the same opinions, and if I didn't, I kept my mouth shut, because he wouldn't have liked it. He used to call me his doll-child, and he played with me the way I played with my dolls. And when I came to live in your house—

Helmer: What kind of way is that to talk about our marriage?

Nora (*undisturbed*): I mean that I was just passed from Papa's hands to yours. You arranged everything according to your own taste, and so I had all the same tastes as you. Or else I pretended to, I'm not really sure which. Sometimes I think it's one way and sometimes the other. When I look back, it's as if I've been living here like a beggar, from hand to mouth. I've supported myself by performing tricks for you, Torvald. But that's the way you wanted it. You and Papa have committed a terrible sin against me. It's your fault that I've done nothing with my life.

Helmer: This is so unfair and ungrateful of you, Nora! Haven't you been happy here?

Nora: No, I've never really been happy. I thought I was, but it wasn't true.

Helmer: Not—not happy!

Nora: No, just cheerful. You've always been very kind to me. But our home's been nothing but a playroom. I've been your doll-wife, the same way that I was Papa's doll-child. And the children have been my dolls. I thought it was great fun when you played with me, the way they thought it was when I played with them. That's what our marriage has been, Torvald.

Helmer: There's some truth in what you're saying, even though your view of it is exaggerated and overwrought. But things will be different from now on. Playtime is over, and now it's lesson-time.

Nora: Whose lessons? Mine, or the children's?

Helmer: Both yours and the children's, my darling Nora.

Nora: I'm sorry, Torvald, but you're not the man to give me lessons on how to be a proper wife to you.

Helmer: How can you say that?

Nora: And as for me, who am I to be allowed to bring up the children?

Helmer: Nora!

Nora: Didn't you say so yourself a little while ago, that you don't dare trust them to me?

Helmer: That was in a moment of anger! Why can't you let it go?

Nora: Because you were absolutely right. I'm not fit for the job. There's another job I have to take on first. I have to try to educate myself. You're not the man to help me with that. I have to do that for myself. And that's why I'm going to leave you now.

Helmer (*jumping up*): What are you saying?

Nora: I have to stand completely on my own, if I'm going to understand myself and everything around me. That's why I can't stay here with you any longer.

Helmer: Nora, Nora!

Nora: I'm leaving right now. I'm sure Kristine will put me up for the night—

Helmer: You're out of your mind! I won't let you go! I forbid it!

Nora: It's no use forbidding me anything anymore. I'm taking only what belongs to me. I won't take anything from you, now or later.

Helmer: This is insanity!

Nora: Tomorrow I'm going home. Back to where I came from, I mean. It'll be easier for me to find something to do there.

Helmer: You're a blind, senseless woman!

Nora: Then I'd better try to get some sense, Torvald.

Helmer: But to desert your home, your husband, and your children! And aren't you concerned about what people will say?

Nora: I can't concern myself with that. I only know that this is what I have to do.

Helmer: This is outrageous! You're just going to walk away from your most sacred duties?

Nora: What do you consider to be my most sacred duties?

Helmer: Do you need me to tell you that? Aren't they your duties to your husband and your children?

Nora: I have other duties just as sacred.

Helmer: No, you do not. What could they be?

Nora: Duties to myself.

Helmer: First and foremost, you're a wife and a mother.

Nora: I don't believe that anymore. I believe that first and foremost I'm a human being, just as you are—or, at least, that I have to try to become one. I know very well, Torvald, that most people would agree with you, and that opinions like yours are in books, but I can't be satisfied anymore with what most people say, or with what's in books. I have to think things through for myself and come to understand them.

Helmer: Why can't you understand your place in your own home? Don't you have an infallible guide in matters like that? What about your religion?

Nora: Torvald, I'm afraid I'm not sure what religion is.

Helmer: What are you saying?

Nora: All I know is what Pastor Hansen said when I was confirmed. He told us that religion was this, that, and the other thing. When I'm away from all this and on my own, I'll look into that subject too. I'll see if what he said is true or not, or at least whether it's true for me.

Helmer: This is unheard of, coming from a young woman like you! But if religion doesn't guide you, let me appeal to your conscience. I assume you have some moral sense. Or do you have none? Answer me.

Nora: Torvald, that's not an easy question to answer. I really don't know. It's very confusing to me. I only know that you and I look at it in very different ways. I'm learning too that the law isn't at all what I thought it was, and I can't convince myself that the law is right. A woman has no right to spare her old dying father or to save her husband's life? I can't believe that.

Helmer: You talk like a child. You don't understand anything about the world you live in.

Nora: No, I don't. But I'm going to try. I'm going to see if I can figure out who's right, me or the world.

Helmer: You're sick, Nora. You're delirious. I'm half convinced that you're out of your mind.

Nora: I've never felt so clearheaded and sure of myself as I do tonight.

Helmer: Clearheaded and sure of yourself—and that's the spirit in which you forsake your husband and your children?

Nora: Yes, it is.

Helmer: Then there's only one possible explanation.

Nora: Which is?

Helmer: You don't love me anymore.

Nora: Exactly.

Helmer: Nora! How can you say that?

Nora: It's very painful for me to say it, Torvald, because you've always been so good to me, but I can't help it. I don't love you anymore.

Helmer (*regaining his composure*): Are you clearheaded and sure of yourself when you say that too?

Nora: Yes, totally clearheaded and sure of myself. That's why I can't stay here.

Helmer: Can you tell me what I did to make you stop loving me?

Nora: Yes, I can. It was tonight, when the miracle didn't happen. That's when I realized you're not the man I thought you were.

Helmer: Can you explain that more clearly? I don't understand you.

Nora: I've been waiting so patiently for the last eight years. Of course I knew that miracles don't happen every day. Then when I found myself in this horrible situation, I was sure that the miracle was about to happen at last. When Krogstad's letter was lying out there, never for a moment did I imagine that you would agree to his conditions. I was absolutely certain that you'd say to him: Go ahead, tell the whole world. And when he had—

Helmer: Yes, what then? After I'd exposed my wife to shame and disgrace?

Nora: When he had, I was absolutely certain you'd come forward and take the whole thing on yourself, and say: I'm the guilty one.

Helmer: Nora—!

Nora: You mean that I would never have let you make such a sacrifice for me? Of course I wouldn't. But who would have believed my word against yours? That was the miracle that I hoped for and dreaded. And it was to keep it from happening that made me want to kill myself.

Helmer: I'd gladly work night and day for you, Nora, and endure sorrow and poverty for your sake. But no man would sacrifice his honor for the one he loves.

Nora: Hundreds of thousands of women have done it.

Helmer: Oh, you think and talk like a thoughtless child.

Nora: Maybe so. But you don't think or talk like the man I want to be with for the rest of my life. As soon as your fear had passed—and it wasn't fear for what threatened me, but for what might happen to you—when the whole thing was past, as far as you were concerned it was just as if nothing at all had happened. I was still your little skylark, your doll, but now you'd handle me twice as gently and carefully as before, because I was so delicate and fragile. (*Getting up.*) Torvald, that's when it dawned on me that for eight years I'd been living here with a stranger and had borne him three children. Oh, I can't bear to think about it! I could tear myself into little pieces!

Helmer (*sadly*): I see, I see. An abyss has opened up between us. There's no denying it. But, Nora, can't we find some way to close it?

Nora: The way I am now, I'm no wife for you.

Helmer: I can find it in myself to become a different man.

Nora: Maybe so—if your doll is taken away from you.

Helmer: But to be apart!—to be apart from you! No, no, Nora, I can't conceive of it.
Nora (*going out to the right*): All the more reason why it has to be done.

    (*She comes back with her coat and hat and a small suitcase which she puts on a chair by the table.*)

Helmer: Nora, Nora, not now! Wait till tomorrow.
Nora (*putting on her cloak*): I can't spend the night in a strange man's room.
Helmer: But couldn't we live here together like brother and sister?
Nora (*putting on her hat*): You know how long that would last. (*Puts the shawl around her.*) Goodbye, Torvald. I won't look in on the children. I know they're in better hands than mine. The way I am now, I'm no use to them.
Helmer: But someday, Nora, someday?
Nora: How can I tell? I have no idea what's going to become of me.
Helmer: But you're my wife, whatever becomes of you.
Nora: Listen, Torvald. I've heard that when a wife deserts her husband's house, the way I'm doing now, he's free of all legal obligations to her. In any event, I set you free from all your obligations. I don't want you to feel bound in the slightest, any more than I will. There has to be complete freedom on both sides. Look, here's your ring back. Give me mine.
Helmer: That too?
Nora: That too.
Helmer: Here it is.
Nora: Good. Now it's all over. I've left the keys here. The maids know all about how to run the house, much better than I do. Kristine will come by tomorrow after I leave her place and pack up my own things, the ones I brought with me from home. I'd like to have them sent to me.
Helmer: All over! All over! Nora, will you ever think about me again?
Nora: I know I'll often think about you, and the children, and this house.
Helmer: May I write to you, Nora?
Nora: No, never. You mustn't do that.
Helmer: But at least let me send you—
Nora: Nothing, nothing.
Helmer: Let me help you if you're in need.
Nora: No. I can't accept anything from a stranger.
Helmer: Nora . . . can't I ever be anything more than a stranger to you?
Nora (*picking up her bag*): Ah, Torvald, for that, the most wonderful miracle of all would have to happen.
Helmer: Tell me what that would be!
Nora: We'd both have to change so much that—Oh, Torvald, I've stopped believing in miracles.
Helmer: But I'll believe. Tell me! Change so much that . . . ?
Nora: That our life together would be a true marriage. Goodbye.

    (*She goes out through the hall.*)

Helmer (*sinks down into a chair at the door and buries his face in his hands*): Nora! Nora! (*Looks around, and stands up.*) Empty. She's gone. (*A hope flashes across his mind.*) The most wonderful miracle of all . . . ?

    (*The heavy sound of a closing door is heard from below.*)

Questions

ACT I

1. From the opening conversation between Helmer and Nora, what are your impressions of him? Of her? Of their marriage?
2. At what moment in the play do you understand why it is called *A Doll's House?*
3. In what ways does Mrs. Linde provide a contrast for Nora?
4. What in Krogstad's first appearance on stage, and in Dr. Rank's remarks about him, indicates that the bank clerk is a menace?
5. Of what illegal deed is Nora guilty? How does she justify it?
6. When the curtain falls on Act I, what problems now confront Nora?

ACT II

1. As Act II opens, what are your feelings on seeing the stripped, ragged Christmas tree? How is it suggestive?
2. What events that soon occur make Nora's situation even more difficult?
3. How does she try to save herself?
4. Why does Nora fling herself into the wild tarantella?

ACT III

1. For what possible reasons does Mrs. Linde pledge herself to Krogstad?
2. How does Dr. Rank's announcement of his impending death affect Nora and Helmer?
3. What is Helmer's reaction to learning the truth about Nora's misdeed? Why does he blame Nora's father? What is revealing (of Helmer's own character) in his remark, "From this moment on happiness is out of the question. All that matters now is to save the bits and pieces, to keep up the appearance—"?
4. When Helmer finds that Krogstad has sent back the note, what is his response? How do you feel toward him?
5. How does the character of Nora develop in this act?
6. How do you interpret her final closing of the door?

General Questions

1. In what ways do you find Nora a victim? In what ways is she at fault?
2. Try to state the theme of the play. Does it involve women's rights? Self-fulfillment?
3. What dramatic question does the play embody? At what moment can this question first be stated?
4. What is the crisis? In what way is this moment or event a "turning point"? (In what new direction does the action turn?)

Suggestions for Writing on Ibsen's A Doll's House

1. How relevant is *A Doll's House* today? Do women like Nora still exist? How about men like Torvald? Build an argument, either that the concerns of *A Doll's House* are timeless and universal or that the issues addressed by the play are historical, not contemporary.
2. Placing yourself in the character of Torvald Helmer, write a defense of him and his attitude as he himself might write it.
3. Write a short account of what you think the next ten years will hold for both Nora and Torvald.

4. Al Capovilla of Folsom Lake Center College has developed an ingenious assignment based on *A Doll's House* that asks you to combine the skills of a literary critic with those of a lawyer. Here is the assignment:

> You are the family lawyer for Torvald and Nora Helmer. The couple comes to you with a request. They want you to listen to an account of their domestic problems and recommend whether they should pursue a divorce or try to reconcile.
>
> You listen to both sides of the argument. (You also know everything that is said by every character.)
>
> Now, it is your task to write a short decision. In stating your opinion, provide a clear and organized explanation of your reasoning. Show both sides of the argument. You may employ as evidence anything said or done in the play.
>
> Conclude your paper with your recommendation. What do you advise under the circumstances—divorce or an attempt at reconciliation?

Suggestions for Writing on *Literature about Personal Identity*

1. Several of the works in this chapter involve parents and children. In some cases there is intergenerational tension or misunderstanding, in others there is connection and legacy; still others include elements of both. Choose at least two works that include a relationship between parents and children, and compare the tensions and the warmer moments. Possible examples are Langston Hughes's "Mother to Son," Charles Bukowski's "my old man," and Virginia Woolf's "What If Shakespeare Had a Sister?"
2. Many of the works in this chapter deal with issues of gender or race. Make an argument for or against the idea that women—or a specific minority group—have achieved full equality in the United States.
3. Several of the pieces in this chapter are written about, or from the point of view of, immigrants. Choose at least two such works and compare how immigration is presented in each. Do the authors see the process and benefits of immigration in the same way? How do they see the United States?
4. Many of the works in this chapter, especially the poems, involve men looking at women, women looking at men, and women and men looking at themselves. Is there a difference in how people see themselves and how they are seen (or think they are seen) by persons of the other sex? Choose at least one work written by a man, and one by a woman, and compare.
5. To what extent do class, education, race, religion, place of birth, or gender affect how someone sees the world? Using two works in this chapter, examine the influence of such factors on the author's worldview.
6. Frederick Douglass wrote more than 150 years ago about the difference that reading and writing made in his life. Choose another work in this chapter and analyze how his observations are—or are not—relevant to the lives of its characters.
7. Describe how *one* element of your own identity—race, religion, region, class, sexual orientation, favorite sport, hobby, current job—influences how you see the world. Give specific examples of situations or issues in which your identity has had a role in how you've responded or felt.
8. What, to you, is the most significant legacy you have received from your family? What characteristics or stories from your family have been most deeply influential on your own sense of self?

17 NATURE AND THE ENVIRONMENT

The goal of life is living in agreement with nature.

—ZENO

Nature and the environment are subjects that inspire strong reactions. Many people—both secular and religious—bring a deep sense of reverence to the natural world. Other people—ironically, both secular and religious—have little patience for such concerns. They feel that the physical world should be developed and used by humanity, and they consider it silly to value an endangered plant or animal above the economic needs of human beings. The Russian novelist Ivan Turgenev said, "Nature's not a temple but a workshop, and man's the workman in it." The poet Robinson Jeffers, however, believed that humanity distorts nature by trying to put itself at the center of things. "We must uncenter our minds from ourselves," he advised. "Not man apart" he wrote, in words that became a rallying cry for environmentalists. Everything in the natural world is connected, Jeffers believed, and humanity is no exception.

In some ways, "nature and the environment" is the broadest of our themes because nature—unlike such themes as "family" and "love"—encompasses not only humans but the entire world, including inanimate matter. The theme of this chapter also has a number of subcategories, including humankind's relationship to the natural world, the importance of all living things, and the tension between preserving natural spaces and developing them for human activity.

Let's consider the relationship of humans to nature. Depending on your own upbringing and experience, you might value the beauty of mountains, rivers, deserts, and beaches, and appreciate that they were shaped by forces beyond human influence. You might thrill—as John Muir does in his essay in this chapter—to the power and majesty of a huge storm; or you may be dazzled, as Elizabeth Bishop is in "The Fish," by the intricate beauty of a single animal. On the other hand, maybe you see the natural world as remote from your own interests—or alternatively, as frightening and indifferent, unappealing precisely because you can't control it. Some people who have spent their entire lives in big cities find the quiet, open space of the wilderness disconcerting or perhaps boring. As the comedian George Carlin once observed, "Some national parks have long waiting lists for camping reservations. When you have to wait a year to sleep next to a tree, something is wrong."

Yet people do—literally and figuratively—make the effort to sleep next to a tree. On a hot day, you can find flocks of people of all ages and backgrounds at beaches, lakes, and rivers. In the winter, people sled, ski, or simply romp in the snow. Families—especially those with children—crowd the local zoos. Millions of people spend their vacations visiting Yosemite, the Grand Canyon, the Everglades, and Niagara Falls. Other people save all year to go on excursions to Africa or Alaska in order to see wildlife in vast, unspoiled tracts of land. All of this suggests that there is something deeply ingrained, in us that is attracted to the natural world. A few of us go even further and embark on quests—to climb mountains or sail around the world—that test our mettle and put us on more intimate terms with nature. Sometimes these quests seem quixotic, even suicidal: Timothy Treadwell, the subject of the movie *Grizzly Man*, spent thirteen years in the wilds of Alaska communing with the bears who eventually killed him.

But what happens when our respect for the natural world collides with other human needs? What is the impact on a landscape when a new highway is built, or on a river when a factory is opened? What happens to a forest when logging is permitted, or to an ocean when there's drilling for oil? Can such undertakings be done in ways that minimize their impact on the environment? Who gets to make the decisions? Is something inherently valuable in the preservation of animals or wild places? Or is the question even more basic than that—do we as people lose something when species or vistas are lost?

These issues, and others like them, have long been the subjects of debate—and where people stand is not always predictable. Today we often associate environmental protection with liberal politics, but the most influential early environmental champions were political conservatives such as President Theodore Roosevelt, who once accompanied John Muir on a backpacking trip in Yosemite and created the national park system, or John D. Rockefeller, the founder of Standard Oil, who donated most of the land that became Grand Teton National Park. Today's conservation groups include The Nature Conservancy and the Sierra Club, as well as some evangelical Christian groups who see nature—as many early explorers did—as the work of God, and believe that humanity must act responsibly as stewards of the earth that it does not own but must pass on to the future.

Even as you read this anthology, policymakers, environmentalists, and business leaders are probably debating these questions: When and where should offshore drilling take place? What animals belong on the endangered species list—and should there even be such a list? Should the federal government designate more wilderness areas? Should natural resources be developed to create more jobs? Should snowmobiles and ATVs be allowed in national forests? Should commercial fishing be restricted to protect the fish population? Should we build nuclear power plants, and if so, where? What should we do to reduce air pollution? "What exactly is the purpose of nature, anyway?" one might reasonably ask. We don't pretend to have definitive answers to any of these questions. With the exception of the essays, the works in this chapter don't give direct answers, either. But they do present a variety of views on the power, difficulty, beauty, danger, appeal, and mystery of the natural world.

THE SELECTIONS IN THIS CHAPTER

Jack London's "To Build a Fire" and Stephen Crane's "The Open Boat" depict the awesome power of nature—and the folly of trying to master it. Leslie Marmon Silko's "The Man to Send Rain Clouds" presents characters who have a deep and abiding connection to the places where they live. Short animal fables from Aesop, Bidpai, and Chuang Tzu use animal characters to point out human foibles. Poems by Wallace Stevens, Robinson Jeffers, and Kay Ryan describe the mysterious power of animals, while Elizabeth Bishop's "The Fish" captures the splendor of one small creature. Essays by John Muir and Wallace Stegner present portraits of a nature that should be valued and preserved, and bell hooks addresses the historical connection between African Americans and the natural world.

As you read these selections, think about your own relationship with nature—whether it's something as grand as the Rocky Mountains or as small as a bird outside your window. Think about your own corner of the world, the places you consider home. Having a deeper appreciation for where you are—the particular sights and sounds, the views, the sensations and smells—may not change your mind about environmental issues, but it will enable you to live more fully in the world around you.

Things to Think About

1. How do you feel about wild places such as mountains, deserts, or oceans? Do you find them beautiful and relaxing? Threatening or unpleasant? Uncomfortable or boring? Why?
2. Have you had a formative experience, either positive or negative, in nature? What element of the natural world (stars, air, weather, animals, scenery) has had the greatest impact on you?
3. Think about the physical or geographical aspects of the place (or places) where you grew up. How did growing up where you did influence your views of nature and of the world?
4. Do you prefer the city or the country? Why? If you like both, what do you enjoy about the different places?
5. Are you drawn to animals? Do you have pets? If you enjoy animals, what is it about them that appeals to you? If you don't, what fails to draw you in?
6. Are you conscious of environmental issues in your everyday life? If so, how? Do you recycle? Do you use particular modes of transportation? Do you opt for energy-saving lights or appliances? If you do these kinds of things, why do you do them? If you don't, why not?
7. Do you see the natural world as something that we should try to fit in with, or as something that we should use for our own needs?

FICTION

HUMANITY VERSUS NATURE

Jack London	*To Build a Fire*
Stephen Crane	*The Open Boat*
T. Coraghessan Boyle	*Greasy Lake*

People have struggled against nature for as long as we have lived on earth. Many human tragedies have been caused by natural events, including, just in recent years, Hurricane Katrina in New Orleans, earthquakes in Haiti and Chile, floods in Australia, and the tsunami in Thailand. On a smaller scale, people challenge or are challenged by nature on a regular basis—in jobs such as farming, fishing, and mining; in sports such as mountain climbing, surfing, and scuba diving. Injuries and deaths in such ventures are not uncommon: hikers get lost in snowstorms; fishing boats sink in rough seas. From a comfortable distance, nature seems beautiful and serene, but when people are caught up in its immense forces, when lives are at stake, it seems ominous and threatening. Is nature indifferent to us? Is it an adversary, or is it just a setting or circumstance whose power we must recognize and adjust to? How should we respond in the face of its challenges—by trying to defeat it, or by working within its parameters? The stories in this section all involve characters who struggle with nature. In Jack London's "To Build a Fire," a man overestimates his own ability and resourcefulness in the face of the Alaskan wilderness. In Stephen Crane's "The Open Boat," several men who have survived the sinking of their ship are pushed beyond their limits. In T. C. Boyle's "Greasy Lake," the harsh indifference of nature seems to inspire a similar lack of empathy in the story's main characters.

Jack London

Jack London (1876–1916), born in San Francisco, won a large popular audience for his novels of the sea and the Yukon: The Call of the Wild *(1903),* The Sea-Wolf *(1904), and* White Fang *(1906). Like Ernest Hemingway, he was a writer who lived a strenuous life. In 1894, he marched cross-country in Coxey's Army, an organized protest of the unemployed; in 1897, he took part in the Klondike gold rush; and later, as a reporter, he covered the Russo-Japanese War and the Mexican Revolution. Son of an unmarried mother and a father who denied his paternity, London grew up in poverty. At fourteen, he began holding hard jobs: working in a canning factory and a jute-mill, serving as a deckhand, pirating oysters in San Francisco Bay. These experiences persuaded him to join the Socialist Labor Party and*

Jack London

crusade for workers' rights. In his political novel The Iron Heel (1908), London envisions a grim totalitarian America. Like himself, the hero of his novel Martin Eden (1909) is a man of brief schooling who gains fame as a writer, works for a cause, loses faith in it, and finds life without meaning. Though endowed with immense physical energy—he wrote fifty volumes—London drank hard, spent fast, and played out early. While his reputation as a novelist may have declined since his own day, some of his short stories have lasted triumphantly.

To Build a Fire 1910

Day had broken cold and gray, exceedingly cold and gray, when the man turned aside from the main Yukon trail and climbed the high earth-bank, where a dim and little-travelled trail led eastward through the fat spruce timberland. It was a steep bank, and he paused for breath at the top, excusing the act to himself by looking at his watch. It was nine o'clock. There was no sun nor hint of sun, though there was not a cloud in the sky. It was a clear day, and yet there seemed an intangible pall over the face of things, a subtle gloom that made the day dark, and that was due to the absence of sun. This fact did not worry the man. He was used to the lack of sun. It had been days since he had seen the sun, and he knew that a few more days must pass before that cheerful orb, due south, would just peep above the sky line and dip immediately from view.

The man flung a look back along the way he had come. The Yukon lay a mile wide and hidden under three feet of ice. On top of this ice were as many feet of snow. It was all pure white, rolling in gentle undulations where the ice jams of the freeze-up had formed. North and south, as far as the eye could see, it was unbroken white, save for a dark hairline that curved and twisted from around the spruce-covered island to the south, and that curved and twisted away into the north, where it disappeared behind another spruce-covered island. This dark hairline was the trail—the main trail—that led south five hundred miles to the Chilcoot Pass, Dyea, and salt water; and that led north seventy miles to Dawson, and still on to the north a thousand miles to Nulato, and finally to St. Michael, on Bering Sea, a thousand miles and half a thousand more.

But all this—the mysterious, far-reaching hairline trail, the absence of sun from the sky, the tremendous cold, and the strangeness and weirdness of it all—made no impression on the man. It was not because he was long used to it. He was a newcomer in the land, a *chechaquo,* and this was his first winter. The trouble with him was that he was without imagination. He was quick and alert in the things of life, but only in the things, and not in the significances. Fifty degrees below zero meant eighty-odd degrees of frost. Such fact impressed him as being cold and uncomfortable, and that was all. It did not lead him to meditate upon his frailty as a creature of temperature, and upon man's frailty in general, able only to live within certain narrow limits of heat and cold; and from there on it did not lead him to the conjectural field of immortality and man's place in the universe. Fifty degrees below zero stood for a bite of frost that hurt and that must be guarded against by the use of mittens, ear flaps, warm moccasins, and thick socks. Fifty degrees below zero was to him just precisely fifty degrees below zero. That there should be anything more to it than that was a thought that never entered his head.

As he turned to go on, he spat speculatively. There was a sharp, explosive crackle that startled him. He spat again. And again, in the air, before it could fall to the snow, the spittle crackled. He knew that at fifty below spittle crackled on the snow, but this spittle had crackled in the air. Undoubtedly it was colder than fifty below—how much colder he did not know. But the temperature did not matter. He was bound for the old claim on the left fork of Henderson Creek, where the boys were already. They had come over across the divide from the Indian Creek country, while he had come the roundabout way to take a look at the possibilities of getting out logs in the spring from the islands in the Yukon. He would be in to camp by six o'clock; a bit after dark, it was true, but the boys would be there, a fire would be going, and a hot supper would be ready. As for lunch, he pressed his hand against the protruding bundle under his jacket. It was also under his shirt, wrapped up in a handkerchief and lying against the naked skin. It was the only way to keep the biscuits from freezing. He smiled agreeably to himself as he thought of those biscuits, each cut open and sopped in bacon grease, and each enclosing a generous slice of fried bacon.

He plunged in among the big spruce trees. The trail was faint. A foot of snow had fallen since the last sled had passed over, and he was glad he was without a sled, travelling light. In fact, he carried nothing but the lunch wrapped in the handkerchief. He was surprised, however, at the cold. It certainly was cold, he concluded, as he rubbed his numb nose and cheekbones with his mittened hand. He was a warm-whiskered man, but the hair on his face did not protect the high cheekbones and the eager nose that thrust itself aggressively into the frosty air.

At the man's heels trotted a dog, a big native husky, the proper wolf dog, gray-coated and without any visible or temperamental difference from its brother, the wild wolf. The animal was depressed by the tremendous cold. It knew that it was no time for travelling. Its instinct told it a truer tale than was told to the man by the man's judgment. In reality, it was not merely colder than fifty below zero; it was colder than sixty below, than seventy below. It was seventy-five below zero. Since the freezing point is thirty-two above zero, it meant that one hundred and seven degrees of frost obtained. The dog did not know anything about thermometers. Possibly in its brain there was no sharp consciousness of a condition of very cold such as was in the man's brain. But the brute had its instinct. It experienced a vague but menacing apprehension that subdued it and made it slink along at the man's heels, and that made it question eagerly every unwonted movement of the man as if expecting him to go into camp or to seek shelter somewhere and build a fire. The dog had learned fire, and it wanted fire, or else to burrow under the snow and cuddle its warmth away from the air.

The frozen moisture of its breathing had settled on its fur in a fine powder of frost, and especially were its jowls, muzzle, and eyelashes whitened by its crystalled breath. The man's red beard and mustache were likewise frosted, but more solidly, the deposit taking the form of ice and increasing with every warm, moist breath he exhaled. Also, the man was chewing tobacco, and the muzzle of ice held his lips so rigidly that he was unable to clear his chin when he expelled the juice. The result was that a crystal beard of the color and solidity of amber was increasing its length on his chin. If he fell down it would shatter itself, like glass, into brittle fragments. But he did not mind the appendage. It was the penalty all tobacco chewers paid in that country, and he had been out before in two cold snaps. They had not been so cold as this, he knew, but by the spirit thermometer at Sixty Mile he knew they had been registered at fifty below and at fifty-five.

He held on through the level stretch of woods for several miles, crossed a wide flat, and dropped down a bank to the frozen bed of a small stream. This was Henderson Creek, and he knew he was ten miles from the forks. He looked at his watch. It was ten o'clock. He was making four miles an hour, and he calculated that he would arrive at the forks at half-past twelve. He decided to celebrate that event by eating his lunch there.

The dog dropped in again at his heels, with a tail drooping discouragement, as the man swung along the creek bed. The furrow of the old sled trail was plainly visible, but a dozen inches of snow covered the marks of the last runners. In a month no man had come up or down that silent creek. The man held steadily on. He was not much given to thinking, and just then particularly he had nothing to think about save that he would eat lunch at the forks and that at six o'clock he would be in camp with the boys. There was nobody to talk to; and, had there been, speech would have been impossible because of the ice muzzle on his mouth. So he continued monotonously to chew tobacco and to increase the length of his amber beard.

Once in a while the thought reiterated itself that it was very cold and that he had never experienced such cold. As he walked along he rubbed his cheekbones and nose with the back of his mittened hand. He did this automatically, now and again changing hands. But, rub as he would, the instant he stopped his cheekbones were numb, and the following instant the end of his nose went numb. He was sure to frost his cheeks; he knew that, and experienced a pang of regret that he had not devised a nose strap of the sort Bud wore in cold snaps. Such a strap passed across the cheeks, as well, and saved them. But it didn't matter much, after all. What were frosted cheeks? A bit painful, that was all; they were never serious.

Empty as the man's mind was of thoughts, he was keenly observant, and he noticed the changes in the creek, the curves and bends and timber jams, and always he sharply noted where he placed his feet. Once, coming around a bend, he shied abruptly, like a startled horse, curved away from the place where he had been walking, and retreated several paces back along the trail. The creek he knew was frozen clear to the bottom—no creek could contain water in that arctic winter—but he knew also that there were springs that bubbled out from the hillsides and ran along under the snow and on top the ice of the creek. He knew that the coldest snaps never froze these springs, and he knew likewise their danger. They were traps. They hid pools of water under the snow that might be three inches deep, or three feet. Sometimes a skin of ice half an inch thick covered them, and in turn was covered by the snow. Sometimes there were alternate layers of water and ice skin, so that when one broke through he kept on breaking through for a while, sometimes wetting himself to the waist.

That was why he had shied in such panic. He had felt the give under his feet and heard the crackle of a snow-hidden ice skin. And to get his feet wet in such a temperature meant trouble and danger. At the very least it meant delay, for he would be forced to stop and build a fire, and under its protection to bare his feet while he dried his socks and moccasins. He stood and studied the creek bed and its banks, and decided that the flow of water came from the right. He reflected awhile, rubbing his nose and cheeks, then skirted to the left, stepping gingerly and testing the footing for each step. Once clear of the danger, he took a fresh chew of tobacco and swung along at his four-mile gait.

In the course of the next two hours he came upon several similar traps. Usually the snow above the hidden pools had a sunken, candied appearance that advertised the danger. Once again, however, he had a close call; and once, suspecting danger, he compelled the dog to go on in front. The dog did not want to go. It hung back until the man shoved it forward, and then it went quickly across the white, unbroken surface. Suddenly it broke through, floundered to one side, and got away to firmer footing. It had wet its forefeet and legs, and almost immediately the water that clung to it turned to ice. It made quick efforts to lick the ice off its legs, then dropped down in the snow and began to bite out the ice that had formed between the toes. This was a matter of instinct. To permit the ice to remain would mean sore feet. It did not know this. It merely obeyed the mysterious prompting that arose from the deep crypts of its being. But the man knew, having achieved a judgment on the subject, and he removed the mitten from his right hand and helped tear out the ice particles. He did not expose his fingers more than a minute, and was astonished at the swift numbness that smote them. It certainly was cold. He pulled on the mitten hastily, and beat the hand savagely across his chest.

At twelve o'clock the day was at its brightest. Yet the sun was too far south on its winter journey to clear the horizon. The bulge of the earth intervened between it and Henderson Creek, where the man walked under a clear sky at noon and cast no shadow. At half-past twelve, to the minute, he arrived at the forks of the creek. He was pleased at the speed he had made. If he kept it up, he would certainly be with the boys by six. He unbuttoned his jacket and shirt and drew forth his lunch. The action consumed no more than a quarter of a minute, yet in that brief moment the numbness laid hold of the exposed fingers. He did not put the mitten on, but, instead, struck the fingers a dozen sharp smashes against his leg. Then he sat down on a snow-covered log to eat. The sting that followed upon the striking of his fingers against his leg ceased so quickly that he was startled. He had had no chance to take a bite of biscuit. He struck the fingers repeatedly and returned them to the mitten, baring the other hand for the purpose of eating. He tried to take a mouthful, but the ice muzzle prevented. He had forgotten to build a fire and thaw out. He chuckled at his foolishness, and as he chuckled he noted the numbness creeping into the exposed fingers. Also, he noted that the stinging which had first come to his toes when he sat down was already passing away. He wondered whether the toes were warm or numb. He moved them inside the moccasins and decided that they were numb.

He pulled the mitten on hurriedly and stood up. He was a bit frightened. He stamped up and down until the stinging returned into the feet. It certainly was cold, was his thought. That man from Sulphur Creek had spoken the truth when telling how cold it sometimes got in the country. And he had laughed at him at the time! That showed one must not be too sure of things. There was no mistake about it, it *was* cold. He strode up and down, stamping his feet and threshing his arms, until reassured by the returning warmth. Then he got out matches and proceeded to make a fire. From the undergrowth, where high water of the previous spring had lodged a supply of seasoned twigs, he got his firewood. Working carefully from a small beginning, he soon had a roaring fire, over which he thawed the ice from his face and in the protection of which he ate his biscuits. For the moment the cold of space was outwitted. The dog took satisfaction in the fire, stretching out close enough for warmth and far enough away to escape being singed.

When the man had finished, he filled his pipe and took his comfortable time over a smoke. Then he pulled on his mittens, settled the ear flaps of his cap firmly about his ears, and took the creek trail up the left fork. The dog was disappointed and yearned back toward the fire. This man did not know cold. Possibly all the generations of his ancestry had been ignorant of cold, of real cold, of cold one hundred and seven degrees below freezing point. But the dog knew; all its ancestry knew, and it had inherited the knowledge. And it knew that it was not good to walk abroad in such fearful cold. It was the time to lie snug in a hole in the snow and wait for a curtain of cloud to be drawn across the face of outer space whence this cold came. On the other hand, there was no keen intimacy between the dog and the man. The one was the toil slave of the other, and the only caresses it had ever received were the caresses of the whip lash and of harsh and menacing throat sounds that threatened the whip lash. So the dog made no effort to communicate its apprehension to the man. It was not concerned in the welfare of the man; it was for its own sake that it yearned back toward the fire. But the man whistled, and spoke to it with the sound of whip lashes, and the dog swung in at the man's heels and followed after.

The man took a chew of tobacco and proceeded to start a new amber beard. Also, his moist breath quickly powdered with white his mustache, eyebrows, and lashes. There did not seem to be so many springs on the left fork of the Henderson, and for half an hour the man saw no signs of any. And then it happened. At a place where there were no signs, where the soft, unbroken snow seemed to advertise solidity beneath, the man broke through. It was not deep. He wet himself halfway to the knees before he floundered out to the firm crust.

He was angry, and cursed his luck aloud. He had hoped to get into camp with the boys at six o'clock, and this would delay him an hour, for he would have to build a fire and dry out his footgear. This was imperative at that low temperature—he knew that much; and he turned aside to the bank, which he climbed. On top, tangled in the underbrush about the trunks of several small spruce trees, was a high-water deposit of dry firewood—sticks and twigs, principally, but also larger portions of seasoned branches and fine, dry, last year's grasses. He threw down several large pieces on top of the snow. This served for a foundation and prevented the young flame from drowning itself in the snow it otherwise would melt. The flame he got by touching a match to a small shred of birch bark that he took from his pocket. This burned even more readily than paper. Placing it on the foundation, he fed the young flame with wisps of dry grass and with the tiniest dry twigs.

He worked slowly and carefully, keenly aware of his danger. Gradually, as the flame grew stronger, he increased the size of the twigs with which he fed it. He squatted in the snow, pulling the twigs out from their entanglement in the brush and feeding directly to the flame. He knew there must be no failure. When it is seventy-five below zero, a man must not fail in his first attempt to build a fire—that is, if his feet are wet. If his feet are dry, and he fails, he can run along the trail for half a mile and restore his circulation. But the circulation of wet and freezing feet cannot be restored by running when it is seventy-five below. No matter how fast he runs, the wet feet will freeze the harder.

All this the man knew. The old-timer on Sulphur Creek had told him about it the previous fall, and now he was appreciating the advice. Already all sensation had gone out of his feet. To build the fire he had been forced to remove his mittens, and the fingers had quickly gone numb. His pace of four miles an hour had kept his heart pumping blood to the surface of his body and to all the extremities. But the instant he stopped, the action of the pump eased down. The cold of space smote the unprotected tip of the planet, and he, being on that unprotected tip, received the full force of the blow. The blood of his body recoiled before it. The blood was alive, like the dog, and like the dog it wanted to hide away and cover itself up from the fearful cold. So long as he walked four miles an hour, he pumped that blood, willy-nilly, to the surface; but now it ebbed away and sank down into the recesses of his body. The extremities were the first to feel its absence. His wet feet froze the faster, and his exposed fingers numbed the faster, though they had not yet begun to freeze. Nose and cheeks were already freezing, while the skin of all his body chilled as it lost its blood.

 But he was safe. Toes and nose and cheeks would be only touched by the frost, for the fire was beginning to burn with strength. He was feeding it with twigs the size of his finger. In another minute he would be able to feed it with branches the size of his wrist, and then he could remove his wet footgear, and, while it dried, he could keep his naked feet warm by the fire, rubbing them at first, of course, with snow. The fire was a success. He was safe. He remembered the advice of the old-timer on Sulphur Creek, and smiled. The old-timer had been very serious in laying down the law that no man must travel alone in the Klondike after fifty below. Well, here he was; he had had the accident; he was alone; and he had saved himself. Those old-timers were rather womanish, some of them, he thought. All a man had to do was to keep his head, and he was all right. Any man who was a man could travel alone. But it was surprising, the rapidity with which his cheeks and nose were freezing. And he had not thought his fingers could go lifeless in so short a time. Lifeless they were, for he could scarcely make them move together to grip a twig, and they seemed remote from his body and from him. When he touched a twig, he had to look and see whether or not he had hold of it. The wires were pretty well down between him and his finger ends.

 All of which counted for little. There was the fire, snapping and crackling and promising life with every dancing flame. He started to untie his moccasins. They were coated with ice; the thick German socks were like sheaths of iron halfway to the knees; and the moccasin strings were like rods of steel all twisted and knotted as by some conflagration. For a moment he tugged with his numb fingers, then, realizing the folly of it, he drew his sheath knife.

 But before he could cut the strings, it happened. It was his own fault or, rather, his mistake. He should not have built the fire under the spruce tree. He should have built it in the open. But it had been easier to pull the twigs from the brush and drop them directly on the fire. Now the tree under which he had done this carried a weight of snow on its boughs. No wind had blown for weeks, and each bough was fully freighted. Each time he had pulled a twig he had communicated a slight agitation to the tree— an imperceptible agitation, so far as he was concerned, but an agitation sufficient to bring about the disaster. High up in the tree one bough capsized its load of snow. This fell on the boughs beneath, capsizing them. This process continued, spreading out and involving the whole tree. It grew like an avalanche, and it descended without warning upon the man and the fire, and the fire was blotted out! Where it had burned was a mantle of fresh and disordered snow.

 The man was shocked. It was as though he had just heard his own sentence of death. For a moment he sat and stared at the spot where the fire had been. Then he grew very calm. Perhaps the old-timer on Sulphur Creek was right. If he had only had a trail mate he would have been in no danger now. The trail mate could have built the fire. Well, it was up to him to build the fire over again, and this second time there must be no failure. Even if he succeeded, he would most likely lose some toes. His feet must be badly frozen by now, and there would be some time before the second fire was ready.

Such were his thoughts, but he did not sit and think them. He was busy all the time they were passing through his mind. He made a new foundation for a fire, this time in the open, where no treacherous tree could blot it out. Next he gathered dry grasses and tiny twigs from the high-water flotsam. He could not bring his fingers together to pull them out, but he was able to gather them by the handful. In this way he got many rotten twigs and bits of green moss that were undesirable, but it was the best he could do. He worked methodically, even collecting an armful of the larger branches to be used later when the fire gathered strength. And all the while the dog sat and watched him, a certain yearning wistfulness in its eye, for it looked upon him as the fire provider, and the fire was slow in coming.

When all was ready, the man reached in his pocket for a second piece of birch bark. He knew the bark was there, and, though he could not feel it with his fingers, he could hear its crisp rustling as he fumbled for it. Try as he would, he could not clutch hold of it. And all the time, in his consciousness, was the knowledge that each instant his feet were freezing. This thought tended to put him in a panic, but he fought against it and kept calm. He pulled on his mittens with his teeth, and threshed his arms back and forth, beating his hands with all his might against his sides. He did this sitting down, and he stood up to do it; and all the while the dog sat in the snow, its wolf brush of a tail curled around warmly over its forefeet, its sharp wolf ears pricked forward intently as it watched the man. And the man, as he beat and threshed with his arms and hands, felt a great surge of envy as he regarded the creature that was warm and secure in its natural covering.

After a time he was aware of the first faraway signals of sensation in his beaten fingers. The faint tingling grew stronger till it evolved into a stinging ache that was excruciating, but which the man hailed with satisfaction. He stripped the mitten from his right hand and fetched forth the birch bark. The exposed fingers were quickly going numb again. Next he brought out his bunch of sulphur matches. But the tremendous cold had already driven the life out of his fingers. In his effort to separate one match from the others, the whole bunch fell in the snow. He tried to pick it out of the snow, but failed. The dead fingers could neither touch nor clutch. He was very careful. He drove the thought of his freezing feet, and nose, and cheeks, out of his mind, devoting his whole soul to the matches. He watched, using the sense of vision in place of that of touch, and when he saw his fingers on each side the bunch, he closed them—that is, he willed to close them, for the wires were down, and the fingers did not obey. He pulled the mitten on the right hand, and beat it fiercely against his knee. Then, with both mittened hands, he scooped the bunch of matches, along with much snow, into his lap. Yet he was no better off.

After some manipulation he managed to get the bunch between the heels of his mittened hands. In this fashion he carried it to his mouth. The ice crackled and snapped when by a violent effort he opened his mouth. He drew the lower jaw in, curled the upper lip out of the way, and scraped the bunch with his upper teeth in order to separate a match. He succeeded in getting one, which he dropped on his lap.

He was no better off. He could not pick it up. Then he devised a way. He picked it up in his teeth and scratched it on his leg. Twenty times he scratched before he succeeded in lighting it. As it flamed he held it with his teeth to the birch bark. But the burning brimstone went up his nostrils and into his lungs, causing him to cough spasmodically. The match fell into the snow and went out.

The old-timer on Sulphur Creek was right, he thought in the moment of controlled despair that ensued: after fifty below, a man should travel with a partner. He beat his hands, but failed in exciting any sensation. Suddenly he bared both hands, removing the mittens with his teeth. He caught the whole bunch between the heels of his hands. His arm muscles not being frozen enabled him to press the hand heels tightly against the matches. Then he scratched the bunch along his leg. It flared into flame, seventy sulphur matches at once! There was no wind to blow them out. He kept his head to one side to escape the strangling fumes, and held the blazing bunch to the birch bark. As he so held it, he became aware of sensation in his hand. His flesh was burning. He could smell it. Deep down below the surface he could feel it. The sensation developed into pain that grew acute. And still he endured it, holding the flame of the matches clumsily to the bark that would not light readily because his own burning hands were in the way, absorbing most of the flame.

At last, when he could endure no more, he jerked his hands apart. The blazing matches fell sizzling into the snow, but the birch bark was alight. He began laying dry grasses and the tiniest twigs on the flame. He could not pick and choose, for he had to lift the fuel between the heels of his hands. Small pieces of rotten wood and green moss clung to the twigs, and he bit them off as well as he could with his teeth. He cherished the flame carefully and awkwardly. It meant life, and it must not perish. The withdrawal of blood from the surface of his body now made him begin to shiver, and he grew more awkward. A large piece of green moss fell squarely on the little fire. He tried to poke it out with his fingers, but his shivering frame made him poke too far, and he disrupted the nucleus of the little fire, the burning grasses and tiny twigs separating and scattering. He tried to poke them together again, but in spite of the tenseness of the effort, his shivering got away from him, and the twigs were hopelessly scattered. Each twig gushed a puff of smoke and went out. The fire provider had failed. As he looked apathetically about him, his eyes chanced on the dog, sitting across the ruins of the fire from him, in the snow, making restless, hunching movements, slightly lifting one forefoot and then the other, shifting its weight back and forth on them with wistful eagerness.

The sight of the dog put a wild idea into his head. He remembered the tale of the man, caught in the blizzard, who killed a steer and crawled inside the carcass, and so was saved. He would kill the dog and bury his hands in the warm body until the numbness went out of them. Then he could build another fire. He spoke to the dog, calling it to him; but in his voice was a strange note of fear that frightened the animal, who had never known the man to speak in such a way before. Something was the matter, and its suspicious nature sensed danger—it knew not what danger, but somewhere, somehow, in its brain arose an apprehension of the man. It flattened its ears down at the sound of the man's voice, and its restless, hunching movements and the liftings and shiftings of its forefeet became more pronounced; but it would not come to the man. He got on his hands and knees and crawled toward the dog. This unusual posture again excited suspicion, and the animal sidled mincingly away.

The man sat up in the snow for a moment and struggled for calmness. Then he pulled on his mittens, by means of his teeth, and got upon his feet. He glanced down at first in order to assure himself that he was really standing up, for the absence of sensation in his feet left him unrelated to the earth. His erect position in itself started to drive the webs of suspicion from the dog's mind; and when he spoke peremptorily, with the sound of whip lashes in his voice, the dog rendered its customary allegiance and came to him. As it came within reaching distance, the man lost his control. His arms flashed out to the dog, and he experienced genuine surprise when he discovered that his hands could not clutch, that there was neither bend nor feeling in the fingers. He had forgotten for the moment that they were frozen and that they were freezing more and more. All this happened quickly, and before the animal could get away, he encircled its body with his arms. He sat down in the snow, and in this fashion held the dog, while it snarled and whined and struggled.

But it was all he could do, hold its body encircled in his arms and sit there. He realized that he could not kill the dog. There was no way to do it. With his helpless hands he could neither draw nor hold his sheath knife nor throttle the animal. He released it, and it plunged wildly away, with tail between its legs, and still snarling. It halted forty feet away and surveyed him curiously, with ears sharply pricked forward.

The man looked down at his hands in order to locate them, and found them hanging on the ends of his arms. It struck him as curious that one should have to use his eyes in order to find out where his hands were. He began threshing his arms back and forth, beating the mittened hands against his sides. He did this for five minutes, violently, and his heart pumped enough blood up to the surface to put a stop to his shivering. But no sensation was aroused in the hands. He had an impression that they hung like weights on the ends of his arms, but when he tried to run the impression down, he could not find it.

A certain fear of death, dull and oppressive, came to him. This fear quickly became poignant as he realized that it was no longer a mere matter of freezing his fingers and toes, or of losing his hands and feet, but that it was a matter of life and death with the chances against him. This threw him into a panic, and he turned and ran up the creek bed along the old, dim trail. The dog joined in behind and kept up with him. He ran blindly, without intention, in fear such as he had never known in his life. Slowly, as he plowed and floundered through the snow, he began to see things again—the banks of the creek, the old timber jams, the leafless aspens, and the sky. The running made him feel better. He did not shiver. Maybe, if he ran on, his feet would thaw out; and anyway, if he ran far enough, he would reach camp and the boys. Without doubt he would lose some fingers and toes and some of his face; but the boys would take care of him, and save the rest of him when he got there. And at the same time there was another thought in his mind that said he would never get to the camp and the boys; that it was too many miles away, that the freezing had too great a start on him, and that he would soon be stiff and dead. This thought he kept in the background and refused to consider. Sometimes it pushed itself forward and demanded to be heard, but he thrust it back and strove to think of other things.

It struck him as curious that he could run at all on feet so frozen that he could not feel them when they struck the earth and took the weight of his body. He seemed to himself to skim along above the surface, and to have no connection with the earth. Somewhere he had once seen a winged Mercury, and he wondered if Mercury felt as he felt when skimming over the earth.

His theory of running until he reached the camp and the boys had one flaw in it: he lacked the endurance. Several times he stumbled, and finally he tottered, crumpled up, and fell. When he tried to rise, he failed. He must sit and rest, he decided, and next time he would merely walk and keep on going. As he sat and regained his breath, he noted that he was feeling quite warm and comfortable. He was not shivering, and it even seemed that a warm glow had come to his chest and trunk. And yet, when he touched his nose and cheeks, there was no sensation. Running would not thaw them out. Nor would it thaw out his hands and feet. Then the thought came to him that the frozen portions of his body must be extending. He tried to keep this thought down, to forget it, to think of something else; he was aware of the panicky feeling that it caused, and he was afraid of the panic. But the thought asserted itself, and persisted, until it produced a vision of his body totally frozen. This was too much, and he made another wild run along the trail. Once he slowed down to a walk, but the thought of the freezing extending itself made him run again.

And all the time the dog ran with him, at his heels. When he fell down a second time, it curled its tail over its forefeet and sat in front of him, facing him, curiously eager and intent. The warmth and security of the animal angered him, and he cursed it till it flattened down its ears appeasingly. This time the shivering came more quickly upon the man. He was losing in his battle with the frost. It was creeping into his body from all sides. The thought of it drove him on, but he ran no more than a hundred feet, when he staggered and pitched headlong. It was his last panic. When he had recovered his breath and control, he sat up and entertained in his mind the conception of meeting death with dignity. However, the conception did not come to him in such terms. His idea of it was that he had been making a fool of himself, running around like a chicken with its head cut off—such was the simile that occurred to him. Well, he was bound to freeze anyway, and he might as well take it decently. With this new-found peace of mind came the first glimmerings of drowsiness. A good idea, he thought, to sleep off to death. It was like taking an anesthetic. Freezing was not so bad as people thought. There were lots worse ways to die.

He pictured the boys finding his body next day. Suddenly he found himself with them, coming along the trail and looking for himself. And, still with them, he came around a turn in the trail and found himself lying in the snow. He did not belong with himself any more, for even then he was out of himself, standing with the boys and looking at himself in the snow. It certainly was cold, was his thought. When he got back to the States he could tell the folks what real cold was. He drifted on from this to a vision of the old-timer on Sulphur Creek. He could see him quite clearly, warm and comfortable, and smoking a pipe.

"You were right, old hoss; you were right," the man mumbled to the old-timer of Sulphur Creek.

Then the man drowsed off into what seemed to him the most comfortable and satisfying sleep he had ever known. The dog sat facing him and waiting. The brief day drew to a close in a long, slow twilight. There were no signs of a fire to be made, and, besides, never in the dog's experience had it known a man to sit like that in the snow and make no fire. As the twilight drew on, its eager yearning for the fire mastered it, and with a great lifting and shifting of forefeet, it whined softly, then flattened its ears down in anticipation of being chidden by the man. But the man remained silent. Later the dog whined loudly. And still later it crept close to the man and caught the scent of death. This made the animal bristle and back away. A little longer it delayed, howling under the stars that leaped and danced and shone brightly in the cold sky. Then it turned and trotted up the trail in the direction of the camp it knew, where were the other food providers and fire providers.

Questions

1. What details of the story's setting are memorable? To what extent does setting determine what happens in this story? To what extent does character determine what happens?
2. From what point of view is London's story told? What effect does this have on your understanding of the story?
3. The man is the protagonist of the story. Who is the antagonist against whom he struggles?
4. London never gives the protagonist a name. What is the effect of his being called simply "the man" throughout the story?
5. In paragraph 21, the man thinks, "Any man who was a man could travel alone." Does this turn out to be true? How does his opinion differ from that of the "old-timer"? What does the "old-timer" understand that the man doesn't?
6. What are the most serious mistakes the man makes? To what factors do you attribute these errors?
7. How do you compare the dog's reading of the man to the man's reading of his surroundings and circumstance? To what do you attribute the difference?
8. What does this story suggest to us about the relation of humanity to nature?

Stephen Crane

Stephen Crane (1871–1900) was born in Newark, New Jersey, a Methodist minister's fourteenth and last child. After flunking out of both Lafayette College and Syracuse University, he became a journalist in New York, specializing in the grim lives of the down-and-out, such as the characters of his early self-published novel Maggie: A Girl of the Streets (1893). Restlessly generating material for stories, Crane trekked to the Southwest, New Orleans, and Mexico. "The Open Boat" is based on personal experience. En route to Havana to report on the Cuban revolution for the New York Press, Crane was shipwrecked when the SS Commodore sank in heavy seas east of New Smyrna, Florida, on January 2, 1897. He escaped in a ten-foot lifeboat with the captain and two members of the crew. Later that year, Crane moved into a stately home in England with Cora Taylor, former madam of a Florida brothel, hobnobbed with literary greats, and lived beyond his means. Hounded by creditors, afflicted by tuberculosis, he died in Germany at twenty-eight. Crane has been called the first writer of American realism. His classic novel The Red Badge of Courage (1895) gives an imagined but convincing account of a young Union soldier's initiation into battle. A handful of his short stories appear immortal. He was also an original poet, writing terse, sardonic poems in open forms, considered radical at the time. In his short life, Crane greatly helped American literature to come of age.

The Open Boat   1897

A tale intended to be after the fact:
Being the experience of four men from the sunk steamer **Commodore**

I

None of them knew the color of the sky. Their eyes glanced level, and were fastened upon the waves that swept toward them. These waves were of the hue of slate, save for the tops, which were of foaming white, and all of the men knew the colors of the sea. The horizon narrowed and widened, and dipped and rose, and at all times its edge was jagged with waves that seemed thrust up in points like rocks.

Many a man ought to have a bathtub larger than the boat which here rode upon the sea. These waves were most wrongfully and barbarously abrupt and tall, and each froth-top was a problem in small-boat navigation.

The cook squatted in the bottom, and looked with both eyes at the six inches of gunwale which separated him from the ocean. His sleeves were rolled over his fat forearms, and the two flaps of his unbuttoned vest dangled as he bent to bail out the boat. Often he said, "Gawd! that was a narrow clip." As he remarked it he invariably gazed eastward over the broken sea.

The oiler, steering with one of the two oars in the boat, sometimes raised himself suddenly to keep clear of water that swirled in over the stern. It was a thin little oar, and it seemed often ready to snap.

The correspondent,° pulling at the other oar, watched the waves and wondered why he was there.

The injured captain, lying in the bow, was at this time buried in that profound dejection and indifference which comes, temporarily at least, to even the bravest and most enduring when, willy-nilly, the firm fails, the army loses, the ship goes down. The mind of the master of a vessel is rooted deep in the timbers of her, though he command for a day or a decade; and this captain had on him the stern impression of a scene in the grays of dawn of seven turned faces, and later a stump of a topmast with a white ball on it, that slashed to and fro at the waves, went low and lower, and down. Thereafter there was something strange in his voice. Although steady, it was deep with mourning, and of a quality beyond oration or tears.

"Keep 'er a little more south, Billie," said he.

"A little more south, sir," said the oiler in the stern.

A seat in this boat was not unlike a seat upon a bucking broncho, and by the same token a broncho is not much smaller. The craft pranced and reared and plunged like an animal. As each wave came, and she rose for it, she seemed like a horse making at a fence outrageously high. The manner of her scramble over these walls of water is a mystic thing, and, moreover, at the top of them were ordinarily these problems in white water, the foam racing down from the summit of each wave requiring a new leap, and a leap from the air. Then, after scornfully bumping a crest, she would slide and race and splash down a long incline, and arrive bobbing and nodding in front of the next menace.

A singular disadvantage of the sea lies in the fact that after successfully surmounting one wave you discover that there is another behind it just as important and just as

---

correspondent: foreign correspondent, newspaper reporter.

nervously anxious to do something effective in the way of swamping boats. In a ten-foot dinghy one can get an idea of the resources of the sea in the line of waves that is not probable to the average experience, which is never at sea in a dinghy. As each slaty wall of water approached, it shut all else from the view of the men in the boat, and it was not difficult to imagine that this particular wave was the final outburst of the ocean, the last effort of the grim water. There was a terrible grace in the move of the waves, and they came in silence, save for the snarling of the crests.

In the wan light the faces of the men must have been gray. Their eyes must have glinted in strange ways as they gazed steadily astern. Viewed from a balcony, the whole thing would doubtless have been weirdly picturesque. But the men in the boat had no time to see it, and if they had had leisure, there were other things to occupy their minds. The sun swung steadily up the sky, and they knew it was broad day because the color of the sea changed from slate to emerald green streaked with amber lights, and the foam was like tumbling snow. The process of the breaking day was unknown to them. They were aware only of this effect upon the color of the waves that rolled toward them.

In disjointed sentences the cook and the correspondent argued as to the difference between a life-saving station and a house of refuge. The cook had said: "There's a house of refuge just north of the Mosquito Inlet Light, and as soon as they see us they'll come off in their boat and pick us up."

"As soon as who see us?" said the correspondent.

"The crew," said the cook.

"Houses of refuge don't have crews," said the correspondent. "As I understand them, they are only places where clothes and grub are stored for the benefit of shipwrecked people. They don't carry crews."

"Oh, yes, they do," said the cook.

"No, they don't," said the correspondent.

"Well, we're not there yet, anyhow," said the oiler, in the stern.

"Well," said the cook, "perhaps it's not a house of refuge that I'm thinking of as being near Mosquito Inlet Light; perhaps it's a life-saving station."

"We're not there yet," said the oiler in the stern.

II

As the boat bounced from the top of each wave the wind tore through the hair of the hatless men, and as the craft plopped her stern down again the spray slashed past them. The crest of each of these waves was a hill, from the top of which the men surveyed for a moment a broad tumultuous expanse, shining and wind-riven. It was probably splendid, it was probably glorious, this play of the free sea, wild with lights of emerald and white and amber.

"Bully good thing it's an on-shore wind," said the cook. "If not, where would we be? Wouldn't have a show."

"That's right," said the correspondent.

The busy oiler nodded his assent.

Then the captain, in the bow, chuckled in a way that expressed humor, contempt, tragedy, all in one. "Do you think we've got much of a show now, boys?" said he.

Whereupon the three were silent, save for a trifle of hemming and hawing. To express any particular optimism at this time they felt to be childish and stupid, but they all doubtless possessed this sense of the situation in their minds. A young man thinks doggedly at such times. On the other hand, the ethics of their condition was decidedly against any open suggestion of hopelessness. So they were silent.

"Oh, well," said the captain, soothing his children, "we'll get ashore all right."

But there was that in his tone which made them think; so the oiler quoth, "Yes! if this wind holds."

The cook was bailing. "Yes! if we don't catch hell in the surf."

Canton-flannel gulls flew near and far. Sometimes they sat down on the sea, near patches of brown seaweed that rolled over the waves with a movement like carpets on a line in a gale. The birds sat comfortably in groups, and they were envied by some in the dinghy, for the wrath of the sea was no more to them than it was to a covey of prairie chickens a thousand miles inland. Often they came very close and stared at the men with black bead-like eyes. At these times they were uncanny and sinister in their unblinking scrutiny, and the men hooted angrily at them, telling them to be gone. One came, and evidently decided to alight on the top of the captain's head. The bird flew parallel to the boat and did not circle, but made short sidelong jumps in the air in chicken-fashion. His black eyes were wistfully fixed upon the captain's head. "Ugly brute," said the oiler to the bird. "You look as if you were made with a jacknife." The cook and the correspondent swore darkly at the creature. The captain naturally wished to knock it away with the end of the heavy painter, but he did not dare do it, because anything resembling an emphatic gesture would have capsized this freighted boat; and so, with his open hand, the captain gently and carefully waved the gull away. After it had been discouraged from the pursuit the captain breathed easier on account of his hair, and others breathed easier because the bird struck their minds at this time as being somehow gruesome and ominous.

In the meantime the oiler and the correspondent rowed. And also they rowed. They sat together in the same seat, and each rowed an oar. Then the oiler took both oars; then the correspondent took both oars; then the oiler; then the correspondent. They rowed and they rowed. The very ticklish part of the business was when the time came for the reclining one in the stern to take his turn at the oars. By the very last star of truth, it is easier to steal eggs from under a hen than it was to change seats in the dinghy. First the man in the stern slid his hand along the thwart and moved with care, as if he were of Sèvres.° Then the man in the rowing-seat slid his hand along the other thwart. It was all done with the most extraordinary care. As the two sidled past each other, the whole party kept watchful eyes on the coming wave, and the captain cried: "Look out, now! Steady, there!"

The brown mats of seaweed that appeared from time to time were like islands, bits of earth. They were travelling, apparently, neither one way nor the other. They were, to all intents, stationary. They informed the men in the boat that it was making progress slowly toward the land.

The captain, rearing cautiously in the bow after the dinghy soared on a great swell, said that he had seen the lighthouse at Mosquito Inlet. Presently the cook remarked that he had seen it. The correspondent was at the oars then, and for some reason he too wished to look at the lighthouse; but his back was toward the far shore, and the waves were important, and for some time he could not seize an opportunity to

Sèvres: chinaware made in this French town.

turn his head. But at last there came a wave more gentle than the others, and when at the crest of it he swiftly scoured the western horizon.

"See it?" said the captain.

"No," said the correspondent, slowly; "I didn't see anything."

"Look again," said the captain. He pointed. "It's exactly in that direction."

At the top of another wave the correspondent did as he was bid, and this time his eyes chanced on a small, still thing on the edge of the swaying horizon. It was precisely like the point of a pin. It took an anxious eye to find a lighthouse so tiny.

"Think we'll make it, Captain?"

"If this wind holds and the boat don't swamp, we can't do much else," said the captain.

The little boat, lifted by each towering sea and splashed viciously by the crests, made progress that in the absence of seaweed was not apparent to those in her. She seemed just a wee thing wallowing, miraculously top up, at the mercy of five oceans. Occasionally a great spread of water, like white flames, swarmed into her.

"Bail her, cook," said the captain, serenely.

"All right, Captain," said the cheerful cook.

III

It would be difficult to describe the subtle brotherhood of men that was here established on the seas. No one said that it was so. No one mentioned it. But it dwelt in the boat, and each man felt it warm him. They were a captain, an oiler, a cook, and a correspondent, and they were friends—friends in a more curiously iron-bound degree than may be common. The hurt captain, lying against the water-jar in the bow, spoke always in a low voice and calmly; but he could never command a more ready and swiftly obedient crew than the motley three of the dinghy. It was more than a mere recognition of what was best for the common safety. There was surely in it a quality that was personal and heartfelt. And after this devotion to the commander of the boat, there was this comradeship, that the correspondent, for instance, who had been taught to be cynical of men, knew even at the time was the best experience of his life. But no one said that it was so. No one mentioned it.

"I wish we had a sail," remarked the captain. "We might try my overcoat on the end of an oar, and give you two boys a chance to rest." So the cook and the correspondent held the mast and spread wide the overcoat; the oiler steered; and the little boat made good way with her new rig. Sometimes the oiler had to scull sharply to keep a sea from breaking into the boat, but otherwise sailing was a success.

Meanwhile the lighthouse had been growing slowly larger. It had now almost assumed color, and appeared like a little gray shadow on the sky. The man at the oars could not be prevented from turning his head rather often to try for a glimpse of this little gray shadow.

At last, from the top of each wave, the men in the tossing boat could see land. Even as the lighthouse was an upright shadow on the sky, this land seemed but a long black shadow on the sea. It certainly was thinner than paper. "We must be about opposite New Smyrna," said the cook, who had coasted this shore often in schooners. "Captain, by the way, I believe they abandoned that life-saving station there about a year ago."

"Did they?" said the captain.

The wind slowly died away. The cook and the correspondent were not now obliged to slave in order to hold high the oar. But the waves continued their old impetuous swooping at the dinghy, and the little craft, no longer under way, struggled woundily over them. The oiler or the correspondent took the oars again.

Shipwrecks are apropos of nothing. If men could only train for them and have them occur when the men had reached pink condition, there would be less drowning at sea. Of the four in the dinghy none had slept any time worth mentioning for two days and two nights previous to embarking in the dinghy, and in the excitement of clambering about the deck of a foundering ship they had also forgotten to eat heartily.

For these reasons, and for others, neither the oiler nor the correspondent was fond of rowing at this time. The correspondent wondered ingenuously how in the name of all that was sane could there be people who thought it amusing to row a boat. It was not an amusement; it was a diabolical punishment, and even a genius of mental aberrations could never conclude that it was anything but a horror to the muscles and a crime against the back. He mentioned to the boat in general how the amusement of rowing struck him, and the weary-faced oiler smiled in full sympathy. Previously to the foundering, by the way, the oiler had worked double watch in the engine-room of the ship.

"Take her easy now, boys," said the captain. "Don't spend yourselves. If we have to run a surf you'll need all your strength, because we'll sure have to swim for it. Take your time."

Slowly the land arose from the sea. From a black line it became a line of black and a line of white—trees and sand. Finally the captain said that he could make out a house on the shore. "That's the house of refuge, sure," said the cook. "They'll see us before long, and come out after us."

The distant lighthouse reared high. "The keeper ought to be able to make us out now, if he's looking through a glass," said the captain. "He'll notify the life-saving people."

"None of those other boats could have got ashore to give word of the wreck," said the oiler, in a low voice, "else the life-boat would be out hunting us."

Slowly and beautifully the land loomed out of the sea. The wind came again. It had veered from the northeast to the southeast. Finally a new sound struck the ears of the men in the boat. It was the low thunder of the surf on the shore. "We'll never be able to make the lighthouse now," said the captain. "Swing her head a little more north, Billie."

"A little more north, sir," said the oiler.

Whereupon the little boat turned her nose once more down the wind, and all but the oarsman watched the shore grow. Under the influence of this expansion doubt and direful apprehension were leaving the minds of the men. The management of the boat was still most absorbing, but it could not prevent a quiet cheerfulness. In an hour, perhaps, they would be ashore.

Their backbones had become thoroughly used to balancing in the boat, and they now rode this wild colt of a dinghy like circus men. The correspondent thought that he had been drenched to the skin, but happening to feel in the top pocket of his coat, he found therein eight cigars. Four of them were soaked with seawater; four were perfectly scatheless. After a search, somebody produced three dry matches; and thereupon the four waifs rode impudently in their little boat and, with an assurance of an impending rescue shining in their eyes, puffed at the big cigars, and judged well and ill of all men. Everybody took a drink of water.

IV

"Cook," remarked the captain, "there don't seem to be any signs of life about your house of refuge."

"No," replied the cook. "Funny they don't see us!"

A broad stretch of lowly coast lay before the eyes of the men. It was of low dunes topped with dark vegetation. The roar of the surf was plain, and sometimes they could see the white lip of a wave as it spun up the beach. A tiny house was blocked out black upon the sky. Southward, the slim lighthouse lifted its little gray length.

Tide, wind, and waves were swinging the dinghy northward. "Funny they don't see us," said the men.

The surf's roar was here dulled, but its tone was nevertheless thunderous and mighty. As the boat swam over the great rollers the men sat listening to this roar. "We'll swamp sure," said everybody.

It is fair to say here that there was not a life-saving station within twenty miles in either direction; but the men did not know this fact, and in consequence they made dark and opprobrious remarks concerning the eyesight of the nation's life-savers. Four scowling men sat in the dinghy and surpassed records in the invention of epithets.

"Funny they don't see us."

The light-heartedness of a former time had completely faded. To their sharpened minds it was easy to conjure pictures of all kinds of incompetency and blindness and, indeed, cowardice. There was the shore of the populous land, and it was bitter and bitter to them that from it came no sign.

"Well," said the captain, ultimately, "I suppose we'll have to make a try for ourselves. If we stay out here too long, we'll none of us have strength left to swim after the boat swamps."

And so the oiler, who was at the oars, turned the boat straight for the shore. There was a sudden tightening of muscles. There was some thinking.

"If we don't all get ashore," said the captain—"if we don't all get ashore, I suppose you fellows know where to send news of my finish?"

They then briefly exchanged some addresses and admonitions. As for the reflections of the men, there was a great deal of rage in them. Perchance they might be formulated thus: "If I am going to be drowned—if I am going to be drowned—if I am going to be drowned, why, in the name of the seven mad gods who rule the sea, was I allowed to come thus far and contemplate sand and trees? Was I brought here merely to have my nose dragged away as I was about to nibble the sacred cheese of life? It is preposterous. If this old ninny-woman, Fate, cannot do better than this, she should be deprived of the management of men's fortunes. She is an old hen who knows not her intention. If she has decided to drown me, why did she not do it in the beginning and save me all this trouble? The whole affair is absurd. . . . But no; she cannot mean to drown me. She dare not drown me. She cannot drown me. Not after all this work." Afterward the man might have had an impulse to shake his fist at the clouds. "Just you drown me, now, and then hear what I call you!"

The billows that came at this time were more formidable. They seemed always just about to break and roll over the little boat in a turmoil of foam. There was a preparatory and long growl in the speech of them. No mind unused to the sea would have concluded that the dinghy could ascend these sheer heights in time. The shore was still afar. The oiler was a wily surfman. "Boys," he said swiftly, "she won't live three minutes more, and we're too far out to swim. Shall I take her to sea again, Captain?"

"Yes; go ahead!" said the captain.

This oiler, by a series of quick miracles and fast and steady oarsmanship, turned the boat in the middle of the surf and took her safely to sea again.

There was a considerable silence as the boat bumped over the furrowed sea to deeper water. Then somebody in gloom spoke: "Well, anyhow, they must have seen us from the shore by now."

The gulls went in slanting flight up the wind toward the gray, desolate east. A squall, marked by dingy clouds and clouds brick-red, like smoke from a burning building, appeared from the southeast.

"What do you think of those life-saving people? Ain't they peaches?"

"Funny they haven't seen us."

"Maybe they think we're out here for sport! Maybe they think we're fishin'. Maybe they think we're damned fools."

It was a long afternoon. A changed tide tried to force them southward, but wind and wave said northward. Far ahead, where coast-line, sea, and sky formed their mighty angle, there were little dots which seemed to indicate a city on the shore.

"St. Augustine?"

The captain shook his head. "Too near Mosquito Inlet."

And the oiler rowed, and then the correspondent rowed; then the oiler rowed. It was a weary business. The human back can become the seat of more aches and pains than are registered in books for the composite anatomy of a regiment. It is a limited area, but it can become the theatre of innumerable muscular conflicts, tangles, wrenches, knots, and other comforts.

"Did you ever like to row, Billie?" asked the correspondent.

"No," said the oiler; "hang it!"

When one exchanged the rowing-seat for a place in the bottom of the boat, he suffered a bodily depression that caused him to be careless of everything save an obligation to wiggle one finger. There was cold sea-water swashing to and fro in the boat, and he lay in it. His head, pillowed on a thwart, was within an inch of the swirl of a wave-crest, and sometimes a particularly obstreperous sea came inboard and drenched him once more. But these matters did not annoy him. It is almost certain that if the boat had capsized he would have tumbled comfortably upon the ocean as if he felt sure that it was a great soft mattress.

"Look! There's a man on the shore!"

"Where?"

"There! See 'im? See 'im?"

"Yes, sure! He's walking along."

"Now he's stopped. Look! He's facing us!"

"He's waving at us!"

"So he is! By thunder!"

"Ah, now we're all right! Now we're all right! There'll be a boat out here for us in half an hour."

"He's going on. He's running. He's going up to that house there."

The remote beach seemed lower than the sea, and it required a searching glance to discern the little black figure. The captain saw a floating stick, and they rowed to it. A bath towel was by some weird chance in the boat, and, tying this on the stick, the captain waved it. The oarsman did not dare turn his head, so he was obliged to ask questions.

"What's he doing now?"

"He's standing still again. He's looking, I think. . . . There he goes again. Toward the house. . . . Now he's stopped again."

"Is he waving at us?"

"No, not now; he was, though."

"Look! There comes another man!"

"He's running."

"Look at him go, would you!"

"Why, he's on a bicycle. Now he's met the other man. They're both waving at us. Look!"

"There comes something up the beach."

"What the devil is that thing?"

"Why, it looks like a boat."

"Why, certainly, it's a boat."

"No; it's on wheels."

"Yes, so it is. Well, that must be the life-boat. They drag them along shore on a wagon."

"That's the life-boat, sure."

"No, by God, it's—it's an omnibus."

"I tell you it's a life-boat."

"It is not! It's an omnibus. I can see it plain. See? One of the these big hotel omnibuses."

"By thunder, you're right. It's an omnibus, sure as fate. What do you suppose they are doing with an omnibus? Maybe they are going around collecting the life-crew, hey?"

"That's it, likely. Look! There's a fellow waving a little black flag. He's standing on the steps of the omnibus. There come those other two fellows. Now they're all talking together. Look at the fellow with the flag. Maybe he ain't waving it!"

"That ain't a flag, is it? That's his coat. Why, certainly, that's his coat."

"So it is; it's his coat. He's taken it off and is waving it around his head. But would you look at him swing it!"

"Oh, say, there isn't any life-saving station there. That's just a winter-resort hotel omnibus that has brought over some of the boarders to see us drown."

"What's that idiot with the coat mean? What's he signalling, anyhow?"

"It looks as if he were trying to tell us to go north. There must be a life-saving station up there."

"No; he thinks we're fishing. Just giving us a merry hand. See? Ah, there, Willie!"

"Well, I wish I could make something out of those signals. What do you suppose he means?"

"He don't mean anything; he's just playing."

"Well, if he'd just signal us to try the surf again, or to go to sea and wait, or go north, or go south, or go to hell, there would be some reason in it. But look at him! He just stands there and keeps his coat revolving like a wheel. The ass!"

"There come more people."

"Now there's quite a mob. Look! Isn't that a boat?"

"Where? Oh, I see where you mean. No, that's no boat."

"That fellow is still waving his coat."

"He must think we like to see him do that. Why don't he quit it? It don't mean anything."

"I don't know. I think he is trying to make us go north. It must be that there's a life-saving station there somewhere."

"Say, he ain't tired yet. Look at 'im wave!"

"Wonder how long he can keep that up. He's been revolving his coat ever since he caught sight of us. He's an idiot. Why aren't they getting men to bring a boat out? A fishing boat—one of those big yawls—could come out here all right. Why don't he do something?"

"Oh, it's all right now."

"They'll have a boat out here for us in less than no time, now that they've seen us."

A faint yellow tone came into the sky over the low land. The shadows on the sea slowly deepened. The wind bore coldness with it, and the men began to shiver.

"Holy smoke!" said one, allowing his voice to express his impious mood, "If we keep on monkeying out here! If we've got to flounder out here all night!"

"Oh, we'll never have to stay here all night! Don't you worry. They've seen us now, and it won't be long before they'll come chasing out after us."

The shore grew dusky. The man waving a coat blended gradually into this gloom, and it swallowed in the same manner the omnibus and the group of people. The spray, when it dashed uproariously over the side, made the voyagers shrink and swear like men who were being branded.

"I'd like to catch the chump who waved the coat. I feel like socking him one, just for luck."

"Why? What did he do?"

"Oh, nothing, but then he seemed so damned cheerful."

In the meantime the oiler rowed, and then the correspondent rowed, and then the oiler rowed. Gray-faced and bowed forward, they mechanically, turn by turn, plied the leaden oars. The form of the lighthouse had vanished from the southern horizon, but finally a pale star appeared, just lifting from the sea. The streaked saffron in the west passed before the all-merging darkness, and the sea to the east was black. The land had vanished, and was expressed only by the low and drear thunder of the surf.

"If I am going to be drowned—if I am going to be drowned—if I am going to be drowned, why, in the name of the seven mad gods who rule the sea, was I allowed to come thus far and contemplate sand and trees? Was I brought here merely to have my nose dragged away as I was about to nibble the sacred cheese of life?"

The patient captain, drooped over the water-jar, was sometimes obliged to speak to the oarsman.

"Keep her head up! Keep her head up!"

"Keep her head, up, sir." The voices were weary and low.

This was surely a quiet evening. All save the oarsman lay heavily and listlessly in the boat's bottom. As for him, his eyes were just capable of noting the tall black waves that swept forward in a most sinister silence, save for an occasional subdued growl of a crest.

The cook's head was on a thwart, and he looked without interest at the water under his nose. He was deep in other scenes. Finally he spoke. "Billie," he murmured, dreamfully, "what kind of pie do you like best?"

V

"Pie!" said the oiler and the correspondent, agitatedly. "Don't talk about those things, blast you!"

"Well," said the cook, "I was just thinking about ham sandwiches, and—"

A night on the sea in an open boat is a long night. As darkness settled finally, the shine of the light, lifting from the sea in the south, changed to full gold. On the northern horizon a new light appeared, a small bluish gleam on the edge of the waters. These two lights were the furniture of the world. Otherwise there was nothing but waves.

Two men huddled in the stern, and distances were so magnificent in the dinghy that the rower was enabled to keep his feet partly warm by thrusting them under his companions. Their legs indeed extended far under the rowing-seat until they touched the feet of the captain forward. Sometimes, despite the efforts of the tired oarsman, a wave came piling into the boat, an icy wave of the night, and the chilling water soaked them anew. They would twist their bodies for a moment and groan, and sleep the dead sleep once more, while the water in the boat gurgled about them as the craft rocked.

The plan of the oiler and the correspondent was for one to row until he lost the ability, and then arouse the other from his sea-water couch in the bottom of the boat.

The oiler plied the oars until his head drooped forward and the overpowering sleep blinded him; and he rowed yet afterward. Then he touched a man in the bottom of the boat, and called his name. "Will you spell me for a little while?" he said meekly.

"Sure, Billie," said the correspondent, awaking and dragging himself to a sitting position. They exchanged places carefully, and the oiler, cuddling down in the sea-water at the cook's side, seemed to go to sleep instantly.

The particular violence of the sea had ceased. The waves came without snarling. The obligation of the man at the oars was to keep the boat headed so that the tilt of the roller would not capsize her, and to preserve her from filling when the crests rushed past. The black waves were silent and hard to be seen in the darkness. Often one was almost upon the boat before the oarsman was aware.

In a low voice the correspondent addressed the captain. He was not sure that the captain was awake, although this iron man seemed to be always awake. "Captain, shall I keep her making for that light north, sir?"

The same steady voice answered him. "Yes. Keep it about two points off the port bow."

The cook had tied a life-belt around himself in order to get even the warmth which this clumsy cork contrivance could donate, and he seemed almost stove-like when a rower, whose teeth invariably chattered wildly as soon as he ceased his labor, dropped down to sleep.

The correspondent, as he rowed, looked down at the two men sleeping underfoot. The cook's arm was around the oiler's shoulders, and, with their fragmentary clothing and haggard faces, they were the babes of the sea—a grotesque rendering of the old babes in the wood.

Later he must have grown stupid at his work, for suddenly there was a growling of water, and a crest came with a roar and a swash into the boat, and it was a wonder that it did not set the cook afloat in his life-belt. The cook continued to sleep, but the oiler sat up, blinking his eyes and shaking with the new cold.

"Oh, I'm awful sorry, Billie," said the correspondent, contritely.

"That's all right, old boy," said the oiler, and lay down again and was asleep.

Presently it seemed that even the captain dozed, and the correspondent thought that he was the one man afloat on all the oceans. The wind had a voice as it came over the waves, and it was sadder than the end.

There was a long, loud swishing astern of the boat, and a gleaming trail of phosphorescence, like blue flame, was furrowed on the black waters. It might have been made by a monstrous knife.

Then there came a stillness, while the correspondent breathed with open mouth and looked at the sea.

Suddenly there was another swish and another long flash of bluish light, and this time it was alongside the boat, and might almost have been reached with an oar. The correspondent saw an enormous fin speed like a shadow through the water, hurling the crystalline spray and leaving the long glowing trail.

The correspondent looked over his shoulder at the captain. His face was hidden, and he seemed to be asleep. He looked at the babes of the sea. They certainly were asleep. So, being bereft of sympathy, he leaned a little way to one side and swore softly into the sea.

But the thing did not then leave the vicinity of the boat. Ahead or astern, on one side or the other, at intervals long or short, fled the long sparkling streak, and there was to be heard the *whirroo* of the dark fin. The speed and power of the thing was greatly to be admired. It cut the water like a gigantic and keen projectile.

The presence of this biding thing did not affect the man with the same horror that it would if he had been a picnicker. He simply looked at the sea dully and swore in an undertone.

Nevertheless, it is true that he did not wish to be alone with the thing. He wished one of his companions to awake by chance and keep him company with it. But the captain hung motionless over the water-jar, and the oiler and the cook in the bottom of the boat were plunged in slumber.

VI

"If I am going to be drowned—if I am going to be drowned—if I am going to be drowned, why, in the name of the seven mad gods who rule the sea, was I allowed to come thus far and contemplate sand and trees?"

During this dismal night, it may be remarked that a man would conclude that it was really the intention of the seven mad gods to drown him, despite the abominable injustice of it. For it was certainly an abominable injustice to drown a man who had worked so hard, so hard. The man felt it would be a crime most unnatural. Other people had drowned at sea since galleys swarmed with painted sails, but still—

When it occurs to a man that nature does not regard him as important, and that she feels she would not maim the universe by disposing of him, he at first wishes to throw bricks at the temple, and he hates deeply the fact that there are no bricks and no temples. Any visible expression of nature would surely be pelleted with his jeers.

Then, if there be no tangible thing to hoot, he feels, perhaps, the desire to confront a personification and indulge in pleas, bowed to one knee, and with hands supplicant, saying, "Yes, but I love myself."

A high cold star on a winter's night is the word he feels that she says to him. Thereafter he knows the pathos of his situation.

The men in the dinghy had not discussed these matters, but each had, no doubt, reflected upon them in silence and according to his mind. There was seldom any expression upon their faces save the general one of complete weariness. Speech was devoted to the business of the boat.

To chime the notes of his emotion, a verse mysteriously entered the correspondent's head. He had even forgotten that he had forgotten this verse, but it suddenly was in his mind.

> A soldier of the Legion lay dying in Algiers;
> There was lack of woman's nursing, there was dearth of woman's tears;
> But a comrade stood beside him, and he took that comrade's hand,
> And he said, "I never more shall see my own, my native land."°

In his childhood the correspondent had been made acquainted with the fact that a soldier of the Legion lay dying in Algiers, but he had never regarded the fact as important. Myriads of his school-fellows had informed him of the soldier's plight, but the dinning had naturally ended by making him perfectly indifferent. He had never considered it his affair that a soldier of the Legion lay dying in Algiers, nor had it appeared to him as a matter for sorrow. It was less to him than the breaking of a pencil's point.

Now, however, it quaintly came to him as a human, living thing. It was no longer merely a picture of a few throes in the breast of a poet, meanwhile drinking tea and warming his feet at the grate; it was an actuality—stern, mournful, and fine.

The correspondent plainly saw the soldier. He lay on the sand with his feet out straight and still. While his pale left hand was upon his chest in an attempt to thwart the going of his life, the blood came between his fingers. In the far Algerian distance, a city of low square forms was set against a sky that was faint with the last sunset hues. The correspondent, plying the oars and dreaming of the slow and slower movements of the lips of the soldier, was moved by a profound and perfectly impersonal comprehension. He was sorry for the soldier of the Legion who lay dying in Algiers.

The thing which had followed the boat and waited had evidently grown bored at the delay. There was no longer to be heard the slash of the cutwater, and there was no longer the flame of the long trail. The light in the north still glimmered, but it was apparently no nearer to the boat. Sometimes the boom of the surf rang in the correspondent's ears, and he turned the craft seaward then and rowed harder. Southward, some one had evidently built a watch-fire on the beach. It was too low and too far to be seen, but it made a shimmering, roseate reflection upon the bluff in back of it, and this could be discerned from the boat. The wind came stronger, and sometimes a wave suddenly raged out like a mountain cat, and there was to be seen the sheen and sparkle of a broken crest.

A soldier of the Legion . . . native land: The correspondent remembers a Victorian ballad about a German dying in the French Foreign Legion, "Bingen on the Rhine" by Caroline Norton.

The captain, in the bow, moved on his water-jar and sat erect. "Pretty long night," he observed to the correspondent. He looked at the shore. "Those life-saving people take their time."

"Did you see that shark playing around?"

"Yes, I saw him. He was a big fellow, all right."

"Wish I had known you were awake."

Later the correspondent spoke into the bottom of the boat.

"Billie!" There was a slow and gradual disentanglement. "Billie, will you spell me?"

"Sure," said the oiler.

As soon as the correspondent touched the cold, comfortable sea-water in the bottom of the boat and had huddled close to the cook's life-belt he was deep in sleep, despite the fact that his teeth played all the popular airs. This sleep was so good to him that it was but a moment before he heard a voice call his name in a tone that demonstrated the last stages of exhaustion. "Will you spell me?"

"Sure, Billie."

The light in the north had mysteriously vanished, but the correspondent took his course from the wide-awake captain.

Later in the night they took the boat farther out to sea, and the captain directed the cook to take one oar at the stern and keep the boat facing the seas. He was to call out if he should hear the thunder of the surf. This plan enabled the oiler and the correspondent to get respite together. "We'll give those boys a chance to get into shape again," said the captain. They curled down and, after a few preliminary chatterings and trembles, slept once more the dead sleep. Neither knew they had bequeathed to the cook the company of another shark, or perhaps the same shark.

As the boat caroused on the waves, spray occasionally bumped over the side and gave them a fresh soaking, but this had no power to break their repose. The ominous slash of the wind and the water affected them as it would have affected mummies.

"Boys," said the cook, with the notes of every reluctance in his voice, "she's drifted in pretty close. I guess one of you had better take her to sea again." The correspondent, aroused, heard the crash of the toppled crests.

As he was rowing, the captain gave him some whisky and water, and this steadied the chills out of him. "If I ever get ashore and anybody shows me even a photograph of an oar—"

At last there was a short conversation.

"Billie! . . . Billie, will you spell me?"

"Sure," said the oiler.

VII

When the correspondent again opened his eyes, the sea and sky were each of the gray hue of the dawning. Later, carmine and gold was painted upon the waters. The morning appeared finally, in its splendor, with a sky of pure blue, and the sunlight flamed on the tips of the waves.

On the distant dunes were set many little black cottages, and a tall white windmill reared above them. No man, nor dog, nor bicycle appeared on the beach. The cottages might have formed a deserted village.

The voyagers scanned the shore. A conference was held in the boat. "Well," said the captain, "if no help is coming, we might better try a run through the surf right away. If we stay out here much longer we will be too weak to do anything for ourselves at all." The others silently acquiesced in this reasoning. The boat was headed for the beach. The correspondent wondered if none ever ascended the tall wind-tower, and if they never looked seaward. This tower was a giant, standing with its back to the plight of the ants. It represented in a degree, to the correspondent, the serenity of nature amid the struggles of the individual— nature in the wind, and nature in the vision of men. She did not seem cruel to him then, nor beneficent, nor treacherous, nor wise. But she was indifferent, flatly indifferent. It is, perhaps, plausible that a man in this situation, impressed with the unconcern of the universe, should see the innumerable flaws of life, and have them taste wickedly in his mind, and wish for another chance. A distinction between right and wrong seems absurdly clear to him, then, in this new ignorance of the grave-edge, and he understands that if he were given another opportunity he would mend his conduct and his words, and be better and brighter during an introduction or at a tea.

"Now, boys," said the captain, "she is going to swamp sure. All we can do is to work her in as far as possible, and then when she swamps, pile out and scramble for the beach. Keep cool now, and don't jump until she swamps sure."

The oiler took the oars. Over his shoulders he scanned the surf. "Captain," he said, "I think I'd better bring her about and keep her head-on to the seas and back her in."

"All right, Billie," said the captain. "Back her in." The oiler swung the boat then, and, seated in the stern, the cook and the correspondent were obliged to look over their shoulders to contemplate the lonely and indifferent shore.

The monstrous inshore rollers heaved the boat high until the men were again enabled to see the white sheets of water scudding up the slanted beach. "We won't get in very close," said the captain. Each time a man could wrest his attention from the rollers, he turned his glance toward the shore, and in the expression of the eyes during this contemplation there was a singular quality. The correspondent, observing the others, knew that they were not afraid, but the full meaning of their glances was shrouded.

As for himself, he was too tired to grapple fundamentally with the fact. He tried to coerce his mind into thinking of it, but the mind was dominated at this time by the muscles, and the muscles said they did not care. It merely occurred to him that if he should drown it would be a shame.

There were no hurried words, no pallor, no plain agitation. The men simply looked at the shore. "Now, remember to get well clear of the boat when you jump," said the captain.

Seaward the crest of a roller suddenly fell with a thunderous crash, and the long white comber came roaring down upon the boat.

"Steady now," said the captain. The men were silent. They turned their eyes from the shore to the comber and waited. The boat slid up the incline, leaped at the furious top, bounced over it, and swung down the long back of the wave. Some water had been shipped, and the cook bailed it out.

But the next crest crashed also. The tumbling, boiling flood of white water caught the boat and whirled it almost perpendicular. Water swarmed in from all sides.

The correspondent had his hands on the gunwale at this time, and when the water entered at that place he swiftly withdrew his fingers, as if he objected to wetting them.

The little boat, drunken with this weight of water, reeled and snuggled deeper into the sea.

"Bail her out, cook! Bail her out!" said the captain.

"All right, Captain," said the cook.

"Now, boys, the next one will do for us sure," said the oiler. "Mind to jump clear of the boat."

The third wave moved forward, huge, furious, implacable. It fairly swallowed the dinghy, and almost simultaneously the men tumbled into the sea. A piece of life-belt had lain in the bottom of the boat, and as the correspondent went overboard he held this to his chest with his left hand.

The January water was icy, and he reflected immediately that it was colder than he had expected to find it off the coast of Florida. This appeared to his dazed mind as a fact important enough to be noted at the time. The coldness of the water was sad; it was tragic. This fact was somehow mixed and confused with his opinion of his own situation, so that it seemed almost a proper reason for tears. The water was cold.

When he came to the surface he was conscious of little but the noisy water. Afterward he saw his companions in the sea. The oiler was ahead in the race. He was swimming strongly and rapidly. Off to the correspondent's left, the cook's great white and corked back bulged out of the water; and in the rear the captain was hanging with his one good hand to the keel of the overturned dinghy.

There is a certain immovable quality to a shore, and the correspondent wondered at it amid the confusion of the sea.

It seemed also very attractive; but the correspondent knew that it was a long journey, and he paddled leisurely. The piece of life-preserver lay under him, and sometimes he whirled down the incline of a wave as if he were on a hand-sled.

But finally he arrived at a place in the sea where travel was beset with difficulty. He did not pause swimming to inquire what manner of current had caught him, but there his progress ceased. The shore was set before him like a bit of scenery on a stage, and he looked at it and understood with his eyes each detail of it.

As the cook passed, much farther to the left, the captain was calling to him, "Turn over on your back, cook! Turn over on your back and use the oar."

"All right, sir." The cook turned on his back, and, paddling with an oar, went ahead as if he were a canoe.

Presently the boat also passed to the left of the correspondent, with the captain clinging with one hand to the keel. He would have appeared like a man raising himself to look over a board fence if it were not for the extraordinary gymnastics of the boat. The correspondent marvelled that the captain could still hold to it.

They passed on nearer to shore—the oiler, the cook, the captain—and following them went the water-jar, bouncing gaily over the seas.

The correspondent remained in the grip of this strange new enemy—a current. The shore, with its white slope of sand and its green bluff topped with little silent cottages, was spread like a picture before him. It was very near to him then, but he was impressed as one who, in a gallery, looks at a scene from Brittany or Algiers.

He thought: "I am going to drown? Can it be possible? Can it be possible? Can it be possible?" Perhaps an individual must consider his own death to be the final phenomenon of nature.

But later a wave perhaps whirled him out of this small deadly current, for he found suddenly that he could again make progress toward the shore. Later still he was aware that the captain, clinging with one hand to the keel of the dinghy, had his face turned away from the shore and toward him, and was calling his name. "Come to the boat! Come to the boat!"

In his struggle to reach the captain and the boat, he reflected that when one gets properly wearied drowning must really be a comfortable arrangement—a cessation of hostilities accompanied by a large degree of relief; and he was glad of it, for the main thing in his mind for some moments had been horror of the temporary agony. He did not wish to be hurt.

Presently he saw a man running along the shore. He was undressing with most remarkable speed. Coat, trousers, shirt, everything flew magically off him.

"Come to the boat!" called the captain.

"All right, Captain." As the correspondent paddled, he saw the captain let himself down to bottom and leave the boat. Then the correspondent performed his one little marvel of the voyage. A large wave caught him and flung him with ease and supreme speed completely over the boat and far beyond it. It struck him even then as an event in gymnastics and a true miracle of the sea. An overturned boat in the surf is not a plaything to a swimming man.

The correspondent arrived in water that reached only to his waist, but his condition did not enable him to stand for more than a moment. Each wave knocked him into a heap, and the undertow pulled at him.

Then he saw the man who had been running and undressing, and undressing and running, come bounding into the water. He dragged ashore the cook, and then waded toward the captain; but the captain waved him away and sent him to the correspondent. He was naked—naked as a tree in winter; but a halo was about his head, and he shone like a saint. He gave a strong pull, and a long drag, and a bully heave at the correspondent's hand. The correspondent, schooled in the minor formulae, said, "Thanks, old man." But suddenly the man cried, "What's that?" He pointed a swift finger. The correspondent said, "Go."

In the shallows, face downward, lay the oiler. His forehead touched sand that was periodically, between each wave, clear of the sea.

The correspondent did not know all that transpired afterward. When he achieved safe ground he fell, striking the sand with each particular part of his body. It was as if he had dropped from a roof, but the thud was grateful to him.

It seems that instantly the beach was populated with men with blankets, clothes, and flasks, and women with coffee-pots and all the remedies sacred to their minds. The welcome of the land to the men from the sea was warm and generous; but a still and dripping shape was carried slowly up the beach, and the land's welcome for it could only be the different and sinister hospitality of the grave.

When it came night, the white waves paced to and fro in the moonlight, and the wind brought the sound of the great sea's voice to the men on the shore, and they felt that they could then be interpreters.

Questions

1. In actuality, Crane, the captain of the *Commodore*, and the two crew members spent nearly thirty hours in the open boat. William Higgins, the oiler, was drowned as Crane describes. Does a knowledge of these facts in any way affect your response to the story? Would you admire the story less—or more—if you believed it to be pure fiction?
2. Sum up the personalities of each of the four men in the boat: captain, cook, oiler, and correspondent.
3. Notice some of the ways in which Crane, as a storyteller conscious of plot, builds suspense. What enemies or obstacles do the men in the boat confront? What is the effect of the episode of the men who wave from the beach (paragraphs 86–141)? What is the climax of the story?
4. In paragraph 70 (and again in paragraph 143), the men wonder, "Was I brought here merely to have my nose dragged away as I was about to nibble the sacred cheese of life?" What variety of irony do you find in this quotation? What does it imply about the powers of man versus the powers of nature?
5. Why does the scrap of verse about the soldier dying in Algiers (paragraph 178) suddenly come to mean so much to the correspondent?
6. What theme in "The Open Boat" seems most important to you? Where is it stated?
7. What secondary themes also enrich the story? See for instance paragraph 43 (the thoughts on comradeship).
8. How do you define *heroism*? Who is a hero in "The Open Boat"?

T. Coraghessan Boyle

T. Coraghessan Boyle (the T. stands for Tom) was born in 1948 in Peekskill, New York, the son of Irish immigrants. He grew up, he recalls, "as a sort of pampered punk" who did not read a book until he was eighteen. After a brief period as a high school teacher, he studied in the University of Iowa Writers' Workshop, submitting a collection of stories for his Ph.D. His stories in Esquire, Paris Review, the Atlantic, and other magazines quickly won him notice for their outrageous macabre humor and bizarre inventiveness. Boyle has published nine volumes of short stories, including Greasy Lake (1985), T. C. Boyle Stories (1998), and Tooth and Claw (2005). He has also published thirteen novels that are quite unlike anything else in contemporary American fiction. The subjects of some Boyle novels reveal his wide-ranging and idiosyncratic interests. Budding Prospects (1984) is a picaresque romp among adventurous marijuana growers. East Is East (1990) is a half-serious, half-comic story of a Japanese fugitive in an American writers' colony. The Road to Wellville (1993) takes place in 1907 in a sanitarium run by Dr. John Harvey Kellogg of corn flakes fame, with cameo appearances by Henry Ford, Thomas Edison, and Harvey Firestone. Boyle's most recent novel is When the Killing's Done (2011). He is Distinguished Professor of English at the University of Southern California.

Greasy Lake

1985

> It's about a mile down on the dark side of Route 88.
>
> —BRUCE SPRINGSTEEN

There was a time when courtesy and winning ways went out of style, when it was good to be bad, when you cultivated decadence like a taste. We were all dangerous characters then. We wore torn-up leather jackets, slouched around with toothpicks in our mouths, sniffed glue and ether and what somebody claimed was cocaine. When we wheeled our parents' whining station wagons out onto the street we left a patch of rubber half a block long. We drank gin and grape juice, Tango, Thunderbird, and Bali Hai. We were nineteen. We were bad. We read André Gide° and struck elaborate poses to show that we didn't give a shit about anything. At night, we went up to Greasy Lake.

Through the center of town, up the strip, past the housing developments and shopping malls, street lights giving way to the thin streaming illumination of the headlights, trees crowding the asphalt in a black unbroken wall: that was the way out to Greasy Lake. The Indians had called it Wakan, a reference to the clarity of its waters. Now it was fetid and murky, the mud banks glittering with broken glass and strewn with beer cans and the charred remains of bonfires. There was a single ravaged island a hundred yards from shore, so stripped of vegetation it looked as if the air force had strafed it. We went up to the lake because everyone went there, because we wanted to snuff the rich scent of possibility on the breeze, watch a girl take off her clothes and plunge into the festering murk, drink beer, smoke pot, howl at the stars, savor the incongruous full-throated roar of rock and roll against the primeval susurrus of frogs and crickets. This was nature.

I was there one night, late, in the company of two dangerous characters. Digby wore a gold star in his right ear and allowed his father to pay his tuition at Cornell; Jeff was thinking of quitting school to become a painter/musician/head-shop proprietor. They were both expert in the social graces, quick with a sneer, able to manage a Ford with lousy shocks over a rutted and gutted blacktop road at eighty-five while rolling a joint as compact as a Tootsie Roll Pop stick. They could lounge against a bank of booming speakers and trade "man"s with the best of them or roll out across the dance floor as if their joints worked on bearings. They were slick and quick and they wore their mirror shades at breakfast and dinner, in the shower, in closets and caves. In short, they were bad.

I drove. Digby pounded the dashboard and shouted along with Toots & the Maytals while Jeff hung his head out the window and streaked the side of my mother's Bel Air with vomit. It was early June, the air soft as a hand on your cheek, the third night of summer vacation. The first two nights we'd been out till dawn, looking for something we never found. On this, the third night, we'd cruised the strip sixty-seven times, been in and out of every bar and club we could think of in a twenty-mile radius, stopped twice for bucket chicken and forty-cent hamburgers, debated going to a party at the house of a girl Jeff's sister knew, and chucked two dozen raw eggs at mailboxes and hitchhikers. It was 2:00 A.M.; the bars were closing. There was nothing to do but take a bottle of lemon-flavored gin up to Greasy Lake.

André Gide: controversial French writer (1869–1951) whose novels, including *The Counterfeiters* and *Lafcadio's Adventures*, often show individuals in conflict with accepted morality.

The taillights of a single car winked at us as we swung into the dirt lot with its tufts of weed and washboard corrugations; '57 Chevy, mint, metallic blue. On the far side of the lot, like the exoskeleton of some gaunt chrome insect, a chopper leaned against its kickstand. And that was it for excitement: some junkie halfwit biker and a car freak pumping his girlfriend. Whatever it was we were looking for, we weren't about to find it at Greasy Lake. Not that night.

But then all of a sudden Digby was fighting for the wheel. "Hey, that's Tony Lovett's car! Hey!" he shouted, while I stabbed at the brake pedal and the Bel Air nosed up to the gleaming bumper of the parked Chevy. Digby leaned on the horn, laughing, and instructed me to put my brights on. I flicked on the brights. This was hilarious. A joke. Tony would experience premature withdrawal and expect to be confronted by grim-looking state troopers with flashlights. We hit the horn, strobed the lights, and then jumped out of the car to press our witty faces to Tony's windows; for all we knew we might even catch a glimpse of some little fox's tit, and then we could slap backs with red-faced Tony, roughhouse a little, and go on to new heights of adventure and daring.

The first mistake, the one that opened the whole floodgate, was losing my grip on the keys. In the excitement, leaping from the car with the gin in one hand and a roach clip in the other, I spilled them in the grass—in the dark, rank, mysterious nighttime grass of Greasy Lake. This was a tactical error, as damaging and irreversible in its way as Westmoreland's decision to dig in at Khe Sanh.° I felt it like a jab of intuition, and I stopped there by the open door, peering vaguely into the night that puddled up round my feet.

The second mistake—and this was inextricably bound up with the first—was identifying the car as Tony Lovett's. Even before the very bad character in greasy jeans and engineer boots ripped out of the driver's door, I began to realize that this chrome blue was much lighter than the robin's-egg of Tony's car, and that Tony's car didn't have rear-mounted speakers. Judging from their expressions, Digby and Jeff were privately groping toward the same inevitable and unsettling conclusion as I was.

In any case, there was no reasoning with this bad greasy character—clearly he was a man of action. The first lusty Rockette° kick of his steel-toed boot caught me under the chin, chipped my favorite tooth, and left me sprawled in the dirt. Like a fool, I'd gone down on one knee to comb the stiff hacked grass for the keys, my mind making connections in the most dragged-out, testudineous way, knowing that things had gone wrong, that I was in a lot of trouble, and that the lost ignition key was my grail and my salvation. The three or four succeeding blows were mainly absorbed by my right buttock and the tough piece of bone at the base of my spine.

Meanwhile, Digby vaulted the kissing bumpers and delivered a savage kung-fu blow to the greasy character's collarbone. Digby had just finished a course in martial arts for phys-ed credit and had spent the better part of the past two nights telling us apocryphal tales of Bruce Lee types and of the raw power invested in lightning blows shot from coiled wrists, ankles, and elbows. The greasy character was unimpressed.

Westmoreland's decision . . . Khe Sanh: General William C. Westmoreland commanded U.S. troops in Vietnam (1964–68). In late 1967 the North Vietnamese and Viet Cong forces attacked Khe Sanh (or Khesanh) with a show of strength, causing Westmoreland to expend great effort to defend a plateau of relatively little tactical importance. *Rockette:* member of a dance troupe in the stage show at Radio City Music Hall, New York, famous for its ability to kick fast and high with wonderful coordination.

He merely backed off a step, his face like a Toltec mask, and laid Digby out with a single whistling roundhouse blow . . . but by now Jeff had got into the act, and I was beginning to extricate myself from the dirt, a tinny compound of shock, rage, and impotence wadded in my throat.

Jeff was on the guy's back, biting at his ear. Digby was on the ground, cursing. I went for the tire iron I kept under the driver's seat. I kept it there because bad characters always keep tire irons under the driver's seat, for just such an occasion as this. Never mind that I hadn't been involved in a fight since sixth grade, when a kid with a sleepy eye and two streams of mucus depending from his nostrils hit me in the knee with a Louisville slugger,° never mind that I'd touched the tire iron exactly twice before, to change tires: it was there. And I went for it.

I was terrified. Blood was beating in my ears, my hands were shaking, my heart turning over like a dirtbike in the wrong gear. My antagonist was shirtless, and a single cord of muscle flashed across his chest as he bent forward to peel Jeff from his back like a wet overcoat. "Motherfucker," he spat, over and over, and I was aware in that instant that all four of us—Digby, Jeff, and myself included—were chanting "motherfucker, motherfucker," as if it were a battle cry. (What happened next? the detective asks the murderer from beneath the turned-down brim of his porkpie hat. I don't know, the murderer says, something came over me. Exactly.)

Digby poked the flat of his hand in the bad character's face and I came at him like a kamikaze, mindless, raging, stung with humiliation—the whole thing, from the initial boot in the chin to this murderous primal instant involving no more than sixty hyperventilating, gland-flooding seconds—I came at him and brought the tire iron down across his ear. The effect was instantaneous, astonishing. He was a stunt man and this was Hollywood, he was a big grimacing toothy balloon and I was a man with a straight pin. He collapsed. Wet his pants. Went loose in his boots.

A single second, big as a zeppelin, floated by. We were standing over him in a circle, gritting our teeth, jerking our necks, our limbs and hands and feet twitching with glandular discharges. No one said anything. We just stared down at the guy, the car freak, the lover, the bad greasy character laid low. Digby looked at me; so did Jeff. I was still holding the tire iron, a tuft of hair clinging to the crook like dandelion fluff, like down. Rattled, I dropped it in the dirt, already envisioning the headlines, the pitted faces of the police inquisitors, the gleam of handcuffs, clank of bars, the big black shadows rising from the back of the cell . . . when suddenly a raw torn shriek cut through me like all the juice in all the electric chairs in the country.

It was the fox. She was short, barefoot, dressed in panties and a man's shirt. "Animals!" she screamed, running at us with her fists clenched and wisps of blow-dried hair in her face. There was a silver chain round her ankle, and her toenails flashed in the glare of the headlights. I think it was the toenails that did it. Sure, the gin and the cannabis and even the Kentucky Fried may have had a hand in it, but it was the sight of those flaming toes that set us off—the toad emerging from the loaf in *Virgin Spring*,° lipstick smeared on a child; she was already tainted. We were on her like Bergman's deranged brothers—see no evil, hear none, speak none—panting, wheezing, tearing at her clothes, grabbing for flesh. We were bad

---

Louisville slugger: a brand of baseball bat.　　*Virgin Spring:* film by Swedish director Ingmar Bergman about a rape (1960).

characters, and we were scared and hot and three steps over the line—anything could have happened.

It didn't.

Before we could pin her to the hood of the car, our eyes masked with lust and greed and the purest primal badness, a pair of headlights swung into the lot. There we were, dirty, bloody, guilty, dissociated from humanity and civilization, the first of the Ur-crimes behind us, the second in progress, shreds of nylon panty and spandex brassiere dangling from our fingers, our flies open, lips licked—there we were, caught in the spotlight. Nailed.

We bolted. First for the car, and then, realizing we had no way of starting it, for the woods. I thought nothing. I thought escape. The headlights came at me like accusing fingers. I was gone.

Ram-bam-bam, across the parking lot, past the chopper and into the feculent undergrowth at the lake's edge, insects flying up in my face, weeds whipping, frogs and snakes and red-eyed turtles splashing off into the night: I was already ankle-deep in muck and tepid water and still going strong. Behind me, the girl's screams rose in intensity, disconsolate, incriminating, the screams of the Sabine women,° the Christian martyrs, Anne Frank° dragged from the garret. I kept going, pursued by those cries, imagining cops and bloodhounds. The water was up to my knees when I realized what I was doing: I was going to swim for it. Swim the breadth of Greasy Lake and hide myself in the thick clot of woods on the far side. They'd never find me there.

I was breathing in sobs, in gasps. The water lapped at my waist as I looked out over the moon-burnished ripples, the mats of algae that clung to the surface like scabs. Digby and Jeff had vanished. I paused. Listened. The girl was quieter now, screams tapering to sobs, but there were male voices, angry, excited, and the high-pitched ticking of the second car's engine. I waded deeper, stealthy, hunted, the ooze sucking at my sneakers. As I was about to take the plunge—at the very instant I dropped my shoulder for the first slashing stroke—I blundered into something. Something unspeakable, obscene, something soft, wet, moss-grown. A patch of weed? A log? When I reached out to touch it, it gave like a rubber duck, it gave like flesh.

In one of those nasty little epiphanies for which we are prepared by films and TV and childhood visits to the funeral home to ponder the shrunken painted forms of dead grandparents, I understood what it was that bobbed there so inadmissibly in the dark. Understood, and stumbled back in horror and revulsion, my mind yanked in six different directions (I was nineteen, a mere child, an infant, and here in the space of five minutes I'd struck down one greasy character and blundered into the waterlogged carcass of a second), thinking, The keys, the keys, why did I have to go and lose the keys? I stumbled back, but the muck took hold of my feet—a sneaker snagged, balance lost—and suddenly I was pitching face forward into the buoyant black mass, throwing out my hands in desperation while simultaneously conjuring the image of reeking

20

Sabine women: members of an ancient tribe in Italy, according to legend, forcibly carried off by the early Romans under Romulus to be their wives. The incident is depicted in a famous painting, "The Rape of the Sabine Women," by seventeenth-century French artist Nicolas Poussin.   *Anne Frank*: German Jewish girl (1929–1945) whose diary written during the Nazi occupation of the Netherlands later became world-famous. She hid with her family in a secret attic in Amsterdam, but was caught by the Gestapo and sent to the concentration camp at Belsen, where she died.

frogs and muskrats revolving in slicks of their own deliquescing juices. AAAAArrrgh! I shot from the water like a torpedo, the dead man rotating to expose a mossy beard and eyes cold as the moon. I must have shouted out, thrashing around in the weeds, because the voices behind me suddenly became animated.

"What was that?"

"It's them, it's them: they tried to, tried to . . . *rape* me!" Sobs.

A man's voice, flat Midwestern accent. "You sons a bitches, we'll kill you!"

Frogs, crickets.

Then another voice, harsh, *r*-less, Lower East Side: "Motherfucker!" I recognized the verbal virtuosity of the bad greasy character in the engineer boots. Tooth chipped, sneakers gone, coated in mud and slime and worse, crouching breathless in the weeds waiting to have my ass thoroughly and definitively kicked and fresh from the hideous stinking embrace of a three-days-dead-corpse, I suddenly felt a rush of joy and vindication: the son of a bitch was alive! Just as quickly, my bowels turned to ice. "Come on out of there, you pansy mothers!" the bad greasy character was screaming. He shouted curses till he was out of breath.

The crickets started up again, then the frogs. I held my breath. All at once there was a sound in the reeds, a swishing, a splash: thunk-a-thunk. They were throwing rocks. The frogs fell silent. I cradled my head. Swish, swish, thunk-a-thunk. A wedge of feldspar the size of a cue ball glanced off my knee. I bit my finger.

It was then that they turned to the car. I heard a door slam, a curse, and then the sound of the headlights shattering—almost a good-natured sound, celebratory, like corks popping from the necks of bottles. This was succeeded by the dull booming of the fenders, metal on metal, and then the icy crash of the windshield. I inched forward, elbows and knees, my belly pressed to the muck, thinking of guerrillas and commandos and *The Naked and the Dead*.° I parted the weeds and squinted the length of the parking lot.

The second car—it was a Trans-Am—was still running, its high beams washing the scene in a lurid stagy light. Tire iron flailing, the greasy bad character was laying into the side of my mother's Bel Air like an avenging demon, his shadow riding up the trunks of the trees. Whomp. Whomp. Whomp-whomp. The other two guys—blond types, in fraternity jackets—were helping out with tree branches and skull-sized boulders. One of them was gathering up bottles, rocks, muck, candy wrappers, used condoms, poptops, and other refuse and pitching it through the window on the driver's side. I could see the fox, a white bulb behind the windshield of the '57 Chevy. "Bobbie," she whined over the thumping, "come on." The greasy character paused a moment, took one good swipe at the left taillight, and then heaved the tire iron halfway across the lake. Then he fired up the '57 and was gone.

Blond head nodded at blond head. One said something to the other, too low for me to catch. They were no doubt thinking that in helping to annihilate my mother's car they'd committed a fairly rash act, and thinking too that there were three bad characters connected with that very car watching them from the woods. Perhaps other possibilities occurred to them as well—police, jail cells, justices of the peace, reparations, lawyers, irate parents, fraternal censure. Whatever they were thinking, they suddenly dropped branches, bottles, and rocks and sprang for their car in unison, as if they'd choreographed it. Five seconds. That's all it took. The engine shrieked,

---

The Naked and the Dead: novel (1948) by Norman Mailer, about U.S. Army life in World War II.

the tires squealed, a cloud of dust rose from the rutted lot and then settled back on darkness.

I don't know how long I lay there, the bad breath of decay all around me, my jacket heavy as a bear, the primordial ooze subtly reconstituting itself to accommodate my upper thighs and testicles. My jaws ached, my knee throbbed, my coccyx was on fire. I contemplated suicide, wondered if I'd need bridgework, scraped the recesses of my brain for some sort of excuse to give my parents—a tree had fallen on the car, I was blinded by a bread truck, hit and run, vandals had got to it while we were playing chess at Digby's. Then I thought of the dead man. He was probably the only person on the planet worse off than I was. I thought about him, fog on the lake, insects chirring eerily, and felt the tug of fear, felt the darkness opening up inside me like a set of jaws. Who was he, I wondered, this victim of time and circumstance bobbing sorrowfully in the lake at my back. The owner of the chopper, no doubt, a bad older character come to this. Shot during a murky drug deal, drowned while drunkenly frolicking in the lake. Another headline. My car was wrecked; he was dead.

When the eastern half of the sky went from black to cobalt and the trees began to separate themselves from the shadows, I pushed myself up from the mud and stepped out into the open. By now the birds had begun to take over for the crickets, and dew lay slick on the leaves. There was a smell in the air, raw and sweet at the same time, the smell of the sun firing buds and opening blossoms. I contemplated the car. It lay there like a wreck along the highway, like a steel sculpture left over from a vanished civilization. Everything was still. This was nature.

I was circling the car, as dazed and bedraggled as the sole survivor of an air blitz, when Digby and Jeff emerged from the trees behind me. Digby's face was crosshatched with smears of dirt; Jeff's jacket was gone and his shirt was torn across the shoulder. They slouched across the lot, looking sheepish, and silently came up beside me to gape at the ravaged automobile. No one said a word. After a while Jeff swung open the driver's door and began to scoop the broken glass and garbage off the seat. I looked at Digby. He shrugged. "At least they didn't slash the tires," he said.

It was true: the tires were intact. There was no windshield, the headlights were staved in, and the body looked as if it had been sledge-hammered for a quarter a shot at the county fair, but the tires were inflated to regulation pressure. The car was drivable. In silence, all three of us bent to scrape the mud and shattered glass from the interior. I said nothing about the biker. When we were finished, I reached in my pocket for the keys, experienced a nasty stab of recollection, cursed myself, and turned to search the grass. I spotted them almost immediately, no more than five feet from the open door, glinting like jewels in the first tapering shaft of sunlight. There was no reason to get philosophical about it: I eased into the seat and turned the engine over.

It was at that precise moment that the silver Mustang with the flame decals rumbled into the lot. All three of us froze; then Digby and Jeff slid into the car and slammed the door. We watched as the Mustang rocked and bobbed across the ruts and finally jerked to a halt beside the forlorn chopper at the far end of the lot. "Let's go," Digby said. I hesitated, the Bel Air wheezing beneath me.

Two girls emerged from the Mustang. Tight jeans, stiletto heels, hair like frozen fur. They bent over the motorcycle, paced back and forth aimlessly, glanced once or twice at us, and then ambled over to where the reeds sprang up in a green fence round the perimeter of the lake. One of them cupped her hands to her mouth. "Al," she called. "Hey, Al!"

"Come on," Digby hissed. "Let's get out of here."

But it was too late. The second girl was picking her way across the lot, unsteady on her heels, looking up at us and then away. She was older—twenty-five or -six—and as she came closer we could see there was something wrong with her: she was stoned or drunk, lurching now and waving her arms for balance. I gripped the steering wheel as if it were the ejection lever of a flaming jet, and Digby spat out my name, twice, terse and impatient.

"Hi," the girl said.

We looked at her like zombies, like war veterans, like deaf-and-dumb pencil peddlers.

She smiled, her lips cracked and dry. "Listen," she said, bending from the waist to look in the window, "you guys seen Al?" Her pupils were pinpoints, her eyes glass. She jerked her neck. "That's his bike over there—Al's. You seen him?"

Al. I didn't know what to say. I wanted to get out of the car and retch, I wanted to go home to my parents' house and crawl into bed. Digby poked me in the ribs. "We haven't seen anybody," I said.

The girl seemed to consider this, reaching out a slim veiny arm to brace herself against the car. "No matter," she said, slurring the *t*'s, "he'll turn up." And then, as if she'd just taken stock of the whole scene—the ravaged car and our battered faces, the desolation of the place—she said: "Hey, you guys look like some pretty bad characters—been fightin', huh?" We stared straight ahead, rigid as catatonics. She was fumbling in her pocket and muttering something. Finally she held out a handful of tablets in glassine wrappers: "Hey, you want to party, you want to do some of these with me and Sarah?"

I just looked at her. I thought I was going to cry. Digby broke the silence. "No, thanks," he said, leaning over me. "Some other time."

I put the car in gear and it inched forward with a groan, shaking off pellets of glass like an old dog shedding water after a bath, heaving over the ruts on its worn springs, creeping toward the highway. There was a sheen of sun on the lake. I looked back. The girl was still standing there, watching us, her shoulders slumped, hand outstretched.

Questions

1. What is it about Digby and Jeff that inspires the narrator to call them "bad"? What details contradict or undercut the three characters' seeming rebelliousness?
2. Twice in "Greasy Lake"—in paragraphs 2 and 32—appear the words "This was nature." What contrasts do you find between the "nature" of the narrator's earlier and later views?
3. What makes the narrator and his friends run off into the woods?
4. How does the young men's encounter with the two girls at the end of the story differ from their earlier encounter with the girl from the blue Chevy? How do you account for the difference? When at the end of the story the girl offers to party with the three friends, what makes the narrator say, "I thought I was going to cry"?
5. How important to what happens in this story is Greasy Lake itself? What details about the lake and its shores strike you as particularly memorable (whether funny, disgusting, or both)?
6. How much of the atmosphere of Greasy Lake is created by the natural world? How much of it is attributable to human influence?

Suggestions for Writing

1. How would you describe nature in London's "To Build a Fire" and Crane's "The Open Boat"? Specifically, what is the relationship between nature and humankind? How do the characters in these two stories react to nature? Do the different ways in which they respond to nature have an effect on their respective fates?
2. What is the theme of Boyle's "Greasy Lake"? How does the description of the lake relate to the theme? Write an essay analyzing the story's theme and how the narrator has (or has not) changed or developed as a result of the story's events.
3. Select a story in this section and discuss how the author's descriptions of nature support the story's theme.
4. "To Build a Fire" and "The Open Boat" both address the theme of a human being pitted against indifferent nature. Contrast the stories' approaches to this theme. How do the tone and atmosphere of the stories differ? How do these differences help to communicate theme?

LIVING WITH NATURE

Ursula K. Le Guin *She Unnames Them*
Leslie Marmon Silko *The Man to Send Rain Clouds*
Terry Bisson *Bears Discover Fire*

We all live with nature. Even if you have never been outside the city, you've experienced heat waves or snowstorms, and walked past flowers and trees. If you live in the country, you might be surrounded by forests or fields, or see wildlife on a regular basis. But whether people live in the city or the country, they seem to crave contact with the natural world—as evidenced by the crowds at lakes and beaches in the summer and the millions who travel to the national parks each year. This seeking out of nature suggests that there is something fundamental about the natural world that appeals to human beings. It is, after all, our natural home, however much we try to change it. Indeed, research has shown that people who are cut off from sunlight, fresh air, and greenery are significantly less healthy than those who experience them on a regular basis. But some people go beyond sampling nature to seek a deeper communion with the natural world for their spiritual nourishment, or recreation, or livelihood. Far from fearing nature, these people acknowledge and honor its power and find ways to live appropriately within it. The stories in this section all feature characters who have respectful and fulfilling relationships with nature. They struggle less with the natural world than with people who have lost their connection to nature, or who perhaps never had one at all.

Ursula K. Le Guin

Ursula Le Guin (b. 1929) receives a capsule biography on page 914, prefacing her story "The Ones Who Walk Away from Omelas." She is a writer who is fascinated by myth, legend, and folklore. Here is her radical revision of a very old story.

She Unnames Them   1985

Most of them accepted namelessness with the perfect indifference with which they had so long accepted and ignored their names. Whales and dolphins, seals and sea otters consented with particular grace and alacrity, sliding into anonymity as into their element. A faction of yaks, however, protested. They said that "yak" sounded right, and that almost everyone who knew they existed called them that. Unlike the ubiquitous creatures such as rats and fleas, who had been called by hundreds or thousands of different names since Babel, the yaks could truly say, they said, that they had a *name*. They discussed the matter all summer. The councils of the elderly females finally agreed that though the name might be useful to others it was so redundant from the yak point of view that they never spoke it themselves and hence might as well dispense with it. After they presented the argument in this light to their bulls, a full consensus was delayed only by the onset of severe early blizzards. Soon after the beginning of the thaw, their agreement was reached and the designation "yak" was returned to the donor.

Among the domestic animals, few horses had cared what anybody called them since the failure of Dean Swift's° attempt to name them from their own vocabulary. Cattle, sheep, swine, asses, mules, and goats, along with chickens, geese, and turkeys, all agreed enthusiastically to give their names back to the people to whom—as they put it—they belonged.

A couple of problems did come up with pets. The cats, of course, steadfastly denied ever having had any name other than those self-given, unspoken, ineffably personal names which, as the poet named Eliot° said, they spend long hours daily contemplating—though none of the contemplators has ever admitted that what they contemplate is their names and some onlookers have wondered if the object of that meditative gaze might not in fact be the Perfect, or Platonic, Mouse. In any case, it is a moot point now. It was with the dogs, and with some parrots, lovebirds, ravens, and mynahs, that the trouble arose. These verbally talented individuals insisted that their names were important to them, and flatly refused to part with them. But as soon as they understood that the issue was precisely one of individual choice, and that anybody who wanted to be called Rover, or Froufrou, or Polly, or even Birdie in the personal sense, was perfectly free to do so, not one of them had the least objection to parting with the lowercase (or, as regards German creatures, uppercase) generic appellations "poodle," "parrot," "dog," or "bird," and all the Linnaean qualifiers° that had trailed along behind them for two hundred years like tin cans tied to a tail.

The insects parted with their names in vast clouds and swarms of ephemeral syllables buzzing and stinging and humming and flitting and crawling and tunnelling away.

As for the fish of the sea, their names dispersed from them in silence throughout the oceans like faint, dark blurs of cuttlefish ink, and drifted off on the currents without a trace.   5

None were left now to unname, and yet how close I felt to them when I saw one of them swim or fly or trot or crawl across my way or over my skin, or stalk me in the night, or go along beside me for a while in the day. They seemed far closer than when their names had stood between myself and them like a clear barrier: so close that my fear of them and their fear of me became one same fear. And the attraction that many of us felt, the desire to smell one another's smells, feel or rub or caress one another's scales or skin or feathers or fur, taste one another's blood or flesh, keep one another warm—that attraction was now all one with the fear, and the hunter could not be told from the hunted, nor the eater from the food.

This was more or less the effect I had been after. It was somewhat more powerful than I had anticipated, but I could not now, in all conscience, make an exception for myself. I resolutely put anxiety away, went to Adam, and said, "You and your father lent me this—gave it to me, actually. It's been really useful, but it doesn't exactly seem to fit very well lately. But thanks very much! It's really been very useful."

It is hard to give back a gift without sounding peevish or ungrateful, and I did not want to leave him with that impression of me. He was not paying much attention, as

---

Dean Swift: Jonathan Swift, author of *Gulliver's Travels* (1726), in which the Houyhnhnms, a race of intelligent horses, run the most reasonable kingdom on earth.   *ineffably personal names . . . Eliot:* Le Guin makes a playful allusion here to T. S. Eliot's poem "The Naming of Cats," in which he claims that cats have secret individual names that they contemplate.   *Linnean qualifiers:* their scientific names. Carolus Linnaeus (1707–1778) invented the system of scientific classification of plants and animals.

it happened, and said only, "Put it down over there, O.K.?" and went on with what he was doing.

One of my reasons for doing what I did was that talk was getting us nowhere, but all the same I felt a little let down. I had been prepared to defend my decision. And I thought that perhaps when he did notice he might be upset and want to talk. I put some things away and fiddled around a little, but he continued to do what he was doing and to take no notice of anything else. At last I said, "Well, goodbye, dear. I hope the garden key turns up."

He was fitting parts together, and said, without looking around, "O.K., fine, dear. When's dinner?"

"I'm not sure," I said. "I'm going now. With the—" I hesitated, and finally said, "With them, you know," and went on out. In fact, I had only just then realized how hard it would have been to explain myself. I could not chatter away as I used to do, taking it all for granted. My words now must be as slow, as new, as single, as tentative as the steps I took going down the path away from the house, between the dark-branched, tall dancers motionless against the winter shining.

Questions

1. Who is the speaker of the story?
2. Who had originally given the animal creatures names?
3. How did most of the creatures feel about their names? Were there exceptions?
4. How does unnaming the creatures change the speaker's relationship with them?
5. Why does the speaker want to take away the names of animals? Cite her specific reason or reasons.

Leslie Marmon Silko

Leslie Marmon Silko was born in Albuquerque, New Mexico, in 1948. Her mixed ancestry included Laguna Pueblo Indian, Mexican, and white, but she grew up on the Laguna Pueblo Reservation, where some part of her family had lived for generations. After attending Indian Affairs schools in Laguna Pueblo and Catholic schools in Albuquerque, Silko graduated from the University of New Mexico–Albuquerque in 1969. She briefly attended law school before deciding to devote herself full-time to writing. "The Man to Send Rain Clouds" was—amazingly—Silko's first published story. Appearing in 1969 when the author was still in college, it shows her sensibility already fully formed. "The Man to Send Rain Clouds" was later incorporated in Storyteller (1981), a miscellany of stories, memoirs, anecdotes, poems, and photographs that portray her native Laguna Pueblo in New Mexico. Silko became known as a poet with Laguna Woman (1974). Her first novel, Ceremony, was published in 1977 to critical acclaim. She has continued to publish poetry, fiction, and nonfiction. Her most recent book is The Turquoise Ledge: A Memoir (2010). Silko lives in Tucson, Arizona.

The Man to Send Rain Clouds (1969) 1981

They found him under a big cottonwood tree. His Levi jacket and pants were faded light blue so that he had been easy to find. The big cottonwood tree stood apart from a small grove of winterbare cottonwoods which grew in the wide, sandy arroyo. He had been dead for a day or more, and the sheep had wandered and scattered up and down the arroyo. Leon and his brother-in-law, Ken, gathered the sheep and left them in the pen at the sheep camp before they returned to the cottonwood tree. Leon waited under the tree while Ken drove the truck through the deep sand to the edge of the arroyo. He squinted up at the sun and unzipped his jacket—it sure was hot for this time of year. But high and northwest the blue mountains were still in snow. Ken came sliding down the low, crumbling bank about fifty yards down, and he was bringing the red blanket.

Before they wrapped the old man, Leon took a piece of string out of his pocket and tied a small gray feather in the old man's long white hair. Ken gave him the paint. Across the brown wrinkled forehead he drew a streak of white and along the high cheekbones he drew a strip of blue paint. He paused and watched Ken throw pinches of corn meal and pollen into the wind that fluttered the small gray feather. Then Leon painted with yellow under the old man's broad nose, and finally, when he had painted green across the chin, he smiled.

"Send us rain clouds, Grandfather." They laid the bundle in the back of the pickup and covered it with a heavy tarp before they started back to the pueblo.

They turned off the highway onto the sandy pueblo road. Not long after they passed the store and post office they saw Father Paul's car coming toward them. When he recognized their faces he slowed his car and waved for them to stop. The young priest rolled down the car window.

"Did you find old Teofilo?" he asked loudly.

Leon stopped the truck. "Good morning, Father. We were just out to the sheep camp. Everything is O.K. now."

"Thank God for that. Teofilo is a very old man. You really shouldn't allow him to stay at the sheep camp alone."

"No, he won't do that any more now."

"Well, I'm glad you understand. I hope I'll be seeing you at Mass this week—we missed you last Sunday. See if you can get old Teofilo to come with you." The priest smiled and waved at them as they drove away.

Louise and Teresa were waiting. The table was set for lunch, and the coffee was boiling on the black iron stove. Leon looked at Louise and then at Teresa.

"We found him under a cottonwood tree in the big arroyo near sheep camp. I guess he sat down to rest in the shade and never got up again." Leon walked toward the old man's bed. The red plaid shawl had been shaken and spread carefully over the bed, and a new brown flannel shirt and pair of stiff new Levi's were arranged neatly beside the pillow. Louise held the screen door open while Leon and Ken carried in the red blanket. He looked small and shriveled, and after they dressed him in the new shirt and pants he seemed more shrunken.

It was noontime now because the church bells rang the Angelus. They ate the beans with hot bread, and nobody said anything until after Teresa poured the coffee.

Ken stood up and put on his jacket. "I'll see about the gravediggers. Only the top layer of soil is frozen. I think it can be ready before dark."

Leon nodded his head and finished his coffee. After Ken had been gone for a while, the neighbors and clanspeople came quietly to embrace Teofilo's family and to leave food on the table because the gravediggers would come to eat when they were finished.

The sky in the west was full of pale yellow light. Louise stood outside with her hands in the pockets of Leon's green army jacket that was too big for her. The funeral was over, and the old men had taken their candles and medicine bags and were gone. She waited until the body was laid into the pickup before she said anything to Leon. She touched his arm, and he noticed that her hands were still dusty from the corn meal that she had sprinkled around the old man. When she spoke, Leon could not hear her.

"What did you say? I didn't hear you."

"I said that I had been thinking about something."

"About what?"

"About the priest sprinkling holy water for Grandpa. So he won't be thirsty."

Leon stared at the new moccasins that Teofilo had made for the ceremonial dances in the summer. They were nearly hidden by the red blanket. It was getting colder, and the wind pushed gray dust down the narrow pueblo road. The sun was approaching the long mesa where it disappeared during the winter. Louise stood there shivering and watching his face. Then he zipped up his jacket and opened the truck door. "I'll see if he's there."

Ken stopped the pickup at the church, and Leon got out; and then Ken drove down the hill to the graveyard where people were waiting. Leon knocked at the old carved door with its symbols of the Lamb. While he waited he looked up at the twin bells from the king of Spain with the last sunlight pouring around them in their tower.

The priest opened the door and smiled when he saw who it was. "Come in! What brings you here this evening?"

The priest walked toward the kitchen, and Leon stood with his cap in his hand, playing with the earflaps and examining the living room—the brown sofa, the green armchair, and the brass lamp that hung down from the ceiling by links of chain. The priest dragged a chair out of the kitchen and offered it to Leon.

"No thank you, Father. I only came to ask you if you would bring your holy water to the graveyard."

The priest turned away from Leon and looked out the window at the patio full of shadows and the dining-room windows of the nuns' cloister across the patio. The curtains were heavy, and the light from within faintly penetrated; it was impossible to see the nuns inside eating supper. "Why didn't you tell me he was dead? I could have brought the Last Rites anyway."

Leon smiled. "It wasn't necessary, Father."

The priest stared down at his scuffed brown loafers and the worn hem of his cassock. "For a Christian burial it was necessary."

His voice was distant, and Leon thought that his blue eyes looked tired.

"It's O.K., Father, we just want him to have plenty of water."

The priest sank down into the green chair and picked up a glossy missionary magazine. He turned the colored pages full of lepers and pagans without looking at them.

"You know I can't do that, Leon. There should have been the Last Rites and a funeral Mass at the very least."

Leon put on his green cap and pulled the flaps down over his ears. "It's getting late, Father. I've got to go."

When Leon opened the door Father Paul stood up and said, "Wait." He left the room and came back wearing a long brown overcoat. He followed Leon out the door and across the dim churchyard to the adobe steps in front of the church. They both stooped to fit through the low adobe entrance. And when they started down the hill to the graveyard only half of the sun was visible above the mesa.

The priest approached the grave slowly, wondering how they had managed to dig into the frozen ground; and then he remembered that this was New Mexico, and saw the pile of cold loose sand beside the hole. The people stood close to each other with little clouds of steam puffing from their faces. The priest looked at them and saw a pile of jackets, gloves, and scarves in the yellow, dry tumbleweeds that grew in the graveyard. He looked at the red blanket, not sure that Teofilo was so small, wondering if it wasn't some perverse Indian trick—something they did in March to ensure a good harvest—wondering if maybe old Teofilo was actually at sheep camp corralling the sheep for the night. But there he was, facing into a cold dry wind and squinting at the last sunlight, ready to bury a red wool blanket while the faces of his parishioners were in shadow with the last warmth of the sun on their backs.

His fingers were stiff, and it took him a long time to twist the lid off the holy water. Drops of water fell on the red blanket and soaked into dark icy spots. He sprinkled the grave and the water disappeared almost before it touched the dim, cold sand; it reminded him of something—he tried to remember what it was, because he thought if he could remember he might understand this. He sprinkled more water; he shook the container until it was empty, and the water fell through the light from sundown like August rain that fell while the sun was still shining, almost evaporating before it touched the wilted squash flowers.

The wind pulled at the priest's brown Franciscan robe and swirled away the corn meal and pollen that had been sprinkled on the blanket. They lowered the bundle into the ground, and they didn't bother to untie the stiff pieces of new rope that were tied around the ends of the blanket. The sun was gone, and over on the highway the east-bound lane was full of headlights. The priest walked away slowly. Leon watched him climb the hill, and when he had disappeared within the tall, thick walls, Leon turned to look up at the high blue mountains in the deep snow that reflected a faint red light from the west. He felt good because it was finished, and he was happy about the sprinkling of the holy water; now the old man could send them big thunderclouds for sure.

Questions

1. Why don't Ken and Leon tell Father Paul that Teofilo is dead?
2. Why does Louise tell Leon her thoughts about sprinkling holy water? Do they see this ritual in the same light that Father Paul does?
3. How are the experience and aftermath of death described in this story?

4. How would you describe Ken's and Leon's beliefs and attitudes toward nature? How might Father Paul's beliefs differ from theirs?
5. Native American and Roman Catholic beliefs about both nature and death seem to differ significantly in this story. Do these differences reflect larger differences?

Terry Bisson

Terry Bisson (b. 1942) grew up in Owensboro, Kentucky, and attended Grinnell College and the University of Louisville. After earning his B.A. in 1964, he worked as a comic book writer, an auto mechanic, and an editor with Berkley Books. Bisson has published more than a dozen book-length works of science fiction, including the novels Wyrldmaker (1981), Talking Man (1986), Pirates of the Universe (1996), and The Pickup Artist (2001), as well as several short story collections, including Bears Discover Fire (1993), In the Upper Room (2000), and TVA Baby (2011). He has won almost every major award for science fiction—some of them repeatedly—including the Locus, Nebula, and Hugo. In addition to science fiction, Bisson has written novelizations of several movies, a series of NASCAR-related books for children, two young adult novels, a memoir, and numerous articles and reviews for publications as varied as the Nation, Glamour, Automotive News, and Writer's Digest. He has also written several screenplays. Bisson has taught science fiction writing at the New School in New York, and currently lives with his wife in Oakland, California. His story "Bears Discover Fire" took every major award in science fiction when it was first published.

Bears Discover Fire   1993

I was driving with my brother, the preacher, and my nephew, the preacher's son, on I-65 just north of Bowling Green when we got a flat. It was Sunday night and we had been to visit Mother at the Home. We were in my car. The flat caused what you might call knowing groans since, as the old-fashioned one in my family (so they tell me), I fix my own tires, and my brother is always telling me to get radials and quit buying old tires.

But if you know how to mount and fix tires yourself, you can pick them up for almost nothing.

Since it was a left rear tire, I pulled over to the left, onto the median grass. The way my Caddy stumbled to a stop, I figured the tire was ruined. "I guess there's no need asking if you have any of that FlatFix in the trunk," said Wallace.

"Here, son, hold the light," I said to Wallace Jr. He's old enough to want to help and not old enough (yet) to think he knows it all. If I'd married and had kids, he's the kind I'd have wanted.

An old Caddy has a big trunk that tends to fill up like a shed. Mine's a '56. Wallace was wearing his Sunday shirt, so he didn't offer to help while I pulled magazines, fishing tackle, a wooden tool box, some old clothes, a comealong wrapped in a grass sack, and a tobacco sprayer out of the way, looking for my jack. The spare looked a little soft.

The light went out. "Shake it, son," I said.

It went back on. The bumper jack was long gone, but I carry a little quarter-ton hydraulic. I found it under Mother's old *Southern Livings*, 1978–1986. I had been meaning to drop them at the dump. If Wallace hadn't been along, I'd have let Wallace Jr. position the jack under the axle, but I got on my knees and did it myself. There's nothing wrong with a boy learning to change a tire. Even if you're not going to fix and mount them, you're still going to have to change a few in this life. The light went off again before I had the wheel off the ground. I was surprised at how dark the night was already. It was late October and beginning to get cool. "Shake it again, son," I said.

It went back on but it was weak. Flickery.

"With radials you just don't *have* flats," Wallace explained in that voice he uses when he's talking to a number of people at once; in this case, Wallace Jr. and myself. "And even when you *do*, you just squirt them with this stuff called FlatFix and you just drive on. Three ninety-five the can."

"Uncle Bobby can fix a tire hisself," said Wallace Jr., out of loyalty, I presume.

"Himself," I said from halfway under the car. If it was up to Wallace, the boy would talk like what Mother used to call "a helot from the gorges of the mountains." But drive on radials.

"Shake that light again," I said. It was about gone. I spun the lugs off into the hubcap and pulled the wheel. The tire had blown out along the sidewall. "Won't be fixing this one," I said. Not that I cared. I have a pile as tall as a man out by the barn.

The light went out again, then came back better than ever as I was fitting the spare over the lugs. "Much better," I said. There was a flood of dim orange flickery light. But when I turned to find the lug nuts, I was surprised to see that the flashlight the boy was holding was dead. The light was coming from two bears at the edge of the trees, holding torches. They were big, three-hundred-pounders, standing about five feet tall. Wallace Jr. and his father had seen them and were standing perfectly still. It's best not to alarm bears.

I fished the lug nuts out of the hubcap and spun them on. I usually like to put a little oil on them, but this time I let it go. I reached under the car and let the jack down and pulled it out. I was relieved to see that the spare was high enough to drive on. I put the jack and the lug wrench and the flat into the trunk. Instead of replacing the hubcap, I put it in there too. All this time, the bears never made a move. They just held the torches, whether out of curiosity or helpfulness, there was no way of knowing. It looked like there may have been more bears behind them, in the trees.

Opening three doors at once, we got into the car and drove off. Wallace was the first to speak. "Looks like bears have discovered fire," he said.

When we first took Mother to the Home almost four years (forty-seven months) ago, she told Wallace and me she was ready to die. "Don't worry about me, boys," she whispered, pulling us both down so the nurse wouldn't hear. "I've drove a million miles and I'm ready to pass over to the other shore. I won't have long to linger here." She drove a consolidated school bus for thirty-nine years. Later, after Wallace left, she told me about her dream. A bunch of doctors were sitting around in a circle discussing her case. One said, "We've done all we can for her, boys, let's let her go."

They all turned their hands up and smiled. When she didn't die that fall she seemed disappointed, though as spring came she forgot about it, as old people will.

In addition to taking Wallace and Wallace Jr. to see Mother on Sunday nights, I go myself on Tuesdays and Thursdays. I usually find her sitting in front of the TV, even though she doesn't watch it. The nurses keep it on all the time. They say the old folks like the flickering. It soothes them down.

"What's this I hear about bears discovering fire?" she said on Tuesday. "It's true," I told her as I combed her long white hair with the shell comb Wallace had brought her from Florida. Monday there had been a story in the Louisville *Courier-Journal*, and Tuesday one on NBC or CBS *Nightly News*. People were seeing bears all over the state, and in Virginia as well. They had quit hibernating, and were apparently planning to spend the winter in the medians of the interstates. There have always been bears in the mountains of Virginia, but not here in western Kentucky, not for almost a hundred years. The last one was killed when Mother was a girl. The theory in the *Courier-Journal* was that they were following I-65 down from the forests of Michigan and Canada, but one old man from Allen County (interviewed on nationwide TV) said that there had always been a few bears left back in the hills, and they had come out to join the others now that they had discovered fire.

"They don't hibernate anymore," I said. "They make a fire and keep it going all winter."

"I declare," Mother said. "What'll they think of next!" The nurse came to take her tobacco away, which is the signal for bedtime.

Every October, Wallace Jr. stays with me while his parents go to camp. I realize how backward that sounds, but there it is. My brother is a Minister (House of the Righteous Way, Reformed) but he makes two thirds of his living in real estate. He and Elizabeth go to a Christian Success Retreat in South Carolina, where people from all over the country practice selling things to one another. I know what it's like not because they've ever bothered to tell me, but because I've seen the Revolving Equity Success Plan ads late at night on TV.

The school bus let Wallace Jr. off at my house on Wednesday, the day they left. The boy doesn't have to pack much of a bag when he stays with me. He has his own room here. As the eldest of our family, I hung on to the old home place near Smiths Grove. It's getting run-down, but Wallace Jr. and I don't mind. He has his own room in Bowling Green, too, but since Wallace and Elizabeth move to a different house every three months (part of the Plan), he keeps his .22 and his comics, the stuff that's important to a boy his age, in his room here at the home place. It's the room his dad and I used to share.

Wallace Jr. is twelve. I found him sitting on the back porch that overlooks the interstate when I got home from work. I sell crop insurance.

After I changed clothes I showed him how to break the bead on a tire two ways, with a hammer, and by backing a car over it. Like making sorghum, fixing tires by hand is a dying art. The boy caught on fast, though. "Tomorrow I'll show you how to mount your tire with the hammer and a tire iron," I said.

"What I wish is I could see the bears," he said. He was looking across the field to I-65, where the northbound lanes cut off the corner of our field. From the house at night, sometimes the traffic sounds like a waterfall.

"Can't see their fire in the daytime," I said. "But wait till tonight." That night CBS or NBC (I forget which is which) did a special on the bears, which were becoming a story of nationwide interest. They were seen in Kentucky, West Virginia, Missouri, Illinois (southern), and, of course, Virginia. There have always been bears in Virginia. Some characters there were even talking about hunting them. A scientist said they were heading into the states where there is some snow but not too much, and where there is enough timber in the medians for firewood. He had gone in with a video camera, but his shots were just blurry figures sitting around a fire. Another scientist said the bears were attracted by the berries on a new bush that grew only in the medians of the interstates. He claimed this berry was the first new species in recent history, brought about by the mixing of seeds along the highway. He ate one on TV, making a face, and called it a "newberry." A climatic ecologist said that the warm winters (there was no snow last winter in Nashville, and only one flurry in Louisville) had changed the bears' hibernation cycle, and now they were able to remember things from year to year. "Bears may have discovered fire centuries ago," he said, "but forgot it." Another theory was that they had discovered (or remembered) fire when Yellowstone burned, several years ago.

The TV showed more guys talking about bears than it showed bears, and Wallace Jr. and I lost interest. After the supper dishes were done I took the boy out behind the house and down to our fence. Across the interstate and through the trees, we could see the light of the bears' fire. Wallace Jr. wanted to go back to the house and get his .22 and go shoot one, and I explained why that would be wrong. "Besides," I said, "a twenty-two wouldn't do much more to a bear than make it mad.

"Besides," I added, "it's illegal to hunt in the medians."

The only trick to mounting a tire by hand, once you have beaten or pried it onto the rim, is setting the bead. You do this by setting the tire upright, sitting on it, and bouncing it up and down between your legs while the air goes in. When the bead sets on the rim, it makes a satisfying "pop." On Thursday, I kept Wallace Jr. home from school and showed him how to do this until he got it right. Then we climbed our fence and crossed the field to get a look at the bears.

In northern Virginia, according to *Good Morning America*, the bears were keeping their fires going all day long. Here in western Kentucky, though, it was still warm for late October and they only stayed around the fires at night. Where they went and what they did in the daytime, I don't know. Maybe they were watching from the newberry bushes as Wallace Jr. and I climbed the government fence and crossed the northbound lanes. I carried an axe and Wallace Jr. brought his .22, not because he wanted to kill a bear but because a boy likes to carry some kind of a gun. The median was all tangled with brush and vines under the maples, oaks, and sycamores. Even though we were only a hundred yards from the house, I had never been there, and neither had anyone else that I knew of. It was like a created country. We found a path in the center and followed it down across a slow, short stream that flowed out of one grate and into another. The tracks in the gray mud were the first bear signs we saw. There was a musty, but not really unpleasant smell. In a clearing under a big hollow beech, where the fire had been, we found nothing but ashes. Logs were drawn up in a rough circle and the smell was stronger. I stirred the ashes and found enough coals to start a new flame, so I banked them back the way they had been left.

I cut a little firewood and stacked it to one side, just to be neighborly.

Maybe the bears were watching us from the bushes even then. There's no way to know. I tasted one of the newberries and spit it out. It was so sweet it was sour, just the sort of thing you would imagine a bear would like.

That evening after supper I asked Wallace Jr. if he might want to go with me to visit Mother. I wasn't surprised when he said yes. Kids have more consideration than folks give them credit for. We found her sitting on the concrete front porch of the Home, watching the cars go by on I-65. The nurse said she had been agitated all day. I wasn't surprised by that, either. Every fall as the leaves change, she gets restless, maybe the word is "hopeful," again. I brought her into the dayroom and combed her long white hair. "Nothing but bears on TV anymore," the nurse complained, flipping the channels. Wallace Jr. picked up the remote after the nurse left, and we watched a CBS or NBC Special Report about some hunters in Virginia who had gotten their houses torched. The TV interviewed a hunter and his wife whose $117,500 Shenandoah Valley home had burned. She blamed the bears. He didn't blame the bears, but he was suing for compensation from the state since he had a valid hunting license. The state hunting commissioner came on and said that possession of a hunting license didn't prohibit ("enjoin," I think, was the word he used) *the hunted* from striking back. I thought that was a pretty liberal view for a state commissioner. Of course, he had a vested interest in not paying off. I'm not a hunter myself.

"Don't bother coming on Sunday," Mother told Wallace Jr. with a wink. "I've drove a million miles and I've got one hand on the gate." I'm used to her saying stuff like that, especially in the fall, but I was afraid it would upset the boy. In fact, he looked worried after we left and I asked him what was wrong.

"How could she have drove a million miles?" he asked. She had told him forty-eight miles a day for thirty-nine years, and he had worked it out on his calculator to be 336,960 miles.

"Have *driven*," I said. "And it's forty-eight in the morning and forty-eight in the afternoon. Plus there were the football trips. Plus, old folks exaggerate a little." Mother was the first woman school-bus driver in the state. She did it every day and raised a family, too. Dad just farmed.

I usually get off the interstate at Smiths Grove, but that night I drove north all the way to Horse Cave and doubled back so Wallace Jr. and I could see the bears' fires. There were not as many as you would think from the TV—one every six or seven miles, hidden back in a clump of trees or under a rocky ledge. Probably they look for water as well as wood. Wallace Jr. wanted to stop, but it's against the law to stop on the interstate and I was afraid the state police would run us off.

There was a card from Wallace in the mailbox. He and Elizabeth were doing fine and having a wonderful time. Not a word about Wallace Jr., but the boy didn't seem to mind. Like most kids his age, he doesn't really enjoy going places with his parents.

On Saturday afternoon the Home called my office (Burley Belt Drought & Hail) and left word that Mother was gone. I was on the road. I work Saturdays. It's the only day a lot of part-time farmers are home. My heart literally missed a beat when I called in and got the message, but only a beat. I had long been prepared. "It's a blessing," I said when I got the nurse on the phone.

"You don't understand," the nurse said. "Not *passed* away, gone. *Ran* away, gone. Your mother has escaped." Mother had gone through the door at the end of the corridor when no one was looking, wedging the door with her comb and taking a bedspread which belonged to the Home. What about her tobacco? I asked. It was gone. That was a sure sign she was planning to stay away. I was in Franklin, and it took me less than an hour to get to the Home on I-65. The nurse told me that Mother had been acting more and more confused lately. Of course they are going to say that. We looked around the grounds, which is only a half acre with no trees between the interstate and a soybean field. Then they had me leave a message at the sheriff's office. I would have to keep paying for her care until she was officially listed as Missing, which would be Monday.

It was dark by the time I got back to the house, and Wallace Jr. was fixing supper. This just involves opening a few cans, already selected and grouped together with a rubber band. I told him his grandmother had gone, and he nodded, saying, "She told us she would be." I called Florida and left a message. There was nothing more to be done. I sat down and tried to watch TV, but there was nothing on. Then, I looked out the back door, and saw the firelight twinkling through the trees across the northbound lane of I-65, and realized I just might know where to find her.

It was definitely getting colder, so I got my jacket. I told the boy to wait by the phone in case the sheriff called, but when I looked back, halfway across the field, there he was behind me. He didn't have a jacket. I let him catch up. He was carrying his .22 and I made him leave it leaning against our fence. It was harder climbing the government fence in the dark, at my age, than it had been in the daylight. I am sixty-one. The highway was busy with cars heading south and trucks heading north.

Crossing the shoulder, I got my pants cuffs wet on the long grass, already wet with dew. It is actually bluegrass.

The first few feet into the trees it was pitch-black and the boy grabbed my hand. Then it got lighter. At first I thought it was the moon, but it was the high beams shining like moonlight into the treetops, allowing Wallace Jr. and me to pick our way through the brush. We soon found the path and its familiar bear smell.

I was wary of approaching the bears at night. If we stayed on the path we might run into one in the dark, but if we went through the bushes we might be seen as intruders. I wondered if maybe we shouldn't have brought the gun.

We stayed on the path. The light seemed to drip down from the canopy of the woods like rain. The going was easy, especially if we didn't try to look at the path but let our feet find their own way.

Then through the trees I saw their fire.

The fire was mostly of sycamore and beech branches, the kind that puts out very little heat or light and lots of smoke. The bears hadn't learned the ins and outs of wood yet. They did okay at tending it, though. A large cinnamon-brown northern-looking bear was poking the fire with a stick, adding a branch now and then from a pile at his side. The others sat around in a loose circle on the logs. Most were smaller black or honey bears, one was a mother with cubs. Some were eating berries from a hubcap. Not eating, but just watching the fire, my mother sat among them with the bedspread from the Home around her shoulders.

If the bears noticed us, they didn't let on. Mother patted a spot right next to her on the log and I sat down. A bear moved over to let Wallace Jr. sit on her other side.

The bear smell is rank but not unpleasant, once you get used to it. It's not like a barn smell, but wilder. I leaned over to whisper something to Mother and she shook her head. *It would be rude to whisper around these creatures that don't possess the power of speech,* she let me know without speaking. Wallace Jr. was silent too. Mother shared the bedspread with us and we sat for what seemed hours, looking into the fire.

The big bear tended the fire, breaking up the dry branches by holding one end and stepping on them, like people do. He was good at keeping it going at the same level. Another bear poked the fire from time to time but the others left it alone. It looked like only a few of the bears knew how to use fire, and were carrying the others along. But isn't that how it is with everything? Every once in a while, a smaller bear walked into the circle of firelight with an armload of wood and dropped it onto the pile. Median wood has a silvery cast, like driftwood.

Wallace Jr. isn't fidgety like a lot of kids. I found it pleasant to sit and stare into the fire. I took a little piece of Mother's Red Man, though I don't generally chew. It was no different from visiting her at the Home, only more interesting, because of the bears. There were about eight or ten of them. Inside the fire itself, things weren't so dull, either: little dramas were being played out as fiery chambers were created and then destroyed in a crashing of sparks. My imagination ran wild. I looked around the circle at the bears and wondered what *they* saw. Some had their eyes closed. Though they were gathered together, their spirits still seemed solitary, as if each bear was sitting alone in front of its own fire.

The hubcap came around and we all took some newberries. I don't know about Mother, but I just pretended to eat mine. Wallace Jr. made a face and spit his out. When he went to sleep, I wrapped the bedspread around all three of us. It was getting colder and we were not provided, like the bears, with fur. I was ready to go home, but not Mother. She pointed up toward the canopy of trees, where a light was spreading, and then pointed to herself. Did she think it was angels approaching from on high? It was only the high beams of some southbound truck, but she seemed mighty pleased. Holding her hand, I felt it grow colder and colder in mine.

Wallace Jr. woke me up by tapping on my knee. It was past dawn, and his grandmother had died sitting on the log between us. The fire was banked up and the bears were gone and someone was crashing straight through the woods, ignoring the path. It was Wallace. Two state troopers were right behind him. He was wearing a white shirt, and I realized it was Sunday morning. Underneath his sadness on learning of Mother's death, he looked peeved.

The troopers were sniffing the air and nodding. The bear smell was still strong. Wallace and I wrapped Mother in the bedspread and started with her body back out to the highway. The troopers stayed behind and scattered the bears' fire ashes and flung their firewood away into the bushes. It seemed a petty thing to do. They were like bears themselves, each one solitary in his own uniform.

There was Wallace's Olds 98 on the median, with its radial tires looking squashed on the grass. In front of it there was a police car with a trooper standing beside it, and behind it a funeral home hearse, also an Olds 98.

"First report we've had of them bothering old folks," the trooper said to Wallace. "That's not hardly what happened at all," I said, but nobody asked me to explain.

They have their own procedures. Two men in suits got out of the hearse and opened the rear door. That to me was the point at which Mother departed this life. After we put her in, I put my arms around the boy. He was shivering even though it wasn't that cold. Sometimes death will do that, especially at dawn, with the police around and the grass wet, even when it comes as a friend.

We stood for a minute watching the cars and trucks pass. "It's a blessing," Wallace said. It's surprising how much traffic there is at 6:22 A.M.

That afternoon, I went back to the median and cut a little firewood to replace what the troopers had flung away. I could see the fire through the trees that night.

I went back two nights later, after the funeral. The fire was going and it was the same bunch of bears, as far as I could tell. I sat around with them a while but it seemed to make them nervous, so I went home. I had taken a handful of newberries from the hubcap, and on Sunday I went with the boy and arranged them on Mother's grave. I tried again, but it's no use, you can't eat them.

Unless you're a bear.

Questions

1. How would you describe the tone of this story?
2. How would you characterize the narrator? How does he feel about modern conveniences such as radial tires? What are his relationships with his mother and his nephew like?
3. What is the role of humor in this story?
4. How are the bears described? Why is the narrator's mother so fascinated by them, and what do you make of her actions at the end of the story?
5. What is the significance of the bears, and of their discovery of fire? What is the theme of the story?

Suggestions for Writing on Stories about Living with Nature

1. In Silko's "The Man to Send Rain Clouds" and Le Guin's "She Unnames Them," some characters have a deep connection to nature, and others don't. How would you describe the authors' attitudes toward the characters who are not close to nature? Are the characters who are closer to nature alike in how they relate to it? Or are there differences, and if so, what are they?
2. In Bisson's "Bears Discover Fire," the narrator seems to imply that bears have retained certain values or ways of being that most humans have lost. How does he describe the bears and their systems of action and belief? Why might some of the characters in the story prefer the company of bears to the company of people?
3. Both "The Man to Send Rain Clouds" and "Bears Discover Fire" involve a character's death. How is the process of death, and the ritual around death, similar in the two stories? How is it different?
4. In "The Man to Send Rain Clouds" a younger character is influenced by an older character's beliefs about, and relationships with, nature and land. What defining people have you known or experiences have you had that shaped your own feelings toward nature? Write an essay describing a person or an event that influenced your interaction with the natural world.

ANIMALS AS ALLEGORY: THREE FABLES

Aesop   *The Grasshopper and the Ant*

Bidpai   *The Camel and His Friends*

Chuang Tzu   *Independence*

Fables—as distinct from the more complex form of short stories—are brief, sometimes funny narratives that illustrate a moral. Often the characters in fables are animals that represent a particular human quality or trait. Such stories are sketched directly and quickly, with the moral either stated explicitly or strongly implied. The following classic fables by Aesop, Bidpai, and Chuang Tzu end with clear lessons about preparation and industry, trust and nobility, and personal freedom. Why do fable writers use animals as characters? Perhaps because it's easier for readers to see the folly of certain actions when they are committed by animals rather than people. Or perhaps it's just the opposite—that despite our human intelligence and complexities, we know that people, when pared down to our essential natures, are not so different from other creatures as we'd like to believe. Whether we see ourselves as totally separate from animals or closely related to them, one thing is clear: these writers effectively use their animal characters' fates and foibles to help us think about our own.

Aesop

Very little is known with certainty about the man called Aesop, but several accounts and many traditions survive from antiquity. According to the Greek historian Herodotus, Aesop was a slave on the island of Samos. He gained great fame from his fables, but he somehow met his death at the hands of the people of Delphi. According to one tradition, Aesop was an ugly and misshapen man who charmed and amused people with his stories. No one knows if Aesop himself wrote down any of his fables, but they circulated widely in ancient Greece and were praised by Plato, Aristotle, and many other authors. His short and witty tales with their incisive morals have remained constantly popular and influenced innumerable writers.

The Grasshopper and the Ant   6th century B.C.

Retold by Grace Ortiz

    One warm summer day a Grasshopper was happily jumping about in a field, chirping and singing. He noticed an Ant passing by who, with great difficulty, was carrying a kernel of wheat to his nest.

    "Why don't you put down that load and come play with me?" the Grasshopper said. "We can dance and sing."

    "I am busy laying up food for winter," said the Ant. "I recommend that you do the same."

    "Why worry about winter?" said the Grasshopper. "I've got more food than I can eat right now."

    The Ant picked up his load and lumbered toward his nest, and the grasshopper went on chirping cheerfully.

The grasshopper and the ant.

When winter came the Grasshopper could find no food, and he was dying of hunger. He came to the ant nest and saw that it was full of grain. When he begged for a morsel, the Ant refused. "If you spent your summer singing," he replied, "you must spend the winter dancing."

Moral: *One must prepare for the future.*

Questions

1. How would you characterize the Grasshopper and the Ant? Do you know people like them?
2. Why would Aesop make his point with a story that involves animals rather than people? What effect do animals have here that humans would not have?
3. It's clear that the Grasshopper should have made different choices. What do you think of the Ant's choices, particularly its decision not to help the Grasshopper in winter?

Bidpai

The Panchatantra (Pañca-tantra), a collection of beast fables from India, is attributed to its narrator, a sage named Bidpai, who is a legendary figure about whom almost nothing is known for certain. The Panchatantra, which means the Five Chapters in Sanskrit, is based on earlier oral folklore. The collection was composed sometime between 100 B.C. and 500 A.D. in a Sanskrit original now lost, and is primarily known through an Arabic version from the eighth century and a twelfth-century Hebrew translation, which is the source of most Western versions of the tales. Other translations spread the fables as far as central Europe, Asia, and Indonesia.

Like many collections of fables, The Panchatantra is a frame tale, with an introduction containing verse and aphorisms spoken by an eighty-year-old Brahmin teacher named Vishnusharman, who tells the stories over a period of six months for the edification of three foolish princes named Rich-Power, Fierce-Power, and Endless-Power. The stories are didactic, teaching *niti, the wise conduct of life,* and *artha, practical wisdom that stresses cleverness and self-reliance above more altruistic virtues.*

The Camel and His Friends

c. 4th century

Retold in English by Arundhati Khanwalkar

Once a merchant was leading a caravan of heavily-laden camels through a jungle when one of them, overcome by fatigue, collapsed. The merchant decided to leave the camel in the jungle and go on his way. Later, when the camel recovered his strength, he realized that he was alone in a strange jungle. Fortunately there was plenty of grass, and he survived.

One day the king of the jungle, a lion, arrived along with his three friends—a leopard, a fox, and a crow. The king lion wondered what the camel was doing in the jungle! He came near the camel and asked how he, a creature of the desert, had ended up in the hostile jungle. The camel tearfully explained what happened. The lion took pity on him and said, "You have nothing to fear now. Henceforth, you are under my protection and can stay with us." The camel began to live happily in the jungle.

Then one day the lion was wounded in a fight with an elephant. He retired to his cave and stayed there for several days. His friends came to offer their sympathy. They tried to catch prey for the hungry lion but failed. The camel had no problem as he lived on grass while the others were starving.

The fox came up with a plan. He secretly went to the lion and suggested that the camel be sacrificed for the good of the others. The lion got furious, "I can never kill an animal who is under my protection."

The Lion, the King of the Animals **from "The Fables of Bidpai," c.1480 (vellum). Musée Condé, Chantilly, France/The Bridgeman Art Library.**

The fox humbly said, "But Lord, you have provided us food all the time. If any one of us voluntarily offered himself to save your life, I hope you won't mind!" The hungry lion did not object to that and agreed to take the offer.

The fox went back to his companions and said, "Friends, our king is dying of starvation. Let us go and beg him to eat one of us. It is the least we can do for such a noble soul."

So they went to the king and the crow offered his life. The fox interrupted, and said, "You are a small creature, the master's hunger will hardly be appeased by eating you. May I humbly offer my life to satisfy my master's hunger."

The leopard stepped forward and said, "You are no bigger than the crow, it is me whom our master should eat."

The foolish camel thought, "Everyone has offered to lay down their lives for the king, but he has not hurt any one. It is now my turn to offer myself." So he stepped forward and said, "Stand aside friend leopard, the king and you have close family ties. It is me whom the master must eat."

An ominous silence greeted the camel's offer. Then the king gladly said, "I accept your offer, O noble camel." And in no time he was killed by the three rogues, the false friends.

Moral: Be careful in choosing your friends.

Questions

1. How would you characterize each animal? Do any of the characters change in the course of the story?
2. Is any character truly noble in this story? Is anyone falsely noble? What is the difference?
3. Do you think the moral stated at the end captures the complexity of what the story has just described? Why or why not?

Chuang Tzu

Zhuang Zi [Chuang Tzu] dreaming of a butterfly, by Ike Taiga (1723–1776).

Chuang Chou, usually known as Chuang Tzu (c. 390–365 B.C.), was one of the great philosophers of the Chou period in China. He was born in the Sung feudal state and received an excellent education. Unlike most educated men, however, Chuang Tzu did not seek public office or political power. Influenced by Taoist philosophy, he believed that individuals should transcend their desire for success and wealth, as well as their fear of failure and poverty. True freedom, he maintained, came from escaping the distractions of worldly affairs. Chuang Tzu's writings have been particularly praised for their combination of humor and wisdom. His parables and stories are classics of Chinese literature.

Independence

Chou Dynasty (4th century B.C.)

Translated by Herbert Giles

Chuang Tzu was one day fishing, when the Prince of Ch'u sent two high officials to interview him, saying that his Highness would be glad of Chuang Tzu's assistance in the administration of his government. The latter quietly fished on, and without looking round, replied, "I have heard that in the State of Ch'u there is a sacred tortoise, which has been dead three thousand years, and which the prince keeps packed up in a box on the altar in his ancestral shrine. Now do you think that tortoise would rather be dead and have its remains thus honored, or be alive and wagging its tail in the mud?" The two officials answered that no doubt it would rather be alive and wagging its tail in the mud; whereupon Chuang Tzu cried out "Begone! I too elect to remain wagging my tail in the mud."

Questions

1. Why doesn't Chuang Tzu answer the officials' request directly and immediately? Why does he change the subject and talk about the sacred tortoise? Does it serve any purpose that he makes the officials answer a question to which he knows the answer?
2. What does this story tell us about the protagonist Chuang Tzu's personality?
3. Based on Chuang Tzu's reply, what do you think he values most in life? Why? Do you agree with his way of thinking?

Suggestions for Writing on Animals as Allegory

1. Choose a character in Aesop's "The Grasshopper and the Ant" or Bidpai's "The Camel and His Friends" and write a paper defending its actions.
2. Write an essay about a real-life situation that proves or personifies the moral of one of the fables in this section. The real-life situation can be drawn from your own life or from events in the larger world. Make explicit connections between elements of the real-life story and elements of the fable.
3. Write a brief animal fable modeled on "The Grasshopper and the Ant" or "The Camel and His Friends." Begin with a familiar proverb—"A penny saved is a penny earned" or "Too many cooks spoil the broth"—and invent a story to make the moral convincing.

POETRY

NATURE

William Blake	*To see a world in a grain of sand*
Gerard Manley Hopkins	*God's Grandeur*
William Butler Yeats	*The Lake Isle of Innisfree*
H.D.	*Storm*
Elizabeth Bishop	*The Fish*
Dana Gioia	*California Hills in August*
Benjamin Alire Sáenz	*To the Desert*

Witnessing the extraordinary beauty of nature can be a humbling and moving experience. Countless people have been drawn to the majesty of the Grand Canyon and Niagara Falls, and many visitors describe having feelings of awe—sometimes even breaking into tears—when they first enter Yosemite Valley. But experiencing the superhuman scale and power of nature isn't just about being impressed; such moments can be calming and restorative. Coming upon an astonishing landscape or sublime vista, we may, paradoxically, become more aware of ourselves and our own humanity. Whether we're looking at a mountain, a coastline, a waterfall, or a desert, contemplating a landscape allows us to pause and experience where and who we are. When we're in the presence of something so vast, so old, so primal, our own lives and problems seem insignificant. We are part of the natural order of things, but only an infinitesimal part. The world itself goes on despite our deadlines and pressures, our squabbles and worries. We even take an ironic comfort in knowing that the world endures while our own tiny troubles will eventually pass. The poems in this section all capture this sense of wonder, humility, and connection to the natural world. Although the landscapes that are celebrated here vary, the poets' responses are similar. They feel awe, appreciation, and a deep understanding of their own place in the order of things.

William Blake

A biography of William Blake (1757–1827) appears on page 796, along with his poem "London." Blake's early poems—especially those that make up Songs of Innocence *(1789) and* Songs of Experience *(1794)—tend, for the most part, to be easy to understand and to enjoy. "To see a world in a grain of sand" is taken from a notebook written about 1800–1803, where it appears as a sort of prologue to "Auguries of Innocence," a grouping of often obscure, highly personal "proverb-couplets."*

To see a world in a grain of sand (about 1803)

To see a world in a grain of sand
And a heaven in a wild flower,
Hold infinity in the palm of your hand
And eternity in an hour.

Questions

1. What figure of speech is used in each of the poem's four lines?
2. In what ways does the world physically resemble a grain of sand? What other meanings might be found in the opening line?

Gerard Manley Hopkins

Gerard Manley Hopkins (1844–1889) was born in Essex, England, the eldest son of middle-class Anglican parents. At twenty, a student at Oxford, he converted to Roman Catholicism—against the wishes of his family— and was received into that church by Cardinal Newman. All of Hopkins's mature poems were rejected by editors during his lifetime. He died of typhoid in 1889 at the age of forty-four, a seemingly forgotten man. Nearly thirty years after Hopkins's death, his friend Robert Bridges finally published his Poems (1918), having thought the innovative and idiosyncratic poems too demanding for earlier readers. Hopkins was soon recognized as one of the great lyric poets in English literature.

Gerard Manley Hopkins

God's Grandeur (1877)

The world is charged with the grandeur of God.
    It will flame out, like shining from shook foil;
    It gathers to a greatness, like the ooze of oil
Crushed. Why do men then now not reck his rod?
Generations have trod, have trod, have trod;   5
    And all is seared with trade; bleared, smeared with toil;
    And wears man's smudge and shares man's smell: the soil
Is bare now, nor can foot feel, being shod.

And for all this, nature is never spent;
    There lives the dearest freshness deep down things;   10
And though the last lights off the black West went
    Oh, morning, at the brown brink eastward, springs—
Because the Holy Ghost over the bent
    World broods with warm breast and with ah! bright wings.

GOD'S GRANDEUR 1 *charged:* as though with electricity. 3–4 *It gathers . . . Crushed:* The grandeur of God will rise and be manifest, as oil rises and collects from crushed olives or grain. 4 *reck his rod:* heed His law. 10 *deep down things:* Tightly packing the poem, Hopkins omits the preposition *in* or *within* before *things.*   11 *last lights . . . went:* When in 1534 Henry VIII broke ties with the Roman Catholic Church and created the Church of England.

Questions

1. In a letter Hopkins explained "shook foil" (line 2): "I mean foil in its sense of leaf or tinsel. . . . Shaken goldfoil gives off broad glares like sheet lightning and also, and this is true of nothing else, owing to its zigzag dints and creasings and network of small many cornered facets, a sort of fork lightning too."
2. What instances of internal rime does the poem contain? How would you describe their effects?
3. According to lines 4–8, what is humanity's present relationship to the natural world?
4. Why do you suppose Hopkins, in the last two lines, says "over the bent / World" instead of (as we might expect) *bent over the world*? How can the world be bent? Can you make any sense out of this wording?

William Butler Yeats

A biography of William Butler Yeats (1865–1939) appears on page 510, along with his poem "When You Are Old." As a young man Yeats often wrote poems of a dreamy and escapist nature, drawing on themes from Irish legend and folklore. Later, an unreciprocated romantic fixation on the Irish patriot Maud Gonne and an involvement in the day-to-day business of operating a series of Dublin theaters led to greater plainspokenness and depth of feeling in his work. Later still, inspired by his study of history and a lifelong interest in the occult, he engaged political and social issues, sometimes by way of an involved symbolic system of his own devising. In the last decade of his life, he wrote poems of a sometimes startling simplicity and directness. In every phase of his career he created masterpieces, one of them the early—and perennially popular—"The Lake Isle of Innisfree."

The Lake Isle of Innisfree   1892

I will arise and go now, and go to Innisfree,
And a small cabin build there, of clay and wattles made:
Nine bean-rows will I have there, a hive for the honey-bee,
And live alone in the bee-loud glade.

And I shall have some peace there, for peace comes dropping slow,   5
Dropping from the veils of the morning to where the cricket sings;
There midnight's all a glimmer, and noon a purple glow,
And evening full of the linnet's wings.

I will arise and go now, for always night and day
I hear lake water lapping with low sounds by the shore;   10
While I stand on the roadway, or on the pavements gray,
I hear it in the deep heart's core.

Questions

1. Where is the poem's speaker presently living? What details tell you so?
2. How literally should line 10 be taken? Explain.
3. How realistic does the poem seem to you, in terms of both the description of the imagined life on Innisfree and the likelihood of the speaker's fulfilling his resolution to "arise and go" there?

H.D. (Hilda Doolittle)

Hilda Doolittle (1886–1961) was born in Bethlehem, Pennsylvania. In 1905, while attending Bryn Mawr College, she met fellow fledging poets Marianne Moore, William Carlos Williams, and Ezra Pound, to whom she became briefly engaged. (Pound would later print her first poems in Poetry magazine, using her initials only, a signature that she used thereafter.) She went to London in 1911 and spent the remaining fifty years of her life living in England and on the European continent. Early in her career she was closely involved with the Imagist movement, which emphasized brevity and chiseled description; "Storm," a representative poem of this period, appeared in Sea Garden (1916), her first collection.

Storm   1916

You crash over the trees,
you crack the live branch—
the branch is white,
the green crushed,
each leaf is rent like split wood.   5

You burden the trees
with black drops,
you swirl and crash—
you have broken off a weighted leaf
in the wind,   10
it is hurled out,
whirls up and sinks,
a green stone.

Questions

1. What effect is achieved by the speaker's addressing the storm directly?
2. It could be maintained that the poem communicates principally through its verbs. Discuss the basis for this claim.

Elizabeth Bishop

Because she suffered from asthma, Elizabeth Bishop (1911–1979) received scant elementary education, but she read widely and deeply at home. At sixteen, she entered Walnut Hill, a boarding school, and later graduated from Vassar College in Poughkeepsie, New York. Fond of travel and flower-filled climates, Bishop lived for nine years in Key West, Florida, then for fifteen years in Brazil, dividing her time between the mountains and Rio de Janeiro. Her sharp-eyed poems, full of vivid images and apt metaphors, have influenced the work of other poets, among them her friends Randall Jarrell and Robert Lowell. "The Fish," an outstanding example of her art, is her most popular and most frequently reprinted poem.

The Fish   1946

I caught a tremendous fish
and held him beside the boat
half out of water, with my hook
fast in a corner of his mouth.
He didn't fight.   5
He hadn't fought at all.
He hung a grunting weight,
battered and venerable
and homely. Here and there
his brown skin hung in strips   10
like ancient wallpaper,
and its pattern of darker brown
was like wallpaper:
shapes like full-blown roses
stained and lost through age.   15
He was speckled with barnacles,
fine rosettes of lime,
and infested
with tiny white sea-lice,
and underneath two or three   20
rags of green weed hung down.
While his gills were breathing in
the terrible oxygen
—the frightening gills,
fresh and crisp with blood,   25
that can cut so badly—
I thought of the coarse white flesh
packed in like feathers,
the big bones and the little bones,
the dramatic reds and blacks   30
of his shiny entrails,
and the pink swim-bladder
like a big peony.
I looked into his eyes
which were far larger than mine   35
but shallower, and yellowed,
the irises backed and packed
with tarnished tinfoil
seen through the lenses
of old scratched isinglass.   40
They shifted a little, but not
to return my stare.
—It was more like the tipping
of an object toward the light.
I admired his sullen face,   45

the mechanism of his jaw,
and then I saw
that from his lower lip
—if you could call it a lip—
grim, wet, and weaponlike, 50
hung five old pieces of fish-line,
or four and a wire leader
with the swivel still attached,
with all their five big hooks
grown firmly in his mouth. 55
A green line, frayed at the end
where he broke it, two heavier lines,
and a fine black thread
still crimped from the strain and snap
when it broke and he got away. 60
Like medals with their ribbons
frayed and wavering,
a five-haired beard of wisdom
trailing from his aching jaw.
I stared and stared 65
and victory filled up
the little rented boat,
from the pool of bilge
where oil had spread a rainbow
around the rusted engine 70
to the bailer rusted orange,
the sun-cracked thwarts,
the oarlocks on their strings,
the gunnels—until everything
was rainbow, rainbow, rainbow! 75
And I let the fish go.

Questions

1. What is the speaker's attitude toward the fish? Comment in particular on lines 61–64.
2. What do the images of the rainbow of oil (line 69), the orange bailer (bailing bucket, line 71), and the sun-cracked thwarts (line 72) convey? Does the poet expect us to feel mournful because the boat is in such sorry condition?
3. What is meant by "rainbow, rainbow, rainbow" (line 75)?
4. Why does the speaker let the fish go?

Dana Gioia

Born in Hawthorne, California, in 1950, Dana Gioia earned a B.A. from Stanford University in 1973, an M.A. from Harvard in 1975, and an M.B.A. from Stanford Business School in 1977. For fifteen years he was an executive with General Foods Corporation, before quitting to become a full-time writer, and from 2003 to 2009 he was Chairman of the National Endowment for the Arts. He is the author of four collections of poetry: Daily

Horoscope (1986), The Gods of Winter (1991), Interrogations at Noon (2001, winner of the American Book Award), and Pity the Beautiful (2012), as well as three collections of essays, most notably Can Poetry Matter? (1991). In a note accompanying this poem, Gioia has written: "'California Hills in August' was conceived as a defense of the special beauty of the dry landscape of California and the American Southwest."

California Hills in August 1986

I can imagine someone who found
these fields unbearable, who climbed
the hillside in the heat, cursing the dust,
cracking the brittle weeds underfoot,
wishing a few more trees for shade.   5

An Easterner especially, who would scorn
the meagerness of summer, the dry
twisted shapes of black elm,
scrub oak, and chaparral, a landscape
August has already drained of green.   10

One who would hurry over the clinging
thistle, foxtail, golden poppy,
knowing everything was just a weed,
unable to conceive that these trees
and sparse brown bushes were alive.   15

And hate the bright stillness of the noon
without wind, without motion,
the only other living thing
a hawk, hungry for prey, suspended
in the blinding, sunlit blue.   20

And yet how gentle it seems to someone
raised in a landscape short of rain—
the skyline of a hill broken by no more
trees than one can count, the grass,
the empty sky, the wish for water.   25

Questions

1. From what—or whose—perspective is the landscape viewed in lines 1–20? Does the speaker share that perspective?
2. Describe each of the two imaginary people in the poem. How do their views of the landscape differ?
3. What are the chief features of this landscape, according to the first four stanzas?
4. How is the last stanza related to what has come before?

Benjamin Alire Sáenz

Benjamin Alire Sáenz (b. 1954) was born in Old Picacho, New Mexico, and went to work at an early age to help support his family. After completing formal studies at the University of Louvain in Belgium, he was ordained a Catholic priest but left the clergy after three years. In 1985 he returned to college to study English and creative writing, which he presently teaches at the University of Texas at El Paso. His first book of poems, Calendar of Dust (1991), won the American Book Award. Four other collections have followed, the most recent of which is The Book of What Remains (2010). Sáenz has also published four novels, three novels for young adults, and several children's books. "To the Desert" is representative of his work in its Southwestern setting, its spiritual concerns, and its emphasis on the harsh beauty of nature.

To the Desert   1995

I came to you one rainless August night.
You taught me how to live without the rain.
You are thirst and thirst is all I know.
You are sand, wind, sun, and burning sky,
The hottest blue. You blow a breeze and brand   5
Your breath into my mouth. You reach—then bend
Your force, to break, blow, burn, and make me new.
You wrap your name tight around my ribs
And keep me warm. I was born for you.
Above, below, by you, by you surrounded.   10
I wake to you at dawn. Never break your
Knot. Reach, rise, blow, *Sálvame, mi dios,*
Trágame, mi tierra. Salva, traga, Break me,
I am bread. I will be the water for your thirst.

To the Desert. 6–7 bend . . . make me new: quoted from John Donne's "Batter my heart." 12–13 *Sálvame, mi dios . . . traga:* Spanish for "Save me, my god, / Take me, my land. Save me, take me." (*Trágame* literally means "swallow me.")

Questions

1. How does the speaker feel about the land being described? What words in the poem suggest or convey those feelings?
2. What effect does the speaker's sudden switch into Spanish create? What is the tone of the Spanish?
3. Of what kind of language do the last few lines of the poem remind you?

Suggestions for Writing on *Poems about Nature*

1. In William Blake's tiny poem "To see a world in a grain of sand," the speaker asserts that vast vistas can be experienced by studying small objects. Do you agree with this paradoxical insight? State your case pro or con.
2. Consider "The Lake Isle of Innisfree" in terms of its idealization of a particular landscape. What qualities are associated with that landscape? How are those qualities contrasted with the ones associated with humanity?
3. In both "The Fish" and "To the Desert," the speaker forms a bond with the natural element mentioned in the title. Discuss the two poems in this regard. What characteristics do the speakers associate with the fish and with the desert? On what basis, and in what spirit, does each speaker connect with nature?
4. In H.D.'s "Storm" the poet describes an external event in nature. Discuss how her description suggests certain emotional events as well.
5. "California Hills in August" draws a contrast of sorts between the natural world and people's responses to that world. Discuss the poem along these lines. Which opposing view is ultimately affirmed?
6. "To the Desert" and "California Hills in August" describe similarly harsh landscapes. How does the speaker in each poem ultimately respond to the terrain he depicts, and why? Be as specific as possible in your references to the poems.
7. In "God's Grandeur" Gerard Manley Hopkins asserts that all aspects of nature suggest a supernatural reality behind or beyond it. Write a defense or critique of Hopkins's idea. Does his poem illuminate our sense of nature or needlessly complicate it?

ANIMALS: SYMBOLIC AND REAL

William Blake	*The Tyger*
Lewis Carroll	*Jabberwocky*
Thomas Hardy	*The Darkling Thrush*
Wallace Stevens	*Thirteen Ways of Looking at a Blackbird*
Robinson Jeffers	*Rock and Hawk*
Phillis Levin	*Brief Bio*
Kay Ryan	*Turtle*

Judging from the millions who visit zoos, aquariums, and wildlife preserves, and the popularity of such television programs as *Meerkat Manor*, *River Monsters*, and *Wild Kingdom*, people find animals fascinating. Humans are rightly curious about the many creatures with whom we share the planet. For thousands of years people have domesticated animals, most notably cats and dogs. Why are humans so drawn to the animal world? Is it because, as *Animal Planet* claims in its tagline, animals are "Surprisingly Human"? Or is it precisely because they're so different from us? There is nothing unusual in owning a dog, a cat, a fish, or a bird; it is our most direct way of having a bit of wildlife right in our households. Observing other animals—in the wild, in zoos, even in our neighborhoods—perhaps gives us access to a beautiful, yet mysterious part of the world we might otherwise lose touch with. Historically, poets have turned to animals to ask questions about the nature of life and of humankind. Animals might be seen as symbols of creativity or joy, of nature's indifference to the plight of humans, of modesty and steadfastness, of destruction and danger.

The poems in this section all invoke animals to explore questions about our own existence. In some such as Robinson Jeffers's "Rock and Hawk," animals are celebrated, even envied. In others, such as Wallace Stevens's "Thirteen Ways of Looking at a Blackbird," the inscrutability of the animal suggests haunting enigmas about human life. But whether the animals in these poems are admired, pitied, or feared, they are all intriguing and mysterious. They live both within the circle of human experience and comfortably outside it. Even as the writers use them for their own purposes, they remain steadfastly themselves.

William Blake

A biography of William Blake (1757–1827) appears on page 796, along with his poem "London." Blake was an unusual and astonishing genius. In addition to being a striking poet, he was a visionary and a remarkable and original graphic artist whose only formal training came from a few months at the Royal Academy. He published his own poems, engraving them in a careful script embellished with hand-colored illustrations and decorations. His most popular pieces are to be found in Songs of Innocence *(1789) and* Songs of Experience *(1794), brief lyrics written from a child's point of view. Many of them are clear and straightforward, but others, such as "The Tyger," raise troubling and often unresolved issues beneath their deceptively simple surfaces.*

Detail of William Blake's *The Tyger*.

The Tyger 1794

Tyger! Tyger! burning bright
In the forests of the night,
What immortal hand or eye
Could frame thy fearful symmetry?

In what distant deeps or skies 5
Burnt the fire of thine eyes?
On what wings dare he aspire?
What the hand dare seize the fire?

And what shoulder, and what art,
Could twist the sinews of thy heart? 10
And when thy heart began to beat,
What dread hand? and what dread feet?

What the hammer? what the chain?
In what furnace was thy brain?
What the anvil? what dread grasp 15
Dare its deadly terrors clasp?

When the stars threw down their spears,
And watered heaven with their tears,
Did he smile his work to see?
Did he who made the Lamb make thee? 20

Tyger! Tyger! burning bright
In the forests of the night,
What immortal hand or eye
Dare frame thy fearful symmetry?

Questions

1. What seems to be the speaker's attitude toward the tyger? Which details in the poem lead you to that conclusion?
2. Compare the first stanza to the last. What is the significance of the change in wording?

Lewis Carroll (Charles Lutwidge Dodgson)

The son of an Anglican clergyman in Cheshire, England, Charles Lutwidge Dodgson (1832–1898) was taught at home until he was twelve. After attending Rugby School, in 1854 he earned an undergraduate degree from Christ Church College of Oxford University, where he then became a lecturer in mathematics. A very accomplished amateur photographer, he also published a number of works on mathematics under his own name. But it is as Lewis Carroll that his fame endures, the beloved author of Alice's Adventures in Wonderland *(1865) and its sequel,* Through the Looking Glass *(1871). "Jabberwocky," a nonsense classic that added at least one word to the English language, first appeared in* Through the Looking Glass.

Jabberwock illustration by John Tenniel, 1872.

Jabberwocky 1871

'Twas brillig, and the slithy toves
   Did gyre and gimble in the wabe:
All mimsy were the borogoves,
   And the mome raths outgrabe.

"Beware the Jabberwock, my son!
   The jaws that bite, the claws that catch!
Beware the Jubjub bird, and shun
   The frumious Bandersnatch!"

He took his vorpal sword in hand:
   Long time the manxome foe he sought—
So rested he by the Tumtum tree
   And stood awhile in thought.

And, as in uffish thought he stood,
　　The Jabberwock, with eyes of flame,
Came whiffling through the tulgey wood,　　　　　　　　　　　　　　　　15
　　And burbled as it came!

One, two! One, two! And through and through
　　The vorpal blade went snicker-snack!
He left it dead, and with its head
　　He went galumphing back.　　　　　　　　　　　　　　　　　　　　　　20

"And hast thou slain the Jabberwock?
　　Come to my arms, my beamish boy!
O frabjous day! Callooh, Callay!"
　　He chortled in his joy.

'Twas brillig, and the slithy toves　　　　　　　　　　　　　　　　　　25
　　Did gyre and gimble in the wabe:
All mimsy were the borogoves,
　　And the mome raths outgrabe.

JABBERWOCKY. Fussy about pronunciation, Carroll in his preface to *The Hunting of the Snark* declares: "The first 'o' in 'borogoves' is pronounced like the 'o' in 'borrow.' I have heard people try to give it the sound of the 'o' in 'worry.' Such is Human Perversity." *Toves*, he adds, rimes with *groves*.

Questions

1. Does the Jabberwock remind you of any familiar (real or mythical) creature?
2. Even if you can't precisely define them, some of the words in the poem make a kind of sense through the way they sound and the context in which they appear. Along these lines, what meanings do you derive from the terms "frumious," "uffish," "galumphing," "beamish," and "frabjous"?

Thomas Hardy

Thomas Hardy (1840–1928) trained as an architect, and worked as a young man in the restoration of churches. But his main ambition was to be a writer, and in 1871 he published Desperate Remedies, *the first of his fourteen novels, a body of work that includes such tragic masterpieces as* The Mayor of Casterbridge *(1886)*, Tess of the d'Urbervilles *(1891), and* Jude the Obscure *(1896). In the last thirty years of his life Hardy wrote no more novels, devoting himself to what he described as his "first love"—poetry. Many modern poets have credited Hardy with teaching them a good deal (probably about irony and the use of spoken language), among them W. H. Auden, Philip Larkin, and Dylan Thomas. In both fiction and poetry, Hardy's view of the universe is somber: God appears to have forgotten us and happiness usually arrives too late. Despite seeming indications to the contrary, a careful reading of "The Darkling Thrush" will show that its thematic emphasis is not inconsistent with this worldview.*

The Darkling Thrush　　　　　　　　　　　　　　　　　　　　　　1900

I leant upon a coppice gate
　　When Frost was specter-gray,
And Winter's dregs made desolate
　　The weakening eye of day.

The tangled bine-stems scored the sky
   Like strings of broken lyres,
And all mankind that haunted nigh
   Had sought their household fires.

The land's sharp features seemed to be
   The Century's corpse outleant,
His crypt the cloudy canopy,
   The wind his death-lament.
The ancient pulse of germ and birth
   Was shrunken hard and dry,
And every spirit upon earth
   Seemed fervorless as I.

At once a voice arose among
   The bleak twigs overhead
In a full-hearted evensong
   Of joy illimited;
An aged thrush, frail, gaunt, and small,
   In blast-beruffled plume,
Had chosen thus to fling his soul
   Upon the growing gloom.

So little cause for carolings
   Of such ecstatic sound
Was written on terrestrial things
   Afar or nigh around,
That I could think there trembled through
   His happy good-night air
Some blessed Hope, whereof he knew
   And I was unaware.

THE DARKLING THRUSH. Hardy set this poem on December 31, 1900, the last day of the nineteenth century.

Questions

1. What is the setting of the poem, in terms of time of day, time of year, etc.?
2. What mood is created in the first two stanzas? Which words in those stanzas serve to communicate that mood?
3. How does the thrush come into the poem? How does the thrush's song relate to the surrounding landscape?
4. Paraphrase the last stanza as precisely as possible.

Wallace Stevens

Wallace Stevens (1879–1955) was born in Reading, Pennsylvania, the son of a lawyer and a former schoolteacher. After graduating from Harvard he became a lawyer himself, and in 1916 joined the legal staff of the Hartford Accident and Indemnity Company; he became a vice president of the firm in 1936. Once asked how he was able to combine poetry and insurance, he replied that the two occupations had an element in common: "calculated risk."

He did not publish a book until *Harmonium* in 1923, when he was forty-four. He was extraordinarily prolific in the last two decades of his life; his *Collected Poems* (1954), published on his seventy-fifth birthday, won several important awards and belated recognition for Stevens as a major American poet. "Thirteen Ways of Looking at a Blackbird," like much of his finest work, is fanciful and teasingly indirect, continuing to haunt the reader's mind long after it has been read.

Thirteen Ways of Looking at a Blackbird   1923

I

Among twenty snowy mountains,
The only moving thing
Was the eye of the blackbird.

II

I was of three minds,
Like a tree   5
In which there are three blackbirds.

III

The blackbird whirled in the autumn winds.
It was a small part of the pantomime.

IV

A man and a woman
Are one.   10
A man and a woman and a blackbird
Are one.

V

I do not know which to prefer,
The beauty of inflections
Or the beauty of innuendoes,   15
The blackbird whistling
Or just after.

VI

Icicles filled the long window
With barbaric glass.
The shadow of the blackbird   20
Crossed it, to and fro.
The mood
Traced in the shadow
An indecipherable cause.

VII

O thin men of Haddam,
Why do you imagine golden birds?
Do you not see how the blackbird
Walks around the feet
Of the women about you?

VIII

I know noble accents
And lucid, inescapable rhythms;
But I know, too,
That the blackbird is involved
In what I know.

IX

When the blackbird flew out of sight,
It marked the edge
Of one of many circles.

X

At the sight of blackbirds
Flying in a green light,
Even the bawds of euphony
Would cry out sharply.

XI

He rode over Connecticut
In a glass coach.
Once, a fear pierced him,
In that he mistook
The shadow of his equipage
For blackbirds.

XII

The river is moving.
The blackbird must be flying.

XIII

It was evening all afternoon.
It was snowing
And it was going to snow.
The blackbird sat
In the cedar-limbs.

THIRTEEN WAYS OF LOOKING AT A BLACKBIRD. 25 *Haddam*: This biblical-sounding name is that of a town in Connecticut.

Questions

1. What is the speaker's attitude toward the men of Haddam? What attitude toward this world does he suggest they lack? What is implied by calling them "thin" (line 25)?
2. What do the landscapes of winter contribute to the poem's effectiveness? If Stevens had chosen images of summer lawns, what would have been lost?
3. In which sections of the poem does Stevens suggest that a unity exists between human being and blackbird, between blackbird and the entire natural world? Can we say that Stevens "philosophizes"? What role does imagery play in Stevens's statement of his ideas?
4. What qualities of the blackbirds might be suggested by the description in section X?

Robinson Jeffers

No American poet was closer to nature than Robinson Jeffers (1887–1962), who lived for many years in a stone house he himself had built—now a national historic monument—on the edge of the Pacific Ocean. His poetry reflects the presence of nature in his daily life. Jeffers was the first major American poet to espouse environmental concerns. His philosophy of "Inhumanism" refused to put humanity above the rest of nature; he demanded that we see ourselves as part of the vast interdependent reality of nature (a message that has made his poetry esteemed by environmentalists). He defined his philosophy in "The Answer": "the greatest beauty is / Organic wholeness, the wholeness of life and things, the divine beauty of the universe. Love that, not man / Apart from that." "Rock and Hawk" is a succinct and memorable embodiment of these views.

Rock and Hawk   1935

Here is a symbol in which
Many high tragic thoughts
Watch their own eyes.

This gray rock, standing tall
On the headland, where the sea-wind   5
Lets no tree grow,

Earthquake-proved, and signatured
By ages of storms: on its peak
A falcon has perched.

I think, here is your emblem   10
To hang in the future sky;
Not the cross, not the hive,

But this; bright power, dark peace;
Fierce consciousness joined with final
Disinterestedness;   15

Life with calm death; the falcon's
Realist eyes and act
Married to the massive

Mysticism of stone,
Which failure cannot cast down   20
Nor success make proud.

Questions

1. What characteristics does the poem associate with the rock? With the hawk?
2. What is represented by the cross in line 12? By the hive?
3. At what or whom does the speaker direct the poem's last two lines?

Phillis Levin

Born in 1954 and raised in Paterson, New Jersey, Phillis Levin earned a bachelor's degree from Sarah Lawrence College in 1976 and a master's degree from Johns Hopkins University in 1977. She has published four volumes of poetry, Temples and Fields (1988), The Afterimage (1995), Mercury (2001), and May Day (2008), and is the editor of The Penguin Book of the Sonnet (2001). A professor of English and the Poet-in-Residence at Hofstra University, she lives in New York. "Brief Bio" displays, in concentrated form, the imaginative reach and lyrical quality of her work.

Brief Bio   1995

Bearer of no news
Under the sun, except
The spring, I quicken
Time, drawing you to see
Earth's lightest pamphlet,   5
Reeling mosaic of rainbow dust,
Filament hinging a new set of wings,
Lord of no land, subject to flowers and wind,
Yesterday born in a palace that hangs by a thread.

Questions

1. What does the poem describe? (How can we know for sure?)
2. What is the form of the poem? (Pay attention to the first letter of each line.)
3. How does the title relate to the rest of the poem?
4. Does the visual shape of the poem on the page suggest any image from the poem itself?

Kay Ryan

Kay Ryan was born in San Jose, California, in 1945, and raised in the dry landscapes of the San Joaquin Valley and Mojave Desert. She studied literature at UCLA, where she earned a bachelor's and a master's degree, but never took a creative writing course. She has taught at the College of Marin, and she has taught writing at San Quentin Prison. Although Ryan's first book was privately printed, her reputation grew slowly but steadily with the publication of subsequent volumes, the most recent of which are The Niagara River (2005) and The Best of It: New and Selected Poems (2010). Her fame accelerated with the winning of the Ruth Lilly Poetry Prize (2004) and especially with her appointment as U.S. Poet Laureate (2008–2010).

Kay Ryan

Like all of her work, "Turtle" delights in intricate wordplay, ingenious (and frequently hidden) rimes, and extravagant metaphors to convey a serious theme.

Turtle

1994

Who would be a turtle who could help it?
A barely mobile hard roll, a four-oared helmet,
she can ill afford the chances she must take
in rowing toward the grasses that she eats.
Her track is graceless, like dragging   5
a packing-case places, and almost any slope
defeats her modest hopes. Even being practical,
she's often stuck up to the axle on her way
to something edible. With everything optimal,
she skirts the ditch which would convert   10
her shell into a serving dish. She lives
below luck-level, never imagining some lottery
will change her load of pottery to wings.
Her only levity is patience,
the sport of truly chastened things.   15

Questions

1. The tone of this poem is lively, almost playful. How does that tone relate to the poem's content and its theme?
2. In what ways is the turtle like a human being? In what ways is it different? Which ultimately predominate, the similarities or the differences?
3. What do you understand the last two lines to mean?

Suggestions for Writing on *Poems about Animals*

1. Choose one poem from this section that—overtly or implicitly—suggests similarities between humanity and the animal it depicts, and one poem that draws a fundamental distinction between humanity and the animal in question. Discuss the two poems, as specifically as possible, in terms of these contrasting viewpoints.
2. "The Darkling Thrush" contrasts the speaker's depression with the title bird's joyful song. To what degree does the bird cheer the speaker? Does the experience described in the poem create any significant or lasting difference in the speaker's mood and outlook?
3. Both "The Tyger" and "Turtle" depict their subjects in less than rapturous terms. Discuss the two poems in this regard. What are the negative qualities associated with the animal in each poem? Does either poem demonstrate anything resembling respect or affection for the animal it describes?
4. In their very different ways, both "Rock and Hawk" and "Thirteen Ways of Looking at a Blackbird" present the bird of the title as some sort of object lesson for humanity. Discuss the two poems in this context. What characteristics of the bird, according to each author, would human beings do well to adopt?

JUST FOR FUN: PET HAIKU

Anonymous   *Dog Haiku*

Anonymous   *Cat Haiku*

Humans love the company of animals for a number of reasons, not least because they make us laugh. Dogs, in their efforts to please us, often act like furry comedians. Cats, who are generally more reserved and independent than their canine counterparts, can be equally amusing in their aloof antics. Pets—no matter what our species of choice—improve our sense of well-being both by providing companionship and taking our minds off our own worries. Several recent studies have shown that the benefits of having pets range from decreases in anxiety and depression to the lowering of blood pressure levels. No wonder pets are celebrated in so many ways, from movies and art to "Dogbook" (the Facebook application for canines) and cat calendars, and also, of course, to literature. The anonymous haiku in this section are a light-hearted testament to the humor, silliness, and joy we receive from our animal companions.

Anonymous

Dog Haiku (2001)

Today I sniffed
Many dog behinds—I celebrate
By kissing your face.

**

I sound the alarm!
Garbage man—come to kill us all—
Look! Look! Look! Look! Look!

**

How do I love thee?
The ways are numberless as
My hairs on the rug.

**

I sound the alarm!
Paper boy—come to kill us all—
Look! Look! Look! Look! Look!

**

I am your best friend,
Now, always, and especially
When you are eating.

Anonymous

Cat Haiku   (2005)

The food in my bowl
Is old, and more to the point
Contains no tuna.

* *

So you want to play.
Will I claw at dancing string?
Your ankle's closer.

* *

Am I in your way?
You seem to have it backwards:
This pillow's taken.

* *

I don't mind being
Teased, any more than you mind
A skin graft or two.

* *

Toy mice, dancing yarn
Meowing sounds. I'm convinced:
You're an idiot.

Suggestions for Writing on Pet Haiku

1. Take any of the dog or cat haiku and relate it to your own experience with a pet. (Your pet does not have to be a dog or cat.) Write two or three short paragraphs about your pet.
2. Write a short paper explaining why you prefer a dog or a cat (or any other animal) as a pet. Or explain why you choose not to have a pet.
3. Write an animal haiku of your own. (Remember, a haiku is traditionally three lines long, with five syllables in the first line, seven in the second, and five in the final line.)

ESSAYS

OUR PLACE IN NATURE

John Muir	*A Wind-Storm in the Forests*
Wallace Stegner	*Wilderness Letter*
bell hooks	*Earthbound: On Solid Ground*

What is humanity's proper relation to the natural world? What do we gain by living in close contact with a natural environment unspoiled by human interference? What do we lose when we cut ourselves off from the natural world? The essays in this chapter ponder these fundamental questions that shape our individual and collective lives. John Muir's famous account of "A Wind-Storm in the Forests" depicts a lone man coming dangerously face to face with the vast power of nature. Wallace Stegner's "Wilderness Letter" is an appeal, written to a public official, which advocates the preservation of land in its natural state. Stegner argues that Americans need wilderness to provide us with a clarifying perspective on "our technological termite-life, the Brave New World of a completely man-controlled environment." In "Earthbound: On Solid Ground," bell hooks addresses why it is important for African Americans to renew their relationship with their historical rural roots and regain their connections to the earth.

These influential essays have inspired artists, scientists, activists, politicians, and millions of ordinary citizens to see the world differently. They cultivate in us a respect and reverence not only for the natural landscape in all its immense diversity, but for life itself in all its forms. These authors show us that the natural world is humanity's purest and most essential source of beauty, reflection, self-discovery, testing, and renewal.

John Muir

John Muir (1838–1914) was born in Dunbar, Scotland, and lived there until his family immigrated to Wisconsin when he was ten. He worked on his family's farm and attended, but never graduated from, the University of Wisconsin. In 1867, Muir resolved to spend his life closer to nature and began a series of long, rambling trips, including a walk of a thousand miles on a "botanical journey" from Indianapolis to the Gulf of Mexico. Muir also hiked throughout the Sierra Nevada and, an accomplished mountaineer, was the first white man to ascend many of its peaks. Later in his life he focused on writing, publishing over three hundred articles and ten books, including The Mountains of California (1894), My First Summer in the Sierra (1911), The Yosemite (1912), and Travels in Alaska (posthumously published in 1915).

John Muir

These works, which were beautifully descriptive and tinged with spirituality, had a profound effect on the public's understanding of the natural world and inspired both everyday people and national leaders. Muir became an activist out of concern for what human activities and industrial interests were doing to the country's wild places. On a camping trip with President Theodore Roosevelt in Yosemite, he convinced the president to make Yosemite a national park, and helped shape Roosevelt's later national conservation efforts. He also founded the Sierra Club and served as its first president. When Muir died in 1914, he was the most important voice for environmental concerns in America, and his legacy stands to this day. His image graces the California state quarter, and many places—including the 211-mile John Muir Trail in the Sierra Nevada, Muir Beach, and Muir Woods National Monument—have been named in his honor. "A Wind-Storm in the Forests" is from his book The Mountains of California.

A Wind-Storm in the Forests 1894

One of the most beautiful and exhilarating storms I ever enjoyed in the Sierra occurred in December, 1874, when I happened to be exploring one of the tributary valleys of the Yuba River. The sky and the ground and the trees had been thoroughly rain-washed and were dry again. The day was intensely pure, one of those incomparable bits of California winter, warm and balmy and full of white sparkling sunshine, redolent of all the purest influences of the spring, and at the same time enlivened with one of the most bracing wind-storms conceivable. Instead of camping out, as I usually do, I then chanced to be stopping at the house of a friend. But when the storm began to sound, I lost no time in pushing out into the woods to enjoy it. For on such occasions Nature has always something rare to show us, and the danger to life and limb is hardly greater than one would experience crouching deprecatingly beneath a roof.

It was still early morning when I found myself fairly adrift. Delicious sunshine came pouring over the hills, lighting the tops of the pines, and setting free a steam of summery fragrance that contrasted strangely with the wild tones of the storm. The air was mottled with pine-tassels and bright green plumes, that went flashing past in the sunlight like birds pursued. But there was not the slightest dustiness, nothing less pure than leaves, and ripe pollen, and flecks of withered bracken and moss. I heard trees falling for hours at the rate of one every two or three minutes; some uprooted, partly on account of the loose, water-soaked condition of the ground; others broken straight across, where some weakness caused by fire had determined the spot. The gestures of the various trees made a delightful study. Young Sugar Pines, light and feathery as squirrel-tails, were bowing almost to

A wind-storm in the California forests (after a sketch by the author), 1894.

the ground; while the grand old patriarchs, whose massive boles had been tried in a hundred storms, waved solemnly above them, their long, arching branches streaming fluently on the gale, and every needle thrilling and ringing and shedding off keen lances of light like a diamond. The Douglas Spruces, with long sprays drawn out in level tresses, and needles massed in a gray, shimmering glow, presented a most striking appearance as they stood in bold relief along the hilltops. The madroños in the dells, with their red bark and large glossy leaves tilted every way, reflected the sunshine in throbbing spangles like those one so often sees on the rippled surface of a glacier lake. But the Silver Pines were now the most impressively beautiful of all. Colossal spires 200 feet in height waved like supple goldenrods chanting and bowing low as if in worship, while the whole mass of their long, tremulous foliage was kindled into one continuous blaze of white sun-fire. The force of the gale was such that the most steadfast monarch of them all rocked down to its roots with a motion plainly perceptible when one leaned against it. Nature was holding high festival, and every fiber of the most rigid giants thrilled with glad excitement.

    I drifted on through the midst of this passionate music and motion, across many a glen, from ridge to ridge; often halting in the lee of a rock for shelter, or to gaze and listen. Even when the grand anthem had swelled to its highest pitch, I could distinctly hear the varying tones of individual trees,—Spruce, and Fir, and Pine, and leafless Oak,—and even the infinitely gentle rustle of the withered grasses at my feet. Each was expressing itself in its own way,—singing its own song, and making its own peculiar gestures,—manifesting a richness of variety to be found in no other forest I have yet seen. The coniferous woods of Canada, and the Carolinas, and Florida, are made up of trees that resemble one another about as nearly as blades of grass, and grow close together in much the same way. Coniferous trees, in general, seldom possess individual character, such as is manifest among Oaks and Elms. But the California forests are made up of a greater number of distinct species than any other in the world. And in them we find, not only a marked differentiation into special groups, but also a marked individuality in almost every tree, giving rise to storm effects indescribably glorious.

    Toward midday, after a long, tingling scramble through copses of hazel and ceanothus, I gained the summit of the highest ridge in the neighborhood; and then it occurred to me that it would be a fine thing to climb one of the trees to obtain a wider outlook and get my ear close to the Æolian° music of its topmost needles. But under the circumstances the choice of a tree was a serious matter. One whose instep was not very strong seemed in danger of being blown down, or of being struck by others in case they should fall; another was branchless to a considerable height above the ground, and at the same time too large to be grasped with arms and legs in climbing; while others were not favorably situated for clear views. After cautiously casting about, I made choice of the tallest of a group of Douglas Spruces that were growing close together like a tuft of grass, no one of which seemed likely to fall unless all the rest fell with it. Though comparatively young, they were about 100 feet high, and their lithe, brushy tops were rocking and swirling in wild ecstasy. Being accustomed to climb trees in making botanical studies, I experienced no difficulty in reaching the top of this one, and never before did I enjoy so noble an exhilaration of motion. The slender tops fairly flapped and swished in the passionate torrent, bending and swirling backward

    Æolian: relating to or caused by wind. In Greek mythology, Æolus was the ruler of the winds.

and forward, round and round, tracing indescribable combinations of vertical and horizontal curves, while I clung with muscles firm braced, like a bobolink° on a reed.

In its widest sweeps my tree-top described an arc of from twenty to thirty degrees, but I felt sure of its elastic temper, having seen others of the same species still more severely tried—bent almost to the ground indeed, in heavy snows—without breaking a fiber. I was therefore safe, and free to take the wind into my pulses and enjoy the excited forest from my superb outlook. The view from here must be extremely beautiful in any weather. Now my eye roved over the piny hills and dales as over fields of waving grain, and felt the light running in ripples and broad swelling undulations across the valleys from ridge to ridge, as the shining foliage was stirred by corresponding waves of air. Oftentimes these waves of reflected light would break up suddenly into a kind of beaten foam, and again, after chasing one another in regular order, they would seem to bend forward in concentric curves, and disappear on some hillside, like sea-waves on a shelving shore. The quantity of light reflected from the bent needles was so great as to make whole groves appear as if covered with snow, while the black shadows beneath the trees greatly enhanced the effect of the silvery splendor.

Excepting only the shadows there was nothing somber in all this wild sea of pines. On the contrary, notwithstanding this was the winter season, the colors were remarkably beautiful. The shafts of the pine and libocedrus were brown and purple, and most of the foliage was well tinged with yellow; the laurel groves, with the pale undersides of their leaves turned upward, made masses of gray; and then there was many a dash of chocolate color from clumps of manzanita, and jet of vivid crimson from the bark of the madroños, while the ground on the hillsides, appearing here and there through openings between the groves, displayed masses of pale purple and brown.

The sounds of the storm corresponded gloriously with this wild exuberance of light and motion. The profound bass of the naked branches and boles booming like waterfalls; the quick, tense vibrations of the pine-needles, now rising to a shrill, whistling hiss, now falling to a silky murmur; the rustling of laurel groves in the dells, and the keen metallic click of leaf on leaf—all this was heard in easy analysis when the attention was calmly bent.

The varied gestures of the multitude were seen to fine advantage, so that one could recognize the different species at a distance of several miles by this means alone, as well as by their forms and colors, and the way they reflected the light. All seemed strong and comfortable, as if really enjoying the storm, while responding to its most enthusiastic greetings. We hear much nowadays concerning the universal struggle for existence, but no struggle in the common meaning of the word was manifest here; no recognition of danger by any tree; no deprecation; but rather an invincible gladness as remote from exultation as from fear.

I kept my lofty perch for hours, frequently closing my eyes to enjoy the music by itself, or to feast quietly on the delicious fragrance that was streaming past. The fragrance of the woods was less marked than that produced during warm rain, when so many balsamic buds and leaves are steeped like tea; but, from the chafing of resiny branches against each other, and the incessant attrition of myriads of needles, the gale was spiced to a very tonic degree. And besides the fragrance from these local sources there were traces of scents brought from afar. For this wind came first from the sea, rubbing against its fresh, briny waves, then distilled through the redwoods, threading

---

bobolink: migratory songbird whose breeding habitats are open grassy fields across North America.

rich ferny gulches, and spreading itself in broad undulating currents over many a flower-enameled ridge of the coast mountains, then across the golden plains, up the purple foot-hills, and into these piny woods with the varied incense gathered by the way.

Winds are advertisements of all they touch, however much or little we may be able to read them; telling their wanderings even by their scents alone. Mariners detect the flowery perfume of land-winds far at sea, and sea-winds carry the fragrance of dulse and tangle far inland, where it is quickly recognized, though mingled with the scents of a thousand land-flowers. As an illustration of this, I may tell here that I breathed sea-air on the Firth of Forth, in Scotland, while a boy; then was taken to Wisconsin, where I remained nineteen years; then, without in all this time having breathed one breath of the sea, I walked quietly, alone, from the middle of the Mississippi Valley to the Gulf of Mexico, on a botanical excursion, and while in Florida, far from the coast, my attention wholly bent on the splendid tropical vegetation about me, I suddenly recognized a sea-breeze, as it came sifting through the palmettos and blooming vine-tangles, which at once awakened and set free a thousand dormant associations, and made me a boy again in Scotland, as if all the intervening years had been annihilated.°

Most people like to look at mountain rivers, and bear them in mind; but few care to look at the winds, though far more beautiful and sublime, and though they become at times about as visible as flowing water. When the north winds in winter are making upward sweeps over the curving summits of the High Sierra, the fact is sometimes published with flying snow-banners a mile long. Those portions of the winds thus embodied can scarce be wholly invisible, even to the darkest imagination. And when we look around over an agitated forest, we may see something of the wind that stirs it, by its effects upon the trees. Yonder it descends in a rush of waterlike ripples, and sweeps over the bending pines from hill to hill. Nearer, we see detached plumes and leaves, now speeding by on level currents, now whirling in eddies, or, escaping over the edges of the whirls, soaring aloft on grand, upswelling domes of air, or tossing on flame-like crests. Smooth, deep currents, cascades, falls, and swirling eddies, sing around every tree and leaf, and over all the varied topography of the region with telling changes of form, like mountain rivers conforming to the features of their channels.

After tracing the Sierra streams from their fountains to the plains, marking where they bloom white in falls, glide in crystal plumes, surge gray and foam-filled in boulder-choked gorges, and slip through the woods in long, tranquil reaches—after thus learning their language and forms in detail, we may at length hear them chanting all together in one grand anthem, and comprehend them all in clear inner vision, covering the range like lace. But even this spectacle is far less sublime and not a whit more substantial than what we may behold of these storm-streams of air in the mountain woods.

We all travel the milky way together, trees and men; but it never occurred to me until this storm-day, while swinging in the wind, that trees are travelers, in the ordinary sense. They make many journeys, not extensive ones, it is true; but our own little journeys, away and back again, are only little more than tree-wavings—many of them not so much.

When the storm began to abate, I dismounted and sauntered down through the calming woods. The storm-tones died away, and, turning toward the east, I beheld the countless hosts of the forests hushed and tranquil, towering above one another on

---

I walked quietly, alone . . . as if all the intervening years had been annihilated: At age 29, Muir walked from Indiana to the Gulf of Mexico on a "botanical journey," recounted in *A Thousand-Mile Walk to the Gulf* (1916).

the slopes of the hills like a devout audience. The setting sun filled them with amber light, and seemed to say, while they listened, "My peace I give unto you."

As I gazed on the impressive scene, all the so-called ruin of the storm was forgotten, and never before did these noble woods appear so fresh, so joyous, so immortal.

15

Questions

1. What details and descriptions are most striking to you? Why?
2. Muir uses terms such as "high festival" and "passionate music and motion" to describe the wind-storm. Why does he see such beauty and life in the storm, even as he acknowledges the destruction it causes?
3. Why does Muir think that the winds are more important to forests than snow, lightning, or avalanches?
4. Why does Muir climb 100 feet up a pine tree? Does he feel he is in danger when the storm arrives?
5. Late in the piece, Muir writes, "We all travel the milky way together, trees and men." What does he mean by this? What is the insight that Muir arrives at about the relationship between trees and men?

Wallace Stegner

Wallace Stegner (1909–1993) was born in Iowa and grew up in North Dakota, Washington, Saskatchewan, Montana, and Utah. Neither of his parents had gone beyond eighth grade, and the family moved all over the West in their attempts to make a living. After several unsuccessful ventures, including a failed wheat farm, Stegner's father started a bootlegging operation and illegal saloon in the family home. These challenging experiences sparked in Stegner a yearning for stable family and community ties, as well as a deep affection for the natural places that sustained him. After earning a B.A. at the University of Utah (1930) and both an M.A. and a Ph.D. at the University of Iowa (1932, 1935), Stegner taught at a number of colleges, including the University of Utah and Harvard University. But the majority of his career was spent at Stanford University, where he taught from 1945 to 1971 and founded the university's creative writing program. A prolific and versatile author, Stegner produced more than thirty books of fiction, nonfiction, and biography. His work is deeply rooted in the American West—the beauty of its regions, the relationships between humans and the land, and the ways that people shape, and are shaped by, geography and history. His novels include Angle of Repose *(1971), which won the Pulitzer Prize;* The Spectator Bird *(1976), winner of the National Book Award; and* Crossing to Safety *(1987). Stegner was an avid spokesperson for environmental causes. His 1960 "Wilderness Letter," which helped to bolster testimony in favor of the 1964 Wilderness Act and was later included in Stegner's essay collection* The Sound of Mountain Water *(1969), remains a classic of environmental literature.*

Wallace Stegner

Wilderness Letter

Los Altos, Calif.
Dec. 3, 1960

David E. Pesonen
Wildland Research Center
Agricultural Experiment Station
243 Mulford Hall
University of California
Berkeley 4, Calif.

Dear Mr. Pesonen:

  I believe that you are working on the wilderness portion of the Outdoor Recreation Resources Review Commission's report. If I may, I should like to urge some arguments for wilderness preservation that involve recreation, as it is ordinarily conceived, hardly at all. Hunting, fishing, hiking, mountain-climbing, camping, photography, and the enjoyment of natural scenery will all, surely, figure in your report. So will the wilderness as a genetic reserve, a scientific yardstick by which we may measure the world in its natural balance against the world in its man-made imbalance. What I want to speak for is not so much the wilderness uses, valuable as those are, but the wilderness *idea*, which is a resource in itself. Being an intangible and spiritual resource, it will seem mystical to the practical-minded—but then anything that cannot be moved by a bulldozer is likely to seem mystical to them.

  I want to speak for the wilderness idea as something that has helped form our character and that has certainly shaped our history as a people. It has no more to do with recreation than churches have to do with recreation, or than the strenuousness and optimism and expansiveness of what historians call the "American Dream" have to do with recreation. Nevertheless, since it is only in this recreation survey that the values of wilderness are being compiled, I hope you will permit me to insert this idea between the leaves, as it were, of the recreation report.

  Something will have gone out of us as a people if we ever let the remaining wilderness be destroyed; if we permit the last virgin forests to be turned into comic books and plastic cigarette cases; if we drive the few remaining members of the wild species into zoos or to extinction; if we pollute the last clear air and dirty the last clean streams and push our paved roads through the last of the silence, so that never again will Americans be free in their own country from the noise, the exhausts, the stinks of human and automotive waste. And so that never again can we have the chance to see ourselves single, separate, vertical and individual in the world, part of the environment of trees and rocks and soil, brother to the other animals, part of the natural world and competent to belong in it. Without any remaining wilderness we are committed wholly, without chance for even momentary reflection and rest, to a headlong drive into our technological termite-life, the Brave New World of a completely man-controlled environment. We need wilderness preserved—as much of it as is still left, and as many kinds—because it was the challenge against which our character as a people was formed. The reminder and the reassurance that it is still there is good for our spiritual health even if we never once in ten years set foot in it. It is good for us when we are young, because of the incomparable sanity it can bring briefly, as vacation and rest, into our insane lives. It is important to us when we are old simply because it is there—important, that is, simply as idea.

We are a wild species, as Darwin pointed out. Nobody ever tamed or domesticated or scientifically bred us. But for at least three millennia we have been engaged in a cumulative and ambitious race to modify and gain control of our environment, and in the process we have come close to domesticating ourselves. Not many people are likely, any more, to look upon what we call "progress" as an unmixed blessing. Just as surely as it has brought us increased comfort and more material goods, it has brought us spiritual losses, and it threatens now to become the Frankenstein that will destroy us. One means of sanity is to retain a hold on the natural world, to remain, insofar as we can, good animals. Americans still have that chance, more than many peoples; for while we were demonstrating ourselves the most efficient and ruthless environment-busters in history, and slashing and burning and cutting our way through a wilderness continent, the wilderness was working on us. It remains in us as surely as Indian names remain on the land. If the abstract dream of human liberty and human dignity became, in America, something more than an abstract dream, mark it down at least partially to the fact that we were in subtle ways subdued by what we conquered.

The Connecticut Yankee,° sending likely candidates from King Arthur's unjust kingdom to his Man Factory for rehabilitation, was over-optimistic, as he later admitted. These things cannot be forced, they have to grow. To make such a man, such a democrat, such a believer in human individual dignity, as Mark Twain himself, the frontier was necessary, Hannibal and the Mississippi and Virginia City,° and reaching out from those the wilderness; the wilderness as opportunity and as idea, the thing that has helped to make an American different from and, until we forget it in the roar of our industrial cities, more fortunate than other men. For an American, insofar as he is new and different at all, is a civilized man who has renewed himself in the wild. The American experience has been the confrontation by old peoples and cultures of a world as new as if it had just risen from the sea. That gave us our hope and our excitement, and the hope and excitement can be passed on to newer Americans, Americans who never saw any phase of the frontier. But only so long as we keep the remainder of our wild as a reserve and a promise—a sort of wilderness bank.

As a novelist, I may perhaps be forgiven for taking literature as a reflection, indirect but profoundly true, of our national consciousness. And our literature, as perhaps you are aware, is sick, embittered, losing its mind, losing its faith. Our novelists are the declared enemies of their society. There has hardly been a serious or important novel in this century that did not repudiate in part or in whole American technological culture for its commercialism, its vulgarity, and the way in which it has dirtied a clean continent and a clean dream. I do not expect that the preservation of our remaining wilderness is going to cure this condition. But the mere example that we can as a nation apply some other criteria than commercial and exploitative considerations would be heartening to many Americans, novelists or otherwise. We need to

5

Connecticut Yankee: in Mark Twain's famous adventure, *A Connecticut Yankee in King Arthur's Court* (1889), a modern American is transported back in time to King Arthur's Camelot. *Hannibal and the Mississippi and Virginia City*: the places where Mark Twain spent his formative years. Hannibal, Missouri, was his boyhood home; the Mississippi was where he worked on steamboats. In Virginia City, Nevada, Twain worked with miners and started writing journalism. These early experiences, Stegner implies, formed Twain's adult character.

demonstrate our acceptance of the natural world, including ourselves; we need the spiritual refreshment that being natural can produce. And one of the best places for us to get that is in the wilderness where the fun houses, the bulldozers, and the pavements of our civilization are shut out.

Sherwood Anderson, in a letter to Waldo Frank° in the 1920's, said it better than I can. "Is it not likely that when the country was new and men were often alone in the fields and the forest they got a sense of bigness outside themselves that has now in some way been lost . . . Mystery whispered in the grass, played in the branches of trees overhead, was caught up and blown across the American line in clouds of dust at evening on the prairies . . . I am old enough to remember tales that strengthen my belief in a deep semi-religious influence that was formerly at work among our people. The flavor of it hangs over the best work of Mark Twain . . . I can remember old fellows in my home town speaking feelingly of an evening spent on the big empty plains. It had taken the shrillness out of them. They had learned the trick of quiet . . ."

We could learn it too, even yet; even our children and grandchildren could learn it. But only if we save, for just such absolutely non-recreational, impractical, and mystical uses as this, all the wild that still remains to us.

It seems to me significant that the distinct downturn in our literature from hope to bitterness took place almost at the precise time when the frontier officially came to an end, in 1890,° and when the American way of life had begun to turn strongly urban and industrial. The more urban it has become, and the more frantic with technological change, the sicker and more embittered our literature, and I believe our people, have become. For myself, I grew up on the empty plains of Saskatchewan and Montana and in the mountains of Utah, and I put a very high valuation on what those places gave me. And if I had not been able periodically to renew myself in the mountains and deserts of western America I would be very nearly bughouse. Even when I can't get to the back country, the thought of the colored deserts of southern Utah, or the reassurance that there are still stretches of prairie where the world can be instantaneously perceived as disk and bowl, and where the little but intensely important human being is exposed to the five directions and the thirty-six winds, is a positive consolation. The idea alone can sustain me. But as the wilderness areas are progressively exploited or "improved," as the jeeps and bulldozers of uranium prospectors scar up the deserts and the roads are cut into the alpine timberlands, and as the remnants of the unspoiled and natural world are progressively eroded, every such loss is a little death in me. In us.

I am not moved by the argument that those wilderness areas which have already been exposed to grazing or mining are already deflowered, and so might as well be "harvested." For mining I cannot say much good except that its operations are generally short-lived. The extractable wealth is taken and the shafts, the tailings, and the ruins left, and in a dry country such as the American West the wounds men make in the earth do not quickly heal. Still, they are only wounds; they aren't absolutely mortal. Better a wounded wilderness than none at all. And as for grazing, if it is strictly controlled so that it does not destroy the ground cover, damage the ecology, or

10

Sherwood Anderson . . . to Waldo Frank: Sherwood Anderson (1876–1941), a fiction writer who depicted small-town life; Waldo Frank (1889–1967), a novelist and critic who explored American spiritual and political issues.   *frontier officially came to an end, in 1890:* the U.S. Census of 1890 declared that the American frontier, as unsettled territory, no longer existed.

compete with the wildlife it is in itself nothing that need conflict with the wilderness feeling or the validity of the wilderness experience. I have known enough range cattle to recognize them as wild animals; and the people who herd them have, in the wilderness context, the dignity of rareness; they belong on the frontier, moreover, and have a look of rightness. The invasion they make on the virgin country is a sort of invasion that is as old as Neolithic man, and they can, in moderation, even emphasize a man's feeling of belonging to the natural world. Under surveillance, they can belong; under control, they need not deface or mar. I do not believe that in wilderness areas where grazing has never been permitted, it should be permitted; but I do not believe either that an otherwise untouched wilderness should be eliminated from the preservation plan because of limited existing uses such as grazing which are in consonance with the frontier condition and image.

Let me say something on the subject of the kinds of wilderness worth preserving. Most of those areas contemplated are in the national forests and in high mountain country. For all the usual recreational purposes, the alpine and forest wildernesses are obviously the most important, both as genetic banks and as beauty spots. But for the spiritual renewal, the recognition of identity, the birth of awe, other kinds will serve every bit as well. Perhaps, because they are less friendly to life, more abstractly nonhuman, they will serve even better. On our Saskatchewan prairie, the nearest neighbor was four miles away, and at night we saw only two lights on all the dark rounding earth. The earth was full of animals—field mice, ground squirrels, weasels, ferrets, badgers, coyotes, burrowing owls, snakes. I knew them as my little brothers, as fellow creatures, and I have never been able to look upon animals in any other way since. The sky in that country came clear down to the ground on every side, and it was full of great weathers, and clouds, and winds, and hawks. I hope I learned something from knowing intimately the creatures of the earth; I hope I learned something from looking a long way, from looking up, from being much alone. A prairie like that, one big enough to carry the eye clear to the sinking, rounding horizon, can be as lonely and grand and simple in its forms as the sea. It is as good a place as any for the wilderness experience to happen; the vanishing prairie is as worth preserving for the wilderness idea as the alpine forests.

So are great reaches of our western deserts, scarred somewhat by prospectors but otherwise open, beautiful, waiting, close to whatever God you want to see in them. Just as a sample, let me suggest the Robbers' Roost country in Wayne County, Utah, near the Capitol Reef National Monument. In that desert climate the dozer and jeep tracks will not soon melt back into the earth, but the country has a way of making the scars insignificant. It is a lovely and terrible wilderness, such a wilderness as Christ and the prophets went out into; harshly and beautifully colored, broken and worn until its bones are exposed, its great sky without a smudge of taint from Technocracy, and in hidden corners and pockets under its cliffs the sudden poetry of springs. Save a piece of country like that intact, and it does not matter in the slightest that only a few people every year will go into it. That is precisely its value. Roads would be a desecration, crowds would ruin it. But those who haven't the strength or youth to go into it and live can simply sit and look. They can look two hundred miles, clear into Colorado; and looking down over the cliffs and canyons of the San Rafael Swell and the Robbers' Roost they can also look as deeply into themselves as anywhere I know.

And if they can't even get to the places on the Aquarius Plateau where the present roads will carry them, they can simply contemplate the *idea*, take pleasure in the fact that such a timeless and uncontrolled part of earth is still there.

These are some of the things wilderness can do for us. That is the reason we need to put into effect, for its preservation, some other principle than the principles of exploitation or "usefulness" or even recreation. We simply need that wild country available to us, even if we never do more than drive to its edge and look in. For it can be a means of reassuring ourselves of our sanity as creatures, a part of the geography of hope.

Very sincerely yours,
Wallace Stegner

Questions

1. What is the difference, according to Stegner, between the concepts "wilderness uses" and the "wilderness *idea*"? Do you agree that this idea is important?
2. In several instances, Stegner refers to people as part of the natural world. What does he mean by this? What does he think has been lost?
3. Stegner describes a wilderness area where people "can also look as deeply into themselves as anywhere I know." How does nature, to Stegner, make it possible for people to look into themselves?
4. What, in Stegner's opinion, happened to the American imagination when the frontier came to an end?
5. What do you think Stegner means by his final phrase, "the geography of hope"?

bell hooks

bell hooks was born Gloria Jean Watkins in 1952, and raised in Hopkinsville, Kentucky, a small, segregated town in a rural area of the state. This social and geographic setting would help to shape both her understanding of race and her love for the natural world. The daughter of a janitor and a maid, hooks excelled in a segregated school where most of her teachers were single black women. She went on to earn a scholarship to Stanford University, where she began working on her first book. Graduating in 1973, she later received an M.A. from the University of Wisconsin (1976) and a Ph.D. from the University of California, Santa Cruz (1983). The book she began at Stanford—Ain't I a Woman: Black Women and Feminism—was published in 1981, and in 1992 Publishers Weekly ranked it among the "twenty most influential women's books of the last twenty years." The author, who writes under the pen name "bell hooks" in honor of her mother and grandmother, has taught at a number of universities. She is presently Distinguished Professor in Residence in Appalachian Studies at Berea College in Kentucky. She has published over thirty books, including

Feminist Theory: From Margin to Center *(1984)*, Talking Back: Thinking Feminist, Thinking Black *(1989)*, Black Looks: Race and Representation *(1992)*, and Belonging: A Culture of Place *(2009)*. *A scholar who writes extensively about race, class, and gender, hooks continues to expound the belief that, for African Americans, a connection to the land is instrumental in black self-definition and self-reliance.*

Earthbound: On Solid Ground   2002

Kentucky hills were the place of my early childhood. Surrounded by a wilderness of honeysuckle, wild asparagus, and sheltering trees, bushes shielding growing crops, the huge garden of a black landowner. Our concrete house on the hill, a leftover legacy from oil drilling, from the efforts of men to make the earth yield greater and greater profit stood as a citadel to capitalism's need for a new frontier. A child of the hills, I was taught early on in my life the power in nature. I was taught by farmers that wilderness land, the untamed environment can give life and it can take life. In my girlhood I learned to watch for snakes, wildcats roaming, plants that irritate and poison. I know instinctively; I know because I am told by all knowing grown-ups that it is humankind and not nature that is the stranger on these grounds. Humility in relationship to nature's power made survival possible.

Coming from "backwoods" folks, Appalachian outlaws, as a child I was taught to understand that those among us who lived organically, in harmony and union with nature were marked with a sensibility that was distinct, and downright dangerous. Backwoods folks tend to ignore the rules of society, the rules of law. In the backwoods one learned to trust only the spirit, to follow where the spirit moved. Ultimately, no matter what was said or done, the spirit called to us from a place beyond words, from a place beyond man made law. The wild spirit of unspoiled nature worked its way in to the folk of the backwoods, an ancestral legacy, handed down from generation to generation. And its fundamental gift the cherishing of that which is most precious, freedom. And to be fully free one had to embrace the organic rights of the earth.

Humankind, no matter how powerful, cannot take away the rights of the earth. Ultimately, nature rules. That is the great democratic gift earth offers us—that sweet death to which we all inevitably go—into that final communion. No race, no class, no gender, nothing can keep any of us from dying into that death where we are made one. To tend the earth is always then to tend our destiny, our freedom and our hope.

These lessons of my girlhood were the oppositional narratives that taught me to care for the earth, to respect country folk. This respect for the earth, for the country girl within, stood me in good stead when I left this environment and entered a world beyond the country town I was raised in. It was only when I left home, that country place where nature's splendors were abundant and not yet destroyed, that I understood for the first time the contempt for country folk that abounds in our nation. That contempt has led to the cultural disrespect for the farmer, for those who live simply in harmony with nature. Writer, sometime farmer, and poet Wendell Berry, another Kentuckian, who loves our land, writes in *Another Turn of the Crank* in the essay "Conserving Communities" that: "Communists and capitalists are alike in their contempt for country people, country life, and country places."

Before the mass migrations to northern cities in the early nineteen hundreds, more than ninety percent of all black folks lived in the agrarian South. We were indeed a people of the earth. Working the land was the hope of survival. Even when that land was owned by white oppressors, master and mistress, it was the earth itself that protected exploited black folks from dehumanization. My sharecropping granddaddy Jerry would walk through neat rows of crops and tell me, "I'll tell you a secret little girl. No man can make the sun or the rains come—we can all testify. We can all see that ultimately we all bow down to the forces of nature. Big white boss may think he can outsmart nature but the small farmer know. Earth is our witness." This relationship to the earth meant that southern black folks, whether they were impoverished or not, knew firsthand that white supremacy, with its systemic dehumanization of blackness, was not a form of absolute power.

In that world country black folks understood that though powerful white folks could dominate and control people of color they could not control nature or divine spirit. The fundamental understanding that white folks were not gods (for if they were they could shape nature) helped imbue black folks with an oppositional sensibility. When black people migrated to urban cities, this humanizing connection with nature was severed; racism and white supremacy came to be seen as all powerful, the ultimate factors informing our fate. When this thinking was coupled with a breakdown in religiosity, a refusal to recognize the sacred in everyday life, it served the interests of white supremacist capitalist patriarchy.

Living in the agrarian South, working on the land, growing food, I learned survival skills similar to those hippies sought to gain in their back to the earth movements in the late sixties and early seventies. Growing up in a world where my grandparents did not hold regular jobs but made their living digging and selling fishing worms, growing food, raising chickens, I was evermindful of an alternative to the capitalist system that destroyed nature's abundance. In that world I learned experientially the concept of interbeing, which Buddhist monk Thich Nhat Hanh talks about as that recognition of the connectedness of all human life.

That sense of interbeing was once intimately understood by black folks in the agrarian South. Nowadays it is only those who maintain our bonds to the land, to nature, who keep our vows of living in harmony with the environment, who draw spiritual strength from nature. Reveling in nature's bounty and beauty has been one of the ways enlightened poor people in small towns all around our nations stay in touch with their essential goodness even as forces of evil, in the form of corrupt capitalism and hedonistic consumerism, work daily to strip them of their ties with nature.

Journalists from the *New York Times* who interviewed Kentucky po' rural folk getting by with scarce resources were surprised to find these citizens expressing connection to nature. In a recent article in the *Times* titled "Forget Washington. The Poor Cope Alone" reporter Evelyn Nieves shared: "People time and again said they were blessed to live in a place as beautiful as Kentucky, where the mountains are green and lush and the trees look as old as time." Maintaining intimacy gives us a concrete place of hope. It is nature that reminds us time and time again that "this too will pass." To look upon a tree, or a hilly waterfall, that has stood the test of time can renew the spirit. To watch plants rise from the earth with no special tending reawakens our sense of awe and wonder.

More than ever before in our nation's history black folks must collectively renew our relationship to the earth, to our agrarian roots. For when we are forgetful and participate in the destruction and exploitation of dark earth, we collude with the domination of the earth's dark people, both here and globally. Reclaiming our history, our relationship to nature, to farming in America, and proclaiming the humanizing restorative of living in harmony with nature so that earth can be our witness is meaningful resistance.

When I leave my small flat in an urban world where nature has been so relentlessly assaulted that it is easy to forget to look at a tree, a sky, a flower emerging in a sea of trash, and go to the country, I seek renewal. To live in communion with the earth fully acknowledging nature's power with humility and grace is a practice of spiritual mindfulness that heals and restores. Making peace with the earth we make the world a place where we can be one with nature. We create and sustain environments where we can come back to ourselves, where we can return home, stand on solid ground, and be a true witness.

Questions

1. What was lost, in hook's view, when African Americans migrated in large numbers from the rural south to large cities in the north? Why does she see life in the rural south as healthier than life in the industrial north? Do you agree with this argument?
2. "Black folks," hooks writes, "must collectively renew our relationship to the earth, to our agrarian roots." What does she mean by this injunction? Do you agree?
3. What does hooks argue is the connection between "black folks" and nature? Why is this relationship to rural life, in her view, particularly important for African Americans?
4. Elsewhere, hooks points out that many urban black people do not see the relevance of environmental concerns to their lives. How and why might this be true? Is it simply that they have forgotten that "black people were first and foremost a people of the land, farmers"? Or are current discussions about nature and the environment conducted in a way that fails to engage African Americans and other people of color?

Suggestions for Writing on Essays about Our Place in Nature

1. Choose two of these essays and compare and contrast how they present humankind's relationship with the natural world. How are the views of the authors different, and how are they similar?
2. Consider the essay by Wallace Stegner. Identify the theme and the arguments it sets forth; discuss how they could be applied to a present-day environmental issue.
3. Choose one of the essays in this section and write a paper making an argument from a different point of view. Be sure to use specific points and examples to support your argument.
4. Write about an experience you had in the natural world, a positive or a negative one. How did it affect you or change you? What did you learn? What does the experience mean to you now?

Suggestions for Writing on *Literature about Nature and the Environment*

1. Many works in this chapter explore what happens when we accept the natural order of things, even when it might seem harsh or frightening. Take one or two works such as "Rock and Hawk," "The Open Boat," or "To Build a Fire," and analyze what the speaker or protagonist seems to learn from the primal experience.
2. Choose a current environmental issue that is the subject of debate. (For example: offshore drilling, the status of wolves near Yellowstone National Park, the use of ATVs and snowmobiles on public lands.) Write an essay that takes a stand, being sure to provide evidence for your point of view.
3. Write about a time when you were impressed, moved, or frightened by a phenomenon of nature. What did you learn from it? Did it change how you see (or live in) the world today? (Note: you can write about this no matter where you live. Even if you've spent your whole life in New York City, you will have encountered animals, park spaces, snowstorms, and heat waves.)
4. Write about the place where you grew up or that you consider home. Describe it physically and geographically, and discuss its history if you know it. How did this place help to shape you and your views? Do you feel attached to it now? How did growing up there have an impact on you, as opposed to the effect other places might have had?
5. Pretend that a large open area is being developed for a sizable new housing and shopping complex. Write a letter to your city council or town officials giving your advice on how they might be sensitive to the natural landscape and local environmental concerns.
6. Choose one species of animal or plant and write a short appreciation of how its presence enriches the natural world.

18

WAR AND PEACE

War is hell.

—GENERAL WILLIAM TECUMSEH SHERMAN

War literature is often neglected in English classes today, probably on the assumption that such writings glorify militarism and violence. It is better, we are told, to focus on peace and justice. But one could make a compelling case that war and peace, conflict and reconciliation, are ideas best considered together: the study of war sharpens one's hunger for peace, justice, and reconciliation. It is not surprising that Leo Tolstoy, author of *War and Peace*, a historical epic about Russia during the Napoleonic wars, dedicated his later life to pacifism. Few artists who meditate on the brutality and suffering of war can refrain from imagining the alternative. War creates the imperative for peace. Founded one month after the end of World War II, the United Nations, for example, began its charter with the declaration that it was "Determined to save succeeding generations from the scourge of war."

War has been a central literary subject as long as there has been literature. The earliest masterpiece of the Western tradition, Homer's *Iliad*, portrays the heroism and human cost of the Trojan War; its companion poem, *The Odyssey*, recounts one veteran's long and difficult homecoming. The great national epics of imperial Rome (*The Aeneid*), France (*The Song of Roland*), Spain (*El Cid*), and Iran (*The Shahnama*) all commemorate the decisive military encounters that shaped each culture's history.

Many great authors have been soldiers. The Greek playwright Sophocles, creator of *Antigonê*, served as an Athenian general in the Peloponnesian War. The Roman poet Horace fought at the Battle of Philippi (and had to flee for his life when his side lost). Shakespeare's friend and fellow playwright Ben Jonson served in the infantry in the Flemish Wars. The two Renaissance poets who first brought the sonnet to English—Sir Thomas Wyatt and Henry Howard, Earl of Surrey—were both soldiers. Other great writers have continued this tradition, from Spain's Miguel de Cervantes, author of *Don Quixote*, to Russia's Nobel laureate, Alexander Solzhenitsyn, author of *The Gulag Archipelago*.

War has also inspired its civilian witnesses to great literature. Tending to wounded Union soldiers in the makeshift hospitals of Washington, D.C., the poet Walt Whitman wrote about the devastation of the American Civil War with heartfelt understanding. During World War I, Ernest Hemingway served as a volunteer ambulance driver for the American Red Cross on the Austro-Italian front and was hospitalized with shrapnel injuries; he fictionalized his war experiences in his novel *A Farewell to Arms*. While many American writers served in World War I, few participated in sustained combat. For most of them, the war was a great storm in the distance that rolled past without touching down. Not so for the British troops, who spent years in brutal trench warfare. The best British poets, especially Wilfred Owen, created a war poetry that spoke for peace rather than victory.

Some writers have refused to serve in the military. Even in World War II, when public opinion supporting America's involvement was overwhelmingly strong, many men became conscientious objectors. Among them, the well-known poets William Stafford, Kenneth Rexroth, William Everson, and Robert Lowell were made to spend years in prisons or civilian work camps. Pacifism is a longstanding American tradition, rooted in many of the Protestant sects whose members came to the United States for religious freedom. The Quakers, Amish, Mennonites, and Church of the Brethren all object to military service, as do the Jehovah's Witnesses, a later American-born denomination. Pacifism is as deeply rooted in American history as is military service, and the dialogue between the two—sometimes productive, often acrimonious—is an essential part of our complex national consciousness.

Few soldiers return from combat without scars, both emotional and physical. To witness the complete breakdown of human civility into organized violence and deadly force, often aimed at civilians as well as enemy soldiers, inverts all normal morality. In battle, human existence is reduced to animal survival. Many veterans return to their previous lives numbed, confused, angry, or depressed, in a condition that has been observed by writers for centuries but only recently has been clinically understood as post-traumatic stress disorder.

Returned to civilian society, soldiers have often been the most eloquent advocates for peace, cooperation, and reconciliation. They understand only too well the horror of the alternatives. Leo Tolstoy, who fought with the Russian Army in the Caucasus, ended his days as a spokesman for Christian pacifism; Vietnam veteran and sci-fi writer Joe Haldeman became an antiwar activist. As all veterans agree, the experience of combat changes a person. St. Francis of Assisi decided to give up worldly possessions and serve the poor after he had fought in battle. Four years after the Civil War, General William Tecumseh Sherman told a graduation class of military cadets, many of whom probably dreamed of glorious battlefield careers:

> War is at its best barbarism. . . . Its glory is all moonshine. It is only those, who have never fired a shot nor heard the shrieks and groans of the wounded, who cry aloud for blood, more vengeance, more desolation. War is hell.

Violence tends to create an escalating cycle of retribution and revenge. Only when the competing parties—be they nations or individuals—break the destructive cycle can there be peace and reconciliation. Such figures in modern history as Mohandas Gandhi, Martin Luther King Jr., Lech Walesa, and Nelson Mandela have shown the power of nonviolent change and reconciliation. The greatest legacy of the Roman Empire was not the many wars it waged but the *Pax Romana*, the Roman peace, that lasted within the borders of the Empire for nearly three hundred years, establishing order and allowing prosperity to flourish. A civilization is not remembered for what it conquers or destroys, but for what it builds, preserves, and fosters.

THE SELECTIONS IN THIS CHAPTER

The stories, poems, dramatic speeches, and essays in this chapter explore the themes of war, violence, peace, and reconciliation from diverse points of view. Many of the works, such as Tim O'Brien's harrowing story "The Things They Carried" and Wilfred Owen's powerful poems, vividly present the experience of war from the soldier's perspective. Other warriors' accounts range from Richard Lovelace's elegant idealization of military honor from the seventeenth century to Richard Eberhart's terrifying account of modern mechanized warfare in World War II and Yusef Komunyakaa's tribute to the Vietnam Veterans Memorial. Ryan Kelly's two letters to his mother from Iraq give voice to the soldiers serving in a recent conflict. Meanwhile, the voices of civilian and military families, often full of pain and anxiety, are presented in stories by Mary Yukari Waters and Guy de Maupassant, poems by Marilyn Nelson and R. S. Gwynn, and Myrna Bein's heartbreaking short memoir "A Journey Taken with My Son." Additionally, two short excerpts from Shakespeare present the cases for and against the notion of military glory. Personal violence and crime are explored in Andre Dubus's "A Father's Story" and Edgar Allan Poe's "The Cask of Amontillado."

Having presented the harsh realities of war and violence, the rest of the chapter investigates theories and visions of peace, especially the influential concepts of nonviolence and passive resistance as the strongest moral tools for social change. Two classic statements of principle by Leo Tolstoy and Mohandas Gandhi, and a gallery of poems from William Blake to Denise Levertov, envision the path to peace.

We hope that these powerful readings will help you think through the important issues posed by war, violence, peace, and reconciliation. Few questions are more significant or pressing, whether one considers them locally or globally. Even when a reading doesn't change your mind on a subject, it should deepen your awareness of what is at stake. The diverse views of these readings will also help you understand the perspectives of other people, from soldiers and veterans to reformers and pacifists—and what better way to begin a journey toward peace and reconciliation than by understanding each other?

Things to Think About

1. Have you or any member of your family served in the military? Or did someone close to you experience war as a civilian? Do you observe any effect of such an experience on someone's life?
2. If you were asked to defend your country in time of war, would you serve in the military? What principles would influence your decision?
3. From your experience of crime or domestic violence, have you learned anything about the perpetrators?
4. When you read or see depictions of violence—either in war or crime—do you watch or turn away? Why do some people refuse to look at these depictions? Why do other people eagerly watch?
5. Is universal human love really possible? Is it just a religious or political myth, or do you believe it is an achievable goal?
6. Is nonviolence always the best means of political reform? Isn't armed violence sometimes the only way of creating change? What are the hidden dangers of violence as a political tool? Can they be worse than a repressive status quo?

FICTION
WAR AND VIOLENCE

Tim O'Brien — *The Things They Carried*
Ambrose Bierce — *An Occurrence at Owl Creek Bridge*
Mary Yukari Waters — *Shibusa*

Wars are vast events that engulf whole countries and continents, but they are also experienced by people one at a time. Historians try to cover the broad sweep of political circumstances and public events, but fiction writers know that they can convey the reality of history most vividly by telling the stories of individual lives. The stories in this section present the experience of war in the lives, imaginations, and memories of specific people. Tim O'Brien's celebrated short story "The Things They Carried" introduces a diverse company of American soldiers on combat patrol during the Vietnam War. Brilliantly, he depicts the profound individuality of these young men whom an outside observer might see as indistinguishable from one another. Ambrose Bierce's classic tale of a wartime execution shows a man desperately hoping to escape death and rejoin his family. Finally, Mary Yukari Waters's "Shibusa" portrays war and its aftermath through the eyes of a civilian survivor: a Japanese woman who lived through World War II.

Tim O'Brien

Tim O'Brien was born in 1946 in Austin, Minnesota. Immediately after graduating summa cum laude from Macalester College in 1968, he was drafted into the U.S. Army. Serving as an infantryman in Vietnam, O'Brien attained the rank of sergeant and won a Purple Heart after being wounded by shrapnel. Upon his discharge in 1970, he began graduate work at Harvard. In 1973 he published If I Die in a Combat Zone, Box Me Up and Ship Me Home, *a mixture of memoir and fiction about his wartime experiences. His 1978 novel* Going After Cacciato *won the National Book Award and is considered by some critics to be the best book of American fiction about the Vietnam War. "The Things They Carried" was first published in* Esquire *in 1986, and later became the title piece in a book of interlocking short stories published in 1990. O'Brien's other novels include* The Nuclear Age *(1985),* In the Lake of the Woods *(1994),* Tomcat in Love *(1998) and* July, July *(2002). He currently teaches at Texas State University–San Marcos.*

The Things They Carried   1990

First Lieutenant Jimmy Cross carried letters from a girl named Martha, a junior at Mount Sebastian College in New Jersey. They were not love letters, but Lieutenant Cross was hoping, so he kept them folded in plastic at the bottom of his rucksack. In the late afternoon, after a day's march, he would dig his foxhole, wash his hands under a canteen, unwrap the letters, hold them with the tips of his fingers, and spend the last hour of light pretending. He would imagine romantic camping trips into the White Mountains in New Hampshire. He would sometimes taste the envelope flaps, knowing her tongue had been there. More than anything, he wanted Martha to love him as he loved her, but the letters were mostly chatty, elusive on the matter of love. She was a virgin, he was almost sure. She was an English major at Mount Sebastian, and she wrote beautifully about her professors and roommates and midterm exams, about her respect for Chaucer and her great affection for Virginia Woolf. She often quoted lines of poetry; she never mentioned the war, except to say, Jimmy, take care of yourself. The letters weighed 10 ounces. They were signed Love, Martha, but Lieutenant Cross understood that Love was only a way of signing and did not mean what he sometimes pretended it meant. At dusk, he would carefully return the letters to his rucksack. Slowly, a bit distracted, he would get up and move among his men, checking the perimeter; then at full dark he would return to his hole and watch the night and wonder if Martha was a virgin.

The things they carried were largely determined by necessity. Among the necessities or near-necessities were P-38 can openers, pocket knives, heat tabs, wristwatches, dog tags, mosquito repellent, chewing gum, candy, cigarettes, salt tablets, packets of Kool-Aid, lighters, matches, sewing kits, Military Payment Certificates, C rations, and two or three canteens of water. Together, these items weighed between 15 and 20 pounds, depending upon a man's habits or rate of metabolism. Henry Dobbins, who was a big man, carried extra rations; he was especially fond of canned peaches in heavy syrup over pound cake. Dave Jensen, who practiced field hygiene, carried a toothbrush, dental floss, and several hotel-sized bars of soap he'd stolen on R&R° in Sydney, Australia. Ted Lavender, who was scared, carried tranquilizers until he was shot in the head outside the village of Than Khe in mid-April. By necessity, and because it was SOP,° they all carried steel helmets that weighed 5 pounds including the liner and camouflage cover. They carried the standard fatigue jackets and trousers. Very few carried underwear. On their feet they carried jungle boots—2.1 pounds—and Dave Jensen carried three pairs of socks and a can of Dr. Scholl's foot powder as a precaution against trench foot. Until he was shot, Ted Lavender carried six or seven ounces of premium dope, which for him was a necessity. Mitchell Sanders, the RTO,° carried condoms. Norman Bowker carried a diary. Rat Kiley carried comic books. Kiowa, a devout Baptist, carried an illustrated New Testament that had been presented to him by his father, who taught Sunday school in Oklahoma City, Oklahoma. As a hedge against bad times, however, Kiowa also carried his grandmother's distrust of

---

R&R: the military abbreviation for "rest and rehabilitation," a brief vacation from active service.   *SOP*: standard operating procedure.   *RTO*: radio and telephone operator.

the white man, his grandfather's old hunting hatchet. Necessity dictated. Because the land was mined and booby-trapped, it was SOP for each man to carry a steel-centered, nylon-covered flak jacket, which weighed 6.7 pounds, but which on hot days seemed much heavier. Because you could die so quickly, each man carried at least one large compress bandage, usually in the helmet band for easy access. Because the nights were cold, and because the monsoons were wet, each carried a green plastic poncho that could be used as a raincoat or groundsheet or makeshift tent. With its quilted liner, the poncho weighed almost two pounds, but it was worth every ounce. In April, for instance, when Ted Lavender was shot, they used his poncho to wrap him up, then to carry him across the paddy, then to lift him into the chopper that took him away.

They were called legs or grunts.

To carry something was to hump it, as when Lieutenant Jimmy Cross humped his love for Martha up the hills and through the swamps. In its intransitive form, to hump meant to walk, or to march, but it implied burdens far beyond the intransitive.

Almost everyone humped photographs. In his wallet, Lieutenant Cross carried two photographs of Martha. The first was a Kodacolor snapshot signed Love, though he knew better. She stood against a brick wall. Her eyes were gray and neutral, her lips slightly open as she stared straight-on at the camera. At night, sometimes, Lieutenant Cross wondered who had taken the picture, because he knew she had boyfriends, because he loved her so much, and because he could see the shadow of the picture-taker spreading out against the brick wall. The second photograph had been clipped from the 1968 Mount Sebastian yearbook. It was an action shot—women's volleyball—and Martha was bent horizontal to the floor, reaching, the palms of her hands in sharp focus, the tongue taut, the expression frank and competitive. There was no visible sweat. She wore white gym shorts. Her legs, he thought, were almost certainly the legs of a virgin, dry and without hair, the left knee cocked and carrying her entire weight, which was just over one hundred pounds. Lieutenant Cross remembered touching that left knee. A dark theater, he remembered, and the movie was *Bonnie and Clyde*, and Martha wore a tweed skirt, and during the final scene, when he touched her knee, she turned and looked at him in a sad, sober way that made him pull his hand back, but he would always remember the feel of the tweed skirt and the knee beneath it and the sound of the gunfire that killed Bonnie and Clyde, how embarrassing it was, how slow and oppressive. He remembered kissing her good night at the dorm door. Right then, he thought, he should've done something brave. He should've carried her up the stairs to her room and tied her to the bed and touched that left knee all night long. He should've risked it. Whenever he looked at the photographs, he thought of new things he should've done.

What they carried was partly a function of rank, partly of field specialty.

As a first lieutenant and platoon leader, Jimmy Cross carried a compass, maps, code books, binoculars, and a .45-caliber pistol that weighed 2.9 pounds fully loaded. He carried a strobe light and the responsibility for the lives of his men.

As an RTO, Mitchell Sanders carried the PRC-25 radio, a killer, 26 pounds with its battery.

As a medic, Rat Kiley carried a canvas satchel filled with morphine and plasma and malaria tablets and surgical tape and comic books and all the things a medic must carry, including M&M's° for especially bad wounds, for a total weight of nearly 20 pounds.

As a big man, therefore a machine gunner, Henry Dobbins carried the M-60, which weighed 23 pounds unloaded, but which was almost always loaded. In addition, Dobbins carried between 10 and 15 pounds of ammunition draped in belts across his chest and shoulders.

As PFCs or Spec 4s, most of them were common grunts and carried the standard M-16 gas-operated assault rifle. The weapon weighed 7.5 pounds unloaded, 8.2 pounds with its full 20-round magazine. Depending on numerous factors, such as topography and psychology, the riflemen carried anywhere from 12 to 20 magazines, usually in cloth bandoliers, adding on another 8.4 pounds at minimum, 14 pounds at maximum. When it was available, they also carried M-16 maintenance gear—rods and steel brushes and swabs and tubes of LSA oil—all of which weighed about a pound. Among the grunts, some carried the M-79 grenade launcher, 5.9 pounds unloaded, a reasonably light weapon except for the ammunition, which was heavy. A single round weighed 10 ounces. The typical load was 25 rounds. But Ted Lavender, who was scared, carried 34 rounds when he was shot and killed outside Than Khe, and he went down under an exceptional burden, more than 20 pounds of ammunition, plus the flak jacket and helmet and rations and water and toilet paper and tranquilizers and all the rest, plus the unweighed fear. He was dead weight. There was no twitching or flopping. Kiowa, who saw it happen, said it was like watching a rock fall, or a big sandbag or something—just boom, then down—not like the movies where the dead guy rolls around and does fancy spins and goes ass over teakettle—not like that, Kiowa said, the poor bastard just flat-fuck fell. Boom. Down. Nothing else. It was a bright morning in mid-April. Lieutenant Cross felt the pain. He blamed himself. They stripped off Lavender's canteens and ammo, all the heavy things, and Rat Kiley said the obvious, the guy's dead, and Mitchell Sanders used his radio to report one U.S. KIA° and to request a chopper. Then they wrapped Lavender in his poncho. They carried him out to a dry paddy, established security, and sat smoking the dead man's dope until the chopper came. Lieutenant Cross kept to himself. He pictured Martha's smooth young face, thinking he loved her more than anything, more than his men, and now Ted Lavender was dead because he loved her so much and could not stop thinking about her. When the dustoff arrived, they carried Lavender aboard. Afterward they burned Than Khe. They marched until dusk, then dug their holes, and that night Kiowa kept explaining how you had to be there, how fast it was, how the poor guy just dropped like so much concrete. Boom-down, he said. Like cement.

In addition to the three standard weapons—the M-60, M-16, and M-79—they carried whatever presented itself, or whatever seemed appropriate as a means of killing or staying alive. They carried catch-as-catch-can. At various times, in various situations, they carried M-14s and CAR-15s and Swedish Ks and grease guns and captured AK-47s and Chi-Coms and RPGs and Simonov carbines and black market Uzis and .38-caliber Smith & Wesson handguns and 66 mm LAWs and shotguns and silencers and blackjacks and bayonets and C-4 plastic explosives. Lee Strunk carried a

M&M's: comic slang for medical supplies.   KIA: killed in action.

slingshot; a weapon of last resort, he called it. Mitchell Sanders carried brass knuckles. Kiowa carried his grandfather's feathered hatchet. Every third or fourth man carried a Claymore antipersonnel mine—3.5 pounds with its firing device. They all carried fragmentation grenades—14 ounces each. They all carried at least one M-18 colored smoke grenade—24 ounces. Some carried CS or tear gas grenades. Some carried white phosphorus grenades. They carried all they could bear, and then some, including a silent awe for the terrible power of the things they carried.

In the first week of April, before Lavender died, Lieutenant Jimmy Cross received a good-luck charm from Martha. It was a simple pebble, an ounce at most. Smooth to the touch, it was a milky white color with flecks of orange and violet, oval-shaped, like a miniature egg. In the accompanying letter, Martha wrote that she had found the pebble on the Jersey shoreline, precisely where the land touched water at high tide, where things came together but also separated. It was this separate-but-together quality, she wrote, that had inspired her to pick up the pebble and to carry it in her breast pocket for several days, where it seemed weightless, and then to send it through the mail, by air, as a token of her truest feelings for him. Lieutenant Cross found this romantic. But he wondered what her truest feelings were, exactly, and what she meant by separate-but-together. He wondered how the tides and waves had come into play on that afternoon along the Jersey shoreline when Martha saw the pebble and bent down to rescue it from geology. He imagined bare feet. Martha was a poet, with the poet's sensibilities, and her feet would be brown and bare, the toenails unpainted, the eyes chilly and somber like the ocean in March, and though it was painful, he wondered who had been with her that afternoon. He imagined a pair of shadows moving along the strip of sand where things came together but also separated. It was phantom jealousy, he knew, but he couldn't help himself. He loved her so much. On the march, through the hot days of early April, he carried the pebble in his mouth, turning it with his tongue, tasting sea salt and moisture. His mind wandered. He had difficulty keeping his attention on the war. On occasion he would yell at his men to spread out the column, to keep their eyes open, but then he would slip away into daydreams, just pretending, walking barefoot along the Jersey shore, with Martha, carrying nothing. He would feel himself rising. Sun and waves and gentle winds, all love and lightness.

What they carried varied by mission.

When a mission took them to the mountains, they carried mosquito netting, machetes, canvas tarps, and extra bug juice.

If a mission seemed especially hazardous, or if it involved a place they knew to be bad, they carried everything they could. In certain heavily mined AOs,° where the land was dense with Toe Poppers and Bouncing Betties, they took turns humping a 28-pound mine detector. With its headphones and big sensing plate, the equipment was a stress on the lower back and shoulders, awkward to handle, often useless because of the shrapnel in the earth, but they carried it anyway, partly for safety, partly for the illusion of safety.

On ambush, or other night missions, they carried peculiar little odds and ends. Kiowa always took along his New Testament and a pair of moccasins for silence. Dave Jensen carried night-sight vitamins high in carotene. Lee Strunk carried his slingshot; ammo, he claimed, would never be a problem. Rat Kiley carried brandy and M&M's

---

AOs: areas of operation.

candy. Until he was shot, Ted Lavender carried the starlight scope, which weighed 6.3 pounds with its aluminum carrying case. Henry Dobbins carried his girlfriend's pantyhose wrapped around his neck as a comforter. They all carried ghosts. When dark came, they would move out single file across the meadows and paddies to their ambush coordinates, where they would quietly set up the Claymores and lie down and spend the night waiting.

Other missions were more complicated and required special equipment. In mid-April, it was their mission to search out and destroy the elaborate tunnel complexes in the Than Khe area south of Chu Lai. To blow the tunnels, they carried one-pound blocks of pentrite high explosives, four blocks to a man, 68 pounds in all. They carried wiring, detonators, and battery-powered clackers. Dave Jensen carried earplugs. Most often, before blowing the tunnels, they were ordered by higher command to search them, which was considered bad news, but by and large they just shrugged and carried out orders. Because he was a big man, Henry Dobbins was excused from tunnel duty. The others would draw numbers. Before Lavender died there were 17 men in the platoon, and whoever drew the number 17 would strip off his gear and crawl in headfirst with a flashlight and Lieutenant Cross's .45-caliber pistol. The rest of them would fan out as security. They would sit down or kneel, not facing the hole, listening to the ground beneath them, imagining cobwebs and ghosts, whatever was down there—the tunnel walls squeezing in—how the flashlight seemed impossibly heavy in the hand and how it was tunnel vision in the very strictest sense, compression in all ways, even time, and how you had to wiggle in—ass and elbows—a swallowed-up feeling—and how you found yourself worrying about odd things: Will your flashlight go dead? Do rats carry rabies? If you screamed, how far would the sound carry? Would your buddies hear it? Would they have the courage to drag you out? In some respects, though not many, the waiting was worse than the tunnel itself. Imagination was a killer.

On April 16, when Lee Strunk drew the number 17, he laughed and muttered something and went down quickly. The morning was hot and very still. Not good, Kiowa said. He looked at the tunnel opening, then out across a dry paddy toward the village of Than Khe. Nothing moved. No clouds or birds or people. As they waited, the men smoked and drank Kool-Aid, not talking much, feeling sympathy for Lee Strunk but also feeling the luck of the draw. You win some, you lose some, said Mitchell Sanders, and sometimes you settle for a rain check. It was a tired line and no one laughed.

Henry Dobbins ate a tropical chocolate bar. Ted Lavender popped a tranquilizer and went off to pee.

After five minutes, Lieutenant Jimmy Cross moved to the tunnel, leaned down, and examined the darkness. Trouble, he thought—a cave-in maybe. And then suddenly, without willing it, he was thinking about Martha. The stresses and fractures, the quick collapse, the two of them buried alive under all that weight. Dense, crushing love. Kneeling, watching the hole, he tried to concentrate on Lee Strunk and the war, all the dangers, but his love was too much for him, he felt paralyzed, he wanted to sleep inside her lungs and breathe her blood and be smothered. He wanted her to be a virgin and not a virgin, all at once. He wanted to know her. Intimate secrets: Why poetry? Why so sad? Why that grayness in her eyes? Why so alone? Not lonely, just alone—riding her bike across campus or sitting off by herself in the cafeteria—even dancing, she danced alone—and it was the aloneness that filled him with love. He remembered telling her that one evening. How she nodded and looked away. And how, later, when he kissed her, she received the kiss without returning it, her eyes wide open, not afraid, not a virgin's eyes, just flat and uninvolved.

Lieutenant Cross gazed at the tunnel. But he was not there. He was buried with Martha under the white sand at the Jersey shore. They were pressed together, and the pebble in his mouth was her tongue. He was smiling. Vaguely, he was aware of how quiet the day was, the sullen paddies, yet he could not bring himself to worry about matters of security. He was beyond that. He was just a kid at war, in love. He was twenty-four years old. He couldn't help it.

A few moments later Lee Strunk crawled out of the tunnel. He came up grinning, filthy but alive. Lieutenant Cross nodded and closed his eyes while the others clapped Strunk on the back and made jokes about rising from the dead.

Worms, Rat Kiley said. Right out of the grave. Fuckin' zombie.

The men laughed. They all felt great relief.

Spook city, said Mitchell Sanders.

Lee Strunk made a funny ghost sound, a kind of moaning, yet very happy, and right then, when Strunk made that high happy moaning sound, when he went *Ahhooooo,* right then Ted Lavender was shot in the head on his way back from peeing. He lay with his mouth open. The teeth were broken. There was a swollen black bruise under his left eye. The cheekbone was gone. Oh shit, Rat Kiley said, the guy's dead. The guy's dead, he kept saying, which seemed profound—the guy's dead. I mean really.

The things they carried were determined to some extent by superstition. Lieutenant Cross carried his good-luck pebble. Dave Jensen carried a rabbit's foot. Norman Bowker, otherwise a very gentle person, carried a thumb that had been presented to him as a gift by Mitchell Sanders. The thumb was dark brown, rubbery to the touch, and weighed four ounces at most. It had been cut from a VC corpse, a boy of fifteen or sixteen. They'd found him at the bottom of an irrigation ditch, badly burned, flies in his mouth and eyes. The boy wore black shorts and sandals. At the time of his death he had been carrying a pouch of rice, a rifle, and three magazines of ammunition.

You want my opinion, Mitchell Sanders said, there's a definite moral here.

He put his hand on the dead boy's wrist. He was quiet for a time, as if counting a pulse, then he patted the stomach, almost affectionately, and used Kiowa's hunting hatchet to remove the thumb.

Henry Dobbins asked what the moral was.

Moral?

You know. *Moral.*

Sanders wrapped the thumb in toilet paper and handed it across to Norman Bowker. There was no blood. Smiling, he kicked the boy's head, watched the flies scatter, and said, It's like with that old TV show—Paladin. Have gun, will travel.

Henry Dobbins thought about it.

Yeah, well, he finally said. I don't see no moral.

There it *is,* man.

Fuck off.

*

They carried USO stationery and pencils and pens. They carried Sterno, safety pins, trip flares, signal flares, spools of wire, razor blades, chewing tobacco, liberated joss sticks and statuettes of the smiling Buddha, candles, grease pencils, *The Stars and Stripes*, fingernail clippers, Psy Ops leaflets, bush hats, bolos, and much more. Twice a week, when the resupply choppers came in, they carried hot chow in green mermite cans and large canvas bags filled with iced beer and soda pop. They carried plastic water containers, each with a two-gallon capacity. Mitchell Sanders carried a set of starched tiger fatigues for special occasions. Henry Dobbins carried Black Flag insecticide. Dave Jensen carried empty sandbags that could be filled at night for added protection. Lee Strunk carried tanning lotion. Some things they carried in common. Taking turns, they carried the big PRC-77 scrambler radio, which weighed 30 pounds with its battery. They shared the weight of memory. They took up what others could no longer bear. Often, they carried each other, the wounded or weak. They carried infections. They carried chess sets, basketballs, Vietnamese-English dictionaries, insignia of rank, Bronze Stars and Purple Hearts, plastic cards imprinted with the Code of Conduct. They carried diseases, among them malaria and dysentery. They carried lice and ringworm and leeches and paddy algae and various rots and molds. They carried the land itself—Vietnam, the place, the soil—a powdery orange-red dust that covered their boots and fatigues and faces. They carried the sky. The whole atmosphere, they carried it, the humidity, the monsoons, the stink of fungus and decay, all of it, they carried gravity. They moved like mules. By daylight they took sniper fire, at night they were mortared, but it was not battle, it was just the endless march, village to village, without purpose, nothing won or lost. They marched for the sake of the march. They plodded along slowly, dumbly, leaning forward against the heat, unthinking, all blood and bone, simple grunts, soldiering with their legs, toiling up the hills and down into the paddies and across the rivers and up again and down, just humping, one step and then the next and then another, but no volition, no will, because it was automatic, it was anatomy, and the war was entirely a matter of posture and carriage, the hump was everything, a kind of inertia, a kind of emptiness, a dullness of desire and intellect and conscience and hope and human sensibility. Their principles were in their feet. Their calculations were biological. They had no sense of strategy or mission. They searched the villages without knowing what to look for, not caring, kicking over jars of rice, frisking children and old men, blowing tunnels, sometimes setting fires and sometimes not, then forming up and moving on to the next village, then other villages, where it would always be the same. They carried their own lives. The pressures were enormous. In the heat of early afternoon, they would remove their helmets and flak jackets, walking bare, which was dangerous but which helped ease the strain. They would often discard things along the route of march. Purely for comfort, they would throw away rations, blow their Claymores and grenades, no matter, because by nightfall the resupply choppers would arrive with more of the same, then a day or two later still more, fresh watermelons and crates of ammunition and sunglasses and woolen sweaters—the resources were stunning—sparklers for the Fourth of July, colored eggs for Easter—it was the great American war chest—the fruits of science, the smokestacks, the canneries, the arsenals at Hartford, the Minnesota forests, the machine shops, the vast fields of corn and wheat—they carried like freight trains; they carried it on their backs and shoulders—and for all the ambiguities of Vietnam, all the mysteries and unknowns, there was at least the single abiding certainty that they would never be at a loss for things to carry.

After the chopper took Lavender away, Lieutenant Jimmy Cross led his men into the village of Than Khe. They burned everything. They shot chickens and dogs, they trashed the village well, they called in artillery and watched the wreckage, then they marched for several hours through the hot afternoon, and then at dusk, while Kiowa explained how Lavender died, Lieutenant Cross found himself trembling.

He tried not to cry. With his entrenching tool, which weighed five pounds, he began digging a hole in the earth.

He felt shame. He hated himself. He had loved Martha more than his men, and as a consequence Lavender was now dead, and this was something he would have to carry like a stone in his stomach for the rest of the war.

All he could do was dig. He used his entrenching tool like an ax, slashing, feeling both love and hate, and then later, when it was full dark, he sat at the bottom of his foxhole and wept. It went on for a long while. In part, he was grieving for Ted Lavender, but mostly it was for Martha, and for himself, because she belonged to another world, which was not quite real, and because she was a junior at Mount Sebastian College in New Jersey, a poet and a virgin and uninvolved, and because he realized she did not love him and never would.

Like cement, Kiowa whispered in the dark. I swear to God—boom, down. Not a word.

I've heard this, said Norman Bowker.

A pisser, you know? Still zipping himself up. Zapped while zipping.

All right, fine. That's enough.

Yeah, but you had to see it, the guy just—

I *heard*, man. Cement. So why not shut the fuck *up*?

Kiowa shook his head sadly and glanced over at the hole where Lieutenant Jimmy Cross sat watching the night. The air was thick and wet. A warm dense fog had settled over the paddies and there was the stillness that precedes rain.

After a time Kiowa sighed.

One thing for sure, he said. The lieutenant's in some deep hurt. I mean that crying jag—the way he was carrying on—it wasn't fake or anything, it was real heavy-duty hurt. The man cares.

Sure, Norman Bowker said.

Say what you want, the man does care.

We all got problems.

Not Lavender.

No, I guess not, Bowker said. Do me a favor, though.

Shut up?

That's a smart Indian. Shut up.

Shrugging, Kiowa pulled off his boots. He wanted to say more, just to lighten up his sleep, but instead he opened his New Testament and arranged it beneath his head as a pillow. The fog made things seem hollow and unattached. He tried not to think about Ted Lavender, but then he was thinking how fast it was, no drama, down and dead, and how it was hard to feel anything except surprise. It seemed unchristian. He wished he could find some great sadness, or even anger, but the emotion wasn't there and he couldn't make it happen. Mostly he felt pleased to be alive. He liked the smell of the New Testament under his cheek, the leather and ink and paper and glue, whatever the chemicals were. He liked hearing the sounds of night. Even his fatigue, it felt fine, the stiff muscles and the prickly awareness of his own body, a floating feeling. He enjoyed not being dead. Lying there, Kiowa admired Lieutenant Jimmy Cross's capacity for grief. He wanted to share the man's pain, he wanted to care as Jimmy Cross cared. And yet when he closed his eyes, all he could think was Boom-down, and all he could feel was the pleasure of having his boots off and the fog curling in around him and the damp soil and the Bible smells and the plush comfort of night.

After a moment Norman Bowker sat up in the dark.

What the hell, he said. You want to talk, *talk*. Tell it to me.

Forget it.

No, man, go on. One thing I hate, it's a silent Indian.

For the most part they carried themselves with poise, a kind of dignity. Now and then, however, there were times of panic, when they squealed or wanted to squeal but couldn't, when they twitched and made moaning sounds and covered their heads and said Dear Jesus and flopped around on the earth and fired their weapons blindly and cringed and sobbed and begged for the noise to stop and went wild and made stupid promises to themselves and to God and to their mothers and fathers, hoping not to die. In different ways, it happened to all of them. Afterward, when the firing ended, they would blink and peek up. They would touch their bodies, feeling shame, then quickly hiding it. They would force themselves to stand. As if in slow motion, frame by frame, the world would take on the old logic—absolute silence, then the wind, then sunlight, then voices. It was the burden of being alive. Awkwardly, the men would reassemble themselves, first in private, then in groups, becoming soldiers again. They would repair the leaks in their eyes. They would check for casualties, call in dustoffs, light cigarettes, try to smile, clear their throats and spit and begin cleaning their weapons. After a time someone would shake his head and say, No lie, I almost shit my pants, and someone else would laugh, which meant it was bad, yes, but the guy had obviously not shit his pants, it wasn't that bad, and in any case nobody would ever do such a thing and then go ahead and talk about it. They would squint into the dense, oppressive sunlight. For a few moments, perhaps, they would fall silent, lighting a joint and tracking its passage from man to man, inhaling, holding in the humiliation. Scary stuff, one of them might say. But then someone else would grin or flick his eyebrows and say, Roger-dodger, almost cut me a new asshole, *almost*.

There were numerous such poses. Some carried themselves with a sort of wistful resignation, others with pride or stiff soldierly discipline or good humor or macho zeal. They were afraid of dying but they were even more afraid to show it.

They found jokes to tell.

They used a hard vocabulary to contain the terrible softness. *Greased*, they'd say. *Offed, lit up, zapped while zipping*. It wasn't cruelty, just stage presence. They were actors. When someone died, it wasn't quite dying, because in a curious way it seemed scripted, and because they had their lines mostly memorized, irony mixed with tragedy, and because they called it by other names, as if to encyst and destroy the reality of death itself. They kicked corpses. They cut off thumbs. They talked grunt lingo. They told stories about Ted Lavender's supply of tranquilizers, how the poor guy didn't feel a thing, how incredibly tranquil he was.

There's a moral here, said Mitchell Sanders.

They were waiting for Lavender's chopper, smoking the dead man's dope.

The moral's pretty obvious, Sanders said, and winked. Stay away from drugs. No joke, they'll ruin your day every time.

Cute, said Henry Dobbins.

Mind blower, get it? Talk about wiggy. Nothing left, just blood and brains.

They made themselves laugh.

There it is, they'd say. Over and over—there it is, my friend, there it is—as if the repetition itself were an act of poise, a balance between crazy and almost crazy, knowing without going, there it is, which meant be cool, let it ride, because Oh yeah, man, you can't change what can't be changed, there it is, there it absolutely and positively and fucking well *is*.

They were tough.

They carried all the emotional baggage of men who might die. Grief, terror, love, longing—these were intangibles, but the intangibles had their own mass and specific gravity, they had tangible weight. They carried shameful memories. They carried the common secret of cowardice barely restrained, the instinct to run or freeze or hide, and in many respects this was the heaviest burden of all, for it could never be put down, it required perfect balance and perfect posture. They carried their reputations. They carried the soldier's greatest fear, which was the fear of blushing. Men killed, and died, because they were embarrassed not to. It was what had brought them to the war in the first place, nothing positive, no dreams of glory or honor, just to avoid the blush of dishonor. They died so as not to die of embarrassment. They crawled into tunnels and walked point and advanced under fire. Each morning, despite the unknowns, they made their legs move. They endured. They kept humping. They did not submit to the obvious alternative, which was simply to close the eyes and fall. So easy, really. Go limp and tumble to the ground and let the muscles unwind and not speak and not budge until your buddies picked you up and lifted you into the chopper that would roar and dip its nose and carry you off to the world. A mere matter of falling, yet no one ever fell. It was not courage, exactly; the object was not valor. Rather, they were too frightened to be cowards.

By and large they carried these things inside, maintaining the masks of composure. They sneered at sick call. They spoke bitterly about guys who had found release by shooting off their own toes or fingers. Pussies, they'd say. Candy-asses. It was fierce, mocking talk, with only a trace of envy or awe, but even so the image played itself out behind their eyes.

They imagined the muzzle against flesh. So easy: squeeze the trigger and blow away a toe. They imagined it. They imagined the quick, sweet pain, then the evacuation to Japan, then a hospital with warm beds and cute geisha nurses.

And they dreamed of freedom birds.

At night, on guard, staring into the dark, they were carried away by jumbo jets. They felt the rush of takeoff. *Gone!* they yelled. And then velocity—wings and engines—a smiling stewardess—but it was more than a plane, it was a real bird, a big sleek silver bird with feathers and talons and high screeching. They were flying.

The weights fell off; there was nothing to bear. They laughed and held on tight, feeling the cold slap of wind and altitude, soaring, thinking *It's over, I'm gone!*—they were naked, they were light and free—it was all lightness, bright and fast and buoyant, light as light, a helium buzz in the brain, a giddy bubbling in the lungs as they were taken up over the clouds and the war, beyond duty, beyond gravity and mortification and global entanglements—*Sin loi!*° they yelled. *I'm sorry, mother-fuckers, but I'm out of it, I'm goofed, I'm on a space cruise, I'm gone!*—and it was a restful, unencumbered sensation, just riding the light waves, sailing that big silver freedom bird over the mountains and oceans, over America, over the farms and great sleeping cities and cemeteries and highways and the golden arches of McDonald's, it was flight, a kind of fleeing, a kind of falling, falling higher and higher, spinning off the edge of the earth and beyond the sun and through the vast, silent vacuum where there were no burdens and where everything weighed exactly nothing—*Gone!* they screamed. *I'm sorry but I'm gone!*—and so at night, not quite dreaming, they gave themselves over to lightness, they were carried, they were purely borne.

On the morning after Ted Lavender died, First Lieutenant Jimmy Cross crouched at the bottom of his foxhole and burned Martha's letters. Then he burned the two photographs. There was a steady rain falling, which made it difficult, but he used heat tabs and Sterno to build a small fire, screening it with his body, holding the photographs over the tight blue flame with the tips of his fingers.

He realized it was only a gesture. Stupid, he thought. Sentimental, too, but mostly just stupid.

Lavender was dead. You couldn't burn the blame.

Besides, the letters were in his head. And even now, without photographs, Lieutenant Cross could see Martha playing volleyball in her white gym shorts and yellow T-shirt. He could see her moving in the rain.

When the fire died out, Lieutenant Cross pulled his poncho over his shoulders and ate breakfast from a can.

There was no great mystery, he decided.

In those burned letters Martha had never mentioned the war, except to say, Jimmy, take care of yourself. She wasn't involved. She signed the letters Love, but it wasn't love, and all the fine lines and technicalities did not matter. Virginity was no longer an issue. He hated her. Yes, he did. He hated her. Love, too, but it was a hard, hating kind of love.

The morning came up wet and blurry. Everything seemed part of everything else, the fog and Martha and the deepening rain.

He was a soldier, after all.

Half smiling, Lieutenant Jimmy Cross took out his maps. He shook his head hard, as if to clear it, then bent forward and began planning the day's march. In ten minutes, or maybe twenty, he would rouse the men and they would pack up and head west, where the maps showed the country to be green and inviting. They would do what they had always done. The rain might add some weight, but otherwise it would be one more day layered upon all the other days.

He was realistic about it. There was that new hardness in his stomach. He loved her but he hated her.

Sin loi: Vietnamese for sorry.

No more fantasies, he told himself.

Henceforth, when he thought about Martha, it would be only to think that she belonged elsewhere. He would shut down the daydreams. This was not Mount Sebastian, it was another world, where there were no pretty poems or midterm exams, a place where men died because of carelessness and gross stupidity. Kiowa was right. Boom-down, and you were dead, never partly dead.

Briefly, in the rain, Lieutenant Cross saw Martha's gray eyes gazing back at him.

He understood.

It was very sad, he thought. The things men carried inside. The things men did or felt they had to do.

He almost nodded at her, but didn't.

Instead he went back to his maps. He was now determined to perform his duties firmly and without negligence. It wouldn't help Lavender, he knew that, but from this point on he would comport himself as an officer. He would dispose of his good-luck pebble. Swallow it, maybe, or use Lee Strunk's slingshot, or just drop it along the trail. On the march he would impose strict field discipline. He would be careful to send out flank security, to prevent straggling or bunching up, to keep his troops moving at the proper pace and at the proper interval. He would insist on clean weapons. He would confiscate the remainder of Lavender's dope. Later in the day, perhaps, he would call the men together and speak to them plainly. He would accept the blame for what had happened to Ted Lavender. He would be a man about it. He would look them in the eyes, keeping his chin level, and he would issue the new SOPs in a calm, impersonal tone of voice, a lieutenant's voice, leaving no room for argument or discussion. Commencing immediately, he'd tell them, they would no longer abandon equipment along the route of march. They would police up their acts. They would get their shit together, and keep it together, and maintain it neatly and in good working order.

He would not tolerate laxity. He would show strength, distancing himself.

Among the men there would be grumbling, of course, and maybe worse, because their days would seem longer and their loads heavier, but Lieutenant Jimmy Cross reminded himself that his obligation was not to be loved but to lead. He would dispense with love; it was not now a factor. And if anyone quarreled or complained, he would simply tighten his lips and arrange his shoulders in the correct command posture. He might give a curt little nod. Or he might not. He might just shrug and say, Carry on, then they would saddle up and form into a column and move out toward the villages west of Than Khe.

Questions

1. How many soldiers are there in the platoon? Name them all.
2. Throughout the story the narrator uses the phrase "the things they carried" or some variation of it. What effect does it have to characterize people by the physical objects they bear?
3. O'Brien fills the story with military terminology from official acronyms such as SOP and AO to nicknames like Toe Poppers and Bouncing Betties. What effect does this specialized language have on the reader?
4. How does O'Brien build an atmosphere of realism in the story?
5. Take any character in the story and list several of the things he carries. What do they tell us about his personality and values?
6. What nonphysical things do the men carry?

7. Why does the lieutenant, Jimmy Cross, burn Martha's photographs and letters the morning after Lavender's death?
8. What does this story suggest about what troops carry home with them when they return from war?

Ambrose Bierce

Ambrose Bierce (1842–1914?) was born in Horse Cave Creek, Ohio, the youngest child of nine in an impoverished farm family. A year at Kentucky Military Academy was his only formal schooling. Enlisting as a drummer boy in the Union Army, Bierce saw action at Shiloh and Chickamauga, took part in Sherman's March to the Sea, and came out of the army a brevet major. Then he became a writer, later an editor, for San Francisco newspapers. For a while Bierce thrived. He and his wife, on her ample dowry, lived five years in London, where Bierce wrote for London papers, honed his style, and cultivated his wit. But his wife left him, his two sons died (one of gunfire and the other of alcoholism), and late in life Bierce came to deserve his nickname "Bitter Bierce." In 1913, at seventy-one, he trekked off to Mexico and

Ambrose Bierce

vanished without a trace, although one report had him riding with the forces of revolutionist Pancho Villa. Bierce, who regarded the novel as "a short story padded," favored shorter lengths: short story, fable, newspaper column, aphorism. Sardonically, in The Devil's Dictionary *(1911), he defines* diplomacy *as "the patriotic art of lying for one's country" and* saint *as "a dead sinner revised and edited." Master of both realism and the ghost story, he collected his best Civil War fiction, including "An Occurrence at Owl Creek Bridge," in* Tales of Soldiers and Civilians *(1891), later retitled* In the Midst of Life.

An Occurrence at Owl Creek Bridge   1891

I

A man stood upon a railroad bridge in northern Alabama, looking down into the swift water twenty feet below. The man's hands were behind his back, the wrists bound with a cord. A rope closely encircled his neck. It was attached to a stout cross-timber above his head and the slack fell to the level of his knees. Some loose boards laid upon the sleepers supporting the metals of the railway supplied a footing for him and his executioners—two private soldiers of the Federal army, directed by a sergeant who in civil life may have been a deputy sheriff. At a short remove upon the same temporary platform was an officer in the uniform of his rank, armed. He was a captain. A sentinel at each end of the bridge stood with his rifle in the position known as "support," that is to say, vertical in front of the left shoulder, the hammer resting on the forearm thrown straight across the chest—a formal and unnatural position, enforcing an erect carriage of the body. It did not appear to be the duty of these two men to know what was occurring at the center of the bridge; they merely blockaded the two ends of the foot planking that traversed it.

Beyond one of the sentinels nobody was in sight; the railroad ran straight away into a forest for a hundred yards, then, curving, was lost to view. Doubtless there was an outpost farther along. The other bank of the stream was open ground—a gentle acclivity topped with a stockade of vertical tree trunks, loop-holed for rifles, with a single embrasure through which protruded the muzzle of a brass cannon commanding the bridge. Midway of the slope between bridge and fort were the spectators—a single company of infantry in line, at "parade rest," the butts of the rifles on the ground, the barrels inclining slightly backward against the right shoulder, the hands crossed upon the stock. A lieutenant stood at the right of the line, the point of his sword upon the ground, his left hand resting upon his right. Excepting the group of four at the center of the bridge, not a man moved. The company faced the bridge, staring stonily, motionless. The sentinels, facing the banks of the stream, might have been statues to adorn the bridge. The captain stood with folded arms, silent, observing the work of his subordinates, but making no sign. Death is a dignitary who when he comes announced is to be received with formal manifestations of respect, even by those most familiar with him. In the code of military etiquette silence and fixity are forms of deference.

The man who was engaged in being hanged was apparently about thirty-five years of age. He was a civilian, if one might judge from his habit, which was that of a planter. His features were good—a straight nose, firm mouth, broad forehead, from which his long, dark hair was combed straight back, falling behind his ears to the collar of his well-fitting frock-coat. He wore a mustache and pointed beard, but no whiskers; his eyes were large and dark gray, and had a kindly expression which one would hardly have expected in one whose neck was in the hemp. Evidently this was no vulgar assassin. The liberal military code makes provision for hanging many kinds of persons, and gentlemen are not excluded.

The preparations being complete, the two private soldiers stepped aside and each drew away the plank upon which he had been standing. The sergeant turned to the captain, saluted and placed himself immediately behind that officer, who in turn moved apart one pace. These movements left the condemned man and the sergeant standing on the two ends of the same plank, which spanned three of the cross-ties of the bridge. The end upon which the civilian stood almost, but not quite, reached a fourth. This plank had been held in place by the weight of the captain; it was now held by that of the sergeant. At a signal from the former the latter would step aside, the plank would tilt and the condemned man go down between two ties. The arrangement commended itself to his judgment as simple and effective. His face had not been covered nor his eyes bandaged. He looked a moment at his "unsteadfast footing," then let his gaze wander to the swirling water of the stream racing madly beneath his feet. A piece of dancing driftwood caught his attention and his eyes followed it down the current. How slowly it appeared to move! What a sluggish stream!

He closed his eyes in order to fix his last thoughts upon his wife and children. The water, touched to gold by the early sun, the brooding mists under the banks at some distance down the stream, the fort, the soldiers, the piece of drift—all had distracted him. And now he became conscious of a new disturbance. Striking through the thought of his dear ones was a sound which he could neither ignore nor understand, a sharp, distinct, metallic percussion like the stroke of a blacksmith's hammer upon the anvil; it had the same ringing quality. He wondered what it was, and whether immeasurably distant or near by—it seemed both. Its recurrence was regular, but as slow as the tolling of a death knell. He awaited each stroke with impatience and—he knew not why—apprehension. The intervals of silence grew progressively longer; the delays became maddening. With their greater infrequency the sounds increased in strength and sharpness. They hurt his ear like the thrust of a knife; he feared he would shriek. What he heard was the ticking of his watch.

He unclosed his eyes and saw again the water below him. "If I could free my hands," he thought, "I might throw off the noose and spring into the stream. By diving I could evade the bullets and, swimming vigorously, reach the bank, take to the woods and get away home. My home, thank God, is as yet outside their lines; my wife and little ones are still beyond the invader's farthest advance."

As these thoughts, which have here to be set down in words, were flashed into the doomed man's brain rather than evolved from it the captain nodded to the sergeant. The sergeant stepped aside.

II

Peyton Farquhar was a well-to-do planter, of an old and highly respected Alabama family. Being a slave owner and like other slave owners a politician he was naturally an original secessionist and ardently devoted to the Southern cause. Circumstances of an imperious nature, which it is unnecessary to relate here, had prevented him from taking service with the gallant army that had fought the disastrous campaigns ending with the fall of Corinth, and he chafed under the inglorious restraint, longing for the release of his energies, the larger life of the soldier, the opportunity for distinction. That opportunity, he felt, would come, as it comes to all in war time. Meanwhile he did what he could. No service was too humble to him to perform in aid of the South, no adventure too perilous for him to undertake if consistent with the character of a civilian who was at heart a soldier, and who in good faith and without too much qualification assented to at least a part of the frankly villainous dictum that all is fair in love and war.

One evening while Farquhar and his wife were sitting on a rustic bench near the entrance to his grounds, a gray-clad soldier rode up to the gate and asked for a drink of water. Mrs. Farquhar was only too happy to serve him with her own white hands. While she was fetching the water her husband approached the dusty horseman and inquired eagerly for news from the front.

"The Yanks are repairing the railroads," said the man, "and are getting ready for another advance. They have reached the Owl Creek bridge, put it in order and built a stockade on the north bank. The commandant has issued an order, which is posted everywhere, declaring that any civilian caught interfering with the railroad, its bridges, tunnels or trains will be summarily hanged. I saw the order."

"How far is it to the Owl Creek bridge?" Farquhar asked.

"About thirty miles."

"Is there no force on this side the creek?"

"Only a picket post half a mile out, on the railroad, and a single sentinel at this end of the bridge."

"Suppose a man—a civilian and student of hanging—should elude the picket post and perhaps get the better of the sentinel," said Farquhar, smiling, "what could he accomplish?"

The soldier reflected. "I was there a month ago," he replied. "I observed that the flood of last winter had lodged a great quantity of driftwood against the wooden pier at this end of the bridge. It is now dry and would burn like tow."

The lady had now brought the water, which the soldier drank. He thanked her ceremoniously, bowed to her husband and rode away. An hour later, after nightfall, he repassed the plantation, going northward in the direction from which he had come. He was a Federal scout.

III

As Peyton Farquhar fell straight downward through the bridge he lost consciousness and was as one already dead. From this state he was awakened—ages later, it seemed to him—by the pain of a sharp pressure upon his throat, followed by a sense of suffocation. Keen, poignant agonies seemed to shoot from his neck downward through every fiber of his body and limbs. These pains appeared to flash along well-defined lines of ramification and to beat with an inconceivably rapid periodicity. They seemed like streams of pulsating fire heating him to an intolerable temperature. As to his head, he was conscious of nothing but a feeling of fulness—of congestion. These sensations were unaccompanied by thought. The intellectual part of his nature was already effaced; he had power only to feel, and feeling was torment. He was conscious of motion. Encompassed in a luminous cloud, of which he was now merely the fiery heart, without material substance, he swung through unthinkable arcs of oscillation, like a vast pendulum. Then all at once, with terrible suddenness, the light about him shot upward with the noise of a loud plash; a frightful roaring was in his ears, and all was cold and dark. The power of thought was restored; he knew that the rope had broken and he had fallen into the stream. There was no additional strangulation; the noose about his neck was already suffocating him and kept the water from his lungs. To die of hanging at the bottom of a river!—the idea seemed to him ludicrous. He opened his eyes in the darkness and saw above him a gleam of light, but how distant, how inaccessible! He was still sinking, for the light became fainter and fainter until it was a mere glimmer. Then it began to grow and brighten, and he knew that he was rising toward the surface—knew it with reluctance, for he was now very comfortable. "To be hanged and drowned," he thought, "that is not so bad; but I do not wish to be shot. No; I will not be shot; that is not fair."

He was not conscious of an effort, but a sharp pain in his wrist apprised him that he was trying to free his hands. He gave the struggle his attention, as an idler might observe the feat of a juggler, without interest in the outcome. What splendid effort!—what magnificent, what superhuman strength! Ah, that was a fine endeavor! Bravo! The cord fell away; his arms parted and floated upward, the hands dimly seen on each side in the growing light. He watched them with a new interest as first one and then the other pounced upon the noose at his neck. They tore it away and thrust it fiercely aside, its undulations resembling those of a water-snake. "Put it back, put it back!" He thought he shouted these words to his hands, for the undoing of the noose had been succeeded by the direst pang that he had yet experienced. His neck ached horribly; his brain was on fire; his heart, which had been fluttering faintly, gave a great leap, trying to force itself out at his mouth. His whole body was racked and wrenched with an insupportable anguish! But his disobedient hands gave no heed to the command. They beat the water vigorously with quick, downward strokes, forcing him to the surface. He felt his head emerge; his eyes were blinded by the sunlight; his chest expanded convulsively, and with a supreme and crowning agony his lungs engulfed a great draught of air, which instantly he expelled in a shriek!

He was now in full possession of his physical senses. They were, indeed, preternaturally keen and alert. Something in the awful disturbance of his organic system had so exalted and refined them that they made record of things never before perceived. He felt the ripples upon his face and heard their separate sounds as they struck. He looked at the forest on the bank of the stream, saw the individual trees, the leaves and the veining of each leaf—saw the very insects upon them: the locusts, the brilliant-bodied flies, the gray spiders stretching their webs from twig to twig. He noted the prismatic colors in all the dewdrops upon a million blades of grass. The humming of the gnats that danced above the eddies of the stream, the beating of the dragon-flies' wings, the strokes of the water-spiders' legs, like oars which had lifted their boat—all these made audible music. A fish slid along beneath his eyes and he heard the rush of its body parting the water.

He had come to the surface facing down the stream; in a moment the visible world seemed to wheel slowly round, himself the pivotal point, and he saw the bridge, the fort, the soldiers upon the bridge, the captain, the sergeant, the two privates, his executioners. They were in silhouette against the blue sky. They shouted and gesticulated, pointing at him. The captain had drawn his pistol, but did not fire; the others were unarmed. Their movements were grotesque and horrible, their forms gigantic.

Suddenly he heard a sharp report and something struck the water smartly within a few inches of his head, spattering his face with spray. He heard a second report, and saw one of the sentinels with his rifle at his shoulder, a light cloud of blue smoke rising from the muzzle. The man in the water saw the eye of the man on the bridge gazing into his own through the sights of the rifle. He observed that it was a gray eye and remembered having read that gray eyes were keenest, and that all famous marksmen had them. Nevertheless, this one had missed.

A counter-swirl had caught Farquhar and turned him half round; he was again looking into the forest on the bank opposite the fort. The sound of a clear, high voice in a monotonous singsong now rang out behind him and came across the water with a distinctness that pierced and subdued all other sounds, even the beating of the ripples in his ears. Although no soldier, he had frequented camps enough to know the dread significance of that deliberate, drawling, aspirated chant; the lieutenant on shore was taking a part in the morning's work. How coldly and pitilessly—with what an even, calm intonation, presaging, and enforcing tranquility in the men—with what accurately measured intervals fell those cruel words:

"Attention, company! . . . Shoulder arms! . . . Ready! . . . Aim! . . . Fire!"

Farquhar dived—dived as deeply as he could. The water roared in his ears like the voice of Niagara, yet he heard the dulled thunder of the volley and, rising again toward the surface, met shining bits of metal, singularly flattened, oscillating slowly downward. Some of them touched him on the face and hands, then fell away, continuing their descent. One lodged between his collar and neck; it was uncomfortably warm and he snatched it out.

As he rose to the surface, gasping for breath, he saw that he had been a long time under water; he was perceptibly farther down stream—nearer to safety. The soldiers had almost finished reloading; the metal ramrods flashed all at once in the sunshine as they were drawn from the barrels, turned in the air, and thrust into their sockets. The two sentinels fired again, independently and ineffectually.

The hunted man saw all this over his shoulder; he was now swimming vigorously with the current. His brain was as energetic as his arms and legs; he thought with the rapidity of lightning.

"The officer," he reasoned, "will not make that martinet's error a second time. It is as easy to dodge a volley as a single shot. He has probably already given the command to fire at will. God help me, I cannot dodge them all!"

An appalling plash within two yards of him was followed by a loud, rushing sound, *diminuendo*,° which seemed to travel back through the air to the fort and died in an explosion which stirred the very river to its deeps! A rising sheet of water curved over him, fell down upon him, blinded him, strangled him! The cannon had taken a hand in the game. As he shook his head free from the commotion of the smitten water he heard the deflected shot humming through the air ahead, and in an instant it was cracking and smashing the branches in the forest beyond.

"They will not do that again," he thought; "the next time they will use a charge of grape. I must keep my eye upon the gun; the smoke will apprise me—the report arrives too late; it lags behind the missile. That is a good gun."

Suddenly he felt himself whirled round and round—spinning like a top. The water, the banks, the forests, the now distant bridge, fort and men—all were commingled and blurred. Objects were represented by their colors only; circular horizontal streaks of color—that was all he saw. He had been caught in a vortex and was being whirled on with a velocity of advance and gyration that made him giddy and sick. In a few moments he was flung upon the gravel at the foot of the left bank of the stream—the southern bank—and behind a projecting point which concealed him from his enemies. The sudden arrest of his motion, the abrasion of one of his hands on the gravel, restored him, and he wept with delight. He dug his fingers into the sand, threw it over himself in handfuls and audibly blessed it. It looked like diamonds, rubies, emeralds; he could think of nothing beautiful which it did not resemble. The trees upon the bank were giant garden plants; he noted a definite order in their arrangement, inhaled the fragrance of their blooms. A strange, roseate light shone through the spaces among their trunks and the wind made in their branches the music of aeolian harps. He had no wish to perfect his escape—was content to remain in that enchanting spot until retaken.

A whiz and rattle of grapeshot among the branches high above his head roused him from his dream. The baffled cannoneer had fired him a random farewell. He sprang to his feet, rushed up the sloping bank, and plunged into the forest.

All that day he traveled, laying his course by the rounding sun. The forest seemed interminable; nowhere did he discover a break in it, not even a woodman's road. He had not known that he lived in so wild a region. There was something uncanny in the revelation.

By nightfall he was fatigued, footsore, famishing. The thought of his wife and children urged him on. At last he found a road which led him in what he knew to be the right direction. It was as wide and straight as a city street, yet it seemed untraveled. No fields bordered it, no dwelling anywhere. Not so much as the barking of a dog suggested human habitation. The black bodies of the trees formed a straight wall on both sides, terminating on the horizon in a point, like a diagram in a lesson in perspective. Overhead, as he looked up through this rift in the wood, shone great golden stars looking unfamiliar and grouped in strange constellations. He was sure they were arranged in some order which had a secret and malign significance. The wood on either side was full of singular noises, among which—once, twice, and again—he distinctly heard whispers in an unknown tongue.

His neck was in pain and lifting his hand to it he found it horribly swollen. He knew that it had a circle of black where the rope had bruised it. His eyes felt congested;

---

diminuendo: diminishing (Italian); a term from music indicating a gradual decrease in loudness or force.

he could no longer close them. His tongue was swollen with thirst; he relieved its fever by thrusting it forward from between his teeth into the cold air. How softly the turf had carpeted the untraveled avenue—he could no longer feel the roadway beneath his feet!

Doubtless, despite his suffering, he had fallen asleep while walking, for now he sees another scene—perhaps he has merely recovered from a delirium. He stands at the gate of his own home. All is as he left it, and all bright and beautiful in the morning sunshine. He must have traveled the entire night. As he pushes open the gate and passes up the wide white walk, he sees a flutter of female garments; his wife, looking fresh and cool and sweet, steps down from the veranda to meet him. At the bottom of the steps she stands waiting, with a smile of ineffable joy, an attitude of matchless grace and dignity. Ah, how beautiful she is! He springs forward with extended arms. As he is about to clasp her he feels a stunning blow upon the back of the neck; a blinding white light blazes all about him with a sound like the shock of a cannon—then all is darkness and silence!

Peyton Farquhar was dead; his body, with a broken neck, swung gently from side to side beneath the timbers of the Owl Creek bridge.

Questions

1. Why has Peyton Farquhar been condemned to death?
2. From what point of view is "An Occurrence at Owl Creek Bridge" told?
3. Are you surprised by the story's conclusion? Can you find hints along the way that Farquhar's escape is an illusion?
4. At what point in the narrative does reality end and fantasy begin?
5. At several places in the story Bierce calls attention to Farquhar's heightened sensibility. How would you explain those almost mystical responses to ordinary stimuli?
6. Where in Bierce's story do you find examples of irony?
7. Do you think the story would have been better had Bierce told it in chronological order? Why or why not?

Mary Yukari Waters

The only child of a Japanese mother and an Irish American physicist, Mary Yukari Waters was born in 1965 in Kyoto, Japan. She lived in Japan until the age of nine, when her family moved to Red Bluff, a small town in Northern California. She attended the University of California at Santa Barbara, where she studied economics. For ten years Waters worked as a certified public accountant, specializing in corporate tax, for Deloitte Touche in Los Angeles. Unsettled by her father's death, she started writing fiction at the age of thirty. She earned an M.F.A. from the University of California at Irvine. In 2003, Waters published her first collection of short stories, The Laws of Evening, *in which "Shibusa" appears. These stories focus on the lives of people in Japan after the country's*

Mary Yukari Waters

catastrophic defeat in World War II. The stories are not autobiographical, but Waters borrowed details from the lives of her grandmother and other elderly people she knew in Japan. Her first novel, The Favorites, was published in 2009. Waters was the recipient of a 2002 National Endowment for the Arts literature grant and a 2004 Kiriyama Prize Notable Book Award. She lives in Los Angeles.

Shibusa   2003

"You have a sensibility for elegant manners," my tea ceremony teacher once told me, "the way a musician has an ear for pitch." Even before I could read, mothers were pointing out my floor bows as examples to their daughters: spine straight, its line barely breaking even when my head approached the floor; rear end clamped to heels the entire time with tensed quadriceps. As a teenager I performed the "admiration of vessel" step at tea ceremonies with an artistry beyond my years. I held out the ceramic bowl before me with arms neither straight nor bent, but rounded in a pleasing curve. Tilting my head just so, rotating the bowl in my hands the requisite three times, I lost myself in the countless subtle ways glaze changes color when shot through with sunlight. Such rituals of etiquette lifted me to an aesthetic plane, where often I had the sense—though I could not have articulated it then—of life being a dance, to be performed with stately grace.

But my bearing lacked that ultimate essence of refinement, described by elders as *shibusa*. It had to do with something more than mere maturity and was hard to define. The Buddha's smile of sorrowful sentience had this quality. A maple leaf in autumn, slowly twisting during its long fall to earth, evoked *shibusa*; that same leaf in midsummer, growing healthy and green from its branch, did not. "Aaa, it will come—" I remember my teacher saying with a sigh.

As a young bride, I was besotted with my husband, Yukio. He was square of face, with a firm straight line of a mouth and hair slicked back from his brow with immaculate comb lines. More than once, others commented on his likeness to those fine three-quarter profiles of samurai painted on New Year's kites. Like a samurai, Yukio was well versed in martial arts—fifteen years of kendo training—and displayed, unconsciously, those fluid transitions of movement so prized in Noh theater.° He was successful in business as well: a fast-rising executive at Kokusai Kogyo, an import-export conglomerate. Years later this company would be disbanded in the aftermath of our military defeat, but at the time it had the clout and prestige of today's Mitsubishi.

Early in our marriage Yukio was transferred overseas, to the Chinese province of Pei-L'an. It was 1937, seven months after the province had fallen to Japanese rule. "Don't forget to write!" my girlfriends clamored; then, in hushed tones, "And give us details! Those women's bound feet . . ."

One would think that sailing away to China would have exposed me to the cruelties of life. Today there is fervent talk on the radio of our soldiers' atrocities there: villages burned, women raped, soldiers butchered in prison camps. But all I knew of Pei-L'an province was our executives' housing compound: nineteen eaves sweeping up, pagoda-style, their ceramic roof shingles glazed a deep Prussian blue. The high wall enclosing our compound was white stucco, and the large main gate (through

---

°*Noh theater*: a traditional form of Japanese theater in which the actors' movements are so highly stylized that they resemble dance.

which we women passed only when escorted by our husbands) was topped with a miniature stylized roof in matching blue tile. I had little curiosity about how the region beyond had been defeated, and it would have been ungallant, ill-bred even, for Yukio to disclose the morbid details of war to a young bride. I wonder now how much he, as a mere civilian, knew of all this at the time. At any rate, I was more interested in immediate events, like the ripening of persimmons in autumn. That fine play of color—bright orange globes against the dark blue—gave me stabs of delight; it added an exotic touch to this new foreign experience.

The company had hired nineteen housemaids from the local village—one for each house. They arrived each day at dawn and were let in by the compound guards. Sometimes Yukio and I, drowsing under our futon, heard their faint voices coming up the main path, the harsh grating of consonants making the women sound as if they were perpetually quarreling.

Xi-Dou, the maid assigned to our home, was about my age. I sneaked curious looks at her while she worked; back home, domestic servants were rare. Her feet, far from being bound, were even bigger than mine. But despite her callused hands and faded mandarin tunic, she had a pleasing face, with full lips and wide-set eyes. She never laughed and only rarely smiled—wistfully, with a slight pucker of brows. Those smiles caused me intense guilt over my own newlywed bliss, which seemed selfish and indulgent in contrast. "Yukio," I said one night when we were lying in bed gazing up at the shadowed beams of the ceiling, "I wish Xi-Dou could join us for dinner."

I heard the slow crunch of his buckwheat-husk pillow as he turned his head in my direction. "Xi-Dou? The maid?"

"I saw the poor thing crouching on a stool in the kitchen," I said, "eating our leftovers. It ruins the harmony of this home for me, seeing something like that."

"Maa, such a gentle heart you have . . . ," Yukio murmured, his forefinger along my cheek as slow and deft as the rest of his movements. "And a face to match . . . . But"— his finger trailed away—"that's the procedure with servants. I assure you she doesn't take it personally. The food here is a lot better than what she's getting at home."

"It seems impolite, when she's already right here in the house," I said.

Yukio propped himself up on his elbow, looking down at me with his handsome samurai face. "Darling?" he said; in the moonlight his brows lifted in amusement like dark wings. "We just defeated these people in a *war*."

I did not reply.

"I'm not suggesting," Yukio said finally, "that etiquette—or consideration, whatever— shouldn't exist in wartime. Far from it. People need it to cope with life. But your nebulous gesture isn't practical. Ne? It would give her false hopes, make her life look bleaker in contrast."

"Wouldn't it give her—dignity? Or—" my voice trailed off in embarrassment. He was right, I saw that now; what would Xi-Dou want with the company of Japanese strangers?

"True kindness, in my opinion," said Yukio, "is good pay." He kissed my forehead once, twice, then fell back on his pillow with a scrunch. "Give her occasional tips, how about that? It'll do you both good." In a moment I heard his soft snore.

I was not fully satisfied by Yukio's solution. On the one hand it pleased my sense of order: for each situation, there should be a proper and logical course of action. Yet some additional dimension was missing, though I could not have defined it.

His comment interested me: *people need it to cope with life.* That had not been my own experience. I had never used etiquette to "cope." But I understood how its ethereal quality, like temple incense, might lift one out from the realm of daily cares.

I continued gazing up at the ceiling. These Chinese roofs were lower than I was used to, pressing down upon me in the darkness. Maa—I thought—whether in kendo or in matters of judgment, Yukio always hits the heart of a matter with one sure blow.

Yukio soon became friends with another executive in our compound, Mr. Nishitani. They were the only two men in management who were still in their thirties. Both were tall and striking, with that genial assurance that comes from a lifetime of excellent schooling and privileged treatment. Nishitani-san, a bachelor, began dining frequently at our house.

In certain ways Nishitani-san was the opposite of my husband. With Yukio one got the impression that behind each word or motion was a hidden reserve of strength, of discipline. It was evident in the way he told jokes at company parties: so deadpan that when he delivered his punch line it took a moment for his audience to react. Only after they burst into laughter, roaring and shrieking, did Yukio give in to laughter himself, his rich baritone notes pealing forth from well-conditioned lungs.

Nishitani-san, by contrast, carried all his energy on the surface. His smiles were dazzling, sudden and unexpected like flashes of sunlight on water; the older wives whispered among themselves that those smiles took your breath away, quite! Somebody once said that even the air around Nishitani-san seemed to shimmer. In excitement his voice rose and his cowlick shot up like a tuft of grass; in a burst of good humor he was not above breaking into some Kabuki chant—right in public—or improvising a silly jig. "Won't you ever learn to behave—" I chided him with motherly resignation, though I was five years younger than he. Compared to Yukio, Nishitani-san was just a bit boyish for my taste. But that quality would later endear him to my little boy Kin-chan, with whom I had recently learned I was pregnant.

Xi-Dou, our maid, fancied Nishitani-san. On the evenings he came over she plaited her hair loosely, draping it over one shoulder in a long gleaming braid instead of pinning it up into a bun. On a few occasions I could have sworn her lips were faintly stained with lipstick. One of mine? I wondered. I never mentioned this to Yukio, but it did occur to me, once or twice, that "coping with life" was not such a clear-cut business as he had implied. Certain needs, however impractical, will transcend all others. From the corner of my eye I watched Xi-Dou as she backed away from our table, clutching the empty serving tray to her chest, then turned to the door with one last look over her shoulder at Nishitani-san. As far as I could tell, he was oblivious to her presence.

Nishitani-san brought out a side of Yukio that I did not often see. When it was just the two of us, my husband was reverently tender or else serious and philosophical. But when Nishitani-san came to dinner he became witty, full of one amusing anecdote after another. Nishitani-san, who flushed easily when drinking sake, responded in kind, determined not to be outdone. I would laugh and laugh, gasping for breath, forgetting even to cover my mouth with my hand, till the muscles in my cheeks ached.

Those were such happy times, right before the Second World War.

Sometimes I left them—either to give Xi-Dou instructions or else to use the bathroom, something I did frequently now that I was expecting. I was not yet far enough along to feel the baby inside me, but surely it was soaking up all this laughter, growing stronger and finer as a result. In the privacy of the hallway I often stopped to tuck in wisps of hair which, on such evenings, invariably came loose from my chignon. Before me was a small window with a view of the Xiang-Ho mountains. Beyond the pagoda-style roofs I could make out their blue outline in the gathering dusk, high and jagged in the distance. And I, heartbeat still high from the hilarity of the evening, would stand in the hallway and gaze out for a while before going on my way. I thought of Yukio's deep laughter, of his large hands; of this coming child and of business continuing to boom—and I forced myself to be calm, to concentrate on those somber mountains darkening and fading beyond the compound walls that enclosed us.

From the next room I could hear the men's deep voices, laughing.

I have learned since that no experience lives on in memory. Not in the true sense. It becomes altered, necessarily, by subsequent events. My memory of China is steeped in a sense of encroaching doom that was surely not present then, like a scene flooded with the last rays of sunset.

War was declared in 1941, when Kin-chan was three years old. Kokusai Kogyo pulled up its Pei-L'an branch, and we employees sailed back in shifts to our various homes in Japan. Nishitani-san sailed home to some town near Nagasaki; the three of us came home to Ueno. Bombs dropped on our city; there were fires. One day, while I was standing in a rationing line on the other side of town, a bomb dropped on our neighborhood. What terrible luck that Yukio was home on leave that week; I had left him and Kin-chan in the garden, playing hide-and-seek. Our son was five years old.

Over the decades, this period has faded in my memory. Only occasionally now will it seep out into my body, staining my saliva with a faint coppery taste, which makes me think that somewhere, within the tissues and nerves of my body, I am bleeding.

One morning a year after the surrender—Kin-chan would have turned eight by now—an odd thing happened.

I was crouched beside the kitchen door out in the alley, watering my potted chrysanthemums. In one hand I held the watering can; with the other, I was twisting off a browned leaf here and there. Hearing the slow *k'sha k'sha* of gravel, I turned around to see a seafood peddler pass me in the alley, bowed under the yoke of his pannier. His blue jacket looked unfamiliar; he was not from our neighborhood.

This was not unusual; residents of other areas often used our alley as a shortcut to Kamogawa Bridge on their way downtown.

As the man bowed slightly, in gratitude and apology for using this shortcut, our eyes met briefly. Then he stopped, a startled look on his face. He lowered his baskets, brimming with shijimi shells and pickled seaweed, onto the gravel before me. Something about him looked familiar—perhaps the shape of his lips, curled up slightly at the ends as if to get a jump start on a smile. But I could not place him.

The peddler stepped toward me, then bowed deeply. It was a well-trained bow, slow and straight-backed, unsettling in a man of his station. I hurriedly rose, still holding my watering can. "Goto-san, do you remember me?" he said. "I'm Nishitani. I once had the pleasure of your friendship, and your husband's, back in Pei-L'an."

Again our eyes met, and I glanced away. The shame in his look made my heart contract with pain. Even for such times, this was extreme misfortune. I fancied I could feel his loss of face pulsing out toward me, like heat waves.

We exchanged pleasantries. Nishitani-san had lines on either side of his mouth, like parentheses. Had they been there before? Something seemed different about his features—he had lost that shimmer, I think now, which had once played upon them.

"Nishitani-san, do you have a moment to sit down?" I sank down onto the kitchen step. "Here with me?" My voice came from far away. Even the weather had a surreal quality to it, I remember. It was overcast. The sky was not gray but whitish, like thick membrane, and light glowed behind it with a brightness almost brutal.

"Saa, that would be fine," he said. A faint version of his old smile brought back China to me, like a whiff of old scent. "Just for a few minutes."

Nishitani-san offered no explanation of his situation, nor did he mention what he was doing in this part of the country. I avoided looking in the direction of his baskets, for I wanted to spare him as much discomfort as possible; I kept my gaze trained on his face and never once glanced down at the hip-length vendor jacket he wore, cobalt blue with the store owner's name written in white brushstrokes down the length of its collar. Nishitani-san smelled so strongly of fish blood, sitting beside me, that my temples were tightening into a headache. And he had once used such lovely cologne, from Paris.

He asked after Yukio and Kin-chan, and I told him, in the briefest terms. "Aaa, here too . . . ," he murmured. I remembered then that he had lived near Nagasaki. "How you must have suffered," he said after a silence, gazing at my face. I knew he was registering the premature streaks of white in my hair, the sun damage on my once flawless complexion.

"Do you remember," Nishitani-san said abruptly, and he began to reminisce about the delicious roast duck at our dinners, Yukio's old jokes, the comical quirks of our compound neighbors. I heard in his voice a new gravity, a new tenderness, that seemed to lift up each memory—like some precious jewel—and hold it up in wonderment to the light.

"You know," I said, "Kin-chan missed you for almost a month after we sailed home. 'Uncle *Nee*-tani,' he kept saying with that lisp of his, and he looked so worried, with his little forehead all wrinkled up, that everybody just had to *laugh*—"

"A whole month, really?" Nishitani-san said. His lips curved up into his old dazzling smile. "That was unusually long for a three-year-old!"

"You see, hora, you're the type," I said with my old playful air, "who makes a huge impression on everyone he meets!" I froze then at my choice of words, for it skirted a little too close to the impression he would be leaving me with today. But Nishitani-san seemed not to mind, for he tipped back his head and laughed.

I pictured him back in China, on a sunny Sunday afternoon a few months before war was declared. He had been striding away after luncheon at our home, a tall, confident man; the force of his gait made the back of his white shirt, always immaculately starched, balloon out above his belt like a full sail. "Uncle *Nee*-tani! Uncle *Nee*-tani!" Kin-chan had shrieked, running after him through the dappled light beneath the persimmon trees, losing his red sandal in the dirt, fumbling to put it back on, then losing it again after a few steps.

Nishitani-san had glanced back. "Escape, Nishitani-san, escape!" I called out to him, laughing and shooing him away with both hands. He had flashed me a big white smile and, with a boyish laugh, trotted away in mock haste, leaving Kin-chan bawling in the middle of the path.

Remembering all this, I felt the prickle of approaching tears and lowered my eyes to hide it. Nishitani-san was still laughing; it surprised me that his hands, red and raw like a laborer's, were trembling on his knees.

"The aristocrats of the ancient court," I say, "were devout Buddhists." It is decades later, and I am lecturing to my older tea ceremony students on the origins of etiquette.

"Buddha taught that life is filled with pain," I tell them. And suddenly an image of Nishitani-san's hands comes to mind, as they looked one day in the year 1946. There were dark scabs on his knuckles, hard as horn and soon to become calluses; on the rest of his hands were thin red scratches. I remembered my first glimpse of his baskets, full to the brim despite the lateness of the morning hour.

Clearly he was new to this, and struggling; he had not yet perfected that peculiar air vendors have, the bland unthinking cheerfulness which attracts customers.

"Filled with pain," I say to my students, "and sorrow."

"Hai, Teacher," the girls murmur in their high-pitched voices.

On that long-ago morning I pulled out my coin purse from my apron pocket—my hands, too, were trembling now—but before I could speak, Nishitani-san shook his head no. It was quick, a mere jerk—the imperceptible warning one gives in the presence of a third party. I slipped the purse back in my pocket.

"Those aristocrats, influenced by Buddha's teachings," I tell my students, "felt that nobility of spirit was the grace—or ability—to move through this world voluntarily, as a game or dance. And they passed down their ideal through the rituals of etiquette, ne? Polite speech, for example. Even today we refer to an honorable person not as having been killed, but as having condescended to play at dying."

The girls nod politely, blankly.

Today, what strikes me most about that morning—for memory will always shift focus—is our wordless farewell as Nishitani-san and I bowed to each other. It would be many years before I linked the essence of our bow with that of Kenryu's famous poem about a rice plant: *weighed down with grain / making graceful bows / in the wind.* How lovely our bows would have seemed to a casual onlooker: stately, seasoned, like movements in a sacred dance.

Questions

1. This story covers most of the narrator's life. What are the four main periods presented in the story?
2. What does "*shibusa*" mean? (See paragraph 2.)
3. The period in the Pei-L'an province of China seems peaceful and prosperous for the narrator. How would it have seemed for her servant?
4. The narrator describes her son's and her husband's deaths in only three sentences. Why do you think she does not say more?
5. The story begins and ends with a discussion of etiquette. Does that seem odd for a story that contains so much personal and historical tragedy in the middle? What do those discussions suggest about the narrator and her society?
6. How does Buddha's teaching that life is full of pain influence the traditional Japanese response to suffering and death?
7. Why do you think Waters titled her story "Shibusa"?

Suggestions for Writing on *Stories about War and Violence*

1. Write a short essay listing and justifying four personal items you would carry with you on a military mission. (If you are opposed to imagining yourself on a military mission, then describe what you would take along on a year in the Peace Corps in a very remote location.)
2. In Mary Yukari Waters's story "Shibusa," the protagonist espouses a formal etiquette that keeps suffering in place. Have you ever known anyone who has done something similar—using a routine or a ritual to get through difficult circumstances? If so, describe the person and the activity in a short essay.
3. Imagine that, like the protagonist of Bierce's "An Occurrence at Owl Creek Bridge," you face execution. Nothing you do can change your fate. What things and people in your life would you want to remember in your last moments?
4. Take one of the stories in this section and analyze its setting (time and place). How does the setting contribute to the total effect of the story? Why would the story be less effective in a different setting?

CRIME AND PUNISHMENT

Andre Dubus	*A Father's Story*
Edgar Allan Poe	*The Cask of Amontillado*
Guy de Maupassant	*Mother Savage*

Most of us will never face the violence of combat in war, but many will experience either personal violence or the threat of violence from crime. In cities and suburbs, people lead their daily lives conscious of potential threats to their safety and the safety of their families: they lock doors, monitor children, walk in groups, avoid deserted locations. Violence is not an idle fantasy but a possibility, however slim, be it street crime, domestic abuse, a hit-and-run accident, a drive-by shooting, or workplace rage. In war, soldiers are compelled to fight by political authority, but what motivates an individual to commit a robbery, murder, rape, or arson in civilian society? The selections in this section present three very different tales of personal violence. In Andre Dubus's deeply moving "A Father's Story," a good and religious man is forced to violate his most cherished values to cover up a crime committed by someone he loves. The amoral narrator of Edgar Allan Poe's "A Cask of Amontillado" is not bothered by matters of conscience; he executes an elaborate plan for ghoulish revenge without the slightest guilt. In Guy de Maupassant's gripping "Mother Savage," we see a good and loving woman transformed into a heartless monster by tragic circumstances.

Andre Dubus

Andre Dubus (1936–1999)—pronounced Dub-YOOSE—was born into a Cajun Irish Catholic family in Lake Charles, Louisiana. After graduating from McNeese State College in his hometown, he joined the Marine Corps, thinking it would be "a romantic way" to earn a living while learning to be a writer. He spent six years in the military, eventually being promoted to captain. He left the marines in 1964 to attend the University of Iowa Writers' Workshop. Dubus's first book was a novel, The Lieutenant *(1967), but thereafter he concentrated on short fiction, beginning with* Separate Flights *(1975). This book and its successor,* Adultery, and Other Choices *(1977), set the general tone of Dubus's fiction, with its emphasis on the complexities of male-female relationships and the emotional costs of infidelity.*

Andre Dubus

In 1983 Dubus published The Times Are Never So Bad; *it contained his Pushcart Prize-winner "A Father's Story," which has become his signature work. Three years later Dubus, while trying to help a woman who had been in an automobile accident, was struck by an oncoming car. As a result, his left leg was amputated, and he spent the rest of his life in a wheelchair. Overcome by depression and a failed third marriage, Dubus gave up writing for a* time. The publication of his Selected Stories *and a grant from the MacArthur Foundation in 1988 served to revive his career. He even claimed that his accident was "a blessing" that helped him become a better writer. When Dubus was sixty-two, happily remarried and with a new child on the way, he died of a heart attack at his home in Haverhill, Massachusetts.*

A Father's Story 1983

My name is Luke Ripley, and here is what I call my life: I own a stable of thirty horses, and I have young people who teach riding, and we board some horses too. This is in northeastern Massachusetts. I have a barn with an indoor ring, and outside I've got two fenced-in rings and a pasture that ends at a woods with trails. I call it my life because it looks like it is, and people I know call it that, but it's a life I can get away from when I hunt and fish, and some nights after dinner when I sit in the dark in the front room and listen to opera. The room faces the lawn and the road, a two-lane country road. When the cars come around the curve northwest of the house, they light up the lawn for an instant, the leaves of the maple out by the road and the hemlock closer to the window. Then I'm alone again, or I'd appear to be if someone crept up to the house and looked through a window: a big-gutted gray-haired guy, drinking tea and smoking cigarettes, staring out at the dark woods across the road, listening to a grieving soprano.

My real life is the one nobody talks about anymore, except Father Paul LeBoeuf, another old buck. He has a decade on me: he's sixty-four, a big man, bald on top with gray at the sides; when he had hair, it was black. His face is ruddy, and he jokes about being a whiskey priest, though he's not. He gets outdoors as much as he can, goes for a long walk every morning, and hunts and fishes with me. But I can't get him on a horse anymore. Ten years ago I could badger him into a trail ride; I had to give him a western saddle, and he'd hold the pommel and bounce through the woods with me, and be sore for days. He's looking at seventy with eyes that are younger than many I've seen in people in their twenties. I do not remember ever feeling the way they seem to; but I was lucky, because even as a child I knew that life would try me, and I must be strong to endure, though in those early days I expected to be tortured and killed for my faith, like the saints I learned about in school.

Father Paul's family came down from Canada, and he grew up speaking more French than English, so he is different from the Irish priests who abound up here. I do not like to make general statements, or even to hold general beliefs, about people's blood, but the Irish do seem happiest when they're dealing with misfortune or guilt, either their own or somebody else's, and if you think you're not a victim of either one, you can count on certain Irish priests to try to change your mind. On Wednesday nights Father Paul comes to dinner. Often he comes on other nights too, and once, in the old days when we couldn't eat meat on Fridays, we bagged our first ducks of the season on a Friday, and as we drove home from the marsh, he said: For the purposes of Holy Mother Church, I believe a duck is more a creature of water than land, and is not rightly meat. Sometimes he teases me about never putting anything in his Sunday collection, which he would not know about if I hadn't told him years ago. I would like to believe I told him so we could have philosophical talk at dinner, but probably the truth is I suspected he knew, and I did not want him to think I so loved money that I would not even give his church a coin on Sunday. Certainly the ushers who pass the baskets know me as a miser.

I don't feel right about giving money for buildings, places. This starts with the Pope, and I cannot respect one of them till he sells his house and everything in it, and that church too, and uses the money to feed the poor. I have rarely, and maybe never, come across saintliness, but I feel certain it cannot exist in such a place. But I admit, also, that I know very little, and maybe the popes live on a different plane and are tried in ways I don't know about. Father Paul says his own church, St. John's, is hardly the Vatican. I like his church: it is made of wood, and has a simple altar and crucifix, and no padding on the kneelers. He does not have to lock its doors at night. Still it is a place. He could say Mass in my barn. I know this is stubborn, but I can find no mention by Christ of maintaining buildings, much less erecting them of stone or brick, and decorating them with pieces of metal and mineral and elements that people still fight over like barbarians. We had a Maltese woman taking riding lessons, she came over on the boat when she was ten, and once she told me how the nuns in Malta used to tell the little girls that if they wore jewelry, rings and bracelets and necklaces, in purgatory snakes would coil around their fingers and wrists and throats. I do not believe in frightening children or telling them lies, but if those nuns saved a few girls from devotion to things, maybe they were right. That Maltese woman laughed about it, but I noticed she wore only a watch, and that with a leather strap.

The money I give to the church goes in people's stomachs, and on their backs, down in New York City. I have no delusions about the worth of what I do, but I feel it's better to feed somebody than not. There's a priest in Times Square giving shelter to runaway kids, and some Franciscans who run a bread line; actually it's a morning line for coffee and a roll, and Father Paul calls it the continental breakfast for winos and bag ladies. He is curious about how much I am sending, and I know why: he guesses I send a lot, he has said probably more than tithing, and he is right; he wants to know how much because he believes I'm generous and good, and he is wrong about that; he has never had much money and does not know how easy it is to write a check when you have everything you will ever need, and the figures are mere numbers, and represent no sacrifice at all. Being a real Catholic is too hard; if I were one, I would do with my house and barn what I want the Pope to do with his. So I do not want to impress Father Paul, and when he asks me how much, I say I can't let my left hand know what my right is doing.

He came on Wednesday nights when Gloria and I were married, and the kids were young; Gloria was a very good cook (I assume she still is, but it is difficult to think of her in the present), and I liked sitting at the table with a friend who was also a priest. I was proud of my handsome and healthy children. This was long ago, and they were all very young and cheerful and often funny, and the three boys took care of their baby sister, and did not bully or tease her. Of course they did sometimes, with that excited cruelty children are prone to, but not enough so that it was part of her days. On the Wednesday after Gloria left with the kids and a U-Haul trailer, I was sitting on the front steps, it was summer, and I was watching cars go by on the road, when Father Paul drove around the curve and into the driveway. I was ashamed to see him because he is a priest and my family was gone, but I was relieved too. I went to the car to greet him. He got out smiling, with a bottle of wine, and shook my hand, then pulled me to him, gave me a quick hug, and said: "It's Wednesday, isn't it? Let's open some cans."

With arms about each other we walked to the house, and it was good to know he was doing his work but coming as a friend too, and I thought what good work he had. I have no calling. It is for me to keep horses.

In that other life, anyway. In my real one I go to bed early and sleep well and wake at four forty-five, for an hour of silence. I never want to get out of bed then, and every morning I know I can sleep for another four hours, and still not fail at any of my duties. But I get up, so have come to believe my life can be seen in miniature in that struggle in the dark of morning. While making the bed and boiling water for coffee, I talk to God: I offer Him my day, every act of my body and spirit, my thoughts and moods, as a prayer of thanksgiving, and for Gloria and my children and my friends and two women I made love with after Gloria left. This morning offertory is a habit from my boyhood in a Catholic school; or then it was a habit, but as I kept it and grew older it became a ritual. Then I say the Lord's Prayer, trying not to recite it, and one morning it occurred to me that a prayer, whether recited or said with concentration, is always an act of faith.

I sit in the kitchen at the rear of the house and drink coffee and smoke and watch the sky growing light before sunrise, the trees of the woods near the barn taking shape, becoming single pines and elms and oaks and maples. Sometimes a rabbit comes out of the treeline, or is already sitting there, invisible till the light finds him. The birds are awake in the trees and feeding on the ground, and the little ones, the purple finches and titmice and chickadees, are at the feeder I rigged outside the kitchen window; it is too small for pigeons to get a purchase. I sit and give myself to coffee and tobacco, that get me brisk again, and I watch and listen. In the first year or so after I lost my family, I played the radio in the mornings. But I overcame that, and now I rarely play it at all. Once in the mail I received a questionnaire asking me to write down everything I watched on television during the week they had chosen. At the end of those seven days I wrote in *The Wizard of Oz* and returned it. That was in winter and was actually a busy week for my television, which normally sits out the cold months without once warming up. Had they sent the questionnaire during baseball season, they would have found me at my set. People at the stables talk about shows and performers I have never heard of, but I cannot get interested; when I am in the mood to watch television, I go to a movie or read a detective novel. There are always good detective novels to be found, and I like remembering them next morning with my coffee.

I also think of baseball and hunting and fishing, and of my children. It is not painful to think about them anymore, because even if we had lived together, they would be gone now, grown into their own lives, except Jennifer. I think of death too, not sadly, or with fear, though something like excitement does run through me, something more quickening than the coffee and tobacco. I suppose it is an intense interest, and an outright distrust: I never feel certain that I'll be here watching birds eating at tomorrow's daylight. Sometimes I try to think of other things, like the rabbit that is warm and breathing but not there till twilight. I feel on the brink of something about the life of the senses, but either am not equipped to go further or am not interested enough to concentrate. I have called all of this thinking, but it is not, because it is unintentional; what I'm really doing is feeling the day, in silence, and that is what Father Paul is doing too on his five-to-ten-mile walks.

When the hour ends I take an apple or carrot and I go to the stable and tack up a horse. We take good care of these horses, and no one rides them but students, instructors, and me, and nobody rides the horses we board unless an owner asks me to. The barn is dark and I turn on lights and take some deep breaths, smelling the hay and horses and their manure, both fresh and dried, a combined odor that you either like or you don't. I walk down the wide space of dirt between stalls, greeting the horses, joking with them about their quirks, and choose one for no reason at all other than the way it looks at me that morning. I get my old English saddle that has smoothed and darkened through the years, and go into the stall, talking to this beautiful creature who'll swerve out of a canter if a piece of paper blows in front of him, and if the barn catches fire and you manage to get him out he will, if he can get away from you, run back into the fire, to his stall. Like the smells that surround them, you either like them or you don't. I love them, so am spared having to try to explain why. I feed one the carrot or apple and tack up and lead him outside, where I mount, and we go down the driveway to the road and cross it and turn northwest and walk then trot then canter to St. John's.

A few cars are on the road, their drivers looking serious about going to work. It is always strange for me to see a woman dressed for work so early in the morning. You know how long it takes them, with the makeup and hair and clothes, and I think of them waking in the dark of winter or early light of other seasons, and dressing as they might for an evening's entertainment. Probably this strikes me because I grew up seeing my father put on those suits he never wore on weekends or his two weeks off, and so am accustomed to the men, but when I see these women I think something went wrong, to send all those dressed-up people out on the road when the dew hasn't dried yet. Maybe it's because I so dislike getting up early, but am also doing what I choose to do, while they have no choice. At heart I am lazy, yet I find such peace and delight in it that I believe it is a natural state, and in what looks like my laziest periods I am closest to my center. The ride to St. John's is fifteen minutes. The horses and I do it in all weather; the road is well plowed in winter, and there are only a few days a year when ice makes me drive the pickup. People always look at someone on horseback, and for a moment their faces change and many drivers and I wave to each other. Then at St. John's, Father Paul and five or six regulars and I celebrate the Mass.

Do not think of me as a spiritual man whose every thought during those twenty-five minutes is at one with the words of the Mass. Each morning I try, each morning I fail, and know that always I will be a creature who, looking at Father Paul and the altar, and uttering prayers, will be distracted by scrambled eggs, horses, the weather, and memories and daydreams that have nothing to do with the sacrament I am about to receive. I can receive, though: the Eucharist, and also, at Mass and at other times, moments and even minutes of contemplation. But I cannot achieve contemplation, as some can; and so, having to face and forgive my own failures, I have learned from them both the necessity and wonder of ritual. For ritual allows those who cannot will themselves out of the secular to perform the spiritual, as dancing allows the tongue-tied man a ceremony of love. And, while my mind dwells on breakfast, or Major or Duchess tethered under the church eave, there is, as I take the Host from Father Paul and place it on my tongue and return to the pew, a feeling that I am thankful I have not lost in the forty-eight years since my first Communion. At its center is excitement; spreading out from it is the peace of certainty. Or the certainty of peace. One night Father Paul and I talked about faith. It was long ago, and all I remember is him saying: Belief is believing in God; faith is believing that God believes in you. That is the excitement, and the peace; then the Mass is over, and I go into the sacristy and we have a cigarette and chat, the mystery ends, we are two men talking like any two men on a morning in America, about baseball, plane crashes, presidents, governors, murders, the sun, the clouds. Then I go to the horse and ride back to the life people see, the one in which I move and talk, and most days I enjoy it.

*

It is late summer now, the time between fishing and hunting, but a good time for baseball. It has been two weeks since Jennifer left, to drive home to Gloria's after her summer visit. She is the only one who still visits; the boys are married and have children, and sometimes fly up for a holiday, or I fly down or west to visit one of them. Jennifer is twenty, and I worry about her the way fathers worry about daughters but not sons. I want to know what she's up to, and at the same time I don't. She looks athletic, and she is: she swims and runs and of course rides. All my children do. When she comes for six weeks in summer, the house is loud with girls, friends of hers since childhood, and new ones. I am glad she kept the girl friends. They have been young company for me and, being with them, I have been able to gauge her growth between summers. On their riding days, I'd take them back to the house when their lessons were over and they had walked the horses and put them back in the stalls, and we'd have lemonade or Coke, and cookies if I had some, and talk until their parents came to drive them home. One year their breasts grew, so I wasn't startled when I saw Jennifer in July. Then they were driving cars to the stable, and beginning to look like young women, and I was passing out beer and ashtrays and they were talking about college.

When Jennifer was here in summer, they were at the house most days. I would say generally that as they got older they became quieter, and though I enjoyed both, I sometimes missed the giggles and shouts. The quiet voices, just low enough for me not to hear from wherever I was, rising and falling in proportion to my distance from them, frightened me. Not that I believed they were planning or recounting anything really wicked, but there was a female seriousness about them, and it was secretive, and of course I thought: love, sex. But it was more than that: it was womanhood they were entering, the deep forest of it, and no matter how many women and men too are saying these days that there is little difference between us, the truth is that men find their way into that forest only on clearly marked trails, while women move about in it like birds. So hearing Jennifer and her friends talking so quietly, yet intensely, I wanted very much to have a wife.

But not as much as in the old days, when Gloria had left but her presence was still in the house as strongly as if she had only gone to visit her folks for a week. There were no clothes or cosmetics, but potted plants endured my neglectful care as long as they could, and slowly died; I did not kill them on purpose, to exorcize the house of her, but I could not remember to water them. For weeks, because I did not use it much, the house was as neat as she had kept it, though dust layered the order she had made. The kitchen went first: I got the dishes in and out of the dishwasher and wiped the top of the stove, but did not return cooking spoons and pot holders to their hooks on the wall, and soon the burners and oven were caked with spillings, the refrigerator had more space and was spotted with juices. The living room and my bedroom went next; I did not go into the children's rooms except on bad nights when I went from room to room and looked and touched and smelled, so they did not lose their order until a year later when the kids came for six weeks. It was three months before I ate the last of the food Gloria had cooked and frozen: I remember it was a beef stew, and very good. By then I had four cookbooks, and was boasting a bit, and talking about recipes with the women at the stables, and looking forward to cooking for Father Paul. But I never looked forward to cooking at night only for myself, though I made myself do it; on some nights I gave in to my daily temptation, and took a newspaper or detective novel to a restaurant. By the end of the second year, though, I had stopped turning on the radio as soon as I woke in the morning, and was able to be silent and alone in the evening too, and then I enjoyed my dinners.

It is not hard to live through a day, if you can live through a moment. What creates despair is the imagination, which pretends there is a future, and insists on predicting millions of moments, thousands of days, and so drains you that you cannot live the moment at hand. That is what Father Paul told me in those first two years, on some of the bad nights when I believed I could not bear what I had to: the most painful loss was my children, then the loss of Gloria, whom I still loved despite or maybe because of our long periods of sadness that rendered us helpless, so neither of us could break out of it to give a hand to the other. Twelve years later I believe ritual would have healed us more quickly than the repetitious talks we had, perhaps even kept us healed. Marriages have lost that, and I wish I had known then what I know now, and we had performed certain acts together every day, no matter how we felt, and perhaps then we could have subordinated feeling to action, for surely that is the essence of love. I know this from my distractions during Mass, and during everything else I do, so that my actions and feelings are seldom one. It does happen every day, but in proportion to everything else in a day, it is rare, like joy. The third most painful loss, which became second and sometimes first as months passed, was the knowledge that I could never marry again, and so dared not even keep company with a woman.

On some of the bad nights I was bitter about this with Father Paul, and I so pitied myself that I cried, or nearly did, speaking with damp eyes and breaking voice. I believe that celibacy is for him the same trial it is for me, not of the flesh, but the spirit; the heart longing to love. But the difference is he chose it, and did not wake one day to a life with thirty horses. In my anger I said I had done my service to love and chastity, and I told him of the actual physical and spiritual pain of practicing rhythm: nights of striking the mattress with a fist, two young animals lying side by side in heat, leaving the bed to pace, to smoke, to curse, and too passionate to question, for we were so angered and oppressed by our passion that we could see no further than our loins. So now I understand how people can be enslaved for generations before they throw down their tools or use them as weapons, the form of their slavery—the cotton fields, the shacks and puny cupboards and untended illnesses—absorbing their emotions and thoughts until finally they have little or none at all to direct with clarity and energy at the owners and legislators. And I told him of the trick of passion and its slaking: how during what we had to believe were safe periods, though all four children were conceived at those times, we were able with some coherence to question the tradition and reason and justice of the law against birth control, but not with enough conviction to soberly act against it, as though regular satisfaction in bed tempered our revolutionary as well as our erotic desires. Only when abstinence drove us hotly away from each other did we receive an urge so strong it lasted all the way to the drugstore and back; but always, after release, we threw away the remaining condoms; and after going through this a few times, we knew what would happen, and from then on we submitted to the calendar she so precisely marked on the bedroom wall. I told him that living two lives each month, one as celibates, one as lovers, made us tense and short-tempered, so we snapped at each other like dogs.

To have endured that, to have reached a time when we burned slowly and could gain from bed the comfort of lying down at night with one who loves you and whom you love, could for weeks on end go to bed tired and peacefully sleep after a kiss, a touch of the hands, and then to be thrown out of the marriage like a bundle from a moving freight car, was unjust, was intolerable, and I could not or would not muster the strength to endure it. But I did, a moment at a time, a day, a night, except twice, each time with a different woman and more than a year apart, and this was so long ago that I clearly see their faces in my memory, can hear the pitch of their voices, and the way they pronounced words, one with a Massachusetts accent, one midwestern, but I feel as though I only heard about them from someone else. Each rode at the stables and was with me for part of an evening; one was badly married, one divorced, so none of us was free. They did not understand this Catholic view, but they were understanding about my having it, and I remained friends with both of them until the married one left her husband and went to Boston, and the divorced one moved to Maine. After both those evenings, those good women, I went to Mass early while Father Paul was still in the confessional, and received his absolution. I did not tell him who I was, but of course he knew, though I never saw it in his eyes. Now my longing for a wife comes only once in a while, like a cold: on some late afternoons when I am alone in the barn, then I lock up and walk to the house, daydreaming, then suddenly look at it and see it empty, as though for the first time, and all at once I'm weary and feel I do not have the energy to broil meat, and I think of driving to a restaurant, then shake my head and go on to the house, the refrigerator, the oven; and some mornings when I wake in the dark and listen to the silence and run my hand over the cold sheet beside me; and some days in summer when Jennifer is here.

Gloria left first me, then the Church, and that was the end of religion for the children, though on visits they went to Sunday Mass with me, and still do, out of respect for my life that they manage to keep free of patronage. Jennifer is an agnostic, though I doubt she would call herself that, any more than she would call herself any other name that implied she had made a decision, a choice, about existence, death, and God. In truth she tends to pantheism, a good sign, I think; but not wanting to be a father who tells his children what they ought to believe, I do not say to her that Catholicism includes pantheism, like onions in a stew. Besides, I have no missionary instincts and do not believe everyone should or even could live with the Catholic faith. It is Jennifer's womanhood that renders me awkward. And womanhood now is frank, not like when Gloria was twenty and there were symbols: high heels and cosmetics and dresses, a cigarette, a cocktail. I am glad that women are free now of false modesty and all its attention paid the flesh; but, still, it is difficult to see so much of your daughter, to hear her talk as only men and bawdy women used to, and most of all to see in her face the deep and unabashed sensuality of women, with no tricks of the eyes and mouth to hide the pleasure she feels at having a strong young body. I am certain, with the way things are now, that she has very happily not been a virgin for years. That does not bother me. What bothers me is my certainty about it, just from watching her walk across a room or light a cigarette or pour milk on cereal.

She told me all of it, waking me that night when I had gone to sleep listening to the wind in the trees and against the house, a wind so strong that I had to shut all but the lee windows, and still the house cooled; told it to me in such detail and so clearly that now, when she has driven the car to Florida, I remember it all as though I had been a passenger in the front seat, or even at the wheel. It started with a movie, then beer and driving to the sea to look at the waves in the night and the wind, Jennifer and Betsy and Liz. They drank a beer on the beach and wanted to go in naked but were afraid they would drown in the high surf. They bought another six-pack at a grocery store in New Hampshire, and drove home. I can see it now, feel it: the three girls and the beer and the ride on country roads where pines curved in the wind and the big deciduous trees swayed and shook as if they might leap from the earth. They would have some windows partly open so they could feel the wind; Jennifer would be playing a cassette, the music stirring them, as it does the young, to memories of another time, other people and places in what is for them the past.

She took Betsy home, then Liz, and sang with her cassette as she left the town west of us and started home, a twenty-minute drive on the road that passes my house. They had each had four beers, but now there were twelve empty bottles in the bag on the floor at the passenger seat, and I keep focusing on their sound against each other when the car shifted speeds or changed directions. For I want to understand that one moment out of all her heart's time on earth, and whether her history had any bearing on it, or whether her heart was then isolated from all it had known, and the sound of those bottles urged it. She was just leaving the town, accelerating past a night club on the right, gaining speed to climb a long, gradual hill, then she went up it, singing, patting the beat on the steering wheel, the wind loud through her few inches of open window, blowing her hair as it did the high branches alongside the road, and she looked up at them and watched the top of the hill for someone drunk or heedless coming over it in part of her lane. She crested to an open black road, and there he was: a bulk, a blur, a thing running across her headlights, and she swerved left and her foot went for the brake and was stomping air above its pedal when she hit him, saw his legs and body in the air, flying out of her light, into the dark. Her brakes were screaming into the wind, bottles clinking in the fallen bag, and with the music and wind inside the car was his sound, already a memory but as real as an echo, that car-shuddering thump as though she had struck a tree. Her foot was back on the accelerator. Then she shifted gears and pushed it. She ejected the cassette and closed the window. She did not start to cry until she knocked on my bedroom door, then called: "Dad?"

Her voice, her tears, broke through my dream and the wind I heard in my sleep, and I stepped into jeans and hurried to the door, thinking harm, rape, death. All were in her face, and I hugged her and pressed her cheek to my chest and smoothed her blown hair, then led her, weeping, to the kitchen and sat her at the table where still she could not speak, nor look at me; when she raised her face it fell forward again, as of its own weight, into her palms. I offered tea and she shook her head, so I offered beer twice, then she shook her head, so I offered whiskey and she nodded. I had some rye that Father Paul and I had not finished last hunting season, and I poured some over ice and set it in front of her and was putting away the ice but stopped and got another glass and poured one for myself too, and brought the ice and bottle to the table where she was trying to get one of her long menthols out of the pack, but her fingers jerked like severed snakes, and I took the pack and lit one for her and took one for myself. I watched her shudder with her first swallow of rye, and push hair back from her face, it is auburn and gleamed in the overhead light, and I remembered how beautiful she looked riding a sorrel; she was smoking fast, then the sobs in her throat stopped, and she looked at me and said it, the words coming out with smoke: "I hit somebody. With the *car*."

Then she was crying and I was on my feet, moving back and forth, looking down at her, asking *Who? Where? Where?* She was pointing at the wall over the stove, jabbing her fingers and cigarette at it, her other hand at her eyes, and twice in horror I actually looked at the wall. She finished the whiskey in a swallow and I stopped pacing and asking and poured another, and either the drink or the exhaustion of tears quieted her, even the dry sobs, and she told me; not as I tell it now, for that was later as again and again we relived it in the kitchen or living room, and, if in daylight, fled it on horseback out on the trails through the woods and, if at night, walked quietly around in the moonlit pasture, walked around and around it, sweating through our clothes. She told it in bursts, like she was a child again, running to me, injured from play. I put on boots and a shirt and left her with the bottle and her streaked face and a cigarette twitching between her fingers, pushed the door open against the wind, and eased it shut. The wind squinted and watered my eyes as I leaned into it and went to the pickup.

When I passed St. John's I looked at it, and Father Paul's little white rectory in the rear, and wanted to stop, wished I could as I could if he were simply a friend who sold hardware or something. I had forgotten my watch but I always know the time within minutes, even when a sound or dream or my bladder wakes me in the night. It was nearly two; we had been in the kitchen about twenty minutes; she had hit him around one-fifteen. Or her. The road was empty and I drove between blowing trees; caught for an instant in my lights, they seemed to be in panic. I smoked and let hope play its tricks on me: it was neither man nor woman but an animal, a goat or calf or deer on the road; it was a man who had jumped away in time, the collision of metal and body glancing not direct, and he had limped home to nurse bruises and cuts. Then I threw the cigarette and hope both out the window and prayed that he was alive, while beneath that prayer, a reserve deeper in my heart, another one stirred: that if he were dead, they would not get Jennifer.

From our direction, east and a bit south, the road to that hill and the night club beyond it and finally the town, is for its last four or five miles, straight through farming country. When I reached that stretch I slowed the truck and opened my window for the fierce air; on both sides were scattered farmhouses and barns and sometimes a silo, looking not like shelters but like unsheltered things the wind would flatten. Corn bent toward the road from a field on my right, and always something blew in front of me: paper, leaves, dried weeds, branches. I slowed approaching the hill, and went up it in second, staring through my open window at the ditch on the left side of the road, its weeds alive, whipping, a mad dance with the trees above them. I went over the hill and down and, opposite the club, turned right onto a side street of houses, and parked there, in the leaping shadows of trees. I walked back across the road to the club's parking lot, the wind behind me, lifting me as I strode, and I could not hear my boots on pavement. I walked up the hill, on the shoulder, watching the branches above me, hearing their leaves and the creaking trunks and the wind. Then I was at the top, looking down the road and at the farms and fields; the night was clear, and I could see a long way; clouds scudded past the half-moon and stars, blown out to sea.

I started down, watching the tall grass under the trees to my right, glancing into the dark of the ditch, listening for cars behind me; but as soon as I cleared one tree, its sound was gone, its flapping leaves and rattling branches far behind me, as though the greatest distance I had at my back was a matter of feet, while ahead of me I could see a barn two miles off. Then I saw her skid marks: short, and going left and downhill, into the other lane. I stood at the ditch, its weeds blowing; across it were trees and their moving shadows, like the clouds. I stepped onto its slope, and it took me sliding on my feet, then rump, to the bottom, where I sat still, my body gathered to itself, lest a part of me should touch him. But there was only tall grass, and I stood, my shoulders reaching the sides of the ditch, and I walked uphill, wishing for the flashlight in the pickup, walking slowly, and down in the ditch I could hear my feet in the grass and on the earth, and kicking cans and bottles. At the top of the hill I turned and went down, watching the ground above the ditch on my right, praying my prayer from the truck again, the first one, the one I would admit, that he was not dead, was in fact home, and began to hope again, memory telling me of lost pheasants and grouse I had shot, but they were small and the colors of their home, while a man was either there or not; and from that memory I left where I was and while walking in the ditch under the wind was in the deceit of imagination with Jennifer in the kitchen, telling her she had hit no one, or at least had not badly hurt anyone, when I realized he could be in the hospital now and I would have to think of a way to check there, something to say on the phone. I see now that, once hope returned, I should have been certain what it prepared me for: ahead of me, in high grass and the shadows of trees, I saw his shirt. Or that is all my mind would allow itself: a shirt, and I stood looking at it for the moments it took my mind to admit the arm and head and the dark length covered by pants. He lay face down, the arm I could see near his side, his head turned from me, on its cheek.

"Fella?" I said. I had meant to call, but it came out quiet and high, lost inches from my face in the wind. Then I said, "Oh God," and felt Him in the wind and the sky moving past the stars and moon and the fields around me, but only watching me as He might have watched Cain or Job, I did not know which, and I said it again, and wanted to sink to the earth and weep till I slept there in the weeds. I climbed, scrambling up the side of the ditch, pulling at clutched grass, gained the top on hands and knees, and went to him like that, panting, moving through the grass as high and higher than my face, crawling under that sky, making sounds too, like some animal, there being no words to let him know I was here with him now. He was long; that is the word that came to me, not tall. I kneeled beside him, my hands on my legs. His right arm was by his side, his left arm straight out from the shoulder, but turned, so his palm was open to the tree above us. His left cheek was cleanshaven, his eye closed, and there was no blood. I leaned forward to look at his open mouth and saw the blood on it, going down into the grass. I straightened and looked ahead at the wind blowing past me through grass and trees to a distant light, and I stared at the light, imagining someone awake out there, wanting someone to be, a gathering of old friends, or someone alone listening to music or painting a picture, then I figured it was a night light at a farmyard whose house I couldn't see. *Going,* I thought. *Still going.* I leaned over again and looked at dripping blood.

So I had to touch his wrist, a thick one with a watch and expansion band that I pushed up his arm, thinking *he's left-handed,* my three fingers pressing his wrist, and all I felt was my tough fingertips on that smooth underside flesh and small bones, then relief, then certainty. But against my will, or only because of it, I still don't know, I touched his neck, ran my fingers down it as if petting, then pressed, and my hand sprang back as from fire. I lowered it again, held it there until it felt that faint beating that I could not believe. There was too much wind. Nothing could make a sound in it.

A pulse could not be felt in it, nor could mere fingers in that wind feel the absolute silence of a dead man's artery. I was making sounds again; I grabbed his left arm and his waist, and pulled him toward me, and that side of him rose, turned, and I lowered him to his back, his face tilted up toward the tree that was groaning, the tree and I the only sounds in the wind. Turning my face from his, looking down the length of him at his sneakers, I placed my ear on his heart, and heard not that but something else, and I clamped a hand over my exposed ear, heard something liquid and alive, like when you pump a well and after a few strokes you hear air and water moving in the pipe, and I knew I must raise his legs and cover him and run to a phone, while still I listened to his chest, thinking *raise with what? cover with what?* and amid the liquid sound I heard the heart, then lost it, and pressed my ear against bone, but his chest was quiet, and I did not know when the liquid had stopped, and do not know now when I heard air, a faint rush of it, and whether under my ear or at his mouth or whether I heard it at all. I straightened and looked at the light, dim and yellow. Then I touched his throat, looking him full in the face. He was blond and young. He could have been sleeping in the shade of a tree, but for the smear of blood from his mouth to his hair, and the night sky, and the weeds blowing against his head, and the leaves shaking in the dark above us.

    I stood. Then I knelt again and prayed for his soul to join in peace and joy all the dead and living; and, doing so, confronted my first sin against him, not stopping for Father Paul, who could have given him the last rites, and immediately then my second one, or, I saw then, my first, not calling an ambulance to meet me there, and I stood and turned into the wind, slid down the ditch and crawled out of it and went up the hill and down it, across the road to the street of houses whose people I had left behind forever, so that I moved with stealth in the shadows to my truck.

    When I came around the bend near my house, I saw the kitchen light at the rear. She sat as I had left her, the ashtray filled, and I looked at the bottle, felt her eyes on me, felt what she was seeing too: the dirt from my crawling. She had not drunk much of the rye. I poured some in my glass, with the water from melted ice, and sat down and swallowed some and looked at her and swallowed some more, and said: "He's dead."

    She rubbed her eyes with the heels of her hands, rubbed the cheeks under them, but she was dry now.

"He was probably dead when he hit the ground. I mean, that's probably what killed—"

"Where was he?"

"Across the ditch, under a tree."

"Was he—did you see his face?"

"No. Not really. I just felt. For life, pulse. I'm going out to the car."

"What for? Oh."

I finished the rye, and pushed back the chair, then she was standing too.

"I'll go with you."

"There's no need."

"I'll go."

    I took a flashlight from a drawer and pushed open the door and held it while she went out. We turned our faces from the wind. It was like on the hill, when I was walking, and the wind closed the distance behind me: after three or four steps I felt there was no house back there. She took my hand, as I was reaching for hers. In the garage we let go, and squeezed between the pickup and her little car, to the front of it, where we had more room, and we stepped back from the grill and I shone the light on the fender, the smashed headlight turned into it, the concave chrome staring to the right, at the garage wall.

"We ought to get the bottles," I said.

She moved between the garage and the car, on the passenger side, and had room to open the door and lift the bag. I reached out, and she gave me the bag and backed up and shut the door and came around the car. We sidled to the doorway, and she put her arm around my waist and I hugged her shoulders.

"I thought you'd call the police," she said.

We crossed the yard, faces bowed from the wind, her hair blowing away from her neck, and in the kitchen I put the bag of bottles in the garbage basket. She was working at the table: capping the rye and putting it away, filling the ice tray, washing the glasses, emptying the ashtray, sponging the table.

"Try to sleep now," I said.

She nodded at the sponge circling under her hand, gathering ashes. Then she dropped it in the sink and, looking me full in the face, as I had never seen her look, as perhaps she never had, being for so long a daughter on visits (or so it seemed to me and still does: that until then our eyes had never seriously met), she crossed to me from the sink and kissed my lips, then held me so tightly I lost balance, and would have stumbled forward had she not held me so hard.

I sat in the living room, the house darkened, and watched the maple and hemlock. When I believed she was asleep I put on *La Boheme*, and kept it at the same volume as the wind so it would not wake her. Then I listened to *Madame Butterfly*, and in the third act had to rise quickly to lower the sound: the wind was gone. I looked at the still maple near the window, and thought of the wind leaving farms and towns and the coast, going out over the sea to die on the waves. I smoked and gazed out the window. The sky was darker, and at daybreak the rain came. I listened to *Tosca*, and at six-fifteen went to the kitchen where Jennifer's purse lay on the table, a leather shoulder purse crammed with the things of an adult woman, things she had begun accumulating only a few years back, and I nearly wept, thinking of what sandy foundations they were: driver's license, credit card, disposable lighter, cigarettes, checkbook, ballpoint pen, cash, cosmetics, comb, brush, Kleenex, these the rite of passage from childhood, and I took one of them—her keys—and went out, remembering a jacket and hat when the rain struck me, but I kept going to the car, and squeezed and lowered myself into it, pulled the seat belt over my shoulder and fastened it and backed out, turning in the drive, going forward into the road, toward St. John's and Father Paul.

Cars were on the road, the workers, and I did not worry about any of them noticing the fender and light. Only a horse distracted them from what they drove to. In front of St. John's is a parking lot; at its far side, past the church and at the edge of the lawn, is an old pine, taller than the steeple now. I shifted to third, left the road, and, aiming the right headlight at the tree, accelerated past the white blur of church, into the black trunk growing bigger till it was all I could see, then I rocked in that resonant thump she had heard, had felt, and when I turned off the ignition it was still in my ears, my blood, and I saw the boy flying in the wind. I lowered my forehead to the wheel. Father Paul opened the door, his face white in the rain.

"I'm all right."

"What happened?"

"I don't know. I fainted."

I got out and went around to the front of the car, looked at the smashed light, the crumpled and torn fender.

"Come to the house and lie down."

"I'm all right."

"When was your last physical?"

"I'm due for one. Let's get out of this rain."

"You'd better lie down."

"No. I want to receive."

That was the time to say I want to confess, but I have not and will not. Though I could now, for Jennifer is in Florida, and weeks have passed, and perhaps now Father Paul would not feel that he must tell me to go to the police. And, for that very reason, to confess now would be unfair. It is a world of secrets, and now I have one from my best, in truth my only, friend. I have one from Jennifer too, but that is the nature of fatherhood.

Most of that day it rained, so it was only in early evening, when the sky cleared, with a setting sun, that two little boys, leaving their confinement for some play before dinner, found him. Jennifer and I got that on the local news, which we listened to every hour, meeting at the radio, standing with cigarettes, until the one at eight o'clock; when she stopped crying, we went out and walked on the wet grass, around the pasture, the last of sunlight still in the air and trees. His name was Patrick Mitchell, he was nineteen years old, was employed by CETA,° lived at home with his parents and brother and sister. The paper next day said he had been at a friend's house and was walking home, and I thought of that light I had seen, then knew it was not for him; he lived on one of the streets behind the club. The paper did not say then, or in the next few days, anything to make Jennifer think he was alive while she was with me in the kitchen. Nor do I know if we—I—could have saved him.

In keeping her secret from her friends, Jennifer had to perform so often, as I did with Father Paul and at the stables, that I believe the acting, which took more of her than our daylight trail rides and our night walks in the pasture, was her healing. Her friends teased me about wrecking her car. When I carried her luggage out to the car on that last morning, we spoke only of the weather for her trip—the day was clear, with a dry cool breeze—and hugged and kissed, and I stood watching as she started the car and turned it around. But then she shifted to neutral and put on the parking brake and unclasped the belt, looking at me all the while, then she was coming to me, as she had that night in the kitchen, and I opened my arms.

I have said I talk with God in the mornings, as I start my day, and sometimes as I sit with coffee, looking at the birds, and the woods. Of course He has never spoken to me, but that is not something I require. Nor does He need to. I know Him, as I know the part of myself that knows Him, that felt Him watching from the wind and the night as I kneeled over the dying boy. Lately I have taken to arguing with Him, as I can't with Father Paul, who, when he hears my monthly confession, has not heard and will not hear anything of failure to do all that one can to save an anonymous life, of injustice to a family in their grief, of deepening their pain at the chance and mystery of death by giving them nothing—no one—to hate. With Father Paul I feel lonely about this, but not with God. When I received the Eucharist while Jennifer's

---

CETA: Acronym for Comprehensive Employment and Training Act, 1970s government public service jobs program.

car sat twice-damaged, so redeemed, in the rain, I felt neither loneliness nor shame, but as though He were watching me, even from my tongue, intestines, blood, as I have watched my sons at times in their young lives when I was able to judge but without anger, and so keep silent while they, in the agony of their youth, decided how they must act; or found reasons, after their actions, for what they had done. Their reasons were never as good or as bad as their actions, but they needed to find them, to believe they were living by them, instead of the awful solitude of the heart.

I do not feel the peace I once did: not with God, nor the earth, or anyone on it. I have begun to prefer this state, to remember with fondness the other one as a period of peace I neither earned nor deserved. Now in the mornings while I watch purple finches driving larger titmice from the feeder, I say to Him: I would do it again. For when she knocked on my door, then called me, she woke what had flowed dormant in my blood since her birth, so that what rose from the bed was not a stable owner or a Catholic or any other Luke Ripley I had lived with for a long time, but the father of a girl.

And he says: I am a Father too.

Yes, I say, as You are a Son Whom this morning I will receive; unless You kill me on the way to church, then I trust You will receive me. And as a Son You made Your plea.

Yes, He says, but I would not lift the cup.

True, and I don't want You to lift it from me either. And if one of my sons had come to me that night, I would have phoned the police and told them to meet us with an ambulance at the top of the hill.

Why? Do you love them less?

I tell Him no, it is not that I love them less, but that I could bear the pain of watching and knowing my sons' pain, could bear it with pride as they took the whip and nails. But You never had a daughter and, if You had, You could not have borne her passion.

So, He says, you love her more than you love Me.

I love her more than I love truth.

Then you love in weakness, He says.

As You love me, I say, and I go with an apple or carrot out to the barn.

Questions

1. Who is the father in the title? Is there anyone else to whom the title might refer?
2. What is the significance of the priest's statement that "Belief is believing in God; faith is believing that God believes in you."
3. Why does Ripley refuse to give money to maintain church buildings and instead gives money to clothe and feed the poor? Why does the author include this detail in the story?
4. In the first paragraph Ripley says "here is what I call my life," and he describes his stable, house, and self. In the second paragraph he says "My real life is the one nobody talks about anymore, except Father Paul LeBoeuf." What is Ripley's real life? Why does Dubus distinguish between Ripley's secular and spiritual lives?
5. Do you accept the different treatment of sons and daughters that Ripley defends in his conversation with God?
6. Is Ripley a static or a dynamic character? If dynamic, describe the change that occurs in him. Does he have an antagonist?
7. Is Ripley a reliable narrator? How would you characterize his narrative voice; for example, is it strong, dominant, sad, weary, peaceful, tense, objective, neutral?

8. What aspect of Ripley's character does his relationship with his wife and later with two other women reveal? Do those relationships tell us anything about how he balances his sexual desire with his religious beliefs?
9. What does Ripley mean when he tells God that He could not bear a daughter's passion? What does "passion" mean in the context of the story?

Edgar Allan Poe

A biographical note about Edgar Allan Poe (1809–1849) appears on page 38 along with his chilling story "The Tell-Tale Heart." Here is another Poe story, a dark tale of revenge that mixes ironic humor and gothic horror to explore a world where evil and hypocrisy triumph.

The Cask of Amontillado   1846

    The thousand injuries of Fortunato I had borne as I best could, but when he ventured upon insult, I vowed revenge. You, who so well know the nature of my soul, will not suppose, however, that I gave utterance to a threat. *At length* I would be avenged; this was a point definitively settled—but the very definitiveness with which it was resolved precluded the idea of risk. I must not only punish, but punish with impunity. A wrong is unredressed when retribution overtakes its redresser. It is equally unredressed when the avenger fails to make himself felt as such to him who has done the wrong.

    It must be understood that neither by word nor deed had I given Fortunato cause to doubt my good-will. I continued, as was my wont, to smile in his face, and he did not perceive that my smile *now* was at the thought of his immolation.

    He had a weak point—this Fortunato—although in other regards he was a man to be respected and even feared. He prided himself on his connoisseurship in wine. Few Italians have the true virtuoso spirit. For the most part their enthusiasm is adopted to suit the time and opportunity—to practice imposture upon the British and Austrian *millionaires*. In painting and gemmary, Fortunato, like his countrymen, was a quack—but in the matter of old wines he was sincere. In this respect I did not differ from him materially: I was skilful in the Italian vintages myself, and bought largely whenever I could.

    It was about dusk, one evening during the supreme madness of the carnival season, that I encountered my friend. He accosted me with excessive warmth, for he had been drinking much. The man wore motley.° He had on a tight-fitting parti-striped dress, and his head was surmounted by the conical cap and bells. I was so pleased to see him, that I thought I should never have done wringing his hand.

    I said to him: "My dear Fortunato, you are luckily met. How remarkably well you are looking to-day! But I have received a pipe° of what passes for Amontillado,° and I have my doubts."

    "How?" said he. "Amontillado? A pipe? Impossible! And in the middle of the carnival!"

    "I have my doubts," I replied; "and I was silly enough to pay the full Amontillado price without consulting you in the matter. You were not to be found, and I was fearful of losing a bargain."

    "Amontillado!"

    "I have my doubts."

    "Amontillado!"

---

motley: the multicolored suit of a court jester (Fortunato has dressed for carnival in the costume of a fool).
pipe: wine barrel.   *amontillado*: dry, pale, expensive sherry from the Montilla region of Spain.

"And I must satisfy them."

"Amontillado!"

"As you are engaged, I am on my way to Luchesi. If any one has a critical turn, it is he. He will tell me—"

"Luchesi cannot tell Amontillado from Sherry."

"And yet some fools will have it that his taste is a match for your own."

"Come, let us go."

"Whither?"

"To your vaults."

"My friend, no; I will not impose upon your good nature. I perceive you have an engagement. Luchesi—"

"I have no engagement;—come."

"My friend, no. It is not the engagement, but the severe cold with which I perceive you are afflicted. The vaults are insufferably damp. They are encrusted with nitre."°

"Let us go, nevertheless. The cold is merely nothing. Amontillado! You have been imposed upon. And as for Luchesi, he cannot distinguish Sherry from Amontillado."

Thus speaking, Fortunato possessed himself of my arm. Putting on a mask of black silk and drawing a *roquelaire*° closely about my person, I suffered him to hurry me to my palazzo.

There were no attendants at home; they had absconded to make merry in honor of the time. I had told them that I should not return until the morning, and had given them explicit orders not to stir from the house. These orders were sufficient, I well knew, to insure their immediate disappearance, one and all, as soon as my back was turned.

I took from their sconces two flambeaux,° and giving one to Fortunato bowed him through several suites of rooms to the archway that led into the vaults. I passed down a long and winding staircase, requesting him to be cautious as he followed. We came at length to the foot of the descent, and stood together on the damp ground of the catacombs of the Montresors.

The gait of my friend was unsteady, and the bells upon his cap jingled as he strode.

"The pipe?" said he.

"It is farther on," said I; "but observe the white webwork which gleams from these cavern walls."

He turned towards me and looked into my eyes with two filmy orbs that distilled the rheum of intoxication.

"Nitre?" he asked, at length.

"Nitre," I replied. "How long have you had that cough!"

"Ugh! ugh! ugh!—ugh! ugh! ugh!—ugh! ugh! ugh!—ugh! ugh! ugh!—ugh! ugh! ugh!"

My poor friend found it impossible to reply for many minutes.

"It is nothing," he said, at last.

"Come," I said, with decision, "we will go back; your health is precious. You are rich, respected, admired, beloved; you are happy, as once I was. You are a man to be missed. For me it is no matter. We will go back; you will be ill, and I cannot be responsible. Besides, there is Luchesi—"

"Enough," he said; "the cough is a mere nothing; it will not kill me. I shall not die of a cough."

"True—true," I replied; "and, indeed, I had no intention of alarming you unnecessarily; but you should use all proper caution. A draught of this Medoc° will defend us from the damps."

---

nitre: white mineral deposit; saltpeter.   *roquelaire:* cloak.   *flambeaux:* lighted torches or candlesticks.   *Medoc:* a red wine.

Here I knocked off the neck of a bottle which I drew from a long row of its fellows that lay upon the mould.

"Drink," I said, presenting him the wine.

He raised it to his lips with a leer. He paused and nodded to me familiarly, while his bells jingled.

"I drink," he said, "to the buried that repose around us."

"And I to your long life."

He again took my arm, and we proceeded.

"These vaults," he said, "are extensive."

"The Montresors," I replied, "were a great and numerous family."

"I forget your arms."°

"A huge human foot d'or, in a field azure; the foot crushes a serpent rampant whose fangs are imbedded in the heel."

"And the motto?"

"*Nemo me impune lacessit.*"°

"Good!" he said.

The wine sparkled in his eyes and the bells jingled. My own fancy grew warm with the Medoc. We had passed through walls of piled bones, with casks and puncheons intermingling, into the inmost recesses of the catacombs. I paused again, and this time I made bold to seize Fortunato by an arm above the elbow.

"The nitre!" I said; "see, it increases. It hangs like moss upon the vaults. We are below the river's bed. The drops of moisture trickle among the bones. Come, we will go back ere it is too late. Your cough—"

"It is nothing," he said; "let us go on. But first, another draught of the Medoc."

I broke and reached him a flagon of De Grâve.° He emptied it at a breath. His eyes flashed with a fierce light. He laughed and threw the bottle upwards with a gesticulation I did not understand.

I looked at him in surprise. He repeated the movement—a grotesque one.

"You do not comprehend?" he said.

"Not I," I replied.

"Then you are not of the brotherhood."°

"How?"

"You are not of the masons."

"Yes, yes," I said "yes, yes."

"You? Impossible! A mason?"

"A mason," I replied.

"A sign," he said.

"It is this," I answered, producing a trowel from beneath the folds of my *roquelaire*.

"You jest," he exclaimed, recoiling a few paces. "But let us proceed to the Amontillado."

"Be it so," I said, replacing the tool beneath the cloak, and again offering him my arm. He leaned upon it heavily. We continued our route in search of the Amontillado. We passed through a range of low arches, descended, passed on, and descending again, arrived at a deep crypt, in which the foulness of the air caused our flambeaux rather to glow than flame.

your arms: family coat of arms, the conventional symbol of a noble family.   *Nemo me impune lacessit*: Latin for "No one attacks me with impunity" (Montresor's family motto suggests the narrator's vengeful nature).   *De Grâve*: another fine red wine.   *brotherhood*: Fortunato wants to know if Montresor is a member of the Masons, a secret fraternal organization.

At the most remote end of the crypt there appeared another less spacious. Its walls had been lined with human remains, piled to the vault overhead, in the fashion of the great catacombs of Paris. Three sides of this interior crypt were still ornamented in this manner. From the fourth the bones had been thrown down, and lay promiscuously upon the earth, forming at one point a mound of some size. Within the wall thus exposed by the displacing of the bones, we perceived a still interior recess, in depth about four feet, in width three, in height six or seven. It seemed to have been constructed for no especial use within itself, but formed merely the interval between two of the colossal supports of the roof of the catacombs, and was backed by one of their circumscribing walls of solid granite.

It was in vain that Fortunato, uplifting his dull torch, endeavored to pry into the depths of the recess. Its termination the feeble light did not enable us to see.

"Proceed," I said; "herein is the Amontillado. As for Luchesi—"

"He is an ignoramus," interrupted my friend, as he stepped unsteadily forward, while I followed immediately at his heels. In an instant he had reached the extremity of the niche, and finding his progress arrested by the rock, stood stupidly bewildered. A moment more and I had fettered him to the granite. In its surface were two iron staples, distant from each other about two feet, horizontally. From one of these depended a short chain, from the other a padlock. Throwing the links about his waist, it was but the work of a few seconds to secure it. He was too much astounded to resist. Withdrawing the key I stepped back from the recess.

"Pass your hand," I said, "over the wall; you cannot help feeling the nitre. Indeed it is *very* damp. Once more let me *implore* you to return. No? Then I must positively leave you. But I must first render you all the little attentions in my power."

"The Amontillado!" ejaculated my friend, not yet recovered from his astonishment.

"True," I replied; "the Amontillado."

As I said these words I busied myself among the pile of bones of which I have before spoken. Throwing them aside, I soon uncovered a quantity of building stone and mortar. With these materials and with the aid of my trowel, I began vigorously to wall up the entrance of the niche.

I had scarcely laid the first tier of the masonry when I discovered that the intoxication of Fortunato had in a great measure worn off. The earliest indication I had of this was a low moaning cry from the depth of the recess. It was *not* the cry of a drunken man. There was then a long and obstinate silence. I laid the second tier, and the third, and the fourth; and then I heard the furious vibrations of the chain. The noise lasted for several minutes, during which, that I might hearken to it with the more satisfaction, I ceased my labors and sat down upon the bones. When at last the clanking subsided, I resumed the trowel, and finished without interruption the fifth, the sixth, and the seventh tier. The wall was now nearly upon a level with my breast. I again paused, and holding the flambeaux over the mason-work, threw a few feeble rays upon the figure within.

A succession of loud and shrill screams, bursting suddenly from the throat of the chained form, seemed to thrust me violently back. For a brief moment I hesitated—I trembled. Unsheathing my rapier, I began to grope with it about the recess; but the thought of an instant reassured me. I placed my hand upon the solid fabric of the catacombs, and felt satisfied. I reapproached the wall. I replied to the yells of him who clamored. I re-echoed—I aided—I surpassed them in volume and in strength. I did this, and the clamorer grew still.

It was now midnight, and my task was drawing to a close. I had completed the eighth, the ninth, and the tenth tier. I had finished a portion of the last and the

"The Cask of Amontillado" illustration by Arthur Rackham, 1935.

eleventh; there remained but a single stone to be fitted and plastered in. I struggled with its weight; I placed it partially in its destined position. But now there came from out the niche a low laugh that erected the hairs upon my head. It was succeeded by a sad voice, which I had difficulty in recognizing as that of the noble Fortunato. The voice said—

"Ha! ha! ha!—he! he!—a very good joke indeed—an excellent jest. We will have many a rich laugh about it at the palazzo—he! he! he!—over our wine—he! he! he!"

"The Amontillado!" I said.

"He! he! he!—he! he! he!—yes, the Amontillado. But is it not getting late? Will not they be awaiting us at the palazzo, the Lady Fortunato and the rest? Let us be gone."

"Yes," I said "let us be gone."

"For the love of God, Montresor!"

"Yes," I said, "for the love of God!"

But to these words I hearkened in vain for a reply. I grew impatient. I called aloud—

"Fortunato!"

No answer. I called again:

"Fortunato!"

No answer still. I thrust a torch through the remaining aperture and let it fall within. There came forth in return only a jingling of the bells. My heart grew sick—on account of the dampness of the catacombs. I hastened to make an end of my labor. I forced the last stone into its position; I plastered it up. Against the new masonry I re-erected the old rampart of bones. For the half of a century no mortal has disturbed them. *In pace requiescat!*°

In pace requiescat!: Latin for "Rest in peace!"

Questions

1. What is Fortunato's crime? Does it seem to be commensurate with Montresor's deadly punishment?
2. Why does the narrator pretend to be so agreeable to Fortunato?
3. How does Poe prefigure the narrator's dark motives?
4. What does this story suggest about the nature of hypocrisy and evil?

Guy de Maupassant

Henri René Albert Guy de Maupassant (1850–1893) was born in a rented castle in Normandy. The son of minor aristocrats (the de in his surname denotes a noble family), Maupassant grew up overshadowed by his parents' unhappy marriage. His mother was a friend of the novelist Gustave Flaubert, who took the teenage boy under his tutelage: "He is my disciple," Flaubert declared, "and I love him like a son." Maupassant studied law, but the Franco-Prussian war of 1870 inspired him to enlist as a solider. After the war he worked briefly as a minor bureaucrat while continuing to study privately with Flaubert. In 1880 he published his first short story, "Boule de Suif" ("Ball of Fat"), the tale of a prostitute, which caused a literary sensation. Maupassant quit his government job and dedicated himself to literature, writing over three hundred short stories, six novels—most notably Pierre and Jean *(1888)—and three travel books in the decade before his untimely death. Becoming wealthy and internationally famous from his stories, the hardworking author lived a luxurious and often dissipated life. Having contracted syphilis (then incurable) in his twenties, Maupassant watched his own health and sanity deteriorate. He died one month before his forty-third birthday.*

Maupassant ranks not only as France's greatest writer of short fiction, but also as one of the key inventors of the modern short story. Concise, clear, and often ironic, his stories present well-plotted and engaging incidents without imposing moral judgment on the characters. A master of the Realist mode, he used narrative as a means of exploring class, character, and culture.

Mother Savage   1884

Translated by Lafcadio Hearn; edited and revised by R. S. Gwynn

I

It had been fifteen years since I had visited Virelogne. One autumn I returned to do some hunting and stayed with my friend Serval, who had finally rebuilt the château that the Prussians had destroyed.

I was madly in love with the area. It is one of those delightful corners of the world that possess a sensual appeal for the eyes. This is almost a physical kind of love. Those of us who are easily seduced by landscapes retain fond memories of certain springs, certain woods, certain streams, and certain hills which have become familiar to us and which can move our hearts like happy events. Sometimes our day-dreams return to a wooded spot, or a riverbank, or an orchard bursting into blossom, seen only once on a lovely day but held in our hearts like images of women strolling the streets on a spring morning with fresh, clean faces, stirring body and soul with unrequited desire, with the unforgettable sensation of fleeting joy.

At Virelogne, I loved the whole countryside, dotted with little woods and traversed by streams that course through the soil like veins carrying blood to the earth. We fished for crawfish, for trout and eels. Such blessed happiness! There were spots to swim, and we could flush snipe from the tall weeds that grew along the banks of these narrow ribbons of water.

I walked along, lightly as a goat, watching my two dogs range in front of me. Serval, a hundred meters to my right, beat through a field of high grass. As I came around the bushes that mark the border of the Saudres Forest, I saw a thatched cottage in ruins.

Suddenly I recalled that I had seen it before, the last time in 1869, well kept up, covered with vines, and with a few chickens around the front door. What can be sadder than a dead house with its skeleton still standing, ruined and sinister?

I also recalled that the good woman who lived there had asked me in, one day when I was bone-tired, for a glass of wine, and that Serval had later told me the family history. The father, an old poacher, had been shot by the police. The son, whom I had seen before, was a tall, wiry fellow who also had a reputation as a fierce killer of game. They were called the Savages.

Was this their name or nickname?

I called out to Serval. He walked over to me with his long, ambling stride.

I asked him:

"What's become of the people who lived here?"

And he told me this story.

II

When the war broke out, Mother Savage's son, who was then thirty-three years old, volunteered, leaving his mother all alone. However, no one felt sorry for the old woman because everybody knew that she had money.

So she lived by herself in her isolated cottage, far from the village at the edge of the forest. But she was not a bit afraid, being made of the same stuff as the men of the countryside—a hardy old woman, tall and gaunt, who seldom laughed and whom nobody dared to cross. The women of the countryside do not laugh much. That's the men's business! The souls of these women are melancholy and narrow, for their lives are dismal and rarely brightened by an hour of joy. The peasant husbands or sons enjoy a little noisy gaiety in taverns, but their wives or mothers remain serious, with perpetually severe expressions. The muscles of their faces have never learned the movements of laughter.

Mother Savage continued to live as she always had in her cottage, which was soon covered with snow. Once a week she used to come to the village to buy bread and meat, after which she would return home. As there was quite a bit of talk about wolves, she never went out without a gun slung on her shoulder, her son's rifle, a rusty weapon whose stock was quite worn from the hands that had rubbed against it; she made a strange sight, that tall old woman, a little stooped by age, walking with slow steps through the snow with the barrel of the gun sticking up behind the black scarf which covered her head and concealed the white hair that no one had ever seen.

One day the Prussians came. They were billeted with the people of the area, according to the wealth and resources of each family. The old woman had to take four of them because she was known to be rich.

These were four big fellows with fair skin, blond beards, and blue eyes who had not grown thin in spite of all the wear and tear they had endured; they seemed to be good boys, even though they were in a conquered country. Finding themselves alone with the old woman, they took pains to show her all possible consideration and did everything they could save her trouble or expense. You could see them every morning, all four of them, washing up at the well in their shirt sleeves, pouring great quantities of cold water over that fair, rosy Northern skin of theirs even on the days when it was snowing most heavily—while Mother Savage came and went, getting their soup ready. Later they could be seen cleaning up the kitchen, washing windows, chopping wood, peeling potatoes, washing linen—in short, doing all the chores like four good boys working for their own mother.

But the old woman was always thinking of her own son—her tall, gaunt boy with his hooked nose and brown eyes and thick mustache that seemed to cover his upper lip like a pelt of black fur. And every day she used to ask the four soldiers quartered in her home, "Do you know where that French regiment is, the 23rd of the line? My son is in it."

They would reply, "No, not know, not nothing." And sensing her pain and fear, they, who had mothers far away themselves, showed her a thousand little courtesies. She liked them well enough, too, those four enemies of hers; for country people do not as a rule feel patriotic hatred—those feelings are reserved for the upper classes. The humble folk—those who pay the most because they are poor and are always being weighed down with new burdens, those who are slaughtered wholesale, those who make up the real cannon fodder because there are so many of them, those who, to tell the truth, suffer most hideously from the miserable atrocities of war because they are the most vulnerable and the least powerful—such people do not understand war fever or the fine points of military honor or, even less, those so-called political necessities which exhaust two nations in six months, both victor and vanquished alike.

Speaking of Mother Savage's Germans, folks in the area would say, "Well, those four landed in a safe enough spot."

One morning while Mother Savage was at home alone, she caught sight of a man far off across the fields, hurrying towards her gate. He soon came near enough for her to recognize him: it was the rural postman. He handed her a sheet of folded paper, and she took her glasses, which she always wore when sewing, out of their case, and read:

Madam Savage,

This letter has a sad story to tell you. Your boy Victor was killed yesterday by a cannonball, which cut him practically in two. I was right there when it happened, for we stood next to each other in line and he was always talking to me about you so that I could let you know at once if he had any bad luck.

I took his watch out of his pocket to bring to you when the war is over.

I salute you amicably.

Césaire Rivot,
Private Second Class in the
Twenty-third Regiment of the Line

*

The letter was dated three weeks earlier.

She did not cry. She remained motionless, so overwhelmed, so stupefied by the blow that she did not immediately feel anything. She thought, "There's Victor, and now he's been killed." Then, little by little, tears slowly rose in her eyes, and sorrow invaded her heart. Thoughts came to her, one after the other—frightful, torturing ones. She would never kiss him again, her only child, her big, tall boy—never! The police had killed his father, and now the Prussians had killed the son . . . he had been cut in two by a cannonball. And it seemed to her she could see it all, the whole horrible thing: his head falling with his eyes wide open, his teeth still gnawing the corners of his thick mustache the way he used to do when he was angry.

What had they done afterward with his body? Couldn't they have brought her son back the same way they brought her husband back to her, with a bullet hole in the middle of his forehead?

But then she heard the sound of loud voices. It was the Prussians returning from the village. Quickly she hid the letter in her pocket and met them very calmly with her usual expression, for she had managed to wipe her eyes.

All four of them were laughing, quite delighted that they had been able to bring home a fine rabbit—doubtless stolen—and they made signs to the old woman that they were all going to have something really good to eat.

She set to work at once to prepare their dinner, but when the time came to kill the rabbit she did not have the heart to do it. Yet surely this wasn't the first rabbit she had ever been given to kill! One of the soldiers knocked it out by striking it behind the ears with his hand. Once it was dead she pulled the red body out of its skin, but the sight of the blood she was handling, which covered her fingers—the warm blood that she could feel cooling and coagulating—made her tremble from head to toe; all the while she kept seeing her tall son, cut in two and all red just like the body of the still quivering animal.

She sat down at the table with her Prussians, but she could not eat, not so much as a mouthful. They devoured the rabbit without paying any attention to her. Meanwhile she watched them from the corners of her eyes, not speaking—turning an idea over and over in her head, but with such an impassive face that none of them noticed anything unusual.

All of a sudden she said, "I don't even know your names, and we've been together for a whole month." They understood, with some difficulty, what she wanted and told her their names. But that was not enough; she made them write them down on a piece of paper along with the addresses of their families, and, placing her reading glasses on her big nose, she looked over the foreign writing; then she folded up the paper and put it into her pocket, next to the letter which had told her about the death of her son.

When the meal was over she said to them:

"Now I'm going to do something for you."

And she started carrying straw up into the loft where they slept.

They thought this was rather strange, but when she explained to them that it would keep them warmer they helped her. They stacked the bales all the way up to the thatched ceiling and made themselves a sort of large room with four walls of forage, warm and fragrant, where they could sleep peacefully.

At supper one of them became worried that Mother Savage still had not eaten anything. She told him that she had stomach cramps. Then she lit a good fire to warm herself, and the four Germans climbed up into their loft on the ladder they used every evening.

As soon as they had closed the trapdoor, the old woman took away the ladder, and, going outside without a sound, she began to collect straw and filled her kitchen with it. She walked barefoot through the snow—so softly that no one could hear her. From time to time she heard the loud and fitful snoring of the four sleeping soldiers.

When she decided that her preparations were complete, she thrust one of the bundles of straw into the fire, then flung the burning handful on top of the others and went outside to watch.

In several seconds a fierce glare lit the inside of the cottage; then the whole thing became a terrible furnace, a gigantic oven whose violent light blazed through the single narrow window and sent a bright ray reflecting over the snow.

Loud cries rang out from the upper part of the house. Then they were followed by a clamor of human screams full of agony and terror. Then, the trapdoor having been lifted, a storm of flame roared up into the loft, burnt through the roof of straw, rose up to the heavens like a vast bonfire, and the whole cottage went up in flames.

Nothing could now be heard but the crackling of the fire, the crumbling of the walls, the falling of the beams. The last fragments of the roof fell in, and the red-hot shell of the dwelling flung a huge shower of sparks skyward through clouds of thick smoke.

The snow-covered fields, lit up by the fire, shone like a sheet of silver tinged with crimson.

Far away, a bell began to ring.

Old Mother Savage stood at attention in front of the ruins of her home, armed with a gun, her dead son's rifle, to make sure that none of them could escape.

When she saw that it was all over, she threw the weapon into the fire. A single shot rang out.

People came running to the scene—the neighbors, the Prussian soldiers.

They found the old woman sitting on a tree stump, calm and satisfied.

A German officer, who spoke French like a son of France, asked her:

"Where are your soldiers?"

She stretched out her skinny arm towards the smoldering mass of ruins where the fire was dying down at last and answered in a strong voice:

"There! Inside!"

Everyone gathered around her. The Prussian asked:

"How did the fire start?"

She answered:

"I started it."

They could not believe her, and they thought that the disaster had driven her mad. Then, when everyone had moved closer to listen to her, she told the whole story from beginning to end—from the arrival of the letter down to the final screams of the burning men inside her house. She did not leave out a single detail of what she had felt and what she had done.

When she finished, she took two pieces of paper out of her pocket and, so she could tell one from the other by the last light of the fire, adjusted her glasses and announced, holding up one piece of paper, "This one is Victor's death." Holding up the other, she added, nodding her head towards the still-red ruins, "This one has their names on it so you can write home about them." She calmly handed the white sheet to the officer, who was now holding her by the shoulders, and she continued:

"You can write them how this all happened, and you can tell their parents that I was the one who did it—I, Victoire Simon, the Savage! Never forget it."

The officer screamed some orders in German. They seized her and pushed her up against the still-warm walls of her house. Then a dozen men lined up in front of her, twenty meters away. She never blinked an eye. She knew what was coming, and she waited.

An order rang out, followed by a loud volley. One shot echoed all by itself after the others.

The old woman did not fall. She sank straight down as though her legs had been cut away from under her.

The Prussian officer approached to look. She had been cut almost in two, and her stiffened fingers still clutched the letter, bathed in blood.

III

My friend Serval added, "In reprisal, the Germans destroyed the local château, which I owned."

For my own part, I thought about the mothers of those four poor boys who had burned inside, and of the terrible heroism of that other mother, shot dead against that wall.

And I picked up a little stone, which still bore the scorch marks of the fire.

Questions

1. "Mother Savage" begins with a narrator telling how he came to hear the main story. How does this introductory section emphasize the brutality of war?
2. Note the narrator's description of the countryside around Virelogne. What kind of imagery does he use to describe its effect on him?
3. When the narrator learns that the family "were called the Savages," he asks, "Was this their name or nickname?" Is this question ever answered in the story?
4. Discuss the symbolism in the scene where Mother Savage prepares the soldiers' dinner.
5. Could Mother Savage's act be called patriotic? Or is it simply an act of private revenge? Is her action comparable to contemporary acts of political terrorism?

Suggestions for Writing on Stories about Crime and Punishment

1. In Poe's "The Cask of Amontillado," an evil man commits a terrible crime and goes unpunished. The story makes no moral judgment of his action and even offers comic moments along the way. Do you think it is morally dangerous to read such violent stories that entertain through shock and horror? Support or critique the horror genre and state your reasons.
2. Have you ever been the victim of a crime? Write a short account of the experience, discussing what you learned from it or how it changed you.
3. In Dubus's "A Father's Story," Ripley covers up the killing of a teenager. Although the killing was accidental, his daughter was clearly intoxicated and negligent. Imagine that Ripley were found out and brought to trial as an accomplice to manslaughter. Write an opening statement for either the prosecution or the defense.
4. Both Maupassant's Mother Savage and Dubus's Ripley commit crimes that contradict their basic nature and seem to be motivated by deep parental love. Compare and contrast the two crimes. Are there any similarities beyond parental love?

POETRY

SOLDIERS AND WARFARE

Richard Lovelace	*To Lucasta*
Henry Reed	*Naming of Parts*
Richard Eberhart	*The Fury of Aerial Bombardment*
Marilyn Nelson	*Star-Fix*
Yusef Komunyakaa	*Facing It*
R. S. Gwynn	*Body Bags*

War has always been a central subject for poetry, but its treatment has changed radically over time. The heroism and glory of ancient wars was based on traditions of individual combat and valor that seem mostly alien to modern warfare, which involves huge numbers of personnel and machines and battles that may be fought by computers, drones, satellites, and smart bombs under the command of leaders thousands of miles away. The poems in this section display a range of responses to war, many of their writers having served in combat or grown up in military families. Richard Lovelace's "To Lucasta" presents a traditional concept of military duty and bravery. Richard Eberhart and Henry Reed, both World War II veterans, re-create moments from their own military experience, while Marilyn Nelson portrays her father, one of the legendary Tuskegee Airmen. Finally, Yusef Komunyakaa and R. S. Gwynn commemorate Vietnam veterans who never made it home.

Richard Lovelace

Richard Lovelace (1618–1658) was born into a wealthy landowning family in Woolwich, England; his father, Sir William Lovelace, was killed in battle in Holland in 1628. As a teenager, Lovelace was prominent in artistic circles at Oxford University, as well as attending at the court of King Charles I, whose cause he later loyally espoused both in political controversies and on the field of battle. During the English Civil War he was imprisoned twice, an experience that inspired his famous lyric "To Althea, from Prison," with its familiar opening lines, "Stone walls do not a prison make, / Nor iron bars a cage." Freed after the execution of the king in 1649, Lovelace spent his remaining years in poverty and bitterness, dying at the age of forty. "To Althea" and "To Lucasta" stand out from the mass of his work for their beauty, wit, and technical perfection.

To Lucasta 1649

    On Going to the Wars

Tell me not, Sweet, I am unkind
    That from the nunnery
Of thy chaste breast and quiet mind,
    To war and arms I fly.

True, a new mistress now I chase,
    The first foe in the field;
And with a stronger faith embrace
    A sword, a horse, a shield.

Yet this inconstancy is such
    As you too shall adore;
I could not love thee, Dear, so much,
    Loved I not Honor more.

Questions

1. What point does the speaker make in the first stanza?
2. What metaphor is the second stanza built upon? What does the speaker mean by "a stronger faith"?
3. The poem is witty, but is it also sarcastic? In what spirit are the last two lines intended?

Henry Reed

Henry Reed (1914–1986) was born in Birmingham, England. He graduated from Birmingham University, where he wrote his master's thesis on Thomas Hardy. During World War II he was in the British Army for a time and was then transferred to the Foreign Office to work in Naval Intelligence. After the war, he worked principally for the BBC as a radio broadcaster and playwright. Reed's poetry was published in two small clusters: A Map of Verona appeared in 1946; it contains both "Naming of Parts" and "Chard Whitlow" (which T. S. Eliot considered the best parody of his poetry). A quarter of a century later came Lessons of the War (1970), the complete five-poem sequence that begins with "Naming of Parts," followed by two volumes of short radio plays, both published in 1971. Reed's Collected Poems, edited by Jon Stallworthy, appeared in 1991.

Naming of Parts   1946

Today we have naming of parts. Yesterday,
We had daily cleaning. And tomorrow morning,
We shall have what to do after firing. But today,
Today we have naming of parts. Japonica
Glistens like coral in all of the neighboring gardens,
      And today we have naming of parts.

This is the lower sling swivel. And this
Is the upper sling swivel, whose use you will see,
When you are given your slings. And this is the piling swivel,
Which in your case you have not got. The branches
Hold in the gardens their silent, eloquent gestures,
      Which in our case we have not got.

This is the safety-catch, which is always released
With an easy flick of the thumb. And please do not let me
See anyone using his finger. You can do it quite easy   15
If you have any strength in your thumb. The blossoms
Are fragile and motionless, never letting anyone see
            Any of them using their finger.

And this you can see is the bolt. The purpose of this
Is to open the breech, as you see. We can slide it   20
Rapidly backwards and forwards: we call this
Easing the spring. And rapidly backwards and forwards
The early bees are assaulting and fumbling the flowers:
            They call it easing the Spring.

They call it easing the Spring: it is perfectly easy   25
If you have any strength in your thumb: like the bolt,
And the breech, and the cocking-piece, and the point of balance,
Which in our case we have not got; and the almond-blossom
Silent in all of the gardens and the bees going backwards and forwards,
            For today we have naming of parts.   30

Questions

1. How many speakers are there in the poem? Who are they?
2. How would you differentiate between the speakers in terms of tone?
3. What plays on words do you find in the poem?
4. Who is the speaker of the final stanza? What is the larger point being made there?

Richard Eberhart

Richard Eberhart (1904–2005) was born in Austin, Minnesota, the son of a well-to-do businessman who worked in the meat-packing industry. After graduating from Dartmouth College in 1926, he sailed on a tramp streamer, worked as a private tutor to the son of the King of Siam, studied at Cambridge University in England and at Harvard, and taught at St. Mark's School in Massachusetts, where one of his students was Robert Lowell. During World War II he was a naval gunnery instructor. He married the daughter of the owner of a prosperous floor-wax company, for which he worked for a time and served on its board of directors. Eberhart published some thirty volumes of poetry and won both the Pulitzer Prize and the National Book Award.

The Fury of Aerial Bombardment   1947

You would think the fury of aerial bombardment
Would rouse God to relent; the infinite spaces
Are still silent. He looks on shock-pried faces.
History, even, does not know what is meant.

You would feel that after so many centuries
God would give man to repent; yet he can kill
As Cain could, but with multitudinous will,
No farther advanced than in his ancient furies.

Was man made stupid to see his own stupidity?
Is God by definition indifferent, beyond us all?
Is the eternal truth man's fighting soul
Wherein the Beast ravens in its own avidity?

Of Van Wettering I speak, and Averill,
Names on a list, whose faces I do not recall
But they are gone to early death, who late in school
Distinguished the belt feed lever from the belt holding pawl.

Questions

1. As a naval officer during World War II, Richard Eberhart was assigned for a time as an instructor in a gunnery school. How has this experience apparently contributed to the diction of his poem?
2. In his *Life of John Dryden,* complaining about a description of a sea fight Dryden had filled with nautical language, Samuel Johnson argued that technical terms should be excluded from poetry. Is this criticism applicable to Eberhart's last line? Can a word succeed for us in a poem, even though we may not be able to define it? (For more evidence, see the technical terms in Henry Reed's "Naming of Parts.")
3. Some readers have found a contrast in tone between the first three stanzas of this poem and the last stanza. How would you describe this contrast? What does diction contribute to it?
4. What thematic point is made in the poem's last two lines?

Marilyn Nelson

Marilyn Nelson was born in Cleveland in 1946. Her late father, to whom "Star-Fix" is dedicated, was one of the Tuskegee Airmen, the first African American aviators in the U.S. military, famous for their heroism and exploits during the Second World War. Their story is the basis of Nelson's "Wings," a six-poem sequence (which includes "Star-Fix") that appears in her book The Homeplace (1990), which was a finalist for the National Book Award. Nelson is a distinguished poet and teacher, a professor emerita at the University of Connecticut, a past Poet Laureate of the State of Connecticut, and founder and director of Soul Mountain Retreat in East Haddam, Connecticut, which offers brief residencies to poets. In her essay "The Fruit of Silence," she talks about having taught poetry and meditation at West Point, and describes lessons from that experience that she passed on to her later college classes: "I've told my students that it seems important that at least some Americans pay attention to what our soldiers are going through; that we shouldn't change the channel when news of the war comes on, and pretend—as I've read many American college students do—it isn't happening. I've told them that people will be coming home from this war as severely traumatized as Wilfred Owen . . . I loved my cadets, and have maintained contact with several of them, all of whom have been deployed to Iraq."

Star-Fix   1990

For Melvin M. Nelson, Captain USAF (ret.) (1917–1966)

At his cramped desk
under the astrodome,
the navigator looks
thousands of light-years
everywhere but down.   5
He gets a celestial fix,
measuring head-winds;
checking the log;
plotting wind-speed,
altitude, drift   10
in a circle of protractors,
slide-rules, and pencils.

He charts in his Howgozit
the points of no alternate
and of no return.   15
He keeps his eyes on the compass,
the two altimeters, the map.
He thinks, *Do we have enough fuel?*
What if my radio fails?

He's the only Negro in the crew.   20
The only black flier on the whole base,
for that matter. Not that it does:
this crew is a team.
Bob and Al, Les, Smitty, Nelson.

Smitty, who said once   25
after a poker game,
I love you, Nelson.
I never thought I could love
a colored man.
When we get out of this man's Air Force,   30
if you ever come down to Tuscaloosa,
look me up and come to dinner.
You can come in the front door, too;
hell, you can stay overnight!
Of course, as soon as you leave,   35
I'll have to burn down my house.
Because if I don't
my neighbors will.

The navigator knows where he is
because he knows where he's been   40
and where he's going.
At night, since he can't fly

by dead-reckoning,
he calculates his position
by shooting a star.   45

The octant tells him
the angle of a fixed star
over the artificial horizon.
His position in that angle
is absolute and true: 50
Where the hell are we, Nelson?
Alioth, in the Big Dipper.
Regulus. Antares, in Scorpio.

He plots their lines
of position on the chart,   55
gets his radio bearing,
corrects for lost time.

Bob, Al, Les, and Smitty
are counting on their navigator.
If he sleeps,   60
they all sleep.
If he fails
they fall.

The navigator keeps watch
over the night and the instruments,   65
going hungry for five or six hours
to give his flight-lunch
to his two little girls.

STAR-FIX. 2 *astrodome*: a transparent dome on top of an aircraft. 13 *Howgozit*: from the phrase "how goes it," a plotted chart by which the navigator determines how much fuel is required for a given action. 43 *dead-reckoning*: a way of determining a plane or a ship's position without astronomical observation.

Questions

1. What is meant by "Not that it does" in line 22?
2. Do you take Smitty's claim (in lines 27–38) that he loves Captain Nelson at face value? Why or why not?
3. Might lines 39–41 have any larger reference to Captain Nelson's life and personality beyond his immediate situation?
4. How do the last five lines of the poem relate to what we already know about Nelson's character?

Yusef Komunyakaa

Yusef Komunyakaa was born in Bogalusa, Louisiana, in 1947. He served in the U.S. Army from 1968 to 1970; his service included a tour of duty in Vietnam, where he was a correspondent and managing editor of the Southern Cross, for which he was awarded a Bronze Star. He earned a B.A. at the University of Colorado Springs in 1975, and advanced degrees in writing from Colorado State University and the University of California at Irvine. He has taught at several universities, including Princeton, and is presently the Distinguished Senior Poet in New York University's graduate creative writing program. Beginning in 1977, he has published more than a dozen volumes of poetry. Toys in a Field (1986) and Dien Cai Dau (1988) deal directly with his Vietnam experiences; the latter volume has been widely praised as containing some of the finest poetry to have been written about that war. Neon Vernacular: New and Selected Poems (1993) won the Pulitzer Prize.

Facing It   1988

My black face fades,
hiding inside the black granite.
I said I wouldn't
dammit: No tears.
I'm stone. I'm flesh.   5
My clouded reflection eyes me
like a bird of prey, the profile of night
slanted against morning. I turn
this way—the stone lets me go.
I turn that way—I'm inside   10
the Vietnam Veterans Memorial
again, depending on the light
to make a difference.
I go down the 58,022 names,
half-expecting to find   15
my own in letters like smoke.
I touch the name Andrew Johnson;
I see the booby trap's white flash.
Names shimmer on a woman's blouse
but when she walks away   20
the names stay on the wall.
Brushstrokes flash, a red bird's
wings cutting across my stare.
The sky. A plane in the sky.
A white vet's image floats   25
closer to me, then his pale eyes
look through mine. I'm a window.
He's lost his right arm
inside the stone. In the black mirror
a woman's trying to erase names: 30
No, she's brushing a boy's hair.

Questions

1. How does the title of "Facing It" relate to the poem? Does it have more than one meaning?
2. The narrator describes the people around him by their reflections on the polished granite rather than by looking at them directly. What does this indirect way of scrutinizing contribute to the poem?
3. Why does the name mentioned in line 17 lead to the visual image in the following line?
4. Lines 19–21 and 29–31 describe women's reflections in the wall of the memorial. What do these descriptions have in common with one another?
5. Do you find the last line of the poem hopeful ("life goes on") or depressing (a suggestion that "history repeats itself")?

R. S. Gwynn

R. S. "Sam" Gwynn was born in Leaksville (now Eden), North Carolina, in 1948, where his father managed several theaters, including the one pictured on the front cover of Gwynn's first full-length collection, The Drive-In (1986). After graduating from Davidson College in 1969, he earned an M.A. and an M.F.A. from the University of Arkansas. Since 1976, he has taught at Lamar University in Beaumont, Texas, where he is a University Professor. "Body Bags" was the title poem of Gwynn's section of the collaborative volume Texas Poets in Concert: A Quartet (1990). His most recent collection is No Word of Farewell: Selected Poems 1970–2000 (2001). A widely acknowledged master of traditional verse forms, he often combines formal elegance with colloquial diction. Though much of his work is driven by a Swiftian savage indignation, he is also capable of great tenderness and compassion. "Body Bags" portrays three hometown friends from the Vietnam era—each one commemorated in a separate sonnet.

Body Bags   1990

I

Let's hear it for Dwayne Coburn, who was small
And mean without a single saving grace
Except for stealing—home from second base
Or out of teammates' lockers, it was all
The same to Dwayne. The Pep Club candy sale,   5
However, proved his downfall. He was held
Briefly on various charges, then expelled
And given a choice: enlist or go to jail.

He finished basic and came home from Bragg
For Christmas on his reassignment leave   10
With one prize in his pack he thought unique,
Which went off prematurely New Year's Eve.
The student body got the folded flag
And flew it in his memory for a week.

II

Good pulling guards were scarce in high-school ball. 15
The ones who had the weight were usually slow
As lumber trucks. A scaled-down wild man, though,
Like Dennis "Wampus" Peterson, could haul
His ass around right end for me to slip
Behind his blocks. Played college ball a year— 20
Red-shirted when they yanked his scholarship
Because he majored, so he claimed, in Beer.

I saw him one last time. He'd added weight
Around the neck, used words like "grunt" and "slope,"
And said he'd swap his Harley and his dope 25
And both balls for a 4-F knee like mine.
This happened in the spring of '68.
He hanged himself in 1969.

III

Jay Swinney did a great Roy Orbison
Impersonation once at Lyn-Rock Park, 30
Lip-synching to "It's Over" in his dark
Glasses beside the jukebox. He was one
Who'd want no better for an epitaph
Than he was good with girls and charmed them by
Opening his billfold to a photograph: 35
Big brother. The Marine. Who didn't die.

He comes to mind, years from that summer night,
In class for no good reason while I talk
About Thoreau's remark that one injustice
Makes prisoners of us all. The piece of chalk 40
Splinters and flakes in fragments as I write,
To settle in the tray, where all the dust is.

BODY BAGS. 39 *Thoreau's remark*: in his 1849 essay "Civil Disobedience," in which he recounts his refusal to pay taxes because of his opposition to slavery and to the Mexican War, Henry David Thoreau (1817–1862) wrote: "Under a government which imprisons any unjustly, the true place for a just man is also a prison."

Questions

1. How would you characterize the three young men described in the poem? Do you find a progression through the three parts, in terms of personality?
2. How many of the three actually go to Vietnam? How many of them die—apparently—in combat?
3. Should the phrase "for no good reason" (line 38) be taken at face value? Explain.
4. What do the breaking of the piece of chalk and the chalk dust in the tray of the blackboard (lines 40–42) have to do with the rest of the poem?
5. How does giving each veteran a separate sonnet add to the total emotional effectiveness of the poem?

Suggestions for Writing on *Poems about Soldiers and Warfare*

1. Both "To Lucasta" and "Naming of Parts" involve a contrast between life's pleasures and the demands of war. Discuss the two poems along these lines. How does each one specifically develop this contrast? What attitude does each take, explicitly or implicitly, to the obligation of military service?
2. "The Fury of Aerial Bombardment" and "Star-Fix" are both concerned with bomber planes in World War II. How does each poem treat this subject? What contrasts do they present in terms of tone, theme, and acceptance of the situations they describe?
3. Both "Facing It" and "Body Bags" deal indirectly with the Vietnam War, one from the perspective of a veteran of that war and the other from that of one who did not serve. Do you find similarities between the two poems? How do they differ in their treatment of the subject?
4. Most of the poems in this section express a clear attitude toward war—its morality or immorality, the demands it makes and the sacrifices it compels, the ways in which the living think and feel about it afterward. On the surface, "Star-Fix" seems silent on these subjects. But does a careful reading of this poem yield insight into the speaker's or author's views on these issues?

PEACE AND SOCIAL JUSTICE

William Blake	*A Poison Tree*
Emma Lazarus	*The New Colossus*
Claude McKay	*If We Must Die*
William Stafford	*At the Un-National Monument Along the Canadian Border*
Denise Levertov	*Making Peace*

The savagery and destruction of war often leave its survivors with a profound desire for peace and justice. Understanding only too well the consequences of violent conflict, many war veterans dedicate themselves to preventing future conflict. Sometimes their most sincere efforts, such as the League of Nations created after World War I, fail to prevent war. But often their efforts serve to improve the world, as the Marshall Plan did when the United States helped to rebuild the economies of the nations that lost World War II. Victory, the modern age has learned, should be a call for reconciliation, not an excuse for retribution. When Nelson Mandela became the first democratically elected president after the end of Apartheid in South Africa, he resisted the political pressure to punish the ruling class of the old regime. Instead he sought to reconcile the many mutually hostile and suspicious factions of the new state into a diverse community that could work together to build a common future. The poems in this section explore the ideas of justice, peace, and reconciliation. William Blake's powerful parable "A Poison Tree" presents two alternatives—revenge and forgiveness—and their consequences. Emma Lazarus's "The New Colossus" contrasts an older political philosophy of power and subjugation with America's inclusive vision. Claude McKay reminds us that the oppressed will eventually revolt against injustice. William Stafford employs irony to celebrate and commemorate the longstanding peace between the United States and Canada. Finally, Denise Levertov asks us to cultivate the "imagination of peace."

William Blake

A brief biography of William Blake (1757–1827) appears with his poem "The Tyger" on page 1269. "A Poison Tree" appears in Blake's Songs of Experience *(1794), the successor and complement to his earlier* Songs of Innocence *(1789). These were two of the books that he issued with hand-lettered texts and illustrations, as shown in the accompanying reproduction.*

A Poison Tree   1794

I was angry with my friend;
I told my wrath, my wrath did end.
I was angry with my foe:
I told it not, my wrath did grow.

Blake's illustration, first printed in *Songs of Experience* (1794).

And I waterd it in fears, 5
Night & morning with my tears:
And I sunned it with smiles,
And with soft deceitful wiles.

And it grew both day and night.
Till it bore an apple bright. 10
And my foe beheld it shine,
And he knew that it was mine.

And into my garden stole,
When the night had veild the pole;°   *the pole star: Polaris, the North Star*
In the morning glad I see; 15
My foe outstretchd beneath the tree.

Questions

1. Blake originally called this poem "Christian Forbearance." How might that title apply to the text?
2. Is there symbolic significance in the position of the body in Blake's illustration for the poem?
3. What is the speaker's attitude at the end of the poem? Does the author seem to share that view?

Emma Lazarus

Emma Lazarus (1849–1887) was born in New York into a well-to-do Jewish family, both sides of which had been in New York at least since the Revolution. Her father paid for the publication of her first volume, Poems and Translations (1866), when she was only seventeen. Her first mature work was Admetus and Other Poems (1871). In addition to her poetry, she wrote a novel, two verse plays, and a number of essays. In the last years of her brief life, which was cut short by cancer, she was extremely active on behalf of oppressed Jews overseas. Quite well known as an author during her lifetime (Ralph Waldo Emerson was a friend), for many years she was remembered only for "The New Colossus." But recent decades have seen a steady rise in her reputation, with the appearance of several biographies, volumes of selections from her writings, and the republication of several of her books.

The New Colossus° 1883

Not like the brazen giant of Greek fame,
With conquering limbs astride from land to land;
Here at our sea-washed, sunset gates shall stand
A mighty woman with a torch, whose flame
Is the imprisoned lightning, and her name 5
Mother of Exiles. From her beacon-hand
Glows world-wide welcome; her mild eyes command
The air-bridged harbor that twin cities frame.
"Keep, ancient lands, your storied pomp!" cries she
With silent lips. "Give me your tired, your poor, 10
Your huddled masses yearning to breathe free,
The wretched refuse of your teeming shore.
Send these, the homeless, tempest-tost to me,
I lift my lamp beside the golden door!"

THE NEW COLOSSUS. In 1883, a committee was formed to raise funds to build a pedestal for what would be the largest statue in the world, "Liberty Enlightening the World" by Frédéric-Auguste Bartholdi, which was a gift from the French people to celebrate America's centennial. American authors were asked to donate manuscripts for a fund-raising auction. The poet Emma Lazarus sent in this sonnet composed for the occasion. When President Grover Cleveland unveiled the Statue of Liberty in October 1886, Lazarus's sonnet was read at the ceremony. In 1903, the poem was carved on the statue's pedestal. The reference in the opening line to "the brazen giant of Greek fame" is to the famous Colossus of Rhodes, a huge bronze statue that once stood in the harbor on the Aegean island of Rhodes. Built to commemorate a military victory, it was one of the so-called Seven Wonders of the World.

Questions

1. What contrasts does the poem draw or suggest between the New Colossus and the original one?
2. What contrasts does the poem draw between the New World and the old one?
3. Frédéric-Auguste Bartholdi, the sculptor of the Statue of Liberty, titled his work "Liberty Enlightening the World." How does Lazarus modify Bartholdi's original conception?

Claude McKay

Claude McKay (1889–1948) was born in Jamaica, the youngest of eight children and the grandson of slaves. At twenty he joined the Jamaican Constabulary, but hated it and soon resigned. In 1912 he published two volumes of dialect verse, Songs of Jamaica and Constab Ballads. In that same year he came to Alabama, where he was shocked by the institutionalized racism he discovered. McKay subsequently moved to Kansas and then New York. He went to London in 1919, commencing a fifteen-year period of living in Europe that was his most productive time as a writer. In those years he published two collections of poetry, three novels, and a book of short stories. A Communist in his thirties, McKay repudiated the party in 1937 and subsequently became a Catholic. "If We Must Die" was written in 1919 in response to a wave of racial unrest that led to riots in a number of American communities, including New York City.

If We Must Die   1922

If we must die, let it not be like hogs
Hunted and penned in an inglorious spot,
While round us bark the mad and hungry dogs,
Making their mock at our accursed lot.
If we must die, O let us nobly die,   5
So that our precious blood may not be shed
In vain; then even the monsters we defy
Shall be constrained to honor us though dead!
O kinsmen! we must meet the common foe!
Though far outnumbered let us show us brave,   10
And for their thousand blows deal one deathblow!
What though before us lies the open grave?
Like men we'll face the murderous, cowardly pack,
Pressed to the wall, dying, but fighting back!

Questions

1. Who are the "we" of the first line?
2. Can you describe the form of this poem?
3. Does "If We Must Die" have a wider application beyond the circumstances that inspired it?
4. How would you interpret lines 7–8? Do you find the view expressed there to be plausible?

William Stafford

Born in Hutchinson, Kansas, William Stafford (1914–1993) graduated from the University of Kansas in 1937. Drafted into the armed forces in 1941, he registered as a conscientious objector and for four years performed alternative service in forestry and soil conservation in Arkansas, California, and Illinois. Beginning in 1948, he taught for many years at Lewis and Clark College in Portland, Oregon. His second book of poetry and first major collection, Traveling Through the Dark (1962), appeared when he was forty-eight years old. It won the National Book Award and established him as a major figure in the poetic landscape, and it was followed by many other books and chapbooks of poetry. In 1970 he was named Consultant in Poetry for the Library of Congress. In much of his work he traced the landscapes of the Midwest and the Pacific Northwest. He described his poetry as "much like talk, with some enhancement," a description that fits "At the Un-National Monument Along the Canadian Border."

At the Un-National Monument Along the Canadian Border   1977

This is the field where the battle did not happen,
where the unknown soldier did not die.
This is the field where grass joined hands,
where no monument stands,
and the only heroic thing is the sky.   5

Birds fly here without any sound,
unfolding their wings across the open.
No people killed—or were killed—on this ground
hallowed by neglect and an air so tame
that people celebrate it by forgetting its name.   10

Questions

1. What nonevent does this poem celebrate? What is the speaker's attitude toward it?
2. The speaker describes an empty field. What is odd about the way in which he describes it?
3. What words does the speaker appear to use ironically?

Denise Levertov

Denise Levertov's father, born a Hasidic Jew, had converted to Christianity as a university student in Germany, and by the time of her birth he was a minister in the Church of England. His daughter Denise (1923–1997) would later follow in his footsteps both by resettling in another country—the United States—and becoming a Christian in 1984 and converting to Catholicism 1989, after many years of agnosticism. Levertov also displayed a tendency toward social involvement from an early age, serving as a nurse in London during World War II, when the city was under frequent bombardment by German aircraft. Beginning with her passionate opposition to the Vietnam War in the 1960s, she wrote poems of active political engagement for several decades. In 2006, her longtime publisher, New Directions, issued a small volume of poems, selected from among her many collections, on issues of war and the alternatives to it; the book was titled *Making Peace*.

Denise Levertov

Making Peace   1987

A voice from the dark called out,
         "The poets must give us
imagination of peace, to oust the intense, familiar
imagination of disaster. Peace, not only
the absence of war."   5
                    But peace, like a poem,
is not there ahead of itself,
can't be imagined before it is made,
can't be known except

in the words of its making, 10
grammar of justice,
syntax of mutual aid.
                A feeling towards it,
dimly sensing a rhythm, is all we have
until we begin to utter its metaphors, 15
learning them as we speak.
                A line of peace might appear
if we restructured the sentence our lives are making,
revoked its reaffirmation of profit and power,
questioned our needs, allowed 20
long pauses . . .
                A cadence of peace might balance its weight
on that different fulcrum; peace, a presence,
an energy field more intense than war,
might pulse then, 25
stanza by stanza into the world,
each act of living
one of its words, each word
a vibration of light—facets
of the forming crystal. 30

Questions

1. In what sense might peace be "not only / the absence of war" (lines 4–5)?
2. What is the controlling simile of this poem? What are the most prominent likenesses between the two things being compared?
3. What are the implications of lines 19–21 in terms of how we live now and how we might live instead?
4. Explain the metaphor that concludes the poem.

Suggestions for Writing on *Poems about Peace and Social Justice*

1. Discuss "The New Colossus" and "If We Must Die" in terms of the spirit of America that Lazarus's sonnet promises, and the degree to which that promise has been fulfilled according to McKay's poem. Must one view be affirmed at the expense of the other, or can both contain elements of truth?
2. "A Poison Tree" and "If We Must Die" describe responses—acted upon or recommended—to perceived injustice or oppression. What is each poem's response to mistreatment? What seems to be each author's attitude toward that response?
3. "At the Un-National Monument Along the Canadian Border" and "Making Peace" assert attitudes opposed to the traditional celebration of martial heroism. Discuss the two poems in terms of the specifics of each one's rejection of traditional views of patriotism, and the values that each one puts forward, directly or indirectly, as an alternative.
4. Which of the poems in this section are you most impressed by? For which one do you have the least affinity? In both instances, explain the reasons for your response.

Poet in Depth
Wilfred Owen

"THE PITY OF WAR"

The Pity of War (prose introduction)

Dulce et Decorum Est

Anthem for Doomed Youth

Futility

World War I marked a turning point in both world history and Western literature. The unprecedented scale of violence across Europe, the role of new technology in accelerating the violence, and the powerlessness of Western governments to avoid or even curb the conflict shattered traditional notions of progress and civilization. The impact was strongest on the young soldiers who had gone to war with dreams of glory, only to see their generation slaughtered in vast, mechanized, inhuman battles. A number of British poets saw action in the front lines and memorably recorded their experiences in verses that were sometimes compassionate, sometimes scathing, sometimes both at once. The greatest English-language poet of the war is generally considered to be Wilfred Owen.

    A nervous, intellectual, and religious young man, equally interested in botany and poetry, deeply concerned by the suffering of the poor and troubled by homosexual longings, Owen made an unlikely soldier. Perhaps it was that complex outsider identity that gave him his deep sense of the historical and human tragedy that was unfolding as the "civilized" nations of Europe slaughtered their young men by the millions. Other poets captured the brutality of modern warfare, but Owen connected the catastrophe to humanity's deepest historical and religious failures. In "Dulce et Decorum Est" he contrasts the brutality of modern warfare with ancient notions of glorious death in battle. In "Anthem for Doomed Youth," the slaughter of young soldiers is presented as a grotesque parody of a Christian funeral, and in "Futility" Owen questions the purpose of life itself if it must end only in sudden and pointless death.

Wilfred Owen

Wilfred Owen (1893–1918) was born in Shropshire, England, the son of a railway stationmaster and a devoutly evangelical mother. The young Owen was a serious student, but he failed to earn a scholarship to London University and had to seek employment. Working as the lay assistant to an Anglican vicar, he attended lectures at Reading University, but after two years he left, claiming he was on the verge of a nervous breakdown. He was employed as a tutor in France when World War I broke out, and in September 1915 he went home to enlist. In 1917 Owen was injured and returned to England with "shell-shock." He recovered in a hospital on

Wilfred Owen

the outskirts of Edinburgh, where some of his best poems were written, and where he met Siegfried Sassoon, a wealthy soldier-poet who had been confined temporarily to the sanitarium because of his outspoken opposition to the war. Owen had written poetry for years, but the harsh experience of trench warfare transformed him from a minor versifier to a powerfully original poet of pacifist vision.

In August 1918 Owen returned to combat. He was put in charge of a platoon and later awarded the Military Cross for a successful attack on the German lines. Tragically, on November 4—one week before the war's end—Owen was killed in battle by German machine guns. A volume of his Poems was published posthumously in 1920, edited by Sassoon. His reputation has grown steadily since then, and he is often regarded as the major English-language war poet of the twentieth century.

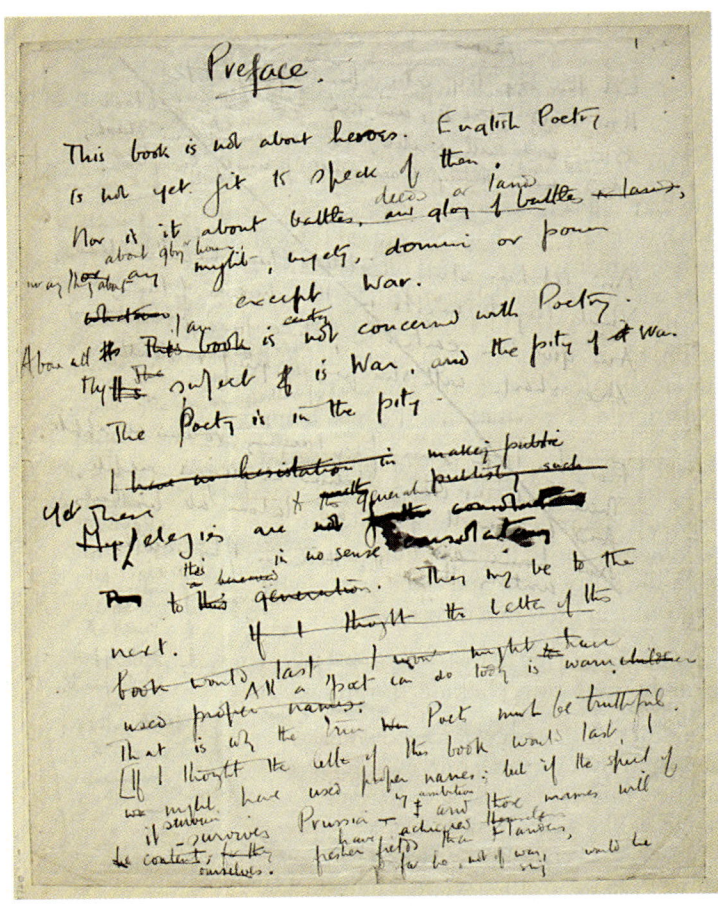

Manuscript draft for the Preface found in Owen's papers.

The Pity of War   1918(?)

This book is not about heroes. English poetry is not yet fit to speak of them.

Nor is it about deeds, or lands, nor anything about glory, honour, might, majesty, dominion, or power, except War.

Above all I am not concerned with Poetry.

My subject is War, and the pity of War.

The Poetry is in the pity.

Yet these elegies are to this generation in no sense consolatory. They may be to the next. All a poet can do today is warn. That is why the true Poets must be truthful.

[If I thought the letter of this book would last, I might have used proper names; but if the spirit of it survives—survives Prussia—my ambition and those names will have achieved themselves fresher fields than Flanders . . .]

THE PITY OF WAR. This is a preface Owen drafted to a book of war poetry he was working on. It was found, unfinished, among Wilfred Owen's papers.

Questions

1. What do you think Owen means by the now famous statement "The Poetry is in the pity"?
2. What does he mean when he says "All the poet can do today is to warn"?
3. What distinction does he seem to draw between the letter and the spirit of his book?

Dulce et Decorum Est   1920

Bent double, like old beggars under sacks,
Knock-kneed, coughing like hags, we cursed through sludge,
Till on the haunting flares we turned our backs
And towards our distant rest began to trudge.
Men marched asleep. Many had lost their boots   5
But limped on, blood-shod. All went lame; all blind;
Drunk with fatigue; deaf even to the hoots
Of tired, outstripped Five-Nines that dropped behind.

Gas! GAS! Quick, boys!—An ecstasy of fumbling,
Fitting the clumsy helmets just in time;   10
But someone still was yelling out and stumbling
And flound'ring like a man in fire or lime . . .
Dim, through the misty panes and thick green light,
As under a green sea, I saw him drowning.

In all my dreams, before my helpless sight,   15
He plunges at me, guttering, choking, drowning.

If in some smothering dreams you too could pace
Behind the wagon that we flung him in,
And watch the white eyes writhing in his face,
His hanging face, like a devil's sick of sin;   20
If you could hear, at every jolt, the blood
Come gargling from the froth-corrupted lungs,

Obscene as cancer, bitter as the cud
Of vile, incurable sores on innocent tongues,—
My friend, you would not tell with such high zest 25
To children ardent for some desperate glory,
The old Lie: Dulce et decorum est
Pro patria mori.

DULCE ET DECORUM EST.   Owen's title is the beginning of the famous Latin quotation from the Roman poet Horace with which he ends his poem: "*Dulce et decorum est pro patria mori.*" It is translated as "It is sweet and proper to die for your country."   8 Five-Nines: German howitzers often used to shoot poison gas shells.   17 *you too*: Some manuscript versions of this poem carry the dedication "To Jessie Pope" (a writer of patriotic verse) or "To a certain Poetess."

Questions
1. What is happening to the soldier in lines 11–12?
2. What is the meaning of the reference to "misty panes and dim green light" in line 13?
3. Why might the dying soldier's face resemble "a devil's sick of sin"?
4. What characteristics of children besides age might be relevant to line 26?

Anthem for Doomed Youth (1917)

What passing-bells for these who die as cattle?
　　Only the monstrous anger of the guns.
　　Only the stuttering rifles' rapid rattle
Can patter out their hasty orisons.
No mockeries now for them; no prayers nor bells, 5
　　Nor any voice of mourning save the choirs,—
The shrill, demented choirs of wailing shells;
　　And bugles calling for them from sad shires.°　　　　　counties

What candles may be held to speed them all?
　　Not in the hands of boys, but in their eyes 10
　　Shall shine the holy glimmers of good-byes.
The pallor of girls' brows shall be their pall;
Their flowers the tenderness of patient minds,
And each slow dusk a drawing-down of blinds.

Questions
1. Who are "these who die as cattle" (line 1), and what is the speaker asking? What implicit comparison does the entire poem turn upon? (Hint: What is meant by "passing-bells"?)
2. Why would the speaker consider traditional funeral rites to be "mockeries" (line 5) under these circumstances?
3. Do you detect a shift in tone between the first eight lines and the last six? How appropriate is the tone of each part of the poem to what is being said there?

Futility

1918

Move him into the sun—
Gently its touch awoke him once,
At home, whispering of fields unsown.
Always it woke him, even in France,
Until this morning and this snow.   5
If anything might rouse him now
The kind old sun will know.

Think how it wakes the seeds,—
Woke, once, the clays of a cold star.
Are limbs so dear-achieved, are sides   10
Full-nerved,—still warm,—too hard to stir?
Was it for this the clay grew tall?
—O what made fatuous sunbeams toil
To break earth's sleep at all?

Questions

1. Is the first stanza purely a poetic fancy, or might there be a reason for thinking that the man might be wakened in the sunlight?
2. What does line 3 suggest about the previous occupation of the subject of the poem? Does the phrase "fields unsown" take on other implications in the larger context?
3. What do you think "for this" (line 12) means?
4. Does this poem suggest that all human existence is futile because of the inevitability of death? If not, what more specific situation might the title refer to?

Suggestions for Writing on *Wilfred Owen's Poetry*

1. What is Owen saying in his unfinished preface, "The Pity of War"? How well does this preface apply to the Owen poems included in this selection?
2. As is made clear in "Dulce et Decorum Est," Owen opposes the customary celebration of war and heroism. Accordingly, none of the poems presented here describe feats of military bravery. How are the soldiers in his poems depicted? What seems to be his attitude toward these men?
3. William Butler Yeats famously excluded Owen and others from his anthology *The Oxford Book of Modern Verse* (1936) with this explanation: "The writers of these poems were invariably officers of exceptional courage and capacity . . . but felt bound, in the words of the best known, to plead the suffering of their men. In poems that had for a time considerable fame, written in the first person, they made that suffering their own. I have rejected these poems . . . passive suffering is not a theme for poetry." How persuasive do you find this view, both as a general proposition and as an estimate of Owen's merits as a poet?

NONFICTION
THE COST OF WAR

Abraham Lincoln *Second Inaugural Address*

Ryan Kelly *A Quick Look at Who Is Fighting This War; This Is Not a Game*

Myrna E. Bein *A Journey Taken with My Son*

Political speech is often weighed down with slogans, clichés, euphemisms, and vague abstractions, all designed to make a quick positive impression (but rarely capable of surviving close analysis). George Orwell observed that "the great enemy of clear language is insincerity," adding that political language was designed "to give an appearance of solidity to pure wind." Yet great language and clear expression can have enormous impact on a society, especially in times of crisis. As the lives of such leaders as Winston Churchill, Martin Luther King Jr., and Václav Havel demonstrate, the right words and the right ideas can change history. This section presents eloquent and effective language—both public and private—written in time of war. We begin with Abraham Lincoln's extraordinary "Second Inaugural Address," delivered toward the end of the Civil War (still the bloodiest conflict in American history) and shortly before the President's assassination. In this prophetic and poetic speech, he predicted that the nation would have to pay the full price for the evils of slavery. Lincoln's powerful account of the cost of America's deadliest war is followed by two pieces produced during the recent wars in Iraq and Afghanistan—one from the battlefront, the other from the home front. Captain Ryan Kelly writes his mother about his fellow troops. Myrna E. Bein, the mother of an infantryman, unforgettably describes a moment in the long and difficult adjustment to her son's heartbreaking battlefield injury.

Abraham Lincoln

Abraham Lincoln's Second Inaugural Address was delivered on the steps of the U.S. Capitol in Washington, D.C., on March 4, 1865. The Civil War, which had been raging since April 1861, was now almost over. The South would surrender on April 9, 1865, at Appomattox, Virginia. The savage and sustained fighting, however, had destroyed much of the South and resulted in horrendous human losses on both sides. (More Americans died in the Civil War than in World War I, World War II, Korea, and Vietnam combined—although the U.S. population then was only one-tenth of what it is now.) In this historic speech Lincoln asserted that the war had been the result of the sin of slavery. The South was guilty of this crime, but the North was not free of culpability. In his final words he proclaimed that only charity and reconciliation could bind the nation's wounds. Addressing a broken and suffering nation, Lincoln knew that even though the war was finally coming to an end, the political, material, and spiritual damage inflicted would not soon be repaired. The Union had been saved, but at a price far heavier than anyone could have predicted. What Lincoln did not know was that a few days after the truce was signed at Appomattox he would be assassinated by a Southern sympathizer.

Abraham Lincoln (center) delivering Inaugural Address on east portico of U.S. Capitol.

Second Inaugural Address

Saturday, March 4, 1865

Fellow-Countrymen:

At this second appearing to take the oath of the presidential office, there is less occasion for an extended address than there was at the first. Then a statement somewhat in detail of a course to be pursued seemed fitting and proper. Now, at the expiration of four years, during which public declarations have been constantly called forth on every point and phase of the great contest which still absorbs the attention and engrosses the energies of the nation, little that is new could be presented. The progress of our arms, upon which all else chiefly depends, is as well known to the public as to myself, and it is, I trust, reasonably satisfactory and encouraging to all. With high hope for the future, no prediction in regard to it is ventured.

On the occasion corresponding to this four years ago, all thoughts were anxiously directed to an impending civil war. All dreaded it, all sought to avert it. While the inaugural address was being delivered from this place, devoted altogether to *saving* the Union without war, insurgent agents were in the city seeking to *destroy* it without war—seeking to dissolve the Union and divide effects by negotiation. Both parties deprecated war, but one of them would *make* war rather than let the nation survive, and the other would *accept* war rather than let it perish. And the war came.

One-eighth of the whole population were colored slaves, not distributed generally over the Union, but localized in the Southern part of it. These slaves constituted a peculiar and powerful interest. All knew that this interest was somehow the cause of the war. To strengthen, perpetuate, and extend this interest was the object for which the insurgents would rend the Union even by war, while the government claimed no right to do more than to restrict the territorial enlargement of it. Neither party expected for the war the magnitude or the duration which it has already attained. Neither anticipated that the *cause* of the conflict might cease with or even before the conflict itself should cease. Each looked for an easier triumph, and a result less fundamental and astounding. Both read the same Bible, and pray to the same God; and each invokes

His aid against the other. It may seem strange that any men should dare to ask a just God's assistance in wringing their bread from the sweat of other men's faces; but let us judge not, that we be not judged. The prayers of both could not be answered. That of neither has been answered fully. The Almighty has His own purposes. "Woe unto the world because of offenses; for it must needs be that offenses come, but woe to that man by whom the offense cometh."° If we shall suppose that American Slavery is one of those offenses which, in the providence of God, must needs come, but which, having continued through His appointed time, He now wills to remove, and that He gives to both North and South this terrible war as the woe due to those by whom the offense came, shall we discern therein any departure from those divine attributes which the believers in a living God always ascribe to Him? Fondly do we hope—fervently do we pray—that this mighty scourge of war may speedily pass away. Yet, if God wills that it continue until all the wealth piled by the bondsman's two hundred and fifty years of unrequited toil shall be sunk, and until every drop of blood drawn with the lash shall be paid by another drawn with the sword, as was said three thousand years ago, so still it must be said "the judgments of the Lord are true and righteous altogether."°

With malice toward none, with charity for all, with firmness in the right as God gives us to see the right, let us strive on to finish the work we are in; to bind up the nation's wounds, to care for him who shall have borne the battle and for his widow and his orphan—to do all which may achieve and cherish a just and lasting peace among ourselves and with all nations.

Questions

1. What does Lincoln identify as the cause of the war?
2. In what ways did Lincoln believe that the harsh reality of the war surprised both sides?
3. How does Lincoln fear that God will punish "the bondsman's two hundred and fifty years of unrequited toil"?
4. How would you characterize the tone of the speech?

"Woe unto the world . . .": quoting Matthew 18:7.   as was said three thousand years ago . . . "the judgments of the Lord . . ." : quoting Psalm 19:9.

Ryan Kelly

Ryan Kelly was born in Wyoming in 1970. He worked as a journalist while serving in the Army National Guard. He did not serve in a war zone, however, until 2004, when the married Army captain, now a Black Hawk helicopter pilot, was put in charge of a mechanized infantry company consisting of New Jersey Army National Guard personnel deployed in Iraq. Kelly's candid and observant reports from Iraq were featured in Operation Homecoming, the National Endowment for the Arts *project to encourage U.S. troops and their spouses to write about their wartime experience. Kelly was also featured in two documentary films on Iraq. He brought all seventy-seven members of his company safely back home. The excerpts that follow are from letters Kelly wrote to his mother in Colorado in 2004 and 2005.*

A Quick Look at Who Is Fighting This War 2004

A quick look around my tent will show you who is fighting this war. There's Ed, a 58-year-old grandfather from Delaware. He never complains about his age, but his body does, in aches and creaks and in the slowness of his movements on late nights and cold mornings....

There's Lindon, a 31-year-old black-as-coal ex-Navy man from Trinidad who speaks every word with a smile. His grandfather owned an animal farm and lived next to his grandmother, who owned an adjacent cocoa field. They met as children.

There's Sgt. Lilian, a single mother who left her five-year-old daughter at home with a frail and aging mother because nobody else was there to help.

There's Melissa and Mike, two sergeants who got married inside the Ft. Dix chapel a month before we deployed—so in love, yet forbidden, because of fraternization policies, even to hold hands in front of other soldiers. But if you watch them closely, you can catch them stealing secret glances at each other. Sometimes I'll see them sitting together on a box of bottled water tenderly sharing a lunch. They are so focused on each other, that the world seems to dissolve around them. If they were on a picnic in Sheep's Meadow in Central Park, instead of here, surrounded by sand and war machines, it would be the same. War's a hell of a way to spend your honeymoon.

There's SFC° Ernesto, 38, a professional soldier whose father owns a coffee plantation in Puerto Rico and whose four-year-old daughter cries when he calls. 5

There's Noah, a 23-year-old motorcross stuntman, who wears his hair on the ragged edge of army regulations. He's been asking me for months to let him ship his motorcycle to the desert. I keep telling him no.

There's CW4° Jerry, the "Linedog" of aviation maintenance, whose father was wounded in WWII a month after he arrived in combat. On D-Day, a bouncing betty popped up from behind a hedge grove near Normandy Beach and spewed burning white phosphorus all over his body, consigning the man to a cane and a stutter for the rest of his life. CW4 Jerry lives out on the flight line, going from aircraft to aircraft with his odd bag of tools, like a doctor making house calls. He works so hard I often have to order him to take a day off.

There's Martina, 22, a jet-black-haired girl, who fled Macedonia with her family to escape the genocide of the Bosnia-Croatian civil war. Her family ran away to prevent the draft from snatching up her older brother and consuming him in a war they considered absurd and illegal. A few years later, the family, with no place else to run, watched helplessly as the US flew their daughter into Iraq. She's not even a US citizen, just a foreigner fighting for a foreign country on foreign soil for a foreign cause. She has become one of my best soldiers.

There is William "Wild Bill," a 23-year-old kid from Jersey with a strong chin and a James Dean-like grin. The day before we went on leave, he roared up in front of the barracks and beamed at me from behind the wheel of a gleaming-white monster truck that he bought for $1500. Three days later, he drove it into the heart of Amish country where the transmission clanked and clattered it to a stop. He drank beer all night at some stranger's house, and in the morning, sold them the truck. Kicker is, he made it back to post in time for my formation.

SFC: Sergeant first class. *CW4*: Chief Warrant Officer 4.

There is my 1SG,° my no-nonsense right-hand man. He's my counsel, my confidant, my friend. He's the top enlisted man in the company with 28 years in the army, and would snap his back, and anybody else's for that matter, for any one of our men. Last year, his pit bull attacked his wife's smaller dog—a terrier of some sort, I think. As she tried to pry them apart, the pit bit off the tip of her ring finger. Top punched the pit bull in the skull and eventually separated the two. A hospital visit and a half a pack of cigarettes later, he learned the blow broke his hand. He bought her a new wedding ring in Kuwait.

And on, and on and on. . . .

I hope you are doing well, mom. I'm doing my best. For them. For me. For you. I hope it's good enough.

Tell everyone I said hello and that I love and miss them. Talk to you soon.

Love, Ryan

This Is Not a Game

2005

Dear Ma,

They are called HERO missions. And they are the worst kind.

It's the body bag in the back that makes the flight hard. No jovial banter among the crew. No jokes of home. No wisecracks about the origin of the meat served at the chow hall, just the noise of the flight—the scream of the engines, the whir of the blades clawing at the air, the voice crackling over the radio and echo of your own thoughts about the boy in the bag in the back.

Yesterday I was in the TOC (tactical operations center)—it's where all the mission planning happens, briefings, maps on the wall, etc. Normally, after flying missions, pilots drift around the TOC with an air of satisfied indifference—similar to lions after devouring a zebra. I was talking with the operations officer, complaining that my pilots weren't flying enough, when a heavy-set, three pieces of cake after dinner man came in. Instead of the usual swagger, he was dazed. I asked him what was wrong. He told me he just finished flying one of the HERO missions. When we pick up friendly KIAs (killed in action), that is what we call it.

He told me he picked up a US kid killed in a car bomb. He tried to shrug it off as just another mission, but it was obviously bothering him. A few seconds later he left, but his look stayed with me.

Body bags must have been in the stars because later the Colonel announced that the heaters in the medevac helicopters were not working that well. In response, the medics, operating on a "corn husk theory," started zipping their live patients inside body bags to keep them warm during the flight. It can get very cold in the back of the Black Hawk because the wind seeps in through cracks in the window seals. However, the medics forgot to explain this to their patients who understandably freaked out. It's kind of funny, in a twisted sort of way. I guess being in a body bag is better than freezing on the way to the hospital. Why is death always so cold?

Things have hardened into routine here, like an old artery that's carried the same, tired blood along the same, tired path for years. Pump, return, pump, return, wake up, eat, work, sleep, wake up—back and forth, back and forth, BOOOM! Rocket attack. Pump, return, pump, return . . . We've worn a trail through the gravel with our boots plodding back and forth to the hangar.

1SG: First sergeant.

If it weren't for the Army uniforms and the constant noise of the helicopters taking off and landing, and the Russian 747-like jets screaming overhead every hour of the day, and the F-16s screeching around looking for something to kill, and the rockets exploding and the controlled blasts shaking the windows and the "thump, thump, thump" sound of the Apache gun ships shooting their 30mm guns in the middle of the night, and the heat and the cold, and the hero missions and the body bags and the stress, and the soldiers fraught with personal problems—child custody battles fought from 3000 miles away, surgeries on ovaries, hearts, breasts, brains, cancers, transplants, divorces, Dear John letters, births, deaths, miscarriages, and missmarriages—and the scorpions and the spiders who hide under the toilet seats, and the freakish bee-sized flies humming around like miniature blimps, and the worst: the constant pang of home, the longing for family, the knowledge that life is rolling past you like an unstoppable freight train, an inevitable force, reinforcing the desire for something familiar, the longing for something beautiful, for something safe, to be somewhere safe, with love and laughter and poetry and cold lemonade and clean sheets, if it weren't for all that Iraq would be just like home. Almost.

Last night, one of my soldiers showed up at the chow hall. I was surprised because he's been gone for a while. Two months ago he volunteered to be part of a security detail that escorts convoys to and from Kuwait and back again. The drive is a perilous 600-mile, one-way trip with roadside bombs, RPG° attacks, ambushes and small arms fire.

The convoys are made up of security teams who speed down the highway in armored HMMVs,° like cowboys herding columns of trucks stuffed with food, fans, etc. Foreigners—Japanese, Turks, you name it—drive the giant semis and risk capture and beheadings because the job pays big money. Some drivers earn $100,000 or more. Men like mine do it because they want to or because commanders like me order them to. My man earns about $40,000 a year.

The convoy escort mission passed to me like a foul smelling egg. The Army hatched the mission in an effort to spare more people the risk of convoying. The idea was to get a few permanent escort teams together instead of making whole units drive. It's a good idea, if you don't happen to be one of the poor suckers on one of the teams. Three men they wanted, three men. I was not happy. I was pissed off. Weren't we done with these awful convoys? I passed the news like a kidney stone to my first sergeant. We went through the horrible process of selection. Who would it be? Who could I afford to lose? Who was worth more to me alive? NO one should ever have to ask these questions. Fortunately, my men volunteered, sparing me the decision. I was—and am—so very proud of their bravery, mom. It nearly brought me to tears. After about two weeks, two of them returned unharmed and wide-eyed from the experience.

But not one man. He's still out there. The guys in the TOC tell me he'll be on a team for up to three months. That's a long time to let someone take shots at you. But it's war, and in comparison to what grandpa went through, a tame one. My man's missions are unpredictable. I never know if he's coming or going. He'll drift around the CP (command post) or the hangar for a week or so, turn a few wrenches on a helicopter and then suddenly I'll get a knock on my door at three o'clock in the morning. I'll open it and see him standing there donned in his body armor, helmet and rifle. He'll tell me he's leaving and my first sergeant and I will wish him good luck and God speed.

RPG: Rocket-propelled grenade.   HMMV: High mobility multipurpose vehicle.

We'll all shake hands, I'll slap him on the back and he'll disappear. Then I won't see him for a few weeks. That's how it goes. That's our routine. Every time I send him off I feel like a father sending a kid off into the world, wondering when he'll be back again or if I'm going to write a death letter to his family.

For weeks I won't know if he's dead or alive, shot or blown up. All I will know is that he is somewhere between here, Kuwait, death, and home. Then, as suddenly as he left, he'll reappear.

The last time he returned, he was flush with confidence and adrenaline. I caught him about three weeks ago regaling the guys about this latest trip; some Iraqi kids chucked a brick off an overpass and shattered a semi's windshield. The driver lost control and flipped the truck upside down. It crushed him to death. My man was unable to return fire because the kids melted into a crowd.

Despite the horror inflicted on someone else, the trip excited him. He announced that he liked driving on the convoys better than working in maintenance. He asked me if he could stay on the escort mission for the rest of our tour. I said, "hell, no" and that he could join the Goddamned infantry later, after we were safely back home. That exchange has become our second routine. He asks to go, I say, no. We both laugh and he leaves on another mission. He said he really likes it.

That was until last night.

I was eating dinner, like I usually do, when he appeared, interrupting me in the middle of a forkful of coleslaw. Something dark had happened. He was somber, deliberate, and scared. Before I could say, "Welcome back," and "hell, no, you can't be an infantryman," he blurted out: "Sir, can I talk to you for a second?" When people say that to me there's a problem. Soldiers don't usually talk to me unless they are bitching or have something troubling them. God, mom, I've heard that phrase so many times.

He said he was driving back in a column of 12 armored gun trucks, secured by the fantasy that the enemy would never dare attack such a bristling display of American industrial might—replete with machine guns and automatic grenade launchers. He was thinking this when a huge roadside bomb exploded, engulfing a semi truck in flames, killing the driver and his passenger and spraying my man's HMMV with dirt.

The experience didn't rattle him. Worse, it changed him. He realized that this is not a game. He understands that there are people who are trying to kill him, and me, and anyone else unfortunate enough to stray down the wrong street. I think he wanted me to pull him off the mission and tell him he didn't have to go out on the road anymore.

But I didn't. He's become proficient, more of an expert on the tactics and tells of the enemy than anyone I could replace him with. So I made him stay. It's a cold decision, but the right one. Again, I felt like his father. "I think he's learning what this is all about," my sergeant said. Maybe we all are.

This morning I went to work and found a VFW° magazine on the conference table. On the front cover was a picture of an injured 20-something soldier, his face and forehead purpled with bruises, his lips swollen and cut, his left eye half-closed, his arm in a sling, fingernails black with dried blood, his thighs blotched with red abrasions and his leg wrapped in an ace bandage, amputated below the knee. He was sitting in a hospital bed with a half smile on his face. A blazing bold yellow headline scrawled across his chest read, "wounded vets rebound." I opened the magazine and flipped to

°VFW: Veterans of Foreign Wars, a congressionally chartered veterans' organization.

the story and saw a second picture of a wounded amputee. This one was of a young Navy guy lying in a hospital bed. His wife was sitting beside him. She was not smiling.

The caption under the picture read: "Navy Corpsman Joe Worley visits with his wife, Angel, while recovering at Walter Reed. A rocket-propelled grenade ripped off his left leg, but he said it was 'a fair trade for getting out of Iraq alive.'" The cut-line continued: "His sense of humor and positive outlook make him a favorite on the amputee ward."

Christ. What a terrible attempt at positive spin.

Tell everyone that I miss them. I think about them and you every day. I hope I'll be home soon. Peace is such a great and delicate thing.

Questions

1. What is unusual about the troops under Captain Ryan's command? Do they fit the stereotypes most Americans have about the troops in combat?
2. What are HERO missions? Why are they so somber?
3. What ironic use are the body bags put to by the helicopter medics?
4. Why is it difficult for Ryan to select personnel for the convoy escort mission team?
5. When does the third member of the convoy escort team realize that "this is not a game"? What is his response when returning to base?

Myrna E. Bein

On the morning of May 2, 2004, Myrna Bein learned that her twenty-six-year-old son, Charles, a U.S. Army infantryman, had been badly wounded in an ambush in Iraq a few hours earlier. Charles was riding in a truck convoy in Kirkuk when insurgents detonated a roadside bomb and then unleashed a barrage of gunfire. One soldier was killed, and ten others were injured. The bomb blast shredded the lower half of Charles's right leg, which was amputated. Myrna Bein began e-mailing friends and family with updates on Charles's progress—as well as her own state of mind. Here is one of her powerfully written e-mails.

Myrna Bein

A Journey Taken with My Son

June 10, 2004

A sock did me in a few nights ago, a plain white sock. I'm doing so much better with the grief, but sometimes I just get blindsided again in a totally unexpected way. Some memory or sharp realization will prick at the places healing in my heart, and I feel the grief wash over me in a massive wave. Sometimes I almost feel I could double over with the pain of it. That's what happened with the sock.

I had brought Charles' soiled clothes home from Walter Reed to wash. Everything had gone through the wash and dry cycles and I had dumped the freshly laundered clothes onto the bed to fold them. It was late and I was quite weary, so I wanted to finish and get to bed to try for a better night's sleep than I've been having lately. I found one sock . . . just one. I folded all the rest of the clothes and still, just one sock. Without even thinking, I walked back to the laundry room and searched the dryer for the mate. Nothing was there. I looked between the washer and dryer and all around the floor, in case I'd dropped the other sock somewhere during the loading and unloading processes. Still, my tired and pre-occupied brain didn't get it. As I walked back to the bedroom with the one sock in hand, it hit me like a punch to the gut. There was no other sock. There was also no other foot, or lower leg, or knee. I stood there in my bedroom and clutched that one clean sock to my breast and an involuntary moan came from my throat; but it originated in my heart.

    I guess as a nurse, I know too much. I know all the details of the physical difficulties and long-term complications of life for an amputee that most others have no reason to comprehend. I know about the everyday activities of daily living that the rest of us take for granted, and for which we never give a moment's consideration, that Charles will now always have to struggle to accomplish. I do know he will eventually win the struggle; he is made of very strong stuff. I'm in awe and so proud of his strength and determination. But my "mother's heart" still feels very tender and sore. The wounds there are fresh and bleed easily when disturbed. God's peace to you all.

Myrna

Questions

1. In what ways does the first sentence help establish the mood of surprise in this piece? What does it tell us and what doesn't it tell us about what will follow?
2. How does the everyday setting of this account contribute to its impact?
3. Does the sock develop a symbolic power by the end of this piece? If so, what sorts of meanings are associated with this symbol?

Suggestions for Writing on *Nonfiction about the Cost of War*

1. A modern political media advisor would probably judge Lincoln's Second Inaugural Address too depressing and fatalistic. Should Lincoln have delivered a more optimistic and positive speech? Defend or critique his approach, giving examples from the text.
2. Write a 1–2 page description of the people you currently work with or share classes with, similar to Captain Ryan Kelly's account of the people in his company.
3. Describe a small incident (such as Myrna Bein's search for the "missing" sock) that contained a strong emotional surprise for you.
4. Is war ever worth the terrible cost it inflicts? What advice would you give a person who wanted to join the military during wartime and seek combat? State your reasons why that person should or should not embark on this significant course of action.

VISIONS OF PEACE

Mohandas Gandhi *Non-Violence—The Greatest Force*

Leo Tolstoy *from The Kingdom of God Is Within You*

Much of the history of humanity has been the search for peace and justice in an unstable and violent world. How can individuals, communities, and nations resolve conflicts without resorting to violence? How can opposed parties be reconciled without one of them defeating the other? Visions of peace have been at the center of the major religions, each of which offers its own version of the Hebrew prophet Isaiah's depiction of the Peaceable Kingdom, where "the wolf also shall dwell with the lamb . . . and the lion shall eat straw like the ox." There have been many great thinkers in the quest for peace and reconciliation, and two of the most influential modern figures are probably the Russian writer Leo Tolstoy and the Indian leader Mohandas Gandhi. In his old age Tolstoy was probably the most famous author in the world, but he abandoned fiction, the literary form which had won him early celebrity, and devoted himself to religious and moral issues, especially pacifism and passive resistance. Tolstoy passionately wanted social and political reform in Russia and elsewhere, but he believed that achieving it by violence would only create a different sort of evil system. (The barbaric history of Soviet Communism born from the bloody Russian Revolution confirms his theory.) Tolstoy argued that positive social change can be achieved only through nonviolent action. He articulated his theory on nonviolent resistance most fully in *The Kingdom of God Is Within You* (1894), which appeared first in Germany because its publication was banned in Russia. Gandhi read this book as a young man. The experience "overwhelmed" him, and later he listed Tolstoy's volume as one of the three most important books of his life. In 1909 Gandhi wrote Tolstoy for advice, and the two continued corresponding until Tolstoy's death in 1910. Gandhi absorbed the Russian's ideas and used them to formulate his plans for Indian independence. Tolstoy's and Gandhi's ideas subsequently had an enormous impact on Martin Luther King Jr., Nelson Mandela, Lech Walesa, Václav Havel, and other modern champions of democracy and equality. Here we present two excerpts from the classic statements of nonviolence and pacifism by these giants of ethical thought.

Mohandas Gandhi

Mohandas Gandhi (1869–1948), a political and spiritual leader often called "Mahatma" ("Great Soul" in Sanskrit), was the preeminent champion of an independent India. He was born in a coastal city then part of the Bombay province, the son of a state official. At thirteen he entered into an arranged marriage to a fourteen-year-old bride. At nineteen he traveled to England to study law. Failing to establish a practice in India, he relocated to South Africa, which like India was then part of the British Empire. In South Africa, Gandhi led

Mohandas Gandhi

a civil rights movement for the Indian population. Returning to India in 1915, he soon emerged as the leader of the nationalist independence movement, seeking to end British rule not through armed rebellion but—deeply influenced by Leo Tolstoy's ideas—through passive resistance. Gandhi also preached the unity of mankind under one God, often quoting Christian and Muslim texts along with Hindu sources. The British repeatedly jailed him, but his political and moral influence became so vast that the colonial government was always forced to release him—often as the result of a widely publicized hunger strike. During World War II Gandhi was jailed one last time because of his pacifism and his campaign for the British to "Quit India." In 1947 the British finally granted independence to India but partitioned the country into two nations—India (primarily Hindu) and Pakistan (primarily Muslim)—which resulted in violence and mass migration. Gandhi did not take an official position in the government, preferring a spiritual role in the new India. In January 1948, while walking to a prayer meeting, he was assassinated by a Hindu who was enraged by Gandhi's toleration of Muslims. In India, Gandhi is called the Father of the Nation, but across the world he is honored as a champion of nonviolent passive resistance, peaceful social change, and religious tolerance.

Non-Violence—The Greatest Force July 15, 1926

Non-violence is the greatest force man has been endowed with. Truth is the only goal he has. For God is none other than Truth. But Truth cannot be, never will be, reached except through non-violence.

That which distinguishes man from all other animals is his capacity to be non-violent. And he fulfils his mission only to the extent that he is non-violent and no more. He has no doubt many other gifts. But if they do not subserve the main purpose—the development of the spirit of non-violence in him—they but drag him down lower than the brute, a status from which he has only just emerged.

The cry for peace will be a cry in the wilderness, so long as the spirit of non-violence does not dominate millions of men and women.

An armed conflict between nations horrifies us. But the economic war is no better than an armed conflict. This is like a surgical operation. An economic war is prolonged torture. And its ravages are no less terrible than those depicted in the literature on war properly so called. We think nothing of the other because we are used to its deadly effects.

Many of us in India shudder to see blood spilled. Many of us resent cow-slaughter, but we think nothing of the slow torture through which by our greed we put our people and cattle. But because we are used to this lingering death, we think no more about it.

The movement against war is sound. I pray for its success. But I cannot help the gnawing fear that the movement will fail, if it does not touch the root of all evil—man's greed.

Will America, England and the other great nations of the West continue to exploit the so-called weaker or uncivilized races and hope to attain peace that the whole world is pining for? Or will Americans continue to prey upon one another, have commercial rivalries and yet expect to dictate peace to the world?

Not till the spirit is changed can the form be altered. The form is merely an expression of the spirit within. We may succeed in seemingly altering the form but the alteration will be a mere make-believe if the spirit within remains unalterable. A whited sepulchre still conceals beneath it the rotting flesh and bone.

Far be it from me to discount or under-rate the great effort that is being made in the West to kill the war-spirit. Mine is merely a word of caution as from a fellow-seeker who has been striving in his own humble manner after the same thing, may be in a different way, no doubt on a much smaller scale. But if the experiment demonstrably succeeds on the smaller field and, if those who are working on the larger field have not overtaken me, it will at least pave the way for a similar experiment on a large field.

I observe in the limited field in which I find myself, that unless I can reach the hearts of men and women, I am able to do nothing. I observe further that so long as the spirit of hate persists in some shape or other, it is impossible to establish peace or to gain our freedom by peaceful effort. We cannot love one another, if we hate Englishmen. We cannot love the Japanese and hate Englishmen. We must either let the Law of Love rule us through and through or not at all. Love among ourselves based on hatred of others breaks down under the slightest pressure. The fact is such love is never real love. It is an armed peace. And so it will be in this great movement in the West against war. War will only be stopped when the conscience of mankind has become sufficiently elevated to recognize the undisputed supremacy of the Law of Love in all the walks of life. Some say this will never come to pass. I shall retain the faith till the end of my earthly existence that it shall come to pass.

Questions

1. Why does Gandhi believe that the capacity for nonviolence is a distinguishing feature of humanity?
2. What human vice does Gandhi see as the root of both war and economic injustice?
3. In the final paragraph, what negative emotion does Gandhi feel inhibits the spread of peace?
4. What does Gandhi mean by "armed peace"?

Leo Tolstoy

The complex and contradictory Leo Nikolaevich Tolstoy (1828–1910) is generally considered the greatest Russian novelist. Born on his aristocratic family's country estate, Yasnaya Polyana, in central Russia, he was orphaned at nine and raised by his aunts. After briefly studying law, the young count took off for St. Petersburg and Moscow, where he led a profligate life—while carefully listing his moral transgressions in his diary. In 1851 Tolstoy joined the army and fought in the Caucasus. It was there that he completed his first book, Childhood *(1852), a lyrical memoir. Having served in the Crimean War, he left the army in 1856 to become a writer. For the next six decades the brilliant and perpetually dissatisfied Tolstoy tried to settle in Yasnaya Polyana, but frequently escaped to St. Petersburg and Western Europe.*

Leo Tolstoy

In 1862 he wed Sonya Bers, an intellectual middle-class woman. Initially happy, the marriage was eventually undermined by the sex-obsessed and guilt-ridden Tolstoy, who engaged in many infidelities (which were sometimes followed by his unsuccessful renunciation of sex).

Despite its many problems, the marriage produced thirteen children. At Yasnaya Polyana, Tolstoy wrote his two greatest novels, War and Peace (1863–1869) and Anna Karenina (1877). As he grew older, he became obsessed with early Christianity. He formulated his own version of Christ's teachings, stressing simplicity, love, nonviolence, and community property. Excommunicated by the Orthodox Church, the count, who now dressed in peasant clothing, preached his "Christian anarchism" and nonviolence to an international audience. Upset by his ruined marriage and his inability to renounce his personal wealth, the eighty-two-year-old Tolstoy fled home one night to enter a monastery. He died of pneumonia a few days later in a provincial railway station, surrounded by reporters from around the world. Much of Tolstoy's writing examines a tragic predicament of human existence: the difficult search for truth and justice in a world of limited knowledge and ethical imperfection. Tolstoy resolutely believed in the moral development of humanity, but he was also painfully aware of the obstacles to genuine progress.

from The Kingdom of God Is Within You 1894
Translated by Constance Garnett

Governments and the ruling classes no longer take their stand on right or even on the semblance of justice, but on a skillful organization carried to such a point of perfection by the aid of science that everyone is caught in the circle of violence and has no chance of escaping from it. This circle is made up now of four methods of working upon men, joined together like the lines of a chain ring.

The first and oldest method is intimidation. This consists in representing the existing state organization—whatever it may be, free republic or the most savage despotism—as something sacred and immutable, and therefore following any efforts to alter it with the cruelest punishments. This method is in use now—as it has been from olden times—wherever there is a government: in Russia against the so-called Nihilists, in America against Anarchists, in France against Imperialists, Legitimists, Communards, and Anarchists.

Railways, telegraphs, telephones, photographs, and the great perfection of the means of getting rid of men for years, without killing them, by solitary confinement, where, hidden from the world, they perish and are forgotten, and the many other modern inventions employed by government, give such power that when once authority has come into certain hands, the police, open and secret, the administration and prosecutors, jailers and executioners of all kinds, do their work so zealously that there is no chance of overturning the government, however cruel and senseless it may be.

The second method is corruption. It consists in plundering the industrious working people of their wealth by means of taxes and distributing it in satisfying the greed of officials, who are bound in return to support and keep up the oppression of the people. These bought officials, from the highest ministers to the poorest copying clerks, make up an unbroken network of men bound together by the same interest—that of living at the expense of the people. They become the richer the more submissively they carry out the will of the government; and at all times and places, sticking at nothing, in all departments support by word and deed the violence of government, on which their own prosperity also rests.

The third method is what I can only describe as hypnotizing the people. This consists in checking the moral development of men, and by various suggestions keeping them back in the ideal of life, outgrown by mankind at large, on which the power of government rests. This hypnotizing process is organized at the present in the most complex manner, and starting from their earliest childhood, continues to act on men till the day of their death. It begins in their earliest years in the compulsory schools, created for this purpose, in which the children have instilled into them the ideas of life of their ancestors, which are in direct antagonism with the conscience of the modern world. In countries where there is a state religion, they teach the children the senseless blasphemies of the Church catechisms, together with the duty of obedience to their superiors. In republican states they teach them the savage superstition of patriotism and the same pretended obedience to the governing authorities.

The process is kept up during later years by the encouragement of religious and patriotic superstitions.

The religious superstition is encouraged by establishing, with money taken from the people, temples, processions, memorials, and festivals, which, aided by painting, architecture, music, and incense, intoxicate the people, and above all by the support of the clergy, whose duty consists in brutalizing the people and keeping them in a permanent state of stupefaction by their teaching, the solemnity of their services, their sermons, and their interference in private life—at births, deaths, and marriages. The patriotic superstition is encouraged by the creation, with money taken from the people, of national fêtes, spectacles, monuments, and festivals to dispose men to attach importance to their own nation, and to the aggrandizement of the state and its rulers, and to feel antagonism and even hatred for other nations. With these objects under despotic governments there is direct prohibition against printing and disseminating books to enlighten the people, and everyone who might rouse the people from their lethargy is exiled or imprisoned. Moreover, under every government without exception everything is kept back that might emancipate and everything encouraged that tends to corrupt the people, such as literary works tending to keep them in the barbarism of religious and patriotic superstition, all kinds of sensual amusements, spectacles, circuses, theaters, and even the physical means of inducing stupefaction, as tobacco and alcohol, which form the principal source of revenue of states. Even prostitution is encouraged, and not only recognized, but even organized by the government in the majority of states. So much for the third method.

The fourth method consists in selecting from all the men who have been stupefied and enslaved by the three former methods a certain number, exposing them to special and intensified means of stupefaction and brutalization, and so making them into a passive instrument for carrying out all the cruelties and brutalities needed by the government. This result is attained by taking them at the youthful age when men have not had time to form clear and definite principles of morals, and removing them from all natural and human conditions of life, home, family and kindred, and useful labor. They are shut up together in barracks, dressed in special clothes, and worked upon by cries, drums, music, and shining objects to go through certain daily actions invented for this purpose, and by this means are brought into an hypnotic condition in which they cease to be men and become mere senseless machines, submissive to the hypnotizer. These physically vigorous young men (in these days of universal conscription, all young men), hypnotized, armed with murderous weapons, always obedient to the governing authorities and ready for any act of violence at their command, constitute the fourth and principal method of enslaving men.

By this method the circle of violence is completed.

Intimidation, corruption, and hypnotizing bring people into a condition in which they are willing to be soldiers; the soldiers give the power of punishing and plundering them (and purchasing officials with the spoils), and hypnotizing them and converting them in time into these same soldiers again.

The circle is complete, and there is no chance of breaking through it by force.

Some persons maintain that freedom from violence, or at least a great diminution of it, may be gained by the oppressed forcibly overturning the oppressive government and replacing it by a new one under which such violence and oppression will be unnecessary, but they deceive themselves and others, and their efforts do not better the position of the oppressed, but only make it worse. Their conduct only tends to increase the despotism of government. Their efforts only afford a plausible pretext for governments to strengthen their power.

Even if we admit that under a combination of circumstances specially unfavorable for the government, as in France in 1870, any government might be forcibly overturned and the power transferred to other hands, the new authority would rarely be less oppressive than the old one; on the contrary, always having to defend itself against its dispossessed and exasperated enemies, it would be more despotic and cruel, as has always been the rule in all revolutions.

While socialists and communists regard the individualistic, capitalistic organization of society as an evil, and the anarchists regard as an evil all government whatever, there are royalists, conservatives, and capitalists who consider any socialistic or communistic organization or anarchy as an evil, and all these parties have no means other than violence to bring men to agreement. Whichever of these parties were successful in bringing their schemes to pass, must resort to support its authority to all the existing methods of violence, and even invent new ones.

The oppressed would be another set of people, and coercion would take some new form; but the violence and oppression would be unchanged or even more cruel, since hatred would be intensified by the struggle, and new forms of oppression would have been devised. So it has always been after all revolutions and all attempts at revolution, all conspiracies, and all violent changes of government. Every conflict only strengthens the means of oppression in the hands of those who happen at a given moment to be in power.

Questions

1. What four factors does Tolstoy believe governments use to maintain their rule of their subjects?
2. How does official corruption work to undermine freedom?
3. Tolstoy asserts that governments "hypnotize" their people. How can this possibly be? What does he mean by "hypnotism"?
4. Why does Tolstoy reject violence as a means of reforming a corrupt state?
5. What aspects of Tolstoy's analysis do you find reasonable? Do you find any ideas you reject? Explain why you agree or disagree.

Suggestions for Writing on Nonfiction about Visions of Peace

1. Many modern leaders reject violence as a means of political reform. Summarize what you think are the two or three central ideas behind nonviolence and passive resistance. After stating the ideas, provide your personal critique as to whether you find them reasonable or not.
2. Both Tolstoy and Gandhi were deeply religious thinkers. (The same was true of the Reverend Martin Luther King Jr.) Defend or critique the assertion that the ideas of nonviolent resistance can work only in a nation that is religious. Does passive resistance also work as a secular political method? State your reasons, pro or con.
3. Take any one of Tolstoy's "four methods" by which governments "enslave" their citizens and rewrite his description in contemporary American terms. Change the details to reflect today's society and economy. Does Tolstoy's theory feel accurate? Or does it ring false in today's society?

DRAMA

WAR IN DRAMA: TWO CONTRASTING SPEECHES FROM SHAKESPEARE

William Shakespeare   *"We Happy Few, We Band of Brothers"*: King Henry's Speech from *Henry V*

William Shakespeare   *"The Better Part of Valor Is Discretion"*: Falstaff's Speech from *Henry IV, Part I*

Shakespeare presents war in most of his tragedies and historical plays. His theatrical imagination was drawn to violent episodes of social and political change—from ancient stories of the Trojan War and the Roman Civil War to the conflicts that shaped the history of his native England. There was nothing uniform, however, about Shakespeare's treatment of war or warriors. He understood that war brought out the best and worst, the noblest and stupidest in humanity. His warriors are variously courageous, generous, wicked, tricky, comic, and cowardly—as diverse, that is to say, as humanity itself. Here are a pair of famous speeches from two of Shakespeare's history plays about Henry V—first as Prince Hal (in *Henry IV, Part I*) and later as the newly crowned King of England in *Henry V*. In the latter play, on the eve of a great battle King Henry speaks to his outnumbered troops about heroism and the brotherhood of men who bear arms together. In the second monologue, which Shakespeare wrote in prose to emphasize its comic qualities, Falstaff, a cowardly knight, makes a cogent case for avoiding combat and keeping himself safe on the battlefield.

"We Happy Few, We Band of Brothers"   1598–1599
Henry V (4.3.16–67)
Edited by David Bevington

Laurence Olivier as Henry V at Agincourt.

SCENE SYNOPSIS

The English knights and soldiers gathering before the Battle of Agincourt know that the French army outnumber them five to one. When Lord Westmorland wishes the British forces included some of the men who sit idly back in England, King Henry interrupts and delivers the most celebrated inspirational speech in all Shakespeare. Despite the odds, the Battle of Agincourt proved to be an overwhelming victory for the English.

Westmorland: O, that we now had here 15
   But one ten thousand of those men in England
   That do no work today!

Henry: What's° he that wishes so?
   My cousin Westmorland? No, my fair cousin.
   If we are marked to die, we are enough 20
   To do our country loss;° and if to live,
   The fewer men, the greater share of honor.
   God's will, I pray thee, wish not one man more.
   By Jove, I am not covetous for gold,
   Nor care I who doth feed upon my cost;° 25
   It yearns° me not if men my garments wear;
   Such outward things dwell not in my desires.
   But if it be a sin to covet honor
   I am the most offending soul alive.
   No, faith, my coz,° wish not a man from England. 30
   God's peace, I would not lose so great an honor
   As one man more, methinks, would share from me°
   For the best hope I have. O, do not wish one more!
   Rather proclaim it, Westmorland, through my host°
   That he which hath no stomach to° this fight, 35
   Let him depart; his passport shall be made
   And crowns for convoy° put into his purse.
   We would not die in that man's company
   That fears his fellowship to die with us.°
   This day is called the Feast of Crispian.° 40
   He that outlives this day and comes safe home
   Will stand a-tiptoe when the day is named
   And rouse him at the name of Crispian.
   He that shall see this day and live° old age
   Will yearly on the vigil° feast his neighbors 45

---

18 *What's* who is   20–21 *enough . . . loss* enough loss for our country to suffer   25 *upon my cost* at my expense   26 *yearns* grieves   30 *coz* cousin, kinsman   32 *share from me* take from me as his share   34 *host* army   35 *stomach to* appetite for   37 *crowns for convoy* travel money   39 *That . . . us* that is afraid to risk his life in my company   40 *Feast of Crispian* Saint Crispin's Day, October 25. (Cripinus and Crispianus were martyrs who fled from Rome in the third century; according to legend they disguised themselves as shoemakers and afterward became the patron saints of that craft.)   44 *live* live to see   45 *vigil* evening before a feast day

And say, "Tomorrow is Saint Crispian."
Then will he strip his sleeve and show his scars,
And say, "These wounds I had on Crispin's Day."
Old men forget; yet° all shall be forgot,
But he'll remember with advantages°   50
What feats he did that day. Then shall our names,
Familiar in his mouth as household words—
Harry the King, Bedford and Exeter,
Warwick and Talbot, Salisbury and Gloucester—
Be in their flowing° cups freshly remembered.   55
This story shall the good man teach his son;
And Crispin Crispian shall ne'er go by,
From this day to the ending of the world,
But we in it shall be rememberèd—
We few, we happy few, we band of brothers.   60
For he today that sheds his blood with me
Shall be my brother; be he ne'er so vile,°
This day shall gentle his condition.°
And gentlemen in England now abed
Shall think themselves accursed they were not here,   65
And hold their manhoods cheap whiles any speaks
That fought with us upon Saint Crispin's Day.

49 *yet* in time   50 *advantages* additions of his own   55 *flowing* overflowing   62 *vile* lowly   63 *gentle his condition* raise him to the rank of gentleman

Questions

1. Why does King Henry argue that it is good that there are so few men going into battle?
2. Since Henry needs every soldier, why does he offer to pay the costs back to England for anyone who wants to leave before the battle? Isn't this offer counterproductive?
3. How does Henry motivate his soldiers to visualize their victory?
4. Does Henry make a plausible case that his outnumbered troops are really a "happy few, we band of brothers . . ."?
5. What does Henry's speech suggest about male bonding in battle? What does Henry suggest all of the English will have in common?

"The Better Part of Valor Is Discretion"   1597

Henry IV, Part I (5.4.111–122)

Edited by David Bevington

SCENE SYNOPSIS

The climax of Shakespeare's Henry IV, Part I *is the battle between the rebel army led by Sir Henry Percy (nicknamed Hotspur) and the forces loyal to King Henry IV, led by his son Prince Hal. In the midst of the battle Shakespeare brings the fat, cowardly, and comic knight Sir John Falstaff into the scene. Attacked by a rebel Scot knight, Falstaff falls and pretends to be dead. After Prince Hal kills Hotspur, Falstaff rises to find himself alone with Hotspur's body. Falstaff stabs the dead body and weaves a story that Hotspur had only been temporarily stunned on the battlefield, and that he, Falstaff, delivered the mortal blow.*

Orson Welles as Falstaff.

Falstaff (Rising up): Embowelled!° If thou embowel me today, I'll give you leave to powder° me and eat me too tomorrow. 'Sblood,° 'twas time to counterfeit, or that hot termagant° Scot had paid° me, scot and lot° too. Counterfeit? I lie, I am no counterfeit. To die is to be a counterfeit, for he is but the counterfeit of a man who hath not the life of a man; but to counterfeit dying, when a man thereby liveth, is to be no counterfeit but the true and perfect image of life indeed. The better part° of valor is discretion, in the which better part I have saved my life. Zounds, I am afraid of this gunpowder Percy, though he be dead. How, if he should counterfeit too and rise? By my faith, I am afraid he would prove the better counterfeit. Therefore I'll make him sure; yea, and I'll swear I killed him. Why may not he rise as well as I? Nothing confutes me but eyes,° and nobody sees me. Therefore, sirrah [*Stabbing him*], with a new wound in your thigh, come you along with me. 111 115 120

He takes up Hotspur on his back.

---

111 *Emboweled* disemboweled, i.e. for embalming and burial   112 *powder* salt.   *'Sblood* Contraction for "God's blood," an Elizabethan oath   113 *termagant* violent and blustering, like the heathen god of the Saracens in medieval and Renaissance lore.   *paid* i.e., killed.   *scot and lot* i.e., completely. (Originally the phrase was the term for a parish tax.)   117 *part* constituent part, quality, role   121 *Nothing . . . eyes* i.e., nothing can contradict me but an eyewitness

Questions

1. Why does Falstaff think it is reasonable to "counterfeit" death to escape injury? Reconstruct his logic.
2. What does Falstaff mean by "the better part of valor is discretion"?
3. Why does Falstaff call Henry Percy "gunpowder Percy"? What aspects of Hotspur's personality does he describe?
4. Is Falstaff's behavior reasonable or dishonorable? Take a position and support it.

Suggestions for Writing on *Shakespeare's Contrasting Speeches on War*

1. How would you motivate a group of people to perform an important but seemingly impossible task? Analyze Henry V's speech at Agincourt, then list and critique the strategies the king uses.
2. Write a short defense of volunteering for military duty in time of war, or refusing to volunteer. State your reasons.
3. Paraphrase Falstaff's argument for "discretion" in battle. What are the points of his defense of his "counterfeit"? Explain and analyze them without making a moral judgment.

Suggestions for Writing on *Literature about War and Peace*

1. William Stafford imagines building a memorial to the wars that were not fought between the United States and Canada. Write a short essay about a monument you would like to see built to commemorate something you think worth celebrating. Explain your reasons.
2. Compare one of Wilfred Owen's poems to Richard Lovelace's "To Lucasta." How do their attitudes about combat differ? Cite specific passages in each text.
3. Andre Dubus, Edgar Allan Poe, and Guy de Maupassant all describe violent deaths or murders. Select one of these crimes and explain the perpetrator's motivation and justification for the act.
4. Shakespeare's speech from *Henry V*, Tim O'Brien's "The Things They Carried," Yusef Komunyakaa's "Facing It," Marilyn Nelson's "Star-Fix," and Ryan Kelly's letters all describe a deep emotional bonding shared by troops in combat. Taking any of these texts, propose and justify a theory of why you think troops experience these deep emotions.
5. Take any two poems in the "Peace and Justice" section and compare their ideas and imagery for communicating the idea of a just society. (Possible selections are Emma Lazarus's "The New Colossus," William Stafford's "At the Un-National Monument Along the Canadian Border," and Denise Levertov's "Making Peace.")
6. Describe your own vision of peace. Write about two or three major changes in the nation or in the world that you believe could bring peace and reconciliation to people.

Tobias Wolff with his dog Paddy.

CRITICAL STRATEGIES

19 CRITICAL APPROACHES TO LITERATURE

Literary criticism should arise out of a debt of love.
—GEORGE STEINER

Literary criticism is not an abstract, intellectual exercise; it is a natural human response to literature. If a friend informs you she is reading a book you have just finished, it would be odd indeed if you did not begin swapping opinions. Literary criticism is nothing more than discourse—spoken or written—about literature. A student who sits quietly in a morning English class, intimidated by the notion of literary criticism, will spend an hour that evening talking animatedly about the meaning of rock lyrics or comparing the relative merits of the *Star Wars* trilogies. It is inevitable that people will ponder, discuss, and analyze the works of art that interest them.

The informal criticism of friends talking about literature tends to be casual, unorganized, and subjective. Since Aristotle, however, philosophers, scholars, and writers have tried to create more precise and disciplined ways of discussing literature. Literary critics have borrowed concepts from other disciplines, such as philosophy, history, linguistics, psychology, and anthropology, to analyze imaginative literature more perceptively. Some critics have found it useful to work in the abstract area of **literary theory,** criticism that tries to formulate general principles rather than discuss specific texts. Mass media critics, such as newspaper reviewers, usually spend their time evaluating works—telling us which books are worth reading, which plays not to bother seeing. But most serious literary criticism is not primarily evaluative; it assumes we know that *Othello* or *The Metamorphosis* is worth reading. Instead, such criticism is analytic; it tries to help us better understand a literary work.

In the following pages you will find overviews of ten critical approaches to literature. While these ten methods do not exhaust the total possibilities of literary criticism, they represent the most widely used contemporary approaches. Although presented separately, the approaches are not necessarily mutually exclusive; many critics mix methods to suit their needs and interests. For example, a historical critic may use formalist techniques to analyze a poem; a biographical critic will frequently use psychological theories to analyze an author. The summaries try neither to provide a history of each approach nor to present the latest trends in each school. Their purpose is to give you a practical introduction to each critical method and then provide a representative example of it. If one of these critical methods interests you, why not try to write a class paper using the approach?

FORMALIST CRITICISM

Formalist criticism regards literature as a unique form of human knowledge that needs to be examined on its own terms. "The natural and sensible starting point for work in literary scholarship," René Wellek and Austin Warren wrote in their influential *Theory of Literature*, "is the interpretation and analysis of the works of literature themselves." To a formalist, a poem or story is not primarily a social, historical, or biographical document; it is a literary work that can be understood only by reference to its intrinsic literary features—that is, those elements found in the text itself. To analyze a poem or story, therefore, the formalist critic focuses on the words of the text rather than facts about the author's life or the historical milieu in which the text was written. The critic pays special attention to the formal features of the text—the style, structure, imagery, tone, and genre. These features, however, are usually not examined in isolation, because formalist critics believe that what gives a literary text its special status as art is how all its elements work together to create the reader's total experience. As Robert Penn Warren commented, "Poetry does not inhere in any particular element but depends upon the set of relationships, the structure, which we call the poem."

A key method that formalists use to explore the intense relationships within a poem is **close reading,** a careful step-by-step analysis and explication of a text. The purpose of close reading is to understand how various elements in a literary text work together to shape its effects on the reader. Since formalists believe that the various stylistic and thematic elements of a literary work influence each other, these critics insist that form and content cannot be meaningfully separated. The complete interdependence of form and content is what makes a text literary. When we extract a work's theme or paraphrase its meaning, we destroy the aesthetic experience of the work.

Michael Clark (b. 1946)

Light and Darkness in "Sonny's Blues" 1985

"Sonny's Blues" by James Baldwin is a sensitive story about the reconciliation of two brothers, but it is much more than that. It is, in addition, an examination of the importance of the black heritage and of the central importance of music in that heritage. Finally, the story probes the central role that art must play in human existence. To examine all of these facets of human existence is a rather formidable undertaking in a short story, even in a longish short story such as this one. Baldwin not only undertakes this task, but he does it superbly. One of the central ways that Baldwin fuses all of these complex elements is by using a metaphor of childhood, which is supported by ancillary images of light and darkness. He does the job so well that the story is a *tour de force*, a penetrating study of American culture.

• • •

Sonny's quest is best described by himself when he writes to the narrator: "I feel like a man who's been trying to climb up out of some deep, real deep and funky hole and just saw the sun up there, outside. I got to get outside." Sonny is a person who finds his life a living hell, but he knows enough to strive for the "light." As it is chronicled in this story, his quest is for regaining something from the past—from his own childhood and from the pasts of all who have come before him. The means for doing this is his music, which is consistently portrayed in terms of light imagery. When Sonny has a discussion with the narrator about the future, the narrator describes Sonny's face as a mixture of concern and hope: "[T]he worry, the thoughtfulness, played on it still, the way shadows play on a face which is staring into the fire." This fire image is reinforced shortly afterward when the narrator describes Sonny's aspirations once more in terms of light: "[I]t was as though he were all wrapped up in some cloud, some fire, some vision all his own." To the narrator and to Isabel's family, the music that Sonny plays is simply "weird and disordered," but to Sonny, the music is seen in starkly positive terms: his failure to master the music will mean "death," while success will mean "life."

The light and dark imagery culminates in the final scene, where the narrator, apparently for the first time, listens to Sonny play the piano. The location is a Greenwich Village club. Appropriately enough, the narrator is seated "in a dark corner." In contrast, the stage is dominated by light, which Baldwin reiterates with a succession of images: "light . . . circle of light . . . light . . . flame . . . light." Although Sonny has a false start, he gradually settles into his playing and ends the first set with some intensity: "Everything had been burned out of [Sonny's face], and at the same time, things usually hidden were being burned in, by the fire and fury of the battle which was occurring in him up there."

The culmination of the set occurs when Creole, the leader of the players, begins to play "Am I Blue?" At this point, "something began to happen." Apparently, the narrator at this time realizes that this music *is* important. The music is central to the experience of the black experience, and it is described in terms of light imagery:

> Creole began to tell us what the blues were all about. They were not about anything very new. He and his boys up there were keeping it new, at the risk of ruin, destruction, madness, and death, in order to find new ways to make us listen. For, while the tale of how we suffer, and how we are delighted, and how we may triumph is never new, it always must be heard. There isn't any other tale to tell, it's the only light we've got in all this darkness.

From "James Baldwin's 'Sonny's Blues': Childhood, Light, and Art"

BIOGRAPHICAL CRITICISM

Biographical criticism begins with the simple but central insight that literature is written by actual people and that understanding an author's life can help readers more thoroughly comprehend the work. Anyone who reads the biography of a writer quickly sees how much an author's experience shapes—both directly and indirectly—what he or she creates. Reading that biography will also change (and usually deepen) our response to the work. Sometimes even knowing a single important fact illuminates our reading of a poem or story. Learning, for example, that the poet Josephine Miles was confined to a wheelchair or that Weldon Kees committed suicide at forty-one will certainly make us pay attention to certain aspects of their poems we might otherwise have missed or considered unimportant. A formalist critic might complain that we would also have noticed those things through careful textual analysis, but biographical information provides the practical assistance of underscoring subtle but important meanings in the poems. Though many literary theorists have assailed biographical criticism on philosophical grounds, the biographical approach to literature has never disappeared because of its obvious practical advantage in illuminating literary texts.

It may be helpful here to make a distinction between biography and biographical criticism. **Biography** is, strictly speaking, a branch of history; it provides a written account of a person's life. To establish and interpret the facts of a poet's life, for instance, a biographer would use all the available information—not just personal documents such as letters and diaries but also the poems—for the possible light they might shed on the subject's life. A biographical *critic*, however, is not concerned with re-creating the record of an author's life. Biographical criticism focuses on explicating the literary work by using the insight provided by knowledge of the author's life. Quite often, biographical critics, such as Brett C. Millier in her discussion of Elizabeth Bishop's "One Art," will examine the drafts of a poem or story to see both how the work came into being and how it might have been changed from its autobiographical origins.

Brett C. Millier (b. 1958)

On Elizabeth Bishop's "One Art" 1993

Elizabeth Bishop left seventeen drafts of the poem "One Art" among her papers. In the first draft, she lists all the things she's lost in her life—keys, pens, glasses, cities—and then she writes "One might think this would have prepared me / for losing one average-sized not exceptionally / beautiful or dazzlingly intelligent person . . . / But it doesn't seem to have at all. . . ." By the seventeenth draft, nearly every word has been transformed, but most importantly, Bishop discovered along the way that there might be a way to master this loss.

One way to read Bishop's modulation between the first and last drafts from "the loss of you is impossible to master" to something like "I am still the master of losing even though losing you looks like a disaster" is that in the writing of such a disciplined, demanding poem as this villanelle ("[*Write* it!]") lies the potential mastery of the loss. Working through each of her losses—from the bold, painful catalog of the first draft to the finely-honed and privately meaningful final version—is the way to overcome them or, if not to overcome them, then to see the way in which she might possibly master herself in the face of loss. It is all, perhaps "one art"—writing elegy, mastering loss, mastering grief, self-mastery. Bishop had a precocious familiarity with loss. Her father died before her first birthday, and four years later her mother disappeared into a sanitarium, never to be seen by her daughter again. The losses in the poem are real: time in the form of the "hour badly spent" and, more tellingly for the orphaned Bishop, "my mother's watch": the lost houses, in Key West, Petrópolis, and Ouro Prêto, Brazil. The city of Rio de Janeiro and the whole South American continent (where she had lived for nearly two decades) were lost to her with the suicide of her Brazilian companion. And currently, in the fall of 1975, she seemed to have lost her dearest friend and lover, who was trying to end their relationship. But each version of the poem distanced the pain a little more, depersonalized it, moved it away from the tawdry self-pity and "confession" that Bishop disliked in so many of her contemporaries.

Bishop's friends remained for a long time protective of her personal reputation, and unwilling to have her grouped among lesbian poets or even among the other great poets of her generation—Robert Lowell, John Berryman, Theodore Roethke—as they seemed to self-destruct before their readers' eyes. Bishop herself taught them this reticence by keeping her private life to herself, and by investing what "confession" there was in her poems deeply in objects and places, thus deflecting biographical inquiry. In the development of this poem, discretion is both a poetic method and a part of a process of self-understanding, the seeing of a pattern in her own life.

Adapted by the author from *Elizabeth Bishop: Life and the Memory of It*

HISTORICAL CRITICISM

Historical criticism seeks to understand a literary work by investigating the social, cultural, and intellectual context that produced it—a context that necessarily includes the artist's biography and milieu. Historical critics are less concerned with explaining a work's literary significance for today's readers than with helping us understand the work by recreating, as nearly as possible, the exact meaning and impact it had for its original audience. A historical reading of a literary work begins by exploring the possible ways in which the meaning of the text has changed over time. An analysis of William Blake's poem "London," for instance, carefully examines how certain words had different connotations for the poem's original readers than they do today. It also explores the probable associations an eighteenth-century English reader would have made with certain images and characters, such as the poem's persona, the chimney sweep—a type of exploited child laborer who, fortunately, no longer exists in our society.

No one doubts the value of historical criticism in reading ancient literature. There have been so many social, cultural, and linguistic changes that some older texts are incomprehensible without scholarly assistance. But historical criticism can also help one better understand modern texts. Considering Weldon Kees's "For My Daughter," for example, one learns a great deal by contemplating two rudimentary historical facts—the year in which the poem was first published (1940) and the nationality of its author (American)—and then asking how this information has shaped the meaning of the poem. In 1940 war had already broken out in Europe, and most Americans realized that their country, still recovering from the Depression, would soon be drawn into it. For a young man like Kees, the future seemed bleak, uncertain, and personally dangerous. Even this simple historical analysis helps explain at least part of the bitter pessimism of Kees's poem, though a psychological critic would rightly insist that Kees's dark personality also played a crucial role. In writing a paper on a poem, you might explore how the time and place of its creation affect its meaning.

Joseph Moldenhauer (b. 1934)

"To His Coy Mistress" and the Renaissance Tradition   1968

Obedient to the neoclassical aesthetic which ruled his age, Andrew Marvell strove for excellence within established forms rather than trying to devise unique forms of his own. Like Herrick, Ben Jonson, and Campion, like Milton and the Shakespeare of the sonnets, Marvell was derivative. He held imitation to be no vice; he chose a proven type and exploited it with a professionalism rarely surpassed even in a century and a land as amply provided with verse craftsmen as his. Under a discipline so willingly assumed, Marvell's imagination flourished, producing superb and enduring examples of the verse types he attempted.

• • •

When he undertook to write a *carpe diem* lyric in "To His Coy Mistress," Marvell was working once more within a stylized form, one of the favorite types in the Renaissance lyric catalogue. Again he endowed the familiar model with his own special sensibility, composing what for many readers is the most vital English instance of the *carpe diem* poem. We can return to it often, with undiminished enthusiasm—drawn not by symbolic intricacy, though it contains two or three extraordinary conceits, nor by philosophical depth, though it lends an unusual seriousness to its theme—but drawn rather by its immediacy and concreteness, its sheer dynamism of statement within a controlled structure.

The *carpe diem* poem, whose label comes from a line of Horace and whose archetype for Renaissance poets was a lyric by Catullus, addresses the conflict of beauty and sensual desire on the one hand and the destructive force of time on the other. Its theme is the fleeting nature of life's joys; its counsel, overt or implied, is Horace's "seize the present," or, in the language of Herrick's "To the Virgins,"

> Gather ye rose-buds while ye may,
>   Old Time is still a flying.

It takes rise from that most pervasive and aesthetically viable of all Renaissance preoccupations, man's thralldom to time, the limitations of mortality upon his senses, his pleasures, his aspirations, his intellectual and creative capacities. Over the exuberance of Elizabethan and seventeenth-century poetry the pall of death continually hovers, and the lyrics of the age would supply a handbook of strategies for the circumvention of decay. The birth of an heir, the preservative balm of memory, the refuge of Christian resignation or Platonic ecstasy—these are some solutions which the poets offer. Another is the artist's ability to immortalize this world's values by means of his verse. Shakespeare's nineteenth and fifty-fifth sonnets, for example, employ this stratagem for the frustration of "Devouring Time," as does Michael Drayton's "How Many Paltry, Foolish, Painted Things." In such poems the speaker's praise of the merits of the beloved is coupled with a celebration of his own poetic gift, through which he can eternize those merits as a "pattern" for future men and women.

The *carpe diem* lyric proposes a more direct and immediate, if also more temporary, solution to the overwhelming problem. Whether subdued or gamesome in tone, it appeals to the young and beautiful to make time their own for a while, to indulge in the "harmless folly" of sensual enjoyment. Ordinarily, as in "To His Coy Mistress" and Herrick's "Corinna's Going A-Maying," the poem imitates an express invitation to love, a suitor's immodest proposal to his lady. Such works are both sharply dramatic and vitally rhetorical; to analyze their style and structure is, in effect, to analyze a persuasive appeal.

From "The Voices of Seduction in 'To His Coy Mistress'"

PSYCHOLOGICAL CRITICISM

Modern psychology has had an immense effect on both literature and literary criticism. The psychoanalytic theories of the Austrian neurologist Sigmund Freud changed our notions of human behavior by exploring new or controversial areas such as wish fulfillment, sexuality, the unconscious, and repression. Perhaps Freud's greatest contribution to literary study was his elaborate demonstration of how much human mental process was unconscious. He analyzed language, often in the form of jokes and conversational slips of the tongue (now often called "Freudian slips"), to show how it reflected the speaker's unconscious fears and desires. He also examined symbols, not only in art and literature but also in dreams, to study how the unconscious mind expressed itself in coded form to avoid the censorship of the conscious mind. His theory of human cognition asserted that much of what we apparently forget is actually stored deep in the unconscious mind, including painful traumatic memories from childhood that have been repressed.

Freud admitted that he himself had learned a great deal about psychology from studying literature. Sophocles, Shakespeare, Goethe, and Dostoyevsky were as important to the development of his ideas as were his clinical studies. Some of Freud's most influential writing was, in a broad sense, literary criticism, such as his psychoanalytic examination of Sophocles' Oedipus in *The Interpretation of Dreams* (1900). In analyzing Sophocles' tragedy *Oedipus the King*, Freud paid the classical Greek dramatist the considerable compliment that the playwright had such profound insight into human nature that his characters display the depth and complexity of real people. In focusing on literature, Freud and his disciples such as Carl Jung, Ernest Jones, Marie Bonaparte, and Bruno Bettelheim endorsed the belief that great literature truthfully reflects life.

Psychological criticism is a diverse category, but it often employs three approaches. First, it investigates the creative process of the arts: what is the nature of literary genius, and how does it relate to normal mental functions? Such analysis may also focus on literature's effects on the reader. How does a particular work register its impact on the reader's mental and sensory faculties? The second approach involves the psychological study of a particular artist. Most modern literary biographers employ psychology to understand their subject's motivations and behavior. Diane Middlebrook's controversial *Anne Sexton: A Biography* (1991) even used tapes of the poet's sessions with her psychiatrist as material for the study. The third common approach is the analysis of fictional characters. Freud's study of Oedipus is the prototype for this approach, which tries to bring modern insights about human behavior into the study of how fictional people act. While psychological criticism carefully examines the surface of the literary work, it customarily speculates on what lies underneath the text—the unspoken or perhaps even unspeakable memories, motives, and fears that covertly shape the work, especially in fictional characterizations.

Daniel Hoffman (b. 1923)

The Father-Figure in "The Tell-Tale Heart" — 1972

There are no parents in the tales of Edgar Poe, nary a Mum nor a Dad. Instead all is symbol. And what does this total repression of both sonhood and parenthood signify but that to acknowledge such relationships is to venture into territory too dangerous, too terrifying, for specificity. Desire and hatred are alike insatiable and unallayed. But the terrible war of superego upon the id, the endless battle between conscience and impulse, the unsleeping enmity of the self and its Imp of the Perverse—these struggles are enacted and reenacted in Poe's work, but always in disguise.

Take "The Tell-Tale Heart," surely one of his nearly perfect tales. It's only four pages long, a triumph of the art of economy:

> How, then, am I mad? Hearken! and observe how healthily—how calmly I can tell you the whole story.

When a narrator commences in *this* vein, we know him to be mad already. But we also know his author to be sane. For with such precision to portray the methodicalness of a madman is the work not of a madman but of a man who truly understands what it is to be mad. Artistic control is the warrant of auctorial sanity. It is axiomatic in the psychiatric practice of our century that self-knowledge is a necessary condition for the therapeutic process. Never using the language of the modern diagnostician—which was unavailable to him in the first place, and which in any case he didn't need—Poe demonstrates the extent of his self-knowledge in his manipulation of symbolic objects and actions toward ends which his tales embody.

The events are few, the action brief. "I" (in the story) believes himself sane because he is so calm, so methodical, so fully aware and in control of his purpose. Of course his knowledge of that purpose is limited, while his recital thereof endows the reader with a greater knowledge than his own. "The disease," he says right at the start, "had sharpened my senses. . . . Above all was the sense of hearing acute. I heard all things in the heavens and in the earth. I heard many things in hell." Now of whom can this be said but a delusional person? At the same time, mad as he is, this narrator is *the hero of sensibility*. His heightened senses bring close both heaven and hell.

His plot is motiveless. "Object there was none. Passion there was none. I loved the old man. He had never wronged me. He had never given me insult. For his gold I had no desire." The crime he is about to commit will be all the more terrible because apparently gratuitous. But let us not be lulled by this narrator's lack of admitted motive. He may have a motive—one which he cannot admit, even to himself.

Nowhere does this narrator explain what relationship, if any, exists between him and the possessor of the Evil Eye. We do, however, learn from his tale that he and the old man live under the same roof—apparently alone together, for there's no evidence of anyone else's being in the house. Is the young man the old man's servant? Odd that he would not say so. Perhaps the youth is the old man's son. Quite natural that he should not say so. "I loved the old man. He had never wronged me. . . . I was never kinder to the old man than during the whole week before I killed him." Such the aggressive revulsion caused by the old man's Evil Eye!

What can this be all about? The Evil Eye is a belief as old and as dire as any in man's superstitious memory, and it usually signifies the attribution to another of a power wished for by the self. In this particular case there are other vibrations emanating from the vulture-like eye of the benign old man. Insofar as we have warrant—which I think we do—to take him as a father-figure, his Eye becomes the all-seeing surveillance of the child by the father, even by The Father. This surveillance is of course the origin of the child's conscience, the inculcation into his soul of the paternal principles of right and wrong. As such, the old man's eye becomes a ray to be feared. For if the boy deviates ever so little from the strict paths of rectitude, *it will find him out*.

• • •

Could he but rid himself of its all-seeing scrutiny, he would then be free of his subjection to time.

All the more so if the father-figure in this tale be, in one of his aspects, a Father-Figure. As, to an infant, his own natural father doubtless is. As, to the baby Eddie, his foster-father may have been. Perhaps he had even a subliminal memory of his natural father, who so early deserted him, eye and all, to the hard knocks experience held in store. So, the evil in that Evil Eye is likely a mingling of the stern reproaches of conscience with the reminder of his own subjection to time, age, and death.

From *Poe Poe Poe Poe Poe Poe Poe*

MYTHOLOGICAL CRITICISM

Mythological critics look for the recurrent universal patterns underlying most literary works. **Mythological criticism** is an interdisciplinary approach that combines the insights of anthropology, psychology, history, and comparative religion. If psychological criticism examines the artist as an individual, mythological criticism explores the artist's common humanity by tracing how the individual imagination uses symbols and situations—consciously or unconsciously—in ways that transcend its own historical milieu and resemble the mythology of other cultures or epochs.

A central concept in mythological criticism is the **archetype,** a symbol, character, situation, or image that evokes a deep universal response. The idea of the archetype came into literary criticism from the Swiss psychologist Carl Jung, a lifetime student of myth and religion. Jung believed that all individuals share a "collective unconscious," a set of primal memories common to the human race, existing below each person's conscious mind. Archetypal images (which often relate to experiencing primordial phenomena such as the sun, moon, fire, night, and blood), Jung believed, trigger the collective unconscious. We do not need to accept the literal truth of the collective unconscious, however, to endorse the archetype as a helpful critical concept. Northrop Frye defined the archetype in considerably less occult terms as "a symbol, usually an image, which recurs often enough in literature to be recognizable as an element of one's literary experience as a whole."

Identifying archetypal symbols and situations in literary works, mythological critics almost inevitably link the individual text under discussion to a broader context of works that share an underlying pattern. In discussing Shakespeare's *Hamlet*, for instance, a mythological critic might relate Shakespeare's Danish prince to other mythic sons avenging the deaths of their fathers, such as Orestes from Greek myth or Sigmund of Norse legend; or, in discussing *Othello*, relate the sinister figure of Iago to the devil in traditional Christian belief. Critic Joseph Campbell took such comparisons even further; his compendious study *The Hero with a Thousand Faces* demonstrates how similar mythic characters appear in virtually every culture on every continent.

Edmond Volpe (1922–2007)

Myth in Faulkner's "Barn Burning"   1964

"Barn Burning" however is not really concerned with class conflict. The story is centered upon Sarty's emotional dilemma. His conflict would not have been altered in any way if the person whose barn Ab burns had been a simple poor farmer, rather than an aristocratic plantation owner. The child's tension, in fact, begins to surface during the hearing in which a simple farmer accuses Ab of burning his barn. The moral antagonists mirrored in Sarty's conflict are not sharecropper and aristocrat. They are the father, Ab Snopes, versus the rest of mankind. Major De Spain is not developed as a character; his house is important to Sarty because it represents a totally new and totally different social and moral entity. Within the context of the society Faulkner is dealing with, the gap between the rich aristocrat and the poor sharecropper provides a viable metaphor for dramatizing the crisis Sarty is under going. Ab Snopes is by no means a social crusader. The De Spain manor is Sarty's first contact with a rich man's house, though he can recall, in the short span of his life, at least a dozen times the family had to move because Ab burned barns. Ab does not discriminate between rich and poor. For him there are only two categories: blood kin and "they," into which he lumps all the rest of mankind. Ab's division relates to Sarty's crisis and only by defining precisely the nature of the conflict the boy is undergoing can we determine the moral significance Faulkner sees in it. The clue to Sarty's conflict rests in its resolution.

• • •

The boy's anxiety is created by his awakening sense of his own individuality. Torn between strong emotional attachment to the parent and his growing need to assert his own identity, Sarty's crisis is psychological and his battle is being waged far below the level of his intellectual and moral awareness.

Faulkner makes this clear in the opening scene with imagery that might be described as synesthesia. The real smell of cheese is linked with the smell of the hermetic meat in the tin cans with the scarlet devils on the label that his "intestines believed he smelled coming in intermittent gusts momentary and brief between the other constant one, the smell and sense just a little of fear because mostly of despair and grief, the old fierce pull of blood." The smells below the level of the olfactory sense link the devil image and the blood image to identify the anxiety the father creates in the child's psyche. Tension is created by the blood demanding identification with his father against *"our enemy he thought in that despair; ourn! mine and hisn both! He's my father!"* Sarty's conflict is played out in terms of identification, not in moral terms. He does not think of his father as bad, his father's enemies as good.

Ab unjustly accuses Sarty of intending to betray him at the hearing, but he correctly recognizes that his son is moving out of childhood, developing a mind and will of his own and is no longer blindly loyal. In instructing the boy that everyone is the enemy and his loyalty belongs to his blood, Ab's phrasing is revealing: "'Don't you know all they wanted was a chance to get at me because they knew I had them beat?'" Ab does not use the plural "us." It is "I" and "they." Blood loyalty means total identification with Ab, and in the ensuing scenes, Snopes attempts to make his son an extension of himself by taking him to the De Spain house, having him rise up before dawn to be with Ab when he returns the rug, having him accompany Ab to the hearing against De Spain and finally making him an accomplice in the burning of De Spain's barn.

The moral import of Ab's insistence on blood loyalty is fully developed by the satanic imagery Faulkner introduces in the scene at the mansion. As they go up the drive, Sarty follows his father, seeing the stiff black form against the white plantation house. Traditionally the devil casts no shadow, and Ab's figure appears to the child as having "that impervious quality of something cut ruthlessly from tin, depthless, as though sidewise to the sun it would cast no shadow." The cloven hoof of the devil is suggested by Ab's limp upon which the boy's eyes are fixed as the foot unwaveringly comes down into the manure. Sarty's increasing tension resounds in the magnified echo of the limping foot on the porch boards, "a sound out of all proportion to the displacement of the body it bore, as though it had attained to a sort of vicious and ravening minimum not to be dwarfed by anything." At first Sarty thought the house was impervious to his father, but his burgeoning fear of the threat the father poses is reflected in his vision of Ab becoming magnified and monstrous as the black arm reaches up the white door and Sarty sees "the lifted hand like a curled claw."

The satanic images are projected out of the son's nightmarish vision of his father, but they are reinforced by the comments of the adult narrator. Sarty believes Snopes fought bravely in the Civil War, but Ab, we are told, wore no uniform, gave his fealty to no cause, admitted the authority of no man. He went to war for booty. Ab's ego is so great it creates a centripetal force into which everything must flow or be destroyed. The will-less, abject creature who is his wife symbolizes the power of his will. What Ab had done to his wife, he sets out to do to the emerging will of his son. Ab cannot tolerate any entity that challenges the dominance of his will. By allowing his hog to forage in the farmer's corn and by dirtying and ruining De Spain's rug, he deliberately creates a conflict that requires the assertion of primacy. Fire, the element of the devil, is the weapon for the preservation of his dominance. Ab's rage is not fired by social injustice. It is fired by a pride, like Lucifer's, so absolute it can accept no order beyond its own. In the satanic myth, Lucifer asserts his will against the divine order and is cast out of heaven. The angels who fall with Lucifer become extensions of his will. In the same way, Ab is an outcast and pariah among men. He accepts no order that is not of his blood.

From "'Barn Burning': A Definition of Evil"

SOCIOLOGICAL CRITICISM

Sociological criticism examines literature in the cultural, economic, and political context in which it is written or received. "Art is not created in a vacuum," critic Wilbur Scott observed, "it is the work not simply of a person, but of an author fixed in time and space, answering a community of which he is an important, because articulate part." Sociological criticism explores the relationships between the artist and society. Sometimes it looks at the sociological status of the author to evaluate how the profession of the writer in a particular milieu affected what was written. Sociological criticism also analyzes the social content of literary works—what cultural, economic, or political values a particular text implicitly or explicitly promotes. Finally, sociological criticism examines the role the audience has in shaping literature. A sociological view of Shakespeare, for example, might look at the economic position of Elizabethan playwrights and actors; it might also study the political ideas expressed in the plays or discuss how the nature of an Elizabethan theatrical audience (which was usually all male unless the play was produced at court) helped determine the subject, tone, and language of the plays.

An influential type of sociological criticism has been Marxist criticism, which focuses on the economic and political elements of art. Marxist criticism, as in the work of the Hungarian philosopher Georg Lukacs, often explores the ideological content of literature. Whereas a formalist critic would maintain that form and content are inextricably blended, Lukacs believed that content determines form and that, therefore, all art is political. Even if a work of art ignores political issues, it makes a political statement, Marxist critics believe, because it endorses the economic and political status quo. Consequently, Marxist criticism is frequently evaluative and judges some literary work better than others on an ideological basis; this tendency can lead to reductive judgment, as when Soviet critics rated Jack London a novelist superior to William Faulkner, Ernest Hemingway, Edith Wharton, and Henry James, because he illustrated the principles of class struggle more clearly. London was America's first major working-class writer. To examine the political ideas and observations found in his fiction can be illuminating, but to fault other authors for lacking his instincts and ideas is not necessarily helpful in understanding their particular qualities. There is always a danger in sociological criticism—Marxist or otherwise—of imposing the critic's personal politics on the work in question and then evaluating it according to how closely it endorses that ideology. As an analytical tool, however, Marxist criticism and sociological methods can illuminate political and economic dimensions of literature that other approaches overlook.

Kathryn Lee Seidel

The Economics of Zora Neale Hurston's "Sweat" — 1991

"Sweat" functions at one level as a documentary of the economic situation of Eatonville in the early decades of the twentieth century. Hurston uses a naturalistic narrator to comment on the roles of Delia and Sykes Jones as workers as well as marriage partners, but ultimately the story veers away from naturalistic fiction and becomes a modernist rumination on Delia as an artist figure. The story's coherence of theme and structure makes it one of Hurston's most powerful pieces of fiction.

Preserved not only as a place but as an idea of a place, Eatonville, Florida, retains the atmosphere of which Hurston wrote. As putatively the oldest town in the United States incorporated by blacks, Eatonville possesses understandable pride in its unique history. When Hurston writes of Eatonville in "How It Feels To Be Colored Me," she implies that her childhood place was idyllic because "it is exclusively a colored town," one in which the young Zora was happily unaware of the restrictions that race conferred elsewhere. However, this gloss of nostalgia can be read simultaneously with "Sweat," published only two years earlier . . . [where] Hurston reveals the somber and multifaced variations of life in Eatonville in the first part of this century.

Economically Eatonville in "Sweat" exists as a twin, a double with its neighbor, the town of Winter Park. Far from being identical, the twin towns are configured like Siamese twins, joined as they are by economic necessity. Winter Park is an all-white, wealthy town that caters to rich northerners from New England who journey south each fall to "winter" in Florida—"snowbirds," as the natives call them. Winter Park then as now boasts brick streets, huge oaks, landscaped lakes, and large, spacious houses. To clean these houses, tend these gardens, cook the meals, and watch the children of Winter Park, residents of Eatonville made a daily exodus across the railroad tracks on which Amtrak now runs to work as domestics. . . . What is unique about Eatonville and Winter Park is that they are not one town divided in two but two towns. Eatonville's self-governance, its pride in its historic traditions, and its social mores were thus able to develop far more autonomously than those in the many towns . . . where the black community had to struggle to develop a sense of independent identity.

In "Sweat" we see the results of this economic situation. On Saturdays the men of the town congregate on the porch of the general store chewing sugarcane and discussing the lamentable marriage of Delia and Sykes Jones. Although these men may be employed during the week, Sykes is not. Some working people mentioned besides Joe Clarke, the store owner, are the woman who runs a rooming house where Bertha, Sykes's mistress, stays, the minister of the church Delia attends, and the people who organize dances that Sykes frequents. Work as farm laborers on land owned by whites is probably available, but it pays very little and is seasonal. Jacqueline Jones points out that in 1900, not long before the time of the story, 50 to 70 percent of adult black women were employed full time as compared to only 20 percent of men.[1] A black man might be unemployed 50 percent of the time. One reason that unemployed men congregated at the local general store was not merely out of idleness, as whites alleged, nor out of a desire to create oral narratives, as we Hurston critics would like to imagine, but there they could be "visible to potential employers," as Jones asserts.

There is not enough work for the men as it is, but the townspeople discuss Sykes's particular aversion to what work is available. Old man Anderson reports that Sykes was always "ovahbearin' . . . but since dat white 'oman from up north done teached 'im how to run a automobile, he done got too biggety to live—an' we oughter kill im." The identity of this woman and her exact role in Sykes's life is not referred to again, but if she was a Winter Park woman, then perhaps Sykes worked for a time as a driver for residents there. All the more ironic, then, his comment to Delia in which

---

[1]Jacqueline Jones, *Labor of Love, Labor of Sorrow: Black Women, Work, and the Family from Slavery to the Present* (New York: Basic Books, 1985) 113.

he berates her for doing white people's laundry: "ah done tole you time and again to keep them white folks' clothes outa this house." The comment suggests that Sykes does not work out of protest against the economic system of Eatonville in which blacks are dependent on whites for their livelihood. Has he chosen to be unemployed to resist the system? Within the story, this reading is fragile at best. The townspeople point out that Sykes has used and abused Delia; he has "squeezed" her dry, like a piece of sugarcane. They report that she was in her youth a pert, lively, and pretty girl, but that marriage to a man like Sykes has worn her out.

In fact, Delia's work is their only source of income. In the early days of their marriage Sykes was employed, but he "took his wages to Orlando," the large city about ten miles from Eatonville, where he spent every penny. At some point Sykes stopped working and began to rely entirely on Delia for income. As she says, "Mah tub of suds is filled yo' belly with vittles more times than yo' hands is filled it. Mah sweat is done paid for this house." Delia's sense of ownership is that of the traditional work ethic; if one works hard, one can buy a house and support a family. That Delia is the breadwinner, however, is a role reversal but not ostensibly a liberation; her sweat has brought her some meager material rewards but has enraged her husband.

Although she may at one time have considered stopping work so that Sykes might be impelled to "feel like man again" and become a worker once more, at the time of the story that possibility is long past. Sykes wants her to stop working so she can be dainty, not sweaty, fat, not thin. Moreover, he wants to oust her from the house so that he and his girlfriend can live there. . . . Sykes's brutality is a chosen compensation because he does not participate in the work of the community. He chooses instead to become the town's womanizer and bully who spends his earnings when he has them; he lives for the moment and for himself.

. . . With her house she possesses not only a piece of property, but she also gains the right to declare herself as a person, not a piece of property. Because Sykes has not shared in the labor that results in the purchase of this property, he remains in a dependent state. He is rebellious against Delia who he feels controls him by denying him the house he feels ought to be his; his only reason for this assertion is that he is a man and Delia is his wife.

Thus, the economics of slavery in "Sweat" becomes a meditation on marriage as an institution that perpetuates the possession of women for profit. Indeed, Sykes is the slaveholder here; he does not work, he is sustained by the harsh physical labor of a black woman, he relies on the work of another person to obtain his own pleasure (in this case buying presents for his mistress Bertha). He regards Delia's property and her body as his possessions to be disposed of as he pleases. Sykes's brutal beatings of Delia and his insulting remarks about her appearance are the tools with which he perpetuates her subordination to him for the sixteen years of their marriage.

From "The Artist in the Kitchen: The Economics of Creativity in Hurston's 'Sweat'"

GENDER CRITICISM

Gender criticism examines how sexual identity influences the creation and reception of literary works. Gender studies began with the feminist movement and was influenced by such works as Simone de Beauvoir's *The Second Sex* (1949) and Kate

Millett's *Sexual Politics* (1970) as well as sociology, psychology, and anthropology. Feminist critics believe that culture has been so completely dominated by men that literature is full of unexamined "male-produced" assumptions. They see their criticism correcting this imbalance by analyzing and combating patriarchal attitudes. **Feminist criticism** has explored how an author's gender influences—consciously or unconsciously—his or her writing. While a formalist critic such as Allen Tate emphasized the universality of Emily Dickinson's poetry by demonstrating how powerfully the language, imagery, and mythmaking of her poems combine to affect a generalized reader, Sandra M. Gilbert, a leading feminist critic, has identified attitudes and assumptions in Dickinson's poetry that she believes are essentially female. Another important theme in feminist criticism is analyzing how sexual identity influences the reader of a text. If Tate's hypothetical reader was deliberately sexless, Gilbert's reader sees a text through the eyes of his or her sex. Finally, feminist critics carefully examine how the images of men and women in imaginative literature reflect or reject the social forces that have historically kept the sexes from achieving total equality.

Recently, gender criticism has expanded beyond its original feminist perspective. In the last twenty years or so, critics in the field of gay and lesbian studies—some of whom describe their discipline as "queer theory"—have explored the impact of different sexual orientations on literary creation and reception. Seeking to establish a canon of classic gay and lesbian authors, these critics argue that sexual orientation is so central a component of human personality (especially when it necessarily puts one at odds with established social and moral norms) that to ignore it in connection with such writers amounts to a fundamental misreading and misunderstanding of their work. A men's movement has also emerged in response to feminism, seeking not to reject feminism but to rediscover masculine identity in an authentic, contemporary way. Led by the poet Robert Bly, the men's movement has paid special attention to interpreting poetry and fables as myths of psychic growth and sexual identity.

Richard R. Bozorth (b. 1965)

"Tell Me the Truth About Love" 2001

The 1994 film *Four Weddings and a Funeral* has probably done more to popularize Auden than any other recent event. It is also an instructive moment in his reception, for where the academy has often praised his work for its universality, the film invokes him as a gay sage: before reciting "Funeral Blues" at his lover's funeral, the character Matthew prefaces it by calling Auden "another splendid bugger" like the late Gareth.

This scene makes visible a number of significant occlusions in Auden's love poetry, including those he himself instigated. This lyric first appeared in Auden and Isherwood's play *The Ascent of* F6 (1936), recited to "A Blues" at the death of James Ransom, the protagonist's brother.[2] The version used in the film dates from 1938 and gained the title "Funeral Blues" in *Another Time* (1940). Included there as one of "Four Cabaret Songs for Miss Hedli Anderson," it is presented as an exercise in light verse. As Mendelson notes, its dedication to Benjamin Britten's favorite soprano was a form of disguise Auden used only for love poems

[2] W. H. Auden and Christopher Isherwood, *Plays and Other Dramatic Writings by W. H. Auden, 1928–1938*, ed. Edward Mendelson (Princeton: Princeton UP, 1988) 350–51.

with masculine pronouns.[3] By putting the text in the voice of a gay male character, *Four Weddings and a Funeral* outs the poem, much as Matthew uses it to affirm before the mourners the romantic nature of his relationship with Gareth. Auden's words become a poignant utterance about the public unspeakability of gay love:

> Let aeroplanes circle moaning overhead
> Scribbling on the sky the message He Is Dead,
> Put crêpe bows round the white necks of the public doves,
> Let the traffic policemen wear black cotton gloves.[4]

In cinematic context, such extravagance is not just an effect of the conventions of light verse, or an expression of anguish that the world goes blithely on—a feeling hardly limited, of course, to gay mourners. For these campy pleas for public ritual point up a gap between gay romantic loss and official forms of lament.

To read "Funeral Blues" as expressing a universal sense of the unfairness of death is to be so taken by Auden's facility with romantic commonplace as to be deaf to its sexual-political implications. For its part, *Four Weddings and a Funeral* risks another illusion in recovering Auden as a master of gay pathos. Perhaps his most touching line came with the 1938 revision: "I thought that love would last forever; I was wrong." Auden was evidently responding not to death but to the end of the affair that had generated most of his love poetry since 1932.[5] But while it is almost irresistible to see the poem as voicing utter desolation at a breakup, impermanence had always haunted Auden's love poems. "Certainty" and "fidelity," in his famous words, are delusions of lovers "in their ordinary swoon."[6] From this angle, "Funeral Blues" might sound contrived or even cruel, since it mourned someone still living. But the poem might also be read as a confession that grief can be a self-indulgent performance, as manipulative of oneself as it is of others. Rather than obscuring the personal, Auden's title invites moral reflection: grieving can indeed be "Funeral Blues"—a way of acting out romantic pathos.

Both universalizing and "gay-positive" readings of "Funeral Blues" find it confirming what we—however "we" may be defined—already feel: we sentimentally construe the mourning voice as echoing our own desires. To read the poem instead as Auden's private response to the end of a homosexual love affair is to see its expression of grief as a means for reflection on love. We have seen how Auden used "parable" to articulate the social value of poetry as an antiuniversalizing form, and this chapter extends my concern with his poetic theory. My largest claim is that Auden came to treat poetry itself as a kind of lovers' discourse: a site of intimate relation between poet and reader in all their particularities. Poetry would be an erotic "game of knowledge," as Auden writes in the 1948 essay "Squares and Oblongs": "a bringing to consciousness . . . of emotions and their hidden relationships."[7]

From *Auden's Games of Knowledge: Poetry and the Meanings of Homosexuality*

---

[3]Edward Mendelson, *Later Auden* (New York: Farrar, 1999) 32.
[4]W. H. Auden, *The English Auden: Poems, Prose and Dramatic Writings* (London: Faber, 1977) 163.
[5]Mendelson, *Later Auden* 32.
[6]Auden, *English Auden* 207.
[7]W. H. Auden, "Squares and Oblongs," *Poets at Work*, ed. Charles D. Abbot (New York: Harcourt, 1948) 173.

READER-RESPONSE CRITICISM

Reader-response criticism attempts to describe what happens in the reader's mind while interpreting a text. If traditional criticism assumes that imaginative writing is a creative act, reader-response theory recognizes that reading is also a creative process. Reader-response critics believe that no text provides self-contained meaning; literary texts do not exist independently of readers' interpretations. A text, according to this critical school, is not finished until it is read and interpreted. As Oscar Wilde remarked in the preface to his novel *The Picture of Dorian Gray* (1891), "It is the spectator, and not life, that art really mirrors." The practical problem then arises, however, that no two individuals necessarily read a text in exactly the same way. Rather than declare one interpretation correct and the other mistaken, reader-response criticism recognizes the inevitable plurality of readings. Instead of trying to ignore or reconcile the contradictions inherent in this situation, it explores them.

The easiest way to explain reader-response criticism is to relate it to the common experience of rereading a favorite book after many years. Rereading a novel as an adult, for example, that "changed your life" as an adolescent, is often a shocking experience. The book may seem substantially different. The character you remembered liking most now seems less admirable, and another character you disliked now seems more sympathetic. Has the book changed? Very unlikely, but *you* certainly have in the intervening years. Reader-response criticism explores how different individuals (or classes of individuals) see the same text differently. It emphasizes how religious, cultural, and social values affect readings; it also overlaps with gender criticism in exploring how men and women read the same text with different assumptions.

While reader-response criticism rejects the notion that there can be a single correct reading for a literary text, it doesn't consider all readings permissible. Each text creates limits to its possible interpretations. As Stanley Fish admits in the following critical selection, we cannot arbitrarily place an Eskimo in William Faulkner's story "A Rose for Emily" (though Professor Fish does ingeniously imagine a hypothetical situation in which this bizarre interpretation might actually be possible).

Stanley Fish (b. 1938)

An Eskimo "A Rose for Emily"   1980

The fact that it remains easy to think of a reading that most of us would dismiss out of hand does not mean that the text excludes it but that there is as yet no elaborated interpretive procedure for producing that text. . . . Norman Holland's analysis of Faulkner's "A Rose for Emily" is a case in point. Holland is arguing for a kind of psychoanalytic pluralism. The text, he declares, is "at most a matrix of psychological possibilities for its readers," but, he insists, "only some possibilities . . . truly fit the matrix": "One would not say, for example, that a reader of . . . 'A Rose for Emily' who thought the 'tableau' [of Emily and her father in the doorway] described an Eskimo was really responding to the story at all—only pursuing some mysterious inner exploration."

Holland is making two arguments: first, that anyone who proposes an Eskimo reading of "A Rose for Emily" will not find a hearing in the literary community. And that, I think, is right. ("We are right to rule out at least some readings.") His second argument is that the unacceptability of the Eskimo reading is a function of the text, of what he calls its "sharable promptuary," the public "store of structured language" that sets limits to the interpretations the words can accommodate. And that, I think, is wrong. The Eskimo reading is unacceptable because there is at present no interpretive strategy for producing it, no way of "looking" or reading (and remember, all acts of looking or reading are "ways") that would result in the emergence of obviously Eskimo meanings. This does not mean, however, that no such strategy could ever come into play, and it is not difficult to imagine the circumstances under which it would establish itself. One such circumstance would be the discovery of a letter in which Faulkner confides that he has always believed himself to be an Eskimo changeling. (The example is absurd only if one forgets Yeats's *Vision* or Blake's Swedenborgianism° or James Miller's recent elaboration of a homosexual reading of *The Waste Land*.) Immediately the workers in the Faulkner industry would begin to reinterpret the canon in the light of this newly revealed "belief" and the work of reinterpretation would involve the elaboration of a symbolic or allusive system (not unlike mythological or typological criticism) whose application would immediately transform the text into one informed everywhere by Eskimo meanings. It might seem that I am admitting that there is a text to be transformed, but the object of transformation would be the text (or texts) given by whatever interpretive strategies the Eskimo strategy was in the process of dislodging or expanding. The result would be that whereas we now have a Freudian "A Rose for Emily," a mythological "A Rose for Emily," a Christological "A Rose for Emily," a regional "A Rose for Emily," a sociological "A Rose for Emily," a linguistic "A Rose for Emily," we would in addition have an Eskimo "A Rose for Emily," existing in some relation of compatibility or incompatibility with the others.

Again the point is that while there are always mechanisms for ruling out readings, their source is not the text but the presently recognized interpretive strategies for producing the text. It follows, then, that no reading, however outlandish it might appear, is inherently an impossible one.

From *Is There a Text in This Class?*

DECONSTRUCTIONIST CRITICISM

Deconstructionist criticism rejects the traditional assumption that language can accurately represent reality. Language, according to deconstructionists, is a fundamentally unstable medium; consequently, literary texts, which are made up of words, have no fixed, single meaning. Deconstructionists insist, according to the critic Paul de Man, on "the impossibility of making the actual expression coincide with what has to be expressed, of making the actual signs coincide with what is signified." Since they believe that literature cannot definitively express its subject matter, deconstructionists tend to shift their attention away from *what* is being said to *how* language is being used in a text.

Paradoxically, deconstructionist criticism often resembles formalist criticism; both methods usually involve close reading. But while a formalist usually tries to

---

Yeats's Vision *or* Blake's Swedenborgianism: Irish poet William Butler Yeats and Swedish mystical writer Emanuel Swedenborg both claimed to have received revelations from the spirit world; some of Swedenborg's ideas are embodied in the long poems of William Blake.

demonstrate how the diverse elements of a text cohere into meaning, the deconstructionist approach attempts to show how the text "deconstructs," that is, how it can be broken down—by a skeptical critic—into mutually irreconcilable positions. A biographical or historical critic might seek to establish the author's intention as a means to interpreting a literary work, but deconstructionists reject the notion that the critic should endorse the myth of authorial control over language. Deconstructionist critics like Roland Barthes and Michel Foucault have therefore called for "the death of the author," that is, the rejection of the assumption that the author, no matter how ingenious, can fully control the meaning of a text. They have also announced the death of literature as a special category of writing. In their view, poems and novels are merely words on a page that deserve no privileged status as art; all texts are created equal—equally untrustworthy, that is.

Deconstructionists focus on how language is used to achieve power. Since they believe, in the words of the critic David Lehman, that "there are no truths, only rival interpretations," deconstructionists try to understand how some "interpretations" come to be regarded as truth. A major goal of deconstruction is to demonstrate how those supposed truths are at best provisional and at worst contradictory.

Deconstruction, as you may have inferred, calls for intellectual subtlety and skill. If you pursue your literary studies beyond the introductory stage, you will want to become more familiar with its assumptions. Deconstruction may strike you as a negative, even destructive, critical approach, and yet its best practitioners are adept at exposing the inadequacy of much conventional criticism. By patient analysis, they can sometimes open up the most familiar text and find unexpected significance.

Roland Barthes (1915–1980)

The Death of the Author 1968

Translated by Stephen Heath

Succeeding the Author, the scriptor no longer bears within him passions, humours, feelings, impressions, but rather this immense dictionary from which he draws a writing that can know no halt: life never does more than imitate the book, and the book itself is only a tissue of signs, an imitation that is lost, infinitely deferred.

Once the Author is removed, the claim to decipher a text becomes quite futile. To give a text an Author is to impose a limit on that text, to furnish it with a final signified, to close the writing. Such a conception suits criticism very well, the latter then allotting itself the important task of discovering the Author (or its hypostases: society, history, psyché, liberty) beneath the work: when the Author has been found, the text is "explained"—victory to the critic. Hence there is no surprise in the fact that, historically, the reign of the Author has also been that of the Critic, nor again in the fact that criticism (be it new) is today undermined along with the Author. In the multiplicity of writing, everything is to be *disentangled*, nothing *deciphered*; the structure can be followed, "run" (like the thread of a stocking) at every point and at every level, but there is nothing beneath: the space of writing is to be ranged over, not pierced; writing ceaselessly posits meaning ceaselessly to evaporate it, carrying out a systematic exemption of meaning. In precisely this way literature (it would be better from now on to say *writing*), by refusing to assign a "secret," an ultimate meaning, to the text (and to the world as text), liberates what may be called an anti-theological activity, an activity that is truly revolutionary since to refuse to fix meaning is, in the end, to refuse God and his hypostases—reason, science, law.

From "The Death of the Author"

CULTURAL STUDIES

Unlike the other critical approaches discussed in this chapter, cultural criticism (or **cultural studies**) does not offer a single way of analyzing literature. No central methodology is associated with cultural studies. Nor is cultural criticism solely, or even mainly, concerned with literary texts in the conventional sense. Instead, the term *cultural studies* refers to a relatively recent interdisciplinary field of academic inquiry. This field borrows methodologies from other approaches to analyze a wide range of cultural products and practices.

To understand cultural studies, it helps to know a bit about its origins. In the English-speaking world, the field was first defined at the Centre for Contemporary Cultural Studies of Birmingham University in Britain. Founded in 1964, this graduate program tried to expand the range of literary study beyond traditional approaches to canonic literature in order to explore a broader spectrum of historical, cultural, and political issues. The most influential teacher at the Birmingham Centre was Raymond Williams (1921–1983), a Welsh socialist with wide intellectual interests. Williams argued that scholars should not study culture as a canon of great works by individual artists but rather examine it as an evolutionary process that involves the entire society. "We cannot separate literature and art," Williams said, "from other kinds of social practice." The cultural critic, therefore, does not study fixed aesthetic objects so much as dynamic social processes. The critic's challenge is to identify and understand the complex forms and effects of the process of culture.

A Marxist intellectual, Williams called his approach cultural materialism (a reference to the Marxist doctrine of dialectical materialism), but later scholars soon discarded that name for two broader and more neutral terms, cultural criticism and cultural studies. From the start, this interdisciplinary field relied heavily on literary theory, especially Marxist and feminist criticism. It also employed the documentary techniques of historical criticism combined with political analysis focused on issues of social class, race, and gender. (This approach flourished in the United States, where it is called New Historicism.) Cultural studies is also deeply antiformalist because the field concerns itself with investigating the complex relationships among history, politics, and literature. Cultural studies rejects the notion that literature exists in an aesthetic realm separate from ethical and political categories.

A chief goal of cultural studies is to understand the nature of social power as reflected in "texts." For example, if the object of analysis were a sonnet by Shakespeare, the cultural studies adherent might investigate the moral, psychological, and political assumptions reflected in the poem and then deconstruct them to see what individuals, social classes, or gender might benefit from having those assumptions perceived as true. The relevant mission of cultural studies is to identify both the overt and covert values reflected in a cultural practice. The cultural studies critic also tries to trace out and understand the structures of meaning that hold those assumptions in place and give them the appearance of objective representation. Any analytical technique that helps illuminate these issues is employed.

In theory, a cultural studies critic might employ any methodology. In practice, however, he or she will most often borrow concepts from deconstruction, Marxist analysis, gender criticism, race theory, and psychology. Each of these earlier methodologies provides particular analytical tools that cultural critics find useful. What cultural studies borrows from deconstructionism is its emphasis on uncovering conflict, dissent, and contradiction in the works under analysis. Whereas traditional critical approaches often sought to demonstrate the unity of a literary work, cultural studies often seeks to portray social, political, and psychological conflicts that the work masks. What cultural studies borrows from Marxist analysis is an attention to the ongoing struggle between social classes, each seeking economic (and therefore political) advantage. Cultural studies often asks questions about what social class created a work of art and what class (or classes) served as its audience. Among the many things that cultural studies borrowed from gender criticism and race theory is a concern with social inequality between the sexes and races. It seeks to investigate how these inequities have been reflected in the texts of a historical period or a society. Cultural studies is, above all, a political enterprise that views literary analysis as a means of furthering social justice.

Since cultural studies does not adhere to any single methodology (or even a consistent set of methodologies), it is impossible to characterize the field briefly, because there are exceptions to every generalization offered. What one sees most clearly are characteristic tendencies, especially the commitment to examining issues of class, race, and gender. There is also the insistence on expanding the focus of critical inquiry beyond traditional high literary culture. British cultural studies guru Anthony Easthope can, for example, analyze with equal aplomb Gerard Manley Hopkins's "The Windhover," Edgar Rice Burroughs' *Tarzan of the Apes,* a Benson and Hedges cigarette advertisement, and Sean Connery's eyebrows. Cultural studies is infamous—even among its practitioners—for its habitual use of literary jargon. It is also notorious for its complex intellectual analysis of mundane materials, such as Easthope's analysis of a cigarette ad, which may be interesting in its own right but remote from most readers' literary experience. Some scholars, such as Camille Paglia, however, use the principles of cultural studies to provide new social, political, and historical insights into canonic texts such as William Blake's "London." Omnivorous, iconoclastic, and relentlessly analytic, cultural criticism has become a major presence in contemporary literary studies.

Camille Paglia (b. 1947)

A Reading of William Blake's "London" 2005

Wandering through London's hell, Blake follows the model of Dante as poet-quester cataloging the horrors of the Inferno. A visitor to the storied British capital in 1793 would have seen a grand, expanding city in economic boom. But the poet, with telepathic hearing and merciless X-ray eyes, homes in on the suffering, dislocation, and hidden spiritual costs of rapid social transformation. The Industrial Revolution, which began in England in the 1770s and would spread globally over the next two centuries, profoundly altered community, personal identity, and basic values in ways we are still sorting out.

"London" is darkly paranoid, as claustrophobic and hallucinatory as an Expressionist nightmare. Everyone and everything in it are in bondage to obscure, malevolent Forces. The streets and even the river Thames are "charter'd"—mapped, licensed, controlled, and choked with commerce (1–2). (Boats, buses, and airplanes in the United States are still "chartered"—reserved and rented—in this sense.) In Blake's vast system, the mathematical grid, produced by the draftsman's compass, is identified with reason, law, and an oppressor Father-God who curtails human imagination and natural energy. When "London" was written, the threat of revolutionary agitation from France, then plunging into the Reign of Terror, had moved the British government to suspend liberties considered "charter'd" by the medieval Magna Carta (Latin for "Great Charter").

As the people flow through London's streets, a moral darkness seems to hang over the land. The poem may begin in the workday but ends in the pitch of night, so that the poet's walking tour seems haunted and driven. "I . . . mark in every face I meet / Marks of weakness, marks of woe": he notes (to "mark" means to remark or observe) the signs and scars of illness, exhaustion, anxiety, and despair, the afflictions of the damned in a city rushing to its doom (3–4). Working-class faces had indeed changed: Blake's generation was the first to see the pasty pallor of factory workers cut off, as their farmer forebears had never been, from the sun's burnishing, life-giving rays.

From *Break, Blow, Burn*

GLOSSARY OF LITERARY TERMS

Abstract diction See **Diction**.

Accent An emphasis or stress placed on a syllable in speech. Clear pronunciation of polysyllabic words almost always depends on correct placement of their accents (e.g., *de*-sert and de-*sert* are two different words and parts of speech, depending on their accent). Accent or speech stress is the basis of most meters in English. (*See also* **Meter**.)

Accentual meter A meter that uses a consistent number of strong speech stresses per line. The number of unstressed syllables may vary, as long as the accented syllables do not. Much popular poetry, such as rap and nursery rimes, is written in accentual meter.

Allegory A narrative in verse or prose in which the literal events (persons, places, and things) consistently point to a parallel sequence of symbolic ideas. This narrative strategy is often used to dramatize abstract ideas, historical events, religious systems, or political issues. An allegory has two levels of meaning: a literal level that tells a surface story and a symbolic level on which the abstract ideas unfold. The names of allegorical characters often hint at their symbolic roles. For example, in Nathaniel Hawthorne's "Young Goodman Brown," Faith is not only the name of the protagonist's wife but also a symbol of the protagonist's religious faith.

Alliteration The repetition of two or more consonant sounds in successive words in a line of verse or prose. Alliteration can be used at the beginning of words ("cool cats"—**initial alliteration**) or internally on stressed syllables ("In kitchen cups concupiscent curds"—which combines initial and **internal alliteration**). Alliteration was a central feature of Anglo-Saxon poetry and is still used by contemporary writers.

Allusion A brief (and sometimes indirect) reference in a text to a person, place, or thing—fictitious or actual. An allusion may appear in a literary work as an initial quotation, a passing mention of a name, or a phrase borrowed from another writer—often carrying the meanings and implications of the original. Allusions imply a common set of knowledge between reader and writer, and operate as a literary shorthand to enrich the meaning of a text.

Analogy A comparison between two things that points out one or more meaningful similarity. Analogy is a key rhetorical device often used to support some new idea or unfamiliar thing by comparing it to a more established concept or fact.

Analysis The examination of a piece of literature as a means of understanding its subject or structure. An effective analysis often clarifies a work by focusing on a single element such as tone, irony, symbolism, imagery, or rhythm in a way that enhances the reader's understanding of the whole. *Analysis* comes from the Greek word meaning to "undo," to "loosen."

Anapest A metrical foot in verse in which two unstressed syllables are followed by a stressed syllable, as in "on a *boat*" or "in a *slump*" (⌣⌣ ′). (*See also* **Meter**.)

Antagonist The most significant character or force that opposes the protagonist in a narrative or drama. The antagonist may be another character, society itself, a force of nature, or even—in modern literature—conflicting impulses within the protagonist.

Anticlimax An unsatisfying and trivial turn of events in a literary work that occurs in place of a genuine climax. An anticlimax often involves a surprising shift in tone from the lofty or serious into the petty or ridiculous. The term is often used negatively to denote a feeble moment in a plot in which an author fails to create an intended effect. Anticlimax, however, can also be a strong dramatic device when a writer uses it for humorous or ironic effect.

Antihero A protagonist who is lacking in one or more of the conventional qualities attributed to a hero. Instead of being dignified, brave, idealistic, or purposeful, for instance, the antihero may be buffoonish, cowardly, self-interested, or weak. The antihero is often considered an essentially modern form of characterization, a satiric or frankly realistic commentary on traditional portrayals of idealized heroes or heroines. Modern examples range from Kafka's many protagonists to Beckett's tramps in *Waiting for Godot*.

Antithesis A figure of speech that contrasts things (ideas, persons, places) by parallel arrangements of words, clauses, or sentences. This rhetorical device underscores the striking difference between the two parallel items (e.g., "Give us *action*, not *words*" or Samuel Johnson's "It is better to *live* rich than to *die* rich.").

Archetype A recurring symbol, character, landscape, or event found in myth and literature across different cultures and eras. The idea of the archetype came into literary criticism from the Swiss psychologist Carl Jung, who believed that all individuals share a "collective unconscious," a set of primal memories common to the human race

1419

that exists in our subconscious. An example of an archetypal character is the devil who may appear in pure mythic form (as in John Milton's *Paradise Lost*) but occurs more often in a disguised form like Fagin in Charles Dickens's *Oliver Twist* or Abner Snopes in William Faulkner's "Barn Burning."

Argumentative essay An essay that attempts to convince the reader by stating a particular case and supporting it through effective argumentation. Argumentative essays can range from short newspaper editorials to longer pieces such as Martin Luther King's "Letter From Birmingham Jail," which makes carefully justified political and moral recommendations.

Aside In drama, a few words or a short passage spoken in an undertone or to the audience. By convention, other characters onstage are deaf to the aside.

Assonance The repetition of two or more vowel sounds in successive words, which creates a kind of rime. Like alliteration, the assonance may occur initially ("all the *aw*ful *au*guries") or internally ("wh*i*te l*i*lacs"). Assonance may be used to focus attention on key words or concepts. Assonance also helps make a phrase or line more memorable.

Atmosphere The dominant mood or feeling that pervades all or part of a literary work. Atmosphere is the total effect conveyed by the author's use of language, images, and physical setting. Atmosphere is often used to foreshadow the ultimate climax in a narrative.

Auditory imagery A word or sequence of words that refers to the sense of hearing. (*See also* **Imagery**.)

Biographical criticism The practice of analyzing a literary work by using knowledge of the author's life to gain insight.

Biography A factual account of a person's life, examining all available information or texts relevant to the subject.

Blank verse The most common and well-known meter of unrimed poetry in English. Blank verse contains five iambic feet per line and is never rimed. (*Blank* means "unrimed.") Many literary works have been written in blank verse, including Tennyson's "Ulysses" and Frost's "Mending Wall." Shakespeare's plays are written primarily in blank verse. (*See also* **Iambic pentameter**.)

Burlesque Incongruous imitation of either the style or subject matter of a serious genre, humorous because of the disparity between the treatment and the subject. On the nineteenth-century English stage, the burlesque was a broad caricature, parody, travesty, or take-off of popular plays, opera, or current events. Gilbert and Sullivan's Victorian operettas, for example, burlesqued grand opera.

Cacophony A harsh, discordant sound often mirroring the meaning of the context in which it is used. For example, "Grate on the scrannel pipes of wretched straw" (Milton's "Lycidas"). The opposite of cacophony is **euphony**.

Caesura, cesura A pause within a line of verse. Traditionally, caesuras appear near the middle of a line, but their placement may be varied to create expressive rhythmic effects. A caesura will usually occur at a mark of punctuation, but there can be a caesura even if no punctuation is present.

Carpe diem Latin for "seize the day." Originally used in Horace's famous *Odes* I (11), this phrase has been applied to characterize much lyric poetry concerned with human mortality and the passing of time.

Character An imagined figure inhabiting a narrative or drama. By convention, the reader or spectator endows the fictional character with moral, dispositional, and emotional qualities expressed in what the character says—the dialogue—and by what he or she does—the action. What a character says and does in any particular situation is motivated by his or her desires, temperament, and moral nature. (*See also* **Dynamic character** and **Flat character**.)

Characterization The techniques a writer uses to create, reveal, or develop the characters in a narrative. (*See also* **Character**.)

Climax The moment of greatest intensity in a story, which almost inevitably occurs toward the end of the work. The climax often takes the form of a decisive confrontation between the protagonist and the antagonist. In a conventional story, the climax is followed by the **resolution** or **dénouement**, in which the effects and results of the climactic action are presented. (*See also* **Falling action**, **Rising action**.)

Close reading A method of analysis involving careful step-by-step explication of a poem in order to understand how various elements work together. Close reading is a common practice of formalist critics in the study of a text.

Closed dénouement One of two types of conventional dénouement or resolution in a narrative. In closed dénouement, the author ties everything up at the end of the story so that little is left unresolved. (*See also* **Open dénouement**.)

Closed form A generic term that describes poetry written in some preexisting pattern of meter, rime, line, or stanza. A closed form produces a prescribed structure, as in the triolet, with a set rime scheme and line length. Closed forms include the sonnet, sestina, villanelle, ballade, and rondeau.

Colloquial English The casual or informal but correct language of ordinary native speakers, which may include contractions, slang, and shifts in grammar, vocabulary, and diction. Wordsworth helped introduce colloquialism into English poetry, challenging the past constraints of highly formal language in verse and calling for the poet to become "a man speaking to men." Conversational in tone, *colloquial* is derived from the Latin *colloquium*, "speaking together." (*See also* **Diction**, **Levels of diction**.)

Comedy A literary work aimed at amusing an audience. Comedy is one of the basic modes of storytelling and can be adapted to most literary forms—from poetry to film. In traditional comic plotting, the action often involves the adventures of young lovers, who face obstacles and complications that threaten disaster but are overturned at the last moment to produce a happy ending. Comic situations or comic characters can provide humor in tragicomedy and even in tragedies (the gravediggers in *Hamlet*).

Comedy of manners A realistic form of comic drama that flourished with seventeenth-century playwrights such as Molière and English Restoration dramatists. It deals with the social relations and sexual intrigues of sophisticated, intelligent, upper-class men and women, whose verbal fencing and witty repartee produce the principal comic effects.

Comic relief The appearance of a comic situation, character, or clownish humor in the midst of a serious action that introduces a sharp contrast in mood. The drunken porter in *Macbeth*, who imagines himself the doorkeeper of Hell, not only provides comic relief but intensifies the horror of Macbeth's murder of King Duncan.

Coming-of-age story *See* **Initiation story**.

Commedia dell'arte A form of comic drama developed by guilds of professional Italian actors in the mid-sixteenth century. Playing stock characters, masked *commedia* players improvised dialogue around a given scenario (a brief outline marking entrances of characters and the main course of action). In a typical play a pair of young lovers (played without masks), aided by a clever servant (Harlequin), outwit older masked characters.

Comparison In the analysis or criticism of literature, one may place two works side-by-side to point out their similarities. The product of this, a comparison, may be more meaningful when paired with its counterpart, a **contrast**.

Complication The introduction of a significant development in the central conflict in a drama or narrative between characters (or between a character and his or her situation). Traditionally, a complication begins the rising action of a story's plot. Dramatic conflict (motivation versus obstacle) during the complication is the force that drives a literary work from action to action. Complications may be *external* or *internal* or a combination of the two. A fateful blow such as an illness or an accident that affects a character is a typical example of an *external* complication—a problem the characters cannot turn away from. An *internal* complication, in contrast, might not be immediately apparent, such as the result of some important aspect of a character's values or personality.

Conclusion In plotting, the logical end or outcome of a unified plot, shortly following the climax. Also called **resolution** or **dénouement** ("the untying of the knot"), as in resolving or untying the knots created by plot complications during the rising action. The action or intrigue ends in success or failure for the protagonist, the mystery is solved, or misunderstandings are dispelled. Sometimes a conclusion is ambiguous; at the climax of the story the characters are changed, but the conclusion suggests different possibilities for what that change is or means.

Concrete diction *See* **Diction**.

Conflict In Greek, *agon,* or contest. The central struggle between two or more forces in a narrative. Conflict generally occurs when some person or thing prevents the protagonist from achieving his or her intended goal. Opposition can arise from another character, external events, preexisting situations, fate, or even some aspect of the main character's own personality. Conflict is the basic material out of which most plots are made. (*See also* **Antagonist, Character, Complication, Rising action**.)

Connotation An association or additional meaning that a word, image, or phrase may carry, apart from its literal denotation or dictionary definition. A word picks up connotations from all the uses to which it has been put in the past. For example, an owl in literature is not merely the literal bird. It also carries the many associations (connotations, that is) attached to it.

Consonance Also called **Slant rime**. A kind of rime in which the linked words share similar consonant sounds but different vowel sounds, as in *reason* and *raisin*, *mink* and *monk*. Sometimes only the final consonant sound is identical, as in *fame* and *room*, *crack* and *truck*. Used mostly by modern poets, consonance often registers more subtly than exact rime, lending itself to special poetic effects.

Contrast A contrast of two works of literature is developed by placing them side-by-side to point out their differences. This method of analysis works well with its opposite, a **comparison**, which focuses on likenesses.

Convention Any established feature or technique in literature that is commonly understood by both authors and readers. A convention is something generally agreed on to be appropriate for its customary uses, such as the sonnet form for a love poem or the opening "Once upon a time" for a fairy tale.

Conventional symbols Literary symbols that have a conventional or customary effect on most readers. We would respond similarly to a black cat crossing our path or a young bride in a white dress. These are conventional symbols because they carry recognizable connotations and suggestions.

Cosmic irony Also called **irony of fate**, it is the irony that exists between a character's aspiration and the treatment he or she receives at the hands of fate. Oedipus's ill-destined relationship with his parents is an example of cosmic irony.

Couplet A two-line stanza in poetry, usually rimed, which tends to have lines of equal length. Shakespeare's sonnets were famous for ending with a summarizing, rimed couplet: "Give my love fame faster than Time wastes life; / So thou prevent'st his scythe and crookèd knife."

Crisis The point in a drama when the crucial action, decision, or realization must occur, marking the turning point or reversal of the protagonist's fortunes. From the Greek word *krisis*, meaning "decision." In *Oedipus*, the crisis occurs as the hero presses forward to face the horrible truth, to realize he is an incestuous parricide and to take responsibility by blinding himself.

Cultural studies A contemporary interdisciplinary field of academic study that focuses on understanding the social power encoded in "texts." Cultural studies defines "texts" more broadly than literary works; they include any analyzable phenomenon from a traditional poem to an advertising image or an actor's face. Cultural studies has no central critical methodology but uses whatever intellectual tools are appropriate to the analysis at hand.

Dactyl A metrical foot of verse in which one stressed syllable is followed by two unstressed syllables (′ ⌣ ⌣, as in *bat*-ter-y or *par*-a-mour). The dactylic meter is less common to English than it was to classical Greek and Latin verse. Longfellow's *Evangeline* is the most famous English-language long dactylic poem.

Deconstructionist criticism A school of criticism that rejects the traditional assumption that language can accurately represent reality. Deconstructionists believe that literary texts can have no single meaning; therefore, they concentrate their attention on *how* language is being used in a text, rather than on *what* is being said.

Denotation The literal, dictionary meaning of a word. (*See also* **Connotation**.)

Dénouement The resolution or conclusion of a literary work as plot complications are unraveled after the climax. In French, *dénouement* means "unknotting" or "untying." (*See also* **Closed dénouement, Conclusion, Open dénouement**.)

Descriptive essay An essay that tries to present a particular time, place, or person with careful and evocative description. Descriptive essays often provide sensory details (sounds, sights, smell, and taste) to recreate the physical sense of being in their settings.

Dialect A particular variety of language spoken by an identifiable regional group or social class of persons. Dialects are often used in literature in an attempt to present a character more realistically and to express significant differences in class or background.

Dialogue The direct representation of the conversation between two or more characters. (*See also* **Monologue**.)

Diction Word choice or vocabulary. Diction refers to the class of words that an author decides is appropriate to use in a particular work. Literary history is the story of diction being challenged, upheld, and reinvented. **Concrete diction** involves a highly specific word choice in the naming of something or someone. **Abstract diction** contains words that express more general ideas or concepts. More concrete diction would offer *boxer puppy* rather than *young canine*, *Lake Ontario* rather than *body of fresh water*. Concrete words refer to what we can immediately perceive with our senses. (*See also* **Levels of diction**.)

Dimeter A verse meter consisting of two metrical feet, or two primary stresses, per line.

Double plot Also called **subplot**. Familiar in Elizabethan drama, a second story or plotline that is complete and interesting in its own right, often doubling or inverting the main plot. By analogy or counterpoint, a skillful subplot broadens perspective on the main plot to enhance rather than dilute its effect. In Shakespeare's *Othello*, for instance, Iago's duping of Rodrigo reflects the main plot of Iago's treachery to Othello.

Drama Derived from the Greek *dran*, "to do," *drama* means "action" or "deed." Drama is the form of literary composition designed for performance in the theater, in which actors take the roles of the characters, perform the indicated action, and speak the written dialogue. In the *Poetics*, Aristotle described tragedy or dramatic enactment as the most fully evolved form of the impulse to imitate or make works of art.

Dramatic irony A special kind of suspenseful expectation, when the audience or reader understands the implication and meaning of a situation onstage and foresees the oncoming disaster (in tragedy) or triumph (in comedy) but the character does not. The irony forms between the contrasting levels of knowledge of the character and the audience. Dramatic irony is pervasive throughout Sophocles's *Oedipus the King*, for example, because we know from the beginning what Oedipus does not. We watch with dread and fascination the spectacle of a morally good man, committed to the salvation of his city, unwittingly preparing undeserved suffering for himself.

Dramatic monologue A poem written as a speech made by a character at some decisive moment. The speaker is usually addressing a silent listener, as in T. S. Eliot's "The Love Song of J. Alfred Prufrock".

Dramatic poetry Any verse written for the stage, as in the plays of classical Greece, the Renaissance (Shakespeare), and the neoclassical period (Molière, Racine). Also a kind of poetry that presents the voice of an imaginary character (or characters) speaking directly, without additional narration by the author. In poetry, the term usually refers to the dramatic monologue, a lyric poem written as a speech made by a character at some decisive moment, such as Alfred Lord Tennyson's "Ulysses." (*See also* **Dramatic monologue**.)

Dramatic point of view A point of view in which the narrator merely reports dialogue and action with minimal interpretation or access to the characters' minds. The dramatic point of view, as the name implies, uses prose fiction to approximate the method of plays (where readers are provided only with set descriptions, stage directions, and dialogue, and thus must supply motivations based solely on this external evidence).

Dramatic question The primary unresolved issue in a drama as it unfolds. The dramatic question is the result of artful plotting, raising suspense and expectation in a play's action as it moves toward its outcome. Will the Prince in *Hamlet*, for example, achieve what he has been instructed to do and what he intends to do?

Dramatic situation The basic conflict that initiates a work or establishes a scene. It usually describes both a protagonist's motivation and the forces that oppose its realization. (*See also* **Antagonist, Character, Complication, Plot, Rising action**.)

Dynamic character A character who, during the course of the narrative, grows or changes in some significant way.

Editing The act of rereading a draft in order to correct mistakes, cut excess words, and make improvements.

Editorial omniscience When an omniscient narrator goes beyond reporting the thoughts of his or her characters to make a critical judgment or commentary, making explicit the narrator's own thoughts or philosophies.

Editorial point of view Also called **Authorial intrusion**. The effect that occurs when a third-person narrator adds his or her own comments (which presumably represent the ideas and opinions of the author) into the narrative.

End rime Rime that occurs at the ends of lines, rather than within them (as internal rime does). End rime is the most common kind of rime in English-language poetry.

End-stopped line A line of verse that ends in a full pause, usually indicated by a mark of punctuation.

English sonnet Also called **Shakespearean sonnet**. The English sonnet has a rime scheme organized into three quatrains with a final couplet: *abab cdcd efef gg*. The poem may turn—that is, shift in mood or tone—between any of the quatrains (although it usually occurs on the ninth line). (*See also* **Sonnet**.)

Epic A long narrative poem usually composed in an elevated style tracing the adventures of a legendary or mythic hero. Epics are usually written in a consistent form and meter throughout. Famous epics include Homer's *Iliad* and *Odyssey*, Virgil's *Aeneid*, and Milton's *Paradise Lost*.

Epigram A very short poem, often comic, usually ending with some sharp turn of wit or meaning.

Epigraph A brief quotation preceding a story or other literary work. An epigraph usually suggests the subject, theme, or atmosphere the work will explore.

Epiphany A moment of insight, discovery, or revelation by which a character's life is greatly altered. An epiphany generally occurs near the end of a story. The term, which means "showing forth" in Greek, was first used in Christian theology to signify the manifestation of God's presence in the world. This theological idea was first borrowed by James Joyce to refer to a heightened moment of secular revelation.

Essay A short piece of nonfiction prose written in a personal style that focuses on a particular subject. There is no standard length or style for the form. Essays can be serious, comic, visionary, informative, or nostalgic. Their style can range from formal to casual. The freest of all literary forms, essays generally explore a topic without trying to treat it comprehensively.

Ethos *See* **Rhetoric**.

Euphony The harmonious effect when the sounds of the words connect with the meaning in a way pleasing to the ear and mind. An example is found in Tennyson's lines, "The moan of doves in immemorial elms, / And murmuring of innumerable bees." The opposite of euphony is cacophony.

Exact rime A full rime in which the sounds following the initial letters of the words are identical in sound, as in *follow* and *hollow*, *go* and *slow*, *disband* and *this hand*.

Explication Literally, an "unfolding." In an explication an entire poem is explained in detail, addressing every element and unraveling any complexities as a means of analysis.

Exposition The opening portion of a narrative or drama. In the exposition, the scene is set, the protagonist is introduced, and the author discloses any other background information necessary to allow the reader to understand and relate to the events that are to follow.

Expository essay An essay that attempts to explain something in an organized and comprehensible manner. Expository essays are the most straightforward type of nonfiction prose. Their primary aim is to give the reader information in a clear and effective way.

Eye rime Rime in which the spelling of the words appears alike, but the pronunciations differ, as in *laughter* and *daughter*, *idea* and *flea*.

Fable A brief, often humorous narrative told to illustrate a moral. The characters in fables are traditionally animals whose personality traits symbolize human traits. Particular animals have conventionally come to represent specific human qualities or values. For example, the ant represents industry, the fox craftiness, and the lion nobility. A fable often concludes by summarizing its moral message in abstract terms. For example, Aesop's fable "The North Wind and the Sun" concludes with the moral "Persuasion is better than force." (*See also* **Allegory**.)

Fairy tale A traditional form of short narrative folklore, originally transmitted orally, that features supernatural characters such as witches, giants, fairies, or animals with human personality traits. Fairy tales often feature a hero or heroine who seems destined to achieve some desirable fate—such as marrying a prince or princess, becoming wealthy, or destroying an enemy.

Falling action The events in a narrative that follow the climax and bring the story to its conclusion, or dénouement.

Farce A type of comedy featuring exaggerated character types in ludicrous and improbable situations, provoking belly laughs with sexual mix-ups, crude verbal jokes, pratfalls, and knockabout horseplay (like the comic violence of the Punch and Judy show).

Feminist criticism *See* **Gender criticism**.

Fiction From the Latin *ficio*, "act of fashioning, a shaping, a making." Fiction refers to any literary work that—although it might contain factual information—is not bound by factual accuracy, but creates a narrative shaped or made up by the author's imagination. Drama and poetry (especially narrative poetry) can be considered works of fiction, but the term now usually refers more specifically to prose stories and novels. Historical and other factual writing also requires shaping and making, but it is distinct from fiction because it is not free to invent people, places, and events; forays from documented fact must identify themselves as conjecture or hypothesis. Nonfiction, as the name suggests, is a category conventionally separate from fiction. Certainly an essay or work of literary journalism is "a made thing," and writers of nonfiction routinely employ the techniques used by fiction writers (moving forward and backward in time, reporting the inner thoughts of characters, etc.), but works of nonfiction must be not only true but factual. The truth of a work of fiction depends not on facts, but on how convincingly the writer creates the world of the story.

Figure of speech An expression or comparison that relies not on its literal meaning, but rather on its connotations and suggestions. For example, "He's dumber than dirt" is not literally true; it is a figure of speech. Major figures of speech include **metaphor** and **simile**.

First-person narrator Refers to a story in which the narrator is a participant in the action. Such a narrator refers to himself or herself as "I" and may be a major or minor character in the story. His or her attitude and understanding of characters and events shape the reader's perception of the story being told.

Fixed form A traditional verse form requiring certain predetermined elements of structure, for example, a stanza pattern, set meter, or predetermined line length. The sonnet, for instance, must have no more or less than fourteen lines, rimed according to certain conventional patterns. (*See also* **Closed form**.)

Flashback A scene relived in a character's memory. Flashbacks may be related by the narrator in a summary or they may be experienced by the characters themselves. Flashbacks allow the author to include events that occurred before the opening of the story, which may show the reader something significant that happened in the character's past or give an indication of what kind of person the character used to be.

Flat character A term coined by the English novelist E. M. Forster to describe a character with only one outstanding trait. Flat characters are rarely the central characters in a narrative and are often based on **stock characters**. Flat characters stay the same throughout a story. (*See also* **Dynamic character**.)

Folklore The body of traditional wisdom and customs—including songs, stories, myths, and proverbs—of a people as collected and continued through oral tradition.

Folktale A short narrative drawn from folklore that has been passed down through an oral tradition. (*See also* **Fairy tale**, **Legend**.)

Foot The unit of measurement in metrical poetry. Different meters are identified by the pattern and order of stressed and unstressed syllables in their foot, usually containing two or three syllables, with one syllable accented.

Foreshadowing In plot construction, the technique of arranging events and information in such a way that later events are prepared for, or shadowed, beforehand. The author may introduce specific words, images, or actions in order to suggest significant later events. The effective use of foreshadowing by an author may prevent a story's outcome from seeming haphazard or contrived.

Form The means by which a literary work conveys its meaning. Traditionally, form refers to the way in which an artist expresses meaning rather than the content of that meaning, but it is now commonplace to note that form and content are inextricably related. Form, therefore, is more than the external framework of a literary work. It includes the totality of ways in which it unfolds and coheres as a structure of meaning and expression.

Formal English The heightened, impersonal language of educated persons, usually only written, although possibly spoken on dignified occasions. (*See also* **Levels of diction**.)

Formalist criticism A school of criticism which argues that literature may only be discussed on its own terms; that is, without outside influences or information. A key method that formalists use is close reading, a step-by-step analysis of the elements in a text.

Free verse From the French *vers libre*. Free verse describes poetry that organizes its lines without meter. It may be rimed (as in some poems by H.D.), but it usually is not. There is no one means of organizing free verse, and different authors have used irreconcilable systems. What unites the two approaches is a freedom from metrical regularity. (*See also* **Open form**.)

Gender criticism Gender criticism examines how sexual identity influences the creation, interpretation, and evaluation of literary works. This critical approach began with feminist criticism in the 1960s and 1970s which stated that literary study had been so dominated by men that it contained many unexamined "male-produced" assumptions. Feminist criticism sought to address this imbalance in two ways: first, by insisting that sexless interpretation was impossible, and, second, by articulating responses to the texts that were explicitly male or female. More recently, gender criticism has focused on gay and lesbian literary identity as interpretive strategies.

General English The ordinary speech of educated native speakers. Most literate speech and writing is general English. Its diction is more educated than **colloquial English**, yet not as elevated as **formal English**. (*See also* **Levels of diction**.)

Genre A conventional combination of literary form and subject matter, usually aimed at creating certain effects. A genre implies a preexisting understanding between the artist and the reader about the purpose and rules of the work. A horror story, for example, combines the form of the short story with certain conventional subjects, styles, and themes with the expectation of frightening the reader. Major short story genres include science fiction, gothic, horror, and detective tales.

Haiku A Japanese verse form that has three unrimed lines of five, seven, and five syllables. Traditional haiku is often serious and spiritual in tone, relying mostly on imagery, and usually set in one of the four seasons.

Hamartia Greek for "error." An offense committed in ignorance of some material fact (without deliberate criminal intent) and therefore free of blameworthiness. A great mistake unintentionally made as a result of an intellectual error (not vice or criminal wickedness) by a morally good person, usually involving the identity of a blood relation. The *hamartia* of Oedipus, quite simply, is based on his ignorance of his true parentage; inadvertently and unwittingly, then, he commits the *hamartia* of patricide and incest.

Heptameter A verse meter consisting of seven metrical feet, or seven primary stresses, per line.

Hero The central character in a narrative. The term is derived from the Greek epic tradition, in which *heroes* were the leading warriors among the princes. By extension, *hero* and *heroine* have come to mean the principal male and female figures in a narrative or dramatic literary work, although many today call protagonists of either sex *heroes*. When a critic terms the protagonist a *hero*, the choice of words often implies a positive moral assessment of the character. (*See also* **Antihero**.)

Hexameter A verse meter consisting of six metrical feet, or six primary stresses, per line.

High comedy A comic genre evoking so-called intellectual or thoughtful laughter from an audience that remains emotionally detached from the play's depiction of the folly, pretense, and incongruity of human behavior. The French playwright Molière and the English dramatists of the Restoration period developed a special form of high comedy in the **comedy of manners**, focused on the social relations and amorous intrigues of sophisticated upper-class men and women, conducted through witty repartee and verbal combat.

Historical criticism The practice of analyzing a literary work by investigating the social, cultural, and intellectual context that produced it—a context that necessarily includes the artist's biography and milieu. Historical critics strive to recreate the exact meaning and impact a work had on its original audience.

Hubris Overweening pride, outrageous behavior, or the insolence that leads to ruin, hubris was in the Greek moral vocabulary the antithesis of moderation or rectitude. Creon, in Sophocles' *Antigonê*, is a good example of a character brought down by his hubris.

Hyperbole A deliberate exaggeration made in order to emphasize a point. People use hyperbole in everyday conversation, as in the saying, "I'm so hungry I could eat a horse." Hyperbole can be used for comic effect as well as more serious purposes.

Iamb A metrical foot in verse in which an unaccented syllable is followed by an accented one, as in "ca-*ress*" or "a *cat*" ($\smile\prime$). The iambic measure is the most common meter used in English poetry.

Iambic meter A verse meter consisting of a specific recurring number of iambic feet per line. (*See also* **Iamb**, **Iambic pentameter**.)

Iambic pentameter The most common meter in English verse—five iambic feet per line. Many fixed forms, such as the sonnet and heroic couplets, are written in iambic pentameter. Unrimed iambic pentameter is called **blank verse**.

Image A word or series of words that refers to any sensory experience (usually sight, although also sound, smell, touch, or taste). An image is a direct or literal recreation of physical experience; it adds immediacy to literary language.

Imagery The collective set of images in a poem or other literary work.

Impartial omniscience Refers to an omniscient narrator who, although he or she presents the thoughts and actions of the characters, does not judge them or comment on them. (Contrasts with **Editorial omniscience**.)

Implied metaphor A metaphor that uses neither connectives nor the verb *to be*. If we say, "John crowed over his victory," we imply metaphorically that John is a rooster but do not say so specifically. (*See also* **Metaphor**.)

Initial alliteration *See* **Alliteration**.

Initiation story Also called **coming-of-age story**. A narrative in which the main character, usually a child or adolescent, undergoes an important experience or rite of passage—often a difficult or disillusioning one—that prepares him or her for adulthood. James Joyce's "Araby" is a classic example of an initiation story.

In medias res A Latin phrase meaning "in the midst of things" that refers to a narrative device of beginning a story midway in the events it depicts (usually at an exciting or significant moment) before explaining the context or preceding actions. Epic poems such as Virgil's *Aeneid* and John Milton's *Paradise Lost* commonly begin *in medias res*, but the technique is also found in modern fiction.

Innocent narrator Also called **naive narrator**. A character who fails to understand all the implications of the story he or she tells. Of course, virtually any narrator has some degree of innocence or naiveté, but the innocent narrator—often a child or childlike adult—is used by an author trying to generate irony, sympathy, or pity by creating a gap between what the narrator knows and what the reader knows. Mark Twain's Huckleberry Finn—despite his mischievous nature—is an example of an innocent narrator.

Interior monologue An extended presentation of a character's thoughts in a narrative. Usually written in the present tense and printed without quotation marks, an interior monologue reads as if the character were speaking aloud to himself or herself, for the reader to overhear. A famous example of interior monologue comes at the end of *Ulysses* when James Joyce gives us the rambling memories and reflections of Molly Bloom.

Internal alliteration See **Alliteration**.

Internal refrain A refrain that appears within a stanza, generally in a position that stays fixed throughout a poem. (*See also* **Refrain**.)

Internal rime Rime that occurs within a line of poetry, as opposed to **end rime**. Read aloud, these Wallace Stevens lines are rich in internal rime: "Chieftain Iffucan of Azcan in caftan / Of tan with henna hackles, halt!" (from "Bantams in Pine-Woods").

Ironic point of view The perspective of a character or narrator whose voice or position is rich in ironic contradictions. (*See also* **Irony**.)

Irony A literary device in which a discrepancy of meaning is masked beneath the surface of the language. Irony is present when a writer says one thing but means something quite the opposite. There are many kinds of irony, but the two major varieties are **verbal irony** (in which the discrepancy is contained in words) and **situational irony** (in which the discrepancy exists when something is about to happen to a character or characters who expect the opposite outcome). (*See also* **Cosmic irony, Irony of fate, Sarcasm, Verbal irony**.)

Irony of fate A type of situational irony that can be used for either tragic or comic purposes. Irony of fate is the discrepancy between actions and their results, between what characters deserve and what they get, between appearance and reality. In Sophocles's tragedy, for instance, Oedipus unwittingly fulfills the prophecy even as he takes the actions a morally good man would take to avoid it. (*See also* **Cosmic irony**.)

Italian sonnet Also called **Petrarchan sonnet**, a sonnet with the following rime pattern for the first eight lines (the **octave**): *abba, abba*; the final six lines (the **sestet**) may follow any pattern of rimes, as long as it does not end in a couplet. The poem traditionally turns, or shifts in mood or tone, after the octave. (*See also* **Sonnet**.)

Katharsis, **catharsis** Often translated as purgation or purification, the term is drawn from the last element of Aristotle's definition of tragedy, relating to the final cause or purpose of tragic art. Catharsis generally refers to the feeling of emotional release or calm the spectator feels at the end of tragedy. In Aristotle *katharsis* is the final effect of the playwright's skillful use of plotting, character, and poetry to elicit pity and fear from the audience. Through *katharsis*, drama taught the audience compassion for the vulnerabilities of others and schooled it in justice and other civic virtues.

Legend A traditional narrative handed down through popular oral tradition to illustrate and celebrate a remarkable character or an important event, or to explain the unexplainable. Legends, unlike other folktales, claim to be true and usually take place in real locations, often with genuine historical figures.

Levels of diction In English, there are conventionally four basic levels of formality in word choice, or four levels of diction. From the least formal to the most elevated they are **vulgate, colloquial English, general English**, and **formal English**. (*See also* **Diction**.)

Limerick A short and usually comic verse form of five anapestic lines usually riming *aabba*. The first, second, and fifth lines traditionally have three stressed syllables each; the third and fourth have two stresses each (3, 3, 2, 2, 3).

Limited omniscience Also called third-person limited point of view. A type of point of view in which the narrator sees into the minds of some but not all of the characters. Most typically, limited omniscience sees through the eyes of one major or minor character. In limited omniscience, the author can compromise between the immediacy of first-person narration and the flexibility of third person.

Literary fiction Fiction that is written with serious artistic intent and doesn't rely on the conventions or formulas of popular genres (such as romance, horror, mystery, or science fiction).

Literary genre See **Genre**.

Literary theory Literary criticism that tries to formulate general principles rather than discuss specific texts. Theory operates at a high level of abstraction and often focuses on understanding basic issues of language, communication, art, interpretation, culture, and ideological content.

Local color The use of specific regional material—unique customs, dress, habits, and speech patterns of ordinary people—to create atmosphere or realism in a literary work.

Locale The location where a story takes place.

Logos *See* **Rhetoric**.

Low comedy A comic style arousing laughter through jokes, slapstick humor, sight gags, and boisterous clowning. Unlike **high comedy**, it has little intellectual appeal. (*See also* **Comedy**.)

Lyric A short poem expressing the thoughts and feelings of a single speaker. Often written in the first person, lyric poetry traditionally has a song-like immediacy and emotional force.

Melodrama Originally a stage play featuring background music and sometimes songs to underscore the emotional mood of each scene. Melodramas were notoriously weak in characterization and motivation but famously strong on action, suspense, and passion. Melodramatic characters were stereotyped villains, heroes, and young lovers. When the term *melodrama* is applied to fiction, it is almost inevitably a negative criticism implying that the author has sacrificed psychological depth and credibility for emotional excitement and adventurous plotting.

Metaphor A statement that one thing *is* something else, which, in a literal sense, it is not. By asserting that a thing is something else, a metaphor creates a close association between the two entities and usually underscores some important similarity between them. An example of metaphor is "Richard is a doll."

Meter A recurrent, regular, rhythmic pattern in verse. When stresses recur at fixed intervals, the result is meter. Traditionally, meter has been the basic organizational device of world poetry. There are many existing meters, each identified by the different patterns of recurring sounds. In English most common meters involve the arrangement of stressed and unstressed syllables.

Mixed metaphor A metaphor that trips—usually unconsciously—over another metaphor already in the statement. Mixed metaphors are the result of combining two or more incompatible metaphors, resulting in ridiculousness or nonsense. For example, "Mary was such a tower of strength that she breezed her way through all the work" ("towers" do not "breeze").

Monologue An extended speech by a single character. The term originated in drama, where it describes a solo speech that has listeners (as opposed to a **soliloquy**, where the character speaks only to himself or herself). A short story or even a novel can be written in monologue form if it is an unbroken speech by one character to another silent character or characters.

Monometer A verse meter consisting of one metrical foot, or one primary stress, per line.

Monosyllabic Foot A foot, or unit of meter, that contains only one syllable.

Moral A paraphrasable message or lesson implied or directly stated in a literary work. Commonly, a moral is stated at the end of a fable.

Motif An element that recurs significantly throughout a narrative. A motif can be an image, idea, theme, situation, or action (and was first commonly used as a musical term for a recurring melody or melodic fragment). A motif can also refer to an element that recurs across many literary works, such as a beautiful lady in medieval romances who turns out to be an evil fairy or three questions that are asked a protagonist to test his or her wisdom.

Motivation What a character in a story or drama wants. The reasons an author provides for a character's actions. Motivation can be either *explicit* (in which reasons are specifically stated in a story) or *implicit* (in which the reasons are only hinted at or partially revealed).

Myth A traditional narrative of anonymous authorship that arises out of a culture's oral tradition. The characters in traditional myths are usually gods or heroic figures. Myths characteristically explain the origins of things—gods, people, places, plants, animals, and natural events—usually from a cosmic view. A culture's values and belief systems are traditionally passed from generation to generation in myth. In literature, myth may also refer to boldly imagined narratives that embody primal truths about life. Myth is usually differentiated from legend, which has a specific historical base.

Mythological criticism The practice of analyzing a literary work by looking for recurrent universal patterns. Mythological criticism explores the artist's common humanity by tracing how the individual imagination uses myths and symbols that are shared by different cultures and epochs.

Naive narrator *See* **Innocent narrator**.

Narrative essay An essay built around a story, sometimes autobiographical, that draws important insights from the telling. Narrative essays usually both present a story and offer an interpretation of it.

Narrative poem A poem that tells a story. Narrative is one of the traditional modes of poetry, along with lyric and dramatic. Ballads and epics are two common forms of narrative poetry.

Narrator A voice or character that provides the reader with information and insight about the characters and incidents in a narrative. A narrator's perspective and personality can greatly affect how a story is told. (*See also* **Omniscient narrator, Point of view**.)

Nonparticipant narrator A narrator who does not appear in the story as a character but is capable of revealing the thoughts and motives of one or more characters. A nonparticipant narrator is also capable of moving from place to place in order to describe action and report dialogue. (*See also* **Omniscient narrator**.)

Novel An extended work of fictional prose narrative. The term *novel* usually implies a book-length narrative (as compared to more compact forms of prose fiction such as the short story). Because of its extended length, a novel usually has more characters, more varied scenes, and a broader coverage of time than a short story.

Novella In modern terms, a prose narrative longer than a short story but shorter than a novel (approximately 30,000 to 50,000 words). Unlike a short story, a novella is long enough to be published independently as a brief book. Classic modern novellas include Franz Kafka's *The Metamorphosis*, Joseph Conrad's *Heart of Darkness*, and Thomas Mann's *Death in Venice*. During the Renaissance, however, the term *novella* originally referred to short prose narratives such as those found in Giovanni Boccaccio's *Decameron*.

Objective point of view See **Dramatic point of view**.

Observer A type of first-person narrator who is relatively detached from or plays only a minor role in the events described.

Octameter A verse meter consisting of eight metrical feet, or eight primary stresses, per line.

Octave A stanza of eight lines. *Octave* is a term usually used when speaking of sonnets to indicate the first eight-line section of the poem, as distinct from the *sestet* (the final six lines). Some poets also use octaves as separate stanzas, as in W. B. Yeats's "Sailing to Byzantium," which employs the *ottava rima* ("eighth rime") stanza—*abababcc*.

Off rime See **Slant rime**.

Omniscient narrator Also called **all-knowing narrator**. A narrator who has the ability to move freely through the consciousness of any character. The omniscient narrator also has complete knowledge of all of the external events in a story. (See also **Nonparticipant narrator**.)

Onomatopoeia A literary device that attempts to represent a thing or action by a word that imitates the sound associated with it (e.g., *crash, bang, pitter-patter*).

Open dénouement One of the two conventional types of dénouement or resolution. In open dénouement, the author ends a narrative with a few loose ends, or unresolved matters, on which the reader is left to speculate. (See also **Closed dénouement**.)

Open form Verse that has no set formal scheme—no meter, rime, or even set stanzaic pattern. Open form is always in free verse. (See also **Free verse**.)

Oral tradition The tradition within a culture that transmits narratives by word of mouth from one generation to another. Fables, folktales, ballads, and songs are examples of narratives found originally in an oral tradition.

Overstatement Also called **hyperbole**. Exaggeration used to emphasize a point.

Parable A brief, often allegorical narrative that teaches a moral. The parables found in Christian literature, such as "The Parable of the Prodigal Son" (Luke 15:11–32), are classic examples of the form. In parables, unlike fables (where the moral is explicitly stated within the narrative), the moral themes are implicit and can often be interpreted in several ways. Modern parables can be found in the works of Franz Kafka and Jorge Luis Borges.

Paradox A statement that at first strikes one as self-contradictory, but that on reflection reveals some deeper sense. Paradox is often achieved by a play on words.

Parallelism An arrangement of words, phrases, clauses, or sentences side-by-side in a similar grammatical or structural way. Parallelism organizes ideas in a way that demonstrates their coordination to the reader.

Paraphrase The restatement in one's own words of what we understand a literary work to say. A paraphrase is similar to a summary, although not as brief or simple.

Parody A mocking imitation of a literary work or individual author's style, usually for comic effect. A parody typically exaggerates distinctive features of the original for humorous purposes.

Participant narrator A narrator that participates as a character within a story. (See also **First-person narrator**.)

Pathos See **Rhetoric**.

Pentameter A verse meter consisting of five metrical feet, or five primary stresses, per line. In English, the most common form of pentameter is iambic.

Persona Latin for "mask." A fictitious character created by an author to be the speaker of a poem, story, or novel. A persona is always the narrator of the work and not merely a character in it.

Personification A figure of speech in which a thing, an animal, or an abstract term is endowed with human characteristics. Personification allows an author to dramatize the nonhuman world in tangibly human terms.

Petrarchan sonnet See **Italian sonnet**.

Play See **Drama**.

Play review A critical account of a performance, providing the basic facts of the production, a brief summary, and an evaluation (with adequate rationale) of the chief elements of performance, including the acting, the direction, scene and light design, and the script, especially if the play is new or unfamiliar.

Plot The particular arrangement of actions, events, and situations that unfold in a narrative. A plot is not merely the general story of a narrative but the author's artistic pattern made from the parts of the narrative, including the exposition, complications, climax, and dénouement. How an author chooses to construct the plot determines the way the reader experiences the story. Manipulating a plot, therefore, can be the author's most important expressive device when writing a story. More than just a story made up of episodes or a bare synopsis of the temporal order of events, the plotting is the particular embodiment of an action that allows the audience to see the causal relationship between the parts of the action. (*See also* **Climax, Falling action, Rising action**.)

Poetic diction Strictly speaking, poetic diction means any language deemed suitable for verse, but the term generally refers to elevated language intended for poetry rather than common use. Poetic diction often refers to the ornate language used in literary periods such as the Augustan age, when authors employed a highly specialized vocabulary for their verse. (*See also* **Diction**.)

Point of view The perspective from which a story is told. There are many types of point of view, including first-person narrator (a story in which the narrator is a participant in the action) and third-person narrator (a type of narration in which the narrator is a nonparticipant).

Protagonist The central character in a literary work. The protagonist usually initiates the main action of the story, often in conflict with the antagonist. (*See also* **Antagonist**.)

Psychological criticism The practice of analyzing a literary work through investigating three major areas: the nature of literary genius, the psychological study of a particular artist, and the analysis of fictional characters. This methodology uses the analytical tools of psychology and psychoanalysis to understand the underlying motivations and meanings of a literary work.

Pun A play on words in which one word is substituted for another similar or identical sound, but of very different meaning, e.g., Hilaire Belloc's "When I am dead, I hope it may be said: His sins were scarlet, but his books were read." A pun can also play on different meanings of the *same* word, as in Benjamin Franklin's statement at the signing of the Declaration of Independence: "We must all hang together, or assuredly we shall all hang separately."

Quatrain A stanza consisting of four lines. Quatrains are the most common stanzas used in English-language poetry.

Rap A popular style of music that emerged in the 1980s, in which lyrics are spoken or chanted over a steady beat, usually sampled or prerecorded. Rap lyrics are almost always rimed and very rhythmic—syncopating a heavy metrical beat in a manner similar to jazz. Originally an African American form, rap is now international. In that way, rap can be seen as a form of popular poetry.

Reader-response criticism The practice of analyzing a literary work by describing what happens in the reader's mind while interpreting the text. Reader-response critics believe that no literary text exists independently of readers' interpretations and that there is no single fixed interpretation of any literary work.

Repetition Repeating words or phrases to create deliberate effect so as to emphasize an important point. A common form of repetition is to repeat the same words at the beginning of sentences, phrases, paragraphs, or (in verse) lines of poetry. Repetition has always been a central feature of poetry and public speech, since it combines a simple musical effect with a clear emphasis of meaning.

Resolution The final part of a narrative, the concluding action or actions that follow the climax. (*See also* **Conclusion, Dénouement**.)

Rhetoric The art of eloquence and persuasion. As a discipline of study, rhetoric dates back to ancient Greek civilization and was employed in areas ranging from the training of lawyers to the assessment of a politician's moral nature. Since Aristotle, scholars have broken rhetoric up into three parts: **logos**, the logical content of a verbal expression; **ethos**, the character or credibility of the speaker as derived from the words and the speaker's reputation; and **pathos**, the emotional appeal of the words. Because of the power of the latter two—rhetoric often succeeds not by its logic but by its ethical and emotional pull—rhetorical analysis usually concentrates on those aspects of language that are the least based on reasoning, such as anecdotes, logical fallacies, figures of speech, and rhythms. Rhetoricians in ancient times composed manuals of composition for instructing readers in verbal techniques of persuasion.

Rhetorical question A question asked to make a point, not to elicit a reply. The answer to a rhetorical question is usually obvious. For example, "Is the Pope Catholic?" is not a question that invites serious theological discussion. It is another way of saying that the answer to the previous question is obvious. Rhetorical questions are dramatic and disruptive rhetorical devices that are effective, but should not be overused.

Rhythm The pattern of stresses and pauses in a poem. A fixed and recurring rhythm in a poem is called **meter**.

Rime, Rhyme Two or more words that contain an identical or similar vowel sound, usually accented, with following consonant sounds (if any) identical as well: *queue* and *stew, prairie schooner* and *piano tuner*. (*See also* **Consonance, Exact rime**.)

Rime scheme, Rhyme scheme Any recurrent pattern of rime within an individual poem or fixed form. A rime scheme is usually described by using small letters to represent each end rime—*a* for the first rime, *b* for the second, and so on. The rime scheme of a stanza of **common meter** or hymn meter, for example, would be notated as *abab*.

Rising action That part of the play or narrative, including the exposition, in which events start moving toward a climax. In the rising action the protagonist usually faces the complications of the plot to reach his or her goal. In *Hamlet*, the rising action develops the conflict between Hamlet and Claudius, with Hamlet succeeding in controlling the course of events. Because the mainspring of the play's first half is the mystery of Claudius's guilt, the rising action reaches a climax when Hamlet proves the king's guilt by the device of the play within a play (3.2—the "mousetrap" scene), when Hamlet as heroic avenger has positive proof of Claudius's guilt.

Romantic comedy A form of comic drama in which the plot focuses on one or more pairs of young lovers who overcome difficulties to achieve a happy ending (usually marriage). Shakespeare's *A Midsummer Night's Dream* is a classic example of the genre.

Round character A term coined by the English novelist E. M. Forster to describe a complex character who is presented in depth and detail in a narrative. Round characters are those who change significantly during the course of a narrative. Most often, round characters are the central characters in a narrative. (*See also* **Flat character**.)

Run-on line A line of verse that does not end in punctuation, but carries on grammatically to the next line. Such lines are read aloud with only a slight pause at the end. A run-on line is also called *enjambment*.

Sarcasm A conspicuously bitter form of irony in which the ironic statement is designed to hurt or mock its target. (*See also* **Irony**.)

Satiric comedy A genre using derisive humor to ridicule human weakness and folly or to attack political injustices and incompetence. Satiric comedy often focuses on ridiculing characters or killjoys, who resist the festive mood of comedy. Such characters, called humors, are often characterized by one dominant personality trait or ruling obsession.

Scansion A practice used to describe rhythmic patterns in a poem by separating the metrical feet, counting the syllables, marking the accents, and indicating the pauses. Scansion can be very useful in analyzing the sound of a poem and how it should be read aloud.

Scene In drama, the scene is a division of the action in an act of the play. There is no universal convention as to what constitutes a scene, and the practice differs by playwright and period. Usually, a scene represents a single dramatic action that builds to a climax (often ending in the entrance or exit of a major character). In this last sense of a vivid and unified action, the term can be applied to fiction.

Selective omniscience The point of view that sees the events of a narrative through the eyes of a single character. The selectively omniscient narrator is usually a nonparticipant narrator.

Sentimentality A usually pejorative description of the quality of a literary work that tries to convey great emotion but fails to give the reader sufficient grounds for sharing it.

Sestet A poem or stanza of six lines. *Sestet* is a term usually used when speaking of sonnets, to indicate the final six-line section of the poem, as distinct from the octave (the first eight lines). (*See also* **Sonnet**.)

Setting The time and place of a literary work. The setting may also include the climate and even the social, psychological, or spiritual state of the participants.

Shakespearean sonnet *See* **English sonnet**.

Short story A prose narrative too brief to be published as a separate volume—as novellas and novels frequently are. The short story is usually a focused narrative that presents one or two main characters involved in a single compelling action.

Simile A comparison of two things, indicated by some connective, usually *like*, *as*, *than*, or a verb such as *resembles*. A simile usually compares two things that initially seem unlike but are shown to have a significant resemblance. "Cool as a cucumber" and "My love is like a red, red rose" are examples of similes.

Situational irony *See* **Irony**.

Sketch A short, static, descriptive composition. Literary sketches can be either fiction or nonfiction. A sketch usually focuses on describing a person or place without providing a narrative.

Slack syllable An unstressed syllable in a line of verse.

Slant rime A rime in which the final consonant sounds are the same but the vowel sounds are different, as in *letter* and *litter*, *bone* and *bean*. Slant rime may also be called near rhyme, off rhyme, or imperfect rhyme. (*See also* **Consonance**.)

Slapstick comedy A kind of farce, featuring pratfalls, pie throwing, fisticuffs, and other violent action. It takes its name originally from the slapstick carried by the *commedia dell'arte*'s main servant type, Harlequin.

Sociological criticism The practice of analyzing a literary work by examining the cultural, economic, and political context in which it was written or received. Sociological criticism primarily explores the relationship between the artist and society.

Soliloquy In drama, a speech by a character alone onstage in which he or she utters his or her thoughts aloud. The soliloquy is important in drama because it gives the audience insight into a character's inner life, private motivations, and uncertainties.

Sonnet From the Italian *sonnetto*: "little song." A traditional and widely used verse form, especially popular for love poetry. The sonnet is a fixed form of fourteen lines, traditionally written in iambic pentameter, usually made up of an **octave** (the first eight lines) and a concluding **sestet** (six lines). There are, however, several variations, most conspicuously the Shakespearean, or English sonnet, which consists of three quatrains and a concluding couplet. Most sonnets turn, or shift in tone or focus, after the first eight lines, although the placement may vary. (*See also* **English sonnet, Italian sonnet**.)

Stage business Nonverbal action that engages the attention of an audience. Expressing what cannot be said, stage business became a particularly important means of revealing the inner thoughts and feelings of a character in the development of Realism.

Stanza From the Italian, meaning "stopping-place" or "room." A recurring pattern of two or more lines of verse, poetry's equivalent to the paragraph in prose. The stanza is the basic organizational principle of most formal poetry.

Static character *See* **Flat character.**

Stock character A common or stereotypical character that occurs frequently in literature. Examples of stock characters are the mad scientist, the battle-scarred veteran, and the strong-but-silent cowboy. (*See also* **Archetype**.)

Stream of consciousness Not a specific technique, but a type of modern narration that uses various literary devices, especially interior monologue, in an attempt to duplicate the subjective and associative nature of human consciousness. Stream of consciousness often focuses on imagistic perception in order to capture the preverbal level of consciousness.

Stress An emphasis or accent placed on a syllable in speech. Clear pronunciation of polysyllabic words almost always depends on correct placement of their stress. (For instance, *de*-sert and de-*sert* are two different words and parts of speech, depending on their stress.) Stress is the basic principle of most English-language meter.

Style All the distinctive ways in which an author, genre, movement, or historical period uses language to create a literary work. An author's style depends on his or her characteristic use of diction, imagery, tone, syntax, and figurative language. Even sentence structure and punctuation can play a role in an author's style.

Subject The main topic of a poem, story, or play.

Subplot *See* **Double plot.**

Summary A brief condensation of the main idea or plot of a literary work. A summary is similar to a paraphrase, but less detailed.

Suspense Enjoyable anxiety created in the reader by the author's handling of plot. When the outcome of events is unclear, the author's suspension of resolution intensifies the reader's interest, particularly if the plot involves characters to whom the reader or audience is sympathetic. Suspense is also created when the fate of a character is clear to the audience, but not to the character. The suspense results from the audience's anticipation of how and when the character will meet his or her inevitable fate.

Symbol A person, place, or thing in a narrative that suggests meanings beyond its literal sense. Symbol is related to allegory, but it works more complexly. In an allegory an object has a single additional significance. By contrast, a symbol usually contains multiple meanings and associations. In Herman Melville's *Moby-Dick*, for example, the great white whale does not have just a single significance but accrues powerful associations as the narrative progresses.

Symbolic act An action whose significance goes well beyond its literal meaning. In literature, symbolic acts usually involve some conscious or unconscious ritual element like rebirth, purification, forgiveness, vengeance, or initiation.

Symbolic characters Characters, usually minor figures, who make brief but significant appearances to convey symbolic meaning in the work. Symbolic characters are not well rounded or fully known, but seen fleetingly, and they usually remain quite mysterious.

Synopsis A brief summary or outline of a story or dramatic work.

Tactile imagery A word or sequence of words that refers to the sense of touch. (*See also* **Imagery**.)

Tale A short narrative without a complex plot, the word originating from the Old English *talu*, or "speech." Tales are an ancient form of narrative found in folklore, and traditional tales often contain supernatural elements. A tale differs from a short story by its tendency toward less developed characters and linear plotting.

Tall tale A humorous short narrative that provides a wildly exaggerated version of events. Originally an oral form, the tall tale assumes that its audience knows the narrator is distorting the events. The form is often associated with the American frontier.

Tercet A group of three lines of verse, usually all ending in the same rime. (*See also* **Terza rima**.)

Terza rima A verse form made up of three-line stanzas that are connected by an overlapping rime scheme (*aba, bcb, cdc, ded*, etc.). Dante employs *terza rima* in *The Divine Comedy*.

Tetrameter A verse meter consisting of four metrical feet, or four primary stresses, per line.

Theme A generally recurring subject or idea conspicuously evident in a literary work. A short didactic work such as a fable may have a single obvious theme, but longer works can contain multiple themes. Not all subjects in a work can be considered themes, only the central subject or subjects.

Thesis sentence A summing up of the one main idea or argument that an essay or critical paper will embody.

Third-person narrator A type of narration in which the narrator is a nonparticipant. In a third-person narrative the characters are referred to as "he," "she," or "they." Third-person narrators are most commonly omniscient, but the level of their knowledge may vary from total omniscience (the narrator knows everything about the characters and their lives) to limited omniscience (the narrator is limited to the perceptions of a single character).

Tone The attitude toward a subject conveyed in a literary work. No single stylistic device creates tone; it is the net result of the various elements an author brings to creating the work's feeling and manner. Tone may be playful, sarcastic, ironic, sad, solemn, or any other possible attitude. A writer's tone plays an important role in establishing the reader's relationship to the characters or ideas presented in a literary work.

Total omniscience A type of point of view in which the narrator knows everything about all of the characters and events in a story. A narrator with total omniscience can also move freely from one character to another. Generally, a totally omniscient narrative is written in the third person.

Tragedy The representation of serious and important actions that lead to a disastrous end for the protagonist. The final purpose of tragedy in Aristotle's formulation is to evoke **katharsis** by means of events involving pity and fear. A unified tragic action, from beginning to end, brings a morally good but not perfect tragic hero from happiness to unhappiness because of a mistaken act, to which he or she is led by **hamartia**, an error in judgment. Tragic heroes move us to pity because their misfortunes are greater than they deserve, because they are not evil, having committed the fateful deed or deeds unwittingly and involuntarily. They also move us to fear, because we recognize in ourselves similar possibilities of error. We share with the tragic hero a common world of mischance. (*See also* **Tragic flaw**.)

Tragic flaw A fatal weakness or moral flaw in the protagonist that brings him or her to a bad end. Sometimes offered as an alternative translation of **hamartia**, in contrast to the idea that the tragic hero's catastrophe is caused by an error in judgment, the idea of a protagonist's being ruined by a tragic flaw makes more sense in relation to the Greek idea of **hubris**, commonly translated as "outrageous behavior," involving deliberate transgressions against moral or divine law.

Tragic hero Generally a person of power and position (e.g. a king, queen, or prince) who is the protagonist of a tragedy. The tragic hero falls from power and happiness, usually because of some **tragic flaw**. Although doomed, the tragic hero valiantly struggles against his or her fate and eloquently expresses insights into the dark side of the human condition. (*See also* **Tragic flaw**.)

Tragic irony A form of **dramatic irony** that ultimately arrives at some tragedy.

Tragicomedy A type of drama that combines elements of both tragedy and comedy. Usually, it creates potentially tragic situations that bring the protagonists to the brink of disaster but then ends happily. Tragicomedy can be traced as far back as the Renaissance (in plays like Shakespeare's *Measure for Measure*), but it also refers to modern plays such as Chekhov's *Cherry Orchard* and Beckett's *Waiting for Godot*.

Trimeter A verse meter consisting of three metrical feet, or three primary stresses, per line.

Trochaic, trochee A metrical foot in which a stressed syllable is followed by an unstressed syllable (′ ˘) as in the words *sum*-mer and *chor*-us. The trochaic meter is often associated with songs, chants, and magic spells in English.

Understatement An ironic figure of speech that deliberately describes something in a way that is less than the true case.

Unities The three formal qualities recommended by Italian Renaissance literary critics to unify a plot in order to give it a cohesive and complete integrity. Traditionally, good plots honored the three unities—of action, time, and place. The action in neoclassical drama, therefore, was patterned by cause and effect to occur within a 24-hour period. The setting took place in one unchanging locale. In the *Poetics*, Aristotle urged only the requirement of unity of plot, with events patterned in a cause-and-effect relationship from beginning through middle to the end of the single action imitated.

Unreliable narrator A narrator who—intentionally or unintentionally—relates events in a subjective or distorted manner. The author usually provides some indication early on in such stories that the narrator is not to be completely trusted.

Verbal irony A statement in which the speaker or writer says the opposite of what is really meant. For example, a friend might comment, "How graceful you are!" after you trip clumsily on a stair.

Verse From the Latin *versum*, "to turn." Verse has two major meanings. First, it refers to any single line of poetry. Second, it refers to any composition in lines of more or less regular rhythm—in contrast to prose.

Vers libre *See* **Free verse**.

Visual imagery A word or sequence of words that refers to the sense of sight or presents something one may see.

Voice Voice can refer either to the person (or personality) narrating a literary work or to the characteristic and identifiable style of an author. In either case, it describes the recognizable personal quality of the voice speaking to the reader. Voice is a crucial element of literary style. A credible and compelling voice can make a story, poem, or essay seem real and immediate. An awkward or unconvincing voice can leave the reader doubtful about the work's insights and reliability.

Vulgate From the Latin word *vulgus*, "mob" or "common people." The lowest level of formality in language, vulgate is the diction of the common people with no pretensions to refinement or elevation. The vulgate is not necessarily vulgar in the sense of containing foul or inappropriate language; it refers simply to unschooled, everyday language.

CREDITS

Literary

Achebe, Chinua: "Dead Man's Path" from GIRLS AT WAR by Chinua Achebe. Copyright © 1953, 1972 by Chinua Achebe, used by permission of The Wylie Agency LLC. Copyright © 1972, 1973 by Chinua Achebe, from GIRLS AT WAR AND OTHER STORIES by Chinua Achebe. Used by permission of Doubleday, a division of Random House, Inc.

Addonizio, Kim: "First Poem for You" from THE PHILOSOPHER'S CLUB by Kim Addonizio. Copyright © 1994 by Kim Addonizio. Reprinted by permission of the author.

Alarcón, Francisco: "The X in My Name" from NO GOLDEN GATE FOR US by Francisco X. Alarcón. Copyright © 1993 by Francisco X. Alarcón. Reprinted by permission of Pennywhistle Press.

Alexie, Sherman: "This Is What It Means to Say Phoenix, Arizona" from THE LONE RANGER AND TONTO FISTFIGHT IN HEAVEN, copyright © 1993 by Sherman Alexie. Used with permission of Grove/Atlantic, Inc.

Alvarez, Julia: "By Accident" from THE WOMAN I KEPT TO MYSELF. Copyright © 2004 by Julia Alvarez. Published by Algonquin Books of Chapel Hill in 2004. First published in A POEM OF HER OWN: VOICES OF AMERICAN WOMEN YESTERDAY AND TODAY (Harry N. Abrams, 2003). By permission of Susan Bergholz Literary Services, New York, NY and Lamy, NM. All rights reserved.

Apple, Max: "Vegetable Love," from THE ORANGING OF AMERICA by Max Apple, copyright © 1974, 1975, 1976 by Max Apple. Used by permission of Viking Penguin, a division of Penguin Group (USA) Inc.

Atwood, Margaret: "Happy Endings" from GOOD BONES AND SIMPLE MURDERS © 1983, 1992, 1994 by O.W.Toad Ltd. Published by McClelland & Stewart. Used with permission of the author and publisher. All rights reserved. Published in the U.S. as a Nan A. Talese book. Used with permission of Doubleday, a division of Random House, Inc.

Atwood, Margaret: "Siren Song" from SELECTED POEMS, 1965-1975 by Margaret Atwood. Copyright © 1976 by Margaret Atwood Reprinted by permission of Houghton Mifflin Harcourt Publishing Company. All rights reserved.

Atwood, Margaret: From Atwood, Margaret. "You are Happy" from SELECTED POEMS 1966-1984. Copyright © Oxford University Press Canada 1990. Reprinted by permission of the publisher.

Auden, W.H.: "Funeral Blues," copyright 1940 and renewed 1968 by W. H. Auden, "The Unknown Citizen," copyright 1940 and renewed 1968 by W. H. Auden, from COLLECTED POEMS OF W. H. AUDEN by W. H. Auden. Used by permission of Random House, Inc.

Auden, W.H.: "The Joker in the Pack," copyright © 1960 by W.H. Auden and renewed 1988 by The Estate of W.H. Auden, from THE DYER'S HAND AND OTHER ESSAYS by W.H. Auden. Used by permission of Random House, Inc.

Baldwin, James: "Notes of a Native Son" from NOTES OF A NATIVE SON by James Baldwin. Copyright © 1955, renewed 1983, by James Baldwin. Reprinted by permission of Beacon Press, Boston.

Baldwin, James: "Sonny's Blues" © 1957 by James Baldwin was originally published in PARTISAN REVIEW. Copyright renewed. Collected in GOING TO MEET THE MAN published by Vintage Books. Reprinted with the permission of the James Baldwin Estate.

Barthes, Roland: "The Death of the Author" from IMAGE/MUSIC/TEXT by Roland Barthes, translated by Stephen Heath. English translation copyright © 1977 by Stephen Heath. Reprinted by permission of Farrar, Straus and Giroux, LLC.

Bein, Myrna E.: "A Journey Taken with My Son" by Myrna E. Bein. Reprinted by permission of the author.

Bishop, Elizabeth: "One Art" and "The Fish" from THE COMPLETE POEMS 1927-1979 by Elizabeth Bishop. Copyright © 1979, 1983 by Alice Helen Methfessel. Reprinted by permission of Farrar, Straus and Giroux, LLC.

Bisson, Terry: "Bears Discover Fire" by Terry Bisson. Copyright © by Terry Bisson. Reproduced by permission of the author.

Bodkin, Maud: "Lucifer in Shakespeare's 'Othello'" by Maud Bodkin, from ARCHETYPAL PATTERNS IN POETRY. Copyright © 1934. By permission of Oxford University Press.

Boyle, T. Coraghessan: "Greasy Lake," from GREASY LAKE AND OTHER STORIES by T. Coraghessan Boyle, copyright © 1979, 1981, 1982, 1983, 1984, 1985 by T. Coraghessan Boyle. Used by permission of Viking Penguin, a division of Penguin Group (USA) Inc.

1433

Bozorth, Richard R.: "Tell Me the Truth About Love" from AUDEN'S GAMES OF KNOWLEDGE: POETRY AND THE MEANINGS OF HOMOSEXUALITY by Richard R. Bozorth. Copyright © 2001 Columbia University Press. Reprinted with permission of the publisher.

Brooks, Gwendolyn: "Sadie and Maud" from A STREET IN BRONZEVILLE by Gwendolyn Brooks, published by Harper and Row. Copyright © 1945. Reprinted By Consent of Brooks Permissions.

Brooks, Gwendolyn: "Speech to the Young. Speech to the Progress-Toward" from BLACKS by Gwendolyn Brooks. Copyright © 1991 by Gwendolyn Brooks Blakely. Reprinted By Consent of Brooks Permissions.

Brooks, Gwendolyn: "The Bean Eaters" from SELECTED POEMS by Gwendolyn Brooks. Copyright © 1944, 1945, 1949, 1959, 1960, 1963 by Gwendolyn Brooks Blakely. Reprinted By Consent of Brooks Permissions.

Brooks, Gwendolyn: "the mother," "We Real Cool," and "the rites for Cousin Vit" from BLACKS by Gwendolyn Brooks. Copyright © 1987 by Gwendolyn Brooks Blakely. Reprinted By Consent of Brooks Permissions.

Bukowski, Charles: "Dostoevsky" from BONE PALACE BALLET by Charles Bukowski. Copyright © 1997 by Linda Lee Bukowski. Reprinted by permission of HarperCollins Publishers.

Bukowski, Charles: "my old man" from LOVE IS A DOG FROM HELL: POEMS 1974-1977 by Charles Bukowski. Copyright © 1977 by Charles Bukowski. Reprinted by permission of HarperCollins Publishers.

Burgess, Anthony: "An Asian Culture Looks at Shakespeare" excerpted from remarks on the "Importance of Translation" at a June 4, 1982 conference, as published in the Columbia University journal TRANSLATION. Copyright © 1982 by the Estate of Anthony Burgess. Reprinted by permission of Artellus, Ltd. (UK).

Buson, Taniguchi: "Moonrise on mudflats" translation by Michael Stillman. Copyright © 2009 by Michael Stillman. Reprinted with permission of the author.

Campo, Rafael: "For J.W." is reprinted with permission from the publisher of THE OTHER MAN WAS ME: A VOYAGE TO THE NEW WORLD by Rafael Campo (©1994 Arte Publico Press - University of Houston).

Carver, Raymond: "Cathedral" from CATHEDRAL by Raymond Carver, copyright © 1981, 1982, 1983 by Raymond Carver. Used by permission of Alfred A. Knopf, a division of Random House, Inc.

Carver, Raymond: "My Father's Life" from FIRES by Raymond Carver. Copyright © "My Father's Life" from FIRES by Raymond Carver, originally published in ESQUIRE. Copyright © 1968, 1969, 1970. 1971, 1972, 1973, 1974, 1975, 1976, 1977, 1978, 1979, 1980, 1981, 1982, 1983 by Raymond Carver. Copyright © 1983, 1984 by the Estate of Raymond Carver used by permission of The Wylie Agency LLC.

Chabon, Michael: "The Little Knife" by Michael Chabon, from A MODEL WORLD. Copyright © 1991 by Michael Chabon. Reprinted by permission of HarperCollins Publishers.

Cheever, John: "The Swimmer" from THE STORIES OF JOHN CHEEVER by John Cheever, copyright © 1978 by John Cheever. Used by permission of Alfred A. Knopf, a division of Random House, Inc.

Christian, Barbara T.: " 'Everyday Use' and the Black Power Movement" excerpted from Christian, Barbara T., ed. EVERYDAY USE: ALICE WALKER. Copyright © 1994 by Rutgers, the State University. Reprinted by permission of Rutgers University Press.

Clark, Michael: "James Baldwin's 'Sonny's Blues': Childhood Light and Art" by Michael Clark, from CLA JOURNAL 29.2, December 1985, pp. 197–205. Copyright © 1989 by the College Language Association. Reprinted by permission of the College Language Association.

Cofer, Judith Ortiz: "Quinceañera" is reprinted with permission from the publisher of TERMS OF SURVIVAL by Judith Ortiz Cofer (©1987 Arte Publico Press - University of Houston).

Cofer, Judith Ortiz: "I Fell in Love, or My Hormones Awakened" is reprinted with permission from the publisher of SILENT DANCING: A PARTIAL REMEMBRANCE OF A PUERTO RICAN CHILDHOOD by Judith Ortiz Cofer (©1990 Arte Publico Press - University of Houston).

Cope, Wendy: "Lonely Hearts" from MAKING COCOA FOR KINGSLEY AMIS by Wendy Cope. Copyright © 1986 by Wendy Cope. Reprinted by permission of United Agents on behalf of Wendy Cope.

Cullen, Countee: "Incident" from MY SOUL'S HIGH SONG by Countee Cullen. Copyrights held by Amistad Research Center, Tulane University. Administered by Thompson and Thompson, Brooklyn, NY.

Cummings, E.E.: "Buffalo Bill 's." Copyright 1923, 1951, © 1991 by the Trustees for the E. E. Cummings Trust. Copyright © 1976 by George James Firmage, "in Just-." Copyright 1923, 1951, © 1991 by the Trustees for the E. E. Cummings Trust. Copyright © 1976 by George James Firmage, "somewhere i have never travelled,gladly beyond." Copyright 1931, © 1959, 1991 by the Trustees for the E. E. Cummings Trust. Copyright 1931, © 1959, 1991 by the Trustees for the E. E. Cummings Trust. Copyright © 1979 by George James Firmage, "anyone lived in a pretty how town." Copyright 1940, © 1968, 1991 by the Trustees for the E. E. Cummings Trust, from COMPLETE POEMS: 1904-1962 by E. E. Cummings, edited by George J. Firmage. Used by permission of Liveright Publishing Corporation.

Daly, Brenda O.: "An Unfilmable Conclusion: Joyce Carol Oates at the Movies" by Brenda O. Daly, from JOURNAL OF POPULAR CULTURE, Volume 23(3), Winter 1989. Copyright © 1989 by John Wiley and Sons. Reprinted with permission.

Dickinson, Emily: Reprinted by permission of the publishers and the Trustees of Amherst College from THE POEMS OF EMILY DICKINSON, Thomas H. Johnson, ed., pp. xi, xviii, xix, xxxix, Cambridge, Mass.: The Belknap Press of Harvard University Press, Copyright © 1951, 1955, 1979, 1983 by the President and Fellows of Harvard College.

Didion, Joan: "On Morality" from SLOUCHING TOWARDS BETHLEHEM by Joan Didion. Copyright © 1966, 1968, renewed 1996 by Joan Didion. Reprinted by permission of Farrar, Straus and Giroux, LLC.

Dillard, Annie: Excerpt from AN AMERICAN CHILDHOOD by Annie Dillard. Copyright © 1987 by Annie Dillard. Reprinted by permission of HarperCollins Publishers.

Dove, Rita and Marilyn Nelson. "The Voices in Langston Hughes" excerpted from "A Black Rainbow: Modern Afro-American Poetry" from POETRY AFTER MODERNISM, edited by Robert McDowell. Reprinted by permission of the publisher.

Dubus, Andre: "A Father's Story" from THE TIMES ARE NEVER SO BAD by Andre Dubus. Reprinted by permission of David R. Godine, Publisher, Inc. Copyright © 1983 by Andre Dubus.

Eberhart, Richard: "The Fury of Aerial Bombardment" from COLLECTED POEMS 1930-1976 by Richard Eberhart. Copyright © 1976 by Richard Eberhart. Used by permission of Oxford University Press, Inc.

Erdrich, Louise: "The Red Convertible," from the book LOVE MEDICINE, New and Revised by Louise Erdrich. Copyright © 1984, 1993 by Louise Erdrich. Reprinted by permission of Henry Holt and Company, LLC.

Espaillat, Rhina P.: "Bilingual / *Bilingüe*" from WHERE HORIZONS GO by Rhina P. Espaillat, published by Truman State University Press. Copyright © 1998. Reprinted by permission of the author.

Espaillat, Rhina: "Bodega" from LAPSING TO GRACE: POEMS AND DRAWINGS by Rhina Espaillat. Copyright © 1992 by Rhina Espaillat. Reprinted by permission of the author.

Evans, Abbie Huston: "Wing-Spread" from COLLECTED POEMS, by Abbie Huston Evans, © 1950, 1952, 1953, 1956, 1960, 1961, 1966, 1970. Reprinted by permission of the University of Pittsburgh Press.

Faulkner, William: "A Rose for Emily," copyright 1930 and renewed 1958 by William Faulkner, "Barn Burning," copyright 1950 by Random House, Inc. Copyright renewed 1977 by Jill Faulkner Summers, from COLLECTED STORIES OF WILLIAM FAULKNER by William Faulkner. Used by permission of Random House, Inc.

Fish, Stanley: Reprinted by permission of the publisher from IS THERE A TEXT IN THIS CLASS? : THE AUTHORITY OF INTERPRETIVE COMMUNITIES by Stanley Fish, pp. 345–347, Cambridge, Mass.: Harvard University Press, Copyright © 1980 by the President and Fellows of Harvard College.

Frost, Robert: "Acquainted with the Night," "Desert Places," "Design," "Fire and Ice," and "Stopping by Woods on a Snowy Evening" all from THE POETRY OF ROBERT FROST edited by Edward Connery Lathem. Copyright © 1923, 1928, 1969 by Henry Holt and Company, copyright © 1936, 1942, 1951, 1956 by Robert Frost, copyright © 1964, 1970 by Lesley Frost Ballantine. Reprinted by arrangement with Henry Holt and Company, LLC.

Gilbert, Sandra M. and Susan Gubar: "Editors' Introduction to Emily Dickinson," from THE NORTON ANTHOLOGY OF LITERATURE BY WOMEN: THE TRADITION IN ENGLISH by Sandra M. Gilbert and Susan Gubar. Copyright © 1985 by Sandra M. Gilbert and Susan Gubar. Used by permission of W. W. Norton & Company, Inc.

Ginsberg, Allen: All lines from "A Supermarket in California" from COLLECTED POEMS 1947–1980 by Allen Ginsberg. Copyright © 1955 by Allen Ginsberg. Reprinted by permission of HarperCollins Publishers.

Gioia, Dana: Dana Gioia, "California Hills in August" from DAILY HOROSCOPE. Copyright © 1986 by Dana Gioia. Reprinted with the permission of The Permissions Company, Inc. on behalf of Graywolf Press, Minneapolis, Minnesota, www.graywolfpress.org.

Gwynn, R. S.: "Body Bags" from NO WORD OF FAREWELL: POEMS 1970-2000 by R. S. Gwynn. Copyright © 2001 by R. S. Gwynn. Reprinted by permission of the author.

Hansberry, Lorraine: From A RAISIN IN THE SUN by Lorraine Hansberry, copyright © 1958 by Robert Nemiroff, as an unpublished work. Copyright © 1959, 1966, 1984 by Robert Nemiroff. Copyright renewed 1986, 1987 by Robert Nemiroff. Used by permission of Random House, Inc.

Hayden, Robert: "Those Winter Sundays." Copyright © 1966 by Robert Hayden, "The Whipping." Copyright © 1966 by Robert Hayden, from COLLECTED POEMS OF ROBERT HAYDEN by Robert Hayden, edited by Frederick Glaysher. Used by permission of Liveright Publishing Corporation.

Heaney, Seamus: "Digging" from OPENED GROUND: SELECTED POEMS 1966-1996 by Seamus Heaney. Copyright © 1998 by Seamus Heaney. Reprinted by permission of Farrar,

1436 Credits

Straus and Giroux, LLC and Faber and Faber Limited.

Hemingway, Ernest: "A Clean, Well-Lighted Place" reprinted with the permission of Scribner, a Division of Simon & Schuster, Inc., from THE SHORT STORIES OF ERNEST HEMINGWAY by Ernest Hemingway. Copyright © 1933 by Charles Scribner's Sons. Copyright renewed 1961 by Mary Hemingway. All rights reserved.

Hoffman, Daniel: "The Father-Figure in 'The Tell-Tale Heart'" from POE POE POE POE POE POE POE, © 1992 by Daniel Hoffman, repr. 1998 Louisiana State University Press. Reprinted by permission of the author.

hooks, bell: "Earthbound: On Solid Ground" from BELONGING: A CULTURE OF PLACE by bell hooks. Copyright © 2009. Reproduced by permission of Taylor & Francis Group LLC; permission conveyed through Copyright Clearance Center, Inc.

Hughes, Langston: "Dream Boogie," "Harlem (2)," "I, Too," "Theme for English B" from THE COLLECTED POEMS OF LANGSTON HUGHES by Langston Hughes, edited by Arnold Rampersad with David Roessel, Associate Editor, copyright © 1994 by the Estate of Langston Hughes. Used by permission of Alfred A. Knopf, a division of Random House, Inc.

Hughes, Langston: "The Harlem Renaissance" from THE BIG SEA by Langston Hughes. Copyright © 1940 by Langston Hughes. Copyright renewed 1968 by Arna Bontemps and George Houston Bass. Reprinted by permission of Hill and Wang, a division of Farrar, Straus and Giroux, LLC.

Hughes, Langston: "The Negro Artist and the Racial Mountain" by Langston Hughes. Reprinted by permission of Harold Ober Associates Incorporated. First published in THE NATION. Copyright © 1926 by Langston Hughes.

Ibsen, Henrik: "A Doll's House," translated by R. Farquharson Sharp and Eleanor Marx-Aveling, revised 2008 by Viktoria Michelsen. Copyright © 2008 by Viktoria Michelsen. Reprinted by permission.

Issa, Kobayashi: Kobayashi Issa's "only one guy" is reprinted from ONE MAN'S MOON, POEMS FROM BASHO & OTHER JAPANESE POETS published by Gnomon Press. Copyright © 1984. Used with permission.

Ives, David: "Sure Thing" copyright © 1989, 1990, 1992 by David Ives, from ALL IN THE TIMING: FOURTEEN PLAYS by David Ives. Used by permission of Vintage Books, a division of Random House, Inc.

Ives, Mike: "Would Hemingway Cry?" by Mike Ives. From the NEW YORK TIMES, October 3, 2010 © 2010 The New York Times. All rights reserved. Used by permission and protected by the Copyright Laws of the United States. The printing, copying, redistribution, or retransmission of this Content without express written permission is prohibited.

Jackson, Shirley: "The Lottery" from THE LOTTERY by Shirley Jackson. Copyright © 1948, 1949 by Shirley Jackson. Copyright renewed 1976, 1977 by Laurence Hyman, Barry Hyman, Mrs. Sarah Webster and Mrs. Joanne Schnurer. Reprinted by permission of Farrar, Straus and Giroux, LLC.

Jeffers, Robinson: "Rock and Hawk," copyright 1934 and renewed 1962 by Donnan Jeffers and Garth Jeffers, from SELECTED POETRY OF ROBINSON JEFFERS by Robinson Jeffers. Used by permission of Random House, Inc.

Jin, Ha: "Saboteur," from THE BRIDEGROOM by Ha Jin, copyright © 2000 by Ha Jin. Used by permission of Pantheon Books, a division of Random House, Inc.

Justice, Donald: "Men at Forty," from COLLECTED POEMS OF DONALD JUSTICE by Donald Justice, copyright © 2004 by Donald Justice. Used by permission of Alfred A. Knopf, a division of Random House, Inc.

Kafka, Franz: "The Metamorphosis" by Franz Kafka, translated by John Siscoe. Reprinted by permission of the author.

Kelly, Ryan: "A Quick Look at Who is Fighting This War; This Is Not a Game" from LETTERS TO MY MOTHER FROM IRAQ by Ryan Kelly. Copyright © by Ryan Kelly. Reprinted by permission of the author.

King, Martin Luther, Jr.: "Letter from Birmingham Jail" reprinted by arrangement with The Heirs to the Estate of Martin Luther King Jr., c/o Writers House as agent for the proprietor New York, NY. Copyright 1963 Dr. Martin Luther King Jr; copyright renewed 1991 Coretta Scott King.

Kingston, Maxine Hong: "No Name Woman" from THE WOMAN WARRIOR, by Maxine Hong Kingston, copyright © 1975, 1976 by Maxine Hong Kingston. Used by permission of Alfred A. Knopf, a division of Random House, Inc.

Komunyakaa, Yusef: "Facing It" from PLEASURE DOME by Yusef Komunyakaa (Wesleyan University Press 2001). © 2001 by Yusef Komunyakaa and reprinted by permission of Wesleyan University Press.

Kooser, Ted: "So This Is Nebraska" from SURE SIGNS: NEW AND SELECTED POEMS, by Ted Kooser, © 1980. Reprinted by permission of the University of Pittsburgh Press.

Kübler-Ross, Elisabeth: Reprinted with the permission of Scribner, a Division of Simon & Schuster, Inc., from ON DEATH AND DYING by Elisabeth Kübler-Ross. Copyright © 1969 by Elisabeth Kübler-Ross; copyright renewed © 1997 by Elisabeth Kubler-Ross. All rights reserved.

Lahiri, Jhumpa: "Interpreter of Maladies" from INTERPRETER OF MALADIES by Jhumpa Lahiri. Copyright © 1999 by Jhumpa Lahiri. Reprinted by permission of Houghton Mifflin

Harcourt Publishing Company. All rights reserved.

Le Guin, Ursula K.: "The Ones Who Walk Away from Omelas" by Ursula K. Le Guin. Copyright © 1973, 2001 by Ursula K. Le Guin; first appeared in NEW DIMENSIONS 3; from the author's collection, THE WIND'S TWELVE QUARTERS; reprinted by permission of the author and the author's agents, the Virginia Kidd Agency, Inc.

Le Guin, Ursula K.: "She Unnames Them" by Ursula K. Le Guin. Copyright © 1985 by Ursula K. Le Guin; first appeared in THE NEW YORKER; from the author's own collection, BUFFALO GALS AND OTHER ANIMAL PRESENCES; reprinted by permission of the author and the author's agents, the Virginia Kidd Agency, Inc.

Leavitt, David: "A Place I've Never Been," copyright © 2003 by David Leavitt. From: COLLECTED STORIES by David Leavitt. Reprinted with permission from Bloomsbury USA.

Lee, Li-Young: Li-Young Lee, "The Gift" from ROSE. Copyright © 1986 by Li-Young Lee. Reprinted with the permission of The Permissions Company, Inc. on behalf of BOA Editions Ltd., www.boaeditions.org.

Levertov, Denise: "The Ache of Marriage" from POEMS 1960-1967, copyright © 1964 by Denise Levertov. Reprinted by permission of New Directions Publishing Corp.

Levertov, Denise: "Making Peace" from BREATHING THE WATER, copyright © 1987 by Denise Levertov. Reprinted by permission of New Directions Publishing Corp.

Levin, Phyllis: "Brief Bio" from THE AFTERIMAGE by Phyllis Levin. Reprinted by permission of Copper Beech Press.

Lim, Shirley Geok-lin: Shirley Geok-lin Lim, "Learning to love America" from WHAT THE FORTUNE TELLER DIDN'T SAY. Copyright © 1998 by Shirley Geok-lin Lim. Reprinted with the permission of The Permissions Company, Inc., on behalf of West End Press, Albuquerque, New Mexico, www.westendpress.org.

Maugham, W. Somerset: "The Appointment in Samarra," from SHEPPEY by W. Somerset Maugham, copyright © 1933 by W. Somerset Maugham. Used by permission of A P Watt Ltd on behalf of The Royal Literary Fund and by permission of Doubleday, a division of Random House, Inc.

Maupassant, Guy de: "Mother Savage" by Guy de Maupassant, translated by Lafcadio Hearn, as appeared in LONGMAN ANTHOLOGY OF SHORT FICTION, Edited by Dana Gioia, R. S. Gwynn. Copyright © 2001. Reprinted by permission of the editor.

McClane, Kenneth: "Sonny's Blues Saved My Life" by Kenneth McClane, from YOU'VE GOT TO READ THIS: CONTEMPORARY AMERICAN WRITERS INTRODUCE STORIES THAT HELD THEM IN AWE, Edited by Ron Hansen and Jim Shepard. Copyright © 1994. Reprinted by permission of the author.

McNally, Terence: "ANDRE'S MOTHER" Copyright © 1995 by Terrence McNally. All rights reserved. CAUTION: Professionals and amateurs are hereby warned that "Andre's Mother" is subject to a royalty. It is fully protected under the copyright laws of the United States of America and of all countries covered by the International Copyright Union (including the Dominion of Canada and the rest of the British Commonwealth), the Berne Convention, the Pan-American Copyright Convention and the Universal Copyright Convention as well as all countries with which the United States has reciprocal copyright relations. All rights, including professional/amateur stage rights, motion picture, recitation, lecturing, public reading, radio broadcasting, television, video or sound recording, all other forms of mechanical or electronic reproduction, such as CD-ROM, CD-I, information storage and retrieval systems and photocopying, and the rights of translation into foreign languages, are strictly reserved. Particular emphasis is laid upon the matter of readings, permission for which must be secured from the Author's agent in writing. Originally Produced by The Manhattan Theatre Club.

Millier, Brett C.: "On Elizabeth Bishop's 'One Art'" copyright © 1993 by Brett C. Millier. Used by permission of the author. A fuller treatment of the subject appears in ELIZABETH BISHOP: LIFE AND THE MEMORY OF IT by Brett C. Millier (University of California Press, 1993). Lines from the first draft of "One Art" are quoted by permission of the Special Collections, Vassar College Libraries.

Moldenhauer, Joseph: "'To His Coy Mistress' and the Renaissance Tradition" from THE VOICES OF SEDUCTION IN 'TO HIS COY MISTRESS' by Joseph Moldenhauer. Reprinted by permission of the author.

Moser, Don: Don Moser, "The Pied Piper of Tucson: He Cruised in a Golden Car, Looking for Action" from LIFE, March 4, 1966. Copyright © 1966. The Picture Collection Inc. Used with permission. All rights reserved.

Nelson, Marilyn: "The Ballad of Aunt Geneva" and "Star-Fix" from THE HOMEPLACE by Marilyn Nelson Waniek. Copyright © 1990 by Marilyn Nelson Waniek. Reprinted by permission of Louisiana State University Press.

Neruda, Pablo: "Mucho Somos/We Are Many" from EXTRAVAGARIA by Pablo Neruda, translated by Alastair Reid. Translation copyright © 1974 by Alastair Reid. Reprinted by permission of Farrar, Straus and Giroux, LLC.

Oates, Joyce Carol: "Where Are You Going, Where Have You Been?: SMOOTH TALK: Short Story Into Film," from WOMAN WRITER:

OCCASIONS AND OPPORTUNITIES by Joyce Carol Oates, copyright © 1988 by The Ontario Review. Used by permission of Dutton, a division of Penguin Group (USA) Inc.

Oates, Joyce Carol: "Where Are You Going, Where Have You Been?" by Joyce Carol Oates. Copyright © 1970 Ontario Review. Reprinted by permission of John Hawkins & Associates, Inc.

O'Brien, Tim: "The Things They Carried" from THE THINGS THEY CARRIED by Tim O'Brien. Copyright © 1990 by Tim O'Brien. Reprinted by permission of Houghton Mifflin Harcourt Publishing Company. All rights reserved.

O'Connor, Flannery: "A Good Man is Hard to Find" from A GOOD MAN IS HARD TO FIND AND OTHER STORIES, copyright 1953 by Flannery O'Connor and renewed 1981 by Regina O'Connor, reprinted by permission of Harcourt, Inc.

O'Connor, Flannery: "Parker's Back" from THE COMPLETE STORIES by Flannery O'Connor. Copyright © 1971 by the Estate of Mary Flannery O'Connor. Reprinted by permission of Farrar, Straus and Giroux, LLC.

Olds, Sharon: "Rite of Passage" copyright © 1987 by Sharon Olds, from THE DEAD AND THE LIVING by Sharon Olds. Used by permission of Alfred A. Knopf, a division of Random House, Inc.

Oliver, Mary: "Wild Geese" from DREAM WORK by Mary Oliver. Copyright © 1986 by Mary Oliver. Used by permission of Grove/Atlantic, Inc.

Orwell, George: SHOOTING AN ELEPHANT AND OTHER ESSAYS by George Orwell (Copyright © George Orwell, 1946) Reprinted by permission of Bill Hamilton as the Literary Executor of the Estate of the Late Sonia Brownell Orwell and Secker & Warburg Ltd.

Orwell, George: "Shooting an Elephant" from SHOOTING AN ELEPHANT AND OTHER ESSAYS by George Orwell, copyright 1950 by Sonia Brownell Orwell and renewed 1978 by Sonia Pitt-Rivers, reprinted by permission of Harcourt, Inc.

Ozick, Cynthia: "Lovesickness" from QUARREL & QUANDARY by Cynthia Ozick, copyright © 2000 by Cynthia Ozick. Used by permission of Alfred A. Knopf, a division of Random House, Inc.

Pacheco, José Emilio: "La Ceniza" and "Ashes" from CITY OF MEMORY AND OTHER POEMS by José Emilio Pacheco. Copyright © 1990, 2001 by La Ceniza Pacheco. All rights reserved. Translation copyright © 1997 by Cynthia Steele and David Laver. Reprinted by permission of City Lights Books.

Packer, ZZ: "Brownies," from DRINKING COFFEE ELSEWHERE by ZZ Packer, copyright © 2003 by ZZ Packer. Used by permission of Riverhead Books, an imprint of Penguin Group (USA) Inc.

Paglia, Camille: From BREAK, BLOW, BURN by Camille Paglia, copyright © 2005 by Camille Paglia. Used by permission of Pantheon Books, a division of Random House, Inc.

Piercy, Marge: "Barbie Doll" from CIRCLES ON THE WATER by Marge Piercy, copyright © 1982 by Middlemarsh, Inc. Used by permission of Alfred A. Knopf, a division of Random House, Inc.

Pinckney, Darryl: "Black Identity in Langston Hughes" by Darryl Pinckney. Excerpted from "Suitcase in Harlem" by Darryl Pinckney, from THE NEW YORK REVIEW OF BOOKS, Vol. 36, Issue 2, Feb. 16, 1989. Reprinted with permission from The New York Review of Books. Copyright © 1989 NYREV, Inc.

Plath, Sylvia: "Daddy" and "Lady Lazarus" from ARIEL: POEMS by Sylvia Plath. Copyright © 1961, 1962, 1963, 1964, 1965, 1966 by Ted Hughes. Reprinted by permission of HarperCollins Publishers and Faber and Faber Limited.

Plath, Sylvia: "Metaphors" from CROSSING THE WATER by Sylvia Plath. Copyright © 1971 by Ted Hughes. Reprinted by permission of HarperCollins Publishers and Faber and Faber Limited.

Rampersad, Arnold: "Hughes as an Experimentalist" from AFRICAN AMERICAN WRITERS, 2E. © Gale, a part of Cengage Learning, Inc. Reproduced by permission. www.cengage.com/permissions.

Reed, Henry: "Naming of Parts" from A MAP OF VERONA by Henry Reed. © 1946 The executor of the Estate of Henry Reed. Reprinted by permission of John Tydeman.

Rich, B. Ruby: "Good Girls, Bad Girls: Joyce Chopra's SMOOTH TALK" by B. Ruby Rich, from VILLAGE VOICE, April 15, 1986. Reprinted by permission of the author.

Rodriguez, Richard: "'Blaxicans' and Other Reinvented Americans" by Richard Rodriguez. Copyright © 2003 by Richard Rodriguez. (Originally appeared in THE CHRONICLE OF HIGHER EDUCATION, September 12, 2003.) Reprinted by permission of Georges Borchardt, Inc., on behalf of the author.

Roethke, Theodore: "My Papa's Waltz," copyright © 1942 by Hearst Magazines, Inc., from COLLECTED POEMS OF THEODORE ROETHKE by Theodore Roethke. Used by permission of Doubleday, a division of Random House, Inc.

Ryan, Kay: "Turtle" from FLAMINGO WATCHING by Kay Ryan. Reprinted by permission of Copper Beech Press.

Sáenz, Benjamin Alire: "To the Desert" from DARK AND PERFECT ANGLES by Benjamin Alire Saenz, published by Cinco Puntos Press. Copyright © 1995 by Benjamin Alire Saenz. Reprinted by permission of the author.

Satyamurti, Carole: "I Shall Paint My Nails Red" from STITCHING THE DARK: NEW &

SELECTED POEMS by Carole Satyamurti. Copyright © 2005 by Bloodaxe Books. Reprinted by permission of the publisher.

Scoblic, Sacha Z.: "Rock Star, Meet Teetotaler" by Sacha Z. Scoblic, from NEW YORK TIMES BLOG SITE, March 1, 2009. Copyright © 2009 by Sacha Z. Scoblic. Reprinted with permission of the author.

Scripture taken from the New King James Version®. Copyright © 1982 by Thomas Nelson, Inc. Used by permission. All rights reserved.

Seidel, Kathryn L.: "The Economics of Zora Neale Hurston's 'Sweat'" by Kathryn L. Seidel from SWEAT, edited by Cheryl Wall. Reprinted with permission of the University Press of Florida.

Sexton, Anne: "Her Kind" from TO BEDLAM AND PART WAY BACK by Anne Sexton. Copyright © 1960 by Anne Sexton, renewed 1988 by Linda G. Sexton. Reprinted by permission of Houghton Mifflin Harcourt Publishing Company. All rights reserved.

Shakespeare, William: Bevington, David, THE COMPLETE WORKS OF SHAKESPEARE UPDATED, 4th Edition, © 1997, Reprinted by permission of Pearson Education, Inc., Upper Saddle River, NJ.

Showalter, Elaine: "Quilt as Metaphor in 'Everyday Use'" from SISTER'S CHOICE: TRADITION AND CHANGE IN AMERICAN WOMEN'S WRITING by Elaine Showalter. Copyright © 1991 by Elaine Showalter. Reprinted by permission of Oxford University Press.

Silko, Leslie Marmon: "The Man to Send Rain Clouds" by Leslie Marmon Silko. Copyright © 1981 by Leslie Marmon Silko, used by permission of The Wylie Agency LLC.

Smith, Stevie: "Not Waving or Drowning" by Stevie Smith, from COLLECTED POEMS OF STEVIE SMITH, copyright © 1957 by Stevie Smith. Reprinted by permission of New Directions Publishing Corp.

Sophocles: "Antigonê" from THE ANTIGONÊ OF SOPHOCLES, AN ENGLISH VERSION by Dudley Fitts and Robert Fitzgerald, copyright 1939 by Houghton Mifflin Harcourt Publishing Company and renewed 1967 by Dudley Fitts and Robert Fitzgerald, reprinted by permission of the publisher.

Stafford, William: William Stafford, "At the Un-National Monument Along the Canadian Border" from THE WAY IT IS: NEW AND SELECTED POEMS. Copyright © 1975, 1998 by William Stafford and the Estate of William Stafford. Reprinted with the permission of The Permissions Company, Inc. on behalf of Graywolf Press, Minneapolis, Minnesota, www.graywolfpress.org.

Staples, Brent: "The Runaway Son" by Brent Staples, copyright © 1996 by Brent Staples, from FAMILY by Sharon Sloan Fiffer and Steve Fiffer. Used by permission of Pantheon Books, a division of Random House, Inc.

Stegner, Wallace: "Wilderness Letter" from THE SOUND OF MOUNTAIN WATER by Wallace Stegner, copyright © 1969 by Wallace Stegner. Used by permission of Doubleday, a division of Random House, Inc.

Steinbeck, John: "The Chrysanthemums," copyright 1937, renewed © 1965 by John Steinbeck, from THE LONG VALLEY by John Steinbeck. Used by permission of Viking Penguin, a division of Penguin Group (USA) Inc.

Tan, Amy: "A Pair of Tickets," from THE JOY LUCK CLUB by Amy Tan, copyright © 1989 by Amy Tan. Used by permission of G.P. Putnam's Sons, a division of Penguin Group (USA) Inc.

Tan, Amy: "Mother Tongue" from THE OPPOSITE OF FATE: A BOOK OF MUSINGS by Amy Tan. Copyright © 1989. First appeared in THREEPENNY REVIEW. Reprinted by permission of the author and the Sandra Dijkstra Literary Agency.

Thiel, Diane: "The Minefield" from ECHOLOCATIONS: POEMS by Diane Thiel (Story Line Press, 2000). Reprinted by permission of the author.

Thomas, Dylan: "Fern Hill" by Dylan Thomas, from THE POEMS OF DYLAN THOMAS, copyright © 1945 by The Trustees for the Copyrights of Dylan Thomas. Reprinted by permission of New Directions Publishing Corp.

Thomas, Dylan: "Do not go gentle into that good night" by Dylan Thomas, from THE POEMS OF DYLAN THOMAS, copyright © 1952 by Dylan Thomas. Reprinted by permission of New Directions Publishing Corp.

Trethewey, Natasha: Natasha Trethewey, "White Lies" from DOMESTIC WORK. Copyright © 1998, 2000 by Natasha Trethewey. Reprinted with the permission of The Permissions Company, Inc. on behalf of Graywolf Press, Minneapolis, Minnesota, www.graywolfpress.org.

Updike, John: "A & P" from PIGEON FEATHERS AND OTHER STORIES by John Updike, copyright © 1962 and renewed 1990 by John Updike. Used by permission of Alfred A. Knopf, a division of Random House, Inc.

Updike, John: "Ex-Basketball Player" from COLLECTED POEMS 1953-1993 by John Updike, copyright © 1993 by John Updike. Used by permission of Alfred A. Knopf, a division of Random House, Inc.

Valdés, Gina: "English con Salsa" by Gina Valdés, first appeared in THE AMERICAS REVIEW. Copyright © 1993 by Gina Valdés. Reprinted by permission of the author.

Volpe, Edmond: "Myth in Faulkner's 'Barn Burning'" by Edmond Volpe from A READERS GUIDE TO WILLIAM FAULKNER, edited by Edmond Volpe. Copyright © 2004 by Syracuse University Press. Reprinted by permission of the publisher.

Vonnegut, Kurt, Jr.: "Harrison Bergeron," from WELCOME TO THE MONKEY HOUSE by

Kurt Vonnegut, Jr, copyright © 1961 by Kurt Vonnegut, Jr. Used by permission of Dell Publishing, a division of Random House, Inc.

Walker, Alice: Alice Walker, "The Black Woman Writer in America" from INTERVIEWS WITH BLACK WRITERS, edited by John O'Brien. Reprinted by permission of The Wendy Weil Agency, Inc. First published by Liveright Publishing Corp. © 1973 by Alice Walker.

Walker, Alice: "Everyday Use" from IN LOVE & TROUBLE: STORIES OF BLACK WOMEN, copyright © 1973 by Alice Walker, reprinted by permission of Harcourt, Inc.

Washington, Mary Helen: "'Everyday Use' as a Portrait of the Artist" excerpted from Christian, Barbara T., ed. EVERYDAY USE: ALICE WALKER, Copyright © 1994 by Rutgers, the State University. Reprinted by permission of Rutgers University Press.

Waters, Mary Yukari: "Shibusa" by Mary Yukari Waters. Reprinted with the permission of Scribner, a Division of Simon & Schuster, Inc., from THE LAWS OF EVENING: STORIES by Mary Yukari Waters. Copyright © 2003 by Mary Yukari Waters. All rights reserved.

Welty, Eudora: "Why I Live at the P.O." from A CURTAIN OF GREEN AND OTHER STORIES copyright 1941 and renewed 1969 by Eudora Welty, reprinted by permission of Houghton Mifflin Harcourt Publishing Company.

Wilbur, Richard: "The Three Privations of Emily Dickinson" excerpted from "Sumptuous Destitution" from RESPONSES: PROSE PIECES, 1953–1976. Reprinted by permission of the author.

Williams, Tennessee: "The Glass Menagerie" by Tennessee Williams. Copyright © 1945, renewed 1973 The University of the South. Reprinted by permission of Georges Borchardt, Inc. for the Estate of Tennessee Williams.

Wolff, Tobias: "The Rich Brother" from BACK IN THE WORLD by Tobias Wolff. Copyright © 1985 by Tobias Wolff. Reprinted by permission of International Creative Management, Inc.

Woolf, Virginia: "What if Shakespeare Had a Sister?" from A ROOM OF ONE'S OWN by Virginia Woolf, copyright 1929 Harcourt, Inc. and renewed 1957 by Leonard Woolf, reprinted by permission of Houghton Mifflin Harcourt Publishing Company.

Photos

1: Michael Brennan/Corbis All Rights Reserved; 33: Associated Press; 38: World History Archive/Newscom; 42: Alfred A. Knopf, Inc.; 51: Corbis All Rights Reserved; 85: The Granger Collection; 88: AP Wide World; 96: Kate Mendelowitz, University of Alaska Fairbanks Theatre Department; 114: Associated Press; 117: Associated Press; 125: Nancy Kaszerman/ZUMA Press/Newscom; 208: Musée d'Art Ancient, Musées Royaux des Beaux-Arts, Brussels, Belgium/Art Resource; 235: Slim Aarons/Getty Images; 240: Amy Tierney/Getty Images; 254: Bettmann/Corbis All Rights Reserved; 276: Harcourt, Inc.; 277: Heather S. Hughes/Associated Press; 279: Suzanne England; 282: Roland L. Freeman; 284: Christies Images/Bridgeman Art; 286: Nancy Kaye/Associated Press; 308: Lynn Goldsmith/Corbis; 321: ZUMA Press/Newscom; 330: Photoshot/Everett Collection; 341: Bettmann/Corbis; 351: Courtesy of Diane Thiel; 353: Bettmann/Corbis All Rights Reserved; 358: Courtesy of Brent Staples; 366: Sophie Bassouls/Sygma/Corbis; 372: Phyllis Rose; 376: Associated Press; 378: Everett Collection; 379: Courtesy Sony Pictures; 448: Bernd Thissen/DPA /Newscom; 451: Bettmann/Corbis All Rights Reserved; 455: Courtesy Max Apple; 466: Bettmann/Corbis All Rights Reserved; 473: Bettmann/Corbis All Rights Reserved; 482: GCSU Library and Instructional Technology Center; 497: Missouri Historical Society; 510: Culver Pictures, Inc.; 518: Bettmann/Corbis All Rights Reserved; 519: Harvard University, The Houghton Reading Library Reading Room; 525: Courtesy Kim Addonizio; 527: National Portrait Gallery, London; 532: AP Photo/Kathy Willens; 538: Melissa Cooperman/Heinemann; 541: Courtesy Mike Ives; 546: Courtesy David Ives; 547: T. Charles Erickson; 557: Northwind Picture Archives; 558-658 (all): T. Charles Erickson; 663: Moviestore Collection Ltd./Alamy Ltd; 664: Robert Stainforth/ALAMY Ltd.; 666: top left, A.F. Archive/Alamy Ltd., top right, Moviestore Collection Ltd./Alamy Ltd., bottom left, Geraint Lewis/Alamy Ltd., bottom right, Everett Collection; 667: AP/Associated Press; 675: Bernice Abbott/Commerce Graphics Ltd. Inc.; 680: Charles Hopkinson Camera Press/Retna Ltd.; 694: Marcio Jose Sanchez/Associated Press; 700: Peabody Essex Museum; 710: Flannery O'Connor Collection, Georgia College & State University Library; 721: Bernard Gotfryd/Getty Images; 734: International Spectra Film/Everett Collection; 736: Time/Life; 743: International Spectrafilm/Everett Collection; 746: Everett Collection; 752: Everett Collection; 753: Brown Brothers; 756: ZUMA Press/Newscom; 760: AP Wide World Photos; 793: The Granger Collection; 802: AP Wide World Photos; 807: Bettmann/Corbis All Rights Reserved; 808: Jeff Towns/Dylan's Bookstore; 815: Eric Schaal/Time-Life Pictures/Getty Images; 821: United States Postal Service; 834: CSU Archives/Everett Collection/Alamy; 840: Courtesy of Sacha Z. Scoblic; 842: Associated Press; 849: Bettmann/Corbis All Rights Reserved; 851: Everett Collection; 895: Getty Images; 896: Everett Collection; 904: Laurence Hyman; 909: Oliver Morris/Hulton Archive/Getty Images; 914: Marian Wood; 920: Bettmann/Corbis All Rights

Reserved; 925: Bettmann/Corbis All Rights Reserved; 933: Associated Press; 942: Library of Congress; 946: Alamy Ltd.; 957: Amherst College Library; 960: John Sherrifus, Courtesy of the National Endowment for the Arts; 961: Alvin-San Whaley; 962: United States Postal Service; 966: Carol Lollis/Associated Press; 968: Bob Adelman/Magnum Photos; 981: Alamy Ltd.; 989: Eric Risberg/Associated Press; 1000: Martha Swope Studio; 1034: The Granger Collection; 1046: Tanya Tribble; 1057: Christopher Felver/Corbis All Rights Reserved; 1067: Pearson Scott Foresman; 1075: Bob Adelman/Magnum Photos; 1086: ZUMA Wire Photos/Newscom; 1111: Courtesy of Shirley Geok-lin Lim; 1117: Beinecke Rare Book & Manuscript Library, Yale University; 1122: Beinecke Rare Book & Manuscript Library, Yale University; 1123: USPS/Associated Press; 1125: Underwood & Underwood/Corbis All Rights Reserved; 1126: Beinecke Rare Book & Manuscript Library, Yale University; 1128: Beinecke Rare Book & Manuscript Library, Yale University; 1132: Alamy Ltd.; 1136: Beresford/Corbis All Rights Reserved; 1141: Newscom; 1147: Hulton-Deutsch/Corbis All Rights Reserved; 1150: The Harvard Theatre Collection, Houghton Library; 1151: Everett Collection; 1205: J.E. Purdy/Corbis All Rights Reserved; 1215: Newark Public Library; 1232: Alamy Ltd.; 1244: Christopher Felver/Corbis All Rights Reserved; 1247: Rosalie Winard; 1256: Bridgeman Art; 1257: Bridgeman Art; 1258: Bridgeman Art; 1261: The Granger Collection; 1270: The New York Public Library/Art Resource; 1271: Wikipedia Commons; 1277: The Marin Independent Journal; 1281: Library of Congress; 1282: Wikipedia Commons; 1286: Associated Press; 1291: Carl Posey/Corbis OUTLINE; 1299: ZUMA Photos/Newscom; 1312: The Granger Collection; 1318: Beth Herzhaft Photo; 1326: Associated Press; 1341: The Image Works; 1346: Alamy Ltd.; 1363: Alamy Ltd.; 1366: Associated Press; 1368: Imperial War Museum, London; 1369: The British Library; 1374: The Granger Collection; 1375: Courtesy of Ryan Kelly; 1380: Courtesy of Myrna Bein; 1382: Alamy Ltd.; 1384: Lebrecht Photo Library; 1389: Everett Collection; 1392: Everett Collection; 1393: Katy Raddatz/Corbis All Rights Reserved

INDEX OF FIRST LINES OF POETRY

A dented spider like a snow drop white, 188
A voice from the dark called out, 1366
Abortions will not let you forget, 355
against the wall, the firing squad ready, 15
Among twenty snowy mountains, 1274
anyone lived in a pretty how town, 943
As the guests arrive at my son's party, 344
Ashes beg no one's pardon, 809
At his cramped desk, 1356

Bearer of no news, 1277
Because a bit of color is a public service, 1103
Because I could not stop for Death, 807
because it has no pure products, 1111
Bent double, like old beggars under sacks, 1370
Between my finger and my thumb, 348
Bitter coffee, musty beans, 1113
Buffalo Bill 's, 810

Caminante, son tus huellas, 804
Can someone make my simple wish come true?, 513
Carried her unprotesting out the door, 356

De tantos hombres que soy, que somos, 947
Death be not proud, though some have callèd thee, 807
Do not go gentle into that good night, 808

Geneva was the wild one, 523
Good morning, daddy!, 1120

Had we but world enough, and time, 515
He was found by the Bureau of Statistics to be, 953
He was running with his friend from town to town, 351
Heat-lightning streak—, 71
Here is a symbol in which, 1276
Here where the wind is always north-north-east, 1112
How do I love thee? Let me count the ways, 509

I, too, sing America, 1118
I came to you one rainless August night, 1267
I can imagine someone who found, 1266
I caught a tremendous fish, 1264
I found a dimpled spider, fat and white, 170
I have been one acquainted with the night, 817
I have done it again, 811
I have gone out, a possessed witch, 946
I hear America singing, the varied carols I hear, 950
I know exactly what I want to say, 512
I know what the caged bird feels, alas!, 951
I leant upon a coppice gate, 1272
I like to touch your tattoos in complete, 525
I wander through each chartered street, 796
I was angry with my friend, 1362
I will arise and go now, and go to Innisfree, 1262
If ever two were one, then surely we, 508
If we must die, let it not be like hogs, 1365
I'm a riddle in nine syllables, 1103
I'm Nobody! Who are you?, 957
in Just-, 74
I've known rivers, 1117

La ceniza no pide excusas a nadie, 809
Let me not to the marriage of true minds, 529
Let us go then, you and I, 519
Let's hear it for Dwayne Coburn, who was small, 1359

Mark but this flea, and mark in this, 517
Maud went to college, 354
Men at forty, 1108
Moonrise on mudflats, 72
Move him into the sun, 1372
Much Madness is divinest Sense, 958
My black face fades, 1358
My dolls have been put away like dead, 795
My father liked them separate, one there, 340
My mistress' eyes are nothing like the sun, 529

Nature's first green is gold, 60, 128
Nobody heard him, the dead man, 944
Not like the brazen giant of Greek fame, 1364
Now as I was young and easy under the apple boughs, 797

Of the many men who I am, who we are, 947
Once riding in old Baltimore, 794
only one guy and, 72

Pearl Avenue runs past the high-school lot, 801

Say to them, 357
Shall I compare thee to a summer's day?, 528
16 years old, 1104
Snow falling and night falling fast, oh, fast, 818
Some keep the Sabbath going to Church, 959
Some say the world will end in fire, 817
Something there is that doesn't love a wall, 952
Sometimes I think I became the woman, 349

1443

somewhere i have never travelled,gladly beyond, 511
Stop all the clocks, cut off the telephone, 51
Stranger, approach this spot with gravity, 72
Sundays too my father got up early, 338

Tell me not, Sweet, I am unkind, 1352
Temple bells die out, 71
The ache of marriage, 1106
The art of losing isn't hard to master, 802
The food in my bowl, 1280
The gravel road rides with a slow gallop, 1114
The instructor said, 1118
The lies I could tell, 803
The midge spins out to safety, 183
The old woman across the way, 346
the poor, 1109
The Soul selects her own Society, 958
The whiskey on your breath, 339
The world is charged with the grandeur of God, 1261
There is no Frigate like a Book, 16
They eat beans mostly, this old yellow pair, 356
This girlchild was born as usual, 1107
This is my letter to the World, 958
This is the field where the battle did not happen, 1366
This is the one song everyone, 53
To pull the metal splinter from my palm, 350
To see a world in a grain of sand, 1260
Today I sniffed, 1279
Today we have naming of parts. Yesterday, 1353
Traveler, your footsteps are, 804

'Twas brillig, and the slithy toves, 1271
Two roads diverged in a yellow wood, 816
Tyger! Tyger! burning bright, 1270

We real cool. We, 794
We wear the mask that grins and lies, 1110
Welcome to ESL 100, English Surely Latinized, 58
Well, son, I'll tell you, 1120
What happens to a dream deferred?, 61
What lips my lips have kissed, and where, and why, 518
What passing-bells for these who die as cattle?, 1371
What thoughts I have of you tonight, Walt Whitman, 945
When, in disgrace with Fortune and men's eyes, 528
When I have fears that I may cease to be, 70
When I was one-and-twenty, 800
When my love swears that she is made of truth, 530
When you are old and grey and full of sleep, 510
Whenever Richard Cory went down town, 52
Who would be a turtle who could help it?, 1278
Whose woods these are I think I know, 818
Wild Nights – Wild Nights!, 56

You crash over the trees, 1263
You do not do, you do not do, 341
You do not have to be good, 954
You would think the fury of aerial bombardment, 1354

INDEX OF AUTHORS AND TITLES

A & P, 33
Ache of Marriage, The, 1106
ACHEBE, CHINUA, 756
   Dead Men's Path, 756
Acquainted with the Night, 817
ADDONIZIO, KIM, 525
   First Poem for You, 525
AESOP, 1255
   Grasshopper and the Ant, The, 1255
ALARCÓN, FRANCISCO X., 1109
   X in My Name, The, 1109
ALEXIE, SHERMAN, 1057
   This Is What It Means to Say Phoenix, Arizona, 1057
ALVAREZ, JULIA, 349
   By Accident, 349
American Childhood, An, 373
Andre's Mother, 896
ANONYMOUS
   Cat Haiku, 1280
   Dog Haiku, 1279
   Epitaph on a Dentist, 72
Anthem for Doomed Youth, 1371
Antigonê, 1000
anyone lived in a pretty how town, 943
APPLE, MAX, 455
   Vegetable Love, 456
Appointment in Samarra, The, 753
Araby, 676
Ashes / La Ceniza, 809
Asian Culture Looks at Shakespeare, An, 667
At the Un-National Monument Along the Canadian Border, 1366
ATWOOD, MARGARET, 448
   Happy Endings, 449
   Siren Song, 53
AUDEN W. H., 953
   Funeral Blues, 51
   Iago as a Triumphant Villain, 668
   Unknown Citizen, The, 953

BALDWIN, JAMES, 286, 820
   Notes of a Native Son, 821
   Sonny's Blues, 287
Ballad of Aunt Geneva, The, 523
Barbie Doll, 1107
Barn Burning, 254
BARTHES, ROLAND
   Death of the Author, The, 1415
BASHO, MATSUO
   Heat-lightning streak, 71
   Temple bells die out, 71

Bean Eaters, The, 356
Bears Discover Fire, 1247
Because I could not stop for Death, 807
BEIN, MYRNA E., 1380
   Journey Taken with My Son, A, 1380
   "The Better Part of Valor Is Discretion," 1391
BIBLE
   "The Greatest of These Is Love": 1 Corinthians 13, 531
   Parable of the Prodigal Son, 267
BIDPAI, 1256
   Camel and His Friends, The, 1257
BIERCE, AMBROSE, 1312
   Occurrence at Owl Creek Bridge, An, 1312
Bilingual / Bilingüe, 340
BISHOP, ELIZABETH, 802, 1263
   Fish, The, 1264
   One Art, 802
BISSON, TERRY, 1247
   Bears Discover Fire, 1247
Black and White in *Othello*, 669
Black Identity in Langston Hughes, 1129
Black Woman Writer in America, The, 277
BLAKE, WILLIAM, 796, 1260, 1269, 1362
   London, 796
   Poison Tree, A, 1362
   To see a world in a grain of sand, 1260
   Tyger, The, 1270
"Blaxicans" and Other Reinvented Americans, 1141
Bodega, 1113
BODKIN, MAUD
   Lucifer in Shakespeare's *Othello*, 669
Body Bags, 1359
BOYLE, T. CORAGHESSAN, 1232
   Greasy Lake, 1233
BOZORTH, RICHARD R.
   "Tell Me the Truth About Love," 1411
BRADSTREET, ANNE, 508
   To My Dear and Loving Husband, 508
Brief Bio, 1277
BROOKS, GWENDOLYN, 235, 353, 794
   Bean Eaters, The, 356
   mother, the, 355
   rites for Cousin Vit, the, 356
   Sadie and Maud, 354
   Speech to the Young. Speech to the Progress-Toward, 357
   We Real Cool, 794
Brownies, 680
BROWNING, ELIZABETH BARRETT, 509
   How Do I Love Thee? Let Me Count the Ways, 509

1445

Buffalo Bill 's, 810
BUKOWSKI, CHARLES, 1104
   Dostoevsky, 15
   my old man, 1104
BURGESS, ANTHONY
   Asian Culture Looks at Shakespeare, An, 667
BUSON, TANIGUCHI
   Moonrise on mudflats, 72
By Accident, 349

California Hills in August, 1266
Camel and His Friends, The, 1257
Caminante / Traveler, 804
CAMPO, RAFAEL, 512
   For J. W., 512
CARROLL, LEWIS, 1271
   Jabberwocky, 1271
CARVER, RAYMOND, 366, 1075
   Cathedral, 1076
   My Father's Life, 366
Cask of Amontillado, The, 1341
Cat Haiku, 1280
Cathedral, 1076
CHABON, MICHAEL, 694
   Little Knife, The, 694
CHEEVER, JOHN, 924
   Swimmer, The, 925
CHOPIN, KATE, 497
   Désirée's Baby, 503
   Storm, The, 500
   Story of an Hour, The, 498
CHRISTIAN, BARBARA T.
   "Everyday Use" and the Black Power Movement, 278
Chrysanthemums, The, 1068
CHUANG TZU, 1258
   Independence, 1259
Civil Disobedience, 982
CLARK, MICHAEL
   Light and Darkness in "Sonny's Blues," 1398
Clean, Well-Lighted Place, A, 921
COFER, JUDITH ORTIZ, 537, 795
   I Fell in Love, or My Hormones Awakened, 538
   Quinceañera, 795
COPE, WENDY, 513
   Lonely Hearts, 513
CRANE, STEPHEN, 1215
   Open Boat, The, 1216
CULLEN, COUNTEE, 793
   Incident, 794
CUMMINGS, E. E., 511, 810, 942
   anyone lived in a pretty how town, 943
   Buffalo Bill 's, 810
   in Just-, 74
   somewhere i have never travelled,gladly beyond, 511

Daddy, 341
DALY, BRENDA O.
   Unfilmable Conclusion: Joyce Carol Oates at the Movies, An, 747

Darkling Thrush, The, 1272
Dead Men's Path, 756
Death be not proud, 807
Death of the Author, The, 1415
Desert Places, 818
Design, 170
Désirée's Baby, 503
DICKINSON, EMILY, 807, 956,
   Because I could not stop for Death, 807
   I'm Nobody! Who are you?, 957
   Much Madness is divinest Sense, 958
   Recognizing Poetry, 961
   Self-Description, 961
   Some keep the Sabbath going to Church, 959
   Soul selects her own Society, The, 958
   There is no Frigate like a Book, 16
   This is my letter to the World, 958
   Wild Nights – Wild Nights!, 56
DIDION, JOAN, 114
   On Morality, 114
Digging, 348
DILLARD, ANNIE, 372
   American Childhood, An, 373
Discovery of Emily Dickinson's Manuscripts, The, 963
Do not go gentle into that good night, 808
Dog Haiku, 1279
Doll's House, A, 1147
DONNE, JOHN, 517, 806
   Death be not proud, 807
   Flea, The, 517
DOOLITTLE, HILDA. See **H.D.**
Dostoevsky, 15
DOUGLASS, FREDERICK, 1131
   Learning to Read and Write, 1132
DOVE, RITA
   Voices in Langston Hughes, The, 1127
Dream Boogie, 1120
Dream Deferred. See Harlem
DUBUS, ANDRE, 1326
   Father's Story, A, 1327
Dulce et Decorum Est, 1370
DUNBAR, PAUL LAURENCE, 950, 1110
   Sympathy, 951
   We Wear the Mask, 1110

Earthbound: On Solid Ground, 1292
EBERHART, RICHARD, 1354
   Fury of Aerial Bombardment, The, 1354
Economics of Zora Neale Hurston's "Sweat," The, 1408
ELIOT, T. S., 519
   Love Song of J. Alfred Prufrock, The, 519
English con Salsa, 58
Epitaph on a Dentist, 72
ERDRICH, LOUISE, 330
   Red Convertible, The, 330
Eskimo "A Rose for Emily," An, 1413
ESPAILLAT, RHINA P., 340, 1113
   Bilingual / *Bilingüe*, 340
   Bodega, 1113

EVANS, ABBIE HUSTON
 Wing-Spread, 183
Everyday Use, 268
"Everyday Use" and the Black Power Movement, 278
"Everyday Use" as a Portrait of the Artist, 281
Ex-Basketball Player, 801

Facing It, 1358
Father's Story, A, 1327
Father-Figure in "The Tell-Tale Heart," The, 1404
FAULKNER WILLIAM, 254, 466
 Barn Burning, 254
 Rose for Emily, A, 467
Fern Hill, 797
Fire and Ice, 817
First Poem for You, 525
FISH, STANLEY
 Eskimo "A Rose for Emily," An, 1413
Fish, The, 1264
Flea, The, 517
For J. W., 512
Freedom of Emily Dickinson, The, 965
FROST, ROBERT, 815, 951
 Acquainted with the Night, 817
 Desert Places, 818
 Design, 170
 Fire and Ice, 817
 In White, 188
 Mending Wall, 952
 Nothing Gold Can Stay, 60, 128
 Road Not Taken, The, 816
 Stopping by Woods on a Snowy Evening, 818
Funeral Blues, 51
Fury of Aerial Bombardment, The, 1354
Futility, 1372

GANDHI, MOHANDAS, 1382
 Non-Violence—The Greatest Force, 1383
Gift of the Magi, The, 452
Gift, The, 350
GILBERT, SANDRA M.
 Freedom of Emily Dickinson, The, 965
GILMAN, CHARLOTTE PERKINS, 1034
 Yellow Wallpaper, The, 1035
GINSBERG, ALLEN, 944
 Supermarket in California, A, 945
GIOIA, DANA, 1265
 California Hills in August, 1266
GLASPELL, SUSAN, 88
 Trifles, 88
Glass Menagerie, The, 850
God's Grandeur, 1261
Godfather Death, 754
Good Girls, Bad Girls: Joyce Chopra's *Smooth Talk*, 745
Good Man Is Hard to Find, A, 711
Grasshopper and the Ant, The, 1255
"The Greatest of These Is Love": 1 Corinthians 13, 531
Greasy Lake, 1233

GRIMM, WILHELM AND JAKOB, 753
 Godfather Death, 754
GUBAR, SUSAN
 Freedom of Emily Dickinson, The, 965
GWYNN, R. S., 1359
 Body Bags, 1359

H.D. (HILDA DOOLITTLE), 1263
 Storm, 1263
HANSBERRY, LORRAINE, 376
 Raisin in the Sun, A, 377
Happy Endings, 449
HARDY, THOMAS, 1272
 Darkling Thrush, The, 1272
Harlem [Dream Deferred], 61
Harlem Renaissance, The, 1124
Harrison Bergeron, 909
HAWTHORNE, NATHANIEL, 700
 Young Goodman Brown, 701
HAYDEN, ROBERT, 338, 346
 Those Winter Sundays, 338
 Whipping, The, 346
HEANEY, SEAMUS, 347
 Digging, 348
Heat-lightning streak, 71
HEMINGWAY, ERNEST, 920
 Clean, Well-Lighted Place, A, 921
HENRY (WILLIAM SYDNEY PORTER), O., 451
 Gift of the Magi, The, 452
Henry IV, Part I (*Scene*), 1391
Henry V (*Scene*), 1389
Her Kind, 946
HOFFMAN, DANIEL
 Father-Figure in "The Tell-Tale Heart," The, 1404
HOOKS, BELL, 1291
 Earthbound: On Solid Ground, 1292
HOPKINS, GERARD MANLEY, 1261
 God's Grandeur, 1261
HOUSMAN, A. E., 800
 When I was one-and-twenty, 800
How Do I Love Thee? Let Me Count the Ways, 509
HUGHES, LANGSTON, 1116
 Dream Boogie, 1120
 Dream Deferred. *See* Harlem
 Harlem [Dream Deferred], 61
 Harlem Renaissance, The, 1124
 I, Too, 1118
 Mother to Son, 1120
 Negro Artist and the Racial Mountain, The, 1123
 Negro Speaks of Rivers, The, 1117
 Theme for English B, 1118
Hughes as an Experimentalist, 1125
HURSTON, ZORA NEALE, 473
 Sweat, 474

I, Too, 1118
I Fell in Love, or My Hormones Awakened, 538
I Hear America Singing, 950
I Shall Paint My Nails Red, 1103

Iago as a Triumphant Villain, 668
IBSEN, HENRIK, 1146
 Doll's House, A, 1147
If We Must Die, 1365
I'm Nobody! Who are you?, 957
in Just-, 74
In White, 188
Incident, 794
Independence, 1259
Interpreter of Maladies, 1086
ISSA, KOBAYASHI
 only one guy, 72
IVES, DAVID, 546
 Sure Thing, 547
IVES, MIKE, 542
 Would Hemingway Cry?, 542

Jabberwocky, 1271
JACKSON, SHIRLEY, 902
 Lottery, The, 903
JEFFERS, ROBINSON, 1276
 Rock and Hawk, 1276
JIN, HA, 933
 Saboteur, 933
JOHNSON, THOMAS H.
 Discovery of Emily Dickinson's Manuscripts, The, 963
Journey Taken with My Son, A, 1380
JOYCE, JAMES, 675
 Araby, 676
JUSTICE, DONALD, 1107
 Men at Forty, 1108

KAFKA, FRANZ, 760
 Metamorphosis, The, 761
KEATS, JOHN
 When I have fears that I may cease to be, 70
KELLY, RYAN, 1375
 Quick Look at Who Is Fighting this War; This Is Not a Game, A, 1376
KING, MARTIN LUTHER, JR., 968
 Letter from Birmingham Jail, 969
Kingdom of God Is Within You, The, 1385
KINGSTON, MAXINE HONG, 989
 No Name Woman, 989
KOMUNYAKAA, YUSEF, 1358
 Facing It, 1358
KOOSER, TED, 1113
 So This Is Nebraska, 1114
KÜBLER-ROSS, ELISABETH, 842
 On the Fear of Death, 842

La Ceniza / Ashes, 809
Lady Lazarus, 811
LAHIRI, JHUMPA, 1086
 Interpreter of Maladies, 1086
Lake Isle of Innisfree, The, 1262
LAZARUS, EMMA, 1364
 New Colossus, The, 1364
LE GUIN, URSULA K., 914, 1241
 Ones Who Walk Away from Omelas, The, 915

She Unnames Them, 1241
Learning to Love America, 1111
Learning to Read and Write, 1132
LEAVITT, DAVID, 1046
 Place I've Never Been, A, 1046
LEE, LI-YOUNG, 350
 Gift, The, 350
Let me not to the marriage of true minds, 529
Letter from Birmingham Jail, 969
LEVERTOV, DENISE, 1106, 1366
 Ache of Marriage, The, 1106
 Making Peace, 1366
LEVIN, PHILLIS, 1277
 Brief Bio, 1277
Light and Darkness in "Sonny's Blues," 1398
LIM, SHIRLEY GEOK-LIN, 1111
 Learning to Love America, 1111
LINCOLN, ABRAHAM, 1373
 Second Inaugural Address, 1374
Little Knife, The, 694
London, 796
LONDON, JACK, 1204
 To Build a Fire, 1205
Lonely Hearts, 513
Lottery, The, 903
Love Song of J. Alfred Prufrock, The, 519
LOVELACE, RICHARD, 1352
 To Lucasta, 1352
Lovesickness, 533
Lucifer in Shakespeare's *Othello*, 669
LUKE, 266
 Parable of the Prodigal Son, The, 267

MACHADO, ANTONIO, 804
 Caminante / Traveler, 804
Making Peace, 1366
Man to Send Rain Clouds, The, 1244
MANSFIELD, KATHERINE, 42
 Miss Brill, 43
MARVELL, ANDREW, 515
 To His Coy Mistress, 515
MAUGHAM, SOMERSET, 752
 Appointment in Samarra, The, 753
MAUPASSANT, GUY DE, 1346
 Mother Savage, 1346
MCCLANE, KENNETH
 "Sonny's Blues" Saved My Life, 13
MCKAY, CLAUDE, 1364
 If We Must Die, 1365
MCNALLY, TERRENCE, 895
 Andre's Mother, 896
Men at Forty, 1108
Mending Wall, 952
Metamorphosis, The, 761
Metaphors, 1103
MILLAY, EDNA ST. VINCENT, 518
 What lips my lips have kissed, and where, and why, 518
MILLIER, BRETT C.
 On Elizabeth Bishop's "One Art," 1400
Minefield, The, 351
Miss Brill, 43

MOLDENHAUER, JOSEPH
    "To His Coy Mistress" and the Renaissance Tradition, 1402
Moonrise on mudflats, 72
MOSER, DON
    Pied Piper of Tucson: He Cruised in a Golden Car, Looking for the Action, The, 735
mother, the, 355
Mother Savage, 1346
Mother to Son, 1120
Mother Tongue, 117
Much Madness is divinest Sense, 958
Muchos Somos / We Are Many, 947
MUIR, JOHN, 1281
    Wind-Storm in the Forests, A, 1282
My Father's Life, 366
My mistress' eyes are nothing like the sun, 529
my old man, 1104
My Papa's Waltz, 339
Myth in Faulkner's "Barn Burning," 1406

Naming of Parts, 1353
Negro Artist and the Racial Mountain, The, 1123
Negro Speaks of Rivers, The, 1117
NELSON, MARILYN, 523, 1355
    Ballad of Aunt Geneva, The, 523
    Star-Fix, 1356
    Voices in Langston Hughes, The, 1127
NERUDA, PABLO, 947
    Muchos Somos / We Are Many, 947
New Colossus, The, 1364
New England, 1112
No Name Woman, 989
Non-Violence—The Greatest Force, 1383
Not Waving but Drowning, 944
Notes of a Native Son, 821
Nothing Gold Can Stay, 60, 128

OATES, JOYCE CAROL, 721
    Where Are You Going, Where Have You Been?, 722
    "Where Are You Going, Where Have You Been?" and *Smooth Talk*: Short Story into Film, 742
O'BRIEN, TIM, 1299
    Things They Carried, The, 1300
Occurrence at Owl Creek Bridge, An, 1312
O'CONNOR, FLANNERY, 482, 710
    Good Man Is Hard to Find, A, 711
    Parker's Back, 483
OLDS, SHARON, 344
    Rite of Passage, 344
OLIVER, MARY, 954
    Wild Geese, 954
On Elizabeth Bishop's "One Art," 1400
On Morality, 114
On the Fear of Death, 842
One Art, 802
Ones Who Walk Away from Omelas, The, 915
only one guy, 72
Open Boat, The, 1216

ORWELL, GEORGE, 834
    Shooting an Elephant, 835
Othello, the Moor of Venice, 560
OWEN, WILFRED, 1368
    Anthem for Doomed Youth, 1371
    Dulce et Decorum Est, 1370
    Futility, 1372
    Pity of War, The, 1370
OZICK, CYNTHIA, 532
    Lovesickness, 533

PACHECO, JOSÉ EMILIO, 809
    La Ceniza / Ashes, 809
PACKER, ZZ, 680
    Brownies, 680
PAGLIA, CAMILLE
    Reading of William Blake's "London," A, 1417
Pair of Tickets, A, 241
Parable of the Prodigal Son, The, 267
Parker's Back, 483
PAUL, 531
    "The Greatest of These Is Love": 1 Corinthians 13, 531
Pied Piper of Tucson: He Cruised in a Golden Car, Looking for the Action, The, 735
PIERCY, MARGE, 1106
    Barbie Doll, 1107
PINCKNEY, DARRYL
    Black Identity in Langston Hughes, 1129
Pity of War, The, 1370
Place I've Never Been, A, 1046
PLATH, SYLVIA, 341, 811, 1102
    Daddy, 341
    Lady Lazarus, 811
    Metaphors, 1103
POE, EDGAR ALLAN, 38, 1341
    Cask of Amontillado, The, 1341
    Tell-Tale Heart, The, 39
Poison Tree, A, 1362
PORTER, WILLIAM SYDNEY. See HENRY, O.

Quick Look at Who Is Fighting this War; This Is Not a Game, A, 1376
Quilt as Metaphor in "Everyday Use," 283
Quinceañera, 795

Raisin in the Sun, A, 377
RAMPERSAD, ARNOLD
    Hughes as an Experimentalist, 1125
Reading of William Blake's "London," A, 1417
Recognizing Poetry, 961
Red Convertible, The, 330
REED, HENRY, 1353
    Naming of Parts, 1353
RICH, B. RUBY
    Good Girls, Bad Girls: Joyce Chopra's *Smooth Talk*, 745
Rich Brother, The, 309
Richard Cory, 52
Rite of Passage, 344
rites for Cousin Vit, the, 356

Road Not Taken, The, 816
ROBINSON, EDWIN ARLINGTON, 1112
　New England, 1112
　Richard Cory, 52
Rock and Hawk, 1276
Rock Star, Meet Teetotaler, 840
RODRIGUEZ, RICHARD, 1141
　"Blaxicans" and Other Reinvented Americans, 1141
ROETHKE, THEODORE, 339
　My Papa's Waltz, 339
Rose for Emily, A, 467
Runaway Son, The, 359
RYAN, KAY, 1277
　Turtle, 1278

Saboteur, 933
Sadie and Maud, 354
SÁENZ, BENJAMIN ALIRE, 1267
　To the Desert, 1267
SATYAMURTI, CAROLE, 1103
　I Shall Paint My Nails Red, 1103
SCOBLIC, SACHA Z., 840
　Rock Star, Meet Teetotaler, 840
Second Inaugural Address, 1374
SEIDEL, KATHRYN LEE
　Economics of Zora Neale Hurston's "Sweat," The, 1408
Self-Description, 961
SEXTON, ANNE, 946
　Her Kind, 946
SHAKESPEARE, WILLIAM, 527, 557
　"The Better Part of Valor Is Discretion" (from Henry IV, Part I), 1391
　Let me not to the marriage of true minds, 529
　My mistress' eyes are nothing like the sun, 529
　Othello, the Moor of Venice, 560
　Shall I compare thee to a summer's day?, 528
　"We Happy Few, We Band of Brothers" (from Henry V), 1389
　When, in disgrace with Fortune and men's eyes, 528
　When my love swears that she is made of truth, 530
Shall I compare thee to a summer's day?, 528
She Unnames Them, 1241
Shibusa, 1319
Shooting an Elephant, 835
SHOWALTER, ELAINE
　Quilt as Metaphor in "Everyday Use," 283
SILKO, LESLIE MARMON, 1243
　Man to Send Rain Clouds, The, 1244
Siren Song, 53
SMITH, STEVIE, 944
　Not Waving but Drowning, 944
So This Is Nebraska, 1114
Some keep the Sabbath going to Church, 959
somewhere i have never travelled,gladly beyond, 511
Sonny's Blues, 287
"Sonny's Blues" Saved My Life, 13

SOPHOCLES, 999
　Antigonê, 1000
Soul selects her own Society, The, 958
Speech to the Young. Speech to the Progress-Toward, 357
STAFFORD, WILLIAM, 1365
　At the Un-National Monument Along the Canadian Border, 1366
STAPLES, BRENT, 358
　Runaway Son, The, 359
Star-Fix, 1356
STEGNER, WALLACE, 1286
　Wilderness Letter, 1287
STEINBECK, JOHN, 1067
　Chrysanthemums, The, 1068
STEVENS, WALLACE, 1273
　Thirteen Ways of Looking at a Blackbird, 1274
Stopping by Woods on a Snowy Evening, 818
Storm (H.D.), 1263
Storm (Chopin), The, 500
Story of an Hour, The, 498
STUDENT PAPERS
　Analysis Paper: The Design of Robert Frost's "Design," 181
　Analysis Paper: The Hearer of the Tell-Tale Heart, 159
　Argument Paper: Lost Innocence in Robert Frost's "Nothing Gold Can Stay," 143
　Comparison and Contrast Paper: "Wing-Spread" Does a Dip, 184
　Comparison and Contrast Paper: Successful Adaptation in "A Rose for Emily" and "Miss Brill," 163
　Drama Review: Trifles Scores Mixed Success in Monday Players Production, 194
　Explication Paper: An Unfolding of Robert Frost's "Design," 178
　Explication Paper: By Lantern Light: An Explication of a Passage in Poe's "The Tell-Tale Heart," 156
　Research Paper: Kafka's Greatness, 222
　Response Paper: "Perfect Balance and Perfect Posture": Reflecting on "The Things They Carried," 165
Supermarket in California, A, 945
Sure Thing, 547
Sweat, 474
Swimmer, The, 925
Sympathy, 951

TAN, AMY, 125, 240
　Mother Tongue, 117
　Pair of Tickets, A, 241
"Tell Me the Truth About Love," 1411
Tell-Tale Heart, The, 39
Temple bells die out, 71
Theme for English B, 1118
There is no Frigate like a Book, 16
THIEL, DIANE, 351
　Minefield, The, 351
Things They Carried, The, 1300

Thirteen Ways of Looking at a Blackbird, 1274
This is my letter to the World, 958
This Is What It Means to Say Phoenix, Arizona, 1057
THOMAS, DYLAN, 797, 808
    Do not go gentle into that good night, 808
    Fern Hill, 797
THOREAU, HENRY DAVID, 981
    from Civil Disobedience, 982
Those Winter Sundays, 338
Three Privations of Emily Dickinson, The, 964
To Build a Fire, 1205
To His Coy Mistress, 515
"To His Coy Mistress" and the Renaissance Tradition, 1402
To Lucasta, 1352
To My Dear and Loving Husband, 508
To see a world in a grain of sand, 1260
To the Desert, 1267
TOLSTOY, LEO, 1384
    from The Kingdom of God Is Within You, 1385
Traveler / Caminante, 804
TRETHEWEY, NATASHA, 803
    White Lies, 803
Trifles, 88
Turtle, 1278
Tyger, The, 1270

Unfilmable Conclusion: Joyce Carol Oates at the Movies, An, 747
Unknown Citizen, The, 953
UPDIKE, JOHN, 1, 33, 801
    A & P, 33
    Ex-Basketball Player, 801

VALDÉS, GINA
    English con Salsa, 58
VAUGHAN, VIRGINIA MASON
    Black and White in Othello, 669
Vegetable Love, 456
Voices in Langston Hughes, The, 1127
VOLPE, EDMOND
    Myth in Faulkner's "Barn Burning," 1406
VONNEGUT, KURT, JR., 909
    Harrison Bergeron, 909

WALKER, ALICE, 268
    Black Woman Writer in America, The, 277
    Everyday Use, 268
WASHINGTON, MARY HELEN
    "Everyday Use" as a Portrait of the Artist, 281

WATERS, MARY YUKARI, 1318
    Shibusa, 1319
We Are Many / Muchos Somos, 947
"We Happy Few, We Band of Brothers," 1389
We Real Cool, 794
We Wear the Mask, 1110
WELTY, EUDORA, 321
    Why I Live at the P.O., 321
What If Shakespeare Had a Sister?, 1136
What lips my lips have kissed, and where, and why, 518
When, in disgrace with Fortune and men's eyes, 528
When I have fears that I may cease to be, 70
When I was one-and-twenty, 800
When my love swears that she is made of truth, 530
When You Are Old, 510
Where Are You Going, Where Have You Been?, 722
"Where Are You Going, Where Have You Been?" and Smooth Talk: Short Story into Film, 742
Whipping, The, 346
White Lies, 803
WHITMAN, WALT, 949
    I Hear America Singing, 950
Why I Live at the P.O., 321
WILBUR, RICHARD
    Three Privations of Emily Dickinson, The, 964
Wild Geese, 954
Wild Nights – Wild Nights!, 56
Wilderness Letter, 1287
WILLIAMS, TENNESSEE, 849
    Glass Menagerie, The, 850
Wind-Storm in the Forests, A, 1282
Wing-Spread, 183
WOLFF, TOBIAS, 308, 1395
    Rich Brother, The, 309
WOOLF, VIRGINIA, 1136
    What If Shakespeare Had a Sister?, 1136
Would Hemingway Cry?, 542

X in My Name, The, 1109

YEATS, WILLIAM BUTLER, 510, 1262
    Lake Isle of Innisfree, The, 1262
    When You Are Old, 510
Yellow Wallpaper, The, 1035
Young Goodman Brown, 701